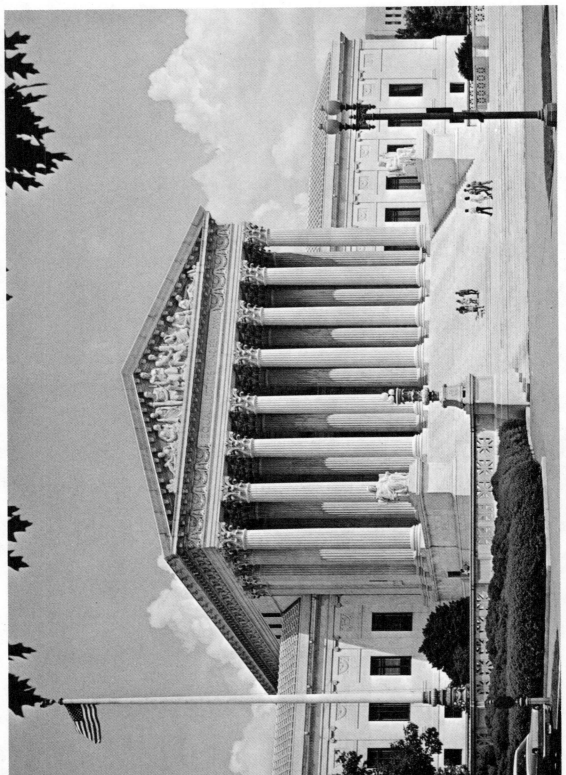

The Supreme Court of the United States, Washington, D.C. From Equal Justice Under Law. Copyright © 1970 the Foundation of the Federal Bar Association.

The Supreme Court and the Criminal Process—

Cases and Comments

PETER W. LEWIS

Associate Professor, University of South Florida, Tampa

KENNETH D. PEOPLES

State of Missouri, Department of Education, Jefferson City

1978

W. B. SAUNDERS COMPANY

Philadelphia / London / Toronto

W. B. Saunders Company: West Washington Square
Philadelphia, PA   19105

1 St. Anne's Road
Eastbourne, East Sussex BN21 3UN, England

1 Goldthorne Avenue
Toronto, Ontario M8Z 5T9, Canada

Library of Congress Cataloging in Publication Data

Lewis, Peter W

The Supreme Court and the criminal process —
cases and comments.

1. Criminal justice, Administration of — United States.
2. United States. Supreme Court.   I. Peoples, Kenneth D.,
joint author.   II. Title.   III. Title: The Supreme
Court and the criminal process.

KF9223.L49   345′.73′05   76–50155

ISBN 0–7216–5769–9

The Supreme Court and the Criminal Process —
Cases and Comments   ISBN   0-7216-5769-9

Last digit is the print number: 9   8   7   6   5   4   3   2   1

To the women in our lives,

Hilda, Kelly and Paige Lewis
and
Kathie and Kelly Peoples

"In a government of laws, existence of the government will be imperilled if it fails to observe the law scrupulously. Our government is the potent, the omnipresent teacher. For good or for ill, it teaches the whole people by its example. Crime is contagious. If the Government becomes a lawbreaker, it breeds contempt for law; it invites every man to become a law unto himself; it invites anarchy. To declare that in the administration of the criminal law the end justifies the means —to declare that the Government may commit crimes in order to secure the conviction of a private criminal—would bring terrible retribution. Against that pernicious doctrine this Court should resolutely set its face."

Olmstead v. United States, 277 U.S. 438, 471, 485 (1928), Brandeis, J. (dissenting)

PREFACE

On June 7, 1977, the voters of Dade County (Miami), Florida, by a margin of 70 to 30 per cent, repealed a city ordinance that prohibited discrimination against homosexuals in employment and housing—the so-called Gay Rights Ordinance. The Anita Bryant–Save Our Children, Inc., forces had prevailed. Later, when questioned by the press, a leader of a gay group to save the ordinance boldly asserted, "We're not worried about the outcome. We intend to take this issue directly to the United States Supreme Court."

The nescience of the gay spokesman on the subjects of federal jurisdiction and Supreme Court review is not surprising. Unfortunately, many persons erroneously believe that our highest federal court can and will give plenary consideration to many of the legal problems arising from the daily activities of our citizens. It has become fashionable to attempt to make a "federal case" out of legal grievances that clearly involve questions of state and local law.*

We are not suggesting that the issues involving sexual preference cannot give rise to substantial federal questions.† But to *assume* that the United States Supreme Court has the constitutional authority (jurisdiction), desire, and resources to resolve every highly publicized legal dispute is, at best, naive. It is the hope of the authors that this text will help to dispell such notions.‡

---

*During the spring of 1977, the Virginia Supreme Court refused to hear a 55-year-old petitioner's appeal of a court order requiring him to get rid of his perfumed pig "sweet lips." The petitioner had raised the 400-pound pet at his combination restaurant and home and claimed that his pig was "as clearn as 90 per cent of the people I know." The pig owner stated, "I'll go all the way to the Supreme Court if I have to."

†But see, e.g., *Gaylord v. Tacoma School District,* 559 P.2d 1340 (Wash. 1977) (public school teacher's status as known and admitted homosexual sufficiently impairs his status as teacher as to justify his dismissal), cert. denied, 46 U.S.L.W. 3206 (1977); see also *Gish v. Board of Education of Paramus,* 377 A.2d 658 (N.J. 1977) (public school board order requiring teacher who became president of statewide gay organization and who participated in public promotion of organization to submit to psychiatric examination does not violate teacher's First Amendment or due process rights), cert. denied, 46 U.S.L.W. 3206 (1977), and *Doe v. Commonwealth's Attorney for City of Richmond,* 403 F. Supp. 1199 (E.D. Va. 1975) (three-judge) (Virginia sodomy statute that punishes, inter alia, consensual homosexual acts in private held not unconstitutional), affirmed, 425 U.S. 985 (1976).

‡During a spring, 1975, course in criminal procedure at Loyola University in Louisiana, a college student asserted, "Everybody knows that the Burger Court has been overruling the decisions of the Warren Court." The student was asked if he was familiar with the story of the young boy who refused to eat his spinach at dinner. His mother said, "Johnny, you should eat all your food because millions of people in India are dying every day of starvation." Whereupon Johnny responded, "Oh yeah, name three." Likewise the student, when asked to name three decisions of the Burger Court that overruled decisions of the Warren Court (in the area of criminal procedure) responded as did Johnny's mother—he said nothing!

This book is written for a basic one- or two-term first course in criminal procedure. It is designed as a teaching tool, presenting more than 170 leading Supreme Court decisions relevant to the fields of criminal justice and political science. Every effort has been made to include those decisions that contribute most to an understanding of the constitutional issues important to the criminal process.

Several chapters in the text provide a framework for advanced courses in more specialized topics. For example, a special topics course or seminar might focus on those chapters that deal with federal jurisdiction, the equal protection of the laws, the juvenile justice process, the legal rights of convicted felons, the constitutional rights of law enforcement authorities, the death penalty, the First Amendment, and the military justice process.

The publisher has most generously permitted us to add cases handed down by the United States Supreme Court while the book was in production. Accordingly, most significant decisions from the 1976–1977 Term are included in the text. Other important cases are included in the annual supplement.

The area of constitutional law that deals with the criminal process (known as criminal procedure) focuses on the legal steps in the processing of criminal prosecutions—from prearrest investigatory problems through trial, conviction, appeals, and postconviction remedies (Chapter Two). Often, but not always, the legal issues involved in the study of the criminal process give rise to federal constitutional questions. These issues are often resolved by the United States Supreme Court in light of the first ten Amendments to the federal Constitution (the Bill of Rights)* and the Fourteenth Amendment. The latter Amendment has two important provisions—the Due Process Clause and the Equal Protection Clause—which are directed specifically to state proceedings.† They are discussed in Chapters Three and Four.

We have attempted to concentrate on those decisions of the United States Supreme Court that have had the greatest impact on the American system of criminal justice. Accordingly, special attention is necessarily devoted to those constitutional guarantees found in the Fourth, Fifth, Sixth, Eighth, and Fourteenth Amendments. In addition, an understanding of the historical development and interpretation of the Bill of Rights and the Fourteenth Amendment is essential to the study of the Supreme Court's role in the criminal process.‡ In this regard, Professor Robert Cord's articles, especially that concerning the Burger Court's neo-incorporation approach, are instructive (Chapter One).

Because many teachers may not wish to cover the entire text in a single term, it is recommended that Chapters One through Seven and Chapter Thirteen be excluded in a one-term course. In some instances the background and interests of the clientele (student-consumers) may dictate that certain topics be covered.

---

*On the historical development of the Bill of Rights, see Schwartz, *The Great Rights of Mankind—A History of the American Bill of Rights* (1977), and Brant, *The Bill of Rights—Its Origin and Meaning* (1965).

†Berger, *Government by Judiciary—The Transformation of the Fourteenth Amendment* (1977).

‡Id. In this controversial book. Professor Berger makes a scholarly argument that the Supreme Court, most notable under Chief Justice Warren, has engaged in a "continuing revision of the Constitution under the guise of interpretation"; that the framers of the Fourteenth Amendment excluded both suffrage and segregation from its reach; and that the Bill of Rights was never intended to apply to state criminal proceedings. For a critical assessment of the Supreme Court's role in society, see Cox, *The Role of the Supreme Court in American Government* (1976).

Therefore, five chapters, covering areas usually reserved for separate courses, may be of special interest to certain groups of students and teachers: Chapter Eight—the Juvenile Justice Process; Chapter Nine—the Legal Rights of Convicted Offenders; Chapter Ten—the Constitutional Rights of Law Enforcement Authorities; Chapter Fifteen—the First Amendment in its Criminal Context;* and Chapter Sixteen—the Military Justice Process. These chapters may be considered optional in a single-term course.

Because of the limitations imposed in keeping the text to a manageable size, many relevant Supreme Court decisions are, by necessity, mentioned only in the Comments following the principal cases. In many instances we have raised questions in the Comments not specifically answered in the principal cases. Teachers may wish to use these queries as a pedagogical tool for classroom discussion, or they may prefer to develop their own critical analyses of the cases. Because many students tend to interpret Supreme Court decisions rather broadly, we have found it useful to ask our students to write down three or four questions after reading a case that raise relevant and collateral issues that were not reached by the Court. This approach enables students to more fully comprehend the Court's self-imposed rule that cases be decided on the most narrow constitutional grounds. It has been our experience, first as law students and later as teachers, that once this principle is grasped, it becomes more meaningful.

The emphasis of the text upon cases is one of practical necessity. We have found that students cannot fully grasp or critically analyze the decisions of the Supreme Court without carefully reading its opinions. In our view, the nuances, the tenor, and the mood of the Court, as well as the constitutional significance and implications of the decisions, cannot be fully appreciated by reading about or listening to lectures on the Court's opinions. One cannot learn to play a musical instrument by listening to another's performance; the instrument itself must be practiced. Likewise, a thorough appreciation of the role of the Supreme Court in the criminal process requires a careful reading of its opinions. We have not found an effective substitute for this endeavor.

We have attempted to carefully edit each opinion to avoid confusing or boring the student with unnecessary dicta and repetition. The inherent risks of such a task are obvious; teachers can, and often do, differ as to the importance of certain statements or phraseology of the Court. Most footnotes from the opinions have been omitted; those that have been retained are indicated by letters. To indicate our own footnotes, we have used bracketed symbols in Supreme Court cases and numbers elsewhere in the text.

A word about the organization and breadth of coverage of the text is in order. Chapter One is designed to acquaint students with the constitutional and statutory limitations on the jurisdiction and powers of review of the Supreme Court. The Court's own self-imposed limitations on judicial review are also noted. We felt it important to present these limitations on federal judicial review in this criminal procedure text because many college students never take a traditional course in constitutional law.

We consider Chapters One through Four to be the "introductory" part of the text—and for the most part, these chapters can be read and digested by students without the necessity of extensive classroom instruction. The background and priorities of the teachers and students will dictate the depth of treatment to be given these chapters. Our practice has been to cover the introductory chapters

---

*For a comprehensive study of the law of obscenity, see Schauer, *The Law of Obscenity* (1976).

during the first two to three weeks of the course, emphasizing federal jurisdiction and judicial review, due process, equal protection of the laws and the nationalization of the Bill of Rights. Some of the materials in Chapter One can be considered "light" reading but are instructive on the "inside" decision-making processes of the Supreme Court. Three of the articles in Chapter One were written by present members of the Supreme Court—Justices Brennan, Rehnquist, and Powell.*

Chapters Five through Seven represent the "essential centralizing" part of the text. These chapters are long because of "manifest necessity" (to borrow a Supreme Court phrase). The Supreme Court has written hundreds of opinions involving Amendments IV through VI, and we have attempted to provide a reasonably thorough presentation of these constitutional issues.†

In several instances, principal cases are preceded by a summary of the oral arguments before the Supreme Court. Some teachers enjoy predicting the outcome of a case based on a careful reading of the questions and answers at oral arguments. However, it should be noted that such second-guessing of the Court, no matter how gratifying, is risky because oral argument is by nature an adversary proceeding.

Although the terms "liberal" and "conservative" sometimes appear in the text (especially in Chapter One), it is important to keep in mind the limited scope of these labels. Many, and perhaps most, decisions of the Supreme Court cannot and should not be categorized as liberal or conservative. On occasion, we have fallen into the "trap" of using such labels at the risk of oversimplification. Parenthetically, Eugene McCarthy has suggested that a liberal is one who throws a 25-foot rope to a drowning man 40 feet away, saying, "I've met you more than half way."

For assistance in the preparation of the manuscript we thank Gary Krautman, Carol Allman, Cathy Hopper, Al De Foor, Jeannette Owen, Pamela Campbell, Paulette Ford, Gary Trichter, and Jerry Vermette for their valuable and capable research and secretarial assistance. To Magdalene Deutsch, whose talents in the art of manuscript preparation are unparalleled, our gratitude. Special appreciation is extended to John Snyder, our former editor, and to Juliana Kremer, his assistant, whose expertise and patience are unmatched. We also wish to thank Susan Loring, our present editor, who graciously and competently assisted us in the final processing of the manuscript. To Ellen Murray, our legally trained copy editor who spent hundreds of hours on the manuscript, our sincere appreciation. Her contribution resulted in a finer product.

We are grateful to Professor Robert Cord, whose knowledge of constitutional law is exceeded only by his commitment to scholarly research, for his helpful comments and suggestions. To the authors and publishers who granted copyright permission for their materials, our thanks. Appreciation is extended to the staff of the Missouri Supreme Court Library for their research assistance, and a special thank you is in order to staff member Bruce Frost, who graciously helped

---

*For recent works on the philosophies of Chief Justice Warren and Justices Black and Douglas, see Warren, *The Memoirs of Chief Justice Earl Warren* (1977), Dunne, *Hugo Black and the Judicial Revolution* (1977), and Countryman (ed.), *The Douglas Opinions* (1977). See also Countryman, *The Judicial Record of Justice William O. Douglas* (1974), and Douglas, *Go East, Young Man* (1974).

†Two excellent recent works on the criminal process are Weinreb, *The Denial of Justice* (1977), and Frankel and Naftalis, *The Grand Jury—An Institution on Trial* (1977).

the authors to locate various case citations and law review articles. Finally, a note of thanks to Professors Harry Allen, Henry Mannle, Harold Vetter, and William Blount, whose insights and encouragement in the preparation of the manuscript are sincerely appreciated.

PETER W. LEWIS

KENNETH D. PEOPLES

SUMMARY OF CONTENTS

CONTENTS

2

STEPS IN THE CRIMINAL PROCESS   73

3

DUE PROCESS AND THE FIFTH AND FOURTEENTH AMENDMENTS... 91

4

PART TWO   CONSTITUTIONAL SAFEGUARDS OF AN ACCUSED: FOURTH, FIFTH, AND SIXTH AMENDMENT PROBLEMS

5

6

**FIFTH AMENDMENT PROBLEMS: DOUBLE JEOPARDY,
SELF–INCRIMINATION, AND THE GRAND JURY** 374

7

SIXTH AMENDMENT PROBLEMS: THE RIGHT TO COUNSEL, JURY TRIALS, SPEEDY TRIALS, THE CONFRONTATION CLAUSE, DEFENSE WITNESSES, AND PUBLIC TRIALS

PART THREE JUVENILE JUSTICE, LEGAL RIGHTS OF THE CONVICTED FELON, THE CIVIL RIGHTS ACT OF 1964, AND THE CONSTITUTIONAL RIGHTS OF LAW ENFORCEMENT AUTHORITIES

8

9

LEGAL RIGHTS OF CONVICTED OFFENDERS

10

THE CIVIL RIGHTS ACT OF 1964 AND THE CONSTITUTIONAL RIGHTS OF LAW ENFORCEMENT AUTHORITIES

PART FOUR SPECIAL PROBLEMS IN THE ADMINISTRATION OF JUSTICE

11

12

13

14

15

THE FIRST AMENDMENT IN ITS CRIMINAL CONTEXT:
FREEDOM OF THE PRESS, SPEECH, RELIGION, AND
ASSEMBLY

16

TABLE OF FIGURES AND TABLES

TABLE OF CASES

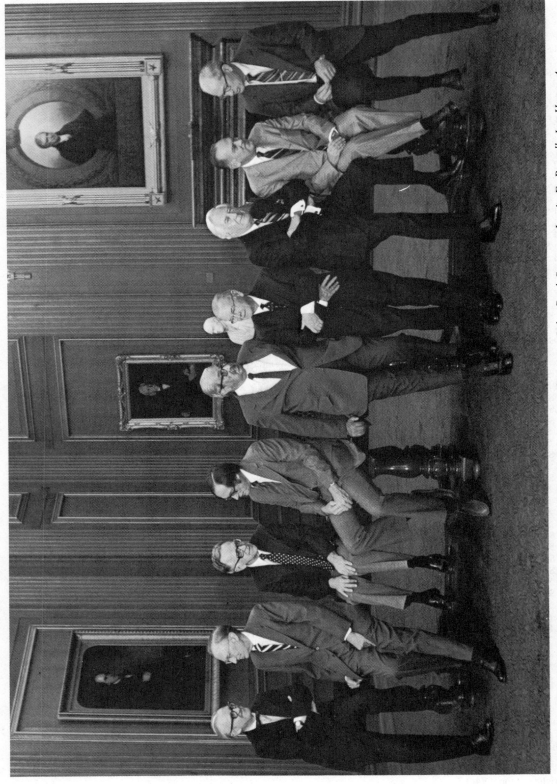

The Supreme Court, 1977–1978 Term. From left: Associate Justices John Paul Stevens, Lewis F. Powell, Jr., Harry A. Blackmun, William H. Rehnquist, Thurgood Marshall, William J. Brennan, Jr., Chief Justice Warren E. Burger, Associate Justices Potter Stewart and Byron R. White.

Part One

THE FEDERAL COURTS, THE BILL OF RIGHTS,
THE CRIMINAL PROCESS, DUE PROCESS,
AND EQUAL PROTECTION OF THE LAWS

1

INSIDE THE SUPREME COURT: JUDICIAL REVIEW, THE DECISION-MAKING PROCESS, AND THE BILL OF RIGHTS

1.01 THE MODERN SUPREME COURT

Many casual, and even faithful, observers of the United States Supreme Court have fixed and sometimes adamant beliefs about how that august body decides cases that involve the criminal process. Often these perceptions are congruent with either a Crime Control or Due Process Model[1] or a liberal or conservative philosophy. By mid-1977, the Burger Court[2] had overruled few of the decisions in this area made by its predecessor, the Warren Court (1953–1969).[3] However, this does not mean that important doctrinal changes are not presently being made by the Court; on the contrary, substantial changes are taking place and the Burger Court appears to be slowly undermining many of the doctrinal underpinnings of certain constitutional pronouncements of the Warren Court affecting the criminal process.

The Warren Court

In 1969, when Warren E. Burger was appointed by President Nixon to the Supreme Court as its fifteenth Chief Justice (replacing Earl Warren),[4] he joined a body later described as one of "uncommon talent."[5] According to scholars who in 1972 rated all the justices who had served on the Court

---

[1]Packer, H., *The Limits of the Criminal Sanction* 149–173 (1968). The Crime Control and Due Process Models describe two competing systems of values in the criminal process. The Crime Control Model stresses the repression of crime and places a high value on bureaucratic efficiency that results in a high rate of apprehension and conviction with an emphasis on speed and finality. Extrajudicial processes are preferred to judicial processes, and informal operations to formal ones. Proponents of this model believe that while the constitutional rights of criminals are important, the guilty should not go free because of legal technicalities. (Most persons arrested are factually guilty.) The Due Process Model, on the other hand, stresses quality control rather than bureaucratic efficiency. Here, extra concern is given to the protection of the constitutional rights of an

Footnote continued on page 4

3

from its beginning in 1789 until 1969 (see Appendix B), Burger joined a Supreme Court that had recently been composed of a "great" Chief Justice (Warren), two "great" associate justices (Black and Frankfurter), and four associate justices who rated as "near great" (Douglas, Harlan, Brennan, and Fortas). Justice Stewart, along with Justices White, Clark, and Marshall, was rated as "average." Thus, the newer members of the Court have had to fill some large judicial shoes. Although these newer appointees (Chief Justice Burger and Associate Justices Blackmun [replacing Fortas in 1970], Powell [replacing Black in 1972], Rehnquist[6] [replacing Harlan in 1972], and Stevens[7] [replacing Douglas in 1975]) have not been subjected to the same critical ratings because of the comparative brevity of their service on the Court, it is possible to assess (albeit subjectively) the judicial philosophies of and rate the present justices of the Burger Court through a careful reading of the opinions of its members.[8] Although, as mentioned, few decisions of the Warren Court have been overruled by the Burger Court

during the period from 1969 to 1977,[9] this does not mean that the present Court has been operating as a mere "rubberstamp" for the pronouncements of its predecessor. In fact, nothing could be further from the truth, although in many instances judicial consistency demands an adherence to earlier doctrine.

The Basic Dilemma*

Political storms have raged around the Supreme Court of the United States almost from the beginning. John Marshall, now

---

*Excerpted by permission of the author and publishers from pp. 1–5, *The Warren Court: Constitutional Decision as an Instrument of Reform* by Archibald Cox, Cambridge, Massachusetts: Harvard University Press. Copyright © 1968 by the President and Fellows of Harvard College.

---

accused to ensure against mistakes. Belief in the reliability of factual determinations made in procedurally regular fashion is an integral part of the Due Process Model.

[2]The Supreme Court is often named after its Chief Justice. Because the Constitution is silent as to the number of justices who shall serve on the Court at any one time, the size of the membership was left to Congress. In the beginning, the Judiciary Act of 1789 (1 Stat. 73) provided for a Chief Justice and five associate justices. The size of the Court was increased to seven in 1807; to nine in 1837; and to ten in 1864. In 1869 Congress set the size of the Supreme Court at nine members, where it has since remained. In 1937 President Roosevelt, unhappy with the Supreme Court's pronouncements, attempted to persuade Congress to increase the size of the Court to fifteen members, thus giving him six new appointments—the famous "Court-packing plan"—but the Senate refused. Today, on occasion, a member of Congress will introduce a bill seeking to increase the size of the Court, usually on the grounds that some of the justices are "too old" to continue to serve on the Court. Such justifications are often rather transparent disguises for displeasure with the judicial philosophies of certain justices. The present membership of nine justices is likely to remain indefinitely.

At present, the federal judiciary consists of approximately 535 active members and 125 senior or semiretired members who were subject to the appointive method as specified in Article III of the Constitution. The President nominates the candidates and the Senate may confirm with a simple majority vote. Even though every state has requirements for some judicial posts, no statutory requirements for a federal judgeship exist. The Constitution is silent with regard to qualifications for the federal judiciary. As a matter of practicality though, a nominee must possess a bachelor of laws degree to be confirmed by the Senate; and no nonlawyer has ever served on the United State Supreme Court. Abraham, H., *Justices and Presidents* (1974).

The Judiciary Act of 1789 established federal district courts throughout the nation, as the first tier of the federal court system. The Supreme Court, as the final court of appeals, was to reside in the nation's capital. The members of the Supreme Court, led by John Jay, the first Chief Justice, first assembled on February 1, 1790, in New York City—then the nation's capital. Because the first cases did not reach the Supreme Court until the following year, it was not until 1792, the Court's third year, that the Justices handed down their first formal written opinions.

Since 1800, the Supreme Court has sat in

Footnote continued on opposite page

universally hailed as our preeminent Chief Justice, was the victim of more vitriolic attacks than Earl Warren almost from the time he ascended the bench in 1801. The difference is that, although the demands for the impeachment of Chief Justice Warren come from a handful of extremists, the plan to impeach Chief Justice Marshall was a plank in the political program of the Jeffersonian Democrats, who held the Presidency and controlled, with large majorities, both houses of Congress. The House of Representatives voted to impeach Marshall's colleague, Samuel Chase, and the Senate acquitted him only because a few Senators ignored party discipline in order to preserve the independence of the judiciary. Had the vote been the reverse, Marshall's impeachment would surely have followed. . . .

One great issue beneath the controversy between Jefferson and Marshall was much like the fundamental question that lies at the bottom of the storm over the Warren Court. What role should the judicial branch play in the government of the American people? Should the Court play an active, creative role in shaping our destiny, equally with the executive and legislative branches? Or should it be characterized by self-restraint, deferring to the legislative branch whenever there is room for policy judgment and leaving new departures to the initiative of others?

Under Marshall the Court staked out an active role in government, building up the power of the federal judiciary and shaping the relation between the Nation and the States according to Marshall's nationalism. *Marbury* v. *Madison* asserted judicial power to issue decrees requiring the Secretary of State to take action contrary to the direct orders of the President, and exercised the authority to declare acts of Congress unconstitutional. The Jeffersonians — the liberals of the early nineteenth century — believed that the Court was too active and should be subordinated to the will of the people. In their view, impeachment implied no wrong-

---

Washington, D.C. Each term begins on the first Monday in October and usually ends toward the end of June (a "term of Court"). The Chief Justice sets the final day of the term, which is determined, in large part, by its workload. 28 U.S.C. § 2.

Under 28 U.S.C. § 1, six justices are necessary to constitute a quorum. 28 U.S.C. § 2109 governs the disposition of cases in the event a quorum is lacking. If a case comes by direct appeal from a district court, the Chief Justice will order the case remanded to the appropriate court of appeals to be heard by that court *en banc* (all the judges in the circuit) or by its three senior judges, as the order directs; and the decision of the court of appeals will be final. In all other cases, the Court will enter an order affirming the judgment of the court below with the same effect as if by an equally divided court. This disposes of the case, but the decision of the Supreme Court carries no precedential weight. See *Neil* v. *Biggers*, 409 U.S. 188 (1972) (Chapter Six, § 6.03). The most authoritative work on Supreme Court procedures is Stern, R. L., and Gressman, E., *Supreme Court Practice* (4th ed. 1969).

Those cases that four of the nine Justices believe present substantial federal questions are usually given plenary review, including oral arguments. The general practice is for the Court in each term to hear oral arguments for two weeks and then recess for two weeks to hold conferences, write opinions, and review petitions for review until about the end of April. Variations in this pattern occur from time to time. Oral arguments are heard Monday through Thursday of the week scheduled from 10:00 A.M. to 12:00 noon, and from 1:00 P.M. to 3:00 P.M. Cases are heard continually through the day, and each side is usually granted 30 minutes to present its position. Extensions in the time permitted each side are permissible under the Rules of the Supreme Court, usually with a maximum of one hour for each side. Supreme Court Rule 44. No oral arguments are heard on Fridays. The justices conduct private conferences on Fridays (during argument and preceding argument weeks) to discuss and vote on petitions for judicial review as well as cases already argued. During oral argument there is a large clock in front of the arguing attorneys. The Supreme Court Marshal acts as a timekeeper, and when counsel has only five minutes left, a white warning light goes on on the lectern immediately in front of him; a red light goes on when time has expired. Counsel must then stop his argument immediately unless he is answering a question posed by one of the justices. Counsel are not required to consume all the time available and should sit down when all the important points of the case have been covered. Several summaries of oral arguments before the Supreme Court are presented in the text, infra.

An opinion of the Court is announced orally in open Court by its author. From 1857 to 1965,

Footnote continued on page 6

doing: it was simply a mechanism for removing a judge whose views were contrary to the wishes of the electorate.

Defining the Court's role in government

also became a major issue early in the present century. Both the Supreme Court and inferior courts used the power to declare laws unconstitutional in order to inval-

---

opinions of the Court were announced only at the beginning of the Monday sessions, following the admission of attorneys to the Supreme Court bar—these were known as "Decision Mondays." Since 1965, decisions are reported as they become ready at any session of the Court, and no announcement of decisions to be reported is made prior to their rendition in open Court. Any Justice who has written a concurring or dissenting opinion is free to announce his views orally. When more than one opinion is ready for announcement, the justices writing the opinions for the Court make their announcements in reverse order of seniority. Most often a justice who has written an opinion for the Court will summarize the written opinion rather than read all or large portions of it.

[3]During the first half of the Warren Court (1953–1960), few important decisions affecting the criminal process were directed at the states, and not a single provision in the Bill of Rights was made applicable to the states through the Fourteenth Amendment. (See Table 1.2.)

[4]Earl Warren, C.J., was appointed to the Court by President Eisenhower (replacing Vinson, C.J.) and served from October 5, 1953, to June 23, 1969. Warren Burger, C.J., was sworn in on June 23, 1969. Prior to his appointment, Burger served as a judge on the United States Court of Appeals (D.C. Cir.) from 1956 to 1969. In all, only 15 Chief Justices have sat on the Supreme Court since 1789, averaging 15 years service apiece. Four Chief Justices served previously as associate justices.

[5]Levy, L., *Against the Law: The Nixon Court and Criminal Justice* 36 (1974). See also Goldberg, A., *Equal Justice: The Warren Era of the Supreme Court* (1971); Cox, A., *The Warren Court: Constitutional Decision as an Instrument of Reform* (1968); Sayler, R., Boyer, B., and Gooding, R. (eds.), *The Warren Court: A Critical Analysis* (1969).

[6]For an interesting examination of the opinions of Mr. Justice Rehnquist, see Shapiro, D., *Mr. Justice Rehnquist: A Preliminary View*, 90 Harv. L. Rev. 293 (1976) ("[w]hile he is a man of considerable intellectual power and independence of mind, the unyielding character of his ideology has had a substantial adverse impact on his judicial product"), at 293. See also Rehnquist, W., *The Notion of a Living Constitution*, 54 Tex. L. Rev. 693 (1976) ("the authority of the Justices to strike down laws as unconstitutional must be somehow tied to the language of the Constitution"), at 698; and Rydell, *Mr. Justice Rehnquist*

and Judicial Self-Restraint, 26 Hast. L.J. 875 (1975).

[7]Mr. Justice John Paul Stevens, the newest member of the Court, was appointed by President Ford and was sworn in on December 19, 1975. Prior to his appointment, Justice Stevens served on the United States Court of Appeals (7th Cir.) from 1970 to 1975. From 1947 to 1948, he was a law clerk for Justice Wiley Rutledge of the United States Supreme Court. Stevens is the 101st justice and the 90th associate justice to serve on the Court. Every president who has served at least one full term has appointed at least one justice to the Supreme Court. President Washington appointed ten (including the original six justices); President F. D. Roosevelt, nine; President Eisenhower, five; President Kennedy, two; President Johnson, two; and President Nixon, four. President Ford, who served less than a full term, appointed one justice.

In 1977, the average age of the justices was 65 years, with a range of 53 years (Rehnquist) to 71 years (Brennan). Five of the justices (Burger, Brennan, Blackmun, Powell, and Marshall) are close to 70 years of age.

[8]Professor Shapiro has listed three qualities that are essential to the craftsmanship of an appellate judge: "(1) reasoned elaboration in the writing of judicial opinions; (2) meticulousness in insuring the appropriate disposition of the case in light of the questions presented and decided, the record, and the governing law; and (3) the avoidance of judicial pronouncements on controversial questions not presented in the case at hand or not necessary to its disposition." Shapiro, D., *Mr. Justice Rehnquist: A Preliminary Review*, 90 Harv. L. Rev. 293, 328 (1976).

[9]*Cardwell* v. *Lewis*, 417 U.S. 583 (1974) (Chapter Five, § 5.04), overruling (sub silentio) *Preston* v. *United States*, 376 U.S. 364 (1964). See Hartman, M., *Foreward—The Burger Court—1973: Leaving the Sixties Behind Us*, 65 J. Crim. L. & C. 439 (1975); *Stone* v. *Powell*, 96 S. Ct. 3037 (1976) (Chapter Five, § 5.03), overruling *Kaufman* v. *United States*, 394 U.S. 217 (1969); *Gregg* v. *Georgia*, 428 U.S. 153 (1976) and *Woodson* v. *North Carolina*, 428 U.S. 280 (1976) (Chapter Eleven, § 11.03), both overruling *McGautha* v. *California*, 402 U.S. 183 (1971). Although the Court did not expressly overrule *Preston*, *Kaufman*, and *McGautha*, the continuing constitutional validity of these cases is doubtful. For a list of Supreme Court decisions involving the criminal process that were subsequently overruled, see Appendix C.

idate much of the modern legislation that we now accept as a normal governmental function—laws on minimum wages and maximum hours, on price regulation, and on labor relations and consumer protection. Most people thought such measures were required by our transformation into a modern industrial and predominantly urban community. Most judges regarded them as dangerous innovations threatening the American way of life. Their judicial activism prevailed until the mid-1930's. It is often associated with the name of Chief Justice Taft.

In reaction, there developed the theory of judicial self-restraint with which the senior generation of lawyers was generally indoctrinated. The theory sprang from the soil of the old Jeffersonian philosophy but was more sophisticated because it allowed room for judicial review in a narrow class of cases. . . .

The philosophy of self-restraint came to be associated with the names of Brandeis, Holmes, Learned Hand, and Felix Frankfurter. It was so far dominant within the Supreme Court after 1937 that by the mid-forties it had hardly any critics.

But the issue concerning the proper role of the Supreme Court never lies quiet very long. The appointment of Earl Warren as Chief Justice of the United States marked the beginning of an era of extraordinarily rapid development in our constitutional law during which the Court has broken new ground for the States and other branches of the federal government. Its defenders rightly point out that the Court has spearheaded the progress in civil rights, administration of criminal justice, protection of individual liberty, and the strengthening and extension of political democracy. The critics charge the Court with subordinating law to personal political preferences, and with acting like a legislature or an omnipotent council of not-so-wise men instead of a court.

[C]onstitutional adjudication presents an insoluble dilemma. The extraordinary character of the questions put before the Court means that the Court cannot ignore the political aspects of its task—the public consequences of its decisions—yet the answer to the question "what substantive result is best for the country?" is often inconsistent with the responses obtained by asking

"what is the decision according to law?" The Court may incline to one direction or the other, but no one could wisely and permanently grasp either horn of the dilemma. . . .

The Controversial Warren Court*

The diversity of views about the Warren Court involves more than disagreements on the values asserted in its decisions or the style that the Court displayed in performing its functions. The very concept of a "Warren Court" is uncertain and elusive. From September, 1953, when Earl Warren first assumed his duties on the Court, until May, 1969, when he resigned, seventeen judges sat on the Court, a group distinctive for its diversity in experience, outlook, and talent. Moreover, the impression one gets from these years is affected by one's interests and by the segments of the Court's work that have attracted his concerns. These impressions vary depending on whether one associates the Warren Court primarily with its contributions to the law of race relations and to more generalized problems of equality under the law, or to criminal justice, or to other areas of its docket. During these years there were several "Warren Courts," each with differing life spans. Thus, in the criminal law area it was perhaps not until 1961 and the decision of *Mapp* v. *Ohio* that a majority of the bench began consistently to reflect those positions that one today considers distinctive of the Warren Court. Although the evidence is less clear, the Warren Court in the criminal cases came to an end a year or two before Chief Justice Warren stepped down. In the area of race relations, on the other hand, the new Chief Justice was confronted by *Brown* v. *Board of Education* in his first year on the bench; and the movement for racial liberation presented

*From Allen, Francis A., *The Judicial Quest For Penal Reform: The Warren Court and the Criminal Cases.* U. Ill. L.F. 518–521 (1975). Reprinted by permission of the University of Illinois Law Forum. Copyright 1975 by the Board of Trustees, University of Illinois.

issues that commanded the Court's attention throughout his entire tenure.

The Warren Court, then, is a complex phenomenon, and one that is still capable of engendering controversy and emotion. Underlying the polemics, however, is a common acceptance of the significance of the phenomenon. The history of the Supreme Court during the years in question is widely believed to afford significant evidence about the nature of American society, its political and legal institutions, its values, and its pathologies. This conviction leads one to anticipate that the Warren Court, however defined or appraised, will continue to be an object of inquiry and reflection in the years ahead.

In the sixteen years of Chief Justice Warren's tenure, the Supreme Court decided upwards of 600 criminal cases. Yet the reputation of the Warren Court for judicial activism in the criminal area—as a tribunal dedicated to the enhancement of the rights of defendants and to the expansion of federal judicial authority—rests largely on the results reached and the opinions rendered in hardly more than two dozen cases. . . . But by far the larger part of the Court's work in the criminal area are the cases in which it was concerned with the routine judicial function of supervising the federal system of criminal justice. Here one finds the Court interpreting federal legislation and the Federal Rules of Criminal Procedure or devising rules of evidence. . . .

. . . Yet it is well to remember as one considers the Court's performance in the highly publicized and controversial cases, that while these cases were under consideration, the Court was week by week disposing of less dramatic issues involving the decency and efficiency of the criminal process. The cumulative importance of this latter activity is very great, and its actual impact may well rival that of the more celebrated adjudications.

There was a time when college students received instruction on the principle of continuity in history. History, it was said, is a continuous stream of events with no abrupt turns or sudden changes. The implication of this proposition for the matters under consideration is that the performance of the Warren Court in the criminal cases has both prologue and epilogue. Contemporary com-

mentary suggests that some persons are unaware that the Supreme Court had concerned itself with establishing constitutional minima for state systems of criminal justice long before the Warren Court came into existence. . . .

Handcuffing the Cops?*

The Warren Court did "handcuff the cops," in some respects; its job was to do just that by keeping the police within the law they enforced. The Constitution deliberately provided for this conflict between the courts and the law-enforcement agencies. When a defendant has the benefit of legal counsel or demands trial by jury or invokes any other constitutional right, police power is circumscribed. The Warren Court enlarged the rights of the criminally accused, evoking strenuous protests from responsible as well as hysterical opponents. Every expansion of the rights of the criminally accused in American history has confronted the warning that handicapping the state makes conviction of the guilty more difficult. More than six decades ago, an essay by a prosecutor on "Coddling the Criminal" attributed the failures of law enforcement to judicial observance of the constitutional protections against double jeopardy and compulsory self-incrimination. The presumption of innocence, trial by jury, writ of habeas corpus, and every other procedural safeguard has been blamed at one time or another for causing crime or hampering the police.

The courts would have little reason to reverse convictions if the police did not break the law in order to enforce it. The argument against the Warren Court's strict observance of the Bill of Rights was essentially an argument that the police should be above the law in order to protect society

---

*From pp. 5–6, *Against the Law: The Nixon Court and Criminal Justice* by Leonard W. Levy. Copyright © 1974 by Clio Enterprises Co. By permission of Harper & Row, Publishers, Inc.

from those who violate it. Our constitutional law is intended to secure all of us from improper, even criminal, police conduct and from prosecutorial shortcuts with the law. The object of the criminal law is to assess guilt or innocence according to canons of fairness and see that justice is done; the object is not simply to convict the guilty by whatever means. "If the exercise of constitutional rights will thwart the effectiveness of a system of law enforcement," as the Warren Court said, "then there is something very wrong with that system." We should not fear if an accused person receives the assistance of a lawyer, if he learns what his rights are and exercises them.

In *Miranda,* his most controversial criminal-justice opinion, Chief Justice Warren quoted these words:

> Law enforcement, however, in defeating the criminal, must maintain inviolate the historic liberties of the individual. To turn back the criminal, yet, by so doing, destroy the dignity of the individual, would be a hollow victory....
> We can have the Constitution, the best laws in the land, and the most honest reviews by courts—but unless the law enforcement profession is steeped in the democratic tradition, maintains the highest in ethics, and makes its work a career of honor, civil liberties will continually—and without end—be violated.... The best protection of civil liberties is an alert, intelligent and honest law enforcement agency.

The author of that statement, made before Warren joined the Court, was no permissive judge or soft-headed social theorist; he was the director of the FBI, J. Edgar Hoover....

Richard Nixon and "Strict Constructionism"

When President Nixon announced the appointments of Chief Justice Burger (1969) and Associate Justices Blackmun (1970), Powell (1971), and Rehnquist (1971), he stated that he desired to see "strict constructionists" serve on the Court. In legal parlance, "strict constructionism" refers to a judicial philosophy that requires that the words of the Constitution be interpreted literally and precisely. It is doubtful that this is what Nixon had in mind,[10] however, since he apparently used the term "strict constructionists" to refer to justices who would alter and reverse the liberal tide of the Warren Court. Nevertheless, Nixon appointed four men whose judicial philosophies, he believed, would be in dramatic opposition to those of many of the justices of the liberal Warren Court. Recent pronouncements by the Burger Court suggest that Nixon may have succeeded.

The Burger Court: Beginning*

For three and a half years, from June 1968 until December 1971, the attention of the American public was drawn to the highest court of the land more closely than at any time since the epic "Court-packing" battle between Franklin D. Roosevelt and the United States Senate in 1937. On June 26, 1968, President Lyndon B. Johnson an-

*From pp. 3–12, *Justices and Presidents: A Political History of Appointments to the Supreme Court* by Henry J. Abraham. Copyright © 1974 by Oxford University Press, Inc. Reprinted by permission.

[10]As an example, the First Amendment provides, inter alia, that "Congress shall make no law ... abridging the freedom of speech, or of the press. ..." Consequently, a strict constructionist would essentially hold that pornographic and obscene materials are constitutionally protected, i.e., removed from the sanctions of the criminal law. As strict constructionists (at least in the area of the First Amendment), Justices Black and Douglas refused to attend the movie showings in the basement of the Supreme Court Building to view the evidence in obscenity cases. To them, the First Amendment should be interpreted in absolute terms. See, e.g., *Roth* v. *United States,* 354 U.S. 476, 508 (1957) (Douglas, J., joined by Black, J., dissenting). See also Countryman, V., *The Judicial Record of Justice William O. Douglas* 382 (1974) ("when Nixon announced his intention to staff the Supreme Court with 'strict constructionists' it may be fairly concluded that what Nixon was seeking was 'niggardly constructionists' of the Bill of Rights"); and Ball, *The Vision and Dream of Justice Hugo L. Black* (1975).

nounced Mr. Chief Justice Earl Warren's intention to resign from the seat he had occupied since 1953 and the nomination of Associate Justice Abe Fortas as his successor. It was a historic event, the start of a fascinating epoch of political maneuvering that would not be resolved until December 10, 1971, when William H. Rehnquist was confirmed as an Associate Justice of the Supreme Court by the less than overwhelming margin of 68:26. When the Senate, after more than three months of partisan and often acrimonious debate, had defeated a motion to vote on the Fortas nomination in the fall of 1968, Fortas requested the President to withdraw his name from further consideration. In turn the Chief Justice withdrew his resignation, commenting: "[S]ince they wouldn't confirm Abe they will have me." And so they did for another full term of Court until late May 1969, when Earl Warren stepped down and was replaced by Warren Earl Burger, Chief Judge of the U.S. Court of Appeals for the District of Columbia. Burger's investiture was President Richard M. Nixon's first of four successful nominations—but the four came from a total of eight attempts.

Judge Burger, sixty-one years old at the time of his appointment and of impeccable Republican credentials, was the prototype of the kind of individual Presidential candidate Nixon had promised the country he would nominate to the bench upon his election: one whose work on the Court would "strengthen the peace forces as against the criminal forces of the land"; one who would have an appreciation of the basic tenets of "law and order," being "thoroughly experienced and versed in the criminal laws of the country"; one who would see himself as a "caretaker" of the Constitution and not as a "super-legislator with a free hand to impose . . . social and political view-points upon the American people"; one who was a "strict constructionist" of the basic document; and one who had had broad experience as an appeals judge on a lower judicial level. Burger's confirmation by a vote of 74:3 was both speedy and decisive. The President was jubilant: not only had *his* kind of candidate overcome the hurdle of Senate confirmation with all but *pro forma* ease, but he had a second vacancy to fill.

Earlier, in May of 1969, Mr. Justice Fortas, under intense public and private at-

tack as a result of revelations concerning his relationship with convicted financier Louis Wolfson, had resigned from the Court—the first Supreme Court jurist to do so under that type of pressure. Fortas had broken no law and he fervidly protested his innocence, but his highly questionable judgment and the integrity and prestige of the Court had clearly mandated his move. The not-inconsiderable number of Warren Court haters in the Senate were delighted, and the President—again publicly citing his criteria for Supreme Court nominees—accepted Attorney General John N. Mitchell's suggestion of Chief Judge Clement F. Haynsworth, Jr., of the U.S. Court of Appeals for the Fourth Circuit. Haynsworth was a native of South Carolina and a Harvard Law School alumnus. To his basic specifications Mr. Nixon had added the desire of choosing a Southern jurist of conservative judicial bent. Of course the Court already had at least one Southern strict constructionist, indeed a constitutional literalist of the first magnitude, in the person of the distinguished Mr. Justice Hugo Lafayette Black of Alabama, but that was not exactly what the President had in mind. Judge Haynsworth, a relatively able jurist meriting a "B-minus" in the minds of most Court-watchers, fit all of the President's specifications to date and, perhaps even more significantly, those of such influential Southern Senators as Strom Thurmond (R.-S.C.), James O. Eastland (D.-Miss.), and John L. McClellan (D.-Ark.).

Indeed, most of the Senate seemed disposed to confirm Judge Haynsworth for the Fortas vacancy. But to the President's anger, frustration, and embarrassment, the hearings of the Senate Committee on the Judiciary provided clear evidence of the nominee's patent insensitivity to financial and conflict-of-interest improprieties. Apparently, as with Fortas, no actual legal infractions had taken place—but how could the Senate confirm Haynsworth when it had played such an activist role in causing Fortas's resignation? It could not, and among those who vocally opposed the South Carolinian and voted against his confirmation were such anti-Fortas, strict-constructionist leaders as Senators Robert Griffin (R.-Mich.) and Jack Miller (R.-Iowa). Down went the Haynsworth nomination by a vote of 55:45 on November 21,

1969—largely for the reasons indicated, although the candidate had also drawn considerable fire from labor and minority groups for allegedly anti-civil libertarian and anti-civil rights stands. A livid President Nixon, however, chose to lay the blame for his nominee's defeat upon "anti-Southern, anti-conservative, and anti-constructionist" prejudice, and he vowed to select another "worthy and distinguished protagonist" of Southern, conservative, and strict-constructionist persuasion.

To the dismay of those Senators who had counseled confirmation of Judge Haynsworth lest a successor-nominee be even less worthy of the high post, the President—again on the recommendation of his Attorney General—quickly countered by nominating Judge G. Harrold Carswell of Florida, a little-known and little-distinguished ex-judge with six months of experience on the U.S. Court of Appeals for the Fifth Circuit. "He is almost too good to be true," Mr. Mitchell was reported to have said. The appointment was an act of vengeance—one intended to teach the Senate a lesson and to downgrade the Court. The Senate, intimidated by the President and the Attorney General, was disposed to confirm him. But suspicious reporters and researchers soon cast serious doubt on that "almost too good to be true" rating of the nominee. Immediately damaging was the discovery of a statement Carswell made to a meeting of the American Legion on August 2, 1948, while running for a seat on the Georgia legislature. "I yield to no man as a fellow candidate or as a fellow citizen in the firm, vigorous belief in the principles of White Supremacy, and I shall always be so governed." To be sure, the nominee, pointing to his youth and inexperience (he was twenty-eight at the time), now disavowed that statement and any racism as well. But an examination of his record on the bench cast further doubt on his objectivity in racial matters: while serving as U.S. Attorney in Florida, Carswell had been involved in the transfer of a public, municipally owned Tallahassee golf course, built with $35,000 of federal funds, to the status of a private club. The transfer was obviously designed to circumvent a contemporary Supreme Court decision proscribing segregation in municipal recreation facilities.

Still, the Administration appeared to have the votes for Senate confirmation given the vivid memories of the Haynsworth battle, the intensive wooing of doubtful Senators by the White House and the Justice Department, and the natural predisposition to give the President his choice, all things being equal. But things were far from equal, for as the Carswell opponents continued their attack it became apparent that—quite apart from the controversy surrounding his civil rights record—the candidate was patently inferior, simply on the basis of fundamental juridical and legal qualifications. If Judge Haynsworth had merited a "B-minus," Judge Carswell scarcely merited a "D" on the scale of relevant ability. Senator Roman Hruska (R.-Neb.), the President's floor manager of the nomination, made a pathetic fumbling attempt to convert the candidate's mediocrity into an asset: "Even if he is mediocre there are a lot of mediocre judges and people and lawyers. They are entitled to a little representation, aren't they, and a little chance? We can't have all Brandeises, Cardozos, and Frankfurters, and stuff like that there." Hruska's remarkable assertion was seconded by Carswell-supporter Senator Russell Long (D.-La.), who observed: "Does it not seem to the Senator that we have had enough of those upside down, corkscrew thinkers? Would it not appear that it might be well to take a B student or a C student who was able to think straight, compared to one of those A students who are capable of the kind of thinking that winds up getting us a 100-percent increase in crime in this country?"

This line of argument failed to convince the doubtful Senators. Instead they became increasingly aware of the lack of ability of the nominee—who, among other debilitating features, held the dubious record of having been reversed by appellate courts more than any of the other then sitting federal jurists except eight! Yale Law School Dean Louis H. Pollak styled the Carswell nomination as one of "more slender credentials than any Supreme Court nominee put forth in this century"; perhaps even more tellingly, the distinguished William Van Alstyne, Professor of Law at Duke University, opposed the nomination. Van Alstyne, an ardent and vocal backer of the Haynsworth nomination, now testified: "There is, in candor, nothing in the quality of the nominee's work to warrant any expectation whatever that he could serve with distinction on the Supreme Court of the United States." When the final vote on confirmation came on April 9, 1970—three months after the nomination—the President's choice went down by a vote of 51:45. Among the "noes" were such significant Republican votes as those of Margaret Chase Smith of Maine, Winston L. Prouty of Vermont, Marlow W. Cook of Kentucky, and Richard S. Schweiker of Pennsylvania.

It was indeed a bitter defeat for the President. Not only had he seen two nominees rejected within less than five months, but his carefully devised "Southern strategy" had suffered a serious blow. His reaction was swift and vitriolic. Conveniently ignoring the basic issues for his candidates' defeat, he blamed it instead on sectional prejudice, abject politics, and philosophical negations, and told the country:

I have reluctantly concluded that—with the Senate as presently constituted—I cannot successfully nominate to the Supreme Court any federal appellate judge from the South who believes as I do in the strict construction of the Constitution.... Judges Carswell and Haynsworth have endured with admirable dignity vicious assaults on their intelligence, their honesty, and their character.... When all the hypocrisy is stripped away, the real issue was their philosophy of strict construction of the Constitution—a philosophy that I share.

Quite to the contrary, several distinguished federal jurists in the South were eminently qualified to serve, jurists who indeed shared the President's philosophy of government and politics, and whom the Senate assuredly would have confirmed. It could not, in good conscience—given the Fortas precedent, the public concern, and the nature and role of the Supreme Court—have confirmed Haynsworth and Carswell, especially not Carswell. The latter, in an ironic footnote, was soon to be defeated by his constituents in the Florida Senatorial primary, during which he was photographed with a lettered sign around his neck, "Heah Come de Judge." It is an intriguing thought that had Haynsworth been nominated *after* Carswell he might well have been confirmed.

President Nixon followed up his blast against the rejections with the petulant suggestion in a publicized letter to Senator William B. Saxbe (R.-Ohio) that the Senate had denied him the right to see his choices appointed. That right, he insisted, had been accorded all previous presidents—a patently false statement: since 1789, 26 of the 136 nominees formally sent to the Senate for confirmation have been rejected—close to one out of five candidates (one out of three in the nineteenth century). Moreover, the President's collateral suggestion to Saxbe and the nation, that Senatorial advice and consent to nominations (expressly provided for in Article II, Section 2, Clause 2 of the Constitution) is merely a *pro forma* requirement, is utterly incorrect with regard to nominations to the judiciary and the Supreme Court. Mr. Nixon, who was fully familiar with the contrary judgment of practically all students of constitutional law and history, as well as with Hamilton's equally contrary assertions in *The Federalist Papers* (#76 and #77), must have known how wrong he was. His anger and frustrations were understandable, but his historical misstatement was a distinct disservice to country, Constitution, and Court.

Announcing that the Senate would never confirm a Southern strict constructionist, President Nixon now turned to a Northerner, Harry A. Blackmun, sixty-one, of Minnesota, judge of the U.S. Court of Appeals for the Eighth Circuit. An old and close friend and ideological ally of Mr. Chief Justice Burger, Blackmun had served for eleven years on the federal bench. His nomination was as anticlimactic as it was non-controversial. To the relief of the Senate he appeared to have impeccable credentials and, although he did not rank with the country's most distinguished jurists, he was quickly confirmed on June 22, 1970, by a vote of 94:0.

It was too late for Blackmun to participate in the remaining decisions of the 1969–70 term of Court, which had functioned with but eight Justices since May 1969, but at last the Fortas seat had been filled. There would be no further vacancies for fifteen months, but when they came President Nixon would find himself in another and multiple imbroglio.

In September 1971 terminal illness compelled the resignations of Justices Hugo Lafayette Black and John Marshall Harlan, the two most influential figures then on the highest bench. Both were veritable giants of the law, often on different jurisprudential tracks but imbued with dedication, intelligence, and judicial excellence. Their places would be incredibly hard to fill, and the President would have to search long and diligently for worthy successors. Yet he did neither. Instead he resorted to the "trial balloon" method and had names leaked to the press.

Thus in early October it became apparent that his first choice was Republican Representative Richard H. Poff of Virginia. Although Poff had less than two years' experience in legal practice, he was an able and fair member of the House Committee on the Judiciary and apparently filled the President's "Southern seat" prescriptions. But newsmen were quick to uncover civil-rights skeletons in the Poff closet, and while the Senate might have confirmed him, given his over-all ability and his popularity among his colleagues, it would not have done so without a battle. Poff asked the President to withdraw his name from consideration in order to save his family and himself from an embarrassing, damaging experience. (In 1972 he resigned from Congress to become a Justice of the Supreme Court of Appeals of Virginia, the highest tribunal of that state.)

The President now decided to send for appraisal a list of six potential nominees to the Committee on the Judiciary of the American Bar Association, the influential group that had endorsed the Haynsworth and Carswell candidacies. The list, which was widely publicized in the media, was singularly marginal in terms of distinction and stature. It was headed by California State Court of Appeals Judge Mildred Lillie (the first woman to be considered for nomination) and Arkansas municipal-bond lawyer Herschel H. Friday, a good friend of Attorney General and Mrs. John N. Mitchell and recommended by Mr. Chief Justice Burger and Mr. Justice Blackmun. The other four potential nominees were Sylvia Bacon, a judge on the Superior Court of the District of Columbia (seven months of bench experience) and part-author of the "no knock" search and "preventive detection" provisions of the District of Columbia crime bill; Senator Robert C. Byrd (D.-W.Va.), longtime opponent of civil rights legislation and ex-member of the Ku Klux Klan who, although a graduate of law school, had never

practiced law; and two recent Nixon appointees to the U.S. Court of Appeals for the Fifth Circuit, Charles Clark of Mississippi and Paul H. Roney of Florida, with a combined total of three years of judicial experience. It is not surprising that the President's selections were widely criticized as manifesting a "relentless pursuit of mediocrity." The American Bar Association, in an uncharacteristically frank statement, urged the President to "add some people with stature," and its Committee on the Judiciary quickly ranked the Administration's two top choices, Mrs. Lillie and Mr. Friday, "unqualified" and "not opposed," respectively. When the Committee's action became public—it and the Department of Justice accused each other of leaking the data to the media—the President angrily withdrew the list of "The Six," and the Attorney General announced that he would no longer submit Supreme Court nominees (as contrasted with lower federal judicial candidates) to the Committee for rating purposes. The Committee, in turn, announced that it would not be prevented from issuing evaluative post-nomination commentaries.

In a dramatic television broadcast President Nixon subsequently revealed to the country his "formal" nominees, whom he had evidently held in reserve. Possibly, as a number of commentators had charged, he did not really expect support of his initial slate and assuredly not of the first two—although the Administration indignantly and conceivably quite truthfully denied any such assumption. The two new selectees were of infinitely higher calibre than "The Six." This was especially true of the person the President identified first, Lewis F. Powell, Jr., of Richmond, Virginia. Powell was a past President of the American Bar Association, a distinguished member of the legal profession in the Harlan mold with recorded views on criminal justice and governmental "paternalism" akin to those of the President. Here then was the President's "Southern strict constructionist"! And not only was his designation received enthusiastically but it was confirmed rapidly by a vote of 89:1, the sole negative vote being cast by Senator Fred R. Harris (D.-Okla.). It was thus crystal clear that the Senate would not refuse to confirm a qualified nominee from the South.

For the second vacancy Mr. Nixon nominated a far more controversial figure: the relatively youthful (forty-seven) William H. Rehnquist of Arizona, an U.S. Assistant Attorney General. Rehnquist was a brilliant ideological conservative who had been one of Senator Barry Goldwater's chief aides in the latter's unsuccessful 1964 campaign for the Presidency. Rehnquist's career had been chiefly political, but his legal credentials were considerable, including a stint as a law clerk on the Supreme Court to Mr. Justice Robert H. Jackson—one of the truly coveted posts for a young attorney. A fine lawyer with a quick, lucid mind, he stood considerably to the right of both Powell and perhaps the President himself. It was thus not surprising that his nomination would engender opposition from a number of segments in and out of the Senate—including the American Civil Liberties Union which, for the first time in its fifty-two-year history, formally fought a nominee for public office. Rehnquist came under strong attack, especially for his championship of such "law and order" issues as preventive detention, limited immunity against compulsory self-incrimination, "no knock" police entries, and wire tapping and eavesdropping; for his hawkish defense posture and advocacy of broad-gauged Presidential war powers; and for his tough stance against street demonstrators. But these were, after all, ideological commitments shared by a great many members of the body politic—quite conceivably by a plurality. Thus, although his confirmation was delayed for a number of weeks it came with a margin of forty-two votes in December 1971.

The country seemed to breathe a sigh of relief at being spared another Haynsworth-Carswell episode, which almost certainly would have resulted had the President persisted in selecting nominees from "The Six." Had it not been for the many wounds sustained by the governmental and confidence process, and had the preceding two years not been so potentially damaging to the prestige and posture of the Supreme Court, one might have regarded these struggles as a salutary educational experience for America's citizenry. They had certainly served to alert the public to both the substance and the procedure of the power struggle that periodically brushes the system

of separation of powers and its attendant checks and balances....

The Burger Court Moves Cautiously

Those who predicted (or hoped) for an immediate counterrevolution by the Burger Court in the area of the criminal process may have been disappointed. Several reasons for the Court's failure to make quick and decisive reversals of Warren Court decisions have been advanced. First, although the Supreme Court has written well over 10,000 opinions since 1789, filling more than 430 volumes, it has overruled itself in fewer than 150 cases.[11] Second, the doctrine of *stare decisis* (let the precedent stand) has always been an integral part of the functioning and operation of the Supreme Court.[12] The Warren Court overruled comparatively few earlier decisions[13]; many of the issues rele-

---

[11]Ernst, M., *The Great Reversals* (1973); Friedman, L., and Israel, F., *The Justices of the United States Supreme Court: 1789–1969* at 3257–3265 (vol. IV 1969), listing 133 decisions overruled as of June, 1969. See also Appendix C.

[12]Cardozo, B., *The Nature of the Judicial Process* (1928). For a view that the Supreme Court has departed too far from the respect for precedent, see Bischoff, R., *The Role of Official Precedents*, in Cahn, E. (ed.), *Supreme Court and Supreme Law* (1954). For a more recent view that the Court has abrogated the principles of *stare decisis*, see Fleming, M., *The Price of Perfect Justice* (1974). See also the dissenting opinion of Mr. Justice Brennan in *Stone* v. *Powell*, 428 U.S. 465 (1976) (Chapter Five, § 5.03).

[13]Among those prior decisions overruled by the Warren Court are *Wolf* v. *Colorado*, 338 U.S. 25 (1949) (overruled by *Mapp* v. *Ohio*, 367 U.S. 643 [1961] [Chapter Five, § 5.03]); *Frank* v. *Maryland*, 359 U.S. 360 (1959) (overruled by *Camara* v. *Municipal Court*, 387 U.S. 523 [1967] and *See* v. *City of Seattle*, 387 U.S. 541 [1967] [Chapter Five, § 5.02]); *Olmstead* v. *United States*, 277 U.S. 438 (1928) (overruled by *Katz* v. *United States*, 389 U.S. 347 [1967] [Chapter Five, § 5.01]); *Twining* v. *New Jersey*, 211 U.S. 78 (1908) (overruled by *Malloy* v. *Hogan*, 378 U.S. 1 [1964] [Chapter Six, § 6.03]); *Adamson* v. *California*, 332 U.S. 46 (1947) (Chapter Three, § 3.04) (overruled by *Griffin* v. *California*, 380 U.S. 609 [1965]); *Betts* v. *Brady*, 316 U.S. 455 (1942) (overruled by *Gideon* v. *Wainwright*, 372 U.S. 335 [1963] [Chapter

Footnote continued on opposite page

vant to the criminal process that were decided by the Warren Court were being examined for the first time. Third, the Supreme Court is a governmental-political institution and must maintain an image of stability and relative predictability,[14] since otherwise, it is argued, no person could rely on principles of constitutional law over time with any degree of certainty. The judicial process and judicial integrity demand no less. Fourth, as Professor Amsterdam notes,[15] the Supreme Court is a committee, and a group is less likely than a single individual to be despotic in its decision-making and is more likely to ponder all the relevant facts before reaching a decision. It is often said that a camel is actually a horse drafted by a committee. According to Professor Amsterdam, the Supreme Court, in attempting to draw a horse, puts very short lines on a large sheet of paper, and all the while the membership of the Court is constantly changing. Parenthetically, some critics of the Court might suggest (perhaps unfairly) that today's camel has become a jackass. Fifth, the Supreme Court has a long-standing (although self-imposed) rule that it will not decide cases on broader legal grounds than are necessary.[16] This use of the narrowest possible grounds often enables the Court to distinguish between cases that at first blush appear to present very similar issues. By individualizing cases in this way, the Court limits the number of overruled decisions, since a reversal in the case may have little or no effect on other cases. Finally, the Supreme Court, in most instances, will not decide a case on constitutional grounds if other (nonconstitutional) legal grounds will suffice. The Court can avoid constitutional decisions (1) if it finds that a state court decided an issue on adequate state grounds[17]; (2) on the basis of its supervisory power over the federal courts[18]; (3) by refusing to grant certiorari (p. 24); or (4) by dismissing a case because of jurisdictional problems (p. 21). Thus, the Burger Court has not, to date, found it necessary to overrule many of the more controversial decisions of the Warren Court. However, a number of decisions by the Burger Court in the area of the criminal process have been the subject of considerable controversy among many critics of the Court (including some of its members).[19] The degree to which the newest member of the Court, Mr. Justice Stevens, will join the ranks of the "conservative" Nixon wing (Burger, Black-

---

Seven, § 7.02]); *Palko* v. *Connecticut*, 302 U.S. 319 (1937) (overruled by *Benton* v. *Maryland*, 395 U.S. 784 [1969] [Chapter Three, § 3.04]); *Delli Paoli* v. *United States*, 352 U.S. 232 (1957) (overruled by *Bruton* v. *United States*, 391 U.S. 123 [1968] [Chapter Seven, § 7.03]); *Rabinowitz* v. *United States*, 339 U. S. 56 (1959) (overruled by *Chimel* v. *California*, 395 U.S. 752 [1969] [Chapter Five, § 5.04]); *Pace* v. *Alabama*, 106 U.S. 583 (1883) (overruled by *McLaughlin* v. *Florida*, 379 U.S. 184 [1964]). A complete list of overruled decisions involving criminal procedure is presented in Appendix C.

[14]Jackson, R., *The Supreme Court in the American System of Government* (1955). See also Pfeffer, L., *This Honorable Court: A History of the United States Supreme Court* (1965); Levy, L. (ed.), *Judicial Review and the Supreme Court* (1967); Cahn, E. (ed.), *Supreme Court and Supreme Law* (1954); McCloskey, R., *The Modern Supreme Court* (1972); Wasby, S., *The Impact of the United States Supreme Court: Some Perspectives* (1970).

[15]Amsterdam, A., *Perspectives on the Fourth Amendment*, 58 Minn. L. Rev. 349 (1974).

[16]*Ashwander* v. *Tennessee Valley Authority*, 297 U.S. 288, 345–348 (1936) (Brandeis, J., con-

curring). See §1.05, infra. Professor Shapiro has listed three factors that should govern judicial restraint in judicial pronouncements: "(1)... an opinion of the Court should not normally rule or express views on controversial issues that are not necessary to disposition of the case; (2)... while it is appropriate for a concurring opinion to point out questions not decided or necessary to the decision, it is far less appropriate for a concurrence to attempt to resolve these questions; and (3)... it is a highly questionable tactic for a dissenter to accuse the majority of adopting a rationale that it has not used, or of deciding cases it has purported not to decide, or to take a stand on issues not considered by the Court and not necessary to the dissent." Shapiro, D., note 6 supra, at 341.

[17]See, e.g., *Murdock* v. *Memphis,* 87 U.S. 596 (1874); *Fay* v. *Noia,* 372 U.S. 391 (1963); *California* v. *Krivda,* 409 U.S. 33 (1972).

[18]See, e.g., *McNabb* v. *United States,* 318 U.S. 332 (1943) and *Mallory* v. *United States,* 354 U.S. 449 (1959) (Chapter Six, § 6.03, Comments, p. 419; *United States* v. *Russell,* 411 U.S. 423 (1973) and *Hampton* v. *United States* 96 S. Ct. 1646 (1976) (Chapter Six, § 6.03).

[19]For example, in the words of Mr. Justice Brennan, the 1975–1976 term marked a "con-

Footnote continued on page 16

mun, Powell, and Rehnquist) or will be influenced by the more "liberal" wing of the Court (Brennan and Marshall) is unclear. A preliminary analysis suggests that Stevens' judicial philosophy may be closer to that of Justices White and Stewart (the so-called "swing voters").[20] However, such an assessment of Justice Stevens may be premature.[21]

Although it can hardly be said that the members of the Burger Court are "strict constructionists" in the traditional sense of the term,[22] a careful reading of its opinions suggests that a "law and order" mood has become a dominant characteristic of the present court.[23]

The Burger Court: Law and Order Philosophy?*

In a figurative sense, Richard M. Nixon now and for an indefinite period in the future casts four votes in criminal-justice

*Abridgement of pp. 421–423, 437–441, *Against the Law: The Nixon Court and Criminal Justice* by Leonard W. Levy. Copyright © 1974 by Clio Enterprises Co. By permission of Harper & Row, Publishers, Inc.

tinuing evisceration of Fourth Amendment protections." *United States* v. *Martinez-Fuerte*, 96 S. Ct. 3074 (1976) (Brennan, J., joined by Marshall, J., dissenting) (Chapter Five, § 5.04).

[20] For example, during Mr. Justice Stevens' first term on the Court (1975–1976), he participated in 19 decisions relevant to the criminal process (involving 14 constitutional issues). Stevens joined the majority in 10 of these issues, while the Nixon appointees (Burger, C.J., Blackmun, Powell, and Rehnquist, JJ.) voted together on all 14 issues resolved by the Court. For a prediction that Justice Stevens will be a "centralist, a moderate, a balancer," see Beytagh, *Mr. Justice Stevens and the Burger Court's Uncertain Trumpet*, 50 Notre Dame Lawyer 946, 951 (1976). See also Note, *Interpretation of Narrow Construction and Policy: Mr. Justice Stevens' Circuit Opinions*, 13 San Diego L. Rev. 899 (1976).

[21] The majority of the justices who served on the latter half of the Warren Court (1961–1969) were, for the most part, labeled as "liberal" by most commentators. Specifically, Chief Justice Warren and Associate Justices Brennan, Marshall, Fortas, Goldberg, Douglas, and Black were consistently labeled as having a "liberal" judicial philosophy with respect to cases involving the criminal process. Spaeth, H., *The Warren Court: Cases and Commentary* (1966). In contrast, Chief Justice Burger and Associate Justices Blackmun, Powell, and Rehnquist are said to be "conservative" with respect to issues involving the criminal process. Levy, L., *Against the Law: The Nixon Court and Criminal Justice* (1974). See note 5, supra.

[22] If there is such a judicial philosophy as "strict constructionism" perhaps Mr. Justice

Black (1937–1972) came the closest to adhering to that view. Besides viewing the First Amendment in absolute terms, Black could find no exclusionary rule in the Fourth Amendment (Chapter Five). Rather, he held that evidence illegally seized by law enforcement authorities and used against a defendant at trial violated the Fifth Amendment privilege against self-incrimination. See *Mapp* v. *Ohio*, 367 U.S. 643, 662 (1961) (Chapter Five, § 5.03). See also *Katz* v. *United States*, 389 U.S. 347, 364 (1967) (dissenting opinion) (eavesdropping by electronic means does not constitute a search and seizure within the meaning of the Fourth Amendment) (Chapter Five, § 5.01); *Griswold* v. *Connecticut*, 381 U.S. 479, 508 (1965) (dissenting opinion) (no constitutional right of privacy) (Chapter Three, § 3.04, Comments, p. 000); *In re Winship*, 397 U.S. 358, 377 (1970) (dissenting opinion) (proof of guilt beyond a reasonable doubt in criminal cases not constitutionally required) (Chapter Eight, § 8.03).

[23] For example, not a single defendant's claim prevailed with a majority of the Court in the nine Fourth Amendment cases decided during the 1975–1976 term, and none of these decisions was unanimous. For a view that the Burger Court is committed to eroding the scope of Fourth Amendment protections, see Nakell, B., *Search of a Person Incident to a Traffic Arrest: A Comment on Robinson and Gustafson*, 10 Crim. L. Bull. 827 (1974). Arthur Goldberg, former Associate Justice of the United States Supreme Court, contends that constitutional rights expand while a "liberal court" is sitting but never contract. Goldberg, A., *Equal Justice: The Warren Era of the Supreme Court* (1971).

cases decided by the Supreme Court. The Court under Burger has not veered dramatically away from the Court under Warren in other areas of constitutional law. Criminal justice is the one field that Nixon expressly desired to influence by appointing men who shared his law-and-order philosophy. Cases that deal with the rights of the criminally accused under the Fourth, Fifth, and Sixth Amendments are the largest category of cases on constitutional law decided by the Court. The trend of decision in such cases by mid-1972 was abundantly clear. By then the four Nixon appointees had been together for six months. When the term of the Court closed, in June 1972, a reporter at a press conference, referring to the President's objective of balancing the Court to strengthen the "peace forces" against the "criminal forces," asked him whether the Court was balanced yet or needed "another dose of strict constructionism if that occasion should arise." Nixon replied, ". . . I feel at the present time that the Court is as balanced as I have had an opportunity to make it." . . .

That the Nixon Court favored law-enforcement values is no surprise. Burger, Blackmun, Powell, and Rehnquist got their seats on the bench because of their supposed or known lack of sympathy for the rights of the criminally accused. In one respect they have been remarkably forbearing to date — and shrewd. They have avoided dramatic overrulings of precedents in the area of criminal justice. Precipitous repudiations of established doctrines would appear too much as an act of arbitrary will; decisions should not look like the obvious result of subjective choices. In the art of judging, a proper regard for appearances counts. One must seem to appreciate the values of coherence, stability, and continuity with the past. Judges, especially judges who are reputedly conservative, ought to avoid sudden, radical shifts in constitutional doctrine. Any man who reaches the highest court is sophisticated enough to appreciate the strategic and political values of achieving desired objectives by indirection. Overruling is a device of last resort, employed when other alternatives have failed. The Nixon Court has raised the use of alternative routes to a high art by relying on more subtle means than overruling in order to alter the course of the law. It reinterprets precedents, distinguishes them away, blunts them, obliterates them, ignores them, and makes new law without the need of overruling or being bound by the past. It nourishes the impression that it is a standpat Court, which merely refuses to endorse further expansions of the rights of the criminally accused. It cultivates the illusion, suitable to the image of a conservative court, of having some respect for precedents; at the same time, it narrows them until they become meaningless and moribund. When new cases arise it finds factual distinctions, always available, that allegedly warrant watering down the constitutional right at issue. New decisions have a corrosive effect on previous ones. While the Nixon Court goes about its quiet business of creating its own regressive "revolution" in the criminal law, striking a pose of doing no more than refusing to open new frontiers, it has systematically closed old frontiers and made daring incursions that cripple many rights of the criminally accused. . . .

The way the Court reasons or reaches its results is as important as the result itself; in the long run, perhaps, the Court's reasoning is even more important because a decision based on an unsound rationale is not likely to survive. A rationale may be unsound because it plays fast and loose with the relevant precedents or with truth; it may be overbroad, illogical, or biased; or, it may be one-dimensional by ignoring opposing arguments. The Court's respect for the judicial process, for the need to strive for objectivity even if unattainable, and for the requirements of professional expertise, in short, its craftsmanship, is a vital aspect of its work. Assessment of the Nixon Court's craftsmanship is as subjective as the art of judging, and experts will doubtless disagree, as they have about the Warren Court's craftsmanship. Concern for the validity of the route by which the Court reached its decisions is a major theme of Archibald Cox's book *The Warren Court,* the most sympathetic account yet published. Again and again, Cox subjects the Court's opinions to the scrutiny of an analytical, questioning mind, and again and again he fretted because the Court, though having reached the just result, failed to convince its critics. Nevertheless, Charles Alan Wright, a conservative constitutional lawyer, writing when criticism of the Warren Court reached a fever pitch, asked, "What Court in the past achieved a higher level of professional craftsmanship than the present Court? The great opinions of Chief Justice Marshall surely fail the test. . . . Has any later Court done better?"

The Nixon Court has done a lot worse in its criminal-justice opinions. It does not confront complicated constitutional questions with appropriate disinterestedness. Its opinions do not provide intellectually convincing explanations for its results. Far too often the majority simply issues edicts. Its fiat cannot command respect when the majority abuses or ignores precedents or refuses to consider fairly and seriously the arguments advanced by dissenting opinions. The majority faces away from, instead of facing, opposing views. There is too little debate in majority opinions. They fail to weigh criticisms. In brief, they do not develop carefully reasoned judgments. The majority seems to engage in result-oriented adjudication which is a corruption of the judicial process that leaves too far behind the idea of the rule of law enforced by impersonal and impartial judges. In constitutional cases, as in any other, the judge who first chooses what the outcome should be and then reasons backwards to supply a rationalization, replete with rules and precedents, has betrayed his calling: Having decided on the basis of prejudice or prejudgment, he has made constitutional law little more than the embodiment of his own policy preferences.

The Nixon Court writes opinions that have the sound of stump speeches for the prosecution. The majority Justices stand for law and order, but there is little reason to respect their work when they do not respect their dissenting brethren or critics who ask if there is something called law and the Constitution to which decisions should conform. The decisions of the Court represent what the majority at the moment happen to think is best for the country, but they do not persuade anyone who believes that a judge who does his job faithfully will with some regularity reach judgments that conflict with his personal views as a private citizen. . . .

The Bill of Rights requires an ardently sympathetic if not a liberal activist Court. There is no way for the guarantees of the Bill of Rights to have real meaning if not enforced by unstinting judicial affirmations

that keep restraints upon government. No one wants to hobble law enforcement, no one wants the Bill of Rights to rot, and no one has ever proved that law enforcement cannot be effective against crime and be observant of the Bill of Rights at the same time. The fundamental law is an instrument of society, existing not as art does for art's sake but as a means for the sake of society's ends. Society requires a risky degree of freedom as well as an unremitting attack on the causes of crime and on lawbreakers, even when the culprit is a policeman, a prosecutor, or a President. If officials protect society by any means at hand, they trade freedom for security. Any means to a justifiable end is, in a free society, a noxious and dangerous doctrine.

The Nixon Court surrendered to that doctrine when it condoned admittedly illegal police practices, sanctioned the use of illegal evidence, allowed warrantless searches and seizures unrelated to the cause of arrest, upheld the prosecution's failure to disclose evidence of value to the accused, permitted unknowing waivers of rights, and denied the effective assistance of counsel. Regrettably, one can expand this list showing the Court's determination to find means to sanitize or legitimize law-enforcement conduct that brings shame on the administration of the criminal-justice system. Stunting the Fourth, Fifth, and Sixth Amendment rights of the criminally accused may increase the prison population but will not have any effect on crime nor help solve its causes, any more than the Nixon Administration's habitual juggling of crime statistics can prove that crime is no longer a problem.

The trouble with the Administration's reports of crime statistics is, as *Time* said, that they are "like a set of crooked corporate books — deceptive." The President himself assured the nation that "the hour of crisis has passed" because of the dip in the urban crime rate. He did not mention that the cities to which he referred declined in population or that violent crime was still on the increase, especially in the suburbs, although the rate of increase is slowing down. Only a week later, in another speech scorning "soft-headed judges," Nixon recommended extremely harsh penalties for criminals. Despite the supposed passing of the crime crisis, there has been an unprecedented government crime wave, prompting a wag to suggest that Nixon took crime off the streets and put it in the White House.

There is a subtle danger that the Nixonian ethic may penetrate the chambers of the Supreme Court. After the close of the 1972–73 term, one Washington lawyer ominously remarked, "The Court has been Nixonized." He meant only that "Nixon has left his stamp on the Court, and consequently on American law. It could last for a generation." But the Court's fidelity to the Bill of Rights has become dangerously attenuated. Its integrity is at issue when it winks at official lawlessness, warps precedents, or reasons woefully.

A hieromancer can read the entrails of a sacrificial chicken for portents of the future. Anyone adept at that art knows that the Nixon Court will continue to undermine many criminal-justice achievements of the Warren Court. Those not skilled at reading entrails predicted that the Nixon appointees, being conservative jurists, would respect not subvert precedents. All of us who possess perfect hindsight can now decipher the writings in the ashes of an increasing number of opinions that for all practical purposes are dead. . . .

1.02   THE FEDERAL COURTS

Federal Judicial Review

It is well settled that federal courts do not have jurisdiction beyond that authorized by the United States Constitution. Federal courts have **limited jurisdiction,** as opposed to state courts, which often have general jurisdiction over various claims and disputes between parties. As noted by a federal district court[24]:

For the federal courts, jurisdiction is not automatic and cannot be presumed. Thus, the presumption in each instance is that a federal court lacks jurisdiction until it can be shown that a specific grant of jurisdiction applies. Federal courts may exercise only that judicial power provided by the Constitution in Article III and conferred by Congress. All other judicial power or jurisdiction is reserved to the states. And . . . it seems settled that federal courts may assume only that portion of the Article III judicial power which Congress, by statute, entrusts to them. Simply

stated, Congress may impart as much or as little of the judicial power as it deems appropriate and the Judiciary may not thereafter on its own motion recur to the Article III storehouse for additional jurisdiction. When it comes to jurisdiction of the federal courts, truly, to paraphrase the Scripture, the Congress giveth, and the Congress taketh away.

In addition, federal court jurisdiction must be proved by a party seeking to invoke its jurisdiction and cannot be conferred or established by consent of both parties or by waiver of either party. "Absent federal jurisdiction, no judgment of a federal court can stand."

State courts in some instances have concurrent jurisdiction with the federal courts; that is, state courts are often called upon to resolve certain federal questions. For example, in a state criminal trial, the trial court is often asked to decide whether a search and seizure by the police was unreasonable in light of the Fourth Amendment to the United States Constitution. Many other federal questions are often decided by state courts; however, state court resolutions of federal questions are often reviewed by the federal courts. One might ask how it is possible that the lowest federal court (United States district court) has jurisdiction to review and perhaps overturn a decision of a state's highest court? Article VI, Section 2 of the United States Constitution provides, inter alia: "This Constitution and the Laws of the United States which shall be made in Pursuance thereof . . . shall be the *supreme law of the Land. . .*" (emphasis added). (This provision is known as the Supremacy Clause.) While the Constitution does not expressly provide which branch or agency of government shall have the authority to interpret its provisions and laws and enforce the Supremacy Clause, this issue was resolved early in our judicial history in the landmark decision *Marbury* v. *Madison,* 1 Cranch 137 (1803).

In that case, Chief Justice John Marshall, writing for the Court, held that the federal courts have the authority to hold acts of Congress unconstitutional and that it is the "duty of the judicial department, to say what the law is." Thus, the doctrine of judicial review was established, crystallizing the role of the United States Supreme Court as the final interpreter of the Constitution with respect to all-important federal issues. Indeed, *Marbury* has never been overruled,

---

[24]*Senate Select Committee on Presidential Campaign Activities* v. *Nixon,* 366 F. Supp. 51, 55 (D.D.C. 1973).

and the principles announced in that case were reiterated in *United States* v. *Nixon,* 418 U.S. 683 (1974), in which a unanimous Supreme Court rejected a presidential claim of an absolute, unqualified executive privilege and consequent immunity from the judicial process. Although some legal historians have suggested that shortly after the *Marbury* decision was announced Chief Justice Marshall was willing to abandon the doctrine of judicial supremacy in return for security against impeachment, the doctrine of judicial review has survived the legal debates it was bound to generate, and its demise is not likely to occur in the foreseeable future.

In the 50 years following the *Marbury* decision, not a single act of Congress was declared unconstitutional until the famous *Dred Scott* decision in 1857.[25] Shortly after *Marbury*, the Supreme Court held the doctrine of judicial review to be applicable to the acts of state legislatures[26] and decisions of state courts[27] in order to implement the supremacy of the United States Constitution. From 1803 to 1857, only 36 state statutes were declared unconstitutional by the Supreme Court. However, these cases represented only a small percentage of those in which the constitutionality of a state statute was contested, because acts of legislatures (Congress and state) are *presumed to be constitutional* and the burden of proving a constitutional infirmity usually lies with the party seeking to have the legislation overturned. Despite this often heavy bur-

den, of the 177 cases argued before the Court during the 1972–1973 term, 57 involved claims that a state or federal statute (or city ordinance) was in conflict with the federal Constitution, and many of these claims were sustained by the Court. Today, the increasing number of such cases coming before the Supreme Court has become a matter of increasing concern to some legal authorities—most notably Chief Justice Burger.[28] Although Burger obviously doesn't favor abandoning the doctrine of judicial review (he wrote the opinion for the unanimous Court in *United States* v. *Nixon,* supra), he is greatly concerned over what seems to him to be an overloaded Supreme Court docket. (See Table 1.1, § 1.06.) However, at the same time, Mr. Justice Douglas felt that the Court should review more cases.[29]

Article III of the United States Constitution (1787)

Section 1. The judicial Power of the United States, shall be vested in one supreme Court, and in such inferior Courts as

---

[25]The court held that slaves were not "citizens" within the meaning of the United States Constitution. *Dred Scott* v. *Sanford,* 60 U.S. (19 How.) 393.

From the beginning until June, 1969, the Supreme Court held 86 acts of Congress unconstitutional. See Friedman and Israel, note 11 supra, at 3240–3256. In examining the period from June, 1969, through January, 1977, the authors found six additional acts of Congress that were declared unconstitutional by the Burger Court. See *Schacht* v. *United States,* 398 U.S. 58 (1970); *Oregon* v. *Mitchell,* 400 U.S. 112 (1970) (in part); *Blount* v. *Rizzi,* 400 U.S. 410 (1971); *U.S. Dept. of Agriculture* v. *Moreno,* 413 U.S. 528 (1973); and *Jiminez* v. *Weinberger,* 417 U.S. 628 (1974).

[26]*Fletcher* v. *Peck,* 10 U.S. 87 (1810).

[27]*Martin* v. *Hunter's Lessee,* 14 U.S. 562 (1816); *Cohens* v. *Virginia,* 19 U.S. 82 (1921).

---

[28]See Burger, W., *State of the Federal Judiciary* (Aug. 10, 1970), 90 S. Ct. 2381 (1970).

[29]Douglas, W. O., *Go East Young Man* (1974). See § 1.05, infra. See also *Tidewater Oil Company* v. *United States,* 409 U.S. 151, 174, 177 (Douglas, J., dissenting) ("the case for our 'overwork' is a myth"; "members of the Court have vast leisure time") and Countryman, V., *The Judicial Record of Justice William O. Douglas* (1974). It is worth noting that Justice Douglas has stated that he has a photographic memory.

The Court's caseload has increased steadily, reaching a total of 4,761 cases on the docket for the term ending July, 1976 (see Table 1.1, infra). The increase has been rapid in recent years. In 1960, only 2,313 cases were on the docket, and in 1945, only 1,460. Plenary (full) review, with oral arguments by attorneys, is granted in about 150 to 180 cases per term. Formal written opinions are delivered in about 125 to 160 cases. Approximately 200 additional cases, primarily on appeal (as opposed to certiorari), are disposed of without granting plenary review. The written opinions in a term, including concurring and dissenting opinions and memorandum orders, sometimes exceed 5,000 pages. Some opinions are revised a dozen or more times before they are announced.

the Congress may from time to time ordain and establish. . . .

Section 2. (1) The judicial Power shall extend to all Cases, in Law and Equity, arising under this Constitution, and the Laws of the United States, and Treaties made, or which shall be made, under their Authority; — to all Cases affecting Ambassadors, other public Ministers and Consuls; — to all Cases of admiralty and maritime Jurisdiction; — to Controversies to which the United States shall be a Party; — to Controversies between two or more states; — between a State and Citizens of another State; — between Citizens of different States; — between Citizens of the same State claiming Lands under the Grants of different States, and between a State, or the Citizens thereof, and foreign States, Citizens or Subjects.

(2) In all Cases affecting Ambassadors, other public Ministers and Consuls, and those in which a State shall be a Party, the supreme Court shall have original Jurisdiction. In all other Cases before mentioned, the supreme Court shall have appellate Jurisdiction, both as to Law and Fact, with such Exceptions, and under such Regulations as the Congress shall make.

Jurisdiction of the Supreme Court

Article III of the Constitution, supra, confers the primary jurisdiction of the Supreme Court; and that Court is the only judicial tribunal specifically mentioned in that document. Section 1 of Article III provides that "the judicial Power of the United States, shall be vested in one supreme Court, and in such inferior Courts as the Congress may from time to time ordain and establish." Section 8 of Article I gives the Congress power "to constitute Tribunals inferior to the supreme Court." Accordingly, the Congress (under the Judiciary Act of 1789) divided the United States into thirteen districts and provided for a district court in each district. In 1891, the Congress created new circuit courts of appeals with jurisdiction to review most district court decisions. In 1925, the Congress (under the "Judges Bill") introduced the discretionary writ of certiorari, which narrowed the mandatory jurisdiction of the Supreme Court. Today, the (Article III) federal courts consist of United States district courts (94), courts of appeals (11) (Fig. 1–1), and the Supreme Court. There is at least one district court in each state and the District of Columbia and larger states (e.g., New York, California) have four district courts. The district courts are the principal federal trial courts. The courts of appeals primarily review district court decisions and many types of federal administrative orders. The jurisdiction of the United States Supreme Court is, for the most part, appellate and discretionary. The Supreme Court alone (as a rule) has authority to review directly the decisions of the highest state courts on federal questions. In addition to these courts, the Congress has, through the years, created various specialized federal courts.[30]

Other sections of Article III are relevant to the jurisdiction of federal courts. Section 2 extends the "judicial Power" to "all Cases . . . arising under this Constitution, the Laws of the United States [federal laws], and Treaties made, or which shall be made, under their Authority" and to "all Cases of admiralty and maritime Jurisdiction." In addition, Article III states that the Supreme Court shall have *original jurisdiction* under certain circumstances (see p. 23) — most importantly, in "those in which a State shall be a Party." In all other cases "the supreme Court shall have appellate Jurisdiction, both as to Law and Fact, with such Exceptions, and under such Regulations as the Congress shall make." In the only significant case[31] in which Congress attempted to restrict the Supreme Court's jurisdiction, the Court deferred to the congressional will. However, most attempts to override some of the Supreme Court's "unpopular" decisions through contrary federal legislation have failed. It is clear that Congress cannot confer jurisdiction on the Supreme Court greater than that authorized by Article III.

Today, Article III and 28 U.S.C. §§ 1251– 1257 and 18 U.S.C. § 3731 (which implement

---

[30]Other "inferior courts" created by Congress include the United States Tax Court, Court of Customs and Patent Appeals, and Court of Claims. These courts, for the most part, are unimportant to the criminal process.

[31]*Ex parte McCardle*, 74 U.S. 506 (1869).

Figure 1–1 The eleven federal judicial circuits. (See 28 U.S.C.A. § 41.) From Forrester, R., Currier, T. S., and Moye, J. E., *Federal Jurisdiction and Procedure*. St. Paul, West Publishing Co., 1970, p. 6.

Article III) provide for the basic jurisdiction of the Supreme Court, and these statutes have given rise to a highly technical body of jurisprudence. In summary, the Supreme Court has jurisdiction to review all lower federal court and state court cases as to the effect or meaning of a federal statute, a constitutional right or immunity, or a treaty when such an issue is properly raised.

In the remainder of this section, we will discuss the four principal methods by which a "Case" or "Controversy" can reach the Supreme Court.

Original Jurisdiction. Article III of the United States Constitution makes it clear that the Supreme Court possesses two types of jurisdiction: *original* and *appellate.*

The original jurisdiction of the Supreme Court grants the Court the power to be the trier of fact and law in certain cases and controversies. This jurisdiction is rarely exercised and almost never involves an issue relevant to the criminal process. The most numerous class of suits decided by the Supreme Court under its original jurisdiction consists of suits by one state against another. Most often the Court is asked to resolve disputes as to boundaries or water rights between states. During the 1975–1976 Term, in only one instance did the Court exercise its original jurisdiction to decide a case on the merits.

Appellate Jurisdiction. Under its appellate jurisdiction, the Supreme Court may receive cases in one of three principal ways: *by certification, on appeal,* or *by a writ of certiorari.*

Certification. On occasion, a United States court of appeals (an intermediate federal appellate court) will request that the Supreme Court review a case in which a point of law is unclear. *Certification* may involve instructions on any question of law in either a civil or criminal case and is governed by federal statute.[32] It is generally accepted that only the courts of appeals may request certification, not the parties to the lawsuit. Although the federal statutes governing certification purport to make it obligatory for the Supreme Court to decide cases sent up in this manner, there are many instances in which the Supreme Court might find jurisdiction on certificate to be improper. Thus, the granting of review by the court on certificate is, in fact, *discretionary.* Few important criminal cases are reviewed by the Supreme Court on certificate.

Appeal (Direct Appeal). In some instances, appellate review by the Supreme Court (as a matter of right) is made obligatory via congressional acts. With this type of review, cases come to the Supreme Court *on appeal* (or *on direct appeal*) in which review of decisions of lower federal courts, as well as of state courts of last resort, is sought. The Supreme Court will review, *on appeal,* final judgments of the highest court of a state in which a decision could be rendered (1) when a state court has held a treaty or federal statute to be unconstitutional; or (2) when a state court has upheld a state law or provision in a state constitution against a challenge that it is in conflict with a federal statute or the United States Constitution.[33]

Within the federal system, the Supreme Court will review cases *on direct appeal* from a lower federal court when (1) a district court has held that a federal statute is invalid and accordingly dismissed an indictment or arrested a judgment upon which the indictment was founded; (2) when a court of appeals has held that a state law is repugnant to a federal statute or the United States Constitution; (3) when a three-judge district court has granted or denied an interlocutory or permanent injunction in any civil action, suit, or proceeding; or (4) when a federal court has held any act of Congress to be unconstitutional in any civil action, suit, or proceeding in which the United States is a party. (See "Selected Federal Statutes," infra.)

In each instance, review by the Supreme Court on direct appeal is available only when a *substantial federal question* is presented and at least four (out of nine) of the justices agree on that point. Otherwise, the appeal will be dismissed for any of a variety of reasons. Two commonly given reasons are (1) "for want of a substantial federal question," and (2) "for want of jurisdiction." However, when a case presented for review comes on direct appeal, a dismissal

---

[32] See 28 U.S.C.A. § 1254(3), infra.

[33] See 28 U.S.C. § 1257, infra.

by summary action is a decision *on the merits*[34]; that is, the judgment of the last court is considered a disposition on the merits and carries precedential weight. Thus, so-called "Mandatory review" by the Supreme Court on direct appeal is actually discretionary to a large extent, as is the remaining method by which a case comes to the Supreme Court for review, the *writ of certiorari.*

Writ of Certiorari. Most cases decided by the Supreme Court under its appellate jurisdiction come on writ of certiorari, a *discretionary writ* authorized by Congress in 1925. The major purpose of this method of gaining appellate review is to allow the Supreme Court authority to control, to some extent, its own docket and to review only those cases that present substantial constitutional or federal questions. In all but a few cases, the Court declines to accept for review those lower court decisions (federal and state) brought up on certiorari. For example, in the 1975–1976 Term, only 221 of the 3,806 cases filed with the Supreme Court were granted certiorari (5 per cent). The reason for dismissal is generally one of *judicial economy* (the Court simply does not have the resources to fully review the large number of cases filed) or the lack of *significant federal issues* that deserve the Court's attention.

As with cases filed on direct appeal, the so-called "rule of four" prevails. Four justices must agree that a case presents a substantial federal or constitutional question before certiorari will be granted. However, unlike dismissal on direct appeal, a dismissal from a writ of certiorari is *not* a decision on the merits of the case. The dismissal's only legal effect is to allow the decision of the last lower court to stand; it is not a disposition on the merits and it does not signify that the Supreme Court agrees with the legal conclusions of the lower courts. Such a dismissal simply means that four justices, for various reasons usually not disclosed, were unwilling to review that particular case.

---

[34]*Hicks* v. *Miranda*, 422 U.S. 332, 343–345 (1975).

Selected Federal Statutes

28 U.S.C.A. § 1251. Original jurisdiction

(a) The Supreme Court shall have original and exclusive jurisdiction of:

(1) All controversies between two or more States;

(2) All actions or proceedings against ambassadors or other public ministers of foreign states or their domestics or domestic servants, not inconsistent with the law of nations.

(b) The Supreme Court shall have original but not exclusive jurisdiction of:

(1) All actions or proceedings brought by ambassadors or other public ministers of foreign states or to which consuls or vice consuls of foreign states are parties;

(2) All controversies between the United States and a State;

(3) All actions or proceedings by a State against the citizens of another State or against aliens.

28 U.S.C.A. § 1252. Direct appeals from decisions invalidating Acts of Congress

Any party may appeal to the Supreme Court from an interlocutory or final judgment, decree or order of any court of the United States ... holding an Act of Congress unconstitutional in any civil action, suit, or proceeding to which the United States ... is a party.

28 U.S.C.A. § 1254. Courts of appeals; certiorari; appeal; certified questions

Cases in the courts of appeals may be reviewed by the Supreme Court by the following methods:

(1) By writ of certiorari granted upon the petition of any party to any civil or criminal case, before or after rendition of judgment or decree;

(2) By appeal by a party relying on a State statute held by a court of appeals to be invalid as repugnant to the Constitution, treaties or laws of the United States, but such appeal shall preclude review by writ of

certiorari at the instance of such appellant, and the review on appeal shall be restricted to the Federal questions presented[35];

(3) By certification at any time by a court of appeals of any question of law in any civil or criminal cases as to which instructions are desired, and upon such certification the Supreme Court may give binding instructions or require the entire record to be sent up for decision of the entire matter in controversy.[36]

28 U.S.C.A. § 1257. State courts; appeal; certiorari

Final judgments or decrees rendered by the highest court of a State in which a decision could be had, may be reviewed by the Supreme Court as follows:

(1) By appeal, where is drawn in question the validity of a treaty or statute of the United States and the decision is against its validity.

(2) By appeal, where is drawn in question the validity of a statute of any State on the ground of its being repugnant to the Constitution, treaties or laws of the United States, and the decision is in favor of its validity.

(3) By writ of certiorari, where the validity of a treaty or statute of the United States is drawn in question on the ground of its being repugnant to the Constitution, treaties or laws of the United States, or where any title, right, privilege or immunity is specially set up or claimed under the Constitution, treaties or statutes of, or commission held or authority exercised under, the United States.

28 U.S.C.A. § 1651. Writs

(a) The Supreme Court and all courts established by Act of Congress may issue all writs necessary or appropriate in aid of their respective jurisdictions and agreeable to the usages and principles of law.

(b) An alternative writ ... may be issued

by a justice or judge of a court which has jurisdiction.

28 U.S.C.A. § 2103. Appeal from State court or from a United States court of appeals improvidently taken regarded as petition for writ of certiorari

If an appeal to the Supreme Court is improvidently taken ... in a case where the proper mode of review is by petition for certiorari, this alone shall not be grounds for dismissal; but the papers whereon the appeal was taken shall be regarded and acted on as a petition for writ of certiorari and as if duly presented to the Supreme Court at the time the appeal was taken....

18 U.S.C.A. § 3731. Appeal by United States

An appeal may be taken by and on behalf of the United States from the district courts direct to the Supreme Court of the United States in all *criminal cases* [emphasis added] in the following instances:

From a decision or judgment setting aside or dismissing any indictment or information, or any count thereof, or arresting judgment, where the decision is based on the invalidity of the statute upon which the indictment or information is founded.

From a decision arresting a judgment of conviction for insufficiency of the indictment or information, where such decision is based upon the invalidity or construction of the statute upon which the indictment or information is founded.

An appeal may be taken by and on behalf of the United States from the district courts to a court of appeals in all *criminal cases* [emphasis added] in the following instances:

From a decision arresting a judgment of conviction except where a direct appeal to the Supreme Court of the United States is provided by this section.

The appeal in all such cases shall be taken within thirty days after the decision or judgment has been rendered and shall be diligently prosecuted.

Pending the prosecution and determination of the appeal in the foregoing instances, the defendant shall be admitted to bail on his own recognizance.

---

[35]See, e.g., *Doran* v. *Salem Inn, Inc.*, 422 U.S. 922 (1975).

[36]See, e.g., *Moody* v. *Albemarle Paper Co.*, 417 U.S. 622 (1974).

Three-Judge Federal District Courts

Under some circumstances a three-judge federal district court may (or must) hear a dispute involving a federal question. Until recently, only a three-judge court could issue a temporary or permanent injunction restraining the enforcement, operation, or execution of any state statute on the grounds of unconstitutionality[37] or restrain the enforcement, operation, or execution of any act of Congress for repugnance to the Constitution.[38] The establishment of the three-judge requirement of 28 U.S.C.A. §§ 2281 and 2282 was a direct response by the Congress in 1910 to the Supreme Court decision *Ex parte Young,* 209 U.S. 123 (1908), which upheld the power of federal courts to enjoin the enforcement of state laws. The intent of Congress in enacting this law was to reduce the possibility that a single federal judge could tie the hands of a state. Congress in 1910 also provided for an automatic appeal from a decision of the three-judge court directly to the Supreme Court, bypassing the court of appeals and circumventing the certiorari process,[39] thus guaranteeing a speedy review by the Supreme Court.

The requirement of a three-judge court under §§ 2281 and 2282 placed an increasingly heavy administrative burden on the federal court system. For example, 140 cases were heard under these sections in 1975 that reached the Supreme Court on direct appeal. The increasing number of three-judge court decisions in recent years has caused a considerable drain on the limited resources of the Supreme Court. As Chief Justice Burger noted[40]:

Three-judge district courts should be substantially reduced or eliminated and direct appeals to the Supreme Court should be eliminated. These changes would confirm and restore the Supreme Court's power, established by law 50 years ago, to select for review only the most important cases of broad general importance.

On August 12, 1976, the 94th Congress repealed §§ 2281 and 2282, eliminating, for the most part, three-judge federal district courts.[41] However, Congress provided that the requirement be retained when "required by an act of Congress" or in a case involving congressional reapportionment or the reapportionment of any statewide legislative body. In addition, suits filed under the 1964 Civil Rights Act and the 1965 Voting Rights Act are not affected by the act. Needless to say, the number of three-judge suits going to the Supreme Court on direct appeal has been sharply curtailed.

Federal Statutes Concerning Three-Judge Courts

28 U.S.C.A. § 2284. Three-judge court; when required; composition; procedure [amended August 12, 1976]

(a) A district court of three judges shall be convened when otherwise required by act of Congress, or when an action is filed challenging the constitutionality of the apportionment of congressional districts or the apportionment of any statewide legislative body.

In any action or proceeding required by Act of Congress to be heard and determined by a district court of three judges the composition and procedure of the court, except as otherwise provided by law, shall be as follows:

(1) Upon the filing of a request for three judges, the judge to whom the request is presented shall, unless he determines that three judges are not required, immediately notify the chief judge of the circuit, who shall designate two other judges, at least one of whom shall be a circuit judge. . . .

28 U.S.C.A. § 1253. Direct appeals from decisions of three-judge courts

Except as otherwise provided by law, any party may appeal to the Supreme Court from an order granting or denying, after notice and hearing, an interlocutory or permanent injunction in any civil action, suit or proceeding required by any Act of Congress to be heard and determined by a district court of three judges.

---

[37] 28 U.S.C.A. § 2281.

[38] 28 U.S.C.A. § 2282.

[39] See 28 U.S.C.A. § 1253, infra.

[40] Speech before the American Bar Association Meeting, February, 1975.

[41] Public Law 94-381, 5.537.

Federal-State Relations

Removal of State Criminal Prosecutions to Federal Courts

28 U.S.C.A. § 1443.   Civil rights cases

Any of the following civil actions or criminal prosecutions, commenced in a State court, may be removed by the defendant to the district court of the United States for the district and division embracing the place wherein it is pending:

(1) Against any person who is denied or cannot enforce in the courts of such State a right under any law providing for the equal civil rights of citizens of the United States, or of all persons within the jurisdiction thereof;

(2) For any act under color of authority derived from any law providing for equal rights, or for refusing to do any act on the ground that it would be inconsistent with such law.

On its face, § 1443 would seem to provide an effective remedy to protect a person's federally guaranteed rights against abuses by the state criminal process. But despite the broad language of this century-old civil rights provision and its potential for remedying many possible abuses of the state criminal process, the Supreme Court has construed the statute very narrowly. Although § 1443(1) applies to "any person" whose rights are denied under a federal civil rights law, it has been most often utilized by criminal defendants. Removal of a state criminal prosecution to a federal court has several advantages: (1) it allows a much quicker adjudication of federal issues; (2) it shortens by months or years the prejudicial consequences a defendant suffers while under indictment or in prison; (3) it avoids the expensive and time-consuming burden of appealing a state conviction through the state courts; and (4) removal may diminish the chilling effect an illegal prosecution can have on federally protected rights.[42]

The leading Supreme Court decisions under § 1443(1)[43] are *City of Greenwood* v. *Peacock,* 384 U.S. 808 (1966), *Georgia* v. *Rachel,* 384 U.S. 780 (1966), and, more recently, *Johnson* v. *Mississippi,* 421 U.S. 213 (1975). In *Peacock* and *Rachel,* the Supreme Court established that a removal petition under § 1443(1) must satisfy a two-pronged test: First, it must be shown by the petitioner that the right allegedly denied arises under a federal law that provides for specific civil rights stated in terms of racial equality.[44] Thus, claims arising under constitutional or statutory provisions having general applicability or under statutes not protecting against racial discrimination do not permit removal under § 1443(1). An allegation by the petitioner that he will be denied due process because the law under which he is being prosecuted is vague or that the prosecution is a sham, corrupt, or without an evidentiary basis will likewise not suffice under § 1443(1).

Second, it must be shown by the removal petitioner that he is being denied or cannot enforce a specified federal right in the state courts.[45] Generally, as a condition for removal, it must appear that a discriminatory state statute or constitutional provision on its face abrogates the petitioner's rights. The Supreme Court has stated that it cannot be

---

[42]Note, *Removal of State Court Prosecutions to Federal Court Under 28 U.S.C. § 1443,* 64 J. Crim. L. & C. 76 (1973).

[43]Subsection (2) has not been applied in many cases, and has been held not to apply to private citizens but only to federal officers acting pursuant to their duties under a federal law providing for equality of civil rights. See *City of Greenwood* v. *Peacock,* 384 U.S. 808, 814–824 (1966), and note 45, infra.

[44]In *Rachel,* the defendants were civil rights demonstrators in Atlanta, Georgia, who were charged with trespass under a state statute making it a crime to refuse to leave premises when requested to do so by the owner or person in charge. The defendants alleged that they had attempted to obtain service at restaurants, and their arrests were designed to promulgate a policy of racial discrimination in public accommodations. The defendants petitioned the federal district court for removal, alleging that § 201 of the Civil Rights Act of 1964 protects the right of equal access to public restaurants without regard to race. The Supreme Court agreed and held that removal was proper if the allegations were true and any criminal prosecutions against the defendants must be dismissed.

[45]In *City of Greenwood* v. *Peacock,* the defendants were being prosecuted for various local crimes, including obstructing public streets, as-

Footnote continued on page 28

presumed that a state court would fail to redress an alleged wrong. Thus, removal under § 1443(1) is not easily accomplished.[46] Until Congress is willing to broaden the remedies under § 1443 or the Supreme Court is more willing to liberally construe this removal provision,[47] few petitions by state defendants for removal to federal court are likely to be granted.

Comity

28 U.S.C.A. § 2283. Stay of state court proceedings

A court of the United States may not grant an injunction to stay proceedings in a State court except as expressly authorized by Act of Congress, or where necessary in aid of its jurisdiction, or to protect or effectuate its judgments.

28 U.S.C.A. § 2283, also known as the "Anti-Injunction Act," expressly forbids a federal court from issuing an injunction (stay) against a pending state court proceeding in the absence of a recognized exception. The three statutory exceptions are (1) "except as expressly authorized by Act of Congress,"[48] (2) "where necessary in aid of its jurisdiction," and (3) "to protect or effectuate its judgments." In addition, the Supreme Court has created a judicial exception when a person about to be prosecuted in a state court can show that he will, unless the proceedings are enjoined, suffer irreparable damage.[49]

The principal reasons against federal court interference in state court proceedings are based on the public policy (1) that courts should not enjoin a criminal prosecution when the petitioner has an adequate

---

sault and battery, and disturbing the peace. They sought removal to a federal court under § 1443(1), stating that they were members of a civil rights group that had been engaged in a drive to encourage blacks to register to vote and that they were lawfully protesting the conditions of racial discrimination and segregation in Mississippi. The defendants, in seeking removal under § 1443, alleged that their federal right to vote without discrimination on the grounds of race and color and their rights guaranteeing all persons equal access to specified rights enjoyed by white persons were violated. The Supreme Court held that removal under § 1443 would not lie under these circumstances. The Court stated that removal would not be proper where the petition merely alleged that equal civil rights have been denied by state officials in advance of trial, that the charges are false, or that the defendants could not receive a fair trial in a particular state court. The Court noted that there had been no showing that the petitioners would be denied or could not enforce their rights in the state courts and that no federal law conferred immunity from prosecution for the conduct with which the defendants had been charged.

[46]More recently, in *Johnson* v. *Mississippi*, the petitioners, six blacks who had been picketing and urging boycott of certain business establishments in Vicksburg because of alleged racial discrimination in hiring, were arrested and charged with unlawfully conspiring to bring about a boycott. The defendants sought removal to a federal court under § 1443, alleging that the charges were unconstitutional and alleging violation of their federal rights under Title I of the Civil Rights Act of 1968, which, under 18 U.S.C.A. § 245(b)(5), makes it a crime to injure, intimidate,

or interfere with a person because he participates lawfully in speech or peaceful assembly opposing racial discrimination in employment. The Supreme Court, on certiorari, held that removal under § 1443 was not warranted based solely on petitioners' allegations that the state statutes underlying the charges were unconstitutional, or that there was no basis for the charges, or that their arrest and prosecution otherwise denied them their constitutional rights. In addition, the Supreme Court held that § 245 does not furnish an adequate basis for removal under § 1443(1) because the legislative history of § 245 evidenced no intent by Congress to interfere with state criminal prosecutions.

[47]Chief Justice Burger has stated that new rules and procedures need to be formulated "to reduce the flood of federal-state cases to a small stream." Burger, W., Speech to the National Association of Attorneys General, February 6, 1970.

[48]The Supreme Court has recognized several legislative exceptions under the statute, including: (1) legislation allowing federal courts to stay state court proceedings that interfere with the administration of a federal bankruptcy proceeding; (2) acts of Congress providing for removal of litigation from state to federal courts; (3) acts of Congress limiting the liability of shipowners; (4) acts of Congress providing for federal interpleader actions; (5) legislation governing federal habeas corpus proceedings; (6) legislation conferring federal jurisdiction over farm mortgages; (7) legislation providing for control of prices; and (8) legislation under § 1983 of the Civil Rights Act of 1964 (42 U.S.C.A.). See *Mitchum* v. *Foster,* 407 U.S. 225, 233–235 (1972).

[49]*Ex parte Young,* 209 U.S. 123 (1908).

remedy at law and will not suffer irreparable injury if equitable relief is denied; (2) that a duplication of legal proceedings is to be avoided when a single suit would protect the rights of the petitioner; and (3) that a proper respect for state functions—the notion of *comity*—requires that states should normally be left free to perform their legitimate functions without undue interference from federal courts.[50]

Under the principle of comity, federal courts should not enjoin pending proceedings in state courts in the absence of "special circumstances." Only when it is "absolutely necessary" for the protection of constitutional rights and when the danger of irreparable loss is both "great and immediate" will a federal court be permitted to enjoin state proceedings.[51] The existence of a "chilling effect" on a petitioner's constitutional rights—even in the area of free speech—is not a sufficient basis for prohibiting state action, unless the statute directly abridges free speech[52]; nor will an injunction lie when the statute is allegedly unconstitutional on its face but the state attempts in good faith to enforce it.[53] However, allegations of a "bad faith" prosecution in which the defendant is subjected to harassment or repeated prosecutions when there is no real hope of securing a valid conviction are sufficient to bring federal relief into play.[54]

---

[50]*Younger* v. *Harris,* 401 U.S. 37 (1971), is the leading case in this area. Plaintiff Harris was indicted under the California Criminal Syndicalism Act (forbidding the advocacy, teaching, or aiding and abetting of the commission of crime, sabotage, or unlawful acts of force and violence or terrorism as a means of accomplishing a change in industrial ownership or control, or effecting any political change—Cal. Penal Code §§ 11400, 11401) for distributing leaflets advocating a change in industrial ownership through political action. A three-judge federal district court held the California statute facially void for vagueness and overbreadth and enjoined the pending prosecution of Harris. On appeal, the Supreme Court reversed, Mr. Justice Douglas dissenting. The Court held that Harris had failed to show the "special circumstances" necessary for federal intervention in state proceedings. Justice Douglas stated in his dissent that special circumstances warrant federal intervention in a state criminal proceeding where a statute being enforced is unconstitutional on its face.

[51]The Court in *Younger,* id. at 46, did not define "irreparable injury" but did state that it must be more than the cost, anxiety, and inconvenience of defending a single criminal prosecution. See also *Dombrowski* v. *Pfister,* 380 U.S. 479 (1965) (injunction proper under § 2282 against criminal prosecution threatened under Louisiana subversive activities statute to discourage defendants from continuing their civil rights activities without awaiting state court interpretation of the statute).

[52]Id. at 51.

[53]Id. at 54. See also *Steffel* v. *Thompson,* 415 U.S. 452 (1974), holding that when a prosecution under a state criminal statute has been threatened but is not pending, declaratory relief (a judicial order that states the rights of a party without awarding damages or ordering that anything be done) is not precluded in a federal court action where the constitutionality of the state statute is challenged even though there is no showing of bad faith enforcement or special circumstances. Where only declaratory relief is sought, no *Younger* showing need be made. See also *Allee* v. *Medrano,* 416 U.S. 802 (1974), and *Huffman* v. *Pursue, Ltd.,* 420 U.S. 592 (1975).

[54]Id. at 49. Five companion cases were decided with *Younger.* In *Samuels* v. *Mackell,* 401 U.S. 66 (1971), the Supreme Court held that a federal district court should deny declaratory relief (under 28 U.S.C. § 2202) without considering the merits of a challenge to the constitutionality of state statutes where (1) criminal proceedings based on violations of such statutes are pending in state courts, and (2) the petitioners do not show that they would suffer immediate irreparable injury. In *Boyle* v. *Landry,* 401 U.S. 77,80 (1971), the Supreme Court held that injunctive and declaratory relief by a federal court against the enforcement of a state criminal statute is improper where no plaintiffs "had even been prosecuted, charged, or even arrested" under the statute and allegations of harassment amounted to "mere speculation." In *Perez* v. *Ledesma,* 401 U.S. 82 (1971), *Dyson* v. *Stein,* 401 U.S. 200 (1971), and *Byrne* v. *Karalexis,* 401 U.S. 216 (1971), the Supreme Court held that it is improper for a federal district court to order the suppression of evidence in a pending state criminal prosecution and the return of allegedly obscene materials which were seized where there are no facts present in the record to show the plaintiffs would suffer the kind of irreparable injury necessary for federal injunctive interference. See also *Doran* v. *Salem Inn, Inc.,* 422 U.S. 922 (1975); *Kugher* v. *Helfant,* 421 U.S. 117 (1975); and *Hicks* v. *Miranda,* 422 U.S. 332 (1975) (in the absence of "extraordinary circumstances" a federal court cannot intervene in a pending state criminal proceeding where the proceeding against the federal plaintiff is begun after the federal complaint is filed but before any proceedings on the merits have taken place in federal courts).

1.03 SELECTED PROVISIONS OF THE UNITED STATES CONSTITUTION

Amendment IV [1791]

The right of the people to be secure in their persons, houses, papers, and effects, against unreasonable searches and seizures, shall not be violated, and no Warrants shall issue, but upon probable cause, supported by Oath or affirmation, and particularly describing the place to be searched, and the persons or things to be seized.

Amendment V [1791]

No person shall be held to answer for a capital or otherwise infamous crime, unless on a presentment or indictment of a Grand Jury, except in cases arising in the land or naval forces, or in the Militia, when in actual service in time of War or public danger; nor shall any person be subject for the same offense to be twice put in jeopardy of life or limb; nor shall be compelled in any criminal case to be a witness against himself; nor be deprived of life, liberty, or property, without due process of law; nor shall private property be taken for public use, without just compensation.

Amendment VI [1791]

In all criminal prosecutions, the accused shall enjoy the right to a speedy and public trial, by an impartial jury of the State and district wherein the crime shall have been committed, which district shall have been previously ascertained by law, and to be informed of the nature and cause of the accusation; to be confronted with the witnesses against him; to have compulsory process for obtaining witnesses in his favor, and to have the Assistance of Counsel for his defense.

Amendment VIII [1791]

Excessive bail shall not be required, nor excessive fines imposed, nor cruel and unusual punishments inflicted.

Amendment IX [1791]

The enumeration in the Constitution, of certain rights, shall not be construed to deny or disparage others retained by the people.

Amendment X [1791]

The powers not delegated to the United States by the Constitution, nor prohibited by it to the States, are reserved to the States respectively, or to the people.

Amendment XIII [1865]

Section 1.   Neither slavery nor involuntary servitude, except as a punishment for crime whereof the party shall have been duly convicted, shall exist within the United States, or any place subject to their jurisdiction.

Section 2.   Congress shall have the power to enforce this article by appropriate legislation.

Amendment XIV [1868]

Section 1.   All persons born or naturalized in the United States, and subject to the jurisdiction thereof, are citizens of the United States and of the State wherein they reside. No State shall make or enforce any law which shall abridge the privileges or immunities of citizens of the United States; nor shall any state deprive any person of life, liberty, or property, without due process of law; nor deny to any person within its jurisdiction the equal protection of the laws.

* * *

Section 5.   The Congress shall have the power to enforce, by appropriate legislation, the provisions of this article.

Article I, Section 9 [1787]

* * *

(2) The privilege of the Writ of Habeas Corpus shall not be suspended, unless when in Cases of Rebellion or Invasion the public Safety may require it.

(3) No Bill of Attainder or ex post facto Law shall be passed.

* * *

1.04 GRANTING SUPREME COURT REVIEW

Supreme Court Review*

The Supreme Court has a great deal of discretion in deciding whether to review a case. In the case of an application for a writ of certiorari, that discretion is explicitly given by statute, and a denial of the writ expresses no judgment on the merits of the issues: the Court simply refuses to review the case. Similarly, if the writ of certiorari is granted, it does not follow that the decision of the lower court will be reversed, only that the Court will give the issues full consideration on written briefs and oral argument.

The second major group of cases coming to the Court is called "appeals." This term is confusing, for the "appeal" and the writ of certiorari are both forms of an appeal as that term is generally understood. The Judicial Code describes those kinds of cases which are brought before the Court by a petition for a writ of certiorari, and those cases in which an appeal is the appropriate form. In theory, the Court has no discretion to refuse to decide an appeal, and a litigant seeking an appeal files a jurisdictional statement—a statement showing that his case falls within the statutory criteria for an appeal rather than a writ of certiorari. Even though the Court must decide an appeal, there is no requirement that it do so after submission of written briefs and oral argu-

ment. If resolution of the issue is clear, the Court may affirm or, less often, reverse in a summary order.

The decision to grant a full hearing on the issues raised in a jurisdictional statement, like the decision to grant a writ of certiorari, is made on the vote of only four Justices. Because that decision is made by a minority of the Court, and because it expresses only an intention to hear a case and not the way it is to be decided, ordinarily no dissenting opinions are written. On occasion, however, there are exception. *Frank* v. *Maryland*[†] was a case in which the Court upheld the right of a city health inspector, who had reasonable cause to believe that a particular area was rat-infested, to search the houses in that area without a search warrant. While the decision in *Frank* was pending, the jurisdictional statement in *Ohio ex rel. Eaton* v. *Price,* which presented similar issues, was filed. Disposition of the jurisdictional statement in this case was held pending the decision in *Frank,* which was ultimately decided on a 5–4 vote. When the Court then decided to consider *Price,* Mr. Justice Stewart, who had been in the majority in *Frank,* did not participate because his father was one of the Justices of the Ohio Supreme Court who had decided the case below. Apparently the four dissenters in *Frank* voted to bring this case on for a full hearing. Mr. Justice Clark thought that this was merely a back-door way of reversing the Court's decision in *Frank,* and wrote an opinion so stating in dissent from the order granting a full hearing. Mr. Justice Brennan wrote an opinion discussing the reasons for forbearance in dissenting from such orders [infra].

---

*From *An Affair with Freedom,* edited by Stephen J. Friedman, pp. 343–344. Copyright © 1967 by Stephen J. Friedman. Reprinted by permission of Atheneum Publishers.

†359 U.S. 360 (1959). *Frank* was subsequently overruled by *Camara* v. *Municipal Court,* 387 U.S. 360 (1967), and *See* v. *City of Seattle,* 387 U.S. 541 (1967).

OHIO ex rel. EATON v. PRICE

360 U.S. 246, 79 S. Ct. 978, 3 L. Ed. 2d 1200 (1959)

Memorandum by Mr. Justice BRENNAN.

The Court's practice, when considering a jurisdictional statement whereby a litigant attempts to invoke the Court's jurisdiction

on appeal, is quite similar to its well-known one on applications for writs of certiorari. That is, if four Justices or more are of opinion that the questions presented by the appeal should be fully briefed and argued orally, an order noting probable jurisdiction or postponing further consideration of the jurisdictional questions to a hearing on the merits is entered. Even though this action is taken on the votes of only a minority of four of the Justices, the Court then approaches plenary consideration of the case anew as a Court; votes previously cast in Conference that the judgment of the court appealed from be summarily affirmed, or that the appeal be dismissed for want of a substantial federal question, do not conclude the Justices casting them, and every member of the Court brings to the ultimate disposition of the case his judgment based on the full briefs and the oral arguments. Because of this, disagreeing Justices do not ordinarily make a public notation, when an order setting an appeal for argument is entered, that they would have summarily affirmed the judgment below, or have dismissed the appeal from it for want of a substantial federal question. Research has not disclosed any instance of such notations until today.[a]

The reasons for such forbearance are obvious. Votes to affirm summarily, and to dismiss for want of a substantial federal question, it hardly needs comment, are votes on the merits of a case, and public expression of views on the merits of a case by a Justice before argument and decision may well be misunderstood; the usual practice in judicial adjudication in this country, where hearings are held, is that judgment follow, and not precede them. Public respect for the judiciary might well suffer if any basis were given for an assumption, however wrong in fact, that this were not so. Thus, the practice of not noting dissents from such orders has been followed, regardless of how strongly Justices may have felt

as to the merits of a case or how clearly they have thought decision in it controlled by past precedent.[b] A precedent which appears to some Justices, upon the preliminary consideration given a jurisdictional statement, to be completely controlling may not appear to be so to other Justices. Plenary consideration can change views strongly held, and on close, reflective analysis precedents may appear inapplicable to varying fact situations. I believe that this approach will obtain in this case despite the unusual notation made today by four of my colleagues.

Guidelines for Granting Certiorari

Supreme Court Rule 19 governs, in part, the types of cases for which certiorari will be granted. However, there are instances in which the Court does not adhere strictly to the rules and decides cases of great social importance, e.g., state criminal abortion statutes.

Rule 19. Considerations governing review on certiorari

1. A review on writ of certiorari is not a matter of right, but of sound judicial discretion, and will be granted only where there are special and important reasons therefore. The following, while neither controlling nor fully measuring the court's discretion, indicate the character of reasons which will be considered:

(a) Where a state court has decided a federal question of substance not theretofore determined by this court, or has decided it in a way probably not in accord with applicable decisions of this court.

(b) Where a court of appeals has rendered a decision in conflict with the decision of another court of appeals on the same matter; or has decided an important state or territorial question in a way in conflict with

---

[a]Likewise, dissents from orders granting certiorari are ordinarily not publicly noted, even though the grant or denial of certiorari ... expresses no intimation as to the merits of the case. The sole exception found appears to be *Youngstown Sheet & Tube Co.* v. *Sawyer*, 343 U.S. 937 (1952), where the extraordinary power to grant certiorari before judgment in the Court of Appeals was exercised.... Of course, in these circumstances, the notation could not possibly have implied or have been taken to imply any view of the case on the merits.

[b]Notation of dissent from a denial of certiorari, or from a summary disposition of an appeal, is a completely different matter. Such notations occur with some frequency and I have made them myself. They are expressions of a Justice's view that a case should be heard when the Court decides not to have a hearing....

applicable state or territorial law; or has decided an important question of federal law which has not been, but should be, settled by this court; or has decided a federal question in a way in conflict with applicable decisions of this court; or has so far departed from the accepted and usual course of judicial proceedings, or so far sanctioned such a departure by a lower court, as to call for an exercise of this court's power of supervision.

2. The same general considerations outlined above will control in respect of petitions for writs of certiorari to review judgments of the Court of Claims, of the Court of Customs and Patent Appeals, or of any other court whose determinations are by law reviewable on writ of certiorari.

1.05 SOME ADDITIONAL LIMITATIONS ON SUPREME COURT REVIEW

In addition to the constitutional constraints that limit judicial review by the federal courts, the Supreme Court has, for many years, had self-imposed limitations on the exercise of its own judicial power. These rules operate even though a "case" or "controversy" may be within the jurisdiction of the Court, and many are formulated on policy considerations rather than on constitutional grounds. These rules of self-governance are applicable to all cases, including criminal cases, for which judicial review by the Supreme Court is sought.

Advisory Opinions

Because the Constitution (Article III, Section 2) limits the judicial power of the federal courts to real "cases" and "controversies," a *definite, real,* and *concrete* dispute between two bona fide adversaries is necessary for any federal court action. No federal court, including the United States Supreme Court, can constitutionally decide what the law might be based upon a hypothetical set of facts.[55] Even though state

courts may render advisory opinions, federal courts cannot. This rule against advisory opinions usually does not come up in criminal cases.

Collusive Cases

The Supreme Court will not decide constitutional issues when the lawsuit is collusive, friendly, or nonadversary in nature.[56] Each party must have a personal stake in the outcome of the litigation. For example, it is collusion if two persons secretly agree that one will sue the other because the second party carries insurance, and the federal courts will not review such cases.

Mootness

It is well settled that federal courts will not decide a case that has become *moot*.[57] A moot case is one in which there is no longer a real dispute that can be adjudicated. For example, if an inmate dies in prison while his appeal is pending, the case

---

[55]*Muskrat* v. *United States,* 219 U.S. 346 (1911); *Aetna Life Insurance Co.* v. *Haworth,* 300 U.S. 299 (1937); *United States* v. *Fruehauf,* 365 U.S. 146 (1961).

[56]*Chicago & Grand Trunk R. Co.* v. *Wellman,* 143 U.S. 339 (1892); *Lord* v. *Veazie,* 8 How. 251 (1850).

[57]*Mills* v. *Green,* 159 U.S. 651, 653 (1895) ("the duty of this court ... is to decide actual controversies by a judgment which can be carried into effect, and not to give opinions on moot questions..."); *California* v. *San Pablo & T.R.R.,* 149 U.S. 308, 314 (1893) (courts are "not empowered to decide moot questions"); *SEC* v. *Medical Committee for Human Rights,* 404 U.S. 403, 407 (1972); *Powell* v. *McCormack,* 395 U.S. 486, 496 (1969); *Spomer* v. *Littleton,* 414 U.S. 514 (1974) (challenge to selective prosecutions based on race by one prosecutor remanded to determine if the new prosecutor was engaging in similar racial discrimination and/or whether the case was moot); see also *Sosna* v. *Iowa,* 419 U.S. 393 (1975). A leading case involving the mootness doctrine is *DeFunis* v. *Odegaard,* 416 U.S. 312 (1974), which involved a white applicant to the University of Washington Law School who was denied admission. The applicant filed suit in a Washington state court alleging that he was denied admission to law school solely on the grounds of his race (so-called "reverse discrimination") and that his Law School Admission Test (LSAT) scores and grade point average (GPA) were higher than those of the 37 minority persons admitted to the law school. The trial court granted the requested relief, and DeFunis was admitted to law school.

Footnote continued on page 34

will be dismissed as moot.[58] The usual rule in federal cases is that an actual controversy must exist at each stage of appellate review, not simply at the date the lawsuit is initiated. However, the Supreme Court has noted several exceptions to the mootness doctrine. For example, in pregnancy litigation (e.g., abortion cases)[59] a case will not be rendered moot simply because a litigant has given birth to a child. And the fact that an inmate has completed his sentence in prison does not necessarily render his appeal moot—especially if there are any collateral consequences of the conviction (e.g., loss of civil rights).[60] The major exception to the mootness doctrine comes into play when an issue is "capable of repetition, yet evad[es] review."[61]

On appeal, the Washington State Supreme Court reversed, upholding the constitutionality of the law school's admissions policy, which gave preferential treatment to applicants from certain minority racial groups. The Washington State Supreme Court, however, allowed DeFunis to remain in law school pending a final review by the United States Supreme Court. By the time the case came before the Supreme Court, DeFunis was a third year law student and graduation was only a couple of months away. In a 5–4 decision, the Supreme Court declined to review the case on its merits; that is, it refused to decide the issue of whether the state had violated DeFunis' equal protection rights under the Fourteenth Amendment, and dismissed the case as being moot. The majority noted that "an actual controversy must exist at stages of appellate or certiorari review, and not simply at the date the action is initiated" (at 319). For a discussion of law school admission procedures in general, see the dissenting opinion of Mr. Justice Douglas in *DeFunis*, at 327–333. See also Winterbottom, W., *A Study of the Criteria for Legal Education and Admission to the Bar*, 21 J. Legal Ed. 75 (1968); Ransey, *Law School Admissions: Science, Art, or Hunch?*, 12 J. Legal Ed. 503 (1960); Lunneborg and Radford, *The LSAT: A Survey of American Practice*, 18 J. Legal Ed. 313 (1966); Rosen, *Equalizing Access to Legal Education: Special Programs for Law Students Who Are Not Admissible by Traditional Criteria*, 321 Toledo L. Rev. (1970).

[58] *Dove* v. *United States*, 423 U.S. 325 (1976). When the Supreme Court has entertained doubt about the continuing nature of a case or controversy, it has often remanded the case to the lower court for consideration of the possibility of mootness. See, e.g., *Indiana Employment Division* v. *Burney*, 409 U.S. 540 (1973); *Scott* v. *Kentucky Parole Board*, 97 S. Ct. 343 (1976) (court of appeals holding that Fourteenth Amendment due process does not apply to state parole release proceedings remanded for consideration of mootness question where petitioner has been granted parole following grant of certiorari by Supreme Court); *Weinstein* v. *Bradford*, 423 U.S. 147 (1975).

[59] *Roe* v. *Wade*, 410 U.S. 113 (1973); *Doe* v. *Bolton*, 410 U.S. 179 (1973) ("if [birth] makes a case moot, pregnancy litigation seldom will sur-

vive much beyond the trial stage, and appellate review will be effectively denied. Our law should not be that rigid" [at 125]).

[60] *Sibron* v. *New York*, 392 U.S. 40 (1968). Potential legal and related disabilities following a conviction may include (1) disenfranchisement (loss of voting rights), (2) loss of right to hold federal or state office, (3) loss of right to join certain professional organizations (e.g., legal or medical profession), (4) being subject to possible impeachment when testifying as a witness, (5) loss of right to serve as a juror, (6) being subject to divorce, (7) possible loss of employment, and (8) possible increased sentence if later convicted on a different charge. These collateral consequences of conviction vary from jurisdiction to jurisdiction. See *North Carolina* v. *Rice*, 404 U.S. 244, 247 n. 1 (1971); Comment, *Civil Disabilities of Felons*, 53 Va. L. Rev. 403 (1967); Note, *The Effect of Expungement on a Criminal Conviction*, 40 S. Cal. L. Rev. 127 (1967); Special Project, *The Collateral Consequences of a Criminal Conviction*, 23 Vand. L. Rev. 929, 954 n. 97 (1970). See also Chapter Nine, § 9.04, Comments.

[61] *Southern Pacific Terminal Co.* v. *ICC*, 219 U.S. 498, 515 (1911); *Moore* v. *Ogilvie*, 394 U.S. 814, 816 (1969); *SEC* v. *Medical Committee for Human Rights*, 404 U.S. 403 (1972). Since 1964 the Supreme Court has based its mootness decisions on the "case" or "controversy" requirement of Article III, so that the question of mootness in the federal courts is now of a constitutional dimension. *Liner* v. *Jafco, Inc.*, 374 U.S. 301, 306 n. 3 (1964). However, the Court has never explained why the mootness doctrine was elevated to a constitutional status.

The mootness doctrine serves at least four purposes: (1) it continues the common law rule that courts lack jurisdiction to decide abstract questions where no dispute exists; (2) it prevents useless expenditures of judicial resources—i.e., government should not be burdened with the expense of trying unimportant controversies; (3) it assures that courts will not intrude prematurely into policymaking, which might unnecessarily constrain other branches of government; and (4) it prevents creation of unnecessary precedents and allows flexibility in the law. See Note, *Mootness in the Supreme Court*, 88 Harv. L. Rev. 373 (1974).

Political Questions

The Supreme Court will not decide a case that presents a "political question."[62] Political questions, the Supreme Court has held, are those that involve the separation of powers doctrine and would bring the Court into collision with a coordinate branch of the federal government (i.e., the President or the Congress).[63] Consequently, challenges to the legality of the Viet Nam War were routinely dismissed by the Supreme Court because they involved political questions and were therefore not appropriate for judicial review.[64] However, the mere fact that a suit seeks protection of a political right does not mean it presents a political question. For example, the Supreme Court has held that the issue of *reapportionment* (one-man, one-vote) does not involve a political question, because there is a judicial remedy for unequal protection of the law under the Fourteenth Amendment.[65] Like-

wise, the issue of whether the Congress could exclude a Congressman (Adam Clayton Powell) duly elected by the voters of his district was held by the Supreme Court not to involve a political question.[66] In general, questions that are best left to the political arms of government are usually not subject to judicial review. In any event, questions of a political nature are uncommon in most criminal cases.

Standing

Standing refers to *who* is a proper person to request an adjudication of a particular issue — not whether the issue itself is reviewable.[67] A party seeking judicial relief must have a personal stake in the outcome to assure that the controversy will be presented in a truly adversary context. In general, a third party may not assert the constitutional rights of another party because he lacks

---

[62]*Coleman* v. *Miller,* 307 U.S. 433 (1939); *Baker* v. *Carr,* 369 U.S. 186 (1962); *Flast* v. *Cohen,* 392 U.S. 83 (1968).

[63]*Marbury* v. *Madison,* 1 Cranch 137, 164–166 (1803) (courts will not entertain political questions even though such questions involve actual controversies); *Coleman* v. *Miller,* 307 U.S. 433, 454–455 (1939) ("in determining whether a question falls within [the political question] category, the appropriateness under our system of government of attributing finality to the action of political departments and also the lack of satisfactory criteria for a judicial determination are dominant considerations"). See also *Oetjen* v. *Central Leather Co.,* 246 U.S. 297 (1918) (the conduct of the foreign relations of our government is left to the executive and legislative branches of government, and is not subject to judicial review).

[64]See, e.g., *Massachusetts* v. *Laird,* 400 U.S. 886 (1970).

[65]*Baker* v. *Carr,* 369 U.S. 186 (1962) (reapportionment of state legislature); *Wesberry* v. *Sanders,* 376 U.S. 1 (1964) (apportionment of congressional seats); *Reynolds* v. *Sims,* 377 U.S. 533 (1964) (standards for apportioning seats in a state legislature); *Avery* v. *Midland County, Texas,* 390 U.S. 474 (1968) (representation on local governing board); *Fortson* v. *Morris,* 385 U.S. 231 (1966) (standards for choosing a governor if no candidate has received a majority vote); *Powell* v. *McCormack,* 395 U.S. 486 (1969) (refusal of House of Representatives to seat a person elected to that body); *Bond* v. *Floyd,* 385 U.S. 116 (1966) (refusal of state legislature to

seat person elected to that body); *Williams* v. *Rhodes,* 393 U.S. 23 (1968) (obstacles a state may impose on an attempt by a new political party to win a place on the ballot).

[66]*Powell* v. *McCormack,* 395 U.S. 486 (1969). The Court noted that political questions involve at least one of the following: (1) "a textually demonstrable constitutional commitment of the issue to a coordinate political department"; or (2) "a lack of judicially discoverable and manageable standards for resolving it"; or (3) "the impossibility of deciding without an initial policy determination of a kind clearly for nonjudicial discretion"; or (4) "the impossibility of a court's undertaking independent resolution without expressing lack of the respect due coordinate branches of government"; or (5) "an unusual need for unquestioning adherence to a political decision already made"; or (6) "the potentiality of embarrassment from multifarious pronouncements by various departments on one question," at 518–519.

[67]*Tileston* v. *Ullman,* 318 U.S. 44 (1943); *Frothingham* v. *Mellon,* 262 U.S. 447 (1923); *Flast* v. *Cohen,* 392 U.S. 83 (1968). In *Baker* v. *Carr,* 369 U.S. 186 (1962), the Court noted that "the 'gist of the question of standing' is whether the party seeking relief has 'alleged such a personal stake in the outcome of the controversy as to assure that concrete adverseness which sharpens the presentation of issues upon which the court so largely depends for illumination of difficult constitutional questions,' " at 204.

standing to assert those claims.[68] In order for a party to have standing, it must be shown that the claimant has suffered or will suffer a direct injury or impairment of his own constitutional rights.[69] For example, in the abortion case of *Roe* v. *Wade,* 410 U.S. 113 (1973), the Supreme Court held that (1) a pregnant woman has standing to challenge a criminal abortion statute; (2) a physician who wishes to perform an abortion has standing to challenge an abortion statute, as his constitutional rights are immediately threatened; but (3) a childless couple who contemplate the possibility of a future pregnancy lacks standing to challenge an abortion statute since there is no immediate threat of direct harm.

The issue of standing sometimes arises in the criminal context, and it will be further discussed in Chapter Five.

Ripeness

Ripeness refers to *when* a claim may be asserted, i.e., the timeliness of the claim. Simply stated, the ripeness doctrine precludes judicial review if the issues are prematurely before the court.[70] Most often the ripeness doctrine comes into the play when administrative policies are challenged. For example, a group of drug manufacturers challenges regulations promulgated under the federal Food, Drug, and Cosmetic Act (21 U.S.C. § 301 et seq.). The rationale of the ripeness doctrine is to protect agencies from judicial interference "until an administrative decision has been formalized and its effects felt in a concrete way by the challenging parties."[71] An issue must be "ripe" before there will be judicial review.

Sometimes the Court will dismiss a case it had accepted because judicial review was *improvidently granted.*[72] By this the Court usually means that the case is not "ripe" for judicial resolution or the Justices acted prematurely. In some cases, the Supreme Court may be unclear as to the legal or factual grounds on which a lower federal or state court based its decision. Such a case may be sent back to the lower court to develop the record for possible later review by the Supreme Court, especially if the defect is jurisdictional in nature.[73]

Ripeness is rarely a problem in most

---

[68]See, e.g., *Eisenstadt* v. *Baird*, 405 U.S. 438, 443–446 (1972); *NAACP* v. *Alabama ex rel. Patterson*, 357 U.S. 449, 459 (1958). However, the Supreme Court has created numerous exceptions to this general rule. See Note, *Standing to Assert Constitutional Jus Tertii*, 88 Harv. L. Rev. 423 (1974). See also Chapter Five, § 5.06.

[69]See, e.g., *Association of Data Processing Service Organizations, Inc.* v. *Camp*, 397 U.S. 150 (1970) (injury in fact required). But see statement of Douglas, J., in *Camp* that "generalizations about standing to sue are largely worthless as such," at 151. See also *Barlow* v. *Collins*, 397 U.S. 159 (1970); *Arnold Tours, Inc.* v. *Camp*, 400 U.S. 45 (1970); *Sierra Club* v. *Morton*, 405 U.S. 727 (1972). See Scott, K., *Standing in the Supreme Court—A Functional Analysis*, 86 Harv. L. Rev. 645 (1973). For an interesting article on standing in environmental issues, see Stone, *Should Trees Have Standing? Toward Legal Rights for Natural Objects*, 45 Calif. L. Rev. 450 (1972). In the Sierra Club case, supra, Mr. Justice Douglas stated that the Court should "fashion a federal rule that allow[s] environmental issues to be litigated before federal agencies or federal courts in the name of the inanimate object about to be despoiled, defaced, or invaded by roads and bulldozers and where injury is the subject of public outrage," at 741.

[70]See *Abbott Laboratories* v. *Gardner*, 387 U.S. 136 (1967). See also *International Longshoremen's Union* v. *Boyd*, 347 U.S. 222 (1954).

[71]*Abbott Laboratories* v. *Gardner*, 387 U.S. 136, 148–149 (1967).

[72]The Supreme Court has indicated that the circumstances that constitute adequate grounds for dismissing a writ of certiorari as improvidently (prematurely) granted must be those that were not fully apprehended by the justices when certiorari was granted. See, e.g., *Rogers* v. *Missouri, Pacific R. Co.,* 352 U.S. 500 (1957) (opinion of Harlan, J.). See also *Iowa Beef Packers, Inc.* v. *Thompson*, 405 U.S. 228 (1972); *Duncan* v. *Tennessee*, 405 U.S. 127 (1972); *Guinn* v. *Muscare,* ____ U.S. ____, 48 L. Ed. 2d 165 (1976) (certiorari to review decision that fireman suspended for violating personal appearance regulations (beard) was denied procedural due process dismissed as improvidently granted because of a change in regulations governing civil service employees). In *Rogers,* supra, Mr. Justice Frankfurter noted in his dissent that "improvidently granted" is a term of art simply meaning that on full consideration, it becomes manifest that the case is not the type of case that should have been brought to the Supreme Court.

[73]See, e.g., *Ohio* v. *Gallagher*, 425 U.S. 257, 47 L. Ed. 2d 722 (1976) (case remanded to Ohio

Footnote continued on opposite page

criminal cases decided by the Supreme Court.

Justiciability

Justiciability refers to *whether* a particular issue is a proper subject for judicial review.[74] Put another way, the issue of justiciability relates to whether or not there exists with the courts a *remedy* to resolve the dispute. The federal courts cannot decide some controversies for want of a proper judicial remedy. For example, an action seeking to increase (or decrease) the number of men in the armed forces would be nonjusticiable because under the Constitution that power rests with the Congress — a political, not a judicial, body.

Justiciability often becomes intertwined with the other limitations previously noted. For example, cases that are moot or that present political questions and those in which the parties lack standing or ask for an advisory opinion are often said to be nonjusticiable.[75]

Supreme Court to determine whether that court rested its decision on federal constitutional law or on state law, or both). Although the Supreme Court has traditionally followed the "rule of four," the Court has not stated definitively whether and under what circumstances five justices may, consistent with the rule of four, have a writ of certiorari dismissed as improvidently granted and dissent from the dismissal of certiorari. This occurred recently in *Burrell* v. *McCray*, _____ U.S. _____ (decided June 14, 1976) where one member of the Court initially voted to grant certiorari but subsequently voted to dismiss the case. The justice was not identified. Several justices have offered various conflicting opinions on whether the rule of four is judicially impaired when certiorari is dismissed as improvidently granted. These stated opinions include the following: (1) It is always improper, as defeating the rule of four, to permit the five other Justices, despite four dissents, to have certiorari dismissed as improvidently granted. See, e.g., *United States* v. *Shannon*, 342 U.S. 288 (1952) (Douglas, J., dissenting). (2) Certiorari should be dismissed as improvidently granted "only" in exceptional circumstances and where all nine [members of the Supreme Court] agree." *Iowa Beef Packers, Inc.* v. *Thompson*, 405 U.S. 228 (1972) (Douglas, J., dissenting). (3) It is proper for five justices, over the dissents of the other four, to dismiss a case on the grounds that certiorari was improvidently granted when based on circumstances that were not fully apprehended when certiorari was granted. *Rogers* v. *Missouri Pacific R. Co.*, 352 U.S. 500 (1957) (opinion of Harlan, J.). See also concurring opinion of Mr. Justice Stevens in *Burrell* v. *McCray*, supra. (4) When a certain class of cases is systematically taken for review on certiorari, and if five justices believe that such cases raise insignificant and unimportant questions and that the Supreme Court's time is being unduly drained by adjudication of such cases, these five justices may properly dismiss the writ of certiorari as improvidently granted, since the reason for deference to

a minority view under the rule of four does not apply in such circumstances. See dissenting opinion of Justice Frankfurter in *Rogers*, supra.

The Supreme Court has relied upon the following grounds in dismissing writs of certiorari as improvidently granted: (1) The lack of a final judgment by the highest state court in which a judgment could be had. See, e.g., *Dresner* v. *Tallahassee*, 378 U.S. 539 (1964). See also 28 U.S.C.A. § 1257(3), supra, § 1.02. (2) The lack of a substantial federal question. See, e.g., *Duncan* v. *Tennessee*, 405 U.S. 127 (1972). (3) The presence of an adequate independent state ground as a basis for supporting the judgment below. See, e.g., *Jankovich* v. *Indiana Toll Road Commission*, 379 U.S. 487 (1965). (4) The lack of a conflict between the circuit courts of appeals. See, e.g., *Layne & Bowler Corp.* v. *Western Well Works, Inc.*, 261 U.S. 387 (1923). (5) A failure of the record to present the same question that the Supreme Court had expected to answer when it granted certiorari. See, e.g., *McClanahan* v. *Moraver & Hartzell, Inc.*, 404 U.S. 16 (1971). (6) A failure by the petitioner to raise or preserve an issue in the lower courts. See, e.g., *Monks* v. *New Jersey*, 398 U.S. 71 (1970). (7) A subsequent change in the law such that, having been fully aware of its implications, the Supreme Court would not have granted certiorari. See, e.g., *Piccirillo* v. *New York*, 400 U.S. 548 (1971). (8) The issues before the Supreme Court are merely factual ones of no important legal consequence. See, e.g., *Rudolph* v. *United States*, 370 U.S. 269 (1969). (9) The final degree by a trial court is based on the parties' express compromise agreement. See, e.g., *Furness, Withy & Co.* v. *YangTsze Ins. Assoc.*, 242 U.S. 430 (1917). (10) It appears that the petitioner was not a party to the record. See, e.g., *Posner* v. *Anderson*, 293 U.S. 531 (1934). (11) The issues presented to the Supreme Court are not ripe. See, e.g., *Taggart* v. *Weinacker's, Inc.*, 397 U.S. 223 (1970). (12) The petitioner could not show that he would suffer irreparable injury for which he had no adequate remedy at

Footnote continued on page 38

Other Self-Imposed Limitations

The Supreme Court has developed several additional rules that place limitations on judicial review. In 1936, in his concurring opinion in *Ashwander* v. *Tennessee Valley Authority,* 297 U.S. 288, 345–348 (1936), Mr. Justice Brandeis listed the following seven rules developed by the Supreme Court "for its own governance" to avoid passing prematurely on constitutional questions:

1. The Court will not pass upon the constitutionality of legislation in a friendly, nonadversary proceeding, declining because to decide such questions "is legitimate only in the last resort, and as a necessity in the determination of a real, earnest, and vital controversy between individuals. It never was thought that, by means of the friendly suit, a party beaten in the legislature could transfer to the courts an inquiry as to the constitutionality of the legislative act."

2. The Court will not "anticipate a question of constitutional law in advance of the necessity of deciding it." . . . "It is not the habit of the Court to decide questions of a constitutional nature unless absolutely necessary to a decision of the case." . . .

3. The Court will not "formulate a rule of con-

stitutional law broader than is required by the precise facts to which it is to be applied." . . .

4. The Court will not pass upon a constitutional question although properly presented by the record, if there is also present some other ground upon which the case may be disposed of. This rule has found most varied application. Thus, if a case can be decided on either of two grounds, one involving a constitutional question, the other a question of statutory construction or general law, the Court will decide only the latter. . . . Appeals from the highest court of a state challenging its decision of a question under the Federal Constitution are frequently dismissed because the judgment can be sustained on an independent state ground. . . .

5. The Court will not pass upon the validity of a statute upon complaint of one who fails to show that he is injured by its operation. . . . Among the many applications of this rule, none is more striking than the denial of the right of challenge to one who lacks a personal or property right. . . .

6. The Court will not pass upon the constitutionality of a statute at the instance of one who has availed himself of its benefits. . . .

7. "When the validity of an act of the Congress is drawn in question, and even if a serious doubt of constitutionality is raised, it is a cardinal principle that this Court will first ascertain whether a

---

law. See, e.g., *Moor* v. *Texas & N.O.R. Co.,* 297 U.S. 101 (1936). (13) The record is unclear. See, e.g., *Johnson* v. *Massachusetts,* 390 U.S. 511 (1968).

Note that the Supreme Court has stated that if the reason for dismissing the writ is jurisdictional in nature, the case can be restored to the docket if the defect can be removed. *Jones* v. *Opelika,* 315 U.S. 782 (1943). Also, the rule of four applies to appeals as well as to petitions for certiorari. See Stern, R. L., and Gressman, E., *Supreme Court Practice,* § 5.16 (4th ed. 1969). As noted by former Associate Justice Clark, "If four of us vote to have an argument, it is scheduled; if not, the appeal is affirmed or dismissed and the petition for certiorari is denied. In short, in the vernacular, you must knock on the door and unless four Justices answer and let you enter, your case cannot be argued." Clark, T., *The Decisional Processes of the Supreme Court,* 50 Cornell L.Q. 385, 389 (1965).

[74]*Flast* v. *Cohen,* 392 U.S. 83 (1968). In *Flast,* the Court noted: "Embodied in the words 'cases' and 'controversies' are two complementary but somewhat different limitations. In part those words limit the business of federal courts to questions presented in an adversary context and

in a form historically viewed as capable of resolution through the judicial process. And in part those words define the role assigned to the judiciary in a tripartite allocation of power to assure that the federal courts will not intrude into areas committed to the other branches of government. Justiciability is the term of art employed to give expression to this dual limitation placed upon federal courts by the case and controversy doctrine. Justiciability is itself a concept of uncertain meaning and scope," at 95. See also *Poe* v. *Ullman,* 367 U.S. 496 (1961), where the Court stated that "[j]usticiability is . . . not a legal concept with a fixed content susceptible to scientific verification," at 508. And in *Aetna Life Insurance Co.* v. *Haworth,* 300 U.S. 227 (1937), the Court stated: "A justiciable controversy is . . . distinguished from a difference or dispute of a hypothetical or abstract character; from one that is academic or moot. The controversy must be definite and concrete, touching the legal relations of the parties having adverse legal interests. It must be a real and substantial controversy admitting of specific relief through a decree of a conclusive character, as distinguished from an opinion advising what the law would be upon a hypothetical state of facts," at 240.

[75]*Flast* v. *Cohen,* 392 U.S. 83 (1968).

construction of the statute is fairly possible by which the question may be avoided...."

In the next section, seven articles are presented that explore the decision-making process and the nature of the Supreme Court. Three of the selections were written by present justices of the Supreme Court; a fourth presents a well-known journalist's view of the writing style of the justices; in another, a clerk gives his view of the Supreme Court; the decision-making process is examined in the sixth selection; and the section ends with a newspaper report of Justice Burger's "blast" at long-winded attorneys. Finally, in § 1.06, Professor Robert L. Cord's articles on the nationalization of the Bill of Rights are presented.

1.06 DECISION-MAKING IN THE SUPREME COURT

INSIDE VIEW OF THE HIGH COURT*

William J. Brennan, Jr.†

Throughout its history the Supreme Court has been called upon to face many of the dominant social, political, economic and even philosophical issues that confront the nation. But Solicitor General Cox only recently reminded us that this does not mean that the Court is charged with making social, political, economic or philosophical decisions. Quite the contrary. The Court is not a council of Platonic guardians for deciding our most difficult and emotional questions according to the Justices' own notions of what is just or wise or politic. To the extent that this is a governmental function at all, it is the function of the people's elected representatives.

The Justices are charged with deciding

---

*From *The New York Times Magazine*, October 6, 1963. © 1963 by The New York Times Co. Reprinted by permission.

†Justice Brennan has served on the Supreme Court since 1956. This article was adapted from an address he gave in September, 1963, at Maxwell Air Force Base, Montgomery, Alabama.

according to law. Because the issues arise in the framework of concrete litigation they must be decided on facts embalmed in a record made by some lower court or administrative agency. And while the Justices may and do consult history and the other disciplines as aids to constitutional decision, the text of the Constitution and relevant precedents dealing with that text are their primary tools.

It is indeed true, as Judge Learned Hand once said, that the judge's authority "depends upon the assumption that he speaks with the mouth of others: the momentum of his utterances must be greater than any which his personal reputation and character can command; if it is to do the work assigned to it—if it is to stand against the passionate resentments arising out of the interests he must frustrate—he must preserve his authority by cloaking himself in the majesty of an over-shadowing past, but he must discover some composition with the dominant trends of his times."

However, we must keep in mind that, while the words of the Constitution are binding, their application to specific problems is not often easy. The Founding Fathers knew better than to pin down their descendants too closely. Enduring principles rather than petty details were what they sought. Thus the Constitution does not take the form of a litany of specifics. There are, therefore, very few cases where the constitutional answers are clear, all one way or all the other, and this is also true of the current cases raising conflicts between the individual and governmental power—an area increasingly requiring the Court's attention.

Ultimately, of course, the Court must resolve the conflicts of competing interests in these cases, but all Americans should keep in mind how intense and troubling these conflicts can be. Where the police have ample external evidence of a man's guilt, but to be sure of their case put into evidence a confession obtained through coercion, the conflict arises between his right to a fair prosecution and society's right to protection against his depravity. Where the orthodox Jew wishes to open his shop and do business on the day which non-Jews have chosen, and the Legislature has sanctioned, as a day of rest, the Court cannot escape a difficult problem of reconciling opposed interests. Finally, the claims of the Negro citizen, to borrow Solicitor General Cox's words, present a "conflict between the ideal of liberty and equality expressed in the Declaration of Independence, on the one hand, and, on the other hand, a way of life rooted in the customs of many of our people."

If all segments of our society can be made to appreciate that there are such conflicts, and that cases which involve constitutional rights often require difficult choices, if this alone is accomplished, we will have immeasurably enriched our common understanding of the meaning and significance of our freedoms. And we will have a better appreciation of the Court's function and its difficulties.

How conflicts such as these ought to be resolved constantly troubles our whole society. There should be no surprise, then, that how properly to resolve them often produces sharp division within the Court itself. When problems are so fundamental, the claims of the competing interests are often nicely balanced, and close divisions are almost inevitable.

Supreme Court cases are usually one of three kinds: the "original" action brought directly in the Court by one state against another state or states, or between a state or states and the Federal Government. Only a handful of such cases arise each year, but they are an important handful. A recent example was the contest between Arizona and California over the waters of the lower basin of the Colorado River. Another was the contest between the Federal Government and the newest state of Hawaii over the ownership of lands in Hawaii.

The second kind of case seeks review of the decisions of a Federal Court of Appeals — there are 11 such courts — or of a decision of a Federal District Court — there is a Federal District Court in each of the 50 states.

The third kind of case comes from a state court — the Court may review a state court judgment by the highest court of any of the 50 states, if the judgment rests on the decision of a Federal question.

When I came to the Court seven years ago the aggregate of the cases in the three classes was 1,600. In the term just completed there were 2,800, an increase of 75 per cent in seven years. Obviously, the volume will have doubled before I complete 10 years of service. How is it possible to manage such a huge volume of cases? The answer is that we have the authority to screen them and select for argument and decision only those which, in our judgment, guided by pertinent criteria, raise the most important and far-reaching questions. By that device we select annually around 6 per cent — between 150 and 170 cases — for decision. That screening process works like this: When nine Justices sit, it takes five to decide a case on the merits. But it takes only the votes of four of the nine to put a case on the argument calendar for argument and decision. Those four votes are hard to come by — only an exceptional case raising a significant Federal question commands them.

Each application for review is usually in the form of a short petition, attached to which are any opinions of the lower courts in the case. The adversary may file a response — also, in practice, usually short. Both the petition and response identify the Federal questions allegedly involved, argue their substantiality, and whether they were properly raised in the lower courts. Each Justice receives copies of the petition and response and such parts of the record as the parties may submit. Each Justice then, without any consultation at this stage with the others, reaches his own tentative conclusion whether the application should be granted or denied.

The first consultation about the case comes at the Court conference at which the case is listed on the agenda for discussion. We sit in conference almost every Friday during the term. Conferences begin at 10 in the morning and often continue until 6, except for a half-hour recess for lunch. Only the Justices are present. There are no law clerks, no stenographers, no secretaries, no pages — just the nine of us. The junior Justice acts as guardian of the door, receiving and delivering any messages that come in or go from the conference.

* * *

Each of us has his copy of the agenda of the day's cases before him. The agenda lists the cases applying for review. Each of us before coming to the conference has noted on his copy his tentative view whether or not review should be granted in each case. The Chief Justice begins the discussion of each case. He then yields to the senior Associate Justice and discussion proceeds down the line in order of seniority until each Justice has spoken. Voting goes the other way. The junior Justice votes first and voting then proceeds up the line to the Chief Justice, who votes last. Each of us has a docket containing a sheet for each case with appropriate places for recording the votes. When any case receives four votes for review, that case is transferred to the oral argument list. Applications in which none of us sees merit may be passed over without discussion.

Now how do we process the decisions we agree to review? There are rare occasions when the question is so clearly controlled by an earlier decision of the Court that a reversal of the lower court judgment is inevitable. In these rare instances we may summarily reverse without oral argument. The case must very clearly justify summary disposition, however, because our ordinary practice is not to reverse a decision without oral argument. Indeed, oral argument of cases taken for review, whether from the state or Federal courts, is the usual practice. We rarely accept submissions of cases on briefs.

Oral argument ordinarily occurs about four months after the application for review is granted. Each party is usually allowed one hour, but in recent years we have limited oral argument to a half-hour in cases thought to involve issues not requiring longer argument. Counsel submit their briefs and record in sufficient time for the distribution of one set to each Justice two or three weeks before the oral argument. Most of the members of the present Court follow the practice of reading the briefs before the argument. This memorandum digests the facts and the arguments of both sides, highlighting the matters about which we may want to question counsel at the argument. Often I have independent research done in advance of argument and incorporate the results in the bench memorandum. . . .

. . . The argued cases are listed on the conference agenda on the Friday following argument. Conference discussion follows the same procedure I have described for the discussion of certiorari petitions. Of course, it is much more extended. Not infrequently discussion of particular cases may be spread over two or more conferences.

Not until the discussion is completed and a vote taken is the opinion assigned. The assignment is not made at the conference but formally in writing some few days after the conference. The Chief Justice assigns the opinions in those cases in which he has voted with the majority. The senior Associate Justice voting with the majority assigns the opinions in the other cases. The dissenters agree among themselves who shall write the dissenting opinion. Of course, each Justice is free to write his own opinion, concurring or dissenting.

The writing of an opinion always takes weeks and sometimes months. The most painstaking research and care are involved. Research, of course, concentrates on relevant legal materials—precedents particularly. But Supreme Court cases often require some familiarity with history, economics, the social and other sciences, and authorities in these areas, too, are consulted when necessary.

When the author of an opinion feels he has an unanswerable document he sends it to a print shop, which we maintain in our building. The printed draft may be revised several times before his proposed opinion is circulated among the other Justices. Copies are sent to each member of the Court, those in the dissent as well as those in the majority.

Now the author often discovers that his work has only begun. He receives a return, ordinarily in writing, from each Justice who voted with him and sometimes also from the Justices who voted the other way. He learns who will write the dissent if one is to be written. But his particular concern is whether those who voted with him are still of his view and what they have to say about his proposed opinion. Often some who voted with him at conference will advise that they reserve final judgment pending the circulation of the dissent. It is a common experience that dissents change votes, even enough votes to become the majority. I have had to convert more than one of my proposed majority opinions into a dissent before the final decision was announced. I have also, however, had the more satisfying experience of rewriting a dissent as a majority opinion for the Court.

Before everyone has finally made up his mind a constant interchange by memoranda, by telephone, at the lunch table, continues while we hammer out the final form of the opinion. I had one case during the past term in which I circulated 10 printed drafts before one was approved as the Court opinion.

The point of this procedure is that each Justice, unless he disqualifies himself in a particular case, passes on every piece of business coming to the Court. The Court does not function by means of committees or panels. Each Justice passes on each petition, each item, no matter how drawn, in longhand, by typewriter, or on a press. Our Constitution vests the judicial power in only one Supreme Court. This does not permit Supreme Court action by committees, panels, or sections.

The method that the Justices use in meeting an enormous caseload varies. There is one uniform rule: Judging is not delegated. Each Justice studies each case in sufficient detail to resolve the question for himself. In a very real sense, each decision is an individual decision of every Justice. The process can be a lonely, troubling experience for fallible human beings conscious that their best may not be adequate to the challenge. "We are not unaware" the late Justice Jackson said, "that we are not final because we are infallible: we know that we are infallible only because we are final." One does not forget how much may depend on his decision. He knows that usually more than the litigants may be affected, that the course of vital social, economic and political currents may be directed.

This then is the decisional process in the Supreme Court. It is not without its tensions, of course—indeed, quiet agonizing tensions at times. I would particularly emphasize that, unlike the case of a Congressional or White House decision, Americans demand of their Supreme Court judges that they produce a written opinion, the collective expression of the judges subscribing to it, setting forth the reasons which led them to the decision. These opinions are the exposition, not just to lawyers, legal scholars and other judges, but to our whole society, of the bases upon which a particular result rests—why a problem, looked at as disinterestedly and dispassionately as nine human beings trained in a tradition of the disinterested and dispassionate approach can look at it, is answered as it is.

It is inevitable, however, that Supreme Court decisions—and the Justices themselves—should be caught up in public debate and be the subjects of bitter controversy. An editorial in The Washington Post did not miss the mark by much in saying that this was so because "one of the primary functions of the Supreme Court is to keep the people of the country from doing what they would like to do—at times when what they would like to do runs counter to the Constitution.... The function of the Supreme Court is not to count constituents; it is to interpret a fundamental charter which imposes restraints on constituents. Independence and integrity, not popularity, must be its standards."

Certainly controversy over its work has attended the Court throughout its history. As Professor Paul A. Freund of Harvard remarked, this has been true almost since the Court's first decision:

"When the Court held, in 1793, that the State of Georgia could be sued on a contract in the Federal courts, the outraged Assembly of that state passed a bill declaring that any Federal marshal who should try to collect the judgment would be guilty of a felony and would suffer death, without benefit of clergy, by being hanged. When the Court decided that state criminal convictions could be reviewed in the Supreme Court, Chief Justice Roane of Virginia exploded, calling it a 'most monstrous and unexampled decision. It can only be accounted for by that love of power which history informs us infects and corrupts all who possess it, and from which even the eminent and upright judges are not exempt.'"

But public understanding has not always been lacking in the past. Perhaps it exists today. But surely a more informed knowledge of the decisional process should aid a better understanding.

It is not agreement with the Court's decisions that I urge. Our law is the richer and the wiser because academic and informed lay criticism is part of the stream of development. It is only a greater awareness of the nature and limits of the Supreme Court's function that I seek. I agree fully with the Solicitor General: It is essential, just because the public questions which the Court faces are pressing and divisive, that they be thoroughly canvassed in public, each step at a time, while the Court is evolving new principles. The ultimate resolution of questions fundamental to the whole community must be based on a common consensus of understanding of the unique responsibility assigned to the Supreme Court in our society.

The lack of that understanding led Mr. Justice Holmes to say 50 years ago: "We are very quiet there, but it is the quiet of a storm center, as we all know. Science has taught the world skepticism and has made it legitimate to put everything to the test of proof. Many beautiful and noble reverences are impaired, but in these days no one can complain if any institution, system, or belief is called on to justify its continuance in life. Of course we are not excepted and have not escaped. Doubts are expressed that go to our very being. Not only are we told that when Marshall pronounced an Act of Congress unconstitutional he usurped a power that the Constitution did not give, but we are told that we are the representatives of a class—a tool of the money power. I get letters, not always anonymous, intimating

TABLE 1.1 The Supreme Court's Workload: 1975–1976 Term*

FINAL DISPOSITION OF CASES

	Disposed of	Remaining on Docket
Original Docket	7	7
On Merits	4	
Leave to File Complaint Denied	3	
Appellate Docket	1810	542
On Merits	272†	
Appeals and Petitions for Review Denied or Dismissed‡	1538	
(*Review Granted: 154 (9.1%)*)§		
Miscellaneous Docket	1989	406
On Merits	86†	
Appeals and Petitions for Review Denied or Dismissed‡	1903	
(*Review Granted: 18 (1.0%)*)§		
Total	**3806**	**955**

Method of Disposition

By Written Opinion	184‖	By Denial or Dismissal of Appeals or Petitions for Review‡	3441
(*Number of Written Opinions:* 159)¶			
By Per Curiam Decision	178	By Denial of Leave to File Complaint— Original Cases	3
Total			**3806**

Disposition of Cases Reviewed on Writ of Certiorari

	Reversed**	Vacated††	Affirmed	Total
Full Opinions	82(64.5%)	17(13.4%)	28(22.1%)	127
Memorandum Orders	3(3.2%)	91(96.8%)	0(0.0%)	94
Total	**85(38.5%)**	**108(48.8%)**	**28(12.7%)**	**221**

*From *The Supreme Court, 1975 Term,* Table II, 90 Harv. L. Rev. 279 (1976). Copyright 1976 by The Harvard Law Review Association.

†Including cases summarily affirmed, reversed, or vacated.

‡This category primarily includes dismissals of appeals and denials of petitions for certiorari. It also includes denials of other applications for review, such as petitions for writs of habeas corpus or writs of mandamus.

§In computing the percentage of cases granted review last Term, the divisor is obtained by adding the number of cases denied or dimissed to the number of cases granted review. Petitions remaining on the docket on which no action has been taken are not included.

‖Including 24 cases disposed of in 21 per curiam opinions containing sufficient legal reasoning to be considered "written opinions" and not included in the per curiam decision figures.

¶Including 21 per curiam opinions containing substantial legal reasoning.

**Including two cases reversed in part and affirmed in part.

††Including one case affirmed in part and vacated in part, and one case reversed in part and vacated in part.

that we are corrupt. Well, gentlemen, I admit that it makes my heart ache. It is very painful, when one spends all the energies of one's soul in trying to do good work, with no thought but that of solving a problem according to the rules by which one is bound, to know that many see sinister motives and would be glad of evidence that one was consciously bad. But we must take such things philosophically and try to see what we can learn from hatred and distrust and whether behind them there may not be a germ of inarticulate truth.

"The attacks upon the court are merely an expression of the unrest that seems to wonder vaguely whether law and order pay. When the ignorant are taught to doubt they do not know what they safely may believe. And it seems to me that at this time we need education in the obvious more than investigation of the obscure."

High Court Justices Lack Literacy*

WASHINGTON, D.C. — The United States Supreme Court winds up its annual term this week, leaving to others the wearisome task of reading what the court hath wrought. After four hours of groping through the ground fog of jurisprudential prose, I am minded to grumble a journalist's word or two. Why do judges write such wretched stuff?

Many of my lawyer friends privately share this layman's critical view. They venture several reasons. Most judicial opinions are hard to read, they say, because the subject matter is complex; opinions cannot be simplified without sacrificing precision to clarity. The language of the law is in part an unknown tongue to ordinary readers. Finally, most of the high court's majority opinions are the end products of the committee process; and in the history of mankind, no committee ever wrote anything that could be enjoyably read.

Doubtless such reasons explain a good

*From Kilpatrick, James J., *The Washington Star,* July 5, 1976. Reprinted by permission of The Washington Star Syndicate, Inc.

deal. Allowing for all that, I still am minded to grouse. High court opinions don't have to be tedious. The country has known good judges who were good writers also. Go back, sometime, and read the collected opinions of John Marshall. The great Virginian wrote sentences that fell like shafts of sunlight, illuminating the whole of the law. Holmes and Brandeis and Jackson turned many a fine phrase; more recently, Frankfurter, Douglas and Black exhibited pith and punch. They were lively writers. Alas, we have a dull lot now.

Between June 10 and June 25, the court delivered itself of 22 opinions. On a recent rainy afternoon I read them all, from Tennessee vs. Dunlap through Massachusetts vs. Murgia. It would have been easier work to cut high grass in the noon day sun. In the whole turgid mass was not a single good sentence. Not one. Rehnquist almost made it. In a dissenting opinion involving the Serbian Orthodox church, he twice came close to a lucid line. In the first attempt he lost to verbosity, in the second he left an orphaned antecedent.

Otherwise, the afternoon was altogether grim. It would be pleasant if the chief justice, as first among the nine, would introduce his brothers to the interesting punctuation point that follows this word. That dot, he might say, is known as a period. Sad to say, the chief has yet to be introduced to it himself. He writes a sentence of 65 words as soddenly as he writes a sentence of only 58.

Rehnquist, bless his conservative heart, tries hard. At least he breaks up his long sentences with short ones. But he cannot resist the out-of-town word. Thus he speaks of "a lacuna in the statute." In ordinary parlance, a lacuna is a gap, a hole, a blank space. Why not say so? Acknowledging the rule against splitting infinitives, I nominate Rehnquist for a special award: He splits 'em in Latin. He posed the question whether "the power of Congress may be thought to *ex proprio vigore* apply to the power of the Puerto Rican legislature."

All of the justices except Blackmun have trouble with "since." In its primary meaning — the meaning that comes first to the eye and mind — "since" denotes the passing of time. It means from then till now, or from some particular past time to the present. When "since" is used in place of the honest "because," the eye flickers and the mind stumbles.

Stevens, the newest member of the court, is the worst offender on "since." He is addicted not only to the single since, but to the double and even the triple since. Perhaps Blackmun might take him to lunch, for Blackmun gets it right: "*Because* the New Hampshire statutes speak in such a way...." Work on him, Harry!

Other members of the court slip slovenly into "claim," when they mean "contend," "charge," "allege," or simply, "say." Careful writers do not claim the reasons were false. Stewart cannot resist the temptation to say, "the fact is that...." Marshall forgets that "none" is singular.... "None of the cases are to the contrary." White has it right: "None of the cases reaches...."

Is such criticism mere nit-picking? I deny it. These birds are busy writing the supreme law of the land. They are dealing with the great gut issues of our country—racial tensions, sexual discrimination, employment, education, politics, religious freedom, criminal trials. Yes, they must try to write precisely, but do they have to write precisely turgidly? Can't they write precisely lucidly instead?

Query: After reading several Supreme Court opinions, do you agree with Mr. Kilpatrick's statement that "most judicial opinions are hard to read"?

A Clerk's View of the Court*

For a case the Supreme Court has decided to hear, written briefs are but one part of counsel's contribution. The other is oral

---

*From Wilkinson, J. Harvie, III, *Serving Justice: A Supreme Court Clerk's View.* New York, Charterhouse Books, Inc., 1974, pp. 31–34, 45–47, 151–154. Reprinted by permission of the author. Mr. Wilkinson served as a law clerk to Mr. Justice Powell during the 1971 and 1972 terms of the Court. He is now an Associate Professor of Law at the University of Virginia.

argument by counsel to the Court, in many ways the most dramatic and challenging part of the appellate process. I was once told, by someone who ought to have known better, that oral argument at the Court was of secondary importance to the briefs, little more than formality for justices "who have already decided what they're going to do." His view was sadly unfounded: the Justices would hardly devote such time to oral argument—the better part of eight days a month—merely to indulge a pointless exercise.

It was Justice Harlan who best underscored the importance of oral argument in an article written shortly after he came to Court. "Judges," he said, "have different work habits. There are some judges who listen better than they read and who are more receptive to the spoken than the written word." Unlike the written brief, good oral argument is give-and-take between counsel and bench; a tough, probing exchange can uncover facts or grounds of decision the briefs might obscure and allow a Justice to test on counsel his misgivings and concerns about a case. From counsel's point of view, oral argument is his only chance to address the Justices collectively and face-to-face. They become for one hour a captive audience to every case, and the opportunity for persuasion can be choice.

It is on days of oral argument that the Supreme Court is most alive. The small first-floor cafeteria becomes a hub of activity, with its swarms of tourists and dark suited lawyers huddling intently at their tables. Members of the press, perhaps John MacKenzie, of the *Washington Post,* or Fred Graham, formerly of *The New York Times,* and now with CBS, might stroll through. Occasionally, Solicitor General Griswold would appear, bedecked in form tux and tails. Eating breakfast there, I would sometimes be interrupted by friends dropping by and wanting to know what seats in the courtroom were available that day.

The courtroom itself, where argument takes place, is elegant in its simplicity. It is of clean, rectangular composition, somewhat higher than it is wide, and ringed about with twenty-four columns of Italian marble. It is imposing but at the same time sufficiently intimate to give dialogue between counsel and Court a conversational tone, not one of formal debate. Institutions of government, even in a democracy, require an aura of drama and ceremony, and the Supreme Court, on a day of argument, is no exception. The courtroom is a theatrical creation, with its high, ornate ceiling, its bench of rich, deep mahogany behind which are the highbacked black leather chairs of the Justices and the red velvet curtain from which they emerge, black-robed, promptly at 10:00 a.m. as the marshal bangs his gavel and announces solemnly:

The Honorable, the Chief Justice, and the Associate Justices of the Supreme Court of the United States. Oyez! Oyez! Oyez! All persons having business before the Honorable, the Supreme Court of the United States, are admonished to draw near and give their attention, for the Court is now sitting. God save the United States and this Honorable Court.

Again the gavel falls, the Justices and all others take their seats, and the day's business begins.

The spotlight at oral argument is on counsel and the Court. The clerks sit in an alcove on the south side of the courtroom, a forgotten part of the whole proceeding. As a clerk, I was generally kept too busy to observe more than a fraction of the cases argued. When I did listen, I witnessed counsel of all ages and skills, from the youngest to the most prestigious elder statesmen of the bar, from the most urbane lawyers to the most roughhewn.

Argument at its best is an illuminating and rapid-paced exercise, at its worst pedantic and unprofitable, sending spectators and judges alike into bouts of drowsiness. Argument before the Court can also take a most unpredictable bent, such as when one celebrated lawyer, after several evasions, finally answered, "I don't know, your honor," to a question on a critical fact of his case; or when an Assistant Attorney General from a Midwestern state failed to cite, when asked, a single federal precedent for his position; or, more pleasantly, when a young, green-looking attorney still in his twenties gave a plucky argument in the face of stiff questioning by the Justices in a significant search and seizure case.

I never sat long in that courtroom, however, without recognizing that effective oral argument before the Supreme Court of the United States demands the very best from a lawyer. Personally he has to communicate candor and directness, confidence but not arrogance, and, in the case of the great advocates, an appropriate touch of humor and eloquence. Intellectually, he needs a determined instinct for the jugular of his case, and the agility of mind to take advantage of play as it develops, to synchronize the questions of the Justices with the logic and momentum of his own argument. Model appellate advocates are exceedingly rare; when one does perform, it is a thing of exquisite grace and power, a view of a master artist at work....

Part of my job as clerk was an attempt to stay on top of detail and paperwork. *Time* magazine once ran a cartoon showing the Justices of the Supreme Court thrashing and choking in a sea of paperwork, something that evoked an appreciative chuckle from employees at the Court. The Clerk's Office, under the direction of Michael Rodak, does an admirable job processing the Court's papers and the submissions of the litigants, and the Court itself is revising its procedures to better cope with the problem. But the number of items, with their sheer volume of paper, that pass through the Supreme Court each term is enormous. As a starter, the Court now handles in a term some 3,600 petitions for certiorari and appeals, each of which, no matter how frivolous, requires in most chambers at least the brief attention of a clerk and a Justice. Then there are various and sundry motions, applications to stay decisions of lower courts, petitions of criminal defendants seeking bail, none of which in and of itself is overwhelming but which collectively peck further away at a Justice's time. Finally, there are the argued cases, decisions which alone would constitute an impressive year's work for the Court.

Each case argued before the Court is in a constant state of evolution, and in the manner of a snowball rolling downhill, each day accumulates unto itself more papers and material: first the briefs of the parties, then the reply, supplementary and amicus briefs and motions, next—after argument and conference—the written opinion drafts, next the concurring and dissenting opinions, then notes from other Justices joining or commenting upon these various opinions, until at last the case is handed down. This process is not intimidating in any one case, but the Court hands down not one, but a bit over a hundred cases with signed opinions each term. During the term, especially from December until late May, the Supreme Court may become something of a marathon, with seventy or so cases alive at any one time and in varying stages of progress, all the way from those scheduled for an upcoming argument to those decided and ready to be handed down. The job of simultaneously keeping abreast of so many items is challenging enough for a clerk, though in our chambers at least, Justice Powell preferred all cases to be divided among us, with one law clerk primarily responsible to him on a third of them. For the Justice himself, with a final responsibility for every matter before the Court, keeping current with developments obviously was a demanding task.

The volume of business before the Supreme Court does not mean that it is choked to the point of paralysis. Justices are able to deal quickly with matters of relatively little importance and with those where they have acquired a background or expertise. What the volume does mean, however, is that much of the work of the Supreme Court is of the "stop and go" variety, and that sustained and uninterrupted periods of time for a single difficult problem or opinion are often hard to come by. As a clerk, I found the chances of interruption during any half hour to be impressive, and I seldom returned to my desk without some new matter demanding attention. I was grateful to be able to block off an entire day to do the quality of research Justice Powell wanted and that a complex case required. Some commentators on the Court's work interpret a particular case or opinion as if the Justice who authored it had nothing to do the whole year but sit back and ponder that single problem. But at times the Court's term might more accurately call to mind the proverbial small boy with his spinning tops, running to keep them all going.

The pace and workload at the Supreme Court has increasingly disturbed those who see the need there for a more reflective atmosphere, who understand the vast importance of the Court's judgements, the human limitations of its personnel, and the philosophic element of its decisions. But the Supreme Court is also a branch of modern government upon which are constantly thrust many of the nation's most complex and burning problems and where a keen activity and bustle seem almost necessary if it is not to be left cold or in the lurch. The Court, in fact, is a place of diverse moods, whose most harassed and feverish moments are yet framed by a more profound character....

The Supreme Court, I was convinced, is the most fascinating branch of American government. Lacking an elective mandate, the Court is perennially vulnerable; I have often wondered how it managed to survive. Beethoven's Fourth Symphony is a beautiful and serene piece between the more boisterous themes of the Third and Fifth. Schumann even called the symphony "a slender Greek maiden between two 'Norse giants.'" That image might aptly describe the place in government of the United States Supreme Court.

Justice Douglas once said in a speech that "the voice of conscience is more compelling than the clamor of a mob." The statement can as easily be thought to mean that the conscience of a Supreme Court Justice is more exalted than the wishes of the people of the country. That does not make Justice Douglas' statement illegitimate; it merely underscores the elitist edge of the Supreme Court's job. To take an example: the root causes of crime run deep, and Supreme Court decisions one way or another may not greatly change them. But the Supreme Court, in relation to the crime issue, is clearly the tip of the iceberg, and as the tip, its decisions are visible. To continue in the late 1960's its reversal of criminal convictions in the name of individual rights at a time of rising public concern over crime was an explosive course. Was such action the "voice of conscience" or a disdainful disregard of public opinion?

The Warren Court continually raised such questions about the Supreme Court as an institution. The irony of its decisions [is] apparent. Its purpose of revitalizing state government in the reapportionment cases may not square with the fact that through variously named constitutional doctrines and clauses such as preemption, incorporation, habeas corpus, and equal protection, the Warren Court stimulated the greatest drain of power from state to federal government since the New Deal. The enhancement of the democratic faith through one-man, one-vote put into question the activism of an "antidemocratic" institution such as the Supreme Court in other areas. The protection of blacks and indigent criminal suspects raised questions as to the relationship between a Supreme Court and majority welfare, as to whether any governing institution, in a democracy, could or should remain actively and permanently committed to minority causes.

The basic nature of the Constitution and Bill of Rights demands that the Supreme Court protect minorities of all sorts from political injustice. Yet the Supreme Court is purposely not put beyond range of political retribution, and there are and always have been distinctive limits to its powers. Not surprisingly, the leader of the Court's most activist era, Chief Justice Warren, all along claimed that the Supreme Court was essentially a passive institution. . . . :

"But the Court is not a self-starter. . . . It can never reach out and grab any issue and bring it into the court and decide it, no matter how strongly it may feel about the condition it's confronted with. It is a creature of the litigation that is brought to it. . . . And so many people can't understand that, because they believe that a lot of the people come there committed to a definite course of conduct and action depending upon their views, their political views. And they think if they see something they don't like, they just pull it into the court and decide it. But that is not true, the Court is very limited in its jurisdiction."

Warren's comments hit an important point: that whatever the lay of its decisions, the Court's strength lay in its continuance as a court and in an institutional posture of passive virtuosity. The passivity does not merely relate to the fact that the Supreme Court is a creature of the cases that come to it or that the Court may often prefer to decide those cases in the narrowest possible way. The passive virtues apply to the conduct of Justices as well.

Justices do not, as a rule, engage in public debate or offer gratuitous opinions on political issues or candidates; their public speeches very often have a bland and abstract ring. Such abstinence and nonpartisanship also extends to their clerks. Justice Powell tactfully let it be known that he did not want me to attend partisan political gatherings while working for him; he would have been disappointed had I, while a law clerk, so much as signed my name to a public petition.

At times a passive state is very difficult to maintain. One evening, on the radio news, I heard the following bulletin: "Today the Supreme Court ruled that police must get a search warrant in certain circumstances." The statement was not altogether inaccurate; it was just that what the radio said the Supreme Court was doing today had been true of its cases for almost the last hundred years. The bulletin bore almost no connection with the day's actual search and seizure case which had held that consent to a police search might be valid, even though the object of the search had not been warned by the police of his right to refuse such consent. The bulletin made me wonder. I was convinced that the Court, possibly because of the legal and technical nature of much of its business, was the most misinterpreted and misunderstood branch of government. Yet it did not, except in the rarest instances, reply to such misunderstanding or itself seek to correct it. It endured all sorts of distortion and malignment; and yet, the Justices stayed silent, relying I suppose, upon friends and followers of the Court's work to set things straight. I could not imagine a Justice attacking the press, even in tones far more moderate than those of Spiro Agnew. The Supreme Court was, in many ways, a mute branch of government. I asked myself why.

Again, the answer seemed that whatever the "political" tenor of its decisions, the Supreme Court must remain a court. That it must somehow seem to be above the give and take between the press and the political branches, or between the political branches themselves. Perhaps the key to its legitimacy and moral authority lay in a kind of institutional asceticism. Again the Beethoven analogy came to mind: amidst Congress and President, the Court must continue the "slender Greek maiden," pristine, pure, restrained, but with a certain elite and elegant touch. Or was it too late in the day to fool anybody? Was the Court, despite its whited veil, bruised from decades of hard and controversial political acts?

The Decision-Making Process in the Supreme Court*

Decision-making by the Supreme Court is a group process. Solo performances are unknown. No single member, be he the Chief or Associate Justice, dictates his private reason or personal views to his independent-minded brethren. Individually and independently they work together to arrive at a group decision for the Court. The fact that the decisions of the Supreme Court are group decisions is trite, but easily overlooked. It is highly important and carries with it some interesting and frequently beneficial consequences. For example, one easily ignored implication is that a group decision probably produced a final judgment having a viewpoint of greater breadth and depth, and fewer extremes, than most individual decisions. This point is particularly applicable when one considers the quality of the individual members of the Supreme Court. When Justices are endowed with high quality intellects and breadth of understanding, they can collectively bring to bear an awesome combination of sweeping brain power and extensive learning on a legal question.

Another feature frequently associated with the group decision process is that of stability. Because of this, the Supreme Court decisions tend to conform to the configurations of the past more than they otherwise might. Radical breaks with history seem not to appear often. Any Justice can raise a point of constitutional tradition and demand that it be met by his colleagues. Collectively, they can record doubts and qualifications which a person, working alone, can easily overlook. The fact that the Court must write group opinions, satisfactory to each member of the majority, although, perhaps, not fully satisfactory to each Justice entirely, the fact that the Court must justify its decisions within the framework of the Constitution, and the fact that

dissents to these opinions are freely filed, all go a long way toward insuring the integrity and reliability of the group decision process. This process can produce court opinions which are not fully satisfactory to the probing minds of legal scholars because the opinions must sometimes represent a compromise among some Justices, with no one Justice's view completely and rigorously followed. Occasionally, therefore, the group decision process can produce an unaesthetic opinion. But the group decision process also aids the Court to produce stable and, frequently, wise decisions which, in turn, are beneficial to our Nation and which can withstand the fickle breezes of a changing wind. One must always keep in mind: the judicial process in the Supreme Court is a group process. The Court does not function by using either committees or panels of Justices. Unless he disqualifies himself for some reason, each Justice passes on each case that seeks a hearing and on the merits of each case after the hearing has been held. The Constitution puts the judicial power in only one Supreme Court, not in its committees, panels or sections. One invariant rule prevails: judging is always an individual matter for each Justice and is never delegated; yet, too, the judicial process of the Supreme Court results in a group process.

What are the outlines of this judicial process? This question intrigues almost everyone who is seriously interested in the Supreme Court, and its answer is somewhat frustrating. The only honest answer is that no one, outside the Court members themselves, can be absolutely sure of everything that takes place inside the chambers. The reason for this situation is a simple one—the actual deliberations and intellectual interchanges of the Justices while they are in conference are, quite properly, not released to the press and are not made the subject of public curiosity. However, a few things are known, and they, in turn, allow some reasonable speculations regarding others.

A term of Court is well known, although its actual duration may vary slightly. It usually lasts about thirty-six weeks with the first session day being the first Monday of each October and continuing in session usually until about July 1. This means then, that, since the average Justice works six days a week and between eight and ten hours per day, each member of the Court

---

*From Morris, Arval A., *The Constitution and American Education*. St. Paul, West Publishing Co., 1974, pp. 71–75. Reprinted by permission.

puts in about 1,800 total hours per court term on court business. These hours are spent listening to lawyer arguments on cases, discussing court business in conference sessions, writing or studying opinions, reading other types of petitions, reading the briefs submitted by attorneys, and engaging in other collateral matters affecting the Court.

Officially, when the courtroom is open, the Court is in session only four days a week, Monday through Thursday, and the Justices listen to arguments only four hours per day. This schedule is usually followed by a recess period of about two weeks. During the days of argument the cases are called promptly, and the formal argument is held. Each case is usually given one hour for oral argument, one-half hour for each side. This is a critical time for the lawyer. He cannot read his argument to the Court. He must be able to pull together his side of a complex case, and to present it in a coherent and convincing way. Yet, there is a constant hurdle for him because he must also answer the probing questions which Justices ask, interrupting his argument, and which are based on their reading of the written materials in the case; that is, the briefs and other materials submitted by the attorneys. After hearing arguments, the Court recesses for two or three weeks for purposes of studying briefs, writing opinions and passing on other petitions.

One day has special significance for a student of the Supreme Court. Each Friday of the oral argument weeks finds the members of the Court in conference. During the usual conference session, the members of the Court spend most of their time discussing and voting, although they sometimes go over final drafts of opinions. The bulk of time in conference is probably spent on the cases which recently have been orally argued on their merits. Yet, the Court also must pass on those cases in which lawyers have asked that its discretion be exercised and that the case be granted a hearing by the Court. In these cases, the lawyers have asked that the Court grant their cases a hearing; that is, they have filed a petition requesting a grant of certiorari, or if the case is on appeal, they have filed a petition in support of the Court's jurisdiction over the case. The conference sessions begin sharply at eleven o'clock on Friday morning and

last until five-thirty. One might be curious about what goes on in the conference.

On Fridays, at eleven, the Justices meet at their conference room, which is a beautifully oak paneled chamber with one side lined with books from the floor to the ceiling. An exquisite marble fireplace is at one end of the chamber and over it hangs the only adornment in the room—a portrait of Mr. Chief Justice Marshall, the "Great Chief Justice." There is a rectangular table that stands in the middle of the conference room. The Justices are called to the conference by a buzzer that rings in each Justice's chamber about five minutes before the appointed hour. Religiously, the Justices follow a long held tradition. Meeting near Chief Justice Marshall's portrait, they greet each other in a friendly fashion and shake hands all around before beginning their work. The reason for this rite is that it helps to maintain the necessary working friendships among the Justices when they take up the court business, which usually consists of very difficult and controversial cases. The observance is important. It shows that a harmony of aims if not views is the guiding principle of the Court. One should always remember that an independent Justice can be the possessor of a mind which has been honed to a keen cutting edge like a scalpel's, and, occasionally, he may have a rapier tongue to match. But reason prevails, and the Court deliberations seem not to get out of hand, despite the burning issues found in a case and the courage and convictions about them which a Justice may have. After cordialities have been exchanged the members of the Court seat themselves around a large conference table. The session ensues.

Seated at the head of the table is the Chief Justice and directly across from him, at the other end of the table, sits the Senior Associate Justice. The rest of the members sit on either side of the table according to their rank in seniority, descending in seniority away from the Chief Justice. No one else ever is allowed in the room, and, if necessary, the most recently appointed Justice serves as a "messenger boy," carrying messages in and out of the conference room. This is a security device. It insures a full, frank and free discussion of all issues and ideas with the complete assurance of privacy. Consequently, no one, other than the

Justices, really knows the substantive content of what actually transpires during a conference. However, it is known that each Justice has an agenda of the day's cases; that the Chief Justice calls the items on for discussion and that he has the first opportunity to discuss the matter, if he so chooses. Discussion of the matter under consideration then passes from Justice to Justice according to his seniority, those having more seniority speaking first, until each of them has said all that he wishes. After discussion, the Chief Justice calls for the vote. If the case is one that has already been accepted by the Court and has had its hearing it takes a majority vote, usually five of the nine votes, to dispose of the case on its merits. But, if the case is one in which the question is whether the Court will grant a full hearing, it takes only four votes to bring the case to the Court for its initial hearing. Thus, a vote of four Justices is necessary to fix the cases onto the calendar of the Supreme Court and a majority vote, usually a vote of five Justices, is necessary to decide the merits of the case, removing it from the Court's calendar. If a Justice disqualifies himself in a case which has had a full hearing and if the remaining eight Justices split in their vote four-to-four, then the decision of the majority in the lower court is affirmed by the Supreme Court. While such a decision is binding on the parties, it does not become a precedent. Interestingly, the voting proceeds by an order opposite to that of the discussion. The first vote is cast by the Justice who has most recently been appointed to the Court and so on up the seniority ladder, with the Chief Justice voting last. This procedure has been designed to eliminate the influence of a senior Justice's vote on a junior Justice. It should be noted that the discussion preceding the vote need not indicate the way a senior Justice will vote, but rather, it may very well consist only of an analytical and dispassionate discussion of the problems involved in a case as they have been seen by a Justice.

After the voting is concluded the case must be assigned to a Justice for opinion writing. This assignment is made by the Chief Justice if he has voted with the majority. If not, then the senior Justice voting with the majority assigns the case to a Justice for an opinion. The Justices are notified that evening by messenger of their assignments. No official assignments are made for dissenting or concurring opinions. These lie solely within the discretion of the Justices, and are freely filed. When the majority opinion has been written, to the satisfaction of the individual Justice doing the initial work, it is then circulated to other members of the Court, majority and dissenting Justices, for their comments. This is a time of agonizing scrutiny. The cracks, crevices and loopholes of an opinion are revealed to its author by the discerning views of his brethren, who pass on them with piercing eyes. Frequently, with due contrition, the opinion must be drastically rewritten by its original author and sent again upon its journey to the Justices. The dissenting opinions are also fully circulated among the Justices, and sometimes the dissenting opinions will change votes, occasionally enough votes to make that opinion the majority opinion. Before each Justice finally makes up his mind there has been a constant interchange among them by memoranda, telephone and at the lunch table. Majority opinions have been rewritten as many as ten to twenty times before final agreement was reached. Finally, after receiving approval from the majority, the opinion, accompanied by its dissents, is filed in open court. Thus, in summary, it can be seen that the work of the Supreme Court Justices falls into four broad categories: reading various papers (petitions for certiorari, motions, etc.), listening to oral arguments, the conference and tentative voting, and writing opinions and ultimate decision.

WHO WRITES DECISIONS OF THE SUPREME COURT?

William H. Rehnquist*

Reprinted from *U.S. News & World Report,* December 13, 1957, pp. 74–75.

Each year some 18[†] young men who recently graduated from law school serve as clerks to the Justices of the Supreme Court

---

*William H. Rehnquist has served on the Supreme Court since 1972.

†Since 1970, each justice may hire three clerks, usually for a one-year period, at an annual salary of $18,000.

of the United States. Some of the mystery and rumor which shroud their work so far as the general public is concerned must necessarily remain. The clerk is primarily a trusted subordinate. Not only information as to how or why a particular decision came to be made—which by Court tradition is confidential—but much else by way of conversations and expressions of opinion on the part of the Justice ought not to be revealed on the initiative of the subordinate.

In addition, each clerk is in a position to offer only a worm's-eye view of the Justice-clerk relation. He will know well the system used by the Justice for whom he works, but his knowledge about the use to which other Justices put their clerks will necessarily be sketchy. I commit my limited knowledge of the nonconfidential aspects of the system to public print because recent controversy about the Court's decisions may make it of general interest.

During my tenure as law clerk for Justice Robert H. Jackson, from February, 1952, until June, 1953, he and six of the other Justices had two law clerks apiece. Chief Justice Vinson had three clerks and Justice Douglas one. Then, as now, there were two branches of the Court's business: first, choosing what cases it would decide, and, second, deciding them.

Each year more than a thousand requests are made to the Supreme Court to decide a case that has been decided by a lower State or federal court. By law the Court is free to grant or deny most of them as it sees fit. These requests for hearing are usually called "petitions for certiorari," and custom has established the rule that when four of the nine Justices vote to "grant" the petition, that is, vote to decide the case, the Court will hear argument on it and decide it. The Court usually grants less than 10 per cent of these petitions for certiorari, so its work of choosing what cases it will decide is neither a small nor an unimportant part of its job.

Each of these petitions for certiorari generally comprises a "brief" urging the Court to hear the case, another "brief" urging the Court not to hear the case, and an often lengthy record of all the proceedings in the lower courts. It is not surprising, therefore, that during my time the majority of Justices delegated substantial responsibilities to their clerks in the digesting of these petitions.

In Justice Jackson's office, the petitions for certiorari which were scheduled to be discussed at the next conference of the Justices were split between the two clerks. Each clerk would then prepare memoranda on the petitions assigned to him. These would include the facts of the case, the law as declared by the lower courts, and a brief summary of previous cases involving the same point. They concluded with a recommendation by the clerk either that the petition be granted or that it be denied. Aided by this data, the Justice himself would then study the petitions in order to determine his vote. I believe that a procedure substantially similar to that just outlined was followed in the offices of a majority of the other Justices during the time that I was a clerk.

The role of the clerks in the preparation of written opinions deciding cases ... which the Court had already agreed to decide varied far more from Justice to Justice than did their role in the handling of petitions for certiorari. Likewise, where the end product was to be a written opinion carrying the name of a Justice as its author, rather than merely an oral vote in conference, individual clerks were rightly far more close-mouthed in talking about procedure in their particular offices. For these reasons, I can fairly describe only the system used by Justice Jackson in this branch of the Court's work.

Robert H. Jackson had one of the finest literary gifts in the history of the Supreme Court. Even a casual acquaintance with his opinions during the 13 years he served on the Court indicates that he neither needed nor used ghost writers. The great majority of opinions which he wrote were drafted originally by him and submitted to his clerks for their criticism and suggestions. Frequently such a draft would be batted back and forth between the Justice and the particular clerk working on it several times. The contributions of the clerk by way of research, organization and, to a lesser extent, method of approach, [were] often substantial. But the end product was unquestionably the Justice's own, both in form and in substance.

On a couple of occasions each term, Justice Jackson would ask each clerk to draft an opinion for him along lines which he suggested. If the clerk were reasonably faithful to his instructions and reasonably diligent in his work, the Justice could be quite charitable with his black pencil and paste pot. The result reached in these opinions was no less the product of Justice Jackson than those he drafted himself; in literary style, these opinions generally suffered by comparison with those which he had drafted.

The conclusions to be drawn from these observations as to the "influence" of the clerks on the work of the Court will necessarily suffer from the worm's-eye point of view referred to above; nonetheless, some tentative ones will be ventured.

The specter of the law clerk as a legal Rasputin, exerting an important influence on the cases actually decided by the Court, may be discarded at once. No published biographical materials dealing with any of the Justices suggest any such influence. I certainly learned of none during the time I spent as a clerk.

Granted that this is the sort of thing that biographers and commentators might not readily learn of, the complete absence of any known evidence of such influence is surely aided by the common-sense view of the relationship between Justice and clerk. It is unreasonable to suppose that a lawyer of middle age or older, of sufficient eminence in some walk of life to be appointed as one of nine judges of the world's most powerful court, would consciously abandon his own views as to what is right and what is wrong in the law because a stripling clerk just graduated from law school tells him to.

Finally, in this area of opinions with which the Court decides cases, a Justice to whom an opinion is assigned generally is able to take sufficient time to examine as carefully as he believes necessary the materials which are to go into the opinion; he is not forced by pressure of time to take the word of a subordinate clerk on any important point.

Passing from the question of influence on written opinions to influence on the Court's action in granting or denying certiorari, no such easy answer is possible. Because of the great number of these petitions, sheer pressure of time often prevents a Justice from personally investigating every fact involved. The clerk's memorandum is usually supposed not only to digest the relevant matter

in the case which the Court is being asked to consider, but to summarize research of other cases on this point. Most of the Justices will base their vote in conference as to whether a petition should be granted at least in part on legal materials digested for him by a subordinate.

Obviously, if the clerk has erred in carrying out this digestive process, or if the clerk has consciously or unconsciously slanted the result of this process in a way different from the way the Justice himself might have done, the Justice may cast his vote in conference in a way different from that which he would have done if properly informed. I do not believe it can be debated that the possibility for influence by the clerks exists in this realm of the jurist's activities.

Because of the generally high level capability among the clerks, factual errors on their part may be discounted as influencing the Court's work. I would likewise rule out conscious slanting of the clerk's work as playing any significant role in the Court's work. An ideal clerk ought, in most aspects of his official capacity, to mirror as best he can the mind of the Justice for whom he works. There is room for sensibly presented difference of opinion when the lines of dispute are clearly drawn and in the open, but there is no room for the clerk's deliberate use of his position as research assistant to champion a cause to which his Justice does not subscribe. It would be an extraordinary reflection on the Justices, the clerks and the law schools if there were many deliberate, conscious departures from this ideal standard by the clerks. I knew of none, and would expect to learn of any here no more than to learn of analogous breaches of faith among honor graduates of schools of medicine, engineering or divinity.

This leaves *unconscious* slanting of material by clerks as the sole remaining possible source of influence by the clerks on the Court's certiorari work. Here, unfortunately, no such clean bill of health is possible.

Any subordinate who briefs his superior is bound to have or acquire ideas of his own regarding the matters briefed. Unless each of the nine Justices is to be utterly without professional assistance, the Court, like many other institutions, is bound to be exposed to the risk of such subordinate bias.

However, there are some facets peculiar to the clerks as a group which accentuate the problem of subordinate bias in their case.

Most of the clerks are recent honor graduates of law schools, and, as might be expected, are an intellectually high-spirited group. Some of them are imbued with deeply held notions about right and wrong in various fields of the law, and some in their youthful exuberance permit their notions to engender a cynical disrespect for the capabilities of anyone, including Justices, who may disagree with them.

The bias of the clerks, in my opinion, is not a random or hit-and-miss bias. From my observations of two sets of Court clerks during the 1951 and 1952 terms, the political and legal prejudices of the clerks were by no means representative of the country as a whole nor of the Court which they served.

After conceding a wide diversity of opinion among the clerks themselves, and further conceding the difficulties and possible inaccuracies inherent in political cataloguing of people, it is nonetheless fair to say that the political cast of the clerks as a group was to the "left" of either the nation or the Court.

Some of the tenets of the "liberal" point of view which commanded the sympathy of a majority of the clerks I knew were: extreme solicitude for the claims of Communists and other criminal defendants, expansion of federal power at the expense of State power, great sympathy toward any government regulation of business—in short, the political philosophy now espoused by the Court under Chief Justice Earl Warren.

There is the possibility of the bias of clerks affecting the Court's certiorari work because of the volume factor described above. I cannot speak for any clerk other than myself in stating as a fact that unconscious bias *did* creep into his work. Looking back, I must admit that I was not guiltless on this score, and I greatly doubt if many of my fellow clerks were much less guiltless than I. And where such bias did have any effect, because of the political outlook of the group of clerks that I knew, its direction would be to the political "left."

Myths and Misconceptions About the Supreme Court*

There are many myths and misconceptions that appear to exist—in varying degrees—about the United States Supreme Court. It is not surprising that there are mistaken views and ideas about what goes on within our cloistered walls. An article in *The New York Times Sunday Magazine* of March 16, 1975, declared that: "There is probably no more secret society in America than the Supreme Court."

Despite the current emphasis on "openness" in government, few would suggest that the conferences of the Court should be conducted in public or that the evolution of our opinions—often going through a dozen or more drafts—should be open to public view. Attorney General Levi recently commented that "the product of the Supreme Court is primarily its words, [and] the words it speaks publicly must be shaped and nurtured with care." This could hardly be accomplished in a "town hall" atmosphere.

But the judiciary is the third branch of government, and it is important for the public to be informed accurately as to nonconfidential facts about its highest tribunal. There is no secret as to how the Court functions. . . . Yet the myths and misconceptions persist, even among lawyers.

Myths and misconceptions are, of course, a necessary price we pay for free and open criticism of our government. Misconceptions would be all the greater if government alone were to dispense "the truth." The fact remains, however, that the Supreme Court is less free to identify errors or to reply to public criticism than our two political branches. And sometimes erroneous impressions can impair public confidence.

---

*From Powell, Lewis F., 48 N.Y. St. B.J. 6 (1976). Reprinted by permission of the New York State Bar Journal. Justice Powell has served on the Supreme Court since 1972.

The Case of the Chopped-Up Conference Table

I start with a frivolous example of an attempt to portray Chief Justice Burger as doing carpentry work on our conference room table. A serious book authored by a political scientist on a university faculty stated as a fact that the table—a huge slab of Honduran mahogany—was cut into three pieces and restructured into an inverted "U." The purpose, attributed to the chief justice, was to denigrate the "role of leadership of the liberal opposition." This is sheer fiction. The conference table retains its pristine shape; there has been no hacking or sawing; the justices occupy their seats in the traditional order of seniority.

Various stories and myths about the Court are commonplace. They often circulate orally and usually are recognized as a rumor or gossip. The story of the chopped-up conference table would properly be classified as malicious gossip were it not enshrined in a serious book.

The Case of the Long "Vacations"

A perennial misconception relates to when and how much the justices work. It is widely believed that the Court enjoys a three- to four-month vacation each year. To the average citizen, "vacation" implies that we are relieved of all work responsibilities and are simply free to enjoy ourselves. The question most frequently asked Court personnel, especially the police officers and staff personnel who serve the thousands of visitors who come to the Court, is why should the justices have protracted vacations.

Lawyers and judges are primarily responsible for the belief that judges work only part time. We inherited from English practice the terminology of courts being "in term" and "in vacation." No wonder we have confused the public. But I would expect responsible newsmen to know better. Yet as recently as last year, a nationally known C.B.S. radio commentator reported that "Supreme Court justices who are paid $60,000 a year and above for life traditionally take off almost four months; that's right, four months during the summer and fall, every year. This is considered by many to be Washington's ranking boondoggle."

Apart from the fact that the Court is not "in vacation" that long, there is simply no truth to the implication that the work of the Court ceases when the term ends.

To be sure, we do not have the burden of arguments and opinion writing. But major responsibilities continue throughout every week of the year. Petitions and appeals are filed at the same rate in the summer as during the rest of the year—some seventy to eighty per week; applications for stays and other relief continue to come in from the circuits; and there is the advance study of major cases already set for argument during the next term. Wherever a justice may be, petitions, memoranda from his clerks, and briefs are regularly sent to him for study or action. Moreover, we remain constantly on call for emergency matters.

This so-called vacation also affords us what little time we have for general background reading and reflection. If the Court is not simply to act on problems but also is to think and ponder them, we must have a period when our daily demands are less intense and consuming. The quality of the Court's work and judgment would surely suffer if the entire year were to be spent in the pressured atmosphere of hearing arguments and meeting opinion deadlines.

The Case of the Mysteriously Light Workload

There is also misunderstanding as to the workload of the Court when we are in term. One of our brothers[*] thinks that "we are vastly underworked" at the Court. In his view, "no justice . . . need work more than four days a week to carry his burden." *Warth* v. *Seldin,* [422 U.S. 490, 519] (June 25, 1975); *Tidewater Oil Co.* v. *United States,* 409 U.S. 151, 174, 177 (1972). But this opinion assumes an equality of experience, capacity and application that simply does not exist. No other justice works only four days a week. Each of us must carry his own responsibilities in his own way, utilizing time and resources, as well as experience and ability, as best one can. And we must function as an institution.

The magnitude of the Court's responsibilities has been the subject recently of a

---

*Mr. Justice Douglas.

thorough study by the Commission on Revision of the Federal Court Appellate System. The facts as to cases filed and disposed of are on the public record. [See Table 1.1, supra.] There is no comparable published data on the work habits of justices, but personnel at the Court know the facts, as do the press reporters who are based there. There is no such thing as a four-day—or even a five-day—work week for most justices.

I dwell on these misconceptions for no personal reason. Respect for and confidence in the Court as an institution, essential to its ultimate authority, is not enhanced either by the popular belief that we enjoy several months' vacation or by the view that we are paid for a full week's work when our duties require much less.

The Case of Law Clerk Influence

A subject closely related to the work of the justices is the role of the law clerks. There is a mistaken but persistent belief that law clerks exercise an undue influence on the decision-making process. It is indeed true that the law clerks play a vital part in the Court's work, but their role is widely misunderstood.

The Court simply could not function without the assistance of these extremely bright and dedicated young lawyers. They come to us each year with superb academic credentials, and usually with experience clerking for a circuit or district judge. The selection process is exacting and arduous. I received 172 applications for the 1975 term. These were reviewed with care, and I personally interviewed more than two dozen applicants and checked references before making final choices.

There is a legend that Justice Holmes insisted that his clerks, in addition to other qualifications, be "socially acceptable." The clerks then usually lived with the justices. John Chipman Gray selected Holmes' clerks for many years. Francis Biddle wrote in *Mr. Justice Holmes* that Gray "knew the kind of boys Holmes wanted—they must be able to deal with certiorari petitions, balance his checkbooks, and listen to his tall talk." Although social acceptability is no longer a criterion, the relationship between clerk and justice remains, as in the interest of the

Court it should, an intimate one of mutual respect and confidence.

In general, law clerks perform essentially the same function for judges that the ablest young associate lawyers perform for partners in a law firm. One of the most gratifying aspects of my service on the Court has been the association, professionally and personally, with the clerks in my chambers. If the attitude and sense of responsibility of these young people is typical of their generation, we may have confidence that the future of our country, despite seemingly intractable problems, is in good hands.

But having said all of this, I emphasize that law clerks do not decide cases. Each justice, conscious of the Court's long tradition of personal decision, recognizes the function of judging as his supreme responsibility. As Paul Freund has noted, when Justice Brandeis was asked to explain the great prestige of the Court, he replied, "because we do our own work." In the same vein, Alexander M. Bickel wrote in the February 17, 1973, *New Republic,* not too long before his tragic death: "Astonishing as the phenomena may appear in Washington, the justices have done their own work in the past, and [they] do it now, and the burden is crushing."

Although in a broad sense the Supreme Court is a collegial body, we recognize and respect the tradition that each justice in the end makes his own decision without pressure from other justices and certainly not from law clerks.

The Case of the Five-Four Decisions

I turn now to the five-four decisions. Many of the great cases, especially in recent years, have been decided by a margin of one vote. Misconceptions persist about these decisions. Should momentous issues of vast consequence to our country be resolved by that narrow a margin? Why should a result be accepted as the "law of the land" when four justices say it is not and often express their dissent in ungenerous language that seems to reflect on the legal ability if not the rationality of the majority?

The answer, quite simply, is that this is our system, and one that has survived the test of time and much criticism. It is well to remember that the cases we take for argument and formal decision represent less than 5 percent of the cases filed. These usually are the "hard" cases: those that involve major unsettled issues and often those that, under our constitutional system, require delicate judgments more related to one's philosophy of government than to familiar issues of private litigation. The Constitution itself is a charter of principles and concepts, not a Code Napoleon. Its meaning rarely is self-evident, especially when we are called on to apply doctrines such as federalism and separation of powers, concepts such as justiciability and standing to sue, and the ideals of a free society represented by due process and equal protection of the laws.

Differences of opinion as to such matters, indeed the strong differences evidenced by our dissents, are inevitable, and in my view reflect a strength—not a weakness—of the Court. The very process of dissent tends to minimize arbitrary decision making, assures a rigorous internal testing of the majority view, and bespeaks the vitality of the Court as an institution.

When the Court splits five-four in an important case, public attention is focused on the division. This tends to exaggerate the public's perception of the frequency of one-vote margins. An examination of recent terms, including four of the Warren Court and four of the Burger Court indicates that only about 13 per cent of the total number of cases decided by the Court in those eight terms were five-four decisions. This examination also refutes the view that these splits have increased significantly under the Burger Court. For the terms examined, the Court divided five-four in less than 15 per cent of its cases in the terms from 1970 through 1973, as compared with about 12 per cent of the cases during the terms from 1965 to 1968. The relatively minor difference in the frequency of five-four decisions for these two sets of terms suggests that changes in the personnel of the Court have had little effect on the most criticized division of the Justices.

It is of interest that in the eight terms examined, the Court tended to divide five-four more often in cases involving the constitutional rights of persons accused of crime than in any other category of cases. First Amendment rights and issues of federal jurisdiction and procedure also frequently produced such a division.

The Case of "Discord" and "Blocs"

News stories sometimes portray a picture of discord among the justices. A strong dissenting opinion is often characterized as "bitter," and a five-four decision is said to reflect deep-seated personal animosities among the justices. These stories are wide of the mark. They result perhaps from failure to understand that judges, like lawyers, may disagree strongly without personal rancor or ill will. The fact is that a genuine cordiality exists among the justices. As Justice Douglas has put it: "We have fierce ideological clashes, but at the same time we are a happy, harmonious group. That is true now, and it has been true all of my days [on the Court]."

Not infrequently, those who write about the Court refer to "blocs" among the justices. It is said that there is a "liberal bloc" and a "conservative bloc." There are intimations, contrary to the history of the Court, that justices tend to vote as a "bloc" according to which president appointed them. One could agree that there *are* liberal justices and conservative justices, if the elasticity of these abused labels is duly recognized. But use of the term "bloc" reflects a serious misconception of the way the Court functions and suggests some invidious degree of collaboration in the decisional process.

By definition, a "bloc" is a number of persons who act in concert or as "a unit." There are no blocs on the Court in this sense, or indeed, in any accurate sense of that term. Of course, justices differ in their perceptions of issues, in what is sometimes called their judicial philosophy, and in basic assumptions as to the meaning of some provisions of the Constitution. On some of these issues, depending on the context, one may rationally guess as to how a brother justice will vote. But on most of the closest issues advance predictions are hazardous, even for those of us who serve together. Independence of thought is indispensable to judging, and no man who wears the robe, whatever his court, is worthy of his office if he compromises this independence.

No Escape From History

We are appointed for life. We are under obligation to no man, to no party, and to no political constituency. Justices are fallible human beings, but our primary allegiance is to our oath of office and duty as we perceive it. Professor Freund wrote in *On Understanding the Supreme Court,* "The taking of the robe, an experience both emancipating and humbling, is apt to dissolve old ties and to quicken the sense that there is no escape from that judgment which is called history."

For me, old ties were quickly dissolved, and service on the Court continues to be a humbling experience. Each of us well knows that there is no escape "from that judgment which is called history."

Burger Blasts Long Briefs by Lawyers*

WASHINGTON (UPI)—Chief Justice Warren Burger Tuesday angrily criticized lawyers practicing before the Supreme Court for being too wordy, and suggested a rule limiting court petitions to 50 pages may be needed.

In a rare outburst from the bench, Burger told a Wake Forest law professor that three briefs totaling 298 pages he had filed were far too long, and said they are "exhibit A" on behalf of a new rule limiting wordage.

"You filed a 216-page brief when 75 pages easily would have done it," Burger told Sylvester Petro of Winston-Salem, N.C.

Burger's complaint came shortly after Justice Harry Blackmun criticized Petro for overwriting. It was the second time this term that Blackmun had publicly warned a lawyer during argument before a crowded courtroom to follow the high court's rules.

The rules say briefs should be "succinct," "precise," "clear" and free of "unnecessary detail."

There is no limit on length now, but the justices could institute one by a simple majority vote. Several justices have complained about the court's workload, and Burger has suggested the quality of advocacy is so low that special qualifications should be established for admission to the Supreme Court bar.

Yesterday's criticisms by Blackmun and Burger may signal the justices' intent to begin rigid enforcement of court rules, sending back for rewriting any briefs they consider rambling or overly long.

As Petro was concluding his argument against an agency shop provision in a Detroit teachers union contract, Burger told him his time was up, and said:

"I want to follow up on what my brother Blackmun said a few moments ago. You filed a 216-page brief and I address this not as a criticism to you personally, but as an observation to the bar.

"In this case there are 600 pages of material filed with us, which means that if every case heard today (four) was treated the same way, we would have 2,400 pages to read. . . .

"I think you may have done a service to the court. You have furnished Exhibit A why the court should activate a rule limiting briefs to 50 pages unless the court grants special leave."

1.07 NATIONALIZATION OF THE BILL OF RIGHTS

The Bill of Rights and the States*

Today, by virtue of the restraining nature of the due process clause of the Fourteenth Amendment, all of the liberties of the First Amendment; the Fourth Amendment guarantee against unreasonable searches and seizures, together with the exclusionary rule; the Fifth Amendment guarantee

---

*From the *Tampa Tribune,* November 11, 1976, p. 7-A. Copyright © 1976 by United Press International. Reprinted by permission of UPI.

*From *Protest, Dissent and the Supreme Court* by Robert L. Cord, pp. 19–29. Copyright © 1971 by Winthrop Publishers, Inc. Reprinted by permission of Winthrop Publishers, Inc., and the author.

against double jeopardy; the Fifth Amendment privilege against self-incrimination accompanied by the "no comment rule"; the Fifth Amendment just compensation clause; the Sixth Amendment right to a speedy and public trial, the right of confrontation, the right of compulsory process, and the effective assistance of counsel; the Eighth Amendment's cruel and unusual punishment clause; and the right of privacy derived from Amendments One, Four, Five, and Nine, have in some form or another been held to be enforceable against the states. [See Table 1.2, infra.]

The following is a brief historical account of how the "nationalization" of *most* of the Bill of Rights guarantees has occurred.

The Barron Doctrine

When the initial eight amendments became part of the Federal Constitution in 1791, it was understood that they constituted prohibitions on the federal government only. Indeed, many of the state ratifying conventions had formed them as a condition for their ratifying the original body of the Constitution. However, it was not clear whether the Bill of Rights also constituted limitations on state authority. The Supreme Court initially addressed itself to this question in the celebrated case of *Barron* v. *Baltimore,* 7 Peters 247 (1833).

Barron, who owned a wharf, sued the City of Baltimore for compensation resulting from what he claimed was a taking of his property for a public purpose. The city, in paving its streets, diverted the water of several streams which carried large amounts of sand and deposited them around Barron's wharf. The sand deposits made the area around the wharf so shallow that ships were unable to approach it for the loading and unloading of cargo.

Barron's constitutional claim assumed that the Fifth Amendment obligated the states (and their creations such as the City of Baltimore) to provide just compensation when they took private property for a public purpose. Mr. Chief Justice John Marshall, speaking for the Court, dismissed the case as beyond the Court's jurisdiction in that it did not present a valid federal question. The *Barron* claim failed to qualify as a federal question, Marshall held, because the Fifth Amendment had to be understood as a restraint *solely* upon the national government. The Court's opinion further implied that Amendments One through Eight were not conceived of as limitations on state power. State authority was to be principally limited by the State Constitution. . . .

Initially then, the Supreme Court construed the prohibitions of the Bill of Rights narrowly.

If there was any doubt as to the clear meaning of the *Barron* decision, it should have been dispelled by the Court's decision in *Permoli* v. *New Orleans* 3 Howard 589 (1845). Permoli, a Catholic priest, had been fined $50.00 for violation of a New Orleans health ordinance forbidding the exposure of dead persons in a public place. Officiating at a funeral, the priest had exposed and blessed the deceased. He claimed the ordinance was passed in violation of the First Amendment. The Supreme Court, speaking through Mr. Justice Catron, held that the First Amendment did not protect state citizens from intrusion into their religious life by state authority:

The ordinances complained of must violate the Constitution or laws of the United States, or some authority exercised under them; if they do not we have no power by the 25th section of the Judiciary Act to interfere. *The Constitution makes no provision for protecting the citizens of the respective States in their religious liberties; this is left to the State Constitutions and laws: nor is there any inhibition imposed by the Constitution of the United States. . . .* [Editor's emphasis.]

In our judgment, the question presented by the record is exclusively of state cognizance, and equally so in the old States and the new ones; and that the writ of error must be dismissed.

The constitutional principles had thus been set and the precedents provided. The Federal Bill of Rights did not in any way legally limit the authority of the states. The prohibitions of Amendments One through Eight were binding on federal power alone. In sum, the *Barron* doctrine held that these Amendments were simply not relevant to the exercise of state governmental power.

After the passage of the Fourteenth Amendment (1868), new attempts were made to apply the limitations of the Federal Bill of Rights to the states. The two clauses of section one (of the Fourteenth Amendment) that served as the principal vehicles for these new attempts at "nationalization" of the Bill of Rights were the "privileges or immunities" clause, and the "due process" clause.

The Privileges or Immunities Clause

In the *Slaughter-House Cases,* 16 Wallace 36 (1873), the first to reach the Supreme Court requiring an interpretation of the Fourteenth Amendment, the hopes for a broad construction of the privileges or immunities clause were dealt a blow from which they have not to this day recovered. The appellants, who were butchers in New Orleans, challenged the constitutionality of a Louisiana statute which conferred exclusive slaughtering rights in the state on a newly chartered slaughter-house company. It was claimed that the state law creating the monopoly violated the privileges and immunities of U.S. citizens engaged in the butchering business.

Mr. Justice Miller in the opinion of a narrowly divided Court (5–4) indicated that the dual citizenship recognized by the first section of the Amendment conferred diverse rights upon Americans. An individual residing in a state had rights which flowed from his state citizenship as well as rights which flowed from his U.S. citizenship. However, only the latter was protected from state intrusion by the privileges or immunities clause. Emphatically, Justice Miller rejected the proposition that the privileges or immunities clause had shifted the responsibility for the protection of civil liberties from the states to the federal government as follows:

> . . . Was it the purpose of the 14th Amendment, by the simple declaration that no state should make or enforce any law which shall abridge the privileges and immunities of citizens of the United States, to transfer the security and protection of all the civil rights which we have mentioned, from the states to the Federal Government? And where it is declared that Congress shall have the power to enforce that article, was it intended to bring within the power of Congress the entire domain of civil rights heretofore belonging exclusively to the states?

*   *   *

> We are convinced that no such results were intended by the Congress which proposed these amendments, nor by the legislatures of the states, which ratified them.

In short, the majority of the Court did not see the Fourteenth Amendment as changing the pattern established under the *Barron* case. The civil liberties of most Americans continued to be guaranteed primarily by the state constitutions because those liberties, the Court declared, derived from state citizenship.

The dissenting opinions reflected the theory that the privileges and immunities designated for federal protection by this Fourteenth Amendment clause were "those which of right belong to the citizens of all free governments." The implications were that many of these immunities corresponded with those specified in the Bill of Rights. This theory was subsequently rejected several times by the Court and has never been given the sanction of a majority.

The fact that the Supreme Court had, since 1873, rejected the claim of the interrelationship between the Bill of Rights and the privileges or immunities clause so often led Mr. Justice Cardozo in *Palko* v. *Connecticut,* 302 U.S. 319 (1937), to dismiss that assertion with but one terse sentence.

Due Process under the Fourteenth Amendment

Initially, the Fourteenth Amendment's due process clause did not fare any better as a vehicle by which the guarantees of the Bill of Rights would become enforceable against the states.

Prior to the adoption of the Fourteenth Amendment, the due process clause of the Fifth Amendment had been the subject of little litigation. That clause had been generally recognized as a guarantee only in the narrow sense that the Congress was required to provide due process for the enforcement of law. The sole notable exception to this early restrictive interpretation of due process appears to have been in the *Dred Scott* case, 19 Howard 393 (1857), where the Court held the Missouri Compromise of 1820 unconstitutional as depriving persons of their property (slaves) without due process of law.

In light of the foregoing, it is not surprising that Mr. Justice Miller in *Davidson* v. *New Orleans,* 96 U.S. 97 (1878), expressed amazement at the breadth of the prohibitions which claimants before the Court now urged in the name of due process:

> It is not a little remarkable that while this provision has been in the Constitution of the United States, as a restraint upon the authority

of the Federal government, for nearly a century, and while during all that time, the manner in which the powers of that government have been exercised has been watched with jealousy, and criticism in all its branches, this special limitation upon its powers has rarely been invoked in the judicial forum or the more enlarged theatre of public discussion. But while it has been part of the Constitution, as a restraint upon the power of the States, only a very few years, the docket of this Court is crowded with cases in which we are asked to hold that State courts and State legislatures have deprived their own citizens of life, liberty, or property without due process of law. There is here abundant evidence that there exists some strange misconception of the scope of this provision as found in the Fourteenth Amendment.

The Miller commentary on the departure from the conventional interpretation of the clause is the more comprehendible when one recalls that the Fourteenth Amendment clause is an exact copy of the Fifth Amendment statement, and was considered to carry the same meaning. That this point had great importance for the Court is abundantly clear in the landmark case of *Hurtado* v. *California*, 110 U.S. 516 (1884).

The Hurtado Case: A Narrow Construction of Fourteenth Amendment Due Process

Hurtado was indicted for murder in California by means of an *information*. He was tried in a California county court, found guilty, and was sentenced to death. His appeal from conviction eventually reached the U.S. Supreme Court, where the conviction was challenged as a violation of his right to indictment by grand jury protected from federal encroachment by the Fifth Amendment and now equally protected from state invasion by the due process clause of the Fourteenth Amendment.

Rejecting this assertion, Mr. Justice Matthews speaking for the Court removed any doubt that the Court was about to accept the nationalization of the Bill of Rights via the due process clause with less reluctance than it had accepted similar claims under the privileges or immunities clause. . . .

The logical extension of Justice Matthew's rule of construction in *Hurtado* led to the conclusion that none of the procedural or substantive freedoms specifically mentioned in Amendments One through Eight were included in the due process clause or else there was wordiness in the U.S. Constitution.

Within sixteen years after its ratification, the Court had explicitly rejected two attempts to make the Fourteenth Amendment a successful vehicle through which the prohibitions of the Bill of Rights would be enforced against the states. Many subsequent cases raised allied questions which allowed the Court to continue to speak its collective mind about the relationship between the Fourteenth Amendment and the Bill of Rights. Its position on the prohibitions of the Bill of Rights remained the same as in *Barron* v. *Baltimore, supra*. The passage of the Fourteenth Amendment apparently had not affected the *Barron* doctrine:

That the first ten Articles of Amendment were not intended to limit the powers of the state governments in respect to their own people, but to operate on the National Government alone, was decided more than a half century ago, and that decision has been steadily adhered to since. . . . [*Spies* v. *Illinois*, 123 U.S. 131 (1887).]

The cases which followed these precedents seem too numerous to indicate anything other than that this constitutional controversy was settled. As late as 1922 in *U.S.* v. *Lanza*, 260 U.S. 377, the Court had invoked the *Barron* case to hold that "the Fifth Amendment, like all the other guarantees in the first eight amendments, applied only to proceedings by the Federal Government."

The Emergence of Substantive Due Process

The *Hurtado* case, however, did not preclude the due process clause of the Fourteenth Amendment from taking on a greater substantive content than had previously been identified with its Fifth Amendment counterpart. Simultaneous with the many decisions reaffirming the *Hurtado* denial of any relationship between the "liberty" of the Fourteenth Amendment and the substantive specific guarantees of the Bill of Rights; the Supreme Court in other cases *accepted* the contention that there were substantive economic freedoms under the Fourteenth Amendment's protection.

In the hope of curtailing certain corporate abuses and making private enterprise more socially responsible, some states had established regulatory commissions to supervise intrastate rail rates, and had enacted laws guaranteeing reasonable minimal standards for production and conditions of employment. The *laissez-faire* economic philosophy, prevalent in America during the late nineteenth century, found expression in United States Supreme Court decisions which struck at the constitutionality of these legislative and administrative attempts to regulate private enterprise and property.

Taken together these decisions established a category of substantive rights understood to be "liberties" guaranteed by the due process clause of the Fourteenth Amendment. The constitutional precedents for a substantive rights concept attributed to a due process clause—unique and novel in the *Dred Scott* case—became commonplace as many judicial opinions were written to support *laissez-faire* philosophy against state economic regulatory legislation after the turn of the twentieth century.

In retrospect, it seems clear that the substantive economic liberties entrusted to the Fourteenth Amendment's care were only a step away from the substantive liberties of speech and press.

A "Settled" Constitutional Principle Eroded: The Demise of the Barron Doctrine

In 1925 the Court handed down the precedent shattering opinion which first related some of the substantive liberties of the First Amendment to the Fourteenth Amendment. The persistent efforts to relate the Bill of Rights to the states over the preceding fifty years resulted in what was to develop into a constitutional revolution in federal-state relations.

In *Gitlow* v. *New York,* 268 U.S. 652 (1925), the Court charted a new course in the interpretation of the Fourteenth Amendment due process clause, which would eventually sweep away most of the rationale and nullify the holding of the *Hurtado* decision. All the earlier decisions to the contrary notwithstanding, Mr. Justice Sanford held:

For present purposes we may and do assume that freedom of speech and of the press—which are protected by the First Amendment from abridgement by Congress—are among the fundamental personal rights and "liberties" protected by the Due Process Clause of the Fourteenth Amendment from impairment by the states. We

do not regard the incidental statement in *Prudential Insurance Company* v. *Cheek,* 259 U.S. 530, that the Fourteenth Amendment imposes no restrictions on the states concerning freedom of speech, as determinative of this question.

As Mr. Justice Brennan was to put it almost thirty years later, the Court "initiated a series of decisions which today hold immune from state invasion every First Amendment protection for the cherished rights of mind and spirit—the freedoms of speech, press, religion, assembly, association, and petition for redress of grievances."

In the *Gitlow* case Justice Sanford was in effect saying that because freedom of speech and press are fundamental liberties, they are part of the "liberty" protected from abridgement by the due process clause of the Fourteenth Amendment. Thus, the term "liberty" in the Fourteenth Amendment's due process clause was, for the first time, understood to embrace some of the specific fundamental liberties protected by the First Amendment from federal invasion. As the Brennan reference above indicates, the fundamental liberties of the Fourteenth Amendment soon grew in number.

In *Near* v. *Minnesota,* 283 U.S. 697 (1931), the "assumption" of *Gitlow* became fixed constitutional law:

. . . It is no longer open to doubt that the liberty of the press and of speech is within the liberty safeguarded by the due process clause of the Fourteenth Amendment from invasion by state action. . . .

Six years later in *DeJonge* v. *Oregon,* 299 U.S. 353 (1937), Mr. Chief Justice Hughes, speaking for the Court, added the right of peaceful assembly to the growing list of fundamental liberties in the Fourteenth Amendment:

Freedom of speech and of the press are fundamental rights which are safeguarded by the due process clause of the Fourteenth Amendment of the Federal Constitution. . . . The right of peaceable assembly is a right cognate to those of free speech and free press and is equally fundamental.

In *Cantwell* v. *Connecticut,* 310 U.S. 296 (1940), the Court further supplemented the list of fundamental rights with the two-fold religious guarantees of the First Amendment.

If the right of association was not clearly considered fundamental as an incident of the right of assembly, it acquired an autono-

TABLE 1.2   The Twelve Provisions in the Bill of Rights Applicable to the Criminal Process

	Amendment	Applicable to States?	Case*
IV	Unreasonable searches and seizures	Yes	*Wolf* v. *Colorado*, 338 U.S. 25 (1949); *Mapp* v. *Ohio*, 367 U.S. 643 (1961)
V	Grand jury indictment	No	*Hurtado* v. *California*, 110 U.S. 516 (1884)
	Double jeopardy	Yes	*Benton* v. *Maryland*, 395 U.S. 784 (1969)
	Privilege against self-incrimination	Yes	*Malloy* v. *Hogan*, 378 U.S. 1 (1964)
VI	Speedy trial	Yes	*Klopfer* v. *North Carolina*, 386 U.S. 213 (1967)
	Public trial	Yes	*In re Oliver*, 330 U.S. 257 (1948)
	Jury trial	Yes	*Duncan* v. *Louisiana*, 391 U.S. 145 (1968)
	Confrontation of Witnesses	Yes	*Pointer* v. *Texas*, 380 U.S. 400 (1965)
	Compulsory process	Yes	*Washington* v. *Texas*, 388 U.S. 14 (1967)
	Right to counsel	Yes	*Gideon* v. *Wainwright*, 372 U.S. 335 (1963) (felonies); *Angersinger* v. *Hamlin*, 407 U.S. 25 (1972) (all offenses; before imprisonment may be imposed)
VIII	Excessive bail and fines	No	None
	Cruel and unusual punishment	Yes	*Robinson* v. *California*, 370 U.S. 660 (1962)

*Most of these cases are presented in the text.

mous fundamental status as a basic right in *N.A.A.C.P.* v. *Alabama,* 357 U.S. 449 (1958).

... It is beyond debate that freedom to engage in assocation for the advancement of beliefs and ideas is an inseparable aspect of the "liberty" assured by the Due Process Clause of the Fourteenth Amendment, which embraces freedom of speech.

The list of rights enforced against the states through the due process clause was not exhausted, however, when all of the liberties protected by the First Amendment were applied. Many procedural rights considered essential to the concept of justice and to due process itself were also ranked as fundamental by the Court and thus became binding on the states.

* * *

It should be reemphasized that *not all* of the provisions of Amendments One through Eight are enforceable against the states. The controversy about the relationship of the remaining particulars of the Bill of Rights and the Fourteenth Amendment continues. Still to be determined is whether all of the Bill of Rights guarantees, in all their particulars and with all their vitality, circumscribe state governmental actions in *precisely* the same way as they limit federal authority. The basic purpose of this section has not been to exhaust those questions, but rather

to trace briefly the legal evolution of the relationship between the Bill of Rights and legitimate state governmental power. This was partially in order to provide a historical perspective; partially to set forth the shifting legal facts governing that relationship; and finally to indicate that law—even constitutional law—is not able to be reduced to static formulation.

NEO-INCORPORATION: THE BURGER COURT AND THE DUE PROCESS CLAUSE OF THE FOURTEENTH AMENDMENT*

Robert L. Cord†

I. Introduction

Over three decades have passed since Justice Black wrote that "(t)he scope and operation of the Fourteenth Amendment

*From 44 Ford. L. Rev. 215 (1975). Reprinted by permission of the Fordham Law Review and the author.

†Professor of Political Science, Northeastern University, Boston, Massachusetts.

have been fruitful sources of controversy in our constitutional history."[1] Today, the procedural guarantees of the fourteenth amendment are at the center of that controversy. An analysis of the Burger Court's contributions to this long-standing dispute requires an exploration of earlier approaches.

During the 1940's and 1950's two basic approaches to the relationship between the Bill of Rights—particularly the procedural guarantees of the fourth, fifth, sixth, and eighth amendments—and the fourteenth amendment emerged.... An examination of these two viewpoints is important to an understanding of their development and modification.

The first school ... embraces a philosophy which envisions the due process clause of the fourteenth amendment as incorporating specific guarantees detailed in the first eight amendments, thus protecting them from state power. Justices who subscribe to this theory hereafter will be referred to as "incorporationists." The other school subscribes to an independent meaning of due process, *not specifically* derived from any particular amendments, which protects from state infringement all "fundamental rights" essential to the "concept of ordered liberty." The Justices who subscribe to this theory will be referred to as the "ordered liberty" [*] school. . . .

II. The Ordered Liberty Approach [*Fundamental Fairness*]

The ordered liberty approach to the meaning and content of the fourteenth amendment due process clause can be traced to within two decades after the amendment's ratification in 1868. In *Hurtado* v. *California*,[7] Justice Matthews, delivering the opinion of the Court, stated that the due process clause of the fourteenth amendment, like that of the fifth amendment, required that governmental power be "exerted within the limits of those fundamental principles of liberty and justice

---

*This concept of "ordered liberty" is also known as the "fundamental fairness" view. See, e.g., *Lisenba* v. *California,* 314 U.S. 219, 236 (1941) (the state must guarantee to the defendant "that fundamental fairness essential to the very concept of justice").

which lie at the base of all our civil and political institutions. . . ." This phrase grew in importance after the Supreme Court's decision in *Twining* v. *New Jersey*.[9] Justice Moody, speaking for the Court, used the *Hurtado* language to define the protection of the fourteenth amendment. *Twining,* however, did not define those principles which are fundamental to liberty and justice, nor did it specify where they might be found.

The first major attempt by the Supreme Court to answer these inquiries was undertaken by Justice Cardozo in *Palko* v. *Connecticut*.[11] He began by rejecting the total incorporationist approach which holds that all of the immunities of the Bill of Rights are liberties protected by the fourteenth amendment. To substantiate this rejection, Justice Cardozo listed several immunities protected by the Bill of Rights that the Court explicitly had held not to be protected from state intrusion by the fourteenth amendment.[13] He then stated that some of the protections of the Bill of Rights are guaranteed by the fourteenth amendment. The essence of the opinion was Justice Cardozo's attempt to clarify the Court's method of determining which immunities found in amendments one through eight are also protected by the fourteenth amendment. In so doing he instituted the "ordered liberty" approach to the meaning of the fourteenth amendment due process clause. All the protections against government that are "implicit in the concept of ordered liberty," Justice Cardozo held, are protected from invasion by state power. Under this approach the courts would have to identify those fundamental liberties through a case-by-case analysis.

The Court's rationale in *Palko* illustrates the essentials of the ordered liberty approach. The due process clause has a comprehensive meaning distinctively its own. The immunities considered fundamental to liberty and justice are embodied in the meaning of "ordered liberty" and "due process," both of which restrict state power through the fourteenth amendment. Although all the specific guarantees of the Bill of Rights have value and importance, only those provisions of the first eight amendments which are fundamental rights—essential to a concept of ordered liberty—are protected from the states by the fourteenth amendment. Finally, Justice Cardozo catalogued those rights which the Court, at that time, held to be fundamental and thus protected by the fourteenth amendment: freedom of thought, freedom of speech, and the right to a fair trial.

In *Palko,* Justice Cardozo's analysis of *Powell* v. *Alabama*[19] illustrates the ordered liberty approach to the relationship between a particular procedural right—which might also be specified in one of the first eight amendments—and the fundamental right to a fair trial inherent in the fourteenth amendment. Justice Cardozo noted that, in *Powell,* the sixth amendment right to counsel, *as such,* was not made applicable to the states by the fourteenth amendment. Rather, the right to counsel under the circumstances of *Powell* was constitutionally required. . . .

By holding that "(d)ue process of law requires that the proceedings shall be fair," and that fairness is a "relative, not an absolute concept," the justices adopting an ordered liberty approach to the due process clause have resisted listing all of the procedural safeguards that make for a fair trial; they maintain that in some circumstances a procedure may be vital, and in others inconsequential. In 1942, for instance, the Court held that the sixth amendment right to counsel in all serious criminal cases was not essential to due process. . . .

A significant characteristic of the ordered liberty school is its dynamic concept of due process. Spokesmen for this approach, such as Justice Frankfurter, have not provided an exhaustive definition of due process. . . . Justice Frankfurter, the dean of the ordered liberty school until his retirement in 1962, viewed due process as embodying the principles of justice commonly held throughout western civilization in general and by the English-speaking peoples in particular. Interpreting the due process clause and the fair trial concept as generative principles, the ordered liberty school rejects a rigid incorporation concept that limits these principles to the particulars of the first eight amendments.

Justice Frankfurter nevertheless recognized that the lack of an authoritative formulation of the content of the due process clause raised serious problems. How are the states to determine what the fourteenth amendment demands in terms of state criminal procedures? What role does the ordered liberty approach to due process demand of the Supreme Court and lower court judges in discovering the canons of decency and fairness inherent in this historical concept? Does this approach to due process allow judges unlimited discretion in the interpretation of constitutional law by substitution of personal predilections for fixed legal principles?

Justice Frankfurter often addressed himself to these questions; he understood the Court's role to be that of carefully giving content to the due process clause through a case-by-case analysis. Viewing the Court's role in a particular case narrowly, Justice Frankfurter and the other ordered liberty justices consistently have urged that the Court not engraft a rigid set of procedures onto the due process clause. Judicial self-restraint, they argued, would preclude the Court from using a specific case to address itself to a host of unlitigated issues not properly before the Court. On the other hand, for Justice Frankfurter, case-by-case analysis of due process did not mean that constitutional law is to be declared on an ad hoc basis. Rather, there are guiding principles, not procrustean rules, to delimit the interpretations of the Court;

The vague contours of the Due Process Clause do not leave judges at large. We may not draw on our merely personal and private notions and disregard the limits that bind judges in their judicial function. Even though the concept of due process of law is not final and fixed, these limits are derived from considerations that are fused in the whole nature of our judicial process.[29]

Justice Frankfurter recognized that a flexible and dynamic concept of due process could be a source of judicial confusion and uncertainty. He warned that judges may be tempted to rely upon their own ideas of social or legal justice if they fail to realize that their proper judicial role is to reflect, rather than to renovate, the historical sense of justice as seen in the light of contemporary needs. Essentially, ordered liberty justices should be viewed as seekers and proclaimers of the law, and not as creators of the law.

Justice Frankfurter was also concerned that the basic limitations on federal judicial authority inherent in the division of power established by a federal system must not be altered by the due process guarantee. "Due process of law . . . is not to be turned into a destructive dogma against the States in the administration of their systems of criminal justice." The ordered liberty justices have maintained that jurisdiction over criminal justice originally was left with the states by the Constitution and was delimited only in general terms by the addition of the fourteenth amendment. Primary responsibility in criminal affairs, although circumscribed somewhat by the demands of due process, remains with states. Incorporation by the fourteenth amendment of the specific criminal procedures of amendments one through eight could mean a serious limitation, if not an end, to state authority in these matters. Thus, incorporation is viewed by this school of justices as harmful to the principles of federalism.

Another argument advanced against the incorporation approach to the fourteenth amendment is that it would be a grand act of judicial legislation contrary to the Constitution. . . . As Justice Frankfurter noted, the short answer to the theory that the due process clause is legislative short-hand for the Bill of Rights is that "it is a strange way of saying it."

To review, the ordered liberty approach to the due process clause of the fourteenth amendment reveals adherence to the following principles: due process has its own meaning independent of other parts of the Constitution; due process protects from state intrusion the fundamental rights "implicit in the concept of ordered liberty"; the indefinable concept of due process necessitates a case-by-case analysis which gives contemporary content to this constitutional guarantee; the primary role of the courts is to articulate the blend of historical values and current standards which satisfy the due process requirements; in the process of performing this judicial function, judges must be extremely careful lest they elevate their own predilections to constitutional dogma; the justices should avoid altering the division of judicial power created by the federal system; and the due process clause should not be used to implement judicial usurpation of legislative functions. Thus, the ordered liberty justices are concerned with both the constitutional guarantees of the individual as represented by the standards of the due process clause and the restriction of judicial authority in our constitutional system.

The ordered liberty justices initially subscribed to a small list of procedural essentials common to all fair trials. Such rights as effective notice of the charge, an adequate opportunity to defend, "an impartial tribunal, an impartial jury untainted by interest or dominated by fear, and a jury selected without racial discrimination" were held to be ingredients essential to a fair trial. Generally, however, the ordered liberty justices saw the fair trial guarantee of *Palko* as mandating different procedural safeguards in diverse circumstances. . . .

* * *

III. The Incorporation Approach

A. Justice Black and Total Incorporation. "I believe that the Fourteenth Amendment made the Sixth applicable to the states,"[49] wrote Justice Black in a 1942 dissenting opinion that represented the first clear embrace of the "incorporation theory" by a contemporary Supreme Court justice.[50] Justice Black, as a total incorporationist, saw the first section of the fourteenth amendment as literally embodying all of the wording and content of the specific guarantees of the first eight amendments. Consequently, he maintained that section one and especially the due process clause of the fourteenth amendment circumscribed state authority in precisely the same manner as the Bill of Rights conditions federal actions.

According to Justice Black, an examination of the debates leading to the adoption of the fourteenth amendment in the Senate and House showed that its sponsors had as their purpose "to make secure against invasion by the states the fundamental liberties and safeguards set out in the Bill of Rights." Incorporation, far from being an act of judicial expansion, was viewed by Justice Black as judicial obedience to the clear historical command of the amendment's proponents in the Congress.

The foundations of the incorporationist approach were not limited to a technical analysis of the legislative history of the fourteenth amendment. Additionally, Justice Black was concerned that if the ordered liberty concept should prevail, due process would remain a vague phrase interpreted to embody the Court's own changing notions of decency and justice. . . .

Justice Black often attacked the ordered

liberty concept of due process as a "natural law" theory that expands the Supreme Court's power unwisely, unconstitutionally and unnecessarily. For him, the due process clause, if understood as a shorthand formula for the specific guarantees of the Bill of Rights, would eliminate the case-by-case review necessary under the ordered liberty approach. The continual necessity of review by the Supreme Court to determine the nebulous content of the fourteenth amendment guarantees was challenged by Justice Black as failing to provide adequate guidelines for state legislatures and for state courts. In fact, Justice Black decried as vague, inadequate and somewhat baffling the very process by which the Supreme Court justices themselves were to determine the commands of the due process clause.

Justice Black also saw the ordered liberty doctrine as seriously harming the federal division of power by subjecting the states to the whim and caprice of the federal judiciary. He argued that, under the ordered liberty approach, constitutional law was not fixed in the area provided with sufficiently precise federal opinions to allow them to predict when a criminal proceeding should be reversed for want of a "fair trial." More importantly, since the finding of a denial of fundamental fairness in a proceeding is based upon the particular facts in that case alone, reversals do not necessarily set adequate general standards for the states to follow.

Essentially Justice Black believed that only total incorporation was consistent with "the great design of a written Constitution." Otherwise "the accordion-like qualities of (the ordered liberty) philosophy (would) inevitably imperil all the individual liberty safeguards specifically enumerated in the Bill of Rights." The fourteenth amendment, Justice Black contended, did not protect any fewer nor any *more* rights than those specified in amendments one through eight. This closed-ended concept of due process distinguished Justice Black from all other incorporationists. Justices who embraced an open-ended concept of due process were categorized by Justice Black as holding a natural law theory of due process. Consequently, Justice Black rejected not only an ordered liberty approach to due process, but also all "emanation" or "penumbra" theories which hold that fundamental rights other than those specifically enumerated in the first eight amendments are also protected by the due process guarantee.

Ultra-Incorporation [Total Incorporation Plus*]. Since the incorporation theory was adopted by Justice Black in 1942, three justices[63] have embraced a variation on the incorporation theme which appropriately might be labeled ultra-incorporation. Unlike the total incorporation position of Justice Black, the ultra-incorporationists accept as a *minimum* guarantee of due process the rights protected by the first eight amendments. Looking beyond those particular guarantees, the ultra-incorporationists believed that the due process protection may well embrace other fundamental rights not specified in the Bill of Rights. These rights may "emanate" from other rights specified in amendments one through eight or they may have an independent existence. Ultra-incorporation might be viewed as somewhat of an amalgam of the total incorporation position and an open-ended approach to due process. As such it was viewed as an evil by Justice Black, as was any theory with a flexible concept of due process.

The earliest judicial embodiment of ultra-incorporation is contained in Justice Murphy's dissent in *Adamson* v. *California*.[65] . . . The position of Justice Rutledge paralleled that of Justice Murphy. He concurred in Justice Murphy's dissenting statement in *Adamson,* and like Justice Murphy, did not join Justice Black's dissent. The inflexibility of the Black opinion seems to have been unacceptable to both of them.

Had Justice Douglas passed from the judicial scene at the end of the 1940's as did Justice Murphy and Rutledge, one would classify him as a total incorporationist similar to Justice Black. Prior to the early 1960's, there was little reason to suspect that they might part company philosophically over the scope of the due process clause. . . .

In 1961, evidence emerged that Justice Douglas had abandoned the rigid total incorporation position held by Justice Black. Dissenting in *Poe* v. *Ullman*,[72] Justice

---

*The ultra-incorporation approach is also known as the "total-incorporation plus" view. See Israel and LaFave, *Criminal Procedure: Constitutional Limitations* (1975), p. 10.

Douglas stated that "(t)hough I believe that due process as used in the Fourteenth Amendment includes all of the first eight Amendments, I do not think it is restricted and confined to them." Justice Douglas noted that the Court in previous cases had used an "emanation" theory to expand protected "liberty" to include such rights as the freedom to travel, the freedom of privacy and the freedom to bring up one's children. Although these liberties as such are not mentioned in the Constitution, Justice Douglas maintained that they derive from specific constitutional guarantees or from the conditions essential for the perpetuation of a free society.

There was no immediate reaction from Justice Black. His brief dissent was confined to an expression of regret that the constitutional issues were not "reached and decided." The difference between Justices Douglas and Black concerning the scope of the due process protection became clearer, however, in *Griswold* v. *Connecticut*.[77] In that case, Justice Douglas, speaking for the Court, embraced an "emanation" theory, whereas Justice Black dissented, sharply denouncing the "emanation" theory and its flexible due process approach as a revived version of natural law.

Taken together, *Poe* and *Griswold* indicated that in 1965 Justice Douglas embraced an ultra-incorporationist position. In 1973, however, in *Roe* v. *Wade*,[80] Justice Douglas specifically denied subscribing to the Murphy-Rutledge due process approach:

"There are, of course, those who have believed that the reach of due process in the Fourteenth Amendment included all of the Bill of Rights but went further. Such was the view of Mr. Justice Murphy and Mr. Justice Rutledge. . . . Perhaps they were right; but it is a bridge that neither I nor those who joined the Court's opinion in *Griswold* crossed."[81]

The apparent distinction is that Justice Douglas' emanations and penumbras are derived from specific rights found in the first eight amendments, whereas the fundamental rights discussed by Justices Murphy and Rutledge in *Adamson* may exist independently of the Bill of Rights.

Selective Incorporation. The incorporation majority which emerged on the Supreme Court in the early 1960's contained several justices who regarded the relationship between the Bill of Rights and the four-teenth amendment in a way perhaps most suitably described as a fundamental rights approach to selective incorporation.

Abstractly stated, this view of the fourteenth amendment rests on two basic maxims. First, the due process clause of the fourteenth amendment incorporates *only* those guarantees in the first eight amendments that are fundamental to justice and a free society. Second, the due process clause protects other fundamental rights which may not be mentioned in the Bill of Rights. Implicit in the first proposition has been the assumption that some of the guarantees of the first eight amendments are not incorporated into the fourteenth amendment. Implicit in the second proposition is the belief that due process is not delimited by the Bill of Rights. Consequently, selective incorporationists subscribe to a flexible due process theory which resembles the ultra-incorporationist and the ordered liberty approaches to due process. The basic distinction between a justice who subscribes to an ultra-incorporation position and one who embraces the fundamental rights approach of selective incorporation seems to be that the former begins with a total incorporation position and adds other fundamental rights, while the latter selectively incorporates from amendments one through eight only those rights deemed fundamental and then adds other fundamental rights. Each theory is essentially open-ended and, as such, is irreconcilable with the closed-ended due process doctrine characteristic of total incorporation.

In the early 1960's the spokesmen for selective incorporation were Justices Brennan and Goldberg. Justice Brennan subscribed to the principles of incorporation as early as 1960. In a dissent in *Ohio ex rel. Eaton* v. *Price*,[86] joined by Chief Justice Warren and Justices Douglas and Black, Justice Brennan rejected the ordered liberty doctrine, stating that, although he neither "accepted nor rejected" the proposition that all the guarantees of the Bill of Rights are enforceable against the States, it was clear that the process of "absorption" used by Justice Cardozo in *Palko* was an early manifestation of selective incorporation. Then, focusing on the major tenet of all traditional incorporation approaches to due process, Justice Brennan pointed out that once the fourteenth amendment absorbs a Bill of Rights guarantee, it is applied against the states with a force equal to that exerted upon the federal government.

Justice Brennan elaborated his *Eaton* position the following term. In *Cohen* v. *Hurley*,[89] he wrote a lengthy dissent which set forth his view of the judicial history of selective incorporation. Repudiating once again the ordered liberty approach to due process, Justice Brennan repeated that a right "absorbed" from the Bill of Rights into the fourteenth amendment does not have diminished efficacy. Further, he charged that those justices who believed that due process has an "independent potency" not reliant upon the Bill of Rights were simply refusing to accept the reality of incorporation, a process the Court had, in fact, been employing selectively for many decades. This interpretation of *Palko* became the view of the Court's majority when Justice Goldberg, in 1964, joined Justices Black and Douglas and Chief Justice Warren to support Justice Brennan's opinion in *Malloy* v. *Hogan*.[91]

In *Pointer* v. *Texas*,[92] his earliest statement on incorporation, Justice Goldberg subscribed to Justice Brennan's analysis of judicial history. "I adhere to and support the process of absorption by means of which the Court holds that certain fundamental guarantees of the Bill of Rights are made obligatory on the States through the Fourteenth Amendment." By holding that only certain guarantees of the Bill of Rights are obligatory against the states, Justice Goldberg's opinion in *Pointer* had the ring of selective incorporation. In *Griswold* v. *Connecticut*[94] Justice Goldberg noted, "I do not take the position of my Brother Black in his dissent in *Adamson* . . . that the entire Bill of Rights is incorporated in the Fourteenth Amendment. . . ." Justice Goldberg's concurring opinion in *Griswold* is typical of the selective incorporation approach. Not only did he discard any notion of total incorporation, but, with Chief Justice Warren and Justice Brennan joining him, he also endorsed the incorporation of only fundamental rights. Further, he argued in favor of an open-ended due process concept. First, Justice Goldberg indicated that although he had "not accepted the view that 'due process' as used in the Fourteenth Amendment incorporates all of the first eight Amendments," he did agree that "the concept of liberty protects those personal rights that are fundamental, and is not confined to the specific

terms of the Bill of Rights." Then, citing James Madison and Justice Story to buttress his flexible due process stance against Justice Black's dissent, Justice Goldberg argued that the ninth amendment[98] was written in response to fears that the explicit protection of certain rights in the Constitution could be interspersed as negating the existence of rights not specified. Thus, Justice Goldberg reasoned, the very presence of the ninth amendment bears witness that its framers recognized the existence of fundamental rights other than those specified in the first eight amendments.

It can be concluded that the judicial development of the fourteenth amendment has placed primary emphasis on the flexibility of the due process clause. The ordered liberty justices, the ultra-incorporationists and the selective incorporationists all have agreed that the due process clause is not a mere shorthand version of the Bill of Rights. Only Justice Black equated the two constitutional concepts. His consistent adherence to the total incorporationist approach placed him in the anomalous position of advocating an expansive reading of the due process clause during the 1940's and 1950's and a restrictive reading of the due process clause during the 1960's. Through it, however, his preeminent concern was the preservation of the virtues of a written constitution. Justice Black believed that the strictures of a written constitution would restrain the members of the Court from introducing their own notions of constitutional right and wrong into the vague contours of the due process clause. As noted by Justice Harlan, however, it would appear that Justice Black's formula for implementing judicial self-restraint was unrealistic.

While I could not more heartily agree that judicial "self restraint" is an indispensable ingredient of sound constitutional adjudication, I do submit that the formula suggested for achieving it is more hollow than real. "Specific" provisions of the Constitution, no less than "due process," lend themselves as readily to "personal" interpretations by judges whose constitutional outlook is simply to keep the Constitution in supposed "tune with the times"....[102]

IV. The Genesis of Neo-Incorporation

A crucial axiom of the ordered liberty approach to due process represented by Justice Harlan must be explored further. If a particular procedural right—which also happens to be protected by the Bill of Rights—is held to be "implicit in the concept of ordered liberty," federal guidelines defining that right in a federal criminal proceeding do not automatically apply to the states.... Under an ordered liberty approach, the states should be free to develop their own criminal procedures—or to adopt the federal rules *if they choose*—so as to guarantee the procedural rights held implicit in the concept of ordered liberty. For example, under Justice Harlan's approach the exact nature of the right to counsel can vary from state to state under the fourteenth amendment as long as the right is sufficiently implemented to be effective.

Precisely the opposite principle is rejected in all the traditional incorporation approaches to the fourteenth amendment. Justice Brennan's majority opinion in *Malloy* v. *Hogan*,[107] incorporating the fifth amendment privilege against self-incrimination, stated this incorporation principle succinctly: "The Court ... has rejected the notion that the Fourteenth Amendment applies to the States only a 'watered-down, subjective version of the individual guarantees of the Bill of Rights'...." The *traditional* incorporationist justices believe that when a right, whether procedural or substantive, is incorporated from the Bill of Rights into the fourteenth amendment, it limits state power with exactly the same force as the particular amendment conditions federal power. The erosion of this basic maxim of the traditional incorporation approach characterizes the development of "neo-incorporation."

* * *

Neo-incorporation appears to embrace the terminology of the traditional incorporation approach but not its substance. According to the neo-incorporation approach, a procedural right, which is admittedly incorporated from the Bill of Rights into the fourteenth amendment, may have a different effect on procedures in state criminal cases than the original right has on procedures in federal criminal prosecutions.

An example of neo-incorporation is Justice Fortas' concurring opinion in *Duncan* v. *Louisiana*.[136] After joining the Court's opinion incorporating the sixth amendment's guarantee of trial by jury in all non-petty criminal prosecutions, Justice Fortas in his own opinion disagreed with the interpretation that the fourteenth amendment required following "not only the Sixth Amendment but all of its bag and baggage, however securely or insecurely affixed they may be by law and precedent to federal proceedings." Arguing that the states should have leeway to develop their own concept of trial by jury, Justice Fortas saw no reason whatever to assume that the incorporation of this sixth amendment right required imposition on the states of ancillary federal rules or "federal requirements such as unanimous verdicts or a jury of 12...."

Justice White, like Justice Stewart, a holdover from the Warren Court, has also followed a neo-incorporationist fourteenth amendment approach....

* * *

V. The Rise of Neo-Incorporation: The Burger Court

Of the judges on the Burger Court, the due process approaches of Justice Marshall and the four Nixon appointees remain to be considered.

Justice Marshall is an incorporationist—most likely a selective incorporationist. His opinion for the Court in *Benton* v. *Maryland*[147] rejected the philosophy of and overruled the holding of *Palko*. Justice Marshall noted that the Court has "increasingly looked to the specific guarantees of the (Bill of Rights) to determine whether a state criminal trial was conducted with due process of law."

Justice Marshall also is a traditional incorporationist, as distinct from neo-incorporationist, because of his view that "(o)nce it is decided that a particular Bill of Rights guarantee is 'fundamental to the American scheme of justice' ... the same constitutional standards apply against both the State and Federal Government."

At first glance it appears that the four Nixon appointees[151] have also embraced some kind of incorporationist approach, and several of the Burger Court's decisions support this conclusion.

* * *

Though (several) cases establish the incorporationist tendencies of the Nixon appointees, the evidence is ample that, regarding several important Bill of Rights procedural guarantees, they are not *traditional* incorporationists. Together with the votes of Justices White or Stewart or both, a neo-incorporationist majority in procedural rights now dominates the Burger Court.

In *Williams* v. *Florida*,[164] Justice White, again speaking for the Court, held that "the 12-man panel is not a necessary ingredient of 'trial by jury'. . . ." Justices Douglas and Black agreed to this holding which allowed for a de facto double standard for jury membership in federal and state trials. Only Justice Marshall dissented based on his belief that the sixth amendment does require a twelve person jury. Thus, for Justice Marshall the fourteenth amendment also requires a panel of twelve in state criminal cases.

Johnson v. *Louisiana*[168] and *Apodaca* v. *Oregon*[169] are true Burger Court decisions, Justices Powell and Rehnquist having succeeded Justices Black and Harlan. In both cases a neo-incorporationist approach replaced traditional incorporation principles. In *Johnson,* Justice White, speaking for a majority which included all the Nixon appointees, addressed the issue of whether the fourteenth amendment's incorporated right to trial by jury required a unanimous verdict. Noting that the Court had "never held jury unanimity to be a requisite of due process of law," Justice White upheld the state trial court's nine to three verdict of guilty.

*   *   *

In both *Johnson* and *Apodaca,* the three traditional incorporationists—Justices Douglas, Brennan and Marshall—dissented. Their objections were expressed in Justice Douglas' dissenting opinion which denounced the neo-incorporationist principles at work. Seeing the unanimity rule as part of the constitutional guarantee of trial by jury, Justice Douglas argued that "(t)he result of today's decision is anomalous: though unanimous jury decisions are not required in state trials, they are constitutionally required in federal prosecutions. How can that be possible when both decisions stem from the Sixth Amendment?" Reviewing several of the previous cases which incorporated Bill of Rights guarantees, Justice Douglas emphasized the frequently repeated *Malloy* phrase—that the fourteenth amendment does not impose upon the states a "watered-down" version of the Bill of Rights. Justice Douglas concluded by stating, "I would construe the Sixth Amendment, when applicable to the States, precisely as I would when applied to the Federal Government." Lack of common subscription to this principle separates the traditional and neo-incorporationists in other procedural rights cases as well.

*   *   *

Conclusion

It may be tempting to equate neo-incorporation with a "warmed-over" ordered liberty approach to the fourteenth amendment. Yet, it has been characteristic of all the varieties of incorporationist justices, including the neo-incorporationists, to use federal cases establishing the substance of amendments four, five, six and eight to determine, in part, the procedural guarantees of the fourteenth amendment. Because all ordered liberty justices have invariably insisted that the fourteenth amendment has meaning and content independent of the Bill of Rights, federal cases could not be used to define the guarantees of the fourteenth amendment, and fourteenth amendment state cases could not be used to determine the scope of federal procedural rights under amendments four, five, six and eight. The Burger Court majority has exhibited this distinguishing characteristic of incorporation by using federal cases to determine the scope and meaning of fourteenth amendment procedural guarantees and the converse. They have thus displayed some kind of incorporation approach as distinct from an ordered liberty approach.

Neo-incorporation as manifested by the Burger Court in state procedural rights cases appears to be a "half-way house" between the substance of ordered liberty and that of traditional incorporation as expressed in the Warren Court decisions of the 1960's. At this point in the history of the Burger Court, it seems that the thrust for congruency in federal and state criminal procedures—the central goal of traditional incorporationists since 1942 — is being decreased. The extent to which the neo-incorporation approach will permit different procedures to be used in state criminal cases is not certain after only a few years of the Supreme Court's new procedural rights voting alignment.

Speculation about the future of the incorporation approach to due process brings to mind a concern long expressed by former Justice Harlan. In a number of opinions, Justice Harlan predicted that in the long run, the incorporation approach to due process would not lead to strengthened criminal procedures in state courts, but, instead, would lead to a "derogation of law enforcement standards in the federal system. . . ." . . .

The prospect of the Supreme Court undoing procedural safeguards in the federal court system to satisfy the ritual of incorporation is not a pleasant one. . . . By using the language of incorporation, the Burger Court majority appears to pay deference to stare decisis, while eroding the substance of traditional incorporation so as not to burden the states with the stricter federal procedural standards. At this point in time, one conclusion seems certain. The neo-incorporationist approach to the fourteenth amendment due process clause illustrates at least one Burger Court procedural rights revisionist policy in conflict with the Warren Court legacy. [See Chapter Three, Tables 3.1 and 3.2.]

References*

1. *Chambers* v. *Florida,* 309 U.S. 227, 235 (1940). . . .
7. 110 U.S. 516 (1884).
9. 211 U.S. 78 (1908). *Twining* held that the fourteenth amendment does not include the protection against self-incrimination. Essentially, *Twining* has been overruled. *Malloy* v. *Hogan,* 378 U.S. 1 (1964). [See Chapter Six, § 6.03.]
11. 302 U.S. 319 (1937). *Palko,* which held that the fourteenth amendment does not include the fifth amendment guarantee against double jeopardy, was overruled in *Benton* v. *Maryland,* 395 U.S. 784 (1969). [See Chapter Three, § 3.04.]
13. 302 U.S. at 323–324. *Hurtado* was cited for the proposition that the fourteenth amendment

*The original footnote numbers as printed in the Fordham Law Review have been retained; numbers do not follow in consecutive order owing to deletion of portions of the original article.

does not compel the states to indict solely by grand jury. *Twining* and subsequent similar cases were listed to show that a state may compel a person to be a witness against himself in a criminal case without violating the fourteenth amendment. Cases indicating that provisions of the fourth, sixth, and seventh amendments were inapplicable to the states also were catalogued. . . .

19. 287 U.S. 45 (1932). [See Chapter Seven, § 7.02.]
29. *Rochin* v. *California,* 342 U.S. 165, 170 (1952) (footnote omitted).
49. *Betts* v. *Brady,* 316 U.S. 455, 474 (1942) (footnote omitted) (Black, J., dissenting), overruled in *Gideon* v. *Wainright,* 372 U.S. 355 (1963). Justices Douglas and Murphy joined in Justice Black's dissent. [See Chapter Seven, § 7.02.]
50. The incorporation theory, however, did not originate with Justice Black. See Landynski, "Due Process and the Concept of Ordered Liberty: A Screen of Words Expressing Will in the Service of Desire?", 2 Hofstra L. Rev. 1, 38 n. 186 (1974).
63. Justices Murphy, Rutledge and Douglas.
65. 332 U.S. 46, 123 (1947) (Murphy, J., dissenting). [See Chapter Three, § 3.04.]
72. 367 U.S. 497, 509 (1961).
77. 381 U.S. 479 (1965).
80. 410 U.S. 113 (1973).
81. Id. at 212 n. 4 (Douglas, J., concurring). . . .
86. 364 U.S. 263 (1960).
89. 366 U.S. 117, 154 (1961) (Brennan, J., dissenting), overruled in *Spevack* v. *Klein,* 385 U.S. 511 (1967). Chief Justice Warren joined in Justice Brennan's dissent.
91. 378 U.S. 1, 10–11 (1964). [See Chapter Six, § 6.03.]
92. 380 U.S. 400, 410 (1965) (Goldberg, J., concurring). In *Pointer,* the sixth amendment right of confrontation was incorporated into the fourteenth amendment. Justice Goldberg also joined in the opinion of the Court. [See Chapter Seven, § 7.03.]
94. 381 U.S. 479 (1956).
98. U.S. Const. amend IX: "The enumeration in the Constitution, of certain rights, shall not be construed to deny or disparage others retained by the people."
102. *Griswold* v. *Connecticut,* 381 U.S. 479, 501 (1965) (Harlan, J., concurring).
107. 378 U.S. 1 (1964). [See Chapter Six, § 6.03.]
136. 391 U.S. 145, 211 (1968). [See Chapter Three, § 3.04.]
147. 395 U.S. 784 (1969), noted in 23 Vand. L. Rev. 835 (1970). [See Chapter Three, § 3.04.]
151. Chief Justice Burger, appointed June 23, 1969, replaced Chief Justice Warren; Justice Blackmun, appointed May 14, 1970, replaced Justice Fortas; Justice Powell, appointed December 9, 1971, replaced Justice Black; Justice Rehnquist, appointed December 16, 1971, replaced Justice Harlan.
164. 399 U.S. 78 (1970); see *Note,* The Preclusion Sanction — A Violation of the Constitutional Right to Present a Defense, 81 Yale L.J. 1342 (1972). [See also Chapter Seven, § 7.03.]
168. 406 U.S. 356 (1972), noted in 61 Geo. L.J. 223 (1972). [See Chapter Seven, § 7.83.]
169. 406 U.S. 404 (1972).

2

STEPS IN THE
CRIMINAL PROCESS

2.01 PRETRIAL STEPS IN THE PROCESSING OF A DEFENDANT ACCUSED OF COMMITTING A CRIME

The legal steps involved in the processing of a person accused of committing a crime vary according to the nature of the charge (i.e., felony or misdemeanor) and the procedural requirements of the situs of the offense (i.e., prosecutor's bill of information or indictment by a grand jury).

Misdemeanors

The processing of a person arrested for a *misdemeanor* is a relatively simple procedure in most jurisdictions. Upon being arrested, the accused is taken to a local lockup, booked, and given an opportunity to post bond, and a trial date is then set. The trial itself is usually held in a court of inferior jurisdiction, often called the magistrate's court, city court, or police court. The presiding judge (magistrate) may be a justice of the peace, a United States magistrate (federal system), or a city judge. Usually no transcript of the trial proceedings is made, and the defendant, if convicted, may be fined, given a suspended sentence, or sentenced to a jail term not to exceed one year. In most jurisdictions, it is the *possible* sen-

tence a convicted offender may receive that distinguishes felonies from misdemeanors. Felonies are usually punishable by a term of more than one year in prison, while misdemeanors carry a maximum jail sentence of up to one year. In a few jurisdictions (e.g., California), the *actual* sentence imposed may determine whether the conviction is for a felony or misdemeanor. Persons convicted of misdemeanors have a right to an appeal in most jurisdictions. Usually this involves a new trial (de novo) in a court of general jurisdiction.

Felonies

The processing of a person accused of a *felony* is more complex, and the procedure varies from jurisdiction to jurisdiction. Basically, there are two types of felony procedures in the United States. One type, found in about one half the states, including California and most western states, involves the filing of a *bill of information* by the prosecutor. (These states are sometimes known collectively as *information states*.) Here, in all but rare instances, the decision to prosecute is left entirely to the prosecutor, leaving the defendant without the shield of the grand jury process. In some information states, however, a grand jury indictment is required before a defendant can be tried for a capital offense. This exception is made because the crime charged and the possible

73

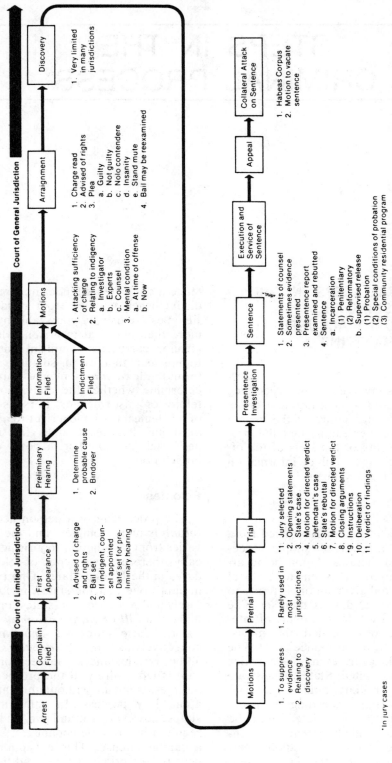

Figure 2–1 Typical Progression of Criminal Felony Litigation. From *The Courts: Fulcrum of the Justice System,* H. Ted Rubin, p. 189. Copyright © 1976 by Goodyear Publishing Company. Reprinted by permission.

sentence are considered too serious to be left entirely to the discretion of the prosecutor. It is considered more desirable to spread the responsibility among a group of 16 to 23 citizens (the *grand jury*), who are thought to represent a cross section of the community in terms of experiences and viewpoints.

The other type of felony procedure found in the United States involves the *grand jury process.* The Fifth Amendment to the United States Constitution requires that the grand jury process be utilized in felony cases brought in the federal courts, but the Supreme Court has held that states have the option to bring cases up on an information. About one half of the states require indictments in felony cases (see note 10, infra).

Before discussing the legal steps involved in the processing of a felony, it should be noted that most defendants do not complete all of the available legal steps in the criminal process. Between 80 and 90 per cent of all persons accused of a crime plead guilty, usually to a lesser offense or in return for a recommended lighter sentence. Plea bargaining takes the defendant out of the criminal process at a much earlier stage (see Chapter Thirteen). However, some defendants do exhaust their legal remedies, and for them, the entire process may take many years. The following discussion traces the various steps in a prosecution in a typical large city of a defendant charged with a serious crime, and the various stages of a typical criminal trial under our system of justice (Fig. 2–1).

Prearrest Investigation.[1] The investigation of a specific crime by the police may be initiated in a variety of ways. The police may become alerted that a crime has taken place because of the complaint of a victim or a witness, or the police may observe the commission of a crime during the course of patrol duty. In addition, the police may obtain information from an informer, undercover agents, or continued surveillance. Most violent crimes and property crimes come to the attention of the police through a complaint by a victim or witness, whereas the investigation of most "victimless crimes" (e.g., drug abuse, prostitution, gambling, consensual deviant sexual behavior) often requires the use of informers and undercover agents. These latter crimes involve a transaction between a willing seller and a willing buyer and normally are not brought to the attention of the police by one of the participants. The "victim" of such a crime is often a satisfied customer or is unwilling to report the transaction for fear of revealing his own deviant behavior. For example, the married man who is the victim of larceny or robbery by a prostitute or her pimp will carefully contemplate the consequences of reporting the crime.

The majority of police-suspect encounters (1) relate to a possible misdemeanor (85%), (2) occur on the street, (3) do not involve an arrest, and (4) cause the suspect to be detained for less than five minutes. In some large cities, police-suspect encounters in a given year may exceed several hundred thousand (not including traffic offenses).

In one third of all police-suspect encounters, the questioning goes beyond mere identification of the person. That is, the person detained becomes a bona fide suspect.

In certain high crime areas, 20 per cent of all encounters lead to some form of search. Of these, 85 per cent involve a search of the person-suspect, which is usually justified by the police as a valid "stop and frisk" (Chapter Five, § 5.04). Only 15 per cent of all searches involve a home or vehicle.

The majority of searches are not made under a search warrant. Usually the police seek to justify a warrantless search on the basis of the suspect's consent or as incident to a lawful arrest. (These and related Fourth Amendment problems are discussed in Chapter Five.)

Arrest. The legal definition of "arrest" varies from jurisdiction to jurisdiction, but the most common definition is the "taking in custody of a person for purposes of charging with a crime."[2] As noted by Professor Perkins, no actual touching of the person is required;[3] only an assertion of authority and submission is necessary for an arrest.

---

[1]The statistics in this section are taken largely from Wright, J., and Lewis, P., *Modern Criminal Justice* 146–152 (1978) and from Kamisar, Y., LaFave, W., and Israel, J., *Modern Criminal Procedure* 1–15 (4th ed. 1974).

[2]Restatement (Second) of Torts, § 112 (1965).

[3]Perkins, R., *Criminal Law and Procedure: Cases and Materials* 864–866 (1972).

Upon being arrested, a person is usually taken to a local police station to be booked.

Booking. *Booking* is essentially a clerical process conducted at the police station in which the police record the charges against the person, fingerprint and photograph him, and make an inventory search. Sometimes charges are dropped at this point because of a procedural error by the police, such as an illegal search and seizure, or because probable cause for the arrest is wanting. Usually the decision to dismiss charges at this point is made by an assistant prosecutor, although someone higher in the police hierarchy than the arresting officer (e.g., the desk sergeant) may make this decision. Charges are often dropped if the suspect has been arrested for a nonviolent misdemeanor.

If a person has been arrested for a felony without an arrest warrant (as occurs in the majority of cases), bail is usually not set until the "initial appearance" or the arraignment (a later stage). In these cases, bail must be set by a magistrate. If a person has been arrested pursuant to an arrest warrant, the warrant usually specifies the amount of bail required and the person can be released upon paying it. In misdemeanor arrests, bail schedules are used and the arrestee usually can be released immediately after the booking process. (Bail is discussed in greater detail in Chapter Twelve, § 12.01.)

Decision to Prosecute. At some point after the booking process, a formal decision must be made whether to prosecute the arrested person. This decision is entirely at the discretion of the prosecutor, although on rare occasions a court may *enjoin* (prevent) the prosecutor from prosecuting a case when he has abused his discretion. It is not unusual in larger cities for 30 to 50 per cent of all persons arrested for a crime to go unprosecuted for lack of evidence or for other reasons cited in the previous section.

In some cities, the decision whether to prosecute a minor misdemeanor is left to the police. The case is prosecuted by a police officer before a magistrate. There, at the initial appearance, a plea is made, and if the defendant pleads not guilty, a trial is held shortly thereafter. The rules of evidence are frequently relaxed in these proceedings, especially in nonjury trials.

Initial Appearance. If a decision has been made to prosecute, the defendant is taken before a magistrate for the first time—the *initial appearance.* Often, this stage is erroneously called the "arraignment": such a label is technically wrong if no plea is taken at this stage of the criminal process.

Statutes in many states require an arrested person to be taken before a local magistrate "without unnecessary delay," which is often interpreted to mean within a few hours. (See, e.g., Federal Rules of Criminal Procedure 5(a).) Although the "unnecessary delay" rule is not constitutionally required, it is rigidly followed in the federal system because of two United States Supreme Court decisions often referred to together as the *McNabb-Mallory* rule[4] (Chapter Six).

At the initial appearance, a defendant is informed of the nature of the charges against him, of his constitutional rights, including his right to counsel, and, depending on the jurisdiction, of his right to a preliminary hearing. Here bail is usually set, often by a schedule, although bail may be delayed until the arraignment.

Preliminary Hearing. Following the initial appearance, a defendant has a statutory right to a preliminary hearing in most jurisdictions. Here the state must introduce evidence to show that it has *probable cause* to believe that the defendant committed the crime for which he is charged.

The major purpose of the preliminary hearing is to protect defendants against unwarranted prosecutions. A preliminary hearing performs a function similar to that of the grand jury, i.e., at both stages a finding of probable cause is required before the accused can be bound over for trial. However, more legal rights are afforded a defendant at the preliminary hearing than a potential defendant during a grand jury investigation. For example, the preliminary hearing is considered a "critical stage" and the defendant therefore has a constitutional right to be represented by counsel[5] (Chapter Seven).

---

[4]*McNabb* v. *United States,* 318 U.S. 332 (1943); *Mallory* v. *United States,* 354 U.S. 449 (1957) (Chapter Six, § 6.03, Comments, p. 419).

[5]*Coleman* v. *Alabama,* 399 U.S. 1 (1970) (Chapter Seven, § 7.02, Comments).

Further, a defendant may, at the preliminary hearing, cross-examine prosecution witnesses and introduce evidence on his own behalf,[6] pursuant to the Confrontation Clause of the Sixth Amendment (Chapter Seven). During this stage, the rules of evidence are more strictly adhered to, as in a trial, and a transcript of the proceeding is often made for possible use at the later trial.

In the majority of cases, the magistrate finds probable cause and binds the defendant over for trial. It should be noted that the preliminary hearing is usually conducted by a magistrate of a court of inferior jurisdiction (e.g., a justice of the peace in a municipal court), but the defendant is actually tried in a court of general jurisdiction (e.g., a criminal court).

Although a preliminary hearing is not constitutionally required in most instances,[7] many states provide for such a hearing pursuant to a statute or the state constitution. Defendants can waive the preliminary hearing, and in large cities it is not unusual for 70 per cent or more of them to do so. If a defendant is indicted by a grand jury, it is generally assumed that he has no right to a preliminary hearing since they both serve the same basic purpose of protecting the defendant from unwarranted prosecutions by requiring a finding of probable cause.

There are several reasons why a defendant may wish to have a preliminary hearing. First, there is always the possibility that the state lacks sufficient evidence for a determination of probable cause. Second, the defendant may use such a hearing as a discovery device; that is, the state will be required to produce in advance of trial some of its evidence. This discovery can be useful in preparing a later defense. Third, the defendant may wish to "freeze" the testimony of the prosecution witnesses so that if a witness changes his testimony at trial from what he gave at the preliminary hearing, he can be *impeached*, i.e., his credibility can be attacked.

Sometimes defense counsel doesn't want a preliminary hearing. If it appears that the prosecution witnesses are aged, ill, or likely to leave the jurisdiction, it may be desirable to waive the preliminary hearing because testimony at the preliminary hearing may be admissible at trial if a witness is bona fide absent at the time of the trial.[8] (This is one of the few exceptions to the defendant's constitutional right to face his accusers at trial.) If a defendant has committed several criminal acts sufficient for a multiple count information or indictment and has been charged with only one count, by waiving the preliminary hearing he might persuade the prosecutor not to file the additional counts.

In the majority of states, the prosecution may demand a preliminary hearing even though the defendant wishes to waive it, but such a prosecutorial request is unusual.

If a magistrate dismisses the charges at the preliminary hearing, a grand jury can still indict the defendant for the same crime without running the risk of violating the defendant's Fifth Amendment protection against double jeopardy (Chapter Six).

In the majority of states, hearsay evidence that would be inadmissible at trial is admissible at the preliminary hearing to establish probable cause. Although the Supreme Court has not decided whether probable cause can be established entirely through hearsay evidence at a preliminary hearing, the Court has approved the use of hearsay at a federal administrative agency hearing[9] and at grand jury proceedings (Chapter Seven).

If a magistrate has found probable cause at the preliminary hearing, the defendant is "bound over" for trial and the prosecutor will file a bill of information.

Grand Jury Indictment. As mentioned

---

[6]*Pointer* v. *Texas,* 380 U.S. 400 (1965) (Chapter Seven, § 7.03).

[7]See, e.g., *Lem Woon* v. *Oregon,* 229 U.S. 586 (1930). The following thirteen states require a preliminary hearing as a prerequisite to prosecution by information rather than by grand jury indictment: Arizona, California, Kansas, Michigan, Minnesota, Montana, Nebraska, Nevada, New Mexico, North Dakota, South Dakota, Utah, and Wisconsin. Steele, *Right to Counsel at the Grand Jury Stage of Criminal Proceedings,* 36 Mo. L. Rev. 193 (1971). See also *Gerstein* v. *Pugh,* 420 U.S. 103 (1975) (person arrested pursuant to a prosecutor's bill of information is constitutionally entitled to a judicial hearing on the issue of probable cause for pretrial restraint of liberty).

---

[8]*Mancusi* v. *Stubbs,* 408 U.S. 204 (1972).

[9]*Richardson* v. *Perales,* 402 U.S. 389 (1971).

previously, in about one half of the states and in the federal system, every felony charge requires a grand jury indictment before the defendant can be tried unless the defendant elects to waive the grand jury process.[10] However, even in information states, the prosecutor can usually elect to take his case before the grand jury (Chapter Six).

The grand jury is composed of 16 to 23 citizens who meet behind closed doors in secret to consider evidence introduced by the prosecutor. As in the preliminary hearing, a finding of probable cause must be made by the grand jury before it can formally charge a defendant. Usually a majority vote is sufficient. When a majority of the grand jury votes in support of the indictment they are said to have returned a *true bill.* See, e.g., Federal Rules of Criminal Procedure 6(f).

During a grand jury hearing, the potential defendant probably enjoys fewer legal rights than at any other stage of the criminal process. The subject of a grand jury investigation has no constitutional right to be represented by counsel, to present evidence

---

[10]The following seven states require, by state statute, grand jury indictments in *all* felony cases: Hawaii, Kentucky, Massachusetts, Mississippi, New York, Texas, and West Virginia.

The following 17 states require grand jury indictments in all felony cases but permit a defendant to waive indictment; however, many of these states permit such waivers only in noncapital cases: Alabama, Alaska, Delaware, Georgia, Illinois, Maine, Maryland, New Hampshire, New Jersey, North Carolina, Ohio, Oregon, Pennsylvania, Rhode Island, South Carolina, Tennessee, and Virginia.

In the following 26 states, the prosecution of felony cases may be commenced by the filing of an information or a grand jury indictment at the option of the prosecutor: Arizona, Arkansas, California, Colorado, Connecticut, Florida, Idaho, Indiana, Iowa, Kansas, Louisiana, Michigan, Minnesota, Missouri, Montana, Nebraska, Nevada, New Mexico, North Dakota, Oklahoma, South Dakota, Utah, Vermont, Washington, Wisconsin, and Wyoming. See Steele, supra note 7, at 194. See also Katz, et al., *Justice Is the Crime* 247–365 (1973).

The following 11 states do not permit filing of a bill of information in capital cases; i.e., a grand jury indictment is required: Connecticut, Florida, Hawaii, Idaho, Kentucky, Massachusetts, Mississippi, New York, Texas, Vermont, and West Virginia.

on his own behalf, or to cross-examine the prosecutor's witnesses. In fact, the person being investigated often is not notified that he is the subject of a grand jury inquiry. While a person subpoenaed to appear before a grand jury may bring his retained counsel, his counsel does not usually have a right to represent his client in the hearing room and must wait outside the closed doors. It should be noted that a person subpoenaed to appear before a grand jury does not lose his constitutional privilege against self-incrimination unless he waives it. He *can* refuse to testify. However, if he is given *immunity* so that his testimony cannot later be used against him, he may be required to testify, subject to contempt of court if he refuses (Chapter Six).

The Supreme Court has held that a grand jury indictment can be based *entirely* on hearsay evidence that would not be admissible at trial,[11] and evidence illegally seized in violation of the Fourth Amendment is admissible at grand jury proceedings.[12]

The grand jury has been attacked by legal commentators for many years. It has often been accused of being a "rubber stamp" or "sword" of the prosecutor, although historically its primary purpose was to act as a "shield" against unwarranted prosecutions.[13] In spite of this criticism, the Fifth Amendment to the federal Constitution expressly provides for grand juries, although this provision is not presently applicable to the states.[14] In any event, the grand jury is likely to be with us for many years because of the Fifth Amendment.

Arraignment. After probable cause has been established, a defendant is brought before a trial judge for an arraignment. Here, the defendant is informed of the charges, counsel is appointed by the court if this has not been done previously (and if the defendant is indigent), and bail is set (if not done previously). Perhaps the most important function of the arraignment is that here the plea is taken. The plea itself usually

---

[11]*Costello* v. *United States,* 350 U.S. 359 (1956) (Chapter Six, § 6.04).

[12]*United States* v. *Calandra,* 414 U.S. 338 (1974) (Chapter Six, § 6.04).

[13]*Wood* v. *Georgia,* 370 U.S. 375, 390 (1962); Morse, D. W., *A Survey of the Grand Jury Systems,* 10 Ore. L. Rev. 101 (1931).

[14]*Hurtado* v. *California,* 110 U.S. 516 (1884).

takes one of four general forms: (1) *guilty*, (2) *not guilty*, (3) *not guilty by reason of insanity*, or (4) *nolo contendere* (no contest). In the event that the defendant refuses to enter a plea, the court will enter a plea of not guilty. See Federal Rules of Criminal Procedure 11(a).

At the arraignment, 70 to 85 per cent of defendants plead guilty — usually because of the plea bargaining process. About 15 to 30 per cent plead not guilty, and in 5 to 10 per cent of these cases the prosecutor drops charges. A relatively uncommon plea is *nolo contendere*, which can be made only with the consent of the court. In making this plea, the defendant neither admits nor denies his guilt. If this plea is accepted, the legal effect is the same as that of a guilty plea, and the defendant can be convicted on that basis. The main purpose of the nolo contendere plea is to prevent evidence of a criminal conviction from being admitted at any subsequent civil trial arising out of the crime committed. Because the majority of defendants convicted of a felony are poor, they need not worry about any subsequent civil litigation. They are, in effect, "judgment proof." Probably the best known plea of nolo contendere in recent years was that of former Vice President Agnew, which resulted in his conviction for violation of federal income tax laws. In federal courts, the nolo contendere plea may be accepted by the court only after due consideration of the views of the parties and the public's interest in the effective administration of justice [see Federal Rules of Criminal Procedure 11(b)], and some states do not permit such pleas under any circumstances.

Assuming a defendant has pleaded not guilty to the felony charge, the next step in the criminal process is the pretrial motions.

Pretrial Motions. Various pretrial motions are available to a defendant who has pleaded not guilty, although they are filed in only 12 to 20 per cent of all cases. Four of the more common pretrial motions are (1) motion to quash, set aside, or dismiss an indictment or information, (2) motion for a change of venue, (3) motion for a bill of particulars, and (4) motion to suppress evidence.

The *motion to quash, set aside, or dismiss an indictment or information* alleges that the indictment or information is insufficient for a variety of reasons. For example, the motion may state that the indictment or information does not state a crime; that jeopardy has attached (in violation of the prohibition against double jeopardy); that the statute of limitations has run; or that the composition of the grand jury is improper (e.g., racial imbalance).

The least commonly filed pretrial motion is for a *change of venue*. Here, the defendant alleges that he cannot get a fair trial in a particular district because of massive pretrial publicity. The defendant in his motion for a change of venue asks that the trial be moved to another jurisdiction where less or no publicity has tainted his case. The motion for a change of venue is rarely granted. Several of the Watergate defendants being tried in Washington, D.C., requested a change of venue; Judge Sirica's denial of this motion was subsequently affirmed in 1976 by the Court of Appeals (D.C. Cir.), sitting en banc, in the case of *United States v. Haldeman*, 45 U.S.L.W. 2232.

Another pretrial motion is for a *bill of particulars*. By this motion, the defendant seeks to obtain information about the details of the charge against him in order to prepare his defense and to avoid prejudicial surprise at trial. This motion is often granted by the trial judge, who has the discretion also to deny it.

One of the most commonly filed pretrial motions is a *motion to suppress evidence*. Most often the defendant alleges that the evidence to be used against him was illegally obtained, usually in some type of search. In some large cities, up to 75 per cent of these motions are successful, and after such a ruling, the case is often dismissed by the prosecutor for lack of evidence. For example, if a defendant is charged with the illegal possession of contraband and a judge has held on a motion to suppress that the contraband will not be admissible at trial, the prosecutor may have little choice but to *nolle prosequi* (dismiss) the case.

In some states, the prosecutor can take an appeal to an appellate court challenging an adverse pretrial decision by a judge, but these *interlocutory appeals* are rare.

Other pretrial motions may include a motion to inspect grand jury minutes, motion for psychiatric examination, motion for continuance, motion for severance of defendants, motion for inspection and disclosure of evidence in the possession of the prosecution, and motion to discover statements by prospective prosecution witnesses.

Assuming that the defendant's pretrial motions have been either denied or granted in part, the next step in the criminal process is the trial itself.

2.02 THE TRIAL

The trial of a defendant charged with a criminal offense often draws much public attention. The drama surrounding criminal trials has fascinated people since Christ was tried before Pontius Pilate; the trials of the Watergate defendants and Patricia Hearst provide more recent examples.

Even though only 10 to 20 per cent (and probably closer to 10 per cent)[15] of all criminal cases actually go to trial, the trial is an integral part of our system of justice. The major functions of the criminal trial are to produce reliable facts and to separate the guilty from the innocent under strict rules of evidence in an atmosphere of fairness to both the defendant and the government. Although certain criminal justice proceedings take place behind closed doors (e.g., the grand jury hearing), in a criminal trial the government is required to *openly* produce evidence before impartial fact-finders (judge or jury). Secret trials not open to the public are a violation of due process (the Sixth Amendment guarantees a speedy and *public* trial).[16] Sixty per cent of all criminal cases that go to trial are tried by a jury; the remaining 40 per cent are bench trials.

The stages of the criminal trial are as follows:

Voir Dire

The selection of the jurors who will hear the evidence and attempt to reach a verdict is known as the *voir dire* ("to tell the truth"). Here each attorney (prosecutor and defense counsel) is interested in selecting those jurors most favorable to his position. During the voir dire, each attorney attempts to present his side of the case to the potential jurors and prepare them for certain events that will happen during the course of the trial. For example, a defense attorney during the voir dire may inquire of a prospective juror whether he will hold it against the defendant if he invokes his Fifth Amendment right not to testify. This defense tactic is designed to prepare the jury for the fact that the defendant will not be testifying and thereby to minimize the harm his silence will cause, because jurors often believe that defendants who do not testify have something to hide. Moreover, at the end of the trial, the defense attorney can remind the jury of their promise not to condition their verdict on the absence of testimony by the defendant.

The potential jurors are called the *veniremen* and are usually selected by elected or appointed jury commissioners who draw their names from the lists of registered or actual voters from the political subdivision within the district of the court. It has been suggested that voter registration lists seldom provide a representative cross section of the community and that census data should be utilized instead.

All jurisdictions have certain minimal qualifications for eligibility to serve on a jury. These include American citizenship, residency in the locality, minimum age, knowledge of English, good character, and ordinary intelligence. Most states disqualify convicted felons and insane persons. Further, all states provide statutory exemptions from jury service for certain occupational groups, such as attorneys, physicians, law enforcement personnel, housewives with very young children, and certain governmental officials. Such exclusions have generally been upheld by the Supreme Court.[17] The Supreme Court has held that the Sixth Amendment requirement of an "impartial jury" is not violated by a jury made up entirely of federal employees.[18]

---

[15] Burger, W., *Address at American Bar Association Annual Convention,* The New York Times, August 11, 1970, p. 24, col. 4. It has been estimated that American criminal jury trials account for at least 80 per cent of all such trials in the world. In 1955, approximately 60,000 criminal jury trials were tried through to a verdict, and another 20,000 criminal jury trials did not result in a verdict. In England, criminal jury trials are available only for those being tried for "indictable offenses" (felonies); persons accused of petty offenses are tried before a lay magistrate without a jury. Only a few countries outside the Anglo-American orbit provide for jury trials. Kalven and Zeisel, *The American Jury* 12–15 (1966).

[16] *In re Oliver,* 333 U.S. 257 (1948) (Chapter Seven, § 7.03).

---

[17] *Rawlins* v. *Georgia,* 201 U.S. 638 (1906).

[18] *Frazier* v. *United States,* 335 U.S. 479 (1948).

It is often said that a defendant in a criminal case has a right to be tried by a jury of his peers. Today, a "jury of one's peers" means a *random cross section of the community*.[19] However, the Supreme Court has held that "neither the jury roll nor the venire need be a perfect mirror of the community or accurately reflect the proportionate strength of every identifiable group."[20] Thus, an accused police officer is not entitled to a jury of policemen, and a black defendant is not entitled to be tried by a black jury nor to representation of his race on any particular jury panel.[21] However, it is a denial of equal protection to arbitrarily discriminate against and eliminate members of a defendant's race from a jury panel[22] (Chapter Seven, § 7.03).

The usual method of selecting the jury during the voir dire is to summon the veniremen in groups of 12 in order to ascertain their competency to sit on the final jury selected. Following the usual order, the trial judge first asks questions of the group or in some cases of individual veniremen to determine if they are qualified to sit on the jury. Next, the prosecutor conducts the voir dire, followed by the defense attorney. The procedure for conducting the voir dire varies, however, from jurisdiction to jurisdiction. For example, in the federal system and in about 10 states, the trial judge has discretion either to conduct the voir dire himself or to permit counsel to do so.[23] In about one half of the states, both the judge and counsel have a right to examine prospective jurors.

Veniremen can be disqualified from sitting on a jury in two ways: (1) by the peremptory challenge, and (2) by the challenge for cause.[24] The *peremptory challenge* allows counsel (prosecutor or defense attorney) to have a prospective juror excused from serving on the jury *without* specifying a reason. The prospective juror may be excused because of the color of his shirt or because he has a beard, or for any other reason, rational or not, if counsel wishes to excuse him. Each side has a limited number of peremptory challenges, depending on the seriousness of the offense charged. For example, in noncapital felony cases, the federal courts allow each side five peremptory challenges. However, in most states, the defendant is granted more peremptory challenges than the prosecution. In cases in which the imposition of the death penalty or life imprisonment is a possibility, a greater number of peremptory challenges are usually allowed each side. In federal prosecutions in which the offense charged is punishable by death, each side is permitted twelve peremptory challenges. See Federal Rules of Criminal Procedure 24(b).

The second method if disqualifying veniremen is known as the *challenge for cause*. If the peremptory challenges have been exhausted by both sides, a potential juror may be excused *only* for cause; that is, a *legally* sufficient reason must be articulated by the attorney seeking to excuse a prospective juror. Under this type of challenge, a prospective juror would virtually have to admit that he is prejudiced against one side or admit that he has information about the case that would preclude him from reaching a fair verdict based on the evidence presented in court. Other examples of legally sufficient challenges for cause include (1) mental and physical infirmities, (2) prior service on a jury with respect to the same charge, (3) relationship to one of the parties or witnesses to the case, and (4) moral or ethical convictions that might preclude impartiality. In most cases, few challenges for cause are invoked, although such challenges are frequently utilized in capital and highly publicized cases.

Although the problem of pretrial publicity is raised in only a small number of cases, this issue presents a conflict between two important constitutional rights—the right of the press to print the news (First Amendment) and the right of a defendant to receive a fair trial by an impartial jury (Sixth Amendment). The major problem in highly publicized cases is that the prospective

---

[19] *Glasser* v. *United States,* 315 U.S. 60 (1942); Federal Jury Selection and Service Act of 1968 (28 U.S.C.A. § 1861).

[20] *Swaim* v. *Alabama,* 380 U.S. 202 (1965) (Chapter Seven, § 7.03).

[21] *Bush* v. *Kentucky,* 107 U.S. 110 (1883).

[22] *Strauder* v. *West Virginia,* 100 U.S. 303 (1880).

[23] Tone, *Voir Dire, New Supreme Court Rule 24-1: How It Works,* 47 Ill. B.J. 140, 142 (1958); Fed. R. Crim. P. 24(a).

[24] Note, 52 Va. L. Rev. 1069, 1072–1080 (1966).

jurors are already familiar with many of the facts of the case. Most Americans had heard of Charles Manson, Sirhan Sirhan, James Earl Ray, Richard Speck, Jack Ruby, Patty Hearst, and the Watergate defendants by the time they came to trial. Millions of people saw the television films of the killing of Lee Harvey Oswald and the shooting of Governor George Wallace.

Because freedom of the press is a *fundamental constitutional right*, it would be difficult (and undesirable) to prevent the press from reporting the news, even to insure a defendant a "fair trial." As the Supreme Court has stated, "Any prior restraint of expression comes to this Court bearing a heavy presumption against its constitutional validity, and a party who seeks to have such a restraint upheld thus carries a heavy burden for showing justification for the imposition of such a restraint."[25] The Supreme Court has dealt with the issue of prejudicial publicity in several cases (Chapter Seven, § 7.03).

It is not required that all veniremen be totally ignorant of the facts surrounding a highly publicized case. If a potential juror states that he is willing to set aside his preconceived notions of the defendant's guilt or innocence and reach a verdict solely upon the evidence presented, a challenge on the grounds of prejudicial publicity may properly be denied by the court. As a rule, the jury should be *sequestered* (held in protective custody) in highly publicized cases.

There are at least two other viable solutions for the problems presented by highly publicized cases: a continuance and a change of venue. A major purpose of a *continuance* in a highly publicized case is to delay the trial so that prospective jurors will forget or be less likely to come in contact with news accounts dealing with the facts surrounding the crime charged. However, continuances are not always effective, because as soon as the case is reinstated on the trial calendar, the press often recapitulates its earlier stories. Also, too long a delay, without the defendant's consent, may

arguably result in a denial of a speedy trial, which is also guaranteed by the Sixth Amendment (see Chapter Seven, § 7.03).

The other solution is to grant a *change of venue*, which allows the trial to be moved to another area of the state or county. In state cases, the case can be transferred to another county, but it cannot be moved to another state. Jurisdiction in state criminal cases is restricted to that state in which a defendant is lawfully charged. In federal cases, the case theoretically can be transferred to any part of the United States or its possessions (e.g., Canal Zone, Virgin Islands, Guam).

In the most highly publicized cases, even a change of venue will not be helpful. In what area of the United States could the Watergate defendants have been tried by a jury untainted by the news accounts surrounding the case?

Other cases dealing with prejudicial publicity include those in which jurors have been exposed to information about a defendant's prior criminal record or other inadmissible, prejudicial, or immaterial evidence. This alone may be a basis for a reversal of a conviction.[26]

After the jury is impaneled and sworn, the indictment or bill of information is read by the clerk of the court to the jury. The next stage of the trial is the opening statements.

Opening Statement by the Prosecutor

Before evidence is formally presented in court, the prosecutor is permitted to address the jury. In his opening statement, he is "limited to a statement of facts which the government in good faith intends to prove. [Opening] should not be argumentative in character, nor should it be designed to destroy the character of the defendant before the introduction of any evidence on the crime charged. . . ."[27] Thus, the major purpose of the opening statement by the prosecutor is to explain to the jury the issues to be tried.

On occasion, the prosecutor will promise

---

[25] *New York Times Company* v. *United States*, 403 U.S. 713, 723 (1971). See also *Nebraska Press Association* v. *Stuart*, 427 U.S. 539 (1976) (Chapter Seven, § 7.03).

[26] *Marshall* v. *United States*, 360 U.S. 310 (1959).

[27] *Leonard* v. *United States*, 277 F.2d 843 (9th Cir. 1960).

more to the jury than he can deliver in the way of evidence. The prevailing view is that if the prosecutor during opening states more than he is able to prove, it is not reversible error so long as such remarks are made in "good faith." Conversely, it is improper for the prosecutor during opening to state that certain evidence will be admitted during the course of the trial when he already knows that such evidence will be inadmissible. Whether the prosecutor acted in "good faith" is within the discretion of the trial judge.[28]

The opening statement by the prosecutor also serves as a discovery device to the defendant because it may put the defendant on notice as to the scope of the issues to which he may have to defend. It has been held that "improper suggestions, insinuations, and . . . assertions of personal knowledge" by a prosecutor on opening are improper.[29]

Reversals of convictions based on improper opening statements are uncommon, and such errors are generally cured by the trial judge's admonition and instruction to the jury to disregard the improper remarks. However, if a defendant fails to object to erroneous opening statements at trial, he may be deemed to have waived such errors unless they rise to a level of "plain error."[30]

In most jurisdictions, if the prosecutor overstates his case during the opening statement, the defense attorney may rebut during closing argument by pointing out that the prosecutor failed to keep his "promises." Since the prosecutor may thereby lose some of his credibility with the jury, it may be tactically advantageous for him to confine his remarks to succinct but general statements as to what the prosecution intends to prove and enumeration of the elements of the crime charged without going into much detail.

The amount of time allocated to opening is discretionary with the trial judge, and opening statements are not evidence to be considered in deciding guilt or innocence.[31]

Finally, in most jurisdictions, an opening statement by the prosecutor is not required in nonjury trials.[32]

The next stage of the trial is the opening statement by the defense.

Opening Statement by the Defense

Upon completion of the prosecution's opening statement, the defendant (or his counsel) is permitted to immediately address the jury and state his theories concerning the applicable legal issues. The major purpose of the opening statement is to allow the defense to outline the facts upon which an acquittal will be sought. As with the prosecutor's opening statement, the defense's opening may serve as a discovery device for the prosecutor: the defense attorney's opening remarks may give the prosecution advance notice of the intended defense.

The rules covering the scope of the opening statement by the defense are similar to those governing the prosecutor's statement. The remarks must be made in "good faith" as to what the defense intends to offer as evidence. It is therefore improper for defense counsel to assert in "bad faith" that he will introduce certain evidence that he knows, or should know, is inadmissible and to later complain to the jury that the trial judge's ruling prevented a fair defense.

Because the defense attorney might promise the jury a defense that he cannot deliver later during the trial, the opening statement is sometimes waived.[33] For tactical reasons, the defense may want to delay its opening until the close of the prosecutor's case. However, such delays are discretionary with the trial court in most jurisdictions; and requiring a defendant to choose between making his opening statement immediately after the opening statement of the prosecutor or not making it at all is likewise within a trial judge's discretion.[34]

Sometimes a defense attorney, during his opening statement, will make flagrant, erroneous, and misleading remarks designed to

[28]*Gladden* v. *Frazier*, 388 F.2d 777 (9th Cir. 1968) affirmed sub nom. *Frazier* v. *Cupp*, 394 U.S. 731 (1969).
[29]*Berger* v. *United States*, 295 U.S. 78 (1935).
[30]Fed. R. Crim. P. 52(b)
[31]*Leonard* v. *United States*, 277 F.2d 843 (9th Cir. 1960).

[32]See generally Mendelson, I., *Defending Criminal Cases* 68–69 (1967).
[33]Id.
[34]Bailey, F. L., and Rothblatt, H. B., *Successful Techniques for Criminal Trials* § 116 (1971).

divert the jury from the material issues of the trial, and sometimes, as a consequence, the jury subsequently acquits the defendant. Because the state normally cannot appeal an acquittal and the defendant cannot be retried for the same offense because of the Fifth Amendment prohibition against double jeopardy,[35] what prevents an unscrupulous defense attorney from employing such tactics? Probably the only means of countering such improper conduct are for the trial judge to declare a mistrial or to find the attorney in contempt of court and punish him, or for the state bar association to suspend or disbar him from the practice of law, although the latter is highly unlikely.

In this connection, the American Bar Association standard on the opening statement provides:[36]

In his opening statement the prosecutor (or defense attorney) should confine his remarks to evidence he intends to offer which he believes in good faith will be available and admissible and a brief statement of the issues in the case. It is unprofessional conduct to allude to any evidence unless there is a good faith and reasonable basis for believing that such evidence will be tendered and admitted in evidence.

Upon completion of opening statements, the prosecutor presents his evidence.

The Prosecutor's Case-in-Chief

It is axiomatic that a defendant charged with a criminal offense (state or federal) is *presumed innocent,*[37] and an accused is protected against conviction "except upon *proof beyond a reasonable doubt* of every fact necessary to constitute the crime with which he is charged" (emphasis added).[38] Thus, a prosecutor seeking to convince a jury of a defendant's guilt bears a heavy burden of persuasion. In civil proceedings, the plaintiff need only prove his case by a *preponderance of evidence,* but the more rigid requirement of proof beyond a reasonable doubt is necessary in criminal cases to protect the accused from "unjust convic-

tions with resulting forfeitures of life, liberty and property."[39]

How then is "proof beyond a reasonable doubt" defined? A frequently cited definition of this burden of proof is found in *Commonwealth* v. *Webster,*[40] decided by the Supreme Court of Massachusetts:

It [reasonable doubt] is a term often used, probably pretty well understood, but not easily defined. It is not mere possible doubt; because everything relating to human affairs, and depending on moral evidence, is open to some possible or imaginary doubt. It is that state of the case, which, after the entire comparison and consideration of all the evidence, leaves the minds of the jurors in that condition and *they cannot say they feel an abiding conviction, to a moral certainty, of the truth of the charge* [emphasis added].

Thus, the prosecutor must introduce competent evidence proving a defendant's guilt beyond a reasonable doubt in order to obtain a conviction. Questions on the legality or admissibility of the prosecutor's evidence do not require proof beyond a reasonable doubt in most jurisdictions. For example, the Supreme Court has held that the burden of proof to establish the voluntariness of a confession in a state criminal case is a preponderance of the evidence.[41]

After the prosecutor has completed his main case (case-in-chief), the defense will ask for a directed verdict by the trial judge.

Motion for a Directed Verdict

At the conclusion of the prosecutor's case, it is common practice in most jurisdictions for defense counsel to request the judge to have the jury removed from the courtroom. Upon the jury's absence, defense counsel will ask the court for a directed verdict; that is, the judge is requested to find the defendant not guilty (on counsel's motion) because the prosecutor has not produced sufficient evidence for the case to go to the jury. The jury is removed from the courtroom because of the possible prejudicial effect of hearing the judge deny the motion.

---

[35] *Benton* v. *Maryland,* 395 U.S. 784 (1969).
[36] A.B.A. Standards, 5.5 (7.4).
[37] *Coffin* v. *United States,* 156 U.S. 432 (1895).
[38] *In re Winship,* 397 U.S. 358, 364 (1970) (Chapter Eight, § 8.03).

[39] *Davis* v. *United States,* 160 U.S. 469, 488 (1895).
[40] 59 Mass. 205 (1850).
[41] *Lego* v. *Twomey,* 404 U.S. 477 (1972).

The directed verdict is always requested in order to preserve some rights on appeal in the event of a conviction, and it will be requested even though the defendant's fingerprints were discovered all over the scene of the crime and 50 Baptist ministers have testified that they saw the defendant commit the crime.

Although a directed verdict is rare, occasionally the motion will be granted when the prosecutor has failed to prove one vital element of the crime charged. For example, common law burglary requires a breaking and entering into a dwelling at night with intent to commit a felony. Failure of the prosecutor to introduce sufficient evidence that *all* these elements were present prohibits a legally sufficient burglary conviction, and a directed verdict would be proper under these circumstances.

Sometimes, in a multiple-count indictment, certain *counts* (charges) will result in an acquittal following a motion for a directed verdict. However, the trial will proceed on the remaining counts.

It is the duty of the trial court to direct an acquittal when there is insufficient evidence of the defendant's guilt. The standard on a motion for a directed verdict is whether a reasonable fact-finder (judge or jury) interpreting the evidence most favorably to the prosecution could not find that the defendant was guilty beyond a reasonable doubt. However, the trial judge is without authority to direct a verdict of guilty at the end of the prosecutor's case before the defense has had an opportunity to present its case.

Assuming that the motion for the directed verdict has been denied, the next stage of the trial is the presentation of the defense's case.

The Case for the Defense

The Fifth Amendment to the Constitution provides, inter alia, that "no person . . . shall be compelled in any criminal case to be a witness against himself." As noted earlier, the privilege against self-incrimination is applicable to the states[42] and is coextensive in both federal and state criminal proceedings[43] (Chapter Six).

Because of this Fifth Amendment protection, a defendant is not required to personally testify on his own behalf[44] or to present any defense evidence during the course of the trial. Accordingly, defense counsel may elect to "rest" his case and allow the prosecutor's evidence to go to the jury unrebutted because (1) he may feel that the prosecutor's case is simply too weak to sustain a conviction, so that the "defense" will rest on the unfulfilled proof of the prosecutor; or (2) the defendant has a prior criminal record, which will be brought out by the prosecutor on cross-examination (impeachment) if the defendant testifies and there are no reliable witnesses available to testify on behalf of the defendant; or (3) the defendant simply may not have a good defense to the crime charged, and offering a generalized, vague defense might be more damaging than helpful. Also, in some states, the defendant has a right to open and close final arguments if no defense has been offered during the evidentiary part of the trial.

Nevertheless, in most felony criminal trials the defendant will offer some evidentiary defense to the crimes with which he is charged. Defense counsel may have the defendant testify and deny his guilt outright, or he may produce character witnesses who attempt to exculpate the defendant by testifying to his good reputation in the community for truthfulness. Other defenses commonly asserted include (1) alibi, (2) self-defense, (3) insanity, (4) entrapment, and (5) lack of intent (mistake of fact or involuntary acts). There are many other defenses available to defendants, and the reader should refer to appropriate criminal law texts.[45]

Next, the prosecutor rebuts the defense's case.

The Prosecutor's Rebuttal

In all jurisdictions, the prosecutor is permitted to rebut any new evidence or testimony presented during the defendant's case.[46] The purpose of *rebuttal* is to weaken the defendant's case. An obvious ques-

---

[42]*Malloy* v. *Hogan*, 378 U.S. 1 (1964) (Chapter Six, § 6.03).

[43]*Murphy* v. *Waterfront Commission*, 378 U.S. 52 (1964) (Chapter Six, § 6.03)

[44]*Griffin* v. *California*, 380 U.S. 609 (1965), overruling *Adamson* v. *California*, 332 U.S. 46 (1947) (Chapter Three, § 3.04).

[45]See, e.g., LaFave, W., and Scott, A., *Criminal Law* (1972); Perkins, R., *Criminal Law* (1969).

[46]*McCormick on Evidence* § 4 (1972); Fed. R. Crim. P. 29(a).

tion is why is the prosecutor allowed to rebut the defendant's case? The basic reason is one of fairness. The prosecution must shoulder a heavy burden of proof (i.e., beyond a reasonable doubt) in order to obtain a conviction. If the prosecutor could not rebut, the defense could present new evidence that, going uncontested, might be sufficient to sustain a reasonable doubt, thereby allowing a guilty defendant to be acquitted. For example, in those states that do not provide for a notice-of-alibi rule, the appearance of an unexpected alibi witness could put the prosecutor at a serious disadvantage if he has no opportunity to offer rebuttal evidence. Cross-examination of the alibi witness might prove ineffective, and the prosecutor might require additional state witnesses to undermine the credibility of the "surprise" defense witness.

The defendant's surrebuttal follows rebuttal by the prosecution.

Defendant's Surrebuttal (Rejoinder)

If the prosecutor has introduced new evidence or gone into new matters during the rebuttal stage of the trial, the defense, at the discretion of the court, may be allowed to rebut this new evidence.[47] This stage is called the *surrebuttal*, or *rejoinder*. However, surrebuttal is limited to new defense evidence that is offered to refute the prosecutor's rebuttal. As a practical matter, surrebuttal evidence is not commonly introduced by the defense and when permitted usually occurs in cases involving complex issues in which many witnesses have testified. The court's decision to exclude surrebuttal evidence is not a basis for a reversal of a conviction in most cases.

When both sides have exhausted their case, the evidentiary part of the trial is over.

In summary, the evidentiary part of a criminal trial may have four stages: (1) the prosecutor's case (case-in-chief), (2) the defendant's case, (3) the prosecutor's rebuttal, and (4) the defendant's surrebuttal. Further, there may be four stages in the examination of each witness: (1) direct examination, (2) cross-examination, (3) redirect examination, and (4) recross-examination.

During the next stage of the trial, the attorneys for both sides work out the judge's instructions on the law.

Working Out Instructions on the Law

Before the jury retires to deliberate, the trial judge must "charge the jury"; i.e., he must explain the applicable law and indicate the essential elements of the crime charged and the applicable defenses in the context of the evidentiary issues presented. It is obvious that each attorney would like the judge to base his instructions to the jury on an interpretation of the law most favorable to his side. Accordingly, prior to closing arguments (the next stage of the trial), the attorneys may request the judge to include certain points in his charge to the jury. Often, the attorneys will submit written instructions to the judge at this point, and normally the judge will rule on each requested instruction prior to closing arguments. Such requests are designed to allow counsel to know the details of the charge in order to make a proper closing argument, although this is not necessary in the jurisdictions in which closing arguments follow the charge to the jury.

A current trend in state courts is for jury instructions to be taken from a uniform work, *Standard Jury Instructions,* which has been approved by the state supreme court in those jurisdictions in which it is utilized. Standardized instructions are designed to implement in an intelligible and uniform manner the objectives of accuracy, efficiency, and impartiality.

Rule 30 of the Federal Rules of Criminal Procedure governs jury instructions in the federal courts. This rule allows the parties to file suggested written instructions at the close of the evidentiary portion of the trial, although they are not required to do so.

After the judge and the attorneys have agreed to the instructions, the closing arguments are made.

Closing Arguments (Summation)

Normally, the last opportunity for counsel on both sides to personally address the jury occurs at that stage of the trial known as the *closing arguments.*[48] (It should be noted that the Supreme Court has held that defense counsel has a right to make a closing argument even in a nonjury trial.[49]) As with the

---

[47]Id.

[48]Vess, H. B., *Walking a Tightrope: A Survey of Limitations on the Prosecutor's Closing Argument,* 64 J. Crim. L. & Criminol. 22 (1973).
[49]*Herring* v. *New York,* 422 U.S. 853 (1975).

opening statements, such remarks on closing are *not evidence* to be used by the jury in deciding the guilt or innocence of the defendant, and the jury will be so instructed by the court.

The time limit for closing arguments is discretionary with the court and can vary from a few minutes to several hours or, in extreme cases, to days.

Usually the prosecutor begins the closing arguments, and in most cases he is allowed to rebut the closing of the defense. This is because of the heavy burden of proof placed on the prosecution. However, the prosecution's rebuttal is usually restricted to those areas argued on closing by the defense so that no new lines of argument may be introduced by the prosecutor. As mentioned, in a few states, the defense is entitled to first and last closing arguments if no defense witnesses have testified.

During closing arguments, each side attempts to convince the jury that his position should prevail. Sometimes great emotion and drama are employed, and it is not unusual for counsel to read Bible passages, poems, and the like. Such tactics should be somehow relevant to the issues in question; however, most judges permit much latitude here.

As a rule of thumb for defense attorneys on closing, it has been said: "When the facts are against you, tell the jury about the law. If the law is against you, stress the facts to the jury. If both the law and the facts are against you, attack the prosecutor." However, attacking the prosecutor is specifically condemned by the American Bar Association unless justified by the record.

Defense counsel at closing should (1) stress to the jury their responsibilities regarding reasonable doubt and the presumption of innocence; (2) present the facts in a manner most favorable to the defendant; (3) anticipate and counter the prosecutor's arguments; (4) pose questions for the prosecutor to answer so that he will have to spend more time answering those questions than developing his own arguments; (5) encourage the jury to reject mere speculation and suspicion regarding the guilt of the defendant; (6) lead the jury to conclusions most favorable to the defendant; (7) minimize the prosecutor's case and histrionics; (8) highlight favorable evidence for the defense; (9) discredit unfavorable witnesses; (10) personal-ize and humanize the defendant; (11) be colorful, frank, and sincere; (12) emphasize, where applicable, the good character of the defendant; (13) explain any weaknesses in the defense; (14) implore each juror to think individually; and (15) describe the prospective fate of the defendant if convicted.

One of the major concerns of the prosecutor on closing is to avoid violating the so-called **Griffin** *rule*, which forbids a prosecutor to comment to the jury on a defendant's failure to testify.[50] However, the *Griffin* rule is not absolute: It is common practice in some jurisdictions for the prosecutor to summarize the evidence presented by the government and to note that it went unrebutted by the defense—without specifically drawing attention to the fact that the defendant has not testified—and of course an adverse inference is there to be picked up by the jury.

If the defendant testified but refused to answer certain questions when he was not privileged to do so, the prosecutor may properly comment on the defendant's failure to answer *those* questions. Further, if the defense attorney on closing talks about what the defendant *would have testified* to (when he did not testify at all), the prosecutor may properly comment on the defendant's failure to testify. The prosecutor at closing is also permitted to (1) accurately summarize the evidence presented, (2) note discrepancies and conflicts in the defense testimony, (3) argue that the evidence in the record supports and justifies a conviction, (4) make statements as to the evils of crime on society, (5) argue for a fearless administration of law and order, and (6) comment on the *conduct* of the defendant.[51]

It is improper for the prosecutor to make remarks not based directly on the evidence or to draw conclusions that cannot reasonably be inferred from the evidence. Further, remarks that are irrelevant to the issues being tried or that misstate the evidence in the record are improper. For example, in a recent Illinois case,[52] the prosecutor's remark during closing that "I am just the thirteenth juror in the case, ladies and gentlemen, nothing more," was held to be

---

[50] *Griffin* v. *California*, 380 U.S. 609 (1965).

[51] Vess, H., supra, note 46.

[52] *People* v. *Vasquez*, 291 N.E.2d 5 (1972).

prejudicial to the defendant since it tended to convey the impression that the prosecutor was impartial.

Although improper arguments alone can be a basis for a reversal of a conviction on appeal, only 10 per cent of cases are reversed on this basis.[53] In most jurisdictions, few improper remarks on closing are per se reversible error; the prejudicial effect on the defendant must be examined in light of the facts of the case.

The Supreme Court has held that a violation of the *Griffin* rule can be "harmless error" if the improper comment by the prosecutor did not, beyond a reasonable doubt, affect the verdict.[54]

If counsel makes an improper comment on closing, the other party must make a *timely, specific objection* to that improper comment. Failure to do so *waives* the objection unless the error is such that it could not be cured, i.e., *plain error.* Normally, an improper remark is cured if the objection is sustained and the trial judge properly instructs the jury to disregard it. However, if the improper remark is so prejudicial that the defendant cannot get a fair trial, a motion for a mistrial should be sustained.

At the completion of the closing arguments, the trial judge charges the jury.

Charge to the Jury

At this stage of the trial, the judge will read to the jury instructions on how to reach a verdict—often called the *charge to the jury.* The major purpose of the charge (instructions) is to inform the jury as to which rules of law apply to the case. The jury is instructed to apply the law to the facts presented during the evidentiary stage of the trial. Generally, the instructions will include such matters as the presumption of innocence, the burden of proof, the elements of the crime charged, how to evaluate the credibility of the witnesses, applicable defenses, and the procedures to be followed while deliberating.

The instructions should be given as clear and concise statements of law. Inaccurate statements of law are a basis for reversible error. It has been said that erroneous instructions to the jury are the greatest single source of reversible error in criminal cases.[55] However, erroneous instructions must be prejudicial to the defendant in order to be reversible. In determining prejudicial error, appellate courts generally focus on the charge as a whole rather than upon an isolated instruction.

In several states and in the federal courts, the trial judge, in instructing the jury, may summarize or comment on the evidence. It is improper for a judge, while commenting on the evidence, to be an advocate or to urge his own view of the defendant's guilt or innocence. Such comments are designed only to aid the jury in seeking the truth, and the jurors must be informed unequivocally that they are the final decision-makers.

At the conclusion of the charge, the jury is excused from the courtroom and taken to the jury room to begin their deliberations.

The Jury Deliberates

Once the jury begins its deliberations, nobody can check on them after they have entered the jury room. Consequently, it is difficult to discover how the jury arrived at its verdict. Further, it is well settled that a juror cannot impeach his own verdict and that he is *incompetent* (unqualified) to testify as to what evidence at trial supported the verdict.[56] Thus, a juror may not testify postverdict as to matters that necessarily inhered in his own consciousness. This is because jurors are *presumed* to have done their duty in accordance with their oaths. However, jurors are competent to testify as to any improper external influences on the jury during its deliberations (e.g., prejudicial newspaper article in jury room, threat by bailiff to reach a certain verdict, rolling dice for verdict, attempts at bribing jurors). In short, in the absence of jury misconduct, a jury cannot *impeach* its own verdict (change its mind after the verdict).

Sometimes a jury is unable to reach a verdict after deliberating many hours or days. In such a case of a *hung jury*, the trial judge has discretion to declare a *mistrial*,

---

[53]Vess, H., supra note 48, at 24 n.18.

[54]*Chapman* v. *California*, 386 U.S. 18 (1967) (Chapter Fourteen, § 14.02).

[55]*Skidmore* v. *Baltimore & Ohio R. Co.*, 167 F.2d 54, 65 (2d Cir. 1948).

[56]*Hyde* v. *United States*, 225 U.S. 347 (1912); *McDonald* v. *Pless*, 238 U.S. 264 (1915).

and the defendant can be tried again by a new jury; otherwise the jury may be ordered to continue its deliberations.

In many jurisdictions, before declaring a mistrial when the jury is unable to reach a verdict, the trial judge will stress to the jury the importance of reaching a verdict through a supplemental instruction known as the **Allen** *charge* ("dynamite charge"). The *Allen* charge encourages deadlocked juries to reach an agreement: The jurors are informed that no juror is expected to yield a conscientiously held opinion, but if a majority of the jury is for either conviction or acquittal, the minority ought to consider whether the majority view may be reasonable and correct.

The *Allen* charge was originally approved by the United States Supreme Court in 1896,[57] but it has recently come under attack by some federal courts as being coercive on the minority members of the jury.[58] Although no federal court has held the *Allen* charge to be unconstitutional, some state and federal courts have prohibited its future use. These courts recommend that trial judges conform to the American Bar Association Standards, Trial by Jury,[59] which provide:

(a) Before the jury retires for deliberation, the court may give an instruction which informs the jury:
  (i) that in order to return a verdict, each juror must agree thereto;
  (ii) that jurors have a duty to consult with one another and to deliberate with a view to reaching an agreement, if it can be done without violence to individual judgment;
  (iii) that each juror must decide the case for himself, but only after an impartial consideration of the evidence with his fellow jurors;
  (iv) that in the course of deliberations, a juror should not hesitate to reexamine his own views and change his opinion if convinced it is erroneous; and
  (v) that no juror should surrender his honest conviction as to the weight or effect of the evidence solely because of the opinion of his fellow jurors, or for the mere purpose of returning a verdict.
(b) If it appears to the court that the jury has been unable to agree, the court may require the jury to continue their deliberations and may give or repeat an instruction as provided in subsection (a). The court shall not require or threaten to require the jury to deliberate for an unreasonable length of time or for unreasonable intervals.

Once the jury has reached a decision, the trial judge and counsel are notified that a verdict has been reached.

The Verdict

The types of verdicts that a jury may reach in a criminal trial depend upon several factors, including the plea given by the defendant (e.g., not guilty by reason of insanity), the number of crimes charged (counts), the number of defendants, and whether a finding of guilt for a lesser included offense is a responsive verdict (e.g., guilty of second degree murder when charged with first degree murder).

The foreman of the jury (selected by other jurors at the beginning of the deliberations) or the bailiff will read the verdict(s) in open court. A verdict can range from not guilty to each charge, to not guilty to some charges, to guilty of a lesser included offense, to guilty to all charges, or to not guilty by reason of insanity (if pleaded). If the verdict is one of not guilty, that ends the case as far as the prosecution is concerned. The defendant may not be tried a second time for the *same offense* because of the double jeopardy bar. However, a defendant may appeal a verdict of guilty in all jurisdictions (Chapter Six). A verdict of guilty is rendered in approximately 65 per cent of all jury trials, and about 5 per cent end in a hung jury. (See Chapter Seven, § 7.03.)

Once the verdict(s) has been read in open court, counsel or the court may request that the jury be *polled*. Each juror is asked by the judge or clerk of the court if that verdict "was then and is now" his verdict. Jurors, however, are not asked to state the reasons for their verdict. In all jurisdictions, the defendant has a right to have the jury polled. Under the American Bar Association Standards, Trial by Jury, if the poll reveals a lack of unanimity, the court may order a

[57]*Allen* v. *United States*, 164 U.S. 492 (1896).
[58]*United States* v. *Fioravanti*, 412 F.2d 407 (3rd Cir. 1969); *United States* v. *Thomas*, 449 F.2d 1177 (D.C. Cir. 1971).
[59]A.B.A. Standards, 5.4. See also Note, 53 Va. L. Rev. 123 (1967).

mistrial or require the jury to deliberate further.[60]

At this point, the trial ends. Post-trial stages may include a motion for a new trial, sentencing, appeals, and petitions for certain postconviction remedies.

Assuming that a defendant has gone to trial and been convicted, the next step in the criminal process is sentencing.

Sentencing

The *sentence* imposed by the court is a crucial part of the criminal justice system to the convicted defendant. Although the court has much discretion throughout the criminal process (e.g., setting bail, admitting or excluding evidence) the judge has the greatest discretion in the area of sentencing. As a general rule, the sentence must be within the limits set by the applicable statute under which the defendant was convicted. Criminal sentences may include probation, a suspended sentence, a fine, incarceration in jail or prison, or capital punishment. In most jurisdictions, an appellate court will not overturn a sentence imposed unless the trial judge has abused his statutory discretion.

The sentence imposed usually reflects the judge's own commitment to a particular sentencing philosophy: retribution, rehabilitation, isolation, or deterrence. Some judges are especially rough on drunk drivers, others on "hot-check" artists. If the defendant has decided to plead guilty, defense attorneys often try to schedule sentencing so that the defendant can appear before a sympathetic judge. The sentencing process will be examined in more detail in Chapter Fourteen.

After sentencing, some defendants appeal their conviction.

Appeals

Of the 80 to 90 per cent of defendants who plead guilty to a felony charge, relatively few appeal their convictions, in part because a guilty plea substantially reduces the legal grounds for a reversal of a conviction (Chapter Thirteen). Of the 10 to 20 per cent who plead not guilty to a felony charge, about two thirds are convicted. Of these, 20 to 40 per cent appeal their convictions to an appellate court. The rate of reversal varies by jurisdiction but is probably around 10 to 20 per cent. To illustrate, suppose that we have 100 criminal defendants who, for various reasons, have decided to plead not guilty to the offenses charged and go to trial (bearing in mind that of every 1,000 criminal defendants, 900 plead guilty as part of a plea-bargaining arrangement). Of the 100 "not guilty" defendants, approximately 66 will be convicted (of the substantive offense charged or a lesser included offense), and of these, only 13 to 26 (20 to 40 per cent) will appeal their convictions. Of these defendants, only 3 to 5 (taking the higher figure of a 20 per cent reversal rate) will have their convictions reversed by the appellate court.[61] We are assuming that the reversal rate on appeal for those defendants who have pleaded guilty is even lower, because in most jurisdictions, a conviction based on a guilty plea insulates from appellate review most procedural irregularities (e.g., illegal search and seizure or coerced confession) and waives all non-jurisdictional errors.[62] (See Chapter Thirteen.)

In short, most defendants do not appeal their convictions, and only a small percentage of persons convicted of a felony have their convictions reversed by an appellate court. In those instances in which an appellate court has overturned a conviction, the case is usually *reversed* and *remanded* to the trial court for a new trial.

After exhausting the appeal process, a defendant may seek postconviction remedies, such as federal habeas corpus. This process is discussed in Chapter Fourteen.

In summary, the legal steps involved in the processing of a person accused of committing a misdemeanor are relatively simple in most jurisdictions. The suspect is arrested, usually booked, given an opportunity to post bond, and a trial is held within a reasonably short time. On the other hand, the processing of a person accused of committing a felony can be quite complicated and lengthy. The procedures followed depend, in part, on whether the accused is charged by a bill of information or via the grand jury process. The legal steps involved vary by jurisdiction and range from a prearrest investigation through complicated postconviction remedies.

---

[60]In a study of 3,576 jury trials, it was found that the judge and jury agreed on the verdict in 75 per cent of the cases. Kalven and Zeisel, supra note 15, at 56.

[61]See Meador, D., *Appellate Courts* (1974); and Kalven and Zeisel, supra, note 15.
[62]See Bond, J., *Plea Bargaining and Guilty Pleas* 8–9 (1975).

DUE PROCESS AND THE FIFTH AND FOURTEENTH AMENDMENTS

3.01 INTRODUCTION

The Fifth Amendment to the United States Constitution provides, inter alia, that "no person shall be ... deprived of life, liberty, or property, without *due process* of law..." (emphasis added). Thus, the Fifth Amendment Due Process Clause is a limitation on the powers of the federal government and the Congress. The Fourteenth Amendment provides, inter alia, that "no *State* shall ... deprive any person of life, liberty, or property, without *due process* of law..." (emphasis added). Accordingly, the Fourteenth Amendment is a limitation on state governmental power. Thus, for the purposes of criminal procedure, all persons charged with a federal offense are guaranteed due process under the Fifth Amendment; and persons charged with a non-federal (e.g., state or local) offense are guaranteed due process under the Fourteenth Amendment. In effect, these Due Process Clauses suggest that a person may be executed, imprisoned, or deprived of his property by the government (state or federal) so long as he is first afforded due process. BUT WHAT PROCESS IS DUE a person under the Fifth and Fourteenth Amendments?

This question is not easy to answer because the doctrinal concept of due process is not self-defining, and the United States Supreme Court has never attempted to give a precise and fixed definition of due process. As noted by Justice Frankfurter, "Due process of law, as a historic and generative principle, *precludes defining,* and thereby confining, these standards of conduct more precisely than to say that convictions cannot be brought about by methods that offend 'a sense of justice' "[1] (emphasis added). The Supreme Court has defined due process according to the facts and circumstances of each case, and accordingly, what is due process today may be quite something else on another day.

In general terms, due process can be operationally defined as *law in the regular course of judicial proceedings that is in accordance with natural, inherent, and fundamental principles of justice.* Thus, one could argue that due process simply means that a defendant must receive all the substantive and procedural protections that the law presently provides. But suppose the *law* is unfair? It might then be argued that due process is that which is *fundamentally*

---

[1] *Rochin* v. *California,* 342 U.S. 165 (1952) (pumping defendant's stomach, without search warrant, to obtain contraband is a denial of due process).

fair under our adversary system of American jurisprudence.

Even though the doctrinal underpinnings of this elusive concept are difficult to state with any degree of precision, it is axiomatic that every accused (federal or state offense) is entitled to due process at every stage of the criminal process. It is generally settled that there are two types of due process: (1) *substantive due process* and (2) *procedural due process*, although, on occasion, the differences between them are not easily discernible.

3.02 SUBSTANTIVE DUE PROCESS

Substantive due process is violated by legislation that can destroy the basic enjoyment of *life, liberty,* or *property*—regardless of the fairness of the procedures employed. In general, substantive due process protects all persons against unreasonable, arbitrary, or capricious laws and acts as a limitation against arbitrary governmental actions so that no court or governmental agency may exercise powers beyond those authorized by the Constitution. Due process requirements are binding on all federal and state governments, as well as on all branches, tribunals, officials, and agencies of those governments.

Earlier in our history, the doctrine of substantive due process was generally applied only to protect economic rights. In a series of cases, the Supreme Court struck down certain regulatory legislation, such as minimum wage and child labor laws, that it deemed *unfair on their face.*

A state may pass laws under its *police powers* that are designed to promote the *health, welfare, safety,* or *morality* of its citizens. Prior to the 1930's, the Supreme Court employed a restrictive view of the state's police powers. For example, in 1905, the Supreme Court struck down a New York state law that purported to regulate maximum hours for bakers because it viewed this statute as an unreasonable limitation on the liberty of contract.[2] Sub-

sequently, however, the Court altered that view, and today statutes are *presumed to be constitutional.* As long as a regulation is *reasonable* and is not arbitrary or capricious, it will pass the test of substantive due process. As an illustration, the Supreme Court has upheld the following enactments under the police powers of a state: (1) regulations of the sale of drugs, foods, etc.;[3] (2) legislation regarding building construction requirements;[4] (3) statutes prohibiting picketing and strike activities;[5] and (4) regulations governing working conditions, hours, and wages.[6] This list is not inclusive.

The Supreme Court has indicated that any statute that appears to be a proper exercise of the state's police power and is reasonably related to a legitimate governmental purpose will be upheld on due process grounds. Most Supreme Court decisions that deal with the criminal process are not decided on substantive due process grounds.

Void-for-Vagueness Doctrine

One facet of substantive due process is closely related to the criminal process: Due process requires that a criminal law must not be so vague and uncertain that "men of common intelligence must necessarily guess at its meaning and differ as to its application."[7] This is known as the *void-for-vagueness* doctrine. To avoid being unduly vague and therefore unconstitutional, a statute must be *definite, certain,* and give *fair warning* regarding (1) the class of persons who fall within its scope, (2) the conduct that is forbidden, and (3) the authorized punishment.[8] Although the doctrine is also

---

[2]*Lochner* v. *New York,* 198 U.S. 45 (1905). *Lochner* was subsequently overruled in *Bunting* v. *Oregon,* 243 U.S. 426 (1917).

[3]*Nebbia* v. *New York,* 291 U.S. 502 (1934). See also *United States* v. *Carolene Products Co.,* 304 U.S. 144 (1938) (federal statute excluding "filled milk" from interstate commerce upheld).

[4]*Block* v. *Hirsh,* 256 U.S. 135 (1921).

[5]*Senn* v. *Tile Layers,* 301 U.S. 468 (1937).

[6]*West Coast Hotel* v. *Parrish,* 300 U.S. 379 (1937); *United States* v. *Darby,* 312 U.S. 100 (1941); *Olsen* v. *Nebraska* ex rel. *Western Ref. & Bond Assoc.,* 313 U.S. 236 (1941).

[7]*Connolly* v. *General Construction Co.,* 269 U.S. 385, 391 (1926).

[8]*Scull* v. *Commonwealth,* 359 U.S. 344, 353 (1959) (fundamental fairness requires that a person cannot be sent to jail for a crime that he

Footnote continued on opposite page

applicable to common law crimes, administrative regulations carrying criminal sanctions, and noncriminal statutes,[9] our discussion is necessarily restricted largely to criminal statutes.[10]

The Supreme Court has struck down for vagueness, among others, criminal statutes and ordinances that make it unlawful (1) to conduct oneself on city sidewalks in a manner "annoying" to passersby[11]; (2) to wander city streets late at night "without lawful business and [without giving] a satis-

---

could not with reasonable certainty know he was committing); *United States* v. *Klarriss,* 347 U.S. 612, 617 (1954) (no man shall be held criminally responsible for conduct that he could not reasonably understand to be proscribed); *Wright* v. *Georgia,* 373 U.S. 284, 293 (1963) (a conviction under a criminal statute that does not give adequate notice that the conduct charged is prohibited is violative of due process); *Bouie* v. *Columbia,* 378 U.S. 347, 351 (1964) (the constitutional requirement of definiteness is violated by a criminal statute that fails to give a person of ordinary intelligence fair notice that his contemplated conduct is forbidden by the statute); *United States* v. *National Dairy Products,* 372 U.S. 29, 32 (1963) ("void for vagueness" means that criminal responsibility should not attach where one could not reasonably understand that his contemplated conduct is proscribed); *Giaccio* v. *Pennsylvania,* 382 U.S. 399, 402 (1966) (a law fails to meet the requirements of due process if it is so vague and standardless that it leaves the public uncertain as to the conduct it prohibits or leaves judges and jurors free to decide, without any legally fixed standards, what is prohibited and what is not in each particular case); *Raley* v. *Ohio,* 360 U.S. 423, 438 (1959) (a state may not issue commands to its citizens, under criminal sanctions, in language so vague and undefined as to afford no fair warning).

[9]It is well-settled that noncriminal statutes that are vague are also violative of the Due Process Clause. However, a statute (criminal or noncriminal) will be upheld by the Supreme Court against an attack on the grounds of vagueness where an appropriate construction of the statute by a state court has removed the alleged vagueness. See, e.g., *Minnesota* ex rel. *Pearson* v. *Probate Court of Ramsey County,* 309 U.S. 270 (1940) (state statute providing for the commitment of persons having a "psychopathic personality" not vague in light of the construction placed thereon by the highest court of the state).

The following noncriminal statutes have been upheld by the Supreme Court as not unconstitutionally vague: *Barsky* v. *Board of Regents,* 347 U.S. 422 (1954) (statute authorizing the suspension or revocation of the license of a physician who "has been convicted in a court of competent jurisdiction, either within or without this state, of a crime"); *Old Dearborn Distributing* v. *Seagram-Distillers Corp.,* 299 U.S. 183 (1936)

(statute making anyone willfully and knowingly advertising "any commodity" at less than the price stipulated in "any contract entered into pursuant to the provisions of [the Illinois Fair Trade Act]" liable for damages for unfair competition); *Neblett* v. *Carpenter,* 305 U.S. 297 (1938) (state statute authorizing the insurance commissioner to mutualize or reinsure the business of a company "or enter into rehabilitation agreements"); *Plymouth Coal Co.* v. *Pennsylvania,* 232 U.S. 531 (1914) (state statute requiring owners of coal properties to leave a pillar of coal in each vein of coal worked by them of such width that will be a sufficient barrier for the safety of the employees of either mine in case the other should be abandoned); *Bandini Petroleum Co.* v. *Superior Court, Los Angeles County,* 284 U.S. 8 (1931) (state statute prohibiting the "unreasonable waste" of natural gas); *Miller* v. *Schoene,* 276 U.S. 272 (1928) (state statute requiring state entomologist to determine whether any trees in a "locality" constitute a menace to the health of any apple orchard); *Edgar A. Levy Leasing Co.* v. *Siegel,* 258 U.S. 242 (1922) (state statute providing that it shall be a defense to an action for rent that such rent is "unjust" and "unreasonable"); *Hicklin* v. *Coney,* 290 U.S. 169 (1933) (state statute requiring private contract motor vehicle carriers to execute an indemnity bond); *Arnett* v. *Kennedy,* 416 U.S. 134 (1974) (federal statute authorizing the removal or suspension of a federal employee "for such case as will promote the efficiency of the service"); *United States Civil Service Commission* v. *National Association of Letter Carriers,* 413 U.S. 548 (1973) (federal statute prohibiting federal employees from taking "an active part in political management or in political campaigns").

[10]The following criminal laws have been upheld by the Supreme Court as not being impermissibly vague: *United States* v. *Powell,* 423 U.S. 87 (1976) (federal statute prohibiting the mailing of "firearms capable of being concealed on the person"); *Examining Board* v. *Otero,* 426 U.S. 572 (1976) (Puerto Rico statute prohibiting aliens from engaging in the private practice of engineering); *Planned Parenthood of Missouri* v. *Danforth,* 428 U.S. 52 (1976) (state abortion statute defining "viability" as the stage of fetal development in which the life of the unborn child may be continued indefinitely outside the womb); *McLucas* v. *DeChamplain,* 421 U.S. 21 (1975)

Footnote continued on page 94

factory account of [oneself][12]; (3) to use "opprobrious words or language, tending to cause a breach of the peace"[13]; (4) to "abuse another by using menacing, insulting, slanderous or profane language"[14]; (5) to "wantonly curse or revile or use obscene or opprobrious language toward or with reference to any member of the city police while in the actual performance of his duty"[15]; (6) to be a "rogue, vagabond or dissolute person"[16]; (7) "to exhibit an ob-

scene motion picture with knowledge of its contents"[17]; (8) to "treat contemptuously the American flag"[18]; (9) to willfully "obstruct public passages"[19]; (10) for "two or more persons to assemble for the purpose of disturbing the public peace"[20]; (11) to disturb the peace in a manner that would "foreseeably disturb or alarm the public"[21]; (12) to "stand or loiter upon any street or sidewalk after having been requested by a police officer to move on"[22]; and (13) to aid

---

(Article of United States Code of Military Justice (UCMJ) that courts-martial may try and punish "crimes and offenses not capital"); *United States* v. *Mazurie,* 419 U.S. 544 (1975) (federal statute prohibiting the unauthorized introduction of liquor into "Indian country"); *Parker* v. *Levy,* 417 U.S. 733 (1974) (Article of UCMJ prohibiting "conduct unbecoming an officer or gentleman"); *Spence* v. *Washington,* 418 U.S. 405 (1974) (state statute providing that nothing may be "affixed to or superimposed on" an American flag); *Secretary of the Navy* v. *Aurech,* 418 U.S. 676 (1974) (article of UCMJ which permits punishment for "all disorders and neglects to the prejudice of good order and discipline in the armed forces"); *Hamling* v. *United States,* 418 U.S. 87 (1974) (federal statute prohibiting the use of mails for sending "obscene, lewd, lascivious, indecent, filthy, or vile" materials); *Wainwright* v. *Stone,* 414 U.S. 21 (1973) (state statute prohibiting "the abominable and detestable crime against nature, either with mankind or with beast"); *Grayned* v. *City of Rockford,* 408 U.S. 104 (1972) (antinoise ordinance forbidding any person on public or private grounds adjacent to any building in which a school or any class is in session from willfully making any noise which disturbs the peace or good order of a school session); *Colten* v. *Kentucky,* 407 U.S. 104 (1972) (state statute providing that a person is guilty of disorderly conduct if he congregates with other persons in a public place and refuses to comply with a lawful police order to disperse); *Zicarelli* v. *New Jersey State Commission of Investigation,* 406 U.S. 472 (1972) (word "responsive" in immunity statute not impermissibly vague); *Cole* v. *Richardson,* 405 U.S. 676 (1972) (state loyalty oath requiring public employees to "uphold and defend" the federal and state constitutions); *Ginsberg* v. *New York,* 390 U.S. 629 (1968) (state statute prohibiting the sale of obscene materials to minors, requiring knowledge of the "character" of the material therein); *Boutilier* v. *Immigration Service,* 387 U.S. 118 (1967) (federal statute declaring aliens "afflicted with psychopathic personality" as "excludable" from admission to the U.S.); *Adderly* v. *Florida,* 385 U.S. 39 (1966) (state

statute penalizing every trespass upon the property of another made with a "malicious and mischievous intent"); *Shuttlesworth* v. *City of Birmingham,* 382 U.S. 85 (1965) (ordinance penalizing persons standing on a sidewalk and obstructing free passage only if they refuse to obey a request by a police officer); *Scales* v. *United States,* 367 U.S. 203 (1961) (federal statute making a felony the acquisition or holding of knowing "membership" in any organization that advocates the overthrow of the government by force or violence); *McGowan* v. *Maryland,* 366 U.S. 420 (1961) (state Sunday closing law that exempts the Sunday retail sale of "merchandise essential to, or customarily sold at, or incidental to the operation of" bathing beaches, amusement parks, etc.); *United States* v. *Korpan,* 354 U.S. 271 (1957) (federal statute defining gaming devices as "slot machines" that operate by means of insertion of a coin and that by application of the element of chance may deliver cash, premiums, merchandise or tokens); *United States* v. *Five Gambling Devices,* 346 U.S. 441 (1953) (federal statute requiring every dealer of gambling devices to register with the Attorney General and to file information "in such district"); *United States* v. *Harriss,* 347 U.S. 612 (1954) (federal statute requiring disclosure of all contributions and expenditures having the purpose of attempting to influence legislation through direct communication with Congress).

[11]*Coates* v. *City of Cincinnati,* 402 U.S. 611 (1971).

[12]*Palmer* v. *City of Euclid,* 402 U.S. 544 (1971).

[13]*Gooding* v. *Wilson,* 405 U.S. 510 (1972).

[14]*Plummer* v. *Columbus,* 414 U.S. 2 (1973).

[15]*Lewis* v. *City of New Orleans,* 415 U.S. 130 (1974).

[16]*Papachristou* v. *City of Jacksonville,* 405 U.S. 156 (1972).

[17]*Rabe* v. *Washington,* 405 U.S. 313 (1972).

[18]*Smith* v. *Goguen,* 415 U.S. 566 (1974).

[19]*Cox* v. *Louisiana,* 379 U.S. 536 (1965).

[20]*Wright* v. *Georgia,* 373 U.S. 284 (1963).

[21]*Garner* v. *Louisiana,* 368 U.S. 157 (1961).

[22]*Shuttlesworth* v. *City of Birmingham,* 382 U.S. 87 (1965).

in the support of "any subversive organization."[23] In addition, the Supreme Court found the following unconstitutional: (1) a municipal ordinance authorizing an administrative board to classify motion pictures as "not suitable for young persons"[24]; (2) a state law prohibiting the sale of magazines that would appeal to the lust of persons under 18 years of age[25]; (3) a state loyalty oath requiring a statement that an employee is not engaged "in one way or another" in an attempt to overthrow the government[26]; (4) a state statute barring the employment in a state university of any person who "by word of mouth or writing willfully and deliberately advocates, advises or teaches the doctrine" of the forceful overthrow of the government[27]; (5) a state statute authorizing a jury to "assess costs" against an accused whom the jury has acquitted[28]; (6) state statutes requiring all teachers to swear that they are not "subversive persons," and that they "will by precept and example promote respect for the flag"[29]; (7) a state statute requiring all state employees to execute a written oath that they have never lent "aid, support, advice, counsel, or influence to the Communist Party"[30]; (8) a federal statute that makes punishable the mailing of material that is "obscene, lewd, lascivious, or filthy, or of an indecent character"[31]; and (9) a municipal ordinance requiring that advance written notice be given to local police by "any person desiring to canvass, solicit or call from house to house for a recognized charitable cause."[32]

While this list is not exhaustive, it is clear that the elements of *certainty* and *fair warning* of what *conduct* is prohibited are constitutionally required. In addition, criminal statutes must not be overly broad and must not infringe on constitutional rights, such as the First Amendment guarantees of freedom of press, religion, speech, and association.[33] As noted by the Supreme Court, "Because First Amendment freedoms need breathing space to survive, government may regulate in the area only with narrow specificity."[34] The *overbreadth doctrine* states that statutes that are invalid because of overbreadth, either on their face or as applied, are violative of the First Amendment[35] (see Chapter Fifteen, § 15.03, Comments).

---

[23]*Dombrowski* v. *Pfister*, 380 U.S. 479 (1965).

[24]*Interstate Circuit, Inc.* v. *City of Dallas*, 390 U.S. 676 (1968).

[25]*Rabeck* v. *New York*, 391 U.S. 462 (1968).

[26]*Whitehill* v. *Elkins*, 389 U.S. 54 (1967).

[27]*Keyishian* v. *Board of Regents*, 385 U.S. 589 (1967).

[28]*Giaccio* v. *Pennsylvania*, 382 U.S. 399 (1966).

[29]*Baggett* v. *Bullitt*, 377 U.S. 360 (1964).

[30]*Cramp* v. *Board of Public Instruction*, 368 U.S. 278 (1961).

[31]*Roth* v. *United States*, 354 U.S. 476 (1957).

[32]*Hynes* v. *Mayor of Oradell*, 425 U.S. 610 (1976).

[33]*NAACP* v. *Button*, 371 U.S. 415 (1963).

[34]*Id.* at 433.

[35]The "overbreadth doctrine" is applicable primarily in the First Amendment area and applies even to laws written with clarity and precision, whereas the void-for-vagueness doctrine rests upon the Due Process Clauses of the Fifth and Fourteenth Amendments and is applicable only to laws that lack clarity and precision. The Supreme Court, in some instances, has struck down laws as both overbroad and vague. See, e.g., *Plummer* v. *City of Columbus*, 414 U.S. 2 (1973); *Coates* v. *City of Cincinnati*, 402 U.S. 611 (1971); *Cox* v. *Louisiana*, 379 U.S. 536 (1965); *NAACP* v. *Button*, 371 U.S. 415 (1963).

Under the overbreadth doctrine, the Supreme Court has carved out exceptions to the general requirement of standing, which is based on the doctrine that constitutional rights are personal and may not be asserted vicariously (Chapter One, § 1.05). Thus, even though a statute or ordinance is neither vague nor overbroad as applied to the conduct charged against a particular defendant, he is permitted to raise the issue of its unconstitutional vagueness or overbreadth as applied to other persons in situations not before the court. See, e.g., *Bigelow* v. *Virginia*, 421 U.S. 809 (1975); *Broadrick* v. *Oklahoma*, 413 U.S. 601 (1973); *Plummer* v. *City of Columbus*, 414 U.S. 2 (1973); *Gooding* v. *Wilson*, 405 U.S. 518 (1972); *Grayned* v. *City of Rockford*, 408 U.S. 104 (1972); *Doran* v. *Salem Inn, Inc.*, 422 U.S. 922 (1975). However, the Supreme Court has indicated that in order for an individual to have standing, he must present more than an allegation that the statute has merely a subjective "chilling effect" on his First Amendment rights: He must make a claim of a specific present harm or of a threat of a specific future harm; that the alleged overbreadth is substantial; and that he is not raising the hypothetical rights of third parties. See *Bigelow* v. *Virginia*, 421 U.S. 809, 816–817 (1975); Note, *Standing to Assert Constitutional*

Footnote continued on page 96

Jus Tertii, 88 Harv. L. Rev. 423 (1974); Note, *The First Amendment Overbreadth Doctrine,* 83 Harv. L. Rev. 844 (1970).

Related to the overbreadth doctrine is the so-called "doctrine of abstention" under which, as a general rule, a federal court when confronted with constitutional issues that implicate or depend upon unsettled questions of state law should abstain and stay the proceedings until those state law questions have been resolved by the state courts. See *Gibson* v. *Berryhill,* 411 U.S. 564 (1973), and 28 U.S.C. § 2283 (Chapter One, § 1.02). State legislation may be saved from invalidation on the ground of overbreadth by a narrowing construction of state laws by the state court, as federal courts lack jurisdiction to authoritatively construe state legislation. Thus, a federal court cannot judge the facial constitutionality of a state statute until the state court has determined what the statute means. See, e.g., *Broadrick* v. *Oklahoma,* 413 U.S. 601 (1973). However, federal legislation may be saved from "overbreadth" by a narrowing construction given that legislation by the Supreme Court. *United States* v. *Thirty-Seven Photographs,* 402 U.S. 363 (1971). And the Supreme Court will narrowly construe a federal statute to avoid constitutional questions where such a construction is reasonable. *Arnett* v. *Kennedy,* 416 U.S. 134 (1974). Finally, the doctrine of abstention is not applicable where a state statute is clear and precise and is not susceptible to a narrowing construction that could avoid or modify the federal constitutional questions involving overbreadth. *Zwickler* v. *Koota,* 389 U.S. 241 (1971).

The following cases decided by the Supreme Court illustrate the overbreadth doctrine: *Gooding* v. *Wilson,* 405 U.S. 510 (1972) (Georgia statute making it a crime for any person to use "opprobrious words or abusive language, tending to cause a breach of the peace" held overly broad); *Broadrick* v. *Oklahoma,* 413 U.S. 601 (1973) (state statute forbidding state employees to solicit or receive any assessment or contribution, inter alia, "for any political organization, candidacy or other political purpose," held not substantially overbroad); *Lewis* v. *City of New Orleans,* 415 U.S. 130 (1974) (to "wantonly curse or revile or use obscene or opprobrious language toward . . . any member of the city police" held overbroad); *Bigelow* v. *Virginia,* 421 U.S. 809 (1975) (state statute prohibiting any publication "to encourage or prompt the procuring of an abortion," held overbroad); *Eisenstadt* v. *Baird,* 405 U.S. 438 (1972) (recognizing that the overbreadth doctrine is applicable to the Equal Protection Clause); *Freedman* v. *Maryland,* 380 U.S. 51 (1965) (recognizing standing of a person on ground of overbreadth whether or not his conduct could be proscribed by a properly drawn statute) — to the same effect

is *Dombrowski* v. *Pfister,* 380 U.S. 479 [1965]); *Parker* v. *Levy,* 417 U.S. 733 (1974) (rule permitting standing with no requirement that person making claim of overbreadth demonstrate that his conduct could not be regulated by a sufficiently narrow statute to be given a good deal less weight in military context); *Grayned* v. *City of Rockford,* 408 U.S. 104 (1972) (antinoise ordinance prohibiting demonstrations within 150 feet of any school building not overly broad); *Plummer* v. *City of Columbus,* 414 U.S. 2 (1973) (ordinance punishing the use of "menacing, insulting, slanderous, or profane language," held overbroad); *Colten* v. *Kentucky,* 407 U.S. 104 (1972) (state disorderly conduct statute which prohibits, inter alia, a refusal to comply with a lawful police order to disperse held not overbroad); *NAACP* v. *Button,* 371 U.S. 415 (1963) (state statute making it a crime to, inter alia, advise another that his legal rights have been infringed and refer him to an attorney for assistance held overly broad); *Coates* v. *City of Cincinnati,* 402 U.S. 611 (1971) (city ordinance making it a crime for three or more persons to assemble on a sidewalk and "conduct themselves in a manner annoying to persons passing by" held overbroad); *Elfbrandt* v. *Russell,* 384 U.S. 11 (1966) (Arizona statute prohibiting a knowing membership in the Communist Party held overbroad); *Cameron* v. *Johnson,* 390 U.S. 611 (1968) (Mississippi statute prohibiting, inter alia, picketing in such a manner as to obstruct the free ingress or egress to and from any courthouse or other public building held not overly broad); *Law Students Research Council* v. *Wadmond,* 401 U.S. 154 (1971) (New York rule requiring that applicants to the state bar furnish satisfactory proof that they believe in the form of the government of the U.S. and are loyal to such government held not overbroad); *Street* v. *New York,* 394 U.S. 576 (1969) (state statute that makes it a crime to "publicly mutilate, deface, defile, trample upon, or cast contempt upon an American flag" is overly broad if it permits a conviction merely for speaking defiantly about the American flag); *Buckley* v. *Valeo,* 424 U.S. 1 (1976) (provisions of federal statute imposing a $1000 limitation on contributions by individuals and groups to any single candidate for election to a federal office held not overbroad); *Young* v. *American Mini Theatres,* 427 U.S. 50 (1976) (City of Detroit ordinance requiring, inter alia, that adult movie theatres may not be located within 1,000 feet of any two other regulated establishments held not overbroad); *Aptheker* v. *Secretary of State,* 378 U.S. 500 (1964) (federal statute making it a crime for any member of a Communist organization, with notice that the organization has been ordered to register with the Subversive Activities Control Board, to apply for a U.S. passport held overbroad); *Erznoznik* v.

Footnote continued on opposite page

"Crimes Against Nature" and the Void-for-Vagueness Doctrine

ROSE v. LOCKE

Supreme Court of the United States, 1975
423 U.S. 48, 96 S. Ct. 243, 46 L. Ed. 2d 243

Harold Locke, the respondent, was convicted in a Tennessee state court of having committed a "crime against nature" in violation of Tenn. Code Ann. 39–707, which provides, "Crimes against nature, either with mankind or any beast, are punishable by imprisonment in the penitentiary not less than five (5) years nor more than fifteen (15) years." The evidence showed that Locke entered the apartment of a female neighbor late at night on the pretext of using the telephone. Once inside, he produced a butcher knife, forced his neighbor to partially disrobe, and compelled her to submit to his twice performing cunnilingus upon her. He was sentenced to five years' imprisonment. The Tennessee Court of Appeals affirmed the conviction, rejecting respondent's claim that the Tennessee statute did not encompass cunnilingus, as well as his claim that the statute was unconstitutionally vague. The Tennessee Supreme Court denied review. Thereafter, Locke's constitutional claim was renewed in a petition for a writ of habeas corpus in the U.S. District Court (E.D. Tenn.). That court denied the petition, but the Court of Appeals (6th Cir.) reversed, holding that the Tennessee statute failed to give the "fair warning" necessary to withstand a charge of unconstitutional vagueness. The United States Supreme Court granted certiorari.

PER CURIAM.

* * *

It is settled that the fair-warning requirement embodied in the Due Process Clause prohibits the States from holding an individual "criminally responsible for conduct which he could not reasonably understand to be proscribed." United States v. Harris, 347 U.S. 612, 617 (1954); see Wainwright

---

City of Jacksonville, 422 U.S. 205 (1975) (ordinance prohibiting the showing of films containing nudity by a drive-in movie theatre when its screen is visible from a public street or place held overbroad); *Talley* v. *California*, 362 U.S. 60 (1960) (ordinance making it a crime to distribute "any hand-bill in any place under any circumstances" held overbroad); *Lovell* v. *Griffin*, 303 U.S. 444 (1938) (ordinance prohibiting the distribution, without a permit by the city manager, of circulars, handbooks, advertising, or literature of any kind, whether delivered free or sold, held overbroad); *Communist Party of Indiana* v. *Whitcomb*, 414 U.S. 441 (1974) (state statute prohibiting any political party or its candidate from being placed on the ballot until it has filed an affidavit that it does not advocate the overthrow of the government by force or violence held overbroad); *United States* v. *12 200-ft. Reels of Super 8 mm. Film*, 413 U.S. 123 (1973) (federal statute prohibiting the importation from any foreign country of any obscene material held not overbroad); *United States* v. *Orito*, 413 U.S. 139 (1973) (federal statute prohibiting any person from knowingly transporting any obscene material in interstate or foreign commerce by means of a common carrier held not overbroad); *United States Civil Service Commission* v. *National Association of Letter Carriers*, 413 U.S. 548 (1973) (federal statute prohibiting federal employees from taking "an active part in political management or in political campaigns" held not overbroad); *Shelton* v. *Tucker*, 364 U.S. 479 (1960) (state statute requiring teachers to annually file affidavit listing every organization to which they belonged or regularly contributed within the preceding 5 years held overbroad); *Arnett* v. *Kennedy*, 416 U.S. 134 (1974) (federal statute authorizing removal or suspension without pay of federal employees "for such cause as will promote the efficiency of the service" held not overbroad); *United States* v. *Robel*, 389 U.S. 258 (1967) (federal statute providing that when a Communist-action organization is under a final order to register, it is a crime for any member of the organization, with knowledge that such order has become final, to become employed in any defense facility held overbroad).

v. Stone, 414 U.S. 21 (1973). But this prohibition against excessive vagueness does not invalidate every statute which a reviewing court believes could have been drafted with greater precision. Many statutes will have some inherent vagueness, for "in most English words and phrases there lurk uncertainties." . . . Even trained lawyers may find it necessary to consult legal dictionaries, treatises, and judicial opinions before they may say with any certainty what some statutes may compel or forbid. . . . All the Due Process Clause requires is that the law give sufficient warning that men may conform their conduct so as to avoid that which is forbidden.

Viewed against this standard, the phrase "crime against nature" is no more vague than many other terms used to describe criminal offenses at common law and now codified in state and federal penal codes. The phrase has been in use among English-speaking people for many centuries . . . and a substantial number of jurisdictions in this country continue to utilize it. . . . Anyone who cared to do so could certainly determine what particular acts have been considered crimes against nature, and there can be no contention that the respondent's acts were ones never before considered as such. . . .

Respondent argued that the vice in the Tennessee statute derives from the fact that jurisdictions differ as to whether "crime against nature" is to be narrowly applied to only those acts constituting the common-law offense of sodomy, or is to be broadly interpreted to encompass additional forms of sexual aberration. We do not understand him to contend that the broad interpretation is itself impermissibly vague; nor do we think he could successfully do so. We have twice before upheld statutes against similar challenges. In State v. Crawford, 478 S.W.2d 314 (Mo. 1972), the Supreme Court of Missouri rejected a claim that its crime against nature statute was so devoid of definition as to be unconstitutional, pointing out its provision was derived from early English law and broadly embraced sodomy, bestiality, buggery, fellatio, and cunnilingus within its terms. We dismissed the appeal from this judgment as failing to present a substantial federal question. Crawford v. Missouri, 409

U.S. 811 (1972). . . . And in Wainwright v. Stone, supra, we held that a Florida statute proscribing "the abominable and detestable crime against nature" was not unconstitutionally vague. . . .

* * *

Respondent seems to argue instead that because some jurisdictions have taken a narrow view of "crime against nature" and some a more broad interpretation, it could not be determined which approach Tennessee would take, making it therefore impossible for him to know [that the Tennessee statute] covered forced cunnilingus. But even assuming the correctness of such an argument if there were no indication of which interpretation Tennessee might adopt, it is not available here. Respondent is simply mistaken in his view of Tennessee law. As early as 1955 Tennessee had expressly rejected a claim that "crime against nature" did not cover fellatio, repudiating those jurisdictions which had taken a "narrow restrictive definition of the offense." . . . And four years later the Tennessee Supreme Court reiterated its view of the coverage intended by [the statute]. Emphasizing that the Tennessee statute's proscription encompasses the broad meaning, the court quoted from a Maine decision it had earlier cited with approval to the effect that " 'the prohibition brings all unnatural copulation with mankind or beast, including sodomy, within its scope.' " . . . And the Maine statute, which the Tennessee Court had at that point twice equated with its own, had been applied to cunnilingus before either Tennessee decision. . . . Thus, we think the Tennessee Supreme Court had given sufficiently clear notice that [the Tennessee statute] would receive the broader of two plausible interpretations, and would be applied to acts such as those committed here when such a case arose.

* * *

The judgment of the Court of Appeals is reversed.

[Justices BRENNAN, MARSHALL, and STEWART dissented.]

Comments

1. If the victim in the *Rose* case had given Locke two hours to stop, would that behavior be proscribed within the meaning of the Tennessee "crimes against nature" statute? Should consensual cunnilingus be a crime? If so, under what conditions? *Rose* makes it clear that a criminal statute is not necessarily void for vagueness merely because the statute might have been drafted with greater precision.

2. Court decisions involving sexual offenses abound in lower state and federal courts. Some recent examples include *Colorado Springs Amusement, Ltd.* v. *Rizzo*, 524 F.2d 571 (3rd Cir. 1975) (City of Philadelphia ordinance prohibiting intersex massages upheld). To the same effect is *Smith* v. *Keator*, 419 U.S. 1043 (1974), *Rubenstein* v. *Cherry Hill*, 417 U.S. 1136 (1974), and *Kisley* v. *City of Falls Church*, 409 U.S. 907 (1972) (appeal dismissed in all three cases "for want of substantial federal question"). See also *Hicks* v. *Miranda*, 422 U.S. 332 (1974) (dismissal of an appeal for want of a substantial federal question is a decision on the merits); *Flannery* v. *City of Norfolk*, 218 S.E.2d 730 (Va. 1975) (city ordinance prohibiting the keeping of a "disorderly house" held applicable to massage parlor offering prostitution and sodomy services); *Connick* v. *Lucky Pierre's, Inc.*, 331 So. 2d 431 (La. 1976) (Louisiana statute permitting the closing of "a place in which assignation, prostitutions and solicitations, is practiced, initiated, solicited for and permitted to exist as a practice," if the owners "have maintained a nuisance or knowingly permitted it to exist without instituting legal proceedings to enjoin it," held void for vagueness); *People* v. *Barger*, 550 P.2d 1281 (Col. 1976) (state statute prohibiting "gross sexual imposition" upheld as a lesser included offense of rape where defendant was charged with rape for binding the hands and feet of his 17-year-old companion and then having sexual intercourse with her); *People* v. *Boyer*, 349 N.E.2d 50 (Ill. 1976) (state statute imposing more severe penalties for fathers convicted of incest with their daughters than for other forms of incest held not unconstitutional); *Campbell* v. *State*, 331 So.2d 289 (Fla. 1976) (waiter at gay bar who fondled a patron's pubic area with one hand while balancing a tray full of glasses on the other held not "lewd and lascivious behavior" under Florida law); *State* v. *Bateman*, 547 P.2d 6 (Ariz. 1976) (state sodomy statute held constitutional even between consenting married adults); *Commonwealth* v. *Heinbaugh*, 354 A.2d 244 (Pa. 1976) (state statute making it a crime to do "any lewd act which [the actor] knows is likely to be observed by others who would be affronted or alarmed" held constitutional as applied to a defendant who was arrested for masturbating in a parked car on a shopping center parking lot); *State* v. *J.O.*, 355 A.2d 195 (N.J. 1976) (two consenting adults discovered committing sodomy in a parked car after dark cannot be convicted under a New Jersey statute prohibiting indecent exposure); *Hanrahan* v. *LaSalle*, 348 N.E.2d 220 (Ill. 1976) (Chicago massage parlor owner's contempt conviction for violating an injunction against maintaining a public nuisance upheld on the basis of the arresting officer's testimony that a mas-

seuse fondled his genitals after he offered her $10 to commit fellatio on him); *People* v. *Fixler*, 128 Cal. Rptr. 363 (1976) (conviction for pandering of photo editor who hired young girls to engage in a variety of sexual acts in front of a camera upheld over a contention that his finished product was protected by the First Amendment); *B.A.A.* v. *State*, 333 So. 2d 552 (La. #1976) (teenage mother who hung out at a certain intersection and persisted in approaching motorists stopped at a traffic light and engaging the drivers in conversation properly convicted for "prowling and loitering"); *Lovisi* v. *Slayton*, 539 F.2d 349 (4th cir. 1976) (married couple's acts of sodomy in another's presence are punishable by the state and dissolve any federally protected right of privacy); *State* v. *Elliott*, 551 P.2d 1352 (N.Mex. 1976) (state sodomy statute includes acts between consenting adults); *United States* v. *Eisner*, 533 F.2d 987 (6th cir. 1976) (conviction of nightclub owner upheld where customers engaged in backstage sex with exotic dancers and paid for the pleasures with checks which traveled in interstate commerce in violation of the Travel Act); *People* v. *Oliver*, 347 N.E.2d 865 (Ill. App. 1975) (state dangerous sexual offender statute upheld which permits the commitment of a person convicted of sexual offenses on a showing by a preponderance of evidence because of the civil nature of the statute); *Young* v. *State*, 531 S.W.2d 560 (Tenn. 1975) (state statute prohibiting crimes against nature held to include cunnilingus); *United States* v. *Roeder*, 526 F.2d 736 (10th cir. 1975) (director and producer of pornographic films who transported his female "star" around the country to play opposite and under and upon him is criminally liable under the Mann Act, which prohibits the taking of women across state lines for immoral purposes); *Doe* v. *Commonwealth's Attorney*, 403 F. Supp. 1199 (E.D. Va., three-judge, 1976) (Virginia sodomy statute not unconstitutional when applied to private consensual homosexual acts; affirmed, 425 U.S. 901 [1976]); *Moffett* v. *State*, 340 So. 2d 1155 (Fla. 1976) (state statute making topless sunbathing on public beaches "disorderly conduct" held not unconstitutional); *People* v. *Salinas*, 551 P.2d 703 (Col. 1976) (state rape statute that applies only to minors held not violative of the equal protection of the laws); *Johnson* v. *State*, 332 So. 2d 69 (Fla. 1976) (statute proscribing unnatural and lascivious acts held not unconstitutionally vague); *People* v. *Pilcher*, 242 N.W.2d 348 (Iowa 1976) (statute prohibiting sodomy, if applied to sexual acts committed in private between consenting married persons, held unconstitutional); *People* v. *Clark*, 241 N.W.2d 756 (Mich. App. 1976) (the "gross, indecent" standard of conduct prohibits oral and manual sexual acts committed without consent or with a person under age of consent); *State* v. *Natzke*, 544 P.2d 1121 (Ariz. Appl. 1976) (statute that prohibits lewd and lascivious acts held to include cunnilingus); *People* v. *Howell*, 238 N.W.2d 148 (Mich. 1976) ("act of gross indecency" held not unconstitutionally vague when applied to forced fellatio or fellatio with a minor); *Dinkens* v. *State*, 546 P.2d 228 (Nev. 1976) (statute proscribing "infamous crime against nature" held not unconstitutionally vague); *Attwood* v. *Purcell*, 402 F. Supp. 231 (D. Ariz. 1975) ("exposure of private parts" held unconstitutionally vague); *State* v. *Lemire*, 345 A.2d 906 (N.H. 1975) (statute prohibiting deviate sexual relations held not unconstitutionally vague even though it is conceded that acts such as cunnilingus and fellatio are no longer considered "unnatural").

Due Process and Private Action

The Due Process Clause is *not* applicable to the actions of private persons unless there is some interplay between government and that private action. Thus, some state action or federal governmental action is required before the Due Process Clause is applicable. If a private citizen assaults you on the street, he has not violated your due process rights (although he may have violated certain of your civil rights; see Chapter Ten). However, if the government wishes to deprive a citizen of his life, liberty, or property, that result is not permissible absent certain safeguards that we call due process. Finally, due process is applicable to all persons within the jurisdiction of the United States (including aliens and corporations). However, the Supreme Court has indicated that the unborn are not "persons" within the meaning of the Fourteenth Amendment.[36]

3.03 PROCEDURAL DUE PROCESS

The vast majority of due process cases decided by the Supreme Court in the area of

---

[36]*Roe* v. *Wade,* 410 U.S. 113, 158 (1973).

criminal procedure deal with *procedural due process.* This concerns the *notice, hearings,* and *procedure* required before the life, liberty, or property of a person may be taken by the government.

In general, procedural due process requires the following:

1. notice of the proceedings,
2. a hearing,
3. and an opportunity to present a defense
4. before an impartial tribunal
5. in an atmosphere of fairness.

Most of the guarantees in the Bill of Rights that are applicable to the criminal process also relate to procedural due process. For example, the prohibition against double jeopardy, the privilege against self-incrimination, the right to a speedy trial, and the right to counsel have been held by the Supreme Court to involve procedural due process guarantees.

In his two articles in Chapter One, Professor Robert Cord indicated that the relationship between the Fourteenth Amendment (due process) and those guarantees found in the Bill of Rights presented the justices of the Supreme Court with some of their more vexing problems and that out of this troublesome area have evolved five different approaches to the nationalization of

---

TABLE 3.1   Individual Justices' Views on the Nationalization of the Bill of Rights

Ordered Liberty (Fundamental Fairness)	Total Incorporation	Total Incorporation Plus (Ultra-Incorporation)	Selective Incorporation	Neo-Incorporation
Cardozo, J.[1]	Black, J.[5]	Murphy, J.[7]	Brennan, J.[10]	Fortas, J.[14]
Frankfurter, J.[2]	Douglas, J. (initially)[6]	Rutledge, J.[8]	Marshall, J.[11]	Stewart, J.[15]
Harlan, J.[3]		Douglas. J.[9]	Goldberg, J.[12]	White, J.[16]
Stewart, J. (initially)[4]			Warren, C.J.[13]	Burger, C.J. ⎫ [17]
				Powell, J. ⎪
				Blackmun, J. ⎬
				Rehnquist, J. ⎭

[1]E.g., *Palko* v. *Connecticut,* 302 U.S. 319 (1937).
[2]E.g., *Adamson* v. *California,* 332 U.S. 46, 67 (1947) (concurring).
[3]E.g., *Duncan* v. *Louisiana,* 391 U.S. 145 (1968) (dissenting).
[4]E.g., *Stoner* v. *California,* 376 U.S. 483 (1964).
[5]E.g., *Adamson* v. *California,* 332 U.S. 46, 71–72 (1947) (dissenting).
[6]Id. (joined in dissenting opinion of Black, J.).
[7]Id. (concurring).
[8]Id. (joined in concurring opinion of Murphy, J.).
[9]E.g., *Griswold* v. *Connecticut,* 381 U.S. 479 (1965).
[10]E.g., *Cohen* v. *Hurley,* 366 U.S. 117, 154 (1961) (dissenting).
[11]E.g., *Duncan* v. *Louisiana,* 391 U.S. 145 (1968).
[12]E.g., *Griswold* v. *Connecticut,* 381 U.S. 479, 492 (1965) (concurring).
[13]Id. (joined in concurring opinion of Goldberg, J.).
[14]E.g., *Duncan* v. *Louisiana,* 391 U.S. 145, 211 (1968) (concurring).
[15]E.g., *Griffin* v. *California,* 380 U.S. 609, 623 (1965) (dissenting).
[16]E.g., *Williams* v. *Florida,* 399 U.S. 78 (1970).
[17]By implication. See, e.g., *Johnson* v. *Louisiana,* 406 U.S. 356 (1972); *Apodaca* v. *Oregon,* 406 U.S. 404 (1972); *Cupp* v. *Naughten,* 414 U.S. 141 (1973).

TABLE 3.2 Summary of Basic Interpretations of the Due Process Clause of the Fourteenth Amendment

Ordered Liberty (Fundamental Fairness)	Total Incorporation	Total Incorporation Plus (Ultra-Incorporation)	Selective Incorporation	Neo-Incorporation
The Due Process Clause applies only those "traditional notions" of due process, such as freedom of religion, speech, and press and procedural rights, that are "implicit in the concept of ordered liberty." The Fourteenth Amendment incorporates none of the guarantees of the Bill of Rights as such.	The Due Process Clause includes *all* rights found in the Bill of Rights, but limits the inclusion to *only* those rights enumerated therein. No unenumerated rights are recognized.	The Due Process Clause encompasses *all* of the specific guarantees of the Bill of Rights *plus* any additional fundamental unenumerated rights that are properly classified as essential to "fairness and individual liberty"; e.g., the right of privacy	Combines aspects of both "ordered liberty" and "total incorporation" interpretations of the Fourteenth Amendment. Accepts the basic premise that the Due Process Clause encompasses *all* rights that are "fundamental to the American system of justice." Recognizes that *not all* rights enumerated in the Bill of Rights are necessarily fundamental, e.g., grand jury indictments. However, this view also recognizes that other rights may be fundamental even though not specifically enumerated in the Bill of Rights; e.g., the right to terminate a pregnancy.	A "half-way house" between the ordered liberty and traditional incorporation approaches. According to this view, the fact that a procedural right is incorporated into the Bill of Rights does *not* make federal procedures binding on state criminal trials; e.g., unanimous jury verdicts required in federal criminal trials, but not in state criminal trials.

Implicit in these traditional incorporation views is the notion that once any Bill of Rights' guarantee is "incorporated," it limits state authority in precisely the same way that the Bill of Rights directly limits federal authority. This is not true for neo-incorporation.

the Bill of Rights: (1) the ordered liberty concept (fundamental fairness), (2) total incorporation, (3) total incorporation plus (ultra-incorporation), (4) selective incorporation, and (5) neo-incorporation (Tables 3.1 and 3.2).

In the next section, selections from four Supreme Court decisions amply demonstrate the differing views espoused by the justices on the relationship between the Fourteenth Amendment Due Process Clause and the Bill of Rights. The concurring opinion of Justice Fortas in *Duncan* v. *Louisiana* exemplifies the neo-incorporation view. *Drope* v. *Missouri* is included as a more recent criminal case decided by the Supreme Court on Fourteenth Amendment due process grounds.

3.04 DUE PROCESS AND THE CRIMINAL PROCESS

Fundamental Fairness and the Prosecutor's Comment on Defendant's Failure To Testify

ADAMSON v. CALIFORNIA
Supreme Court of the United States, 1947
332 U.S. 46, 67 S. Ct. 1672, 91 L. Ed. 1903

The California constitution and criminal code permitted the trial judge and prosecutors to comment on the failure of a defendant to testify on his own behalf. Juries were allowed to infer guilt from such a failure to testify. Adamson was tried and convicted of first degree murder and sentenced to death. He did not testify at trial. During the trial, the prosecutor suggested to the jury that the defendant's failure to testify was a strong indication of his guilt. The California Supreme Court affirmed Adamson's conviction. On appeal to the United States Supreme Court, Adamson challenged the constitutionality of the California provision allowing comment on a defendant's failure to testify. He claimed, inter alia, that such a procedure violated his due process rights under the Fourteenth Amendment.

Mr. Justice REED delivered the opinion of the Court.

* * *

[A]ppellant relies upon the due process of law clause of the Fourteenth Amendment to invalidate provisions of the California law ... and as applied (a) because comment on failure to testify is permitted, (b) because appellant was forced to forego testimony in person because of danger of disclosure of his past convictions through cross-examination, and (c) because the presumption of innocence was infringed by the shifting of the burden of proof to appellant in permitting comment on his failure to testify.

* * *

Appellant ... contends that if the privilege against self-incrimination is not a right protected by the privileges and immunities clause of the Fourteenth Amendment against state action, this privilege, to its full scope under the Fifth Amendment, inheres in the right to a fair trial. A right to a fair trial is a right admittedly protected by the due process clause of the Fourteenth Amendment. Therefore, appellant argues, the due process clause of the Fourteenth Amendment protects his privilege against self-incrimination. The due process clause of the Fourteenth Amendment, however, does not draw all the rights of the federal Bill of Rights under its protection. That contention was made and rejected in Palko v. Connecticut, 302 U.S. 319, 323 (1937). It was rejected with citation of the cases excluding several of the rights, protected by the Bill of Rights, against infringement by the National Government. Nothing has been called to our attention that either the framers of the Fourteenth Amendment or the states that adopted intended its due process clause to draw within its scope the earlier amendments to the Constitution. Palko held that such provisions of the Bill of Rights as were "implicit in the concept of ordered liberty" ... became secure from state interference by the clause. But it held nothing more.

... For a state to require testimony from an accused is not necessarily a breach of a state's obligation to give a fair trial. Therefore, we must examine the effect of the California law applied in this trial to see whether the comment on failure to testify violated the protection against state action that the due process clause does grant to an accused. The due process clause forbids compulsion to testify by fear of hurt, torture or exhaustion. It forbids any other type of coercion that falls within the scope of due process.... So our inquiry is directed, not at the broad question of the constitutionality of compulsory testimony from the accused under the due process clause, but to the constitutionality of the provision of the California law that permits comment upon his failure to testify.

... California ... is one of a few states that permit limited comment upon a defendant's failure to testify. That permission is narrow. The California law ... authorizes comment by the court and counsel upon the "failure of the defendant to explain or deny by his testimony any evidence or facts in the case against him." This does not involve any presumption, rebuttable or irrebuttable, either of guilt or of the truth of any fact, that is offered in evidence.... It allows inferences to be drawn from proven facts. Because of this clause, the court can direct the jury's attention to whatever evidence there may be that a defendant could deny and the prosecution can argue as to inferences that may be drawn from the accused's failure to testify.

... California has prescribed a method for advising the jury in the search for truth. However sound may be the legislative conclusion that an accused should not be compelled in any criminal case to be a witness against himself, we see no reason why comment should not be made upon his silence. It seems quite natural that when a defendant has opportunity to deny or explain facts and

determines not to do so, the prosecution should bring out the strength of the evidence by commenting upon defendant's failure to explain or deny it. The prosecution evidence may be of facts that may be beyond the knowledge of the accused. If so, his failure to testify would have little if any weight. But the facts may be such as are necessarily in the knowledge of the accused. In that case a failure to explain would point to an inability to explain.

* * *

It is true that if comment were forbidden, an accused in this situation could remain silent and avoid evidence of former crimes and comment upon his failure to testify. We are of the view, however, that a state may control such a situation in accordance with its own ideas of the most efficient administration of criminal justice. The purpose of due process is not to protect an accused against a proper conviction but against an unfair conviction. When evidence is before a jury that threatens conviction, it does not seem unfair to require him to choose between leaving the adverse evidence unexplained and subjecting himself to impeachment through disclosure of former crimes. Indeed, this is a dilemma with which any defendant may be faced. If facts, adverse to the defendant, are proven by the prosecution, there may be no way to explain them favorably to the accused except by a witness who may be vulnerable to impeachment on cross-examination. The defendant must then decide whether or not to use such a witness. The fact that the witness may also be the defendant makes the choice more difficult but a denial of due process does not emerge from the circumstances.

* * *

Affirmed.

Mr. Justice FRANKFURTER (concurring).

* * *

For historical reasons a limited immunity from the common duty to testify was written into the Federal Bill of Rights, and I am prepared to agree that, as part of that immunity, comment on the failure of an accused to take the witness stand is forbidden in federal prosecutions.... But to suggest that such a limitation can be drawn out of "due process" in its protection of ultimate decency in a civilized society is to suggest that the Due Process Clause fastened fetters of unreason upon the States....

Between the incorporation of the Fourteenth Amendment into the Constitution and the beginning of the present membership of the Court—a period of seventy years—the scope of that Amendment was passed upon by forty-three judges. Of all these judges, only one, who may respectfully be called an eccentric exception, ever indicated the belief that the Fourteenth Amendment was a shorthand summary of the first eight Amendments theretofore limiting only the Federal Government, and that due process incorporated those eight Amendments as restrictions upon the powers of the States....

...The notion that the Fourteenth Amendment was a covert way of imposing upon the States all the rules which it seemed important to Eighteenth Century statesmen to write into the Federal Amendments, was rejected by judges who were themselves witnesses of the process by which the Fourteenth Amendment became part of the Constitution. Arguments that may now be adduced to prove that the first eight Amendments were concealed within the historic phrasing of the Fourteenth Amendment were not unknown at the time of its adoption. A surer estimate of their bearing was possible for judges at the time than distorting distance is likely to vouchsafe. Any evidence of design or purpose not contemporaneously known could hardly have influenced those who ratified the Amendment. Remarks of a particular proponent of the Amendment, no matter how influential, are not to be deemed part of the Amendment. What was submitted for ratification was his proposal, not his speech. Thus, at the time of the ratification of the Fourteenth Amendment the constitutions of nearly half of the ratifying States did not have the rigorous requirements of the Fifth Amendment for instituting criminal proceedings through a grand jury. It could hardly have occurred to these States that by ratifying the Amendment they uprooted their established methods for prosecuting crime and fastened upon themselves a new prosecutorial system.

Indeed, the suggestion that the Fourteenth Amendment incorporates the first eight Amendments as such is not unambiguously urged. Even the boldest innovator would shrink from suggesting to more than half the States that they may no longer initiate prosecutions without indictment by grand jury, or that thereafter all the States of the Union must furnish a jury of twelve for every case involving a claim above twenty dollars. There is suggested merely a selective incorporation of the first eight Amendments into the Fourteenth Amendment. Some are in and some are out, but we are left in the dark as to which are in and which are out. Nor are we given the calculus for determining which go in and which stay out. If the basis of selection is merely that those provisions of the first eight Amendments are incorporated which commend themselves to individual justices as indispensable to the dignity and happiness of a free man, we are thrown back to a merely subjective test.... If all that is meant is that due process contains within itself certain minimal standards which are "of the very essence of a scheme of ordered liberty" ... putting upon this Court the duty of applying these standards from time to time, then we have merely arrived at the insight which our predecessors long ago expressed.... The Due Process Clause of the Fourteenth Amendment has an independent potency, precisely as does the Due Process Clause of the Fifth Amendment in relation to the Federal Government. It ought not to require argument to reject the notion that due process of law meant one thing in the Fifth Amendment and another in the Fourteenth. ... Are Madison and his contemporaries in the framing of the Bill of Rights to be charged with writing into it a meaningless clause? To consider "due process of law" as merely a shorthand statement of other specific clauses in the same amendment is to attribute to the authors and proponents of this Amendment ignorance of, or indifference to, a historic conception which was one of the great instruments in the arsenal of constitutional freedom which the Bill of Rights was to protect and strengthen.

* * *

Mr. Justice BLACK, with whom Mr. Justice DOUGLAS concurs (dissenting).

* * *

This decision reasserts a constitutional theory spelled out in Twining v. New Jersey, 211 U.S. 78 (1908), that this Court is endowed by the Constitution with boundless power under "natural law" periodically to expand and contract constitutional standards to conform to the Court's conception of what at a particular time constitutes "civilized decency" and "fundamental liberty and justice." Invoking this Twining rule, the Court concluded that although comment upon testimony in a federal court would violate the Fifth Amendment, identical comment in a state court does not violate today's fashion in civilized decency and fundamentals and is therefore not prohibited by the Federal Constitution as amended.

... I would not reaffirm the Twining decision. I think that decision and the "natural law" theory of the Constitution upon which it relies degrade the constitutional safeguards of the Bill of Rights and simultaneously appropriate for this Court a broad power which we are not authorized by the Constitution to exercise....

* * *

My study of the historical events that culminated in the Fourteenth Amendment, and the expressions of those who sponsored and favored, as well as those who opposed its submission and passage, persuades me that one of the chief objects that the provisions of the Amendment's first section, separately and as a whole, were intended to accomplish was to make the Bill of Rights applicable to the states. With full knowledge of the import of the Barron decision, the framers and backers of the Fourteenth Amendment proclaimed its purpose to be to overturn the constitutional rule that case had announced. This historical purpose has never received full consideration or exposition in any opinion of this Court interpreting the Amendment....

I cannot consider the Bill of Rights to be an outworn 18th Century "strait jacket" as the Twining opinion did. Its provisions may be thought outdated abstractions by some. And it is true that they were designed to meet ancient evils. But they are the same kind of human evils that have emerged from century to century wherever excessive power is sought by the few at the expense of the many. In my judgement the people of no nation can lose their liberty so long as a Bill of Rights like ours survives and its basic purposes are conscientiously interpreted, enforced and respected so as to afford continuous protection against old, as well as new, devices and practices which might thwart those purposes. I fear to see the consequences of the Court's practice of substituting its own concepts of decency and fundamental justice for the language of the Bill of Rights as its point of departure in interpreting and enforcing that Bill of Rights. If the choice must be between the selective process of the Palko decision applying some of the Bill of Rights to the States, or the Twining rule applying none of them, I would choose the Palko selective process. But rather than accept either of these choices, I would follow what I believe was the original purpose of the Fourteenth Amendment—to extend to all the people of the nation the complete protection of the Bill of Rights. To hold that this Court can determine what, if any, provisions of the Bill of Rights will be enforced, and if so to what degree, is to frustrate the great design of a written Constitution.

Conceding the possibility that this Court is now wise enough to improve on the Bill of Rights by substituting natural law concepts for the Bill of Rights, I think the possibility is entirely too speculative to agree to take that course. I would therefore hold in this case that the full protection of the Fifth Amendment's proscription against compelled testimony must be afforded by California. This I would do because of reliance upon the original purpose of the Fourteenth Amendment....

Mr. Justice MURPHY, with whom Mr. Justice RUTLEDGE concurs (dissenting).

While in substantial agreement with the views of Mr. Justice BLACK, I have one reservation and one addition to make.

I agree that the specific guarantees of the Bill of Rights should be carried over intact into the first section of the Fourteenth Amendment. But I am not prepared to say that the latter is entirely and necessarily limited by the Bill of Rights. Occasions may arise where a proceeding falls so far short of conforming to fundamental standards of procedure as to warrant constitutional condemnation in terms of a lack of due process despite the absence of a specific provision in the Bill of Rights.

* * *

Comments

1. *Adamson* exemplifies the *fundamental fairness (ordered liberty)* view of the nationalization of the Bill of Rights. This view commanded a majority of the Court for many years. Why was it fundamentally fair to allow a state prosecutor to adversely comment on a defendant's silence while a federal prosecutor could not?

2. The now classic dissenting opinion of Justice Black in *Adamson* represents the first modern-day pronouncement by a justice of the Supreme Court suggesting that all of the Bill of Rights should be applicable to the states—the *total incorporation view*. In a 1968 television interview, Justice Black stated that his dissent in *Adamson* represented his most important opinion. The approach taken by Justices Murphy and Rutledge (dissenting) in *Adamson* represents the so-called *total incorporation plus (ultra-incorporation)* view. *Adamson* was subsequently overruled by *Malloy* v. *Hogan*, 378 U.S. 1 (1964), and specifically in *Griffin* v. *California*, 380 U.S. 609 (1965), as violative of the Fifth Amendment privilege against self-incrimination.

3. Many, if not most, criminal defendants who do not testify at trial do so to avoid having the prosecutor reveal any of their prior convictions on cross-examination—especially in jury trials. Perhaps it is more prudent, in some cases, to allow the jury to imagine what one's past is rather than to testify and leave no doubt. For the criminal defendant with a prior record, the decision whether to testify may be crucial. If he fails to testify, the jury may infer that he has "something to hide"—even though today the prosecutor cannot comment on an accused's silence. If he does testify and the jury learns of his prior convictions, the jury may use that evidence to convict him of the present charge—even though the jury will be instructed (if requested) that evidence of an accused's prior conviction introduced on cross-examination is offered solely to impeach (discredit) the testimony of the witness, and cannot be used as substantive proof of his guilt or innocence. The jury may feel that "if he did it once, he probably would do it again." Because the credibility of *any* witness is always material, evidence of prior convictions on cross-examination is usually relevant. What other factors should the defense attorney consider before he advises his client whether to testify or not? May a prosecutor on closing argument state to the jury, "The state produced overwhelming evidence of the defendant's guilt—and this evidence went unrefuted by the defense"? Would that be an impermissible "comment" on the defendant's silence?

Selective Incorporation and the Right to a Jury Trial

DUNCAN v. LOUISIANA

Supreme Court of the United States, 1968
391 U.S. 145, 88 S. Ct. 1444, 20 L. Ed. 2d 491

The defendant, Gary Duncan, was convicted by a Louisiana court of simple battery (a misdemeanor punishable by a maximum sentence of two years' imprisonment and a $300 fine). Duncan's request for a jury trial was denied because under

the then Louisiana law jury trials were permitted only when hard labor or capital punishment might be imposed. Duncan was convicted and sentenced to 60 days in jail and fined $150. His petition for relief was denied by the Louisiana Supreme Court, whereupon Duncan appealed to the United States Supreme Court contending that the Sixth and Fourteenth Amendments granted an accused the right to a trial by jury in state criminal proceedings for crimes punishable by two years' imprisonment or more.

Mr. Justice WHITE delivered the opinion of the Court.

* * *

The Fourteenth Amendment denies the States the power to "deprive any person of life, liberty, or property, without due process of law." In resolving conflicting claims concerning the meaning of this spacious language, the Court has looked increasingly to the Bill of Rights for guidance; many of the rights guaranteed by the first eight Amendments to the Constitution have been held to be protected against state action by the Due Process Clause of the Fourteenth Amendment. That clause now protects the right to compensation for property taken by the State; the rights of speech, press, and religion covered by the First Amendment; the Fourth Amendment rights to be free from unreasonable searches and seizures and to have excluded from criminal trials any evidence illegally seized; the right guaranteed by the Fifth Amendment to be free of compelled self-incrimination; and the Sixth Amendment rights to counsel, to a speedy and public trial, to confrontation of opposing witnesses, and to compulsory process for obtaining witnesses.

The test for determining whether a right extended by the Fifth and Sixth Amendments with respect to federal criminal proceedings is also protected against state action by the Fourteenth Amendment has been phrased in a variety of ways in the opinions of this Court. The question has been asked whether a right is among those " 'fundamental principles of liberty and justice which lie at the base of all our civil and political institutions,' " . . . whether it is "basic in our system of jurisprudence" . . . and whether it is "a fundamental right, essential to a fair trial." . . . The claim before us is that the right to trial by jury guaranteed by the Sixth Amendment meets these tests. The position of Louisiana, on the other hand, is that the Constitution imposes upon the States no duty to give a jury trial in any criminal case, regardless of the seriousness of the crime or the size of the punishment which may be imposed. Because we believe that trial by jury in criminal cases is *fundamental to the American scheme of justice* [emphasis added], we hold that the Fourteenth Amendment guarantees a right of jury trial in all criminal cases which — were they to be tried in a federal court — would come within the Sixth Amendment's guarantee. Since we consider the appeal before us to be such a case, we hold that the Constitution was violated when appellant's demand for jury trial was refused.

The history of trial by jury in criminal cases has been frequently told. It is sufficient for present purposes to say that by the time our Constitution was written, jury trial in criminal cases had been in existence in England for several centuries and carried impressive credentials traced by many to Magna Carta. . . .

Jury trial continues to receive strong support. The laws of every State guarantee a right to jury trial in serious criminal cases; no State has dispensed with it; nor are there significant movements underway to do so. . . .

* * *

The guarantees of jury trial in the Federal and State Constitutions reflect a profound judgment about the way in which law should be enforced and justice administered. A right to jury trial is granted to criminal defendants in order to prevent oppression by the Government. . . .

* * *

The State of Louisiana urges that holding that the Fourteenth Amendment assures a right to jury trial will cast doubt on the integrity of every trial conducted without a jury. Plainly, this is not the import of our holding. Our conclusion is that in the American States, as in the federal judicial system, a general grant of jury trial for serious offenses is a fundamental right, essential for preventing miscarriages of justice and for assuring that fair trials are provided for all defendants. We would not assert, however, that every criminal trial or any particular trial held before a judge alone is unfair or that a defendant may never be as fairly treated by a judge as he would be by a jury. Thus we hold no constitutional doubts about the practices, common in both federal and state courts, of accepting waivers of jury trial and prosecuting petty crimes without extending a right to jury trial. However, the fact is that in most places more trials for serious crimes are to juries than to a court alone; a great many defendants prefer the judgment of a jury to that of a court. Even where defendants are satisfied with bench trials, the right to a jury trial very likely serves its intended purpose of making judicial or prosecutorial unfairness less likely.

Louisiana's final contention is that even if it must grant jury trials in serious criminal cases, the conviction before us is valid and constitutional because here the petitioner was tried for simple battery and was sentenced to only 60 days in the parish prison. We are not persuaded. It is doubtless true that there is a category of petty crimes or offenses which is not subject to the Sixth Amendment jury trial provision and should not be subject to the Fourteenth Amendment jury trial requirement here applied to the States. Crimes carrying possible penalties up to six months do not require a jury trial if they otherwise qualify as petty offenses....

* * *

...We need not, however, settle in this case the exact location of the line between petty offenses and serious crimes. It is sufficient for our purposes to hold that a crime punishable by two years in prison is, based on past and contemporary standards in this country, a serious crime and not a petty offense. Consequently, appellant was entitled to a jury trial and it was error to deny it.

* * *

Reversed and remanded.

Mr. Justice BLACK, with whom Mr. Justice DOUGLAS joins (concurring).

The Court today holds that the right to trial by jury guaranteed defendants in criminal cases in federal courts by Art. III of the United States Constitution and by the Sixth Amendment is also guaranteed by the Fourteenth Amendment to defendants tried in state courts. With this holding I agree for reasons given by the Court. I also agree because of reasons given in my dissent in Adamson v. California, 332 U.S. 46, 68 (1947)....

* * *

It seems to me totally inconsistent to advocate on the one hand the power of this Court to strike down any state law or practice which it finds "unreasonable" or "unfair" and, on the other hand, urge that the States be given maximum power to develop their own laws and procedures. Yet the due process approach of my Brothers HARLAN and FORTAS [see subsequent concurring and dissenting opinions] does just that since in effect it restricts the States to practices which a majority of this Court is willing to approve on a case-by-case basis. No one is more concerned than I that the States be allowed to use the full scope of their powers as their citizens see fit. And that is why I have continually fought against the expansion of this Court's authority over the States through the use of a broad, general interpretation of due process that permits judges to strike down state laws they do not like.

In closing I want to emphasize that I believe as strongly as ever that the Fourteenth Amendment was intended to make the Bill of Rights applicable to the States. I have been willing to support the selective incorporation doctrine, however, as an alternative, although perhaps less historically supportable than complete incorporation. The selective incorporation process, if used properly, does limit the Supreme Court in the Fourteenth Amendment field to specific Bill of Rights' protections only and keeps judges from roaming at will in their own notions of what policies outside the Bill of Rights are desirable and what are not. And, most importantly for me, the selective incorporation process has the virtue of having already worked to make most of the Bill of Rights' protections applicable to the States.

Mr. Justice FORTAS, concurring.

* * *

[A]lthough I agree with the decision of the Court, I cannot agree with the implication . . . when we hold, influenced by the Sixth Amendment, that "due process" requires that the States accord the right of jury trial for all but petty offenses, we automatically import all of the ancillary rules which have been or may hereafter be developed incidental to the right to jury trial in the federal courts. I see no reason whatever, for example, to assume that our decision today should require us to impose federal requirements such as unanimous verdicts or a jury of 12 upon the States. We may well conclude that these and other features of federal jury practice are by no means fundamental — that they are not essential to due process of law — and that they are not obligatory on the States.

I would make these points clear today. Neither logic nor history nor the intent of the draftsmen of the Fourteenth Amendment can possibly be said to require that the Sixth Amendment or its jury trial provision be applied to the States together with the total gloss that this Court's decisions have supplied. The draftsmen of the Fourteenth Amendment intended what they said, not more or less: that no State shall deprive any person of life, liberty, or property without due process of law. It is ultimately the duty of this Court to interpret, to ascribe specific meaning to this phrase. There is no reason whatever for us to conclude that, in so doing, we are bound slavishly to follow not only the Sixth Amendment but all of its bag and baggage, however securely or insecurely affixed they may be by law and precedent to federal proceedings. To take this course, in my judgment, would be not only unnecessary but mischievous because it would inflict a serious blow upon the principle of federalism. The Due Process Clause commands us to apply its great standard to state court proceedings to assure basic fairness. It does not command us rigidly and arbitrarily to impose the exact pattern of federal proceedings upon the 50 States. . . . [T]he Constitution's command, in my view, is that in our insistence upon state observance of due process, we should, so far as possible, allow the greatest latitude for state differences. It requires, within the limits of the lofty basic standards that it prescribes for the States as well as the Federal Government, maximum opportunity for diversity and minimal imposition of uniformity of method and detail upon the States. Our Constitution sets up a federal union, not a monolith.

* * *

Mr. Justice HARLAN, with whom Mr. Justice STEWART joins (dissenting).

* * *

The Court's approach to this case is an uneasy and illogical compromise among the views of various Justices on how the Due Process Clause should be interpreted. The Court does not say that those who framed the Fourteenth Amendment intended to make the Sixth Amendment applicable to the States. And the Court concedes that it finds nothing unfair about the procedure by which the present appellant was tried. Nevertheless, the Court reverses his conviction: it holds, for some reason not apparent to me, that the Due Process Clause incorporates the particular clause of the Sixth Amendment that requires trial by jury in federal criminal cases — including, as I read its opinion, the sometimes trivial accompanying baggage of judicial interpretation in federal contexts. I have raised my voice many times before against the Court's continuing undiscriminating insistence upon fastening on the States federal notions of criminal justice, and I must do so again in this instance. With all respect, the Court's approach and its reading of history are altogether topsy-turvy.

I believe I am correct in saying that every member of the Court for at least the last 135 years has agreed that our Founders did not consider the requirements of the Bill of Rights so fundamental that they should operate directly against the States. They were wont to believe rather that the security of liberty in America rested primarily upon the dispersion of governmental power across a federal system. The Bill of Rights was considered unnecessary by some but insisted upon by others to curb the possibility of abuse of power by the strong central government they were creating.

* * *

A few members of the Court have taken the position that the intention of those who drafted the first section of the Fourteenth Amendment was simply, and exclusively, to make the provisions of the first eight Amendments applicable to state action. This view has never been accepted by this Court. In my view, often expressed elsewhere, the first section of the Fourteenth Amendment was meant neither to incorporate, nor to be limited to, the specific guarantees of the first eight Amendments. The overwhelming historical evidence ... demonstrates, to me conclusively, that the Congressmen and state legislators who wrote, debated, and ratified the Fourteenth Amendment did not think they were "incorporating" the Bill of Rights, and the very breadth and generality of the Amendment's provisions suggest that its authors did not suppose that the Nation would always be limited to mid-19th century conceptions of "liberty" and "due process of law" but that the increasing experience and evolving conscience of the American people would add new "intermediate premises." In short, neither history, nor sense, supports using the Fourteenth Amendment to put the States in a constitutional strait jacket with respect to their own development in the administration of criminal or civil law.

* * *

Today's Court still remains unwilling to accept the total incorporationists' view of the history of the Fourteenth Amendment. This, if accepted, would afford a cogent reason for applying the Sixth Amendment to the States. The Court is also, apparently, unwilling to face the task of determining whether denial of trial by jury in the situation before us, or in other situations, is fundamentally unfair. Consequently, the Court has compromised on the ease of the incorporationist position, without its internal logic. It has simply assumed that the question before us is whether the Jury Trial Clause of the Sixth Amendment should be incorporated into the Fourteenth, jot-for-jot, and case-for-case, or ignored. Then the Court merely declares that the clause in question is "in" rather than "out."

The Court has justified neither its starting place nor its conclusion. If the problem is to discover and articulate the rules of fundamental fairness in criminal proceedings, there is no reason to assume that the whole body of rules developed in this Court constituting Sixth Amendment jury trial must be regarded as a unit. . . .

The argument that jury trial is not a requisite of due process is quite simple. The central proposition of Palko, supra, a proposition to which I would adhere, is that "due process of law" requires only that criminal trials be fundamentally fair. [A]part from the theory that it was historically intended as a mere shorthand for the Bill of Rights, I do not see what else "due process of law" can intelligibly be thought to mean. If due process of law requires only fundamental fairness, then the inquiry in each case must be whether a state trial process was a fair one. The Court has held, properly I think, that in an adversary process it is a requisite of fairness, for which there is no adequate substitute, that a criminal defendant be afforded a right to counsel and to cross-examine opposing witnesses. But it simply has not been demonstrated, nor, I think, can it be demonstrated, that trial by jury is the only fair means of resolving issues of fact.

* * *

That trial by jury is not the only fair way of adjudicating criminal guilt is well attested by the fact that it is not the prevailing way, either in England or in this country. . . .

. . . I . . . see no reason why this Court should reverse the conviction of appellant, absent any suggestion that his particular trial was in fact unfair, or compel the State of Louisiana to afford jury trial in an as yet unbounded category of cases that can, without unfairness, be tried to a court.

* * *

In sum, there is a wide range of views on the desirability of trial by jury, and on the ways to make it most effective when it is used; there is also considerable variation from State to State in local conditions such as the size of the criminal caseload, the ease or difficulty of summoning jurors, and other trial conditions bearing on fairness. We have before us, therefore, an almost perfect example of a situation in which the celebrated dictum of Mr. Justice Brandeis should be invoked. It is, he said, "one of the happy incidents of the federal system that a single courageous State may, if its citizens choose, serve as a laboratory. . ." New State Ice Company v. Liebman, 285 U.S. 262, 280 (1932) (dissenting opinion). This Court, other courts, and the political process are available to correct any experiments in criminal procedure that prove fundamentally unfair to defendants. That is not what is being done today: instead, and quite without reason, the Court has chosen to impose upon every State one means of trying crimi-nal cases; it is a good means, but it is not the only fair means, and it is not demonstrably better than the alternatives States might devise.

I would affirm the judgment of the Supreme Court of Louisiana.

Comments

1. *Duncan* represents the so-called *selective incorporation* view of the nationalization of the Bill of Rights — a compromise position between the ordered liberty and total incorporation views. Selective incorporation represents the current approach by the Court to the nationalization of the Bill of Rights.

2. *Duncan* made the Sixth Amendment right to a jury trial applicable to the states through the Due Process Clause of the Fourteenth Amendment for "serious crimes." The Court in *Duncan* did not define "serious crime." Two years later, in *Baldwin* v. *New York,* 399 U.S. 66 (1970), the Court held that "no offense can be deemed 'petty' for purposes of the right to a trial by jury where imprisonment for more than six months is authorized," at 69. Thus an accused has no Sixth Amendment right to a jury trial if the maximum sentence cannot exceed six months' imprisonment.

3. Suppose a criminal statute authorizes as punishment a heavy fine (e.g., $10,000) but not imprisonment. Is the crime a "serious offense" for purposes of the *Duncan–Baldwin* decisions? See *Muniz* v. *Hoffman,* 422 U.S. 454 (1975) (labor union had no right to a jury trial in criminal contempt proceedings that resulted in a $10,000 fine). Suppose an accused is charged with two or more petty offenses that could result in a combined penalty in excess of six months' imprisonment. See *Codispoti* v. *Pennsylvania,* 418 U.S. 506 (1974) (right to jury trial in contempt proceedings if the sentences imposed aggregate more than six months, even though no single sentence imposed is for more than six months).

4. The American Bar Association considers the use of juries to be advantageous for the following reasons: "(1) a group judgment is better than that of a single person; (2) there is value in citizen participation in the administration of justice; (3) juries, in contrast to at least some trial judges, have the confidence of the community; (4) juries perform an important mitigating function; and (5) juries can best apply imprecise legal standards, such as the 'reasonable man' test." A.B.A. Standards, *Trial by Jury,* 40. See also Kalven and Zeisel, *The American Jury* (1966).

What factors should defense counsel consider in deciding whether to waive a jury trial? Does a defendant have a constitutional right to demand a trial before a judge sitting alone? See *Patton* v. *United States,* 281 U.S. 276 (1930) (no absolute federal right to a bench trial). See also *Singer* v. *United States,* 380 U.S. 24 (1965) (upholding Fed. R. Crim. P. 23(a) requiring trials by jury unless the defendant waives a jury trial in writing with the approval of the court and the consent of the government). Forty-four states

TABLE 3.3 Jury Waiver for Major Crimes in Selected States*

State	Per Cent Jury Waiver (Bench Trials) of All Trials
Wisconsin	79
Connecticut	74
California	64
New Hampshire	58
New Jersey	57
Kansas	56
Ohio	50
North Dakota	50
Wyoming	45
Iowa	36
Pennsylvania	34
Massachusetts	33
South Dakota	24
Texas	18
Colorado	17
Oregon	15
New Mexico	13
Idaho	12
Washington	7
Minnesota	5
Utah	5
District of Columbia	3
Montana	0
Average all states	40%

*See Kalven and Zeisel, *The American Jury,* Little, Brown and Co. (Inc.); Boston, 1966, p. 25. Data from U.S. Bureau of the Census, Judicial Criminal Statistics (1945).

permit a defendant to waive a jury trial (Table 3.3). Of these, 27 states require the approval of either the court or the prosecutor or both, and 17 require no approval. Note, 51 Cornell L. Rev. 339, 342–343 (1966). What federally protected interests of a defendant are infringed upon by "forcing" a jury trial on him?

Selective Incorporation and Double Jeopardy

BENTON v. MARYLAND

Supreme Court of the United States, 1969
395 U.S. 784, 89 S. Ct. 2056, 23 L. Ed. 2d 707

John Benton was tried in a Maryland state court for burglary and larceny. He was found not guilty of larceny but was convicted of burglary and sentenced to 10 years' imprisonment. Because of a subsequent change in Maryland law, the defendant was given the option of being retried or leaving his conviction for burglary intact. He chose to be retried. At his second trial, he was again tried for both larceny and burglary. Over the defendant's objections that a retrial on the

larceny charge violated the constitutional prohibition against double jeopardy, he was convicted of both offenses. He was denied relief by the Maryland courts and the United States Supreme Court granted certiorari.

Mr. Justice MARSHALL delivered the opinion of the Court.

* * *

"(1) Is the double jeopardy clause of the Fifth Amendment applicable to the States through the Fourteenth Amendment?"

"(2) If so, was the petitioner 'twice put in jeopardy' in this case?"

After consideration of all the questions before us ... we hold that the Double Jeopardy Clause of the Fifth Amendment is applicable to the States through the Fourteenth Amendment, and we reverse petitioner's conviction for larceny.

* * *

In 1937, this Court decided the landmark case of Palko v. Connecticut, 302 U.S. 319. Palko, although indicted for first-degree murder, had been convicted of murder in the second degree after a jury trial in a Connecticut state court. The State appealed and won a new trial. Palko argued that the Fourteenth Amendment incorporated, as against the States, the Fifth Amendment requirement that no person "be subject for the same offense to be twice put in jeopardy of life or limb." The Court disagreed. Federal double jeopardy standards were not applicable against the States. Only when a kind of jeopardy subjected a defendant to "a hardship so acute and shocking that our policy will not endure it" ... did the Fourteenth Amendment apply. The order for a new trial was affirmed. In subsequent appeals from state courts, the Court continued to apply this lesser Palko standard....

Recently, however, this Court has "increasingly looked to the specific guarantees of the [Bill of Rights] to determine whether a state criminal trial was conducted with due process of law." ... In an increasing number of cases, the Court "has rejected the notion that the Fourteenth Amendment applies to the States only a 'watered-down, subjective version' of the individual guarantees of the Bill of Rights. ..." ... Only last Term we found that the right to trial by jury in criminal cases was "fundamental to the American scheme of justice" ... and held that the Sixth Amendment right to a jury trial was applicable to the States through the Fourteenth Amendment. For the same reasons, we today find that the double jeopardy prohibition of the Fifth Amendment represents a fundamental idea in our constitutional heritage, and that it should apply to the States through the Fourteenth Amendment. Insofar as it is inconsistent with this holding, Palko v. Connecticut is overruled.

Palko represented an approach to basic constitutional rights which this Court's recent decisions have rejected. It was cut of the same cloth as Betts v. Brady, 316 U.S. 455 (1942), the case which held that a criminal defendant's right to counsel was to be determined by deciding in each case whether the denial of that right was "shocking to the universal sense of justice." ...

It relied upon Twining v. New Jersey, 211 U.S. 78 (1908), which held that the right against compulsory self-incrimination was not an element of Fourteenth Amendment due process. Betts was overruled by Gideon v. Wainwright, 372 U.S. 335 (1963); Twining, by Malloy v. Hogan, 378 U.S. 1 (1964). Our recent cases have thoroughly rejected the Palko notion that basic constitutional rights can be denied by the States as long as the totality of the circumstances does not disclose a denial of "fundamental fairness." Once it is decided that a particular Bill of Rights guarantee is "fundamental to the American scheme of justice" ... the same constitutional standards apply against both the State and Federal Governments. Palko's roots had thus been cut away years ago. We today only recognize the inevitable.

The fundamental nature of the guarantee against double jeopardy can hardly be doubted. Its origins can be traced to Greek and Roman times, and it became established in the common law of England long before this Nation's independence. . . . Today, every State incorporates some form of the prohibition in its constitution or common law. As this Court [has said] ... "[t]he underlying idea, one that is deeply ingrained in at least the Anglo-American system of jurisprudence, is that the State with all its resources and power should not be allowed to make repeated attempts to convict an individual for an alleged offense, thereby subjecting him to embarrassment, expense and ordeal and compelling him to live in a continuing state of anxiety and insecurity, as well as enhancing the possibility that even though innocent he may be found guilty." This underlying notion has from the very beginning been part of our constitutional tradition. Like the right to trial by jury, it is clearly *"fundamental to the American scheme of justice"* (emphasis added). The validity of petitioner's larceny conviction must be judged, not by the watered-down standard enunciated in Palko, but under this Court's interpretation of the Fifth Amendment double jeopardy provision.

It is clear that petitioner's larceny conviction cannot stand once federal double jeopardy standards are applied. Petitioner was acquitted of larceny in his first trial. Because he decided to appeal his burglary conviction, he is forced to suffer retrial on the larceny count as well.... This cannot do. Petitioner's larceny conviction cannot stand....

Vacated and remanded.

[Mr. Justice WHITE wrote a concurring opinion.]

Mr. Justice HARLAN, with whom Mr. Justice STEWART joins (dissenting).

* * *

I would hold, in accordance with Palko v. Connecticut ... that the Due Process Clause of the Fourteenth Amendment does not take over the Double Jeopardy Clause of the Fifth, as such. Today Palko becomes another casualty in the so far unchecked march toward "incorporating" much, if not all, of the Federal Bill of Rights into the Due Process Clause. This march began, with a Court majority, in 1961 when Mapp v. Ohio [Chapter Five, § 5.03] was decided, and before the present decision, found its last stopping point in Duncan v. Louisiana [supra] decided at the end of last Term (1968). I have at each step in the march expressed my opposition ... to show that the "selective incorporation" doctrine finds no support either in history or in reason....

* * *

The principle that an accused should not be tried twice for the same offense is deeply rooted in Anglo-American law. In this country, it is presently embodied in the Fifth Amendment to the Federal Constitution and in the constitution or common law of every State. The Palko Court found it unnecessary to decide "[w]hat the answer would have to be if the State were permitted after a trial free from error to try the accused over again or to bring another case against him...." ... However, I have no hesitation in stating that it would be a denial of due process at least for a State to retry one previously acquitted following an errorless trial. The idea that the State's interest in convicting wrongdoers is entirely satisfied by one fair trial ending in an acquittal, and that the accused's interest in repose must thereafter be given precedence, is indubitably a "'principle of justice so rooted in the traditions and conscience of our people as to be ranked as fundamental.'" ... The State had no more interest in compelling petitioner to stand trial again for larceny, of which he had been acquitted, than in retrying any other person declared innocent after an error-free trial. His retrial on the larceny count therefore, in my opinion, denied due process, and on that ground reversal would be called for under Palko.

Comments

1. In *Benton*, note the *selective incorporation* approach taken by the majority of the Court and the continuing adherence by Justice Harlan (joined by Justice Stewart) in favor of *fundamental fairness*. *Benton* overruled *Palko* v. *Connecticut* (1937). The *Palko* Court, utilizing the fundamental fairness approach, had rejected the application of the Double Jeopardy Clause to the states. *Benton* was the last decision, to date, to incorporate a provision of the Bill

of Rights through the Fourteenth Amendment Due Process Clause and make it applicable to the states. Is it surprising that, prior to 1969, the Double Jeopardy Clause was not applicable to the states? (Other problems involving double jeopardy will be considered in Chapter Six.)

2. After reading the *Adamson, Duncan,* and *Benton* decisions, which view, in your opinion, is the most persuasive on the nationalization of the Bill of Rights? Can you think of a sixth approach that might have been adopted by the Court?

3. The difficulties the Supreme Court encountered in deciding which, if any, procedural due process guarantees are incorporated through the Fourteenth Amendment arose again in the context of substantive due process with the issue of the right of privacy. Although the Supreme Court has stated that the right of privacy is of a constitutional dimension, it remains unclear exactly which constitutional provision(s) embodies this right. For example in *Griswold* v. *Connecticut,* 381 U.S. 479 (1965), Justice Douglas wrote the following oft-quoted passage: "Specific guarantees in the Bill of Rights have penumbras, formed from emanations from those guarantees that help give them life and substance.... Various guarantees create zones of privacy," at 484. Douglas went on to state that a right of privacy is contained in the penumbras of the First, Third, Fourth, Fifth, and Ninth Amendments. In *Griswold,* the Court struck down a state statute prohibiting the use of contraceptives and the giving of information or medical advice to married, as well as single, persons as to methods of preventing conception. Thus, the Court recognized that a right of privacy is encompassed in marital relationships. Later in *Griswold,* the Court said, "We deal with a right of privacy older than the Bill of Rights—older than our political parties, older than our school system. Marriage is a coming together for better or for worse, hopefully enduring, and intimate to the degree of being sacred. It is an association that promotes a way of life, not causes; a harmony in living, not political faiths; a bilateral loyalty, not commercial or social projects. Yet it is an association for as noble a purpose as any involved in our prior decisions," at 486. Dicta in earlier cases made reference to a right of privacy. See, e.g., *Boyd* v. *United States,* 116 U.S. 616, 630 (1886) ("privacies of life"); *Mapp* v. *Ohio,* 367 U.S. 643, 656 (1961) (Fourth Amendment creates a right to privacy). But see dissenting opinion of Justice Black (joined by Stewart, J.) in *Griswold,* where he wrote, "The Court talks about a constitutional 'right of privacy' as though there is some constitutional provision or provisions forbidding any law ever to be passed which might abridge the 'privacy' of individuals. But there is not," at 508.... I get nowhere ... by talk about a constitutional 'right of privacy' as an emanation from one or more constitutional provisions. I like my privacy as well as the next one, but I am nevertheless compelled to admit that government has a right to invade it unless prohibited by some specific constitutional provision," at 509–510. In a concurring opinion in *Griswold,* Justice Goldberg (joined by Warren, C. J., and Brennan, J.) relied heavily on the Ninth Amendment: "To hold that a right so basic and fundamental and so deep-rooted in our society as the right of privacy in marriage may be infringed because that right is not guaranteed in so many words by the first eight amendments to the Constitution is to ignore the Ninth Amendment and to give

it no effect whatsoever. Moreover, a judicial construction that this fundamental right is not protected by the Constitution because it is not mentioned in explicit terms ... would violate the Ninth Amendment, which specifically states that '(t)he enumeration in the Constitution, of certain rights, shall not be *construed* to deny or disparage others retained by the people,'" at 491–492.... "I believe that the right of privacy in the marital relation is fundamental and basic—a personal right 'retained by the people' within the meaning of the Ninth Amendment," at 499.

The view that a right of privacy is encompassed within the Ninth Amendment has never commanded the support of a majority of the Court. Justice White, concurring in *Griswold,* stated that the right of privacy is a "liberty" interest within the meaning of the Due Process Clause of the Fourteenth Amendment. Thus it is unclear on what constitutional grounds *Griswold* was decided, beyond the fact that the majority recognized a constitutional right of privacy.

In *Eisenstadt* v. *Baird,* 405 U.S. 438 (1972), a majority of the Court struck down a Massachusetts statute making it a felony to distribute contraceptives, except by registered physicians and pharmacists to married persons. Although the Court reaffirmed the view that a constitutional right of privacy is inherent in the marital relationship, the statute in *Eisenstadt* was struck down on equal protection grounds.

The following year in *Roe* v. *Wade,* 410 U.S. 113 (1973), and *Doe* v. *Bolton,* 410 U.S. 179 (1973), the Court struck down as violative of Fourteenth Amendment due process state criminal abortion statutes. In an opinion written by Justice Blackmun, the majority of the Court noted that although "the Constitution does not explicitly mention any right of privacy," the Court has recognized that "a right of personal privacy, or a guarantee of certain areas or zones of privacy, does exist under the Constitution," at 152. "This right of privacy, whether it be founded in the Fourteenth Amendment's concept of personal liberty and restrictions upon state action, *as we feel it is,* or ... in the Ninth Amendment's reservation of rights to the people, is broad enough to encompass a woman's decision whether or not to terminate a pregnancy," at 153 (emphasis added).

In *Planned Parenthood of Central Missouri* v. *Danforth,* 428 U.S. 52 (1976), the Court held, inter alia, that (1) a statutory requirement that a woman, prior to submitting to abortion during the first trimester of pregnancy, give written "informed" consent to the procedure is not an unconstitutional state interference with the abortion decision; (2) a state may not constitutionally require the consent of the husband as a condition for abortion during the first trimester of pregnancy; and (3) a state may not constitutionally impose a blanket parental consent requirement as a condition for an abortion during the first trimester of an unmarried minor's pregnancy. In light of the abortion decisions, the majority of the Supreme Court apparently views the "right of privacy" as encompassed within the Due Process Clause of the Fourteenth Amendment. The Ninth Amendment argument, first suggested by Justice Goldberg (concurring) in *Griswold,* supra, has never commanded a majority of the Court. References to a "right of privacy" have been made by the Court in other constitutional areas: *Stanley* v. *Georgia,* 394 U.S. 557, 564 (1969) (right to possession of obscene materials through First Amendment); *Katz* v. *United States,* 389

U.S. 347, 350 (1967) (right of privacy in Fourth Amendment); *Loving* v. *Virginia*, 388 U.S. 1, 12 (1967) (right of privacy in marriage); *Skinner* v. *Oklahoma,* 316 U.S. 535, 541–542 (1942) (right to procreate); *Eisenstadt* v. *Baird,* 405 U.S. 438, 453–454 (1972) (contraceptives); *Pierce* v. *Society of Sisters,* 268 U.S. 510, 535 (1925) (child rearing and education); and *Fisher* v. *United States,* 425 U.S. 391 (1976) (compelled testimony within meaning of Fifth Amendment is an invasion of privacy). A constitutional "right to privacy" is compatible with the *total incorporation plus* interpretation of the nationalization of the Bill of Rights first suggested by Justice Murphy (joined by Rutledge, J.) in *Adamson* v. *California* (dissenting opinion), supra. Interestingly, the "plus" has arrived ahead of total incorporation.

Even "Mad" Defendants Are Entitled to Due Process

DROPE v. MISSOURI

Supreme Court of the United States, 1975
420 U.S. 162, 95 S. Ct. 896, 43 L. Ed. 2d 103

James Drope, the petitioner, was indicted, with two others, for the forcible rape of petitioner's wife. He filed a motion for a continuance so that he might receive psychiatric treatment, but the motion was denied and the case proceeded to trial. Petitioner's wife testified that her husband participated with four of his acquaintances in forcibly raping her and subjecting her to other bizarre abuse and indignities. She also testified about petitioner's "strange behavior" and stated that she had changed her mind about not wanting to prosecute petitioner because he had tried to kill her on the Sunday prior to trial. On the second day of the trial petitioner shot himself in a suicide attempt and was hospitalized. Despite his absence, the trial court denied a motion for a mistrial on the ground that his absence was voluntary, and the trial continued. Petitioner was convicted and sentenced to life imprisonment. The Missouri Court of Appeals and Supreme Court affirmed, and the United States Supreme Court granted certiorari.

Mr. Chief Justice BURGER delivered the opinion of the Court.

We granted certiorari in this case to consider petitioner's claims that he was deprived of due process of law by the failure of the trial court to order a psychiatric examination with respect to his competence to stand trial and by the conduct in his absence of a portion of his trial on an indictment charging a capital offense.

* * *

It has long been accepted that a person whose mental condition is such that he lacks the capacity to understand the nature and object of the proceedings against him, to consult with counsel, and to assist in preparing his defense may not be subjected to a trial. ... One who became "mad" after the commission of an offense should not be arraigned for it "because he is not able to plead to it with the advice and caution that he ought." Similarly, if he became "mad" after pleading, he should not be tried, "for how can he make his defense?" ... Some have viewed the common-law prohibition "as a by-product of the ban against trials in absentia; the mentally incompetent defendant, though physically present in the courtroom, is in reality afforded no opportunity to defend himself." ... For our purpose, it suffices to note that the prohibition is fundamental to an adversary system of justice. . . . Accordingly, as to federal cases, we have approved a test of incompetence which seeks to ascertain whether a criminal defendant "had sufficient present ability to consult with his lawyer with a reasonable degree of rational understanding—and whether he has a rational as well as factual understanding of the proceedings against him." . . .

. . . The failure to observe procedures adequate to protect a defendant's right not to be tried or convicted while incompetent to stand trial deprives him of his due process right to a fair trial. . . .

* * *

In the present case there is no dispute as to the evidence possibly relevant to petitioner's mental condition that was before the trial court prior to trial and thereafter. Rather, the dispute concerns the inferences that were to be drawn from the undisputed evidence and whether, in light of what was then known, the failure to make further inquiry into petitioner's competence to stand trial, denied him a fair trial. . . .

The sentencing judge and the Missouri Court of Appeals concluded that the psychiatric evaluation of petitioner attached to his pretrial motion for a continuance did not contain sufficient indicia of incompetence to stand trial to require further inquiry. Both courts mentioned aspects of the report suggesting competence, such as the impressions that petitioner did not have "any delusions, illusions, hallucinations . . . ," was "well oriented in all spheres," and "was able, without trouble, to answer questions testing judgment," but neither court mentioned the contrary data. The report also showed that petitioner, although cooperative in the examination, "had difficulty in participating well," "had a difficult time relating," and that he "was markedly circumstantial and irrelevant in his speech." In addition, neither court felt that petitioner's episodic irrational acts described in the report or the psychiatrist's diagnoses of "borderline mental deficiency" and "chronic anxiety reaction with depression" created a sufficient doubt of competence to require further inquiry.

It does not appear that the examining psychiatrist was asked to address himself to medical facts bearing specifically on the issue of petitioner's competence to stand trial, as distinguished from his mental and emotional condition generally. Thus, it is not surprising that before this Court the dispute centers on the inferences that could or should properly have been drawn from the report. Even where the issue is in focus we have recognized "the uncertainty of diagnosis in this field and the tentativeness of professional judgment." . . .

. . . The motion for a continuance did not clearly suggest that petitioner's competence to stand trial was the question sought to be resolved. . . . Petitioner's somewhat inartfully drawn motion for a continuance probably fell short of appropriate assistance to the trial court in that regard. However, we are constrained to disagree with the sentencing judge that counsel's pretrial contention that "the defendant is not a person of sound mind and should have a further psychiatric examination before the case should be forced to trial," did not raise the issue of petitioner's competence to stand trial. This statement also may have tended to blur the aspect of petitioner's mental condition which would bear on his criminal responsibility and that which would bear on his competence to stand trial. However, at that stage, and with the obvious advantages of hindsight, it seems to us that it would have been, at the very least, the better practice to order an immediate examination. . . . It is unnecessary for us to decide whether such examination was constitutionally required on the basis of what was then known to the trial court, since in our view the question was settled by later events.

The state courts viewed the evidence as failing to show that during trial petitioner had acted in a manner that would cause the trial court to doubt his competence. The testimony of petitioner's wife, some of which repeated and confirmed information contained in the psychiatric evaluation attached to petitioner's motion for a continuance, was given little weight. Finally, the sentencing judge, relying on his finding on petitioner's motion for a new trial and although stating "that it does not take a psychiatrist to know that such a man has a problem and indicated poor judgment," concluded that the "fact that Mr. Drope shot himself to avoid trial suggests very strongly an awareness of what was going on." The Court of Appeals, accepting arguendo petitioner's contention that his was "a bona fide attempt at suicide," refused to conclude "that as a matter of law an attempt at suicide creates a reasonable doubt as to the movant's competency to stand trial."

... We conclude that the record reveals a failure to give proper weight to the information suggesting incompetence which came to light during trial.... Although a defendant's demeanor during trial may be such as to obviate "the need for extensive reliance on psychiatric prediction concerning his capabilities" ... this reasoning offers no justification for ignoring the uncontradicted testimony of ... a history of pronounced irrational behavior." ... We believe the Missouri courts failed to consider and give proper weight to the record evidence. Too little weight was given to the testimony of petitioner's wife that on the Sunday prior to trial he tried to choke her to death. For a man whose fate depended in large measure on the indulgence of his wife, who had hesitated about pressing the prosecution, this hardly could be regarded as rational conduct. We conclude that when considered together with the information available prior to trial and the testimony of petitioner's wife at trial, the information concerning petitioner's suicide attempt created a sufficient doubt of his competence to stand trial so as to require further inquiry on the question.

Evidence of a defendant's irrational behavior, his demeanor at trial, and any prior medical opinion on competence to stand trial are all relevant in determining whether further inquiry is required, but that even one of these factors standing alone may, in some circumstances, be sufficient. There are, of course, no fixed or immutable signs which invariably indicate the need for further inquiry to determine fitness to proceed; the question is often a difficult one in which a wide range of manifestations and subtle nuances are implicated. That they are difficult to evaluate is suggested by the varying opinions trained psychiatrists can entertain on the same facts.

... Even when a defendant is competent at the commencement of his trial, a trial court must always be alert to circumstances suggesting a change that would render the accused unable to meet the standards of competence to stand trial. Whatever the relationship between mental illness and incompetency to stand trial, in this case the bearing of the former on the latter was sufficiently likely that, in light of the evidence of petitioner's behavior, including his suicide attempt, and there being no opportunity without his presence to evaluate that bearing in fact, the correct course was to suspend the trial until such an evaluation could be made. That this might have aborted the trial is a hard reality, but we cannot fail to note that such a result might have been avoided by prompt psychiatric examination before trial, when it was sought by petitioner.

Our resolution of the first issue raised by petitioner makes it unnecessary to decide whether, as he contends, it was constitutionally impermissible to conduct the remainder of his trial on a capital offense in his enforced absence from a self-inflicted wound....

The question remains whether petitioner's due process rights would be adequately protected by remanding the case now for a psychiatric examination aimed at establishing whether petitioner was in fact competent to stand trial in 1969. Given the inherent difficulties of such a nunc pro tunc determination under the most favorable circumstance ... we cannot conclude that such a procedure would be adequate here.... The State is free to retry petitioner, assuming, of course, that at the time of such trial he is competent to be tried.

Reversed and remanded.

Comments

1. A man engages other men to rape his wife and later attempts suicide —aren't these sufficient facts to raise a doubt as to his competence to stand trial? The *Drope* Court noted that "a trial court must always be alert to circumstances suggesting a change that would render the accused unable to meet the standards of competence to stand trial." What "circumstances" beyond the *Drope*

case is the Court referring to? Physical violence in the courtroom? Cursing the judge? Acute depression manifested by defendant's sitting throughout the trial with his head on the defense table? Does the *Drope* case mean that a trial judge should order psychiatric examinations, even when not requested, for those defendants he suspects might be incompetent? Under what circumstances might a defendant be tried in absentia? In *Taylor* v. *United States*, 414 U.S. 17 (1973), the Supreme Court held that if a defendant is present at the start of his trial, but later *voluntarily* absents himself, the trial may continue in his absence since he has thereby waived the right to be present. Does an attempted suicide by a defendant constitute a voluntary or involuntary absence from trial? May an unruly defendant be removed from the courtroom and the trial continued in his absence? See *Illinois* v. *Allen*, 397 U.S. 337 (1970), Chapter Seven, § 7.03.

2. Other Supreme Court decisions related to the criminal process decided on due process grounds (Fifth and Fourteenth Amendments) during the past decade include *O'Connor* v. *Donaldson*, 422 U.S. 563 (1975) (state may not confine in a mental hospital without more than a finding of mental illness a nondangerous person who is capable of surviving safely in freedom); *Goss* v. *Lopez*, 419 U.S. 565 (1975) (students facing temporary suspension from public school have a due process right to notice and a hearing prior to suspension); *Donnelly* v. *DeChristoforo*, 416 U.S. 637 (1974) (prosecutor's remark during his closing argument to jury in state first degree murder trial about defendant's expectations as to the degree of murder of which he might be convicted held not sufficiently prejudicial as to deny due process); *Cupp* v. *Naughten*, 414 U.S. 141 (1973) (use of jury instructions that every witness is presumed to speak the truth not violative of due process even though only prosecution witnesses testified at the trial); *Eaton* v. *City of Tulsa*, 415 U.S. 697 (1974) (defendant's single use of expletive "chicken shit" during prosecution for violation of local ordinance held not constitutionally punishable as criminal contempt); *Vachon* v. *New Hampshire*, 414 U.S. 478 (1974) (state conviction for contributing to delinquency of a minor by selling to a 14-year-old girl a button inscribed "copulation not masturbation" held denial of due process where the evidence failed to show the defendant sold the button, knew it had been sold to a minor, authorized such sales to minors, or was even in the store at the time of the sale); *Douglas* v. *Buder*, 412 U.S. 430 (1973) (failure of a probationer to report traffic citation does not violate condition of probation that probationer report "all arrests" without delay where the mere issuance of a traffic citation does not constitute an arrest under state law); *United States* v. *Gaddis*, 424 U.S. 544 (1976) (under federal statute defendant may not be convicted of both robbing a bank and possessing the funds from the robbery); *Calero-Toledo* v. *Pearson Yacht Leasing Co.*, 416 U.S. 663 (1974) (seizure and forfeiture of yacht used by one of two lessees for transportation of marijuana without affording lessor or lessee preseizure notice and hearing not violative of due process); *Wardius* v. *Oregon*, 412 U.S. 470 (1973) (enforcement of state law requiring that defendant give pretrial notice of alibi and identity of alibi witnesses but not providing for reciprocal discovery by the defendant held violative of due process); *Dean* v. *Gadsden Times Publishing Corp.*, 412 U.S. 543 (1973) (state law

providing that employee excused from his employment for jury duty is entitled to his usual salary less any fees received for serving as a juror held not a denial of due process to employer); *Tollett* v. *Henderson*, 411 U.S. 258 (1973) (guilty plea bars federal habeas corpus relief for discrimination in selection of grand jury, absent showing of incompetent advice of counsel); *Chambers* v. *Mississippi*, 410 U.S. 284 (1973) (state evidentiary voucher rule ˜which precludes defendant from impeaching his own witness who had repudiated a prior written confession held violative of due process); *Robinson* v. *Hanrattan*, 409 U.S. 38 (1972) (mailing of notice of forfeiture proceedings to home address of property owner who is confined in jail held violative of due process); *Ward* v. *Village of Monroeville*, 409 U.S. 57 (1972) (trial of traffic case before village mayor who is responsible for village finances derived in large part from the fines he imposes violative of due process); *Beecher* v. *Alabama*, 408 U.S. 234 (1972) (use of defendant's confession in state murder trial made in hospital after he had received morphine for wound received upon arrest one hour earlier held denial of due process); *McNeil* v. *Director, Patuxent Institution*, 407 U.S. 245 (1972) (state law that permits the holding of a prisoner beyond his term of sentence because of his refusal to talk to psychiatrists held violative of due process); *Giglio* v. *United States*, 405 U.S. 150 (1972) (government's failure to disclose its promise not to prosecute the defendant's co-conspirator if he became a government witness a denial of due process); *Rabe* v. *Washington*, 405 U.S. 313 (1972) (due process violated where state statute making it a crime to show obscene films fails to give notice that criminal liability is dependent on the place where an obscene film is shown); *Loper* v. *Beto*, 405 U.S. 473 (1972) (the Due Process Clause precludes the use for impeachment purposes of a prior conviction that is constitutionally invalid because the defendant was denied the right to counsel); *Lego* v. *Twomey*, 404 U.S. 477 (1972) (due process requires that the prosecution prove the voluntariness of a confession only by a preponderance of evidence and not beyond a reasonable doubt) (plurality opinion); *Groppi* v. *Leslie*, 404 U.S. 496 (1972) (state assembly's punishment of defendant for contempt without notice or opportunity to respond violative of due process); *Bell* v. *Burson*, 402 U.S. 535 (1971) (due process requires that when a state seeks to suspend a motorist's license, it must first afford the motorist notice and an opportunity for a hearing); *Wisconsin* v. *Constantineau*, 400 U.S. 433 (1971) (due process violated by failure to provide notice and hearing before posting notice naming person to whom sale of liquor is forbidden); *Leary* v. *United States*, 395 U.S. 6 (1969) (federal statute authorizing jury to infer from defendant's possession of marijuana that he knew of the illegal importation of the marijuana held violative of due process); *In re Ruffalo*, 390 U.S. 544 (1968) (due process requires that charges in a disbarment proceeding must be known before the proceedings commence); *Specht* v. *Patterson*, 386 U.S. 605 (1967) (state procedure authorizing judge to impose indeterminate sentence on convicted sex offender without granting him a hearing or right of confrontation a denial of due process); *Pate* v. *Robinson*, 383 U.S. 375 (1966) (failure of trial court to conduct hearing as to accused's competency to stand trial is violative of due process). While the above list is not inclusive, the range of interests protected by the Due Process Clause indicates that the scope of this constitutional guarantee is quite broad.

TABLE 3.4 Voting Patterns of the Justices in Criminal Cases, 1965–66 Term (the Warren Court)

Case	Issue	Proportion of Cases in Which Each Justice Favored the Defendant's Claim									Vote
		Douglas .983	Fortas .866	Warren .833	Black .790	Brennan .774	Stewart .661	Clark .612	White .607	Harlan .435	
James v. Louisiana, 382 U.S. 36	Search and seizure	+*	+	+	+	+	+	+	+	+	9:0
Shuttlesworth v. Birmingham, 382 U.S. 87	Due process	+	+	+	+	+	+	+	+	+	9:0
U.S. v. Romano, 382 U.S. 136	Federal statute	+	+	+	+	+	+	+	+	+	9:0
California v. Buzard, 382 U.S. 386	Due process	+	+	+	+	+	+	+	+	+	9:0
Giaccio v. Pennsylvania, 382 U.S. 399	Due process	+	+	+	+	+	+	+	+	+	9:0
Baxstrom v. Herold, 383 U.S. 107	Equal protection	+	+	+	+	+	+	+	+	+	9:0
Ashton v. Kentucky, 384 U.S. 195	Due process	+	+	+	+	+	+	+	+	+	9:0
Mills v. Alabama, 384 U.S. 214	Freedom of press	+	+	+	+	+	+	+	+	+	9:0
Gojack v. U.S., 384 U.S. 702	Contempt	+	+	+	+	+	+	+	+	+	9:0
U.S. v. Johnson, 383 U.S. 169	Speech or debate clause	+	+	+	NP*	+	+	+	NP	+	7:0
Brookhart v. Janis, 384 U.S. 1	Sixth Amendment	+	+	+	+	+	+	+	+	—*	8:1
Rinaldi v. Yeager, 384 U.S. 305	Equal protection	+	+	+	+	+	+	+	+	—	8:1
Sheppard v. Maxwell, 384 U.S. 333	Due process	+	+	+	—	+	+	+	+	+	8:1
Shillitani v. U.S., 384 U.S. 364	Due process	+	+	+	+	+	+	+	NP	—	7:1
Stevens v. Marks, 383 U.S. 234	Self-incrimination	+	+	+	+	+	— (in part)	+	+	— (in part)	7:2
Pate v. Robinson, 383 U.S. 375	Due process	+	+	+	—	+	+	+	+	—	7:2
Davis v. North Carolina, 384 U.S. 737	Due process	— (in part)	+	+	+	+	+	—	+	—	7:2
Dennis v. U.S., 384 U.S. 855	Discovery	+	+	+	— (in part)	+	+	+	—	—	7:2
DeGregory v. Attorney Gen., 383 U.S. 825	Self-incrimination	+	+	+	+	+	+	—	—	—	6:3
Harris v. U.S., 382 U.S. 162	Contempt	+	+	+	+	+	—	—	—	—	5:4
Brown v. Louisiana, 383 U.S. 169	First Amendment	+	+	+	—	+	+	—	—	—	5:4
Kent v. U.S., 383 U.S. 541	Due process	+	+	+	+	+	—	—	—	—	5:4
Elfbrandt v. Russell, 384 U.S. 11	First Amendment	+	+	+	+	+	—	—	—	—	5:4
Miranda v. Arizona, 384 U.S. 436	Self-incrimination	+	+	+	+	+	—	—	—	—	5:4
Ginsburg v. U.S., 383 U.S. 463	First Amendment	+	—	—	+	—	+	—	—	+	4:5
Schmerber v. California, 384 U.S. 757	Search and seizure	+	+	+	+	—	—	—	—	—	4:5
Mishkin v. New York, 383 U.S. 502	First Amendment	+	+	—	+	—	+	—	—	+	4:5
Teltan v. Short, 382 U.S. 406	Retroactivity	+	NP	NP	+	—	—	—	—	—	2:5
Cheff v. Schnackenberg, 384 U.S. 373	Contempt	+	—	—	+	—	—	—	NP	—	2:6
U.S. v. Ewell, 382 U.S. 116	Speedy trial	+	—	—	+	—	—	—	—	—	2:7
Johnson v. New Jersey, 384 U.S. 719	Retroactivity	+	—	—	+	—	—	—	—	—	2:7
(N = 31) Number of cases participated in		31	30	30	31	31	31	31	28	31	
Number of cases in which favored defendant's claim		30+ (1 in part)	26	25	24+ (1 in part)	24	20+ (1 in part)	19	17	13+ (1 in part)	

(The Court was unanimous in 32.2% of the cases.)

*Key: + Favored defendant's claim
— Did not favor defendant's claim
NP Did not participate

TABLE 3.5 Voting Patterns of the Justices in Criminal Cases, 1975–76 Term (the Burger Court)

Case	Issue	Proportion of Cases in Which Each Justice Favored the Defendant's Claim									Vote*
		Brennan .785	Marshall .780	Stewart .380	White .226	Burger .142	Powell .190	Blackmun .166	Rehnquist .119	Stevens* .294	
U.S. v. Gaddis	Multiple conviction	++	+	+	+	+	+	+	+	NP†	8:0
McKinney v. Alabama	First Amendment	+	+	+	+	+	+	+	+	NP	8:0
Geders v. U.S.	Right to counsel	+	+	+	+	+	+	+	+	NP	8:0
Goldberg v. U.S.	Discovery	+	+	+	+	+	+	+	+	NP	8:0
Henderson v. Morgan	Plea bargaining	+	+	+	+	—†	+	+	—	+	7:2
Hynes v. Mayor	First Amendment	+	+	+	+	+	+	+	—	NP	7:1
Woodson v. North Carolina‡	Capital punishment	+	+	+	—	—	+	+	—	+	5:4
U.S. v. MacCollum	Transcripts—Post-conviction	+	+	—	+	—	—	—	—	NP	4:5
Young v. Am. Mini Theatres	First Amendment	+	+	+	+	—	—	+	—	+	4:5
Ludwig v. Massachusetts	Double jeopardy	+	+	+	—	+	+	+	—	—	4:5
Paul v. Davis	Civil Rights Act	+	+	—	+ (in part)	—	—	—	—	NP	3:5
Middendorf v. Henry	Right to counsel	+	+	+	—	—	—	—	—	NP	3:5
Hampton v. U.S.	Entrapment	+	+	+	—	—	—	—	—	NP	3:5
Doyle v. Ohio	Self-incrimination	+	+	+	—	—	—	—	—	+	3:6
Meachum v. Fano	Due process	+	+	+	—	—	—	—	—	—	3:6
South Dakota v. Opperman	Search and seizure	+	+	—	+	—	—	—	—	—	3:6
U.S. v. Janis	Search and seizure	+	+	+	+	—	—	—	—	—	3:6
Stone v. Powell	Search and seizure	+	+	+	—	—	—	—	—	—	3:6
Baxter v. Palmigiano	Due process	+	+	—	—	—	—	—	—	NP	2:6
Estelle v. Williams	Due process	—	+	+	—	—	—	—	—	NP	2:6
Michigan v. Mosley	Self-incrimination	+	+	—	+	—	—	—	—	NP	2:6
Barrett v. U.S.	Federal statute	+	—	+	—	—	—	+	+	NP	2:6
U.S. v. Watson	Search and seizure	+	+	+	—	—	—	—	—	NP	2:6
Ristaino v. Ross	Due process	+	+	—	—	—	—	—	—	NP	2:6
U.S. v. Dinitz	Double jeopardy	+	+	—	+	—	—	—	—	NP	2:6
Greer v. Spock	First Amendment	—	+	+	—	—	—	—	—	—	2:7
North v. Russell	Due process	+	+	—	—	—	—	—	—	—	2:7
U.S. v. Martinez-Fuerte	Search and seizure	+	—	+	—	—	—	—	—	—	2:7
U.S. v. Miller	Search and seizure	+	—	—	—	—	—	—	—	—	2:7
U.S. v. Santana	Search and seizure	+	—	—	—	—	—	—	—	—	2:7
U.S. v. Agurs	Due process	+	+	—	—	—	—	—	—	—	2:7
Andresen v. Maryland	Search and seizure	+	+	—	—	—	—	—	—	—	2:7
Gregg v. Georgia§	Capital punishment	+	+	—	—	—	—	—	—	—	1:6
Francis v. Henderson	Federal habeas corpus	+	NP	—	—	—	—	—	—	—	1:7
Beckwith v. U.S.	Self-incrimination	+	—	—	—	—	—	—	—	—	1:7
U.S. v. Powell	Due process	—	—	—	—	—	—	—	—	NP	0:8
U.S. v. Moore	Federal statute	—	—	—	—	—	—	—	—	NP	0:8
Imbler v. Pachtman	Civil Rights Act	—	—	—	—	—	—	—	—	NP	0:8
Garner v. U.S.	Self-incrimination	—	—	—	—	—	—	—	—	NP	0:8
Fisher v. U.S.	Self-incrimination	—	—	—	—	—	—	—	—	NP	0:8
U.S. v. Mandujano	Self-incrimination	—	—	—	—	—	—	—	—	NP	0:8
Nebraska Press Assoc. v. Stuart	First Amendment	—	—	—	—	—	—	—	—	—	0:9
(N = 42) Number of cases participated in		42	41	42	42	42	42	42	42	17	
Number of cases in which favored defendant's claim		33	32	16	9 (1 in part)	6	8	7	5	5	

(The Court was unanimous in 26.1% of the cases.)

*Did not join the Court until December 19, 1975.   †Key: + Favored defendants' claim   ‡Alone with *Roberts v. Louisiana*

4

EQUAL PROTECTION OF THE LAWS AND THE CRIMINAL PROCESS

4.01 INTRODUCTION

In this chapter, we will briefly discuss the application of the Fourteenth Amendment Equal Protection Clause to the criminal process. This overview is designed merely to indicate how the Supreme Court, on occasion, utilizes the Equal Protection Clause to resolve decisions involving the criminal process. For a more in-depth study of equal protection problems, especially in the noncriminal area, the student should consult appropriate texts in constitutional law.

The Fourteenth Amendment to the United States Constitution provides, inter alia, that "no State shall . . . deny to any person within its jurisdiction the equal protection of the laws." The intent of the framers of the Fourteenth Amendment was to guarantee to blacks and other minority groups full enjoyment of their constitutional rights. Today that amendment protects all persons without regard to color, class, religion, or sex and prohibits any *state act* that has the effect of arbitrarily denying any race, class, or person the equal protection of the laws. However, discrimination is not per se unlawful.

4.02 INVIDIOUS CLASSIFICATIONS

When a legislative body enacts laws, it necessarily creates legal categories that, to some extent, are inherently unequal. Disparity in the treatment of some citizens is not uncommon, and legal categories, as such, necessarily discriminate. For example, all states have established a minimum age before which a person may not lawfully drive a vehicle, serve on a jury, vote in an election, become married, or be a party to a valid contract. These statutes, on their face, discriminate against a class of persons *because* of their age. All states have minimal educational requirements for certain professional occupations. To practice law or medicine one must, in almost all jurisdictions, have graduated from an accredited professional school and passed board examinations given by the state. On its face this is discrimination based on maturity, education, and training. Tax laws affect persons differently according to their incomes. Military conscription laws were applicable only to males.

Thus, equal protection of the laws does

not mean that all persons must be treated equally at all times. Rather, equal protection means that discrimination among groups must have a rational and constitutional basis. To avoid a finding of invidious discrimination, the statutory classification must be *reasonable*. Classifications based on race,[1] nationality,[2] religion,[3] income,[4] and sex[5] are said to be *suspect* and receive stricter scrutiny by the United States Supreme Court. Through the years the Su-

preme Court has developed two distinct standards for determining the reasonableness of a legal classification for equal protection purposes: (1) the "reasonable-rational basis test," and (2) the "compelling state interest" test.

"Reasonable-Rational Basis" Test

The first test evolved by the Supreme Court to determine whether a statutory clas-

---

[1]*Loving* v. *Virginia*, 388 U.S. 1 (1967) (state antimiscegenation laws prohibiting interracial marriage violate Equal Protection Clause); *Washington* v. *Davis*, 426 U.S. 229 (1976) (a law or other governmental act is not unconstitutional solely because it has a racially disproportionate impact); *Milliken* v. *Bradley*, 418 U.S. 717 (1974) (desegregation, in the sense of dismantling a dual school system, does not require a particular racial balance in each school, grade, or classroom); *Alexander* v. *Louisiana*, 405 U.S. 625 (1972) (procedures in grand jury selection that are not racially neutral are violative of the Equal Protection Clause); *Palmer* v. *Thompson*, 403 U.S. 217 (1971) (city council's closing of public swimming pools rather than desegregating them does not violate Equal Protection Clause); *Adricks* v. *Kress & Co.*, 398 U.S. 144 (1970) (state law requiring a private person to refuse restaurant service to a customer because of his race violates the equal protection of the laws); *Turner* v. *Fouche*, 396 U.S. 346 (1970) (state law conferring discretion on county officials in the selection of prospective grand jurors does not violate equal protection of the laws even though opportunity exists for officials to discriminate on the basis of race); *Evans* v. *Abney*, 396 U.S. 435 (1970) (state supreme court ruling that upon failure of testamentary trust of land to city for unconstitutional purpose of providing a park for whites only trust property reverted to heirs of testator held not violative of Equal Protection Clause); *Hunter* v. *Erickson*, 393 U.S. 385 (1969) (a state may not disadvantage any particular racial group by making it more difficult to enact legislation in the group's behalf); *Coleman* v. *Alabama*, 389 U.S. 22 (1967) (prima facie case of denial of equal protection established where evidence showed no black had ever served on a grand jury and few blacks had ever served on petit juries) (to the same effect is *Jones* v. *Georgia*, 389 U.S. 24 [1967], *Whitus* v. *Georgia*, 385 U.S. 545 [1967], *Arnold* v. *North Carolina*, 376 U.S. 773 [1964], and *Hernandez* v. *Texas*, 347 U.S. 475 [1954]); *Reitman* v. *Mulkey*, 387 U.S. 369 (1967) (state law allowing any person to discriminate on racial grounds in sale or rental

of residential property violates the equal protection of the laws); *Evans* v. *Newton*, 382 U.S. 296 (1966) (a city may not act as a trustee under a private will that serves to promote racial segregation in a private park); *McLaughlin* v. *Florida*, 379 U.S. 184 (1964) (state statute making it a crime for a white person and a black person of opposite sexes to habitually live in the same room violates the Equal Protection Clause); *Swain* v. *Alabama*, 380 U.S. 202 (1965) (an accused is not entitled to proportionate representation of his race on a jury that tries him); *Griffin* v. *School Board of Prince Edward County*, 377 U.S. 218 (1964) (the closing of public schools in one county for the purpose of avoiding desegregation ordered by the Supreme Court, while public schools in all other counties remain open, deprives black students of the equal protection of the laws); *Griffin* v. *Maryland*, 378 U.S. 130 (1964) (state may not enforce a private policy of racial discrimination); *Anderson* v. *Martin*, 375 U.S. 399 (1964) (state law requiring that nomination papers and ballots designate race of candidates violates the Equal Protection Clause); *Robinson* v. *Florida*, 378 U.S. 153 (1964) (Equal Protection Clause bars state conviction of blacks and whites for remaining in restaurant after being requested by manager to leave); *Johnson* v. *Virginia*, 373 U.S. 61 (1963) (state-compelled segregation in courtroom violates Equal Protection Clause); *Peterson* v. *City of Greenville*, 373 U.S. 244 (1963) (blacks' trespass convictions at lunch counter held violative of Equal Protection Clause) (to the same effect is *Lombard* v. *Louisiana*, 373 U.S. 267 [1967], and *Wright* v. *Georgia*, 373 U.S. 284 [1963]); *Gross* v. *Board of Education*, 373 U.S. 683 (1963) (classifications based on race for purposes of transfers between public schools held unconstitutional); *Taylor* v. *Louisiana*, 370 U.S. 154 (1962) (Equal Protection Clause forbids a state to segregate persons according to race in interstate transportation facilities); *Bailey* v. *Patterson*, 369 U.S. 31 (1962) (state may not require racial segregation of interstate or intrastate transportation facilities); *Turner* v. *City of Memphis*, 369 U.S. 350 (1962) (state regulation requiring segregation of

Footnote continued on opposite page

sification violates the Equal Protection Clause is the *"rational basis"* test. Under this test, a statute may discriminate and classify persons only if (1) the classification bears a rational relation to the purposes of the legislation; (2) the classification furthers a proper governmental purpose; (3) all persons within the class are treated equally; and (4) the classification is not expressly forbidden by the Constitution.

The Supreme Court has specifically held that the "rational basis" test is applicable to classifications related to economic and social regulations. For example, in *United States Department of Agriculture* v. *Moreno,* 413 U.S. 528 (1973), the Federal Food Stamp Act (7 U.S.C. § 2012[e]) excluded "any household containing an individual who is unrelated to any other member of the household." The Supreme Court concluded that the intent of this legislation was to prevent "hippie communes"

---

municipal restaurant unconstitutional); *Burton* v. *Wilmington Parking Authority,* 365 U.S. 715 (1961) (Equal Protection Clause violated by refusal of restaurant operated in premises leased from a state agency to serve black patrons); *Cooper* v. *Aaron,* 358 U.S. 1 (1958) (public hostility does not entitle school board to suspend plan to integrate public schools); *Eubanks* v. *Louisiana,* 356 U.S. 584 (1958) (unconstitutional for a defendant to be indicted by a grand jury or tried by a petit jury from which members of his race have been systematically excluded because of their race); *Commonwealth of Pennsylvania* v. *Board of Directors of City Trusts of the City of Philadelphia,* 353 U.S. 230 (1957) (unconstitutional for a state board operating a private college to refuse to admit qualified blacks even though a testator provided in a trust that such school be limited to qualified white students); *Brown* v. *Board of Education,* 347 U.S. 483 (1954) (separate but equal public school facilities are unconstitutional); *Strauder* v. *West Virginia,* 100 U.S. 303 (1880) (state law forbidding blacks from serving on grand or petit juries unconstitutional); *Mayor of Philadelphia* v. *Educational Equality League,* 415 U.S. 605 (1974) (complaint alleging racial discrimination in appointment of school board nominating committee held properly dismissed for lack of proof); *Lee* v. *Washington,* 390 U.S. 333 (1968) (segregation of inmates by race unconstitutional); *McDonald* v. *Santa Fe Trail Transportation Co.,* 427 U.S. 273 (1976) (federal civil rights statutes applicable to racial discrimination in private employment against white persons); *Runyon* v. *McCrary,* 427 U.S. 160 (1976) (federal civil rights statute, 42 U.S.C. § 1981, prohibits private schools from excluding black children solely on racial grounds).

[2]*Graham* v. *Richardson,* 403 U.S. 365 (1971) (state statutes denying welfare benefits to resident aliens who have not resided in the U.S. for a specified number of years held violative of equal protection of the laws); *Sugarman* v. *Dougall,* 413 U.S. 634 (1973) (state statute barring all aliens from state's classified competitive civil service held unconstitutional); *In re Griffiths,* 413 U.S. 717 (1973) (state rule barring resident aliens from admission to bar held unconstitutional); *Takahashi* v. *Fish and Game Commission,* 334 U.S. 410 (1948) (state law prohibiting aliens from making a living by fishing off state's shores held unconstitutional); *Truax* v. *Raich,* 239 U.S. 33 (1915) (state law restricting employment of aliens held unconstitutional) (but see *Crane* v. *New York,* 239 U.S. 195 [1915] [state law prohibiting employment of aliens on public works project upheld]); *Yick Wo* v. *Hopkins,* 118 U.S. 356 (1886) (city ordinance making it a crime to operate a laundry without the consent of the board of supervisors held denial of equal protection of the laws as discriminatory against Chinese aliens).

[3]*Hunter* v. *Erickson,* 393 U.S. 385 (1969) (state may not disadvantage any particular religious group). See also cases cited in Chapter Fifteen, Comments.

[4]*Griffin* v. *Illinois,* 351 U.S. 12 (1956), infra, § 4.04. See also note 14, infra.

[5]*Frontiero* v. *Richardson,* 411 U.S. 677 (1973) (plurality opinion) (difference in treatment of servicewomen and servicemen under statutes governing claims of spouse as dependent for increased benefits held unconstitutional); *Stanton* v. *Stanton,* 421 U.S. 7 (1975) (Utah statute specifying greater age of majority for males than females denies equal protection of the laws); *Kahn* v. *Shevin,* 416 U.S. 351 (1974) (Florida statute granting widows, but not widowers, annual $500 property tax exemption held constitutional); *Geduldig* v. *Aiello,* 417 U.S. 484 (1974) (state disability insurance program excluding coverage for disability accompanying normal pregnancy and childbirth upheld); *Reed* v. *Reed,* 404 U.S. 71 (1971) (state statute giving mandatory preference to male applicants over female applicants as administrator of decedent's estate held unconstitutional); *Hoyt* v. *Florida,* 368 U.S. 57 (1961) (state statute granting women exemption from jury duty does not violate the Equal Protection Clause) (but see *Taylor* v. *Louisiana,* 419 U.S. 522 [1975] [Louisiana's practice of excluding women from jury service unless a written declaration indicating a desire to serve is filed held violative of Sixth Amendment right to a jury trial]).

from participating in the food stamp program and held that portion of the statute to be violative of the Equal Protection Clause since it failed to serve a legitimate governmental purpose in discriminating against "hippies" and was wholly without any rational basis. However, statutory categories based on "natural classifications" such as age, geographical location, or education and training are likely to be upheld as rational. In the relatively few criminal cases decided by the Supreme Court on equal protection grounds, the "rational basis" test has been employed.

"Compelling State Interest" Test

The second test applied by the Supreme Court when a statutory classification is alleged to be violative of the Equal Protection Clause is the *"compelling state interest"* test. In cases that involve a *suspect classification* or touch on *fundamental interests,* the state is required to bear the burden of establishing that it has a compelling interest that justifies the law and that such a law is necessary to further a legitimate purpose of the state. The Supreme Court has designated as *fundamental* the right to travel,[6] the right to vote,[7] the right to procreate,[8] a woman's right to terminate a pregnancy,[9] and freedom of speech,[10] press,[11] and religion.[12] The following have been classed as *nonfundamental rights,* thereby requiring the less strict "rational basis" test: the right to an education,[13] the right to receive public welfare benefits,[14] the right to housing,[15] and the right to discharge one's debts through bankruptcy proceedings.[16]

---

[6]*Shapiro* v. *Thompson,* 394 U.S. 618 (1969) (state statutes conditioning welfare benefits on one year's residency unconstitutional); *Memorial Hospital* v. *Maricopa County,* 415 U.S. 250 (1974) (state statute requiring one year's residency in county as condition to receiving nonemergency medical care at county expense held unconstitutional); *Village of Belle Terre* v. *Boraas,* 416 U.S. 1 (1974) (village zoning ordinance prohibiting occupancy of one-family dwellings by more than two unrelated persons, but allowing occupancy by any number of persons related by blood, adoption, or marriage upheld); *Sosna* v. *Iowa,* 419 U.S. 393 (1975) (one-year residency requirement for divorce action held not to violate equal protection of the laws); *Airport Authority* v. *Delta Airlines,* 405 U.S. 707 (1972) (state and municipal charges imposed on commercial passengers to defray the costs of airport construction and maintenance upheld as not an unconstitutional burden on the right to travel); *Martin* v. *Walton,* 368 U.S. 25 (1961) (state statute permitting an out-of-state lawyer to practice before state courts only if he associates a member of the state bar with him as attorney of record held not violative of Equal Protection Clause).

[7]*Williams* v. *Rhodes,* 393 U.S. 23 (1968) (state election laws imposing undue burdens on placing new or small political parties on state ballots held unconstitutional); *Hill* v. *Stone,* 421 U.S. 289 (1975) (Texas laws restricting voters in local bond elections to persons who reported property for taxation held violative of the Equal Protection Clause); *Kramer* v. *Union Free School District No. 15,* 395 U.S. 621 (1969) (requirements other than residency, age, and citizenship for vot-

ing in general election must promote a compelling state interest); *Cipriano* v. *City of Houma,* 395 U.S. 701 (1969) (restricting eligible voters in local revenue bond elections to "property taxpayers" held unconstitutional); *City of Phoenix* v. *Kolodziejski,* 399 U.S. 204 (1970) (restricting voting on general obligation bond issue to real property taxpayers violates the equal protection of the laws); *Rosario* v. *Rockefeller,* 410 U.S. 752 (1973) (neutral requirement that a voter register a party preference 30 days in advance of general election upheld); *Dunn* v. *Blumstein,* 405 U.S. 330 (1972) (state laws requiring one year's state residence and three month's county residence for voting in state elections held unconstitutional); *McDonald* v. *Board of Election,* 394 U.S. 802 (1969) (state absentee voting statute does not violate Equal Protection Clause in failing to provide means to vote for pretrial jail inmates unable to post bail or held on nonbailable charges); *Bullock* v. *Carter,* 405 U.S. 134 (1972) (state laws requiring candidates to pay large election fees as a condition to appearing on the ballot in primary elections held unconstitutional); *Lubin* v. *Panish,* 415 U.S. 709 (1974) (state election laws requiring candidates to pay filing fees to get their names placed on primary ballot but not providing alternative means of access to ballot held denial of equal protection of laws to indigent candidates); *Storer* v. *Brown,* 415 U.S. 724 (1974) (state law prohibiting ballot position in general election for independent candidate who had been registered with political party within one year prior to preceding primary upheld); *American Party of Texas* v. *White,* 415 U.S. 767 (1974) (Texas law requiring minority political parties and independent candidates to file nomin-

Footnote continued on opposite page

ating petitions signed by 1 per cent of voters at previous general election upheld); *O'Brien* v. *Skinner*, 414 U.S. 524 (1974) (state law denying jailed persons right to register and vote in general elections held to violate the equal protection of the laws); *Gaffney* v. *Cummings*, 412 U.S. 735 (1973) (minor deviations from mathematical equality among state legislative districts under reapportionment plan held insufficient to prove prima facie case of invidious discrimination under Equal Protection Clause) (to the same effect is *White* v. *Regester*, 412 U.S. 755 [1973]); *Mahan* v. *Howell*, 410 U.S. 375 (1973) (state legislative apportionment plan having population deviation of 16.4 per cent between highest and lowest districts held constitutional); *Marston* v. *Lewis*, 410 U.S. 679 (1973) (state law imposing 50-day voter residency and registration requirements for state and local elections held constitutional) (to the same effect is *Burns* v. *Fortson*, 410 U.S. 686 [1973]); *Jenness* v. *Fortson*, 403 U.S. 431 (1971) (state election law requiring candidates who do not enter and win party primary but who wish to have names printed on ballots must obtain signatures of at least 5 per cent of registered voters on nominating petitions upheld); *Oregon* v. *Mitchell*, 400 U.S. 112 (1970) (Voting Rights Act amendments lowering minimum voting age from 21 to 18 in federal elections upheld, but not as applied to state and local elections under Equal Protection Clause); *Richardson* v. *Ramirez*, 418 U.S. 24 (1974) (state law disqualifying from voting convicted felons who have completed their sentences and paroles held not violative of the equal protection of the laws); *Evans* v. *Cornman*, 398 U.S. 419 (1970) (a state may not, consistent with the Equal Protection Clause, exclude from the polls all persons living on federally tax-exempt property); *Hadley* v. *Junior College District*, 397 U.S. 50 (1970) (one man–one vote rule held applicable to election of trustees of junior college district); *Moore* v. *Ogilvie*, 394 U.S. 814 (1969) (state law requiring 200 signatures of voters from each of at least 50 of 102 counties on independent candidates' nominating petitions held unconstitutional); *Hadnott* v. *Amos*, 394 U.S. 358 (1969) (state law increasing barriers to black independent candidates' gaining place on ballot held violative of the equal protection of the laws); *Avery* v. *Midland County*, 390 U.S. 474 (1968) (one man–one vote rule held applicable to election of county commissioners); *Sailors* v. *Kent Board of Education*, 387 U.S. 105 (1967) (one man–one vote rule not applicable to nonelective selection of county school board); *Dusch* v. *Davis*, 387 U.S. 112 (1967) (one man–one vote rule does not invalidate requirement that city councilmen elected at large be residents of certain boroughs); *Fortson* v. *Morris*, 385 U.S. 231 (1966) (state law requiring legislature to select governor when no candidate received a majority of votes held

constitutional); *Harper* v. *Virginia Board of Elections*, 383 U.S. 663 (1966) (state statute requiring payment of poll tax as a condition to vote held violative of the Equal Protection Clause); *Carrington* v. *Rash*, 380 U.S. 89 (1965) (state law which denies servicemen the right to vote on the sole ground of their military status held unconstitutional); *Reynolds* v. *Sims*, 377 U.S. 533 (1964) (Equal Protection Clause requires apportionment of both houses of state legislature substantially on a population basis) (to the same effect is *WMCA* v. *Lomenzo*, 377 U.S. 633 [1964]; *Maryland Committee* v. *Tawes*, 377 U.S. 656 [1964], *Williams* v. *Moss*, 378 U.S. 558 [1964], *Davis* v. *Mann*, 377 U.S. 678 [1964], *Roman* v. *Sincock*, 377 U.S. 695 [1964], *Lucas* v. *Colorado General Assembly*, 377 U.S. 713 [1974], *Meyers* v. *Thigpen*, 378 U.S. 554 [1964]; *Gray* v. *Sanders*, 372 U.S. 368 (1963) (Equal Protection Clause violated by use of county unit system in counting votes which results in disproportionate vote weighting); *Baker* v. *Carr*, 369 U.S. 186 (1962) (complaint that state apportionment statute effected a debasement of votes held to state a justiciable cause of action); *Nixon* v. *Condon*, 286 U.S. 73 (1932) (resolution of state executive committee of a political party limiting voting rights to white persons held denial of equal protection of the laws).

[8]*Skinner* v. *Oklahoma*, 316 U.S. 535 (1942) (state law providing for sterilization of those persons convicted two times for felonies involving "moral turpitude" but not for those convicted of other felonies held to violate the Equal Protection Clause). See also *Eisenstadt* v. *Baird*, 405 U.S. 438 (1972) (state law restricting the distribution of contraceptives to married persons held a denial of equal protection of the laws).

[9]*Roe* v. *Wade*, 410 U.S. 113 (1973) (right to abortion fundamental but not absolute); *Doe* v. *Bolton*, 410 U.S. 179 (1973). See also Chapter Three, § 3.04, Comments, p. 117.

[10]E.g., *Brandenburg* v. *Ohio*, 395 U.S. 444 (1969) (free speech is a fundamental right and may not be abridged except under compelling circumstances) (overruling *Whitney* v. *California*, 274 U.S. 357 [1927]). See Chapter Fifteen, § 15.03, Comments.

[11]E.g., *New York Times Co.* v. *United States*, 403 U.S. 713 (1971) (any system of prior restraints on the freedom of expression bears a heavy presumption against its constitutionality). See Chapter Fifteen, § 15.02, Comments.

[12]E.g., *Engel* v. *Vitale*, 307 U.S. 421 (1962) (inclusion of a classroom prayer composed by state officials for daily use in public schools violates Establishment Clause of First Amendment). To the same effect is *Abington School District* v. *Schempp*, 374 U.S. 203 (1963). See Chapter Fifteen, § 15.04, Comments.

[13]*San Antonio Independent School District* v. *Rodriguez*, 411 U.S. 1 (1973) (state system for

Footnote continued on page 130

financing public schools which resulted in disparities in per-pupil expenditures not violative of Equal Protection Clause). See also *Wisconsin* v. *Yoder*, 406 U.S. 205 (1972) (Chapter Fifteen, § 15.04); *McCollum* v. *Board of Education*, 333 U.S. 203 (1948); *Pierce* v. *Society of Sisters*, 268 U.S. 510 (1925); *Meyer* v. *Nebraska*, 262 U.S. 390 (1923); *Interstate Consolidated Street R. Co.* v. *Massachusetts*, 207 U.S. 79 (1907).

[14]*Dandridge* v. *Williams*, 397 U.S. 471 (1970) (state regulation imposing maximum limit on the total amount of welfare aid which one family could receive held not violative of equal protection of the laws).

Supreme Court cases involving economic and welfare benefits decided on equal protection grounds abound: *Weber* v. *Aetna Casualty & Surety Co.*, 406 U.S. 164 (1972) (state workmen's compensation law denying equal recovery rights to dependent illegitimate children held a denial of equal protection of the laws); *New Jersey Welfare Rights Organization* v. *Cahill*, 411 U.S. 619 (1973) (state may not exclude illegitimate children from sharing equally with other children in recovery of workmen's compensation benefits for the death of a parent); *Gomez* v. *Perez*, 409 U.S. 535 (1973) (denial under state law of illegitimate child's right to support from natural father unconstitutional); *City of New Orleans* v. *Dukes*, 427 U.S. 297 (1976) ("grandfather clause" in ordinance exempting 8-year operators from prohibition against selling foodstuffs from pushcarts not violative of Equal Protection Clause as against 2-year operator); *Hughes* v. *Alexandria Scrap Corp.*, 426 U.S. 794 (1976) (Maryland statute providing for state bounties for destruction of Maryland-titled junk automobiles while requiring stricter proof of ownership for out-of-state processors held constitutional); *City of Charlotte* v. *Firefighters*, 426 U.S. 283 (1976) (city's refusal to withhold union dues while withholding for other organizations that benefited all city or departmental employees not in violation of equal protection of the laws); *LeHuHausen* v. *Lake Shore Auto Parts Co.*, 410 U.S. 356 (1973) (state law requiring corporations, but not individuals, to pay ad valorem personal property taxes not unconstitutional); *Ortwein* v. *Schwab*, 410 U.S. 656 (1973) (state law requiring payment of $25 appellate court filing fee before judicial review permitted from adverse agency decision as to public assistance not in violation of Equal Protection Clause); *Jefferson* v. *Hackney*, 406 U.S. 535 (1972) (state decision to provide lower welfare benefits to AFDC [Aid to Families and Dependent Children] recipients than for aged and infirm in other categories not unconstitutional); *Lindsey* v. *Normet*, 405 U.S. 56 (1972) (state law in eviction proceedings requiring tenant-appellant to post double bond held unconstitutional); *Stanley* v. *Illinois*, 405 U.S. 645 (1972)

(a denial to unwed fathers of a hearing on parental fitness which is accorded to all other parents whose custody of their children is challenged by the state held unconstitutional); *Labine* v. *Vincent*, 401 U.S. 532 (1971) (state law barring illegitimate child from sharing with legitimate heirs in intestate father's estate not unconstitutional); *WHYY* v. *Glassboro*, 393 U.S. 117 (1968) (foreign nonprofit corporation licensed to do business in a taxing state may not be denied state property tax exemption where domestic corporations are granted such exemption on the ground that the foreign corporation was organized under the laws of another state); *Levy* v. *Louisiana*, 391 U.S. 68 (1968) (denial to illegitimate children of the right to maintain lawsuit for mother's wrongful death held unconstitutional); *Glona* v. *American Guarantee and Liability Insurance Co.*, 391 U.S. 73 (1968) (denial to mother of illegitimate child a right to maintain lawsuit for child's wrongful death held unconstitutional); *Florida Avocado Growers* v. *Paul*, 373 U.S. 132 (1963) (state law prohibiting transportation or sale in state of avocados containing less than 8 per cent oil not unconstitutional); *Central R. Co. of Pennsylvania* v. *Pennsylvania*, 370 U.S. 607 (1962) (state does not violate Equal Protection Clause by reasonably differentiating for tax purposes between railroads having tracks which lie only within its borders and railroads whose tracks lie both within and without the state); *Cohen* v. *Hurley*, 366 U.S. 117 (1961) (disbarment of attorney for refusal to answer questions in investigation of professional misconduct not violative of Equal Protection Clause); *McGowan* v. *Maryland*, 366 U.S. 420 (1961) (a state Sunday closing law does not violate the Equal Protection Clause merely because it exempts the retail sale of certain products) (to the same effect is *Gallagher* v. *Crown Kosher Super Market*, 366 U.S. 617 [1961], and *Two Guys From Harrison-Allentown, Inc.* v. *McGinley*, 366 U.S. 582 [1961]); *Allied Stores of Ohio* v. *Bowers*, 358 U.S. 522 (1959) (state law exempting from property tax merchandise belonging to nonresident if held in storage warehouse for storage only not unconstitutional) (to the same effect is *Youngstown Sheet & Tube Co.* v. *Bowers*, 358 U.S. 534 [1959]); *Nelson* v. *City of New York*, 352 U.S. 103 (1956) (default judgments by city in foreclosing its liens on real property for water charges and subsequent sale thereof are not violative of equal protection even though the city had available other remedies for collecting such taxes); *Schware* v. *Board of Bar Examiners*, 353 U.S. 232 (1957) (state may not exclude a person from the practice of law or any other occupation merely because he is a member of a particular political party, religion, or race) (to the same effect is *Konisberg* v. *State Bar of California*, 353 U.S. 252 [1957]); *Morey* v. *Doud*, 354 U.S. 457 (Equal Protection Clause

Footnote continued on opposite page

In summary, if a state classification alleged to be violative of equal protection involves a fundamental right (e.g., voting) or is a suspect classification (e.g., race), the Supreme Court in reviewing that classification will utilize the stricter "compelling state interest" test.

Statutes involving classifications that affect fundamental rights are suspect, and are *not* presumed to be constitutional. The state must prove that the classification is *necessary* to promote some compelling state interest; and the statute must be *narrowly drawn* so that it is the *least burdensome alternative available.*[17]

More recently, the Supreme Court has added an intermediate, or third-tier, standard for equal protection purposes in the area of sex-based discrimination, which the Court refers to as "gender-based discrimination." In *Craig* v. *Boren,*[18] a majority of the Court held that a classification based on sex must "serve important governmental objectives and must be substantially related to achievement of those objectives." Apparently in future cases, a gender-based classification, while not "suspect," will be measured against a standard that is stricter than the "rational basis" test but less strict than the "compelling state interest" test.

4.03 THE "STATE ACTION" REQUIREMENT

There is no Equal Protection Clause in the United States Constitution specifically directed at the federal government — the Fourteenth Amendment is applicable only to the states. However, the United States Supreme Court has held that a denial of the equal protection of the laws by the federal government violates the Fifth Amendment Due Process Clause,[19] and invidious classifications promulgated by the federal government are therefore unconstitutional.

Because the Fourteenth Amendment

---

does not require that every state regulatory statute apply to all in same business); *Williamson* v. *Lee Optical Co.,* 348 U.S. 483 (1955) (state statute preventing opticians, but not optometrists or ophthalmologists, from fitting or duplicating lenses in eyeglasses, held not violative of Equal Protection Clause); *Watson* v. *City of St. Louis,* 347 U.S. 231 (1954) (city ordinance specifying different treatment for taxpayers deriving income from salary and wages and for taxpayers deriving profits from self-employment does not per se violate Equal Protection Clause); *Salsburg* v. *Maryland,* 346 U.S. 545 (1954) (state may prescribe substantive restrictions and variations for procedures related to concentrations of populations which are not uniform throughout all parts of the state); *James* v. *Valtierra,* 402 U.S. 137 (1971) (state law providing that no low-rent public housing project could be developed unless approved by referendum in locality not unconstitutional).

[15]*Lindsey* v. *Normet,* 405 U.S. 56 (1972) (there is no federal constitutional guarantee of access to dwellings of a particular quality). See also *Grant Timber & Mfg. Co.* v. *Gray,* 236 U.S. 133 (1915), and *Bianchi* v. *Morales,* 262 U.S. 170 (1923).

[16]*United States* v. *Kras,* 409 U.S. 434 (1973) (requirement that indigent petitioner for voluntary bankruptcy pay filing fees up to $50 does not deny him the equal protection of the laws). But see *Boddie* v. *Connecticut,* 401 U.S. 371 (1971) (filing fee of $60 to initiate divorce proceedings held to deny the equal protection of the laws to indigents).

[17]E.g., *Procunier* v. *Martinez,* 416 U.S. 396 (1974) (Chapter Nine, § 9.03) (state prison regulations censoring prisoners' mail justifiable under the freedom of speech guarantee only if such regulations further an important or substantial governmental interest unrelated to the suppression of expression and impose no greater limitation than is necessary to protect the particular governmental interest involved). See also *United States* v. *O'Brien,* 391 U.S. 367 (1968) (First Amendment free speech guarantee not violated by conviction of defendant who publicly burned his draft card).

[18]429 U.S. 190 (1976) (state statute prohibiting sale of 3.2% beer to males under age 21 and to females under age 18 held violative of equal protection of the laws).

[19]*Bolling* v. *Sharpe,* 347 U.S. 497 (1954) (Due Process Clause of the Fifth Amendment prohibits racial segregation in the public schools of the District of Columbia); *Hampton* v. *Mow Sun Wong,* 426 U.S. 88 (1976) (Civil Service Commission regulation barring resident aliens from civil service employment violative of Due Process Clause); *Mathews* v. *Diaz,* 426 U.S. 67 (1976) (Medicare eligibility requirements that 65-year-old aliens must be admitted for permanent residence and must reside in U.S. for 5 years held violative of due process); *Examining Board* v. *Otero,* 426 U.S. 572 (1976) (Puerto Rico statute prohibiting aliens from engaging in the private practice of engineering violative of the equal protection component of the Fifth Amendment Due Process Clause); *Mathews* v. *Lucas,* 427 U.S. 495 (1976) (Social Security Act which con-

Footnote continued on page 132

Equal Protection Clause is directed at the states, it is generally conceded that discrimination by *private persons* is not prohibited by the Fourteenth Amendment.[20] (For equal protection purposes, corporations[21] and aliens[22] are "persons" within the meaning of the Fourteenth Amendment.) An alleged Fourteenth Amendment equal protection violation usually must involve *state action* of some sort. Thus, the Fourteenth Amendment is applicable to any department of a state (legislative, executive, or judicial), or any officer, agency, or instrumentality of a state.

Private persons who willfully engage in *joint activity* with state officials are, how-ever, subject to the constraints of the Fourteenth Amendment.[23] In addition, the Fourteenth Amendment contains an *enabling clause* that grants Congress the power to enforce that amendment "by appropriate legislation." For example, the 1964 Civil Rights Act authorizes civil damage judgments and/or criminal convictions against any persons, *acting under color of state law*, who deprive others of their constitutional rights.[24] Moreover, even in the absence of federal legislation, the Supreme Court has recognized a cause of action against federal agents who violate the constitutional rights of others[25] (see Chapter Ten).

---

ditions illegitimate child's survivorship benefits on proof of dependency of deceased not violative of due process); *Ng Fung Hoe* v. *White*, 259 U.S. 276 (1922) (alien subject to deportation proceedings is entitled to judicial determination of claim that he is a citizen); *Washington* v. *Legrant*, 394 U.S. 618 (1969) (congressionally imposed requirement of one year's residence within the District of Columbia for receipt of welfare benefits violative of due process); *Schlesinger* v. *Ballard*, 419 U.S. 498 (1975) (federal statutes providing for mandatory discharge of Naval officers who have been twice passed over for promotion but guaranteeing women 13 years of service not violative of due process); *Weinberger* v. *Wisenfeld*, 420 U.S. 636 (1975) (provision in Social Security Act granting survivors' benefits to widows and minor children but only to minor children and not to widower when a husband survives his working spouse held violative of due process); *Johnson* v. *Robison*, 415 U.S. 361 (1974) (denial of educational benefits to conscientious objectors who performed alternate civilian service not violative of due process); *Richardson* v. *Belcher*, 404 U.S. 78 (1971) (provision of Social Security Act requiring reduction of benefits to persons also receiving workmen's compensation not violative of due process); *Jimenez* v. *Weinberger*, 417 U.S. 628 (1974) (Social Security Act provision denying benefits to certain illegitimate children born after parent's disability violative of due process). Equal protection of the laws under the Fifth and Fourteenth Amendments requires the same type of analysis. See *Buckley* v. *Valeo*, 424 U.S. 1 (1976).

[20]See, e.g., *Shelley* v. *Kramer*, 334 U.S. 13 (1948), infra, note 26; *Jackson* v. *Metropolitan Edison Co.*, 419 U.S. 345 (1974) (termination of electrical service to household, without notice or hearing, by privately owned and operated utility company not sufficient "state action" for Fourteenth Amendment requirements to apply); *Gilmore* v. *City of Montgomery*, 417 U.S. 556 (1974) (discrimination by otherwise private entity not violative of equal protection merely because the entity receives some sort of benefit or service by the state or because it is subject to some state regulation); *Barrows* v. *Jackson*, 346 U.S. 249 (1953) (state court's award of damages in an action for breach of covenant restricting the use of real property to white persons is "state action" under the Fourteenth Amendment).

[21]*Santa Clara County* v. *South Pacific R. Co.*, 118 U.S. 394 (1886) (without discussion).

[22]See cases cited in note 2, supra.

[23]*Burton* v. *Wilmington Parking Authority*, 365 U.S. 715 (1961), supra, note 1; *Anderson* v. *Martin*, 375 U.S. 399 (1964), supra, note 1; *Evans* v. *Newton*, 382 U.S. 296 (1966), supra, note 1; *Gilmore* v. *City of Montgomery*, 417 U.S. 556 (1974), supra, note 19 (each case recognizing the rule).

[24]42 U.S.C. § 1983 (1964) provides: "Every person who, under color of any statute, ordinance, regulation, custom, or usage, of any State or Territory, subjects, or causes to be subjected, any citizen of the United States or other person within jurisdiction thereof to the deprivation of any rights, privileges, or immunities, secured by the Constitution and laws, shall be liable to the party injured in any action at law, suit in equity, or other proper proceeding for redress." See also Chapter Ten.

18 U.S.C. §§ 241–242 prescribe criminal penalties for the violation of a person's federal civil rights.

[25]*Bivens* v. *Six Unknown Agents*, 403 U.S. 388

Footnote continued on opposite page

During the past 30 years, the Court has expanded the concept of "state action" and in so doing has struck down literacy tests limiting the right of minorities to vote;[26] private covenants authorizing persons to discriminate in the sale or lease of their property;[27] and a state law granting financial aid to racially discriminatory private schools.[28] More recently, however, the Court has held that the mere granting of a liquor license or the provision of essential services (e.g., police, fire, water, electricity) by a state to a private facility that practices racial discrimination in admitting members does not significantly involve state action in violation of the Equal Protection Clause.[29] Similarly, the closing of a public swimming pool by a city to avoid integration does not involve a denial of the equal protection of the laws.[30]

As we have indicated, in most cases involving the criminal process the Supreme Court has not dealt with questions of equal protection of the laws, but in most of the cases that have been decided on those grounds, the less strict rational basis test was applied. In the next section, four criminal cases decided by the Supreme Court on equal protection grounds are presented. These cases were selected because they involve different stages in the criminal process. Other Supreme Court cases decided on equal protection grounds can be found in later chapters.

4.04 EQUAL PROTECTION AND THE CRIMINAL PROCESS

The Right of Indigent Defendants to Free Trial Transcripts on Appeal

GRIFFIN v. ILLINOIS

Supreme Court of the United States, 1956
351 U.S. 12, 76 S. Ct. 585, 100 L. Ed. 891

Griffin was convicted of armed robbery in Chicago in the Cook County Criminal Court. Following the conviction he asked the trial court for a certified copy of the entire record (transcript) in order to pursue an appeal. Because he was without funds, he requested a free copy of the transcript. The trial court denied the request on the grounds that Illinois law permitted free transcripts only in capital

---

(1971) (Chapter Ten, § 10.02) (a violation of the Fourth Amendment by a federal agent acting under color of federal authority gives rise to a federal cause of action for damages).

[26]*Katzenbach* v. *Morgan,* 384 U.S. 641 (1966) (§ 4(e) of the Voting Rights Act of 1965 prohibiting English literacy tests for citizens educated in American flag schools upheld). But see *Lassiter* v. *Northampton County Board of Elections,* 360 U.S. 45 (1959) (literacy test, fair on its face, may be employed).

[27]*Shelley* v. *Kramer,* 334 U.S. 1 (1948) (enforcement by state courts of racially restrictive covenants in the sale or lease of property sufficient state action inconsistent with the equal protection of the laws).

[28]*Griffin* v. *County School Board,* 377 U.S. 218 (1964) (closing of public schools in one county to avoid desegregation so that white students could attend private schools which received state grants and tax credits held violative of Equal Protection Clause).

[29]*Moose Lodge 107* v. *Irvis,* 407 U.S. 163 (1972) (refusal of lodge, a private club licensed by a state to serve alcoholic beverages on its premises, to serve a black solely because of his race held not violative of Equal Protection Clause unless the state is significantly involved in the invidious discrimination).

[30]*Palmer* v. *Thompson,* 403 U.S. 217 (1971) (a state act is not violative of the equal protection of the laws solely because of the motivations of the persons supporting a discriminatory policy).

cases. Griffin appealed to the Illinois Supreme Court on the grounds that a denial of a free transcript to poor defendants violated the Fourteenth Amendment's guarantee of equal protection of the laws. The Illinois Supreme Court denied him relief, and the United States Supreme Court granted certiorari.

Mr. Justice BLACK announced the judgment of the Court and an opinion in which the CHIEF JUSTICE (WARREN), Mr. Justice DOUGLAS and Mr. Justice CLARK join.

* * *

Counsel for Illinois concedes that these petitioners needed a transcript in order to get adequate appellate review of their alleged trial errors. There is no contention that petitioners were dilatory in their efforts to get appellate review, or that the Illinois Supreme Court denied review on the ground that the allegations of trial error were insufficient. We must therefore assume for purposes of this decision that errors were committed in the trial which would merit reversal, but that the petitioners could not get appellate review of those errors solely because they were too poor to buy a stenographic transcript. . . .

Providing equal justice for poor and rich, weak and powerful alike is an age-old problem. . . . Our own constitutional guaranties of due process and equal protection both called for procedures in criminal trials which allow no invidious discriminations between persons and different groups of persons. Both equal protection and due process emphasize the central aim of our entire judicial system—all people charged with crime must, so far as the law is concerned, "stand on an equality before the bar of justice in every American court." . . .

Surely no one would contend that either a State or the Federal Government could constitutionally provide that defendants unable to pay court costs in advance should be denied the right to plead not guilty or to defend themselves in court. Such a law would make the constitutional promise of a fair trial a worthless thing. Notice, the right to be heard, and the right to counsel would under such circumstances be meaningless promises to the poor. In criminal trials a State can no more discriminate on account of poverty than on account of religion, race, or color. Plainly the ability to pay costs in advance bears no rational relationship to a defendant's guilt or innocence and could not

be used as an excuse to deprive a defendant of a fair trial. . . .

There is no meaningful distinction between a rule which would deny the poor the right to defend themselves in a trial court and one which effectively denies the poor an adequate appellate review accorded to all who have money enough to pay the costs in advance. It is true that a State is not required by the Federal Constitution to provide appellate courts or a right to appellate review at all. . . . But that is not to say that a State that does grant appellate review can do so in a way that discriminates against some convicted defendants on account of their poverty. Appellate review has now become an integral part of the Illinois trial system for finally adjudicating the guilt or innocence of a defendant. Consequently at all stages of the proceedings the Due Process and Equal Protection Clauses protect persons like petitioners from invidious discriminations. . . .

All of the States now provide some method of appeal from criminal convictions, recognizing the importance of appellate review to a correct adjudication of guilt or innocence. Statistics show that a substantial proportion of criminal convictions are reversed by state appellate courts. Thus to deny adequate review to the poor means that many of them may lose their life, liberty or property because of unjust convictions which appellate courts would set aside. Many States have recognized this and provided aid for convicted defendants who have a right to appeal and need a transcript but are unable to pay for it. A few have not. Such a denial is a misfit in a country dedicated to affording equal justice to all and special privileges to none in the administration of its criminal law. There can be no equal justice where the kind of trial a man gets depends on the amount of money he has. Destitute defendants must be afforded as adequate appellate review as defendants who have money enough to buy transcripts.

The Illinois Supreme Court denied these petitioners relief under the Post-Conviction Act because of its holding that no constitutional rights were violated. In view of our holding to the contrary the State Supreme Court may decide that petitioners are now entitled to a transcript. . . . We do not hold, however, that Illinois must purchase a stenographer's transcript in every case where a defendant cannot buy it. The Supreme Court may find other means of affording adequate and effective appellate review to indigent defendants. For example, it may be that bystanders' bills of exceptions or other methods of reporting trial proceedings could be used in some cases. The Illinois Supreme Court appears to have broad power to promulgate rules of procedure and appellate practice. We are confident that the State will provide corrective rules to meet the problem which this case lays bare.

Vacated and remanded.

Mr. Justice FRANKFURTER, concurring in the judgment.

* * *

. . . It is now settled that due process of law does not require a State to afford review of criminal judgments.

Nor does the equal protection of the laws deny a State the right to make classifications in law when such classifications are rooted in reason. . . .

But neither the fact that a State may deny the right of appeal altogether nor the right of a State to make an appropriate classification, based on differences in crimes and their punishment, nor the right of a State to lay down conditions it deems appropriate for criminal appeals, sanctions differentiations by a State that have no relation to a rational policy of criminal appeal or authorizes the imposition of conditions that offend the deepest presuppositions of our society. Surely it would not need argument to conclude that a State could not, within its wide scope of discretion in these matters, allow an appeal for persons convicted of crimes punishable by imprisonment of a year or more, only on payment of a fee of $500. Illinois, of course, has done nothing so crude as that. But Illinois has said, in effect, that the Supreme Court of Illinois can consider alleged errors occurring in a criminal trial only if the basis for determining whether there were errors is brought before it by a bill of exceptions and not otherwise. From this it follows that Illinois has decreed that only defendants who can afford to pay

for the stenographic minutes of a trial may have trial errors reviewed on appeal by the Illinois Supreme Court. . . . It has thereby shut off means of appellate review for indigent defendants.

This Court would have to be willfully blind not to know that there have in the past been prejudicial trial errors which called for reversal of convictions of indigent defendants, and that the number of those who have not had the means for paying for the cost of a bill of exceptions is not so negligible as to invoke whatever truth there may be in the maxim de minimis.

Law addresses itself to actualities. It does not face actuality to suggest that Illinois affords every convicted person, financially competent or not, the opportunity to take an appeal, and that it is not Illinois that is responsible for disparity in material circumstances. Of course a State need not equalize economic conditions. A man of means may be able to afford the retention of an expensive, able counsel not within reach of a poor man's purse. Those are contingencies of life which are hardly within the power, let alone the duty, of a State to correct or cushion. But when a State deems it wise and just that convictions be susceptible to review by an appellate court, it cannot by force of its exactions draw a line which precludes convicted indigent persons, forsooth erroneously convicted, from securing such a review merely by disabling them from bringing to the notice of an appellate tribunal errors of the trial court which would upset the conviction were practical opportunity for review not foreclosed.

* * *

. . . If (the State) has a general policy of allowing criminal appeals, it cannot make lack of means an effective bar to the exercise of this opportunity. The State cannot keep the word of promise to the ear of those illegally convicted and break it to their hope. But in order to avoid or minimize abuse and waste, a State may appropriately hedge about the opportunity to prove a conviction wrong. When a State not only gives leave for appellate correction of trial errors but must pay for the cost of its exercise by the indigent, it may protect itself so that frivolous appeals are not subsidized and public moneys not needlessly spent. The growing experience of reforms in appellate procedure and sensible, economic modes for securing review still to be devised, may be drawn upon to the end that the State will neither bolt the door to equal justice nor support a wasteful abuse of the appellate process.

It follows that the petitioners must be accorded an appeal from their conviction, either by having the State furnish them a transcript of the proceedings in the trial court, or by any other means, of which we have not been advised, that may be available under Illinois law, so that the errors of which they complain can effectively be brought for review to the Illinois Supreme Court. It is not for us to tell Illinois what means are open to the indigent and must be chosen. Illinois may prescribe any means that are within the wide area of its constitutional discretion.

*   *   *

Mr. Justice BURTON and Mr. Justice MINTON, whom Mr. Justice REED and Mr. Justice HARLAN join, dissenting.

While we do not disagree with the desirability of the policy of supplying an indigent defendant with a free transcript of testimony in a case like this, we do not agree that the Constitution of the United States compels each State to do so with the consequence that, regardless of the State's legislation and practice to the contrary, this Court must hold invalid state appellate proceedings wherever a required transcript has not been provided without cost to an indigent litigant who has requested that it be so provided. It is one thing for Congress and this Court to prescribe such procedure for the federal courts. It is quite another for this Court to hold that the Constitution of the United States has prescribed it for all state courts.

*   *   *

Whether the Illinois statute denies equal protection depends upon whether, first, it is an arbitrary and unreasonable distinction for the legislature to make, between those convicted of a capital offense and those convicted of a lesser offense, as to their right to a free transcript. It seems to us the whole practice of criminal law teaches that there are valid distinctions between the ways in which criminal cases may be looked upon

and treated without violating the Constitution. Very often we have cases where the convicted seek only to avoid the death penalty. As all practicing lawyers know, who have defended persons charged with capital offenses, often the only goal possible is to avoid the death penalty. There is something pretty final about a death sentence.

If the actual practice of law recognizes this distinction between capital and noncapital cases, we see no reason why the legislature of a State may not extend the full benefit of appeal to those convicted of capital offenses and deny it to those convicted of lesser offenses. It is the universal experience in the administration of criminal justice that those charged with capital offenses are granted special considerations. Examples of such will readily occur. All States allow a larger number of peremptory challenges of jurors in capital cases than in other cases. Most States permit changes of venue in capital cases on different terms than in other criminal cases. Some States require a verdict of 12 jurors for conviction in a capital case but allow less than 12 jurors to convict in noncapital cases. On the other side of the coin, most States provide no statute of limitations in capital cases. We think the distinction here made by the Illinois statute between capital cases and noncapital cases is a reasonable and valid one.

Secondly, certainly Illinois does not deny equal protection to convicted defendants when the terms of appeal are open to all, although some may not be able to avail themselves of the full appeal because of their poverty. Illinois is not bound to make the defendants economically equal before its bar of justice. For a State to do so may be a desirable social policy, but what may be a good legislative policy for a State is not necessarily required by the Constitution of the United States. Persons charged with crimes stand before the law with varying degrees of economic and social advantage. Some can afford better lawyers and better investigations of their cases. Some can afford bail, some cannot. Why fix bail at any reasonable sum if a poor man can't make it?

The Constitution requires the equal protection of the law, but it does not require the States to provide equal financial means for all defendants to avail themselves of such laws.

*   *   *

Comments

1. In *Mayer* v. *City of Chicago,* 404 U.S. 189 (1971), the defendant was convicted of two misdemeanors (ordinance violations) and fined $250 on each offense. Because he wished to take an appeal, the defendant petitioned the trial court for a free transcript of the proceedings to support his appeal. Although the trial court found that he was indigent, his request was denied because, under Illinois law, such transcripts were available only to defendants convicted of a felony. The Illinois Supreme Court denied him relief. A unanimous United States Supreme Court, per Brennan, J., held that a state must afford an indigent appellant a "record of sufficient completeness to permit proper consideration of his claims," but that a complete verbatim transcript need not be furnished in all cases because adequate alternatives may provide effective appellate review. However, when the defendant states a colorable need for a full transcript, the state has the burden of showing that less than the complete transcript is required or that an "alternative" will suffice.

2. How can an appellate court adequately review trial proceedings without a sufficiently complete transcript? Does the *Griffin-Mayer* rationale require that convicted defendants be informed of their right to a free transcript on appeal if they are indigent? In many jurisdictions, especially in misdemeanor or ordinance violation cases, no transcript is made of the proceedings unless the defendant hires a court stenographer. Is this practice a denial of equal protection to indigent defendants?

3. The *Griffin-Mayer* principle has been applied rather broadly: *Burns* v. *Ohio,* 360 U.S. 252 (1959) (state may not require indigent defendant to pay a filing fee before being allowed to appeal in one of its courts); *Smith* v. *Bennett,* 365 U.S. 708 (1961) (state may not require indigent defendant to pay filing fee for state habeas corpus petition); *Lane* v. *Brown,* 372 U.S. 477 (1963) (state may not confine to the public defender the final decision as to whether a transcript shall be available to defendant who collaterally attacks his conviction); *Draper* v. *Washington,* 372 U.S. 487 (1963) (state may not withhold transcript from indigent defendant wishing to appeal his conviction on the sole ground that the trial judge concluded the appeal was frivolous) (see also *Eskridge* v. *Washington State Board,* 357 U.S. 214 [1958]); *Long* v. *District Court,* 385 U.S. 192 (1966) (indigent must be given a free transcript for use on appeal of prior hearing in which state habeas corpus was denied); *Gardner* v. *California,* 393 U.S. 367 (1969) (indigent state prisoner petitioning appellate court for habeas corpus entitled to free transcript of lower court's habeas corpus hearing). *Boddie* v. *Connecticut,* 401 U.S. 371 (state filing fee of $60 in divorce cases is denial of equal protection to indigents); *Roberts* v. *LaVallee,* 389 U.S. 40 (1967) (indigent defendant entitled to free transcript of preliminary hearing for use at trial); *Williams* v. *Oklahoma City,* 395 U.S. 814 (1969) (state court's refusal to provide convicted indigent with trial transcript at public expense for purposes of appeal held violative of Equal Protection Clause); *Rinaldi* v. *Yeager,* 384 U.S. 305 (1966) (state law requiring reimbursement to county from inmates' prison work pay for cost of transcripts furnished held violative of Equal

Protection Clause); *Norvell* v. *Illinois,* 373 U.S. 420 (1963) (Equal Protection Clause violated by state court's denial of post-conviction relief to indigent defendant where no trial transcript available due to death of court reporter); *Britt* v. *North Carolina,* 404 U.S. 226 (1971) (state's refusal to furnish indigent defendant with free transcript of prior mistrial held not violative of equal protection where adequate alternative remedy available); *Entsminger* v. *Iowa,* 386 U.S. 748 (1967) (clerk's transcript procedure in which, in the absence of request for full review, modified transcript filed does not contain transcript of evidence or briefs or argument of counsel held denial of equal protection of the laws).

4. In *United States* v. *MacCollom,* 426 U.S. 317 (1976), a majority of the Supreme Court held that (1) an indigent criminal defendant is entitled to a free transcript *on appeal* as a matter of right; but (2) an indigent federal prisoner who collaterally attacks his conviction (under 28 U.S.C. § 2255 — see Appendix A) has no similar right to such a transcript unless he meets the prerequisites of 28 U.S.C. § 753(f), which requires that (1) the indigent defendant convince the trial judge that his § 2255 claim is nonfrivolous, and (2) that the transcript is needed to decide the issues presented. Mr. Justice Stevens (joined in his dissent by Justices Brennan, White, and Marshall) stated that a defendant's right to a transcript should survive even if he fails to take a direct appeal. See Chapter Fourteen, § 14.03.

5. Other equal protection–related decisions by the Supreme Court involving the criminal process include *McGinnis* v. *Royster,* 410 U.S. 263 (1973) (Chapter Fourteen, § 14.01) (state statute denying state prisoners "good time" credit for presentence incarceration in county jails not violative of the equal protection of the laws; *Jackson* v. *Indiana,* 406 U.S. 715 (1972) (the mere filing of criminal charges against a person is insufficient under the Equal Protection Clause to justify providing fewer procedural and substantive protections against indefinite commitment in a mental hospital than are available to all others); *James* v. *Strange,* 407 U.S. 128 (1972) (state statute allowing state to recover expenses from indigent defendant's legal expenses but denying such defendants protective exemptions available to other judgment debtors held denial of equal protection); *Schilb* v. *Kuebel,* 404 U.S. 357 (1971) (Chapter Twelve, § 12.01) (state pretrial bail statute providing for court clerk's retention of part of 10 per cent bail deposit as bail bond costs held constitutional); *North Carolina* v. *Pearce,* 395 U.S. 711 (1969) (Chapter Fourteen, § 14.01) (Equal Protection Clause does not impose an absolute bar to a more severe sentence upon reconviction for same offense); *Johnson* v. *Avery,* 393 U.S. 483 (1969) (prison regulation barring inmates from helping other inmates in preparing legal briefs and petitions for postconviction review held violative of equal protection of the laws) (see also Chapter Nine); *Baxstrom* v. *Herold,* 383 U.S. 107 (1966) (state may not deny jury review for persons civilly committed to a mental hospital at expiration of penal sentence while allowing such review to all other persons); *Ferguson* v. *Skrupa,* 372 U.S. 726 (1963) (state law making it a crime for any person to engage in the business of "debt adjusting" except as incident to the lawful practice of law held constitutional); *Beck* v. *Washington,* 369 U.S. 541 (1962) (failure of a state to follow certain procedures in questioning grand jurors as to their

bias or prejudice against an accused without more not violative of equal protection); *Oyler* v. *Boles,* 368 U.S. 448 (1962) (policy of selective enforcement does not violate equal protection of the laws where selection is not deliberately based on some unjustifiable standard such as race, religion, or other arbitrary classification); *Douglas* v. *Green,* 363 U.S. 192 (1960) (failure of highest court of a state to provide an indigent defendant with adequate remedy to present appeal without paying docket fees is violative of equal protection); *Police Department of City of Chicago* v. *Mosley,* 408 U.S. 92 (1972) (city ordinance prohibiting all picketing within 150 feet of a school except the peaceful picketing of any school involved in a labor dispute held violative of equal protection of the laws) (to the same effect is *Grayned* v. *City of Rockford,* 408 U.S. 104 [1972]); *Massachusetts Board of Retirement* v. *Murgia,* 427 U.S. 307 (1976) (Chapter Ten, § 10.03) (mandatory retirement of uniformed state police officers at age 50 held constitutional); *Ross* v. *Moffitt,* 417 U.S. 600 (1974) (Chapter Seven, § 7.02) (Equal Protection Clause does not require that court-appointed counsel be provided to indigent defendants in discretionary appeals following counsel on first appeal as a matter of right); *Douglas* v. *California,* 372 U.S. 353 (1963) (denial of counsel to indigent defendant on first appeal as a matter of right violative of equal protection of the laws); *Estelle* v. *Williams,* 425 U.S. 501 (1976) (Chapter Seven, § 7.03) (compelling incarcerated defendant to stand trial in jail clothes while defendants released on bail prior to trial permitted to wear civilian clothes held violative of Equal Protection Clause).

Fines and the Indigent

TATE v. SHORT

Supreme Court of the United States, 1971
401 U.S. 396, 92 S. Ct. 410, 28 L. Ed. 2d 130

The facts are stated in the opinion.

Mr. Justice BRENNAN delivered the opinion of the Court.

Petitioner accumulated fines of $425 on nine convictions in the Corporation Court of Houston, Texas, for traffic offenses. He was unable to pay the fines because of indigency and the Corporation Court, which otherwise has no jurisdiction to impose prison sentences, committed him to the municipal prison farm according to the provisions of a state statute and municipal ordinance which required that he remain there a sufficient time to satisfy the fines at the rate of five dollars for each day; this required that he serve 85 days at the prison farm. After 21 days in custody, petitioner was released on bond when he applied to the County Criminal Court of Harris County for a writ of habeas corpus. He alleged that: "Because I am too poor, I am, therefore, unable to pay the accumulated fine of $425." The county court held that "legal cause has been shown for the imprisonment," and denied the application. The Court of Criminal Appeals of Texas affirmed, stating: "We overrule appellant's contention that because he is too poor to pay the fines his imprisonment is unconstitutional." 445 S.W.2d 210 (1969). . . . We reverse on the authority of our decision in Williams v. Illinois, 399 U.S. 235 (1970) [Chapter Twelve, § 12.02].

* * *

Although the instant case involves offenses punishable by fines only, petitioner's imprisonment for nonpayment constitutes precisely the same unconstitutional discrimination since . . . petitioner was subjected to imprisonment solely because of his indigency. . . . "[T]he Constitution prohibits the State from imposing a fine as a sei tence and then automatically converting it into a jail term solely because the defendant is indigent and cannot forthwith pay the fine in full."

* * *

There are, however, other alternatives to which the State may constitutionally resort to serve its concededly valid interest in enforcing payment of fines. We repeat our observation in Williams in that regard: . . .

"The State is not powerless to enforce judgments against those financially unable to pay a fine; indeed, a different result would amount to inverse discrimination since it would enable an indigent to avoid both the fine and imprisonment for nonpayment whereas other defendants must always suffer one or the other conviction.

"It is unnecessary for us to canvass the numerous alternatives to which the State by legislative enactment — or judges within the scope of their authority — may resort in order to avoid imprisoning an indigent beyond the statutory maximum for involuntary nonpayment of a fine or court costs. Appellant has suggested several plans, some of which are already utilized in some States, while others resemble those proposed by various studies. The State is free to choose from among the variety of solutions already proposed and, of course, it may devise new ones."

We emphasize that our holding today does not suggest any constitutional infirmity in imprisonment of a defendant with the means to pay a fine who refuses or neglects to do so. Nor is our decision to be understood as precluding imprisonment as an enforcement method when alternative means are unsuccessful despite the defendant's reasonable efforts to satisfy the fines by those means; the determination of the constitutionality of imprisonment in that circumstance must await the presentation of a concrete case.

Reversed and remanded.

Mr. Justice BLACKMUN, concurring.

The Court's opinion is couched in terms of being constitutionally protective of the indigent defendant. I merely add the observation that the reversal of this Texas judgment may well encourage state and municipal legislatures to do away with the fine and to have the jail term as the only punishment for a broad range of traffic offenses. Eliminating the fine whenever it is prescribed as alternative punishment avoids the equal protection issue that indigency occasions and leaves only possible Eighth Amendment considerations. If, as a nation, we ever reach that happy point where we are willing to set our personal convenience to one side and we are really serious about resolving the problems of traffic irresponsibility and the frightful carnage it spews upon our highways, a development of that kind may not be at all undesirable.

Comment

1. In *Williams* v. *Illinois* (1970) (Chapter Twelve, § 12.02), which was cited in *Tate,* the Court held that an indigent defendant who is unable to pay a fine imposed cannot be incarcerated beyond the *maximum term* of imprisonment allowed by statute. In light of *Williams-Tate,* is it constitutionally permissible for a judge to sentence a defendant to "$60 or 60 days" and sentence him to 60 days, or any days, in jail if he is indigent? What are some of the "numerous alternatives" available to the states to avoid imprison-

ing an indigent beyond the statutory maximum for involuntary non-payment of a fine? Which is a more severe punishment, a $1,000 fine to a man of moderate means or 60 days in jail to an indigent?

Repaying the State for the Cost of Legal Services

FULLER v. OREGON

Supreme Court of the United States, 1974
417 U.S. 40, 94 S. Ct. 2116, 40 L. Ed. 2d 642

Fuller pleaded guilty to sodomy in the third degree in an Oregon state court. Because he was indigent, he was represented by court-appointed counsel, who hired an investigator to aid in gathering facts for his defense. The investigator's fees were paid by the state. Fuller was sentenced to five years' probation on the condition, in part, that he reimburse the county for the fees and expenses of the attorney and investigator whose services had been provided for him because of his indigent status and under an Oregon recoupment statute. The Oregon Court of Appeals rejected his claim on appeal that the recoupment statute violated the Fourteenth Amendment guarantee of equal protection of the laws. The United States Supreme Court granted certiorari.

Mr. Justice STEWART delivered the opinion of the Court.

* * *

Oregon mandates that every defendant in a criminal case be assigned a lawyer at state expense if "[i]t appears to the court that the defendant is without means and is unable to obtain counsel." ... As part of a recoupment statute passed in 1971, Oregon requires that in some cases all or part of the "expenses specially incurred by the state in prosecuting the defendant" ... be repaid to the State, and that when a convicted person is placed on probation, repayment of such expenses may be made a condition of probation. These expenses include the costs of the convicted person's legal defense.

As the Oregon appellate court noted in its opinion in this case, however, the requirement of repayment "is never mandatory." ... Rather, several conditions must be satisfied before a person may be required to repay the costs of his legal defense. First, a requirement of repayment may be imposed only upon a *convicted* defendant; those who are acquitted, whose trials end in mistrial or dismissal, and those whose convictions are overturned upon appeal face no possibility

of being required to pay. ... Second, a court may not order a convicted person to pay these expenses unless he "is or will be able to pay them." ... The sentencing court must "take account of the financial resources of the defendant and the nature of the burden that payment of costs will impose." As the Oregon court put the matter in this case, no requirement to repay may be imposed if it appears at the time of sentencing that "there is no likelihood that a defendant's indigency will end." ... Third, a convicted person under an obligation to repay "may at any time petition the court which sentenced him for remission of the payment of costs or of any unpaid portion thereof." ... The court is empowered to remit if payment "will impose manifest hardship on the defendant or his immediate family...."

Finally, no convicted person may be held in contempt for failure to repay if he shows that "his default was not attributable to an intentional refusal to obey the order of the court or to a failure on his part to make a good faith effort to make the payment...."

Thus, the recoupment statute is quite clearly directed only at those convicted defendants who are indigent at the time of the criminal proceedings against them but who subsequently gain the ability to pay the expenses of legal representation. Defendants with no likelihood of having the means to repay are not put under even a conditional obligation to do so, and those upon whom a conditional obligation is imposed are not subjected to collection procedures until their indigency has ended and no "manifest hardship" will result. The contrast with appointment of counsel procedures in States without recoupment requirements is thus relatively small: a lawyer is provided at the expense of the State to all defendants who are unable, even momentarily, to hire one, and the obligation to repay the State accrues only to those who later acquire the means to do so without hardship.

The petitioner's first contention is that Oregon's recoupment system violates the Equal Protection Clause of the Fourteenth Amendment because of various classifications explicitly or implicitly drawn by the legislative provisions. He calls attention to our decision in James v. Strange, 407 U.S. 128 (1972), which held invalid under the Equal Protection Clause a law enacted by Kansas that was somewhat similar to the legislation now before us. But the offending aspect of the Kansas statute was its provision that in an action to compel repayment of counsel fees "[n]one of the exemptions provided for in the code of civil procedure (for collection of other judgment debts) shall apply to any such judgment...," ... a provision which "strip[ped] from indigent defendants the array of protective exemptions Kansas has erected for other civil judgment debtors...." ... The Court found that the elimination of the exemptions normally available to judgment debtors "embodie[d] elements of punitiveness and discrimination which violate the rights of citizens to equal treatment under the law." ...

The Oregon statute under consideration here suffers from no such infirmity. As the Oregon Court of Appeals observed, "[n]o denial of the exemptions from execution afforded to other judgment debtors is included in the Oregon statutes." ... Indeed, a separate provision directs that "[a] judgment that the defendant pay money, either as a fine or as costs and disbursements of the action, or both, shall be docketed as a judgment in a civil action and with like effect." ... The convicted person from whom recoupment is sought thus retains all the exemptions accorded other judgment debtors,

in addition to the opportunity to show at any time that recovery of the costs of his legal defense will impose "manifest hardship." ... The legislation before us, therefore, is wholly free of the kind of discrimination that was held in James v. Strange to violate the Equal Protection Clause.

The petitioner contends further, however, that the Oregon statute denies equal protection of the laws in another way — by discriminating between defendants who are convicted, on the one hand, and those who are not convicted or whose convictions are reversed, on the other. Our review of this distinction, of course, is a limited one. As the Court stated in James v. Strange: "We do not inquire whether this statute is wise or desirable.... Misguided laws may nonetheless be constitutional." ... Our task is merely to determine whether there is "some rationality in the nature of the class singled out." Rinaldi v. Yeager, 384 U.S. 305 (1966).... In Rinaldi the Court found impermissible New Jersey's decision to single out prisoners confined to state institutions for imposition of an obligation to repay to the State costs incurred in providing free transcripts of trial court proceedings required by this Court's decision in Griffin v. Illinois [supra]. The legislative decision to tax those confined to prison but not those also convicted but given a suspended sentence, probation, or a fine without imprisonment was found to be invidiously discriminatory and thus violative of the requirements of the Equal Protection Clause. In the case before us, however, the sole distinction is between those who are ultimately convicted and those who are not.

We conclude that this classification is wholly noninvidious. A defendant whose trial ends without conviction or whose conviction is overturned on appeal has been seriously imposed upon by society without any conclusive demonstration that he is criminally culpable. His life has been interrupted and subjected to great stress, and he may have incurred financial hardship through loss of job or potential working hours. His reputation may have been greatly damaged. The imposition of such dislocations and hardships without an ultimate conviction is, of course, unavoidable in a legal system that requires proof of guilt beyond a reasonable doubt and guarantees important procedural protections to every defendant in a criminal trial. But Oregon could surely decide with objective rationality that when a defendant has been forced to submit to a criminal prosecution that does not end in conviction, he will be freed of any potential liability to reimburse the State for the costs of his defense. This legislative decision reflects no more than an effort to achieve elemental fairness and is a far cry from the kind of invidious discrimination that the Equal Protection Clause condemns.

* * *

...Oregon's recoupment statute merely provides that a convicted person who later becomes able to pay for his counsel may be required to do so. Oregon's legislation is tailored to impose an obligation only upon those with a foreseeable ability to meet it, and to enforce that obligation only against those who actually become able to meet it without hardship.

Affirmed.

[Mr. Justice DOUGLAS concurred.]

Mr. Justice MARSHALL, with whom Mr. Justice BRENNAN joins, dissenting.

In my view, the Oregon recoupment statute at issue in this case discriminates against indigent defendants in violation of the Equal Protection Clause and the principles established by this Court in James v. Strange, 407 U.S. 128 (1972). In that case we held unconstitutional under the Equal Protection Clause a Kansas recoupment statute because it failed to provide equal treatment between indigent defendants and other civil judgment debtors. We relied on the fact that indigent defendants were not entitled to the protective exemptions Kansas had erected for other civil judgment debtors.

The Oregon recoupment statute at issue here similarly provides unequal treatment between indigent defendants and other civil judgment debtors. The majority obfuscates the issue in this case by focusing solely on the question whether the Oregon statute affords an indigent the same protective exemptions provided other civil debtors. True, as construed by the Oregon Court of Appeals, the statute does not discriminate in this regard. But the treatment it affords indigent defendants remains unequal in another, even more fundamental, respect. The important fact which the majority ignores is that under Oregon law, the repayment of the indigent defendant's debt to the State can be made a condition of his probation, as it was in this case. Petitioner's failure to pay his debt can result in his being sent to prison. In this respect the indigent defendant in Oregon, like the indigent defendant in James v. Strange, is treated quite differently from other civil judgment debtors.

Petitioner's "predicament under this statute comes into sharper focus when compared with that of one who has hired counsel in his defense." ... Article 1, § 19, of the Oregon Constitution provides that "[t]here shall be no imprisonment for debt, except in case of fraud or absconding debtors." Hence, the nonindigent defendant in a criminal case in Oregon who does not pay his privately retained counsel, even after he obtains the means to do so, cannot be imprisoned for such failure. The lawyer in that instance must enforce his judgment through the normal routes available to a creditor—by attachment, lien, garnishment, or the like. Petitioner, on the other hand, faces five years behind bars if he fails to pay his "debt" arising out of the appointment of counsel.

Article 1, § 19 of the Oregon Constitution is representative of a fundamental state policy consistent with the modern rejection of the practice of imprisonment for debt as unnecessarily cruel and essentially counterproductive.

Since Oregon chooses not to provide imprisonment for debt for well-heeled defendants who do not pay their retained counsel, I do not believe it can, consistent with the Equal Protection Clause, imprison an indigent defendant for his failure to pay the costs of his appointed counsel. For as we held in James v. Strange, a State may not "impose unduly harsh or discriminatory terms merely because the obligation is to the public treasury rather than to a private creditor." ...

I would therefore hold the Oregon recoupment statute unconstitutional under the Equal Protection Clause insofar as it permits payment of the indigent defendant's debt to be made a condition of his probation. I respectfully dissent.

Comment

1. Suppose a state recoupment statute requires *both* convicted and acquitted defendants to repay the costs of state-provided legal services — would that be a denial of due process? Can a legally innocent defendant be required to repay the state for the costs of legal services provided him? Does the Oregon recoupment statute encourage indigents who are convicted and ordered to repay the state the cost of legal services to avoid employment or otherwise secrete their income? Which, in your opinion, is the more persuasive argument in *Fuller* — the majority or dissenting position?

Escape of an Inmate During Pendency of His Appeal

ESTELLE v. DORROUGH

Supreme Court of the United States, 1975
420 U.S. 534, 95 S. Ct. 1173, 43 L. Ed. 2d 790

Jerry Mack Dorrough was convicted in a Texas state court of robbery and sentenced to 25 years' imprisonment. After he had filed an appeal to the Texas Court of Criminal Appeals, he escaped from jail. He was recaptured two days later. After his recapture, the Texas Court of Criminal Appeals dismissed his appeal pursuant to a Texas law (Art. 44.09 Texas Code of Criminal Procedure) which provides for the automatic dismissal of such a pending appeal by an escaped felon unless the felon voluntarily surrenders within 10 days of his escape. His petition for a writ of habeas corpus in the United States District Court (N.D. Tex.) on the grounds that the dismissal of his appeal denied him equal protection of the laws under the Fourteenth Amendment was denied. The United States Court of Appeals (5th Cir.) reversed and held that the Texas law permitting automatic dismissals of appeals denied Dorrough equal protection of the law. The United States Supreme Court granted certiorari.

PER CURIAM.

* * *

The Court of Appeals correctly recognized that there is no federal constitutional right to state appellate review of state criminal convictions.... Disposition by dismissal of pending appeals of escaped prisoners is a longstanding and established principle of American law.... This Court itself has long followed the practice of declining to review the convictions of escaped criminal defendants. ... Thus in Molinaro v. New Jersey, 396 U.S. 365 (1970), we dismissed the appeal of an escaped criminal defendant, stating that no persuasive reason exists to adjudicate the merits of such a case and that

an escape "disentitles the defendant to call upon the resources of the Court for determination of his claims." ... In Allen v. Georgia, 166 U.S. 128 (1897), we upheld as against a constitutional due process attack a state court's dismissal of the appeal of an escaped prisoner and its refusal to reinstate the appeal upon his later recapture....

The Texas courts have found similar ends served by Art. 44.09. It discourages the felony of escape and encourages voluntary surrenders. It promotes the efficient, dignified operation of the Texas Court of Criminal Appeals.

The Court of Appeals, however, found two classifications created by the statute to lack any rational relation to its purposes and hence concluded that the statute was unconstitutional as violative of the Equal Protection Clause. That court recognized that appeals from state criminal convictions are not "explicitly or implicitly guaranteed by the Constitution," ... and that this Court in dealing with equal protection challenges to state regulation of the right of appeal in criminal cases had applied the traditional rational basis test.... [T]his Court [has] said: " 'The Constitution does not require things which are different in fact ... to be treated in law as though they were the same.' ... Hence, legislation may impose special burdens upon defined classes in order to achieve permissible ends. But the Equal Protection Clause does require that, in defining a class subject to legislation, the distinctions that are drawn have 'some relevance to the purpose for which the classification is made.' " ...

The Court of Appeals thought that this test rendered the statute invalid for two reasons. First, while the statute provides for reinstatement of the appeal of most escaped felons only if they voluntarily surrender within 10 days, the Texas Court of Criminal Appeals may in its discretion reinstate the appeals of prisoners under a sentence of life imprisonment or death if they are returned to custody within 30 days. Second, the statute applies only to those prisoners with appeals pending at the time of their escape; prisoners who have not invoked the appellate process by filing an appeal at the time of their escape may still appeal after recapture if applicable appellate time limits have not run. We disagree with the analysis of the Court of Appeals, and find that neither of these distinctions offends the Equal Protection Clause.

Insofar as the separate treatment of prisoners under a sentence of life imprisonment or death is concerned, we see no reason why the Texas Legislature was not free to separate out these two most severe sentences from other terms of imprisonment, and provide an additional period of discretionary review for them but not for the remainder. The Court of Appeals determined that under Texas law a prisoner serving a sentence for a term greater than 60 years would not be eligible for parole any sooner than a prisoner under life sentence, and from that fact concluded that there could be no rational distinction between those serving a life term and those serving a term in excess of 60 years. It is not altogether clear how respondent, who himself has been sentenced to 25 years, could assert the rights of those under term sentences of 60 years or more. But apart from this difficulty, we see no reason why the Texas legislature could not focus on the actual severity of the sentence imposed in making distinctions, rather than on the collateral consequence of sentence elaborated by the Court of Appeals. The State of Texas could reasonably balance its concern with deterring escapes and encouraging surrenders with its alternate interest in allowing the validity of particularly severe sentences to be tested by appellate review. In doing so, it was not required to draw lines with "mathematical nicety." ...

Nor do we find the statutory limitation of the dismissal requirement to those prisoners with appeals pending at the time of their escape violative of the Equal Protection Clause. The Court of Appeals felt that the statute was "underinclusive" for this reason, since a prisoner who had not invoked the appellate process by filing an appeal at the time of his escape might still appeal after recapture if the prescribed times for filing an appeal had not expired.

Criminal defendants in Texas are subject to relatively stringent time limits for filing their appeals. Since an escaped defendant cannot comply with the required appellate steps during the time he is not confined, these time limits serve much the same function as Art. 44.09. Whatever difference in treatment exists between the class of prisoners who escape, return, and are nonetheless able to file an appeal, and those whose appeals are dismissed pursuant to Art. 44.09, is sufficiently rational to withstand a challenge based on the Equal Protection Clause. Texas was free to deal more severely with those who simultaneously invoked the appellate process within the time permitted by law. While each class of prisoners sought to escape, the first did so in the very midst of their invocation of the appellate process, while the latter did so before returning to custody and commencing that process. If Texas is free to adopt a policy which deters escapes by prisoners, as all of our cases make clear it is, it is likewise free to impose more severe sanctions on those whose escape is reasonably calculated to

disrupt the very appellate process which they themselves have set in motion....
Reversed.

Mr. Justice STEWART, with whom Mr. Justice BRENNAN and Mr. Justice MARSHALL join, dissenting.

* * *

... I think the Court has failed to come to grips with the real constitutional defect in the challenged statute.

In summarily reversing the judgment before us the Court relies upon decisions establishing the long-settled "practice of declining to review the convictions of escaped criminal defendants." ... But these decisions have universally been understood to mean only that a court may properly dismiss an appeal of a fugitive convict when, and because, he is not within the custody and control of the court. Until today, this Court has never intimated that under the rule of [our decisions] a court might dismiss an appeal of an escaped criminal defendant at a time when he has been returned to custody, and thus to the court's power and control.

The rationale for the dismissal of an appeal when the appellant is at large is clearly stated in [another] decision:

"It is clearly within our discretion to refuse to hear a criminal case in error, unless the convicted party, suing out the writ, is where he can be made to respond to any judgment we may render. In this case it is admitted that the plaintiff in error has escaped, and is not within the control of the court below, either actually, by being in custody, or constructively, by being out on bail. If we affirm the judgment, he is not likely to appear to submit to his sentence. If we reverse it and order a new trial, he will appear or not, as he may consider most for his

interest. Under such circumstances, we are not inclined to hear and decide what may prove to be only a moot case." ...

Here, as the Court notes, Dorrough was recaptured two days after his flight. And, as the Court also notes, his appeal was dismissed after his recapture. In this situation, the rule of [our earlier decisions] provides no support whatever for the Texas law that deprived Dorrough of his right to appeal.

If the challenged statute can be sustained, it must rest upon the alternative ground advanced by the Court—that, as a punitive and deterrent measure enacted in the exercise of the State's police power, it "discourages the felony of escape and encourages voluntary surrender." But the statute imposes totally irrational punishments upon those subject to its application. If an escaped felon has been convicted in violation of law, the loss of his right to appeal results in his serving a sentence that under law was erroneously imposed. If, on the other hand, his trial was free of reversible error, the loss of his right to appeal results in no punishment at all. And those whose convictions would have been reversed if their appeals had not been dismissed serve totally disparate sentences, dependent not upon the circumstances of their escape, but upon whatever sentences may have been meted out under their invalid convictions. In my view, this random pattern of punishment cannot be considered a rational means of enforcing the State's interest in deterring and punishing escapes....

* * *

I would affirm the judgment of the Court of Appeals.

[Mr. Justice DOUGLAS wrote a dissenting opinion.]

Comments

1. Suppose the right of appeal from a criminal conviction was of a constitutional dimension. Would the Texas law allowing a dismissal of an appeal following a defendant's escape from jail survive constitutional scrutiny as a "voluntary, intelligent, and knowing" waiver of a constitutional right?

2. In recent years, the Supreme Court has indicated by dicta that there is no constitutional right to an appeal following a criminal conviction. Suppose a state decided to abolish all appeals in crimi-

nal cases to lighten the docket of its appellate courts and to save the often heavy costs of defending such appeals? Would that be a denial of equal protection, since all other jurisdictions permit criminal appeals? Suppose a state abolished all appeals except in capital cases. Would that be a denial of equal protection to defendants convicted of noncapital offenses? Suppose a state permitted an appeal following felony but not misdemeanor convictions?

3. Some recent lower federal and state court decisions involving the equal protection of the laws include: *Commonwealth* v. *MacKenzie,* 334 N.E.2d 613 (Mass. 1975) (state statute which imposes criminal liability on a man found guilty of fathering an illegitimate child, but not on the mother, held denial of equal protection of the laws); *People* v. *Williams,* 336 N.E.2d 26 (Ill. App. 1975) (state statute restricting aggravated incest to fathers and stepfathers held not violative of the Equal Protection Clause); *State* v. *Donovan,* 344 A.2d 401 (Me. 1975) (state's prohibiting of marijuana use while permitting use of alcohol and tobacco held not violative of the Equal Protection Clause); *United States* v. *American Theatre Corp.,* 526 F.2d 48 (8th Cir. 1975) (government has a right under federal law to tax an unsuccessful nonindigent defendant for the cost of prosecution as long as it does so in a nondiscriminatory manner); *Call* v. *McKenzie,* 220 S.E.2d 665 (W. Va. App. 1975) (indigent defendants who plead guilty are entitled upon request to a free transcript for appeal purposes); *Britt* v. *McKenney,* 529 F.2d 44 (1st Cir. 1976) (no equal protection right to a transcript of a state probable cause hearing); *In re Podesto,* 544 P.2d 1297 (Calif. 1976) (state law which makes bail pending appeal discretionary for convicted felons but mandatory for convicted misdemeanants held not violative of the Equal Protection Clause); *City of Minneapolis* v. *Buschette,* 240 N.W.2d 500 (Minn. 1976) (police department's policy of arresting and prosecuting female prostitutes but not their male clients held not violative of equal protection of the laws); *People* v. *Pembrock,* 342 N.E.2d 28 (Ill. App. 1976) (state statute which permits commitment of persons who have suffered from a mental disorder for more than one year, display propensities to commit sex offenses, and have propensities to commit sexual assaults on children held not violative of the Equal Protection Clause); *Liistro* v. *Warden,* 365 A.2d 109 (Conn. 1976) (state statute extending bail to alleged probation violators but not to alleged parole violators not denial of equal protection); *Davis* v. *Director,* 351 A.2d 905 (Md. Ct. Spec. App. 1976) (application of preponderance of the evidence standard for defective delinquents not violative of Equal Protection Clause); *Commonwealth* v. *McQuoid,* 344 N.E.2d 179 (Mass. 1976) (state mandatory jail sentence for possession of unlicensed gun held not violative of the equal protection of the laws); *United States* v. *Ecker,* 479 F.2d 1206 (D.C. Cir. 1976) (defendant confined in mental hospital following insanity-based acquittal may be subjected to release provisions different from those applied to involuntary civil committees); *People* v. *Easton,* 353 N.E.2d 587 (N.Y. Ct. App. 1976) (state statute requiring prosecutorial recommendation as a precondition to a minimum sentence of probation for drug offenders held not violative of equal protection of the laws); *Tucker* v. *Kostos,* 356 N.E.2d 798 (Ill. App. 1976) (equal protection requires that state parolees awaiting a final revocation hearing be afforded the same bail right that probationers awaiting final revocation hearings

have); *Ex parte Tullos*, 541 S.W.2d 167 (Tex. Crim. App. 1976) (state statute which permits confinement for 17-year-old males convicted of DWI [driving while under the influence] but does not permit confinement for females of same age held violative of the Equal Protection Clause); *Autry* v. *Mitchell*, 420 F. Supp. 967 (E.D. N.C. 1976) (state law which requires judge to proclaim as an "outlaw" any person accused of having committed a felony and then having fled to avoid arrest held denial of equal protection); *Thompson* v. *South Carolina Commission on Alcoholism and Drug Abuse*, 229 S.E.2d 718 (S.C. 1976) (state law limiting application of alcoholism treatment act only to those counties with treatment facilities held denial of equal protection of laws); *People* v. *Horan*, ___ P.2d ___ (Col. 1976) (trial before nontenured judge held not violative of Equal Protection Clause) (see also *Palmore* v. *United States*, 411 U.S. 389 [1973] [defendant not denied equal protection when he was found guilty in the Superior Court for the District of Columbia before a judge without lifetime tenure even though federal district judges hold lifetime tenure]); *State* v. *Wolery*, 348 N.E.2d 351 (Ohio 1976) (fact that prosecutor granted immunity to defendant's accomplice but not to defendant held not a denial of equal protection); *State* v. *Hinkle*, 550 P.2d 115 (Ariz. App. 1976) (fact that defendant was indicted by grand jury rather than proceeded against by prosecutor's information not a denial of equal protection); *United States* v. *Bergdoll*, 412 F. Supp. 1308 (D. Del. 1976) (federal statute that prohibits use of marijuana but allows consumption of alcohol and tobacco held not a denial of equal protection); *Sandiford* v. *Commonwealth*, 225 S.E. 409 (Va. 1976) (statute which authorizes presumption that possession of sawed-off shotgun by unnaturalized foreign-born person was "for an offensive or aggressive purpose" held violative of Equal Protection Clause); *Ellis* v. *State*, 227 S.E.2d 304 (S.C. 1976) (rule allowing trial in absentia limited to misdemeanants does not result in denial of equal protection to misdemeanants); *Fant* v. *Fisher*, 414 F. Supp. 807 (D. Okla. 1976) (prisoner not denied equal protection by virtue of fact that he was required to pay for dental treatment received at prison when he was receiving VA benefits totaling $300 per month); *Guan Chow Tok* v. *Immigration and Naturalization Service*, 538 F.2d 36 (2d Cir. 1976) (statute which mandates deportation of aliens who have been convicted of narcotics offenses held not violative of the equal protection of the laws); *Karr* v. *Blay*, 413 F. Supp. 579 (D. Ohio 1976) (state may not imprison indigent defendant for failure to make immediate total payment of a fine); *Foster* v. *Smith*, 384 N.Y.S.2d 591 (N.Y. App. Div. 1976) (statute providing that a parole violator returned with less than one year remaining of his maximum term is ineligible for good behavior time credit held not violative of the equal protection of the laws); *Thomale* v. *Schoen*, 244 N.W.2d 51 (Minn. 1976) (statue authorizing up to $100 for "gate-pay" to prisoner upon his release if he does not have at least $100 in his work fund held not a denial of equal protection of the laws); *Gould* v. *People*, 128 Cal. Rptr. 743 (Cal. App. 1976) (state obscenity statute which exempts motion picture projectionists from punishment held not violative of the Equal Protection Clause); *People* v. *Scott*, 343 N.E.2d 517 (Ill. App. 1976) (evaluation which must be made by trial judge with respect to trial of a misdemeanant for which no imprisonment may be imposed unless accused is represented by counsel held not violative of the equal protection of the laws); *People* v. *Smith*, 548 P.2d 603 (Colo. 1976) (rule providing that notice of right to review shall be given to defendants except in cases following a plea of guilty or nolo contendere held not a violation of the equal protection of the laws); *State* v. *Bolton*, 223 S.E.2d 863 (S.C. 1976) (failure to record closing arguments and make them available to defendant held not a denial of equal protection); *Wooten* v. *State*, 332 So.2d 15 (Fla. 1976) (requirement of mandatory adjudication in DWI cases held not violative of the Equal Protection Clause); *Colvin* v. *State*, 346 N.E.2d 737 (Ind. 1976) (state law under which an accused is entitled to have a presentence report considered prior to sentencing if he is sentenced by a judge but not if sentence is fixed by a jury not violative of equal protection); *People* v. *Estes*, 346 N.E.2d 469 (Ill. App. 1976) (armed robbery statute denying probation for armed robbery not violative of equal protection); *State* v. *Loveland*, 240 N.W.2d 326 (Minn. 1976) (credit given for time served on parole but not for probation, held not violative of the equal protection of the laws); *People* v. *Riddle*, 237 N.W.2d 491 (Mich. App. 1975) (statute prohibiting possession, use, and delivery of marijuana not violative of the equal protection of the laws); *People* v. *McAller*, 341 N.E.2d 72 (Ill. App. 1975) (failure of state to allow defendant to prove his innocence by means of polygraph held not violative of the equal protection of the laws); *State* v. *Patterson*, 220 S.E.2d 600 (N.C. 1975) (indigent defendant not entitled to have the court appoint a psychiatrist of his own choosing); *State* v. *Savin*, 238 N.W.2d 911 (Neb. 1976) (imposition of sentence of imprisonment for 1 to 3 years on defendant convicted of embezzlement held not to violate the equal protection of the laws against contention that greater sentence was imposed on him because he was a lawyer); *People* v. *Williams*, 238 N.W.2d 407 (Mich. App. 1975) (probation condition of payment of cash based on actual ability to pay held not violative of Equal Protection Clause); *State* v. *Lucero*, 541 P.2d 430 (N.M. 1975) (exemption of those standing in close relationship to a felon from scope of statute making it an offense to harbor or aid a felon does not violate the equal protection of the laws); *State* v. *Renfro*, 542 P.2d 366 (Hawaii 1975) (statute criminalizing possession of marijuana while possession of alcohol remained noncriminal held not violative of Equal Protection Clause) (in accord is *State* v. *Leins*, 234 N.W.2d 645 [Iowa 1975]); *State* v. *Callaway*, 542 P.2d 1147 (Ariz. App. 1975) (statutes prohibiting sodomy which are not applicable to consenting married persons but are applicable to consenting unmarried persons held violative of the equal protection of the laws); *State* v. *Lemire*, 345 A.2d 906 (N.H. 1975) (discrepancies in sentences imposed on various defendants for similar crimes committed on the same victim not violative of the Equal Protection Clause); *Nelson* v. *Tullos*, 323 So.2d 539 (Miss. 1975) (imprisonment of indigent defendant for failure to pay traffic fines held violative of the Equal Protection Clause).

The Fable of a Fatty*

by Gilbert Geis, Ph.D.

I have studiously attended to the debates between those who would permit—nay, even encourage—the promiscuous use of pharmaceutical agents such as marihuana and LSD throughout the social order, and those of us who demand that all Americans face up to their decent responsibility to live cleanly, with neither their bodies nor their minds contaminated by artificial exhilarants. The recent public pronouncement by the director of the Food and Drug Administration that he would as soon have his daughter smoke cannabis sativa ("pot") as drink ethyl hydroxide ("booze")—the one legally proscribed, the other, however meretricious, legally sanctioned—only underscores the imperative necessity to outlaw equivalently all forms of self-indulgent and intolerable behavior. Fairness and justice demand no less.

To this end, I am proposing that a new criminal offense be created during the next sessions of the state legislatures and the federal Congress. The new crime will be overweightedness, and it shall be divided into two classes—first-degree obesity and second-degree obesity.

Unlike the narcotic laws, enforcement of the obesity statutes should provide only a minimum number of difficulties. The offender will carry his offense with him, as it were, and he cannot expeditiously shed the tell-tale signs of his culpability in the manner that the narcotic addict flushes away his heroin or disposes of his hypodermic needle.

The degrees of the crime of obesity will also readily yield to precise determination. Persons ten to twenty percent over the normal weight for their height and sex will be guilty of the crime in the second degree. Those twenty percent or more above that weight maintained by normal, law-abiding citizens will be guilty of obesity in the first degree. Juries, if they wish, may regard such factors as bone structure and metabolism rate as mitigating circumstances when they come to recommend dispositions. Certainly factors of temptation, such as those relating to notorious proximity to products of great culinary skill, should provide no legally acceptable excuse for violation. As Justice Holmes once sagely observed: "Laws do not merely require that every man should get as near as he can to the best conduct possible for him. They require him at his own peril to come up to a certain height. They take no account of incapacities, unless the weakness is so marked as to fall into the well-known exceptions, such as lunacy and madness."

Nevertheless, traditional legal standards of mens rea, requiring a guilty mind and a culpable intent, must be scrupulously observed. Normally, it may be assumed that the criminal intent inheres in consequences that reasonable persons might ordinarily anticipate. He or she who consumes items of high caloric content, without compensating energy output, should appreciate that sooner or later the limits of legal tolerance will be transgressed. On occasion, however, an accused may be able to demonstrate satisfactorily that coercion or duress—say a form of force-feeding—precipitated the violation. It is not beyond belief that the intravenous introduction of food substances into an unconscious or otherwise helpless person could adequately excuse the violation. Care should be exercised, however, to see that the defense of irresistible impulse is not abused. It has been wisely noted that no impulse is apt to go unresisted if a policeman is standing behind the potential offender. In addition, morphine addicts clearly are preempted from effectively alleging that prior medical experience with the drug created an overwhelming impulse to repeat the experience. The same may be said about fortuitous introduction to cheese cake, mashed potatoes, and similar items, all of which, it might be noted, are lethal if taken in overdoses. From the viewpoint of law students, it may be hoped that a benign history will protect them from a case in which an offense of first-degree obesity is the product of cannibalism, committed on a raft afloat on the high seas by men in fear of imminent death unless they ingest one of their fellows. Of cases such as this it is truly said, "hard cases make bad law."

The preeminent necessity for new legislation outlawing obesity is so self-evident that it hardly needs detailed exposition. It has been clearly shown that the overweight person represents a serious threat, with a potentially shortened life span. The crime may seemingly be one without a "real" victim, but all of us are the victims of the overweight man or woman who prematurely deprives us of his company and his talents, not to mention his taxes. Overweightedness is a crime of epidemic proportions; its perpetrators characteristically are persons of deceptive conviviality who assiduously inveigh into their ranks the unwary through blandishments of quick, irresponsible pleasure. Families suffer from overweight members just as surely as they suffer from members who are gamblers,

*From *Issues in Criminology*, Vol. 3, No. 2 (1968). Reprinted by permission of the publisher.

adulterers or narcotic addicts. There is the terrible tension of the supper table, all persons intent upon seeing whether the offender has learned to control his habit or whether he is slipping irretrievably into recidivism.

National considerations amply support the call for creation of the new criminal offense and forceful federal and state action against those violators undercutting the virility and vitality of the Nation. Obese persons detract from the war effort. They tend to be sluggish, to indulge in self-satisfied after-meal naps, and more passive pursuits. Research indicates that the obese spend approximately four percent more time at each meal then normal individuals — a finding which, if multiplied out, provides a staggering loss of constructive investment of time and energy. The obese are readily diverted from a task at hand by the nearness of times set aside for good ingestion. Their habits make them particularly vulnerable to enemy blackmail, since they demonstrably lack the will-power and internal strength necessary for self-control so that, tortured by promises of surcease, they will, if permitted to gain positions of trust, divulge those secrets to the preservation of our free society.

It is perhaps not altogether necessary to take cognizance of reports, most of which have not as yet been fully de-classified, that foreign powers may stand behind the flood of high caloric poisons entering our cities and sapping the strength of children and adults alike. We would urge the creation of a new agency to work alongside the United States Customs Service and the Federal Bureau of Narcotics, an agency which would be charged with surveillance of imports; among other items, Israeli halvah, Swiss chocolate, and Italian spaghetti must be turned aside at the borders, and all conceivable efforts must be undertaken to see that a flourishing underworld traffic in these and similar items does not become established. It goes without saying that it will take the concerted efforts of all federal and local authorities to see that spaghetti, in particular, is kept under tight control, for organizations already exist with a special expertise in the handling of such noxious substances.

Standard police practices should prove adequate for apprehending most food addicts. A core of informers will obviously come forward to help identify and ferret out those violators who secrete themselves rather than submit to the procedures society will set up for its own protection. Such informers may reasonably be rewarded by being allowed a certain leeway in their own weight, perhaps a percent or two, and they might on occasion be permitted to keep goods that form part of the underworld commerce in black-market food. A newly created internal cadre of enforcement agents, called the S.S. (for Supermarket Surveillance), could monitor grocery outlets and confectionery stores, placed where there is the greatest likelihood of criminal activity occurring.

It may be anticipated that the courts will come to declare that obesity is not really a crime, and that imprisonment of obese persons is violative of the eighth amendment stipulation concerning "cruel and unusual punishment." Precedent exists in the case of narcotics for such a stand. In the *Robinson* case, Justice Stewart noted that "A state might determine that the general health and welfare required that the victims of these and other human afflictions be dealt with by compulsory treatment, involving quarantine, confinement, or sequestration. But, in the light of the contemporary human knowledge, a law which made a criminal offense of such a disease would doubtless be universally thought to be an affliction of cruel and unusual punishment."

There is always the possibility that the minority opinion in *Robinson* might come to prevail in the manner that dissenting views have so often in Supreme Court history proven over the course of time to be superior to transient responses to immediate problems. The minority stand of Justice Clark is clearly applicable to the obese: "Even if interpreted as penal," Clark said, "the sanction of incarceration for three to twelve months is not unreasonable when applied to a person who has voluntarily placed himself in a condition posing a serious threat to the state."

If the courts are determined to declare obesity a "sickness" rather than a crime, the legislative response is clear. Civil commitment programs can be established at once to treat the obese. Since craving for illegal nourishment is one of the obvious characteristics of this type of offender, it will be necessary for the civil commitment hospitals to be fenced, preferably with barbed wire, and carefully guarded. Commitment to the program will follow the testimony of two duly registered physicians that the felon is indeed beyond the tolerable weight. The accused may, of course, cross-examine all witnesses, and scrupulous care will be taken to see that he is not deprived of this or other of his inalienable rights under the Constitution.

Once institutionalized, the patient will at once be detoxified; that is, various dietetic substances will be given to him in place of his habitual fare. This therapeutic regime will be supplemented by intensive group therapy, which will concentrate upon intrapsychic conditions which have led to the failure to control his emotional dependence. Studies already point to the fact that oedipal complexes, sibling rivalry, oral and anal fixations — particularly these — as well as similar aberrant syndromes are typical of the obese when contrasted to a normal sample of the American population.

It is hardly to be expected that efforts to

enact the necessary legislation will go unopposed. But it seems evident that there exists a widespread foundation from which support may be expected. Theological doctrines have traditionally inveighed against self-indulgence and over-indulgence. Military authorities, beleaguered by the Vietnam campaign, can be expected to see in the new law a return to those fundamental principles which will revitalize our fighting capacities. Opposition may be expected to arise from diverse sources, and to be sizeable. It will undoubtedly have the support of our enemies abroad, who desire to undermine our resolution. Given the obvious good sense of the law, however, there should be only a slim chance of its defeat. The experience and the depth of conviction of those forces behind the present narcotic laws, all of which will undoubtedly be in the forefront of the new campaign, should be more than enough to assure early success.

Rejoinder to Geis*

by Richard R. Korn, Ph.D.

As one of the more obvious members of the new class of offenders which would be created by the new penal law proposed by Geis, I have asked for the privilege of making a brief rejoinder.

As is not infrequently the case with "radical" innovations, Geis's proposal is far from radical enough. Nor is it new. As early as 1886 Samuel Butler, author of *Erewhon*, suggested that all forms of illness caused by overindulgence (including indulgence in bad luck) be treated as crimes. (Actual crimes would, of course, be treated sympathetically, as social illnesses.)

Geis is correct to cite obesity as a national disgrace, an assault on the sanctity of the home, an undermining of the body politic. But why only obesity? To come to the point: if obesity should be a crime, so should emaciation. The one extreme is as culpable as the other. Moreover, emaciation selectively affects a far more criminalistic cohort of the population—the poor—whom everyone knows are by nature more depraved. But the poor are not the only offenders.

In recent years we have all observed a most sinister attack on the natural human figure—particularly the female figure. Any citizen with eyes can confirm this for himself. One of the most scandalous examples is the notorious Twiggy. Twiggy is presented to us as the emerging form of the New Woman. Woman indeed! If Twiggy is a woman, then Venus de Milo is a wart-hog. The subversiveness of this assault on the human psyche can hardly be overemphasized. Psychologists have established beyond doubt the crucial importance of breast feeding for the young. It is not merely the ingestion of the milk that is important: the whole visual and tactile complex of the experience is equally essential. Twiggy and her ilk would condemn the infants of America to a universal experience of breast feeding without breasts; we might as well have our babies suck milk from straws as from those stunted spigots!

The issue is clear. Our holiest tradition demands equal protection of the laws. If obesity is criminal, so is flat-chestedness. What is sauce for the Geis must be sauce for the gender.

*From *Issues in Criminology*, Vol. 3, No. 2 (1968). Reprinted by permission of the publisher.

Part Two

5

FOURTH AMENDMENT PROBLEMS: THE LAW OF ARREST, SEARCH AND SEIZURE

These [Fourth Amendment rights], I protest, are not mere second-class rights but belong in the catalog of indispensable freedoms. Among deprivations of rights, none is so effective in cowing a population, crushing the spirit of the individual and putting terror in every heart. Uncontrolled search and seizure is one of the first and most effective weapons in the arsenal of every arbitrary government.[1]

The right of privacy — the right to be let alone — is perhaps the most cherished right of a free society. The Fourth Amendment provides that the people have a *right* "to be secure in their persons, houses, papers, and effects, against unreasonable searches and seizures." Of course not all searches are prohibited; only those that are *unreasonable*. A search is considered unreasonable if probable cause is lacking, or, absent a showing of "exigent circumstances," if a search or seizure is conducted without a valid search warrant having first been obtained via the judicial process.

Since it is a part of the Bill of Rights, it is axiomatic that the Fourth Amendment represents a restraint on the power of the government to search and seize; hence it serves as a constitutional safeguard against unreasonable governmental invasions of privacy. As Professor Amsterdam noted, "The Bill of Rights in general and the fourth amend-

ment in particular are profoundly anti-government documents."[2] Likewise, the United States Supreme Court specifically noted the amendment's intended application in *Burdeau* v. *McDowell,* 256 U.S. 465, 475 (1921):

The Fourth Amendment gives protection against unlawful searches and seizures, and . . . its protection applies to *government action*. Its origin and history clearly show that it was intended to be a *limitation upon the activities of sovereign authority,* and was not intended to be a limitation upon other than governmental agencies [emphasis added].

In further refining the Fourth Amendment's practical application, the United States Supreme Court in a series of deci-

---

[1]*Brinegar* v. *United States,* 338 U.S. 160, 180 (1949) (Jackson, J., dissenting).

[2]Amsterdam, A., *Perspectives on the Fourth Amendment,* 58 Minn. L. Rev. 349, 353 (1974). Presented as the Oliver Wendell Holmes Lecture Series at the University of Minnesota School of Law, January 22–24, 1974.

sions has noted that "searches conducted outside the judicial process, without prior approval by judge or magistrate, are per se unreasonable . . . subject only to a few specifically established and well-delineated exceptions."[3] The test "is not whether it is reasonable to procure a search warrant, but whether the search was unreasonable."[4]

5.01 HISTORY AND SCOPE OF THE FOURTH AMENDMENT

The primary purpose of the Fourth Amendment was to protect what its framers believed to be the fundamental right to privacy of the citizens of the United States. It should be noted that the subject of freedom from unreasonable searches and seizures was absent from both the Articles of Confederation and the original Constitution of 1787, and the protections afforded by the amendment were not guaranteed until the adoption of the Bill of Rights in 1791.

Although search and seizure abuses did not become of primary concern to the American colonists until the mid 1700's, antecedent problems in England can be traced back to the reign of Henry VIII. From 1538 until 1679, a system of licensing printers existed in England, and to implement enforcement of that system, vast powers of search were conferred upon those responsible for uncovering violators and evidence.[5]

After the Printing Act expired and Parliament failed to renew it, these harsh search and seizure powers were granted to those enforcing various tax laws. Jacob Landynski noted that this transition did not take place without opposition:

One tax law was abolished by Parliament specially on the ground that the searches required "a badge of slavery upon the whole people, exposing every man's house to be entered into, and searched by persons unknown to him."[6]

Perhaps the most notable outcry against the power of the king to search and seize came from William Pitt the Elder in 1763 when he proclaimed:

The poorest man may in his cottage bid defiance to all the force of the Crown. It may be frail; its roof may shake; the wind may blow through it; the storm may enter; the rain may enter—but the King of England cannot enter; all his forces dare not cross the threshold of that ruined tenement![7]

At about the same time that William Pitt was denouncing the enforcement provisions of the cider tax, the American colonies began to feel the strong hand of the Crown through the issuance of the so-called "Writs of Assistance." Becoming quite common after 1750, the Writs of Assistance were issued to officers, usually customs officers, who wanted search warrants good at all times so that places could be searched for contraband both day and night. Under the writs, the inspectors could search any place they chose and seize any property or papers they desired. Of course, with such wide search and seizure powers, the officers readily uncovered violations of the revenue laws, to the pleasure of the Crown and the displeasure of the colonists.

Records indicate that search warrants were common in America at least 100 years before the colonists began to experience the abuses of the Writs of Assistance. In the Massachusetts Colony, for example, the law entitled "Burglary and Theft of 1650" provided that:

When any goods were stolen, the constable "by warrant from authority" was to search any suspect places or houses and if he found the goods or any part thereof or had any ground of suspicion, he was to bring the delinquent or the suspected party to a magistrate to be proceeded against according to law.[8]

Although by 1750 general warrants (Writs of Assistance) were being used and abused, it appears that, despite royal pressure, not all judges were eager to issue writs. As Mr. Justice Douglas pointed out:

Colonial judges were usually appointed at the pleasure of the King, and were customarily

---

[3]*Katz* v. *United States,* 389 U.S. 347, 357 (1967). (See § 5.01, infra).

[4]*McDonald* v. *United States,* 335 U.S. 451, 456 (1948). See also *United States* v. *Rabinowitz,* 339 U.S. 56, 66 (1950), and *Jones* v. *United States,* 357 U.S. 493, 499 (1960).

[5]Landynski, J. W., *Search and Seizure and the Supreme Court* (1966), at 20, 21.

[6]Id. at 25.

[7]Quoted by Justice Douglas in *Frank* v. *Maryland,* 359 U.S. 360, 378–379 (1959) (dissenting opinion).

[8]Smith, J. (ed.), *Colonial Justice in Western Massachusetts, 1639–1702* (1961), at 142.

Tories. Great pressure was put on them to bow to royal will. . . . Prominent in the opposition was Chief Justice William Allen of Pennsylvania, who said, "If you (custom officer) will make oath that you have had an information that they (taxable goods) are in any particular place, I will grant you a writ to search that place, but no general writ to search every house."[9]

One of the first to publicly denounce the use of the writs was James Otis. On February 24, 1761, Otis, representing 63 Boston merchants, made a historic argument to the Boston court, urging that applications for Writs of Assistance be denied. Otis reminded the judges that the security of one's house is an essential liberty: "A man in his home must be as secure as a prince in his castle. A law which violates that privacy is an instrument of slavery and villany."[10] Protesting the ease with which a writ could be obtained, he stated, "Bare suspicion without oath is sufficient. . . . Every man, prompted by revenge, ill-humor, or wantonness to inspect the inside of his neighbor's house, may get a writ of assistance."[11] Otis went on to show that the writs were negotiable, that is, they could be passed from one officer to another, and that once a writ was granted no one could be called to account for its use. Of James Otis' speech, John Adams wrote, "Then and there the child Independence was born."[12]

Although Otis lost his clients' case, the legislature (then called the General Court of Massachusetts) came to his assistance by producing a bill that outlawed general warrants and authorized special writs only. However, the bill was vetoed by the Governor, and thereafter the writs were executed without difficulty in Massachusetts until riots broke out in opposition to the Stamp Act in 1765. Thereafter, it became almost impossible to enforce the writs.[13]

It is interesting to note that while Virginia's Declaration of Rights contained language in opposition to the general writ, the Declaration of Independence, written one month later, did not. While the constitution of Massachusetts provided for the right to be secure from unreasonable searches and seizures, the United States Constitution contained no such provision. In the Massachusetts Constitution of 1780, the right of privacy was specifically set out:

Every subject[14] has a right to be secure from all unreasonable searches, and seizures of his person, his house, his papers, and all his possessions. . . . All warrants [must be] previously supported by oath or affirmation . . . [and] be accompanied with a special designation of the persons or objects of search, arrest, or seizure; and no warrant ought to be issued but in cases, and with formalities, prescribed by the laws.[15]

When the United States Constitution was written in 1787, no bill of rights was included, much less a specific provision to secure protection against unreasonable searches and seizures. Finally, after much outcry from various states including Rhode Island, Virginia, and North Carolina, James Madison proposed a federal bill of rights in Congress on June 8, 1789. Included in that proposal was an amendment calling for protection against unreasonable searches and seizures:

The right of the people to be secure in their persons, their houses, their papers, and their other property, from all unreasonable searches, and seizures, shall not be violated by warrants issued without probable cause, supported by oath or affirmation, or not particularly describing the places to be searched, or the persons or things to be seized.[16]

With minor alterations in wording, the amendment, along with the rest of the Bill of Rights, was submitted to the states for ratification in September, 1789. Finally in December, 1791, Virginia cast the final vote needed for ratification, and the Fourth Amendment became law. At last the weight of the Constitution was placed behind the right of privacy—the right Mr. Justice Brandeis described as "the right to be let alone—the most comprehensive of rights

---

[9]Douglas, W. O., *An Almanac of Liberty* (1954), at 51.

[10]Id. at 247.

[11]Id.

[12]Id.

[13]Landynski, J. W., supra note 6, at 37.

---

[14]It is interesting to note that the word "subject" is used rather than "person" or "citizen."

[15]Taylor, R. J. (ed.), *Massachusetts, Colony to Commonwealth* (1961), at 130.

[16]Schwartz, B., *A Documentary History of the Bill of Rights* (vol. II 1971), at 1016.

and the right most valued by civilized men."[17]

From an examination of the history of the Fourth Amendment, it appears that the amendment was written (1) to end the conflict over the extent of the government's power to search and seize, and (2) to guard against the abuse of the warrant requirement.

In response to the first problem, the opening language of the amendment makes explicit the absolute right of the people to be secure against unreasonable governmental invasions: "The right . . . against unreasonable searches and seizures, shall not be violated. . . ." To guard against abuses of the warrant requirement, the framers were very specific as to what conditions were necessary before judicial authorization was justified: ". . . no Warrants shall issue, but upon probable cause, supported by Oath or affirmation. . . ." Finally, care was taken to outline the content and scope of a search warrant: ". . . particularly describing the place to be searched, and the person or things to be seized."

From a procedural standpoint, the document declared that when conditions existed that would necessitate the issuance of a search warrant (probable cause), and when the warrant was constructed properly (particularized descriptions of persons, places, and things to be seized) and sanctioned by judicial authority (signed by a judge or magistrate after careful review of the facts before him), then a search and seizure conducted in accordance with an official warrant was considered *reasonable* within the meaning of the Fourth Amendment.

Such a "traditional" view of the Fourth Amendment's proscriptions appears to have dominated the thought of legal scholars throughout most of the nineteenth century. In fact, almost no judicial attention was afforded the Fourth Amendment until 1878.[18] In that year the United States Supreme

Court delivered its opinion in the case of *Ex parte Jackson*, 96 U.S. 727. In dictum, the *Jackson* Court noted that the Fourth Amendment prohibited the United States Post Office from opening sealed letters in the mails except when authorized by a warrant.

In 1886, the Supreme Court was again faced with Fourth Amendment interpretation problems, this time in *Boyd* v. *United States*, 116 U.S. 616. Considering the language of the amendment and the problems associated with deliberate violations of its proscriptions by the police, the Court in *Boyd* plainly suggested that evidence gathered in violation of the Fourth Amendment should be excluded from federal criminal trials. Although the Court's suggestion took the form of illustration and argument and was never considered to be a command to the lower courts, the *Boyd* dicta did contribute to the later development of the so-called "exclusionary rule," which was made binding on all federal courts by the Supreme Court's decision in *Weeks* v. *United States*, 232 U.S. 383 (1914). (The exclusionary rule will be discussed further in § 5.03, infra.)

Because a strict interpretation of the Fourth Amendment severely limits the investigatory powers of law enforcement officials, many persons, officials as well as laymen, began to seriously question whether the language of the amendment implied that *only* searches conducted *with warrants* were to be considered "reasonable." Did the Fourth Amendment declare *all* searches conducted without a warrant to be "unreasonable"?

By 1930, support for the proposition that only searches accompanied by a warrant were "reasonable" began to decline. Accordingly, absent any constitutional language appropriate to determine the reasonableness of a search conducted with or without a warrant, the United States Supreme Court assumed the duty of declaring what the law is on a case-by-case basis. As the Court noted in *Go-Bart Import Co.* v. *United States*, 282 U.S. 344 (1931), and again in *United States* v. *Rabinowitz*, 399 U.S. 56 (1950), "What is a reasonable search must be resolved in the facts and circumstances of each case." The net result of this statement, and of the constitutional interpretation underlying it, has been the judi-

---

[17]*Olmstead* v. *United States*, 227 U.S. 438, 478 (1928) (dissenting opinion).

[18]Limited attention was afforded the Fourth Amendment in *Ex parte Burford*, 3 Cranch 448 (1805), *Smith* v. *Maryland*, 18 How. 71 (1855), and *Murray* v. *Hoboken Land Company*, 18 How. 272 (1855).

cial creation of many exceptions to the warrant requirement of the Fourth Amendment.

The scope of the Fourth Amendment's protections represented the focal point in *Katz* v. *United States*, 389 U.S. 347 (1967). Rejecting the so-called "protected places" principle as being too narrow and restrictive, the majority of the *Katz* Court sought to give the Fourth Amendment a more lib-

eral interpretation by identifying a broader range of governmental intrusions that the amendment was designed to prevent. The Court paid particular attention to what parameters might be sufficient to delineate the "right of privacy" concept.[19]

---

[19] For an extended discussion of *Katz,* see generally Amsterdam, A., supra note 1.

"The Fourth Amendment Protects Persons, Not Places"

KATZ v. UNITED STATES

Supreme Court of the United States, 1967
389 U.S. 347, 88 S. Ct. 507, 19 L. Ed. 2d 576

In February, 1965, FBI agents placed microphones on the tops of two public telephone booths after they discovered that Katz used them routinely in suspected gambling activities. Incriminating conversations were recorded and later introduced at trial over Katz's objection. Petitioner was convicted in the United States District Court for the Southern District of California on eight counts of interstate transmission of bets and wagers by telephone in violation of 18 U.S.C. § 1084, and he appealed. The Court of Appeals (9th Cir.) affirmed and the Supreme Court granted certiorari.

Mr. Justice STEWART delivered the opinion of the Court.

The petitioner was convicted ... [of] transmitting wagering information by telephone from Los Angeles to Miami and Boston in violation of a federal statute. At trial the Government was permitted, over the petitioner's objection, to introduce evidence of the petitioner's end of the telephone conversations, overheard by FBI agents who had attached an electronic listening and recording device to the outside of the public telephone booth from which he had placed his calls. In affirming his conviction, the Court of Appeals rejected the contention that the recordings had been obtained in violation of the Fourth Amendment, because "[t]here was no physical entrance into the area occupied by [the petitioner]." We granted certiorari in order to consider the constitutional questions thus presented. Petitioner has phrased those questions as follows:

"A. Whether a public telephone booth is a constitutionally protected area so that evidence obtained by attaching an electronic listening recording device to the top of such a booth is obtained in violation of the right to privacy of the user of the booth.

"B. Whether physical penetration of a constitutionally protected area is necessary before a search and seizure can be said to be violative of the Fourth Amendment to the United States Constitution."

We decline to adopt this formulation of the issues. In the first place the correct solution of Fourth Amendment problems is not necessarily promoted by incantation of the phrase "constitutionally protected area." Secondly, the Fourth Amendment cannot be translated into a general constitutional "right to privacy." That Amendment protects individual privacy against certain kinds of governmental intrusion, but its protections go further, and often have nothing to do with privacy at all. . . . Other provisions of the Constitution protect personal privacy from other forms of governmental invasion.[e] But the protection of a person's *general* right to privacy—his right to be let alone by other people—is, like the protection of his property and of his very life, left largely to the law of the individual states.

Because of the misleading way the issues have been formulated, the parties have attached great significance to the characterization of the telephone booth from which the petitioner placed his calls. The petitioner has strenuously argued that the booth was a "constitutionally protected area." The Government has maintained with equal vigor that it was not. But this effort to decide whether or not a given "area," viewed in the abstract, is "constitutionally protected" deflects attention from the problem presented by this case. For the Fourth Amendment protects people, not places. What a person knowingly exposes to the public, even in his own home or office, is not a subject of Fourth Amendment protection.... But what he seeks to preserve as private, even in an area accessible to the public, may be constitutionally protected....

The Government stresses the fact that the telephone booth from which the petitioner made his calls was constructed partly of glass, so that he was as visible after he entered it as he would have been if he had remained outside. But what he sought to exclude when he entered the booth was not the intruding eye—it was the uninvited ear. He did not shed his right to do so simply because he made his calls from a place where he might be seen. No less than an individual in a business office, in a friend's apartment, or in a taxicab, a person in a telephone booth may rely upon the protection of the Fourth Amendment. One who occupies it, shuts the door behind him, and

---

[e] The First Amendment, for example, imposes limitations upon governmental abridgement of "freedom to associate and privacy in one's associations."... The Third Amendment's prohibition against the unconsented peacetime quartering of soldiers protects another aspect of privacy from government intrusion. To some extent, the Fifth Amendment too "reflects the Constitution's concern for ... '... the right of each individual "to a private enclave where he may lead a private life." ' "...

pays the toll that permits him to place a call is surely entitled to assume that the words he utters into the mouthpiece will not be broadcast to the world. To read the Constitution more narrowly is to ignore the vital role that the public telephone has come to play in private communication.

The Government contends, however, that the activities of its agents in this case should not be tested by Fourth Amendment requirements, for the surveillance technique they employed involved no physical penetration of the telephone booth from which the petitioner placed his calls. It is true that the absence of such penetration was at one time thought to foreclose further Fourth Amendment inquiry, Olmstead v. United States, 277 U.S. 438 (1928), and Goldman v. United States, 316 U.S. 129 (1942), for that Amendment was thought to limit only searches and seizures of tangible property. But "[t]he premise that property interests control the right of the Government to search and seize has been discredited.".... Thus, although a closely divided Court supposed in Olmstead that surveillance without any trespass and without the seizure of any material object fell outside the ambit of the Constitution, we have since departed from the narrow view on which that decision rested. Indeed, we have expressly held that the Fourth Amendment governs not only the seizure of tangible items, but extends as well to the recording of oral statements overheard without any "technical trespass under ... local property law."... Once this much is acknowledged, and once it is recognized that the Fourth Amendment protects people—and not simply "areas"—against unreasonable searches and seizures it becomes clear that the reach of that Amendment cannot turn upon the presence or absence of a physical intrusion into any given enclosure.

We conclude that the underpinnings of Olmstead and Goldman have been so eroded by our subsequent decisions that the "trespass" doctrine there enunciated can no longer be regarded as controlling. The Government's activities in electronically listening to and recording the petitioner's words violated the privacy upon which he justifiably relied while using the telephone booth and thus constituted a "search and seizure" within the meaning of the Fourth Amendment. The fact that the electronic device employed to achieve that end did not happen to penetrate the wall of the booth can have no constitutional significance.

The question remaining for decision ... is whether the search and seizure conducted in this case complied with constitutional standards. In that regard, the Government's position is that its agents acted in an entirely defensible manner: They did not begin their electronic surveillance until investigation of the petitioner's activities had established a strong probability that he was using the telephone in question to transmit gambling information to persons in other States, in violation of federal law. Moreover, the surveillance was limited, both in scope and in duration, to the specific purpose of establishing the contents of the petitioner's unlawful telephonic communications. The agents confined their surveillance to the brief periods during which he used the telephone booth, and they took great care to overhear only the conversation of the petitioner himself.

Accepting this account of the Government's actions as accurate, it is clear that this surveillance was so narrowly circumscribed that a duly authorized magistrate, properly notified of the need for such investigation, specifically informed of the basis on which it was to proceed, and clearly apprised of the precise intrusion it would entail, could constitutionally have authorized, with appropriate safeguards, the very limited search and seizure that the Government asserts in fact took place. Only last Term we sustained the validity of such an authorization, holding that, under sufficiently "precise and discriminate circumstances," a federal court may empower government agents to employ a concealed electronic device "for the narrow and particularized purpose of ascertaining the truth of the ... allegations" of a "detailed factual affidavit alleging the commission of a specific criminal offense." ... [T]he Court in Berger v. State of New York, 388 U.S. 41 (1967), said that "the order authorizing the use of the electronic device" in Osborn "afforded similar protections to those ... of conventional warrants authorizing the seizure of tangible evidence." Through those protections, "no greater invasion of privacy was permitted than was necessary under the circumstances." ... Here, too, a similar judicial order could have accommodated "the legitimate needs of law enforcement" by authorizing the carefully limited use of electronic surveillance.

The Government urges that, because its agents relied upon the decisions in Olmstead and Goldman, and because they did no more here than they might properly have done with prior judicial sanction, we should retroactively validate their conduct. That we cannot do.... They were not required, before commencing the search, to present their estimate of probable cause for detached scrutiny by a neutral magistrate. They were not compelled, during the conduct of the search itself, to observe precise limits established in advance by a specific court order. Nor were they directed, after the search had been completed, to notify the authorizing magistrate in detail of all that had been seized. In the absence of such safeguards, this Court has never sustained a search upon the sole ground that officers reasonably expected to find evidence of a particular crime and voluntarily confined their activities to the least intrusive means consistent with that end.... Searches conducted outside the judicial process, without prior approval by judge or magistrate, are per se unreasonable under the Fourth Amendment—subject only to a few specifically established and well-delineated exceptions....

It is difficult to imagine how any of those exceptions [see § 5.04, infra] could ever apply to the sort of search and seizure involved in this case....

The Government does not question these basic principles. Rather, it urges the creation of a new exception to cover this case. It argues that surveillance of a telephone booth should be exempted from the usual requirement of advance authorization by a magistrate upon a showing of probable cause. We cannot agree. Omission of such authorization "bypasses the safeguards provided by an objective predetermination of probable cause, and substitutes instead the far less reliable procedure of an after-the-event justification for the ... search, too likely to be subtly influenced by the familiar shortcomings of hindsight judgment." ...

* * *

These considerations do not vanish when the search in question is transferred from the setting of a home, an office, or a hotel room to that of a telephone booth. Wherever a man may be, he is entitled to know that he will remain free from unreasonable searches and seizures. The government agents here ignored "the procedure of antecedent justification . . . that is central to the Fourth Amendment," a procedure that we hold to be a constitutional precondition of the kind of electronic surveillance involved in this case. . . .

Judgment reversed.

Mr. Justice DOUGLAS, with whom Mr. Justice BRENNAN joins, concurring.

While I join the opinion of the Court, I feel compelled to reply to the separate concurring opinion of my Brother WHITE, which I view as a wholly unwarranted green light for the Executive Branch to resort to electronic eavesdropping without a warrant in cases which the Executive Branch itself labels "national security" matters.

Neither the President nor the Attorney General is a magistrate. In matters where they believe national security may be involved they are not detached, disinterested, and neutral as a court or magistrate must be. Under the separation of powers created by the Constitution, the Executive Branch is not supposed to be neutral and disinterested. Rather it should vigorously investigate and prevent breaches of national security and prosecute those who violate the pertinent federal laws. The President and Attorney General are properly interested parties, cast in the role of adversary, in national security cases. They may even be the intended victims of subversive action. Since spies and saboteurs are as entitled to the protection of the Fourth Amendment as suspected gamblers like petitioner, I cannot agree that where spies and saboteurs are involved adequate protection of Fourth Amendment rights is assured when the President and Attorney General assume both the position of adversary-and-prosecutor and disinterested, neutral magistrate.

There is, so far as I understand constitutional history, no distinction under the Fourth Amendment between types of crimes. Article III, § 3, gives "treason" a very narrow definition and puts restrictions on its proof. But the Fourth Amendment draws no lines between various substantive offenses. The arrests in cases of "hot pursuit" and the arrests on visible or other evidence of probable cause cut across the board and are not peculiar to any kind of crime.

I would respect the present lines of distinction and not improvise because a particular crime seems particularly heinous. When the Framers took that step, as they did with treason, the worst crime of all, they made their purpose manifest.

Mr. Justice HARLAN, concurring.

I join the opinion of the Court, which I read to hold only (a) that an enclosed telephone booth is an area where like a home . . . and unlike a field . . . a person has a constitutionally protected reasonable expectation of privacy; (b) that electronic as well as physical intrusion into a place that is in this sense private may constitute a violation of the Fourth Amendment; and (c) that the invasion of a constitutionally protected area by federal authorities is, as the Court has long held, presumptively unreasonable in the absence of a search warrant.

As the Court's opinion states, "the Fourth Amendment protects people, not places." The question, however, is what protection it affords to those people. Generally, as here, the answer to that question requires reference to a "place." My understanding of the rule that has emerged from prior decisions is that there is a twofold requirement, first that a person have exhibited an actual (subjective) expectation of privacy and, second, that the expectation be one that society is prepared to recognize as "reasonable." Thus a man's home is, for most purposes, a place where he expects privacy, but objects, activities, or statements that he exposes to the "plain view" of outsiders are not "protected" because no intention to keep them to himself has been exhibited. On the other hand, conversations in the open would not be protected against being overheard, for the expectation of privacy under the circumstances would be unreasonable. . . .

The critical fact in this case is that "[o]ne who occupies [a telephone booth], shuts the door behind him, and pays the toll that permits him to place a call is surely entitled to assume" that his conversation is not being intercepted.... The point is not that the booth is "accessible to the public" at other times ... but that it is a temporarily private place whose momentary occupants' expectations of freedom from intrusion are recognized as reasonable....

In Silverman v. United States, 365 U.S. 505 (1961), we held that eavesdropping accomplished by means of an electronic device that penetrated the premises occupied by petitioner was a violation of the Fourth Amendment.... This case requires us to reconsider Goldman, and I agree that it should now be overruled. Its limitation on Fourth Amendment protection is, in the present, day, bad physics as well as bad law, for reasonable expectations of privacy may be defeated by electronic as well as physical invasion.

Finally, I do not read the Court's opinion to declare that no interception of a conversation one-half of which occurs in a public telephone booth can be reasonable in the absence of a warrant. As elsewhere under the Fourth Amendment, warrants are the general rule, to which the legitimate needs of law enforcement may demand specific exceptions. It will be time enough to consider any such exceptions when an appropriate occasion presents itself, and I agree with the Court that this is not one.

Mr. Justice WHITE, concurring.

I agree that the official surveillance of petitioner's telephone conversation in a public booth must be subject to the test of reasonableness under the Fourth Amendment and that on the record now before us the particular surveillance undertaken was unreasonable absent a warrant properly authorizing it. This application of the Fourth Amendment need not interfere with legitimate needs of law enforcement....

I note the Court's acknowledgment that there are circumstances in which it is reasonable to search without a warrant. In this connection, ... the Court points out that today's decision does not reach national security cases. Wiretapping to protect the security of the Nation has been authorized by successive Presidents....

We should not require the warrant procedure and the magistrate's judgment if the President of the United States or his chief legal officer, the Attorney General, has considered the requirements of national security and authorized electronic surveillance as reasonable.

[Mr. Justice BLACK wrote a dissenting opinion.]

[Mr. Justice MARSHALL took no part in the consideration or decision of this case.]

Comments

1. Although *Katz* is most often associated with electronic eavesdropping problems, it might also be argued that the decision has had a far greater impact on the overall development of search and seizure law. Why is this true?

2. Under the so-called "plain view" doctrine (infra, § 5.04), most courts hold that as long as the officer makes his observation from a place where he has a lawful right to be, such an observation does not constitute a search under the Fourth Amendment. Does the language in *Katz* serve to reinforce this "public exposure" concept as being outside the protection of the Fourth Amendment?

3. The *Katz* Court did not seem to take issue with the "manner" in which the actual recordings were obtained (i.e., the FBI showed considerable restraint), but rather the Court attacked the lack of prior judicial authorization. What is the likelihood that *Katz* would have been granted Supreme Court review had the government not "bypassed" the warrant requirement?

4. In rejecting the protection of *places* in favor of protection of *people,* the Court seemed compelled to dismiss the *Olmstead* "tres-

pass doctrine." Are the concepts mutually exclusive? Doesn't the Fourth Amendment mention both persons and places?

5. Read in its strictest sense, the language of the Fourth Amendment severely limits the investigatory powers of law enforcement officials. In attempting to protect the basic right to privacy while also providing law enforcement authorities with reasonable search power for legitimate ends, the Supreme Court has attempted to balance the right and need of the government to search without a warrant against the individual's right to privacy. Thus, the "well-delineated exceptions" noted by the *Katz* majority have become increasingly more important in the day-to-day policing activities in the United States.

6. In order to justify certain types of warrantless invasions of privacy, "the burden is on those seeking the exception to show a need for it," *United States* v. *Jeffers*, 342 U.S. 48, 51 (1951). Since available data suggest that more searches occur outside the parameters of the judicial process (see generally Ringel, W., *Searches and Seizures, Arrests and Confessions* [1972]), the Supreme Court, through an extended series of decisions, has upheld warrantless searches when the government has been able to show "a need for the exception." To date, warrantless searches have been sanctioned under the following exceptions: incident to a lawful arrest, *Chimel* v. *California*, 395 U.S. 752 (1969), infra, § 5.04; "hot pursuit," *Warden* v. *Hayden*, 387 U.S. 294 (1967), infra, § 5.04; "emergency situation," *Carroll* v. *United States*, 267 U.S. 132 (1925); valid consent, *Schneckloth* v. *Bustamonte*, 412 U.S. 218 (1973), infra, § 5.04; border searches, *Aleimda-Sanchez* v. *United States*, 413 U.S. 266 (1973), infra, § 5.04; evidence found in "plain view," *Harris* v. *United States*, 390 U.S. 234 (1968), infra, § 5.04; *Coolidge* v. *New Hampshire*, 403 U.S. 443 (1971), infra, § 5.04; "stop and frisk," *Terry* v. *Ohio*, 392 U.S. 1 (1968), infra, § 5.04; abandoned property, *Abel* v. *United States*, 362 U.S. 217 (1960); certain administrative-type searches involving fire, health, and safety violations, *United States* v. *Biswell*, 406 U.S. 311 (1972); *Colonnade Catering Corporation* v. *United States*, 397 U.S. 72 (1970); and the actions of private citizens not acting in concert with government officials, *Burdeau* v. *McDowell*, 256 U.S. 465 (1921).

7. Although most warrantless intrusions must, in retrospect, be able to stand the primary test of probable cause (see § 5.02, infra), the Supreme Court, under at least three of the exceptions just mentioned (e.g., most border searches, "stop and frisk" cases, and certain administrative searches), has sanctioned warrantless searches without a showing of probable cause prior to the privacy invasion. So long as the search is *reasonable*, or in the case of the administrative search, is conducted pursuant to an authorized statute, a prior showing of probable cause is not necessary. It is also interesting to note that in several of the more recent Burger Court decisions, the majority of Justices have shown a tendency to expand the "few specifically ... and well-delineated exceptions" beyond those noted in *Katz*. See, e.g., *Cady* v. *Dombrowski*, 413 U.S. 433 (1973) (Comments, § 5.04, infra, p. 247); *United States* v. *Edwards*, 417 U.S. 800 (1974); *Cardwell* v. *Lewis*, 417 U.S. 583 (1974); *United States* v. *Robinson*, 414 U.S. 218 (1973); and *Cupp* v. *Murphy*, 412 U.S. 291 (1973) (infra, § 5.04).

8. Much has been said about the right to be free from unreasonable searches and seizures of "things." But what about the *person*? The Fourth Amendment provides that the people shall "be secure in their persons" as well. An arrest is a "seizure of the person." After nearly four centuries the law of arrest has changed very little. The fact that the Fourth Amendment was intended to apply to arrests was noted early in our judicial history, e.g., *Ex parte Burford,* 3 Cranch 448 (1805). (See also *Beck* v. *Ohio,* 379 U.S. 89 [1964]; *Ker* v. *California* 374 U.S. 23 [1963]; *Giordenello* v. *United States,* 357 U.S. 480 [1958]; and *Draper* v. *United States,* 358 U.S. 307 [1959] [infra, § 5.02]). Having its roots in English common law, the modern concept of lawful arrest is analogous to that of search and seizure; i.e., it can occur with or without a warrant but must be grounded upon probable cause. (The cases in the next section focus on the probable cause issues germane to both arrests and searches.)

9. In *Katz,* the Court stated, "What a person knowingly exposes to the public, even in his home or office, is not a subject of Fourth Amendment protection. But what he seeks to preserve as private, even in an area accessible to the public, may be constitutionally protected." Suppose a police officer, while on duty in a public park, overhears a conversation between two men planning to commit a robbery. If the officer records the conversation with a recording device, may evidence of the conversation be admitted at a subsequent trial for conspiracy to commit robbery? At any rate, may the officer testify as to what he heard? Can it be said that the two conversants *knowingly* exposed their conversation to the public; or did they seek to preserve as private their conversation even though it took place in an area accessible to the public (the park)? Is a conversation subject to a seizure under the so-called "plain-view" doctrine? (See § 5.04, infra.)

10. Some recent lower federal and state court decisions involving the right to privacy include *Gedko* v. *Heer,* 406 F. Supp. 609 (W.D. Wis. 1975) (suspected marijuana farmer has a reasonable expectation of privacy with respect to his 160-acre farm, and police who trespassed on his land cannot rely on the "open fields" doctrine of *Hester* v. *United States,* 265 U.S. 57 [1924], or *Katz* v. *United States,* 389 U.S. 347 [1967] [supra], to legitimize their activity); *Ochs* v. *State,* 543 S.W.2d 355 (Tex. Crim. App. 1976) (Fourth Amendment rights of a husband and wife dealing in marijuana outside of their house were violated by state officers who observed their activity from a place on their property about 50 yards from the house); *Carey* v. *Covelli,* 336 N.E.2d 759 (Ill. 1975) (Fourth Amendment rights of murder victim's family are no bar to a warrant-authorized state examination of the victim's papers and effects); *People* v. *McKunes,* 124 Cal. Rptr. 126 (Cal. App. 1975) (securing records of a suspect's telephone calls from telephone company without subpoena or other court order held violative of suspect's constitutional right of privacy) (but see *United States* v. *Riddick,* 519 F.2d 645 [8th Cir. 1975] [there is no violation of right to privacy when lawful legal processes have been employed to subpoena bank records]); *Venner* v. *State,* 354 A.2d 483 (Md. Ct. Special App. 1976) (police who had probable cause to believe that suspect swallowed numerous balloons filled with marijuana did not violate Fourth Amendment by waiting for

nature to take its course, as feces and their contents constitute abandoned property); *State* v. *Ferrari*, 344 A.2d 332 (N.J. Super. Ct., App. Div., 1976) (assistant police chief whose erratic behavior had troubled his chief had a reasonable expectation of privacy against intrusion into his locked desk by law enforcement officers investigating his possible criminal activity, and warrantless search was violative of Fourth Amendment) (but see *United States* v. *Speights*, 413 F. Supp. 1221 [D.N.J. 1976] [police officer who stored unregistered sawed-off shotgun belonging to him in his stationhouse locker held to have no reasonable expectation of privacy against departmental search]); *United States* v. *Haughn*, 414 F. Supp. 37 (D.N.J. 1976) (landing outside defendant's apartment held not sufficiently removed and private in character that he could reasonably expect privacy within the meaning of the Fourth Amendment); *Magda* v. *Benson*, 536 F.2d 111 (6th Cir. 1976) (no reasonable expectation of privacy in garbage that has been placed outside a residence for collection) (in accord are *United States* v. *Dzialak*, 441 F.2d 212 [2nd Cir. 1971], *United States* v. *Stroeble*, 431 F.2d 1273 [6th Cir. 1970], *People* v. *Huddleston*, 347 N.E.2d 76 [Ill. App. 1976]; *Nathanson* v. *State*, 554 P.2d 456 (Alas. 1976) (Alaska Fish and Game officials not bound by Fourth Amendment's requirements when checking out crab pots for compliance with state regulations as no reasonable expectation of privacy exists in commercial fishing for king crab where pots are highly visible in the waters); *United States* v. *Pagan*, 537 F.2d 554 (1st Cir. 1976) (person cannot have a reasonable expectation of privacy in a well-traveled common area of a condominium garage); *People* v. *Henderson*, 245 N.W.2d 72 (Mich. App. 1976) (the method by which a state may obtain a voice exemplar is subject to the reasonableness requirements of the Fourth Amendment); *Vargas* v. *State*, 543 S.W.2d 151 (Tex. Crim. App. 1976) (police officer's warrantless search of clothes of hospital patient who had overdosed, and in whose pants pocket a nurse had found a .22 pistol, held reasonable under *South Dakota* v. *Opperman*, 428 U.S. 364 [1976] [infra, § 5.04]; *United States* v. *Choate*, 422 F. Supp. 261 (C.D. Cal. 1976) (warrantless mail cover authorized by postal officials at the request of a customs agent who "felt" that suspect was using the mails as part of a drug smuggling conspiracy held violative of Fourth Amendment); *Commonwealth* v. *Wallington*, 357 A.2d 598 (Pa. Super. 1976) (prison officials may search prisoners and seize evidence without warrant or probable cause absent a showing that the search and seizure is solely for purposes of harassment); *Hodges* v. *Klein*, 412 F. Supp. 896 (D.N.J. 1976) (prison regulation requiring inmates to submit to anal searches upon entering or leaving the institution and following personal contact visits with other inmates, friends, and relatives held not violative of Fourth Amendment) (in accord is *Penn* v. *Riddle*, 399 F. Supp. 1059 [D. Va. 1976] [body cavity searches held to be within discretion of prison officials and do not constitute violations of prisoners' Fourth Amendment rights]); *United States* v. *Carriger*, 541 F.2d 545 (6th Cir. 1976) (federal agents' warrantless entry into a locked apartment building to arrest narcotics supplier in his apartment held unreasonable in light of occupants' reasonable expectations of privacy of common area of apartment building); *United States* v. *Kim*, 415 F. Supp. 1252 (D. Hawaii 1976) (police use of telescope or binoculars to observe a suspect's activities within the confines of his residence constitutes a search within the meaning of the Fourth Amendment) (contra, *State* v. *Manly*, 530 P.2d 306 [Wash. 1975] [where second floor apartment window was not curtained and plants resembling marijuana were observed by a detective using binoculars from his auto parked across the street, court held that officer's observation did not amount to an illegal search, and defendants did not have a reasonable expectation of privacy under the circumstances]); *United States* v. *Coplen*, 541 F.2d 211 (9th Cir. 1976) (federal agents' use of a flashlight to peer into windows of marijuana suspects' airplane not a search and not violative of suspects' reasonable expectation of privacy); *United States* v. *Hufford*, 539 F.2d 32 (9th Cir. 1976) (federal agent's installation of electronic "beeper" on drum of caffeine that was transported by drug suspect held not a search within the meaning of the Fourth Amendment); *United States* v. *Emery*, 541 F.2d 887 (1st Cir. 1976) (federal agents who inserted electronic beeper into cocaine packages that were being mailed held not violative of Fourth Amendment's right of privacy even though beeper enabled agents to maintain their surveillance of package after it reached the recipient's apartment); *United States* v. *Padilla*, 520 F.2d 526 (1st Cir. 1975) (undercover agent's bugging of defendant's hotel room and recording of conversations concerning narcotics without prior consent or court authorization held invasion of privacy); *Tamex* v. *State*, 534 W.2d 686 (Tex. Crim. App. 1976) (probation condition that required probationer to submit to a search and seizure "at any time of day or night, with or without a search warrant, whenever requested to do so by the probation officer or any law enforcement officer" held violative of Fourth Amendment); in accord is *United States* v. *Consuelo-Gonzales*, 521 F.2d 259 [1975] (contra, *Simpson* v. *Simpson*, 490 F.2d 803 [5th Cir. 1974]) (see also *United States ex rel. Coleman* v. *Smith*, 395 F. Supp. 1155 [S.D.N.Y. 1975] [a "general consent to search" given by parolee as part of parole held to be an invalid consent, and parole officer was not justified in conducting search of parolee's residence]) (but cf. *Latta* v. *Fitzharris*, 521 F.2d 246 [9th Cir. 1975] [parole officer's warrantless search of parolee's house some time after his arrest for a parole violation held not improper when officer reasonably believed that a search was necessary, and a parolee's expectation of privacy held to be less than that of other citizens] and *Connelly* v. *Parkinson*, 405 F. Supp. 811 [D.S.D. 1975] [neither parole or probation officers are bound by Fourth Amendment warrant requirements that apply to law enforcement authorities]); *State* v. *Williams*, 486 S.W.2d 468 (Mo. 1972) (warrantless search of room at halfway house by parole officer who was suspicious but did not have probable cause not violative of the Fourth Amendment) (to the same effect is *United States* v. *Lewis*, 400 F. Supp. 1046 [S.D.N.Y. 1975]); *United States* v. *Solis*, 536 F.2d 880 (9th Cir. 1976) (customs agents' use of dogs in public area to sniff semi-trailer they suspected contained marijuana was reasonable and did not constitute a search within the meaning of the Fourth Amendment, but rather constituted a "minimal" invasion based on founded suspicion) (cf. *United States* v. *Bronstein*, 521 F.2d 459 [2nd Cir. 1975], and *United States* v. *Fulero*, 498 F.2d 748 [D.C. Cir. 1974]) (compare *Solis*, supra, with *People* v. *Williams*,

124 Cal. Rptr. 523 [Cal. App. 1975] [sheriff's deputies were trespassing when they entered airlines *nonpublic* baggage room with a trained dog without probable cause and screened baggage, and drugs sniffed out were ruled inadmissible]) (for a decision involving the use of detection dogs on military posts, see *United States* v. *Unrue,* 22 U.S.C.M.A. 466 [1973], and see also Lederer and Lederer, *Marijuana Dog Searches after United States* v. *Unrue,* The Army Lawyer 6 [December 1973]); *United States* v. *Milroy,* 538 F.2d 1033 (4th Cir. 1976) (Fourth Amendment protections do not extend against customs officials to first class envelopes mailed at APO in a foreign country) (accord, *United States* v. *King,* 517 F.2d 350 [5th Cir. 1975] [envelopes mailed from abroad with APO return address], *United States* v. *Odland,* 502 F.2d 148 [7th Cir. 1974], cert. den. 419 U.S. 1088 [1974] [first class mail sent to U.S. from Colombia], *United States* v. *Doe,* 472 F.2d 982 [2nd Cir. 1973] [package mailed to U.S. from Colombia], *United States* v. *Beckley,* 335 F.2d 86 [6th Cir. 1964] [sealed parcel post package mailed in U.S. Mail from Canal Zone to Detroit], *United States* v. *Various Articles of Obscene Merchandise, Schedule No. 896,* 363 F. Supp. 165 [S.D.N.Y. 1973] [envelopes mailed to U.S. from Europe], *United States* v. *Sohnen,* 298 F. Supp. 51 [E.D.N.Y. 1969] [package mailed to U.S. from Switzerland]).

5.02 PROBABLE CAUSE: ARREST AND SEARCH WARRANTS

A. INFORMANTS, PROBABLE CAUSE, AND ARRESTS

The Reasonable Police Officer Test

DRAPER v. UNITED STATES

Supreme Court of the United States, 1959
358 U.S. 307, 70 S. Ct. 329, 3 L. Ed. 2d 327

James Draper was convicted of violating federal narcotic laws in the United States District Court for the District of Colorado. The Court of Appeals (10th Cir.) affirmed, and The United States Supreme Court granted certiorari. The record revealed that one Marsh, a federal agent, was told by a previously reliable informer (one Hereford) that Draper, who was peddling narcotics to several addicts in Denver, would be arriving from Chicago by train on the morning of September 8 or 9, bringing with him a quantity of heroin. The informant advised Marsh that Draper, who was unknown to the agent, would be wearing certain clothing, walking fast, and would be carrying a tan zipper bag. In addition, a very detailed physical description of Draper was provided by the informant. On September 9, Marsh and a Denver police officer observed a person (Draper), with the "exact physical attributes and wearing the precise clothing" described by the informant, alight from an incoming Chicago train and start walking "fast" toward the exit. He was carrying a tan zipper bag. The two law enforcement officers arrested Draper and a subsequent search of his person uncovered heroin.

Mr. Justice WHITTAKER delivered the opinion of the Court.

*   *   *

The crucial question for us ... is whether knowledge of the related facts and circumstances gave Marsh "probable cause" within the meaning of the Fourth Amendment ... to believe that petitioner had committed or was committing a violation of the narcotic laws. If it did, the arrest, though without a warrant, was lawful and the subsequent search of petitioner's person and the seizure of the found heroin were validly made incident to a lawful arrest, and therefore the motion to suppress was properly overruled and the heroin was competently received in evidence at the trial. . . .

[Petitioner] ... contends (1) that the information given by Hereford to Marsh was "hearsay" and, because hearsay is not legally competent evidence in a criminal trial, could not legally have been considered, but should have been put out of mind, by Marsh in assessing whether he had "probable cause" and "reasonable grounds" to arrest petitioner without a warrant, and (2) that, even if hearsay could lawfully have been considered, Marsh's information should be held insufficient to show "probable cause" and "reasonable grounds" to believe that petitioner had violated or was violating the narcotic laws and to justify his arrest without a warrant.

Considering the first contention, we find petitioner entirely in error. Brinegar v. United States, 338 U.S. 160 (1949) has settled the question the other way. There, in a similar situation, the convict contended "that the factors relating to inadmissibility of the evidence [for] *purposes of proving guilt at the trial,* deprive[d] the evidence as a whole of sufficiency to show probable cause for the search. . . ." . . . But this Court, rejecting that contention, said: "[T]he so-called distinction places a wholly unwarranted emphasis upon the criterion of admissibility in evidence, to prove the accused's guilt, of the facts relied upon to show probable cause. That emphasis we think, goes much too far in confusing and disregarding the difference between what is required to prove guilt in a criminal case and what is required to show probable cause for arrest or search. It approaches requiring

[if it does not in practical effect require] proof sufficient to establish guilt in order to substantiate the existence of probable cause. There is a large difference between the two things to be proved [guilt and probable cause], as well as between the tribunals which determine them, and therefore a like difference in the quanta and modes of proof required to establish them." . . .

Nor can we agree with petitioner's second contention that Marsh's information was insufficient to show probable cause and reasonable grounds to believe that petitioner had violated or was violating the narcotic laws and to justify his arrest without a warrant. The information given to narcotic agent Marsh by "special employee" Hereford may have been hearsay to Marsh, but coming from one employed for that purpose and whose information had always been found accurate and reliable, it is clear that Marsh would have been derelict in his duties had he not pursued it. And when, in pursuing that information, he saw a man, having the exact physical attributes and wearing the precise clothing and carrying the tan zipper bag that Hereford had described, alight from one of the very trains from the very place stated by Hereford and start to walk at a "fast" pace toward the station exit, Marsh had personally verified every facet of the information given him by Hereford except whether petitioner had accomplished his mission and had the three ounces of heroin on his person or in his bag. And surely, with every other bit of Hereford's information being thus personally verified, Marsh had "reasonable grounds" to believe that the remaining unverified bit of Hereford's information — that Draper would have the heroin with him — was likewise true.

"In dealing with probable cause ... we deal with probabilities. These are not technical; they are the factual and practical considerations of everyday life on which reasonable and prudent men, not legal technicians, act." . . . Probable cause exists where "the facts and circumstances within [the arresting officers'] knowledge and of which they had reasonably trustworthy information are sufficient in themselves to warrant a man of reasonable caution in the belief that" an offense has been or is being committed. . . .

We believe that, under the facts and circumstances here, Marsh had probable cause and reasonable grounds to believe that petitioner was committing a violation of the laws of the United States relating to narcotic drugs at the time he arrested him. The arrest was therefore lawful, and the subsequent search and seizure, having been made incident to that lawful arrest, were likewise valid. It follows that petitioner's motion to suppress was properly denied and that the seized heroin was competent evidence lawfully received at the trial.

Affirmed.

[Mr. Justice DOUGLAS wrote a dissenting opinion.]

[Mr. Chief Justice WARREN and Mr. Justice FRANKFURTER took no part in the consideration or decision of this case.]

Warrantless Arrests and Probable Cause

UNITED STATES v. WATSON

Supreme Court of the United States, 1976
423 U.S. 411, 96 S. Ct. 820, 46 L. Ed. 2d 598

A government informant received a stolen credit card from the respondent (Watson) and delivered it to a postal inspector. At the inspector's suggestion, the informant arranged a second meeting with Watson a few days later, which took place in a restaurant. Believing that Watson had additional stolen credit cards, the informant gave the postal officers a prearranged signal and they moved in to make a warrantless arrest of Watson. Respondent was taken outside the restaurant and a search of his person was conducted, but no cards were found. However, a search, based on his consent, of his nearby parked auto produced two stolen cards. Watson was subsequently convicted of possessing stolen mail in violation of federal law. The Court of Appeals (9th Cir.) reversed, finding, inter alia, that notwithstanding probable cause Watson's arrest was invalid because the postal inspector had ample time to secure an arrest warrant but did not do so. The United States Supreme Court granted certiorari.

The portions of the Court's opinion that concern the consent search of Watson's automobile are presented in § 5.04, infra.

Mr. Justice WHITE delivered the opinion of the Court.

* * *

A major part of the Court of Appeals' opinion was its holding that Watson's warrantless arrest violated the Fourth Amendment. Although it did not expressly do so, it may have intended to overturn the conviction on the independent ground that the two credit cards were the inadmissible fruits of an unconstitutional arrest. . . .

Contrary to the Court of Appeals' view, Watson's arrest was not invalid because executed without a warrant. Section 3061(a) of Title 18 U.S.C. expressly empowers the Board of Governors of the Postal Service to authorize Postal Service officers and employees "performing duties related to the inspection of postal matters" to "(3) make arrests without warrant for felonies cognizable under the laws of the United States if they have reasonable grounds to believe that the person to be arrested has committed or is committing such a felony."

By regulation, 39 CFT § 232.5(a) (1975), and in identical language the Board of Governors has exercised that power and authorized warrantless arrests. There being probable cause in this case to believe that Watson had violated § 1708 [possessing stolen mail], the inspector and his subordinates, in arresting Watson, were acting strictly in accordance with the governing statute and regulations. The effect of the judgment of the Court of Appeals was to invalidate the statute as applied in this case and as applied to all the situations where a court fails to find exigent circumstances justifying a warrantless arrest. We reverse that judgment.... Section 3061 represents a judgment by Congress that it is not unreasonable under the Fourth Amendment for postal inspectors to arrest without a warrant provided they have probable cause to do so. This was not an isolated or quixotic judgment of the legislative branch. Other Federal law enforcement officers have been expressly authorized by statute for many years to make felony arrests on probable cause but without a warrant....

Because there is a "strong presumption of constitutionality due to an Act of Congress, especially when it turns on what is 'reasonable,'... [o]bviously the Court should be reluctant to decide that a search thus authorized by Congress was unreasonable and that the Act was therefore unconstitutional."... Moreover, there is nothing in the Court's prior cases indicating that under the Fourth Amendment a warrant is required to make a valid arrest for a felony. Indeed, the relevant prior decisions are uniformly to the contrary.

* * *

The cases construing the Fourth Amendment ... reflect the ancient common-law rule that a peace officer was permitted to arrest without a warrant for a misdemeanor or felony committed in his presence as well as for a felony not committed in his presence if there was reasonable grounds for making the arrest.

* * *

Because the common-law rule authorizing arrests without warrant generally prevailed in the States, it is important for present purposes to note that in 1792 Congress invested United States Marshals and their deputies with "the same powers in executing the laws of the United States, as sheriffs and their deputies in their several states have by law, in executing the laws of their respective states." Act of May 2, 1792, c. 18, § 9, 1 Stat. 265. The Second Congress thus saw no inconsistency between the Fourth Amendment and giving United States Marshals the same power as local peace officers to arrest for a felony without a warrant. This provision equating the power of federal marshals to those of local sheriffs was several times re-enacted and is today § 570 of Title 28. That provision,

however, was supplemented in 1935 by § 504a of the Judicial Code, which in its essential elements is now 18 U.S.C. § 3053 and which expressly empowered marshals to make felony arrests without warrant and on probable cause. It was enacted to furnish a federal standard independent of the vagaries of state laws, the Committee Report remarking that under existing law a "marshal or deputy marshal may make an arrest without a warrant within his district in all cases where the sheriff might do so under the State statutes."...

The balance struck by the common law in generally authorizing felony arrests on probable cause, but without warrant, has survived substantially intact. It appears in almost all of the States in the form of express statutory authorization. In 1963, the American Law Institute undertook the task of formulating a model statute governing police powers and practice in criminal law enforcement and related aspects of pretrial procedure. In 1975, after years of discussion, a Model Code of Pre-arraignment Procedure was proposed. Among its provisions was § 120.1 which authorized an officer to take a person into custody if the officer has reasonable cause to believe that the person to be arrested has committed a felony, or has committed a misdemeanor or petty misdemeanor in his presence. The commentary to this section said: "The Code thus adopts the traditional and almost universal standard for arrest without a warrant."

This is the rule Congress has long directed its principal law enforcement officers to follow. Congress has plainly decided against conditioning warrantless arrest power on proof of exigent circumstances. Law enforcement officers may find it wise to seek arrest warrants where practicable to do so, and their judgments about probable cause may be more readily accepted where backed by a warrant issued by a magistrate. ... But we decline to transform this judicial preference into a constitutional rule when the judgment of the Nation and Congress has for so long been to authorize warrantless public arrests on probable cause rather than to encumber criminal prosecutions with endless litigation with respect to the existence of exigent circumstances, whether it was practicable to get a warrant, whether the suspect was about to flee, and the like.

Watson's arrest did not violate the Fourth

Amendment, and the Court of Appeals erred in holding to the contrary.

* * *

[Mr. Chief Justice BURGER, Mr. Justice BLACKMUN, Mr. Justice POWELL, and Mr. Justice REHNQUIST joined in the opinion of the Court.]

[Mr. Justice POWELL and Mr. Justice STEWART wrote concurring opinions.]

Mr. Justice MARSHALL, with whom Mr. Justice BRENNAN joins, dissenting.

By granting police broad powers to make warrantless arrests, the Court today sharply reverses the course of our modern decisions construing the Warrant Clause of the Fourth Amendment.

* * *

Before addressing what the Court does today, I note what it does not do. It does not decide this case on the narrow question that is presented. That is unfortunate for this is, fundamentally, a simple case.

* * *

The signal of the reliable informant that Watson was in possession of stolen credit cards gave the postal inspectors probable cause to make the arrest. This probable cause was separate and distinct from the probable cause relating to the offense six days earlier, and provided an adequate independent basis for the arrest. Whether or not a warrant ordinarily is required prior to making an arrest, no warrant is required when exigent circumstances are present. When law enforcement officers have probable cause to believe that an offense is taking place in their presence and that the suspect is at that moment in possession of the evidence, exigent circumstances exist. Delay could cause the escape of the suspect or the destruction of the evidence. Accordingly, Watson's warrantless arrest was valid under the recognized exigent circumstances exception to the warrant requirement, and the Court has no occasion to consider whether a warrant would otherwise be necessary.

* * *

Since, for reasons it leaves unexpressed, the Court does not take this traditional course, I am constrained to express my views on the issues it unnecessarily decides. The Court reaches its conclusion that a warrant is not necessary for a police officer to make an arrest in a public place, so long as he has probable cause to believe a felony has been committed, on the basis of its views of precedent and history.... None of the cases cited by the Court squarely confronted the issue decided today. Moreover, an examination of the history relied on by the Court shows that it does not support the conclusion laid upon it. ...

* * *

The Court ... relies on the English common-law rule of arrest and the many state and federal statutes following it. There are two serious flaws in this approach. First, as a matter of factual analysis, the substance of the ancient common-law rule provides no support for the far-reaching modern rule that the Court fashions on its model. Second, as a matter of doctrine, the long-standing existence of a Government practice does not immunize the practice from scrutiny under the mandate of our Constitution.

The common-law rule was indeed as the Court states it:

"[A] peace officer was permitted to arrest without a warrant for a misdemeanor or felony committed in his presence as well as for a felony not committed in his presence if there was reasonable grounds for making the arrest." ...

To apply the rule blindly today, however, makes as much sense as attempting to interpret Hamlet's admonition to Ophelia, "Get thee to a nunnery, go," without understanding the meaning of Hamlet's words in the context of their age. For the fact is that a felony at common law and a felony today bear only slight resemblance, with the result that the relevance of the common-law rule of arrest to the modern interpretation of our Constitution is minimal.

Both at common law and today, felonies find definition in the penal consequences of crime rather than the nature of the crime itself. At common law, as this Court has several times recognized:

"No crime was considered a felony which did not occasion a total forfeiture of the offender's lands, or goods, or both."

* * *

At present, on the other hand:

"Any offense punishable by death or imprisonment for a term exceeding one year is a felony." 18 U.S.C. § 1(1).

This difference reflects more than changing notions of penology. It reflects a substantive change in the kinds of crimes called felonies.... Only the most serious crimes were felonies at common law, and many crimes now classified as felonies under federal or state law were treated as misdemeanors. Professor Wilgus has summarized and documented the cases:

"At common law an assault was a misdemeanor and it was still only such even if made with the intent to rob, murder, or rape. Affrays, abortion, barratry, bribing voters, challenging to fight, compounding felonies, cheating by false weights or measures, escaping from lawful arrest, eavesdropping, forgery, kidnapping, libel, mayhem, maliciously killing valuable animals, obstructing justice, public nuisance, perjury, riots, and routs, etc. were misdemeanors...." Wilgus, Arrests Without a Warrant, 22 Mich. L. Rev. 541, 572–573 (1923).... To make an arrest for any of these crimes at common law, the police officer was required to obtain a warrant, unless the crime was committed in his presence. Since many of these same crimes are commonly classified as felonies today, however, under the Court's holding a warrant is no longer needed to make such arrests, a result in contravention of the common law.

Thus the lesson of the common law, and those courts in this country that have accepted its rule, is an ambiguous one. Applied in its original context, the common-law rule would allow the warrantless arrest of some, but not all, of those we call felons today. Accordingly, the Court is simply historically wrong when it tells us that "[t]he balance struck by the common law in generally authorizing felony arrests on probable cause, but without a warrant, has survived substantially intact."

* * *

I do not mean by this that a modern warrant requirement should apply only to arrests precisely analogous to common-law misdemeanors, and be inapplicable to analogues of common-law felonies. Rather, the point is simply that the Court's unblinking literalism cannot replace analysis of the constitutional interests involved. While we can learn from the common law, the ancient rule does not provide a simple answer directly transferable to our system. Thus, in considering the applicability of the common-law rule to our present constitutional scheme, we must consider *both* of the rule's two opposing constructs: the presumption favoring warrants, as well as the exception allowing immediate arrests of the most dangerous criminals. The Court's failure to do so, indeed its failure to recognize any tension in the common-law rule at all, drains all validity from its historical analysis.

Lastly, the Court relies on the numerous state and federal statutes codifying the common-law rule. But this, too, is no substitute for reasoned analysis. True enough, the national and state legislatures have steadily ratified the drift of the balance struck by the common-law rule past the bounds of its original intent. And it is true as well, as the Court observes, that a presumption of constitutionality attaches to every Act of Congress. But neither observation is determinative of the constitutional issue, and the doctrine of deference that the Court invokes is contrary to the principles of constitutional analysis practiced since Marbury v. Madison, 1 Cranch 137 (1803). The Court's error on this score is far more dangerous than its misreading of history, for it is well settled that the mere existence of statutes or practice, even of longstanding, is no defense to an unconstitutional practice. "[N]o one acquires a vested or protected right in violation of the Constitution by long use, even when the span of time covers our entire national existence and indeed predates it."... Our function in constitutional cases is weightier than the Court today suggests: where reasoned analysis shows a practice to be constitutionally deficient, our obligation is to the Constitution, not the Congress.

In sum, the Court's opinion is without foundation. It relies on precedents that are not precedents. It relies on history that offers no clear rule to impose, but only conflicting interests to balance. It relies on statutes that constitute, at best, no more than an aid to construction. The Court never grapples with the warrant requirement of the Fourth Amendment and the cases construing it. It simply announces, by ipse dixit, a rule squarely rejecting the warrant requirement we have favored for so long.

* * *

[Mr. Justice Stevens took no part in the consideration or decision of the case.]

Comments

1. The majority in *Draper* asserted that probable cause can be found in what they term "the factual and practical considerations of everyday life on which reasonable and prudent men must act." Can we assume that all policemen are reasonable and prudent? Can it be argued that policemen (as a group) are less prudent than "legal technicians"? If not, then why does the Fourth Amendment promote the use of a warrant? Is it a question of prudence or impartiality? What about the informer's reliability and credibility; i.e., might the policeman and the judge differ on those points if the officer chooses to seek a warrant prior to the arrest? See *Aguilar* v. *Texas,* 378 U.S. 108 (1964). Finally, is it significant that Marsh had some 48 to 72 hours in which to obtain an arrest warrant prior to his encounter with Draper?

2. What if a policeman "seizes" a person only to have the court find, in retrospect, a lack of probable cause? What recourse does the citizen have against the officer? Would any recourse be available had the officer acted pursuant to a warrant issued by a "legal technician"?

3. In *Henry* v. *United States,* 364 U.S. 98 (1959), the issue of probable cause for a warrantless arrest was again before the Court. The majority opinion, written by Justice Douglas (who dissented in *Draper*), held that "good faith on the part of the arresting officer is not enough to establish probable cause." What "factual and practical considerations" are "guilt-laden" enough to help establish probable cause? For a list of facts and circumstances which the courts have recognized as sufficient to establish probable cause see Creamer, J. S., *The Law of Arrest, Search and Seizure* (2nd ed. 1975), at 19.

4. The *Watson* case represents a departure from past Supreme Court cases in which a strong preference was expressed for arrest warrants when practical, e.g., *Aguilar* v. *Texas,* 378 U.S. 108, 110–111 (1964), and *Beck* v. *Ohio,* 379 U.S. 89, 96 (1964). The *Watson* majority declined "to transform this judicial preference into a constitutional rule. . . ." Instead of relying upon one of the recognized exceptions to the warrant requirement, i.e., "exigent circumstances," the Court validated the arrest by looking to the federal statute involved. The congressional rule, according to the Court, has its roots in "ancient common law." What, according to the Court, would be the disadvantages of conditioning warrantless arrest powers only upon proof of exigent circumstances?

5. Although *Watson* may be viewed as a "plus" decision by many law enforcement officers, what problems does the officer encounter when he arrests a person without a warrant? Is it important that "prior approval" by a magistrate will serve to protect the officer against false arrest and false imprisonment suits under the Civil Rights Act, 42 U.S.C. § 1983 (Chapter Ten, § 10.01)? If practical, why not allow the "quantum of evidence" to be assessed by a judicial officer? Even Mr. Justice White notes in *Watson,* "Law enforcement officers may find it wise to seek arrest warrants, and their judgments about probable cause may be more readily accepted

where backed by a warrant issued by a magistrate." See also *Jones* v. *United States,* 362 U.S. 257 (1960) (infra, § 5.06). Of course, in the final analysis, both practices [(i.e., assessment of probable cause by police or by magistrate)] may be challenged at a suppression hearing. See *Rooker* v. *Commonwealth,* 508 S.W.2d 570 (1974).

6. The majority/minority disagreement in *Watson* centered on the issues of *how* probable cause is to be determined and *who* shall make that determination. Both seemed to be in agreement that in the instant case there was probable cause for the arrest. Thus, the *Watson* case does support the proposition that the informer, if reliable, is a valuable asset to the officer who wishes to establish probable cause for arrest. The dissenting justices saw *Watson* as a simple "exigent circumstances" case. However, they made it clear that in the absence of exigent circumstances, they favor the arrest warrant. Why did the minority argue that the history of the common law rule of arrest without warrant "offers no clear rule ... but only conflicting interests to balance"? What is the significance of Mr. Justice Marshall's remark that "it is well settled that the mere existence of statutes or practice, even of long standing, is no defense to an unconstitutional practice"?

7. Among recent lower federal and state court decisions involving informants, probable cause, and arrests are *United States* v. *Scott,* 545 F.2d 38 (8th Cir. 1976) (suspected drug courier's own answer to federal agents' questions after they stopped her on the basis of reliable informer's tip contained sufficient facts to constitute probable cause for her arrest); *United States* v. *Branch,* 545 F.2d 177 (D.C. Cir. 1976) (even though police officers executing a warrant to search apartment had been told by their reliable informant that a new shipment of drugs was expected that evening, they lacked probable cause to arrest person who showed up at the apartment carrying a canvas bag that was big enough to transport a large quantity of drugs); *United States* v. *Wingate,* 520 F.2d 309 (2nd Cir. 1975) (probable cause for arrest established when, at police direction, an informer telephoned defendant to arrange a heroin buy at a New York airport and defendant was arrested when he arrived at the location); *Burbank* v. *Warden, Illinois State Penitentiary,* 535 F.2d 361 (7th Cir. 1976) (police officer's knowledge of his beat and his own neighborhood should be given more than minimal weight in assessing probable cause); *United States* v. *Shavers,* 524 F.2d 1094 (8th Cir. 1975) (generalized description of a suspect's height, race, and walking pace held insufficient probable cause for arrest) (see also *United States* v. *Nicholas,* 448 F.2d 622, 625–626 [8th Cir. 1971] [presence of black men in predominately black area at "reasonable hour" does not give probable cause for investigatory stop], *Holloway* v. *Wolff,* 482 F.2d 110, 115–116 [8th Cir. 1973] [mere presence at suspected criminal hangout not sufficient to justify arrest], *United States* v. *Strickler,* 490 F.2d 378, 380 (9th Cir. 1974) [proximity to scene of crime does not provide probable cause to arrest]); *United States* v. *Race,* 529 F.2d 12 (1st Cir. 1976) (trained dog's singling out two crates from among 300 in airport warehouse as containing marijuana, along with federal agents' knowledge that the crates were extremely heavy and came from a border state, held sufficient probable cause to arrest the recipient of the crates) (but cf. *People* v. *Williams,* 124 Cal. Rptr. 253 [1975] [see § 5.01, Comments,

supra]); *State* v. *Evans*, 548 S.W.2d 772 (Kan. 1976) (police officer's misdemeanor arrest of three drug theft suspects on the basis of druggist's tip held valid, upholding Kansas statute permitting arrests, even though the officers did not witness the misdemeanor) (but see *In re Thierry*, 132 Cal. Rptr. 194 [Cal. Ct. App. 1976] [California law permits warrantless arrests of juveniles for misdemeanor-type offenses committed out of the presence of the arresting officer, but warrant required for arrest of adults under same circumstances]) (see also *Mass* v. *Weaver*, ____ F.2d ____ [5th Cir. 1976] [preliminary hearing to determine probable cause applicable to juvenile detainees]); *United States* v. *Richard*, 535 F.2d 246 (3rd Cir. 1976) (presence of two black males cruising in a car in a predominately white neighborhood is insufficient without more for a belief that those persons participated in a recent crime in the neighborhood); *State* v. *Goldberg*, 540 P.2d 674 (Ariz. 1975) (although arrest authority of federal fish and game agents is limited to fish and game violations, agents who smelled and discovered marijuana hidden on a motorbike they had followed into a restricted area had authority to make a citizen's arrest of the bike operator).

B. INFORMANTS, PROBABLE CAUSE, AND SEARCH WARRANTS

When the Defendant is a "Known" Criminal

SPINELLI v. UNITED STATES

Supreme Court of the United States, 1969
393 U.S. 410, 89 S. Ct. 584, 21 L. Ed. 2d 637

William Spinelli was convicted in the United States Court for the Eastern District of Missouri of interstate travel in aid of racketeering. Based on their own surveillance and information supplied by an informer, FBI agents secured a search warrant for petitioner's apartment. The search uncovered evidence which led to petitioner's conviction. On appeal, a majority of the Court of Appeals (8th Cir.) held that the warrant was issued without probable cause. However, after an en banc rehearing, the court of appeals affirmed the conviction by a vote of 6 to 2. The United States Supreme Court granted certiorari to determine if the informant's tip was sufficient to establish probable cause for the issuance of the search warrant.

Mr. Justice HARLAN delivered the opinion of the Court.

* * *

In Aguilar [v. Texas, 378 U.S. 108 (1964)], a search warrant had issued upon an affidavit of police officers who swore only that they had "received reliable information from a credible person and do believe" that narcotics were being illegally stored on the premises. While recognizing that the constitutional requirement of probable cause can be satisfied by hearsay information, this Court held the affidavit inadequate for two reasons. First, the application failed to set forth any of the "underlying circumstances" necessary to enable the magistrate independently to judge of the validity of the informant's conclusion that the narcotics were where he said they were. Second, the affiant-officers did not attempt to support their claim that their informant was " 'credible' or his information 'reliable.' " The Government is, however, quite right in saying that the FBI affidavit in the present case is more ample than that in Aguilar. Not only does it contain a report from an anonymous informant, but it also contains a report of an independent FBI investigation which is said to corroborate the informant's tip. We are, then, required to delineate the manner in which Aguilar's two-pronged test should be applied in these circumstances.

In essence, the affidavit ... contained the following allegations:

1. The FBI had kept track of Spinelli's movements on five days during the month of August 1965. On four of these occasions, Spinelli was seen crossing one of two bridges leading from Illinois into St. Louis, Missouri, between 11 A.M. and 12:15 P.M. On four of the five days, Spinelli was also seen parking his car in a lot used by residents of an apartment house at 1108 Indian Circle Drive in St. Louis, between 3:30 P.M. and 4:45 P.M. On one day, Spinelli was followed further and seen to enter a particular apartment in the building.

2. An FBI check with the telephone company revealed that this apartment contained two telephones listed under the name of Grace P. Hagen, and carrying the numbers WYdown 4-0029 and WYdown 4-0136.

3. The application stated that "William Spinelli is known to this affiant and to federal law enforcement agents and local law enforcement agents as a bookmaker, an associate of bookmakers, a gambler, and an associate of gamblers."

4. Finally it was stated that the FBI "has been informed by a confidential reliable informant that William Spinelli is operating a handbook and accepting wagers and disseminating wagering information by means of the telephones which have been assigned the numbers WYdown 4-0029 and WY-down 4-0136."

There can be no question that the last item mentioned, detailing the informant's tip, has a fundamental place in this warrant application. Without it, probable cause could not be established. The first two items reflect only innocent-seeming activity and data. Spinelli's travels to and from the apartment building and his entry into a particular apartment on one occasion could hardly be taken as bespeaking gambling activity; and there is surely nothing unusual about an apartment containing two separate telephones. Many a householder indulges himself in this petty luxury. Finally, the allegation that Spinelli was "known" to the affiant and to other federal and local law enforcement officers as a gambler and an associate of gamblers is but a bald and unilluminating assertion of suspicion that is entitled to no weight in appraising the magistrate's decision. . . .

So much indeed the Government does not deny. Rather, following the reasoning of the Court of Appeals, the Government claims that the informant's tip gives a suspicious color to the FBI's reports detailing Spinelli's innocent-seeming conduct and that, conversely, the FBI's surveillance corroborates the informant's tip, thereby entitling it to more weight. It is true, of course, that the magistrate is obligated to render a judgment based upon a common-sense reading of the entire affidavit. . . . We believe, however, that the "totality of circumstances" approach taken by the Court of Appeals paints with too broad a brush. Where, as here, the informer's tip is a necessary element in a finding of probable cause, its proper weight must be determined by a more precise analysis.

The informer's report must first be measured against Aguilar's standards so that its probative value can be assessed. If the tip is found inadequate under Aguilar, the other allegations which corroborate the information contained in the hearsay report should then be considered. At this stage as well, however, the standards enunciated in Aguilar must inform the magistrate's decision. He must ask: Can it fairly be said that the tip, even when certain parts of it have been corroborated by independent sources, is as trustworthy as a tip which would pass Aguilar's tests without independent corroboration? Aguilar is relevant at this stage of the inquiry as well because the tests it establishes were designed to implement the long-standing principle that probable cause must be determined by a "neutral and detached magistrate" and not by "the officer engaged in the often competitive enterprise of ferreting out crime." . . . A magistrate cannot be said to have properly discharged his constitutional duty if he relies on an informer's tip which—even when partially corroborated—is not as reliable as one which passes Aguilar's requirements when standing alone.

Applying these principles to the present case, we first consider the weight to be given the informer's tip when it is considered apart from the rest of the affidavit. It is clear that a Commissioner could not credit it without abdicating his constitutional function. Though the affiant swore that his confidant was "reliable," he offered the magistrate no reason in support of this conclusion. Perhaps even more important is the fact that Aguilar's other test has not been satisfied. The tip does not contain a sufficient statement of the underlying circumstances from which the informer concluded that Spinelli was running a bookmaking operation. We are not told how the FBI's source received his information—it is not alleged that the informant personally observed Spinelli at work or that he had ever placed a bet with him. Moreover, if the informant came by the information indirectly, he did not explain why his sources were reliable.... In the absence of a statement detailing the manner in which the information was gathered, it is especially important that the tip describe the accused's criminal activity in sufficient detail that the magistrate may know that he is relying on something more substantial than a casual rumor circulating in the underworld or an accusation based merely on an individual's general reputation.

The detail provided by the informant in Draper v. United States [supra] . . . provides a suitable benchmark. While Hereford, the Government's informer in that case, did not state the way in which he had obtained his information, he reported that Draper had gone to Chicago the day before by train and that he would return to Denver by train with three ounces of heroin on one of two specified mornings. Moreover, Hereford went on to describe, with minute particularity, the clothes that Draper would be wearing upon his arrival at the Denver station. A magistrate, when confronted with such detail, could reasonably infer that the informant had gained his information in a reliable way. Such an inference cannot be made in the present case. Here, the only facts supplied were that Spinelli was using two specified telephones and that these phones were being used in gambling opera-

tions. This meager report could easily have been obtained from an offhand remark heard at a neighborhood bar.

Nor do we believe that the patent doubts Aguilar raises as to the report's reliability are adequately resolved by a consideration of the allegations detailing the FBI's independent investigative efforts. At most, these allegations indicated that Spinelli could have used the telephones specified by the informant for some purpose. This cannot by itself be said to support both the inference that the informer was generally trustworthy and that he had made his charge against Spinelli on the basis of information obtained in a reliable way. Once again, Draper provides a relevant comparison. Independent police work in that case corroborated much more than one small detail that had been provided by the informant. There, the police, upon meeting the inbound Denver train on the second morning specified by informer Hereford, saw a man whose dress corresponded precisely to Hereford's detailed description. It was then apparent that the informant had not been fabricating his report out of whole cloth; since the report was of the sort which in common experience may be recognized as having been obtained in a reliable way, it was perfectly clear that probable cause had been established.

We conclude, then, that in the present case the informant's tip—even when corroborated to the extent indicated—was not sufficient to provide the basis for a finding of probable cause. This is not to say that the tip was so insubstantial that it could not properly have counted in the magistrate's determination. Rather, it needed some further support. When we look to the other parts of the application, however, we find nothing alleged which would permit the suspicions engendered by the informant's report to ripen into a judgment that a crime was probably being committed. As we have already seen, the allegations detailing the FBI's surveillance of Spinelli and its investigation of the telephone company records contain no suggestion of criminal conduct when taken by themselves—and they are not endowed with an aura of suspicion by virtue of the informer's tip. Nor do we find that the FBI's reports take on a sinister color when read in light of common knowledge that bookmaking is often carried on over the telephone and from premises ostensibly used by others for perfectly normal purposes. Such an argument would carry weight in a situation in which the premises contain an unusual number of telephones or abnormal activity is observed ... but it does not fit this case where neither of these factors is present. All that remains to be considered is the flat statement that Spinelli was "known" to the FBI and others as a gambler. But just as a simple assertion of police suspicion is not itself a sufficient basis for a magistrate's finding of probable cause, we do not believe it may be used to give additional weight to allegations that would otherwise be insufficient.

The affidavit, then, falls short of the standards set forth in Aguilar, Draper, and our other decisions that give content to the notion of probable cause. In holding as we have done, we do not retreat from the established propositions that only the probability, and not a prima facie showing, of criminal activity is the standard of probable

cause; ... that affidavits of probable cause are tested by much less rigorous standards than those governing the admissibility of evidence at trial; ... that in judging probable cause issuing magistrates are not to be confined by niggardly limitations or by restrictions on the use of their common sense; ... and that their determination of probable cause should be paid great deference by reviewing courts.... But we cannot sustain this warrant without diluting important safeguards that assure that the judgment of a disinterested judicial officer will interpose itself between the police and the citizenry.

Reversed and remanded.

[Mr. Justice WHITE wrote a concurring opinion.]

[Mr. Justice BLACK and Mr. Justice FORTAS wrote dissenting opinions and Mr. Justice STEWART also dissented.]

[Mr. Justice MARSHALL took no part in the consideration or decision of this case.]

The Supreme Court Revisits *Aguilar* and *Spinelli*

UNITED STATES v. HARRIS

Supreme Court of the United States, 1971
403 U.S. 573, 91 S. Ct. 2075, 29 L. Ed. 2d 723

Roosevelt Harris was convicted in the United States District Court for the Eastern District of Kentucky of possessing non–tax-paid liquor. The search that uncovered incriminatory evidence was conducted by a federal tax investigator and a local constable pursuant to a warrant issued by a federal magistrate. The Court of Appeals (6th Cir.), relying on *Aguilar* v. *Texas* (1964) and *Spinelli* v. *United States* (1969), reversed, and the United States Supreme Court granted certiorari to consider again the question of what showing is constitutionally required before a magistrate can find there is a substantial basis for crediting the report of a police informant.

Mr. Chief Justice BURGER announced the judgment of the Court in an opinion in which Mr. Justice BLACK and Mr. Justice BLACKMUN join, and in Part I of which Mr. Justice STEWART joins, and in Part III of which Mr. Justice WHITE joins.

* * *

In 1967 a federal tax investigator and a local constable entered the premises of re-

spondent Harris, pursuant to a search warrant issued by a federal magistrate, and seized jugs of whiskey upon which the federal tax had not been paid. The warrant had been issued solely on the basis of the investigator's affidavit, which recited the following:

"Roosevelt Harris has had a reputation with me for over four years as being a trafficker of nontaxpaid distilled spirits, and over this period I have received numerous information from all types of persons as to his activities. Constable Howard Johnson located a sizeable stash of illicit whiskey in an abandoned house under Harris' control during this period of time. This date, I have received information from a person who fears for their life and property should their name be revealed. I have interviewed this person, found this person to be a prudent person, and have, under a sworn verbal statement, gained the following information: This person has personal knowledge of and has purchased illicit whiskey from within the residence described, for a period of more than two years, and most recently within the past two weeks, has knowledge of a person who purchased illicit whiskey within the past two days from the house, has personal knowledge that the illicit whiskey is consumed by purchasers in the outbuilding known as and utilized as the 'dance hall,' and has seen Roosevelt Harris go to the other outbuilding, located about 50 yards from the residence, on numerous occasions, to obtain the whiskey for this person and other persons."

Respondent was subsequently charged with possession of nontaxpaid liquor, in violation of 26 U.S.C. § 5205(a) (2) . . . and he was convicted after a jury trial and sentenced to two years' imprisonment. The Court of Appeals for the Sixth Circuit reversed the conviction, holding that the information in the affidavit was insufficient to enable the magistrate to assess the informant's reliability and trustworthiness. . . .

* * *

In evaluating the showing of probable cause necessary to support a search warrant, against the Fourth Amendment's prohibition of unreasonable searches and seizures, we would do well to heed the sound admonition of United States v. Ventresca, 380 U.S. 102 (1965):

"[T]he Fourth Amendment's commands, like all constitutional requirements, are practical and not abstract. If the teachings of the Court's cases are to be followed and the constitutional policy served, affidavits for search warrants, such as the one involved here, must be tested and interpreted by magistrates and courts in a common-sense and realistic fashion. They are normally drafted by nonlawyers in the midst and

haste of a criminal investigation. Technical requirements of elaborate specificity once exacted under common law pleadings have no proper place in this area. A grudging or negative attitude by reviewing courts toward warrants will tend to discourage police officers from submitting their evidence to a judicial officer before acting." . . .

Aguilar in no way departed from these sound principles. There a warrant was issued on nothing more than an affidavit reciting:

"Affiants have received reliable information from a credible person and do believe that heroin, marijuana, barbiturates and other narcotics and narcotic paraphernalia are being kept at the above described premises for the purpose of sale and use contrary to the provisions of the law."

* * *

The affidavit, therefore, contained none of the underlying "facts or circumstances" from which the magistrate could find probable cause. . . . On the contrary, the affidavit was a "mere affirmation of suspicion and belief." . . .

Significantly, the Court in Aguilar cited with approval the affidavit upheld in Jones v. United States, 362 U.S. 257 (1960). That affidavit read in pertinent part as follows:

"In the late afternoon of Tuesday, August 20, 1957, I, Detective Thomas Didone, Jr., received information that Cecil Jones and Earline Richardson were involved in the illicit narcotic traffic and that they kept a ready supply of heroin on hand in the above mentioned apartment. The source of information also relates that the two aforementioned persons kept these same narcotics either on their person, under a pillow, on a dresser or on a window ledge in said apartment. The source of information goes on to relate that on many occasions the source of information has gone to said apartment and purchased narcotic drugs from the above mentioned persons and that the narcotics were secreated [sic] in the above mentioned places. The last time being August 20, 1957." . . .

The substance of the tip, held sufficient in Jones, closely parallels that here held insufficient by the Court of Appeals. Both recount personal and recent observations by an unidentified informant of criminal activity, factors showing that the information had been gained in a reliable manner, and serving to distinguish both tips from that held insufficient in Spinelli, supra, in which the affidavit failed to explain how the informant came by his information. . . .

The Court of Appeals seems to have believed, however, that there was no substantial basis for believing that the tip was truthful. Indeed, it emphasized that the affiant had never alleged that the informant was truthful, but only "prudent," a word that "signifies that he is circumspect in the conduct of his affairs, but reveals nothing about his credibility." . . . While a bare statement by an affiant that he believed the informant to be truthful would not, in itself, provide a *factual* basis for crediting the report of an unnamed informant, we conclude that the affidavit in the present case contains an ample factual basis for believing the informant which, when coupled with affiant's own knowledge of the respondent's background, afforded a basis upon which a magistrate could reasonably issue a warrant. The accusation by the informant was plainly a declaration against interest since it could readily warrant a prosecution and could sustain a conviction against the informant himself. . . .

In determining what quantum of information is necessary to support a belief that an unidentified informant's information is truthful, Jones v. United States, supra, is a suitable benchmark. The affidavit in Jones recounted the tip of an anonymous informant, who claimed to have recently purchased narcotics from the defendant at his apartment, and described the apartment in some detail.

* * *

Mr. Justice Frankfurter, writing for the Court in Jones, upheld the warrant. Although the information in the affidavit was almost entirely hearsay, he concluded that there was "substantial basis" for crediting the hearsay. The informant had previously given accurate information; his story was corroborated by "other sources" [albeit unnamed]; additionally the defendant was known to the police as a user of narcotics. Justice Frankfurter emphasized the last two of these factors:

"Corroboration through other sources of information reduced the chances of a reckless or prevaricating tale; that petitioner was a known user of narcotics made the charge against him much less subject to skepticism than would be such a charge against one without such a history."

* * *

Aguilar cannot be read as questioning the "substantial basis" approach of Jones. And unless Jones has somehow, without acknowledgment, been overruled by Spinelli, there would be no basis whatever for a holding that the affidavit in the present case is wanting. The affidavit in the present case, like that in Jones, contained a substantial basis for crediting the hearsay. Both affidavits purport to relate the personal observations of the informant—a factor that clearly distinguishes Spinelli, in which the affidavit failed to explain how the informant came by his information. Both recite prior events within the affiant's own knowledge—the needle marks in Jones and Constable Johnson's prior seizure in the present case—indicating that the defendant had previously trafficked in contraband. These prior events again distinguish Spinelli, in which no facts were supplied to support the assertion that Spinelli was "known . . . as a bookmaker, an associate of bookmakers, a gambler, and an associate of gamblers." . . .

To be sure there is no averment in the present affidavit, as there was in Jones, that the informant had previously given "correct information," but this Court in Jones never suggested that an averment of previous reliability was necessary. Indeed . . . the inquiry is, as it always must be in determining probable cause, whether the informant's *present* information is truthful or reliable. . . . Were it not for some language in Spinelli, it is doubtful that any . . . reputation attributes of the informant could be said to reveal any more about his present reliability than is afforded by the support of the officer's personal knowledge of the suspect. In Spinelli, however, the Court rejected as entitled to no weight the "bald and unilluminating" assertion that the suspect was known to the affiant as a gambler. . . . For this proposition the Court relied on Nathanson v. United States, 290 U.S. 41 (1933). But a careful examination of Nathanson shows that the Spinelli opinion did not fully reflect the critical points of what Nathanson held since it was limited to holding that reputation, *standing alone,* was insufficient; it surely did not hold it irrelevant when supported by other information. This reading of Nathanson is confirmed by Brinegar v. United States, 338 U.S. 160 (1949) in which the Court, in sustaining a finding of probable cause for a warrantless arrest, held proper the assertion of the searching officer that he had previously arrested the defendant for a similar offense and that the defendant had a reputation for hauling liquor. Such evidence would rarely be admissible at trial, but the Court took pains to emphasize the very different functions of criminal trials and preliminary determinations of probable cause. Trials are necessarily surrounded with evidentiary rules "developed to safeguard men from dubious and unjust convictions." ... But before the trial we deal only with probabilities that "are not technical; they are the factual and practical considerations of everyday life on which reasonable and prudent men, not legal technicians, act." ...

We cannot conclude that a policeman's knowledge of a suspect's reputation — something that policemen frequently know and a factor that impressed such a "legal technician" as Mr. Justice Frankfurter — is not a "practical consideration of everyday life" upon which an officer (or a magistrate) may properly rely in assessing the reliability of an informant's tip. To the extent that Spinelli prohibits the use of such probative information, it has no support in our prior cases, logic, or experience and we decline to apply it to preclude a magistrate from relying on a law enforcement officer's knowledge of a suspect's reputation.

Quite apart from the affiant's own knowledge of respondent's activities, there was an additional reason for crediting the informant's tip. Here the warrant's affidavit recited extrajudicial statements of a declarant, who feared for his life and safety if his identity was revealed, that over the past two years he had many times and recently purchased "illicit whiskey." These statements were against the informant's penal interest, for he thereby admitted major elements of an offense under the Internal Revenue Code. Section 5205(a) (2), Title 26, United States Code, proscribes the sale, purchase, or possession of unstamped liquor.

Common sense in the important daily affairs of life would induce a prudent and disinterested observer to credit these statements. People do not lightly admit a crime and place critical evidence in the hands of the police in the form of their own admissions. Admissions of crime, like admissions against proprietary interests, carry their own indicia of credibility — sufficient at least to support a finding of probable cause to search. That the informant may be paid or promised a "break" does not eliminate the residual risk and opprobrium of having admitted criminal conduct. Concededly admissions of crime do not always lend credibility to contemporaneous or later accusations of another. But here the informant's admission that over a long period and currently he had been buying illicit liquor on certain premises, itself and without more, implicated that property and furnished probable cause to search.

* * *

It will not do to say that warrants may not issue on uncorroborated hearsay. This only avoids the issue of whether there is reason for crediting the out-of-court statement. Nor is it especially significant that neither the name nor the person of the informant was produced before the magistrate. The police themselves almost certainly knew his name, the truth of the affidavit is not in issue, and McCray v. Illinois, 386 U.S. 300 (1967) disposed of the claim that the informant must be produced whenever the defendant so demands.

Reversed.

Mr. Justice BLACK, concurring.

While I join the opinion of the CHIEF JUSTICE which distinguishes this case from Aguilar v. Texas ... and Spinelli v. United States ... I would go further and overrule those two cases and wipe their holdings from the books for the reasons, among others, set forth in the dissent of Mr. Justice Clark in Aguilar, which I joined, and my dissent in Spinelli.

Mr. Justice BLACKMUN, concurring.

I joint the opinion of the CHIEF JUSTICE and the judgment of the Court, but I add a personal comment in order to make very clear my posture as to Spinelli v. United States ... cited in several places in that opinion. I was a member of the 6–2 majority of the United States Court of Appeals for the Eighth Circuit in Spinelli v. United States . . . which this Court by a 5–3 vote reversed, with the pivotal Justice concluding his concurring opinion . . . by the observation that, "Pending full-scale reconsideration of that case (Draper v. United States . . .) on the one hand, or of the Nathanson-Aguilar cases on the other, I join the opinion of the Court and the judgment of reversal, especially since a vote to affirm would produce an evenly divided Court." Obviously, I then felt that the Court of Ap-

peals had correctly decided the case. Nothing this Court said in Spinelli convinced me to the contrary. I continue to feel today that Spinelli at this level was wrongly decided and, like Mr. Justice BLACK, I would overrule it.

[Mr. Justice HARLAN, Mr. Justice DOUGLAS, Mr. Justice BRENNAN, and Mr. Justice MARSHALL all joined in a dissenting opinion.]

Comments

1. There is little doubt that the Court granted certiorari in *Spinelli* in order to further explicate the principles of *Aguilar* v. *Texas,* 378 U.S. 108 (1964). *Aguilar's* "two-pronged test" provides that in order for an affidavit to establish probable cause to issue a search warrant the government must convince the magistrate that (1) the informant is both trustworthy and reliable, and (2) there is other evidence that tends to support the informant's conclusions. Although the affidavit in *Spinelli* was more ample than that in *Aguilar,* it was still not sufficient to meet the *Aguilar* test. In *Aguilar,* the Court, per Mr. Justice Goldberg, concluded: "Although an affidavit may be based on hearsay . . . the magistrate must be informed of some of the *underlying circumstances* from which the informant concluded that the narcotics were where he claimed they were and some of the *underlying circumstances* from which the officer concluded that the informant, whose identity need not be disclosed, . . . was 'credible' or his information 'reliable,'" at 114 (emphasis added).

2. It should be understood that probable cause for arrest warrants and probable cause for search warrants can be distinguished — i.e., probable cause for one does not necessarily give rise to probable cause for the other. This can be more easily understood when consideration is given to what conclusions are necessary to establish probable cause for each. For a search, the magistrate must find that the items are subject to seizure, i.e., contraband, etc., and that the items will be found in the *particular place* to be searched. In contrast, the affidavit for an arrest warrant must show the judicial officer that an offense has been committed and that the person against whom the warrant is sought probably committed it.

3. The *Spinelli* Court declined to attach any weight to a suspect s reputation in establishing probable cause. Although the FBI's application stated that "William Spinelli is known . . . as a bookmaker, an associate of bookmakers, a gambler, and an associate of gamblers," such information was insufficient to establish the requisite "underlying circumstances." The Supreme Court changed its position on "reputation information" in *United States* v. *Harris.* The *Spinelli* Court also rejected the Court of Appeals' "totality of the circumstances" approach. Why? Could an informer's tip that fails the *Aguilar* standards be rehabilitated through the use of corrobo-

rative evidence? If so, does the Court suggest what measure of *reliability* the corroborating evidence must meet? Might "reliable" and "trustworthy" information from additional sources, i.e., police officers and their informers, be "pooled" in order to help corroborate the informer's tip? See *Hood* v. *United States,* 422 F.2d 737 (7th Cir. 1970), cert. denied, 400 U.S. 820.

4. Regarding *Harris,* it should be noted that there was a pronounced lack of unanimity among both the plurality and the dissenters. However, the plurality does succeed in distinguishing *Harris* from both *Aguilar* and *Spinelli.* In contrast to those cases, the Court found that the Harris affidavit more closely resembled the one found in *Jones* v. *United States,* 362 U.S. 257 (1960). In doing so, the *Harris* plurality suggested that it may no longer be necessary to establish the "previous reliability" of an informer, the test being "whether the informer's *present* information is truthful and reliable." Would adoption of that test by a majority of the justices have a substantial impact on current police practices of "developing" informer reliability over protracted periods of times?

5. Why does the *Harris* Court conclude that *Spinelli* was wrong in excluding a suspect's prior reputation for criminal activities? Does the ruling make it easier to corroborate an informant's tip? Is it likely that there will be more affidavits using declarations against penal interest? If so, why?

6. What seems to be the overall impact of *Harris*? Does it serve to seriously question the viability of *Aguilar* and *Spinelli*? Are both cases likely to be overruled as Burger and Blackmun suggest? Or does *Harris* do little to clarify the informant's role? Is there a likelihood that the Court will adopt a "totality of the circumstances" test in the future? Would such a test make the warrant standard any clearer? What factors might be included in such a test? Can you write an affidavit for a search warrant that satisfies the *Aguilar-Spinelli-Harris* standards?

7. The following is an affidavit filed by a police officer in support of his application for a warrant to search for stolen property:

STATE OF MISSOURI
COUNTY OF_____

IN THE MAGISTRATE COURT WITHIN AND FOR
SAID COUNTY

_____ being duly sworn, deposes and states that certain personal property, to-wit: two mahogony-style stereo speakers; General Electric television (Black & White Model # SE2208 WDE, Serial # 5750-26386); Arthur Fulmer Auto Stereo & Speaker (Model CP-3710, Serial # B270149); Electronic Range, Tappan (Model 56-1139); and a Sylvania Stereo Combination dark brown in color (Model # CST9735, Serial # 3837393, Chassis IDR 520801-3542085) of the goods and chattels of Mr. _____ of _____ _____, City of _____, Lot # 106, _____ _____ Trailer Court, has been heretofore unlawfully stolen, and that said property is now being held and kept at the following place in the said county and state, to-wit: a white metal house trailer with blue trim located on a private drive north of the tavern commonly

known as the _____ House on Route _____,
such trailer having a rear door with step and front door with step, also
having a parking space on the west end of said trailer with an entrance
on the south side of such trailer being one of two trailers at such
location to-wit: the second trailer on the east side of the lane.

Wherefore complainant prays that a search warrant be issued as
provided by law.

_____

Subscribed and sworn to before me this ____th day of March, 197__.

_____

JUDGE OF SAID COURT

Query: Is this affidavit sufficient for the issuance of a search
warrant? (The warrant *was* issued in this case.)

8.   CONNALLY v. GEORGIA
                        Supreme Court of the United States, 1977
                        429 U.S. 245, 97 S. Ct. 546, 51 L. Ed. 2d 444

PER CURIAM.

Appellant John Connally was indicted, tried, and convicted in
the Superior Court of Walker County, Ga., for possession of
marijuana in violation of the Georgia Controlled Substances Act,
Ga. Code Ann. c. 79A-8.... The Supreme Court of Georgia affirmed, with two justices dissenting ... 237 Ga. 203, 227 S.E.2d
352 (1976).

Pursuant to a search warrant issued by a justice of the peace, appellant's house was raided and marijuana found there was seized.
Connally was arrested. At his trial he moved to suppress the evidence so seized on the grounds that the justice who had issued the
warrant was not "a neutral and detached magistrate" because he
had a pecuniary interest in issuing the warrant. The trial court denied that motion, and the Supreme Court of Georgia, in affirming,
rejected the constitutional challenge.

Under Ga. Code Ann. § 24–1601, the fee for the issuance of a
search warrant by a Georgia justice of the peace "shall be" $5,
"and it shall be lawful for said justices of the peace to charge and
collect the same." If the requested warrant is refused, the justice of
the peace collects no fee for reviewing and denying the application.
The fee so charged apparently goes into county funds and from
there to the issuing justice as compensation.

At a pretrial hearing in Connally's case, the issuing justice testified on cross-examination that he was a justice primarily because
he was "interested in a livelihood"; that he received no salary; that
his compensation was "directly dependent on how many warrants"
he issued; that since January 1, 1973, he had issued "some
10,000" warrants for arrests or searches; and that he had no legal
background other than attendance at seminars and reading law.

Fifty years ago, in Tumey v. Ohio, 273 U.S. 510 (1927), the
Court considered state statutes that permitted a charge of violating
the State's prohibition laws to be tried without a jury before a vil-

lage mayor. Any fine imposed was divided between the State and the village. The latter's share was used to hire attorneys and detectives to arrest offenders and prosecute them before the mayor. When the mayor convicted, he received fees and costs, and these were in addition to his salary. The Court, in an opinion by Mr. Chief Justice Taft, unanimously held that subjecting a defendant to trial before a judge having "a direct, personal, pecuniary interest in convicting the defendant," that is in the $12 of fees and costs imposed . . . effected a denial of due process in violation of the Fourteenth Amendment.

This approach was reiterated in Ward v. Village of Monroeville, 409 U.S. 57 (1972). There, an Ohio statute authorized mayors to sit as judges of ordinance violations and certain traffic offenses. The petitioner was so convicted and fined by the mayor of Monroeville. Although the mayor had no direct personal financial stake in the outcome of cases before him, a major portion of the village's income was derived from the fines, fees, and costs imposed in the mayor's court. This Court . . . cited Tumey and repeated the test formulated in that case, namely, "whether the mayor's situation is one 'which would offer a possible temptation to the average man as a judge to forget the burden of proof required to convict the defendant, or which might lead him not to hold the balance nice, clear and true between the State and the accused. . . .' " 409 U.S., at 60. Dugan v. Ohio, 277 U.S. 61 (1928), where a mayor had judicial functions but only "very limited executive authority," and the executive power rested in a city manager and a commission, was distinguished as a situation where "the Mayor's relationship to the finances and financial policy of the city was too remote to warrant a presumption of bias toward conviction in prosecutions before him as a judge," 409 U.S., at 60–61, and the possibility of a later de novo trial in another court was held to be of no constitutional relevance because the defendant was "entitled to a neutral and detached judge in the first instance." . . .

The present case, of course, is not precisely the same as Tumey or as Ward, but the principle of those cases, we conclude, is applicable to the Georgia system for the issuance of search warrants by justices of the peace. The justice is not salaried. He is paid, so far as search warrants are concerned, by receipt of the fee prescribed by statute for his *issuance* of the warrant, and he receives nothing for his *denial* of the warrant. His financial welfare, therefore, is enhanced by positive action and is not enhanced by negative action. The situation, again, is one which offers "a possible temptation to the average man as a judge . . . or it might lead him not to hold the balance nice, clear and true between the State and the accused." It is, in other words, another situation where the defendant is subjected to what surely is judicial action by an officer of a court who "has a direct, personal, substantial, pecuniary interest" in his conclusion to issue or deny the warrant. See Bennett v. Cottingham, 290 F. Supp. 759, 762–763 (N.D. Ala. 1968), aff'd, 393 U.S. 317 (1969).

Shadwick v. City of Tampa, 407 U.S. 345 (1972), does not weight to the contrary. The issue there centered in the qualification of municipal court clerks to issue arrest warrants for breaches of ordinances. The Court held that the clerks, although laymen, worked within the Judicial Branch under the supervision of judges and were qualified to determine the existence of probable cause.

They were, therefore, "neutral and detached magistrates for purposes of the Fourth Amendment." Id., at 346. There was no element of personal financial gain in the clerks' issuance or nonissuance of arrest warrants. Cf. Coolidge v. New Hampshire, 403 U.S. 443, 449–453 (1971).

We disagree with the Supreme Court of Georgia's rulings ... that the amount of the search warrant fee is de minimis in the present context, that the unilateral character of the justice's adjudication of probable cause distinguishes the present case from Tumey, and that, instead, this case equates with Bevan v. Krieger, 289 U.S. 459–466 (1933), where a notary public's fee for taking a deposition was measured by the folios of testimony taken.

We therefore hold that the issuance of the search warrant by the justice of the peace in Connally's case effected a violation of the protections afforded him by the Fourth and Fourteenth Amendments of the United States Constitution. The judgment of the Supreme Court of Georgia is vacated and the case is remanded for further proceedings not inconsistent with this opinion.

9. Court decisions involving informants, probable cause, and search warrants abound in lower federal and state courts. Some recent examples are *United States* v. *Pond*, 523 F.2d 210 (2nd Cir. 1975) (search warrant based on railroad baggage agent's report of marijuana odor upheld); *People* v. *Williams*, 541 P.2d 76 (Colo. 1975) (reliable informer's failure to explain how he came by his information about a heroin courier was overcome by the ample detail of his tip, its verification, and the suspicious behavior of the courier himself, which satisfied *Aguilar-Spinelli* test); *People* v. *Thomas*, 342 N.E.2d 383 (Ill. 1975) (search warrant affidavit which read, "Said informant has furnished affiant with information on four prior occasions which information has resulted in four purchases of marijuana or dangerous drugs and that arrests are pending on these four purchases," held to satisfy the *Aguilar-Spinelli* informant test); *Mapp* v. *Warden*, 531 F.2d 1167 (2nd Cir. 1976) (untested informer's tip which was corroborated by police officers overhearing suspect's statement that she was engaged in narcotics traffic held sufficient probable cause to search her New York apartment—this is the same Dollree Mapp as in *Mapp* v. *Ohio*, 367 U.S. 643 [1961] [infra, § 5.03]); *State* v. *Gerber*, 241 N.W.2d 720 (S.D. 1976) (three different tips from anonymous long-distance callers accusing four named persons of drug peddling and describing their activities, when corroborated as to certain details by independent police investigation, held to furnish probable cause for search warrant for suspect's car); *United States* v. *Myers*, 538 F.2d 424 (D.C. Cir. 1976) (independent police knowledge of a heroin suspect's activities when added to a reliable informer's insufficiently detailed tip held sufficient probable cause); *United States* v. *Watts*, 540 F.2d 1093 (D.C. Cir. 1976) (although "bare recital" in affidavit that an unnamed informant is "credible" or "reliable" or "prudent" without offering any factual basis for that conclusion is insufficient probable cause, an assertion that the source had previously given correct information is entitled to weight as a factor in establishing previous reliability); *State* v. *Houlf*, 557 P.2d 565 (Ariz. App. 1976) (for purposes of probable cause, police and courts can assume the inherent reliability of "citizen-informers" as opposed to paid or habitual informers who operate on the fringe of the un-

derworld); *People* v. *Rogers,* 332 N.E.2d 562 (Ill. 1975) (prior reliability of informants does not apply to ordinary citizens who, without seeking anonymity, give information, and officers are justified in relying on such information); *Lawson* v. *Commonwealth,* 228 S.E.2d 685 (Va. 1976) (police officer who followed up a telephone tip from an unidentified informer that two persons known to the officer were selling heroin held to have probable cause to make warrantless search of their car after he saw them trying to conceal a small bag); *State* v. *Sullivan,* 230 S.E.2d 621 (S.C. 1976) (affidavit for search warrant which stated that the manager of an apartment saw a large quantity of plant material, plastic bags, and small scales in a certain apartment and detected a "peculiar odor," and which also alleged that the manager was "believable, because she is known to deponent to be a businesswoman and a truthful person," upheld); *State* v. *Collins,* 317 So. 2d 846 (Fla. 1975) (*Aguilar-Spinelli* hearsay principles are inapplicable where informant appears before magistrate and personally swears to facts contained in the affidavit); *United States* v. *Moore,* 522 F.2d 1068 (9th Cir. 1975) (in camera hearing conducted by trial judge held to be proper after defendant moved for disclosure of informant's identity, alleging falsehoods in a search warrant affidavit); *United States* v. *Bravo,* 403 F. Supp. 297 (S.D.N.Y. 1975) (attempts by defendants to bribe their way out of a minor bust for possession of marijuana supplied independent probable cause to justify the issuance of a warrant for a more thorough search); *United States* v. *Boswell,* 347 A.2d 270 (D.C. App. 1975) (police officers with reason to be suspicious of two men carrying a large object covered by a blanket but without probable cause to believe a crime was being committed held not justified in sneaking a look at what it concealed, and stolen color T.V. set was thus not admissible); *United States* v. *Giles,* 536 F.2d 136 (6th Cir. 1976) (telex message from airline employees in Philadelphia describing bag which one of the employees had inadvertently discovered filled with pills and plastic bags gave police at bag's destination in Detroit probable cause to believe it contained contraband); *State* v. *Turner,* 337 So. 2d 1090 (La. 1976) (search warrant affidavit which contained admission made by a possessor of stolen clothes to informer held entitled to weight in determining probable cause for search warrant); *Stief* v. *Sande,* 540 P.2d 968 (Mont. 1975) (search warrant directed to "any police officer of this state" rather than to a "peace officer" as required under Montana law held invalid); *United States* v. *Luna,* 525 F.2d 4 (6th Cir. 1975) (false statement on an affidavit which is facially sufficient to provide probable cause for a search warrant is fatal only if the false statement was knowingly used or was recklessly included in the affidavit); *State* v. *Gillin,* 541 P.2d 1156 (Ariz. 1975) (evidence seized pursuant to search of Apartment "B" when search warrant called for a search of Apartment "C" held inadmissible); *State* v. *Chaffin,* 324 So. 2d 369 (La. 1975) (50-day lapse from the time a search warrant affiant obtained facts giving him probable cause to seize drugs and application for warrant does not render the information stale and the warrant invalid) (see also *People* v. *Hanlon,* 330 N.E.2d 631 [N.Y. 1975] [affiant was introduced to informant in early September but did not submit affidavit until November 14th, held not so stale as to violate reliability of information]); *United States* v. *Prout,* 526 F.2d 380 (5th Cir. 1976) (slight inaccuracy in address stated on search warrant not fatal) (cf. *United*

States v. *Darensbourg,* 520 F.2d 985 [5th Cir. 1975] [warrant to search Apartment 70 at 3101 X Street held to be reasonable identification of the place intended to be searched even though Apartment 70 was in another building complex separated by a canal from X Street—there was only one apartment 70 in the complex]); *State* v. *Luciow,* 240 N.W.2d 833 (Minn. 1976) (defendants are entitled to challenge the truthfulness and accuracy of statements in a search warrant affidavit even though affidavit is facially valid); *United States* v. *Dauphinee,* 536 F.2d (1st Cir. 1976) (federal agent's inaccurate statement in his return on search warrant authorizing search for grenades that no property had been seized when revolver had been discovered and taken held not to require suppression of the handgun); *United States* v. *Sevier,* 539 F.2d 599 (6th Cir. 1976) (affidavit in support of application for search warrant need not allege specific facts sufficient to establish probable cause as to each and every element of the crime under investigation) (cf. *United States* v. *Marchildon,* 519 F.2d 337 [8th Cir. 1975] [affidavit need establish only the probable cause of criminal activity and secreting of evidence on specific premises, not proof beyond a reasonable doubt]); *People* v. *Marshall,* 244 N.W.2d 451 (Mich. Ct. App. 1976) (warrant is the only appropriate device for authorizing search, not a court order authorizing detention of a suspect for the purpose of a search) (contra, *Wise* v. *Murphy,* 275 A.2d 205 [D.C. App. 1971], and *Merola* v. *Fico,* 365 N.Y.S.2d 743 [1975]) (see also *United States* v. *Grummel,* 452 F.2d 789 [9th Cir. 1976] [valid arrest and the securing of house while search warrant is sought held permissible]); *State* v. *Shelton,* 554 P.2d 404 (Alas. 1976) (trial judge's failure to strike language limiting the hours of execution of a late-night search warrant issued does not require suppression of the evidence seized pursuant to the warrant) (see also *State* v. *Stephenson,* 245 N.W.2d 621 [Minn. 1976] [warrant-authorized search that began during the daytime but continued after sunset held valid despite fact that warrant did not authorize nighttime searches]); *People* v. *Smith,* 553 P.2d 557 (Cal. 1976) (police officer's failure to specify in his affidavit for search warrant that his informer was a juvenile makes warrant invalid) (plurality opinion); (see also *People* v. *Hill,* 528 P.2d 1 [1974]); *State* v. *Briggs,* 556 P.2d 247 (Wash. Ct. App. 1976) (jacket left behind by drug defendant who arrived at suspected dealer's house while police were executing a search warrant held properly searched by police as once he departed it came under scope of the warrant); *State* v. *Santillanes,* 557 P.2d 576 (N.M. App. 1976) (police officers who had a warrant to search a specified residence, a specified vehicle, and a named person, held to have acted properly in searching the purse belonging to that person's wife when she was found in the car with him); *Commonwealth* v. *Smith,* 348 N.E.2d 101 (Mass. 1976) (warrant issued to search a drug dealer's apartment and "any person present" held not overbroad given the detailed nature of the affidavit); *United States* v. *Bedford,* 519 F.2d 650 (3rd Cir. 1975) (under federal rules, a search warrant is valid if it specifies name of the occupant of the apartment against which it is directed despite the absence of a particularized physical description of the apartment) (but cf. *United States* v. *Besase,* 521 F.2d 1306 [6th Cir. 1975] [Fourth Amendment specificity requirement is directed against the place to be searched and "things" to be seized and not to the person who owns or occupies the named premises]).

5.03   THE EXCLUSIONARY RULE: WHEN THE CONSTABLE BLUNDERS

"We hold that all evidence obtained by searches and seizures in violation of the Constitution is, by that same authority, inadmissible..." *Mapp* v. *Ohio,* 367 U.S. 643, 655 (1961).

A.   THE *WEEKS* REMEDY AND STATE PROSECUTIONS

The "Nonessential" Test: The Fourth Amendment Becomes an "Empty Promise"

WOLF v. COLORADO

Supreme Court of the United States, 1949
388 U.S. 25, 69 S. Ct. 1359, 93 L. Ed. 1782

Colorado police officers, acting without a warrant, entered the office of Dr. Julius Wolf and seized certain appointment books, which were later introduced as evidence against him at trial. Wolf was convicted of conspiring with others to commit illegal abortions. The Supreme Court of Colorado affirmed the conviction, and Wolf successfully petitioned the United States Supreme Court for certiorari. Counsel for Wolf argued that the Fourteenth Amendment's Due Process Clause prohibited the state police of Colorado from violating Dr. Wolf's right against unreasonable searches and seizures under the Fourth Amendment. The issue facing the Supreme Court was whether the exclusionary rule, made enforceable against federal courts in *Weeks* v. *United States,* 232 U.S. 383 (1914), should be made applicable to state criminal trials.

Mr. Justice FRANKFURTER delivered the opinion of the Court.

The precise question for consideration is this: Does a conviction by a State Court for a State offense deny the "due process of law" required by the Fourteenth Amendment, solely because evidence that was admitted at the trial was obtained under circumstances which would have rendered it inadmissible in a prosecution for violation of a federal law in a court of the United States because there was deemed to be an infraction of the Fourth Amendment as applied in Weeks v. United States ...?

* * *

The security of one's privacy against arbitrary intrusion by the police — which is at the core of the Fourth Amendment — is basic to a free society. It is therefore im-

plicit in "the concept of ordered liberty" and as such enforceable against the States through the Due Process Clause.

* * *

Accordingly, we have no hesitation in saying that were a State affirmatively to sanction such police incursion into privacy it would run counter to the guaranty of the Fourteenth Amendment. But the ways of enforcing such a basic right raise questions of a different order. How such arbitrary conduct should be checked, what remedies against it should be afforded, the means by which the right should be made effective, are all questoins that are not to be so dogmatically answered as to preclude the varying solutions which spring from an allowable range of judgment on issues not susceptible of quantitative solution.

In Weeks v. United States ... this Court

held that in a federal prosecution the Fourth Amendment barred the use of evidence secured through an illegal search and seizure. This ruling . . . was not derived from the explicit requirements of the Fourth Amendment; it was not based on legislation expressing Congressional policy in the enforcement of the Constitution. The decision was a matter of judicial implication. Since then it has been frequently applied and we stoutly adhere to it. But the immediate question is whether the basic right to protection against arbitrary intrusion by the police demands the exclusion of logically relevant evidence obtained by an unreasonable search and seizure because, in a federal prosecution for a federal crime, it would be excluded. As a matter of inherent reason, one would suppose this to be an issue as to which men with complete devotion to the protection of the right of privacy might give different answers. When we find that in fact most of the English-speaking world does not regard as vital to such protection the exclusion of evidence thus obtained, we must hesitate to treat this remedy as an essential ingredient of the right. The contrariety of views of the States is particularly impressive in view of the careful reconsideration which they have given the problem in light of the Weeks decision.

As of today 30 States reject the Weeks doctrine, 17 States are in agreement with it. . . . Of 10 jurisdictions within the United Kingdom and the British Commonwealth of Nations which have passed on the question, none has held evidence obtained by illegal search and seizure inadmissible. . . .

The jurisdictions which have rejected the Weeks doctrine have not left the right to privacy without other means of protection. Indeed, the exclusion of evidence is a remedy which directly serves only to protect those upon whose person or premises something incriminating has been found. We cannot, therefore, regard it as a departure from basic standards to remand such persons, together with those who emerge scatheless from a search, to the remedies of private action and such protection as the internal discipline of the police, under the eyes of an alert public opinion, may afford. Granting that in practice the exclusion of evidence may be an effective way of deterring unreasonable searches, it is not for this Court to condemn as falling below the minimal standards assured by the Due Process Clause a

State's reliance upon other methods which, if consistently enforced, would be equally effective. Weighty testimony against such an insistence on our own view is the opinion of Mr. Justice (then Judge) Cardozo in People v. Defore, 130 N.E. 585 (1926). We cannot brush aside the experience of States which deem the incidence of such conduct by the police too slight to call for a deterrent remedy not by way of disciplinary measures but by overriding the relevant rules of evidence. There are, moreover, reasons for excluding evidence unreasonably obtained by the federal police which are less compelling in the case of police under State or local authority. The public opinion of a community can far more effectively be exerted against oppressive conduct on the part of police directly responsible to the community itself than can local opinion, sporadically aroused, be brought to bear upon remote authority pervasively exerted throughout the country.

We hold, therefore, that in a prosecution in a State court for a State crime the Fourteenth Amendment does not forbid the admission of evidence obtained by an unreasonable search and seizure. And though we have interpreted the Fourth Amendment to forbid the admission of such evidence, a different question would be presented if Congress under its legislative powers were to pass a statute purporting to negate the Weeks doctrine. We would then be faced with the problem of the respect to be accorded by legislative judgement of an issue as to which, in default of that judgement, we have been forced to depend upon our own. Problems of a converse character, also not before us, would be presented should Congress under §5 of the Fourteenth Amendment undertake to enforce the rights there guaranteed by attempting to make the Weeks doctrine binding upon the States.

Affirmed.

Mr. Justice BLACK, concurring.

* * *

. . . I agree with the conclusion of the Court that the Fourth Amendment's prohibition of "unreasonable searches and seizures" is enforceable against the states. Consequently, I should be for reversal of this case if I thought the Fourth Amendment not only prohibited "unreasonable searches and seizures," but also, of itself, barred the use of evidence so unlawfully obtained. But I agree with what appears to be a plain implication of the Court's opinion that the federal exclusionary rule is not a command of the Fourth Amendment but is a judicially created rule of evidence which Congress might negate....

Mr. Justice RUTLEDGE, with whom Mr. Justice MURPHY joins, dissenting.

...I think that all "the specific guarantees of the Bill of Rights should be carried over intact into the first section of the Fourteenth Amendment"....

* * *

...I reject the Court's...conclusion that the mandate embodied in the Fourth Amendment, although binding on the states, does not carry with it the one sanction—exclusion of evidence taken in violation of the Amendment's terms—failure to observe which means that "the protection of the Fourth Amendment...might as well be stricken from the Constitution."...

* * *

The version of the Fourth Amendment today held applicable to the states hardly rises to the dignity of a form of words; at best it is a pale and frayed carbon copy of the original, bearing little resemblance to the Amendment the fulfillment of whose command I had heretofore thought to be "an indispensable need for a democratic society."

* * *

Mr. Justice MURPHY, with whom Mr. Justice RUTLEDGE joins, dissenting.

* * *

Imagination and zeal may invent a dozen methods to give content to the commands of the Fourth Amendment. But this Court is limited to the remedies currently available. It cannot legislate the ideal system. If we would attempt the enforcement of the search and seizure clause in the ordinary case today, we are limited to three devices: judicial exclusion of the illegally obtained evidence; criminal prosecution of violators; and civil action against violators in the action of trespass.

* * *

...Little need be said concerning the possibilities of criminal prosecution. Self-scrutiny is a lofty ideal, but its exaltation reaches new heights if we expect a District Attorney to prosecute himself or his associates for well-meaning violations of the search and seizure clause during a raid the District Attorney or his associates have ordered. But there is an appealing ring in another alternative. A trespass action for damages is a venerable means of securing reparation for unauthorized invasion of the home....

But what an illusory remedy this is, if by "remedy" we mean a positive deterrent to police and prosecutors tempted to violate the Fourth Amendment. The appealing ring softens when we recall that in a trespass action the measure of damages is simply the extent of the injury to physical property. If the officer searches with care, he can avoid all but nominal damages—a penny, or a dollar. Are punitive damages possible? Perhaps. But a few states permit none, whatever the circumstances. In those that do, the plaintiff must show the real ill will or malice of the defendant, and surely it is not unreasonable to assume that one in honest pursuit of crime bears no malice toward the search victim....

* * *

The conclusion is inescapable that but one remedy exists to deter violations of the search and seizure clause. That is the rule which excludes illegally obtained evidence. Only by exclusion can we impress upon the zealous prosecutor that violation of the Constitution will do him no good.

* * *

Mr. Justice DOUGLAS, dissenting.

I believe for the reasons stated by Mr. Justice BLACK in his dissent in Adamson v. California, 332 U.S. 46 (1947), that the Fourth Amendment is applicable to the States. I agree with Mr. Justice MURPHY that the evidence obtained in violation of it must be excluded in state prosecutions as well as in federal prosecutions, since in absence of that rule of evidence the Amendment would have no effective sanction. I also agree with him that under that test this evidence was improperly admitted and that the judgments of conviction must be reversed.

Application of the Exclusionary Rule to the States

MAPP v. OHIO

Supreme Court of the United States, 1961
367 U.S. 643, 81 S. Ct. 1684, 6 L. Ed. 2d 1081

Appellant, Dollree Mapp, was convicted in an Ohio Common Pleas Court of knowingly having in her possession and under her control obscene materials in violation of Ohio law. Although the Supreme Court of Ohio found that the evidence had been seized during an unlawful search of her home (the facts are stated in the opinion), her conviction was affirmed. Miss Mapp appealed to the United States Supreme Court urging that the Court review its holding in *Wolf* v. *Colorado*, supra.

Mr. Justice CLARK delivered the opinion of the Court.

* * *

On May 23, 1957, three Cleveland police officers arrived at appellant's residence in that city pursuant to information that "a person [was] hiding out in the home, who was wanted for questioning in connection with a recent bombing, and that there was a large amount of policy paraphernalia being hidden in the home." Miss Mapp and her daughter by a former marriage lived on the top floor of the two-family dwelling. Upon their arrival at that house, the officers knocked on the door and demanded entrance but appellant, after telephoning her attorney, refused to admit them without a search warrant. They advised their headquarters of the situation and undertook a surveillance of the house.

The officers again sought entrance some three hours later when four or more additional officers arrived on the scene. When Miss Mapp did not come to the door immediately, at least one of the several doors to the house was forcibly opened and the policemen gained admittance. Meanwhile Miss Mapp's attorney arrived, but the officers, having secured their own entry, and continuing in their defiance of the law, would permit him neither to see Miss Mapp nor to enter the house. It appears that Miss Mapp was halfway down the stairs from the upper floor to the front door when the officers, in this high-handed manner, broke into the hall. She demanded to see the search warrant. A paper, claimed to be a warrant, was held up by one of the officers. She grabbed the "warrant" and placed it in her bosom. A struggle ensued in which the officers recovered the piece of paper and as a result of which they handcuffed appellant because she had been "belligerent" in resisting their official rescue of the "warrant" from her person. Running roughshod over appellant, a policeman "grabbed" her, "twisted [her] hand," and she "yelled [and] pleaded with him" because "it was hurting." Appellant, in handcuffs, was then forcibly taken upstairs to her bedroom where the officers searched a dresser, a chest of drawers, a closet and some suitcases. They also looked into a photo album and through personal papers belonging to the appellant. The search spread to the rest of the second floor including the child's bedroom, the living room, the kitchen and a dinette. The basement of the building and a trunk found therein were also searched. The obscene materials for possession of which she was ultimately convicted were discovered in the course of that widespread search.

At the trial no search warrant was produced by the prosecution, nor was the failure to produce one explained or accounted for. At best, "[t]here is, in the record, considerable doubt as to whether there ever was any warrant for the search of defendant's home." ... The Ohio Supreme Court believed a "reasonable argument" could be made that the conviction should be reversed "because the 'methods' employed to obtain the [evidence] were such as to 'offend "a sense of justice,"'" but the court found determinative the fact that the evidence had not been taken "from defendant's person by the use of brutal or offensive physical force against defendant."...

The State says that even if the search were made without authority or otherwise unreasonably, it is not prevented from using the unconstitutionally seized evidence at trial, citing Wolf v. People of the State of Colorado ... in which this Court did indeed hold "that in a prosecution in a State court for a State crime the Fourteenth Amendment does not forbid the admission of evidence obtained by an unreasonable search and seizure." On this appeal ... it is urged once again that we review that holding.

* * *

Since the Fourth Amendment's right of privacy has been declared enforceable against the States through the Due Process Clause of the Fourteenth, it is enforceable against them by the same sanction of exclusion as is used against the Federal Government. Were it otherwise, then just as without the Weeks rule the assurance against unreasonable federal searches and seizures would be "a form of words," valueless and undeserving of mention in a perpetual charter of inestimable human liberties, so too, without that rule the freedom from all brutish means of coercing evidence as not to merit this Court's high regard as a freedom "implicit in 'the concept of ordered liberty.'" At the time that the Court held in Wolf that the Amendment was applicable to the States through the Due Process Clause, the cases of this Court, as we have seen, had steadfastly held that as to federal officers the Fourth Amendment included the exclusion of the evidence seized in violation of its provisions. Even Wolf "stoutly adhered" to that proposition. The right to privacy, when conceded operatively enforceable against the States, was not susceptible of destruction by avulsion of the sanction upon which its protection and enjoyment had always been deemed dependent under the ... [earlier] cases. Therefore, in extending the substantive protections of due process to all constitutionally unreasonable searches — state or federal — it was logically and constitutionally necessary that the exclu-

sion doctrine — an essential part of the right to privacy — be also insisted upon as an essential ingredient of the right newly recognized by the Wolf case. In short, the admission of the new constitutional right by Wolf could not consistently tolerate denial of its most important constitutional privilege, namely, the exclusion of the evidence which an accused had been forced to give by reason of the unlawful seizure. To hold otherwise is to grant the right but in reality to withhold its privilege and enjoyment. Only last year the Court itself recognized that the purpose of the exclusionary rule "is to deter — to compel respect for the constitutional guaranty in the only effectively available way — by removing the incentive to disregard it."...

Indeed, we are aware of no restraint, similar to that rejected today, conditioning the enforcement of any other basic constitutional right. The right to privacy, no less important than any other right carefully and particularly reserved to the people, would stand in marked contrast to all other rights declared as "basic to a free society." This Court has not hesitated to enforce as strictly against the States as it does against the Federal Government the rights of free speech and of a free press, the rights to notice and to a fair, public trial, including, as it does, the right not to be convicted by use of a coerced confession, however logically relevant it be, and without regard to its reliability.... And nothing could be more certain than that when a coerced confession is involved, "the relevant rules of evidence" are overridden without regard to "the incidence of such conduct by the police," slight or frequent. Why should not the same rule apply to what is tantamount to coerced testimony by way of unconstitutional seizure of goods, papers, effects, documents, etc.? We find that, as to the Federal Government, the Fourth and Fifth Amendments and, as to the States, the freedom from unconscionable invasions of privacy and the freedom from convictions based upon coerced confessions do enjoy an "intimate relation" in their perpetuation of "principles of humanity and civil liberty [secured] ... only after years of struggle." ... They express "supplementing phrases of the same constitutional purpose — to maintain inviolate large areas of personal privacy." ... The philosophy of each Amendment and of each freedom is complementary to, although not dependent upon, that of the other in its sphere of influence—the very least that together they assure in either sphere is that no man is to be convicted on unconstitutional evidence. . . .

Moreover, our holding that the exclusionary rule is an essential part of both the Fourth and Fourteenth Amendments is not only the logical dictate of prior cases, but it also makes very good sense. There is no war between the Constitution and common sense. Presently, a federal prosecutor may make no use of evidence illegally seized, but a State's attorney across the street may, although he supposedly is operating under the enforceable prohibitions of the same Amendment. Thus the State, by admitting evidence unlawfully seized, served to encourage disobedience to the Federal Constitution which it is bound to uphold. Moreover, as was said in Elkins "[t]he very essence of a healthy federalism depends upon the avoidance of needless conflict between state and federal courts." . . . Such a conflict, hereafter needless, arose this very Term, in Wilson v. Schnettler, 365 U.S. 381 (1961), in which, and in spite of the promise made by Rea, we gave full recognition to our practice in this regard by refusing to restrain a federal officer from testifying in a state court as to evidence unconstitutionally seized by him in the performance of his duties. Yet the double standard recognized until today hardly put such a thesis into practice. In non-exclusionary States, federal officers, being human, were by it invited to and did, as our cases indicate, step across the street to the State's attorney with their unconstitutionally seized evidence. Prosecution on the basis of that evidence was then had in a state court in utter disregard of the enforceable Fourth Amendment. If the fruits of an unconstitutional search had been inadmissible in both state and federal courts, this inducement to evasion would have been sooner eliminated. There would be no need to reconcile such cases as Rea and Schnettler, each pointing up the hazardous uncertainties of our heretofore ambivalent approach.

Federal-state cooperation in the solution of crime under constitutional standards will be promoted, if only by recognition of their now mutual obligation to respect the same fundamental criteria in their approaches.

"However much in a particular case insistence upon such rules may appear as a technicality that inures to the benefit of a guilty person, the history of the criminal law proves that tolerance of shortcut methods in law enforcement impairs its enduring effectiveness." . . . Denying shortcuts to only one of two cooperating law enforcement agencies tends naturally to breed legitimate suspicion of "working arrangements" whose results are equally tainted. . . .

There are those who say, as did Justice [then Judge] Cardozo, that under our constitutional exclusionary doctrine "[t]he criminal is to go free because the constable has blundered." . . . In some cases this will undoubtedly be the result. But, as was said in Elkins, "there is another consideration—the imperative of judicial integrity." . . . The criminal goes free, if he must, but it is the law that sets him free. Nothing can destroy a government more quickly than its failure to observe its own laws, or worse, its disregard of the charter of its own existence. As Mr. Justice Brandeis, dissenting, said in Olmstead v. United States . . . "Our government is the potent, the omnipresent teacher. For good or for ill, it teaches the whole people by its example. . . . If the government becomes a lawbreaker, it breeds contempt for law; it invites every man to become a law unto himself; it invites anarchy." Nor can it lightly be assumed that, as a practical matter, adoption of the exclusionary rule fetters law enforcement. Only last year this Court expressly considered that contention and found that "pragmatic evidence of a sort" to the contrary was not wanting. . . . [In Elkins the] Court noted that "The federal courts themselves have operated under the exclusionary rule of Weeks for almost half a century; yet it has not been suggested either that the Federal Bureau of Investigation has thereby been rendered ineffective, or that the administration of criminal justice in the federal courts has thereby been disrupted. Moreover, the experience of the states is impressive. . . . The movement towards the rule of exclusion has been halting but seemingly inexorable." . . .

The ignoble shortcut to conviction left open to the States tends to destroy the entire system of constitutional restraints on which the liberties of the people rest. Having once recognized that the right to privacy embodied in the Fourth Amendment is enforceable against the States, and that the right to be secure against rude invasions of privacy by state officers is, therefore, constitutional in origin, we can no longer permit that right to remain an empty promise. Because it is enforceable in the same manner and to like effect as other basic rights secured by the Due Process Clause, we can no longer permit it to be revocable at the whim of any police officer who, in the name of law enforcement itself, chooses to suspend its enjoyment. Our decision, founded on reason and truth, gives to the individual no more than that which the Constitution guarantees him, to the police officer no less than that to which honest law enforcement is entitled, and, to the courts, that judicial integrity so necessary in the true administration of justice.

Reversed and remanded.

Mr. Justice BLACK, concurring.

* * *

I am still not persuaded that the Fourth Amendment, standing alone, would be enough to bar the introduction into evidence against an accused of papers and effects seized from him in violation of its commands. For the Fourth Amendment does not itself contain any provision expressly precluding the use of such evidence, and I am extremely doubtful that such a provision could properly be inferred from nothing more than the basic command against unreasonable searches and seizures. Reflection on the problem, however, in the light of cases coming before the Court since Wolf, has led me to conclude that when the Fourth Amendment's ban against unreasonable searches and seizures is considered together with the Fifth Amendment's ban against compelled self-incrimination, a constitutional basis emerges which not only justifies but actually requires the exclusionary rule.

The close interrelationship between the Fourth and Fifth Amendments, as they apply to this problem, has long been recognized and, indeed, was expressly made the ground for this Court's holding in Boyd v. United States. There the Court fully discussed this relationship and declared itself unable to perceive that the seizure of a man's private books and papers to be used in evidence against him is substantially different from compelling him to be a witness against himself. It was upon this ground that Mr. Justice Rutledge largely relied in his dissenting opinion in the Wolf case. And, although I rejected the argument at that time, its force has, for me at least, become compelling with the more thorough understanding of the problem brought on by recent cases. . . .

* * *

[Mr. Justice DOUGLAS wrote a concurring opinion.]

[Mr. Justice STEWART wrote a memorandum but declined to express a view as to the merits of the constitutional issue before the Court.]

Mr. Justice HARLAN, whom Mr. Justice FRANKFURTER and Mr. Justice WHITTAKER join, dissenting.

* * *

I would not impose upon the States this federal exclusionary remedy. The reasons given by the majority for now suddenly turning its back on Wolf seem to me notably unconvincing.

. . . It is said that "the factual grounds upon which Wolf was based" have since changed, in that more States now follow the Weeks exclusionary rule than was so at the time Wolf was decided. While that is true, a recent survey indicates that at present one-half of the States still adhere to the common-law non-exclusionary rule, and one, Maryland, retains the rule as to felonies. . . . But in any case surely all this is beside the point, as the majority itself indeed seems to recognize. Our concern here, as it was in Wolf, is not with the desirability of that rule but only with the question whether the States are Constitutionally free to follow it or not as they may themselves determine, and the relevance of the disparity of views among the States on this point lies simply in the fact that the judgment involved is a debatable one. Moreover, the very fact on which the majority relies, instead of lending support to what is now being done, points away from the need of replacing voluntary state action with federal compulsion.

The preservation of a proper balance between state and federal responsibility in the administration of criminal justice demands patience on the part of those who might like to see things move faster among the States in this respect. Problems of criminal law enforcement vary widely from State to State. One State, in considering the totality of its legal picture, may conclude that the need for embracing the Weeks rule is pressing because other remedies are unavailable or inadequate to secure compliance with the substantive Constitutional principle involved. Another, though equally solicitous of Constitutional rights, may choose to pursue one purpose at a time, allowing all evidence relevant to guilt to be brought into a criminal trial, and dealing with Constitutional infractions by other means. Still another may consider the exclusionary rule too rough-and-ready a remedy, in that it reaches only unconstitutional intrusions which eventuate in criminal prosecution of the victims. Further, a State after experimenting with the Weeks rule for a time may, because of unsatisfactory experience with it, decide to revert to a non-exclusionary rule. And so on. From the standpoint of Constitutional permissibility in pointing a State in one direction or another, I do not see at all why "time has set its face against" the considerations which led Mr. Justice Cardozo, then chief judge of the New York Court of Appeals, to reject for New York . . . the Weeks exclusionary rule. For us the question remains, as it has always been, one of state power, not one of passing judgment on the wisdom of one state course or another. In my view this Court should continue to forbear from fettering the States with an adamant rule which

may embarrass them in coping with their own peculiar problems in criminal law enforcement.

. . . I do not believe that the Fourteenth Amendment empowers this Court to mold state remedies effectuating the right to freedom from "arbitrary intrusion by the police" to suit its own notions of how things should be done, as, for instance, the California Supreme Court did in People v. Cahan (1955) with reference to procedures in the California courts or as this Court did in Weeks for the lower federal courts.

Finally, it is said that the overruling of Wolf is supported by the established doctrine that the admission in evidence of an involuntary confession renders a state conviction Constitutionally invalid. Since such a confession may often be entirely reliable, and therefore of the greatest relevance to the issue of the trial, the argument continues, this doctrine is ample warrant in precedent that the way evidence was obtained, and not just its relevance, is Constitutionally significant to the fairness of a trial. I believe this analogy is not a true one. The "coerced confession" rule is certainly not a rule that any illegally obtained statements may not be used in evidence. I would suppose that a statement which is procured during a period of illegal detention . . . is, as much as unlawfully seized evidence, illegally obtained, but this Court has consistently refused to reverse state convictions resting on the use of such statements. . . .

* * *

Is the Fourth Amendment in Danger of Becoming a "Dead Letter"?

ORAL ARGUMENTS BEFORE THE U.S. SUPREME COURT*

Wolff v. Rice, No. 74-1222; argued 2/24/76

In what could be the most important criminal cases of the present Term and

perhaps the most significant Fourth Amendment cases since *Mapp* v. *Ohio*, 367 U.S. 643 (1961), the Court last week was asked to limit both the exclusionary rule and the availability of federal habeas corpus to state prisoners claiming Fourth Amendment violations. State attorneys representing wardens in Nebraska and California urged the Court to hold that the exclusionary rule should not be applied where police officers acted in good faith but for one reason or another

*From 18 Crim. L. Rptr. 4176–4179 (1976). Reprinted by permission of the Bureau of National Affairs, Inc.

their actions resulted in a violation of Fourth Amendment rights.

The Nebraska case involved a search pursuant to a warrant that was later declared invalid because the affidavit offered to support it failed to establish probable cause. 513 F.2d 1280. Melvin Kent Kammerlohr, Assistant Attorney General of Nebraska, explained that the police officers here, after arriving at the home of a murder suspect and receiving no answer, sent two of their number back to obtain a search warrant. The warrant was issued by a magistrate who, the federal habeas court later held, erred in finding probable cause. In this case, counsel said, it was the magistrate, not the police, who made the error.

The Fourth Amendment's exclusionary rule is primarily a rule of deterrence, Kammerlohr argued. Its objective is to deter unlawful conduct by law enforcement agencies. That deterrent purpose is not served when the rule is applied in cases where the police act in good faith but are guilty of Fourth Amendment violations because of a magisterial error. In fact, applying the rule to such cases will discourage the police from obtaining search warrants.

The appropriate course, he said, should be to abolish or limit the exclusionary rule, provided some other remedy for redressing Fourth Amendment violations is supplied.

Mr. Justice Stewart: "There are other remedies available aren't there? And these remedies are not alternatives to the exclusionary rule but additional remedies."

Counsel thought the Court should require the states to provide a tort remedy for persons aggrieved by Fourth Amendment violations, perhaps setting a minimum recovery.

Mr. Justice Stewart: "Do you think we should refrain from reconsidering the exclusionary rule until the states have all acted to provide such a remedy?

"You could impose that as a requirement in your holding."

The Chief Justice: "You mean a conditional holding." Mr. Justice Stewart: "Wouldn't it be your guess that most states already have such remedies available?"

"Not with a minimum recovery. What I'm advocating in this case is that the Court should not apply the exclusionary rule in cases where the police, in good faith, seek and obtain a warrant before acting."

Mr. Justice Stewart: "No matter how inept the warrant?"

"In the absence of fraud or collusion, yes." In cases where the magistrate makes the mistake, he added, the sanction should be imposed on the magistrate.

"Are you suggesting that he should be civilly or criminally liable?"

"If he is grossly negligent, his immunity should be removed."

"Wouldn't that seriously erode the doctrine of judicial immunity?"

"Yes, it would."

The exclusionary rule as it now stands, Kammerlohr argued, operates to release the guilty in many cases but offers no remedy to the innocent and in effect punishes society. At any rate, if the exclusionary rule is designed to deter the policeman, it should be noted that it is not the policeman who suffers when the evidence is suppressed.

What is especially significant, he maintained, is the element of deterrence in this case. Here the police acted in good faith and obtained a warrant. They did what the Fourth Amendment required them to do. How, he wondered, is application of the exclusionary rule here going to deter these officers in the future?

Michigan v. *Tucker,* 417 U.S. 433 (1974), although arising in a Fifth Amendment context, offers guidance. Significantly, Kammerlohr noted, for purposes of the issues involved in this case, *Tucker* stressed that the concept of deterrence of improper police conduct, upon which the exclusionary rule is based, and the question of whether the police were acting in good faith are inextricably intertwined. The *Tucker* majority noted that where the official action involved was pursued in good faith, the deterrence rationale loses much of its force.

This, counsel said, "lies at the heart of the instant case. We submit that it would be difficult to discover a case in which the people were acting in more good faith or one in which the supposed deterrent against future 'misconduct' would be less, should the decision of the lower court suppressing the evidence in this case be sustained."

No Habeas Relief

The second aspect of the state's argument was that habeas relief should not be available at all in cases of this type. On this point, Kammerlohr urged the Court to adopt the position outlined by Mr. Justice Powell in his concurring opinion in *Schneckloth* v. *Bustamonte*, 412 U.S. 218 (1973). "That federal courts would actually redetermine constitutional claims bearing no relation to the prisoner's innocence with the possibility of releasing him from custody if the search is held unlawful not only defeats our societal interest in a rational legal system but serves no compensating ends of personal justice." 412 U.S. at 258.

Mr. Justice White: "If we agree with you on this point, then we do not have to consider your first argument, do we?"

"The first argument is a fallback argument, your honor."

This argument, Kammerlohr explained, is that federal habeas relief should not be available to raise Fourth Amendment violations where there is no colorable claim of innocence and an adequate remedy under state law exists to resolve the alleged Fourth Amendment violation.

Also an important consideration in this area, counsel concluded, is Mr. Justice Powell's observation in *Schneckloth* that the exclusionary rule on collateral attack not only retains its major liabilities, but its hoped-for deterrent function is even more weakened coming months or years after the claimed Fourth Amendment violation.

Guilt or Innocence

William C. Cunningham, Santa Barbara, California, began his argument for the defendant by placing special stress on the need for habeas relief. The importance of independent review of constitutional claims is no less present in cases involving the exclusionary rule, where guilt or innocence is not central to the right violated, than in cases where the right goes directly to guilt or innocence. Previous decisions of the Court holding that federal habeas corpus reaches all constitutional errors are consistent with the history and underlying purpose of the Habeas Corpus Act. And when *Mapp* v. *Ohio* held the Fourth Amendment exclusionary rule applicable to the states, it brought state search and seizure cases within the ambit of federal habeas corpus.

Mr. Justice Stewart: "This case could not have arisen, then, if *Mapp* had not been decided?"

"No, your honor."

The federal courts, counsel continued, are better situated to evaluate questions arising under the federal Constitution.

Mr. Justice Stewart: "How can we denigrate the state courts by saying that they don't have a sufficient understanding of the federal Constitution?"

"To make such an assumption would be irresponsible," Cunningham replied. However, he added, a survey of Nebraska Supreme Court cases indicates that that court has been less than disposed to find a want of probable cause in the issuance of a search warrant and some of its holdings have been in direct conflict with decisions of this Court.

If the scope of federal habeas relief is to be changed, Cunningham said, then it is Congress which should change it.

The Chief Justice: "Do you believe that a murderer going scot-free is the right price to pay for a mistake by a magistrate?"

"I would not say it that way." Guilt or innocence has never been a consideration in the evaluation of claimed violations of constitutional rights.

"Taking this whole record, is it not a fair statement to say that a murderer is to go free because the constable blundered?"

The real question, counsel replied, is whether a man is to be imprisoned if his trial was lacking in constitutional fairness.

Mr. Justice Powell: "Is it your position that the exclusionary rule is compelled by the Constitution?"

"It is judicially created, but, yes, I believe it is constitutionally compelled."

Effective Sanction

In the absence of an effective sanction against the officer who transgresses the Constitution, namely an exclusionary rule, the officer will be encouraged to do so again. And, to make the operation of the exclusionary rule depend on the absence of good faith upon the part of the police officers would substantially diminish its deterrent effect, Cunningham said. At any rate, the rule is not aimed at past conduct, but at future conduct. Furthermore, the adoption of a "situationally rooted good faith test" would render future application of the exclusionary rule highly unpredictable.

Mr. Justice Powell: "Does Congress have

the authority to change the rule? Could they revise it with respect to the federal courts?"

"Yes, but it would require a constitutional amendment."

Stone v. Powell, No. 74-1055; argued 2/24/76.

The California case involves the suppression of a murder weapon which had been seized by a Nevada police officer when he searched the defendant after arresting him under a local vagrancy ordinance which the Ninth Circuit found unconstitutional on appeal from the district court's denial of habeas relief. 507 F.2d 93.

The Court of Appeals decision in this case, Robert R. Granucci, Deputy Attorney General of California, argued, represents "a triumph of logic over justice."

A fundamental question presented, he said, is whether a California murder defendant is to go free because Nevada policemen, acting in good faith, arrested him under an ordinance which had not yet been held unconstitutional. The second question is whether searches made in reasonable reliance upon a coordinate branch of government should be cognizable under federal habeas corpus.

Granucci maintained that Fourth Amendment claims of state prisoners should be cognizable on habeas corpus only if the state has not afforded an adequate corrective process or if the habeas petitioner can allege his innocence in good faith.

Mr. Justice White: "What if the issue is never litigated in the state courts?"

"We would argue that where there was an opportunity to litigate it or the petitioner had a possibility to litigate it, habeas relief should not be available."

Mr. Justice Stewart: "You don't argue that if there is no state procedure for litigating the claim, habeas is not available, do you?"

"No, sir. We don't."

Mr. Justice White: "Suppose the state hearing is flawed. Would you still say that federal habeas is closed to him?"

Counsel thought this would be a due process violation and that the district court should send the case back to the state courts for another hearing. Habeas corpus, he argued, should be limited to the vindication of due process rights. The benefit of the exclusionary rule as a device to deter un-lawful police conduct is speculative, counsel maintained, and the cost of federal habeas review in terms of misallocation of resources, duplication of effort, friction between the state and federal courts, the state's interest in the finality of its judgements, and the freeing of guilty persons is "manifest and unacceptable." This is especially true in this case where the Fourth Amendment violation is technical in nature. "We would urge the Court to adopt Mr. Justice Powell's analysis in *Schneckloth*."

No Personal Right

Turning his attention to the exclusionary rule, Granucci argued that *Calandra* and *U.S.* v. *Peltier*, 422 U.S. 531 (1974), indicate that the rule is a judicially created remedy designed to deter unlawful police conduct. It is not a personal right but a remedy for the benefit of society.

Calandra, he noted, involved a balancing analysis of the effect of applying the rule to the grand jury on the one hand, and the benefit to society on the other. Where personal rights are involved a balancing approach is not appropriate; thus *Calandra* indicates that the exclusion of evidence is not a personal right. Where a societal interest is involved, a balancing of interests and benefit is acceptable.

Mr. Justice White: "Would you apply the same rule to Fifth Amendment claims?"

"The Fifth Amendment privilege against self-incrimination is a trial right. The right is not violated until the confession or statement is introduced."

Mr. Justice Stewart: "Do you argue that someone from whom a confession is extracted by force has no remedy if that confession is not introduced at trial?"

"No, sir, he has a right to sue under (42 USC) 1983." Assuming the Court is willing to hold that the exclusionary rule should not be applied here, Granucci offered, that holding could be limited to situations where the search is made on reasonable good faith reliance on the actions of coordinate branches of government such as legislative bodies or magistrates. Application of the rule should be limited to cases where its deterrent purposes will be served.

Applying it to the facts of this case, he said, would be counterproductive. It would be totally inappropriate to apply the rule to deter legislatures from enacting invalid laws. No tenable purpose can be served by applying the rule here. It could not deter police misconduct because there was no misconduct here in any sense of the word. The officer discovered the weapon in a lawful search incident to an arrest under an ordinance he had no reason to believe was invalid. Exclusion of the evidence, here, counsel argued, would only cause police officers to be reluctant to enforce laws whose validity had not yet been authoritatively determined.

No Probable Cause

Regardless of the validity of the ordinance, Robert W. Peterson, Santa Clara, California, argued, the arrest in this case was invalid because the officer did not have probable cause to arrest the defendant for violating the ordinance. While he conceded that the officer may have had a right to make a *Terry* v. *Ohio,* 392 U.S. 1 (1968), stop under the circumstances here, counsel did not believe the officer had a right to demand answers to his questions about the defendant's identity and business.

Mr. Justice Marshall: "Didn't he have a right to frisk the defendant?"

"Not unless he had a founded suspicion to believe that criminal activity was afoot."

The ordinance under which this defendant was arrested is not only vague, Peterson said, it violates both the Fourth and Fifth Amendments. It violates the Fourth Amendment because it authorizes a full custodial arrest, and the attendant search, for conduct which under *Terry* would only justify a brief stop. It violates the Fifth Amendment because it makes criminal an individual's refusal to give a narrative account of his conduct. A person's refusal to answer questions may not be considered as a factor justifying his arrest. In this respect the ordinance exacts a penalty for the individual's exercise of his right to remain silent.

Counsel also questioned the officer's good faith in this case by noting that federal and state courts had struck down similar ordinances in the past and the officer should have been aware that this ordinance too was infirm.

Mr. Justice Stewart wondered whether it is a police officer's duty not to enforce an ordinance if he believes it is invalid.

Mr. Justice Brennan: "Do you lose if we uphold the ordinance?"

"No, sir. Then we argue that the officer lacked probable cause to arrest this defendant for violating it."

The Chief Justice: "Does *Terry* hold that there must be an arrest before there can be a patdown?"

"No, sir. A patdown may be made if the officer has founded suspicion."

Mr. Justice Powell: "Do you think the respondent has a cause of action under 1983 for an unlawful arrest?"

Peterson replied that there is a cause of action against the police officer, but not against the city council for enacting the ordinance.

The reasons for the exclusionary rule apply even more clearly to an arrest under an ordinance that violates the Fourth, Fifth and Fourteenth Amendments than they do to an arrest which is unconstitutional only because the individual officer makes a mistake. The existence and enforcement of unconstitutional ordinances and laws threaten the security of every individual, and the rule must be available to deter the enactment of such laws.

Furthermore, giving judicial approval to evidence obtained in this manner impugns the integrity of the courts.

Peterson argued that habeas corpus has existed in its present form since 1867, and the Habeas Corpus Act has been interpreted consistently with its plain meaning to reach all imprisonment in violation of the Constitution. Congress has steadfastly refused to change the scope of habeas corpus, he said, and reconfirmed its scope by reenacting the statute in 1966.

Since the exclusionary rule is designed to accomplish both special and general deterrence, arguments that habeas corpus relief often comes too late to achieve that goal are not well founded. Also, Fourth Amendment claims are particularly appropriate for habeas review because they do not go to the question of guilt or innocence and are therefore less likely to be given sympathetic treatment by the state courts. Finally, Peterson argued, any friction which may exist between the state and federal courts is the result of the Fourth Amendment, not federal habeas corpus.

If the Court decides to cut back on federal habeas relief, Peterson concluded, it should do so in a purely prospective opinion. It would be unconscionable to deprive this defendant of all access to the federal courts by applying the rule to his case.

STONE v. POWELL, No. 74-1055
WOLFF v. RICE, No. 74-1222

Supreme Court of the United States, 1976
428 U.S. 465, 96 S. Ct. 3037, 49 L. Ed. 2d 1067

Respondent Lloyd Powell was convicted of murder in a California state court, in part, on the basis of testimony concerning a revolver found on his person when he was arrested for violating a vagrancy ordinance. The trial court specifically rejected respondent's claim that the testimony should have been excluded because the ordinance was unconstitutional and the arrest therefore illegal. The California District Court of Appeal affirmed, finding it unnecessary to pass upon the legality of the arrest and search because it concluded that the error, if any, in admitting the testimony was harmless beyond a reasonable doubt. Powell sought federal habeas corpus relief in the United States District Court (N.D. Cal.), which concluded that the arresting officer had probable cause, and that even if the ordinance was unconstitutional, the deterrent purpose of the exclusionary rule did not require that it be applied to bar admission of evidence seized incident to an otherwise lawful arrest. The Court of Appeals (9th Cir.) reversed, 507 F.2d 93, finding that (1) the questioned ordinance was unconstitutional, (2) Powell's arrest was therefore illegal, and (3) although exclusion of the evidence would serve no deterrent purpose with regard to police officers who were enforcing laws in good faith, exclusion would serve to deter legislators from enacting unconstitutional statutes. The court concluded that the admission of the evidence was not harmless error.

Respondent David Rice was convicted of murder in a Nebraska state court, in part, on the basis of evidence seized pursuant to a search warrant. The trial court's denial of Rice's motion to suppress was upheld by the Nebraska Supreme Court. Rice filed a petition for writ of habeas corpus in the United States District Court for Nebraska. The court concluded that the warrant was invalid and rejected the state's contention that, in any event, probable cause justified the search. The Court of Appeals (8th Cir.) affirmed, 513 F.2d 1280. Petitioners Stone and Wolff, the wardens of the respective state prisons where Powell and Rice were incarcerated, petitioned for review, and the Supreme Court granted certiorari.

Mr. Justice POWELL delivered the opinion of the Court.

. . . The question presented is whether a federal court should consider, in ruling on a petition for habeas corpus relief filed by a state prisoner, a claim that evidence obtained by an unconstitutional search or seizure was introduced at his trial, when he has previously been afforded an opportunity for full and fair litigation of his claim in the state courts. The issue is of considerable importance to the administration of criminal justice.

* * *

. . . Prior to the Court's decision in Kaufman v. United States, 394 U.S. 217 (1969), . . . a substantial majority of the federal courts of appeals had concluded that collateral review of search-and-seizure claims was inappropriate on motions filed by federal prisoners under 28 U.S.C. § 2255, the modern post-conviction procedure available to federal prisoners in lieu of habeas corpus [see Appendix A]. The primary rationale advanced in support of those decisions was that Fourth Amendment violations are different in kind from denials of Fifth or Sixth Amendment rights in that claims of illegal search and seizure do not "impugn the integrity of the fact-finding process or challenge evidence as inherently unreliable; rather, the exclusion of illegally seized evidence is simply a prophylactic device intended generally to deter Fourth Amendment violations by law enforcement officers." ...

Kaufman rejected this rationale and held that search-and-seizure claims are cognizable in § 2255 proceedings. The Court noted that "the federal habeas remedy extends to state prisoners alleging that unconstitutionally obtained evidence was admitted against them at trial," ... and concluded, as a matter of statutory construction, that there was no basis for restricting "access by federal prisoners with illegal search-and-seizure claims to federal collateral remedies, while placing no similar restriction on access by state prisoners". . . . Although in recent years the view has been expressed that the Court should re-examine the substantive scope of federal habeas jurisdiction and limit collateral review of search-and-seizure claims "solely to the question of whether the petitioner was provided with a fair opportunity to raise and have adjudicated the question in state courts" ... the Court, without discussion or consideration of the issue, has continued to accept jurisdiction in cases raising such claims. ...

The discussion in Kaufman of the scope of federal habeas corpus rests on the view that the effectuation of the Fourth Amendment, as applied to the States through the Fourteenth Amendment, required the granting of habeas corpus relief when a prisoner has been convicted in state court on the basis of evidence obtained in an illegal search or seizure since those Amendments were held in Mapp v. Ohio, 367 U.S. 643 (1961), to require exclusion of such evidence at trial and reversal of conviction upon direct review. Until this case we have not had occasion fully to consider the validity of this view. . . . Upon examination, we conclude, in light of the nature and purpose of the Fourth Amendment exclusionary rule, that this view is unjustified. We hold, therefore, that where the State has provided an opportunity for full and fair litigation of a Fourth Amendment claim, the Constitution does not require that a state prisoner be granted federal habeas corpus relief on the ground that evidence obtained in an unconstitutional search or seizure was introduced at his trial.

* * *

Decisions prior to Mapp advanced two principal reasons for application of the rule in federal trials. The Court in [Elkins v. United States, 364 U.S. 206 (1960)] ... referred to the "imperative of judicial integrity," suggesting that exclusion of illegally seized evidence prevents contamination of the judicial process. ... But ... a more pragmatic ground was emphasized: "The rule is calculated to prevent, not to repair. Its purpose is to deter—to compel respect for the constitutional guaranty in the only effectively available way—by removing the incentive to disregard it." Id. at 217. The Mapp majority justified the application of the rule to the States on several grounds, but relied principally upon the belief that exclusion would deter future unlawful police conduct.

* * *

The primary justification for the exclusionary rule then is the deterrence of police conduct that violates Fourth Amendment rights. Post-Mapp decisions have established that the rule is not a personal constitutional right. It is not calculated to redress the injury to the privacy of the victim of the search or seizure, for any "[r]eparation comes too late." ... Instead, "the rule is a judicially created remedy designed to safeguard Fourth Amendment rights generally through its deterrent effect...." United States v. Calandra, [414 U.S. at 348].

Mapp involved the enforcement of the exclusionary rule at state trials and on direct review. The decision in Kaufman, as noted above, is premised on the view that implementation of the Fourth Amendment also requires the consideration of search-and-seizure claims upon collateral review of state convictions. But despite the broad deterrent purpose of the exclusionary rule, it has never been interpreted to proscribe the introduction of illegally seized evidence in all proceedings or against all persons. As in the case of any remedial device, "the application of the rule has been restricted to those areas where its remedial objectives are thought most efficaciously served." ... Refusal to extend the exclusionary rule to grand jury proceedings was based on a balancing of the potential injury to the historic role and function of the grand jury by such extension against the potential contribution to the effectuation of the Fourth Amendment through deterrence of police misconduct....

We turn now to the specific question presented by these cases. Respondents allege violations of Fourth Amendment rights guaranteed them through the Fourteenth Amendment. The question is whether state prisoners—who have been afforded the opportunity for full and fair consideration of their reliance upon the exclusionary rule with respect to seized evidence by the state courts at trial and on direct review—may invoke their claim again on federal habeas corpus review. The answer is to be found by weighing the utility of the exclusionary review of Fourth Amendment claims.

The costs of applying the exclusionary rule even at trial and on direct review are well known: the focus of the trial, and the attention of the participants therein, is diverted from the ultimate question of guilt or innocence that should be the central concern in a criminal proceeding. Moreover, the physical evidence sought to be excluded is typically reliable and often the most probative information bearing on the guilt or innocence of the defendant. As Mr. Justice Black emphasized in his dissent in Kaufman: "A claim of illegal search and seizure under the Fourth Amendment is crucially different from many other constitutional rights; ordinarily the evidence seized can in no way have been rendered untrustworthy by the means of its seizure and indeed often this evidence alone establishes beyond virtually any shadow of a doubt that the defendant is guilty" 394 U.S., at 237. Application of the rule thus deflects the truthfinding process and often frees the guilty. The disparity in particular cases between the error committed by the police officer and the windfall afforded a guilty defendant by application of the rule is contrary to the idea of proportionality that is essential to the concept of justice. Thus, although the rule is thought to deter unlawful police activity in part through the nurturing of respect for Fourth Amendment values, if applied indiscriminately it may well have the opposite effect of generating disrespect for the law and administration of justice. These long-recognized costs of the rule persist when a criminal conviction is sought to be overturned on collateral review on the ground that a search-and-seizure claim was erroneously rejected by two or more tiers of state courts.

Evidence obtained by police officers in violation of the Fourth Amendment is excluded at trial in the hope that the frequency of future violations will decrease. Despite the absence of supportive empirical evidence, we have assumed that the immediate effect of exclusion will be to discourage law enforcement officials from violating the Fourth Amendment by removing the incentive to disregard it. More importantly, over the long term, this demonstration that our society attaches serious consequences to violation of constitutional rights is thought to encourage those who formulate law enforcement policies, and the officers who implement them, to incorporate Fourth Amendment ideals into their value system.

We adhere to the view that these considerations support the implementation of the exclusionary rule at trial and its enforcement on direct appeal of the state court convictions. But the additional contribution, if any, of the consideration of search-and-seizure claims of state prisoners on collateral review is small in relation to the costs. To be sure, each case in which such claim is considered may add marginally to an awareness of the values protected by the Fourth Amendment. There is no reason to believe, however, that the overall educative effect of the exclusionary rule would be appreciably diminished if search-and-seizure claims could not be raised in federal habeas corpus review of state convictions. Nor is there reason to assume that any specific disincentive already created by the risk of exclusion of evidence at trial or the reversal of convictions on direct review would be enhanced if there were the further risk that a conviction obtained in state court and affirmed on direct review might be overturned in collateral proceedings often occurring years after the incarceration of the defendant. The view that the deterrence of Fourth Amendment violations would be furthered rests on the dubious assumption that law enforcement authorities would fear that federal habeas review might reveal flaws in a search or seizure that went undetected at trial and on appeal. Even if one rationally could assume that some additional incremental deterrent effect would be present in isolated cases, the resulting advance of the legitimate goal of furthering Fourth Amendment rights would be outweighed by the acknowledged costs to other values vital to a rational system of criminal justice.

In sum, we conclude that where the State has provided an opportunity for full and fair litigation of a Fourth Amendment claim, a state prisoner may not be granted federal habeas corpus relief on the ground that evidence obtained in an unconstitutional search or seizure was introduced at his trial. In this context the contribution of the exclusionary rule, if any, to the effectuation of the Fourth Amendment is minimal and the substantial societal costs of application of the rule persist with special force. . . .

Reversed.

Mr. Chief Justice BURGER, concurring.

I concur in the Court's opinion. By way of dictum, and somewhat hesitantly, the Court notes that the holding in this case leaves undisturbed the exclusionary rule as applied to criminal trials. . . . [I]t seems clear to me that the exclusionary rule has been operative long enough to demonstrate its flaws. The time has come to modify its reach, even if it is retained for a small and limited category of cases.

Over the years, the strains imposed by reality, in terms of the costs to society and the bizarre miscarriages of justice that have been experienced because of the exclusion of reliable evidence when the "constable blunders," have led the Court to vacillate as to the rationale to the point where the rule has become a doctrinaire result in search of validating reasons.

In evaluating the exclusionary rule, it is important to bear in mind exactly what the rule accomplishes. Its function is simple — the exclusion of truth from the fact-finding process. . . . The operation of the rule is therefore unlike that of the Fifth Amendment's protection against compelled self-incrimination. A confession produced after intimidating or coercive interrogation is inherently dubious. If a suspect's will has been overborne, a cloud hangs over his custodial admissions; the exclusion of such statements is based essentially on their lack of reliability. This is not the case as to *reliable* evidence — a pistol, a packet of heroin, counterfeit money, or the body of a murder victim — which may be judicially declared to be the result of an "unreasonable" search. The reliability of such evidence is beyond question; its probative value is certain.

This remarkable situation — one unknown to the common-law tradition — had its genesis in a case calling for the protection of private papers against governmental intru-

sions. . . . In Boyd, the Court held that private papers were inadmissible because of the Government's violation of the Fourth and Fifth Amendments. In Weeks, the Court excluded private letters seized from the accused's home by a federal official acting without a warrant. In both cases, the Court had a clear vision of what it was seeking to protect. What the Court said in Boyd shows how far we have strayed from the original path: "The search for and seizure of stolen or forfeited goods, or goods liable to duties and concealed to avoid the payment thereof, *are totally different things from a search for and seizure of a man's private books and papers* for the purpose of obtaining information therein contained, or of using them as evidence against him. The two things differ toto coelo." 116 U.S., at 623. (Emphasis added.) In Weeks, the Court emphasized that the Government, under settled principles of common law, had no right to keep a person's *private papers.* The Court noted that the case did not involve "burglar's tools or other *proofs of guilt . . . .*" 232 U.S., at 392. (Emphasis added.)

From this origin, the exclusionary rule has been changed in focus entirely. It is now used almost exclusively to exclude from evidence articles which are unlawful to be possessed or tools and instruments of crime. Unless it can be rationally thought that the Framers considered it essential to protect the liberties of the people to hold that which it is unlawful to possess, then it becomes clear that our constitutional course has taken a most bizarre tack.

The drastically changed nature of judicial concern — from the protection of personal papers or effects in one's private quarters, to the exclusion of that which the accused had no right to possess — is only one of the more recent anomalies of the rule. The original incongruity was the rule's inconsistency with the general proposition that "our legal system does not attempt to do justice incidentally and to enforce penalties by indirect means." . . . The rule is based on the hope that events in the courtroom or appellate chambers, long after the crucial acts took place, will somehow modify the way in which policemen conduct themselves. A more clumsy, less direct means of imposing sanctions is difficult to imagine, particularly since the issue whether the policeman did indeed run afoul of the Fourth Amendment is often not resolved until years after the event. The "sanction" is particularly indirect when, ... the police go before a magistrate, who issues a warrant. Once the warrant issues, there is literally nothing more the policeman can do in seeking to comply with the law. Imposing an admittedly indirect "sanction" on the police officer in that instance is nothing less than sophisticated nonsense.

Despite this anomaly, the exclusionary rule now rests upon its purported tendency to deter police misconduct ... although, as we know, the rule has long been applied to wholly good-faith mistakes and to purely technical deficiencies in warrants. Other rhetorical generalizations, including the "imperative of judicial integrity," have not withstood analysis as more and more critical appraisals of the rule's operation have appeared. . . . Indeed, settled rules demonstrate that the "judicial integrity" rationalization is fatally flawed. First, the Court has refused to entertain claims that evidence was unlawfully seized unless the claimant could demonstrate that he had standing to press the contention. Alderman v. United States, 394 U.S. 165 (1969). If he could not, the evidence, albeit secured in violation of the Fourth Amendment, is admissible. Second, as one scholar has correctly observed: "[I]t is difficult to accept the proposition that the exclusion of improperly obtained evidence is necessary for 'judicial integrity' when no such rule is observed in other common law jurisdictions such as England and Canada, whose courts are otherwise regarded as models of judicial decorum and fairness." ... Despite its avowed deterrent objective, proof is lacking that the exclusionary rule, a purely judge-created device based on "hard cases," serves the purpose of deterrence. Notwithstanding Herculean efforts, no empirical study has been able to demonstrate that the rule does in fact have any deterrent effect. In the face of dwindling support for the rule some would go so far as to extend it to *civil* cases. United States v. Janis [infra, Comments].

To vindicate the continued existence of this judge-made rule, it is incumbent upon those who seek its retention—and surely its *extension*—to demonstrate that the results outweigh the rule's heavy costs to rational enforcement of the criminal law. . . .

* * *

Mr. Justice BRENNAN, with whom Mr. Justice MARSHALL concurs, dissenting.

The Court today holds "that where the State has provided an opportunity for full and fair litigation of a Fourth Amendment claim, a state prisoner may not be granted federal habeas corpus relief on the ground that evidence obtained in an unconstitutional search or seizure was introduced at his trial." . . . To be sure, my Brethren are hostile to the continued vitality of the exclusionary rule as part and parcel of the Fourth Amendment's prohibition of unreasonable searches and seizures, as today's decision in United States v. Janis confirms. . . .

. . .The Court insists that its holding is based on the Constitution. . . but in light of the explicit language of 28 U.S.C. § 2254[b] (significantly not even mentioned by the Court), I can only presume that the Court intends to be understood to hold either that respondents are not, as a matter of statutory construction, "in custody in violation of the Constitution or laws of the United States," or that "considerations of comity and concerns for the orderly administration of criminal justice" . . . are sufficient to allow this Court to rewrite jurisdictional statutes enacted by Congress. Neither ground of decision is tenable; the former is simply illogical, and the latter is an arrogation of power committed solely to the Congress.

Much of the Court's analysis implies that respondents are not entitled to habeas relief because they are not being unconstitutionally detained. Although purportedly adhering to the principle that the Fourth and Fourteenth Amendments "require exclusion" of evidence seized in violation of their commands ... the Court informs us that there has merely been a "view" in our cases that "the effectuation of the Fourth Amendment ... requires the granting of habeas corpus relief when a prisoner has been convicted in state court on the basis of evidence obtained in an illegal search or seizure. . . ." ... Applying a "balancing test" ... the

_____

[b]28 U.S.C. § 2254 provides:
"§ 2254. State custody; remedies in State courts. (a) The Supreme Court, a Justice thereof, a circuit judge, or a district court shall entertain an application for a writ of habeas corpus in behalf of a person in custody pursuant to the judgment of a State court only on the ground that he is in custody in violation of the Constitution or laws or treaties of the United States."

Court then concludes that this "view" is unjustified and that the policies of the Fourth Amendment would not be implemented if claims to the benefits of the exclusionary rule were cognizable in collateral attacks on the state court convictions.

Understandably the Court must purport to cast its holding in constitutional terms, because that avoids a direct confrontation with the incontrovertible facts that the habeas statutes have heretofore always been construed to grant jurisdiction to entertain Fourth Amendment claims of both state and federal prisoners, that Fourth Amendment principles have been applied in decisions on the merits in numerous cases on collateral review of final convictions, and that Congress has legislatively accepted our interpretation of congressional intent as to the necessary scope and function of habeas relief. Indeed, the Court reaches its result without explicitly overruling any of our plethora of precedents inconsistent with that result or even discussing principles of stare decisis. Rather, the Court asserts, in essence, that the Justices joining those prior decisions or reaching the merits of Fourth Amendment claims simply overlooked the obvious constitutional dimension to the problem in adhering to the "view" that granting collateral relief when state courts erroneously decide Fourth Amendment issues would effectuate the principles underlying that Amendment. But shorn of the rhetoric of "interest balancing" used to obscure what is at stake in this case, it is evident that today's attempt to rest the decision on the Constitution must fail so long as Mapp v. Ohio, 367 U.S. 643 (1961), remains undisturbed.

Under Mapp, as a matter of federal constitutional law, a state court *must* exclude evidence from the trial of an individual whose Fourth and Fourteenth Amendment rights were violated by a search or seizure that directly or indirectly resulted in the acquisition of that evidence. As United States v. Calandra, 414 U.S. 338, 347 (1974), reaffirmed, "evidence obtained in violation of the Fourth Amendment cannot be used in a criminal proceeding against the victim of the illegal search and seizure." When a state court admits such evidence, it has committed a *constitutional* error, and unless that error is harmless under federal standards ... it follows ineluctably that the defendant has been placed "in custody in

violation of the Constitution" within the comprehension of 28 U.S.C. § 2254. In short, it escapes me as to what logic can support the assertion that the defendant's unconstitutional confinement obtains during the process of direct review, no matter how long that process takes, but that the unconstitutionality then suddenly dissipates at the moment the claim is asserted in a collateral attack on the conviction.

The only conceivable rationale upon which the Court's "constitutional" thesis might rest is the statement that "the [exclusionary] rule is not a personal constitutional right. . . . Instead, 'the rule is a judicially created remedy designed to safeguard Fourth Amendment rights generally through its deterrent effect.' " ... Although my dissent in Calandra [infra, § 6.04] rejected, in light of contrary decisions establishing the role of the exclusionary rule, the premise that an individual has no constitutional right to have unconstitutionally seized evidence excluded from all use by the government, I need not dispute that point here. For today's holding is not logically defensible even under Calandra. However the Court reinterprets Mapp, and whatever the rationale now attributed to Mapp's holding or the purpose ascribed to the exclusionary rule, the prevailing constitutional *rule* is that unconstitutionally seized evidence *cannot be admitted* in the criminal trial of a person whose federal constitutional rights were violated by the search or seizure. The erroneous admission of such evidence is a violation of the Federal Constitution — Mapp inexorably means at least this much, or there would be no basis for applying the exclusionary rule in state criminal proceedings — and an accused against whom such evidence is admitted has been convicted in derogation of rights mandated by, and is "in custody in violation of," the Constitution of the United States. Indeed, since state courts violate the strictures of the Federal Constitution by admitting such evidence, then even if federal habeas review did not directly effectuate Fourth Amendment values, a proposition I deny, that review would nevertheless serve to effectuate what is concededly a constitutional principle concerning admissibility of evidence at trial.

The Court, assuming without deciding that respondents were convicted on the basis of unconstitutionally obtained evidence erroneously admitted against them by the state trial courts, acknowledges that respondents had the right to obtain a reversal of their convictions on appeal in the state courts or on certiorari to this Court. Indeed, since our rules relating to the time limits for applying for certiorari in criminal cases are nonjurisdictional, certiorari could be granted respondents even today and their convictions could be reversed despite today's decisions.... And the basis for reversing those convictions would of course have to be that the States, in rejecting respondents' Fourth Amendment claims, had deprived them of a right in derogation of the Federal Constitution. It is simply inconceivable that the constitutional deprivation suddenly vanishes after the appellate process has been exhausted. And as between this Court on certiorari, and federal district courts on habeas, it is for *Congress* to decide what the most efficacious method is for enforcing *federal* constitutional rights and asserting the primacy of federal law. ... The Court, however, simply ignores the settled principle that for purposes of adjudicating constitutional claims Congress, which has the power to do so under Art. III of the Constitution, has effectively cast the district courts sitting in habeas in the role of surrogate Supreme Courts.[j]

---

[j]The failure to confront this fact forthrightly is obviously a core defect in the Court's analysis. For to the extent Congress has accorded the Federal District Courts a role in our constitutional scheme functionally equivalent to that of the Supreme Court with respect to review of state court resolutions of federal constitutional claims, it is evident that the Court's direct/collateral review distinction for constitutional purposes simply collapses. Indeed, logically extended, the Court's analysis, which basically turns on the fact that law enforcement officials cannot anticipate a second court finding constitutional errors after one court has fully and fairly adjudicated the claim and found it to be meritless, would preclude any Supreme Court review on direct appeal or even state appellate review if the trial court fairly addressed the Fourth Amendment claim on the merits. The proposition is certainly frivolous if Mapp is constitutionally grounded; yet such is the essential thrust of the Court's view that the unconstitutional admission of evidence is tolerable merely because police officials cannot be deterred from unconstitutional conduct by the possibility that a favorable "admission" decision would be followed by an unfavorable "exclusion" decision.

* * *

The Court adheres to the holding of Mapp that the Constitution "require[d] exclusion" of the evidence admitted at respondents' trials.... However, the Court holds that the Constitution "does not require" that respondents be accorded habeas relief if they were accorded "an opportunity for full and fair litigation of [their] Fourth Amendment claim[s]" in state courts. ... Yet once the Constitution was interpreted by Mapp to require exclusion of certain evidence at trial, the Constitution became irrelevant to the manner in which that constitutional right was to be enforced in the federal courts; *that* inquiry is only a matter of respecting Congress' allocation of federal judicial power between this Court's appellate jurisdiction and a federal district court's habeas jurisdiction. Indeed, by conceding that today's "decision does not mean that the federal [district] court lacks jurisdiction over [respondents'] claim[s "... the Court admits that respondents have sufficiently alleged that they are "in custody in violation of the Constitution" within the meaning of § 2254 and that there is no "constitutional" rationale for today's holding. Rather, the constitutional "interest balancing" approach to this case is untenable, and I can only view the constitutional garb in which the Court dresses its result as a disguise for rejection of the longstanding principle that there are no "second class" constitutional rights for purposes of federal habeas jurisdiction; it is nothing less than an attempt to provide a veneer of respectability for an obvious usurpation of Congress' Art. III power to delineate the jurisdiction of the federal courts.

* * *

... If today's decision were only that erroneous state court resolution of Fourth Amendment claims did not render the defendant's resultant confinement "in violation of the Constitution," these pronouncements would have been wholly irrelevant and unnecessary. I am therefore justified in apprehending that the groundwork is being laid today for a drastic withdrawal of federal habeas jurisdiction, if not for all grounds of alleged unconstitutional detention, then at least for claims—for example, of double jeopardy, entrapment, self-incrimination, Miranda violations, and use of invalid identification procedures—that this Court later decides are not "guild-related."

To the extent the Court is actually premising its holding on an interpretation of 28 U.S.C. § 2243 or § 2254, it is overruling the heretofore settled principle that federal habeas relief is available to redress *any* denial of asserted constitutional rights, whether or not denial of the right affected the truth or fairness of the fact-finding process. . . .

* * *

. . . [T]he Court's failure to limit today's ruling to prospective application stands in sharp contrast to recent cases that have so limited decisions expanding or affirming constitutional rights. Respondents, relying on the explicit holding of Fay v. Noia . . . , that a petition for a writ of certiorari is not a necessary predicate for federal habeas relief, and accepting at face value the clear import of our prior habeas cases that all unconstitutional confinements may be challenged on federal habeas, contend that any new restriction on state prisoners' ability to obtain habeas relief should be held to be prospective only. The Court, however, dismisses respondents' effective inability to have a single federal court pass on their federal constitutional claims with the offhand remark that "respondents were, of course, free to file a timely petition for certiorari prior to seeking federal habeas relief." . . . To be sure, the fact that the time limits for invoking our certiorari jurisdiction with respect to criminal cases emanating from state courts are *non*-jurisdictional would dictate that respondents are at least free to file out-of-time certiorari petitions; under the Court's "direct review" distinction delineated today, we would still have authority to address the substance of respondents' eminently and concededly meritorious Fourth Amendment claims. Of course, federal review in this Court is a matter of grace, and it is grace now seldom bestowed at the behest of a criminal defendant. I have little confidence that three others of the Brethren would join in voting to grant such petitions, thereby reinforcing the notorious fact that our certiorari jurisdiction is inadequate for containing state criminal proceedings within constitutional bounds and underscoring Congress' wisdom in mandating a broad federal habeas jurisdiction for the District Courts. In any event, since we are fully familiar with the records in these cases, respondents are owed at least review in this Court, particularly since it shuts the doors of the District Courts in a decision that marks such a stark break with our precedents on the scope of habeas relief; indeed, if the Court were at all disposed to safeguard constitutional rights and educate state and federal judges concerning the contours of Fourth Amendment jurisprudence in various situations, it would decide these cases on the merits rather than employ a procedural ruse that ensures respondents continued unconstitutional confinement. . . .

* * *

Mr. Justice WHITE, dissenting.

For many of the reasons stated by Mr. Justice BRENNAN I cannot agree that the writ of habeas corpus should be any less available to those convicted of state crimes where they allege Fourth Amendment violations than where other constitutional issues are presented to the federal court. Under the amendments to the habeas corpus statute, which were adopted after Fay v. Noia, 372 U.S. 391 (1963), and represented an effort by Congress to lend a modicum of finality to state criminal judgments, I cannot distinguish between Fourth Amendment and other constitutional issues.

* * *

I feel constrained to say, however, that I would join four or more other Justices in substantially limiting the reach of the exclusionary rule as presently administered under the Fourth Amendment in federal and state criminal trials.

Whether I would have joined the Court's opinion in Mapp v. Ohio, 367 U.S. 643 (1961), had I then been a Member of the Court, I do not know. But as time went on after coming to this bench, I became convinced that both Weeks v. United States, 232 U.S. 383 (1914), and Mapp v. Ohio had overshot their mark insofar as they aimed to deter lawless action by law enforcement personnel and that in many of its applications the exclusionary rule was not advancing that aim in the slightest and that in this respect it was a senseless obstacle to arriving at the truth in many criminal trials. . . .

* * *

When law enforcement personnel have acted mistakenly, but in good faith and on reasonable grounds, and yet the evidence they have seized is later excluded, the exclusion can have no deterrent effect. The officers, if they do their duty, will act in similar fashion in similar circumstances in the future; and the only consequence of the rule as presently administered is that unimpeachable and probative evidence is kept from the trier of fact and the truth-finding function of proceedings is substantially impaired or a trial totally aborted. . . .

* * *

If the defendant in criminal cases may not recover for a mistaken but good-faith invasion of his privacy, it makes even less sense to exclude the evidence solely on his behalf. He is not at all recompensed for the invasion by merely getting his property back. It is often contraband and stolen property to which he is not entitled in any event. He has been charged with crime and is seeking to have probative evidence against him excluded, although often it is the instrumentality of the crime. There is very little equity in the defendant's side in these circumstances. The exclusionary rule, a judicial construct, seriously shortchanges the public interest as presently applied. I would modify it accordingly.

Comments

1. In *Wolf* the majority suggested a willingness to regard a state's "affirmative" sanction of unlawful police intrusions as running "counter to . . . the Fourteenth Amendment." Can it be argued that *Wolf* suffered "less of a deprivation" merely because the Colorado courts chose to tacitly accept the police conduct rather than "affirmatively" sanction it? What is the significance of Mr. Justice Frankfurter's conclusion that the *Weeks* rule "was a matter of judicial implication" and was "not derived from the explicit requirements of the Fourth Amendment" nor based on "Congressional policy in the enforcement of the Constitution"? It is interesting to note how accurate Mr. Justice Murphy's prophecy has proved to be in regard to the ineffectiveness of criminal and civil actions against Fourth Amendment violators. See, e.g., Amsterdam, A., *The Supreme Court and the Rights of Suspects in Criminal Cases,* 45 N.Y.U.L. Rev. 785 (1970). One notable exception has been the relief afforded under 42 U.S.C. § 1983. For a look at the so-called "constitutional tort," see Chapter Ten.

2. The majority in *Mapp* briefly stated the content of the exclusionary rule: "We hold that all evidence obtained by searches and seizures in violation of the Constitution is, by that same authority, inadmissible in a state court." 367 U.S. at 655. It should be noted that with the exception of the Court's unanimous decision in *Weeks* v. *United States,* 232 U.S. 383 (1914), the application of the exclusionary rule has been marked by sharp divisions within the Court: The cases of *Wolf* v. *Colorado,* 338 U.S. 25 (1949), *Lustig* v. *United States,* 388 U.S. 74 (1949), *Irvine* v. *California,* 347 U.S. 128 (1954), *Elkins* v. *United States,* 364 U.S. 206 (1960), *Mapp* v. *Ohio,* 367 U.S. 643 (1961), *Bivens* v. *Six Unknown Agents,* 403 U.S. 388 (1971), *Coolidge* v. *New Hampshire,* 403 U.S. 443 (1971), *United States* v. *Calandra,* 414 U.S. 338 (1974), *Stone* v. *Powell,* 428 U.S. 465, supra, and *United States* v. *Janis,* 428 U.S. 433, infra, have produced a total of 37 separate opinions or statements.
   The exclusionary rule has traditionally been justified on two grounds: (1) that by excluding evidence the rule serves to "deter" illegal police conduct, and (2) that the rule serves to "shield" the government from participation in illegal conduct. See generally Oaks,

Studying the Exclusionary Rule in Search and Seizure, 37 U. Chi. L. Rev. 665 (1970). Whatever justification might be advanced, the exclusionary rule has never been very popular, particularly with state law enforcement agencies. In his book *Our Handcuffed Police* (1968), Edward J. Van Allen asserted that the *Mapp* decision represented a "legal stumbling block tossed in front of policemen seeking to do their duty," at 220. He further asserted that "policing the police is an unconstitutional act by the Supreme Court." Mr. Justice Jackson noted in *Irvine* v. *California,* 347 U.S. 128, 136 (1954), "[I]t protects one against whom incriminatory evidence is discovered, but does nothing to protect innocent persons who are the victims of illegal but fruitless searches." For other opposition views, see Wilson and Alprin, *Controlling Police Conduct: Alternatives to the Exclusionary Rule,* 36 Law & Contemp. Prob. 488 (1971); Wingo, *Growing Disillusionment with the Exclusionary Rule,* 25 S.W.L.J. 573 (1971); Wright, *Must the Criminal Go Free if the Constable Blunders?,* 50 Texas L. Rev. 736 (1972); and Quintana, *The Erosion of the Fourth Amendment Exclusionary Rule,* 17 How. L.J. 805 (1973).

3.   The Supreme Court held in *Stone* v. *Powell,* supra, that a state prisoner who has had an opportunity in state court for a full and fair litigation of his Fourth Amendment claims is not entitled to federal habeas corpus consideration of his claim that evidence obtained in an unconstitutional search or seizure was introduced at his trial. If a state defendant knows that he might not be granted habeas review, can he immediately seek a federal court's injunction against the use of unconstitutionally seized evidence against him at his state trial? Such relief has been foreclosed to state defendants in the past, primarily because the defendant has had ultimate review available either on direct review or collaterally through habeas. See, e.g., *Dombrowski* v. *Pfister,* 380 U.S. 479, 485 n. 3 (1965); *Younger* v. *Harris,* 401 U.S. 37 (1971). In addition, the "exhaustion requirement" of 28 U.S.C. § 2254 has generally dictated that federal habeas corpus review be delayed until an ultimate determination is made in state court. Section 2254(b) provides: "An application for a writ of habeas corpus in behalf of a person in custody pursuant to the judgment of a State court shall not be granted unless it appears that the applicant has exhausted the remedies available in the courts of the State, or that there is either an absence of available State corrective process or the existence of circumstances rendering such process ineffective to protect the rights of the prisoner." Mr. Justice Brennan argued in a footnote that what the majority had really done in *Stone* was to "convert" the "delay rule" into a doctrine "producing" federal review. He commented, "Although the federal courts could have been the forum for the initial 'opportunity for a full and fair hearing' of Fourth Amendment claims of state prisoners that the Court finds constitutionally sufficient, nonconstitutional concerns dictated temporary abstention; but having so abstained, federal courts are now ousted by this Court from ever determining the claims, since the courts to which they initially deferred are all that this Court deems necessary for protecting rights essential to preservation of the Fourth Amendment. Such hostility to federal jurisdiction to redress violations of rights secured by the Federal Constitution, despite congressional conferral of that jurisdiction, is profoundly disturbing."

In *Stone,* the Court supported the proposition that state prisoners have ample opportunity to redress constitutional claims via direct review and petitions for certiorari. Given the present views of the majority with regard to Fourth Amendment claims, is it reasonable to assume that a large number of petitions will be granted? Consider the following remark by the majority in a footnote: "Despite differences in institutional environment and the unsympathetic attitude to federal constitutional claims of some state judges in years past, we are unwilling to assume that there now exists a general lack of appropriate sensitivity to constitutional rights in the trial and appellate courts of the several States."

What effect, if any, will *Stone* have on *Kaufman* v. *United States,* 394 U.S. 217 (1969)? The majority never affirmatively answered that question. However, in a footnote the Court observed: "The issue in Kaufman was the scope of §2255. Our decision today rejects the dictum in Kaufman concerning the applicability of the exclusionary rule in federal habeas corpus review of state court decisions pursuant to §2254. To the extent the application of the exclusionary rule in Kaufman did not rely upon the supervisory role of this Court over the lower federal courts, cf. Elkins v. United States, 364 U.S. 206 (1960), . . . the rationale for its application in that context is also rejected. . . ."

4. It is clear that in *Stone* Mr. Chief Justice Burger (concurring) was concerned primarily with the continued application of the exclusionary rule. He argued that the time has come to "modify its reach, *even if* it is retained for a *small* and *limited* category of cases" (emphasis added). It isn't clear what specific types of cases the Chief Justice might choose to retain within the rule's reach. Perhaps the following proposals might be considered when seeking to limit the scope of the rule: "The rule [would] not apply in the most serious cases—treason, espionage, murder, armed robbery, and kidnapping by organized groups, . . . or . . . to cases where the police department in question has taken seriously its responsibility to adhere to the Fourth Amendment." Kaplan, *The Limits of the Exclusionary Rule,* 26 Stan. L. Rev. 1027 (1974). Certainly the latter "good faith" option would appeal to Mr. Justice White (dissenting in *Stone,* supra). See also *United States* v. *Peltier,* 422 U.S. 531 (1975). Burger asserted that all the rule accomplishes is the "exclusion of truth," and "the operation of the rule is therefore unlike that of the Fifth Amendment's protection against compelled self-incrimination." Although his view never commanded a majority of the Court, consider, in light of the above statement, the following remarks made by Mr. Justice Black (concurring) in *Mapp* v. *Ohio* 367 U.S. 643, 662 (1961): "[C]ases . . . since *Wolf* [have] led me to conclude that when the Fourth Amendment's ban against searches and seizures is considered together with the Fifth Amendment's ban against compelled self-incrimination, a *constitutional basis* emerges which not only *justifies* but actually *requires* the exclusionary rule. . . . In *Boyd* v. *United States* . . . the Court . . . declared itself 'unable to perceive that the seizure of a man's private books and papers to be used in evidence against him is substantially different from compelling him to be a witness against himself'" (emphasis added). Does the language of the Fourth Amendment indicate a concern with *how* the government seizes as well as *what* it takes? Does the exclusionary rule reinforce Fourth Amendment concern with how evidence is taken? Consider the following: "As the exclusionary rule is applied time after time,

it seems that its deterrent efficacy at some stage reaches a point of diminishing return, and beyond that point its continued application is a public nuisance." Amsterdam, *Search, Seizure, and Section 2255: A Comment,* 112 U. Pa. L. Rev. 378, 389 (1964). Burger also contended that the rule serves to exclude "reliable" evidence. While it is true that seized contraband such as narcotics and weapons might be considered highly reliable and probative at a defendant's trial for possession of drugs or armed robbery, what about the question of the "constitutional *competency"* of that same evidence if seized in violation of the Fourth Amendment? Of course, the answer seems to revolve around how the individual members of the Court view the rule itself, i.e., should it be viewed as a "right"? In *United States* v. *Calandra* [Chapter Six, § 6.04], the Supreme Court, per Powell, J., noted that the exclusionary rule "is a judicially created remedy designed to safeguard Fourth Amendment rights generally through its deterrent effect, rather than a personal constitutional right. . . ." Dissenting in *Calandra,* Justice Brennan, joined by Justices Douglas and Marshall, argued that the rule should be viewed as "part and parcel of the Fourth Amendment's limitations upon government encroachment . . . ," 414 U.S. at 360. Regarding the argument that exclusion is necessary for "judicial integrity," Burger cited one authority who maintains that such a proposition is questionable because no exclusionary rule operates in "England and Canada, whose courts are otherwise regarded as models of judicial decorum and fairness." How persuasive is that argument in light of the fact that neither nation has similar Fourth Amendment protections to consider and hence has no *constitutional obligation* to safeguard similar personal liberties? Finally, given the present posture of the Court, what is the future of the exclusionary rule? Will it be limited or modified? Is it possible that it will be discarded completely? Is Mr. Justice Brennan fearful of the latter? Is that why he was careful in *Stone* to reiterate the holding in *Mapp?* Consider Brennan's comment in a footnote: ". . . I take seriously this Court's continuing incursions on constitutionally guaranteed rights. '[I]llegitimate and unconstitutional practices get their first footing in that way, namely, by silent approaches and slight deviations from legal modes of procedure. . . . It is the duty of courts to be watchful for the constitutional rights of the citizen, and against any stealthy encroachments thereon.' *Boyd* v. *United States,* 116 U.S. 616, at 635 (1886)."

5. The issue presented in *United States* v. *Janis,* 428 U.S. 433, infra, decided the same day as *Stone,* supra, also provided the members of the Court with ample opportunity to express divergent views regarding the purpose and scope of the exclusionary rule: Is evidence seized by a state criminal law enforcement officer in good faith, but nonetheless unconstitutionally, inadmissible in a civil proceeding by or against the United States? Based upon the affidavit of a Los Angeles police officer, a Los Angeles municipal court judge issued a search warrant, pursuant to which the police seized from Max Janis $4,940 in cash and certain wagering records. The police notified the Internal Revenue Service of respondent's arrest, and using a calculation based upon the seized evidence, the IRS assessed Janis for wagering excise taxes and levied upon the $4,940 in cash in partial satisfaction of that assessment. In the subsequent state criminal proceeding against respondent, the trial court granted his motion to quash the warrant as defective and ordered the seized material returned, except for the

$4,940. When Janis filed a refund claim for the $4,940, the government counterclaimed for the unpaid balance of the assessment. Respondent then moved to suppress the evidence and quash the assessment. The District Court found that the assessment "was based in substantial part, if not completely, on illegally procured evidence," ordered the assessment quashed, and concluded that Janis was entitled to a refund of the $4,940. The United States Court of Appeals (9th Cir.) affirmed. The Supreme Court granted certiorari, and the opinion is set out below.

UNITED STATES v. JANIS
Supreme Court of the United States, 1976
428 U.S. 433, 96 S. Ct. 3021, 49 L. Ed. 2d 1046

Mr. Justice BLACKMUN delivered the opinion of the Court.

* * *

In the present case we are asked to create judicially a deterrent sanction by holding that evidence obtained by a state criminal law enforcement officer in good-faith reliance on a warrant that later proved to be defective shall be inadmissible in a federal civil tax proceeding. Clearly, the enforcement of admittedly valid laws would be hampered by so extending the exclusionary rule, and, as is nearly always the case with the rule, concededly relevant and reliable evidence would be rendered unavailable.

In evaluating the need for a deterrent sanction, one must first identify those who are to be deterred. In this case it is the state officer who is the primary object of the sanction. It is his conduct that is to be controlled. Two factors suggest that a sanction in addition to those that presently exist is unnecessary. First, the local law enforcement official is already "punished" by the exclusion of the evidence in the state criminal trial. That, necessarily, is of substantial concern to him. Second, the evidence is also excludable in the federal criminal trial, Elkins v. United States, [364 U.S. 206 (1960)], so that the entire criminal enforcement process, which is the concern and duty of these officers, is frustrated.

Jurists and scholars uniformly have recognized that the exclusionary rule imposes a substantial cost on the societal interest in law enforcement by its proscription of what concededly is relevant evidence. . . . [A]lternatives that would be less costly to societal interests have been the subject of extensive discussion and exploration.

Equally important, although scholars have attempted to determine whether the exclusionary rule in fact does have any deterrent effect, each empirical study on the subject, in its own way, appears to be flawed. It would not be appropriate to fault those who have attempted empirical studies for their lack of convincing data. The number of variables is substantial, and many cannot be measured or subjected to effective controls. Recordkeeping before Mapp was spotty at best, and thus severely hampers before-and-after studies. Since Mapp, of course, all possibility of broad-scale controlled or even semi-controlled comparison studies has been eliminated. "Response" studies are hampered by the presence of the respondents' interests. And extrapolation studies are rendered highly inconclusive by the changes in legal doctrines and police-citizen relationships that have taken place in the 15 years since Mapp was decided.

We find ourselves, therefore, in no better position than the Court was in 1960 when it said: "Empirical statistics are not available to show that the inhabitants of states which follow the exclusionary rule suffer less from lawless searches and seizures than do those of states which admit evidence unlawfully obtained. Since as a practical matter it is never easy to prove a negative, it is hardly likely that conclusive factual data could ever be assembled. For much the same reason, it cannot positively be demonstrated that enforcement of the criminal law is either more or less effective under either rule." Elkins v. United States, 364 U.S., at 218.

If the exclusionary rule is the strong medicine that its proponents claim it to be, then its use in the situations in which it is now applied (resulting, for example, in this case in frustration of the Los Angeles police officers' good-faith duties as enforcers of the criminal laws) must be assumed to be a substantial and efficient deterrent. Assuming this efficacy, the additional marginal deterrence provided by forbidding a different sovereign from using the evidence in a civil proceeding surely does not outweigh the cost to society of extending the rule to that situation. If, on the other hand, the exclusionary rule does not result in appreciable deterrence, then, clearly, its use in the instant situation is unwarranted. Under either assumption, therefore, the extension of the rule is unjustified.

In short, we conclude that exclusion from federal civil proceedings of evidence unlawfully seized by a state criminal enforcement officer has not been shown to have a sufficient likelihood of deterring the conduct of the state police so that it outweighs the societal costs imposed by the exclusion. This Court, therefore, is not justified in so extending the exclusionary rule.

* * *

Mr. Justice BRENNAN, with whom Mr. Justice MARSHALL concurs, dissenting.

I adhere to my view that the exclusionary rule is a necessary and inherent constitutional ingredient of the protections of the Fourth Amendment. . . . Repetition or elaboration of the reasons supporting that view in this case would serve no useful purpose. My view of the exclusionary rule would of course require an affirmance of the Court of Appeals. Today's decisions in this case and in Stone v. Powell, post, continue the Court's business of slow strangulation of the rule." . . .

[Mr. Justice STEWART wrote a separate dissenting opinion.]

6. The Court in *Janis,* supra, declined to use the exclusionary rule as a means to prevent the use of illegally seized evidence by state law enforcement officers in federal civil proceedings. This type of federal-state search and seizure practice is commonly known as the "silver platter" doctrine. The name stems from Mr. Justice Frankfurter's plurality opinion in *Lustig* v. *United States,* 388 U.S. 74 (1949): "The crux of that doctrine is that a search is a search by a

federal official if he had a hand in it; it is not a search by a federal official if evidence secured by state authorities is turned over to the federal authorities on a silver platter." 388 U.S. at 78–79. Prior to *Janis* the Court had never had occasion to rule on the propriety of the practice with regard to civil proceedings. However, the Court did condemn the practice in criminal investigations in *Elkins* v. *United States*, 364 U.S. 206 (1960). Writing for the majority, Mr. Justice Stewart concluded that a continuation of the doctrine would serve as "inducement to subterfuge and evasion . . . in criminal investigations." 364 U.S. at 222. See also *Rios* v. *United States*, 364 U.S. 253 (1960). It should be noted that in 1921 the Supreme Court specifically held in *Burdeau* v. *McDowell*, 256 U.S. 465, that the Fourth Amendment's protection did not apply when evidence was seized by private persons not acting in concert with police. Hence, the exclusionary rule has been inapplicable in such situations.

7. It should be noted that *Stone* v. *Powell*, supra, was held retroactive in *Rigsbee* v. *Parkinson*, 545 F.2d 56 (8th Cir. 1976); accord, *Bracco* v. *Reed*, 540 F.2d 1019 (9th Cir. 1976) and *Chavez* v. *Rodriquez*, 540 F.2d 500 (10th Cir. 1976). See also *Tisnado* v. *United States*, 547 F.2d 452 (9th Cir. 1976) (federal prisoners may not attack sentence by seeking habeas corpus relief on the ground that a prior state conviction considered by the sentencing judge suffered from Fourth Amendment problems). Other recent lower federal and state court decisions that illustrate some of the legal issues surrounding the scope of the exclusionary rule include *Gundlach* v. *Janing*, 401 F. Supp. 1089 (D. Neb. 1975) (defendant seeking to suppress evidence seized as the result of an unlawful entry by a private party must show that the government instigated or encouraged the search, not merely that the government had knowledge of the entry); *In the matter of J.M.A.*, 542 P.2d 170 (Alas. 1975) (search of child's room by foster parent held not sufficient governmental action to implicate the Fourth Amendment); *State* v. *Crum*, 323 So. 2d 673 (Fla. Ct. App. 1975) (officer who leaves his jurisdiction and seizes evidence is acting in the capacity of a private citizen as long as he does not hold himself out as a police officer); *State* v. *McDaniel*, 337 N.E. 2d 173 (Ohio Ct. App. 1975) (exclusionary rule does not apply to searches conducted by department store security officers); *State* v. *Stump*, 547 P.2d 305 (Alas. 1976) (airline employee's removal of a package of cocaine from a shipment of T-shirts, after he had alerted police to the suspicious package and after officer had arrived, held an act of a private citizen and not that of a law enforcement officer); *United States* v. *Sherwin*, 539 F.2d 1 (9th Cir. 1976) (en banc) (federal agents did not violate the Fourth Amendment by failing to obtain a search warrant before accepting copies of two allegedly obscene books from a trucker who discovered them and called the FBI after the shipment was damaged); *United States* v. *Dudek*, 530 F.2d 684 (6th Cir. 1976) (exclusionary rule is not applicable to evidence seized pursuant to a warrant which, following completed search, was not processed in accordance with state procedural requirements to make a prompt return and verify the inventory); *United States* v. *Buck*, 548 F.2d 871 (9th Cir. 1977) (Texas federal court's finding that an illegally seized weapon purchased in Cali-

fornia was the product of an illegal search collaterally estops the government from trying to introduce the same weapon in an Oregon federal prosecution); *State* v. *Landry,* 339 So. 2d 8 (Fla. 1976) (trial judge who granted defendant's motion to suppress allegedly unlawfully seized evidence may not subsequently grant the state's rehearing motion and receive more evidence on the issue) (but see *United States* v. *Raftery,* 534 F.2d 854 [9th Cir. 1976] [exclusionary rule does not prohibit illegally seized drugs which were suppressed at narcotics trial from being used against defendant to prove perjury before grand jury in later prosecution for perjury]); *State* v. *Barajas,* 238 N.W.2d 913 (Neb. 1976) (American sheriff's request of Mexican police that they conduct search of residence in Juarez for murder weapon held not sufficient involvement by U.S. officials to constitute a joint venture under Fourth Amendment); *United States* v. *Jordon,* _____ U.S.M.C.A. _____ (1976) (evidence obtained directly or indirectly from a search conducted by foreign officials is admissible upon a showing that the search complied with the law of the nation in which it took place); *State* v. *Danko,* 548 P.2d 819 (Kan. 1976) (even though federal statute prohibits the unauthorized use of military troops to enforce civilian law [Posse Comitatus Act, 18 U.S.C. § 1385] exclusionary rule not applicable in state trial where evidence was obtained during search by joint patrol that included civilian police officer and military policeman); *United States* v. *Marzano,* 537 F.2d 257 (7th Cir. 1976) (federal agents' enlisting the aid of a City of Grand Cayman policeman, who tracked down Chicago bank burglary suspects on his own and arrested them, held not sufficient federal involvement to trigger exclusionary rule); *United States* v. *Jones,* 518 F.2d 384 (7th Cir. 1975) (the fact that federal agents accompanied Chicago police officers to execute state-issued search warrant and seized evidence which was later used to convict defendants in federal court of conspiracy to possess, distribute, and use a communication facility to facilitate distribution of narcotics did not invalidate the search since possession and distribution of narcotics violate the laws of both sovereignties); *People* v. *Wilkerson,* 541 P.2d 896 (Colo. 1975) (exclusionary rule not applicable at probation revocation hearings) (to the same effect are *United States* v. *Winsett,* 518 F.2d 51 [9th Cir. 1975], *United States* v. *Farmer,* 512 F.2d 100 [6th Cir. 1975], *United States* v. *Brown,* 488 F.2d 94 [5th Cir. 1973], *United States* v. *Hill,* 447 F.2d 817 [7th Cir. 1971], *Sterling* v. *Fitzpatrick,* 426 F.2d 1161 [2nd Cir. 1970], *Lombardino* v. *Heyd,* 318 F. Supp. 648 [E.D. La. 1970], *State* v. *Caron,* 334 A.2d 495 [Me. 1975], *People* v. *Coleman,* 535 P.2d 1025 [Cal. 1975], *State* v. *Thorsness,* 528 P.2d 16 [Mont. 1974], *People* v. *Atencio,* 525 P.2d 461 [Colo. 1975], *Commonwealth* v. *Kanes,* 305 A.2d 701 [Pa. 1973], *Stone* v. *Shea,* 304 A.2d 647 [N.H. 1973], *Reeves* v. *Turner,* 501 P.2d 1212 [Utah 1972], *Baker* v. *State,* 483 S.W. 2d 586 [Tenn. 1972], *State* v. *Kuhn,* 499 P.2d 49 [Wash. 1972], *People* v. *Dowery,* 340 N.E.2d 529 [Ill. 1975], and *State* v. *Sears,* 553 P.2d 907 [Alas. 1976]) (cf. *Croteau* v. *State,* 334 So. 2d 577 [Fla. 1976] [probationer charged with possession of marijuana discovered during probation officer's illegal search held entitled to have the pot excluded at his trial but not at probation revocation hearing]); *United States* v. *Lee,* 540 F.2d 1205 (4th Cir. 1976) (exclusionary rule not applicable to judicial sentencing).

5.04 WARRANTLESS SEARCHES AND SEIZURES: EXCEPTIONS TO THE WARRANT REQUIREMENT OF THE FOURTH AMENDMENT

A. SEARCH INCIDENT TO LAWFUL ARREST

Narrowing the Scope

CHIMEL v. CALIFORNIA

Supreme Court of the United States, 1969
395 U.S. 752, 89 S. Ct. 2034, 23 L. Ed. 2d 685

Los Angeles police officers, armed with an arrest warrant (but no search warrant), were admitted to Chimel's house by his wife. When Chimel arrived he was arrested. Although he denied a request by the officers to "look around," the officers proceeded to conduct a search of the entire house. At his trial for burglary, items that were taken during the search were introduced over his objection and admitted as evidence secured during a search incident to a lawful arrest. The California Supreme Court affirmed, and the United States Supreme Court granted certiorari.

Mr. Justice STEWART delivered the opinion of the Court.

*　*　*

Approval of a warrantless search incident to a lawful arrest seems first to have been articulated by the Court in 1914 as dictum in Weeks v. United States . . . in which the Court stated:

"What then is the present case? Before answering that inquiry specifically it may be well by a process of exclusion to state what it is not. It is not an assertion of the right on the part of the Government, always recognized under English and American law, to search the person of the accused when legally arrested to discover and seize the fruits of evidences of crime." . . .

That statement made no reference to any right to search the *place* where an arrest occurs, but was limited to a right to search the "person." Eleven years later the case of Carroll v. United States, 267 U.S. 132 (1925), brought the following embellishment of the Weeks statement:

"When a man is legally arrested for an offense, whatever is found upon his person or

in his control which it is unlawful for him to have and which may be used to prove the offense may be seized and held as evidence in the prosecution." (Emphasis added.). . .

Still, that assertion too was far from a claim that the "place" where one is arrested may be searched so long as the arrest is valid. Without explanation, however, the principle emerged in expanded form a few months later in Agnello v. United States, 269 U.S. 20 (1925)—although still by way of dictum:

"The right without a search warrant contemporaneously to search persons lawfully arrested while committing crime and to search the place where the arrest is made in order to find and seize things connected with the crime as its fruits or as the means by which it was committed, as well as weapons and other things to effect an escape from custody, is not to be doubted." And in Marron v. United States two years later, the dictum of Agnello appeared to be the foundation of the Court's decision. In that case federal agents had secured a search warrant authorizing the seizure of liquor and certain articles used in its manufacture. When they arrived at the premises to be searched, they say "that the place was used for retailing and drinking intoxicating liquors." They proceeded to arrest the person in charge and to execute the warrant. In searching a closet for the items listed in the warrant they came across an incriminating ledger, concededly not covered by the warrant, which they also seized. The Court upheld the seizure of the ledger by holding that since the agents had made a lawful arrest, "[t]hey had a right without a warrant contemporaneously to search the place in order to find and seize the things used to carry on the criminal enterprise." ...

That the Marron opinion did not mean all that it seemed to say became evident, however, a few years later in Go-Bart Importing Company v. United States, 282 U.S. 344 (1931), and United States v. Lefkowitz, 285 U.S. 452 (1932). ... In Go-Bart, agents had searched the office of persons whom they had lawfully arrested and had taken several papers from a desk, a safe, and other parts of the office. The Court noted that no crime had been committed in the agents' presence, and that although the agent in charge "had an abundance of information and time to swear out a valid [search] warrant, he failed to do so." . . . In holding the search and seizure unlawful, the Court stated:

"Plainly the case before us is essentially different from Marron v. United States. . . . There, officers executing a valid search warrant for intoxicating liquors found and arrested one Birdsall who in pursuance of a conspiracy was actually engaged in running a saloon. As an incident to the arrest they seized a ledger in a closet where the liquor or some of it was kept and some bills beside the cash register. These things were visible and accessible and in the offender's immediate custody. There was no threat of force or general search or rummaging of the place." . . .

This limited characterization of Marron was reiterated in Lefkowitz, a case in which the Court held unlawful a search of desk drawers and cabinet despite the fact that the search had accompanied a lawful arrest. . . .

The limiting views expressed in Go-Bart and Lefkowitz were thrown to the winds, however, in Harris v. United States, 331 U.S. 145, decided in 1947. In that case, officers had obtained a warrant for Harris' arrest on the basis of his alleged involvement with the cashing and interstate transportation of a forged check. He was arrested in the living room of his four-room apartment, and in an attempt to recover two canceled checks thought to have been used in effecting the forgery, the officers undertook a thorough search of the entire apartment. Inside a desk drawer they found a sealed envelope marked "George Harris, personal papers." The envelope, which was then torn open, was found to contain altered Selective Service documents, and those documents were used to secure Harris' conviction for violating the Selective Training and Service Act of 1940. The Court rejected Harris' Fourth Amendment claim, sustaining the search as "incident to arrest." . . .

Only a year after Harris, however, the pendulum swung again. In Trupiano v. United States, 334 U.S. 699 (1948), agents raided the site of an illicit distillery, saw one of several conspirators operating the still, and arrested him, contemporaneously "seiz[ing] the illicit distillery." . . . The Court held that the arrest and others made subsequently had been valid, but that the unexplained failure of the agents to procure a search warrant—in spite of the fact that they had had more than enough time before the raid to do so—rendered the search unlawful. The opinion stated:

"It is a cardinal rule that, in seizing goods and articles, law enforcement agents must secure and use search warrants wherever reasonably practicable. . . . This rule rests upon the desirability of having magistrates rather than police officers determine when searches and seizures are permissible and what limitations should be placed upon such activities. . . . To provide the necessary security against unreasonable intrusions upon the private lives of individuals, the framers of the Fourth Amendment required adherence to judicial processes wherever possible. And subsequent history has confirmed the wisdom of that requirement.

* * *

"A search or seizure without a warrant as an incident to a lawful arrest had always been considered to be a strictly limited right. It grows out of the inherent necessities of the situation at the time of the arrest. But there must be something more in the way of necessity than merely a lawful arrest." . . .

In 1950, two years after Trupiano, came United States v. Rabinowitz, 339 U.S. 56, the decision upon which California primarily relies in the case now before us. In Rabinowitz, federal authorities had been informed that the defendant was dealing in stamps bearing forged overprints. On the basis of that information they secured a warrant for his arrest, which they executed at his one-room business office. At the time of the arrest, the officers "searched the desk, safe, and file cabinets in the office for about an hour and a half" . . . and seized 573 stamps with forged overprints. The stamps were admitted into evidence at the defendant's trial, and this Court affirmed his conviction, rejecting the contention that the warrantless search had been unlawful. The Court held that the search in its entirety fell within the principle giving law enforcement authorities "[t]he right 'to search the place where the arrest is made in order to find and seize things connected with the crime. . . .'" . . . Harris was regarded as "ample authority" for that conclusion. . . . The opinion rejected the rule of Trupiano that "in seizing goods and articles, law enforcement agents must secure and use search warrants wherever reasonably practicable." The test, said the Court, "is not whether it is reasonable to procure a search warrant, but whether the search was reasonable." . . .

Rabinowitz has come to stand for the proposition, inter alia, that a warrantless search "incident to a lawful arrest" may generally extend to the area that is considered to be in the "possession" or under the "control" of the person arrested. And it was on the basis of that proposition that the California courts upheld the search of the petitioner's entire house in this case. That doctrine, however, at least in the broad sense in which it was applied by the California courts in this case, can withstand neither historical nor rational analysis.

Even limited to its own facts, the Rabinowitz decision was, as we have seen, hardly founded on an unimpeachable line of authority. As Mr. Justice Frankfurter commented in dissent in that case, the "hint" contained in Weeks was, without persuasive justification, "loosely turned into dictum and finally elevated to a decision." . . . And the approach taken in cases such as Go-Bart, Lefkowitz, and Trupiano was essentially disregarded by the Rabinowitz Court.

Nor is the rationale by which the State seeks here to sustain the search of the petitioner's house supported by a reasoned view of the background and purpose of the Fourth Amendment. Mr. Justice Frankfurter wisely pointed out in his Rabinowitz dissent that the Amendment's proscription of "unreasonable searches and seizures" must be read in light of "the history that gave rise to the words"—history of "abuses so deeply felt by the Colonies as to be one of the potent causes of the Revolution. . . ." The Amendment was in large part a reaction to the general warrants and warrantless searches that had so alienated the colonists and had helped speed the movement for independence. In the scheme of the Amendment, therefore, the requirement that "no Warrants shall issue, but upon probable cause," plays a crucial part. As the Court put it in McDonald v. United States, 335 U.S. 451 (1948):

"We are not dealing with formalities. The presence of a search warrant serves a high function. Absent some grave emergency, the Fourth Amendment has interposed a magistrate between the citizen and the police. This was done not to shield criminals nor to make the home a safe haven for illegal activities. It was done so that an objective mind might weigh the need to invade that privacy in order to enforce the law. The right of privacy was deemed too precious to entrust to the discretion of those whose job is the detection of crime and the arrest of criminals. . . . And so the Constitution requires a magistrate to pass on the desires of the police before they violate the privacy of the home. We cannot be true to that constitutional requirement and excuse the absence of a search warrant without a showing by those who seek exemption from the constitutional mandate that the exigencies of the situation made that course imperative." . . . Even in the Agnello case the Court relied upon the rule that "[b]elief, however well founded, that an article sought is concealed in a dwelling house, furnishes no justification for a search of that place without a warrant. And such searches are held unlawful notwithstanding facts unquestionably showing probable cause." . . . Clearly, the general requirement that a search warrant be obtained is not lightly to be dispensed with, and "the burden is on those seeking

[an] exemption [from the requirement] to show the need for it. . . ."

* * *

. . . When an arrest is made, it is reasonable for the arresting officer to search the person arrested in order to remove any weapons that the latter might seek to use in order to resist arrest or effect his escape. Otherwise, the officer's safety might well be endangered, and the arrest itself frustrated. In addition, it is entirely reasonable for the arresting officer to search for and seize any evidence on the arrestee's person in order to prevent its concealment or destruction. And the area into which an arrestee might reach in order to grab a weapon or evidentiary items must, of course, be governed by a like rule. A gun on a table or in a drawer in front of one who is arrested can be as dangerous to the arresting officer as one concealed in the clothing of the person arrested. There is ample justification, therefore, for a search of the arrestee's person and the area "within his immediate control"—construing that phrase to mean the area from within which he might gain possession of a weapon or destructible evidence.

There is no comparable justification, however, for routinely searching any room other than that in which an arrest occurs—or, for that matter, for searching through all the desk drawers or other closed or concealed areas in that room itself. Such searches, in the absence of well-recognized exceptions, may be made only under the authority of a search warrant. The "adherence to judicial processes" mandated by the Fourth Amendment requires no less.

* * *

It is argued in the present case that it is "reasonable" to search a man's house when he is arrested in it. But that argument is founded on little more than a subjective view regarding the acceptability of certain sorts of police conduct, and not on considerations relevant to Fourth Amendment interests. Under such an unconfined analysis, Fourth Amendment protection in this area would approach the evaporation point. It is not easy to explain why, for instance, it is less subjectively "reasonable" to search a man's house when he is arrested on his front lawn—or just down the street—than it is

when he happens to be in the house at the time of arrest.

* * *

It would be possible, of course, to draw a line between Rabinowitz and Harris on the one hand, and this case on the other. For Rabinowitz involved a single room, and Harris a four-room apartment, while in the case before us an entire house was searched. But such a distinction would be highly artificial. The rationale that allowed the searches and seizures in Rabinowitz and Harris would allow the searches and seizures in this case. No consideration relevant to the Fourth Amendment suggests any point of rational limitation, once the search is allowed to go beyond the area from which the person arrested might obtain weapons or evidentiary items. The only reasoned distinction is one between a search of the person arrested and the area within his reach on the one hand, and more extensive searches on the other.

The petitioner correctly points out that one result of decisions such as Rabinowitz and Harris is to give law enforcement officials the opportunity to engage in searches not justified by probable cause, by the simple expedient of arranging to arrest suspects at home rather than elsewhere. We do not suggest that the petitioner is necessarily correct in his assertion that such a strategy was utilized here, but the fact remains that had he been arrested earlier in the day, at his place of employment rather than at home, no search of his house could have been made without a search warrant. In any event, even apart from the possibility of such police tactics, the general point so forcefully made by Judge Learned Hand in United States v. Kirschenblatt remains:

"After arresting a man in his house, to rummage at will among his papers in search of whatever will convict him, appears to us to be indistinguishable from what might be done under a general warrant; indeed, the warrant would give more protection, for presumably it must be issued by a magistrate. True, by hypothesis the power would not exist, if the supposed offender were not found on the premises; but it is small consolation to know that one's papers are safe only so long as one is not at home." . . .

Rabinowitz and Harris have been the subject of critical commentary for many years, and have been relied upon less and less in our own decisions. It is time, for the reasons we have stated, to hold that on their own facts, and insofar as the principles they stand for are inconsistent with those that we have endorsed today, they are no longer to be followed.

Application of sound Fourth Amendment principles to the facts of this case produces a clear result. The search here went far beyond the petitioner's person and the area from within which he might have obtained either a weapon or something that could have been used as evidence against him. There was no constitutional justification, in the absence of a search warrant, for extending the search beyond that area. The scope of the search was, therefore, "unreasonable" under the Fourth and Fourteenth Amendments and the petitioner's conviction cannot stand.

Reversed.

[Mr. Justice HARLAN wrote a concurring opinion.]

[Mr. Justice WHITE, with whom Mr. Justice BLACK joined, dissented.]

Comments

1. Historically, the Supreme Court has held that in order to justify a search incident to arrest, the arrest itself must be lawful and the accompanying search must be *reasonable*, both in scope and in conduct. Consequently, the constitutional validity of the search depends first upon the constitutional validity of the arrest. See, e.g., *Rios* v. *United States,* 364 U.S. 253 (1960).

2. Although some state courts have held that the arrest need not necessarily precede the search, the Supreme Court has not indicated that the traditional sequence should be altered in "search incident" cases. The Court has, however, hinted that altering the sequence in so-called "hot pursuit" situations would be permissible. See *Warden* v. *Hayden,* infra. But these searches conducted under the so-called "emergency doctrine" can be readily distinguished from those conducted incident to arrest and therefore provide no justification for any attempt to vary the arrest-search sequence of the ordinary search incident case.

3. *Chimel* was a "landmark" decision in the history of warrantless searches and seizures. It involved a complete re-evaluation and redefinition of the search incident exception. Of particular import is the establishment of very narrow restrictions on the *scope* of searches conducted incident to arrest. In setting these limits, the Court overruled the earlier leading cases of *Rabinowitz* and *Harris*. The *Chimel* Court concluded that the search must be limited to the "immediate area of control of the arrestee." The phrase "immediate area of control" was generally defined as the area within which the arrestee may be able to reach for a weapon or destroy evidence.

4. Although the Court declined to apply *Chimel* retroactively in *Vale* v. *Louisiana,* 399 U.S. 30 (1970), the same basic principles were followed. In *Vale* the defendant was arrested outside his house and a search was conducted inside the house incident to the arrest. The majority concluded that if such a search was to be upheld as incident to an arrest, the arrest must take place inside the house. The Court said in *Vale*, "If a search of a house is to be upheld as incident to an arrest, that arrest must take place inside the house,"

399 at 33–34. "We decline to hold that an arrest on the street can provide its own 'exigent circumstance' so as to justify a warrantless search of [an] arrestee's house," at 35. Likewise, in *Coolidge* v. *New Hampshire*, 403 U.S. 443 (1971) (infra), the Court denied the validity of a similar search where the police attempted to justify a search of an automobile outside a house by arguing that the search was incidental to an arrest made inside the house.

Extending the *Chimel* Rationale to "Investigatory Detentions"

CUPP v. MURPHY

Supreme Court of the United States, 1973
412 U.S. 291, 93 S. Ct. 2000, 36 L. Ed. 2d 900

During a station-house questioning of respondent Murphy in connection with the strangulation-murder of his wife, Portland, Oregon, police noticed a dark spot on respondent's finger which they suspected was dried blood. Over respondent's protest and without a warrant, the police took sample scrapings from his fingernails and discovered evidence later used to convict him. Murphy was not under arrest at the time the samples were obtained, and in fact, was not formally arrested until one month later. Subsequently, after respondent's conviction was affirmed by the Oregon Court of Appeals and his petition for federal habeas corpus was rejected by the United States District Court (D. Ore.), the Court of Appeals (9th Cir.) reversed his conviction, holding that in the absence of an arrest or other exigent circumstances, the search violated the Fourth Amendment. The Supreme Court granted the State of Oregon certiorari. Additional facts are stated in the opinion.

Mr. Justice STEWART delivered the opinion of the Court.

*　*　*

The respondent, Daniel Murphy, was convicted by a jury in an Oregon Court of the second-degree murder of his wife. The victim died by strangulation in her home in the city of Portland, and abrasions and lacerations were found on her throat. There was no sign of a break-in or robbery. Word of the murder was sent to the respondent, who was not then living with his wife. Upon receiving the message, Murphy promptly telephoned the Portland police and voluntarily came into Portland for questioning. Shortly after the respondent's arrival at the station house, where he was met by retained counsel, the police noticed a dark spot on the respondent's finger. Suspecting that the spot might be dried blood and knowing that evidence of strangulation is often found under the assailant's fingernails, the police

asked Murphy if they could take a sample of scrapings from his fingernails. He refused. Under protest and without a warrant, the police proceeded to take the samples, which turned out to contain traces of skin and blood cells, and fabric from the victim's nightgown. This incriminating evidence was admitted at the trial.

*　*　*

The trial court, the Oregon Court of Appeals, and the Federal District Court all agreed that the police had probable cause to arrest the respondent at the time they detained him and scraped his fingernails. As the Oregon Court of Appeals said,

"At the time the detectives took these scrapings they knew:

"The bedroom in which the wife was found dead showed no signs of disturbance, which fact tended to indicate a killer known to the victim rather than a burglar or other stranger.

"The decedent's son, the only other person in the house that night, did not have fingernails which could have made the lacerations observed on the victim's throat.

"The defendant and his deceased wife had had a stormy marriage and did not get along well.

"The defendant had, in fact, been at his home on the night of the murder. He left and drove back to central Oregon claiming that he did not enter the house or see his wife. He volunteered a great deal of information without being asked, yet expressed no concern or curiosity about his wife's fate." . . .

The Court of Appeals for the Ninth Circuit did not disagree with the conclusion that the police had probable cause to make an arrest . . . nor do we.

It is also undisputed that the police did not obtain an arrest warrant or formally "arrest" the respondent, as that term is understood under Oregon law.[a] The respondent was detained only long enough to take the fingernail scrapings, and was not formally "arrested" until approximately one month later. Nevertheless, the detention of the respondent against his will constituted a seizure of his person, and the Fourth Amendment guarantee of freedom from "unreasonable searches and seizures" is clearly implicated. . . . As the Court said in Davis v. Mississippi, 394 U.S. 721 (1969), "Nothing is more clear than that the Fourth Amendment was meant to prevent wholesale intrusions upon the personal security of our citizenry, whether these intrusions be termed 'arrests' or 'investigatory detentions.'"

In Davis, the Court held that fingerprints obtained during the brief detention of persons seized in a police dragnet procedure, without probable cause, were inadmissible in evidence. Though the Court recognized that fingerprinting "involves none of the probing into an individual's private life and thoughts that marks an interrogation or search," . . . the Court held the stationhouse detention in that case to be violative of the Fourth and Fourteenth Amendments.

"Investigatory seizures would subject unlimited numbers of innocent persons to the harassment and ignominy incident to involuntary detention." . . .

The respondent in this case, like Davis, was briefly detained at the station house. Yet, here, there was, as three courts have found, probable cause to believe that the respondent had committed the murder. The vice of the detention in Davis is therefore absent in the case before us. . . .

The inquiry does not end here, however, because Murphy was subjected to a search as well as a seizure of his person. Unlike the fingerprinting in Davis, the voice exemplar obtained in United States v. Dionisio, 410 U.S. 1 (1973), or the handwriting exemplar obtained in United States v. Mara, 410 U.S. 19 (1973), the search of the respondent's fingernails went beyond mere "physical characteristics . . . constantly exposed to the public," and constituted the type of "severe, though brief, intrusion upon cherished personal security" that is subject to constitutional scrutiny. Terry v. Ohio, 392 U.S. 1, 1968.

We believe this search was constitutionally permissible under the principles of Chimel v. California, 395 U.S. 752 (1969). Chimel stands in a long line of cases recognizing an exception to the warrant requirement when a search is incident to a valid arrest. . . . The basis for this exception is that when an arrest is made, it is reasonable for a police officer to expect the arrestee to use any weapons he may have and to attempt to destroy any incriminating evidence then in his possession. . . . The Court recognized in Chimel that the scope of a warrantless search must be commensurate with the rationale that excepts the search from the warrant requirement. Thus, a warrantless search incident to arrest, the Court held in Chimel, must be limited to the area "into which an arrestee might reach." . . .

Where there is no formal arrest, as in the case before us, a person might well be less hostile to the police and less likely to take conspicuous, immediate steps to destroy incriminating evidence on his person. Since he knows he is going to be released, he might be likely instead to be concerned with diverting attention away from himself. Accordingly, we do not hold that a full Chimel search would have been justified in this case

---

[a]Oregon defines arrest as "the taking of a person into custody so that he may be held to answer for a crime." Ore. Rev. Stat. § 133.210.

without a formal arrest and without a warrant. But the respondent was not subjected to such a search.

At the time Murphy was being detained at the station house, he was obviously aware of the detectives' suspicions. Though he did not have the full warning of official suspicion that a formal arrest provides, Murphy was sufficiently apprised of his suspected role in the crime to motivate him to attempt to destroy what evidence he could without attracting further attention. Testimony at trial indicated that after he refused to consent to the taking of fingernail samples, he put his hands behind his back and appeared to rub them together. He then put his hands in his pockets, and a "metallic sound, such as keys or change rattling" was heard. The rationale of Chimel, in these circumstances, justified the police in subjecting him to the very limited search necessary to preserve the highly evanescent evidence they found under his fingernails. . . .

On the facts of this case, considering the existence of probable cause, the very limited intrusion undertaken incident to the station house detention, and the ready destructibility of the evidence, we cannot say that this search violated the Fourth and Fourteenth Amendments. Accordingly, the judgment of the Court of Appeals is reversed.

* * *

Mr. Justice WHITE joins the opinion of the Court but does not consider the issue of probable cause to have been decided here or to be foreclosed on remand to the Court of Appeals where it has never been considered.

* * *

[Mr. Justice MARSHALL wrote a concurring opinion.]
[Mr. Justice BLACKMUN and Mr. Chief Justice BURGER joined, concurring.]
[Mr. Justice POWELL, with whom Mr. Chief Justice BURGER and Mr. Justice REHNQUIST joined, wrote a concurring opinion.]

Mr. Justice DOUGLAS, dissenting in part.

I agree with the Court that exigent circumstances existed making it likely that the fingernail scrapings of suspect Murphy might vanish if he were free to move about. The police would therefore have been justified in detaining him while a search warrant was sought from a magistrate. None was sought and the Court now holds there was probable cause to search or arrest, making a warrant unnecessary.

Whether there was or was not probable cause is difficult to determine on this record. It is a question that the Court of Appeals never reached. We should therefore remand to it for a determination of that question.

The question is clouded in my mind because the police did not arrest Murphy until a month later. It is a case not covered by Chimel v. California . . . on which the Court relies, for in Chimel an arrest had been made.

As the Court states, Oregon defines arrest as "the taking of a person into custody so that he may be held to answer for a crime." Ore. Rev. Stat. § 133.210. No such arrest was made until a month after Murphy's fingernails were scraped. As we stated in Johnson v. United States, 333 U.S. 10 . . . "State law determines the validity of arrests without warrant." The case is therefore on all fours with Davis v. Mississippi, 394 U.S. 721 (1969) [Comments, infra] . . . .

The reason why no arrest of Murphy was made on the day his fingernails were scraped creates a nagging doubt that they did not then have probable cause to make an arrest and did not reach that conclusion until a month later. Why was Murphy allowed to roam at will, a free man, for the next month? The evolving pattern of a conspiracy offense might induce the police to turn a suspect loose in order to tail him and see that other suspects could be brought into their net. But no such circumstances were present here.

What the decision made today comes down to, I fear, is that "suspicion" is the basis for a search of the person without a warrant. Yet "probable cause" is the requirement of the Fourth Amendment which is applicable to the States by reason of the Fourteenth Amendment. . . . Suspicion has never been sufficient for a warrantless search, save for the narrow situation of searches incident to an arrest as was involved in Chimel. That exception is designed . . . to protect the officer against assaults through weapons within easy reach of the accused or to save evidence within that narrow zone from destruction. However, this is a case where a warrant might have been sought but was not. It is therefore governed by the rule that the rights of a person "against unlawful search and seizure are to be protected even if the same result might have been achieved in a lawful way." Silverthorne Lumber Co. v. United States, 251 U.S. 385 (1939). No warrant could have been issued by the police, for as we held in Coolidge v. New Hampshire, 403 U.S. 443 (1971), a warrant must be issued by "the neutral and detached magistrate required by the Constitution." As stated in Johnson v. United States, 333 U.S., at 14, "When the right of privacy must reasonably yield to the right of search is, as a rule, to be decided by a judicial officer, not by a policeman or Government enforcement agent."

* * *

Moreover, the Fourth Amendment guarantees the right of the people to be secure "in their persons." Scraping a man's fingernails is an invasion of that privacy and it is tolerable, constitutionally speaking, only if there is a warrant for a search or seizure issued by a magistrate on a showing of "probable cause" that the suspect had committed a crime. There was time to get a warrant; Murphy could have been detained while one was sought; and that detention would have preserved the perishable evidence the police sought. A suspect on the loose could get rid of it; but a suspect closely detained until a warrant is obtained plainly could not.

Our approval of the shortcut taken to avoid the Fourth and Fifth Amendments may be typical of this age. Erosions of constitutional guarantees usually start slowly, not in dramatic onsets. . . .

The issue of probable cause should be considered by the Court of Appeals. On the record before us and the arguments based on it I cannot say there was "probable cause" for an arrest and for a search, since the arrest came after a month's delay. The only weight we can put in the scales to turn suspicion into probable cause is Murphy's conviction by a jury based on the illegally obtained evidence. That is but a simple way of making the end justify the means—a principle wholly at war with our constitutionally enshrined adversary system.

Mr. Justice BRENNAN, dissenting in part.

Without effecting an arrest, and without first seeking to obtain a search warrant from a magistrate, the police decided to scrape respondent's fingernails for destructible evidence. In upholding this search, the Court engrafts another, albeit limited, exception on the warrant requirement. Before we take the serious step of legitimating even limited searches merely upon probable cause—without a warrant or as incident to an arrest—we ought first be certain that such probable cause in fact existed. Here, as my Brother DOUGLAS convincingly demonstrates "[w]hether there was or was not probable cause is difficult to determine on this record." And, since the Court of Appeals did not consider that question, the proper course would be to remand to that court so that it might decide in the first instance whether there was probable cause to arrest or search. There is simply no need for this Court to decide, upon a disputed record and at this stage of the litigation, whether the instant search would be permissible if probable cause existed.

Comments

1. The majority's analysis in *Murphy* is puzzling in that the warrantless search of the defendant preceded his arrest by a month, yet his Fourth Amendment claims were defeated on the basis of *Chimel*, which involved a warrantless search incident to a formal lawful arrest. Perhaps the majority in *Murphy* was of the view that the "emergency" nature of the situation, i.e., the limited intrusion together with the ready destructibility of the evidence, made the

warrantless search permissible. Arguably, the limited intrusion under these circumstances might have been more justifiable under the emergency doctrine of *Schmerber* v. *California,* infra, rather than the principles enunciated in *Chimel.* In *Schmerber,* a majority of the Supreme Court upheld the warrantless taking of a blood sample by a physician from a suspect when the arresting officer had probable cause to believe that the defendant was under the influence of intoxicating liquor and the blood test involved only a "minor intrusion into [the] individual's body." However, even *Schmerber* may be inapposite in that, in contrast to *Murphy,* Schmerber was formally arrested prior to the warrantless intrusion. In addition, *Schmerber's* blood alcohol level would have diminished regardless of any precautionary procedures employed by the police prior to the blood test. Arguably *Murphy* involved less of an emergency than *Schmerber,* and as noted by Mr. Justice Douglas (dissenting in *Murphy*), "There was time to get a warrant; Murphy could have been detained while one was sought; and that detention would have preserved the perishable evidence the police sought." Presumably it would have been necessary to handcuff or otherwise physically restrain Murphy to prevent a destruction of the evidence under his fingernails. Yet Justice Douglas had a "nagging doubt" about whether the police had probable cause to physically detain Murphy. In *Davis* v. *Mississippi,* 304 U.S. 721 (1969), the Court left open the issue whether under narrowly defined circumstances the Fourth Amendment might permit the taking of fingerprints from a suspect for whom there is no probable cause to arrest. Perhaps this is what Justice Douglas had in mind in his dissenting opinion in *Murphy.*

2. The result in *Murphy* is questionable because it reflects a willingness by the Court to let the protection of substantial individual rights turn on the practical difficulties of law enforcement. Cf. *Chambers* v. *Maroney,* 399 U.S. 42 (1970) (where police have probable cause to conduct warrantless search of automobile on highway, warrantless search of same car at police station not unreasonable); *Cady* v. *Dombrowski,* 413 U.S. 433 (1973) (warrantless search of automobile at private garage 2½ hours after defendant's arrest not unreasonable where danger to public safety outweighed the driver's interest in the privacy of the car's contents); *South Dakota* v. *Opperman,* 428 U.S. 364 (1976) (infra) (warrantless general inventory search of impounded automobile following seizure of car involved in parking violations not unreasonable); *United States* v. *Watson,* 423 U.S. 411 (1976) (supra) (warrantless arrest of defendant with probable cause not unreasonable notwithstanding that agents had sufficient time to obtain warrant prior to arrest); *Texas* v. *White,* 423 U.S. 67 (1975) (warrantless search of automobile after it was removed to police station following defendant's arrest not unreasonable under *Chambers* even though defendant specifically refused to consent to search); *United States* v. *Santana,* 427 U.S. 38 (1976) (infra) (warrantless felony arrest of defendant after she fled into house not unreasonable where agents had probable cause to make arrest). It is nevertheless clear that the reach of *Murphy* as a precedent should extend only to cases in which (a) the police have probable cause to arrest, (b) an emergency is involved in which evidence could be readily destroyed, and (c) the warrantless intrusion is very limited in scope.

"Reasonable Delay": Extending the Temporal and Geographic Scope

UNITED STATES v. EDWARDS

Supreme Court of the United States, 1974
415 U.S. 800, 94 S. Ct. 1234, 39 L. Ed. 2d 771

Respondent, Eugene Edwards, and an alleged confederate (one William Livesay, who was co-respondent in this case but died after the petition for certiorari was granted) were arrested shortly after 11 P.M. on May 31, 1970, for attempting to break into a post office. They were taken to a local jail and placed in a cell. Shortly thereafter, investigation at the scene revealed that paint chips had been left on the window sill in which the attempted entry had been made, and the police had probable cause to believe that Edward's clothes were themselves material evidence of the crime for which he had been arrested. The next morning (approximately 10 hours after his arrest) Edwards was given substitute clothing for the clothing he had been wearing since the time of his arrest, which was seized and held as evidence. A subsequent examination of the clothing revealed paint chips matching samples taken from the window sill. Over respondent's objections, this evidence and his clothing were admitted at trial, which resulted in his conviction. The United States Court of Appeals (6th Cir.) reversed the conviction, holding that the warrantless seizure of his clothing "after the administrative process and the mechanics of the arrest [had] come to a halt" was unreasonable under the Fourth Amendment. The Supreme Court granted the United States government certiorari.

Mr. Justice WHITE delivered the opinion of the Court.

The question here is whether the Fourth Amendment should be extended to exclude from evidence certain clothing taken from respondent Edwards while he was in custody at the city jail approximately 10 hours after his arrest.

* * *

The prevailing rule under the Fourth Amendment that searches and seizures may not be made without a warrant is subject to various exceptions. One of them permits warrantless searches incident to custodial arrests ... and has traditionally been justified by the reasonableness of searching for weapons, instruments of escape, and evidence of crime when a person is taken into official custody and lawfully detained. . . .

It is also plain that searches and seizures that could be made on the spot at the time of arrest may legally be conducted later when the accused arrives at the place of de-

tention. If need be, Abel v. United States, 362 U.S. 217 (1960), settled this question. There the defendant was arrested at his hotel, but the belongings taken with him to the place of detention were searched there. In sustaining the search, the Court noted that a valid search of the property could have been made at the place of arrest and perceived little difference "when the accused decides to take the property with him, for the search of it to occur instead at the first place of detention when the accused arrives there, especially as the search of property carried by an accused to the place of detention has additional justifications, similar to those which justify a search of the person of one who is arrested." Id., at 239. The courts of appeals have followed this same rule, holding that both the person and the property in his immediate possession may be searched at the station house after the arrest has occurred at another place and if evidence of crime is discovered, it may be seized and admitted in evidence. Nor is there any doubt that clothing or other belongings may be seized upon arrival of the accused at the place of detention and later subjected to laboratory analysis or that the test results are admissible at trial.

Conceding all this, the Court of Appeals in this case nevertheless held that a warrant is required where the search occurs after the administrative mechanics of arrest have been completed and the prisoner is incarcerated. But even on these terms, it seems to us that the normal processes incident to arrest and custody had not been completed when Edwards was placed in his cell on the night of May 31. With or without probable cause, the authorities were entitled at that point not only to search Edwards' clothing but also to take it from him and keep it in official custody. There was testimony that this was the standard practice in this city. The police were also entitled to take from Edwards any evidence of the crime in his immediate possession, including his clothing. And the Court of Appeals acknowledged that contemporaneously with or shortly after the time Edwards went to his cell, the police had probable cause to believe that the articles of clothing he wore were themselves material evidence of the crime for which he had been arrested.... But it was late at night; no substitute clothing was then available for Edwards to wear, and it would certainly have been unreasonable for the police to have stripped respondent of his clothing and left him exposed in his cell throughout the night.... When the substitutes were purchased the next morning, the clothing he had been wearing at the time of arrest was taken from him and subjected to laboratory analysis. This was no more than taking from respondent the effects in his immediate possession that constituted evidence of crime. This was and is a normal incident of a custodial arrest, and reasonable delay in effectuating it does not change the fact that Edwards was no more imposed upon than he could have been at the time and place of the arrest or immediately upon arrival at the place of detention. The police did no more on June 1 than they were entitled to do incident to the usual custodial arrest and incarceration.

Other closely related considerations sustain the examination of the clothing in this case. It must be remembered that on May 31 and June 1 the police had lawful custody of Edwards and necessarily of the clothing he wore. When it became apparent that the articles of clothing were evidence of the crime for which Edwards was being held, the police were entitled to take, examine, and preserve them for use as evidence, just as they are normally permitted to seize evidence of crime when it is unlawfully encountered.... Surely, the clothes could have been brushed down and vacuumed while Edwards had them on in the cell, and it was similarly reasonable to take and examine them as the police did, particularly in view of the existence of probable cause linking the clothes to the crime. Indeed, it is difficult to perceive what is unreasonable about the police's examining and holding as evidence those personal effects of the accused that they already have in their lawful custody as the result of a lawful arrest....

[In] United States v. Caruso, 358 F.2d 184 ... [the] defendant's clothes were not taken until six hours after his arrival at a place of detention. The Court of Appeals properly held that no warrant was required:

"He and his clothes were constantly in custody from the moment of his arrest, and the inspection of his clothes and the holding of them for use in evidence were, under the circumstances, reasonable and proper." 358 F.2d, at 185 (citations omitted).

Caruso is typical of most cases in the courts of appeals that have long since concluded that once the accused is lawfully arrested and is in custody, the effects in his possession at the place of detention that were subject to search at the time and place of his arrest may lawfully be searched and seized without a warrant even though a substantial period of time has elapsed between the arrest and subsequent administrative processing, on the one hand, and the taking of the property for use as evidence, on the other. This is true where the clothing or effects are immediately seized upon arrival at the jail, held under the defendant's name in the "property room" of the jail, and at a later time searched and taken for use at the subsequent criminal trial. The result is the same where the property is not physically taken from the defendant until sometime after his incarceration.

In upholding this search and seizure, we do not conclude that the Warrant Clause of the Fourth Amendment is never applicable to postarrest seizures of the effects of an arrestee. But we do think that the Court of Appeals for the First Circuit captured the essence of situations like this when it said in United States v. DeLeo, 422 F.2d 487, 493 (1970) (footnote omitted):

"While the legal arrest of a person should not destroy the privacy of his premises, it does—for at least a reasonable time and to a reasonable extent—take his own privacy out of the realm of protection from police interest in weapons, means of escape, and evidence."

The judgement of the Court of Appeals is reversed.

Mr. Justice STEWART, with whom Mr. Justice DOUGLAS, Mr. Justice BRENNAN, and Mr. Justice MARSHALL join, dissenting.

The Court says that the question before us "is whether the Fourth Amendment should be extended" to prohibit the warrantless seizure of Edwards' clothing. I think, on the contrary, that the real question in this case is whether the Fourth Amendment is to be ignored. For in my view the judgment of the Court of Appeals can be reversed only by disregarding established Fourth Amendment principles firmly embodied in many previous decisions of this Court.

As the Court has repeatedly emphasized in the past, "the most basic constitutional rule in this area is that 'searches conducted outside the judicial process, without prior approval by judge or magistrate, are per se unreasonable under the Fourth Amendment—subject only to a few specifically established and well-delineated exceptions.'" ... Since it is conceded here that the seizure of Edwards' clothing was not made pursuant to a warrant, the question becomes whether the Government has met its burden of showing that the circumstances of this seizure brought it within one of the "jealously and carefully drawn" exceptions to the warrant requirement.

The Court finds a warrant unnecessary in this case because of the custodial arrest of the respondent. It is, of course, well settled that the Fourth Amendment permits a warrantless search or seizure incident to a constitutionally valid custodial arrest.... But the mere fact of an arrest does not allow the police to engage in warrantless searches of unlimited geographic or temporal scope. Rather, the search must be spatially limited

to the person of the arrestee and the area within his reach ... and must, as to time, be "substantially contemporaneous with the arrest"....

Under the facts of this case, I am unable to agree with the Court's holding that the search was "incident" to Edwards' custodial arrest. The search here occurred fully 10 hours after he was arrested, at a time when the administrative processing and mechanics of arrest had long since come to an end. His clothes were not seized as part of an "inventory" of a prisoner's effects, nor were they taken pursuant to a routine exchange of civilian clothes for jail garb.[b] And the considerations that typically justify a warrantless search incident to a lawful arrest were wholly absent here....

* * *

Accordingly, I see no justification for dispensing with the warrant requirement here. The police had ample time to seek a warrant, and no exigent circumstances were present to excuse their failure to do so. Unless the exceptions to the warrant requirement are to be "enthroned into the rule," ... this is precisely the sort of situation where the Fourth Amendment requires a magistrate's prior approval for a search.

The Court says that the relevant question is "not whether it was reasonable to procure a search warrant, but whether the search itself was reasonable."... Precisely such a view, however, was explicitly rejected in Chimel v. California ... where the Court characterized the argument as "founded on little more than a subjective view regarding the acceptability of certain sorts of police conduct, and not on considerations relevant to Fourth Amendment interests." As they were in Chimel, the words of Mr. Justice Frankfurter are again most relevant here:

"To say that the search must be reasonable is to require some criterion of reason. It is no guide at all either for a jury or for district judges or the police to say that an 'unreasonable search' is forbidden—that the search must be reasonable. What is the test

_____

[b]The Government conceded at oral argument that the seizure of the clothing was not a matter of routine jail procedure, but was undertaken solely for the purpose of searching for the incriminating paint chips.

of reason which makes a search reasonable? The test is the reason underlying and expressed by the Fourth Amendment: the history and the experience which it embodies and the safeguards afforded by it against the evils to which it was a response. There must be a warrant to permit search, barring only inherent limitations upon that requirement when there is a good excuse for not getting a search warrant. . . ." United States v. Rabinowitz, [339 U.S. 56, 83 (1950)] (dissenting opinion).

The intrusion here was hardly a shocking one, and it cannot be said that the police acted in bad faith. The Fourth Amendment, however, was not designed to apply only to situations where the intrusion is massive and the violation of privacy shockingly flagrant. . . .

* * *

Because I believe that the Court today unjustifiably departs from well-settled constitutional principles, I respectfully dissent.

Comments

1. In *Edwards,* the majority of the Court left open the issue whether a warrantless seizure of the clothing of an arrestee would be reasonable under the Fourth Amendment absent probable cause that the clothing itself was material criminal evidence. (Presumably probable cause that the clothing seized from an arrestee in jail is material evidence would not be required because such proof is not required in searches immediately following a lawful arrest. However, a significant passage of time between the arrest and the completion of the administrative processing could give rise to a requirement of probable cause under the Fourth Amendment,) Mr. Justice Stewart (joined by Justices Douglas, Brennan, and Marshall) dissented in *Edwards,* stating that the warrantless seizure of the clothing was unreasonable in that there were no "jealously and carefully drawn" exigent circumstances for dispensing with the warrant requirement of the Fourth Amendment. In addition, the dissenting justices stated that the administrative processing and mechanics of Edwards' arrest had "long since come to an end"; that the clothes were not seized as part of an "inventory" search nor taken pursuant to a routine exchange of civilian clothes for jail garb; and that the reasons which typically justify a warrantless arrest following a custody arrest were "wholly absent here." Justice Stewart quoted from the opinion of Mr. Justice Black in *Preston* v. *United States,* 376 U.S. 364, 367 (1967), in which it was stated that warrantless searches following custodial arrest are justified by the need to seize weapons which might be used to assault an officer or effect an escape and to prevent the destruction of criminal evidence, at 811. "But these justifications are absent where a search is remote in time or place from the arrest," quoting *Preston* at 367. In *Edwards,* the government did not contend that the defendant possessed a weapon, was planning to destroy the paint chips, or was even aware of the existence of the evidence on his clothing, at 811, n.3. However, it should be noted that at least one writer has observed that *Preston* was overruled (sub silentio) by *Cardwell* v. *Lewis,* infra. See Hartman, M., *Foreword — The Burger Court — 1973 Term: Leaving the Sixties Behind Us,* 65, J. Crim. L. & C. 439 (1975). For an analysis of Justice Stewart's views on Fourth Amendment probable cause, see Lewis, P., *Justice Stewart and Fourth Amendment Probable Cause: 'Swing Voter' or Participant in a 'New Majority'?* 22 Loyola L. Rev. 713 (1976).

2. Perhaps the most noteworthy feature of the majority's opinion in *Edwards* concerns the apparent change in temporal scope of a search following an arrest. Prior to *Edwards,* the Court had often stated the familiar rule that a search of a person following custodial arrest must be, as to time, "substantially contemporaneous with the arrest." See *Carroll* v. *United States,* 267 U.S. 132, 158 (1925); *Weeks* v. *United States,* 232 U.S. 383, 392 (1914); *Agnello* v. *United States,* 269 U.S. 20 (1925); *Stoner* v. *California,* 376 U.S. 483, 486 (1964); *Preston* v. *United States,* 376 U.S. 364, 367–368 (1964). *Edwards* appears to have somewhat relaxed the earlier "substantially contemporaneous" standard, and now warrantless searches following a custodial arrest may not be unreasonable "even though a substantial period of time has elapsed between the arrest and the administrative processing." In view of the majority's language in *Edwards,* it seems unlikely that the Court meant to confine searches of an arrestee to a 10-hour period. It is unclear whether a search warrant would have been required had the police seized Edwards' clothing 24 hours or later following his arrest. *Edwards* represents a subtle, arguably significant, modification in the application of Fourth Amendment standards following a custodial arrest and indicates a willingness on the part of the Burger Court to allow the practical problems of law enforcement to take precedence over strict Fourth Amendment standards — as long as the intrusion is "minor" in scope.

Applying the Exception to Traffic Arrests

UNITED STATES v. ROBINSON

Supreme Court of the United States, 1973
414 U.S. 218, 94 S. Ct. 467, 38 L. Ed. 2d 427

Respondent Robinson was convicted in the United States District Court for the District of Columbia of the possession and facilitation of concealment of heroin in violation of federal law. Robinson appealed to the Court of Appeals (D.C. Cir.) and his conviction was reversed. The court of appeals found that the contraband used to convict Robinson had been obtained as the result of an unlawful search. The Supreme Court granted the United States government certiorari. Additional facts are stated in the opinion.

Mr. Justice REHNQUIST delivered the opinion of the Court.

* * *

On April 23, 1968, at approximately 11 P.M., Officer Richard Jenks, a 15-year veteran of the District of Columbia Metropolitan Police Department, observed the respondent driving a 1965 Cadillac near the intersection of 8th and C Streets, N.E., in the District of Columbia. Jenks, as a result of previous investigation following a check of respondent's operator's permit four days earlier, determined there was reason to believe that respondent was operating a motor vehicle after the revocation of his operator's permit. This is an offense defined by statute in the District of Columbia which carries a mandatory minimum jail term, a mandatory minimum fine, or both. . . .

Jenks signaled respondent to stop the automobile, which respondent did, and all three of the occupants emerged from the car. At that point Jenks informed respondent that he was under arrest for "operating after revocation and obtaining a permit by misrepresentation." It was assumed by the Court of Appeals, and is conceded by the respondent here, that Jenks had probable cause to arrest respondent, and that he effected a full-custody arrest.

In accordance with procedures prescribed in police department instructions, Jenks then began to search respondent. He explained at a subsequent hearing that he was "face-to-face" with the respondent, and "placed [his] hands on [the respondent], my right hand to his left breast like this [demonstrating] and proceeded to pat him down thus [with the right hand]." During this patdown, Jenks felt an object in the left breast pocket of the heavy coat respondent was wearing, but testified that he "couldn't tell what it was" and also that he "couldn't actually tell the size of it." Jenks then reached into the pocket and pulled out the object, which turned out to be a "crumpled up cigarette package." Jenks testified that at this point he still did not know what was in the package:

"As I felt that package I could feel objects in the package but I couldn't tell what they were ... I knew they weren't cigarettes."

The officer then opened the cigarette pack and found 14 gelatin capsules of white powder which he thought to be, and which later analysis proved to be, heroin. Jenks then continued his search of respondent to completion, feeling around his waist and trouser legs, and examined the remaining pockets. The heroin seized from the respondent was admitted into evidence at the trial, which resulted in his conviction in the District Court.

* * *

It is well settled that a search incident to a lawful arrest is a traditional exception to the warrant requirement of the Fourth Amendment. This general exception has historically been formulated into two distinct propositions. The first is that a search may be made of the *person* of the arrestee by virtue of the lawful arrest. The second is that a search may be made of the area within the control of the arrestee.

Examination of this Court's decisions shows that these two propositions have been treated quite differently. The validity of the search of a person incident to a lawful arrest has been regarded as settled from its first enunciation, and has remained virtually unchallenged until the present case. The validity of the second proposition, while likewise conceded in principle, has been subject to differing interpretations as to the extent of the area which may be searched.

* * *

Throughout the series of cases in which the Court has addressed the second proposition relating to a search incident to a lawful arrest—the permissible area beyond the person of the arrestee which such a search may cover—no doubt has been expressed as to the unqualified authority of the arresting authority to search the person of the arrestee.

* * *

In its decision of this case, the Court of Appeals decided that even after a police officer lawfully places a suspect under arrest for the purpose of taking him into custody, he may not ordinarily proceed to fully search the prisoner. He must, instead, conduct a limited frisk of the outer clothing and remove such weapons that he may, as a result of that limited frisk, reasonably believe and ascertain that the suspect has in his possession. ... Terry v. Ohio, 392 U.S. 88 (1968) [infra], dealt with a permissible "frisk" incident to an investigative stop based on less than probable cause to arrest; the Court of Appeals felt that the principles of that case should be carried over to this probable-cause arrest for driving while one's license is revoked. Since there would be no further evidence of such a crime to be obtained in a search of the arrestee, the court held that only a search for weapons could be justified.

Terry v. Ohio ... did not involve an arrest for probable cause, and it made quite clear that the "protective frisk" for weapons which it approved might be conducted without probable cause. ... This Court's opinion explicitly recognized that there is a "distinction in purpose, character, and extend between a search incident to an arrest and a limited search for weapons."

* * *

". . . [A]n arrest is a wholly different kind of intrusion upon individual freedom from a limited search for weapons, and the interests each is designed to serve are likewise quite different. An arrest is the initial stage of a criminal prosecution. It is intended to vindicate society's interest in having its laws obeyed, and it is inevitably accompanied by future interference with the individual's freedom of movement, whether or not trial or conviction ultimately follows. The protective search for weapons, on the other hand, constitutes a brief, though far from inconsiderable, intrusion upon the sanctity of the person." . . .

Terry, therefore, affords no basis to carry over to a probable-cause arrest the limitations this Court placed on a stop-and-frisk search permissible without probable cause.

* * *

The Court of Appeals in effect determined that the *only* reason supporting the authority for a *full* search incident to lawful arrest was the possibility of discovery of evidence or fruits. Concluding that there could be no evidence or fruits in the case of an offense such as that with which respondent was charged, it held that any protective search would have to be limited by the conditions laid down in Terry for a search upon less than probable cause to arrest. Quite apart from the fact that Terry clearly recognized the distinction between the two types of searches, and that a different rule governed one than governed the other, we find additional reason to disagree with the Court of Appeals.

The justification or reason for the authority to search incident to a lawful arrest rests quite as much on the need to disarm the suspect in order to take him into custody as it does on the need to preserve evidence on his person for later use at trial. . . . The standards traditionally governing a search incident to lawful arrest are not, therefore, commuted to the stricter Terry standards by the absence of probable fruits or further evidence of the particular crime for which the arrest is made.

Nor are we inclined, on the basis of what seems to us to be a rather speculative judgment, to qualify the breadth of the general authority to search incident to a lawful custodial arrest on an assumption that persons arrested for the offense of driving while their licenses have been revoked are less likely to possess dangerous weapons than are those arrested for other crimes. It is scarcely open to doubt that the danger to an officer is far greater in the case of the extended exposure which follows the taking of a suspect into custody and transporting him to the police station than in the case of the relatively fleeting contact resulting from the typical Terry-type stop. This is an adequate basis for treating all custodial arrests alike for purposes of search justification.

But quite apart from these distinctions, our more fundamental disagreement with the Court of Appeals arises from its suggestion that there must be litigated in each case the issue of whether or not there was present one of the reasons supporting the authority for a search of the person incident to a lawful arrest. We do not think the long line of authorities of this Court dating back to Weeks, or what we can glean from the history of practice in this country and in England, requires such a case-by-case adjudication. A police officer's determination as to how and where to search the person of a suspect whom he has arrested is necessarily a quick ad hoc judgment which the Fourth Amendment does not require to be broken down in each instance into an analysis of each step in the search. The authority to search the person incident to a lawful custodial arrest, while based upon the need to disarm and to discover evidence, does not depend on what a court may later decide was the probability in a particular arrest situation that weapons or evidence would in fact be found upon the person of the suspect. A custodial arrest of a suspect based on probable cause is a reasonable intrusion under the Fourth Amendment; that intrusion being lawful, a search incident to the arrest requires no additional justification. It is the fact of the lawful arrest which establishes the authority to search, and we hold that in the case of a lawful custodial arrest a full search of the person is not only an exception to the warrant requirement of the Fourth Amendment, but is also a "reasonable" search under that Amendment.

The search of respondent's person conducted by Officer Jenks in this case and the seizure from him of the heroin were permissible under established Fourth Amendment law. . . . Since it is the fact of custodial arrest which gives rise to the authority to search, it is of no moment that Jenks did not indicate any subjective fear of the respondent or that he did not himself suspect that respondent was armed. Having in the course of a lawful search come upon the crumpled package of cigarettes, he was entitled to inspect it; and when his inspection revealed the heroin capsules, he was entitled to seize them as "fruits, instrumentalities, or contraband" probative of criminal conduct. . . .

Reversed.

[Mr. Justice POWELL wrote a concurring opinion.]

Mr. Justice MARSHALL, with whom Mr. Justice DOUGLAS and Mr. Justice BRENNAN join, dissenting.

Certain fundamental principles have characterized this Court's Fourth Amendment jurisprudence over the years. Perhaps the most basic of these was expressed by Mr. Justice Butler, speaking for a unanimous Court in Go-Bart Import Company v. United States (1931). "There is no formula for the determination of reasonableness. Each case is to be decided on its own facts and circumstances." . . .

In the present case, however, the majority turns its back on these principles, holding that "the fact of the lawful arrest" always establishes the authority to conduct a full search of the arrestee's person, regardless of whether in a particular case "there was present one of the reasons supporting the authority for a search of the person incident to a lawful arrest." . . . The majority's approach represents a clear and marked departure from our long tradition of case-by-case adjudication of the reasonableness of searches and seizures under the Fourth Amendment.

* * *

. . . [T]he majority, rather than focusing on the facts of this case, places great emphasis on the police department order which instructed Officer Jenks to conduct a full search and to examine carefully everything he found whenever making an in-custody arrest. . . . But this mode of analysis was explicitly rejected in Sibron v. New York, 392 U.S. 40 (1968), . . . "Our constitutional inquiry," we concluded, "would not be furth-

ered here by an attempt to pronounce judgment on the words of the statute. We must confine our review instead to the reasonableness of the searches and seizures which underlie these two convictions." . . .

The majority also suggests that the Court of Appeals reached a novel and unprecedented result by imposing qualifications on the historically recognized authority to conduct a full search incident to a lawful arrest. Nothing could be further from the truth, as the Court of Appeals itself was so careful to point out.

The fact is that this question has been considered by several state and federal courts, the vast majority of which have held that, absent special circumstances, a police officer has no right to conduct a full search of the person incident to a lawful arrest for violation of a motor vehicle regulation.

* * *

The majority's attempt to avoid case-by-case adjudication of Fourth Amendment issues is not only misguided as a matter of principle, but is also doomed to fail as a matter of practical application. As the majority itself is well aware . . . the powers granted the police in this case are strong ones, subject to potential abuse. Although, in this particular case, Officer Jenks was required by police department regulations to make an in-custody arrest rather than to issue a citation, in most jurisdictions and for most traffic offenses the determination of whether to issue a citation or effect a full arrest is discretionary with the officer. There is always the possibility that a police officer, lacking probable cause to obtain a search warrant, will use a traffic arrest as a pretext to conduct a search. . . . I suggest this possibility not to impugn the integrity of our police, but merely to point out that case-by-case adjudication will always be necessary to determine whether a full arrest was effected for purely legitimate reasons, or, rather, as a pretext for searching the arrestee.

* * *

The majority states that "[a] police officer's determination as to how and where to search the person of a suspect whom he has arrested is necessarily a quick ad hoc judgment which the Fourth Amendment does not require to be broken down in each instance into an analysis of each step in the search.'' . . .

This Court has held in the past that a search which is reasonable at its inception may violate the Fourth Amendment by virtue of its intolerable intensity and scope.'' As we there concluded, "in determining whether the seizure and search were 'unreasonable' our inquiry is a dual one — whether the officer's action was justified at its inception, and whether it was reasonably related in scope to the circumstances which justified the interference in the first place.'' . . .

As I view the matter, the search in this case divides into three distinct phases: the patdown of respondent's coat pocket; the removal of the unknown object from the pocket; and the opening of the crumpled-up cigarette package.

No question is raised here concerning the lawfulness of the patdown of respondent's coat pocket. The Court of Appeals unanimously affirmed the right of a police officer to conduct a limited frisk for weapons when making an in-custody arrest, regardless of the nature of the crime for which the arrest was made.

* * *

With respect to the removal of the unknown object from the coat pocket, the first issue presented is whether that aspect of the search can be sustained as part of the limited frisk for weapons. The weapons search approved by the Court of Appeals was modeled upon the narrowly drawn protective search for weapons authorized in Terry, which consists "of a limited patting of the outer clothing of the suspect for concealed objects which might be used as instruments of assault.'' . . .

It appears to have been conceded by the Government below that the removal of the object from respondent's coat pocket exceeded the scope of a Terry frisk for weapons, since, under Terry, an officer may not remove an object from the suspect's pockets unless he has reason to believe it to be a dangerous weapon. . . .

In the present case, however, Officer Jenks had no reason to believe and did not in fact believe that the object in respondent's coat pocket was a weapon. . . . Since the removal of the object from the pocket cannot be justified as part of a limited Terry weapons frisk, the question arises whether it is reasonable for a police officer, when effecting an in-custody arrest of a traffic offender, to make a fuller search of the person than is permitted pursuant to Terry.

. . . A search incident to arrest, as the majority indicates, has two basic functions: the removal of weapons the arrestee might use to resist arrest or effect an escape, and the seizure of evidence or fruits of the crime for which the arrest is made, so as to prevent their concealment or destruction. . . .

The Government does not now contend that the search of respondent's pocket can be justified by any need to find and seize evidence in order to prevent its concealment or destruction, for, as the Court of Appeals found, there is no evidence or fruits of the offense with which respondent was charged. The only rationale for a search in this case, then, is the removal of weapons which the arrestee might use to harm the officer and attempt an escape. This rationale, of course, is identical to the rationale of the search permitted in Terry. . . . Since the underlying rationale of a Terry search and the search of a traffic violator are identical, the Court of Appeals held that the scope of the searches must be the same.

* * *

The problem with this approach, however, is that it ignores several significant differences between the context in which a search incident to arrest for a traffic violation is made, and the situation presented in Terry. Some of these differences would appear to suggest permitting a more thorough search in this case than was permitted in Terry; other differences suggest a narrower, more limited right to search than was there recognized.

The most obvious difference between the two contexts relates to whether the officer has cause to believe that the individual he is dealing with possesses weapons which might be used against him. . . . While the policeman who arrests a suspected rapist or robber may well have reason to believe he is dealing with an armed and dangerous person, certainly this does not hold true with equal force with respect to a person arrested for a motor vehicle violation of the sort involved in this case.

Nor was there any particular reason in this case to believe that respondent was dangerous. He had not attempted to evade arrest, but had quickly complied with the police both in bringing his car to a stop after being signaled to do so and in producing the documents Officer Jenks requested. In fact, Jenks admitted that he searched respondent face to face rather than in spread-eagle fashion because he had no reason to believe respondent would be violent.

While this difference between the situation presented in Terry and the context presented in this case would tend to suggest a lesser authority to search here than was permitted in Terry, other distinctions between the two cases suggest just the opposite. As the Court of Appeals noted, a crucial feature distinguishing the in-custody arrest from the Terry context " 'is not the greater likelihood that a person taken into custody is armed, but rather the increased likelihood of danger to the officer *if* in fact the person is armed.' " ... A Terry stop involves a momentary encounter between officer and suspect, while an in-custody arrest places the two in close proximity for a much longer period of time. If the individual happens to have a weapon on his person, he will certainly have much more opportunity to use it against the officer in the in-custody situation. The prolonged proximity also makes it more likely that the individual will be able to extricate any small hidden weapon which might go undetected in a weapons frisk, such as a safety pin or razor blade. In addition, a suspect taken into custody may feel more threatened by the serious restraint on his liberty than a person who is simply stopped by an officer for questioning and may therefore be more likely to resort to force.

Thus, in some senses there is less need for a weapons search in the in-custody traffic arrest situation than in a Terry context; while in other ways, there is a greater need.

The majority opinion fails to recognize that the search conducted by Officer Jenks did not merely involve a search of respondent's person. It also included a separate search of effects found on his person. And even were we to assume, arguendo, that it was reasonable for Jenks to remove the object he felt in respondent's pocket, clearly there was no justification consistent with the Fourth Amendment which would authorize his opening the package and looking inside.

To begin with, after Jenks had the cigarette package in his hands, there is no indication that he had reason to believe or did in fact believe that the package contained a weapon. More importantly, even if the crumpled-up cigarette package had in fact contained some sort of small weapon, it would have been impossible for respondent to have used it once the package was in the officer's hands. Opening the package, therefore, did not further the protective purpose of the search.

* * *

... Chimel established the principle that the lawful right of the police to interfere with the security of the person did not, standing alone, automatically confer the right to interfere with the security and privacy of his house. Hence, the mere fact of an arrest should be no justification, in and of itself, for invading the privacy of the individual's personal effects.

The Government argues that it is difficult to see what constitutionally protected "expectation of privacy" a prisoner has in the interior of a cigarette pack. One wonders if the result in this case would have been the same were respondent a businessman who was lawfully taken into custody for driving without a license and whose wallet was taken from him by the police. Would it be reasonable for the police officer, because of the possibility that a razor blade was hidden somewhere in the wallet, to open it, remove all the contents, and examine each item carefully? Or suppose a lawyer lawfully arrested for a traffic offense is found to have a sealed envelope on his person. Would it be permissible for the arresting officer to tear open the envelope in order to make sure that it did not contain a clandestine weapon—perhaps a pin or a razor blade? ... Would it not be more consonant with the purpose of the Fourth Amendment and the legitimate needs of the police to require the officer, if he has any question whatsoever about what the wallet or letter contains, to hold on to it until the arrestee is brought to the precinct station?

I, for one, cannot characterize any of these intrusions into the privacy of an individual's papers and effects as being negligible incidents to the more serious intrusion into the individual's privacy stemming from the arrest itself. Nor can any principled distinction be drawn between the hypothetical searches I have posed and the search of the cigarette package in this case. The only reasoned distinction is between warrantless searches which serve legitimate protective and evidentiary functions and those that do not.

The search conducted by Officer Jenks in this case went far beyond what was reason-ably necessary to protect him from harm or to ensure that respondent would not effect an escape from custody. In my view, it therefore fell outside the scope of a properly drawn "search incident to arrest" exception to the Fourth Amendment's warrant requirement.

* * *

Luggage, Baggage, and the Fourth Amendment Right of Privacy

ORAL ARGUMENTS BEFORE THE U.S. SUPREME COURT*

U.S. v. Chadwick, No. 75-1721; argued 4/26/77

The federal government asked the Court last week to lay down a broad rule concerning the Fourth Amendment law governing the search of a container that has been lawfully seized in a public place. There should be no presumptive requirement of a warrant in such a situation, the government argued. Instead, such a search should be upheld if it is based on probable cause and is otherwise reasonable. Defense counsel on the other hand, saw this as an attempt to "amend the Fourth Amendment" and argued that the government's position has no basis in history or the Court's decisions.

A. Raymond Randolph, Jr., of the Solicitor General's Office, set forth the case's factual background in some detail. (See also the opinions of the courts below, 532 F.2d 773 and 393 F. Supp. 763.) Federal agents in Boston received information from other agents in California that a footlocker, suspected of containing marijuana, was being shipped to Boston by Amtrak train. The original tip came from an Amtrak official, who noted that the footlocker was leaking talcum powder and was unusually heavy for its size. Moreover, the shipper of the footlocker, defendant Machado, fit a "profile" for drug traffickers used by Amtrak.

Six agents met the train in Boston and observed the footlocker's being taken from the train to the station. It was claimed by Machado and a female companion, Leary. They proceeded to sit on the footlocker. The agents never saw the footlocker opened but a trained dog sniffed it and gave an "alert response"—he scratched it.

Chadwick entered the station and talked to Machado and Leary. The three had a porter put the footlocker into the trunk of Chadwick's car. When the porter left the three were arrested, and Machado and Chadwick were frisked. The footlocker was opened at the agents' office, and 200 pounds of marijuana was seized. The U.S. Court of Appeals for the First Circuit ruled that, while the seizure of the footlocker was proper, the agents should not have opened it without a warrant.

The situation faced by the agents is a common one in law enforcement, Randolph said, and there is need for a coherent legal analysis. The courts of appeals have generally approved warrantless searches of this type, he claimed, but their reasons have varied widely.

The Chief Justice wanted to know how much time elapsed from the seizure to the search. Randolph indicated that 20–30 minutes went by.

*From 21 Crim. L. Rptr. 4040–4042 (1976). Reprinted by permission of the Bureau of National Affairs, Inc.

When Randolph asserted that the seizure of the trunk was unquestionably legal, Mr. Justice Stewart asked whether that point was contested.

Yes, Randolph said, Chadwick and Machado sought to suppress the footlocker itself as well as its contents. But the First Circuit ruled against them, and they took no cross-petition to this Court. So the legality of the seizure is a given here.

Automobile Analogy

We say that the reasons underlying the automobile exception to the warrant requirement are just as applicable here, counsel continued. The footlocker was movable—indeed it had just traversed the entire continent and was still moving. "There was no reason for the agents to treat it like a child treats a package on Christmas Eve—shake it but put it down unopened."

Randolph stressed that while the seizure of the footlocker is not an issue, "it is important that the seizure occurred." The footlocker's use in the scheme rendered it subject to forfeiture, and it was evidence in its own right. The government could have kept it for an extended period.

Mr. Justice Stewart: "For a long, long time—long enough to get a warrant."

Randolph: "That's not the test."

The Chief Justice was curious about how the footlocker was opened. There is some indication that the agents picked the lock, he said. Counsel said he wasn't sure.

Randolph referred to *Preston* v. *U.S.,* 376 U.S. 364, 366, where Mr. Justice Black said, "[c]ommon sense dictates ... that questions involving searches of motor cars or other things readily moved cannot be treated as identical to questions arising out of searches of fixed structures like houses." This supports our distinction between searches in houses and other protected zones and those in public places, as well as our analogy between car searches and searches of the type represented here, counsel said.

Mr. Justice Marshall: "How movable was the footlocker once it was in the agents' office?"

Admittedly it was not movable then, Randolph answered. But the cars in *Chambers* v. *Maroney,* 399 U.S. 42 (1970), and *Texas* v. *White,* 423 U.S. 67 (1975), were not movable either. The seizure justifies the search. There is no difference between the footlocker here and the locked car trunk in *Cady* v. *Dombrowski,* 413 U.S. 433 (1973), the front seat console in *Texas* v. *White,* or the glove compartment in *Chambers* v. *Maroney.* On the other hand there is a crucial distinction between the footlocker and a house—the latter implicates the core values of the Fourth Amendment.

Incident-to-Arrest Rationale

Mr. Justice White posed some hypotheticals under the incident-to-arrest rationale. Suppose an arrestee is found to have a small locked box in his possession, or a sealed envelope—could it be opened without a warrant?

Randolph thought the box, at least, could be opened. He cited *U.S.* v. *Robinson,* 414 U.S. 218 (1973), and *Gustafson* v. *Florida,* 414 U.S. 206 (1973), in which the opening of cigarette packages found on arrestees was upheld.

What about a locked briefcase? Mr. Justice White asked.

Draper v. *U.S.,* 358 U.S. 307 (1959), indicates that it could be opened, Randolph said.

Mr. Justice White: "If that approach is sound, then you don't have to go any farther than the search-incident theory."

But the defendants reject that rationale on the ground that the footlocker wasn't within their immediate reach or control, Randolph answered.

Counsel cited the familiar language in *Katz* v. *U.S.,* 389 U.S. 347 (1967), about "reasonable expectation of privacy" and asked, "Could anyone reasonably expect privacy here? Could anyone expect that the footlocker would remain inviolate?"

Mr. Justice Rehnquist: "If we agree, then the next person who ships a footlocker will not have an expectation of privacy, and you can search it. But then your position becomes a self-fulfilling prophecy. The reasonable expectation of privacy must mean more than that."

The government has used the *Katz* rationale in this fashion before, Randolph said.

Mr. Justice Rehnquist: "But not in such a tautological way."

Randolph replied that the expectation of privacy in the footlocker is no greater than that in a glove compartment or car trunk.

In response to Mr. Justice Stewart, counsel conceded that the case fell into none of the established exceptions to the warrant requirement.

But Mr. Justice Rehnquist adverted to counsel's analogy to car search cases and remarked, "This Court hasn't upset a car search in the last five years where there was probable cause."

Automobile Analogy Disputed

Martin G. Weinberg, of Boston, Massachusetts, presented the argument for the defendants. Contrary to what the government has said, he maintained, there is already a coherent standard for searches of this kind—the standard of *Katz*. He also noted that, while the government is now urging the formulation of a new rule, its unsuccessful approach in the courts below was to force the case into the mold of previously existing exceptions.

Disputing the government's analogy between cars and the footlocker, Weinberg said that a container of this kind is often the depository of a person's private effects. Moreover, a footlocker does not have the kind of non-investigative contacts with police to which cars are commonly subjected. The Court relied on these special attributes of cars in *Cady* v. *Dombrowski* and *South Dakota* v. *Opperman,* 428 U.S. 346 (1976), he stressed.

Counsel also said that mobility is a justification for a stop but not for a search. It is the lesser expectation of privacy in a car that justifies its search.

Mr. Justice Rehnquist referred again to the seeming quandary raised by the application of *Katz*. If we rule against you, he said, then the expectation of privacy in a shipped footlocker will be reduced—but again this is a self-fulfilling prophecy.

The real question, Weinberg replied, is whether constitutional standards justify the search.

Mr. Justice Rehnquist: "But some of the same arguments you are making were advanced in *Cady* and *Opperman,* and we rejected them."

I would have made them myself had I argued those cases, Weinberg replied. But there are reasons, not present here, that justified the Court's decisions in *Cady* and *Opperman*. What the Court should do now is to establish that there is a reasonable expectation of privacy in a situation such as this.

Mr. Justice Stewart: "If the Fourth Amendment were repealed, then nobody would have any expectation of privacy anywhere."

That's right, counsel replied. Up to now, he added, the warrant requirement has not been limited to searches of homes and offices.

Searches and Arrests

Mr. Justice White repeated the questions he had put to the government. What is the established rule on searches of closed containers found in arrestees' possession? he asked.

The relevant line of cases begins with *Chimel* v. *California,* 395 U.S. 752 (1969), Weinberg replied. The courts have frozen the situation as of the time of the arrest and asked whether the arrestee could retrieve evidence or a weapon from the container. There is no coherent rule, however; nor is there one for a sealed container in a locked automobile trunk.

Mr. Justice White: "If the police can open a locked container found on an arrestee, would that rule govern here?"

No, Weinberg replied; the question of accessibility must also be considered. Nor would a rule permitting the opening of containers found in cars govern, because the expectation of privacy in a car is reduced.

Counsel distinguished the situation in *Draper* in two ways. The footlocker here was double-locked, not just zipped. Also, it was too heavy to be moved by one person, whereas the bag in *Draper* was in the arrestee's hand.

The Chief Justice expressed doubt that size has anything to do with the matter.

Counsel stressed that the police had no reason to fear that the defendants would destroy evidence or go into the footlocker for a weapon. This brought a response from Mr. Justice Rehnquist; *U.S.* v. *Robinson,* he said, held that there is no need in each case to show the reasons for a search incident to arrest.

But *Robinson* did not expand the area that *Chimel* said could be searched, Weinberg replied. If *Chimel* is to be expanded, we must go back to the reasons for allowing such searches. The government's position would practically take us back to the pre-*Chimel* regime of *U.S.* v. *Rabinowitz,* 339 U.S. 56 (1950).

Neither history nor the current needs of our mobile society support the government's distinction between homes and public places, Weinberg continued.

Mr. Justice Rehnquist thought the distinction had some basis in fact, and he cited *Coolidge* v. *New Hampshire.*

Coolidge and other cases do distinguish between seizures and searches, Weinberg said. The home is important to the extent that a warrantless seizure is involved. *Coolidge,* for instance, invalidated the seizure of a car parked on the defendant's driveway.

Mr. Justice Marshall: "Your problem is the dog. Once the dog scratched the footlocker your clients should have said, 'I wonder whose trunk this is.'"

Nonetheless, counsel insisted, "it is of the highest constitutional significance" that the police did not leave the footlocker in the station and get a warrant.

Counsel also agreed with an observation of Mr. Justice Stevens, that the *Draper* opinion contained no holding as to the search of the bag.

In response to questioning from Mr. Justice Powell, counsel said the fact that a warrant could have been obtained cannot save the case against the defendants. The same fact was present in *Katz* and many other cases in which the exclusionary rule has been applied.

Weighing Intrusions

The Chief Justice: "If innocent substances were found in the footlocker, your clients could have gone on their way with apologies and perhaps a potential lawsuit. Isn't it a greater intrusion to delay them until a warrant is obtained?"

That's what the consent exception is for, Weinberg replied.

The Chief Justice: I suppose you say that the contents of the footlocker make no difference—whether it's marijuana, heroin, or a small atomic bomb.

Nor diaries, papers, or other private possessions, counsel agreed.

Mr. Justice White asked what the basis was for the decision in *Cooper* v. *California,* 386 U.S. 56 (1967), in which the Court upheld a belated warrantless search of a narcotics suspect's car that had been seized pursuant to a state forfeiture statute at the time of the defendant's arrest.

Weinberg answered that the police caretaking function plus the reduced expectation of privacy in a car justified the search. The forfeiture statute went only to the seizure, he emphasized.

Mr. Justice White: "Then why did the Court say that, once seized, the car could be searched?"

Because of the reduced expectation of privacy, Weinberg answered. The privacy interest in a footlocker is much greater than that in a car.

Mr. Justice Rehnquist asked if the privacy expectation would be changed were the ICC to permit carriers to open shipped footlockers for inspection.

There would be no change in one's expectation as to whether the government intended to open the container to find evidence of a crime, Weinberg replied.

On rebuttal, Randolph said that the courts of appeals, with the exception of the First Circuit, are unanimous that a closed container in an arrestee's possession may be opened. It is true, however, that no court has specifically embraced a "luggage exception" to the warrant requirement.

He also said the defendants' contrary rule has a "delusive exactness" about it and is unworkable. Many distinctions would have to be made—such as how much the container weighed, and whether the car in which it was placed was pulling away. This breeds litigation and leaves the police unsure of the bounds of permissible conduct. Most important, such distinctions reduce the seriousness of the warrant requirement.

UNITED STATES v. CHADWICK

Supreme Court of the United States, 1977
433 U.S. 1, 96 S. Ct. 2476, 52 L. Ed. 2d 538

Amtrak railroad officials in San Diego observed respondents Gregory Machado and Bridget Leary load a brown, double-locked footlocker onto a train bound for Boston. They were suspicious of the trunk because of its unusual heaviness and because it was leaking talcum powder, a substance often used to mask the odor of marijuana or hashish. In addition, Machado matched a profile used to spot drug traffickers. Federal narcotics agents met the train when it arrived in Boston two days later. Respondent Chadwick joined Machado and Leary, and the footlocker and their luggage were moved outside to Chadwick's waiting automobile. The 200-pound footlocker was put into the trunk of the car. While the trunk was still open and before the car engine had been started, all three respondents were arrested. A search of respondents disclosed no weapons, but the keys to the footlocker were taken from Machado. Respondents, together with the automobile and footlocker, which admittedly were under the agents' exclusive control, were taken to the federal building in Boston. About an hour and a half later, the agents opened the footlocker and luggage without a search warrant, and large amounts of marijuana were found in the footlocker. Respondents were subsequently indicted for possession of marijuana with intent to distribute, 21 U.S.C. § 841(a)(1), and for conspiracy, in violation of 21 U.S.C. § 846. The district court granted their pretrial motion to suppress the marijuana, holding that warrantless searches are per se unreasonable under the Fourth Amendment unless they fall within some established exception to the warrant requirement. The Court of Appeals (1st Cir.) agreed with the district court that the footlocker search was not justified under the "automobile exception" or as a search incident to a lawful arrest. The United States Supreme Court granted certiorari.

Mr. Chief Justice BURGER delivered the opinion of the Court.

We granted certiorari in this case to decide whether a search warrant is required before federal agents may open a locked footlocker which they have lawfully seized at the time of the arrest of its owners, when there is probable cause to believe the footlocker contains contraband.

* * *

II

[T]he Government ... contends that the Fourth Amendment Warrant Clause protects only interests traditionally identified with the home. Recalling the colonial writs of assistance, which were often executed in searches of private dwellings, the Government claims that the Warrant Clause was adopted primarily, if not exclusively, in response to unjustified intrusions into private homes on the authority of general warrants.

The Government argues there is no evidence that the Framers of the Fourth Amendment intended to disturb the established practice of permitting warrantless searches outside the home, or to modify the initial clause of the Fourth Amendment by making warrantless searches supported by probable cause per se unreasonable.

* * *

We do not agree that the Warrant Clause protects only dwellings and other specifically designated locales. As we have noted before, the Fourth Amendment "protects people, not places." Katz v. United States, 389 U.S. 347, 351 (1967); more particularly, it protects people from unreasonable government intrusions into their legitimate expectations of privacy. In this case, the Warrant Clause makes a significant contribution to that protection. The question, then, is whether a warrantless search in these circumstances was unreasonable.

III

* * *

[I]t would be a mistake to conclude, as the Government contends, that the Warrant Clause was therefore intended to guard only against intrusions into the home. First, the Warrant Clause does not in terms distinguish between searches conducted in private homes and other searches. There is also a strong historical connection between the Warrant Clause and the initial clause of the Fourth Amendment, which draws no distinctions among "persons, houses, papers, and effects" in safeguarding against unreasonable searches and seizures. See United States v. Rabinowitz, 339 U.S. 56, 68 (1950) (Frankfurter, J., dissenting).

Moreover, if there is little evidence that the Framers intended the Warrant Clause to operate outside the home, there is no evidence at all that they intended to exclude from protection of the Clause all searches occurring outside the home. . . .

. . . Our fundamental inquiry in considering Fourth Amendment issues is whether or not a search or seizure is reasonable under all the circumstances. Cooper v. California, 386 U.S. 58 (1967). The judicial warrant has a significant role to play in that it provides the detached scrutiny of a neutral magistrate, which is a more reliable safeguard against improper searches than the hurried judgment of a law enforcement officer "engaged in the often competitive enterprise of ferreting out crime." Johnson v. United States, 333 U.S. 10, 14 (1948). Once a lawful search has begun, it is also far more likely that it will not exceed proper bounds when it is done pursuant to a judicial authorization "particularly describing the place to be searched and the persons or things to be seized." Further, a warrant assures the individual whose property is searched or seized of the lawful authority of the executing officer, his need to search and the limits of his power to search. Camara v. Municipal Court, 387 U.S. 523, 532 (1967).

Just as the Fourth Amendment "protects people, not places," the protections a judicial warrant offers against erroneous governmental intrusions are effective whether applied in or out of the home. Accordingly, we have held warrantless searches unreasonable, and therefore unconstitutional, in a variety of settings. . . .

. . . Judicial warrants have been required for other searches conducted outside the home. E.g., Katz v. United States, 389 U.S. 347 (1963) (electronic interception of conversation in public telephone booth); Coolidge v. New Hampshire, 403 U.S. 443 (1971) (automobile on private premises); Preston v. United States, 376 U.S. 364 (1964) (automobile in custody); United States v. Jeffers, 342 U.S. 48 (1951) (hotel room); G. M. Leasing Corp. v. United States, [97 S. Ct. 619] (1977) (office); Mancusi v. DeForte, 392 U.S. 364 (1968) (office). These cases illustrate the applicability of the Warrant Clause beyond the narrow limits suggested by the Government. They also reflect the settled constitutional principle . . . that a fundamental purpose of the Fourth Amendment is to safeguard individuals from unreasonable government invasions of legitimate privacy interests, and not simply those interests found inside the four walls of the home. Wolf v. Colorado, 338 U.S. 25, 27 (1949).

In this case, important Fourth Amendment privacy interests were at stake. By placing personal effects inside a double-locked footlocker, respondents manifested an expectation that the contents would remain free from public examination. No less than one who locks the doors of his home against intruders, one who safeguards his personal possessions in this manner is due the protection of the Fourth Amendment Warrant Clause. There being no exigency, it was unreasonable for the Government to conduct this search without the safeguards a judicial warrant provides.

IV

. . . [T]he Government views . . . luggage as analogous to motor vehicles for Fourth Amendment purposes. It is true that, like the footlocker in issue here, automobiles are "effects" under the Fourth Amendment, and searches and seizures of automobiles are therefore subject to the constitutional standard of reasonableness. But this Court has recognized significant differences between motor vehicles and other property which permit warrantless searches of automobiles in circumstances in which warrantless searches would not be reasonable in other contexts. Carroll v. United States, 267 U.S. 132 (1925); Preston v. United States, 376 U.S., at 366–367 (1964);

Chambers v. Maroney, 399 U.S. 42 (1970). See also South Dakota v. Opperman, 428 U.S., at 367.

Our treatment of automobiles has been based in part on their inherent mobility, which often makes obtaining a judicial warrant impracticable. Nevertheless, we have also sustained "warrantless searches of vehicles ... in cases in which the possibilities of the vehicle's being removed or evidence in it destroyed were remote, if not non-existent." Cady v. Dombrowski, 413 U.S. 433, 441–442 (1973); accord, South Dakota v. Opperman, supra, at 367; see Texas v. White, 423 U.S. 67 (1975); Chambers v. Maroney, supra; Cooper v. California, 386 U.S. 58 (1967).

The answer lies in the diminished expectation of privacy which surrounds the automobile:

"One has a lesser expectation of privacy in a motor vehicle because its function is transportation and it seldom serves as one's residence or as the repository of personal effects.... It travels public thoroughfares where both its occupants and its contents are in plain view." Cardwell v. Lewis, 417 U.S. 583, 590 (1974) (plurality opinion).

Other factors reduce automobile privacy. "All States require vehicles to be registered and operators to be licensed. States and localities have enacted extensive and detailed codes regulating the condition and manner in which motor vehicles may be operated on public streets and highways." Cady v. Dombrowski, 413 U.S., at 441. Automobiles periodically undergo official inspection, and they are often taken into police custody in the interests of public safety. South Dakota v. Opperman, 428 U.S., at 368.

The factors which diminish the privacy aspects of an automobile do not apply to respondents' footlocker. Luggage contents are not open to public view, except as a condition to a border entry or common carrier travel; nor is luggage subject to regular inspections and official scrutiny on a continuing basis. Unlike an automobile whose primary function is transportation, luggage is intended as a repository of personal effects. In sum, a person's expectations of privacy in personal luggage are substantially greater than in an automobile.

Nor does the footlocker's mobility justify dispensing with the added protections of the Warrant Clause. Once the federal agents had seized it at the railroad station and had safely transferred it to the Boston federal building under their exclusive control, there was not the slightest danger that the footlocker or its contents could have been removed before a valid search warrant could be obtained. The initial seizure and detention of the footlocker, the validity of which respondents do not contest, were sufficient to guard against any risk that evidence might be lost. With the footlocker safely immobilized, it was unreasonable to undertake the additional and greater intrusion of a search without a warrant.

Finally, the Government urges that the Constitution permits the warrantless search of any property in the possession of a person arrested in public, so long as there is probable cause to believe that the property contains contraband or evidence of crime. Although recognizing that the footlocker was not within respondents' immediate control, the Government insists that the search was reasonable because the footlocker was seized contemporaneously with respondents' arrests and was searched as soon thereafter as was practicable. The reasons justifying search in a custodial arrest are quite different. When a custodial arrest is made, there is always some danger that the person arrested may seek to use a weapon, or that evidence may be concealed or destroyed. To safeguard himself and others, and to prevent the loss of evidence, it has been held reasonable for the arresting officer to conduct a prompt, warrantless "search of the arrestee's person and the area 'within his immediate control'—construing that phrase to mean the area from within which he might gain possession of a weapon or destructible evidence." Chimel v. California, 395 U.S., at 763. See also Terry v. Ohio, 392 U.S. 1 (1968).

Such searches may be conducted without a warrant, and they may also be made whether or not there is probable cause to believe that the person arrested may have a weapon or is about to destroy evidence. The potential dangers lurking in all custodial arrests make warrantless searches of items within the "immediate control" area reasonable without requiring the arresting officer to calculate the probability that weapons or destructible evidence may be involved.

United States v. Robinson, 414 U.S. 218 (1973); Terry v. Ohio, supra. However, warrantless searches of luggage or other property seized at the time of an arrest cannot be justified as incident to that arrest either if the "search is remote in time or place from the arrest," Preston v. United States, 376 U.S., at 367, or no exigency exists. Once law enforcement officers have reduced luggage or other personal property not immediately associated with the person of the arrestee to their exclusive control, and there is no longer any danger that the arrestee might gain access to the property the search is no longer an incident of the arrest.

Here the search was conducted more than an hour after federal agents had gained exclusive control of the footlocker and long after respondents were securely in custody; the search therefore cannot be viewed as incidental to the arrest or as justified by any other exigency. Even though on this record the issuance of a warrant by a judicial officer was reasonably predictable, a line must be drawn. In our view, when no exigency is shown to support the need for an immediate search, the Warrant Clause places the line at the point where the property to be searched comes under the exclusive dominion of police authority. Respondents were therefore entitled to the protection of the Warrant Clause with the evaluation of a neutral magistrate, before their privacy interests in the contents of the footlocker were invaded.

Affirmed.

[Mr. Justice BRENNAN wrote a concurring opinion.]

Mr. Justice BLACKMUN, with whom Mr. Justice REHNQUIST joins, dissenting.

* * *

One line of recent decisions establishes that no warrant is required for the arresting officer to search the clothing and effects of one placed in custodial arrest. The rationale for this was explained in United States v. Robinson, 414 U.S. 218 (1973). . . .

. . . Under this doctrine, a search of personal effects need not be contemporaneous with the arrest, and indeed may be delayed a number of hours while the suspect remains in lawful custody. United States v. Edwards, 415 U.S. 800 (1974).

A second series of decisions concerns the consequences of custodial arrest of a person driving an automobile. The car may be impounded and, with probable cause, its contents (including locked compartments) subsequently examined without a warrant. Texas v. White, 423 U.S. 67 (1975); Cady v. Dombrowski, 413 U.S. 433, 439–448 (1973); Chambers v. Maroney, 399 U.S. 42, 47–52 (1970). Moreover, once a car has been properly impounded for any reason, the police may follow a standard procedure of inventorying its contents without any showing of probable cause. South Dakota v. Opperman, 428 U.S. 364 (1976).

I would apply the rationale of these two lines of authority and hold generally that a warrant is not required to seize and search any movable property in the possession of a person properly arrested in a public place. A person arrested in a public place is likely to have various kinds of property with him; items inside his clothing, a briefcase or suitcase, packages, or a vehicle. In such instances the police cannot very well leave the property on the sidewalk or street while they go to get a warrant. The items may be stolen by a passer-by or removed by the suspect's confederates. Rather than requiring the police to "post a guard" over such property, I think it is surely reasonable for the police to take the items along to the station with the arrested person.

* * *

. . . The agents probably could have avoided having the footlocker search held unconstitutional either by delaying the arrest for a few minutes or by conducting the search on the spot rather than back at their office. Probable cause for the arrest was present from the time respondents Machado and Leary were seated on the footlocker inside Boston's South Station. . . . Rather than make an arrest at this moment, the agents commendably sought to determine the possible involvement of others in the illegal scheme. They waited a short time until respondent Chadwick arrived and the footlocker had been loaded into the trunk of his car, and then made the arrest. But if the agents had postponed the arrest just a few minutes longer until the respondents started to drive away, then the car could have been seized, taken to the agents' office, and all its contents—including the footlocker—searched without a warrant.

Alternatively, the agents could have made a search of the footlocker at the time and place of the arrests. Machado and Leary were standing next to an open automobile trunk containing the footlocker, and thus it was within the area of their "immediate control." And certainly the footlocker would have been properly subject to search at the time if the arrest had occurred a few minutes earlier while Machado and Leary were seated on it.

... [I] see no way that these alternative courses of conduct, which likely would have been held constitutional under the Fourth Amendment, would have been any more solicitous of the privacy or well-being of the respondents. ... It is decisions of this kind made by the Court today that make criminal law a trap for the unwary policeman and detract from the important activities of detecting criminal activity and protecting the public safety.

Comments

1. In *Robinson,* the Court fundamentally disagreed with the court of appeals on at least three important points: (1) Based on available statistical data concerning assaults on officers who are in the course of making arrests, the Court could not agree that persons arrested for traffic violations are less likely to possess dangerous weapons than those arrested for other offenses. (2) The Court could not agree that the search was invalid because the officer was not likely to find probable fruits or further evidence of the offense for which the arrest was made. And (3) the Court disagreed with the court of appeals' suggestion that each of the above issues must be litigated in each case in order to determine whether the officers had authority to make a search incident to arrest. The Court went on to note: "A custodial arrest of a suspect based on probable cause is a reasonable intrusion under the Fourth Amendment; that intrusion being lawful, a search incident to the arrest requires no additional justification. It is the fact of the lawful arrest which establishes the authority to search. ..." The statement is interesting because, as noted in *Chimel,* the search incident to arrest had previously been considered reasonable as a means for the arresting officer to assure his own safety, to prevent escape, and to prevent the destruction of evidence. "Thus, from a historical standpoint, it has been the connection between the items sought and the nature of the crime that has made such searches reasonable." See, e.g., *Searches of the Person Incident to Lawful Arrest,* 69 Colum. L. Rev. 868 (1969). How can *Robinson* be squared with *Chimel?*

What is the possibility of subterfuge arrests occurring? In the companion case of *Gustafson* v. *Florida,* 414 U.S. 260 (1973), the petitioner was arrested for driving without a driver's license, and a search incident to the lawful arrest uncovered a cigarette box containing marijuana. Although Gustafson argued that (1) the officer had no reason to suspect that he was dangerous, and (2) the officer was under no duty to take petitioner into custody (i.e., there were no police regulations such as those in *Robinson*), the Court nevertheless concluded that the differences were not "determinative of the constitutional issue." The Court, per Rehnquist, J., found the search to be reasonable on the basis of *Robinson.* It is important to note that the court in *Robinson* and *Gustafson* was careful to limit the full-scale search to (1) only the *person* of the arrestee, and (2) only arrests that are *custodial* in character. It is important to note that *Gustafson* is *clearly distinguishable* from *Robinson* with regard to the fact that the officer's actions were *discretionary* rather than required by established police regulations; hence, it is interesting that the Court passed over the factual differences so lightly. As one Fourth Amendment scholar observed: "In the first case [*Robinson*], both the decision of the officer to make a 'full custody arrest' rather than to issue a citation and his decision to conduct a full 'field type search' . . . were apparently dictated by local police regulations. In the second case [*Gustafson*] both decisions were left entirely to the discretion of the officer. If the Court had distinguished the two cases on this ground, it would, in my judgment, have made by far the greatest contribution to the jurisprudence of the Fourth Amendement since James Otis argued against the writs of assistance in 1761. . . ." Amsterdam, A., *Perspectives on the Fourth Amendment,* 58 Minn. L. Rev. 349, 416 (1974). See also Nakell, B., *Search of the Person Incident to a Traffic Arrest: A Comment on Robinson and Gustafson,* 10 Crim. L. Bull. 827 (1974). What if state law governing traffic "arrests" *required* that persons stopped for misdemeanor traffic violations merely be issued a citation or summons to appear? Presumably the officer in such a state could not conduct a *Robinson*-type search absent independent probable cause to take the violator into custody.

2. The Supreme Court noted in *Weeks* v. *United States* that there is "a right on the part of the government. . ., under English and American law, to search the person of the accused when legally arrested," 235 U.S. 383 at 392. However, the Court also observed in 1948: "The mere fact that there is a valid arrest does not ipso facto legalize a search or seizure without a warrant. . . ." *Trupiano* v. *United States,* 334 U.S. 669 at 708 (1948). In *Robinson* the Court held that an officer's authority to make a full-custody search incident to a lawful arrest requires no justification beyond the fact of arrest itself. Why did the Court reverse its stand? What was the Court's intent in including the above language in *Trupiano*?

3. In *Robinson* (and the companion case *Gustafson*) and *Murphy* and *Edwards* (supra)—the only major opinions of the Burger Court during the period 1972 to 1977 that involved searches incident to a custodial arrest—the Supreme Court demonstrated a willingness to narrow the scope of Fourth Amendment protections afforded an accused that had been expanded by the Warren Court. In each case the Burger Court found the warrantless intrusion to be either "routine" or "minor" or both. Although *Robinson, Murphy,* and *Edwards* did not serve to specifically overrule any earlier pronouncements of the Supreme Court, taken together, they may indicate that the Burger Court is about to significantly alter the doctrinal safeguards that for many years were thought to be required by the Fourth Amendment.

    In *Robinson* and *Gustafson* the Court declined to discuss the permissible scope of a search of an automobile incident to an incustody traffic arrest. Many lower courts have applied the *Chimel* standards to car searches justified as incident to an arrest. See 23 Okla. L. Rev. 447 (1970); 87 Harv. L. Rev. 835, n.8 (1974); and *Adams* v. *Williams,* 407 U.S. 143, 149 (1972) (without discussion allowing warrantless search of car). The locked trunk situation is a thorny one, and the Court has so far declined to lay down any Fourth Amendment standards on that issue. See *Cady* v. *Dombrowski,* 413 U.S. 433 (1973), which is one of the few contemporary Supreme Court opinions dealing with a warrantless search of the locked trunk of an automobile. However, the seizure of evidence in *Dombrowski* was not justified on the basis of a search incident to a lawful arrest. In addition, the *Robinson-Gustafson* Court left open the issue whether a *Terry*-type frisk or full-field search of a person briefly detained following a routine traffic investigation (non-custodial) might be reasonable under the Fourth Amendment. Presumably, the Court would decline to lay down any per se rules in such situations and would adopt the "balancing test" of *Terry* v. *Ohio,* 392 U.S. 1 (1968), infra.

4. In *Murphy* the Court seemed more concerned with the reasonableness of the intrusion than whether the officers had probable cause to arrest the defendant. Perhaps the Court was hinting that it is reordering its Fourth Amendment priorities so that the "reasonableness" of the intrusion stands on a higher footing than the probable cause requirement. Although the Fourth Amendment does not, on its face, distinguish in terms of priorities between the reasonableness and probable cause requirements, a relaxation of the latter standard could result in a greater intrusion on Fourth Amendment protections if the Court chooses to continue to balance these safeguards against each other. In *Edwards,* the Court appeared to have abolished or seriously modified the heretofore contemporaneous requirement for a warrantless search following a valid arrest. Apparently the principal reasons which have traditionally justified such a search continue to operate long past the probable cause which gives rise to the initial intrusion. By focusing on the reasonableness of the intrusion in *Edwards* and largely ignoring the probable cause issue (a majority of the Court accepted, without discussion, the court of appeals' conclusion that probable cause existed for the search and seizure of Edwards' clothing at the time of the intrusion at the jail, at 808, n.9.), the Court may have inadvertently placed itself in the unenviable position of having to balance reasonableness against probable cause in future similar cases. While such an approach can be supported without seriously eroding Fourth Amendment principles, the ultimate effect could be an inverse concomitant relationship such that the greater the reasonableness of the search and seizure following the arrest, the less the need for a clear finding of probable cause to justify the subsequent intrusion. Yet the Fourth Amendment and the prior decisions of the Court would seem not to permit a *balancing* between reasonableness and probable cause. Rather, earlier established doctrine required reasonableness and probable cause to go hand-in-hand, so that a warrantless search following an arrest could not be justified on the basis of reasonableness alone where probable cause had been greatly reduced because of the extended temporal or geographic scope of the intrusion. The so-called "calculus" model of *Katz* v. *United States* (supra § 5.01), i.e., "searches conducted outside the judicial process, without prior approval by judge or magistrate, are per se unreasonable — subject only to a few specifically established and well-delineated exceptions," 389 U.S. 347, 357, would seem to better serve the Fourth Amendment interests of parties, but the triology of *Robinson-Murphy-Edwards* represents somewhat of a departure from the *Katz* per se rule. Yet, as noted by Justice Douglas in his dissent in *Edwards,* "Erosions of constitutional guarantees start slowly, not in dramatic onsets." See also *Boyd* v. *United States,* 116 U.S. 616,

635 (1896) ("illegitimate and unconstitutional practices get their first footing ... by silent approaches and slight deviations from legal modes of procedure").

5. In *United States* v. *Chadwick,* supra, the Court held that luggage and baggage are entitled to a greater degree of privacy than are automobiles. Note that Chief Justice Burger was careful not, for Fourth Amendment purposes, to equate one's "effects" seized outside the home with items seized within a dwelling. Is the Court stating that on a privacy continuum luggage falls between items seized in a home and those taken from an automobile? Is the fact that the footlocker in *Chadwick* was double locked significant? Are the size and weight (200 pounds) of the luggage important? Could the federal agents have searched the footlocker immediately following the arrest? Suppose the footlocker was much smaller and lighter and was unlocked? Is the Court saying that luggage can never be searched without a warrant? Do you agree with Justices Blackmun and Rehnquist (dissenting in *Chadwick*) that the agents probably could have avoided an illegal search by delaying the arrest until the respondents drove away or conducting a search immediately following the arrest? Note that the dissenting justices did not cite any previous decisions of the Supreme Court to support that contention. Is an unlocked suitcase subject to a warrantless search away from the place of arrest? Is it permissible for airport officials to conduct warrantless searches at random in the baggage room without the knowledge or consent of the owners? Is X-raying luggage a "search" within the meaning of the Fourth Amendment?

    In *Katz* v. *United States* (supra, § 5.01), cited with approval in *Chadwick,* the Court held that "[s]earches conducted outside the judicial process, without prior approval by judge or magistrate, are per se unreasonable under the Fourth Amendment — subject only to a few specifically established and delineated exceptions," 389 U.S. at 357. Yet Chief Justice Burger and several other justices have refused to cite this per se rule in other Fourth Amendment decisions. Is the *Katz* "per se" rule a bit "too strong" for them to adopt? Does the "per se" rule erode the scope of warrantless searches?

6. At least two states (Hawaii and California) have refused to follow *United States* v. *Robinson,* which permits full searches of persons incident to custodial arrests for traffic offenses. See *State* v. *Kaluna,* 520 P.2d 51 (Hawaii 1974) and *People* v. *Brisendine,* 531 P.2d 1099 (Cal. 1975). The following recent cases involved the traditional time, place, and scope considerations of "search incident" cases: *United States* v. *Mason,* 523 F.2d 1122 (D.C. Cir. 1975) (even though arrested suspect was handcuffed, it was not unreasonable for FBI agents to conduct warrantless search of a partially opened suitcase in closet from which suspect was about to take his jacket); *State* v. *Noles,* 546 P.2d 814 (Ariz. 1976) (police officers who entered motel room with knowledge that armed robbery suspect within had two loaded revolvers with him held justified under *Chimel* in searching a nearby nightstand after they had handcuffed the suspect and told him to sit on the floor in the middle of the room); *United States* v. *Griffith,* 537 F.2d 900 (7th Cir. 1976) (search of bathroom and closed suitcase in another room following warrantless arrest of drug suspect in motel room held beyond the scope of *Chimel*); *State* v. *Kennel,* 546 P.2d 1156 (Ariz. Ct. App.

1976) (police officers who took highly intoxicated person into custody in order to transport him to a local treatment center held justified under *Robinson-Gustafson* rationale in conducting full search of his person before placing him in patrol car); *Beck* v. *State*, 547 S.W. 2d 266 (Tex. Ct. Crim. App. 1976) (police officer's search of trunk of traffic violator's auto after arrest for making an illegal turn held beyond scope of search incident to arrest when not necessary for officer's protection); *United States* v. *Sellers*, 520 F.2d 1281 (4th Cir. 1975) (federal agents' search of defendant's apartment for armed associates made after his arrest outside his apartment on a federal fugitive warrant held valid since officers had reasonable grounds to suspect the presence of others who might present a security risk); *United States* v. *Harris*, 528 F.2d 1327 (10th Cir. 1975) (warrantless seizure of evidence following arrest of defendants at a public fun and games establishment held not unreasonable even though the agents had sufficient time to obtain a warrant); *Hopkins* v. *Alabama*, 524 F.2d 473 (5th Cir. 1975) (warrantless search of defendant's house following his arrest outside his home and following gun battle with the police held justified to determine that no one remained in the house); *Commonwealth* v. *Getz*, 344 A.2d 686 (1975) (search of defendant's apartment upstairs after his arrest at the foot of the stairs held violative of Fourth Amendment since apartment was not in the immediate vicinity of the arrest).

B. THE "PLAIN VIEW" DOCTRINE

On a Clear Day You Can Seize Forever

HARRIS v. UNITED STATES

Supreme Court of the United States, 1968
390 U.S. 234, 88 S. Ct. 992, 19 L. Ed. 2d 1067

The facts are stated in the opinion.

PER CURIAM.

Petitioner was charged with robbery under the District of Columbia Code. . . . At his trial in the United States District Court for the District of Columbia, petitioner moved to suppress an automobile registration card belonging to the robbery victim, which the Government sought to introduce in evidence. The trial court, after a hearing, ruled that the card was admissible. Petitioner was convicted of the crime charged and sentenced to imprisonment for a period of two to seven years. On appeal a panel of the United States Court of Appeals for the District of Columbia Circuit reversed, holding that the card had been obtained by means of an unlawful search. The Government's petition for rehearing en banc was, however, granted, and the full Court of Appeals affirmed petitioner's conviction, with two judges dissenting. We granted certiorari to consider the problem presented under the Fourth Amendment. . . .

Petitioner's automobile had been seen leaving the site of the robbery. The car was traced and petitioner was arrested as he was entering it near his home. After a cursory search of the car, the arresting officer took petitioner to a police station. The police decided to impound the car as evidence, and a crane was called to tow it to the precinct. It reached the precinct about an hour and a quarter after petitioner. At this moment, the windows of the car were open and the door unlocked. It had begun to rain.

A regulation of the Metropolitan Police Department requires the officer who takes an impounded vehicle in charge to search the vehicle thoroughly, to remove all valuables from it, and to attach to the vehicle a property tag listing certain information about the circumstances of the impounding. Pursuant to this regulation, and without a warrant, the arresting officer proceeded to the lot to which petitioner's car had been towed, in order to search the vehicle, to place a property tag on it, to roll up the windows, and to lock the doors. The officer entered on the driver's side, searched the car, and tied a property tag on the steering wheel. Stepping out of the car, he rolled up an open window on one of the back doors. Proceeding to the front door on the passenger side, the officer opened the door in order to secure the window and door. He then saw the registration card, which lay face up on the metal stripping over which the door

closes. The officer returned to the precinct, brought petitioner to the car, and confronted petitioner with the registration card. Petitioner disclaimed all knowledge of the card. The officer then seized the card and brought it into the precinct. Returning to the car, he searched the trunk, rolled up the windows, and locked the doors.

The sole question of our consideration is whether the officer discovered the registration card by means of illegal search. We hold that he did not. The admissibility of evidence found as a result of a search under the police regulation is not presented by this case. The precise and detailed findings of the District Court, accepted by the Court of Appeals, were to the effect that the discovery of the card was not the result of a search of the car, but of a measure taken to protect the car while it was in police custody. Nothing in the Fourth Amendment requires the police to obtain a warrant in these narrow circumstances.

Once the door had lawfully been opened, the registration card, with the name of the robbery victim on it, was plainly visible. It has long been settled that objects falling in the plain view of an officer who has a right to be in the position to have that view are subject to seizure and may be introduced in evidence. . . .

[Mr. Justice DOUGLAS wrote a concurring opinion.]

[Mr. Justice MARSHALL took no part in the consideration or decision of this case.]

Comment

1. *United States* v. *Harris* represents the only decision, to date, in which the Court has upheld the seizure of evidence from an auto *solely* under the "plain view" exception. The Court found that the police officer did not discover the card during a search, but rather while he was engaged in activity designed to protect the auto and its contents while in police custody. The Court left open the question of whether police may routinely conduct warrantless general inventory searches of autos by virtue of the fact that the car is in lawful custody and therefore subject to impoundment. However, that issue was ultimately resolved in *South Dakota* v. *Opperman*, 428 U.S. 364 (1976), infra.

An Exercise in Ambiguity

COOLIDGE v. NEW HAMPSHIRE

Supreme Court of the United States, 1971
403 U.S. 443, 91 S. Ct. 2022, 29 L. Ed. 2d 564

New Hampshire Police obtained an arrest warrant for petitioner and a search warrant for his automobile. Following petitioner's arrest inside his house, his auto was seized from his driveway and towed to the police station where, two days later, it was searched and vacuumed. Vacuum sweepings from the vehicle were admitted in evidence at Coolidge's trial for murder. The New Hampshire Supreme Court affirmed petitioner's conviction, and the United States Supreme Court granted certiorari.

After the Supreme Court found that the original search warrant was invalid because it had not been issued by a "neutral and detached magistrate" (the warrant had been issued by the state attorney general who was also the chief investigator in the case), the state proposed three theories to justify the warrantless search and seizure of the automobile: (1) the seizure and subsequent search were incident to arrest; (2) the search and seizure were based on "exigent circumstances"; and (3) since the auto itself was an instrumentality of the crime, it could be seized and searched because it was in "plain view."

Finding that the search was not substantially contemporaneous with the arrest nor confined to the immediate vicinity of the arrest, Mr. Justice Stewart, writing for the plurality (and joined by Douglas, Brennan, and Marshall, JJ.), rejected the "search incident" theory. Likewise, the Court rejected the state's second theory and held that no "exigent circumstances" existed to justify the warrantless search. Finally, the Court turned its attention to the "plain view" theory advanced by the state.

Mr. Justice STEWART delivered the opinion of the Court.

* * *

The State's third theory in support of the warrantless seizure and search of the Pontiac car is that the car itself was an "instrumentality of the crime," and as such might be seized by the police on Coolidge's property because it was in plain view.... Of course, the distinction between an "instrumentality of crime" and "mere evidence" was done away with by Warden v. Hayden, 387 U.S. 294 (1967) [infra], and we may assume that the police had probable cause to seize the automobile. But, for the reasons that follow, we hold that the "plain view" exception to the warrant requirement is inapplicable to this case.

It is well established that under certain circumstances the police may seize evidence in plain view without a warrant. But it is important to keep in mind that, in the vast majority of cases, *any* evidence seized by the police will be in plain view, at least at the moment of seizure. The problem with the "plain view" doctrine has been to identify the circumstances in which plain view has legal significance rather than being simply the normal concomitant of any search, legal or illegal.

An example of the applicability of the "plain view" doctrine is the situation in which the police have a warrant to search a given area for specified objects, and in the course of the search come across some other article of incriminating character....

Where the initial intrusion that brings the police within plain view of such an article is supported, not by a warrant, but by one of the recognized exceptions to the warrant requirement, the seizure is also legitimate. Thus the police may inadvertently come across evidence while in "hot pursuit" of a fleeing suspect. Warden v. Hayden.... And an object that comes into view during a search incident to arrest that is appropriately limited in scope under existing law may be seized without a warrant. Chimel v. California [supra]. . . . Finally, the "plain view" doctrine has been applied where a police officer is not searching for evidence against the accused, but nonetheless inadvertently comes across an incriminating object. Harris v. United States [supra]. . . .

What the "plain view" cases have in common is that the police officer in each of them had a prior justification for an intrusion in the course of which he came inadvertently across a piece of evidence incriminating the accused. The doctrine serves to supplement the prior justification—whether it be a warrant for another object, hot pursuit, search incident to lawful arrest, or some other legitimate reason for being present unconnected with a search directed against the accused—and permits the warrantless seizure. Of course, the extension of the original justification is legitimate only where it is immediately apparent to the police that they have evidence before them; the "plain view" doctrine may not be used to extend a general exploratory search from one object to another until something incriminating at last emerges. . . .

The rationale for the "plain view" exception is evident if we keep in mind the two distinct constitutional protections served by the warrant requirement. First, the magistrate's scrutiny is intended to eliminate altogether searches not based on probable cause. The premise here is that *any* intrusion in the way of search or seizure is an evil, so that no intrusion at all is justified without a careful prior determination of necessity. . . . The second, distinct objective is that those searches deemed necessary should be as limited as possible. Here, the specific evil is the "general warrant" abhorred by the colonists, and the problem is not that of intrusion per se but of a general, exploratory rummaging in a person's belongings. . . . The warrant accomplishes this second objective by requiring a "particular description" of the things to be seized.

The "plain view" doctrine is not in conflict with the first objective because plain view does not occur until a search is in progress. In each case, this initial intrusion is justified by a warrant or by an exception such as "hot pursuit" or search incident to a lawful arrest, or by an extraneous valid reason for the officer's presence. And, given the initial intrusion, the seizure of an object in plain view is consistent with the second objective, since it does not convert the search into a general or exploratory one. As against the minor peril to Fourth Amendment protections, there is a major gain in effective law enforcement. Where, once an otherwise lawful search is in progress, the police inadvertently come upon a piece of evidence, it would often be a needless inconvenience, and sometimes dangerous—to the evidence or to the police themselves—to require them to ignore it until they have obtained a warrant particularly describing it.

The limits on the doctrine are implicit in the statement of its rationale. The first of these is that plain view *alone* is never enough to justify the warrantless seizure of evidence. This is simply a corollary of the familiar principle discussed above, that no amount of probable cause can justify a warrantless search or seizure absent "exigent circumstances." Incontrovertible testimony of the senses that an incriminating object is on premises belonging to a criminal suspect may establish the fullest possible measure of probable cause. But even where the object is contraband, this Court has repeatedly stated and enforced the basic rule that the police may not enter and make a warrantless seizure.

* * *

The second limitation is that the discovery of evidence in plain view must be inadvertent. The rationale of the exception to the warrant requirement, as just stated, is that a plain-view seizure will not turn an initially valid (and therefore limited) search into a "general" one, while the inconvenience of procuring a warrant to cover an inadvertent discovery is great. But where the discovery is anticipated, where the police know in advance the location of the evidence and intend to seize it, the situation is altogether different. The requirement of a warrant to seize imposes no inconvenience whatever, or at least none which is constitutionally cognizable in a legal system that regards warrantless searches as "per se unreasonable" in the absence of "exigent circumstances."

If the initial intrusion is bottomed upon a warrant that fails to mention a particular object, though the police know its location and intend to seize it, then there is a violation of the express constitutional requirement of "Warrants ... particularly describing ... (the) things to be seized." The initial intrusion may, of course, be legitimated not by a warrant but by one of the exceptions to the warrant requirement, such as hot pursuit or search incident to lawful arrest. But to extend the scope of such an intrusion to the seizure of objects — not contraband nor stolen nor dangerous in themselves — which the police know in advance they will find in plain view and intend to seize, would fly in the face of the basic rule that no amount of probable cause can justify a warrantless seizure.

In the light of what has been said, it is apparent that the "plain view" exception cannot justify the police seizure of the Pontiac car in this case. The police had ample opportunity to obtain a valid warrant; they knew the automobile's exact description and location well in advance; they intended to seize it when they came upon Coolidge's property. And this is not a case involving contraband or stolen goods or objects dangerous in themselves.

The seizure was therefore unconstitutional, and so was the subsequent search at the station house. Since evidence obtained in the course of the search was admitted at Coolidge's trial, the judgment must be reversed and the case remanded to the New Hampshire Supreme Court....

In his dissenting opinion today, Mr. Justice WHITE marshals the arguments that can be made against our interpretation of the "automobile" and "plain view" exceptions to the warrant requirement. Beyond the unstartling proposition that when a line is drawn there is often not a great deal of difference between the situations closest to it on either side, there is a single theme that runs through what he has to say about the two exceptions. Since that theme is a recurring one in controversies over the proper meaning and scope of the Fourth Amendment, it seems appropriate to treat his views in this separate section, rather than piecemeal.

Much the most important part of the conflict that has been so notable in this Court's attempts over a hundred years to develop a coherent body of Fourth Amendment law has been caused by disagreement over the importance of requiring law enforcement officers to secure warrants. Some have argued that a determination by a magistrate of probable cause as a precondition of any search or seizure is so essential that the Fourth Amendment is violated whenever the police might reasonably have obtained a warrant but failed to do so. Others have argued with equal force that a test of reasonableness, applied after the fact of search or seizure when the police attempt to introduce the fruits in evidence, affords ample safeguard for the rights in question, so that "(t)he relevant test is not whether it is reasonable to procure a search warrant, but whether the search was reasonable."

Both sides to the controversy appear to recognize a distinction between searches and seizures that take place on a man's property — his home or office — and those carried out elsewhere. It is accepted, at least as a matter of principle, that a search or seizure carried out on a suspect's premises without a warrant is per se unreasonable, unless the police can show that it falls within one of a carefully defined set of exceptions based on the presence of "exigent circumstances." As to other kinds of intrusions, however, there has been disagreement about the basic rules to be applied, as our cases ... make clear.

* * *

Reversed and remanded.

Mr. Justice BLACK, concurring and dissenting.

* * *

I believe the seizure of petitioner's automobile was valid under the well-established right of the police to seize evidence in plain view at the time and place of arrest. The majority concedes that the police were rightfully at petitioner's residence to make a valid arrest at the time of the seizure. To use the majority's words, the "initial intrusion" which brought the police within plain view of the automobile was legitimate. The majority also concedes that the automobile was "plainly visible both from the street and from inside the house where Coolidge was actually arrested" [and] ... that the automobile itself was evidence which the police had probable cause to seize.... Indeed, the majority appears to concede that the seizure of petitioner's automobile was valid under the doctrine upholding seizures of evidence in plain view at the scene of arrest, at least as it stood before today. . . .

However, even after conceding that petitioner's automobile itself was evidence of the crime, that the police had probable cause to seize it as such, and that the automobile was in plain view at the time and place of arrest, the majority holds the seizure to be a violation of the Fourth Amendment because the discovery of the automobile was not "inadvertent." The majority confidently states: "What the 'plain view' cases have in common is that the police officer in each of them had a prior justification for an intrusion in the course of which he came inadvertently across a piece of evidence incriminating the accused." But the prior holdings of this Court not only fail to support the majority's statement, they flatly contradict it. One need look no further than the cases cited in the majority opinion to discover the invalidity of that assertion.

* * *

The majority confuses the historically justified right of the police to seize visible evidence of the crime in open view at the scene of arrest with the "plain view" exception to the requirement of particular description in search warrants. The majority apparently reasons that unless the seizure made pursuant to authority conferred by a warrant is limited to the particularly described object of seizure, the warrant will become a general writ of assistance. Evidently, as a check on the requirement of particular description in search warrants, the majority announces a new rule that items not named in a warrant cannot be seized unless their discovery was unanticipated or "inadvertent." The majority's concern is with the scope of the intrusion authorized by a warrant. But the right to seize items properly subject to seizure because in open view at the time of arrest is quite independent of any power to search for such items pursuant to a warrant. The entry in the present case did not depend for its authority on a search warrant but was concededly authorized by probable cause to effect a valid arrest. The intrusion did not exceed that authority. The intrusion was limited in scope to the circumstances which justified the entry in the first place—the arrest of petitioner. There was no general search; indeed, there was no

search at all. The automobile itself was evidence properly subject to seizure and was in open view at the time and place of arrest.

Only rarely can it be said that evidence seized incident to an arrest is truly unexpected or inadvertent. Indeed, if the police officer had no expectation of discovering weapons, contraband, or other evidence, he would make no search. It appears to me that the rule adopted by the Court today, for all practical purposes, abolishes seizure incident to arrest. The majority rejects the test of reasonableness provided in the Fourth Amendment and substitutes a per se rule—if the police could have obtained a warrant and did not, the seizure, no matter how reasonable, is void. But the Fourth Amendment does not require that every search be made pursuant to a warrant. It prohibits only "unreasonable searches and seizures." The relevant test is not the reasonableness of the opportunity to procure a warrant, but the reasonableness of the seizure under all the circumstances. The test of reasonableness cannot be fixed by per se rules; each case must be decided on its own facts.

For all the reasons stated above, I believe the seizure and search of petitioner's car was reasonable and, therefore, authorized by the Fourth Amendment. The evidence so obtained violated neither the Fifth Amendment which does contain an exclusionary rule, nor the Fourth Amendment which does not.

* * *

Mr. Justice WHITE, with whom the CHIEF JUSTICE [BURGER] joins, concurring and dissenting.

I would affirm the judgment. In my view, Coolidge's Pontiac was lawfully seized as evidence of the crime in plain sight and thereafter was lawfully searched under Cooper v. California, 386 U.S. 58 (1967).

* * *

[O]fficers may be on a suspect's premises executing a search warrant and in the course of the authorized search discover evidence of crime not covered by the warrant. . . . Apparently the majority agrees, for it lumps plain-sight seizure in such circumstances along with other situations where seizures are made after a legal entry.

* * *

... [I]n these various circumstances, at least where the discovery of evidence is "inadvertent," the Court would permit the seizure because, it is said, "the minor peril to Fourth Amendment protections" is overridden by the "major gain in effective law enforcement" inherent in avoiding the "needless inconvenience" of procuring a warrant. ... I take this to mean that both the possessory interest of the defendant and the importance of having a magistrate confirm that what the officer saw with his own eyes is in fact contraband or evidence of crime are not substantial constitutional considerations. Officers in these circumstances need neither guard nor ignore the evidence while a warrant is sought. Immediate seizure is justified and reasonable under the Fourth Amendment.

The Court would interpose in some or all of these situations, however, a condition that the discovery of the disputed evidence be "inadvertent." If it is "anticipated," that is if "the police know in advance the location of the evidence and intend to seize it," the seizure is invalid. ...

I have great difficulty with this approach. Let us suppose officers secure a warrant to search a house for a rifle. While staying well within the range of a rifle search, they discover two photographs of the murder victim, both in plain sight in the bedroom. Assume also that the discovery of the one photograph was inadvertent but finding the other was anticipated. The Court would permit the seizure of only óne of the photographs. But in terms of the "minor" peril to Fourth Amendment values there is surely no difference between these two photographs: the interference with possession is the same in each case and the officers' appraisal of the photograph they expected to see is no less reliable than their judgment about the other. And in both situations the actual inconvenience and danger to evidence remain identical if the officers must depart and secure a warrant. The Court, however, states that the State will suffer no constitutionally cognizable inconvenience from invalidating anticipated seizures since it had probable cause to search for the items seized and could have included them in a warrant.

This seems a punitive and extravagant application of the exclusionary rule. If the police have probable cause to search for a photograph as well as a rifle and they proceed to seek a warrant, they could have no possible motive for deliberately including the rifle but omitting the photograph. Quite the contrary is true. Only oversight or careless mistake would explain the omission in the warrant application if the police were convinced they had probable cause to search for the photograph. Of course, they may misjudge the facts and not realize they have probable cause for the picture, or the magistrate may find against them and not issue a warrant for it. In either event the officers may validly seize the photograph for which they had no probable cause to search but the other photograph is excluded from evidence when the Court subsequently determines that the officers, after all, had probable cause to search for it.

More important, the inadvertence rule is unnecessary to further any Fourth Amendment ends and will accomplish nothing. Police with a warrant for a rifle may search only places where rifles might be and must terminate the search once the rifle is found; the inadvertence rule will in no way reduce the number of places into which they may lawfully look.

* * *

In the case before us, the officers had probable cause both to arrest Coolidge and to seize his car. In order to effect his arrest, they went to his home—perhaps the most obvious place in which to look for him. They also may have hoped to find his car at home and, in fact, when they arrived on the property, to make the arrest, they did find the 1951 Pontiac there. Thus, even assuming that the Fourth Amendment protects against warrantless seizures outside the house ... the fact remains that the officers had legally entered Coolidge's property to effect an arrest and that they seized the car only after they observed it in plain view before them. The Court, however, would invalidate this seizure on the premise that officers should not be permitted to seize effects in plain sight when they have anticipated they will see them.

Even accepting this premise of the Court, seizure of the car was not invalid. The majority makes an assumption that, when the police went to Coolidge's house to arrest him, they anticipated that they would also find the 1951 Pontiac there. In my own reading of the record, however, I have found no evidence to support this assumption. For all the record shows, the police, although they may have hoped to find the Pontiac at Coolidge's home, did not know its exact location when they went to make the arrest, and their observation of it in Coolidge's driveway was truly inadvertent.

* * *

It is evident on the facts of this case that Coolidge's Pontiac was subject to seizure if proper procedures were employed. It is also apparent that the Pontiac was in plain view of the officers who had legally entered Coolidge's property to effect his arrest. I am satisfied that it was properly seized whether or not the officers expected that it would be found where it was. And, since the Pontiac was legally seized as evidence of the crime for which Coolidge was arrested, Cooper v. California ... authorizes its warrantless search while in lawful custody of the police. "It would be unreasonable to hold that the police, having to retain the car in their custody for such a length of time, had no right, even for their own protection, to search it. It is no answer to say that the police could have obtained a search warrant, for '[t]he relevant test is not whether it is reasonable to procure a search warrant, but whether the search was reasonable.'" ...

* * *

[Mr. Justice HARLAN wrote a concurring opinion.]

WARRANTLESS SEARCHES AND THE "PLAIN VIEW" DOCTRINE: THE CURRENT PERSPECTIVE*

Peter W. Lewis and Henry W. Mannle

* * *

The Future of the Plain View Doctrine

Prior to *Coolidge,* it was thought that a warrantless seizure of evidence under the plain view doctrine required an inadvertent

*12 Crim. L. Bull. 5, 17–24 (1976). Reprinted by permission of Warren, Gorham and Lamont, Inc.

discovery.[63] Thus, if the police had a reasonable suspicion—but less than probable cause—that criminal evidence would be found at a particular place, a warrantless seizure of the evidence could not be justified under the Fourth Amendment in the absence of "exigent circumstances."[64] But only a plurality of the Court in *Coolidge* was willing to uphold the inadvertent-discovery requirement. Justice Stewart, writing for the plurality, defended the inadvertence requirement by arguing that the Fourth Amendment's twin goals of (1) encouraging the police to obtain warrants and (2) limiting the authorized intrusion to the smallest extent possible by requiring a "particular description of the things to be seized"[65] would be subverted without the rule. Yet, nowhere did Justice Stewart state the degree of expectation that is required before the discovery of evidence by the police will be deemed not inadvertent. This ambiguity is both puzzling and unsound.[66] Some illustrations follow.

Hypothetical Problems. Suppose the police have probable cause to arrest a suspect for robbery, and they have "some information"—but no probable cause—that the suspect has been dealing in drugs and that such contraband may be found on his premises. Further, assume that the police know the suspect is a "loner" and rarely has visitors at his residence. There is little doubt that the police will seek to arrest the suspect at his residence in the expectation of discovering contraband.[67] Suppose after placing the suspect under arrest in his living room, an officer sees, in plain view, a bottle of suspicious looking pills lying on a dresser in the suspect's bedroom. The pills are later discovered to be heroin capsules. Further, assume that the bedroom is beyond the scope of a search incident to a lawful arrest under the *Chimel* standards.[68] Obviously, the police will seize the evidence anyway and seek to justify the seizure as discovered in plain view. But is the contraband admissible against the defendant under the plain view doctrine, in view of the plurality's approach in *Coolidge?*

Interpreting the Inadvertence Rule. If Justice Stewart's inadvertence rule means that the plain view doctrine is not applicable when the police have probable cause to believe that evidence will be found at a particular place, and they failed to obtain a warrant absent "exigent circumstances," the rule will only have a limited effect. On the other hand, the inadvertence rule will be far more significant if it is interpreted to mean that when the police have *some expectation* that evidence will be found on the premises, but lack probable cause, a warrantless seizure cannot be justified on the basis of the plain view doctrine absent exigent circumstances. Justice Stewart stated in *Coolidge* that exigent circumstances include emergencies, such as a discovery of evidence during "hot pursuit" of a suspect,[69] a fleeing automobile on the highway,[70] a likelihood that the evidence would be destroyed if the police delayed the seizure,[71] or evidence seized within the permissible scope incident to a lawful arrest.[72] In the hypothetical situation posed, exigent circumstances justifying the warrantless seizure appear to be wanting—at least under the *Coolidge* plurality's approach.[73] Yet Justice Stewart indicated in *Coolidge* that:

"Where, once an otherwise lawful search is in progress, the police inadvertently come upon a piece of evidence, it would be a needless inconvenience, and sometimes dangerous—to the evidence or to themselves—to require them to ignore it until they have obtained a warrant particularly describing it."[74]

Again, referring to our hypothetical illustration, it would be an obvious waste of resources to require the police to ignore the suspicious evidence and first seek prior judical approval. Without a doubt, the police could obtain a warrant under these circumstances. Yet there is little reason to believe that the evidence would not be destroyed in the interim. If noninadvertence is equated with probable cause, then the seizure of the heroin might be justified as discovered in plain view. If, on the other hand, noninadvertence is equated with less than probable cause, then the warrantless seizure could not be justified under the doctrine in the absence of exigent circumstances—missing in our hypothetical.

It would be difficult for the police to establish that they had no expectation of discovering evidence at the suspect's residence. Indeed, the inadvertence rule invites false testimony. Perhaps Justice Stewart was concerned that the police would purposely delay arresting a suspect until he was at his residence, in the anticipation of seizing evidence which they could not obtain with a warrant; or having probable cause for one offense, but making a deliberately timed arrest, hoping to discover evidence of another crime. The plurality opinion in *Coolidge* did not make this clear.

Clearly, the probable cause interpretation under the inadvertence rule is the most desirable. Otherwise, valuable evidence may be lost. And the police will deny that they anticipated the discovery of evidence sought to be admitted under the plain view doctrine.

Impounded Automobile Searches.
Sometimes, a seizure of evidence sought to be admitted under the plain view doctrine is inextricably intertwined with other theories which might otherwise justify a governmental intrusion. Suppose a police officer at night legitimately stops a "known drug addict" for a routine traffic investigation and places him under custodial arrest for a traffic offense. A search of the arrestee's person under the *Robinson*[75]-*Gustafson*[76] standards reveals what appears to be heroin in two glassine envelopes. Further, the arresting officer, using his flashlight, sees several burglary tools under the front seat which are seized. The car is impounded and taken to a local police station, and pursuant to police regulations, a general inventory search is conducted. The inventory reveals two "suspicious looking" color television sets in the trunk of the car. The serial numbers have been filed off. A subsequent investigation reveals the television sets have recently been reported as stolen. Finally, the evidence fails to support a finding that the initial encounter with the arrestee was a "pretext arrest."[77]

What should be the results of a motion to suppress filed by the defendant? Should a prosecutor argue for the admissibility of the burglary tools found in the car under the plain view doctrine? Or as incident to a lawful arrest under *Chimel* standard?[78] Or under the "emergency" doctrine of *Carroll*[79]-*Chambers*?[80] Are the televisions in the trunk seizable under a general inventory search of impounded automobiles? Does the defendant lack *standing,* since he could not have a legitimate possessory interest in the properties seized?[81] Are the items taken from the trunk seizable under the plain view doctrine, notwithstanding a possible rejection by the Supreme Court of general inventory searches of automobiles? Perhaps a prosecutor would find it advantageous to argue all of the above theories. However, the plain view theory would seem to be inapposite to a warrantless general inventory theory and could place the prosecutor in several inconsistent positions. We shall confine our practical analysis in this hypothetical to a discussion of the interplay between general inventory searches and the plain view doctrine.

Earlier, we indicated that Supreme Court has not explicitly held that warrantless general inventory searches of impounded automobiles comport with Fourth Amendment requirements.[*] In *Cooper* v. *California*,[82] the Court upheld an inventory search of a vehicle (required under state law) being held for a *forfeiture hearing*. Accordingly, the Supreme Court could, in the future, hold that general inventory searches of impounded automobiles, even though not being held for a forfeiture hearing, are not "searches" within the meaning of the Fourth Amendment; that such inventories are simply measures designed to protect the car while in police custody;[83] and that in the absence of any evidence indicating that an inventory was a subterfuge to conduct exploratory searches, such general inventory searches are an exception to the Fourth Amendment warrant requirements.

If a general inventory theory is justifiable under these circumstances, the plain view doctrine would not be applicable or necessary.

Most courts have upheld a general inventory of the *arrestee's person* as a part of the booking process to insure that weapons or contraband would not be introduced into the jail.[84] Is this theory applicable to automobile inventories on the ground that it is a reasonable governmental intrusion, supplying the "exigent circumstances" requirement? Or should the *scope* of a general inventory automobile search be restricted to the *interior* of the car and not a *locked trunk?* Arguably, the need to protect the seized property (as found by the *Cooper* Court) under these circumstances would not be present.[85]

_____

[*]This article was written prior to *South Dakota* v. *Opperman*, 428 U.S. 364 (1976), infra.

If, on the other hand, general inventory searches of impounded automobiles (not held for forfeiture) are held to run afoul of the Fourth Amendment, the prior justification requirement of the plain view doctrine would not be met. On its face, the seizing officer would not have a right to be in that position to have that view, absent exigent circumstances. In addition, if the arrestee is a "known addict," is it reasonable to assume that the seizure of the evidence discovered in the trunk of the car (even if, arguably, found in "plain view") was truly inadvertent? It is also arguable whether the "suspicious looking" television sets provide the "nexus . . . between the item seized and criminal behavior" apparently required by the doctrine.[86] Do television sets in the trunk of an impounded car automatically provide that nexus? Or does the nexus requirement allow general exploratory investigations of items seized pursuant to the plain view doctrine based on the slightest suspicion? Finally, the seizure of the burglary tools from under the car seat would not seem to be justifiable under the plain view doctrine since they were discovered pursuant to a search. The use of the flashlight and the concealed nature of the evidence (under the seat) may negative a plain view seizure.[87] In the absence of a constitutional warrant exception allowing general inventory searches of impounded automobiles, the apparently rigid but unclear status of the plain view doctrine is likely to become the focus of more attention by the Supreme Court, especially in view of the changing membership of the Court since *Coolidge*.

Subterfuge Seizures. Sometimes, the police have probable cause to search premises with respect to certain items but not others. Yet there may be some suspicion that criminal evidence other than that specified in the warrant is on the premises; and it is not unusual for the primary focus of attention by the police to be directed at the nondescribed evidence, which the police do not have probable cause to search for or seize. Suppose, for example, the police have probable cause to search a suspect's premises for stolen property, but they also have some reason to believe (but not probable cause) that illicitly possessed narcotics are on the premises. A search warrant for the stolen property is issued, and the scope of the search by the police is restricted to those items specified in the warrant.[88] How, then, may the police justify seizing any narcotics found on the premises in the absence of exigent circumstances?

One method often utilized by the police is to announce to the householders, "You know what we're after! Bring it out or we'll tear your house apart!" Sometimes, much criminal evidence not specified in the warrant is brought forth in "plain view" — and sometimes from areas the police could not justify searching under the warrant. A prosecutor could seek to justify the warrantless seizure under the plain view theory — and he might be successful. Arguably, at least three of the four requirements of the doctrine have been satisfied. The narcotics were not discovered pursuant to a search; the articles seized were of an incriminating character; and the police, by virtue of the search warrant, had a prior justification for the intrusion.

The vexation is the inadvertent discovery rule. If *Coolidge* means that the discovery must be totally inadvertent, and if the police testify in accordance with their oath requirements, the narcotics, under these circumstances, are not admissible under the plain view theory. If inadvertence means less than probable cause, the seized narcotics may be admissible under the doctrine, and the subterfuge would have been successful. Moreover, since most criminal defendants plead guilty through plea bargaining,[89] there is a good possibility that the legality of the seizure would never be tested in court. (A guilty plea, in most jurisdictions, waives all nonjurisdictional errors. Collateral attacks on any defects in the prior proceedings, such as the legality of a search and seizure, are disallowed.[90]) Thus, the present status of the plain view doctrine may invite subterfuge seizures and false testimony by the police.

* * *

References*

63. See, *e.g., Trupiano* v. *United States,* 334 U.S. 699 (1948), and *McDonald* v. *United States,* 335 U.S. 451 (1948).

*The original footnote numbers as printed in the Criminal Law Bulletin have been retained; numbers begin with "63" owing to deletion of the first part of the article.

64. *Trupiano* v. *United States,* note 63 *supra.*
65. *Coolidge* v. *United States,* ... [403 U.S. 443 (1971)], at 467.
66. See, *e.g., Note* 85 Harv. L. Rev. 237–250 (Nov. 1, 1971).
67. *Note, The Neglected Fourth Amendment Problem in Arrest Entries,* 23 Stan. L. Rev. 995, 997 (1971).
68. *Chimel* v. *California,* 395 U.S. 752 (1969), held that a search incident to a lawful arrest must be restricted to a search of the arrestee's person and the area wtihin his immediate control.
69. *Warden* v. *Hayden,* 387 U.S. 294 (1967).
70. *Carroll* v. *United States,* ... [267 U.S. 132 (1925)].
71. *Coolidge* v. *New Hampshire,* ... [403 U.S. 443 (1971)], at 478.
72. *Chimel* v. *California,* note 68 *supra.*
73. In our hypothetical, there would be little danger that the evidence would be destroyed, since the suspect was known to be a "loner and rarely had visitors." In addition, the "fleeing automobile" exception would not be applicable here.
74. *Coolidge* v. *New Hampshire,* ... [403 U.S. 443 (1971)], at 467, 468.
75. *United States* v. *Robinson,* 414 U.S. 218 (1973), holding that a police officer who subjects a suspect to a custodial arrest for a noncitation traffic offense may conduct a full-field search of the person incident to that arrest.
76. *Gustafson* v. *Florida,* 414 U.S. 260 (1973), is to the same effect. For an interesting analysis of the *Robinson-Gustafson* decision, see Nakell, *Search of the Person Incident to a Traffic Arrest: A Comment on Robinson and Gustafson,* 10 Crim. L. Bull. 9 (1974).
77. The leading case on "pretext arrests" is *Green* v. *United States,* 386 F.2d 953 (10th Cir. 1967), where the Court disapproved of a local vagrancy ordinance as a pretext to arrest and justify a search incident to that arrest.
78. *Chimel* v. *California,* note 68 *supra.*
79. *Carroll* v. *United States,* 267 U.S. 132 (1925). ...
80. *Chambers* v. *Maroney,* 399 U.S. 42 (1970), holding that if the police have probable cause to search an automobile at one place, a search of that automobile at another place and time does not violate the Fourth Amendment.
81. Apparently, the defendant would have "automatic standing" in our hypothetical since possession alone would be sufficient to convict. See *Jones* v. *United States,* 362 U.S. 257, 263 (1960), holding, *inter alia,* that where "possession both convicts and confers standing, [that] eliminates any necessity for a preliminary showing of an interest in the premises searched or the property seized, which ordinarily is required when standing is challenged." See also *Mancusi* v. *DeForte,* 392 U.S. 364 (1968); *Simmons* v. *United States,* 390 U.S. 377 (1968); *Alderman* v. *United States,* 394 U.S. 165 (1969); *Brown* v. *United States,* 411 U.S. 223 (1973).
82. 386 U.S. 58 (1967). The *Cooper* Court held that it "would be unreasonable to hold that the police, having to retain the car in their garage for such length of time, had no right, even for their own protection, to search it." (At 61, 62) (Opinion by Black, J.)
83. *Id.*

84. Kamisar, LaFave, and Israel, *Modern Criminal Procedure* 330 (1974).
85. See dissenting opinion in *Cooper* by Douglas, J., joined by Warren, C. J., Brennan and Fortas, JJ., at 62–65.
86. *Warden* v. *Hayden*, note 69 *supra*, at 307 (opinion by Brennan, J.). See also *Stanley* v. *Georgia*, 394 U.S. 557, 571 (concurring opinion by Stewart, J.).
87. The Court has, in several instances, indicated that the plain view doctrine is not applicable where evidence is discovered pursuant to a search. See,

e.g., Ker v. *California*, 374 U.S. 23 (1963), and *Harris* v. *United States*, 390 U.S. 234 (1968). However, the seizure of the burglary tools is probably within the scope of *Chimel* v. *California*, note 68 *supra*.
88. U.S. Const. amend. IV. See, *e.g., Stanford* v. *Texas*, 379 U.S. 476 (1965).
89. President's Commission on Law Enforcement and Administration of Justice, *Task Force Report: The Courts* (1967).
90. Bond, *Plea Bargaining and Guilty Pleas* 8–9 (1975).

Comment

1. A few recent decisions in the lower federal and state courts involving the "plain view" doctrine include: *United States* v. *Wilson*, 524 F.2d 595 (8th Cir. 1975) (warrantless station-house search of an accident victim's padlocked duffle bag from which a sawed-off shotgun barrel protruded held not unreasonable); *United States* v. *Montiell*, 526 F.2d 1008 (2nd Cir. 1975) (plain view doctrine justified narcotic agents' warrantless seizure of drug evidence found in toilet as they rushed inside upon hearing toilet flush after they had knocked and announced their presence); *United States* v. *Wysong*, 528 F.2d 345 (9th Cir. 1976) (ledger discovered unexpectedly by federal agents during warrant-authorized search of a drug suspect's suitcase held admissible under plain view doctrine); *Anderson* v. *State*, 555 P.2d 251 (Alas. 1976) (police officer with warrant authorizing him to search for marijuana in defendant's home violated the Fourth Amendment by seeing slide negatives, which contained pictures of naked boys, and lifting them to a light for examination since slides held not in plain view); *State* v. *Mollberg*, 246 N.W. 2d 463 (Minn. 1976) (police officers with valid search warrant to search for poaching evidence who found marijuana in kitchen in plain view held justified in seizing marijuana from closet); *United States* v. *Truitt*, 521 F.2d 1174 (6th Cir. 1975) (seizure of sawed-off shotgun by police who discovered it while conducting a warrant-authorized search of a gun shop for gambling paraphernalia held valid under the plain view exception to the Fourth Amendment); *State* v. *Johnson*, 232 N.W.2d 477 (Iowa 1975) (police seizure of stolen T.V. and hi-fi after warrant-authorized entry of defendant's house to make arrest for robbery held valid as officers had a right to be where they were and the contraband was in plain view); *Smith* v. *State*, 365 A.2d 53 (Md. App. 1976) (police officers executing a warrant to search a suspect's home for motorcycle boots and bolt cutters held to have exceeded the scope of the warrant by seizing several construction tools, even though in plain view, because they had no reason to believe they were stolen); *People* v. *Allende*, 348 N.E.2d 416 (N.Y. Ct. App. 1976) (police officers who approached double-parked car with drawn guns, but without reasonable suspicion, held to have seized the vehicle, and officer's plain view observation of a gun after ordering occupant out was fatally tainted by the illegality of the initial seizure); *Application of Richard Martuzas*, 400 F. Supp. 1305 (S.D.N.Y. 1975) (in case in which policeman testified that while he was talking to speeder at rear of violator's auto and in front of police car,

he flashed his light into stopped vehicle and saw marijuana on floor, plain view doctrine held not to apply because only logical conclusion was that officer had to approach side of auto and flash his light in, and plain view demands that the officer be in a place where he has a valid reason to be, and since operator's papers were in order, officer had no right to make the flashlight search); *Pinkney* v. *United States,* ____ F.2d ____ (D.C. Cir. 1976) (police officers with the right to seize an auto driven by suspect whom they had a warrant to arrest may check car by looking inside it before releasing it to suspect's friend, and any objects falling in plain view may be seized). For an interesting case on jail mail and the plain view exception see *United States* v. *Baumgarten,* 517 F.2d 1020 (8th Cir. 1975), in which, pursuant to jail policy, a jailer opened a prisoner's letter written to him by the defendant, copied it, and made it available to the police who introduced the letter in evidence at defendant's trial for conspiracy. The court held that screening the letter was proper for security reasons, and the plain view doctrine justified the copying and dissemination of the letter).

C. "HOT PURSUIT" AND OTHER EMERGENCIES

The Demise of the "Mere Evidence" Rule

WARDEN, MARYLAND PENITENTIARY v. HAYDEN

Supreme Court of the United States, 1967
387 U.S. 294, 87 S. Ct. 1642, 18 L. Ed. 2d 782

Respondent Hayden was convicted of robbery in a Maryland court. After unsuccessful state court proceedings, he sought and was denied federal habeas corpus relief in the District Court for Maryland. However, the Court of Appeals (4th Cir.) reversed, and the State of Maryland was granted certiorari.
Additional facts are stated in the opinion.

Mr. Justice BRENNAN delivered the opinion of the Court.

* * *

About 8 A.M. on March 17, 1962, an armed robber entered the business premises of the Diamond Cab Company in Baltimore, Maryland. He took some $363 and ran. Two cab drivers in the vicinity, attracted by shouts of "holdup," followed the man to 2111 Cocoa Lane. One driver notified the company dispatcher by radio that the man was a Negro about 5' 8" tall, wearing a light cap and dark jacket, and that he had entered the house on Cocoa Lane. The dispatcher relayed the information to police who were proceeding to the scene of the robbery. Within minutes, police arrived at the house in a number of patrol cars. An officer knocked and announced their presence. Mrs. Hayden answered, and the officers told her they believed that a robber had entered the house, and asked to search the house. She offered no objection.

The officers spread out through the first and second floors and the cellar in search of the robber. Hayden was found in an upstairs bedroom feigning sleep. He was arrested when the officers on the first floor and in the cellar reported that no other man was in the house. Meanwhile, an officer was attracted to an adjoining bathroom by the noise of running water, and discovered a shotgun and a pistol in a flush tank; another officer, who, according to the District Court, "was searching the cellar for a man or the money" found in a washing machine a jacket and trousers of the type the fleeing man was said to have worn. A clip of ammunition for the pistol and a cap were found under the mattress of Hayden's bed, and ammunition for the shotgun was found in a bureau drawer in Hayden's room. All these items of evidence were introduced against respondent at his trial.

We agree with the Court of Appeals that neither the entry without warrant to search for the robber, nor the search for him without warrant was invalid. Under the circumstances of this case, "the exigencies of the situation made that course imperative." ... The police were informed that an armed robbery had taken place, and that the suspect had entered 2111 Cocoa Lane less than five minutes before they reached it. They acted reasonably when they entered the house and began to search for a man of the description they had been given and for weapons which he had used in the robbery or might use against them. The Fourth Amendment does not require police officers to delay in the course of an investigation if to do so would gravely endanger their lives or the lives of others. Speed here was essential, and only a thorough search of the house for persons and weapons could have insured that Hayden was the only man present and that the police had control of all weapons which could be used against them or to effect an escape.

We do not rely upon Harris v. United States, ... (1947), in sustaining the validity of the search. The principal issue in Harris was whether the search there could properly be regarded as incident to the lawful arrest, since Harris was in custody before the search was made and the evidence seized. Here, the seizures occurred prior to or immediately contemporaneous with Hayden's arrest, as part of an effort to find a suspected felon, armed, within the house into which he had run only minutes before the police arrived. The permissible scope of search must, therefore, at the least, be as broad as may reasonably be necessary to prevent the dangers that the suspect at large in the house may resist or escape.

It is argued that, while the weapons, ammunition, and cap may have been seized in the course of a search for weapons, the officer who seized the clothing was searching neither for the suspect nor for weapons when he looked into the washing machine in which he found the clothing. But even if we assume, although we do not decide, that the exigent circumstances in this case made lawful a search without warrant only for the suspect or his weapons, it cannot be said on this record that the officer who found the clothes in the washing machine was not searching for weapons. He testified that he was searching for the man or the money, but his failure to state explicitly that he was searching for weapons, in the absence of a specific question to that effect, can hardly be accorded controlling weight. He knew that the robber was armed and he did not know that some weapons had been found at the time he opened the machine. In those circumstances the inference that he was in fact also looking for weapons is fully justified.

We come, then, to the question whether, even though the search was lawful, the Court of Appeals was correct in holding that that seizure and introduction of the items of clothing violated the Fourth Amendment because they are "mere evidence." The distinction made by some of our cases between seizure of items of evidential value only and seizure of instrumentalities, fruits, or contraband has been criticized by courts and commentators. The Court of Appeals, however, felt "obligated to adhere to it." ... We today reject the distinction as based on premises no longer accepted as rules governing the application of the Fourth Amendment.

We have examined on many occasions the history and purposes of the Amendment. It was a reaction to the evils of the use of the general warrant in England and the writs of assistance in the Colonies, and was intended to protect against invasions of "the sanctity of a man's home and the privacies of life," Boyd v. United States, ... (1886), from searches under indiscriminate, general authority. Protection of these interests was assured by prohibiting all "unreasonable" searches and seizures, and by requiring the use of warrants, which particularly describe "the place to be searched, and the persons or things to be seized," thereby interposing "a magistrate between the citizen and the police." ...

Nothing in the language of the Fourth Amendment supports the distinction between "mere evidence" and instrumentalities, fruits of crime, or contraband. On its face, the provision assures the "right of the people to be secure in their persons, houses, papers and effects . . ." without regard to the use to which any of these things are applied. This "right of the people" is certainly unrelated to the "mere evidence" limitation. Privacy is disturbed no more by a search directed to a purely evidentiary object than it is by a search directed to an instrumentality, fruit, or contraband. A magistrate can intervene in both situations, and the requirements of probable cause and specificity can be preserved intact. Moreover, nothing in the nature of property seized as evidence renders it more private than property seized, for example, as an instrumentality; quite the opposite may be true. Indeed, the distinction is wholly irrational, since, depending on the circumstances, the same "papers and effects" may be "mere evidence" in one case and "instrumentality" in another. . . .

In Gouled v. United States, 255 U.S. 298 (1921), the Court said that search warrants "may not be used as a means of gaining access to a man's house or office and papers solely for the purpose of making search to secure evidence to be used against him in a criminal or penal proceeding. . . ." The Court derived from Boyd v. United States, supra, the proposition that warrants "may be resorted to only when a primary right to such search and seizure may be found in the interest which the public or the complainant may have in the property to be seized, or in the right to the possession of it, or when a valid exercise of the police power renders possession of the property by the accused unlawful and provides that it may be taken" . . . that is, when the property is an instrumentality or fruit of crime, or contraband. Since it was "impossible to say, on the record . . . that the Government had any interest" in the papers involved "other than

as evidence against the accused . . .," "to permit them to be used in evidence would be, in effect, as ruled in the Boyd case, to compel the defendant to become a witness against himself." . . .

The items of clothing involved in this case are not "testimonial" or "communicative" in nature, and their introduction therefore did not compel respondent to become a witness against himself in violation of the Fifth Amendment. . . . This case thus does not require that we consider whether there are items of evidential value whose very nature precludes them from being the object of a reasonable search and seizure.

* * *

. . . The requirements of the Fourth Amendment can secure the same protection of privacy whether the search is for "mere evidence" or for fruits, instrumentalities or contraband. There must, of course, be a nexus — automatically provided in the case of fruits, instrumentalities or contraband — between the item to be seized and criminal behavior. Thus in the case of "mere evidence," probable cause must be examined in terms of cause to believe that the evidence sought will aid in a particular conviction. In doing so, consideration of police purposes will be required. Cf. Kremen v. United States, 353 U.S. 346 (1957). But no such problem is presented in this case. The clothes found in the washing machine matched the description of those worn by the robber and the police therefore could reasonably believe that the items would aid in the identification of the culprit.

* * *

Reversed.

[Mr. Justice FORTAS, with whom Mr. Chief Justice BURGER joined, concurred.]

[Mr. Justice BLACK wrote a concurring opinion.]

[Mr. Justice DOUGLAS dissented.]

The Forcible Taking of the Defendant's Blood

SCHMERBER v. CALIFORNIA

Supreme Court of the United States, 1966
384 U.S. 757, 86 S. Ct. 1826, 16 L. Ed. 2d 908

Petitioner Schmerber was convicted by a Los Angeles municipal court of the criminal offense of driving an automobile while under the influence of intoxicating liquor and he appealed. The Appellate Department of the California Superior

Court affirmed and certiorari was granted. The record reveals that Schmerber was arrested at a hospital while receiving treatment for injuries suffered in an accident involving the auto he had apparently been driving. At the direction of police, and over the objection of the petitioner, a physician extracted a sample of Schmerber's blood. The results of the laboratory examination were later introduced at his trial. On certiorari, the petitioner contended, inter alia, that the withdrawal of the blood and the admission of the analysis in evidence violated his Fourth Amendment rights.

The Court's discussion of Schmerber's Fifth Amendment claim of self-incrimination and Sixth Amendment claim of right to counsel are presented in Chapter Six, § 6.03.

Mr. Justice BRENNAN delivered the opinion of the Court.

* * *

THE SEARCH AND SEIZURE CLAIM

. . . The question is squarely presented whether the chemical analysis introduced as evidence in this case should have been excluded as the product of an unconstitutional search and seizure. . . . It could not reasonably be argued, and indeed respondent does not argue, that the administration of the blood test in this case was free of the constraints of the Fourth Amendment. Such testing procedures plainly constitute searches of "persons" and depend antecedently upon seizures of "persons" within the meaning of that Amendment.

Because we are dealing with intrusions into the human body rather than with state interferences with property relationships or private papers — "houses, papers, and effects" — we write on a clean slate. Limitations on the kinds of property which may be seized under warrant, as distinct from the procedures for search and the permissible scope of search, are not instructive in this context. We begin with the assumption that once the privilege against self-incrimination has been found not to bar compelled intrusions into the body for blood to be analyzed for alcohol content, the Fourth Amendment's proper function is to constrain, not against all intrusions as such, but against intrusions which are not justified in the circumstances, or which are made in an improper manner. In other words, the questions we must decide in this case are whether the police were justified in requiring petitioner to submit to the blood test, and

whether the means and procedures employed in taking his blood respected relevant Fourth Amendment standards of reasonableness.

In this case, as will often be true when charges of driving under the influence of alcohol are pressed, these questions arise in the context of an arrest made by an officer without a warrant. Here, there was plainly probable cause for the officer to arrest petitioner and charge him with driving an automobile while under the influence of intoxicating liquor. The police officer who arrived at the scene shortly after the accident smelled liquor on petitioner's breath, and testified that petitioner's eyes were "blood-shot, watery, sort of a glassy appearance." The officer saw petitioner again at the hospital, within two hours of the accident. There he noticed similar symptoms of drunkenness. He thereupon informed petitioner "that he was under arrest and that he was entitled to the services of an attorney, and that he could remain silent, and that anything that he told me would be used against him in evidence."

* * *

Although the facts which established probable cause to arrest in this case also suggested the required relevance and likely success of a test of petitioner's blood for alcohol, the question remains whether the arresting officer was permitted to draw these inferences himself, or was required instead to procure a warrant before proceeding with the test. Search warrants are ordinarily required for searches of dwellings, and absent an emergency, no less could be required where intrusions into the human body are concerned. The requirement that a warrant be obtained is a requirement that inferences to support the search "be drawn by a neutral and detached magistrate instead of being judged by the officer engaged in the often competitive enterprise of ferreting out crime." . . . The importance of informed, detached and deliberate determinations of the issue whether or not to invade another's body in search of evidence of guilt is indisputable and great.

The officer in the present case, however, might reasonably have believed that he was confronted with an emergency, in which the delay necessary to obtain a warrant, under the circumstances, threatened "the destruction of evidence". . . . We are told that the percentage of alcohol in the blood begins to diminish shortly after drinking stops, as the body functions to eliminate it from the system. Particularly in a case such as this, where time had to be taken to bring the accused to a hospital and to investigate the scene of the accident, there was no time to seek out a magistrate and secure a warrant. Given these special facts, we conclude that the attempt to secure evidence of blood-alcohol content in this case was an appropriate incident to petitioner's arrest.

Similarly, we are satisfied that the test chosen to measure petitioner's blood-alcohol level was a reasonable one. Extraction of blood samples for testing is a highly effective means of determining the degree to which a person is under the influence of alcohol. . . . Such tests are a commonplace in these days of periodic physical examinations and experience with them teaches that the quantity of blood extracted is minimal, and that for most people the procedure involves virtually no risk, trauma, or pain. Petitioner is not one of the few who on grounds of fear, concern for health, or religious scruple might prefer some other means of testing, such as the "breathalyzer" test petitioner refused. . . . We need not decide whether such wishes would have to be respected.

Finally, the record shows that the test was performed in a reasonable manner. Petitioner's blood was taken by a physician in a hospital environment according to accepted medical practices. We are thus not presented with the serious questions which would arise if a search involving use of a medical technique, even of the most rudimentary sort, were made by other than medical personnel or in other than a medical environment—for example, if it were administered by police in the privacy of the stationhouse. To tolerate searches under these conditions might be to invite an unjustified element of personal risk of infection and pain.

We thus conclude that the present record shows no violation of petitioner's right under the Fourth and Fourteenth Amendments to be free of unreasonable searches and seizures. It bears repeating, however, that we reach this judgment only on the facts of the present record. The integrity of an individual's person is a cherished value of our society. That we today hold that the Constitution does not forbid the States minor intrusions into an individual's body under stringently limited conditions in no way indicates that it permits more substantial intrusions, or intrusions under other conditions.

Affirmed.

* * *

[Mr. Justice HARLAN, with whom Mr. Justice STEWART joined, concurred.]

MR. JUSTICE DOUGLAS, dissenting.

* * *

We are dealing with the right of privacy which, since the Breithaupt case, we have held to be within the penumbra of some specific guarantees of the Bill of Rights. Griswold v. State of Connecticut, 381 U.S. 479 (1965). The Fourth Amendment recognizes that right when it guarantees the right of the people to be secure "in their persons." No clearer invasion of this right of privacy can be imagined than forcible blood-letting of the kind involved here.

[Mr. Justice BLACK, with whom Mr. Justice DOUGLAS joined, dissented.]
[Mr. Justice FORTAS wrote a dissenting opinion.]

When the Suspect Retreats

UNITED STATES v. SANTANA

Supreme Court of the United States, 1976
427 U.S. 38, 96 S. Ct. 2406, 49 L. Ed. 2d 300

One Patricia McCafferty met an undercover agent for the purpose of selling the agent heroin. McCafferty got into the officer's car and directed him to respondent Santana's residence. McCafferty took marked money from the officer, went into the house, and returned with several envelopes containing a brownish white powder. The officer placed McCafferty under arrest, and asked where the money was. McCafferty indicated that Santana had it. Armed with that information, police officers returned to Santana's house, where she was standing in the doorway holding a paper bag. When the officers identified themselves, she retreated into the vestibule of her house, where she was caught. When she tried to escape, envelopes containing heroin fell to the floor, and she was found to have been carrying some of the marked money on her person. Respondent Alejandro, who had been sitting on the front steps, was caught when he tried to escape with the dropped envelopes of heroin. After their indictment for possessing heroin with intent to distribute, the respondents moved to suppress the evidence. The district court granted the motion, finding that although there was probable cause to make the arrest, Santana's retreat into the house did not justify a warrantless entry into the house on the ground of "hot pursuit." The Court of Appeals (3rd Cir.) affirmed without opinion and the Supreme Court granted certiorari.

Mr. Justice REHNQUIST delivered the opinion of the Court.

* * *

In United States v. Watson [supra, § 5.02], we held that the warrantless arrest of an individual in a public place upon probable cause did not violate the Fourth Amendment. Thus the first question we must decide is whether, when the police first sought to arrest Santana, she was in a public place.

While it may be true that under the common law of property the threshold of one's dwelling is "private," as is the yard surrounding the house, it is nonetheless clear that under the cases interpreting the Fourth Amendment Santana was in a "public" place. She was not in an area where she had any expectation of privacy. "What a person knowingly exposes to the public, even in his own house or office, is not a subject of Fourth Amendment protection." Katz v. United States [supra § 5.01]. She was not merely visible to the public but as exposed to public view, speech, hearing and touch as

if she had been standing completely outside her house. Hester v. United States, 265 U.S. 57, 59 (1924). Thus, when the police, who concededly had probable cause to do so, sought to arrest her, they merely intended to perform a function which we have approved in Watson.

The only remaining questions is whether her act of retreating into her house could thwart an otherwise proper arrest. We hold that it could not. In Warden v. Hayden [supra], we recognized the right of police, who had probable cause to believe that an armed robber had entered a house a few minutes before, to make a warrantless entry to arrest the robber and to search for weapons. This case, involving a true "hot pursuit," is clearly governed by Warden; the need to act quickly here is even greater than in that case while the intrusion is much less. The District Court was correct in concluding that "hot pursuit" means some sort of a chase, but it need not be an extended hue and cry "in and out (the) public streets." The fact that the pursuit here ended almost as soon as it began did not render it any less a "hot pursuit" sufficient to justify the warrantless entry into Santana's house. Once Santana saw the police, there was likewise a realistic expectation that any delay would result in destruction of evidence. . . . Once she had been arrested the search, incident to that arrest, which produced the drugs and money was clearly justified. . . .

We thus conclude that a suspect may not defeat an arrest which has been set in motion in a public place, and is therefore proper under Watson, by the expedient of escaping to a private place. . . .

Reversed.

Mr. Justice STEVENS, with whom Mr. Justice STEWART joins, concurring.

When Officer Gilletti placed McCafferty under arrest, the police had sufficient information to obtain a warrant for the arrest of Santana in her home. It is therefore important to note that their failure to obtain a warrant at that juncture was both (a) a justifiable police decision, and (b) even if not justifiable, harmless.

The decision was justified by the significant risk that the marked money would no longer be in Santana's possession if the police waited until a warrant could be obtained. The failure to seek a warrant was harmless, because it would have been proper to keep the Santana residence under surveillance while the warrant was being sought; since she ventured into plain view, a warrantless arrest would have been justified before the warrant could have been procured.

I therefore join the opinion of the Court.

[Mr. Justice WHITE wrote a separate concurring opinion.]

Mr. Justice MARSHALL, with whom Mr. Justice BRENNAN joins, dissenting.

Earlier this Term, I expressed the view that, in the absence of exigent circumstances, the police may not arrest a suspect without a warrant. United States v. Watson . . . [supra, § 5.02] (Marshall, J., dissenting). For this reason, I cannot join either the opinion of the Court or that of Mr. Justice White, each of which disregards whether exigency justified the police decision to approach Santana's home without a warrant for the purpose of arresting her. Nor can I accept Mr. Justice Stevens' approach, for while acknowledging that some notion of exigency must be asserted to justify the police conduct in this case, Mr. Justice Stevens fails to consider that the exigency present in this case was produced solely by police conduct. I would remand the case to allow the District Court to determine whether the police conduct was justifiable or was solely an attempt to circumvent the warrant requirement.

The Court declines today to settle the oft-reserved question of whether and under what circumstances a police officer may enter the home of a suspect in order to make a warrantless arrest. . . . Seizing upon the fortuity that Santana was standing in her doorway when the police approached her home for the purpose of entering and arresting her, the Court ignores Mr. Justice White's repeated advocacy of the common-law rule on warrantless entries and treats this case as a simple application of Watson.

It is somewhat more than that, for the Court takes the opportunity to refine the contours of that decision. Thus, if I correctly read the Court's citation to the "open fields" doctrine of Hester v. United States . . . , the Court holds that the police may enter upon private property to make warrantless arrests of persons who are in plain view and outdoors; and the Court applies that doctrine today to persons who are arguably within their homes but who are "as exposed" to the public as if they were outside. But the Court's encroachment upon the reserved question is limited. Thus, the Court's citation of Katz v. United States . . . does not suggest that a plain view of a suspect is alone sufficient to justify warrantless entry and seizure in the home. Indeed, the Court's rejection of sight alone as a basis for warrantless entry and arrest is made patent, in Mr. Justice Stewart's phrase, by negative implication from the Court's need to elaborate a hot pursuit justification for the police following Santana into her home. . . . Presumably, if plain view were the touchstone, Santana would have been just as liable to warrantless arrest as she retreated several feet inside her open door as she was when standing in the doorway.

The Court's doctrine, then, appears sui generis, useful only in arresting persons who are "as exposed to public view, speech, hearing and touch" . . . as though in the unprotected outdoors. Narrow though it may be, however, the Court's approach does not depend on whether exigency justifies an arrest on private property and thus I cannot join it.

Mr. Justice Stevens focuses on what I believe to be the right question in this case—whether there were exigent circumstances—and reaches an affirmative answer because he finds a "significant risk that the marked money would no longer be in Santana's possession if the police waited until a warrant could be obtained." . . .

I agree that there were exigent circumstances in this case. McCafferty was arrested a block and a half down the street from Santana's home. Although the arresting officers did not see anyone in Santana's home watching the arrest, one officer testified, "We were a block and a half from her home when the arrest was made. I am sure that the word would have been back within a matter of seconds or minutes." That is undoubtedly a reasonable conclusion to draw from the facts of the arrest; and the danger that the evidence would be destroyed and the suspects gone before a warrant could be obtained would ordinarily justify the police's quick return to Santana's home and the warrantless entry and arrest. If that is the basis of the "significant risk" to which Mr. Justice Stevens refers, I have no difference with him on that score.

I do not believe, however, that these exigent circumstances automatically validate Santana's arrest. The exigency that justified the entry and arrest was solely a product of police conduct. Had Officer Gilletti driven McCafferty to a more remote location before arresting her, it appears that no exigency would have been created by the arrest; in such an event a warrant would have been necessary in my view, before Santana could have been arrested. United States v. Watson . . . (Marshall, J., dissenting). . . . While a police decision that the time is right to arrest a suspect should properly be given great deference . . . the power to arrest is an awesome one and is subject to abuse. An arrest may permit a search of premises incident to the arrest; a search that otherwise could be carried out only upon probable cause and pursuant to a search warrant. Likewise, an arrest in circumstances such as those presented here may create exigency that may justify a search or another arrest. When an arrest is so timed that it is no more than an attempt to circumvent the warrant requirement, I would hold the subsequent arrest or search unlawful. . . . Accordingly, I would remand this case for consideration of whether the police decision to arrest McCafferty a block and a half from Santana's home was for the sole purpose of creating the exigent circumstances that otherwise would justify Santana's subsequent arrest.

Comments

1. The majority in *Hayden* reaffirmed the basic concept that police may make a lawful entry into a premises without the aid of a warrant when the entry is made in response to an emergency. Although the law recognizes the necessity for speed when emergency situations arise, the mere fact that the initial entry is lawful will not justify a subsequent search of the premises absent a showing of "compelling reasons" and "exceptional circumstances." See *Johnson* v. *United States*, 333 U.S. at 13, 14 (1948); *McDonald* v. *United States*, 335 U.S. at 454, 455 (1948). In *Hayden*, the Court concluded that "only a thorough search of the house for weapons and for persons" could have assured the police that Hayden was the only person present and that they had all weapons under control. Hence, "compelling reasons" and "exceptional circumstances" were found to exist.

   Convinced that the officers had probable cause for the entry and search, the *Hayden* Court also proceeded to outline the broad scope considered reasonable for searches in "hot pursuit" situations. It should be remembered, however, that the *Hayden* scope must be read as that which is permissible *prior* to the apprehension of a suspect. The scope *after* arrest is restricted to a very limited area. See, e.g., *Chimel* v. *California,* supra.

Hayden objected to the seizure of what he termed "mere evidence." To support his claim he relied primarily on *Gouled* v. *United States,* 255 U.S. 298 (1921). The *Gouled* case rested upon the premise that the government may seize only evidence that is "connected" to the crime, i.e., fruits of the crime, contraband, or instrumentalities. However, the Court in *Hayden* concluded that if evidence will somehow aid in identifying or otherwise connecting the suspect with the crime it may be lawfully seized. In rejecting the so-called "mere evidence" rule found in *Gouled,* the Court emphasized four points:

a. Nothing in the language of the Fourth Amendment supports a distinction between "mere evidence" on the one hand and contraband, fruits, or instrumentalities on the other.

b. Hayden's "property interest" in the items selected was not relevant because under the Fourth Amendment privacy, not property, is protected.

c. Privacy is disturbed no more by a search for evidentiary material than for other items.

d. The distinction between "mere evidence" and the other traditional types of physical evidence is an illogical one which has spawned numerous exceptions and great confusion.

Must there be probable cause to believe that an item to be seized is criminal evidence before the *Hayden* "nexus" requirement is met?

2. The majority in *Schmerber* relied heavily on the 1948 case of *Johnson* v. *United States,* 333 U.S. 10. The Court in *Johnson* noted at 13, 14; "There are *exceptional circumstances* in which, on balancing the need for effective law enforcement against the right of privacy, it may be contended that a ... warrant for search may be dispensed with. For example ... [when] contraband [is] threatened with removal or destruction. . . ." (Emphasis added.) In the same year, the Court reiterated the rule in *McDonald* v. *United States,* 335 U.S. 451, in which, in contrast to *Johnson,* the Court could find no exceptional circumstances from the record and therefore concluded that the warrantless search had been improper. Although both 1948 cases involved searches of premises rather than invasions of the body, the Court nevertheless had no problems in applying the "exceptional circumstances" rule to the fact situation in *Schmerber.* Essentially, the *Schmerber* Court reasoned that (1) the officer might reasonably have believed that he was confronted with an emergency in which delay in obtaining a warrant threatened the destruction of evidence since the level of alcohol in the blood begins to diminish after drinking stops as the body eliminates it from the system; and (2) the search was reasonable because the test used to measure the blood-alcohol level was a reasonable one, and the test was performed by a physician in a hospital environment according to accepted medical practices.

3. Although the majority in *Santana* did not dispute the existence of the common law property concept of "curtilage," it is clear that exposing one's self to "public view," even while still on private property, serves to eliminate any expectation of privacy upon which one might justifiably rely. Hence, for purposes of arrest, an officer

with probable cause may enter on private property when the subject of the arrest is "visible" or "exposed to public view." Would the result have been different if Santana had retreated into the house *prior* to the police officer's arrival? Or, could the Court simply have utilized the argument made by justices Stevens and Stewart to justify the warrantless entry, i.e., the entry was justified as a proper "police decision" because (1) probable cause existed for Santana's arrest, and (2) a significant risk existed that the marked money would be destroyed? If the entry and arrest could be justified solely by a showing of exigency, would Justice Marshall's objection that the emergency was in fact a "police-initiated" one have had more force?

4. Regarding *Santana*, it is interesting to note that although the district court did find that the police acted under an "extreme emergency" condition, the facts in the case do not show a "true" or "pure" hot pursuit situation, i.e., "a chase on and about public streets." Apparently the Court of Appeal's (3rd Cir.) interpretation of the facts was the same, since it affirmed the lower court's decision. However, the Supreme Court, citing *Warden* v. *Hayden* (infra), concluded that although the "pursuit here ended almost as soon as it began," it did not render the situation any less of a hot pursuit for purposes of justifying the warrantless entry.

5. The following recent decisions by lower federal and state courts involved hot pursuit, warrantless entry, and other emergencies: *People* v. *Etcheverry*, 347 N.E.2d 654 (N.Y. Ct. App. 1976) (warrantless police search of dresser and closet in house where an armed fugitive was believed to be upheld under *Warden* v. *Hayden*); *United States* v. *Bishop*, 530 F.2d 1156 (5th Cir. 1976) (local plice officers who utilized electronic "beeper" in robbed bank's "bait" money to trail robbers were in hot pursuit for purposes of Louisiana statute that allows officers in such pursuit to make arrests outside their jurisdiction); *Edwards* v. *United States*, ____ F.2d ____ (D.C. Cir. 1976) (police officers with articulable suspicion that two men walking through a residential area during the early hours of the morning were carrying stolen goods held justified in following the men into an apartment after they fled); *United States* v. *Scott*, 520 F.2d 697 (9th Cir. 1975) (police were justified in making warrantless entry and search of defendant's apartment during pursuit that began ten minutes after robbery when they had probable cause to believe armed suspects were inside the apartment); *United States* v. *Flores*, 540 F.2d 432 (9th Cir. 1976) (federal agents' compliance with federal "knock and announce" statute, 18 U.S.C. § 3109, does not strip agents' warrantless entry of house occupied by retreating drug suspects of its hot pursuit quality); *Young* v. *Superior Court*, 129 Cal. Rptr. 422 (Cal. Ct. App. 1976) (police officers who obtained permission to enter mobile home from one of the residents were required to comply with California's "knock and announce" statute before opening a bathroom door to arrest two bad check suspects, as statute applies to both inner and outer doors of a house); *State* v. *Anaya*, 551 P.2d 992 (N.M. Ct. App. 1976) (police officer who prior to execution of search warrant crawled beneath a house trailer and sawed through the sewer pipe and then later recovered two packets of heroin after the warrant had been executed, held to have acted reasonably in not knocking and announcing prior to crawling under trailer); *United States* v. *Fluker*, 543 F.2d 709 (9th

Cir. 1976) (federal statute, 18 U.S.C. § 3109, requiring officer to knock and announce prior to entry applies to privately controlled outer doorway which leads inside an apartment building to defendant's unit); *Bell* v. *State,* 330 N.E.2d 752 (Ind. 1975) (police entry through open door without knocking held valid because officers had identified themselves before entering and announced that they had a warrant to search the house); *United States* v. *Smith,* 520 F.2d 74 (D.C. Cir. 1975) (in case in which, after knocking and stating "police officers, we have a search warrant," officers broke open door when it was not opened by occupant after a 30-second wait, court held that an officer executing a search warrant may forcibly enter only if he is denied admittance after giving notice of his authority and purpose, but case was remanded for determination of the issue of refusal of admittance); *United States* v. *Hickman,* 523 F.2d 323 (9th Cir. 1975) (warrantless search of boat by customs agents upheld where the possibility of movement and need for information provided exigent circumstances); *People* v. *Mitchell,* 347 N.E.2d 607 (N.Y. Ct. App. 1976) ("emergency search" exception to warrant requirement requires a finding that police had reasonable belief that an emergency existed, that there was a need to protect life or property, that the primary police motive was not to arrest or seize evidence, and that police had reason approximating probable cause to associate the emergency with place to be searched); *State* v. *Mankel,* 555 P.2d 1124 (Ariz. Ct. App. 1976) (police officers who entered a house to investigate a suspected burglary and thereby gained probable cause to believe that the occupant was a major drug dealer held not justified in conducting immediate warrantless search of house despite the officers' inability to contact a magistrate); *United States* v. *Phifer,* 400 F. Supp. 719 (E.D. Pa. 1975) (exigent circumstances justified the warrantless search of an airplane stopped on public airport with access to runway ramps since confederates might have been alerted by plane radio to come and remove the plane and its contraband); *United States* v. *McLaughlin,* 525 F.2d 517 (9th Cir. 1975) (where federal agents have probable cause to arrest defendant and co-defendant is arrested outside defendant's home, it is not unreasonable for agents to make warrantless entry of home to arrest defendant and prevent destruction of evidence); *State* v. *Lasley,* 236 N.W.2d 604 (Minn. 1975) (warrantless entry of suspect's house was justified where police officers were searching for robbery-murder suspect and he had been identified earlier as the "probable killer"); *People* v. *Ramey,* 545 P.2d 1333 (Cal. 1976) (absent exigent circumstances, a warrantless entry of suspect's home to arrest held violative of Fourth Amendment and California constitution); *Sheff* v. *State,* 329 So. 2d 270 (Fla. 1976) (evidence seized from motel room following illegal entry held admissible where arrest was predicated upon evidence independent of the illegal entry); *United States* v. *Murrie,* 534 F.2d 695 (6th Cir. 1976) (upon defendant's allegation that federal agents suddenly and unannounced broke into his dwelling in violation of 18 U.S.C. § 3109, which requires prior announcement, the burden shifts to the prosecution to prove that the federal statute was complied with); *United States* v. *Guidry,* 534 F.2d 1220 (6th Cir. 1976) (exigent circumstances justified warrantless entry of house known to conceal counterfeit operation after undercover agent's cover had been blown and carport adjoining residence had been set on fire 15 minutes earlier since entry was necessary to prevent destruction of counterfeit money) (accord,

United States v. *Rubin*, 474 F.2d 262 [3rd Cir. 1973], *United States* v. *Blake*, 484 F.2d 50 [8th Cir. 1973], *Thomas* v. *Parett*, 524 F.2d 779 [8th Cir. 1975], *United States* v. *Rosselli*, 506 F.2d 627 [7th Cir. 1974]); *People* v. *Vaccaro*, 348 N.E.2d 886 (N.Y. Ct. App. 1976) (informer's warning that a shipment of illegal guns cached at restaurant was rapidly being depleted and that the dealer was fearful of police intervention held to justify immediate raid by police without a warrant); *State* v. *Fenske*, 244 N.W.2d 743 (Minn. 1976) (police officers violated Fourth Amendment when, in checking on mother's belief that her 14-year-old daughter might be with a man rumored to be furnishing marijuana to teenaged girls, they walked into the man's apartment and seized marijuana); *Brooks* v. *United States*, ___ F.2d ___ (D.C. Cir. 1976) (police officers responding to a woman's complaint that she had been taken to a certain apartment and raped held justified in entering the apartment without a warrant in order to arrest the suspect) (see also *Dunston* v. *United States*, 315 A.2d 563 [D.C. Ct. App. 1974], *Dorman* v. *United States*, 435 F.2d 385 [D.C. Cir. 1970], and *United States* v. *Lindsay*, 306 F.2d 166 [1974]); *People* v. *Bracamonte*, 540 P.2d 624 (Cal. 1975) (where police used their warrant authorizing a search of defendant's person to have a physician pump her stomach and recover several swallowed balloons of heroin, warrant was ineffective to justify search beyond the body's surface, and further, search was not proper incident to arrest under *Schmerber* because there was no danger that the evidence might be quickly destroyed); *State* v. *Gordon*, 549 P.2d 886 (Kan. 1976) (blood sample taken by physician who was deputy coroner from driver in fatal accident before police arrived at hospital held illegal search since the driver was not under arrest or in custody and physician was acting as an agent of the state); *People* v. *Morse*, 242 N.W.2nd 47 (Mich. App. 1976) (police officer's directing hospital personnel to take blood sample from unconscious driver involved in fatal accident held not unreasonable even absent a formal arrest) (accord, *Filmon* v. *State*, 336 S. 2d 586 [Fla. 1976]); *United States* v. *Crowder*, 543 F.2d 312 (D.C. Cir. 1976) (court-ordered removal of .32 slug from underneath the skin of a murder suspect's arm for purpose of ballistics comparison with slugs in victim's body held reasonable since defendant was afforded an adversary hearing on the question of the minor surgery and because police had probable cause to believe the defendant was the killer).

D. AUTOMOBILE SEARCHES: REAFFIRMATION OF THE *CARROLL* DOCTRINE

The Constitutional Difference Between Houses and Automobiles

CHAMBERS v. MARONEY

Supreme Court of the United States, 1970
399 U.S. 42, 90 S. Ct. 1975, 26 L. Ed. 2d 419

Petitioner Chambers was convicted of two armed robberies in a Pennsylvania state court. Chambers did not take a direct appeal, but later sought habeas corpus relief through the state court system. Unsuccessful in the state courts, he

then sought a writ of habeas corpus in the United States District Court for the Western District of Pennsylvania. The District Court denied the petition without a hearing and the Court of Appeals (3rd Cir.) affirmed. The United States Supreme Court granted certiorari.

Additional facts are stated in the opinion.

Mr. Justice WHITE delivered the opinion of the Court.

The principal question in this case concerns the admissibility of evidence seized from an automobile, in which petitioner was riding at the time of his arrest, after the automobile was taken to a police station and was there thoroughly searched without a warrant. The Court of Appeals for the the Third Circuit found no violation of petitioner's Fourth Amendment rights. We affirm.

During the night of May 20, 1963, a Gulf service station in North Braddock, Pennsylvania, was robbed by two men, each of whom carried and displayed a gun. The robbers took the currency from the cash register; the service station attendant, one Stephen Kovacich, was directed to place the coins in his right-hand glove, which was then taken by the robbers. Two teen-agers, who had earlier noticed a blue compact station wagon circling the block in the vicinity of the Gulf station, then saw the station wagon speed away from a parking lot close to the Gulf station. About that time they learned that the Gulf station had been robbed. They reported to police, who arrived immediately, that four men were in the station wagon and one was wearing a green sweater. Kovacich told the police that one of the men who robbed him was wearing a green sweater and the other was wearing a trench coat. A description of the car and the two robbers was broadcast over the police radio. Within an hour, a light blue compact station wagon answering the description and carrying four men was stopped by the police about two miles from the Gulf station. Petitioner was one of the men in the station wagon. He was wearing a green sweater and there was a trench coat in the car. The occupants were arrested and the car was driven to the police station. In the course of a thorough search of the car at the station, the police found concealed in a compartment under the dashboard two .38-caliber revolvers (one loaded with dumdum bullets), a right-hand glove containing small change, and certain cards bearing the name of Raymond Havicon, the attendant at a Boron service station in McKeesport, Pennsylvania, who had been robbed at gunpoint on May, 13, 1963. In the course of a warrant-authorized search of petitioner's home the day after petitioner's arrest, police found and seized certain .38-caliber ammunition, including some dumdum bullets similar to those found in one of the guns taken from the station wagon.

Petitioner was indicted for both robberies. His first trial ended in a mistrial but he was convicted of both robberies at the second trial. . . . The materials taken from the station wagon were introduced into evidence. . . . We pass over quickly the claim that the search of the automobile was the fruit of an unlawful arrest. Both the courts below thought the arresting officers had probable cause to make the arrest. We agree. Having talked to the teen-age observers and to the victim Kovacich, the police had ample cause to stop a light blue compact station wagon carrying four men and to arrest the occupants, one of whom was wearing a green sweater and one of whom had a trench coat with him in the car.

Even so, the search that produced the incriminating evidence was made at the police station some time after the arrest and cannot be justified as a search incident to an arrest: "Once an accused is under arrest and in custody, then a search made at another place, without a warrant, is simply not incident to the arrest." . . .

There are, however, alternative grounds arguably justifying the search of the car in this case. . . . Here . . . the police had probable cause to believe that the robbers, carrying guns and the fruits of the crime, had fled the scene in a light blue compact station wagon which would be carrying four men, one wearing a green sweater and another wearing a trench coat. As the state courts correctly held, there was probable cause to arrest the occupants of the station wagon that the officers stopped; just as obviously was there probable cause to search the car for guns and stolen money.

In terms of the circumstances justifying a warrantless search, the Court has long distinguished between an automobile and a home or office. In Carroll v. United States, . . . (1925), the issue was the admissibility in evidence of contraband liquor seized in a warrantless search of a car on the highway. After surveying the law from the time of the adoption of the Fourth Amendment onward, the Court held that automobiles and other conveyances may be searched without a warrant in circumstances that would not justify the search without a warrant of a house or an office, provided that there is probable cause to believe that the car contains articles that the officers are entitled to seize. The Court expressed its holding as follows:

"We have made a somewhat extended reference to these statutes to show that the guaranty of freedom from unreasonable searches and seizures by the Fourth Amendment has been construed, practically since the beginning of the government, as recognizing a necessary difference between a search of a store, dwelling house, or other structure in respect of which a proper official warrant readily may be obtained and a search of a ship, motor boat, wagon, or automobile for contraband goods, where it is not practicable to secure a warrant, because the vehicle can be quickly moved out of the locality or jurisdiction in which the warrant must be sought.

"Having thus established that contraband goods concealed and illegally transported in an automobile or other vehicle may be searched for without a warrant, we come now to consider under what circumstances such search may be made. . . . [T]hose lawfully within the country, entitled to use the public highways, have a right to free passage without interruption or search unless there is known to a competent official, authorized to search, probable cause for believing that their vehicles are carrying contraband or illegal merchandise. . . .

* * *

"The measure of legality of such a seizure is, therefore, that the seizing officer shall have reasonable or probable cause for believing that the automobile which he stops and seizes has contraband liquor therein which is being illegally transported." . . .

The Court also noted that the search of an auto on probable cause proceeds on a theory wholly different from that justifying the search incident to an arrest:

"The right to search and the validity of the seizure are not dependent on the right to arrest. They are dependent on the reasonable cause the seizing officer has for belief that the contents of the automobile offend against the law." . . .

* * *

Neither Carroll . . . nor other cases in this Court require or suggest that in every conceivable circumstance the search of an auto even with probable cause may be made without the extra protection for privacy that a warrant affords. But the circumstances that furnish probable cause to search a particular auto for particular articles are most often unforeseeable; moreover, the opportunity to search is fleeting since a car is readily movable. Where this is true, as in Carroll and the case before us now, if an effective search is to be made at any time, either the search must be made immediately without a warrant or the car itself must be seized and held without a warrant for whatever period is necessary to obtain a warrant for the search.

In enforcing the Fourth Amendment's prohibition against unreasonable searches and seizures, the Court has insisted upon probable cause as a minimum requirement for a reasonable search permitted by the Constitution. As a general rule, it has also required the judgment of a magistrate on the probable-cause issue and the issuance of a warrant before a search is made. Only in exigent circumstances will the judgment of the police as to probable cause serve as a sufficient authorization for a search. Carroll holds a search warrant unnecessary where there is probable cause to search an automobile stopped on the highway; the car is movable, the occupants are alerted, and the car's contents may never be found again if a warrant must be obtained. Hence an immediate search is constitutionally permissible.

Arguably, because of the preference for a magistrate's judgment, only the immobilization of the car should be permitted until a search warrant is obtained; arguably, only the "lesser" intrusion is permissible until the magistrate authorizes the "greater." But which is the "greater" and which the "lesser" intrusion is itself a debatable question and the answer may depend on a variety of circumstances. For constitutional purposes, we see no difference between on the one hand seizing and holding a car before presenting the probable cause issue to a magistrate and on the other hand carrying out an immediate search without a warrant. Given probable cause to search, either course is reasonable under the Fourth Amendment.

On the facts before us, the blue station wagon could have been searched on the spot when it was stopped since there was probable cause to search and it was a fleeting target for a search. The probable-cause factor still obtained at the station house and so did the mobility of the car unless the Fourth Amendment permits a warrantless seizure of the car and the denial of its use to anyone until a warrant is secured. In that event there is little to choose in terms of practical consequences between an immediate search without a warrant and the car's immobilization until a warrant is obtained.[j] The same consequences may not follow where there is unforeseeable cause to search a house. . . . But as Carroll held, for the purposes of the Fourth Amendment there is a constitutional difference between houses and cars.

* * *

[Mr. Justice STEWART wrote a concurring opinion.]

[Mr. Justice HARLAN concurred in part and dissented in part.]

[Mr. Justice BLACKMUN took no part in the consideration or decision of this case.]

---

[j] It was not unreasonable in this case to take the car to the station house. All occupants in the car were arrested in a dark parking lot in the middle of the night. A careful search at that point was impractical and perhaps not safe for the officers, and it would serve the owner's convenience and the safety of his car to have the vehicle and the keys together at the station house.

Public Parking Lots, the Exterior of an Automobile, and the Right to Privacy

CARDWELL v. LEWIS

Supreme Court of the United States, 1974
417 U.S. 583, 94 S. Ct. 2464, 41 L. Ed. 2d 325

In July, 1967, police interviewed respondent Lewis in connection with a murder and viewed his auto, which was believed to have been used in the commission of the crime. On October 10, respondent appeared at the police station for questioning in response to the request of the police. Lewis drove to the station house and left his vehicle in a nearby parking lot. Although the police already had an arrest warrant, the respondent was not arrested until late in the afternoon of October 10. Following the arrest, police towed his car to an impoundment lot. On October 11, a technician from the Ohio Bureau of Criminal Investigation examined the auto and found that the tread of its right rear tire matched the cast of a tire impression made at the scene of the crime. In addition, paint samples taken from respondent's car were found to be similar to foreign paint taken from the murder victim's car. Evidence taken on October 11 was introduced at respondent's trial for murder. Lewis was convicted and the Ohio State courts affirmed on appeal. The federal district court, on a habeas application, reversed respondent's conviction, finding that the examination of his auto violated his Fourth and Fourteenth Amendment rights. The Court of Appeals (6th Cir.) affirmed, and the State of Ohio successfully sought certiorari.

Mr. Justice BLACKMUN delivered the opinion of the Court.

* * *

This case is factually different from prior car search cases decided by this Court. The evidence with which we are concerned is not the product of a "search" that implicates traditional considerations of the owner's privacy interest. It consisted of paint scrapings from the *exterior* and an observation of the tread of a tire on an operative wheel. The issue, therefore, is whether the examination of an automobile's exterior upon probable cause invades a right to privacy which the interposition of a warrant requirement is meant to protect. This is an issue this Court has not previously addressed.

* * *

At least since Carroll v. United States, . . . (1925), the Court has recognized a distinction between the warrantless search and seizure of automobiles or other movable vehicles, on the one hand, and the search of a home or office on the other hand. Generally, less stringent warrant requirements have been applied to vehicles. In Chambers v. Maroney, . . . (1970), the Court chronicled the development of car searches and seizures. An underlying factor in the Carroll-Chambers line of decisions has been the exigent circumstances that exist in connection with movable vehicles. "[T]he circumstances that furnish probable cause to search a particular auto for particular articles are most often unforeseeable; moreover, the opportunity to search is fleeting since the car is readily movable." Chambers v. Maroney. . . . This is strikingly true where the automobile's owner is alerted to police intentions and, as a consequence, the motivation to remove evidence from official grasp is heightened.

There is still another distinguishing factor. "The search of an automobile is far less intrusive on the rights protected by the Fourth Amendment than the search of one's person or of a building." . . . One has a lesser expectation of privacy in a motor vehicle because its function is transportation and it seldom serves as one's residence or as the repository of personal effects. A car has little capacity for escaping public

scrutiny. It travels public thoroughfares where both its occupants and its contents are in plain view. . . . "What a person knowingly exposes to the public, even in his own home or office, is not a subject of Fourth Amendment protection." . . . This is not to say that no part of the interior of an automobile has Fourth Amendment protection; the exercise of a desire to be mobile does not, of course, waive one's right to be free of unreasonable government intrusion. But insofar as Fourth Amendment protection extends to a motor vehicle, it is the right to privacy that is the touchstone of our inquiry.

In the present case, nothing from the interior of the car and no personal effects, which the Fourth Amendment traditionally has been deemed to protect, were searched or seized and introduced in evidence. With the "search" limited to the examination of the tire on the wheel and the taking of paint scrapings from the exterior of the vehicle left in the public parking lot, we fail to comprehend what expectation of privacy was infringed. Stated simply, the invasion of privacy, "if it can be said to exist, is abstract and theoretical." . . . Under circumstances such as these, where probable cause exists, a warrantless examination of the exterior of a car is not unreasonable under the Fourth and Fourteenth Amendments.

* * *

Concluding, as we have, that the examination of the exterior of the vehicle upon probable cause was reasonable, we have yet to determine whether the prior impoundment of the automobile rendered that examination a violation of the Fourth and Fourteeth Amendments. We do not think that, because the police impounded the car prior to the examination, which they could have made on the spot, there is a constitutional barrier to the use of the evidence obtained thereby. Under the circumstances of this case, the seizure itself was not unreasonable.

Respondent asserts that this case is indistinguishable from Coolidge v. New Hampshire. . . . We do not agree. The present case differs from Coolidge both in the scope of the search and in the circumstances of the seizure. Since the Coolidge car was parked on the defendant's driveway, the seizure of that automobile required an entry upon private property. Here, as in Chambers v. Maroney ... the automobile was seized from a public place where access was not meaningfully restricted.

* * *

The fact that the car in Chambers was seized after being stopped on a highway, whereas Lewis' car was seized from a public parking lot, has little, if any legal significance. The same arguments and considerations of exigency, immobilization on the spot, and posting a guard obtain. In fact, because the interrogation session ended with awareness that Lewis had been arrested and that his car constituted incriminating evidence, the incentive and potential for the car's removal substantially increased. There was testimony at the federal hearing that Lewis asked one of his attorneys to see that his wife and family got the car, and that the attorney relinquished the keys to the police in order to avoid a physical confrontation. . . . In Chambers, all occupants of the car were in custody and there was no means of relating this fact or the location of the car (if it had not been impounded) to a friend or confederate. Chambers also stated that a search of the car on the spot was impractical because it was dark and the search could not be carefully executed. . . . Here too, the seizure facilitated the type of close examination necessary.

Repondent contends that here, unlike Chambers, probable cause to search the car existed for some time prior to arrest and that, therefore, there were no exigent circumstances. Assuming that probable cause previously existed, we know of no case or principle that suggests that the right to search on probable cause and the reasonableness of seizing a car under exigent circumstances are foreclosed if a warrant was not obtained at the first practicable moment. Exigent circumstances with regard to vehicles are not limited to situations where probable cause is unforeseeable, and arises only at the time of arrest. . . . The exigency may arise at any time, and the fact that the police might have obtained a warrant earlier does not negate the possibility of a current situation's necessitating prompt police action.

The judgment of the Court of Appeals is reversed.

[Mr. Justice POWELL wrote a concurring opinion.]

Mr. Justice STEWART, with whom Mr. Justice DOUGLAS, Mr. Justice BRENNAN and Mr. Justice MARSHALL join, dissenting.

The most fundamental rule in this area of constitutional law is that "Searches conducted outside the judicial process, without prior approval by judge or magistrate, are per se unreasonable under the Fourth Amendment—subject only to a few specifically established and well-delineated exceptions." . . . Since there was no warrant authorizing the search and seizure in this case, and since none of the "specifically established and delineated exceptions" to the warrant requirement here existed, I am convinced the judgment of the Court of Appeals must be affirmed.

In casting about for some way to avoid the impact of our previous decisions, the plurality opinion first suggests . . . that no "search" really took place in this case, since all that the police did was to scrape paint from the respondent's car and make observations of its tires. Whatever merit this argument might possess in the abstract, it is irrelevant in the circumstances disclosed by this record. The argument is irrelevant for the simple reason that the police, before taking the paint scrapings and looking at the tires, first took possession of the car itself. The Fourth and Fourteenth Amendments protect against "unreasonable searches and *seizures*," and there most assuredly was a seizure here.

The plurality opinion next seems to suggest that the basic constitutional rule can be overlooked in this case because the subject of the seizure was an automobile. It is true, of course, that a line of decisions, beginning with Carroll v. United States . . . have recognized a so-called "automobile exception" to the constitutional requirement of a warrant. But "(t)he word 'automobile' is not a talisman in whose presence the Fourth Amendment fades away and disappears." . . . Rather, the Carroll doctrine simply recognizes the obvious—that a *moving* automobile on the open road presents a situation "where it is not practicable to secure a warrant because the vehicle can be quickly moved out of the locality or jurisdiction in

which the warrant must be sought." ...
Where there is no reasonable likelihood that
the automobile would or could be moved,
the Carroll doctrine is simply inapplicable.
...

The facts of this case make clear beyond
peradventure that the "automobile exception" is not available to uphold the warrantless seizure of the respondent's car. Well
before the time that the automobile was
seized, the respondent—and the keys to his
car—were securely within police custody.
There was thus absolutely no likelihood that
the respondent could have either moved the
car or meddled with it during the time necessary to obtain a search warrant. And there
was no realistic possibility that anyone else
was in a position to do so either. I am at a
loss, therefore, to understand the plurality
opinion's conclusion ... that there was a "potential for the car's removal" during the
period immediately preceding the car's seizure. The facts of record can only support a
diametrically opposite conclusion.

Finally, the plurality opinion suggests that
other "exigent circumstances" might have
excused the failure of the police to procure
a warrant. The opinion nowhere states what
these mystical exigencies might have been,
and counsel for the petitioner has not been
so inventive as to suggest any. Since the
authorities had taken care to procure an arrest warrant even before the respondent arrived for questioning, it can scarcely be said
that probable cause was not discovered until
so late a point in time as to prevent the obtaining of a warrant for seizure of the automobile. And, with the automobile effectively immobilized during the period of the
respondent's interrogation, the fear that evidence might be destroyed was hardly an exigency, particularly when it is remembered
that no such fear prompted a seizure during
all the preceding months while the defendant, though under investigation, had been in
full control of the car. This is, quite simply,
a case where no exigent circumstances existed.

Until today it has been clear that "(n)ei-
ther Carroll ... nor other cases in this Court
require or suggest that in every conceivable
circumstance the search of an auto even
with probable cause may be made without
the extra protection of privacy that a warrant affords." ... I would follow the settled
constitutional law established in our decisions and affirm the judgment of the Court
of Appeals.

Auto Inventory Searches

SOUTH DAKOTA v. OPPERMAN

Supreme Court of the United States, 1976
428 U.S. 364, 96 S. Ct. 3092, 49 L. Ed. 2d 1000

**On December 10, 1973, Donald Opperman's auto was impounded by Vermillion
police officers for multiple parking violations. At the impoundment lot, a police
officer observed from outside the car certain items of personal property located
on the dashboard, back seat, and back floorboard. Following standard procedures, the police inventoried the contents of the auto. In doing so, they discovered
marijuana in the unlocked glove compartment. Respondent was subsequently arrested for possession of marijuana. His motion to suppress the evidence yielded by
the inventory search was denied; he was convicted after a jury trial, fined $100,
and incarcerated in the county jail for 14 days. The South Dakota Supreme Court
reversed on appeal, concluding that the evidence had been obtained in violation of
the Fourth and Fourteenth Amendments. The United States Supreme Court
granted certiorari.**

Mr. Chief Justice BURGER delivered the opinion of the court.

We review the judgment of the Supreme Court of South Dakota, holding that local police violated the Fourth Amendment to the Federal Constitution as applicable to the States under the Fourteenth Amendment, when they conducted a routine inventory search of an automobile lawfully impounded by police for violations of municipal parking ordinances.

* * *

II

This Court has traditionally drawn a distinction between automobiles and homes or offices in relation to the Fourth Amendment. Although automobiles are "effects" and thus within the reach of the Fourth Amendment, Cady v. Dombrowski, 413 U.S. 433, 439 (1973), warrantless examinations of automobiles have been upheld in circumstances in which a search of a home or office would not. . . .

The reason for this well-settled distinction is twofold. First, the inherent mobility of automobiles creates circumstances of such exigency that, as a practical necessity, rigorous enforcement of the warrant requirement is impossible. . . . But the Court has also upheld warrantless searches where no immediate danger was presented that the car would be removed from the jurisdiction. . . . Besides the element of mobility, less rigorous warrant requirments govern because the expectation of privacy with respect to one's automobile is significantly less than that relating to one's home or office. In discharging their varied responsibilities for ensuring the public safety, law enforcement officials are necessarily brought into frequent contact with automobiles. Most of this contact is distinctly noncriminal in nature. . . . Automobiles, unlike homes, are subjected to pervasive and continuing governmental regulation and controls, including periodic inspection and licensing requirements. As an everyday occurrence, police stop and examine vehicles when license plates or inspections stickers have expired, or if other violations, such as exhaust fumes or excessive noise, are noted, or if headlights or other safety equipment are not in proper working order.

The expectation of privacy as to autos is further diminished by the obviously public nature of automobile travel. Only two Terms ago, the Court noted:

"One has a lesser expectation of privacy in a motor vehicle because its function is transportation and it seldom serves as one's residence or as the repository of personal effects. It travels public thoroughfares where both its occupants and its contents are in plain view." Cardwell v. Lewis, 417 U.S. at 590.

In the interests of public safety and as part of what the Court has called "community caretaking functions" . . . automobiles are frequently taken into police custody. Vehicle accidents present one such occasion. To permit the uninterrupted flow of traffic and in some circumstances to preserve evidence, disabled or damaged vehicles will often be removed from the highways or streets at the behest of police engaged solely in caretaking and traffic-control activities. Police will also frequently remove and impound automobiles which violate parking ordinances and which thereby jeopardize both the public safety and the efficient movement of vehicular traffic. The authority of police to seize and remove from the streets vehicles impeding traffic or threatening public safety and convenience is beyond challenge.

When vehicles are impounded, local police departments generally follow a routine practice of securing and inventorying the automobiles' contents. These procedures developed in response to three distinct needs: The protection of the owner's property while it remains in police custody . . .; the protection of the police against claims or disputes over lost or stolen property . . .; and the protection of the police from potential danger. . . . The practice has been viewed as essential to respond to incidents of theft or vandalism. . . . In addition, police frequently attempt to determine whether a vehicle has been stolen and thereafter abandoned.

These caretaking procedures have almost uniformly been upheld by the state courts, which by virtue of the localized nature of traffic regulation have had considerable occasion to deal with the issue: applying the Fourth Amendment standard of "reasonableness"[e] the state courts have overwhelmingly concluded that, even if an inventory is characterized as a "search," the intrusion is constitutionally permissible. . . . Even the seminal state decision relied on by the South Dakota Supreme Court in reaching the contrary result . . . expressly approved police caretaking activities resulting in the securing of property within the officer's plain view.

The majority of the federal Courts of Appeals have likewise sustained inventory procedures as reasonable police intrusions. . . .

These cases have recognized that standard inventories often include an examination of the glove compartments since it is a customary place for documents of ownership and registration . . . as well as a place for the temporary storage of valuables.

III

The decisions of this Court point unmistakedly to the conclusion reached by both federal and state courts that inventories pursuant to standard police procedures are reasonable. In the first such case, Justice

---

[e]In analyzing the issue of reasonableness vel non, the courts have not sought to determine whether a protective inventory was justified by "probable cause." The standard of probable cause is peculiarly related to criminal investigations, not routine, noncriminal procedures. The probable-cause approach is unhelpful when analysis centers upon the reasonableness of routine administrative caretaking functions, particularly when no claim is made that the protective procedures are a subterfuge for criminal investigations.

In view of the noncriminal context of inventory searches, and the inapplicability of such a setting of the requirement of probable cause, courts have held—and quite correctly—that search warrants are not required, linked as the warrant requirement textually is to the probable-cause concept.

We have frequently observed that the warrant requirement assures that legal inferences and conclusions as to probable cause will be drawn by a neutral magistrate unrelated to the criminal investigative-enforcement process. With respect to noninvestigative police inventories of automobiles lawfully within governmental custody, however, the policies underlying the warrant requirement to which Mr. Justice Powell refers are inapplicable.

Black made plain the nature of the inquiry before us:

"But the question here is not whether the search was *authorized* by state law. The question is rather whether the search was *reasonable* under the Fourth Amendment." Cooper v. California, 386 U.S. 58, 61 (1967) (emphasis added).

And, in his last writing on the Fourth Amendment, Justice Black said:

"[T]he Fourth Amendment does not require that every search be made pursuant to a warrant. It prohibits only *unreasonable* searches and seizures. The relevant test *is not the reasonableness of the opportunity to procure a warrant,* but the reasonableness of the seizure under all the circumstances. The test of reasonableness cannot be fixed by per se rules; each case must be decided on its own facts." Coolidge v. New Hampshire, 403 U.S. at 509–510 (concurring and dissenting) (emphasis added).

In applying the reasonableness standard adopted by the Framers, this Court has consistently sustained police intrusions into automobiles impounded or otherwise in lawful police custody where the process is aimed at securing or protecting the car and its contents. In Cooper v. California, supra, the Court upheld the inventory of a car impounded under the authority of a state forfeiture statute. Even though the inventory was conducted in a distinctly criminal setting and carried out a week after the car had been impounded, the Court nonetheless found that the car search, including examination of the glove compartment where contraband was found, was reasonable under the circumstances. This conclusion was reached despite the fact that no warrant had issued and probable cause to search for the contraband in the vehicle had not been established. The Court said in language explicitly applicable here:

"It would be unreasonable to hold that the police, having to retain the car in their custody for such a length of time, had no right, even for their own protection, to search it." 386 U.S. at 61, 62.

In the following Term, the Court in Harris v. United States, . . . (1968), upheld the introduction of evidence, seized by an officer who, after conducting an inventory search of a car and while taking means to safeguard it, observed a car registration card lying on the metal stripping of the car door. Rejecting the argument that a warrant was necessary, the Court held that the intrusion was justifiable since it was "taken to protect the car while it was in police custody." ...

Finally, in Cady v. Dombrowski, supra, the Court upheld a warrantless search of an auto towed to a private garage even though no probable cause existed to believe that the vehicle contained fruits of a crime. The sole justification for the warrantless incursion was that it was incident to the caretaking function of the local police to protect the community's safety. Indeed, the protective search was instituted solely because local police "were under the impression" that the incapacitated driver, a Chicago police officer, was required to carry his service revolver at all times; the police had reasonable grounds to believe a weapon might be in the car, and thus available to vandals. ... The Court carefully noted that the protective search was carried out in accordance with *standard procedures* in the local police department, a factor tending to ensure that the intrusion would be limited in scope to the extent necessary to carry out the caretaking function. In reaching this result, the Court in Cady distinguished Preston v. United States, ... (1964), on the grounds that the holding, invalidating a car search conducted after a vagrancy arrest, "stands only for the proposition that the search challenged there could not be justified as one incident to an arrest." ... Preston therefore did not raise the issue of the constitutionality of protective inventory of a car lawfully within police custody.

The holdings in Cooper, Harris, and Cady point the way to the correct resolution of this case. None of the three cases, of course, involves the precise situation presented here; but, as in all Fourth Amendment cases, we are obliged to look to all the facts and circumstances of this case in light of the principles set forth in these prior decisions.

"[W]hether a search and seizure is unreasonable within the meaning of the Fourth Amendment depends upon the facts and circumstances of each case. ...." Cooper v. California, supra, at 59.

The Vermillion police were indisputably engaged in a caretaking search of a lawfully impounded automobile. ... The inventory was conducted only after the car had been impounded for multiple parking violations. The owner, having left his car illegally parked for an extended period, and thus subject to impoundment, was not present to make other arrangements for the safekeeping of his belongings. The inventory itself was prompted by the presence in plain view of a number of valuables inside the car. As in Cady, there is no suggestion whatever that this standard procedure, essentially like that followed throughout the country, was a pretext concealing an investigatory police motive.

On this record we conclude that in following standard police procedures prevailing throughout the country and approved by the overwhelming majority of courts, the conduct of the police was not "unreasonable" under the Fourth Amendment. ...

Reversed and remanded.

Mr. Justice POWELL, concurring.

* * *

I

The central purpose of the Fourth Amendment is to safeguard the privacy and security of individuals against arbitrary invasions by government officials. ... None of our prior decisions is dispositive of the issue whether the Amendment permits routine inventory "searches" of automobiles. Resolution of this question requires a weighing of the governmental and societal interests advanced to justify such intrusions against the constitutionally protected interest of the individual citizen in the privacy of his effects. ... As noted in the Court's opinion, three interests generally have been advanced in support of inventory searches: (i) protection of the police from danger; (ii) protection of the police against claims and disputes over lost or stolen property; and (iii) protection of the owner's property while it remains in police custody.

* * *

Against these interests must be weighed the citizen's interest in the privacy of the contents of his automobile. Although the expectation of privacy in an automobile is significantly less than the traditional expectation of privacy associated with the home . . ., the unrestrained search of an automobile and its contents would constitute a serious intrusion upon the privacy of the individual in many circumstances. But such a search is not at issue in this case. As the Court's opinion emphasizes, the search here was limited to an inventory of the unoccupied automobile, and was conducted strictly in accord with the regulations of the Vermillion Police Department. Upholding searches of this type provides no general license for the police to examine all the contents of such automobiles.[g]

I agree with the Court that the Constitution permits routine inventory searches, and turn next to the question whether they must be conducted pursuant to a warrant.

II

While the Fourth Amendment speaks broadly in terms of "unreasonable searches and seizures," the decisions of this Court have recognized that the definition of "reasonableness" turns, at least in part, on the more specific dictates of the warrant clause. . . .

Although the Court has validated warrantless searches of automobiles in circumstances that would not justify a search of a home or office, Cady v. Dombrowski, supra, Chambers v. Maroney, . . . (1970), Carroll v. United States, . . . (1925), these decisions establish no general "automobile exception" to the warrant requirement. . . . Rather, they demonstrate that "for the purpose of the Fourth Amendment there is a constitutional difference between houses and cars" . . . a

difference that may in some cases justify a warrantless search.

* * *

The routine inventory search under consideration in this case does not fall within any of the established exceptions to the warrant requirement. But examination of the interests which are protected when searches are conditioned on warrants issued by a judicial officer reveals that none of these is implicated here. A warrant may issue only upon "probable cause." In the criminal context the requirement of a warrant protects the individual's legitimate expectation of privacy against the overzealous police officer. "Its protection consists in requiring that those inferences (concerning probable cause) be drawn by a neutral and detached magistrate instead of being judged by the officer engaged in the often competitive enterprise of ferreting out crime." . . . Inventory searches, however, are not conducted in order to discover evidence of crime. The officer does not make a discretionary determination to search based on a judgment that certain conditions are present. Inventory searches are conducted in accordance with established police department rules or policy and occur whenever an automobile is seized. There are thus no special facts for a neutral magistrate to evaluate.

A related purpose of the warrant requirement is to prevent hindsight from affecting the evaluation of the reasonableness of a search. In the case of an inventory search conducted in accordance with standard police department procedures, there is no significant danger of hindsight justification. The absence of a warrant will not impair the effectiveness of post-search review of the reasonableness of a particular inventory search.

Warrants also have been required outside the context of a criminal investigation. In Camara v. Municipal Court, 387 U.S. 523 (1967), the Court held that absent consent, a warrant was necessary to conduct an area-wide building code inspection, even though the search could be made absent cause to believe that there were violations in the particular buildings being searched. In requiring a warrant the Court emphasized that "[t]he practical effect of [the existing warrantless search procedures had been] to leave the occupant subject to the discretion

---

[g]As part of their inventory search the police may discover materials such as letters or checkbooks that "touch upon intimate areas of an individual's personal affairs," and "reveal much about a person's activities, associations, and beliefs." California Bankers Assn. v. Shultz, 416 U.S. 21, 78 (1974) (Powell, J., concurring). See also Fisher v. United States, 425 U.S. 391, (1976). In this case the police found, inter alia, "miscellaneous papers," a checkbook, an installment loan book, and a social security status card. There is, however, no evidence in the record that in carrying out their established inventory duties the Vermillion police do other than search for and remove for storage such property without examining its contents.

of the official in the field," since "when [an] inspector demands entry, the occupant ha[d] no way of knowing whether enforcement of the municipal code involved require[d] inspection of his premises, no way of knowing the limits of the inspector's power to search, and no way of knowing whether the inspector himself [was] acting under proper authorization." Id., at 532.

In the inventory search context these concerns are absent. The owner or prior occupant of the automobile is not present, nor, in many cases, is there any real likelihood that he could be located within a reasonable period of time. More importantly, no significant discretion is placed in the hands of the individual officer: he usually has no choice as to the subject of the search or its scope. . . .

Mr. Justice MARSHALL, with whom Mr. Justice BRENNAN and Mr. Justice STEWART join, dissenting.

The Court today holds that the Fourth Amendment permits a routine police inventory search of the closed glove compartment of a locked automobile impounded for ordinary traffic violations. Under the Court's holding, such a search may be made without attempting to secure the consent of the owner and without any particular reason to believe the impounded automobile contains contraband, evidence, or valuables or presents any danger to its custodians or the public. Because I believe this holding to be contrary to sound elaboration of established Fourth Amendment principles, I dissent.

As Mr. Justice POWELL recognizes, the requirement of a warrant aside, resolution of the question whether an inventory search of closed compartment inside a locked automobile can ever be justified as a constitutionally "reasonable" search depends upon a reconciliation of the owner's constitutionally protected privacy interests against governmental intrusion, and legitimate governmental interests furthered by securing the car and its contents. . . . The Court fails clearly to articulate the reasons for its reconciliation of these interests in this case, but it is at least clear to me that the considerations alluded to by the Court, and further discussed by Mr. Justice POWELL, are insufficient to justify the Court's result in this case.

To begin with, the Court appears to suggest by reference to a "diminished" expectation of privacy . . . that a person's constitutional interest in protecting the integrity of closed compartments of his locked automobile may routinely be sacrificed to governmental interests requiring interference with that privacy that are less compelling than would be necessary to justify a search of similar scope of the person's home or office. This has never been the law. The Court correctly observes that some prior cases have drawn distinctions between automobiles and homes or offices in Fourth Amendment cases; but even as the Court's discussion makes clear, the reasons for distinction in those cases are not present here. Thus, while Chambers v. Maroney, . . . (1970), and Carroll v. United States, . . . (1925), permitted certain probable cause searches to be carried out without warrants in view of the exigencies created by the mobility of automobiles, both decisions reaffirmed that the standard of probable cause necessary to authorize such a search was no less than the standard applicable to search of a home or office. In other contexts the Court has recognized that automobile travel sacrifices some privacy interests to the publicity of plain view, e.g., Cardwell v. Lewis, . . . (1974) (plurality opinion) . . . But this recognition, too, is inapposite here, for there is no question of plain view in this case. Nor does this case concern intrusions of the scope the Court apparently assumes would ordinarily be permissible in order to insure the running safety of a car. While it may be that privacy expectations associated with automobile travel are in some regards less than those associated with a home or office . . . it is equally clear that "[t]he word 'automobile' is not a talisman in whose presence the Fourth Amendment fades away . . ." Coolidge v. New Hampshire, . . . (1971). Thus, we have recognized that "[a] search even of an automobile, is a substantial invasion of privacy" . . . and accordingly our cases have consistently recognized that the nature and substantiality of interest required to justify a search of private areas of an automobile is no less than that necessary to justify an intrusion of similar scope into a home or office. . . .

The Court's opinion appears to suggest that its result may in any event be justified because the inventory search procedure is a "reasonable" response to "three distinct needs: the protection of the owner's property while it remains in police custody . . . ; the protection of the police against claims or disputes over lost or stolen property . . . ; and the protection of the police from potential danger." This suggestion is flagrantly misleading however, because the record of this case explicitly belies any relevance of the last two concerns. In any event it is my view that none of these "needs," separately or together, can suffice to justify the inventory search procedure approved by the Court.

First, this search cannot be justified in any way as a safety measure, for—though the Court ignores it—the sole purpose given by the State for the Vermillion police's inventory procedure was to secure *valuables* . . . . Nor is there any indication that the officer's search in this case was tailored in any way to safety concerns, or that ordinarily it is so circumscribed. Even aside from the actual basis for the police practice in this case, however, I do not believe that any blanket safety argument could justify a program of routine searches of the scope permitted here. As Mr. Justice POWELL recognizes, ordinarily "there is little danger associated with impounding unsearched automobiles" . . . . Thus, while the safety rationale may not be entirely discounted when it is actually relied upon, it surely cannot justify the search of every car upon the basis of undifferentiated possibility of harm; on the contrary, such an intrusion could ordinarily be justified only in those individual cases where the officer's inspection was prompted by specific circumstances indicating the possibility of a particular danger. . . .

Second, the Court suggests that the search for valuables in the closed glove compartment might be justified as a measure to protect the police against lost property claims. Again, this suggestion is belied by the record, since—although the Court declines to discuss it—the South Dakota Supreme Court's interpretation of state law explicitly absolves the police, as "gratuitous depositors," from any obligation beyond inventorying objects in plain view and locking the car. . . . Moreover, as Mr. Justice POWELL notes . . . it may well be doubted that an inventory procedure would in any

event work significantly to minimize the frustrations of false claims.

Finally, the Court suggests that the public interest in protecting valuables that may be found inside a closed compartment of an impounded car may justify the inventory procedure. I recognize the genuineness of this governmental interest in protecting property from pilferage. But even if I assume that the posting of a guard would be fiscally impossible as an alternative means to the same protective end, I cannot agree with the Court's conclusion. The Court's result authorizes—indeed it appears to require—the routine search of nearly every car impounded. In my view, the Constitution does not permit such searches as a matter of routine; absent specific consent, such a search is permissible only in exceptional circumstances of particular necessity.

It is at least clear that any owner might prohibit the police from executing a protective search of his impounded car, since by hypothesis the inventory is conducted for the owner's benefit. Moreover, it is obvious that not everyone whose car is impounded would want to be searched. Respondent himself proves this; but one need not carry contraband to prefer that the police not examine one's private possessions. Indeed, that preference is the premise of the Fourth Amendment. Nevertheless, according to the Court's result the law may presume that each owner in respondent's position consents to the search. I cannot agree. In my view, the Court's approach is squarely contrary to the law of consent;[n] it ignores the duty in the absence of consent to analyze in each individual case whether there is a need to search a particular car for the protection of its owner which is sufficient to outweigh the particular invasion. It is clear to me under established principles that in order to override the absence of explicit consent, such a search must at least be conditioned upon the fulfillment of two requirements. First, there must be specific cause to believe

---

[n] Even if it may be true that many persons would ordinarily consent to a protective inventory of their car upon its impoundment, this fact is not dispositive since even a majority lacks authority to consent to the search of *all* cars in order to assure the search of theirs.

that a search of the scope to be undertaken is necessary in order to preserve the integrity of particular valuable property threatened by the impoundment; "in justifying the particular intrusion the police officer must be able to point to specific and articulable facts which . . . reasonably warrant that intrusion." Terry v. Ohio., 392 U.S. at 21. Such a requirement of "specificity in the information upon which police action is predicated is the central teaching of this Court's Fourth Amendment jurisprudence" . . . for "(t)he basic purpose of this Amendment, as recognized by countless decisions of this Court, is to safeguard the privacy and security of individuals against arbitrary invasions by governmental officials." Second, even when a search might be appropriate, such an intrusion may only follow the exhaustion and failure of reasonable efforts under the circumstances to identify and reach the owner of the property in order to facilitate alternative means of security or to obtain his consent to the search, for in this context the right to refuse the search remains with the owner. . . .

Because the record in this case shows that the procedures followed by the Vermillion police in searching respondent's car fall far short of these standards, in my view the search was impermissible and its fruits must be suppressed. . . .

* * *

The Court's result in this case elevates the conservation of property interests — indeed mere possibilities of property interests — above the privacy and security interests protected by the Fourth Amendment. For this reason I dissent. On the remand it should be clear in any event that this Court's holding does not preclude a contrary resolution of this case or others involving the same issues under any applicable state law. . . .

Statement of Mr. Justice WHITE.

Although I do not subscribe to all of my Brother MARSHALL's dissenting opinion, particularly some aspects of his discussion concerning the necessity for obtaining the consent of the car owner, I agree with most of his analysis and conclusions and consequently dissent from the judgment of the Court.

Comments

1. The rule outlining a police officer's power to seize and search motor vehicles was first announced in the 1925 case of *Carroll* v. *United States,* 267 U.S. 132; i.e., so long as the officer has probable cause to believe that the automobile contains contraband he can make an immediate warrantless search. Searches conducted in this manner are considered reasonable because of the mobility of motor vehicles; the fact that the vehicle can be quickly and easily moved out of the jurisdiction establishes the exigent circumstances necessary to justify such a search. Moreover, if contraband is secreted in the auto, there is a probability that such evidence will be destroyed or removed before a search warrant can be obtained. The *Chambers* case served to revitalize the *Carroll* doctrine by extending it to cover station-house searches. Although petitioner argued that the auto was no longer mobile and could have simply been held until a warrant was obtained, the Court could not see that any greater protection of privacy would be afforded by doing so. The Court reasoned that since the search could have been conducted in the parking lot at the time petitioner was arrested, there was no difference between carrying out an immediate warrantless search and holding the auto until the probable cause issue could be presented to a magistrate; such a requirement was perceived as being substantially inconvenient to the searching officers.

2. The Supreme Court again relied upon the concept of "continuing probable cause" to justify the station-house search of an auto in the following case:

TEXAS v. WHITE
Supreme Court of the United States, 1975
423 U.S. 67, 96 S. Ct. 304, 46 L. Ed. 2d 209

PER CURIAM.

Respondent was arrested at 1:30 P.M. by Amarillo, Texas, police officers while attempting to pass fraudulent checks at a drive-in window of the First National Bank of Amarillo. Only 10 minutes earlier, the officers had been informed by another bank that a man answering respondent's description and driving an automobile exactly matching that of respondent had tried to negotiate four checks drawn on a nonexistent account. Upon arrival at the First National Bank pursuant to a telephone call from that bank, the officers obtained from the drive-in teller other checks that respondent had attempted to pass there. The officers directed respondent to park his automobile at the curb. While parking the car, respondent was observed by a bank employee and one of the officers attempting to "stuff" something between the seats. Respondent was arrested and one officer drove him to the station house while the other drove respondent's car there. At the station house, the officers questioned respondent for 30 to 45 minutes and, pursuant to their normal procedure, requested consent to search the automobile. Respondent refused to consent to the search. The officers then proceeded to search the automobile anyway. During the search, an officer discovered four wrinkled checks that corresponded to those respondent had attempted to pass at the first bank. The trial judge, relying on Chambers v. Maroney, 399 U.S. 42 (1970), admitted over respondent's objection the four checks seized during the search of respondent's automobile at the station house. The judge expressly found probable cause both for the arrest and for the search of the vehicle, either at the scene or at the station house. Respondent was convicted after a jury trial of knowingly attempting to pass a forged instrument. The Texas Court of Criminal Appeals, in a 3–2 decision, reversed respondent's conviction on the ground that the evidence of the four wrinkled checks was obtained without a warrant in violation of respondent's Fourth Amendment right. . . . We reverse.

In Chambers v. Maroney . . ., we held that police officers with probable cause to search an automobile on the scene where it was stopped could constitutionally do so later at the station house without first obtaining a warrant. There, as here, "[t]he probable cause factor" that developed on the scene "still obtained at the station house." . . . The Court of Criminal Appeals erroneously excluded the evidence seized from the search at the station house in light of the trial judge's finding, undisturbed by the appellate court, that there was probable cause to search respondent's car.

The petition for certiorari and the motion of respondent to proceed in forma pauperis are granted, the judgment of the Court of Criminal Appeals is reversed, and the case is remanded to that court for further proceedings not inconsistent with this opinion.

[Mr. Justice MARSHALL, with whom Mr. Justice BRENNAN joined, dissented.]

3. It should be noted that prior to *Chambers*, the Court had placed certain limitations on the *Carroll* doctrine; e.g., in *Preston* v. *United States*, 376 U.S. 364 (1964), and *Dyke* v. *Taylor Implement Manufacturing Company*, 391 U.S. 216 (1968), vehicle searches that occurred *after* the vehicle had been taken into custody were disallowed. The drivers had been arrested for vagrancy and speeding, respectively. Finding that neither offense implied that weapons or other contraband might be found in the vehicles, the Court invalidated the warrantless searches. Although the Court did approve a delayed search in *Cooper* v. *California*, 386 U.S. 58 (1967), the majority did so only because the auto was subject to forfeiture pursuant to a California statute. Since a considerable length of time was involved before forfeiture proceedings could begin, the Court concluded that it "would be unreasonable to hold that the police, having to retain the car in their garage for such a length of time, had no right, even for their own protection, to search it."

What if the driver is arrested but is afforded the opportunity to immediately make bail and reclaim his automobile? See *Dyke* v. *Taylor Implement Manufacturing Company*, supra, where the search of a vehicle after a traffic arrest was declared to be unlawful because (1) the car had not been impounded, and (2) the defendant was immediately taken before the court to make bail.

4. *Cardwell* v. *Lewis* points out the continued viability of the *Carroll* distinction between homes and automobiles for purposes of a warrantless search and seizure. However, there are factual differences between the trilogy of *Carroll*, *Chambers*, and *Cardwell*. Of greatest import is the fact that in *Carroll* only the *exterior* of respondent's auto was examined. Since the auto had "little capacity for escaping public scrutiny" and it was "knowingly exposed," the plurality reasoned that the examination was not a "search" within the meaning of the Fourth Amendment. Likewise, the Court found the initial "seizure" of the vehicle to be constitutionally permissible. Recognizing that Chambers' auto was seized after it was stopped on the highway, whereas the Lewis vehicle was taken from a parking lot, the Court nevertheless found exigency to be equally apparent in both. In doing so, the Court was quick to note that autos not only represent emergencies at the time of arrest but at any time. Consider, however, the following note to the minority opinion: "It can hardly be argued that the questioning of the respondent by the police for the first time alerted him to their intentions, thus suddenly providing him with a motivation to remove the car from 'official grasp.' Even putting to one side the question of how the respondent could have acted to destroy any evidence while he was in police custody, the fact is that he was fully aware of official suspicion during several months preceding the interrogation. He had been questioned on several occasions prior to his arrest, and he had been alerted on the day before the interrogation that the police wished to see him. Nonetheless, he voluntarily drove his car to Columbus to keep his appointment with the investigators."

5. In *South Dakota* v. *Opperman,* the distinction between automobiles and homes or offices again provided the springboard for the Court's decision. Writing for the majority, the Chief Justice acknowledged that autos are "effects" and thus within the reach of the Fourth Amendment. However, he also concluded that automobiles can be subjected to warrantless searches under circumstances in which a search of a home or office could not be conducted. In addition to recognizing that the inherent mobility of the auto creates exigent conditions, the Court also suggested that there exists a "diminished" expectation of privacy with regard to automobiles, i.e., the expectation of privacy with respect to one's auto is "significantly less" than that relating to one's office or home.

Prior to *Opperman,* the Court had not squarely faced the question of whether a routine police inventory search of a lawfully impounded vehicle was permissible under the Fourth Amendment. Clearly, such a search did not seem to fall within any of the previously established exceptions to the warrant requirement. The majority advanced three interests in support of routine inventory searches: (1) protection of the police officer from danger; (2) protection of the police against claims and disputes over lost or stolen property; and (3) protection of the owner's property while it remains in police custody. It appears that the Court's opinion rests primarily upon the last stated need. If inventory searches are to be justified, in part, as a simple "caretaker function," is it reasonable to assume that everyone whose car is impounded would want it to be inventoried? What if an owner specifically instructs the police *not* to conduct a protective inventory search of his vehicle? Would it make any difference if the owner could not make other arrangements for the safekeeping of the auto's contents? If the owner is in custody, or at least in communication with the police, should police seek his consent before the search takes place? What if permission is sought by the police and the owner refuses to consent? May the search proceed? Would the owner's refusal to consent give rise to probable cause to believe that the auto contains contraband? On the other hand, do most automobile owners desire to preserve as private their car's contents? If police are always permitted to conduct protective inventory searches, how can the administrative-custodial procedure be distinguished from a subterfuge to conduct a search for incriminating articles? The Court observed that non-criminal inventory searches represent a general routine practice in the Vermillion police department. If it is not the usual practice of a police department to conduct such searches, would a deviation from the "nonsearch" routine require a different result? Finally, what effect does the Court's "diminished expectation of privacy" pronouncement have on owners of motor homes or vanlike mobile offices? What if the owner of the auto is poor and is forced to actually live in his automobile? Does *Opperman* permit an inventory of a locked car trunk? May an inventory be made at the place where the car is impounded, e.g., the street?

6. It should be noted that on remand the South Dakota Supreme Court expressly declined to follow the United States Supreme Court's pronouncement in *Opperman* and elected instead to afford greater protection under state law than that required by the federal Constitution. See *State* v. *Opperman,* 247 N.W.2d 673 (S.D.

1976) (holding automobile inventory upheld by United States Supreme Court to be unreasonable under South Dakota's state constitution). Some other recent lower federal and state court decisions involving automobile stops, searches, inventories, and forfeitures include *United States* v. *Diggs,* 522 F.2d 1310 (D.C. Cir. 1975) (FBI agents who had earlier arrested the driver of a distinctive Cadillac that had been used as a robbery get-away car held to have probable cause to stop that vehicle when they learned that it had just been spotted near the scene of a bank hold-up); *Patrick* v. *Commonwealth,* 535 S.W.2d 88 (Ky. 1976) (suspicious patrolman's opening of a motorist's parked car and shining his flashlight inside held a full search under the Fourth Amendment and invalid absent probable cause); *Joyce* v. *State,* 327 So. 2d 255 (Miss. 1976) (police officers who verified informer's tip that an airline passenger would be arriving in Jackson, Mississippi, from Phoenix with 60 pounds of marijuana and would be met by a particularly described individual held justified in stopping their car and conducting warrantless search, as tip was received only three hours earlier); *Winberly* v. *Superior Court,* 547 P.2d 417 (Cal. 1976) (highway patrol officer's plain view discovery of marijuana seeds and a pipe on the front seat of car that had been stopped for reckless driving gave officer probable cause to search passenger compartment but not the trunk); *Hilleary* v. *Wallace,* 519 F.2d 786 (4th Cir. 1975) (exigent circumstances and probable cause justified policeman's warrantless seizure of auto found behind a television store that had been broken into at 3 o'clock in the morning, since key was found in the auto's ignition and radiator was still warm); *United States* v. *Blanton,* 520 F.2d 907 (6th Cir. 1975) (where reliable informant described auto as 1973 beige Torino and reported that auto contained stolen money and a machine gun, police stop and search of auto was valid as there was probable cause for arrest of defendant and it was impractical for officers to obtain a warrant because of exigency of the circumstances); *Haefeli* v. *Chernoff,* 526 F.2d 1314 (1st Cir. 1975) (warrantless search of auto at stationhouse following arrest of suspects held justified under *Carroll-Chambers* doctrine); *United States* v. *Chulengarian,* 538 F.2d 553 (4th Cir. 1976) (warrantless search of impounded car at stationhouse in which officers had earlier seen marijuana in plain view during reckless driving investigation upheld under *Carroll-Chambers* doctrine); *State* v. *Barber,* 241 N.W.2d 476 (Minn. 1976) (police officers had sufficient reason to stop car for routine traffic investigation because license plates were attached in an unusual, though legal, manner, i.e., clean plates affixed by wire on a dirty car); *United States* v. *Robinson,* 536 F.2d 1298 (9th Cir. 1976) (showing at trial of "founded suspicion" necessary for a police officer's stop of a vehicle cannot rest solely on a radio dispatch to make the stop, absent any proof of the factual foundation for the message); *Pinkey* v. *United States,* ___ F.2d ___ (D.C. Cir. 1976) (police officers with the right to seize an auto driven by suspect whom they had a warrant to arrest could check car by looking inside it before releasing it to suspect's friend, and any incriminating objects in plain view could be seized); *People* v. *Lemmons,* 354 N.E.2d 836 (N.Y. App. 1976) (police officers who stopped car for speeding and then arrested driver when radio check indicated he was wanted in another state were justified in checking the identity of his three traveling companions); *United States* v. *Mor-*

row, 541 F.2d 1229 (7th Cir. 1976) (federal agent's impoundment of a stolen vehicle from a private garage where its driver had parked it and where two male occupants in the house could have driven it away held justified); *State* v. *Stockert*, 245 N.W.2d 266 (N.D. 1976) (warrantless entry and search of snowbound car that was immobile held unreasonable in the absence of exigent circumstances); *United States* v. *Kressin*, ____ U.S.A.F. Mil. Rev. ____ (1976) (base commander's order directing Air Force security police to randomly search vehicles entering or operating on base for weapons or contraband upheld); *Scott* v. *State*, 543 S.W.2d 128 (Tex. Ct. Crim. App. 1976) (policeman on late-night patrol who saw two black males driving in a normal manner through a new, partially occupied development of apartments and expensive townhouses did not have sufficient cause to pull the car over for an investigative stop, and stolen oil paintings found in front seat and trunk were not admissible); *United States* v. *Zaicek*, 519 F.2d 412 (2nd Cir. 1975) (when auto is seized pursuant to a New York statute allowing police officer with good reason to believe auto stolen to seize it, the officer also has the authority to search the vehicle without a warrant); *People* v. *Valoppi*, 233 N.W.2d 41 (Mich. 1975) (police inspection of a vehicle identification number does constitute a search within the meaning of the Fourth Amendment); *Cabbler* v. *Superintendent, Virginia State Penitentiary*, 528 F.2d 1142 (4th Cir. 1975) (police officer's impoundment of defendant's auto and inventory of the car's trunk held not unreasonable); *Altman* v. *State*, 335 So. 2d 626 (Fla. App. 1976) (inventory of traffic offender's slightly damaged vehicle when friend of driver was willing and able to take care of it held unnecessary and unreasonable); *Robertson* v. *State*, 541 S.W.2d 608 (Tex. Crim. App. 1976) (policemen acted properly under *South Dakota* v. *Opperman* in inventorying a damaged auto after injured driver had been taken to the hospital and before car had been towed to a private lot, and marijuana found in glove compartment was admissible); *People* v. *Counterman*, 556 P.2d 481 (Colo. 1976) (unreasonable for police to open a knapsack found in plain view during an inventory of an impounded automobile, and narcotics discovered should be suppressed); *State* v. *Clark*, 556 P.2d 851 (N.M. App. 1976) (policeman who seized a rented truck that matched the description of one that had been reported stolen and then turned it over to the local agent of the rental firm held to have acted unlawfully in going to the firm's garage and conducting an inventory of the truck's contents); *United States* v. *Mitchell*, 525 F.2d 1275 (5th Cir. 1976) (en banc) (federal agents who conducted elaborate summer investigation of an international drug-smuggling operation culminating in arrests in October held justified in seizing truck without a warrant); *Johnson* v. *United States*, ____ F.2d ____ (D.C. Cir. 1976) (police officer who stopped motorist for running red light held justified in examining a grocery bag on the floor between the driver's legs on the basis of the officer's "fear for his safety"); *United States* v. *Robinson*, 533 F.2d 578 (D.C. Cir. 1976) (warrantless search of parked get-away car by police "hot on trail" of four armed robbers held justified in order to learn the identity and whereabouts of the robbers); *United States* v. *Boyd*, 530 F.2d 1269 (5th Cir. 1976) (threat to public safety posed by presence of liquor in car of motorist stopped for routine registration and license check justified trooper's minimal intrusion in reaching into auto to seize and inspect liquor bottle, and conviction for possession of non-tax paid liquor upheld); *United States* v. *Farnkoff*, 535 F.2d 661 (1st Cir. 1976) ("exigent circumstances" are essential requisite for warrantless searches of automobiles) (accord, *Fuqua* v. *Armour,* 543 S.W.2d 64 [Tenn. 1976] [warrantless searches of automobiles absent exigent circumstances are violative of the Fourth Amendment]); *Castleberry* v. *Alcohol, Tobacco and Firearms Division,* 530 F.2d 672 (5th Cir. 1976) (an owner whose property has been seized and is subject to forfeiture under the Contraband Seizure Act, 49 U.S.C. § 781, and who believes the government is unnecessarily delaying the forfeiture proceedings may request the district court to order the government to begin the proceedings immediately or return the property—here, a Cadillac in which a sawed-off shotgun was found—and abandon the seizure); *State* v. *One 1972 Pontiac Grand Prix,* 242 N.W.2d 660 (S.D. 1976) (South Dakota forfeiture statute held not applicable to cars in which 0.4 ounce of marijuana seeds found, a misdemeanor).

7.   In a recent case, *G. M. Leasing Corp.* v. *United States,* 97 S. Ct. 619 (1977), the United States Supreme Court granted certiorari to consider, in part, the Fourth Amendment issue arising in context of the warrantless seizure of several automobiles in partial satisfaction of income tax assessments. The facts revealed that George I. Norman, Jr., general manager of the G. M. Leasing Corporation, was convicted in 1971 in the United States District Court for the District of Colorado on two counts of aiding and abetting a misapplication of funds from a federally insured bank in violation of 18 U.S.C. §§ 2 and 656. The Court of Appeals (10th Cir.) affirmed, and the United States Supreme Court denied certiorari. Thereafter, in March, 1973, he surrendered to the U.S. Marshal to serve his sentence. By a stratagem, however, he immediately disappeared. Because of Norman's failure to file appropriate income tax returns in 1970 and 1971 and because of his fugitive status, collection of taxes in the amount of $951,409.93 was regarded by the Internal Revenue Service as in jeopardy; the deficiencies, therefore, were assessed pursuant to the authority granted under § 6861(a) of the Internal Revenue Code of 1954, 26 U.S.C. § 6861(a). On March 21, two days after the jeopardy assessments, IRS agents, without a warrant, seized several automobiles, including a 1972 Stutz, a Rolls Royce Phantom V, a 1930 Rolls Royce Phantom I, two 1971 Stutzes and a Jaguar. Petitioner corporation was determined to be the alter ego of Norman, and the autos seized were registered in petitioner's name. Petitioner corporation filed suit in district court alleging that the assessments were arbitrary, that it was not an alter ego of Norman, and that the levy violated the Fourth Amendment. Although the district court found that the revenue officers committed an illegal seizure of the autos, the Court of Appeals (10th Cir.) disagreed, finding that appellant officers were acting pursuant to statute and did not commit an illegal search. Section 6331(a) of the 1954 IRS Code provides, inter alia, "If any person liable to pay any tax neglects or refuses to pay the same within 10 days after notice and demand, it shall be lawful for [IRS agents] to collect such tax . . . by levy upon all property belonging to such person or on which there is a lien for the payment of such tax . . . ." If IRS officials find that "the collection of such tax is in jeopardy, notice and demand for immediate payment of such tax may be made . . . and, upon fail-

ure or refusal to pay such tax, collection thereof by levy shall be lawful. . . ." Sections 6331(b) and 7701(a)(21) define "levy" as including "the power of distraint and seizure [of both real and personal property] by any means." The Supreme Court granted certiorari, 432 U.S. 1031 (1975), and Mr. Justice Blackmun, writing for the majority, concluded that the seizure of the automobiles took place on public streets, parking lots, or other open places, and did not violate the Fourth Amendment. The majority, relying on *Murray's Lessee* v. *Hoboken Land and Improvement Co.,* 18 How. 272 (1856), held that a judicial warrant is not required for the seizure of a debtor's property in satisfaction of a claim of the United States; hence "the warrantless seizure of the automobiles . . . are governed by . . . [those] principles and therefore were not unconstitutional."

E. CONSENT SEARCHES

The "Voluntariness" and "Totality of Circumstances" Tests

SCHNECKLOTH v. BUSTAMONTE

Supreme Court of the United States, 1973
412 U.S. 218, 93 S. Ct. 2041, 36 L. Ed. 2d 854

The facts are stated in the opinion.

Mr. Justice STEWART delivered the opinion of the Court.

* * *

The respondent was brought to trial in a California court upon a charge of possessing a check with intent to defraud. He moved to suppress the introduction of certain material as evidence against him on the ground that the material had been acquired through an unconstitutional search and seizure. In response to the motion, the trial judge conducted an evidentiary hearing where it was established that the material in question had been acquired by the State under the following circumstances:

While on routine patrol in Sunnyvale, California, at approximately 2:40 in the morning, Police Officer James Rand stopped an automobile when he observed that one headlight and its license plate light were burned out. Six men were in the vehicle. Joe

Alcala and the respondent, Robert Bustamonte, were in the front seat with Joe Gonzales, the driver. Three older men were seated in the rear. When, in response to the policeman's question, Gonzales could not produce a driver's license, Officer Rand asked if any of the other five had any evidence of identification. Only Alcala produced a license, and he explained that the car was his brother's. After the six occupants had stepped out of the car at the officer's request, and after two additional policemen had arrived, Officer Rand asked Alcala if he could search the car. Alcala replied, "Sure, go ahead." Prior to the search no one was threatened with arrest and, according to Officer Rand's uncontradicted testimony, it "was all very congenial at this time." Gonzales testified that Alcala actually helped in the search of the car, by opening the trunk and glove compartment. In Gonzales' words: "[T]he police officer asked Joe (Alcala), he goes, 'Does the trunk open?' And Joe said 'Yes.' He went to the car and got the keys and opened up the trunk." Wadded up under the left rear seat, the police officers found three checks that had previously been stolen from a car wash.

The trial judge denied the motion to suppress, and the checks in question were admitted in evidence at Bustamonte's trial. On the basis of this and other evidence he was convicted, and the California Court of Appeal for the First Appellate District affirmed the conviction. . . . In agreeing that the search and seizure were constitutionally valid, the appellate court applied the standard earlier formulated by the Supreme Court of California in an opinion by then Justice Traynor: "Whether in a particular case an apparent consent was in fact voluntarily given or was in submission to an express or implied assertion of authority, is a question of fact to be determined in the light of all the circumstances."

* * *

... The California Supreme Court denied review.

Thereafter, the respondent sought a writ of habeas corpus in a federal district court. It was denied. On appeal, the Court of Appeals for the Ninth Circuit . . . set aside the District Court's order. . . . We granted certiorari to determine whether the Fourth and Fourteenth Amendments require the showing thought necessary by the Court of Appeals.

It is important to make it clear at the outset what is not involved in this case. The respondent concedes that a search conducted pursuant to a valid consent is constitutionally permissible. . . . And similarly the State concedes that "[w]hen a prosecutor seeks to rely upon consent to justify the lawfulness of a search, he has the burden of proving that the consent was, in fact, freely and voluntarily given." . . .

The precise question in this case, then, is what must the prosecution prove to demonstrate that a consent was "voluntarily" given. And upon that question there is a square conflict of views between the state and federal courts that have reviewed the search involved in the case before us. The Court of Appeals for the Ninth Circuit concluded that it is an essential part of the State's initial burden to prove that a person

knows he has a right to refuse consent. The California courts have followed the rule that voluntariness is a question of fact to be determined from the totality of all the circumstances, and that the state of a defendant's knowledge is only one factor to be taken into account in assessing the voluntariness of a consent. . . .

The most extensive judicial exposition of the meaning of "voluntariness" has been developed in those cases in which the Court has had to determine the "voluntariness" of a defendant's confession for purposes of the Fourteenth Amendment. . . . It is to that body of case law to which we turn for initial guidance on the meaning of "voluntariness" in the present context.

* * *

The significant fact about all of these decisions is that none of them turned on the presence or absence of a single controlling criterion; each reflected a careful scrutiny of all the surrounding circumstances. . . . In none of them did the Court rule that the Due Process Clause required the prosecution to prove as part of its initial burden that the defendant knew he had a right to refuse to answer the questions that were put. While the state of the accused's mind, and the failure of the police to advise the accused of his rights, were certainly factors to be evaluated in assessing the "voluntariness" of an accused's responses, they were not in and of themselves determinative. . . .

Similar considerations lead us to agree with the courts of California that the question whether a consent to a search was in fact "voluntary" or was the product of duress or coercion, express or implied, is a question of fact to be determined from the totality of all the circumstances. While knowledge of the right to refuse consent is one factor to be taken into account, the government need not establish such knowledge as the sine qua non of an effective consent. As with police questioning, two competing concerns must be accommodated in determining the meaning of a "voluntary" consent—the legitimate need for such searches and the equally important requirement of assuring the absence of coercion.

In situations where the police have some evidence of illicit activity, but lack probable cause to arrest or search, a search authorized by a valid consent may be the only means of obtaining important and reliable evidence. In the present case for example, while the police had reason to stop the car for traffic violations, the State does not contend that there was probable cause to search the vehicle or that the search was incident to a valid arrest of any of the occupants. Yet the search yielded tangible evidence that served as a basis for prosecution, and provided some assurance that others, wholly innocent of the crime, were not mistakenly brought to trial. And in those cases where there is probable cause to arrest or search, but where the police lack a warrant, a consent search may still be valuable. If the search is conducted and proves fruitless, that in itself may convince the police that an arrest with its possible stigma and embarrassment is unnecessary, or that a far more extensive search pursuant to a warrant is not justified. In short, a search pursuant to consent may result in considerably less inconvenience for the subject of the search, and, properly conducted, is a constitutionally permissible and wholly legitimate aspect of effective police activity.

But the Fourth and Fourteenth Amendments require that a consent not be coerced, by explicit or implicit means, by implied threat or covert force. For, no matter how subtly the coercion was applied, the resulting "consent" would be no more than a pretext for the unjustified police intrusion against which the Fourth Amendment is directed.

* * *

The problem of reconciling the recognized legitimacy of consent searches with the requirement that they be free from any aspect of official coercion cannot be resolved by any infallible touchstone. To approve such searches without the most careful scrutiny would sanction the possibility of official coercion; to place artificial restrictions upon such searches would jeopardize their basic validity. Just as was true with confessions, the requirement of a "voluntary" consent reflects a fair accommodation of the constitutional requirements involved. In examining all the surrounding circumstances to determine if in fact the consent to search was coerced, account must be taken of subtly coercive police questions, as well as the possibly vulnerable subjective state of

the person who consents. Those searches that are the product of police coercion can thus be filtered out without undermining the continuing validity of consent searches. In sum, there is no reason for us to depart in the area of consent searches, from the traditional definition of "voluntariness."

The approach of the Court of Appeals for the Ninth Circuit finds no support in any of our decisions that have attempted to define the meaning of "voluntariness." Its ruling, that the State must affirmatively prove that the subject of the search knew that he had a right to refuse consent, would, in practice, create serious doubt whether consent searches could continue to be conducted. There might be rare cases where it could be proved from the record that a person in fact affirmatively knew of his right to refuse — such as a case where he announced to the police that if he didn't sign the consent form, "you [police] are going to get a search warrant" or a case where by prior experience and training a person had clearly and convincingly demonstrated such knowledge. But more commonly where there was no evidence of any coercion, explicit or implicit, the prosecution would nevertheless be unable to demonstrate that the subject of the search in fact had known of his right to refuse consent.

The very object of the inquiry — the nature of a person's subjective understanding — underlines the difficulty of the prosecution's burden under the rule applied by the Court of Appeals in this case. Any defendant who was the subject of a search authorized solely by his consent could effectively frustrate the introduction into evidence of the fruits of that search by simply failing to testify that he in fact knew he could refuse to consent. And the near impossibility of meeting this prosecutorial burden suggests why this Court has never accepted any such litmus-paper test of voluntariness.

* * *

One alternative that would go far toward proving that the subject of a search did know he had a right to refuse consent would be to advise him of that right before eliciting his consent. That, however, is a suggestion that has been almost universally repudiated by both federal and state courts, and, we think, rightly so. For it would be thoroughly impractical to impose on the normal consent search the detailed requirements of an effective warning. Consent searches are part of the standard investigatory techniques of law enforcement agencies. They normally occur on the highway, or in a person's home or office, and under informal and unstructured conditions. The circumstances that prompt the initial request to search may develop quickly or be a logical extension of investigative police questioning. The police may seek to investigate further suspicious circumstances or to follow up leads developed in questioning persons at the scene of a crime. These situations are a far cry from the structured atmosphere of a trial where, assisted by counsel if he chooses, a defendant is informed of his trial rights. And, while surely a closer question, these situations are still immeasurably far removed from "custodial interrogation" where, in Miranda v. Arizona . . . [Chapter Six, § 6.03], we found that the Constitution required certain now familiar warnings as a prerequisite to police interrogation.

* * *

Consequently, we cannot accept the position of the Court of Appeals in this case that proof of knowledge of the right to refuse consent is a necessary prerequisite to demonstrating a "voluntary" consent. Rather it is only by analyzing all the circumstances of an individual consent that it can be ascertained whether in fact it was voluntary or coerced. It is this careful sifting of the unique facts and circumstances of each case that is evidenced in our prior decisions involving consent searches.

* * *

It is said, however, that a "consent" is a "waiver" of a person's rights under the Fourth and Fourteenth Amendments. The argument is that by allowing the police to conduct a search, a person "waives" whatever right he had to prevent the police from searching. It is argued that under the doctrine of Johnson v. Zerbst, 304 U.S. 458 (1938), to establish such a "waiver" the State must demonstrate "an intentional relinquishment or abandonment of a known right or privilege."

* * *

Almost without exception, the requirement of a knowing and intelligent waiver has been applied only to those rights which the Constitution guarantees to a criminal defendant in order to preserve a fair trial. Hence, and hardly surprisingly in view of the facts of Johnson itself, the standard of a knowing and intelligent waiver has most often been applied to test the validity of a waiver of counsel, either at trial, or upon a guilty plea. And the Court has also applied the Johnson criteria to assess the effectiveness of a waiver of other trial rights such as the right to confrontation, to a jury trial, and to a speedy trial, and the right to be free from twice being placed in jeopardy. Guilty pleas have been carefully scrutinized to determine whether the accused knew and understood all the rights to which he would be entitled at trial, and that he had intentionally chosen to forgo them. And the Court has evaluated the knowing and intelligent nature of the waiver of trial rights in trial-type situations, such as the waiver of the privilege against compulsory self-incrimination before an administrative agency or a congressional committee, or the waiver of counsel in a juvenile proceeding.

The guarantees afforded a criminal defendant at trial also protect him at certain stages before the actual trial, and any alleged waiver must meet the strict standard of an intentional relinquishment of a "known" right. But the "trial" guarantees that have been applied to the "pretrial" stage of the criminal process are similarly designed to protect the fairness of the trial itself.

* * *

There is a vast difference between those rights that protect a fair criminal trial and the rights guaranteed under the Fourth Amendment. . . .

The protections of the Fourth Amendment are of a wholly different order, and have nothing whatever to do with promoting the fair ascertainment of truth at a criminal trial. . . . The Fourth Amendment "is not an adjunct to the ascertainment of truth." The guarantees of the Fourth Amendment stand "as a protection of quite different constitutional values — values reflecting the concern of our society for the right of each individual to be let alone. To recognize this is no more than to accord those values undiluted respect."

* * *

It would be unrealistic to expect that in the informal, unstructured context of a consent search, a policeman, upon pain of tainting the evidence obtained, could make the detailed type of examination demanded by Johnson. . . .

Similarly, a "waiver" approach to consent searches would be thoroughly inconsistent with our decisions that have approved "third party consents." . . . Yet it is inconceivable that the Constitution could countenance the waiver of a defendant's right to counsel by a third party, or that a waiver could be found because a trial judge reasonably, though mistakenly, believed a defendant had waived his right to plead not guilty.

* * *

Much of what has already been said disposes of the argument that the Court's decision in the Miranda case requires the conclusion that knowledge of a right to refuse is an indispensable element of a valid consent. The considerations that informed the Court's holding in Miranda are simply inapplicable in the present case. In Miranda the Court found that the techniques of police questioning and the nature of custodial surroundings produce an inherently coercive situation. . . .

Indeed, since consent searches will normally occur on a person's own familiar territory, the specter of incommunicado police interrogation in some remote station house is simply inapposite. . . .

It is also argued that the failure to require the Government to establish knowledge as a prerequisite to a valid consent will relegate the Fourth Amendment to the special province of "the sophisticated, the knowledgeable and the privileged." We cannot agree. The traditional definition of voluntariness we accept today has always taken into account evidence of minimal schooling, low intelligence, and the lack of any effective warnings to a person of his rights; and the voluntariness of any statement taken under those conditions has been carefully scrutinized to determine whether it was in fact voluntarily given.

Our decision today is a narrow one. We hold that when the subject of a search is not in custody and the State attempts to justify a search on the basis of his consent, the Fourth and Fourteenth Amendments require that it demonstrate that the consent was in fact voluntarily given, and not the result of duress or coercion, express or implied. Voluntariness is a question of fact to be determined from all the circumstances, and while the subject's knowledge of a right to refuse is a factor to be taken into account, the prosecution is not required to demonstrate such knowledge as a prerequisite to establishing a voluntary consent. . . .

The judgment of the Court of Appeals is reversed.

[Mr. Justice POWELL wrote a concurring opinion, in which Mr. Justice REHNQUIST and Mr. Chief Justice BURGER joined.]

[Mr. Justice BLACKMUN wrote a separate concurring opinion.]

[Mr. Justice BRENNAN, Mr. Justice MARSHALL, and Mr. Justice DOUGLAS wrote separate dissenting opinions.]

Third-Party Consent

UNITED STATES v. MATLOCK

Supreme Court of the United States, 1974
415 U.S. 164, 94 S. Ct. 988, 39 L. Ed. 2d 242

Respondent Matlock was arrested in the front yard of a house in which he lived along with a Mrs. Graff (daughter of the lessees) and others. The arresting officers were admitted to the house by Mrs. Graff, and with her consent but absent a warrant, they searched the house, including a bedroom which Mrs. Graff told them was jointly occupied by Matlock and herself. In the closet of the bedroom officers found and seized stolen money. Matlock was indicted for bank robbery

and moved to suppress as evidence the seized money. The District Court for the Western District of Wisconsin suppressed the evidence when it concluded that the government had not satisfactorily proved Mrs. Graff's actual authority to consent to the search. The Court of Appeals (7th Cir.) affirmed, and certiorari was granted.]

Mr. Justice WHITE delivered the opinion of the Court.

* * *

It has been assumed by the parties and the courts below that the voluntary consent of any joint occupant of a residence to search the premises jointly occupied is valid against the occupant, permitting evidence discovered in the search to be used against him at a criminal trial.... This Court left open, in Amos v. United States, 255 U.S. 313 (1921), the question whether a wife's permission to search the residence in which she lived with her husband could "waive his constitutional rights," but more recent authority here clearly indicates that the consent of one who possesses common authority over premises or effects is valid as against the absent, nonconsenting person with whom that authority is shared. In Frazier v. Cupp, 394 U.S. 731 (1969), the Court "dismissed rather quickly" the contention that the consent of the petitioner's cousin to the search of a duffel bag, which was being used jointly by both men and had been left in the cousin's home, would justify the seizure of petitioner's clothing found inside; joint use of the bag rendered the cousin's authority to consent to its search clear. Indeed, the Court was unwilling to engage in the "metaphysical subtleties" raised by Frazier's claim that his cousin only had permission to use one compartment within the bag. By allowing the cousin the use of the bag, and by leaving it in his house, Frazier was held to have assumed the risk that his cousin would allow someone else to look inside. ... More generally, in Schneckloth v. Bustamonte ... we noted that our prior recognition of the constitutional validity of "third party consent" searches in cases like Frazier and Coolidge v. New Hampshire ... supported the view that a consent search is fundamentally different in nature from the waiver of a trial right. These cases at least make clear that when the prosecution seeks to justify a warrantless search by proof of voluntary consent, it is not limited to proof that consent was given by the defendant, but may show that permission to search was obtained from a third party who possessed common authority over or other sufficient relationship to the premises or effects sought to be inspected. The issue now before us is whether the Government made the requisite showing in this case.

The District Court excluded from evidence at the suppression hearings, as inadmissible hearsay, the out-of-court statements of Mrs. Graff with respect to her and respondent's joint occupancy and use of the east bedroom, as well as the evidence that both respondent and Mrs. Graff at various times and to various persons had represented themselves as husband and wife. The Court of Appeals affirmed the ruling. Both courts were in error.

As an initial matter we fail to understand why, on any approach to the case, the out-of-court representations of respondent himself that he and Gayle Graff were husband and wife were considered to be inadmissible against him. Whether or not Mrs. Graff's statements were hearsay, the respondent's own out-of-court admissions would surmount all objections based on the hearsay rule both at the suppression hearings and at the trial itself, and would be admissible for whatever inferences the trial judge could reasonably draw concerning joint occupancy of the east bedroom. ...

As for Mrs. Graff's statements to the searching officers, it should be recalled that the rules of evidence normally applicable in criminal trials do not operate with full force at hearings before the judge to determine the admissibility of evidence. ... "There is a large difference between the two things to be proved, as well as between the tribunals which determine them, and therefore a like difference in the quanta and modes of proof required to establish them." ...

* * *

There is, therefore, much to be said for the proposition that in proceedings where the judge himself is considering the admissibility of evidence, the exclusionary rules, aside from rules of privilege, should not be applicable; and the judge should receive the evidence and give it such weight as his judgment and experience counsel. However that may be, certainly there should be no automatic rule against the reception of hearsay evidence in such proceedings, and it seems equally clear to us that the trial judge should not have excluded Mrs. Graff's statements in the circumstances present here.

In the first place, the court was quite satisfied that the statements had in fact been made. Second, there is nothing in the record to raise serious doubts about the truthfulness of the statements themselves. Mrs. Graff harbored no hostility or bias against respondent that might call her statements into question. Indeed, she testified on his behalf at the suppression hearings. Mrs. Graff responded to inquiry at the time of the search that she and respondent occupied the east bedroom together. A few minutes later, having led the officers to the bedroom, she stated that she and respondent shared the one dresser in the room and that the woman's clothing in the room was hers. Later the same day, she stated to the officers that she and respondent had slept together regularly in the room, including the early morning of that very day.

* * *

If there is remaining doubt about the matter, it should be dispelled by another consideration: cohabitation out of wedlock would not seem to be a relationship that one would falsely confess. Respondent and Gayle Graff were not married, and cohabitation out of wedlock is a crime in the State of Wisconsin. Mrs. Graff's statements were against her penal interest and they carried their own indicia of reliability. This was sufficient in itself, we think, to warrant admitting them to evidence for consideration by the trial judge. . . .

Finally, we note that Mrs. Graff was a witness for the respondent at the suppression hearings. As such, she was available for cross-examination, and the risk of prejudice, if there was any, from the use of hearsay was reduced. Indeed, she entirely denied that she either gave consent or made the November 12 statements to the officers that the District Court excluded from evidence. When asked whether in fact she and respondent had lived together, she claimed her privilege against self-incrimination and declined to answer.

It appears to us, given the admissibility of Mrs. Graff's and respondent's out-of-court statements, that the Government sustained its burden of proving by the preponderance of the evidence that Mrs. Graff's voluntary consent to search the east bedroom was legally sufficient to warrant admitting into evidence the $4,995 found in the diaper bag. But we prefer that the District Court first reconsider the sufficiency of the evidence in the light of this decision and opinion.

Reversed and remanded.

[Mr. Justice DOUGLAS dissented.]
[Mr. Justice BRENNAN, with whom Mr. Justice MARSHALL joined, dissented.]

A Return to Voluntariness

UNITED STATES v. WATSON

Supreme Court of the United States, 1976
423 U.S. 411, 96 S. Ct. 820, 46 L. Ed. 2d 598

Following respondent Watson's arrest outside a restaurant by a postal inspector, the respondent consented to a search of his nearby automobile. The search uncovered two stolen credit cards, and Watson was subsequently convicted of possessing stolen mail. A divided panel of the Court of Appeals (9th Cir.) reversed,

finding that, based on the totality of the circumstances, one of which was the illegality of the arrest, Watson's consent to the search had been coerced and hence was not valid. The government was granted certiorari.

Additional facts and the portions of the Court's opinion that concerned the legality of the arrest are presented in § 5.02, supra.

Mr. Justice WHITE delivered the opinion of the Court.

* * *

Because our judgment is that Watson's arrest comported with the Fourth Amendment, Watson's consent to the search of his car was not the product of an illegal arrest. To the extent that the issue of the voluntariness of Watson's consent was resolved on the premise that his arrest was illegal, the Court of Appeals was also in error.

We are satisfied in addition that the remaining factors relied upon by the Court of Appeals to invalidate Watson's consent are inadequate to demonstrate that, in the totality of the circumstances, Watson's consent was not his own "essentially free and unconstrained choice" because his "will ha(d) been . . . overborne and his capacity for self-determination critically impaired." Schneckloth v. Bustamonte.... There was no overt act or threat of force against Watson proved or claimed. There were no promises made to him and no indication of more subtle forms of coercion that might flaw his judgment. He had been arrested and was in custody, but his consent was given while on a public street, not in the confines of the police station. Moreover, the fact of custody alone has never been enough in itself to demonstrate a coerced confession or consent to search. Similarly, under Schneckloth, the absence of proof that Watson knew he could withhold his consent, though it may be a factor in the overall judgment, is not to be given controlling significance. There is no indication in this record that Watson was a newcomer to the law, mentally deficient or unable in the face of a custodial arrest to exercise a free choice. He was given Miranda warnings and was further cautioned that the results of the search of his car could be used against him. He persisted in his consent.

In these circumstances, to hold that illegal coercion is made out from the fact of arrest and the failure to inform the arrestee that he could withhold consent would not be consistent with Schneckloth and would distort the voluntariness standard that we reaffirmed in that case.

* * *

[Mr. Chief Justice BURGER, Mr. Justice POWELL, Mr. Justice BLACKMUN, and Mr. Justice REHNQUIST joined the opinion of the Court.]

[Mr. Justice STEWART wrote a concurring opinion.]

Mr. Justice MARSHALL, with whom Mr. Justice BRENNAN joins, dissenting.

* * *

Having disposed of the suggestion that the Fourth Amendment requires a warrant of arrest before the police may seize our persons, the Court turns its attention, briefly, to whether Watson voluntarily consented to the search of his automobile. I have suggested . . . that because this issue is of some complexity and has not been thoroughly briefed for us I would remand this case for initial consideration of the question by the Court of Appeals. The Court, however, finds the question simplicity itself. It applies the "totality of the circumstances" test established in Schneckloth v. Bustamonte and treats the question as merely requiring the application of settled law to the facts before us.

That is not the case. Watson was in custody when his consent was obtained. The lack of custody was of decisional importance in Schneckloth which repeatedly distinguished the case before it from one involving a suspect in custody. . . . The Court held:

"Our decision today is a narrow one. We hold only that *when the subject is not in custody* and the State attempts to justify a search on the basis of his consent, the Fourth and Fourteenth Amendments require that it demonstrate that the consent was in fact voluntarily given, and not the result of duress or coercion, express or implied" . . . (emphasis added).

Not once, but twice, the question the Court today treats as settled was expressly reserved:

"[T]he present case does not require a determination of the proper standard to be applied in assessing the validity of a search authorized solely by an alleged consent that is obtained from a person after he has been placed in custody. . . .

I adhere to the views expressed in my dissent in Schneckloth, and therefore believe that the Government must always show that a person who consented to a search did so knowing he had the right to refuse. But even short of this position, there are valid reasons for application of such a rule to consents procured from suspects held in custody. It was, apparently, the force of those reasons that prompted the Court in Schneckloth to reserve the question. Most significantly, we have previously accorded constitutional recognition to the distinction between custodial and noncustodial police contacts. Miranda v. Arizona. . . . Indeed, Schneckloth directly relied on Miranda's articulation of that distinction to reach its conclusion. . . . Thus, while custodial interrogation is inherently coercive, and any consent thereby obtained necessarily suspect, Miranda (and Schneckloth) expressly rejects the notion that there is anything inherently coercive about general noncustodial interrogation. . . . For this reason it is entirely appropriate to place a substantially greater burden on the Government to validate a consent obtained from a suspect following custodial interrogation, however brief. Indeed, it is difficult, if not impossible, to square a contrary conclusion with Miranda. A substantially greater burden on the Government means, quite obviously, that the fact of custody is not merely another factor to be considered in the "totality of the circumstances." And, in my view, it means that the Government must show that the suspect knew he was not obligated to consent to the search. . . .

[Mr. Justice STEVENS took no part in the consideration or decision of the case.]

Comments

1. Generally, consent can be given in three ways: (1) expressed consent, either orally or by a written waiver; (2) implied consent, by the action of the one being searched — e.g., when a person voluntarily opens his property for inspection, or (3) by law — e.g., consent implicit in licensing laws, or by virtue of the employment of the one being searched. See Tobias, M., and Peterson, R., *Pre-Trial Criminal Procedure* 84–86 (1972). See also *Zap* v. *United States*, Comment 2, infra.

   Comparatively few cases concerning consent searches have reached the United States Supreme Court; of those that did, the majority were heard in the decade 1959 to 1969. During the last half century, the Supreme Court has adjudged such diverse issues as who may lawfully consent to a search, what constitutes an intelligent waiver of Fourth Amendment rights, and who may waive constitutional rights. The decisions reached have served as guidelines to lower federal courts, which have heard the bulk of the consent search cases. For an extended discussion of the many consent cases decided in the federal courts of appeals, see Fisher, E., *Search and Seizure* 111–130 (1970) and Tobias and Petersen, supra, at 83–97.

2. In 1921, the United States Supreme Court first recognized that peaceful submission to law enforcement officers' demands to search will not, by itself, constitute a valid consent. In *Amos v. United*

States, 255 U.S. 313, federal revenue agents went to defendant's home. Finding him not at home but finding a woman who claimed she was his wife, they identified themselves and said they had come to search the premises "for violations of the revenue law." The woman opened the door, and during the course of the search the agents found two bottles of illegal distilled whiskey. The evidence was introduced at trial and Amos was convicted of violating revenue laws. The Supreme Court reversed the conviction. Delivering the opinion of the Court, Mr. Justice Clarke pointed out the coercive nature of the search: "The contention that the constitutional rights of defendant were waived when his wife admitted to his home the government officers, who came, without warrant, demanding admission to make search of it under government authority, cannot be entertained.... [I]t is perfectly clear that under the implied coercion here presented, no waiver was intended or effected." 255 U.S. at 317.

Again, in *Johnson* v. *Zerbst,* 304 U.S. 458 (1938), the Supreme Court pointed out the intentional, voluntary nature required of a waiver of constitutional rights. Although the *Johnson* case involved the issue of whether a federal prisoner had waived his Sixth Amendment right to counsel, the Supreme Court in dictum spelled out some guidelines that were particularly valuable to the lower federal courts in resolving the issue of the voluntariness of waivers in Fourth Amendment cases. The Court noted that a waiver "is ordinarily an intentional relinquishment or abandonment of a known right or privilege." In addition, the Court proceeded to outline the burden placed on the prosecution in showing that a waiver had, in fact, been given: "Courts indulge every reasonable presumption against waiver" of fundamental constitutional rights, and we "do not presume acquiescence in the loss of fundamental rights." 304 U.S. at 464.

The Supreme Court held in *Zap* v. *United States,* 328 U.S. 624 (1946), that consent to a search may be given by law as well as orally or in writing. The defendant, Zap, was under contract to do experimental work for the Navy, and under the terms of the contract he agreed to allow the government to audit his books and records. Pursuant to the terms of the contract and authority delegated to them, FBI agents audited the defendant's books at his place of business during business hours with the consent and cooperation of defendant's employees. Zap's bookkeeper, upon request from one of the agents, turned over a cancelled check that was later used to convict Zap of defrauding the government. Zap appealed, charging that his Fourth Amendment rights had been violated. Mr. Justice Douglas delivered the opinion of the Court that Zap's rights had not been infringed upon: "[T]he law of searches and seizures as revealed in the decisions of this Court is the product of the interplay of the Fourth and Fifth Amendments. But those rights may be waived.... [When,] in order to obtain the Government's business, [petitioner] agreed to permit inspection of his accounts and records, he voluntarily waived such claim to privacy which he otherwise might have had as respects business documents related to those contracts." 328 U.S. at 628.

3. It is well established that in consent searches the important consideration is possession and not ownership. This doctrine was spelled out in 1959 when the United States Supreme Court heard the case of *Abel* v. *United States,* 362 U.S. 217. The facts related that Im-

migration and Naturalization Service officers arrested Abel on a warrant for deportation. Incident to arrest, petitioner's hotel room was searched. After Abel had checked out of his room, the hotel management gave consent to an FBI agent who conducted a second search of the room without a warrant. Based upon articles seized during the second search, Able was convicted of conspiracy to commit espionage. The issue before the Supreme Court was whether Abel's constitutional rights had been violated when the hotel management consented to a search of the room that petitioner had occupied. In affirming the conviction, the Supreme Court outlined the importance of the possession issue: "It [the search] was entirely lawful, although undertaken without a warrant .... [A]t the time of the search, petitioner had *vacated* the room. The hotel then had the exclusive right to its *possession*, and the hotel management freely gave its consent that the search be made. Nor was it unlawful to seize the entire contents of the wastebasket .... [P]etitioner had abandoned these articles." 262 U.S. at 241. (Emphasis added.)

The question of the constitutional rights of a hotel guest again came before the United States Supreme Court in *Stoner* v. *California,* 376 U.S. 483 (1964). The results, however, were quite different. The facts in *Stoner* showed that the police, in following up a robbery lead, searched petitioner's hotel room without a warrant after having been given consent to do so by the hotel clerk. Certain articles seized during the search of the room led to Stoner's conviction for robbery. The Supreme Court of the United States reversed petitioner's conviction, holding that the clerk had no authority to consent to the search of Stoner's room: "It is important to bear in mind that it was the petitioner's constitutional right which was at stake here, and not the night clerk's nor the hotel's. It was a right, therefore, which *only petitioner could waive* ... No less than a tenant of a house, or the occupant of a room in a boarding house, a guest in a hotel is entitled to constitutional protection against unreasonable searches and seizures." 376 U.S. at 489–490. (Emphasis added.)

The same considerations regarding possession that apply in hotel consent searches seem to permeate the law relating to the question of who may consent in landlord-tenant situations. The leading case in this area is *Chapman* v. *United States,* 365 U.S. 610 (1961).

In that case, state police officers, without a warrant but with consent from Chapman's landlord, entered the petitioner's rented dwelling and found an illegal still. When Chapman returned home he was arrested by the state officers. Shortly thereafter federal agents arrived and, without a warrant, seized Chapman and samples of the illegal mash. The mash samples were admitted into evidence in federal court, and Chapman was convicted of violating federal liquor laws. Petitioner appealed to the United States Supreme Court, asserting that his Fourth Amendment rights had been violated. The Supreme Court found that the search and seizure were unlawful. In delivering the opinion of the Court, Mr. Justice Whittaker noted that the government "cites no Georgia or other case holding that a landlord, in the absence of an express covenant so permitting, has a right forcibly to enter the demised premises without the consent of the tenant." 365 U.S. at 614. Since the landlord had originally summoned the authorities and entered the dwelling with them, the government attempted to claim that the landlord has a right to enter to "view waste." The Court countered by pointing out that "their purpose in entering was [not to view waste] but to search for distilling equipment" and that such an entry, search, and seizure "without a warrant would reduce the [Fourth] Amendment to a nullity and leave [tenants'] homes secure only in the discretion of [landlords]." 365 U.S. at 616.

4. As part of the necessary proof that a valid consent has been made, evidence must be produced supporting the proposition that the waiver was voluntarily given by the prosecution and that no threats or coercion was employed. A showing of mere acquiescence to a claim of lawful authority does not satisfy the burden placed on the prosecution. The validity of these rules became a central issue in June 1968, when the United States Supreme Court heard the case of *Bumper* v. *North Carolina,* 391 U.S. 543 (1968). The record showed that petitioner was found guilty of rape, and that prior to his arrest, four law enforcement officers came to the home of his 66-year-old grandmother where Bumper lived. The officers announced that they *had a search warrant,* and Bumper's grandmother told them to go ahead and search. In the kitchen the officers found a rifle that was later introduced in evidence at the defendant's trial. At a hearing on a motion to suppress the rifle, the prosecutor acknowledged that he had relied on consent rather than a warrant to justify the search. On appeal, the Supreme Court of North Carolina found that consent had been given and affirmed the conviction. The United States Supreme Court granted certiorari to consider whether the search had in fact been based on consent, and the Court could find no evidence that the grandmother had consented: "The issue thus presented is whether a search can be justified as lawful on the basis of consent when that "consent" has been given only after the official conducting the search has asserted that he possesses a warrant. We hold that there can be no consent under such circumstances." 391 U.S. at 548. In a footnote to the opinion the Court observed: "Mrs. Leath [the grandmother] owned both the house and the rifle. The petitioner concedes that her voluntary consent to the search would have been binding upon him. Conversely, there can be no question of the petitioner's standing to challenge the lawfulness of the search." 391 U.S. 548 n.11. In reaffirming basic consent concepts, the Court noted: "When a prosecutor seeks to rely upon consent to justify the lawfulness of a search, he has the burden of proving that the consent was, in fact, freely and voluntarily given.... A search conducted in reliance upon a warrant cannot later be justified on the basis of consent . . . when it turns out that the State does not even attempt to rely upon the validity of the warrant." 391 U.S. at 548–549.

In 1969, the case of *Frazier* v. *Cupp,* 394 U.S. 731, reached the United States Supreme Court. The petitioner claimed that a number of his constitutional rights were violated in his 1965 trial in which he was convicted for murder along with his cousin, one Rawls. One of his claims to the Court was that certain articles of clothing that officers had seized from his duffel bag should not have been admitted in evidence. This bag was used jointly by both petitioner and his cousin Rawls, and it was in Rawls' home at the time the police arrived to arrest Rawls. The officers asked for permission to take clothing belonging to Rawls from the bag, and Rawls consented. During the search, officers also seized petitioner's clothing from the bag. The petitioner argued before the

Supreme Court that the clothing had been illegally seized in violation of the Fourth and Fourteenth Amendments. The issue of who
may consent in joint-ownership situations was swiftly disposed of
by the Court. While affirming on all other points of error raised by
petitioner, the Court noted: "Petitioner's final contention can be
dismissed rather quickly.... Since Rawls was a joint user of the
bag, he clearly had authority to consent to its search. The officers
therefore found evidence against petitioner while in the course of
an otherwise lawful search... [and] they were clearly permitted
to seize it." 394 U.S. at 740. In response to Frazier's claim that
Rawls only had *actual permission* to use one compartment of the
bag and was not authorized to consent to the search of other compartments, the Court concluded: "We will not . . . engage in such
metaphysical subtleties in judging the efficacy of Rawls' consent.
Petitioner, in allowing Rawls to use the bag and in leaving it in his
house, must be taken to have assumed the risk that Rawls would
allow someone else to look inside." Id.

A consent issue was also raised in *Coolidge* v. *New Hampshire,*
403, U.S. 443 (1971). The facts revealed that while petitioner was
being interrogated at the police station, two policemen came to his
house and questioned his wife in order to corroborate certain information they had received. Unaware that other officers who had
visited the petitioner at his home some days earlier had been shown
guns, the police asked Mrs. Coolidge about any guns that might be in
the house. They were shown four guns by petitioner's wife, which
she offered to let them take. At first the officers declined the offer,
but they later decided to take along the guns and some articles of
clothing made available to them. The petitioner contended before
the Supreme Court that the guns and clothing were obtained
through an unlawful search and seizure in violation of his Fourth
and Fourteenth Amendment rights. He asserted that (1) when Mrs.
Coolidge handed over the guns and clothing "she was acting as an
'instrument' of the officials, complying with a 'demand' made by
them," and (2) Mrs. Coolidge "could not or did not 'waive' her
husband's Fourth Amendment rights." In considering petitioner's
first assertion that his wife acted as an "instrument" or agent of the
state, the Court concluded: "There is not the slightest implication
of an attempt on their [the officer's] part to coerce or dominate her,
or, for that matter, to direct her actions by the more subtle techniques of suggestion that are available to officials in circumstances
like these. To hold that the conduct of the police here was a search
and seizure would be to hold, in effect, that a criminal suspect has
constitutional protection against the adverse consequences of a
spontaneous, good-faith effort by his wife to clear him of suspicion." 403 U.S. at 489–490. Because the Court could not find that
the conduct of the police constituted a search and seizure, petitioner's second assertion became a moot issue. In response to it
the Court noted: "Since we cannot accept this interpretation of the
facts, we need not consider the petitioner's further argument that
Mrs. Coolidge could not or did not "waive" her husband's constitutional protection against unreasonable searches and seizures."
403 U.S. at 487. Finding error on other grounds, the Court reversed the conviction and remanded the case back to the New
Hampshire Supreme Court.

5. As noted above, two general principles apply in all consent
searches: (1) consent must be given by the person who is in lawful

possession at the time of the search, or in the case of a search of the person, consent must be given by the one being searched, and (2) the consent must be given voluntarily without duress or coercion. The first of these two principles becomes very important when third-party consent or joint-occupancy situations arise. See, e.g., *United States* v. *Matlock, supra.* Therefore, it is important to understand that *possession* and not *ownership* is the important consideration for the law enforcement officer. *Bustamonte* leaves this principle undisturbed but does focus on the issue of voluntariness and how it is to be shown by the prosecution. Although a consent search can prove to be very valuable to law enforcement officials, the same kind of search may prove to be a nightmare for the prosecution when it comes time to introduce in evidence any results of the search. If the defendant claims that he did not consent or that he consented under coercion, the search will be condemned and the fruits will be excluded. Consequently, *Bustamonte* has been a plus to law enforcement since the decision does give the prosecutor greater latitude in showing voluntariness when the subject of the search denies that he consented.

6. It should be noted that in *Bustamonte* the Court rejected the idea that consent searches can occur only when the subject understands his right to *refuse* and *intentionally waives* that right. For example, in the 1966 case of *Stoner* v. *California, supra,* the Court noted at 489–490: "[P]etitioner's constitutional right was at stake here ... [and] *only petitioner could waive* [it]. . . ." (Emphasis added.) The Court in *Bustamonte* held that such a waiver approach "would be thoroughly inconsistent with our decisions." Consequently, the Court concluded that in *noncustody* consent situations the prosecutor is not required to prove that the subject *knew* he had the right to refuse. Although such knowledge should be taken into account, the Court announced that voluntariness is to be determined from the "totality of circumstances." Ultimately, the same test was applied in *Watson, supra,* to a suspect who *was in custody* at the time consent was given.

7. Actually, the *Watson* decision should have come as a little surprise in light of recent post-*Bustamonte* decisions by various courts of appeals in which the "totality of circumstances" test was applied to custodial consents. See, e.g., *United States* v. *Cage,* 494 F.2d 740 (10 Cir. 1974); *Hayes* v. *Cady,* 500 F.2d 1212 (7th Cir. 1974); *United States* v. *Hearn and Taylor,* 496 F.2d 236 (6th Cir. 1974), and, of course, *United States* v. *Watson,* 504 F.2d 849 (9th Cir. 1974). It should be noted, however, that at least one state supreme court has refused to follow *Schneckloth* v. *Bustamonte.* See *State* v. *Johnson,* 346 A.2d 66 (N.J. 1975) (New Jersey Constitution requires that person from whom consent for a search is to be obtained first be informed of his right to refuse). Other recent lower federal and state court decisions involving consent issues include *Santos* v. *Bayley,* 400 F. Supp. 784 (M.D. Pa. 1975) (warrantless search upheld on the basis of consent even though preceded by an illegal arrest because *Miranda* warnings were given two times and defendant was informed of right to refuse to consent); *State* v. *Cox,* 330 So. 2d 284 (La. 1975) (police officer's statement to detained suspect that "your van will have to be searched and it would be better if you gave us any objectionable items" held to result in coerced consent); *United States* v. *Griffin,* 530 F.2nd 739 (7th Cir.

1976) (where defendant in opening door allowed police officers to follow him into living room where stolen mail was strewn about a table, court held that voluntary consent was manifested by the defendant's conduct); *Johnson* v. *State,* 352 A.2d 349 (Md. Ct. Special App. 1976) (consent coerced when three carloads of heavily armed police apprehended defendant, handcuffed him, obtained his permission at gunpoint to search his apartment, and briefly freed his hands so he could sign the consent form); *State* v.*Middleton,* 222 S.E.2d 763 (S.C. 1976) (admission of testimony at defendant's rape trial that he refused to consent to a combing of his pubic area for samples of his hairs and any alien hairs held not violative of Fourth or Fifth Amendment); *People* v. *Reynolds,* 127 Cal. Rptr. 561 (Ca.. Ct. App. 1976) (prosecution has burden of proving by "clear and convincing" evidence that a warrantless search was procured by consent); *People* v. *Taylor,* 333 N.E.2d 41 (Ill. 1975) (son not living in same house occupied by mother and brother may not consent to search of room in mother's house occupied by brother); *United States* v. *Diggs,* 396 F. Supp. 610 (E.D.Pa. 1975) (fact that defendant and girlfriend left *locked* metal box with her uncle for safekeeping following bank robbery strongly negated any implication that they intended to waive right of privacy or to consent to opening the box, and uncle did not have right to allow FBI agents to open box without a warrant, so the government's claim of consent was invalid); *Lawton* v. *State,* 320 So. 2d 463 (Fla. App. 1975) (warrantless search cannot be based on consent when the wife consents but the husband, who is present, objects) (cf. *State* v. *Deputy,* 319 So. 2d 299 [La. 1975] [consent of a spouse to search on the basis of *United States* v. *Matlock*]); *Butler* v. *Commonwealth,* 536 S.W.2d 139 (Ky. 1976) (babysitter's consent to search of residence held valid with respect to suspected armed robber in hiding); *United States* v. *Harris,* 534 F.2d 95 (7th Cir. 1976) (government required to prove by a preponderance of evidence that police had reason to believe that robbery suspect's accomplice had necessary common authority over suspect's apartment to validly consent to warrantless search of it).

F. BORDER SEARCHES

The "Border or Its Functional Equivalent" Test

ALMEIDA-SANCHEZ v. UNITED STATES

Supreme Court of the United States, 1973
413 U.S. 266, 93 S. Ct. 2535, 37 L. Ed. 2d 596

Petitioner, a Mexican citizen holding a valid American work permit, was stopped some 25 air miles north of the Mexican border by the United States Border Patrol, and his automobile was thoroughly searched. The search, made without probable cause or consent, uncovered marijuana which was used to convict petitioner of a federal crime. The Court of Appeals (9th Cir.) upheld the validity of the search on the basis of § 287(a)(3) of the Immigration and Nationality Act, 66 Stat. 233, 8 U.S.C. § 1357(a)(3). Petitioner successfully sought certiorari.

Mr. Justice STEWART delivered the opinion of the Court.

* * *

... It is undenied that the Border Patrol had no search warrant, and that there was no probable cause of any kind for the stop or the subsequent search—not even the "reasonable suspicion" found sufficient for a street detention and weapons search in Terry v. Ohio . . . [infra] and Adams v. Williams [infra]. . . .

The only asserted justification for this extravagant license to search is § 287(a)(3) of the Immigration and Nationality Act, 66 Stat. 233, 8 U.S.C. § 1357(a)(3), which simply provides for warrantless searches of automobiles and other conveyances "within a reasonable distance from any external boundary of the United States," as authorized by regulations to be promulgated by the Attorney General. The Attorney General's regulation, 8 C.F.R. § 287.1, defines "reasonable distance" as "within 100 air miles from any external boundary of the United States." . . .

No claim is made, nor could one be, that the search of the petitioner's car was constitutional under any previous decision of this Court involving the search of an automobile. It is settled, of course, that a stop and search of a moving automobile, can be made without a warrant. That narrow exception to the warrant requirement was first established in Carroll v. United States.... The Court recognized that a moving automobile on the open road presents a situation "where it is not practicable to secure a warrant because the vehicle can be quickly moved out of the locality or jurisdiction in which the warrant must be sought." . . . Carroll has been followed in a line of subsequent cases, but the Carroll doctrine does not declare a field day for the police in searching automobiles. Automobile or no automobile there must be probable cause for the search. . . .

In seeking a rationale for the validity of the search in this case, the Government thus understandably sidesteps the automobile search cases. Instead, the Government relies heavily on cases dealing with administrative inspections. But these cases fail to support the constitutionality of this search.

In Camara v. Municipal Court, 387 U.S. 523 (1967), the Court held that administrative inspections to enforce community health and welfare regulations could be made on less than probable cause to believe that particular dwellings were the sites of particular violations.... Yet the Court insisted that the inspector obtain either consent or a warrant supported by particular physical and demographic characteristics of the areas to be searched. ... The search in the present case was conducted in the unfettered discretion of the members of the Border Patrol, who did not have a warrant, probable cause, or consent. The search thus embodied precisely the evil the Court saw in Camara when it insisted that the "discretion of the official in the field" be circumscribed by obtaining a warrant prior to the inspection. ...

Two other administrative inspection cases relied upon by the Government are equally inapposite. Colonnade Catering Corporation v. United States, 397 U.S. 72 (1970), and United States v. Biswell 406 U.S. 311 (1972), both approved warrantless inspections of commercial enterprises engaged in businesses closely regulated and licensed by the Government. ...

A central difference between those cases and this one is that businessmen engaged in such federally licensed and regulated enterprises accept the burdens as well as the benefits of their trade, whereas the petitioner here was not engaged in any regulated or licensed business.

Moreover, in Colonnade and Biswell, the searching officers knew with certainty that the premises searched were in fact utilized for the sale of liquor or guns. In the present case, by contrast, there was no such assurance that the individual searched was within the proper scope of official scrutiny—that is, there was no reason whatever to believe that he or his automobile had even crossed the border, much less that he was guilty of the commission of an offense.

Since neither this Court's automobile search decisions nor its administrative inspection decisions provide any support for the constitutionality of the stop and search in the present case, we are left simply with the statute that purports to authorize automobiles to be stopped and searched without a warrant and "within a reasonable distance from any external boundary of the United States." It is clear, of course, that no Act of Congress can authorize a violation of the Constitution. But under familiar principles of constitutional adjudication, our duty is to construe the statute, if possible, in a manner consistent with the Fourth Amendment. . . .

It is undoubtedly within the power of the Federal Government to exclude aliens from the country. . . . It is also without doubt that this power can be effectuated by routine inspections and searches of individuals or conveyances seeking to cross our borders. As the Court stated in Carroll v. United States: "Travellers may be so stopped in crossing an international boundary because of national self-protection reasonably requiring one entering the country to identify himself as entitled to come in, and his belongings as effects which may be lawfully brought in." . . .

Whatever the permissible scope of intrusiveness of a routine border search might be, searches of this kind may in certain circumstances take place not only at the border itself, but at its functional equivalents as well. For example, searches at an established station near the border, at a point marking the confluence of two or more roads that extend from the border, might be functional equivalents of border searches. For another example, a search of the passengers and cargo of an airplane arriving at a St. Louis airport after a nonstop flight from Mexico City would clearly be the functional equivalent of a border search.

But the search of the petitioner's automobile by a roving patrol, on a California road that lies at all points at least 20 miles north of the Mexican border, was of a wholly different sort. In the absence of probable cause or consent, that search violated the petitioner's Fourth Amendment right to be free of "unreasonable searches and seizures."

It is not enough to argue, as does the Government, that the problem of deterring unlawful entry by aliens across long expanses of national boundaries is a serious one. The needs of law enforcement stand in constant tension with the Constitution's protections of the individual against certain exercises of official power. . . .

The Court that decided Carroll v. United States . . . sat during a period in our history when the Nation was confronted with a law enforcement problem of no small magnitude — the enforcement of the Prohibition laws. But that Court resisted the pressure of official expedience against the guarantee of the Fourth Amendment. Mr. Chief Justice Taft's opinion for the Court distinguished between searches at the border and in the interior, and clearly controls the case at bar:

"It would be intolerable and unreasonable if a prohibition agent were authorized to stop every automobile on the chance of finding liquor and thus subject all persons lawfully using the highways to the inconvenience and indignity of such a search. Travellers may be so stopped in crossing an international boundary because of national self-protection reasonably requiring one entering the country to identify himself as entitled to come in, and his belongings as effects which may be lawfully brought in. But those lawfully within the country, entitled to use the public highways, have a right to free passage without interruption or search unless there is known to a competent official authorized to search, probable cause for believing that their vehicles are carrying contraband or illegal merchandise."

Reversed.

Mr. Justice WHITE, with whom the Chief Justice [BURGER], Mr. Justice BLACKMUN, and Mr. Justice REHNQUIST join, dissenting.

* * *

In 1946, it was represented to Congress that "[i]n the enforcement of the immigration laws it is at times desirable to stop and search vehicles within a reasonable distance from the boundaries of the United States and the legal right to do so should be conferred by law." . . . The House Committee on Immigration and Naturalization was "of the opinion that the legislation is highly desirable," and its counterpart in the Senate . . . stated that "[t]here is no question but that this is a step in the right direction." The result was express statutory authority, Act of Aug. 7, 1946, 60 Stat. 865, to conduct searches of vehicles for aliens within a reasonable distance from the border without warrant or possible cause. Moreover, in the

Immigration and Nationality Act of 1952, 66 Stat. 163, Congress permitted the entry onto private lands, excluding dwellings, within a distance of 25 miles from any external boundaries of the country "for the purpose of patrolling the border to prevent the illegal entry of aliens into the United States ..." § 287(a)(3), 66 Stat. 233.

The judgment of Congress obviously was that there are circumstances in which it is reasonably necessary, in the enforcement of the immigration laws, to search vehicles and other private property for aliens, without warrant or probable cause and at locations other than at the border. To disagree with this legislative judgment is to invalidate 8 U.S.C. § 1357(a)(3) in the face of the contrary opinion of Congress that its legislation comported with the standard of reason-

ableness of the Fourth Amendment. This I am quite unwilling to do.

* * *

Guided by the principles of Camara, Colonnade, and Biswell [see Comments, infra], I can not but uphold the judgment of Congress that for purposes of enforcing the immigration laws it is reasonable to treat the exterior boundaries of the country as a zone, not a line, and that there are recurring circumstances in which the search of vehicular traffic without warrant and without probable cause may be reasonable under the Fourth Amendment although not carried out at the border itself.

[Mr. Justice POWELL wrote a concurring opinion.]

Stopping Automobiles at Fixed Checkpoints

UNITED STATES v. MARTINEZ-FUERTE

Supreme Court of the United States, 1976
428 U.S. 543, 96 S. Ct. 3070, 49 L. Ed. 2d 1116

The Supreme Court granted certiorari in two cases, Nos. 74-1560 and 75-5387, involving criminal prosecutions for offenses relating to the transportation of illegal aliens. The cases were consolidated. Respondents in No. 74-1560 were defendants in three separate prosecutions resulting from arrests made on three different occasions at the permanent immigration checkpoint 66 road miles north of the Mexican border near San Clemente, California. Petitioner in No. 75-5387, Rodolfo Sifuentes, was arrested at the permanent immigration checkpoint on U.S. Highway 77 near Sarita, Texas. The Sarita checkpoint is approximately 65 to 90 miles from the nearest point of the Mexican border.

Additional facts are stated in the opinion.

Mr. Justice POWELL delivered the opinion of the court.

I.

* * *

A.

* * *

....Respondent Amado Martinez-Fuerte approached the checkpoint driving a vehicle containing two female passengers. The

women were illegal Mexican aliens who entered the United States at the San Ysidro port of entry by using false papers and rendezvoused with Martinez-Fuerte in San Diego to be transported northward. At the checkpoint their car was directed to the secondary inspection area. Martinez-Fuerte produced documents showing him to be a lawful resident alien, but his passengers admitted being present in the country unlawfully. He was charged with two counts of illegally transporting aliens in violation of 8

U.S.C. § 1324(a)(2). He moved before trial to suppress all evidence stemming from the stop on the ground that the operation of the checkpoint was in violation of the Fourth Amendment. The motion to suppress was denied, and he was convicted on both counts after a jury trial.

Respondent Jose Jiminez-Garcia attempted to pass through the checkpoint while driving a car containing one passenger. He had picked the passenger up by prearrangement in San Ysidro after the latter had been smuggled across the border. Questioning at the secondary inspection area revealed the illegal status of the passenger, and Jiminez-Garcia was charged in two counts with illegally transporting an alien, 8 U.S.C. § 1324(a)(2), and conspiring to commit that offense. 18 U.S.C. § 371. His motion to suppress the evidence derived from the stop was granted.

Respondents Raymond Guillen and Fernando Medrano-Barragan approached the checkpoint with Guillen driving and Medrano-Barragan and his wife as passengers. Questioning at the secondary inspection area revealed that Medrano-Barragan and his wife were illegal aliens. A subsequent search of the car uncovered three other illegal aliens in the trunk. Medrano-Barragan had led the other aliens across the border at the beach near Tijuana, Mexico, where they rendezvoused with Guillen, a United States citizen. Guillen and Medrano-Barragan were jointly indicted on four counts of illegally transporting aliens, 8 U.S.C. § 1324(a)(2), four counts of inducing the illegal entry of aliens, id., § 1324(a)(4), and one conspiracy count. 18 U.S.C. § 371. The District Court granted the defendants' motion to suppress.

Martinez-Fuerte appealed his conviction, and the Government appealed the granting of the motions to suppress in the respective prosecutions of Jiminez-Garcia and of Guillen and Medrano-Barragan. The Court of Appeals for the Ninth Circuit consolidated the three appeals, which presented the common question whether routine stops and interrogations at checkpoints are consistent with the Fourth Amendment. The Court of Appeals held, with one judge dissenting, that these stops violated the Fourth Amendment, concluding that a stop for inquiry is constitutional only if the Border Patrol reasonably suspects the presence of illegal aliens on the basis of articulable facts. It reversed Martinez-Fuerte's conviction and affirmed the orders to suppress the other cases. . . .

B.

Petitioner . . . Rodolfo Sifuentes was arrested at the permanent immigration checkpoint . . . near Sarita, Tex[as]. . . .

Sifuentes drove up to the checkpoint without any visible passengers. When an agent approached the vehicle, however, he observed four passengers, one in the front seat and the other three in the rear, slumped down in the seats. Questioning revealed that each passenger was an illegal alien, although Sifuentes was a United States citizen. The aliens had met Sifuentes in the United States, by prearrangement, after swimming across the Rio Grande.

Sifuentes was indicted on four counts of illegally transporting aliens. 8 U.S.C. § 1324(a)(2). He moved on Fourth Amendment grounds to suppress the evidence derived from the stop. The motion was denied and he was convicted after a jury trial. Sifuentes renewed his Fourth Amendment argument on appeal, contending primarily that stops made without reason to believe a car is transporting aliens illegally are unconstitutional. The United States Court of Appeals for the Fifth Circuit affirmed. . . .

* * *

II.

* * *

B.

We are concerned here with permanent checkpoints, the locations of which are chosen on the basis of a number of factors. The Border Patrol believes that to assure effectiveness, a checkpoint must be (i) distant enough from the border to avoid interference with traffic in populated areas near the border, (ii) close to the confluence of two or more significant roads leading away from the border, (iii) situated in terrain that restricts vehicle passage around the checkpoint, (iv) on a stretch of highway compatible with safe operation, and (v) beyond the 25-mile zone in which "border passes" . . . are valid. . . .

The record in No. 74-1560 provides a rather complete picture of the effectiveness of San Clemente checkpoint. Approximately 10 million cars pass the checkpoint location each year, although the checkpoint actually is in operation only about 70% of the time. In calendar year 1973, approximately 17,000 illegal aliens were apprehended there. During an eight-day period in 1974 that included the arrests involved in No. 74-1560, roughly 146,000 vehicles passed through the checkpoint during 124 1/6 hours of operation. Of these, 820 vehicles were referred to the secondary inspection area, where Border Patrol agents found 725 deportable aliens in 171 vehicles. In all but two cases, the aliens were discovered without a conventional search of the vehicle. A similar rate of apprehensions throughout the year would have resulted in an annual total of over 33,000, although the Government contends that many illegal aliens pass through the checkpoint undetected. The record in No. 75-5387 does not provide comparable statistical information regarding the Sarita checkpoint. While it appears that fewer illegal aliens are apprehended there, it may be assumed that fewer pass by undetected, as every motorist is questioned.

III.

The Fourth Amendment imposes limits on search and seizure powers in order to prevent arbitrary and oppressive interference by enforcement officials with the privacy and personal security of individuals.... In delineating the constitutional sageguards applicable in particular contexts, the Court has weighed the public interest against the Fourth Amendment interest of the individual ... a process evident in our previous cases dealing with Border Patrol traffic-checking operations. . . .

IV.

It is agreed that checkpoint stops are "seizures" within the meaning of the Fourth Amendment. The defendants contend primarily that the routine stopping of vehicles at a checkpoint is invalid because [United States v.] Brignoni-Ponce [422 U.S. 873 (1975)] must be read as proscribing any stops in the absence of reasonable suspicion. Sifuentes alternatively contends in No. 75-5387 that routine checkpoint stops are

permissible only when the practice has the advance judicial authorization of a warrant. There was a warrant authorizing the stops at San Clemente but none at Sarita. As we reach the issue of a warrant requirement only if reasonable suspicion is not required, we turn first to whether reasonable suspicion is a prerequisite to a valid stop, a question to be resolved by balancing the interests at stake.

A.

Our previous cases have recognized that maintenance of a traffic-checking program in the interior is necessary because the flow of illegal aliens cannot be controlled effectively at the border. We note here only the substantiality of the public interest in the practice of routine stops for inquiry at permanent checkpoints, a practice which the Government identifies as the most important of the traffic-checking operations.... These checkpoints are located on important highways; in their absence such highways would offer illegal aliens a quick and safe route into the interior. Routine checkpoint inquiries apprehend many smugglers and illegal aliens who succumb to the lure of such highways. And the prospect of such inquiries forces others onto less efficient roads that are less heavily travelled, slowing their movement and making them more vulnerable to detection by roving patrols. . . .

A requirement that stops on major routes inland always be based on reasonable suspicion would be impractical because the flow of traffic tends to be too heavy to allow it to be identified as a possible carrier of illegal aliens. In particular, such a requirement would largely eliminate any deterrent to the conduct of well-disguised smuggling operations, even though smugglers are known to use these highways regularly.

B.

While the need to make routine checkpoint stops is great, the consequent intrusion on the Fourth Amendment interests is quite limited. The stop does intrude to a limited extent on motorists' right to "free passage without interruption" ... and arguably on their right to personal security. But it involves only a brief detention of travelers during which " '(a)ll that is required of the vehicle's occupants is a response to a brief question or two and possibly the production of a document evidencing a right to be in the United States.' " United States v. Brignoni-Ponce, supra, at 880. Neither the vehicle nor its occupants are searched, and visual inspection of the vehicle is limited to what can be seen without a search. This objective intrusion—the stop itself, the questioning, and the visual inspection—also existed in roving-patrol stops. But we view checkpoint stops in a different light because the subjective intrusion—the generating of concern or even fright on the part of lawful travelers—is appreciably less in the case of a checkpoint stop. ...

In Brignoni-Ponce, we recognized that Fourth Amendment analysis in this context also must take into account the overall degree of interference with legitimate traffic. ... We concluded there that random roving-patrol stops could not be tolerated because they "would subject the residents of ... (border) areas to potentially unlimited interference with their use of the highways, solely at the discretion of Border Patrol officers.... (They) could stop motorists at random for questioning, day or night, anywhere within 100 air miles of the 2,000 mile border, on a city street, a busy highway, or a desert road...." ... There also was a grave danger that such unreviewable discretion would be abused by some officers in the field. ...

Routine checkpoint stops do not intrude similarly on the motoring public. First, the potential interference with legitimate traffic is minimal. Motorists using these highways are not taken by surprise as they know, or may obtain knowledge of, the location of the checkpoints and will not be stopped elsewhere. Second, checkpoint operations both appear to and actually involve less discretionary enforcement activity. The regularized manner in which established checkpoints are operated is visible evidence, reassuring to law-abiding motorists, that the stops are duly authorized and believed to serve the public interest. The location of a fixed checkpoint is not chosen by officers in the field, but by officials responsible for making overall decisions as to the most effective allocation of limited enforcement resources. We may assume that such officials will be unlikely to locate a checkpoint where it bears arbitrarily or oppressively on motorists as a class. And since field officers

may stop only those cars passing the checkpoint, there is less room for abusive or harassing stops of individuals than there was in the case of roving-patrol stops. Moreover, a claim that a particular exercise of discretion in locating or operating a checkpoint is unreasonable is subject to post-stop judicial review.

The defendants arrested at the San Clemente checkpoint suggest that its operation involves a significant extra element of intrusiveness in that only a small percentage of cars are referred to the secondary inspection area, thereby "stigmatizing" those diverted and reducing the assurances provided by equal treatment of all motorists. We think defendants overstate the consequences. Referrals are made for the sole purpose of conducting a routine and limited inquiry into residence status that cannot feasibly be made of every motorist where the traffic is heavy. The objective intrusion of the stop and inquiry thus remains minimal. Selective referral may involve some annoyance, but it remains true that the stops should not be frightening or offensive because of their public and relatively routine nature. Moreover, selective referrals—rather than questioning the occupants of every car—tend to advance some Fourth Amendment interests by minimizing the intrusion on the general motoring public.

C.

The defendants note correctly that to accommodate public and private interests some quantum of individualized suspicion is usually a prerequisite to a constitutional search or seizure.... But the Fourth Amendment imposes no irreducible requirement of such suspicion. This is clear from Camara v. Municipal Court, 387 U.S. 523 (1967). ... In Camara the Court required an "area" warrant to support the reasonableness of inspecting private residences within a particular area for building code violations, but recognized that "specific knowledge of the conditions of the particular dwelling" was not required to enter any given residence. ... In so holding, the Court examined the government interests advanced to justify such routine intrusions "upon the constitutionally protected interests of the private citizen" ... and concluded that under the circumstances the government interests outweighed those of the private citizen.

We think the same conclusion is appropriate here, where we deal neither with searches nor with the sanctity of private dwellings, ordinarily afforded the most stringent Fourth Amendment protection. . . . As we have noted earlier, one's expectation of privacy in an automobile and of freedom in its operation are significantly different from the traditional expectation of privacy and freedom in one's residence. . . . And the reasonableness of the procedures followed in making these checkpoint stops makes the resulting intrusion on the interests of motorists minimal. On the other hand, the purpose of the stops is legitimate and in the public interest, and the need for this enforcement technique is demonstrated by the records in the cases before us. Accordingly, we hold that the stops and questioning at issue may be made in the absence of any individualized suspicion at reasonably located checkpoints.

* * *

V.

Sifuentes' alternative argument is that routine stops at a checkpoint are permissible only if a warrant has given judicial authorization to the particular checkpoint location and the practice of routine stops. A warrant requirement in these circumstances draws some support from Camara, where the Court held that, absent consent, an "area" warrant was required to make a building code inspection, even though the search could be conducted absent cause to believe that there were violations in the building searched.

We do not think, however, that Camara is an apt model. It involved the search of private residences, for which a warrant traditionally has been required. . . . As developed more fully above, the strong Fourth Amendment interests that justify the warrant requirement in that context are absent here. The degree of intrusion upon privacy that may be occasioned by a search of a house hardly can be compared with the minor interference with privacy resulting from the mere stop for questioning as to residence. Moreover, the warrant requirement in Camara served specific Fourth Amendment interests to which a warrant require-

ment here would make little contribution. The Court there said:

"[W]hen [an] inspector [without a warrant] demands entry, the occupant has no way of knowing whether enforcement of the municipal code involved requires inspection of his premises, no way of knowing the lawful limits of the inspector's power to search, and no way of knowing whether the inspector himself is acting under proper authorization." 387 U.S. at 532.

A warrant provided assurance to the occupant on these scores. We believe that the visible manifestations of the field officers' authority at a checkpoint provide substantially the same assurances in this case.

Other purposes served by the requirement of a warrant also are inapplicable here. One such purpose is to prevent hindsight from coloring the evaluation of the reasonableness of a search or seizure. . . . The reasonableness of checkpoint stops, however, turns on factors such as the location and method of operation of the checkpoint, factors that are not susceptible to the distortion of hindsight, and therefore will be open to post-stop review notwithstanding the absence of a warrant. Another purpose for a warrant requirement is to substitute the judgment of the magistrate for that of the searching or seizing officer. . . . But the need for this is reduced when the decision to "seize" is not entirely in the hands of the officer in the field, and deference is to be given to the administrative decisions of higher ranking officials.

VI.

In summary, we hold that stops for brief questioning routinely conducted at permanent checkpoints are consistent with the Fourth Amendment and need not be authorized by warrant. The principal protection of Fourth Amendment rights at checkpoints lies in appropriate limitations on the scope of the stop. . . . We have held that checkpoint searches are constitutional only if justified by consent or probable cause to search. United States v. Ortiz. . . . And our holding today is limited to the type of stops described in this opinion. "[A]ny further detention . . . must be based on consent or probable cause." United States v. Brignoni-Ponce, supra, at 882. None of the defendants in these cases argues that the stopping officers exceeded these limitations. Consequently, we affirm the judgment of the Court of Appeals for the Fifth Circuit, which had affirmed the conviction of Sifuentes. We reverse the judgment of the Court of Appeals for the Ninth Circuit and remand the case with directions to affirm the conviction of Martinez-Fuerte and to remand the other cases to the District Court for further proceedings.

Mr. Justice BRENNAN, with whom Mr. Justice MARSHALL joins, dissenting.

* * *

Consistent with [its] purpose to debilitate Fourth Amendment protections, the Court's decision today virtually empties the Amendment of its reasonableness requirement by holding that law enforcement officials manning fixed checkpoint stations who make standardless seizures of persons do not violate the Amendment. This holding cannot be squared with this Court's recent decisions in United States v. Ortiz, 422 U.S. 891 (1975); United States v. Brignoni-Ponce, 422 U.S. 873 (1975); and Almeida-Sanchez v. United States, 413 U.S. 266 (1973) [supra]. I dissent.

While the requisite justification for permitting a search or seizure may vary in certain contexts, . . . even in the exceptional situations permitting intrusions on less than probable cause, it has long been settled that justification must be measured by objective standards. Thus in the seminal decision justifying intrusions on less than probable cause, Terry v. Ohio, [392 U.S. 1 (1968)] [infra], the Court said:

"The scheme of the Fourth Amendment becomes meaningful only when it is assured that at some point the conduct of those charged with enforcing the laws can be subjected to the more detached, neutral scrutiny of a judge who must evaluate the reasonableness of a particular search or seizure in light of the particular circumstances. And in making that assessment it is imperative that the facts be judged against an objective standard. . . . Anything less would invite intrusions upon constitutionally guaranteed rights based on nothing more substantial than inarticulate hunches, a result this Court has consistently refused to sanction." Terry v. Ohio, supra, at 21–22.

"This demand for specificity in the information upon which police action is predicated is the central teaching of this Court's Fourth Amendment jurisprudence." Id., at 21 n. 18.

Terry thus made clear what common sense teaches: conduct, to be reasonable, must pass muster under objective standards applied to specific facts.

We are told today, however, that motorists without number may be individually stopped, questioned, visually inspected, and then further detained without even a showing of articulable suspicion . . . let alone the heretofore constitutional minimum of reasonable suspicion, a result that permits search and seizure to rest upon "nothing more substantial than inarticulate hunches." This defacement of Fourth Amendment protections is arrived at by a balancing process that overwhelms the individual's protection against unwarranted official intrusion by a governmental interest said to justify the search and seizure. But that method is only a convenient cover for condoning arbitrary official conduct, for the governmental interests relied on as warranting intrusion here are the same as those in Almeida-Sanchez and Ortiz, which required a showing of probable cause for roving-patrol and fixed checkpoint searches, and Brignoni-Ponce, which required at least a showing of reasonable suspicion based on specific articulable facts to justify roving-patrol stops. Absent some difference in the nature of the intrusion, the same minimal requirement should be imposed for checkpoint stops.

The Court assumes, and I certainly agree, that persons stopped at fixed checkpoints, whether or not referred to a secondary detention area, are "seized" within the meaning of the Fourth Amendment. Moreover, since the vehicle and its occupants are subjected to a "visual inspection," the intrusion clearly exceeds mere physical restraint, for officers are able to see more in a stopped vehicle than in vehicles traveling at normal speeds down the highway. As the Court concedes . . . the checkpoint stop involves essentially the same intrusions as a roving-patrol stop, yet the Court provides no principled basis for distinguishing checkpoint stops.

* * *

In abandoning any requirement of a minimum of reasonable suspicion, or even articulable suspicion, the Court in every practical sense renders meaningless, as applied to checkpoint stops, the Brignoni-Ponce holding that "standing alone [Mexican appearance] does not justify stopping all Mexican-Americans to ask if they are aliens." ... Since the objective is almost entirely the Mexican illegally in the country, checkpoint officials, uninhibited by any objective standards and therefore free to stop any or all motorists without explanation or excuse, wholly on whim, will perforce target motorists of Mexican appearance. The process will then inescapably discriminate against citizens of Mexican ancestry and Mexican aliens lawfully in this country for no other reason than that they unavoidably possess the same "suspicious" physical and grooming characteristics of illegal Mexican aliens.

Every American citizen of Mexican ancestry and every Mexican alien lawfully in this country must know after today's decision that he travels the fixed checkpoint highways at the risk of being subjected not only to a stop, but also to detention and interrogation, both prolonged and to an extent far more than for non-Mexican appearing motorists. ...

As an initial matter, whatever force this argument may have, it cannot apply to the secondary detentions that occurred in No. 74-1560. Once a vehicle has been slowed and observed at a checkpoint, ample opportunity exists to formulate the reasonable suspicion which, if it actually exists, would justify further detention. Indeed, though permitting roving stops based on reasonable suspicion which, if it actually exists, would justify further detention, Brignoni-Ponce required that "any further detention or search must be based on (the greater showing of) consent or probable cause." ... The Court today, however, does not impose a requirement of even reasonable suspicion for these secondary stops.

* * *

Finally, the Court's argument fails for more basic reasons. There is no principle in the jurisprudence of fundamental rights which permits constitutional limitations to be dispensed with merely because they cannot be conveniently satisfied. Dispensing with reasonable suspicion as a prerequisite to stopping and inspecting motorists because the inconvenience of such a requirement would make it impossible to identify a given car as a possible carrier of aliens is no more justifiable than dispensing with probable cause as prerequisite to the search of an individual because the inconvenience of such a requirement would make it impossible to identify a given person in a high-crime area as a possible carrier of concealed weapons. "The needs of law enforcement stand in constant tension with the Constitution's protections of the individual against certain exercises of official power. It is precisely the predictability of these pressures that counsels a resolute loyalty to constitutional safeguards." ...

The Court also attempts to justify its approval of standardless conduct on the ground that checkpoint stops "involve less discretionary enforcement activity" than roving stops. ... This view is at odds with its later more revealing statement that "officers must have wide discretion in selecting the motorists to be diverted for the brief questioning involved." ... Similarly unpersuasive is the statement that "since field officers may stop only those cars passing the checkpoint, there is less room for abusive or harassing stops of individuals than there was in the case of roving-patrol stops." ... The Fourth Amendment standard of reasonableness admits of neither intrusion at the discretion of law enforcement personnel nor abusive or harassing stops, however infrequent. Action based merely on whatever may pique the curiosity of a particular officer is the antithesis of the objective standards requisite to reasonable conduct and to avoiding abuse and harassment. Such action, which the Court now permits, has expressly been condemned as contrary to basic Fourth Amendment principles. Certainly today's holding is far removed from the proposition emphatically affirmed in United States v. United States District Court, 407 U.S. 297, 317 (1972), that "those charged with ... investigative and prosecutorial duty should not be the sole judges of when to utilize constitutionally sensitive means of pursuing their tasks. The historical judgment, which the Fourth Amendment accepts, is that unreviewed executive discretion may yield too readily to pressures to obtain incriminating evidence and overlook potential invasions of privacy. ...." Indeed, it is far removed from the even more recent affirmation that "the central concern of the Fourth Amendment is to protect liberty and privacy from arbitrary and oppressive interference by government officials." ...

The cornerstone of this society, indeed of any free society, is orderly procedure. The Constitution, as originally adopted, was therefore, in great measure, a procedural document. For the same reasons the drafters of the Bill of Rights largely placed their faith in procedural limitations on government action. The Fourth Amendment's requirement that searches and seizures be reasonable enforces this fundamental understanding in erecting its buffer against the arbitrary treatment of citizens by government. But to permit, as the Court does today, police discretion to supplant the objectivity of reason and, thereby, expediency to reign in the place of order, is to undermine Fourth Amendment safeguards and threaten erosion of the cornerstone of our system of government, for as Mr. Justice Frankfurter reminded us, "The history of American freedom is, in no small measure, the history of procedure." Malinski v. New York, 324 U.S. 401, 414 (1945).

International Mail and Border Searches

ORAL ARGUMENTS BEFORE THE U.S.
SUPREME COURT*

U.S. v. Ramsey, No. 76-167; argued 3/30/77

In a case from the D.C. Circuit, the U.S. Supreme Court was asked to decide whether probable cause and a search warrant are required before customs officers may open an envelope entering this country from abroad, if the officers suspect that the envelope contains smuggled goods. The government relied on the border search exception to justify this official conduct. Counsel for the defendants, on the other hand, questioned the very existence of the border search exception and argued that, in any event, no such exception could apply to letter class mail.

Kenneth F. Geller, of the Solicitor General's Office, explained the background of the case. The envelopes were opened by a customs officer whose duty it was to ferret out "suspicious" items from the international letter class mail entering this country at New York. He removed the eight envelopes from the normal flow of mail, because

they were from Thailand—a known heroin source—and were bulky. Without obtaining a warrant, he opened the envelopes and found heroin.

In response to questioning from the Chief Justice and Mr. Justice Blackmun, Geller said the envelopes were of normal size but were substantially heavier than the normal letter.

Mr. Justice Stewart: "Are you asking us to find that there was probable cause?"

Our position, counsel replied, is that probable cause is not necessary.

Mr. Justice Stewart said that reversal of the court of appeals would be required were the Court to apply the probable cause but not the warrant requirement to this situation. He referred to footnote 8 of the D.C. Circuit's opinion, where the court said, "We believe that the facts in this case are such that, had they been presented to a magistrate, issuance of a search warrant permitting opening of the envelopes would have been appropriate."

Despite the appeals court's apparent decision in this regard, however, counsel was unsure whether there was probable cause.

The Chief Justice pointed out that an international passenger may be subjected to

*From 21 Crim. L. Rptr. 4026–4028 (1976). Reprinted by permission of the Bureau of National Affairs, Inc.

search without probable cause as he disembarks from an international flight.

Counsel agreed, citing 19 U.S.C. 482. He went on to say, in response to a question from Mr. Justice Stevens, that 482 should be taken to cover mail as well.

(In pertinent part, 482 provides as follows: "Any of the officers or persons authorized to board or search vessels may stop, search, examine . . . any vehicle, beast, or person, on which or whom he or they shall suspect there is merchandise which is subject to duty, or shall have been introduced into the United States in any manner contrary to law, whether by the person in possession or charge, or by, in, or upon such vehicle, beast, or otherwise, and to search any trunk or envelope, wherever found, in which he may have a reasonable cause to suspect there is merchandise which was imported contrary to law; . . . .")

Mr. Justice Stevens said the statute appears to refer only to envelopes carried by someone.

Someone must have carried them, Geller responded, even if that person was a postal clerk. Moreover, other courts of appeal have said that 482 covers this situation.

Statute Necessary?

The Chief Justice and Mr. Justice Rehnquist both wondered whether any statute at all is necessary.

A federal agency may not operate without statutory authority, counsel replied. The statute is necessary only to allocate the government's sovereign power to search at the border.

The Chief Justice again voiced his view that the government need not show probable cause or any other quantum of cause to conduct a search at the border.

Counsel agreed but noted that the government could decide to limit this authority through a statute.

Mr. Justice Rehnquist wondered whether the Fourth Amendment applies at the border at all.

Counsel responded that the reasonableness requirement applies. But it is hard to say how a border search would be unreasonable, except as to manner.

Mr. Justice Stewart expanded on this suggestion: "So you can't hang someone up by the toes and shake him."

Geller emphasized that there was no written matter in the envelopes that the customs officer opened.

The border search power is clearly established, Geller said. Both the government's need to control its borders and the minimal intrusion involved point to the necessity for maintaining this power. People, luggage, and packages are concededly searchable. There is no reason to carve out an exception for letter mail.

While the court below noted the absence of exigent circumstances, the border search exception does not depend on the presence of such circumstances, Geller said. Exigent circumstances are recognized as a substitute for a warrant but do not excuse the absence of probable cause. The court also noted that only limited kinds of contraband can be introduced into the country through letter class mail. But some such contraband is important—drugs and pornography, for instance. Indeed most illicit drugs come into the country this way, Geller asserted.

Third, the D.C. Circuit said that the practice of conducting warrantless searches of envelopes would have a chilling effect on First Amendment rights. There is nothing at all to this concern, Geller said. Customs officers are prohibited from reading correspondence; their authority is limited to opening envelopes as to which there is a reasonable belief that merchandise is inside.

Mr. Justice Marshall asked what an officer does with a letter once an envelope is opened.

It is stamped as having been opened and is sent on its way, Geller replied.

Geller also said one can avoid having his correspondence opened simply by sending it in letters of normal weight. There may be a privacy interest involved here. But that interest would be sufficiently served by the formulation of a narrow exclusionary rule for correspondence or the fruits of correspondence.

The defendants cite statistics from which they conclude that 80 percent of the opened envelopes contain correspondence. This is not true, Geller asserted. Most of the envelopes that are opened contain non-dutiable goods.

Mr. Justice Rehnquist asked whether a customs officer can open an ordinary looking envelope if he thinks it contains currency, microfilm, or the like.

He could, counsel answered, but under current regulations and procedures he would have to have a tip.

Procedures Changed

In response to a question from Mr. Justice Blackmun, counsel said that in 1971 the procedures governing the opening of mail were changed. Under prior practice, suspicious-looking mail was set aside and the addressee was notified that he should come to the post office, where the mail would be opened in his presence. The change to the present procedure was not a radical one, Geller said. At no time has the sender or addressee ever had an expectation that the letter would not be opened. Geller also said that the increased government efforts against the narcotics trade were partly responsible for the 1971 change of procedure.

Statutes and Carroll

Allen M. Palmer, of Washington, D.C., presented the argument for defendant Charles Ramsey. He contended that 482 does not allow the opening of letter mail. Historically this statute has only been applied to envelopes and trunks that were carried over the border by international travelers. Indeed, the general counsel of the Post Office Department told Congress in 1970 that at that time there were no statutory provisions dealing specifically with the customs treatment of any type of incoming foreign mail.

The Chief Justice: "Maybe that individual did not know about the statute on which the government relies. When counsel found that hard to believe, the Chief Justice suggested that the individual did not agree with the statute."

But Palmer thought the Post Office counsel viewed the statute in historical perspective and considered that it did not apply to this situation.

Referring to *Carroll* v. *U.S.*, 267 U.S. 132 (1925), Palmer said that even when dealing with border searches, the foundation statute distinguished between things that could and could not disappear into the country. Thus the Court viewed the border search concept as inseparably intertwined with the element of exigence.

Mr. Justice Rehnquist drew counsel's attention to page 154 of the *Carroll* decision. The Court said that while it would be "intolerable and unreasonable" to permit any person lawfully using the highway to be searched on the chance of finding illicit liquor, "travelers may be so stopped in crossing an international boundary, because of national self-protection reasonably requiring one entering the country to identify himself as entitled to come in, and his belongings as effects which may be lawfully brought in." I don't get any sense of "disappearance" from that language, the Justice said.

But in the opinion as a whole, the Court was concerned with this distinction, counsel replied.

Mr. Justice Rehnquist remarked that *Carroll* seems to take quite different views of car and border searches.

Replying to the government's argument that the practice involved here does not chill expression, counsel said that the customs service's "no reading" requirement is not enough. Palmer pointed out that in *Wolff* v. *McDonnell*, 418 U.S. 539 (1974), the Court upheld the opening of prisoner mail and noted that the prison's requirement that the addressee be present would insure that correspondence would not be read. By inference, he argued, it can be argued that the customs officer's private opening of the mail does not provide sufficient protection. If a prisoner is entitled to the safeguard relied on by the Court, a free individual should expect no less.

The Chief Justice: "Don't you see the difference between domestic attorney-client mail and mail coming from overseas?"

Counsel responded that he did not. I have the same right of privacy whatever the source, he said.

The Chief Justice remarked that it was a good deal easier for the Court to say that a prisoner can be there when his mail is opened, than to rely on such a practice in general.

But Palmer pointed out that until 1971, opening suspicious mail in the addressee's presence was the practice.

Noting that the envelopes involved here contained no written matter whatsoever, Mr. Justice Blackmun told counsel that his argument had "a hollow sound."

The hollowness recedes somewhat when the rights of the public at large are considered, Palmer responded.

Border Exception Challenged

Argument for the other defendant in this case, James Kelly, was presented by Irving R. M. Panzer, of Washington, D.C. He stressed that the Court has never before been presented with any question of the government's power to open letter class mail from abroad.

Panzer took the view that the "border search exception" much relied upon by the lower federal courts in fact has no basis in the Supreme Court's decisions. In *Carroll,* he said, the only question was the search of a car. The Court's language about border searches was mere dictum.

Even if there is a border search exception, counsel said, it cannot be a blunderbuss one, permitting the government to do anything it wants at the border. And a border search exception is inapplicable in the context of this case.

Counsel's theory drew sharp responses from the Chief Justice and Mr. Justice Rehnquist. Both noted that the question at the border is whether someone or something is to be admitted into the country.

Mr. Justice Marshall: "Why is mail so magic? Isn't it privacy that is important?"

Counsel answered that when mail is sent in from abroad it rises to a different level. He stressed that this case implicates First as well as Fourth Amendment rights. Even if there is a border exception for a traveler, luggage, or mailed package, there should be none for a letter.

The government turns the Fourth Amendment on its head, counsel said, by advising senders to use smaller envelopes. The affirmative duty should be on the government, and that duty is to obtain a warrant when the opening of a letter is proposed.

In response to questions from Mr. Justice Stevens, Panzer said that, in his view, there would not have been probable cause to obtain a warrant for the opening of these envelopes. He exhibited to the Court several envelopes he had prepared, saying they were identical to those involved in the case. He stressed the fact that the postal inspector called them "letters," and he chided the government for constantly referring to them as "envelopes."

The government is trying a familiar intimidation tactic, Panzer continued. It would have you believe that the power to conduct warrantless intrusions of this kind is the only way it can fulfill its mission. But the court of appeals had a different view, and the burden must be on the government to prove that it needs this power. Judge McGowan offered some possibilities. The administrative search outlined in *Camara* v. *Municipal Court,* 387 U.S. 523 (1967), or the "area warrant" discussed in Mr. Justice Powell's concurrence in *Almeida-Sanchez* v. *U.S.,* 413 U.S. 266 (1973), are other possibilities.

UNITED STATES v. RAMSEY

Supreme Court of the United States, 1977
431 U.S. 606, 96 S. Ct. 1972, 52 L. Ed. 2d 617

Title 19 U.S.C. § 482 and implementing postal regulations authorize customs officials to inspect incoming international mail when they have a "reasonable cause to suspect" that the mail contains illegally imported merchandise, although the regulations prohibit the reading of correspondence absent a search warrant. Acting pursuant to the statute and regulations, a customs inspector, noting that certain in-coming letter-sized airmail envelopes were from Thailand, a known source of narcotics, and were bulky and much heavier than normal airmail letters, opened the envelopes for inspection at the General Post Office in New York City, considered a "border" for border search purposes. The envelopes ultimately were found to contain heroin. Respondents were subsequently indicted for and con-

victed of narcotics offenses, the district court having denied their motion to suppress the heroin. The Court of Appeals (D.C. Cir.) reversed, holding that the border search exception to the Fourth Amendment's warrant requirement applicable to persons, baggage, and mailed packages does not apply to the opening of international mail and that the Constitution requires that before such mail is opened a showing of probable cause must be made and a warrant obtained. The United States Supreme Court granted certiorari.

Mr. Justice REHNQUIST delivered the opinion of the Court.

*   *   *

Congress and the applicable postal regulations authorized the actions undertaken in this case. 19 U.S.C. § 482 (1970), a recodification of Rev. Stat. § 3061, and derived from § 3 of the Act of July 18, 1866, 14 Stat. 178, explicitly deals with the search of an "envelope":

"Any of the officers or persons authorized to board or search vessels may ... search any trunk or envelope, wherever found, in which he may have a reasonable cause to suspect there is merchandise which was imported contrary to law...."

This provision authorizes customs officials to inspect, under the circumstances therein stated, incoming international mail. The "reasonable cause to suspect" test adopted by the statute is, we think, a practical test which imposes a less stringent requirement than that of "probable cause" imposed by the Fourth Amendment as a requirement for the issuance of warrants. See United States v. King, 517 F.2d 350, 352 (5th Cir. 1975); cf. Terry v. Ohio, 392 U.S. 18, 21–22, 27 (1968). Inspector Kallnischkies, at the time he opened the letters, knew that they were from Thailand, were bulky, were many times the weight of a normal airmail letter, and "felt like there was something in there." Under these circumstances, we have no doubt that he had reasonable "cause to suspect" that there was merchandise or contraband in the envelopes. The search, therefore, was plainly authorized by the statute.

Since the search in this case was authorized by statute, we are left simply with the question of whether the search, although authorized by statute, violated the Constitution. Cf. United States v. Brignoni-Ponce, 422 U.S. 873, 877 (1975). Specifically, we need not decide whether Congress con-

ceived the statute as a necessary precondition to the validity of the search or whether it was viewed, instead, as a limitation on otherwise existing authority of the executive.[k] Having acted pursuant to, and within the scope of, a congressional act, Inspector Kallnischkies' searches were permissible unless they violated the Constitution.

That searches made at the border, pursuant to the longstanding right of the sovereign to protect itself by stopping and examining persons and property crossing into this country, are reasonable simply by virtue of the fact that they occur at the border, should, by now, require no extended demonstration. The Congress which proposed the Bill of Rights, including the Fourth Amendment, to the state legislatures on September 25, 1789, 1 Stat. 97, had, some two months prior to that proposal, enacted the first customs statute, Act of July 31, 1789, c.5, 1 Stat. 29, 43. Section 24 of this statute granted customs officials "full power and authority" to enter and search "any ship or vessel in which they shall have reason to suspect any goods, wares or merchandise subject to duty shall be concealed.

---

[k]Although the statutory authority authorizes searches of envelopes "wherever found," 19 U.S.C. § 482 (1970), the envelopes were searched at the New York City Post Office as the mail was entering the United States. We, therefore, do not have before us the question, recently addressed in other contexts, of the geographical limits to border searches. See United States v. Brignoni-Ponce, 422 U.S. 873 (1975); Almeida-Sanchez v. United States, 413 U.S. 266 (1973). Nor do we need to decide whether the broad statutory authority subjects such mail to customs inspection at a place other than the point of entry into this country. See United States v. King, 517 F.2d 350, 354 (5th Cir. 1975) ("the envelopes had passed an initial customs stage in the customs process when they were routed to Alabama, but they were still in the process of being delivered, and still subject to customs inspection").

..." This acknowledgement of the plenary customs power was differentiated from the more limited power to enter and search "any particular dwelling-house, store, building, or other place..." where a warrant upon "cause to suspect" was required. The historical importance of the enactment of this customs statute by the same Congress which proposed the Fourth Amendment is, we think, manifest. This Court so concluded almost a century ago....

* * *

Border searches ... from before the adoption of the Fourth Amendment, have been considered to be "reasonable" by the single fact that the person or item in question had entered into our country from outside. There has never been any additional requirement that the reasonableness of a border search depended on the existence of probable cause. This longstanding recognition that searches at our borders without probable cause and without a warrant are nonetheless "reasonable" has a history as old as the Fourth Amendment itself. We reaffirm it now.

Respondents urge upon us, however, the position that mailed letters are somehow different, and, whatever may be the normal rule with respect to border searches, different considerations, requiring the full panoply of Fourth Amendment protections, apply to international mail. The Court of Appeals agreed, and felt that whatever the rule may be with respect to travelers, their baggage, and even mailed packages, it would not "extend" the border search exception to include mailed letter size envelopes. 538 F.2d, at 421. We do not agree that this inclusion of letters within the border search exception represents any "extension" of that exception.

The border search exception is grounded in the recognized right of the sovereign to control, subject to substantive limitations imposed by the Constitution, who and what may enter the country. It is clear that there is nothing in the rationale behind the border search exception which suggests that the mode of entry will be critical. It was conceded at oral argument that customs officials could search, without probable cause and without a warrant, envelopes carried by an entering traveler, whether in his luggage or on his person. (Tr. of Oral Arg., at 43–

44.) Surely no different constitutional standard should apply simply because the envelopes were mailed, not carried. The critical fact is that the envelopes cross the border and enter this country, not that they are brought in by one mode of transportation rather than another. It is their entry into this country from without it that makes a resulting search "reasonable."

* * *

The historically recognized scope of the border search doctrine, suggests no distinction in constitutional doctrine stemming from the mode of transportation across our borders. The contrary view of the Court of Appeals and respondents stems, we think, from an erroneous reading of Carroll v. United States, 267 U.S., at 153, under which the Court of Appeals reasoned that "the rationale of the border search exception ... is based upon ... the difficulty of obtaining a warrant when the subject of the search is mobile, as a car or person...." 538 F.2d, at 418.

The fundamental difficulty with this position is that the "border search" exception is not based on the doctrine of "exigent circumstances" at all. It is a longstanding, historically recognized exception to the Fourth Amendment's general principle that a warrant be obtained, and in this respect is like the similar "search incident to arrest" exception treated in United States v. Robinson, 414 U.S. 218, 224 (1973)....

The Court of Appeals also relied upon what it described as this Court's refusal in recent years twice "to take an expansive view of the border search exception or the authority of the Border Patrol. See United States v. Brignoni-Ponce, 422 U.S. 873 (1975); Almeida-Sanchez v. United States, 413 U.S. 266 (1973)." 538 F.2d, at 420. But as the language from each of these opinions suggests, 422 U.S., at 876, 884; 413 U.S., at 272–273, plenary border search authority was not implicated by our refusal to uphold searches and stops made at places in the interior of the country; the express premise for each holding was that the checkpoint or stop in question was not the border or its "functional equivalent."

In view of the wealth of authority establishing the border search as "reasonable" within the Fourth Amendment even though there be neither probable cause nor a warrant, we reject the distinctions made by the Court of Appeals in its opinion.

Nor do we agree that, under the circumstances presented by this case, First Amendment considerations dictate a full panoply of Fourth Amendment rights prior to the border search of mailed letters. There is, again, no reason to distinguish between letters mailed into the country, and letters carried on the traveler's person. More fundamentally, however, the existing system of border searches has not been shown to invade protected First Amendment rights, and hence there is no reason to think that the potential presence of correspondence makes the otherwise constitutionally reasonable search "unreasonable."

The statute in question requires that there be "reasonable cause to believe" the customs laws are being violated prior to the opening of envelopes. Applicable postal regulations flatly prohibit, under all circumstances, the reading of correspondence absent a search warrant, 19 C.F.R. § 145.3 (1976)....

We are unable to agree with the Court of Appeals that the opening of international mail in search of customs violation, under the above guidelines, impermissibly chills the exercise of free speech. Accordingly, we find it unnecessary to consider the constitutional reach of the First Amendment in this area in the absence of the existing statutory and regulatory protection. Here envelopes are opened at the border only when the customs officers have reason to believe they contain other than correspondence, while the reading of any correspondence inside the envelopes is forbidden. Any "chill" that might exist under these circumstances may fairly be considered not only "minimal," United States v. Martinez-Fuerte, 428 U.S. 543, 560, 562 (1972); cf. United States v. Biswell, 406 U.S. 311, 316–317 (1972), but also wholly subjective.

We therefore conclude that the Fourth Amendment does not interdict the actions taken by Inspector Kallnischkies in opening and searching the eight envelopes. The judgment of the Court of Appeals is, therefore,

Reversed.

Mr. Justice POWELL, concurring.

...In view of the necessarily enhanced power of the Federal Government to en-

force customs laws at the border, I have no doubt that this statute—requiring as a precondition to the opening of mail "reasonable cause to suspect" a violation of law—adequately protects both First and Fourth Amendment rights.

I therefore join in the judgment of the Court. On the understanding that the precedential effect of today's decision does not go beyond the validity of mail searches at the border pursuant to the statute, I also join the opinion of the Court.

Mr. Justice STEVENS, with whom Mr. Justice BRENNAN and Mr. Justice MARSHALL join, dissenting.

* * *

...There are five reasons why I am convinced that Congress did not authorize the kind of secret searches of private mail that the executive here conducted.

First, throughout our history Congress has respected the individual's interest in private communication. The notion that private letters could be opened and inspected without notice to the sender or the addressee is abhorrent to the tradition of privacy and freedom to communicate protected by the Bill of Rights. I cannot believe that any member of the Congress would grant such authority without considering its constitutional implications.

Second, the legislative history of the 1866 statute unambiguously discloses that this very concern was voiced during debate by Senator Howe, and that he was assured by the sponsor of the legislation that the bill would not authorize the examination of the United States mails. This colloquy is too plain to be misunderstood:

"Mr. Howe. The second and third sections of this bill speak of the seizure, search, and examination of all trunks, packages, and envelopes. It seems to me that language is broad enough to cover the United States mails. I suppose it is not the purpose of the bill to authorize the examination of the United States mails.

"Mr. Morrill. [Sponsor of the bill.] Of course not.

"Mr. Howe. I propose to offer an amendment to prevent such a construction.

"Mr. Edmunds. There is no danger of

such a construction being placed upon this language. It is the language usually employed in these bills.

"Mr. Howe. If gentlemen are perfectly confident that it will bear no such construction, and will receive no such construction, I do not care to press it.

"The Presiding Officer. The Senator from Wisconsin withdraws his amendment."

Third, the language of the statute itself, when read in its entirety, quite plainly has reference to packages of the kind normally used to import dutiable merchandise. It is true that buried deep in the first long sentence in § 3 of the Act to prevent smuggling there is an authorization to "search any trunk, or envelope, wherever found." I do not believe, however, that the word "envelope" as there used was intended to refer to ordinary letters. Contemporary American dictionaries emphasize the usage of the word as descriptive of a package or wrapper as well as an ordinary letter. This emphasis is consistent with the text of the bill as originally introduced, which used the phrase "any trunk, or other envelope." ...

Fourth, the consistent construction of the statutory authorization by a series of changing administrations over a span of 105 years must be accorded great respect. NLRB v. Bell Aerospace Co., 416 U.S. 267, 274–275; Helvering v. Reynolds Co., 306 U.S. 110, 114–115. If the executive perceives that new conditions and problems justify enlargement of the authority that had been found adequate for over a century, then these matters should be brought to the attention of Congress. ...

Finally, the asserted justification for the broad power claimed is so weak that it is difficult to believe that Congress would accept it without the most searching analysis. The fear the new practice is intended to overcome is that the addressee of a suspicious item of mail would withhold consent to open foreign mail, thereby necessitating the return of the item to the sender. But the refusal to accept delivery without disclosing the contents of a suspicious letter would itself be a fact which could be considered—along with whatever indicia caused the inspector to regard the item with suspicion in the first place—in a probable cause determination. There is no reason to believe that the alternatives of probable cause or consent would lead to the extensive return of contraband that would otherwise be confiscated on the basis of "reasonable cause to suspect."

If the Government is allowed to exercise the power it claims, the door will be open to the wholesale, secret examination of all incoming international letter mail. No notice would be necessary either before or after the search. Until Congress has made an unambiguous policy decision that such an unprecedented intrusion upon a vital method of personal communication is in the Nation's interest, this Court should not address the serious constitutional question it decides today. ...

Accordingly, I would affirm the judgment of the Court of Appeals.

Comments

1. *Almeida-Sanchez* v. *United States,* supra, supported the broad proposition that border searches made without a warrant may occur only *at the border* or *"its functional equivalent."* This basic concept was reaffirmed in the cases of *United States* v. *Ortiz,* 422 U.S. 891 (1975), and *United States* v. *Brignoni-Ponce,* 422 U.S. 873 (1975). In *Ortiz* the Court declined to allow searches at "traffic checkpoints" some 60 miles from the border absent a showing of probable cause or consent. The Court disagreed with the government's contention that a checkpoint officer's discretion is limited by the location of the checkpoint. The Court noted at 896, "Viewed realistically, this position would authorize the Border Patrol to search vehicles at random, for no officer ever would have to justify his discretion to search a particular car." The Court also rejected the argument that checkpoints are "less intrusive" than roving patrols and noted at 896, "We are not persuaded that the differences between rov-

ing patrols and traffic checkpoints justify dispensing in this case with safeguards we required in Almeida-Sanchez." In the companion case of *Brignoni-Ponce* the Court refused to allow roving patrols to have the authority to stop an auto near the border simply because the occupants appeared to be of Mexican ancestry. The majority concluded that such stops are permissible only if the officer is armed with specific facts which would reasonably warrant suspicion that the automobile was transporting illegal aliens: "[Mexican ancestry] alone would justify neither a reasonable belief that they were aliens, nor a reasonable belief that the car concealed other aliens who were illegally in the country. Large numbers of native-born and naturalized citizens have the physical characteristics identified with Mexican ancestry, and even in the border area a relatively small proportion of them are aliens. The likelihood that any given person of Mexican ancestry is an alien is high enough to make Mexican appearance a relevant factor, but standing alone it does not justify stopping all Mexican-Americans to ask if they are aliens." 422 U.S. at 886. It should be noted that *Almeida-Sanchez* was held to be nonretroactive by the Supreme Court in *United States* v. *Peltier*, 422 U.S. 531 (1975).

2. *United States* v. *Martinez-Fuerte*, supra, stands for the proposition that the Fourth Amendment does not require Border Patrol officers at fixed checkpoints to have either a warrant or reasonable suspicion that an automobile contains illegal aliens before stopping it and conducting a limited interrogation of the occupants. It appears that the majority sought to rely on a type of "balancing test" in which the Court weighed the public interest against the Fourth Amendment interest of the individual — a test not unlike that used in previous cases, e.g., *Camara* v. *Municipal Court of San Francisco*, 387 U.S. 523 (1967), and its companion case, *See* v. *City of Seattle*, 387 U.S. 541 (1967) (see Comment 4), and *Terry* v. *Ohio*, 392 U.S. 1 (1968), infra. The majority took the view that car stops involve only a visual inspection and are limited to "what can be seen without a search." What do the officers expect to see? Surely the answer must be Mexican aliens. Doesn't this suggest that detentions or "secondary referrals" are based largely on physical indications of Mexican ancestry? Such a question prompted the dissenters to conclude in a footnote: "That law in this country should tolerate use of one's ancestry as probative of possible criminal conduct is repugnant under any circumstances." How can this rationale be squared with the *Brignoni-Ponce* holding that appearance indicative of Mexican ancestry is by itself insufficient reason to allow roving patrols the same authority to stop autos? The majority did state, however, that it must be assumed that Border Patrol officers act in "good faith" in referring motorists for secondary detentions, so that such referrals do not depend solely on Mexican ancestry. The "good faith" assumption evoked the following comment by the minority in a footnote: "Even if good faith is assumed, the affront to the dignity of Mexican citizens and Mexican aliens lawfully within the country is in no way diminished. The fact still remains that people of their ancestry are targeted for examination at checkpoints and that the burden of checkpoint intrusions will lie heaviest on them. As the Court observed, the fact that '[l]ess than 1% of the motorists passing the checkpoint are stopped for questioning,' whereas approximately 16% of the population of

California is Spanish speaking or of Spanish surname, has little bearing on this point—or, for that matter, on the integrity of Border Patrol practices. There is no indication how many of the 16% have physical and grooming characteristics identifiable as Mexican. There is no indication what portion of the motoring public in California is of Spanish or Mexican ancestry. Given the socioeconomic status of this portion, it is likely that the figure is significantly less than 16%. Neither is there any indication that those of Mexican ancestry are not subjected to lengthier initial stops than others, even if they are secondarily detained. Finally, there is no indication of the ancestral makeup of the 1% who are referred for secondary detention. If, as is quite likely the case, it is overwhelmingly Mexican, the sense of discrimination which will be felt is only enhanced."

Consider the Court's remark that "selective referrals—rather than questioning the occupants of every car—tend to advance some Fourth Amendment interests by minimizing the intrusion on the general motoring public." Is the majority assuming that intrusions are expected and condoned by the general public and hence the minimization of intrusions serves Fourth Amendment ends? Isn't the better view of Fourth Amendment interests and goals actually described in terms of nonintrusion?

3. Apart from addressing the specific issues in *Martinez-Fuerte,* Mr. Justice Brennan devoted a small measure of his dissenting opinion to reflection on the Court's "track record" on Fourth Amendment cases during the October 1975 Term:

"Today's decision is the ninth this Term marking the continuing evisceration of Fourth Amendment protections against unreasonable searches and seizures. Early in the Term, Texas v. White, 423 U.S. 67 (1976), permitted the warrantless search of an automobile in police custody despite the unreasonableness of the custody and opportunity to obtain a warrant. United States v. Watson, 423 U.S. 411 (1976), held that regardless whether opportunity exists to obtain a warrant, an arrest in a public place for a previously committed felony never requires a warrant, a result certainly not fairly supported by either history or precedent. . . . United States v. Santana, 427 U.S. 38 (1976), went further and approved the warrantless arrest for a felony of a person standing on the front porch of her residence. United States v. Miller, 425 U.S. 435 (1976), narrowed the Fourth Amendment's protection of privacy by denying the existence of a protectible interest in the compilation of checks, deposit slips, and other records pertaining to an individual's bank account. Stone v. Powell, 428 U.S. 465 (1976), precluded the assertion of Fourth Amendment claims in federal collateral relief proceedings. United States v. Janis, 428 U.S. 433 (1976), held that evidence unconstitutionally seized by a state officer is admissible in a civil proceeding by or against the United States. South Dakota v. Opperman, 428 U.S. 364 (1976), approved sweeping inventory searches of automobiles in police custody irrespective of the particular circumstances of the case. Finally, in Andresen v. Maryland, 427 U.S. 463 (1976), the Court, in practical effect, weakened the Fourth Amendment prohibition against general warrants."

The majority countered in a footnote: "Since 1952, Act of June 27, 1952, Stat. 233, Congress has expressly authorized persons believed to be aliens to be interrogated as to residence and vehicles 'within a reasonable distance' from the border to be searched for aliens. . . . Our holding today, approving routine stops for brief questioning (a type of stop familiar to all motorists) is confined to permanent checkpoints. We understand, of course, that neither longstanding congressional authorization nor widely prevailing practice justifies a constitutional violation. We do suggest, however, that against this background and in the context of our recent decisions, the rhetoric of the dissent reflects unjustified concern."

4. In *United States* v. *Ramsey,* supra, the Supreme Court equated international mail with border searches. If this is true, must 19 U.S.C. § 482 be interpreted as requiring that warrantless searches of international mail be supported by "reasonable cause to suspect"? If a person crossing a border to the United States and his luggage may be searched without any prior suspicion, why shouldn't the opening of international mail be governed by the same rule—as long as the contents are not read? Suppose a postal inspector who reasonably suspects that an envelope sent through the international mail contains heroin, opens it and sees a note that reads, "Tonight we blow up Washington, D.C." If the writer of the note is subsequently arrested for conspiracy to destroy government property, would the contents of the note be admissible at his trial? Would a federal statute permitting the warrantless search of domestic mail based on a "reasonable cause to suspect" comply with the Fourth Amendment? Can there ever be any "exigent circumstances" for the warrantless search of domestic mail? What are the quantitative differences between "probable cause" and "reasonable cause to suspect"?

5. Another body of Fourth Amendment case law involves administrative searches. At various times the Supreme Court has been called upon to decide the propriety of limited inspections or regulatory searches with and without warrants. The petitioner in *Frank* v. *Maryland,* 359 U.S. 360 (1959), raised the question of whether his conviction for resisting an inspection of his house without a warrant was obtained in violation of the Due Process Clause of the Fourteenth Amendment. The issue centered on the validity of a Baltimore city code which permitted the Commissioner of Health to demand entry to private dwellings whenever he had cause to suspect that a nuisance existed therein.

The facts disclosed that a Baltimore City health inspector seeking the source of a rat infestation discovered evidence of such at the rear of Frank's home. Without a warrant the inspector requested entry to inspect the basement. Frank refused, and pursuant to § 120 of the city code, Frank was convicted and fined for refusal to allow inspection of his premises. Petitioner complained to the Supreme Court of the United States that the city code authorized "unreasonable" searches within the meaning of the Fourth Amendment, and consequently, a conviction resulting from a violation of the code was obtained in violation of the Due Process Clause of the Fourteenth Amendment.

In affirming the conviction the Supreme Court held that the Baltimore code was valid and a conviction resulting from a violation thereof did not violate Frank's rights under the Due Process Clause of the Fourteenth Amendment. The Court noted: "[T]here is 'a total unlikeness' between official acts and proceedings, for which the legal protection of privacy requires a search warrant under the Fourteenth Amendment, and the situation now under consideration is laid bare by the suggestion that the kind of inspection by a health official with which we are concerned may be satisfied by what is, in effect, a synthetic search warrant, an authorization 'for periodic inspections.' ... Time and experience have forcefully taught that the power to inspect dwelling places ... is of indispensable importance to the maintenance of community health; a power that would be greatly hobbled by the blanket requirement of the safeguards necessary for a search of evidence of criminal acts." 359 U.S. at 372–373.

The United States Supreme Court was again faced with the validity of warrantless administrative inspections of premises for health and safety violations in *Camara* v. *Municipal Court of San Francisco,* 387 U.S. 523 (1967), and the companion case of *See* v. *City of Seattle,* 387 U.S. 541 (1967). In *Camara,* the petitioner was charged with violating the San Francisco housing code by refusing to allow city housing inspectors to conduct a warrantless inspection of his apartment. While awaiting trial, Camara sued in the state superior court for a writ of prohibition, claiming that the inspection code was unconstitutional because it authorized warrantless inspections in violation of the Fourth Amendment. Relying on *Frank* v. *Maryland,* supra, both the superior court and the California Court of Appeal denied the writ. In addition, the state supreme court denied a hearing, and Camara then brought the issue to the United States Supreme Court.

In overruling *Frank* v. *Maryland,* supra, the Supreme Court noted: "We may agree that a routine inspection of the physical condition of private property is a less hostile intrusion than the typical policeman's search for the fruits and instrumentalities of crime. ... We cannot agree that the Fourth Amendment interests ... are merely 'peripheral.' ... Inspections of (this kind) do in fact jeopardize 'self-protection' interests of the property owner. Like most regulatory laws, fire, health, and housing codes are enforced by criminal processes." 387 U.S. at 530–531.

The Court went on to point out the necessity for the intervention of a neutral magistrate: "[T]he occupant has no way of knowing whether enforcement of the municipal code involved requires inspection of his premises, no way of knowing the lawful limits of the inspector's power to search, and no way of knowing whether the inspector himself is acting under proper authorization. ... The practical effect of this system is to leave the occupant subject to the discretion of the official in the field. ... This is precisely the discretion ... we have consistently circumscribed by a requirement that a disinterested party warrant the need to search." 387 U.S. at 532–533.

The Supreme Court thus held that such administrative inspections could not be made without a warrant absent an emergency or consent by the occupant. However, the Court noted that the search warrant for such inspections does not require a showing of probable cause that violations exist on the premises but only that standards do exist that allow such inspections to be conducted. In establishing the special probable cause test, the Court designed a balancing test in which the need, in the public interest, to inspect could be balanced against the invasion of individual privacy inherent in such inspections.

In *See* v. *City of Seattle,* a situation similar to that in *Camara* emerged. The petitioner was convicted for refusing to allow a City of Seattle Fire Department inspector entry to his locked commercial warehouse. The facts related that the inspector had neither a warrant nor probable cause to believe that a violation of a city ordinance existed in the warehouse. The Court agreed that the issue of whether the Fourth Amendment bars prosecution of a person who refuses to consent to a warrantless code inspection of his personal residence was well settled in *Camara.* However, the Court also was faced with the issue of whether the same rationale would apply to similar inspections of commercial structures not used as private dwellings. The Court reversed See's conviction and concluded: "The businessman, like the occupant of a residence, has a constitutional right to go about his business free from unreasonable official entries upon his private commercial property." 387 U.S. at 545.

The combined effect of these two cases produced a substantial change in the law concerning administrative inspections. The Court made it clear that such inspections, whether upon residential or commercial structures, are not permitted absent a warrant unless the occupant consents or an emergency situation exists.

In *Colonnade Catering Corp.* v. *United States,* 397 U.S. 72 (1970), the Supreme Court held that federal revenue agents could not make a forcible, warrantless entry into a locked liquor storeroom pursuant to a valid inspection of a liquor dealer's premises. The government contended that agents had such a right under a federal statute (26 U.S.C. § 7606) which allowed entry of "any building or place where any articles or objects subject to tax are made, produced, or kept, so far as it may be necessary for the purpose of examining said articles or objects." The majority concluded that Congress "resolved the issue not by authorizing forcible, warrantless entries, but by making it [unlawful] for a licensee to refuse admission to the inspector" under 26 U.S.C. § 7342. Inspection of licensed premises was also the issue in *United States* v. *Biswell,* 406 U.S. 311 (1972). Respondent, a licensed gun dealer, refused to submit his locked storeroom to inspection by a federal agent until the official showed him the federal statute (18 U.S.C. § 923(q) authorizing such inspection. The majority, per Mr. Justice White, expressed the view that inspections for compliance with the Gun Control Act "pose only limited threats to the dealer's . . . expectations of privacy." Hence the warrant requirement announced in *See,* supra, was held to be inapplicable where frequent, unannounced inspections are essential. The majority reasoned that "the prerequisite of a warrant could easily frustrate inspection."

The maintenance and inspection of bank records also has given rise to litigation before the Court. In *California Bankers Assoc.* v. *Shultz,* 416 U.S. 21 (1974), the Court, per Mr. Justice Rehnquist, upheld the constitutionality of the record-keeping requirements of the Bank Secrecy Act, 12 U.S.C. § 18296(d), finding that a bank, in complying with the requirement that it keep copies of the checks written by its customers, "neither searches nor seizes records in which depositor has a Fourth Amendment right." However, the Court noted that the government could only obtain records via the "existing legal process." In 1975, the Court held in *United States* v. *Bisceglia,* 420 U.S. 141, that the Internal Revenue Service could properly issue a "John Doe" summons to a bank in order to obtain records necessary to an on-going income tax evasion investigation. For an earlier but related view on the use of an IRS summons in obtaining third-party bank records, see *First National Bank* v. *United States,* 267 U.S. 576 (1925). Finally, the Court, per Mr. Justice Powell, held in *United States* v. *Miller,* 425 U.S. 435 (1976) that respondent, who had been convicted of various federal offenses, possessed no Fourth Amendment interest in subpoenaed bank records and was not entitled to challenge the validity of grand jury subpoenas or the admissibility of the records at his criminal trial. The majority reasoned that (1) the subpoenaed materials were business records of the banks, not respondent's private papers, and (2) there was no legitimate "expectation of privacy" in the contents of the original checks and deposit slips since the checks were not confidential communications but negotiable instruments and all the documents obtained contained only information voluntarily conveyed to the banks and exposed to their employees in the ordinary course of business.

For an extended discussion of administrative searches on university campuses, see Peoples, K., *Dormitory Searches and the Fourth Amendment: Are College Students Second-Rate Citizens?* 25 Chitty's L. J. 56 [Toronto] (1977).

6. Recent examples of border search and other administrative-type search cases in the lower federal and state courts include *United States* v. *Caluillo,* 537 F.2d 158 (5th Cir. 1976) (semipermanent and little used Border Patrol checkpoint located on a busy highway 30 miles from border city is not a "functional equivalent" under *Almeida-Sanchez* v. *United States,* and searches conducted there are not exempt from probable cause requirement); *United States* v. *Brennan,* 538 F.2d 711 (5th Cir. 1976) (law developed in *Almeida-Sanchez* and its progeny applies with equal force to the activities of Customs officials); *United States* v. *Byrd,* 520 F.2d 1101 (5th Cir. 1975) (absent suspicion, a roving border patrol does not have right to stop a car on any road, and any evidence so seized must be suppressed); *United States* v. *Martinez,* 526 F.2d 954 (5th Cir. 1976) (en banc) (border search cases of *United States* v. *Ortiz* and *United States* v. *Brignoni-Ponce* decided by U.S. Supreme Court held retroactive) (see also *United States* v. *Juarez-Rodriguez,* 498 F.2d 7 [9th Cir. 1976] [evidence obtained in fixed-checkpoint searches conducted after *Almeida-Sanchez* but prior to *Bowen* v. *United States* is admissible as long as it was seized reasonably and in good faith]); *United States* v. *Soria,* 519 F.2d 1060 (5th Cir. 1975) (warrantless search of pickup truck headed for border invalid because agents lacked the requisite reasonable suspicion); *United States* v. *Rodriguez,* 525 F.2d 1313 (10th Cir. 1975) (border patrol agents' discovery of marijuana in a U-Haul trailer towed by a small commercial bus based on information from an informant did not justify search of bus passenger's luggage); *United States* v. *Ogilvie,* 527 F.2d 330 (9th Cir. 1975) (border patrol officers violated Fourth Amendment by stopping a vehicle that had reversed its northbound direction and headed back towards the border just before approaching a checkpoint, as such an action, being legal, did not provide officers with the requisite suspicion) (see also *United States* v. *Garcia,* 516 F.2d 318 [9th Cir. 1975]); *United States* v. *Coffey,* 520 F.2d 1103 (5th Cir. 1975) (immigration officer's stop of defendant's auto at checkpoint for routine

check of occupant's citizenship held valid, and when officer detected strong odor of marijuana from the car's interior he had probable cause to then conduct a search of the vehicle); *United States v. Tilton*, 534 F.2d 1363 (9th Cir. 1976) (customs agents with "reasonable certainty" that boat had come from foreign waters properly searched it at the border or its equivalent without probable cause) (see also *United States v. Stanley*, 545 F.2d 661 [9th Cir. 1976] [vessels leaving American waters may be subjected to border-type searches] (cf. *United States v. Bates*, 533 F.2d 466 [9th Cir. 1976], *United States v. One Twin Engine Beech Airplane*, 533 F.2d 1106 [9th Cir. 1976], *United States v. Solmes*, 527 F.2d 1370 [9th Cir. 1975], *United States v. Ingham*, 502 F.2d 1287 [5th Cir. 1974], *Klein v. United States*, 472 F.2d 847 [9th Cir. 1973], and Note, 77 Yale L.J. 1007 [1968]); *United States v. Rocha-Lopez*, 527 F.2d 476 (9th Cir. 1975) ("no substantial difference" between doctrine of "founded suspicion" applicable to the Ninth Circuit for temporary border detentions and the "reasonable suspicion" standard in stop and frisk cases) (see also *Wilson v. Porter*, 361 F.2d 412 [1966]); *United States v. Cameron*, 538 F.2d 254 (9th Cir. 1976) (customs officials who, with aid of a civilian physician, made a heroin trafficker undergo two digital anal probes and two enemas and take a liquid laxative held to have violated Fourth Amendment); *United States v. Salter*, 521 F.2d 1326 (2nd Cir. 1975) (Buffalo, New York, immigration officers' brief interrogation of defendant and two women traveling companions was reasonable when they pronounced "Buffalo" with a Jamaican accent since the Jamaican accent gave reasonable suspicion that defendant was bringing aliens into United States); *United States v. Ensoerro*, 401 F. Supp. 460 (S.D.N.Y. 1975) (1970 Drug Control Act provision for pharmacy inspections requires search warrant in the absence of exigent circumstances — *United States v. Biswell* distinguished); *State v. Wybierala*, 235 N.W.2d 197 (Minn. 1975) (warrantless search of a "second-hand" business establishment held valid even though made without consent under city ordinance which makes submission to such inspections a condition of operating the business); *Picha v. Wielgos*, 419 F. Supp. 1214 (N.D. Ill. 1976) (school officials who subjected female junior high student to fruitless strip search held not immune from liability under the Civil Rights Act, 42 U.S.C. § 1983); *Collier v. Miller*, 414 F. Supp. 1357 (S.D. Tex. 1976) (University of Houston policy calling for warrantless searches at school stadium and auditorium of "containers, packages or bundles that could conceal alcoholic beverages, cans or bottles" and permitting university security police to deny entrance to those who refuse the search held violative of Fourth Amendment); *People v. Rizzo*, 353 N.E.2d 841 (N.Y. Ct. App. 1976) (New York statute authorizing tax authorities to examine records and equipment of a person who occupies premises where cigarettes are stored or sold held to require probable cause for entry and inspection); *United States v. Pugh*, ___ F. Supp. ___ (W.D. Mich. 1976) (although 21 U.S.C. § 800 requires warrant for searches of premises licensed to deal in controlled substances, and § 800(c) permits warrantless search obtained by consent, druggist's signed "consent" to a search of his store that he in fact thought would be only an audit of his records held invalid); *Bloomfield Mechanical Contracting v. Occupational Safety and*

Health Administration, 519 F.2d 1257 (3rd Cir. 1975) (where OSHA inspector inspected construction job and found violations, the contractors could not claim a violation of their Fourth Amendment rights since expectation of privacy extended only to owner of work site, not to contractors doing plumbing work) (see also *Lake Butler Apparel Co.* v. *Secretary of Labor,* 519 F.2d 84 [5th Cir. 1975] [company cannot claim Fourth Amendment violation where president accompanied OSHA compliance officer through plant on routine inspection that uncovered several violations of the Occupational Health and Safety Act since president consented to search and violations were in plain view); *Nelson* v. *State,* 319 So. 2d 154 (Fla. App. 1975) (school officials, at least to a limited degree, stand in loco parentis to their students and hence it was not violative of Fourth Amendment to demand that defendant student found smoking in violation of school rules empty his pockets, as there was reasonable suspicion that they contained marijuana); *United States* v. *Bunkers,* 521 F.2d 1217 (9th Cir. 1975) (supervisor's search of postal employee's locker without warrant did not violate Fourth Amendment as the locker was government property, she had been told her locker was subject to such administrative searches, and there was probable cause to believe she was secreting stolen packages).

G. STOP AND FRISK

When "Criminal Activity is Afoot"

TERRY v. OHIO

Supreme Court of the United States, 1968
392 U.S. 1, 88 S. Ct. 1868, 20 L. Ed. 2d 889

A Cleveland police detective, Martin McFadden, observed two men on a street corner in downtown Cleveland at approximately 2:30 in the afternoon of October 31, 1963. It appeared to Officer McFadden that the two men (one of whom was petitioner Terry) were "casing" a store because each walked up and down peering into the store window, and then both returned to the corner to confer. At one point a third man joined the pair, and then quickly left. After the officer observed the two rejoining the same third man a couple of blocks away, he approached the three, told them who he was, and asked for identification. When a mumbled response was offered, the officer frisked all three men. The frisk revealed that Terry and one of the other two men were carrying handguns. Both the petitioner and one Chilton were convicted of carrying concealed weapons. The Court of Appeals for the Eighth Judicial District, Cuyahoga County, affirmed, and the Supreme Court of Ohio dismissed petitioner's appeal for want of a "substantial constitutional question." Certiorari was granted to consider a number of questions concerning the constitutional validity of the stop-and-frisk practice.

Mr. Chief Justice WARREN delivered the opinion of the Court.

* * *

We have recently held that "the Fourth Amendment protects people, not places." . . . Unquestionably petitioner was entitled to the protection of the Fourth Amendment as he walked down the street in Cleveland.

The question is whether in all the circumstances of this on-the-street encounter, his right to personal security was violated by an unreasonable search and seizure.

We would be less than candid if we did not acknowledge that this question thrusts to the fore difficult and troublesome issues regarding a sensitive area of police activity — issues which have never before been squarely presented to this Court. Reflective of the tensions involved are the practical and constitutional arguments pressed with great vigor on both sides of the public debate over the power of the police to "stop and frisk" — as it is sometimes euphemistically termed — suspicious persons.

On the one hand, it is frequently argued that in dealing with the rapidly unfolding and often dangerous situations on city streets the police are in need of an escalating set of flexible responses, graduated in relation to the amount of information they possess. For this purpose it is urged that distinctions should be made between a "stop" and an "arrest" [or a "seizure" of a person], and between a "frisk" and a "search." Thus, it is argued, the police should be allowed to "stop" a person and detain him briefly for questioning upon suspicion that he may be connected with criminal activity. Upon suspicion that the person may be armed, the police should have the power to "frisk" him for weapons. If the "stop" and the "frisk" give rise to probable cause to believe that the suspect has committed a crime, then the police should be empowered to make a formal "arrest," and a full incident "search" of the person. This scheme is justified in part upon the notion that a "stop" and a "frisk" amount to a mere "minor inconvenience and petty indignity," which can properly be imposed upon the citizen in the interest of effective law enforcement on the basis of a police officer's suspicion.

On the other side the argument is made that the authority of the police must be strictly circumscribed by the law of arrest and search as it has developed to date in the traditional jurisprudence of the Fourth Amendment. . . . The heart of the Fourth Amendment, the argument runs, is a severe requirement of specific justification for any intrusion upon protected personal security, coupled with a highly developed system of judicial controls to enforce upon the agents of the State the commands of the Constitution.

* * *

In this context we approach the issues in this case mindful of the limitations of the judicial function in controlling the myriad daily situations in which policemen and citizens confront each other on the street. The State has characterized the issue here as "the right of a police officer . . . to make an on-the-street stop, interrogate and pat down for weapons [known in street vernacular as 'stop and frisk']." But this is only partly accurate. For the issue is not the abstract propriety of the police conduct, but the admissibility against petitioner of the evidence uncovered by the search and seizure.

* * *

The exclusionary rule has its limitations, however, as a tool of judicial control. It cannot properly be invoked to exclude the products of legitimate police investigative techniques on the ground that much conduct which is closely similar involves unwarranted intrusions upon constitutional protections. Moreover, in some contexts the rule is ineffective as a deterrent. Street encounters between citizens and police officers are incredibly rich in diversity. They range from wholly friendly exchanges of pleasantries or mutually useful information to hostile confrontations of armed men involving arrests, or injuries, or loss of life. Moreover, hostile confrontations are not all of a piece. Some of them begin in a friendly enough manner, only to take a different turn upon the injection of some unexpected element into the conversation. Encounters are initiated by the police for a wide variety of purposes, some of which are wholly unrelated to a desire to prosecute for crime. Doubtless some police "field interrogation" conduct violated the Fourth Amendment.

But a stern refusal by this Court to condone such activity does not necessarily render it responsive to the exclusionary rule. Regardless of how effective the rule may be where obtaining convictions is an important objective of the police, it is powerless to deter invasions of constitutionally guaranteed rights where the police either have no interest in prosecuting or are willing to forgo successful prosecution in the interest of serving some other goal.

Proper adjudication of cases in which the exclusionary rule is invoked demands a constant awareness of these limitations. The wholesale harassment by certain elements of the police community, of which minority groups, particularly Negroes, frequently complain, will not be stopped by the exclusion of any evidence from any criminal trial. Yet a rigid and unthinking application of the exclusionary rule, in futile protest against practices which it can never be used effectively to control, may exact a high toll in human injury and frustration of efforts to prevent crime. No judicial opinion can comprehend the protean variety of the street encounter, and we can only judge the facts of the case before us. Nothing we say today is to be taken as indicating approval of police conduct outside the legitimate investigative sphere. Under our decision, courts still retain their traditional responsibility to guard against police conduct which is overbearing or harassing, or which trenches upon personal security without the objective evidentiary justification which the Constitution requires....

Having thus roughly sketched the perimeters of the constitutional debate over the limits on police investigation conduct in general and the background against which this case presents itself, we turn our attention to the quite narrow question posed by the facts before us: whether it is always unreasonable for a policeman to seize a person and subject him to a limited search for weapons unless there is probable cause for an arrest. Given the narrowness of this question, we have no occasion to canvass in detail the constitutional limitations upon the scope of a policeman's power when he confronts a citizen without probable cause to arrest him.

... There is some suggestion in the use of such terms as "stop" and "frisk" that such police conduct is outside the purview of the Fourth Amendment because neither action rises to the level of a "search" or "seizure" within the meaning of the Constitution.... It is quite plain that the Fourth Amendment governs "seizures" of the person which do not eventuate in a trip to the station house and prosecution for crime—"arrests" in traditional terminology. It must be recognized that whenever a police officer accosts an individual and restrains his freedom to walk away, he has "seized" that person. And it is nothing less than sheer torture of the English language to suggest that a careful exploration of the outer surfaces of a person's clothing all over his or her body in an attempt to find weapons is not a "search." Moreover, it is simply fantastic to urge that such a procedure performed in public by a policeman while the citizen stands helpless, perhaps facing a wall with his hands raised, is a "petty indignity." It is a serious intrusion upon the sanctity of the person, which may inflict great indignity and arouse strong resentment, and it is not to be undertaken lightly.

* * *

The distinctions of classical "stop-and-frisk" theory thus serve to divert attention from the central inquiry under the Fourth Amendment—the reasonableness in all the circumstances of the particular governmental invasion of a citizen's personal security. "Search" and "seizure" are not talismans. We therefore reject the notion that the Fourth Amendment does not come into play at all as a limitation upon police conduct if the officers stop short of something called a "technical arrest" or a "full-blown search."

In this case there can be no question, then, that Officer McFadden "seized" petitioner and subjected him to a "search" when he took hold of him and patted down the outer surfaces of his clothing. We must decide whether at that point it was reasonable for Officer McFadden to have interfered with petitioner's personal security as he did. And in determining whether the seizure and search were "unreasonable" our inquiry is a dual one—whether the officer's action was justified at its inception, and whether it was reasonably related in scope to the circumstances which justified the interference in the first place.

If this case involved police conduct subject to the Warrant Clause of the Fourth Amendment, we would have to ascertain whether "probable cause" existed to justify the search and seizure which took place. However, that is not the case. We do not retreat from our holdings that the police must, whenever practicable, obtain advance judicial approval of searches and seizures through the warrant procedure, ... or that in most instances failure to comply with the warrant requirement can only be excused by exigent circumstances. ... But we deal here with an entire rubric of police conduct — necessarily swift action predicated upon the on-the-spot observations of the officer on the beat — which historically has not been, and as a practical matter could not be, subjected to the warrant procedure. Instead, the conduct involved in this case must be tested by the Fourth Amendment's general proscription against unreasonable searches and seizures.

Nonetheless, the notions which underlie both the warrant procedure and the requirement of probable cause remain fully relevant in this context. In order to assess the reasonableness of Officer McFadden's conduct as a general proposition, it is necessary "first to focus upon the governmental interest which allegedly justifies official intrusion upon the constitutionally protected interests of the private citizen," for there is "no ready test for determining reasonableness other than by balancing the need to search [or seize] against the invasion which the search [or seizure] entails." ... And in justifying the particular intrusion the police officer must be able to point to specific and articulable facts which, taken together with rational inferences from those facts, reasonably warrant that intrusion. The scheme of the Fourth Amendment becomes meaningful only when it is assured that at some point the conduct of those charged with enforcing the laws can be subjected to the more detached, neutral scrutiny of a judge who must evaluate the reasonableness of a particular search or seizure in light of the particular circumstances. And in making that assessment it is imperative that the facts be judged against an objective standard: would the facts available to the officer at the moment of the seizure or the search "warrant a man of reasonable caution in the belief" that the action taken was appropriate? ... Anything less would invite intru-

sions upon constitutionally guaranteed rights based on nothing more substantial than inarticulate hunches, a result this Court has consistently refused to sanction. ...

Applying these principles to this case, we consider first the nature and extent of the governmental interests involved. One general interest is of course that of effective crime prevention and detection; it is this interest which underlies the recognition that a police officer may in appropriate circumstances and in an appropriate manner approach a person for purposes of investigating possibly criminal behavior even though there is no probable cause to make an arrest. It was this legitimate investigative function Officer McFadden was discharging when he decided to approach petitioner and his companions. He had observed Terry, Chilton, and Katz go through a series of acts, each of them perhaps innocent in itself, but which taken together warranted further investigation. ...

It would have been poor police work indeed for an officer of 30 years' experience in the detection of thievery from stores in this same neighborhood to have failed to investigate this behavior further.

The crux of this case, however, is not the propriety of Officer McFadden's taking steps to investigate petitioner's suspicious behavior, but rather whether there was justification for McFadden's invasion of Terry's personal security by searching him for weapons in the course of that investigation. We are now concerned with more than the governmental interest in investigating crime; in addition, there is the more immediate interest of the police officer in taking steps to assure himself that the person with whom he is dealing is not armed with a weapon that could unexpectedly and fatally be used against him. Certainly it would be unreasonable to require that police officers take unnecessary risks in the performance of their duties. ...

In view of these facts, we cannot blind ourselves to the need for law enforcement officers to protect themselves and other prospective victims of violence in situations where they may lack probable cause for an arrest. When an officer is justified in believing that the individual whose suspicious behavior he is investigating at close range is armed and presently dangerous to the officer or to others, it would appear to be clearly unreasonable to deny the officer the power to take necessary measures to determine whether the person is in fact carrying a weapon and to neutralize the threat of physical harm.

We must still consider, however, the nature and quality of the intrusion on individual rights which must be accepted if police officers are to be conceded the right to search for weapons in situations where probable cause to arrest for crime is lacking. Even a limited search of the outer clothing for weapons constitutes a severe, though brief, intrusion upon cherished personal security, and it must surely be an annoying, frightening, and perhaps humiliating experience. . . .

Petitioner does not argue that a police officer should refrain from making any investigation of suspicious circumstances until such time as he has probable cause to make an arrest; nor does he deny that police officers in properly discharging their investigative function may find themselves confronting persons who might well be armed and dangerous. Moreover, he does not say that an officer is always unjustified in searching a suspect to discover weapons. Rather, he says it is unreasonable for the policeman to take that step until such time as the situation evolves to a point where there is probable cause to make an arrest. When that point has been reached, petitioner would concede that officer's right to conduct a search of the suspect for weapons, fruits or instrumentalities of the crime, or "mere" evidence, incident to the arrest.

There are two weaknesses in this line of reasoning however. First, it fails to take account of traditional limitations upon the scope of searches, and thus recognizes no distinction in purpose, character, and extent between a search incident to an arrest and a limited search for weapons. The former, although justified in part by the acknowledged necessity to protect the arresting officer from assault with a concealed weapon . . . is also justified on other grounds and can therefore involve a relatively extensive exploration of the person. A search for weapons in the absence of probable cause to arrest, however, must, like any other search, be strictly circumscribed by the exigencies which justify its initiation. . . . Thus it must be limited to that which is necessary for the discovery of weapons which might be used

to harm the officer or others nearby, and may realistically be characterized as something less than a "full" search, even though it remains a serious intrusion.

A second, and related, objection to petitioner's argument is that it assumes that the law of arrest has already worked out the balance between the particular interests involved here — the neutralization of danger to the policeman in the investigative circumstance and the sanctity of the individual. But this is not so. An arrest is a wholly different kind of intrusion upon individual freedom from a limited search for weapons, and the interests each is designed to serve are likewise quite different. An arrest is the initial stage of a criminal prosecution. It is intended to vindicate society's interest in having its laws obeyed, and it is inevitably accompanied by future interference with the individual's freedom of movement, whether or not trial or conviction ultimately follows. The protective search for weapons, on the other hand, constitutes a brief, though far from inconsiderable, intrusion upon the sanctity of the person. It does not follow that because an officer may lawfully arrest a person only when he is apprised of facts sufficient to warrant a belief that the person has committed or is committing a crime, the officer is equally unjustified, absent that kind of evidence, in making any intrusions short of an arrest. Moreover, a perfectly reasonable apprehension of danger may arise long before the officer is possessed of adequate information to justify taking a person into custody for the purpose of prosecuting him for a crime. Petitioner's reliance on cases which have worked out standards of reasonableness with regard to "seizures" constituting arrests and searches incident thereto is thus misplaced. It assumes that the interests sought to be vindicated and the invasions of personal security may be equated in the two cases, and thereby ignores a vital aspect of the analysis of the reasonableness of particular types of conduct under the Fourth Amendment. . . .

Our evaluation of the proper balance that has to be struck in this type of case leads us to conclude that there must be a narrowly drawn authority to permit a reasonable search for weapons for the protection of the police officer, where he has reason to believe that he is dealing with an armed and dangerous individual, regardless of whether he has probable cause to arrest the individual for a crime. The officer need not be absolutely certain that the individual is armed; the issue is whether a reasonably prudent man in the circumstances would be warranted in the belief that his safety or that of others was in danger.... And in determining whether the officer acted reasonably in such circumstances, due weight must be given, not to his inchoate and unparticularized suspicion or "hunch," but to the specific reasonable inferences which he is entitled to draw from the facts in light of his experience....

We must now examine the conduct of Officer McFadden in this case to determine whether his search and seizure of petitioner were reasonable, both at their inception and as conducted. He had observed Terry, together with Chilton and another man, acting in a manner he took to be preface to a "stick-up." We think on the facts and circumstances Officer McFadden detailed before the trial judge a reasonably prudent man would have been warranted in believing petitioner was armed and thus presented a threat to the officer's safety while he was investigating his suspicious behavior. The actions of Terry and Chilton were consistent with McFadden's hypothesis that these men were contemplating a daylight robbery—which, it is reasonable to assume, would be likely to involve the use of weapons—and nothing in their conduct from the time he first noticed them until the time he confronted them and identified himself as a police officer gave him sufficient reason to negate that hypothesis. Although the trio had departed the original scene, there was nothing to indicate abandonment of an intent to commit a robbery at some point. Thus, when Officer McFadden approached the three men gathered before the display window at Zucker's store he had observed enough to make it quite reasonable to fear that they were armed; and nothing in their response to his hailing them, identifying himself as a police officer, and asking their names served to dispel that reasonable belief. We cannot say his decision at that point to seize Terry and pat his clothing for weapons was the product of a volatile or inventive imagination, or was undertaken simply as an act of harassment; the record evidences the tempered act of a policeman who in the course of an investigation had to make a quick decision as to how to protect himself and others from possible danger, and took limited steps to do so.

The manner in which the seizure and search were conducted is, of course, as vital a part of the inquiry as whether they were warranted at all.

* * *

We need not develop at length ... the limitations which the Fourth Amendment places upon a protective seizure and search for weapons. These limitations will have to be developed in the concrete factual circumstances of individual cases.... Suffice it to note that such a search, unlike a search without a warrant incident to a lawful arrest, is not justified by any need to prevent the disappearance or destruction of evidence of crime.... The sole justification of the search in the present situation is the protection of the police officer and others nearby, and it must therefore be confined in scope to an intrusion reasonably designed to discover guns, knives, clubs, or other hidden instruments for the assault of the police officer.

The scope of the search in this case presents no serious problem in light of these standards. Officer McFadden patted down the outer clothing of petitioner and his two companions. He did not place his hands in their pockets or under the outer surface of their garments until he had felt weapons, and then he merely reached for and removed the guns. He never did invade Katz' person beyond the outer surfaces of his clothes, since he discovered nothing in his patdown which might have been a weapon. Officer McFadden confined his search strictly to what was minimally necessary to learn whether the men were armed and to disarm them once he discovered the weapons. He did not conduct a general exploratory search for whatever evidence of criminal activity he might find.

We conclude that the revolver seized from Terry was properly admitted in evidence against him. At the time he seized petitioner and searched him for weapons, Officer McFadden had reasonable grounds to believe that petitioner was armed and dangerous, and it was necessary for the protection of himself and others to take swift measures to discover the true facts and neutralize the threat of harm if it materialized. The policeman carefully restricted his search to what was appropriate to the discovery of the particular items which he sought. Each case of this sort will, of course, have to be decided on its own facts. We merely hold today that where a police officer observes unusual conduct which leads him reasonably to conclude in light of his experience that criminal activity may be afoot and that the persons with whom he is dealing may be armed and presently dangerous, where in the course of investigating this behavior he identifies himself as a policeman and makes reasonabe inquiries, and where nothing in the initial stages of the encounter serves to dispel his reasonable fear for his own or others' safety, he is entitled for the protection of himself and others in the area to conduct a carefully limited search of the outer clothing of such persons in an attempt to discover weapons which might be used to assault him.

Such a search is a reasonable search under the Fourth Amendment, and any weapons seized may properly be introduced in evidence against the person from whom they were taken.

Affirmed.

[Mr. Justice WHITE, Mr. Justice HARLAN, and Mr. Justice BLACK each wrote separate concurring opinions.]

[Mr. Justice DOUGLAS wrote a dissenting opinion.]

When an Informer Reports Criminal Activity

ADAMS v. WILLIAMS

Supreme Court of the United States, 1972
407 U.S. 143, 92 S. Ct. 1921, 32 L. Ed. 2d 612

Acting on a tip supplied by an informer whom the officer knew, a policeman approached respondent Williams' parked car and asked him to open the door. When Williams rolled down the window, the officer reached into the car and seized a loaded handgun from respondent's waistband—precisely where the informant had told the officer it would be. Williams was then placed under arrest for unlawful possession of the pistol, and a subsequent search incident to arrest produced heroin and other contraband. Williams was convicted in a Connecticut court of illegal possession of the handgun found during the "stop and frisk" encounter, as well as possession of heroin discovered during the full search incident to his weapons arrest. After his conviction was affirmed by the Supreme Court of Connecticut, Williams unsuccessfully sought habeas corpus relief in both the United States District Court for the District of Connecticut and the Court of Appeals (2nd Cir.). However, on rehearing en banc, the court of appeals reversed the conviction, finding that the search and seizure were unlawful. The State of Connecticut was granted certiorari.

Mr. Justice REHNQUIST delivered the opinion of the Court.

* * *

Respondent contends that the initial seizure of his pistol, upon which rested the later search and seizure of other weapons and narcotics, was not justified by the informant's tip to Sgt. Connolly. He claims that absent a more reliable informant, or some corroboration of the tip, the policeman's actions were unreasonable under the standards set forth in Terry v. Ohio. . . .

* * *

Applying [the Terry] principles to the present case, we believe that Sgt. Connolly acted justifiably in responding to his informant's tip. The informant was known to him personally and had provided him with information in the past. This is a stronger case than obtains in the case of an anonymous telephone tip. The informant here came forward personally to give information that was immediately verifiable at the scene. Indeed, under Connecticut law, the informant might have been subject to immediate arrest for making a false complaint had Sgt. Connolly's investigation proved the tip incorrect. Thus, while the Court's decisions indicate that this informant's unverified tip may have been insufficient for a narcotics arrest or search warrant . . . the information carried enough indicia of reliability to justify the officer's forcible stop of Williams.

In reaching this conclusion, we reject respondent's argument that reasonable cause for a stop and frisk can only be based on the officer's personal observation, rather than on information supplied by another person. Informant's tips, like all other clues and evidence coming to a policeman on the scene, may vary greatly in their value and reliability. One simple rule will not cover every situation. Some tips, completely lacking in indicia of reliability, would either warrant no police response or require further investigation before a forcible stop of a suspect would be authorized. But in some situations — for example, when the victim of a street crime seeks immediate police aid and gives a description of his assailant, or when a credible informant warns of a specific impending crime — the subtleties of the hearsay rule should not thwart an appropriate police response.

While properly investigating the activity of a person who was reported to be carrying narcotics and a concealed weapon and who was sitting alone in a car in a high-crime area at 2:15 in the morning, Sgt. Connolly had ample reason to fear for his safety.

When Williams rolled down his window, rather than complying with the policeman's request to step out of the car so that his movements could more easily be seen, the revolver allegedly at Williams' waist became an even greater threat. Under these circumstances the policeman's action in reaching to the spot where the gun was thought to be hidden constituted a limited intrusion designed to insure his safety, and we conclude that it was reasonable. The loaded gun seized as a result of this intrusion was therefore admissible at Williams' trial. . . .

Once Sgt. Connolly had found the gun precisely where the informant had predicted, probable cause existed to arrest Williams for unlawful possession of the weapon. . . . In the present case the policeman found Williams in possession of a gun in precisely the place predicted by the informant. This tended to corroborate the reliability of the informant's further report of narcotics and, together with the surrounding circumstances, certainly suggested no lawful explanation for possession of the gun.

* * *

Under the circumstances surrounding Williams' possession of the gun seized by Sgt. Connolly, the arrest on the weapons charge was supported by probable cause, and the search of his person and of the car incident to that arrest was lawful. . . . The fruits of the search were therefore properly admitted at Williams' trial, and the Court of Appeals erred in reaching a contrary conclusion.

Reversed.

[Mr. Justice DOUGLAS, Mr. Justice MARSHALL, and Mr. Justice BRENNAN each wrote a dissenting opinion.]

Comments

1. In *Terry,* the Court declined to comment on particular statutes or common law interpretations of the stop-and-frisk practice. Instead, the Court examined the particular factual situation before it with an eye to whether the initial contact with Terry was *reasonable* within the meaning of the Fourth Amendment. Convinced that the reasonableness of such a practice must be measured by a special "balancing test," the Court concluded that the need for effective law enforcement must be balanced against the need to protect the individual rights of the person to be detained and frisked.

It is interesting to note that the *Terry* opinion reflects a standard of reasonableness relating to searches for weapons that is quite different from that for other searches. Actually, the reasonableness standard established was "reason to believe" rather than the more common "probable cause to believe." The Court did, however, carefully note "that a search in absence of probable cause to arrest must be strictly circumscribed by the exigencies of the situation."

2. On the same day that it decided *Terry,* the Court also rendered decisions in the companion cases of *Sibron* v. *New York* and *Peters* v. *New York,* 392 U.S. 40. In *Sibron,* a New York policeman observed petitioner conversing with several narcotics addicts during an eight-hour period, and later the same day, the officer saw petitioner with three other known addicts in a restaurant. The officer heard none of the conversation, nor did he see anything being passed among the participants. The officer ordered petitioner outside the restaurant and asked Sibron if he knew who he (the officer) was. Sibron then reached into his pocket and the policeman reached into the same pocket and found some envelopes containing heroin. Convicted of possession of heroin, petitioner appealed to the New York Court of Appeals, charging that the heroin had been illegally seized. The court of appeals affirmed the conviction, justifying the search on the basis of a New York stop-and-frisk law.

Before the Supreme Court of the United States, the District Attorney of New York confessed error. The Court noted: "The prosecution has quite properly abandoned the notion that there was probable cause to arrest Sibron for any crime. . . . Nothing resembling probable cause existed until after the search had turned up the envelope of heroin. . . . Although the Court of Appeals wrote no opinion in this case, it seems to have viewed the search here as a self-protective search for weapons. . . . In the case of the self-protective search for weapons, he [the officer] must be able to point to particular facts from which he reasonably inferred that the individual was armed and dangerous. . . . Patrolman Martin's testimony reveals no such facts." 392 U.S. at 62–64.

Reversing the decision, the Court distinguished the case from *Terry:* "The search for weapons approved in Terry consisted solely of a limited patting of the outer clothing. . . . Only when he discovered (suspect) objects did the officer in Terry place his hands in the pockets of the men he searched." 392 U.S. at 65.

The facts in *Peters* reveal that a police officer, while in his apartment, heard a noise at his door. Looking through the peephole in the door, he saw two men whom he did not know tiptoeing toward the stairs. He called the local police and entered the hallway to investigate. Believing that the pair were attempting a burglary, the officer pursued them when they fled down the stairs. When the officer finally caught Peters in the hallway, Peters explained that he was in the building visiting a married girl friend. When Peters refused to identify himself, the officer frisked him and uncovered burglary tools. Peters was convicted of possessing burglary tools, and the trial court found the frisk reasonable under New York's stop-and-frisk statute. Later the New York Court of Appeals affirmed on the same ground.

Although both sides came before the United States Supreme Court to argue for and against the constitutionality of the New

York statute, the United States Supreme Court declined to consider that particular issue. Instead, the Court concluded: "Our constitutional inquiry would not be furthered here by an attempt to pronounce judgment on the words of the statute. We must confine our review instead to the reasonableness of the searches and seizures. . . . We have held today in Terry v. Ohio . . . that police conduct of the sort with which [the statute] deals must be judged under the Reasonable Search and Seizure Clause of the Fourth Amendment." 392 U.S. at 62.

In affirming Peters' conviction, the Court found that the search was, in fact, properly incident to a lawful arrest. The Court concluded: "By the time Officer Lasky caught up with Peters on the stairway between the fourth and fifth floors . . . he had probable cause to arrest him for attempted burglary. . . . It is difficult to conceive of stronger grounds for an arrest, short of actual eye-witness observation of criminal activity. . . . When the policeman grabbed Peters . . . he seized him to cut short his flight and he searched him primarily for weapons." 392 U.S. at 66, 67.

3. The *Adams* decision is indicative of the continuing strength of *Terry* v. *Ohio*. In *Adams,* the reasonableness standards outlined in *Terry,* including that concerning the basis of the officer's "reasonable belief" that a suspect is armed, were extended to include the observations of others who, in turn, are able to reliably relate such information to the officer himself. The officer's knowledge of the reliability of the informer, coupled with the officer's need to protect himself, seems to be, under appropriate circumstances, enough to justify the stop and frisk of suspicious persons. It should be noted, however, that the *Adams* decision was not unanimous. Justices Marshall, Douglas, and Brennan were opposed to extending the *Terry* doctrine: Mr. Justice Douglas observed that "the easy extension of Terry v. Ohio to 'possessory offenses' is a serious intrusion of Fourth Amendment safeguards."

4. Court decisions involving stop and frisk abound in the lower federal and state courts. Some recent examples include *People* v. *Williams,* 237 N.W.2d 545 (Mich. App. 1975) (police officer who made a warrantless search by taking and examining a wallet from a "suspicious" man whom he had no probable cause to arrest or search held not justified); *United States* v. *Solomon,* 528 F.2d 88 (9th Cir. 1975) ("rational suspicion" as used by California courts, "founded suspicion" as used in the Ninth Circuit, and "reasonable suspicion" as used by the United States Supreme Court in stop-and-frisk cases are substantially the same tests); *People* v. *Taylor,* 544 P.2d 392 (Colo. 1975) (police officers who saw three men in a high-crime area unloading a large pile of clothing from a car, near where a clothing store had been burglarized some weeks before, had the requisite "reasonable suspicion" for a stop and frisk); *People* v. *Harris,* 540 P.2d 632 (Cal. 1975) (temporary detention of a suspect on less than probable cause to arrest does not include the right to take him into custody and transport him for a confrontation with witnesses); *People* v. *Scott,* 546 P.2d 327 (Cal. 1976) (highway patrolman about to drive drunken father and his three-year-old son home held not justified in patting down the father for weapons absent arrest or articulable belief that he was armed and dangerous, so marijuana seen in father's coat pocket as he spread his arms to submit to pat-down inadmissible); *United*

States v. *Tharpe*, 526 F.2d 326 (5th Cir. 1976) (pat-down of suspect's companion held not justified absent showing that police officer had requisite reasonable suspicion under *Terry* v. *Ohio*) (but see *United States* v. *Tharpe*, 536 F.2d 1098 [5th Cir. 1976] [en banc] [reversing *United States* v. *Tharpe*, supra, and holding that where lone police officer makes late-night traffic arrest, search of violator's companions permissible where the officer has a subjective awareness of articulable facts suggesting that the situation is a dangerous one]); *Stanley* v. *State*, 327 So. 2d 243 (Fla. App. 1976) (police officers checking certain road in response to a report about speeding cars and intoxicated juveniles had sufficient cause to stop and frisk passengers in a car that was traveling within speed limit); *Robinson* v. *United States*, 533 F.2d 578 (D.C. Cir. 1976) (police officer who suspected without probable cause that defendant was a peeping Tom and exhibitionist and gave chase and forcibly brought him to a halt held not to have made an arrest but justified in stopping and frisking); *Colding* v. *State*, 536 S.W.2d 106 (Ark. 1976) (policeman during warrant-authorized search of bar for narcotics concealed on premises was justified in removing plastic bag from stranger during frisk); (but see *People* v. *Leib*, 548 P.2d 1105 [Cal. 1976] [police officer's removal of a small plastic pill bottle from stranger who wandered into a drug bust held not justified under *Terry* v. *Ohio* where officer could not articulate facts suggesting the presence of a deadly weapon]); *People* v. *DeBour*, 386 N.E.2d 375 (N.Y. App. 1976) (policeman with less than the degree of suspicion necessary for a *Terry*-type stop can, however, approach a person and request information where he has some "articulable reason" for doing so); *People* v. *Costalis*, 354 N.E.2d 849 (N.Y. App. 1976) (mere fact that raincoat of person who just entered the scene of narcotics raid fell to floor with a thud held not to provide enough suspicion to permit a search of the coat); *United States* v. *Robinson*, 535 F.2d 881 (5th Cir. 1976) (officers who mistook slowly cruising car for a police vehicle exceeded their "stop" authority under *Terry* once they observed two young black males in the auto, and stolen government checks recovered after they saw the driver trying to hide a paper bag under the front seat held not admissible under "fruit of poisonous tree" doctrine); *United States* v. *Jeffers*, 520 F.2d 1256 (7th Cir. 1975) (defendant who claimed she had dropped her purse outside police headquarters when a sudden shooting frightened her away did not have Fourth Amendment rights violated when officer searched the purse for weapons, told her to remove her calf-length boots, and peered and felt inside them, uncovering a capsule that was possibly a narcotic, and search of purse and boots was justified under *Terry* v. *Ohio*); *United States* v. *Schleis*, 543 F.2d 59 (8th Cir. 1976) (off-duty federal officer's stop and frisk of a stumbling, staggering man outside a restaurant after he determined that the man was under the influence of some drug other than alcohol was justified because he had a reasonable suspicion that the man might be carrying a dangerous weapon); *State* v. *Van Suggs*, 246 N.W.2d 206 (Neb. 1976) (police officer who picked up hitchhiker carrying a cigar box in a sack similar to that taken in a café burglary earlier that day justified under *Adams* v. *Williams* in stopping his car, identifying himself, and demanding to see what was in the sack); *Jones* v. *State*, 233 N.W.2d 441 (Wis. 1975) (defendant who accompanied a described armed suspect was properly a subject of police frisk as the crime suggested the likelihood of danger to the officer); *Pleger* v. *Bouwman,* 233 N.W.2d 82 (Mich. 1975) (although furtive gestures alone do not justify the search of a speeder under *Adams* v. *Williams,* furtive gestures late at night generally do, and officer acted properly in ordering defendant out of auto for search and seizure of gun in plain view); *United States* v. *Hill,* 545 F.2d 1191 (9th Cir. 1976) (policeman responding to bank robbery held to have acted reasonably under *Terry* in lifting person's shirt to see what was causing the large bulge at the waistband); *State* v. *Hocker,* 556 P.2d 784 (Ariz. 1976) (car stop by police in area of rumored pot parties held unreasonable under *Terry* v. *Ohio* where officers had no reason to suspect that the vehicle was involved in criminal activity); *State* v. *Clark,* 365 A.2d 1031 (Me. 1976) (stop of person who fit a citizen-informer's highly detailed description of an individual allegedly seen putting a gun in his belt held justified under *Terry-Adams*).

5.05 THE "FRUIT OF THE POISONOUS TREE" DOCTRINE

When the Illegality Has Been Purged of Its Primary Taint, or the "Chinese Fire Drill"

WONG SUN v. UNITED STATES

Supreme Court of the United States, 1963
371 U.S. 471, 83 S. Ct. 407, 9 L. Ed. 2d 441

The facts are given in the opinion.

Mr. Justice BRENNAN delivered the opinion of the Court.

The petitioners were tried without a jury in the District Court for the Northern District of California under a two-count indictment for violation of the Federal Narcotics Laws.... They were acquitted under the first count which charged a conspiracy, but convicted under the second count which charged the substantive offense of fraudulent and knowing transportation and concealment of illegally imported heroin. The Court of Appeals for the Ninth Circuit, one judge dissenting, affirmed the convictions. ... We granted certiorari. ...

About 2 A.M. on the morning of June 4, 1959, federal narcotics agents in San Francisco, after having had one Hom Way under surveillance for six weeks, arrested him and found heroin in his possession. Hom Way, who had not before been an informant, stated after his arrest that he had bought an ounce of heroin the night before from one known to him only as "Blackie Toy," proprietor of a laundry on Leavenworth Street.

About 6 A.M. that morning six or seven federal agents went to a laundry at 1733 Leavenworth Street. The sign above the door of this establishment said "Oye's Laundry." It was operated by the petitioner James Wah Toy. There is, however, nothing in the record which identifies James Wah Toy and "Blackie Toy" as the same person. The other federal officers remained nearby out of sight while Agent Alton Wong, who was of Chinese ancestry, rang the bell. When petitioner Toy appeared and opened the door, Agent Wong told him that he was calling for laundry and dry cleaning. Toy replied that he didn't open until 8 o'clock and told the agent to come back at that time. Toy started to close the door. Agent Wong thereupon took his badge from his pocket and said, "I am a federal narcotics agent." Toy immediately "slammed the door and started running" down the hallway through the laundry to his living quarters at the back where his wife and child were sleeping in a bedroom. Agent Wong and the other federal officers broke open the door and followed Toy down the hallway to the living quarters and into the bedroom. Toy reached into a nightstand drawer. Agent Wong thereupon drew his pistol, pulled Toy's hand out of the drawer, placed him under arrest and handcuffed him. There was nothing in the drawer and a search of the premises uncovered no narcotics.

One of the agents said to Toy ". . . (Hom Way) says he got narcotics from you." Toy responded, "No, I haven't been selling any narcotics at all. However, I do know somebody who has." When asked who that was, Toy said, "I only know him as Johnny. I don't know his last name." However, Toy described a house on Eleventh Avenue where he said Johnny lived; he also described a bedroom in the house where he said "Johnny kept about a piece" of heroin, and where he and Johnny had smoked some of the drug the night before. The agents left immediately for Eleventh Avenue and located the house. They entered and found one Johnny Yee in the bedroom. After a discussion with the agents, Yee took from a bureau drawer several tubes containing in all just less than one ounce of heroin, and surrendered them. Within the hour Yee and Toy were taken to the Office of the Bureau of Narcotics. Yee there stated that the heroin had been brought to him some four days earlier by petitioner Toy and another Chinese known to him only as "Sea Dog."

Toy was questioned as to the identity of "Sea Dog" and said that "Sea Dog" was Wong Sun. Some agents, including Agent Alton Wong, took Toy to Wong Sun's neighborhood where Toy pointed out a multifamily dwelling where he said Wong Sun lived. Agent Wong rang a downstairs door bell and a buzzer sounded, opening the door. The officer identified himself as a nar-

cotics agent to a woman on the landing and asked "for Mr. Wong." The woman was the wife of petitioner Wong Sun. She said that Wong Sun was "in the back room sleeping." Alton Wong and some six other officers climbed the stairs and entered the apartment. One of the officers went into the back room and brought petitioner Wong Sun from the bedroom in handcuffs. A thorough search of the apartment followed, but no narcotics were discovered. . . .

. . . Within a few days, both petitioners and Yee were interrogated at the office of the Narcotics Bureau by Agent William Wong, also of Chinese ancestry. The agent advised each of the three of his right to withhold information which might be used against him, and stated to each that he was entitled to the advice of counsel, though it does not appear that any attorney was present during the questioning of any of the three. The officer also explained to each that no promises or offers of immunity or leniency were being or could be made.

The agent interrogated each of the three separately. After each had been interrogated the agent prepared a statement in English from rough notes. The agent read petitioner Toy's statement to him in English and interpreted certain portions of it for him in Chinese. Toy also read the statement in English aloud to the agent, said there were corrections to be made, and made the corrections in his own hand. Toy would not sign the statement, however; in the agent's words "he wanted to know first if the other persons involved in the case had signed theirs." Wong Sun had considerable difficulty understanding the statement in English and the agent restated its substance in Chinese. Wong Sun refused to sign the statement although he admitted the accuracy of its contents.

* * *

The Government's evidence tending to prove the petitioner's possession (the petitioners offered no exculpatory testimony) consisted of four items which the trial court admitted over timely objections that they were inadmissible as "fruits" of unlawful arrests or of attendant searches: (1) the statements made orally by petitioner Toy in his bedroom at the time of his arrest; (2) the heroin surrendered to the agents by Johnny Yee; (3) petitioner Toy's pretrial unsigned statement; and (4) petitioner Wong Sun's similar statement. The dispute below and here has centered around the correctness of the rulings of the trial judge allowing these items in evidence.

* * *

We believe that significant differences between the cases of the two petitioners require separate discussion of each. We shall first consider the case of petitioner Toy.

The Court of Appeals found there was neither reasonable grounds nor probable cause for Toy's arrest. Giving due weight to that finding, we think it is amply justified by the facts clearly shown on this record. It is basic that an arrest with or without a warrant must stand upon firmer ground than mere suspicion. . . .

* * *

The threshold question in this case, therefore, is whether the officers could, on the information which impelled them to act, have procured a warrant for the arrest of Toy. We think that no warrant would have issued on evidence then available.

The narcotics agents had no basis in experience for confidence in the reliability of Hom Way's information; he had never before given information. And yet they acted upon his imprecise suggestion that a person described only as "Blackie Toy," the proprietor of a laundry somewhere on Leavenworth Street, had sold one ounce of heroin. . . . Hom Way's accusation merely invited the officers to roam the length of Leavenworth Street (some 30 blocks) in search of one "Blackie Toy's" laundry—and whether by chance or other means (the record does not say) they came upon petitioner Toy's laundry which bore not his name over the door, but the unrevealing label "Oye's."

* * *

Agent Wong did eventually disclose that he was a narcotics officer. However, he affirmatively misrepresented his mission at the outset, by stating that he had come for laundry and dry cleaning. And before Toy fled, the officer never adequately dispelled the misimpression engendered by his own ruse. . . .

Moreover, he made no effort at that time, nor indeed at any time thereafter, to ascertain whether the man at the door was the "Blackie Toy" named by Hom Way. . . .

[T]he Government claims no extraordinary circumstances . . . which excused the officer's failure truthfully to state his mission before he broke in.

Thus we conclude that the Court of Appeals' finding that the officers' uninvited entry into Toy's living quarters was unlawful and that the bedroom arrest which followed was likewise unlawful was fully justified on the evidence. It remains to be seen what consequences flow from this conclusion.

It is conceded that Toy's declarations in his bedroom are to be excluded if they are held to be "fruits" of the agents' unlawful action.

* * *

The exclusionary rule has traditionally barred from trial physical, tangible materials obtained either during or as a direct result of an unlawful invasion. It follows from our holding in Silverman v. United States . . . that the Fourth Amendment may protect against the overhearing of verbal statements as well as against the more traditional seizure of "papers and effects." Similarly, testimony as to matters observed during an unlawful invasion has been excluded in order to enforce the basic constitutional policies. . . . Thus, verbal evidence which derives so immediately from an unlawful entry and an unauthorized arrest as the officers' action in the present case is no less the "fruit" of official illegality than the more common tangible fruits of the unwarranted intrusion.

* * *

The Government argues that Toy's statements to the officers in his bedroom, although closely consequent upon the invasion which we hold unlawful, were nevertheless admissible because they resulted from "an intervening independent act of a free will." This contention, however, takes insufficient account of the circumstances. Six or seven officers had broken the door and followed on Toy's heels into the bedroom where his wife and child were sleeping. He had been almost immediately handcuffed and arrested. Under such circumstances it is unreasonable to infer that Toy's response was sufficiently an act of free will to purge the primary taint of the unlawful invasion. . . .

We now consider whether the exclusion

of Toy's declarations requires also the exclusion of the narcotics taken from Yee, to which those declarations led the police. The prosecutor candidly told the trial court that "we wouldn't have found those drugs except that Mr. Toy helped us to." Hence this is not the case envisioned by this Court where the exclusionary rule has no application because the Government learned of the evidence "from an independent source" ... in which the connection between the lawless conduct of the police and the discovery of the challenged evidence has "become so attenuated as to dissipate the taint." ... We need not hold that all evidence is "fruit of the poisonous tree" simply because it would not have come to light but for the illegal actions of the police. Rather, the more apt question in such a case is "whether, granting establishment of the primary illegality, the evidence to which instant objection is made has been come at by exploitation of that illegality or instead by means sufficiently distinguishable to be purged of the primary taint." ... We think it clear that the narcotics were "come at by the exploitation of that illegality" and hence that they may not be used against Toy.

* * *

We turn now to the case of the other petitioner, Wong Sun. We have no occasion to disagree with the finding of the Court of Appeals that his arrest, also, was without probable cause or reasonable grounds. At all events no evidentiary consequences turn upon that question. For Wong Sun's unsigned confession was not the fruit of that arrest, and was therefore properly admitted at trial. On the evidence that Wong Sun had been released on his own recognizance after a lawful arraignment, and had returned voluntarily several days later to make the statement, we hold that the connection between the arrest and the statement had "become so attenuated as to dissipate the taint." ...

We must then consider the admissibility of the narcotics surrendered by Yee. Our holding that this ounce of heroin was inadmissible against Toy does not compel a like result with respect to Wong Sun. The exclusion of the narcotics as to Toy was required solely by their tainted relationship to information unlawfully obtained from Toy, and not by any official impropriety connected with their surrender by Yee. The seizure of this heroin invaded no right of privacy of person or premises which would entitle Wong Sun to object to its use at his trial.

[The Court did, however, reverse and remand Wong Sun's case for a new trial. The Court was of the opinion that Wong Sun's statements to Toy, which Toy put in his own statement to police, were not competent to corroborate Wong Sun's admissions. Since the Court could not determine whether the trial judge had considered the contents of Toy's statements as a source of corroboration, the case was sent back to the district court for retrial.]

[Mr. Justice DOUGLAS wrote a concurring opinion.]

[Mr. Justice CLARK, joined by Mr Justice HARLAN, Mr. Justice STEWART, and Mr. Justice WHITE, dissented.]

The Fifth Amendment Does Not Cure a Fourth Amendment Violation

BROWN v. ILLINOIS

Supreme Court of the United States, 1975
422 U.S. 590, 95 S. Ct. 2254, 45 L. Ed. 2d 416

Petitioner Brown, who was arrested without a warrant and without probable cause after three detectives broke into his apartment and searched it, made two in-custody inculpatory statements after he had been given *Miranda* warnings. He was subsequently indicted for murder. Brown filed a motion to suppress the

statements as the "fruits" of an illegal arrest and detention. The trial court overruled the motion and the statements were used in the trial which resulted in Brown's conviction. The Supreme Court of Illinois recognized the illegality of Brown's arrest but held the statements admissible on the ground that the giving of *Miranda* warnings served to break the causal chain of connection between the arrest and the giving of the statements and that petitioner's act of giving the statements was "sufficiently an act of free will" to purge the primary "taint" of the unlawful arrest. Brown successfully sought certiorari.

Mr. Justice BLACKMUN delivered the opinion of the Court.

* * *

The Illinois courts refrained from resolving the question, as apt here as it was in Wong Sun [supra], whether Brown's statements were obtained by exploitation of the illegality of his arrest. . . .

* * *

Although, almost 90 years ago, the Court observed that the Fifth Amendment is in "intimate relation" with the Fourth . . . the Miranda warnings thus far have not been regarded as a means either of remedying or deterring violations of Fourth Amendment rights. Frequently, as here, rights under the two amendments may appear to coalesce since "the 'unreasonable searches and seizures' condemned in the Fourth Amendment are almost always made for the purpose of compelling a man to give evidence against himself, which in criminal cases is condemned in the Fifth Amendment." . . . The exclusionary rule, however, when utilized to effectuate the Fourth Amendment, serves interests and policies that are distinct from those it serves under the Fifth. It is directed at all unlawful searches and seizures, and not merely those that happen to produce incriminating material or testimony as fruits. In short, exclusion of a confession made without Miranda warnings might be regarded as necessary to effectuate the Fifth Amendment, but it would not be sufficient fully to protect the Fourth. Miranda warnings, and the exclusion of a confession made without them, do not alone sufficiently deter a Fourth Amendment violation.

Thus, even if the statements in this case were found to be voluntary under the Fifth Amendment, the Fourth Amendment issue remains. In order for the causal chain, between the illegal arrest and the statements made subsequent thereto, to be broken, Wong Sun requires not merely that the statement meet the Fifth Amendment standard of voluntariness but that it be "sufficiently an act of free will to purge the primary taint." . . .

If Miranda warnings, by themselves, were held to attenuate the taint of an unconstitutional arrest, regardless of how wanton and purposeful the Fourth Amendment violation, the effect of the exclusionary rule would be substantially diluted. Arrests made without warrant or without probable cause, for questioning or "investigation," would be encouraged by the knowledge that evidence derived therefrom hopefully could be made admissible at trial by the simple expedient of giving Miranda warnings. Any incentive to avoid Fourth Amendment violations would be eviscerated by making the warnings, in effect, a "cure-all," and the constitutional guarantee against unlawful searches and seizures could be said to be reduced to "a form of words." . . .

It is entirely possible, of course, as the State here argues, that persons arrested illegally frequently may decide to confess, as an act of free will unaffected by the initial illegality. But the Miranda warnings, *alone* and *per se,* cannot always make the act sufficiently a product of free will to break, for Fourth Amendment purposes, the causal connection between the illegality and the confession. They cannot assure in every case that the Fourth Amendment violation has not been unduly exploited. . . .

While we therefore reject the per se rule which the Illinois courts appear to have accepted, we also decline to adopt any alternative per se or "but for" rule. The petitioner himself professes not to demand so much. . . . The question whether a confession is the product of a free will under Wong Sun must be answered on the facts of each case. No single fact is dispositive. The workings of the human mind are too complex, and the possibilities of misconduct too diverse, to permit protection of the Fourth Amendment to turn on such a talismanic test. The Miranda warnings are an important factor, to be sure, in determining whether the confession is obtained by exploitation of an illegal arrest. But they are not the only factor to be considered. The temporal proximity of the arrest and the confession, the presence of intervening circumstances ... and, particularly, the purpose and flagrancy of the official misconduct are all relevant.... The voluntariness of the statement is a threshold requirement. And the burden of showing admissibility rests, of course, on the prosecution.

Although the Illinois courts failed to undertake the inquiry mandated by Wong Sun to evaluate the circumstances of this case in the light of the policy served by the exclusionary rule, the trial resulted in a record of amply sufficient detail and depth from which the determination may be made.... We conclude that the State failed to sustain the burden of showing that the evidence in question was admissible under Wong Sun.

Brown's first statement was separated from his illegal arrest by less than two hours, and there was no intervening event of significance whatsoever. In its essentials, his situation is remarkably like that of James Wah Toy in Wong Sun. We could hold Brown's first statement admissible only if we overrule Wong Sun. We decline to do so. And the second statement was clearly the result and the fruit of the first.

The illegality here, moreover, had a quality of purposefulness. The impropriety of the arrest was obvious; awareness of that fact was virtually conceded by the two detectives when they repeatedly acknowledged, in their testimony, that the purpose of their action was "for investigation" or for "questioning."... The manner in which Brown's arrest was affected gives the appearance of having been calculated to cause surprise, fright, and confusion.

We emphasize that our holding is a limited one. We decide only that the Illinois courts were in error in assuming that the Miranda warnings, by themselves, under Wong Sun always purge the taint of an illegal arrest.

Reversed and remanded.

[Mr. Justice WHITE wrote a concurring opinion.]

[Mr. Justice POWELL, with whom Mr. Justice REHNQUIST joined, wrote a concurring opinion.]

Comments

1. The so-called "derivative evidence" rule, or "fruit of the poisonous tree" doctrine, would seem to be a natural extension of the exclusionary rule. Although the exclusionary rule was first applied in 1914 in *Weeks* v. *United States,* 232 U.S. 383, the Court did not consider the exclusion of evidence derived from other illegal or initially "tainted" evidence until 1920. In *Silverthorne Lumber Company* v. *United States,* 251 U.S. 385 (1920), federal law enforcement officers illegally seized documents from the lumber company and presented them to a grand jury. After a district court ordered the federal prosecutor to return the papers and documents that had been unlawfully seized, the grand jury then issued subpoenas demanding that the petitioners produce the returned documents, or face contempt charges. The Supreme Court, per Mr. Justice Holmes, held that the subpoenas were issued as a result of the initial unlawful conduct of the government and that since the grand jury had not gained knowledge of the documents through "independent sources" but as a direct result of the illegal seizure, the subpoenas were therefore invalid. See 43 A.L.R.3d 385; Oaks, D., *Studying the Exclusionary Rule in Search and Seizure,* 37 U. Chi. L. Rev. 665 (1970).

   The fact that the exclusionary rule prohibits "indirect" or "derivative" as well as "direct" use of illegally obtained evidence was reinforced in *Nardone* v. *United States*, 308 U.S. 338 (1939). The majority in *Nardone* referred to secondary evidence as "fruit of the poisonous tree" and demanded its exclusion unless the "taint" could somehow be removed. In addition to applying the rule to situations involving illegal arrests and illegally obtained confessions (as was done in *Wong Sun*), the Court has also recognized its application to pretrial identification procedures. See *United States* v. *Wade*, 388 U.S. 218 (1967). It is worthwhile to note, however, that the Court has declined to extend the rule to exclude guilty pleas resulting from alleged coerced confessions when the defendant was represented by counsel at the pleading. See *McMann* v. *Richardson*, 397 U.S. 759 (1970).

2. In *Wong Sun*, the Court excluded from evidence the statements of "Blackie Toy" as the "fruits" of the illegal entry and bedroom arrest. Thus the Court placed "verbal evidence" under the derivative evidence rule's protective shield. On the other hand, the Court ruled that the unsigned statement of Wong Sun was admissible even though his arrest had been illegal. Based on the fact that Wong Sun had voluntarily returned to the station house to make the statement, the Court held that the "connection between the arrest and the statement had 'become so attenuated as to dissipate the taint.'" In so doing, the Court reaffirmed the strength of the so-called "doctrine of attenuation" first announced in *Nardone* v. *United States*, under which, if it can be shown that the evidence objected to was acquired in a manner that would lessen its virulence, the evidence is said to have been "purged" of the original or "primary taint" and is therefore admissible.

3. In *Brown* v. *Illinois* the court held that *Miranda* warnings do not automatically remedy violations of the Fourth Amendment. In rejecting the state court's view that *Miranda* warnings "*alone and per se*" served to "purge the taint" of the earlier unlawful seizure (arrest), the Court's opinion (1) clearly reaffirmed the viability of the *Wong Sun* "poisonous tree" doctrine, and (2) provided additional clarification and guidance with regard to the exclusion of statements obtained pursuant to an unlawful arrest. The Court concluded that "*Wong Sun* requires not merely that the statement meet the Fifth Amendment standard of voluntariness but that it sufficiently be 'an act of free will to purge the primary taint'.... The *Miranda* warnings are an important factor ... but they are not the only factor...." What if the detectives' actions had been less calculated and flagrant; the impropriety of the arrest less obvious and purposeful? What is the significance of the phrase, "the question whether a confession is the product of a free will under *Wong Sun* must be answered on the facts of each case"? Could the introduction of evidence showing that the police acted in "good faith" serve to negate the effect of the "poisonous tree" rule? See, e.g., *Michigan* v. *Tucker*, 417 U.S. 433 (1974). What if a substantial amount of time separated the arrest from the confession or statement? Would the mere element of time alone serve as an "intervening event" sufficient to "break the causal chain," and hence, allow the state to meet its burden of showing admissibility under *Wong Sun*? Regarding the time element, what is the significance of the Court's reference to "the temporal proximity of the arrest and the confession"?

4. Some related state and lower federal court cases are *Ryon* v. *State*, 349 S.E.2d 393 (Md. Ct. App. 1975) (defective arrest warrant precludes admission of voluntary confession even though *Miranda* warnings given); *People* v. *Bates*, 546 P.2d 491 (Colo. 1976) (arrest of suspect without probable cause makes subsequent confession inadmissible even though *Miranda* warnings given); *United States* v. *Griffin*, 413 F. Supp. 178 (E.D. Mich. 1976) (where arrest of A is lawful and arrest of B is unlawful, evidence seized incident to the arrest of A is admissible against B if it has a source that is free from the taint of the illegality) (see also *United States* v. *Robinson*, 535 F.2d 881 [5th Cir. 1976] [evidence discovered as result of illegal car stop not admissible under fruit of the poisonous tree doctrine]).

5.06 STANDING TO CHALLENGE THE LEGALITY OF THE SEARCH

A Person Lawfully on the Premises Is an "Aggrieved Party"

JONES v. UNITED STATES

Supreme Court of the United States, 1960
362 U.S. 257, 80 S. Ct. 725, 4 L. Ed. 2d 697

Petitioner Jones was arrested in a Washington, D.C., apartment by federal narcotics agents who entered to execute a search warrant. The officer uncovered illicit narcotics and narcotics paraphernalia. Petitioner admitted to the agents that some of the seized evidence was his and that he was living in the apartment. Following arrest, the petitioner moved to suppress the evidence on the ground that the warrant had been issued without probable cause. The government challenged petitioner's standing to make this motion because Jones alleged neither ownership of the evidence nor an interest in the apartment greater than that of an "invitee or guest." The district court agreed to conduct a hearing on the issue of petitioner's standing.

On direct examination Jones maintained that the apartment belonged to a friend, Evans, who had given him a key and permission to use it on the day of the arrest. Jones testified that he had slept there "maybe a night," had paid nothing for the use of the apartment, and had a suit and a shirt there. The district judge ruled that petitioner lacked standing to suppress the evidence. Defendent was convicted of violation of federal narcotics laws. The Court of Appeals (D.C. Cir.) affirmed, and Jones sucessfully sought certiorari.

Mr. Justice FRANKFURTER delivered the opinion of the Court.

* * *

The issue of petitioner's standing is to be decided with reference to Rule 41(e) of the Federal Rules of Criminal Procedure, 18 U.S.C.A. This is a statutory direction governing the suppression of evidence acquired in violation of the conditions validating a search. It is desirable to set forth the Rule.

"A person aggrieved by an unlawful search and seizure may move the district court for the district in which the property was seized for the return of the property and to suppress for use as evidence anything so obtained on the ground that (1) the property was illegally seized without warrant, or (2) the warrant is insufficient on its fact, or (3) the property seized is not that described in the warrant, or (4) there was not probable cause for believing the existence of the grounds on which the warrant was issued, or (5) the warrant was illegally executed. The judge shall receive evidence on any issue of fact necessary to the decision of the motion. If the motion is granted the property shall be restored unless otherwise subject to lawful detention and it shall not be admissible in evidence at any hearing or trial. The motion to suppress evidence may also be made in the district where the trial is to be had. The motion shall be made before trial or hearing unless opportunity therefore did not exist or the defendant was not aware of the grounds for the motion, but the court in its discretion may entertain the motion at the trial or hearing."

In order to qualify as a "person aggrieved by an unlawful search and seizure" one must have been a victim of a search or seizure, one against whom the search was directed, as distinguished from one who claims prejudice only through the use of evidence gathered as a consequence of a search or seizure directed at someone else. Rule 41(e) applies the general principle that a party will not be heard to claim a constitutional protection unless he "belongs to the class for whose sake the constitutional protection is given." ... The restrictions upon searches and seizures were obviously designed for protection against official invasion of privacy and the security of property. They are not exclusionary provisions against the admission of kinds of evidence deemed inherently unreliable or prejudicial. The exclusion in federal trials of evidence otherwise competent but gathered by federal officials in violation of the Fourth Amendment is a means for making effective the protection of privacy.

Ordinarily, then, it is entirely proper to require of one who seeks to challenge the legality of a search as the basis for suppressing relevant evidence that he allege, and if the allegation be disputed that he establish, that he himself was the victim of an invasion of privacy. But prosecutions like this one have presented a special problem. To establish "standing" Courts of Appeals have generally required that the movant claim either to have owned or possessed the seized property or to have had a substantial pos-

sessory interest in the premises searched. Since narcotics charges like those in the present indictment may be established through proof solely of possession of narcotics, a defendant seeking to comply with what has been the conventional standing requirement has been forced to allege facts the proof of which would tend, if indeed not be sufficient, to convict him. At the least, such a defendant has been placed in the criminally tendentious position of explaining his possession of the premises. He has been faced, not only with the chance that the allegations made on the motion to suppress may be used against him at the trial, although that they may is by no means an inevitable holding, but also with the encouragement that he perjure himself if he seeks to establish "standing" while maintaining a defense to the charge of possession.

* * *

... The Government urges us to follow the body of Court of Appeals' decisions and to rule that the lower courts ... have been right in barring a defendant in a case like this from challenging a search because of his failure, when making his motion to suppress, to allege either that he owned or possessed the property seized or that he had a possessory interest in the premises searched greater than the interest of an "invitee or guest."

... Two separate lines of thought effectively sustain defendant's standing in this case. (1) The same element in this prosecution which has caused a dilemma, i.e., that possession both convicts and confers standing, eliminates any necessity for a preliminary showing of an interest in the premises searched or the property seized, which ordinarily is required when standing is challenged. (2) Even were this not a prosecution turning on illicit possession, the legally requisite interest in the premises was here satisfied, for it need not be as extensive a property interest as was required by the courts below.

As to the first ground, we are persuaded by this consideration: to hold to the contrary, that is, to hold that petitioner's failure to acknowledge interest in the narcotics or the premises prevented his attack upon the search, would be to permit the Government to have the advantage of contradictory positions as a basis for conviction. Petitioner's conviction flows from his possession of the narcotics at the time of the search. Yet the fruits of that search, upon which the conviction depends, were admitted into evidence on the ground that petitioner did not have possession of the narcotics at that time. The prosecution here thus subjected the defendant to the penalties meted out to one in lawless possession while refusing him the remedies designed for one in that situation. It is not consonant with the amenities, to put it mildly, of the administration of criminal justice to sanction such squarely contradictory assertions of power by the Government. The possession on the basis of which petitioner is to be and was convicted suffices to give him standing under any fair and rational conception of the requirements of Rule 41(e).

In the interest of normal procedural orderliness, a motion to suppress, under Rule 41(e), must be made prior to trial, if the defendant then has knowledge of the grounds on which to base the motion. . . . As codified, the rule is not a rigid one, for under Rule 41(e) "the court in its discretion may entertain the motion (to suppress) at the trial or hearing." . . . In cases where the indictment itself charges possession, the defendant in a very real sense is revealed as a "person aggrieved by an unlawful search and seizure" upon a motion to suppress evidence prior to trial. Rule 41(e) should not be applied to allow the Government to deprive the defendant of standing to bring a motion to suppress by framing the indictment in general terms, while prosecuting for possession.

As a second ground sustaining "standing" here we hold that petitioner's testimony on the motion to suppress made out a sufficient interest in the premises to establish him as a "person aggrieved" by their search. That testimony established that at the time of the search petitioner was present in the apartment with the permission of Evans, whose apartment it was. The Government asserts that such an interest is insufficient to give standing. The Government does not contend that only ownership of the premises may confer standing. It would draw distinctions among various classes of possessors, deeming some, such as "guests" and "invitees" with only the "use" of the premises, to have too "tenuous" an interest although concededly having "some measure of control" through their "temporary presence," while conceding that others, who in a "realistic sense, have dominion of the apartment" or who are "domiciled" there, have standing. Petitioner, it is insisted by his own testimony falls in the former class.

* * *

. . . Distinctions such as those between "lessee," "licensee," "invitee" and "guest," often only of gossamer strength, ought not to be determinative in fashioning procedures ultimately referable to constitutional safeguards.

. . . No just interest of the Government in the effective and rigorous enforcement of the criminal law will be hampered by recognizing that anyone legitimately on premises where a search occurs may challenge its legality by way of a motion to suppress, when its fruits are proposed to be used against him. This would of course not avail those who, by virtue of their wrongful presence, cannot invoke the privacy of the premises searched. As petitioner's testimony established Evans' consent to his presence in the apartment, he was entitled to have the merits of his motion to suppress adjudicated.

* * *

Vacated and remanded.

A Third Party Doesn't Have A Leg To Stand On

BROWN v. UNITED STATES

Supreme Court of the United States, 1973
411 U.S. 223, 93 S. Ct. 1565, 36 L. Ed. 2d 208

The facts are stated in the opinion.

Mr. Chief Justic BURGER delivered the opinion of the Court.

Petitioners were convicted by a jury of transporting stolen goods and of conspiracy to transport stolen goods in interstate commerce. . . . The central issue now is whether petitioners have standing to challenge the lawfulness of the seizure of merchandise stolen by them but stored in the premises of one Knuckles, a coconspirator. At the time of the seizure from Knuckles, petitioners were in police custody in a different State. Knuckles successfully challenged the introduction of the stolen goods seized from his store under a faulty warrant, and his case was separately tried.

The evidence against petitioners is largely uncontroverted. Petitioner Brown was the manager of a warehouse in Cincinnati, Ohio, owned by a wholesale clothing and household goods company. He was entrusted with the warehouse keys. Petitioner Smith was a truck driver for the company. During 1968 and 1969, the company had experienced losses attributed to pilferage amounting to approximately $60,000 each year. One West, a buyer and supervisor for the company, recovered a slip of paper he had seen drop from Brown's pocket. On the slip, in Brown's handwriting, was a list of warehouse merchandise together with a price on each item that was well below wholesale cost. West estimated that the lowest legitimate wholesale price for these items would have been a total of about $6,400, while the total as priced by Brown's list was $2,200. The police were promptly notified and set up a surveillance of the warehouse. Ten days later, petitioners were observed wheeling carts containing boxes of merchandise from the warehouse to a truck. From a concealed point, the police took 20 photographs of petitioners loading the merchandise into the truck. Petitioners then locked the warehouse, and drove off. They were followed and stopped by the police, placed under arrest, advised of their rights, and, with the loaded truck, taken into custody to police headquarters. The goods in the truck had not been lawfully taken from the warehouse and had a total value of about $6,500.

Following their arrest, and after being fully informed of their constitutional rights, both petitioners made separate confessions to police indicating that they had conspired with Knuckles to steal from the warehouse, that they had stolen goods from the warehouse in the past, and that they had taken these goods, on two occasions about two months before their arrest, to Knuckles' store in Manchester, Kentucky. Petitioners also indicated that they had "sold" the previously stolen goods on delivery to Knuckles for various amounts of cash. Knuckles' store was then searched pursuant to a warrant, and goods stolen from the company, worth over $100,000 in retail value, were discovered. Knuckles was at the store during the search, but petitioners were in custody in Ohio.

Prior to trial, petitioners . . . moved to suppress the stolen merchandise found at Knuckles' store. . . . The District Court held a hearing on petitioners' motion to suppress the evidence. Petitioners, however, alleged no proprietary or possessory interest in Knuckles' premises or in the goods seized there, nor was any evidence of such an interest presented to the District Court. . . . [T]he District Court . . . denied petitioners' motion for lack of standing. . . .

On appeal the Court of Appeals for the Sixth Circuit . . . held that the stolen merchandise seized pursuant to the defective warrant was properly admitted against petitioners, stating:

"This ruling [of the District Court] was correct because appellants claimed no possessory or proprietary rights in the goods or in Knuckles' store, and it is clear that they cannot assert the Fourth Amendment right of another." 452 F.2d 868, 870 (1971).

Petitioners contend that they have "automatic" standing to challenge the search and seizure at Knuckles' store. They rely on the decision of this Court in Jones v. United States (1960) [supra], establishing a rule of "automatic" standing to contest an allegedly illegal search where the same possession needed to establish standing is "an essential element of the offense . . . charged." . . . That case involved (a) a seizure of contraband narcotics, (b) a defendant who was present at the seizure, and (c) an offense in which the defendant's possession of the seized narcotics at the time of the contested search and seizure was a critical part of the Government case. . . . Mr. Justice Frankfurter, writing for the Court in Jones, emphasized the "dilemma" inherent in a defendant's need to allege "possession" to contest a seizure, when such admission of possession could later be used against him. . . .

The self-incrimination dilemma, so central to the Jones decision, can no longer occur under the prevailing interpretation of the Constitution. Subsequent to Jones, in Simmons v. United States, 390 U.S. 377 (1968), we held that a prosecutor may not use against a defendant at trial any testimony given by that defendant at a pretrial hearing to establish standing to move to suppress evidence. . . . Thus, petitioners in this case could have asserted, at the pretrial suppression hearing, a possessory interest in the goods at Knuckles' store without any danger of incriminating themselves. They did not do so.

But it is not necessary for us now to determine whether our decision in Simmons makes Jones' "automatic" standing unnecessary. We reserve that question for a case where possession at the time of the contested search and seizure is "an essential element of the offense . . . charged." . . . Here, unlike Jones, the Government's case against petitioners does not depend on petitioners' possession of the seized evidence at the time of the contested search and seizure. The stolen goods seized had been transported and "sold" by petitioners to Knuckles approximately two months before the challenged search. The conspiracy and transportation alleged by the indictment were carefully limited to the period before the day of the search.

In deciding this case, therefore, it is suf-ficient to hold that there is no standing to contest a search and seizure where, as here, the defendants: (a) were not on the premises at the time of the contested search and seizure; (b) alleged no proprietary or possessory interest in the premises; and (c) were not charged with an offense that includes, as an essential element of the offense charged, possession of the seized evidence at the time of the contested search and seizure. The vice of allowing the Government to allege possession as part of the crime charged, and yet deny that there was possession sufficient for standing purposes, is not present. The Government cannot be accused of taking "advantage of contradictory positions." . . .

Again, we do not decide that this vice of prosecutorial self-contradiction warrants the continued survival of Jones' "automatic" standing now that our decision in Simmons has removed the danger of coerced self-incrimination. We simply see no reason to afford such "automatic" standing where, as here, there was no risk to a defendant of either self-incrimination or prosecutorial self-contradiction. Petitioners were afforded a full hearing on standing and failed to allege any legitimate interest of any kind in the premises searched or the merchandise seized.

* * *

Affirmed.

Comments

1. *Jones* v. *United States* solved the "damned if you do and damned if you don't" dilemma faced by the defendant who wished to suppress evidence but did not wish to claim possessory rights to the evidence seized. In *Jones,* the petitioner had to maintain that the narcotics were taken from *his possession* in order to have "standing" to challenge the validity of the search warrant under which the evidence was seized. But in admitting possession, Jones would have also "convicted" himself of the possessory offense. The Court rejected the argument that dominion or possessory rights must be the basis for the standing. Instead, they held that anyone who is *legitimately* on the premises where the search takes place may properly challenge, by way of the motion to suppress, the introduction of seized evidence against him. Recognizing that defendant was so situated as to qualify as a "person aggrieved by an unlawful search and seizure" under Rule 41(e), the Court found that proper standing had been established to challenge the existence of the probable cause upon which the warrant was issued. Rule 41(e) allows a person to challenge both the warrant itself and

the manner in which it was executed. Also, under the rule, evidence may be suppressed if seized illegally without a warrant, or if seized but not described in the warrant.

2. The facts that (1) there was a seizure of contraband, the possession of which was illegal, (2) Jones was on the premises *legitimately* (one who is there unlawfully, e.g., a burglar, is not protected) at the time of the search, (3) Jones was the person against whom the evidence was to be used, and (4) the offense involving Jones' possession of the narcotics at the time of the search and seizure was a crucial part of the government's case all combined to convince the Court that proper standing had been established. It has been said that under such circumstances the defendant has "automatic" standing to challenge the admission of the evidence. Of course, for one who has possessory interests in the place searched or the items seized, the "legitimate presence on the premises" requirement has no applicability. See *Chapman* v. *United States,* 365 U.S. 610 (1965). However, in *Mancusi* v. *DeForte,* 392 U.S. 364 (1968), the Court suggested that factors other than simple "possessory interests" might serve to justify standing for the defendant who has joint use of the place searched; i.e., the "reasonable expectation of privacy" concept might apply.

3. The need for the "automatic standing" rule may no longer exist. See *Simmons* v. *United States,* 390 U.S. 377 (1968), in which the Court held that the pretrial testimony of an accused given to establish standing cannot be used against him at trial to establish guilt. The Court was careful to note the effect of the *Simmons* ruling in *Brown* v. *United States.*

4. The *Brown* facts differ from those in *Jones* in three distinct ways: (1) petitioners were not present at the contested search but were already in custody in a different state; (2) they claimed no ownership or possessory rights in the premises searched; and (3) the crime for which they were charged (transportation and sale of stolen goods) was not an offense that includes possession at the time of the seizure as an essential element. Because of the Court's ruling in *Simmons,* the *Jones* "automatic" standing rule may be discarded if and when the Court has occasion to hear a case in which possession at the time of the contested search and seizure is an essential element of the crime charged.

5. The following recent decisions in the lower federal and state courts involved the issue of standing to challenge the legality of a search: *United States* v. *Prueitt,* 540 F.2d 995 (9th Cir. 1976) (where defendants are charged with possession of marijuana but only convicted of conspiracy—in which possession is not an element—only those defendants who assert a possessory interest in the marijuana seized have standing on appeal to challenge the legality of the search); *Wing* v. *Anderson,* 398 F. Supp. 197 (D. Okla.) (defendant charged with robbery had no claim to challenge search of deceased accomplice's auto, as defendant claimed no possessory rights to car or its contents, and essential element of armed robbery is not possession of those items seized); *Commonwealth* v. *Corradino,* 332 N.E.2d 907 (Mass. 1975) (part of defendant's burden of proof at suppression hearing is to demonstrate a possessory interest in premises searched or property seized) (accord, *United*

States v. *Stull,* 521 F.2d 687 [6th Cir. 1975] [if at suppression hearing a defendant denies possessory rights in evidence seized, he lacks standing to object to the search]); *United States* v. *Lisk,* 522 F.2d 228 (7th Cir. 1975) (defendant A who stored a bomb in trunk of defendant B's car that was subsequently seized unlawfully from B's auto by police has, by virtue of ownership, standing to challenge the validity of the search and seizure, but bomb was contraband and subject to seizure, and even if seizure was unlawful, evidence is admissible against A even though it could not be used against B); *United States* v. *Cassell,* 542 F.2d 279 (5th Cir. 1976) (defendant held to have no standing to challenge search of apartment in which he and his partner in crime were found, because the partner had no right to be there); *United States* v. *Tortorello,* 533 F.2d 809 (2nd Cir. 1976) (defendant who consented to police search of house garage held to have no standing to challenge legality of search when only evidence seized from house basement was used against him).

5.07 ELECTRONIC SURVEILLANCE AND RELATED PROBLEMS

Meeting the Constitutional Test

BERGER v. NEW YORK

Supreme Court of the United States, 1967
388 U.S. 41, 87 S. Ct. 1873, 18 L. Ed. 2d 1040

Petitioner, Berger, was convicted in the Supreme Court, Special and Trial Term, New York County, on two counts of conspiracy to bribe a public officer of the New York State Liquor Authority. On appeal the Supreme Court, Appellate Division, and the New York Court of Appeals affirmed without opinion. Certiorari was granted.

Additional facts are stated in the opinion.

Mr. Justice CLARK delivered the opinion of the Court.

This writ tests the validity of New York's permissive eavesdrop statute, N.Y. Code Crim. Proc. § 813-a.... The claim is that the statute sets up a system of surveillance which involves trespassory intrusions into private, constitutionally protected premises.

... We have concluded that the language of New York's statute is too broad in its sweep resulting in a trespassory intrusion into a constitutionally protected area and is, therefore, violative of the Fourth and Fourteenth Amendments....

Berger, the petitioner, was convicted on two counts of conspiracy to bribe the Chairman of the New York State Liquor Authority. The case arose out of the complaint of one Ralph Pansini to the District Attorney's office that agents of the State Liquor Authority had entered his bar and grill and without cause seized his books and records. Pansini asserted that the raid was in reprisal for his failure to pay a bribe for a liquor license. Numerous complaints had been filed with the District Attorney's office charging the payment of bribes by applicants for liquor licenses. On the direction of that office, Pansini, while equipped with a "minifon" recording device, interviewed an employee of the Authority. The employee advised Pansini that the price for a license was $10,000 and suggested that he contact attorney Harry Neyer. Neyer subsequently told Pansini that he worked with the Authority employee before and that the latter was aware of the going rate on liquor licenses downtown.

On the basis of this evidence an eavesdrop order was obtained from a Justice of the State Supreme Court, as provided by § 813-a. The order permitted the installation, for a period of 60 days, of a recording device in Neyer's office. On the basis of leads obtained from this eavesdrop a second order permitting the installation, for a period, of a recording device in the office of one Harry Steinman was obtained. After some two weeks of eavesdropping a conspiracy was uncovered involving the issuance of liquor licenses for the Playboy and Tenement Clubs, both of New York City. Petitioner was indicted as "a go-between" for the principal conspirators, who though not named in the indictment were disclosed in a bill of particulars. Relevant portions of the recordings were received in evidence at the trial and were played to the jury, all over the objection of the petitioner. The parties have stipulated that the District Attorney "had no information upon which to proceed to present a case to the Grand Jury, or on the basis of which to prosecute" the petitioner except by the use of the eavesdrop evidence.

* * *

We, therefore, turn to New York's statute to determine the basis of the search and seizure authorized by it upon the order of a state supreme court justice, a county judge or general sessions judge of New York County. Section 813-a authorizes the issuance of an "ex parte order for eavesdropping" upon "oath or affirmation of a district attorney, or of the attorney-general or of an officer above the rank of sergeant of any police department of the state or of any political subdivision thereof...." The oath must state "that there is reasonable ground to believe that evidence of crime may be thus obtained, and particularly describing the person or persons whose communications, conversations or discussions are to be overheard or recorded and the pur-

pose thereof, and ... identifying the particular telephone number or telegraph line involved." The judge "may examine on oath the applicant and any other witness he may produce and shall satisfy himself of the existence of reasonable grounds for the granting of such application." The order must specify the duration of the eavesdrop — not exceeding two months unless extended — and "(a)ny such order together with the papers upon which the application was based, shall be delivered to and retained by the applicant as authority for the eavesdropping authorized therein."

While New York's statute satisfies the Fourth Amendment's requirement that a neutral and detached authority be interposed between the police and the public ... the broad sweep of the statute is immediately observable.

* * *

The Fourth Amendment commands that a warrant issue not only upon probable cause supported by oath or affirmation, but also "particularly describing the place to be searched and the persons or things to be seized." New York's statute lacks this particularization. It merely says that a warrant may issue on reasonable ground to believe that evidence of crime may be obtained by the eavesdrop. It lays down no requirement for particularity in the warrant as to what specific crime has been or is being committed, nor "the place to be searched," or "the persons or things to be seized" as specifically required by the Fourth Amendment. The need for particularity and evidence of reliability in the showing required when judicial authorization of a search is sought is especially great in the case of eavesdropping. By its very nature eavesdropping involves an intrusion on privacy that is broad in scope. As was said in Osborn v. United States, 385 U.S. 326 (1966), the "indiscriminate use of such devices in law enforcement raises grave constitutional questions under the Fourth and Fifth Amendments," and imposes "a heavier responsibility on this Court in its supervision of the fairness of procedures...." ... The recording device [in Osborn] was, as the Court said, authorized "under the most precise and discriminate circumstances, circumstances which fully met the "requirement of particularity" of the Fourth Amendment.

* * *

By contrast, New York's statute lays down no such "precise and discriminate" requirements. Indeed, it authorizes the "indiscriminate use" of electronic devices as specifically condemned in Osborn.... New York's broadside authorization rather than being "carefully circumscribed" so as to prevent unauthorized invasions of privacy actually permits general searches by electronic devices.

First, as we have mentioned, eavesdropping is authorized without requiring belief that any particular offense has been or is being committed; nor that the "property" sought, the conversations, be particularly described. . . . Likewise the statute's failure to describe with particularity the conversations sought gives the officer a roving commission to "seize" any and all conversations. It is true that the statute requires the naming of "the person or persons whose communications, conversations or discussions are to be overheard or recorded. . . ." But this does no more than identify the person whose constitutionally protected area is to be invaded rather than "particularly describing" the communications, conversations, or discussions to be seized. . . . Secondly, authorization of eavesdropping for a two-month period is the equivalent of a series of intrusions, searches, and seizures pursuant to a single showing of probable cause. Prompt execution is also avoided. During such a long and continuous (24 hours a day) period the conversations of any and all persons coming into the area covered by the device will be seized indiscriminately and without regard to their connection with the crime under investigation. Moreover, the statute permits, and there were authorized here, extensions of the original two-month period—presumably for two months each—on a mere showing that such extension is "in the public interest." Apparently the original grounds on which the eavesdrop order was initially issued also form the basis of the renewal. This we believe insufficient without a showing of present probable cause for the continuance of the eavesdrop. Third, the statute places no termination date on the eavesdrop once the conversation sought is seized. This is left entirely in the discretion of the officer. Finally, the statute's procedure, necessarily because its success depends on secrecy, has

no requirement for notice as do conventional warrants, nor does it overcome this defect by requiring some showing of special facts. On the contrary, it permits uncontested entry without any showing of exigent circumstances. Such a showing of exigency, in order to avoid notice would appear more important in eavesdropping, with its inherent dangers, than that required when conventional procedures of search and seizure are utilized. Nor does that statute provide for a return on the warrant thereby leaving full discretion in the officer as to the use of seized conversations of innocent as well as guilty parties. In short, the statute's blanket grant of permission to eavesdrop is without adequate judicial supervision or protective procedures.

* * *

It is said that neither a warrant nor a statute authorizing eavesdropping can be drawn so as to meet the Fourth Amendment's requirements. If that be true then the "fruits" of eavesdropping devices are barred under the Amendment. On the other hand this Court has in the past, under specific conditions and circumstances, sustained the use of eavesdropping devices. In the latter case the eavesdropping device was permitted where the "commission of a specific offense" was charged, its use was "under the most precise and discriminate circumstances" and the effective administration of justice in a federal court was at stake. The States are under no greater restrictions. The Fourth Amendment does not make the "precincts of the home or the office ... sanctuaries where the law can never reach" ... but it does prescribe a constitutional standard that must be met before official invasion is permissible. Our concern with the statute here is whether its language permits a trespassory invasion of the home or office, by general warrant, contrary to the command of the Fourth Amendment. As it is written, we believe that it does.

Reversed.

[Mr. Justice DOUGLAS, with whom Mr. Justice STEWART joined, concurred.]
[Separate dissenting opinions were written by Mr. Justice BRENNAN, Mr. Justice HARLAN, and Mr. Justice WHITE.]

The Use of Secret Agents "Wired for Sound"

ON LEE v. UNITED STATES

Supreme Court of the United States, 1952
343 U.S. 747, 72 S. Ct. 967, 96 L. Ed. 1270

Petitioner On Lee was convicted in the United States District Court for the Southern District of New York of making an illegal sale of opium and of conspiring to sell opium, and he appealed. The Court of Appeals (2nd Cir.) affirmed, and the Supreme Court granted certiorari.

Additional facts are stated in the opinion.

Mr. Justice JACKSON delivered the opinion of the Court.

* * *

Petitioner, On Lee, had a laundry in Hoboken.... Chin Poy, an old acquaintance and former employee, sauntered in and, while customers came and went, engaged the accused in conversation in the course of which petitioner made incriminating statements. He did not know that Chin Poy was what the Government calls "an undercover agent" ... for the Bureau of Narcotics. Neither did he know that Chin Poy was wired for sound, with a small microphone in his inside overcoat pocket and a small antenna running along his arm. Unbeknownst to petitioner, an agent of the Narcotics Bureau named Lawrence Lee had stationed himself outside with a receiving set properly tuned to pick up any sounds the Chin Poy microphone transmitted. Through the large front window Chin Poy could be seen and through the receiving set his conversation, in Chinese, with petitioner could be heard by agent Lee. A few days later, on the sidewalks of New York, another conversation took place between the two, and damaging admissions were again "audited" by agent Lee.

For reasons left to our imagination, Chin Poy was not called to testify about petitioner's incriminating admissions. Against objection, however, agent Lee was allowed to relate the conversations as heard with aid of his receiving set. Of this testimony, it is enough to say that it was certainly prejudicial if its admission was improper.

Petitioner contends that this evidence should have been excluded because the manner in which it was obtained violates both the search and seizure provisions of the Fourth Amendment, and § 605 of the Federal Communications Act....

The conduct of Chin Poy and agent Lee did not amount to an unlawful search and seizure such as is proscribed by the Fourth Amendment. In Goldman v. United States, 316 U.S. 129 (1942), we held that the action of federal agents in placing a detectaphone on the outer wall of defendant's hotel room, and thereby overhearing conversations held within the room, did not violate the Fourth Amendment. There the agents had earlier committed a trespass in order to install a listening device within the room itself. Since the device failed to work, the Court expressly reserved decision as to the effect on the search and seizure question of a trespass in that situation. Petitioner in the instant case has seized upon that dictum, apparently on the assumption that the presence of a radio set would automatically bring him within the reservation if he can show a trespass.

But petitioner cannot raise the undecided question, for here no trespass was committed. Chin Poy entered a place of business with the consent, if not the implied invitation, of the petitioner.

* * *

By the same token, the claim that Chin Poy's entrance was a trespass because consent to his entry was obtained by fraud must be rejected.... The further contention of petitioner that agent Lee, outside the laundry, was a trespasser because by these aids he overheard what went on inside verges on the frivolous. Only in the case of physical entry, either by force, ... by unwilling submission to authority ... or without any express or implied consent ... would the problem left undecided in the Goldman case be before the Court.

Petitioner relies on cases relating to the more common and clearly distinguishable problems raised where tangible property is unlawfully seized. Such unlawful seizure may violate the Fourth Amendment, even though the entry itself was by subterfuge or fraud rather than force.... But such decisions are inapposite in the field of mechanical or electronic devices designed to overhear or intercept conversation, at least where access to the listening post was not obtained by illegal methods.

Petitioner urges that if his claim of unlawful search and seizure cannot be sustained on authority, we reconsider the question of Fourth Amendment rights in the field of overheard or intercepted conversations. This apparently is upon the theory that since there was a radio set involved, he could succeed if he could persuade the Court to overturn the leading case holding wiretapping to be outside the ban of the Fourth Amendment, Olmstead v. United States ... and the cases which have fol-

lowed it. We need not consider this, however, for success in this attempt, which failed in Goldman v. United States ... would be of no aid to petitioner unless he can show that his situation should be treated as wiretapping. The presence of a radio set is not sufficient to suggest more than the most attenuated analogy to wiretapping. Petitioner was talking confidentially and indiscreetly with one he trusted, and he was overheard. This was due to aid from a transmitter and receiver, to be sure, but with the same effect on his privacy as if agent Lee had been eavesdropping outside an open window. The use of bifocals, field glasses or the telescope to magnify the object of a witness' vision is not a forbidden search and seizure, even if they focus without his knowledge or consent upon what one supposes to be private indiscretions. It would be a dubious service to the genuine liberties protected by the Fourth Amendment to make them bedfellows with spurious liberties improvised by farfetched analogies which would liken eavesdropping on a conversation, with the connivance of one of the parties, to an unreasonable search and seizure. We find no violation of the Fourth Amendment here.

[Mr. Justice BURTON, Mr. Justice DOUGLAS, Mr. Justice BLACK, and Mr. Justice FRANKFURTER dissented.]

Assumption of the Risk

UNITED STATES v. WHITE

Supreme Court of the United States, 1971
401 U.S. 745, 91 S. Ct. 1122, 28 L. Ed. 2d 453

Respondent, White, was convicted in 1966 of narcotics violations. At his trial in the United States District Court for the Northern District of Illinois, evidence was admitted of certain incriminating statements he had made that were overheard by means of warrantless electronic eavesdropping. Government agents heard White's statements by means of a transmitter that an informer, Harvey Jackson, consented to wear during several conversations with respondent. Four of the conversations took place in Jackson's home, two in his car, one in a restaurant, and one in respondent's home. The prosecution was unable to locate and produce Jackson at the trial, and over objection, the agents were allowed to testify about the statements they had overheard. Reading *Katz* (supra) as overruling *On Lee* (supra), the Court of Appeals (7th Cir.) reversed and remanded, and the government was granted certiorari.

Mr. Justice WHITE announced the judgment of the Court and an opinion in which the CHIEF JUSTICE [BURGER], Mr. Justice STEWART, and Mr. Justice BLACKMUN join.

* * *

Until Katz v. United States, 389 U.S. 347 (1967), neither wiretapping nor electronic eavesdropping violated a defendant's Fourth Amendment rights "unless there has been an official search and seizure of his person, or such a seizure of his papers or his tangible material effects, or an actual physical invasion of his house 'or curtilage' for the purpose of making a seizure."... But where "eavesdropping was accomplished by means of an unauthorized physical penetration into the premises occupied" by the defendant, although falling short of a "technical trespass under the local property law," the Fourth Amendment was violated and any evidence of what was seen and heard, as well as tangible objects seized, was considered the inadmissible fruit of an unlawful invasion....

Katz v. United States, however, finally swept away doctrines that electronic eavesdropping is permissible under the Fourth Amendment unless physical invasion of a constitutionally protected area produced the challenged evidence.... [T]he Court overruled Olmstead [v. United States, 277 U.S. 438 (1928)] and Goldman [v. United States, 316 U.S. 129 (1942)] and held that the absence of physical intrusion into the telephone booth did not justify using electronic devices in listening to and recording Katz's words, thereby violating the privacy on which he justifiably relied while using the telephone in those circumstances.

The Court of Appeals understood Katz to render inadmissible against White the agents' testimony concerning conversations that Jackson broadcast to them. We cannot agree. Katz involved no revelation to the Government by a party to conversations with the defendant nor did the Court indicate in any way that a defendant has a justifiable and constitutionally protected expectation that a person with whom he is conversing will not then or later reveal the conversation to the police.

Hoffa v. United States, 385 U.S. 293 (1966), which was left undisturbed by Katz held that however strongly a defendant may trust an apparent colleague, his expectations in this respect are not protected by the Fourth Amendment when it turns out that the colleague is a government agent regularly communicating with the authorities....

Conceding that Hoffa, Lewis, and Lopez remained unaffected by Katz, the Court of Appeals nevertheless read both Katz and the Fourth Amendment to require a different result if the agent not only records his conversations with the defendant but instantaneously transmits them electronically to other agents equipped with radio receivers....

To reach this result it was necessary for the Court of Appeals to hold that On Lee v. United States, 343 U.S. 747 (1952), was no longer good law. In that case, which involved facts very similar to the case before us, the Court first rejected claims of a Fourth Amendment violation because the informer had not trespassed when he entered the defendant's premises and conversed with him. To this extent the Court's rationale cannot survive Katz.... But the Court announced a second and independent ground for its decision; for it went on to say that overruling Olmstead and Goldman would be of no aid to On Lee since he "was talking confidentially and indiscreetly with one he trusted, and he was overheard.... It would be a dubious service to the genuine liberties protected by the Fourth Amendment to make them bedfellows with spurious liberties improvised by farfetched analogies which would liken eavesdropping on a conversation, with the connivance of one of the parties, to an unreasonable search or seizure. We find no violation of the Fourth Amendment here."... We see no indication in Katz that the Court meant to disturb the understanding of the Fourth Amendment or to disturb the result reached in the On Lee case, nor are we now inclined to overturn this view of the Fourth Amendment.

Concededly a police agent who conceals his police connections may write down for official use his conversations with a defendant and testify concerning them, without a warrant authorizing his encounters with the defendant and without otherwise violating the latter's Fourth Amendment rights.... For constitutional purposes, no different result is required if the agent instead of immediately reporting and transcribing his conversations with defendant, either (1) simultaneously records them with electronic equipment which he is carrying on his person . . . (2) or carries radio equipment which simultaneously transmits the conversations either to recording equipment located elsewhere or to other agents monitoring the transmitting frequency. . . . If the conduct and revelations of an agent operating without electronic equipment do not invade the defendant's constitutionally justifiable expectations of privacy, neither does a simultaneous recording of the same conversations made by the agent or by others from transmissions received from the agent to whom the defendant is talking and whose trustworthiness the defendant necessarily risks.

Our problem is not what the privacy expectations of particular defendants in particular situations may be or the extent to which they may in fact have relied on the discretion of their companions. Very probably, individual defendants neither know nor suspect that their colleagues have gone or will go to the police or are carrying recorders or transmitters. Otherwise, conversation would cease and our problem with these encounters would be nonexistent or far different from those now before us. Our problem, in terms of the principles announced in Katz, is what expectations of privacy are constitutionally "justifiable"— what expectations the Fourth Amendment will protect in the absence of a warrant. So far, the law permits the frustration of actual expectations of privacy by permitting authorities to use the testimony of those "associates who for one reason or another have determined to turn to the police, as well as by authorizing the use of informants in the manner exemplified by Hoffa and Lewis. If the law gives no protection to the wrongdoer whose trusted accomplice is or becomes a police agent, neither should it protect him when that same agent has recorded or transmitted the conversations which are later offered in evidence to prove the State's case. . . .

Inescapably, one contemplating illegal activities must realize and risk that his companions may be reporting to the police. If he sufficiently doubts their trustworthiness, the association will very probably end or never materialize. But if he has no doubts, or allays them, or risks what doubt he has, the risk is his. In terms of what his course will be, what he will or will not do or say, we are unpersuaded that he would distinguish between probable informers on the one hand and probable informers with transmitters on the other. Given the possibility or probability that one of his colleagues is cooperating with the police, it is only speculation to assert that the defendant's utterances would be substantially different or his sense of security any less if he also thought it possible that the suspected colleague is wired for sound. At least there is no persuasive evidence that the difference in this respect between the electronically equipped and the unequipped agent is substantial enough to require discrete constitutional recognition, particularly under the Fourth Amendment which is ruled by fluid concepts of "reasonableness."

Nor should we be too ready to erect constitutional barriers to relevant and probative evidence which is also accurate and reliable. An electronic recording will many times produce a more reliable rendition of what a defendant has said than will the unaided memory of a police agent. It may also be that with the recording in existence it is less likely that the informant will change his mind, less chance that threat or injury will suppress unfavorable evidence and less chance that cross-examination will confound the testimony. Considerations like these obviously do not favor the defendant, but we are not prepared to hold that a defendant who has no constitutional right to exclude the informer's unaided testimony nevertheless has a Fourth Amendment privilege against a more accurate version of the events in question.

It is thus untenable to consider the activities and reports of the police agent himself, though acting without a warrant, to be a "reasonable" investigative effort and lawful under the Fourth Amendment but to view the same agent with a recorder or transmitter as conducting an "unreasonable" and unconstitutional search and seizure. . . .

No different result should obtain where, as in On Lee and the instant case, the informer disappears and is unavailable at trial; for the issue of whether specified events on a certain day violate the Fourth Amendment should not be determined by what later happens to the informer. His unavailability at trial and proffering the testimony of other agents may raise evidentiary problems or pose issues of prosecutorial misconduct with respect to the informer's disappearance, but they do not appear critical to deciding whether prior events invaded the defendant's Fourth Amendment rights.

* * *

The judgment of the Court of Appeals is reversed.

[Mr. Justice BRENNAN and Mr. Justice BLACK concurred in the result.]

[Mr. Justice HARLAN, Mr. Justice MARSHALL, and Mr. Justice DOUGLAS wrote separate dissenting opinions.]

Comments

1. *Berger* v. *New York* reflects the Court's view on electronic surveillance, particularly wiretapping, during a sort of "quiet before
the storm" period—i.e., prior to the passage of Title III of the Omnibus Crime Control and Safe Streets Act of 1968 and the reassessment of the relationship of electronic surveillance to Fourth
Amendment rights made in *Katz* v. *United States*. In its totality,
the *Berger* decision does establish constitutional criteria important
to wiretap practices:

    a. The decision left little doubt as to the constitutional neces-
sity of interposing a magistrate between the police and the target of
the tap. Hence, the language in *Osborn* v. *United States,* 385 U.S.
323 (1966), was reinforced.

    b. The Court carefully applied the Fourth Amendment's "par-
ticularity" requirement, noting that the New York statute was a
"broadside authorization" rather than being "carefully circumscribed" so as to guard against searches of a general nature.

    c. The Court found the New York statute constitutionally in-
firm because it avoided prompt execution of the warrant by allowing surveillance for an extended period, the "equivalent of a series
of intrusions pursuant to a single showing of probable cause."

    d. Another constitutional infirmity of the statute was its failure
to set limitations on the tap, i.e., a termination date for the tap once
the conversation sought was seized.

    e. Finally the Court required notice, as with conventional war-
rants, unless a showing of exigency was involved.

2. Six months after *Berger,* the Court laid to rest the "prior authorization" issue in *Katz* v. *United States* (supra, § 5.01). In addition,
the *Katz* majority per Mr. Justice Stewart, reaffirmed the necessity
for probable cause, notice, and surveillance limitations as outlined
in *Berger*. More importantly, *Katz* rejected the notion that electronic surveillance required both a "physical trespass" by the
searching officials and the seizure of "tangible property" (see *Olmstead* v. *United States,* 277 U.S. 438 [1928]) before a Fourth
Amendment violation claim could attach. The Court concluded
that any time the government violated the privacy upon which a
person justifiably relied, a "search and seizure" had taken place
within the meaning of the Fourth Amendment; i.e., the Fourth
Amendment protects "*people* and not *places.*"

    In June, 1968, Congress passed the Omnibus Crime Control and
Safe Streets Act, 18 U.S.C. §§ 2510–2520. The act, inter alia,
approves of wiretapping and electronic eavesdropping in certain
limited situations even without requiring notice or the consent of
the person or persons being tapped. The Court has not had occasion to rule on the legality of the act itself (however, the Court of
Appeals [3rd Cir.] held Title III to be constitutional in *United*

States v. *Cafero*, 473 F.2d 489 [1973]) but it would appear to generally meet the criteria suggested in *Katz*, i.e., that limited eavesdropping is permissible if conducted pursuant to judicial authorization:

"To safeguard the privacy of innocent persons, the interception of wire or oral communications where none of the parties to the communication has consented to the interception should be allowed only when authorized by a court of competent jurisdiction and should remain under the control and supervision of the authorizing court. Interception of wire and oral communications should further be limited to certain major types of offenses and specific categories of crime with assurances that the interception is justified and that the information obtained thereby will not be misused." [Section 801(d).]

Section 2516 of the act allows intercept orders to be authorized for the following crimes:

    a.   felonies relating to the Atomic Energy Act of 1954; espionage; sabotage; treason; or riots

    b.   the crimes of kidnapping, robbery, murder, and extortion and crimes dealing with restrictions on payments and loans to labor organizations

    c.   bribery of public officials and witnesses; transmission of wagering information; influencing or injuring a law enforcement or judicial officer, juror, or witness generally; presidential assassinations, kidnapping, and assault; interference with commerce by threats or violence; interstate and foreign travel or transportation in aid of racketeering enterprises; offer, acceptance, or solicitation to influence operations of an employee benefit plan; theft from interstate shipment; embezzlement from pension and welfare funds; and interstate transportation of stolen property

    d.   counterfeiting offenses

    e.   crimes involving narcotic drugs, marijuana, or other dangerous drugs

    f.   any offense involving bankruptcy fraud

    g.   extortionate credit transactions

    h.   conspiracy to commit any of the foregoing offenses

3.   The *On Lee* decision is indicative of the Court's pre-*Katz* approach to eavesdropping cases. Finding that there was no "physical trespass," nor any "tangible objects" seized, the Court applied the *Olmstead* rationale and affirmed the conviction. What is of interest, however, is that *Katz* and post-*Katz* cases have left *On Lee* essentially undisturbed. Compare, for example, *United States* v. *White*, supra, in which the four-man majority relied on *Hoffa* v. *United States*, 385 U.S. 293 (1966), in overruling the court of appeals. Conceding that *Hoffa* was unaffected by the *Katz* decision, the Court found that the instant case was similar to *Hoffa* in that White had had no "reasonable expectation of privacy" when he conversed with Jackson. The implication is that White "assumed the risk" of disclosure when he openly discussed illegal activities with the informant, i.e., his expectation of privacy was unprotected under the circumstances. Although *White* supports the proposition that *On Lee* is still good law, might the result have been different "but for" the ex parte consent of Jackson?

4. The Supreme Court's examination of wiretapping began with the 1928 case of *Olmstead* v. *United States,* 277 U.S. 438, in which the Court was called upon to decide if wiretapping was a violation of the Fourth Amendment prohibition against unreasonable searches and seizures. The petitioners were convicted in the District Court for the Western District of Washington of conspiring to violate the National Prohibition Act by unlawfully possessing, transporting, importing, and selling intoxicating liquors. Olmstead, the leading conspirator and the general manager of the business, maintained an office in a large Seattle office building. Federal officers inserted small wires along telephone lines from the residences of four of the defendants and the office. The taps were made in the basement of the office building and in the streets near the conspirators' houses. Evidence gathered from the taps was used to convict Olmstead and his co-conspirators. In a 5–4 decision, the majority, per Chief Justice Taft, concluded that the federal agents had not violated the Fourth Amendment, reasoning that (1) the officers did not commit a "physical trespass" upon the petitioners' property, homes, or office and thus no "place" had been searched, and (2) because evidence was secured by the use of the sense of hearing alone, only petitioners' conversations were obtained and thus no "things" had been seized. Therefore, the majority concluded, the wiretapping was not violative of the Fourth Amendment because the procedure involved no *searching* or *seizing* of tangible *places* or *things.*

Six years later, in 1934, Congress passed the Federal Communications Act, § 605 of which provided, in part, that "no person not being authorized by the sender shall intercept any communication and divulge or publish the existence, contents, substance, purport, effect, or meaning of such intercepted communication to any person. . . ." In a series of cases, § 605 was held by the Supreme Court to apply to interstate or intrastate communications obtained by state or federal officers. See *Nardone* v. *United States,* 302 U.S. 379 (1937), 308 U.S. 338 (1939); *Weiss* v. *United States,* 308 U.S. 321 (1939); *Goldstein* v. *United States,* 316 U.S. 114 (1942); and *Benanti* v. *United States,* 355 U.S. 96 (1957). In addition, the Court concluded in *Goldstein* that any party to such an intercepted conversation could suppress in a federal prosecution evidence obtained by state or federal law enforcement officers via the wiretap *unless* the interception was done with the consent of one of the parties to the conversation. The holding in *Goldstein* was reinforced by *Rathbun* v. *United States,* 355 U.S. 107 (1957). Although the Supreme Court did hold in *Schwartz* v. *Texas,* 344 U.S. 199 (1952), that evidence secured by a wiretap placed by state officers was admissible in state prosecutions, the practice was eventually prohibited in *Lee* v. *Florida,* 392 U.S. 378 (1968), as being violative of the exclusionary principles announced in *Mapp* v. *Ohio,* 367 U.S. 643 (1961). Hence, state governments were required to follow the same standards as the federal government.

Lee v. *Florida* was the last case decided pursuant to the Federal Communications Act. In June, 1968, the Omnibus Crime Control and Safe Streets Act was passed, which superseded § 605 of the 1934 legislation. It is noteworthy that one portion of the 1968 act actually allows a grand jury witness to properly refuse to testify when his testimony is sought on the basis of an illegal wiretap or other illegal surveillance. Section 2515 provides that if the evidence or testimony sought is evidence derived from a violation of Chapter 119 of Title III of the act, then its use is prohibited. In *Gelbard* v. *United States,* 408 U.S. 41 (1972), petitioners refused under § 2515 to answer questions before a federal grand jury until they had the opportunity to challenge the legality of the intercepted conversations upon which the government was basing their court order compelling testimony from them. A 5–4 majority of the Supreme Court, per Mr. Justice Brennan, held that the witness could refuse to answer if the testimony was sought on the basis of a violation of Title III of the act.

5. When an electronic device is used to intercept communications transmitted by means other than telephone or telegraph, the practice is commonly referred to as "electronic surveillance." Included under this broad term are a variety of techniques for hearing and/or recording conversations, such as "bugging" (using a planted or carried listening and/or recording device); "eavesdropping" (monitoring, transmitting, or recording conversations without the knowledge of the persons conversing); and using a device known as a "pen register" (a device that records the number dialed on a particular telephone, but not the conversation itself). The first "bugging" case to come before the Supreme Court was *Goldman* v. *United States,* 316 U.S. 129 (1942). There, federal officers had placed a detectaphone against the outer wall of petitioner's private office and listened to incriminating conversations within. The petitioner argued that the practice violated his Fourth Amendment right against unreasonable searches and seizures, but the Supreme Court, applying a rationale identical to that used in *Olmstead* v. *United States,* held that because there had been no "physical trespass" such practices did not run afoul of the Fourth Amendment. Ten years later in *On Lee* v. *United States,* supra, a 5–4 majority essentially reinforced the idea that a "physical trespass" was necessary before the Fourth Amendment's protections came into play. Likewise, support for the general premise that there must be an actual physical trespass to have a Fourth Amendment violation can be found (by implication) in the 1961 case of *Silverman* v. *United States,* 365 U.S. 505. In that case, a unanimous Court held that intercepting incriminating conversations within a house by inserting a so-called "spike mike" into a wall (it is actually driven into a wall) and making contact with a heating duct constituted an illegal search and seizure. However, it is interesting to note that the "intrusion" by the spike was never really discussed by the Court. Taken together, *Goldman, On Lee, Silverman,* and of course the earlier case of *Olmstead,* made it clear that the Court intended to base its holdings in wiretap and electronic surveillance cases on whether an "actual physical trespass" occurred. But as noted earlier, *Katz* v. *United States,* (supra, § 5.01) tolled the death knell of the "physical trespass and tangible property" doctrine, replacing it with the proposition that "the Fourth Amendment protects people, not places." The *Katz* holding was made applicable to the states in 1969 in *Kaiser* v. *New York,* 394 U.S. 280.

A different pre-*Katz* approach to eavesdropping was taken in *Lopez* v. *United States,* 373 U.S. 427 (1963). There, an IRS agent equipped with a pocket wire recorder entered petitioner's office with petitioner's consent and secretly recorded his conversation with Lopez, which later formed the basis of an indictment against Lopez for attempted bribery of the IRS agent. Lopez sought to exclude the evidence on the ground that the agent entered his office for the sole purpose of recording the conversation and not to consider a bribe, as petitioner had thought. Hence, Lopez argued, the agent had gained access to the office by "misrepresentation," and therefore the evidence obtained had been "seized" illegally. In a 6–3 decision, the Court rejected Lopez's contention, finding that no "invasion" of his premises had occurred. The Court concluded that "the risk the petitioner took ... included the risk that the offer would be accurately reproduced in court, whether by faultless memory or mechanical recording."

Another interesting pre-*Katz* case involving eavesdropping was decided by the Supreme Court in 1962. In *Lanza* v. *New York,* 370 U.S. 139 (1962), the Court rejected the petitioner's contention that the visitors' room of a public jail was a constitutionally protected area and that surreptitious electronic eavesdropping in it amounted to an illegal search and seizure. A 4–3 majority found petitioner's argument to be a "novel" one because in prison official surveillance "has traditionally been the order of the day." The Court stated that such an argument might have merit only if petitioner could claim a "special relationship" or "particularized confidentiality" inherent in the conversation.

In 1966 the Supreme Court heard a trilogy of cases involving the issue of "access by misrepresentation," which it had considered earlier in *Lopez.* In *Lewis* v. *United States,* 385 U.S. 206 (1966), the petitioner presented the question of whether a federal agent who, after misrepresenting his identity, entered petitioner's home and purchased narcotics from him thereby made an illegal search and seizure within the meaning of the Fourth Amendment. The Court concluded that he had not, finding that since the petitioner was engaged in the unlawful selling of narcotics, the agent, upon entering the house, did not "see, hear, or take anything that was not contemplated and in fact intended by petitioner as a necessary part of his illegal business." *Osborn* v. *United States,* 385 U.S. 323, decided the same day as *Lewis,* involved the use of a tape recorder secreted on an informer's person pursuant to a court order authorizing its concealment. The petitioner, an attorney for Teamster president Jimmy Hoffa, hired one Vick to make background investigations of prospective jurors for Hoffa's federal criminal trial. Without petitioner's knowledge, Vick had agreed to report to federal agents any "illegal activities" he observed. During the course of a conversation with petitioner, Vick mentioned that one of the prospective jurors was his (Vick's) cousin. Petitioner then told Vick to meet with his cousin and see what "arrangements" could be made about the case. Vick reported this to federal agents who had him repeat the information in a sworn statement. The statement was then used to gain authorization to conceal the recorder on Vick's person. During a second visit to petitioner's office, Vick pretended to have talked to his cousin and reported that his cousin might be interested in taking money in exchange for "hanging up" the jury. Osborn then authorized Vick to offer his cousin $10,000 if he became a member of the jury and would agree to "hang" it. The tape recording of the second conversation and Vick's testimony was later used to convict Osborn of attempting to bribe a member of a jury. In a 7–1 decision, the Court held that the use and introduction of the recording itself was proper, finding that the use of the device had not been "indiscriminate" but had been properly authorized under circumstances which fully met the standards of "particularity" and "antecedent justification" required by the Fourth Amendment. Finally, in *Hoffa* v. *United States,* 385 U.S. 293 (1966), the petitioner presented the issue of whether evidence obtained by the placement of a secret informer in the quarters of petitioner and his counsel so violated his Fourth Amendment rights that suppression of the evidence was required in a subsequent trial of petitioner on a different charge. Although the Court found no "hard" evidence that the informant was "placed" in the room by the government, it did "assume" that he was, in fact, working for the government. The government did pay the informant's wife $1200 and also dropped charges that were pending against him. The facts revealed that Edward Partin, the informer, was present, with petitioner's consent, when several incriminating statements were allegedly made by the petitioner. Partin reported the text of the conversation to federal officers, and later testified at petitioner's trial on charges of attempting to bribe members of the jury at the first trial, the so-called "Test Fleet" case, in which Hoffa was charged with violation of the Taft-Hartley Act. (It is noteworthy that the Test Fleet trial ended with a hung jury.) Convicted of jury tampering, Hoffa sought certiorari, arguing that the Government's "planting" of the informer and the subsequent use of his testimony violated his Fourth Amendment rights. Hoffa reasoned that because Partin failed to reveal his true role and subsequently listened in on conversations and reported them to government agents, he was guilty of conducting an "illegal search for verbal evidence." The majority rejected Hoffa's contentions, holding that "the Fourth Amendment protects the *security* a man relies upon when he places himself or his property within a *constitutionally protected area*" (emphasis added). However, the Court could not find that the petitioner had any interest "legitimately protected by the Fourth Amendment." Partin had been present in petitioner's room by invitation, and Hoffa had not been relying on the security of his room when he made the incriminating statements in Partin's presence, but rather was relying "upon his misplaced confidence that Partin would not reveal his wrongdoing."

6. During the 1970's, the Supreme Court has been called upon to interpret various sections of Title III of the Omnibus Crime Control and Safe Streets Act (the Criminal Justice Act, as amended, October 14, 1970). For example, in *United States* v. *United States District Court,* 407 U.S. 297 (1972), the government sought to rely on § 2511(3) to justify a wiretap made without prior judicial authorization. Because the case involved a conspiracy to destroy federal property, the government contended that the wiretap was necessary to protect "domestic security," and that § 2511(3) authorized such procedures as an exception to the court order requirements of Title III when "domestic security" was at issue. Section 2511(3) provides, inter alia, that "nothing contained in [Title III or § 605 of the Federal Communications Act of 1934] shall limit the constitutional power of the President to take such measures as he deems necessary to protect . . . the United States against the overthrow of the government by force or other unlawful means or against any

other clear and present danger to the structure or existence of the government." A unanimous Court, per Mr. Justice Powell, held that neither the powers of the President to defend the government nor § 2511(3) can be used to "justify departure" from the "prior judicial approval" requirement of the Fourth Amendment. The Court concluded that § 2511(3) merely provides that the act shall not be construed as a limit to or disturbance of presidential power under the Constitution, and the act "simply did not legislate with respect to national security surveillances." Although the Court recognized that distinctions can be made between Title III criminal surveillances and those involving domestic security, the latter situation cannot be relied on by the government to justify a departure from the "customary Fourth Amendment requirement of judicial approval prior to initiation of a search or surveillance." Likewise, in *United States* v. *Giordano,* 416 U.S. 505 (1974), the Court was asked to construe the meaning of § 2516(1), which provides that application for a court order to intercept wire or oral communications may be authorized by the Attorney General "specially designated by the Attorney General." The Supreme Court found that § 2516(1) "conditioned the use of intercept procedures upon the judgment of a senior official in the Department of Justice," and thus held that evidence derived from a wiretap application signed by the attorney general's executive assistant was inadmissible because it had been "unlawfully intercepted" within the meaning of § 2518(10)(a)(i). However, in *United States* v. *Chavez,* 416 U.S. 562 (1974), the Court refused to invalidate a court order and suppress evidence in a wiretap case simply because the assistant attorney general had been mistakenly identified as the authorizing official. In *Chavez,* the attorney general had, in fact, authorized the application for the court order; however, the application and court order identified Assistant Attorney General Wilson as the authorizing official. Distinguishing the case from *Giordano,* supra, the Court, per Mr. Justice White, observed that the case did not involve an application authorized by one without the responsibility to do so. Although the Court recognized and supported the identification reporting requirements of § 2518(1)(a) (requiring that each application state the identity of the authorizing officer), it concluded that the government had performed its task of prior approval, and the application provided sufficient information to enable the issuing judge to determine that the statutory preconditions were satisfied.

In *United States* v. *Kahn,* 415 U.S. 143 (1974), a federal judge approved a wiretap application and issued a court order allowing FBI agents to intercept wire communications of one Irving Kahn and "others as yet unknown" from two designated telephones. Evidence gathered by the tap was used to indict Kahn's wife for federal gambling offenses. The petitioner moved to suppress the evidence on the ground that the conversations between her and her husband and between her and a third party were not within the scope of the court order. She relied on the language of § 2518 which provides, inter alia, that each court order shall identify the person, if known, committing the offense and whose communications are to be intercepted [see § 2518(1)(b)(iv) and § 2518(4)(a)], arguing that she was a person "known" within the meaning of the section as one who probably used the Kahn telephone for illegal activities and thus was excluded from the category of "others as yet unknown" within the meaning of § 2518. The Court of Appeals (7th Cir.) affirmed her motion to suppress; the Supreme Court reversed in a 6–3 decision. Mr. Justice Stewart, writing for the majority, observed that the statute requires identification only of those "known" to be committing the offense. The majority went on to note that the government is not required to "fully investigate the possibility that any likely user of a telephone was engaging in criminal activities" before making application for a wiretap order. The government agents had no reason to suspect Mrs. Kahn of complicity in the illegal activity prior to the application, and therefore, she was considered a person "yet unknown" for purposes of the court order.

The identification requirement of § 2518 was again one of the focal points in the more recent case of *United States* v. *Donovan,* 97 S. Ct. 658 (1977). There, a federal judge in Ohio issued a wiretap order authorizing FBI agents to intercept gambling-related conversations at four separate telephones in the cities of North Olmstead and Canton, Ohio. The application specifically named Kotoch, Spaganlo, and Florea (three persons other than the respondents) and "others yet unknown." During the initial tap, FBI agents overheard respondents Donovan, Robbins, and Buzzaco discussing illegal gambling activities with Kotoch, Spaganlo, and Florea. Fifteen days after the initial tap was begun, the government applied for an extension of the order, but did not name respondents in the application even though there was probable cause to believe their conversations would again be intercepted. Likewise, the government neglected to include the names of two other respondents, Merlo and Lauer, in its post-use inventory notice list. When all five respondents were indicted, they moved to suppress evidence derived from the extended tap based on the identification and notice requirements of § 2518. The district court granted their motions and the Court of Appeals (6th Cir.) affirmed. The Supreme Court, per Mr. Justice Powell, agreed that a wiretap application must name an individual if the government has probable cause to believe that the individual is engaged in illegal activity and expects to intercept that person's conversations over the target telephone, and it rejected the government's contention that only the "principal target" of the tap must be identified. However, the majority refused to accept the respondents' contention that the communications were "unlawfully intercepted" within the meaning of § 2518(10)(a)(i) given the government's violations of the notice and identification requirements of § 2518(1)(b)(iv) and § 2518(8)(d). Citing *Giordano* and *Chavez,* supra, the majority held that suppression is required only for a "failure to satisfy any of those statutory requirements that *directly* and *substantially* implement ... congressional intent to limit the use of intercept procedures to those situations clearly calling for the employment of this extraordinary device. United States v. Giordano, 416 U.S. at 527 (emphasis added)." Once the judge determines, in light of information contained in the application, that an order should issue, "failure to identify additional persons likely to be overheard ... could hardly invalidate an otherwise lawful judicial authorization." The Court went on to note that the legislative history of the statute is void of any suggestion that Congress intended the identification requirement to play "a central, or even functional, role in guarding against unwarranted use of wiretapping or electronic surveillance." The

Court also reached the same conclusion with respect to the government's obligation to provide the judge with a list of names, for purposes of post-use notice, of persons whose conversations had been overheard, finding that suppression was not justified "with respect to respondents Merlo and Lauer simply because the government inadvertently omitted their names" from the original inventory notice list provided to the federal judge upon termination of the tap. Nothing in the ... Act or ... [its] legislative history suggests that incriminating conversations are 'unlawfully intercepted' whenever parties to those conversations do not receive discretionary inventory notice as a result of the government's failure to inform the District Court of their identities."

7. The issue of standing to challenge the legality of a search (see Chapter Five, § 5.06), often arises in cases involving illegal electronic surveillance. The leading case in this area is *Alderman* v. *United States*, 394 U.S. 165 (1969). Following their convictions for various federal offenses, Alderman and three other petitioners discovered that the government had engaged in electronic surveillance which, if found to be illegal (and hence inadmissible), might have caused a different result at trial. On certiorari, each of the four petitioners asked for retrial if any of the evidence used to convict him was found to be the product of an unauthorized electronic surveillance, irrespective of *whose* Fourth Amendment rights had been violated by the surveillance. Hence, petitioners were arguing that each of them possessed an "independent" constitutional right to have evidence excluded because it was seized from another unlawfully. The Court, per Mr. Justice White, rejected such a "third party" standing claim, noting that "there is no necessity to exclude evidence against one defendant in order to protect the rights of another. No rights of the victim of an illegal search are at stake when the evidence is offered against some other party." The majority was careful to restate the basic premise that "Fourth Amendment rights are personal rights which ... may not be vicariously asserted." Recognizing, however, that any petitioner would be entitled to the suppression of evidence derived from unauthorized surveillance violative of his *own* Fourth Amendment rights, the Court vacated the judgments against each petitioner and remanded the cases to the district court for hearings to determine (1) if any petitioner's own Fourth Amendment rights had been violated via illegal surveillance and (2) if the evidence derived from the illegal surveillance had tainted his conviction. The Court outlined a procedure to be followed that called for the disclosure, to each petitioner with standing to object, of specified surveillance records without a prior judicial screening. However, this disclosure was limited to the individual petitioner's conversations or those that took place on his own premises.

8. Some recent lower federal and state court decisions involving electronic surveillance include *United States* v. *Holmes,* 537 F.2d 227 (5th Cir. 1975) (en banc) (government agents may not plant a beeper on a primary suspect's van without both probable cause and a warrant) (cf. *United States* v. *Bobisink,* 415 F. Supp. 1334 [D. Mass. 1976] [drug agents' warrantless use of beepers attached to drug suspects' vehicles and package of chemicals which enabled agents to trail suspects held violative of warrant requirement of Fourth Amendment]) (but see *United States* v. *Frazier,* 538 F.2d

1322 [8th Cir. 1976] [federal agents' placement of a beeper on extortion suspect's vehicle without warrant but with probable cause held justified by exigent circumstances], and *United States* v. *Perez*, 526 F.2d 859 [5th Cir. 1976] [warrantless placing of tracking "bug" inside television set given to suspect in exchange for heroin held not violative of Fourth Amendment]); *United States* v. *Pretzinger*, 542 F.2d 517 (9th Cir. 1976) (action of agents who obtained warrant before attaching electronic beeper to airplane held not unreasonable); *United States* v. *Cotroni*, 527 F.2d 708 (2nd Cir. 1975) (wiretap evidence obtained against international drug traffickers by Canadian officials under conditions legal at that time in Canada but not in accordance with U.S. law held admissible in federal courts); *State* v. *Rowman*, 352 A.2d 737 (N.H. 1976) (New Hampshire wiretap statute which does not require postsurveillance notice to subject of tap, although required under federal law, held not unconstitutional—*Berger* v. *New York* not controlling); *People* v. *Sher*, 381 N.E.2d 843 (N.Y. Ct. App. 1976) (prosecution's failure to adequately explain absence of seals on tapes of gambling defendant's intercepted telephone conversations renders the tapes inadmissible) (accord, *United States* v. *Gigante*, 538 F.2d 502 [3rd Cir. 1976] [government's unexplained failure to comply promptly with federal statute requiring judicially supervised sealing of tapes obtained through electronic surveillance requires suppression of the tape-recorded evidence]); *United States* v. *Abraham*, 541 F.2d 624 (6th Cir. 1976) (judge supervising electronic surveillance operation must be present at sealing of the intercept records); *United States* v. *Illinois Bell Telephone Company*, 531 F.2d 809 (7th Cir. 1976) (district court, following authorization of government to use pen register on a tax suspect's phone line, has authority to order the telephone company to cooperate in its installation) (but cf. *In re Application of United States*,___ F.2d ___ [2nd Cir. 1976] [district court may not order phone company to help install pen register for wiretapping purposes following issuance of warrant authorizing installation of such device]); *People* v. *DiStefano*, 345 N.E.2d 548 (N.Y. Ct. App. 1976) (police officers conducting organized crime wiretap on cocktail lounge held justified in recording several unexpected telephone conversations about an unrelated robbery plot, and conversations were properly admitted); *United States* v. *Principie*, 531 F.2d 1132 (2nd Cir. 1976) (police violation of limited wiretap order that tap stop daily at 7:30 P.M. does not require suppression of all the evidence obtained from the tap); *State* v. *Hruska*, 547 S.W.2d 732 (Kan. 1976) (telephone company has authority to monitor the calls of one of its subscribers without court order if it has reason to believe that the customer is using an electronic device to defraud the company out of its charges for long-distance toll calls) (to the same effect is *United States* v. *Clegg*, 509 F.2d 605 [5th Cir. 1975] and *United States* v. *Goldstein*, 532 F.2d 1305 [9th Cir. 1976]) (see also *United States* v. *Glanzer*, 521 F.2d 11 [9th Cir. 1975] [surveillance by telephone company to detect customer using "by-pass" device to avoid paying bills does not violate Fourth Amendment, and wiretap evidence may be admitted in evidence]); *United States* v. *Agrusa*, 541 F.2d 690 (8th Cir. 1976) (federal agents' surreptitious and forcible entry of defendant's unoccupied business premises to plant an electronic bug pursuant to a court order held not unreasonable); *United States* v. *Johnson*, 539 F.2d 181 (D.C. Cir. 1976) (federal law doesn't require police officers to ask for judicial permission before using the fruits of a federally authorized wiretap); *United States* v. *Hall*, ___ F.2d ___ (1st Cir. 1976) (en banc) (introduction of state-gathered wiretap evidence is admissible at federal trial even though not admissible in that state's courts); *United States* v. *Jones*, 542 F.2d 661 (6th Cir. 1976) (Title III of Omnibus Crime Control Act prohibiting unauthorized wiretaps held applicable to husband's wiretapping of his estranged wife's phone conversation to confirm his suspicions about her "infidelity") (see also *United States* v. *Giordano*, 416 U.S. 505 [1974], and *Simpson* v. *Simpson*, 490 F.2d 803 [5th Cir. 1974]) (cf. *United States* v. *Phillips*, 540 F.2d 319 [8th Cir. 1976] [defendant who seeks suppression of electronic surveillance recorded by private party has the burden of showing his conversations were intercepted for a wrongful purpose under a federal statute which makes it unlawful for a private party to intercept conversations to which he is a party for criminal, tortious, or other injurious purposes]).

6

FIFTH AMENDMENT PROBLEMS: DOUBLE JEOPARDY, SELF-INCRIMINATION, AND THE GRAND JURY

6.01 INTRODUCTION

The Fifth Amendment to the United States Constitution has been the focal point for hundreds of Supreme Court decisions, in part because of its rather vague contours. Like other clauses in the Bill of Rights, the guarantees found in the Fifth Amendment are not self-defining and require judicial interpretation. Consequently, the justices of the Supreme Court are not always in agreement as to the parameters of this important Amendment.

The Fifth Amendment provides, in part:

No person shall be held to answer for a capital, or otherwise infamous crime, unless on a presentment or indictment of a Grand Jury ... ; nor shall any person be subject for the same offence to be twice put in jeopardy of life or limb; nor shall be compelled in any criminal case to be a witness against himself....

These three clauses—the guarantee against double jeopardy, the privilege against self-incrimination, and the requirement, in federal courts, of grand jury indictments—are important to the criminal process. Decisions by the Supreme Court involving the Fifth Amendment and the criminal process have centered on such diverse issues as confessions, immunity, entrapment, collateral estoppel, police interrogations, the grand jury, pretrial identification procedures, and the retrial of convicted and acquitted defendants.

6.02 THE GUARANTEE AGAINST DOUBLE JEOPARDY

A. PRIOR CONVICTIONS

Waiving the Guarantee

UNITED STATES v. TATEO

Supreme Court of the United States, 1964
377 U.S. 463, 84 S. Ct. 1587, 12 L. Ed. 2d 448

Tateo was brought to trial in federal district court on a five-count indictment that included charges of bank robbery and kidnapping. On the fourth day of the trial, the judge informed Tateo's counsel that if the jury convicted Tateo, he intended to impose a life sentence for the kidnapping charge and consecutive sentences for

the other charges. Informed of the judge's position, Tateo pleaded guilty and the jury was dismissed. The kidnapping charge was dismissed with the consent of the prosecutor, and Tateo was sentenced to 22 years and 6 months' imprisonment on the other counts. In a later habeas corpus proceeding, another federal judge set aside Tateo's conviction on the grounds that his guilty plea was not voluntary. Tateo was then reindicted on the dismissed kidnapping charge and the four bank robbery charges to which he had pleaded guilty. The federal district court dismissed the kidnapping charge and the four robbery counts on the grounds that the Double Jeopardy Clause precluded the government from retrying Tateo. The United States government appealed to the Supreme Court pursuant to a federal statute that permits direct appeal from a decision of a district court that sustains a motion before a defendant has been put in jeopardy, 18 U.S.C. § 3731.

Mr. Justice HARLAN delivered the opinion of the Court.

* * *

The Fifth Amendment provides that no "person [shall] be subject for the same offense to be twice put in jeopardy of life or limb. . . ."

The principle that this provision does not preclude the Government's retrying a defendant whose conviction is set aside because of an error in the proceedings leading to conviction is a well-established part of our constitutional jurisprudence. In this respect we differ from the practice obtaining in England. The rule in this country was explicitly stated in United States v. Ball, 163 U.S. 662 (1896), a case in which defendants were re-indicted after this Court had found the original indictment to be defective. It has been followed in a variety of circumstances; . . . [for example] (after conviction reversed because of confession of error); . . . (after conviction reversed because of insufficient evidence); . . . (after original conviction reversed for error in instructions to the jury).

* * *

While different theories have been advanced to support the permissibility of retrial, of greater importance than the conceptual abstractions employed to explain the Ball principle are the implications of that principle for the sound administration of justice. Corresponding to the right of an accused to be given a fair trial is the societal interest in punishing one whose guilt is clear after he has obtained such a trial. It would be a high price indeed for society to pay were every accused granted immunity from punishment because of any defect sufficient to constitute reversible error in the proceedings leading to conviction. From the standpoint of a defendant, it is at least doubtful that appellate courts would be as zealous as they now are in protecting against the effects of improprieties at the trial or pretrial stage if they knew that reversal of a conviction would put the accused irrevocably beyond the reach of further prosecution. In reality, therefore, the practice of retrial serves defendants' rights as well as society's interest. The underlying purpose of permitting retrial is as much furthered by application of the rule to this case as it has been in cases previously decided.

Tateo contends that his situation must be distinguished from one in which an accused has been found guilty by a jury, since his involuntary plea of guilty deprived him of the opportunity to obtain a jury verdict of acquittal. We find this argument unconvincing. If a case is reversed because of a coerced confession improperly admitted, a deficiency in the indictment, or an improper instruction, it is presumed that the accused did not have his case fairly put to the jury. A defendant is no less wronged by a jury finding of guilt after an unfair trial than by a failure to get a jury verdict at all; the distinction between the two kinds of wrongs affords no sensible basis for differentiation with regard to retrial. . . .

* * *

. . . If Tateo had *requested* a mistrial on the basis of the judge's comments, there would be no doubt that if he had been successful, the Government would not have been barred from retrying him. . . . Although there may be good reasons why Tateo and his counsel chose not to make such a motion before the trial judge, it would be strange were Tateo to benefit because of his delay in challenging the judge's conduct.

We conclude that this case falls squarely within the reasoning of Ball and subsequent cases allowing the Government to retry persons whose convictions have been overturned.

Reversed and remanded.

[Mr. Justice GOLDBERG, Mr. Justice BLACK, and Mr. Justice DOUGLAS dissented.]

Successive Municipal and State Prosecutions

WALLER v. FLORIDA

Supreme Court of the United States, 1970
397 U.S. 387, 90 S. Ct. 1184, 25 L. Ed. 2d 435

Waller and a number of others removed a canvas mural from inside the St. Petersburg, Florida, city hall. As they carried it through the streets of St. Petersburg, they were confronted by police officers. The mural was found to be damaged. Waller was tried and convicted of violating two City of St. Petersburg ordinances: destruction of city property and disorderly conduct. The municipal court sentenced him to 180 days in jail. Thereafter the State of Florida charged him with grand larceny—a state felony. The State of Florida conceded that the grand larceny charges were based on the same acts that constituted the violations of the two city ordinances. A Florida state court denied Waller's claim that his conviction on the earlier charges precluded, on double jeopardy grounds, his trial on the felony charge, and he was convicted of the felony of grand larceny and sentenced to 6 months to 5 years' imprisonment. The Florida appellate courts denied him postconviction relief, and the United States Supreme Court granted certiorari.

Mr. Chief Justice BURGER delivered the opinion of the Court.

* * *

...What is before us is the asserted power of the two courts within one State to place petitioner on trial for the same alleged crime.

In Benton v. Maryland, 395 U.S. 784 (1969), this Court declared the double jeopardy provisions of the Fifth Amendment applicable to the States....

Florida does not stand alone in treating municipalities and the State as separate sovereign entities, each capable of imposing punishment for the same alleged crime.

Here respondent State of Florida seeks to justify this separate sovereignty theory by asserting that the relationship between a municipality and the State is analogous to the relationship between a State and the Federal Government....

In another context, but relevant here, this Court noted:

"Political subdivisions of States—counties, cities, or whatever—never were and never have been considered as sovereign entities. Rather, they have been traditionally regarded as subordinate governmental instrumentalities created by the State to assist in the carrying out of state governmental functions." ...

Florida has recognized this unity in its Constitution:

"[T]he judicial power of the *State of Florida* is vested in a supreme court ... and such other courts, *including municipal courts* ... as the legislature may from time to time ordain and establish." (Art. V, § 1, Florida Constitution) (1885).

These provisions of the Florida Constitution demonstrate that the judicial power to try petitioner on the first charges in municipal court springs from the same organic law that created the state court of general jurisdiction in which petitioner was tried and convicted for a felony. Accordingly, the apt analogy to the relationship between municipal and state governments is to be found in the relationship between the government of a Territory and the Government of the United States. The legal consequence of that relationship was settled in Grafton v. United States, 206 U.S. 333 (1907), where this Court held that a prosecution in a court of the United States is a bar to a subsequent prosecution in a territorial court, since both are arms of the same sovereign. In Grafton a soldier in the United States Army had been acquitted by a general court-martial convened in the Philippine Islands of the alleged crime of feloniously killing two men. Subsequently, a criminal information in the name of the United States was filed in a Philippine court while those islands were a federal territory, charging the soldier with the same offense committed in violation of local law. When Philippine courts upheld a conviction against a double jeopardy challenge, this Court reversed (holding that): . . .

"An offense against the United States can only be punished under its authority and in the tribunals created by its laws; whereas, an offense against a State can be punished only by its authority and in its tribunals. The same act . . . may constitute two offenses, one against the United States and the other against a State. But these things cannot be predicated on the relations between the United States and the Philippines. The Government of a State does not derive its powers from the United States, while the Government of the Philippines owes its existence wholly to the United States, and its judicial tribunals exert all their powers by authority of the United States. The jurisdiction and authority of the United States over that territory and its inhabitants, for all legitimate purposes of government, is paramount. So that the cases holding that the same acts committed in a State of the Union may constitute an offense against the United States and also a distinct offense against the State, do not apply here where the two tribunals that tried the accused exert all their powers under and by authority of the same government—that of the United States." . . .

* * *

We hold that on the basis of the facts upon which the Florida District Court of Appeal relied petitioner could not lawfully be tried both by the municipal government and by the State of Florida. In this context a "dual sovereignty" theory is an anachronism, and the second trial constituted double jeopardy violative of the Fifth and Fourteenth Amendments to the United States Constitution.

We decide only that the Florida courts were in error to the extent of holding that—"even if a person has been tried in a municipal court for the identical offense with which he is charged in a state court, this would not be a bar to the prosecution of such person in the proper state court."

The second trial of petitioner which resulted in a judgment of conviction in the state court for a felony having no valid basis, that judgment is vacated and the cause remanded. . . .

[Mr. Justice BRENNAN and Mr. Justice BLACK wrote concurring opinions.]

Lesser Included Offenses

ORAL ARGUMENTS BEFORE U.S. SUPREME COURT*

Brown v. Ohio, No. 75-6933; argued 3/21/77

On the same day the Court heard argument in *Jeffers* v. *U.S.,* 20 Cr.L. 4203, a double jeopardy case, it was asked by an Ohio defendant to hold that double jeopardy principles barred his conviction for auto theft after his earlier guilty plea to a joyriding charge. Both offenses arose out of the same incident.

Robert Plautz, of Cleveland, maintained that the State of Ohio violated double jeopardy principles by first convicting petitioner Brown of operating a motor vehicle without the owner's consent, a misde-

*From 21 Crim. L. Rptr. 4005–4006. Reprinted by permission of The Bureau of National Affairs, Inc.

meanor, and later trying him for auto theft, a felony.

On December 8, 1973, Lake County police arrested Brown for the misdemeanor, which amounts to a joyriding offense, Plautz said. Brown waived his right to counsel and then pleaded guilty to the charge. This led to a 30-day jail term and a $100 fine. On December 11, the City of East Cleveland (Cuyahoga County), where the vehicle was taken, charged him with the auto theft offense.

The Chief Justice: "Did the joyriding offense require proof of intent to steal?"

Counsel answered in the negative. He went on to explain that a Cuyahoga County grand jury indicted Brown for auto theft, and the lesser included offense of joyriding, which was later nolled. Brown entered a conditional plea of guilty, reserving his right to challenge the charges on double jeopardy grounds. But the trial court overruled a later motion to dismiss on double jeopardy grounds and sentenced Brown to a suspended six-month jail term. His conviction was affirmed by the Ohio Court of Appeals and the state supreme court denied certiorari.

Mr. Justice Rehnquist: "Would it be constitutional if Ohio enacted a statute prohibiting driving of a car without the owner's permission and put in that each day was a separate offense?"

It might be constitutionally permissible, Plautz answered, if treated as a regulatory statute. But Ohio statutes do not create such an offense, he added.

Mr. Justice Marshall: "What would you do if the state arrested a man who explained that he was joyriding, and then the state later discovered that he was part of a car theft ring?"

Plautz thought that case was factually distinguishable from this one, and might affect the car ring defendant's double jeopardy argument.

Brown had no notice of the second charge at the time of his uncounselled plea, Plautz stated. Moreover, the second charge allegedly occurred prior to the first.

The Chief Justice: "Did the petitioner challenge the indictment before trial?"

"Yes, sir." At the pretrial hearing, Brown entered a conditional plea on the theft charge, and later filed a motion to dismiss on double jeopardy grounds. The main issue at trial was whether the joyriding was a lesser

included offense of auto theft and thus barred the prosecution on the greater offense.

The Ohio Court of Appeals affirmed the conviction, holding that because two different dates were alleged, the two convictions were premised on different acts, Plautz explained. However, the court of appeals did conclude that joyriding was a lesser included offense of auto theft.

Mr. Justice White: "It's just as though two entirely different cars were concerned."

"Yes, sir."

The petitioner is not asking this Court to interpret the Ohio statutes, Plautz stressed. We are asking the Court to look at the proscribed conduct and determine whether double jeopardy principles were violated. Once convicted on the joyriding offense, double jeopardy barred the theft conviction, he stressed.

The Chief Justice: "The criminal law doesn't just punish you for conduct. Sometimes it punishes for conduct covered by a certain kind of intent."

Yes, Plautz replied, that's correct.

This Court need not create any new constitutional doctrine to overturn the defendant's second conviction, Plautz argued. The Court has the same evidence test at its disposal. That rule would bar the subsequent theft prosecution.

In *Jeffers* v. *U.S.*, [*] there was a question about double punishment, Plautz noted. While there apparently was no double punishment in *Jeffers,* there is here. Brown was convicted and sentenced on both charges.

Mr. Justice White: "I think you are making the same argument as in *Jeffers* — that double jeopardy principles preclude trial on the greater offense after trial of the lesser."

Plautz agreed.

Mr. Justice Rehnquist: "If the Ohio Court of Appeals' decision is upheld, not only can Brown be prosecuted twice, but also punished twice."

"Yes, sir."

Mr. Justice Stewart: "What happens if a man stole a car in Ohio, and was picked up in California? Could Ohio try him for stealing the car?"

---

*In Jeffers v. United States, 432 U.S. ___ (1977), decided the same day as *Brown,* the Supreme Court held that there is no double jeopardy violation if a defendant elects to have two separate trials for a greater and a lesser included offense.

Counsel thought so.

Mr. Justice Blackmun: "You said he received six months on the second go-round? You didn't mention it was suspended?"

"I think that I did." The second prosecution took place in another county, Cuyahoga, he added.

Mr. Justice Blackmun: "Did you think the sentence was less severe because of the earlier sentence?"

"No, sir."

Mr. Chief Justice: "Was there an agreement that the second sentence would be suspended?"

No there was not, Plautz replied.

In response to a question from Mr. Justice Blackmun, Plautz explained that Lake County is contiguous to Cuyahoga County.

Mr. Justice Marshall: "How could Lake County have jurisdiction over theft in another county?"

Under state law, defendant can be tried in any county where the car is taken, Plautz replied. He also urged the Court to adopt the same transaction test.

Judicial Notice

George J. Sadd, Chief Appellate Prosecuting Attorney of Cuyahoga County, stressed that the record shows no reason for officials in Cuyahoga and Lake Counties to contact one another about the theft.

The state maintains that the crimes of auto theft and operating a stolen vehicle without consent do not constitute a continuous offense in violation of the Double Jeopardy Clause.

Mr. Justice Marshall: "Do you object to our taking judicial notice of the statutes of Ohio?"

"No, your honor."

Mr. Justice Stevens: "The name and the summons identifies the owner as being from East Cleveland. Was it not proper to infer that the prosecutor knew the owner's location through state vehicle registration and could have contacted the prosecutor there before filing the Lake County charges?"

Counsel was uncertain on this point.

"The fact is that the record shows the officials knew where the car came from," Mr. Justice Stevens observed.

The judicial record is a limited one here, Sadd asserted.

Mr. Justice Marshall: "Don't you have 'hot car sheets' in Ohio?"

Computer records are kept, Sadd answered.

Separate Elements

Ohio urges affirmance of the state court's holding, Sadd said. Here the elements of each statutory offense require proof of additional facts. The Ohio Court of Appeals erred in finding that the joyriding is a lesser included offense of auto theft, he asserted.

Mr. Justice White: "Are we bound by the court of appeals' construction of Ohio law?"

No, Sadd replied. The Ohio Supreme Court has not yet ruled on the point.

Mr. Justice White: "In finding joyriding to be a lesser included offense, I think that the Ohio court found that every fact that was necessary to prove that offense was necessary for the greater."

Counsel disagreed with Mr. Justice White on this point. He added, however that the Court could remand to Ohio as to whether joyriding is a lesser included offense.

The joyriding statute's intent requirement differs from that of the auto theft provision, Sadd stressed. With respect to the misdemeanor offense, "there is no requirement of knowledge that the vehicle was stolen in order to convict." However, the felony statute requires an intent to permanently deprive the owner of his car.

Moreover, the acts prohibited by the two statutes differ. The misdemeanor statute assigns liability based on the vehicle's unauthorized operation, but a physical taking is punished by the felony statute. Sadd also agreed with the government's argument in *Jeffers* that prosecution for a lesser included offense does not always bar a subsequent prosecution for the greater offense.

Mr. Justice White: "Are you supporting the dispositive part of the court of appeals' holding—that these were different offenses even if joyriding is a lesser included?"

Sadd replied that he was.

Mr. Justice Stewart: "You started to tell us about an Ohio Supreme Court decision which was subsequent to this case?"

"Yes, sir." In *State* v. *Ikner*, 44 Ohio St. 2d 132, 134 (1975), the court held that the misdemeanor operation of a motor vehicle without the owner's consent is not a lesser included offense of the felony of concealing a stolen motor vehicle.

Mr. Justice Stewart: "Then isn't it really a function of the courts of Ohio to determine what's a lesser included offense?"

Mr. Justice White: "I don't understand why you don't defend the rationale of the Ohio Court of Appeals. That is, there were two operative acts."

The state feels that there was no double jeopardy violation, Sadd said. This Court should permit multiple convictions for different acts.

Mr. Justice Marshall: "I understand the state's position to be [that] they can still prosecute for both crimes."

On rebuttal, Plautz contended, "I think it was inherently arbitrary to act as the state did here."

BROWN v. OHIO

Supreme Court of the United States, 1977
432 U.S. ___, 97 S. Ct. 2221, 53 L. Ed. 2d 187

The facts are stated in the opinion.

Mr. Justice POWELL delivered the opinion of the Court.

The question in this case is whether the Double Jeopardy Clause of the Fifth Amendment bars prosecution and punishment for the crime of stealing an automobile following prosecution and punishment for the lesser included offense of operating the same vehicle without the owner's consent.

I

On November 29, 1973, the petitioner, Nathaniel Brown, stole a 1965 Chevrolet from a parking lot in East Cleveland, Ohio. Nine days later, on December 8, 1973, Brown was caught driving the car in Wickliffe, Ohio. The Wickliffe police charged him with "joyriding" — taking or operating the car without the owner's consent — in violation of Ohio Rev. Code § 4549.04(D). The complaint charged that "on or about December 8, 1973, . . . Nathaniel H. Brown did unlawfully and purposely take, drive or operate a certain motor vehicle, to wit; a 1965 Chevrolet . . . without the consent of the owner one Gloria Ingram . . ." App. 3. Brown pled guilty to this charge and was sentenced to 30 days in jail and a $100 fine.

Upon his release from jail on January 8, 1974, Brown was returned to East Cleveland to face further charges, and on February 5 he was indicted by the Cuyahoga County grand jury. The indictment was in two counts, the first charging the theft of the car "on or about the 29th day of November 1973," in violation of Ohio Rev. Code § 4549.04(A), and the second charging joyriding on the same date in violation of § 4549.04(D). A bill of particulars filed by the prosecuting attorney specified that "on or about the 29th day of November, 1973, . . . Nathaniel Brown unlawfully did steal a Chevrolet motor vehicle, and take, drive or operate such vehicle without the consent of the owner, Gloria Ingram . . ." App. 10. Brown objected to both counts of the indictment on the basis of former jeopardy.

On March 18, 1974, at a pretrial hearing in the Cuyahoga County Court of Common Pleas, Brown pled guilty to the auto theft charge on the understanding that the court would consider his claim of former jeopardy on a motion to withdraw the plea. Upon submission of the motion, the court overruled Brown's double jeopardy objections. The court sentenced Brown to six months in jail but suspended the sentence and placed Brown on probation for one year.

The Ohio Court of Appeals affirmed. It held that under Ohio law the misdemeanor of joyriding was included in the felony of auto theft:

"Every element of the crime of operating a motor vehicle without the consent of the owner is also an element of the crime of auto theft. 'The difference between the crime of stealing a motor vehicle and operating a motor vehicle without the consent of the owner is that conviction for stealing requires proof of an intent on the part of the thief to permanently deprive the owner of possession.' . . . [T]he crime of operating a motor vehicle without the consent of the owner is a lesser included offense of auto theft. . . ." App. 22.

Although this analysis led the court to agree with Brown that "for purposes of double jeopardy the two prosecutions involve the same statutory offense," id., at 23, it nonetheless held the second prosecution permissible:

"The two prosecutions are based on two separate acts of the appellant, one which occurred on November 29th and one which occurred on December 8th. Since appellant has not shown that both prosecutions are based on the same act or transaction, the second prosecution is not barred by the double jeopardy clause. . . ." Ibid.

The Ohio Supreme Court denied leave to appeal.

We granted certiorari to consider Brown's double jeopardy claim, 429 U.S. 893 (1976), and we now reverse.

II

The Double Jeopardy Clause of the Fifth Amendment, applicable to the States through the Fourteenth, provides that no person shall "be subject for the same offence to be twice put in jeopardy of life or limb." It has been understood that separate statutory crimes need not be identical—either in constituent elements or in actual proof—in order to be the same within the meaning of the constitutional prohibition. Bishop's New Criminal Law § 1051 (1892); Comment, Twice in Jeopardy, 75 Yale L.J. 262, 268–269 (1965). The principal question in this case is whether auto theft and joyriding, a greater and lesser included offense under Ohio law, constitute the "same offence" under the Double Jeopardy Clause.

Because it was designed originally to embody the protection of the common law plea of former jeopardy, see United States v. Wilson, 420 U.S. 332, 339–340 (1975), the Fifth Amendment double jeopardy guarantee serves principally as a restraint on courts and prosecutors. The legislature remains free under the Double Jeopardy Clause to define crimes and fix punishments; but once the legislature has acted courts may not impose more than one punishment for the same offense and prosecutors ordinarily may not attempt to secure that punishment in more than one trial.

The Double Jeopardy Clause "protects against a second prosecution for the same offense after acquittal. It protects against a second prosecution for the same offense after conviction. And it protects against multiple punishments for the same offense." North Carolina v. Pearce, 395 U.S. 711, 717 (1969). Where consecutive sentences are imposed at a single criminal trial, the role of the constitutional guarantee is limited to assuring that the court does not exceed its legislative authorization by imposing multiple punishments for the same offense. See Gore v. United States, 357 U.S. 386 (1958); Bell v. United States, 349 U.S. 81 (1955); Ex parte Lange, 18 Wall. 163 (1873). Where successive prosecutions are at stake, the guarantee serves "a constitutional policy of finality for the defendant's benefit." United States v. Jorn, 400 U.S. 470, 479 (1971) (plurality opinion). That policy protects the accused from attempts to relitigate the facts underlying a prior acquittal, see Ashe v. Swenson, 397 U.S. 436 (1970); cf. United States v. Martin Linen Supply Co. [97 S. Ct. 1349] (1977), and from attempts to secure additional punishment after a prior conviction and sentence, see Green v. United States, 355 U.S. 184, 187–188 (1957); cf. North Carolina v. Pearce, supra.

The established test for determining whether two offenses are sufficiently distinguishable to permit the imposition of cumulative punishment was stated in Blockburger v. United States, 284 U.S. 299, 304 (1932):

"The applicable rule is that where the same act or transaction constitutes a violation of two distinct statutory provisions, the test to be applied to determine whether there are two offenses or only one, is whether each provision requires proof of a fact which the other does not. . . ."

This test emphasizes the elements of the two crimes. "If each requires proof that the other does not, the Blockburger test would be satisfied, notwithstanding a substantial overlap in the proof offered to establish the crimes. . . ." Iannelli v. United States, 420

U.S. 770, 785 n.17 (1975). If two offenses are the same under this test for purposes of barring consecutive sentences at a single trial, they necessarily will be the same for purposes of barring successive prosecutions. See In re Nielsen, 131 U.S. 176, 187–188 (1889); cf. Gavieres v. United States, 220 U.S. 338 (1911). Where the judge is forbidden to impose cumulative punishment for two crimes at the end of a single proceeding, the prosecutor is forbidden to strive for the same result in successive proceedings. Unless "each statute requires proof of an additional fact which the other does not," Morey v. Commonwealth, 108 Mass. 433, 434 (1871), the Double Jeopardy Clause prohibits successive prosecutions as well as cumulative punishments.[f]

We are mindful that the Ohio courts "have the final authority to interpret that State's legislation." Garner v. Louisiana, 368 U.S. 157, 169 (1961). Here the Ohio Court of Appeals has authoritatively defined the elements of the two Ohio crimes: Joyriding consists of taking or operating a vehicle without the owner's consent, and auto theft consists of joyriding with the intent permanently to deprive the owner of possession. App. 22. Joyriding is the lesser included offense. The prosecutor who has established joyriding need only to prove the requisite intent in order to establish auto theft; the prosecutor who has established auto theft necessarily has established joyriding as well.

Applying the Blockburger test, we agree with the Ohio Court of Appeals that joyriding and auto theft, as defined by the court, constitute "the same statutory offense" within the meaning of the Double Jeopardy Clause. App. 23. For it is clearly *not* the case that "each statute requires proof of an additional fact which the other does not." 284 U.S., at 304. As is invariably true of a greater and lesser included offense, the lesser offense—joyriding—requires no proof beyond that which is required for conviction of the greater—auto theft. The greater offense is therefore by definition the "same" for purposes of double jeopardy as any lesser offense included in it.

This conclusion merely restates what has been this Court's understanding of the Double Jeopardy Clause at least since In re Nielsen was decided in 1889. In that case the Court endorsed the rule that "where . . . a person has been tried and convicted for a crime which has various incidents included in it, he cannot be a second time tried for the same offense." 131 U.S., at 188. Although in this formulation the conviction of the greater precedes the conviction of the lesser, the opinion makes it clear that the sequence is immaterial. Thus the Court treated the

---

[f] The Blockburger test is not the only standard for determining whether successive prosecutions impermissibly involve the same offense. Even if two offenses are sufficiently different to permit the imposition of consecutive sentences, successive prosecutions will be barred in some circumstances where the second prosecution requires the relitigation of factual issues already resolved by the first. Thus in Ashe v. Swenson, 397 U.S. 436 (1970), where an acquittal on a charge of robbing one of several participants in a poker game established that the accused was not present at the robbery, the Court held that principles of collateral estoppel embodied in the Double Jeopardy Clause barred prosecutions of the accused for robbing the other victims. And in In re Nielsen, 131 U.S. 176 (1889), the Court held that a conviction of a Mormon on a charge of cohabiting with his two wives over a two-and-one-half year period barred a subsequent prosecution for adultery with one of them on the day following the end of that period. In both cases, strict application of the Block-burger test would have permitted imposition of

consecutive sentences had the charges been consolidated in a single proceeding. In Ashe, separate convictions of the robbery of each victim would have required proof in each case that a different individual had been robbed. See Ebeling v. Morgan, 237 U.S. 625 (1915). In Nielsen, conviction for adultery required proof that the defendant had sexual intercourse with one woman while married to another; conviction for cohabitation required proof that the defendant lived with more than one woman at the same time. Nonetheless, the Court in both cases held the separate offenses to be the "same" for purposes of protecting the accused from having to "run the gantlet a second time." Ashe, supra, at 446, quoting from Green v. United States, 355 U.S. 184, 190 (1957).

Because we conclude today that a lesser included and a greater offense are the same under Blockburger, we need not decide whether the repetition of proof required by the successive prosecutions against Brown would otherwise entitle him to the additional protection offered by Ashe and Nielsen.

formulation as just one application of the rule that two offenses are the same unless each requires proof that the other does not. Id., at 188, 190, citing Morey v. Commonwealth, 108 Mass., at 434. And as another application of the same rule, the Court reported with approval the decision of State v. Cooper, 13 N.J.L. 361 (1833), where the New Jersey Supreme Court held that a conviction for arson barred a subsequent felony-murder indictment based on the death of a man killed in the fire. Cf. Waller v. Florida, 397 U.S. 387, 390 (1970). Whatever the sequence may be, the Fifth Amendment forbids successive prosecution and cumulative punishment for a greater and lesser included offense.

III·

After correctly holding that joyriding and auto theft are the same offense under the Double Jeopardy Clause, the Ohio Court of Appeals nevertheless concluded that Nathaniel Brown could be convicted of both crimes because the charges against him focused on different parts of his 9-day joyride. App. 23. We hold a different view. The Double Jeopardy Clause is not such a fragile guarantee that prosecutors can avoid its limitations by the simple expedient of dividing a single crime into a series of temporal or spatial units. Cf. Braveman v. United States, 317 U.S. 40, 52 (1942). The applicable Ohio statutes, as written and construed in this case, make the theft and operation of a single car a single offense. Although the Wickliffe and East Cleveland authorities may have had different perspectives on Brown's offense, it was still only one offense under Ohio law.[h]

---

[h]We would have a different case if the Ohio Legislature had provided that joyriding is a separate offense for each day in which a motor vehicle is operated without the owner's consent. Cf. Blockburger v. United States, 284 U.S. 299, 302 (1932). We also would have a different case if in sustaining Brown's second conviction the Ohio courts had constructed the joyriding statute to have that effect. We then would have to decide whether the state courts' construction, applied retroactively in this case, was such "an unforeseeable judicial enlargement of a criminal statute" as to violate due process. See Bouie v. City of Columbia, 378 U.S. 347, 353 (1964); cf. In re Snow, 120 U.S. 274, 283–286 (1887); Crepps v. Durden, 2 Cowper 640 (K.B. 1777).

Accordingly, the specification of different dates in the two charges on which Brown was convicted cannot alter the fact that he was placed twice in jeopardy for the same offense in violation of the Fifth and Fourteenth Amendments.

Reversed.

Mr. Justice BRENNAN, with whom Mr. Justice MARSHALL joins, concurring.

I join the Court's opinion, but in any event would reverse on the ground, not addressed by the Court, that the State did not prosecute petitioner in a single proceeding. I adhere to the view that the Double Jeopardy Clause of the Fifth Amendment, applied to the States through the Fourteenth Amendment, requires the prosecution in one proceeding, except in extremely limited circumstances not present here, of "all the charges against a defendant that grow out of single criminal act, occurrence, episode, or transaction." Ashe v. Swenson, 397 U.S. 436, 453–454, and n. 7 (1970) (BRENNAN, J., concurring). See Thompson v. Oklahoma, [97 S. Ct. 768] (1977) (BRENNAN, J., dissenting), and cases collected therein. In my view the Court's suggestion, ante, at 8 [n.h.], that the Ohio Legislature might be free to make joyriding a separate and distinct offense for each day a motor vehicle is operated without the owner's consent would not affect the applicability of the single transaction test. Though under some circumstances a legislature may divide a continuing course of conduct into discrete offenses. I would nevertheless hold that all charges growing out of conduct constituting a "single criminal act, occurrence, episode, or transaction" must be tried in a single proceeding.

Mr. Justice BLACKMUN, with whom The Chief Justice [BURGER] and Mr. Justice REHNQUIST join, dissenting.

* * *

Nine days elapsed between the two incidents that are the basis of petitioner's convictions. During that time the automobile moved from East Cleveland to Wickliffe. It strains credulity to believe that petitioner was operating the vehicle every minute of those nine days. A time must have come when he stopped driving the car. When he operated it again nine days later in a different community, the Ohio courts could properly find, consistently with the Double Jeopardy Clause, that the acts were sufficiently distinct to justify a second prosecution. Only if the Clause requires the Ohio courts to hold that the allowable unit of prosecution is the course of conduct would the Court's result here be correct. On the facts of this case, no such requirement should be inferred, and the state courts should be free to construe Ohio's statute as they did.

This Court, I fear, gives undeserved emphasis . . . to the Ohio Court of Appeals' passing observation that the Ohio misde-meanor of joyriding is an element of the Ohio felony of auto theft. That observation was merely a preliminary statement, indicating that the theft and any simultaneous unlawful operation were one and the same. But the Ohio Court of Appeals then went on flatly to hold that such simultaneity was not present here. Thus, it seems to me, the Ohio courts did precisely what this Court, in its [note h] . . . professes to say they did not do.

In my view, we should not so willingly circumvent an authoritative Ohio holding as to Ohio law. I would affirm the judgment of the Court of Appeals.

Comments

1. Mr. Justice Black observed in *Bartkus* v. *Illinois* that the "fear and abhorrence of governmental power to try people twice for the same conduct . . . [is] one of the oldest ideas found in Western civilization." 359 U.S. at 151 (1959) (dissenting opinion). While the exact origin of the protection against double jeopardy remains obscure, many scholars contend that the concept barring multiple prosecutions for the same offense (nemo debet bis vexari pro eadem causa) can be traced back to ancient Greece and Rome. See, e.g., Sigler, *Double Jeopardy, The Development of a Legal and Social Policy* (1969); Levy, *Origins of the Fifth Amendment* (1968); 11 Scott, *The Civil Law* 17 (1932); and Bachelder, *Former Jeopardy,* 17 Am. L. Rev. 748 (1883). In the thirteenth century, Bracton commented on the existence of a bar against multiple prosecutions even when trial was by combat; see 2 Bracton, *On the Laws and Customs of England* 391 (Thorne trans. 1968), noting that after a defendant had been placed on trial for "one deed . . . he will depart quit (acquitted) against all, also as regards the King's suit, because he thereby proves his innocence against all, as though he had put himself on the country and it had exonerated him completely." By the mid-seventeenth century, the double jeopardy concept had been merged into English common law pleading. Although there was no actual pleading of "former jeopardy," Lord Coke reported that a defendant could exercise the pleas of "former acquittal" (autrefois acquit) or "former conviction" (autrefois convict). 3 Coke, *Institutes of the Laws of England* 213–214 (1797 ed.). By invoking the first plea, a defendant could bar a second prosecution upon proof that he had previously been acquitted on the same charge. The latter plea allowed a defendant to escape a second trial by proving that he had been convicted of the same offense at an earlier proceeding. By the late eighteenth century, Blackstone reported the existence of four pleas: "(1) autrefois acquit, (2) autrefois convict, (3) autrefois attaint (former attaint, founded on the reasoning that 'a second prosecution cannot be to any purpose, for the prisoner is dead in law by the first attainder'), and (4) pardon. In terms that plainly anticipated the Fifth Amendment's language, Blackstone described the protection against double jeopardy

as a 'universal maxim of the common law of England, that no man is to be brought into jeopardy of his life more than once for the same offense.'" *United States* v. *Jenkins,* 400 F.2d 868, 873 (1973), citing 4 Blackstone, *Commentaries on the Laws of England* 335–336 (Sharswood ed. 1873). In a footnote, the court of appeals remarked, "By 1776, defense counsel could assert confidently, 'whenever, and by whatever means, there is an acquittal in a criminal prosecution, the scene is closed and the curtain drops.'" 400 F.2d at 873, n.6, citing *Duchess of Kingston's Case,* 20 Howell, *State Trials* 355, 528 (1776).

Although Coke and Blackstone had attempted to clarify the principle of former jeopardy, there appears to have been considerable misunderstanding about the meaning of the concept at the time the draft of the Double Jeopardy Clause was introduced in the House of Representatives in 1789; see Sigler, supra, at 1–37. The original proposal read: "No persons shall be subject, except in cases of impeachment, to more than one punishment or one trial for the same offense." 1 *Annals of Congress* 434 (1789). One writer noted that the language in the original proposal may have stemmed from an earlier Maryland document proposing that "there be no appeal from a matter of fact, or second trial after acquittal." 2 Schwartz, *The Bill of Rights: A Documentary History* 732 (1971). In the final draft, the Senate substituted the term "jeopardy" for the phrase "more than one punishment in one trial." According to the same commentator, the language of the proposed amendment may have derived from an earlier one submitted by the New York Ratifying Convention, which provided, "That no person ought to be put twice in jeopardy of Life or Limb for one and the same offense." Schwartz, supra, at 912. Still another writer, commenting on the precise language of the Double Jeopardy Clause, concluded: "There is no reason to believe that the phrase 'twice put in jeopardy' was used in the Fifth Amendment for the purpose of introducing a change into this department [common law pleading] of the law. In all likelihood the framers of the Constitution had no more in mind than embodiment of the common-law prohibition against placing a defendant in jeopardy a second time for the same offense after *acquittal* or *conviction*. . . . The common-law principle . . . was that an accused person should not be prosecuted again for the same offense after he had once been convicted or acquitted thereof. The word 'jeopardy' merely happened to be used by Blackstone and others in explanation of this principle." Perkins, *Criminal Law and Procedure* 788–789 (4th ed. 1972).

As now construed, the Fifth Amendment's protection against double jeopardy consists of three separate constitutional protections: (1) "It protects against a second prosecution for the same offense after acquittal; (2) it protects against a second prosecution for the same offense after conviction; and (3) it protects against multiple punishments for the same offense." *North Carolina* v. *Pearce,* 395 U.S. 711, 717 (1969). See also *United States* v. *Engle,* 458 F.2d 1021, 1025 (6th Cir. 1972). See generally Note, *Twice in Jeopardy,* 75 Yale L.J. 262, 264 (1965); Fisher, *Double Jeopardy: Six Common Boners Summarized,* 15 U.C.L.A. 81 (1967). For some earlier but excellent comments on double jeopardy, see Note, *Criminal Law–Double Jeopardy,* 24 Minn. L. Rev. 522 (1940);

Note, *What Constitutes Double Jeopardy?*, 38 J. Crim. L.C. & P.S. 379 (1947); Note, *Statutory Implementation of Double Jeopardy Clauses: New Life for a Moribund Constitutional Guarantee,* 65 Yale L.J. 339 (1956).

2. In *Tateo,* the Court mentioned the "societal interest in punishing" guilty defendants. Accordingly, if a defendant obtains a reversal of his conviction on appeal, he can be retried for the *same offense* on the ground that he has "waived" his right against double jeopardy. By appealing his conviction, a defendant is, in effect, saying that he did not receive a fair trial at the earlier proceeding, and the government normally can retry him for the same offense absent the legal defect that was the basis for the reversal. Likewise, if an intermediate appellate court reverses a defendant's conviction, the government (state or federal), seeking to affirm the conviction, normally can appeal to a higher appellate court. The subsequent appeal by the government is permissible because the defendant "waived" any double jeopardy claims by appealing in the first instance. If there is a retrial, the initial legal defect which occurred at the first trial must be "cured" at the second trial. Otherwise, in the event of a reconviction, the second conviction is subject to reversal on the same grounds. Most appellate court reversals are also remanded (i.e., "reversed and remanded") so that the state can have an opportunity to retry the defendant. A finding of double jeopardy by an appellate court, of course, precludes retrial for the same offense because the trial court normally loses jurisdiction of the case once jeopardy has attached and a conviction has been appealed and reversed on those grounds.

Sometimes the "cure" at retrial requires the exclusion of much of the evidence on which the original prosecution was based, and the prosecution is forced to dismiss the case. For example, if an appellate court reverses a defendant's conviction for possession of heroin because of an unlawful search and seizure in which the heroin was obtained—thereby precluding the introduction at retrial of that evidence—the prosecution has little choice but to dismiss the case on remand since there would not be sufficient admissible evidence to support a conviction.

The *Tateo* Court noted that in England the reversal of a conviction on appeal bars a retrial of the defendant on double jeopardy grounds. If United States law followed the English rule wouldn't most, if not all, defendants appeal their convictions in the hope of obtaining a reversal and thereby being set free? Isn't the Court correct in suggesting that if the English rule were followed in the United States, appellate courts would be less zealous in guarding a defendant's constitutional rights if they knew that reversal of a conviction absolutely precluded a retrial?

All American jurisdictions permit, as a matter of right, a first appeal from a conviction—although such appeals are not constitutionally required. If Tateo's position had prevailed, wouldn't most states reevaluate their positions with regard to appeals from convictions being a matter of right? Is it possible that the *Tateo* Court considered this possibility without saying so? Finally, what *are* the "interests of society" in punishing guilty defendants? For an excellent discussion of this question, see Van Den Haag, E., *Punishing Criminals* (1975) and Von Hirsch, A., *Doing Justice* (1976).

The double jeopardy problems involved in imposition of a greater punishment or reconviction are discussed in *North Carolina* v. *Pearce,* Chapter Fourteen, § 14.02.

3. In *Waller* v. *Florida,* supra, the Court held that municipal and state courts are not separate sovereignties for purposes of the Double Jeopardy Clause. Thus, when a defendant has been convicted of a criminal offense by any *political subdivision of the state* (e.g., city, county, municipality), the state may not retry the defendant for acts that constitute the *same offense.* However, acts that constitute different offenses are apparently not subject to the *Waller* rule. Thus, if a defendant strikes a victim (e.g., simple battery—a misdemeanor) and unlawfully kills a different victim, a trial for the battery-misdemeanor in a municipal court would apparently not bar a subsequent trial by the state for murder.

In *Bartkus* v. *Illinois,* 359 U.S. 121 (1959), the Supreme Court permitted successive prosecutions by the federal and state governments as separate sovereignties. Bartkus was tried in federal district court in Illinois for bank robbery and acquitted by a jury. He was subsequently tried for the same bank robbery in an Illinois state court and convicted. In rejecting Bartkus' claim of double jeopardy, the Supreme Court held that due process does not prohibit successive state and federal prosecutions for a single act violative of both state and federal laws. Although *Bartkus* has never been overruled, the fact that it was decided prior to *Benton* v. *Maryland* (Chapter Three, § 3.04), which made the Double Jeopardy Clause applicable to the states, makes its continuing validity questionable.

In *Abbate* v. *United States,* 359 U.S. 187 (1959), a divided Supreme Court held that the Double Jeopardy Clause did not bar a successive federal prosecution of defendants for conspiracy to destroy federal property after they had been convicted, on identical facts, in an Illinois state court of violating a state statute making it a crime to conspire to destroy the property of another. Like *Bartkus,* the *Abbate* decision has been the subject of much criticism. In *Robinson* v. *Neil,* 409 U.S. 505 (1973), the Supreme Court held *Waller* v. *Florida* to be fully retroactive.

4. In *Brown* v. *Ohio,* supra, the majority of the justices declined to adopt the "same transaction" test espoused by Justices Brennan and Marshall. What would the result have been if the Ohio courts had held that, as a matter of state law, auto theft and operating a motor vehicle without the owner's permission are separate, distinct offenses; i.e., the latter is not a lesser included offense of auto theft? Would the *Blockburger* "same evidence" test have barred the second trial? Note that the United States Supreme Court is bound by state courts' construction of state law.

Applying the facts to the *Brown* case, doesn't auto theft (as opposed to unauthorized use) require "proof of a fact which the other does not"; i.e., intent by the theft to permanently deprive? Why then doesn't the *Blockburger* test permit a subsequent prosecution? Does it matter whether Brown was first convicted of auto theft or of unauthorized use? Applying the reasoning of the Court, wouldn't the result be the same—no prosecution for the other offense? Suppose Brown had been acquitted on the unauthorized use charge. Could he still be prosecuted for auto theft?

B. PRIOR ACQUITTALS

Continuing Jeopardy and "Implicit Acquittals"

PRICE v. GEORGIA

Supreme Court of the United States, 1970
398 U.S. 323, 900 S. Ct. 1757, 26 L. Ed. 2d 300

Earl Price was tried for murder in a Georgia state court. The jury returned a verdict of guilty on the lesser included crime of voluntary manslaughter, and Price was sentenced to 10 to 15 years' imprisonment. On appeal, the Georgia Court of Appeals reversed the conviction because of an erroneous jury instruction and ordered a new trial. Price was tried a second time for murder under the original indictment. The trial court rejected his claim that placing him on trial again for murder would expose him to double jeopardy in view of the conviction for voluntary manslaughter at the first trial. At the close of the trial, the judge gave instructions on the offenses of murder and manslaughter. The jury found Price guilty of manslaughter and he was sentenced to 10 years' imprisonment. The Georgia Court of Appeals affirmed the conviction, rejecting Price's argument that his retrial for murder constituted double jeopardy. The Georgia Supreme Court denied review, and the United States Supreme Court granted certiorari.

Mr. Chief Justice BURGER delivered the opinion of the Court.

* * *

I

In United States v. Ball, 163 U.S. 662, 669 (1896), this Court observed: "The Constitution of the United States, in the Fifth Amendment, declares, 'nor shall any person be subject [for the same offense] to be twice put in jeopardy of life or limb.' The prohibition is not against being twice punished, but against being twice *put* in jeopardy. . . ." The "twice put in jeopardy" language of the Constitution thus relates to a potential, *i.e.*, the risk that an accused for a second time will be convicted of the "same offense" for which he was initially tried.

The circumstances that give rise to such a forbidden potential have been the subject of much discussion in this Court. In the Ball case, for example, the Court expressly rejected the view that the double jeopardy provision prevented a second trial when a conviction had been set aside. In so doing, it effectively formulated a concept of continuing jeopardy that has application where

criminal proceedings against an accused have not run their full course. . . .

The continuing jeopardy principle necessarily is applicable to this case. Petitioner sought and obtained the reversal of his initial conviction for voluntary manslaughter by taking an appeal. Accordingly, no aspect of the bar on double jeopardy prevented his retrial for that crime. However, the first verdict, limited as it was to the lesser included offense, required that the retrial be limited to that lesser offense. Such a result flows inescapably from the Constitution's emphasis on a risk of conviction and the Constitution's explication in prior decisions of this Court.

An early case . . . (dealing) with restrictions on retrials . . . held that the Fifth Amendment's double jeopardy prohibition barred the Government from appealing an acquittal in a criminal prosecution. . . .

[I]n Green v. United States, 355 U.S. 184 (1957), the petitioner had been tried and convicted of first-degree murder after an earlier offense of second-degree murder had been set aside on appeal. A majority of the Court rejected the argument that by appealing the conviction of second-degree murder the petitioner had "waived" his plea of former jeopardy with regard to the charge of first-degree murder.

The Court in the Green case reversed the first-degree murder conviction obtained at the retrial, holding that the petitioner's jeopardy for first-degree murder came to an end when the jury was discharged at the end of his first trial. This conclusion rested on two premises. First, the Court considered the first jury's verdict on the murder charge to be an "implicit acquittal" on the charge of first-degree murder.

Second, and more broadly, the Court reasoned that petitioner's jeopardy on the greater charge had ended when the first jury "was given a full opportunity to return a verdict" on that charge and instead reached a verdict on the lesser charge. . . . Under either of these premises, the holding . . . that there could be no appeal from an acquittal because such a verdict ended an accused's jeopardy was applicable.

The rationale of the Green holding applies here. The concept of continuing jeopardy . . . would allow petitioner's retrial for voluntary manslaughter after his first conviction for that offense had been reversed. . . .

[T]his Court has consistently refused to rule that jeopardy for an offense continues after an acquittal, whether that acquittal is express or implied by a conviction on a lesser included offense when the jury was given a full opportunity to return a verdict on the greater charge. There is no relevant factual distinction between this case and Green v. United States. Although the petitioner was not convicted of the greater charge on retrial, whereas Green was, the risk of conviction on the greater charge was the same in both cases, and the Double Jeopardy Clause of the Fifth Amendment is written in terms of potential or risks of trial and conviction, not punishment.

* * *

II

. . . Because the petitioner was convicted of the same crime at both the first and second trials, and because he suffered no greater punishment on the subsequent conviction, Georgia submits that the second jeopardy was harmless error. . . .

We must reject this contention. The Double Jeopardy Clause, as we have noted, is cast in terms of the risk or hazard of trial and conviction, not of the ultimate legal consequences of the verdict. To be charged and to be subjected to a second trial for first-degree murder is an ordeal not to be viewed lightly. Further, and perhaps of more importance, we cannot determine whether or not the murder charge against petitioner induced the jury to find him guilty of the less serious offense of voluntary manslaughter rather than to continue to debate his innocence. . . .

* * *

Reversed and remanded.

[Mr. Justice BLACKMUN did not participate in the consideration or decision of this case.]

Comments

1. In *Price* v. *Georgia,* supra, the Court held that a defendant cannot be charged on retrial with a *greater offense* than he was convicted of at his first trial. Thus on remand, Price could be retried only for manslaughter, not murder, because he would have been placed in jeopardy on the latter charge. The *Green* case noted in *Price* v. *Georgia* held that the prosecution cannot retry a defendant for a greater degree of the same offense (e.g., no retrial for first degree robbery when jury found defendant guilty of second degree robbery at first trial). Suppose a defendant pleads guilty to a lesser offense (e.g., attempted robbery as opposed to armed robbery) and he is successful in getting his conviction reversed on appeal. Can he be tried for the greater offense of armed robbery? Had he ever been placed in jeopardy on the greater offense?

2. In recent years, the Supreme Court has examined the relation between the Double Jeopardy Clause and governmental appeals. In *United States* v. *Wilson,* 420 U.S. 332 (1975), the Court held that the Double Jeopardy Clause does not bar the government's appeal from a district court's *postverdict dismissal of an indictment.* The majority reasoned that the district court's ruling in favor of the defendant can be acted on by the court of appeals or the United States Supreme Court without subjecting the defendant to a second trial at the behest of the government. That is, if the defendant prevails on appeal, the indictment will remain dismissed and final, and the government cannot retry him for the same offense. If he loses on appeal, the case must go back to the district court for a disposition of the defendant's remaining motions.

In *United States* v. *Jenkins,* 420 U.S. 358 (1975), the Supreme Court held that a district court's dismissal of an indictment *after a bench trial* was not appealable by the government in light of the Double Jeopardy Clause. However, when a jury convicts the defendant and the trial judge thereafter directs an acquittal, a governmental appeal is permitted since a conclusion by an appellate court that the judgment of acquittal was improper does not require the defendant to be subjected to a second trial, since the conviction will be automatically reinstated. If the appellate court finds the judgment of acquittal proper, their decision is final and the defendant must be discharged.

The Court ruled in *Serfass* v. *United States,* 420 U.S. 377 (1975), that the Double Jeopardy Clause does not bar an appeal by the government from a *pretrial order* of a district court dismissing an indictment. The Court reasoned that in that situation, the defendant had not yet been "put to trial before the trier of facts" (judge or jury). The Court noted that jeopardy does not attach until a defendant has been put to trial. In a jury trial, jeopardy attaches when the jury is empaneled and sworn; in a bench trial, jeopardy attaches when the court begins to hear evidence.

3.

UNITED STATES v. MORRISON
Supreme Court of the United States, 1976
429 U.S. 1, 97, S. Ct. 24, 50 L. Ed. 2d 1

PER CURIAM.

On September 27, 1972, a car driven by respondent was stopped by Border Patrol Agents at the permanent immigration traffic checkpoint near Truth or Consequences, N.M. An Agent detected the odor of marihuana; the car was then searched, disclosing a large quantity of marihuana.

Respondent was charged with possessing marihuana with intent to distribute in violation of 21 U.S.C. § 841(a)(1). Respondent filed a pretrial motion to suppress the marihuana on the grounds that the search of his car violated the Fourth Amendment. Respondent waived his right to a jury trial. The motion to suppress was heard during the trial on the merits, and the District Court denied the motion to suppress and found the respondent guilty as charged.

Approximately three months later, we held that a warrantless roving patrol search of vehicles for aliens, conducted without probable cause at a point removed from the border or its functional equivalent, violated the Fourth Amendment. Almeida-Sanchez v.

United States, 413 U.S. 266 (1973). The Court of Appeals for the Tenth Circuit thereafter held that Almeida-Sanchez should be applied retroactively and that its rationale encompasses searches conducted at fixed traffic checkpoints. United States v. King, 485 F.2d 353 (10th Cir., 1973); United States v. Maddox, 485 F.2d 361 (10th Cir., 1973).

Respondent's original motion to suppress was then reconsidered by the District Court in the light of King, supra, and Maddox, supra, and the following order was entered:

"... it is hereby
"ORDERED that the marihuana which is the subject matter of the charge herein shall be and is hereby suppressed.
"The Court will take appropriate action consistent with this Order if this Order is not appealed by the United States of America or if this Order is affirmed on appeal."

Thereupon the Government appealed pursuant to 18 U.S.C. § 3731.[b] While this appeal was pending in the Court of Appeals, we held in Bowen v. United States, 422 U.S. 916 (1975), that Almeida-Sanchez was not to be applied retroactively to checkpoint searches conducted prior to June 21, 1973. After the Government moved for summary reversal of the District Court's suppression order, the Court of Appeals, without benefit of briefing or oral argument, dismissed the Government's appeal for lack of jurisdiction, finding that double jeopardy would bar a retrial. The court, citing United States v. Jenkins, 420 U.S. 358 (1975), felt that double jeopardy would bar further proceedings involving "the resolution of factual matters going to the elements of the offense charged ..." would be required.

We cannot agree. In United States v. Wilson, 420 U.S. 332 (1975), we held:

"We therefore conclude that when a judge rules in favor of the defendant after a verdict of guilty has been entered by the trier of fact, the Government may appeal from that ruling without running afoul of the Double Jeopardy Clause." 420 U.S., at 352–353.

The holding in Wilson applies to the bench trial here, for, as we stated in United States v. Jenkins, supra:

"Since the Double Jeopardy Clause of the Fifth Amendment nowhere distinguishes between bench and jury trials, the principles given expression through that Clause apply to cases tried to a judge....
"A general finding of guilt by a judge may be analogized to a verdict of 'guilty' returned by a jury." 420 U.S., at 365–366.

Thus the District Court's general finding of guilt here is for double jeopardy purposes the same as a jury verdict of guilty. The Government is therefore entitled to appeal the order suppressing

---

[b]The Criminal Appeals Act provides in pertinent part: "In a criminal case an appeal by the United States shall lie to a court of appeals from a decision, judgment, or order of a district court dismissing an indictment or information as to any one or more counts, except that no appeal shall lie where the double jeopardy clause of the United States Constitution prohibits further prosecution."

the evidence, since success on that appeal would result in the reinstatement of the general finding of guilt, rather than in further factual proceedings relating to guilt or innocence. As in Wilson, there would then remain only the imposition of sentence and the entry of a judgment of conviction pursuant to Fed. Rule Crim. Proc. 32.

We grant the petition for certiorari, vacate the judgment of the Court of Appeals and remand for further proceedings consistent with this opinion.

———————

In *United States* v. *Rose*, 97 S. Ct. 26 (1976), decided the same day as *Morrison*, supra, the Supreme Court, in a per curiam opinion, held that a motion to suppress granted following a finding of guilt after a bench trial does not bar an appeal by the government. The Court noted that "the fact that the order of suppression . . . occurred after a general finding of guilt rendered by the court in a bench trial, rather than after a return of a verdict of guilty by a jury, is immaterial" for the purposes of the Double Jeopardy Clause. In accord is *United States* v. *Kopp*, 97 S. Ct. 400 (1976).

4.   UNITED STATES v. SANFORD
Supreme Court of the United States, 1976
429 U.S. 14, 97 S. Ct. 20, 50 L. Ed. 2d 17

PER CURIAM.

Respondents were indicted for illegal game hunting in Yellowstone National Park. A jury trial in the United States District Court for the District of Montana resulted in a hung jury, and the District Court declared a mistrial. Four months later, while the Government was preparing to retry them, respondents moved to dismiss the indictment. The District Court, agreeing that the Government had consented to the activities which formed the basis of the indictment, dismissed it. The Government's appeal pursuant to the Criminal Appeals Act, 18 U.S.C. § 3731 [see Table 6.1] was dismissed by the Court of Appeals because that court thought retrial was barred by the Double Jeopardy Clause of the Fifth Amendment to the United States Constitution. The Government petitioned for certiorari, and we vacated the judgment of the Court of Appeals and remanded for further consideration in the light of our intervening decision in Serfass v. United States, 420 U.S. 377 (1975). 421 U.S. 996 (1975).

On remand, the Court of Appeals, considering the trilogy of Serfass, supra, United States v. Wilson, 420 U.S. 332 (1975), and United States v. Jenkins, 420 U.S. 358 (1975), adhered to its prior determination. The Government now seeks certiorari from that ruling.

The reasoning of the Court of Appeals is best summarized by this language from its opinion:

"Here appellees have undergone trial. There is no question but that jeopardy has attached. That being so, and since the proceedings in the district court have ended in appellees' favor and the

TABLE 6.1 Government Appeals in Criminal Cases Under 18 U.S.C. § 3731

Case	Holding	Comment
United States v. Wilson, 420 U.S. 332 (1975)	Government appeal permitted following trial court ruling in favor of defendant after jury has returned a verdict of guilty.	In accord is *United States* v. *Rose,* 429 U.S. 5 (1976); *United States* v. *Morrison,* 429 U.S. 1 (1976); and *United States* v. *Kopp,* 429 U.S. 121 (1976)
United States v. Jenkins, 420 U.S. 358 (1975)	In a bench trial, if the trial court dismisses the indictment at the close of the evidence, and it is unclear whether the decision rests on a finding of not guilty or is based on errors of law that can be corrected on appeal, no appeal by the government is permitted.	
Serfass v. United States, 420 U.S. 377 (1975)	Jeopardy does not attach when the trial court grants a pretrial motion to dismiss and an appeal by the government is permitted.	
United States v. Sanford, 429 U.S. 14 (1976) (per curiam)	When jury trial ends in a hung jury and district court declares a mistrial, government appeal under 18 U.S.C. § 3731 is permitted following court's dismissal of indictment, and government not barred by Double Jeopardy Clause from retrying defendants.	
United States v. Dieter 429 U.S. 6 (1976) (per curiam)	The 30-day limit for a governmental appeal from an order dismissing an indictment runs from the time of denial of a timely petition in the district court for rehearing.	In accord is *United States* v. *Healy,* 376 U.S. 75 (1964).
United States v. Martin Linen Supply Co., 430 U.S. 564 (1977)	Double Jeopardy Clause bars appeal by the government following a judgment of acquittal under Fed. R. Crim. P. 29(c) after jury has been discharged because it could not reach a verdict.	
Finch v. United States, 433 U.S. —— (1977) (per curiam)	Government appeal under 18 U.S.C. § 3731 not permitted when district court dismisses a bill of information based on stipulated facts after jeopardy has attached, even though no formal finding of guilt or innocence has been entered.	

consequences of a reversal in favor of the Government would be that appellees must be tried again, we conclude that they would, on retrial, be placed twice in jeopardy." 536 F.2d 871, 872 (9th Cir., 1976).

We agree with the Court of Appeals that jeopardy attached at the time of the empanelling of the jury for the first trial of respondents. But we do not agree with that court's conclusion that by reason of the sequence of events in the District Court the Government would be barred by the Double Jeopardy Clause from retrying respondents. The trial of respondents on the indictment terminated not in their favor, but in a mistrial declared, sua sponte, by the District Court. Where the trial is terminated in this manner, the classical test for determining whether the defendants may be retried without violating the Double Jeopardy Clause is stated in Mr. Justice Story's opinion for this Court in United States v. Perez, 9 Wheat., 579, 580 (1824):

"We are of the opinion, that the facts constitute no legal bar to a future trial. The prisoner has not been convicted or acquitted, and may again be put on his defence. We think, that in all cases of this nature, the law has invested courts of justice with the authority to discharge a jury from giving any verdict, whenever, in their opinion, taking all circumstances into consideration, there is a manifest necessity for the act, or the ends of public justice would otherwise be defeated."

The Government's right to retry the defendant, after a mistrial, in the face of his claim of double jeopardy is generally[b] governed by the test laid down in Perez, supra. The situation of a hung jury presented here is precisely the situation that was presented in Perez, supra, and therefore the Double Jeopardy Clause does not bar retrial of these respondents on the indictment which had been returned against them.

The District Court's dismissal of the indictment occurred several months after the first trial had ended in a mistrial, but before the retrial of respondents had begun. This case is, therefore, governed by United States v. Serfass, supra, in which we held that a pretrial order of the District Court dismissing an indictment charging refusal to submit to induction into the Armed Forces was appealable under 18 U.S.C. § 3731. The dismissal in this case, like that in Serfass, was prior to a trial that the Government had a right to prosecute and that the defendant was required to defend. Since in such cases a trial following the Government's successful appeal of a dismissal is not barred by double jeopardy, an appeal from the dismissal is authorized by 18 U.S.C. § 3731.

The petition for certiorari is granted, the judgment of the Court of Appeals is reversed, and the case is remanded for further proceedings consistent with this opinion.

Mr. Justice BRENNAN and Mr. Justice MARSHALL dissent from summary reversal. They would set the case for oral argument.

---

[b]If the mistrial is declared at the behest of the defendant, the manifest necessity test does not apply. See United States v. Dinitz, 424 U.S. 600 (1976) [infra].

C. COLLATERAL ESTOPPEL

Relitigating Issues Based on the Same Transaction

ASHE v. SWENSON

Supreme Court of the United States, 1970
397 U.S. 436, 90 S. Ct. 1189, 25 L. Ed. 2d 469

While playing poker in the basement of a residence, six men were robbed by several masked and armed men who fled in a car belonging to one of the robbery victims. Four persons, including Robert Ashe, were subsequently charged with seven offenses — the armed robbery of each of the six poker players and the theft of the car. Ashe was tried for robbing one of the participants (Knight) in the poker game. At the trial, the state's evidence that Ashe had been one of the robbers was weak, and the jury found him "not guilty due to insufficient evidence." Six weeks later Ashe was brought to trial again, this time for the robbery of another participant (Roberts) in the poker game. Ashe's motion to dismiss on grounds of double jeopardy was denied. This time the jury found him guilty and he was sentenced to 35 years' imprisonment. The Missouri Supreme Court affirmed the conviction. The United States District Court (W.D. Mo.) and the United States Court of Appeals (8th Cir.) denied habeas corpus relief. The United States Supreme Court granted certiorari to determine whether the State of Missouri violated the guarantee against double jeopardy when it prosecuted Ashe a second time for armed robbery.

Mr. Justice STEWART delivered the opinion of the Court.

* * *

As the District Court and the Court of Appeals correctly noted, the operative facts here are virtually identical to those of Hoag v. New Jersey, 356 U.S. 464 (1958). In that case the defendant was tried for the armed robbery of three men who, along with others, had been held up in a tavern. The proof of the robbery was clear, but the evidence identifying the defendant as one of the robbers was weak, and the defendant interposed an alibi defense. The jury brought in a verdict of not guilty. The defendant was then brought to trial again, on an indictment charging the robbery of a fourth victim of the tavern holdup. This time the jury found him guilty. After appeals in the state courts proved unsuccessful, Hoag brought his case here.

Viewing the question presented solely in terms of Fourteenth Amendment due process — whether the course that New Jer-

sey had pursued had "led to fundamental unfairness" ... this Court declined to reverse the judgment of conviction, because "in the circumstances shown by this record, we cannot say that petitioner's later prosecution and conviction violated due process." ...

The Court found it unnecessary to decide whether "collateral estoppel" — the principle that bars relitigation between the same parties of issues actually determined at a previous trial — is a due process requirement in a state criminal trial, since it accepted New Jersey's determination that the petitioner's previous acquittal did not in any event give rise to such an estoppel. ... And in the view the Court took of the issues presented, it did not, of course, even approach consideration of whether collateral estoppel is an ingredient of the Fifth Amendment guarantee against double jeopardy.

The doctrine of Benton v. Maryland ... puts the issues in the present case in a perspective quite different from that in which the issues were perceived in Hoag v.

New Jersey. The question is no longer whether collateral estoppel is a requirement of due process, but whether it is a part of the Fifth Amendment's guarantee against double jeopardy. And if collateral estoppel is embodied in that guarantee, then its applicability in a particular case is no longer a matter to be left for state court determination within the broad bounds of "fundamental fairness," but a matter of constitutional fact we must decide through an examination of the entire record. . . .

"Collateral estoppel" is an awkward phrase, but it stands for an extremely important principle in our adversary system of justice. It means simply that when an issue of ultimate fact has once been determined by a valid and final judgment, that issue cannot again be litigated between the same parties in any future lawsuit. Although first developed in civil litigation, collateral estoppel has been an established rule of federal criminal law. . . .

The federal decisions have made clear that the rule of collateral estoppel in criminal cases is not to be applied with the hypertechnical and archaic approach of a 19th century pleading book, but with realism and rationality. Where a previous judgment of acquittal was based upon a general verdict, as is usually the case, this approach requires a court to "examine the record of a prior proceeding, taking into account the pleadings, evidence, charge, and other relevant matter, and conclude whether a rational jury could have grounded its verdict upon an issue other than that which the defendant seeks to foreclose from consideration." The inquiry "must be set in a practical frame and viewed with an eye to all the circumstances of the proceedings." . . . Any test more technically restrictive would, of course, simply amount to a rejection of the rule of collateral estoppel in criminal proceedings, at least in every case where the first judgment was based upon a general verdict of acquittal.

Straightforward application of the federal rule to the present case can lead to but one conclusion.

* * *

The single rationally conceivable issue in dispute before the jury was whether the petitioner had been one of the robbers. And the jury by its verdict found that he had not.

The federal rule of law, therefore, would make a second prosecution for the robbery of Roberts wholly impermissible.

The ultimate question to be determined, then, in the light of Benton v. Maryland, is whether this established rule of federal law is embodied in the Fifth Amendment guarantee against double jeopardy. We do not hesitate to hold that it is. For whatever else that constitutional guarantee may embrace . . . it surely protects a man who has been acquitted from having to "run the gantlet" a second time. . . .

The question is not whether Missouri could validly charge the petitioner with six separate offenses for the robbery of the six poker players. It is not whether he could have received a total of six punishments if he had been convicted in a single trial of robbing the six victims. It is simply whether, after a jury determined by its verdict that the petitioner was not one of the robbers, the State could constitutionally hale him before a new jury to litigate that issue again.

After the first jury had acquitted the petitioner of robbing Knight, Missouri could certainly not have brought him to trial again upon that charge. Once a jury had determined upon conflicting testimony that there was at least a reasonable doubt that the petitioner was one of the robbers, the State could not present the same or different identification evidence in a second prosecution for the robbery of Knight in the hope that a different jury might find that evidence more convincing. The situation is constitutionally no different here, even though the second trial related to another victim of the same robbery. For the name of the victim, in the circumstances of this case, had no bearing whatever upon the issue of whether the petitioner was one of the robbers.

In this case the State in its brief has frankly conceded that following the petitioner's acquittal, it treated the first trial as no more than a dry run for the second prosecution: "No doubt the prosecutor felt the state had a provable case on the first charge and, when he lost, he did what every good attorney would do—he refined his presentation in light of the turn of events at the first trial." But this is precisely what the constitutional guarantee forbids.

Reversed and remanded.

Mr. Justice BLACK, concurring.

I join in the opinion of the Court although I must reject any implication in that opinion that the so-called due process test of "fundamental fairness" might have been appropriate as a constitutional standard at some point in the past or might have a continuing relevancy today in some areas of constitutional law. In my view it is a wholly fallacious idea that a judge's sense of what is fundamentally "fair" or "unfair" should ever serve as a substitute for the explicit, written provisions of our Bill of Rights. One of these provisions is the Fifth Amendment's prohibition against putting a man twice in jeopardy. On several occasions I have stated my view that the Double Jeopardy Clause bars a State or the Federal Government or the two together from subjecting a defendant to the hazards of trial and possible conviction more than once for the same alleged offense. . . .

The opinion of the Court in the case today amply demonstrates that the doctrine of collateral estoppel is a basic and essential part of the Constitution's prohibition against double jeopardy. Accordingly, for the reasons stated in the Court's opinion I fully agree that petitioner's conviction must be reversed.

Mr. Justice HARLAN, concurring.

If I were to judge this case under the traditional standards of Fourteenth Amendment due process, I would adhere to the decision in Hoag v. New Jersey . . . believing that regardless of the reach of the federal rule of collateral estoppel, it would have been open to a state court to treat the issue differently. However, having acceded . . . to the decision in Benton v. Maryland . . . which, over my dissent, held that the Fourteenth Amendment imposes on the States the standards of the Double Jeopardy Clause of the Fifth Amendment, I am satisfied that on this present record Ashe's acquittal in the first trial brought double jeopardy standards into play. Hence, I join the Court's opinion. In doing so I wish to make explicit my understanding that the Court's opinion in no way intimates that the Double Jeopardy Clause embraces to any degree the "same transaction" concept reflected in the concurring opinion of my Brother BRENNAN.

Mr. Justice BRENNAN, whom Mr. Justice DOUGLAS and Mr. Justice MARSHALL join, concurring.

I agree that the Double Jeopardy Clause incorporates collateral estoppel as a constitutional requirement and therefore join the Court's opinion. However, even if the rule of collateral estoppel had been inapplicable to the facts of this case, it is my view that the Double Jeopardy Clause nevertheless bars the prosecution of petitioner a second time for armed robbery. The two prosecutions, the first for the robbery of Knight and the second for the robbery of Roberts, grew out of one criminal episode, and therefore I think it clear on the facts of this case that the Double Jeopardy Clause prohibited Missouri from prosecuting petitioner for each robbery at a different trial. . . .

* * *

The Double Jeopardy Clause . . . guarantee is expressed as a prohibition against multiple prosecutions for the "same offence. Although the phrase "same offence" appeared in most of the early common-law articulations of the double-jeopardy principle, questions of its precise meaning rarely arose prior to the 18th century, and by the time the Bill of Rights was adopted it had not been authoritatively defined.

When the common law did finally attempt a definition, in The King v. Vandercomb, 2 Leach 708, 720, 168 Eng. Rep. 455, 461 (Crown 1796), it adopted the "same evidence" test, which provided little protection from multiple prosecution:

"[U]nless the first indictment were such as the prisoner might have been convicted upon by proof of the facts contained in the second indictment, an acquittal on the first indictment can be no bar to the second."

The "same evidence" test of "same offence" was soon followed by a majority of American jurisdictions, but its deficiencies are obvious. It does not enforce but virtually annuls the constitutional guarantee. For example, where a single criminal episode involves several victims, under the "same evidence" test a separate prosecution may be brought as to each. . . .

The "same evidence" test permits multiple prosecutions where a single transaction is divisible into chronologically discrete crimes ... (e.g., each of 75 poker hands a separate "offense"). Even a single criminal act may lead to multiple prosecutions if it is viewed from the perspectives of different statutes.... Given the tendency of modern criminal legislation to divide the phases of a criminal transaction into numerous separate crimes, the opportunities for multiple prosecutions for an essentially unitary criminal episode are frightening. And given our tradition of virtually unreviewable prosecutorial discretion concerning the initiation and scope of a criminal prosecution, the potentialities for abuse inherent in the "same evidence" test are simply intolerable.

The "same evidence" test is not constitutionally required. It was first expounded *after* the adoption of the Fifth Amendment, and ... had never been squarely held by this Court to be the required construction of the constitutional phrase "same offence" in a case involving multiple trials; indeed, in that context it has been rejected....

The "same evidence" test may once have been defensible at English common law, which, for reasons peculiar to English criminal procedure, severely restricted the power of prosecutors to combine several charges in a single trial. In vivid contrast, American criminal procedure generally allows a prosecutor freedom, subject to judicial control, to prosecute a person at one trial for all the crimes arising out of a single criminal transaction.

In my view, the Double Jeopardy Clause requires the prosecution, except in most limited circumstances, to join at one trial all the charges against a defendant that grow out of a single criminal act, occurrence, episode, or transaction. This "same transaction" test of "same offence" not only enforces the ancient prohibition against vexatious multiple prosecutions embodied in the Double Jeopardy Clause, but responds as well to the increasingly widespread recognition that the consolidation in one lawsuit of all issues arising out of a single transaction or occurrence best promotes justice, economy, and convenience. Modern rules of criminal and civil procedure reflect this recognition.

... Although in 1935 the American Law Institute adopted the "same evidence" test, it has since replaced it with the "same transaction" test. England, too, has abandoned its surviving rules against joinder of charges

and has adopted the "same transaction" test. The Federal Rules of Criminal Procedure liberally encourage the joining of parties and charges in a single trial. Rule 8(a) provides for joinder of charges that are similar in character, or arise from the same transaction or from connected transactions or form part of a common scheme or plan. Rule 8(b) provides for joinder of defendants. Rule 13 provides for joinder of separate indictments or informations in a single trial where the offenses alleged could have been included in one indictment or information. These rules represent considered modern thought concerning the proper structuring of criminal litigation.

* * *

... Some flexibility in the structuring of criminal litigation is also desirable and consistent with our traditions. But the Double Jeopardy Clause stands as a constitutional barrier against possible tyranny by the overzealous prosecutor. The considerations of justice, economy, and convenience that have propelled the movement for consolidation of civil cases apply with even greater force in the criminal context because of the constitutional principle that no man shall be vexed more than once by trial for the same offense. Yet, if the Double Jeopardy Clause were interpreted by this Court to incorporate the "same evidence" test, criminal defendants would have less protection from multiple trials than civil defendants. This anomaly would be intolerable....

* * *

... Correction of the abuse of criminal process should not in any event be made to depend on the availability of collateral estoppel. Abuse of the criminal process is foremost among the feared evils that led to the inclusion of the Double Jeopardy Clause in the Bill of Rights. That evil will be most effectively avoided, and the Clause can thus best serve its worthy ends, if "same offence" is construed to embody the "same transaction" standard. Then both federal and state prosecutors will be prohibited from mounting successive prosecutions for offenses growing out of the same criminal episode, at least in the absence of a showing of unavoidable necessity for successive prosecutions in the particular case.

Mr. Chief Justice BURGER, dissenting.

The Fifth Amendment to the Constitution of the United States provides in part: "nor shall any person be subject for the same offence to be twice put in jeopardy of life or limb...." Nothing in the language or gloss previously placed on this provision of the Fifth Amendment remotely justifies the treatment that the Court today accords to the collateral-estoppel doctrine. Nothing in the purpose of the authors of the Constitution commands or even justifies what the Court decides today; this is truly a case of expanding a sound basic principle beyond the bounds—or needs—of its rational and legitimate objectives to preclude harassment of an accused.

* * *

The concept of double jeopardy and our firm constitutional commitment is against repeated trials "for the *same offence*." This Court, like most American jurisdictions, has expanded that part of the Constitution into a "same evidence" test. For example, in Blockburger v. United States, 284 U.S. 299, 304 (1932), it was stated, so far as here relevant, that "the test to be applied to determine whether there are two offenses or only one, is whether each provision (i.e., each charge) requires *proof of a fact which the other does not."*

Clearly and beyond dispute the charge against Ashe in the second trial required proof of a fact—robbery of Roberts—which the charge involving Knight did not. The Court, therefore, has had to reach out far beyond the accepted offense-defining rule to reach its decision in this case. What it has done is to superimpose on the same-evidence test a new and novel collateral-estoppel gloss.

The majority rests its holding in part on a series of cases ... which did not involve constitutional double jeopardy but applied collateral estoppel as developed in civil litigation to federal criminal prosecutions as a matter of this Court's supervisory power over the federal court system. The Court now finds the federal collateral estoppel rule to be an "ingredient" of the Fifth Amendment guarantee against double jeopardy and applies it to the States through the Fourteenth Amendment. This is an ingredient that eluded judges and justices for nearly two centuries.

The collateral-estoppel concept—originally a product only of civil litigation—is a strange mutant as it is transformed to control this criminal case. In civil cases the doctrine was justified as conserving judicial resources as well as those of the parties to the actions and additionally as providing the finality needed to plan for the future. It ordinarily applies to parties on each side of the litigation who have the same interest as or who are identical with the parties in the initial litigation. Here the complainant in the second trial is not the same as in the first even though the State is a party in both cases. Very properly, in criminal cases, finality and conservation of private, public, and judicial resources are lesser values than in civil litigation. Also, courts that have applied the collateral-estoppel concept to criminal actions would certainly not apply it to *both* parties, as is true in civil cases, i.e., here, if Ashe had been convicted at the first trial, presumably no court would then hold that he was thereby foreclosed from litigating the identification issue at the second trial.

Perhaps, then, it comes as no surprise to find that the only expressed rationale for the majority's decision is that Ashe has "run the gantlet" once before. This is not a doctrine of the law or legal reasoning but a colorful and graphic phrase, which, as used originally in an opinion of the Court written by Mr. Justice Black, was intended to mean something entirely different. The full phrase is "run the gantlet once *on that charge...*" ... found in Green v. United States, 355 U.S. 184, 190 (1957), where no question of multiple crimes against multiple victims was involved. Green, having been found guilty of second degree murder on a charge of first degree, secured a new trial. This Court held nothing more than that Green, once put in jeopardy—once having "run the gantlet ... on *that charge"*—of first degree murder, could not be compelled to defend against that charge again on retrial.

Today's step in this area of constitutional law ought not be taken on no more basis that casual reliance on the "gantlet" phrase lifted out of the context in which it was originally used. This is decision by slogan.

Some commentators have concluded that the harassment inherent in standing trial a second time is a sufficient reason for use of collateral estoppel in criminal trials. If the Court is today relying on a harassment concept to superimpose a new brand of collateral-estoppel gloss on the "same evidence" test, there is a short answer; this case does not remotely suggest harassment of an accused who robbed six victims and the harassment aspect does not rise to constitutional levels.

Finally, the majority's opinion tells us "that the rule of collateral estoppel in criminal cases is not to be applied with the hypertechnical and archaic approach of a 19th century pleading book, but with realism and rationality." ... With deference I am bound to pose the question: what is reasonable and rational about holding that an acquittal of Ashe for robbing Knight bars a trial for robbing Roberts? To borrow a phrase from the Court's opinion, what could conceivably be more "hypertechnical and archaic" and more like the stilted formalisms of 17th and 18th century common-law England, than to stretch jeopardy for robbing Knight into jeopardy for robbing Roberts?

After examining the facts of this case the Court concludes that the first jury must have concluded that Ashe was not one of the robbers—that he was not present at the time. Also, since the second jury necessarily reached its decision by finding he was present, the collateral-estoppel doctrine applies....

... Even the facts in this case, which the Court's opinion considers to "lead to but one conclusion," are susceptible of an interpretation that the first jury did not base its acquittal on the identity ground which the Court finds so compelling. The Court bases its holding on sheer "guesswork," which should have no place particularly in our review of state convictions by way of habeas corpus....

* * *

The essence of Mr. Justice Brennan's concurrence is that this was all one transaction, one episode, or, if I may so characterize it, one frolic, and, hence, only one crime. His approach, like that taken by the Court, totally overlooks the significance of there being *six entirely separate charges of robbery* against six individuals.

This "single frolic" concept is not a novel notion; it has been urged in various courts including this Court. One of the theses underlying the "single frolic" notion is that the criminal episode is "indivisible." The short answer to that is that to the victims, the criminal conduct is readily divisible and intensely personal; each offense is an offense against *a person*. For me it demeans the dignity of the human personality and individuality to talk of "a single transaction" in the context of six separate assaults on six individuals.

No court that elevates the individual rights and human dignity of the accused to a high place—as we should—ought to be so casual as to treat the victims as a single homogenized lump of human clay. I would grant the dignity of individual status to the victims as much as to those accused, not more but surely no less.

If it be suggested that multiple crimes can be separately punished but must be collectively tried, one can point to the firm trend in the law to allow severance of defendants and offenses into separate trials so as to avoid possible prejudice of one criminal act or of the conduct of one defendant to "spill over" on another.

What the Court holds today must be related to its impact on crimes more serious than ordinary house-breaking, followed by physical assault on six men and robbery of all of them. To understand its full impact we must view the holding in the context of four men who break and enter, rob, and then kill six victims. The concurrence tells us that unless all the crimes are joined in one trial the alleged killers cannot be tried for more than one of the killings even if the evidence is that they personally killed two, three, or more of the victims. Or alter the crime to four men breaking into a college dormitory and assaulting six girls. What the Court is holding is, in effect, that the second and third and fourth criminal acts are "free," unless the accused is tried for the multiple crimes in a single trial—something defendants frantically use every legal device to avoid, and often succeed in avoiding. This is the reality of what the Court holds today; it does not make good sense and it cannot make good law.

I therefore join with the four courts that have found no double jeopardy in this case.

* * *

Comments

1. As noted by Mr. Justice Stewart, the facts in *Ashe* paralleled those in the 1958 case of *Hoag* v. *New Jersey*, 356 U.S. 464. In *Hoag*, however, the defendant chose to challenge his second prosecution not by claiming violation of the federal double jeopardy guarantee, but rather by raising the question of whether the New Jersey procedure denied him "fundamental fairness" in violation of the Due Process Clause of the Fourteenth Amendment. The Court found that the procedure was not violative of due process under fundamental fairness standards and, hence, refused to reverse the conviction. The latter line of attack was necessary in *Hoag* because the Supreme Court had not yet applied the double jeopardy provision of the Fifth Amendment to the states via the Fourteenth Amendment. However, during the 12-year interim between *Hoag* and *Ashe,* the Court made the Double Jeopardy Clause applicable to the states in *Benton* v. *Maryland,* 395 U.S. 784 (1969) (Chapter Three, § 3.04).

2. It should be noted that *Benton* v. *Maryland* did not pose double jeopardy problems for any other states because all except Maryland had already provided their citizens with some form of double jeopardy protection. Forty-five states had done so by way of constitutional provisions; Massachusetts and Vermont by state statutes; and Connecticut and North Carolina by judicial decisions. See Ala. Const. art. I, § 9; Alas. Const. art. I, § 9; Ariz. Const. art. 2, § 10; Ark. Const. art. 2, § 8; Cal. Const. art. I, § 13; Colo. Const. art. II, § 18; Del. Const. art. I, § 8; Fla. Const. art. I, § 9; Ga. Const. § 2-108; Hawaii Const. art. I, § 8; Idaho Const. art. I, § 13; Ill. Const. art. I, § 10; Ind. Const. art. I, § 14; Iowa Const. art. I, § 12; Kan. Const. Bill of Rights, § 10; Ky. Const. § 13; La. Const. art. I, § 9; Me. Const. art. I, § 8; Mich. Const. art. I, § 15; Minn. Const. art. I, § 7; Miss. Const. art. 3, § 22; Mo. Const. art. I, § 19; Mont. Const. art. III, § 18; Neb. Const. art. I, § 12; Nev. Const. art. I, § 8; N.H. Const. pt. 1, art. 16; N.J. Const. art. I, § 11; N.M. Const. art. II, § 15; N.Y. Const. art. I, § 6; N.D. Const. art. I, § 13; Ohio Const. art. I, § 10; Okla. Const. art. 2, § 21; Ore. Const. art. I, § 12; Pa. Const. art. 1, § 10; R.I. Const. amend. XXXIX, § 1; S.C. Const. art. I, § 17 and art. XVI, § 8; S.D. Const. art. VI, § 9; Tenn. Const. art. I, § 10; Tex. Const. art. I, § 14; Utah Const. art. I, § 12; Va. Const. art. I, § 8; Wash. Const. art. 1, § 9; W.Va. Const. art. 3, § 5; Wis. Const. art. I, § 8; Wyo. Const. art. 1, § 11. See also Mass. Gen. Laws Ann. ch. 265, § 5 and ch. 277, § 75 (1958); Vt. Stat. Ann. tit. 13 §§ 6556-57 (1947). The pertinent Connecticut and North Carolina cases are *State* v. *Vincent,* 197 A.2d 79 (Conn. Super. Ct. 1961) and *Kohlfuss* v. *Warden,* 183 A.2d 626 (Conn. 1962); and *State* v. *Crocker,* 80 S.E.2d 243 (N.C. 1954).

3. *Collateral estoppel* is an old common law, civil law concept designed to give finality to litigated issues. It is closely related to another concept, *res judicata,* which, simply stated, means that if a court decides a case so that an issue is decided on its merits, no new lawsuit on the same issue can be brought by the parties involved. Collateral estoppel means that a party may be stopped from asserting claims *(estoppel)* in one lawsuit that have been

decided in a different, prior, proceeding. Thus, if a question of ultimate fact has been decided in one proceeding, that issue may not be relitigated between the same parties in a new lawsuit. See Restatement (Second) of Judgments § 68 (Tent. Draft No. 1, 1973). See also 46 Am. Jur. 2d *Judgments* § 397 (1969). One of the earliest cases in which the Supreme Court discussed the concept of collateral estoppel (in its civil context) was *Cromwell* v. *County of Sac,* 94 U.S. 351 (1876). Mr. Justice Field delivered the opinion of the Supreme Court, noting that:

"... there is a difference between the effect of a judgment as a bar or estoppel against the prosecution of a *second action* upon the *same claim* or demand, and its effect as an estoppel in another action *between the same parties upon a different claim* or cause of action. In the former case, the judgment, if rendered upon the merits, constitutes an absolute bar to a subsequent action. It is a finality as to the claim or demand in controversy, concluding parties and those in privity with them, not only as to every matter which was offered and received to sustain or defeat the claim or demand, but as to any other admissible matter which might have been offered for that purpose.... But where the second action between the same parties is upon a different claim or demand, the judgment in the prior action operates as an estoppel only as to those matters in issue or points controverted, upon the determination of which the finding or verdict was rendered. In all cases, therefore, where it is sought to apply the estoppel of a judgment rendered upon one cause of action to matters arising in a suit upon a different cause of action, the inquiry must always be as to the point or question *actually litigated and determined* in the original action...," at 352–353 (emphasis added).

The Court made it clear in *Cromwell,* supra, that the concept of collateral estoppel embraced the three basic requirements that (1) the second litigation involve the *same parties,* (2) the second action rest upon the *same claim,* and (3) the precise point or question in the second action have been *actually litigated and determined* in the previous lawsuit. See also *Russell* v. *Place,* 94 U.S. 606 (1876). Actually, there is a fourth ingredient that is commonly recognized as part of the civil law concept of collateral estoppel; namely, *mutuality of estoppel,* which requires that "a judgment which is not conclusive as to facts and law as against a party shall not be so considered as to his adversary." *Kirby* v. *Pennsylvania R.R.,* 188 F.2d 793, 797 (3rd Cir. 1951).

In holding that the civil law doctrine was applicable to criminal cases, a majority of the Supreme Court in *Ashe* concluded that collateral estoppel is a part of the Fifth Amendment's guarantee against double jeopardy. Such a determination is interesting in light of the facts that (1) some lower federal courts had previously held collateral estoppel and double jeopardy to be two separate and distinct concepts (see, e.g., *Cosgrove* v. *United States,* 224 F.2d 146 [9th Cir. 1955], and *United States* v. *Kramer,* 289 F.2d 909 [2nd Cir. 1961]); and (2) the Supreme Court itself had earlier refused to consider collateral estoppel in the context of criminal due process in *Hoag* v. *New Jersey,* 356 U.S. at 471 (1958). For more on this issue, see *Collateral Estoppel in Criminal Cases — a Supplement to the Double Jeopardy Protection,* 21 Rutgers L. Rev. 274; Pattinson, *Double Jeopardy and Collateral Estoppel,* 4 Crim. L. Bull. 406 (1968); Schaefer, *Unresolved Issues in the Law of Double Jeopardy: Waller and Ashe,* 58 Cal. L. Rev. 391 (1970); *Ashe* v. *Swenson: A New Look at Double Jeopardy,* 7 Tulsa L.J. 68 (1971); *Collateral Estoppel: Its Application and Misapplication,* 29 Wash. & Lee L. Rev. 100 (1972).

4. The majority in *Ashe* chose to "modify" the civil law concept of collateral estoppel since they did not believe all of its basic ingredients were applicable to the criminal process. Although the basic requirements of same parties and same claim were retained, the Court rejected the so-called mutuality requirement (see, e.g., *Simpson* v. *Florida,* 403 U.S. 384, 386 [1971], "[In Ashe] we specifically noted that 'mutuality' was not an ingredient of the collateral estoppel rule imposed ... upon the States.") In addition, the requirement that the *precise* point or question presented in the second litigation have been *actually litigated and determined* in the first action was supplanted by one grounded upon "realism and rationality," i.e., "collateral estoppel in criminal cases is not to be applied with the hypertechnical approach of [the] 19th century ... but ... a court [should] 'conclude whether a rational jury could have grounded its verdict upon an issue other than that which the defendant seeks to foreclose from consideration.'" Applying these principles, a majority of the Court in *Ashe* held that if the defendant was not guilty of robbing the first victim, the jury must have found that he did not rob the second victim—an "implied acquittal." Which is the more convincing view in *Ashe,* that of the majority or the dissent of Chief Justice Burger?

    Under the "same evidence" test referred to by the Court, if an offense charged in a second trial is in substance the same (both in law and in fact) as the offense charged in the first trial, jeopardy attaches and the defendant may not be retried for that offense. However, when a defendant commits two separate and distinct crimes, an acquittal for one offense does not bar a trial for the second offense. Most jurisdictions follow the "same evidence" test in determining whether a subsequent trial is barred by the Double Jeopardy Clause. Under the "same transaction" test, if an offense charged in a second trial was committed as a part of the same transaction that was the basis for the first prosecution, both offenses must be regarded as the same for purposes of double jeopardy. The operation and application of the doctrine of collateral estoppel and the "same evidence" versus the "same transaction" tests have been a source of confusion because of the absence of Supreme Court decisions in this complicated area of the law.

5. In *Ciucci* v. *Illinois,* 356 U.S. 571 (1958), the defendant was charged in four separate indictments with the murder of his wife and three children on a single occasion. In three successive trials, the defendant was found guilty of the first degree murder of his wife and children. At each trial the prosecutor introduced into evidence details of all four deaths. At the first two trials, involving the deaths of the wife and one of the children, the jury fixed the defendant's penalty at 20 and 45 years' imprisonment respectively. At the third trial, involving the death of the second child, the penalty was fixed at death. The United States Supreme Court affirmed, finding no fundamental unfairness or denial of due process.

Newspapers had reported that the prosecutor was determined to prosecute the defendant until a death sentence was obtained. Because the newspaper reports were not a part of the record, a majority of the justices were unwilling to examine the motives of the prosecutor. What effect, if any, does *Ashe* have on the *Ciucci* decision?

6. Following *Ashe,* the Supreme Court has reversed convictions on collateral estoppel grounds. In *Harris* v. *Washington,* 404 U.S. 55 (1971), the defendant was charged with mailing a bomb that exploded in the residence of Ralph Burdick. The explosion killed Burdick and the defendant's infant son, Mark Harris. The defendant was tried in a Washington state court for the murder of Ralph Burdick and was acquitted by the jury. Thereafter, the defendant was rearrested for the murder of his son, Mark Harris. The Washington Supreme Court rejected the defendant's claims of double jeopardy and collateral estoppel. The United States Supreme Court, in a per curiam decision, reversed, holding that the jury that acquitted the defendant in the first trial had already decided the ultimate issue—whether Harris was the person who mailed the bomb—and that subsequent prosecution was thus barred on the grounds of double jeopardy and collateral estoppel.

7. In *Simpson* v. *Florida,* 403 U.S. 384 (1971), two armed men robbed the manager and a customer in a store. Simpson was tried and convicted by a jury of the armed robbery of the store manager, but the conviction was reversed on appeal because of erroneous instructions to the jury by the trial court. Simpson was retried on the same charge and acquitted. Subsequently, Simpson was charged with the robbery of the customer. His claim of double jeopardy was overruled by the trial court and a jury convicted him of armed robbery. The Florida Courts denied relief. On certiorari, the United States Supreme Court, citing *Ashe* v. *Swenson,* vacated and remanded the case back to the Florida courts. In a per curiam opinion, the Court noted that unless the jury that acquitted the defendant of armed robbery of the store manager could have acquitted him for reasons other than identity, the Double Jeopardy Clause precluded a subsequent trial for the robbery of the customer. In other words, if the sole disputed issue at both trials was the identity of the robber, the second trial was an impermissible violation of the Double Jeopardy Clause.

8. In *Turner* v. *Arkansas,* 407 U.S. 366 (1972), the defendant was tried for the robbery and murder of Larry Yates. A jury returned a general verdict of not guilty. Subsequently, an Arkansas county grand jury indicted the defendant for the robbery, but not the murder, of the same decedent, Yates. Turner's claim of double jeopardy was rejected by the Arkansas courts. On certiorari, the United States Supreme Court reversed and remanded, holding that *Ashe* v. *Swenson* precluded a trial for the robbery charge since the jury that acquitted Turner of murder must have concluded that he was not present at the scene of the murder and robbery. To prosecute Turner for robbery would be to relitigate an issue previously decided by a jury, and the state was estopped on double jeopardy grounds from retrying the defendant under these circumstances.

9. Some recent lower federal and state court decisions involving the doctrine of collateral estoppel include: *Tang* v. *Aetna Life Insur-*

ance Co., 523 F.2d 811 (9th Cir. 1975) (Taiwan court's determination that defendant was sane and was guilty of the California murder of his wife did not give rise to collateral estoppel in the United States regarding defendant's claim, for insurance purposes, that he was insane at the time of the killing); *State* v. *Tanton,* 536 P.2d 269 (N. Mex. 1975) (motorist's drunk driving conviction arising out of his involvement in a fatal accident does not bar, on double jeopardy grounds, a subsequent prosecution for vehicular homicide under the "same evidence" test); *Standlee* v. *Rhay,* 403 F. Supp. 1247 (E.D. Wash. 1975) (parolee acquitted of a new criminal offense cannot be subjected to revocation proceedings based on the facts that gave rise to the criminal charge); *Di Giangiemo* v. *Regan,* 528 F.2d 1262 (2nd Cir. 1975) (granting of a defendant's constitutionally based suppression motion collaterally estops the state from introducing the same evidence at a subsequent trial before a different court); *State* v. *Briggs,* 533 S.W. 2d 290 (Tenn. 1976) (under the "same evidence" test, defendant who commits murder during the course of a robbery can be convicted for both the murder and the robbery), overruling *Acres* v. *State,* 484 S.W. 2d 534 (1972); *Copening* v. *United States,* 353 A.2d 305 (D.C. App. 1976) (fact that jury acquitted a defendant of carrying an unlicensed firearm does not collaterally estop judge from finding him guilty of violating two police regulations based on the same evidence); *Farina* v. *District Court,* 553 P.2d 394 (Col. 1976) (mental hospital patient who was committed after being found not guilty by reason of insanity in two counties on two sets of criminal charges held entitled to benefit of collateral estoppel for purposes of obtaining his release from the institution when the jury in one county determined that he was competent and entitled to be released); (see also *Stockton* v. *State,* 509 P.2d 153 [1973]); *Thomas* v. *State,* 361 A.2d 138 (Md. 1976) (defendant's conviction of assault with intent to commit murder does not bar his later trial for second degree murder after the victim died); *United States* v. *Casper,* 541 F.2d 1275 (8th Cir. 1976) (collateral estoppel does not extend to rulings on law, so that defendants are not entitled to benefits of favorable ruling in another prosecution); *State* v. *Lordan,* 363 A.2d 201 (N.H. 1976) (prosecutor dissatisfied with the sentences imposed on a defendant who pleaded guilty to certain charges may not bring in another indictment on new charges arising out of the same transaction); *Crampton* v. *54-A District Judge,* 245 N.W.2d 28 (Mich. 1976) (under "same transaction" test, successive prosecutions are forbidden if the offenses are part of the same criminal episode and involve laws intended to prevent the same harm or evil); *People* v. *Mordican,* 356 N.E.2d 71 (Ill. 1976) (defendant whose pretrial motion to suppress evidence on Fourth Amendment grounds was denied but who was acquitted at trial held not collaterally estopped from raising the same search and seizure issue at a subsequent armed robbery trial) (see also *People* v. *Hopkins,* 56 Ill. 2d 1 [1972], and *People* v. *Armstrong,* 56 Ill. 2d 159 [1973]); *Harris* v. *State,* 555 P.2d 76 (Okla. Ct. Crim. App. 1976) (defendant already convicted of felony-murder arising from store hold-up not barred on double jeopardy grounds from being tried on the robbery charge); *Douthit* v. *Estelle,* 540 F.2d 800 (5th Cir. 1976) (fact that defendant who took a female on a three-county trip and subjected her to numerous sexual assaults was acquitted of rape in one county does not bar prosecution for sexual assault in another county); *Davis* v. *Commonwealth*, 545 S.W.2d 644 (Ky. 1976) (defendant who picked up girl in County A and had sexual intercourse with her in County B held not protected against prosecution for rape in County B after being acquitted in County A of detaining her against her will).

D. REPROSECUTION FOLLOWING A MISTRIAL

Absence of a Key Witness

DOWNUM v. UNITED STATES

Supreme Court of the United States, 1963
372 U.S. 734, 83 S. Ct. 1033, 10 L. Ed. 2d 100

Raymond Downum was indicted for stealing from the mails and forging and uttering stolen checks in violation of federal laws. During the prosecution, the case was called, both sides announced ready, and a jury was selected and sworn and instructed to return that afternoon. However, the prosecution asked that the jury be discharged because its key witness had not yet been found. Over the defendant's objection, the trial judge discharged the jury. Two days later a second jury was impaneled, which found Downum guilty. Downum appealed his conviction, but the United States Court of Appeals (5th Cir.) affirmed, holding that the impaneling of the second jury did not subject Downum to double jeopardy. The United States Supreme Court granted certiorari.

Mr. Justice DOUGLAS delivered the opinion of the Court.

* * *

...There are occasions when a second trial may be had although the jury impaneled for the first trial was discharged without reaching a verdict and without the defendant's consent. The classic example is a mistrial because the jury is unable to agree.... Discovery by the judge during a trial that a member or members of the jury were biased pro or con one side has been held to warrant discharge of the jury and direction of a new trial.... At times the valued right of a defendant to have his trial completed by the particular tribunal summoned to sit in judgment on him may be subordinated to the public interest—when there is an imperious necessity to do so.... Differences have arisen as to the application of the principle.... Harassment of an accused by successive prosecutions or declaration of a mistrial so

as to afford the prosecution a more favorable opportunity to convict are examples when jeopardy attaches.... But those extreme cases do not mark the limits of the guarantee. The discretion to discharge the jury before it has reached a verdict is to be exercised "only in very extraordinary and striking circumstances."... For the prohibition of the Double Jeopardy Clause is "not against being twice punished; but against being twice put in jeopardy."...

The jury first selected to try petitioner and sworn was discharged because a prosecution witness had not been served with a summons and because no other arrangements had been made to assure his presence. That witness was essential only for two of the six counts concerning petitioner. Yet the prosecution opposed petitioner's motion to dismiss those two counts and to proceed with a trial on the other four counts—a motion the court denied. Here ... we refuse to say that the absence of witnesses "can never justify discontinuance of a trial." Each case must turn on its facts. On this record, however, we think what was said in Cornero v. United States (9th Cir.) 48 F.2d 69 . . . , states the governing principle. There a trial was first continued because prosecution witnesses were not present, and when they had not been found at the time the case was again called, the jury was discharged. A plea of double jeopardy was sustained when a second jury was selected, the court saying:

"The fact is that, when the district attorney impaneled the jury without first ascertaining whether or not his witnesses were present, he took a chance. While their absence might have justified a continuance of the case in view of the fact that they were under bond to appear at that time and place, the question presented here is entirely different from that involved in the exercise of the sound discretion of the trial court in granting a continuance in furtherance of jus-

tice. The situation presented is simply one where the district attorney entered upon the trial of the case without sufficient evidence to convict. This does not take the case out of the rule with reference to former jeopardy. There is no difference in principle between a discovery by the district attorney immediately after the jury was impaneled that his evidence was insufficient and a discovery after he had called some or all of his witnesses."

That view, which has some support in the authorities, is in our view the correct one. We resolve any doubt "in favor of the liberty of the citizen, rather than exercise what would be an unlimited, uncertain, and arbitrary judicial discretion."

Reversed.

[Mr. Justice CLARK, joined by Mr. Justice HARLAN, Mr. Justice STEWART, and Mr. Justice WHITE, dissented.]

"Manifest Necessity" and Defective Indictments

ILLINOIS v. SOMERVILLE

Supreme Court of the United States, 1973
410 U.S. 458, 93 S. Ct. 1066, 35 L. Ed. 2d 425

Somerville was indicted by an Illinois grand jury for the crime of theft. The case was called for trial and a jury was impaneled and sworn. The following day and before any evidence had been presented, the prosecutor realized that the indictment was fatally defective under Illinois law as it failed to state an element of the crime of theft. Under Illinois law this type of defect could not be cured by amendment. The effect of Illinois procedure and substantive law was that the defect could not be waived by the defendant's failure to object and could be asserted on appeal in the event of a final judgment of conviction. The prosecutor asked for a mistrial, which was granted by the trial court. Two days later, Somerville was indicted a second time and over his claim of double jeopardy a second trial was commenced. The jury found Somerville guilty and he was sentenced to prison. The Illinois courts upheld the conviction. The United States District Court (N.D. Ill.) dismissed his petition for habeas corpus, but the United States Court of Appeals (7th Cir.) reversed. The United States Supreme Court granted certiorari.

Mr. Justice REHNQUIST delivered the opinion of the Court.

We must here decide whether declaration of a mistrial over the defendant's objection,

because the trial court concluded that the indictment was insufficient to charge a crime, necessarily prevents a State from subsequently trying the defendant under a valid indictment. We hold that the mistrial met the "manifest necessity" requirement of our cases, since the trial court could reasonably have concluded that the "ends of public justice" would be defeated by having allowed the trial to continue. Therefore, the Double Jeopardy Clause of the Fifth Amendment, made applicable to the States through the Due Process Clause of the Fourteenth Amendment . . . did not bar retrial under a valid indictment.

* * *

The fountainhead decision construing the Double Jeopardy Clause in the context of a declaration of a mistrial over a defendant's objection is United States v. Perez, 9 Wheat. 579, 6 L. Ed. 165 (1824). Mr. Justice Story, writing for a unanimous Court, set forth the standards for determining whether a retrial, following a declaration of a mistrial over a defendant's objection, constitutes double jeopardy within the meaning of the Fifth Amendment. In holding that the failure of the jury to agree on a verdict of either acquittal or conviction did not bar retrial of the defendant, Mr. Justice Story wrote:

"We think, that in all cases of this nature, the law has invested Courts of justice with the authority to discharge a jury from giving any verdict, whenever, in their opinion, taking all the circumstances into consideration, there is a manifest necessity for the act, or the ends of public justice would otherwise be defeated. They are to exercise a sound discretion on the subject; and it is impossible to define all the circumstances which would render it proper to interfere. To be sure, the power ought to be used with the greatest caution, under urgent circumstances, and for very plain and obvious causes; and, in capital cases especially, Courts should be extremely careful how they interfere with any of the chances of life, in favour of the prisoner. But, after all, they have the right to order the discharge; and the security which the public have for the faithful, sound, and conscientious exercise of this discretion, rests, in this, as in other cases, upon the responsibility of the Judges, under their oaths of office."

This formulation, consistently adhered to by this Court in subsequent decisions, abjures the application of any mechanical formula by which to judge the propriety of declaring a mistrial in the varying and often unique situations arising during the course of a criminal trial. The broad discretion reserved to the trial judge in such circumstances has been consistently reiterated in decisions of this Court. . . .

* * *

. . . In Gori v. United States, 367 U.S. 364, (1961), the Court again underscored the breadth of a trial judge's discretion, and the reasons therefore, to declare a mistrial.

"Where, for reasons deemed compelling by the trial judge, who is best situated intelligently to make such a decision, the ends of substantial justice cannot be attained without discontinuing the trial, a mistrial may be declared without the defendant's consent and even over his objection, and he may be retried consistently with the Fifth Amendment."

* * *

In reviewing the propriety of the trial judge's exercise of his discretion, this Court, following the counsel of Mr. Justice Story, has scrutinized the action to determine whether, in the context of that particular trial, the declaration of a mistrial was dictated by "manifest necessity" or the "ends of public justice." The interests of the public in seeing that a criminal prosecution proceed to verdict, either of acquittal or conviction, need not be forsaken by the formulation or application of rigid rules that necessarily preclude the vindication of that interest. This consideration, whether termed the "ends of public justice" . . . or, more precisely, "the public's interest in fair trials designed to end in just judgments" . . . has not been disregarded by this Court.

In United States v. Perez . . . this Court held that "manifest necessity" justified the discharge of juries unable to reach verdicts, and, therefore, the Double Jeopardy Clause did not bar retrial. . . . In Simmons v. United States, 142 U.S. 148 (1891), a trial judge dismissed the jury, over defendant's objection, because one of the jurors had been acquainted with the defendant, and, therefore, was probably prejudiced against the Government; this Court held that the trial judge properly exercised his power "to prevent the defeat of the ends of public justice." . . . In Thompson v. United States, 155 U.S. 271 (1894), a mistrial was declared after the trial judge learned that one of the jurors was disqualified, he having been a member of the grand jury that indicted the defendant. . . .

While virtually all of the cases turn on the particular facts and thus escape meaningful categorization . . . it is possible to distill from them a general approach, premised on the "public justice" policy enunciated in United States v. Perez, to situations such as that presented by this case. A trial judge properly exercises his discretion to declare a mistrial if an impartial verdict cannot be reached, or if a verdict of conviction could be reached but would have to be reversed on appeal due to an obvious procedural error in the trial. If an error would make reversal on appeal a certainty, it would not serve "the ends of public justice" to require that the Government proceed with its proof when, it it succeeded before the jury, it would automatically be stripped of that success by an appellate court. . . . While the declaration of a mistrial on the basis of a rule or a defective procedure that would lend itself to prosecutorial manipulation would involve an entirely different question . . . such was not the situation in the above cases or in the instant case.

In Downum v. United States . . . this Court, in reversing the convictions on the ground of double jeopardy, emphasized that "[e]ach case must turn on its facts" . . . and held that the second prosecution constituted double jeopardy, because the absence of the witness and the reason therefor did not there justify, in terms of "manifest necessity," the declaration of a mistrial.

In United States v. Jorn, 400 U.S. 470 (1971), the Government called a taxpayer witness in a prosecution for willfully assisting in the preparation of fraudulent income tax returns. Prior to his testimony, defense counsel suggested he be warned of his constitutional right against compulsory self-incrimination. The trial judge warned him of his rights, and the witness stated that he was willing to testify and that the Internal Revenue Service agent who first contacted him warned him of his rights. The trial judge, however, did not believe the witness' declaration that the IRS had so warned him, and refused to allow him to testify until after he had consulted with an attorney. After learning from the Government that the remaining four witnesses were "similarly situated," and after surmising that they, too, had not been properly informed of their rights, the trial judge declared a mistrial to give the witnesses the opportunity to consult with attorneys. In sustaining a plea in bar of double jeopardy to an attempted second trial of the defendant, the plurality opinion of the Court, emphasizing the importance to the defendant of proceeding before the first jury sworn, concluded:

"It is apparent from the record that no consideration was given to the possibility of a trial continuance; indeed, the trial judge acted so abruptly in discharging the jury that, had the prosecutor been disposed to suggest a continuance, or the defendant to object to the discharge of the jury, there would have been no opportunity to do so. When one examines the circumstances surrounding the discharge of this jury, it seems abundantly apparent that the trial judge made no effort to exercise a sound discretion to assure that, taking all the circumstances into account, there was a manifest necessity for the sua sponte declaration of this mistrial. . . . Therefore, we must conclude that in the circumstances of this case, appellee's reprosecution would violate the double jeopardy provision of the Fifth Amendment."

Respondent advances two arguments to support the conclusion that the Double Jeopardy Clause precluded the second trial in the instant case. The first is that since United States v. Ball, 163 U.S. 662 (1896), held that jeopardy obtained even though the indictment upon which the defendant was first acquitted had been defective, and since Downum v. United States, supra, held that jeopardy "attaches" when a jury has been selected and sworn, the Double Jeopardy Clause precluded the State from instituting the second proceeding that resulted in respondent's conviction. Alternatively, respondent argues that our decision in United States v. Jorn, supra, which respondent interprets as narrowly limiting the circumstances in which a mistrial is manifestly necessary, requires affirmance. Emphasizing the " 'valued right to have his trial completed by a particular tribunal,' " . . . respondent contends that the circumstances did not justify depriving him of that right.

Respondent's first contention is precisely the type of rigid, mechanical rule which the

Court has eschewed since the seminal decision in Perez. The major premise of the syllogism—that trial on a defective indictment precludes retrial—is not applicable to the instant case. . . .

. . . Only if jeopardy has attached is a court called upon to determine whether the declaration of a mistrial was required by "manifest necessity" or the "ends of public justice."

We believe that in light of the State's established rules of criminal procedure, the trial judge's declaration of a mistrial was not an abuse of discretion. Since this Court's decision in Benton v. Maryland, . . . federal courts will be confronted with such claims that arise in large measure from the often diverse procedural rules existing in the 50 States. Federal courts should not be quick to conclude that simply because a state procedure does not conform to the corresponding federal statute or rule, it does not serve a legitimate state policy. Last Term, recognizing this fact, we dismissed a writ of certiorari as improvidently granted in a case involving a claim of double jeopardy stemming from the dismissal of an indictment under the "rules of criminal pleading peculiar to" an individual State followed by a retrial under a proper indictment. . . .

In the instant case, the trial judge terminated the proceeding because a defect was found to exist in the indictment that was, as a matter of Illinois law, not curable by amendment. The Illinois courts have held that even after a judgment of conviction has become final, the defendant may be released on habeas corpus, because the defect in the indictment deprives the trial court of "jurisdiction." The rule prohibiting the amendment of all but formal defects in indictments is designed to implement the State's policy of preserving the right of each defendant to insist that a criminal prosecution against him be commenced by the action of a grand jury. The trial judge was faced with a situation similar to those in (other cases) in which a procedural defect might or would preclude the public from either obtaining an impartial verdict or keeping a verdict of conviction if its evidence persuaded the jury. If a mistrial were constitutionally unavailable in situations such as this, the State's policy could only be implemented by conducting a second trial after verdict and reversal on appeal, thus wasting time, energy, and money for all concerned. Here, the trial judge's action was a rational determination designed to implement a legitimate state policy, with no suggestion

that the implementation of that policy in this manner could be manipulated so as to prejudice the defendant. This situation is thus unlike Downum, where the mistrial entailed not only a delay for the defendant, but also operated as a post-jeopardy continuance to allow the prosecution an opportunity to strengthen its case. Here, the delay was minimal, and the mistrial was, under Illinois law, the only way in which a defect in the indictment could be corrected. Given the established standard of discretion set forth in Perez, Gori, and Hunter, we cannot say that the declaration of a mistrial was not required by "manifest necessity" and the "ends of public justice."

Our decision in Jorn, relied upon by the court below and respondent, does not support the opposite conclusion. . . . The Court emphasized that the absence of any manifest need for the mistrial had deprived the defendant of his right to proceed before the first jury, but it did not hold that that right may never be forced to yield, as in this case, to "the public's interest in fair trials designed to end in just judgments." . . .

"The double-jeopardy provision of the Fifth Amendment, however, does not mean that every time a defendant is put to trial before a competent tribunal he is entitled to go free if the trial fails to end in a final judgment. Such a rule would create an insuperable obstacle to the administration of justice in many cases in which there is no semblance of the type of oppressive practices at which the double-jeopardy prohibition is aimed. There may be unforeseeable circumstances that arise during a trial making its completion impossible, such as the failure of a jury to agree on a verdict. In such event the purpose of law to protect society from those guilty of crimes frequently would be frustrated by denying courts power to put the defendant to trial again. And there have been instances where a trial judge has discovered facts during a trial which indicated that one or more members of the jury might be biased against the Government or the defendant. It is settled that the duty of the judge in this event is to discharge the jury and direct a retrial. *What has been said is enough to show that a defendant's valued right to have his trial completed by a particular tribunal must in some instances be subordinated to the public's interest in fair trials designed to end in just judgments.*"

The determination by the trial courts to abort a criminal proceeding where jeopardy has attached is not one to be lightly undertaken, since the interest of the defendant in having his fate determined by the jury first impaneled is itself a weighty one. . . . Nor will the lack of demonstrable additional prejudice preclude the defendant's invocation of the double jeopardy bar in the absence of some important countervailing interest of proper judicial administration. But where the declaration of a mistrial implements a reasonable state policy and aborts a proceeding that at best would have produced a verdict that could have been upset at will by one of the parties, the defendant's interest in proceeding to verdict is outweighed by the competing and equally legitimate demand for public justice.

Reversed.

[Mr. Justice WHITE, with whom Mr. Justice DOUGLAS and Mr. Justice BRENNAN joined, dissented.]

[Mr. Justice MARSHALL also wrote a dissenting opinion.]

When the Defendant Requests a Mistrial

UNITED STATES v. DINITZ

Supreme Court of the United States, 1976
424 U.S. 600, 96 S. Ct. 1075, 47 L. Ed. 2d 267

The facts are stated in the opinion.

Mr. Justice STEWART delivered the opinion of the Court.

The question in this case is whether the Double Jeopardy Clause of the Fifth Amendment was violated by the retrial of the respondent after his original trial had ended in a mistrial granted at his request.

I

The respondent, Nathan Dinitz, was arrested on December 8, 1972, following the return of an indictment charging him with conspiracy to distribute LSD and with distribution of that controlled substance. . . . On the day of his arrest, the respondent retained a lawyer named Meldon to represent him. Meldon appeared with the respondent at his arraignment, filed numerous pretrial motions on his behalf, and was completely responsible for the preparation of the case until shortly before trial. Some five days before the trial was scheduled to begin, the respondent retained another lawyer, Maurice Wagner, to conduct his defense. Wagner had not been admitted to practice before the United States District Court for the Northern District of Florida, but on the first day of the trial the court permitted him to appear *pro hac vice*. In addition to Meldon and Wagner, Fletcher Baldwin, a professor of law at the University of Florida, also appeared on the respondent's behalf.

The jury was selected and sworn on February 14, 1973, and opening statements by counsel began on the following afternoon. The prosecutor's opening statement briefly outlined the testimony that he expected an undercover agent named Steve Cox to give regarding his purchase of LSD from the respondent. Wagner then began his opening statement for the defense. After introducing himself and his cocounsel, Wagner turned to the case against the respondent:

"Mr. Wagner: After working on this case over a period of time it appeared to me that if we would have given nomenclature, if we would have named this case so there could be no question about identifying it in the future, I would have called it The Case—

"Mr. Reed (Asst. U.S. Attorney): Your Honor, we object to personal opinions.

"The Court: Objection sustained. The

purpose of the opening statement is to summarize the facts the evidence will show, state the issues, not to give personal opinions. Proceed, Mr. Wagner.

"Mr. Wagner: Thank you, Your Honor. I call this The Case of the Incredible Witness."

The prosecutor again objected and the judge excused the jury. The judge then warned Wagner that he did not approve of his behavior and cautioned Wagner that he did not want to have to remind him again about the purpose of the opening statement.

Following this initial incident, the trial judge found it necessary twice again to remind Wagner of the purpose of the opening statement and to instruct him to relate "the facts that you expect the evidence to show, the admissible evidence." Later on in his statement, Wagner started to discuss an attempt to extort money from the respondent that had occurred shortly after his arrest. The prosecutor objected and the jury was again excused. Wagner informed the trial judge of some of the details of the extortion attempt and assured the court that he would connect it with the prospective government witness Cox. But it soon became apparent that Wagner had no information linking Cox to the extortion attempt, and the trial judge then excluded Wagner from the trial and ordered him to leave the courthouse.

The judge then asked Meldon if he was prepared to proceed with the trial. Upon learning that Meldon had not discussed the case with the witnesses, the judge gave Meldon until 9:00 the following morning to prepare. Meldon informed the judge that the respondent was "in a quandary because he hired Mr. Wagner to argue the case and he feels he needs more time to obtain outside counsel to argue the case for him." The judge responded that "(y)ou are his counsel and have been" but stated that he would consider the matter "between now and 9:00 o'clock tomorrow morning."

The next morning, Meldon told the judge that the respondent wanted Wagner and not himself or Baldwin to try the case. The judge then set forth three alternative courses that might be followed—(1) a stay or recess pending application to the Court of Appeals to review the propriety of expelling Wagner, (2) continuation of the trial

with Meldon and Baldwin as counsel, or (3) a declaration of a mistrial which would permit the respondent to obtain other counsel. Following a short recess, Meldon moved for a mistrial, stating that, after "full consideration of the situation and an explanation of the alternatives before him, (the respondent) feels that he would move for a mistrial and that this would be in his best interest." The government prosecutor did not oppose the motion. The judge thereupon declared a mistrial, expressing his belief that such a course would serve the interest of justice.

Before his second trial, the respondent moved to dismiss the indictment on the ground that a retrial would violate the Double Jeopardy Clause of the Constitution. This motion was denied. The respondent represented himself at the new trial, and he was convicted by the jury on both the conspiracy and distribution counts. A divided panel of the Court of Appeals for the Fifth Circuit reversed the conviction, holding that the retrial violated the respondent's constitutional right not to be twice put in jeopardy. 492 F.2d 53. The appellate court took the view that the trial judge's exclusion of Wagner and his questioning of Meldon had left the respondent no choice but to move for a mistrial. On that basis, the court concluded that the respondent's request for a mistrial should be ignored and the case should be treated as though the trial judge had declared a mistrial over the objection of the defendant. So viewing the case, the court held that the Double Jeopardy Clause barred the second trial of the respondent, because there had been no manifest necessity requiring the expulsion of Wagner. The Court of Appeals granted rehearing en banc and, by a vote of 8–7, affirmed the decision of the panel. 504 F.2d 854. We granted certiorari to consider the constitutional question thus presented....

II

The Double Jeopardy Clause of the Fifth Amendment protects a defendant in a criminal proceeding against multiple punishments or repeated prosecutions for the same offense.... Underlying this constitutional safeguard is the belief that "the State with all its resources and power should not be allowed to make repeated attempts to convict an individual for an alleged offense, thereby subjecting him to embarrassment, expense and ordeal and compelling him to live in a continuing state of anxiety and insecurity, as well as enhancing the possibility that even though innocent he may be found guilty." Green v. United States, 355 U.S. 184, 187–188 (1957). Where, as here, a mistrial has been declared, the defendant's "valued right to have his trial completed by a particular tribunal" is also implicated. . . .

Since Justice Story's 1824 opinion for the Court in United States v. Perez . . . this Court has held that the question whether under the Double Jeopardy Clause there can be a new trial after a mistrial has been declared without the defendant's request or consent depends on whether "there is a manifest necessity for the (mistrial), or the ends of public justice would otherwise be defeated." . . . Different considerations obtain, however, when the mistrial has been declared at the defendant's request. . . .

The distinction between mistrials declared by the court sua sponte and mistrials granted at the defendant's request or with his consent is wholly consistent with the protections of the Double Jeopardy Clause. Even when judicial or prosecutorial error prejudices a defendant's prospects of securing an acquittal, he may nonetheless desire "to go to the first jury and, perhaps, end the dispute then and there with an acquittal." . . . Our prior decisions recognize the defendant's right to pursue this course in the absence of circumstances of manifest necessity requiring a *sua sponte* judicial declaration of mistrial. But it is evident that when judicial or prosecutorial error seriously prejudices a defendant, he may have little interest in completing the trial and obtaining a verdict from the first jury. The defendant may reasonably conclude that a continuation of the tainted proceeding would result in a conviction followed by a lengthy appeal and, if a reversal is secured, by a second prosecution. In such circumstances, a defendant's mistrial request has objectives not unlike the interests served by the Double Jeopardy Clause—the avoidance of the anxiety, expense, and delay occasioned by multiple prosecutions.

* * *

The Double Jeopardy Clause does protect a defendant against governmental actions intended to provoke mistrial requests and thereby subject defendants to the substantial burdens imposed by multiple prosecutions. It bars retrials where "bad-faith conduct by the judge or prosecutor" threatens the "[h]arassment of an accused by successive prosecutions or declaration of a mistrial so as to afford the prosecution a more favorable opportunity to convict" the defendant. . . .

But here the trial judge's banishment of Wagner from the proceedings was not done in bad faith in order to goad the respondent into requesting a mistrial or to prejudice his prospects for an acquittal. . . .

Under these circumstances we hold that the Court of Appeals erred in finding that the retrial violated the respondent's constitutional right not to be twice put in jeopardy.

Reversed and remanded.

Mr. Chief Justice BURGER, concurring.

I concur fully with Mr. Justice STEWART's opinion for the Court. I add an observation only to emphasize what is plainly implicit in the opinion, i.e., a trial judge's plenary control of the conduct of counsel particularly in relation to addressing the jury.

An opening statement has a narrow purpose and scope. It is to state what evidence will be presented to make it easier for the jurors to understand what is to follow, and to relate parts of the evidence and testimony to the whole; it is not an occasion for argument. To make statements which will not or cannot be supported by proof is, if it relates to significant elements of the case, professional misconduct. Moreover, it is fundamentally unfair to an opposing party to allow an attorney, with the standing and prestige inherent in being an officer of the court, to present to the jury statements not susceptible of proof but intended to influence the jury in reaching a verdict.

A trial judge is under a duty, in order to protect the integrity of the trial, to take prompt and affirmative action to stop such professional misconduct. Here the misconduct of the attorney, Wagner, was not only unprofessional per se but contemptuous in that he defied the court's explicit order.

Far from "overreacting" to the misconduct of Wagner, in my view, the trial judge exercised great restraint in not citing Wagner for contempt then and there.

Mr. Justice BRENNAN, with whom Mr. Justice MARSHALL concurs, dissenting.

The Court's premise is that the mistrial was directed at respondent's request or with his consent. I agree with the Court of Appeals that, for purposes of double jeopardy analysis, it was not, but rather that ". . . the trial judge's response to the conduct of defense counsel deprived Dinitz's motion for a mistrial of its necessary consensual character." Therefore the rule that "a motion by the defendant for mistrial is ordinarily assumed to remove any barrier to reprosecution," United States v. Jorn, 400 U.S. 485 (1971), is inapplicable. Accordingly, I agree that respondent's motion, for the reasons expressed in the panel and en banc opinions of the Court of Appeals, did not remove the bar of double jeopardy to reprosecution in "the extraordinary circumstances of the present case, in which judicial error alone, rather than (respondent's) exercise of any option to stop or go forward, took away his 'valued right to have his trial completed by a particular tribunal.' " . . . I also agree with the holding in the panel opinion that "[i]n view of . . . [the] alternatives which would not affect the ability to continue the trial, we cannot say that there was manifest necessity for the trial judge's actions." . . . I would affirm.

[Mr. Justice STEVENS took no part in the consideration or decision of this case.]

Comments

1. In *Downum* v. *United States,* supra, the Court held that the absence of a key prosecution witness was not a sufficient ground for declaring a mistrial over the objections of the defendant and thereby permitting a retrial. Jeopardy had attached by that point in the proceedings, which precluded a retrial on the same charges. Would the Court have reached a similar result if the defendant had consented to the prosecutor's request for a mistrial? Why would a defendant consent to such a request? Normally, if a defendant requests a mistrial on the grounds of "manifest necessity" (e.g., key defense witness becomes ill), the Double Jeopardy Clause does not bar a retrial.

2. In *Illinois* v. *Somerville,* supra, the prosecutor requested and was granted a mistrial, over the objections of the defendant, because of a defective indictment. The *Downum* case would seem to be controlling; however, a majority of the Supreme Court held that the circumstances in *Sommerville* amounted to a "manifest necessity" warranting a mistrial and that a retrial was not precluded by the Double Jeopardy Clause. Do you agree? The majority opinion focused on the "ends of public justice" to justify its holding that a defendant should not be allowed to escape trial simply because of the prosecutor's error in drafting the indictment. Is this equitable?

3. In *United States* v. *Dinitz,* supra, the Court noted that in most instances, if a defendant requests or consents to a mistrial, the Double Jeopardy Clause is not a bar to a retrial for the same offense. Are there any instances in which a defendant's request for a mistrial would, if granted, bar a retrial? The Court noted that in dismissing the defendant's counsel, the trial judge acted in "good faith." Is the Court suggesting that a trial court's actions necessitating a mistrial *could* preclude a retrial if done with less than honest motives? Suppose the prosecutor intentionally engages in misconduct and the trial court grants the defendant's motion for a

mistrial—can the defendant be retried notwithstanding the prosecution's bad faith?

The Court in *Dinitz* referred to the appearance of counsel *pro hac vice*, which means "for this particular occasion only." This situation occurs most frequently when the defendant has retained counsel who is not a member of the local bar. At the direction of the court, defense counsel is usually permitted to represent the defendant pro hac vice. This allows defense attorneys (e.g., F. Lee Bailey) to represent defendants in many states without first passing a bar examination in each state. The reference by the Court in *Dinitz* to a motion by the trial court *sua sponte*, refers to a judge's own motion without a request from one of the parties.

The Double Jeopardy Clause was applied to juvenile proceedings in *Breed* v. *Jones*, Chapter Eight, § 8.03. Cases involving multiple punishments and double jeopardy are found in Chapter Fourteen.

4. Consider the following problems involving the Double Jeopardy Clause: Can a defendant be tried again after a judge has declared a mistrial in the reasonable but mistaken belief that the prosecution has knowingly withheld evidence favorable to the defendant? See *United States* v. *Sedgwick,* 345 A.2d 465 (D.C. App. 1975) (holding retrial permitted). Can a state appeal a trial court's judgment of acquittal notwithstanding the verdict, which can lead to a reinstatement of the jury's guilty verdict? See *State* v. *Kleinwaks,* 345 A.2d 793 (N.J. 1975) (holding yes). Does a sua sponte mistrial entered early in a criminal trial to protect a defendant against his counsel's apparent incompetence raise a double jeopardy bar to retrial? See *United States* v. *Williams,* 521 F. Supp. 950 (S.D.N.Y. 1976) (permitting retrial). Does a mere mention that a defendant sought a polygraph examination constitute manifest necessity for a mistrial? See *People* v. *Johnson,* 240 N.W.2d 729 (Mich. 1976) (holding no). Is it error for a trial judge to declare a mistrial after defense counsel offered to let the jury question the defendant? See *Strawn* v. *Anderberg,* 332 So. 2d 601 (Fla. 1976) (holding not erroneous). Does the prosecution's intentional use of a false exhibit followed by defendant's request for a mistrial bar a mistrial? See *United States* v. *Kessler,* 530 F.2d 1246 (5th Cir. 1976) (holding no retrial allowed). Does a judge's dismissal of a deadlocked jury without declaring a mistrial bar the state from retrying the defendant? See *State* v. *Spillman,* 553 P.2d 686 (N.M. 1976) (holding yes). Can a defendant be retried under a corrected indictment when the first trial was completed but ended in a dismissal because of a technical flaw in the indictment because of which the defendant requested a mistrial? See *United States* v. *Lee,* 539 F.2d 612 (7th Cir. 1976) (permitting retrial) affirmed, 97 S. Ct. 2141 (1977). Is the Double Jeopardy Clause violated where an alien has been deported on grounds that he had twice been convicted of bank robbery? See *LeTourneur* v. *Immigration and Naturalization Service,* 538 F.2d 1368 (9th Cir. 1976) (holding deportation is not criminal punishment). Does the Double Jeopardy Clause bar a governmental appeal from a directed verdict of acquittal following a hung jury mistrial? See *United States* v. *Martin Linen Supply Co.,* 534 F.2d 585 (5th Cir. 1976) (retrial not permitted), affirmed, 430 U.S. 564 (1977). Does the Double Jeopardy Clause prohibit a second trial if the first prosecution was in a court that lacked jurisdiction to try the offense charged? See *Rogers* v. *State,* 336 So. 2d 1233 (Fla. App. 1976) (permitting retrial).

5. Some recent lower federal and state court decisions involving mistrials, "manifest necessity," and the Double Jeopardy Clause are: *State* v. *DeBaca,* 541 P.2d 634 (N. Mex. App. 1975) (trial court's grant of a mistrial after one juror revealed that her sister-in-law received a telephone call asking about the juror's views on drug abuse held erroneous and not done on the grounds of manifest necessity, which bars retrial) (see also *Russo* v. *Superior Court of New Jersey,* 483 F.2d 7 [3rd Cir. 1973], and *United States* v. *Holland,* 378 F. Supp. 144 [E.D. Pa. 1974]); *United States* v. *Durbin,* 542 F.2d 486 (8th Cir. 1976) (once a defendant has begun serving his sentence, the Double Jeopardy Clause forbids increasing his sentence); *People* v. *LeBlanc,* 354 N.E.2d 10 (Ill. 1976) (jeopardy attaches only at adjudication stage of juvenile proceeding); *People* v. *Bastardo,* 554 P.2d 297 (Colo. 1976) (where court wrongfully declares mistrial, retrial of defendant is barred); *People* v. *Morris,* 245 N.W.2d 126 (Mich. 1976) (second trial following hung jury mistrial does not violate Double Jeopardy Clause); *Jones* v. *State,* 336 So.2d 1172 (Fla. 1976) (increase in sentence after sentence has been partially served may constitute double jeopardy).

6.03 THE PRIVILEGE AGAINST SELF-INCRIMINATION

A. CONFESSIONS AND DUE PROCESS

The Older "Totality of Circumstances" Test

BLACKBURN v. ALABAMA

Supreme Court of the United States, 1960
361 U.S. 199, 80 S. Ct. 274, 4 L. Ed. 2d 242

Jessee Blackburn was tried in an Alabama state court for robbery, found guilty, and sentenced to 20 years' imprisonment. The most damaging evidence against Blackburn was his confession — which he insisted was involuntary. There was substantial evidence that Blackburn was insane and incompetent at the time of the confession. Prior to confessing, he was interrogated for a sustained period of eight to nine hours in a tiny room that was occasionally filled with police officers. None of his friends or relatives were permitted to visit him, and legal counsel was not present. Although signed by Blackburn, the confession was written by a deputy sheriff. Nevertheless, the trial court held the confession to be voluntary. The Alabama Supreme Court denied review, and the United States Supreme Court granted certiorari.

Mr. Chief Justice WARREN delivered the opinion of the Court.

* * *

After according all ... deference to the trial judge's decision ... we are unable to escape the conclusion that Blackburn's confession can fairly be characterized only as involuntary. Consequently the conviction must be set aside, since this Court, in a line of decisions beginning in 1936 with Brown v. Mississippi, 297 U.S. 278, and including cases by now too well known and too numerous to bear citation, has established the principle that the Fourteenth Amendment is grievously breached when an involuntary confession is obtained by state officers and introduced into evidence in a criminal prosecution which culminates in a conviction.

... This Court has recognized that coercion can be mental as well as physical, and that the blood of the accused is not the only hallmark of an unconstitutional inquisition. A number of cases have demonstrated, if demonstration were needed, that the efficiency of the rack and the thumbscrew can be matched, given the proper subject, by more sophisticated modes of "persuasion." A prolonged interrogation of an accused who is ignorant of his rights and who has been cut off from the moral support of friends and relatives is not infrequently an effective technique of terror. Thus the range of inquiry in this type of case must be broad, and this Court has insisted that the judgment in each instance be based upon consideration of "[t]he totality of the circumstances."

It is also established that the Fourteenth Amendment forbids "fundamental unfairness in the use of evidence, whether true or false." ... Consequently, we have rejected the argument that introduction of an involuntary confession is immaterial where other evidence establishes guilt or corroborates the confession.... As important as it is that persons who have committed crimes be convicted, there are considerations which transcend the question of guilt or innocence. Thus, in cases involving involuntary confessions, this Court enforces the strongly felt attitude of our society that important human values are sacrificed where an agency of the government, in the course of securing a conviction, wrings a confession out of an accused against his will. This insistence upon putting the government to the task of proving guilt by means other than inquisition was engendered by historical abuses which are quite familiar....

But neither the likelihood that the confession is untrue nor the preservation of the individual's freedom of will is the sole interest at stake. As we said just last Term, "The abhorrence of society to the use of involuntary confessions ... also turns on the deep-rooted feeling that the police must obey the law while enforcing the law; that in the end

life and liberty can be as much endangered from illegal methods used to convict those thought to be criminals as from the actual criminals themselves." ... Thus, a complex of values underlies the stricture against use by the state of confessions which, by way of convenient shorthand, this Court terms involuntary, and the role played by each in any situation varies according to the particular circumstances of the case.

In the case at bar, the evidence indisputably establishes the strongest probability that Blackburn was insane and incompetent at the time he allegedly confessed. Surely in the present state of our civilization a most basic sense of justice is affronted by the spectacle of incarcerating a human being upon the basis of a statement he made while insane; and this judgment can without difficulty be articulated in terms of the unreliability of the confession, the lack of rational choice of the accused, or simply a strong conviction that our system of law enforcement should not operate so as to take advantage of a person in this fashion. And when the other pertinent circumstances are considered — the eight- to nine-hour sustained interrogation in a tiny room which was upon occasion literally filled with police officers; the absence of Blackburn's friends, relatives, or legal counsel; the composition of the confession by the Deputy Sheriff rather than by Blackburn — the chances of the confession's having been the product of a rational intellect and a free will become even more remote and the denial of due process even more egregious.

It is, of course, quite true that we are dealing here with probabilities. It is *possible,* for example, that Blackburn confessed during a period of complete mental competence. Moreover, these probabilities are gauged in this instance primarily by the opinion evidence of medical experts. But this case is novel only in the sense that the evidence of insanity here is compelling, for this Court has in the past reversed convictions where psychiatric evidence revealed that the person who had confessed was "of low mentality, if not mentally ill" ... or had a "history of emotional instability" .... And although facts such as youth and lack of education are more easily ascertained than the imbalance of a human mind, we cannot say that this has any appreciable bearing upon the difficulty of the ultimate judgment as to the effect these various circumstances have upon independence of will, a judgment which must by its nature always be one of probabilities.

* * *

The evidence here clearly establishes that the confession most probably was not the product of any meaningful act of volition. Therefore, the use of that evidence to convict Blackburn transgressed the imperatives of fundamental justice which find their expression in the Due Process Clause of the Fourteenth Amendment, and the judgment must be

Reversed.

The Decline of "Fundamental Fairness"

MALLOY v. HOGAN

Supreme Court of the United States, 1964
378 U.S. 1, 84 S. Ct. 1489, 12 L. Ed. 2d 653

William Malloy, a convicted gambler, was ordered to testify in a Connecticut state investigation of gambling activities. Malloy was asked a number of questions related to events surrounding his prior arrest and conviction. He refused to answer any questions "on the grounds that it may tend to incriminate me." A Connecticut state court held Malloy in contempt and ordered him jailed until he was willing to testify. In habeas corpus proceedings, two state courts denied relief, overruling Malloy's objection that his Fifth Amendment privilege against self-incrimination had been violated. The United States Supreme Court granted certiorari.

Mr. Justice BRENNAN delivered the opinion of the Court.

In this case we are asked to reconsider prior decisions holding that the privilege against self-incrimination is not safeguarded against state action by the Fourteenth Amendment. Twining v. New Jersey, 211 U.S. 78 (1908); Adamson v. California, 322 U.S. 46 (1947).

* * *

We hold today that the Fifth Amendment's exception from compulsory self-incrimination is also protected by the Fourteenth Amendment against abridgment by the States. Decisions of the Court since Twining and Adamson have departed from the contrary view expressed in those cases. . . .

* * *

We turn to the petitioner's claim that the State of Connecticut denied him the protection of his federal privilege. It must be considered irrelevant that the petitioner was a witness in a statutory inquiry and not a defendant in a criminal prosecution, for it has long been settled that the privilege protects witnesses in similar federal inquiries. . . . We recently elaborated the content of the federal standard in Hoffman [v. United States, 341 U.S. 479 (1951)]:

"The privilege afforded not only extends to answers that would in themselves support a conviction . . . but likewise embraces those which would furnish a link in the chain of evidence needed to prosecute. . . . [I]f the witness, upon interposing his claim, were required to prove the hazard . . . he would be compelled to surrender the very protection which the privilege is designed to guarantee. To sustain the privilege, it need only be evident from the implications of the question, in the setting in which it is asked, that a responsive answer to the question or an explanation of why it cannot be answered might be dangerous because injurious disclosure could result." 341 U.S., at 486–487.

We also said that, in applying that test, the judge must be *"perfectly clear,* from a careful consideration of all the circumstances in the case, that the witness is mistaken, and that the answer[s] *cannot possibly* have such tendency to incriminate." 341 U.S., at 488.

... The interrogation was part of a wide-ranging inquiry into crime, including gambling, in Hartford. It was admitted on behalf of the State at oral argument—and indeed it is obvious from the questions themselves—that the State desired to elicit from the petitioner the identity of the person who ran the pool-selling operation in connection with which he had been arrested in 1959. It was apparent that petitioner might apprehend that if this person were still engaged in

unlawful activity, disclosure of his name might furnish a link in a chain of evidence sufficient to connect the petitioner with a more recent crime for which he might still be prosecuted.

... An affirmative answer to the question might well have either connected petitioner with a more recent crime, or at least have operated as a waiver of his privilege with reference to his relationship with a possible criminal. ... We conclude, therefore, that as to each of the questions, it was "evident from the implications of the question, in the setting in which it (was) asked, that a responsive answer to the question or an explanation of why it (could not) be answered might be dangerous because injurious disclosure could result" ....

Reversed.

[Mr. Justice HARLAN and Mr. Justice CLARK dissented.]

Comments

1. Prior to *Malloy* v. *Hogan,* supra, which made the Fifth Amendment privilege against self-incrimination applicable to the states, convictions in state courts based on alleged involuntary confessions were subject to appellate review under the Due Process Clause of the Fourteenth Amendment. As indicated in *Blackburn* v. *Alabama,* supra, the *voluntariness* of a confession was measured by the *"totality of circumstances"* test. For many years a "voluntary" confession was admissible as long as it was deemed "trustworthy" or "probably true." In evaluating the reliability of a confession under the "totality of circumstances" test, the Court looked to the circumstances in which the confession was obtained: these included the defendant's age, prior experience with the criminal justice system, mental and physical condition, and educational background, the methods of interrogation utilized by the police ("police methods" test), and the time and place of the interrogation. Over time, police interrogators began to make greater use of psychological techniques, which made proof of the voluntariness of a confession very difficult. In local courts, the dispute as to the voluntariness of a confession usually resulted in a "swearing contest" between the defendant and police interrogators, and the courts almost invariably resolved the dispute in favor of the police.

    In the federal courts, the Supreme Court attempted to control the interrogation techniques of federal law enforcement officials by use of its *supervisory powers* over the federal courts. The Federal Rules of Criminal Procedure [5(a)] require that an arrestee be taken "without unnecessary delay" before the nearest available magistrate so that he can be formally charged and informed of his rights. In *McNabb* v. *United States,* 318 U.S. 332 (1943), and *Mallory* v. *United States,* 354 U.S. 449 (1957), the Supreme Court held that any confession obtained by federal officials during an unreasonable period of delay was inadmissible in evidence, regardless of its voluntariness or trustworthiness. Because this rule, known as the McNabb–Mallory rule, was based on the Supreme Court's supervisory power over lower federal courts and not on any constitutional provision, the rule was not binding on the states.

In 1968, Congress abolished the McNabb–Mallory rule by means of a provision in the Omnibus Crime Control and Safe Streets Act that stated that a delay in taking an arrestee before a federal judicial officer was only one of many circumstances to be considered in evaluating the voluntariness of a confession. 18 U.S.C. § 3501(a)(b). Under the act, if a defendant makes a voluntary confession within 6 hours following his arrest or detention, it is admissible even though the arrestee has not yet been taken before a magistrate. 18 U.S.C. § 3501(c). This provision of the act is likely to be upheld since the *McNabb–Mallory* rule is not of constitutional dimension. Today most states provide that an arrestee shall be taken before a magistrate "without unnecessary delay," but the time factor varies considerably from jurisdiction to jurisdiction.

2. In *Massiah* v. *United States,* 377 U.S. 201 (1964), the Supreme Court held that any statements, voluntary or not, made by a defendant after he has been formally charged with a crime (e.g., indicted), has been released from custody (e.g., posted bail), and has retained counsel are inadmissible at trial when the police have used an undercover agent to elicit a confession. The *Massiah* Court reasoned that in such circumstances the defendant was denied the right to the assistance of counsel. It is not clear whether the Court would have reached the same result if Massiah had not retained counsel or had otherwise waived counsel at the time of his inculpatory statements. There was no question that the confession by Massiah was voluntary. However, the Court relied upon the Sixth Amendment right to counsel to exclude his statements from trial. The *Massiah* case marked the beginning of the Supreme Court's reliance upon the Sixth Amendment right to counsel to exclude from evidence even voluntary confessions. The holding of *Massiah* was reaffirmed in *Brewer* v. *Williams,* 430 U.S. 387 (1977) (Chapter Seven, § 7.02). But see *United States* v. *Hinton,* 543 F.2d 1002 (2d Cir. 1976) (surreptitiously recorded conversations between defendant in drug prosecution and government witness held admissible despite fact that when recordings were made defendant was under indictment on separate and unrelated state narcotics charge and was represented by counsel in that pending case who was not present when recorded inculpatory statements were made).

3. In *Escobedo* v. *Illinois,* 378 U.S. 478 (1964), the defendant was arrested for the murder of his brother-in-law. During the ensuing police interrogation, Escobedo was not permitted to speak with his retained lawyer, who had arrived at the police station and wished to consult with him. The defendant was not advised of his constitutional rights during the entire interrogation, which lasted several hours. Escobedo made several incriminating statements during the interrogation process, which were admitted at his trial for murder. He was convicted and he appealed. The United States Supreme Court reversed, holding that "when the process shifts from investigatory to accusatory—when its focus is on the accused and its purpose is to elicit a confession—our adversary system begins to operate, and . . . the accused must be permitted to consult with his lawyer," at 492. The *Escobedo* decision is important in that it in-

dicated a shift in the Supreme Court's focus from the traditional "totality of circumstances" and voluntariness tests on the admissibility of confessions to the Sixth Amendment right to counsel. By the time of the *Escobedo* decision, the Court had held that the right to counsel attaches at "critical stages" of the criminal process, and the Court was beginning to find police interrogations to be such a stage. The decision in *Miranda* v. *Arizona*, infra, was the culmination of this shift by the Court from the traditional voluntariness test to an elaborate set of procedural safeguards designed to prevent a circumventing of due process protections by the police and the resultant "swearing contest" in the courts.

4. The following lower federal and state court decisions deal with some of the legal issues surrounding the privilege against self-incrimination: *Commonwealth* v. *Smith*, 344 A.2d 889 (Pa. 1975) (statements from an accused obtained as a result of an unnecessary prearraignment delay are inadmissible only upon a showing of a nexus between the delay and the challenged evidence); *Pearson* v. *State*, 347 A.2d 239 (Md. 1975) (better practice for trial judge to honor the request of an accused to refrain from advising the jury that no inference of guilt should be drawn from his failure to take the stand and testify); *United States* v. *Williams*, 521 F.2d 950 (D.C. Cir. 1975) (trial court's refusal to give general instruction that no inference of guilt should be drawn from the refusal of either of two jointly tried defendants to testify after one defendant requested the instruction and the other objected to it held not reversible error); *Commonwealth* v. *Mitchell*, 346 A.2d 48 (Pa. 1975) (defendant's claim, raised for the first time on appeal, that his confession was the product of an unnecessary prearraignment delay held not to be considered on appeal); *Commonwealth* v. *Mahnke*, 335 N.E.2d 660 (Mass. 1975) (confession of murder defendant made to "concerned group of citizens" who abducted the defendant and subjected him to prolonged and threatening interrogation and held him captive in a remote cabin until he agreed to lead them to the place where the victim was buried held inadmissible); *People* v. *Hayes*, 193 N.W.2d 899 (Mich. App. 1975) (drunk driving defendant's refusal to take a chemical test at the time of arrest cannot be used against him at trial, although the state can revoke his license for such refusal); *Williams* v. *Director, Patuxent Institution*, 347 A.2d 179 (Md. 1975) (convicted felon committed for "defective delinquency" exam held to have no right under Self-incrimination Clause to refuse to cooperate with the examiners, as such treatment is civil rather than criminal); *State* v. *Helker*, 545 P.2d 1028 (N. Mex. App. 1975) (defendant who failed to make a motion for suppression of his confession at pretrial proceedings held to have no right to make a similar motion at trial); *State* v. *Haze*, 542 P.2d 720 (Kan. 1975) (Fifth Amendment doesn't bar use at trial of the fact that a defendant refused to furnish a handwriting exemplar); *Gibson* v. *Commonwealth*, 219 S.E.2d 845 (Va. 1975) (no Fifth Amendment violation in the admission of testimony of a psychiatrist who had conducted a court-ordered exam of a murder defendant that the defendant had admitted the killing to him during the exam); *People* v. *Brown*, _____ N.E.2d _____ (Nassau City Ct., N.Y., 1976) (confession by mentally ill defendant held admissible) (see also *Eisen* v. *Picard*, 452 P.2d 860 [Calif. 1971], *People* v. *MacPherson*, 465 P.2d 17 [Calif. 1970], and *United States* v. *Robinson*, 459 F.2d. 1164 [D.C. Cir. 1972]); *Dempsey* v.

State, 355 A.2d 455 (Md. 1976) (under the "Massachusetts rule" for determining the voluntariness of a confession whereby the judge makes the initial determination out of the jury's presence and then, if he finds the confession voluntary, instructs the jury that it is to make its own voluntariness determination, it is reversible error for the court to inform the jury that he found the confession voluntary) (in accord is *Clifton* v. *United States,* 371 F.2d 354 [D.C. Cir. 1966], and *State* v. *Walter,* 145 S.E.2d 833 [N.C. 1966]); *State* v. *Kaiser,* 534 N.W.2d 19 (Mo. 1976) (judge presiding at drunk driving trial violated defendant's privilege against self-incrimination by requiring him to testify about his two prior convictions for the same offense—a third offense being a felony); *State* v. *Wyman,* 547 P.2d 531 (Utah 1976) (delay of 48 hours in bringing defendant before a magistrate following his arrest does not, in and of itself, require suppression of the defendant's voluntary statements); *Brecheen* v. *Dycus,* 547 P.2d 980 (Okla. Crim. Ct. App. 1976) (municipal judge cannot require a defendant or his attorney to meet with the bailiff and prosecutor at a pretrial conference, unattended by the judge, to disclose all the evidence he intends to use at a forthcoming criminal trial); *Lewis* v. *State,* 329 So.2d 596 (Ala. App. 1976) (admitting confession over defendant's objection without first requiring jury to determine its voluntariness held reversible error); *United States* v. *Cohen,* 530 F.2d 43 (5th Cir. 1976) (compelled court-ordered psychiatric exam of a defendant is not violative of the privilege against self-incrimination when the defendant has raised the insanity defense); *Williamson* v. *State,* 330 So. 2d 272 (Miss. 1976) (inculpatory statements by a defendant to a court-appointed psychiatrist about the events surrounding the crime charged are inadmissible); *United States* v. *Field,* 532 F.2d 404 (5th Cir. 1976) (privilege against self-incrimination not violated where Grand Cayman banker under a grant of immunity is compelled to answer grand jury questions even though it would be illegal to answer them under the Cayman Bank Secrecy Act); *People* v. *Markiewicz,* 348 N.E.2d 240 (Ill. App. 1976) (statements obtained during police officer's bedside questioning of murder suspect who was in a coma from a drug overdose held inadmissible); *People* v. *Gallagher,* 241 N.W.2d 279 (Mich. App. 1976) (presumption that possession of more than 2 ounces of marijuana carries an intent to sell held not violative of the privilege against self-incrimination); *United States* v. *Rose,* 541 F.2d 750 (8th Cir. 1976) (defendant's voluntary confession obtained by federal agents while he was in state custody pursuant to an invalid arrest warrant held admissible, as the agents had probable cause to believe the defendant was involved in the crime); *Asby* v. *State,* 354 N.E.2d 192 (Ind. 1976) (incriminating statements obtained from two defendants who had been told the previous day by police that they would be allowed to plead guilty to lesser charges held inadmissible at their subsequent trial); *United States* v. *Barker,* 542 F.2d 479 (8th Cir. 1976) (fact that defendant gave custodial statement to state officials in return for assurances that the state would not prosecute him raised no Fifth Amendment bar to prosecution by the federal government); *People* v. *Dikeman,* 555 P.2d 519 (Col. 1976) (trial judge erred in permitting defense counsel to question witnesses called by the defendant when defense counsel knew that the witnesses would claim, in the presence of the jury, their valid privilege not to answer on the grounds of self-incrimination).

B. CONFESSIONS AND POLICE INTERROGATIONS

Miranda and its Progeny

MIRANDA v. ARIZONA

Supreme Court of the United States, 1966
384 U.S. 436, 86 S. Ct. 1602, 16 L. Ed. 2d 694

Miranda was decided by the Supreme Court with three other cases, *Vignera* v. *New York*, *Westover* v. *United States*, and *California* v. *Stewart*. All the cases raised the issue of the admissibility of statements taken from the defendants during custodial interrogations in possible violation of their Fifth, Sixth, and Fourteenth Amendment rights.

Ernesto Miranda was arrested at his home in Phoenix and taken to a police station for questioning with regard to a rape and kidnapping that had occurred ten days earlier. At this time, Miranda was 23 years old, poor, and had completed only half the ninth grade. A doctor's report indicated that Miranda had an "emotional illness" of the schizophrenic type. The victim picked him out of a lineup. Two hours later, officers emerged from the interrogation room with a written confession signed by Miranda. The confession was admitted at trial, over Miranda's objections, and he was convicted of rape and kidnapping and sentenced to 20 to 30 years' imprisonment on each count. The Arizona Supreme Court affirmed the conviction.

Michael Vignera was picked up by New York police for questioning in connection with the robbery of a Brooklyn dress shop three days earlier. During questioning, Vignera orally admitted committing the robbery. While at the police station, Vignera was identified by the store owner and saleslady as the person who had robbed the shop. Later that day, Vignera was questioned by an assistant district attorney in the presence of a stenographer. The questions and Vignera's answers were transcribed. At no time was he advised of his right to counsel. At his trial for first degree robbery, Vignera's confessions were admitted in evidence over his objections. He was convicted and sentenced to 30 to 60 years' imprisonment. The New York courts affirmed the conviction.

Carl Westover was arrested by Kansas City police as a suspect in two Kansas City robberies. Subsequently, he was interrogated by three special agents of the FBI with respect to the robbery of a savings and loan association and a bank in Sacramento, California. After about two hours, Westover signed separate confessions to each of the two robberies. Westover had been advised of his rights by the FBI agents but not by the Kansas City police. Subsequently, Westover was tried and found guilty in federal court of the California robberies. The United States Court of Appeals (9th Cir.) affirmed.

Roy Allen Stewart was arrested at his house by Los Angeles police in connection with a series of purse snatchings in which one of the victims had died. A search of his house turned up various items taken from the five robbery victims. Stewart was taken to a local police station, and during the next five days police interrogated him on nine different occasions. During the ninth interrogation, Stewart admitted robbing one of the victims. The record disclosed that he had never been warned of his right to remain silent or his right to counsel. Subsequently, Stewart was charged with kidnapping with intent to commit robbery, rape, and murder. Evidence of his confession was admitted at his trial and he was convicted of robbery and first degree murder. The penalty was fixed at death. The United States Court of Appeals (9th Cir.) reversed, holding that Stewart should have been advised of his right to remain silent and his right to counsel.

In each case, the United States Supreme Court granted certiorari.

Mr. Chief Justice WARREN delivered the opinion of the Court.

The cases before us raise questions which go to the roots of our concepts of American criminal jurisprudence: the restraints society must observe consistent with the Federal Constitution in prosecuting individuals for crime. More specifically, we deal with the admissibility of statements obtained from an individual who is subjected to custodial police interrogation and the necessity for procedures which assure that the individual is accorded his privilege under the Fifth Amendment to the Constitution not to be compelled to incriminate himself.

We dealt with certain phases of this problem recently in Escobedo v. Illinois, 378 U.S. 478 (1964). There, as in the four cases before us, law enforcement officials took the defendant into custody and interrogated him in a police station for the purpose of obtaining a confession. The police did not effectively advise him of his right to remain silent or of his right to consult with his attorney. Rather, they confronted him with an alleged accomplice who accused him of having perpetrated a murder. When the defendant denied the accusation and said "I didn't shoot Manuel, you did it," they handcuffed him and took him to an interrogation room. There, while handcuffed and standing, he was questioned for four hours until he confessed. During this interrogation, the police denied his request to speak to his attorney, and they prevented his retained attorney, who had come to the police station, from consulting with him. At his trial, the State, over his objection, introduced the confession against him. We held that the statements thus made were constitutionally inadmissible.

This case has been the subject of judicial interpretation and spirited legal debate since it was decided two years ago. Both state and federal courts, in assessing its implications, have arrived at varying conclusions. A wealth of scholarly material has been written tracing its ramifications and underpinnings. Police and prosecutor have speculated on its range and desirability. We granted certiorari in these cases . . . in order further to explore some facets of the problems, thus exposed, of applying the privilege against self-incrimination to in-custody interrogation, and to give concrete constitu-tional guidelines for law enforcement agencies and courts to follow.

We start here, as we did in Escobedo, with the premise that our holding is not an innovation in our jurisprudence, but is an application of principles long recognized and applied in other settings. We have undertaken a thorough re-examination of the Escobedo decision and the principles it announced, and we reaffirm it. That case was but an explication of basic rights that are enshrined in our Constitution — that "No person . . . shall be compelled in any criminal case to be a witness against himself," and that "the accused shall . . . have the Assistance of Counsel" — rights which were put in jeopardy in that case through official overbearing. These precious rights were fixed in our Constitution only after centuries of persecution and struggle. And in the words of Chief Justice Marshall, they were secured "for ages to come, and . . . designed to approach immortality as nearly as human institutions can approach it" . . . . Our holding will be spelled out with some specificity in the pages which follow but briefly stated it is this: the prosecution may not use statements, whether exculpatory or inculpatory, stemming from custodial interrogation of the defendant unless it demonstrates the use of procedural safeguards effective to secure the privilege against self-incrimination. By custodial interrogation, we mean questioning initiated by law enforcement officers after a person has been taken into custody or otherwise deprived of his freedom of action in any significant way.[d] As for the procedural safeguards to be employed, unless other fully effective means are devised to inform accused persons of their right of silence and to assure a continuous opportunity to exercise it, the following measures are required. Prior to any questioning, the person must be warned that he has a right to remain silent, that any statement he does make may be used as evidence against him, and that he has a right to the presence of an attorney, either retained or appointed. The defendant may waive effectuation of these rights, provided the waiver is made voluntarily, knowingly and intelligently. If, how-

---

[d]This is what we meant in *Escobedo* when we spoke of an investigation which had focused on an accused.

ever, he indicates in any manner and at any stage of the process that he wishes to consult with an attorney before speaking there can be no questioning. Likewise, if the individual is alone and indicates in any manner that he does not wish to be interrogated, the police may not question him. The mere fact that he may have answered some questions or volunteered some statements on his own does not deprive him of the right to refrain from answering any further inquiries until he has consulted with an attorney and thereafter consents to be questioned.

I

The constitutional issue we decide in each of these cases is the admissibility of statements obtained from a defendant questioned while in custody or otherwise deprived of his freedom of action in any significant way. In each, the defendant was questioned by police officers, detectives, or a prosecuting attorney in a room in which he was cut off from the outside world. In none of these cases was the defendant given a full and effective warning of his rights at the outset of the interrogation process. In all the cases, the questioning elicited oral admissions, and in three of them, signed statements as well which were admitted at their trials. They all thus share salient features—incommunicado interrogation of individuals in a police-dominated atmosphere, resulting in self-incriminating statements without full warnings of constitutional rights.

An understanding of the nature and setting of this in-custody interrogation is essential to our decisions today. The difficulty in depicting what transpires at such interrogations stems from the fact that in this country they have largely taken place incommunicado. From extensive factual studies undertaken in the early 1930's, including the famous Wickersham Report to Congress by a Presidential Commission, it is clear that police violence and the "third degree" flourished at that time. In a series of cases decided by this Court long after these studies, the police resorted to physical brutality—beating, hanging, whipping—and to sustained and protracted questioning incommunicado in order to extort confessions. The Commission on Civil Rights in 1961 found much evidence to indicate that "some policemen still resort to physical force to obtain confessions," 1961 Comm'n. on Civil Rights Rep., Justice, pt. 5, 17. The use of

physical brutality and violence is not, unfortunately, relegated to the past or to any part of the country. Only recently in Kings County, New York, the police brutally beat, kicked and placed lighted cigarette butts on the back of a potential witness under interrogation for the purpose of securing a statement incriminating a third party. . . .

The examples given above are undoubtedly the exception now, but they are sufficiently widespread to be the object of concern. Unless a proper limitation upon custodial interrogation is achieved—such as these decisions will advance—there can be no assurance that practices of this nature will be eradicated in the foreseeable future. . . .

* * *

. . . [W]e stress that the modern practice of in-custody interrogation is psychologically rather than physically oriented. As we have stated before . . . this Court has recognized that "coercion can be mental as well as physical, and that the blood of the accused is not the only hallmark of an unconstitutional inquisition." . . . Interrogation still takes place in privacy. Privacy results in secrecy and this in turn results in a gap in our knowledge as to what in fact goes on in the interrogation rooms. A valuable source of information about present police practices, however, may be found in various police manuals and texts which document procedures employed with success in the past, and which recommend various other effective tactics. These texts are used by law enforcement agencies themselves as guides. It should be noted that these texts professedly present the most enlightened and effective means presently used to obtain statements through custodial interrogation. . . .

* * *

From . . . representative samples of interrogation techniques, the setting prescribed by the manuals and observed in practice becomes clear. In essence, it is this: To be alone with the subject is essential to prevent distraction and to deprive him of any outside support. The aura of confidence in his guilt undermines his will to resist. He merely confirms the preconceived story the police seek to have him describe. Patience and persistence, at times relentless questioning, are employed. To obtain a confession, the interrogator must "patiently maneuver himself or his quarry into a position from which the desired objective may be attained." When normal procedures fail to produce the needed result, the police may resort to deceptive stratagems such as giving false legal advice. It is important to keep the subject off balance, for example, by trading on his insecurity about himself or his surroundings. The police then persuade, trick, or cajole him out of exercising his constitutional rights.

Even without employing brutality, the "third degree" or the specific stratagems described above, the very fact of custodial interrogation exacts a heavy toll on individual liberty and trades on the weakness of individuals. . . .

* * *

. . . [T]he constitutional foundation underlying the privilege is the respect a government — state or federal — must accord to the dignity and integrity of its citizens. To maintain a "fair state-individual balance," to require the government "to shoulder the entire load" . . . to respect the inviolability of the human personality, our accusatory system of criminal justice demands that the government seeking to punish an individual produce the evidence against him by its own independent labors, rather than by the cruel, simple expedient of compelling it from his own mouth. . . .

. . . We are satisfied that all the principles embodied in the privilege apply to informal compulsion exerted by law-enforcement officers during in-custody questioning. An individual swept from familiar surroundings into police custody, surrounded by antagonistic forces, and subjected to the techniques of persuasion described above cannot be otherwise than under compulsion to speak. As a practical matter, the compulsion to speak in the isolated setting of the police station may well be greater than in courts or other official investigations, where there are often impartial observers to guard against intimidation or trickery.

* * *

III

Today, then, there can be no doubt that the Fifth Amendment privilege is available outside of criminal court proceedings and serves to protect persons in all settings in which their freedom of action is curtailed in any significant way from being compelled to incriminate themselves. We have concluded that without proper safeguards the process of in-custody interrogation of persons suspected or accused of crime contains inherently compelling pressures which work to undermine the individual's will to resist and to compel him to speak where he would not otherwise do so freely. In order to combat these pressures and to permit a full opportunity to exercise the privilege against self-incrimination, the accused must be adequately and effectively apprised of his rights and the exercise of those rights must be fully honored.

It is impossible for us to foresee the potential alternatives for protecting the privilege which might be devised by Congress or the States in the exercise of their creative rule-making capacities. Therefore we cannot say that the Constitution necessarily requires adherence to any particular solution for the inherent compulsions of the interrogation process as it is presently conducted. Our decision in no way creates a constitutional straitjacket which will handicap sound efforts at reform, nor is it intended to have this effect. We encourage Congress and the States to continue their laudable search for increasingly effective ways of protecting the rights of the individual while promoting efficient enforcement of our criminal laws. However, unless we are shown other procedures which are at least as effective in apprising accused persons of their right of silence and in assuring a continuous opportunity to exercise it, the following safeguards must be observed.

At the outset, if a person in custody is to be subjected to interrogation, he must first be informed in clear and unequivocal terms that he has the right to remain silent. For those unaware of the privilege, the warning is needed simply to make them aware of it — the threshold requirement for an intelligent decision as to its exercise. More important, such a warning is an absolute prerequisite in overcoming the inherent pressures of the interrogation atmosphere. It is not just the subnormal or woefully ignorant who succumb to an interrogator's imprecations, whether implied or expressly stated, that the interrogation will continue until a confession is obtained or that silence in the face of accusation is itself damning and will bode ill when presented to a jury. Further, the warning will show the individual that his interrogators are prepared to recognize his privilege should he choose to exercise it.

* * *

The principles announced today deal with the protection which must be given to the privilege against self-incrimination when the individual is first subjected to police interrogation while in custody at the station or otherwise deprived of his freedom of action in any significant way....

Our decision is not intended to hamper the traditional function of police officers in investigating crime.... When an individual is in custody on probable cause, the police may, of course, seek out evidence in the field to be used at trial against him. Such investigation may include inquiry of persons not under restraint. General on-the-scene questioning as to facts surrounding a crime or other general questioning of citizens in the fact-finding process is not affected by our holding. It is an act of responsible citizenship for individuals to give whatever information they may have to aid in law enforcement. In such situations the compelling atmosphere inherent in the process of in-custody interrogation is not necessarily present.

In dealing with statements obtained through interrogation, we do not purport to find all confessions inadmissible. Confessions remain a proper element in law enforcement. Any statement given freely and voluntarily without any compelling influences is, of course, admissible in evidence. The fundamental import of the privilege while an individual is in custody is not whether he is allowed to talk to the police without the benefit of warnings and counsel, but whether he can be interrogated. There is no requirement that police stop a person who enters a police station and states that he wishes to confess a crime, or a person who calls the police to offer a confession or any other statement he desires to make. Volunteered statements of any kind are not barred by the Fifth Amendment and their admissibility is not affected by our holding today.

To summarize, we hold that when an individual is taken into custody or otherwise deprived of his freedom by the authorities in any significant way and is subjected to questioning, the privilege against self-incrimination is jeopardized. Procedural safeguards must be employed to protect the privilege, and unless other fully effective means are adopted to notify the person of his right of silence and to assure that the exercise of the right will be scrupulously honored, the following measures are required. He must be warned prior to any questioning that he has the right to remain silent, that anything he says can be used against him in a court of law, that he has the right to the presence of an attorney, and that if he cannot afford an attorney one will be appointed for him prior to any questioning if he so desires. Opportunity to exercise these rights must be afforded to him throughout the interrogation. After such warnings have been given, and such opportunity afforded him, the individual may knowingly and intelligently waive these rights and agree to answer questions or make a statement. But unless and until such warnings and waiver are demonstrated by the prosecution at trial, no evidence obtained as a result of interrogation can be used against him.

IV

* * *

If the individual desires to exercise his privilege, he has the right to do so. This is not for the authorities to decide. An attorney may advise his client not to talk to police until he has had an opportunity to investigate the case, or he may wish to be present with his client during any police questioning. In doing so an attorney is merely exercising the good professional judgment he has been taught. This is not cause for considering the attorney a menace to law enforcement. He is merely carrying out what he is sworn to do under his oath—to protect to the extent of his ability the rights of his client. In fulfilling this responsibility the attorney plays a vital role in the administration of criminal justice under our Constitution.

In announcing these principles, we are not unmindful of the burdens which law enforcement officials must bear, often under trying circumstances. We also fully recognize the obligation of all citizens to aid in enforcing the criminal laws....

Therefore, in accordance with the foregoing, the judgments of the Supreme Court of

Arizona ..., of the New York Court of Appeals ... and of the Court of Appeals for the Ninth Circuit ... are reversed. The judgment of the Supreme Court of California ... is affirmed.

Mr. Justice HARLAN, whom Mr. Justice STEWART and Mr. Justice WHITE join, dissenting.

I believe the decision of the Court represents poor constitutional law and entails harmful consequences for the country at large. How serious these consequences may prove to be only time can tell. But the basic flaws in the Court's justification seem to me readily apparent now once all sides of the problem are considered.

* * *

While the fine points of this scheme are far less clear than the Court admits, the tenor is quite apparent. The new rules are not designed to guard against police brutality or other unmistakably banned forms of coercion. Those who use third-degree tactics and deny them in court are equally able and destined to lie as skillfully about warnings and waivers. Rather, the thrust of the new rules is to negate all pressures, to reinforce the nervous or ignorant suspect, and ultimately to discourage any confession at all. The aim in short is toward "voluntariness" in a utopian sense, or to view it from a different angle, voluntariness with a vengeance.

To incorporate this notion into the Constitution requires a strained reading of history and precedent and a disregard of the very pragmatic concerns that alone may on occasion justify such strains. I believe that reasoned examination will show that the Due Process Clauses provide an adequate tool for coping with confessions and that, even if the Fifth Amendment privilege against self-incrimination be invoked, its precedents taken as a whole do not sustain the present rules. Viewed as a choice based on pure policy, these new rules prove to be a highly debatable, if not one-sided, appraisal of the competing interests, imposed over widespread objection, at the very time when judicial restraint is most called for by the circumstances.

* * *

Without at all subscribing to the generally black picture of police conduct painted by the Court, I think it must be frankly recognized at the outset that police questioning allowable under due process precedents may inherently entail some pressure on the suspect and may seek advantage in his ignorance or weaknesses. The atmosphere and questioning techniques, proper and fair though they be, can in themselves exert a tug on the suspect to confess, and in this light "(t)o speak of any confessions of crime made after arrest as being 'voluntary' or 'uncoerced' is somewhat inaccurate, although traditional. A confession is wholly and incontestably voluntary only if a guilty person gives himself up to the law and becomes his own accuser." Ashcraft v. Tennessee, 322 U.S. 143, (Jackson, J., dissenting). Until today, the role of the Constitution has been only to sift out *undue* pressure, not to assure spontaneous confessions.

* * *

What the Court largely ignores is that its rules impair, if they will not eventually serve wholly to frustrate, an instrument of law enforcement that has long and quite reasonably been thought worth the price paid for it. There can be little doubt that the Court's new code would markedly decrease the number of confessions. To warn the suspect that he may remain silent and remind him that his confession may be used in court are minor obstructions. To require also an express waiver by the suspect and an end to questioning whenever he demurs must heavily handicap questioning. And to suggest or provide counsel for the suspect simply invites the end of the interrogation.

How much harm this decision will inflict on law enforcement cannot fairly be predicted with accuracy. Evidence on the role of confessions is notoriously incomplete.... We do know that some crimes cannot be solved without confessions, that ample expert testimony attests to their importance in crime control, and that the Court is taking a real risk with society's welfare in imposing its new regime on the country. The social costs of crime are too great to call the new rules anything but a hazardous experimentation.

While passing over the costs and risks of its experiment, the Court portrays the evils of normal police questioning in terms which I think are exaggerated. Albeit stringently confined by the due process standards interrogation is no doubt often inconvenient and unpleasant for the suspect. However, it is no less so for a man to be arrested and jailed, to have his house searched, or to stand trial in court, yet all this may properly happen to the most innocent given probable cause, a warrant, or an indictment. Society has always paid a stiff price for law and order, and peaceful interrogation is not one of the dark moments of the law.

This brief statement of the competing considerations seems to me ample proof that the Court's preference is highly debatable at best and therefore not to be read into the Constitution. . . .

* * *

. . . Nothing in the letter or the spirit of the Constitution or in the precedents squares with the heavy-handed and one-sided action that is so precipitously taken by the Court in the name of fulfilling its constitutional responsibilities. . . .

[Mr. Justice CLARK wrote a separate dissenting opinion.]

Comments

1. In light of the *Miranda* decision, consider the Supreme Court's holding in *Michigan* v. *Tucker,* 417 U.S. 433 (1974). Respondent, Tucker, was convicted of rape by a Michigan state court and sentenced to 20 to 40 years in prison. His conviction was affirmed by both the Michigan Court of Appeals and the Michigan Supreme Court. However, when Tucker sought habeas corpus relief in federal district court (E.D. Mich.), that court, noting that respondent had not received his full *Miranda* warnings and that the police had learned of a prosecution witness' identity only through Tucker's answers during interrogation, concluded that the witness' testimony should have been excluded from trial. Consequently, the district court granted the petition provided Michigan did not retry Tucker within 90 days. The Court of Appeals (6th Cir.) affirmed. The facts revealed that although the police asked Tucker prior to questioning if he understood the crime for which he was arrested, whether he wanted an attorney, and whether he understood his constitutional rights, he was not advised that he would be furnished counsel free of charge if he could not afford one. The interrogation occurred prior to the Supreme Court's ruling in *Miranda* v. *Arizona,* but Tucker's trial occurred after *Miranda.* The Supreme Court granted certiorari to consider whether the testimony of the witness should have been excluded simply because "full" *Miranda* warnings were not given prior to questioning. Writing for the majority, Mr. Justice Rehnquist noted, citing *Miranda* v. *Arizona,* 384 U.S. at 467, "These procedural safeguards were not themselves *rights* protected by the Constitution but were instead *measures* to insure that the right against compulsory self-incrimination was protected. . . . [T]hey were not intended to 'create a constitutional straightjacket' . . . but rather to provide *practical reinforcement* for the right. . ." (emphasis added). The majority went on to conclude that "the police conduct at issue here did not abridge respondent's constitutional privilege against compulsory self-incrimination, but *departed only from the prophylactic standards* later laid down . . . to safeguard that privilege" (emphasis added). Finally, the majority suggested that a balancing test of sorts might be in order: "In this particular case we also 'must consider society's interest in the ef-

fective prosecution of criminals in light of the protection our *Miranda* standards afford criminal defendants,' [*Jenkins* v. *Delaware*, 395 U.S. 213 (1969)]. These interests may be outweighed by the need to provide an effective sanction to a constitutional right ... but they must in any event be valued."

What is the significance of the reference to *Miranda* warnings as "prophylactic standards"? If they are to be effective as a protective or preventive device, is it sound practice to "circumvent" them, or to give them in less than their totality? What are the warnings designed to protect? On the other hand, what are they designed to prevent? Likewise, consider the statement by Mr. Justice Rehnquist that "a failure to give interrogated suspects full *Miranda* warnings does not entitle the suspect to insist that statements made by him be excluded in every conceivable context." How can that be squared with the following blanket holding by the majority of the Court in *Miranda*? "Our holding ... briefly stated ... is this: the prosecution *may not use* statements, whether exculpatory or inculpatory, stemming from custodial interrogation of the defendant *unless it demonstrates* the use of procedural safeguards to secure the privilege against self-incrimination. ... In order *fully* to apprise a person interrogated of the extent of his rights ... it is necessary to warn him not only that he has the right to consult with an attorney, but also that *if he is indigent a lawyer will be appointed to represent him*" (emphasis added).

2. Chief Justice Warren, writing for the majority in *Miranda,* observed that "'the principal psychological factor contributing to a successful interrogation is *privacy*—being alone with the person under interrogation' [citing Inbau and Reid, *Criminal Interrogation and Confessions* 1 (1962)]. ... Privacy results in secrecy and this in turn results in a gap in our knowledge as to what in fact goes on in the interrogation rooms." It would appear that the majority of the Court in *Miranda* believed that the existence of the warnings would enable those who are apprised of their rights to reap the benefits derived from those rights. Is the assumption that a man who knows his rights will exercise them a sound one? Is *Miranda* simply an attempt to get the police to behave "better" toward suspects in the sense of being less violent? For a discussion of these and other hypotheses concerning the *Miranda* decision, see Jacobs, *Miranda: The Right to Silence,* Trial, March-April 1975, Vol. II, p. 69. See generally Kamisar, *A Dissent from the Miranda Dissents: Some Comments on the "New" Fifth Amendment and the "Old" Voluntariness Test,* 65 Mich. L. Rev. 59 (1966); Pepinsky, *A Theory of Police Reaction to Miranda v. Arizona,* 16 Crime & Delin. 379 (1970).

3. In *Miranda* the Court held that the appropriate warnings are required *prior to custodial interrogation,* and "custodial" was defined as referring to the situation of a person who is "in custody [under arrest] or *otherwise deprived of his freedom of action in any significant way.*" Thus, it may not be necessary for an arresting officer to give a suspect his *Miranda* warnings *if* the officer does not intend to question or otherwise interrogate the suspect—the "silent approach"; and if a suspect voluntarily makes incriminating statements not in response to custodial interrogation, the *Miranda* decision would seem to have no bearing on their admissibility. Many arresting officers quickly read the *Miranda* warnings as soon

as the suspect has been placed under arrest for fear that any subsequent statements made by the defendant will be inadmissible at trial. A fair reading of *Miranda* does not suggest that this is the case. The *Miranda* Court emphasized that *"prior to custodial interrogation"* the warnings are required. Surely the *Miranda* Court did not mean that if a suspect has *not* been subjected to custodial interrogation and he voluntarily makes disserving statements, the police are obligated to interrupt him and warn him that such statements are admissible against him.

Although the *Miranda* decision has been severely criticized by many authorities, including the four justices who dissented, the Court could have said that no questioning of suspects will be permitted following an arrest, a *per se* rule obviating the necessity of determining whether preinterrogation procedures were followed. The actual holding of *Miranda* seems rather mild compared to the latter possibility. Perhaps critics of *Miranda* should feel blessed that the Court did not take that more stringent approach. Empirical studies measuring the effect of the *Miranda* decision have consistently found that the rate of confessions has not changed significantly since that decision. There is some evidence that most defendants do not fully appreciate the significance of their constitutional rights and quickly waive the *Miranda* warnings because they are eager to tell "their side of the story," which often turns out to be damaging evidence because of their unfamiliarity with the law of accessories and the liability of parties under the substantive criminal law (e.g., "I only tied up the victim, my partner shot him"). Further, perhaps it is difficult for many defendants to tell an arresting officer that "I don't understand my constitutional rights." After all the *Miranda* warnings are rather straightforward and, on the surface, appear to be easily comprehensible. A defendant might feel foolish admitting to the arresting officer that he does not understand the legal ramifications of the *Miranda* warnings; moreover, the "fuzz" are not regarded by the criminal element as persons who gave up scholarships at Harvard to become police officers. In actual practice many defendants will interrupt an officer while he is reciting the *Miranda* warnings with "Yea, I know my rights!" The fact is that the legal implications of *Miranda* are complex, as evidenced by the hundreds of lower court decisions attempting to interpret that case—decisions that are far from uniform. Subsequent pronouncements by the Supreme Court interpreting and further elaborating on the *Miranda* decision have been relatively few.

In *Mathis* v. *United States,* 391 U.S. 1 (1968), an Internal Revenue agent visited the defendant at the Florida State Penitentiary to question him about possible income tax violations. The defendant was serving a state sentence for an unrelated charge. During the interview, the IRS agent did not inform the defendant of his *Miranda* rights. The defendant made some incriminating statements that were admitted in evidence at his subsequent trial for filing false federal income tax returns. His conviction was affirmed by the United States Court of Appeals (5th Cir.). The United States Supreme Court reversed and remanded, holding that when a defendant is in custody, even on an unrelated charge, he is entitled to the *Miranda* warnings. In *Orozco* v. *Texas,* 394 U.S. 324 (1969), the Court held that "custodial interrogations" are not limited to those that take place at the police station and that *whenever* a defendant is "in custody or otherwise deprived of his freedom of action in any significant way," he is entitled to the *Miranda* warnings prior to custodial interrogation — even after being placed under arrest in his own home. See also *United States* v. *Robson*, 477 F.2d 13 (9th Cir. 1973); *United States* v. *Dickerson*, 413 F.2d 111 (7th Cir. 1969); *Cohen* v. *United States*, 405 F.2d 34 (8th Cir. 1968), cert. denied, 394 U.S. 943 (1969); *United States* v. *Squeri*, 398 F.2d 785 (2d Cir. 1968).

Although the Supreme Court has not had occasion to rule on the issue, the overwhelming majority of lower federal and state courts have held that general on-the-scene questioning by police officers does not constitute a custodial interrogation requiring the giving of *Miranda* warnings. The following cases support this view: *Sciberras* v. *United States*, 380 F.2d 732 (10th Cir. 1967); *Arnold* v. *United States*, 382 F.2d 4 (9th Cir. 1967); *United States* v. *Thomas*, 396 F.2d 310 (2d Cir. 1968); *Chevez-Montez* v. *Hernandez*, 291 F.Supp. 712 (D. Cal. 1968); *United States* v. *Littlejohn*, 260 F. Supp. 278 (D.N.Y. 1966); *United States* v. *Kuntz*, 265 F. Supp. 543 (D.N.Y. 1967); *United States* v. *Montez-Hernandez*, 291 F. Supp. 712 (D. Cal. 1968); *United States* v. *Clark*, 294 F. Supp. 1108 (D. Pa. 1968), aff'd, 425 F.2d 827 (3rd Cir. 1970), cert. denied, 400 U.S. 820 (1970); *United States* v. *Hatchel*, 329 F. Supp. 113 (D. Mass. 1971); *United States* v. *Shafer*, 384 F. Supp. 486 (N.D. Ohio 1974); *Ison* v. *State*, 200 So. 2d 511 (Ala. 1967); *State* v. *Telley*, 431 P.2d 691 (Ariz. 1967); *State* v. *Hunt*, 447 P.2d 896 (Ariz. App. 1968); *Stout* v. *State*, 426 S.W.2d 800 (Ark. 1968); *People* v. *Hazel*, 60 Cal. Rptr. 437 (Cal. App. 1967); *Lockridge* v. *Superior Court*, 80 Cal. Rptr. 233 (Cal. App. 1969); *State* v. *Corrigan*, 228 A.2d 568 (Conn. 1967); *Keith* v. *United States*, 232 A.2d 92 (D.C. App. 1967); *Montgomery* v. *United States*, 268 A.2d 271 (D.C. App. 1970); *Melero* v. *State*, 306 So. 2d 603 (Fla. App. 1975); *People* v. *Bailey*, 304 N.E.2d 668 (Ill. App. 1973); *Owens* v. *State*, 266 N.E.2d 612 (Ind. 1971); *State* v. *Carlson*, 533 P.2d 1342 (Kan. 1975); *State* v. *Amphy*, 249 So.2d 560 (La. 1971); *People* v. *Jackson*, 195 N.W.2d 312 (Mich. App. 1972); *State* v. *Martin*, 212 N.W.2d 847 (Minn. 1973); *Nevels* v. *State*, 216 So. 2d 529 (Miss. 1968); *State* v. *Gosser*, 236 A.2d 377 (N.J. 1967); *People* v. *Yukl*, 256 N.E.2d 172 (N.Y. App. 1970); *State* v. *Shedd*, 161 S.E.2d 477 (N.C. 1968); *State* v. *Archible*, 212 S.E.2d 44 (N.C. App. 1975); *State* v. *Perry*, 237 N.E.2d 891 (Ohio 1968); *State* v. *Taylor*, 437 P.2d 853 (Ore. 1968); *Commonwealth* v. *Lopinson*, 234 A.2d 552 (Pa. 1967); *State* v. *Watts*, 152 S.E.2d 684 (S.C. 1967); *Cole* v. *State*, 512 S.W.2d 598 (Tenn. 1974); *Graham* v. *State*, 486 S.W.2d 92 (Tex. Crim. App. 1972); *State* v. *Cloud*, 498 P.2d 907 (Wash. App. 1972); and *Britton* v. *State*, 170 N.W.2d 785 (Wisc. 1969). The cases are collected in 31 A.L.R.3d 565.

Generally, no *Miranda* warnings are required when a suspect has been interrogated by his relatives, friends, or acquaintances. See, e.g., *Truex* v. *State*, 210 So. 2d 424 (Ala. 1968); *Edington* v. *State*, 418 S.W.2d 637 (Ark. 1967); *People* v. *Petker*, 62 Cal. Rptr. 215 (Cal. App. 1967); *State* v. *Fisk*, 448 P.2d 768 (Idaho 1968); *Skinner* v. *State*, 432 P.2d 675 (Nev. 1967); and *Commonwealth* v. *Butler*, 309 A.2d 720 (Pa. 1973).

Most courts have held that spontaneous or volunteered statements by a suspect do not fall under the custodial interrogation requirement of *Miranda*. See, e.g., *People* v. *Vargas*, 111 Cal. Rptr. 745 (Cal. App. 1974); *United States* v. *Martin*, 511 F.2d 148 (8th Cir. 1975); *State* v. *Levy*, 292 So. 2d 226 (La. 1974); and *Cork* v. *State*, 282 So. 2d 107 (Ala. App. 1973).

The majority of lower federal and state courts have applied the following principles regarding *Miranda* requirements (see 31 A.L.R.3d 565–696): (1) police station interrogations are usually regarded as custodial unless the person questioned is present as a witness, has been invited to the police station, or has walked into the station on his own initiative; (2) questioning in police vehicles is usually characterized as custodial; (3) the questioning of a suspect at his place of employment or business without an arrest is not custodial interrogation; (4) police interrogations of suspects at the residences of third parties (e.g., friend's home) are not usually characterized as custodial; (5) interrogations of suspects by IRS agents at IRS offices are generally not regarded as custodial; (6) interrogations in nonpolice vehicles are usually held to be noncustodial; (7) lengthy interrogations using accusatory, leading, and persistent questioning are usually regarded as custodial; (8) where the suspect initiates the interview with the police, the questioning is usually regarded as noncustodial; (9) routine questioning of a defendant during the booking process by the booking officer is usually held to be noncustodial; (10) *Miranda* warnings are usually held not required in misdemeanor cases involving short jail terms; (11) *Miranda* is not applicable to interviews by probation or parole officers; (12) *Miranda* warnings are usually held applicable to juvenile proceedings (see *In re Gault*, Chapter Eight, § 8.03); (13) *Miranda* warnings are usually not required at grand jury proceedings (see *United States* v. *Washington*, 328 A.2d 98 [D.C. App. 1975], rev'd on other grounds, 97 S. Ct. 1815 (1977); (14) private citizens not working as agents of or in cooperation with the police are not required to give *Miranda* warnings, and damaging statements made by a suspect in response to such questioning are usually admissible.

Whether the questioning of a suspect by the police at his residence constitutes custodial interrogation sufficient to require *Miranda* warnings depends on the facts and circumstances of the case. Most courts look to see if the suspect was in custody or was otherwise deprived of his freedom of action in any significant way. In the following situations, the courts found sufficient custodial interrogation to require *Miranda* warnings: *Rosario* v. *Guam*, 391 F.2d 869 (9th Cir. 1968) (questioning of suspect by commissioner of village in Territory of Guam where commissioner's duty as peace officer was to enforce the law); *State* v. *Intogna*, 419 F.2d 59 (9th Cir. 1966) (police officer's asking suspect why he had shot the victim when the officer was standing with his gun drawn 3 feet from the suspect); *State* v. *Anderson*, 428 P.2d 672 (Ariz. 1967) (the defendant was an "obvious suspect" in a murder investigation); *People* v. *Payton*, 62 Cal. Rptr. 865 (Cal. App. 1967) (questioning of a defendant at her home after she had already confessed); *People* v. *Wilson*, 74 Cal. Rptr. 131 (Cal. App. 1968) (questioning of a suspect while police officers searched a residence pursuant to a search warrant); *Jiminez* v. *State*, 208 So. 2d 124 (Fla. App. 1968) (questioning of a suspect at her home after the police had already questioned her at police headquarters); *State* v. *Peters*, 231 N.E.2d 91 (Ohio App. 1967) (defendant made statements following questioning by a police officer in the presence of another police officer and a codefendant after having been arrested 10 blocks away and brought to the apartment by the interrogating officer); *Commonwealth* v. *Sites*, 235 A.2d 387 (Pa. 1967) (questioning of a prime suspect where officer admitted being engaged in a police custodial investigation designed to elicit a confession); *Windsor* v. *United States*, 389 F.2d 530 (5th Cir. 1968) (defendant confessed in his hotel room before his arrest but after his accomplice had already implicated him); *South Dakota* v. *Hale*, 465 F.2d 65 (8th Cir. 1972), cert. denied, 409 U.S. 1130 (1973), (deputies stopped and searched defendant's car and later questioned him in his dormitory room); *People* v. *Reed*, 224 N.W.2d 867 (Mich. 1975), cert. denied, 422 U.S. 1044 (1975) (during homicide investigation, police searching suspect's apartment with consent discovered mop in red-tinged water and trousers soaking in the water and asked suspect who owned the trousers); *Agius* v. *United States*, 413 F.2d 915 (5th Cir. 1969) (FBI agents questioned suspect at his home about a bank robbery and when the suspect took them to his car they noticed a toy gun in the glove compartment); *United States* v. *Bekowies*, 432 F.2d 8 (9th Cir. 1970) (defendant made statements to FBI agent who was searching his apartment for federal fugitive); *People* v. *Wright*, 78 Cal. Rptr. 75 (Cal. App. 1969) (police officers who received tip went to defendant's house, inspected defendant's arms, asked if there were any narcotics on the premises, and seized same); *People* v. *Paulin*, 255 N.E.2d 164 (N.Y. App. 1969) (suspect confessed to police officer who had been called to her home by son who had discovered decomposed body of defendant's husband in closet); *State* v. *Myers*, 487 P.2d 663 (Ore. App. 1971) (police officers arrived at house armed with indictment and arrest warrant and questioned defendant 30 to 40 minutes).

In the following cases, the courts found no custodial interrogation requiring *Miranda* warnings: *United States* v. *Essex*, 275 F. Supp. 393 (D. Tenn.), rev'd on other grounds, 407 F.2d 214 (6th Cir. 1967) ("entirely investigatory interview" at suspect's home); *Menendez* v. *United States*, 393 F.2d 312 (5th Cir. 1968) (FBI agents' investigation was exploratory and not at accusatory stage); *Ison* v. *State*, 200 So. 2d 511 (Ala. 1967) (suspect was asked whether he had shot the victim); *State* v. *Hunt*, 447 P.2d 896 (Ariz. App. 1968) (conversation with victim's father as to the circumstances of the crime); *Staut* v. *State*, 426 S.W.2d 800 (Ark. 1968) (questioning of defendant following shooting as to "what was going on"); *People* v. *Butterfield*, 65 Cal. Rptr. 765 (Cal. App. 1968) (15-minute interview with 19-year-old boy with the boy's mother in an adjoining room); *People* v. *Merchant*, 67 Cal. Rptr. 459 (Cal. App. 1968) (questioning of suspect through a closed screen door of his home); *People* v. *Routt*, 241 N.E.2d 206 (Ill. App. 1968) (police officer who arrived in response to emergency telephone call asked the defendant what happened) (in accord is *State* v. *Gosser*, 236 A.2d 377 [N.J. 1967]); *United States* v. *Thompson*, 463 F.2d 258 (D.C. Cir. 1972) (defendant who claimed to be victim made incriminating statements during interview); *United States* v. *Hall*, 493 F.2d 904 (5th Cir. 1974) (defendant had telephoned threat to President, and FBI agent had not heard the telephone conversation and could not link voice on phone with that of man who answered the door); *Sims* v. *State,* 283 So. 2d 635 (Ala. App. 1973) (defendant questioned in his front yard but was not under arrest and was free to leave); *State* v. *Melot,* 502 P.2d 1346 (Ariz. 1972) (officer summoned to defendant's home to investigate shooting asked, "What happened?" and defendant answered, "I just shot my brother"); *Lovell* v. *State,* 250 So. 2d 915 (Fla. App. 1971) (questions of a general investigatory nature); *Colocado* v. *State,* 251 So. 2d 721 (Fla. App. 1971) (officers during valid search asked who was in charge of the premises); *People* v. *Hall,* 275 N.E.2d 196 (Ill. App. 1971) (officer finding searched-for girl unconscious asked suspect what happened); *Walker* v. *State,* 203 S.E.2d 890 (1974) (officers having description of defendant suspected of burglary went to his room and questioned him as to his identity); *Commonwealth* v. *Valliere,* 321 N.E.2d 625 (1974) (police interviewed suspect whom they did not believe they could arrest and abstained from threatening arrest); *Roberts* v. *State,* 301 So. 2d 859 (Miss. 1974) (defendant questioned in her front yard before arrest); *State* v. *Chappell,* 211 S.E.2d 828 (1975) (officer investigating shooting was admitted to house by defendant who made incriminating statements in response to nonaccusatory statements); *Graham* v. *State,* 486 S.W.2d 92 (Tex. Crim. App. 1972) (officer came upon defendant standing in street holding rifle and learned that defendant had shot another); *State* v. *Werry,* 494 P.2d 1002 (Wash. App. 1972) (officers during valid search stopped defendant as he was leaving house and asked whether he was a renter); *Government of Virgin Islands* v. *Berne,* 412 F.2d 1055 (3rd Cir. 1969), cert. denied, 396 U.S. 837 (suspect questioned in presence of his wife and parents and acknowledged presence of physical evidence in trunk of car); *United States* v. *Hall,* 421 F.2d 540 (2nd Cir. 1969), cert. denied, 397 U.S. 990 (1970) (suspect voluntarily admitted FBI agents into his apartment and gave false exculpatory statement); *United States* v. *Littlepage,* 435 F.2d 498 (5th Cir. 1970), cert. denied, 402 U.S. 915 (1971) (defendant not under arrest nor threatened with arrest); *Dickson* v. *State,* 492 S.W.2d 895 (Ark. 1973) (officer's investigation had not reached accusatory stage); *People* v. *Miller,* 455 P.2d 377 (Cal. App. 1969) (defendant questioned in front yard during investigative stage); *Hubbard* v. *State,* 181 S.E.2d 890 (Ga. App. 1971) (investigation had not focused on suspect); *Stallings* v. *State,* 264 N.E.2d 618 (Ind. 1970) (police officer on arriving at scene of shooting asked defendant if he shot victim and defendant answered affirmatively); *Jackson* v. *State,* 259 A.2d 587 (Md. App. 1969) (questioning of defendant during house-to-house investigation to discover owner of hat found at scene of crime); *Coward* v. *State,* 268 A.2d 508 (Md. App. 1970) (rape victim identified license plate number and police interviewed owner of car but did not regard him as a likely suspect); *Bernos* v. *State,* 268 A.2d 568 (Md. App. 1970) (police officer asked defendant what happened and defendant made incriminating statements); *State* v. *Wiley,* 205 N.W.2d 667 (Minn. 1973) (statement by defendant three days before arrest claiming possessory interest in premises on which marijuana was found); *People* v. *Neulist,* 338 N.Y.S.2d 794 (Nassau Co. Ct. 1972), rev'd on other grounds, 43 App. Div. 150 (1972) (questioning of murder victim's husband at his home); *State* v. *O'Hora,* 182 S.E.2d 823 (N.C. App. 1971), appeal dismissed, 183 S.E.2d 690 (1971) (officers executing warrant to search truck not required to give *Miranda* warnings before asking suspect whether he owned the truck); *Grist* v. *State*, 510 P.2d 964 (Okla. Crim. App. 1973) (officer responding to report of shooting asked defendant what happened); *State* v. *Crossen*, 499 P.2d 1357 (Ore. App. 1972) (questioning during investigative stage); *State* v. *Douglas*, 488 P.2d 1366 (Ore. 1971) (burglary suspect questioned in his motel room and one officer testified he was free to leave but other officer testified he was not free to leave); *State* v. *Martinez*, 457 P.2d 613 (Utah 1969) (police invited defendant to voluntarily attend a lineup and asked if he owned a trenchcoat); *State* v. *Lacallade*, 303 A.2d 131 (Utah 1973) (general investigation of traffic accident); *Gelhaar* v. *State*, 207 N.W.2d 88 (Wisc. 1973) (defendant made inculpatory statement while his freedom of action was not impaired).

4. Should the requirements of *Miranda* be applicable to traffic offenses? This problem has been discussed in the following cases: *State* v. *Tellez*, 431 P.2d 69 (Ariz. App. 1967) (*Miranda* not applicable to traffic offenses generally); *State* v. *Bliss*, 238 A.2d 848 (Del. 1968) (not applicable to drunken drivers); *Capler* v. *Greenville*, 207 So. 2d 339 (Miss. 1968) (drunken driver need not be advised of his right to counsel); *People* v. *Ceccone*, 260 Cal. App. 2d 886 (Cal. App. 1968) (*Miranda* applicable to some traffic offenses); *United States* v. *LeQuire*, 424 F.2d 341 (5th Cir. 1970) (*Miranda* warnings not required prior to questioning about driver's license and car registration); *Campbell* v. *Superior Court*, 479 P.2d 685 (Ariz. 1971) (*Miranda* not applicable to routine traffic offenses where citation is given); *People* v. *Walsh*, 183 N.W.2d 360 (Mich. App. 1970) (*Miranda* not applicable to driver stopped for speeding and asked for license and registration); *Dayton* v. *Nugent*, 265 N.E.2d 826 (Ohio 1970) (*Miranda* not applicable to misdemeanor offenses); *Allen* v. *United States*, 390 F.2d 476 (D.C. Cir. 1960) (*Miranda* not applicable to traffic situations in which no custodial interrogation is involved) (accord, *People* v. *Bolinski*, 260 Cal. App. 347 [Cal. App. 1968]); *People* v. *Grant*, 70 Cal. Rptr. 801 (Cal. App. 1968) (*Miranda* not applicable to traffic offenses when defendant is not in custody) (accord, *State* v. *Everett*, 157 N.W.2d 144 [Iowa 1968], *People* v. *Ricketson*, 264 N.E.2d 220 [Ill. 1970], *State* v. *Sykes*, 203 S.E.2d 849 [N.C. 1969], *United States* v. *Chase*, 414 F.2d 780 [9th Cir. 1969], *Lowe* v. *United States*, 415 F.2d 167 [10th Cir. 1969], *United States* v. *Smith*, 441 F.2d 539 [9th Cir. 1971], *People* v. *Hubbard*, 88 Cal. Rptr. 411 [Cal. App. 1970], *Gustafson* v. *State*, 243 So. 2d 615 [Fla. App. 1971], rev'd on other grounds, 258 So. 2d 1 [1972], *People* v. *Tate*, 259 N.E.2d 791 [Ill. 1970], *People* v. *Pullum*, 295 N.E.2d 315 [Ill. App. 1973], *State* v. *Dubany*, 167 N.W.2d 556 [Neb. 1969], *State* v. *Twitty*, 246 N.E.2d 556 [Ohio App. 1969], *Davis* v. *State*, 516 S.W.2d 157 [Tex. Crim. App. 1974], *State* v. *Darnell*, 508 P.2d 613 [Wash. App. 1973]). The cases are collected in 25 A.L.R.3d 1076–1086. See also *Chay* v. *Riddle*, 541 F.2d 456 (4th Cir. 1974) (*Miranda* not applicable to custodial questioning of traffic offenders). Accord, *State* v. *Gabrielson*, 192 N.W.2d 792 (Iowa 1971); *State* v. *Pyle*, 249 N.E.2d 826 (Ohio 1969); *State* v. *Angelo*, 203 So. 2d 710 (La. 1967); and *Capler* v. *City of Greenville*, 207 So. 2d 339 (Miss. 1968).

5.   OREGON v. MATHIASON
                        Supreme Court of the United States, 1977
                        429 U.S. 492, 97 S. Ct. 711, 51 L. Ed. 2d 714

PER CURIAM

Respondent Carl Mathiason was convicted of first-degree burglary after a bench trial in which his confession was critical to the
State's case. At trial he moved to suppress the confession as the
fruit of questioning by the police not preceded by the warnings
required in Miranda v. Arizona, 384 U.S. 436 (1966). The trial
court refused to exclude the confession because it found that
Mathiason was not in custody at the time of the confession.

The Oregon Court of Appeals affirmed respondent's conviction,
but on his petition for review in the Supreme Court of Oregon that
court by a divided vote reversed the conviction. It found that although Mathiason had not been arrested or otherwise formally detained, "the interrogation took place in a 'coercive environment' "
of the sort to which Miranda was intended to apply. The court
conceded that its holding was contrary to decisions in other jurisdictions, and referred in particular to People v. Yukl, 25 N.Y.2d
585, 256 N.E.2d 172 (1969). The State of Oregon has petitioned
for certiorari to review the judgment of the Supreme Court of
Oregon. We think that court has read Miranda too broadly, and we
therefore reverse its judgment.

The Supreme Court of Oregon described the factual situation
surrounding the confession as follows:

"An officer of the State Police investigated a theft at a residence
near Pendleton. He asked the lady of the house which had been
burglarized if she suspected anyone. She replied that the defendant
was the only one she could think of. The defendant was a parolee
and a 'close associate' of her son. The officer tried to contact defendant on three or four occasions with no success. Finally, about
25 days after the burglary, the officer left his card at defendant's
apartment with a note asking him to call because "I'd like to
discuss something with you.' The next afternoon the defendant did
call. The officer asked where it would be convenient to meet. The
defendant had no preference; so the officer asked if the defendant
could meet him at the state patrol office in about an hour and a
half, about 5:00 p.m. The patrol office was about two blocks from
defendant's apartment. The building housed several state agencies.

"The officer met defendant in the hallway, shook hands and took
him into an office. The defendant was told he was not under arrest.
The door was closed. The two sat across a desk. The police radio
in another room could be heard. The officer told defendant he
wanted to talk to him about a burglary and that his truthfulness
would possibly be considered by the district attorney or judge. The
officer further advised that the police believed defendant was involved in the burglary and [falsely stated that] defendant's fingerprints were found at the scene. The defendant sat for a few minutes
and then said he had taken the property. This occurred within five
minutes after defendant had come to the office. The officer then advised defendant of his Miranda rights and took a taped confession.

"At the end of the taped conversation the officer told defendant he was not arresting him at this time; he was released to go about his job and return to his family. The officer said he was referring the case to the district attorney for him to determine whether criminal charges would be brought. It was 5:30 p.m. when the defendant left the office.

"The officer gave all the testimony relevant to this issue. The defendant did not take the stand either at the hearing on the motion to suppress or at the trial." State v. Mathiason, 549 P.2d 673, 674 (1976).

The Supreme Court of Oregon reasoned from these facts that:

"We hold the interrogation took place in a 'coercive environment.' The parties were in the offices of the State Police; they were alone behind closed doors; the officer informed the defendant he was a suspect in a theft and the authorities had evidence incriminating him in the crime; and the defendant was a parolee under supervision. We are of the opinion that this evidence is not overcome by the evidence that the defendant came to the office in response to a request and was told he was not under arrest." Id., at 675.

Our decision in *Miranda* set forth rules of police procedure applicable to "custodial interrogation." "By custodial interrogation, we mean questioning initiated by law enforcement officers after a person has been taken into custody or otherwise deprived of his freedom of action in any significant way." 384 U.S. at 444. Subsequently we have found the Miranda principle applicable to questioning which takes place in a prison setting during a suspect's term of imprisonment on a separate offense, Mathis v. United States, 391 U.S. 1 (1968), and to questioning taking place in a suspect's home, after he has been arrested and is no longer free to go where he pleases. Orozco v. Texas, 394 U.S. 324 (1969).

In the present case, however, there is no indication that the questioning took place in a context where respondent's freedom to depart was restricted in any way. He came voluntarily to the police station, where he was immediately informed that he was not under arrest. At the close of a one half-hour interview respondent did in fact leave the police station without hindrance. It is clear from these facts that Mathiason was not in custody "or otherwise deprived of his freedom of action in any significant way."

Such a noncustodial situation is not converted to one in which Miranda applies simply because a reviewing court concludes that, even in the absence of any formal arrest or restraint on freedom of movement, the questioning took place in a "coercive environment." Any interview of one suspected of a crime by a police officer will have coercive aspects to it, simply by virtue of the fact that the police officer is part of a law enforcement system which may ultimately cause the suspect to be charged with a crime. But police officers are not required to administer Miranda warnings to everyone whom they question. Nor is the requirement of warnings to be imposed simply because the questioned person is one whom the police suspect. Miranda warnings are required only where there has been such a restriction on a person's freedom as to render him "in custody." It was that sort of coercive environment to which Miranda by its terms was made applicable, and to which it is limited.

The officer's false statement about having discovered Mathiason's fingerprints at the scene was found by the Supreme Court of Oregon to be another circumstance contributing to the coercive environment which makes the Miranda rationale applicable. Whatever relevance this fact may have to other issues in the case, it has nothing to do with whether respondent was in custody for purposes of the *Miranda* rule.

The petition for certiorari is granted, the judgment of the Oregon Supreme Court is reversed, and the case is remanded for proceedings not inconsistent with this opinion.

[Mr. Justice BRENNAN would have granted the writ but dissented from the summary disposition and would have set the case for oral argument.]

Mr. Justice STEVENS, dissenting.

In my opinion the issues presented by this case are too important to be decided summarily. Of particular importance is the fact that the respondent was on parole at the time of his interrogation in the police station. This fact lends support to inconsistent conclusions.

On the one hand, the State surely has greater power to question a parolee about his activities than to question someone else. Moreover, as a practical matter, it seems unlikely that a Miranda warning would have much effect on a parolee's choice between silence and responding to police interrogation. Arguably, therefore, Miranda warnings are entirely inappropriate in the parole context.

On the other hand, a parolee is technically in legal custody continuously until his sentence has been served. Therefore, if a formalistic analysis of the custody question is to determine when the Miranda warning is necessary, a parolee should always be warned. Moreover, Miranda teaches that even if a suspect is not in custody, warnings are necessary if he is "otherwise deprived of his freedom of action in any significant way." If a parolee being questioned in a police station is not described by that language, today's decision qualifies that part of Miranda to some extent. I believe we would have a better understanding of the extent of that qualification, and therefore of the situations in which warnings must be given to a suspect who is not technically in custody, if we had the benefit of full argument and plenary consideration.

I therefore respectfully dissent from the Court's summary disposition.

[Mr. Justice MARSHALL dissented on the merits.]

6. ERNESTO MIRANDA IS SLAIN*

PHOENIX, ARIZ. (AP) — Ernesto Miranda, for whom the landmark Miranda decision was named — requiring police to inform arrested persons of their rights — was stabbed to death yesterday in what police said appeared to be a bar fight.

Miranda, 34, received numerous stab wounds and was pronounced dead at a Phoenix hospital, police said. They said no one

---

*From the *Kansas City Star,* February 1, 1976. Copyright 1976 by the Associated Press.

had been arrested and there were no other details available immediately.

The decision involving Miranda was issued by the U.S. Supreme Court in 1966 after the justices overturned his conviction for rape and kidnapping on grounds that he was not advised of his rights at the time of his arrest.

Miranda was later retried, convicted and resentenced to 20 to 30 years in prison for the 1963 crimes. He also served a consecutive term for an unrelated $8 robbery of a housewife.

Miranda was paroled in 1972. In July, 1974, he was arrested on a charge of possession of a firearm while on parole. The arrest came after he was stopped for a routine traffic violation. That charge was later dropped.

When he was arrested in 1963, Miranda was 23 years old and had just rented a house in Phoenix.

He said officers promised to drop robbery charges if he would confess to a kidnapping.

"So I made the statement," Miranda said.

But when he got to court he was told he was still charged with robbery. Miranda said he repeatedly asked for a lawyer but was denied one. Eventually an attorney was appointed by the court.

Miranda was convicted of robbery, then was brought to trial for kidnapping and rape, for which he also was convicted.

Unknown to Miranda, his case had caught the eye of other Phoenix lawyers. His case was argued before the U.S. Supreme Court by John Flynn, who thought the crux of the case rested on a violation of the Fifth Amendment which guarantees the right to remain silent.

He also argued that the Sixth Amendment, the right to counsel, had been violated.

On June 13, 1966, the Supreme Court in a 5–4 decision, upheld the Fifth and Sixth Amendment rights of Miranda and other prisoners in other states.

By chance, Miranda's name was the first on the list, and the ruling came to be known as the Miranda decision. Most police officers now carry a "Miranda card" with the now famous words, beginning, "You have the right to remain silent...."

7. Some other recent lower federal and state court decisions involving *Miranda* warnings and interrogations are: *Commonwealth* v. *Hosey,* 334 N.E.2d 44 (Mass. 1975) (*Miranda* waiver invalid where the defendant was drunk, highly agitated, and obviously not mentally normal); *Rowpotham* v. *State,* 542 P.2d 610 (Okla. Crim. App. 1975) (*Miranda* warning that included statement that the police cannot presently obtain a lawyer for the suspect "but one will be appointed for you, if you wish, when you got to court," held adequate); *State* v. *Malvia,* 539 P.2d 1200 (Hawaii 1975) (waiver-of-*Miranda*-rights form that informs a suspect that if he cannot afford an attorney "the court will appoint one for you" held to adequately inform a defendant that his right to a lawyer attaches immediately); *People* v. *White,* 338 N.E.2d 81 (Ill. 1975) (confession made two days after interrogation admissible even though police failed to obtain lawyer for in-custody suspect after he first stated he would rather have an attorney and was given *Miranda* warnings several times); *People* v. *Parnell,* 334 N.E.2d 403 (Ill. App. 1975) (when there is a request for an attorney prior to any questioning, a

knowing and intelligent waiver of a right to an attorney is impossible, and all questioning must cease); *Commonwealth* v. *Romberger*, 347 A.2d 460 (Pa. 1975) (*Miranda-Tucker* exclusionary rule that *Miranda* does not apply to custodial statements obtained prior to Miranda held inapplicable in Pennsylvania); *United States* v. *Olof*, 527 F.2d 752 (9th Cir. 1975) (Federal agents' resumption of their custodial interrogation of a defendant who had refused to make a statement three hours earlier held violative of *Miranda* as they questioned him about the same subject matter); *United States* v. *Clayton*, 407 F. Supp. 204 (E.D. Wisc. 1976) (*Michigan* v. *Mosley* [infra] not applicable to a statement obtained from a defendant who was twice questioned within an hour by the same officer regarding the same crime); *United States* v. *Johnson*, 529 F.2d 581 (8th Cir. 1976) (statements of a defendant who agreed to answer questions of federal agents but refused to sign a waiver-of-*Miranda*-rights form held admissible); *State* v. *McNeal*, 337 So. 2d 178 (La. 1976) (police officers who had provided defendant with a written explanation of his rights under *Miranda* held not required to supplement the written form with oral explanations despite the defendant's contention that he was too nervous to read or understand the writing); *Jordon* v. *Commonwealth*, 222 S.E.2d 573 (Va. 1976) (police officer's questioning of those present at the scene of a fatal shooting after responding to an emergency call held not custodial interrogation in the *Miranda* sense); *Hearne* v. *State*, 534 S.W.2d. 703 (Tex. Ct. Crim. App. 1976) (police officer's persistence in questioning in-custody defendant after the defendant had first expressed his desire to remain silent and in persuading the defendant to confess held violative of *Miranda*); *People* v. *Medina*, 347 N.E.2d 424 (Ill. App. 1976) (police resumption of questioning after in-custody defendant expressed a desire to remain silent renders the defendant's oral and written statements in response to the resumed questioning inadmissible); *State* v. *Robbins*, 547 P.2d 288 (Wash. App. 1976) (defendant's refusal on Friday to make statement following *Miranda* warnings and to sign "Acknowledgement and Waiver" form did not bar the police from requesting the defendant to sign form on Monday, and her subsequent oral statements are admissible); *People* v. *Hobson*, 348 N.E.2d 894 (N.Y. Ct. App. 1976) (once a defendant obtains counsel he cannot waive his right to counsel unless he relinquishes that right in his attorney's presence, and any statements taken by the police at interrogation prior to the waiver are inadmissible); *Commonwealth* v. *Yates*, 357 A.2d 134 (Pa. 1976) (statement from in-custody defendant in the absence of retained counsel following a waiver of his *Miranda* rights is admissible); *People* v. *Ridley*, 242 N.W.2d. 402 (Mich. 1976) (police officers responding to a radio report of a B & E in progress, held not required to give *Miranda* warnings to a man found parked near the house several citizens had directed them to); *United States* v. *Toral*, 536 F.2d 893 (9th Cir. 1976) (defendant's statements made after he was given proper *Miranda* warnings not tainted by his earlier statements improperly obtained in the absence of warnings) (see also *Knott* v. *Howard*, 511 F.2d 1060 [1st Cir. 1975], *United States* v. *Knight*, 395 F.2d 971 [2nd Cir. 1968], cert. denied, 395 U.S. 930 [1969], *Cotton* v. *United States*, 371 F.2d 385, 393 [9th Cir. 1967]); *People* v. *Morgan*, 350 N.E.2d 27 (Ill. App. 1976) (inculpatory statement of in-custody defendant after he first requested counsel but later decided to talk held admissible); *State* v. *Johnson*, 226 S.E.2d 442 (W. Va. App. 1976) (spontaneously uttered statement by a defendant not in custody held admissible without the trial court first determining its voluntariness); *United States* v. *Satterfield*, 417 F. Supp. 293 (S.D.N.Y. 1976) (statements obtained from indicted defendant without the benefit of counsel held inadmissible despite the giving of *Miranda* warnings since the defendant was not first warned of the implications of waiving counsel); *People* v. *Norwood*, 245 N.W.2d 170 (Mich. App. 1976) (deputy who went to woman's home after she said, over the telephone, that she had shot her former husband should not have questioned her without first advising her of her *Miranda* rights); *United States* v. *Flores-Calvillo*, 540 F.2d 432 (9th Cir. 1976) (defendant's assertion of right to counsel following *Miranda* warnings precludes a later interrogation even though preceded by new warnings); *State* v. *Magby*, 554 P.2d 1272 (Ariz. 1976) (in-custody statements about a later crime made without *Miranda* warnings to a parole officer held inadmissible if the parolee is prosecuted for that crime); *Sanville* v. *State*, 553 P.2d 1386 (Wyo. 1976) (police officer who arrived at a burglary victim's house at the same time as a man trying to return stolen items to the victim held not required to give *Miranda* warnings before asking him where he had gotten the tools); *Lamb* v. *Commonwealth*, 227 S.E.2d 737 (Va. 1976) (custodial interrogation of a defendant who had his attorney arrange for his surrender and warn the police about interrogating him upheld as a valid waiver); *United States* v. *Pheaster*, 544 F.2d 353 (9th Cir. 1976) (suspect's insistence upon seeing a lawyer does not preclude agents from informing him of the evidence against him, and his subsequent cooperation is a valid waiver of *Miranda* rights); *People* v. *Sandovall*, 353 N.E. 2d 715 (Ill. App. 1976) (police may interrogate an in-custody defendant even though he has already been provided with the assistance of a public defender) (see also *United States* v. *Springer*, 460 F.2d 1344 [2nd Cir. 1972], and *United States* v. *Crisp*, 435 F.2d 354 [7th Cir. 1971]); *State* v. *Carl*, 246 N.W.2d 192 (Minn. 1976) (police officers investigating kidnapping of man's son did not preclude them from further questioning the father after he said, "Don't bother me," as the officers at that time had no reason to suspect the father); *People* v. *Wong*, 555 P.2d 297 (Calif. 1976) (custodial interrogation of a defendant without first notifying and obtaining the consent of the attorney who is representing the defendant is proper); *State* v. *Snethen*, 245 N.W.2d 308 (Iowa 1976) (admissibility of statements of person in custody who has decided to remain silent depends on whether his right to cut off questioning under *Miranda* was scrupulously honored); *Commonwealth* v. *Fielding*, 353 N.E.2d 719 (Mass. 1976) (voluntary statements by a defendant are admissible if *Miranda* warnings have been given between an illegal arrest and the statement); *State* v. *Snethen*, 245 N.W.2d 308 (Iowa 1976) (interrogation within the meaning of *Miranda* includes police conduct which is designed to elicit admissions); *Lamb* v. *Commonwealth*, 227 S.E.2d 737 (Va. 1976) (the right to have counsel present during interrogation is a right of the defendant not of defendant's counsel); *State* v. *Strong*, 245 N.W.2d 277 (S.D. 1976) (undercover agent not required to give *Miranda* warnings to defendant since drug investigation focused on him); *United States* v. *Calhoun*, 363 A.2d 277 (D.C. App. 1976) (*Miranda* warnings not required prior to all interviews with suspect after investigation has focused on him); *State* v. *McNeal,* 337 So. 2d 178 (La. 1976) (*Miranda* rights need not be orally explained to an accused); *Commonwealth* v. *Borodine,* 353 N.E.2d 649 (Mass. 1976) (in giving *Miranda* rights to defendant, police do not have to tell him he is a suspect); *State* v. *Thomas,* 553 P.2d 1357 (Wash. App. 1976) (collateral inquiry relative to a defendant's awareness of his *Miranda* rights may not be substituted for giving *Miranda* warnings); *People* v. *Sandoval,* 353 N.E.2d 715 (Ill. App. 1976) (retention or appointment of counsel does not absolutely preclude defendant from waiving *Miranda* rights without counsel being present or notified); *Grimes* v. *State,* 354 N.E.2d 500 (Ind. App. 1976) (there is no requirement that a defendant sign a written waiver of his *Miranda* rights).

How to Circumvent Miranda

"PARTICIPATING MIRANDA" An Attempt to Subvert Certain Constitutional Safeguards*†

Peter W. Lewis and Harry E. Allen

* * *

About ten years ago the United States Supreme Court held that the Fifth Amendment privilege against self-incrimination requires that procedural guidelines be implemented before the custodial interrogation of a suspect by law enforcement agents. Specifically, in 1966 the Court held, in *Miranda* v. *Arizona,*[1] that before any questioning, a suspect must be informed that he has the right to remain silent; that anything he says can be used against him in a subsequent criminal proceeding; that he has the right to the presence of an attorney during the interrogation; and that, if he cannot afford an at-

torney, one will be appointed for him at the state's expense.

The doctrinal underpinnings of *Miranda* were an extension of *Escobedo* v. *Illinois,*[2] decided two years earlier, which held that a suspect (detained at a police station) has a Sixth Amendment right to the *presence* of his *retained* counsel during a custodial interrogation. Both decisions (and especially *Miranda*) have been the subject of much debate and criticism, most notably by law enforcement authorities.[3] Indeed, four justices on the *Miranda* Court did not agree that the Fifth Amendment requires such procedural safeguards.[4] To date, the Supreme Court has decided few cases involving alleged *Miranda* violations, although there is a plethora of lower federal and state court decisions involving these issues.[5]

This article describes and demonstrates a method of interrogation, utilized by some members of the homicide division in a large metropolitan police force, which attempts to subvert *Miranda* safeguards, and it indicates how this modified procedure is accomplished with relative success and impunity—at least in one jurisdiction.

What Miranda Means

Before *Miranda,* a confession was admissible only if it was voluntary. Involuntary confessions were and are *per se* inadmissible at trial; and voluntariness was determined by the "totality of circumstances" surrounding the confession.[6] Thus, the time and place of the alleged confession, the defendant's background (including his intelligence, education, and mental status), and the length and conditions of the interrogation were considered on the question of ad-

*From 23 Crime and Delinquency 75 (January, 1977). Reprinted by permission of the National Council on Crime and Delinquency.

†This article was written before some other *Miranda*-type cases were decided by the Supreme Court. See, *Michigan* v. *Mosley,* 423 U.S. 96 (1975); *Beckwith* v. *United States,* 425 U.S. 341 (1976); *United States* v. *Mandujano,* 425 U.S. 564 (1976); and *Doyle* v. *Ohio,* 426 U.S. 610 (1976). See also *Brewer* v. *Williams,* 430 U.S. 387 (1977), infra.

missibility of a confession.[7] Only when the trier-of-fact concluded that an alleged confession was the voluntary product of an unfettered free will could a defendant's inculpatory or exculpatory statements be used in determining his guilt or innocence. The same year that *Escobedo* was decided, the Court, in an attempt to screen against a possible misuse of an involuntary confession by the jury, held that the initial determination of the voluntariness of a confession was to be decided by the trial judge outside the presence of the jury in what is often referred to as a *Jackson-Denno* hearing.[8] Only if the judge concluded that the confession was voluntary could the jury utilize this evidence in its decision-making process, and it was free to reject the judge's initial determination that the confession was voluntary. Later, in *Lego* v. *Twomey*,[9] a plurality Court held that the burden of proof regarding the voluntariness of a confession was by a "preponderance of evidence" (rather than the "proof beyond a reasonable doubt" required for a conviction).

Clearly, the intent of *Miranda* was to undermine subversive attempts by the police to obtain confessions which might be less than voluntary and reliable. In addition, the Court recognized that a suspect should be given an opportunity to exercise his Fifth Amendment right to remain silent and understand the legal consequences of a waiver. As an additional safeguard, the Court recognized the importance of the role of counsel during a police interrogation. However, a defendant can waive these Fifth and Sixth Amendment rights provided the waiver is made "voluntarily, knowingly and intelligently."[10]

Following *Miranda* several empirical studies demonstrated that the decision did not "handcuff" the police in the apprehension and conviction of criminals and that the rate of confessions by suspects in custody has remained substantially the same as the pre-*Miranda* confession rate.[11] These studies indicated that often *Miranda* warnings are read from a card by a police officer in rapid succession and in bureaucratic tones and that most defendants do not, in fact, understand the nature of the constitutional rights given and often quickly waive these procedural safeguards. Despite these findings, it is not uncommon for many law enforcement authorities to complain that *Miranda* serves only to "handcuff" effective law enforcement activities and ultimately allows "dangerous criminals to be set free on the streets." Some of them have gone beyond the point of verbal dissatisfaction with *Miranda* and have attempted to skirt the parameters of the rule. Before explaining how this is done, we shall review the conditions under which the *Miranda* rules become operational.

Miranda (and the three cases decided with it)[12] involved custodial interrogations of suspects at police stations. Although there was no evidence that the suspects had been subjected to physical brutality during the interrogation process, the police had used a variety of psychological techniques designed to encourage the suspects to waive their right to remain silent. As noted by the *Miranda* court:

> The modern practice of in-custody interrogation is psychologically rather than physically oriented.... Interrogation still takes place in privacy.[13]

The *Miranda* court noted and quoted from, or described tactics recommended in, various police manuals and texts which documented procedures utilizing various psychological ploys that had been successfully used to obtain confessions. Such practices included *inter alia* the so-called "Mutt and Jeff" (friendly-unfriendly) act, the "reverse line-up," offering the suspect legal excuses for his actions, and suggesting to the suspect that refusing to talk could have an incriminating significance. The Court summarized the then-existing interrogation techniques as follows:

> To be alone with the subject is essential to prevent distraction and to deprive him of any outside support. The aura of confidence in his guilt undermines his will to resist. He merely confirms the preconceived story the police seek to have him describe. Patience and persistence, at times relentless questioning, are employed. To obtain a confession, the interrogator must "patiently maneuver himself or his quarry into a position from which the desired objective may be obtained." When normal procedures fail to produce the needed result, the police may resort to deceptive stratagems such as giving false legal advice. It is important to keep the subject off balance, for example, by trading on his insecurity about himself or his surroundings. The police then persuade, trick, or cajole him out of exercising his constitutional rights.[14]

In order to protect suspects against incommunicado interrogations in a police-dominated atmosphere resulting in self-incriminating statements without full warnings of constitutional rights, the Court held that a custodial interrogation is one that occurs "after a person has been taken into custody or otherwise deprived of his freedom of action in any significant way."[15] Subsequently, the Court held that *Miranda* warnings are not restricted to police station interrogations and that such procedural safeguards are applicable to interrogations in a home[16] or even in jail where a suspect is being held on another charge.[17] However, such warnings are apparently not required in the absence of questioning by law enforcement agents designed to elicit statements (inculpatory and exculpatory) by the suspect. Thus, if a suspect decides to appear at a police station and make a confession, *Miranda* does not preclude the police from receiving his statements before the giving of such warnings. Nor has the Court suggested that a suspect must be given *Miranda* warnings *immediately* following an arrest. *Miranda* and its progeny suggest only that the warnings must *precede* custodial interrogations.

How Miranda is Subverted

There is one interrogation procedure presently utilized by some police in a large metropolitan area designed to elicit a voluntary confession (in the pre-*Miranda* tradition) from a suspect charged with a homicide offense. This procedure is known as "Participating Miranda" and operates in the following manner:

Suppose the police, with probable cause, arrest a suspect ("Sam") at his house or on the street for murder. Sam is transported in a patrol car to the police station. The ride to the police station is made in silence; Sam has not been given any *Miranda* warnings and he has not been questioned. The *Miranda* rules have apparently not been violated—there has been no custodial interrogation. As soon as the booking process is completed, the suspect is taken into a room and a "friendly" officer begins to give him the *Miranda* warnings: "Sam, you have a right to remain silent and anything you say can be used against you." The officer then says, calmly and casually (almost as if talking out loud to himself) that often the police arrest the wrong person; that it is understandable why a person might carry a gun for self-protection (suggesting a legal justification for the suspect's actions); that the victim was probably responsible for his own demise, etc. At this point as much as fifteen to thirty minutes may have passed since the first warnings were given. At no time has the suspect been directly questioned or asked to confess.

Next, Officer Friendly informs the suspect that he has a right to the presence of an attorney during any custodial interrogation. Officer Friendly continues his narration by indicating that retained counsel is often a needless expense and that a suspect with nothing to hide does not need professional service. The narration continues a few more minutes and finally the suspect is informed that counsel will be appointed for him at the state's expense if he cannot afford one. The soliloquy may continue several more minutes. *"Participating Miranda"* may take from thirty minutes to a full hour.

Our sources state that most suspects will voluntarily make inculpatory or exculpatory statements before the final *Miranda* warnings are given and that as soon as the officer is certain that the suspect is willing to discuss the events leading up to his arrest, the officer will remind the suspect that he has been given his full constitutional rights (sometimes they are given in rapid succession when it is clear that the suspect will talk). Next, the suspect is asked whether he understands these rights (most suspects answer affirmatively) and is willing to sign a waiver of his constitutional rights (again, most suspects answer affirmatively). As soon as the waiver is signed by the suspect, the real interrogation begins and discrepancies in the suspect's story are noted in order to obtain a full confession. The suspect is *convinced* he has been given his full constitutional rights (sometimes two times) and he usually has no reason to complain. He is, of course, overlooking the fact that the police have his confession and a signed waiver of his constitutional rights.

Later the suspect, in response to his counsel's inquiry, is *certain* that he has been given his constitutional rights, and the signed waiver is prima facie proof. Given the above, most defense attorneys will consider plea bargaining. It is well known that up to 90 per cent of defendants plead guilty in exchange for a reduced charge or a recommended lighter sentence[18]; and in most jurisdictions acceptance of a guilty plea by the court is a bar to collateral attacks.[19] That is, the method by which the confession was obtained cannot be legally attacked on appeal. Generally, only the issue of whether the guilty plea was made voluntarily or whether the defendant received the aid of effective counsel is open to attack.[20]

In short, the police have successfully subverted the *Miranda* rules and obtained an apparently voluntary confession (in the traditional sense); the defendant has pleaded guilty to the substantive charge or a reduced charge and has been sentenced to prison. The defendant is certain that his *Miranda* rights were not violated (although he may have other complaints); the police are pleased that another "dangerous criminal" is off the streets; the defense attorney and the prosecutor "believe" that the defendant was given his full *Miranda* warnings; the sentencing judge is officially unaware that the defendant was subjected to *"Participating Miranda"* (it was never raised in court); and, in most jurisdictions, an appellate court will not review collateral issues attending a guilty plea. All participants are "satisfied" that justice has been served.

"Participating Miranda," however, does not work in all cases; nor is it used on all defendants. We are told that the police select suspects for subjection to this psychological technique on the basis of prior criminal record, education, intelligence, social class, and, in some cases, race; in addition, the seriousness of the crime charged and other available evidence weigh heavily in the decision whether to invoke the technique. That is, the "poorer" the defendant's background, the more likely is it that he will be subjected to *"Participating Miranda."* The vice, of course, is that this psychological technique strikes at the heart of the doctrinal underpinnings of *Miranda* and allows the Fifth Amendment to become little more than an empty promise. The technique plays on human weaknesses and extracts a heavy toll of individual liberty. Generally the police believe that *technically* the *Miranda* rules were fully complied with (as there was no overt custodial interrogation until a waiver of constitutional rights was secured), although a few police officers freely admit

that the intent of the *Miranda* rules was undermined.

There are no studies which indicate whether and how often *"Participating Miranda"* is used in other jurisdictions. To assume that this technique is confined to a homicide division of a single police force would be no victory for common sense; perhaps it is used elsewhere under a different label. Nevertheless, it is applied in at least one large jurisdiction with increasing frequency and, in the words of a veteran police officer: "We wouldn't do it if we couldn't get away with it. When used, there is a high probability that the technique will work." The police do not believe that the technique can and does result in wrongful convictions. After all, "innocent men do not voluntarily confess."

Despite adverse feelings about *Miranda* by some law enforcement authorities, there seems to be little justification for the police to undermine a suspect's constitutional rights and, by a psychological ploy, subvert the procedural safeguards ordered by the Supreme Court. The defendant has hardly "voluntarily, knowingly and intelligently" waived his constitutional rights. As noted by the *Miranda* court:

We have concluded that without proper safeguards the process of in-custody interrogation of persons suspected or accused of crime contains inherently compelling pressures which work to undermine the individual's will to resist and to compel him to speak where he would not otherwise do so freely. In order to combat these pressures and to permit a full opportunity to exercise the privilege against self-incrimination, the accused must be adequately and effectively apprised of his rights and the exercise of those rights must be fully honored.[21]

References

1. *Miranda* v. *Arizona*, 384 U.S. 436 (1966) [supra].
2. *Escobedo* v. *Illinois*, 378 U.S. 478 (1964).
3. In 1968, Congress purported to "repeal" *Miranda* by 18 U.S.C. § 3501, which purports to make all voluntary confessions admissible. The absence or the giving of *Miranda* warnings is not conclusive on the issue of the voluntariness of a confession. To date, the constitutionality of this statute has not been tested by the Supreme Court.
4. Justices Clark, Harlan, Stewart, and White dissented in *Miranda*.
5. The Supreme Court has recently allowed violation of *Miranda* to be admissible for impeachment purposes at trial. See e.g., *Harris* v. *New York*, 401 U.S. 222 (1971) [infra], and *Oregon* v. *Hass*, 420 U.S. 714 (1975) [infra].

6. See e.g., *Crooker* v. *California,* 357 U.S. 433 (1958); *Cicenia* v. *La Gay,* 357 U.S. 504 (1958); *Spano* v. *New York,* 360 U.S. 315 (1959); *Blackburn* v. *Alabama,* 361 U.S. 199 (1960) [supra].

7. *Ibid.*

8. *Jackson* v. *Denno,* 378 U.S. 368 (1964).

9. *Lego* v. *Twomey,* 404 U.S. 477 (1972).

10. 384 U.S. at 444.

11. *Interrogations in New Haven: The Impact of Miranda,* Yale Alumni Magazine, December 1968 at 18; Seeburger and Wettick, *Miranda in Pittsburgh,* 29 U. Pitt. L. Rev. 1 (1967); Medalie, Leitz, and Alexander, *Custodial Police Interrogation in Our Nation's Capital: The Attempt to Implement Miranda,* 66 Mich. L. Rev. 1347 (1968).

12. *Vignera* v. *New York* (no. 760), *Westover* v. *United States* (no. 761), and *California* v. *Stewart* (no. 584).

13. 384 at 448.

14. 384 at 455.

15. 384 at 477.

16. *Orozco* v. *Texas,* 394 U.S. 324 (1969).

17. *Mathis* v. *United States,* 391 U.S. 1 (1968).

18. President's Commission on Law Enforcement and Administration of Justice, *The Courts* 9 (1967).

19. See *Parker* v. *North Carolina,* 397 U.S. 790, 797 (1970); *McCann* v. *Richardson,* 397 U.S. 757, 770–71 (1970); *Brady* v. *United States,* 397 U.S. 742, 757 (1970); but see *Blackledge* v. *Perry,* 417 U.S. 21 (1974), in which the Supreme Court allowed collateral attack where a claim raised both double jeopardy and due process issues.

20. There are a few other exceptions, not relevant to this hypothetical case. See Note, *The United States Court of Appeals, 1973–1974 Term: Criminal Law and Procedure,* 63 Geo. L.J. 484–87 (1974).

21. *Miranda* v. *Arizona,* 384 U.S. 436, 467 (1966).

When *Miranda* Warnings are "Scrupulously Honored"

MICHIGAN v. MOSLEY

Supreme Court of the United States, 1975
423 U.S. 96, 96 S. Ct. 321, 46 L. Ed. 2d 313

Richard Mosley was arrested in Detroit in connection with certain robberies that had recently occurred. In accordance with *Miranda* v. *Arizona,* Mosley was advised that he was not obligated to answer any questions and that he could remain silent if he wished. Mosley acknowledged, orally and in writing, that he had received his *Miranda* warnings. Mosley declined to discuss the robberies and the arresting officer ceased the interrogation. About two hours later, after giving Mosley his *Miranda* warnings, another officer questioned him about an unrelated murder. Mosley acknowledged, orally and in writing, receiving the *Miranda* warnings from the second officer. During the latter interrogation, Mosley made an incriminating statement that was used, over his objection, in his trial for first degree murder. He was convicted of that offense and sentenced to life imprisonment. On appeal to the Michigan Court of Appeals, Mosley renewed his objections to the use of his incriminating statement at trial. That court reversed his conviction, and the Michigan Supreme Court denied review. The United States Supreme Court granted certiorari.

Mr. Justice STEWART delivered the opinion of the Court.

* * *

In the Miranda case this Court promulgated a set of safeguards to protect the there delineated constitutional rights of persons subjected to custodial police interrogation. In sum, the Court held in that case that unless law enforcement officers give certain specified warnings before questioning a person in custody, and follow certain specified procedures during the course of any subsequent interrogation, any statement made by the person in custody cannot over his objection be admitted in evidence against him as a defendant at trial, even though the statement may in fact be wholly voluntary. . . .

Neither party in the present case challenges the continuing validity of the Miranda decision, nor of any of the so-called guidelines it established to protect what the Court there said was a person's constitutional privilege against compulsory self-incrimination. The issue in this case, rather, is whether the conduct of the Detroit police that led to Mosley's incriminating statement did in fact violate the Miranda "guidelines," so as to render the statement inadmissible in evidence against Mosley at his trial. Resolution of the question turns almost entirely on the interpretation of a single passage in the Miranda opinion, upon which the Michigan appellate court relied in finding a per se violation of Miranda:

"Once warnings have been given, the subsequent procedure is clear. If the individual indicates in any manner, at any time prior to or during questioning, that he wishes to remain silent, the interrogation must cease. At this point he has shown that he intends to exercise his Fifth Amendment privilege; any statement taken after the person invokes his privilege cannot be other than the product of compulsion, subtle or otherwise. Without the right to cut off questioning, the setting of in-custody interrogation operates on the individual to overcome free choice in producing a statement after the privilege has been once invoked." 384 U.S., at 473–474.

This passage states that "the interrogation must cease" when the person in custody indicates that "he wishes to remain silent." It does not state under what circumstances, if any, a resumption of questioning is permissible. The passage could be literally read to mean that a person who has invoked his "right to silence" can never again be subjected to custodial interrogation by any police officer at any time or place on any subject. Another possible construction of the passage would characterize "any statement taken after the person invokes his privilege" as "the product of compulsion" and would therefore mandate its exclusion from evidence, even if it were volunteered by the person in custody without any further interrogation whatever. Or the passage could be interpreted to require only the immediate cessation of questioning, and to permit a resumption of interrogation after a momentary respite.

It is evident that any of these possible literal interpretations would lead to absurd and unintended results. To permit the continuation of custodial interrogation after a momentary cessation would clearly frustrate the purposes of Miranda by allowing repeated rounds of questioning to undermine the will of the person being questioned. At the other extreme, a blanket prohibition against the taking of voluntary statements or a permanent immunity from further interrogation regardless of the circumstances, would transform the Miranda safeguards into wholly irrational obstacles to legitimate police investigative activity, and deprive suspects of an opportunity to make informed and intelligent assessments of their interests. Clearly, therefore, neither this passage nor any other passage in the Miranda opinion can sensibly be read to create a per se proscription of indefinite duration upon any further questioning by any police officer on any subject, once the person in custody has indicated a desire to remain silent.

A reasonable and faithful interpretation of the Miranda opinion must rest on the intention of the Court in that case to adopt "fully effective means . . . to notify the person of his right of silence and to assure that the exercise of the right will be scrupulously honored. . . ." 384 U.S., at 479. The critical safeguard identified in the passage at issue is a person's "right to cut off questioning." Through the exercise of his option to terminate questioning he can control the time at which questioning occurs, the subjects discussed, and the duration of the interrogation. The requirement that law enforcement authorities must respect a person's exercise of that option counteracts the coercive pressures of the custodial setting. We therefore conclude that the admissibility of statements obtained after the person in custody has decided to remain silent depends under Miranda on whether his "right to cut off questioning" was "scrupulously honored."

A review of the circumstances leading to Mosley's confession reveals that his "right to cut off questioning" was fully respected in this case. Before his initial interrogation, Mosley was carefully advised that he was under no obligation to answer any questions and could remain silent if he wished. He orally acknowledged that he understood the Miranda warnings and then signed a printed notification of rights form. When Mosley stated that he did not want to discuss the robberies, Detective Cowie immediately ceased the interrogation and did not try either to resume the questioning or in any way to persuade Mosley to reconsider his position. After an interval of more than two hours, Mosley was questioned by another police officer at another location about an unrelated holdup murder. He was given full and complete Miranda warnings at the outset of the second interrogation. He was thus reminded again that he could remain silent and could consult with a lawyer, and was carefully given a full and fair opportunity to exercise these options. The subsequent questioning did not undercut Mosley's previous decision not to answer Detective Cowie's inquiries. Detective Hill did not resume the interrogation about the (robberies) but instead focused exclusively on the homicide, a crime different in nature and in time and place of occurrence from the robberies for which Mosley had been arrested and interrogated by Detective Cowie. Although it is not clear from the record how much Detective Hill knew about the earlier interrogation, his questioning of Mosley about an unrelated homicide was quite consistent with a reasonable interpretation of Mosley's earlier refusal to answer any questions about the robberies.

This is not a case, therefore, where the police failed to honor a decision of a person in custody to cut off questioning, either by refusing to discontinue the interrogation upon request or by persisting in repeated efforts to wear down his resistance and make him change his mind. In contrast to such practices, the police here immediately ceased the interrogation, resumed questioning only after the passage of a significant period of time and the provision of a fresh set of warnings, and restricted the second interrogation to a crime that had not been a subject of the earlier interrogation.

* * *

Here ... the police gave full "Miranda warnings" to Mosley at the very outset of each interrogation, subjected him to only a brief period of initial questioning, and suspended questioning entirely for a significant period before beginning the interrogation that led to his incriminating statement.... The failure of the police officers to give any warnings whatever to the person in their custody before embarking on an intense and prolonged interrogation of him was simply not present in this case....

For these reasons, we conclude that the admission in evidence of Mosley's incriminating statement did not violate the principles of *Miranda* v. *Arizona, supra.* . . .

Vacated and remanded.

Mr. Justice WHITE, concurring.

I concur in the result and in much of the majority's reasoning. However, it appears to me that, in an effort to make only a limited holding in this case, the majority has implied that some custodial confessions will be suppressed even though they follow an informed and voluntary waiver of the defendant's rights. The majority seems to say that a statement obtained within some unspecified time after an assertion by an individual of his "right to silence" is always inadmissible, even if it was the result of an informed and voluntary decision—following, for example, a disclosure to such an individual of a piece of information bearing on his waiver decision which the police had failed to give him prior to his assertion of the privilege but which they gave him immediately thereafter. Indeed ... the majority characterizes as "absurd" any contrary rule. I disagree. I don't think the majority's conclusion is compelled by Miranda v. Arizona ... and I suspect that in the final analysis the majority will adopt voluntariness as the standard by which to judge the waiver of the right to silence by a properly informed defendant. I think the Court should say so now.

* * *

Mr. Justice BRENNAN, with whom Mr. Justice MARSHALL joins, dissenting.

* * *

... The process of eroding Miranda rights, begun with Harris v. New York, 401 U.S. 222 (1971), continues with today's holding that police may renew the questioning of a suspect who has once exercised his right to remain silent, provided the suspect's right to cut off questioning has been "scrupulously honored." Today's distortion of Miranda's constitutional principles can be viewed only as yet another step toward the erosion and, I suppose, ultimate overruling of Miranda's enforcement of the privilege against self-incrimination.

* * *

... As to statements which are the product of renewed questioning, Miranda established a virtually irrebuttable presumption of compulsion ... and that presumption stands strongest where, as in this case, a suspect, having initially determined to remain silent, is subsequently brought to confess his crime. Only by adequate procedural safeguards could the presumption be rebutted.

In formulating its procedural safeguard, the Court skirts the problem of compulsion and thereby fails to join issue with the dictates of Miranda. The language which the Court finds controlling in this case teaches that renewed questioning is itself part of the process which invariably operates to overcome the will of a suspect. That teaching is embodied in the form of a proscription on any further questioning once the suspect has exercised his right to remain silent. Today's decision uncritically abandons that teaching. The Court assumes, contrary to the controlling language, that "scrupulously honoring" an initial exercise of the right to remain silent preserves the efficaciousness of initial and future warnings despite the fact that the suspect has once been subjected to interrogation and then has been detained for a lengthy period of time.

Observing that the suspect can control the circumstances of interrogation "[t]hrough the exercise of his option to terminate questioning," the Court concludes "that the admissibility of statements obtained after the person in custody has decided to remain silent depends . . . on whether his 'right to cut off questioning' was 'scrupulously honored.'" But scrupulously honoring exercises of the right to cut off questioning is only meaningful insofar as the suspect's will to exercise that right remains wholly unfettered. . . .

I agree that Miranda is not to be read, on the one hand, to impose an absolute ban on resumption of questioning "at any time or place on any subject," or on the other hand, "to permit a resumption of interrogation after a momentary respite," ibid. But this surely cannot justify adoption of a vague and ineffective procedural standard that falls somewhere between those absurd extremes, for Miranda in flat and unambiguous terms requires that questioning "cease" when a suspect exercises the right to remain silent. Miranda's terms, however, are not so uncompromising as to preclude the fashioning of guidelines to govern this case. . . .

* * *

... Today's decision, however, virtually empties Miranda of principle, for plainly the decision encourages police asked to cease interrogation to continue the suspect's detention until the police station's coercive atmosphere does its work and the suspect responds to resumed questioning. Today's rejection of that reality of life contrasts sharply with the Court's acceptance only two years ago that "[i]n Miranda the Court found that the techniques of police questioning and the nature of custodial surroundings produce an inherently coercive situation." Schneckloth v. Bustamonte, 412 U.S. 218 (1973). I can only conclude that today's decision signals rejection of Miranda's basic premise.

Miranda and Tax Collectors

BECKWITH v. UNITED STATES

Supreme Court of the United States, 1976
425 U.S. 341, 96 S. Ct. 1612, 48 L. Ed. 2d 1

The facts are stated in the opinion.

Mr. Chief Justice BURGER delivered the opinion of the Court.

The important issue presented in this case is whether a special agent of the Internal Revenue Service, investigating potential criminal income tax violations, must, in an interview with a taxpayer, not in custody, give the warnings called for by this Court's decision in Miranda v. Arizona, 394 U.S.

436 (1966). We granted certiorari to resolve the conflict between the holding of the Court of Appeals in this case, which is consistent with the weight of authority on the issue, and the position adopted by the United States Court of Appeals for the Seventh Circuit.

. . . After a considerable amount of investigation, two special agents of the Intelligence Division of the Internal Revenue Service met with petitioner in a private home where petitioner occasionally stayed. The senior agent testified that they went to see petitioner at this private residence at 8 a.m. in order to spare petitioner the possible embarrassment of being interviewed at his place of employment which opened at 10 a.m. Upon their arrival, they identified themselves to the person answering the door and asked to speak to petitioner. The agents were invited into the house and, when petitioner entered the room where they were waiting, they introduced themselves. . . . Petitioner then sat down at the dining room table with the agents; they presented their credentials and stated they were attached to the Intelligence Division and that one of their functions was to investigate the possibility of criminal tax fraud. They then informed petitioner that they were assigned to investigate his federal income tax liability for the years 1966 through 1971. The senior agent then read to petitioner from a printed card the following:

"As a special agent, one of my functions is to investigate the possibility of criminal violations of the Internal Revenue laws, and related offenses.

"Under the Fifth Amendment to the Constitution of the United States, I cannot compel you to answer any questions or to submit any information if such answers or information might tend to incriminate you in any way. I also advise you that anything which you say and any information which you submit may be used against you in any criminal proceeding which may be undertaken. I advise you further that you may, if you wish, seek the assistance of an attorney before responding."

Petitioner acknowledged that he understood his rights. The agents then interviewed him until about 11 o'clock. The agents described the conversation as "friendly" and "relaxed." The petitioner noted that the agents did not "press" him on any question he could not or chose not to answer.

Prior to the conclusion of the interview, the senior agent requested that petitioner permit the agents to inspect certain records. Petitioner indicated that they were at his place of employment. The agents asked if they could meet him there later. Traveling separately from petitioner the agents met petitioner approximately 45 minutes later and the senior agent advised the petitioner that he was not required to furnish any books or records; petitioner, however, supplied the books to the agents.

Prior to trial, petitioner moved to suppress all statements he made to the agents or evidence derived from those statements on the ground that petitioner had not been given the warnings mandated by Miranda. The District Court rules that he was entitled to such warnings "when the court finds as a fact that there were custodial circumstances." The District Judge went on to find that "on this record . . . there is no evidence whatsoever of any such situation." The Court of Appeals affirmed the judgment of conviction. 510 F.2d 751 (D.C. Cir. 1975). It noted that the reasoning of Miranda was based "in crucial part" on whether the suspect " 'has been taken into custody or otherwise deprived of his freedom in any significant way,' " . . . citing Miranda . . . and agreed with the District Court that "Beckwith was neither arrested nor detained against his will." We agree with the analysis of the Court of Appeals and, therefore, affirm its judgment.

* * *

. . . The narrow issue before the Court in Miranda was presented very precisely in the opening paragraph of that opinion — "the admissibility of statements obtained from an individual who is subjected to *custodial* police interrogation." 348 U.S., at 439. (Emphasis supplied.) The Court concluded that compulsion "is inherent in custodial surroundings," id., at 458, and, consequently, that special safeguards were required in the case of "incommunicado interrogation of individuals in a police-dominated atmosphere, resulting in self-incrimination statements without full warnings of constitutional rights." Id., at 455. In subsequent decisions, the Court specifically stressed that it was the *custodial* nature of the interrogation which triggered the necessity for adherence in the specific requirements of its Miranda holding. . . .

Petitioner's argument that he was placed in the functional and, therefore, legal equivalent of the Miranda situation asks us now to ignore completely that Miranda was grounded squarely in the Court's explicit and detailed assessment of the peculiar "nature and setting of . . . in-custody interrogation," 386 U.S., at 455. . . . Mathis v. United States, 391 U.S. 1 (1968), directly supports this conclusion in holding that the Miranda requirements are applicable to interviews with Internal Revenue agents concerning tax liability, *when the subject is in custody;* the Court thus squarely grounded its holding on the custodial aspects of the situation, not the subject matter of the interview.

An interview with government agents in a situation such as the one shown by this record simply does not present the elements which the Miranda Court found so inherently coercive as to require its holding. . . . Miranda specifically defined "focus," for its purposes, as "questioning initiated by law enforcement officers *after* a person has been taken into custody or otherwise deprived of his action in any significant way." 384 U.S., at 444. (Emphasis supplied.) . . .

We recognize, of course, that noncustodial interrogation might possibly in some situations, by virtue of some special circumstances, be characterized as one where "the behavior of . . . law enforcement officials was such as to overbear petitioner's will to resist and bring about confessions not freely self-determined. . . ." Rogers v. Richmond, 365 U.S. 534, 544 (1961). When such a claim is raised, it is the duty of an appellate court, including this Court, "to examine the entire record and make an independent determination of the ultimate issue of voluntariness." . . . Proof that some kind of warnings were given or that none were given would be relevant evidence only on the issue of whether the questioning was in fact coercive. . . . In the present case . . . "[t]he

entire interview was free of coercion," 510 F.2d, at 743 [footnote omitted].

Accordingly, the judgment of the Court of Appeals is
Affirmed.

Mr. Justice MARSHALL, concurring in the judgment.

. . . Under the circumstances of this case, in which petitioner was not under arrest and the interview took place in a private home . . . the warning recited [by the special agent] satisfied the requirements of the Fifth Amendment. If this warning had not been given, however, I would not join the judgment of the Court.

Mr. Justice BRENNAN, dissenting.

I respectfully dissent. In my view the District Court should have granted petitioner's motion to suppress all statements made by him to the agents because the agents did not give petitioner the warnings mandated by Miranda v. Arizona, 384 U.S. 436 (1966). . . . [T]he fact that Beckwith had not been taken into formal "custody" is not determinative of the question whether the agents were required to give him the Miranda warnings. I agree with the Court of Appeals for the Seventh Circuit that the warnings are also mandated when the taxpayer is, as here, interrogated by Intelligence Division agents of the Internal Revenue Service in surroundings where, as in the case of the subject in "custody," the practical compulsion to respond to questions about his tax returns is comparable to the psychological pressures described in *Miranda.* . . . Interrogation under conditions that have the practical consequence of compelling the taxpayer to make disclosures, and interrogation in "custody" having the same consequence, are in my view peas from the same pod. . . .

[Mr. Justice STEVENS took no part in the consideration or decision of this case.]

Comments

1. *Michigan* v. *Mosley,* supra, represents what might be called a further erosion of the *Miranda* principles. Although the holding of that decision was rather narrow and probably will not affect many subsequent cases, *Mosley* invites perhaps a more interesting ques-

tion. Suppose the second interrogating officer did not give the *Miranda* warnings to Mosley—knowing that the warnings had been given to him by the first interrogating officer. And suppose Mosley had voluntarily confessed to a crime unrelated to the one about which he had initially been interrogated. Would the Supreme Court have held the statements admissible? The touchstone of *Mosley* is that if *Miranda* rights are "scrupulously honored," the voluntary statements of a defendant will not be excluded on the basis of the *Miranda* decision.

2. In *Beckwith* v. *United States,* supra, a majority of the Court held that *Miranda* warnings are not required when a suspect is not in custody or when there is no evidence that the questioning was in fact coercive. The *Beckwith* interrogation took place in the privacy of his home. Is that controlling? Suppose Beckwith had been asked to come to the IRS office to discuss his tax returns. Is that the type of psychological coercion that *Miranda* was designed to protect against in the absence of adequate warnings? Suppose Beckwith had not been given any warnings at all. Would his answers have been compelled testimony within the meaning of the Fifth Amendment? Suppose Beckwith had refused to answer any questions. Could his silence have been used to impeach his credibility if he elected to testify at trial? See *Doyle* v. *Ohio,* infra, § 6.03. Would the *Beckwith* Court have reached a similar result if police officers, rather than IRS agents, had interviewed Beckwith at his home? The type of law enforcement agent is probably immaterial because the majority in *Beckwith* focused on the nature of the interrogation rather than the occupational classification of the agents involved. The majority opinion noted that *Miranda* presented a "narrow issue." If *Miranda* was decided on narrow grounds, doesn't that give the Court broad grounds to find exceptions to the requirements of *Miranda*? Although *Beckwith* in no way overrules *Miranda,* is the decision a further indication that a majority of the present Court is unwilling to expand the principles of *Miranda*?

A majority of the Court may be on the verge of overruling *Miranda* and returning to the older voluntariness test. The present Court seems to be saying, "We won't overrule *Miranda* yet, but in the meantime we won't necessarily exclude the voluntary statements of the defendants even though taken in violation of *Miranda*." The initial "sting" of *Miranda* has been assuaged. There are other constitutional devices that the Court might utilize to further weaken the impetus of *Miranda*. For example, the Court, in an appropriate case, could hold that an inadvertent violation of *Miranda* might be "harmless error"—permitting incriminating statements to be admitted and used as part of the prosecutor's case in chief (instead of allowing them to be used for impeachment purposes only). By 1976, only three of the justices who participated in the *Miranda* decision were still serving on the Court (Brennan, Stewart, and White), and, of them, only Justice Brennan supported the original decision. All the Nixon appointees (Chief Justice Burger, and Justices Powell, Blackmun, and Rehnquist) supported the decisions in *Harris* and *Hass* (infra). It should be noted that the Supreme Court has overruled itself in about 150 cases (out of tens of thousands of decisions), with an average span of about 20 years between decisions that overruled earlier cases. Thus, it is not surprising that the Court, out of respect for stare decisis ("let the precedent stand"), has not yet overruled *Miranda*. But as noted by Justice Brennan (dissenting in *Michigan* v. *Mosley,* supra) an actual overruling of *Miranda* may be forthcoming, and in the not too distant future.

3. In *Fisher* v. *United States,* 425 U.S. 391 (1976), a unanimous Supreme Court held that enforcement of an IRS summons to a taxpayer's attorney for the production of an accountant's work papers that had been transferred through the taxpayer to the attorney does not violate the taxpayer's privilege against self-incrimination. The Court reasoned that because the work papers would not have been protected in the taxpayer's hands by the Fifth Amendment, they were not protected in the attorney's hands by the attorney-client privilege. However, a taxpayer's papers not subject to subpoena are, by virtue of the attorney-client privilege, unobtainable from an attorney to whom the taxpayer has transferred the papers in order to obtain legal assistance.

4. In *Andresen* v. *Maryland,* 427 U.S. 463 (1976), a majority of the Supreme Court rejected the view that the admission into evidence of one's personal and private papers properly seized pursuant to a valid search warrant involves "compulsion" within the meaning of the Fifth Amendment privilege against self-incrimination. The Court noted that the Fifth Amendment prohibition against compelling a person to be a witness against himself is a personal privilege which adheres basically to the person. The privilege is not transgressed simply because the defendant is made the source of the incriminating evidence, so long as the evidence is not secured by means of testimonial compulsion.

5. In *Garner* v. *United States,* 424 U.S. 64 (1976), a unanimous Supreme Court held that the Fifth Amendment privilege against self-incrimination does not bar use of a defendant's federal income tax returns in which he stated, instead of claiming the privilege, that he was a professional gambler and derived substantial income as such. The Court applied the general rule that if a witness does not claim the privilege, his disclosures will not be considered as having been "compelled" within the meaning of the Fifth Amendment.

6. In *Couch* v. *United States,* 409 U.S. 322 (1973), a majority of the Supreme Court held that a taxpayer's records given to an accountant for use in preparing the taxpayer's income tax returns are outside the taxpayer's privilege against self-incrimination and are therefore subject to production pursuant to an IRS summons. The Court reasoned that since the taxpayer had voluntarily surrendered possession of the records to the accountant, no personal compulsion was exercised against the taxpayer to produce the records.

The administrative summons used in *Couch* demanded the production of "books, records, bank statements, cancelled checks, deposit ticket copies, workpapers and all pertinent documents pertaining to the tax liability" of the defendant, 409 U.S. at 323. The summons was authorized pursuant to Internal Revenue Code of 1954, § 7602, which provides, in part: "For the purpose of ascertaining the correctness of any return . . . the Secretary or his delegate is authorized: (1) To examine any books, papers, records . . . relevant or material to such inquiry; (2) To summon the person liable for tax or required to perform the act, or any officer or employee of such person, or any person having possession, custody, or care of books of account containing entries relating to the business of the person liable for tax or required to perform the act, or any other person the Secretary or his delegate may deem proper, to appear . . . and to produce such [materials], and to give such testimony, under oath, as may be relevant or material to such inquiry. . . ." In addition, § 7604(a) provides that any person summoned under § 7602 to appear or to produce records can be compelled to do so, by appropriate process, by "the United States district court for the district in which such person resides or is found." Finally if any person summoned under § 7602 neglects or refuses to obey the summons, § 7604(b) provides that "the Secretary or his delegate may apply to the judge of the district court or to a United States commissioner for the district within which the person so summoned resides or is found for an attachment against him as for a contempt . . . and, [upon] satisfactory proof [the judge or commissioner may] issue an attachment . . . for the arrest of such person. . . ." For a discussion of the investigatory powers of the IRS, see Ritholz, *The Commissioner's Inquisitorial Powers,* 45 Taxes 782 (1967); Note, *Criminal Tax Fraud Investigations: Limitations on the Scope of the Section 7602 Summons,* 25 U. Fla. L. Rev. 114 (1972). See also Lipton, *Constitutional Protection for Books and Records in Tax Fraud Investigations,* N.Y.U. 29th Institute on Fed. Tax 945 (1971); Lipton, *Constitutional Issues in Tax Fraud Cases,* 55 A.B.A.J. 731 (1969); Duke, *Prosecutions for Attempts to Evade Income Tax: A Discordant View of a Procedural Hybrid,* 76 Yale L.J. 1 (1966); Taylor, *The Commissioner's Summons—Its Scope—Who May Object,* N.Y.U. 27th Institute on Fed. Tax 1383 (1969); Garbis and Burke, *Fifth Amendment Protection of the Accountant's Workpapers in Tax Fraud Investigations,* 47 Taxes 12 (1969).

C. USE OF ILLEGALLY SEIZED EVIDENCE FOR IMPEACHMENT PURPOSES

When an Accused Is Not Warned of His Right to Counsel

HARRIS v. NEW YORK

Supreme Court of the United States, 1971
401 U.S. 222, 91 S. Ct. 643, 28 L. Ed. 2d 1

Harris was charged by the State of New York in a two count indictment with twice selling heroin to an undercover police officer. After being taken into custody, Harris was not warned of his right to counsel, in violation of *Miranda* v. *Arizona.* At the subsequent trial, the undercover police officer testified as to the details of the two sales. Corroborating testimony as to the sales and the chemical analysis of the heroin was also introduced. Harris testified in his own defense but denied making the first sale and claimed the second sale was only part of a scheme to defraud the purchaser—that the contents of a glassine bag contained only baking powder. On cross-examination, Harris was asked whether he made statements immediately following his arrest that contradicted his testimony on direct examination at trial. Harris testified that he could not remember. The prior inconsistent statements which Harris had made to the police were admitted in evidence for the purpose of impeaching his credibility. The jury was instructed that such statements could be considered only in weighing Harris' credibility and not as evidence of guilt. Harris was convicted of the first sale. The New York courts affirmed the conviction. The United States Supreme Court granted certiorari.

Mr. Chief Justice BURGER delivered the opinion of the Court.

We granted the writ in this case to consider petitioner's claim that a statement made by him to police under circumstances rendering it inadmissible to establish the prosecution's case in chief under Miranda v. Arizona, 384 U.S. 436 (1966), may not be used to impeach his credibility.

* * *

Some comments in the Miranda opinion can indeed be read as indicating a bar to use of an uncounseled statement for any purpose, but discussion of that issue was not at all necessary to the Court's holding and cannot be regarded as controlling. Miranda barred the prosecution from making its case with statements of an accused made while in custody prior to having or effectively waiving counsel. It does not follow from Miranda that evidence inadmissible against an accused in the prosecution's case in chief is barred for all purposes, provided of course that the trustworthiness of the evidence satisfies legal standards.

In Walder v. United States, 347 U.S. 62 (1954), the Court permitted physical evidence, inadmissible in the case in chief, to be used for impeachment purposes.

"It is one thing to say that the Government cannot make an affirmative use of evidence unlawfully obtained. It is quite another to say that the defendant can turn the illegal method by which evidence in the Government's possession was obtained to his own advantage, and provide himself with a shield against contradiction of his untruths. Such an extension of the Weeks doctrine would be a perversion of the Fourth Amendment.

"[T]here is hardly justification for letting the defendant affirmatively resort to perjurious testimony in reliance on the Government's disability to challenge his credibility." 347 U.S., at 65.

It is true that Walder was impeached as to collateral matters included in his direct examination, whereas petitioner here was impeached as to testimony bearing more directly on the crimes charged. We are not persuaded that there is a difference in principle that warrants a result different from that reached by the Court in Walder. Petitioner's testimony in his own behalf concerning the events of January 7 contrasted sharply with what he told the police shortly after his arrest. The impeachment process here undoubtedly provided valuable aid to the jury in assessing petitioner's credibility, and the benefits of this process should not be lost, in our view, because of the speculative possibility that impermissible police conduct will be encouraged thereby. Assuming that the exclusionary rule has a deterrent effect on proscribed police conduct, sufficient deterrence flows when the evidence in question is made unavailable to the prosecution in its case in chief.

Every criminal defendant is privileged to testify in his own defense, or to refuse to do so. But that privilege cannot be construed to include the right to commit perjury. . . . Having voluntarily taken the stand, petitioner was under an obligation to speak truthfully and accurately, and the prosecution here did no more than utilize the traditional truth-testing devices of the adversary process. Had inconsistent statements been made by the accused to some third person, it could hardly be contended that the conflict could not be laid before the jury by way of cross-examination and impeachment.

The shield provided by Miranda cannot be perverted into a license to use perjury by way of a defense, free from the risk of confrontation with prior inconsistent utterances. We hold, therefore, that petitioner's credibility was appropriately impeached by use of his earlier conflicting statements.

Affirmed.

Mr. Justice BRENNAN, with whom Mr. Justice DOUGLAS and Mr. Justice MARSHALL join, dissenting.

It is conceded that the question-and-answer statement used to impeach petitioner's direct testimony was, under Miranda v. Arizona ... constitutionally inadmissible as part of the State's direct case against petitioner. I think that the Constitution also denied the State the use of the statement on cross-examination to impeach the credibility of petitioner's testimony given in his own defense. The decision in Walder v. United States ... is not, as the Court today holds, dispositive to the contrary. Rather, that case supports my conclusion.

* * *

The objective of deterring improper police conduct is only part of the larger objective of safeguarding the integrity of our adversary system. The "essential mainstay" of that system ... is the privilege against self-incrimination, which for that reason has occupied a central place in our jurisprudence since before the Nation's birth. Moreover, "we may view the historical development of the privilege as one which groped for the proper scope of governmental power over the citizen.... All these policies point to one overriding thought: the constitutional foundation underlying the privilege is the respect a government ... must accord to the dignity and integrity of its citizens." These values are plainly jeopardized if an exception against admission of tainted statements is made for those used for impeachment purposes. Moreover, it is monstrous that courts should aid or abet the lawbreaking police officer. It is abiding truth that "[n]othing can destroy a government more quickly than its failure to observe its own laws, or worse, its disregard of the charter of its own existence." ... Thus, even to the extent that Miranda was aimed at deterring police practices in disregard of the Constitution, I fear that today's holding will seriously undermine the achievement of that objective. The Court today tells the police that they may freely interrogate an accused incommunicado and without counsel and know that although any statement they obtain in violation of Miranda cannot be used on the State's direct case, it may be introduced if the defendant has the temerity to testify in his own defense. This goes far toward undoing much of the progress made in conforming police methods to the Constitution. I dissent.

[Mr. Justice BLACK wrote a separate dissenting opinion.]

Prior Inconsistent Statements Taken in Violation of *Miranda*

OREGON v. HASS

Supreme Court of the United States, 1975
420 U.S. 714, 95 S. Ct. 1215, 43 L. Ed. 2d 570

William Hass was arrested by an Oregon police officer on suspicion of burglary and was given his *Miranda* warnings. While being transported to the police station, Hass stated that he wished to telephone his attorney. The officer replied that Hass could do so as soon as they arrived at the police station. Thereafter Hass made some inculpatory statements, which were apparently taken in violation of *Miranda* since Hass had first expressed a desire to speak with his attorney. At his trial for burglary, Hass testified and maintained his innocence. The arresting officer, Officer Osterholme, called in rebuttal by the prosecution, repeated the inculpatory information supplied to him by Hass. The latter testimony was admitted solely for the purpose of impeaching Hass' credibility—not on the issue of his guilt—and the jury was so instructed. The jury returned a verdict of guilty and Hass received a sentence of 2 years' probation and a $250 fine. The Oregon Court of Appeals reversed the conviction, and the Oregon Supreme Court affirmed. The United States Supreme Court granted certiorari.

Mr. Justice BLACKMUN delivered the opinion of the Court.

This case presents a variation of the fact situation encountered by the Court in Harris v. New York, 401 U.S. 222 (1971). When a suspect, who is in the custody of a state police officer, has been given full Miranda warnings and accepts them, and then later states that he would like to telephone a lawyer but is told that this cannot be done until the officer and the suspect reach the station, and the suspect then provides inculpatory information, is that information admissible in evidence solely for impeachment purposes after the suspect has taken the stand and testified contrarily to the inculpatory information, or is it inadmissible under the Fifth and Fourteenth Amendments?

* * *

We see no valid distinction to be made in the application of the principles of Harris to his case and to Hass' case. Hass' statements were made after the defendant knew Osterholme's opposing testimony had been ruled inadmissible for the prosecution's case in chief.

As in Harris, it does not follow from Miranda that evidence inadmissible against Hass in the prosecution's case in chief is barred for all purposes, always provided that "the trustworthiness of the evidence satisfied legal standards." Again, the impeaching material would provide valuable aid to the jury in assessing the defendant's credibility; again, "the benefits of this process should not be lost"; and, again, making the deterrent effect assumption, there is sufficient deterrence when the evidence in question is made unavailable to the prosecution in its case in chief. If all this sufficed for the result in Harris, it supports and demands a like result in Hass' case. Here, too, the shield provided by Miranda is not to be perverted to a license to testify inconsistently, or even perjuriously, free from the risk of confrontation with prior inconsistent utterances.

We are, after all, always engaged in a search for truth in a criminal case so long as the search is surrounded with the safeguards provided by our Constitution. There is no evidence or suggestion that Hass' statements to Officer Osterholme on the way to Moyina Heights were involuntary or coerced. He properly sensed, to be sure, that he was in "trouble"; but the pressure on him was no greater than that on any person in like custody or under inquiry by any investigating officer.

The only possible factual distinction between Harris and this case lies in the fact that the Miranda warnings given Hass were proper whereas those given Harris were defective. The deterrence of the exclusionary rule, of course, lies in the necessity to give the warnings. That these warnings, in a given case, may prove to be incomplete, and therefore defective, as in Harris, does not mean that they have not served as a deterrent to the officer who is not then aware of their defect; and to the officer who is aware of the defect the full deterrence remains. The effect of inadmissibility in the Harris case and in this case is the same: inadmissibility would pervert the constitutional right into a right to falsify free from the embarrassment of impeachment evidence from the defendant's own mouth.

One might concede that when proper Miranda warnings have been given, and the officer then continues his interrogation after the suspect asks for an attorney, the officer may be said to have little to lose and perhaps something to gain by way of possibly uncovering impeachment material. This speculative possibility, however, is even greater where the warnings are defective and the defect is not known to the officer. In any event, the balance was struck in Harris, and we are not disposed to change it now. If, in a given case, the officer's conduct amounts to abuse, that case, like those involving coercion or duress, may be taken care of when it arises measured by the traditional standards for evaluating voluntariness and trustworthiness.

We therefore hold that the Oregon appellate courts were in error when they ruled that Officer Osterholme's testimony on rebuttal was inadmissible on Fifth and Fourteenth Amendment grounds for purposes of Hass' impeachment. The judgment of the Supreme Court of Oregon is reversed.

Mr. Justice BRENNAN, with whom Mr. Justice MARSHALL joins, dissenting.

* * *

I adhere to my dissent in Harris in which I stated that Miranda "completely disposes of any distinction between statements used on direct as opposed to cross-examination." . . .

The Court's decision today goes beyond Harris in undermining Miranda. Even after Harris, police had some incentive for following Miranda by warning an accused of his right to remain silent and his right to counsel. If the warnings were given, the accused might still make a statement which could be used in the prosecution's case in chief. Under today's holding, however, once the warnings are given, police have almost no incentive for following Miranda's requirement that "[i]f the individual states that he wants an attorney, the interrogation must cease until an attorney is present." Miranda, supra, at 474. If the requirement is followed there will almost surely be no statement since the attorney will advise the accused to remain silent. If, however, the requirement is disobeyed, the police may obtain a statement which can be used for impeachment if the accused has the temerity to testify in his own defense. Thus, after today's decision, if an individual states that he wants an attorney, police interrogation will doubtless now be vigorously pressed to obtain statements before the attorney arrives. I am unwilling to join this fundamental erosion of Fifth and Sixth Amendment rights and therefore dissent. . . .

Mr. Justice MARSHALL, with whom Mr. Justice BRENNAN joins, dissenting.

. . . I think it appropriate to add a word about this Court's increasingly common practice of reviewing state court decisions upholding constitutional claims in criminal cases. . . .

In my view, we have too often rushed to correct state courts in their view of federal constitutional questions without sufficiently considering the risk that we will be drawn into rendering a purely advisory opinion. Plainly, if the Oregon Supreme Court had expressly decided that Hass' statement was inadmissible as a matter of state as well as federal law, this Court could not upset that judgment. . . . The sound policy behind this rule was well articulated by Mr. Justice

Jackson in Herb v. Pitcairn, 324 U.S. 117 (1945):

"This Court from the time of its foundation has adhered to the principle that it will not review judgments of state courts that rest on adequate and independent state grounds. The reason is so obvious that it has rarely been thought to warrant statement. It is found in the partitioning of power between the state and federal judicial systems and in the limitations of our own jurisdiction. Our only power over state judgments is to correct them to the extent that they incorrectly adjudge federal rights. And our power is to correct wrong judgments, not to revise opinions. We are not permitted to render an advisory opinion, and if the same judgment would be rendered by the state court after we corrected its views of federal laws, our review could amount to nothing more than an advisory opinion." Id., at 125–126 (citations omitted).

Where we have been unable to say with certainty that the judgment rested solely on federal law grounds, we have refused to rule on the federal issue in the case; the proper course is then either to dismiss the writ as improvidently granted or to remand the case to the state court to clarify the basis of its decision. . . .

* * *

In addition to the importance of avoiding jurisdictional difficulties, it seems much the better policy to permit the state court the freedom to strike its own balance between individual rights and police practices, at least where the state court's ruling violates no constitutional prohibitions. It is peculiarly within the competence of the highest court of a state to determine that in its jurisdiction the police should be subject to more stringent rules than are required as a federal constitutional minimum.

* * *

I dissent.

[Mr. Justice DOUGLAS took no part in the consideration or decision of this case.]

When an Accused is Silent Following *Miranda* Warnings

DOYLE v. OHIO

Supreme Court of the United States, 1976
426 U.S. 610, 96 S. Ct. 2240, 49 L. Ed. 2d 91

Jefferson Doyle and Richard Wood were arrested together and charged with selling 10 pounds of marijuana to a local narcotics bureau informant. Each of the petitioners remained silent after they were given the *Miranda* warnings immediately following the arrest. In separate trials, each petitioner took the stand and stated that he had been "framed" by the informant. This exculpatory story had not previously been told to the police or the prosecutor. Over defense objections, the petitioners were cross-examined by the prosecutor as to why they had not given the arresting officer the exculpatory explanations immediately following their arrest. Petitioners were convicted and their convictions were affirmed on appeal in Ohio state courts. The United States Supreme Court granted certiorari.

Mr. Justice POWELL delivered the opinion of the Court.

The question in these consolidated cases is whether a state prosecutor may seek to impeach a defendant's exculpatory story, told for the first time at trial, by cross-examining the defendant about his failure to have told the story after receiving Miranda warnings at the time of his arrest. We conclude that use of the defendant's post-arrest silence in this matter violates due process, and therefore reverse the convictions of both petitioners.

* * *

The State pleads necessity as justification for the prosecutor's action in these cases. It argues that the discrepancy between an exculpatory story at trial and silence at time of arrest gives rise to an inference that the story was fabricated somewhere along the way, perhaps to fit within the seams of the State's case as it was developed at pretrial hearings. Noting that the prosecution usually has little else with which to counter such an exculpatory story, the State seeks only the right to cross-examine a defendant as to post-arrest silence for the limited purpose of impeachment. In support of its position the State emphasizes the importance of cross-examination in general ... and relies upon those cases in which this Court has

permitted use for impeachment purposes of post-arrest statements that were inadmissible as evidence of guilt because of an officer's failure to follow Miranda's dictates. Harris v. New York, 401 U.S. 222 (1971); Oregon v. Hass, 420 U.S. 714 (1975); see also Walder v. United States, 347 U.S. 62 (1954). Thus, although the State does not suggest petitioners' silence could be used as evidence of guilt, it contends that the need to present to the jury all information relevant to the truth of petitioners' exculpatory story fully justifies the cross-examination that is at issue.

Despite the importance of cross-examination, we have concluded that the Miranda decision compels rejection of the State's position. The warnings mandated by that case, as a prophylactic means of safeguarding Fifth Amendment rights, see Michigan v. Tucker, 417 U.S. 433, 443–444 (1974), require that a person taken into custody be advised immediately that he has the right to remain silent, that anything he says may be used against him, and that he has a right to retained or appointed counsel before submitting to interrogation. Silence in the wake of these warnings may be nothing more than the arrestee's exercise of these Miranda rights. Thus, every post-arrest silence is insolubly ambiguous because of what the State is required to advise the person arrested. . . . Moreover, while it is true that the Miranda warnings contain no express assurance that silence will carry no penalty, such assurance is implicit to any person who receives the warnings. In such circumstances, it would be fundamentally unfair and a deprivation of due process to allow the arrested person's silence to be used to impeach an explanation subsequently offered at trial. Mr. Justice WHITE, concurring in the judgment in United States v. Hale, 422 U.S., at 182–183, put it very well:

"[W]hen a person under arrest is informed, as Miranda requires, that he may remain silent, that anything he says may be used against him, and that he may have an attorney if he wishes, it seems to me that it does not comport with due process to permit the prosecution during the trial to call attention to his silence at the time of arrest and to insist that because he did not speak about the facts of the case at that time, as he was told he need not do, an unfavorable inference might be drawn as to the truth of his trial testimony. . . . Surely Hale was not informed here that his silence, as well as his words, could be used against him at trial. Indeed, anyone would reasonably conclude from Miranda warnings that this would not be the case."

We hold that the use for impeachment purposes of petitioners' silence, at the time of arrest and after receiving Miranda warnings, violated the Due Process Clause of the Fourteenth Amendment.[k] The State has not claimed that such use in the circumstances of this case might have been harmless error.

Reversed and remanded.

Mr. Justice STEVENS, with whom Mr. Justice BLACKMUN and Mr. Justice REHNQUIST join, dissenting.

---

[k] It goes almost without saying that the fact of post-arrest silence could be used by the prosecution to contradict a defendant who testifies to an exculpatory version of events and claims to have told the police the same version upon arrest. In that situation the fact of earlier silence would not be used to impeach the exculpatory story, but rather to challenge the defendant's testimony as to his behavior following arrest. Cf. United States v. Fairchild, 505 F.2d 1378, 1383 (5th Cir. 1975).

Petitioners assert that the prosecutor's cross-examination about their failure to mention the purported "frame" until they testified at trial violated their constitutional right to due process and also their constitutional privilege against self-incrimination. I am not persuaded by the first argument; though there is merit in a portion of the second, I do not believe it warrants reversal of these state convictions.

. . . The key to the Court's analysis is apparently a concern that the Miranda warning, which is intended to increase the probability that a person's response to police questioning will be intelligent and voluntary, will actually be deceptive unless we require the State to honor an unstated promise not to use the accused's silence against him.

In my judgment there is nothing deceptive or prejudicial to the defendant in the Miranda warning. Nor do I believe that the fact that such advice is given to the defendant lessens the probative value of his silence, or makes the prosecutor's cross-examination about his silence any more unfair than if he had received no such warning.

This is a case in which the defendants' silence at the time of their arrest was graphically inconsistent with their trial testimony that they were the unwitting victims of a "frame" in which the police did not participate. If defendants had been framed, their failure to mention that fact at the time of their arrest is almost inexplicable; for that reason, under accepted rules of evidence, their silence is tantamount to a prior inconsistent statement and admissible for purposes of impeachment.

Indeed, there is irony in the fact that the Miranda warning provides the only plausible explanation for their silence. If it were the true explanation, I should think that they would have responded to the questions on cross-examination about why they had remained silent by stating that they relied on their understanding of the advice given by the arresting officers. Instead, however, they gave quite a different jumble of responses. Those responses negate the Court's presumption that their silence was induced by reliance on deceptive advice.

Since the record requires us to put to one side the Court's presumption that the defendants' silence was the product of reliance on the Miranda warning, the Court's entire due process rationale collapses. For without reliance on the waiver, the case is no different than if no warning had been given, and nothing in the Court's opinion suggests that there would be any unfairness in using petitioners' prior inconsistent silence for impeachment purposes in such a case.

Indeed, as a general proposition, if we assume the defendant's silence would be admissible for impeachment purposes if no Miranda warning had been given, I should think that the warning would have a tendency to salvage the defendant's credibility as a witness. If the defendant is a truthful witness, and if his silence is the consequence of his understanding of the Miranda warning, he may explain that fact when he is on the stand. Even if he is untruthful, the availability of that explanation puts him in a better position than if he had received no warning. In my judgment, the risk that a truthful defendant will be deceived by the Miranda warning and also will be unable to explain his honest misunderstanding is so much less than the risk that exclusion of the evidence will merely provide a shield for perjury that I cannot accept the Court's due process rationale.

Accordingly, if we assume that the use of a defendant's silence for impeachment purposes would be otherwise unobjectionable, I find no merit in the notion that he is denied due process of law because he received a *Miranda* warning.

II

Petitioners argue that the State violated their Fifth Amendment privilege against self-incrimination by asking the jury to draw an inference of guilt from their constitutionally protected silence. They challenge both the prosecutor's cross-examination and his closing argument.

A

Petitioners claim that the cross-examination was improper because it referred to their silence at the time of their arrest, to their failure to testify at the preliminary hearing, and to their failure to reveal the "frame" prior to trial. Their claim applies to the testimony of each defendant at his own trial, and also to the testimony each gave as a witness at the trial of the other. Since I think it quite clear that a defendant may not object to the violation of another person's privilege, I shall only discuss the argument

that a defendant may not be cross-examined about his own prior inconsistent silence.

In support of their objections to the cross-examination about their silence at the time of arrest, petitioners primarily rely on the statement in Miranda v. Arizona, 384 U.S. 436, that the prosecution may not use at trial the fact that the defendant stood mute or claimed the privilege in the face of accusations during custodial interrogation. There are two reasons why that statement does not adequately support petitioners' argument.

First, it is not accurate to say that the petitioners "stood mute or claimed the privilege in the face of accusations." Neither petitioner claimed the privilege and petitioner Doyle did not even remain silent. The case is not one in which a description of the actual conversation between the defendants and the police would give rise to any inference of guilt if it were not so flagrantly inconsistent with their trial testimony. Rather than a claim of privilege, we simply have a failure to advise the police of a "frame" at a time when it most surely would have been mentioned if petitioners' trial testimony were true. That failure gave rise to an inference of guilty only because it belied their trial testimony.

Second, the dictum in the footnote in Miranda relies primarily upon Griffin v. California, 380 U.S. 609 (1965), which held that the Fifth Amendment, as incorporated in the Fourteenth, prohibited the prosecution's use of the defendant's silence in its case in chief. But as long ago as Raffel v. United States, 271 U.S. 494 (1926), this Court recognized the distinction between the prosecution's affirmative use of the defendant's prior silence and the use of prior silence for impeachment purposes. Raffel expressly held that the defendant's silence at a prior trial was admissible for purposes of impeachment despite the application in federal prosecutions of the prohibition that Griffin found in the Fifth Amendment.

Moreover, Chief Justice Warren, the author of the Court's opinion in Miranda joined the opinion in Walder v. United States, 347 U.S. 62 (1954), which squarely held that a valid constitutional objection to the admissibility of evidence as part of the Government's case-in-chief did not bar the use of that evidence to impeach the defendant's trial testimony. The availability of an objection to the affirmative use of improper evidence does not provide the defendant "with a shield against contradiction of his untruths." Id., at 65. The need to ensure the integrity of the truth-determining function of the adversary trial process has provided the predicate for an unbroken line of decisions so holding.

Although I have no doubt concerning the propriety of the cross-examination about petitioners' failure to mention the purported "frame" at the time of their arrest, a more difficult question is presented by their objection to the questioning about their failure to testify at the preliminary hearing and their failure generally to mention the "frame" before trial. Unlike the failure to make the kind of spontaneous comment that discovery of a "frame" would be expected to prompt, there is no significant inconsistency between petitioners' trial testimony and their adherence to counsel's advice not to take the stand at the preliminary hearing; moreover, the decision not to divulge their defense prior to trial is probably attributable to counsel rather than to petitioners. Nevertheless, unless and until this Court overrules Raffel v. United States, . . . I think a state court is free to regard the defendant's decision to take the stand as a waiver of his objection to the use of his failure to testify at an earlier proceeding or his failure to offer his version of the events prior to trial.

B

In my judgment portions of the prosecutor's argument to the jury overstepped permissible bounds. In each trial, he commented upon the defendant's silence not only as inconsistent with his testimony that he had been "framed," but also as inconsistent with the defendant's innocence. Comment on the lack of credibility of the defendant is plainly proper; it is not proper, however, for the prosecutor to ask the jury to draw a direct inference of guilt from silence — to argue, in effect, that silence is inconsistent with innocence. But since the two inferences — perjury and guilt — are inextricably intertwined because they have a common source, it would be unrealistic to permit comment on the former but to find reversible error in the slightest reference to the latter. In the context of the entire argument and the entire trial, I am not persuaded that the rather sophisticated distinction between permissible comment on credibility and impermissible comment on an inference of guilt justifies a reversal of these state convictions.

Accordingly, although I have some doubt concerning the propriety of the cross-examination about the preliminary hearing and consider a portion of the closing argument improper, I would affirm these convictions.

Comments

1. In *Harris* v. *New York* and *Oregon* v. *Hass*, supra, a majority of the Court held that the voluntary statements of a defendant, even though taken in violation of *Miranda*, are admissible in rebuttal by the prosecution if the defendant takes the stand and testifies at variance with the disserving statements. The Court reasoned that *Miranda* should not become a shield against the possible perjury of a defendant — a compelling argument even though it seems to go against the original intent of the *Miranda* Court. But as Mr. Justice Brennan points out in his dissent in *Harris* v. *New York,* why should the police now be overly concerned with obeying the technicalities of *Miranda,* since any voluntary statements of a defendant (albeit taken in violation of *Miranda*) will be admissible to impeach him if he elects to take the stand and his testimony is in conflict with those statements?

2. Consider the significance of these statements by Justice Marshall in his dissent in *Hass*: "[I]f a [state supreme court] had expressly decided that [a defendant's statement] was inadmissible as a matter of state as well as federal law, this Court could not upset that judgment [citations omitted]," at 420 U.S. 714, 726. "It is peculiarly

within the competence of the highest court of a state to determine that in its jurisdiction the police should be subject to more stringent rules than are required as a federal constitutional minimum," at 728. Contrast these statements with the pronouncement by Justice Blackmun, speaking for the majority in *Hass*: "[A] state may not impose such greater restrictions as a matter of federal constitutional law when this Court specifically refrains from imposing them," at 719. In *Hass*, the majority specifically repudiated a statement by the Oregon Supreme Court (in another case) that "we can interpret the Fourth Amendment more restrictively than interpreted by the United States Supreme Court," at 719, n.4.

3. A minority of jurisdictions have expressly decided not to follow certain Supreme Court pronouncements and have afforded defendants greater constitutional protections under state law than are required by the federal Constitution. Some examples are: *State* v. *Opperman*, 547 P.2d 673 (S.D. 1976) (refusing to follow *South Dakota* v. *Opperman*, Chapter Five, § 5.04); *People* v. *Disbrow*, 545 P.2d 272 (Calif. 1976) (rejecting *Harris* v. *New York* and *Oregon* v. *Hass*, supra); *Commonwealth* v. *Romberger*, 347 A.2d 460 (Pa. 1975) (rejecting *Miranda-Tucker* exclusionary rule that *Miranda* does not apply to custodial statements obtained prior to the date of the *Miranda* decision); *State* v. *Talbot*, 343 A.2d 777 (N.J. 1976) (rejecting *Hampton* v. *United States*, infra); *People* v. *Duran*, 545 P.2d 1322 (Calif. 1976) (restrictive reading of *Illinois* v. *Allen*, Chapter Seven, § 7.03); *Van Cleaf* v. *State*, 339 So. 2d 1193 (Fla. App. 1976) (permitting counsel at probation revocation hearings despite standards under *Gagnon* v. *Scarpelli*, Chapter Nine, § 9.02); *People* v. *Jackson*, 217 N.W.2d 22 (Mich. 1974) (rejecting *Kirby* v. *Illinois* and *United States* v. *Ash*); *Commonwealth* v. *Richman*, 320 A.2d 35 (Pa. 1974) (rejecting *United States* v. *Ash*); *Commonwealth* v. *Triplett*, 341 A.2d 62 (Pa. 1975) (rejecting *Harris* v. *New York*, supra) (in accord is *State* v. *Santiago*, 492 P.2d 657 [Hawaii 1971]); *State* v. *Johnson*, 346 A.2d 66 (N.J. 1975) (refusing to follow *Schneckloth* v. *Bustamonte*, Chapter Five, § 5.04); *State* v. *Kaluna*, 520 P.2d 51 (Hawaii 1975) (rejecting *United States* v. *Robinson*, Chapter Five, § 5.04); *People* v. *Beavers*, 227 N.W.2d 511 (Mich. 1975) (refusing to follow *United States* v. *White*); *People* v. *Brisendine*, 531 P.2d 1099 (Calif. 1975) (declining to follow *United States* v. *Robinson*, Chapter Five, § 5.04, and *Gustafson* v. *Florida*).

4. In *Doyle* v. *Ohio*, supra, a majority of the Court held that a defendant's postarrest silence following *Miranda* warnings cannot be used to impeach him once he has elected to take the stand. Was the decision reached on Fifth Amendment self-incrimination grounds, on Fourteenth Amendment due process grounds, or both? That aspect of the decision is not entirely clear, and this could become important in subsequent decisions involving the issue of a defendant's postarrest silence. Was the majority decision based solely on the idea that it would be "fundamentally unfair" to admit a defendant's silence, even for impeachment purposes, since the *Miranda* warnings imply that silence will carry no penalty? Or is introduction of evidence of postarrest silence a violation of the privilege against self-incrimination irrespective of *Miranda*? What would be the effect of the holding of *Doyle* if *Miranda* was someday overruled in light of the Court's statement that "[d]espite the impor-

tance of cross-examination, we have concluded that the *Miranda* decision compels rejection of the State's position" (at 460)? Is the Court suggesting that had the defendants not been given the *Miranda* warnings, evidence of their postarrest silence would have been admissible at trial for impeachment purposes?

5.   *Doyle* was decided on narrow grounds, and it would probably be unwise to suggest that the decision stands for the proposition that a defendant's postarrest silence is inadmissible at trial for any purpose. Under evidentiary rules, evidence is often admissible for one purpose but not another; for example, evidence used to impeach a witness (to weaken his credibility) is usually admissible only for that purpose and is inadmissible to prove guilt. There seems to be little doubt that had the prosecution attempted to use the defendant's postarrest silence as substantive proof of guilt, the *Doyle* case would never have reached the Supreme Court, because the trial court would have disallowed the evidence. Are there any conditions in which a defendant's postarrest silence could be used as substantive evidence of guilt? What did the Court mean when it said in the footnote, "It goes almost without saying that the fact of post-arrest silence could be used by the prosecution to contradict a defendant who testifies to an exculpatory version of events and claims to have told the police the same version upon arrest. In that situation, the fact of earlier silence would not be used to impeach the exculpatory story, but rather to challenge the defendant's testimony as to his behavior following arrest"? Why didn't Ohio as an alternative argument urge that the use of the defendant's silence at trial was "harmless error"? Would the Supreme Court have reached a similar or different result? As a practice pointer, the prosecution should always argue on appeal that even if there was error committed during the proceedings, the error was harmless. For a discussion of the harmless error doctrine, see Chapter Fourteen, § 14.02.

6.   The dissenting argument of Mr. Justice Stevens in *Doyle* is interesting and should not be written off as merely the eccentric view of another "conservative" justice. According to Justice Stevens, a defendant's silence does have probative value (and is not "insolubly ambiguous" as suggested by the majority) and should be admissible at least for impeachment purposes as the equivalent of a prior inconsistent statement. Interestingly, a prior inconsistent statement of a witness is not considered as hearsay evidence (under federal rules of evidence) and is admissible to prove the truth of the matter asserted; in other words, a prior inconsistent statement by a witness is not admissible for other than impeachment purposes. See Federal Rules of Evidence for United States Courts and Magistrates 801(d)(1). Justice Stevens stated in his dissent that the majority held the evidence of defendant's silence to be inadmissible for impeachment purposes *because* the *Miranda* warnings were given. Is that an accurate reading of the majority position? If Justice Stevens correctly interpreted the rationale of majority, why should police officers be concerned with *Miranda* warnings in the future since: (1) evidence of a defendant's postarrest silence *might* be admissible at trial for impeachment purposes if no warnings were given; and (2) any statements by a defendant taken in violation of *Miranda* are admissible for impeachment purposes? *Harris* v. *New York* and *Oregon* v. *Hass,* supra. How is

the integrity of *Miranda* upheld when a defendant's silence following the warnings is not admissible at trial, but any statements taken in violation of *Miranda* are admissible for impeachment purposes. In light of the majority's hint that a defendant's silence might be admissible absent the warnings, could *Doyle* arguably be read as undermining *Miranda* rather than as a "prophylactic means of safeguarding Fifth Amendment rights"? Is it a denial of the privilege against self-incrimination for the prosecution to cross-examine a defendant as to why he had not told his exculpatory story at the preliminary hearing or at any other time prior to trial? The Court did not reach this issue, and even if it had, it would probably have had to be decided on different constitutional grounds.

7. Some recent lower federal and state court decisions involving the use of illegally taken evidence for impeachment purposes and a defendant's silence are: *People* v. *Wright*, 336 N.E.2d 18 (Ill. App. 1975) (state's impeachment reference to murder defendant's invocation of his *Miranda* rights when questioned by the police at his home held reversible error); *Bird* v. *State*, 527 S.W.2d 891 (Tex. Ct. Crim. App. 1975) (prosecutor's referring to silencer used on a murder weapon and looking directly at the defendant and asking "Where did you get it?" held improper comment on defendant's right to remain silent); *State* v. *Wright*, 542 P.2d 63 (Idaho 1975) (no fundamental error in admission, without objection, of police officer's testimony that the defendant refused to divulge his name at the time of arrest and stated that he wanted to see an attorney) (contra is *People* v. *Mingo*, 509 P.2d 800 [Col. 1973], and *State* v. *Ritson*, 504 P.2d 605 [Kan. 1972]); *Minor* v. *Black*, 527 F.2d 1 (6th Cir. 1975) (impeachment of a defendant by evidence of his silence at the time of his arrest violates the Fifth Amendment); *United States* v. *Yates*, 524 F.2d 1282 (Cir. D.C. 1975) (rebuttal testimony about a defendant's silence at the time of his arrest in face of a codefendant's statement inculpating the defendant held violative of the Fifth Amendment); *People* v. *Disbrow*, 545 P.2d 1282 (Calif. 1976) (state constitution forbids impeachment of a defendant by an inculpatory statement taken in violation of *Miranda—Harris* v. *New York* not followed), (overruling *People* v. *Nudd*, 12 Col. 3d 204 [1974]); *Booker* v. *State*, 326 So. 2d 791 (Miss. 1976) (defendant may not be impeached by the use of a confession unless it is first shown that the confession was freely and voluntarily given, but if the only objection to its use is that it was obtained following a defective *Miranda* warning, the state may use the confession to impeach the defendant's testimony without first establishing that the confession was freely and voluntarily given) (see also *Ladner* v. *State*, 95 So. 2d 468 [Miss. 1956]); *Braden* v. *State*, 534 S.W.2d 657 (Tenn. 1975) (reversible error for prosecution on cross-examination to put into evidence a defendant's silence following his arrest and prodding him into admitting that he had not told police officers about the alibi he offered at trial); *State* v. *Deatore*, 358 A.2d 163 (N.J. 1976) (error for prosecutor to ask a defendant who testified in support of his alibi defense why he kept silent at the time of his arrest); *State* v. *Alston*, 346 A.2d 622 (N.J. 1976) (cross-examination of a defendant about his failure to raise his alibi defense at the time of arrest and defendant's response that "they didn't ask me" held improper but harmless error); *United States* v. *Impson*, 531 F.2d 274 (5th Cir.

1976) (federal prosecutor committed prejudicial error by questioning a police officer about the defendant's silence following his arrest); *State* v. *Smith,* 336 So. 2d 867 (La. 1976) (police officer's inadvertent reference at trial to a defendant's refusal to talk at the time of arrest held harmless error where the state did not deliberately exploit the issue); *Clark* v. *State,* 336 So. 2d 469 (Fla. 1976) (police officer's reference to a defendant's silence at the time of his arrest cannot be harmless error); *State* v. *Denny,* 555 P.2d 111 (Ariz. App. 1976) (*Harris* v. *New York* not applicable where statements are obtained by deceit or trickery); *Booton* v. *Hanover,* 541 F.2d 296 (1st Cir. 1976) (introduction of a defendant's refusal to continue to answer further questions during interrogation held error); *Greenfield* v. *State,* 337 So. 2d 1021 (Fla. App. 1976) (proper to admit a police officer's testimony about a defendant's invocation of his *Miranda* rights against the defendant's claim of insanity); *State* v. *Pisauro,* 233 N.W.2d 109 (Mich. App. 1975) (admissions by silence prior to arrest are competent evidence); *People* v. *Matonti,* 385 N.Y.S.2d 992 (N.Y. App. Div. 1976) (defendant's failure to offer explanation or to lay out alibi at time of his arrest may not be considered by the jury); *United States* v. *Flecha,* 539 F.2d 874 (2nd Cir. 1976) (when *Miranda* warnings have been given, the prosecution cannot introduce evidence as to a defendant's silence at that time).

D. IMMUNITY

The "Coextensive" Requirement

MURPHY v. WATERFRONT COMMISSION

Supreme Court of the United States, 1964
378 U.S. 52, 84 S. Ct. 1594, 12 L. Ed. 2d 678

William Murphy and James Moody were subpoenaed to testify before the Waterfront Commission of New York in regard to a work stoppage at certain piers in New Jersey. They refused to answer on the ground of self-incrimination but were granted immunity from prosecution under the laws of New Jersey and New York. Notwithstanding the grant of immunity, they still refused to answer on the ground that their answers might tend to incriminate them and subject them to a federal prosecution — to which the grant of immunity did not extend. Murphy and Moody were thereafter held in civil and criminal contempt of court. The New Jersey Supreme Court affirmed the civil contempt judgments, holding that a state may compel a witness to give testimony even though such testimony might later be used in a federal prosecution against him. The United States Supreme Court granted certiorari.

Mr. Justice GOLDBERG delivered the opinion of the Court.

* * *

Since a grant of immunity is valid only if it is coextensive with the scope of the privilege against self-incrimination, ... we must now decide the fundamental constitutional question of whether, absent an immunity protection, one jurisdiction in our federal structure may compel a witness to give testimony which might incriminate him under the laws of another jurisdiction. . . .

* * *

[T]here is no continuing legal vitality to, or historical justification for, the rule that one jurisdiction within our federal structure may compel a witness to give testimony which could be used to convict him of a crime in another jurisdiction.

* * *

. . . We hold that the constitutional privilege against self-incrimination protects a state witness against incrimination under federal as well as state law and a federal witness against incrimination under state as well as federal law.

* * *

. . . [A] state witness may not be compelled to give testimony which may be incriminating under federal law unless the compelled testimony and its fruits cannot be used in any manner by federal officials in connection with a criminal prosecution against him. We conclude, moreover, that in order to implement this constitutional rule and accommodate the interests of the State and Federal Governments in investigating and prosecuting crime, the Federal Government must be prohibited from making any

such use of compelled testimony and its fruits. This exclusionary rule, while permitting the States to secure information necessary for effective law enforcement, leaves the witness and the Federal Government in substantially the same position as if the witness had claimed his privilege in the absence of a state grant of immunity.

It follows that petitioners here may now be compelled to answer the questions propounded to them. At the time they refused to answer, however, petitioners had a reasonable fear . . . that the federal authorities might use the answers against them in connection with a federal prosecution. . . . The Federal Government may make no such use of the answers. Fairness dictates that petitioners should now be afforded an opportunity, in light of this development, to answer the questions. . . . Accordingly, the judgment of the New Jersey courts ordering petitioners to answer the questions may remain undisturbed.

Vacated and remanded.

[Mr. Justice BLACK concurred.]

[Mr. Justice HARLAN, with whom Mr. Justice CLARK joined, wrote a concurring opinion.]

[Mr. Justice WHITE, with whom Mr. Justice STEWART joined, wrote a concurring opinion.]

Use and Transactional Immunity

KASTIGAR v. UNITED STATES

Supreme Court of the United States, 1972
406 U.S. 441, 92 S. Ct. 1653, 32 L. Ed. 2d 212

Charles Kastigar and Michael Stewart were subpoenaed to appear before a federal grand jury in California. The United States District Court (C.D. Calif.) granted them use (limited) immunity. The grant of use immunity, pursuant to a federal statute, provided that neither the compelled testimony nor any information directly or indirectly derived from such testimony could be used against the witnesses. Notwithstanding the grant of immunity, Kastigar and Stewart refused to answer the grand jury's questions. They contended that the scope of the immunity provided by the statute was not coextensive with the scope of the privilege against self-incrimination. The district court found them in civil contempt and ordered them jailed until they answered the questions of the grand jury or the term of the grand jury expired. The United States Court of Appeals (9th Cir.) affirmed, and the United States Supreme Court granted certiorari.

Mr. Justice POWELL delivered the opinion of the Court.

* * *

... This Court granted certiorari to resolve the important question whether testimony may be compelled by granting immunity from the use of compelled testimony and evidence derived therefrom ("use and derivative use" immunity), or whether it is necessary to grant immunity from prosecution for offenses to which compelled testimony relates ("transactional" immunity). ...

I

The power of government to compel persons to testify in court or before grand juries and other governmental agencies is firmly established in Anglo-American jurisprudence. ... The power to compel testimony, and the corresponding duty to testify, are recognized in the Sixth Amendment requirements that an accused be confronted with the witnesses against him, and have compulsory process for obtaining witnesses in his favor. ...

* * *

But the power to compel testimony is not absolute. There are a number of exemptions from the testimonial duty, the most important of which is the Fifth Amendment privilege against compulsory self-incrimination. The privilege reflects a complex of our fundamental values and aspirations, and marks an important advance in the development of our liberty. It can be asserted in any proceeding, civil or criminal, administrative or judicial, investigatory or adjudicatory; and it protects against any disclosures that the witness reasonably believes could be used in a criminal prosecution or could lead to other evidence that might be so used. This Court has been zealous to safeguard the values that underlie the privilege.

Immunity statutes, which have historical roots deep in Anglo-American jurisprudence, are not incompatible with these values. Rather, they seek a rational accommodation between the imperatives of the privilege and the legitimate demands of government to compel citizens to testify. The existence of these statutes reflects the importance of testimony, and the fact that many offenses are of such a character that the only persons capable of giving useful testimony are those implicated in the crime. Indeed, their origins were in the context of such offenses, and their primary use has been to investigate such offenses. ... [E]very State in the Union, as well as the District of Columbia and Puerto Rico, has one or more such statutes. The commentators, and this Court on several occasions, have characterized immunity statutes as essential to the effective enforcement of various criminal statutes. ...

II

Petitioners contend, first, that the Fifth Amendment's privilege against compulsory self-incrimination, which is that "[n]o person ... shall be compelled in any criminal case to be a witness against himself," deprives Congress of power to enact laws that compel self-incrimination, even if complete immunity from prosecution is granted prior to the compulsion of the incriminatory testimony. In other words, petitioners assert that no immunity statute, however drawn, can afford a lawful basis for compelling incriminatory testimony. ... We find no merit to this contention. ...

III

Petitioners' second contention is that the scope of immunity provided by the federal witness immunity statute, 18 U.S.C. § 6002, is not coextensive with the scope of the Fifth Amendment privilege against compulsory self-incrimination, and therefore is not sufficient to supplant the privilege and compel testimony over a claim of the privilege. The statute provides that when a witness is compelled by district court order to testify over a claim of the privilege: "the witness may not refuse to comply with the order on the basis of his privilege against self-incrimination; but no testimony or other information compelled under the order (or any information directly or indirectly derived from such testimony or other information) may be used against the witness in any criminal case, except a prosecution for perjury, giving a false statement, or otherwise failing to comply with the order." 18 U.S.C. § 6002.

The constitutional inquiry ... is whether the immunity granted under this statute is coextensive with the scope of the privilege.

If so, petitioners' refusals to answer based on the privilege were unjustified, and the judgments of contempt were proper, for the grant of immunity has removed the dangers against which the privilege protects.... If, on the other hand, the immunity granted is not as comprehensive as the protection afforded by the privilege, petitioners were justified in refusing to answer, and the judgments of contempt must be vacated....

Petitioners draw a distinction between statutes that provide transactional immunity and those that provide, as does the statute before us, immunity from use and derivative use. They contend that a statute must at a minimum grant full transactional immunity in order to be coextensive with the scope of the privilege....

* * *

The statute's explicit proscription of the use in any criminal case of "testimony or other information compelled under the order (or any information directly or indirectly derived from such testimony or other information)" is consonant with Fifth Amendment standards. We hold that such immunity from use and derivative use is coextensive with the scope of the privilege against self-incrimination, and therefore is sufficient to compel testimony over a claim of the privilege. While a grant of immunity must afford protection commensurate with that afforded by the privilege, it need not be broader. Transactional immunity, which accords full immunity from prosecution for the offense to which the compelled testimony relates, affords the witness considerably broader protection than does the Fifth Amendment privilege. The privilege has never been construed to mean that one who invokes it cannot subsequently be prosecuted. Its sole concern is to afford protection against being "forced to give testimony leading to the infliction of 'penalties affixed to ... criminal acts.' " Immunity from the use of compelled testimony, as well as evidence derived directly and indirectly therefrom, affords this protection. It prohibits the prosecutorial authorities from using the compelled testimony in *any* respect, and it therefore insures that the testimony cannot lead to the infliction of criminal penalties on the witness.

* * *

IV

Although an analysis of prior decisions and the purpose of the Fifth Amendment privilege indicate that use and derivative-use immunity is coextensive with the privilege, we must consider additional arguments advanced by petitioners against the sufficiency of such immunity. We start from the premise, repeatedly affirmed by this Court, that an appropriately broad immunity grant is compatible with the Constitution.

Petitioners argue that use and derivative-use immunity will not adequately protect a witness from various possible incriminating uses of the compelled testimony: for example, the prosecutor or other law enforcement officials may obtain leads, names of witnesses, or other information not otherwise available that might result in a prosecution. It will be difficult and perhaps impossible, the argument goes, to identify, by testimony or cross-examination, the subtle ways in which the compelled testimony may disadvantage a witness, especially in the jurisdiction granting the immunity.

This argument presupposes that the statute's prohibition will prove impossible to enforce. The statute provides a sweeping proscription of any use, direct or indirect, of the compelled testimony and any information derived therefrom:

"[N]o testimony or other information compelled under the order (or any information directly or indirectly derived from such testimony or other information) may be used against the witness in any criminal case...." 18 U.S.C. § 6002.

This total prohibition on use provides a comprehensive safeguard, barring the use of compelled testimony as an "investigatory lead," and also barring the use of any evidence obtained by focusing investigation on a witness as a result of his compelled disclosures.

A person accorded this immunity under 18 U.S.C. § 6002, and subsequently prosecuted, is not dependent for the preservation of his rights upon the integrity and good faith of the prosecuting authorities. As stated in Murphy [v. Waterfront Commission]:

"Once a defendant demonstrates that he has testified, under a state grant of immunity, to matters related to the federal prosecution, the federal authorities have the burden of showing that their evidence is not tainted by establishing that they had an independent legitimate source for the disputed evidence." 378 U.S., at 79.

This burden of proof, which we reaffirm as appropriate, is not limited to a negation of taint; rather, it imposes on the prosecution the affirmative duty to prove that the evidence it proposes to use is derived from a legitimate source wholly independent of the compelled testimony.

This is very substantial protection, commensurate with that resulting from invoking the privilege itself. The privilege assures that a citizen is not compelled to incriminate himself by his own testimony. It usually operates to allow a citizen to remain silent when asked a question requiring an incriminatory answer. This statute, which operates after a witness has given incriminatory testimony, affords the same protection by assuring that the compelled testimony can in no way lead to the infliction of criminal penalties. The statute, like the Fifth Amendment, grants neither pardon nor amnesty. Both the statute and the Fifth Amendment allow the government to prosecute using evidence from legitimate independent sources.

The statutory proscription is analogous to the Fifth Amendment requirement in cases of coerced confessions. A coerced confession, revealing of leads as testimony given in exchange for immunity, is inadmissible in a criminal trial, but it does not bar prosecution. Moreover, a defendant against whom incriminating evidence has been obtained through a grant of immunity may be in a stronger position at trial than a defendant who asserts a Fifth Amendment coerced-confession claim. One raising a claim under this statute need only show that he testified under a grant of immunity in order to shift to the government the heavy burden of proving that all of the evidence it proposes to use was derived from legitimate independent sources. On the other hand, a defendant raising a coerced-confession claim under the Fifth Amendment must first prevail in a voluntariness hearing before his confession and evidence derived from it become inadmissible.

There can be no justification in reason or policy for holding that the Constitution requires an amnesty grant where, acting pursuant to statute and accompanying safeguards, testimony is compelled in exchange for immunity from use and derivative use when no such amnesty is required where the government, acting without colorable right, coerces a defendant into incriminating himself.

We conclude that the immunity provided by 18 U.S.C. § 6002 leaves the witness and the prosecutorial authorities in substantially the same position as if the witness had claimed the Fifth Amendment privilege. The immunity therefore is coextensive with the privilege and suffices to supplant it. . . .

Affirmed.

Mr. Justice DOUGLAS, dissenting.

The Self-Incrimination Clause says: "No person . . . shall be compelled in any criminal case to be a witness against himself." I see no answer to the proposition that he is such a witness when only "use" immunity is granted.

* * *

As Mr. Justice BRENNAN has also said:

"Transactional immunity . . . provides the individual with an assurance that he is not testifying about matters for which he may later be prosecuted. No question arises of tracing the use or non-use of information gleaned from the witness' compelled testimony. The sole question presented to a court is whether the subsequent prosecution is related to the substance of the compelled testimony. Both witness and government know precisely where they stand. Respect for law is furthered when the individual knows his position and is not left suspicious that a later prosecution was actually the fruit of his compelled testimony." 400 U.S., at 568–569 (dissenting).

When we allow the prosecution to offer only "use" immunity we allow it to grant far less than it has taken away. For while the precise testimony that is compelled may not be used, leads from that testimony may be pursued and used to convict the witness. My view is that the framers put it beyond the power of Congress to *compel* anyone to confess his crimes. The Self-Incrimination Clause creates, as I have said before, "the federally protected right of silence," making it unconstitutional to use a law "to pry open one's lips and make him a witness against himself." . . . That is indeed one of the chief procedural guarantees in our accusatorial system. Government acts in an ignoble way when it stoops to the end which we authorize today.

I would . . . hold that this attempt to dilute the Self-Incrimination Clause is unconstitutional.

[Mr. Justice MARSHALL also wrote a dissenting opinion.]

[Mr. Justice BRENNAN and Mr. Justice REHNQUIST took no part in the consideration or decision of this case.]

Public Officials and Immunity

LEFKOWITZ v. CUNNINGHAM

Supreme Court of the United States, 1977
431 U.S. 801, 97 S. Ct. 2132, 53 L. Ed. 2d 1

Section 22 of the New York Election Law provides that if an officer of a political party who is subpoenaed by a grand jury or other authorized tribunal to testify regarding the conduct of his office refuses to testify or waive immunity against subsequent criminal prosecution, his term of office shall terminate. Further, he shall be disqualified from holding any other party or public office for five years.

Patrick Cunningham, appellee and an attorney, after being subpoenaed to testify before the grand jury, refused to sign a waiver of immunity. Cunningham's refusal to waive his constitutional immunity automatically divested him of all party offices and activated the five year ban on holding any public or party office.

Cunningham then brought suit in Federal District Court, which granted him declaratory and injunctive relief against enforcement of the statute on the ground that it violated his Fifth and Fourteenth Amendment rights. On appeal by the State of New York, the United States Supreme Court noted probable jurisdiction.

Mr. Chief Justice BURGER delivered the opinion of the Court.

* * *

II

[T]he Fifth Amendment privilege against compelled self-incrimination protects grand jury witnesses from being forced to give testimony which may later be used to convict them in a criminal proceeding. . . . Moreover, since the test is whether the testimony might later subject the witness to criminal prosecution, the privilege is available to a witness to criminal prosecution. Malloy v. Hogan, 378 U.S. 1, 11 (1964). In either situation the witness may "refuse to answer unless and until he is protected at least against the use of his compelled answers and evidence derived therefrom in any subsequent criminal case in which he is a defendant." Lefkowitz v. Turley, 414 U.S. 70, 78 (1973).

Thus, when a state compels testimony by threatening to inflict potent sanctions unless the constitutional privilege is surrendered, that testimony is obtained in violation of the Fifth Amendment and cannot be used against the declarant in a subsequent criminal prosecution. In Garrity v. New Jersey, 385 U.S. 493 (1967), for example, police officers under investigation were told that if they declined to answer potentially incriminating questions they would be removed from office, but that any answers they did give could be used against them in a criminal prosecution. We held that statements given under such circumstances were made involuntarily and could not be used to convict the officers of crime.

Similarly, our cases have established that a state may not impose substantial penalties because a witness elects to exercise his Fifth Amendment right not to give incriminating testimony against himself. In Gardner v. Broderick, 392 U.S. 273 (1968), a police officer appearing before a grand jury investigating official corruption was subject to discharge if he did not waive his Fifth Amendment privilege and answer, without immunity, all questions asked of him. When he refused, and his employment was terminated, this Court held that the officer could not be discharged solely for his refusal to forfeit the rights guaranteed him by the Fifth Amendment; the privilege against compelled self-incrimination could not abide any "attempt, regardless of its ultimate effectiveness, to coerce a waiver of the immunity it confers on penalty of the loss of employment." Id., at 279. Accord, Uniformed Sanitation Men Ass'n., Inc. v. Commissioner of Sanitation, 392 U.S. 280 (1968). At the same time, the Court provided for effectuation of the important public interest in securing from public employees an accounting of their public trust. Public employees may constitutionally be discharged for refusing to answer potentially incriminating questions concerning their official duties if they have not been required to surrender their constitutional immunity. Gardner, supra, at 278–279.

We affirmed the teaching of Gardner more recently in Lefkowitz v. Turley, supra, where two architects who did occasional work for the State of New York refused to waive their Fifth Amendment privilege before a grand jury investigating corruption in public contracting practices. State law provided that if a contractor refused to surrender his constitutional privilege before a grand jury, his existing state contracts would be canceled, and he would be barred from future contracts with the State for five years. The Court saw no constitutional distinction between discharging a public employee and depriving an independent contractor of the opportunity to secure public contracts; in both cases the State had sought to compel testimony by imposing a sanction as the price of invoking the Fifth Amendment right.

These cases settle that government cannot penalize assertion of the constitutional privilege against compelled self-incrimina-tion by imposing sanctions to compel testimony which has not been immunized. It is true, as appellant points out, that our earlier cases were concerned with penalties having a substantial economic impact. But the touchstone of the Fifth Amendment is compulsion, and direct economic sanctions and imprisonment are not the only penalties capable of forcing the self-incrimination which the Amendment forbids.

III

Section 22 confronted appellee with grave consequences solely because he refused to waive immunity from prosecution and give self-incriminating testimony. Section 22 is therefore constitutionally indistinguishable from the coercive provisions we struck down in Gardner, Uniformed Sanitation Men and Turley. Appellee's party offices carry substantial prestige and political influence, giving him a powerful voice in recommending or selecting candidates for office and in other political decisions. The threatened loss of such widely sought positions, with their power and perquisites, is inherently coercive. Additionally, compelled forfeiture of these posts diminishes appellee's general reputation in his community.

There are also economic consequences; appellee's professional standing as a practicing lawyer would suffer by his removal from his political offices under these circumstances. Further, § 22 bars appellee from holding any other party or public office for five years. Many such offices carry substantial compensation. . . .

Section 22 is coercive for yet another reason: it requires appellee to forfeit one constitutionally protected right as the price for exercising another. See Simmons v. United States, 390 U.S. 377, 394 (1968). As an officer in a private political party, appellee is in a far different position from a government policymaking official holding office at the pleasure of the President or governor. By depriving appellee of his offices, § 22 impinges on his right to participate in private, voluntary political associations. That right is an important aspect of First Amendment freedom which this Court has consistently found entitled to constitutional protection. Kusper v. Pontikes, 414 U.S. 51 (1973); William v. Rhodes, 393 U.S. 23 (1968).

Appellant argues that even if § 22 is violative of Fifth Amendment rights, the State's overriding interest in preserving public confidence in the integrity of its political process justifies the constitutional infringement. We have already rejected the notion that citizens may be forced to incriminate themselves because it serves a governmental need. E.g., Lefkowitz v. Turley, supra, at 78–79. Government has compelling interests in maintaining an honest police force and civil service, but this Court did not permit those interests to justify infringement of Fifth Amendment rights in Garrity, Gardner and Uniformed Sanitation Men, where alternate methods of promoting state aims were no more apparent than here.

IV

It may be, as appellant contends, that "[a] State forced to choose between an accounting from or a prosecution of a party officer is in an intolerable position." Brief for Appellant 12–13. But this dilemma is created by New York's transactional immunity law, which immunizes grand jury witnesses from prosecution for any transaction about which they testify. The more limited use immunity required by the Fifth Amendment would permit the State to prosecute appellee for any crime of which he may be guilty in connection with his party office, provided only that his own compelled testimony is not used to convict him. Once proper use immunity is granted, the State may use its contempt powers to compel testimony concerning the conduct of public office, without forfeiting the opportunity to prosecute the witness on the basis of evidence derived from other sources.

Affirmed.

Mr. Justice BRENNAN, with whom Mr. Justice MARSHALL joins, concurring in part.

I join the Court's judgment, for the reasons stated in Parts I, II and III of its opinion. I cannot, however, join Part IV, because I continue to believe that "the Fifth Amendment privilege against self-incrimination requires that any jurisdiction that compels a man to incriminate himself grant him absolute immunity under its laws from prosecution for any transaction revealed in that testimony." Piccirillo v. New York, 400 U.S. 548, 562 (1971) (Brennan, J., dissenting). See also Kastigar v. United States, 406 U.S. 441, 462 (1972) (Douglas, J., dissent-

ing) [supra]; id., at 467 (Marshall J., dissenting). . . .

Mr. Justice STEVENS, dissenting.

The First Amendment protects the individual's right to speak and to believe in accordance with the dictates of his own conscience. But if he believes in peace at any price and speaks out against a strong military, the President may decide not to nominate him for the office of Secretary of Defense. If he already occupies a comparable policymaking office, the President may remove him as a result of his exercise of First Amendment rights. The fact that the Constitution protects the exercise of the right does not mean that it also protects the speaker's "right" to hold high public office.[a]

The Fifth Amendment protects the individual's right to remain silent. The central purpose of the privilege against compulsory self-incrimination is to avoid unfair criminal trials. It is an expression of our conviction that the defendant in a criminal case must be presumed innocent, and that the State has the burden of proving guilt without resorting to an inquisition of the accused.

Just as constitutionally protected speech may disclose a valid reason for terminating the speaker's employment, so may constitutionally protected silence provide a valid reason for refusing or terminating employment in certain sensitive public positions. Thus a person nominated to an office which may not be filled without the consent of the Senate could exercise his right not to incriminate himself during questioning by a Senate committee, but no one would doubt the Senate's constitutional power to withhold its consent for that very reason. Nor can there be any doubt concerning the President's power to discharge any White House

---

[a] It is often incorrectly assumed that whenever an individual right is sufficiently important to receive constitutional protection, that protection implicitly guarantees that the exercise of the right shall be cost free. Nothing could be further from the truth. The right to representation by counsel of one's choice, for example, may require the defendant in a criminal case to pay a staggering price to employ the lawyer he selects. Insistence on a jury trial may increase the cost of defense. The right to send one's children to a private school, Meyer v. Nebraska, 262 U.S. 390, may be exercised only by one prepared to pay the associated tuition cost.

aide who might assert his Fifth Amendment privilege in response to a charge that he had used his office to conceal wrongdoing or to solicit illegal campaign contributions.

I see no reason why there should be any greater doubt concerning a state governor's power to discharge an appointed member of his personal staff who asserts his Fifth Amendment privilege before a grand jury investigating accusations of influence peddling in state government. And since a constitutional limitation on the power of the "government," . . . applies equally to the legislature and the executive, a statutory restriction is no more objectionable than an executive order. . . .

[C]onditions may appropriately be attached to the holding of high public office that would be entirely inappropriate for the vast majority of government employees whose work is not significantly different from that performed in the private sector.

The Court has decided in the past that workers such as sanitation men employed by a state-chartered municipality may not be threatened with the loss of their livelihood in order to compel them to waive their privilege against self-incrimination. Neither that decision, nor any in its line, controls this case. For rules which protect the rights of government workers whose jobs are not fundamentally different from positions in other areas of society are not automatically

applicable to policymaking officials of government.

* * *

The State has a legitimate interest, not only in preventing actual corruption, but also in avoiding the appearance of corruption among those it favors with sensitive, policymaking office. If such a person wishes to exercise his constitutional right to remain silent and refuses to waive his privilege against compulsory self-incrimination, I see no reason why the State should not have the power to remove him from office.

I recognize that procedures are available by which the State may compel *any* of its employees to render an accounting of his or her office in exchange for a grant of immunity. But the availability of that alternative does not require us to conclude that our highest public officers may refuse to respond to legitimate inquiries and remain in office unless they are first granted immunity from criminal prosecution. The Fifth Amendment does not require the State to pay such a price to effect the removal of an officer whose claim of privilege can only erode the public's confidence in its government.

* * *

[Mr. Justice REHNQUIST took no part in the consideration or decision of this case.]

Comments

1. In *Murphy* v. *Waterfront Commission,* supra, the Court noted that to be valid, a grant of immunity must be coextensive with the scope of the privilege against self-incrimination—the "coextensive" requirement. Since the scope of the privilege is subject to debate, the enactment and implementation of immunity laws have been a source of considerable controversy in recent years. Although the use of immunity to compel testimony may appear to violate the Fifth Amendment privilege against self-incrimination, the witness is not compelled to testify against *himself* since his testimony cannot later be used against him in a criminal proceeding. In *Murphy,* the Court was concerned that the testimony of a witness given under a grant of immunity in one jurisdiction might be used against him in another jurisdiction where he had not been granted immunity—a situation analogous to the "silver platter" doctrine (p. 215). Note that if a witness has been granted valid immunity, he is not given an option to accept or reject the immunity; he must testify or be held in contempt of court. Usually, when a witness refuses to testify after being granted immunity, a judgment of *civil contempt* of court follows. That is, the witness is jailed until he agrees to comply with the order of the court, but he can "purge"

himself of contempt by agreeing to testify. *Criminal contempt* of court is used to punish a witness for disobeying the lawful order of a court, and thus no purge is permitted.

2. In *Kastigar* v. *United States,* supra, the Court had to decide whether use immunity was coextensive with the privilege against self-incrimination. In general, there are two types of immunity: transactional and use. *Use immunity* (limited immunity) prohibits the government only from *using* a witness' compelled testimony in a subsequent criminal proceeding. It does not prohibit a prosecution on the transaction about which the witness testified if the later evidence was obtained from a legitimate independent source. Thus, if a grand jury witness has been granted use immunity, his compelled testimony cannot be used against him as direct evidence or as an "investigatory lead" in a subsequent criminal proceeding, and the prosecutor has an affirmative duty to prove that the evidence he proposes to use against the immunity-granted witness was derived from a source wholly independent of the compelled testimony. For example, if a grand jury witness has been given use immunity and his compelled testimony reveals that he was a participant in a bank robbery, the witness may nevertheless be prosecuted for that crime *if* the prosecution is able to produce at trial evidence wholly independent of the witness' grand jury testimony. Thus, use immunity is not total immunity in that a witness can later be prosecuted about any transaction (crime) about which he was compelled to testify.

Transactional immunity (complete immunity) prohibits the government from *prosecuting* any witness on account of any "transaction, matter or thing" concerning which he was compelled to testify after claiming his Fifth Amendment privilege. Thus, if a grand jury witness has been given transactional immunity and his compelled testimony reveals that he was responsible for several brutal homicides and a half dozen bank robberies, he cannot be prosecuted for those crimes regardless of any evidence independent of his testimony that the prosecution is able to procure. Thus, the type of immunity that a witness receives is important to both the witness and the prosecutor. In light of *Kastigar,* which held that only use, not transactional, immunity is constitutionally required, only use immunity is authorized in federal proceedings today. Although a state or the federal government may constitutionally grant either type of immunity, the prosecutorial limitations attending a grant of transactional immunity are obvious. And in view of *Kastigar,* many states are likely to follow the more limited federal use-immunity statute. See *Symposium on Witness Immunity,* 67 J. Crim. L. & Criminol. 129 (1976).

3. In light of previous Supreme Court pronouncements regarding a grand jury witness' compelled self-incrimination, the *Cunningham* decision comes as little surprise. It certainly is not a "landmark" decision, or even a particularly remarkable one; the case simply affirms the earlier holdings in *Garrity* [infra, Chapter Ten, § 10.03], *Gardner, Turley, Washington* (infra, § 6.04), et al. The majority reaffirmed the basic propositions that the Fifth Amendment privilege against compelled self-incrimination protects grand jury witnesses from being forced to give testimony that may later be used to convict them in a criminal proceeding; and that the government may not penalize assertion of the privilege by imposing sanctions to compel testimony that has not been immunized.

According to the majority, Section 22 of the New York Election Law posed at least three "grave consequences" for the defendant: the economic consequence that the appellee's standing as a practicing lawyer would be jeopardized by his removal from political office, and the noneconomic consequences that he would lose prestige and political influence as well as his good name in the community, and he would have to sacrifice his right to participate in political associations in order to exercise his right against self-incrimination or vice versa.

It is interesting to note that Justices Brennan and Marshall used their concurring opinion to take issue with the concept of use immunity (see Comment 2, supra). While Justice Marshall dissented in *Kastigar,* Justice Brennan, along with Justice Rehnquist, declined to take part in consideration of the *Kastigar* case. However, Justice Brennan chose to join Justice Marshall in stating their belief that only absolute, or transactional, immunity can satisfy the Fifth Amendment.

Finally, consider Justice Stevens' dissent in *Cunningham.* Do you believe that his analogy concerning removal of a "public official" by the President or a governor is a reasonable one? Does it matter that officials such as the secretary of defense are appointed by and serve at the pleasure of the President? Appellee was elected to his political positions by his fellow Democratic Party members. Likewise, is it significant that the First Amendment guarantees to all persons the right to participate in private, voluntary political associations? Is it reasonable to enforce a law that requires a person to choose between silence and public service?

E. ENTRAPMENT

The Defendant's "Predisposition to Commit the Crime"

UNITED STATES v. RUSSELL

Supreme Court of the United States, 1973
411 U.S. 423, 93 S. Ct. 1637, 36 L. Ed. 2d 366

After a trial in federal district court in the state of Washington, Richard Russell was convicted on three counts of a five count indictment for unlawfully manufacturing and selling methamphetamine ("speed"). His sole defense was entrapment, on the ground that a government undercover agent (Shapiro) supplied an essential ingredient in the manufacture of methamphetamine. The United States Court of Appeal (9th Cir.) reversed the conviction holding that "a defense to a criminal charge may be founded upon an intolerable degree of governmental participation in the criminal enterprise." The United States Supreme Court granted certiorari.

Mr. Justice REHNQUIST delivered the opinion of the Court.

*   *   *

This Court first recognized and applied the entrapment defense in Sorrells v. United States, 287 U.S. 435 (1932). In Sorrells, a federal prohibition agent visited the defendant while posing as a tourist and engaged him in conversation about their common war experiences. After gaining the defendant's confidence, the agent asked for some liquor, was twice refused, but upon asking a third time the defendant finally capitulated, and was subsequently prosecuted for violating the National Prohibition Act.

Mr. Chief Justice Hughes, speaking for the Court, held that as a matter of statutory construction the defense of entrapment should have been available to the defendant. Under the theory propounded by the Chief Justice, the entrapment defense prohibits law enforcement officers from instigating a criminal act by persons "otherwise innocent in order to lure them to its commission and to punish them." . . . Thus, the thrust of the entrapment defense was held to focus on the intent of predisposition of the defendant to commit the crime. If the defendant seeks acquittal by reason of entrapment he cannot complain of an appropriate and searching inquiry into his own conduct and predisposition as bearing upon that issue. . . .

Mr. Justice Roberts concurred but was of the view "that courts must be closed to the trial of a crime instigated by the government's own agents. . . . The difference in the view of the majority and the concurring opinion is that in the former the inquiry focuses on the predisposition of the defendant, whereas in the latter the inquiry focuses on whether the government "instigated the crime."

In 1958 the Court again considered the theory underlying the entrapment defense and expressly reaffirmed the view expressed by the Sorrells majority. Sherman v. United States. . . . In Sherman the defendant was convicted of selling narcotics to a Government informer. As in Sorrells, it appears that the Government agent gained the confidence of the defendant and, despite initial reluctance, the defendant finally acceded to the repeated importunings of the agent to commit the criminal act. On the basis of Sorrells, this Court reversed the affirmance of the defendant's conviction.

In affirming the theory underlying Sorrells, Mr. Chief Justice Warren for the Court, held that "[to] determine whether entrapment has been established, a line must be drawn between the trap for the unwary innocent and the trap for the unwary criminal." 356 U.S., at 372. Mr. Justice Frankfurter stated in an opinion concurring in the result that he believed Mr. Justice Roberts had the better view in Sorrells and would have framed the question to be asked in an entrapment defense in terms of "whether the police conduct revealed in the particular case falls below standards . . . for the proper use of governmental power." Id., at 382.

In the instant case, respondent asks us to reconsider the theory of the entrapment defense as it is set forth in the majority opinions in Sorrells and Sherman. His principal contention is that the defense should rest on constitutional grounds . . . [and that] the level of Shapiro's involvement in the manufacture of the methamphetamine was so high that a criminal prosecution for the drug's manufacture violates the fundamental principles of due process. The respondent contends that the same factors that led this Court to apply the exclusionary rule to illegal searches and seizures, Weeks v. United States, 232 U.S. 383 (1914), Mapp v. Ohio, 367 U.S. 643 (1961), and confessions, Miranda v. Arizona, 384 U.S. 436 (1966), should be considered here. . . . But he would have the Court go further in deterring undesirable official conduct by requiring that any prosecution be barred absolutely because of the police involvement in criminal activity. The analogy is imperfect in any event. . . .

The Government's conduct here violated no independent constitutional right of the respondent. Nor did Shapiro violate any federal statute or rule or commit any crime in infiltrating the respondent's drug enterprise.

Respondent would overcome this basic weakness in his analogy to the exclusionary rule cases by having the Court adopt a rigid constitutional rule that would preclude any prosecution when it is shown that the criminal conduct would not have been possible had not an undercover agent "supplied an indispensable means to the commission of the crime that could not have been obtained otherwise, through legal or illegal channels." Even if we were to surmount the difficulties attending the notion that due process of law can be embodied in fixed rules, and those attending respondent's particular formulation, the rule he proposes would not appear to be of significant benefit to him. For, on the record presented, it appears that he cannot fit within the terms of the very rule he proposes.

* * *

While we may some day be presented with a situation in which the conduct of law enforcement agents is so outrageous that due process principles would absolutely bar the government from invoking judicial processes to obtain a conviction ... the instant case is distinctly not of that breed. ... The law enforcement conduct here stops far short of violating that "fundamental fairness, shocking to the universal sense of justice," mandated by the Due Process Clause of the Fifth Amendment. ...

The illicit manufacture of drugs is not a sporadic, isolated criminal incident, but a continuing, though illegal, business enterprise. In order to obtain convictions for illegally manufacturing drugs, the gathering of evidence of past unlawful conduct frequently proves to be an all but impossible task. Thus in drug related offenses law enforcement personnel have turned to one of the only practicable means of detection: the infiltration of drug rings and a limited participation in their unlawful present practices. Such infiltration is a recognized and permissible means of investigation; if that be so, then the supply of some item of value that the drug ring requires must, as a general rule, also be permissible. For an agent will not be taken into the confidence of the illegal entrepreneurs unless he has something of value to offer them. Law enforcement tactics such as this can hardly be said to violate "fundamental fairness" or be "shocking to the universal sense of justice." ... This Court's opinion in Sorrells v. United States, supra, and Sherman v. United States, supra, held that the principal element in the defense of entrapment was the defendant's predisposition to commit the crime. Respondent conceded in the Court of Appeals, as well he might, "that he may have harbored a predisposition to commit the charged offenses." 459 F.2d, at 672. Yet he argues that the jury's refusal to find entrapment under the charge submitted to it by the trial court should be overturned and the views of Justices Roberts and Frankfurter, in Sorrells and Sherman, respectively, which make the essential element of the defense turn on the type and degree of governmental conduct, be adopted as the law.

We decline to overrule these cases. Sorrells is a precedent of long standing that has already been once reexamined in Sherman and implicitly there reaffirmed. Since the defense is not of a constitutional dimension, Congress may address itself to the question and adopt any substantive definition of the defense that it may find desirable.

* * *

Those cases establish that entrapment is a relatively limited defense. It is rooted not in any authority of the Judicial Branch to dismiss prosecutions that it feels to have been "overzealous law enforcement," but instead in the notion that Congress could not have intended criminal punishment for a defendant who has committed all the elements of a prescribed offense but was induced to commit them by the government.

Sorrells and Sherman both recognize "that the fact that officers or employees of the Government merely afford opportunities or facilities for the commission of the offense does not defeat the prosecution." ... Nor will the mere fact of deceit defeat a prosecution ... for there are circumstances when the use of deceit is the only practicable law enforcement technique available. It is only when the Government's deception actually implants the criminal design in the mind of the defendant that the defense of entrapment comes into play.

Respondent's concession in the Court of Appeals that the jury finding as to predisposition was supported by the evidence is, therefore, fatal to his claim of entrapment. He was an active participant in an illegal drug manufacturing enterprise which began before the Government agent appeared on the scene and continued after the Government agent had left the scene. He was, in the words of Sherman, supra, not an "unwary innocent" but an "unwary criminal." The Court of Appeals was wrong, we believe, when it sought to broaden the principle laid down in Sorrels and Sherman. Its judgment is therefore

Reversed.

Mr. Justice DOUGLAS, with whom Mr. Justice BRENNAN concurs, dissenting.

* * *

Federal agents play a debased role when they become the instigators of the crime, or partners in its commission, or the creative brain behind the illegal scheme. That is what the federal agent did here when he furnished the accused with one of the chemical ingredients needed to manufacture the unlawful drug.

Mr. Justice STEWART, with whom Mr. Justice BRENNAN and Mr. Justice MARSHALL join, dissenting.

* * *

... The Government cannot be permitted to instigate the commission of a criminal offense in order to prosecute someone for committing it.... The Government "may not provoke or create a crime and then punish the criminal its creature." ... It is to prevent this situation from occurring in the administration of federal criminal justice that the defense of entrapment exists. ...

* * *

Under the objective approach that I would follow, this respondent was entrapped, regardless of his predisposition or "innocence."

* * *

I would affirm the judgment of the Court of Appeals.

When a Government Informer Supplies Contraband

HAMPTON v. UNITED STATES

Supreme Court of the United States, 1976
425 U.S. 484, 96 S. Ct. 1646, 48 L. Ed. 2d 113

The facts are stated in the opinion.

Mr. Justice REHNQUIST announced the judgment of the Court in an opinion in which the Chief Justice [BURGER] and Mr. Justice WHITE join.

This case presents the question of whether a defendant may be convicted for the sale of contraband which he procured from a government informer or agent. The Court of Appeals for the Eighth Circuit held he could be, and we agree.

Petitioner was convicted of two counts of distributing heroin in violation of 21 U.S.C. § 841(a)(1) in the United States District Court for the Eastern District of Missouri and sentenced to concurrent terms of five years' imprisonment (suspended).[a] The case arose from two sales of heroin by petitioner to agents of the Federal Drug Enforcement Administration (DEA) in St. Louis on February 25 and 26, 1974. The sales were arranged by one Hutton, who was a pool-play-ing acquaintance of petitioner at the Pud bar in St. Louis and also a DEA informant.

According to the government's witnesses, in late February 1974, Hutton and petitioner were shooting pool at the Pud when petitioner, after observing "track" (needle) marks on Hutton's arms told Hutton that he needed money and knew where he could get some heroin. Hutton responded that he could find a buyer and petitioner suggested that he "get in touch with those people." Hutton then called DEA agent Terry Sawyer and arranged a sale for 10 p.m. on February 25.

At the appointed time, Hutton and petitioner went to a prearranged meeting place and were met by agent Sawyer and DEA agent McDowell, posing as narcotics dealers. Petitioner produced a tinfoil packet from his cap and turned it over to the agents who tested it, pronounced it "okay" and negotiated a price of $145 which was paid to petitioner. Before they parted, petitioner told Sawyer that he could obtain larger quantities of heroin and gave Sawyer a phone number where he could be reached.

The next day Sawyer called petitioner

---

[a] Petitioner was placed on five years' probation which was to run concurrently with the remainder of a 28 to 30 year state armed robbery sentence from which petitioner had escaped.

and arranged for another "buy" that afternoon. Petitioner got Hutton to go along and they met the agents again near where they had been the previous night.

They all entered the agents' car and petitioner again produced a tinfoil packet from his cap. The agents again tested it and pronounced it satisfactory. Petitioner then asked for $500 which agent Sawyer said he would get from the trunk. Sawyer got out and opened the trunk which was a signal to other agents to move in and arrest petitioner, which they did.

Petitioner's version of events was quite different. According to him, in response to petitioner's statement that he was short of cash, Hutton said that he had a friend who was a pharmacist who could produce a non-narcotic counterfeit drug which would give the same reaction as heroin. Hutton proposed selling this drug to gullible acquaintances who would be led to believe they were buying heroin. Petitioner testified that they successfully duped one buyer with this fake drug and that the sale which led to the arrest was "solicited" by petitioner[c] in an effort to profit further from this ploy.

Petitioner contended that he neither intended to sell, nor knew that he was dealing in heroin and that all of the drugs he sold were supplied by Hutton. His account was at least partially disbelieved by the jury which was instructed that in order to convict petitioner they must find that the Government proved "that the defendant knowingly did an act which the law forbids, purposely intending to violate the law." Thus the guilty verdict necessarily implies that the jury rejected petitioner's claim that he did not know the substance was heroin, and petitioner himself admitted both soliciting and carrying out sales. The only relevance of his version of the facts, then, lies in his having requested an instruction embodying that version. He did not request a standard entrapment instruction but he did request the following:

"The defendant asserts that he was the

victim of entrapment as to the crimes charged in the indictment.

"If you find that the defendant's sales of narcotics were sales of narcotics supplied to him by an informer in the employ of or acting on behalf of the government, then you must acquit the defendant because the law as a matter of policy forbids his conviction in such a case.

"Furthermore, under this particular defense, you need not consider the predisposition of the defendant to commit the offense charged, because if the governmental involvement through its informer reached the point that I have just defined in your own minds, then the predisposition of the defendant would not matter."

The trial court refused the instruction and petitioner was found guilty. He appealed to the United States Court of Appeals for the Eighth Circuit, claiming that if the jury had believed that the drug was supplied by Hutton he should have been acquitted. The Court of Appeals rejected this argument and affirmed the conviction, relying on our opinion in United States v. Russell, 411 U.S. 423 (1973).

In Russell we held that the statutory defense of entrapment was not available where it was conceded that a government agent supplied a necessary ingredient in the manufacture of an illicit drug. We reaffirmed the principle of Sorrells v. United States, 287 U.S. 435 (1932), and Sherman v. United States, 356 U.S. 369 (1958), that the entrapment defense "focus[es] on the intent or predisposition of the defendant to commit the crime," Russell, supra, at 429, rather than upon the conduct of the Government's agents. We ruled out the possibility that the defense of entrapment could ever be based upon governmental misconduct in a case, such as this one, where the predisposition of the defendant to commit the crime was established.

In holding that "it is only when the Government's deception actually implants the criminal design in the mind of the defendant that the defense of entrapment comes into play," 411 U.S., at 436, we of course rejected the contrary view of the dissents in that case and the concurrences in Sorrells and Sherman. In view of these holdings, petitioner correctly recognizes that his case does not qualify as one involving "entrap-

---

[c]On appeal, petitioner's counsel, who was also his counsel at trial, conceded that petitioner was predisposed to commit this offense, United States v. Hampton, 507 F.2d 832, 836 n.5 (8th Cir. 1974).

ment" at all. He instead relies on the language in Russell that "we may some day be presented with a situation in which the conduct of law enforcement agents is so outrageous that due process principles would absolutely bar the government from invoking judicial processes to obtain a conviction, cf. Rochin v. California, 342 U.S. 165 (1952)...." 411 U.S., at 431–432.

In urging that this case involves a violation of his due process rights, petitioner misapprehends the meaning of the quoted language in Russell, supra. Admittedly petitioner's case is different from Russell's but the difference is one of degree, not of kind. In Russell the ingredient supplied by the government agent was a legal drug which the defendants demonstrably could have obtained from other sources besides the Government. Here the drug which the government informant allegedly supplied to petitioner was both illegal and constituted the corpus delicti for the sale of which the petitioner was convicted. The Government obviously played a more significant role in enabling petitioner to sell contraband in this case than it did in Russell.

But in each case the government agents were acting in concert with the defendant, and in each case either the jury found or the defendant conceded that he was predisposed to commit the crime for which he was convicted. The remedy of the criminal defendant with respect to the acts of government agents, which, far from being resisted, are encouraged by him, lies solely in the defense of entrapment. But, as noted, petitioner's conceded predisposition rendered this defense unavailable to him.

To sustain petitioner's contention here would run directly contrary to our statement in Russell that the defense of entrapment is not intended "to give the federal judiciary a 'chancellor's foot' veto over law enforcement practices of which it did not approve. The execution of the federal laws under our Constitution is confided primarily to the executive branch of the government, subject to applicable constitutional and statutory limitations and to judicially fashioned rules to enforce those limitations."...

The limitations of the Due Process Clause of the Fifth Amendment, and of those portions of the Bill of Rights which it has been held to incorporate, come into play only when the government activity in question violates some protected right of the *defendant*. Here, as we have noted, the police, the government informer, and the defendant acted in concert with one another. If the result of the governmental activity is to "implant in the mind of an innocent person the disposition to commit the alleged offense and induce its commission..." Sorrells, supra, at 442, the defendant is protected by the defense of entrapment. If the police engage in illegal activity in concert with a defendant beyond the scope of their duties the remedy lies, not in freeing the equally culpable defendant, but in prosecuting the police under the applicable provisions of state or federal law.... But the police conduct here no more deprived defendant of any right secured to him by the United States Constitution than did the police conduct in Russell deprive Russell of any rights.

Affirmed.

Mr. Justice POWELL, with whom Mr. Justice BLACKMUN joins, concurring in the judgment.

Petitioner, Charles Hampton, contends that the Government's supplying of contraband to one later prosecuted for trafficking in contraband constitutes a per se denial of due process. As I do not accept this proposition, I concur in the judgment of the Court and much of the plurality opinion directed specifically to Hampton's contention. I am not able to join the remainder of the plurality opinion, as it would unnecessarily reach and decide difficult questions not before us.

... Hampton would distinguish Russell on the ground that here contraband itself was supplied by the Government, while the phenyl-2-propanone supplied in Russell was not contraband. Given the characteristics of phenyl-2-propanone, this is a distinction without a difference and Russell disposes of this case.

But the plurality opinion today does not stop there. In discussing Hampton's due process contention, it enunciates a per se rule:

"[In Russell,] [w]e ruled out the possibility that the defense of entrapment could *ever* be based upon governmental misconduct in a case, such as this one, where the predisposition of the defendant to commit the crime was established...."

"The remedy of the criminal defendant with respect to the acts of government agents, which ... are encouraged by him, lies *solely* in the defense of entrapment." ...

The plurality thus says that the concept of fundamental fairness inherent in the guarantee of due process would never prevent the conviction of a predisposed defendant, regardless of the outrageousness of police behavior in light of the surrounding circumstances.

I do not understand Russell or earlier cases delineating the predisposition-focused defense of entrapment to have gone so far, and there was no need for them to do so. In those cases the Court was confronted with specific claims of police "over-involvement" in criminal activity involving contraband. Disposition of those claims did not require the Court to consider whether overinvolvement of government agents in contraband offenses could ever reach such proportions as to bar conviction of a predisposed defendant as a matter of due process. Nor have we had occasion yet to confront Government overinvolvement in areas outside the realm of contraband offenses.... In these circumstances, I am unwilling to conclude that an analysis other than one limited to predisposition would never be appropriate under due process principles.

* * *

I am not unmindful of the doctrinal and practical difficulties of delineating limits to police involvement in crime that do not focus on predisposition, as government participation ordinarily will be fully justified in society's "war with the criminal classes." ... This undoubtedly is the concern that prompts the plurality to embrace an absolute rule. But we left these questions open in Russell, and this case is controlled completely by Russell. I therefore am unwilling to join the plurality in concluding that, no matter what the circumstances, neither due process principles nor our supervisory power could support a bar to conviction in any case where the Government is able to prove predisposition.

Mr. Justice BRENNAN, with whom Mr. Justice STEWART and Mr. Justice MARSHALL concur, dissenting.

... The "subjective" approach to the defense of entrapment — followed by the Court today and in Sorrells, Sherman, and Russell — focuses on the conduct and propensities of the particular defendant in each case and, in the absence of a conclusive showing, permits the jury to determine as a question of fact the defendant's "predisposition" to the crime. The focus of the view espoused by Mr. Justice Roberts, Mr. Justice Frankfurter, and my Brother STEWART "is not on the propensities and predisposition of a specific defendant, but on 'whether the police conduct revealed in the particular case falls below standards, to which common feelings respond, for the proper use of governmental power'.... Under this approach, the determination of the lawfulness of the Government's conduct must be made — as it is on all questions involving the legality of law enforcement methods — by the trial judge, not the jury." Petitioner's claims in this case allege a course of police conduct that, under this view, would plainly be held to constitute entrapment as a matter of law.

In any event, I think that reversal of petitioner's conviction is also compelled for those who follow the "subjective" approach to the defense of entrapment.... In my view, the police activity in this was beyond permissible limits.

Two facts significantly distinguish this case from Russell. First, the chemical supplied in that case was not contraband. It is legal to possess and sell phenyl-2-propanone and, although the Government there supplied an ingredient that was essential to the manufacture of methamphetamine, it did not supply the contraband itself. In contrast, petitioner claims that the very narcotic he is accused of selling was supplied by an agent of the Government....

Second, the defendant in Russell "was an active participant in an illegal drug manufacturing enterprise which began before the Government agent appeared on the scene, and continued after the Government agent had left the scene." ... Russell was charged with unlawfully manufacturing and processing methamphetamine, ... and his crime was participation in an ongoing operation. In contrast, the two sales for which petitioner was convicted were allegedly instigated by Government agents and completed by the Government's purchase. The beginning and end of this crime thus coincided exactly with the Government's entry into and withdrawal from the criminal activity involved in this case, while the Government was not similarly involved in Russell's crime. . . .

Whether the differences from the Russell situation are of degree or of kind, . . . I think they clearly require a different result. Where the Government's agent deliberately sets up the accused by supplying him with contraband and then bringing him to another agent as a potential purchaser, the Government's role has passed the point of toleration. . . . The Government is doing nothing less than buying contraband from itself through an intermediary and jailing the intermediary. . . . There is little, if any, law enforcement interest promoted by such conduct; plainly it is not designed to discover ongoing drug traffic. Rather, such conduct deliberately entices an individual to commit a crime. That the accused is "predisposed" cannot possibly justify the action of government officials in purposefully creating the crime. No one would suggest that the police would round up and jail all "predisposed" individuals, yet that is precisely what set-ups like the instant one are intended to accomplish. . . . Thus, this case is nothing less than an instance of "the Government . . . seeking to punish for an alleged offense which is the product of the creative activity of its own officials.". . .

These considerations persuaded the Court of Appeals for the Fifth Circuit to hold that where the Government has provided the contraband that the defendant is convicted of selling, there is entrapment as a matter of law. . . . I agree with my Brother POWELL that "entrapment" under the "subjective" approach is only one possible defense — he suggests due process or appeal to our supervisory power as alternatives — in cases where the Government's conduct is as egregious as in this case. . . . I would at a minimum . . . hold that conviction is barred as a matter of law where the subject of the criminal charge is the sale of contraband provided to the defendant by a Government agent. . . .

[Mr. Justice STEVENS took no part in the consideration or decision of this case.]

Comments

1. The Supreme Court has never held that freedom from entrapment is of a constitutional dimension; therefore, state law governs entrapment. The few decisions by the Supreme Court involving entrapment were decided on the basis of the Court's "supervisory power" over lower federal courts. In each of these cases the justices were sharply divided on the definition of entrapment. The majority of justices focused on the defendants' predisposition to commit the crime—the *"origin of intent" test.* Under this test, a subjective determination is made of whether the original intent to commit the criminal act was the product of the creative activity of law enforcement officers or the defendant. It is not sufficient for the police merely to afford the defendant an opportunity to commit an offense; the defendant must lack a predisposition to commit the crime in order to be entrapped. Thus, entrapment becomes a question of fact for the jury rather than a question of law for the court. The minority view (espoused by the dissenting justices in *Russell* and *Hampton*) is known as the *"police conduct" theory*. Under this test, an objective determination is made of whether the police conduct in a particular case constitutes a proper use of governmental power; i.e., was the conduct of the police reprehensible? In this view, entrapment is a question of law to be decided by the court (not the jury). Most states utilize the "defendants' predisposition" test, and only a few states the "police conduct" theory. Entrapment may not always be an appealing defense, because in some states a defendant who denies the commission of the offense

charged cannot claim entrapment as a defense. This places the defendant in the unenviable position of having to admit committing the offense charged, while claiming that "the police induced me to do it." Juries may not be willing to separate the criminal act from the overzealous behavior of the police.

2. In *Russell,* the Court held that entrapment is not proved simply because a governmental undercover agent supplies an essential chemical necessary for the unlawful manufacture of a drug ("speed"). The defendant's downfall was his admission in oral arguments before the court of appeals that he might have had a "predisposition to commit the crime." (Actually it was the defendant's counsel who made the concession before the court of appeals — defendants normally do not appear before appellate courts.) Since defense counsel represents the defendant, any statements by counsel are usually binding on the defendant under agency principles. We have to assume that defense counsel was authorized by the defendant to make the concession. Suppose he wasn't? Is the defendant being treated fairly when his counsel "gives away" the case on appeal? Could this arguably be a denial of effective counsel? The Supreme Court took the defendant's concession at face value, which, in part, resulted in the affirmation of the conviction. This was not the first case in which the Supreme Court adopted the admissions of a defendant. In *Ginzburg* v. *United States,* 383 U.S. 463 (1966), the defendant advertised that he was selling obscene materials, and the Supreme Court affirmed his conviction by taking him at his word without deciding whether the materials sold were obscene as a matter of constitutional law. The practical lesson of the *Russell* and *Ginzburg* cases for defense attorneys seems to be "never concede guilt at any stage of the criminal process."

3. In *Hampton* v. *United States,* supra, only three justices (a plurality) were willing to foreclose the defense of entrapment when government agents, a government informer, and a defendant act "in concert" with one another and the defendant concedes a predisposition to commit the crime in question. But the plurality went one step further and stated that a predisposition to commit a crime bars a defense of denial of due process regardless of how outrageous the government's conduct is. However, Justices Powell and Blackmun (concurring) found that the plurality opinion went further than was necessary for a disposition of the case. For Justices Powell and Blackmun, the fact that a government informer supplied contraband pursuant to an unlawful sale wasn't sufficiently outrageous to warrant a denial of due process. What type of police conduct would require a finding of a denial of due process notwithstanding the defendant's predisposition to commit the crime? What result if a defendant denies a predisposition and the conduct of the police is outrageous? Do you agree with the view of Mr. Justice Brennan (dissenting) that "the Government is doing nothing less than buying contraband from itself through an intermediary and jailing the intermediary"? The 3–2–3 split by the *Hampton* Court did little to settle the issue of outrageous police conduct and entrapment and invites further litigation in this area.

4. Some recent lower federal and state court decisions involving the issue of entrapment are: *United States* v. *Gurule,* 522 F.2d 20 (10th Cir. 1975) (accused's undisputed claim that he was aiding

federal officials in breaking up a drug ring doesn't, in and of itself, establish entrapment as a matter of law); *United States* v. *Demma*, 523 F.2d 981 (9th Cir. 1975) (en banc) (defendant may assert entrapment without being required to concede that he committed the crime charged or any of its elements) (overruling *Eastman* v. *United States*, 212 F.2d 320 [9th Cir. 1954]); *State* v. *Curtis*, 542 P.2d 744 (Utah 1975) (47-year-old defendant who alleged that a sexually intimate relationship was instigated by a 24-year-old undercover policewoman to induce him to obtain drugs for her use and not for his profit held not entitled, over her denial, to a finding of entrapment as a matter of law under the "police conduct" test); *People* v. *Cushman*, 237 N.W.2d 228 (Mich. 1976) (judge, not jury, decides question of entrapment under the "police conduct" theory); *State* v. *Basham*, 223 S.E.2d 53 (W. Va. 1976) (junkyard operator who admitted knowingly buying stolen goods but claimed he did so pursuant to an agreement with the police held entitled to entrapment instruction at trial); *People* v. *Jensen*, 347 N.E.2d 371 (Ill. App. 1976) (defendant accused of driving with a suspended license entitled to entrapment instruction where his uncontradicted testimony indicated that he drove his car only because a park ranger ordered him to do so); *State* v. *Talbot*, 343 A.2d 777 (N.J. 1976) (proof that the government was both the supplier and buyer of contraband establishes entrapment as a matter of law); *United States* v. *Boone*, 543 F.2d 512 (D.C. Cir. 1976) (lesser degree of criminal involvement takes a lesser showing of inducement in order to entitle a defendant to an entrapment instruction); *United States* v. *Ramirez*, 533 F.2d 138 (5th Cir. 1976) (by asserting defense of entrapment, defendant necessarily admitted acts charged against him); *People* v. *Wurbs*, 347 N.E.2d 879 (Ill. App. 1976) (defendant may not deny commission of the offense and still claim entrapment); *United States* v. *Martin*, 533 F.2d 268 (5th Cir. 1976) (entrapment exists only where the government has implanted the criminal design in the mind of the defendant); *State* v. *Tomlinson*, 243 N.W.2d 551 (Iowa 1976) (conduct merely affording person opportunity to commit offense is not entrapment); *State* v. *Jordan*, 551 P.2d 733 (Kan. 1976) (accused can rely on defense of entrapment when he is induced to commit a crime which he had no previous disposition to commit) (in accord is *State* v. *Stein*, 360 A.2d 347 [N.J. 1976]); *United States* v. *Onori*, 535 F.2d 938 (5th Cir. 1976) (fact that informer was paid on a contingent fee basis after drug transaction does not alone establish entrapment as a matter of law); *Orkin* v. *State*, 223 S.E.2d 61 (Ga. 1976) (entrapment requires that idea of committing act must have originated with the police and accused would not have committed the act except for conduct of police) (in accord is *State* v. *Basham*, 223 S.E.2d 53 [W. Va. 1976]); *State* v. *Padgett*, 224 S.E.2d 211 (N.C. App. 1976) (the mere affording of opportunities for commission of crime by police officers does not constitute entrapment); *United States* v. *McClain*, 531 F.2d 431 (9th Cir. 1976) (entrapment depends on the predisposition of the defendant to commit the offense) (in accord is *State* v. *Fiechter*, 547 P.2d 555 [N.M. 1976], and *State* v. *Kiser*, 546 P.2d 831 [Ariz. App. 1976]); *Willis* v. *United States*, 530 F.2d 308 (7th Cir. 1976) (mere fact of deceit by government agents does not establish entrapment); *State* v. *Matheson*, 363 A.2d 716 (Me. 1976) (when defendant's predisposition is established, governmental misconduct can never be a basis of an entrapment defense); *People* v. *Morris,* 545 P.2d 151 (Colo. 1976) (entrapment is not a defense of constitutional proportion); *People* v. *Cushman,* 237 N.W.2d 228 (Mich. App. 1975) (conduct of the police is the test for entrapment, not the predisposition of the defendant to commit the act); *Kimmons* v. *State,* 322 So. 2d 366 (Fla. App. 1975) (entrapment defense does not arise from federal Constitution, but from public policy); *Saienni* v. *State,* 346 A.2d 152 (Del. 1975) (entrapment defense not available to defendant where the causing or threatening of physical injury is an element of the offense charged); *State* v. *Farris,* 542 P.2d 725 (Kan. 1975) (entrapment defense is not available when acts of inducement are committed by persons who are not public officers or acting as agents of public officers); *Mullins* v. *State,* 323 So. 2d 109 (Ala. App. 1975) (entrapment is not established merely because a police officer affords the defendant an opportunity to commit the crime).

F. PRETRIAL IDENTIFICATION PROCEDURES

The Forcible Taking of a Suspect's Blood

SCHMERBER v. CALIFORNIA

Supreme Court of the United States, 1966
384 U.S. 757, 86 S. Ct. 1826, 16 L. Ed. 2d 908

Armando Schmerber was convicted in Los Angeles Municipal Court of the criminal offense of driving an automobile while under the influence of liquor (a misdemeanor). After leaving a tavern about midnight, Schmerber and a companion were injured when Schmerber's car skidded, crossed the road, and struck a tree. They were taken to a hospital for treatment, where Schmerber was arrested. A blood sample was withdrawn by a physician at the direction of a police officer, over Schmerber's objections on the advice of his counsel. The report of the chemical analysis of the test, indicating intoxication, was admitted in evidence at trial over Schmerber's objections that the compulsory blood test and the admission of the evidence violated his right to due process under the Fourteenth Amendment, his privilege against self-incrimination under the Fifth Amendment, his right to counsel under the Sixth Amendment, and his right against unreasonable searches and seizures under the Fourth Amendment. The Appellate Department of the California Superior Court affirmed. The United States Supreme Court granted certiorari.

Mr. Justice BRENNAN delivered the opinion of the Court.

* * *

I

The Due Process Claim

[A majority of the Court rejected Schmerber's claim that his due process

rights under the Fourteenth Amendment had been violated.]

II

The Privilege Against Self-Incrimination Claim

* * *

...We therefore must now decide whether the withdrawal of the blood and admission in evidence of the analysis involved in this case violated petitioner's privilege. We hold that the privilege protects an accused only from being compelled to testify against himself, or otherwise provide the State with evidence of a testimonial or communicative nature, and that the withdrawal of blood and use of the analysis in question in this case did not involve compulsion to these ends.

It could not be denied that in requiring petitioner to submit to the withdrawal and chemical analysis of his blood the State compelled him to submit to an attempt to discover evidence that might be used to prosecute him for a criminal offense. He submitted only after the police officer rejected his objection and directed the physician to proceed. The officer's direction to the physician to administer the test over petitioner's objection constituted compulsion for the purposes of the privilege. The critical question, then, is whether petitioner was thus compelled "to be a witness against himself."

If the scope of the privilege coincided with the complex of values it helps to protect, we might be obliged to conclude that the privilege was violated.... The withdrawal of blood necessarily involves puncturing the skin for extraction, and the percent by weight of alcohol in that blood, as established by chemical analysis, is evidence of criminal guilt. Compelled submission fails on one view to respect the "inviolability of the human personality." Moreover, since it enables the State to rely on evidence forced from the accused, the compulsion violates at least one meaning of the requirement that the State procure the evidence against an accused "by its own independent labors."

* * *

The privilege has never been given the full scope which the values it helps to protect suggest. History and a long line of authorities in lower courts have consistently limited its protection to situations in which the State seeks to submerge those values by obtaining the evidence against an accused through "the cruel, simple expedient of compelling it from his own mouth.... In sum, the privilege is fulfilled only when the person is guaranteed the right 'to remain silent unless he chooses to speak in the unfettered exercise of his own will.'" ... It is clear that the protection of the privilege reaches an accused's communications, whatever form they might take, and the compulsion of responses which are also communications, for example, compliance with a subpoena to produce one's papers. ...

On the other hand, both federal and state courts have usually held that it offers no protection against compulsion to submit to fingerprinting, photographing, or measurements, to write or speak for identification, to appear in court, to stand, to assume a stance, to walk, or to make a particular gesture. The distinction which has emerged, often expressed in different ways, is that the privilege is a bar against compelling "communications" or "testimony," but that compulsion which makes a suspect or accused the source of "real or physical evidence" does not violate it.

Although we agree that this distinction is a helpful framework for analysis, we are not to be understood to agree with past applications in all instances. There will be many cases in which such a distinction is not readily drawn. Some test seemingly directed to obtain "physical evidence," for example lie detector tests measuring changes in body function during interrogation, may actually be directed to eliciting responses which are essentially testimonial. To compel a person to submit to testing in which an effort will be made to determine his guilt or innocence on the basis of physiological responses, whether willed or not, is to evoke the spirit and history of the Fifth Amendment. ...

In the present case, however, no such problem of application is presented. Not even a shadow of testimonial compulsion upon or enforced communication by the accused was involved either in the extraction or in the chemical analysis. Petitioner's testimonial capacities were in no way implicated; indeed, his participation, except as a donor, was irrelevant to the results of the test, which depend on chemical analysis and on that alone. Since the blood test evidence, although an incriminating product of compulsion, was neither petitioner's testimony nor evidence relating to some communicative act or writing by the petitioner, it was not inadmissible on privilege grounds.

III

The Right to Counsel Claim

This conclusion also answers petitioner's claim that in compelling him to submit to the test in the face of the fact that his objection was made on the advice of counsel, he was denied his Sixth Amendment right to the assistance of counsel. Since petitioner was not entitled to assert the privilege, he has no greater right because counsel erroneously advised him that he could assert it. His claim is strictly limited to the failure of the police to respect his wish, reinforced by counsel's advice to be left inviolate. No issue of counsel's ability to assist petitioner in respect of any rights he did possess is presented. The limited claim thus made must be rejected.

IV

The Search and Seizure Claim

[This part of the opinion was presented in Chapter Five, § 5.04.]

* * *

Affirmed.

[Mr. Justice HARLAN and Mr. Justice STEWART concurred.]

Mr. Justice BLACK, with whom Mr. Justice DOUGLAS joins, dissenting.

I would reverse petitioner's conviction. . . . I disagree with the Court's holding that California did not violate the petitioner's constitutional right against self-incrimination when it compelled him, against his will, to allow a doctor to puncture his blood vessels in order to extract a sample of blood and analyze it for alcoholic content, and then used that analysis as evidence to convict petitioner of a crime. The Court admits that "the State compelled [petitioner] to submit to an attempt to discover the evidence [in his blood] that might be [and was] used to prosecute him for a criminal offense." To reach the conclusion that compelling a person to give his blood to help the State convict him is not equivalent to compelling him to be a witness against himself strikes me as quite an extraordinary feat. The Court, however, overcomes what had seemed to me to be an insuperable obstacle to its conclusion by holding that ". . . the privilege protects an accused only from being compelled to testify against himself, or otherwise provide the State with evidence of a testimonial or communicative nature, and that the withdrawal of blood and use of the analysis in question in this case did not involve compulsion to these ends."

I cannot agree that this distinction and reasoning of the Court justify denying petitioner his Bill of Rights guarantee that he must not be compelled to be a witness against himself.

In the first place it seems to me that the compulsory extraction of petitioner's blood for analysis so that the person who analyzed it could give evidence to convict him had both a "testimonial" and a "communicative nature." The sole purpose of this project which proved to be successful was to obtain "testimony" from some person to prove that petitioner had alcohol in his blood at the time he was arrested. And the purpose of the project was certainly "communicative" in that the analysis of the blood was to supply information to enable a witness to communicate to the court and jury that petitioner was more or less drunk.

I think it unfortunate that the Court rests so heavily for its very restrictive reading of the Fifth Amendment's privilege against self-incrimination on the words "testimonial" and "communicative." These words are not models of clarity and precision as the Court's rather labored explication shows. Nor can the Court, so far as I know, find precedent in the former opinions of this Court for using these particular words to limit the scope of the Fifth Amendment's protection. . . .

* * *

. . . It is a strange hierarchy of values that allows the State to extract a human being's blood to convict him of a crime because of the blood's content but proscribes compelled production of his lifeless papers. Certainly there could be few papers that would have any more "testimonial" value to convict a man of drunken driving than would an analysis of the alcoholic content of a human being's blood introduced in evidence at a trial for driving while under the influence of alcohol. In such a situation blood, of course, is not oral testimony given by an accused but it can certainly "communicate" to a court and jury the fact of guilt.

* * *

A basic error in the Court's holding and opinion is its failure to give the Fifth

Amendment's protection against compulsory self-incrimination the broad and liberal construction that . . . other opinions of this Court have declared it ought to have.

* * *

. . . The closing sentence in the Fifth Amendment section of the Court's opinion in the present case is enough by itself, I think, to expose the unsoundness of what the Court here holds. That sentence reads:

"Since the blood test evidence, although an incriminating product of compulsion, was neither petitioner's testimony nor evidence relating to some communicative act or writing by the petitioner, it was not inadmissible on privilege grounds."

How can it reasonably be doubted that the blood test evidence was not in all respects the actual equivalent of "testimony" taken from petitioner when the result of the test was offered as testimony, was considered by the jury as testimony, and the jury's verdict of guilt rests in part on that testimony? The refined, subtle reasoning and balancing process used here to narrow the scope of the Bill of Rights' safeguard against self-incrimination provides a handy instrument for further narrowing of that constitutional protection, as well as others in the future. Believing with the Framers that these constitutional safeguards broadly construed by independent tribunals of justice provide our best hope for keeping our people free from governmental oppression, I deeply regret the Court's holding. . . . I dissent from the Court's holding and opinion in this case.

Mr. Justice DOUGLAS dissenting.

* * *

We are dealing with the right of privacy which, since the Breithaupt case, we have held to be within the penumbra of some specific guarantees of the Bill of Rights. Griswold v. Connecticut, 381 U.S. 479 (1967). The Fifth Amendment marks "a zone of privacy" which the Government may not force a person to surrender. . . . Likewise the Fourth Amendment recognizes that right when it guarantees the right of the people to be secure "in their persons." No clearer invasion of this right of privacy can be imagined than forcible blood-letting of the kind involved here.

Mr. Justice FORTAS, dissenting.

I would reverse. In my view, petitioner's privilege against self-incrimination applies. I would add that, under the Due Process Clause, the State in its role as prosecutor, has no right to extract blood from an accused or anyone else, over his protest. As prosecutor, the State has no right to commit any kind of violence upon the person, or to utilize the results of such a tort, and the extraction of blood, over the protest, is an act of violence. . . .

[Mr. Chief Justice WARREN wrote a separate dissenting opinion.]

Preindictment Lineups, Physical Characteristics, and the Right to Counsel

UNITED STATES v. WADE

Supreme Court of the United States, 1967
388 U.S. 218, 87 S. Ct. 1926, 18 L. Ed. 2d 1149

The facts are given in the opinion.

Mr. Justice BRENNAN delivered the opinion of the Court.

The question here is whether courtroom identifications of an accused at trial are to be excluded from evidence because the accused was exhibited to the witnesses before trial at a post-indictment lineup conducted for identification purposes without notice to and in the absence of the accused's appointed counsel.

The federally insured bank in Eustace, Texas, was robbed on September 21, 1964. A man with a small strip of tape on each side of his face entered the bank, pointed a pistol at the female cashier and the vice-president, the only persons in the bank at the time, and forced them to fill a pillowcase with the bank's money. The man then drove away with an accomplice who had been waiting in a stolen car outside the bank. On March 23, 1965, an indictment was returned against respondent, Wade, and two others for conspiring to rob the bank, and against Wade and the accomplice for the robbery itself. Wade was arrested on April 2, and counsel was appointed to represent him on April 26. Fifteen days later an FBI agent, without notice to Wade's lawyer, arranged to have the two bank employees observe a lineup made up of Wade and five or six other prisoners and conducted in a courtroom of the local county courthouse. Each person in the line wore strips of tape such as allegedly worn by the robber and upon direction each said something like "put the money in the bag," the words allegedly uttered by the robber. Both bank employees identified Wade in the lineup as the bank robber.

At trial, the two employees, when asked on direct examination if the robber was in the courtroom, pointed to Wade. The prior lineup identification was then elicited from both employees on cross-examination. At the close of testimony, Wade's counsel moved for a judgment of acquittal or, alternatively, to strike the bank officials' courtroom identifications on the ground that conduct of the lineup, without notice to and in the absence of his appointed counsel, violated his Fifth Amendment privilege against self-incrimination and his Sixth Amendment right to the assistance of counsel. The motion was denied, and Wade was convicted. The Court of Appeals for the Fifth Circuit reversed the conviction and ordered a new trial at which the in-court identification evidence was to be excluded, holding that, though the lineup did not violate Wade's Fifth Amendment rights, "the lineup, held as it was, in the absence of counsel, already chosen to represent appellant, was a violation of his Sixth Amendment rights...." 358 F2d 557, 560. We granted certiorari....

I

Neither the lineup itself nor anything shown by this record that Wade was required to do in the lineup violated his privilege against self-incrimination. We have only recently reaffirmed that the privilege "protects an accused only from being compelled to testify against himself, or otherwise provide the State with evidence of a testimonial or communicative nature . . ." Schmerber v. California [supra].

We there held that compelling a suspect to submit to a withdrawal of a sample of his blood for analysis for alcohol content and the admission in evidence of the analysis report were not compulsion to those ends. . . .

* * *

We have no doubt that compelling the accused merely to exhibit his person for observation by a prosecution witness prior to trial involves no compulsion of the accused to give evidence having testimonial significance. It is compulsion of the accused to exhibit his physical characteristics, not compulsion to disclose any knowledge he might have. It is no different from compelling Schmerber to provide a blood sample or Holt to wear the blouse, and, as in those instances, is not within the cover of the privilege. Similarly, compelling Wade to speak within hearing distance of the witnesses, even to utter words purportedly uttered by the robber, was not compulsion to utter statements of a "testimonial" nature; he was required to use his voice as an identifying physical characteristic, not to speak his guilt. We held in Schmerber, supra . . . that the distinction to be drawn under the Fifth Amendment privilege against self-incrimination is one between an accused's "communications" in whatever form, vocal or physical, and "compulsion which makes a suspect or accused the source of 'real or physical evidence.' " . . . We recognize that "both federal and state courts have usually held that . . . (the privilege) offers no protection against compulsion to submit to fingerprinting, photography, or measurements, to write or speak for identification, to appear in court, to stand, to assume a stance, to walk, or to make a particular gesture." . . . None of these activities becomes testimonial within the scope of the privilege because required of the accused in a pretrial lineup.

Moreover, it deserves emphasis that this case presents no question of the admissibility in evidence of anything Wade said or did at the lineup which implicates his privilege. The Government offered no such evidence as part of its case, and what came out about the lineup proceedings on Wade's cross-examination of the bank employees involved no violation of Wade's privilege.

II

The fact that the lineup involved no violation of Wade's privilege against self-incrimination does not, however, dispose of his contention that the courtroom identifications should have been excluded because the lineup was conducted without notice to and in the absence of his counsel. Our rejection of the right to counsel claim in Schmerber rested on our conclusion in that case that "no issue of counsel's ability to assist petitioner in respect of any rights he did possess is presented." ... In contrast, in this case it is urged that the assistance of counsel at the lineup was indispensable to protect Wade's most basic right as a criminal defendant—his right to a fair trial at which the witnesses against him might be meaningfully cross-examined.

* * *

... [O]ur cases have construed the Sixth Amendment guarantee to apply to "critical" stages of the proceedings. The guarantee reads:

"In all criminal prosecutions, the accused shall enjoy the right ... to have the Assistance of Counsel *for his defence*." The plain wording of this guarantee thus encompasses counsel's assistance whenever necessary to assure a meaningful "defence."

* * *

... It is central to that principle that in addition to counsel's presence at trial, the accused is guaranteed that he need not stand alone against the State at any stage of the prosecution, formal or informal, in court or out, where counsel's absence might derogate from the accused's right to a fair trial. The security of that right is as much the aim of the right to counsel as it is of the other guarantees of the Sixth Amendment—the right of the accused to a speedy and public trial by an impartial jury, his

right to be informed of the nature and cause of the accusation, and his right to be confronted with the witnesses against him and to have compulsory process for obtaining witnesses in his favor. The presence of counsel at such critical confrontations, as at the trial itself, operates to assure that the accused's interests will be protected consistently with our adversary theory of criminal prosecution. ...

* * *

III

The Government characterizes the lineup as a mere preparatory step in the gathering of the prosecution's evidence, not different—for Sixth Amendment purposes—from various other preparatory steps, such as systematized or scientific analyzing of the accused's fingerprints, blood sample, clothing, hair, and the like. We think there are differences which preclude such stages being characterized as critical stages at which the accused has the right to the presence of his counsel. Knowledge of the techniques of science and technology is sufficiently available, and the variables in techniques few enough, that the accused has the opportunity for a meaningful confrontation of the Government's case at trial through the ordinary processes of cross-examination of the Government's expert witnesses and the presentation of evidence of his own experts. The denial of a right to have his counsel present at such analyses does not therefore violate the Sixth Amendment; they are not critical stages since there is minimal risk that his counsel's absence at such stages might derogate from his right to a fair trial.

IV

But the confrontation compelled by the State between the accused and the victim or witnesses to a crime to elicit identification evidence is peculiarly riddled with innumerable dangers and variable factors which might seriously, even crucially, derogate from a fair trial. The vagaries of eyewitness identification are well-known; the annals of criminal law are rife with instances of mistaken identification.

* * *

The pretrial confrontation for purpose of identification may take the form of a lineup, also known as an "identification parade" or "showup," as in the present case, or presentation of the suspect alone to the witness, as in Stovall v. Denno [infra]. . . . It is obvious that risks of suggestion attend either form of confrontation and increase the dangers inhering in eyewitness identification. But as is the case with secret interrogations, there is serious difficulty in depicting what transpires at lineups and other forms of identification confrontations: "Privacy results in secrecy and this in turn results in a gap in our knowledge as to what in fact goes on. . . ." Miranda v. Arizona [supra]. . . .

For the same reasons, the defense can seldom reconstruct the manner and mode of lineup identification for judge or jury at trial. Those participating in a lineup with the accused may often be police officers, in any event, the participants' names are rarely recorded or divulged at trial. The impediments to an objective observation are increased when the victim is the witness. Lineups are prevalent in rape and robbery prosecutions and present a particular hazard that a victim's understandable outrage may excite vengeful or spiteful motives. In any event, neither witnesses nor lineup participants are apt to be alert for conditions prejudicial to the suspect. And if they were, it would likely be of scant benefit to the suspect since neither witnesses nor lineup participants are likely to be schooled in the detection of suggestive influences. Improper influences may go undetected by a suspect, guilty or not, who experiences the emotional tension which we might expect in one being confronted with potential accusers. Even when he does observe abuse, if he has a criminal record he may be reluctant to take the stand and open up the admission of prior convictions. Moreover, any protestations by the suspect of the fairness of the lineup made at trial are likely to be in vain; the jury's choice is between the accused's unsupported version and that of the police officers present. In short, the accused's inability effectively to reconstruct at trial any unfairness that occurred at the lineup may deprive him of his only opportunity meaningfully to attack the credibility of the witness' courtroom identification.

What facts have been disclosed in specific cases about the conduct of pretrial confrontations for identification illustrate both the potential for substantial prejudice to the ac-cused at that stage and the need for its revelation at trial. . . .

The lineup in Gilbert [v. California, Comments, infra] . . . was conducted in an auditorium in which some 100 witnesses to several alleged state and federal robberies charged to Gilbert made wholesale identifications of Gilbert as the robber in each other's presence, a procedure said to be fraught with dangers of suggestion. And the vice of suggestion created by the identification in Stovall was the presentation to the witness of the suspect alone handcuffed to police officers. It is hard to imagine a situation more clearly conveying the suggestion to the witness that the one presented is believed guilty by the police. . . .

* * *

Since it appears that there is grave potential for prejudice, intentional or not, in the pretrial lineup, which may not be capable of reconstruction at trial, and since presence of counsel itself can often avert prejudice and assure a meaningful confrontation at trial, there can be little doubt that for Wade the post-indictment lineup was a critical stage of the prosecution at which he was "as much entitled to such aid [of counsel] . . . as at the trial itself." Powell v. Alabama, 287 U.S. 45. Thus both Wade and his counsel should have been notified of the impending lineup, and counsel's presence should have been a requisite to conduct of the lineup, absent an "intelligent waiver." . . . [W]e leave open the question whether the presence of substitute counsel might not suffice where notification and presence of the suspect's own counsel could result in prejudicial delay. And to refuse to recognize the right to counsel for fear that counsel will obstruct the course of justice is contrary to the basic assumptions upon which this Court had operated in Sixth Amendment cases. We rejected similar logic in Miranda v. Arizona. . . .

In our view counsel can hardly impede legitimate law enforcement; on the contrary, for the reasons expressed, law enforcement may be assisted by preventing the infiltration of taint in the prosecution's identification evidence. That result cannot help the guilty avoid conviction but can only help assure that the right man has been brought to justice.

* * *

V

We come now to the question whether the denial of Wade's motion to strike the courtroom identification by the bank witnesses at trial because of the absence of his counsel at the lineup required, as the Court of Appeals held, the grant of a new trial at which such evidence is to be excluded. We do not think this disposition can be justified without first giving the Government the opportunity to establish by clear and convincing evidence that the in-court identifications were based upon observations of the suspect other than the lineup identification. . . . Where, as here, the admissibility of evidence of the lineup identification itself is not involved, a per se rule of exclusion of courtroom identification would be unjustified. . . .

A rule limited solely to the exclusion of testimony concerning identification at the lineup itself, without regard to admissibility of the courtroom identification, would render the right to counsel an empty one. The lineup is most often used, as in the present case, to crystallize the witnesses' identification of the defendant for future reference. We have already noted that the lineup identification will have that effect. The State may then rest upon the witnesses' unequivocal courtroom identification, and not mention the pretrial identification as part of the State's case at trial. Counsel is then in the predicament in which Wade's counsel found himself—realizing that possible unfairness at the lineup may be the sole means of attack upon the unequivocal courtroom identification, and having to probe in the dark in an attempt to discover and reveal unfairness, while bolstering the government witness' courtroom identification by bringing out and dwelling upon his prior identification. Since counsel's presence at the lineup would equip him to attack not only the lineup identification but the courtroom identification as well, limiting the impact of violation of the right to counsel to exclusion of evidence only of identification at the lineup itself disregards a critical element of that right.

We think it follows that the proper test to be applied in these situations is that quoted in Wong Sun v. United States . . . [Chapter Five, § 5.05], " '[W]hether, granting establishment of the primary illegality, the evidence to which instant objection is made has been come at by exploitation of that illegality or instead by means sufficiently distinguishable to be purged of the primary taint.' " . . . Application of this test in the present context requires consideration of various factors; for example, the prior opportunity to observe the alleged criminal act, the existence of any discrepancy between any pre-lineup description and the defendant's actual description, any identification prior to lineup of another person, the identification by picture of the defendant prior to the lineup, failure to identify the defendant on a prior occasion, and the lapse of time between the alleged act and the lineup identification. It is also relevant to consider those facts which, despite the absence of counsel, are disclosed concerning the conduct of the lineup.

We doubt that the Court of Appeals applied the proper test for exclusion of the in-court identification of the two witnesses. The court stated that "it cannot be said with any certainty that they would have recognized appellant at the time of trial if this intervening lineup had not occurred," and that the testimony of the two witnesses "may well have been colored by the illegal procedure [and] was prejudicial." . . .

Moreover, the court was persuaded, in part, by the "compulsory verbal responses made by Wade at the instance of the Special Agent." This implies the erroneous holding that Wade's privilege against self-incrimination was violated so that the denial of counsel required exclusion.

On the record now before us we cannot make the determination whether the in-court identifications had an independent origin. This was not an issue at trial, although there is some evidence relevant to a determination. That inquiry is most properly made in the District Court. We therefore think the appropriate procedure to be followed is to vacate the conviction pending a hearing to determine whether the in-court identifications had an independent source, or whether, in any event, the introduction of the evidence was a harmless error, Chapman v. California [Chapter Fourteen, § 14.02] . . . and for the District Court to reinstate the conviction or order a new trial, as may be proper. . . .

Vacated and remanded.

[Mr. Justice BLACK dissented from parts I and V and concurred in parts II, III, and IV.]

[Mr. Justice WHITE, joined by Mr. Justice HARLAN and Mr. Justice STEWART, concurred in parts I and III and dissented in parts II, IV, and V.]

[Mr. Justice FORTAS, joined by Mr. Chief Justice WARREN and Mr. Justice DOUGLAS, dissented from part I above.]

Comments

1. The police use a variety of identification procedures, including lineups, showups and on-the-scene, in-court, and photographic identifications. While an identification procedure can be attacked as being violative of a specific constitutional right, such as the privilege against self-incrimination, a defendant can also allege, and prove, that a pretrial or in-court identification procedure was so inherently unfair that it constituted a denial of due process.

2. In *Schmerber* v. *California,* the Court, per Mr. Justice Brennan, held that "the privilege protects an accused only from being compelled to testify against himself, or *otherwise provide the State with evidence of a testimonial or communicative nature."* The Court went on to state that the forcible withdrawal of blood from Schmerber did not provide the State with evidence of a testimonial or communicative nature. What did the blood sample provide the State with? Don't the results of a blood analysis communicate something to the trier of fact? Why couldn't Schmerber have been convicted of DWI without a blood sample? The Court noted that the blood sample procedure was done by a physician. Is that important? What if the procedure had been done by a nurse? an intern? a medical student? a medical technician? an orderly? a police sergeant trained as a paramedic? Is it surprising that the Court rejected each of the four constitutional objections (violation of Fourth, Fifth, Sixth, and Fourteenth Amendments) raised by the defendant? Do you have the feeling that Mr. Justice Black was utterly shocked by the decision of the Court? Isn't it rather surprising that the *Schmerber* case was decided by the "liberal" Warren Court? On the other hand, drunken drivers are responsible for more than 25,000 traffic deaths a year. Was this a factor the Court took into account in reaching the decision? A broader holding of *Schmerber* is that compulsion that makes a suspect a source of physical evidence does not violate the privilege against self-incrimination. Accordingly, the Court has held that forcing a suspect to provide voice exemplars, *United States* v. *Dionisio,* 410 U.S. 1 (1973), or handwriting exemplars, *United States* v. *Mara,* 410 U.S. 19 (1973), or to display other physical characteristics, *Wade* and *Schmerber,* supra, does not provide the state with evidence of a "testimonial or communicative nature." Would *Schmerber* and its progeny allow a physician, at the direction of the police, to take a urine sample from a suspect over the suspect's objection? Does a catheterization involve a serious invasion of the body? What about minor surgery?

3. In *United States* v. *Wade,* supra, the Court held that a postindictment lineup was a "critical stage" requiring the assistance of counsel. The only function of counsel in these situations would be to insure that the lineup procedure was fair—to be a "watchman over the police." In *Gilbert* v. *California,* 388 U.S. 263 (1967), decided the same day as *Wade,* the Court held that requiring a suspect to

give handwriting exemplars in the absence of counsel does not violate his Fifth or Sixth Amendment rights. In addition the Court noted that an *in-court identification* may be admissible even though a pretrial identification procedure is shown to be tainted by a denial of counsel or a violation of due process so long as the in-court identification is shown to be derived from a source *independent* of the tainted pretrial procedure. This is, in essence, the *Wade-Gilbert* rule.

4. In *Kirby* v. *Illinois,* 406 U.S. 682 (1972), the Court refused to extend the right to counsel to *preindictment* lineups. The Court held that the Sixth Amendment right to counsel attaches only at or after the initiation of judicial criminal proceedings. In *United States* v. *Ash,* 413 U.S. 300 (1973), the Court held that "the Sixth Amendment does not grant the right to counsel at photographic displays conducted by the Government for the purpose of allowing a witness to attempt an identification of the offender." The *Ash* rule is applicable to pre- and postindictment photographic sessions. However, in *Kirby* and *Ash,* the Court noted that even though counsel is not required at preindictment lineups or at photographic sessions, any pretrial identification procedure that is "unnecessarily suggestive and conducive to irreparable mistaken identification" is subject to the Due Process Clause of the Fifth and Fourteenth Amendments and may be excluded as evidence at trial.

5. The results of polygraph (lie-detector) examinations are largely inadmissible in American jurisdictions, mainly because the polygraph has failed to conform to the so-called "*Frye* doctrine." In *Frye* v. *United States,* 293 F.2d 1013 (D.C. Cir. 1923), the court stated that before the results of scientific tests will be admissible as evidence in a trial, the procedures used "must be sufficiently established to have gained general acceptance in the particular field in which it belongs." However, many jurisdictions will admit the results of polygraph tests when both parties have stipulated that they will accept the results of such tests and they are not objected to at trial. In the following jurisdictions, the results of polygraph tests are inadmissible as evidence: *United States* v. *Jenkins,* 470 F.2d 1061 (9th Cir. 1972), cert. denied 411 U.S. 920 (1973); *United States* v. *Zeiger,* 475 F.2d 1280 (D.C. Cir. 1972); *United States* v. *Frogge,* 476 F.2d 369 (5th Cir. 1973), cert. denied 414 U.S. 849 (1973); *Marks* v. *United States,* 260 F.2d 377 (10th Cir. 1958), cert. denied 358 U.S. 929 (1959); *McCroskey* v. *United States,* 339 F.2d 895 (8th Cir. 1965); *Pulakis* v. *State,* 476 P.2d 474 (Alas. 1970); *Flurry* v. *State,* 289 So. 2d 632 (Ala. App. 1973); *State* v. *Bowen,* 449 P.2d 603 (Ariz. 1969); *Smith* v. *State,* 402 S.W.2d 412 (Ark. 1966), cert. denied 385 U.S. 980 (1966); *People* v. *Ferguson,* 81 Cal. Rptr. 418 (Cal. App. 1969); *State* v. *Carnegie,* 259 A.2d 628 (Conn. 1969); *Larkin* v. *United States,* 144 A.2d 100 (D.C. App. 1958); *State* v. *Jones,* 521 P.2d 978 (Ariz. 1974), cert. denied 419 U.S. 1004 (1974); *Sullivan* v. *State,* 303 So. 2d 632 (Fla. 1974); *Cagle* v. *State,* 207 S.E.2d 703 (Ga. App. 1974); *State* v. *Chang,* 374 P.2d 5 (Hawaii 1962); *People* v. *Gargano,* 295 N.E.2d 342 (Ill. App. 1973); *Robinson* v. *State,* 317 N.E.2d 850 (Ind. 1974); *State* v. *Galloway,* 187 N.W.2d 725 (Iowa 1971); *State* v. *Hemminger,* 502 P.2d 791 (Kan. 1972); *Henderson* v. *Commonwealth,* 507 S.W.2d 454 (Ky. 1974); *State* v. *Corbin,* 285 So. 2d 234 (La. 1973); *State* v. *Mottram,* 184 A.2d

225 (Me. 1962); *Smith* v. *State,* 318 A.2d 568 (Md. App. 1974), cert. denied 420 U.S. 909 (1975); *People* v. *Levelston,* 221 N.W.2d 235 (Mich. App. 1974); *State* v. *Perry,* 142 N.W.2d 573 (Minn. 1966); *Mattox* v. *State,* 128 So. 2d 368 (Miss. 1961); *State* v. *Bibee,* 496 S.W.2d 305 (Mo. App. 1973); *State* v. *Hollywood,* 358 P.2d 437 (Mont. 1960); *State* v. *Temple,* 222 N.W.2d 356 (Neb. 356); *State* v. *Clark,* 331 A.2d 257 (N.J. Sup. 1974); *State* v. *Varos,* 363 P.2d 629 (N.M. 629); *People* v. *Dodge,* 338 N.Y.S.2d 690 (N.Y. 1972); *United States ex rel. Sadowy* v. *Fay,* 284 F.2d 426 (2nd Cir. 1960); *Cherry* v. *State,* 518 P.2d 324 (Okla. Crim. App. 1974); *State* v. *Pope,* 210 S.E.2d 267 (N.C. App. 1974), cert. denied 211 S.E.2d 799 (N.C. 1975); *State* v. *Hill,* 317 N.E.2d 233 (Ohio 1974); *Commonwealth* v. *Talley,* 318 A.2d 922 (Pa. 1974); *State* v. *Britt,* 111 S.E.2d 669 (S.C. 1974); *State* v. *O'Connor,* 194 N.W.2d 246 (S.D. 1972); *King* v. *State,* 511 S.W.2d 32 (Tex. Crim. App. 1974); *Marable* v. *State,* 313 S.W.2d 451 (Tenn. 1958); *Jones* v. *Commonwealth,* 204 S.E.2d 247 (Va. 1973).

6. In recent years the use of physical detection devices for identification and other purposes has given rise to a number of legal issues. Some recent lower federal and state court decisions are illustrative: *Fulton* v. *State,* 541 P.2d 871 (Okla. Ct. Crim. App. 1975) (polygraph evidence not admissible at trial for any purpose) (overruling *Castleberry* v. *State,* 522 P.2d 257 [1973], and *Jones* v. *State,* 527 P.2d 169 [1974]); *State* v. *Olderman,* 336 N.E.2d 442 (Ohio Ct. App. 1975) (prosecution may use for identification purposes spectrographic voiceprint exemplar if operator is properly qualified and test shown to be reliable) (in accord is *Commonwealth* v. *Lykus,* 327 N.E.2d 671 [Mass. 1975], *Hodo* v. *Superior Court,* 30 Cal. App. 3d 778 [1973], *Alea* v. *State,* 265 So. 2d 96 [Fla. App. 1972], *Worley* v. *State,* 263 So. 2d 613 [Fla. App. 1972], *State ex rel. Trimble* v. *Hedman,* 291 Minn. 442 [1971] [as to probable cause for arrest warrant], *State* v. *Andretta,* 61 N.J. 544 [1972], *United States* v. *Wright,* 17 U.S.C.M.A. 183 [1967], *United States* v. *Franks,* 511 F.2d 25 [6th Cir. 1975], *United States* v. *Askins,* 351 F.2d 408 [D. Md. 1972]); *United States* v. *Oliver,* 525 F.2d 731 (8th Cir. 1975) (defendant's stipulation that the government could use test results of a polygraph if the test indicated that he was lying upheld); *United States* v. *Alexander,* 526 F.2d 161 (8th Cir. 1975) (results of unstipulated polygraph examinations not admissible in criminal trials); *People* v. *Reagan,* 235 N.W.2d 581 (Mich. 1975) (court order resulting from prosecutor's agreement to dismiss charges against a defendant should he pass a polygraph test bars the prosecution from reinstating the charges after the defendant passed the test)); *State* v. *Lassley,* 545 P.2d 383 (Kan. 1976) (use at trial of polygraph results which the parties had stipulated would be admissible and which are supported by a showing that the expert was qualified and the tests were conducted under proper conditions upheld) (in accord is *State* v. *Stanislawski,* 216 N.W.2d 8 [Wisc. 1974], *State* v. *Towns,* 301 N.E.2d 700 [Ohio 1973], *State* v. *Freeland,* 125 N.W.2d 825]Iowa 1964], and *State* v. *Valdez,* 371 P.2d 894 [Ariz. 1962]); *People* v. *Rodgers,* 239 N.W.2d 701 (Mich. Ct. App. 1976) (prosecution's effort to enhance a witness' credibility by bringing out the fact that charges against the witness

had been dropped after he took a polygraph test held reversible error); *Johnson* v. *State*, 355 A.2d 504 (Md. 1976) (jury should be permitted to determine whether police use of a polygraph in questioning a defendant affected the voluntariness of his statements once those statements are admitted into evidence); *United States* v. *Fine*, 413 F. Supp. 740 (W.D. Wisc. 1976) (defendant's Fifth Amendment rights not violated by his being required to furnish voice exemplars for purposes of comparing his voice with that of an anonymous caller who threatened a bombing); *United States* v. *McDaniel*, 538 F.2d 408 (D.C. Cir. 1976) (results of voiceprint spectrographic analysis not admissible at trial) (see also *United States* v. *Addison*, 498 F.2d 741 [D.C. Cir. 1974], and *United States* v. *Baller*, 519 F.2d 463 [4th Cir. 1975]); *Hutchins* v. *State*, 334 So. 2d 112 (Fla. App. 1976) (results of lie detector examinations not admissible in evidence) (in accord is *Harris* v. *State*, 226 S.E.2d 462 [Ga. App. 1976], *People* v. *Barlow*, 350 N.E.2d 554 [Ill. App. 1976], *Bush* v. *State*, 348 N.E.2d [Ind. App. 1976], *State* v. *Fowler*, 225 S.E.2d 110 [N.C. App. 1976], *People* v. *Towns*, 245 N.W.2d 97 [Mich. App. 1976], and *State* v. *Moore*, 353 N.E.2d 866 [Ohio App. 1976]); *Banks* v. *State*, 351 N.E.2d 4 (Ind. 1976) (results of polygraph test are inadmissible absent any waiver or stipulation that would permit testimony on the test results); *Commonwealth* v. *Juvenile* (No. 1), 348 N.E.2d 760 (Mass. 1976) (polygraph evidence offered by defendant as indication of innocence not admissible over objection of prosecutor); *Anderson* v. *State*, 551 P.2d 1155 (Okla. App. 1976) (defendant in murder trial cannot demand polygraph test); *State* v. *Young*, 550 P.2d 1 (Wash. 1976) (in the absence of stipulation of parties, results of polygraph tests are inadmissible); *In re J.P.B.*, 362 A.2d 1183 (N.J. Sup. App. Div. 1976) (police may not lawfully administer polygraph test to juvenile without proper consent from parents); *State* v. *Baskerville*, 354 A.2d 328 (N.J. Sup. App. Div. 1976) (where defendant agreed to submit to polygraph test and stipulated that the results of such exam could be used against him at trial results admissible); *Major* v. *State*, 358 A.2d 609 (Md. App. 1976) (defendant arrested for drunken driving held entitled to select chemical test to be performed on him, whether it be breathalyzer, blood, or urine test); *State* v. *Thomas*, 536 S.W.2d 529 (Mo. App. 1976) (evidence of tracking by dog admissible); *People* v. *Reed*, 384 N.Y.S.2d 555 (N.Y. App. Div. 1976) (corpus delicti in a drug case may be proved by chemist who tested substance in question).

Identification by Showups

STOVALL v. DENNO

Supreme Court of the United States, 1967
388 U.S. 293, 87 S. Ct. 1967, 18 L. Ed. 2d 1199

The facts are stated in the opinion.

Mr. Justice BRENNAN delivered the opinion of the Court.

* * *

Dr. Paul Behrendt was stabbed to death in the kitchen of his home in Garden City, Long Island, about midnight August 23,

1961. Dr. Behrendt's wife, also a physician, had followed her husband to the kitchen and jumped at the assailant. He knocked her to the floor and stabbed her 11 times. The police found a shirt on the kitchen floor and keys in a pocket which they traced to petitioner. They arrested him on the afternoon of August 24. An arraignment was promptly held but was postponed until petitioner could retain counsel.

Mrs. Behrendt was hospitalized for major surgery to save her life. The police, without affording petitioner time to retain counsel, arranged with her surgeon to permit them to bring petitioner to her hospital room about noon of August 25, the day after surgery. Petitioner was handcuffed to one of five police officers who, with two members of the staff of the District Attorney, brought him to the hospital room. Petitioner was the only Negro in the room. Mrs. Behrendt identified him from her hospital bed after being asked by an officer whether he "was the man" and after petitioner repeated at the direction of an officer a "few words for voice identification." None of the witnesses could recall the words that were used. Mrs. Behrendt and the officers testified at the trial to her identification of the petitioner in an in-court identification of petitioner in the courtroom. Petitioner was convicted and sentenced to death. The New York Court of Appeals affirmed without opinion, 13 N.Y.2d. 1094. Petitioner pro se sought federal habeas corpus in the District Court for the Southern District of New York. He claimed that among other constitutional rights allegedly denied him at his trial, the admission of Mrs. Behrendt's identification testimony violated his rights under the Fifth, Sixth and Fourteenth Amendments because he had been compelled to submit to the hospital room confrontation without the help of counsel and under circumstances which unfairly focused the witness' attention on him as the man believed by the police to be the guilty person. The District Court dismissed the petition after hearing argument on an unrelated claim of an alleged invalid search and seizure. On appeal to the Court of Appeals for the Second Circuit a panel of that court initially reversed the dismissal after reaching the issue of the admissibility of Mrs. Behrendt's identification evidence and holding it inadmissible on the ground that the hospital room identification violated petitioner's constitutional right to the assistance of counsel. The Court of Appeals thereafter heard the case en banc, vacated the panel decision, and affirmed the District Court. 355 F.2d 731. We granted certiorari ... and set the case for argument with Wade and Gilbert. We hold that Wade and Gilbert affect only those cases and all future cases which involve confrontations for identification purposes conducted in the absence of counsel after this date. The rulings of Wade and Gilbert are therefore inapplicable in the present case. We think also that on the facts of this case petitioner was not deprived of due process of law in violation of the Fourteenth Amendment. . . .

* * *

II

We turn now to the question whether petitioner, although not entitled to the application of Wade and Gilbert to his case, is entitled to relief on his claim that in any event the confrontation conducted in this case was so unnecessarily suggestive and conducive to irreparable mistaken identification that he was denied due process of law. This is a recognized ground of attack upon a conviction independent of any right to counsel claim. . . . The practice of showing suspects singly to persons for the purpose of identification and not as part of a lineup has been widely condemned. However, a claimed violation of due process of law in the conduct of a confrontation depends on the totality of the circumstances surrounding it, and record in the present case reveals that the showing of Stovall to Mrs. Behrendt in an immediate hospital confrontation was imperative. The Court of Appeals en banc stated, 355 F.2d, at 735, "Here was the only person in the world who could possibly exonerate Stovall. Her words, and only her words, 'He is not the man' could have resulted in freedom for Stovall. The hospital was not far distant from the courthouse and jail. No one knew how long Mrs. Behrendt might live. Faced with the responsibility of identifying the attacker, with the need for immediate action and with the knowledge that Mrs. Behrendt could not visit the jail, the police followed the only feasible procedure and took Stovall to the hospital room. Under these circumstances, the usual police station line-up,

which Stovall now argues he should have had, was out of the question."
Affirmed.

[Mr. Justice HARLAN, Mr. Justice STEWART, and Mr. Justice WHITE concurred in the result.]

[Mr. Justice BLACK, Mr. Justice DOUGLAS, and Mr. Justice FORTAS dissented.]

The Unfair Lineup

FOSTER v. CALIFORNIA

Supreme Court of the United States, 1969
394 U.S. 440, 89 S. Ct. 1127, 22 L. Ed. 2d 402

The facts are stated in the opinion.

Mr. Justice FORTAS delivered the opinion of the Court.

Petitioner was charged by information with the armed robbery of a Western Union office in violation of California Penal Code 211a. The day after the robbery one of the robbers, Clay, surrendered to the police and implicated Foster and Grice. Allegedly, Foster and Clay had entered the office while Grice waited in a car. Foster and Grice were tried together. Grice was acquitted. Foster was convicted. The California District Court of Appeal affirmed the conviction; the State Supreme Court denied review. We granted certiorari, limited to the question whether the conduct of the police lineup resulted in a violation of petitioner's constitutional rights. . . .

Except for the robbers themselves, the only witness to the crime was Joseph David, the late-night manager of the Western Union office. After Foster had been arrested, David was called to the police station to view a lineup. There were three men in the lineup. One was petitioner. He is a tall man—close to six feet in height. The other two men were short—five feet, five or six inches. Petitioner wore a leather jacket which David said was similar to the one he had seen underneath the coveralls worn by the robber. After seeing this lineup, David could not positively identify petitioner as the robber. He "thought" he was the man, but he was not sure. David then asked to speak to petitioner, and petitioner was

brought into an office and sat across from David at a table. Except for prosecuting officials there was no one else in the room. Even after this one-to-one confrontation David still was uncertain whether petitioner was one of the robbers: "truthfully, I was not sure," he testified at trial. A week or 10 days later, the police arranged for David to view a second lineup. There were five men in that lineup. Petitioner was the only person in the second lineup who had appeared in the first lineup. This time David was "convinced" petitioner was the man.

At trial, David testified to his identification of petitioner in the lineups as summarized above. He also repeated his identification of petitioner in the courtroom. The only evidence against petitioner which concerned the particular robbery with which he was charged was the testimony of the alleged accomplice Clay.

In United States v. Wade, . . . (1967), and Gilbert v. California, . . . (1967), this Court held that because of the possibility of unfairness to the accused in the way a lineup is conducted, a lineup is a "critical stage" in the prosecution, at which the accused must be given the opportunity to be represented by counsel. That holding does not, however, apply to petitioner's case, for the lineups in which he appeared occurred before June 12, 1967. Stovall v. Denno [supra]. . . . But in declaring the rule of Wade and Gilbert to be applicable only to lineups conducted after those cases were decided, we recognized that, judged by the "totality of the circumstances," the conduct of identification procedures may be "so unnecessarily suggestive and conducive to irreparable mistaken identification" as to be a denial of due process of law....

Judged by that standard, this case presents a compelling example of unfair lineup procedures. In the first lineup arranged by the police, petitioner stood out from the other men by the contrast of his height and by the fact that he was wearing a leather jacket similar to that worn by the robber.... When this did not lead to positive identification, the police permitted a one-to-one confrontation between petitioner and the witness. This Court pointed out in Stovall that "[t]he practice of showing suspects singly to persons for the purpose of identification, and not as part of a lineup, has been widely condemned." ... Even after this the witness' identification of petitioner was tentative. So some days later another lineup was arranged. Petitioner was the only person in this lineup who had also participated in the first lineup.... This finally produced a definite identification.

The suggestive elements in this identification procedure made it all but inevitable that David would identify petitioner whether or not he was in fact "the man." In effect, the police repeatedly said to the witness, "This is the man." ... This procedure so undermined the reliability of the eyewitness identification as to violate due process.

* * *

The respondent invites us to hold that any error was harmless under Chapman v. California [see Comments, infra]....We decline to rule upon this question in the first instance.

Reversed and remanded.

[Mr. Justice WHITE, with whom Mr. Justice HARLAN and Mr. Justice STEWART concurred, being unwilling in this case to disagree with the jury on the weight of evidence, would have voted to affirm the judgment.]

[Mr. Justice BLACK dissented.]

The "Substantial Likelihood of Misidentification" Test

NEIL v. BIGGERS

Supreme Court of the United States, 1972
409 U.S. 188, 93 S. Ct. 375, 34 L. Ed. 2d 401

The facts are stated in the opinion.

Mr. Justice POWELL delivered the opinion of the Court.

In 1965, after a jury trial in a Tennessee court, respondent was convicted of rape and was sentenced to 20 years' imprisonment. The State's evidence consisted in part of testimony concerning a station-house identification of respondent by the victim. The Tennessee Supreme Court affirmed.... On certiorari, the judgment of the Tennessee Supreme Court was affirmed by an equally divided Court. Biggers v. Tennessee, 390 U.S. 404 (1968) (Marshall, J., not participa-

ting). Respondent then brought a federal habeas corpus action raising several claims. ... The District Court held that the claims were not barred and, after a hearing, held in an unreported opinion that the station-house identification procedure was so suggestive as to violate due process. The Court of Appeals affirmed. 448 F.2d 91 (1971). We granted certiorari to decide whether an affirmance by an equally divided Court is an actual adjudication barring subsequent consideration on habeas corpus, and, if not, whether the identification procedure violated due process....

I

* * *

...We review our cases explicating the disposition "affirmed by an equally divided Court." ... [I]t is the appellant or petitioner who asks the Court to overturn a lower court's decree.

"If the judges are divided, the reversal cannot be made. The judgment of the court below, therefore, stands in full force. It is, indeed, the settled practice in such case to enter a judgment of affirmance; but this is only the most convenient mode of express-ing the fact that the cause is finally disposed of in conformity with the action of the court below, and that that court can proceed to enforce its judgment. The legal effect would be the same if the appeal, or writ of error, were dismissed." Durant v. Essex Co., 7 Wall. 107 (1869). Nor is an affirmance by an equally divided Court entitled to preceden-tial weight. Ohio ex rel. Eaton v. Price, 364 U.S. 263 (1960). ...

II

We proceed, then, to consider respon-dent's due process claim. As the claim turns upon facts, we must first review the relevant testimony at the jury trial and at the habeas corpus hearing regarding the rape and the identification. The victim testifies at trial that on the evening of January 22, 1965, a youth with a butcher knife grabbed her in the doorway to her kitchen:

"A. [H]e grabbed me from behind, and grappled—twisted me on the floor. Threw me down on the floor.

"Q. And there was no light in that kitch-en?

"A. Not in the kitchen.

"Q. So you couldn't have seen him then?

"A. Yes, I could see him when I looked up in his face.

"Q. In the dark?

"A. He was right in the doorway—it was enough light from the bedroom shining through. Yes, I could see who he was.

"Q. You could see? No light? And you could see him and know him then?

"A. Yes."

When the victim screamed, her 12-year-old daughter came out of her bedroom and also began to scream. The assailant directed the victim to "tell her [the daughter] to shut up, or I'll kill you both." She did so, and was then walked at knifepoint about two blocks along a railroad track, taken into a woods, and raped there. She testified that "the moon was shining brightly, full moon." After the rape, the assailant ran off, and she returned home, the whole incident having taken between 15 minutes and half an hour.

She then gave police what the Federal District Court characterized as "only a very general description," describing him as "being fat and flabby with smooth skin, bushy hair and a youthful voice." Addition-ally, though not mentioned by the District Court, she testified at the habeas corpus hearing that she had described her assailant as being between 16 and 18 years old and between five feet ten inches and six feet tall, as weighing between 180 and 200 pounds, and as having a dark brown complexion. This testimony was substantially corrobo-rated by that of a police officer who was tes-tifying from his notes.

On several occasions over the course of the next seven months, she viewed suspects in her home or at the police station, some in lineups, and others in showups, and was shown between 30 and 40 photographs. She told police that a man pictured in one of the photographs had features similar to those of her assailant, but identified none of the sus-pects. On August 17, the police called her to the station to view respondent, who was being detained on another charge. In an ef-fort to construct a suitable lineup, the police checked the city jail and the city juvenile home. Finding no one at either place fitting respondent's unusual physical description, they conducted a showup instead.

The showup itself consisted of two detec-tives walking respondent past the victim. At the victim's request, the police directed the respondent to say "shut up or I'll kill you." The testimony at trial was not altogether clear as to whether the victim first identified him and then asked that he repeat the words or made her identification after he had spo-ken. In any event, the victim testified that she had "no doubt" about her identification. At the habeas corpus hearing, she elab-orated in response to questioning.

"A. That I have no doubt, I mean that I am sure that when I—see, when I first laid eyes on him, I knew that it was the individu-al, because his face—well, there was just something that I don't think I could ever forget. I believe —

"Q. You say when you first laid eyes on him, which time are you referring to?

"A. When I identified him — when I seen him in the courthouse when I was took up to view the suspect."

We must decide whether, as the courts below held, his identification and the circumstances surrounding it failed to comport with due process requirements.

III

We have considered on four occasions the scope of due process protection against the admission of evidence deriving from suggestive identification procedures. In Stovall v. Denno, 388 U.S. 293 (1967), the Court held that the defendant could claim that "the confrontation conducted ... was so unnecessarily suggestive and conducive to irreparable mistaken identification that he was denied due process of law." ... This, we held, must be determined "on the totality of the circumstances." We went on to find that on the facts of the case then before us, due process was not violated, emphasizing that the critical condition of the injured witness justified a showup in her hospital room. At trial, the witness, whose view of the suspect at the time of the crime was brief, testified to the out-of-court identification, as did several police officers present in her hospital room, and also made an in-court identification.

Subsequently, in a case where the witness made in-court identifications arguably stemming from previous exposure to a suggestive photographic array, the Court restated the governing test:

"[W]e hold that each case must be considered on its own facts, and that convictions based on eye-witness identification at trial following a pretrial identification by photograph will be set aside on that ground only if the photographic identification procedure was so impermissibly suggestive as to give rise to a very substantial likelihood of irreparable mis-identification." Simmons v. United States, 390 U.S. 377 (1968).

Again we found the identification procedure to be supportable, relying both on the need for prompt utilization of other investigative leads and on the likelihood that the photographic identifications were reliable, the witnesses having viewed the bank robbers for periods of up to five minutes under good lighting conditions at the time of the robbery.

The only case to date in which this Court has found identification procedures to be violative of due process is Foster v. California [supra]. There, the witness failed to identify Foster the first time he confronted him, despite a suggestive lineup. The police then arranged a showup, at which the witness could make only a tentative identification. Ultimately, at yet another confrontation, this time a lineup, the witness was able to muster a definite identification. We held all of the identifications inadmissible, observing that the identifications were "all but inevitable" under the circumstances. . . .

* * *

Some general guidelines emerge from these cases as to the relationship between suggestiveness and misidentification. It is, first of all, apparent that the primary evil to be avoided is "a very substantial likelihood of irreparable misidentification." Simmons v. United States. . . . While the phrase was coined as a standard for determining whether an in-court identification would be admissible in the wake of a suggestive out-of court identification, with the deletion of "irreparable" it serves equally well as a standard for the admissibility of testimony concerning the out-of-court identification itself. It is the likelihood of misidentification which violates a defendant's right to due process, and it is this which was the basis of the exclusion of evidence in Foster. Suggestive confrontations are disapproved because they increase the likelihood of misidentification, and unnecessarily suggestive ones are condemned for the further reason that the increased chance of misidentification is gratuitous. But as Stovall makes clear, the admission of evidence of a showup without more does not violate due process.

What is less clear from our cases is whether, as intimated by the District Court, unnecessary suggestiveness alone requires the exclusion of evidence. While we are inclined to agree with the courts below that the police did not exhaust all possibilities in seeking persons physically comparable to respondent, we do not think that the evidence must therefore be excluded. The purpose of a strict rule barring evidence of unnecessarily suggestive confrontations would be to deter the police from using a less reliable procedure where a more reliable one may be available, not because in every instance the admission of evidence of such a confrontation offends due process.... Such a rule would have no place in the present case, since both the confrontation and the trial preceded Stovall v. Denno, supra, when we first gave notice that the suggestiveness of confrontation procedures was anything other than a matter to be argued to the jury.

We turn, then, to the central question, whether under the "totality of the circumstances" the identification was reliable though the confrontation procedure was suggestive. As indicated by our cases, the factors to be considered in evaluating the likelihood of misidentification include the opportunity of the witness to view the criminal at the time of the crime, the witness' degree of attention, the accuracy of the witness' prior description of the criminal, the level of certainty demonstrated by the witness at the confrontation, and the length of time between the crime and the confrontation. Applying these factors, we disagree with the District Court's conclusion.

* * *

We find that the District Court's conclusions on the critical facts are unsupported by the record and clearly erroneous. The victim spent a considerable period of time with her assailant, up to half an hour. She was with him under adequate artificial light in her house and under a full moon outdoors, and at least twice, once in the house and later in the woods, facing him directly and intimately. She was no casual observer, but rather the victim of one of the most personally humiliating of all crimes. Her description to the police, which included the assailant's approximate age, height, weight, complexion, skin texture, build and voice, might not have satisfied Proust but was more than ordinarily thorough. She had "no doubt" that respondent was the person who raped her. In the nature of the crime, there are rarely witnesses to a rape other than the victim, who often has a limited opportunity of observation. The victim here, a practical nurse by profession, had an unusual opportunity to observe and identify her assailant. She testified at the habeas corpus hearing that there was something about his face "I don't think I could ever forget."

There was, to be sure, a lapse of seven months between the rape and the confrontation. This would be a seriously negative factor in most cases. Here, however, the testimony is undisputed that the victim made no previous identification at any of the showups, lineups, or photographic showings. Her record for reliability was thus a good one, as she had previously resisted whatever suggestiveness inheres in a showup. Weighing all the factors, we find no substantial likelihood of misidentification. The evidence was properly allowed to go to the jury.

Affirmed in part, reversed in part, and remanded.

[Mr. Justice BRENNAN wrote an opinion concurring in part and dissenting in part, which Mr. Justice DOUGLAS and Mr. Justice STEWART joined.]

[Mr. Justice MARSHALL took no part in the consideration or decision of this case.]

"Reliability is the Linchpin" in Identification Procedures

ORAL ARGUMENTS BEFORE THE U.S. SUPREME COURT*

Manson v. Brathwaite, No. 75–871; argued 11/29/76

*From 20 Crim. L. Rptr. 4094–4096. Reprinted by permission of the Bureau of National Affairs, Inc.

The State of Connecticut asked the Court ... to overturn a Second Circuit holding which granted habeas relief to a narcotics defendant who claimed that his out-of-court identification by means of a single-photo display created a substantial likelihood of misidentification.

Bernard D. Gaffney, Assistant State's Attorney, began his argument for the state by setting forth the facts of the case. Connecticut undercover agent Jimmy D. Glover, accompanied by an informer, went to an apartment building to purchase narcotics from a suspected seller. A black man eased open the door to his apartment about 12 or 18 inches, after Glover's knock. After the informer identified himself to the man, Glover asked to buy some heroin. Glover repeated his request, and the man held out his hands. Glover handed him $20 and received two glassine bags containing heroin. Glover then left. During the sale, which took five to seven minutes, Glover got a good look at the seller. The sale took place at about 7:45 p.m.

Mr. Justice Stewart: "What date?"

On May 5, 1970, Gaffney answered. It had not yet become dark, he added, and natural light shining through the hall window lit the hallway. Glover had no problems seeing in the hallway. Returning to the factual setting, counsel explained that Glover left the apartment building after the sale. Later that evening, he described the seller, whom he did not know, to Detective Michael D'Onofrio of the Hartford Police Department. Glover described the seller as a dark-skinned black, about 5'11", with a heavy build, high cheek bones, and an Afro. D'Onofrio recognized the description as that of Nowell Brathwaite, the respondent. D'Onofrio obtained Brathwaite's photo from the Hartford Police Department and left it on Glover's desk at the State Police Headquarters.

Returning to his headquarters two days later, Glover viewed the photo for the first time and unequivocally identified Brathwaite as the seller. D'Onofrio, who was not present at the identification, brought no pressures on Glover to identify Brathwaite, counsel asserted.

Mr. Justice Marshall: "No pressure except for the picture?"

"Yes, sir, your honor."

More than two months later, Brathwaite was arrested at the same apartment in which the sale occurred. At trial, the photo on which Glover based his identification was admitted into evidence without objection. Glover, who had not seen Brathwaite since the purchase, also identified him in court. Brathwaite's conviction for illegal sale and possession of narcotics was affirmed by the Connecticut Supreme Court. On federal habeas, a district court dismissed Brathwaite's petition but the Second Circuit reversed and granted habeas relief, 527 F.2d 363 (1975).

The Second Circuit, speaking through Judge Friendly, concluded that the single photo identification procedure was unnecessarily and impermissibly suggestive. Fashioning an exclusionary rule of its own, the Second Circuit held that such an out-of-court identification was excludable at trial without regard to its reliability, counsel said. Alternatively, the Second Circuit concluded that even under the totality of the circumstances test, the admitting of the out-of-court identification evidence was prejudicial.

Totality of Circumstances

Gaffney conceded that the single-photo display was unnecessarily suggestive, but argued that, on the facts here, no great likelihood of misidentification existed. He took issue with the exclusionary rule fashioned by the Second Circuit. "Nowhere in *Stovall* v. *Denno,* 338 U.S. 293, do the words 'exclusionary rule' appear." In *Stovall,* this Court looked to the totality of the circumstances in judging the effects of an improper identification. Later Supreme Court holdings also indicate that the totality of the circumstances approach governs.

One year after *Stovall,* the Court again applied that approach in assessing the reliability of an identification procedure, see *Simmons* v. *U.S.,* 390 U.S. 377. More recently, in *Neil* v. *Biggers,* 409 U.S. 188 (1972), the Court pointed out that the essential question is the reliability of the identification evidence under all the circumstances, Gaffney told the Justices. "If the *Biggers* criteria are applied here, Glover's identification is wholly reliable." Sufficient opportunity existed for Glover, a trained officer, to view the suspect, whom he looked at directly and with an eye toward details, counsel stated.

Experienced Officer

Mr. Justice Rehnquist: "Was Glover a full-time police officer?"

"Yes, sir. A state police officer."

In response to a question from Mr. Justice Stevens, Gaffney explained that

Glover's conversation with the seller was brief.

Mr. Justice Stevens: "Is it your view that the conversation took two or three minutes?"

Counsel thought so. Glover, an experienced officer, was thorough in observing the defendant. He positively identified Brathwaite as the seller.

Mr. Justice Marshall: "Why did Glover wait two days to pick up the photo of this 'hardened criminal'?"

"It was two days before he found the photo on his desk." He did not return to his office until then.

The Chief Justice: "I suppose this was not the only narcotics investigation at that time?"

"Right, your honor." As to the delay in the arrest, an arrest ordinarily occurs after the state conducts a toxicological examination of a substance. That did not happen here until July. The arrest delay relates to the "worklog," counsel pointed out.

No Compelling Need

Returning to the exclusionary rule, counsel explained that no "compelling need" exists for such a strict rule in these circumstances. "Police abuses today are minimal." The Second Circuit's exclusionary rule would effectively "keep out relevant evidence."

Moreover, jurors would be confused by an exclusionary rule. "The state won't look good," counsel told the Court. On cross-examination, a defense counsel would draw out the reasons for the exclusion of the evidence.

Mr. Justice Stevens: "I am not quite sure that I understand the argument that you are making."

The argument highlights the difficulties which a broad-based exclusionary rule would visit on the prosecution, and the resulting confusion to the jurors, counsel replied.

Jury Instructions

A trial judge can cure any defects in an out-of-court identification by advising the jury of "the weaknesses and dangers of pretrial identification," Gaffney maintained, repeating that the key question is the reliability of the identification. Judged by all the circumstances, Officer Glover's identification was reliable. Gaffney also contended that the Second Circuit should not have substituted its judgment on Glover's reliability for that of the district court.

Tainted Evidence

David S. Golub, of Stamford, Connecticut, counsel for respondent, told the Court that the Second Circuit properly concluded that identification evidence derived from the impermissibly suggestive photographic showup was excludable.

Mr. Justice White: "You don't say that the in-court identification is automatically excludable along with the out-of-court?"

"No, your honor." But the Second Circuit found Officer Glover's identification testimony unreliable.

Mr. Justice Rehnquist questioned counsel about defense counsel's failure to object to the identification testimony at the state trial.

Counsel acknowledged that trial counsel made no contemporaneous objection, but he asserted that the trial lawyer's action was not part of a plan to deliberately bypass the state courts on this point. Moreover, trial counsel's failure to object actually prejudiced Brathwaite.

Exclusionary Rule

The Second Circuit acted properly in fashioning an exclusionary rule to remedy the situation here. Even if the totality of the circumstances approach applies, Golub maintained, Judge Friendly was correct in his conclusion on the unreliability of the identification procedure.

Mr. Justice Marshall: "How much time would it take for me to look at you before I could identify you later?"

"It depends on the situation, your honor."

Mr. Justice Marshall: "Would two or three minutes be enough?"

Counsel repeated that it would depend on the situation.

Mr. Justice Stevens: "Is the fact that the defendant was arrested in the same apartment (as the sale) relevant to the question whether the identification was reliable?"

Golub found substantial problems with the identification procedure. D'Onofrio received a very general description from

Glover that could have applied to many black men. He did not think that the arrest at the apartment, rented by a friend, relates to Brathwaite's guilt or innocence.

The Chief Justice: "Did the court of appeals attempt to review the witnesses' credibility?"

Judge Friendly simply pointed out some of the problems he had with some of the testimony, Golub answered.

Mr. Justice Marshall: "Which court should we follow on the facts?"

"I would say the court of appeals."

Mr. Justice White: "Was there an evidentiary hearing in the district court?"

"No, sir."

In response to a question from the Chief Justice, Golub stated that Judge Friendly felt that the officer's identification testimony posed a high risk of misidentification.

Strict Rule

An exclusionary rule directed at officers would avoid the problems which accompany the totality of the circumstances approach. "The impact on the officers would be clear."

The Chief Justice: "Do you think there was something wrong with showing the witness the photo?"

The prosecution should have taken all steps to avoid prejudice, Golub answered.

Mr. Justice Marshall: "You are not urging us to turn him (Brathwaite) loose, are you?"

"Yes, sir, I am." A genuine question exists as to his guilt or innocence. No other evidence supports Brathwaite's conviction.

Mr. Justice White asked counsel whether the Second Circuit had determined if an independent basis existed for the in-court identification of Brathwaite.

Counsel thought the Second Circuit's opinion confusing on that point.

Retrial

Mr. Justice Brennan: "On retrial, if there is an in-court identification by Glover, would the state have to show an independent ground (free of any alleged taint from the out-of-court procedure)?"

"Yes, sir."

Mr. Justice White: "Do you think the state may retry him?"

"No, sir," in light of the reliability problems with Glover's testimony.

Rebuttal

On rebuttal, Gaffney pointed out that single mug shots are often used by officers to confirm identifications by another officer.

Returning to the exclusionary rule issue, Mr. Justice White asked: "Wouldn't the admissibility of the out-of-court identification be critical in lots of cases?"

"Yes, sir." Such evidence is often essential. Even if the out-of-court identification was improper, Gaffney asserted that an independent basis existed for Glover's in-court identification of Brathwaite.

MANSON v. BRATHWAITE

Supreme Court of the United States, 1977
432 U.S. 98, 97 S. Ct. 2243, 53 L. Ed. 2d 140

Jimmy Glover, a trained black undercover Connecticut State Police officer, purchased heroin from a seller through the open doorway of an apartment. During this transaction, he stood for two to three minutes within two feet of the seller in a hallway illuminated by natural light from a window in the third floor hallway. A few minutes later, Glover described the seller to another police officer, D'Onofrio, as being "a colored man, approximately five feet eleven inches tall, dark complexion, black hair, short Afro style, and having high cheekbones, and a heavy build." Officer D'Onofrio, suspecting from the description that the respondent, Nowell Brathwaite, might be the seller, obtained a photograph of respondent from the Records Division of the Hartford Police Department. He left it on Glover's desk. Glover viewed it two days later and identified it as the picture of

the seller. Respondent was tried in a Connecticut court eight months later and convicted of possession and sale of heroin. At his trial, the photograph was received in evidence without objection; Glover testified that there was no doubt that the person shown in the photograph was respondent, and made a positive in-court identification without objection. The conviction was affirmed by the Connecticut Supreme Court. *State* v. *Brathwaite*, 325 A.2d 284 (1973). Fourteen months later, respondent filed a petition for habeas corpus in the United States District Court (D. Conn.), alleging that the admission of the identification testimony at his trial deprived him of due process of law under the Fourteenth Amendment. The district court dismissed the petition, but the court of appeals reversed, holding that the photographic evidence should have been excluded, regardless of its reliability, because the examination of the single photograph was unnecessary and suggestive. 527 F.2d 363 (2d Cir. 1975). The United States Supreme Court granted certiorari.

Mr. Justice BLACKMUN delivered the opinion of the Court.

This case presents the issue as to whether the Due Process Clause of the Fourteenth Amendment compels the exclusion, in a state criminal trial, apart from any consideration of reliability, of pretrial identification evidence obtained by a police procedure that was both suggestive and unnecessary. This Court's decisions in Stovall v. Denno, 388 U.S. 293 (1967), and Neil v. Biggers, 409 U.S. 188 (1972), are particularly implicated.

* * *

II

Stovall v. United States, supra, decided in 1967, concerned a petitioner who had been convicted in a New York court of murder. He was arrested the day following the crime and was taken by the police to a hospital where the victim's wife, also wounded in the assault, was a patient. After observing Stovall and hearing him speak, she identified him as the murderer. She later made an in-court identification. On federal habeas, Stovall claimed the identification testimony violated his Fifth, Sixth, and Fourteenth Amendment rights. The District Court dismissed the petition, and the Court of Appeals, en banc, affirmed. This Court also affirmed. On the identification issue, the Court reviewed the practice of showing a suspect singly for purposes of identification and the claim that this was so unnecessarily suggestive and conducive to irreparable mistaken identification that it constituted a denial of due process of law. The Court noted that the practice "has been widely con-

demned," 388 U.S., at 302, but it concluded that "a claimed violation of due process of law in the conduct of a confrontation depends on the totality of the circumstances surrounding it."

Neil v. Biggers, supra, decided in 1972, concerned a respondent who had been convicted in a Tennessee court of rape, on evidence consisting in part of the victim's visual and voice identification of Biggers at a station-house showup seven months after the crime. The victim had been in her assailant's presence for some time and had directly observed him indoors and under a full moon outdoors. She testified that she had "no doubt" that Biggers was her assailant. She previously had given the police a description of the assailant. She had made no identification of others presented at previous showups, lineups, or through photographs. On federal habeas, the District Court held that the confrontation was so suggestive as to violate due process. The Court of Appeals affirmed. This Court reversed on that issue, and held that the evidence properly had been allowed to go to the jury. The Court reviewed Stovall and certain later cases where it had considered the scope of due process protection against the admission of evidence derived from suggestive identification procedures, namely, Simmons v. United States, 390 U.S. 377 (1968); Foster v. California, 394 U.S. 440 (1969); and Coleman v. Alabama, 399 U.S. 1 (1970). The Court concluded that general guidelines emerged from these cases "as to the relationship between suggestiveness and misidentification." The "admission of evidence of a showup without more does not violate due process." 409 U.S., at 198. The

Court expressed concern about the lapse of seven months between the crime and the confrontation and observed that this "would be a seriously negative factor in most cases." Id., at 201. The "central question," however, was "whether under the 'totality of the circumstances' the identification was reliable even though the confrontation procedure was suggestive." Applying that test, the Court found "no substantial likelihood of misidentification. The evidence was properly allowed to go to the jury." Ibid.

Biggers well might be seen to provide an unambiguous answer to the question before us: the admission of testimony concerning a suggestive and unnecessary identification procedure does not violate due process so long as the identification possesses sufficient aspects of reliability. In one passage, however, the Court observed that the challenged procedure occurred pre-Stovall and that a strict rule would make little sense with regard to a confrontation that preceded the Court's first indication that a suggestive procedure might lead to the exclusion of evidence. Id., at 199. One perhaps might argue that, by implication, the Court suggested that a different rule could apply post-Stovall. The question before us, then, is simply whether the Biggers analysis applies to post-Stovall confrontations as well as to those pre-Stovall.

* * *

IV

The State at the outset acknowledges that "the procedure in the instant case was suggestive [because only one photograph was used] and unnecessary" [because there was no emergency or exigent circumstance]. ... The respondent, in agreement with the Court of Appeals, proposes a per se rule of exclusion that he claims is dictated by the demands of the Fourteenth Amendment's guarantee of due process. He rightly observes that this is the first case in which this Court has had occasion to rule upon strictly post-Stoval out-of-court identification evidence of the challenged kind.

Since the decision in Biggers, the courts of appeals appear to have developed at least two approaches to such evidence. See Pulaski, Neil v. Biggers: The Supreme Court Dismantles the Wade Trilogy's Due Process Protection, 26 Stan. L. Rev. 1097,

1111–1114 (1974). The first, or per se, approach, employed by the Second Circuit in the present case, focuses on the procedures employed and requires exclusion of the out-of-court identification evidence, without regard to reliability, whenever it has been obtained through unnecessarily suggestive confrontation procedures. The justifications advanced are the elimination of evidence of uncertain reliability, deterrence of the police and prosecutors, and the stated "fair assurance against the awful risks of misidentification." 527 F.2d, at 371. See Smith v. Coiner, 473 F.2d 877, 882 (4th Cir.), cert. denied sub nom. Wallace v. Smith, 414 U.S. 1115 (1973).

The second, or more lenient, approach is one that continues to rely on the totality of the circumstances. It permits the admission of the confrontation evidence if, despite the suggestive aspect, the out-of-court identification possesses certain features of reliability. Its adherents feel that the per se approach is not mandated by the Due Process Clause of the Fourteenth Amendment. This second approach, in contrast to the other, is ad hoc and serves to limit the societal costs imposed by a sanction that excludes relevant evidence from consideration and evaluation by the trier of fact. ...

* * *

The respondent here stresses the ... need for deterrence of improper identification practices, a factor he regards as preeminent. Photographic identification, it is said, continues to be needlessly employed. He notes that the legislative regulation "the Court hoped Wade [388 U.S. 218, 239 (1967)] would engender" ... has not been forthcoming. He argues that a totality rule cannot be expected to have a significant deterrent impact; only a strict rule of exclusion will have direct and immediate impact on law enforcement agents. Identification evidence is so convincing to the jury that sweeping exclusionary rules are required. Fairness of the trial is threatened by suggestive confrontation evidence, and thus, it is said, an exclusionary rule has an established constitutional predicate.

There are, of course, several interests to be considered and taken into account. The driving force behind United States v. Wade, 388 U.S. 218 (1967), and Gilbert v. California, 388 U.S. 263 (1967) [right to counsel at a post-indictment lineup], and Stovall, all decided on the same day, was the Court's concern with the problems of eyewitness identification. Usually the witness must testify about an encounter with a total stranger under circumstances of emergency or emotional stress. The witness' recollection of the stranger can be distorted easily by the circumstances or by later actions of the police. Thus, Wade and its companion cases reflect the concern that the jury not hear eyewitness testimony unless that evidence has aspects of reliability. It must be observed that both approaches before us are responsive to this concern. The per se rule, however, goes too far since its application automatically and peremptorily, and without consideration of alleviating factors, keeps evidence from the jury that is reliable and relevant.

The second factor is deterrence. Although the per se approach has the more significant deterrent effect, the totality approach also has an influence on police behavior. The police will guard against unnecessarily suggestive procedures under the totality rule, as well as the per se one, for fear that their actions will lead to the exclusion of identifications as unreliable.

The third factor is the effect on the administration of justice. Here the per se approach suffers serious drawbacks. Since it denies the trier reliable evidence, it may result, on occasion, in the guilty going free. Also, because of its rigidity, the per se approach may make error by the trial judge more likely than the totality approach. And in those cases in which the admission of identification evidence is error under the per se approach but not under the totality approach—cases in which the identification is reliable despite an unnecessarily suggestive identification procedure—reversal is a draconian sanction. Certainly, inflexible rules of exclusion that may frustrate rather than promote justice have not been viewed recently by this Court with unlimited enthusiasm. See, for example, the several opinions in Brewer v. Williams [97 S. Ct. 1232 (1977) (Chapter Seven, § 7.03)]. See also United States v. Janis, 428 U.S. 433 (1976 [Chapter Five, § 5.03, Comments].

It is true, as has been noted, that the Court in Biggers referred to the pre-Stovall character of the confrontation in that case. 409 U.S., at 199. But that observation was only one factor in the judgmental process. It does not translate into a holding that post-Stovall confrontation evidence automatically is to be excluded.

The standard, after all, is that of fairness as required by the Due Process Clause of the Fourteenth Amendment. See United States v. Lovasco [97 S. Ct. 2044 (1977) (Chapter Seven, § 7.03)]; Rochin v. California, 342 U.S. 165, 170–172 (1952). Stovall, with its reference to "the totality of the circumstances," 388 U.S., at 302, and Biggers, with its continuing stress on the same totality, 409 U.S., at 199, did not, singly or together, establish a strict exclusionary rule or new standard of due process. Judge Leventhal, although speaking pre-Biggers and of a pre-Wade situation, correctly has described Stovall as protecting an *evidentiary* interest and, at the same time, as recognizing the limited extent of that interest in our adversary system.

We therefore conclude that reliability is the lynchpin in determining the admissibility of identification testimony for both pre- and post-Stovall confrontations. The factors to be considered are set out in Biggers. 409 U.S., at 199–200. These include the opportunity of the witness to view the criminal at the time of the crime, the witness' degree of attention, the accuracy of his prior description of the criminal, the level of certainty demonstrated at the confrontation, and the time between the crime and the confrontation. Against these factors is to be weighed the corrupting effect of the suggestive identification itself.

V

We turn, then, to the facts of this case and apply the analysis:

1. The opportunity to view. Glover testified that for two to three minutes he stood at the apartment door, within two feet of the respondent. The door opened twice, and each time the man stood at the door. The moments passed, the conversation took place, and payment was made. Glover looked directly at his vendor. It was near sunset, to be sure, but the sun had not yet set, so it was not dark or even dusk or twilight. Natural light from outside entered the hallway through a window. There was natural light, as well, from inside the apartment.

2. The degree of attention. Glover was not a casual or passing observer, as is so

often the case with eyewitness identification. Trooper Glover was a trained police officer on duty — and specialized and dangerous duty — when he called at the third floor of 201 Westland in Hartford on May 5, 1970. Glover himself was a Negro and unlikely to perceive only general features of "hundreds of Hartford black males," as the Court of Appeals stated. 527 F.2d, at 371. It is true that Glover's duty was that of ferreting out narcotics offenders and that he would be expected in his work to produce results. But it is also true that, as a specially trained, assigned, and experienced officer, he could be expected to pay scrupulous attention to detail, for he knew that subsequently he would have to find and arrest his vendor. In addition, he knew that his claimed observations would be subject later to close scrutiny and examination at any trial.

3. The accuracy of the description. Glover's description was given to D'Onofrio within minutes after the transaction. It included the vendor's race, his height, his build, the color and style of his hair, and the high cheekbone facial feature. It also included clothing the vendor wore. No claim has been made that respondent did not possess the physical characteristics so described. D'Onofrio reacted positively at once. Two days later, when Glover was alone, he viewed the photograph D'Onofrio produced and identified its subject as the narcotics seller.

4. The witness' level of certainty. There is no dispute that the photograph in question was that of respondent. Glover, in response to a question whether the photograph was that of the person from whom he made the purchase, testified: "There is no question whatsoever." Tr. 38. This positive assurance was repeated. Id., at 41–42.

5. The time between the crime and the confrontation. Glover's description of his vendor was given to D'Onofrio within minutes of the crime. The photographic identification took place only two days later. We do not have here the passage of weeks or months between the crime and the viewing of the photograph.

These indicators of Glover's ability to make an accurate identification are hardly outweighed by the corrupting effect of the challenged identification itself. Although

identifications arising from single-photograph displays may be viewed in general with suspicion, see Simmons v. United States, 390 U.S., at 383, we find in the instant case little pressure on the witness to acquiesce in the suggestion that such a display entails. D'Onofrio had left the photograph at Glover's office and was not present when Glover first viewed it two days after the event. There thus was little urgency and Glover could view the photograph at his leisure. And since Glover examined the photograph alone, there was no coercive pressure to make an identification arising from the presence of another. The identification was made in circumstances allowing care and reflection.

Although it plays no part in our analysis, all this assurance as to the reliability of the identification is hardly undermined by the facts that respondent was arrested in the very apartment where the sale had taken place, and that he acknowledged his frequent visits to that apartment.

Surely, we cannot say that under all the circumstances of this case there is "a very substantial likelihood of irreparable misidentification." Simmons v. United States, 390 U.S., at 384. Short of that point, such evidence is for the jury to weigh. We are content to rely upon the good sense and judgment of American juries, for evidence with some element of untrustworthiness is customary grist for the jury mill. Juries are not so susceptible that they cannot measure intelligently the weight of identification testimony that has some questionable feature.

Of course, it would have been better had D'Onofrio presented Glover with a photographic array including "so far as practicable ... a reasonable number of persons similar to any person then suspected whose likeness is included in the array." ... The use of that procedure would have enhanced the force of the identification at trial and would have avoided the risk that the evidence would be excluded as unreliable. But we are not disposed to view D'Onofrio's failure as one of constitutional dimension to be enforced by a rigorous and unbending exclusionary rule. The defect, if there be one, goes to weight and not to substance.

We conclude that the criteria laid down in Biggers are to be applied in determining the admissibility of evidence offered by the prosecution concerning a post-Stovall identification, and that those criteria are satisfactorily met and complied with here.

The judgment of the Court of Appeals is reversed.

It is so ordered.

[Mr. Justice STEVENS wrote a concurring opinion.]

Mr. Justice MARSHALL, with whom Mr. Justice BRENNAN joins, dissenting.

Today's decision can come as no surprise to those who have been watching the Court dismantle the protections against mistaken eyewitness testimony erected a decade ago in United States v. Wade, 388 U.S. 218 (1967); Gilbert v. California, 388 U.S. 263 (1967); and Stovall v. Denno, 388 U.S. 293 (1967). But it is still distressing to see the Court virtually ignore the teaching of experience embodied in those decisions and blindly uphold the conviction of a defendant who may well be innocent.

The magnitude of the Court's error can be seen by analyzing the cases in the Wade trilogy and the decisions following it. The foundation of the Wade trilogy was the Court's recognition of the "high incidence of miscarriage of justice" resulting from the admission of mistaken eyewitness identification evidence at criminal trials. United States v. Wade, supra, 388 U.S., at 228. Relying on numerous studies made over many years by such scholars as Professor Wigmore and Mr. Justice Frankfurter, the Court concluded that "[t]he vagaries of eyewitness identification are well-known; the annals of criminal law are rife with instances of mistaken identification." ...

* * *

Apparently, the Court does not consider Biggers controlling in this case. I entirely agree, since I believe that Biggers was wrongly decided. The Court, however, concludes that Biggers is distinguishable because it, like the identification decisions that preceded it, involved a pre-Stovall confrontation, and because a paragraph in Biggers itself, 409 U.S., at 198–199, seems to distinguish between pre- and post-Stovall confrontations. Accordingly, in determining the admissibility of the post-Stovall identification in this case, the Court considers two alternatives, a per se exclusionary rule and a totality of the circumstances approach.... The Court weighs three factors in deciding that the totality approach, which is essentially the test used in Biggers, should be applied.... In my view, the Court wrongly evaluates the impact of these factors.

First, the Court acknowledges that one of the factors, deterrence of police use of unnecessarily suggestive identification procedures, favors the per se rule. Indeed, it does so heavily, for such a rule would make it unquestionably clear to the police that they must never use a suggestive procedure when a fairer alternative is available. I have no doubt that conduct would quickly conform to the rule.

Second, the Court gives passing consideration to the dangers of eyewitness identification recognized in the Wade trilogy. It concludes, however, that the grave risk of error does not justify adoption of the per se approach because that would too often result in exclusion of relevant evidence. In my view, this conclusion totally ignores the lessons of Wade. The dangers of mistaken identification are, as Stovall held, simply too great to permit unnecessarily suggestive identifications. Neither Biggers nor the Court's opinion today points to any contrary empirical evidence. Studies since Wade have only reinforced the validity of its assessment of the dangers of identification testimony. While the Court is "content to rely on the good sense and judgment of American juries," ... the impetus for Stovall and Wade was repeated miscarriages of justice resulting from juries' willingness to credit inaccurate eyewitness testimony.

Finally, the Court errs in its assessment of the relative impact of the two approaches on the administration of justice. The Court relies most heavily on this factor, finding that "reversal is a draconian sanction" in cases where the identification is reliable despite an unnecessarily suggestive procedure used to obtain it. Relying on little more than a strong distaste for "inflexible rules of exclusion," the Court disregards two significant distinctions between the per se rule advocated in this case and the exclusionary remedies for certain other constitutional violations.

First, the per se rule here is not "inflexible." Where evidence is suppressed, for example, as the fruit of an unlawful search, it may well be forever lost to the prosecution. Identification evidence, however, can by its very nature be readily and effectively reproduced. The in-court identification, permitted under Wade and Simmons if it has a source independent of an uncounseled or suggestive procedure, is one example. Similarly, when a prosecuting attorney learns that there has been a suggestive confrontation, he can easily arrange another lineup conducted under scrupulously fair conditions. . . .

Second, other exclusionary rules have been criticized for preventing jury consideration of relevant and usually reliable evidence in order to serve interests unrelated to guilt or innocence, such as discouraging illegal searches or denial of counsel. Suggestively obtained eyewitness testimony is excluded, in contrast, precisely because of its unreliability and concomitant irrelevance. Its exclusion both protects the integrity of the truth-seeking function of the trial and discourages police use of needlessly inaccurate and ineffective investigatory methods.

Indeed, impermissibly suggestive identifications are not merely worthless law enforcement tools. They pose a grave threat to society at large in a more direct way than most governmental disobedience of the law, see Olmstead v. United States, 277 U.S. 438, 471, 485 (1928) (Brandeis, J., dissenting). For if the police and the public erroneously conclude, on the basis of an unnecessarily suggestive confrontation, that the right man has been caught and convicted, the real outlaw must still remain at large. Law enforcement has failed in its primary function and has left society unprotected from the depredations of an active criminal.

For these reasons, I conclude that adoption of the per se rule would enhance, rather than detract from, the effective administration of justice. In my view, the Court's totality test will allow seriously unreliable and misleading evidence to be put before juries. Equally important, it will allow dangerous criminals to remain on the streets while citizens assume that police action has given them protection. According to my calculus, all three factors upon which the Court relies point to acceptance of the per se approach.

Even more disturbing than the Court's reliance on the totality test, however, is the analysis it uses, which suggests a reinterpretation of the concept of due process of law in criminal cases. The decision suggests that due process violations in indentification procedures may not be measured by whether the Government employed procedures violating standards of fundamental fairness. By relying on the probable accuracy of a challenged identification, instead of the necessity for its use, the Court seems to be ascertaining whether the defendant was probably guilty. Until today, I had thought that "equal justice under law" meant that the existence of constitutional violations did not depend on the race, sex, religion, nationality or likely guilt of the accused. The Due Process Clause requires adherence to the same high standard of fundamental fairness in dealing with every criminal defendant, whatever his personal characteristics and irrespective of the strength of the State's case against him. Strong evidence that the defendant is guilty should be relevant only to the determination whether an error of constitutional magnitude was nevertheless harmless beyond a reasonable doubt. See Chapman v. California, 386 U.S. 18 (1967). By importing the question of guilt into the initial determination of whether there was a constitutional violation, the apparent effect of the Court's decision is to undermine the protection afforded by the Due Process Clause. . . .

The use of a single picture (or the display of a single live suspect, for that matter) is a grave error, of course, because it dramatically suggests to the witness that the person shown must be the culprit. Why else would the police choose the person? And it is deeply ingrained in human nature to agree with the expressed opinions of others — particularly others who should be more knowledgeable — when making a difficult decision. In this case, moreover, the pressure was not limited to that inherent in the display of a single photograph. Glover, the identifying witness, was a State Police officer on special assignment. He knew that D'Onofrio, an experienced Hartford narcotics detective, presumably familiar with local drug operations, believed respondent to be the seller. There was at work, then, both loyalty to another police officer and deference to a better informed colleague. Finally, of course, there was Glover's knowledge that without an identification and arrest, government funds used to buy heroin had been wasted.

The Court discounts this overwhelming

evidence of suggestiveness, however. It reasons that because D'Onofrio was not present when Glover viewed the photograph, there was "little pressure on the witness to acquiesce in the suggestion." ... That conclusion blinks psychological reality. There is no doubt in my mind that even in D'Onofrio's absence, a clear and powerful message was telegraphed to Glover as he looked at respondent's photograph. He was emphatically told, "*This* is the man," and he responded by identifying respondent then and at trial "whether or not he was in fact 'the man.'" Foster v. California, supra, 394 U.S., at 443.

I must conclude that this record presents compelling evidence that there was "a very substantial likelihood of misidentification" of respondent Brathwaite. The suggestive display of respondent's photograph to the witness Glover likely erased any independent memory that Glover had retained of the seller from his barely adequate opportunity to observe the criminal.

Since I agree with the distinguished panel of the Court of Appeals that the legal standard of Stovall should govern this case, but that even if it does not, the facts here reveal a substantial likelihood of misidentification in violation of respondent's right to due process of law, I would affirm the grant of habeas corpus relief. Accordingly, I dissent from the Court's reinstatement of respondent's conviction.

Comments

1. In *Stovall,* the Court held that the *Wade-Gilbert* rule requiring counsel at postindictment lineups was not retroactive and was applicable only to confrontations occurring after June 12, 1967. The *Stovall* test for the fairness of a pretrial identification procedure — whether it was "so unnecessarily suggestive and conducive to irreparable mistaken identification" — was adopted from a United States court of appeals decision, *Palmer* v. *Peyton,* 350 F.2d 199 (4th Cir. 1966). The fairness of the procedure is measured by the "totality of circumstances" surrounding the confrontation. An unfair identification procedure is a denial of due process, and the results are subject to exclusion at trial on that basis. Although the *Stovall* Court noted that the use of *showups* (a one-man lineup in which a single suspect is shown to a witness for the purpose of identification) is generally disapproved of, there are circumstances in which such a procedure does not violate due process. Suppose the police pick up a suspect shortly after receiving a report of a robbery and take the suspect to the store and ask the manager, "Do you recognize this man?" Is this showup so inherently unfair or, in the words of the Court, "so unnecessarily suggestive and conducive to irreparable mistaken misidentification" as measured by the "totality of circumstances" as to deny the suspect due process? The words used by the police at a showup may be critical. Suppose the police asked the store manager, "This is the man who robbed you, isn't it?"

2. *Foster* v. *California,* supra, is the only Supreme Court decision, to date, in which a pretrial lineup procedure was found to be unfair and a denial of due process. The *Foster* Court declined to rule on whether the unfair lineup procedure utilized constituted a "harmless error." The "harmless error" rule originated in *Chapman* v. *California,* 386 U.S. 18 (1967), in which the Court held that not all errors of constitutional dimension require reversal; that is, there can be harmless constitutional error. Whether a constitutional error is harmless is governed by federal, not state, law. In

order for an error involving the denial of a federal constitutional right to be held harmless in a state criminal case, the state must prove beyond a reasonable doubt that the error did not contribute to the defendants' conviction. The concept of "harmless constitutional error" is also known as the *Chapman* rule. Some constitutional errors cannot be harmless and require an ***automatic reversal***. For example, the use of an involuntary confession at trial is never deemed harmless and is per se reversible error. *Haynes* v. *Washington,* 373 U.S. 503 (1963). Likewise, a denial of a fair trial requires an automatic reversal. However, the Court has held that the following constitutional errors may be harmless: (1) a violation of *Griffin* v. *California* (comment by a prosecutor on a defendant's failure to testify at trial), *Chapman* v. *California,* supra; (2) in-court identifications based on invalid pretrial identification procedures, *United States* v. *Wade,* supra; (3) evidence seized in violation of the Fourth Amendment, *Chambers* v. *Maroney,* 399 U.S. 42 (1970); (4) a denial of counsel at a preliminary hearing, *Coleman* v. *Alabama,* 399 U.S. 1 (1970); (5) obtaining a confession from a defendant after indictment without expressly informing the defendant of his right to counsel, in violation of *Massiah* v. *United States,* 377 U.S. 201 (1964), *Milton* v. *Wainwright,* 407 U.S. 371 (1972); and (6) a violation of the *Bruton* rule (Chapter Seven, § 7.03) in which a co-defendant's confession implicating the defendant was erroneously admitted into evidence, *Harrington* v. *California,* 393 U.S. 250 (1969). The Supreme Court has not decided whether a violation of *Miranda* can be a harmless error, but presumably it can be.

3. In *Neil* v. *Biggers,* supra, it was held that a decision by an equally divided Supreme Court (e.g., 4–4) is "no decision" on the merits and may not be cited as precedent in later cases. It does, however, have the procedural effect of affirming the most recent lower court decision on the case.

   On the merits of the case, the *Neil* Court held that even if a pretrial identification procedure is unnecessarily suggestive, there must be a *very substantial likelihood of misidentification* before the evidence of identification will be excluded. The "very substantial likelihood" test actually derives from an earlier case, *Simmons* v. *United States,* 390 U.S. 377, 384 (1968), which involved a photographic identification procedure. The *Neil* Court's reliance on *Simmons* may be misplaced since the procedure in *Neil* involved a showup rather than a photographic display. It seems doubtful that many defendants will be able to meet the burden of proof required under the "very substantial likelihood" test for showing a denial of due process. And even if the burden is met, there is always the possibility that the Court will find the improper identification procedure to be a harmless error.

4. *Manson* v. *Brathwaite,* supra, reaffirms the rule set out in the *Stovall-Simmons-Biggers* trilogy that the admissibility of identifications is measured by the "totality of circumstances" surrounding the procedure, and that unnecessary suggestiveness *alone* does not amount to a denial of due process. Would the Court have reached the same result if a single photograph had been shown to the victim of a crime (for example, robbery) two days later?

   The majority's refusal to accept a per se rule of exclusion for unnecessarily suggestive identification procedures is hardly surprising in light of the Burger Court's increasingly jaundiced view of the exclusionary rule. See, e.g., *United States* v. *Calandra,* infra, § 6.04; *Stone* v. *Powell,* Chapter Five, § 5.03; and *United States* v. *Janis,* Chapter Five, § 5.03, Comments. Is the "totality of circumstances" test as weak as Justices Marshall and Brennan suggested? Recall that this test has been utilized by the Supreme Court for a variety of purposes, e.g., for determining the voluntariness of a consent to a search, the voluntariness of a confession, and the validity of a guilty plea.

5. Some recent lower federal and state court decisions involving pretrial and in-court identification procedures are: *United States* v. *Dailey,* 524 F.2d 911 (8th Cir. 1975) (showing photos of a robbery defendant to an eyewitness on the morning he was to testify held impermissibly suggestive); *Bennett* v. *State,* 530 S.W.2d 788 (Tenn. 1975) (showing mug shots or photographs to witnesses immediately prior to a lineup or showup held improper); *United States* v. *Green,* 526 F.2d 212 (8th Cir. 1975) (trial court acted within its discretion in allowing FBI photographic analyst to testify as expert witness and compare surveillance film of a bank robber with black and white photographs of a model dressed in clothing belonging to one of the defendants) (see also *United States* v. *Brown,* 501 F.2d 146 [9th Cir. 1974], and *United States* v. *Cairns,* 424 F.2d 643 [9th Cir. 1970]); *United States* v. *Grose,* 525 F.2d 1115 (7th Cir. 1975) (no impermissible suggestiveness in bank robbery witnesses' exposure to a newspaper photograph of a robber taken by an automatic bank camera when the witnesses testified that their identification at trial was based on their own observations during the robbery); *Cannon* v. *Smith,* 527 F.2d 702 (2nd Cir 1975) (requiring suspect in a lineup to wear the only type of clothing described by the victim held impermissibly suggestive); *Harris* v. *State,* 350 A.2d 769 (Del. 1975) (reliability standard of *Neil* v. *Biggers* applies to showups that took place before as well as after *Stovall* v. *Denno*) (in accord is *Kirby* v. *Sturgis,* 510 F.2d 397 [7th Cir. 1975], *Pierce* v. *Cannon,* 508 F.2d 197 [7th Cir. 1974], *Dobson* v. *State,* 335 A.2d 124 [Md. 1975]) (contra is *Smith* v. *Coiner,* 473 F.2d 877 [7th Cir. 1973] [single-suspect composite drawing and photos shown to victim, while unnecessarily suggestive, not reversible error where the victim accurately described the defendant before the suggestive drawing and photo showings]); *Sanchell* v. *Parrah,* 530 F.2d 286 (8th Cir. 1976) (bringing victim into a courtroom on two occasions when the defendant was being arraigned on robbery charges and was the only black male fitting the general description given by the victim held impermissibly suggestive); *State* v. *Williams,* 239 N.W.2d 222 (Minn. 1976) (robbery defendant's Fifth Amendment rights not violated by his being ordered in the jury's presence to put on a hat which was worn by the robber and lost during the getaway); *Manis* v. *Miller,* 327 So. 2d 117 (Fla. App. 1976) (defendant in a civil suit not liable for damages to plaintiff where the defendant made a good faith, honest mistake as to the identity of a party in a criminal proceeding); *United States* v. *Russell,* 532 F.2d 1063 (6th Cir. 1976) (eyewitness to bank robbery who selected another man's mug shot as that of the robber but at trial identified the defendant as the holdup man held improperly influenced by federal agent who, after the witness selected the photo, pointed to the defendant's mug shot and iden-

tified him as the government's prime suspect); *United States* v. *Higginbotham*, 539 F.2d 17 (9th Cir. 1976) (federal defendant's conviction affirmed even though local police department lost the photos that formed the array from which he was identified); *Williams* v. *State*, 352 N.E.2d 732 (Ind. 1976) (witness permitted to make in-court identification independent of a pretrial orientation session at which police officers set aside the defendant's photos to refresh his recollection even though the procedure was suggestive); *Buchanan* v. *State*, 554 P.2d 1153 (Ala. 1976) (police officer's remark that gave a 9-year-old victim of a sexual assault the impression that a picture of her assailant would be found in a 6-person photographic array held not impermissibly suggestive); *State* v. *Boettcher*, 338 So. 2d 1357 (La. 1976) (although a defendant has no constitutional right to an out-of-court pretrial lineup, trial judge has discretion to grant such a defense request).

6.04 THE GRAND JURY

A. SOME EVIDENTIARY PROBLEMS

Indictments Based on Hearsay Evidence

COSTELLO v. UNITED STATES

Supreme Court of the United States, 1953
350 U.S. 359, 76 S. Ct. 406, 100 L. Ed. 397

Frank Costello, a well known figure in organized crime, was indicted by a federal grand jury for income tax evasion for the years 1947 to 1949. He was charged with falsely and fraudulently reporting less income than he actually received during the taxable years in question. Costello filed a motion to dismiss the indictment on the ground that it had been based solely on the hearsay evidence of three government witnesses who had no firsthand knowledge of the transaction upon which they based their computations showing that Costello had received a greater income than he had reported. The motion was denied. After a trial in which 144 witnesses testified and 368 exhibits were introduced, Costello was convicted. The United States Court of Appeals (2d Cir.) affirmed, holding that the indictment was valid even though the sole evidence before the grand jury was hearsay. The United States Supreme Court granted certiorari.

Mr. Justice BLACK delivered the opinion of the Court.

* * *

Petitioner here urges: (1) that an indictment based solely on hearsay evidence violates that part of the Fifth Amendment providing that "No person shall be held to answer for a capital, or otherwise infamous crime, unless on a presentment or indictment of a Grand Jury..." and (2) that if the Fifth Amendment does not invalidate an indictment based solely on hearsay we should now lay down such a rule for the guidance of federal courts....

The Fifth Amendment provides that federal prosecutions for capital or otherwise infamous crimes must be instituted by presentments or indictments of grand juries. But neither the Fifth Amendment nor any other constitutional provision prescribes the kind of evidence upon which grand juries must act. The grand jury is an English institution, brought to this country by the early colonists and incorporated in the Constitution by the Founders. There is every reason to believe that our constitutional grand jury was intended to operate substantially like its English progenitor. The basic purpose of the English grand jury was to provide a fair method for instituting criminal proceedings against persons believed to have committed crimes. Grand jurors were selected from the body of the people and their work was not hampered by rigid procedural or evidential rules. In fact, grand jurors could act on their own knowledge and were free to make their presentments or indictments on such information as they deemed satisfactory. Despite its broad power to institute criminal proceedings the grand jury grew in popular favor with the years. It acquired an independence in England free from control by the Crown or judges. Its adoption in our Constitution as the sole method for preferring charges in serious criminal cases shows the high place it held as an instrument of justice. And in this country as in England of old the grand jury has convened as a body of laymen, free from technical rules, acting in secret, pledged to indict no one because of prejudice and to free no one because of special favor. . . .

* * *

If indictments were to be held open to challenge on the ground that there was inadequate or incompetent evidence before the grand jury, the resulting delay would be great indeed. The result of such a rule would be that before trial on the merits a defendant could always insist on a kind of preliminary trial to determine the competency and adequacy of the evidence before the grand jury. This is not required by the Fifth Amendment. An indictment returned by a legally constituted and unbiased grand jury, like an information drawn by the prosecutor, if valid on its face, is enough to call for trial of the charge on the merits. The Fifth Amendment requires nothing more.

Petitioner urges that this Court should exercise its power to supervise the administration of justice in federal courts and establish a rule permitting defendants to challenge indictments on the ground that they are not supported by adequate or competent evidence. No persuasive reasons are advanced for establishing such a rule. It would run counter to the whole history of the grand jury institution, in which laymen conduct their inquiries unfettered by technical rules. Neither justice nor the concept of a fair trial requires such a change. In a trial on the merits, defendants are entitled to a strict observance of all the rules designed to bring about a fair verdict. Defendants are not entitled, however, to a rule which would result in interminable delay but add nothing to the assurance of a fair trial.

Affirmed.

[Mr. Justice BURTON wrote a concurring opinion.]

The Exclusionary Rule and Grand Jury Proceedings

UNITED STATES v. CALANDRA

Supreme Court of the United States, 1974
414 U.S. 338, 94 S. Ct. 613, 38 L. Ed. 2d 561

Federal agents obtained a warrant to search John Calandra's place of business, a machine and tool company in Cleveland. The object of the search was to discover evidence of bookmaking records and gambling paraphernalia. Federal agents executed the warrant and conducted a thorough search of the premises. Although no gambling paraphernalia was discovered, evidence of a loan-sharking enter-

prise was found. Subsequently, a special federal grand jury was convened and Calandra was subpoenaed to answer questions based on the evidence seized at his place of business. He refused to testify on Fifth Amendment grounds and on the grounds that the search and seizure of his premises was in violation of the Fourth Amendment—that the affidavit supporting the warrant was defective and the search exceeded the scope of the warrant. The district court ordered the evidence suppressed and further ordered that Calandra need not answer any questions of the grand jury based on the seized evidence. The court found that the search warrant had been issued without probable cause and that the search had exceeded the scope of the warrant. The United States Court of Appeals (6th Cir.) affirmed, holding that the exclusionary rule may be invoked by a witness before the grand jury to bar questioning based on evidence obtained as a result of an unlawful search and seizure. The United States Supreme Court granted certiorari.

Mr. Justice POWELL delivered the opinion of the Court.

This case presents the question whether a witness summoned to appear and testify before a grand jury may refuse to answer questions on the ground that they are based on evidence obtained from an unlawful search and seizure. The issue is of considerable importance to the administration of criminal justice.

* * *

II

The institution of the grand jury is deeply rooted in Anglo-American history. In England, the grand jury served for centuries both as a body of accusers sworn to discover and present for trial persons suspected of criminal wrongdoing and as a protector of citizens against arbitrary and oppressive governmental action. In this country the Founders thought the grand jury so essential to basic liberties that they provided in the Fifth Amendment that federal prosecution for serious crimes can only be instituted by "a presentment or indictment of a Grand Jury." Costello v. United States, [supra]. . . . The grand jury's historic functions survive to this day. Its responsibilities continue to include both the determination whether there is probable cause to believe a crime has been committed and the protection of citizens against unfounded criminal prosecutions. Branzburg v. Hays, [infra]. . . .

Traditionally the grand jury has been accorded wide latitude to inquire into violations of criminal law. No judge presides to monitor its proceedings. It deliberates in secret and may determine alone the course of its inquiry. The grand jury may compel the production of evidence or the testimony of witnesses as it considers appropriate, and its operation generally is unrestrained by the technical procedural and evidentiary rules governing the conduct of criminal trials. . . .

The scope of the grand jury's powers reflects its special role in insuring fair and effective law enforcement. A grand jury proceeding is not an adversary hearing in which the guilt or innocence of the accused is adjudicated. Rather, it is an ex parte investigation to determine whether a crime has been committed and whether criminal proceedings should be instituted against any person. The grand jury's investigative power must be broad if its public responsibility is adequately to be discharged. . . .

* * *

The grand jury's sources of information are widely drawn, and the validity of an indictment is not affected by the character of the evidence considered. Thus, an indictment valid on its face is not subject to challenge on the ground that the grand jury acted on the basis of inadequate or incompetent evidence . . . or even on the basis of information obtained in violation of a defendant's Fifth Amendment privilege against self-incrimination. . . .

The power of a federal court to compel persons to appear and testify before a grand jury is also firmly established. Kastigar v. United States, [supra]. . . . The duty to testify has long been recognized as a basic obligation that every citizen owes his Government. [T]he Court [has] noted that "[c]itizens generally are not constitutionally immune from grand jury subpoenas..." and that "the longstanding principle that 'the public ... has a right to every man's evidence' ... is particularly applicable to grand jury proceedings." The duty to testify may on occasion be burdensome and even embarrassing. It may cause injury to a witness' social and economic status. Yet the duty to testify has been regarded as "so necessary to the administration of justice" that the witness' personal interest in privacy must yield to the public's overriding interest in full disclosure.... Furthermore, a witness may not interfere with the course of the grand jury's inquiry. He "is not entitled to urge objections of incompetency or irrelevancy, such as a party might raise, for this is no concern of his." ... Nor is he entitled "to challenge the authority of the court or of the grand jury" or "to set limits to the investigation that the grand jury may conduct."

Of course, the grand jury's subpoena power is not unlimited. It may consider incompetent evidence, but it may not itself violate a valid privilege, whether established by the Constitution, statutes, or the common law.... Although, for example, an indictment based on evidence obtained in violation of a defendant's Fifth Amendment privilege is nevertheless valid, Lawn v. United States, 355 U.S. 339 (1958), the grand jury may not force a witness to answer questions in violation of that constitutional guarantee. Rather, the grand jury may override a Fifth Amendment claim only if the witness is granted immunity coextensive with the privilege against self-incrimination. Kastigar v. United States, supra. Similarly, a grand jury may not compel a person to produce books and papers that would incriminate him.... The grand jury is also without power to invade a legitimate privacy interest protected by the Fourth Amendment. A grand jury's subpoena duces tecum will be disallowed if it is "far too sweeping in its terms to be regarded as reasonable" under the Fourth Amendment.... Judicial supervision is properly exercised in such cases to prevent the wrong before it occurs.

III

In the instant case, the Court of Appeals held that the exclusionary rule of the Fourth Amendment limits the grand jury's power to compel a witness to answer questions based on evidence obtained from a prior unlawful search and seizure. The exclusionary rule was adopted to effectuate the Fourth Amendment right of all citizens "to be secure in their persons, houses, papers, and effects, against unreasonable searches and seizures...." Under this rule, evidence obtained in violation of the Fourth Amendment cannot be used in a criminal proceeding against the victim of the illegal search and seizure.... This prohibition applies as well to the fruits of the illegally seized evidence....

* * *

[T]he rule's prime purpose is to deter future unlawful police conduct and thereby effectuate the guarantee of the Fourth Amendment against unreasonable searches and seizures:

"The rule is calculated to prevent, not to repair. Its purpose is to deter—to compel respect for the constitutional guaranty in the only effectively available way—by removing the incentive to disregard it." Elkins v. United States, 365 U.S. 206 (1960).

In sum, the rule is a judicially created remedy designed to safeguard Fourth Amendment rights generally through its deterrent effect, rather than a personal constitutional right of the party aggrieved.

Despite its broad deterrent purpose, the exclusionary rule has never been interpreted to proscribe the use of illegally seized evidence in all proceedings or against all persons. As with any remedial device, the application of the rule has been restricted to those areas where its remedial objectives are thought most efficaciously served....

IV

In deciding whether to extend the exclusionary rule to grand jury proceedings, we must weigh the potential injury to the historic role and functions of the grand jury against the potential benefits of the rule as applied in this context. It is evident that this extension of the exclusionary rule would seriously impede the grand jury. Because the grand jury does not finally adjudicate guilt or innocence, it has traditionally been allowed to pursue its investigative and accusatorial functions unimpeded by the evidentiary and procedural restrictions applicable to a criminal trial. Permitting witnesses to invoke the exclusionary rule before a grand jury would precipitate adjudication of issues hitherto reserved for the trial on the merits and would delay and disrupt grand jury proceedings. Suppression hearings would halt the orderly progress of an investigation and might necessitate extended litigation of issues only tangentially related to the grand jury's primary objective. The probable result would be "protracted interruption of grand jury proceedings" ... effectively transforming them into preliminary trials on the merits. In some cases the delay might be fatal to the enforcement of the criminal law. Just last Term we reaffirmed our disinclination to allow litigious interference with grand jury proceedings:

"Any holding that would saddle a grand jury with minitrials and preliminary showings would assuredly impede its investigation and frustrate the public's interest in the fair and expeditious administration of the criminal laws." United States v. Dionisio, 410 U.S. 1 (1973).

In sum, we believe that allowing a grand jury witness to invoke the exclusionary rule would unduly interfere with the effective and expeditious discharge of the grand jury's duties.

Against this potential damage to the role and functions of the grand jury, we must weigh the benefits to be derived from this proposed extension of the exclusionary rule. Suppression of the use of illegally seized evidence against the search victim in a criminal trial is thought to be an important method of effectuating the Fourth Amendment. But it does not follow that the Fourth Amendment requires adoption of every proposal that might deter police misconduct. ...

Any incremental deterrent effect which might be achieved by extending the rule to grand jury proceedings is uncertain at best. Whatever deterrence of police misconduct may result from the exclusion of illegally seized evidence from criminal trials, it is unrealistic to assume that application of the rule to grand jury proceedings would significantly further that goal. Such an extension would deter only police investigation consciously directed toward the discovery of evidence solely for use in a grand jury investigation. The incentive to disregard the requirement of the Fourth Amendment solely to obtain an indictment from a grand jury is substantially negated by the inadmissibility of the illegally seized evidence in a subsequent criminal prosecution of the search victim. For the most part, a prosecutor would be unlikely to request an indictment where a conviction could not be obtained. We therefore decline to embrace a view that would achieve a speculative and undoubtedly minimal advance in the deterrence of police misconduct at the expense of substantially impeding the role of the grand jury.

V

Respondent also argues that each and every question based on evidence obtained from an illegal search and seizure constitutes a fresh and independent violation of the witness' constitutional rights. Ordinarily, of course, a witness has no right of privacy before the grand jury. Absent some recognized privilege of confidentiality, every man owes his testimony. He may invoke his Fifth Amendment privilege against compulsory self-incrimination, but he may not decline to answer on the grounds that his responses might prove embarrassing or result in an unwelcome disclosure of his personal affairs. ... Respondent's claim must be, therefore, not merely that the grand jury's questions invade his privacy but that, because those questions are based on illegally obtained evidence, they somehow constitute distinct violations of his Fourth Amendment rights. We disagree.

The purpose of the Fourth Amendment is to prevent unreasonable governmental intrusions into the privacy of one's person, house, papers, or effects. The wrong condemned is the unjustified governmental invasion of these areas of an individual's life. That wrong, committed in this case, is fully accomplished by the original search without probable cause. Grand jury questions based on evidence obtained thereby involve no independent governmental invasion of one's person, house, papers, or effects, but rather the usual abridgment of personal privacy common to all grand jury questioning. Questions based on illegally obtained evidence are only a derivative use of the product of a past unlawful search and seizure. They work no new Fourth Amendment wrong. Whether such derivative use of illegally obtained evidence by a grand jury should be proscribed presents a question, not of rights, but of remedies.

In the usual context of a criminal trial, the

defendant is entitled to the suppression of, not only the evidence obtained through an unlawful search and seizure, but also any derivative use of that evidence. The prohibition of the exclusionary rule must reach such derivative use if it is to fulfill its function of deterring police misconduct. In the context of a grand jury proceeding, we believe that the damage to that institution from the unprecedented extension of the exclusionary rule urged by respondent outweighs the benefit of any possible incremental deterrent effect. Our conclusion necessarily controls both the evidence seized during the course of an unlawful search and seizure and any question or evidence derived therefrom (the fruits of the unlawful search). The same considerations of logic and policy apply to both the fruits of an unlawful search and seizure and derivative use of that evidence, and we do not distinguish between them.

The judgment of the Court of Appeals is Reversed.

Mr. Justice BRENNAN, with whom Mr. Justice DOUGLAS and Mr. Justice MARSHALL join, dissenting.

The Court holds that the exclusionary rule in search-and-seizure cases does not apply to grand jury proceedings because the principal objective of the rule is "to deter future unlawful police conduct" ... [and] "it is unrealistic to assume that application of the rule to grand jury proceedings would significantly further that goal."

... This downgrading of the exclusionary rule to a determination whether its application in a particular type of proceeding furthers deterrence of future police misconduct reflects a startling misconception, unless it is a purposeful rejection, of the historical objective and purpose of the rule.

The commands of the Fourth Amendment are, of course, directed solely to public officials. Necessarily, therefore, only official violations of those commands could have created the evil that threatened to make the Amendment a dead letter. But curtailment of the evil, if a consideration at all, was at best only a hoped-for effect of the exclusionary rule, not its ultimate objective. Indeed, there is no evidence that the possible deterrent effect of the rule was given any attention by the judges chiefly responsible for

its formulation. Their concern as guardians of the Bill of Rights was to fashion an enforcement tool to give content and meaning to the Fourth Amendment's guarantees....

*　*　*

The judges who developed the exclusionary rule were well aware that it embodied a judgment that it is better for some guilty persons to go free than for the police to behave in forbidden fashion....

*　*　*

[T]o allow Calandra to be subjected to questions derived from the illegal search of his office and seizure of his files is "to thwart the [Fourth and Fourteenth Amendments' protection] of ... individual privacy ... and to entangle the courts in the illegal acts of Government agents." Ibid. "And for a court, on petition of the executive department, to sentence a witness, who is [himself] the victim of the illegal [search and seizure], to jail for refusal to participate in the exploitation of that [conduct in violation of the explicit command of the Fourth Amendment] is to stand our whole system of criminal justice on its head." In re Evans, 452 F.2d 1239, 1252 (1971) (Wright, J., concurring).

*　*　*

In Mapp, the Court thought it had "close[d] the only courtroom door remaining open to evidence secured by official lawlessness" in violation of Fourth Amendment rights.... The door is again ajar. As a consequence, I am left with the uneasy feeling that today's decision may signal that a majority of my colleagues have positioned themselves to reopen the door still further and abandon altogether the exclusionary rule in search-and-seizure cases; for surely they cannot believe that application of the exclusionary rule at trial furthers the goal of deterrence, but that its application in grand jury proceedings will not "significantly" do so. Unless we are to shut our eyes to the evidence that crosses our desks every day, we must concede that official lawlessness has not abated and that no empirical data distinguishes trials from grand jury proceedings. I thus fear that when next we confront a case of a conviction rested on illegally seized evidence, today's decision will be invoked to sustain the conclusion in that case also that "it is unrealistic to assume" that application of the rule at trial would "significantly further" the goal of deterrence — though, if the police are presently undeterred, it is difficult to see how removal of the sanction of

exclusion will induce more lawful official conduct.

* * *

I dissent and would affirm the judgment of the Court of Appeals.

B. THE GRAND JURY, THE FIRST AMENDMENT, AND SELF-INCRIMINATION

Every Man Owes His Testimony, Including Reporters

BRANZBURG v. HAYES

Supreme Court of the United States, 1972
408 U.S. 665, 92 S. Ct. 2646, 33 L. Ed. 2d 626

Branzburg was decided by the Supreme Court together with two other cases, *In re Pappas* and *United States* v. *Caldwell*. All three cases raised the First Amendment issue of whether news reporters can be compelled to testify before grand juries and reveal their confidential sources of information.

Paul Branzburg was a staff reporter for a daily newspaper in Louisville, Kentucky. The newspaper carried a story written by Branzburg describing in detail two young men who regularly engaged in synthesizing hashish from marijuana, which earned them $5,000 in three weeks. The article stated that Branzburg had promised not to reveal the identities of the two hashish makers. Shortly thereafter, Branzburg was summoned to testify before a local grand jury and was asked to reveal the names of the two persons described in the article. He refused to reveal the sources of his information on First Amendment grounds. The Kentucky courts rejected his contention that he did not have to answer the questions of the grand jury.

Paul Pappas, a television newsman-reporter for a Massachusetts television station was summoned to appear before a county grand jury to testify about the activities of a local Black Panther group from which he had gained confidential information. His motion to quash the summons on First Amendment grounds was denied by the Massachusetts courts.

Earl Caldwell, a reporter for the New York Times, was assigned in California to write a story on the Black Panther Party and other black militant groups. Caldwell was subpoenaed by a federal grand jury to testify and bring with him notes and tape recordings of interviews given him for publication by officers of the Black Panther Party. Caldwell's motion to quash the subpoena on First Amendment grounds was denied by the District Court (N.D. Calif.). Subsequently, Caldwell was held in contempt of court for refusing to appear before the grand jury and was ordered to jail until he complied with the court's order or until the expiration of the term of the grand jury. Caldwell appealed the contempt order, and the United States Court of Appeals (9th Cir.) reversed, holding that the First Amendment provided a qualified testimonial privilege to newsmen.

In each of these cases, the United States Supreme Court granted certiorari.

Mr. Justice WHITE delivered the opinion of the Court.

The issue in these cases is whether requiring newsmen to appear and testify before state or federal grand juries abridges the freedom of speech and press guaranteed by the First Amendment. We hold that it does not.

* * *

II

* * *

The sole issue before us is the obligation of reporters to respond to grand jury subpoenas as other citizens do and to answer questions relevant to an investigation into the commission of crime. Citizens generally are not constitutionally immune from grand jury subpoenas; and neither the First Amendment nor any other constitutional provision protects the average citizen from disclosing to a grand jury information that he has received in confidence. The claim is, however, that reporters are exempt from these obligations because if forced to respond to subpoenas and identify their sources or disclose other confidences, their informants will refuse or be reluctant to furnish news-worthy information in the future. This asserted burden on news gathering is said to make compelled testimony from newsmen constitutionally suspect and to require a privileged position for them.

It is clear that the First Amendment does not invalidate every incidental burdening of the press that may result from the enforcement of civil or criminal statutes of general applicability. Under prior cases, otherwise valid laws serving substantial public interests may be enforced against the press as against others, despite the possible burden that may be imposed. The Court has emphasized that "[t]he publisher of a newspaper has no special immunity from the application of general laws. He has no special privilege to invade the rights and liberties of others." . . .

The prevailing view is that the press is not free to publish with impunity everything and anything it desires to publish. Although it may deter or regulate what is said or published, the press may not circulate knowing or reckless falsehoods damaging to private reputation without subjecting itself to liability for damages, including punitive damages, or even criminal prosecution. . . . A newspaper or a journalist may also be punished for contempt of court, in appropriate circumstances. . . .

It has generally been held that the First Amendment does not guarantee the press a constitutional right of special access to information not available to the public generally. . . .

Despite the fact that news gathering may be hampered, the press is regularly excluded from grand jury proceedings, our own conferences, the meetings of other official bodies gathered in executive session, and the meetings of private organizations. Newsmen have no constitutional right of access to the scenes of crime or disaster when the general public is excluded, and they may be prohibited from attending or publishing information about trials if such restrictions are necessary to assure a defendant a fair trial before an impartial tribunal. . . .

It is thus not surprising that the great weight of authority is that newsmen are not exempt from the normal duty of appearing before a grand jury and answering questions relevant to a criminal investigation. At common law, courts consistently refused to recognize the existence of any privilege authorizing a newsman to refuse to reveal confidential information to a grand jury. . . .

* * *

A number of States have provided newsmen a statutory privilege of varying breadth, but the majority have not done so, and none has been provided by federal statute. Until now the only testimonial privilege for unofficial witnesses that is rooted in the Federal Constitution is the Fifth Amendment privilege against compelled self-incrimination. We are asked to create another by interpreting the First Amendment to grant newsmen a testimonial privilege that other citizens do not enjoy. This we decline to do. . . .

* * *

[N]ews gathering is not without its First Amendment protections, and grand jury investigations if instituted or conducted other than in good faith, would pose wholly different issues for resolution under the First Amendment. Official harassment of the press undertaken not for purposes of law enforcement but to disrupt a reporter's relationship with his news sources would have no justification. Grand juries are subject to judicial control and subpoenas to motions to quash. We do not expect courts will forget that grand juries must operate within the limits of the First Amendment as well as the Fifth.

* * *

[Affirmed.]

[Mr. Justice POWELL concurred.]

Mr. Justice DOUGLAS, dissenting.

* * *

It is my view that there is no "compelling need" that can be shown which qualifies the reporter's immunity from appearing or testifying before a grand jury, unless the reporter himself is implicated in a crime. His immunity in my view is therefore quite complete, for, absent his involvement in a crime, the First Amendment protects him against an appearance before a grand jury and if he is involved in a crime, the Fifth Amendment stands as a barrier. Since in my view there is no area of inquiry not protected by a privilege, the reporter need not appear for the futile purpose of invoking one to each question. And, since in my view a newsman has an absolute right not to appear before a grand jury, it follows for me that a journalist who voluntarily appears before that body may invoke his First Amendment privilege to specific questions.

The basic issue is the extent to which the First Amendment (which is applicable to investigating committees) . . . must yield to the Government's asserted need to know a reporter's unprinted information.

Mr. Justice STEWART, with whom Mr. Justice BRENNAN and Mr. Justice MARSHALL join, dissenting.

The Court's crabbed view of the First Amendment reflects a disturbing insensitivity to the critical role of an independent press in our society. The question whether a reporter has a constitutional right to a confidential relationship with his source is of first impression here, but the principles that should guide our decision are as basic as any to be found in the Constitution. While Mr. Justice Powell's enigmatic concurring opinion gives some hope of a more flexible view in the future, the Court in these cases holds that a newsman has no First Amendment right to protect his sources when called before a grand jury. The Court thus invites state and federal authorities to undermine the historic independence of the press by attempting to annex the journalistic profession as an investigative arm of government. Not only will this decision impair performance of the press' constitutionally protected functions, but it will, I am convinced, in the long run harm rather than help the administration of justice.

I respectfully dissent.

* * *

[The three dissenting justices went on to state that, in their view, the First Amendment requires that before a newsman can be compelled to appear before a grand jury and reveal confidences, the government must show (1) probable cause to believe that the newsman has information clearly relevant to a specific violation of law, (2) that the information cannot be obtained by alternate means less destructive of First Amendment rights, and (3) that there is a compelling and overriding need for the information.]

C. RACIAL DISCRIMINATION AND THE SELECTION OF GRAND JURORS

The Requirement of Neutral Selection Criteria

ALEXANDER v. LOUISIANA

Supreme Court of the United States, 1972
405 U.S. 625, 92 S. Ct. 1221, 31 L. Ed. 2d 536

The facts are stated in the opinion.

Mr. Justice WHITE delivered the opinion of the Court.

After a jury trial in the District Court for the Fifteenth Judicial District of Lafayette Parish, Louisiana, petitioner, a Negro, was convicted of rape and sentenced to life imprisonment. His conviction was affirmed on appeal by the Louisiana Supreme Court, and this Court granted certiorari. Prior to trial, petitioner had moved to quash the indictment because (1) Negro citizens were included on the grand jury list and venire in only token numbers, and (2) female citizens were systematically excluded from the grand jury list, venire, and impaneled grand jury. Petitioner therefore argued that the indictment against him was invalid because it was returned by a grand jury impaneled from a venire made up contrary to the requirements of the Equal Protection Clause and the Due Process Clause of the Fourteenth Amendment. Petitioner's motions were denied.

According to 1960 U.S. census figures admitted into evidence below, Lafayette Parish contained 44,986 persons over 21 years of age and therefore presumptively eligible for grand jury service; of this total, 9,473 persons (21.06%) were Negro. At the hearing on petitioner's motions to quash the indictment, the evidence revealed that the Lafayette Parish jury commission consisted of five members, all of whom were white, who had been appointed by the court. The commission compiled a list of names from various sources (telephone directory, city directory, voter registration rolls, lists prepared by the school board, and by the jury commissioners themselves) and sent questionnaires to the persons on this list to determine those qualified for grand jury service. The questionnaire included a space to indicate the race of the recipient. Through this process, 7,374 questionnaires were returned, 1,015 of which (13.76%) were from Negroes, and the jury commissioners attached to each questionnaire an information card designating, among other things, the race of the person, and a white slip indicating simply the name and address of the person. The commissioners then culled out about 5,000 questionnaires, ostensibly on the ground that these persons were not qualified for grand jury service or were exempted under state law. The remaining 2,000 sets of papers were placed on a table, and the papers of 400 persons were selected, purportedly at random, and placed in a box from which the grand jury panels of 20 of Lafayette Parish were drawn. Twenty-seven of the persons thus selected were Negro (6.75%). On petitioner's grand jury venire, one of the 20 persons drawn was Negro (5%), but none of the 12 persons on the grand jury that indicted him, drawn from this 20, was Negro.

I

For over 90 years, it has been established that a criminal conviction of a Negro cannot stand under the Equal Protection Clause of the Fourteenth Amendment if it is based on an indictment of a grand jury from which Negroes were excluded by reason of their race. Strauder v. West Virginia, 100 U.S. 303 (1880). . . . Although a defendant has no right to demand that members of his race be included on the grand jury that indicts him . . . he is entitled to require that the State not deliberately and systematically deny to members of his race the right to participate as jurors in the administration of justice. . . . It is only the application of these settled principles that is at issue here.

This is not a case where it is claimed that there have been no Negroes called for service within the last 30 years . . .; only one Negro chosen within the last 40 years . . .; or no Negroes selected "within the memory of witnesses who had lived [in the area] all their lives." . . . Rather, petitioner argues that, in his case, there has been a consistent process of progressive and disproportionate reduction of the number of Negroes eligible to serve on the grand jury at each stage of the selection process until ultimately an all-white grand jury was selected to indict him.

In Lafayette Parish, 21% of the population was Negro and 21 or over, therefore presumptively eligible for grand jury service. Use of questionnaires by the jury commissioners created a pool of possible grand jurors which was 14% Negro, a reduction by one-third of possible black grand jurors. The commissioners then twice culled this group to create a list of 400 prospective jurors, 7% of whom were Negro—a further reduction by one-half.

The percentage dropped to 5% on petitioner's grand jury venire and to zero on the grand jury that actually indicted him. Against this background, petitioner argues that the substantial disparity between the proportion of blacks chosen for jury duty and the proportion of blacks in the eligible population raises a strong inference that racial discrimination and not chance has produced this result because elementary principles of probability make it extremely unlikely that a random selection process would, at each stage, have so consistently reduced the number of Negroes.

This Court has never announced mathematical standards for the demonstration of "systematic" exclusion of blacks but has, rather, emphasized that a factual inquiry is necessary in each case that takes into account all possible explanatory factors. The progressive decimaton of potential Negro grand jurors is indeed striking here, but we do not rest our conclusion that petitioner has demonstrated a prima facie case of invidious racial discrimination on statistical improbability alone, for the selection procedures themselves were not racially neutral. The racial designation on both the questionnaire and the information card provided a clear and easy opportunity for racial discrimination. At two crucial steps in the selection process, when the number of returned questionnaires was reduced to 2,000 and when the final selection of the 400 names was made, these racial identifications were visible on the forms used by the jury commissioners, although there is no evidence that the commissioners consciously selected by race. The situation here is thus similar to Avery v. Georgia, 345 U.S. 559 (1953), where the Court sustained a challenge to an array of petit jurors in which the names of prospective jurors had been selected from segregated tax lists. Juror cards were prepared from these lists, yellow cards being used for Negro citizens and white cards for whites. Cards were drawn by a judge, and there was no evidence of specific discrimination. The Court held that such evidence was unnecessary, however, given the fact that no Negroes had appeared on the final jury: "Obviously that practice makes it easier for those to discriminate who are of a mind to discriminate." . . . Again, in Whitus v. Georgia, 385 U S 545 (1967), the Court reversed the conviction of a defendant who had been tried before an all-white petit jury. Jurors had been selected from a one-volume tax digest divided into separate sections of Negroes and whites; black taxpayers also had a "(c)" after their names as required by Georgia law at the time. The jury commissioners testified that they were not aware of the "(c)" appearing after the names of the Negro taxpayer; that they had never included or excluded anyone because of race;

that they had placed on the jury list only those persons whom they knew personally; and that the jury list they compiled had had no designation of race on it. The county from which jury selection was made was 42% Negro, and 27% of the county's taxpayers were Negro. Of the 33 persons drawn for the grand jury panel, three (9%) were Negro, while on the 19-member grand jury only one was Negro; and in the 90-man venire from which the petit jury was selected, there were seven Negroes (8%), but no Negroes appeared on the actual jury that tried petitioner. The Court held that this combination of factors constituted a prima facie case of discrimination, and a similar conclusion is mandated in the present case.

Once a prima facie case of invidious discrimination is established the burden of proof shifts to the State to rebut the presumption of unconstitutional action by showing that permissible racially neutral selection criteria and procedures have produced the monochromatic result. Turner v. Fouche, 396 U.S. 346 (1970). . . . The State has not carried this burden in this case; it has not adequately explained the eliminating of Negroes during the process of selecting the grand jury that indicted petitioner. As in Whitus v. Georgia, supra, the clerk of the court, who was also a member of the jury commission, testified that no consideration was given to race during the selection procedure. The Court has squarely held, however, that affirmations of good faith in making individual selections are insufficient to dispel a prima facie case of systematic exclusion. . . . "The result bespeaks discrimination, whether or not it was a conscious decision on the part of any individual jury commissioner." Hernandez v. Texas, 347 U.S. at 482 (1954). . . . The clerk's testimony that the mailing list for questionnaires was compiled from nonracial sources is not, in itself, adequate to meet the State's burden of proof, for the opportunity to discriminate was presented at later stages in the process. The commissioners, in any event, had a duty "not to pursue a course of conduct in the administration of their office which would operate to discriminate in the selection of jurors on racial grounds." Hill v. Texas, 316 U.S. 400 (1942). . . . We conclude, therefore, that "the opportunity for discrimination was present and [that it cannot be said] on this record that it was not resorted to by the commissioners." Whitus v. Georgia, supra.

II

Petitioner also challenges the Louisiana statutory exemption of women who do not volunteer for grand jury service. Article 402, La. Code Crim. Proc. This claim is novel in this Court and, when urged by a male, finds no support in our past cases. The strong constitutional and statutory policy against racial discrimination has permitted Negro defendants in criminal cases to challenge the systematic exclusion of Negroes from the grand juries that indicted them. Also, those groups arbitrarily excluded from grand or petit jury service are themselves afforded an appropriate remedy. But there is nothing in past adjudications suggesting that petitioner himself has been denied equal protection by the alleged exclusion of women from grand jury service.

Although the Due Process Clause guarantees petitioner a fair trial, it does not require the States to observe the Fifth Amendment's provision for presentment or indictment by a grand jury. . . .

[B]ecause petitioner's conviction has been set aside on other grounds, we follow our usual custom of avoiding decision of constitutional issues unnecessary to the decision of the case before us. . . . The State may or may not recharge petitioner, a properly constituted grand jury may or may not return another indictment, and petitioner may or may not be convicted again. . . .

Reversed.

[Mr. Justice POWELL and Mr. Justice REHNQUIST did not participate in the consideration or decision of this case.]

[Mr. Justice DOUGLAS wrote a concurring opinion.]

D. WARNING WITNESSES OF THEIR RIGHT TO REMAIN SILENT

Rights of a "Putative" Defendant

UNITED STATES v. MANDUJANO

Supreme Court of the United States, 1976
425 U.S. 564, 96 S. Ct. 1768, 48 L. Ed. 2d 212

Roy Mandujano, the respondent, was subpoenaed to testify before a federal grand jury in San Antonio, Texas, with regard to his alleged attempted sale of heroin to a federal undercover narcotics officer. At the grand jury proceeding Mandujano was warned by the prosecutor that (1) he was not required to answer any questions that might incriminate him; (2) he must answer questions truthfully or be subject to a charge of perjury; (3) if he desired retained counsel he could have one; but (4) his lawyer could not appear inside the grand jury room. During the questioning, Mandujano admitted that 15 years earlier he had been convicted of distributing drugs, that he had recently used heroin himself, and that he had purchased heroin five months earlier. However, he steadfastly denied either selling or attempting to sell heroin since his conviction and specifically disclaimed discussing the sale of heroin with anyone during the preceding year. Subsequently, Mandujano was indicted for perjury for making false statements to the grand jury about his involvement in the attempted heroin sale. The District Court (W.D. Tex. 1973) granted Mandujano's motion to suppress his testimony before the grand jury because he had not been given the full *Miranda* warnings when called before the grand jury. The Court of Appeals (5th Cir. 1974) affirmed, and the United States Supreme Court granted certiorari.

Mr. Chief Justice BURGER announced the judgment of the Court in an opinion in which Mr. Justice WHITE, Mr. Justice POWELL, and Mr. Justice REHNQUIST join.

This case presents the question whether the warnings called for by Miranda v. United States, 384 U.S. 436 (1966), must be given to a grand jury witness who is called to testify about criminal activities in which he may have been personally involved; and, whether absent such warnings, false statements made to the grand jury must be suppressed in a prosecution for perjury based on those statements.

The grand jury is an integral part of our constitutional heritage which was brought to this country with the common law. The Framers, most of them trained in the English law and traditions, accepted the grand jury as a basic guarantee of individual liberty; notwithstanding periodic criticism, much of which is superficial, overlooking relevant history, the grand jury continues to function as a barrier to reckless or unfounded charges.... Its historic office has been to provide a shield against arbitrary or oppressive action, by insuring that serious criminal accusations will be brought only upon the considered judgment of a representative body of citizens acting under oath and under judicial instruction and guidance.

* * *

When called by the grand jury, witnesses are thus legally bound to give testimony.... This principle has long been recognized. In United States v. Barr, 25 Fed. Cases No. 14,692e, at 38, Chief Justice Marshall drew on English precedents, aptly described by Lord Chancellor Hardwick in the 18th Century, and long accepted in America as a hornbook proposition: "The public has a right to every man's evidence." This Court has repeatedly invoked this fundamental proposition when dealing with the powers of the grand jury....

The grand jury's authority to compel testimony is not, of course, without limits. The same Amendment that established the grand jury also guarantees that "no person ... shall be compelled in any criminal case to be a witness against himself...." The duty to give evidence to a grand jury is therefore conditional; every person owes society his testimony, unless some recognized privilege is asserted.

Under settled principles, the Fifth Amendment does not confer an absolute right to decline to respond in a grand jury inquiry; the privilege does not negate the duty to testify but simply conditions that duty. The privilege cannot, for example, be asserted by a witness to protect others from possible criminal prosecution.... Nor can it be invoked simply to protect the witness' interest in privacy. "Ordinarily, of course, a witness has no right of privacy before the grand jury."...

The very availability of the Fifth Amendment privilege to grand jury witnesses, recognized by this Court in Counselman v. Hitchcock, 142 U.S. 547 (1892), suggests that occasions will often arise when potentially incriminating questions will be asked in the ordinary course of the jury's investigation. Probing questions to all types of witnesses is the stuff that grand jury investigations are made of; the grand jury's mission is, after all, to determine whether to make a presentment or return an indictment....

It is in keeping with the grand jury's historic function as a shield against arbitrary accusations to call before it persons suspected of criminal activity, so that the investigation can be complete. This is true whether the grand jury embarks upon an inquiry focused upon individuals suspected of wrongdoing, or is directed at persons suspected of no misconduct but who may be able to provide links in a chain of evidence relating to criminal conduct of others, or is centered upon broader problems of concern to society. It is entirely appropriate—indeed imperative—to summon individuals who may be able to illuminate the shadowy precincts of corruption and crime. Since the subject matter of the inquiry is crime, and often organized, systematic crime—as is true with drug traffic—it is unrealistic to assume that all of the witnesses capable of providing useful information will be pristine pillars of the community untainted by criminality.

* * *

Accordingly, the witness, though possibly engaged in some criminal enterprise, can be required to answer before a grand jury, so long as there is no compulsion to answer questions that are self-incriminating; the witness can, of course, stand on the privilege, assured that its protection "is as broad as the mischief against which it seeks to guard." Counselman v. Hitchcock, 142 U.S., at 562. The witness must invoke the privilege, however, as the "Constitution does not forbid the asking of criminative questions." United States v. Monia, 317 U.S., at 433 (Frankfurter, J., dissenting). . . . Absent a claim of the privilege, the duty to give testimony remains absolute.

The stage is therefore set when the question is asked. If the witness interposes his privilege, the grand jury has two choices. If the desired testimony is of marginal value, the grand jury can pursue other avenues of inquiry; if the testimony is thought sufficiently important, the grand jury can seek a judicial determination as to the bona fides of the witness' Fifth Amendment claim . . . in which case the witness must satisfy the presiding judge that the claim of privilege is not a subterfuge. If in fact "there is reasonable ground to apprehend danger to the witness from his being compelled to answer" . . . the prosecutor must then determine whether the answer is of such overriding importance as to justify a grant of immunity to the witness.

If immunity is sought by the prosecutor and granted by the presiding judge, the witness can then be compelled to answer, on pain of contempt, even though the testimony would implicate the witness in criminal activity. . . . Immunity is the Government's ultimate tool for securing testimony that otherwise would be protected; unless immunity is conferred, however, testimony may be suppressed, along with its fruits, if it is compelled over an appropriate claim of privilege. United States v. Blue, 384 U.S. 251, 255 (1966). On the other hand, when granted immunity, a witness once again owes the obligation imposed upon all citizens—the duty to give testimony—since immunity substitutes for the privilege.

In this constitutional process of securing a witness' testimony, perjury simply has no place whatever. Perjured testimony is an obvious and flagrant affront to the basic concepts of judicial proceedings. Effective restraints against this type of egregious offense are therefore imperative. The power of subpoena, broad as it is, and the power of contempt for refusing to answer, drastic as that is—and even the solemnity of the oath—cannot insure truthful answers. Hence, Congress has made the giving of false answers a criminal act punishable by severe penalties; in no other way can criminal conduct be flushed into the open where the law can deal with it.

Similarly, our cases have consistently—indeed without exception—allowed sanctions for false statements or perjury; they have done so even in instances where the perjurer complained that the Government exceeded its constitutional powers in making the inquiry. . . .

* * *

Even where a statutory scheme granted blanket immunity from further use of testimony the Court has found perjured statements to fall outside the grant. . . .

In this case, the Court of Appeals required the suppression of perjured testimony given by respondent. . . . The court reached this result because the prosecutor failed to give Miranda warnings at the outset of Mandujano's interrogation. Those warnings were required, in the Court of Appeals' view, because Mandujano was a "virtual" or "putative" defendant—that is, the prosecutor had specific information concerning Mandujano's participation in an attempted sale of heroin and the focus of the grand jury interrogation, as evidenced by the prosecutor's questions, centered on Mandujano's involvement in narcotics traffic. The fundamental error of the prosecutor, in the court's view, was to treat respondent in such a way as to "smack of entrapment"; as a consequence, the court concluded that "elemental fairness" required the perjured testimony to be suppressed.

The court's analysis, premised upon the prosecutor's failure to give Miranda warnings, erroneously applied the standards fashioned by this Court in Miranda. Those warnings were aimed at the evils seen by the Court as endemic to police interrogation of a person in custody. Miranda addressed extra-judicial confessions or admissions procured in a hostile, unfamiliar environment which lacked procedural safeguards. The decision expressly rested on the privilege against compulsory self-incrimination; the prescribed warnings sought to negate the "compulsion" thought to be inherent in police station interrogation. But the Miranda Court simply did not perceive judicial inquiries and custodial interrogation as equivalents: "... the compulsion to speak in the isolated setting of the police station may well be greater than in courts or other official investigations, where there are often impartial observers to guard against intimidation or trickery." Miranda, supra, at 461.

The Court thus recognized that many official investigations, such as grand jury questioning, take place in a setting wholly different from custodial police interrogation. ... To extend these concepts to questioning before a grand jury inquiring into criminal activity under the guidance of a judge is an extravagant expansion never remotely contemplated by this Court in Miranda; the dynamics of constitutional interpretation do not compel constant extension of every doctrine announced by the Court.

* * *

The warnings volunteered by the prosecutor to respondent in this case were more than sufficient to inform him of his rights—and his responsibilities—and particularly of the consequences of perjury. To extend the concepts of Miranda, as contemplated by the Court of Appeals, would require that the witness be told that there was an absolute right to silence, and obviously any such warning would be incorrect, for there is no such right before a grand jury. Under Miranda, a person in police custody has, of course, an absolute right to decline to answer any question, incriminating or innocuous ... whereas a grand jury witness, on the contrary, has an absolute duty to answer all questions, subject only to a valid Fifth Amendment claim. And even when the grand jury witness asserts the privilege, questioning need not cease, except as to the particular subject to which the privilege has been addressed....

Respondent was also informed that if he desired he could have the assistance of counsel, but that counsel could not be inside the grand jury room. That statement was plainly a correct recital of the law. No criminal proceedings had been instituted against respondent, hence the Sixth Amendment right to counsel had not come into play.... A witness "before a grand jury cannot insist, as a matter of constitutional right, on being represented by counsel...." In re Groban, 352 U.S., at 333. Under settled principles the witness may not insist upon

the presence of his attorney in the grand jury room. Fed. Rule Crim. Proc. 6(d).

Respondent, by way of further explanation, was also warned that he could be prosecuted for perjury if he testified falsely. Since respondent was already under oath to testify truthfully, this explanation was redundant; it served simply to emphasize the obligation already imposed by the oath.

* * *

Similarly, a witness subpoenaed to testify before a petit jury and placed under oath has never been entitled to a warning that, if he violates the solemn oath to "tell the truth," he may be subject to a prosecution for perjury, for the oath itself is the warning. Nor has any case been cited to us holding that the absence of such warnings before a petit jury provides a shield against use of false testimony in a subsequent prosecution for perjury or in contempt proceedings.

In any event, a witness sworn to tell the truth before a duly constituted grand jury will not be heard to call for suppression of false statements made to that jury, any more than would be the case with false testimony before a petit jury or other duly constituted tribunal....

The fact that here the grand jury interrogation had focused on some of respondent's specific activities does not require that these important principles be jettisoned; nothing remotely akin to "entrapment" or abuse of process is suggested by what occurred here.... Assuming, arguendo, that respondent was indeed a "putative defendant," that fact would have no bearing on the validity of a conviction for testifying falsely.

Respondent was free at every stage to interpose his constitutional privilege against self-incrimination, but perjury was not a permissible option....

The judgment of the Court of Appeals is therefore reversed, and the cause is remanded for further proceedings consistent with this opinion.

Reversed.

Mr. Justice BRENNAN, with whom Mr. Justice MARSHALL joins, concurring in the judgment.

I concur in the result reached by the Court, for "even when the privilege against self-incrimination permits an individual to refuse to answer questions asked by the Government, if false answers are given the individual may be prosecuted for making false statements." . . . Although the Fifth Amendment guaranteed respondent the right to refuse to answer the potentially incriminating questions put to him before the grand jury, in answering falsely he took "a course that the Fifth Amendment gave him no privilege to take." . . . "Our legal system provides methods for challenging the Government's right to ask questions—lying is not one of them." . . . Further, the record satisfies me that the respondent's false answers were not induced by governmental tactics or procedures so inherently unfair under all the circumstances as to constitute a prosecution for perjury a violation of the Due Process Clause of the Fifth Amendment.

* * *

[However], I would hold that, in the absence of an intentional and intelligent waiver by the individual of his known right to be free from compulsory self-incrimination, the Government may not call before a grand jury one whom it has probable cause—as measured by an objective standard—to suspect committed a crime, and by use of judicial compulsion compel him to testify with regard to that crime. In the absence of such a waiver, the Fifth Amendment requires that any testimony obtained in this fashion be unavailable to the Government for use at trial. Such a waiver could readily be demonstrated by proof that the individual was warned prior to questioning that he is currently subject to possible criminal prosecution for the commission of a stated crime, that he has a constitutional right to refuse to answer any and all questions that may tend to incriminate him, and by record evidence that the individual understood the nature of his situation and privilege prior to giving testimony.

* * *

Certainly to the extent that our task is to "weigh the potential benefits" to be derived from this requirement against the "potential injury to the role and functioning of the grand jury" . . . we must come down on the side of imposing this requirement if subversion of the adversary process is to be avoided where suspected persons are ignorant of their rights. In no way does the requirement of a knowing waiver "interfere with the effective and expeditious discharge of the grand jury's duties" . . . or "saddle a grand jury with minitrials and preliminary showings that would . . . impede its investigation"; or "delay and disrupt grand jury proceedings." . . . And plainly the requirements of an effective warning and an intelligent waiver by a putative defendant prior to attempts to elicit potentially incriminating information impose no onerous duty on the prosecutor. The reported decisions of the lower federal courts are replete with examples of prosecuting officials proffering such warnings as an essential element of our fundamental liberties. Where uncertain whether the situation requires it, the prosecutor may safely err on the side of ensuring the knowing and intentional nature of the waiver, for he does no more than discharge his responsibility to safeguard a constitutional guarantee calculated to ensure the liberty of us all. . . .

A . . . disturbing facet of the plurality opinion today is its statement that "[n]o criminal proceedings had been instituted against respondent, hence the Sixth Amendment right to counsel had not come into play." . . .

It is true that dictum in In re Groban, 352 U.S. 330, 333 (1957), denied there is any constitutional right of a witness to be represented by counsel when testifying before a grand jury. But neither Groban nor any other case in this Court has squarely presented the question. . . . Given the inherent danger of subversion of the adversary system in the case of a putative defendant called to testify before a grand jury, and the peculiarly critical role of the Fifth Amendment privilege as the bulwark against such abuse, it is plainly obvious that some guidance by counsel is required. This conclusion entertains only the "realistic recognition of the obvious truth that the average [putative] defendant does not have the professional legal skill to protect himself when brought before a tribunal . . . wherein the prosecution is [represented] by experienced and learned counsel." . . . Under such conditions it "would indeed be strange were this Court" to hold that a putative defendant, called before a grand jury and interrogated concerning the substance of the crime for which he is in imminent danger of being criminally charged, is simply to be left to "fend for himself." . . .

It may be that a putative defendant's Fifth Amendment privilege will be adequately preserved by a procedure whereby, in addition to warnings, he is told that he has a right to consult with an attorney prior to questioning, that if he cannot afford an attorney one will be appointed for him, that during the questioning he may have that attorney wait outside the grand jury room, and that he may at any and all times during questioning consult with the attorney prior to answering any question posed.... At least if such minimal protections were present, a putative defendant would be able to consult with counsel prior to answering any question that he might in any way suspect may incriminate him. Thereafter, if the privilege is invoked and contested, a hearing on the propriety of its invocation will take place in open court before an impartial judicial officer and the putative defendant will there have his counsel present.... If the invocation of the privilege is disallowed, the putative defendant will then have the opportunity to answer the question posed prior to the imposition of sanctions for contempt....

There is clearly no argument that a procedure allowing a putative defendant called to testify before a grand jury to consult at will with counsel outside the grand jury room prior to answering any given question would in any way impermissibly "delay and disrupt grand jury proceedings." United States v. Calandra, 414 U.S., at 349. This is clearly manifested by the plethora of reported instances in which just such procedures have been followed. Nor would such a procedure damage the constitutional "role and functioning of the grand jury," ... for the only effect on its investigative function is to secure a putative defendant's Fifth Amendment privilege and thereby avoid subversion of the adversary system.

It is of course unnecessary in this case to define the exact dimensions of the right to counsel since the testimony obtained by the grand jury interrogation was not introduced as evidence at respondent's trial on the charge concerning which he was questioned. I write only to make plain my disagreement with the implication in the plurality opinion that constitutional rights to counsel are not involved in a grand jury proceeding, and my disagreement with the further implication that there is a right to have counsel present for consultation outside the grand jury room but that it is not constitutionally derived and therefore may be enjoyed only by those wealthy enough to hire a lawyer....

Mr. Justice STEWART, with whom Mr. Justice BLACKMUN joins, concurring in the judgment.

The Fifth Amendment privilege against compulsory self-incrimination provides no protection for the commission of perjury.... The respondent's grand jury testimony is relevant only to his prosecution for perjury and was not introduced in the prosecution for attempting to distribute heroin. Since this is not a case where it could plausibly be argued that the perjury prosecution must be barred because of prosecutorial conduct amounting to a denial of due process, I would reverse the judgment without reaching the other issues explored in the CHIEF JUSTICE's opinion and by Mr. Justice BRENNAN in his separate opinion.

[Mr. Justice STEVENS took no part in the consideration or decision of this case.]

On the Horns of a Dilemma — Perjury and the Fifth Amendment

UNITED STATES v. WONG

Supreme Court of the United States, 1977
431 U.S. 174, 97 S. Ct. 1823, 52 L. Ed. 2d 231

The facts are contained in the opinion.

Mr. Chief Justice BURGER delivered the opinion of the Court.

We granted certiorari to decide whether a witness who is called to testify before a grand jury while under investigation for possible criminal activity, and who is later indicted for perjury committed before the grand jury is entitled to have the false testimony suppressed on the ground that no effective warning of the Fifth Amendment privilege to remain silent was given.

I

Rose Wong, the respondent, came to the United States from China in early childhood. She was educated in public schools in San Francisco, where she completed eight grades of elementary education. Because her husband does not speak English, respondent generally speaks in her native tongue in her household.

In September 1973 respondent was subpoenaed to testify before a federal grand jury in the Northern District of California. The grand jury was investigating illegal gambling and obstruction of state and local law enforcement in San Francisco. At the time of her grand jury appearance, the Government had received reports that respondent paid bribes to two undercover San Francisco police officers and agreed to make future payments to them. Before any interrogation began, respondent was advised of her Fifth Amendment privilege; she then denied having given money or gifts to police officers or having discussed gambling activities with them. It is undisputed that this testimony was false.

II

Respondent was indicted for perjury in violation of 18 U.S.C. § 1623. She moved to dismiss the indictment on the ground that, due to her limited command of English, she had not understood the warning of her right not to answer incriminating questions. At a suppression hearing, defense counsel called an interpreter and two language specialists as expert witnesses and persuaded the District Judge that respondent had not comprehended the prosecutor's explanation of the Fifth Amendment privilege; on the contrary, the court accepted respondent's testimony that she was required to answer all questions. Based upon informal oral findings to this effect, the District Court ordered the testimony suppressed as evidence of perjury.

Accepting the District Court's finding that respondent had not understood the warning, the Court of Appeals held that due process required suppression where "... the procedure employed by the government was fraught with the danger ... of placing [respondent] in the position of either perjuring or incriminating herself." 553 F.2d 576 (9th Cir. 1974). Absent effective warnings of the right to remain silent, the court concluded, a witness suspected of criminal involvement by the Government will" ... not understand the right to remain silent, and [will] be compelled by answering to subject himself to criminal liability." Id., at 578. In the Court of Appeals' view, the ineffectiveness of the prosecutor's warning meant that "the unfairness of procedures remained undissipated and due process requires the testimony be suppressed." Id., at 579.

Following our decision in United States v. Mandujano, [425 U.S. 564 (1976)], we granted certiorari. 426 U.S. 905 (1976). We now reverse.

III

Under findings which the Government does not challenge, respondent, in legal effect, was unwarned of her Fifth Amendment privilege. Resting on the finding that no effective warning was given, respondent contends that both the Fifth Amendment privilege and Fifth Amendment due process require suppression of her false testimony. As to her claim under the Fifth Amendment testimonial privilege, respondent argues that, without effective warnings, she was in effect forced by the Government to answer all questions, and that her choice was confined either to incriminating herself or lying under oath. From this premise, she contends that such testimony, even if knowingly false, is inadmissible against her as having been obtained in violation of the constitutional privilege. With respect to her due process claim, she contends and the Court of Appeals held, that absent warnings a witness is placed in the dilemma of engaging either in self-incrimination or perjury, a situation so inherently unfair as to require suppression of perjured testimony. We reject both contentions.

As our holding in Mandujano makes clear, and indeed as the Court of Appeals recognized, the Fifth Amendment privilege does not condone perjury. It grants a privilege to remain silent without risking contempt, but it "does not endow the person who testifies with a license to commit perjury." Glickstein v. United States, 222 U.S. 139, 142 (1911). The failure to provide a warning of the privilege, in addition to the oath to tell the truth, does not call for a different result. The contention is that warnings inform the witness of the availability of the privilege and thus eliminate the claimed dilemma of self-incrimination or perjury. Cf. Garner v. United States, 424 U.S. 648, 657–658 (1976). However, in United States v. Knox, 396 U.S. 77 (1969), the Court held that even the predicament of being forced to choose between incriminatory truth and falsehood, as opposed to refusing to answer, does not justify perjury. In that case, a taxpayer was charged with filing false information on a federal wagering tax return. At the time of the offense, federal law commanded the filing of a tax return even though the effect of that requirement, in some circumstances, was to make it a crime not to supply the requested information to the Government. To justify the deliberate falsehood contained in his tax return, Knox, like respondent here, argued that the false statements were not made voluntarily, but were compelled by the tax laws and therefore violated the Fifth Amendment. The Court rejected that contention. Although it recognized that tax laws which compelled filing the returns injected an "element of pressure into Knox's predicament at the time he filed the forms," id., at 82, the Court held that by answering falsely the taxpayer took "a course that the Fifth Amendment gave him no privilege to take." Ibid.

In this case respondent stands in no better position than Knox; her position, in fact, is weaker since respondent's refusal to give inculpatory answers, unlike Knox, would not have constituted a crime. It follows that our holding in Mandujano, that the Fifth Amendment privilege does not protect perjury, is equally applicable to this case.

Respondent also relies on the Court of Appeals' holding that the failure to inform a prospective defendant of the constitutional privilege of silence at the time of a grand jury appearance is so fundamentally unfair as to violate due process. In the Court of Appeals' view, the Government's conduct in this case, although in good faith, so thwarted the adversary model of our criminal justice system as to require suppression of the testimony in any subsequent perjury case based on the falsity of the sworn statement. We disagree.

First, the "unfairness" urged by respondent was also present in the taxpayer's predicament in Knox, yet the Court there found no constitutional infirmity in the taxpayer's conviction for making false statements on his returns. Second, accepting arguendo respondent's argument as to the dilemma posed in the grand jury procedures here, perjury is nevertheless not a permissible alternative. The "unfairness" perceived by the respondent is not the act of calling a prospective defendant to testify before a grand jury but rather the failure effectively to inform a prospective defendant of the Fifth Amendment privilege. Thus, the core of respondent's due process argument, and of the Court of Appeals' holding, in reality relates to the protection of values served by the Fifth Amendment privilege, a privilege which does not protect perjury.

Finally, to characterize these proceedings as "unfair" by virtue of inadequate Fifth Amendment warnings is essentially to say that the Government acted unfairly or oppressively by asking searching questions of a witness uninformed of the privilege. But, as the Court has consistently held, perjury is not a permissible way of objecting to the Government's questions. "Our legal system provides methods for challenging the Government's right to ask questions—lying is not one of them." Bryson v. United States, 396 U.S. 64, 72 (1969); United States v. Mandujano, supra, at 577, 585 (Brennan, J., concurring in the judgment), 609 (Stewart, J., concurring in the judgment). Indeed, even if the Government could, on pain of criminal sanctions, compel an answer to its incriminating questions, a citizen is not at liberty to answer falsely. United States v. Knox, supra, at 82–83. If the citizen answers the question, the answer must be truthful.

The judgment of the Court of Appeals is reversed and the case is remanded for further proceedings consistent with this opinion.

Reversed and remanded.

Warning a Potential Defendant

UNITED STATES v. WASHINGTON

Supreme Court of the United States, 1977
431 U.S. 181, 97 S. Ct. 1814, 52 L. Ed. 2d 238

Gregory Washington, the respondent, who was suspected of possible implication in the theft of a motorcycle, was subpoenaed to appear before a federal grand jury in the District of Columbia. The prosecutor did not advise Washington before his appearance that he might be indicted for the theft. However, he was given a series of warnings, one of which was that he had a right to remain silent. Washington nevertheless testified and subsequently was indicted for the theft. The Superior Court for the District of Columbia suppressed the testimony and dismissed the indictment, holding that before the government could use respondent's grand jury testimony at trial it first had to demonstrate that the respondent had knowingly waived his privilege against compulsory self-incrimination. The District of Columbia Court of Appeals affirmed the suppression order, holding that the prosecutor should have advised respondent that he was a potential defendant and that the warnings should have been given prior to the grand jury hearing. 328 A.2d 98 (1974). The United States Supreme Court granted certiorari.

Mr. Chief Justice BURGER delivered the opinion of the Court.

The question presented in this case is whether testimony given by a grand jury witness suspected of wrongdoing may be used against him in a later prosecution for a substantive criminal offense when the witness was not informed in advance of his testimony that he is a potential defendant in danger of indictment.

*   *   *

[T]his Court has not decided that the grand jury setting presents coercive elements which compel witnesses to incriminate themselves. Nor have we decided whether any Fifth Amendment warnings whatever are constitutionally required for grand jury witnesses; moreover, we have no occasion to decide these matters today, for even assuming that the grand jury setting exerts some pressures on witnesses generally or on those who may later be indicted, the comprehensive warnings respondent received in this case plainly satisfied any possible claim to warnings. Accordingly, respondent's grand jury testimony may properly be used against him in a subsequent trial for theft of the motorcycle.

Although it is well settled that the Fifth Amendment privilege extends to grand jury proceedings, Counselman v. Hitchcock, 142 U.S. 547 (1892), it is also axiomatic that the Amendment does not automatically preclude self-incrimination, whether spontaneous or in response to questions put by government officials. "It does not preclude a witness from testifying voluntarily in matters which may incriminate him," United States v. Monia, 317 U.S. 424, 427 (1943), for "those competent and freewilled to do so may give evidence against the whole world, themselves included." United States v. Kimball, 117 F. 156, 163 (C.C.S.D.N.Y. 1902); accord, Miranda [v. Arizona, 384 U.S. 436 (1966)] . . . , at 478; Michigan v. Tucker, 417 U.S. 433 (1974); Hoffa v. United States, 385 U.S. 293 (1966). Indeed, far from being prohibited by the Constitution, admissions of guilt by wrongdoers, if not coerced, are inherently desirable. In addition to guaranteeing the right to remain silent unless immunity is granted, the Fifth Amendment proscribes only self-incrimination obtained by a "genuine compulsion of testimony." Michigan v. Tucker, supra, at 440. Absent some officially coerced self-accusation, the Fifth Amendment privilege is not violated by even the most damning admissions. Accordingly, unless the record reveals some compulsion, respondent's incriminating testimony cannot conflict with any constitutional guarantees of the privilege.

The Constitution does not prohibit every element which influences a criminal suspect to make incriminating admissions. . . . The constitutional guarantee is only that the witness be not *compelled* to give self-incriminating testimony. The test is whether, considering the totality of the circumstances, the free will of the witness was overborne. Rogers v. Richmond, 365 U.S. 534, 544 (1961).

After being sworn, respondent was explicitly advised that he had a right to remain silent and that any statements he did make could be used to convict him of crime. It is inconceivable that such a warning would fail to alert him to his right to refuse to answer any question which might incriminate him. This advice also eliminated any possible compulsion to self-incrimination which might otherwise exist. To suggest otherwise is to ignore the record and reality. Indeed, it seems self-evident that one who is told he is free to refuse to answer questions is in a curious posture to later complain that his answers were compelled. Moreover, any possible coercion or unfairness resulting from a witness' misimpression that he must answer truthfully even questions with incriminatory aspects is completely removed by the warnings given here. Even in the presumed psychologically coercive atmosphere of police custodial interrogation, Miranda does not require that any additional warnings be given simply because the suspect is a potential defendant; indeed, such suspects are potential defendants more often than not. United States v. Binder, 453 F.2d 805, 810 (2d Cir. 1971), cert. denied, 407 U.S. 920 (1972).

* * *

Respondent points out that unlike one subject to custodial interrogation, whose arrest should inform him only too clearly that he is a potential criminal defendant, a grand jury witness may well be unaware that he is targeted for possible prosecution. While this may be so in some situations, it is an overdrawn generalization. In any case, events here clearly put respondent on notice that he was a suspect in the motorcycle theft. He knew that the grand jury was investigating that theft and that his involvement was known to the authorities. Respondent was made abundantly aware that his exculpatory version of events had been disbelieved by the police officer, and that his friends, whose innocence his own story supported, were to be prosecuted for the theft. The interview with the prosecutor put him on additional notice that his implausible story was not accepted as true. The warnings he received in the grand jury room served further to alert him to his own potential criminal liability. In sum, by the time he testified respondent knew better than anyone else of his potential defendant status.

However, all of this is largely irrelevant since we do not understand what constitutional disadvantage a failure to give potential defendant warnings could possibly inflict on a grand jury witness, whether or not he has received other warnings. It is firmly settled that the prospect of being indicted does not entitle a witness to commit perjury, and witnesses who are not grand jury targets are protected from compulsory self-incrimination to the same extent as those who are. Because target witness status neither enlarges nor diminishes the constitutional protection against compelled self-incrimination, potential defendant warnings add nothing of value to protection of Fifth Amendment rights.

The judgment of the Court of Appeals is reversed, and the cause is remanded for further proceedings not inconsistent with this opinion.

Reversed.

Mr. Justice BRENNAN, with whom Mr. Justice MARSHALL joins, dissenting.

The general rule that a witness must affirmatively claim the privilege against compulsory self-incrimination must in my view admit of an exception in the case of a grand jury witness whom the prosecutor interrogates with the express purpose of getting evidence upon which to base a criminal charge against him. In such circumstances, even warnings before interrogation of his right to silence do not suffice. The privilege is emptied of substance unless the witness is further advised by the prosecutor that he is a potential defendant. Only if the witness then nevertheless intentionally and intelligently waives his right to be free from compulsory self-incrimination and submits to further interrogation should use of his grand jury testimony against him be sanctioned. . . .

* * *

The ancient privilege of a witness against being compelled to incriminate himself is precious to free men as a shield against high-handed and arrogant inquisitorial practices. It has survived centuries of controversies, periodically kindled by popular impatience that its protection sometimes allows the guilty to escape punishment. But it has endured as a wise and necessary protection of the individual against arbitrary power, and the price of occasional failures of justice is pain in the larger interest of general personal security.

I would hold that a failure to warn the witness that he is a potential defendant is fatal to an indictment of him when it is made unmistakably to appear, as here, that the grand jury inquiry became an investigation directed against the witness and was pursued with the purpose of compelling him to give self-incriminating testimony upon which to indict him. I would further hold that without such prior warning and the witness' subsequent voluntary waiver of his privilege, there is such gross encroachment upon the witness' privilege as to render worthless the values protected by it unless the self-incriminating testimony is unavailable to the Government for use at any trial brought pursuant to even a valid indictment.

It should be remarked that of course today's decision applies only to application of the privilege against self-incrimination secured by the Fifth Amendment to the United States Constitution. The holding does not affect the authority of state courts to construe counterpart provisions of state constitutions—even identically phrased provisions—"to give the individual greater protection than is provided" by the federal provision. State v. Johnson, 68 N.J. 349, 353, 346 A.2d 66, 67–68 (1975). See generally Brennan, "State Constitutions and the Protection of Individual Rights," 90 Harv. L. Rev. 489 (1977).

Comments

1. *Costello* v. *United States,* supra, established the rule that a defendant can be indicted by a federal grand jury solely on the basis of hearsay evidence—even though the hearsay would not be admissible at a subsequent trial. The constitutional protections that safeguard grand jury witnesses and potential defendants are few. For a long time, the Supreme Court asserted that Fourth Amendment rights need not be sacrificed in a grand jury investigation. However, recent cases have underscored the conflict between the grand jury's investigative powers and a citizen's right to be free from unreasonable searches and seizures. In 1970, Congress passed the Omnibus Crime Control and Safe Streets Act (18 U.S.C. §§ 2510–2520). Title III of the act provided for judicial authorization of wiretapping but made unauthorized wiretaps illegal and their fruits (products) inadmissible in any proceeding, including grand jury hearings. In *Gelbard* v. *United States,* 408 U.S. 41 (1972), the Court held that a grand jury witness can refuse to answer questions that are based on information that was the fruit of illegal electronic surveillance. However, in other Fourth Amendment cases, the Court has been less generous to grand jury witnesses. In *United States* v. *Mara,* 410 U.S. 19 (1973), the Court held that compelling a grand jury witness to furnish a sample of his handwriting was not a "seizure" within the meaning of the Fourth Amendment and that the government was not required to make a preliminary showing of "reasonableness" in requiring the exemplar since one's handwriting is a physical characteristic constantly exposed to the public. Similarly, the Court has held that a grand jury witness cannot refuse, on Fourth Amendment grounds, to furnish an exemplar of his voice to a grand jury, *United States* v. *Dionisio,* 410 U.S. 1 (1973).

In *United States* v. *Calandra,* supra, a divided Court held that the exclusionary rule is not applicable to grand jury proceedings and that a grand jury witness cannot refuse to answer questions on the ground that they are based on the products of an illegal search and seizure. Do you agree with the statement by the Court that the exclusionary rule would "unduly interfere with the effective and expeditious discharge of the grand jury's duties" or with the dissenting view that a "downgrading" of the exclusionary rule threatens to make the Fourth Amendment a "dead letter"? Refer to *Stone* v. *Powell,* Chapter Five, § 5.03.

2. In the federal courts, a witness' counsel is not permitted to be present in the grand jury room, and a similar rule exists in most other jurisdictions. However, the grand jury witness is allowed to consult with his attorney outside the grand jury room. This rule is designed to prevent a disruption of the grand jury process by the witness' lawyer (see Comment 3, infra). The absence of counsel at the grand jury proceeding may lead a witness, because of his unfamiliarity with the law, to inadvertently waive his constitutional rights. Once a witness has answered any questions, even if inadvertently, he can be cited for contempt if he then claims the privilege against self-incrimination for an area that he has opened up by his testimony. Accordingly, most attorneys advise their clients, when the privilege is to be invoked, to "take the Fifth" in response to *all* questions asked (even if only their name and address) to prevent an inadvertent waiver of the privilege.

3. As mentioned, the traditional rule is that a grand jury witness does not have a Sixth Amendment right to have counsel with him in the grand jury room. This rule was reinforced by the 1957 decision *In re Groban,* 352 U.S. 330, in which Mr. Justice Reed, speaking for a five man majority, stated, "A witness before a grand jury cannot insist, as a matter of constitutional right, on being represented by his counsel, nor can a witness before other investigatory bodies," at 333. However, *Groban* involved a proceeding conducted by a state fire marshall to determine the causes of a fire, and therefore the statement that counsel is not required at grand jury proceedings is dictum. In addition, Justice Brennan is the only member of the present Court who participated in the *Groban* decision and post-*Groban* pronouncements by the Supreme Court extending the right to counsel to other stages of the criminal process appear to have reopened the issue of the right to counsel at grand jury proceedings. See, e.g., Comment, *Right to Counsel in Grand Jury Proceedings,* 26 Wash. & Lee L. Rev. 97 (1969). However, in light of the trend of the Burger Court to refuse to extend the right of counsel to other stages of the criminal process (e.g., preindictment lineups, parole revocation hearings, prison disciplinary hearings, summary courts-martial, photographic identification displays, and subsequent appeals following a first appeal as a matter of right — see Chapter Seven), the argument favoring counsel at grand jury proceedings is not likely, at this time, to persuade a majority of the justices of the Burger Court.

    In many jurisdictions, the grand jury witness is allowed to consult with counsel outside the confines of the grand jury room. The decision of the New York Court of Appeals in *People* v. *Ianniello,* 255 N.E.2d 439 (1968), raises questions concerning the existence and scope of a grand jury witness' right to consult with counsel outside the grand jury room. There the defendant was subpoenaed to appear before the grand jury as a witness in connection with an investigation of a bribery conspiracy involving the police and officials of the New York State Liquor Authority. At the outset Ianniello refused to be sworn on the ground that he was a defendant in a pending criminal prosecution. The prosecutor, Mr. Scotti, informed Ianniello that he had been called solely in the role of a witness in a bribery conspiracy investigation and that the grand jury had voted to confer immunity upon him. When questioned by the prosecutor about certain conversations with a person under investigation, Ianniello answered that he could not recall such conversations. Pressed by the prosecutor to confirm or deny that the conversations took place, the defendant asked to be allowed to leave the grand jury room to consult with his attorney to determine the propriety of the question. The request was denied, and the prosecutor suggested that they go into open court and make an application for a ruling on the propriety of the question. The colloquy went as follows:*

Q. Does that enable you to be able to deny ever having such a conversation with Benny Cohen? A. Could I excuse myself to see my attorney for a minute?

By Mr. Scotti:

Q. Your attorney doesn't know the answer. You are the one who knows. A. I want to ask him if it's a proper question.

Q. I'm telling you, as legal advisor to this grand jury, it's a proper question. A. May I ask the foreman of the grand jury if I may excuse myself for a minute, please?

Q. Mr. Ianniello, we are not going to consent to the practice of your excusing yourself to confer ostensibly with your attorney in order to find out what kind of an answer you should make. You are the one that is legally obligated to give testimony and not your attorney.

Now, are you refusing to answer the question? A. I'm not refusing.

Q. After you answer the question you can confer— A. I'd like to confer with my attorney because I think it's an improper question.

Q. Why? A. I don't know.

Q. Why? Why is it improper? You said you think it's improper. A. I wouldn't need an attorney outside if I knew why. I think it's an improper question.

Q. Why do you think it's improper, why? A. I don't know why.

Q. Because it's a very, very serious matter. It involves your knowledge of payoffs, your knowledge of the fact that you were receiving information, confidential information from certain members of the Police Department, is that the reason why it bothers you? A. Mr. Scotti—

Q. You are on the spot, is that the reason? Is that the reason why you hesitate because an answer to that question, an affirmative answer, would mean to this grand jury that you are admitting that you do have information from the police and that you do business with the police? Is that what you are worried about? Is that what you are— A. Mr. Scotti, you are drawing conclusions. You made your statements, you might as well indict me. You have all the evidence.

---

*Petitioner's brief for certiorari at 8–9. Cert. denied, 393 U.S. 827 (1968).

Q. Why don't you want to answer the question? A. There is no use to go any further unless I consult my attorney.

The Witness: Mr. Foreman, do I have your permission to leave this room and consult my attorney?

Mr. Scotti: Shall we go to court for a direction?

The Witness: Go to court. I don't understand the question.

Mr. Scotti: We will go in open court, then, and make an application. You don't understand the question. Mr. Reporter, read the question.

The Witness: I didn't—

Mr. Scotti: Now, he said he doesn't understand the question.

The Witness: I didn't say—I said, "Will you please repeat the question." Don't jump to conclusions.

Mr. Scotti: Read the question. Mr. Reporter, will you be good enough to read what the witness said a little while ago.

[Whereupon, the reporter read as follows:

"Question: Why don't you want to answer the question? Answer: There is no use to go any further unless I consult my attorney.

The Witness: Mr. Foreman, do I have your permission to leave this room and consult my attorney?

Mr. Scotti: Shall we go to court for a direction?

The Witness: Go to court. I don't understand the question.

Mr. Scotti: We will go in open court, then, and make an application."]

Q. Now, has your memory been refreshed that you said you didn't understand the question? A. Yes, sir.

Q. We accept your apology. A. Thank you.

Q. Now, are you willing to answer the question?

The Witness: Mr. Foreman, may I please leave the room to consult with my attorney as to the significance of the question?

The Foreman: I can't give you permission to do so without consent of Mr. Scotti.

Mr. Scotti: I advise the grand jury that this is a proper question and that there is no legal question involved.

Now, Mr. Foreman, I ask that you direct this witness to answer the question.

The Foreman: I so direct you to answer.

A. I don't recall the conversation.

Ianniello was indicted for contempt on the basis of his evasive testimony. The indictment was upheld by the New York Court of Appeals on the ground that, although a grand jury witness has a right to consult with his attorney concerning questions of "legal rights," he has no right to consult his attorney concerning "matters of strategy." The court stated that the phrase "legal rights" includes such things as (1) the decision to assert or waive the privilege against self-incrimination, (2) the right to refuse to answer improper questions (i.e., those having no relevancy to the subject of the investigation), and (3) the right to refuse to answer a question involving a testimonial privilege (e.g., attorney-client, husband-wife, physician-patient), 235 N.E.2d at 443.

Federal Judge Wilkey has noted that the coming and going of a grand jury witness makes a "mockery" of the grand jury system. In one proceeding he noted that "at one point the witness left the grand jury room at 1:59 p.m., returned at 3:48 p.m., was asked the same question, again left the room, and finally, on her return, read a prepared statement raising every conceivable objection," *In re Evans,* 452 F.2d 1239, 1253 (D.C. Cir. 1971) (dissenting opinion). But one commentator has noted that the grand jury witness without counsel is subjected to a "cruel trilemma" "patently unfair to the witness" in which the witness can (1) incriminate himself, (2) risk a perjury prosecution, or (3) subject himself to a contempt finding. See Boudin, *The Federal Grand Jury,* 61 Georgetown L.J. 1, 16–17 (1972). It is perhaps noteworthy that England, the mother of the grand jury system, abolished that institution in 1933. Plucknett, *A Concise History of the Common Law* 112, n.1 (5th ed. 1956).

4. During the last decade, the expansive use of the grand jury for investigation into allegedly dissident political groups has become a focus of concern for legal commentators and scholars. It is said that the subpoena power of the grand jury is being used to subvert the First Amendment rights of citizens—specifically, freedom of speech, press, and assembly. The Supreme Court has held on many occasions that First Amendment rights have a preferred position in the hierarchy of constitutional rights and that any governmental actions that have a "chilling effect" on these guarantees are subject to judicial intervention.

The grand jury investigations of the Black Panthers, Weathermen, and other dissident groups have posed First Amendment problems because of the breadth and scope of their inquiries. It has been charged that the Nixon administration abused the power of the grand jury process to further the political status of the executive branch of government, Clark, *The Grand Jury: Use and Abuse of Political Power* (1975). Many Americans are not aware of the constitutional challenges posed by the grand jury process. This is understandable in view of the fact that most of the publicity given grand jury proceedings has focused on the successful indictments of such public figures as the Watergate defendants and Patricia Hearst, while the harassment of ordinary citizens by grand juries has often gone unreported. For a laymen's view of these complex issues, see Harris, *Freedom Spent* (1976).

Branzburg v. *Hayes,* supra, represents the most celebrated case involving a clash between the First Amendment right of a newspaper reporter to protect his news sources and the necessity for a grand jury investigation. Do you agree with the statement of the Court majority that "[there appears to be] no basis why the public interest in law enforcement and in insuring effective grand jury proceedings is insufficient to override the consequential, but uncertain, burden on news gathering" or with the dissenting view that "the Court thus invites state and federal authorities to undermine the historic independence of the press by attempting to annex the journalistic profession as an investigative arm of government"?

5. *Alexander* v. *Louisiana,* supra, provides an excellent summary of previous cases dealing with racial discrimination in the selection of grand jurors. The Court noted that the selection process must employ "racially neutral" procedures. Is it possible for a defendant to demonstrate a prima facie case of invidious racial discrimination based on statistical improbability if the selection process is racially neutral? The Court has seemed much more interested in the selection process used than in the resulting ratio of white and black jurors. The Court noted that once a prima facie case of invidious racial discrimination is presented, the burden is on the state to

overcome this evidence and prove that the selection criteria utilized were racially neutral. Is it likely, or even possible, that the state could prove racial nondiscrimination after a defendant demonstrated a prima facie case of invidious racial discrimination? In *Peters* v. *Kiff*, 407 U.S. 493 (1972), the Court held that a white defendant is entitled to judicial relief upon proof that blacks have been systematically excluded from the state grand and petit juries that indicted and convicted him. The Court also held that the random cross section of the community requirement for petit jurors is also applicable to grand jurors.

6. The following is a facsimile of a "true bill" grand jury indictment:

IN THE CIRCUIT COURT OF THE _____ JUDICIAL CIRCUIT IN AND FOR _____ COUNTY STATE OF FLORIDA THE _____ DAY OF JULY, 19_____.

THE STATE OF FLORIDA   :

                                    NO. _____

            V.   :

                                DIVISION _____

    [Name of Defendant]   :

IN THE NAME AND BY THE AUTHORITY OF THE STATE OF FLORIDA:

The Grand Jurors of the County of _____, State of Florida, charge that [name of defendant] on the _____ day of July, 19_____, in the County and State aforesaid, unlawfully and from a premeditated design to effect the death of [name of victim] did murder the said [name of victim] by stabbing him to death with a knife, a more detailed description of which knife is to the Grand Jurors unknown, contrary to the form of the Statute in such case made and provided, to-wit: Florida Statute 782.04.

****
   INDICTMENT FOR FIRST DEGREE MURDER
****

   A TRUE BILL:

_____

   Foreman of the Grand Jury

   A NO TRUE BILL:

_____

   Foreman of the Grand Jury

I, _____, State Attorney for the _____ Judicial Circuit in and for _____ County, State of Florida, do hereby aver, as authorized and required by law, that I have acted in an advisory capacity to the Grand Jurors of _____ County previous to their returning the above indictment in the above styled cause.

_____

   State Attorney

7. In *United States* v. *Mandujano,* supra, a plurality of the Court refused to extend the requirements of *Miranda* to a "putative" (virtual) defendant at a grand jury proceeding, and all the justices agreed that even absent such warnings false testimony given before a grand jury is admissible at a subsequent perjury trial, a holding further explicated in *United States* v. *Wong,* supra. *Mandujano,* however, did not specifically decide the question whether there are any conditions under which *Miranda* warnings — or any warnings (e.g., of the privilege against self-incrimination) — might be required of putative defendants subpoenaed to testify before a grand jury. The plurality suggests that *Miranda* warnings are not required under any circumstances. Do you agree with this conclusion? Suppose an illiterate putative defendant is subpoenaed to testify before a grand jury and is given no warnings whatsoever and makes incriminating, but truthful, statements. Is that arguably the kind of prosecutorial misconduct referred to in *Mandujano*? Do illiterate putative defendants "assume the risk" of subsequent prosecution by testifying notwithstanding their ignorance of the privilege against self-incrimination? Is it fundamentally fair that the uninformed must suffer because of their ignorance? Are some constitutional rights available only to the educated and knowledgeable? Mr. Justice Brennan (joined by Marshall, J., concurring) suggested that some "minimal" warnings should be given to putative defendants, although he did not go so far as to suggest that full *Miranda* warnings are required. Do you agree with that view? Is the subpoenaed grand jury witness subjected to "custodial interrogation" within the meaning of *Miranda*? Can it be said that a grand jury proceeding is "highly coercive"? Do you agree with Justices Brennan and Marshall that the right to counsel attaches to grand jury proceedings? A plurality of the Court assumed a negative answer. In a substantial number (albeit a minority) of jurisdictions, counsel is permitted at grand jury hearings (outside the grand jury room). Mr. Justice Brennan listed those jurisdictions as: *United States* v. *George,* 444 F.2d 310, 315 (6th Cir. 1971) (right to consult with attorney "after every question"); *United States* v. *Weinberg,* 439 F.2d 743, 745 (9th Cir. 1971) (right to confer with attorney exercised "after almost every question"); *United States* v. *Capaldo,* 402 F.2d 821, 824 (2nd Cir. 1968), cert. denied, 394 U.S. 989 (1969) (permitted to consult with counsel "whenever he so desired"); *United States* v. *Isaacs,* 347 F. Supp. 743, 759 (N.D. Ill. 1972) ("provided every opportunity to consult with counsel"); *Application of Caldwell,* 311 F. Supp. 358, 362 (N.D. Cal. 1970) (permitted to consult with counsel "at any time he wishes"); *United States* v. *Di Sapio,* 299 F. Supp. 436, 440 (S.D.N.Y. 1969) ("could consult with counsel during the interrogation if he so desired"); *United States* v. *Leighton,* 265 F. Supp. 27, 37 (S.D.N.Y. 1967) (right to consult with counsel "at any time he chose"); *United States* v. *Hoffa,* 156 F. Supp. 495, 512 (S.D.N.Y. 1957) ("given every opportunity to consult with [his] lawyer"). See also *Levine* v. *United States,* 362 U.S. 610, 611 (1960); *United States* v. *Nickels,* 502 F.2d 1173 (7th Cir., 1974), *United States* v. *Daniels,* 461 F.2d 1076, 1077 (5th Cir. 1972); *Perrone* v. *United States,* 416 F.2d 464, 466 (2d Cir. 1969); *United States* v. *Corallo,* 413 F.2d 1306, 1328 (2d Cir.), cert. denied, 396 U.S. 958 (1969); *United States* v. *Di Michele,* 375 F.2d

959, 960 (3d Cir.), cert. denied, 389 U.S. 838 (1967); *United States* v. *Irwin*, 354 F.2d 192, 199 (2d Cir. 1965); cert. denied, 383 U.S. 967 (1966); *Kitchell* v. *United States*, 354 F.2d 715, 720 (1st Cir.), cert. denied, 384 U.S. 1011 (1966); *United States* v. *Tramunti*, 343 F.2d 548, 551 (2d Cir. 1965), vacated 384 U.S. 886 (1966); *United States* v. *Kane*, 243 F. Supp. 746, 753 (S.D.N.Y. 1965); *United States* v. *Grunewald*, 164 F. Supp. 640, 641–642, at n.21 (S.D.N.Y. 1958).

8. In addition, many jurisdictions require that all grand jury witnesses be informed of their privilege against self-incrimination prior to testifying. These jurisdictions include: *United States* v. *Washington*, 328 A.2d 98, 100 (Ct. App. D.C. 1974), (requiring a knowing and intelligent waiver of the privilege by a "potential" defendant); *United States* v. *Luxenberg*, 374 F.2d 241, 246 (6th Cir. 1967) (warning concerning the privilege required for one "virtually in the position of a defendant"); *United States* v. *Orta*, 253 F.2d 312, 314 (5th Cir.), cert. denied, 357 U.S. 905 (1958) (knowing and intelligent waiver of privilege required for "a witness"); *Stanley* v. *United States*, 245 F.2d 427, 434 (6th Cir. 1957) (protection afforded a defendant in custody extended to witnesses "virtually in the position of a defendant"); *United States* v. *Pepe*, 367 F. Supp. 1365, 1369 (Conn. 1973) (warning required for a "potential" defendant); *In re Kelly*, 350 F. Supp. 1198, 1205 (E.D. Ark. 1972) (warning required if "even a remote possibility of prosecution"); *United States* v. *Kreps*, 349 F. Supp. 1049, 1053–1054 (W.D. Wis. 1972) (*Miranda* warnings required for "prime suspect"); *United States* v. *Fruchtman*, 282 F. Supp. 534, 536 (N.D. Ohio 1968) (warning required for one "virtually in the position of a defendant"); *Mattox* v. *Carson*, 295 F. Supp. 1054, 1059 (M.D. Fla. 1969) (*Miranda* warnings required for "potential defendants"), rev'd on other grounds, 424 F.2d 202 (5th Cir.), cert. denied, 400 U.S. 822 (1970); *United States* v. *Haim*, 218 F. Supp. 922, 932 (S.D.N.Y. 1963) (warning required for "potential" defendant); *United States* v. *Di Grazia*, 213 F. Supp. 232, 234 (N.D. Ill. 1963) (warning and execution of formal waiver required for "any witness"); *United States* v. *Grossman*, 154 F. Supp. 813, 816 (N.J. 1957) (warning required at least for "target" defendant). See also *Powell* v. *United States*, 96 U.S. App. D.C. 367, 226 F.2d 269, 274 (1955) (serious constitutional question whether prosecutor may call before grand jury "person against whom an indictment is being sought"); *United States* v. *Scully*, 225 F.2d 113, 116 (2d Cir.), cert. denied, 350 U.S. 897 (1955) ("suppos[ing] . . . as a matter of ethics or fair play or policy, a prosecutor would . . . refrain from calling as a witness before a grand jury any person who is de jure or de facto an accused"); id., at 117 (Frank, J., concurring) (suggesting a warning for any person called whom the prosecutor intends to indict); *United States* v. *Grunewald*, 233 F.2d 556, 576 n.10 (2d Cir. 1956) (Frank, J., dissenting) rev'd., 353 U.S. 391 (1957) (warning required for any witness); *Connelly* v. *United States*, 249 F.2d 576, 581 (8th Cir. 1957), cert. denied, 356 U.S. 921 (1958) (ap-

proving the suppression of all testimony, even in presence of warnings, after point at which prosecutor decided to indict); *United States* v. *Nickels*, 502 F.2d 1173, 1176 (7th Cir., 1974) (*Miranda* warning required by implication for "potential defendant"); *Kitchell* v. *United States*, 354 F.2d 715, 720 (1st Cir.), cert. denied, 384 U.S. 1011 (1966) (warning required by implication for person "clearly suspected"); *United States* v. *Di Sapio*, 299 F. Supp. 436, 440, at n.19 (S.D.N.Y. 1969) (warning required by implication for "target" defendant).

9. Consider the following problems involving the grand jury process: Does a prosecutor have an affirmative duty to inform the grand jury of any evidence favorable to a potential indictee? See *Johnson* v. *Superior Court*, 539 P.2d 792 (Cal. 1975) (holding yes). Does a prosecutor have authority to ignore a grand jury's indictment and file a bill of information charging a higher grade offense than that charged by the grand jury? See *Dresner* v. *County Court*, 540 P.2d 1085 (Colo. 1975) (holding yes). Does a state official subpoenaed to testify before a federal grand jury and fully warned of his privilege against self-incrimination have a Fifth Amendment privilege against the state's use of his testimony to indict him on state charges? See *State* v. *Wallace*, 321 So. 2d 349 (La. 1975) (holding no privilege). Does a potential indictee have a right to have his grand jury testimony recorded and transcribed at his own expense and made available to him? See *Lawless* v. *Commonwealth*, 539 S.W.2d 101 (Ky. 1976) (holding no). May a reporter refuse to answer grand jury's questions about her source of information when the purpose was to plug grand jury leaks and not to discover information needed in a criminal investigation? See *Morgan* v. *State*, 337 So.2d 951 (Fla. 1976) (holding answers not required). May a grand jury indict a defendant on the basis of hearsay testimony of a police officer who testified on behalf of eight witnesses who were out of state? See *State* v. *Gieffels*, 554 P.2d 460 (Alaska 1976) (holding no, absent a compelling justification for its use). Is a grand jury illegally constituted because a member of the grand jury that indicted a murder defendant was awaiting trial on three criminal charges? See *Stevens* v. *State*, 354 N.E.2d 727 (Ind. 1976) (holding grand jury legally impaneled). Is a John Doe indictment valid that describes the indictee as "a/k/a Leo, a white male approx. 23 years old, approx. 5'7" tall, approx. 135 pounds, with black hair, brown eyes and a black mustache?" See *United States* v. *Doe*, 401 F. Supp. 63 (E.D. Wis. 1975) (holding valid indictment). Is a grand jury witness entitled to warnings about the right to remain silent when he isn't faced with a choice between perjury and self-incrimination? See *United States* v. *Chevoor*, 526 F.2d 178 (1st Cir. 1975) (holding no warnings required). Is it improper for a federal court to permit FBI access to possibly incriminating business records that have been subpoenaed by a grand jury? See *United States* v. *Universal Mfg. Co.*, 525 F.2d 808 (5th Cir. 1975) (holding not improper). Is a defendant denied due process or equal protection rights by fact that persons 18–20 years of age were excluded from grand jury that indicted him? See *Gibson* v. *State*, 226 S.E.2d 63 (Ga. 1976) (holding no violation). Are the equal protection rights of a defendant violated by a state statute that permits

public officials to appear before a grand jury prior to a return of an indictment against them? See *Orkin* v. *State,* 223 S.E.2d 61 (Ga. 1976) (holding no denial of equal protection).

10. The following recent lower federal and state court decisions are illustrative of some additional legal issues involving the grand jury process: *People* v. *Castro,* 327 P.2d 596 (Cal. Sup. Ct. 1975) (indictment quashed where little effort was made to include names of low income persons in master grand jury list); *In re Grand Jury Proceedings,* 522 F.2d 196 (5th Cir. 1975) (grand jury witness with no self-incrimination problems has no right to an adversary hearing on the legality of a facially valid court order for electronic surveillance on which questions to him were based); *Marston's Inc.* v. *Strand,* 560 P.2d 778 (Ariz. 1977) (grand jury witness is not entitled to set limits on investigation that grand jury may conduct and burden is on witness to show that there is an abuse on the grand jury process); *Lawless* v. *Commonwealth,* 539 S.W.2d 101 (Ky. 1976) (potential indictee has no right to have his testimony before a grand jury recorded and transcribed at his expense and made available to him); *United States* v. *Echols,* 542 F.2d 948 (5th Cir. 1976) (presence in grand jury room of a movie projector operator hired by the government who was not a grand jury witness in an obscenity indictment requires dismissal of the indictment); *State* v. *Wallace,* 321 S.2d 349 (La. 1975) (state official subpoenaed to testify before federal grand jury and fully warned of his privilege against self-incrimination held to have no Fifth Amendment privilege against the state's use of his testimony to indict him on state charges); *United States* v. *Chanen,* 549 F.2d 1306 (9th Cir. 1977) (prosecutors are charged with a high duty to screen out unreliable grand jury witnesses); *United States* v. *Test,* 550 F.2d 577 (10th Cir. 1976) (defendent has no right to grand jury of any given demographic composition); *In re Melvin,* 550 F.2d 674 (1st Cir. 1977) (grand jury has power to order person suspected of crime to participate in a lineup); *United States* v. *Knight,* (8th Cir. 1976) (recording of all grand jury proceedings is not required) (in accord is *United States* v. *Bresley,* 548 F.2d 223 [8th Cir. 1977]; *In re Grand Jury No. 76-3 (MIA) Subpoena Duces Tecum,* 555 F.2d 1306 (5th Cir. 1977) (cost of reproduction of documents sought by grand jury subpoena duces tecum rests with the holder); *In re Cueto,* 554 F.2d 14 (2d Cir. 1977) (witnesses' status as lay Episcopalian ministers gave them no right to be treated differently from other citizens before grand jury); *State* v. *O'Blanc,* 346 S. 2d 686 (La. 1977) (testimony taken before grand jury cannot be used in any trial other than a prosecution for perjury); *Davis* v. *Traub,* 565 P.2d 1015 (N.M. 1977) (presence of unauthorized person before grand jury requires dismissal of indictment without necessity of showing prejudice); *United States* v. *Gomez,* 553 F.2d 958 (5th Cir. 1977) (fear for personal and family's safety is no defense to crime of refusing to testify before grand jury); *United States* v. *Potter,* 552 F.2d 901 (9th Cir. 1977) (Jury Selection Act of 1968 establishes as a national policy the right of all litigants to have grand juries selected at random from a fair cross section of the local community); *United States* v. *Smith,* 552 F.2d 25 (8th Cir.

1977) (a defendant has no absolute right to appear before a grand jury or to have his counsel present); *United States* v. *Beasley*, 550 F.2d 261 (5th Cir. 1977) (prosecution may not use the grand jury for the primary purpose of strengthening its case on a pending indictment); *State ex rel. Brackman* v. *District Court of First Judicial District*, 560 P.2d 523 (Mont. 1977) (there is no constitutional right to counsel at grand jury proceedings); *McCrory* v. *State*, 342 So. 2d 897 (Miss. 1977) (grand jury has authority to interrogate accused following his arrest by the police).

7

SIXTH AMENDMENT PROBLEMS: THE RIGHT TO COUNSEL, JURY TRIALS, SPEEDY TRIALS, THE CONFRONTATION CLAUSE, DEFENSE WITNESSES, AND PUBLIC TRIALS

7.01 INTRODUCTION

Of the twelve Bill of Rights guarantees that are applicable to the criminal process, six are found in the Sixth Amendment. That Amendment provides:

> In all criminal prosecutions, the accused shall enjoy the right to a speedy and public trial, by an impartial jury ...; to be confronted with the witnesses against him; to have compulsory process for obtaining witnesses in his favor, and to have the Assistance of Counsel for his defence.

Each of these constitutional safeguards has been the subject of numerous Supreme Court decisions, and each is today applicable to the states through the Due Process Clause of the Fourteenth Amendment.

7.02 THE RIGHT TO COUNSEL

History of the Right

The Right at Common Law. The right to the assistance of counsel had its beginnings in the Middle Ages. It should be noted, however, that the modern concept of "assistance of counsel" is not broad enough to encompass the different kinds of legal assistance that were available during this period. By the end of the thirteenth century, defendants commonly were availing themselves of three different modes of legal representation. The first type of legal practitioner, known as the *pleader,* was a person learned in the law who did not act as a representative of the defendant but merely stood at the defendant's side and spoke for his cause. The second type, the *attornatus,* actually represented his client and acted as an authorized deputy who appeared in his place. The third type, the *advocatus,* represented the defendant as a surety or warrantor. The advocatus was usually the defendant's lord, and he made the defense not on the accused's behalf but on his own.[1]

Two distinctions appeared in English law

---

[1] Pollack and Maitland, *The History of English Law Before the Time of Edward I* (1968).

549

between the fifteenth and sixteenth centuries that created restraints on the right to counsel that lasted until the early nineteenth century. The first was a facts-law distinction whereby the defendant would present the facts that were particularly within his knowledge and his counsel would plead the law and apply it to the facts. The exact origin of this rule is still a matter of debate, but by the time of Lord Coke it had become a firmly established rule that the accused was required to plead to the indictment and make his defense with regard to the facts by himself without the aid of counsel. In matters of law, however, the accused could employ the aid of counsel. The second distinction limiting the right to counsel was the prohibition of legal assistance to a defendant accused of committing a felony.[2] However, a defendant accused of committing a misdemeanor could secure the assistance of counsel for his defense. The rationale for this anomaly was that a felony defendant was not to be protected because he posed a greater danger to the Crown.[3]

During the next four centuries, the right to counsel expanded slowly but steadily. By an act of Parliament in 1695, the right to counsel was extended to persons accused of treason or misprision of treason. The act provided that in cases of treason, the accused was to have the aid of counsel in matters of both fact and law and if he could not afford counsel, one would be appointed for him by the court. During the eighteenth century, counsel was permitted to perform an increasing number of defense functions until, by the end of the century, he could do everything necessary to aid the defendant except address the jury at the conclusion of the evidence, a privilege reserved for the King's Counsel. In 1836, Parliament again extended the right to counsel. In that year, felons were given the same right to counsel that misdemeanants had previously enjoyed. This act also abolished the facts-law distinction. The Poor Prisoner's Defense Acts of 1903 and 1930 further broadened the right. The Act of 1903 empowered judges to appoint counsel in all indictments in which it was ascertained that the defend-

ant lacked sufficient means to retain counsel or in which it appeared that justice required such an appointment. However, the Act of 1903 proved to be of little value to defendants; it was rarely implemented by English judges, who felt confident of their own ability to even-handedly dispense justice. The Act of 1930 added one major improvement as it required the assignment of counsel whenever the defendant was accused of murder. The greatest advance in the right to counsel made by Parliament came with the Legal Aid and Advice Act of 1949. Under this act, doubts concerning the appointment of counsel were to be resolved in favor of the accused and the accused could request counsel at a stage prior to arraignment.

The Right to Counsel in the United States. Prior to the American Revolution, the colonies of Pennsylvania, Delaware and South Carolina by statute gave the right to counsel a greater scope than the English procedures of the period permitted. Court-appointed counsel was available when a capital crime was charged and the accused requested the appointment. Virginia and Rhode Island also gave statutory recognition to the right to counsel.

The American colonial courts seemed acutely aware that an accused who was undefended by counsel was at a serious disadvantage; and in fact, the accused was at a greater disadvantage in the colonies than in England where the criminal defendant was generally confronted by the injured person or some other interested party rather than by a public prosecutor. The early eighteenth century colonial system of judicial administration differed in that the accused faced a government official whose specific function it was to prosecute, and this prosecutor naturally was more familiar than the defendant with trial procedure, law, and the personnel of the court.

By the time the Sixth Amendment to the United States Constitution was proposed to Congress in 1789, every state but Rhode Island and Georgia had some constitutional provision regarding the right to counsel, and eleven of the states had either directly or impliedly abolished the facts-law distinction. It was against this background that on December 15, 1791, the eleventh state ratified the clause "to have Assistance of Counsel for his defence," making that right part of the Sixth Amendment to the United States Constitution.

---

[2]Beaney, *Right to Counsel in American Courts* 8–9 (1955).

[3]Moore, *The Jury: Tool of Kings, Palladium of Liberty* 71 (1973).

Ostensibly, the framers of the right to counsel guarantees in both state and federal constitutions intended that the right would never again be denied. But as Professor Beaney has commented:[4]

It is extremely difficult, it not impossible, with the available material to reach any positive conclusion concerning the intention of Congress in proposing [the Assistance of Counsel Clause of the Sixth Amendment] or the interpretation given it by the states at the time of ratification. Lack of discussion usually means that there is general agreement ... but the question may well be asked, "To what did the states agree?"

However, another authority has suggested:[5]

[4]Beaney, supra note 2, at 24.
[5]Note, *An Historical Argument for the Right to Counsel During Police Interrogation,* 73 Yale L.J. 1000, 1032, 1033 (1964).

One thing can be said with certainty: the right to counsel was ... one of the basic and continuing procedural rights of a criminal defendant in the common law.... The right ... is not a recent grant of largess by society but an old right which has never completely faded in the face of severe opposition.... [The Framers] appreciated that if a defendant were forced to stand alone against the state, his case was foredoomed.

From 1789, the date of ratification of the United States Constitution, until the mid-nineteenth century, few cases were heard in federal and state courts concerning the right to counsel. However, as American society progressed, the courts were asked with increasing frequency to redress the injustices and hardships faced by indigent and friendless defendants. In 1932, a case that had gained national attention reached the United States Supreme Court—*Powell* v. *Alabama,* one of the famous Scottsboro cases.

Fundamental Fairness in Capital Cases

POWELL v. ALABAMA

Supreme Court of the United States, 1932
287 U.S. 45, 53 S. Ct. 55, 77 L. Ed. 158

Ozzie Powell and two other black defendants were charged in an Alabama state court with the rape of two white girls. Each of the defendants pleaded not guilty to the charges, and each was tried separately in a single day. The juries convicted the defendants, and the death penalty was imposed. The trial court overruled their motions for a new trial, and the judgments were affirmed by the Alabama Supreme Court. Subsequently, the defendants appealed to the United States Supreme Court, alleging a denial of Fourteenth Amendment due process and equal protection of the laws because (1) they had not been given a fair trial; (2) they had been denied the right to counsel; and (3) they had been denied a trial by an impartial jury since blacks were systematically excluded from jury service.

Additional facts appear in the opinion.

Mr. Justice SUTHERLAND delivered the opinion of the Court.

* * *

The record shows that on the day when the offense is said to have been committed, these defendants, together with a number of other negroes, were upon a freight train on its way through Alabama. On the same train were seven white boys and the two white girls. A fight took place between the negroes and the white boys, in the course of which the white boys, with the exception of one named Gilley, were thrown off the train. A message was sent ahead, reporting the fight and asking that every negro be gotten off the train. The participants in the fight, and the two girls, were in an open gondola car. The two girls testified that each of them was assaulted by six different negroes in turn, and they identified the seven defendants as having been among the number. None of the white boys was called to testify, with the exception of Gilley, who was called in rebuttal.

Before the train reached Scottsboro, Alabama, a sheriff's posse seized the defendants and two other negroes. Both girls and the negroes then were taken to Scottsboro, the county seat. Word of their coming and of the alleged assault had preceded them, and they were met at Scottsboro by a large crowd. It does not sufficiently appear that the defendants were seriously threatened with, or that they were actually in danger of, mob violence; but it does appear that the attitude of the community was one of great hostility. The sheriff thought it necessary to call for the militia to assist in safeguarding the prisoners. . . . Every step taken from the arrest and arraignment to the sentence was accompanied by the military. Soldiers took the defendants to Gadsden for safekeeping, brought them back to Scottsboro for arraignment, returned them to Gadsden for safekeeping while awaiting trial, escorted them to Scottsboro for trial a few days later, and guarded the courthouse and grounds at every stage of the proceedings. It is perfectly apparent that the proceedings, from beginning to end, took place in an atmosphere of tense, hostile, and excited public sentiment. During the entire time, the defendants were closely confined or were under military guard. The record does not disclose their ages, except that one of them was nineteen; but the record clearly indicates that most, if not all, of them were youthful, and they were constantly referred to as "the boys." They were ignorant and illiterate. All of them were residents of other states, where alone members of their families or friends resided.

However guilty defendants, upon due inquiry, might prove to have been, they were, until convicted, presumed to be innocent. It was the duty of the court having their cases in charge to see that they were denied no necessary incident of a fair trial. With any error of the state court involving alleged contravention of the state statutes or Constitution we, of course, have nothing to do. The sole inquiry which we are permitted to make is whether the federal Constitution was contravened . . . and as to that, we confine ourselves . . . to the inquiry whether the defendants were in substance denied the right of counsel, and if so, whether such denial infringes the due process clause of the Fourteenth Amendment.

First. The record shows that immediately upon the return of the indictment defendants were arraigned and pleaded not guilty. Apparently they were not asked whether they had, or were able to employ, counsel, or wished to have counsel appointed; or whether they had friends or relatives who might assist in that regard if communicated with. That it would not have been an idle ceremony to have given the defendants reasonable opportunity to communicate with their families and endeavor to obtain counsel is demonstrated by the fact that very soon after conviction, able counsel appeared in their behalf. . . .

It is hardly necessary to say that the right to counsel being conceded, a defendant should be afforded a fair opportunity to secure counsel of his own choice. Not only was that not done here, but such designation of counsel as was attempted was either so indefinite or so close upon the trial as to amount to a denial of effective and substantial aid in that regard. . . .

It thus will be seen that until the very morning of the trial no lawyer had been named or definitely designated to represent the defendants. Prior to that time, the trial judge had "appointed all members of the bar" for the limited "purpose of arraigning the defendants." Whether they would represent the defendants thereafter, if no counsel appeared in their behalf, was a matter of speculation only, or, as the judge indicated, of mere anticipation on the part of the court. Such a designation, even if made for all purposes, would, in our opinion, have fallen far short of meeting, in any proper sense, a requirement for the appointment of counsel. How many lawyers were members of the bar does not appear; but, in the very nature of things, whether many or few, they would not, thus collectively named, have been given that clear appreciation of responsibility or impressed with that individual sense of duty which should and naturally would accompany the appointment of a selected member of the bar, specifically named and assigned.

[T]his action of the trial judge in respect

of appointment of counsel was little more than an expansive gesture, imposing no substantial or definite obligation upon any one. . . .

In any event, the circumstance lends emphasis to the conclusion that during perhaps the most critical period of the proceedings against these defendants, that is to say, from the time of their arraignment until the beginning of their trial, when consultation, thorough-going investigation, and preparation were vitally important, the defendants did not have the aid of counsel in any real sense, although they were as much entitled to such aid during that period as at the trial itself. . . .

The defendants, young, ignorant, illiterate, surrounded by hostile sentiment, haled back and forth under guard of soldiers, charged with an atrocious crime regarded with especial horror in the community where they were to be tried, were thus put in peril of their lives within a few moments after counsel for the first time charged with any degree of responsibility began to represent them. . . . Under the circumstances disclosed, we hold that defendants were not accorded the right of counsel in any substantial sense. To decide otherwise would simply be to ignore actualities. This conclusion finds ample support in the reasoning of an overwhelming array of state decisions. . . .

It is true that great and inexcusable delay in the enforcement of our criminal law is one of the grave evils of our time. Continuances are frequently granted for unnecessarily long periods of time, and delays incident to the disposition of motions for new trial and hearings upon appeal have come in many cases to be a distinct approach to the administration of justice. The prompt disposition of criminal cases is to be commended and encouraged. But in reaching that result a defendant, charged with a serious crime, must not be stripped of his right to have sufficient time to advise with counsel and prepare his defense. To do that is not to proceed promptly in the calm spirit of regulated justice but to go forward with the haste of the mob. . . .

Second. The Constitution of Alabama . . . provides that in all criminal prosecutions the accused shall enjoy the right to have the assistance of counsel; and a state statute . . .

requires the court in a capital case, where the defendant is unable to employ counsel, to appoint counsel for him. The state Supreme Court held that these provisions had not been infringed. . . . The question, however, which it is our duty, and within our power, to decide, is whether the denial of the assistance of counsel contravenes the due process clause of the Fourteenth Amendment to the Federal Constitution. . . .

It never has been doubted by this court, or any other so far as we know, that notice and hearing are preliminary steps essential to the passing of an enforceable judgment, and that they, together with a legally competent tribunal having jurisdiction of the case, constitute basic elements of the constitutional requirement of due process of law. The words of Webster, so often quoted, that by "the law of the land" is intended "a law which hears before it condemns," have been repeated in varying forms of expression in a multitude of decisions. . . .

What, then, does a hearing include? Historically and in practice, in our own country at least, it has always included the right to the aid of counsel when desired and provided by the party asserting the right. The right to be heard would be, in many cases, of little avail if it did not comprehend the right to be heard by counsel. Even the intelligent and educated layman has small and sometimes no skill in the science of law. If charged with crime, he is incapable, generally, of determining for himself whether the indictment is good or bad. He is unfamiliar with the rules of evidence. Left without the aid of counsel he may be put on trial without a proper charge, and convicted upon incompetent evidence, or evidence irrelevant to the issue or otherwise inadmissible. He lacks both the skill and knowledge adequately to prepare his defense, even though he have a perfect one. He requires the guiding hand of counsel at every step in the proceedings against him. Without it, though he be not guilty, he faces the danger of conviction because he does not know how to establish his innocence. If that be true of men of intelligence, how much more true is it of the ignorant and illiterate, or those of feeble intellect. If in any case, civil or criminal, a state or federal court were arbitrarily to refuse to hear a party by counsel, employed by and appearing for him, it reasonably may not be doubted that such a refusal would be a denial of a hearing, and, therefore, of due process in the constitutional sense. . . .

In the light of the facts outlined in the forepart of this opinion—the ignorance and illiteracy of the defendants, their youth, the circumstances of public hostility, the imprisonment and the close surveillance of the defendants by the military forces, the fact that their friends and families were all in other states and communication with them necessarily difficult, and above all that they stood in deadly peril of their lives—we think the failure of the trial court to give them reasonable time and opportunity to secure counsel was a clear denial of due process.

But passing that, and assuming their inability, even if opportunity had been given, to employ counsel, as the trial court evidently did assume, we are of opinion that, under the circumstances just stated, the necessity of counsel was so vital and imperative that the failure of the trial court to make an effective appointment of counsel was likewise a denial of due process within the meaning of the Fourteenth Amendment. Whether this would be so in other criminal prosecutions, or under other circumstances, we need not determine. All that it is necessary now to decide, as we do decide, is that in a capital case, where the defendant is unable to employ counsel, and is incapable adequately of making his own defense because of ignorance, feeble-mindedness, illiteracy, or the like, it is the duty of the court, whether requested or not, to assign counsel for him as a necessary requisite of due process of law; and that duty is not discharged by an assignment at such a time or under such circumstances as to preclude the giving of effective aid in the preparation and trial of the case. To hold otherwise would be to ignore the fundamental postulate, already adverted to, "that there are certain immutable principles of justice which inhere in the very idea of free government which no member of the Union may disregard." . . .

The United States by statute and every state in the Union by express provision of law, or by the determination of its courts, make it the duty of the trial judge, where the accused is unable to employ counsel, to appoint counsel for him. In most states the rule applies broadly to all criminal prosecutions, in others it is limited to the more serious crimes, and in a very limited number, to capital cases. A rule adopted with such unanimous accord reflects, if it does not establish, the inherent right to have counsel appointed at least in cases like the present, and lends convincing support to the conclusion we have reached as to the fundamental nature of that right.

The judgments must be reversed and the causes remanded for further proceedings not inconsistent with this opinion.

Judgments reversed.

[Mr. Justice BUTLER wrote a dissenting opinion in which Mr. Justice MCREYNOLDS joined.]

Application to the States

GIDEON v. WAINWRIGHT

Supreme Court of the United States, 1963
372 U.S. 335, 83 S. Ct. 792, 9 L. Ed. 2d 799

Clarence Gideon was tried and convicted in a Florida state court of the felony of breaking and entering a pool hall with intent to commit a misdemeanor. As Gideon was too poor to hire his own defense attorney, he requested that the trial court appoint counsel to represent him. The request was denied because under Florida law, appointed counsel was available to indigents only in capital cases. Gideon represented himself but was convicted by a jury and sentenced to five years' imprisonment. The Florida Supreme Court denied relief. In *Betts* v. *Brady*, 316 U.S. 455 (1942), a divided United States Supreme Court had held that there was no general right to court-appointed counsel in state felony cases and that such counsel was available only under "special circumstances." In *Gideon*, the Supreme Court granted certiorari and appointed counsel to represent Gideon before the Court. The question presented was "Should this Court's holding in *Betts* v. *Brady* be reconsidered?"

Mr. Justice BLACK delivered the opinion of the Court.

* * *

I

The facts upon which Betts claimed that he had been unconstitutionally denied the right to have counsel appointed to assist him are strikingly like the facts upon which Gideon here bases his federal constitutional claim. Betts was indicted for robbery in a Maryland state court. On arraignment, he told the trial judge of his lack of funds to hire a lawyer and asked the court to appoint one for him. Betts was advised that it was not the practice in that county to appoint counsel for indigent defendants except in murder and rape cases. He then pleaded not guilty, had witnesses summoned, cross-examined the State's witnesses, examined his own, and chose not to testify himself. He was found guilty by the judge, sitting without a jury, and sentenced to eight years in prison.

Like Gideon, Betts sought release by habeas corpus, alleging that he had been denied the right to assistance of counsel in violation of the Fourteenth Amendment. Betts was denied any relief, and on review this Court affirmed. It was held that a refusal to appoint counsel for an indigent defendant charged with a felony did not necessarily violate the Due Process Clause of the Fourteenth Amendment, which for reasons given the Court deemed to be the only applicable federal constitutional provision. The Court said: "Asserted denial [of due process] is to be tested by an appraisal of the totality of facts in a given case. That which may, in one setting, constitute a denial of fundamental fairness, shocking to the universal sense of justice, may, in other circumstances, and in the light of other considerations, fall short of such denial." ...

Treating due process as "a concept less rigid and more fluid than those envisaged in other specific and particular provisions of the Bill of Rights," the Court held that refusal to appoint counsel under the particular facts and circumstances in the Betts case was not so "offensive to the common and fundamental ideas of fairness" as to amount to a denial of due process. Since the facts and circumstances of the two cases are so nearly indistinguishable, we think the Betts v. Brady holding if left standing would require us to reject Gideon's claim that the Constitution guarantees him the assistance of counsel. Upon full reconsideration we conclude that Betts v. Brady should be overruled.

II

The Sixth Amendment provides, "In all criminal prosecutions, the accused shall enjoy the right ... to have the Assistance of Counsel for his defence." We have construed this to mean that in federal courts counsel must be provided for defendants unable to employ counsel unless the right is competently and intelligently waived. Betts argued that this right is extended to indigent defendants in state courts by the Fourteenth Amendment. In response the Court stated that, while the Sixth Amendment laid down "no rule for the conduct of the States, the question recurs whether the constraint laid by the Amendment upon the national courts expresses a rule so fundamental and essential to a fair trial, and so, to due process of law, that it is made obligatory upon the States by the Fourteenth Amendment." ... In order to decide whether the Sixth Amendment's guarantee of counsel is of this fundamental nature, the Court in Betts set out and considered "[r]elevant data on the subject ... afforded by constitutional and statutory provisions subsisting in the colonies and the States prior to the inclusion of the Bill of Rights in the national Constitution, and in the constitutional, legislative, and judicial history of the States to the present date." ... On the basis of this historical data the Court concluded that "appointment of counsel is not a fundamental right, essential to a fair trial." . . . It was for this reason the Betts Court refused to accept the contention that the Sixth Amendment's guarantee of counsel for indigent federal defendants was extended to or, in the words of that Court, "made obligatory upon the States by the Fourteenth Amendment." Plainly, had the Court concluded that appointment of counsel for an indigent criminal defendant was "a fundamental right, essential to a fair trial," it would have held that the Fourteenth Amendment requires appointment of counsel in a state court, just as the Sixth Amendment requires in a federal court. . . .

We accept Betts v. Brady's assumption, based as it was on our prior cases, that a provision of the Bill of Rights which is "fundamental and essential to a fair trial" is made obligatory upon the States by the Fourteenth Amendment. We think the Court in Betts was wrong, however, in concluding that the Sixth Amendment's guarantee of counsel is not one of these fundamental rights. Ten years before Betts v. Brady, this Court, after full consideration of all the historical data examined in Betts, had unequivocally declared that "the right to the aid of counsel is of this fundamental character." Powell v. Alabama. . . . While the Court at the close of its Powell opinion did by its language, as this Court frequently does, limit its holding to the particular facts and circumstances of that case, its conclusions about the fundamental nature of the right to counsel are unmistakable. . . .

In light of these and many other prior decisions of this Court, it is not surprising that the Betts Court, when faced with the contention that "one charged with crime, who is unable to obtain counsel, must be furnished counsel by the State," conceded that "[e]xpressions in the opinions of this court lend color to the argument. . . ." . . . The fact is that in deciding as it did—that "appointment of counsel is not a fundamental right, essential to a fair trial"—the Court in Betts v. Brady made an abrupt break with its own well-considered precedents. In returning to these old precedents, sounder we believe than the new, we but restore constitutional principles established to achieve a fair system of justice. Not only these precedents but also reason and reflection require us to recognize that in our adversary system of criminal justice, any person haled into court, who is too poor to hire a lawyer, cannot be assured a fair trial unless counsel is provided for him. This seems to us to be an obvious truth. Governments, both state and federal, quite properly spend vast sums of money to establish machinery to try defendants accused of crime. Lawyers to prosecute are everywhere deemed essential to protect the public's interest in an orderly society. Similarly, there are few defendants charged with crime, few indeed, who fail to hire the best lawyers they can get to prepare and present their defenses. That government hires lawyers to prosecute and defendants who have the money hire lawyers to defend are the strongest indications of the widespread belief that lawyers in criminal courts are necessities, not luxuries. The right of one charged with crime to counsel may not be deemed fundamental and essential to fair trials in some countries, but it is in ours. From the very beginning, our state and national constitutions and laws have laid great emphasis on procedural and substantive safeguards designed to assure fair trials before impartial tribunals in which every defendant stands equal before the law. This noble ideal cannot be realized if the poor man charged with crime has to face his accusers without a lawyer to assist him. . . .

The Court in Betts v. Brady departed from the sound wisdom upon which the Court's holding in Powell v. Alabama rested. Florida, supported by two other States, has asked that Betts v. Brady be left intact. Twenty-two States, as friends of the Court, argue that Betts was "an anachronism when handed down" and that it should now be overruled. We agree.

The judgment is reversed and the cause is remanded to the Supreme Court of Florida for further action not inconsistent with this opinion.

Reversed.

[Mr. Justice DOUGLAS, Mr. Justice CLARK, and Mr. Justice HARLAN each wrote concurring opinions.]

Extending the Doctrine of *Gideon*

ARGERSINGER v. HAMLIN

Supreme Court of the United States, 1972
407 U.S. 25, 92 S. Ct. 2006, 32 L. Ed. 2d 530

Jon Argersinger, an indigent, was convicted by a Florida state court of carrying a concealed weapon, an offense punishable by imprisonment up to six months, a $1000 fine, or both. At his trial, Argersinger was not represented by counsel. Following his conviction, he was sentenced to serve 90 days in jail. The Florida Supreme Court denied relief on the ground that the Sixth Amendment right to counsel extended only to trials for nonpetty offenses punishable by more than six months' imprisonment. The United States Supreme Court granted certiorari.

Mr. Justice DOUGLAS delivered the opinion of the Court.

* * *

The Sixth Amendment, which in enumerated situations has been made applicable to the States by reason of the Fourteenth Amendment [see Duncan v. Louisiana, 391 U.S. 145 (1968); Washington v. Texas, 388 U.S. 14 (1967); Klopfer v. North Carolina, 386 U.S. 213 (1967); Pointer v. Texas, 380 U.S. 400 (1965); Gideon v. Wainwright, 372 U.S. 335 (1963); and In re Oliver, 333 U.S. 257 (1948)] provides specified standards for "all criminal prosecutions." . . .

The right to trial by jury, also guaranteed by the Sixth Amendment by reason of the Fourteenth, was limited by Duncan v. Louisiana . . . to trials where the potential punishment was imprisonment of six months or more. But, as the various opinions in Baldwin v. New York, 399 U.S. 66 (1970), made plain, the right to trial by jury has a different genealogy and is brigaded with a system of trial to a judge alone. . . .

While there is historical support for limiting the "deep commitment" to trial by jury to "serious criminal cases," there is no such support for a similar limitation on the right to assistance of counsel. . . .

The Sixth Amendment thus extended the right to counsel beyond its common-law dimensions. But there is nothing in the language of the Amendment, its history, or in the decisions of this Court, to indicate that it was intended to embody a retraction of the right in petty offenses wherein the common law previously did require that counsel be provided. . . .

We reject, therefore, the premise that since prosecutions for crimes punishable by imprisonment for less than six months may be tried without a jury, they may also be tried without a lawyer.

The assistance of counsel is often a requisite to the very existence of a fair trial. . . .

In Gideon v. Wainwright, supra [overruling Betts v. Brady, 316 U.S. 455 (1942)], we dealt with a felony trial. But we did not so limit the need of the accused for a lawyer. . . .

Both Powell [v. Alabama, 287 U.S. 45 (1932), supra] and Gideon involved felonies. But their rationale has relevance to any criminal trial, where an accused is deprived of his liberty. Powell and Gideon suggest that there are certain fundamental rights applicable to all such criminal prosecutions, even those . . . where the penalty is 60 days' imprisonment. . . .

The requirement of counsel may well be necessary for a fair trial even in a petty-offense prosecution. We are by no means convinced that legal and constitutional questions involved in a case that actually leads to imprisonment even for a brief period are any less complex than when a person can be sent off for six months or more. . . .

Beyond the problem of trials and appeals is that of the guilty plea, a problem which looms large in misdemeanor as well as in felony cases. Counsel is needed so that the accused may know precisely what he is doing, so that he is fully aware of the prospect of going to jail or prison, and so that he is treated fairly by the prosecution.

In addition, the volume of misdemeanor cases, far greater in number than felony prosecutions, may create an obsession for speedy dispositions, regardless of the fairness of the result. The Report by the President's Commission on Law Enforcement and Administration of Justice, The Challenge of Crime in a Free Society 128 (1967), states: "For example, until legislation last year increased the number of judges, the District of Columbia Court of General Sessions had four judges to process the preliminary stages of more than 1,500 felony cases, 7,500 serious misdemeanor cases, and 38,000 petty offenses and an equal number of traffic offenses per year. An inevitable consequence of volume that large is the almost total preoccupation in such a court with the movement of cases. The calendar is long, speed often is substituted for care, and casually arranged out-of-court compromise too often is substituted for adjudication. Inadequate attention tends to be given to the individual defendant, whether in protecting his rights, sifting the facts at trial, deciding the social risk he presents, or determining how to deal with him after conviction. The frequent result is futility and failure. As Dean Edward Barrett recently observed: "'Wherever the visitor looks at the system, he finds great numbers of defendants being processed by harassed and overworked officials. Police have more cases than they can investigate. Prosecutors walk into courtrooms to try simple cases as they take their initial looks at the files. Defense lawyers appear having had no more than time for hasty conversations with their clients. Judges face long calendars with the certain knowledge that their calendars tomorrow and the next day will be, if anything, longer, and so there is no choice but to dispose of the cases.

Suddenly it becomes clear that for most defendants in the criminal process, there is scant regard for them as individuals. They are numbers on dockets, faceless ones to be processed and sent on their way. The gap between the theory and the reality is enormous.

Very little such observation of the administration of criminal justice in operation is required to reach the conclusion that it suffers from basic ills.' "

That picture is seen in almost every report. "The misdemeanor trial is characterized by insufficient and frequently irresponsible preparation on the part of the defense, the prosecution, and the court. Everything is rush, rush." . . .

There is evidence of the prejudice which results to misdemeanor defendants from this "assembly-line justice." One study concluded that "[m]isdemeanants represented by attorneys are five times as likely to emerge from police court with all charges dismissed as are defendants who face similar charges without counsel." . . .

We must conclude, therefore, that the problems associated with misdemeanor and petty offenses often require the presence of counsel to insure the accused a fair trial. Mr. Justice Powell suggests that these problems are raised even in situations where there is no prospect of imprisonment. . . . We need not consider the requirements of the Sixth Amendment as regards the right to counsel where loss of liberty is not involved, however, for here petitioner was in fact sentenced to jail. And, as we said in Baldwin v. New York . . ., "the prospect of imprisonment for however short a time will seldom be viewed by the accused as a trivial or 'petty' matter and may well result in quite serious repercussions affecting his career and his reputation."

We hold, therefore, that absent a knowing and intelligent waiver, no person may be imprisoned for any offense, whether classified as petty, misdemeanor, or felony, unless he was represented by counsel at his trial. . . .

We do not sit as an ombudsman to direct state courts how to manage their affairs but only to make clear the federal constitutional requirement. How crimes should be classified is largely a state matter. The fact that traffic charges technically fall within the category of "criminal prosecutions" does not necessarily mean that many of them will be brought into the class where imprisonment actually occurs. . . .

Under the rule we announce today, every judge will know when the trial of a misdemeanor starts that no imprisonment may be imposed, even though local law permits it, unless the accused is represented by counsel. He will have a measure of the seriousness and gravity of the offense and therefore know when to name a lawyer to represent the accused before the trial starts.

The run of misdemeanors will not be affected by today's ruling. But in those that end up in the actual deprivation of a person's liberty, the accused will receive the benefit of "the guiding hand of counsel" so necessary when one's liberty is in jeopardy.

Reversed.

[Mr. Justice BRENNAN, joined by Mr. Justice DOUGLAS and Mr. Justice STEWART, wrote a concurring opinion.]

[Chief Justice BURGER wrote a concurring opinion.]

[Mr. Justice POWELL, joined by Mr. Justice REHNQUIST, wrote a concurring opinion.]

Counsel on Appeal

ROSS v. MOFFITT

Supreme Court of the United States, 1974
417 U.S. 600, 94 S. Ct. 2437, 41 L. Ed. 2d 341

Fred Moffitt, an indigent defendant, was tried and convicted of forgery and uttering a forged instrument in two separate criminal prosecutions in North Carolina state courts. Because of his indigency, he was represented at each trial by court-appointed counsel. Pursuant to North Carolina statutes, which permit an appeal as a matter of right, he appealed his convictions to the North Carolina Court of Appeals, again represented by court-appointed counsel. His convictions were affirmed. Thereafter, he sought discretionary review by the North Carolina Supreme Court but was denied the assistance of court-appointed counsel on such appeal. His petitions for federal habeas corpus relief were denied in the district courts. The Court of Appeals (4th Cir.) consolidated the two cases and reversed, holding, in effect, that court-appointed counsel on appeal was available to indigents at all stages of the appellate process—including petitions for certiorari to the United States Supreme Court. The Supreme Court granted certiorari.

Mr. Justice REHNQUIST delivered the opinion of the Court.

We are asked in this case to decide whether Douglas v. California, 372 U.S. 353 (1963), which requires appointment of counsel for indigent state defendants on their first appeal as of right, should be extended to require counsel for discretionary state appeals and for applications for review in this Court. The Court of Appeals for the Fourth Circuit held that such appointment was required by the Due Process and Equal Protection Clauses of the Fourteenth Amendment.

* * *

II

This Court, in the past 20 years, has given extensive consideration to the rights of indigent persons on appeal. In Griffin v. Illinois, 351 U.S. 12 (1956) [supra, Chapter Four, § 4.04], the first of the pertinent cases, the Court had before it an Illinois rule allowing a convicted criminal defendant to present claims of trial error to the Supreme Court of Illinois only if he procured a transcript of the testimony adduced at his trial. No exception was made for the indigent defendant, and thus one who was unable to pay the cost of obtaining such a transcript was precluded from obtaining appellate review of asserted trial error. . . . The Court in Griffin held that this discrimination violated the Fourteenth Amendment.

Succeeding cases invalidated similar financial barriers to the appellate process, at the same time reaffirming the traditional principle that a State is not obliged to provide any appeal at all for criminal defendants.... The cases encompassed a variety of circumstances but all had a common theme.... Each of these state-imposed financial barriers to the adjudication of a criminal defendant's appeal was held to violate the Fourteenth Amendment.

The decisions ... stand for the proposition that a State cannot arbitrarily cut off appeal rights for indigents while leaving open avenues of appeal for more affluent persons. In Douglas v. California, 372 U.S. 353 (1963), ... the Court departed somewhat from the limited doctrine of the transcript and fee cases and undertook an examination of whether an indigent's access to the appellate system was adequate. The Court in Douglas concluded that a State does not fulfill its responsibility towards indigent defendants merely by waiving its own requirements that a convicted defendant procure a transcript or pay a fee in order to appeal, and held that the State must go further and provide counsel for the indigent on his first appeal as of right. It is this decision we are asked to extend today.

Petitioners in Douglas, each of whom had been convicted by a jury on 13 felony counts, took appeals as of right to the California District Court of Appeal. No filing fee was exacted of them, no transcript was required in order to present their arguments to the Court of Appeals, and the appellate process was therefore open to them. Petitioners, however, claimed that they not only had the right to make use of the appellate process, but were also entitled to court-appointed and state-compensated counsel because they were indigent. The California appellate court examined the trial record on its own initiative, following the then-existing rule in California, and concluded that " 'no good whatever could be served by appointment of counsel.' " It therefore denied petitioners' request for the appointment of counsel.

This Court held unconstitutional California's requirement that counsel on appeal would be appointed for an indigent only if the appellate court determined that such appointment would be helpful to the defendant or to the court itself. The Court noted that under this system an indigent's case was initially reviewed on the merits without the benefit of any organization or argument by counsel. By contrast, persons of greater means were not faced with the preliminary "ex parte examination of the record" ... but had their arguments presented to the Court in fully briefed form. The Court noted, however, that its decision extended only to initial appeals as of right. ...

The precise rationale for the Griffin and Douglas lines of cases has never been explicitly stated, some support being derived from the Equal Protection Clause of the Fourteenth Amendment, and some from the Due Process Clause of that Amendment. Neither clause by itself provides an entirely satisfactory basis for the result reached, each depending on a different inquiry which emphasizes different factors. "Due process" emphasizes fairness between the State and the individual dealing with the State, regardless of how other individuals in the same situation may be treated. "Equal protection," on the other hand, emphasizes disparity in treatment by a State between classes of individuals whose situations are arguably indistinguishable. We will address these issues separately in the succeeding sections.

III

* * *

We do not believe that the Due Process Clause requires North Carolina to provide respondent with counsel on his discretionary appeal to the State Supreme Court. At the trial stage of a criminal proceeding, the right of an indigent defendant to counsel is fundamental and binding upon the States by virtue of the Sixth and Fourteenth Amendments. Gideon v. Wainwright, 372 U.S. 335 (1963). But there are significant differences between the trial and appellate stages of a criminal proceeding. The purpose of the trial stage from the State's point of view is to convert a criminal defendant from a person presumed innocent to one found guilty beyond a reasonable doubt. To accomplish this purpose, the State employs a prosecuting attorney who presents evidence to the court, challenges any witnesses offered by the defendant, argues rulings of the court, and makes direct arguments to the court and jury seeking to persuade them of the defendant's guilt. Under these circumstances "reason and reflection require us to recognize that in our adversary system of criminal justice, any person haled into court, who is too poor to hire a lawyer, cannot be assured a fair trial unless counsel is provided for him." ...

By contrast, it is ordinarily the defendant, rather than the State, who initiates the appellate process, seeking not to fend off the efforts of the State's prosecutor but rather to overturn a finding of guilt made by a judge or jury below. The defendant needs an attorney on appeal not as a shield to protect him against being "haled into court" by the State and stripped of his presumption of innocence, but rather as a sword to upset the prior determination of guilt. This difference is significant for, while no one would agree that the State may simply dispense with the trial stage of proceedings without a criminal defendant's consent, it is clear that the State need not provide any appeal at all. McKane v. Durston, 153 U.S. 684 (1894).

The fact that an appeal *has* been provided does not automatically mean that a State then acts unfairly by refusing to provide counsel to indigent defendants at every stage of the way. Douglas v. California, supra. Unfairness results only if indigents are singled out by the State and denied meaningful access to the appellate system because of their poverty. That question is more profitably considered under an equal protection analysis.

IV

Language invoking equal protection notions is prominent both in Douglas and in other cases treating the rights of indigents on appeal. The Court in Douglas, for example, stated: "[W]here the merits of *the one and only appeal* an indigent has as of right are decided without benefit of counsel, we think an unconstitutional line has been drawn between rich and poor." ... The Court in Burns v. Ohio stated the issue in the following terms: "[O]nce the State chooses to establish appellate review in criminal cases, it may not foreclose indigents from access to any phase of that procedure because of their poverty." 360 U.S., at 257 (1959).

Despite the tendency of all rights "to declare themselves absolute to their logical extreme," there are obviously limits beyond which the equal protection analysis may not be pressed without doing violence to principles recognized in other decisions of this Court. The Fourteenth Amendment "does not require absolute equality or precisely equal advantages," San Antonio Independent School District v. Rodriguez, 411 U.S.

1, 24 (1973), nor does it require the State to "equalize economic conditions." Griffin v. Illinois, 351 U.S., at 23 (Frankfurter, J., concurring). It does require that the state appellate system be "free of unreasoned distinctions," Rinaldi v. Yeager, 384 U.S. 305, 310 (1966), and that indigents have an adequate opportunity to present their claims fairly within the adversary system. Griffin v. Illinois, supra.... The State cannot adopt procedures which leave an indigent defendant "entirely cut off from any appeal at all," by virtue of his indigency, Lane v. Brown, 372 U.S., at 481 (1963), or extend to such indigent defendants merely a "meaningless ritual" while others in better economic circumstances have a "meaningful appeal." Douglas v. California, supra. The question is not one of absolutes, but one of degrees. In this case we do not believe that the Equal Protection Clause, when interpreted in the context of these cases, requires North Carolina to provide free counsel for indigent defendants seeking to take discretionary appeals to the North Carolina Supreme Court, or to file petitions for certiorari in this Court.

A. The North Carolina appellate system, as are the appellate systems of almost half the States, is multitiered, providing for both an intermediate Court of Appeals and a Supreme Court. The Court of Appeals was created and, like other intermediate state appellate courts, was intended to absorb a substantial share of the caseload previously burdening the [North Carolina] Supreme Court. In criminal cases, an appeal as of right lies directly to the Supreme Court in all cases which involve a sentence of death or life imprisonment, while an appeal of right in all other criminal cases lies to the Court of Appeals.... A second appeal of right lies to the Supreme Court in any criminal case "(1) [w]hich directly involves a substantial question arising under the Constitution of the United States or of this State, or (2) [i]n which there is a dissent...." ... All other decisions of the Court of Appeals on direct review of criminal cases may be further reviewed in the Supreme Court on a discretionary basis.

The statute governing discretionary appeals to the Supreme Court ... provides, in relevant part, that "[i]n any cause in which appeal has been taken to the Court of Appeals ... the Supreme Court may in its discretion, on motion of any party to the cause or on its own motion, certify the cause for review by the Supreme Court, either before or after it has been determined by the Court of Appeals." The statute further provides that "[i]f the cause is certified for transfer to the Supreme Court after its determination by the Court of Appeals, the Supreme Court reviews the decision of the Court of Appeals." The choice of cases to be reviewed is not left entirely within the discretion of the Supreme Court but is regulated by statutory standards. Subsection (c) of this provision states: "In causes subject to certification under subsection (a) of this section, certification may be made by the Supreme Court after determination of the cause by the Court of Appeals when in the opinion of the Supreme Court (1) The subject matter of the appeal has significant public interest, or (2) The cause involves legal principles of major significance to the jurisprudence of the State, or (3) The decision of the Court of Appeals appears likely to be in conflict with a decision of the Supreme Court."

Appointment of counsel for indigents in North Carolina is governed by [various state statutes]. These provisions, although perhaps on their face broad enough to cover appointments such as those respondent sought here, have generally been construed to limit the right to appointed counsel in criminal cases to direct appeals taken as of right. Thus North Carolina has followed the mandate of Douglas v. California ..., and authorized appointment of counsel for a convicted defendant appealing to the intermediate Court of Appeals, but has not gone beyond Douglas to provide for appointment of counsel for a defendant who seeks either discretionary review in the Supreme Court of North Carolina or a writ of certiorari here.

B. The facts show that respondent, in connection with his Mecklenburg County conviction, received the benefit of counsel in examining the record of his trial and in preparing an appellate brief on his behalf for the state Court of Appeals. Thus, prior to his seeking discretionary review in the State Supreme Court, his claims had "once been presented by a lawyer and passed upon by an appellate court." Douglas v. California. . . . We do not believe that it can be said, therefore, that a defendant in respondent's circumstances is denied meaningful access to the North Carolina Supreme Court simply because the State does not appoint counsel to aid him in seeking review in that court. At that stage he will have, at the very least, a transcript or other record of trial proceedings, a brief on his behalf in the Court of Appeals setting forth his claims of error, and in many cases an opinion by the Court of Appeals disposing of his case. These materials, supplemented by whatever submission respondent may make pro se, would appear to provide the Supreme Court of North Carolina with an adequate basis for its decision to grant or deny review.

We are fortified in this conclusion by our understanding of the function served by discretionary review in the North Carolina Supreme Court. The critical issue in that court, as we perceive it, is not whether there has been "a correct adjudication of guilt" in every individual case . . . but rather whether "the subject matter of the appeal has significant public interest," whether "the cause involves legal principles of major significance to the jurisprudence of the State," or whether the decision below is in probable conflict with a decision of the Supreme Court. The Supreme Court may deny certiorari even though it believes that the decision of the Court of Appeals was incorrect . . . since a decision which appears incorrect may nevertheless fail to satisfy any of the criteria discussed above. Once a defendant's claims of error are organized and presented in a lawyer like fashion to the Court of Appeals, the justices of the Supreme Court of North Carolina who make the decision to grant or deny discretionary review should be able to ascertain whether his case satisfies the standards established by the legislature for such review.

This is not to say, of course, that a skilled lawyer, particularly one trained in the somewhat arcane art of preparing petitions for discretionary review, would not prove helpful to any litigant able to employ him. An indigent defendant seeking review in the Supreme Court of North Carolina is therefore somewhat handicapped in comparison with a wealthy defendant who has counsel assisting him in every conceivable manner at every stage in the proceeding. But both the opportunity to have counsel prepare an initial brief in the Court of Appeals and the nature of discretionary review in the Supreme

Court of North Carolina make this relative handicap far less than the handicap borne by the indigent defendant denied counsel on his initial appeal as of right in Douglas. And the fact that a particular service might be of benefit to an indigent defendant does not mean that the service is constitutionally required. The duty of the State under our cases is not to duplicate the legal arsenal that may be privately retained by a criminal defendant in a continuing effort to reverse his conviction, but only to assure the indigent defendant an adequate opportunity to present his claims fairly in the context of the State's appellate process. We think respondent was given that opportunity under the existing North Carolina system.

V

Much of the discussion in the preceding section is equally relevant to the question of whether a State must provide counsel for a defendant seeking review of his conviction in this Court. North Carolina will have provided counsel for a convicted defendant's only appeal as of right, and the brief prepared by that counsel together with one and perhaps two North Carolina appellate opinions will be available to this Court in order that it may decide whether or not to grant certiorari. This Court's review, much like that of the Supreme Court of North Carolina, is discretionary and depends on numerous factors other than the perceived correctness of the judgment we are asked to review.

There is also a significant difference between the source of the right to seek discretionary review in the Supreme Court of North Carolina and the source of the right to seek discretionary review in this Court. The former is conferred by the statutes of the State of North Carolina, but the latter is granted by statute enacted by Congress. Thus the argument relied upon in the Griffin and Douglas cases, that the State having once created a right of appeal must give all persons an equal opportunity to enjoy the right, is by its terms inapplicable. The right to seek certiorari in this Court is not granted by any State, and exists by virtue of federal statute with or without the consent of the State whose judgment is sought to be reviewed.

The suggestion that a State is responsible for providing counsel to one petitioning this Court simply because it initiated the prosecution which led to the judgment sought to be reviewed is unsupported by either reason or authority. It would be quite as logical under the rationale of Douglas and Griffin, and indeed perhaps more so, to require that the Federal Government or this Court furnish and compensate counsel for petitioners who seek certiorari here to review state judgments of conviction. Yet this Court has followed a consistent policy of denying applications for appointment of counsel by persons seeking to file jurisdictional statements or petitions for certiorari in this Court.... In the light of these authorities, it would be odd, indeed, to read the Fourteenth Amendment to impose such a requirement on the States, and we decline to do so.

VI

We do not mean by this opinion to in any way discourage those States which have, as a matter of legislative choice, made counsel available to convicted defendants at all stages of judicial review. Some States which might well choose to do so as a matter of legislative policy may conceivably find that other claims for public funds within or without the criminal justice system preclude the implementation of such a policy at the present time. North Carolina, for example, while it does not provide counsel to indigent defendants seeking discretionary review on appeal, does provide counsel for indigent prisoners in several situations where such appointments are not required by any constitutional decision of this Court. Our reading of the Fourteenth Amendment leaves these choices to the State, and respondent was denied no right secured by the Federal Constitution when North Carolina refused to provide counsel to aid him in obtaining discretionary appellate review.

The judgment of the Court of Appeals holding to the contrary is

Reversed.

Mr. Justice DOUGLAS, with whom Mr. Justice BRENNAN and Mr. Justice MARSHALL concur, dissenting.

I would affirm the judgment below because I am in agreement with the opinion of Chief Judge Haynsworth for a unanimous panel in the Court of Appeals. 483 F.2d 650.

In Douglas v. California ... [the Court] considered the necessity for appointed counsel on the first appeal as of right, the only issue before us. We did not deal with the appointment of counsel for later levels of discretionary review, either to the higher state courts or to this Court, but we noted that "there can be no equal justice where the kind of an appeal a man enjoys 'depends on the amount of money he has.' " ...

Judge Haynsworth could find "no logical basis for differentiation between appeals of right and permissive review procedures in the context of the Constitution and the right to counsel." ... More familiar with the functioning of the North Carolina criminal justice system than are we, he concluded that "in the context of constitutional questions arising in criminal prosecutions, permissive review in the state's highest court may be predictably the most meaningful review the conviction will receive." The North Carolina Court of Appeals, for example, will be constrained in diverging from an earlier opinion of the State Supreme Court, even if subsequent developments have rendered the earlier Supreme Court decision suspect. "[T]he state's highest court remains the ultimate arbiter of the rights of its citizens."

Judge Haynsworth also correctly observed that the indigent defendant proceeding without counsel is at a substantial disadvantage relative to wealthy defendants represented by counsel when he is forced to fend for himself in seeking discretionary review from the State Supreme Court or from this Court. It may well not be enough to allege error in the courts below in lay-man's terms; a more sophisticated approach may be demanded: "An indigent defendant is as much in need of the assistance of a lawyer in preparing and filing a petition for certiorari as he is in the handling of an appeal as of right. In many appeals, an articulate defendant could file an effective brief by telling his story in simple language without legalisms, but the technical requirements for application for writs of certiorari are hazards which one untrained in the law could hardly be expected to negotiate.

"Certiorari proceedings constitute a highly specialized aspect of appellate work. The factors which [a court] deems important in connection with deciding whether to grant certiorari are certainly not within the normal knowledge of an indigent appellant.... Furthermore, the lawyer who handled the first appeal in a case would be familiar with the facts and legal issues involved in the case. It would be a relatively easy matter for the attorney to apply his expertise in filing a petition for discretionary review to a higher court, or to advise his client that such a petition would have no chance of succeeding."

Douglas v. California was grounded on concepts of fairness and equality. The right to seek discretionary review is a substantial one, and one where a lawyer can be of significant assistance to an indigent defendant. It was correctly perceived below that the "same concepts of fairness and equality, which require counsel in a first appeal of right, require counsel in other and subsequent discretionary appeals." ...

Waiving the Right to Counsel

FARETTA v. CALIFORNIA

Supreme Court of the United States, 1975
422 U.S. 806, 95 S. Ct. 2525, 45L. Ed. 2d 562

Anthony Faretta was charged with grand theft in an information filed in a California state court. Well before the date of the trial, Faretta requested that he be permitted to represent himself. The trial judge to whom the case had been assigned, after questioning the defendant on the hearsay rule and the California law governing the challenge of potential jurors, ruled that Faretta had not made an intelligent and knowing waiver of his right to counsel. The trial judge ruled that

there is no constitutional right to conduct one's own defense and appointed a public defender to represent Faretta. At the conclusion of the trial, Faretta was convicted and sentenced to prison. The California Court of Appeals affirmed the ruling of the trial court that Faretta had no federal or state constitutional right to represent himself. The California Supreme Court denied review, and the United States Supreme Court granted certiorari.

Mr. Justice STEWART delivered the opinion of the Court.

The Sixth and Fourteenth Amendments of our Constitution guarantee that a person brought to trial in any state or federal court must be afforded the right to the assistance of counsel before he can be validly convicted and punished by imprisonment. This clear constitutional rule has emerged from a series of cases decided here over the last 50 years. The question before us now is whether a defendant in a state criminal trial has a constitutional right to proceed *without* counsel when he voluntarily and intelligently elects to do so. Stated another way, the question is whether a State may constitutionally hale a person into its criminal courts and there force a lawyer upon him, even when he wants to conduct his own defense. It is not an easy question....

* * *

II

In the federal courts, the right of self-representation has been protected by statute since the beginnings of our Nation. Section 35 of the Judiciary Act of 1789, 1 Stat. 73, 92, enacted by the First Congress and signed by President Washington one day before the Sixth Amendment was proposed, provided that "in all courts of the United States, the parties may plead and manage their own causes personally or by the assistance of counsel...." The right is currently codified in 28 U.S.C. § 1654.

With few exceptions, each of the several States also accords a defendant the right to represent himself in any criminal case. The constitutions of 36 States explicitly confer that right. Moreover, many state courts have expressed the view that the right is also supported by the Constitution of the United States.

This Court has more than once indicated the same view. In Adams ex rel. McCann v. United States, 317 U.S. 269, 279 (1942), the Court recognized that the Sixth Amend-

ment right to the assistance of counsel implicitly embodies a "correlative right to dispense with a lawyer's help." The defendant in that case, indicted for federal mail fraud violations, insisted on conducting his own defense without benefit of counsel. He also requested a bench trial and signed a waiver of his right to trial by jury. The prosecution consented to the waiver of a jury, and the waiver was accepted by the court. The defendant was convicted, but the Court of Appeals reversed the conviction on the ground that a person accused of a felony could not competently waive his right to trial by jury except on the advice of a lawyer. This Court reversed and reinstated the conviction, holding that "an accused, in the exercise of free and intelligent choice, and with the considered approval of the court, may waive trial by jury, and so likewise may he competently and intelligently waive his Constitutional right to assistance of counsel." Id., at 275.

The Adams case does not, of course, necessarily resolve the issue before us. It held only that "the Constitution does not force a lawyer upon a defendant." Id., at 279. Whether the Constitution forbids a State from forcing a lawyer upon a defendant is a different question. But the Court in Adams did recognize, albeit in dictum, an affirmative right of self-representation: "The right to assistance of counsel and the *correlative right to dispense with a lawyer's help* are not legal formalisms. They rest on considerations that go to the substance of an accused's position before the law....

"What were contrived as protections for the accused should not be turned into fetters.... To deny an accused a choice of procedure in circumstances where he, though a layman, is as capable as any lawyer of making an intelligent choice, is to impair the worth of great Constitutional safeguards by treating them as empty verbalisms.

"... When the administration of the criminal law ... is hedged about as it is by the Constitutional safeguards for the protection of an accused, to deny him in the exercise of his free choice the right to dispense with some of these safeguards . . . is to imprison a man in his privileges and call it the Constitution" . . . (emphasis added).

In other settings as well, the Court has indicated that a defendant has a constitutionally protected right to represent himself in a criminal trial. For example, in Snyder v. Massachusetts, 291 U.S. 97 (1934), the Court held that the Confrontation Clause of the Sixth Amendment gives the accused a right to be present at all stages of the proceedings where fundamental fairness might be thwarted by his absence. This right to "presence" was based upon the premise that the "defense may be made easier if the accused is permitted to be present at the examination of jurors or the summing up of counsel, *for it will be in his power,* if present, to give advice or suggestion or *even to supersede his lawyers altogether and conduct the trial himself.*" Id., at 106 (emphasis added). And in Price v. Johnston, 334 U.S. 266 (1948) the Court, in holding that a convicted person had no absolute right to argue his own appeal, said this holding was in "sharp contrast" to his "recognized privilege of conducting his own defense at the trial." 334 U.S. at 285.

The United States Courts of Appeals have repeatedly held that the right of self-representation is protected by the Bill of Rights. . . . This Court's past recognition of the right of self-representation, the federal court authority holding the right to be of constitutional dimension, and the state constitutions pointing to the right's fundamental nature form a consensus not easily ignored. "[T]he fact that a path is a beaten one," Mr. Justice Jackson once observed, "is a persuasive reason for following it." We confront here a nearly universal conviction, on the part of our people as well as our courts, that forcing a lawyer upon an unwilling defendant is contrary to his basic right to defend himself if he truly wants to do so.

III

This consensus is soundly premised. The right of self-representation finds support in the structure of the Sixth Amendment, as well as in the English and colonial jurisprudence from which the Amendment emerged.

* * *

There can be no blinking the fact that the right of an accused to conduct his own defense seems to cut against the grain of this Court's decisions holding that the Constitution requires that no accused can be convicted and imprisoned unless he has been accorded the right to the assistance of counsel. . . . For it is surely true that the basic thesis of those decisions is that the help of a lawyer is essential to assure the defendant a fair trial. And a strong argument can surely be made that the whole thrust of those decisions must inevitably lead to the conclusion that a State may constitutionally impose a lawyer upon even an unwilling defendant.

But it is one thing to hold that every defendant, rich or poor, has the right to the assistance of counsel, and quite another to say that a State may compel a defendant to accept a lawyer he does not want. The value of state-appointed counsel was not unappreciated by the Founders, yet the notion of compulsory counsel was utterly foreign to them. And whatever else may be said of those who wrote the Bill of Rights, surely there can be no doubt that they understood the inestimable worth of free choice.

It is undeniable that in most criminal prosecutions defendants could better defend with counsel's guidance than by their own unskilled efforts. But where the defendant will not voluntarily accept representation by counsel, the potential advantage of a lawyer's training and experience can be realized, if at all, only imperfectly. To force a lawyer on a defendant can only lead him to believe that the law contrives against him. Moreover, it is not inconceivable that in some rare instances, the defendant might in fact present his case more effectively by conducting his own defense. Personal liberties are not rooted in the law of averages. The right to defend is personal. The defendant, and not his lawyer or the State, will bear the personal consequences of a conviction. It is the defendant, therefore, who must be free personally to decide whether in his particular case counsel is to his advantage. And although he may conduct his own defense ultimately to his own detriment, his choice must be honored out of "that respect for the individual which is the life-blood of the law." Illinois v. Allen, 397 U.S. 337, 350–351 (1970).

When an accused manages his own defense, he relinquishes, as a purely factual matter, many of the traditional benefits associated with the right to counsel. For this reason, in order to represent himself, the accused must "knowingly and intelligently" forego those relinquished benefits.... Although a defendant need not himself have the skill and experience of a lawyer in order competently and intelligently to choose self-representation, he should be made aware of the dangers and disadvantages of self-representation, so that the record will establish that "he knows what he is doing and his choice is made with eyes open."...

Here, weeks before trial, Faretta clearly and unequivocally declared to the trial judge that he wanted to represent himself and did not want counsel. The record affirmatively shows that Faretta was literate, competent, and understanding, and that he was voluntarily exercising his informed free will. The trial judge had warned Faretta that he thought it was a mistake not to accept the assistance of counsel, and that Faretta would be required to follow all the "ground rules" of trial procedure. We need make no assessment of how well or poorly Faretta had mastered the intricacies of the hearsay rule and the California code provisions that govern challenges of potential jurors on voir dire. For his technical legal knowledge, as such, was not relevant to an assessment of his knowing exercise of the right to defend himself.

In forcing Faretta, under these circumstances, to accept against his will a state-appointed public defender, the California courts deprived him of his constitutional right to conduct his own defense.

Vacated and remanded.

Mr. Chief Justice BURGER, with whom Mr. Justice BLACKMUN and Mr. Justice REHNQUIST join, dissenting.

This case ... is another example of the judicial tendency to constitutionalize what is thought "good." That effort fails on its own terms here, because there is nothing desirable or useful in permitting every accused person, even the most uneducated and inexperienced, to insist upon conducting his own defense to criminal charges. Moreover, there is no constitutional basis for the Court's holding and it can only add to the problems of an already malfunctioning criminal justice system. I therefore dissent.

Society has the right to expect that, when courts find new rights implied in the Constitution, their potential effects upon the resources of our criminal justice system will be considered. However, such considerations are conspicuously absent from the Court's opinion in this case.

It hardly needs repeating that courts at all levels are already handicapped by the unsupplied demand for competent advocates, with the result that it often takes far longer to complete a given case than experienced counsel would require. If we were to assume that there will be widespread exercise of the newly discovered constitutional right to self-representation, it would almost certainly follow that there will be added congestion in the courts and that the quality of justice will suffer. Moreover, the Court blandly assumes that once an accused has elected to defend himself he will be bound by his choice and not be heard to complain of it later. This assumption ignores the role of appellate review, for the reported cases are replete with instances of a convicted defendant being relieved of a deliberate decision even when made *with the advice of counsel*.... It is totally unrealistic, therefore, to suggest that an accused will always be held to the consequences of a decision to conduct his own defense. Unless, as may be the case, most persons accused of crime have more wit than to insist upon the dubious benefit that the Court confers today, we can expect that many expensive and good-faith prosecutions will be nullified on appeal for reasons that trial courts are now deprived of the power to prevent.

Mr. Justice BLACKMUN, with whom the Chief Justice and Mr. Justice REHNQUIST join, dissenting.

Today the Court holds that the Sixth Amendment guarantees to every defendant in a state criminal trial the right to proceed without counsel whenever he elects to do so. I find no textual support for this conclusion in the language of the Sixth Amendment. I find the historical evidence relied upon by the Court to be unpersuasive, especially in light of the recent history of criminal procedure. Finally, I fear that the right to self-representation constitutionalized today frequently will cause procedural confusion without advancing any significant strategic interest of the defendant. I therefore dissent.

* * *

[I] note briefly the procedural problems that, I suspect, today's decision will visit upon trial courts in the future. Although the Court indicates that a pro se defendant necessarily waives any claim he might otherwise make of ineffective assistance of counsel ... the opinion leaves open a host of other procedural questions. Must every defendant be advised of his right to proceed pro se? If so, when must that notice be given? Since the right to assistance of counsel and the right to self-representation are mutually exclusive, how is the waiver of each right to be measured? If a defendant has elected to exercise his right to proceed pro se, does he still have a constitutional right to assistance of standby counsel? How

soon in the criminal proceeding must a defendant decide between proceeding by counsel or pro se? Must he be allowed to switch in midtrial? May a violation of the right to self-representation ever be harmless error? Must the trial court treat the pro se defendant differently than it would professional counsel? I assume that many of these questions will be answered with finality in due course. Many of them, however, such as the standards of waiver and the treatment of the pro se defendant, will haunt the trial of every defendant who elects to exercise his right to self-representation. The procedural problems spawned by an absolute right to self-representation will far outweigh whatever tactical advantage the defendant may feel he has gained by electing to represent himself.

If there is any truth to the old proverb that "one who is his own lawyer has a fool for a client," the Court by its opinion today now bestows a *constitutional* right on one to make a fool of himself.

The "Christian Burial" Case

ORAL ARGUMENTS BEFORE THE U.S. SUPREME COURT*

Brewer v. Williams, No. 74-1263; argued 10/4/76

On the opening day of the new Term, the Court was urged either to disapprove or limit *Miranda* v. *Arizona,* 384 U.S. 436. Richard C. Turner, Attorney General of Iowa, told the Justices that the 10-year-old *Miranda* rule should be replaced by a voluntariness standard. The crucial inquiry in determining whether or not to admit a defendant's inculpatory statement should be: whether under the totality of the circumstances it was voluntarily made.

A jury convicted Robert Williams of the murder of a 10-year-old girl. His conviction

*From 20 Crim. L. Rptr. 4033–4034. Reprinted by permission of the Bureau of National Affairs, Inc.

was affirmed by the Iowa Supreme Court. But on federal attack, a district court granted him habeas relief, and a divided U.S. Court of Appeals affirmed the district court's decision that Williams' statements were not voluntary.

After a child stealing warrant had been issued for Williams' arrest, he called a Des Moines attorney who advised him to surrender to Davenport, Iowa, police. Brewer, who lived in Des Moines, had gone to Davenport. A little later, the lawyer went to the Des Moines police station and again spoke to Williams by phone. In the presence of the chief of police and Detective Leaming, he told Williams by phone that Williams would be driven to Des Moines from Davenport by officers. He was also told not to make any statements. Detectives Leaming and Nelson transported Williams to Des Moines.

Before leaving, the officers gave Williams *Miranda* warnings. These warnings were not repeated during the trip. Leaming knew that Williams was an escapee from a Missouri mental institution. During this trip, Williams revealed the location of the young girl's body.

"How far is it from Davenport to Des Moines?" one of the Justices asked.

"About 163 miles, your honor," counsel replied.

Turner told the Justices that the officers talked with Williams during the trip, but did not question him directly about the girl's murder.

Mr. Justice Stevens: "Is it correct to say that the officers wanted the defendant to reveal [the location of] the child's body?"

"Yes, sir."

The dialogue between the officers and Williams was spurred, in part, by the length of the long drive on the icy Iowa roads and the weather outside, Turner said. As the car drove along, Williams spontaneously volunteered to the officers: "Did you find her shoes?" Later at a rest stop, Williams asked: "Did you find the blanket?" Witnesses earlier had told police that Williams might have wrapped her body in a blanket.

Not far out of Davenport, Leaming told Williams that it would be very difficult to locate the girl's body due to weather conditions. He suggested that if Williams knew the location of the body, they could find it so that the girl could get a "Christian burial." Leaming did not accuse Williams of the murder.

Agreement?

The Justices' attention soon shifted to the question of the existence of an agreement between officers and defense attorneys that ostensibly barred interrogation of Williams during the trip.

"I submit that the officers didn't agree to anything," Turner said.

Mr. Justice Rehnquist: "Is that sort of an agreement enforceable under Iowa law?"

Turner thought not, even assuming the existence of the agreement.

Mr. Justice Stewart: "I thought we had to accept that there was an agreement." Both the district court and the state trial judge concluded that such an agreement existed, he pointed out.

The state trial court record was incomplete on this point, Turner observed, but he reiterated his view that there was no such agreement.

Mr. Justice Rehnquist: "How did the Supreme Court of Iowa rest on that point [the agreement]?"

"The Iowa Supreme Court made no rulings on that point," Turner replied.

Mr. Justice Marshall: "As the record stands now, everybody agrees there was an agreement except you."

"Yes sir, that's correct."

Mr. Justice Powell: "What is your view on whether or not the agreement was broken?"

Assuming its existence, Turner asserted that the agreement was not broken.

Turning to Leaming's "monologue" about the "Christian burial," Mr. Justice Powell asked if those statements amounted to "interrogation."

Mr. Justice Powell: "Isn't the point that the officer wanted to elicit information from the defendant?"

"Yes, sir."

On the "agreement" point, Mr. Justice Powell asked if an understanding of this nature would have been binding if entered into between a prosecutor and a defense attorney.

Counsel thought so.

Mr. Justice Stevens: "Does your position depend on the fact that the police rather than a prosecutor [made this agreement]?"

"Yes, sir."

Waiver?

Mr. Justice Marshall then focused on the question of the defendant's waiver of his right to counsel. "Did he waive his right to a lawyer?"

"Yes, sir, I think that he did," Turner answered.

Mr. Justice Marshall: "Did he say anything about a waiver?"

A waiver does not have to be explicit, Turner argued. It can be accomplished by conduct.

Mr. Justice Marshall continued on this point. "When did he waive his right to a lawyer?"

"Sir, he never expressly said: 'I waive.' "

"Nonetheless, did defendant say or do

anything that could be interpreted as a waiver?" Mr. Justice Marshall asked.

Turner thought that Williams' own questions to the officers indicated a waiver of his rights. He pointed to Williams question: "Did you find her shoes?"

Williams knew his constitutional rights, Turner explained. Both of his lawyers had warned him not to talk. He made his inculpatory statements in spite of those warnings. The Chief Justice: "He waives his rights by talking [on substantive elements of the crime]?"

"I think he does." A defendant can waive his rights by proceeding without counsel, Turner submitted.

The Chief Justice: "Did he waive his right to remain silent?"

"Yes, sir."

In response to questioning from Mr. Justice Stevens, Turner told the Court that the officers' conduct here did not rise to the level of a constitutional violation. Williams' actions were completely voluntary. This case is simply distinguishable from the gross misconduct in *Escobedo* v. *Illinois*, 378 U.S. 478 (1964).

Mr. Justice Blackmun: "Would *Stone* v. *Powell* affect this case?"

The defendant was granted habeas relief before the *Stone* decision. But Turner noted that the defendant had received a full and fair adjudication of his claims in the Iowa courts. *Stone* should be extended to these facts, he urged.

Turning to *Miranda,* counsel argued that this case points up the need for disapproval or limitation of *Miranda.* The officers did nothing wrong here.

Voluntariness

Robert Bartels, counsel for the defendant, began his argument by noting that the police had been warned against interrogating Williams. Nothing in this case indicates that the defendant waived his right to counsel. There is sufficient support in the record for the district court's finding that these inculpatory statements were made involuntarily.

While the Iowa Supreme Court made no explicit finding on the existence of an agreement between the police and the defense lawyers, it left the trial court's findings on that point undisturbed.

The Chief Justice: "Assuming the [existence of an] agreement, in the attorney-client relationship, who is the master, the servant?"

"Sir, the client is master; the attorney the servant."

The Chief Justice: "Can a defendant change an agreement made by his attorney?"

In certain circumstances, a client may modify or change such an agreement, Bartels replied. But here, Williams neither rejected the agreement nor waived its terms later.

Bartels explained that Leaming's "Christian burial" speech was the turning point for the defendant. Before that monologue, Williams had given little or no information that might incriminate him.

Counsel told Mr. Justice Rehnquist that the "Christian burial" remarks were coercive. The reference to a "Christian burial" was obviously designed to play on Williams' strong religious feelings.

As to the agreement, Bartels pointed out that the defense attorneys relied on the officers' promises. The lawyers were misled by the officers into forgoing other means to assure that their client's rights would be protected.

Mr. Justice Rehnquist: "Is that agreement enforceable?"

As to the defendant, counsel noted, it is enforceable.

Mr. Justice Rehnquist: "What you are saying is that it's enforceable as a constitutional right, not as a contract?"

"Yes, sir."

Counsel went on to assert that the officers' purposeful attempts to obtain information were violative of the defendant's right to counsel, quite apart from any consideration of *Miranda.* While the Eighth Circuit ostensibly rested its decision on *Miranda,* Bartels noted that it did not disturb the district judge's finding on the voluntariness point. "The Eighth Circuit was faced with equally persuasive theories."

Mr. Justice Rehnquist: "There is not a sentence in the Eighth Circuit opinion's referring to voluntariness."

"Yes, sir, that's correct."

But counsel pointed out that Williams relied strongly on *Escobedo, Massiah* v. *U.S.,* 377 U.S. 201 (1963), and the Sixth and Fourteenth Amendments. The defendant simply did not waive his right to counsel.

Nor did counsel think *Stone* v. *Powell* should be extended here. "To apply *Stone* here would be to go beyond the Court's holding in that case."

Under the state's view, law enforcement officers may do anything short of violence to obtain information. That view simply emasculates the Fifth, Sixth, and Fourteenth Amendments, he said.

BREWER v. WILLIAMS

Supreme Court of the United States, 1977
430 U.S. 387, 97 S. Ct. 1232, 51 L. Ed. 2d 424

The facts appear in the opinion.

Mr. Justice STEWART delivered the opinion of the Court.

An Iowa trial jury found the respondent, Robert Williams, guilty of murder. The judgment of conviction was affirmed in the Iowa Supreme Court by a closely divided vote. In a subsequent habeas corpus proceeding a federal district court ruled that under the United States Constitution Williams is entitled to a new trial, and a divided Court of Appeals for the Eighth Circuit agreed. The question before us is whether the District Court and the Court of Appeals were wrong.

I

On the afternoon of December 24, 1968, a 10-year-old girl named Pamela Powers went with her family to the YMCA in Des Moines, Iowa, to watch a wrestling tournament in which her brother was participating. When she failed to return from a trip to the washroom, a search for her began. The search was unsuccessful.

Robert Williams, who had recently escaped from a mental hospital, was a resident of the YMCA. Soon after the girl's disappearance Williams was seen in the YMCA lobby carrying some clothing and a large bundle wrapped in a blanket. He obtained help from a 14-year-old boy in opening the street door of the YMCA and the door to his automobile parked outside. When Williams placed the bundle in the front seat of his car the boy "saw two legs in it and they were skinny and white." Before anyone could see what was in the bundle Williams drove away. His abandoned car was found the following day in Davenport, Iowa, roughly 160 miles east of Des Moines. A warrant was then issued in Des Moines for his arrest on a charge of abduction.

On the morning of December 26, a Des Moines lawyer named Henry McKnight went to the Des Moines police station and informed the officers present that he had just received a long distance call from Williams, and that he had advised Williams to turn himself in to the Davenport police. Williams did surrender that morning to the police in Davenport, and they booked him on the charge specified in the arrest warrant and gave him the warnings required in Miranda v. Arizona, 384 U.S. 436 (1966). The Davenport police then telephoned their counterparts in Des Moines to inform them that Williams had surrendered. McKnight, the lawyer, was still at the Des Moines police headquarters, and Williams conversed with McKnight on the telephone. In the presence of the Des Moines Chief of Police and a Police Detective named Leaming, McKnight advised Williams that Des Moines police officers would be driving to Davenport to pick him up, that the officers would not interrogate him or mistreat him, and that Williams was not to talk to the officers about Pamela Powers until after consulting with McKnight upon his return to Des Moines. As a result of these conversations, it was agreed between McKnight and the Des Moines police officials that Detective Leaming and a fellow officer would drive to Davenport to pick up Williams, that they would bring him directly back to Des Moines, and that they would not question him during the trip.

In the meantime Williams was arraigned before a judge in Davenport on the outstanding arrest warrant. The judge advised him of his Miranda rights and committed him to jail. Before leaving the courtroom, Williams conferred with a lawyer named Kelly, who advised him not to make any statements until consulting with McKnight back in Des Moines.

Detective Leaming and his fellow officer arrived in Davenport about noon to pick up Williams and return him to Des Moines. Soon after their arrival they met with Williams and Kelly, who, they understood, was acting as Williams' lawyer. Detective Leaming repeated the Miranda warnings, and told Williams:

"[W]e both know that you're being represented here by Mr. Kelly and you're being represented by Mr. McKnight in Des Moines, and . . . I want you to remember this because we'll be visiting between here and Des Moines."

Williams then conferred again with Kelly alone, and after this conference Kelly reiterated to Detective Leaming that Williams was not to be questioned about the disappearance of Pamela Powers until after he had consulted with McKnight back in Des Moines. When Leaming expressed some reservations, Kelly firmly stated that the agreement with McKnight was to be carried out — that there was to be no interrogation of Williams during the automobile journey to Des Moines. Kelly was denied permission to ride in the police car back to Des Moines with Williams and the two officers.

The two Detectives, with Williams in their charge, then set out on the 160-mile drive. At no time during the trip did Williams express a willingness to be interrogated in the absence of an attorney. Instead, he stated several times that "[w]hen I get to Des Moines and see Mr. McKnight, I am going to tell you the whole story." Detective Leaming knew that Williams was a former mental patient, and knew also that he was deeply religious.

The Detective and his prisoner soon embarked on a wide-ranging conversation covering a variety of topics, including the subject of religion. Then, not long after leaving Davenport and reaching the interstate highway, Detective Leaming delivered what has been referred to in the briefs and oral arguments as the "Christian burial speech." Addressing Williams as "Reverend," the Detective said:

"I want to give you something to think about while we're traveling down the road . . . . Number one, I want you to observe the weather conditions, it's raining, it's sleeting, it's freezing, driving is very treacherous, visibility is poor, it's going to be dark early this evening. They are predicting several inches of snow for tonight, and I feel that you yourself are the only person that knows where this little girl's body is, that you yourself have only been there once, and if you get a snow on top of it you yourself may be unable to find it. And, since we will be going right past the area on the way into Des Moines, I feel that we could stop and locate the body, that the parents of this little girl should be entitled to a Christian burial for the little girl who was snatched away from them on Christmas Eve and murdered. And I feel we should stop and locate it on the way in rather than waiting until morning and trying to come back out after a snow storm and possibly not being able to find it at all."

Williams asked Detective Leaming why he thought their route to Des Moines would be taking them past the girl's body, and Leaming responded that he knew the body was in the area of Mitchellville — a town they would be passing on the way to Des Moines. Leaming then stated: "I do not want you to answer me. I don't want to discuss it further. Just think about it as we're riding down the road."

As the car approached Grinnell, a town approximately 100 miles west of Davenport Williams asked whether the police had found the victim's shoes. When Detective Leaming replied that he was unsure, Williams directed the officers to a service station where he said he had left the shoes; a search for them proved unsuccessful. As they continued towards Des Moines, Williams asked whether the police had found the blanket, and directed the officers to a rest area where he said he had disposed of the blanket. Nothing was found. The car continued towards Des Moines, and as it approached Mitchellville, Williams said that he would show the officers where the body was. He then directed the police to the body of Pamela Powers.

Williams was indicted for first-degree murder. Before trial, his counsel moved to suppress all evidence relating to or resulting from any statements Williams had made during the automobile ride from Davenport to Des Moines. After an evidentiary hearing the trial judge denied the motion. He found that "an agreement was made between defense counsel and the police officials to the effect that the Defendant was not to be questioned on the return trip to Des Moines," and that the evidence in question had been elicited from Williams during a "critical stage in the proceedings requiring the presence of counsel on his request." The judge ruled, however, that Williams had "waived his right to have an attorney present during the giving of such information."

The evidence in question was introduced over counsel's continuing objection at the subsequent trial. The jury found Williams guilty of murder, and the judgment of conviction was affirmed by the Iowa Supreme Court, a bare majority of whose members agreed with the trial court that Williams had "waived his right to the presence of his counsel" on the automobile ride from Davenport to Des Moines. State v. Williams, 182 N.W.2d 396, 402. The four dissenting justices expressed the view that "when counsel and police have agreed defendant is not to be questioned until counsel is present and defendant has been advised not to talk and repeatedly has stated he will tell the whole story after he talks with counsel, the state should be required to make a stronger showing of intentional voluntary waiver than was made here." Id, at 408.

Williams then petitioned for a writ of habeas corpus in the United States District Court for the Southern District of Iowa. Counsel for the State and for Williams stipulated "that the case would be submitted on the record of facts and proceedings in the trial court, without taking of further testimony." The District Court made findings of fact as summarized above, and concluded as a matter of law that the evidence in question had been wrongly admitted at Williams' trial. This conclusion was based on three alternative and independent grounds: (1) that Williams had been denied his constitutional right to the assistance of counsel; (2) that he had been denied the constitutional protections defined by this Court's decisions in Escobedo v. Illinois, 378 U.S. 478 (1964), and Miranda v. Arizona, 384 U.S. 436 (1966); and (3) that in any event, his self-incriminatory statements on the automobile trip from Davenport to Des Moines had been involuntarily made. Further, the District Court ruled that there had been no waiver by Williams of the constitutional protections in question. Williams v. Brewer, 375 F. Supp. 174.

The Court of Appeals for the Eighth Circuit, with one judge dissenting, affirmed this judgment, 509 F.2d 227, and denied a petition for rehearing en banc. We granted certiorari to consider the constitutional issues presented. 423 U.S. 1031.

II

[T]here is no need to review in this case the doctrine of Miranda v. Arizona, supra, a doctrine designed to secure the constitutional privilege against compulsory self-incrimination, Michigan v. Tucker, 417 U.S. 433, 438–439 (1974). It is equally unnecessary to evaluate the ruling of the District Court that Williams' self-incriminating statements were, indeed, involuntarily made. Cf. Spano v. New York, 360 U.S. 315 (1959). For it is clear that the judgment before us must in any event be affirmed upon the ground that Williams was deprived of a different constitutional right—the right to the assistance of counsel.

This right, guaranteed by the Sixth and Fourteenth Amendments, is indispensable to the fair administration of our adversary system of criminal justice. . . .

There has occasionally been a difference of opinion within the Court as to the peripheral scope of this constitutional right. See Kirby v. Illinois, 406 U.S. 682 (1972). Coleman v. Alabama, 399 U.S. 1 (1970). But its basic contours, which are identical in state and federal contexts, Gideon v. Wainwright, 372 U.S. 335 (1963) [supra], Argersinger v. Hamlin, 407 U.S. 25 (1972) [supra], are too well established to require extensive elaboration here. Whatever else it may mean, the right to counsel granted by the Sixth and Fourteenth Amendments means at least that a person is entitled to the help of a lawyer at or after the time that judicial proceedings have been initiated against him—"whether by way of formal charge, preliminary hearing, indictment, information, or arraignment.". . .

There can be no doubt in the present case that judicial proceedings had been initiated against Williams before the start of the automobile ride from Davenport to Des Moines. A warrant had been issued for his arrest, he had been arraigned on that warrant before a judge in a Davenport courtroom, and he had been committed by the court to confinement in jail. The State does not contend otherwise.

There can be no serious doubt, either, that Detective Leaming deliberately and designedly set out to elicit information from Williams just as surely as—and perhaps more effectively than—if he had formally interrogated him. Detective Leaming was fully aware before departing from Des Moines that Williams was being represented in Davenport by Kelly and in Des Moines by McKnight. Yet he purposely sought during Williams' isolation from his lawyers to obtain as much incriminating information as possible. Indeed, Detective Leaming conceded as much when he testified at Williams' trial:

"Q. In fact, Captain, whether he was a mental patient or not, you were trying to get all the information you could before he got to his lawyer, weren't you?

"A. I was sure hoping to find out where that little girl was, yes, sir.

"Q. Well, I'll put it this way: You was hoping to get all the information you could before Williams got back to McKnight, weren't you?

"A. Yes, sir."

The State courts clearly proceeded upon the hypothesis that Detective Leaming's "Christian burial speech" had been tantamount to interrogation. Both courts recognized that Williams had been entitled to the assistance of counsel at the time he made the incriminating statements. Yet no such constitutional protection would have come into play if there had been no interrogation.

The circumstances of this case are thus constitutionally indistinguishable from those presented in Massiah v. United States, 377 U.S. 201 (1964). The petitioner in that case was indicted for violating the federal narcotics law. He retained a lawyer, pleaded not guilty, and was released on bail. While he was free on bail a federal agent succeeded by surreptitious means in listening to incriminating statements by him. Evidence of these statements was introduced against the petitioner at his trial, and he was convicted. This Court reversed the conviction, holding "that the petitioner was denied the basic protections of that guarantee [the right to counsel] when there was used against him at his trial evidence of his own incriminating words, which federal agents had deliberately solicited from him after he had been indicted and in the absence of his counsel." 377 U.S., at 206.

That the incriminating statements were elicited surreptitiously in the Massiah case, and otherwise here, is constitutionally irrelevant. . . . Rather, the clear rule of Massiah is that once adversary proceedings have commenced against an individual, he has a right to legal representation when the government interrogates him. It thus requires no wooden or technical application of the Massiah doctrine to conclude that Williams was entitled to the assistance of counsel guaranteed to him by the Sixth and Fourteenth Amendments.

III

The Iowa courts recognized that Williams had been denied the constitutional right to the assistance of counsel. They held, however, that he had waived that right during the course of the automobile trip from Davenport to Des Moines. . . .

In its lengthy opinion affirming this determination, the Iowa Supreme Court applied "the totality-of-circumstances test for a showing of waiver of constitutionally protected rights in the absence of an express waiver," and concluded "that evidence of the time element involved on the trip, the general circumstances of it, and the absence of any request or expressed desire for the aid of counsel before or at the time of giving information, were sufficient to sustain a conclusion that defendant did waive his constitutional rights as alleged." 182 N.W.2d, at 402.

In the federal habeas corpus proceeding the District Court, believing that the issue of waiver was not one of fact but of federal law, held that the Iowa courts had "applied the wrong constitutional standards" in ruling that Williams had waived the protections that were his under the Constitution. 375 F.

Supp., at 182. The court held "that it is the *government* which bears a heavy burden . . . but that is the burden which explicitly was placed on [Williams] by the state courts." Ibid. (emphasis in original). . . .

The Court of Appeals approved the reasoning of the District Court:

"A review of the record here . . . discloses no facts to support the conclusion of the state court that [Williams] had waived his constitutional rights other than that [he] had made incriminating statements. . . . The District Court here properly concluded that an incorrect constitutional standard had been applied by the state court in determining the issue of waiver. . . .

"[T]his court recently held that an accused can voluntarily, knowingly and intelligently waive his right to have counsel present at an interrogation after counsel has been appointed. . . . The prosecution, however, has the weighty obligation to show that the waiver was knowingly and intelligently made. We quite agree with [the District Court] that the state here failed to so show." 509 F.2d, at 233.

The District Court and the Court of Appeals were correct in the view that the question of waiver was not a question of historical fact, but one which . . . requires "application of constitutional principles to the facts as found. . . ." . . .

The District Court and the Court of Appeals were also correct in their understanding of the proper standard to be applied in determining the question of waiver as a matter of federal constitutional law—that it was incumbent upon the State to prove "an intentional relinquishment or abandonment of a known right or privilege." Johnson v. Zerbst, 304 U.S. 458, 464 (1938). That standard has been reiterated in many cases. We have said that the right to counsel does not depend upon a request by the defendant . . . and that courts indulge in every reasonable presumption against waiver. . . . This strict standard applies equally to an alleged waiver of the right to counsel whether at trial or at a critical stage of pretrial proceedings. . . .

We conclude, finally, that the Court of Appeals was correct in holding that, judged by these standards, the record in this case falls far short of sustaining the State's burden. It is true that Williams had been informed of and appeared to understand his right to counsel. But waiver requires not merely comprehension but relinquishment, and Williams' consistent reliance upon the advice of counsel in dealing with the authorities refutes any suggestion that he waived that right. He consulted McKnight by long distance telephone before turning himself in. He spoke with McKnight by telephone again shortly after being booked. After he was arraigned Williams sought out and obtained legal advice from Kelly. Williams again consulted with Kelly after Detective Leaming and his fellow officer arrived in Davenport. Throughout, Williams was advised not to make any statements before seeing McKnight in Des Moines, and was assured that the police had agreed not to question him. His statements while in the car that he would tell the whole story *after* seeing McKnight in Des Moines were the clearest expressions by Williams himself that he desired the presence of an attorney before any interrogation took place. But even before making these statements, Williams had effectively asserted his right to counsel by having secured attorneys at both ends of the automobile trip, both of whom, acting as his agents, had made clear to the police that no interrogation was to occur during the journey. Williams knew of that agreement and, particularly in view of his consistent reliance on counsel, there is no basis for concluding that he disavowed it.

Despite Williams' express and implicit assertions of his right to counsel, Detective Leaming proceeded to elicit incriminating statements from Williams. Leaming did not preface this effort by telling Williams that he had a right to the presence of a lawyer, and made no effort at all to ascertain whether Williams wished to relinquish that right. The circumstances of record in this case thus provide no reasonable basis for finding that Williams waived his right to the assistance of counsel.

The Court of Appeals did not hold, nor do we, that under the circumstances of this case Williams *could not,* without notice to counsel, have waived his rights under the Sixth and Fourteenth Amendments. It only held, as do we, that he did not.

IV

The crime of which Williams was convicted was senseless and brutal, calling for swift and energetic action by the police to apprehend the perpetrator and gather evidence with which he could be convicted. No mission of law enforcement officials is more important.... Although we do not lightly affirm the issuance of a writ of habeas corpus in this case, so clear a violation of the Sixth and Fourteenth Amendments as here occurred cannot be condoned. The pressures on state executive and judicial officers charged with the administration of the criminal law are great, especially when the crime is murder and the victim a small child. But it is precisely the predictability of those pressures that makes imperative a resolute loyalty to the guarantees that the Constitution extends to us all.

The judgment of the Court of Appeals is affirmed.

Mr. Justice MARSHALL, concurring.

I concur wholeheartedly in my Brother STEWART's opinion for the Court, but add these words in light of the dissenting opinions filed today. The dissenters have, I believe, lost sight of the fundamental constitutional backbone of our criminal law. They seem to think that Detective Leaming's actions were perfectly proper, indeed laudable, examples of "good police work." In my view, good police work is something far different from catching the criminal at any price. It is equally important that the police, as guardians of the law, fulfill their responsibility to obey its commands scrupulously. For "in the end life and liberty can be as much endangered from illegal methods used to convict those thought to be criminals as from the actual criminals themselves." Spano v. New York, 360 U.S. 315, 320–321 (1959).

Leaming knowingly isolated Williams from the protection of his lawyers and during that period he intentionally "persuaded" him to give incriminating evidence. It is this intentional police misconduct—not good police practice—that the Court rightly condemns. The heinous nature of the crime is no excuse, as the dissenters would have it, for condoning knowing and intentional police transgression of the constitutional rights of a defendant. If Williams is to go free—and given the ingenuity of Iowa prosecutors on retrial or in a civil commitment proceeding, I doubt very much that there is any chance a dangerous criminal will be loosed on the streets, the bloodcurdling

cries of the dissenters notwithstanding—it will hardly be because he deserves it. It will be because Detective Leaming, knowing full well that he risked reversal of Williams' conviction, intentionally denied Williams the right of *every* American under the Sixth Amendment to have the protective shield of a lawyer between himself and the awesome power of the State.

I think it appropriate here to recall ... the closing words of Justice Brandeis' great dissent in Olmstead v. United States, 277 U.S. 438, 471, 485 (1928):

"In a government of laws, existence of the government will be imperilled if it fails to observe the law scrupulously. Our government is the potent, the omnipresent teacher. For good or for ill, it teaches the whole people by its example. Crime is contagious. If the Government becomes a lawbreaker, it breeds contempt for law; it invites every man to become a law unto himself; it invites anarchy. To declare that in the administration of the criminal law the end justifies the means—to declare that the Government may commit crimes in order to secure the conviction of a private criminal—would bring terrible retribution. Against that pernicious doctrine this Court should resolutely set its face."

Mr. Justice POWELL, concurring.

[R]esolution of the issues in this case turns primarily on one's perception of the facts. There is little difference of opinion, among the several courts (and numerous judges) who have reviewed the case, as to the relevant constitutional principles: (i) Williams had the right to assistance of counsel; (ii) once that right attached (it is conceded that it had in this case), the State could not properly interrogate Williams in the absence of counsel unless he voluntarily and knowingly waived the right; and (iii) the burden was on the State to show that Williams in fact had waived the right before the police interrogated him.

The critical factual issue is whether there had been a voluntary waiver, and this turns in large part upon whether there was interrogation....

I join the opinion of the Court which ... finds that the efforts of Detective Leaming "to elicit information from Williams," as conceded by counsel for the State at oral argument, ... were a skillful and effective form of interrogation. Moreover, the entire setting was conducive to the psychological coercion that was successfully exploited. Williams was known by the police to be a young man with quixotic religious convictions and a history of mental disorders. The date was Christmas eve, the weather was ominous, the setting appropriate for Detective Leaming's talk of snow concealing the body and preventing a "Christian burial." Williams was alone in the automobile with two police officers for several hours. It is clear from the record, as both of the federal courts below found, that there was no evidence of a knowing and voluntary waiver of the right to have counsel present beyond the fact that Williams ultimately confessed. It is settled law that an inferred waiver of a constitutional right is disfavored. Estelle v. Williams, 425 U.S. 501, 515 (1976) (POWELL, J., concurring). I find no basis in the record of this case—or in the dissenting opinions—for disagreeing with the conclusion of the District Court that "the State has produced no affirmative evidence whatever to support its claim of waiver." 375 F. Supp., at 183.

The dissenting opinion of the CHIEF JUSTICE states that the Court's holding today "conclusively presumes a suspect is legally incompetent to change his mind and tell the truth until an attorney is present." I find no justification for this view. On the contrary, the opinion of the Court is explicitly clear that the right to assistance of counsel may be waived, after it has attached, without notice to or consultation with counsel. We would have such a case here if the State had proved that the police officers refrained from coercion and interrogation, as they had agreed, and that Williams freely on his own initiative had confessed the crime.

* * *

Mr. Justice STEVENS, concurring.

* * *

Nothing that we write, no matter how well reasoned or forcefully expressed, can bring back the victim of this tragedy or undo the consequences of the official neglect which led to the respondent's escape from a State mental institution. The emotional aspects of the case make it difficult to decide dispassionately, but do not qualify our obligation to apply the law with an eye to the future as well as with concern for the result in the particular case before us.

Underlying the surface issue in this case is the question whether a fugitive from justice can rely on his lawyer's advice given in connection with a decision to surrender voluntarily. The defendant placed his trust in an experienced Iowa trial lawyer who in turn trusted the Iowa law enforcement authorities to honor a commitment made during negotiations which led to the apprehension of a potentially dangerous person. Under any analysis, this was a critical stage of the proceeding in which the participation of an independent professional was of vital importance to the accused and to society. At this stage—as in countless others in which the law profoundly affects the life of the individual—the lawyer is the essential medium through which the demands and commitments of the sovereign are communicated to the citizen. If, in the long run, we are seriously concerned about the individual's effective representation by counsel, the State cannot be permitted to dishonor its promise to this lawyer.

Mr. Chief Justice BURGER, dissenting.

The result reached by the Court in this case ought to be intolerable in any society which purports to call itself an organized society. It continues the court—by the narrowest margin—on the much criticized course of punishing the public for the mistakes and misdeeds of law enforcement officers, instead of punishing the officer directly, if in fact he is guilty of wrongdoing. It mechanically and blindly keeps reliable evidence from juries whether the claimed constitutional violation involves gross police misconduct or honest human error. Williams is guilty of the savage murder of a small child; no Member of the Court contends he is not. While in custody, and after no fewer than *five* warnings of his rights to silence and to counsel, he led police to the place where he had buried the body of his victim. The Court now holds the jury must not be told how the police found the body.

The Court concedes Williams was not threatened or coerced and that he acted voluntarily and with full awareness of his constitutional rights when he guided police to the body. In the face of all this, the Court now holds that because Williams was prompted by the detective's statement — not interrogation but a statement — his disclosure cannot be given to the jury. . . . [I] categorically reject the remarkable notion that the police in this case were guilty of unconstitutional misconduct, or any conduct justifying the bizarre result reached by the Court. Apart from a brief comment on the merits, however, I wish to focus on the irrationality of applying the increasingly discredited exclusionary rule to this case.

I

The Court Concedes Williams' Disclosures Were Voluntary

Under well-settled precedents which the Court freely acknowledges, it is very clear that Williams had made a valid waiver of his Fifth Amendment right to silence and his Sixth Amendment right to counsel when he led police to the child's body. Indeed, even under the Court's analysis I do not understand how a contrary conclusion is possible.

The Court purports to apply as the appropriate constitutional waiver standard the familiar "intentional relinquishment or abandonment of a known right or privilege" test of Johnson v. Zerbst, 304 U.S. 458, 464 (1938). The Court assumes, without deciding, that Williams' conduct and statements were voluntary. It concedes, as it must . . . that Williams had been informed of and fully understood his constitutional rights and the consequences of their waiver. Then having either assumed or found every element necessary to make out a valid waiver under its own test, the Court reaches the astonishing conclusion that no valid waiver has been demonstrated.

* * *

The evidence is uncontradicted that Williams had abundant knowledge of his right to have counsel present and of his right to silence. Since the Court does not question Williams' mental competence, it boggles the mind to suggest that he could not understand that leading police to the child's body would have other than the most serious consequences. All of the elements necessary to make out a valid waiver are shown by the record and, paradoxically, acknowledged by the Court; we thus are left to guess how the Court reached its holding.

One plausible but unarticulated basis for the result reached is that once a suspect has asserted his right not to talk without the presence of an attorney, it becomes legally impossible to waive that right until the suspect has seen an attorney. But constitutional rights are *personal,* and an otherwise valid waiver should not be brushed aside by judges simply because an attorney was not present. The Court's holding operates to "imprison a man in his privileges," Adams v. United States ex rel. McCann, 317 U.S. 269, 280 (1942); it conclusively presumes a suspect is legally incompetent to change his mind and tell the truth until an attorney is present. It denigrates an individual to some sort of nonperson whose free will has become hostage to a lawyer so that until a lawyer consents, the suspect is deprived of any legal right or power to decide for himself that he wishes to make a disclosure. It denies that the rights to counsel and silence are *personal,* nondelegable, and subject to a waiver only by that individual. The opinions in support of the Court's judgment do not enlighten us as to why police conduct — whether good or bad — should operate to suspend Williams' right to change his mind and "tell all" at once rather than waiting until he reached Des Moines.

In his concurring opinion Mr. Justice POWELL suggests that the result in this case turns on whether Detective Leaming's remarks constituted "interrogation," as he views them, or whether they were "statements" intended to prick the conscience of the accused. I find it most remarkable that a murder case should turn on judicial interpretation that a statement becomes a question simply because it is followed by an incriminating disclosure from the suspect. The Court seems to be saying that since Williams said he would "tell the whole story" at Des Moines, the police should have been content and waited; of course, that would have been the wiser course, especially in light of the nuances of constitutional jurisprudence applied by the Court, but a murder case ought not turn on such tenuous strands.

In any case, the Court assures us . . . this is not at all what it intends, and that a valid waiver was *possible* in these circumstances, but was not quite made. Here of course Williams did not confess to the murder in so many words; it was his conduct in guiding police to the body, not his words, which incriminated him. And the record is replete with evidence that Williams knew precisely what he was doing when he guided police to the body. The human urge to confess wrongdoing is, of course, normal in all save hardened, professional criminals, as psychiatrists and analysts have demonstrated. T. Reik, The Compulsion to Confess.

II

The Exclusionary Rule Should Not Be Applied to Non-egregious Police Conduct

Even if there was no waiver, and assuming a technical violation occurred, the Court errs gravely in mechanically applying the exclusionary rule without considering whether that draconian judicial doctrine should be invoked in these circumstances, or indeed whether any of its conceivable goals will be furthered by its application here.

The obvious flaws of the exclusionary rule as a judicial remedy are familiar.... Today's holding interrupts what has been a more rational perception of the constitutional and social utility of excluding reliable evidence from the truth-seeking process. In its Fourth Amendment context, we have now recognized that the exclusionary rule is in no sense a *personal* constitutional right, but a judicially conceived remedial device designed to safeguard and effectuate guaranteed legal rights generally.... We have repeatedly emphasized that deterrence of unconstitutional or otherwise unlawful police conduct is the only valid justification for excluding reliable and probative evidence from the criminal factfinding process....

Accordingly, unlawfully obtained evidence is not automatically excluded from the factfinding process in all circumstances. In a variety of contexts we inquire whether application of the rule will promote its objectives sufficiently to justify the enormous cost it imposes on society.

* * *

[I]t is striking that the Court fails even to consider whether the benefits secured by application of the exclusionary rule in this case outweigh its obvious social costs. Perhaps the failure is due to the fact that this case arises not under the Fourth Amendment, but under Miranda v. Arizona, 384 U.S. 436, 86 S. Ct. 1602, 16 L. Ed. 2d 694

(1966), and the Sixth Amendment right to counsel. The Court apparently perceives the function of the exclusionary rule to be so different in these varying contexts that it must be mechanically and uncritically applied in all cases arising outside the Fourth Amendment.

But this is demonstrably not the case where police conduct collides with Miranda's procedural safeguards rather than with the Fifth Amendment privilege against compulsory self-incrimination. Involuntary and coerced admissions are suppressed because of the inherent unreliability of a confession wrung from an unwilling suspect by threats, brutality, or other coercion.

But use of Williams' disclosures and their fruits carries no risk whatever of unreliability, for the body was found where he said it would be found. Moreover, since the Court makes no issue of voluntariness, no dangers are posed to individual dignity or free will. Miranda's safeguards are premised on presumed unreliability long associated with confessions extorted by brutality or threats; they are not personal constitutional rights, but are simply judicially created prophylactic measures.... It will not do to brush this off by calling this a Sixth Amendment right-to-counsel case.

Thus, in cases where incriminating disclosures are voluntarily made without coercion, and hence not violative of the Fifth Amendment, but are obtained in violation of one of the Miranda prophylaxis, suppression is no longer automatic.

* * *

Similarly, the exclusionary rule is not uniformly implicated in the Sixth Amendment, particularly its pretrial aspects. We have held that

"the core purpose of the counsel guarantee was to assure 'Assistance' at trial, when the accused was confronted with both the intricacies of the law and the advocacy of the public prosecutor." United States v. Ash, 413 U.S. 300, 309–310 (1973).

Thus, the right to counsel is fundamentally a "trial" right necessitated by the legal complexities of a criminal prosecution and the need to offset, to the trier of fact, the power of the State as prosecutor.... It is now thought that modern law enforcement involves pretrial confrontations at which the defendant's fate might effectively be sealed before the right of counsel could attach. In order to make meaningful the defendant's opportunity to a fair trial and to assistance of counsel at that trial—the core purposes of the counsel guarantee—the Court formulated a per se rule guaranteeing counsel at what it has characterized as "critical" pretrial proceedings where substantial rights might be endangered. United States v. Wade, 388 U.S. 218, 224–227 (1967); Schneckloth v. Bustamonte, 412 U.S., at 238–239 (1973).

As we have seen in the Fifth Amendment setting, violations of prophylactic rules designed to safeguard other constitutional guarantees and deter impermissible police conduct need not call for the automatic suppression of evidence without regard to the purposes served by exclusion; nor do Fourth Amendment violations merit uncritical suppression of evidence. In other situations we decline to suppress eyewitness identifications which are the products of unnecessarily suggestive lineups or photo displays unless there is a "very substantial likelihood of irreparable misidentification." Simmons v. United States, 390 U.S. 377, 384 (1968). Recognizing that "[i]t is the likelihood of misidentification which violates a defendant's right to due process," Neil v. Biggers, 409 U.S. 188, 198 (1972), we exclude evidence only when essential to safeguard the integrity of the truth-seeking process. The test, in short, is the reliability of the evidence.

So too in the Sixth Amendment sphere, failure to have counsel in a pretrial setting should not lead to the "knee-jerk" suppression of relevant and reliable evidence. Just as even uncounselled "critical" pretrial confrontations may often be conducted fairly and not in derogation of Sixth Amendment values..., evidence obtained in such proceedings should be suppressed only when its use would imperil the core values the Amendment was written to protect. Having extended the Sixth Amendment concepts originally thought to relate to the trial itself to earlier periods when a criminal investigation is focused on a suspect, application of the drastic bar of exclusion should be approached with caution.

In any event, the fundamental purpose of the Sixth Amendment is to safeguard the fairness of the trial and the integrity of the fact finding process. In this case, where the evidence of how the child's body was found is of unquestioned reliability, and since the Court accepts Williams' disclosures as voluntary and uncoerced, there is no issue either of fairness or evidentiary reliability to justify suppression of truth. It appears suppression is mandated here for no other reason than the Court's general impression that it may have a beneficial effect on future police conduct; indeed, the Court fails to say even that much in defense of its holding.

Thus, whether considered under Miranda or the Sixth Amendment, there is no more reason to exclude the evidence in this case than there was in Stone v. Powell; that holding was premised on the utter reliability of evidence sought to be suppressed, the irrelevancy of the constitutional claim to the criminal defendant's factual guilt or innocence, and the minimal deterrent effect of habeas corpus on police misconduct.... Rather than adopting a formalistic analysis varying with the constitutional provision invoked, we should apply the exclusionary rule on the basis of its benefits and costs, at least in those cases where the police conduct at issue is far from being "outrageous" or "egregious."

In his opinion, Mr. Justice POWELL intimates that he agrees there is little sense in applying the exclusionary sanction where the evidence suppressed is "typically reliable and often the most probative information bearing on the guilt or innocence of the defendant." Since he seems to concede that the evidence in question is highly reliable and probative, his joining the Court's opinion can be explained only by an insistence that the "question has not been presented in the briefs or arguments submitted to us." But the State has directly challenged the applicability of the exclusionary rule to this case, Brief for Petitioner, at 31–32, and has invoked principles of comity and federalism against reversal of the conviction. Id., at 69–73. Moreover, at oral argument—the first opportunity to do so—the State argued that our intervening decision in Stone v. Powell should be extended to this case, just as respondent argued that it should not. Tr. of Oral Arg., at 26–27, 49–50.

At the least, if our intervening decision in Stone makes application of the exclusionary rule in this case an open question which "should be resolved only after the implications of such a ruling have been fully explored," the plainly proper course is to vacate the judgment of the Court of Appeals and remand the case for reconsideration in light of that case.... Today, the Court declines either to apply the intervening case of Stone v. Powell, which Mr. Justice POWELL admits may well be controlling, or to remand for reconsideration in light of that case, all the more surprising since Mr. Justice POWELL authored Stone v. Powell and today makes the fifth vote for the Court's judgment.

* * *

Mr. Justice WHITE, with whom Mr. Justice BLACKMUN and Mr. Justice REHNQUIST join, dissenting.

* * *

The consequence of the majority's decision is, as the majority recognizes, extremely serious. A mentally disturbed killer whose guilt is not in question may be released. Why? Apparently, the answer is that the majority believes that the law enforcement officers acted in a way which involves some risk of injury to society and that such conduct should be deterred. However, the officers' conduct did not, and was not likely to, jeopardize the fairness of respondent's trial or in any way risk the conviction of an innocent man—the risk against which the Sixth Amendment guaranty of assistance of counsel is designed to protect.... The police did nothing "wrong" let alone anything "unconstitutional." To anyone not lost in the intricacies of the prophylactic rules of Miranda v. Arizona, the result in this case seems utterly senseless.... [T]he statements made by respondent were properly admitted. [T]he majority's protest that the result in this case is justified by a "clear violation" of the Sixth and Fourteenth Amendments has a distressingly hollow ring. I respectfully dissent.

Mr. Justice BLACKMUN, with whom Mr. Justice WHITE and Mr. Justice REHNQUIST join, dissenting.

The State of Iowa, and 21 States and others, as amici curiae, strongly urge that this Court's procedural (as distinguished from constitutional) ruling in Miranda v. Arizona, 384 U.S. 436 (166), be re-examined and overruled. I, however, agree with the Court that this is not now the case in which that issue need be considered.

What the Court chooses to do here, and with which I disagree, is to hold that respondent Williams' situation was in the mold of Massiah v. United States, 377 U.S. 201 (1964), that is, that it was dominated by a denial to Williams of his Sixth Amendment right to counsel after criminal proceedings had been instituted against him. The Court rules that the Sixth Amendment was violated because Detective Leaming "purposely sought during Williams' isolation from his lawyers to obtain as much incriminating information as possible." I cannot regard that as unconstitutional per se.

First, the police did not deliberately seek to isolate Williams from his lawyers so as to deprive him of the assistance of counsel. Cf. Escobedo v. Illinois, 378 U.S. 478 (1964). The isolation in this case was a necessary incident of transporting Williams to the county where the crime was committed.

Second, Leaming's purpose was not solely to obtain incriminating evidence. The victim had been missing for only two days, and the police could not be certain that she was dead. Leaming, of course, and in accord with his duty, was "hoping to find out where that little girl was," ... but such motivation does not equate with an intention to evade the Sixth Amendment. Moreover, the Court seems to me to place an undue emphasis ... and aspersion on what it and the lower courts have chosen to call the "Christian burial speech," and on Williams' "deeply religious" convictions.

Third, not every attempt to elicit information should be regarded as "tantamount to interrogation." I am not persuaded that Leaming's observations and comments made as the police car traversed the snowy and slippery miles between Davenport and Des Moines that winter afternoon, were an interrogation, direct or subtle, of Williams. Contrary to this Court's statement..., the Iowa Supreme Court appears to have thought and held otherwise, 182 N.W.2d, at 403–405, and I agree. Williams, after all, was counseled by lawyers, and warned by the arraigning judge in Davenport and by the police, and yet it was he who started the travel conversations and brought up the subject of the criminal investigation. Without further reviewing the circumstances of the trip, I would say it is clear there was no interrogation....

In summary, it seems to me that the Court is holding that Massiah is violated whenever police engage in any conduct, in the absence of counsel, with the subjective desire to obtain information from a suspect after arraignment. Such a rule is far too broad. Persons in custody frequently volunteer statements in response to stimuli other than interrogation. . . . When there is no interrogation, such statements should be admissible as long as they are truly voluntary.

The Massiah point thus being of no consequence, I would vacate the judgment of the Court of Appeals and remand the case for consideration of the issue of voluntariness, in the constitutional sense, of Williams' statements, an issue the Court of Appeals did not reach when the case was before it. . . . This was a brutal, tragic, and heinous crime inflicted upon a young girl on the afternoon of the day before Christmas. With the exclusionary rule operating as the Court effectuates it, the decision today probably means that, as a practical matter, no new trial will be possible at this date eight years after the crime, and that this respondent necessarily will go free. That, of course, is not the standard by which a case of this kind strictly is to be judged. But, as Judge Webster in dissent below observed, 509 F.2d, at 237, placing the case in sensible and proper perspective: "The evidence of Williams' guilt was overwhelming. No challenge is made to the reliability of the fact-finding process." I am in full agreement with that observation.

Comments

1. The constitutional right of an indigent defendant to court-appointed counsel (at state expense) is of recent vintage. In *Powell* v. *Alabama,* supra, the Court held that "fundamental fairness" and the Due Process Clause of the Fourteenth Amendment require the appointment of counsel to indigent defendants charged with capital offenses in state proceedings. *Powell* hinted that there might be a general right to appointed counsel in all felony trials, but the Court did not then decide that issue. Six years later, in *Johnson* v. *Zerbst,* 304 U.S. 458 (1938), the Court held that indigent defendants charged with a federal felony have a Sixth Amendment right to appointed counsel in the federal courts. Subsequently, in *Betts* v. *Brady,* 316 U.S. 455 (1942), a majority of the Court refused to extend the *Powell* rationale to state noncapital felony trials absent "special circumstances." During the next 20 years, the Court, on a case-by-case basis, found a number of instances in which "special circumstances" and Fourteenth Amendment due process required the presence of court-appointed counsel in state felony trials. For example, in *Chewning* v. *Cunningham,* 368 U.S. 443 (1962), the Supreme Court held that a charge under a Virginia habitual criminal statute, which carried a long sentence, was serious enough to warrant the assistance of court-appointed counsel. Other "special circumstances" included the sentencing of a convicted defendant, *Townsend* v. *Burke,* 334 U.S. 736 (1948); the entering of a guilty plea in court at any time, *Moore* v. *Michigan,* 355 U.S. 155 (1957); an arraignment at which the defendant is charged with a capital offense, *Hamilton* v. *Alabama,* 368 U.S. 52 (1961); and arraignments for noncapital felonies, *White* v. *Maryland,* 373 U.S. 59 (1963). By 1963, the Court had found so many instances of "special circumstances" requiring the presence of court-appointed counsel that the *Betts* rule was no longer viable. At the time of the *Gideon* decision (1963), only two justices (Black and Douglas) remained on the Court who had participated in *Betts* (1942); and they had dissented in that decision. The time was ripe for the Court to

make the Sixth Amendment right to counsel applicable to the states through the Due Process Clause of the Fourteenth Amendment. Interestingly, after Gideon's petition for certiorari in forma pauperis was granted, the Court appointed Abe Fortas, a well-known Washington, D.C., attorney, and later an associate justice of the Supreme Court, to represent Gideon. Was that appointment a clue as to the type of decision that was forthcoming? See, Lewis, A., *Gideon's Trumpet* (1964).

Only two years before *Gideon,* the Court had made the exclusionary rule applicable to state criminal trials, *Mapp* v. *Ohio,* 367 U.S. 643 (1961) (Chapter Five, § 5.03), and the following year the Court had made the Cruel and Unusual Punishment Clause of the Eighth Amendment applicable to the states, *Robinson* v. *California,* 370 U.S. 660 (1962) (Chapter Eleven, § 11.02). Nine of the ten guarantees in the Bill of Rights that today are applicable to the states were made so by the Supreme Court between 1962 and 1969 — the height of the Warren Court era.

2. The Sixth Amendment right to counsel is not applicable at all stages of the criminal process. Through a long line of decisions, the Supreme Court has held that the right to counsel is applicable at "critical stages" of the criminal process. A "critical stage" occurs when "substantial rights of a defendant are affected." See, e.g., *Mempa* v. *Rhay,* 389 U.S. 128, 134 (1967), Chapter Nine, § 9.02. It can hardly be argued that a poorly educated defendant is a match for a seasoned prosecutor at the trial or at any other stage of the criminal process.

3. Following *Gideon,* and during the next ten or so years, the Court found other stages in the criminal process at which indigent defendants were entitled to appointed counsel at state expense (see Table 7.1, p. 593). In *Miranda* v. *Arizona,* 384 U.S. 436 (1966) (Chapter Six, § 6.03), the Court held that a suspect is entitled to the presence of counsel during custodial interrogation. In *United States* v. *Wade* (1967) (Chapter Six, § 6.03), the Court held that a postindictment lineup is a "critical stage" requiring the presence of counsel. However, in *Kirby* v. *Illinois,* 406 U.S. 682 (1972) (Chapter Six, § 6.03, Comments, p. 496), the Court reached an opposite conclusion with respect to the right to counsel at preindictment lineups. In *Coleman* v. *Alabama,* 399 U.S. 1 (1970), the Court held that the preliminary hearing (where the state must make a showing of probable cause before a defendant may be bound over for a felony trial) is a "critical stage" necessitating counsel.

Argersinger v. *Hamlin,* supra, extended the *Gideon* rationale to grant the right to court-appointed counsel in cases in which the imposition of a jail sentence is a possibility. The *Argersinger* Court left open the issue of whether court-appointed counsel is required when a fine is the only penalty that might be imposed. Should counsel be constitutionally required in such cases?

4. In *Argersinger,* Mr. Justice Powell, with whom Mr. Justice Rehnquist joined concurring, pointed up several problems inherent in implementing that decision: (1) The ruling will tend to "favor defendants classified as indigents over those not so classified, yet who are in low-income groups where engaging counsel in a minor petty-offense case would be a luxury the family could

not afford." (2) Since the Fifth and Fourteenth Amendments guarantee "that property, as well as life and liberty, may not be taken . . . without affording due process . . . the logic [*Argersinger*] advances for extending the right to counsel to all cases in which the penalty of any imprisonment is imposed applies equally well to cases in which other penalties may be imposed"; however, the majority "suggests no constitutional basis for distinguishing between deprivations of liberty and property." (3) The *Argersinger* rule could result in equal protection problems; i.e., "there may be an unfair and unequal treatment of individual defendants, depending on whether the individual judge has determined in advance to leave open the option of imprisonment." And (4) the holding may have an adverse impact on "overburdened local courts . . . [and] may well exacerbate delay and congestion," particularly in communities with few lawyers and limited resources. For an excellent discussion of the practical impact of the *Argersinger* decision, see Simeone, *Gideon II or the Trumpet Blows Again,* 28 J. Missouri Bar 528 (1972). For example, Judge Simeone notes that in Missouri, "in the whole of Lewis County there are approximately 5 lawyers. There were 509 misdemeanors in that county [in 1971]. And in Missouri last year [1971] there were 189,247 misdemeanors," at 532.

5. On the same day that *Gideon* was decided, the Court in *Douglas v. California,* 372 U.S. 353 (1963), held that a state is required to appoint counsel to indigent defendants, if requested, on the first appeal following a felony conviction. The *Douglas* Court noted (in dictum) that although state appellate review is not constitutionally required in criminal cases, an indigent felon is entitled to equal treatment—at least on the first appeal as a matter of right. The Court has not indicated whether the same right to court-appointed counsel on a first appeal is applicable to indigent misdemeanants, but presumably it is. However, most jurisdictions provide a *trial de novo* (completely new trial) on a first appeal following a misdemeanor conviction and thus must grant the assistance of counsel under the *Argersinger* rationale.

6. In *Ross* v. *Moffitt,* supra, a majority of the Court refused to extend the *Douglas* rationale to appeals beyond the first appeal as of right following a felony conviction. Thus, neither the Sixth Amendment nor the Equal Protection Clause requires court-appointed counsel for discretionary state appeals or certiorari applications to the United States Supreme Court. As noted by Mr. Justice Rehnquist in *Ross,* "The Fourteenth Amendment does not require absolute equality or precise equal advantages." Does that square with the often quoted statement of Mr. Justice Black in *Griffin* v. *Illinois,* 351 U.S. 12 (1956) (Chapter Four, § 4.04) that "there can be no equal justice where the kind of an appeal a man enjoys depends on the amount of money he has"? Appellate law has become such a specialized area that only a small percentage of convicted felons can afford to retain an appellate attorney to pursue the often time-consuming appellate process. Was the majority of the Court in *Ross* evidencing a belief that most appeals are "frivolous" without actually saying so? Mr. Justice Clark, dissenting in *Douglas* v. *California,* stated, "We all know that the overwhelming percentage of in forma pauperis appeals [those filed by indigents] are frivolous. Statistics of this Court

show that over 96 per cent of the petitions filed here are of this variety," 373 U.S. 353, 358. Assuming that Justice Clark's statistics are accurate, what happens to the 4 per cent or so of indigent appellants whose appeals are not frivolous? Are their cases always granted full appellate review? Should constitutional questions be decided by the Court, even in part, on the basis of statistical data? Or is empirical data wholly irrelevant to the resolution of constitutional issues?

7. While it is clear that the right to court-appointed counsel applies at many, if not most, pretrial stages of the criminal process, as well as at the trial, indigent defendants are not constitutionally entitled to court-appointed counsel at those stages where there is only a minimal risk of infringement of constitutional rights. These stages include investigative proceedings such as grand jury and legislative hearings, *In re Groban*, 352 U.S. 330 (1957) (dictum); taking defendant's fingerprints, *Davis* v. *Mississippi*, 394 U.S. 721 (1969) (dictum); taking handwriting exemplars, *Gilbert* v. *California*, 388 U.S. 263 (1967); taking blood samples, *Schmerber* v. *California*, 384 U.S. 218 (1966) (Chapter Six, § 6.03); taking voice exemplars at grand jury proceedings, *United States* v. *Dionisio*, 410 U.S. 1 (1973); and taking photographs for identification purposes, *United States* v. *Ash*, 413 U.S. 300 (1973), and summary courts-martial, *Middendorf* v. *Henry*, 425, U.S. 25 (1976) (Chapter Sixteen, § 16.02). However, the Court has extended the right of counsel to the juvenile justice process, *In re Gault*, 387 U.S. 1 (1967) (Chapter Eight, § 8.03).

    Supreme Court decisions involving the right to counsel at post-adjudicatory stages of the criminal process, such as probation and parole revocation hearings, and prison disciplinary hearings are included in Chapter Nine.

8. In *Faretta* v. *California*, supra, the Court held on constitutional grounds that a defendant has a right to self-representation at trial provided the waiver of counsel is made voluntarily and intelligently. In most instances, how can a waiver of counsel be intelligent if the defendant does not have the assistance of counsel in making the initial decision? Or is the Court in using the term "intelligent" referring to an awareness of the risks in waiving counsel analogous to the common law tort concept of *assumption of risk* (acting with knowledge and appreciation of the danger involved)? The *Faretta* Court noted that a defendant who elects to represent himself is expected to comply with the local rules of procedure and substantive law. Presumably, such a defendant could not argue on appeal (in the event of a conviction) that he lacked *effective* assistance of counsel. Are you in agreement with Mr. Justice Blackmun (dissenting) as to the magnitude of the procedural problems that *Faretta* is likely to produce?

9. The *Powell* Court hinted that there is a constitutional right to the *effective* assistance of counsel. Although the Court has more recently suggested that a denial of effective counsel might require a reversal of a conviction on constitutional grounds, that issue has not been faced squarely by the Court. What is effective assistance of counsel? Surely it doesn't mean that every defendant is entitled to an F. Lee Bailey as his counsel. In *McMann* v. *Richardson*, 397 U.S. 759, 771 (1970), the Court stated (by dictum) that "de-

fendants facing felony charges are entitled to the effective assistance of competent counsel." In *McMann* and other decisions, the Court seems to be developing a "normal competency" test of the effectiveness of counsel, i.e., whether counsel's advice and techniques are "within the range of competence demanded of attorneys in criminal cases." Id.

Appellate courts have seemed reluctant to find a denial of the effective assistance of counsel in most cases. In *Chambers* v. *Maroney,* 399 U.S. 42 (1970), the Supreme Court sidestepped the issue of effective counsel and refused to hold that a late appointment of counsel is a violation of the Sixth Amendment or the Fourteenth Amendment Due Process Clause. And where the defendant has retained his own counsel, courts are even more reluctant to find ineffective assistance. The defendant, in effect, assumes the risk of his choice.

10. For many years it has been thought that every criminal defendant has a Sixth Amendment or due process right (or both) to the "effective assistance" of counsel—whether retained or court-appointed. The first suggestion by the Supreme Court that effective assistance of counsel might be constitutionally required was made in *Powell* v. *Alabama,* supra, where the Court stated, in dictum, that the duty to appoint counsel "is not discharged . . . as to preclude the giving of *effective aid* in the preparation and trial of the case," at 57 (emphasis added). However, by the end of the 1976–1977 Term, the issue of effective assistance raised in *Powell* had not been squarely confronted by the Court. In at least three decisions, the Burger Court, while acknowledging a general right to the effective assistance of counsel in criminal cases, failed to develop a precise test and formulate standards for the lower courts. In *McMann* v. *Richardson,* 397 U.S. 759 (1970), in which a majority of the Court held that a defendant who alleges that his guilty plea was the product of a coerced confession is not, without more, entitled to federal habeas corpus relief, Justice White, writing for the Court, spoke of whether the advice of counsel (to plead guilty or not) was "within the range of competence demanded of attorneys in criminal cases," at 771. While acknowledging that "defendants facing felony charges are entitled to the effective assistance of competent counsel" and that "defendants cannot be left to the mercies of incompetent counsel," Justice White said that "[we] think the matter, for the most part, should be left to the good sense and discretion of the trial courts. . . ." In closing, Justice White stated that a plea of guilty will not be set aside unless the defendant can "demonstrate gross error on the part of counsel," at 772, and "can allege and prove serious derelictions on the part of counsel," at 774. In *Chambers* v. *Maroney,* 399 U.S. 42 (1970) (Chapter Five, § 5.04), Justice White, writing for the Court, rejected a petition that alleged that tardy appointment of counsel (a few minutes before trial) was a denial of effective assistance of counsel: "Unquestionably, the courts should make every effort to effect early appointments of counsel in all cases. But we are not disposed to fashion a per se rule requiring reversal of every conviction following tardy appointment of counsel," at 54. Finally, in *Tollett* v. *Henderson,* 411 U.S. 258 (1973), Justice Rehnquist, writing for the Court, said "Counsel's failure to evaluate properly facts giving rise to a constitutional claim, or his failure properly to inform himself of

facts that would have shown the existence of a constitutional claim ... [are] not themselves independent grounds for federal collateral relief," at 266–267.

Understandably, the lower federal and state courts have divided over the constitutional standards for the effective assistance of counsel. A substantial number of courts have adopted the so-called "mockery of justice" test, a standard that looks to determine if counsel's representation has been so poor as to be considered a "farce" or a "sham that shocks the conscience of the court." See Finer, *Ineffective Assistance of Counsel,* 58 Cornell L. Rev. 1077 (1973). But as noted by Chief Justice Bazelon of the United States Court of Appeals for the D.C. Circuit, "A great many — if not most — indigent defendants do not receive the effective assistance of counsel...." Bazelon, *The Defective Assistance of Counsel,* 42 U. Cin. L. Rev. 1, 2 (1973). As examples, Judge Bazelon cited the following: (1) "Defense counsel advised the [trial] judge that he could take only a few minutes for summation because he had to move his car by five o'clock"; (2) "[d]efense counsel based his case on an 1895 decision, and when the [trial] judge asked for a later precedent, the attorney said that he couldn't find a Shepard's citator," id. at 3; and (3) "[in one recent case,] defense counsel was observed to be sound asleep during the examination of prosecution witnesses.... If the lawyer had not been present there would be a reversal without a showing of prejudice; but because the lawyer was merely asleep, an entirely different standard was applied. The [c]ourt found that the presence of a warm, albeit sleeping, body at the defense table satisfied the defendant's sixth amendment right," id. at 30. Another author has reported a case in which "[a] defendant was asked how much money he had in his pocket. He replied, 'Forty cents.' The judge, presumably in jest, told the defendant he 'should hire a forty-cent lawyer.' Missing the joke, the Spanish-speaking accused was tried and convicted without a lawyer." Duke, *The Right to Appointed Counsel: Argersinger and Beyond,* 12 Am. Crim. L. Rev. 601, 621, n.30 (1975). See also Bazelon, *The Realities of Gideon and Argersinger,* 64 Geo. L.J. 811 (1976); Krantz, *The Right to Counsel in Criminal Cases: The Mandate of Argersinger v. Hamlin* (1976); and Note, *Of Trumpeters, Pipers, and Swingmen: What Tune is the Burger Court Playing in Right to Representation Cases?* 29 Vanderbilt L. Rev. 776 (1976).

11. The oral arguments in *Brewer* v. *Williams,* supra, suggested that the decision would be resolved in terms of *Miranda* and the Fifth Amendment privilege against self-incrimination. However, the majority opinion makes only a passing reference to *Miranda,* and a majority of the Court merely reaffirmed the *Massiah* rule that once a defendant has been formally charged with a criminal offense, he has a Sixth Amendment right to counsel when law enforcement authorities interrogate him. *Massiah* v. *United States,* 377 U.S. 201 (1964). As noted by the *Brewer* majority, "There is no need to review in this case the doctrine of *Miranda* v. *Arizona* [384 U.S. 436 (1966)], a doctrine designed to secure the constitutional privilege against compulsory self-incrimination." Why did the majority decide *Brewer* on the narrower grounds of a right to counsel instead of utilizing the case for a broader reevaluation of the *Miranda* safeguards? Is it because a majority of the justices

could not reach a consensus on *Miranda*? Recall that Justice Stewart, who wrote the principal opinion in *Brewer*, dissented in *Miranda* and Justice Powell, who concurred with the *Brewer* majority, has in every post-*Miranda* decision voted against extension of *Miranda*.

Why didn't the majority of the *Brewer* Court simply reaffirm *Massiah* but hold that the defendant had voluntarily waived his right to counsel? Is it because Williams' counsel was not notified that his client wished to waive counsel? Or was it because Williams did not specifically state that he wished to waive counsel? Didn't the Williams' *conduct* indicate a voluntary waiver? Is conduct constitutionally irrelevant in the waiving of the right to counsel? How would a deaf and dumb defendant who is also illiterate waive counsel?

It would appear that Justice Stewart was the "swing voter" in *Brewer*, as he has generally favored the right to counsel after formal charges have been initiated. See, e.g., *Middendorf* v. *Henry*, 425 U.S. 25 (1976) (no Sixth Amendment right to counsel in summary court-martial proceedings (dissenting); *North* v. *Russell*, 427 U.S. 328 (1976) (no denial of right to counsel when defendant is tried before a lay judge) (dissenting); *Herring* v. *New York*, 422 U.S. 853 (1975) (denying defense counsel the right to make closing argument in bench trial is a denial of the right to counsel) (majority opinion); *Gedders* v. *United States*, 425 U.S. 80 (1976) (trial court order preventing defendant from consulting with his counsel during a 17-hour overnight recess violates the defendant's right to the assistance of counsel) (joining Court); *Maness* v. *Meyers*, 419 U.S. 449 (1975) (lawyer may not be held in contempt of court for advising his client to refuse to produce material demanded by a subpoena when the lawyer believes in good faith that the material might tend to incriminate his client); *Faretta* v. *California*, 422 U.S. 806 (1975) (supra) (the right to counsel also includes the right to self-representation) (majority opinion). But see *Ross* v. *Moffitt*, 417 U.S. 600 (1974) (no right to court-appointed counsel beyond the first appeal) (joining majority opinion); *Kirby* v. *Illinois*, 406 U.S. 682 (1972) (no right to counsel at preindictment lineup) (majority opinion); *United States* v. *Ash*, 413 U.S. 300 (1973) (no right to counsel at postindictment photographic display (concurring opinion); *United States* v. *Wade*, 388 U.S. 218 (right to counsel at postindictment lineup) (dissenting opinion). Interestingly, Justice Stewart wrote the majority opinion in *Massiah*, which was the basis for the decision in *Brewer*.

Do some of the words used by Chief Justice Burger (dissenting) in *Brewer* seem overly strong—e.g., "intolerable," "absurd," "bizarre result," "astonishing conclusion," "remarkable result," and "boggles the mind"? Why does Burger describe Justice Powell as the "fifth vote for the Court's judgment"? Because Powell was the principal author of *Stone* v. *Powell*, 428 U.S. 465 (1976), and in Burger's view, *Stone* should have precluded federal habeas corpus review in *Brewer*?

Brewer is not a landmark decision in the sense that it has not served to change or otherwise modify the doctrinal underpinnings of prior Sixth Amendment law. Nor will *Brewer* foreclose the Court from later reexamining the doctrinal underpinnings of *Miranda*.

On July 15, 1977, Anthony Williams was reconvicted in an Iowa state court of first-degree murder. The jury deliberated 15 hours over three days. On August 5, 1977, Williams was sentenced to a mandatory life term at the Iowa State Penitentiary.

12. Some recent lower federal and state court decisions involving the right to counsel include: *United States* v. *Swinton,* 400 F. Supp. 805 (S.D.N.Y. 1975) (defendant already represented by counsel has no right to act as his own co-counsel at trial); *United States* v. *Corrigan,* 401 F. Supp. 795 (D. Wyo. 1975) (defendant has no Sixth Amendment right to be formally represented by a disbarred attorney); *Brown* v. *State,* 193 N.W.2d 613 (Minn. 1972) (standard for ineffective assistance of counsel is whether counsel's incompetence made the proceedings a "farce, sham, or mockery of justice"); *United States* v. *Armedo-Sarmiento,* 524 F.2d 591 (2d Cir. 1975) (right to counsel includes the right to waive effective representation); *Barnes* v. *State,* 528 S.W. 2d 370 (Ark. 1975) (robbery defendant who did not assert his right of self-representation until the morning of his trial should have been permitted to act as his own counsel); *Sheely* v. *Whealon,* 525 F.2d 713 (6th Cir. 1975) (admission of rape defendant's uncounseled and subsequently withdrawn plea of guilty held violative of right to counsel); *Carey* v. *Garrison,* 403 F. Supp. 395 (W.D.N.C. 1975) (state prisoner whose execution date for murder has been postponed so that he can seek certiorari in U.S. Supreme Court must be provided counsel to assist him with his petition); *People* v. *Holcomb,* 235 N.W.2d 343 (Mich. 1975) (*Faretta* v. *California* is fully retroactive); *State* v. *Renshaw,* 347 A.2d 219 (Md. Spec. App. 1975) (defendant who stressed his unhappiness with public defender handling his case held not to have waived his right to counsel, and trial court committed reversible error by having trial proceed with the public defender simply standing by); *People* v. *Lewis,* 235 N.W.2d. 100 (Mich. App. 1975) (to support a claim of ineffective counsel the defendant must show that "defense counsel, through failure to investigate and prepare a substantial defense, has deprived defendant of that substantial defense"); *State* v. *Francis,* 540 P.2d 421 (Wash. 1975) (traffic conviction predating *Argersinger* v. *Hamlin* and obtained without counsel can be considered in a subsequent license revocation proceeding); *Harrison* v. *State,* 337 N.E.2d 533 (Ind. App. 1975) (under "mockery of justice" standard, no denial of effective counsel where defense attorney failed to object to admission of evidence obtained in an illegal search, thereby waiving that Fourth Amendment issue for purposes of appeal); *Turner* v. *American Bar Association,* 407 F. Supp. 451 (N.D. Tex. 1975) (no Sixth Amendment right to unlicensed counsel); *United States* v. *Anderson,* 523 F.2d 1192 (5th Cir. 1975) (*Massiah* v. *United States* violated by federal agents who sent an informer posing as a drug-seeking prostitute to a physician who had been indicted on drug charges and was facing trial in a week); *People* v. *Kester,* 337 N.E.2d 44 (Ill. App. 1975) (defendant entitled to have his guilty plea vacated because his attorney had participated in criminal proceedings against him before going into private practice); *Stepp* v. *Estelle,* 524 F.2d 447 (5th Cir. 1975) (Texas robbery defendant who was antisocial and emotionally unstable but not mentally incompetent held to have made a knowing and intelligent waiver of his right to counsel in

insisting on his right of self-representation); *Hammond* v. *United States*, 528 F.2d 15 (4th Cir. 1975) (defense counsel's giving defendant erroneous advice about possible sentencing consequences of going to trial as opposed to pleading guilty held ineffective assistance of counsel); *State* v. *McCorgary*, 543 P.2d 952 (Kan. 1975) (*Massiah* v. *United States* violated when police placed an informer in the cell of an indicted murder defendant for the purpose of obtaining an inculpatory statement); *United States* v. *Merritts*, 527 F.2d 713 (7th Cir. 1975) (defendant whose statements to turncoat co-defendant constituted new offense held not protected by *Massiah* rule); *People* v. *Metcalf*, 236 N.W.2d 573 (Mich. 1976) (right to counsel at photograph sessions only applies if suspect is in custody and investigation has focused on him); *United States* v. *Merritt*, 528 F.2d 650 (7th Cir. 1976) (Indiana federal judge erred by appointing on behalf of a defendant an attorney who had passed the Iowa bar exam but, unbeknownst to him, had failed the Indiana bar exam three times and had never before represented a client in any capacity); *State* v. *Trivitt*, 548 P.2d 442 (N. Mex. 1976) (test for ineffective counsel is whether the trial was a "sham, farce, or mockery of justice"); *State* v. *Timmons*, 545 P.2d 358 (Kan. 1976) (unmarried drug defendant who had a job paying $60 a week was properly denied appointed counsel); *People* v. *McDaniel*, 545 P.2d 843 (Calif. 1976) (*Faretta* v. *California*, permitting self-representation, held not retroactive); *Webb* v. *State*, 533 S.W.2d 780 (Tex. Crim. App. 1976) (right of self-representation applies at the appellate stage of the criminal process, although there is no right on demand to appear pro se before an appellate court); *United States* v. *Gaines*, 529 F.2d 1038 (7th Cir. 1976) (trial judge has duty to warn defendant of foreseeable dangers posed by his attorney's conflict of interest in representing two co-defendants whose interests ran contrary to those of defendant); *Ingle* v. *State*, 546 P.2d 598 (Nev. 1976) (trial court committed reversible error in refusing to allow defendant to reject his lawyer's advice and not testify on his own behalf); *State* v. *Clark*, 365 A.2d 1167 (Conn. 1976) (test for effective counsel is that the performance "must be reasonably competent or within the range of competence displayed by lawyers with ordinary training and skill in the criminal law"); *Thomas* v. *Superior Court*, 126 Cal. Rptr. 830 (Calif. App. 1976) (right of self-representation extends to capital cases); *Van Cleaf* v. *State*, 328 So. 2d 568 (Fla. App. 1976) (right of counsel is available to indigents facing probation revocation hearings despite standards under *Gagnon* v. *Scarpelli* [Chapter Nine, § 9.02]); *Potts* v. *Estelle*, 529 F.2d 450 (5th Cir. 1976) (whether prior uncounselled misdemeanor convictions are invalid under *Argersinger* depends on whether the defendant faced possible incarceration, not whether he was actually incarcerated); *Callahan* v. *State*, 354 A.2d 191 (Md. Spec. App. 1976) (granting defendant's request for "hybrid representation" so he could appear on his own behalf but with the assistance of counsel on appeal within the discretion of the appellate court); *United States* v. *Fratus*, 530 F.2d 644 (5th Cir. 1976) (failure of robbery defendant's counsel to make a motion for an appointed defense psychiatrist when defendant had already been adjudged competent to stand trial following three psychiatric exams held not denial of effective assistance of counsel); *Stevenson* v. *Reed*, 530 F.2d 1207 (5th

Cir. 1976) (state's duty to assist prisoners in communicating their claims to the courts does not include providing them counsel at its own expense); *Mason* v. *Balcom*, 531 F.2d 717 (5th Cir. 1976) (defendant whose court-appointed counsel allowed him to plead guilty without first familiarizing himself with the facts or investigating possible defenses was denied effective assistance of counsel); *State* v. *Rudolph*, 332 So. 2d 806 (La. 1976) (presence of attorney not required at lineups conducted prior to filing of a bill of information); *People* v. *Martin*, 347 N.E.2d 200 (Ill. App. 1976) (rape defendant was denied effective assistance of counsel by failure of lawyer who represented both him and his co-defendant at their joint trial to take proper steps with respect to the prosecutor's use of a letter written by the co-defendant asking a key prosecution witness to change his testimony since defense counsel could not discredit the co-defendant in any way); *Commonwealth* v. *Tyler*, 360 A.2d 617 (Pa. 1976) (indigent's request for new appointed counsel because of irreconcilable differences of opinion over the conduct of the defense should have been granted provided the request was not made arbitrarily or for the sole purpose of delaying the trial); *United States* v. *Allen*, 542 F.2d 630 (4th Cir. 1976) (defendant's right to counsel held denied when trial court order prevented him from consulting with his attorney during a brief daytime recess at trial); *Garton* v. *Swenson*, 417 F. Supp. 697 (W.D.Mo. 1976) (defendant was denied effective assistance of counsel where his attorney was ignorant of a state statute that would have enabled him to subpoena important out-of-state witnesses); *United States* v. *Easter*, 539 F.2d 663 (8th Cir. 1976) (under the "reasonable competency" test, defendant who was represented by a civil lawyer with limited criminal experience was denied effective assistance when his lawyer failed to file a suppression motion for which there was a factual basis); *Payne* v. *Superior Court*, 553 P.2d 565 (Calif. 1976) (indigent prisoners facing property losses as a result of civil suits must be given appointed counsel if necessary to protect their property rights); *People* v. *Mason*, 132 Cal. Rptr. 265 (Calif. App. 1976) (disappearance of defendant's counsel late in murder trial requires new trial even though substitute counsel made substantial effort to represent defendant); *State* v. *Brooks*, 537 P.2d 574 (Mont. 1976) (defendant who had retained counsel and made no objection to the lawyer's competency throughout the criminal proceedings held to have no claim for ineffective assistance of counsel); *Pinnell* v. *Cauthron*, 540 F.2d 938 (8th Cir. 1976) (standard for effective assistance of counsel is whether trial counsel has exercised the customary skills and diligence which a reasonably competent attorney would employ under similar circumstances); *Ex parte prior*, 540 S.W.2d 723 (Tex. Cr. App. 1976) (constitutional right to counsel does not mean errorless counsel, and adequacy of services will be gauged by the totality of representation); *Hicks* v. *State*, 555 P.2d 889 (Kan. 1976) (attorney representing criminal defendant has a duty to advise defendant as to the law affecting defendant's rights); *United States* v. *LaRiche*, 549 F.2d 1088 (6th Cir. 1977) (where defendant claims ineffective assistance of counsel and alleges conflict of interest, defendant must show conflict and actual prejudice therefrom); *State* v. *Eby*, 342 So. 2d 1087 (Fla. App. 1977) (decision not to raise certain defenses or call certain defense witnesses is ordinarily a matter of strategy and is not proper predicate for collateral attack on competence of counsel unless irresponsibly made); *Haliburton* v. *State*, 546 S.W.2d 771 (Mo. App. 1977) (effective assistance of counsel does not require that counsel interview accused for any specific minimum period of time); *White* v. *State*, 248 N.W.2d 281 (Minn. 1976) (effective assistance of counsel in representation by an attorney exercising the customary skills and diligence that a reasonably competent attorney would use under similar circumstances); *People* v. *Dowd*, 391 N.Y.S.2d 733 (N.Y. App. Div.) (ineffective assistance of counsel means the attorney's conduct made the proceedings a mockery of justice); *Summers* v. *United States*, 538 F.2d 1208 (5th Cir. 1976) (amount of time that counsel spends on defense is one of several relevant factors to be considered in determining whether there has been effective assistance of counsel); *Riley* v. *State*, 226 S.E.2d 922 (Ga. 1976) (standard of effectiveness is not to be judged by hindsight nor by fact that defendant was convicted); *People* v. *Carter*, 354 N.E.2d 482 (Ill. App. 1976) (mere errors of judgment by defense counsel do not amount to incompetence); *Cantrell* v. *Alabama*, 546 F.2d 652 (5th Cir. 1977) (failure of counsel to perfect appeal is a denial of effective assistance of counsel); *People* v. *Chandler*, 358 N.E.2d 1293) (Ill. App. 1976) (appellate counsel's failure to argue that trial counsel was incompetent did not result in ineffective assistance of counsel); *Langkeit* v. *State*, 414 F. Supp. 870 (D. Okla. 1976) (ineffective representation by counsel must have been such as to make the proceedings a mockery, sham, or farce); *State* v. *Smiley*, 554 P.2d 910 (Ariz. App. 1976) (court will not grant relief to criminal defendant because of allegation of ineffective counsel unless it is shown that proceedings were reduced to a farce); *Commonwealth* v. *Cavanaugh*, 353 N.E.2d 732 (Mass. 1976) (defendant's right to counsel is not satisfied by mere presence of competent attorney if attorney is not prepared to try the case); *State* v. *McNicol*, 554 P.2d 203 (Utah 1976) (right of an accused to have counsel is not satisfied by a sham or pretense of an appearance by an attorney who manifests no real concern about the interests of the accused); *Kibler* v. *State*, 227 S.E.2d 199 (S.C. 1976) (mere speculation as to what might have happened had defense counsel independently investigated alleged offense is not sufficient grounds for finding ineffective counsel); *Carter* v. *Bordenkircher*, 226 S.E.2d 711 (W. Va. 1976) (error by counsel that does not affect the outcome of the case is harmless); *Goodrick* v. *State*, 559 P.2d 303 (Idaho 1977) (defense counsel's decision to inform jury of defendant's prior criminal record to forestall any attempt by prosecutor to bring out that information was a strategical decision that could not form the basis of an incompetent counsel claim); *State* v. *Montgomery*, 229 S.E.2d 572 (N.C. 1976) (refusal of trial court to appoint private investigator to assist defense counsel did not deprive defendant of right to counsel); *Watkins* v. *State*, 560 P.2d 921 (Nev. 1977) (on appeal from conviction, reviewing court will not second-guess decisions of defense counsel pertaining to trial strategy); *State* v. *Watson*, 559 P.2d 121 (Ariz. 1976) (ineffective assistance of counsel means the representation was a farce, sham, or mockery of justice); *State* v. *Lythe*, 358 N.E.2d 623 (Ohio 1976) (on issue of counsel's ineffectiveness, defendant has burden of proof, because properly licensed attorney is presumed competent); *Common-*

TABLE 7.1 The Right to Counsel and the Burger Court: 1970–1977

Case	Justices											
	Burger	Blackmun	Powell[1]	Rehnquist[2]	Douglas[3]	Brennan	Marshall	Stewart	White	Black[4]	Harlan[5]	Stevens[6]
Coleman v. Alabama[7]	−(D)	np			+(C)	+(M)	+(m)	−(D)	+(C)	+(C)	+(C)	
Kitchens v. Smith[8]	+(m)	+(m)			+(m)	+(m)	+(m)	+(m)	+(m)	+(m)	+(m)	
U.S. v. Tucker[9]	−(d)	−(D)	np	np	+(m)	+(m)	+(m)	+(M)	+(m)			
Kirby v. Illinois[10]	−(C)	−(m)	−(C)	−(m)	+(d)	+(D)	+(d)	−(M)	+(D)			
Argersinger v. Hamlin[11]	+(C)	+(m)	+(C)	+(C)	+(M)	+(C)	+(m)	+(c)	+(m)			
Gagnon v. Scarpelli[12]	−(m)	−(m)	−(M)	−(m)	+(C)	+(m)	+(m)	−(m)	−(m)			
U.S. v. Ash[13]	−(m)	−(M)	−(m)	−(m)	+(d)	+(D)	+(d)	−(C)	−(m)			
Ross v. Moffitt[14]	−(m)	−(m)	−(m)	−(M)	+(D)	+(D)	+(d)	−(m)	−(m)			
Wolff v. McDonnell[15]	−(m)	−(m)	−(M)	−(D)	+(D)	−(m)	−(m)	−(m)	−(m)			
Faretta v. California[16]	−(D)	−(M)	+(m)	−(d)	+(D)	−(m)	−(m)	+(M)	+(m)			
Herring v. New York[17]	−(d)	−(d)	+(m)	−(d)	+(m)	+(m)	+(m)	+(M)	+(M)			
Middendorf v. Henry[18]	−(m)	−(m)	−(C)	−(M)		+(d)	+(D)	+(D)	−(m)			np

Key: + Voted to extend right to counsel
− Voted not to extend right to counsel
np Did not participate

M Wrote majority opinion
m Joined majority opinion
C Wrote concurring opinion
c Joined concurring opinion

D Wrote dissenting opinion
d Joined dissenting opinion

[1] Sworn in December 9, 1971.
[2] Sworn in December 15, 1971.
[3] Retired November 12, 1975.
[4] Died 1971.
[5] Died 1971.
[6] Sworn in December 19, 1975.
[7] 399 U.S. 1 (1970) (right to counsel at preliminary hearings).
[8] 401 U.S. 847 (1971) (per curiam) (*Gideon v. Wainwright* is fully retroactive).
[9] 404 U.S. 443 (1972) (evidence of prior felony convictions may not be used at sentencing when defendant was not represented by counsel at earlier proceedings).
[10] 406 U.S. 682 (1972) (no right to counsel at preindictment lineups).
[11] 407 U.S. 25 (1972) (right to counsel for all offenses punishable by imprisonment).
[12] 411 U.S. 778 (1973) (no per se right to counsel at probation revocation hearings).
[13] 413 U.S. 300 (1973) (no right to counsel at postindictment photograph displays).
[14] 417 U.S. 600 (1974) (no right to court-appointed counsel after the first appeal as of right).
[15] 418 U.S. 539 (1974) (no right to counsel at prison disciplinary hearings).
[16] 422 U.S. 806 (1975) (right to self-representation in felony trials).
[17] 422 U.S. 853 (1975) (denying counsel right to make closing argument in nonjury trial).
[18] 425 U.S. 1281 (1976) (no right to counsel at summary court-martial proceedings).

wealth v. *Davis,* 368 A.2d 260 (Pa. 1977) (trial counsel was not ineffective in failing to request bill of particulars to determine whether defendant had made any statements to police); *Ellis* v. *State,* 227 S.E.2d 304 (S.C. 1976) (defendant who waived his right to be present at trial cannot assert that his absence resulted in ineffective assistance of counsel); *State* v. *Pina,* 561 P.2d 43 (N. Mex. 1977) (defendant was not entitled to appointed counsel when he refused to fill out, under oath, a certificate of indigency showing his income); *Commonwealth* v. *Taylor,* 370 A.2d 1197 (Pa. 1977) (defendant was denied assistance of counsel when counsel was not informed that lineup was being conducted; *State* v. *Nielsen,* 547 S.W.2d 153 (Mo. App. 1977) (once guilty plea is entered, issue of adequacy of representation of counsel becomes immaterial except to extent that counsel's ineffectiveness bears on issue of voluntariness and understanding of plea); *State* v. *Forsyth,* 560 P.2d 337 (Utah 1977) (defendant who contends that he was not afforded effective assistance of counsel has burden of persuading court that counsel failed in some manner to represent his interests, resulting in prejudice to his defense); *State* v. *Lockett,* 358 N.E.2d 1062 (Ohio 1977) (mere failure of counsel to make objections after the fact does not establish ineffectiveness of counsel); *People* v. *Reeder,* 135 Cal. Rptr. 421 (Cal. App. 1977) (claim of ineffective counsel not supported where counsel stipulated to admissibility of polygraph results and there was no showing that defendant did not accede to stipulation freely and voluntarily).

7.03 THE RIGHT TO A FAIR TRIAL AND AN IMPARTIAL JURY

A. THE RIGHT TO A FAIR TRIAL

Six-Man Juries

WILLIAMS v. FLORIDA

Supreme Court of the United States, 1970
399 U.S. 78, 90 S. Ct. 1893, 26 L. Ed. 2d 446

Johnny Williams was tried and convicted of robbery by a six-man jury in a Florida state court. During the proceedings, he objected to being tried by a six-man jury, which under Florida law was permitted in all cases involving noncapital offenses. Williams asserted that less than a twelve-man jury violated his constitutional rights under the Sixth Amendment as made applicable to the states through the Fourteenth Amendment. This and other motions were denied, and he was sentenced to life imprisonment. The Florida Court of Appeals affirmed the conviction, and the United States Supreme Court granted certiorari.

Mr. Justice WHITE delivered the opinion of the Court.

* * *

[In Part I the Court discussed Florida's notice-of-alibi rule. See Comment 2, infra.]

II

In Duncan v. Louisiana, 391 U.S. 145 (1968), we held that the Fourteenth Amendment guarantees a right to trial by jury in all criminal cases that—were they to be tried in a federal court—would come within the Sixth Amendment's guarantees. Petitioner's trial for robbery on July 3, 1968, clearly falls within the scope of that holding.... The question in this case then is whether the constitutional guarantee of a trial by "jury" necessarily requires trial by exactly 12 persons, rather than some lesser number—in this case six. We hold that the 12-man panel is not a necessary ingredient of "trial by jury," and that respondent's refusal to impanel more than the six members provided for by Florida law did not violate petitioner's Sixth Amendment rights as applied to the States through the Fourteenth.

We had occasion in Duncan v. Louisiana, supra, to review briefly the oft-told history of the development of trial by jury in criminal cases. That history revealed a long tradition attaching great importance to the concept of relying on a body of one's peers to determine guilt or innocence as a safeguard against arbitrary law enforcement. That same history, however, affords little insight into the considerations that gradually led the size of that body to be generally fixed at 12. Some have suggested that the number 12 was fixed upon simply because that was the number of the presentment jury from the hundred, from which the petit jury developed. Other, less circular but more fanciful reasons for the number 12 have been given, "but they were all brought forward after the number was fixed," and rest on little more than mystical or superstitious insights into the significance of "12." Lord Coke's explanation that the "number of twelve is much respected in holy writ, as 12 apostles, 12 stones, 12 tribes, etc." is typical. In short, while sometime in the 14th century the size of the jury at common law came to be fixed generally at 12, that particular feature of the jury system appears to have been a historical accident, unrelated to the great purposes which gave rise to the jury in the first place. The question before us is whether this accidental feature of the jury has been immutably codified into our Constitution.

* * *

While "the intent of the Framers" is often an elusive quarry, the relevant constitutional history casts considerable doubt on the easy assumption in our past decisions that if a given feature existed in a jury at common law in 1789, then it was necessarily preserved in the Constitution. Provisions for jury trial were first placed in the Constitution in Article III's provision that "[t]he Trial of all Crimes ... shall be by Jury; and such Trial shall be held in the State where the said Crimes shall have been committed." The "very scanty history [of this provision] in the records of the Constitutional Convention" sheds little light either way on the intended correlation between Article III's "jury" and the features of the jury at common law....

We do not pretend to be able to divine precisely what the word "jury" imported to the Framers, the First Congress, or the States in 1789. It may well be that the usual expectation was that the jury would consist of 12, and that hence, the most likely conclusion to be drawn is simply that little thought was actually given to the specific questions we face today. But there is absolutely no indication in "the intent of the Framers" of an explicit decision to equate the constitutional and common-law characteristics of the jury. Nothing in this history suggests, then, that we do violence to the letter of the Constitution by turning to other than purely historical considerations to determine which features of the justice system, as it existed at common law, were preserved in the Constitution. The relevant inquiry, as we see it, must be the function that the particular feature performs and its relation to the purposes of the jury trial. Measured by this standard, the 12-man requirement cannot be regarded as an indispensable component of the Sixth Amendment.

The purpose of the jury trial, as we noted in Duncan, is to prevent oppression by the Government. "Providing an accused with the right to be tried by a jury of his peers gave him an inestimable safeguard against the corrupt or overzealous prosecutor and against the compliant, biased, or eccentric judge." ... Given this purpose, the essential feature of a jury obviously lies in the interposition between the accused and his accuser of the commonsense judgment of a group of laymen, and in the community participation and shared responsibility that results from that group's determination of guilt or innocence. The performance of this role is not a function of the particular number of the body that makes up the jury. To be sure, the number should probably be large enough to promote group deliberation, free from outside attempts at intimidation, and to provide a fair possibility for obtaining a representative cross-section of the community. But we find little reason to think that these goals are in any meaningful sense less likely to be achieved when the jury numbers six, than when it numbers 12– particularly if the requirement of unanimity is retained. And certainly the reliability of the jury as a factfinder hardly seems likely to be a function of its size.

It might be suggested that the 12-man jury gives a defendant a greater advantage since he has more "chances" of finding a juror who will insist on acquittal and thus prevent conviction. But the advantage might just as easily belong to the State, which also needs only one juror out of twelve insisting on guilt to prevent acquittal. What few experiments have occurred—usually in the civil area—indicate that there is no discernible difference between the results reached by the two different-sized juries. In short, neither currently available evidence nor theory suggests that the 12-man jury is necessarily more advantageous to the defendant than a jury composed of fewer members.

Similarly, while in theory the number of viewpoints represented on a randomly selected jury ought to increase as the size of the jury increases, in practice the difference between the 12-man and the six-man jury in terms of the cross-section of the community represented seems likely to be negligible. Even the 12-man jury cannot insure representation of every distinct voice in the community, particularly given the use of the peremptory challenge. As long as arbitrary exclusions of a particular class from the jury rolls are forbidden ... the concern that the cross-section will be significantly diminished if the jury is decreased in size from 12 to six seems an unrealistic one.

We conclude, in short, as we began: the fact that the jury at common law was composed of precisely 12 is a historical accident, unnecessary to effect the purposes of the jury system and wholly without significance "except to mystics." ... To read the Sixth Amendment as forever codifying a feature so incidental to the real purpose of the Amendment is to ascribe a blind forma-

lism to the Framers which would require considerably more evidence that we have been able to discover in the history and language of the Constitution or in the reasoning of our past decisions. We do not mean to intimate that legislatures can never have good reasons for concluding that the 12-man jury is preferable to the smaller jury, or that such conclusions—reflected in the provisions of most States and in our federal system—are in any sense unwise. Legislatures may well have their own views about the relative value of the larger and smaller juries, and may conclude that, wholly apart from the jury's primary function, it is desirable to spread the collective responsibility for the determination of guilt among the larger group. In capital cases, for example, it appears that no State provides for less than 12 jurors—a fact that suggests implicit recognition of the value of the larger body as a means of legitimating society's decision to impose the death penalty. Our holding does no more than leave these considerations to Congress and the States, unrestrained by an interpretation of the Sixth Amendment that would forever dictate the precise number that can constitute a jury. Consistent with this holding, we conclude that petitioner's Sixth Amendment rights, as applied to the States through the Fourteenth Amendment, were not violated by Florida's decision to provide a six-man rather than a 12-man jury. The judgment of the Florida District Court of Appeal is

Affirmed.

Mr. Justice BLACK, with whom Mr. Justice DOUGLAS joins, concurring.

The Court today holds that a State can, consistently with the Sixth Amendment to the United States Constitution, try a defendant in a criminal case with a jury of six members. I agree with that decision for substantially the same reasons given by the Court. My Brother HARLAN, however, charges that the Court's decision on this point is evidence that the "incorporation doctrine," through which the specific provisions of the Bill of Rights are made fully applicable to the States under the same standards applied in federal courts, will somehow result in a "dilution" of the protections required by those provisions. He asserts that this Court's desire to relieve the States from the rigorous requirements of the Bill of Rights is bound to cause re-examination and modification of prior decisions interpreting those provisions as applied in federal courts in order simultaneously to apply the provisions equally to the State and Federal Governments and to avoid undue restrictions on the States. This assertion finds no support in today's decision or any other decision of this Court. We have emphatically "rejected the notion that the Fourteenth Amendment applies to the States only a 'watered-down, subjective version of the individual guarantees of the Bill of Rights.' " ... Today's decision is in no way attributable to any desire to dilute the Sixth Amendment in order more easily to apply it to the States but follows solely as a necessary consequence of our duty to re-examine prior decisions to reach the correct constitutional meaning in each case. The broad implications in early cases indicating that only a body of 12 members could satisfy the Sixth Amendment requirement arose in situations where the issue was not squarely presented and were based, in my opinion, on an improper interpretation of that amendment. Had the question presented here arisen in a federal court before our decision in Duncan v. Louisiana ... this Court would still, in my view, have reached the result announced today. In my opinion the danger of diluting the Bill of Rights protections lies not in the "incorporation doctrine," but in the "shock the conscience" test on which my Brother HARLAN would rely instead—a test which depends, not on the language of the Constitution, but solely on the views of a majority of the Court as to what is "fair" and "decent."

* * *

Mr. Justice HARLAN, ... concurring in the result. ...

* * *

The historical argument by which the Court undertakes to justify its view that the Sixth Amendment does not require 12-member juries is, in my opinion, much too thin to mask the true thrust of this decision. The decision evinces, I think, a recognition that the "incorporationist" view of the Due Process Clause of the Fourteenth Amendment, which underlay Duncan and is now

carried forward ... must be tempered to allow the States more elbow room in ordering their own criminal systems. With that much I agree. But to accomplish this by diluting constitutional protections within the federal system itself is something to which I cannot possibly subscribe. Tempering the rigor of Duncan should be done forthrightly, by facing up to the fact that at least in this area the "incorporation" doctrine does not fit well with our federal structure, and by the same token that Duncan was wrongly decided.

* * *

... With all respect, I consider that before today it would have been unthinkable to suggest that the Sixth Amendment's right to a trial by jury is satisfied by a jury of six or less, as is left open by the Court's opinion in Williams, or by less than a unanimous verdict, a question also reserved in today's decision.

The Court, in stripping off the livery of history from the jury trial, relies on a two-step analysis. With arduous effort the Court first liberates itself from the "intent of the Framers" and "the easy assumption in our past decisions that if a given feature existed in a jury at common law in 1789, then it was necessarily preserved in the Constitution." ... Unburdened by the yoke of history the Court then concludes that the policy protected by the jury guarantee does not require its perpetuation in common-law form.

Neither argument is, in my view, an acceptable reason for disregarding history and numerous pronouncements of this Court that have made "the easy assumption" that the Sixth Amendment's jury was one composed of 12 individuals.

* * *

The principle of stare decisis is multifaceted. It is a solid foundation for our legal system; yet care must be taken not to use it to create an unmovable structure. It provides the stability and predictability required for the ordering of human affairs over the course of time and a basis of "public faith in the judiciary as a source of impersonal and reasoned judgments." ... Surely, if the principle of stare decisis means anything in the law, it means that precedent should not be jettisoned when the rule of yesterday remains viable, creates no injustice, and can reasonably be said to be no less sound than the rule sponsored by those who seek change, let alone incapable of being demonstrated wrong. The decision in Williams, however, casts aside workability and relevance and substitutes uncertainty. The only reason I can discern for today's decision that discards numerous judicial pronouncements and historical precedent that sound constitutional interpretation would look to as controlling, is the Court's disquietude with the tension between the jurisprudential consequences wrought by "incorporation" in Duncan . . . and the counterpulls of the situation in Williams which presents the prospect of invalidating the common practice in the States of providing less than a 12-member jury for the trial of misdemeanor cases.

These decisions demonstrate that the difference between a "due process" approach, that considers each particular case on its own bottom to see whether the right alleged is one "implicit in the concept of ordered liberty" . . . and "selective incorporation" is not an abstract one whereby different verbal formulae achieve the same results. The internal logic of the selective incorporation doctrine cannot be respected if the Court is both committed to interpreting faithfully the meaning of the Federal Bill of Rights and recognizing the governmental diversity that exists in this country. The "backlash" in Williams exposes the malaise, for there the Court dilutes a federal guarantee in order to reconcile the logic of "incorporation," the "jot-for-jot and case-for-case" application of the federal right to the States, with the real-

ity of federalism. Can one doubt that had Congress tried to undermine the common-law right to trial by jury before Duncan came on the books the history today recited would have barred such action? Can we expect repeat performances when this Court is called upon to give definition and meaning to other federal guarantees that have been "incorporated"?

* * *

But the best evidence of the vitality of federalism is today's decision in Williams. The merits or demerits of the jury system can, of course, be debated and those States that have diluted the common-law requirements evince a conclusion that the protection as known at common law is not necessary for a fair trial, or is only such marginal assurance of a fair trial that the inconvenience of assembling 12 individuals outweighs other gains in the administration of justice achieved by using only six individuals. . . .

* * *

It is time, I submit, for this Court to face up to the reality implicit in today's holdings and reconsider the "incorporation" doctrine before its leveling tendencies further retard development in the field of criminal procedure by stifling flexibility in the States and by discarding the possibility of federal leadership by example.

[Mr. Justice STEWART wrote a concurring opinion.]
[Mr. Justice MARSHALL dissented.]
[Mr. Justice BLACKMUN took no part in the consideration or decision of this case.]

Nonunanimous Jury Verdicts

JOHNSON v. LOUISIANA

Supreme Court of the United States, 1972
406 U.S. 356, 92 S. Ct. 1620, 32 L. Ed. 2d 152

Frank Johnson was charged with armed robbery in a Louisiana state court. He was tried by a twelve-man jury and convicted by a 9–3 verdict pursuant to Louisiana constitutional and statutory provisions authorizing such a nonunanimous verdict in certain noncapital cases. The defendant conceded that *Duncan* v.

Louisiana, 391 U.S. 145 (1968), which made the Sixth Amendment right to a trial by jury applicable to the states, did not apply to his case because his trial had occurred before the *Duncan* decision. However, Johnson argued that he had been denied a fair trial under Louisiana procedures because a unanimous jury verdict was required under the Due Process Clause to give substance to the reasonable doubt standard of proof made applicable to the states in *In re Winship*, 397 U.S. 358 (1970). The Louisiana Supreme Court affirmed the conviction, and Johnson appealed to the United States Supreme Court.

Mr. Justice WHITE delivered the opinion of the Court.

. . . The principal question in this case is whether these provisions allowing less-than-unanimous verdicts in certain cases are valid under the Due Process and Equal Protection Clauses of the Fourteenth Amendment.

* * *

Appellant argues that in order to give substance to the reasonable-doubt standard, which the State, by virtue of the Due Process Clause of the Fourteenth Amendment, must satisfy in criminal cases . . ., that clause must be construed to require a unanimous jury verdict in all criminal cases. In so contending, appellant does not challenge the instructions in this case. Concededly, the jurors were told to convict only if convinced of guilt beyond a reasonable doubt. Nor is there any claim that, if the verdict in this case had been unanimous, the evidence would have been insufficient to support it. Appellant focuses instead on the fact that less than all jurors voted to convict and argues that, because three voted to acquit, the reasonable-doubt standard has not been satisfied and his conviction is therefore infirm.

We note at the outset that this Court has never held jury unanimity to be a requisite of due process of law. Indeed, the Court has more than once expressly said that "[i]n criminal cases due process of law is not denied by a state law . . . which dispenses with the necessity of a jury of twelve, or unanimity in the verdict." . . .

. . . It is our view that the fact of three dissenting votes to acquit raises no question of constitutional substance about either the integrity or the accuracy of the majority verdict of guilt. Appellant's contrary argument breaks down into two parts, each of which we shall consider separately: first, that nine individual jurors will be unable to vote con-scientiously in favor of guilt beyond a reasonable doubt when three of their colleagues are arguing for acquittal, and second, that guilt cannot be said to have been proved beyond a reasonable doubt when one or more of a jury's members at the conclusion of deliberation still possess such a doubt. Neither argument is persuasive.

* * *

In considering the first branch of appellant's argument, we can find no basis for holding that the nine jurors who voted for his conviction failed to follow their instructions concerning the need for proof beyond such a doubt or that the vote of any one of the nine failed to reflect an honest belief that guilt had been so proved. Appellant, in effect, asks us to assume that, when minority jurors express sincere doubts about guilt, their fellow jurors will nevertheless ignore them and vote to convict even if deliberation has not been exhausted and minority jurors have grounds for acquittal which, if pursued, might persuade members of the majority to acquit. But the mere fact that three jurors voted to acquit does not in itself demonstrate that, had the nine jurors of the majority attended further to reason and the evidence, all or one of them would have developed a reasonable doubt about guilt. We have no grounds for believing that majority jurors, aware of their responsibility and power over the liberty of the defendant, would simply refuse to listen to arguments presented to them in favor of acquittal, terminate discussion, and render a verdict. On the contrary it is far more likely that a juror presenting reasoned argument in favor of acquittal would either have his arguments answered or would carry enough other jurors with him to prevent conviction. A majority will cease discussion and outvote a minority only after reasoned discussion has ceased to have persuasive effect or to serve any other purpose — when a minority, that is, continues to insist upon acquittal without having persuasive reasons in support of its position.... Appellant offers no evidence that majority jurors simply ignore the reasonable doubts of their colleagues or otherwise act irresponsibly in casting their votes in favor of conviction, and before we alter our own longstanding perceptions about jury behavior and overturn a considered legislative judgment that unanimity is not essential to reasoned jury verdicts, we must have some basis for doing so other than unsupported assumptions.

We conclude, therefore, that, as to the nine jurors who voted to convict, the State satisfied its burden of proving guilt beyond any reasonable doubt. The remaining question under the Due Process Clause is whether the vote of three jurors for acquittal can be said to impeach the verdict of the other nine and to demonstrate that guilt was not in fact proved beyond such doubt. We hold that it cannot.

Of course, the State's proof could be regarded as more certain if it had convinced all 12 jurors instead of only nine; it would have been even more compelling if it had been required to convince and had, in fact, convinced 24 or 36 jurors. But the fact remains that nine jurors — a substantial majority of the jury — were convinced by the evidence. In our view disagreement of three jurors does not alone establish reasonable doubt, particularly when such a heavy majority of the jury, after having considered the dissenters' views, remains convinced of guilt. That rational men disagree is not in itself equivalent to a failure of proof by the State, nor does it indicate infidelity to the reasonable doubt standard. Jury verdicts finding guilt beyond a reasonable doubt are regularly sustained even though the evidence was such that the jury would have been justified in having a reasonable doubt; ... even though the trial judge might not have reached the same conclusion as the jury ... and even though appellate judges are closely divided on the issue whether there was sufficient evidence to support a conviction.... That want of jury unanimity is not to be equated with the existence of a reasonable doubt emerges even more clearly from the fact that, when a jury in a federal court, which operates under the unanimity rule is instructed to acquit a defendant if it has a reasonable doubt about his guilt ...

cannot agree unanimously upon a verdict, the defendant is not acquitted, but is merely given a new trial.... If the doubt of a minority of jurors indicates the existence of a reasonable doubt, it would appear that a defendant should receive a directed verdict of acquittal rather than a retrial. We conclude, therefore, that verdicts rendered by nine out of 12 jurors are not automatically invalidated by the disagreement of the dissenting three. Appellant was not deprived of due process of law.

Appellant also attacks as violative of the Equal Protection Clause the provisions of Louisiana law requiring unanimous verdicts in capital and five-man jury cases, but permitting less-than-unanimous verdicts in cases such as his. We conclude, however, that the Louisiana statutory scheme serves a rational purpose and is not subject to constitutional challenge.... Louisiana has permitted less serious crimes to be tried by five jurors with unanimous verdicts, more serious crimes have required the assent of nine of 12 jurors, and for the most serious crimes a unanimous verdict of 12 jurors is stipulated. In appellant's case, nine jurors rather than five or 12 were required for a verdict. We discern nothing invidious in this classification. We have held that the States are free under the Federal Constitution to try defendants with juries of less than 12 men. Williams v. Florida, 399 U.S. 78 (1970). Three jurors have voted to acquit, but from what we have earlier said, this does not demonstrate that appellant was convicted on a lower standard of proof. To obtain a conviction in any of the categories under Louisiana law, the State must prove guilt beyond reasonable doubt, but the number of jurors who must be so convinced increases with the seriousness of the crime and the severity of the punishment that may be imposed. We perceive nothing unconstitutional or invidiously discriminatory, however, in a State's insisting that its burden of proof be carried with more jurors where more serious crimes or more severe punishments are at issue.

Appellant nevertheless insists that dispensing with unanimity in his case disadvantaged him as compared with those who commit less serious or capital crimes. With respect to the latter, he is correct; the State does make conviction more difficult by requiring the assent of all 12 jurors. Appellant might well have been ultimately acquitted had he committed a capital offense. But as we have indicated, this does not constitute a denial of equal protection of the law; the State may treat capital offenders differently without violating the constitutional rights of those charged with lesser crimes. As to the crimes triable by a five-man jury, if appellant's position is that it is easier to convince all of five, he is simply challenging the judgment of the Louisiana legislature. That body obviously intended to vary the difficulty of proving guilt with the gravity of the offense and the severity of the punishment. We remain unconvinced by anything appellant has presented that this legislative judgment was defective in any constitutional sense.

* * *

The judgment of the Supreme Court of Louisiana is therefore
Affirmed.

Mr. Justice BLACKMUN, concurring.

I join the Court's opinion and ... in so doing I do not imply that I regard a State's split-verdict system as a wise one. My vote means only that I cannot conclude that the system is constitutionally offensive. Were I a legislator, I would disfavor it as a matter of policy. Our task here, however, is not to pursue and strike down what happens to impress us as undesirable legislative policy.

I do not hesitate to say, either, that a system employing a 7–5 standard, rather than a 9–3 or 75% minimum, would afford me great difficulty. As Mr. Justice WHITE points out ..., "a substantial majority of the jury" are to be convinced. That is all that is before us in [this case].

Mr. Justice POWELL, concurring. . . .

* * *

I concur in the plurality opinion in this case insofar as it concludes that a defendant in a state court may constitutionally be convicted by less than a unanimous verdict, but I am not in accord with a major premise upon which that judgment is based. Its premise is that the concept of jury trial, as applicable to the States under the Fourteenth Amendment must be identical in every detail to the concept required in federal courts by the Sixth Amendment. I do not think that all of the elements of jury trial within the meaning of the Sixth Amendment are necessarily embodied in or incorporated into the Due Process Clause of the Fourteenth Amendment. . . .

* * *

Mr. Justice DOUGLAS, with whom Mr. Justice BRENNAN and Mr. Justice MARSHALL concur, dissenting.

* * *

I had ... assumed that there was no dispute that the Federal Constitution required a unanimous jury in all criminal cases. After all, it has long been explicit constitutional doctrine that the Seventh Amendment civil jury must be unanimous. . . .

The result of today's [decision] is anomalous: though unanimous jury decisions are not required in state trials, they are constitutionally required in federal prosecutions. How can that be possible when both decisions stem from the Sixth Amendment?

* * *

After today's [decision], a man's property may only be taken away by a unanimous jury vote, yet he can be stripped of his liberty by a lesser standard. How can that result be squared with the law of the land as expressed in the settled and traditional requirements of procedural due process?

... After today a unanimous verdict will be required in a federal prosecution but not in a state prosecution. Yet the source of the right in each case is the Sixth Amendment. I fail to see how with reason we can maintain those inconsistent dual positions.

* * *

It is said, however, that the Sixth Amendment, as applied to the States by reason of the Fourteenth, does not mean what it does in federal proceedings, that it has a "due process" gloss on it, and that that gloss gives the States power to experiment with the explicit or implied guarantees in the Bill of Rights.

* * *

Do[es] today's [decision] mean that States may apply a "watered down" version of the Just Compensation Clause? Or [is] today's [decision] limited to a paring down of civil rights protected by the Bill of Rights and up until now as fully applicable to the States as to the Federal Government?

* * *

...My chief concern is one often expressed by the late Mr. Justice Black, who was alarmed at the prospect of nine men appointed for life sitting as a super legislative body to determine whether government has gone too far. The balancing was done when the Constitution and Bill of Rights were written and adopted. For this Court to determine, say, whether one person but not another is entitled to free speech is a power never granted it. But that is the ultimate reach of decisions that let the States, subject to our veto, experiment with rights guaranteed by the Bill of Rights.

I would construe the Sixth Amendment, when applicable to the States, precisely as I would when applied to the Federal Government.

* * *

Mr. Justice BRENNAN, with whom Mr. Justice MARSHALL joins, dissenting.

* * *

[W]e must view the constitutional requirement that all juries be drawn from an accurate cross section of the community. When verdicts must be unanimous, no member of the jury may be ignored by the others. When less than unanimity is sufficient, consideration of minority views may become nothing more than a matter of majority grace. In my opinion the right of all groups in this Nation to participate in the criminal process means the right to have their voices heard. A unanimous verdict vindicates that right. Majority verdicts could destroy it.

Mr. Justice STEWART, with whom Mr. Justice BRENNAN and Mr. Justice MARSHALL join, dissenting.

...I think the Fourteenth Amendment alone clearly requires that if a State purports to accord the right of trial by jury in a criminal case, then only a unanimous jury can return a constitutionally valid verdict.

The guarantee against systematic discrim-

ination in the selection of criminal court juries is a fundamental of the Fourteenth Amendment. That has been the insistent message of this Court in a line of decisions extending over nearly a century....

The clear purpose of these decisions has been to ensure universal participation of the citizenry in the administration of criminal justice. Yet today's judgment approves the elimination of the one rule that can ensure that such participation will be meaningful—the rule requiring the assent of all jurors before a verdict of conviction or acquittal can be returned. Under today's judgment, nine jurors can simply ignore the views of their fellow panel members of a different race or class.

The constitutional guarantee of an impartial system of jury selection in a state criminal trial rests on the Due Process and Equal Protection Clauses of the Fourteenth Amendment.... Only a jury so selected can assure both a fair criminal trial ... and public confidence in its result.... Today's decision grossly undermines those basic assurances. For only a unanimous jury so selected can serve to minimize the potential bigotry of those who might convict on inadequate evidence, or acquit when evidence of guilt was clear.... And community confidence in the administration of criminal justice cannot but be corroded under a system in which a defendant who is conspicuously identified with a particular group can be acquitted or convicted by a jury split along group lines. The requirements of unanimity and impartial selection thus complement each other in ensuring the fair performance of the vital functions of a criminal court jury.

* * *

I dissent.

Mr. Justice MARSHALL, with whom Mr. Justice BRENNAN joins, dissenting.

Today the Court cuts the heart out of two of the most important and inseparable safeguards the Bill of Rights offers a criminal defendant: the right to submit his case to a jury, and the right to proof beyond a reasonable doubt. Together, these safeguards occupy a fundamental place in our constitutional scheme, protecting the individual defendant from the awesome power of the

State. After today, the skeleton of these safeguards remains, but the Court strips them of life and of meaning. I cannot refrain from adding my protest to that of my Brothers DOUGLAS, BRENNAN, and STEWART, whom I join.

[T]he question is too frighteningly simple to bear much discussion. We are asked to decide what is the nature of the "jury" that is guaranteed by the Sixth Amendment. I would have thought that history provided the appropriate guide . . ., that unanimity is an essential feature of that jury. But the majority has embarked on a "functional" analysis of the jury that allows it to strip away, one by one, virtually all the characteristic features of the jury as we know it. Two years ago, over my dissent, the Court discarded as an essential feature the traditional size of the jury. Williams v. Florida, 399 U.S. 78 (1970) [supra]. Today the Court discards, at least in state trials, the traditional requirement of unanimity. It seems utterly and ominously clear that so long as the tribunal bears the label "jury," it will meet Sixth Amendment requirements as they are presently viewed by this Court. The Court seems to require only that jurors be laymen, drawn from the community without systematic exclusion of any group, who exercise common-sense judgment.

More distressing still than the Court's treatment of the right to jury trial is the cavalier treatment the Court gives to proof beyond a reasonable doubt. The Court asserts that when a jury votes nine to three for conviction, the doubts of the three do not impeach the verdict of the nine. The argument seems to be that since, under Williams, nine jurors are enough to convict, the three dissenters are mere surplusage. But there is all the difference in the world between three jurors who are not there, and three jurors who entertain doubts after hearing all the evidence. In the first case we can never know, and it is senseless to ask, whether the prosecutor might have persuaded additional jurors had they been present. But in the second case we know what has happened: the prosecutor has tried and failed to persuade those jurors of the defendant's guilt. In such circumstances, it does violence to language and to logic to say that the government has proved the defendant's guilt beyond a reasonable doubt.

* * *

A STATISTICAL CASE FOR THE 12-MEMBER JURY*

Alan E. Gelfand†

Proposing alternatives to the traditional 12-member jury with unanimity has become a popular pastime in recent years. Substitutes ranging from five-member and six-member juries which must vote unanimously to 12-member juries which must have 9 of 12 or 10 of 12 votes for conviction are already being used in various civil and criminal venues. Recent U.S. Supreme Court decisions set the stage for such experimentation in jury size and majority requirements for conviction. In *Williams* v. *Florida* (1970), *Johnson* v. *Louisiana* (1972), *Apodaca* v. *Oregon* (1972), and *Colgrove* v. *Battin* (1973), the arguments presented by the court seemed tenuous and inadequately supported. Researchers have been quick to take issue with these opinions, using an assortment of qualitative and quantitative counterarguments.

Although the six-member unanimous jury now is the most common alternative, a growing body of evidence suggests the inferiority of the smaller jury. The research indicates that the long-range impact of this inferiority will be quite significant.

The most striking quantitative results suggest that for 12-member juries, the probability of convicting an innocent person is .0221 and the probability of acquitting a guilty person is .0615. For a six-member jury, these errors are increased by more than 50%—that is, the probabilities become .0325 and .1395 respectively. These figures are based on an elaborate statistical model and are not yet "proven," but assuming this

---

*Reproduced by permission of *Trial* magazine, Vol. 13, No. 2, February, 1977, pp. 41–42.

†Alan E. Gelfand is an associate professor of statistics at the University of Connecticut. This article was abstracted from a paper, *Considerations in Building Jury Behavior Models and in Comparing Jury Schemes: An Argument in Models and in Comparing Jury Schemes,* coauthored by Professor Gelfand and Professor Herbert Solomon of the Department of Statistics, Stanford University.

minimal accuracy, these figures imply that the smaller jury would commit 800 additional errors over a span of 10,000 jury trials.

Before considering the empirical evidence, consider the inherent difficulties in comparing jury schemes and the qualitative argument used to suggest the existence of size effects with regard to jury performance.

Comparisons

How may one analyze data from two jury schemes to make comparisons in performance? The most immediate pertinent measurement data one could obtain would be conviction rates for both the jury sizes. Suppose one takes the court's position—no performance differences between the formats—as the "natural" hypothesis to be tested, and makes a statistical decision based on that data. If the decision is to accept, we may incur one error—claiming no differences exist when they truly do. If the decision is to reject, we may incur a different error—claiming differences exist when they do not.

Classical hypothesis-testing methodology leads to rejection of the hypothesis only upon discovering highly significant findings, hence strongly controlling the chance of making the latter error. How does one assess the costs of making these two errors? This is not a question of favoring acceptance or rejection of the hypothesis. Rather, if we assert no differences between the jury sizes, then we would take advantage of the dollar savings which may accrue in using a smaller jury, while if we assert there are differences, we would protect against the possibility of the abridgement of the defendant's jury rights which may result from use of the smaller jury.

Moreover, ought not the greater burden of proof rest upon the court to argue the truth of the hypothesis that there will be no differences rather than compelling researchers to "prove" there will be?

But there are two further crucial points. First, even if the differences in conviction rate relative to the total number of cases are small, the differences, in cases where differences could be expected to be found in the first place, may be large. In other words, most cases are clear and hearing such a case before any of the proposed jury formats

would result in a common decision. What percentage of the total number of criminal jury trials might be considered to be "close" or "difficult" cases wherein one might expect differing jury structures to reach different conclusions?

Secondly, even if two schemes resulted in identical conviction rates, does this imply that the schemes are performing equivalently? Indeed, the answer is no.

Two jury schemes actually may not convict the same defendants in all cases, even though the conviction and acquittal rates of the two schemes may be identical in terms of total percentages.

Hence the "conditional" quantities, such as the chance of acquitting a guilty defendant or convicting an innocent, vary with different juries, and must be studied to effectively reveal size effects.

Qualitative Arguments

Conceptually, there are two ways in which jury size can be expected to affect performance. The first one involves jury composition and the second one the quality of decision making. "Composition" refers to the representativeness of the jury. Members of a larger group drawn randomly from the same population are likely to be more broadly representative of the population from which the groups are drawn than members of a smaller group. With increasing jury size, decisions are likely to be more consistent across similar cases and more closely approximate decisions that would prevail if the entire community could judge the trial for itself.

As to quality of decision-making, certainly the larger jury enjoys the participation of a greater number of individuals which provides more diverse inputs into the problem-solving efforts. Further, jurors in the minority are subjected to coercive psychological pressure from the majority. In a very large proportion of cases, the initial majority will persuade the minority to capitulate. Moreover, for the group to fail to reach a unanimous decision, i.e., for the jury to hang, a substantial minority is usually needed to hold out against the majority.

Empirical evidence in this vein shows a hung-jury rate of 2.4%[1] for a rather small sample of six-member jury trials compared with the approximately 5.5%[2] figure for the

TABLE 1   Guilty Votes on First Ballot and Jury Decision

Final Verdict	Guilty Votes on First Ballot					
	0	*.1–5*	*6*	*7–11*	*12*	*Total*
Not guilty	100%	91%	50%	5%	0%	32%
Guilty	0	2	50	86	100	62
Hung	0	7	0	9	0	6
Total	100	100	100	100	100	100

The model enables the estimation of the probabilities headed in Table 2 and hence the comparison between jury sizes.

12-member jury. It is apparent that varying jury sizes will vary the chances that minority positions will be maintained.

Quantitative Arguments

Where do the startling probabilities of the higher conviction-error rate for the six-member jury arise? Certainly empirical verification of these estimates of jury conviction error is not possible; one can never deduce the guilt or innocence of a defendant. Rather, they emerge from a complex statistical model of the jury decision-making process, developed and refined by the author and Herbert Solomon of Stanford University over the last five years. The actual decision-making process of a jury cannot be known, but we can gain insight into the process by comparing the first ballot with succeeding ballots. Table 1, taken from the classic University of Chicago study by Hans Zeisel and the late Harry Kalven, describes the results of 225 jury delibera-

tions and illustrates the type of raw data to which the models were fitted.

Table 2 reveals the two key quantitative points of this article; that the conviction rate may be remaining approximately the same between six- and 12-member juries, but that the crucial performance differences will be revealed by a comparison of the quantities in the last two columns.

The increasing body of evidence indicating the potentially adverse results associated with smaller juries reveals that the U.S. Supreme Court rulings on jury size rest on a weak foundation.

References

1. Hans Zeisel, 1971, University of Chicago Law Review, "And Then There Were None: The Diminution of the Federal Jury," vol. 38, pages 710–724.
2. Harry Kalven and Hans Zeisel, 1965, *The American Jury,* a 10-year study based on 3,576 jury trials.

TABLE 2   Comparison of the Effects of Diminution of Jury Size

	Probability of Conviction	Probability of Acquittal	Probability of Hanging
6-member juries	.6347	.3207	.0446
12-member juries	.637	.303	.060

	Probability of Guilt Given Conviction	Probability of Innocence Given Acquittal
6-member juries	.9675	.8605
12-member juries	.9779	.9385

	Probability of Innocence Given Conviction	Probability of Guilt Given Acquittal
6-member juries	.0325	.1395
12-member juries	.0221	.0615

Nondisclosure of Evidence Favorable to the Defendant

UNITED STATES v. AGURS

Supreme Court of the United States, 1976
427 U.S. 97, 96 S. Ct. 2392, 49 L. Ed. 2d 342

Linda Agurs, the respondent, was convicted of second degree murder for killing James Sewell with a knife during a fight in a motel room. Evidence at the trial indicated that the parties had completed an act of intercourse, that Sewell had then gone to the bathroom down the hall, and that the struggle had occurred upon his return. The contents of his pockets were in disarray on the dresser and no money was found, although Sewell had had $360 on his person less than two hours prior to the killing. Additional evidence indicated that just before the killing, Sewell had been carrying two knives, including the one with which the respondent had stabbed him. Sewell had been stabbed repeatedly, but the respondent herself was uninjured. Respondent's sole defense at trial was self-defense. The jury deliberated 25 minutes and returned a verdict of guilty. Three months later, defense counsel filed a motion for a new trial, asserting that he had discovered (1) that Sewell had had a prior criminal record including convictions for assault and carrying a deadly weapon; (2) that such evidence would have supported the theory of self-defense because of Sewell's violent character; and (3) that the prosecutor had failed to disclose this information to the defendant. The district court denied the motion, but the Court of Appeals (D.C. Cir.) reversed, holding that evidence of Sewell's criminal record was material and that its nondisclosure required a new trial because the jury might have returned a different verdict had the evidence been received. The United States Supreme Court granted certiorari to further clarify the decision in *Brady* v. *Maryland*, 373 U.S. 83 (1963), which held that the prosecution may not knowingly withhold evidence favorable to a defendant if such evidence is requested by the defense.

Mr. Justice STEVENS delivered the opinion of the Court.

. . . The question before us is whether the prosecutor's failure to provide defense counsel with certain background information about Sewell, which would have tended to support the argument that respondent acted in self-defense, deprived her of a fair trial under the rule of Brady v. Maryland, 373 U.S. 84 (1963).

The answer to the question depends on (1) a review of the facts, (2) the significance of the failure of defense counsel to request the material, and (3) the standard by which the prosecution's failure to volunteer exculpatory material should be judged.

* * *

The rule of Brady v. Maryland, supra arguably applies in three quite different situations. Each involves the discovery, after trial, of information which had been known to the prosecution but unknown to the defense.

In the first situation, typified by Mooney v. Holohan, 294 U.S. 103 (1935), the undisclosed evidence demonstrates that the prosecution's case includes perjured testimony and that the prosecution knew, or should have known, of the perjury. In a series of subsequent cases, the Court has consistently held that a conviction obtained by the knowing use of perjured testimony is fundamentally unfair[h] and must be set aside

---

[h]Pyle v. Kansas, 317 U.S. 213 (1942); Alcordo v. Texas, 355 U.S. 28 (1963); Napue v. Illinois, 360 U.S. 264 (1959); Miller v. Pate, 386 U.S. 1 (1967); Giglio v. United States (1972); Donnelly v. DeChristoforo, 416 U.S. 637 (1974).

if there is any reasonable likelihood that the false testimony could have affected the judgement of the jury. It is this line of cases on which the Court of Appeals placed primary reliance. . . . Since this case involves no misconduct, and since there is no reason to question the veracity of any of the prosecution witnesses, the test of materiality followed in the Mooney line of cases is not necessarily applicable to this case.

The second situation, illustrated by the Brady case itself, is characterized by a pretrial request for specific evidence. In that case defense counsel had requested the extra-judicial statements made by Brady's accomplice, one Boblit. This Court held that the suppression of one of Boblit's statements deprived Brady of due process, noting specifically that the statement had been requested and that it was "material." A fair analyst of the holding in Brady indicates that implicit in the requirement of materiality is a concern that the suppressed evidence might have affected the outcome of the trial.

* * *

The test of materiality in a case like Brady in which specific information has been requested by the defendant is not necessarily the same as in a case in which no such request has been made. Indeed, this Court has not yet decided whether the prosecutor has any obligation to provide defense counsel with exculpatory information when no request has been made. . . .

Although there is, of course, no duty to provide defense counsel with unlimited discovery of everything known by the prosecutor, if the subject matter of such a request is material, or indeed if a substantial basis for claiming materiality exists, it is reasonable to require the prosecutor to respond by furnishing the information or by submitting the problem to the trial judge. When the prosecutor receives a specific and relevant request, the failure to make any response is seldom, if ever, excusable.

In many cases, however, exculpatory information in the possession of the prosecutor may be unknown to defense counsel. In such a situation he may make no request at all, or possibly ask for "all Brady material" or for "anything exculpatory." Such a request really gives the prosecutor no better notice than if no request was made. If there

is a duty to respond to a general request of that kind, it must derive from the obviously exculpatory character of certain evidence in the hands of the prosecutor. But if the evidence is so clearly supportive of a claim of innocence that it gives the prosecution notice of a duty to produce, that duty should equally arise even if no request is made. Whether we focus on the desirability of a precise definition of the prosecutor's duty or on the potential harm to the defendant, we conclude that there is no significant difference between cases in which there has been merely a general request for exculpatory matter and cases, like the one we must now decide, in which there has been no request at all. The third situation in which the Brady rule arguably applies, typified by this case, therefore embraces the case in which only a general request for "Brady material" has been made.

We now consider whether the prosecutor has any constitutional duty to volunteer exculpatory matter to the defense, and if so, what standard of materiality gives rise to that duty.

We are not considering the scope of discovery authorized by the Federal Rules of Criminal Procedure, or the wisdom of amending those rules to enlarge the defendant's discovery rights. We are dealing with defendant's right to a fair trial mandated by the Due Process Clause of the Fifth Amendment to the Constitution. Our construction of that clause will apply equally to the comparable clause in the Fourteenth Amendment applicable to trials in state courts.

The problem arises in two principal contexts. First, in advance of trial, and perhaps during the course of a trial as well, the prosecutor must decide what, if anything, he should voluntarily submit to defense counsel. Second, after trial a judge may be required to decide whether a nondisclosure deprived the defendant of his right to due process. Logically the same standard must apply at both times. For unless the omission deprived the defendant of a fair trial, there was no constitutional violation requiring that the verdict be set aside; and absent a constitutional violation, there was no breach of the prosecutor's constitutional duty to disclose.

Nevertheless, there is a significant practical difference between the pretrial decision of the prosecutor and the posttrial decision of the judge. Because we are dealing with an inevitably imprecise standard, and because the significance of an item of evidence can seldom be predicted accurately until the entire record is complete, the prudent prosecutor will resolve doubtful questions in favor of disclosure. But to reiterate a critical point, the prosecutor will not have violated his constitutional duty of disclosure unless his omission is of sufficient significance to result in the denial of the defendant's right to a fair trial. . . . If everything that might influence a jury must be disclosed, the only way a prosecutor could discharge his constitutional duty would be to allow complete discovery of his files as a matter of routine practice.

Whether or not a procedural rule authorizing such broad discovery might be desirable, the Constitution surely does not demand that much. . . . [T]his Court recently noted that there is "no constitutional requirement that the prosecution make a complete and detailed accounting to the defense of all police investigatory work on the case." Moore v. Illinois, 408 U.S. 786, 795 (1972). The mere possibility that an item of undisclosed information might have helped the defense, or might have affected the outcome of the trial, does not establish "materiality" in the constitutional sense.

Nor do we believe the constitutional obligation is measured by the moral culpability, or the willfulness, of the prosecutor. If evidence highly probative of innocence is in his files, he should be presumed to recognize its significance even if he has actually overlooked it. . . . Conversely, if evidence actually has no probative significance at all, no purpose would be served by requiring a new trial simply because an inept prosecutor incorrectly believed he was suppressing a fact that would be vital to the defense. If the suppression of evidence results in constitutional error, it is because of the character of the evidence not the character of the prosecutor.

. . . [T]here are situations in which evidence is obviously of such substantial value to the defense that elementary fairness requires it to be disclosed even without a specific request. For though the attorney for the sovereign must prosecute the accused with earnestness and vigor, he must always be faithful to his client's overriding interest "that justice shall be done." He is the "servant of the law, the twofold aim of which is that guilt shall not escape nor innocence suffer." Berger v. United States, 295 U.S. 78, 88 (1935). This description of the prosecutor's duty illuminates the standard of materiality that governs his obligation to disclose exculpatory evidence.

On the one hand, the fact that such evidence was available to the prosecutor and not submitted to the defense places it in a different category than if it had simply been discovered from a neutral source after trial. For that reason the defendant should not have to satisfy the severe burden of demonstrating that newly discovered evidence probably would have resulted in acquittal. . . .

On the other hand, since we have rejected the suggestion that the prosecutor has a constitutional duty routinely to deliver his entire file to defense counsel, we cannot consistently treat every nondisclosure as though it were error. It necessarily follows that the judge should not order a new trial every time he is unable to characterize a nondisclosure as harmless under the customary harmless error standard. Under that standard when error is present in the record, the reviewing judge must set aside the verdict and judgment unless his "conviction is sure that the error did not influence the jury or had but only slight effect." Kotteakos v. United States, 328 U.S. 750, 764 (1946). Unless every nondisclosure is regarded as automatic error, the constitutional standard of materiality must impose a higher burden on the defendant.

The proper standard of materiality must reflect our overriding concern with the justice of the finding of guilt. Such a finding is permissible only if supported by evidence establishing guilt beyond a reasonable doubt. It necessarily follows that if the omitted evidence creates a reasonable doubt that did not otherwise exist, constitutional error has been committed. This means that the omission must be evaluated in the context of the entire record. If there is no reasonable doubt about guilt whether or not the additional evidence is considered, there is no justification for a new trial. On the other hand, if the verdict is already of questionable validity, additional evidence of relatively minor importance might be sufficient to create a reasonable doubt. . . .

Since the arrest record was not requested

and did not even arguably give rise to any inference of perjury, since after considering it in the context of the entire record the trial judge remained convinced of respondent's guilt beyond a reasonable doubt, and since we are satisfied that his firsthand appraisal of the record was thorough and entirely reasonable, we hold that the prosecutor's failure to tender Sewell's record to the defense did not deprive respondent of a fair trial as guaranteed by the Due Process Clause of the Fifth Amendment. Accordingly, the judgment of the Court of Appeals is
Reversed.

Mr. Justice MARSHALL, with whom Mr. Justice BRENNAN joins, dissenting.

The Court today holds that the prosecutor's constitutional duty to provide exculpatory evidence to the defense is not limited to cases in which the defense makes a request for such evidence. But once having recognized the existence of a duty to volunteer exculpatory evidence, the Court so narrowly defines the category of "material" evidence embraced by the duty as to deprive it of all meaningful content.

* * *

...One of the most basic elements of fairness in criminal trials is that available evidence tending to show innocence, as well as that tending to show guilt, be fully aired before the jury; more particularly, it is that the State in its zeal to convict a defendant not suppress evidence that might exonerate him.... This fundamental notion of fairness does not pose any irreconcilable conflict for the prosecutor, for as the Court reminds us, the prosecutor, "must always be faithful to his client's overriding interest 'that justice shall be done.'"... No interest of the State is served, and no duty of the prosecutor advanced, by the suppression of evidence favorable to the defendant. On the contrary, the prosecutor fulfills his most basic responsibility when he fully airs all relevant evidence at his command.

* * *

Under today's ruling, if the prosecution has not made knowing use of perjury, and if the defense has not made a specific request for an item of information, the defendant is entitled to a new trial only if the withheld evidence actually creates a reasonable doubt as to guilt in the judge's mind. With all respect, this rule is completely at odds with the overriding interest in assuring that evidence tending to show innocence is brought to the jury's attention. The rule creates little, if any, incentive for the prosecutor conscientiously to determine whether his files contain evidence helpful to the defense. Indeed, the rule reinforces the natural tendency of the prosecutor to overlook. evidence favorable to the defense, and creates an incentive for the prosecutor to resolve close questions of disclosure in favor of concealment.

More fundamentally, the Court's rule usurps the function of the jury as the trier of fact in a criminal case. The Court's rule explicitly establishes the judge as the trier of fact with respect to evidence withheld by the prosecution. The defendant's fate is sealed so long as the evidence does not create a reasonable doubt as to guilt in the judge's mind, regardless of whether the evidence is such that reasonable men could disagree as to its import—regardless, in other words, of how "close" the case may be.

* * *

This case, however, does not involve deliberate prosecutorial misconduct. Leaving open the question whether a different rule might appropriately be applied in cases involving deliberate misconduct, I would hold that the defendant in this case had met the burden of demonstrating that there is a significant chance that the withheld evidence, developed by skilled counsel, would have induced a reasonable doubt in the minds of enough jurors to avoid a conviction. This is essentially the standard applied by the Court of Appeals, and I would affirm its judgement.

Comments

1. In *Williams* v. *Florida,* supra, the Court, in holding that twelve-man juries are not constitutionally required in state criminal trials, noted that the jury should be large enough (1) "to promote group

deliberation," (2) to be "free from outside attempts at intimidation," and (3) to "provide a fair possibility for obtaining a representative cross-section of the community." Since a six-man jury
apparently satisfies these criteria, would five-, four-, or three-man
juries likewise be permissible? Are six-man juries the barebones
constitutional minimum? Why are twelve-man juries constitutionally required in federal criminal trials but not in state trials?
Aren't six-man juries advantageous to prosecutors since only six
jurors need be convinced of a defendant's guilt rather than twelve?
Is it likely that the Warren Court would have reached the same
result in *Williams?*

2. In Part I of *Williams,* a majority of the Court upheld Florida's
    notice-of-alibi statute. In about one third of the states, a procedural
    rule requires that a defendant give notice to the prosecutor in ad-
    vance of trial if he intends to claim alibi as a defense to the criminal
    charge. Usually the defendant must furnish the prosecutor with
    written information concerning the place where he claims to have
    been at the time of the crime and the names and addresses of the
    alibi witnesses he intends to have testify on his behalf.

    Alibi evidence can provide a powerful defense if the credibility
    of the alibi witnesses can withstand vigorous cross-examination by
    the prosecutor. However, it is well known that alibi witnesses
    often commit perjury. Many defendants are able to obtain the per-
    jured testimony of their friends or relatives in the hope of winning
    an acquittal. In this respect, the prosecutor may be at a marked
    disadvantage if he does not have advance notice that the defendant
    will produce alibi witnesses at trial. Without notice, the prosecutor
    will know little, if anything, about the alibi witnesses prior to trial,
    making impeachment of these "surprise" alibi witnesses difficult. As
    every prosecutor knows, alibi witnesses often remember what they
    and the defendant were doing at the precise time of the crime —
    often many months earlier. However, often these same witnesses
    have difficulty remembering their activities immediately before
    and after the commission of the crime, and some cannot remember
    what they had for dinner the night before the trial. In *Williams,*
    the defendant sought to be excused from Florida's notice-of-
    alibi rule on the ground that the rule operated to "compel" a
    defendant in a criminal case to be a witness against himself in
    violation of his Fifth and Fourteenth Amendment rights. In reject-
    ing Williams' argument, a majority of the Supreme Court held that
    the decision to produce alibi witnesses is voluntary, not compelled,
    within the meaning of the Fifth and Fourteenth Amendments.

    In *Warduis* v. *Oregon,* 412 U.S. 470 (1973), the Court held that
    a state notice-of-alibi statute must make provisions for *reciprocal
    discovery* by the defendant. Under this rule, the state must notify a
    defendant in turn of any prosecution witnesses it proposes to offer
    in rebuttal to the defendant's alibi evidence.

    In some states that have notice-of-alibi statutes, failure of the de-
    fendant to comply with the discovery procedures will result in the
    exclusion of alibi evidence — with the exception that the defendant
    may always testify in his own behalf. The constitutionality of this
    practice was left open in *Williams.*

3. In *Johnson* v. *Louisiana,* supra, the Supreme Court specifically
    approved of conviction by 9–3 jury verdicts in state noncapital
    cases. In *Apodaca* v. *Oregon,* 406 U.S. 404 (1972), decided the

same day as *Johnson,* the Court approved of 10–2 and 11–1 jury verdicts in noncapital felony cases. In each case, the Court noted that a "substantial majority" of the jury had voted for a conviction. Would a jury verdict of 8–4 for conviction satisfy the "substantial majority" test? In view of *Williams* and *Johnson,* would a state law permitting five-man juries and allowing convictions by 4–1 verdicts be constitutional? What about 5–1 verdicts or 4–2 verdicts? If you were convicted of a felony on a 9–3 jury verdict, would you feel that the prosecution had proved your guilt beyond a reasonable doubt? Would a state statute permitting a conviction for a capital offense on less than a unanimous verdict (e.g., 10–2) be constitutional? The issue is not likely to arise in the near future since all jurisdictions presently require unanimous jury verdicts in capital cases. Are twelve-man juries constitutionally required in trials of capital offenses? At present, only Louisiana and Oregon permit nonunanimous jury verdicts in noncapital cases. If you were a state legislator, would you vote to reduce the size of petit juries from twelve in noncapital trials in the interests of fiscal responsibility and judicial economy? Why are unanimous jury verdicts constitutionally required in federal criminal trials but not in state criminal trials? Is the reasoning of the majority in *Johnson* persuasive?

4. The Supreme Court held in *Brady* v. *Maryland,* 373 U.S. 83 (1963) (discussed in the *Agurs* case), that the suppression by the prosecution of evidence favorable to the defendant after it was requested by the defendant is a violation of due process when the evidence is material to either guilt or punishment. Suppose the defendant has no reason to believe that the prosecution has such favorable evidence and therefore doesn't request discovery? Suppose the prosecution does not have actual knowledge of exculpatory evidence but could have discovered such evidence by reasonable means (e.g., it was known to the arresting officer)? Prior to *Brady,* the Court had held in *Mooney* v. *Holohan,* 294 U.S. 103 (1935), that the prosecution's deliberate use of perjured testimony violated a defendant's right to due process and a fair trial. In *Alcorta* v. *Texas,* 355 U.S. 28 (1957), the Court held that a defendant is denied a fair trial when the testimony of a prosecution witness is known to be misleading and thereby creates a false impression. The prosecution has a duty to reveal the misleading nature of testimony even though there is no evidence of outright perjury. In *Napue* v. *Illinois,* 360 U.S. 264 (1959), the Court held that when the prosecution knows that testimony is false, it has a duty to disclose this to the defense. To the same effect is *Miller* v. *Pate,* 386 U.S. 1 (1967). In *Moore* v. *Illinois,* 404 U.S. 812 (1972), the Court reaffirmed *Brady* by stating that the prosecution's suppression of evidence favorable to the defendant violates due process only when the defendant's counsel has requested the disclosure of such evidence. Suppose a defendant waives his right to counsel under *Faretta* v. *California,* supra, and it never occurs to him that the prosecution might have evidence favorable to his defense (e.g., physician's report that the victim had not been raped). Suppose that report is never disclosed at trial and the defendant is convicted of rape—has he obtained a fair trial under *Brady*? Or has the defendant assumed such risks by electing to represent himself? Should a defendant's right to a fair trial and due process be dependent upon his ability to guess what favorable evidence a prosecutor might have knowledge of?

5. In *United States* v. *Agurs,* supra, a majority of the Supreme Court refused to hold that inadvertent, or even willful, nondisclosure by the prosecution of evidence favorable to a defendant is an error of constitutional dimension that automatically entitles the defendant to a new trial. The Court ruled that the omission must be of "sufficient significance" to deprive the defendant of a fair trial; and the evidence omitted must be sufficiently material that nondisclosure creates a reasonable doubt of guilt that would not otherwise exist. Thus, a specific request by the defense for favorable evidence will not always be required. As noted by the Court: "There are situations in which evidence is obviously of such substantial value to the defense that elementary fairness requires it to be disclosed even without a specific request." Suppose the prosecution has evidence that a third party has confessed to the same crime with which the defendant is charged. Would nondisclosure of this evidence in the absence of a defense request be of "sufficient significance" to deprive the defendant of a fair trial? Suppose the police know of the third-party confession, but the prosecutor doesn't? Does the prosecutor have an affirmative duty to be cognizant of *all* evidence favorable to the defense? Is the Court's statement that "if evidence highly probative of innocence is in [the prosecutor's] file, he should be presumed to recognize its significance even if he has actually overlooked it," controlling? Should the police have an affirmative duty to inform the prosecution of all evidence favorable to the defendant? Suppose the defense requests specific materials but the prosecution willfully (or negligently) fails to turn over the materials. Is this nondisclosure automatically constitutional error? Apparently not, in light of the Court's statement that the "character of the evidence, not the character of the prosecutor" is controlling. Thus, willful nondisclosure of immaterial evidence by the prosecutor would probably not be held to be constitutional error.

When the Trial Judge Is Not Legally Trained

NORTH v. RUSSELL

Supreme Court of the United States, 1976
427 U.S. 328, 96 S. Ct. 2709, 49 L. Ed. 2d 534

Lonnie North, the appellant, was arrested in Lynch, Kentucky, and charged with driving while intoxicated in violation of a state statute. North was tried in the Lynch City Police Court before appellee C. B. Russell, a nonlawyer judge. He was found guilty and sentenced to 30 days in jail, a fine of $150, and revocation of his driver's license. Under Kentucky's two-tier court system, police courts (the first tier) have jurisdiction in misdemeanor cases, but an accused has an appeal of right from a police judge's decision to the circuit court (the second tier), where there is a trial de novo. The Kentucky Constitution requires cities to be classified according to population size. There are six classes of cities: fifth-class cities have populations of between 1,000 and 3,000; sixth-class cities have populations of less than 1,000. Police judges in such cities need not be lawyers. Lynch, Kentucky, is a fifth-class city. The Kentucky courts denied North relief on appeal, and the United States Supreme Court noted probable jurisdiction.

Mr. Chief Justice BURGER delivered the opinion of the Court.

The question presented in this case is whether an accused, subject to possible imprisonment, is denied due process when tried before a nonlawyer police court judge with a later trial de novo available under a State's two-tier court system; and whether a State denies equal protection by providing law-trained judges for some police courts and lay judges for others, depending upon the state constitution's classification of cities according to population.

* * *

Appellant's first claim is that when confinement is a possible penalty, a law-trained judge is required by the Due Process Clause of the Fourteenth Amendment whether or not a trial de novo before a lawyer-judge is available.[d]

It must be recognized that there is a wide gap between the functions of a judge of a court of general jurisdiction, dealing with complex litigation, and the functions of a local police court judge trying a typical "drunk" driver case or other traffic violations. However, once it appears that confinement is an available penalty, the process commands scrutiny. See Argersinger v. Hamlin, 407 U.S. 25 (1972).

Appellant argues that the right to counsel articulated in Argersinger v. Hamlin, supra, and Gideon v. Wainwright, 372 U.S. 335 (1963), is meaningless without a lawyer-judge to understand the arguments of counsel. Appellant also argues that the increased complexity of substantive and procedural criminal law requires that all judges now be lawyers in order to be able to rule correctly on the intricate issues lurking even in some simple misdemeanor cases. In the context of

---

[d]Article III of the United States Constitution, of course, unlike provisions of some state constitutions . . . is silent as to any requirement that judges of the United States' courts, including Justices of the Supreme Court, be lawyers or "learned in the law." We note that in excess of 95% of all criminal cases in England are tried before lay judicial officers. See D. Karlen, Judicial Administration: The American Experience 32 (1970); H. Abraham, The Judicial Process 246–247 and n.4 (2d ed. 1968). We also note that many of the States in the United States which utilize nonlawyer judges provide mandatory or voluntary training programs. . . .

the Kentucky procedures, however, it is unnecessary to reach the question whether a defendant could be convicted and imprisoned after a proceeding in which the only trial afforded is conducted by a lay judge. In all instances, a defendant in Kentucky facing a criminal sentence is afforded an opportunity to be tried de novo in a court presided over by a lawyer-judge since an appeal automatically vacates the conviction in police court. . . . The trial de novo is available after either a trial or a plea of guilty in the police court; a defendant is entitled to bail while awaiting the trial de novo. . . .

It is obvious that many defendants charged with a traffic violation or other misdemeanor may be uncounseled when they appear before the police court. They may be unaware of their right to a de novo trial after a judgment is entered since the decision is likely to be prompt. We assume that police court judges recognize their obligation under Argersinger v. Hamlin, 407 U.S. 25 (1972), to inform defendants of their right to a lawyer if a sentence of confinement is to be imposed. The appellee judge testified that informing defendants of a right to counsel was "the usual procedure." . . . We also assume that police court judges in Kentucky recognize their obligation to inform all convicted defendants, including those who waived counsel or for whom imprisonment was not imposed, of their unconditional right to a trial de novo and of the necessity that an "appeal" be filed within 30 days in order to implement that right. . . .

In Colten v. Kentucky, 407 U.S. 104 (1972) [Chapter Fourteen, § 14.01], we considered Kentucky's two-tier system there challenged on other grounds. We noted that:

"The right to a new trial is absolute. A defendant need not allege error in the inferior court proceeding. If he seeks a new trial, the Kentucky statutory scheme contemplates that the slate be wiped clean. Ky. Rule Crim. Proc. 12.06. Prosecution and defense begin anew. . . . The case is to be regarded exactly as if it had been brought there in the first instance." Id., at 113.

We went on to note that the justifications urged by States for continuing such tribunals are the "increasing burdens on state judiciaries" and the "interest of both the defendant and the State to provide speedier and less costly adjudications" than those provided in courts "where the full range of constitutional guarantees is available. . . ." Id., at 114. Moreover, state policy takes into account that it is a convenience to those charged to be tried in or near their own community, rather than travel to a distant court where a law-trained judge is provided, and to have the option, as here, of a trial after regular business hours. . . .

Under Ward v. Village of Monroeville, 409 U.S. 57, 61–62 (1972), appellant argues that he is entitled to a lawyer-judge in the first instance. There the judge was also mayor and the village received a substantial portion of its income from fines imposed by him as judge. Similarly in Tumey v. Ohio, 273 U.S. 510 (1927), the challenge was directed not at the training or education of the judge, but at his possible bias due to interest in the outcome of the case, because as in Monroeville he was both mayor and judge and received a portion of his compensation directly from the fines. Financial interest in the fines was thought to risk a possible bias in finding guilt and fixing the amount of fines and the Court found that potential for bias impermissible.

Under the Kentucky system, as we noted in Colten, a defendant can have an initial trial before a lawyer-judge by pleading guilty in the police court, thus bypassing that court and seeking the de novo trial, "erasing . . . any consequence that would otherwise follow from tendering the guilty plea." . . .

Our concern in prior cases with judicial functions being performed by nonjudicial officers has also been directed at the need for independent neutral and detached judgment, not at legal training. . . . Yet cases such as Shadwick v. City of Tampa, 407 U.S. 345 (1971), are relevant; lay magistrates and other judicial officers empowered to issue warrants must deal with evaluation of such legal concepts as probable cause and the sufficiency of warrant affidavits. Indeed, in Shadwick the probable cause evaluation made by the lay magistrate related to a charge of "impaired driving."[f]

---

[f]In Shadwick we cautioned that: "our federal system warns of converting desirable practice into constitutional commandment. It recognizes in plural and diverse state activities one key to national innovation and vitality. States are entitled to some flexibility and leeway. . . ." Shadwick v. City of Tampa, 407 U.S., at 353–354.

Appellant's second claim is that Kentucky's constitutional provisions classifying cities by population and its statutory provisions permitting lay judges to preside in some cities while requiring law-trained judges in others denies him the equal protection guaranteed by the Fourteenth Amendment. However, all people within a given city and within cities of the same size are treated equally.

The Kentucky Court of Appeals in Ditty v. Hampton, articulated reasons for the differing qualifications of police court judges in cities of different size:

"1. The greater volume of court business in the larger cities requires that judges be attorneys to enable the courts to operate efficiently and expeditiously (not necessarily with more fairness and impartiality).

"2. Lawyers with whom to staff the courts are more available in the larger cities.

"3. The larger cities have greater financial resources with which to provide better qualified personnel and better facilities for the courts." Ditty v. Hampton, 490 S.W.2d, at 776.

That Court of Appeals then noted, "That population and area factors may justify classifications within a court system has long been recognized." . . . The Court of Appeals relied upon Missouri v. Lewis, 101 U.S. 22 (1879), which held that as long as all people within the classified area are treated equally:

"Each State . . . may establish one system of courts for cities and another for rural districts, one system for one portion of its territory and another system for another portion. Convenience, if not necessity, often requires this to be done, and it would seriously interfere with the power of a State to regulate its internal affairs to deny to it this right." Id., at 30–31.

* * *

We conclude that the Kentucky two-tier trial court system with lay judicial officers in the first tier in smaller cities and an appeal of right with a de novo trial before a traditionally law-trained judge in the second does not violate either the due process or equal protection guarantees of the Constitution of the United States; accordingly the judgment before us is

Affirmed.

[Mr. Justice BRENNAN concurred in the result.]

Mr. Justice STEWART, with whom Mr. Justice MARSHALL joins, dissenting.

Lonnie North was haled into a Kentucky criminal court and there tried and convicted, and sentenced to a term of imprisonment by Judge C. B. Russell. Judge Russell is a coal miner without any legal training or education whatever.[a] I believe that a trial before such a judge that results in the imprisonment of the defendant is constitutionally intolerable. It deprives the accused of his right to the effective assistance of counsel guaranteed by the Sixth and Fourteenth Amendments, and deprives him as well of Due Process of Law.[b]

* * *

---

[a]The judge at North's state habeas corpus hearing concluded: "I think the fact has been established that [Judge Russell is] not a lawyer, he doesn't know any law, he hasn't studied any law." Judge Russell testified that he had only a high school education. He had never received any training concerning his duties as a lay judge. This is not a case, therefore, involving a lay judge who has received the kind of special training that several States apparently provide....

A study of California's lay judges made in 1972 showed that 37% had no education beyond high school while 13% had even less formal education. Gordon v. Justice Court, 525 P.2d 72, 176, n.6 (1974). A 1966 survey revealed that only 5% of Virginia's justices of the peace were college graduates, Note, 52 Va. L. Rev. 151, 177, while in 1958 one-half of West Virginia's justices had not completed high school, Note, 69 W. Va. L. Rev. 314, 323. In 1969, the Assistant State Attorney General of Mississippi told the State's Judiciary Commission that "33% of the justices of the peace are limited in educational background to the extent that they are not capable of learning the necessary elements of law." Hearings on Justice of the Peace Courts and Judges before the Mississippi Judiciary Comm'n (testimony of R. Hugo Newcomb, Sr.), quoted in Comment, 44 Miss. L.J. 996, 1000, n. 31.

[b]At least two state courts have held that such a trial violates the United States Constitution, Gordon v. Justice Court, 525 P.2d 72 (1974); Shelmidine v. Jones, Case No. 224948 (Utah 3d Judicial Dist., June 3, 1975). Contemporary studies of American court systems have been unanimous in calling for the elimination of nonlawyer judges....

... [B]eginning with the capital case of Powell v. Alabama, 287 U.S. 45 (1932), extending through the felony case of Gideon v. Wainwright, 372 U.S. 335 (1963), and culminating in the misdemeanor case of Argersinger v. Hamlin, 407 U.S. 25 (1972), the Court's decision firmly established that a person who has not been accorded the constitutional right to the assistance of counsel cannot be sentenced to even one day of imprisonment.

But the essential presupposition of this basic constitutional right is that the judge conducting the trial will be able to understand what the defendant's lawyer is talking about. For if the judge himself is ignorant of the law, then he too will be incapable of determining whether the charge "is good or bad." He too will be "unfamiliar with the rules of evidence."[c] And a lawyer for the defendant will be able to do little or nothing to prevent an unjust conviction. In a trial before such a judge, the constitutional right to the assistance of counsel thus becomes a hollow mockery—"a teasing illusion like a munificent bequest in a pauper's will." Edwards v. California, 314 U.S. 160, 186 (1941) (concurring opinion).

* * *

[E]ven if it were not possible to demonstrate in a particular case that the lay judge had been incompetent or the trial egregiously unfair, I think that *any* trial before a lay judge that results in the defendant's imprisonment violates the Due Process Clause of the Fourteenth Amendment. The Court has never required a showing of specific or individualized prejudice when it was the procedure itself that violated Due Process of Law....

Among the critical functions that a trial judge must frequently perform are the acceptance of a guilty plea ..., the determination of the voluntariness of a confession ..., the advising of the defendant of his trial

---

[c]Judge Russell testified that he had not received any training concerning rules of evidence and that he was not familiar with the Kentucky statutes relating to jury trials, with the Kentucky rules of criminal procedure, or with the rights guaranteed to a defendant in a criminal case under the Fourteenth Amendment....

rights . . ., and the instruction of a jury. . . . A judge ignorant of the law is simply incapable of performing these functions. If he is aware of his incompetence, such a judge will perhaps instinctively turn to the prosecutor for advice and direction.[d] But such a practice no more than compounds the due process violation. . . .

The Kentucky Court of Appeals characterized the kind of trial that took place here as an "absurdity." The trial, in my view, was such an absurdity as to constitute a gross denial of Due Process of Law.[f]

The Court seems to say that these constitutional deficiencies can all be swept under the rug and forgotten because the convicted defendant may have a trial de novo before a qualified judge. I cannot agree.

In Ward v. Village of Monroeville, 409 U.S. 57 (1972), the Court made clear that "the State's trial court procedure [cannot] be deemed constitutionally acceptable simply because the State eventually offers a defendant an impartial adjudication. Petitioner is entitled to a neutral and detached judge in the first instance." Id., at 61–62. . . .

The Court would distinguish the Ward case as "directed at the need for independent, neutral and detached judgment, not at legal training." . . . But surely there can be no meaningful constitutional difference between a trial that is fundamentally unfair

because of the judge's possible bias, and one that is fundamentally unfair because of the judge's ignorance of the law.[g]

And the Court's suggestion that a defendant haled before a lay judge can protect his constitutional rights by simply pleading guilty and immediately seeking a trial de novo is wholly unpersuasive. First, this argument assumes without any factual support that the defendant will be informed of his right to a trial de novo.[h] Second, the procedure would still necessitate multiple court appearances, at the cost of both delay and an increased financial burden for attorneys' fees and court costs. Third, such a practice would turn what should be a solemn court proceeding, see Boykin v. Alabama, 395 U.S. 238 (1969) [Chapter Thirteen, § 13.01], into nothing more than a sham. In short, I cannot accept the suggestion that, as a prerequisite to a constitutionally fair trial, a defendant must stand up in open court and inform a judge that he is guilty when in fact he believes that he is not.

At Runnymede in 1215 King John pledged to his barons that he would "not make any justiciaries, constables, sheriffs or bailiffs but from those who understand the law of the realm." Magna Carta XLV.

---

[d]Judge Russell conceded that he relied on the city attorney for legal advice.

"Q. Prior to your appointment as City Judge . . . had you had any previous legal experience of any kind?"

"Judge Russell: No Sir."

"Q. Have you had any legal training of any kind since your appointment?"

"Judge Russell: Well the only thing I can say, if I have any doubt, I consult with the city lawyer. . . ."

* * *

"Q. And when you receive advice from the city attorney, do you follow that advice?"

"Judge Russell: Yes, sir."

[f]The scarcity of lawyers or legally trained persons in rural areas cannot serve to justify trials such as this. Utah, to cite one example, has managed to devise a constitutionally adequate trial system even though large portions of the State are sparsely populated and 13 of its 29 counties have two or fewer lawyers. . . .

[g]The Court's reliance on Colten v. Kentucky . . . is misplaced. The question in Colten was not whether a trial of the kind challenged here is constitutionally valid, but the quite different question whether a greater sentence can be imposed on a defendant following a trial de novo without violating North Carolina v. Pearce, 395 U.S. 711 (1969) [Chapter Fourteen, § 14.01].

[h]The record indicates that North was taken to jail immediately after sentencing and obtained his freedom only when the state habeas corpus court on the following day signed a writ ordering his release. It is hardly likely that North would have spent the night in jail if he had been told that he could avoid jail simply by asking for a trial de novo.

The Court also states its assumption that Kentucky police court judges will advise defendants of their right to counsel and that counsel will advise their clients of their right to a trial de novo. . . . This assumption is also devoid of support in the present record. Although Judge Russell stated that it was "the standard procedure" to advise defendants of their right to counsel, he was unwilling to state that he advised North of this right, and North unreservedly testified that he was not so advised.

Today, more than 750 years later, the Court leaves that promise unkept.

I respectfully dissent.

[Mr. Justice STEVENS took no part in the consideration or decision of this case.]

The Two-Tier Court System and Jury Trials

LUDWIG v. MASSACHUSETTS

Supreme Court of the United States, 1976
427 U.S. 618, 96 S. Ct. 2781, 49 L. Ed. 2d 732

Richard Ludwig, the appellant, was charged with negligently operating a motor vehicle in violation of Massachusetts law. The offense carries a maximum penalty of a $200 fine, or two years' imprisonment, or both. The appellant pleaded not guilty. On the day of his scheduled trial, appellant moved for a speedy trial by jury. The motion was denied and after a brief trial he was found guilty and fined $20. Thereafter, appellant asserted his statutory right to a trial de novo before a six-man jury in the Massachusetts District Court. After unsuccessfully moving to dismiss the case on the grounds that he had been deprived of his constitutional right to a speedy jury trial in the first instance and had been subjected to double jeopardy, he waived a jury trial and was again convicted and fined $20. The Massachusetts Supreme Court affirmed his conviction. The United States Supreme Court noted probable jurisdiction on appeal.

Mr. Justice BLACKMUN delivered the opinion of the Court.

The Commonwealth of Massachusetts long ago established a "two-tier" system of trial courts for certain crimes. A person accused of such is tried in the first instance in the lower tier. No trial by jury is available there. If convicted, the defendant may take a timely "appeal" to the second tier and, if he so desires, have a trial de novo by jury. The issues here presented are (1) whether, where the Constitution guarantees an accused a jury trial, it also requires that he be permitted to exercise that right at the first trial in the lower tier, and (2) whether the Massachusetts procedure violates the Double Jeopardy Clause of the Fifth Amendment made applicable to the States by the Fourteenth. Benton v. Maryland, 395 U.S. 784 (1969) [Chapter Three, § 3.04].

Massachusetts is one of several States having a two-tier system of trial courts for criminal cases. See Colten v. Kentucky, 407 U.S. 104 (1972) [Chapter Fourteen, § 14.01]. Some states provide a jury trial in each tier; others provide a jury only in the second tier but allow an accused to bypass the first; and still others, like Massachusetts, do not allow an accused to avoid a trial of some sort at the first tier before he obtains a trial by jury at the second.

The first tier of the Massachusetts system is composed of district courts of the State's several counties, and the municipal court of the city of Boston.... These courts have jurisdictions over violations of municipal ordinances, over misdemeanors except criminal libel, over felonies having a maximum potential sentence in excess of five years.

A criminal proceeding in the first-tier court is begun with the issuance of a complaint. An accused then has two statutory alternatives. He may plead guilty at arraignment and be sentenced by the court. If he is dissatisfied with the sentence, he may appeal. In that case, however, the accused is not entitled to a trial de novo respecting his guilt or innocence; he is limited, instead, to a challenge to his sentence....

If on the other hand, the accused pleads not guilty in the first-tier, he is tried by the judge without a jury. An acquittal there terminates the proceeding. After a judgment of guilty, however, he may appeal either to the superior court, where a 12-person jury is available . . ., or to the district court, where a jury of six is available. . . .

Unlike the two-tier Kentucky system under consideration in Colten v. Kentucky, supra, an accused in Massachusetts does not avoid trial in the first instance by pleading guilty. Nevertheless, he achieves essentially the same result by an established, informal procedure known as "admitting sufficient findings of fact." . . . This procedure is used "[i]f the defendant wishes to waive a trial in the District Court and save his right for a trial in the Superior Court on the appeal." . . .

The trial court then hears only enough evidence to assure itself that there is probable cause to believe that the defendant has committed the offense with which he is charged. The court, however, does make a finding of guilt and enter a judgment of conviction.

Once a person convicted in the District Court indicates that he is going to appeal,[a] his conviction is vacated. He may suffer adverse collateral consequences from the conviction, such as revocation of parole or of his driver's license. . . . Moreover, if the accused "fails to enter and prosecute his appeal, he shall be defaulted on his recognizance and the superior court may impose sentence upon him for the crime of which he was convicted as if he had been convicted in said court. . . .

If an accused does appeal and does not default, he may upon request, be tried de novo by a jury. If again, he is found guilty, he may appeal, as of right, to the Massachu-

---

[a] Mass. Gen. Laws Ann., c. 218, § 31, governs the execution of sentence. If a sentence of six months or less is imposed, the convicted defendant apparently must state immediately that he intends to appeal. If the sentence exceeds six months, the defendant has one day, before commitment, in which to decide whether to appeal. Although the statute provides that a defendant be informed of his right to appeal, it is unclear whether he also is to be informed that, by appealing, he may secure a trial by jury. Since appellant Ludwig did appeal and then expressly waived a jury in the second tier, we need not address the question whether a failure to take an appeal would constitute a knowing and intelligent waiver of the right to trial by jury. See Boykin v. Alabama, 395 U.S. 238, 243 (1969). . . .

setts Appeals Court or to the Supreme Judicial Court where he may raise both factual and legal claims of error. . . .

The standard against which we judge whether the Massachusetts two-tier system violates an individual's constitutional right to trial by jury is the Fourteenth Amendment's guarantee that no person may be deprived "of life, liberty, or property without due process of law." In giving content to this sweeping proscription in the jury trial contest, the Court in the past has considered two distinct issues: whether a State is ever obliged to grant an accused a jury trial, and whether certain features of the 18th century common-law jury are inherent in the right.

In Duncan v. Louisiana, 391 U.S. 145 (1968) [Chapter Three, § 3.04], the Court resolved the first issue by reference to, and in the light of, the Sixth Amendment. It held that the right to a jury trial in a "serious" criminal case was "fundamental to the American scheme of justice." Id., at 149. Accordingly, it held that the "Fourteenth Amendment guarantees a right of jury trial in all criminal cases which — were they to be tried in a federal court — would come within the Sixth Amendment's guarantee." Only when an accused is charged with a "petty" offense, usually defined by reference to the maximum punishment that might be imposed, does the Constitution permit the Federal Government and the State to deprive him of his liberty without affording him an opportunity to have his guilt determined by a jury. Baldwin v. New York, 399 U.S. 66 (1970).

In Williams v. Florida, 399 U.S. 78 (1970) [supra], and in Apodaca v. Oregon, 406 U.S. 404 (1972), the Court dealt with the second issue by considering whether particular features of the 18th century common-law jury are essential, or merely incidental to the central purpose of the jury trial requirement. . . .

The Court held in Williams that a jury of 12 is not required in order that this central purpose be served. Similar analysis led to the holding in Apodaca and Johnson v. Louisiana, 406 U.S. 356 (1972) [supra] that the jury's verdict need not be unanimous. . . .

These two issues are not again in controversy in the present case. It is indisputable that the Massachusetts two-tier system does afford an accused charged with a serious offense the absolute right to have his guilt determined by a jury composed and operating in accordance with the Constitution. Within the system, the jury serves its function of protecting against prosecutorial and judicial misconduct. It does so directly at the second tier of the Massachusetts system, and it may also have an indirect effect on first-tier trials. . . .

This is not to say that we are unaware of a remote possibility that an accused in Massachusetts may be faced at his first trial with an overzealous prosecutor and a judge who is either unable or unwilling to control him. But in such a case, he may protect himself from questionable incarceration by appealing, and insisting upon a trial by jury.

Even though the Massachusetts procedure does not deprive an accused of his Fourteenth Amendment right to a jury trial, the question remains whether it unconstitutionally burdens the exercise of that right: (1) by imposing the financial cost of an additional trial; (2) by subjecting an accused to a potentially harsher sentence if he seeks a trial de novo in the second tier; and (3) by imposing the increased psychological and physical hardships of two trials.

Appellant charges that the Massachusetts system financially burdens the accused by requiring that he twice defend himself and by causing a loss of wages if he is employed. Although these burdens are not unreal and although they may, in an individual case, impose a hardship, we conclude that they do not impose an unconstitutional burden on the exercise of the right to a trial by jury expeditiously by invoking the above-described procedure of "admitting sufficient findings of fact," a defense at the lower tier. . . .

The question whether the possibility of a harsher sentence at the second tier impermissibly burdens the exercise of an accused's right to a trial by jury is controlled by the decisions in North Carolina v. Pearce and Colten v. Kentucky [Chapter Fourteen, § 14.01]. These cases establish that the mere possibility of a harsher sentence does not unconstitutionally burden an accused's right to a trial by jury. . . .

We are not oblivious to the adverse psychological and physical effects that delay in obtaining the final adjudication of one's guilt or innocence may engender. Protection against unwarranted delay, with its con-

comitant function of the Speedy Trial Clause of the Sixth Amendment, made applicable to the States by means of the Fourteenth. Klopfer v. North Carolina, 386 U.S. 213 (1967). Appellant does not continue to press the contention, made below, that he was denied his constitutional right to a speedy trial. Further, it is nearly always true that an accused may obtain a faster adjudication of his guilt or innocence by waiving a jury trial even in those States where he may have one in the first instance. No one has seriously charged, however, that the fact that trials by jury are not scheduled so quickly as trials before a judge impermissibly burdens the constitutional right to trial by jury. Finally we are uncertain whether the delay in obtaining a jury trial is increased by the de novo procedure or decreased. Appellant has not presented any evidence to show that there is a greater delay in obtaining a jury in Massachusetts than there would be if the Commonwealth abandoned its two-tier system. We are reluctant to attribute to Massachusetts a perverse determination to maintain an inefficient system whose very purpose is to increase efficiency.

* * *

The modes of exercising federal constitutional rights have traditionally been left, within limits, to state specification. In this case, Massachusetts absolutely guarantees trial by jury to persons accused of serious crimes and the manner it has specified for exercising this right is fair and not unduly burdensome.

The final contention is that the Massachusetts procedure violates the Double Jeopardy Clause. The basis of appellant's contention is that "the de novo procedure forces the accused to the 'risk' of two trials." . . . We agree that there is no double jeopardy violation posed by the Massachusetts system. . . . The Massachusetts system presents no danger of prosecution after an accused has been pardoned; nor is there any doubt that acquittal at the first tier precludes reprosecution. Instead, the argument appears to be that because the appellant has been placed once in jeopardy and convicted, the State may not retry him when he informs the trial court of his decision to "appeal" and to secure a trial de novo.

Appellant's argument is without substance. The decision to secure a new trial rests with the accused alone. A defendant who elects to be tried de novo in Massachusetts is in no different position than is a convicted defendant who successfully appeals on the basis of the trial record and gains a reversal of his conviction and a remand of his case for a new trial. Under these circumstances, it long has been clear that the State may reprosecute. United States v. Ball, 163 U.S. 662 (1896). The only difference between an appeal on the record and an appeal resulting automatically in a new trial is that a convicted defendant in Massachusetts may obtain a "reversal" and a new trial without assignment of error in the proceedings at his first trial. Nothing in the Double Jeopardy Clause prohibits a State from affording a defendant two opportunities to avoid and secure an acquittal.

The judgment is affirmed

Mr. Justice POWELL, concurring.

I join the opinion of the court, as I understand it to be consistent with my view that the right to a jury trial afforded by the Fourteenth Amendment is not indentical to that guaranteed by the Sixth Amendment. . . .

Mr. Justice STEVENS, with whom Mr. Justice BRENNAN, Mr. Justice STEWART, and Mr. Justice MARSHALL join, dissenting.

The question in this case is whether Massachusetts may convict a defendant of a crime and sentence him to prison for a period of five years without a jury trial. The Court answers the question in the affirmative for two reasons. First, the conviction is almost meaningless since the defendant may have it vacated by an immediate appeal; and second, the defendant may minimize the burden of the trial by, in effect, stipulating that the proof need not establish his guilt beyond a reasonable doubt. To put it mildly, I find these reasons unsatisfactory.

* * *

. . . I should think the Court would at least ask why Massachusetts *requires* the defendant to stand trial in the first tier before permitting him to have a jury trial. This is also a requirement which—as far as the record, the briefs, the oral argument, or the opinion announced by the Court today shed any light on the matter—is totally irrational. All

of the legitimate benefits of the two-tier system could be obtained by giving the defendant the right to waive the first-tier trial completely.

The only reason I can perceive for not allowing such a waiver illustrates the vice of the system. A defendant who can afford the financial and psychological burden of one trial may not be able to withstand the strain of a second. Thus, as a practical matter, a finding of guilt in the first-tier proceeding will actually end some cases that would have been tried by a jury if the defendant had the right to waive the first-tier proceeding. And since the nonjury trial is less expensive and time consuming, the State receives the benefit of an expedited disposition in such a case. The Court quite properly does not rely on any such justification because, if valid, it would justify the complete elimination of jury trials.

There are several reasons why I cannot accept the Court's naive assumption that the first-tier proceeding is virtually meaningless. If it is meaningless for the defendant, it must be equally meaningless for the Commonwealth. But if so, why does the Commonwealth insist on the *requirement* that the defendant must submit to the first trial? Only, I suggest, because it believes the number of jury trials that would be avoided by the required practice exceeds the number that would take place in an optional system. In short, the very purpose of the requirement is to discourage jury trials by placing a burden on the exercise of the constitutional right.

The burden, in my opinion, is significant. A second trial of the same case is never the same as the first. Lawyers and witnesses are stale; opportunities for impeachment that may have little or much actual significance are present in the second trial that were not present in the first; a witness may be available at one time but not the other; the tactics on cross-examination, or on the presentation of evidence, in the first trial will be influenced by the judgment of what may happen at the second; the strategy in a nonjury trial may be different than in a proceeding before a jury. Clearly if a defendant has participated in a full first-tier nonjury trial, his jury trial in the second tier is significantly different from the normal jury trial.

The Court responds by indicating that "Massachusetts permits an accused to short-circuit trial in the first tier by admitting to sufficient findings of fact." But if we presume that the defendant is innocent until proven guilty, we must also assume that the innocent defendant would deny or contradict the evidence offered by the prosecutor. The choice between admitting the truth and also the prima facie sufficiency of evidence the defendant considers false or misleading, on the one hand, or insisting on a full nonjury trial on the other, is not an insignificant price to pay for the exercise of a constitutional right.

Nor does the right to a trial de novo by taking an immediate appeal make the judge's guilty finding and sentence entirely meaningless. Apart from any legal consequence, the finding certainly tarnishes the defendant's reputation.[c] The finding, and the first judge's sentencing determination, may

––––––––––

[c]To dramatize this point, we might make the not entirely unrealistic hypothetical assumption that a defendant might suddenly suffer a fatal heart attack when the trial judge announces his finding and sentence. More realistically, we need simply recognize the fact that many convicted defendants will be unwilling to undergo the ordeal of a second trial after being found guilty by a judge.

have a greater impact on the second trial judge than the mere return of an indictment. Moreover, if we presume that at least some laymen have some knowledge of the law, we must also recognize the likelihood that some jurors at the second-tier trial will be aware of the first conviction. Such awareness inevitably compromises the defendant's presumption of innocence. Moreover, a judge's instructions cannot adequately avoid the risk of prejudice without creating the additional risk of letting other jurors know about the first conviction.

Unquestionably in a great majority of proceedings the two-tier system may expedite the disposition of cases and, indeed, may give a defendant two opportunities to establish his innocence. But that fact is of no significance to the individual who wants only one trial and who wants that trial to be conducted before a jury. The Constitution guarantees him that protection; that guarantee is not fulfilled by a State which eventually offers the defendant the kind of trial he is entitled to receive in the first instance. . . . The burden on the right to a jury trial imposed by Massachusetts is especially unacceptable because the Commonwealth has offered no legitimate justification for its *requirement* of a first-tier nonjury trial. . . .

I respectfully dissent.

Comments

1. In *North* v. *Russell,* supra, a majority of the Court held that the misdemeanor trial of an accused before a judge who is not legally trained does not deprive the accused of his right to the effective assistance of counsel or his right to a fair trial *provided* the accused has an absolute right to a trial de novo before a legally trained judge. The majority reached this conclusion despite the evidence that Judge C. B. Russell (1) had only a high school education, (2) had never received any training concerning his duties as a lay judge, (3) was not familiar with the Kentucky statutes relating to jury trials, with the Kentucky rules of criminal procedure, or with the rights guaranteed to a defendant in a criminal case under the Fifth and Fourteenth Amendments, (4) usually relied on and followed the legal advice of the city attorney (prosecutor), and (5) was unwilling to testify that he advised North of his right to counsel (dissenting opinion of Stewart, J.). Is the majority saying (sub silento) that it is permissible for an accused's due process rights to be "watered down" in the first instance under a two-tier court system? Is this because the accused has an absolute right to a trial de novo? Although it may be "standard procedure" in Kentucky for a trial judge to inform an accused of his right to a trial de novo, is it a denial of due process if the record suggests that the accused was not so informed? Suppose an accused pleads guilty at

the initial trial in order to obtain a trial de novo before a legally trained judge, and the de novo judge learns of the accused's guilty plea. Is it a denial of due process for the de novo judge to try the case? In small towns few events are kept secret, especially those involving the criminal process. Mr. Justice Stewart's point (dissenting) is well taken with respect to the majority's "misplaced reliance" on *Colten* v. *Kentucky* (Chapter Fourteen, § 14.01). *Colten* did not in any way deal with the issue of the legal training of the trial judge, involving instead a claim of double jeopardy on resentencing following a reconviction. It is more than incredible that the majority decided such an important issue as that presented in *North* based on the dicta of an earlier case *(Colten)* that involved a claim of double jeopardy on resentencing.

2. The majority opinion failed to note that a substantial number of judges in the United States are not legally trained. For example, "in South Carolina only 16 of 328 magistrates are lawyers. New York has 430 lawyer justices and 1,983 non-lawyer justices. A majority of South Carolina's magistrates have no schooling beyond the 12th grade. Thirty or more states still use lay judges to try minor criminal cases." 32 *Preview of U.S. Supreme Court Cases* (1976). The majority also failed to indicate that most lay judges have additional judicial powers, beyond trying misdemeanor cases, important to the criminal process. These include (1) presiding at the initial appearance of an accused charged with a crime (usually a felony charge), (2) setting the initial bail, (3) presiding at preliminary hearings to determine probable cause (felonies), (4) issuing arrest warrants (misdemeanors and felonies), and (5) issuing search warrants. In addition, as noted by Justice Stewart, trial judges accept guilty pleas, decide the voluntariness of confessions, advise defendants of their trial rights, and instruct juries. Thus, lay judges have extensive judicial power.

3. In practical terms, the convenience of letting the butcher, the baker, or the candlestick maker dispense justice will be appreciated in some quarters, especially in rural areas with few lawyers. But the question that remains unsettled is whether the guarantees of the Constitution can be properly implemented by laymen. Undoubtedly, many lay judges are conscientious and well-meaning; and justice prevails in many of these courts. The best of intentions can go awry, however, if they are unsupported by adequate knowledge. One wonders how many lay judges can recognize hearsay evidence (as opposed to out-of-court statements offered for some purpose other than to prove the truth of the matter asserted). Or are familiar with the numerous exceptions to the hearsay rule (over 30 in some jurisdictions). Or can distinguish the concepts of res judicata and collateral estoppel. Or can distinguish between a proprietary and a penal interest when a third-party declaration against interest is sought to be admitted as an exception to the hearsay rule. Or understand the difference between materiality and relevancy. Or know the limitations on judicial notice. The list could go on and on. Judges who have the power to deprive an accused of his liberty should be trained in the law. It is as simple as that.

4. Does the holding of *North* seem inconsistent with that in *Argersinger* v. *Hamlin,* 407 U.S. 25 (1972) (supra, § 7.02)? In all juris-

dictions prosecutors and defense attorneys must be legally trained; thus it is possible that both lawyers in a criminal trial will be legally trained but the presiding judge will not. Such a situation is no victory for common sense. Are you satisfied with the reasoning of the majority that a trial before a lay judge does not deny the accused the effective assistance of counsel, especially when the evidence suggests that many such judges rely heavily on the legal advice of the prosecutor? Doesn't that assume that the prosecutor's legal advice will always be accurate? What is the probability that an accused will be found innocent by a lay judge if he is represented by a "high-priced, slick, big-city lawyer" in a rural area? How many lay judges would appreciate the complex defense motions and fancy legal oratory of an F. Lee Bailey? Arguably (although sadly), a defendant might fare better before some lay judges without the services of a "superstar" defense attorney. The majority glosses over these practical considerations with bland assurances that the convicted defendant can always take an appeal on a trial de novo. Won't retained counsel charge additional fees for a second trial? Is that the price an accused must pay for justice? Consider the statement of the majority that "it is unnecessary to reach the question whether a defendant could be convicted and imprisoned after a proceeding in which the only trial afforded is conducted by a lay judge." Would the majority permit this? Do you agree with Justice Stewart's statement, "In a trial before such a [lay] judge, the constitutional right to the assistance of counsel . . . becomes a hollow mockery. . ."?

5. The majority in *North* had little difficulty with the equal protection issue because "all people within a given city and within cities of the same size are treated equally," and thus, no invidious classifications were being employed. Apparently even Justices Stewart and Marshall (dissenting) agreed on this point. The appellant's reliance on *Ward* v. *Village of Monroeville,* 409 U.S. 57 (1972), was, according to the majority, equally misplaced even though the Court in *Ward* said, "Petitioner is entitled to a neutral and detached judge in the first instance." Id. at 61–62. In view of all the relevant facts in *North,* can it be said that Judge Russell met the test of due process?

6. In *Ludwig* v. *Massachusetts,* supra, a majority of the Court could find no unconstitutional burden on exercise of the Sixth Amendment right to a jury trial when that right is available only at the second stage (tier) of a two-tier criminal court system. Why is this so? An accused in jurisdictions with such a system must first plead guilty or be convicted at the first tier before a jury trial is available; i.e., waiver of a trial at the first tier is not permitted. If this system doesn't place an unconstitutional burden on the Sixth Amendment, doesn't it at the least have a "chilling effect" on the exercise of one's constitutional rights? Consider the statement of the majority in *United States* v. *Jackson,* 390 U.S. 570 (1968), that if a law has "no other purpose . . . than to chill the assertion of constitutional rights by penalizing them, then it [is] patently unconstitutional," at 581. Does the Massachusetts procedure "penalize" one for exercising constitutional rights or does it serve some other purpose? If so, what is that purpose? In light of *North,* supra, and *Williams* v. *Florida, Apodaca* v. *Oregon, Johnson* v. *Louisiana,* and *Colten* v. *Kentucky* (cited in *Ludwig*), isn't it now possible for an accused in

a two-tier system to be tried without a jury before a lay judge (first tier) and on a trial de novo to be tried before a six-man jury and be convicted by a less than unanimous verdict and receive a harsher punishment? Does such a combination of procedures, upheld by the Supreme Court in separate cases, put an "unconstitutional burden", or, at the very least, have a "chilling effect" on assertion of one's constitutional rights? Or is the answer "no," since twelve-man juries and unanimous verdicts are not constitutionally required? If a jury trial for "serious crimes" is constitutionally required, *Duncan* v. *Louisiana,* 391 U.S. 145 (1968) (Chapter Three, § 3.04), why does an accused have to go through the ordeal of a first trial in order to obtain the benefits of this constitutional right?

B. THE RIGHT TO AN IMPARTIAL JURY

Exclusion of Blacks from Petit Juries

SWAIN v. ALABAMA

Supreme Court of the United States, 1965
380 U.S. 202, 85 S. Ct. 824, 13 L. Ed. 2d 759

Robert Swain, a black, was tried and convicted of rape by an all-white jury in an Alabama state court. He appealed the conviction, asserting that the jury selection process was discriminatory and unconstitutional because of (1) discrimination in the selection of the venire panels of prospective jurors; (2) discrimination in the selection of jurors from the veniremen; and (3) discrimination in the use of the peremptory strike system. The facts showed that no black had served on a petit jury in Talladega County, Alabama (the site of the trial) since 1950. The Alabama Supreme Court affirmed the conviction, and the United States Supreme Court granted certiorari.

Mr. Justice WHITE delivered the opinion of the Court.

* * *

... Although a Negro defendant is not entitled to a jury containing members of his race, a State's purposeful or deliberate denial to Negroes on account of race of participation as jurors in the administration of justice violates the Equal Protection Clause. ...

And it has been consistently and repeatedly applied in many cases coming before this Court. The principle of these cases is broadly based. "For racial discrimination to result in the exclusion from jury service of otherwise qualified groups not only violates

our Constitution and the laws enacted under it but is at war with our basic concepts of a democratic society and a representative government." ...

Further, "jurymen should be selected as individuals, on the basis of individual qualifications and not as members of a race." ... Nor is the constitutional command forbidding intentional exclusion limited to Negroes. It applies to any identifiable group in the community which may be the subject of prejudice. ...

But purposeful discrimination may not be assumed or merely asserted. ... It must be proven ..., the quantum of proof necessary being a matter of federal law. ... It is not the soundness of these principles, which is unquestioned, but their scope and application to the issues in this case that concern us here.

I

We consider first petitioner's claims concerning the selection of grand jurors and the petit jury venire. The evidence was that while Negro males over 21 constitute 26% of all males in the county in this age group, only 10 to 15% of the grand and petit jury panels drawn from the jury box since 1953 have been Negroes, there having been only one case in which the percentage was as high as 23%. In this period of time, Negroes served on 80% of the grand juries selected, the number ranging from one to three. There were four or five Negroes on the grand jury panel of about 33 in this case, out of which two served on the grand jury which indicted petitioner. Although there has been an average of six to seven Negroes on petit jury venires in criminal cases, no Negro has actually served on a petit jury since about 1950. In this case there were eight Negroes on the petit jury venire but none actually served, two being exempt and six being struck by the prosecutor in the process of selecting the jury.

It is wholly obvious that Alabama has not totally excluded a racial group from either grand or petit jury panels. . . . Moreover, we do not consider an average of six to eight Negroes on these panels as constituting forbidden token inclusion within the meaning of the cases in this Court. . . . Nor do we consider the evidence in this case to make out a prima facie case of invidious discrimination under the Fourteenth Amendment.

* * *

Venires drawn from the jury box . . . unquestionably contained a smaller proportion of the Negro community than of the white community. But a defendant in a criminal case is not constitutionally entitled to demand a proportionate number of his race on the jury which tries him nor on the venire or jury roll from which petit jurors are drawn. . . . Neither the jury roll nor the venire need be a perfect mirror of the community or accurately reflect the proportionate strength of every identifiable group. "Obviously the number of races and nationalities appearing in the ancestry of our citizens would make it impossible to meet a requirement of proportional representation. Similarly, since there can be no exclusion of Negroes as a race and no discrimination because of color, proportional limitation is not permissible." . . . We cannot say that purposeful discrimination based on race alone is satisfactorily proved by showing that an identifiable group in a community is underrepresented by as much as 10%. . . . Here the commissioners denied that racial considerations entered into their selections of either their contacts in the community or the names of prospective jurors. There is no evidence that the commissioners applied different standards of qualifications to the Negro community than they did to the white community. Nor was there any meaningful attempt to demonstrate that the same proportion of Negroes qualified under the standards being administered by the commissioners. . . . Undoubtedly the selection of prospective jurors was somewhat haphazard and little effort was made to ensure that all groups in the community were fully represented. . . . An imperfect system is not equivalent to purposeful discrimination based on race. We do not think that the burden of proof was carried by petitioner in this case.

II

Petitioner makes a further claim relating to the exercise of peremptory challenges to exclude Negroes from serving on petit juries.

In Talladega County the petit jury venire drawn in a criminal case numbers about 35 unless a capital offense is involved, in which case it numbers about 100. . . . After excuses and removals for cause, the venire in a capital case is reduced to about 75. The jury is then "struck" — the defense striking two veniremen and the prosecution one in alternating turns, until only 12 jurors remain. . . . This essentially is the Alabama struck-jury system, applicable in all criminal cases and available in civil cases. . . . In this case, the six Negroes available for jury service were struck by the prosecutor in the process of selecting the jury which was to try petitioner.

In the trial court after the jury was selected, petitioner moved to have the jury declared void on Fourteenth Amendment grounds. . . .

The main thrust of the motion according to its terms was the striking of the six Negroes from the petit jury venire. No evidence was taken, petitioner apparently being content to rely on the record which had been made in connection with the motion to quash the indictment. We think the motion, seeking as it did to invalidate the alleged purposeful striking of Negroes from the jury which was to try petitioner, was properly denied.

In providing for jury trial in criminal cases, Alabama adheres to the common-law system of trial by an impartial jury of 12 men who must unanimously agree on a verdict, the system followed in the federal courts by virtue of the Sixth Amendment. As part of this system it provides for challenges for cause and substitutes a system of strikes for the common-law method of peremptory challenge. Alabama contends that its system of peremptory strikes—challenges without cause without explanation and without judicial scrutiny—affords a suitable and necessary method of securing juries which in fact and in the opinion of the parties are fair and impartial. This system, it is said, in and of itself, provides justification for striking any group of otherwise qualified jurors in any given case, whether they be Negroes, Catholics, accountants or those with blue eyes. Based on the history of this system and its actual use and operation in this country, we think there is merit in this position.

* * *

The function of the challenge is not only to eliminate extremes of partiality on both sides, but to assure the parties that the jurors before whom they try the case will decide on the basis of the evidence placed before them, and not otherwise.... Indeed the very availability of peremptories allows counsel to ascertain the possibility of bias through probing questions on the voir dire and facilitates the exercise of challenges for cause by removing the fear of incurring a juror's hostility through examination and challenge for cause.... The essential nature of the peremptory challenge is that it is one exercised without a reason stated, without inquiry and without being subject to the court's control.... While challenges for cause permit rejection of jurors on a narrowly specified, provable and legally cognizable basis of partiality, the peremptory permits rejection for a real or imagined partiality that is less easily designated or demonstrable.... It is often exercised upon the "sudden impressions and unaccountable prejudices we are apt to conceive upon the bare looks and gestures of another,"... upon a juror's "habits and associations"... or upon the feeling that "the bare question [of a juror's] indifference may sometimes provoke a resentment".... It is no less frequently exercised on grounds normally thought irrelevant to legal proceedings or official action, namely, the race, religion, nationality, occupation or affiliations of people summoned for jury duty. For the question a prosecutor or defense counsel must decide is not whether a juror of a particular race or nationality is in fact partial, but whether one from a different group is less likely to be. It is well known that these factors are widely explored during the voir dire, by both prosecutor and accused....

With these considerations in mind, we cannot hold that the striking of Negroes in a particular case is a denial of equal protection of the laws. In the quest for an impartial and qualified jury, Negro and white, Protestant and Catholic, are alike subject to being challenged without cause....

In the light of the purpose of the peremptory system and the function it serves in a pluralistic society in connection with the institution of jury trial, we cannot hold that the Constitution requires an examination of the prosecutor's reasons for the exercise of his challenges in any given case. The presumption in any particular case must be that the prosecutor is using the State's challenges to obtain a fair and impartial jury to try the case before the court. The presumption is not overcome and the prosecutor therefore subjected to examination by allegations that in the case at hand all Negroes were removed from the jury or that they were removed because they were Negroes....

III

Petitioner, however, presses a broader claim in this Court. His argument is that not only were the Negroes removed by the prosecutor in this case but that there never has been a Negro on a petit jury in either a civil or criminal case in Talladega County and that in criminal cases prosecutors have consistently and systematically exercised their strikes to prevent any and all Negroes on petit jury venires from serving on the petit jury itself. This systematic practice, it is claimed, is invidious discrimination for which the peremptory system is insufficient justification.

We agree that this claim raises a different issue and it may well require a different answer. We have decided that it is permissible to insulate from inquiry the removal of Negroes from a particular jury on the assumption that the prosecutor is acting on acceptable considerations related to the case he is trying, the particular defendant involved and the particular crime charged. But when the prosecutor in a county, in case after case, whatever the circumstances, whatever the crime and whoever the defendant or the victim may be, is responsible for the removal of Negroes who have been selected as qualified jurors by the jury commissioners and who have survived challenges for cause, with the result that no Negroes ever serve on petit juries, the Fourteenth Amendment claim takes on added significance.... In these circumstances, giving even the widest leeway to the operation of irrational but trial-related suspicions and antagonisms, it would appear that the purposes of the pe-

remptory challenge are being perverted. If the State has not seen fit to leave a single Negro on any jury in a criminal case, the presumption protecting the prosecutor may well be overcome. Such proof might support a reasonable inference that Negroes are excluded from juries for reasons wholly unrelated to the outcome of the particular case on trial and that the peremptory system is being used to deny the Negro the same right and opportunity to participate in the administration of justice enjoyed by the white population. These ends the peremptory challenge is not designed to facilitate or justify.

We need pursue this matter no further, however, for even if a State's systematic striking of Negroes in the selection of petit juries raises a prima facie case under the Fourteenth Amendment, we think it is readily apparent that the record in this case is not sufficient to demonstrate that the rule has been violated by the peremptory system as it operates in Talladega County....

* * *

Affirmed.

[Mr. Justice HARLAN concurred.]
[Mr. Justice GOLDBERG, joined by Chief Justice WARREN and Mr. Justice DOUGLAS, dissented.]

When the Defendant and Victim Are of Different Races

RISTAINO v. ROSS

Supreme Court of the United States, 1976
424 U.S. 589, 96 S. Ct. 1017, 47 L. Ed. 2d 258

The facts are stated in the opinion.

Mr. Justice POWELL delivered the opinion of the Court.

Respondent is a Negro convicted in a state court of violent crimes against a white security guard. The trial judge denied respondent's motion that a question specifically directed to racial prejudice be asked during voir dire in addition to customary

questions directed to general bias or prejudice. The narrow issue is whether, under our recent decision in Ham v. South Carolina, 409 U.S. 524 (1973), respondent was constitutionally entitled to require the asking of a question specifically directed to racial prejudice. The broader issue presented is whether Ham announced a requirement applicable whenever there may be a confrontation in a criminal trial between persons of different races or different ethnic origins. We answer both of these questions in the negative.

I

Respondent, James Ross, was tried in a Massachusetts court with two other Negroes for armed robbery, assault and battery by means of a dangerous weapon, and assault and battery with intent to murder. The victim of the alleged crimes was a white man employed by Boston University as a uniformed security guard. The voir dire of prospective jurors was to be conducted by the court, which was required by statute to inquire generally into prejudice. Each defendant, represented by separate counsel, made a written motion that the prospective jurors also be questioned specifically about racial prejudice. Each defendant also moved that the veniremen be asked about affiliations with law-enforcement agencies.

The trial judge consulted counsel for the defendants about their motions. After tentatively indicating that he "felt that no purpose would be accomplished by asking such questions in this instance," the judge invited the views of counsel:

"The Court: . . . I thought from something Mr. Donnelly [counsel for a co-defendant] said, he might have wanted on the record something which was peculiar to this case, or peculiar to the circumstances which we are operating under here which perhaps he didn't want to say in open court.

"Is there anything peculiar about it, Mr. Donnelly?

"Mr. Donnelly: No, just the fact that the victim is white, and the defendants are black.

"The Court: This, unfortunately, is a problem with us, and all we can hope and pray for is that the jurors and all of them take their oaths seriously and understand the spirit of their oath and understand the spirit of what the Court says to them—this Judge anyway—and I am sure all Judges of this Court—would take the time to impress upon them before, during, and after the trial, and before their verdict, that their oath means just what it says, that they are to decide the case on the evidence, with no extraneous considerations.

"I believe that that is the best that can be done with respect to the problems which—as I said, I regard as extremely important. . . ." . . .

Further discussion persuaded the judge that a question about law-enforcement affiliations should be asked because of the victim's status as a security guard. But he adhered to his decision not to pose a question directed specifically to racial prejudice.

The voir dire of five panels of prospective jurors then commenced. The trial judge briefly familiarized each panel with the facts of the case, omitting any reference to racial matters. He then explained to the panel that the clerk would ask a general question about impartiality and a question about affiliations with law-enforcement agencies. Consistently with his announced intention to "impress upon the jurors . . . that they are to decide the case on the evidence, with no extraneous considerations," the judge preceded the questioning of the panel with an extended discussion of the obligations of jurors. After these remarks the clerk posed the questions indicated to the panel. Panelists answering a question affirmatively were questioned individually at the bench by the judge, in the presence of counsel. This procedure led to the excusing of 18 veniremen for cause on grounds of prejudice, including one panelist who admitted a racial bias.

The jury eventually impaneled convicted each defendant of all counts. On direct appeal Ross contended that his federal constitutional rights were violated by the denial of his request that prospective jurors be questioned specifically about racial prejudice. This contention was rejected by the Supreme Judicial Court of Massachusetts . . . and Ross sought a writ of certiorari. While his petition was pending, we held in Ham that a trial court's failure on request to question veniremen specifically about racial prejudice had denied Ham due process of law. We granted Ross' petition for certiorari and remanded for reconsideration in light of Ham, 410 U.S. 901 (1973); the Supreme Judicial Court again affirmed Ross' conviction. . . . The court reasoned that Ham turned on the need for questions about racial prejudice presented by its facts and did not announce "a new broad constitutional principle requiring that such questions . . . be put to prospective jurors in all State criminal trials when the defendant is black. . . ." . . . Ross again sought certiorari, but the writ was denied. . . .

In the present case Ross renewed his contention on collateral attack in federal habeas corpus. Relying on Ham, the District Court granted a writ of habeas corpus, and the Court of Appeals for the First Circuit affirmed. ... The Court of Appeals assumed that Ham turned on its facts. But it held that the facts of Ross' case, involving "violence against a white" with "a status close to that of a police officer," presented a need for specific questioning about racial prejudice similar to that in Ham. We think the Court of Appeals read Ham too broadly.

II

The Constitution does not always entitle a defendant to have questions posed during voir dire specifically directed to matters that conceivably might prejudice veniremen against him. Voir dire "is conducted under the supervision of the court, and a great deal must, of necessity, be left to its sound discretion." ... This is so because the "determination of impartiality, in which demeanor plays such an important part, is particularly within the province of the trial judge." ... Thus, the State's obligation to the defendant to impanel an impartial jury generally can be satisfied by less than an inquiry into a specific prejudice feared by the defendant.

In Ham, however, we recognized that some cases may present circumstances in which an impermissible threat to the fair trial guaranteed by due process is posed by a trial court's refusal to question prospective jurors specifically about racial prejudice during voir dire. Ham involved a Negro tried in South Carolina courts for possession of marihuana. He was well known in the locale of his trial as a civil rights activist, and his defense was that law enforcement officials had framed him on the narcotics charge to "get him" for those activities. Despite the circumstances, the trial judge denied Ham's request that the court-conducted voir dire include questions specifically directed to racial prejudice. We reversed the judgment of conviction because "... the essential fairness required by the Due Process Clause of the Fourteenth Amendment requires that under the facts shown by this record the defendant be permitted to have the jurors interrogated during voir dire on the issue of racial bias." ...

By its terms Ham did not announce a requirement of universal applicability. Rather, it reflected an assessment of whether under all of the circumstances presented there was a constitutionally significant likelihood that, absent questioning about racial prejudice, the jurors would not be as "indifferent as they stand unsworne." In this approach Ham was consistent with other determinations by this Court that a State had denied a defendant due process by failing to impanel an impartial jury. ...

The circumstances in Ham strongly suggested the need for voir dire to include specific questioning about racial prejudice. Ham's defense was that he had been framed because of his civil rights activities. His prominence in the community as a civil rights activist, if not already known to the veniremen, inevitably would have been revealed to the members of the jury in the course of his presentation of that defense. Racial issues therefore were inextricably bound up with the conduct of the trial. Further, Ham's reputation as a civil rights activist and the defense he interposed were likely to intensify any prejudice that the individual members of the jury might harbor. In such circumstances we deem a voir dire that included questioning specifically directed to racial prejudice, when sought by Ham, necessary to meet the constitutional requirement that an impartial jury be impaneled.

We do not agree with the Court of Appeals that the need to question veniremen specifically about racial prejudice also rose to constitutional dimensions in this case. The mere fact that the victim of the crimes alleged was a white man and the defendants were Negroes was less likely to distort the trial than were the special factors involved in Ham. The victim's status as a security officer, also relied upon by the Court of Appeals, was cited by respective defense counsel primarily as a separate source of prejudice, not as an aggravating racial factor, ... and the trial judge dealt with it by his question about law-enforcement affiliations. The circumstances thus did not suggest a significant likelihood that racial prejudice might infect Ross' trial. This was made clear to the trial judge when Ross was unable to support his motion concerning voir dire by pointing to racial factors such as existed in Ham or others of comparable significance. In these circumstances, the trial judge acted within the Constitution in determining that the demands of due process could be satisfied by his more generalized but thorough inquiry into the impartiality of the veniremen.

Reversed.

Mr. Justice WHITE concurs in the result on the ground that Ham v. South Carolina, 409 U.S. 524 (1973), announced a new constitutional rule applicable to federal and state criminal trials and that this rule should not be applied retroactively to cases such as this involving trials which occurred prior to the decision in Ham.

[Mr. Justice MARSHALL, with whom Mr. Justice BRENNAN joined, dissented.]

[Mr. Justice STEVENS took no part in the consideration or decision of this case.]

When the Defendant Is Tried in Jail Clothes

ESTELLE v. WILLIAMS

Supreme Court of the United States, 1976
425 U.S. 501, 96 S. Ct. 1691, 48 L. Ed. 2d 126

Harry Lee Williams, the respondent, was convicted in a Texas state court of assault with intent to commit murder. During an argument with his former landlord, Williams had stabbed the landlord with a knife in the neck, chest, and abdomen, severely wounding him. Because he was unable to post bond, Williams was held in jail while awaiting trial. Williams appeared at trial in jail clothes, but neither the respondent nor his counsel raised an objection to the wearing of the jail attire at any time. The Texas Court of Criminal Appeals affirmed the conviction. Williams then sought release in the United States district court on a petition for a writ of habeas corpus. That court held that although it is inherently unfair to try a defendant in jail clothes, such error was harmless. The United States Court of Appeals (5th Cir.) reversed, holding that such error was not harmless. The United States Supreme Court granted certiorari.

Mr. Chief Justice BURGER delivered the opinion of the Court.

We granted certiorari in this case to determine whether an accused who is compelled to wear identifiable prison clothing at his trial by a jury is denied due process or equal protection of the laws.

* * *

I

The right to a fair trial is a fundamental liberty secured by the Fourteenth Amendment. Drope v. Missouri, 420 U.S. 162, 172 (1975). The presumption of innocence, although not articulated in the Constitution, is a basic component of a fair trial under our system of criminal justice. Long ago this Court stated:

"The principle that there is a presumption of innocence in favor of the accused is the undoubted law, axiomatic and elementary, and its enforcement lies at the foundation of the administration of our criminal law." Coffin v. United States, 156 U.S. 432, 453 (1895).

To implement the presumption, courts must be alert to factors that may undermine the fairness of the fact-finding process. In the administration of criminal justice, courts must carefully guard against dilution of the principle that guilt is to be established by probative evidence and beyond a reasonable doubt. In re Winship, 397 U.S. 358, 364 (1970).

The actual impact of a particular practice on the judgment of jurors cannot always be fully determined. But this Court has left no doubt that the probability of deleterious effects on fundamental rights calls for close judicial scrutiny. Estes v. Texas, 381 U.S. 532 (1965). . . . Courts must do the best they can to evaluate the likely effects of a particular procedure, based on reason, principle, and common human experience.

The potential effects of presenting an accused before the jury in prison attire need not, however, be measured in the abstract. Courts have, with few exceptions, determined that an accused should not be compelled to go to trial in prison or jail clothing because of the possible impairment of the presumption so basic to the adversary system. . . . The American Bar Association's Standards for Criminal Justice also disapprove the practice. . . . This is a recognition that the constant reminder of the accused's condition implicit in such distinctive, identifiable attire may affect a juror's judgment. The defendant's clothing is so likely to be a continuing influence throughout the trial that, not unlike placing a jury in the custody of deputy sheriffs who were also witnesses for the prosecution, an unacceptable risk is presented of impermissible factors coming into play. Turner v. Louisiana, 379 U.S. 466, 473 (1965).

* * *

. . . Compelling an accused to wear jail clothing furthers no essential state policy. That it may be more convenient for jail administrators, a factor quite unlike the substantial need to impose physical restraints upon contumacious defendants, provides no justification for the practice. Indeed, the State of Texas asserts no interest whatever in maintaining this procedure.

Similarly troubling is the fact that compelling the accused to stand trial in jail garb operates usually against only those who cannot post bail prior to trial. Persons who can secure release are not subjected to this condition. To impose the condition on one category of defendants, over objection, would be repugnant to the concept of equal justice embodied in the Fourteenth Amendment. Griffin v. Illinois, 351 U.S. 12 (1956).

II

The Fifth Circuit, in this as well as in prior decisions, has not purported to adopt a per se rule invalidating all convictions where a defendant had appeared in identifia-

ble prison clothes. That court has held, for instance, that the harmless-error doctrine is applicable to this line of cases. . . .

* * *

. . . In the present case, the Court of Appeals concluded:

"A different result may be appropriate where the defendant is on trial for an offense allegedly committed while he was in prison, because the jury would learn of his incarceration in any event." 500 F.2d, at 209 n.5. . . .

Consequently, the courts have refused to embrace a mechanical rule vitiating any conviction, regardless of the circumstances, where the accused appeared before the jury in prison garb. Instead, they have recognized that the particular evil proscribed is compelling a defendant, against his will, to be tried in jail attire. The reason for this judicial focus upon compulsion is simple; instances frequently arise where a defendant prefers to stand trial before his peers in prison garments. The cases show, for example, that it is not an uncommon defense tactic to produce the defendant in jail clothes in the hope of eliciting sympathy from the jury. . . . This is apparently an accepted practice in Texas courts . . . including the court where the respondent was tried.

Courts have therefore required an accused to object to being tried in jail garments, just as he must invoke or abandon other rights. The Fifth Circuit has held: "A defendant may not remain silent and willingly go to trial in prison garb and thereafter claim error." Hernandez v. Beto, 443 F.2d, at 637. . . . Similarly, the Ninth Circuit has indicated that the courts must determine whether an accused "was in fact compelled to wear prison clothing at his state court trial." Bently v. Crist, 469 F.2d, at 856. . . .

III

The record is clear that no objection was made to the trial judge concerning the jail attire either before or at any time during the trial. This omission plainly did not result from any lack of appreciation of the issue, for respondent had raised the question with the jail attendant prior to trial. At trial, defense counsel expressly referred to the respondent's attire during voir dire. The trial judge was thus informed that respondent's counsel was fully conscious of the situation.[e]

Despite respondent's failure to raise the issue at trial, the Court of Appeals held: "Waiver of objection cannot be inferred merely from failure to object if trial in prison garb is customary in the jurisdiction." 500 F.2d, at 208. The District Court had concluded that at the time of respondent's trial the majority of nonbailed defendants in Harris County were indeed tried in jail clothes. From this, the Court of Appeals concluded that the practice followed in respondent's case was customary. 500 F.2d, at 208.

However, that analysis ignores essential facts adduced at the evidentiary hearing. Notwithstanding the evidence as to the general practice in Harris County, there was no finding that nonbailed defendants were compelled to stand trial in prison garments if timely objection was made to the trial judge. On the contrary, the District Court concluded that the practice of the particular judge presiding in respondent's case was to permit any accused who so desired to change into civilian clothes: "There is no doubt but that the [judge] had a practice of allowing defendants to stand trial in civilian clothing, if requested, a practice evidently followed by certain of the other judges as well." 364 F. Supp., at 343. The state judge's policy was confirmed at the evidentiary hearing by the prosecutor and by a defense attorney who practiced in the judge's court.

Significantly, at the evidentiary hearing respondent's trial counsel did not intimate that he feared any adverse consequences attending an objection to the procedure. There is nothing to suggest that there would have been any prejudicial effect on defense counsel had he made objection, given the decision on this point in that jurisdiction.

... Prior Texas cases had made it clear that an objection should be interposed. ...

Nothing in this record, therefore, warrants a conclusion that respondent was compelled to stand trial in jail garb or that there was sufficient reason to excuse the failure to raise the issue before trial. Nor can the trial judge be faulted for not asking the respondent or his counsel whether he was deliberately going to trial in jail clothes. ... Under our adversary system, once a defendant has the assistance of counsel the vast array of trial decisions, strategic and tactical, which must be made before and during trial rests with the accused and his attorney. Any other approach would rewrite the duties of trial judges and counsel in our legal system.

Accordingly, although the State cannot, consistent with the Fourteenth Amendment, compel an accused to stand trial before a jury while dressed in identifiable prison clothes, the failure to make an objection to the court as to being tried in such clothes, for whatever reason, is sufficient to negate the presence of compulsion necessary to establish a constitutional violation.[j]

Reversed.

Mr. Justice POWELL, with whom Mr. Justice STEWART joins, concurring.

* * *

As relevant to this case, there are two situations in which a conviction should be left standing despite the claimed infringement of a constitutional right. The first situation arises when it can be shown that the substantive right in question was consensually relinquished. The other situation arises when a defendant has made an "inexcusable procedural default" in failing to object at a time when a substantive right could have been protected. ...

Williams was represented by retained, experienced counsel. It is conceded that his counsel was fully aware of the "prison garb" issue and elected to raise no objection sim-

---

[e]The evidence showed that respondent was a Caucasian in his 60s. At the evidentiary hearing, he testified that he felt he had no real case to present at trial. The testimony of several eyewitnesses was clear and consistent. Under these circumstances, a desire to elicit jury sympathy would have been a reasonable approach and one which the trial judge might reasonably have assumed was deliberately undertaken.

[j]The State has contended in its brief and in oral argument that the Court of Appeals' decision in Hernandez should not be applied retroactively. The petition for certiorari did not raise this issue and our disposition of the case renders it unnecessary to decide it.

ply because he thought objection would be futile. The record also shows that the state judge who presided at Williams' trial "had a practice of allowing defendants to stand trial in civilian clothing, if requested. . . ." 346 F. Supp., at 343. It thus is apparent that had an objection been interposed by Williams to trial in prison garb, the issue here presented would not have arisen.

* * *

It is my view that a tactical choice or procedural default of the nature of that involved here ordinarily should operate, as a matter of federal law, to preclude the later raising of the substantive right. We generally disfavor inferred waivers of constitutional rights. . . . That policy, however, need not be carried to the length of allowing counsel for a defendant deliberately to forego objection to a curable trial defect, even though he is aware of the factual and legal basis for an objection, simply because he thought objection would be futile.

Mr. Justice BRENNAN, with whom Mr. Justice MARSHALL concurs, dissenting.

I dissent. The Court's statement that "The defendant's clothing is so likely to be a continuing influence throughout the trial that . . . an unacceptable risk is presented of impermissible factors" affecting the jurors' judgment, thus presenting the possibility of an unjustified verdict of guilt . . . concedes that respondent's trial in identifiable prison garb[a] constituted a denial of due process of law. The judgment setting aside respondent's conviction is nevertheless reversed on the ground that respondent was not compelled by the State to wear the prison garb. The Court does not—for on this record plainly the Court could not—rest the reversal on a finding that respondent knowingly, voluntarily, and intelligently consented to be tried in such attire, and thus had waived his

due process right. Johnson v. Zerbst, 304 U.S. 458 (1938). Rather, for the first time, the Court confines due process protections by defining a right that materially affects the fairness and accuracy of the fact-finding process in terms of state compulsion, a concept which, although relevant in the context of the Fifth Amendment's privilege against self-incrimination, is simply inapposite to constitutional analysis concerning due process in criminal proceedings. The end result of this definitional approach is to impute the effect of waiver to the failure of respondent or his counsel to apprise the trial judge of respondent's objection to being tried in prison garb. This not only results in an illogical delineation of the particular right involved in this case, but also introduces into this Court's jurisprudence a novel and dangerously unfair test of surrender of basic constitutional rights to which I cannot agree.

* * *

In light of the effect of trial in prison garb in denying the accused the benefit of the presumption of innocence and undercutting the reasonable-doubt standard, it escapes me how the Court can delineate the right established in this case as the right not to be *compelled* to wear prison garb. If, as the Court holds, the clothes of the accused who has unsuccessfully objected to wearing prison garb (and thus is "compelled" to wear them) unconstitutionally disadvantage his case, obviously the prison clothes of the nonobjecting accused are similarly unconstitutionally disadvantageous. From the *jury's* perspective, the situations of the objecting and the nonobjecting defendants are in every respect identical; if the clothes of the accused who has objected to the court will create improper negative inferences in the minds of the jurors, so too must the clothes of the nonobjecting accused. Nothing in logic or experience suggests that jurors, who need have no knowledge that an objection was lodged with the court, will react any differently in the two situations. It baffles me how the Court, having conceded that trial in identifiable prison garb denigrates the accused's presumption of innocence, can then make the constitutional determination turn on whether or not the accused informed the trial court that he objected; since an objec-

---

[a]Respondent appeared at trial wearing a white T-shirt with "Harris County Jail" stenciled across the back, oversized white dungarees that had "Harris County Jail" stenciled down the legs, and shower thongs. Both of the principal witnesses for the State at respondent's trial referred to him as the person sitting in the "uniform." Record on Appeal in Tex. Ct. of Crim. Appl., at 108, 112.

tion is irrelevant to the purpose underlying the prohibition of trial in prison garb, the Court's delineation of the due process right in this case — confining the due process safeguard to situations of state "compulsion" — is irrational on its face.

To be sure, an accused may knowingly, voluntarily, and intelligently consent to be tried in prison garb. Johnson v. Zerbst, 304 U.S. 458 (1938). But the Court, without any reason for departing from this standard, has simply subverted it by promulgating the novel and dangerous doctrine that a basic due process safeguard, affecting the fairness and accuracy of the factfinding procedure, is a contingent right that does not even come into existence until it is affirmatively as-

serted. Is the Court today thus signaling the demise of the Johnson v. Zerbst voluntary waiver test as the standard for determination of the surrender of constitutional protections? For certainly if failure to object to trial in prison garb, even where the accused has not been shown to know that he might object, surrenders so basic a constitutional right as that securing fairness and accuracy of the factfinding process, the Court has totally eviscerated the traditional doctrine that loss of such rights cannot be presumed from inaction.

* * *

[Mr. Justice STEVENS took no part in the consideration or decision of this case.]

Pretrial Publicity and Impartial Juries

MURPHY v. FLORIDA

Supreme Court of the United States, 1975
421 U.S. 794, 95 S. Ct. 2031, 44 L. Ed. 2d 589
The facts are stated in the opinion.

Mr. Justice MARSHALL delivered the opinion of the Court.

The question presented by this case is whether the petitioner was denied a fair trial because members of the jury had learned from news accounts about a prior felony conviction or certain facts about the crime with which he was charged. . . .

I

Petitioner was convicted in the Dade County, Florida, Criminal Court in 1970 of breaking and entering a home, while armed, with intent to commit robbery, and of assault with intent to commit robbery. The charge stemmed from the January 1968 robbery of a Miami Beach home and petitioner's apprehension with three others, while fleeing from the scene.

The robbery and petitioner's arrest received extensive press coverage because petitioner had been much in the news before. He had first made himself notorious for his

part in the 1964 theft of the Star of India sapphire from a museum in New York. His flamboyant life style made him a continuing subject of press interest; he was generally referred to — at least in the media — as "Murph the Surf."

Before the date set for petitioner's trial on the instant charges, he was indicted on two counts of murder in Broward County, Florida. Thereafter the Dade County court declared petitioner mentally incompetent to stand trial; he was committed to a hospital and the prosecutor nolle prossed the robbery indictment. In August 1968 he was indicted by a federal grand jury for conspiring to transport stolen securities in interstate commerce. After petitioner was adjudged competent for trial, he was convicted on one count of murder in Broward County (March 1969) and pleaded guilty to one count of the federal indictment involving stolen securities (December 1969). The indictment for robbery was refiled in August 1969 and came to trial one year later.

The events of 1968 and 1969 drew extensive press coverage. Each new case against petitioner was considered newsworthy, not only in Dade County but elsewhere as well. The record in this case contains scores of articles reporting on petitioner's trials and tribulations during this period; many purportedly relate statements that petitioner or his attorney made to reporters.

Jury selection in the present case began in August 1970. Seventy-eight jurors were questioned. Of these, 30 were excused for miscellaneous personal reasons; 20 were excused peremptorily by the defense or prosecution; 20 were excused by the court as having prejudged petitioner; and the remaining eight served as the jury and two alternates. Petitioner's motions to dismiss the chosen jurors, on the ground that they were aware that he had previously been convicted of either the 1964 Star of India theft or the Broward County murder, were denied, as was his renewed motion for a change of venue based on allegedly prejudicial pretrial publicity.

At trial, petitioner did not testify or put on any evidence; assertedly in protest of the selected jury, he did not cross-examine any of the State's witnesses. He was convicted on both counts, and after an unsuccessful appeal he sought habeas corpus relief in the District Court for the Southern District of Florida.

The District Court denied petitioner relief ... and the Court of Appeals for the Fifth Circuit affirmed.... We granted certiorari ... in order to resolve the apparent conflict between the decision below and that of the Third Circuit in United States ex rel. Doggett v. Yeager, 472 F.2d 229 (1973), over the applicability of Marshall v. United States, 360 U.S. 310 (1959), to state criminal proceedings.

II

The defendant in Marshall was convicted of dispensing certain drugs without a prescription. In the course of the trial seven of the jurors were exposed to various news accounts relating that Marshall had previously been convicted of forgery, that he and his wife had been arrested for other narcotics offenses, and that he had for some time practiced medicine without a license. After interviewing the jurors, however, the trial judge denied a motion for a mistrial, relying on the juror's assurances that they could maintain impartiality in spite of the news articles.

Noting that the jurors had been exposed to information with a high potential for prejudice, this Court reversed the conviction. It did so, however, expressly "in the exercise of its supervisory power to formulate and apply proper standards for enforcement of the criminal law in the federal courts," and not as a matter of constitutional compulsion. . . .

In the face of so clear a statement, it cannot be maintained that Marshall was a constitutional ruling now applicable, through the Fourteenth Amendment, to the States. Petitioner argues, nonetheless, that more recent decisions of this Court have applied to state cases the principle underlying the Marshall decision: that persons who have learned from news sources of a defendant's prior criminal record are presumed to be prejudiced. We cannot agree that Marshall has any application beyond the federal courts.

Petitioner relies principally upon Irvin v. Dowd, 366 U.S. 717 (1961), Rideau v. Louisiana, 373 U.S. 723 (1963), Estes v. Texas, 381 U.S. 532 (1965), and Sheppard v. Maxwell, 384 U.S. 333 (1966). In each of these cases, this Court overturned a state court conviction obtained in a trial atmosphere that had been utterly corrupted by press coverage.

In Irvin v. Dowd the rural community in which the trial was held had been subjected to a barrage of inflammatory publicity immediately prior to trial, including information on the defendant's prior convictions, his confession to 24 burglaries and six murders including the one for which he was tried, and his unaccepted offer to plead guilty in order to avoid the death sentence. As a result, eight of the 12 jurors had formed an opinion that the defendant was guilty before the trial began; some went "so far as to say that it would take evidence to overcome their belief" in his guilt. In these circumstances, the Court readily found actual prejudice against the petitioner to a degree that rendered a fair trial impossible.

Prejudice was presumed in the circumstances under which the trials in Rideau, Estes, and Sheppard were held. In those cases the influence of the news media, either in the community at large or in the court-room itself, pervaded the proceedings. In Rideau the defendant had "confessed" under police interrogation to the murder of which he stood convicted. A 20-minute film of his confession was broadcast three times by a television station in the community where the crime and the trial took place. In reversing, the Court did not examine the voir dire for evidence of actual prejudice because it considered the trial under review "but a hollow formality"—the real trial had occurred when tens of thousands of people, in a community of 150,000, had seen and heard the defendant admit his guilt to the cameras.

The trial in Estes had been conducted in a circus atmosphere, due in large part to the intrusions of the press, which was allowed to sit within the bar of the court and to over-run it with television equipment. Similarly, Sheppard arose from a trial infected not only by a background of extremely inflam-matory publicity but also by a courthouse given over to accommodate the public appe-tite for carnival. The proceedings in these cases were entirely lacking in the solemnity and sobriety to which a defendant is entitled in a system that subscribes to any notion of fairness and rejects the verdict of a mob. They cannot be made to stand for the prop-osition that the juror exposure to informa-tion about a state defendant's prior convic-tions or to news accounts of the crime with which he is charged alone presumptively deprives the defendant of due process. To resolve this case, we must turn, therefore, to any indications in the totality of circum-stances that petitioner's trial was not fun-damentally fair.

III

The constitutional standard of fairness requires that a defendant have "a panel of impartial 'indifferent' jurors." ... Qualified jurors need not, however, be totally ignorant of the facts and issues involved.

"To hold that the mere existence of any preconceived notion as to the guilt or in-nocence of an accused, without more, is suf-ficient to rebut the presumption of a pro-spective juror's impartiality would be to establish an impossible standard. It is suf-ficient if the juror can lay aside his impres-sion or opinion and render a verdict based on the evidence presented in court." ...

At the same time, the juror's assurances that he is equal to this task cannot be dispo-sitive of the accused's rights, and it remains open to the defendant to demonstrate "the actual existence of such an opinion in the mind of the juror as will raise the presump-tion of partiality."

The voir dire in this case indicates no such hostility to petitioner by the jurors who served in his trial as to suggest a partiality that could not be laid aside. Some of the jurors had a vague recollection of the rob-bery with which petitioner was charged and each had some knowledge of petitioner's past crimes, but none betrayed any belief in the relevance of petitioner's past to the present case. Indeed, four of the six jurors volunteered their views of its irrelevance, and one suggested that people who have been in trouble before are too often singled out for suspicion of each new crime—a predisposition that could only operate in pe-titioner's favor.

In the entire voir dire transcript furnished to us, there is only one colloquy on which petitioner can base even a colorable claim of partiality by a juror. In response to a leading and hypothetical question, presupposing a two- or three-week presentation of evidence against petitioner and his failure to put on any defense, one juror conceded that his prior impression of petitioner would dispose him to convict. We cannot attach great sig-nificance to this statement, however, in light of the leading nature of counsel's questions and the juror's other testimony indicating that he had no deep impression of petitioner at all.

The juror testified that he did not keep up with current events and, in fact, had never heard of petitioner until he arrived in the room for prospective jurors where some veniremen were discussing him. He did not know that petitioner was "a convicted jewel thief" even then; it was petitioner's counsel who informed him of this fact. And he volunteered that petitioner's murder convic-tion, of which he had just heard, would not be relevant to his guilt or innocence in the present case, since "we are not trying him for murder."

Even these indicia of impartiality might be disregarded in a case where the general atmosphere in the community or courtroom is sufficiently inflammatory, but the circum-stances surrounding petitioner's trial are not at all of that variety. Petitioner attempts to portray them as inflammatory by reference to the publicity to which the community was exposed. The District Court found, however, that the news articles concerning petitioner had appeared almost entirely during the period between December 1967 and January 1969, the latter date being seven months before the jury in this case was selected.... They were, moreover, largely factual in nature....

The length to which the trial court must go in order to select jurors who appear to be impartial is another factor relevant in evaluating those jurors' assurances of impartiality. In a community where most veniremen will admit to a disqualifying prejudice, the reliability of the others' protestations may be drawn into question; for it is then more probable that they are part of a community deeply hostile to the accused, and more likely that they may unwittingly have been influenced by it. In Irvin v. Dowd, for example, the Court noted that 90% of those examined on the point were inclined to belief in the accused's guilt, and the court had excused for this cause 268 of the 430 veniremen. In the present case, by contrast, 20 of the 78 persons questioned were excused because they indicated an opinion as to petitioner's guilt. This may indeed be 20 more than would occur in the trial of a totally obscure person, but it by no means suggests a community with sentiment so poisoned against petitioner as to impeach the indifference of jurors who displayed no hostile animus of their own.

In sum, we are unable to conclude, in the circumstances presented in this case, that petitioner did not receive a fair trial. Petitioner has failed to show that the setting of the trial was inherently prejudicial or that the jury selection process of which he complains permits an inference of actual prejudice. The judgment of the Court of Appeals must therefore be

Affirmed.

Mr. Chief Justice BURGER, concurring in the judgment.

I agree with Mr. Justice BRENNAN that the trial judge ·was woefully remiss in failing to insulate prospective jurors from the bizarre media coverage of this case and in not taking steps to prevent pretrial discussion of the case among them. Although I would not hesitate to reverse petitioner's conviction in the exercise of our supervisory powers, were this a federal case, I agree with the Court that the circumstances of petitioner's trial did not rise to the level of a violation of the Due Process Clause of the Fourteenth Amendment.

Mr. Justice BRENNAN, dissenting.

I dissent.... Petitioner here was denied a fair trial. The risk that taint of widespread publicity regarding his criminal background, known to all members of the jury, infected the jury's deliberations is apparent, the trial court made no attempt to prevent discussion of the case or petitioner's previous criminal exploits among the prospective jurors, and one juror freely admitted that he was predisposed to convict petitioner.

* * *

Others who ultimately served as jurors revealed similar prejudice toward petitioner on voir dire. One juror conceded that it would be difficult, during deliberations, to put out of his mind that petitioner was a convicted criminal. He also admitted that he did not "hold a convicted felon in the same regard as another person who has never been convicted of a felony," and admitted further that he had termed petitioner a "menace."

A third juror testified that she knew from several sources that petitioner was a convicted murderer, and was aware that the community regarded petitioner as a criminal who "should be put away." She disclaimed having a fixed opinion about the result she would reach, but acknowledged that the fact that petitioner was a convicted criminal would probably influence her verdict....

Still another juror testified that the comments of venire members in discussing the case had made him "sick to his stomach." He testified that one venireman had said that petitioner was "thoroughly rotten," and that another had said, "Hang him, he's guilty."

... The Court ignores the crucial significance of the fact that at no time before or during this daily buildup of prejudice against Murphy did the trial judge instruct the prospective jurors not to discuss the case among themselves. Indeed the trial judge took no steps to insulate the jurors from media coverage of the case or from the many news articles that discussed petitioner's last criminal exploits.

It is of no moment that several jurors ultimately testified that they would try to exclude from their deliberations their knowledge of petitioner's past misdeeds and of his community reputation. Irvin held in like circumstances that little weight could be attached to such self-serving protestations.

* * *

On the record of this voir dire, therefore, the conclusion is to me inescapable that the attitude of the entire venire toward Murphy reflected the "then current community pattern of thought as indicated by the popular news media" . . . and was infected with the taint of the view that he was a "criminal" guilty of notorious offenses, including that for which he was on trial. It is a plain case, from a review of the entire voir dire, where "the extent and nature of the publicity had caused such a buildup of prejudice that excluding the preconception of guilt from the deliberations would be too difficult for the jury to be honestly found impartial." . . . In my view, the denial of a change of venue was therefore prejudicial error, and I would reverse the conviction.

Pretrial Publicity and "Gag" Orders

ORAL ARGUMENTS BEFORE THE U.S. SUPREME COURT*

Nebraska Press Association v. Stuart, No. 75-817; argued 4/19/76

For the first time since Sheppard v. Maxwell, 384 U.S. 333, was decided 10 years ago, the U.S. Supreme Court last week was asked to resolve a direct confrontation between a criminal defendant's Sixth Amendment right to a fair trial and the First Amendment's guarantee of a free press. At issue was a series of "gag" orders limiting press reporting of a widely publicized Nebraska murder trial. . . .

E. Barrett Prettyman, Jr., representing Nebraska press organizations and several individual reporters, explained that the primary issue is the constitutionality of a direct prior restraint on the right of the press to report information concerning a criminal trial and proceedings in open court.

Mr. Justice Stewart: "How much publicity was there in the town where the murders took place?"

Prettyman replied that there is no newspaper in Sutherland but there are a number of papers and a television station in nearby towns, particularly North Platte.

He noted that the initial order in this case was based on the trial judge's belief that there was a reasonable likelihood that prejudicial publicity would make it impossible to impanel an impartial jury. It forbade the news media to disseminate any information other than as set forth in the state's bar-press guidelines.

The Chief Justice inquired whether the pretrial hearings could have been closed to the public at the defendant's request. Prettyman didn't think they could under Nebraska law.

The Chief Justice: "What alternatives were there?"

Prettyman: "The court could have used some of the approaches recommended in Sheppard v. Maxwell."

Mr. Justice Stevens: "Wouldn't it be a prior restraint to impose an order on the prosecutor, defense counsel, and others under the jurisdiction of the court?"

"Absolutely not," Prettyman replied. "You might have a free speech problem then, but you would not have a prior restraint on the press."

"How important is the label?"

Counsel thought it highly important because by its nature an order of this type imposes a direct prior restraint on the right of the press to publish and by indirection the right of the people to be informed.

*From 44 U.S. Law Week 3601 (1976). Reprinted by permission of The Bureau of National Affairs, Inc.

There is no question, Prettyman said, that the court is free to place some restrictions on the prosecutor and defense counsel.

He emphasized that there are four orders involved in this case, the final one, that issued by the Nebraska Supreme Court, being that one immediately at issue. That order prohibited the publication of information strongly implicating the accused, including confessions or other statements made to anyone except representatives of the news media.

All four orders, he noted, effectively prohibited the press from reporting information that appeared in public records or that was obtained during public court proceedings. This is "blatantly unconstitutional," he argued.

Mr. Justice Blackmun: "Has the criminal conviction been appealed?"

"Yes, sir, I believe it has."

"And it could be reversed on appeal?"

"That's true, Mr. Justice Blackmun, but if it's retried, the same type of order could be issued again."

It should be pointed out, Prettyman added, that this was a small town and the community was fully aware of most of the details concerning the crime anyway.

Mr. Justice White: "Is this a live case?"

Repetition

Counsel had no doubt that it was. In the few months since this case arose, he said, many similar orders have been issued and there is nothing to indicate that there will not be a continuous wave of them unless this Court puts a stop to it. It is, Prettyman argued, a case that is capable of repetition yet evading review.

Mr. Justice Rehnquist posed a hypothetical: Suppose every minister, priest, and rabbi in the area got together and decided that Simants [the defendant] was the devil incarnate and decided to reveal that from their pulpits. "Is there any question that the court could not enjoin that?"

Prettyman thought not.

"What if the county bar association did the same thing?"

"They could possibly have been held in contempt but not subjected to a prior restraint."

Prettyman also challenged the assumption underlying these orders that a prospective juror who heard even a confession would not be impartial or, if partial, would not be weeded out. That assumption, he said, just isn't valid. There are numerous cases indicating that a juror who has been exposed to pretrial publicity can still be impartial. The cases of William Calley, Gordon Liddy, John Mitchell, and others indicate that an impartial jury can be impanelled even where publicity is pervasive.

A proper voir dire can weed out those jurors who shouldn't sit and proper instructions can protect against those vestiges of publicity that might remain, counsel argued. Also available are changes of venue and continuances.

The Chief Justice: "Would a protective order preventing the reporters from seeking out stories be constitutional?"

Prettyman did not think so.

"What devices would be constitutional?"

"Continuances, changes of venue, sequestration, foreign juries, to name a few."

Even if every man and woman in the country had seen Jack Ruby shoot Lee Harvey Oswald on television, Prettyman said, it would still have been possible to select an impartial jury.

Although the Sheppard case discussed a number of ways to protect a defendant against pretrial publicity, he noted, it made clear that it was not talking about prior restraints.

"To subject the press to prior restraints is to take away one of our greatest liberties," he concluded, "and would put the courts in the position of deciding what is news and what the public is entitled to hear, see, and read."

Amicus

Floyd Abrams, New York City, appearing as amicus curiae on behalf of the Reporters Committee for Freedom of the Press, noted that the Court has consistently taken the position that the judiciary should not and cannot tell the press what it should not print except in the extremely rare national security case. This position was reflected, Abrams said, in the Pentagon Papers case.

In the past, the courts have indicated that, whatever else they could do to protect against pretrial publicity, they could not impose prior restraints. However, that has changed and prior restraints are becoming commonplace. "What is new?" "What has changed?" he asked. It is not that the press has become irresponsible. It is not that guilty people are walking the streets or innocent people are in jail because of an irresponsible press. Nor is it because juries are less responsible or that studies have shown that some kind of a change is needed. In fact, he said, five studies have shown that prior restraints are constitutionally impermissible, unwise, or both.

What is new, Abrams said, is an apparent growing sense of judicial concern with allegedly irresponsible reporting. However, "the evil of abuse by the press is an evil for which there may be no acceptable cure."

Abrams attributed the number of prior restraint orders to this judicial concern and to a misreading of Sheppard v. Maxwell. These courts are also misreading the heavy burden of justifying prior restraints, he said.

Mr. Justice Stevens: "What do you do about an inadmissible confession that's published?"

"I think we will have to live with that danger but try to deal with it by good jury instructions and the like."

The press fully realizes, counsel said, the difficulty inherent in trying to draw lines in this area. But it also realizes that the power to place prior restraints on the press is the power to destroy a free press. "We urge the Court not to let this practice be born."

Narrow Order

Harold Mosher, Nebraska Assistant Attorney General, argued that the order involved in this case is a very narrow one. He further maintained that any claim that the Nebraska Supreme Court failed to act expeditiously in this case is unfair.

Mr. Justice Blackmun: "Isn't 11 days kind of a long time?"

"Not really, sir."

"Why didn't the court hear it promptly?"

"Because of their case load."

Mr. Justice Stevens: "Would you say this case is exceptional or routine?"

"Exceptional."

"Why couldn't they treat it as exceptional?"

Mosher replied that the court had already scheduled more than 50 cases for argument during the time this case came up. This involved more than 100 lawyers from all over the state. It's impossible to stop everything at that point, he said.

Mr. Justice Marshall wondered if the court couldn't have rescheduled one or two cases.

Mr. Justice Stevens: "Aren't you demonstrating that one defect of the system with respect to prior restraints is that these orders will remain in effect until the system has a chance to work?"

"That's something we have to live with."

The courts need the power to impose such orders, Mosher continued. The fair administration of justice requires a device to protect the integrity of its processes and the media has the power to destroy the right to a fair trial. "No government can endure if it allows one or more individuals or groups to prevent the discharge of governmental obligations."

The press is not above the law, he said. No one is. And freedom of the press is not absolute. Absolute discretion is granted to no one.

Asked under what circumstances such an order could be issued, Mosher replied that where the balance between the right to a fair trial and the right to a free press is upset by reporting, the courts should have the authority to step in and restore equilibrium. The dissemination of damaging information which comes out at a preliminary hearing but which might not be admissible at trial can be devastating to the right to a fair trial, he said. The order in this case was a sincere attempt to balance the rights involved.

Mr. Justice Marshall: "What is the difference between everyone talking about what went on at a preliminary hearing and the press reporting it?"

The difference is one of degree, Mosher replied. While rumor and innuendo might or might not have much weight, the fact that something is reported in the media gives it more weight.

Mr. Justice Stevens: "You say the order here was narrow because of the time element, is that right?"

"Yes, sir. And also because of its content."

"Do you think an order like this would have been appropriate in the Watergate break-in case?"

Watergate, counsel replied, involved extensive government action before the government set the criminal process in motion. It might be a different situation.

"Do you think the Watergate scandal would ever have surfaced if such an order had been issued?"

Counsel thought it might have surfaced eventually, but not right away.

Prosecutor

Milton R. Larson, who prosecuted the Simants case, argued that orders of the type involved here would only arise in the very exceptional case where there is extensive publicity. He explained that an order was requested in this case because as prosecutor he felt it was his duty to take those steps necessary to ensure a fair trial.

At any rate, he said, none of the Court's prior cases have indicated that prior restraints are now constitutionally permissible. And he saw no reason why they should not be available in cases where there is a reasonable likelihood of prejudicial publicity.

He conceded that, prior restraints notwithstanding, it is not possible to stop rumors and innuendo. But, by the same token, rumor and innuendo are not as persuasive as a media report with the sanction of a judicial proceeding.

The record in this case, Larson argued, justifies the narrow and limited restriction on publicity imposed for the purpose of protecting the defendant's right to a fair trial.

Rebuttal

Whatever their constitutional status, prior restraints just don't work, Prettyman said on rebuttal. Rumor and speculation can be and usually are far more damaging to a fair trial than are newspaper or television reports.

The Chief Justice: "Do you think Rideau [v. Louisiana, 373 U.S. 723] is erroneous?"

"No sir, I don't. When you reversed in that case, you didn't order a prior restraint, you simply ordered a fair trial."

No matter how narrow an order this Court approves, Prettyman warned, the result will be a flood of litigation involving more numerous and broader orders.

The Chief Justice: "Why is it essential that information be published immediately instead of later?"

There are three reasons, Prettyman replied. First, the courts could become embroiled in determining how long is too long. Second, the public has a right to be informed contemporaneously with the events being reported. Third, momentum is important to the news. Watergate, he concluded, is a good example of this.

NEBRASKA PRESS ASSOCIATION v. STUART

Supreme Court of the United States, 1976
427 U.S. 539, 96 S. Ct. 2791, 49 L. Ed. 2d 683

The facts are stated in the opinion.

Chief Justice BURGER delivered the opinion of the Court.

The respondent State District Judge entered an order restraining the petitioners from publishing or broadcasting accounts of confessions or admissions made by the accused or facts "strongly implicative" of the accused in a widely reported murder of six persons. We granted certiorari to decide whether the entry of such an order on the showing made before the state court violated the constitutional guarantee of freedom of the press.

I

On the evening of October 18, 1975, local police found the six members of the Henry Kellie family murdered in their home in Sutherland, Neb., a town of about 850 people. Police released the description of a suspect, Erwin Charles Simants, to the reporters who had hastened to the scene of the crime. Simants was arrested and arraigned in Lincoln County Court the following morning, ending a tense night for this small rural community.

The crime immediately attracted widespread news coverage, by local, regional, and national newspapers, radio and television stations. Three days after the crime, the County Attorney and Simants' attorney joined in asking the County Court to enter a restrictive order relating to "matters that may or may not be publicly reported or disclosed to the public," because of the "mass coverage by news media" and the "reasonable likelihood of prejudicial news which would make difficult, if not impossible, the impaneling of an impartial jury and tend to prevent a fair trial."... The County Court granted the prosecutor's motion for a restrictive order and entered it the next day, October 22. The order prohibited everyone in attendance from "releasing or authorizing for public dissemination in any form or manner whatsoever any testimony given or evidence adduced"; the order also required members of the press to observe the Nebraska Bar-Press Guidelines.[a]

Simants' preliminary hearing was held the same day, open to the public but subject to the order. The County Court bound over the defendant for trial to the State District Court. The charges, as amended to reflect the autopsy findings, were that Simants had committed the murders in the course of a sexual assault.

Petitioners — several press and broadcast associations, publishers, and individual reporters — moved on October 23 for leave to intervene in the District Court, asking that the restrictive order imposed by the County Court be vacated.... The District Judge granted petitioners' motion to intervene and, on October 27, entered his own restrictive order. The judge found "because of the nature of the crimes charged in the complaint that there is a clear and present danger that pre-trial publicity could impinge upon the defendant's right to a fair trial." The order

applied only until the jury was impaneled, and specifically prohibited petitioners from reporting five subjects: (1) the existence or contents of a confession Simants had made to law enforcement officers, which had been introduced in open court at arraignment; (2) the fact or nature of statements Simants had made to other persons; (3) the contents of a note he had written the night of the crime; (4) certain aspects of the medical testimony at the preliminary hearing; (5) the identity of the victims of the alleged sexual assault and the nature of the assault. It also prohibited reporting the exact nature of the restrictive order itself. . . .

Four days later, on October 31, petitioners asked the District Court to stay its order. At the same time, they applied to the Nebraska Supreme Court for a writ of mandamus, a stay, and an expedited appeal from the order. The State of Nebraska and the defendant Simants intervened in these actions. . . .

* * *

The Nebraska Supreme Court . . . modified the District Court's order to accommodate the defendant's right to a fair trial and the petitioners' interest in reporting pretrial events. The order as modified prohibited reporting of only three matters: (a) the existence and nature of any confessions or admissions made by the defendant to law enforcement officers, (b) any confessions or admissions made to any third parties, except members of the press, and (c) other facts "strongly implicative" of the accused. . . .

We granted certiorari to address the important issues raised by the District Court order as modified by the Nebraska Supreme Court. . . . We are informed by the parties that since we granted certiorari, Simants has been convicted of murder and sentenced to death. His appeal is pending in the Nebraska Supreme Court.

---

[a]The Nebraska Guidelines are voluntary standards adopted by members of the state bar and news media to deal with the reporting of crimes and criminal trials. They outline the matters of fact that may appropriately be reported, and also list what items are not generally appropriate for reporting, including: confessions, opinions on guilt or innocence, statements that would influence the outcome of a trial, the results of tests or examinations, comments on the credibility of witnesses, and evidence presented in the jury's absence. The publication of an accused's criminal record should, under the Guidelines, be "considered very carefully."...

II

The order at issue in this case expired by its own terms when the jury was impaneled on January 7, 1976. There were no restraints on publication once the jury was selected, and there are now no restrictions on what may be spoken or written about the Simants case. Intervenor Simants argues that for this reason the case is moot.

Our jurisdiction under Art. III, § 2, of the Constitution extends only to actual cases and controversies. . . . The Court has recognized, however, that jurisdiction is not necessarily defeated simply because the order attacked is one "capable of repetition, yet evading review." Pacific Terminal Co. v. ICC, 219 U.S. 498, 515 (1911).

The controversy between the parties to this case is "capable of repetition" in two senses. First, if Simants' conviction is reversed by the Nebraska Supreme Court and a new trial ordered, the District Court may enter another restrictive order to prevent a resurgence of prejudicial publicity before Simants' retrial. Second, the State of Nebraska is a party to this case; the Nebraska Supreme Court's decision authorizes state prosecutors to seek restrictive orders in appropriate cases. The dispute between the State and the petitioners who cover events throughout the State is thus "capable of repetition." Yet, if we decline to address the issues in this case on grounds of mootness, the dispute will evade review, or at considered plenary review in this Court, since these orders are by nature short-lived. . . . We therefore conclude that this case is not moot, and proceed to the merits.

III

The problems presented by this case are almost as old as the Republic. Neither in the Constitution nor in contemporaneous writings do we find that the conflict between these two important rights was anticipated, yet it is unconceivable that the authors of the Constitution were unaware of the potential conflicts between the right to an unbiased jury and the guarantee of freedom of the press. The unusually able lawyers who helped write the Constitution and later drafted the Bill of Rights were familiar with the historic episode in which John Adams defended British soldiers charged with homicide for firing into a crowd of Boston demonstrators; they were intimately familiar with the clash of the adversary system and the part that passions of the populace sometimes play in influencing potential jurors. They did not address themselves directly to the situation presented by this case; their chief concern was the need for freedom of expression in the political arena and the dialogue in ideas. But they recognized that there were risks to private rights from an unfettered press. . . .

* * *

The speed of communication and the pervasiveness of the modern news media have exacerbated these problems, however, as numerous appeals demonstrate. The trial of Bruno Hauptmann in a small New Jersey community, for the abduction and murder of Charles Lindbergh's infant child, probably was the most widely covered trial up to that time, and the nature of the coverage produced widespread public reaction. Criticism was directed at the "carnival" atmosphere that pervaded the community and the courtroom itself. Responsible leaders of the press and the legal profession—including other judges—pointed out that much of this sorry performance could have been controlled by a vigilant trial judge and by other public officers subject to the control of the court. . . .

The excesses of press and radio and lack of responsibility of those in authority in the Hauptmann case and others of that era led to efforts to develop voluntary guidelines for courts, lawyers, press and broadcasters.[c] . . .

In practice, of course, even the most ideal guidelines are subjected to powerful strains when a case such as Simants' arises, with reporters from many parts of the country on the scene. Reporters from distant places are unlikely to consider themselves bound by local standards. They report to editors outside the area covered by the guidelines, and their editors are likely to be guided only by their own standards. To contemplate how a state court can control acts of a newspaper or broadcaster outside its jurisdiction, even though the newspapers and broadcasters reach the very community from which the jurors are to be selected, suggests something of the practical difficulties of managing such guidelines.

The problems presented in this case have a substantial history outside the reported decisions of courts, in the efforts of many responsible people to accommodate the competing interests. We cannot resolve all of them, for it is not the function of this Court to write a code. We look instead to this

---

[c]The Warren Commission conducting an inquiry into the murder of President Kennedy implied grave doubts whether, after the dissemination of "a great deal of misinformation" prejudicial to Oswald, a fair trial could be had. Report of the President's Commission on the Assassination of President Kennedy 231 (1964). Probably the same could be said in turn with respect to a trial of Oswald's murderer even though a multitude were eyewitnesses to the guilty acts. . . .

particular case and the legal context in which it arises.

IV

The Sixth Amendment . . . in terms guarantees "trial by an impartial jury . . ." in federal criminal prosecutions. Because "trial by jury in criminal cases is fundamental to the American scheme of justice," the Due Process Clause of the Fourteenth Amendment guarantees the same right in state criminal prosecutions. Duncan v. Louisiana, 391 U.S. 145, 149 (1968). . . .

In the overwhelming majority of criminal trials, pretrial publicity presents few unmanageable threats to this important right. But when the case is a "sensational" one tensions develop between the right of the accused to trial by an impartial jury and the rights guaranteed others by the First Amendment. . . .

* * *

In Sheppard v. Maxwell, 384 U.S. 333 (1966), the Court focused sharply on the impact of pretrial publicity and a trial court's duty to protect the defendant's constitutional right to a fair trial. With only Justice Black dissenting, and he without opinion, the Court ordered a new trial for the petitioner, even though the first trial had occurred 12 years before. Beyond doubt the press had shown no responsible concern for the constitutional guarantee of a fair trial; the community from which the jury was drawn had been inundated by publicity hostile to the defendant. But the trial judge "did not fulfill his duty to protect the defendant from the inherently prejudicial publicity which saturated the community and to control disruptive influences in the courtroom." Id., at 363. The Court noted that "unfair and prejudicial news comment on pending trials has become increasingly prevalent," id., at 362. . . .

Because the trial court had failed to use even minimal efforts to insulate the trial and the jurors from the "deluge of publicity," . . . the Court vacated the judgment of conviction and a new trial followed, in which the accused was acquitted.

Cases such as these are relatively rare, and we have held in other cases that trials have been fair in spite of widespread publicity. . . .

. . . Pretrial publicity—even pervasive, adverse publicity—does not inevitably lead to an unfair trial. The capacity of the jury eventually impanelled to decide the case fairly is influenced by the tone and extent of the publicity, which is in part, and often in large part, shaped by what attorneys, police, and other officials do to precipitate news coverage. The trial judge has a major responsibility. What the judge says about a case, in or out of the courtroom, is likely to appear in newspapers and broadcasts. More important, the measures a judge takes or fails to take to mitigate the effects of pretrial publicity—the measures described in Sheppard—may well determine whether the defendant receives a trial consistent with the requirements of due process. That this responsibility has not always been properly discharged is apparent from the decisions just reviewed.

* * *

The state trial judge in the case before us acted responsibly, out of a legitimate concern, in an effort to protect the defendant's right to a fair trial. What we must decide is not simply whether the Nebraska courts erred in seeing the possibility of real danger to the defendant's rights, but whether in the circumstances of this case the means employed were foreclosed by another provision of the Constitution.

V

The First Amendment provides that "Congress shall make no law . . . abridging the freedom . . . of the press," and it is "no longer open to doubt that the liberty of the press, and of speech, is within the liberty safeguarded by the due process clause of the Fourteenth Amendment from invasion by state action." Near v. Minnesota, 283 U.S. 697, 707 (1931). . . . The Court has interpreted these guarantees to afford special protection of particular information or commentary—orders that impose a "previous" or "prior" restraint on speech. None of our decided cases on prior restraint involved restrictive orders entered to protect a defendant's right to a fair and impartial jury. . . .

* * *

. . . Prior restraints on speech and publication are the most serious and the least tolerable infringement on First Amendment rights. A criminal penalty or a judgment in a defamation case is subject to the whole panoply of protections afforded by deferring the impact of the judgment until all avenues of appellate review have been exhausted. Only after judgment has become final, correct or otherwise, does the law's sanction become fully operative.

A prior restraint, by contrast and by definition, has an immediate and irreversible sanction. If it can be said that a threat of criminal or civil sanctions after publication "chills" speech, prior restraint "freezes" it at least for the time.

The damage can be particularly great when the prior restraint falls upon the communication of news and commentary on current events. Truthful reports of public judicial proceedings have been afforded special protection against subsequent punishment. . . . For the same reasons the protection against prior restraint should have particular force as applied to reporting of criminal proceedings, whether the crime in question is a single isolated act or a pattern of criminal conduct.

* * *

The extraordinary protections afforded by the First Amendment carry with them something in the nature of a fiduciary duty to exercise the protected rights responsibility — a duty widely acknowledged but not always observed by editors and publishers. It is not asking too much to suggest that those who exercise First Amendment rights in newspapers or broadcasting enterprises direct some effort to protect the rights of an accused to a fair trial by unbiased jurors.

Of course, the order at issue . . . does not prohibit but only postpones publication. Some news can be delayed and most commentary can even more readily be delayed without serious injury, and there often is a self-imposed delay when responsible editors call for verification of information. But such delays are normally slight and they are self-imposed. Delays imposed by governmental authority are a different matter.

* * *

. . . As a practical matter, moreover, the element of time is not unimportant if press coverage is to fulfill its traditional function of bringing news to the public promptly.

The authors of the Bill of Rights did not undertake to assign priorities as between First Amendment and Sixth Amendment rights, ranking one as superior to the other. In this case, the petitioners would have us declare the right of an accused subordinate to their right to publish in all circumstances. But if the authors of these guarantees, fully aware of the potential conflicts between them, were unwilling or unable to resolve the issue by assigning to one priority over the other, it is not for us to rewrite the Constitution by undertaking what they declined. It is unnecessary, after nearly two centuries, to establish a priority applicable in all circumstances. Yet it is nonetheless clear that the barriers to prior restraint remain high unless we are to abandon what the Court has said for nearly a quarter of our national existence and implied throughout all of it. . . .

VI

We turn now to the record in this case to determine whether, as Learned Hand put it, "the gravity of the 'evil,' discounted by its improbability, justifies such invasion of free speech as is necessary to avoid the danger." Dennis v. United States, 183 F.2d 201, 212 (1950), aff'd, 341 U.S. 494 (1951). . . . To do so, we must examine the evidence before the trial judge when the order was entered to determine (a) the nature and extent of pretrial news coverage; (b) whether other measures would be likely to mitigate the effects of unrestrained pretrial publicity; (c) how effectively a restraining order would operate to prevent the threatened danger. The precise terms of the restraining order are also important. We must then consider whether the record supports the entry of a prior restraint on publication, one of the most extraordinary remedies known to our jurisprudence.

A

* * *

Our review of the pretrial record persuades us that the trial judge was justified in concluding that there would be intense and pervasive pretrial publicity concerning this case. He could also reasonably conclude, based on common human experience, that publicity might impair the defendant's right to a fair trial. He did not purport to say more, for he found only "a clear and present danger that pretrial publicity *could* impinge upon the defendant's right to a fair trial." (Emphasis added.) His conclusion as to the impact of such publicity on prospective jurors was of necessity speculative, dealing as he was with factors unknown and unknowable.

B

We find little in the record that goes to another aspect of our task, determining whether measures short of an order restraining all publication would have insured the defendant a fair trial. Although the entry of the order might be read as a judicial determination that other measures would not suffice, the trial court made no express findings to that effect; the Nebraska Supreme Court referred to the issue only by implication. . . .

Most of the alternatives to prior restraint of publication in these circumstances were discussed with obvious approval in Sheppard v. Maxwell, 384 U.S., at 357–362: (a) change of trial venue to a place less exposed to the intense publicity that seemed imminent in Lincoln County; (b) postponement of the trial to allow public attention to subside; (c) use of searching questioning of prospective jurors . . . to screen out those with fixed opinions as to guilt or innocence; (d) the use of emphatic and clear instructions on the sworn duty of each juror to decide the issues only on evidence presented in open court. Sequestration of jurors is, of course, always available. Although that measure insulates jurors only after they are sworn, it also enhances the likelihood of dissipating the impact of pretrial publicity and emphasizes the elements of the jurors' oaths.

This Court has outlined other measures short of prior restraints on publication tending to blunt the impact of pretrial publicity. . . . Professional studies have filled out these suggestions, recommending that trial courts in appropriate cases limit what the contending lawyers, the police and witnesses may say to anyone.[h] . . .

We have noted earlier that pretrial publicity, even if pervasive and concentrated,

cannot be regarded as leading automatically and in every kind of criminal case to an unfair trial. The decided cases "cannot be made to stand for the proposition that juror exposure to information about a state defendant's prior convictions or to news accounts of the crime with which he is charged alone presumptively deprives the defendant of due process." Murphy v. Florida, 421 U.S. 794, 799 (1975). . . .

We have therefore examined this record to determine the probable efficacy of the measures short of prior restraint on the press and speech. There is no finding that alternative measures would not have protected Simants' rights, and the Nebraska Supreme Court did no more than imply that such measures might not be adequate. Moreover, the record is lacking in evidence to support such a finding.

C

We must also assess the probable efficacy of prior restraint on publication, as a workable method of protecting Simants' right to a fair trial, and we cannot ignore the reality of the problems of managing and enforcing pretrial restraining orders. The territorial jurisdiction of the issuing court is limited by concepts of sovereignty. . . . The need for in personam jurisdiction also presents an obstacle to a restraining order that applies to publication at-large as distinguished from restraining publication within a given jurisdiction.[i] . . .

The Nebraska Supreme Court narrowed the scope of the restrictive order, and its opinion reflects awareness of the tensions between the need to protect the accused as fully as possible and the need to restrict publication as little as possible. . . . When a restrictive order is sought, a court can anticipate only part of what will develop that may injure the accused. . . .

Finally, we note that the events disclosed by the record took place in a community of 850 people. It is reasonable to assume that,

---

[h]Closing of pretrial proceedings with the consent of the defendant when required is also recommended in guidelines that have emerged from various studies. At oral argument petitioners' counsel asserted that judicially imposed restraints on lawyers and others would be subject to challenge as interfering with press rights to news sources. . . . We are not now confronted with such issues. . . .

[i]Here, for example, the Nebraska Supreme Court decided that the District Court had no jurisdiction of the petitioners except by virtue of their voluntary submission to the jurisdiction of that court when they moved to intervene. Except for the intervention which placed them within reach of the court, the Nebraska Supreme Court conceded, the petitioners "could have ignored the restraining order. . . ." 194 Neb., at 795.

without any news accounts being printed or broadcast, rumors would travel swiftly by word of mouth. One can only speculate on the accuracy of such reports, given the generative propensities of rumors; they could well be more damaging than reasonably accurate news accounts. But plainly a whole community cannot be restrained from discussing a subject intimately affecting life within it.

Given these practical problems, it is far from clear that prior restraint on publication would have protected Simants' rights.

D

* * *

To the extent that this order prohibited the reporting of evidence adduced at the open preliminary hearing, it plainly violated settled principles: "There is nothing that proscribes the press from reporting events that transpire in the courtroom." Sheppard v. Maxwell, supra, at 362–363. . . . The County Court could not know that closure of the preliminary hearing was an alternative open to it until the Nebraska Supreme Court so construed state law; but once a public hearing had been held, what transpired there could not be subject to prior restraint.

* * *

E

The record demonstrates, as the Nebraska courts held, that there was indeed a risk that pretrial news accounts, true or false, would have some adverse impact on the attitudes of those who might be called as jurors. . . . We cannot say on this record that alternatives to a prior restraint on petitioners would not have sufficiently mitigated the adverse effects of pretrial publicity so as to make prior restraint unnecessary. Nor can we conclude that the restraining order actually entered would serve its intended purpose. . . .

Of necessity our holding is confined to the record before us. But our conclusion is not simply a result of assessing the adequacy of the showing made in this case; it results in part from the problems inherent in meeting the heavy burden of demonstrating, in advance of trial, that without prior restraint a fair trial will be denied. The practical problems of managing and enforcing restrictive orders will always be present. . . . However difficult it may be, we need not rule out the possibility of showing the kind of threat to fair trial rights that would possess the requisite degree of certainty to justify restraint. This Court has frequently denied that First Amendment rights are absolute and has consistently rejected the proposition that a prior restraint can never be employed. . . .

Our analysis ends as it began, with a confrontation between prior restraint imposed to protect one vital constitutional guarantee and the explicit command of another that the freedom to speak and publish shall not be abridged. We reaffirm that the guarantees of freedom of expression are not an absolute prohibition under all circumstances, but the barriers to prior restraint remain high and the presumption against its use continues intact. We hold that, with respect to the order entered in this case prohibiting reporting or commentary on judicial proceedings held in public, the barriers have not been overcome; to the extent that this order restrained publication of such material, it is clearly invalid. To the extent that it prohibited publication based on information gained from other sources, we conclude that the heavy burden imposed as a condition to securing a prior restraint was not met and the judgment of the Nebraska Supreme court is therefore

Reversed.

Mr. Justice BRENNAN, with whom Mr. Justice STEWART and Mr. Justice MARSHALL join, concurring in the judgment.

. . . The right to a fair trial by a jury of one's peers is unquestionably one of the most precious and sacred safeguards enshrined in the Bill of Rights. I would hold, however, that resort to prior restraints on the freedom of the press is a constitutionally impermissible method for enforcing that right; judges have at their disposal a broad spectrum of devices for ensuring that fundamental fairness is accorded the accused without necessitating so drastic an incursion on the equally fundamental and salutary constitutional mandate that discussion of public affairs in a free society cannot depend on the preliminary grace of judicial censors.

* * *

. . . Settled case law concerning the impropriety and constitutional invalidity of prior restraints on the press compels the conclusion that there can be no prohibition on the publication by the press of any information pertaining to pending judicial proceedings or the operation of the criminal justice system, no matter how shabby the means by which the information is obtained. This does not imply, however, any subordination of Sixth Amendment rights, for an accused's right to a fair trial may be adequately assured through methods that do not infringe First Amendment values.

* * *

Respondents correctly contend that "the First Amendment protection even as to prior restraint is not absolutely unlimited." ... However, the exceptions to the rule have been confined to "exceptional cases." The Court in Near, the first case in which we were faced with a prior restraint against the press, delimited three such possible exceptional circumstances. The first two exceptions were that "the primary requirements of decency may be enforced against obscene publications," and that the security of the community may be protected against incitements to acts of violence and the overthrow by force of orderly government for the constitutional guaranty of free speech does not 'protect a man from an injunction against uttering words that have all the effect of force....'" Ibid. These exceptions have since come to be interpreted as situations in which the "speech" involved is not encompassed within the meaning of the First Amendment. . . . And even in these situations, adequate and timely procedures are mandated to protect against any restraint of speech that does come within the ambit of the First Amendment. . . . Thus, only the third category in Near contemplated the possibility that speech meriting and entitled to constitutional protection might nevertheless be suppressed before publication in the interest of some overriding countervailing interest:

"'When a nation is at war many things that might be said in time of peace are such a hindrance to its effort that their utterance will not be endured so long as men fight and that no Court could regard them as protected by any constitutional right.' Schenck v. United States, 249 U.S. 47, 52. No one would question but that a government might prevent actual obstruction to its recruiting service or the publication of the sailing dates

of transports or the number and location of troops." 283 U.S., at 716.

Even this third category, however, has only been adverted to in dictum and has never served as the basis for actually upholding a prior restraint against the publication of constitutionally protected materials. In New York Times Co. v. United States, 403 U.S. 713 (1971), we specifically addressed the scope of the "military security" exception alluded to in Near and held that there could be no prior restraint on publication of the "Pentagon Papers" despite the fact that a majority of the Court believed that release of the documents, which were classified "Top Secret-Sensitive" and which were obtained surreptitiously, would be harmful to the Nation and might even be prosecuted after publication as a violation of various espionage statutes. To be sure, our brief per curiam declared that "any system of prior restraints of expression comes to this Court bearing a heavy presumption against its constitutional validity," id., at 714 ... and that the "Government 'thus carries a heavy burden of showing justification for the imposition of such a restraint.'" 403 U.S., at 714. . . . This language refers to the fact that, as a matter of procedural safeguards and burden of proof, prior restraints even within a recognized exception to the rule against prior restraints will be extremely difficult to justify; but as an initial matter, the purpose for which a prior restraint is sought to be imposed "must fit within one of the narrowly defined exceptions to the prohibition against prior restraints." . . . It is thus clear that even within the sole possible exception to the prohibition against prior restraints on publication of constitutionally protected materials, the obstacles to issuance of such an injunction are formidable. . . .

* * *

I unreservedly agree with Mr. Justice Black that "free speech and fair trials are two of the most cherished policies of our civilization, and it would be a trying task to choose between them." Bridges v. California, 314 U.S. 252, 260 (1961). But I would reject the notion that a choice is necessary, that there is an inherent conflict that cannot be resolved without essentially abrogating one right or the other. To hold that courts cannot impose any prior restraints on the reporting of or commentary upon information revealed in open court proceedings, disclosed in public documents, or divulged by other sources with respect to the criminal justice system is not, I must emphasize, to countenance the sacrifice of precious Sixth Amendment rights on the altar of the First Amendment. For although there may in some instances be tension between uninhibited and robust reporting by the press and fair trials for criminal defendants, judges possess adequate tools short of injunctions against reporting for relieving that tension....

... The press may be arrogant, tyrannical, abusive, and sensationalist, just as it may be incisive, probing, and informative. But at least in the context of prior restraints on publication, the decision of what, when, and how to publish is for editors, not judges....

Mr. Justice WHITE, concurring.

* * *

... There is grave doubt in my mind whether orders with respect to the press such as were entered in this case would ever be justifiable. It may be the better part of discretion, however, not to announce such a rule in the first case in which the issue has been squarely presented here. Perhaps we should go no farther than absolutely necessary until the federal courts, and ourselves, have been exposed to a broader spectrum of cases presenting similar issues. If the recurring result, however, in case after case is to be similar to our judgment today, we should at some point announce a more general rule and avoid the interminable litigation that our failure to do so would necessarily entail.

Mr. Justice POWELL, concurring.

* * *

In my judgment a prior restraint properly may issue only when it is shown to be necessary to prevent the dissemination of prejudicial publicity that otherwise poses a high likelihood of preventing, directly or irreparably, the impaneling of a jury meeting the Sixth Amendment requirement of impartiality. This requires a showing that (i) there is a clear threat to the fairness of trial, (ii) such a threat is posed by the actual publicity to be restrained, and (iii) no less restrictive alternatives are available. Notwithstanding such a showing, a restraint may not issue unless it also is shown that previous publicity or publicity from unrestrained sources will not render the restraint inefficacious. The threat to the fairness of the trial is to be evaluated in the context of Sixth Amendment law on impartiality, and any restraint must comply with the standards of specificity always required in the First Amendment context.

Mr. Justice STEVENS, concurring in the judgment.

For the reasons eloquently stated by Mr. Justice BRENNAN, I agree that the judiciary is capable of protecting the defendant's right to a fair trial without enjoining the press from publishing information in the public domain, and that it may not do so. Whether the same absolute protection would apply no matter how shabby or illegal the means by which the information is obtained, no matter how serious an intrusion on privacy might be involved, no matter how demonstrably false the information might be, no matter how prejudicial it might be to the interests of innocent persons, and no matter how perverse the motivation for publishing it, is a question I would not answer without further argument.... I do, however, subscribe to most of what Mr. Justice BRENNAN says, and if ever required to face the issue squarely, may well accept his ultimate conclusion.

Comments

1. In *Swain* v. *Alabama,* supra, the Court was concerned about alleged discrimination against blacks in petit jury selection. While the Court acknowledged that Alabama's system of drawing *venires* (panels of prospective jurors) was "imperfect," the petitioner (Swain) was unable to carry the burden of proof and establish purposeful discrimination, since blacks were underrepresented by only 10 per cent in the venire. Could Swain have

presented a prima facie case of invidious discrimination by showing underrepresentation of blacks by 20 per cent? 30 per cent? 50 per cent?

The Court rejected Swain's argument that the fact that no black had served on a petit jury in Talladega County since 1950 proved that the Alabama peremptory strike system was discriminatory. *Veniremen* (prospective jurors) can be disqualified from serving on a petit jury in one of two ways: (1) by peremptory challenges, or (2) by challenges for cause. The *peremptory challenge* (strike) allows the prosecutor and defense attorney to have prospective jurors excused from serving on the petit jury without giving any reason. The venireman may be excused because he has a beard, has red hair, or even because he is a member of a minority group. However, each side has only a limited number of peremptory challenges, the number usually increasing with the seriousness of the offense charged. The second means of disqualifying veniremen is the *challenge for cause*. With this type of challenge a legally sufficient reason must be articulated by the attorney seeking to excuse the venireman. After the peremptory challenges have been exhausted, a venireman may be excused only for cause. Examples of sufficient grounds to support a challenge for cause are (1) the statement of a venireman that he is prejudiced against one side and cannot reach a fair verdict based solely on the evidence presented, (2) mental or physical infirmities (e.g., hearing impairment), (3) prior service on a petit jury reviewing the same charge, (4) relationship to one of the parties in the lawsuit, and (5) moral or ethical convictions that may preclude impartiality.

Do you agree with the *Swain* Court that the fact that no black had ever served on a petit jury (civil or criminal) in Talladega County since 1950 was not sufficient proof for a prima facie showing of invidious racial discrimination? Was the absence of blacks on petit juries in Talladega County a "historical accident" like twelve-man juries (see *Williams* v. *Florida*, 399 U.S. 78 [1970] [supra]). Are there any reasons why a black defendant might desire an all-white jury, or a white defendant an all-black jury?

2. In *Taylor* v. *Louisiana*, 419 U.S. 522 (1975) (overruling *Hoyt* v. *Florida*, 368 U.S. 57 [1961]), the Court held that the selection of a petit jury from a representative cross section of the community is an essential component of the Sixth Amendment right to a trial by jury; and Louisiana's system of excluding women from jury service unless they had previously filed a written declaration of their desire to be subject to jury service was violative of the Sixth and Fourteenth Amendments. The systematic exclusion of women in Louisiana from jury service amounted to exclusion of 53 per cent of the citizens eligible for jury service.

3. In *Ristaino* v. *Ross,* supra, the Court refused to hold that if the defendant and victim of a crime are of different races, the defendant is constitutionally entitled to include questions about racial prejudice on *voir dire* (the questioning of prospective jurors). The test formulated is "whether under all of the circumstances presented, there was a significant likelihood that, absent questioning about racial prejudice, the jurors" would remain indifferent as to the races of the concerned parties. In *Ristaino,* the Court distinguished *Ham* v. *South Carolina,* 409 U.S. 524 (1973), in which a need for questions directed to racial

prejudice was demonstrated. What factors should a trial court consider in deciding whether to permit questions about racial prejudice during the voir dire? Suppose the defendant and victim are of different religions? different sexes? widely different ages? different social classes? different ethnic backgrounds? In *Peters* v. *Kiff*, 407 U.S. 493 (1972), the Court held that a white defendant has standing to sue and is entitled to federal relief upon a showing that blacks had been systematically excluded from the petit jury that convicted him.

It is often said that a defendant in a criminal trial has a right to be tried by a "jury of his peers." The Supreme Court has stated that a "jury of one's peers" means a random cross section of the community, *Glasser* v. *United States,* 315 U.S. 60 (1942). However in *Swain,* the Court noted that neither the veniremen nor the jury actually selected "need be a perfect mirror of the community or accurately reflect the proportionate strength of every identifiable group." Suppose a black female defendant is convicted by an all-white, all-male, six-member jury, and there is evidence that no black female has ever served on a petit jury in that jurisdiction—has she a prima facie case of invidious discrimination based on race and sex under the standards formulated by the Court?

In other decisions dealing with discriminatory jury selection, the Supreme Court has held that (1) minority groups excluded from juries may file a class action suit charging such discrimination, *Carter* v. *Jury Comm.,* 396 U.S. 320 (1970); (2) where a defendant shows a prima facie case of systematic exclusion of members of a minority group, the burden is on the state to disprove the alleged discrimination, *Whitus* v. *Georgia,* 385 U.S. 545 (1967); (3) the use of questionnaires by jury commissioners in selecting a venire list that include a space for designation of race may constitute prima facie evidence of discrimination, *Alexander* v. *Louisiana,* 405 U.S. 625 (1972), (Chapter Six, § 6.04); and (4) a state statute requiring jury members to be "upright" and "intelligent" may be implemented so subjectively as to present a prima facie case of discrimination, *Turner* v. *Fouche,* 396 U.S. 346 (1970).

4. In *Estelle* v. *Williams,* supra, a majority of the Court refused to hold that trying a defendant in jail clothes always requires a reversal of conviction, finding that the failure of the defendant or his counsel to object to the wearing of jail clothes waives any due process claims when the defendant was not compelled to wear them. Suppose there was evidence that the trial judge would have overruled any such objection. Would wearing of jail clothes under such conditions amount to "harmless error"? Can it really be said that Williams "knowingly, voluntarily, and intelligently" waived any due process claims by not objecting to the Texas procedure? Suppose counsel is court appointed and a novice at criminal work, and he inadvertently fails to make a timely objection. Is that a denial of effective assistance of counsel? Could the *defendant* be held to have voluntarily relinquished his right to a fair trial? Suppose the defendant isn't very intelligent and it never occurs to him that the wearing of jail clothes might prejudice his case? Suppose a defendant waives a jury trial and is tried in jail clothes before a judge. Is that a denial of due process? Suppose

defendant's objections to the wearing of jail clothes before the judge are overruled?

The Court declined to decide the retroactivity of *Williams*. In this regard see *Stovall* v. *Denno*, 388 U.S. 293 (1967) (Chapter Six, § 6.03), in which the Court held that the retroactivity or nonretroactivity of a rule is governed by the following criteria: "(a) the purpose to be served by the new standards, (b) the extent of the reliance by law enforcement authorities on the old standards, and (c) the effect on the administration of justice of a retroactive application of the new standards" at 297. By these standards, should *Estelle* v. *Williams* be made retroactive?

The Supreme Court has declined to give retroactive effect to the following cases: (1) *Mapp* v. *Ohio*, 367 U.S. 643 (Chapter Five, § 5.03), holding that evidence unconstitutionally obtained is inadmissible in state criminal proceedings. *Linkletter* v. *Walker*, 381 U.S. 618 (1965). (2) *Escobedo* v. *Illinois*, 378 U.S. 478 (1964), and *Miranda* v. *Arizona*, 384 U.S. 436 (1966) (Chapter Six, § 6.03), implementing new self-incrimination safeguards. *Johnson* v. *New Jersey*, 384 U.S. 719 (1966). (3) *Griffin* v. *California*, 380 U.S. 609 (1965), holding that adverse comments by a prosecutor on a defendant's failure to testify violate the privilege against self-incrimination. *Tehan* v. *United States ex rel. Schott*, 382 U.S. 406 (1966). (4) *Katz* v. *United States*, 389 U.S. 347 (1967) (Chapter Five, § 5.01), holding that Fourth Amendment protections are not dependent upon the presence or absence of a physical intrusion into a given area. *Desist* v. *United States*, 394 U.S. 244 (1969). (5) *Duncan* v. *Louisiana*, 391 U.S. 145 (1968) (Chapter Three, § 3.04), holding that the Sixth Amendment right to a trial by jury is applicable to the states. *De Stefano* v. *Woods*, 392 U.S. 631 (1968). (6) *Chimel* v. *California*, 395 U.S. 752 (1969) (Chapter Five, § 5.04), narrowing the permissible scope of searches incident to a lawful arrest. *Williams* v. *United States*, 401 U.S. 646 (1971). (7) *Coleman* v. *Alabama*, 399 U.S. 1 (1970), which held that a preliminary hearing is a "critical stage" requiring the assistance of counsel. *Adams* v. *Illinois*, 405 U.S. 278 (1972). (8) *North Carolina* v. *Pearce*, 395 U.S. 711 (1969), (Chapter Fourteen, § 14.01), imposing restrictions on resentencing following a defendant's successful appeal of his first conviction. *Michigan* v. *Payne*, 412 U.S. 47 (1973).

The Supreme Court has given retroactive effect to the following decisions: (1) *Bruton* v. *United States*, 391 U.S. 123 (1968) (infra), holding that a defendant has a Sixth Amendment right to cross-examine a co-defendant whose extrajudicial statements are admitted in evidence against the defendant. *Roberts* v. *Russell*, 392 U.S. 293 (1968). (2) *Mempa* v. *Rhay*, 399 U.S. 128 (1967) (Chapter Nine, § 9.02), holding that a defendant has a Sixth Amendment right to counsel at a probation revocation hearing when the sentence has been deferred. *McConnell* v. *Rhay*, 393 U.S. 2 (1968). (3) *Gideon* v. *Wainwright*, 372 U.S. 335 (1963) (supra, § 7.02), holding that the Sixth Amendment right to counsel is applicable to state felony trials. *Kitchens* v. *Smith*, 401 U.S. 847 (1971). (4) *Taylor* v. *Louisiana*, 419 U.S. 522 (1975), holding that exclusion of women from jury duty denies a defendant the right to a fair trial. *Daniel* v. *Louisiana*, 420 U.S. 31 (1975). (5) *Barber* v. *Page*, 390 U.S. 719 (1968), holding that a witness is not "unavailable" so as to entitle the prosecution to introduce transcripts of his testimony at an earlier preliminary hearing unless the prosecution has made a "good faith" effort to obtain his presence. *Berger* v. *California,* 393 U.S. 314 (1969). (6) *White* v. *Maryland,* 373 U.S. 59 (1963), holding that there is a Sixth Amendment right to counsel at an arraignment. *Arsenault* v. *Massachusetts,* 393 U.S. 5 (1968). (7) *In re Winship,* 397 U.S. 358 (1970) (Chapter Eight, § 8.03), holding that the standard of proof beyond a reasonable doubt is constitutionally required and applicable to juvenile proceedings. *Ivan* v. *City of New York,* 407 U.S. 203 (1972). (8) *Waller* v. *Florida,* 397 U.S. 387 (1970) (Chapter Six, § 6.02), holding that the Double Jeopardy Clause bars successive state and municipal prosecutions based on the same act or offense. *Robinson* v. *Neil,* 409 U.S. 505 (1973). (9) *Jackson* v. *Denno,* 378 U.S. 368 (1964), holding that the voluntariness of a confession is to be initially decided by the judge out of the presence of the jury. *Lego* v. *Twomey,* 404 U.S. 477 (1972). (10) *United States* v. *Wade,* 388 U.S. 218 (1967) (Chapter Six, § 6.03), requiring counsel at postindictment lineups, and *Gilbert* v. *California,* 388 U.S. 263 (1967), holding that there is no right to counsel at the taking of handwriting exemplars. *Stovall* v. *Denno,* 388 U.S. 293 (1967) (Chapter Six, § 6.03).

5.   Although the problem of pretrial publicity—how to balance the right of the press to report the news with the defendant's right to a fair trial—is raised in only a few cases, it is a difficult one to solve. A major problem in highly publicized cases is that the prospective jurors know many facts about the case. It would be difficult, and undesirable, to stop the press from reporting the news even if we could thereby guarantee the defendant a "fair trial." But we cannot guarantee a defendant a fair trial; we can only attempt to provide one. As noted by the Supreme Court, a defendant is entitled to only a "fair trial, not a perfect one." In *Irvin* v. *Dowd,* 366 U.S. 717 (1961), cited in *Murphy,* the Supreme Court struck down, for the first time, a state conviction solely on the basis of prejudicial pretrial publicity. The Court acknowledged that in highly publicized cases it may be impossible to impanel a jury that has no knowledge of the case. Accordingly, the Court held that the guarantee of an "impartial jury" does not require that the jurors be totally ignorant of the facts of the case. A venireman may serve on a jury if he can "lay aside his impression or opinion and render a verdict based on the evidence presented in court." Id. at 722–723. Thus, if a prospective juror states that he is willing to set aside his preconceived notions of guilt or innocence and can reach a verdict based solely on the evidence presented, a challenge for cause may properly be denied by the trial court.

In *Marshall* v. *United States,* 360 U.S. 310 (1959), cited in *Murphy,* the Court reversed the defendant's conviction because the jurors had been prejudicially exposed to news accounts detailing the defendant's prior criminal record. If Murphy had been tried in a federal criminal court would his conviction have been reversed on the basis of *Marshall*? Why did the Court refuse in *Murphy* to make the rule in *Marshall* applicable to the states? Was Murphy's conviction affirmed because his counsel had made sure that the veniremen were aware of the defendant's prior criminal record? As a tactical move at trial, in protest to the jury selected, Murphy did not testify, offer any defense, or cross-examine any state witnesses. Is it likely that Murphy anticipated a conviction and was hoping for a reversal on appeal?

6. In *Nebraska Press Association* v. *Stuart,* supra, the Court could have avoided a decision on the merits by finding the case to be "moot," since the gag order was no longer in effect by the time the case reached the Supreme Court. Because many issues become moot by the time they reach the Supreme Court and thus no longer meet the "case or controversy" requirement of Article III, § 2, of the Constitution, the Court has had to create a number of exceptions to the mootness rule. The most frequently utilized exception applies when an issue is "capable of repetition, yet evad[es] [judicial] review." *Pacific Terminal Co.* v. *ICC,* 219 U.S. 498, 515 (1911). For an example of perhaps the most flagrant "cop-out" by the Court in recent years, see *De Funis* v. *Odegaard,* 416 U.S. 312 (1974), in which the Court held in a 5–4 decision that the plaintiff's claim of "reverse discrimination" was moot since he had sought and obtained an injunction that enabled him to attend law school and was just a few weeks away from graduating when his case reached the Supreme Court. See Note, *The Mootness Doctrine in the Supreme Court,* 88 Harv. L. Rev. 373 (1974). The leading case in recent years involving the mootness doctrine is *Sosna* v. *Iowa,* 419 U.S. 393 (1975).

7. The Court noted in *Nebraska Press Association* that five alternatives are available to judges to protect an accused's Sixth Amendment right to a fair trial in heavily publicized cases: (1) change of venue, (2) continuance, (3) careful questioning of prospective jurors on voir dire, (4) careful instruction of the jury, and (5) sequestration of the jury. Which of these alternatives is most likely to protect the right to a fair trial? Would a change of venue have enhanced the possibility of a fairer trial in the Watergate defendants' cases? In the cases of Charles Manson and Patricia Hearst? Of what value is a continuance when the press reiterates its earlier stories when the case finally comes to trial? Aren't most veniremen likely to state that they have "open minds and can reach a verdict solely on the evidence presented"? How many prospective jurors are likely to admit that they are so narrow-minded that they could not make a fair and unbiased assessment of guilt or innocence? Sequestration would have a minimal curative effect in cases involving massive pretrial publicity. For these reasons, many courts have concluded that a prior restraint on the press via a gag order is the only solution to protecting the rights of an accused. Interestingly, a majority of the Court was unwilling to hold that gag orders are unconstitutional under all circumstances, stating that "the guarantees of freedom of expression are not an absolute prohibition under all circumstances." Under what circumstances might a gag order in a criminal case be upheld? Would such an order have been upheld in the case of Jack Ruby, who shot Lee Harvey Oswald in full view of millions of persons watching television? Or would prior restraint in that case serve no useful purpose in view of the circumstances? Are gag orders likely to continue to flourish at the trial court level in light of the apparent nonabsolute prohibition announced by the majority? Should Sixth Amendment rights always be secondary to First Amendment rights? Does a state trial court have contempt jurisdiction over extrajurisdictional newspapers that violate re-

straining orders? Suppose a local reporter is found in contempt of court for violating a gag order, but the order is later found to be unlawful. Does the reporter have a right to have the contempt finding expunged from his record? Does the newspaper have a right to a refund in the event a fine was imposed? Suppose the reporter-contemnor spent 30 days in jail. Does he have any legal recourse if the gag order was unconstitutional?

8. **OKLAHOMA PUBLISHING COMPANY v. DISTRICT COURT IN AND FOR OKLAHOMA COUNTY, OKLAHOMA, ET AL.**

Supreme Court of the United States, 1977
430 U.S. 308, 9 S. Ct. 1045, 51 L. Ed. 2d 355

PER CURIAM.

A pretrial order entered by the District Court of Oklahoma County enjoined members of the news media from "publishing, broadcasting, or disseminating, in any manner, the name or picture of [a] minor child" in connection with a juvenile proceeding involving that child then pending in that court. On application for prohibition and mandamus challenging the order as a prior restraint on the press violative of the First and Fourteenth Amendments, the Supreme Court of the State of Oklahoma sustained the order. This Court entered a stay pending the timely filing and disposition of a petition for certiorari. . . . We now grant the petition for certiorari and reverse the decision below.

A railroad switchman was fatally shot on July 26, 1976. On July 29, 1976, an 11-year-old boy, Larry Donnell Brewer, appeared at a detention hearing in Oklahoma County Juvenile Court on charges filed by state juvenile authorities alleging delinquency by second-degree murder in the shooting of this switchman. Reporters, including one from petitioner's newspapers, were present in the courtroom during the hearing and learned the juvenile's name. As the boy was escorted from the courthouse to a vehicle, one of petitioner's photographers took his picture. Thereafter, a number of stories using the boy's name and photograph were printed in newspapers within the county, including petitioner's three newspapers in Oklahoma City; radio stations broadcast his name and television stations showed film footage of him and identified him by name.

On August 3, 1976, the juvenile was arraigned at a closed hearing, at which the judge entered the pretrial order involved in this case. Additional news reports identifying the juvenile appeared on August 4 and 5. On August 16, the District Court denied petitioner's motion to quash the order. The Oklahoma Supreme Court then denied petitioner's writ of prohibition and mandamus, relying on Oklahoma statutes providing that juvenile proceedings are to be held in private "unless specifically ordered by the judge to be conducted in public," and that juvenile records are open to public inspection "only by order of the court to persons having a legitimate interest therein." Okla. Stat. Ann. Tit. 10, §§ 1111, 1125 (Supp. 1976).

As we noted in entering our stay of the pretrial order, petitioner does not challenge the constitutionality of the Oklahoma statutes relied on by the court below. Petitioner asks us only to hold that the First and Fourteenth Amendments will not permit a state court to prohibit the publication of widely disseminated information obtained at court proceedings which were in fact open to the public. We think this result is compelled by our recent decisions in Nebraska Press Assn. v. Stuart, 96 S. Ct. 2791 (1976), and Cox Broadcasting Corp. v. Cohn, 420 U.S. 469 (1975).

In Cox Broadcasting the Court held that a State could not impose sanctions on the accurate publication of the name of a rape victim "which was publicly revealed in connection with the prosecution of the crime." Id., at 471. There, a reporter learned the identity of the victim from an examination of indictments made available by a clerk for his inspection in the courtroom during a recess of court proceedings against the alleged rapists. The Court expressly refrained from intimating a view on any constitutional questions arising from a state policy of denying the public or the press access to official records of juvenile proceedings, id., at 496 n.26, but made clear that the press may not be prohibited from "truthfully publishing information released to the public in official court records." Id., at 496.

This principle was reaffirmed last Term in Nebraska Press Assn. v. Stuart, supra, which held unconstitutional an order prohibiting the press from publishing certain information tending to show the guilt of a defendant in an impending criminal trial. In Part VI (D) of its opinion, the Court focused on the information covered by the order that had been adduced as evidence in a preliminary hearing open to the public and the press; we concluded that, to the extent the order prohibited the publication of such evidence, "It plainly violated settled principles," 427 U.S., at 568, citing Cox Broadcasting v. Cohn, supra; Sheppard v. Maxwell, 384 U.S. 333, 362–363 (1966) ("there is nothing that proscribes the press from reporting events that transpire in the courtroom"); and Craig v. Harney, 331 U.S. 367, 374 (1947) ("[t]hose who see and hear what transpired [in the courtroom] can report it with impunity"). The Court noted that under state law the trial court was permitted in certain circumstances to close pretrial proceedings to the public, but indicated that such an option did not allow the trial judge to suppress publication of information from the hearing if the public was allowed to attend: "[O]nce a public hearing had been held, what transpired there could not be subject to prior restraint." 427 U.S., at 568.

The court below found the rationale of these decisions to be inapplicable here because a state statute provided for closed juvenile hearings unless specifically opened to the public by court order and because "there is no indication that the judge distinctly and expressly ordered the hearing to be public." We think Cox and Nebraska Press are controlling nonetheless. Whether or not the trial judge expressly made such an order, members of the press were in fact present at the hearing with the full knowledge of the presiding judge, the prosecutor, and the defense counsel. No objection was made to the presence of the press in the courtroom or to the photographing of the juvenile as he left the courthouse. There is no evidence that petitioner acquired the information unlawfully or even without the State's implicit approval. The name and picture of the juvenile here were "publicly revealed in connection with the prosecution of the crime" much as the name of the rape victim in Cox Broadcasting was placed in the public domain. Under these circumstances, the District Court's order abridges the freedom of the press in violation of the First and Fourteenth Amendments.

The petition for certiorari is granted and the judgment is reversed.

9. In other decisions involving the Sixth Amendment guarantee of an impartial jury, the Supreme Court has reversed convictions by finding the defendant was denied a fair trial when (1) a change of venue was denied after a community was exposed repeatedly to television films of a defendant personally confessing to the crimes with which he was later charged, *Rideau* v. *Louisiana*, 373 U.S. 723 (1963); (2) a trial was dominated by a mob (e.g., courtroom filled with hooded KKK members at a trial of a defendant accused of killing one of their own), *Moore* v. *Dempsy*, 261 U.S. 86 (1963); (3) the trial judge in a nonjury trial had a direct pecuniary interest in the outcome of the trial (i.e., the judges income came partly from the fines he assessed, *Ward* v. *Village of Monroeville*, 409 U.S. 57 (1972); (4) a jury deliberated in the custody of a deputy sheriff who had given key testimony against the defendant, *Turner* v. *Louisiana*, 397 U.S. 466 (1965); (5) a bailiff assigned to guard a sequestered jury during deliberations suggested to the jury that the defendant was guilty, *Parker* v. *Gladden*, 385 U.S. 363 (1966); (6) a state statute allowed a change of venue in felony cases only and prejudicial pretrial publicity was alleged in a misdemeanor case, *Groppi* v. *Wisconsin*, 400 U.S. 505 (1971); (7) a trial was televised, even though no actual prejudice was shown, *Estes* v. *Texas*, 381 U.S. 532 (1965); (8) a trial judge failed to protect the defendant against the use of the courtroom by the press, to insulate witnesses, and to control the release of information to the press, *Sheppard* v. *Maxwell*, 384 U.S. 333 (1966); and (9) a juror received a private communication during a criminal trial that concerned a matter pending before the jury, *In re Murchison*, 349 U.S. 133 (1955). See also *Remmer* v. *United States*, 347 U.S. 227 (1954). See also *Mattox* v. *United States*, 146 U.S. 140 (1892).

10. Some recent lower federal and state court decisions involving the right to a fair trial include *Ray* v. *State*, 333 N.E.2d 317 (Ind. App. 1975) (fact that bailiff testified as prosecution witness not sufficient to deny defendant a fair trial); *Manuel* v. *State*, 541 P.2d 233 (Okla. Ct. App. 1975) (presence on jury of husband of local chief secretary for district attorney requires reversal of murder conviction, as prosecutor failed to notify defense of the juror's connection with law enforcement); *United States* v. *Smith*, ___ U.S.C.M.A. ___ (1975) (military judge may be replaced prior to assembly of a court-martial without a showing of good cause, but replacement thereafter requires showing of good cause); *Perry* v. *Mulligan*, 399 F. Supp. 1285 (D.N.J. 1975) (prosecutor's references at police officer's extortion trial to the social problems caused by such conduct denies defendant fair trial); *Government of Virgin Islands* v. *Gereau*, 523 F.2d 914 (3d Cir. 1975) (vague, generalized rumors that "further killings would occur on the Islands," held to have had no effect on jury's deliberations; *State* v. *Rios*, 539 P.2d 900 (Ariz. 1975) (where defendants were Mexican nationals unable to speak English and were denied interpreter, fact that they had bilingual defense attorney held not enough to assure them a fair trial); *United States* v. *Corrigan*, 401 F. Supp. 795 (D. Wyo. 1975)

(claim that judge should disqualify himself from trying a criminal case because the defendant had brought a lawsuit against him and every other federal judge held properly denied); *Morgan* v. *Yancy County Department of Corrections,* 527 F.2d 1004 (4th Cir. 1975) (*Peters* v. *Kiff,* under which white defendants may challenge jury selections on the ground that blacks have been systematically excluded, held not retroactive) (in accord is *Watson* v. *United States,* 484 F.2d 34 (5th Cir. 1973); *In the matter of Public Law No. 305,* 334 N.E.2d 659 (Ind. 1975) (new provision in law providing for six-man juries in county courts for civil and criminal cases upheld); *State* v. *Brown,* 319 So. 2d 409 (La. 1975) (prosecutor's remark to defense counsel upon being asked if counsel could question the defendant on a collateral matter that "you can ask him anything you want the way he's lying" held not reversible error); *State* v. *Mims,* 235 N.W.2d 381 (Minn. 1975) (trial judge's unsolicited visit, unaccompanied by defense counsel or prosecutor, to a deliberating jury's room to discuss how long deliberations should continue held reversible error); *United States* v. *Smith,* 523 F.2d 788 (5th Cir. 1975) (defense counsel's assurance, in the defendant's presence, that his client would sign a stipulation waiving his right to a 12-man jury in the event any juror could not complete the trial held adequate waiver despite the absence of written consent); *United States* v. *Perez-Martinez,* 525 F.2d 365 (9th Cir. 1975) (Cuban defendant not entitled to jury voir dire with respect to racial prejudice that was found essential in *Ham* v. *South Carolina*); *United States* v. *Williams,* 523 F.2d 1203 (5th Cir. 1975) (fact that newspaper editor published a first-person account of his kidnapping and gave several radio and television interviews in which he described the mental state of his abductor held to deny the defendant a fair trial); *People* v. *Williams,* 234 N.W.2d 689 (Mich. App. 1975) (trial court that permitted reference to narcotics paraphernalia found on larceny defendant held to deny fair trial); *State* v. *Lindgren,* 235 N.W.2d 379 (Minn. 1975) (lay judges may preside over misdemeanor trials for offenses punishable by incarceration); *United States* v. *Carter,* 523 F.2d 476 (8th Cir. 1975) (use of peremptory challenges to exclude blacks from juries not improper when defendant failed to show that those excluded were challenged "for reasons wholly unrelated to the outcome of the particular case on trial"); *Moore* v. *State,* 530 S.W.2d 536 (Tex. Ct. Crim. App. 1975) (prosecutor's remarks in obscenity prosecution while urging jury to find "Deep Throat" obscene — "And if that is not obscene, we might as well quit. We might as well quit prosecuting obscenity cases if this film here isn't obscene, and concentrate on sex crimes and other matters that arise after people view things like that" — held prejudicial error); *Roth* v. *State,* 543 P.2d 939 (Kan. 1975) (statute providing that veniremen be selected from real and personal property assessment rolls does not, by itself, mean that the poor have been systematically excluded from jury service); *Commonwealth* v. *Brown,* 347 A.2d 716 (Pa. 1975) (rape defendant should have been permitted to ask prospective jurors: "Would you, or do you, get upset or take special note when you see a white girl and a black man walking together, talking together, or holding hands?"); *State* v. *Boone,* 543 P.2d 945 (Kan. 1975) (use of nonlawyer magistrates to make probable cause determinations at preliminary hearings upheld); *Commonwealth* v. *Morgan,* 339 N.E.2d 723

(Mass. 1975) (jury selection provision permitting the exclusion in sex offense cases of women who say they would be embarrassed by hearing or discussing the evidence upheld); *United States* v. *Lamb,* 529 F.2d 1153 (9th Cir. 1975) (trial court's calling alternate juror, who had been discharged and sent home, to return and replace a member of the panel who was excused just as the jury was directed to reconsider its verdict, which was inconsistent with the court's instructions, held reversible error); *Reaves* v. *State,* 324 So. 2d 687 (Fla. App. 1976) (not error for prosecutor to cast doubt on a theft defendant's story by referring to the defendant's indigency when the defendant testified that he went to the robbed store with intent to buy some large appliances and the prosecutor pointed out that the defendant was represented by a public defender and could not have had such large amounts of money to spend); *Sumpter* v. *State,* 340 N.E.2d 764 (Ind. 1976) (trial judge acted properly in taking judicial notice of the sex of Johnnie Marie Sumpter, accused of living in a house of ill repute); *State* v. *Aragon,* 547 P.2d 574 (N. Mex. App. 1976) (trial judge's inquiry into the vote split of a deadlocked jury was reversible error); *Bradley* v. *Judges of Superior Court,* 531 F.2d 413 (9th Cir. 1976) (juries may be drawn from the county as a whole and not restricted to the county subdivision where the crime occurred); *State* v. *Murphy,* 353 A.2d 346 (Vt. 1976) (selection of jurors entirely from one of two counties within a judicial unit upheld); *State* v. *Woodward,* 353 A.2d 321 (Vt. 1976) (juror's continued service on jury after overhearing defendant say on courthouse telephone that he needed an alibi held denial of right to fair trial); *Commonwealth* v. *Scoggins,* 353 A.2d 392 (Pa. 1976) (prosecutor committed nonprejudicial error in case of life prisoner on trial for murder and assault by revealing in his opening argument that the offense for which the defendant was serving a life sentence was first degree murder); *Anderson* v. *Casseles,* 531 F.2d 682 (2d Cir. 1976) (impanelling of jury consisting of approximately 2 per cent black persons when eligible black population was 4.4 per cent did not violate the defendant's constitutional rights); *People* v. *Smith,* 240 N.W.2d 202 (Mich. 1976) (trial judge who specifically foreclosed any opportunity for jury to have testimony read back to it during the course of its deliberations committed reversible error); *United States* v. *Segal,* 534 F.2d 578 (3d Cir. 1976) (defendants charged with conspiracy and bribery of IRS agent should have been permitted to ask whether any of the prospective veniremen or their close relatives were or had been employed by the IRS or its state or local counterparts); *State* v. *Rhone,* 548 P.2d 752 (Kan. 1976) (trial judge acted within his discretion in conducting part of criminal jury trial in the home of a witness who was ill and too close to death to travel to the courtroom); *United States* v. *Mathis,* 535 F.2d 1303 (D.C. Cir. 1976) (trial court's denial of defense counsel's motion to have jurors polled individually rather than as a group after they announced their verdict of guilt held not reversible error); *State* v. *Pfeiffer,* 548 P.2d 174 (Ore. App. 1976) (preliminary hearing before nonlawyer judge upheld); *United States* v. *Coast of Maine Lobster Co., Inc.,* 538 F.2d 899 (1st Cir. 1976) (prosecutor's public statement that sentences for white collar crimes have been too lenient held reversible error in ongoing fraud trial where statements may have reached the jury); *Sharplin* v. *State,* 330 So. 2d 591 (Miss. 1976) (trial judge permitted to ask deadlocked deliberating jury about the vote split as long as the court does not ask whether split favors guilt or innocence) (in accord is *People* v. *Carter,* 442 P.2d 353 [Calif. 1968], rev'd on other grounds, *Joyner* v. *State,* 848 P. 2d 560 [Okla. App. 1971], *Huffaker* v. *State,* 168 S.E.2d 895 [Ga. App. 1969]; *State* v. *Morris,* 476 S.W.2d 485 [Mo. 1971]) (contra is *Taylor* v. *State,* 299 A.2d 841 [Md. 1973], *People* v. *Wilson,* 213 N.W.2d 193 [Mich. 1973], *Kersey* v. *State,* 525 S.W.2d 139 [Tenn. 1975]); *Shelmidine* v. *Jones,* 550 P.2d 207 (Utah 1976) (use of nonlawyers as justices of the peace upheld); *People* v. *McCrary,* 549 P.2d 1320 (Col. 1976) (trial court did not abuse its discretion by denying a motion for a change of venue and refusing to excuse for cause some jurors who had read newspaper articles about the case); *United States* v. *Joseph,* 533 F.2d 282 (5th Cir. 1976) (prosecutor's mention to jury in his closing remarks that two narcotics informers did not testify for the government out of fear for their safety held harmless error); *McCloud* v. *State,* 335 So. 2d 257 (Fla. 1976) (trial judge who pressured a prosecution witness out of the jury's presence to recall the subject matter of his testimony did not abuse his discretion); *McKay* v. *State,* 362 A.2d 666 (Md. App. 1976) (under Maryland law defendant cannot be found guilty by a jury vote that is less than unanimous); *State* v. *Arndt,* 533 P.2d 1328 (Wash. 1976) (unanimous jury verdict that a defendant committed the crime charged need not be supported by unanimity among jurors as to which of the alternate means the defendant used in committing the offense); *State* v. *Upton,* 362 A.2d 738 (Me. 1976) (no fatal inconsistency in jury verdict finding defendant guilty of murder of trading post manager and "not guilty by reason of mental disease or defect" of murdering his wife, who was shot seconds after the manager); *People* v. *Collins,* 552 P.2d 742 (Calif. 1976) (trial judge's substitution of alternate for regular juror who claimed after deliberations were well underway that she was unable to function as required by the instructions requires that instructions be given again and deliberations begin anew); *State* v. *Solem,* 552 P.2d 951 (Kan. 1976) (allowing nonlawyer judge to preside over preliminary hearing upheld); *State* v. *Bauer,* 245 N.W.2d 848 (Minn. 1976) (trial judge has duty to keep a continuous watch for signs that a defendant has become incompetent to stand trial); *Zicarelli* v. *Gray,* 543 F.2d 466 (3d Cir. 1976) (en banc) (Sixth Amendment guarantee of trial by jury of "vicinage" doesn't preclude drawing jury from other counties within same federal judicial district); *United States* v. *Brown,* 547 F.2d 1264 (5th Cir. 1976) (federal judge's alleged remark to a patent lawyer that he was "going to get that nigger," made about a defendant, H. Rap Brown, prior to his trial, held to require reversal of conviction for federal firearms violation); *State* v. *Cage,* 337 So. 2d 1122 (La. 1976) (jury commission's temporary exclusion of an entire housing project with 9,500 residents from its jury selection process on the grounds of concern for the safety of the process servers held unconstitutional); *United States* v. *Green,* 544 F.2d 138 (3d Cir. 1976) (federal judge who attempted to determine competency of hijacking defendant to stand trial did not abuse discretion in discussing defendant's conduct over telephone with expert who had already testified or by having his law clerk keep an eye on the defendant and make notes on his behavior); *Commonwealth* v. *Pana,* 364 A.2d 895 (Pa. 1976) (trial judge's refusal to allow burglary defendants who had considerable difficulty understanding English, to testify in his native Spanish through an interpreter held reversible error); *People* v. *Duran,* 545 P.2d 1322 (Calif. 1976) (prejudicial error to impose physical restraints upon a defendant at trial unless there is "evident necessity" for doing so) (see also *People* v. *Harrington,* 42 Cal. 165 [1871]); *Hazel* v. *United States,* 353 A.2d 280 (D.C. App. 1976) (trial judge committed reversible error in failing to address a robbery defendant in open court after having ejected him for an outburst at the prosecutor when the defendant regained his composure and wished to return to the courtroom).

C. THE RIGHT TO A SPEEDY TRIAL

The Putative Defendant and Preindictment Delays

UNITED STATES v. MARION

Supreme Court of the United States, 1971
404 U.S. 307, 92 S. Ct. 455, 30 L. Ed. 2d 468

William Marion and Samuel Cratch were indicted by a federal grand jury on 19 counts of consumer fraud on April 21, 1970. The period covered by the indictment was March 15, 1965, to February 6, 1967. On June 8, 1970, the United States District Court (D.C.) dismissed the indictment for lack of speedy prosecution, on the ground that the defendants must have been prejudiced by the delay. The United States appealed directly to the United States Supreme Court under a federal statute that permits judicial review when a district court has dismissed an indictment and the defendant has not yet been put in jeopardy.

Mr. Justice WHITE delivered the opinion of the Court.

This appeal requires us to decide whether dismissal of a federal indictment was constitutionally required by reason of a period of three years between the occurrence of the alleged criminal acts and the filing of the indictment.

* * *

Appellees do not claim that the Sixth Amendment was violated by the two-month delay between the return of the indictment and its dismissal. Instead, they claim that their rights to a speedy trial were violated by the period of approximately three years between the end of the criminal scheme charged and the return of the indictment; it is argued that this delay is so substantial and inherently prejudicial that the Sixth Amend-

ment required the dismissal of the indictment. In our view, however, the Sixth Amendment speedy trial provision has no application until the putative defendant in some way becomes an "accused," an event that occurred in this case only when the appellees were indicted on April 21, 1970.

The Sixth Amendment provides that "[i]n all criminal prosecutions, the accused shall enjoy the right to a speedy and public trial. . . ." On its face, the protection of the Amendment is activated only when a criminal prosecution has begun and extends only to those persons who have been "accused" in the course of that prosecution. These provisions would seem to afford no protection to those not yet accused, nor would they seem to require the Government to discover, investigate, and accuse any person within any particular period of time. The Amendment would appear to guarantee to a criminal defendant that the Government will move with the dispatch that is appropriate to assure him an early and proper disposition of the charges against him. . . .

Our attention is called to nothing in the circumstances surrounding the adoption of the Amendment indicating that it does not mean what it appears to say, nor is there more than marginal support for the proposition that, at the time of the adoption of the Amendment, the prevailing rule was that prosecutions would not be permitted if there had been long delay in presenting a charge. The framers could hardly have selected less appropriate language if they had intended the speedy trial provision to protect against preaccusation delay. No opinions of this Court intimate support for appellees' thesis, and the courts of appeals that have considered the question in constitutional terms have never reversed a conviction or dismissed an indictment solely on the basis of the Sixth Amendment's speedy trial provision where only pre-indictment delay was involved.

Legislative efforts to implement federal and state speedy trial provisions also plainly reveal the view that these guarantees are applicable only after a person has been accused of a crime. . . .

* * *

It is apparent also that very little support for appellees' position emerges from a consideration of the purposes of the Sixth Amendment's speedy trial provision, a guarantee that this Court has termed "an important safeguard to prevent undue and oppressive incarceration prior to trial, to minimize anxiety and concern accompanying public accusation and to limit the possibilities that long delay will impair the ability of an accused to defend himself." . . . Inordinate delay between arrest, indictment, and trial may impair a defendant's ability to present an effective defense. But the major evils protected against by the speedy trial guarantee exist quite apart from actual or possible prejudice to an accused's defense. To legally arrest and detain, the Government must assert probable cause to believe the arrestee has committed a crime. Arrest is a public act that may seriously interfere with the defendant's liberty, whether he is free on bail or not, and that may disrupt his employment,

drain his financial resources, curtail his associations, subject him to public obloquy, and create anxiety in him, his family and his friends. . . . So viewed, it is readily understandable that it is either a formal indictment or information or else the actual restraints imposed by arrest and holding to answer a criminal charge that engage the particular protections of the speedy trial provision of the Sixth Amendment.

Invocation of the speedy trial provision thus need not await indictment, information, or other formal charge. But we decline to extend the reach of the amendment to the period prior to arrest. Until this event occurs, a citizen suffers no restraints on his liberty and is not the subject of public accusations: his situation does not compare with that of a defendant who has been arrested and held to answer. Passage of time, whether before or after arrest, may impair memories, cause evidence to be lost, deprive the defendant of witnesses, and otherwise interfere with his ability to defend himself. But this possibility of prejudice at trial is not itself sufficient reason to wrench the Sixth Amendment from its proper context. Possible prejudice is inherent in any delay, however short; it may also weaken the Government's case.

The law has provided other mechanisms to guard against possible as distinguished from actual prejudice resulting from the passage of time between crime and arrest or charge. . . . "[T]he applicable statute of limitations . . . is . . . the primary guarantee against bringing overly stale criminal charges." . . . These statutes provide predictability by specifying a limit beyond which there is an irrebuttable presumption that a defendant's right to a fair trial would be prejudiced. . . .

There is thus no need to press the Sixth Amendment into service to guard against the mere possibility that preaccusation delays will prejudice the defense in a criminal case since statutes of limitation already perform that function.

Since appellees rely only on potential prejudice and the passage of time between the alleged crime and the indictment . . . we perhaps need go no further to dispose of this case, for the indictment was the first official act designating appellees as accused individuals and that event occurred within the statute of limitations. Nevertheless, since a criminal trial is the likely consequence of our judgment and since appellees may claim actual prejudice to their defense, it is appropriate to note here that the statute of limitations does not fully define the appellees' rights with respect to the events occurring prior to indictment. Thus, the Government concedes that the Due Process Clause of the Fifth Amendment would require dismissal of the indictment if it were shown at trial that the preindictment delay in this case caused substantial prejudice to appellees' rights to a fair trial and that the delay was an intentional device to gain tactical advantage over the accused.... However, we need not and could not now, determine when and in what circumstances actual prejudice resulting from preaccusation delays requires the dismissal of the prosecution. Actual prejudice to the defense of a criminal case may result from the shortest and most necessary delay; and no one suggests that every delay-caused detriment to a defendant's case should abort a criminal prosecution. To accommodate the sound administration of justice to the rights of the defendant to a fair trial will necessarily involve a delicate judgment based on the circumstances in each case. It would be unwise at this juncture to attempt to forecast our decision in such cases.

In the case before us, neither appellee was arrested, charged, or otherwise subjected to formal restraint prior to indictment. It was this event, therefore, that transformed the appellees into "accused" defendants who are subject to the speedy trial protections of the Sixth Amendment.

The 38-month delay between the end of the scheme charged in the indictment and the date the defendants were indicted did not extend beyond the period of the applicable statute of limitations here. Appellees have not, of course, been able to claim undue delay pending trial, since the indictment was brought on April 21, 1970, and dismissed on June 8, 1970. Nor have appellees adequately demonstrated that the preindictment delay by the Government violated the Due Process Clause. No actual prejudice to the conduct of the defense is alleged or proved, and there is no showing that the Government intentionally delayed to gain some tactical advantage over appellees or to harass them. Appellees rely solely on the real possibility of prejudice inherent in any extended delay: that memories will dim, witnesses become inaccessible, and evidence be lost. ... Events of the trial may demonstrate actual prejudice, but at the present time appellees' due process claims are speculative and premature.

Reversed.

Mr. Justice DOUGLAS, with whom Mr. Justice BRENNAN and Mr. Justice MARSHALL join, concurring in the result.

I assume that if the three-year delay in this case had occurred *after* the indictment had been returned, the right to a speedy trial would have been impaired and the indictment would have to be dismissed. I disagree with the Court that the guarantee does not apply if the delay was at the pre-indictment stage of a case.

* * *

Preindictment Delays, Good Faith, and Actual Prejudice

UNITED STATES v. LOVASCO

Supreme Court of the United States, 1977
431 U.S. 783, 96 S. Ct. 2044, 52 L. Ed. 2d 752

On March 6, 1975, respondent, Eugene Lovasco, Sr., was indicted by a federal grand jury for possessing eight firearms from the United States Mail and for dealing in firearms without a license. The offenses were alleged to have occurred between July 25 and August 31, 1973, more than 18 months before the indictment was filed. Respondent moved to dismiss the indictment due to the delay.

The district court conducted a hearing on respondent's motion at which the respondent sought to prove that the delay was unnecessary and that it had prejudiced his defense. In an effort to establish the former proposition, respondent presented a postal inspector's report on his investigation, prepared one month after the crimes were committed, which stated that the government had developed a strong case against the respondent. To establish prejudice to his defense, respondent testified that owing to the delay he had lost the testimony of two material witnesses, who had died.

The district court, which concluded that the delay had not been explained or justified and was unnecessary and prejudicial to the respondent, granted the motion to dismiss. The Court of Appeals (8th Cir.) affirmed, and the United States Supreme Court granted certiorari.

Mr. Justice MARSHALL delivered the opinion of the Court.

We granted certiorari in this case to consider the circumstances in which the Constitution requires that an indictment be dismissed because of delay between the commission of an offense and the initiation of prosecution.

I

* * *

II

* * *

Respondent seems to argue that due process bars prosecution whenever a defendant suffers prejudice as a result of preindictment delay. To support that proposition respondent relies on the concluding sentence of the Court's opinion in [United States v.] Marion where, in remanding the case, we stated that "[e]vents at the trial may demonstrate actual prejudice, but at the present time appellees' due process claims are speculative and premature." 404 U.S., at 326. But the quoted sentence establishes only that proof of actual prejudice makes a due process claim automatically valid. Indeed, two pages earlier in the opinion we expressly rejected the argument respondent advances here:

"[W]e need not . . . determine when and in what circumstances actual prejudice resulting from preaccusation delay requires the dismissal of the prosecution. Actual prejudice to the defense of a criminal case may result from the shortest and most necessary delay; and no one suggests that every delay-caused detriment to a defendant's case should abort a criminal prosecution." Id., at 324–325.

Thus Marion makes clear that proof of prejudice is generally a necessary but not

sufficient element of a due process claim, and that the due process inquiry must consider the reasons for the delay as well as the prejudice to the accused. . . .

[T]he Due Process Clause does not permit courts to abort criminal prosecutions simply because they disagree with a prosecutor's judgment as to when to seek an indictment. Judges are not free, in defining "due process," to impose on law enforcement officials our "personal and private notions" of fairness and to "disregard the limits that bind judges in their judicial function." Rachin v. California, 342 U.S. 165, 170 (1952). Our task is more circumscribed. We are to determine only whether the actions complained of—here, compelling respondent to stand trial after the Government delayed indictment to investigate further—violate those "fundamental conceptions of justice which lie at the base of our civil and political institutions," Mooney v. Holohan, 294 U.S. 103, 112 (1935), and which define "the community's sense of fair play and decency." Rachin v. California, supra, at 173. See also Ham v. South Carolina, 409 U.S. 524, 526 (1923); Lisenba v. California, 314 U.S. 219, 236 (1941); Hebert v. Louisiana, 272 U.S. 312, 316 (1926); Hurtado v. California, 110 U.S. 516, 535 (1884).

It requires no extended argument to establish that prosecutors do not deviate from "fundamental conceptions of justice" when they defer seeking indictments until they have probable cause to believe an accused is guilty; indeed it is unprofessional conduct for a prosecutor to recommend an indictment on less than probable cause. It should be equally obvious that prosecutors are under no duty to file charges as soon as probable cause exists but before they are satisfied they will be able to establish the suspect's guilt beyond a reasonable doubt. To impose such a duty "would have a deleterious effect both upon the rights of the accused and upon the ability of society to protect itself." United States v. Ewell, ... 383 U.S., at 120. From the perspective of potential defendants, requiring prosecutions to commence when probable cause is established is undesirable because it would increase the likelihood of unwarranted charges being filed, and would add to the time during which defendants stand accused but untried. These costs are by no means insubstantial since, as we recognized in Marion, a formal accusation may "interfere with the defendant's liberty..., disrupt his employment, drain his financial resources, curtail his associations, subject him to public obloquy, and create anxiety in him, his family and his friends." 404 U.S., at 320. From the perspective of law enforcement officials, a requirement of immediate prosecution upon probable cause is equally unacceptable because it could make obtaining proof of guilt beyond a reasonable doubt impossible by causing potentially fruitful sources of information to evaporate before they are fully exploited. And from the standpoint of the courts, such a requirement is unwise because it would cause scarce resources to be consumed on cases that prove to be insubstantial, or that involve only some of the responsible parties or some of the criminal acts. Thus, no one's interests would be well served by compelling prosecutors to initiate prosecutions as soon as they are legally entitled to do so.

It might be argued that once the Government has assembled sufficient evidence to prove guilt beyond a reasonable doubt, it should be constitutionally required to file charges promptly, even if its investigation of the entire criminal transaction is not complete. Adopting such a rule, however, would have many of the same consequences as adopting a rule requiring immediate prosecution upon probable cause.

First, compelling a prosecutor to file public charges as soon as the requisite proof has been developed against one participant on one charge would cause numerous problems in those cases in which a criminal transaction involves more than one person or more than one illegal act. ...

Second, insisting on immediate prosecution once sufficient evidence is developed to obtain a conviction would pressure prosecutors into resolving doubtful cases in favor of early—and possibly unwarranted—prosecu-

tions. The determination of when the evidence available to the prosecution is sufficient to obtain a conviction is seldom clear-cut, and reasonable persons often will reach conflicting conclusions. ...

Finally, requiring the Government to make charging decisions immediately upon assembling evidence sufficient to establish guilt would preclude the Government from giving full consideration to the desirability of not prosecuting in particular cases. The decision to file criminal charges, with the awesome consequences it entails, requires consideration of a wide range of factors in addition to the strength of the Government's case, in order to determine whether prosecution would be in the public interest. ...

We would be most reluctant to adopt a rule which would have these consequences absent a clear constitutional command to do so. We can find no such command in the Due Process Clause of the Fifth Amendment. In our view, investigative delay is fundamentally unlike delay undertaken by the Government solely "to gain tactical advantage over the accused," United States v. Marion, supra, 404 U.S., at 324, precisely because investigative delay is not so one-sided. Rather than deviating from elementary standards of "fair play and decency," a prosecutor abides by them if he refuses to seek indictments until he is completely satisfied that he should prosecute and will be able promptly to establish guilt beyond a reasonable doubt. Penalizing prosecutors who defer action for these reasons would subordinate the goal of "orderly expedition" to that of "mere speed." Smith v. United States, 360 U.S. 1, 10 (1959). This the Due Process Clause does not require. We therefore hold that to prosecute a defendant following investigative delay does not deprive him of due process, even if his defense might have been somewhat prejudiced by the lapse of time.

* * *

III

In Marion we conceded that we could not determine in the abstract the circumstances in which preaccusation delay would require dismissing prosecutions. 404 U.S., at 324. More than five years later, that statement remains true. Indeed, in the intervening years so few defendants have established that they were prejudiced by delay that neither this Court nor any lower court has had a sustained opportunity to consider the constitutional significance of various reasons for delay. We therefore leave to the lower courts, in the first instance, the task of applying the settled principles of due process that we have discussed to the particular circumstances of individual cases. We simply hold that in this case the lower courts erred in dismissing the indictment.

Reversed.

[Mr. Justice STEVENS, dissented.]

The Balancing Test

BARKER v. WINGO

Supreme Court of the United States, 1972
407 U.S. 514, 92 S. Ct. 2182, 33 L. Ed. 2d 101

The facts are stated in the opinion.

Mr. Justice POWELL delivered the opinion of the Court.

Although a speedy trial is guaranteed the accused by the Sixth Amendment to the Constitution, this Court has dealt with that right on infrequent occasions. . . . The Court's opinion in Klopfer v. North Carolina, 386 U.S. 213 (1967), established that the right to a speedy trial is "fundamental" and is imposed by the Due Process Clause of the Fourteenth Amendment on the States. . . . In none of these cases have we attempted to set out the criteria by which the speedy trial right is to be judged. . . . This case compels us to make such an attempt.

I

On July 20, 1958, in Christian County, Kentucky, an elderly couple was beaten to death by intruders wielding an iron tire tool. Two suspects, Silas Manning and Willie Barker, the petitioner, were arrested shortly thereafter. The grand jury indicted them on September 15. Counsel was appointed on September 17, and Barker's trial was set for October 21. The Commonwealth had a stronger case against Manning, and it believed that Barker could not be convicted unless Manning testified against him. Manning was naturally unwilling to incriminate himself. Accordingly, on October 23, the day

Silas Manning was brought to trial, the Commonwealth sought and obtained the first of what was to be a series of 16 continuances of Barker's trial. Barker made no objection. By first convicting Manning, the Commonwealth would remove possible problems of self-incrimination and would be able to assure his testimony against Barker.

The Commonwealth encountered more than a few difficulties in its prosecution of Manning. The first trial ended in a hung jury. A second trial resulted in a conviction, but the Kentucky Court of Appeals reversed because of the admission of evidence obtained by an illegal search. . . . At his third trial, Manning was again convicted, and the Court of Appeals again reversed because the trial court had not granted a change of venue. . . . A fourth trial resulted in a hung jury. Finally, after five trials, Manning was convicted in March 1962, of murdering one victim, and after a sixth trial, in December 1962, he was convicted of murdering the other.

The Christian County Circuit Court holds three terms each year—in February, June, and September. Barker's initial trial was to take place in the September term of 1958. The first continuance postponed it until the February 1959 term. The second continuance was granted for one month only. Every term thereafter for as long as the Manning prosecutions were in process, the Commonwealth routinely moved to continue Barker's case to the next term. When the case was continued from the June 1959 term until the following September, Barker, having spent 10 months in jail, obtained his release by posting a $5,000 bond. He thereafter remained free in the community until his trial. Barker made no objection, through his counsel, to the first 11 continuances.

When on February 12, 1962, the Commonwealth moved for the twelfth time to continue the case until the following term, Barker's counsel filed a motion to dismiss the indictment. The motion to dismiss was denied two weeks later, and the Commonwealth's motion for a continuance was granted. The Commonwealth was granted further continuances in June 1962 and September 1962, to which Barker did not object.

In February 1963, the first term of court following Manning's final conviction, the Commonwealth moved to set Barker's trial for March 19. But on the day scheduled for trial, it again moved for a continuance until the June term. It gave as its reason the illness of the ex-sheriff who was the chief investigating officer in the case. To this continuance, Barker objected unsuccessfully.

The witness was still unable to testify in June, and the trial, which had been set for June 19, was continued again until the September term over Barker's objection. This time the court announced that the case would be dismissed for lack of prosecution if it were not tried during the next term. The final trial date was set for October 9, 1963. On that date, Barker again moved to dismiss the indictment, and this time specified that his right to a speedy trial had been violated. The motion was denied; the trial commenced with Manning as the chief prosecution witness; Barker was convicted and given a life sentence.

* * *

II

The right to a speedy trial is generically different from any of the other rights enshrined in the Constitution for the protection of the accused. In addition to the general concern that all accused persons be treated according to decent and fair procedures, there is a societal interest in providing a speedy trial which exists separate from, and at times in opposition to, the interests of the accused. The inability of courts to provide a prompt trial has contributed to a large backlog of cases in urban courts which, among other things, enables defendants to negotiate more effectively for pleas of guilty to lesser offenses and otherwise manipulate the system. In addition, persons released on bond for lengthy periods awaiting trial have an opportunity to commit other crimes. It must be of little comfort to the residents of Christian County, Kentucky, to know that Barker was at large on bail for over four years while accused of a vicious and brutal murder of which he was ultimately convicted. Moreover, the longer an accused is free awaiting trial, the more tempting becomes his opportunity to jump bail and escape. Finally, delay between arrest and punishment may have a detrimental effect on rehabilitation.

If an accused cannot make bail, he is generally confined. . . . This contributes to the overcrowding and generally deplorable state of [penal] institutions. Lengthy exposure to these conditions "has a destructive effect on human character and makes the rehabilitation of the individual offender much more difficult." At times the result may even be violent rioting. Finally, lengthy pretrial detention is costly. The cost of maintaining a prisoner in jail varies from $3 to $9 per day, and this amounts to millions across the Nation. In addition, society loses wages which might have been earned, and it must often support families of incarcerated breadwinners.

A second difference between the right to a speedy trial and the accused's other constitutional rights is that deprivation of the right may work to the accused's advantage. Delay is not an uncommon defense tactic. As the time between the commission of the crime and trial lengthens, witnesses may become unavailable or their memories may fade. If the witnesses support the prosecution, its case will be weakened, sometimes seriously so. And it is the prosecution which carries the burden of proof. Thus, unlike the right to counsel or the right to be free from compelled self-incrimination, deprivation of the right to speedy trial does not per se prejudice the accused's ability to defend himself.

Finally, and perhaps most importantly, the right to speedy trial is a more vague concept than other procedural rights. It is, for example, impossible to determine with precision when the right has been denied. We cannot definitely say how long is too long in a system where justice is supposed to be swift but deliberate. As a consequence, there is no fixed point in the criminal process when the State can put the defendant to the choice of either exercising or waiving the right to a speedy trial. If, for example, the State moves for a 60-day continuance, granting that continuance is not a violation of the right to speedy trial unless the circumstances of the case are such that further delay would endanger the values the right protects. It is impossible to do more than generalize about when those circumstances exist. There is nothing comparable to the point in the process when a defendant exercises or waives his right to counsel or his right to a jury trial. . . .

The amorphous quality of the right also leads to the unsatisfactorily severe remedy of dismissal of the indictment when the right has been deprived. This is indeed a serious consequence because it means that a defendant who may be guilty of a serious crime will go free, without having been tried. Such a remedy is more serious than an exclusionary rule or a reversal for a new trial, but it is the only possible remedy.

III

Perhaps because the speedy trial right is so slippery, two rigid approaches are urged upon us as ways of eliminating some of the uncertainty which courts experience in protecting the right. The first suggestion is that we hold that the Constitution requires a criminal defendant to be offered a trial within a specified time period. The result of such a ruling would have the virtue of clarifying when the right is infringed and of simplifying courts' application of it. Recognizing this, some legislatures have enacted laws, and some courts have adopted procedural rules which more narrowly define the right. The United States Court of Appeals for the Second Circuit has promulgated rules for the district courts in that Circuit establishing that the government must be ready for trial within six months of the date of arrest, except in unusual circumstances, or the charge will be dismissed. This type of rule is also recommended by the American Bar Association.

But such a result would require this Court to engage in legislative or rulemaking activity, rather than in the adjudicative process to which we should confine our efforts. We do not establish procedural rules for the States, except when mandated by the Constitution. We find no constitutional basis for holding that the speedy trial right can be quantified into a specified number of days or months. The States, of course, are free to prescribe a reasonable period consistent with constitutional standards, but our approach must be less precise.

The second suggested alternative would restrict consideration of the right to those cases in which the accused has demanded a speedy trial. Most States have recognized what is loosely referred to as the "demand rule," although eight States reject it. It is not clear, however, precisely what is meant by that term. Although every federal court of appeals that has considered the question has endorsed some kind of demand rule, some have regarded the rule within the concept of waiver, whereas others have viewed it as a factor to be weighed in assessing whether there has been a deprivation of the speedy trial right. We shall refer to the former approach as the demand-waiver doctrine. The demand-waiver doctrine provides that a defendant waives any consideration of his right to speedy trial for any period prior to which he has not demanded a trial. Under this rigid approach, a prior demand is a necessary condition to the consideration of the speedy trial right. . . .

Such an approach, by presuming waiver of a fundamental right from inaction, is inconsistent with this Court's pronouncements on waiver of constitutional rights. The Court has defined waiver as "an intentional relinquishment or abandonment of a known right or privilege." . . . Courts should "indulge every reasonable presumption against waiver" . . . and they should "not presume acquiescence in the loss of fundamental rights." . . . In Carnley v. Cochran, 369 U.S. 506 (1962), we held: "Presuming waiver from a silent record is impermissible. The record must show, or there must be an allegation and evidence which show, that an accused was offered counsel but intelligently and understandably rejected the offer. Anything less is not waiver." . . .

In excepting the right to speedy trial from the rule of waiver we have applied to other fundamental rights, courts that have applied the demand-waiver rule have relied on the assumption that delay usually works for the benefit of the accused and on the absence of any readily ascertainable time in the criminal process for a defendant to be given the choice of exercising or waiving his right. But it is not necessarily true that delay benefits the defendant. There are cases in which delay appreciably harms the defendant's ability to defend himself. Moreover, a defendant confined to jail prior to trial is obviously disadvantaged by delay as is a defendant released on bail but unable to lead a normal life because of community suspicion and his own anxiety.

The nature of the speedy trial right does make it impossible to pinpoint a precise time in the process when the right must be asserted or waived, but that fact does not argue for placing the burden of protecting the right solely on defendants. A defendant has no duty to bring himself to trial; the State has that duty as well as the duty of insuring that the trial is consistent with due process. Moreover, for the reasons earlier expressed, society has a particular interest in bringing swift prosecutions, and society's representatives are the ones who should protect that interest.

It is also noteworthy that such a rigid view of the demand-waiver rule places defense counsel in an awkward position. Unless he demands a trial early and often, he is in danger of frustrating his client's right. If counsel is willing to tolerate some delay because he finds it reasonable and helpful in preparing his own case, he may be unable to obtain a speedy trial for his client at the end of that time. Since under the demand-waiver rule no time runs until the demand is made, the government will have whatever time is otherwise reasonable to bring the defendant to trial after a demand has been made. Thus, if the first demand is made three months after arrest in a jurisdiction which prescribes a six-month rule, the prosecution will have a total of nine months—which may be wholly unreasonable under the circumstances. The result in practice is likely to be either an automatic, pro forma demand made immediately after appointment of counsel or delays which, but for the demand-waiver rule, would not be tolerated. Such a result is not consistent with the interests of defendants, society, or the Constitution. We reject,

therefore, the rule that a defendant who fails to demand a speedy trial forever waives his right. This does not mean, however, that the defendant has no responsibility to assert his right. We think the better rule is that the defendant's assertion of or failure to assert his right to a speedy trial is one of the factors to be considered in an inquiry into the deprivation of the right. Such a formulation avoids the rigidities of the demand-waiver rule and the resulting possible unfairness in its application. It allows the trial court to exercise a judicial discretion based on the circumstances including due consideration of any applicable formal procedural rule. It would permit, for example, a court to attach a different weight to a situation in which the defendant knowingly fails to object from a situation in which his attorney acquiesces in long delay without adequately informing his client, or from a situation in which no counsel is appointed. It would also allow a court to weigh the frequency and force of the objections as opposed to attaching significant weight to a purely pro forma objection.

In ruling that a defendant has some responsibility to assert a speedy trial claim, we do not depart from our holdings in other cases concerning the waiver of fundamental rights, in which we have placed the entire responsibility on the prosecution to show that the claimed waiver was knowingly and voluntarily made. Such cases have involved rights which must be exercised or waived at a specific time or under clearly identifiable circumstances, such as the rights to plead not guilty, to demand a jury trial, to exercise the privilege against self-incrimination, and to have the assistance of counsel. We have shown above that the right to a speedy trial is unique in its uncertainty as to when and under what circumstances it must be asserted or may be deemed waived. But the rule we announce today, which comports with constitutional principles, places the primary burden on the courts and the prosecutors to assure that cases are brought to trial. We hardly need add that if delay is attributable to the defendant, then his waiver may be given effect under standard waiver doctrine, the demand rule aside.

We, therefore, reject both of the inflexible approaches—the fixed-time period because it goes further than the Constitution requires; the demand-waiver rule because it is insensitive to a right which we have deemed fundamental. The approach we accept is a balancing test, in which the conduct of both the prosecution and the defendant are weighed.

IV

A balance test necessarily compels courts to approach speedy trial cases on an ad hoc basis. We can do little more than identify some of the factors which courts should assess in determining whether a particular defendant has been deprived of his right. Though some might express them in different ways, we identify four such factors: Length of delay, the reason for the delay, the defendant's assertion of his right, and prejudice to the defendant.

The length of the delay is to some extent a triggering mechanism. Until there is some delay which is presumptively prejudicial, there is no necessity for inquiry into the other factors that go into the balance. Nevertheless, because of the imprecision of the right to speedy trial, the length of delay that will provoke such an inquiry is necessarily dependent upon the peculiar circumstances of the case. To take but one example, ·the delay that can be tolerated for an ordinary street crime is considerably less than for a serious, complex conspiracy charge.

Closely related to length of delay is the reason the government assigns to justify the delay. Here, too, different weights should be assigned to different reasons. A deliberate attempt to delay the trial in order to hamper the defense should be weighed heavily against the government. A more neutral reason such as negligence or overcrowded courts should be weighed less heavily but nevertheless should be considered since the ultimate responsibility for such circumstances must rest with the government rather than with the defendant. Finally, a valid reason, such as a missing witness, should serve to justify appropriate delay.

We have already discussed the third factor, the defendant's responsibility to assert his right. Whether and how a defendant asserts his right is closely related to the other factors we have mentioned. The strength of his efforts will be affected by the length of the delay, to some extent by the reason for the delay, and most particularly by the personal prejudice, which is not always readily iden-

tifiable, that he experiences. The more serious the deprivation, the more likely a defendant is to complain. The defendant's assertion of his speedy trial right, then, is entitled to strong evidentiary weight in determining whether the defendant is being deprived of the right. We emphasize that failure to assert the right will make it difficult for a defendant to prove that he was denied a speedy trial.

A fourth factor is prejudice to the defendant. Prejudice, of course, should be assessed in the light of the interests of defendants which the speedy trial right was designed to protect. This Court has identified three such interests: (i) to prevent oppressive pretrial incarceration; (ii) to minimize anxiety and concern of the accused; and (iii) to limit the possibility that the defense will be impaired. Of these, the most serious is the last, because the inability of a defendant adequately to prepare his case skews the fairness of the entire system. If witnesses die or disappear during a delay, the prejudice is obvious. There is also prejudice if defense witnesses are unable to recall accurately events of the distant past. Loss of memory, however, is not always reflected in the record because what has been forgotten can rarely be shown.

We have discussed previously the societal disadvantages of lengthy pretrial incarceration, but obviously the disadvantages for the accused who cannot obtain his release are even more serious. The time spent in jail awaiting trial has a detrimental impact on the individual. It often means loss of a job; it disrupts family life; and it enforces idleness. Most jails offer little or no recreation or rehabilitative programs. The time spent in jail is simply dead time. Moreover, if a defendant is locked up, he is hindered in his ability to gather evidence, contact witnesses, or otherwise prepare his defense. Imposing those consequences on anyone who has not yet been convicted is serious. It is especially unfortunate to impose them on those persons who are ultimately found to be innocent. Finally, even if àn accused is not incarcerated prior to trial, he is still disadvantaged by restraints on his liberty and by living under a cloud of anxiety, suspicion, and often hostility.

We regard none of the four factors identified above as either a necessary or sufficient condition to the finding of a deprivation of the right of speedy trial. Rather, they are related factors and must be considered together with such other circumstances as may be relevant. In sum, these factors have no talismanic qualities; courts must still engage in a difficult and sensitive balancing process. But, because we are dealing with a fundamental right of the accused, this process must be carried out with full recognition that the accused's interest in a speedy trial is specifically affirmed in the Constitution.

V

The difficulty of the task of balancing these factors is illustrated by this case, which we consider to be close. It is clear that the length of delay between arrest and trial—well over five years—was extraordinary. Only seven months of that period can be attributed to a strong excuse, the illness of the ex-sheriff who was in charge of the investigation. Perhaps some delay would have been permissible under ordinary circumstances, so that Manning could be utilized as a witness in Barker's trial, but more than four years was too long a period, particularly since a good part of that period was attributable to the Commonwealth's failure or inability to try Manning under circumstances that comported with due process.

Two counterbalancing factors, however, outweigh these deficiencies. The first is that prejudice was minimal. Of course, Barker was prejudiced to some extent by living for over four years under a cloud of suspicion and anxiety. Moreover, although he was released on bond for most of the period, he did spend 10 months in jail before trial. But there is no claim that any of Barker's witnesses died or otherwise became unavailable owing to the delay. The trial transcript indicates only two very minor lapses of memory—one on the part of a prosecution witness—which were in no way significant to the outcome.

More important than the absence of serious prejudice, is the fact that Barker did not want a speedy trial. Counsel was appointed for Barker immediately after his indictment and represented him throughout the period. No question is raised as to the competency of such counsel. Despite the fact that counsel had notice of the motions for continuances, the record shows no action whatever taken between October 21, 1958,

and February 12, 1962, that could be construed as the assertion of the speedy trial right. On the latter date, in response to another motion for continuance, Barker moved to dismiss the indictment. The record does not show on what ground this motion was based, although it is clear that no alternative motion was made for an immediate trial. Instead the record strongly suggests that while he hoped to take advantage of the delay in which he had acquiesced, and thereby obtain a dismissal of the charges, he definitely did not want to be tried. Counsel conceded as much at oral argument:

"Your honor, I would concede that Willie Mae Barker probably—I don't know this for a fact—probably did not want to be tried. I don't think any man wants to be tried. And I don't consider this a liability on his behalf. I don't blame him."

The probable reason for Barker's attitude was that he was gambling on Manning's acquittal. The evidence was not very strong against Manning, as the reversals and hung juries suggest, and Barker undoubtedly thought that if Manning were acquitted, he would never be tried. Counsel also conceded this. . . .

That Barker was gambling on Mannings' acquittal is also suggested by his failure, following the pro forma motion to dismiss filed in February 1962, to object to the Commonwealth's next two motions for continuances. Indeed, it was not until March 1963, after Manning's convictions were final, that Barker, having lost his gamble, began to object to further continuances. At that time, the Commonwealth's excuse was the illness of the ex-sheriff, which Barker has conceded justified the further delay.

We do not hold that there may never be a situation in which an indictment may be dismissed on speedy trial grounds where the defendant has failed to object to continuances. There may be a situation in which the defendant was represented by incompetent counsel, was severely prejudiced, or even cases in which the continuances were granted ex parte. But barring extraordinary circumstances, we would be reluctant indeed to rule that a defendant was denied this constitutional right on a record that strongly indicates, as does this one, that the defendant did not want a speedy trial. We hold, therefore, that Barker was not deprived of his due process right to a speedy trial.

The judgment of the Court of Appeals is Affirmed.

[Mr. Justice WHITE, with whom Mr. Justice BRENNAN joined, wrote a concurring opinion.]

Comments

1. The Sixth Amendment right to a speedy trial is applicable only to criminal prosecutions, not to civil proceedings. It was not made applicable to the states until 1967 in *Klopfer* v. *North Carolina*, 386 U.S. 213. In most of the "speedy trial" cases decided by the Supreme Court, the prosecuting officials had used unconscionable delaying tactics. In *Smith* v. *Hooey*, 393 U.S. 379 (1969), the State of Texas refused for six years to bring the defendant to trial on a theft charge even though he made repeated requests that they do so. The United States Supreme Court held that a state has a constitutional duty to try a defendant who has repeatedly demanded that he be brought to trial. The Court further held that the right to a speedy trial cannot be abated simply because the requesting defendant is serving a sentence in another jurisdiction (e.g., a defendant who is serving a federal prison sentence while under state indictment). In *Dickey* v. *Florida*, 398 U.S. 30 (1970), the Court reversed a conviction for armed robbery where the state gave no valid reason for delaying the defendant's trial for seven years, which resulted in actual prejudice to his case since two of his potential witnesses died in the meantime.

   In *United States* v. *Marion* supra, the Court noted that the Sixth Amendment right to a speedy trial is not applicable until the "putative defendant" has become an "accused," and thus it is inapplicable to preindictment delays. However, if a preindictment delay causes substantial prejudice to the defense (e.g., loss of alibi witnesses), the indictment *may* be dismissed on the ground of denial of due process (not denial of a speedy trial). Thus, a defendant must first become an "accused" (usually by being arrested or indicted) before the Sixth Amendment speedy trial guarantee comes into play.

   The degree of prejudice to the defendant's case is only one factor to be considered in deciding whether a delay violated the Sixth Amendment. Suppose a defendant has been the cause of a lengthy preindictment delay (e.g., refused to cooperate with the grand jury). Can he ever successfully argue that the delay caused a substantial prejudice to his defense necessitating a dismissal of the indictment?

2. In *United States* v. *Lovasco,* supra, the Court held that to prosecute a defendant following a good-faith delay for a preindictment investigation is not necessarily a denial of due process, even if the defense is somewhat predjudiced thereby; the reasons for the delay must be considered. Could a defendant ever prove that a lengthy preindictment investigation was not done in good faith? How much prejudice to a defendant's defense is required under *Lovasco?*

3. In *Barker* v. *Wingo,* supra, the Court wisely refused to quantify the right to a speedy trial by limiting allowable delays to a specific number of days or months. Whether a defendant has been denied a

speedy trial is decided by a "balancing test" in which the interests and conduct of the defendant are weighed against those of the prosecution. The *Barker* Court identified four factors to be considered in assessing whether a particular defendant was denied a speedy trial in violation of the Sixth Amendment: (1) the length of the delay; (2) the prosecution's reasons for the delay; (3) the defendant's assertion of the right; and (4) the degree of prejudice to the defendant caused by the delay. The length of the delay is dependent upon the particular circumstances of each case (e.g., a complex conspiracy case would justify a longer delay than would an ordinary street crime). A purposeful delay by the prosecution in an attempt to handicap the defense would weigh heavily in favor of the defendant, whereas a more neutral reason (e.g., crowded court docket) would weigh less heavily. Although it is not absolutely necessary that a defendant assert his right to a speedy trial, his failure to do so will usually count strongly against him. The *Barker* Court indicated further that the degree of prejudice to the defendant caused by the delay should be assessed in light of the interests that the speedy trial right is designed to protect; which are (1) to prevent oppressive pretrial incarceration, (2) to minimize the anxiety and hardship of the defendant, and (3) to avoid hampering the defense. The greatest weight is to be assigned to the latter category since an unusually lengthy delay can result in a denial of a fair trial in violation of the Due Process Clauses of the Fifth and Fourteenth Amendments.

4. Suppose a defendant becomes an "accused" but is not brought to trial for several years. Must he affirmatively prove that the delay caused actual prejudice to his defense in order to successfully argue that his Sixth Amendment right to a speedy trial was violated? In *Marion,* supra, the Court held that such a showing of *actual prejudice* due to delay between arrest and trial is not required; such a showing is neither a necessary nor a sufficient condition for a finding of a denial of a speedy trial. More recently, in *Dillingham* v. *United States,* 423 U.S. 64 (1975), the Court held that a showing of actual prejudice to a defendant from delay between arrest and indictment is likewise not required for showing a violation of the Sixth Amendment right to a speedy trial.

5. In *Jackson* v. *Indiana,* 406 U.S. 715 (1972), the Court held that indefinite commitment of a defendant solely on the ground that he is incompetent to stand trial violates the Due Process Clause of the Fourteenth Amendment. The *Jackson* Court held that a criminal defendant cannot be incarcerated for more than the period of time necessary to determine whether there is a substantial probability that he will become competent to stand trial in the foreseeable future. If it is determined that the defendant is not likely to become competent, the state must either institute civil proceedings for indefinite commitment or release the defendant. Although the *Jackson* Court did not decide the case on Sixth Amendment speedy trial grounds (since Jackson's counsel did not raise the issue), the Court noted that such an argument might be available to an incompetent accused who will never have an opportunity to prove his innocence.

6. The Supreme Court has ruled on other aspects of the right to a speedy trial. In *Strunk* v. *United States,* 412 U.S. 434 (1973), the

Court held that if a defendant has been denied a speedy trial, "the only possible remedy" is for the charges to be dismissed. The Court ruled in *Levine* v. *United States*, 362 U.S. 610 (1960), that a charge of contempt (civil or criminal) is not a "criminal prosecution" for the purposes of the Sixth Amendment, thus removing it from the speedy trial requirement. In *United States* v. *Ewell*, 383 U.S. 116 (1960), the Court held that the right to a speedy trial is not applicable to delays in the appellate process. Given that a denial of a speedy trial requires a dismissal of the charges entirely and bars all further prosecution for the same offense, how likely is it that appellate courts will reverse convictions on that ground? Suppose there is an excessive delay between a verdict of guilty and sentencing—is that a denial of a speedy trial?

7. The Congress has passed into law the Speedy Trial Act of 1974 (18 U.S.C. §§ 3161–3174), which governs federal trials. The provisions of this act, which take effect over a five-year period, impose gradually declining time limits for the periods between arrest and indictment, indictment and arraignment, and arraignment and trial. By 1979, a federal defendant who has not gone to trial within 100 days following his arrest will be able to move for a dismissal of the charges.

8. The following are some recent decisions by lower federal and state courts involving speedy trials and postindictment delays: *United States* v. *Lara*, 520 F.2d 460 (D.C. Cir. 1975) (19-month delay caused by government's effort to obtain a trial in a more favorable court requires dismissal of indictment); *United States* v. *Sarvis*, 523 F.2d 1177 (D.C. Cir. 1975) (no denial of right to speedy trial when delay of 3 years and 10 months between robbery defendant's arrest and his second trial following a reversal of his first conviction was caused by "neutral reasons"); *Singletary* v. *State*, 322 So.2d 551 (Fla. 1975) (service of summons upon defendant who is never actually arrested is the equivalent of an arrest for speedy trial purposes); *Commonwealth* v. *Burhoe*, 337 N.E.2d 913 (Mass. App. 1975) (defendant who wasn't tried until 38 months after his indictment held not denied speedy trial when 11 months of delay caused by clerical error but remainder caused by defendant); *State* v. *Dieffenbach*, 349 A.2d 581 (N.J. Sup. Ct. 1975) (right to speedy trial is applicable to delays arising from extradition proceedings); *Townsend* v. *Superior Court*, 543 P.2d 581 (Calif. 1975) (defendant's statutory right to be brought to trial within 60 days of indictment can be waived only by counsel); *United States* v. *Yagid*, 528 F.2d 962 (2d Cir. 1976) (district court properly dismissed indictment against defendant who wasn't tried within 90 days of the date when he was granted a new trial); *United States* v. *Clendening*, 526 F.2d 842 (5th Cir. 1976) (31-month postindictment delay held not violative of 90-day speedy trial rule when defendant's requests for continuances caused much of the delay); *People* v. *Imbesi*, 345 N.E.2d 333 (N.Y. Ct. App. 1976) (21-month delay from defendant's arrest until trial held not a denial of speedy trial because priority was given other cases involving defendants incarcerated for longer periods and because defendant was at liberty from arrest until trial and failed to object to the delay); *United States* v. *Tirasso*, 532 F.2d 1298 (9th Cir. 1976) (90-day limit set by 1974 Speedy Trial Act, 18 U.S.C. § 3164 not violated where defendant's failure to file timely motions delayed their pretrial hearings); *Sanford* v. *District*

Court, 551 P.2d 1005 (Mont. 1976) (delay of 10 months between arraignment and trial establishes a prima facie case of denial of right to speedy trial); *United States* v. *Salzmann,* 417 F. Supp. 1139 (E.D.N.Y. 1976) (4-year-old indictment of defendant for failure to appear for a preinduction physical and induction following his move to Israel held to require dismissal when government did not make substantial efforts to obtain his presence); *United States* v. *Clardy,* 540 F.2d 439 (9th Cir. 1976) (when prisoners are accused of assaulting another inmate, the speedy-trial time clock begins to run from the date of their indictment, not from the time when they were "arrested" and placed in solitary confinement); *State* v. *Keller,* 553 P.2d 1013 (Mont. 1976) (under *Barker* v. *Wingo* standards, 11-month delay between arrest and trial requires dismissal of charges); *Turner* v. *State,* 545 S.W.2d 133 (Tex. Crim. App. 1976) (unjustified delay of 27 months between indictment and trial held denial of speedy trial); *United States* v. *Avalos,* 541 F.2d 1100 (5th Cir. 1976) (under standards in *Barker* v. *Wingo,* 15-month delay in trial contributed to by both the government and the defendants not a denial of speedy trial).

Recent cases involving prearrest and preindictment delays include: *United States* v. *Jones,* 527 F.2d 817 (D.C. Cir. 1976) (delay of 13 months between narcotics transaction and seller's arrest held not prejudicial to seller's defense); *United States* v. *Barket,* 530 F.2d 189 (8th Cir. 1976) (47-month preindictment delay held prejudicial and indictment dismissed under *United States* v. *Marion*); *United States* v. *Cowsen,* 530 F.2d 734 (7th Cir. 1976) (4½-month delay between drug sale and arrest held not prejudicial); *United States* v. *Guinn,* 540 F.2d 954 (8th Cir. 1976) (under *United States* v. *Marion,* government's preindictment delay of one year did not substantially prejudice the defense); *State* v. *Jojola,* 553 P.2d 1296 (N. Mex. Ct. App. 1976) (defendant claiming denial of due process because of preindictment delay must show substantial prejudice before he is entitled to a dismissal of his case).

D. THE RIGHT TO CONFRONT WITNESSES

Application to the States

POINTER v. TEXAS

Supreme Court of the United States, 1965
380 U.S. 400, 85 S. Ct. 1065, 13 L. Ed. 2d 923

Robert Pointer and one Dillard were arrested in Texas for robbery and taken before a state judge for a preliminary hearing. At the hearing, the chief witness for the prosecution was one Phillips, who gave his version of the robbery in detail, identifying Pointer as the man who had robbed him at gunpoint. Neither of the defendants was represented by counsel. Dillard tried to cross-examine Phillips, but Pointer did not. Pointer was subsequently indicted on a charge of robbery. At some time prior to the trial, Phillips moved to California. At Pointer's robbery trial, the prosecution introduced, over the defendant's objections, the transcript of Phillips'

testimony given at the preliminary hearing. The defendant objected to the use of Phillips' prior testimony on the ground that it was a denial of his right to confront witnesses against him. The objections were overruled and Pointer was convicted. The Texas Court of Criminal Appeals affirmed, and the United States Supreme Court granted certiorari.

Mr. Justice BLACK delivered the opinion of the Court.

The Sixth Amendment provides in part that:

"In all criminal prosecutions, the accused shall enjoy the right ... to be confronted with the witnesses against him ... and to have the Assistance of Counsel for his defense."

Two years ago in Gideon v. Wainwright, 372 U.S. 335 (1963), ... we held that the Fourteenth Amendment makes the Sixth Amendment's guarantee of right to counsel obligatory upon the States. The question we find necessary to decide in this case is whether the Amendment's guarantee of a defendant's right "to be confronted with the witnesses against him," which has been held to include the right to cross-examine those witnesses, is also made applicable to the States by the Fourteenth Amendment.

* * *

In this Court we do not find it necessary to decide one aspect of the question petitioner raises, that is, whether failure to appoint counsel to represent him at the preliminary hearing unconstitutionally denied him the assistance of counsel. ... The objections and arguments in the trial court as well as the arguments in the Court of Criminal Appeals and before us make it clear that petitioner's objection is based not so much on the fact that he had no lawyer when Phillips made his statement at the preliminary hearing, as on the fact that use of the transcript of that statement at the trial denied petitioner any opportunity to have the benefit of counsel's cross-examination of the principal witness against him. It is that latter question which we decide here.

I

The Sixth Amendment is a part of what is called our Bill of Rights. In Gideon v. Wainwright, supra, in which this Court held that the Sixth Amendment's right to the assistance of counsel is obligatory upon the

States, we did so on the ground that "a provision of the Bill of Rights which is 'fundamental and essential to a fair trial' is made obligatory upon the States by the Fourteenth Amendment." ... We hold today that the Sixth Amendment's right of an accused to confront the witnesses against him is likewise a fundamental right and is made obligatory on the States by the Fourteenth Amendment.

It cannot seriously be doubted at this late date that the right of cross-examination is included in the right of an accused in a criminal case to confront the witnesses against him. And probably no one, certainly no one experienced in the trial of lawsuits, would deny the value of cross-examination in exposing falsehood and bringing out the truth in the trial of a criminal case. ... The fact that this right appears in the Sixth Amendment of our Bill of Rights reflects the belief of the Framers of those liberties and safeguards that confrontation was a fundamental right essential to a fair trial in a criminal prosecution. Moreover, the decisions of this Court and other courts throughout the years have constantly emphasized the necessity for cross-examination as a protection for defendants in criminal cases. ...

There are few subjects, perhaps, upon which this Court and other courts have been more nearly unanimous than in their expressions of belief that the right of confrontation and cross-examination is an essential and fundamental requirement for the kind of fair trial which is this country's constitutional goal. Indeed, we have expressly declared that to deprive an accused of the right to cross-examine the witnesses against him is a denial of the Fourteenth Amendment's guarantee of due process of law. ...

... Since Gideon v. Wainwright, it no longer can broadly be said that the Sixth Amendment does not apply to state courts. And as this Court said in Malloy v. Hogan, 378 U.S. 1 (1964), "The Court has not hesitated to re-examine past decisions according the Fourteenth Amendment a less central role in the preservation of basic liberties than that which was contemplated by its Framers when they added the Amendment to our constitutional scheme." ... In the light of Gideon, Malloy, and other cases cited in those opinions holding various provisions of the Bill of Rights applicable to the States by virtue of the Fourteenth Amendment, the statements made in ... similar cases generally declaring that the Sixth Amendment does not apply to the States can no longer be regarded as the law. We hold that petitioner was entitled to be tried in accordance with the protection of the confrontation guarantee of the Sixth Amendment, and that that guarantee, like the right against compelled self-incrimination, is "to be enforced against the States under the Fourteenth Amendment according to the same standards that protect those personal rights against federal encroachment." ...

II

Under this Court's prior decisions, the Sixth Amendment's guarantee of confrontation and cross-examination was unquestionably denied petitioner in this case. As has been pointed out, a major reason underlying the constitutional confrontation rule is to give a defendant charged with crime an opportunity to cross-examine the witness against him. ... This Court has recognized the admissibility against an accused of dying declarations ... and of testimony of a deceased witness who has testified at a former trial. ... Nothing we hold here is to the contrary. The case before us would be quite a different one had Phillips' statement been taken at a full-fledged hearing at which petitioner had been represented by counsel who had been given a complete and adequate opportunity to cross-examine. ... There are other analogous situations which might not fall within the scope of the constitutional rule requiring confrontation of witnesses. The case before us, however, does not present any situation like those mentioned above or others analogous to them. Because the transcript of Phillips' statement offered against petitioner at his trial had not been taken at a time and under circumstances affording petitioner through counsel an adequate opportunity to cross-examine Phillips, its introduction in a federal court in a criminal case against Pointer would have amounted to denial of the privilege of confrontation

guaranteed by the Sixth Amendment. Since we hold that the right of an accused to be confronted with the witnesses against him must be determined by the same standards whether the right is denied in a federal or state proceeding, it follows that use of the transcript to convict petitioner denied him a constitutional right, and that his conviction must be reversed.

Reversed and remanded.

Mr. Justice HARLAN, concurring in the result.

I agree that in the circumstances the admission of the statement in question deprived the petitioner of a right of "confrontation" assured by the Fourteenth Amendment. I cannot subscribe, however, to the constitutional reasoning of the Court.

* * *

For me this state judgment must be reversed because a right of confrontation is "implicit in the concept of ordered liberty," Palko v. Connecticut, 302 U.S. 319 (1937), reflected in the Due Process Clause of the Fourteenth Amendment independently of the Sixth.

* * *

... The "incorporation" doctrines, whether full blown or selective, are both historically and constitutionally unsound and incompatible with the maintenance of our federal system on even course.

Mr. Justice STEWART, concurring in the result.

I join in the judgment reversing this conviction, for the reason that the petitioner was denied the opportunity to cross-examine, through counsel, the chief witness for the prosecution. But I do not join in the Court's pronouncement which makes "the Sixth Amendment's right of an accused to confront the witnesses against him ... obligatory on the States." That questionable tour de force seems to me entirely unnecessary to the decision of this case, which I think is directly controlled by the Fourteenth Amendment's guarantee that no State shall "deprive any person of life, liberty, or property, without due process of law."

* * *

Mr. Justice GOLDBERG, concurring.

I agree with the holding of the Court that "the Sixth Amendment's right of an accused to confront the witnesses against him is . . . a fundamental right and is made obligatory on the States by the Fourteenth Amendment." I therefore join in the opinion and judgment of the Court. . . .

* * *

I adhere to and support the process of absorption by means of which the Court holds that certain fundamental guarantees of the Bill of Rights are made obligatory on the States through the Fourteenth Amendment. Although, as this illustrates, there are differences among members of the Court as to the theory by which the Fourteenth Amendment protects the fundamental liberties of individual citizens, it is noteworthy that there is a large area of agreement, both here and in other cases, that certain basic rights are fundamental — not to be denied the individual by either the state or federal government under the Constitution. . . .

The Disruptive Defendant

ILLINOIS v. ALLEN

Supreme Court of the United States, 1970
397 U.S. 337, 90 S. Ct. 1057, 25 L. Ed. 2d 353

The facts are stated in the opinion.

Mr. Justice BLACK delivered the opinion of the Court.

The Confrontation Clause of the Sixth Amendment to the United States Constitution provides that: "In all criminal prosecutions, the accused shall enjoy the right . . . to be confronted with the witnesses against him. . . ." We have held that the Fourteenth Amendment makes the guarantees of this clause obligatory upon the States. Pointer v. Texas, 380 U.S. 400 (1965). One of the most basic of the rights guaranteed by the Confrontation Clause is the accused's right to be present in the courtroom at every stage of his trial. . . . The question presented in this case is whether an accused can claim the benefit of this constitutional right to remain in the courtroom while at the same time he engages in speech and conduct which is so noisy, disorderly, and disruptive that it is exceedingly difficult or wholly impossible to carry on the trial.

The issue arose in the following way. The respondent, Allen, was convicted by an Illinois jury of armed robbery and was sentenced to serve 10 to 30 years in the Illinois State Penitentiary. The evidence against him showed that on August 12, 1956, he entered a tavern in Illinois and, after ordering a drink, took $200 from the bartender at gunpoint. The Supreme Court of Illinois affirmed his conviction . . . and this Court denied certiorari. . . . Later Allen filed a petition for a writ of habeas corpus in federal court alleging that he had been wrongfully deprived by the Illinois trial judge of his constitutional right to remain present throughout his trial. Finding no constitutional violation, the District Court declined to issue the writ. The Court of Appeals reversed, 413 F.2d 323 (1969), Judge Hastings dissenting.

The facts surrounding Allen's expulsion from the courtroom are set out in the Court of Appeals' opinion sustaining Allen's contention:

"After his indictment and during the pretrial stage, the petitioner [Allen] refused court-appointed counsel and indicated to the trial court on several occasions that he wished to conduct his own defense. After considerable argument by the petitioner, the trial judge told him, 'I'll let you be your own lawyer, but I'll ask Mr. Kelly [court-appointed counsel] [to] sit in and protect the record for you, insofar as possible.'

"The trial began on September 9, 1957. After the State's Attorney had accepted the first four jurors following their voir dire examination, the petitioner began examining the first juror and continued at great length. Finally, the trial judge interrupted the petitioner, requesting him to confine his questions solely to matters relating to the prospective juror's qualifications. At that point, the petitioner started to argue with the judge in a most abusive and disrespectful manner. At last, and seemingly in desperation, the judge asked appointed counsel to proceed with the examination of the jurors. The petitioner continued to talk, proclaiming that the appointed attorney was not going to act as his lawyer. He terminated his remarks by saying, 'When I go out for lunchtime, you're [the judge] going to be a corpse here.' At that point he tore the file which his attorney had and threw the papers on the floor. The judge thereupon stated to the petitioner, 'One more outbreak of that sort and I'll remove you from the courtroom.' This warning had no effect on the petitioner. He continued to talk back to the judge, saying, 'There's not going to be no trial, either. I'm going to sit here and you're going to talk and you can bring your shackles out and straight jacket and put them on me and tape my mouth, but it will do no good because there's not going to be no trial.' After more abusive remarks by the petitioner, the trial judge ordered the trial to proceed in the petitioner's absence. The petitioner was removed from the courtroom. The voir dire examination then continued and the jury was selected in the absence of the petitioner.

"After a noon recess and before the jury was brought into the courtroom, the petitioner, appearing before the judge, complained about the fairness of the trial and his appointed attorney. He also said he wanted to be present in the court during his trial. In reply, the judge said that the petitioner would be permitted to remain in the courtroom if he 'behaved [himself] and [did] not interfere with the introduction of the case.' The jury was brought in and seated. Counsel for the petitioner then moved to exclude the witnesses from the courtroom. The [petitioner] protested this effort on the part of his

attorney, saying: 'There is going to be no proceeding. I'm going to start talking and I'm going to keep on talking all through the trial. There's not going to be no trial like this. I want my sister and my friends here in court to testify for me.' The trial judge thereupon ordered the petitioner removed from the courtroom." . . .

After this second removal, Allen remained out of the courtroom during the presentation of the State's case-in-chief, except that he was brought in on several occasions for purposes of identification. During one of these latter appearances, Allen responded to one of the judge's questions with vile and abusive language. After the prosecution's case had been presented, the trial judge reiterated his promise to Allen that he could return to the courtroom whenever he agreed to conduct himself properly. Allen gave some assurances of proper conduct and was permitted to be present through the remainder of the trial, principally his defense, which was conducted by his appointed counsel.

* * *

The Court of Appeals felt that the defendant's Sixth Amendment right to be present at his own trial was so "absolute" that, no matter how unruly or disruptive the defendant's conduct might be, he could never be held to have lost that right so long as he continued to insist upon it, as Allen clearly did. Therefore the Court of Appeals concluded that a trial judge could never expel a defendant from his own trial and that the judge's ultimate remedy when faced with an obstreperous defendant like Allen who determines to make his trial impossible is to bind and gag him. We cannot agree that the Sixth Amendment, the cases upon which the Court of Appeals relied, or any other cases of this Court so handicap a trial judge in conducting a criminal trial. . . . We accept . . . the statement of Mr. Justice Cardozo who, speaking for the Court in Snyder v. Massachusetts, 291 U.S. 97, 106 (1938), said: "No doubt the privilege [of personally confronting witnesses] may be lost by consent or at times even by misconduct." Although mindful that courts must indulge every reasonable presumption against the loss of constitutional rights . . . we explicitly hold today that a defendant can lose his right to be present at trial if, after he has been warned by the judge that he will be removed if he continues his disruptive behavior, he nevertheless insists on conducting himself in a manner so disorderly, disruptive, and disrespectful of the court that his trial cannot be carried on with him in the courtroom. Once lost, the right to be present can, of course, be reclaimed as soon as the defendant is willing to conduct himself consistently with the decorum and respect inherent in the concept of courts and judicial proceedings.

It is essential to the proper administration of criminal justice that dignity, order, and decorum be the hallmarks of all court proceedings in our country. The flagrant disregard in the courtroom of elementary standards of proper conduct should not and cannot be tolerated. We believe trial judges confronted with disruptive, contumacious, stubbornly defiant defendants must be given sufficient discretion to meet the circumstances of each case. No one formula for maintaining the appropriate courtroom atmosphere will be best in all situations. We think there are at least three constitutionally permissible ways for a trial judge to handle an obstreperous defendant like Allen: (1) bind and gag him, thereby keeping him present; (2) cite him for contempt; (3) take him out of the courtroom until he promises to conduct himself properly.

I

Trying a defendant for a crime while he sits bound and gagged before the judge and jury would to an extent comply with that part of the Sixth Amendment's purposes that accords the defendant an opportunity to confront the witnesses at the trial. But even to contemplate such a technique, much less see it, arouses a feeling that no person should be tried while shackled and gagged except as a last resort. Not only is it possible that the sight of shackles and gags might have a significant effect on the jury's feelings about the defendant, but the use of this technique is itself something of an affront to the very dignity and decorum of judicial proceedings that the judge is seeking to uphold. Moreover, one of the defendant's primary advantages of being present at the trial, his ability to communicate with his counsel, is greatly reduced when the defendant is in a condition of total physical restraint. It is in part because of these inherent disadvantages and

limitations in this method of dealing with disorderly defendants that we decline to hold with the Court of Appeals that a defendant cannot under any possible circumstances be deprived of his right to be present at trial. However, in some situations which we need not attempt to foresee, binding and gagging might possibly be the fairest and most reasonable way to handle a defendant who acts as Allen did here.

II

In a footnote the Court of Appeals suggested the possible availability of contempt of court as a remedy to make Allen behave in his robbery trial, and it is true that citing or threatening to cite a contumacious defendant for criminal contempt might in itself be sufficient to make a defendant stop interrupting a trial. If so, the problem would be solved easily, and the defendant could remain in the courtroom. Of course, if the defendant is determined to prevent *any* trial, then a court in attempting to try the defendant for contempt is still confronted with the identical dilemma that the Illinois court faced in this case. And criminal contempt has obvious limitations as a sanction when the defendant is charged with a crime so serious that a very severe sentence such as death or life imprisonment is likely to be imposed. In such a case the defendant might not be affected by a mere contempt sentence when he ultimately faces a far more serious sanction. Nevertheless, the contempt remedy should be borne in mind by a judge in the circumstances of this case.

Another aspect of the contempt remedy is the judge's power, when exercised consistently with state and federal law, to imprison an unruly defendant such as Allen for civil contempt and discontinue the trial until such time as the defendant promises to behave himself. This procedure is consistent with the defendant's right to be present at trial, and yet it avoids the serious shortcomings of the use of shackles and gags. It must be recognized, however, that a defendant might conceivably, as a matter of calculated strategy, elect to spend a prolonged period in confinement for contempt in the hope that adverse witnesses might be unavailable after a lapse of time. A court must guard against allowing a defendant to profit from his own wrong in this way.

III

The trial court in this case decided under the circumstances to remove the defendant from the courtroom and to continue his trial in his absence until and unless he promised to conduct himself in a manner befitting an American courtroom. As we said earlier, we find nothing unconstitutional about this procedure. Allen's behavior was clearly of such an extreme and aggravated nature as to justify either his removal from the courtroom or his total physical restraint. Prior to his removal he was repeatedly warned by the trial judge that he would be removed from the courtroom if he persisted in his unruly conduct, and ... the record demonstrates that Allen would not have been at all dissuaded by the trial judge's use of his criminal contempt powers. Allen was constantly informed that he could return to the trial when he would agree to conduct himself in an orderly manner. Under these circumstances we hold that Allen lost his right guaranteed by the Sixth and Fourteenth Amendments to be present throughout his trial.

IV

It is not pleasant to hold that the respondent Allen was properly banished from the court for a part of his own trial. But our courts, palladiums of liberty as they are, cannot be treated disrespectfully with impunity. Nor can the accused be permitted by his disruptive conduct indefinitely to avoid being tried on the charges brought against him. It would degrade our country and our judicial system to permit our courts to be bullied, insulted, and humiliated and their orderly progress thwarted and obstructed by defendants brought before them charged with crimes. As guardians of the public welfare, our state and federal judicial systems strive to administer equal justice to the rich and the poor, the good and the bad, the native and foreign born of every race, nationality, and religion. Being manned by humans, the courts are not perfect and are bound to make some errors. But, if our courts are to remain what the Founders intended, the citadels of justice, their proceedings cannot and must not be infected with the sort of scurrilous, abusive language and conduct paraded before the Illinois trial judge in this case. The record shows that the Illinois judge at all times conducted himself with that dignity, decorum, and patience that befit a judge. Even in holding that the trial judge had erred, the Court of Appeals praised his "commendable patience under severe provocation."

We do not hold that removing this defendant from his own trial was the only way the Illinois judge could have constitutionally solved the problem he had. We do hold, however, that there is nothing whatever in this record to show that the judge did not act completely within his discretion. Deplorable as it is to remove a man from his own trial, even for a short time, we hold that the judge did not commit legal error in doing what he did.

The judgment of the Court of Appeals is Reversed.

[Mr. Justice BRENNAN and Mr. Justice DOUGLAS concurred.]

The *Bruton* Rule

BRUTON v. UNITED STATES

Supreme Court of the United States, 1968
391 U.S. 123, 88 S. Ct. 1620, 20 L. Ed. 2d 476

George Bruton and one Evans were jointly tried in federal district court for armed postal robbery. During the trial, a postal inspector testified that Evans orally confessed to him that Evans and Bruton committed the armed robbery. The trial court instructed the jury that the confession was admissible evidence against Evans, but was inadmissible hearsay against Bruton and must be disregarded in

determining Bruton's guilt or innocence. Both were convicted. The United States Court of Appeals (8th Cir.) reversed Evans' conviction on the ground that his oral confession to the postal inspector should not have been received in evidence against him, but affirmed Bruton's conviction because of the trial court's limiting instructions to the jury. The United States Supreme Court granted certiorari to reconsider its earlier decision in *Delli Paoli* v. *United States*, 352 U.S. 232 (1957), which had approved of the procedures utilized in the instant case.

Mr. Justice BRENNAN delivered the opinion of the Court.

This case presents the question, last considered in Delli Paoli v. United States, 352 U.S. 232 (1957), whether the conviction of a defendant at a joint trial should be set aside although the jury was instructed that a codefendant's confession inculpating the defendant had to be disregarded in determining his guilt or innocence.

* * *

...We hold that, because of the substantial risk that the jury, despite instructions to the contrary, looked to the incriminating extrajudicial statements in determining petitioner's guilt, admission of Evans' confession in this joint trial violated petitioner's right of cross-examination secured by the Confrontation Clause of the Sixth Amendment. We therefore overrule Delli Paoli and reverse.

The basic premise of Delli Paoli was that it is "reasonably possible for the jury to follow" sufficiently clear instructions to disregard the confessor's extrajudicial statement that his codefendant participated with him in committing the crime. ... If it were true that the jury disregarded the reference to the codefendant, no question would arise under the Confrontation Clause, because by hypothesis the case is treated as if the confessor made no statement inculpating the nonconfessor. But since Delli Paoli was decided this Court has effectively repudiated its basic premise. Before discussing this, we pause to observe that in Pointer v. Texas, 380 U.S. 400 (1965), we confirmed "that the right of cross-examination is included in the right of an accused in a criminal case to confront the witnesses against him" secured by the Sixth Amendment ...; "a major reason underlying the constitutional confrontation rule is to give a defendant charged with crime an opportunity to cross-examine the witnesses against him." ...

* * *

...Here Evans' oral confessions were in fact testified to, and were therefore actually in evidence. That testimony was legitimate evidence against Evans and to that extent was properly before the jury during its deliberations. Even greater, then, was the likelihood that the jury would believe Evans made the statements and that they were true—not just the self-incriminating portions but those implicating petitioner as well. Plainly, the introduction of Evans' confession added substantial, perhaps even critical, weight to the Government's case in a form not subject to cross-examination, since Evans did not take the stand. Petitioner thus was denied his constitutional right of confrontation.

Delli Paoli assumed that this encroachment on the right to confrontation could be avoided by the instruction to the jury to disregard the inadmissible hearsay evidence. But, as we have said, that assumption has since been effectively repudiated. True, the repudiation was not in the context of the admission of a confession inculpating a codefendant but in the context of a New York rule which submitted to the jury the question of the voluntariness of the confession itself. Jackson v. Denno, 378 U.S. 368 (1964). Nonetheless the message of Jackson for Delli Paoli was clear. We there held that a defendant is constitutionally entitled at least to have the trial judge first determine whether a confession was made voluntarily before submitting it to the jury for an assessment of its credibility. More specifically, we expressly rejected the proposition that a jury, when determining the confessor's guilt, could be relied on to ignore his confession of guilt should it find the confession involuntary. ...

* * *

In addition to Jackson, our action in 1966 in amending Rule 14 of the Federal Rules of Criminal Procedure also evidences our repudiation of Delli Paoli's basic premise. Rule

14 authorizes a severance where it appears that a defendant might be prejudiced by a joint trial. . . . The Advisory Committee on Rules said in explanation of the amendment:

"A defendant may be prejudiced by the admission in evidence against a co-defendant of a statement or confession made by that co-defendant. This prejudice cannot be dispelled by cross-examination if the co-defendant does not take the stand. Limiting instructions to the jury may not in fact erase the prejudice." . . .

* * *

Not every admission of inadmissible hearsay or other evidence can be considered to be reversible error unavoidable through limiting instructions; instances occur in almost every trial where inadmissible evidence creeps in, usually inadvertently. "A defendant is entitled to a fair trial but not a perfect one." . . . It is not unreasonable to conclude that in many such cases the jury can and will follow the trial judge's instructions to disregard such information. Nevertheless, as was recognized in Jackson v. Denno, there are some contexts in which the risk that the jury will not, or cannot, follow instructions is so great, and the consequences of failure so vital to the defendant, that the practical and human limitations of the jury system cannot be ignored. . . . Such a context is presented here, where the powerfully incriminating extrajudicial statements of a codefendant, who stands accused side-by-side with the defendant, are deliberately spread before the jury in a joint trial. Not only are the incriminations devastating to the defendant but their credibility is inevitably suspect, a fact recognized when accomplices do take the stand and the jury is instructed to weigh their testimony carefully given the recognized motivation to shift blame onto others. The unreliability of such evidence is intolerably compounded when the alleged accomplice, as here, does not testify and cannot be tested by cross-examination. It was against such threats to a fair trial that the Confrontation Clause was directed.

We, of course, acknowledge the impossibility of determining whether in fact the jury did or did not ignore Evans' statement inculpating petitioner in determining petitioner's guilt. . . .

Here the introduction of Evans' confession posed a substantial threat to petitioner's right to confront the witnesses against him, and this is a hazard we cannot ignore. Despite the concededly clear instructions to the jury to disregard Evans' inadmissible hearsay evidence inculpating petitioner, in the context of a joint trial we cannot accept limiting instructions as an adequate substitute for petitioner's constitutional right of cross-examination. The effect is the same as if there had been no instruction at all. . . .

Reversed.

Mr. Justice STEWART, concurring.

* * *

. . . I think it clear that the underlying rationale of the Sixth Amendment's Confrontation Clause precludes reliance upon cautionary instructions when the highly damaging out-of-court statement of a codefendant, who is not subject to cross-examination, is deliberately placed before the jury at a joint trial. A basic premise of the Confrontation Clause, it seems to me, is that certain kinds of hearsay . . . are at once so damaging, so suspect, and yet so difficult to discount, that jurors cannot be trusted to give such evidence the minimal weight it logically deserves, *whatever* instructions the trial judge might give. . . . It is for this very reason that an out-of-court accusation is universally conceded to be constitutionally *inadmissible* against the accused, rather than admissible for the little it may be worth. . . .

Mr. Justice WHITE, with whom Mr. Justice HARLAN joins, dissenting.

Whether or not Evans' confession was inadmissible against him, nothing in that confession which was relevant and material to Bruton's case was admissible against Bruton. As to him it was inadmissible hearsay, a presumptively unreliable out-of-court statement of a nonparty who was not a witness subject to cross-examination. Admitting Evans' confession against Bruton would require a new trial unless the error was harmless.

The trial judge in this case had no different view. He admitted Evans' confession only against Evans, not against Bruton, and carefully instructed the jury to disregard it in determining Bruton's guilt or innocence. Contrary to its ruling just a decade ago in

Delli Paoli v. United States, the Court now holds this instruction insufficient and reverses Bruton's conviction. It would apparently also reverse every other case where a court admits a codefendant's confession implicating a defendant, regardless of cautionary instructions and regardless of the circumstances. I dissent from this excessively rigid rule. There is nothing in this record to suggest that the jury did not follow the trial judge's instructions. There has been no new learning since Delli Paoli indicating that juries are less reliable than they were considered in that case to be. There is nothing in the prior decisions of this Court which supports this new constitutional rule.

* * *

Comments

1. The right of confrontation is essentially a guarantee that a defendant may cross-examine the witnesses of the prosecution. Of course the prosecution likewise has the right to cross-examine witnesses for the defense, including the defendant if he elects to testify. In *California* v. *Green,* 399 U.S. 157 (1970), the Supreme Court stated that the Sixth Amendment Confrontation Clause serves three essential purposes: (1) It insures that the witness will give his statement under oath, thus deterring lying by the threat of a perjury charge; (2) it forces the witness to submit to cross-examination, the "greatest legal machine ever invented for the discovery of the truth"; and (3) it permits the jury to observe the demeanor of the witness which aids them in assessing his credibility. Since *Pointer* v. *Texas,* supra, the Supreme Court has decided more than twenty cases involving the Confrontation Clause.

2. In *Illinois* v. *Allen,* supra, the Court held that there are at least three constitutionally permissible ways in which a trial court may deal with a disruptive defendant during a criminal trial: The court can (1) bind and gag him, thereby allowing him to remain in the courtroom; (2) cite him for contempt; or (3) remove him from the courtroom until he promises to conduct himself properly. The *Allen* Court implied, but did not hold, that the alternative of binding and gagging should be used only as a last resort. Are there any circumstances in which a trial judge would commit reversible error by removing a disruptive defendant from the courtroom rather than allowing him to remain while bound and gagged in full view of the jury? Under what circumstances might binding and gagging be the fairest and most reasonable way to handle a disruptive defendant? Suppose a disruptive defendant wishes to testify on his own behalf but has been removed from the courtroom because he refuses to state that he will conduct himself properly. Is that a denial of his Sixth Amendment right to present his own defense witnesses? Suppose a defendant's counsel has been disruptive and is ordered from the courtroom. Is that necessarily a denial of the defendant's Sixth Amendment right to counsel? Can the trial court order a mistrial over the objections of the defendant and have the defendant retried? See *Illinois* v. *Somerville,* Chapter Six, § 6.02, suggesting that it can if there is a "manifest necessity" for doing so. Does *Allen* absolutely require that a trial court first warn a disruptive defendant about the consequences of his conduct before he orders him removed from the courtroom or bound and gagged? Is the threat of a contempt charge likely to be taken seriously by a disruptive defendant who faces a possible lengthy prison sentence?

3.　One of the more noteworthy decisions involving the Confrontation Clause is *Bruton* v. *United States,* supra. The Court held that a defendant's Sixth Amendment right to confront witnesses is violated if a co-defendant's confession implicates the defendant and the co-defendant does not testify at the trial — even though the jury is instructed that the confession is admissible only against the confessor–co-defendant. This *Bruton* rule is clearly applicable to the joint trial of accomplices even when the prosecution tends to use a confession. However, by joining co-defendants in a single trial, the prosecution may be forced to pay the heavy price of an inadmissible confession if the confessor does not intend to testify and subject himself to cross-examination. In *Harrington* v. *California,* 395 U.S. 250 (1969), the Supreme Court held that a violation of the *Bruton* rule can be harmless error if there is other "overwhelming evidence" of the defendant's guilt. To the same effect is *Schneble* v. *Florida,* 405 U.S. 427 (1972).

In other decisions involving the Confrontation Clause the Supreme Court has held that (1) prior inconsistent statements made by a witness at a preliminary hearing are admissible at a subsequent trial if that witness subjects himself to full cross-examination, even though the defendant did not have an opportunity to cross-examine the witness at the earlier hearing (and such statements are admissible as hearsay evidence) (*California* v. *Green,* 399 U.S. 149 [1970]); (2) an accused's confrontation rights are not violated if he voluntarily absents himself during the course of his trial and the trial continues in his absence (*Taylor* v. *United States,* 414 U.S. 17 [1974]); (3) a witness cannot be deemed "unavailable" to testify at trial so as to allow the prosecution to introduce his prior testimony absent a good faith effort by the prosecution to produce the witness at trial (*Barber* v. *Page,* 390 U.S. 719 [1968]); (4) merely showing that a witness is incarcerated in a federal prison outside the state at the time of trial is not a good faith effort to prove "unavailability" (*Barber* v. *Page,* supra); (5) a showing that a witness is bona fide absent (e.g., moved to another country) is sufficient to prove "unavailability" (*Mancusi* v. *Stubbs,* 408 U.S. 204 [1972]); (6) the *Bruton* rule is not applicable when a co-defendant testifies but denies making a confession (thereby testifying favorably for his accomplice) and the co-defendant's confession is later admitted (*Dutton* v. *Evans,* 400 U.S. 74 [1970]); (7) a state rule allowing the use against a defendant of the statements of a co-defendant made after the commission of a crime (and not in furtherance of the crime) does not violate the Confrontation Clause (*Dutton* v. *Evans,* supra); (8) an accused must be allowed to cross-examine a witness as to any matters which may indicate possible bias by the witness against him (*Davis* v. *Alaska,* 415 U.S. 308 [1974]); (9) a witness for the prosecution must reveal his true identity and address on cross-examination — even though he acted as an informant (*Smith* v. *Illinois,* 390 U.S. 129 [1968]); (10) the Sixth Amendment Confrontation Clause is applicable to juvenile proceedings (*In re Gault,* 387 U.S. 1 [1967] [Chapter Eight, § 8.03]); (11) the Confrontation Clause is not applicable to investigative proceedings (e.g., grand jury hearings) (*Hannah* v. *Larche,* 363 U.S. 420 [1960]); (12) an accused has a Sixth Amendment right to cross-examine all adverse witnesses, whether called by the prosecution or the defense (*Chambers* v. *Mississippi,* 410 U.S. 284 [1973]); (13) an accused at a probation or parole revocation hearing has a right to cross-examine all adverse witnesses (*Gagnon* v. *Scarpelli*, 411 U.S. 778 [1973], and *Morrissey* v. *Brewer*, 408 U.S. 471 [1972]); (14) an inmate at a prison disciplinary hearing does not have a Sixth Amendment right to cross-examine any witnesses (*Wolff* v. *McDonnell*, 418 U.S. 539 [1974]); and (15) a convicted defendant at sentencing does not have a Sixth Amendment right to cross-examine persons who have supplied information to the Court in regard to sentencing (*Williams* v. *New York*, 337 U.S. 241 [1949]).

4. Recent lower federal and state court decisions involving the Confrontation Clause of the Sixth Amendment include *State* v. *DeLawder*, 344 A.2d 446 (Md. Ct. Spec. App. 1975) (*Davis* v. *Alaska*, which held that a defendant should be permitted to cross-examine a prosecution witness about his probationary status as a juvenile delinquent in order to impeach his credibility, held retroactive); *State* v. *Shotley*, 233 N.W.2d 755 (Minn. 1975) (use at trial of an absent witness' testimony given at a preliminary hearing jeopardizes the fairness of the trial unless the evidence of guilt is so strong that the preliminary hearing testimony could not affect the outcome of the trial); *Commonwealth* v. *Jackson*, 344 A.2d 842 (Penn. 1975) (admission of young homicide witness' preliminary hearing testimony after the witness disappeared on the way to the courthouse upheld); *In re Arthur*, 218 S.E.2d 869 (N.C. Ct. App. 1975) (certain hearsay statements are admissible in juvenile proceedings if shown to have "indicia of reliability" even though there might be a technical deprivation of the right to confront witnesses); *Stewart* v. *Cowan*, 528 F.2d 79 (6th Cir. 1976) (police officer's testimony about the results of an FBI ballistics test and anonymous phone tips implicating the defendant held denial of right of confrontation); *State* v. *Hewett*, 545 P.2d 1201 (Wash. 1976) (use of properly authenticated video transcript of a robbery victim's testimony in lieu of his appearance at trial held not a denial of the right of confrontation when the accused was present and had an opportunity to cross-examine the victim); *State* v. *Alford*, 222 S.E.2d 222 (N.C. 1976) (joint trial with co-defendant which effectively denied the accused the right to call the co-defendant as a witness because he would have asserted his right to remain silent held violative of the Confrontation Clause); *Broecker* v. *State*, 342 N.E.2d 886 (Ind. Ct. App. 1976) (defendant can validly waive his right to be present at his own trial and thus waive his right of confrontation if he refuses to appear); *United States* v. *Croucher*, 532 F.2d 1042 (5th Cir. 1976) (defendant charged with conspiracy to smuggle marijuana denied right of confrontation under *Davis* v. *Alaska*, supra, by trial judge's refusal to permit counsel to cross-examine a government informer about his recent troubles with the law); *State* v. *Boast*, 553 P.2d 1322 (Wash. 1976) (admission of prosecution witness' testimony about a conversation in which three men, including defendant, talked in a restaurant about their part in a robbery held no denial of right to confront witnesses as the testimony possessed sufficient "indicia of reliability" and defense counsel was able to cross-examine the prosecution witness); *United States* v. *Garrett*, 542 F.2d 23 (6th Cir. 1976) (trial judge committed reversible error in blocking drug defendant's attempts to cross-examine a police officer about the defendant's refusal to take a urine test that would have determined whether he was using narcotics).

E. THE RIGHT TO DEFENSE WITNESSES

Application to the States

WASHINGTON v. TEXAS

Supreme Court of the United States, 1967
388 U.S. 14, 87 S. Ct. 1920, 18 L. Ed. 2d 1019

Jackie Washington was tried and convicted of murder in a Texas state court. At the trial, the prosecutor's evidence showed that Washington became jealous when his girlfriend began dating another boy, the deceased. Washington and several other youths, including one Charles Fuller, who owned a shotgun, drove over to the girlfriend's house, where she, her family, and the deceased were having supper. Bricks were thrown at the house by some of the boys, and Washington and Fuller were left in front of the house with the shotgun. The deceased rushed out of the house to investigate the disturbance and was fatally wounded by either Washington or Fuller. Both youths were arrested for murder, and Washington was convicted and sentenced to 50 years' imprisonment. At his trial, Washington testified that he had tried unsuccessfully to persuade Fuller to leave before the shooting and that Fuller had shot the deceased. Washington's attempt to offer Fuller's testimony in support of this defense was rejected by the trial court in light of two Texas statutes that provided that persons charged or convicted as co-participants in the same crime could not testify for one another (although co-participants in a crime could both testify for the state). The Texas Court of Criminal Appeals affirmed the conviction, and the United States Supreme Court granted certiorari.

Mr. Chief Justice WARREN delivered the opinion of the Court.

We granted certiorari in this case to determine whether the right of a defendant in a criminal case under the Sixth Amendment to have compulsory process for obtaining witnesses in his favor is applicable to the States through the Fourteenth Amendment, and whether that right was violated by a state procedural statute providing that persons charged as principals, accomplices, or accessories in the same crime cannot be introduced as witnesses for each other.

* * *

We have not previously been called upon to decide whether the right of an accused to have compulsory process for obtaining witnesses in his favor, guaranteed in federal trials by the Sixth Amendment, is so fundamental and essential to a fair trial that it is incorporated in the Due Process Clause of the Fourteenth Amendment. At one time, it was thought that the Sixth Amendment had no application to state criminal trials. That view no longer prevails, and in recent years we have increasingly looked to the specific guarantees of the Sixth Amendment to determine whether a state criminal trial was conducted with due process of law. We have held that due process requires that the accused have the assistance of counsel for his defense, that he be confronted with the witnesses against him, and that he have the right to a speedy and public trial.

The right of an accused to have compulsory process for obtaining witnesses in his favor stands on no lesser footing than the other Sixth Amendment rights that we have previously held applicable to the States....

The right to offer the testimony of witnesses, and to compel their attendance, if necessary, is in plain terms the right to present a defense, the right to present the defendant's version of the facts as well as the prosecution's to the jury so it may decide where the truth lies. Just as an accused has the right to confront the prosecution's witnesses for the purpose of challenging their testimony, he has the right to present his own witnesses to establish a defense. This right is a fundamental element of due process of law.

II

Since the right to compulsory process is applicable in this state proceeding, the question remains whether it was violated in the circumstances of this case. The testimony of Charles Fuller was denied to the defense not because the State refused to compel his attendance, but because a state statute made his testimony inadmissible whether he was present in the courtroom or not. We are thus called upon to decide whether the Sixth Amendment guarantees a defendant the right under any circumstances to put his witnesses on the stand, as well as the right to compel their attendance in court. . . .

* * *

It was thought that if two persons charged with the same crime were allowed to testify on behalf of each other, "each would try to swear the other out of the charge." This rule, as well as the other disqualifications for interest, rested on the unstated premises that the right to present witnesses was subordinate to the court's interest in preventing perjury, and that erroneous decisions were best avoided by preventing the jury from hearing any testimony that might be perjured, even if it were the only testimony available on a crucial issue.

* * *

The rule disqualifying an alleged accomplice from testifying on behalf of the defendant cannot even be defended on the ground that it rationally sets apart a group of persons who are particularly likely to commit perjury. The absurdity of the rule is amply demonstrated by the exceptions that have been made to it. For example, the accused accomplice may be called by the prosecution to testify against the defendant. Common sense would suggest that he often has a greater interest in lying in favor of the prosecution rather than against it, especially if he is still awaiting his own trial or sentencing. To think that criminals will lie to save their fellows but not to obtain favors from the prosecution for themselves is indeed to clothe the criminal class with more nobility than one might expect to find in the public at large. Moreover, under the Texas statutes the accused accomplice is no longer disqualified if he is acquitted at his own trial. Presumably, he would then be free to testify on behalf of his comrade, secure in the knowledge that he could incriminate himself as freely as he liked in his testimony, since he could not again be prosecuted for the same offense. The Texas law leaves him free to testify when he has a great incentive to perjury, and bars his testimony in situations where he has a lesser motive to lie.

We hold that the petitioner in this case was denied his right to have compulsory process for obtaining witnesses in his favor because the State arbitrarily denied him the right to put on the stand a witness who was physically and mentally capable of testifying to events that he had personally observed, and whose testimony would have been relevant and material to the defense. The Framers of the Constitution did not intend to commit the futile act of giving to a defendant the right to secure the attendance of witnesses whose testimony he had no right to use.

Reversed.

When the Trial Judge Intimidates the Sole Defense Witness

WEBB v. TEXAS

Supreme Court of the United States, 1972
409 U.S. 95, 93 S. Ct. 351, 34 L. Ed. 2d 330

Alfred Webb was convicted of burglary in a Texas state court and was sentenced to 12 years' imprisonment. At the trial, and after the prosecution had rested its case, the jury was temporarily excused. During the recess, the defendant called his only witness, Leslie Max Mills, who had a prior criminal record and was then serving a

prison sentence. The trial judge on his own initiative admonished the defense witness that he was not required to testify, that if he lied under oath, the court would personally see that his case went to the grand jury, that he would be convicted of perjury and would probably have to serve more time, and that it would be held against him when he was considered for parole. Defendant's counsel objected to these comments on the ground that the judge was coercing the only defense witness into refusing to testify. After the trial judge rejected counsel's objections, the defense witness refused to testify for any purpose and was excused by the court. The Texas Court of Criminal Appeals affirmed the conviction, and the United States Supreme Court granted certiorari.

PER CURIAM.

* * *

On appeal, the petitioner argued that the judge's conduct indicated a bias against the petitioner and deprived him of due process of law by driving his sole witness off the witness stand. The Court of Criminal Appeals rejected this contention, stating that, while it did not condone the manner of the admonition, the petitioner had made no objection until the admonition was completed, and there was no showing that the witness had been intimidated by the admonition or had refused to testify because of it.

The trial judge gratuitously singled out this one witness for a lengthy admonition on the dangers of perjury. But the judge did not stop at warning the witness of his right to refuse to testify and of the necessity to tell the truth. Instead, the judge implied that he expected Mills to lie, and went on to assure him that if he lied, he would be prosecuted and probably convicted for perjury, that the sentence for that conviction would be added on to his present sentence, and that the result would be to impair his chances for parole. At least some of these threats may have been beyond the power of this judge to carry out. Yet, in light of the great disparity between the posture of the presiding judge and that of a witness in these circumstances, the unnecessarily strong terms used by the judge could well have exerted such duress on the witness' mind as to preclude him from making a free and voluntary choice whether or not to testify.

In Washington v. Texas, 388 U.S. 14, 19 (1967), we stated:

"The right to offer the testimony of witnesses, and to compel their attendance, if necessary, is in plain terms the right to present a defense, the right to present the defendant's version of the facts as well as the prosecution's to the jury so it may decide where the truth lies. Just as an accused has the right to confront the prosecution's witnesses for the purpose of challenging their testimony, he has the right to present his own witnesses to establish a defense. This right is a fundamental element of due process of law."

In the circumstances of this case, we conclude that the judge's threatening remarks, directed alone at the single witness for the defense, effectively drove that witness off the stand, and thus deprived the petitioner of due process of law under the Fourteenth Amendment. The admonition by the Texas Court of Criminal Appeals might well have given the trial judge guidance for future cases, but it did not serve to repair the infringement of the petitioner's due process rights under the Fourteenth Amendment.

Reversed.

Mr. Justice BLACKMUN, with whom Mr. Justice REHNQUIST joins, dissenting.

The facts before us do not, in my opinion, justify the Court's summary disposition. Petitioner Webb (who, on a prior occasion, had been convicted on still another burglary charge) was apprehended by the owner of a lumber business. The owner, armed with his shotgun, had driven to his office at three o'clock in the morning upon the activation of a burglar alarm. When he entered the building, the owner observed a broken window and an assortment of what he regarded as burglary tools on his desk. When men emerged from an adjacent room, a gun fight ensued. Two intruders escaped, but the owner, despite his having been shot twice, succeeded in holding the petitioner at gunpoint until police arrived.

Although the admonition given by the state trial judge to the sole witness proffered by the defense is obviously improper, sufficient facts have not been presented to this Court to demonstrate the depth of prejudice that requires a summary reversal. The admonition might prove far less offensive, and the conduct of the trial judge understandable if, for example, . . . the witness was known to have been called for the purpose of presenting an alibi defense. Against the backdrop of being caught on the premises and of apparently overwhelming evidence of guilt, offset only by a bare allegation of prejudice, I would deny the petition for certiorari and, as the Court so often has done, I would remit the petitioner to the relief available to him by way of a post-conviction proceeding with a full evidentiary hearing.

Jury Instructions and the "Negative Pregnant"

COOL v. UNITED STATES

Supreme Court of the United States, 1972
409 U.S. 100, 93 S. Ct. 354, 34 L. Ed. 2d 335

Marilyn Cool was tried and convicted in a district court of possessing and concealing counterfeit obligations of the United States. At trial, she relied primarily on the testimony of an accomplice, one Robert Voyles, who admitted his own guilt but steadfastly insisted that the defendant had had nothing to do with the crime. The trial court, over the objections of the defendant, instructed the jury that an accomplice's testimony is "open to suspicion," and that unless the jury was convinced that such testimony was true "beyond a reasonable doubt," it should "throw this testimony out." The United States Court of Appeals (7th Cir.) affirmed the conviction, and the United States Supreme Court granted certiorari.

PER CURIAM.

In this case, the court below held in effect that in a criminal trial, the jury may be instructed to ignore defense testimony unless it believes beyond a reasonable doubt that the testimony is true. That holding is fundamentally inconsistent with our prior decisions . . . and must therefore be reversed.

* * *

[T]he trial judge gave the jury a lengthy "accomplice instruction" to be used in evaluating Voyles' testimony. After first defining the word "accomplice" and warning that an accomplice's testimony is "open to suspicion," the judge made the following statement: "However, I charge you that the testimony of an accomplice is competent evidence and it is for you to pass upon the credibility thereof. If the testimony carries conviction and you are convinced it is true beyond a reasonable doubt, the jury should give it the same effect as you would to a witness not in any respect implicated in the alleged crime and you are not only justified, but it is your duty, not to throw this testimony out because it comes from a tainted source."

The clear implication of this instruction was that the jury should disregard Voyles' testimony unless it was "convinced it is true beyond a reasonable doubt." Such an instruction places an improper burden on the defense and allows the jury to convict despite its failure to find guilt beyond a reasonable doubt.

Accomplice instructions have long been in use and have been repeatedly approved. . . . In most instances, they represent no more than a commonsense recognition that an accomplice may have a special interest in testifying, thus casting doubt upon his veracity. . . . But in most of the recorded cases, the instruction has been used when the accomplice turned State's evidence and testified against the defendant. . . . No constitutional problem is posed when the judge instructs a jury to receive the prosecution's accomplice testimony "with care and caution." . . .

But there is an essential difference between instructing a jury on the care with which it should scrutinize certain evidence in determining how much weight to accord it and instructing a jury, as the judge did here, that as a predicate to the consideration of certain evidence, it must find it true beyond a reasonable doubt.

In Washington v. Texas, supra, we held that a criminal defendant has a Sixth Amendment right to present to the jury exculpatory testimony of an accomplice. The instruction given below impermissibly obstructs the exercise of that right by totally excluding relevant evidence unless the jury makes a preliminary determination that it is extremely reliable.

Moreover, the instruction also has the effect of substantially reducing the Government's burden of proof. . . . The Constitution requires proof of guilt beyond a reasonable doubt. It is possible that Voyles' testimony would have created a reasonable doubt in the minds of the jury, but that it was not considered because the testimony itself was not believable beyond a reasonable doubt. By creating an artificial barrier to the consideration of relevant defense testimony putatively credible by a preponderance of the evidence, the trial judge reduced the level of proof necessary for the Government to carry its burden. Indeed, where, as here, the defendant's case rests almost entirely on accomplice testimony, the effect of the judge's instructions is to require the defendant to establish his *innocence* beyond a reasonable doubt.

Because such a requirement is plainly inconsistent with the constitutionally rooted presumption of innocence, the conviction must be reversed.

Mr. Justice REHNQUIST, with whom the CHIEF JUSTICE [BURGER] and Mr. Justice BLACKMUN concur, dissenting.

I believe that the Court's fine-spun parsing of the trial judge's charge to the jury turns the appellate review of this case into the sort of "quest for error". . . .

* * *

The trial court gave 36 separate instructions to the jury, which covered some 52 pages of the transcript in this case. The instruction in question covers two pages, and the Court reverses the conviction on the basis of one sentence in that one instruction. The trial judge repeatedly emphasized to the jury that the Government was obligated to prove guilt beyond a reasonable doubt. Typical is the following statement, which is repeated throughout the instructions in at least half a dozen places:

"The entire burden of proof is upon the Government from the beginning to the end of this trial and the burden of proof never shifts from the Government to the defendants, and the defendants are not bound to prove their innocence, offer any excuse, or explain anything. . . ."

The record before us does not indicate that either counsel so much as mentioned the accomplice instruction in his argument to the jury. Nonetheless, the Court concludes that because the instruction contained a "negative pregnant" that could be taken to mean that the jurors should reject Voyles' testimony if they had a reasonable doubt as to its veracity, the conviction is to be reversed.

I had thought the day long past when even appellate courts of the first instance, such as the Court of Appeals in this case, parsed instructions and engaged in nice semantical distinctions in the absence of any showing that would satisfy an ordinary lawyer or layman that substantial rights of one of the parties had been prejudiced by the supposed error. If the nuance of the instruction upon which reversal is now based did not suggest itself to petitioner's trial counsel, it seems doubtful that it suggested itself to the jury either. . . .

Nor, as pointed out above, did this particular instruction of the trial stand alone; it was incorporated into a series of instructions, that had as their predominant theme that the burden of proof was upon the Government at every stage to prove guilt beyond a reasonable doubt. The trial court's instructions are to be taken as a whole, and even if an isolated passage might be error if standing by itself, that alone is not a sufficient ground for reversal. . . .

The Court's reversal on the ground that one of the instructions contained a "negative pregnant" smacks more of scholastic jurisprudence . . . than it does of [a] commonsense approach to appellate review. . . .

Comments

1. The Compulsory Process Clause of the Sixth Amendment requires that a criminal defendant be afforded an opportunity to present his own defense witnesses. In addition, the Sixth Amendment guarantees the defendant a right to present a defense as well as to testify on his own behalf. As indicated in *Washington* v. *Texas,* supra, the right of compulsory process includes the right of a defendant (and his witnesses) to present his own version of the facts. Suppose a state statute forbids the use of the testimony of an accomplice on behalf of or against a defendant if the accomplice-witness has previously been convicted of perjury. Would such a statute be constitutional under the Compulsory Process Clause and *Washington* v. *Texas*? States have a valid interest in preventing perjury, but any undue interference with the defendant's right to compulsory process by local substantive or procedural laws or by the trial court is a violation of the Sixth Amendment and due process.

    What checks are available to keep defendants from subpoenaing their friends from around the country as potential defense witnesses at governmental expense? If the defendant is indigent, he must first obtain the permission of the trial court to subpoena his defense witnesses and must show that the testimony of the potential defense witnesses would be material to his defense. If the defendant is wealthy, he can subpoena his witnesses from near and far without the court's permission, but at his own expense.

2. In *Webb* v. *Texas,* supra, the trial court was obviously anticipating perjurious testimony by the sole defense witness (Mills) in the form of a false alibi. If the trial court had also admonished all the prosecution witnesses concerning the pains and penalties of perjury, would Webb's Sixth Amendment rights have been violated even though Mills refused to testify? Suppose Mills had testified despite the admonition by the trial court. Suppose Mills had testified but the admonition by the trial court was made in the presence of the jury. Do you agree with the dissenting opinion of Mr. Justice Blackmun (joined by Justice Rehnquist) that the admonition by the trial court amounted to "harmless error" because of the evidence of "overwhelming guilt"?

3. In *Cool* v. *United States,* supra, the Supreme Court reversed the defendant's conviction on the basis of erroneous jury instructions, which the dissenting justices called a "negative pregnant." While "cautionary" instructions are common, the *Cool* Court stated that such instructions cannot imply that the burden of proof can shift from the prosecution to the defense. In *Skidmore* v. *Baltimore & Ohio R. Co.,* 167 F.2d 54, 65 (1948), the United States Court of Appeals (2d Cir.) stated that "erroneous jury instructions are the greatest single source of reversible error." The major purpose of the instructions (charge to the jury) is to explain to the jury what rules of law should be applied to the case. The instructions usually include

discussion of the presumption of innocence, the burden of proof, the elements of the crime(s) charged, how to evaluate the credibility of the witnesses, and what procedures are to be followed while deliberating. The instructions should be given as clear and concise statements of law. However, erroneous instructions must be prejudicial to the defendant in order to constitute reversible error. In determining prejudicial error, appellate courts usually focus on the charge as a whole as opposed to an isolated instruction. Did the majority of the Court in *Cool* examine the charge as a whole?

4. Some recent decisions by lower federal and state courts involving jury instructions include *Wilson* v. *State,* 333 N.E.2d 755 (Ind. 1975) (jury instruction during felony-murder trial that "evidence of a low I.Q. in and of itself is not sufficient to negate responsibility for criminal acts" held not erroneous; *Abney* v. *United States,* ___ F.2d ___ (D.C. Cir. 1975) (jury instruction that a member of one race is less likely to be accurate in identifying a member of another race than a member of his own held improper); *Farris* v. *State,* 535 S.W.2d 608 (Tenn. 1976) (statute requiring trial judges in felony prosecutions to instruct jury about a defendant's parole eligibility struck down); *Russell* v. *Commonwealth,* 223 S.E.2d 877 (Va. 1976) (error for trial court during jury instructions to state that "the unexplained failure of a party to produce a material witness raises a presumption that the testimony of such witness would have been adverse to the party thus failing to produce him"); *People* v. *Atkins,* 243 N.W.2d 292 (Mich. 1976) (special cautionary jury instructions regarding the testimony of drug addicts who also serve as paid government informers not required unless requested); *Roberts* v. *State,* 335 So.2d 285 (Fla. 1976) (trial judge committed reversible error in failing to instruct a rape jury on the consequences of a verdict of not guilty by reason of insanity); *Hoskins* v. *State,* 552 P.2d 342 (Wyo. 1976) (trial judge's giving an Allen "dynamite" charge and commenting on the evidence to a deadlocked jury in the absence of defense counsel held not reversible error); *Harding* v. *Marks,* 541 F.2d 402 (ed Cir. 1976) (trial court erred in belittling rape defendant's claim that he never wore a hat, after the victim and her rescuer described the rapist as wearing a blue knit hat, by remarking during instructions: "Now members of the jury, there was testimony that the defendant never wears a hat except when he's going out to rob a bank, or never wears a hat unless he is going ice skating, or never wears a hat unless he is going out to commit some crime, or whatever. So what significance that has I don't know. You must say."); *People* v. *Carter,* 358 N.E.2d 517 (N.Y. Ct. App. 1976) (trial judge's statement to jurors that "unless and until the court is convinced that there is no possibility whatever of a verdict being arrived at, this jury will stay in session—incommunicado, if you know what that means" held coercive and prejudicial). See also *People* v. *Chaney,* 347 N.E.2d 138 (Ill. 1976) (failure of prosecution to reveal ahead of time that a key defense witness was also the informer whose tip had set up the defendant's encounter with the police held reversible error); *United States* v. *Morrison,* 535 F.2d 233 (3d Cir. 1976) (prosecutor's unsolicited out-of-court warnings to defense witness about the legal risks of testifying held reversible error when the witness subsequently declined to testify as to certain areas vital to the defense).

F. THE RIGHT TO A PUBLIC TRIAL

Application to the States

IN RE OLIVER

Supreme Court of the United States, 1948
330 U.S. 257, 68 S. Ct. 499, 92 L. Ed. 682

The facts are stated in the opinion.

Mr. Justice BLACK delivered the opinion of the Court.

A Michigan circuit judge summarily sent the petitioner to jail for contempt of court. We must determine whether he was denied the procedural due process guaranteed by the Fourteenth Amendment.

In obedience to a subpoena the petitioner appeared as a witness before a Michigan circuit judge who was then conducting, in accordance with Michigan law, a "one-man grand jury" investigation into alleged gambling and official corruption. The investigation presumably took place in the judge's chambers. . . . Two other circuit judges were present in an advisory capacity. A prosecutor may have been present. A stenographer was most likely there. The record does not show what other members, if any, of the judge's investigatorial staff participated in the proceedings. It is certain, however, that the public was excluded—the questioning was secret in accordance with the traditional grand jury method.

After petitioner had given certain testimony, the judge-grand jury, still in secret session, told petitioner that neither he nor his advisors believed petitioner's story—that it did not "jell." This belief of the judge-grand jury was not based entirely on what the petitioner had testified. . . . [I]t rested in part on beliefs or suspicions of the judge-jury derived from the testimony of at least one other witness who had previously given evidence in secret. Petitioner had not been present when that witness testified and so far as appears was not even aware that he had

testified. Based on its beliefs thus formed—that petitioner's story did not "jell"—the judge-grand jury immediately charged him with contempt, immediately convicted him, and immediately sentenced him to sixty days in jail. Under these circumstances of haste and secrecy, petitioner, of course, had no chance to enjoy the benefits of counsel, no chance to prepare his defense, and no opportunity either to cross-examine the other grand jury witness or to summon witnesses to refute the charge against him.

Three days later a lawyer filed on petitioner's behalf in the Michigan Supreme Court the petition for habeas corpus now under consideration. . . .

The Supreme Court of Michigan . . . rejected petitioner's contention that the summary manner in which he had been sentenced to jail in the secrecy of the grand jury chamber had deprived him of his liberty without affording him the kind of notice, opportunity to defend himself, and trial which the due process clause of the Fourteenth Amendment requires. . . . We granted certiorari . . . to consider these procedural due process questions.

* * *

The petitioner does not here challenge the constitutional power of Michigan to grant traditional inquisitorial grand jury power to a single judge, and therefore we do not concern ourselves with that question. . . .

Here we are concerned, not with petitioner's rights as a witness in a secret grand jury session, but with his rights as a defendant in a contempt proceeding. The powers of the judge-grand jury who tried and convicted him in secret and sentenced him to jail on a charge of false and evasive swearing must likewise be measured ... by the constitutional standards applicable to court proceedings in which an accused may be sentenced to fine or imprisonment or both. Thus our first question is this: Can an accused be tried and convicted for contempt of court in grand jury secrecy?

First. Counsel have not cited and we have been unable to find a single instance of a criminal trial conducted in camera in any federal, state, or municipal court during the history of this country. Nor have we found any record of even one such secret criminal trial in England since abolition of the Court of Star Chamber in 1641, and whether that court ever convicted people secretly is in dispute. Summary trials for alleged misconduct called contempt of court have not been regarded as an exception to this universal rule against secret trials. . . .

This nation's accepted practice of guaranteeing a public trial to an accused has its roots in our English common law heritage. The exact date of its origin is obscure, but it likely evolved long before the settlement of our land as an accompaniment of the ancient institution of jury trial. In this country the guarantee to an accused of the right to a public trial first appeared in a state constitution in 1776. Following the ratification in 1791 of the Federal Constitution's Sixth Amendment, which commands that "In all criminal prosecutions, the accused shall enjoy the right to a speedy and public trial. . ." most of the original states and those subsequently admitted to the Union adopted similar constitutional provisions. Today almost without exception every state by constitution, statute, or judicial decision requires that all criminal trials be open to the public.

The traditional Anglo-American distrust for secret trials has been variously ascribed to the notorious use of this practice by the Spanish Inquisition, to the excesses of the English Court of Star Chamber, and to the French monarchy's abuse of the lettre de cachet. All of these institutions obviously symbolized a menace to liberty. In the hands of despotic groups each of them had become an instrument for the suppression of political and religious heresies in ruthless disregard of the right of an accused to a fair trial. Whatever other benefits the guarantee to an accused that his trial be conducted in public may confer upon our society, the guarantee has always been recognized as a safeguard against any attempt to employ our courts as instruments of persecution. The knowledge that every criminal trial is subject to contemporaneous review in the forum of public opinion is an effective restraint on possible abuse of judicial power. . . .

[N]o court in this country has ever before held, so far as we can find, that an accused can be tried, convicted, and sent to jail when everybody else is denied entrance to the court, except the judge and his attaches. And without exception all courts have held that an accused is at the very least entitled to have his friends, relatives and counsel present, no matter what offense he may be charged with. . . .

In the case before us, the petitioner was called as a witness to testify in secret before a one-man grand jury conducting a grand jury investigation. In the midst of petitioner's testimony the proceedings abruptly changed. The investigation became a "trial," the grand jury became a judge, and the witness became an accused charged with contempt of court—all in secret. Following a charge, conviction and sentence, the petitioner was led away to prison—still without any break in the secrecy. Even in jail, according to undenied allegations, his lawyer was denied an opportunity to see and confer with him. And that was not the end of the secrecy. His lawyer filed in the State Supreme Court this habeas corpus proceeding. Even there, the mantle of secrecy enveloped the transaction and the State Supreme Court ordered him sent back to jail without ever having seen a record of his testimony, and without knowing all that took place in the secrecy of the judge's chambers. In view of this nation's historic distrust of secret proceedings, their inherent dangers to freedom, and the universal requirement of our federal and state governments that criminal trials be public, the Fourteenth Amendment's guarantee that no one shall be deprived of his liberty without due process of law means at least that an accused cannot be thus sentenced to prison.

Second. We further hold that failure to

afford the petitioner a reasonable opportunity to defend himself against the charge of false and evasive swearing was a denial of due process of law. A person's right to reasonable notice of a charge against him, and an opportunity to be heard in his defense—a right to his day in court—are basic in our system of jurisprudence. . . .

* * *

It is true that courts have long exercised a power summarily to punish certain conduct committed in open court without notice, testimony or hearing. . . .

Except for a narrowly limited category of contempts, due process of law . . . requires that one charged with contempt of court be advised of the charges against him, have a reasonable opportunity to meet them by way of defense or explanation, have the right to be represented by counsel, and have a chance to testify and call other witnesses in his behalf, either by way of defense or explanation. The narrow exception to these due process requirements includes only charges of misconduct, in open court, in the presence of the judge, which disturbs the court's business, where all of the essential elements of the misconduct are under the eye of the court, are actually observed by the court, and where immediate punishment is essential to prevent "demoralization of the court's authority . . . before the public." If some essential elements of the offense are not personally observed by the judge, so that he must depend upon statements made by others for his knowledge about these essential elements, due process requires . . . that the accused be accorded notice and a fair hearing as above set out.

The facts shown by this record put this case outside the narrow category of cases that can be punished as contempt without notice, hearing and counsel. Since the petitioner's alleged misconduct all occurred in secret, there could be no possibility of a demoralization of the court's authority before the public. . . . The traditional grand juries have never punished contempts. The practice that has always been followed with recalcitrant grand jury witnesses is to take them into open court, and that practice, consistent with due process, has not de-

moralized the authority of courts. Reported cases reveal no instances in which witnesses believed by grand juries on the basis of other testimony to be perjurers have been convicted for contempt, or for perjury, without notice of the specific charges against them, and opportunity to prepare a defense, to obtain counsel, to cross-examine the witnesses against them and to offer evidence in their own defense. The right to be heard in open court before one is condemned is too valuable to be whittled away under the guise of "demoralization of the court's authority."

It is "the law of the land" that no man's life, liberty or property be forfeited as a punishment until there has been a charge fairly made and fairly tried in a public tribunal. . . . The petitioner was convicted without that kind of trial.

* * *

Reversed and remanded.

Mr. Justice RUTLEDGE, concurring.

I join the Court's opinion and decision. But there is more which needs to be said.

Michigan's one-man grand jury, as exemplified by this record, combines in a single official the historically separate powers of grand jury, committing magistrate, prosecutor, trial judge and petit jury. This aggregated authority denies to the accused not only the right to a public trial, but also those other basic protections secured by the Sixth Amendment, namely, the rights "to be informed of the nature and cause of the accusation, to be confronted with the witnesses against him, to have compulsory process for obtaining witnesses in his favor, and to have the Assistance of Counsel for his defence." It takes away the security against being twice put in jeopardy for the same offense and denies the equal protection of the laws by leaving to the committing functionary's sole discretion the scope and contents of the record on appeal.

* * *

[Mr. Justice JACKSON, with whom Mr. Justice FRANKFURTER concurred, dissented.]

Comment

1. *In re Oliver,* supra, made the Sixth Amendment right to a public trial applicable to the States through the Fourteenth Amendment Due Process Clause. See *Argersinger* v. *Hamlin,* supra, § 7.02. Secret trials are manifestly contrary to the American system of justice. However, investigative hearings (e.g. grand jury proceedings) are usually closed to the public since they are not trials. In most jurisdictions, it is common practice not to allow spectators to enter or leave the courtroom during the charge to the jury; and a judge may order the courtroom emptied if the trial becomes disrupted. In many juvenile courts the hearings are closed to the public. Is this practice constitutional in light of *In re Gault* (Chapter Eight, § 8.03)? Does the Sixth Amendment right to a public trial belong only to the defendant, or to the public as well? The Supreme Court has never decided this question. If the right belongs only to the defendant, then excluded spectators would arguably not have standing to allege a denial of a constitutional right. Does a defendant have a right to have the public excluded from the courtroom? If he could do so, obviously he could not later complain that his Sixth Amendment rights were violated. Assuming that a one-man grand jury is not unconstitutional, what procedures should the circuit judge have followed to properly find Oliver in contempt? Should the judge have taken Oliver into the courtroom, instead of chambers, and there pronounced him in contempt? In a later decision, *Levine* v. *United States,* 362 U.S. 610 (1960), the Supreme Court held that a contempt charge is not a "criminal prosecution" for the purposes of the Sixth Amendment right to a speedy trial. How can the public trial guarantee apply to contempt charges while the speedy trial guarantee does not? *In re Oliver* is one of the very few decisions by the Supreme Court on the right to a public trial. Others are *Levine* v. *United States,* supra (witness appearing before federal judge in summary proceedings for his refusal to answer questions of grand jury has no right to have general public present while grand jury's questions are read); *Estes* v. *Texas,* 381 U.S. 532 (1965) (defendant is entitled to his day in court, not in a stadium, or a city- or nationwide arena); *Douglas* v. *State,* 328 So. 2d 18 (Fla. 1976) (murder defendant not denied his right to a public trial when judge cleared the public from the courtroom while the victim's wife testified about the degrading sex acts the defendant forced her to perform). See also *Robertson* v. *State,* 60 So. 118 (1912).

Part Three

8

THE JUVENILE JUSTICE PROCESS

8.01 INTRODUCTION

An average of one million persons are arrested each year who, because of their youth, are not processed through the normal criminal justice channels[1] and are not subject to ordinary criminal sanctions and adjudicatory proceedings. Recognizing that youthful offenders should have a special place in our total scheme of criminal justice, each of the states has enacted statutes that classify such persons as "juveniles" and provide special courts and procedures for dealing with their unlawful or "delinquent" conduct.[2]

All states distinguish juveniles from other types of offenders on the basis of chronological age; however, there is considerable difference of opinion as to what the exact age limit should be. The maximum age at which a young person may still be classified as a juvenile generally ranges from a low of 14 years to a high of 18 years. By employing so-called "youth corrections" or "wayward minors" laws, some states have allowed youths who are too old to be classified as juveniles but who are still under the age of 21 to enjoy the benefits of special informal judicial procedures. These persons who are legally neither juveniles nor adults are commonly referred to as "youthful offenders."

Children accused of crimes have not always enjoyed the benefits of special judicial and correctional attention. At common law, children over the age of 14 were subject to adult adjudicatory procedures as a matter of law. In addition, any child between the ages of 7 and 14 years could be subject to adult criminal sanctions if the prosecution could show that he was intelligent enough to form the required mental intent, or *mens rea*, to commit the criminal act. Only children under the age of 7 were presumed by law to be incapable of forming the necessary mental intent and therefore not held accountable for their criminal acts.[3] These common law rules were followed in the United States until well into the nineteenth century, and no effort was made to separate juveniles from adult violators for purposes of trial or punishment. Once children were found guilty, they were

---

[1]Federal Bureau of Investigation, *Uniform Crime Reports* (1968–1975).

[2]Some authoritative works on the juvenile justice process are Fox, S., *Modern Juvenile Justice* (1972); Miller, F., et al., *The Juvenile Justice Process* (1976); Ketcham, O., and Paulsen, M., *Juvenile Courts* (1967); Kobetz, R., and Bosarge, B., *Juvenile Justice Administration* (1973); Senna, J., and Siegel, B., *Juvenile Law* (1976); Faust, F., and Brantingham, P., *Juvenile Justice Philosophy* (1974).

---

[3]LaFave, W., and Scott, A., *Handbook on Criminal Law* 351–355 (1972), and Blackstone, W., *Commentaries on the Laws of England* 23 (Vol. 4 1795).

701

subject to harsh punishments, including protracted prison sentences and even death.

During the latter half of the nineteenth century, a movement began in the United States to improve the general welfare of children. Reformers set out to upgrade the public education system, end child labor abuses, and provide better social services for both dependent and neglected children. The so-called "juvenile justice movement" was a natural extension of this child welfare campaign. Judicial reformers sought to establish a separate and distinct system of justice for young offenders that would provide special courts and detention facilities and informal adjudicatory procedures for juveniles accused of unlawful behavior.

In 1899, Illinois passed the first juvenile court statute,[4] which authorized the establishment of a juvenile court in Cook County (Chicago), Illinois. The purpose of the court was to provide the juvenile with guidance and protection and to assist in redirecting his behavior. To eliminate the "criminal stigma" that previously had been associated with the legal processing of juveniles, flexible and informal proceedings were established. As originally conceived, the court was to exercise a type of chancery (guardianship) jurisdiction over the child. This concept derived from the English doctrine of *parens patriae* (parent of the country), under which the sovereign acted as a "parent" and exercised guardianship powers over certain classes of persons deemed to need such protection.[5] Thus, the state, via the juvenile court, was to act as "parent" or "guardian" to the child.

Along with the new philosophy of juvenile justice came a new vocabulary: the child was "taken into custody," not arrested; a "petition" was filed rather than an indictment handed down by a grand jury; the child was given a "hearing" rather than a trial; the court passed "disposition" on a child rather than a sentence; and the net result was "redirection" and "rehabilitation," not punishment. The hearing was conducted in an informal atmosphere and only the child, the parents, and the professional juvenile workers (i.e., the juvenile judge and juvenile caseworkers) participated. The hearing was intended to be a fact-finding rather than an adversary proceeding, its purpose being to determine what happened and why and to develop a rehabilitation program that would serve the best interests of the child.[6]

Although this philosophy of rehabilitation and guidance still prevails, it is noteworthy that today many states allow juveniles to be tried as adults under certain circumstances. In most states a "certification hearing" is held in which the juvenile judge decides if the case is one that can legally be transferred to the jurisdiction of the adult criminal court under the existing statutory guidelines. If the juvenile is "certified," he will be tried and punished as would an adult convicted of the same offense. The following Missouri law is a typical certification statute:

211.071. (Mo. R.S.) Child prosecuted under general law, when

In the discretion of the judge of the juvenile court, when any petition under this

---

[6]Among the many excellent works on juvenile delinquency are Cohen, A., *Delinquent Boys* (1955); Cloward, R., and Ohlin, L., *Delinquency and Opportunity* (1960); Gibbons, D., *Changing the Lawbreaker* (1965); Gold, M., *Status Forces in Delinquent Boys* (1963); Hirschi, T., and Selvin, H., *False Criteria of Causality in Delinquency Research,* 13 Soc. Prob. 254 (1966); Matza, D., *Delinquency and Drift* (1964); Miller, W., *Lower Class Culture as a Generating Milieu of Gang Delinquency,* 14 J. Soc. Issues 5 (1958); Reckless, W., Dinitz, S., and Murray, E., *Self-Concept as an Insulator Against Delinquency,* 21 Am. Soc. Rev. 744 (1956); Shaw, C., and McKay, H., *Juvenile Delinquency and Urban Areas* (1942); Sykes, G., and Matza, D., *Techniques of Neutralization: A Theory of Delinquency,* 22 Am. Soc. Rev. 664 (1957); Hirschi, T., *Causes of Delinquency* (1970); Schur, E., *Radical Non-Intervention: Rethinking the Delinquency Problem* (1973); Murphy, P., *Our Kindly Parent . . . the State* (1974); Sebald, H., *Adolescence: A Sociological Analysis* (1968); Lerman, P., (ed.), *Delinquency and Social Policy* (1970); Eisner, V., *The Delinquency Label: The Epidemiology of Juvenile Delinquency* (1969); Kassebaum, G., *Delinquency and Social Policy* (1974); Garabedian, P., and Gibbons, D., (eds.), *Becoming Delinquent: Young Offenders and the Correctional System* (1970); Giallombardo, R., (ed.), *Juvenile Delinquency* (1972); Voss, H., (ed.) *Society, Delinquency, and Delinquent Behavior* (1970); Gibbons, D., *Delinquent Behavior* (1970).

---

[4]Faust and Brantingham, supra note 1, at 52–65.

[5]Fox, S., supra note 1, at 19.

chapter alleges that a child of the age of fourteen years or older has committed an offense which would be a felony if committed by an adult, or that the child has violated a state or municipal traffic law or ordinance or that a minor between the ages of seventeen and twenty-one years over whom the juvenile court has jurisdiction has violated any state law or municipal ordinance, the petition may be dismissed and such child or minor may be prosecuted under the general law, whenever the judge after receiving the report of the investigation required by this chapter and hearing evidence finds that such child or minor is not a proper subject to be dealt with under the provisions of this chapter.

8.02 STAGES IN THE JUVENILE JUSTICE PROCESS

The modern juvenile justice process can be divided into four distinct stages: (1) *preadjudicatory,* (2) *adjudicatory,* (3) *postadjudicatory,* and (4) *postadjudicatory review.*

The Preadjudicatory Stage

Preadjudicatory proceedings consist of (1) referral, (2) intake processing, and (3) filing of the formal petition for adjudication. Children may be referred to a juvenile court in a number of ways: A police officer may refer a juvenile whom he apprehends in the course of unlawful activity, takes into custody via a formal complaint, or apprehends as a result of an ongoing investigation. A child also may be referred to the juvenile court by juvenile probation officers, school officials, or his parents or guardian.

Once the child has been referred to the juvenile court, he will initially be handled by the court's intake officer. On the basis of the information before him, the intake officer must decide whether the child's case can be disposed of nonjudicially (i.e., release to the parents with or without a verbal reprimand) or whether, because of an ongoing investigation or other reason, further detention is necessary. If detention is indicated, the intake officer will contact the parents. Many state statutes require that a court order or other authorization be obtained for anything other than very short periods of detention.

If the evidence presented to the intake officer appears to necessitate a juvenile court hearing, the intake officer will consult with the prosecutor assigned to the juvenile court and together they will prepare the formal charges against the juvenile. If a petition is filed, the child's parents must be notified of the charges. The formal request for a court hearing is called a *petition for adjudication.* Once the petition is filed with the court the child must be released to his parents or a court order must be obtained to hold the child in the juvenile detention center until the adjudicatory hearing, the second major step in the process.

The Adjudicatory Stage

The purpose of the adjudicatory hearing is to determine, based on the facts available, whether the child is guilty of the delinquent conduct charged in the petition. Because of the recent United States Supreme Court decisions in *Kent* v. *United States,* 383 U.S. 541 (1966), *In re Gault,* 387 U.S. 1 (1967) (infra, § 8.03), and *In re Winship,* 397 U.S. 358 (1970) (infra, § 8.03), the modern adjudicatory hearing closely resembles the adult trial, in terms of the constitutional protections afforded: The juvenile has the right to confront witnesses against him and the right to be represented by counsel and cannot be adjudicated delinquent except upon proof beyond a reasonable doubt. If the prosecutor can prove beyond a reasonable doubt that the child is guilty of the offense, the judge will adjudicate the child delinquent, which triggers the third stage in the proceedings.

The Postadjudicatory (Dispositional) Stage

Once the judge finds that the child is a "juvenile delinquent in need of supervision," he must determine what form of "supervision" or treatment would be best for the child. To make that determination, the judge will most likely meet informally with the juvenile probation officer (who will have made an investigation into the child's personal history) and the parents, the defense counsel, and the prosecutor. The judge may dispose of the case in a variety of ways: He may (1) dismiss it, (2) release the child to his parents, (3) put the child on probation, (4) take the child from the parents and place him in a supervised foster home, or finally, (5) commit the child to a state juvenile institution.

Postadjudicatory Review

The Supreme Court concluded in *In re Gault* (dictum) that a juvenile has no constitutional right to appeal under the Due Process Clause of the Fourteenth Amendment. However, many state statutes do provide for appeal of an adjudication of delinquency or at least allow for de novo review. The Missouri statute is representative:

211.261. (Mo. R.S.) Appeals

An appeal shall be allowed to the child from any final judgment, order or decree made under the provisions of this chapter and may be taken on the part of the child by its parent, guardian, legal custodian, spouse, relative, or next friend. An appeal shall be allowed to a parent from any final judgement, order or decree made under the provisions of this chapter which adversely affects him. Notice of appeal shall be filed within thirty days after the final judgement, order or decree has been entered but neither the notice of appeal nor any motion filed subsequent to the final judgement acts as a supersedeas unless the court so orders.

8.03 THE SELECTION AND APPLICATION OF DUE PROCESS SAFEGUARDS TO STATE JUVENILE PROCEEDINGS

The "Essential Requirements" at the Adjudicatory Stage

IN RE GAULT

Supreme Court of the United States, 1967
378 U.S. 1, 87 S. Ct. 1428, 18 L. Ed. 2d 527

Gerald Gault, a 15-year-old, and a friend were arrested by the police following a complaint by a neighbor, Mrs. Cook, that they had made lewd and indecent remarks to her over the telephone. Gault's parents were not notified by the police of their son's arrest and they did not receive a copy of the petition filed by the police for a court hearing. Their son was not advised of his right to remain silent or of his right to counsel. No record was made of the proceedings. The juvenile judge declared Gerald to be a juvenile delinquent and he was committed to a state industrial school for a maximum of six years (i.e., until he reached 21 years of age). Because no appeal in juvenile cases was permitted under Arizona law, Gault's parents filed a petition for a writ of habeas corpus in an Arizona state court alleging that Arizona's Juvenile Code was unconstitutional because it failed to provide the same procedural safeguards in juvenile hearings as were afforded under the Fourteenth Amendment in adult criminal trials. A state superior court dismissed the writ, and the Arizona Supreme Court affirmed. The Gaults appealed to the United States Supreme Court.

Mr. Justice FORTAS delivered the opinion of the Court.

* * *

I

* * *

[A]ppellants ... urge that we hold the Juvenile Court of Arizona invalid on its face or as applied in this case because, contrary to the Due Process Clause of the Fourteenth Amendment, the juvenile is taken from the custody of his parents and committed to a state institution pursuant to proceedings in which the Juvenile Court has virtually unlimited discretion, and in which the following basic rights are denied:

1. Notice of the charges;
2. Right to counsel;
3. Right to confrontation and cross-examination;
4. Privilege against self-incrimination;
5. Right to a transcript of the proceedings; and
6. Right to appellate review.

* * *

II

* * *

. . . As to these proceedings, there appears to be little current dissent from the proposition that the Due Process Clause has a role to play. The problem is to ascertain the precise impact of the due process requirement upon such proceedings.

* * *

. . . [I]t would be extraordinary if our Constitution did not require the procedural regularity and the exercise of care implied in the phrase "due process." Under our Constitution, the condition of being a boy does not justify a kangaroo court. . . . Under traditional notions, one would assume that in a case like that of Gerald Gault, where the juvenile appears to have a home, a working mother and father, and an older brother, the Juvenile Judge would have made a careful inquiry and judgment as to the possibility that the boy could be disciplined and dealt with at home, despite his previous transgressions. Indeed, so far as appears in the record before us, except for some conversation with Gerald about his school work and his "wanting to go to . . . Grand Canyon with his father," the points to which the judge directed his attention were little different from those that would be involved in determining any charge of violation of a penal statute. The essential difference between Gerald's case and a normal criminal case is that safeguards available to adults were discarded in Gerald's case. The summary procedure as well as the long commitment was possible because Gerald was 15 years of age instead of over 18.

If Gerald had been over 18, he would not have been subject to Juvenile Court proceedings. For the particular offense immediately involved, the maximum punishment would have been a fine of $5 to $50, or imprisonment in jail for not more than two months. Instead, he was committed to custody for a maximum of six years. If he had been over 18 and had committed an offense to which such a sentence might apply, he would have been entitled to substantial rights under the Constitution of the United States as well as under Arizona's laws and constitution. . . .

In Kent v. United States . . . we stated that the Juvenile Court Judge's exercise of the power of the state as parens patriae was not unlimited. . . . We announced with respect to . . . waiver proceedings that while "We do not mean . . . to indicate that the hearing to be held must conform with all the requirements of a criminal trial or even of the usual administrative hearing; but we do hold that the hearing must measure up to the essentials of due process and fair treatment." We reiterate this view, here in connection with a juvenile court adjudication of "delinquency," as a requirement which is part of the Due Process Clause of the Fourteenth Amendment of our Constitution.

We now turn to the specific issues which are presented to us in the present case.

III

Notice of Charges

. . . No notice was given to Gerald's parents when he was taken into custody on Monday, June 8. On that night, when Mrs. Gault went to the Detention Home, she was orally informed that there would be a hearing the next afternoon and was told the reason why Gerald was in custody. The only written notice Gerald's parents received at any time was a note on plain paper from Officer Flagg delivered on Thursday or Friday, June 11 or 12, to the effect that the judge had set Monday, June 15, "for further Hearings on Gerald's delinquency."

A "petition" was filed with the court on June 9 by Officer Flagg, reciting only that he was informed and believed that "said minor is a delinquent minor and that it is necessary that some order be made by the Honorable Court for said minor's welfare." The applicable Arizona statute provides for a petition to be filed in Juvenile Court, alleging in general terms that the child is "neglected, dependent or delinquent." The statute explicitly states that such a general allegation is sufficient, "without alleging the facts." There is no requirement that the petition be served and it was not served upon, given to, or shown to Gerald or his parents.

The Supreme Court of Arizona ... held that because "the policy of the juvenile law is to hide youthful errors from the full gaze of the public and bury them in the graveyard of the forgotten past," advance notice of the specific charges or basis for taking the juvenile into custody and for the hearing is not necessary. It held that the appropriate rule is that "the infant and his parent or guardian will receive a petition only reciting a conclusion of delinquency. But no later than the initial hearing by the judge, they must be advised of the facts involved in the case. If the charges are denied, they must be given a reasonable period of time to prepare."

We cannot agree with the court's conclusion that adequate notice was given in this case. Notice, to comply with due process requirements, must be given sufficiently in advance of scheduled court proceedings so that reasonable opportunity to prepare will be afforded, and it must "set forth the alleged misconduct with particularity." ... The "initial hearing" in the present case was a hearing on the merits. Notice at that time is not timely; and even if there were a conceivable purpose served by the deferral proposed by the court below, it would have to yield to the requirements that the child and his parents or guardian be notified, in writing, of the specific charge or factual allegations to be considered at the hearing, and that such written notice be given at the earliest practicable time, and in any event sufficiently in advance of the hearing to permit preparation. Due process of law requires notice of the sort we have described — that is, notice which would be deemed constitutionally adequate in a civil or criminal proceeding. It does not allow a hearing to be held in which a youth's freedom and his parents' right to his custody are at stake without giving them timely notice, in advance of the hearing, of the specific issues that they must meet. Nor, in the circumstances of this case, can it reasonably be said that the requirement of notice was waived.

IV

Right to Counsel

Appellants charge that the Juvenile Court proceedings were fatally defective because the court did not advise Gerald or his parents of their right to counsel, and proceeded with the hearing, the adjudication of delinquency and the order of commitment in the absence of counsel for the child and his parents or an express waiver of the right thereto. The Supreme Court of Arizona ... referred to a provision of the Juvenile Code which it characterized as requiring "that the probation officer shall look after the interests of neglected, delinquent and dependent children," including representing their interests in court. The court argued that "the parent and the probation officer may be relied upon to protect the infant's interests." Accordingly it rejected the proposition that "due process requires that an infant have a right to counsel." It said that juvenile courts have the discretion, but not the duty, to allow such representation; it referred specifically to the situation in which the Juvenile Court discerns conflict between the child and his parents as an instance in which this discretion might be exercised. We do not agree. ... The probation officer cannot act as counsel for the child. His role in the adjudicatory hearing, by statute and in fact, is as arresting officer and witness against the child. Nor can the judge represent the child. There is no material difference in this respect between adult and juvenile proceedings of the sort here involved. In adult proceedings, this contention has been foreclosed by decisions of this Court. A proceeding where the issue is whether the child will be found to be "delinquent" and subjected to the loss of his liberty for years is comparable in seriousness to a felony prosecution. The juvenile needs the assistance of counsel to cope with problems of law, to make skilled inquiry into the facts, to insist upon regularity of the proceedings, and to ascertain whether he has a defense and to prepare and submit it. The child "requires the guiding hand of counsel at every step in the proceedings against him." Just as in Kent v. United States ... we indicated ... that the assistance of counsel is essential for purposes of waiver proceedings, so we hold now that it is equally essential for the determination of delinquency, carrying with it the awesome prospect of incarceration in a state institution until the juvenile reaches the age of 21.

We conclude that the Due Process Clause of the Fourteenth Amendment requires that in respect of proceedings to determine delinquency which may result in commitment to an institution in which the juvenile's freedom is curtailed, the child and his parents must be notified of the child's right to be represented by counsel retained by them, or if they are unable to afford counsel, that counsel will be appointed to represent the child.

At the habeas corpus proceeding, Mrs. Gault testified that she knew that she could have appeared with counsel at the juvenile hearing. This knowledge is not a waiver of the right to counsel which she and her juvenile son had, as we have defined it. They had a right expressly to be advised that they might retain counsel and to be confronted with the need for specific consideration of whether they did or did not choose to waive the right. If they were unable to afford to employ counsel, they were entitled in view of the seriousness of the charge and potential commitment, to appointed counsel, unless they chose waiver. Mrs. Gault's knowledge that she could employ counsel was not an "intentional relinquishment or abandonment" of a fully known right.

V

Confrontation, Self-incrimination, Cross-examination

Appellants urge that the writ of habeas corpus should have been granted because of the denial of the rights of confrontation and cross-examination in the Juvenile Court hearings, and because the privilege against self-incrimination was not observed. The Juvenile Court Judge testified at the habeas corpus hearing that he had proceeded on the basis of Gerald's admissions at the two hearings. Appellants attack this on the ground that the admissions were obtained in disregard of the privilege against self-incrimination. If the confession is disregarded, appellants argue that the delinquency conclusion, since it was fundamentally based on a finding that Gerald had made lewd remarks during the phone call to Mrs. Cook, is fatally defective for failure to accord the rights of confrontation and cross-examination which the Due Process Clause of the Fourteenth Amendment of the Federal Constitution guarantees in state proceedings generally.

Our first question, then, is whether Gerald's admission was improperly obtained and relied on as the basis of decision, in conflict with the Federal Constitution. For this purpose, it is necessary briefly to recall the relevant facts.

Mrs. Cook, the complainant, and the recipient of the alleged telephone call, was not called as a witness. Gerald's mother asked the Juvenile Court Judge why Mrs. Cook was not present and the judge replied that "she didn't have to be present." So far as appears, Mrs. Cook was spoken to only once, by Officer Flagg, and this was by telephone. The judge did not speak with her on any occasion. Gerald had been questioned by the probation officer after having been taken into custody. The exact circumstances of this questioning do not appear but any admissions Gerald may have made at this time do not appear in the record. Gerald was also questioned by the Juvenile Court Judge at each of the two hearings. The judge testified in the habeas corpus proceeding that Gerald admitted making "some of the lewd statements . . . [but not] any of the more serious lewd statements." There was conflict and uncertainty among the witnesses . . . as to what Gerald did or did not admit.

We shall assume that Gerald made admissions of the sort described by the Juvenile Court Judge, as quoted above. Neither Gerald nor his parents were advised that he did not have to testify or make a statement, or that an incriminating statement might result in his commitment as a "delinquent."

The Arizona Supreme Court rejected appellants' contention that Gerald had a right to be advised that he need not incriminate himself. . . .

In reviewing this conclusion of Arizona's Supreme Court, we emphasize again that we are here concerned only with a proceeding to determine whether a minor is a "delinquent" and which may result in commitment to a state institution. Specifically, the question is whether, in such a proceeding, an admission by the juvenile may be used against him in the absence of clear and unequivocal evidence that the admission was made with knowledge that he was not obliged to speak and would not be penalized for remaining silent. In light of Miranda v. Arizona, 384 U.S. 436 (1966), we must also consider whether, if the privilege against self-incrimination is available, it can effectively be waived unless counsel is present or the right to counsel has been waived.

This Court has emphasized that admissions and confessions of juveniles require special caution. [See Haley v. Ohio, 332

U.S. 596 (1948).] . . . In notable decisions, the New York of Court of Appeals and the Supreme Court of New Jersey have recently considered decisions of Juvenile Courts in which boys have been adjudged "delinquent" on the basis of confessions obtained in circumstances comparable to those in Haley. In both instances, the State contended before its highest tribunal that constitutional requirements governing inculpatory statements applicable in adult courts do not apply to juvenile proceedings. In each case, the State's contention was rejected, and the juvenile court's determination of delinquency was set aside on the grounds of inadmissibility of the confession. . . .

The privilege against self-incrimination is, of course, related to the question of the safeguards necessary to assure that admissions or confessions are reasonably trustworthy, that they are not the mere fruits of fear or coercion, but are reliable expressions of the truth. The roots of the privilege are, however, far deeper. They tap the basic stream of religious and political principle because the privilege reflects the limits of the individual's attornment to the state and — in a philosophical sense — insists upon the equality of the individual and the state. In other words, the privilege has a broader and deeper thrust than the rule which prevents the use of confessions which are the product of coercion because coercion is thought to carry with it the danger of unreliability. One of its purposes is to prevent the state, whether by force or by psychological domination, from overcoming the mind and will of the person under investigation and depriving him of the freedom to decide whether to assist the state in securing his conviction.

It would indeed be surprising if the privilege against self-incrimination were available to hardened criminals but not to children. The language of the Fifth Amendment, applicable to the States by operation of the Fourteenth Amendment, is unequivocal and without exception. And the scope of the privilege is comprehensive.

* * *

With respect to juveniles, both common observation and expert opinion emphasize that the distrust of confessions made in certain situations" . . . is imperative in the case of children from an early age through adolescence. . . .

The authoritative "Standards for Juvenile and Family Courts" concludes that, "Whether or not transfer to the criminal court is a possibility, certain procedures should always be followed. Before being interviewed [by the police], the child and his parents should be informed of his right to have legal counsel present and to refuse to answer questions or be fingerprinted if he should so decide."

Against the application to juveniles of the right to silence, it is argued that juvenile proceedings are "civil" and not "criminal," and therefore the privilege should not apply. It is true that the statement of the privilege in the Fifth Amendment, which is applicable to the States by reason of the Fourteenth Amendment, is that no person "shall be compelled in any *criminal case* to be a witness against himself." However, it is also clear that the availability of the privilege does not turn upon the type of proceeding in which its protection is invoked, but upon the nature of the statement or admission and the exposure which it invites. The privilege may, for example, be claimed in a civil or administrative proceeding, if the statement is or may be inculpatory.

It would be entirely unrealistic to carve out of the Fifth Amendment all statements by juveniles on the ground that these cannot lead to "criminal" involvement. In the first place, juvenile proceedings to determine "delinquency," which may lead to commitment to a state institution, must be regarded as "criminal" for purposes of the privilege against self-incrimination. To hold otherwise would be to disregard substance because of the feeble enticement of the "civil" label-of-convenience which has been attached to juvenile proceedings. Indeed, in over half of the States, there is not even assurance that the juvenile will be kept in separate institutions, apart from adult "criminals." In those States juveniles may be placed in or transferred to adult penal institutions after having been found "delinquent" by a juvenile court. For this purpose, at least, commitment is a deprivation of liberty. It is incarceration against one's will, whether it is called "criminal" or "civil." And our Constitution guarantees that no person shall be "compelled" to be a witness against himself when he is threatened with deprivation of his liberty. . . .

In addition, apart from the equivalence for this purpose of exposure to commitment as a juvenile delinquent and exposure to imprisonment as an adult offender, the fact of the matter is that there is little or no assurance in Arizona, as in most if not all of the States, that a juvenile apprehended and interrogated by the police or even by the Juvenile Court itself will remain outside of the reach of adult courts as a consequence of the offense for which he has been taken into custody. In Arizona, as in other States, provision is made for Juvenile Courts to relinquish or waive jurisdiction to the ordinary criminal courts. In the present case, when Gerald Gault was interrogated concerning violation of a section of the Arizona Criminal Code, it could not be certain that the Juvenile Court Judge would decide to "suspend" criminal prosecution in court for adults by proceeding to an adjudication in Juvenile Court.

It is also urged . . . that the juvenile and presumably his parents should not be advised of the juvenile's right to silence because confession is good for the child as the commencement of the assumed therapy of the juvenile court process, and he should be encouraged to assume an attitude of trust and confidence toward the officials of the juvenile process. This proposition has been subjected to widespread challenge on the basis of current reappraisals of the rhetoric and realities of the handling of juvenile offenders.

In fact, evidence is accumulating that confessions by juveniles do not aid in "individualized treatment," as the court below put it, and that compelling the child to answer questions, without warning or advice as to his right to remain silent, does not serve this or any other good purpose. . . . It seems probable that where children are induced to confess by "paternal" urgings on the part of officials and the confession is then followed by disciplinary action, the child's reaction is likely to be hostile and adverse—the child may well feel that he has been led or tricked into confession and that despite his confession, he is being punished.

* * *

We conclude that the constitutional privilege against self-incrimination is applicable in the case of juveniles as it is with respect to adults. We appreciate that special problems may arise with respect to waiver of the privilege by or on behalf of children, and that there may well be some difference in technique—but not in principle—depending upon the age of the child and the presence and competence of parents. The participation of counsel will, of course, assist the police, Juvenile Courts and appellate tribunals in administering the privilege. If counsel was not present for some permissible reason when an admission was obtained, the greatest care must be taken to assure that the admission was voluntary, in the sense not only that it was not coerced or suggested, but also that it was not the product of ignorance of rights or of adolescent fantasy, fright or despair.

The "confession" of Gerald Gault was first obtained by Officer Flagg, out of the presence of Gerald's parents, without counsel and without advising him of his right to silence, as far as appears. The judgment of the Juvenile Court was stated by the judge to be based on Gerald's admissions in court. Neither "admission" was reduced to writing, and, to say the least, the process by which the "admissions" were obtained and received must be characterized as lacking the certainty and order which are required of proceedings of such formidable consequences. Apart from the "admissions," there was nothing upon which a judgment or finding might be based. There was no sworn testimony. Mrs. Cook, the complainant, was not present. The Arizona Supreme Court held that "sworn testimony must be required of all witnesses, including police officers, probation officers and others who are part of or officially related to the juvenile court structure." We hold that this is not enough. No reason is suggested or appears for a different rule in respect of sworn testimony in juvenile courts than in adult tribunals. Absent a valid confession adequate to support the determination of the Juvenile Court, confrontation and sworn testimony by witnesses available for cross-examination were essential for a finding of "delinquency" and an order committing Gerald to a state institution for a maximum of six years.

* * *

VI

Appellate Review and Transcript of Proceedings

Appellants urge that the Arizona statute is unconstitutional under the Due Process

Clause because, as construed by its Supreme Court, "there is no right of appeal from a juvenile court order. . . ." The court held that there is no right to a transcript because there is no right to appeal and because the proceedings are confidential and any record must be destroyed after a prescribed period of time. Whether a transcript or other recording is made, it held, is a matter for the discretion of the juvenile court.

This Court has not held that a State is required by the Federal Constitution "to provide appellate courts or a right to appellate review at all." In view of the fact that we must reverse the Supreme Court of Arizona's affirmance of the dismissal of the writ of habeas corpus for other reasons, we need not rule on this question in the present case or upon the failure to provide a transcript or recording of the hearings—or, indeed, the failure of the Juvenile Judge to state the grounds for his conclusion. Cf. Kent v. United States . . . where we said, in the context of a decision of the juvenile court waiving jurisdiction to the adult court, which

by local law, was permissible: ". . . it is incumbent upon the Juvenile Court to accompany its waiver order with a statement of the reasons or considerations therefor." As the present case illustrates, the consequences of failure to provide an appeal, to record the proceedings, or to make findings or state the grounds for the juvenile court's conclusion may be to throw a burden upon the machinery for habeas corpus, to saddle the reviewing process with the burden of attempting to reconstruct a record, and to impose upon the Juvenile Judge the unseemly duty of testifying under cross-examination as to the events that transpired in the hearings before him.

Reversed and remanded.

[Mr. Justice BLACK concurred.]

[Mr. Justice WHITE concurred except for Part V.]

[Mr. Justice HARLAN concurred in part and dissented in part.]

[Mr. Justice STEWART wrote a separate dissenting opinion.]

Comments

1. *Gault* was handed down only a year after *Kent* v. *United States,* 383 U.S. 541 (1966). *Kent* concerned a 16-year-old charged with housebreaking, rape, and robbery. A District of Columbia statute provided for waiver of jurisdiction by the juvenile court, after "full investigation," to the adult criminal court. Kent challenged the propriety of the waiver, and the United States Supreme Court reversed. The Court noted that the waiver process "assumes procedural regularity sufficient . . . to satisfy . . . basic requirements of due process and fairness . . .," 383 U.S., at 553. In regard to the due process requirements, the Court concluded that "as a condition to valid waiver" the juvenile was entitled to (1) a waiver hearing; (2) access to social records and probation reports; and (3) a "statement of reason" for the juvenile court's decision to waive jurisdiction. *Kent* not only established a constitutional basis for applying due process guarantees to juvenile proceedings, but it also suggested a need for counsel at waiver hearings, since it granted the right to inspect records and reports specifically to the juvenile's counsel. Although the *Kent* decision turned upon the interpretation of the District of Columbia statute, the Court, per Mr. Justice Fortas, was careful to emphasize specific requirements that quite obviously were rooted in the Due Process Clause of the Fourteenth Amendment.

2. Building on the foundation provided by *Kent,* the *Gault* majority enumerated certain rights required at the adjudicatory stage by the Fourteenth Amendment Due Process Clause. However, it is noteworthy that *Gault* "intentionally" left a number of due process

questions unanswered. The majority noted in the beginning, "We indicate no opinion . . . as to other issues"—i.e., issues other than the (1) right to notice; (2) right to counsel; (3) right to confrontation of witnesses; (4) privilege against self-incrimination; (5) right to transcripts; and (6) right to appellate review.

3. Although the Supreme Court has decided other issues relating to juvenile proceedings, such as who has the burden of proof, *In re Winship*, 397 U.S. 358 (1970) (infra), and the applicability of both the right to trial by jury, *McKeiver* v. *Pennsylvania*, 403 U.S. 528 (1971) (infra), and the double jeopardy guarantee, *Breed* v. *Jones*, 421 U.S. 519 (1975) (infra), other due process issues have been left to the lower federal and state courts.

    These courts have held that (1) the Fourth Amendment's probable cause standard applies at the time the juvenile is taken into custody, *Baldwin* v. *Lewis*, 300 F. Supp. 1220 (E.D. Wis. 1969), and at the time of the search, *In re Marsh*, 237 N.E.2d 529 (Ill. 1968), *In re Donaldson*, 75 Cal. Rptr. 220 (Calif. 1969), *State* v. *Stein*, 456 P.2d 1 (Kan. 1969); (2) juveniles have the right to a speedy trial, *Piland* v. *Clark County*, 457 P.2d 523 (Nev. 1969); (3) juveniles have a limited right to pretrial discovery, *Joe Z.* v. *Superior Court*, 478 P.2d (Calif. 1970); and (4) the guarantee against double jeopardy bars a second juvenile delinquency petition, *Richard M.* v. *Superior Court*, 482 P.2d 664 (Calif. 1971). The lower federal and state courts have also probed the issues of the voluntariness of waivers of constitutional rights by juveniles, *West* v. *United States*, 399 F.2d 467 (5th Cir. 1968), *Smith* v. *Crouse*, 413 F.2d 979 (10th Cir. 1969), *United States* v. *Miller*, 453 F.2d 634 (4th Cir. 1972), *In re S. H.*, 293 A.2d 181 (N.J. Super. Ct. 1972), and the applicability of *Miranda* warnings to juveniles, *Leach* v. *State*, 428 S.W.2d 817 (Tex. Ct. Civ. App. 1968), *In re Creek*, 243 A.2d 49 (D.C. App. 1968), *Commonwealth* v. *Taper*, 253 A.2d 90 (Pa. 1969), and *State* v. *Maloney*, 433 P.2d 625 (Ariz. 1967).

The Reasonable Doubt Standard Is Also "Essential"

IN RE WINSHIP

Supreme Court of the United States, 1970
397 U.S. 358, 90 S. Ct. 1068, 25 L. Ed. 2d 368

During a 1967 adjudicatory hearing, conducted pursuant to § 742 of the New York Family Court Act, a judge found that appellant, then a 12-year-old boy, had entered a locker and stolen $112 from a woman's purse. The petition that charged appellant with delinquency alleged that his act "if done by an adult would constitute the crime or crimes of Larceny." Under § 744 (b) of the act, the quantum of proof required for a finding of guilt was a preponderance of the evidence, and the judge rejected appellant's contention that the Fourteenth Amendment required that guilt be established beyond a reasonable doubt. At a subsequent dispositional hearing, appellant was ordered placed in a training school for an initial period of 18 months, subject to annual extensions until his 18th birthday. On appeal, his disposition was affirmed by both the Appellate Division of the New York Supreme Court and the New York Court of Appeals. The United States Supreme Court granted appellate review.

Mr. Justice BRENNAN delivered the opinion of the Court.

... This case presents the single, narrow question whether proof beyond a reasonable doubt is among the "essentials of due process and fair treatment" required during the adjudicatory stage when a juvenile is charged with an act which would constitute a crime if committed by an adult.

* * *

I

The requirement that guilt of a criminal charge be established by proof beyond a reasonable doubt dates at least from our early years as a Nation. The "demand for a higher degree of persuasion in criminal cases was recurrently expressed from ancient times, [though] its crystallization into the formula 'beyond a reasonable doubt' seems to have occurred as late as 1798. It is now accepted in common law jurisdictions as the measure of persuasion by which the prosecution must convince the trier of all the essential elements of guilt." ... Although virtually unanimous adherence to the reasonable-doubt standard in common-law jurisdictions may not conclusively establish it as a requirement of due process, such adherence does "reflect a profound judgment about the way in which law should be enforced and justice administered." ...

Expressions in many opinions of this Court indicate that it has long been assumed that proof of a criminal charge beyond a reasonable doubt is constitutionally required.

* * *

The reasonable-doubt standard plays a vital role in the American scheme of criminal procedure. It is a prime instrument for reducing the risk of convictions resting on factual error. The standard provides concrete substance for the presumption of innocence—that bedrock "axiomatic and elementary" principle whose "enforcement lies at the foundation of the administration of our criminal law." ... As the dissenters in the New York Court of Appeals observed, and we agree, "a person accused of a crime ... would be at a severe disadvantage, a disadvantage amounting to a lack of fundamental fairness, if he could be adjudged guilty and imprisoned for years on the strength of the same evidence as would suffice in a civil case." ...

The requirement of proof beyond a reasonable doubt has this vital role in our criminal procedure for cogent reasons. The accused during a criminal prosecution has at stake interests of immense importance, both because of the possibility that he may lose his liberty upon conviction and because of the certainty that he would be stigmatized by the conviction. Accordingly, a society that values the good name and freedom of every individual should not condemn a man for commission of a crime when there is reasonable doubt about his guilt. As we said in Speiser v. Randall, 357 U.S. 513 (1958), "There is always in litigation a margin of error, representing error in factfinding, which both parties must take into account. Where one party has at stake an interest of transcending value—as a criminal defendant his liberty—this margin of error is reduced as to him by the process of placing on the other party the burden of ... persuading the factfinder at the conclusion of the trial of his guilt beyond a reasonable doubt. Due process commands that no man shall lose his liberty unless the Government has borne the burden of ... convincing the factfinder of his guilt." To this end, the reasonable-doubt standard is indispensable; for it "impresses on the trier of fact the necessity of reaching a subjective state of certitude of the facts in issue." ...

Moreover, use of the reasonable-doubt standard is indispensable to command the respect and confidence of the community in applications of the criminal law. It is critical that the moral force of the criminal law not be diluted by a standard of proof that leaves people in doubt whether innocent men are being condemned. It is also important in our free society that every individual going about his ordinary affairs have confidence that his government cannot adjudge him guilty of a criminal offense without convincing a proper factfinder of his guilt with utmost certainty.

Lest there remain any doubt about the constitutional stature of the reasonable-doubt standard, we explicitly hold that the Due Process Clause protects the accused against conviction except upon proof beyond a reasonable doubt of every fact necessary to constitute the crime with which he is charged.

II

We turn to the question whether juveniles, like adults, are constitutionally entitled to proof beyond a reasonable doubt when they are charged with violation of a criminal law. The same considerations that demand extreme caution in factfinding to protect the innocent adult apply as well to the innocent child. . . .

We made clear in [Gault] that civil labels and good intentions do not themselves obviate the need for criminal due process safeguards in juvenile courts, for "a proceeding where the issue is whether the child will be found to be 'delinquent' and subjected to the loss of his liberty for years is comparable in seriousness to a felony prosecution." . . .

Nor do we perceive any merit in the argument that to afford juveniles the protection of proof beyond a reasonable doubt would risk destruction of beneficial aspects of the juvenile process. Use of the reasonable-doubt standard during the adjudicatory hearing will not disturb New York's policies that a finding that a child has violated a criminal law does not constitute a criminal conviction, that such a finding does not deprive the child of his civil rights, and that juvenile proceedings are confidential. Nor will there be any effect on the informality, flexibility, or speed of the hearing at which the factfinding takes place. And the opportunity during the post-adjudicatory or dispositional hearing for a wide-ranging review of the child's social history and for his individualized treatment will remain unimpaired. Similarly, there will be no effect on the procedures distinctive to juvenile proceedings that are employed prior to the adjudicatory hearing.

The Court of Appeals observed that "a child's best interest is not necessarily, or even probably, promoted if he wins in the particular inquiry which may bring him to the juvenile court." . . . It is true, of course, that the juvenile may be engaging in a general course of conduct inimical to his welfare that calls for judicial intervention. But that intervention cannot take the form of subjecting the child to the stigma of a finding that he violated a criminal law and to the possibility of institutional confinement on proof insufficient to convict him were he an adult.

We conclude, as we concluded regarding the essential due process safeguards applied in Gault, that the observance of the standard of proof beyond a reasonable doubt "will not compel the States to abandon or displace any of the substantive benefits of the juvenile process." . . .

Finally, we reject the Court of Appeals' suggestion that there is, in any event, only a "tenuous difference" between the reasonable-doubt and preponderance standards. The suggestion is singularly unpersuasive. In this very case, the trial judge's ability to distinguish between the two standards enabled him to make a finding of guilt that he conceded he might not have made under the standard of proof beyond a reasonable doubt. Indeed, the trial judge's action evidences the accuracy of the observation of commentators that "the preponderance test is susceptible to the misinterpretation that it calls on the trier of fact merely to perform an abstract weighing of the evidence in order to determine which side has produced the greater quantum, without regard to its effect in convincing his mind of the truth of the proposition asserted." . . .

III

In sum, the constitutional safeguard of proof beyond a reasonable doubt is as much required during the adjudicatory stage of a delinquency proceeding as are those constitutional safeguards applied in Gault — notice of charges, right to counsel, the rights of confrontation and examination, and the privilege against self-incrimination. We therefore hold, in agreement with Chief Judge Fuld in dissent in the Court of Appeals, "that, where a 12-year-old child is charged with an act of stealing which renders him liable to confinement for as long as six years, then, as a matter of due process . . . the case against him must be proved beyond a reasonable doubt." . . .

Reversed.

[Mr. Justice HARLAN wrote a concurring opinion.]

Mr. Justice BLACK, dissenting.

. . . The Bill of Rights, which in my view is made fully applicable to the States by the Fourteenth Amendment, . . . does by express language provide for, among other things, a right to counsel in criminal trials, a right to indictment, and the right of a defendant to be informed of the nature of the charges against him. And in two places the Constitution provides for trial by jury, but nowhere in that document is there any statement that conviction of crime requires proof of guilt beyond a reasonable doubt. The Constitution thus goes into some detail to spell out what kind of trial a defendant charged with crime should have, and I believe the Court has no power to add to or subtract from the procedures set forth by the Founders. I realize that it is far easier to substitute individual judges' ideas of "fairness" for the fairness prescribed by the Constitution, but I shall not at any time surrender my belief that that document itself should be our guide, not our own concept of what is fair, decent, and right. That this old "shock-the-conscience" test is what the Court is relying on, rather than the words of the Constitution, is clearly enough revealed by the reference of the majority to "fair treatment" and to the statement by the dissenting judges in the New York Court of Appeals that failure to require proof beyond a reasonable doubt amounts to a "lack of fundamental fairness." . . . As I have said time and time again, I prefer to put my faith in the words of the written Constitution itself rather than to rely on the shifting, day-to-day standards of fairness of individual judges. . . .

* * *

I admit a strong, persuasive argument can be made for a standard of proof beyond a reasonable doubt in criminal cases — and the majority has made that argument well — but it is not for me as a judge to say for that reason that Congress or the States are without constitutional power to establish another standard that the Constitution does not otherwise forbid. It is quite true that proof beyond a reasonable doubt has long been required in federal criminal trials. It is also true that this requirement is almost universally found in the governing laws of the States. And as long as a particular jurisdiction requires proof beyond a reasonable doubt, then the Due Process Clause commands that every trial in that jurisdiction must adhere to that standard. . . . But when, as here, a State through its duly constituted legislative branch decides to apply a different standard, then that standard, unless it is otherwise unconstitutional, must be applied to insure that persons are treated according to the "law of the land." The State of New York has made such a decision, and in my view nothing in the Due Process Clause invalidates it.

[Mr. Justice STEWART, joined by the Chief Justice (BURGER), dissented.]

Comments

1. *In re Winship,* supra, is illustrative of how the Due Process Clause of the Fourteenth Amendment can be used as a vehicle for imposing "essential standards of fair treatment" even when those standards are not readily distinguishable as specific Bill of Rights guarantees. The fact that the standard of "proof beyond a reasonable doubt" is not particularized in the Bill of Rights makes Justice Black's dissent quite powerful. A long-time exponent of the "total incorporation" view (see Black, J., [dissenting opinion] in *Adamson* v. *California,* 332 U.S. 46 [1947] [Chapter Three, § 3.04]), Justice Black rejected the contention that such a standard of proof is constitutionally required because it was not specifically mentioned in the Bill of Rights. He contended that the Due Process Clauses of both the Fifth and Fourteenth Amendments require only that the government proceed according to the "law of the land" as it exists at the time of the proceedings in question. He defined the "law of the land" as "written constitutional or statutory provisions." Thus, given the absence of the requisite constitutional or statutory base, Black concluded that "it is not for me as a judge to say that . . . Congress or the States are without constitutional power to establish another

standard [of proof] that the Constitution does not otherwise forbid."

2. It is clear that the *Winship* majority applied the reasonable doubt standard to juvenile delinquency proceedings. However, it should be recognized that in its totality the decision is as important to adults as it is to juveniles. Prior to *Winship* the reasonable doubt standard was only assumed to be constitutionally required in adult criminal proceedings. This fact is well illustrated by the manner in which the majority, per Mr. Justice Brennan, approached the question, relying not on established case law but on (1) dicta from the earlier cases of *Davis* v. *United States,* 160 U.S. 469 (1895), and *Speiser* v. *Randall,* 357 U.S. 513 (1958); and (2) the "virtually unanimous adherence" to the reasonable doubt standard in common-law jurisdictions. Without acknowledging that the Bill of Rights is silent on the matter, the majority concludes, "Lest there remain any doubt . . . we explicitly hold that the Due Process Clause of the Fourteenth Amendment protects the accused against conviction except upon proof beyond a reasonable doubt. . . ." Thus, *Winship* not only extended the reasonable doubt standard of proof to juveniles, but it also explicitly established it as an essential ingredient of due process.

3. *Winship* held that the Due Process Clause protects the accused by requiring proof beyond a reasonable doubt of *every fact* necessary to constitute the crime charged. The question of whether that principle is applicable to so-called "reductive factors" (those that reduce the crime to a lesser grade) came before the Supreme Court in *Mullaney* v. *Wilbur,* 421 U.S. 684 (1975). The State of Maine required a defendant charged with murder to establish that he acted "in the heat of passion on sudden provocation" by a preponderance of evidence in order to reduce the homicide to manslaughter. The United States Court of Appeals (1st Cir.) held that the *Winship* principle was controlling and that to establish murder the prosecution must prove beyond a reasonable doubt that the defendant did *not* act in the heat of passion on sudden provocation, *Wilbur* v. *Mullaney,* 496 F.2d 1303 (1st Cir. 1974). Maine appealed and the Supreme Court granted certiorari. Mr. Justice Powell, speaking for the majority, affirmed the lower court's decision and noted, "The Due Process Clause requires the prosecution to prove beyond a reasonable doubt the absence of the heat of passion or sudden provocation when the issue is properly presented in a homicide case."

4. Since the decision in *Mullaney* v. *Wilbur,* id., a number of lower federal and state court decisions on the "burden of proof" have been decided, including *City of Chicago* v. *Robinson,* 336 N.E.2d 158 (Ill. App. 1975) (offense of knowingly committing an "unreasonable act" to make or provoke a breach of the peace may be proved by a "clear preponderance of the evidence"); *State* v. *Grady,* 345 A.2d 436 (Md. Ct. Spec. App. 1975) (alibi is an affirmative defense which the accused has the burden of establishing) (in accord is *Smith* v. *Smith,* 454 F.2d 572 [5th Cir. 1971], *Stump* v. *Bennett,* 398 F.2d 111 [5th Cir. 1968] [en banc], *People* v. *Pearson,* 1969 N.E.2d 252 [1960], *State* v. *Jewell,* 285 A.2d 847 [Me. 1972], and *People* v. *Elmore,* 14 N.E.2d 451 [N.Y. 1938]); *Byrd* v. *Hopper,* 402 F. Supp. 787 (N.D. Ga. 1975) (accused's right to presumption of innocence

is violated by state jury instruction that the defendant's possession of a recently stolen vehicle, "if not satisfactorily explained," raises the presumption of guilt"); *Magley* v. *State*, 335 N.E.2d 811 (Ind. 1975) (state must prove beyond a reasonable doubt that confession is voluntary); *Fuentes* v. *State*, 349 A.2d 1 (Del. 1975) (statute which places on first-degree murder defendant the burden of proving "extreme emotional distress" in order to reduce the homicide to manslaughter held unconstitutional); *People* v. *Oliver*, 336 N.E.2d 586 (Ill. App. 1975) (state dangerous offender statute permitting commitment of a person convicted of sexual offenses by a preponderance of evidence upheld); *Castro* v. *Regan*, 525 F.2d 1157 (3d Cir. 1975) (state jury instruction that all unlawful homicides are presumed to have been "committed with malice unless the lack of malice is affirmatively demonstrated by the evidence" upheld); *State* v. *Berry*, 324 So. 2d 822 (La. 1975) (state statute placing burden on defendant to prove his insanity upheld) (see also *Leland* v. *Oregon*, 343 U.S. 960 [1952] [defendant must prove his insanity beyond a reasonable doubt], and *Rivera* v. *State*, 351 A.2d 561 [Del. 1976], appeal dismissed for want of substantial federal question, 96 S. Ct. 226 [1976] [state law classifying mental illness as affirmative defense which defendant must prove by preponderance of evidence upheld]); *Pinkerton* v. *Farr*, 220 S.E.2d 682 (W. Va. App. 1975) (state law which presumes that a defendant convicted of aiding and abetting others in a felonious assault is also guilty of conspiracy unless he proves otherwise held unconstitutional); *Evans* v. *State*, 349 A.2d 300 (Md. Ct. Spec. App. 1975) (*Mullaney* v. *Wilbur* is fully retroactive), aff'd, 352 A.2d 343 (Md. Ct. App. 1976); *Westberry* v. *Mullaney*, 406 F. Supp. 407 (D. Me. 1976) (*Mullaney* v. *Wilbur* is not applicable to felony-murder where an intent to kill is not an element of the offense); *Dinkins* v. *State*, 349 A.2d 676 (Md. Ct. Spec. App. 1976) (unexplained exclusive possession of recently stolen goods permits inference of criminal liability); *Commonwealth* v. *Barnes*, 340 N.E.2d 863 (Mass. 1976) (common law presumption that a wife who acts in her husband's presence acts under his coercion abolished); *James* v. *United States*, 350 A.2d 748 (D.C. App. 1976) (federal statute that punishes the possession of implements of a crime and permits the accused an affirmative defense by showing a satisfactory and innocent reason for possessing the implements upheld); *State* v. *Travis*, 545 P.2d 986 (Ariz. App. 1976) (state law permitting jury to infer malice from use of a deadly weapon does not shift the burden of proof to defendant to prove its absence); *People* v. *Smith*, 379 N.Y.S. 2d 479 (N.Y. Ct. App. 1976) (state statute which presumes that a pistol displayed during a robbery was loaded and operable and places the burden on the defendant to prove that it was not held unconstitutional); *Rumfolo* v. *State*, 535 S.W.2d 16 (Tex. Ct. Crim. App. 1976) (state forfeiture statute which places the burden of proof on the person found in possession of gambling proceeds to show cause why the property should not be forfeited held denial of due process); *People* v. *Reynolds*, 127 Cal. Rptr. 561 (Calif. App. 1976) (warrantless search sought to be justified on the basis of consent requires proof by "clear and convincing evidence"); *Hallowell* v. *Keve*, 412 F. Supp. 681 (D. Del. 1976) (state trial judge's instruction that "the law implies malice and renders it incumbent upon" an accused murderer to show its absence held not violative of *Mullaney* v. *Wilbur*); *State* v. *Keys*, 548 P.2d 205 (Ore. App. 1976)

(*Mullaney* v. *Wilbur* held not applicable to indictment stage of prosecution, and murder indictment need not allege that defendant was not under the influence of extreme emotional disturbance); *Buznski* v. *Oliver*, 538 F.2d 6 (1st Cir. 1976) (state requirement that a criminal defendant prove his insanity by a preponderance of the evidence held constitutional) (in accord is *State* v. *Pendry*, 227 S.E.2d 210 [W. Va. 1976]); *Farrell* v. *Czarnetsky*, 417 F. Supp. 987 (S.D.N.Y. 1976) (state statute that permits a reduction of a robbery charge from first to second degree upon a showing by the defendant that the weapon used was inoperable or not loaded upheld); *Hodge* v. *Commonwealth*, 228 S.E.2d 692 (Va. 1976) (state law that creates rebuttable presumption that an unlawful homicide is second-degree murder once the prosecution makes a prima facie showing of malice upheld); *United States* v. *Hendrix*, 542 F.2d 879 (2d Cir. 1976) (juries should not be informed of the common law presumption of sanity when the defendant has entered an insanity plea) (see also *United States* v. *Arroyave*, 465 F.2d 962 [9th Cir. 1972], *Davis* v. *United States*, 364 F.2d 572 [10th Cir. 1966], *United States* v. *Lawrance*, 480 F.2d 688 [5th Cir. 1973], *United States* v. *Sennett*, 505 F.2d 774 [7th Cir. 1974], *United States* v. *Retolaza*, 398 F.2d 235 [4th Cir. 1968], and *United States* v. *Dube*, 520 F.2d 250 [1st Cir. 1970]); *In re Ames*, 554 P.2d 1084 (Wash. App. 1976) (proof beyond a reasonable doubt that a juvenile violated the law or a condition of probation not required at juvenile probation revocation hearing).

The Court Retreats: Due Process Does Not Require Trial by Jury

McKEIVER v. PENNSYLVANIA

Supreme Court of the United States, 1971
403 U.S. 441, 91 S. Ct. 1976, 29 L. Ed. 2d 677

This case was decided with a companion case, *In re Burrus*. The facts are stated in the opinion.

Mr. Justice BLACKMUN announced the judgments of the Court and an opinion in which the Chief Justice [BURGER], Mr. Justice STEWART, and Mr. Justice WHITE join.

These cases present the narrow but precise issue whether the Due Process Clause of the Fourteenth Amendment assures the right to trial by jury in the adjudicative phase of a state juvenile court delinquency proceeding.

I

* * *

... From [the] cases—Haley [v. Ohio, 332 U.S. 596 (1948)], Gallegos [v. Colorado, 370 U.S. 49 (1962)], Kent [v. United States, 383 U.S. 541 (1966)], [In re] Gault, [387 U.S. 1 (1967)], DeBacker [v. Brainard, 396 U.S. 28 (1969)], and [In re] Winship, [397 U.S. 358 (1970)]—it is apparent that:

1. Some of the constitutional require-

ments attendant upon the state criminal trial have equal application to that part of the state juvenile proceedings that is adjudicative in nature. Among these are the rights to appropriate notice, to counsel, to confrontation and to cross-examination, and the privilege against self-incrimination. Included, also, is the standard of proof beyond a reasonable doubt.

2. The Court, however, has not yet said that *all* rights constitutionally assured to an adult accused of crime also are to be enforced or made available to the juvenile in his delinquency proceeding. Indeed, the Court specifically has refrained from going that far:

"We do not mean by this to indicate that the hearing to be held must conform with all the requirements of a criminal trial or even of the usual administrative hearing; but we do hold that the hearing must measure up to the essentials of due process and fair treatment."

3. The Court, although recognizing the high hopes and aspirations of Judge Julian Mack, the leaders of the Jane Adams School and the other supporters of the juvenile court concept, has also noted the disappointments of the system's performance and experience and the resulting widespread disaffection.... There have been, at one and the same time, both an appreciation for the juvenile court judge who is devoted, sympathetic, and conscientious, and a disturbed concern about the judge who is untrained and less than fully imbued with an understanding approach to the complex problems of childhood and adolescence. There has been praise for the system and its purposes, and there has been alarm over its defects.

4. The Court has insisted that these successive decisions do not spell the doom of the juvenile court system or even deprive it of its "informality, flexibility, or speed." ... On the other hand, a concern precisely to the opposite effect was expressed by two dissenters in Winship....

II

With this substantial background already developed, we turn to the facts of the present cases:

... Joseph McKeiver, then age 16, in May 1968 was charged with robbery, larceny, and receiving stolen goods (felonies under Pennsylvania law, Pa. Stat. Ann., Tit. 18 §§ 4704, 4807, and 4817 [1963]) as acts of juvenile delinquency. At the time of the adjudication hearing he was represented by counsel. His request for a jury trial was denied and his case was heard by Judge Theodore S. Gutowicz of the Court of Common Pleas, Family Division, Juvenile Branch, of Philadelphia County, Pennsylvania. McKeiver was adjudged a delinquent upon findings that he had violated a law of the Commonwealth, Pa. Stat. Ann., Tit. 11, § 243(4)(a) (1965). On appeal, the Superior Court affirmed without opinion. . . .

Edward Terry, then age 15, in January 1969 was charged with assault and battery on a police officer and conspiracy (misdemeanors under Pennsylvania law, Pa. Stat. Ann., Tit. 18 §§ 4708 and 4302 [1963]) as acts of juvenile delinquency. His counsel's request for a jury trial was denied and his case was heard by Judge Joseph C. Bruno of the same Juvenile Branch of the Court of Common Pleas of Philadelphia County. Terry was adjudged a delinquent on the charges. This followed an adjudication and commitment in the preceding week for an assault on a teacher. He was committed, as he had been on the earlier charge, to the Youth Development Center at Cornwells Heights. On appeal, the Superior Court affirmed without opinion. . . .

The Supreme Court of Pennsylvania granted leave to appeal in both cases and consolidated them. The single question considered, as phrased by the court, was "whether there is a constitutional right to a jury trial in juvenile court." The answer, one justice dissenting, was in the negative. . . . We noted probable jurisdiction. . . .

The details of the McKeiver and Terry offenses are set forth in Justice Roberts' opinion for the Pennsylvania court ... and need not be repeated at any length here. It suffices to say that McKeiver's offense was his participating with 20 or 30 youths who pursued three young teenagers and took 25 cents from them; that McKeiver never before had been arrested and had a record of gainful employment; that the testimony of two of the victims was described by the court as somewhat inconsistent and as "weak"; and that Terry's offense consisted of hitting a police officer with his fists and with a stick when the officer broke up a boys' fight Terry and others were watching.

... Barbara Burrus and approximately 45 other black children, ranging in age from 11 to 15 years, were the subjects of juvenile court summonses issued in Hyde County, North Carolina, in January 1969.

The charges arose out of a series of demonstrations in the county in late 1968 by black adults and children protesting school assignments and a school consolidation plan. Petitions were filed by North Carolina state highway patrolmen. Except for one relating to James Lambert Howard, the petitions charged the respective juveniles with wilfully impeding traffic. The charge against Howard was that he wilfully made riotous noise and was disorderly in the O. A. Peay School in Swan Quarter; interrupted and disturbed the school during its regular sessions; and defaced school furniture. The acts so charged are misdemeanors under North Carolina law. N.C. Gen. Stat. §§ 20-174.1 (1965 and Supp. 1969), 14-132(a), 14-273 (1969).

The several cases were consolidated into groups for hearing before District Judge Hallett S. Ward, sitting as a juvenile court. The same lawyer appeared for all the juveniles. Over counsel's objection, made in all except two of the cases, the general public was excluded. A request for a jury trial in each case was denied.

The evidence as to the juveniles other than Howard consisted solely of testimony of highway patrolmen. No juvenile took the stand or offered a witness. The testimony was to the effect that on various occasions the juveniles and adults were observed walking along Highway 64 singing, shouting, clapping, and playing basketball. As a result there was interference with traffic. The marchers were asked to leave the paved portion of the highway and they were warned that they were committing a statutory offense. They either refused or left the roadway and immediately returned. The juveniles and participating adults were taken into custody. Juvenile petitions were then filed with respect to those under the age of 16.

The evidence as to Howard was that on the morning of December 5, he was in the office of the principal of the O. A. Peay School with 15 other persons while school was in session and was moving furniture around; that the office was in disarray; that as a result the school closed before noon; and that neither he nor any of the others was a student at the school or authorized to enter the principal's office.

In each case the court found that the juvenile had committed "an act for which an adult may be punished by law." A custody order was entered declaring the juvenile a delinquent "in need of more suitable guardianship" and committing him to the custody of the County Department of Public Welfare for placement in a suitable institution "until such time as the Board of Juvenile Correction or the Superintendent of said institution may determine, not inconsistent with the laws of this State." The court, however, suspended these commitments and placed each juvenile on probation for either one or two years conditioned upon his violating none of the State's laws, upon his reporting monthly to the County Department of Welfare, upon his being home by 11 p.m. each evening, and upon his attending a school approved by the Welfare Director. None of the juveniles has been confined on these charges.

On appeal, the cases were consolidated into two groups. The North Carolina Court of Appeals affirmed. . . . In its turn the Supreme Court of North Carolina deleted that portion of the order in each case relating to commitment, but otherwise affirmed. . . . Two justices dissented without opinion. We granted certiorari. . . .

III

* * *

IV

The right to an impartial jury "in all criminal prosecutions" under federal law is guaranteed by the Sixth Amendment. Through the Fourteenth Amendment the requirement has now been imposed upon the States "in all criminal cases which — were they to be tried in a federal court — would come within the Sixth Amendment's guarantee." This is because the Court has said it believes "that trial by jury in criminal cases is fundamental to the American scheme of justice." . . .

This, of course, does not automatically provide the answer to the present jury trial issue, if for no other reason than that the juvenile court proceeding has not yet been held to be a "criminal prosecution," within the meaning and reach of the Sixth Amendment, and also has not yet been regarded as devoid of criminal aspects merely because it usually has been given the civil label. . . .

Little, indeed, is to be gained by any attempt simplistically to call the juvenile court proceeding either "civil" or "criminal." The Court carefully has avoided this wooden approach. Before Gault was decided in 1967, the Fifth Amendment's guarantee against self-incrimination had been imposed upon the state criminal trial. . . . So, too, had the Sixth Amendment's rights of confrontation and cross-examination. . . . Yet the Court did not automatically and peremptorily apply those rights to the juvenile proceeding. A reading of Gault reveals the opposite. And the same separate approach to the standard-of-proof issue is evident from the carefully separated application of the standard, first to the criminal trial, and then to the juvenile proceeding, displayed in Winship. . . .

Thus, accepting "the proposition that the Due Process Clause has a role to play," . . . our task here with respect to trial by jury, as it was in Gault with respect to other claimed rights, "is to ascertain the precise impact of the due process requirement." . . .

V

The Pennsylvania juveniles' basic argument is that they were tried in proceedings "substantially similar to a criminal trial." They say that a delinquency proceeding in their State is initiated by a petition charging a penal code violation in the conclusory language of an indictment; that a juvenile detained prior to trial is held in a building substantially similar to an adult prison; that in Philadelphia juveniles over 16 are, in fact, held in the cells of a prison; that counsel and the prosecution engage in plea bargaining; that motions to suppress are routinely heard and decided; that the usual rules of evidence are applied; that the customary common-law defenses are available; that the press is generally admitted in the Philadelphia juvenile courtrooms; that members of the public enter the room; that arrest and prior record may be reported by the press (from police sources, however, rather than from the juvenile court records); that, once adjudged delinquent, a juvenile may be confined until his majority in what amounts to a prison . . . describing the state correctional institution at Camp Hill as a "maximum security prison for adjudged delinquents and youthful criminal offenders"; and that the stigma attached upon delinquency adjudication approximates that resulting from conviction in an adult criminal proceeding.

The North Carolina juveniles particularly urge that the requirement of a jury trial would not operate to deny the supposed benefits of the juvenile court system; that the system's primary benefits are its discretionary intake procedure permitting disposition short of adjudication, and its flexible sentencing permitting emphasis on rehabilitation; that realization of these benefits does not depend upon dispensing with the jury; that adjudication of factual issues on the one hand and disposition of the case on the other are very different matters with very different purposes; that the purpose of the former is indistinguishable from that of the criminal trial; that the jury trial provides an independent protective factor; that experience has shown that jury trials in juvenile courts are manageable; that no reason exists why protection traditionally accorded in criminal proceedings should be denied young people subject to involuntary incarceration for lengthy periods; and that the juvenile courts deserve healthy public scrutiny.

VI

All the litigants here agree that the applicable due process standard in juvenile proceedings, as developed by Gault and Winship, is fundamental fairness. As that standard was applied in those two cases, we have an emphasis on factfinding procedures. The requirements of notice, counsel, confrontation, cross-examination, and standard of proof naturally flowed from this emphasis. But one cannot say that in our legal system the jury is a necessary component of accurate factfinding. There is much to be said for it, to be sure, but we have been content to pursue other ways for determining facts. Juries are not required, and have not been, for example, in equity cases, in workmen's compensation, in probate, or in deportation cases. Neither have they been generally used in military trials. In Duncan [v. Louisiana, 391 U.S. 145 (1968)] the Court stated, "We would not assert, however, that every criminal trial—or any particular trial—held before a judge alone is unfair or that a defendant may never be as fairly treated by a judge as he would be by a jury." . . . In DeStefano [v. Woods, 392 U.S. 631 (1968)], for this reason and others, the Court refrained from retrospective application of Duncan, an action it surely would have not taken had it felt that the integrity of the result was seriously at issue. And in Williams v. Florida, 399 U.S. 78 (1970), . . . the Court saw no particular magic in a 12-man jury for a criminal case, thus revealing that even jury concepts themselves are not inflexible.

We must recognize, as the Court has recognized before, that the fond and idealistic hopes of the juvenile court proponents and early reformers of three generations ago have not been realized. . . .

Despite all these disappointments, all these failures and all these shortcomings, we conclude that trial by jury in the juvenile court's adjudicative stage is not a constitutional requirement. We so conclude for a number of reasons:

1. The Court has refrained, in the cases heretofore decided, from taking the easy way with a flat holding that all rights constitutionally assured for the adult accused are to be imposed upon the state juvenile proceeding. What was done in Gault and in Winship is aptly described in Commonwealth v. Johnson, 211 Pa. Super. 62 (1967):

"It is clear to us that the Supreme Court has properly attempted to strike a judicious balance by injecting procedural orderliness into the juvenile court system. It is seeking to reverse the trend [pointed out in Kent v. United States, 383 U.S., at 556, 86 S. Ct. 1045] whereby 'the child receives the worst of both worlds'. . . ."

2. There is a possibility, at least, that the jury trial, if required as a matter of constitutional precept, will remake the juvenile proceeding into a fully adversary process and will put an effective end to what has been the idealistic prospect of an intimate, informal protective proceeding.

3. The [President's Commission] Task Force Report, although concededly pre-Gault, is notable for its not making any recommendation that the jury trial be imposed upon the juvenile court system. This is so despite its vivid description of the system's deficiencies and disappointments. Had the Commission deemed this vital to the integrity of the juvenile process, or to the handling of juveniles, surely a recommendation or suggestion to this effect would have appeared. The intimations, instead, are quite the other way. . . . Further, it expressly recommends against the return of the juvenile to the criminal courts.

4. The Court specifically has recognized by dictum that a jury is not a necessary part even of every criminal process that is fair and equitable. Duncan v. Louisiana, 391 U.S., at 149–150, n.14, and 158, 88 S. Ct., at 1447, and 1452.

5. The imposition of the jury trial on the juvenile court system would not strengthen greatly, if at all, the factfinding function, and would, contrarily, provide an attrition of the juvenile court's assumed ability to function in a unique manner. It would not remedy the defects of the system. Meager as has been the hoped-for advance in the juvenile field, the alternative would be regressive, would lose what has been gained, and would tend once again to place the juvenile squarely in the routine of the criminal process.

6. The juvenile concept held high promise. We are reluctant to say that, despite disappointments of grave dimensions, it still does not hold promise, and we are particularly reluctant to say, as do the Pennsylvania appellants here, that the system cannot accomplish its rehabilitative goals. So much depends on the availability of resources, on the interest and commitment of the public, on willingness to learn, and on understanding as to cause and effect and cure. In this field, as in so many others, one perhaps learns best by doing. We are reluctant to disallow the States to experiment further and to seek in new and different ways the elusive answers to the problems of the young, and we feel that we would be impeding that experimentation by imposing the jury trial. The States, indeed, must go forward. If in its wisdom, any State feels the jury trial is desirable in all cases, or in certain kinds, there appears to be no impediment to its installing a system embracing that feature. That, however, is the State's privilege and not its obligation.

7. Of course there have been abuses. The Task Force Report has noted them. We refrain from saying at this point that those abuses are of constitutional dimension. They relate to the lack of resources and of dedication rather than to inherent unfairness.

8. There is, of course, nothing to prevent a juvenile court judge, in a particular case where he feels the need, or when the need is demonstrated, from using an advisory jury.

9. "The fact that a practice is followed by a large number of states is not conclusive in a decision as to whether that practice accords with due process, but it is plainly worth considering in determining whether the practice 'offends some principle of justice so

rooted in the traditions and conscience of our people as to be ranked as fundamental.' " . . . It therefore is of more than passing interest that at least 28 States and the District of Columbia by statute deny the juvenile a right to a jury trial in cases such as these. The same result is achieved in other States by judicial decision. In 10 States statutes provide for a jury trial under certain circumstances.

10. Since Gault and since Duncan the great majority of States, in addition to Pennsylvania and North Carolina, that have faced the issue have concluded that the considerations that led to the result in those two cases do not compel trial by jury in the juvenile court. . . .

11. Stopping short of proposing the jury trial for juvenile proceedings are the Uniform Juvenile Court Act, § 24(a), approved in July 1968 by the National Conference of Commissioners on Uniform State Laws; the Standard Juvenile Court Act, Art. V, § 19, proposed by the National Council on Crime and Delinquency. . . .

12. If the jury trial were to be injected into the juvenile court system as a matter of right, it would bring with it into that system the traditional delay, the formality, and the clamor of the adversary system and, possibly, the public trial. It is of interest that these very factors were stressed by the District Committee of the Senate when, through Senator Tydings, it recommended, and Congress then approved, as a provision in the District of Columbia Crime Bill, the abolition of the jury trial in the juvenile court. . . .

13. Finally, the arguments advanced by the juveniles here are, of course, the identical arguments that underlie the demand for the jury trial for criminal proceedings. The arguments necessarily equate the juvenile proceeding—or at least the adjudicative phase of it—with the criminal trial. Whether they should be so equated is our issue. Concern about the inapplicability of exclusionary and other rules of evidence, about the juvenile court judge's possible awareness of the juvenile's prior record and of the contents of the social file; about repeated appearances of the same familiar witnesses in the persons of juvenile and probation officers and social workers—all to the effect that this will create the likelihood of prejudgment—chooses to ignore, it seems to us, every aspect of fairness, of concern, of sympathy, and of paternal attention that the juvenile court system contemplates.

If the formalities of the criminal adjudicative process are to be superimposed upon the juvenile court system, there is little need for its separate existence. Perhaps that ultimate disillusionment will come one day, but for the moment we are disinclined to give impetus to it.

Affirmed.

[Mr. Justice WHITE and Mr. Justice HARLAN concurred.]

[Mr. Justice BRENNAN concurred in *McKeiver* and dissented in *Burrus*.]

[Mr. Justice DOUGLAS, Mr. Justice BLACK, and Mr. Justice MARSHALL joined, dissenting.]

Comment

1. The Public Defender Service for the District of Columbia and the Neighborhood Legal Services Program of Washington, D.C., filed an amicus curiae brief in *McKeiver* outlining various problems associated with providing jury trials and urging the Court not to extend the right to juveniles. In an appendix to his dissenting opinion, Mr. Justice Douglas excerpted part of an opinion by Judge DeCiantis of the Family Court of Providence, Rhode Island, which refuted those specific problems pointed out in the amicus brief. In the Rhode Island case, Judge DeCiantis granted a jury trial to a juvenile charged with rape. Judge DeCiantis' opinion specifically rebutted the following arguments against jury trials for juveniles:

    1. *Jury trial would expose a juvenile to added trauma.*
    Judge DeCiantis concluded that "procedures which are now

followed in juvenile cases are far more traumatic than the potential experience of a jury trial"; i.e., the real traumatic experience is incarceration without due process—the feeling of being deprived of basic rights.

2. Jury trial would cause a great backlog of cases, which would impair the functioning of the juvenile court.

Judge DeCiantis argued that this is not true. He noted that in states that permit jury trials in all juvenile cases, few juries have been demanded, and "there is no suggestion from these courts that jury trials have impeded the system of juvenile justice."

3. To place the child's fate in the hands of a jury would defeat the purpose of the juvenile court by removing the case from the trained judge's authority.

Judge DeCiantis noted that it is at the dispositional hearing that the judge's expertise is most needed; "the granting of a jury trial will not prevent the judge from carrying out the basic philosophy of the juvenile court."

4. Such a procedure would require a jury of peers and thus necessitate a teenage jury.

Judge DeCiantis expressed the opinion that since teenagers (18-year-olds) can vote in many states, it is quite possible that they might serve as jurors. He concluded, "Are we now to say that a juvenile is a second-class citizen, not equal to an adult?"

5. Since delinquency adjudication is not equivalent to a criminal process, the trial by jury is simply not necessary nor in the best interest of the juvenile.

Judge DeCiantis argued that such a position is "spurious." When one is involved in a proceeding that may result in a loss of liberty, the label it is given is unimportant. "Because the legislature dictates that a child who commits a felony shall be called a delinquent does not change the nature of the crime. Murder is murder; robbery is robbery—they are both criminal offenses, not civil, regardless and independent of the age of the doer."

"Same Offense" Test Evokes Double Jeopardy Prohibition

BREED v. JONES

Supreme Court of the United States, 1975
421 U.S. 519, 95 S. Ct. 1779, 44 L. Ed. 2d 346

The facts are stated in the opinion.

Mr. Chief Justice BURGER delivered the opinion of the Court.

We granted certiorari to decide whether the prosecution of respondent as an adult, after juvenile court proceedings which resulted in a finding that respondent had violated a criminal statute and a subsequent finding that he was unfit for treatment as a juvenile, violated the Fifth and Fourteenth

Amendments to the United States Constitution.

On February 9, 1971, a petition was filed in the Superior Court of California, County of Los Angeles Juvenile Court, alleging that respondent, then 17 years of age, was a person described by Cal. Welf. & Inst'ns Code § 602, in that, on or about February 8, while armed with a deadly weapon, he had committed acts which, if committed by an adult, would constitute the crime of robbery in violation of Cal. Penal Code § 211. The following day, a detention hearing was held, at the conclusion of which respondent was ordered detained pending a hearing on the petition.

The jurisdictional or adjudicatory hearing was conducted on March 1, pursuant to Cal. Welf. & Inst'ns Code § 701. After taking testimony from two prosecution witnesses and respondent, the Juvenile Court found that the allegations in the petition were true and that respondent was a person described by § 602, and it sustained the petition. The proceedings were continued for a dispositional hearing, pending which the court ordered that respondent remain detained.

At a hearing conducted on March 15, the Juvenile Court indicated its intention to find respondent "not . . . amenable to the care, treatment and training program available through the facilities of the juvenile court" under Cal. Welf. & Inst'ns Code § 707. Respondent's counsel orally moved "to continue the matter on the ground of surprise," contending that respondent "was not informed that it was going to be a fitness hearing." The court continued the matter for one week, at which time, having considered the report of the probation officer assigned to the case and having heard her testimony, it declared respondent "unfit for treatment as a juvenile," and ordered that he be prosecuted as an adult.

Thereafter, respondent filed a petition for a writ of habeas corpus in Juvenile Court, raising the same double jeopardy claim now presented. Upon the denial of that petition, respondent sought habeas corpus relief in the California Court of Appeal, Second Appellate District. Although it initially stayed the criminal prosecution pending against respondent, that court denied the petition. . . . The Supreme Court of California denied respondent's petition for hearing.

After a preliminary hearing respondent was ordered held for trial in Superior Court, where an information was subsequently filed accusing him of having committed robbery, in violation of Cal. Penal Code § 211, while armed with a deadly weapon, on or about February 8, 1971. Respondent entered a plea of not guilty, and he also pleaded that he had "already been placed once in jeopardy and convicted of the offense charged, by the judgment of the Superior Court of the County of Los Angeles, Juvenile Court, rendered . . . on the 1st day of March, 1971." . . . By stipulation, the case was submitted to the court on the transcript of the preliminary hearing. The court found respondent guilty of robbery in the first degree under Cal. Penal Code § 211a and ordered that he be committed by the California Youth Authority. No appeal was taken from the judgment of conviction.

On December 10, 1971, respondent, through his mother as guardian ad litem, filed the instant petition for a writ of habeas corpus in the United States District Court for the Central District of California. In his petition he alleged that his transfer to adult court pursuant to Cal. Welf. & Inst'ns Code § 707 and subsequent trial there "placed him in double jeopardy." . . . The District Court denied the petition, rejecting respondent's contention that jeopardy attached at his adjudicatory hearing. . . .

The Court of Appeals reversed, concluding . . . the Double Jeopardy Clause "is fully applicable to juvenile court proceedings." . . .

Turning to the question whether there had been a constitutional violation in this case, the Court of Appeals pointed to the power of the Juvenile Court to "impose severe restrictions upon the juvenile's liberty" in support of its conclusion that jeopardy attached in respondent's adjudicatory hearing. It rejected petitioner's contention that no new jeopardy attached when respondent was referred to Superior Court and subsequently tried and convicted, finding "continuing jeopardy" principles advanced by petitioner inapplicable. Finally, the Court of Appeals observed that acceptance of petitioner's position would "allow the prosecution to review in advance the accused's defense and, as here, hear him testify about the crime charged," a procedure it found offensive to "our concepts of basic, even-handed fairness." The court therefore held that once jeopardy attached at the adjudicatory hearing, a minor could not be retried as an adult or a juvenile "absent some exception to the double jeopardy prohibition," and that there "was none here." . . .

We granted certiorari because of a conflict between courts of appeals and the highest courts of a number of States on the issue presented in this case and similar issues and because of the importance of final resolution of the issue to the administration of the juvenile court system.

I

The parties agree that, following his transfer from Juvenile Court, and as a defendant to a felony information, respondent was entitled to the full protection of the Double Jeopardy Clause of the Fifth Amendment, as applied to the States through the Fourteenth Amendment. . . . In addition, they agree that respondent was put in jeopardy by the proceedings on that information, which resulted in an adjudication that he was guilty of robbery in the first degree and in a sentence of commitment. Finally, there is no dispute that the petition filed in Juvenile Court and the information filed in Superior Court related to the "same offence" within the meaning of the constitutional prohibition. The point of disagreement between the parties, and the question for our decision, is whether, by reason of the proceedings in Juvenile Court, respondent was "twice put in jeopardy."

II

Jeopardy denotes risk. In the constitutional sense, jeopardy describes the risk that is traditionally associated with a criminal prosecution. . . . Although the constitutional language, "jeopardy of life or limb," suggests proceedings in which only the most serious penalties can be imposed, the Clause has long been construed to mean something far broader than its literal language. . . . At the same time, however, we have held that the risk to which the Clause refers is not present in proceedings that are not "essentially criminal." . . .

Although the juvenile court system had its genesis in the desire to provide a distinctive procedure and setting to deal with the problems of youth, including those manifested by antisocial conduct, our decisions in recent years have recognized that there is a gap between the originally benign conception of the system and its realities. With the exception of McKeiver v. Pennsylvania, 403 U.S. 528 (1971) . . . the Court's response to that perception has been to make applicable in juvenile proceedings constitutional guarantees associated with traditional criminal prosecutions. . . . In so doing the Court has evinced awareness of the threat which such a process represents to the efforts of the juvenile court system, functioning in a unique manner, to ameliorate the harshness of criminal justice when applied to youthful offenders. That the system has fallen short of the high expectations of its sponsors in no way detracts from the broad social benefits sought or from those benefits that can survive constitutional scrutiny.

We believe it is simply too late in the day to conclude, as did the District Court in this case, that a juvenile is not put in jeopardy at a proceeding whose object is to determine whether he has committed acts that violate a criminal law and whose potential consequences include both the stigma inherent in such a determination and the deprivation of liberty for many years. For it is clear under our cases that determining the relevance of constitutional policies, like determining the applicability of constitutional rights, in juvenile proceedings, requires that courts eschew "the 'civil' label-of-convenience which has been attached to juvenile proceedings" . . . and that "the juvenile process . . . be candidly appraised." . . .

As we have observed, the risk to which the term jeopardy refers is that traditionally associated with "actions intended to authorize criminal punishment to vindicate public justice." . . . The purpose of the Double Jeopardy Clause is to require that he be subject to the experience only once "for the same offence." . . .

[T]here is little to distinguish an adjudicatory hearing such as was held in this case from a traditional criminal prosecution. For that reason, it engenders elements of "anxiety and insecurity" in a juvenile, and imposes a "heavy personal strain." . . . And we can expect that, since our decisions implementing fundamental fairness in the juvenile court system, hearings have been prolonged, and some of the burdens incident to a juvenile's defense increased, as the system has assimilated the process thereby imposed....

We deal here, not with "the formalities of the criminal adjudicative process" ... but with an analysis of an aspect of the juvenile court system in terms of the kind of risk to which jeopardy refers. Under our decisions, we can find no persuasive distinction in that regard between the proceeding conducted in this case pursuant to Cal. Wel. & Inst'ns Code § 701 and a criminal prosecution, each of which is designed "to vindicate [the] very vital interest in enforcement of criminal laws." ... We therefore conclude that respondent was put in jeopardy at the adjudicatory hearing. Jeopardy attached when respondent was "put to trial before the trier of the facts," ... that is, when the Juvenile Court, as the trier of the facts, began to hear evidence. ...

III

* * *

We cannot agree with petitioner that the trial of respondent in Superior Court on an information charging the same offense as that for which he had been tried in Juvenile Court violated none of the policies of the Double Jeopardy Clause. For, even accepting petitioner's premise that respondent "never faced the risk of more than one punishment," we have pointed out that "the Double Jeopardy Clause ... is written in terms of potential or risk of trial and conviction, not punishment."

* * *

Respondent was subjected to the burden of two trials for the same offense; he was twice put to the task of marshaling his resources against those of the State, twice subjected to the "heavy personal strain" which such an experience represents. ... We turn, therefore, to inquire whether either traditional principles or "the juvenile court's assumed ability to function in a unique manner" ... support an exception to the "constitutional policy of finality" to which respondent would otherwise be entitled. ...

In denying respondent's petitions for writs of habeas corpus, the California Court of Appeal first, and the United States District Court later, concluded that no new jeopardy arose as a result of his transfer from Juvenile Court and trial in Superior Court. ... In the view of those courts, the jeopardy that attaches at an adjudicatory hearing continues until there is a final disposition of the case under the adult charge.

The phrase "continuing jeopardy" describes both a concept and a conclusion. As originally articulated by Mr. Justice Holmes in his dissent in Kepner v. United States, 195 U.S. 100 (1904), the concept has proved an interesting model for comparison with the system of constitutional protection which the Court has in fact derived from the rather ambiguous language and history of the Double Jeopardy Clause. ... Holmes' view has "never been adopted by a majority of this Court." ...

The conclusion, "continuing jeopardy," as distinguished from the concept, has occasionally been used to explain why an accused who has secured the reversal of a conviction on appeal may be retried for the same offense. ... Probably a more satisfactory explanation lies in analysis of the respective interests involved. ... [T]he fact that the proceedings against respondent had not "run their full course" ... within the contemplation of the California Welfare and Institutions Code, at the time of transfer, does not satisfactorily explain why respondent should be deprived of the constitutional protection against a second trial. If there is to be an exception to that protection in the context of the juvenile court system, it must be justified by interests of society, reflected in that unique institution, or of juveniles themselves, of sufficient substance to render tolerable the costs and burdens, noted earlier, which the exception will entail in individual cases.

The possibility of transfer from Juvenile Court to a court of general criminal jurisdiction is a matter of great significance to the juvenile. ... At the same time, there appears to be widely shared agreement that not all juveniles can benefit from the special features and programs of the juvenile court system and that a procedure for transfer to an adult court should be available. ... This general agreement is reflected in the fact that an overwhelming majority of jurisdictions permits transfer in certain circumstances. As might be expected, the statutory provisions differ in numerous details. Whatever their differences, however, such transfer provisions represent an attempt to impart to the juvenile court system the flexibility needed to deal with youthful offenders who cannot benefit from the specialized guidance and treatment contemplated by the system.

* * *

We recognize that juvenile courts, perhaps even more than most courts, suffer from the problems created by spiraling caseloads unaccompanied by enlarged resources and manpower.... And courts should be reluctant to impose on the juvenile court system any additional requirements which could so strain its resources as to endanger its unique functions. However, the burdens that petitioner envisions appear to us neither qualitatively nor quantitatively sufficient to justify a departure in

this context from the fundamental prohibition against double jeopardy.

* * *

We hold that the prosecution of respondent in Superior Court, after an adjudicatory proceeding in Juvenile Court, violated the Double Jeopardy Clause of the Fifth Amendment, as applied to the States through the Fourteenth Amendment. The mandate of the Court of Appeals, which was stayed by that court pending our decision, directs the District Court "to issue a writ of habeas corpus directing the state court, within 60 days, to vacate the adult conviction of Jones and either set him free or remand him to the juvenile court for disposition." Since respondent is no longer subject to the jurisdiction of the California Juvenile Court, we vacate the judgment and remand the case to the Court of Appeals for such further proceedings consistent with this opinion as may be appropriate in the circumstances.

Comments

1. After the *Winship* decision in 1970, the Supreme Court underwent a substantial change in membership; by 1976, four new justices—Blackmun, Powell, Rehnquist, and Stevens—had been appointed to the Court. During these six years, there appeared to be a shift toward "conservatism" on the Court, and there was speculation that the Court would now be less inclined to extend additional due process guarantees to juveniles. The Court's retreat in *McKeiver* increased such speculation. However, *Breed* seems to suggest that the Burger Court is willing to extend additional safeguards to juveniles when the "potential consequences" of a questioned procedure would deny them the "fundamental fairness" guaranteed to adults in criminal prosecutions. Although *McKeiver* may be viewed as a setback, the trilogy of *Gault, Winship,* and *Breed* has had a sizable, even a revolutionary, impact on the juvenile justice system. What is uncertain is whether the Court will continue to expand due process guarantees or "hold the line" in response to the increasing outcry that the juvenile courts, "handcuffed" by due process considerations, are "coddling" young offenders and therefore contributing to the ever-increasing crime rates among young people.

2. Recent lower federal and state court decisions involving the juvenile justice process include *People* v. *Superior Court (Carl W.),* 125 Cal. Rptr. 504 (Calif. 1975) (juvenile court has authority to empanel an advisory jury to assist it in the adjudicatory or jurisdictional phase of its proceedings); *Garcia-Zamora* v. *United States,* 524 F.2d 656 (9th Cir. 1975) (federal enactments reducing the voting age and the age of competency to make contracts do not change the meaning of

the word "minority" in the federal statutes to the condition of being less than 18 years of age, rather than 21, as that word has been judicially construed); *Commonwealth* v. *Webster,* 353 A.2d 372 (Pa. 1975) (police must inform parents of in-custody juvenile suspects of the juveniles' *Miranda* rights before they may question the juveniles); *Stokes* v. *Commonwealth,* 336 N.E.2d 735 (Mass. 1975) (*Breed* v. *Jones* is not to be applied retroactively); *In re Morgan,* 341 N.E.2d 19 (Ill. App. 1975) (15-year-old burglary suspect in the ninth grade of vocational school held capable of intelligent waiver of his *Miranda* rights); *J.T.P.* v. *State,* 544 P.2d 1270 (Okla. Ct. Crim. App. 1975) (confession by juvenile which would be inadmissible at trial under *Miranda* and *Gault* cannot be considered in decision whether to certify juvenile for adult trial); *In re Bryan,* 548 P.2d 693 (Calif. 1976) (*Breed* v. *Jones,* held retroactive); *People* v. *Drayton,* 350 N.E.2d 377 (N.Y. Ct. App. 1976) (state law providing mandatory treatment for juveniles charged with misdemeanors in local courts while leaving treatment of juveniles accused of felonies in a superior court to the discretion of the trial court upheld); *In re Welfare I.Q.S.,* 244 N.W.2d 30 (Minn. 1976) (juvenile waiver decisions should be accompanied by a statement of reasons for the decision); *People* v. *Olivas,* 131 Cal. Rptr. 55 (Calif. 1976) (youthful misdemeanants may not be subjected to the control of the Youth Authority for any period of time in excess of the maximum jail term which might be imposed upon a person sentenced as an adult); *In re D. G. W.,* 361 A.2d 513 (N.J. 1976) (juvenile judge has authority to order a youthful offender to make restitution for his acts of vandalism); *State* v. *Williams,* 361 A.2d 122 (Md. Ct. App. 1976) (ultimate diagnosis of "defective delinquency," resulting in confinement in a state institution, cannot be made by psychologists); *In re R. L. W.,* 245 N. W.2d 204 (Minn. 1976) (juvenile found guilty of contempt of court not denied due process resulting when sentenced to 30 days in an adult workhouse without separate accommodations for juveniles); *In re L. J.,* 552 P.2d 1322 (Ore. App. 1976) (juveniles facing delinquency proceedings for offenses that would be crimes if committed by adults are entitled to assert the same affirmative defenses as adults); *In re Thierry,* 132 Cal. Rptr. 194 (Calif. 1976) (state law permitting warrantless arrests of juveniles for misdemeanors commited outside the presence of the arresting officer upheld).

8.04 DUE PROCESS AND NONDELINQUENT JUVENILES

The School Paddling Case

INGRAHAM v. WRIGHT

Supreme Court of the United States, 1977
430 U.S. 651, 97 S. Ct. 1401, 51 L. Ed. 2d 711

Petitioners James Ingraham and Roosevelt Andrews, pupils at a junior high school in Miami, Florida, filed a complaint in federal district court alleging that they and other students had been subjected to disciplinary corporal punishment by paddling in violation of the Eighth Amendment prohibition against cruel and

unusual punishment. The Florida statute authorized corporal punishment after the teacher had consulted with the principal and specified that the punishment was not be to "degrading or unduly severe." A school board regulation contained specific directions and limitations, authorizing punishment administered to a recalcitrant student's buttocks with a wooden paddle. The evidence showed that the paddling of petitioners was exceptionally harsh. The district court dismissed the complaint, and the Court of Appeals (5th Cir.) affirmed. The Supreme Court granted certiorari.

Mr. Justice POWELL delivered the opinion of the Court.

This case presents questions concerning the use of corporal punishment in public schools: first, whether the paddling of students as a means of maintaining school discipline constitutes cruel and unusual punishment in violation of the Eighth Amendment; and second, to the extent that paddling is constitutionally permissible, whether the Due Process Clause of the Fourteenth Amendment requires prior notice and opportunity to be heard.

* * *

The use of corporal punishment in this country as a means of disciplining schoolchildren dates back to the colonial period. It has survived the transformation of primary and secondary education from the colonials' reliance on optional private arrangements to our present system of compulsory education and dependence on public schools. Despite the general abandonment of corporal punishment as a means of punishing criminal offenders, the practice continues to play a role in the public education of schoolchildren in most parts of the country. Professional and public opinion is sharply divided on the practice, and has been for more than a century. Yet we can discern no trend toward its elimination.

At common law a single principle has governed the use of corporal punishment since before the American Revolution: teachers may impose reasonable but not excessive force to discipline a child. . . . To the extent that the force is excessive or unreasonable the educator in virtually all States is subject to possible civil and criminal liability.

* * *

Of the 23 States that have addressed the problem through legislation, 21 have authorized the moderate use of corporal punishment in public schools. Of these States only a few have elaborated on the common law test of reasonableness, typically providing for approval or notification of the child's parents, or for infliction of punishment only by the principal or in the presence of an adult witness. Only two States, Massachusetts and New Jersey, have prohibited all corporal punishment in their public schools. Where the legislatures have not acted, the state courts have uniformly preserved the common law rule permitting teachers to use reasonable force in disciplining children in their charge.

Against this background of historical and contemporary approval of reasonable corporal punishment, we turn to the constitutional questions before us.

The Eighth Amendment provides, "Excessive bail shall not be required, nor excessive fines imposed, nor cruel and unusual punishment inflicted." Bail, fines and punishment traditionally have been associated with the criminal process, and by subjecting the three to parallel limitations the text of the Amendment suggests an intention to limit the power of those entrusted with the criminal law function of government. An examination of the history of the Amendment and the decisions of this Court construing the proscription against cruel and unusual punishment confirms that it was designed to protect those convicted of crimes. We adhere to this longstanding limitation and hold that the Eighth Amendment does not apply to the paddling of children as a means of maintaining discipline in public schools.

* * *

In light of the [the history of the Eighth Amendment], it is not surprising to find that every decision of this Court considering whether a punishment is "cruel and unusual" within the meaning of the Eighth and Fourteenth Amendments has dealt with a criminal punishment. See Estelle v. Gamble, 429 U.S. 190 (1976) (incarceration without medical care) [Chapter Nine, § 9.03]; Gregg v. Georgia, 428 U.S. 153 (1976) (execution for murder) [Chapter Eleven, § 11.03]; Powell v. Texas, 392 U.S. 514 (1968) ($20 fine for drunkenness) [Chapter Eleven, § 11.02]; Robinson v. California, 370 U.S. 660 (1962) (incarceration as a criminal for addiction to narcotics) [Chapter Eleven, § 11.02]; Trop v. Dulles, 356 U.S. 86 (1958) (plurality opinion) (expatriation for desertion); Louisiana ex rel. Francis v. Resweber, 329 U.S. 459 (1947) (execution by electrocution after a failed first attempt); Weems v. United States [217 U.S. 349 (1910)] (15 years' imprisonment and other penalties for falsifying an official document); Howard v. Fleming, 191 U.S. 126 (1903) (10 years' imprisonment for conspiracy to defraud); In re Kemmler [136 U.S. 436 (1890)] (execution by electrocution); Wilkerson v. Utah, 99 U.S. 130 (1879) (execution by firing squad); Pervear v. Commonwealth, 5 Wall. 475 (1867) (fine and imprisonment at hard labor for bootlegging).

These decisions recognize that the Cruel and Unusual Punishments Clause circumscribes the criminal process in three ways: first, it limits the kinds of punishment that can be imposed on those convicted of crimes, . . . second, it proscribes punishment grossly disproportionate to the severity of the crime, . . . and third, it imposes substantive limits on what can be made criminal and punished as such. . . . We have recognized the last limitation as one to be applied sparingly. "The primary purpose of [the Cruel and Unusual Punishment Clause] has always been considered, and properly so, to be directed at the method or kind of punishment imposed for the violation of criminal statutes. . . ." Powell v. Texas, 392 U.S., at 531–532 (plurality opinion).

In the few cases where the Court has had occasion to confront claims that impositions outside the criminal process constituted cruel and unusual punishment, it has had no difficulty finding the Eighth Amendment inapplicable. Thus, in Fong Yue Ting v. United States, 149 U.S. 698 (1893), the Court held the Eighth Amendment inapplicable to the deportation of aliens on the ground that "deportation is not a punishment for crime." Id., at 730; see Mahler v. Eby, 264 U.S. 32 (1924); Bugajewitz v. Adams, 228 U.S. 585 (1913). And in Uphaus v. Wyman, 360 U.S. 72 (1959), the Court sustained a judgment of civil contempt, resulting in incarceration pending compliance with a subpoena, against a claim that the judgment imposed cruel and unusual punishment. It was emphasized that the case involved "essentially a civil remedy designed for the benefit of other parties . . . exercised for centuries to secure compliance with judicial decrees." Id., at 81, quoting Green v. United States, 356 U.S. 165, 197 (1958) (dissenting opinion).

Petitioners acknowledge that the original design of the Cruel and Unusual Punishments Clause was to limit criminal punishments, but urge nonetheless that the prohibition should be extended to ban the paddling of school children. Observing that the Framers of the Eighth Amendment could not have envisioned our present system of public and compulsory education, with its opportunities for noncriminal punishments, petitioners contend that extension of the prohibition against cruel punishments is necessary lest we afford greater protection to criminals than to schoolchildren. It would be anomalous, they say, if school children could be beaten without constitutional redress, while hardened criminals suffering the same beatings at the hands of their jailors might have a valid claim under the Eighth Amendment. See Jackson v. Bishop, 404 F.2d 571 (8th Cir. 1968); cf. Estelle v. Gamble, supra. Whatever force this logic may have in other settings,[kk] we find it an inadequate basis for wrenching the Eighth Amendment from its historical context and extending it to traditional disciplinary practices in the public schools.

The prisoner and the schoolchild stand in wholly different circumstances, separated

---

[kk]Some punishments, though not labeled "criminal" by the State, may be sufficiently analogous to criminal punishments in the circumstances in which they are administered to justify application of the Eighth Amendment. Cf. In re Gault, 387 U.S. 1 (1967). We have no occasion in this case, for example, to consider whether or under what circumstances persons involuntarily confined in mental or juvenile institutions can claim the protection of the Eighth Amendment.

by the harsh facts of criminal conviction and incarceration. The prisoner's conviction entitles the State to classify him as a "criminal," and his incarceration deprives him of the freedom "to be with family and friends and to form the other enduring attachments of normal life." Morrissey v. Brewer, 408 U.S. 471, 482 (1972). See Meachum v. Fano, 427 U.S. 215, 224–225 (1976). Prison brutality, as the Court of Appeals observed in this case, is "part of the total punishment to which the individual is subjected for his crime and, as such, is a proper subject for Eighth Amendment scrutiny." 525 F.2d, at 915. Even so, the protection afforded by the Eighth Amendment is limited. After incarceration, only the "unnecessary and wanton infliction of pain," Estelle v. Gamble, 429 U.S., at 190, quoting Gregg v. Georgia, supra, at 173, constitutes cruel and unusual punishment forbidden by the Eighth Amendment.

The schoolchild has little need for the protection of the Eighth Amendment. Though attendance may not always be voluntary, the public school remains an open institution. Except perhaps when very young, the child is not physically restrained from leaving school during school hours; and at the end of the school day, the child is invariably free to return home. Even while at school, the child brings with him the support of family and friends and is rarely apart from teachers and other pupils who may witness and protest any instances of mistreatment.

The openness of the public school and its supervision by the community afford significant safeguards against the kinds of abuses from which the Eighth Amendment protects the prisoner. In virtually every community where corporal punishment is permitted in the schools, these safeguards are reinforced by the legal constraints of the common law. Public school teachers and administrators are privileged at common law to inflict only such corporal punishment as is reasonably necessary for education and discipline of the child; any punishment going beyond the privilege may result in both civil and criminal liability. As long as the schools are open to public scrutiny, there is no reason to believe that the common law constraints will not effectively remedy and deter excesses such as those alleged in this case.

We conclude that when public school teachers or administrators impose disciplinary corporal punishment, the Eighth Amendment is inapplicable. The pertinent constitutional question is whether the imposition is consonant with the requirements of due process.

The Fourteenth Amendment prohibits any State deprivation of life, liberty or property without due process of law. Application of this prohibition requires the familiar two-stage analysis: we must first ask whether the asserted individual interests are encompassed within the Fourteenth Amendment's protection of "life, liberty or property"; if protected interests are implicated, we then must decide what procedures constitute "due process of law." Morrissey v. Brewer, 408 U.S., at 481; Board of Regents v. Roth, 408 U.S. 564, 569–572 (1972). See Friendly, "Some Kind of Hearing," 123 U. Pa. L. Rev. 1267 (1975). Following that analysis here, we find that corporal punishment in public school implicates a constitutionally protected liberty interest, but we hold that the traditional common law remedies are fully adequate to afford due process.

* * *

"[T]he question remains what process is due." Morrissey v. Brewer, 408 U.S. at 481. Were it not for the common law privilege permitting teachers to inflict reasonable corporal punishment on children in their care, and the availability of the traditional remedies for abuse, the case for requiring advance procedural safeguards would be strong indeed. But here we deal with a punishment—paddling—within that tradition, and the question is whether the common law remedies are adequate to afford due process. . . . Whether in this case the common law remedies for excessive corporal punishment constitute due process of law must turn on an analysis of the competing interests at stake, viewed against the background of "history, reason, [and] the past course of decisions." The analysis requires consideration of three distinct factors: "first, the private interest that will be affected . . . ; second, the risk of an erroneous deprivation of such interest . . . and the probable value, if any, of additional or substitute procedural safeguards; and, finally, the [state] interest, including the function involved and the fiscal and administrative burdens that the additional or substitute procedural requirement would entail." Mathews v. Eldridge, 424 U.S. 319,

335 (1976). Cf. Arnett v. Kennedy, 416 U.S. 134, 167–168 (1974) (Powell, J., concurring).

* * *

. . . In any deliberate infliction of corporal punishment on a child who is restrained for that purpose, there is some risk that the intrusion on the child's liberty will be unjustified and therefore unlawful. In these circumstances the child has a strong interest in procedural safeguards that minimize the risk of wrongful punishment and provide for the resolution of disputed questions of justification.

We turn now to a consideration of the safeguards that are available under applicable Florida Law.

Florida has continued to recognize, and indeed has strengthened by statute, the common law right of a child not to be subjected to excessive corporal punishment in school. Under Florida law the teacher and principal of the school decide in the first instance whether corporal punishment is reasonably necessary under the circumstances in order to discipline a child who has misbehaved. But they must exercise prudence and restraint. For Florida has preserved the traditional judicial proceedings for determining whether the punishment was justified. If the punishment inflicted is later found to have been excessive—not reasonably believed at the time to be necessary for the child's discipline or training—the school authorities inflicting it may be held liable in damages to the child and, if malice is shown, they may be subject to criminal penalties.

Although students have testified in this case to specific instances of abuse, there is every reason to believe that such mistreatment is an aberration. The uncontradicted evidence suggests that corporal punishment in the Dade County schools was, "[w]ith the exception of a few cases . . . unremarkable in physical severity." App. 152. Moreover, because paddlings are usually inflicted in response to conduct directly observed by teachers in their presence, the risk that a child will be paddled without cause is typically insignificant. . . .

In those cases where severe punishment is contemplated, the available civil and criminal sanctions for abuse—considered in light of the openness of the school environment—afford significant protection against unjustified corporal punishment. Teachers and school authorities are unlikely to inflict corporal punishment unnecessarily or excessively when a possible consequence of doing so is the institution of civil or criminal proceedings against them.

* * *

[E]ven if the need for advance procedural safeguards were clear, the question would remain whether the incremental benefit could justify the cost. Acceptance of petitioners' claims would work a transformation in the law governing corporal punishment in Florida and most other States. Given the impracticability of formulating a rule of procedural due process that varies with the severity of the particular imposition, the prior hearing petitioners seek would have to precede any paddling, however moderate or trivial.

Such a universal constitutional requirement would significantly burden the use of corporal punishment as a disciplinary measure. Hearings—even informal hearings—require time, personnel, and a diversion of attention from normal school pursuits. School authorities may well choose to abandon corporal punishment rather than incur the burdens of complying with the procedural requirements. Teachers, properly concerned with maintaining authority in the classroom, may well prefer to rely on other disciplinary measures—which they may view as less effective—rather than confront the possible disruption that prior notice and a hearing may entail. Paradoxically, such an alteration of disciplinary policy is most likely to occur in the ordinary case where the contemplated punishment is well within the common law privilege.

Elimination or curtailment of corporal punishment would be welcomed by many as a societal advance. But when such a policy choice may result from this Court's determination of an asserted right to due process, rather than from the normal processes of community debate and legislative action, the societal costs cannot be dismissed as insubstantial. We are reviewing here a legislative judgment, rooted in history and reaffirmed in the laws of many States, that corporal punishment serves important educational interests. . . . In view of the low incidence of abuse, the openness of our schools, and the common law safeguards that already exist, the risk of error that may result in violation of a school-child's substantive rights can only be regarded as minimal. Imposing additional administrative safeguards as a constitutional requirement might reduce that risk marginally, but would also entail a significant intrusion into an area of primary educational responsibility. We conclude that the Due Process Clause does not require notice and a hearing prior to the imposition of corporal punishment in the public schools, as that practice is authorized and limited by common law.

Petitioners cannot prevail on either of the theories before us in this case. The Eighth Amendment's prohibition against cruel and unusual punishments is inapplicable to school paddlings, and the Fourteenth Amendment's requirement of procedural due process is satisfied by Florida's preservation of common law constraints and remedies. We therefore agree with the Court of Appeals that petitioner's evidence affords no basis for injunctive relief, and that petitioners cannot recover damages on the basis of any Eighth Amendment or procedural due process violation.

Affirmed.

Mr. Justice WHITE, with whom Mr. Justice BRENNAN, Mr. Justice MARSHALL, and Mr. Justice STEVENS join, dissenting.

The Eighth Amendment places a flat prohibition against the infliction of "cruel and unusual punishments." This reflects a societal judgment that there are some punishments that are so barbaric and inhumane that we will not permit them to be imposed on anyone, no matter how opprobrious the offense. See Robinson v. California 370 U.S. 660, 676 (1962) (Douglas, J., concurring). If there are some punishments that are so barbaric that they may not be imposed for the commission of crimes, designated by our social system as the most thoroughly reprehensible acts an individual can commit, then a fortiori, similar punishments may not be imposed on persons for less culpable acts, such as breaches of school discipline. Thus, if it is constitutionally impermissible to cut off someone's ear for the commission of murder, it must be unconstitutional to cut off a child's ear for being late to class. Although there were no ears cut off in this case, the record reveals beatings so severe that if they were in-

flicted on a hardened criminal for the commission of a serious crime, they might not pass constitutional muster.

Nevertheless, the majority holds that the Eighth Amendment "was designed to protect [only] those convicted of crimes," . . . relying on a vague and inconclusive recitation of the history of the Amendment. Yet the constitutional prohibition is against cruel and unusual *punishments*; nowhere is that prohibition limited or modified by the language of the Constitution. Certainly, the fact that the Framers did not choose to insert the word "criminal" into the language of the Eighth Amendment is strong evidence that the Amendment was designed to prohibit all inhumane or barbaric punishments, no matter what the nature of the offense for which the punishment is imposed.

No one can deny that spanking of school children is "punishment" under any reasonable reading of the word, for the similarities between spanking in public schools and other forms of punishment are too obvious to ignore. Like other forms of punishment, spanking of school children involves an institutionalized response to the violation of some official rule or regulation proscribing certain conduct and is imposed for the purpose of rehabilitating the offender, deterring the offender and others like him from committing the violation in the future, and inflicting some measure of social retribution for the harm that has been done.

. . . The relevant inquiry is not whether the offense for which a punishment is inflicted has been labeled as criminal, but whether the purpose of the deprivation is among those ordinarily associated with punishment, such as retribution, rehabilitation, or deterrence.

If this purposive approach were followed in the present case, it would be clear that spanking in the Florida schools is punishment within the meaning of the Eighth Amendment. . . .

* * *

[T]he Eighth Amendment has never been confined to criminal punishments. Nevertheless, the majority adheres to its view that any protections afforded by the Eighth Amendment must have something to do with criminals, and it would therefore confine any exceptions to its general rule that only criminal punishments are covered by the Eighth Amendment to abuses inflicted on prisoners. Thus, if a prisoner is beaten mercilessly for a breach of discipline, he is entitled to the protection of the Eighth Amendment, while a school child who commits the same breach of discipline and is similarly beaten is simply not covered.

* * *

By holding that the Eighth Amendment protects only criminals, the majority adopts the view that one is entitled to the protections afforded by the Eighth Amendment only if he is punished for acts that are sufficiently opprobrious for society to make them "criminal." This is a curious holding in view of the fact that the more culpable the offender the more likely it is that the punishment will not be disproportionate to the offense, and consequently, the less likely it is that the punishment will be cruel and unusual. Conversely, a public school student who is spanked for a mere breach of discipline may sometimes have a strong argument that the punishment does not fit the offense, depending upon the severity of the beating, and therefore that it is cruel and unusual. Yet the majority would afford the student no protection no matter how inhumane and barbaric the punishment inflicted on him might be.

The issue presented in this phase of the case is limited to whether corporal punishment in public schools can *ever* be prohibited by the Eighth Amendment. I am therefore not suggesting that spanking in the public schools is in every instance prohibited by the Eighth Amendment. My own view is that it is not. I only take issue with the extreme view of the majority that corporal punishment in public schools, no matter how barbaric, inhumane, or severe, is never limited by the Eighth Amendment. Where corporal punishment becomes so severe as to be unacceptable in a civilized society, I can see no reason that it should become any more acceptable just because it is inflicted on children in the public schools.

The majority concedes that corporal punishment in the public schools implicates an interest protected by the Due Process Clause—the liberty interest of the student to be free from "bodily restraint and punishment" involving "appreciable physical pain" inflicted by persons acting under color of state law. The question remaining,

as the majority recognizes, is what process is due. . . .

In Goss v. Lopez, 419 U.S. 565 (1975), the Court applied this principle to the school disciplinary process, holding that a student must be given an informal opportunity to be heard before he is finally suspended from public schools:

"*Disciplinarians, although proceeding in utmost good faith, frequently act on the reports and advice of others;* and the controlling facts and the nature of the conduct under challenge are often disputed. *The risk of error is not at all trivial,* and it should be guarded against if that may be done without prohibitive cost or interference with the educational process." Id., at 580. (Emphasis added.)

To guard against this risk of punishing an innocent child, the Due Process Clause requires, not an "elaborate hearing" before a neutral party, but simply "an informal give-and-take between student and disciplinarian" which gives the student "an opportunity to explain his version of the facts." Id., at 580, 582, 584.

The Court now holds that these "rudimentary precautions against unfair or mistaken findings of misconduct," id., at 581, are not required if the student is punished with "appreciable physical pain" rather than with a suspension, even though both punishments deprive the student of a constitutionally protected interest. Although the respondent school authorities provide absolutely *no* process to the student before the punishment is finally inflicted, the majority concludes that the student is nonetheless given due process because he can later sue the teacher and recover damages if the punishment was "excessive."

This tort action is utterly inadequate to protect against erroneous infliction of punishment for two reasons. First, under Florida law, a student punished for an act he did not commit cannot recover damages from a teacher "proceeding in utmost good faith. . . . on the reports and advice of others," p. 10, supra; the student has no remedy at all for punishment imposed on the basis of mistaken facts, at least as long as the punishment was reasonable from the point of view of the disciplinarian, uninformed by any prior hearing. The "traditional common law remedies" on which the majority relies . . . thus do nothing to protect the student from the danger that concerned the Court in Goss—the risk of reasonable, good faith mistake in the school disciplinary process.

Second, and more important, even if the student could sue for good faith error in the infliction of punishment, the lawsuit occurs after the punishment has been finally imposed. The infliction of physical pain is final and irreparable; it cannot be undone in a subsequent proceeding. There is every reason to require, as the Court did in Goss, a few minutes of "informal give-and-take between student and disciplinarian" as a "meaningful hedge" against the erroneous infliction of irreparable injury. 419 U.S., at 583–584.

The majority's conclusion that a damage remedy for excessive corporal punishment affords adequate process rests on the novel theory that the State may punish an individual without giving him any opportunity to present his side of the story, as long as he can later recover damages from a state official if he is innocent. The logic of this theory would permit a State that punished speeding with a one-day jail sentence to make a driver serve his sentence first without a trial and then sue to recover damages for wrongful imprisonment. Similarly, the State could finally take away a prisoner's good time credits for alleged disciplinary infractions and require him to bring a damage suit after he was eventually released. There is no authority for this theory, nor does the majority purport to find any, in the procedural due process decisions of this Court. Those cases have "consistently held that *some kind of hearing is required at some time before a person is finally deprived* of his property interests . . . [and that] a person's liberty is equally protected. . . ." Wolff v. McDonnell, 418 U.S. 539, 557–558 (1974). (Emphasis added.)

* * *

There is . . . no basis in logic or authority for the majority's suggestion that an action to recover damages for excessive corporal punishment "afford[s] substantially greater protection to the child than the informal conference mandated by Goss." The majority purports to follow the settled principle that what process is due depends on "'the risk of an erroneous deprivation of [the protected] interest . . . and the probable value, if any, of additional or substitute procedural safeguards'"; it recognizes, as did Goss, the risk of error in the school disciplinary process and concedes that "the child has a strong interest in procedural safeguards that minimize the risk of wrongful punishment . . . ," . . . ; but it somehow concludes that this risk is adequately reduced by a damage remedy that never has been recognized by a Florida court, that leaves unprotected the innocent student punished by mistake, and that allows the State to punish first and hear the student's version of events later. I cannot agree.

The majority emphasizes, as did the dissenters in Goss, that even the "rudimentary precautions" required by that decision would impose some burden on the school disciplinary process. But those costs are no greater if the student is paddled rather than suspended; the risk of error in the punishment is no smaller; and the fear of "a significant intrusion" into the disciplinary process, ante, at 31 (compare Goss, supra, at 585) (Powell, J., dissenting), is just as exaggerated. The disciplinarians need only take a few minutes to give the student "notice of the charges against him and, if he denies them, an explanation of the evidence the authorities have and an opportunity to present his side of the story." Id., at 581. In this context the Constitution requires, "if anything less than a fair-minded principal would impose upon himself" in order to avoid injustice. Id., at 583.

I would reverse the judgment below.

[Mr. Justice STEVENS wrote a separate dissenting opinion.]

Comments

1. The majority in *Ingraham* v. *Wright,* supra, addressed the issue of the applicability of the Eighth Amendment prohibition against "cruel and unusual" punishment to particular classes of persons, i.e., crim-

inals and noncriminal schoolchildren. Could a juvenile probation officer beat a juvenile delinquent without running afoul of the Eighth Amendment? Are delinquents "criminals" within the meaning of *Ingraham?* Or does a person have to be an adult to be a "criminal"? May a person (adult or child) confined to a mental institution be spanked for violating institutional rules? See footnote kk in the majority opinion.

2. As noted by the Court in *Ingraham,* the legislatures of 21 states have authorized the use of corporal punishment in public schools. The authorizing statutes are: Calif. Education Code, §§ 49000–49001 (1976); Del. Code Ann., Tit. 14 § 701 (1976 Supp.); Fla. Stat. Ann. § 232.27 (1977); Ga. Code Ann. §§ 322–835, 32–836 (1976); Hawaii Rev. Stat. §§ 298–16 (1975 Supp.), 703–309(2) (1975); Ill. Ann. Stat., c. 122 §§ 24–24, 34–84a (1977 Supp.); Ind. Code Ann. § 20–8.1–5–2 (1975); Md. Educ. Code Ann., Art. 77, § 98B (1975) (in specified counties); Mich. Comp. Laws Ann. § 340, 756 (1976); Mont. Rev. Codes Ann. § 75–6109 (1947); Nev. Rev. Stat. § 392.–465 (1973); N.C. Gen. Stat. § 115–146 (1975); Ohio Rev. Code Ann. § 3319.41 (1972); Okla. Stat. Ann., Tit. 70, § 6–114 (1972); Pa. Cons. Stat. Ann., Tit. 24 § 13–1317 (1976–1977 Supp.); S.C. Code § 21–776 (1975 Supp.); S.D. Comp. Laws Ann. § 13–32–2 (1975); Vt. Stat. Ann., Tit. 16, § 1161 (1974); Va. Code Ann. § 22–231.1 (1950); W. Va. Code, § 18A–5–1 (1977); Wyo. Stat. § 21.1–64 (1975 Supp.).

3. In *Goss* v. *Lopez,* 419 U.S. 565 (1974), petitioners, who were public school students, filed a class action suit against Ohio school officials challenging a state statute that permitted the principal of an Ohio public school to suspend any pupil for misconduct for up to ten days without a prior hearing. The complaint sought a declaration that the statute was unconstitutional in that it permitted school administrators to deprive pupils of their right to an education in violation of the Due Process Clause of the Fourteenth Amendment. A three-judge federal district court granted the relief sought. On appeal, the Supreme Court affirmed. In a 5–4 decision authored by Justice White, the Court held that "although Ohio may not be constitutionally obliged to establish and maintain a public school system," a state may not suspend a student on the grounds of misconduct, absent fundamentally fair procedures compatible with the Due Process Clause. The majority went on to hold that a student should be given oral or written notice of the charges against him, and, if denied, an explanation of the evidence to be used and an opportunity to present his version.

4. In *Goss,* supra, the Supreme Court stated that the right to an education, although not constitutionally required, involves a "property" interest under the Due Process Clause, and in *Ingraham,* the Court held that corporal punishment of public school pupils involves a "liberty" interest within the meaning of the Due Process Clause. Yet the Court was unwilling to provide procedural safeguards for the administration of corporal punishment, even if severe, but it was willing to provide minimal due process safeguards in connection with a suspension of ten days or less. Do you agree with these apparently conflicting results?

9

LEGAL RIGHTS OF CONVICTED OFFENDERS

9.01 INTRODUCTION

Criminal offenders lose some, but not all, of their constitutional rights as a result of conviction. It is difficult to state precisely which rights are retained and which lost, in part, because of the lack of definitive United States Supreme Court decisions in this area. Lower federal court opinions proliferate, but there is often substantial disagreement among the circuits.

For various reasons, the number of lawsuits filed by inmates attacking conditions of confinement and prison regulations has increased dramatically in recent years. But before we discuss some of the legal problems raised by these lawsuits, a brief statement of facts regarding correctional institutions and their inmates is appropriate.

Some Facts About Correctional Institutions and Prisoners*

There are approximately 400 institutions for offenders in the United States, ranging

---

*From Modern Criminal Justice by Wright & Lewis. Copyright © 1978 by McGraw-Hill, Inc. Used with permission of McGraw-Hill Book Co. References have been omitted.

from maximum-security prisons to reception centers. Of these, 250 are prisons for adults, housing over two hundred thousand prisoners (federal and state). About 10 percent of all prisoners are confined in federal institutions, and about 3 percent of the adult prison population is made up of women.

Of the 77 maximum-security institutions in America, 45 were built before 1900 (12 were built before 1850); they employ over seventy thousand full-time employees. Of all correctional employees, 87 percent perform only custodial or administrative functions. Only the 31 prisons for women and 58 institutions for men are oriented primarily toward rehabilitation; the remainder are primarily custodial.

In the United States, there are over five thousand jails which house convicted misdemeanants, defendants awaiting trial, and a few people who are serving short felony sentences. More than half of all people in jail have not been convicted of any offense, the majority being pretrial detainees who are unable to make bail. Our jails hold 3 to 4 million people, and in two-thirds of the jails there are no rehabilitation programs. Over a million people served jail sentences in 1965.

It has been estimated that between 20 and 50 million Americans have criminal records and that 50 to 90 percent of the males in high poverty areas have such records. However, only 28 percent of all convicted offenders are in institutions on any given day (72 percent are in community or juvenile programs such as probation, parole, or halfway houses).

The majority of convicted offenders are less than thirty years of age, poor, have less than a high school education, lack salable skills, and come from urban areas. But most of our major correctional institutions are located in rural areas, although there is a trend toward smaller institutions that are nearer urban areas.

A disproportionate number of institutionalized offenders are nonwhite. Blacks make up more than half the inmate population in many large prisons. All but 2 percent of institutionalized offenders are eventually released (either on parole or because they have served their full terms). Although we sentence our offenders to some of the longest prison terms in the world, several polls indicate that most Americans believe that our courts are too lenient with offenders. Yet our recidivism rate is estimated to run between 50 and 80 percent. In view of the above, it is not surprising that prisoners' litigation has continued to rise in recent years. In the words of Chief Justice Burger, our prisons are "a national disgrace."

Few Americans have any substantial knowledge of their prisons; an "out of sight, out of mind" philosophy is dominant in our society. But this attitude may change. One important development has been the suggestion that female criminality has dramatically increased in recent years. Such a trend would make the proportion of incarcerated males to females more equal and would probably draw increased public attention to our correctional institutions.

Federal Jurisdiction and Remedies for Inmates' Complaints

Most prisoners' rights cases are brought in the federal courts because of the many obstacles such suits have encountered in state courts in the past. Historically, the doctrine of *sovereign immunity* (governmental immunity from liability) was a barrier to suits brought by inmates against correctional authorities. Although sovereign immunity has largely been abrogated in most jurisdictions and state remedies (e.g., state habeas corpus petitions, criminal prosecutions of correctional authorities, civil damage suits, contempt of court citations) are available to redress legitimate inmate complaints, most inmate suits are today filed in the federal courts because federal jurisdiction has been broadened in this area.

A federal court can exercise its primary jurisdiction to review state prison practices in two principal ways: (1) via federal habeas corpus petitions,[1] whereby an inmate seeks release from custody on the ground that his conviction was unlawful (see Chapter Fourteen, § 14.03), and (2) via inmate suits filed under 42 U.S.C. § 1983 of the 1964 Civil Rights Act—the so-called 1983 suit (see Chapter Ten, §§ 10.01 and 10.02). Although habeas corpus can be used, most inmate suits challenging prison conditions and regulations are filed in federal courts under § 1983.

The applicable statutes provide:

42 U.S.C.A. § 1343

The district courts shall have original jurisdiction of any civil action authorized by law to be commenced by any person:

(3) To redress the deprivation, under color of any state law, statute, ordinance, regulation, custom or usage, of any right, privilege, or immunity secured by the Constitution of the United States or by any Act of Congress providing for equal rights of citizens or of all persons within the jurisdiction of the United States.

42 U.S.C.A. § 1983

Every person who, under color of any statute, ordinance, regulation, custom, or usage, of any State or Territory, subjects or causes to be subjected, any citizen of the United States or other person within the jurisdiction thereof to the deprivation of any rights, privileges, or immunities secured by

---

[1] 28 U.S.C. §§ 2241–2255.

the Constitution and laws, shall be liable to the party injured in an action at law, suit in equity, or other proper proceeding for redress.

Thus an inmate must allege two claims in a § 1983 suit: (1) that the defendants acted "under color of" state law (acts by state or local officials); and (2) that the defendants deprived the inmate of a constitutional (or federal) right.

The major advantages of a § 1983 suit, as opposed to a habeas corpus petition, are that a § 1983 suit does not require that available state remedies be exhausted before the federal district courts will have jurisdiction (as is the case when state prisoners file federal habeas corpus petitions) and that an award of money damages is possible under a § 1983 suit. Three types of money damages are available to redress the denial of constitutional rights: (1) *actual damages*—to compensate for an inmate's out-of-pocket expenses and mental suffering; (2) *nominal damages*—to vindicate an inmate's rights if no actual damages were sustained; and (3) *punitive damages*—to punish wrongful acts done intentionally and maliciously.

The major disadvantage of a § 1983 suit is that the remedy of release from imprisonment is not available. (It can be obtained only by a writ of habeas corpus.[2]) Thus, federal habeas corpus can be used either to secure release from imprisonment or to challenge prison practices, while a § 1983 suit can be utilized only for the latter purpose.

It should be noted that § 1983 suits are not available to federal prisoners since federal correctional authorities do not act "under color of" state law. However, the Supreme Court, in *Bivens* v. *Six Unknown Named Agents of the Federal Narcotics Bureau*, 403 U.S. 388 (1971) (Chapter Ten, § 10.02), judicially created a federal cause of action for violation of an individual's constitutional rights by a federal agent acting under color of federal law. The narrow holding in that case was that money damages may be obtained upon a showing of a Fourth Amendment violation by federal officials, but presumably all constitutional violations by law enforcement officials acting in their official capacities (with the exception of prosecutors) are actionable in the federal courts.[3]

In addition to money damages and release from confinement, there are other remedies available to inmates bringing suit in the federal courts. For example, the Federal Declaratory Judgment Act (1934) allows a federal court to declare the legal rights, responsibilities, and liabilities of two or more adverse parties prior to the commission of some act that might result in actionable liabilities. The Declaratory Judgment Act provides, inter alia:

28 U.S.C. § 2201

In a case of actual controversy within its jurisdiction . . . any court of the United States, upon the filing of an appropriate pleading, may declare the rights and other legal relations of any interested party seeking such declaration. . . .

Under this act, a federal court may grant "necessary or proper relief."[4] Such relief may take the form of an *injunction*—a judicial order directing some party to do, or refrain from doing, a specific thing, (e.g., removing an inmate from solitary confinement). Criminal prosecutions of correctional authorities are allowed under the 1970 Civil Rights Act.[5] Federal courts can invoke their *contempt power* to enforce any of these remedies.[6]

In summary, inmates usually have a choice of federal or state forums when seeking redress of legitimate complaints against correctional authorities. The remedies available depend upon which forum is chosen.

---

[3]See *Imbler* v. *Pachtman*, 424 U.S. 409 (1976) (Chapter Ten, § 10.02).

[4]28 U.S.C. § 2202.

[5]18 U.S.C.A. § 241–242. See also *Screws* v. *United States,* 325 U.S. 91 (1945); and *United States* v. *Classic*, 313 U.S. 299 (1941).

[6]*White* v. *Commissioner, Alabama Board of Corrections,* 470 F.2d 55 (5th Cir. 1972).

---

[2]*Preiser* v. *Rodriguez,* 411 U.S. 475 (1973).

9.02   DUE PROCESS OUTSIDE THE PRISON WALLS

Revocation of Probation When Sentence Not Previously Imposed

MEMPA v. RHAY

Supreme Court of the United States, 1967
389 U.S. 128, 88 S. Ct. 254, 19 L. Ed. 2d 336

The facts are stated in the opinion.

Mr. Justice MARSHALL delivered the opinion of the Court.

These consolidated cases raise the question of the extent of the right to counsel at the time of sentencing where the sentencing has been deferred subject to probation.

Petitioner Jerry Douglas Mempa was convicted in the Spokane County Superior Court on June 17, 1959, of the offense of "joyriding," Wash. Rev. Code § 9.54.020. This conviction was based on his plea of guilty entered with the advice of court-appointed counsel. He was then placed on probation for two years on the condition, inter alia, that he first spend 30 days in the county jail, and the imposition of sentence was deferred. . . .

About four months later the Spokane County prosecuting attorney moved to have petitioner's probation revoked on the ground that he had been involved in a burglary on September 15, 1959. A hearing was held in the Spokane County Superior Court on October 23, 1959. Petitioner Mempa, who was 17 years old at the time, was accompanied to the hearing by his stepfather. He was not represented by counsel and was not asked whether he wished to have counsel appointed for him. Nor was any inquiry made concerning the appointed counsel who had previously represented him.

At the hearing Mempa was asked if it was true that he had been involved in the alleged burglary and he answered in the affirmative. A probation officer testified without cross-examination that according to his information petitioner had been involved in the burglary and had previously denied participation in it. Without asking petitioner if he had anything to say or any evidence to supply, the court immediately entered an order revoking petitioner's probation and then sentenced him to 10 years in the penitentiary, but stated that it would recommend to the parole board that Mempa be required to serve only a year.

In 1965 Mempa filed a pro se petition for a writ of habeas corpus with the Washington Supreme Court, claiming that he had been deprived of his right to counsel at the proceeding at which his probation was revoked and sentence imposed. The Washington Supreme Court denied the petition. . . .

Petitioner William Earl Walkling was convicted in the Thurston County Superior Court on October 29, 1962, of burglary in the second degree on the basis of his plea of guilty entered with the advice of his retained counsel. He was placed on probation for three years and the imposition of sentence was deferred. As conditions of his probation he was required to serve 90 days in the county jail and make restitution. On May 2, 1963, a bench warrant for his arrest was issued based on a report that he had violated the terms of his probation and had left the State.

On February 24, 1964, Walkling was arrested and charged with forgery and grand larceny. After being transferred back to Thurston County he was brought before the court on May 12, 1964, for a hearing on the petition by the prosecuting attorney to revoke his probation. Petitioner then requested a continuance to enable him to retain counsel and was granted a week. On May 18, 1964, the hearing was called and Walkling appeared without a lawyer. He informed the court that he had retained an attorney who was supposed to be present. After waiting for 15 minutes the court went ahead with the hearing in the absence of petitioner's counsel. He was not offered appointed counsel and would not have had counsel appointed for him had he requested it. Whether he made such a request does not appear from the record.

At the hearing a probation officer presented hearsay testimony to the effect that petitioner had committed the acts alleged in the 14 separate counts of forgery and 14 separate counts of grand larceny that had been charged against petitioner previously at the time of his arrest. The court thereupon revoked probation and imposed the maximum sentence of 15 years on Walkling on his prior second degree burglary conviction. Because of the failure of the State to keep a record of the proceeding, nothing is known as to whether Walkling was advised of his right to appeal. He did not, however, take an appeal.

In May 1966 Walkling filed a habeas corpus petition with the Washington Supreme Court, claiming denial of his right to counsel at the combined probation revocation and sentencing proceeding. The petition was denied. . . . We granted certiorari . . . and the cases were consolidated for argument.

In 1948 this Court held in Townsend v. Burke, 334 U.S. 736, that the absence of counsel during sentencing after a plea of guilty coupled with "assumptions concerning his criminal record which were materially untrue" deprived the defendant in that case of due process. Mr. Justice Jackson there stated in conclusion, "In this case, counsel might not have changed the sentence but he could have taken steps to see that the conviction and sentence were not predicated on misinformation or misreading of court records, a requirement of fair play which absence of counsel withheld from this prisoner." . . . Then in Moore v. Michigan, 355 U.S. 155 (1957), where a denial of due process was found when the defendant did not intelligently and understandingly waive counsel before entering a plea of guilty, this Court emphasized the prejudice stemming from the absence of counsel at the hearing on

the degree of the crime following entry of the guilty plea and stated, "The right to counsel is not a right confined to representation during the trial on the merits." . . .

In Hamilton v. Alabama, 368 U.S. 52 (1961), it was held that failure to appoint counsel at arraignment deprived the petitioner of due process, notwithstanding the fact that he simply pleaded not guilty at that time, because under Alabama law certain defenses had to be raised then or be abandoned. See also . . . White v. Maryland, 373 U.S. 59 (1963).

All the foregoing cases, with the exception of White, were decided during the reign of Betts v. Brady, 316 U.S. 455 (1942), and accordingly relied on various "special circumstances" to make the right to counsel applicable. In Gideon v. Wainwright, 372 U.S. 335 (1963), however, Betts was overruled and this Court held that the Sixth Amendment as applied through the Due Process Clause of the Fourteenth Amendment was applicable to the States and, accordingly, that there was an absolute right to appointment of counsel in felony cases.

There was no occasion in Gideon to enumerate the various stages in a criminal proceeding at which counsel was required, but Townsend, Moore, and Hamilton, when the Betts requirement of special circumstances is stripped away by Gideon, clearly stand for the proposition that appointment of counsel for an indigent is required at every stage of a criminal proceeding where substantial rights of a criminal accused may be affected. In particular, Townsend v. Burke, supra, illustrates the critical nature of sentencing in a criminal case and might well be considered to support by itself a holding that the right to counsel applies at sentencing. Many lower courts have concluded that the Sixth Amendment right to counsel extends to sentencing in federal cases.

The State, however, argues that the petitioners were sentenced at the time they were originally placed on probation and that the imposition of sentence following probation revocation is, in effect, a mere formality constituting part of the probation revocation proceeding. It is true that sentencing in Washington offers fewer opportunities for the exercise of judicial discretion than in many other jurisdictions. The applicable statute requires the trial judge in all cases to sentence the convicted person to the maximum term provided by law for the offense of which he was convicted. The actual determination of the length of time to be served is to be made by the Board of Prison Terms and Paroles within six months after the convicted person is admitted to prison.

On the other hand, the sentencing judge is required by statute, together with the prosecutor, to furnish the Board with a recommendation as to the length of time that the person should serve, in addition to supplying it with various information about the circumstances of the crime and the character of the individual. We were informed during oral argument that the Board places considerable weight on these recommendations, although it is in no way bound by them. Obviously to the extent such recommendations are influential in determining the resulting sentence, the necessity for the aid of counsel in marshaling the facts, introducing evidence of mitigating circumstances and in general aiding and assisting the defendant to present his case as to sentence is apparent.

Even more important in a case such as this is the fact that certain legal rights may be lost if not exercised at this stage. For one, Washington law provides that an appeal in a case involving a plea of guilty followed by probation can only be taken after sentence is imposed following revocation of probation. . . . Therefore in a case where an accused agreed to plead guilty, although he had a valid defense, because he was offered probation, absence of counsel at the imposition of the deferred sentence might well result in loss of the right to appeal. While ordinarily appeals from a plea of guilty are less frequent than those following a trial on the merits, the incidence of improperly obtained guilty pleas is not so slight as to be capable of being characterized as de minimis. . . .

Likewise the Washington statutes provide that a plea of guilty can be withdrawn at any time prior to the imposition of sentence . . . if the trial judge in his discretion finds that the ends of justice will be served. . . . Without undertaking to catalog the various situations in which a lawyer could be of substantial assistance to a defendant in such a case, it can be reiterated that a plea of guilty might well be improperly obtained by the promise to have a defendant placed on the very probation the revocation of which furnishes the occasion for desiring to withdraw the plea. An uncounseled defendant might very likely be unaware of this opportunity.

The two foregoing factors assume increased significance when it is considered that, as happened in these two cases, the eventual imposition of sentence on the prior plea of guilty is based on the alleged commission of offenses for which the accused is never tried.

In sum, we do not question the authority of the State of Washington to provide for a deferred sentencing procedure coupled with its probation provisions. Indeed, it appears to be an enlightened step forward. All we decide here is that a lawyer must be afforded at this proceeding whether it be labeled a revocation of probation or a deferred sentencing. We assume that counsel appointed for the purpose of the trial or guilty plea would not be unduly burdened by being requested to follow through at the deferred sentencing stage of the proceeding.

Reversed and remanded.

The Parole Revocation Hearing

MORRISSEY v. BREWER

Supreme Court of the United States, 1972
408 U.S. 471, 92 S. Ct. 2593, 33 L. Ed. 2d 484

John Morrissey and G. Donald Booker, two Iowa convicts whose paroles were revoked by the Iowa Board of Parole, filed habeas corpus petitions in the United States District Court (S.D. Iowa). Their habeas petitions alleged that they had

been denied due process under the Fourteenth Amendment because their paroles were revoked without a hearing. The district court denied the petitions on the ground that due process did not require a prerevocation parole hearing. The United States Court of Appeals (8th Cir.) affirmed, and the United States Supreme Court granted certiorari.

Mr. Chief Justice BURGER delivered the opinion of the Court.

We granted certiorari in this case to determine whether the Due Process Clause of the Fourteenth Amendment requires that a State afford an individual some opportunity to be heard prior to revoking his parole.

* * *

II

We begin with the proposition that the revocation of parole is not part of a criminal prosecution and thus the full panoply of rights due a defendant in such a proceeding does not apply to parole revocations. . . . Parole arises after the end of the criminal prosecution, including imposition of sentence. Supervision is not directly by the court but by an administrative agency, which is sometimes an arm of the court and sometimes of the executive. Revocation deprives an individual, not of the absolute liberty to which every citizen is entitled, but only of the conditional liberty properly dependent on observance of special parole restrictions.

We turn, therefore, to the question whether the requirements of due process in general apply to parole revocations. . . . Whether any procedural protections are due depends on the extent to which an individual will be "condemned to suffer grievous loss." . . . The question is not merely the "weight" of the individual's interest, but whether the nature of the interest is one within the contemplation of the "liberty or property" language of the Fourteenth Amendment. . . . Once it is determined that due process applies, the question remains what process is due. It has been said so often by this Court and others . . . that due process is flexible and calls for such procedural protections as the particular situation demands. "[C]onsideration of what procedures due process may require under any given set of circumstances must begin with a determination of the precise nature of the government function involved as well as

of the private interest that has been affected by governmental action." . . . To say that the concept of due process is flexible does not mean that judges are at large to apply it to any and all relationships. Its flexibility is in its scope once it has been determined that some process is due; it is a recognition that not all situations calling for procedural safeguards call for the same kind of procedure.

We turn to an examination of the nature of the interest of the parolee in his continued liberty. The liberty of a parolee enables him to do a wide range of things open to persons who have never been convicted of any crime. The parolee has been released from prison based on an evaluation that he shows reasonable promise of being able to return to society and function as a responsible, self-reliant person. Subject to the conditions of his parole, he can be gainfully employed and is free to be with family and friends and to form the other enduring attachments of normal life. Though the State properly subjects him to many restrictions not applicable to other citizens, his condition is very different from that of confinement in a prison. He may have been on parole for a number of years and may be living a relatively normal life at the time he is faced with revocation. The parolee has relied on at least an implicit promise that parole will be revoked only if he fails to live up to the parole conditions. In many cases, the parolee faces lengthy incarceration if his parole is revoked.

We see, therefore, that the liberty of a parolee, although indeterminate, includes many of the core values of unqualified liberty and its termination inflicts a "grievous loss" on the parolee and often on others. It is hardly useful any longer to try to deal with this problem in terms of whether the parolee's liberty is a "right" or a "privilege." By whatever name, the liberty is valuable and must be seen as within the protection of the Fourteenth Amendment. Its termination calls for some orderly process, however informal.

Turning to the question what process is due, we find that the State's interests are several. The State has found the parolee guilty of a crime against the people. That finding justifies imposing extensive restrictions on the individual's liberty. Release of the parolee before the end of his prison sentence is made with the recognition that with many prisoners there is a risk that they will not be able to live in society without committing additional antisocial acts. Given the previous conviction and the proper imposition of conditions, the State has an overwhelming interest in being able to return the individual to imprisonment without the burden of a new adversary criminal trial if in fact he has failed to abide by the conditions of his parole.

Yet, the State has no interest in revoking parole without some informal procedural guarantees. Although the parolee is often formally described as being "in custody," the argument cannot even be made here that summary treatment is necessary as it may be with respect to controlling a large group of potentially disruptive prisoners in actual custody. Nor are we persuaded by the argument that revocation is so totally a discretionary matter that some form of hearing would be administratively intolerable. A simple factual hearing will not interfere with the exercise of discretion. Serious studies have suggested that fair treatment on parole revocation will not result in fewer grants of parole.

This discretionary aspect of the revocation decision need not be reached unless there is first an appropriate determination that the individual has in fact breached the conditions of parole. The parolee is not the only one who has a stake in his conditional liberty. Society has a stake in whatever may be the chance of restoring him to normal and useful life within the law. Society thus has an interest in not having parole revoked because of erroneous information or because of an erroneous evaluation of the need to revoke parole, given the breach of parole conditions. . . . And society has a further interest in treating the parolee with basic fairness: fair treatment in parole revocations will enhance the chance of rehabilitation by avoiding reactions to arbitrariness.

Given these factors, most States have recognized that there is no interest on the part of the State in revoking parole without

any procedural guarantees at all. What is needed is an informal hearing structured to assure that the finding of a parole violation will be based on verified facts and that the exercise of discretion will be informed by an accurate knowledge of the parolee's behavior.

III

We now turn to the nature of the process that is due, bearing in mind that the interest of both State and parolee will be furthered by an effective but informal hearing. In analyzing what is due, we see two important stages in the typical process of parole revocation.

(a) *Arrest of Parolee and Preliminary Hearing.* The first stage occurs when the parolee is arrested and detained, usually at the direction of his parole officer. The second occurs when parole is formally revoked. There is typically a substantial time lag between the arrest and the eventual determination by the parole board whether parole should be revoked. Additionally, it may be that the parolee is arrested at a place distant from the state institution, to which he may be returned before the final decision is made concerning revocation. Given these factors, due process would seem to require that some minimal inquiry be conducted at or reasonably near the place of the alleged parole violation or arrest and as promptly as convenient after arrest while information is fresh and sources are available. . . . Such an inquiry should be seen as in the nature of a "preliminary hearing" to determine whether there is probable cause or reasonable ground to believe that the arrested parolee has committed acts that would constitute a violation of parole conditions. . . .

In our view, due process requires that after the arrest, the determination that reasonable ground exists for revocation of parole should be made by someone not directly involved in the case. It would be unfair to assume that the supervising parole officer does not conduct an interview with the parolee to confront him with the reasons for revocation before he recommends an arrest. It would also be unfair to assume that the parole officer bears hostility against the parolee that destroys his neutrality; realistically the failure of the parolee is in a sense a failure for his supervising officer. However, we need make no assumptions one way or the other to conclude that there should be an uninvolved person to make this preliminary evaluation of the basis for believing the conditions of parole have been violated. The officer directly involved in making recommendations cannot always have complete objectivity in evaluating them. . . .

This independent officer need not be a judicial officer. The granting and revocation of parole are matters traditionally handled by administrative officers. . . . It will be sufficient, therefore, in the parole revocation context, if an evaluation of whether reasonable cause exists to believe that conditions of parole have been violated is made by someone such as a parole officer other than the one who has made the report of parole violations or has recommended revocation. A State could certainly choose some other independent decisionmaker to perform this preliminary function.

With respect to the preliminary hearing before this officer, the parolee should be given notice that the hearing will take place and that its purpose is to determine whether there is probable cause to believe he has committed a parole violation. The notice should state what parole violations have been alleged. At the hearing the parolee may appear and speak in his own behalf; he may bring letters, documents, or individuals who can give relevant information to the hearing officer. On request of the parolee, persons who have given adverse information on which parole revocation is to be based are to be made available for questioning in his presence. However, if the hearing officer determines that the informant would be subjected to risk of harm if his identity were disclosed, he need not be subjected to confrontation and cross-examination.

The hearing officer shall have the duty of making a summary, or digest, of what occurs at the hearing in terms of the responses of the parolee and the substance of the documents or evidence given in support of parole revocation and of the parolee's position. Based on the information before him, the officer should determine whether there is probable cause to hold the parolee for the final decision of the parole board on revocation. Such a determination would be sufficient to warrant the parolee's continued detention and return to the state correctional institution pending the final decision. . . . "The decision maker should state the reasons for his determination and indi-

cate the evidence he relied on . . ." but it should be remembered that this is not a final determination calling for "formal findings of fact and conclusions of law." . . . No interest would be served by formalism in this process; informality will not lessen the utility of this inquiry in reducing the risk of error.

(b) *The Revocation Hearing.* There must also be an opportunity for a hearing, if it is desired by the parolee, prior to the final decision on revocation by the parole authority. This hearing must be the basis for more than determining probable cause; it must lead to a final evaluation of any contested relevant facts and consideration of whether the facts as determined warrant revocation. The parolee must have an opportunity to be heard and to show, if he can, that he did not violate the conditions, or, if he did, that circumstances in mitigation suggest that the violation does not warrant revocation. The revocation hearing must be tendered within a reasonable time after the parolee is taken into custody. A lapse of two months, as the State suggests occurs in some cases, would not appear to be unreasonable.

We cannot write a code of procedure; that is the responsibility of each State. Most States have done so by legislation, others by judicial decision usually on due process grounds. Our task is limited to deciding the minimum requirements of due process. They include (a) written notice of the claimed violations of parole; (b) disclosure to the parolee of evidence against him; (c) opportunity to be heard in person and to present witnesses and documentary evidence; (d) the right to confront and cross-examine adverse witnesses (unless the hearing officer specifically finds good cause for not allowing confrontation); (e) a "neutral and detached" hearing body such as a traditional parole board, members of which need not be judicial officers or lawyers; and (f) a written statement by the factfinders as to the evidence relied on and reasons for revoking parole. We emphasize there is no thought to equate this second stage of parole revocation to a criminal prosecution in any sense. It is a narrow inquiry; the process should be flexible enough to consider evidence including letters, affidavits, and other material that would not be admissible in an adversary criminal trial.

We do not reach or decide the question whether the parolee is entitled to the assistance of retained counsel or to appointed counsel if he is indigent.

We have no thought to create an inflexible structure for parole revocation procedures. The few basic requirements set out above, which are applicable to future revocations of parole, should not impose a great burden on any State's parole system. Control over the required proceedings by the hearing officers can assure that delaying tactics and other abuses sometimes present in the traditional adversary trial situation do not occur. . . .

* * *

Reversed and remanded.

Mr. Justice BRENNAN, with whom Mr. Justice MARSHALL joins, concurring in the result.

I agree that a parole may not be revoked, consistently with the Due Process Clause, unless the parolee is afforded, first, a preliminary hearing at the time of arrest to determine whether there is probable cause to believe that he has violated his parole conditions and, second, a final hearing within a reasonable time to determine whether he has, in fact, violated those conditions and whether his parole should be revoked. . . .

The Court, however, states that it does not now decide whether the parolee is also entitled at each hearing to the assistance of retained counsel or of appointed counsel if he is indigent. Goldberg v. Kelly, 397 U.S. 254 (1970), nonetheless plainly dictates that he at least "must be allowed to *retain* an attorney if he so desires." . . .

The only question open under our precedents is whether counsel must be furnished the parolee if he is indigent.

Mr. Justice DOUGLAS, dissenting in part.

* * *

A parolee, like a prisoner, is a person entitled to constitutional protection, including procedural due process. At the federal level, the construction of regulations of the Federal Parole Board presents federal questions of which we have taken cognizance. . . . At the state level, the construction of parole statutes and regulations is for the States alone, save as they implicate the Federal Constitution, in which even the Supremacy Clause controls.

It is only procedural due process, required by the Fourteenth Amendment, that con-

cerns us in the present cases. Procedural due process requires the following.

If a violation of a condition of parole is involved, rather than the commission of a new offense, there should not be an arrest of the parolee and his return to the prison or to a local jail. Rather, notice of the alleged violation should be given to the parolee and a time set for a hearing. The hearing should not be before the parole officer, as he is the one who is making the charge and "there is inherent danger in combining the functions of judge and advocate." . . . Moreover, the parolee should be entitled to counsel. . . . "A hearing in which counsel is absent or is present only on behalf of one side is inherently unsatisfactory if not unfair. Counsel can see that relevant facts are brought out, vague and insubstantial allegations discounted, and irrelevancies eliminated." . . .

The hearing required is not a grant of the full panoply of rights applicable to a criminal trial. But confrontation with the informer may . . . be necessary for a fair hearing and the ascertainment of the truth. The hearing is to determine the fact of parole violation. The results of the hearing would go to the parole board—or other authorized state agency—for final action, as would cases which involved voluntary admission of violations.

The rule of law is important in the stability of society. Arbitrary actions in the revocation of paroles can only impede and impair the rehabilitative aspects of modern penology. . . . We do not sit as an ombudsman, telling the States the precise procedures they must follow. I would hold that so far as the due process requirements of parole revocation are concerned:

(1) the parole officer—whatever may be his duties under various state statutes . . . —is . . . not qualified as a hearing officer;

(2) the parolee is entitled to a due process notice and a due process hearing of the alleged parole violations including, for example, the opportunity to be confronted by his accusers and to present evidence and argument on his own behalf; and

(3) the parolee is entitled to the freedom granted a parolee until the results of the hearing are known and the parole board—or other authorized state agency—acts.

I would reverse the judgments and remand for further consideration in light of this opinion.

Revocation of Probation When Sentence Previously Imposed

GAGNON v. SCARPELLI

Supreme Court of the United States, 1973
411 U.S. 778, 93 S. Ct. 1756, 36 L. Ed. 2d 656

The facts are stated in the opinion.

Mr. Justice POWELL delivered the opinion of the Court.

This case presents the related questions whether a previously sentenced probationer is entitled to a hearing when his probation is revoked and, if so, whether he is entitled to be represented by appointed counsel at such a hearing.

I

Respondent, Gerald Scarpelli, pleaded guilty in July, 1965, to a charge of armed robbery in Wisconsin. The trial judge sentenced him to 15 years' imprisonment, but suspended the sentence and placed him on probation for seven years in the custody of the Wisconsin Department of Public Welfare (the Deparment). At that time, he signed an agreement specifying the terms of his probation and a "Travel Permit and Agreement to Return" allowing him to reside in Illinois, with supervision there under an interstate compact. On August 5, 1965, he was accepted for supervision by the Adult Probation Department of Cook County, Illinois.

On August 6, respondent was apprehended by Illinois police, who had surprised him and one Fred Kleckner, Jr., in the course of the burglary of a house. After being apprised of his constitutional rights, respondent admitted that he and Kleckner had broken into the house for the purpose of stealing merchandise or money, although he now asserts that his statement was made under duress and is false. Probation was revoked by the Department on September 1, without a hearing. The stated grounds for revocation were that:

"1. [Scarpelli] has associated with known criminals, in direct violation of his probation regulations and his supervising agent's instructions;

"2. [Scarpelli] while associating with a known criminal, namely Fred Kleckner, Jr., was involved in, and arrested for, a burglary . . . in Deerfield, Illinois."

On September 4, 1965, he was incarcerated in the Wisconsin State Reformatory at Green Bay to begin serving the 15 years to which he had been sentenced by the trial judge. At no time was he afforded a hearing.

Some three years later, on December 16, 1968, respondent applied for a writ of habeas corpus. After the petition had been filed, but before it had been acted upon, the Department placed respondent on parole. The District Court found that his status as parolee was sufficient custody to confer jurisdiction on the court and that the petition was not moot because the revocation carried "collateral consequences," presumably including the restraints imposed by his parole. On the merits, the District Court held that revocation without a hearing and counsel was a denial of due process. . . . The Court of Appeals affirmed (7th Cir. 1971) . . . and we granted certiorari. . . .

II

Two prior decisions set the bounds of our present inquiry. In Mempa v. Rhay, 389 U.S. 128 (1967), the Court held that a probationer is entitled to be represented by appointed counsel at a combined revocation and sentencing hearing. Reasoning that counsel is required "at every stage of a criminal proceeding where substantial rights of a criminal accused may be affected"

... and that sentencing is one such stage, the Court concluded that counsel must be provided an indigent at sentencing even when it is accomplished as part of a subsequent probation revocation proceeding. But this line of reasoning does not require a hearing or counsel at the time of probation revocation in a case such as the present one, where the probationer was sentenced at the time of trial.

Of greater relevance is our decision last Term in Morrissey v. Brewer, 408 U.S. 471 (1972). There we held that the revocation of parole is not a part of a criminal prosecution.

* * *

Even though the revocation of parole is not a part of the criminal prosecution, we held that the loss of liberty entailed is a serious deprivation requiring that the parolee be accorded due process. Specifically, we held that a parolee is entitled to two hearings, one a preliminary hearing at the time of his arrest and detention to determine whether there is probable cause to believe that he has committed a violation of his parole and the other a somewhat more comprehensive hearing prior to the making of the final revocation decision.

Petitioner does not contend that there is any difference relevant to the guarantee of due process between the revocation of parole and the revocation of probation, nor do we perceive one. Probation revocation, like parole revocation, is not a stage of a criminal prosecution, but does result in a loss of liberty. Accordingly, we hold that a probationer, like a parolee, is entitled to a preliminary and a final revocation hearing, under the conditions specified in Morrissey v. Brewer, supra.

III

The second, and more difficult, question posed by this case is whether an indigent probationer or parolee has a due process right to be represented by appointed counsel at these hearings. In answering that question, we draw heavily on the opinion in Morrissey. . . .

* * *

. . . Morrissey mandated preliminary and final revocation hearings. At the preliminary hearing, a probationer or parolee is entitled to notice of the alleged violations of probation or parole, an opportunity to appear and to present evidence in his own behalf, a conditional right to confront adverse witnesses, an independent decisionmaker, and a written report of the hearing. . . . The final hearing is a less summary one because the decision under consideration is the ultimate decision to revoke rather than a mere determination of probable cause. . . .

These requirements in themselves serve as substantial protection against ill-considered revocation, and petitioner argues that counsel need never be supplied. What this argument overlooks is that the effectiveness of the rights guaranteed by Morrissey may in some circumstances depend on the use of skills which the probationer or parolee is unlikely to possess. Despite the informal nature of the proceedings and the absence of technical rules of procedure or evidence, the unskilled or uneducated probationer or parolee may well have difficulty in presenting his version of a disputed set of facts where the presentation requires the examining or cross-examining of witnesses or the offering or dissecting of complex documentary evidence.

By the same token, we think that the Court of Appeals erred in accepting respondent's contention that the State is under a constitutional duty to provide counsel for indigents in all probation or parole revocation cases. While such a rule has the appeal of simplicity, it would impose direct costs and serious collateral disadvantages without regard to the need or the likelihood in a particular case for a constructive contribution by counsel. In most cases, the probationer or parolee has been convicted of committing another crime or has admitted the charges against him. And while in some cases he may have a justifiable excuse for the violation or a convincing reason why revocation is not the appropriate disposition, mitigating evidence of this kind is often not susceptible of proof or is so simple as not to require either investigation or exposition by counsel.

The introduction of counsel into a revocation proceeding will alter significantly the nature of the proceeding. If counsel is provided for the probationer or parolee, the State in turn will normally provide its own counsel; lawyers, by training and disposition, are advocates and bound by professional duty to present all available evidence and arguments in support of their clients' positions and to contest with vigor all adverse evidence and views. The role of the hearing body itself, aptly described in Morrissey as being "predictive and discretionary" as well as factfinding, may become more akin to that of a judge at a trial, and less attuned to the rehabilitative needs of the individual probationer or parolee. In the greater self-consciousness of its quasi-judicial role, the hearing body may be less tolerant of marginal deviant behavior and feel more pressure to reincarcerate rather than to continue nonpunitive rehabilitation. Certainly, the decisionmaking process will be prolonged, and the financial cost to the State—for appointed counsel, counsel for the State, a longer record, and the possibility of judicial review—will not be insubstantial.

In some cases, these modifications in the nature of the revocation hearing must be endured and the costs borne because, as we have indicated above, the probationer's or parolee's version of a disputed issue can fairly be represented only by a trained advocate. But due process is not so rigid as to require that the significant interests in informality, flexibility, and economy must always be sacrificed.

In so concluding, we are of course aware that the case-by-case approach to the right to counsel in felony prosecutions adopted in Betts v. Brady, 316 U.S. 455 (1942), was later rejected in favor of a per se rule in Gideon v. Wainwright, 372 U.S. 335 (1963). See also Argersinger v. Hamilin, 407 U.S. 25 (1972). We do not, however, draw from Gideon and Argersinger the conclusion that a case-by-case approach to furnishing counsel is necessarily inadequate to protect constitutional rights asserted in varying types of proceedings: there are critical differences between criminal trials and probation or parole revocation hearings, and both society and the probationer or parolee have stakes in preserving these differences.

* * *

We thus find no justification for a new inflexible constitutional rule with respect to the requirement of counsel. We think, rather, that the decision as to the need for counsel must be made on a case-by-case basis in the exercise of a sound discretion by the state authority charged with responsibility for administering the probation and parole system. Although the presence and participation of counsel will probably be both undesirable and constitutionally unnecessary in most revocation hearings, there will remain certain cases in which fundamental fairness—the touchstone of due process—will require that the State provide at its expense counsel for indigent probationers or parolees.

It is neither possible nor prudent to attempt to formulate a precise and detailed set of guidelines to be followed in determining when the providing of counsel is necessary to meet the applicable due process requirements. . . . Presumptively, it may be said that counsel should be provided in cases where, after being informed of his right to request counsel, the probationer or parolee makes such a request, based on a timely and colorable claim (i) that he has not committed the alleged violation of the conditions upon which he is at liberty; or (ii) that, even if the violation is a matter of public record or is uncontested, there are substantial reasons which justified or mitigated the violation and make revocation inappropriate, and that the reasons are complex or otherwise difficult to develop or present. In passing on a request for the appointment of counsel, the responsible agency also should consider, especially in doubtful cases, whether the probationer appears to be capable of speaking effectively for himself. In every case in which a request for counsel at a preliminary or final hearing is refused, the grounds for refusal should be stated succinctly in the record.

IV

We return to the facts of the present case. Because respondent was not afforded either a preliminary hearing or a final hearing, the revocation of his probation did not meet the standards of due process prescribed in Morrissey, which we have here held applicable to probation revocations. . . .

Affirmed in part, reversed in part, and remanded.

Mr. Justice DOUGLAS, dissenting in part.

I believe that due process requires the appointment of counsel in this case because of the claim that respondent's confession of the burglary was made under duress. . . .

Comments

1. In *Mempa* v. *Rhay*, supra, the Supreme Court reiterated its holding in prior cases that the appointment of counsel is required "at every stage of a criminal proceeding where substantial rights of a criminal accused may be affected"—the so-called "critical stage" test—and that a probation revocation hearing when sentence has not previously been imposed is such a stage. Yet the Court in *Gagnon* v. *Scarpelli*, supra, declined to fashion a per se rule requiring the appointment of counsel at probation revocation hearings when a sentence had previously been imposed and left the decision as to the need for counsel to be made on a case-by-case basis as was done in pre-*Gideon* criminal trials. Is there really a constitutional difference between the *Mempa* and *Gagnon* proceedings in terms of the right to counsel and the "critical stage" test? Aren't "substantial rights of an accused affected" at probation revocation hearings when sentence has previously been imposed? Is the real difference the fact *Mempa* was decided by the Warren Court, and *Gagnon* by the Burger Court? Would the Warren Court have reached the same result in *Gagnon*? If counsel is required at sentencing in a criminal case (see *Townsend* v. *Burke*, 334 U.S. 736 [1948], noted in *Mempa*, why isn't the right to appointed counsel applicable to probation revocation hearings when sentence has previously been imposed? Are the other due process safeguards required in *Gagnon* sufficient to overcome the need for counsel? In *Gagnon* the Court dealt with the issue of appointed counsel for indigents. Does an accused have a constitutional right to retained counsel at a *Gagnon*-type revocation hearing? If not, would that constitute a denial of equal protection of the laws to an indigent accused under *Griffin* v. *Illinois* 351 U.S. 12, 19 (1956) (Chapter Four, § 4.04) in which the Court stated that "there can be no equal justice where the kind of trial a man gets depends on the amount of money he has"?

2. In *Morrissey* v. *Brewer*, supra, the Court left open the issue of the right to appointed counsel at parole revocation hearings. When this issue is resolved, is the Court likely to adopt the *Gagnon* approach and leave the issue of appointed counsel to be decided on a case-by-case basis? Is there a constitutional right to retained counsel at a parole revocation hearing? Which is the more "critical stage" in a parole revocation proceeding—the preliminary hearing or the revocation hearing itself? What is the constitutional standard of proof in a probation or parole revocation hearing? Beyond a reasonable doubt? Preponderance of the evidence? Clear and convincing evidence? Prima facie case? Some other standard?

3.

𝕱𝖑𝖔𝖗𝖎𝖉𝖆 𝕻𝖆𝖗𝖔𝖑𝖊 𝕮𝖔𝖒𝖒𝖎𝖘𝖘𝖎𝖔𝖓
𝕿𝖆𝖑𝖑𝖆𝖍𝖆𝖘𝖘𝖊𝖊, 𝕱𝖑𝖔𝖗𝖎𝖉𝖆

𝕮𝖊𝖗𝖙𝖎𝖋𝖎𝖈𝖆𝖙𝖊 𝖔𝖋 𝕻𝖆𝖗𝖔𝖑𝖊

No. _____

KNOW ALL MEN BY THESE PRESENTS:

Pursuant to thorough investigation and consideration the Florida Parole Commission finds that [*name of inmate*], Prison No. _____, is eligible to be placed on parole under Section 12, Chapter 20519, Laws of Florida, Acts of 1941, as amended, and that there is reasonable probability that said prisoner will live and conduct [him]self as a respectable and law-abiding person, and also that the release of said prisoner will be compatible with [his] own welfare and the welfare of society, and it appearing further that the Florida Parole Commission is satisfied that said prisoner will be suitably employed in self-sustaining employment, or that [he] will not become a public charge on release:

It is hereby ordered that said prisoner be, and hereby is, paroled effective _____, 19____, and that [he] remain under supervision subject to the specific conditions of parole as listed [following] this Order until _____, 19____, unless otherwise released, or until other action may be taken by the Florida Parole Commission.

IN WITNESS WHEREOF this certificate bearing the seal of the Florida Parole Commission is issued this the _____ day of _____, 19____.

𝕱𝖑𝖔𝖗𝖎𝖉𝖆 𝕻𝖆𝖗𝖔𝖑𝖊 𝕮𝖔𝖒𝖒𝖎𝖘𝖘𝖎𝖔𝖓

BY:

_____

_____

_____

Commissioners

The above-named prisoner was released on the _____ *day of* _____, *19*____.

_____

Superintendent or Warden

STATEMENT OF THE CONDITIONS UNDER WHICH
THIS PAROLE IS GRANTED

This Certificate of Parole will not become operative until the following conditions are agreed to by the prisoner, and it is understood that violation of any of these conditions may result in revocation of this parole:

1. I will report immediately upon arrival at my destination, by personal visit, to the Parole Supervisor under whose supervision I am paroled.

The Parole Supervisor's name and address is:

Name_____

Address_____

_____

2. I will not change my residence or employment or leave the county of my residence, without first procuring the consent of the Florida Parole Commission, which consent shall be obtained through my Parole Supervisor.

3. I will, before the fifth day of each month, until my final release, make a full and truthful report to my Parole Supervisor on the form provided for that purpose.

4. I will not use intoxicants of any kind to excess; nor use narcotic drugs; nor visit places where intoxicants or drugs are unlawfully sold, dispensed, or used.

5. I will not visit gambling places or "juke joints" or associate with persons of harmful character or bad reputation.

6. I will in all respects conduct myself honorably; work diligently at a lawful occupation; support my dependents, if any, to the best of my ability; and live within my income.

7. I will not own nor carry with me any weapons, without first securing the consent of my Parole Supervisor.

8. I will live and remain at liberty without violating the law.

9. I hereby waive all extradition rights and process and agree to return to Florida if at any time prior to my release from parole the Florida Parole Commission directs that I do so.

10. I will promptly and truthfully answer all inquiries directed to me by the Commission or by my Parole Supervisor and I will allow the Supervisor to visit me at my home, employment site or elsewhere, and I will carry out all instructions he may give me.

11. If at any time it becomes necessary to communicate with my Parole Supervisor for any purpose and he is not accessible, I will direct my communication to the Commission, at Tallahassee, Florida.

12. I hereby agree not to marry without the consent of the Commission.

13. I understand that I am to remain on parole until released therefrom by the Commission.

14. If at the time of my release, or at any time during my parole term, I am infected with venereal disease, I agree to take regular treatments for same and continue such treatments until cured.

15. I agree not to own or to operate a motor vehicle or to secure a license to operate a motor vehicle without first procuring the consent of

the Florida Parole Commission, which consent shall be obtained through my Parole Supervisor.

I hereby certify that the statement of conditions has been read and explained to the parolee and [he] has agreed and consented to these conditions.

I hereby agree to all the conditions set forth for me in this certificate of parole.

_____
Signature of Parolee

This _____ day of _____, 19___

_____
Supervisor

The Commission realizes that, under the American system, compulsory church attendance may be regarded as an infringement upon the idea of separation of church and state and therefore does not include this as a specific condition of parole. However, the Commission wishes the parolee to know that in its opinion, no more important element enters into the proper rehabilitation of the individual than does religion. The Commission strongly recommends to the parolee that he or she, do, immediately upon release on parole, communicate with a minister, priest, or rabbi of the parolee's own choosing and secure the assistance of such person in helping work out the parolee's problems. The Commission suggests to the parolee regular church attendance and active membership by the parolee in a church of the parolee's choosing.

Query: Are any legal problems posed by these parole conditions?

FLORIDA PAROLE COMMISSION
STATE OF FLORIDA

REVOCATION OF PAROLE

TO ALL TO WHOM THESE PRESENTS
SHALL COME, GREETING:

WHEREAS, [*name of Parolee*] Prison No. _____, an inmate of the State Prison, was sentenced from _____ County on the _____ day of _____, 19 ___, and was thereafter on the _____ day of _____, 19 ___, granted a parole; and

WHEREAS, The Parole Commission, after hearing and consideration in the premises, in accordance with the provisions of Chapter 20519, Laws of Florida, 1941, finds that the said [*name of parolee*] has violated the terms and conditions of his parole

By failing to live and remain at liberty without violating the law as required under Section Eight of his Certificate of Parole; in that on January   1977 he was sentenced to five years in the State Prison by the   County Criminal Court on a charge of Breaking and Entering with Intent to Commit a Felony and Escape. This revocation is to be effective upon the expiration of the sentence which parolee is now serving in the Florida State Prison under No.   namely, a sentence of five years in the State Prison by the   County Criminal Court, Florida on January   1977.

and deems it for the best interests of society and the parolee, that [he] be returned to the custody of the superintendent of the Florida State Prison there to remain not to exceed his sentence or until the further order of the Commission;

NOW THEREFORE, The Parole Commission, by virtue of the authority in it vested by law, does hereby revoke said parole and authorize and direct any parole or probation supervisor, any officer authorized to serve criminal process, or any peace officer of the State of Florida to apprehend and take into custody the said [name of parolee] and hold such person to be returned to said institution in accordance with the instructions of the Parole Commission; and return to said institution is hereby ordered, and the ___superintendent___ of said in-

(Supt., Warden, Jailer)

stitution is hereby ordered to receive such person.

Dated at <u>Tallahassee</u>, Florida, this ___ day of _____, 19 ___

FLORIDA PAROLE COMMISSION

By _____

_____

_____

Members

(SEAL)

4. Some recent lower federal and state court decisions involving the rights of probationers and parolees are *In re Meidinger*, 539 P. 2d 1185 (Mont. 1975) (probationer who remained free pending disposition of probation violation charges held not entitled to a preliminary probable cause hearing under *Morrissey* and *Gagnon*); *People* v. *Peterson*, 234 N.W.2d 692 (Mich. App. 1975) (probation condition that forbids "antisocial conduct" upheld); *People* v. *Harkness*, 339 N.E.2d 545 (Ill. App. 1975) (finding of no probable cause at preliminary hearing of defendant charged with burglary does not preclude subsequent probation revocation hearing based on the same burglary); *Haymes* v. *Regan*, 525 F.2d 540 (2d Cir. 1975) (state parole board need not disclose its release decision criteria to inmates denied parole); *Richerson* v. *Wolff*, 525 F.2d 797 (7th Cir. 1975) (state parole board must provide a statement of reasons to inmates denied parole); *People* v. *Wilkerson*, 541 P.2d 896 (Col. 1975) (evidence obtained as result of an illegal search and seizure is admissible at a probation revocation hearing) (see also *People* v. *Atencio*, 525 P.2d 461 [1971]) (contra is *Thomas* v. *State*, 530 S.W.2d 834 [Tex. Ct. Crim. App. 1976] [evidence illegally seized by the police not admissible at probation revocation hearing]); *Bricker* v. *Michigan Parole Board*, 405 F. Supp. 1340 (E.D. Mich. 1975) (parole conditions forbidding parolee from working for particular company suspected of having mob connections or to work as a self-employed broker in a trash disposal industry held not unconstitutional); *Reese* v. *U.S. Board of Parole*, 530 F.2d 231 (9th Cir. 1976) (federal parolee convicted and imprisoned for new crime need not immediately be given revocation hearing required by *Morrissey* v. *Brewer*); *Brown* v. *Lundgren*, 528 F.2d 1050 (5th Cir. 1976) (parole denial procedures not gov-

erned by due process requirements) (contra is *Childs* v. *U.S. Board of Parole,* 511 F.2d 1270 (D.C. Cir. 1974), and *Bradford* v. *Weinstein,* 519 F.2d 728 (4th Cir. 1974), vacated as moot, 423 U.S. 147 (1975); *Ewing* v. *Wyrick,* 535 S.W.2d 442 (Mo. 1976) (prompt preliminary hearing on criminal charges against a probationer cannot serve as a substitute for the probable cause hearing required by *Morrissey* v. *Brewer* unless the probationer has been so informed); *Beattie* v. *N.Y. State Board of Parole,* 348 N.E.2d 873 (N.Y. Ct. App. 1976) (parolee held on an unrelated criminal charge is entitled to a prompt final revocation hearing); *Hofmann* v. *Wainwright,* 332 So. 2d 18 (Fla. 1976) (*Morrissey* v. *Brewer* does not require immediate parole revocation hearings for parolees convicted of intervening offenses and who are imprisoned elsewhere); *Kloner* v. *United States,* 535 F.2d 730 (2d Cir. 1976) (parole revocation based on two grounds, one of which the parolee was given no notice of prior to the hearing, held violative of *Morrissey* v. *Brewer*); *Dublin* v. *State,* 346 N.E.2d 746 (Ind. App. 1976) (exclusionary rule is not applicable to probation revocation hearings); *Pickus* v. *U.S. Board of Parole,* 507 F.2d 1107 (D.C. Cir. 1976) (federal inmates have no due process right to orally present their views on parole board's proposed rules on the granting and denial of parole); *Creech* v. *U.S. Board of Parole,* 538 F.2d 205 (8th Cir. 1976) (three-month delay between a charge of parole violation and a final revocation hearing held not unreasonable); *People* v. *Richards,* 552 P.2d 97 (Calif. 1976) (absent extraordinary circumstances, probation for a defendant may not be conditioned on restitution of sums involved in a crime for which he was acquitted); *Tucker* v. *Kostos,* 356 N.E.2d 798 (Ill. App. 1976) (state parolees awaiting final revocation hearing must be afforded the same bail right that probationers awaiting final revocation hearings have (contra is *In re Whitney,* 421 F.2d 337 (1st Cir. 1970); *Inmates' Councilmatic Voice* v. *Rogers,* 541 F.2d 633 (6th Cir. 1976) (state parolees who are arrested for new crimes in the state should be afforded a final revocation hearing within a reasonable time if requested by parolee); *Ockel* v. *Riley,* 541 S.W.2d 535 (Mo. 1976) (extension in length of probation does not trigger such due process requirements as notice and hearing); *Coralluzzo* v. *N.Y. State Parole Board,* 420 F. Supp. 592 (W.D.N.Y. 1976) (parole board must give written reasons for its decision as to when an inmate will be considered for parole); *People* v. *Hardin,* 245 N.W.2d 556 (Mich. App. 1976) (prior to trial court's acceptance of a defendant's admission of probation violations, the probationer must first be informed of his right to a revocation hearing); *Billiteri* v. *U.S. Board of Parole,* 541 F.2d 938 (2d Cir. 1976) (federal prisoner seeking parole is not constitutionally entitled to see the presentence report prior to his hearing before the examining panel); *State ex rel. Pizzaro* v. *New York State Parole Board,* 390 N.Y.S.2d 121 (N.Y. App. Div. 1977) (parole records should be disclosed to parole violator unless there is some overriding reason to maintain their confidentiality); *State* v. *Lindsey,* 233 S.E.2d 734 (W. Va. 1977) (one convicted of a crime is never *entitled* to parole); *Mack* v. *McCune,* 551 F.2d 251 (10th Cir. 1977) (possession of a weapon without the knowledge or consent of parolee's supervisor will by itself justify revocation of parole); *Persico* v. *U.S. Dept. of Justice,* 426 F. Supp. 1031 (D. Ill. 1977) (judicial review of parole board's decision to deny parole is ordinarily not available).

9.03 DUE PROCESS INSIDE THE PRISON WALLS

Censorship of Inmates' Mail and Restrictions on Access to the Courts

PROCUNIER v. MARTINEZ

Supreme Court of the United States, 1974
416 U.S. 396, 94 S. Ct. 1800, 40 L. Ed. 2d 224

Robert Martinez and other inmates of California penal institutions brought a class action suit on behalf of themselves and all other inmates similarly situated challenging the constitutionality of certain regulations promulgated by appellant, Raymond Procunier, in his capacity as Director of the California Department of Corrections. The suit challenged the department's regulations relating to the censorship of inmates' incoming and outgoing personal mail and the ban against the use of law students and legal paraprofessionals to conduct attorney-client interviews with inmates. A three-judge United States District Court (N.D. Calif.) was convened to hear appellees' request for declaratory and injunctive relief. That court entered summary judgment and enjoined continued enforcement of the regulations, holding that (1) the mail censorship regulations violated the First Amendment's protection of lawful expression, were void for vagueness, and failed to provide minimum procedural safeguards against arbitrary censorship of protected speech; and (2) the ban on the use of law students or paraprofessionals to conduct attorney-client interviews constituted an unjustifiable restriction on inmates' right of access to the courts. Appellants were ordered to submit new regulations for the court's approval. Procunier and others appealed directly to the United States Supreme Court to contest the decision of the three-judge court.

Mr. Justice POWELL delivered the opinion of the Court.

I

* * *

A

Traditionally, federal courts have adopted a broad hands-off attitude toward problems of prison administration. In part this policy is the product of various limitations on the scope of federal review of conditions in state penal institutions. More fundamentally, this attitude springs from complementary perceptions about the nature of the problems and the efficacy of judicial intervention. . . . The problems of prisons in America are complex and intractable, and, more to the point, they are not readily susceptible of resolution by decree. Most require expertise, comprehensive planning, and the commitment of resources, all of which are peculiarly within the province of the legislative and executive branches of government. For all of those reasons, courts are ill equipped to deal with the increasingly urgent problems of prison administration and reform. Judicial recognition of that fact reflects no more than a healthy sense of realism. Moreover, where state penal institutions are involved, federal courts have a further reason for deference to the appropriate prison authorities.

But a policy of judicial restraint cannot encompass any failure to take cognizance of valid constitutional claims whether arising in a federal or state institution. When a prison regulation or practice offends a fundamental constitutional guarantee, federal courts will discharge their duty to protect constitutional rights. . . .

The issue before us is the appropriate standard of review for prison regulations restricting freedom of speech. This Court has not previously addressed this question, and the tension between the traditional policy of judicial restraint regarding prisoner complaints and the need to protect constitutional rights has led the federal courts to adopt a variety of widely inconsistent approaches to the problem. . . .

[T]he array of disparate approaches and the absence of any generally accepted standard for testing the constitutionality of prisoner mail censorship regulations disserve both the competing interests at stake. On the one hand, the First Amendment interests implicated by censorship of inmate correspondence are given only haphazard and inconsistent protection. On the other, the uncertainty of the constitutional standard makes it impossible for correctional officials to anticipate what is required of them and invites repetitive, piecemeal litigation on behalf of inmates. The result has been unnecessarily to perpetuate the involvement of the federal courts in affairs of prison administration. Our task is to formulate a standard of review for prisoner mail censorship that will be responsive to these concerns.

B

We begin our analysis of the proper standard of review for constitutional challenges to censorship of prisoner mail with a somewhat different premise from that taken by the other federal courts that have considered the question. For the most part, these courts have dealt with challenges to censorship of prison mail as involving broad questions of "prisoners' rights." . . . We have no occasion to consider the extent to which an individual's right to free speech survives incarceration, for a narrower basis of decision is at hand. In the case of direct personal correspondence between inmates and those who have a particularized interest in communicating with them, mail censorship implicates more than the right of prisoners.

Communication by letter is not accomplished by the act of writing words on paper. Rather, it is effected only when the letter is read by the addressee. Both parties to the correspondence have an interest in securing that result, and censorship of the communication between them necessarily impinges on the interest of each. Whatever the status of a prisoner's claim to uncensored correspondence with an outsider, it is plain that the latter's interest is grounded in the First Amendment's guarantee of freedom of speech. And this does not depend on whether the nonprisoner correspondent is the author or intended recipient of a particular letter, for the addressee as well as the sender of direct personal correspondence derives from the First and Fourteenth Amendments a protection against unjustified governmental interference with the intended communication. . . . The wife of a prison inmate who is not permitted to read all that her husband wanted to say to her has suffered an abridgment of her interest in communicating with him as plain as that which results from censorship of her letter to him. In either event, censorship of prisoner mail works a consequential restriction on the First and Fourteenth Amendment rights of those who are not prisoners.

Accordingly, we reject any attempt to justify censorship of inmate correspondence merely by reference to certain assumptions about the legal status of prisoners. . . . We therefore turn for guidance, not to cases involving questions of "prisoners' rights," but to decisions of this Court dealing with the general problem of incidental restrictions on First Amendment liberties imposed in furtherance of legitimate governmental activities.

* * *

. . . One of the primary functions of government is the preservation of societal order through enforcement of the criminal law, and the maintenance of penal institutions is an essential part of that task. The identifiable governmental interests at stake in this task are the preservation of internal order and discipline, the maintenance of institutional security against escape or unauthorized entry, and the rehabilitation of the prisoners. While the weight of professional opinion seems to be that inmate freedom to correspond with outsiders advances rather than retards the goal of rehabilitation, the legitimate governmental interest in the order and security of penal institutions justifies the imposition of certain restraints on inmate correspondence. Perhaps the most obvious example of justifiable censorship of prisoner mail would be refusal to send or deliver letters concerning escape plans or containing other information concerning proposed criminal activity, whether within or without the prison. Similarly, prison officials may properly refuse to transmit encoded messages. Other less obvious possibilities come to mind, but it is not our purpose to survey the range of circumstances in which particular restrictions on prisoner mail might be warranted by the legitimate demands of prison administration as they exist from time to time in the various kinds of penal institutions found in this country. Our task is to determine the proper standard for deciding whether a particular regulation or practice relating to inmate correspondence constitutes an impermissible restraint of First Amendment liberties.

Applying the teachings of our prior decisions to the instant context, we hold that censorship of prisoner mail is justified if the following criteria are met. *First,* the regulation or practice in question must *further an important or substantial governmental interest unrelated to the suppression of expression.* Prison officials may not censor inmate correspondence simply to eliminate unflattering or unwelcome opinions or factually inaccurate statements. Rather, they must show that a regulation authorizing mail censorship furthers one or more of the substantial governmental interests of *security, order, and rehabilitation. Second,* the limitation of First Amendment freedoms *must be no greater than is necessary or essential to the protection of the particular governmental interest involved.* Thus a restriction on inmate correspondence that furthers an important or substantial interest of penal administration will nevertheless be invalid if its sweep is unnecessarily broad. This does not mean, of course, that prison administrators may be required to show with certainty that adverse consequences would flow from the failure to censor a particular letter. Some latitude in anticipating the probable consequences of allowing certain speech in a prison environment is essential to the proper discharge of an administrator's duty. But any regulation or practice that restricts inmate correspondence must be generally necessary to protect one or more of the legitimate governmental interests identified above.

C

On the basis of this standard, we affirm the judgment of the District Court. The regulations invalidated by that court authorized,

inter alia, censorship of statements that "unduly complain" or "magnify grievances," expression of "inflammatory political, racial, religious or other views," and matter deemed "defamatory" or "otherwise inappropriate." These regulations fairly invited prison officials and employees to apply their own personal prejudices and opinions as standards for prisoner mail censorship. Not surprisingly, some prison officials used the extraordinary latitude for discretion authorized by the regulations to suppress unwelcome criticism. . . .

Appellants have failed to show that these broad restrictions on prisoner mail were in any way necessary to the furtherance of a governmental interest unrelated to the suppression of expression. . . .

. . . In short, the Department's regulations authorized censorship of prisoner mail far broader than any legitimate interest of penal administration demands and were properly found invalid by the District Court.

D

We also agree with the District Court that the decision to censor or withhold delivery of a particular letter must be accompanied by *minimum procedural safeguards.* The interest of prisoners and their correspondents in uncensored communication by letter, grounded as it is in the First Amendment, is plainly a "liberty" interest within the meaning of the Fourteenth Amendment even though qualified of necessity by the circumstance of imprisonment. As such, it is protected from arbitrary governmental invasion. . . . The District Court required that an inmate be notified of the rejection of a letter written by him or addressed to him, that the author of that letter be given a reasonable opportunity to protest that decision, and that complaints be referred to a prison official other than the person who originally disapproved the correspondence. These requirements do not appear to be unduly burdensome, nor do appellants so contend. . . .

II

The District Court also enjoined continued enforcement of Administrative Rule MV-IV-02, which provides in pertinent part:

"Investigators for an attorney-of-record will be confined to not more than two. Such investigators must be licensed by the State or must be members of the State Bar. Designation must be made in writing by the Attorney."

By restricting access to prisoners to members of the bar and licensed private investigators, this regulation imposed an absolute ban on the use by attorneys of law students and legal paraprofessionals to interview inmate clients. In fact, attorneys could not even delegate to such persons the task of obtaining prisoners' signatures on legal documents. The District Court reasoned that this rule constituted an unjustifiable restriction on the right of access to the courts. We agree.

[I]nmates must have a reasonable opportunity to seek and receive the assistance of attorneys. Regulations and practices that unjustifiably obstruct the availability of professional representation or other aspects of the right of access to the courts are invalid. Ex parte Hull, 312 U.S. 546 (1941).

* * *

[P]rison administrators are not required to adopt every proposal that may be thought to facilitate prisoner access to the courts. The extent to which that right is burdened by a particular regulation or practice must be weighed against the legitimate interests of penal administration and the proper regard that judges should give to the expertise and discretionary authority of correctional officials. . . .

Appellants' enforcement of the regulation in question . . . created an arbitrary distinction between law students employed by practicing attorneys and those associated with law school programs providing legal assistance to prisoners. While the Department flatly prohibited interviews of any sort by law students working for attorneys, it freely allowed participants of a number of law school programs to enter the prisons and meet with inmates. . . . The arbitrariness of the distinction between the two categories of law students does reveal the absence of any real justification for the sweeping prohibition of Administrative Rule MV-IV-02. We cannot say that the District Court erred in invalidating this regulation.

This result is mandated by our decision in Johnson v. Avery, 393 U.S. 483 (1969). There the Court struck down a prison regulation prohibiting any inmate from advising or assisting another in the preparation of legal documents. Given the inadequacy of alternative sources of legal assistance, the rule had the effect of denying to illiterate or poorly educated inmates any opportunity to vindicate possibly valid constitutional claims. The Court found that the regulation impermissibly burdened the right of access to the courts despite the not insignificant state interest in preventing the establishment of personal power structures by unscrupulous jailhouse lawyers and the attendant problems of prison discipline that follow. The countervailing state interest in Johnson is, if anything, more persuasive than any interest advanced by appellants in the instant case.

The judgment is
Affirmed.

[Mr. Justice MARSHALL wrote a concurring opinion in which Mr. Justice BRENNAN joined.]

[Mr. Justice DOUGLAS wrote a brief concurring opinion in which Mr. Justice BRENNAN and Mr. Justice MARSHALL joined.]

Press Interviews with Inmates

PELL v. PROCUNIER

Supreme Court of the United States, 1974
417 U.S. 817, 95 S. Ct. 2800, 41 L. Ed. 2d 495

Four inmates at San Quentin Penitentiary, California, and three journalists, including Eve Pell, brought suits to enjoin Raymond Procunier, Director of the California Department of Corrections, from enforcing a regulation that prohibited

"press and other media interviews with specific individual inmates." The inmates alleged that the regulation violated their First and Fourteenth Amendment rights to free speech. The journalists contended that the ban constituted an unconstitutional infringement on newsgathering. A three-judge United States District Court (S.D. Calif.) upheld the allegations of the inmates and struck down the regulation prohibiting face-to-face interviews. However, the court rejected the journalists' claim, holding that the press had sufficient opportunity to enter prisons and interview inmates randomly. Director Procunier appealed the judgment of the district court that the regulation infringed upon the inmates' First and Fourteenth Amendment rights; the journalists appealed the district court's rejection of their claims. The United States Supreme Court consolidated the cross-appeals for oral argument.

Mr. Justice STEWART delivered the opinion of the court.

* * *

I

* * *

We start with the familiar proposition that "[l]awful incarceration brings about the necessary withdrawal or limitation of many privileges and rights, a retraction justified by the considerations underlying our penal system." Price v. Johnson, 334 U.S. 266 (1948). In the First Amendment context a corollary of this principle is that a prison inmate retains those First Amendment rights that are not inconsistent with his status as a prisoner or with the legitimate penological objectives of the corrections system. Thus, challenges to prison restrictions that are asserted to inhibit First Amendment interests must be analyzed in terms of the legitimate policies and goals of the corrections system, to whose custody and care the prisoner has been committed in accordance with due process of law.

An important function of the corrections system is the deterrence of crime. The premise is that by confining criminal offenders in a facility where they are isolated from the rest of society, a condition that most people presumably find undesirable, they and others will be deterred from committing additional criminal offenses. This isolation, of course, also serves a protective function by quarantining criminal offenders for a given period of time while, it is hoped, the rehabilitative processes of the corrections system work to correct the offender's demonstrated criminal proclivity. Thus, since most offenders will eventually return to society, another paramount objective of the corrections system is the rehabilitation of

those committed to its custody. Finally, central to all other corrections goals is the institutional consideration of internal security within the corrections facilities themselves. It is in the light of these legitimate penal objectives that a court must assess challenges to prison regulations based on asserted constitutional rights of prisoners.

The regulation challenged here clearly restricts one manner of communication between prison inmates and members of the general public beyond the prison walls. But this is merely to state the problem, not to resolve it. For the same could be said of a refusal by corrections authorities to permit an inmate temporarily to leave the prison in order to communicate with persons outside. Yet no one could sensibly contend that the Constitution requires the authorities to give even individualized consideration to such requests. . . . In order properly to evaluate the constitutionality of § 415.071, we think that the regulation cannot be considered in isolation but must be viewed in the light of the alternative means of communication permitted under the regulations with persons outside the prison. . . .

One such alternative available to California prison inmates is communication by mail. Although prison regulations, until recently, called for the censorship of statements . . ., we recently held that "the Department's regulations authorized censorship of prisoner mail far broader than any legitimate interest of penal administration demands," and accordingly affirmed a district court judgment invalidating the regulations. Procunier v. Martinez, 416 U.S. 396 (1974). . . .

[T]he visitation policy of the California Corrections Department does not seal the inmate off from personal contact with those outside the prison. Inmates are permitted to receive limited visits from members of their families, the clergy, their attorneys, and friends of prior acquaintance. The selection of these categories of visitors is based on the Director's professional judgment that such visits will aid in the rehabilitation of the inmate while not compromising the other legitimate objectives of the corrections system. This is not a case in which the selection is based on the anticipated content of the communication between the inmate and the prospective visitor. If a member of the press fell within any of these categories, there is no suggestion that he would not be permitted to visit with the inmate. More importantly, however, inmates have an unrestricted opportunity to communicate with the press or any other member of the public through their families, friends, clergy, or attorneys who are permitted to visit them at the prison. Thus, this provides another alternative avenue of communication between prison inmates and persons outside the prison.

* * *

In Procunier v. Martinez, supra, we could find no legitimate governmental interest to justify the substantial restrictions that had been imposed on written communication by inmates. When, however, the question involves the entry of people into the prisons for face-to-face communication with inmates, it is obvious that institutional considerations, such as security and related administrative problems, as well as the accepted and legitimate policy objectives of the corrections system itself, require that some limitation be placed on such visitations. So long as reasonable and effective means of communication remain open and no discrimination in terms of content is involved, we believe that, in drawing such lines, "prison officials must be accorded latitude." ...

* * *

[I]n light of the alternative channels of communication that are open to prison inmates, we cannot say on the record in this case that this restriction on one manner in which prisoners can communicate with persons outside of prison is unconstitutional. So long as this restriction operates in a neutral fashion, without regard to the content of the expression, it falls within the "appropriate rules and regulations" to which "prisoners necessarily are subject" ... and does not abridge any First Amendment freedoms retained by prison inmates.

II

[T]he media plaintiffs ask us to hold that the limitation on press interviews imposed by § 415.071 violates the freedom of the press guaranteed by the First and Fourteenth Amendments. They contend that, irrespective of what First Amendment liberties may or may not be retained by prison inmates, members of the press have a constitutional right to interview any inmate who is willing to speak with them, in the absence of an individualized determination that the particular interview might create a clear and present danger to prison security or to some other substantial interest served by the corrections system. In this regard, the media plaintiffs do not claim any impairment of their freedom to publish, for California imposes no restrictions on what may be published about its prisons, the prison inmates, or the officers who administer the prisons. Instead, they rely on their right to gather news without governmental interference, which the media plaintiffs assert includes a right of access to the sources of what is regarded as newsworthy information.

* * *

The sole limitation on newsgathering in California prisons is the prohibition in § 415.071 of interviews with individual inmates specifically designated by representatives of the press. This restriction is of recent vintage, having been imposed in 1971 in response to a violent episode that the Department of Corrections felt was at least partially attributable to the former policy with respect to face-to-face prisoner-press interviews. Prior to the promulgation of § 415.071, every journalist had virtually free access to interview any individual inmate whom he might wish. Only members of the press were accorded this privilege; other members of the general public did not have the benefit of such an unrestricted visitation policy. Thus, the promulgation of § 415.071 did not impose a discrimination against press access, but merely eliminated a special privilege formerly given to representatives of the press vis-a-vis members of the public generally.

* * *

The First and Fourteenth Amendments bar government from interfering in any way with a free press. The Constitution does not, however, require government to accord the press special access to information not shared by members of the public generally. It is one thing to say that a journalist is free to seek out sources of information not available to members of the general public, that he is entitled to some constitutional protection of the confidentiality of such sources . . . and that government cannot restrain the publication of news emanating from such sources. . . . It is quite another thing to suggest that the Constitution imposes upon government the affirmative duty to make available to journalists sources of information not available to members of the public generally. That proposition finds no support in the words of the Constitution or in any decision of this Court. Accordingly, since § 415.071 does not deny the press access to sources of information available to members of the general public, we hold that it does not abridge the protections that the First and Fourteenth Amendments guarantee.

For the reasons stated, we reverse the District Court's judgment that § 415.071 infringes the freedom of speech of the prison inmates and affirm its judgement that the regulation does not abridge the constitutional right of a free press. . . .

Vacated and remanded.

[Mr. Justice POWELL concurred in part and dissented in part.]

Mr. Justice DOUGLAS, with whom Mr. Justice BRENNAN and Mr. Justice MARSHALL join, dissenting.

* * *

It is true that the prisoners are left with other means of expression such as visits by relatives and communication by mail. But the State can hardly defend an overly broad restriction on expression by demonstrating that it has not eliminated expression completely.

* * *

Prisons, like all other public institutions, are ultimately the responsibility of the populace. Crime, like the economy, health, education, defense, and the like, is a matter of grave concern in our society and people have the right and the necessity to know not only of the incidence of crime but of the effectiveness of the system designed to control it. "On any given day, approximately 1,500,000 people are under the authority of [federal, state and local prison] systems. The cost to taxpayers is over one billion dollars annually. Of those individuals sentenced to prisons, 98% will return to society." The public's interest in being informed about prisons is thus paramount.

As with the prisoners' free speech claim, no one asserts that the free press right is such that the authorities are powerless to impose reasonable regulations as to the time, place, and manner of interviews to effectuate prison discipline and order. The only issue here is whether the complete ban on interviews with inmates selected by the press goes beyond what is necessary for the protection of these interests and infringes upon our cherished right of a free press. . . .

* * *

[T]he absolute ban on press interviews with specifically designated federal inmates is far broader than is necessary to protect any legitimate governmental interests and is an unconstitutional infringement on the public's right to know protected by the free press guarantee of the First Amendment. . . .

Prison Disciplinary Hearings and Due Process

BAXTER v. PALMIGIANO

Supreme Court of the United States, 1976
425 U.S. 308, 96 S. Ct. 1551, 47 L. Ed. 2d 810

Nicholas Palmigiano, an inmate at the Rhode Island Adult Correctional Institution serving a life sentence for murder, was charged by prison officials with "inciting a disturbance." He was told by prison officials that he might be prosecuted

under state law, that he should consult an attorney (although his attorney could not be present during the prison disciplinary hearing), and that he had a right to remain silent at the hearing but his silence could be used against him. At the hearing, Palmigiano remained silent and was placed in "punitive segregation" for 30 days. He filed an action under 42 U.S.C. § 1983 for damages and injunctive relief, alleging that the procedures utilized at the disciplinary hearing violated the Due Process Clause of the Fourteenth Amendment. The District Court (D.R.I.) denied relief, but the Court of Appeals (1st Cir.) reversed, holding that (1) an inmate at a prison disciplinary hearing must be informed of his right to remain silent; (2) he must not be questioned further once he exercises that right; (3) such silence may not be used against him at that time or in future proceedings; and (4) when criminal charges are a realistic possibility, prison officials should consider whether defense counsel, if requested, should be permitted at the disciplinary hearing. The United States Supreme Court granted certiorari.

John Clutchette and other inmates at San Quentin filed an action under 42 U.S.C. § 1983 seeking declaratory and injunctive relief, alleging that the procedures used in disciplinary proceedings at San Quentin violated their rights to due process and equal protection of the laws under the Fourteenth Amendment. After an evidentiary hearing, the United States District Court (N.D. Calif.) granted substantial relief, and the Court of Appeals (9th Cir.) affirmed, holding that (1) minimum notice and a right to respond are due an inmate faced with even a temporary suspension of privileges; (2) an inmate at a disciplinary hearing who is denied the privilege of confronting and cross-examining witnesses must receive written reasons therefor or the denial will be deemed prima facie evidence of abuse of discretion; and (3) an inmate facing prison discipline for a violation that might also be punishable in state criminal proceedings has a right to counsel, not merely a counsel substitute, at a prison hearing. The United States Supreme Court granted certiorari.

Mr. Justice WHITE delivered the opinion of the Court.

* * *

I

* * *

II

* * *

Relying on Miranda v. Arizona, 384 U.S. 436 (1966), and Mathis v. United States, 391 U.S. 1 (1968), both Courts of Appeals in these cases held that prison inmates are entitled to representation at prison disciplinary hearings where the charges involve conduct punishable as a crime under state law, not because of the services that counsel might render in connection with the disciplinary proceedings themselves but because statements inmates might make at the hearings would perhaps be used in later state court prosecutions for the same conduct.

Neither Miranda, supra, nor Mathis, supra, has any substantial bearing on the question whether counsel must be provided at "prison disciplinary hearings [which] are not part of a criminal prosecution." Wolff v. McDonnell, 418 U.S. at 566. The Court has never held, and we decline to do so now, that the requirements of those cases must be met to render pretrial statements admissible in other than criminal cases.

We see no reason to alter our conclusion so recently made in Wolff that inmates do not "have a right to either retained or appointed counsel in disciplinary hearings." ... Plainly, therefore, state authorities were not in error in failing to advise Palmigiano to the contrary, i.e., that he was entitled to counsel at the hearing and that the State would furnish counsel if he did not have one of his own.

III

Palmigiano was advised that he was not required to testify at his disciplinary hearing, that he could remain silent but that his silence could be used against him. The Court of Appeals for the First Circuit held that the self-incrimination privilege of the Fifth Amendment, made applicable to the States by reason of the Fourteenth Amendment, forbids drawing adverse inferences against an inmate from his failure to testify. The State challenges this determination and we sustain the challenge.

As the Court has often held, the Fifth

Amendment "not only protects the individual against being involuntarily called as a witness against himself in a criminal prosecution but also privileges him not to answer official inquiries put to him in any other proceeding, civil or criminal, formal or informal, where the answers might incriminate him in state proceedings." Lefkowitz v. Turley, 414 U.S. 70, 77 (1973). Prison disciplinary hearings are not criminal proceedings; but if inmates are compelled in those proceedings to furnish testimonial evidence that might incriminate them in later criminal proceedings, they must be offered "whatever immunity is required to supplant the privilege" and may not be required "to waive such immunity." . . . [In several cases] the States, pursuant to statute, sought to interrogate individuals about their job performance or about their contractual relations with the State; insisted upon waiver of the Fifth Amendment privilege not to respond or to object to later use of the incriminating statements in criminal prosecutions; and, upon refusal to waive, automatically terminated employment or eligibility to contract with the State. Holding that the State could not constitutionally seek to compel testimony that had not been immunized by threats of serious economic reprisal, we invalidated the challenged statutes.

The Court has also plainly ruled that it is constitutional error under the Fifth Amendment to instruct a jury in a criminal case that it may draw an inference of guilt from a defendant's failure to testify about facts relevant to his case. Griffin v. California, 380 U.S. 609 (1965). This holding paralleled the existing statutory policy of the United States, and the governing statutory or constitutional rule in the overwhelming majority of the states. . . .

The Rhode Island prison rules do not transgress the foregoing principles. No criminal proceedings are or were pending against Palmigiano. The State has not, contrary to Griffin, sought to make evidentiary use of his silence at the disciplinary hearing in any criminal proceeding. Neither has Rhode Island insisted or asked that Palmigiano waive his Fifth Amendment privilege. He was notified that he was privileged to remain silent if he chose. He was also advised that his silence could be used against him, but a prison inmate in Rhode Island electing to remain silent during his disciplin-

ary hearing, as respondent Palmigiano did here, is not in consequence of his silence automatically found guilty of the infraction with which he has been charged. Under Rhode Island law, disciplinary decisions "must be based on substantial evidence manifested in the record of the disciplinary proceeding." . . . It is thus undisputed that an inmate's silence in and of itself is insufficient to support an adverse decision by the disciplinary board. In this respect, this case is very different from the circumstances before the Court in the [other decisions, where refusal to submit to interrogation and to waive the Fifth Amendment privilege, standing alone and without regard to the other evidence, resulted in loss of employment or opportunity to contract with the State. There, failure to respond to interrogation was treated as a final admission of guilt. Here, Palmigiano remained silent at the hearing in the face of evidence that incriminated him; and as far as this record reveals, his silence was given no more evidentiary value than was warranted by the facts surrounding his case. This does not smack of an invalid attempt by the State to compel testimony without granting immunity or to penalize the exercise of the privilege. The advice given inmates by the decisionmakers is merely a realistic reflection of the evidentiary significance of the choice to remain silent.

Had the State desired Palmigiano's testimony over his Fifth Amendment objection, we can but assume that it would have extended whatever use immunity is required by the Federal Constitution. Had this occurred and Palmigiano nevertheless refused to answer, it surely would not have violated the Fifth Amendment to draw whatever inference from his silence that the circumstances warranted. Insofar as the privilege is concerned, the situation is little different where the State advises the inmate of his right to silence but also plainly notifies him that his silence will be weighed in the balance.

Our conclusion is consistent with the prevailing rule that the Fifth Amendment does not forbid adverse inferences against parties to civil actions when they refuse to testify in response to probative evidence offered against them: the Amendment "does not preclude the inference where the privilege is claimed by a party to a civil cause."

... In criminal cases, where the stakes are higher and the State's sole interest is to convict, Griffin prohibits the judge and prosecutor from suggesting to the jury that it may treat the defendant's silence as substantive evidence of guilt. Disciplinary proceedings in state prisons, however, involve the correctional process and important state interests other than conviction for crime. We decline to extend the Griffin rule to this context.

It is important to note here that the position adopted by the Court of Appeals is rooted in the Fifth Amendment and the policies which it serves. It has little to do with a fair trial and derogates rather than improves the chances for accurate decisions. Thus, aside from the privilege against compelled self-incrimination, the Court has consistently recognized that in proper circumstances silence in the face of accusation is a relevant fact not barred from evidence by the Due Process Clause. . . . Indeed, as Mr. Justice Brandeis declared . . . "Silence is often evidence of the most persuasive character." . . . And just last Term . . . the Court recognized that "failure to contest an assertion . . . is considered evidence of acquiescence . . . if it would have been natural under the circumstances to object to the insertion of the question." . . .

The short of it is that permitting an adverse inference to be drawn from an inmate's silence at his disciplinary proceedings is not, on its face, an invalid practice; and there is no basis in the record for invalidating it as applied to Palmigiano.

IV

In Wolff v. McDonnell, we held that "the inmate facing disciplinary proceedings should be allowed to call witnesses and present documentary evidence in his defense when permitting him to do so will not be unduly hazardous to institutional safety or correctional goals." . . . We noted that "[o]rdinarily, the right to present evidence is basic to a fair hearing; but the unrestricted right to call witnesses from the prison population carries obvious potential for disruption and for interference with the swift punishment that in individual cases may be essential to carrying out the correctional program of the institution." The right to call witnesses, like other Due Process rights delineated in Wolff, is thus circumscribed by

the necessary "mutual accommodation between institutional needs and objectives and the provisions of the Constitution that are of general application." . . . Within the reasonable limitations necessary in the prison disciplinary context, we suggested, but did not require, that the disciplinary committee "state its reason for refusing to call a witness, whether it be for irrelevance, lack of necessity, or the hazards presented in individual cases." . . .

We were careful to distinguish between this limited right to call witnesses and other due process rights at disciplinary hearings. We noted expressly that, in comparison to the right to call witnesses, "[c]onfrontation and cross-examination present greater hazards to institutional interests." . . . We said:

"If confrontation and cross-examination of those furnishing evidence against the inmate were to be allowed as a matter of course, as in criminal trials, there would be considerable potential for havoc inside the prison walls. Proceedings would inevitably be longer and tend to unmanageability."

We therefore concluded that "[t]he better course at this time, in a period where prisons' practices are diverse and somewhat experimental, is to leave these matters to the sound discretion of the officials of state prisons." . . .

Although acknowledging the strictures of Wolff with respect to confrontation and cross-examination, the Court of Appeals for the Ninth Circuit [in Clutchette] went on to require prison authorities to provide reasons in writing to inmates denied the privilege to cross-examine or confront witnesses against them in disciplinary proceedings; absent explanation, failure to set forth reasons related to the prevention of one or more of the four concerns expressly mentioned in Wolff would be deemed prima facie abuse of discretion.

This conclusion is inconsistent with Wolff. We characterized as "useful," but did not require, written reasons for denying inmates the limited right to call witnesses in their defense. We made no such suggestion with respect to confrontation and cross-examination which, as was there pointed out, stand on a different footing because of their inherent danger and the availability of adequate bases of decision without them. . . . Mandating confrontation and cross-examination, except where prison officials can justify their denial on one or more grounds that appeal to judges, effectively preempts the area that Wolff left to the sound discretion of prison officials. We add that on the record before us there is no evidence of the abuse of discretion by the state prison officials.

V

Finally, the Court of Appeals for the Ninth Circuit [in Clutchette] held that minimum due process — such as notice, opportunity for response, and statement of reasons for action by prison officials — was necessary where inmates were deprived of privileges. 510 F.2d, at 615. We did not reach the issue in Wolff; indeed, we said "[w]e do not suggest, however, that the procedures required by today's decision for the deprivation of good time would also be required for the imposition of lesser penalties such as the loss of privileges." . . . Nor do we find it necessary to reach the issue now in light of the record before us. None of the named plaintiffs in [Clutchette] was subject solely to loss of privileges; all were brought before prison disciplinary hearings for allegations of the type of "serious misconduct" . . . that we held in Wolff to trigger procedures therein outlined. Without such a record, we are unable to consider the degree of "liberty" at stake in loss of privileges and thus whether some sort of procedural safeguards are due when only such "lesser penalties" are at stake. To the extent that the Court of Appeals for the Ninth Circuit required any procedures in such circumstances, the Court of Appeals acted prematurely and its decision on the issue cannot stand.

We said in Wolff v. McDonnell that "[a]s the nature of the prison disciplinary process changes in future years, circumstances may then exist which will require further consideration and reflection by this Court. It is our view, however, that the procedures we have now required in prison disciplinary proceedings represent a reasonable accommodation between the interest of the inmates and the needs of the institution." . . . We do not retreat from that view. However, the procedures required by the Court of Appeals in [Palmigiano] and [Clutchette] are either inconsistent with the "reasonable accommodation" reached in Wolff, or premature on the bases of the records before us. . . .

Reversed.

Mr. Justice BRENNAN, with whom Mr. Justice MARSHALL joints, concurring in part and dissenting in part.

I agree that consideration of the procedural safeguards necessary where an inmate is deprived only of privileges is premature on this record, and thus I join Part V of the Court's opinion, which leaves open whether an inmate may be deprived of privileges in the absence of due process safeguards.

Parts II and IV of the Court's opinion simply reaffirm last Term's Wolff v. McDonnell, 418 U.S. 539 (1974). I continue to believe that Wolff approved procedural safeguards short of the minimum requirements of the Due Process Clause, and I dissent from Parts II and IV for the reasons stated by my Brother MARSHALL, id, at 580.

Part III of the Court's opinion, however, confronts an issue not present in Wolff and in my view reaches an erroneous conclusion. The Court acknowledges that inmates have the right to invoke the privilege against compulsory self-incrimination in prison disciplinary proceedings, but nevertheless holds that "permitting an adverse inference to be drawn from an inmate's silence at his disciplinary proceedings is not, on its face, an invalid practice," and was proper in the circumstances of this case. This conclusion cannot be reconciled with the numerous cases holding that the government is barred from penalizing an individual for exercising the privilege; precedents require the holding that if government officials ask questions of an individual to elicit incriminating information, as happened here, the imposition of any substantial sanction on that individual for remaining silent violates the Fifth Amendment. That principle prohibits reliance on any inference of guilt from the exercise of the privilege in the context of a prison disciplinary hearing.

* * *

. . . I must therefore view today's decision as another regrettable disregard of Mr. Justice Frankfurter's admonition that our interpretation of the privilege is not faithful to the Founding Fathers' purpose when it does not reflect the teaching of history:

"This command of the Fifth Amendment . . . registers an important advance in the development of our liberty — 'one of the great landmarks in man's struggle to make himself civilized.' Time has not shown that protection from the evils against which this safeguard was directed is needless or unwarranted. This constitutional protection must not be interpreted in a hostile or niggardly spirit. Too many, even those who should be better advised, view this privilege as a shelter for wrongdoers. They too readily assume that those who invoke it are either

guilty of crime or commit perjury in claiming the privilege. Such a view does scant honor to the patriots who sponsored the Bill of Rights as a condition to acceptance of the Constitution by the ratifying States." Ullman v. United States, 350 U.S. 422, 426–427 (1956).

[Mr. Justice STEVENS took no part in the consideration or decision of these cases.]

Due Process and Inmate Transfers

MEACHUM v. FANO

Supreme Court of the United States, 1976
427 U.S. 215, 96 S. Ct. 2532, 49 L. Ed. 2d 451

Arthur Fano, an inmate at Massachusetts' Norfolk Correctional Institution, was informed that prison officials had information from reliable informers that he had engaged in criminal conduct at the prison and that a classification hearing would be held. Respondent Fano was represented by counsel at the hearing. The board heard, in camera and out of Fano's presence, the testimony of prison superintendent Meachum. Finding that the evidence supported the allegations the board recommended that Fano be transferred to Walpole Prison. The commissioner of corrections accepted the recommendation and the transfer was carried out. Fano brought action in the federal district court under 42 U.S.C. § 1983, alleging that he was deprived of liberty without due process of law in that he had been ordered transferred to a less favorable institution without an adequate factfinding hearing. Relying on *Wolff* v. *McDonnell*, 418 U.S. 539 (1974), the district court ordered Fano returned to Norfolk until transferred after proper notice and hearing. A divided panel of the Court of Appeals (1st Cir.) affirmed, holding that the transfer from a medium-security institution to a maximum-security one involved "a significant modification of the overall conditions of confinement" and thus was "serious enough to trigger the application of due process protections." The United States Supreme Court granted certiorari.

Mr. Justice WHITE delivered the opinion of the Court.

*   *   *

The Fourteenth Amendment prohibits any State from depriving a person of life, liberty, or property without due process of law. The initial inquiry is whether the transfer of respondent from Norfolk to Walpole and Bridgewater infringed or implicated a "liberty" interest of respondent within the meaning of the Due Process Clause. Contrary to the Court of Appeals, we hold that it did not. We reject at the outset the notion that *any* grievous loss visited upon a person

by the State is sufficient to invoke the procedural protections of the Due Process Clause. In Board of Regents v. Roth, 408 U.S. 564 (1972), a university professor was deprived of his job, a loss which was surely a matter of great substance, but because the professor had no property interest in his position, due process procedures were not required in connection with his dismissal. We there held that the determining factor is the nature of the interest involved rather than its weight.

Similarly, we cannot agree that *any* change in the conditions of confinement having a substantial adverse impact on the prisoner involved is sufficient to invoke the protections of the Due Process Clause. The Due Process Clause by its own force forbids the State from convicting any person of crime and depriving him of his liberty without complying fully with the requirements of the Clause. But given a valid conviction, the criminal defendant has been constitutionally deprived of his liberty to the extent that the State may confine him and subject him to the rules of its prison system so long as the conditions of confinement do not otherwise violate the Constitution. The Constitution does not require that the State have more than one prison for convicted felons; nor does it guarantee that the convicted prisoner will be placed in any particular prison if, as is likely, the State has more than one correctional institution. The initial decision to assign the convict to a particular institution is not subject to audit under the Due Process Clause, although the degree of confinement in one prison may be quite different from that in another. The conviction has sufficiently extinguished the defendant's liberty interest to empower the State to confine him in *any* of its prisons.

Neither, in our view, does the Due Process Clause in and of itself protect a duly convicted prisoner against transfer from one institution to another within the state prison system. Confinement in any of the State's institutions is within the normal limits or range of custody which the conviction has authorized the State to impose. That life in one prison is much more disagreeable than in another does not in itself signify that a Fourteenth Amendment liberty interest is implicated when a prisoner is transferred to the institution with the more severe rules.

Our cases hold that the convicted felon does not forfeit all constitutional protections by reason of his conviction and confinement in prison. He retains a variety of important rights that the courts must be alerted to protect. . . . But none of these cases reaches this one; and to hold as we are urged to do that *any* substantial deprivation imposed by prison authorities triggers the procedural protections of the Due Process Clause would subject to judicial review a wide spectrum of discretionary actions that traditionally have been the business of prison administrators rather than of the federal courts.

Transfers between institutions, for example, are made for a variety of reasons and often involve no more than informed predictions as to what would best serve institutional security or the safety and welfare of the inmate. Yet under the approach urged here, any transfer, for whatever reasons, would require a hearing as long as it could be said that the transfer would place the prisoner in substantially more burdensome conditions than he had been experiencing. We are unwilling to go so far.

Wolff v. McDonnell, 418 U.S. 539 (1974), on which the Court of Appeals heavily relied, is not to the contrary. Under that case, the Due Process Clause entitles a state prisoner to certain procedural protections when he is deprived of good-time credits because of serious misconduct. But the liberty interest there identified did not originate in the Constitution, which "itself does not guarantee good-time credit for satisfactory behavior while in prison." . . . The State itself, not the Constitution, had "not only provided a statutory right to good time but also specifies that it is to be forfeited only for serious misbehavior." . . .

* * *

The liberty interest protected in Wolff had its roots in state law, and the minimum procedures appropriate under the circumstances were held required by the Due Process Clause "to insure that the state-created right is not arbitrarily abrogated."

Here, Massachusetts law conferred no right on the prisoner to remain in the prison to which he was initially assigned, defeasible only upon proof of specific acts of misconduct. Insofar as we are advised, transfers between Massachusetts prisons are not conditioned upon the occurrence of specified events. . . . That an inmate's conduct, in general or in specific instances may often be a major factor in the decision of prison officials to transfer him is to be expected unless it be assumed that transfers are mindless events. A prisoner's past and anticipated future behavior will very likely be taken into account in selecting a prison in which he will be initially incarcerated or to which he will be transferred to best serve the State's penological goals.

A prisoner's behavior may precipitate a transfer; and absent such behavior, perhaps transfer would not take place at all. But, as we have said, Massachusetts prison officials have the discretion to transfer prisoners for any number of reasons. Their discretion is not limited to instances of serious misconduct. . . .

*   *   *

Holding that arrangements like this are within reach of the procedural protections of the Due Process Clause would place the Clause astride the day-to-day functioning of state prisons and involve the judiciary in issues and discretionary decisions that are not the business of federal judges. We decline to so interpret and apply the Due Process Clause. The federal courts do not sit to supervise state prisons, the administration of which is of acute interest to the States. . . .

Reversed.

Mr. Justice STEVENS, with whom Mr. Justice BRENNAN and Mr. Justice MARSHALL join, dissenting.

The Court's rationale is more disturbing than its narrow holding. If the Court had merely held "that the transfer of a prisoner from one penal institution to another does not cause a sufficiently grievous loss to amount to a deprivation of liberty within the meaning of the Due Process Clause of the Fourteenth Amendment," I would disagree with the conclusion but not with the constitutional analysis. The Court's holding today, however, appears to rest on a conception of "liberty" which I consider fundamentally incorrect.

The Court indicates that a "liberty interest" may have either of two sources. According to the Court, a liberty interest may "originate in the Constitution" . . . or it may have "its roots in state law." . . . Apart from those two possible origins, the Court is unable to find that a person has a constitutionally protected interest in liberty.

If a man were a creature of the State, the analysis would be correct. But neither the Bill of Rights nor the laws of sovereign States create the liberty which the Due Process Clause protects. The relevant constitutional provisions are limitations on the power of the sovereign to infringe on the liberty of the citizen. The relevant state laws either create property rights, or they curtail the freedom of the citizen who must live in an ordered society. Of course, law is essen-

tial to the exercise and enjoyment of individual liberty in a complex society. But it is not the source of liberty and surely not the exclusive source.

I had thought it self-evident that all men were endowed by their Creator with liberty as one of the cardinal unalienable rights. It is that basic freedom which the Due Process Clause protects, rather than the particular rights or privileges conferred by specific laws or regulations.

A correct description of the source of the liberty protected by the Constitution does not of course, decide this case. For, by hypothesis, we are dealing with persons who may be deprived of their liberty because they have been convicted of criminal conduct after a fair trial. We should therefore first ask whether the deprivation of liberty which follows conviction is total or partial.

At one time the prevailing view was that deprivation was essentially total. The penitentiary inmate was considered "the slave of the State." . . . Although the wording of the Thirteenth Amendment provided some support for that point of view, courts in recent years have moderated the harsh implications of the Thirteenth Amendment.

The moderating trend culminated in this Court's landmark holding that notwithstanding the continuation of legal custody pursuant to a criminal conviction, a parolee has a measure of liberty that is entitled to constitutional protection. [Morrissey v. Brewer, 408 U.S. 471 (1972).]

Although the Court's opinion was narrowly written with careful emphasis on the permission given to the parolee to live outside the prison walls, the Court necessarily held that the individual possesses a residuum of constitutionally protected liberty while in legal custody pursuant to a valid conviction. For release on parole is merely conditional, and it does not interrupt the State's legal custody. . . .

It demeans the holding in Morrissey—more importantly it demeans the concept of liberty itself—to ascribe to that holding nothing more than a protection of an interest that the State had created through its own prison regulations. For if the inmate's protected liberty interests are no greater than the State chooses to allow, he is really little more than the slave described in the 19th century cases. I think it clear that even the inmate retains an unalienable interest in liberty—at the very minimum the right to be treated with dignity—which the Constitution may never ignore.

This basic premise is not inconsistent with recognition of the obvious fact that the State must have wide latitude in determining the conditions of confinement that will be imposed following conviction of crime. To supervise and control its prison population, the State must retain the power to change the conditions for individuals, or for groups of prisoners, quickly and without judicial review. In many respects the State's problems in governing its inmate population are comparable to those encountered in governing a military force. Prompt and unquestioning obedience by the individual, even to commands he does not understand, may be essential to the preservation of order and discipline. Nevertheless, within the limits imposed by the basic restraints governing the controlled population, each individual retains his dignity, and, in time, acquires a status that is entitled to respect.

Imprisonment is intended to accomplish more than the temporary removal of the offender from society in order to prevent him from committing like offenses during the period of his incarceration. While custody denies the inmate the opportunity to offend, it also gives him an opportunity to improve himself and to acquire skills and habits that will help him to participate in an open society after his release. Within the prison community, if my basic hypothesis is correct, he has a protected right to pursue his limited rehabilitative goals, or at the minimum, to maintain whatever attributes of dignity are associated with his status in a tightly controlled society. It is unquestionably within the power of the State to change that status, abruptly and adversely; but if the change is sufficiently grievous, it may not be imposed arbitrarily. In such case due process must be afforded.

That does not mean, of course, that every adversity amounts to a deprivation within the meaning of the Fourteenth Amendment. There must be grievous loss, and that term itself is somewhat flexible. I would certainly not consider every transfer within a prison system, even to more onerous conditions of confinement, such a loss. On the other hand, I am unable to identify a principled basis for differentiating between a transfer from the general prison population to solitary confinement and a transfer involving equally disparate conditions between one physical facility and another.

In view of the Court's basic holding, I merely note that I agree with the Court of Appeals that the transfer involved in this case was sufficiently serious to invoke the protection of the Constitution.

Medical Malpractice Inside the Prison Walls

ESTELLE v. GAMBLE

Supreme Court of the United States, 1976
429 U.S. 97, 97 S. Ct. 285, 50 L. Ed. 2d 251

J. W. Gamble, the respondent and an inmate of a Texas prison, was injured in November, 1973, when a 600-pound bale of cotton fell on him while he was unloading a truck. Two months later, he filed a civil rights action under 42 U.S.C. § 1983 against Dr. Ralph Gray, the Medical Director of the Texas Department of Corrections, and two corrections officials, the warden and W. J. Estelle, Jr., the Director of the Department of Corrections. The complaint alleged that he was subjected to cruel and unusual punishment in violation of the Eighth Amendment by receiving inadequate medical treatment of the back injury he sustained in the accident. The district court dismissed the complaint for failure to state a claim upon which relief could be granted, but the Court of Appeals (5th Cir.) reversed and remanded with instructions to reinstate the claim. The United States Supreme Court granted certiorari.

Mr. Justice MARSHALL delivered the opinion of the Court.

* * *

The gravamen of respondent's § 1983 complaint is that petitioners have subjected him to cruel and unusual punishment in violation of the Eighth Amendment, made applicable to the States by the Fourteenth. See Robinson v. California, 370 U.S. 660 (1962). We therefore base our evaluation of respondent's complaint on those Amendments and our decisions interpreting them.

The history of the constitutional prohibition of "cruel and unusual punishments" has been recounted at length in prior opinions of the Court and need not be repeated here. See, e.g., Gregg v. Georgia, 428 U.S. 153 (1976) (plurality opinion). . . . It suffices to note that the primary concern of the drafters was to proscribe "tortures" and other "barbarous" methods of punishment. Id., at 842. Accordingly, this Court first applied the Eighth Amendment by comparing challenged methods of execution to concededly inhuman techniques of punishment. See Wilkerson v. Utah, 99 U.S. 130, 136 (1878) ("[I]t is safe to affirm that punishments of torture . . . and all others in the same line of unnecessary cruelty, are forbidden by that amendment. . . ."); In re Kemmler, 136 U.S. 436, 447 (1890) ("Punishments are cruel when they involve torture or a lingering death. . . .")

Our more recent cases, however, have held that the Amendment proscribes more than physically barbarous punishments. See, e.g., Gregg v. Georgia, supra, at 171 (plurality opinion); Trop v. Dulles, 356 U.S. 86, 100–101 (1958); Weems v. United States, 217 U.S. 349, 373 (1910). The Amendment embodies "broad and idealistic concepts of dignity, civilized standards, humanity, and decency . . .," Jackson v. Bishop, 404 F.2d 571, 579 (8th Circ. 1968), against which we must evaluate penal measures. Thus, we have held repugnant to the Eighth Amendment punishments which are incompatible with "the evolving standards of decency that mark the progress of a maturing society," Trop v. Dulles, supra, at 101; . . . or which "involve the unnecessary and wanton infliction of pain," Gregg v. Georgia, supra, at 173 (plurality opinion). . . .

These elementary principles establish the government's obligation to provide medical care for those whom it is punishing by incarceration. An inmate must rely on prison authorities to treat his medical needs; if the authorities fail to do so, those needs will not be met. In the worst cases, such a failure may actually produce physical "torture or a lingering death," . . . the evils of most immediate concern to the drafters of the Amendment. In less serious cases, denial of medical care may result in pain and suffering which no one suggests would serve any penological purpose. . . . The infliction of such unnecessary suffering is inconsistent with contemporary standards of decency as manifested in modern legislation codifying the common law view that "[i]t is but just that the public be required to care for the prisoner, who cannot, by reason of the deprivation of his liberty, care for himself."

We therefore conclude that deliberate indifference to serious medical needs of prisoners constitutes the "unnecessary and wanton infliction of pain," . . . proscribed by the Eighth Amendment. This is true whether the indifference is manifested by prison doctors in their response to the prisoner's needs[j] or by prison guards in intentionally denying or delaying access to medical care or intentionally interfering with the treatment once prescribed. Regardless of how evidenced, deliberate indifference to a prisoner's serious illness or injury states a cause of action under § 1983.

This conclusion does not mean, however, that every claim by a prisoner that he has not received adequate medical treatment states a violation of the Eighth Amendment. An accident, although it may produce added

---

[j]See, e.g., Williams v. Vincent, 508 F.2d 541 (2d Cir. 1974) (doctor's choosing the "easier and less efficacious treatment" of throwing away the prisoner's ear and stitching the stump may be attributable to "deliberate indifference . . . rather than an exercise of professional judgment"); Thomas v. Pate, 493 F.2d 151, 158 (7th Cir.), cert. denied sub nom. Thomas v. Cannon, 419 U.S. 879 (1974) (injection of penicillin with knowledge that prisoner was allergic, and refusal of doctor to treat allergic reaction); Jones v. Lockhart, 484 F.2d 1192 (8th Cir. 1973) (refusal of paramedic to provide treatment); Martinez v. Mancusi, 443 F.2d 921 (2d Cir. 1970), cert. denied, 401 U.S. 983 (1971) (prison physician refuses to administer the prescribed pain killer and renders leg surgery unsuccessful by requiring prisoner to stand despite contrary instructions of surgeon).

anguish, is not on that basis alone to be characterized as a wanton infliction of unnecessary pain. In Louisiana ex rel. Francis v. Resweber, 329 U.S. 459 (1947), for example, the Court concluded that it was not unconstitutional to force a prisoner to undergo a second effort to electrocute him after a mechanical malfunction had thwarted the first attempt. Writing for the plurality, Justice Reed reasoned that the second execution would not violate the Eighth Amendment because the first attempt was an "unforeseeable accident." Id., at 464. . . .

Similarly, in the medical context, an inadvertent failure to provide adequate medical care cannot be said to constitute a "wanton infliction of unnecessary pain" or to be "repugnant to the conscience of mankind." Thus, a complaint that a physician has been negligent in diagnosing or treating a medical condition does not state a valid claim of medical mistreatment under the Eighth Amendment. Medical malpractice does not become a constitutional violation merely because the victim is a prisoner. In order to state a cognizable claim, a prisoner must allege acts or omissions sufficiently harmful to evidence deliberate indifference to serious medical needs. It is only such indifference that can offend "evolving standards of decency" in violation of the Eighth Amendment.

* * *

[G]amble's claims against Dr. Gray, both in his capacity as treating physician and as medical director of the Corrections Department, are not cognizable under § 1983. Gamble was seen by medical personnel on 17 occasions spanning a three-month period: by Dr. Astone five times; by Dr. Gray twice; by Dr. Heaton three times; by an unidentified doctor and inmate nurse on the day of the injury; and by medical assistant Blunt six times. They treated his back injury, high blood pressure, and heart problems. Gamble has disclaimed any objection to the treatment provided for his high blood pressure and his heart problem; his complaint is "based solely on the lack of diagnosis and inadequate treatment of his back injury." . . . The doctors diagnosed his injury as a lower back strain and treated it with bed rest, muscle relaxants and pain relievers. Respondent contends that more should have

been done by way of diagnosis and treatment, and suggests a number of options that were not pursued. . . . The Court of Appeals agreed, stating that "Certainly an x-ray of [Gamble's] lower back might have been in order and other tests conducted that would have led to appropriate diagnosis and treatment for the daily pain and suffering he was experiencing." 516 F.2d., at 941. But the question whether an X-ray—or additional diagnostic techniques or forms of treatment—is indicated is a classic example of a matter for medical judgment. A medical decision not to order an X-ray, or like measures, does not represent cruel and unusual punishment. At most it is medical malpractice, and as such the proper forum is state court under the Texas Tort Claims Act. The Court of Appeals was in error in holding that the alleged insufficiency of the medical treatment required reversal and remand. That portion of the judgment of the District Court should have been affirmed.

The Court of Appeals focused primarily on the alleged actions of the doctors, and did not separately consider whether the allegations against the Director of the Department of Corrections, Estelle, and the warden of the prison, Husbands, stated a cause of action. Although we reverse the judgment as to the doctors, we remand the case to the Court of Appeals to allow it an opportunity to consider, in conformity with this opinion, whether a cause of action has been stated against the other prison officials.

Reversed and remanded.

[Mr. Justice BLACKMUN concurred in the judgment of the Court.]

Mr. Justice STEVENS, dissenting.

* * *

The complaint represents a crude attempt to challenge the system of administering medical care in the prison where Gamble is confined. Fairly construed, the complaint alleges that he received a serious disabling back injury in November 1973, that the responsible prison authorities were indifferent to his medical needs, and that as a result of that indifference he has been mistreated and his condition has worsened.

The indifference is allegedly manifested,

not merely by the failure or refusal to diagnose and treat his injury properly, but also by the conduct of the prison staff. Gamble was placed in solitary confinement for prolonged periods as punishment for refusing to perform assigned work which he was physically unable to perform. The only medical evidence presented to the disciplinary committee was the statement of a medical assistant that he was in first class condition, when in fact he was suffering not only from the back sprain but from high blood pressure. Prison guards refused to permit him to sleep in the bunk that a doctor has assigned. On at least one occasion a medical prescription was not filled for four days because it was lost by staff personnel. When he suffered chest pains and blackouts while in solitary, he was forced to wait 12 hours to see a doctor because clearance had to be obtained from the warden. His complaint also draws into question the character of the attention he received from the doctors and the inmate nurse in response to his 17 attempts to obtain proper diagnosis and treatment for his condition. However, apart from the medical director who saw him twice, he has not sued any of the individuals who saw him on these occasions. In short, he complains that the system as a whole is inadequate.

On the basis of Gamble's handwritten complaint it is impossible to assess the quality of the medical attention he received. As the Court points out, even if what he alleges is true, the doctors may be guilty of nothing more than negligence or malpractice. On the other hand, it is surely not inconceivable that an overworked, undermanned medical staff in a crowded prison is following the expedient course of routinely prescribing nothing more than pain killers when a thorough diagnosis would disclose an obvious need for remedial treatment. . . .

* * *

The principal beneficiaries of today's decision will not be federal judges, very little of whose time will be saved, but rather the "writ-writers" within the prison walls, whose semiprofessional services will be in greater demand. I have no doubt about the ability of such a semiprofessional to embellish this pleading with conclusory allegations which could be made in all good faith and which would foreclose a dismissal without any response from the State. It is unfortunate that today's decision will increase prisoners' dependence on those writ-writers. See Cruz v. Beto, 405 U.S. 319, 327, n.7 (REHNQUIST, J., dissenting).

Like the District Court's decision to dismiss the complaint, this Court's decision to hear this case, in violation of its normal practice of denying interlocutory review, see R. Stern & E. Gressman, Supreme Court Practice 180 (4th ed. 1969), ill serves the interest of judicial economy.

Frankly, I was, and still am puzzled by the Court's decision to grant certiorari.[i] . . .

By its reference to the accidental character of the first unsuccessful attempt to electrocute the prisoner in Louisiana ex rel. Francis v. Resweber, 329 U.S. 459 . . . and by its repeated references to "deliberate indifference" and the "intentional" denial of adequate medical care, I believe the Court improperly attaches significance to the subjective motivation of the defendant as a criterion for determining whether cruel and unusual punishment has been inflicted. Subjective motivation may well determine what, if any, remedy is appropriate against a particular defendant. However, whether the constitutional standard has been violated should turn on the character of the punishment rather than the motivation of the individual who inflicted it. Whether the conditions in Andersonville were the product of design, negligence, or mere poverty, they were cruel and inhuman.

In sum, I remain convinced that the petition for certiorari should have been denied. It having been granted, I would affirm the judgment of the Court of Appeals.

---

[i] "The only remarkable thing about this case is its presence in this Court. For the case involves no more than the application of well-settled principles to a familiar situation, and has little significance except for the respondent. Why certiorari was granted is a mystery to me — particularly at a time when the Court is thought by many to be burdened by too heavy a caseload." Butz v. Glover Livestock Comm'n Co., 411 U.S. 182, 189 (STEWART, J., dissenting).

Prison Law Libraries and Access to the Courts

ORAL ARGUMENTS BEFORE THE U.S. SUPREME COURT*

Bounds v. Smith, No. 75–915; argued 11/1/76

Jacob L. Safron, Special Deputy Attorney General of North Carolina, urged the Court last week to overturn a Fourth Circuit decision requiring state officials to provide indigent prisoners with reasonable access to adequate legal research materials. The Fourth Circuit's ruling, which relied in part on *Johnson* v. *Avery,* 393 U.S. 483 (1969), and *Younger* v. *Gilmore,* 404 U.S. 15 (1971), goes far beyond the intent of those cases, Safron argued.

Recounting the history of this case, counsel explained that both the district court and the Fourth Circuit . . . concluded that the state's failure to provide indigent inmates with adequate research materials or some meaningful alternative effectively denied them access to the courts as guaranteed by the First and Fourteenth Amendments. Pursuant to a court order, the state submitted a plan that would provide access to certain legal materials, including the Federal Supplement and Federal Reporter, to inmates at its widely scattered prisons.

Meaningful Alternative

The Constitution simply does not require North Carolina to furnish its inmates with legal research materials, he said. At any rate, the state provides a meaningful alternative. It has established a complete procedure for collateral review of convictions, including the appointment of counsel if a petition has merit.

Mr. Justice Stewart: "What would be the mechanics for [a petitioner] getting appointed counsel in your state courts?"

Safron explained that all an inmate need do

is file a request in writing. If the court finds merit in the petition, counsel is appointed.

The Chief Justice: "By merit, do you mean that the petition makes out a plausible case?"

"Yes, sir."

In addition to court-appointed counsel, legal aid societies in the state give assistance to inmates. Neither the respondents nor their fellow inmates have been denied access to the courts, he noted. Court records bear out the litigious propensities of these respondents; numerous lawsuits have been filed by them. "These inmates have had their day in court time and time again."

Misreading of Avery

The lower federal courts have simply misread *Johnson* v. *Avery* on the law library point, Safron argued. In *Johnson* v. *Avery,* this Court held that a state could not prohibit "jailhouse" writ writers from assisting other inmates in the preparation of legal materials unless that state provided some meaningful alternative. It held nothing more than that. Reading *Johnson* v. *Avery* with *Ross* v. *Moffit,* 417 U.S. 600 (1974), it becomes clear that the state need not provide an inmate with a law library. Nor is a state required to provide an inmate with the same resources as a private attorney would have available to him, Safron submitted.

Equal Protection

Mr. Justice Stewart asked if a state would violate the Equal Protection Clause by providing a law library at one prison, but not at others.

Counsel thought so. However, he explained that North Carolina would face substantial burdens if it had to provide law libraries at all its widely scattered prisons. Many inmates are housed in small units near their homes. Such a scheme, utilizing small

---

*From 20 Crim. L. Rptr. 4065–4067. Reprinted by permission of the Bureau of National Affairs, Inc.

units, aids rehabilitation. Providing libraries at such units would be costly. Moreover, many rural judges and lawyers do not have access to law libraries in their communities.

Mr. Justice Marshall: "What happens in County A, out in the woods, where judges and the district attorneys don't have law libraries?"

"They call [the Attorney General's Office]." But counsel conceded that inmates ordinarily do not request such services.

Mr. Justice Stevens: "Would providing lawyers be an alternative?"

"That's up to the General Assembly."

The Chief Justice: "Does your state have a limit on the number of prisoners housed in one institution?"

"No, sir." North Carolina prisons are facing an over-crowding problem. There are about 77 "main institutions."

The Chief Justice: "What's the total number of prisoners? Approximately?"

About 13,000, counsel responded.

Returning to the library point, Mr. Justice White asked: "Is a prisoner with means permitted to buy law books?"

"Yes, sir."

Explaining that only a small number of inmates write petitions seeking legal relief, Safron argued that those inmates would use a law library to establish a "power base." These prolific inmates will create more litigation — much of it frivolous — and stir up prison strife.

Understanding Younger

Barry Nakell, counsel for respondent, began his argument by noting that *Younger* v. *Gilmore* was unanimously decided.

Mr. Justice Rehnquist: "It was just a one sentence affirmance, wasn't it?"

Nakell acknowledged that the Court affirmed *Younger* v. *Gilmore* in a per curiam opinion, but explained that the issues there were thoroughly briefed before the Court.

Mr. Justice White: "What do you think the question was in the *Gilmore* case?"

The question, Nakell replied, was whether California had to provide inmates with an adequate law library or a reasonable alternative in light of its restrictions on inmate ownership of law books.

Mr. Justice White: "Would [*Gilmore*] require a lawyer?"

"No, sir."

If the state does not provide a law library, counsel argued, it must establish that the alternative it offers is a reasonable one.

Mr. Justice White: "What does *Johnson* v. *Avery* have to do with this case?"

Johnson v. *Avery* defines, in part, what a reasonable alternative is.

Mr. Justice Rehnquist: "But *Johnson* was talking about a prohibition?"

"Yes, sir." In *Johnson,* Tennessee barred inmates from assisting one another in the preparation of legal documents.

Mr. Justice Rehnquist asked whether *Avery* required the respondents here to show that North Carolina had denied them use of jailhouse lawyers.

Counsel thought not.

With respect to the question of court-appointed counsel on collateral attack, Nakell explained that an inmate is not entitled, under state rules, to counsel unless he presents a petition that has "merit." But the inmate receives no help in preparing a petition at the initial stage. Without access to law materials, therefore, the inmate is effectively hindered in presenting a meritorious claim.

Mr. Justice Stevens: "Do you recall whether, in [*Younger* v. *Gilmore*], California had ruled against inmates helping one another [in preparing cases]?"

"There was no prohibition."

State's Plan

Outlining the state's plan that was approved by the district court, Nakell pointed out that a central law library and several core libraries would be available for inmate use. Copies of legal materials could be requested by inmates who are not housed at the prison in which a library is located.

Mr. Justice Brennan: "Did you say that the plan was submitted by the state?"

"Yes, sir."

The Chief Justice suggested that the state's plan might have "little relevance to what's constitutionally required."

The Chief Justice then asked: "How could you justify having anything less than the same scope of privileges in each library?"

The state's plan assures meaningful access for inmates in every prison, Nakell replied. Materials will be available to all through copying services.

Mr. Justice Rehnquist: "What provision of

the Constitution provides the right to a law library?"

The right to a law library, of course, is not specifically enumerated in the Constitution. But such a right stems from both the First and Fourteenth Amendments, Nakell said.

Mr. Justice Rehnquist: "What case was this?"

Johnson v. *Avery* provides support for this view as does *Procunier* v. *Martinez,* 416 U.S. 396 (1974).

"Would this right extend, as a next step, to having a lawyer interpret cases found in the library?"

"No, sir." All that is required is that an inmate have reasonable access to the courts. The state enjoys flexibility in satisfying the requirement of reasonable access.

"Is North Carolina obligated to furnish trained paralegals?"

The method of complying with the Constitution is up to the state, counsel thought. The plan which the state submitted here measures up to constitutional requirements. Of course, paralegals would be useful.

Mr. Justice Blackmun: "Do you have a position on the state's claim that law libraries create a 'power base'?"

Law libraries aid the general prison population. Having a prison library does not mean that the library will be abused for selfish goals, or even that writ writers will flourish. The state's fear has no basis.

Access to the State Libraries

Mr. Justice Blackmun: "You are not attacking the [state's plan] as submitted?"

"No, sir."

Responding to a question from Justice Stevens, Nakell observed that inmates do not now have access to the state's own libraries.

Counsel repeatedly emphasized that respondents are seeking only reasonable access to facilities that would assure their access to the courts. Moreover, the state has sufficient resources through LEAA grants or other sources to fund such libraries, he concluded.

BOUNDS v. SMITH

Supreme Court of the United States, 1977
430 U.S. 817, 97 S. Ct. 1491, 52 L. Ed. 2d 72

Respondent inmates filed actions under 42 U.S.C.§ 1983 of the Civil Rights Act alleging they were denied access to the courts in violation of the Fourteenth Amendment by North Carolina's failure to provide legal research facilities. The federal district court granted respondents' motion for summary judgment finding that the sole prison library in the state was "severely inadequate" and that there was no other legal assistance available to inmates. The court charged the Department of Corrections with the task of devising a constitutionally sound program to assure inmates access to the courts.

Additional facts appear in the opinion.

Mr. Justice MARSHALL delivered the opinion of the Court.

I

* * *

The State responded [to respondents' complaints] by proposing the establishment of seven libraries in institutions located across the State chosen so as to serve best all prison units. In addition, the State planned to

set up smaller libraries in the Central Prison segregation unit and the Women's Prison. Under the plan, inmates desiring to use a library would request appointments. They would be given transportation and housing, if necessary, for a full day's library work. In addition to its collection of law books, each library would stock legal forms and writing paper and have typewriters and use of copying machines. The State proposed to train inmates as research assistants and typists to aid fellow prisoners. It was estimated that ultimately some 350 inmates per week could use the libraries, although inmates not facing court deadlines might have to wait three or four weeks for their turn at a library. Respondents protested that the plan was totally inadequate and sought establishment of a library at every prison.

The District Court rejected respondents' objections, finding the State's plan "both economically feasible and practicable," and one that, fairly and efficiently run, would "insure each inmate the time to prepare his petitions." . . .

In its final decision, the District Court held that petitioners were not constitutionally required to provide legal assistance as well as libraries. It found that the library plan was sufficient to give inmates reasonable access to the courts and that our decision in Ross v. Moffitt, 417 U.S. 600 (1974), while not directly on point, supported the State's claim that it need not furnish attorneys to bring habeas corpus and civil rights actions for prisoners.

* * *

Both sides appealed from those portions of the District Court orders adverse to them. The Court of Appeals for the Fourth Circuit affirmed in all respects save one. It found that the library plan denied women prisoners the same access rights as men to research facilities. Since there was no justification for this discrimination, the Court of Appeals ordered it eliminated. The State petitioned for review and we granted certiorari. 425 U.S. 910 (1976). We affirm.

II

A

It is now established beyond doubt that prisoners have a constitutional right to access to the courts. This Courst recognized that right more than 35 years ago when it struck down a regulation prohibiting state prisoners from filing petitions for habeas corpus unless they were found "properly drawn" by the "legal investigator" for the parole board. Ex parte Hull, 312 U.S. 546 (1941). We held this violated the principle that "the state and its officers may not abridge or impair petitioner's right to apply to a federal court for a writ of habeas

corpus." Id., at 549. See also Cochran v. Kansas, 316 U.S. 255 (1942).

More recent decisions have struck down restrictions and required remedial measures to insure that inmate access to the courts is adequate, effective and meaningful. Thus, in order to prevent "effectively foreclosed access," indigent prisoners must be allowed to file appeals and habeas corpus petitions without payment of docket fees. Burns v. Ohio, 360 U.S. 252, 257 (1959); Smith v. Bennett, 365 U.S. 708 (1961). Because we recognized that "adequate and effective appellate review" is impossible without a trial transcript or adequate substitute, we held that states must provide trial records to inmates unable to buy them. Griffin v. Illinois, 351 U.S. 12, 20 (1956).[h] Similarly, counsel must be appointed to give indigent inmates "a meaningful appeal" from their convictions. Douglas v. California, 372 U.S. 353, 358 (1963).

Essentially the same standards of access were applied in Johnson v. Avery, 393 U.S. 483 (1969), which struck down a regulation prohibiting prisoners from assisting each

---

[h]See also Eskridge v. Washington Prison Board, 357 U.S. 214 (1958) (provision of trial transcript may not be conditioned on approval of judge); Draper v. Washington, 372 U.S. 487 (1963) (same); Lane v. Brown, 372 U.S. 477 (1963) (public defender's approval may not be required to obtain coram nobis transcript); Rinaldi v. Yeager, 384 U.S. 305 (1966) (unconstitutional to require reimbursement for cost of trial transcript only from unsuccessful imprisoned defendants); Long v. District Court, 385 U.S. 192 (1966) (State must provide transcript of post-conviction proceeding); Roberts v. LaVallee, 389 U.S. 40 (1967) (State must provide preliminary hearing transcript); Gardner v. California, 393 U.S. 367 (1969) (State must provide habeas corpus transcript); Williams v. Oklahoma City, 395 U.S. 458 (1969) (State must provide transcript of petty offense trial); Mayer v. Chicago, 404 U.S. 189 (1971) (State must provide transcript of nonfelony trial).

The only cases that have rejected indigent defendants' claims to transcripts have done so either because an adequate alternative was available but not used, Britt v. North Carolina, 404 U.S. 226 (1971), or because the request was plainly frivolous and a prior opportunity to obtain a transcript was waived, United States v. MacCollom, 426 U.S. 317 (1976).

other with habeas corpus applications and other legal matters. Since inmates had no alternative form of legal assistance available to them, we reasoned that this ban on jailhouse lawyers effectively prevented prisoners who were "unable themselves, with reasonable adequacy, to prepare their petitions," from challenging the legality of their confinements. Id., at 489. Johnson was unanimously extended to cover assistance in civil rights actions in Wolff v. McDonnell, 418 U.S. 539, 577–580 (1974). And even as it rejected a claim that indigent defendants have a constitutional right to appointed counsel for discretionary appeals, the Court reaffirmed that States must "assure the indigent defendant an adequate opportunity to present his claims fairly." Ross v. Moffitt, supra, 417 U.S., at 616. "Meaningful access" to the courts is the touchstone. . . .

Petitioners contend, however, that this constitutional duty merely obliges States to allow inmates "writ writers" to function. They argue that under Johnson v. Avery, supra, as long as inmate communications on legal problems are not restricted, there is no further obligation to expend state funds to implement affirmatively the right of access. This argument misreads the cases.

In Johnson and Wolff v. McDonnell, supra, the issue was whether the access rights of ignorant and illiterate inmates were violated without adequate justification. Since these inmates were unable to present their own claims in writing to the courts, we held that their "constitutional right to help," . . . required at least allowing assistance from their literate inmates. But in so holding, we did not attempt to set forth the full breadth of the right of access. In McDonnell, for example, there was already an adequate law library in the prison. The case was thus decided against a backdrop of availability of legal information to those inmates capable of using it. And in Johnson, although the petitioner originally requested law books . . . the Court did not reach the question, as it invalidated the regulation because of its effect on illiterate inmates. Neither case considered the question we face today and neither is inconsistent with requiring additional measures to assure meaningful access to inmates able to present their own cases.

Moreover, our decisions have consistently required States to shoulder affirmative obligations to assure all prisoners meaningful access to courts. It is indisputable that indigent inmates must be provided at state expense with paper and pen to draft legal documents, with notarial services to authenticate them, and with stamps to mail them. States must forego collection of docket fees otherwise payable to the treasury and expend funds for transcripts. State expenditures are necessary to pay lawyers for indigent defendants at trial, Gideon v. Wainwright, 372 U.S. 335 (1963); Argersinger v. Hamlin, 407 U.S. 25 (1972), and in appeals as of right, Douglas v. California, supra. This is not to say that economic factors may not be considered, for example, in choosing the methods used to provide meaningful access. But the cost of protecting a constitutional right cannot justify its total denial. Thus, neither the availability of jailhouse lawyers nor the necessity for affirmative state action is dispositive of respondents' claims. The inquiry is rather whether law libraries or other forms of legal assistance are needed to give prisoners a reasonably adequate opportunity to present claimed violations of fundamental constitutional rights to the courts.

B

Although it is essentially true, as petitioners argue, that a habeas corpus petition or civil rights complaint need only set forth facts giving rise to the cause of action, but see, Fed. Rule Civ. Proc. 8 (a)(1), (3), it hardly follows that a law library or other legal assistance is not essential to frame such documents. It would verge on incompetence for a lawyer to file an initial pleading without researching such issues as jurisdiction, venue, standing, exhaustion of remedies, proper parties plaintiff and defendant, and types of relief available. Most importantly, of course, a lawyer must know what the law is in order to determine whether a colorable claim exists, and if so, what facts are necessary to state a cause of action.

If a lawyer must perform such preliminary research, it is no less vital for a pro se prisoner. Indeed, despite the "less stringent standards" by which a pro se pleading is judged, Haines v. Kerner, 404 U.S. 519, 520 (1972), it is often more important that a prisoner complaint set forth a nonfrivolous claim meeting all procedural prerequisites, since the court may pass on the complaint's sufficiency before allowing filing in forma pauperis and may dismiss the case if it is deemed frivolous. See 28 U.S.C. § 1915. Moreover, if the State files a response to a pro se pleading, it will undoubtedly contain seemingly authoritative citations. Without a library, an inmate will be unable to rebut the State's argument. It is not enough to answer that the court will evaluate the facts pleaded in light of the relevant law. Even the most dedicated trial judges are bound to overlook meritorious cases without the benefit of an adversarial presentation. . . .

We reject the State's claim that inmates are "ill-equipped to use" "the tools of the trade of the legal profession," making libraries useless in assuring meaningful access. In the first place, the claim is inconsistent with the State's presentations . . . that access is adequately protected by allowing inmates to help each other with legal problems. More importantly, this Court's experience indicates that pro se petitioners are capable of using law books to file cases raising claims that are serious and legitimate even if ultimately unsuccessful. Finally, we note that if petitioners had any doubts about the efficacy of libraries, the District Court's initial decision left them free to choose another means of assuring access.

* * *

We hold, therefore, that the fundamental constitutional right of access to the courts requires prison authorities to assist inmates in the preparation and filing of meaningful legal papers by providing prisoners with adequate law libraries or adequate assistance from persons trained in the law.

C

Our holding today is, of course, a reaffirmation of the result reached in Younger v. Gilmore [404 U.S. 15 (1971)]. . . . The substantive question presented in Gilmore was "Does a state have an affirmative federal constitutional duty to furnish prison inmates with extensive law libraries or, alternatively, to provide inmates with professional or quasi-professional legal assistance?" Jurisdictional Statement, at 5; Brief for Appellants, at 4. This Court explicitly decided that question when it affirmed the judgment of the District Court in reliance on Johnson v. Avery. Cf. Supreme Court Rule 15(c). The affirmative answer was given unani-

mously after full briefing and oral argument. Gilmore has been relied upon without question in our subsequent decisions. . . .

Experience under the Gilmore decision suggests no reason to depart from it. Most States and the Federal Government have made impressive efforts to fulfill Gilmore's mandate by establishing law libraries, prison legal assistance programs, or combinations of both.

It should be noted that while adequate law libraries are one constitutionally acceptable method to assure meaningful access to the courts, our decision here, as in Gilmore, does not foreclose alternative means to achieve that goal. Nearly half the States and the District of Columbia provide some degree of professional or quasi-professional legal assistance to prisoners. . . .

Nevertheless, a legal access program need not include any particular element we have discussed, and we encourage local experimentation. Any plan, however, must be evaluated as a whole to ascertain its compliance with constitutional standards.

* * *

III

* * *

Affirmed.

Mr. Justice POWELL, concurring.

The decision today recognizes that a prison inmate has a constitutional right of access to the courts to assert such procedural and substantive rights as may be available to him under state and federal law. It does not purport to pass on the kinds of claims that the Constitution requires state or federal courts to hear. . . . [T]he holding here implies nothing as to the constitutionally required scope of review of prisoners' claims in state or federal court.

With this understanding, I join the opinion of the Court.

Mr. Chief Justice BURGER, dissenting.

. . . I write only to emphasize the theoretical and practical difficulties raised by the Court's holding. The Court leaves us unenlightened as to the source of the "right of access to the courts" which it perceives or of the requirement that States "foot the bill" for assuring such access for prisoners who want to act as legal researchers and brief writers. The holding, in my view, has far-reaching implications which I doubt have been fully analyzed or their consequences adequately assessed.

It should be noted, first, that the access to the courts which these respondents are seeking is not for the purpose of direct appellate review of their criminal convictions. . . . Rather, the underlying substantive right here is that of prisoners to mount collateral attacks on their state convictions. The Court is ordering the State to expend resources in support of the federally created right of collateral review.

* * *

It is a novel and doubtful proposition, in my view, that the Federal Government can, by statute, give individuals certain rights and then require the State, as a *constitutional* matter, to fund the means for exercise of those rights. Cf. National League of Cities v. Usery, 415 U.S. 833 (1976).

As to the substantive right of state prisoners to collaterally attack in federal court their convictions entered by a state court of competent jurisdiction, it is now clear that there is no broad federal *constitutional* right to such collateral attack, see Stone v. Powell, 428 U.S. 465 (1976); whatever right exists is solely a creation of federal statute. . . . But absent a federal constitutional right to attack convictions collaterally—and I discern no such right—I can find no basis on which a federal court may require States to fund costly law libraries for prison inmates. Proper federal-state relations preclude such intervention in the "complex and intractable" problems of prison administration. Procunier v. Martinez, 416 U.S. 397 (1974).

I can draw only one of two conclusions from the Court's holding; it may be read as implying that the right of prisoners to collaterally attack their convictions is constitutional, rather than statutory, in nature; alternatively, it may be read as holding that States can be compelled by federal courts to subsidize the exercise of federally created statutory rights. Neither of these novel propositions is sustainable and for the reasons stated I cannot adhere to either view and therefore dissent.

Mr. Justice STEWART, dissenting.

* * *

. . . More than 20 years of experience with pro se habeas corpus petitions as a Member of this Court and as a Circuit Judge have convinced me that "meaningful access" to the federal courts can seldom be realistically advanced by the device of making law libraries available to prison inmates untutored in their use. In the vast majority of cases, access to a law library will, I am convinced, simply result in the filing of pleadings heavily larded with irrelevant legalisms—possessing the veneer but lacking the substance of professional competence.

If, on the other hand, Mr. Justice REHNQUIST is correct in his belief that a convict in a state prison pursuant to a final judgment of a court of competent jurisdiction has no constitutional right of "meaningful access" to the federal courts in order to attack his sentence, then a State can be under no constitutional duty to make that access "meaningful." If the extent of the constitutional duty of a State is simply not to deny or obstruct a prisoner's access to the courts, . . . then it cannot have, even arguably, any affirmative constitutional obligation to provide law libraries for its prison inmates.

I respectfully dissent.

Mr. Justice REHNQUIST, dissenting.

* * *

There is nothing in the United States Constitution which requires that a convict serving a term of imprisonment pursuant to a final judgment of a court of competent jurisdiction in a state penal institution have a "right of access" to the federal courts in order to attack his sentence. . . .

. . . The prisoners here in question have all pursued all avenues of direct appeal available to them from their judgments of conviction, and North Carolina imposes no invidious regulations which allow visits from all persons except those knowledgeable in the law. All North Carolina has done in this case is to decline to expend public funds to make available law libraries to those who are incarcerated within its penitentiaries.

If respondent's constitutional arguments were grounded on the Equal Protection Clause, and were in effect that rich prisoners could employ attorneys who could in turn consult law libraries and prepare petitions for habeas corpus, whereas indigent prisoners could not, they would have superficial appeal. . . . I believe that they would nonetheless fail under Ross v. Moffitt, 417 U.S. 600 (1974). There we held that although our earlier cases had required the State to provide meaningful access to state created judicial remedies for indigents, the only right on direct appeal was that "indigents have an adequate opportunity to present their claims fairly within the adversary system." Id., at 612.

In any event, the Court's opinion today does not appear to proceed upon the guarantee of equal protection of the laws, a guarantee which at least has the merit of being found in the Fourteenth Amendment to the Constitution. It proceeds instead to enunciate a "fundamental constitutional right of access to the courts," . . . which is found nowhere in the Constitution. . . . [T]he "fundamental constitutional right of access to the courts" which the Court announces today is created virtually out of whole cloth with little or no reference to the Constitution from which it is supposed to be derived.

Our decisions have recognized on more than one occasion that lawful imprisonment properly results in a "restriction [of rights] justified by the considerations underlying our penal system." Price v. Johnston, 334 U.S. 226, 285 (1948); Pell v. Procunier, 417 U.S. 817, 822 (1974). A convicted prisoner who has exhausted his avenues of direct appeal is no longer to be accorded every presumption of innocence, and his former constitutional

liberties may be substantially restricted by the exigencies of the incarceration in which he has been placed. . . . See Meachum v. Fano, 427 U.S. 215 (1976). . . . If "meaningful access" to the courts is to include law libraries, there is no convincing reason why it should not also include lawyers appointed at the expense of the State. Just as a library may assist some inmates in filing papers which contain more than the bare factual allegations of injustice, appointment of counsel would assure that the legal arguments advanced are made with some degree of sophistication.

I do not believe anything in the Constitution requires this result, although states and federal penal institutions might as a matter of policy think it wise to implement such a program. I conclude by indicating the same respect for Younger v. Gilmore, supra, as has the Court, in relegating it to a final section set apart from the body of the Court's reasoning. Younger supports the result reached by the Court of Appeals in this case, but it is a two paragraph opinion which is most notable for the unbridged distance between its premise and its conclusion. The Court's opinion today at least makes a reasoned defense of the result which it reaches, but I am not persuaded by those reasons. Because of that fact I would not have the slightest reluctance to overrule Younger and reverse the judgment of the Court of Appeals in this case.

Prison Labor Unions

ORAL ARGUMENTS BEFORE THE U.S. SUPREME COURT*

Jones v. North Carolina Prisoners' Labor Union, Inc., No. 75-1874; argued 4/19/77

The Court was asked last week to overturn a three-judge district court's ruling that a prisoners' "labor union" be afforded the same opportunity for mailings, organiza-

tional activities, and membership solicitation as other in-prison organizations. The U.S. District Court for the Eastern District of North Carolina described the union as an eleemosynary institution which seeks to eliminate allegedly unconstitutional or unjust practices within prisons, see 19 Cr.L. 2031, but the state disagreed with this characterization.

Jacob L. Safron, Special Deputy Attorney General of North Carolina, urged the Court

*From 21 Crim. L. Rptr. 4032–4034. Reprinted by permission of the Bureau of National Affairs, Inc.

to overturn the three-judge district court's ruling. The district court, he said "paid lip service" to the Court's holding in *Pell* v. *Procunier*, 417 U.S. 817, by requiring North Carolina prisons to open their doors to the Prisoners' Labor Union (PLU).

As a result of the district court's refusal to stay its order, it became necessary to issue regulations for the in-prison operation of inmate organizations. Of course, the state reserved its right to alter these regulations if this Court modified the trial court's ruling, he explained.

The three-judge court recognized that correctional officers had real and sincere doubts about the PLU, yet the court disregarded those fears. Even now the PLU, Safron maintained, refuses to comply fully with the new regulations.

Mr. Justice Rehnquist: "But that's all post-trial, isn't it? What does it bear on?"

That's correct, Safron said. But the state wishes to emphasize that it promulgated the new regulations because it could not obtain a stay of the trial court's order.

Opening the Doors

According to the three-judge court, Safron went on, we opened the doors to recognizing the PLU by permitting the Jaycees, the Boy Scouts, and Alcoholics Anonymous to actively operate at state prisons. But these organizations, counsel stressed, are national service organizations with valid and proven rehabilitative goals within the prison context. "Now the three-judge court says we can't pick and choose among organizations to receive our resources. If we permit the Jaycees to send in a bundle of materials for its members, we must allow the PLU to do so."

The state's refusal to permit prison meetings and membership solicitation by the PLU involves no real equal protection problem, Safron asserted. The district court found such a problem only by misreading *Ross* v. *Moffitt*, 417 U.S. 600. In *Ross,* the Court observed that the Fourteenth Amendment "does not require absolute equality or precisely equal advantages," counsel pointed out. The state distinguished the PLU from the Jaycees, AA, and the Boy Scouts for purely legitimate reasons. Here a valid fear exists as to possible concerted activities that PLU might undertake.

Mr. Justice Rehnquist: "The district court indicated that relief would be granted the state if the PLU undertook such concerted activities."

But Safron replied that the question is whether correctional authorities must await a catastrophic event before barring the PLU.

Mr. Justice Rehnquist: "That's what we are waiting for you to argue."

The spread of the PLU will naturally increase friction between inmates and prison personnel, Safron submitted. In "Constant Fear" [Reader's Digest Press 1975], a Massachusetts inmate details how introduction of a prison union organization led to full-scale rioting at Walpole Prison.

Mr. Justice Stevens: "Do you dispute the right of prisoners to form a union?"

Not altogether, Safron answered. "We take a moderate position."

Mr. Justice Stevens: "Does this position include objections to the formation of a union?"

Then-existing regulations at the time of this § 1983 suit prevented formation of the Prisoners' Labor Union, Safron answered. "We did not say that you couldn't join the Prisoners' Labor Union, on a one-to-one basis, by writing to the outside organization." But the state did object to its existence as an active organization within its correctional facilities.

Mr. Justice Stevens: "Didn't the district court agree with you that inmates had no right to form an organization for concerted labor activities?"

Safron thought that the district court's holding on this point did not go far enough. The court emasculated the state's authority to exercise its discretion to pick and choose among organizations for representation within its prisons.

Equal Protection

An amicus curiae, Kenneth S. Geller, Assistant to the Solicitor General of the United States, joined the state in seeking reversal of the district court. The lower court required North Carolina to allow inmates to solicit other prisoners for PLU membership and to permit prisoner receipt of PLU correspondence. Moreover, the district court construed the Equal Protection Clause to require mailing opportunities for the PLU to the same extent as provided other organizations.

The problem with the district court's disposition is that it can lead to serious breaches of prison security, Geller asserted. True, the former regulations restricted the prisoner's associational liberties to an extent, but this Court has indicated that not all First Amendment rights are absolute within the prison context. In *Pell* v. *Procunier,* this Court stated that an inmate retains only those First Amendment rights which are not inconsistent with his incarceration.

Mr. Justice Stevens: "Is there a Fourteenth Amendment violation here?"

The district court found that the state must allow mass mailings and meetings for the PLU to the same extent as it does for other groups, Geller replied. The court did not say that the prisoners have a First Amendment right to receive the mailings from the PLU, but that they had a Fourteenth Amendment equal protection right to receive it.

Prisons differ radically from free society, Geller stressed. They are peopled by proven law breakers who live in an atmosphere which is frequently tense and volatile. The presence of concerted activity would make this environment even more dangerous, he said. Ordinarily, prison grievances can be handled without disruption, but inmate unionism would make resolution of problems more difficult and tumultuous. The district court created problems by its holding that the PLU must be allowed to solicit members to the same extent as other groups.

There are obvious differences among organizations, Geller pointed out. Some groups are beneficial and should be allowed to function within the prisons; others are not. Inmates tend to behave more aggressively in groups. A union, because of its nature, would bring an even greater potential for institutional violence.

Mr. Justice Marshall: "What does the organization plan to do?"

Ostensibly, to present grievances, Geller answered.

Mr. Justice Marshall: "What is wrong with that?"

The organization might resort to force to press its demands, Geller replied.

In response to Mr. Justice Stevens, Geller said that the PLU had not officially operated within North Carolina prisons before this suit.

Future Unrest

While the union now may be avowedly dedicated to peaceful change, no barometer exists to forecast what its future course might become, Geller contended.

Mr. Justice Stevens: "Are there findings to that effect?"

Counsel indicated that the three-judge court recognized that the organization's goals might shift.

Mr. Justice Stevens: "The district court found the announced goals harmless."

True, Geller acknowledged, but the district court did not give due respect to *Pell* v. *Procunier* in reaching its decision. We maintain that the district court improperly substituted its judgment for that of the prison officials. "We think the district court gave absolutely no deference to the anticipated fears of prison officials."

The Chief Justice: "Under the judgment, if the state excluded all organizations, it wouldn't be in violation of the court's mandate?"

That's correct with respect to the equal protection point, Geller said.

Mr. Justice Rehnquist: "I thought the prison allowed the inmates to join a union but saw no constitutional right that would allow inmates to do so."

Counsel agreed.

Self-help Group

Norman B. Smith of Greensboro, counsel for the appellee PLU, set forth the group's objectives. The PLU is a prison reform organization, not a labor "union" within the ordinary sense of that term. The PLU seeks to secure public support for reforms and the litigation of prison rights issues.

Mr. Justice Powell: "Is the certificate of incorporation of the union before us?"

"Yes, sir."

Mr. Justice Powell: "Does it allow for concerted activities?"

In part, the articles do, Smith conceded. But nothing in those articles calls for concerted activities that are disruptive or otherwise unlawful.

Mr. Justice Powell: "Is it a fact that after this suit began, the PLU newspaper stated that prisoners should be allowed to bargain collectively?"

PLU realizes that such activities are presently illegal, Smith said, but plans only to work through the system to achieve such bargaining rights. The PLU seeks legislative action. No intent exists to proceed illegally, Smith stressed. Since the district court's judgment, the PLU has published newsletters and undertaken other projects, Smith noted. The state's new regulations apply neutrally to all organizations.

Mr. Justice White: "Do you think the union should be able to solicit authorizations for membership?"

Counsel thought so but noted that the organization has no plans to hold itself out as the prisoners' bargaining unit.

Mr. Justice White: "Now none of the prison facilities may be used by an outsider for solicitation, right?"

That's right, Smith said. But he thought that outsiders should be permitted to solicit within the prison for inmate membership purposes.

The Chief Justice: "Do you agree that if the prison officials excluded every organization from operating within its walls, they would be in compliance with the judgment?"

Counsel thought there were First Amendment associational interests involved as well as the equal protection question. He agreed, however, that the state could prevent outsiders from coming onto the prison grounds for solicitation, absent an equal protection claim.

Mr. Justice Stewart: "How about the Ku Klux Klan?"

"Whether prison officials could bar inmate establishment of the KKK chapter would depend on that organization's aims, Smith submitted.

Mr. Justice Stewart: "I haven's read its constitution."

I have, Smith stated, but its constitution could be inconsistent with its real goals.

Mr. Justice Stewart: "What can you tell from its constitution?"

I would probably be correct in saying its constitution doesn't indicate that the KKK was formed to foment racial hatred, Smith replied.

The Chief Justice: "What if the Palestine Liberation Organization applied to come in?"

Again, it would depend on the organization's aims, Smith said.

The Chief Justice: "But they don't openly advocate terrorism."

Whatever the merits of other organizations, Smith told the Court, the PLU has no expressed or implied goal to create prison violence or unrest.

The Chief Justice: "How do you show that the union could engage in violence?"

Unless an organization has such violent action as a purpose, or has a past history of violence, you have to assume that it won't resort to violence, Smith said. The district court here has given correctional authorities the power to curtail the PLU if violence breaks out.

Mr. Justice White: "If the union indicated that one of its purposes was to form a collective bargaining unit, could the state say it has demonstrated that it's engaging in illegal conduct?"

Under those circumstances, Smith indicated, the state might be able to say that.

Mr. Justice Powell: "Which one of the existing prison organizations is most analogous to the PLU?"

Both the Jaycees and the AA have rehabilitative purposes somewhat akin to the PLU, Smith replied.

Mr. Justice Stevens: "Does the record tell us how the PLU activities are funded?"

The union receives "seed money" from charitable organizations. There is also a provision in the organization's rules for dues.

Mr. Justice White: "How long has the organization been in existence?"

Since Fall, 1974, Smith said.

Mr. Justice White: "Is it a statewide organization?"

Yes, it has more than 2000 members throughout the state, Smith replied.

The Chief Justice: "Suppose prison authorities sought to limit the number of prison organizations to ten groups?"

That could be permissible depending on the circumstances, Smith said. Prison authorities have some discretion to keep prisons from being literally overrun by organizations.

Counsel also expressed satisfaction with the new rules promulgated by the state in response to the district court's order.

Rebuttal

The state has never denied an inmate the right to join an organization, Safron stressed on rebuttal. We perform no lobotomies on them.

The Chief Justice: "Other than the contribution of the AFL-CIO is there any evidence of the PLU's linkage to any other union?"

Counsel thought not.

The Chief Justice: "But there's nothing unusual about the AFL-CIO contributing to a prison group?"

Safron was unsure on this. He went on to argue that *Pell* v. *Procunier* gives officials wide latitude in combatting threats to prison security.

JONES v. NORTH CAROLINA PRISONERS' LABOR UNION, INC.

Supreme Court of the United States, 1977
433 U.S.____, 97 S. Ct. 2532, 53 L. Ed. 2d 629

Appellee prisoner's labor union brought an action in federal district court under 42 U.S.C. § 1983 claiming that its First Amendment and equal protection rights were violated by regulations promulgated by the North Carolina Department of Correction that prohibited prisoners from soliciting other inmates to join the union and barred union meetings and bulk mailings concerning the union to and from outside sources. A three-judge district court found merit in the union's free speech, association, and equal protection arguments and enjoined appellants from preventing inmates from soliciting other prisoners to join the union. Further, the district court granted the union the privilege of bulk mailing, which was afforded other organizations. The United States Supreme Court noted probable jurisdiction.

Mr. Justice REHNQUIST delivered the opinion of the court.

* * *

II

A

The District Court, we believe, got off on the wrong foot in this case by not giving appropriate deference to the decisions of prison administrators and appropriate recognition to the peculiar and restrictive circumstances of penal confinement. While litigation by prison inmates concerning conditions of confinement, challenged other than under the Eighth Amendment, is of recent vintage, this Court has long recognized that "[l]awful incarceration brings about the necessary withdrawal or limitation of many privileges and rights, a retraction justified by the considerations underlying our penal system." Price v. Johnson, 334 U.S. 266, 285 (1948); see also Pell v. Procunier, 417 U.S. 817, 822 (1974): Wolff v. McDonnell, 418 U.S. 539, 555 (1974). The fact of confinement and the needs of the penal institution

impose limitations on constitutional rights, including those derived from the First Amendment, which are implicit in incarceration. . . .

* * *

Because the realities of running a penal institution are complex and difficult, we have also recognized the wide-ranging deference to be accorded the decisions of prison administrators. . . .

B

State correctional officials uniformly testified that the concept of a prisoners' labor union was itself fraught with potential dangers, whether or not such a union intended, illegally, to press for collective-bargaining recognition. Appellant Ralph Edwards, the Commissioner of the Department of Correction, stated in his affidavit that:

"The creation of an inmate union will naturally result in increasing the existing friction between inmates and prison personnel. It can also create friction between union inmates and non-union inmates."

Appellant David Jones, Secretary of the Department of Correction, stated that:

"The existence of a union of inmates can create a devisive element within the inmate population. In a time when the units are already seriously overcrowded, such an element could aggravate already tense conditions. The purpose of the Union may well be worthwhile projects. But it is evident that the inmate organizers could, if recognized as spokesmen for all inmates, make themselves to be powerful figures among the inmates. If the Union is successful, these inmates would be in a position to misuse their influence. After the inmate Union has become established, there would probably be nothing this Department could do to terminate its existence, even if its activities became overtly subversive to the functioning of the Department. Work stoppages and routines are easily foreseeable. Riots and chaos would almost inevitably result. Thus, even if the purposes of the Union are as stated in this Complaint, the potential for a dangerous situation exists, a situation which would not be brought under control."

. . . The necessary and correct result of our deference to the informed discretion of prison administrators permits them, and not the courts, to make the difficult judgments concerning institutional operations in situations such as this.

. . . It is clearly not irrational to conclude that individuals may believe what they want, but that concerted group activity, or solicitation therefor, would pose additional and unwarranted problems and frictions in the operation of the State's penal institutions. The ban on inmate solicitation and group meetings, therefore, was rationally related to the reasonable, indeed to the central, objectives of prison administration. Cf. Pell v. Procunier, 417 U.S., at 822. . . .

* * *

C

An examination of the potential restrictions on speech or association that have been imposed by the regulations under challenge, demonstrates that the restrictions imposed are reasonable, and are consistent with the inmates' status as prisoners and with the legitimate operational considerations of the institution. To begin with, First Amendment speech rights are barely implicated in this case. Mail rights are not themselves implicated; the only question respecting the mail is that of *bulk* mailings. The advantages of bulk mailings to inmates by the Union are those of cheaper rates and convenience. While the District Court relied on the cheaper bulk mailing rates in finding an equal protection violation . . . it is clear that losing these cost advantages does not fundamentally implicate *free speech* values. Since other avenues of outside informational flow by the Union remain available, the prohibition on bulk mailing, reasonable in the absence of First Amendment consideration, remains reasonable. Cf. Pell v. Procunier, supra; Saxbe v. Washington Post, 417 U.S. 843 (1974).

Nor does the prohibition on inmate-to-inmate solicitation of membership trench untowardly on the inmates' First Amendment speech rights. Solicitation of membership itself involves a good deal more than the simple expression of individual views as to the advantages or disadvantages of a Union or its views; it is an invitation to collectively engage in a legitimately prohibited activity. If the prison officials are otherwise entitled to control organized union activity within the prison walls, the prohibition on solicitation for such activity is not then made impermissible on account of First Amendment considerations, for such a prohibition is then not only reasonable but necessary. Pell v. Procunier, 417 U.S., at 822.

First Amendment associational rights, while perhaps more directly implicated by the regulatory prohibitions, likewise must give way to the reasonable considerations of penal management. As already noted, numerous associational rights are necessarily curtailed whenever the institution's officials, in the exercise of their informed discretion, reasonably conclude that such associations, whether through group meetings or otherwise, possess the likelihood of disruption to prison order or stability, or otherwise interfere with the legitimate penological objectives of the prison environment. . . .

Apellant prison officials concluded that the presence, perhaps even the objectives, of a prisoners' labor union would be detrimental to order and security in the prisons. . . . It is enough to say that they have not been conclusively shown to be wrong in this view. The interest in preserving order and authority in the prisons is self-evident. . . . If the appellants' views as the the possible detrimental effects of the organizational activities of the Union are reasonable, as we conclude they are, then the regulations are drafted no more broadly than they need be to meet the perceived threat—which stems directly from group meetings and group organizational activities of the Union. Cf. Procunier v. Martinez, 416 U.S., at 412–416. When weighed against the First Amendment rights asserted, these institutional reasons are sufficiently weighty to prevail.

D

The District Court rested on the Equal Protection Clause of the Fourteenth Amendment to strike down appellants' prohibition against the receipt and distribution of bulk mail from the Union as well as the prohibition of Union meetings among the inmates. It felt that this was a denial of equal protection because bulk mailing and meeting rights had been extended to the Jaycees, Alcoholics Anonymous, and the Boy Scouts. . . .

This analysis is faulty for two reasons. The District Court erroneously treated this case as if the prison environment was essentially a "public forum." We observed last Term in upholding a ban on political meetings at Fort Dix that a government enclave such as a military base was not a public forum. Greer v. Spock, 424 U.S. 828 (1976). . . . A prison may be more easily converted into a public forum than a military base. Thus appellants need only demonstrate a rational basis for their distinctions between organizational groups. Cf. City of Charlotte v. Firefighters, 426 U.S. 283 (1976). Here, appellants' affidavits indicate exactly why Alcoholics Anonymous and the Jaycees have been allowed to operate within the prison. Both were seen as serving a rehabilitative purpose, working in harmony with the goals and desires of the prison administrators, and both had been determined not to pose any threat to the order or security of the institution. The affidavits indicate that the administrators' view of the Union differed critically in both these respects.

Those conclusions are not unreasonable. Prison administrators may surely conclude that the Jaycees and Alcoholics Anonymous differ in fundamental respects from appellee Union, a group with no past to speak of, and

the avowed intent to pursue an adversary relationship with the prison officials. . . .

Since a prison is most emphatically not a "public forum," these reasonable beliefs of appellants are sufficient, cf. Greer v. Spock, supra; City of Charlotte v. Firefighters, supra. The District Court's further requirement of a demonstrable showing that the Union was in fact harmful is inconsistent with the deference federal courts should pay to the informed discretion of prison officials. Procunier v. Martinez, 416 U.S., at 405. It is precisely in matters such as this, the decision as to which of many groups should be allowed to operate within the prison walls, where confronted with claims based on the Equal Protection Clause, the courts should allow the prison administrators the full latitude of discretion, unless it can be firmly stated that the two groups are so similar that discretion has been abused. That is surely not the case here. There is nothing in the Constitution which requires prison officials to treat all inmate groups alike unless differentiation is necessary to avoid an imminent threat of institutional disruption or violence. The regulations of appellants challenged in the District Court offended neither the First nor the Fourteenth Amendments, and the judgment of that Court holding to the contrary is

Reversed.

[Mr. Justice STEVENS concurred in part and dissented in part.]

Mr. Justice MARSHALL, with whom Mr. Justice BRENNAN joins, dissenting.

* * *

I

In Procunier v. Martinez, 416 U.S. 396 (1974), I set forth at some length my understanding of the First Amendment rights of prison inmates. The fundamental tenet I advanced is simply stated: "A prisoner does not shed . . . basic First Amendment rights at the prison gate. Rather, he 'retains all the rights of an ordinary citizen except those expressly, or by necessary implication, taken from him by law.' Coffin v. Reichard, 143 F.2d 443, 445 (6th Cir. 1944)." 416 U.S., at 422 (concurring opinion). It follows from this tenet that a restriction on the First Amendment rights of prisoners, like a restriction on First Amendment rights of non-prisoners, "can only be justified by a substantial government interest and a showing that the means chosen to effectuate the State's purpose are not unnecessarily restrictive of personal freedoms." Id., at 423. . . .

* * *

Nothing in the Court's opinion justifies its wholesale abandonment of traditional principles of First Amendment analysis. I realize, of course, that "the realities of running a penal institution are complex and difficult," . . . and that correctional officers possess considerably more "professional expertise" . . . in prison management than do judges. I do not in any way minimize either the seriousness of the problems or the significance of the expertise. . . . Yet in no First Amendment case of which I am aware has the Court deferred to the judgment of such officials simply because their judgment was "rational." . . . I do not understand why a different rule should apply simply because prisons are involved.

The reason courts cannot blindly defer to the judgment of prison administrators—or any other officials for that matter—is easily understood. Because the prison administrator's business is to maintain order, "there inheres the danger that he may well be less responsive than a court—part of an independent branch of government—to the constitutionally protected interests in free expression." Freedman v. Maryland, 380 U.S. 51, 57–58 (1965). . . .

[T]he ultimate responsibility for evaluating the prison officials' testimony, as well as any other expert testimony, must rest with the courts, which are required to reach an independent judgment concerning the constitutionality of any restriction on expressive activity.

* * *

II

Once it is established that traditional First Amendment principles are applicable in prisoners' rights cases, the dispute here is easily resolved. The three-judge court not only found that there was "not one scintilla of evidence to suggest that the Union had been utilized to disrupt the operation of the penal institutions," North Carolina Prison-

ers' Labor Union Inc. v. Jones 409 F. Supp. 937, 944 (E.D.N.C. 1976), as the Court acknowledges, it also found no evidence "that the inmates intend to operate [the union] to hamper and interfere with proper interest of government," 409 F. Supp., at 944, or that the union posed a "present danger to security and order," id., at 945. In the face of these findings, it cannot be argued that the restrictions on the union are "imperatively justif[ied]."

The regulation barring inmates from soliciting fellow prisoners to join the union is particularly vulnerable to attack. As the late Judge Craven stated for the court below, "To permit an inmate to join a union and forbid his inviting others to join borders on the irrational." 409 F. Supp., at 943. . . . Because the actual regulation at issue here needlessly bars solicitation for an activity—joining the union—which is not and presumably could not be prohibited, I would hold it unconstitutional.

Once the rule outlawing solicitation is invalidated, the prohibition on bulk mailing by the Union must fall with it. Since North Carolina allows the Union to mail its newsletters to prisoners individually, the State cannot claim that the bulk mail rule serves to keep "subversive material" out of the prison. Rather, the primary purpose of the rule must be to supplement the ban on solicitation; overturning that ban would sap all force from the rationale for excluding bulk mailings. The exclusion would then be left as one that unnecessarily increases the cost to the Union of exercising its First Amendment rights while allowing other inmate groups such as the Jaycees to exercise their rights at a lower price. It would, therefore, be plainly unconstitutional.

The regulation prohibiting the Union from holding meetings within the prison is somewhat more justifiable than the regulations previously considered. Once the Union is permitted to hold meetings it will become operational within the prisons. . . .

[I] believe that where, as here, meetings would not pose an immediate and substantial threat to the security or rehabilitative functions of the prisons, the First Amendment guarantees Union members the right to associate freely, and the Fourteenth Amendment guarantees them the right to be treated as favorably as members of other inmate organizations. The State can surely regulate the time, place, and manner of the meetings, and perhaps can monitor them to assure that disruptions are not planned, but the State cannot outlaw such assemblies altogether.

III

If the mode of analysis adopted in today's decision were to be generally followed, prisoners eventually would be stripped of all constitutional rights, and would retain only those privileges that prison officials, in their "informed discretion," deigned to recognize. The sole constitutional constraint on prison officials would be a requirement that they act rationally. Ironically, prisoners would be left with a right of access to the courts . . . but no substantive rights to assert once they get there. . . . I therefore believe that the tension between today's decision and our prior cases ultimately will be resolved not by the demise of the earlier cases, but by the recognition that the decision today is an aberration, a manifestation of the extent to which the very phrase "prisoner union" is threatening to those holding traditional conceptions of the nature of penal institutions.

I respectfully dissent.

Comments

1. As noted by the Supreme Court in *Procunier* v. *Martinez, supra,* federal courts traditionally adhered to a "hands-off" policy with regard to inmate complaints about prison regulations and practices, especially those by inmates in state custody. The rationale was that correctional authorities were "experts" in the custodial and institutionalization process. Several reasons were advanced in support of this policy: (1) the maintenance of the correctional system is an executive function and should not be subject to federal review; (2) judicial review of the correctional system violates the doctrine of separation of powers; (3) the judicial branch lacks the expertise to review the decisions of correctional authorities; and (4) the judicial branch lacks jurisdiction to review such cases because prisoners do not have any constitutional rights. Singer and Statsky, *Rights of the Imprisoned* (1974).

   However, in recent years, and especially since the adoption of the 1964 Civil Rights Act (42 U.S.C. § 1983), the problem of prisoners' rights has received increased attention from the federal courts. Sections of the Civil Rights Act give state prisoners direct access to the federal courts to redress their legitimate grievances on prison conditions and practices. Although there has been a steady decrease in the population of prisons (see Rothman, *The Discovery of the Asylum* [1971]), the number of lawsuits filed by inmates attacking the conditions of confinement and prison regulations has increased dramatically. Today the constitutional rights of prisoners is becoming the subject of courses in universities because of the increasing volume of appellate court decisions in this area. Although the United States Supreme Court has not responded as quickly as other federal courts to the demise of the "hands-off" policy, recent Supreme Court pronouncements give strong evidence that the earlier reasons given for judicial restraint in this area are no longer viable.

2. In *Procunier* v. *Martinez,* the Supreme Court left no doubt that the First Amendment reaches inside prison walls. However, the full scope of the First Amendment is not enjoyed by prison inmates. Federal courts, in dealing with these issues, have attempted to strike a balance between First Amendment rights and legitimate penologic goals, which may necessitate some restrictions on these

fundamental rights. In order for a state to restrict an inmate's First Amendment rights, it must show that (1) the prison regulation is necessary under a "balancing of interests" test, and (2) the limitation on the right is the least restrictive alternative available.

Inmates have filed lawsuits in federal court alleging a denial of First Amendment rights with regard to (1) visitation, *Rowland* v. *Wolff*, 336 F. Supp. 257 (N.D. Neb. 1971); (2) personal physical appearance, *Blake* v. *Pryse*, 315 F. Supp. 625 (D. Minn. 1970), aff'd 444 F.2d 218 (8th Cir. 1971); (3) receipt of publication, *Sostre* v. *Otis*, 330 F. Supp. 941 (S.D.N.Y. 1971); (4) prisoners' manuscripts, *Berrigan* v. *Norton*, 451 F.2d 790 (2d Cir. 1971); (5) freedom of expression in prison, *Roberts* v. *Pepersack*, 256 F. Supp. 415 (D. Md. 1966); and (6) freedom of religion in prison, *Sostre* v. *McGinnis*, 334 F.2d 906 (2d Cir. 1964). In most cases, the federal courts have struck down prison regulations that are not shown to serve a legitimate governmental purpose and that have a "chilling effect" on First Amendment rights.

What practical problems are likely to arise in light of the *Martinez* and *Pell* decisions?

3. In *Pell*, the Supreme Court identified four "legitimate penal objectives": (1) deterrence (specific and general); (2) protection (isolation); (3) rehabilitation; and (4) internal security. Which, if any, of these objectives is furthered by a state regulation prohibiting face-to-face interviews with specific inmates by news reporters? Does the press have a First Amendment right to witness an execution that the general public is excluded from? Would the Supreme Court uphold "secret" executions? Does the press have a right to televise or otherwise record the proceedings at an execution? Does the general public have a right to be informed about prison conditions? Could a state enforce a statute that denied the press access to death row inmates under all circumstances?

   In *Saxbe* v. *Washington Post Co.*, 417 U.S. 843 (1974), decided the same day as *Pell*, a 5–4 Supreme Court held that a policy statement of the Federal Bureau of Prisons prohibiting interviews between newsmen and individually named inmates of federal prisons other than minimum security institutions did not abridge the freedom of the press guaranteed under the First Amendment because the policy statement did not deny the press access to sources of information available to the general public. Some penal institutions have an unwritten policy of making it difficult to obtain information about them. How do such policies square with the *Pell-Saxbe* decisions? Reconsider the statement of the Court in *Pell*, which was reiterated in *Saxbe*, that "newsmen have no constitutional right of access to prisons or their inmates beyond that afforded the general public," 417 U.S. 817, 134 (1974).

4. The Supreme Court granted certiorari in *Baxter* v. *Palmigiano*, supra, in order to clarify the earlier holding in *Wolff* v. *McDonnell*, 418 U.S. 539 (1974), that some minimal due process safeguards that "reasonably accommodate" the interests of the inmates and the needs of the institution are required at prison disciplinary hearings. In *Wolff*, the Court held that the minimal due process requirements include (1) advance written notice of the charges given to the inmate at least 24 hours prior to the disciplinary hear-

ing, and (2) a written statement by the factfinders as to the evidence relied on and reasons for the disciplinary action. *Baxter* makes it clear that under the *Wolff* "reasonable accommodation" standard, the Sixth Amendment right to confront and cross-examine witnesses and the right to counsel are not constitutionally required at prison disciplinary hearings. What did the *Wolff* Court mean by the statement that "as the nature of the prison disciplinary process changes in future years, circumstances may exist which will require further consideration and reflection by this Court" (at 572)? What changes? What circumstances? Can you think of a situation in which a denial of the right to confront witnesses at a prison disciplinary proceeding would be a denial of due process? Suppose the accuser is a convicted perjurer, a notorious liar or a guard who "has it in" for the inmates?

5. In *Montanye* v. *Haymes*, 427 U.S. 236 (1976), a companion case to *Meachum* v. *Fano,* supra, the Supreme Court, in a 6–3 decision, reversed an earlier ruling by the Court of Appeals (2d Cir.) requiring appropriate hearings under the Due Process Clause of the Fourteenth Amendment prior to the disciplinary transfer of a New York State prisoner. Unlike the court of appeals in *Meachum*, the *Montanye* court of appeals did not hold that every disadvantageous transfer triggered procedural due process protections: "administrative" transfers were exempt from the ruling. However, the court of appeals thought that "when harsh treatment is meted out to reprimand, deter or reform an individual, elementary fairness demands that the one punished be given a satisfactory opportunity to establish he is not deserving of such handling." 505 F.2d, at 980. The Supreme Court, per Mr. Justice White, held that the Due Process Clause does not automatically require hearings when a prisoner is transferred because of a breach of prison rules. The majority concluded that "as long as the conditions or degree of confinement . . . are within the sentence imposed . . . and are not otherwise violative of the Constitution, . . . the Clause does not require hearings in connection with transfers whether or not they are the result of the inmate's misbehavior or may be labeled as disciplinary or punitive."

6. *Meachum* and *Montanye* involved transfers within the same state system, but prisoners can also be transferred from one state to another under the Interstate Corrections Compact. In *Gomes* v. *Travisono*, 353 F. Supp. 457 (1973), a Rhode Island District Court upheld the constitutionality of such transfers, but ruled that they required *Morrissey*-type safeguards. However, the Court of appeals (1st Cir.) declined to apply such a broad range of constitutional protections, narrowing the due process requirements for interstate transfers to (1) notice of proposed transfer and reasons therefor; (2) a hearing; and (3) a reasonable opportunity to challenge the evidence or allegations made to support the proposed transfer. *Gomes* was vacated by the Supreme Court and remanded to the court of appeals for consideration in light of *Wolff* v. *McDonnell*, 418 U.S. 539 (1974). The First Circuit affirmed, 510 F.2d 537 (1st Cir. 1974). If *Gomes* were to come to the Supreme Court for reconsideration now, would *Wolff* still apply to punitive interstate transfers in light of the Court's holdings in *Meachum* and *Montanye*?

7. In *Meachum*, the majority noted, "The Due Process Clause in and of itself [does not] protect a duly convicted prisoner against transfer from one institution to another." What if prison officials transferred all inmates of a particular race, religion, nationality, or political belief to one particular institution? Would such a practice invoke the protections of the Due Process Clause? What if prison officials argued that the transfers involved only troublemakers? Consider the National Advisory Commission on Criminal Justice Standards and Goals Standard 2.8 – Nondiscriminatory Treatment: "Each correctional agency should develop . . . policies and procedures assuring the right of offenders not to be subjected to discriminatory treatment based on race, religion, nationality, sex, or political beliefs." In light of the above hypothetical situations, consider the Supreme Court's language in *Wolff* v. *McDonnell* that "the touchstone of due process is protection of the individual against arbitrary action of government," *Dent* v. *West Virginia*, 129 U.S. 114, 123 (1889).

8. In *Estelle* v. *Gamble*, supra, a majority of the Supreme Court held that medical malpractice by prison health officials does not per se give rise to a cause of action under the Civil Rights Act (42 U.S.C. § 1983) even though the government has an obligation to provide medical care to inmates; only a showing of "deliberate indifference to serious medical needs" by correctional officials is sufficient to bring the Eighth Amendment into play. Suppose the quality of care is clearly below acceptable medical standards. Would that be sufficient evidence of "deliberate indifference" under the *Gamble* standards? Or is medical care in prisons and in the community outside to be judged by different standards? Should they be in theory? For practical reasons? Do inmates with special medical and psychological problems have an Eighth Amendment right to treatment? Incarcerated alcoholics? Heroin addicts? Homosexuals? Sexual psychopaths? Would failure to render any treatment at all to inmates with special problems constitute the type of "deliberate indifference" required by *Gamble?* In light of the holding in *Gamble*, should the inmate-respondent have sued the prison physicians under the Texas Tort Claims Act, under which medical malpractice gives rise to a cause of action in negligence? See Prosser, W., *The Laws of Torts* 161–166 (1971). In all states an inmate may be sued, but in a few states an inmate may not sue in his own name or may not bring a lawsuit under any circumstances while he is imprisoned. Accordingly, an injured inmate claiming intentional medical malpractice in those states may sue only in federal court under the Civil Rights Act. Do you agree with the statement by Mr. Justice Stevens (dissenting) that the decision in *Gamble* will increase federal litigation by inmate "writ-writers"?

9. Complaints from inmates that they have been denied medical care or have received inadequate care are increasing in the federal courts. See Zalman, M., *Prisoners' Rights to Medical Care*, 63 J. Crim. Law, Criminol. Pol. Sci. 185 (1972). Most courts have held that correctional officials have a duty to provide medical care of ordinary and reasonable quality, but they generally have not been receptive to complaints from individual inmates that they were denied proper medical treatment. As noted by one federal district court, the courts are reluctant to "second guess a licensed physician as to the propriety of a particular course of medical

treatment afforded a prisoner-patient in his care." *Mayfield* v. *Craven,* 299 F. Supp. 111 (E.D. Calif. 1969), affirmed 443 F.2d 873 (9th Cir. 1970). However, one federal district court has held that the medical care program in the Alabama Penal System constitutes cruel and unusual punishment. *Newman* v. *State,* 349 F. Supp. 278 (M.D. Ala. 1972).

10. In *Bounds* v. *Smith,* supra, a majority of the Court held that state inmates have a "fundamental constitutional right" to "meaningful access" to the federal courts. But as noted by Justice Rehnquist (dissenting), on what constitutional grounds was *Bounds* decided? Fourteenth Amendment due process? Equal protection? The majority does not tell us. Presumably, the decision was grounded on the Fourteenth Amendment Due Process Clause. That clause prohibits the taking of life, liberty, or property without some procedural safeguards, and logic dictates that the Court must have based its decision on the "liberty" provision of the clause. But if this is the case, why didn't the majority say so?

Anyone familiar with pro se habeas corpus petitions filed by inmates knows that the vast majority of the claims presented are frivolous. Is that immaterial in determining what constitutes "meaningful access" to the courts? Wouldn't inmates have more "meaningful access" if counsel were appointed at state expense? Will, or should, the Court go that far?

11. In *Gilmore* v. *Lynch,* 319 F. Supp. 105 (N.D. Calif. 1970), aff'd sub nom. *Younger* v. *Gilmore,* 404 U.S. 15 (1971), the critical precedent upon which the majority relied in *Bounds,* the Supreme Court, on appeal, summarily affirmed a lower federal court decision that held that states must provide law libraries for inmates who want them. Recall that a summary decision without opinion by the Supreme Court on appeal (rather than on certiorari) is a decision on the merits (see Chapter One). In response to *Gilmore,* many states spent hundreds of thousands of dollars to create law libraries for inmates. Jailhouse lawyers have filed an enormous number of actions, usually in the federal courts. For example, inmate petitions account for 18 per cent of all civil actions filed in the federal district courts. See Shapiro, D., *Federal Habeas Corpus: A Study in Massachusetts,* 87 Harv. L. Rev. 321 (1973). In North Carolina in 1975, 41 per cent of all civil actions were filed by inmates. The burden on the courts is enormous.

12. The *Bounds* decision will create some practical problems for death row inmates. Such inmates are usually not permitted to associate with inmates in the general prison population, and consequently, they can do legal research (out of their cell) only on an individual basis. Some states, like Florida, have nearly 100 inmates on death row: Given these regulations, how are these inmates going to have "meaningful access" to the prison law library? In addition, Florida's Death Row is a mile away from the prison library which is in a building that is already overcrowded, and two correctional officers must accompany every death row inmate who is taken off the Row. Will the *Bounds* decision necessitate the closing down of the law library for long periods daily while a single death row inmate conducts legal research? Wouldn't the inmates in general population then be denied "meaningful access" to the law library? In short, is there a constitutional right of "meaningful access" to prison law libraries? Note the statement by Chief Justice Burger

(dissenting in *Bounds*) that the Court's opinion raises "theoretical and practical difficulties." Which legal texts, if any, might a prison be constitutionally required to stock in a library? All state and federal reporters? Is a North Dakota inmate denied access to the courts if the prison library doesn't contain the *Florida Reports*? The implications of *Bounds* v. *Smith* are enormous.

13. It is difficult to believe that when the framers of the Bill of Rights wrote the First Amendment in 1787 they intended inmates to have a constitutional right to form and join prison unions. Which is the more persuasive reason for not giving constitutional sanction to prison unions: That such organizations would tend to disrupt the orderly administration of the correctional process; that the decisions of correctional authorities should be given great deference by the courts; or that the primary purpose of incarceration is punishment and that prisons are not "public forums" designed to foster free speech? Note that the majority of the Court in *Jones* v. *North Carolina Prisoners' Labor Union, Inc.*, supra, failed to discuss the possible rehabilitative benefits of prison unions. Would the implementation of such organizations serve to enhance or defeat the ideals of rehabilitation? Could members of a prison union lawfully strike in protest of poor working conditions? To demand higher wages? To demand a right to collective bargaining? To set up a union pension fund? Could Congress permit prison unions to come under the jurisdiction of the National Labor Relations Act? Do inmates have a First Amendment right to form various nonunion clubs or organizations such as "Lifer's Inc." or "Gay Guys"?

THE IDENTIFICATION AND TREATMENT OF INCARCERATED DANGEROUS OFFENDERS AND THE POLITICIZATION OF INMATE POPULATIONS: REHABILITATION OR REPRESSION?*

Henry W. Mannle

Approximately 400 correctional institutions of varying size and organizational complexity exist throughout U.S. jurisdictions (Goldfarb and Singer, 1973: 47) which have as objectives—relative to their respective legislative mandates—the provision of custody, instruction, discipline, treatment, rehabilitation and safekeeping of those committed to them as the consequence of a felony conviction (see also Sourcebook of Criminal Justice Statistics, 1974: 129).[1] In addition, such facilities have a legislatively derived objective, either implicitly or explicitly stated, to insure the safety of the public. Thus, with the apparent mutually supportive goals of (1) providing for the safekeeping of those in custody and (2) protecting the public, especially from gross predatory behavior, much attention has been focused upon identification and treatment of the dangerous offender.[2] For example, the National Advisory Commission on Criminal Justice Standards and Goals, in its document on corrections (1973), devoted a section to "Special Offender Types" in which it called for the development of provisions for dangerous and "recalcitrant" inmates.

Few would challenge the necessity of developing programs and institutional policies aimed at the protection of inmates from each other. Respectable arguments do exist which support the proposition that the protection of those in custody from violence perpetrated by fellow inmates is a strict legal responsibility of the "keepers." However, inmate efforts to have correctional officials held legally responsible for assaults by other

---

*From 24 Chitty's L. J. 281 (1976).

inmates while institutionalized have not been, in general, very successful. Defendants in such civil actions (jailers, prison administrators, etc.) have tended to include, as part of their defense, the argument that they had no way of knowing in advance that the alleged assaulters were "aggressive types." Without arguing the merits of that defense, such repeated claims by administrators do suggest a need for developing valid, reliable and *apolitical* criteria that will enable correctional personnel to identify and treat, *with qualifications*, those who pose a threat to themselves and others while institutionalized.

However, it is suggested that these qualifications should be clearly delineated and monitored in view of the mounting concern over the role and scope of criminal justice administration within correctional facilities housing an apparently politicized population.

* * *

That corrections and its attendant treatment model are currently under critical re-examination is, no doubt, related to recent challenges to the traditional paradigm of criminology, *i.e.*, positivism, a school of thought which represents a commitment to science and the rehabilitative ideal. Until very recently positivism has gone unchallenged as the dominant paradigm in criminology and corrections in spite of the criticisms and critiques of this bias that began to emerge a few decades ago.

* * *

Competing paradigms are now evident in criminology which emphasize the need for criminology to study *crime* and its relationship to the law rather than persist in a deterministic myopic focus upon the criminal, *i.e.*, the discovery of those personal attributes which are alleged to discriminate between criminals and non-criminals. Studying crime as well as the criminal brings to the arena such issues as (1) the political nature of law and its administration (2) the effect of interest group activity upon all levels of criminal justice administration and (3) a critical assessment of treatment ideologies as integral to the "therapeutic state" which, through professional expertise, may promote repressive authoritarianism over the individ-

ual, especially evident in total institutions, *i.e.*, corrections.

* * *

Treatment schemes, which frequently fall under the category of "behavior mod," may have the greatest potential for abuse in total institutions. These programs, reduced to their essentials, center around three basic strategies: (1) the provision of negative reinforcements for undesirable behavior (2) the administration of rewards for desirable behavior and (3) treatment aimed at alteration of the offender's personality structure (Sage, 1974: 18).[3]

The professional and lay community alike were "shocked" to learn of the "Tucker Telephone" used in the Arkansas penal system, *i.e.*, the practice of connecting the wires of a telephone generator to the genitals of recalcitrant inmates in order to promote inmate compliance. However, when such essentially similar practices are carried out under the cloak of treatment in "progressive" institutions one's sensibilities can be easily salved. For example, Sage (1974) relates how sex offenders are shown films of crime situations similar to their previous criminogenic encounters and then given electrical shocks in the groin; the aim, of course, being that of making the offender repulsed even at the *thought* of committing such behavior in the future. (Sage, 1974: 18). Not only do such practices catalyze purely ethical considerations, such as the right and ability of inmates to refuse the "treatment," but also raise significant constitutionally related issues. For example, in *Stanley* v. *Georgia* (394 U.S. 557:565–566) [Chapter Fifteen, § 15.02] (involving the right of the citizen to possess "pornography" in the privacy of his home) the U.S. Supreme Court may have alluded to the dangers of treatments which have the objective of altering a person's cognitive processes, thus, perhaps, infringing upon the individual's reception and dissemination of communication (First Amendment rights).

A more sensational tactic is the use of psychosurgical techniques to change, very directly, undesirable behavior. Originally, in the 1920's and 1930's, psychosurgery involved the practice of performing rather crude lobotomies which, today, does not appear to be in the mainstream of neurological practice. However, the Liberation News Service (1973) has produced policy statements smuggled out of the California system which indicate that this procedure has not been ruled out for use on "selected" inmates at the state's Vacaville Center. In response to growing concern, a Michigan court recently enjoined the use of experimental psychosurgery where based on the informed consent of involuntarily detained mental patients (*Kaimowitz* v. *Department of Mental Health for the State of Michigan*, Civ. Action No. 73–19434–AW [Cir. Ct. for Wayne City, Mich. 1974].) The court held that such consent is permissible for *accepted* neurological procedures, but that the state of medical knowledge was inadequate to show that such psychosurgery would have any direct therapeutic effect in controlling aggressive behavior.

Pertinent to the topic of identifying and treating the dangerous offender is the current cycle of prison riots and the possible adoption of unbridled behavior modification programs, given the politicization of significant portions of the inmate population.

Prison violence is not a new pattern in the history of corrections. Without belaboring that history, suffice to say that three cycles of disruptive behavior have been discerned by students of corrections. During the late 19th and early 20th centuries, prison disturbances were largely sporadic, with the goals of inmates being limited primarily to improving internal conditions and securing the amenities of life (better food, visiting privileges and, in general, more humane treatment).

Riots occurring during the mid 1950's appeared to be more clustered and patterned. . . . In 1952 and 1953, for example, there were approximately 45 such riots which occurred in about half of the states. For the next few decades these episodes declined until 1969 when the cycle of violence and injury increased; the most dramatic example being that of Attica in the fall of 1971.

Thus, it is evident that disturbances behind the walls have not been restricted to time and place. What may be significant is that the character or nature of this phenomenon has undergone considerable change. . . .

Observations of recent collective disturbances have led to the conclusion that there may be varying levels of inmate commitment to, and involvement in, "revolutionary" ideologies. Thus, prisons may still house a substantial population whose chief concerns focus upon the improvement of internal conditions. Indications are that prisons also house elite groupings of ideologists who view their incarceration as a status rendered by an unjust social system and illegitimate legal order. It is this elite which, no doubt, has contributed (although not, in any sense, exclusively) to the increased politicization of inmate populations — more significantly, perhaps, for minority group members.

Given the clandestine nature of a closed institution, prison disturbances may appear to many inmates as the only viable mode of expressing grievances. . . . It may be that perceived inability to express grievances is not a necessary *and* sufficient cause for riots. Nevertheless, institutional controls and motivations to maintain order may go beyond the traditional symbiotic social relationships between inmates and staff when segments of the inmate population feel that collective disturbances are necessary and legitimate behavior.

It is within this context that caution regarding the introduction of programs aimed at the identification of "dangerous and violent" offenders is warranted. More specifically, the potential for abuse is escalated when certain types of programs, in the name of treatment, become instruments by which the institution attempts to neutralize politically motivated inmate "trouble-makers."

Recent dramatic revelations by a California psychiatrist, Michael Serber (Sage, 1974), point to the potential consequences when a supply of "therapies" is placed in the hands of "scientific criminologists" employed by the state. For example, Serber charges that certain black militants, sexual deviants and other "undesirable" inmates in California are being treated with Anectine (a drug which simulates death, and, incidentally, one which was outlawed for use in Vietnam as a war crime). Under the influence of Anectine, inmates receive conditioning suggestions designed to alter behavior. Upon examination of the program, Serber found that "when placed in the hands of paraprofessionals, the experiment degenerated into blatant torture." Further, the experiment, according to Serber, was methodologically wanting to say the least, *i.e.*, no base-line data was gathered, there were no controls, no objective ratings and no follow-up studies.

In some instances, when the courts have

become aware of chemotherapy being practiced in an institutional setting, legal restrictions have been imposed. In a recent Iowa case (*Knecht* v. *Gillman,* 488 F.2d 1136 [8th Cir. 1973]), a federal Court of Appeals enjoined the use of the drug apomorphine — an emetic which causes vomiting for fifteen minutes to one hour after intra-muscular injection into an inmate — for violating behavior protocol established by the staff without certain procedural guidelines. The court held, inter alia, that informed consent by the inmate was permissible but that consent could be revoked (by the subjects) at any time.

Other non-chemotherapeutic programs, designed to modify the behavior of inmates who are "*manipulative, assaultive, aggressive leaders of prison subcultures . . .* [inmates for whom] the general level of intelligence and cunning is high" (Sage, 1974: 20), have been introduced into the federal system. Asklepion therapy, which includes sprinklings of transactional analysis and psychodrama, is being proposed for use on selected inmates in certain federal penitentiaries (Sage, 1974: 20). Inmates have smuggled out reports on Asklepion which paint a different picture than that of its chief architect, psychiatrist Martin Groder. Accordingly, Asklepion represents a concerted effort to undermine character structures of troublesome inmates in which the goal is to reduce those individuals to a state of total non-involvement (Sage, 1974: 21). The new federal facility at Butner, North Carolina (and, reportedly, at several other institutions which are on the drawing board), calls for operant conditioning tactics, similar to Asklepion, as integral to their "treatment" programs. Ironically, the completion of these treatment milieu installations is scheduled for 1984 (Sage, 1974: 18).

The Correctional Dilemma

Prisons continue to exist for a variety of reasons; both manifest and latent. One manifest function of prisons concerns the intended purpose of protecting the public *and* institutional populations from acts of violence. Increasing proposals for victim compensation legislation often place the burden of payment (quite logically) upon the state. When citizens are constrained from using unqualified efforts to protect themselves and that since the duty to insure public safety rests with the state, it follows, then, that the state must provide some form of remuneration to those who have obviously not been protected. As a state agency, it may be that the inability to rehabilitate dangerous offenders could serve, through victim compensation awards, as a financially delineated example of the failure of correctional agencies to serve their intended functions.

Concerning the protection of the inmate population, the courts have recently become inundated with petitions from prisoners requesting relief from deprivations of immunity as granted by the U.S. Constitution, *e.g.,* provision of safety for inmates from other aggressive inmates. . . . Chief Justice Burger has suggested that federal courts should not deny prisoners protection, but that new procedures are required. These include: (1) having new federal statutes provide for administrative hearings within prison and require that these procedures be exhausted before a petition may be filed in federal court, or (as an alternative), (2) have federal courts refer writs of habeas corpus and civil rights claims brought by inmates so that they will be dealt with initially by a U.S. Magistrate sitting as a Special Master and reporting to the Supreme Court.[4]

A possible latent function of prisons is that they provide ideal captive subjects for research, be it conventional drug experimentation or exotic behavior mod programs designed to test game plans for the "Americanization of 1984." Thus, with growing legal demands for protection of human life without and within the walls, plus an apparent obligation to insure the preservation of basic human rights of convicted felons, prisons may be faced with an extremely complex responsibility. It is suggested that a guideline to assist corrections out of its present dilemma may lie somewhere within the bounds of a Therapeutic Bill of Rights.[5] In particular:

(1) No person shall be compelled to undergo treatment except for the defense of society, further

(2) Man's innate right to remain free of excessive forms of human modification shall be inviolable, further

(3) No social sanctions may be invoked unless the person subjected to treatment has demonstrated a clear and present danger through truly harmful behavior which is immediately forthcoming or has already

occurred. Generally an *overt act* should be required, further

(4) No person shall be subjected to involuntary incarceration or treatment on the basis of a finding of a general condition or status alone. Nor shall the mere conviction of a crime or a finding of not guilty by reason of insanity suffice to have a person automatically committed or treated, further

(5) No social sanctions, whether designated criminal, civil or therapeutic, may be invoked in the absence of the previous right to a judicial or other independent hearing, appointed counsel, and an opportunity to confront those testifying about one's past conduct or therapeutic needs.

References

1. In addition, there are about 2,500 municipal and county jails in the U.S. serving primarily as places of confinement for convicted misdemeanants, persons awaiting trial, and convicted felons awaiting transfer to other institutions (*Sourcebook of Criminal Justice Statistics*, 1974).
2. However, according to the F.B.I. only about 10 per cent of all reported offenses involve violent, predatory crimes. The vast majority of offenses reported annually involve property crimes.
3. Sage, Wayne (1974) *Crime and Clockwork Lemon.* Human Behavior (September): 16–25.
4. However, see *Wingo* v. *Wedding*, 418 U.S. 461 (1974) holding that: the Federal Magistrates Act (28 USC §§ 631–639) requires district judges to personally conduct evidentiary hearings in all federal habeas corpus cases—rejecting such hearings before full-time magistrates. "Report on the Federal Judicial Branch," delivered before the American Bar Association, Washington, D.C., August 6, 1974.
5. Kittrie, Nicholas N. (1971) *The Right to Be Different.* Baltimore: The Johns Hopkins Press.

9.04 THE COLLATERAL CONSEQUENCES OF CONVICTION

RESTORING THE EX-OFFENDER'S RIGHT TO VOTE: BACKGROUND AND DEVELOPMENTS*

When an offender is sent to prison for the commission of a crime, his punishment does

*From 11 Am. Crim. L. Rev. 721, 721–729 (1973). Reproduced by permission from the American Bar Association.

not end with his release. In most states, the ex-convict who has completed his prison term is subject to a variety of civil disabilities that remain in force for the rest of his life.

One such disability is loss of the right to vote. Yet, according to the Supreme Court, "no right is more precious" than suffrage because "other rights, even the most basic, are illusory if the right to vote is undermined." Nonetheless, participation in the electoral process is denied to those citizens who have broken the law, even though they may have been incarcerated for years to repay society for their wrongs.

* * *

History of Disenfranchisement and Other Civil Disabilities

The first recorded instances of disenfranchisement as a consequence of crime can be found in the ancient civilizations of Greece and Rome. In Greece, a criminal who had committed a heinous crime was denied such fundamental rights of Greek citizenship as the right to vote and to appear in court. In Rome, a citizen could be deprived of such valued rights as suffrage and service in the Roman legions if the label of "infamia" were placed upon him. This pronouncement of moral censure occurred when a citizen committed an act considered either criminal or immoral and could be rendered by Roman administrative authorities such as the censors as well as magistrates in their civil or criminal judgments.

After the fall of the Roman Empire, the Germanic tribes of continental Europe and England used "outlawry" to punish those who committed particular crimes involving serious harm to the society and to compel wrongdoers to obey orders of the courts. The offender was expelled from the community and completely deprived of his civil rights and society's protection. Thus, the consequences of outlawry were severe: resulting in a denouncement as "infamous," the deprivation of all rights, confiscation of property, exposure to injury and even to death, since the outlaw could be killed with impunity by anyone.

In the period that followed the Middle Ages, the tradition of outlawry survived and was expanded by statutory enactment in various communes, principalities and monarchies. The outlaw now found himself declared "civilly dead," an expression first evidenced in Roman law but developed fully in later times to describe the offender deprived of his legal existence. While the deprivation of rights inherent in the status of civil death coincided with the punishment of outlawry, it was extended to those convicted of crimes termed "capital" and rendered their punishments more severe by imposing dishonor and incapacity on the offender's descendants.

Moreover, lesser criminals were now subjected to loss of civil rights through another vestige of Roman law: infamy. Similar but less severe in its consequences than civil death, infamy could be imposed by operation of law ("juris") or by commission of an act which diminished public esteem ("facti") and resulted in the deprivation of many but not all civil and political rights.

While the sanctions of outlawry, civil death and infamy evolved in continental Europe, England developed its own method of imposing civil disabilities: attainder. Under the English system, a person pronounced "attainted" after conviction for a felony or the crime of treason was subject to three penalties: forfeiture, corruption of the blood and loss of civil rights.

"Forfeiture" resulted in confiscation of chattel and other goods upon criminal conviction and surrender of real property upon judgment of attainder. "Corruption of the blood" left the attainted person unfit to inherit, possess or devise his estate to his heirs, and his land escheated to the lord of the fee, subject to the king's superior right of forfeiture. Finally, because the criminal was considered "dead in law," he was prevented from appearing as a witness in court, bringing suit or performing any other legal function. As on the continent, such loss of civil and property rights was known as "civil death."

In the course of settling North America, the English colonists transplanted much of their common law heritage, including the imposition of civil disabilities and forfeiture of property that resulted from the procedure of attainder. In some colonies, the concepts of infamy and outlawry were introduced.

Following the American Revolution, the newly independent states rejected some of their inherited legal tradition. The United States Constitution specifically prohibited forfeiture and corruption of the blood except during the life of a person convicted of treason.[35] Civil death was rejected as part of the common law and existed only in states which passed civil death statutes. This did not, however, dislodge civil disabilities from a place in American law. Eleven state constitutions adopted between 1776 and 1821 denied voting rights to convicted felons or authorized their state legislatures to do so.[37] Before the Civil War, 19 of the 34 states in the Union excluded serious offenders from the franchise.

Thus the history of civil disabilities can be traced from the ancient civilizations of Greece and Rome to 18th century America, appearing in such forms as infamy, outlawry, civil death and attainder. Although the consequences varied in detail, each sanction was imposed for violations of social norms, legal or moral, and each deprived the offender of whatever civil rights the society offered its inhabitants. Therefore, disenfranchisement was included among the civil disabilities in countries that gave the right of suffrage to their citizens.

Disenfranchisement in the United States Today

Currently only four states—Arkansas, Maine, Michigan and Tennessee—do not deprive criminals of their right to vote, while still another 25 jurisdictions have some form of general automatic restoration procedures. This leaves almost one-half of the states with provisions disenfranchising ex-criminals for the rest of their lives. Only if the offender has the perseverance, financial resources and perhaps political contacts necessary to utilize successfully state pardon procedures will he ever regain that right.

Although the vast majority of states have provisions that prohibit offenders from casting their ballots, these provisions vary greatly in their specific terms. Twenty-nine states plus the District of Columbia disenfranchise felons, while 15 states deny suffrage to those who have committed treason. Approximately one-third of the states list specific offenses for which criminals can be prohibited from registering to vote—frequently including bribery and larceny, but occasionally more unusual crimes such as duelling and bigamy. Eleven states disenfranchise merely for convictions of "infamous crimes," two states for crimes involving "moral turpitude," and 18 for commission of election offenses. Although the preceding analysis indicates a variety of categories, it should be noted that approximately one-half of the states that disenfranchise criminals have a combination of the above provisions in their constitutions and statutory codes.

States with disenfranchisement provisions may also provide procedures for restoration of suffrage rights. The most common provision is the executive pardon; the least, automatic restoration. The power to grant a pardon generally rests with the governor, although some states require an initial recommendation by a board of pardons. Usually the governor has authority to grant pardons for most categories of crime, although pardons for treason or impeachment must generally be secured from the state legislature. In a few states, it is not the governor but the board of pardons, a court or the state legislature which dispenses pardons resulting in the restoration of civil rights.

Approximately half of the states also provide some form of automatic restoration. Nineteen states have various disenfranchisement provisions but also have specific provisions which restore civil rights automatically upon termination of imprisonment, parole or probation. Five more states, plus the District of Columbia, deny offenders their voting rights for a fixed period of time only. For example, Massachusetts disenfranchises only those convicted of election crimes for a period of three years following the date of conviction. North Carolina, which denies suffrage to those convicted of felonies or other crimes punishable by imprisonment, restores rights automatically two years from the offender's release by the Department of Correction, "including probation or parole," if he "has not been convicted of a criminal offense" during that period. Three other states disenfranchise for determinate periods for certain specified crimes but disenfranchise permanently for others.

* * *

References*

35. U.S. Const. art. III, § 3.
37. In order of their enactment: Va. Const. art. 3, § 1 (1776); Ky. Const. art. 8, § 8 (1799); Ohio Const. art. 4, § 4 (1802); La. Const. art. 6, § 4 (1812); Ind. Const. art. 6, § 4 (1816); Miss. Const. art. 6, § 5 (1817); Conn. Const. art. 6, § 2 (1818); Ill. Const. art. 2, § 30 (1818); Ala. Const. art. 6, § 5 (1819); Mo. Const. art. 3, § 14 (1820); N.Y. Const. art. 2, § 2 (1821). See *Green* v. *Bd. of Elections,* 380 F. 2d 445, 450 (2d Cir. 1967) (compiling statutes).

---

*Most references in this excerpt have been omitted.

Disenfranchisement of Ex-felons

RICHARDSON v. RAMIREZ

Supreme Court of the United States, 1974
418 U.S. 24, 94 S. Ct. 2655, 41 L. Ed. 2d 551

The facts are stated in the opinion.

Mr Justice REHNQUIST delivered the opinion of the Court.

The three individual respondents in this case were convicted of felonies and have completed the service of their respective sentences and paroles. They filed a petition for a writ of mandate in the Supreme Court of California to compel California county election officials to register them as voters. They claimed, on behalf of themselves and others similarly situated, that application to them of the provisions of the California Constitution and implementing statutes which disenfranchised persons convicted of an "infamous crime" denied them the right to equal protection of the laws under the Federal Constitution. The Supreme Court of

California held that "as applied to all ex-felons whose terms of incarceration and parole have expired, the provisions . . . of the California Constitution denying the right of suffrage to persons convicted of crime, together with the several sections of the Elections Code implementing that disqualification . . . violate the equal protection clause of the Fourteenth Amendment." 9 Cal. 3d 199, 216–217, 507 P.2d 1345, 1357 (1973). We granted certiorari. . . .

Article XX, § 11, of the California Constitution has provided since its adoption in 1879 that "[l]aws shall be made" to exclude from voting persons convicted of bribery, perjury, forgery, malfeasance in office, "or other high crimes." At the time respondents were refused registration, former Art. II, § 1, of the California Constitution provided in part that "no alien ineligible to citizenship, no idiot, no insane person, no person convicted of any infamous crime, no person hereafter convicted of embezzlement or misappropriation of public money, and no person who shall not be able to read the Constitution in the English language and write his or her name, shall ever exercise the privileges of an elector in this State." Sections 310 and 321 of the California Elections Code provide that an affidavit of registration shall show whether the affiant has been convicted of "a felony which disqualifies [him] from voting." Sections 383, 389, and 390 direct the county clerk to cancel the registration of all voters who have been convicted of "any infamous crime or of the embezzlement or misappropriation of any public money." Sections 14240 and 14246 permit a voter's qualifications to be challenged on the ground that he has been convicted of "a felony" or of the "embezzlement or misappropriation of public money." California provides by statute for restoration of the right to vote to persons convicted of crime either by court order after the completion of probation, or, if a prison term was served, by executive pardon after completion of rehabilitation proceedings. California also provides a procedure by which a person refused registration may obtain judicial review of his disqualification.

Each of the individual respondents was convicted of one or more felonies, and served some time in jail or prison followed by a successfully terminated parole. . . . All three respondents were refused registration because of their felony convictions.

In May 1972 respondents filed a petition for a writ of mandate in the Supreme Court of California. . . . They named as defendants below the three election officials of San Luis Obispo, Monterey, and Stanislaus Counties who had refused to allow them to register. . . . The petition for a writ of mandate challenged the constitutionality of respondents' exclusion from the voting rolls on two grounds. First, it was contended that California's denial of the franchise to the class of ex-felons could no longer withstand scrutiny under the Equal Protection Clause of the Fourteenth Amendment. Relying on the Court's recent voting-rights cases, respondents argued that a compelling state interest must be found to justify exclusion of a class from the franchise, and that California could assert no such interest with respect to ex-felons. Second, respondents contended that application of the challenged California constitutional and statutory provisions by election officials of the State's 58 counties was so lacking in uniformity as to itself deny them due process and "geographical . . . equal protection." They appended a report by respondent California Secretary of State, and the questionnaires returned by county election officials on which it was based. The report concluded that there was wide variation in the county election officials' interpretation of the challenged voting exclusions. The Supreme Court of California upheld the first contention and therefore did not reach the second one.

* * *

Unlike most claims under the Equal Protection Clause, for the decision of which we have only the language of the Clause itself as it is embodied in the Fourteenth Amendment, respondents' claim implicates not merely the language of the Equal Protection Clause of § 1 of the Fourteenth Amendment, but also the provisions of the less familiar § 2 of the Amendment:

"Representatives shall be apportioned among the several States according to their respective numbers, counting the whole number of persons in each State, excluding Indians not taxed. But when the right to vote at any election for the choice of electors for President and Vice President of the United

States, Representatives in Congress, the Executive and Judicial officers of a State, or the members of the Legislature thereof, is denied to any of the male inhabitants of such State, being twenty-one years of age, and citizens of the United States, or in any way abridged, *except for participation in rebellion, or other crime,* the basis of representation therein shall be reduced in the proportion which the number of such male citizens shall bear to the whole number of male citizens twenty-one years of age in such State." (Emphasis supplied.)

Petitioner contends that the italicized language of § 2 expressly exempts from the sanction of that section disenfranchisement grounded on prior conviction of a felony. She goes on to argue that those who framed and adopted the Fourteenth Amendment could not have intended to prohibit outright in § 1 of that Amendment that which was expressly exempted from the lesser sanction of reduced representation imposed by § 2 of the Amendment. This argument seems to us a persuasive one unless it can be shown that the language of § 2, "except for participation in rebellion, or other crime," was intended to have a different meaning than would appear from its face.

. . . The legislative history bearing on the meaning of the relevant language of § 2 is scant indeed; the framers of the Amendment were primarily concerned with the effect of reduced representation upon the States, rather than with the two forms of disenfranchisement which were exempted from that consequence by the language with which we are concerned here. Nonetheless, what legislative history there is indicates that this language was intended by Congress to mean what it says.

* * *

[T]he historical understanding of the Fourteenth Amendment is confirmed by the decisions of this Court which have discussed the constitutionality of provisions disenfranchising felons. Although the Court has never given plenary consideration to the precise question of whether a State may constitutionally exclude some or all convicted felons from the franchise, we have indicated approval of such exclusions on a number of occasions. In two cases decided toward the end of the last century, the Court approved ex-

clusions of bigamists and polygamists from the franchise under territorial laws of Utah and Idaho. Murphy v. Ramsey, 114 U.S. 15 (1885); Davis v. Beason, 133 U.S. 333 (1890). Much more recently we have strongly suggested in dicta that exclusion of convicted felons from the franchise violates no constitutional provision. In Lassiter v. Northhampton County Board of Elections, 360 U.S. 45 (1959), where we upheld North Carolina's imposition of a literacy requirement for voting, the Court said: "Residence requirements, age, previous criminal record . . . are obvious examples indicating factors which a State may take into consideration in determining the qualifications of voters."

Still more recently, we have summarily affirmed two decisions of three-judge District Courts rejecting constitutional challenges to state laws disenfranchising convicted felons. . . .

Despite this settled historical and judicial understanding of the Fourteenth Amendment's effect on state laws disenfranchising convicted felons, respondents argue that our recent decisions invalidating other state-imposed restrictions on the franchise as violative of the Equal Protection Clause require us to invalidate the disenfranchisement of felons as well. . . .

[T]he exclusion of felons from the vote has an affirmative sanction in § 2 of the Fourteenth Amendment, a sanction which was not present in the case of the other restrictions on the franchise which were invalidated in the cases on which respondents rely. We hold that the understanding of those who adopted the Fourteenth Amendment, as reflected in the express language of § 2 and in the historical and judicial interpretation of the Amendment's applicability to state laws disenfranchising felons, is of controlling significance in distinguishing such laws from those other state limitations on the franchise which have been held invalid under the Equal Protection Clause by this Court. . . .

Pressed upon us by the respondents, and by amici curiae, are contentions . . . that the more modern view is that it is essential to the process of rehabilitating the ex-felon that he be returned to his role in society as a fully participating citizen when he has completed the serving of his term. We would by no means discount these arguments if addressed to the legislative forum which may properly weigh and balance them against those advanced in support of California's present constitutional provisions. But it is not for us to choose one set of values over the other. If respondents are correct, and the view which they advocate is indeed the more enlightened and sensible one, presumably the people of the State of California will ultimately come around to that view. And if they do not do so, their failure is some evidence, at least, of the fact that there are two sides to the argument.

We therefore hold that the Supreme Court of California erred in concluding that California may no longer, consistent with the Equal Protection Clause of the Fourteenth Amendment, exclude from the franchise convicted felons who have completed their sentences and paroles. . . .

Reversed and remanded.

[Mr. Justice MARSHALL, joined by Mr. Justice BRENNAN and Mr. Justice DOUGLAS, dissented.]

Comments

1. In *Richardson* v. *Ramirez*, supra, the Supreme Court upheld the right of a state to disenfranchise convicted felons on the basis of § 2 of the Fourteenth Amendment, which provides such disenfranchisement "for participation in rebellion, or other crime." Could a state consistent with § 2 disenfranchise convicted misdemeanants? Don't such offenders participate in crimes? What about nonconvicted participants? Or does "participation" imply a lawful conviction? Would the Supreme Court have upheld the California disenfranchisement provision if the issue had been decided on traditional equal protection tests; i.e., "reasonable-rational basis" or "compelling state interest" tests? What is the rational basis for denying an offender the right to vote, especially if the crime involved had nothing to do with the ballot box? What compelling state interests are advanced by the disenfranchisement of all convicted felons?

2. Convicted felons are subject to other disabilities and disqualifications apart from the possible loss of liberty and the right to vote. These additional legal deprivations are known as the *collateral consequences* of conviction. Whether certain civil rights are lost or retained following a felony conviction depends, for the most part, on the laws of each jurisdiction. Only the most generalized statements about the collateral consequences of conviction can be made absent an intensive study of the laws within a particular jurisdiction, and such a study is difficult because the applicable statutes are often scattered throughout the statute books rather than being collected in a single section. The Vanderbilt Law Review has made an exhaustive study of the collateral consequences of a criminal conviction throughout the United States; it is reported in *The Collateral Consequences of Criminal Convictions,* 23 Vand. L. Rev. 929 (1970).

Civil rights other than the right to vote that may be lost following a criminal conviction include the right (1) to serve on a jury, (2) to hold public office, (3) to make or enforce a contract, (4) to sue, (5) to make a will or inherit property, (6) to collect insurance, pension, or workmen's compensation benefits, and (7) to obtain a license for certain occupations. Ex-offenders may be denied licenses to practice the trades of (1) barber, (2) architect, (3) engineer, (4) teacher, (5) realtor, (6) cosmetologist, (7) physician, (8) attorney, (9) dentist, (10) dry cleaner, (11) pharmacist, (12) nurse, (13) undertaker, (14) notary public, (15) insurance adjustor, (16) liquor dealer,

(17) private detective, and (18) law enforcement officer. Almost all states have some licensing restrictions for ex-offenders.

Some studies have shown that unemployment is a major factor in the increase in crime and that regular employment is directly related to a low recidivism rate. Glasser, D., *The Effectiveness of a Prison and Parole System* (1964). In light of this, barriers to employment in the form of licensing restrictions are particularly significant since most offenders already have low employability. It is a cruel hoax to train an inmate in prison for a certain occupation as part of the rehabilitation process and then deny him the right to practice that occupation upon release because of licensing regulations.

3. The civil disabilities incurred following a criminal conviction may be permanent or may apply only during the period of imprisonment. All jurisdictions provide methods for restoring civil rights. The oldest form of relief is the *pardon.* The pardoning process is usually the responsibility of the governor, the pardoning board, or both. The pardon is generally reserved for cases in which the evidence shows probable innocence or in which the judicial process has produced an unfair result. Pardons given prior to a criminal conviction (as in the case of President Nixon) are extremely rare. Why did President Ford pardon President Nixon? Probable innocence? Unfair result? In *Burdick* v. *United States*, 236 U.S. 79 (1915), the Supreme Court held that the acceptance of a pardon is an implied admission of guilt.

    In approximately one fourth of the states, an offender's civil rights are automatically restored upon the successful completion of probation, parole, or sentence. In other jurisdictions, the civil rights of an offender are restored at the discretion of the parole board or the court in which the sentence was imposed. Unfortunately, the restoration procedures are often ineffective because so many offenders lack the knowledge or ability to utilize them.

4. Most states permanently deny the right to vote to convicted felons. The underlying rationale is that incarcerated offenders have no compelling personal interest in the outcome of the election and that disenfranchisement prevents election fraud and keeps ex-felons from voting to repeal provisions of the criminal code. Are these fears justified?

10

THE CIVIL RIGHTS ACT OF 1964 AND THE CONSTITUTIONAL RIGHTS OF LAW ENFORCEMENT AUTHORITIES

10.01 INTRODUCTION: THE CONSTITUTIONAL TORT — 42 U.S.C. § 1983

The Fourteenth Amendment to the United States Constitution was proposed to the states by Congress in April, 1866. Sometimes called the "Civil War Amendment," it was enacted primarily to guarantee blacks and other minority groups full enjoyment of their constitutional rights. The Fourteenth Amendment provides, inter alia: "No State shall . . . deny to any person within its jurisdiction the equal protection of the laws."

The nucleus of the Fourteenth Amendment was the Civil Rights Act of 1865. Designed to protect the rights of freedmen in the South, the legislation called for extension of the jurisdiction of the federal district courts and charged federal marshals and federal attorneys with enforcement of the act.[1] Although the act was vetoed by President Johnson, Congress was able to muster the two-thirds vote necessary to override the

veto. Thereafter, concerned that the United States Supreme Court might strike down the new law, Congress submitted to the states a proposed constitutional amendment that embodied the provisions of the original Civil Rights Act. On the advice of President Johnson, all southern states except Tennessee initially rejected the new amendment; however, it was finally ratified on July 28, 1868.

The draftsmen of the Fourteenth Amendment, determined to "give teeth" to the amendment, included an *enabling clause* that granted Congress power to enforce the amendment through legislation. Section 5 provides: "The Congress shall have power to enforce, by appropriate legislation, the provisions of this article." In 1880, the Supreme Court acknowledged the constitutional validity of § 5 in *Ex parte Virginia,* 100 U.S. 399 (1880). In that case, the Supreme Court noted that "some legislation was contemplated to make the amendment *fully effective*" (emphasis added), and that view was most recently reaffirmed in *Katzenbach v. Morgan,* 384 U.S. 641 (1966).

During Reconstruction, secret organizations arose in the South that used terror and force to deny to blacks their newly bestowed

---

[1]Fielding, R. K., *The United States: An Interpretive History* 301 (1964).

political franchise. Their names are legion—Knights of the Black Cross, Knights of the White Camellia, the White Brotherhood, the Red Jackets, Native Sons of the South—but none became as famous as the Ku Klux Klan. The Klan engaged in shootings and lynchings and used various means of intimidation to keep blacks from the polls. In addition, they drove out carpetbaggers and silenced teachers and preachers whom they considered disloyal to southern traditions.[2]

Apprised of the lawless conditions in the South, Congress, on April 20, 1871, chose to exercise the power vested in it by § 5 of the Fourteenth Amendment. To enforce the provisions of the amendment, Congress passed the famous Civil Rights Act of 1871 (17 Stat. 13), often referred to as the Ku Klux Act. Section 1 of the Act (later codified in 1875 as R.S. § 1979) established a federal remedy for violations of an individual's constitutional rights done under color of state law, and provided that the violators would "be liable to the party injured in any action at law, suit in equity, or other proper proceeding for redress; such proceeding to be prosecuted in the . . . district or circuit courts of the United States." The 1871 legislation was later incorporated in the Civil Rights Act of 1964, under which the earlier § 1 (R.S. § 1979) was retitled 42 U.S.C. § 1983. (The text of § 1983 is presented on p. 738.)

The purpose of § 1983 is to provide a civil action for damages for persons injured by the misuse of power vested in the defendant by state law and made possible because the defendant was clothed with the authority of the state.[3] Although such civil actions can be brought in state courts,[4] most are filed in the United States district courts under 28 U.S.C. § 1343(c).[5] Since § 1983 allows for redress of a private and personal wrong (in contrast to a crime, which is perceived as a public and societal wrong) it is often referred to as the "constitutional tort" statute.

The term "tort" is from the Latin "tortquere," which means "to twist" or "to wrest aside."[6] A tort can be described as a civil wrong that results in harm, or that is about to result in harm, that can be compensated in an action at law. The action brought is referred to as a *damage suit* and its purpose is to redress wrongs done to the individual. The Supreme Court noted in *Monroe* v. *Pape,* 365 U.S. 167 (1961) (infra, § 10.02), that 42 U.S.C. § 1983 "should be read against the background of tort liability that makes a man responsible for the natural consequences of his actions."

To bring a successful tort action, a plaintiff must show three essential elements: (1) the existence of a legal duty owed by the defendant to the plaintiff, (2) a breach of that duty, and (3) injury suffered as the proximate result.[7] Although most tort actions require the showing of a tangible physical injury to the plaintiff or his property, a tort can also be committed when there is a direct invasion of a legal right of the plaintiff. It is for such intangible injuries that § 1983 provides redress.

The elements of a cause of action under 42 U.S.C. § 1983 include (1) conduct engaged in under color of law (2) that deprived the plaintiff of rights, privileges, or immunities secured to him by the federal Constitution or federal statutes Otherwise to maintain an action under § 1983, the plaintiff must allege and prove the denial of a federally protected right. Relief available under § 1983 includes injunctions, writs of mandamus, declaratory judgments and monetary damages.[8] A plaintiff who can prove actual damages can recover such damages from a defendant who deprived him of his civil rights. On the other hand, nominal damages can be recovered without a showing of actual damages; the plantiff need only show that he was deprived of a right to which he was entitled. Finally, exemplary, or punitive, damages are available to the injured party

---

[2]Id. at 307.

[3]Antieau, C. J., *Federal Civil Rights Act* 49 (1971), citing *Davis* v. *Johnson,* 138 F. Supp. 572 (D. Ill. 1955), and *Jobson* v. *Henne,* 355 F.2d 129 (2d Cir. 1966).

[4]*Hirych* v. *State,* 376 Mich. 384, 136 N.W.2d 910 (1965).

[5]28 U.S.C. § 1343 provides, inter alia: "The district courts shall have original jurisdiction of any civil action authorized by law to be commenced by any person."

[6]*Black's Law Dictionary* 1660 (4th ed. 1968).

[7]Id., citing *City of Mobile* v. *McClure,* 127 So. 832, at 835.

[8]Kerper, H. B., and Kerper, J., *Legal Rights of the Convicted* 368, 371 (1974). See also *Marshall* v. *Sawyer,* 301 F.2d 639 (9th Cir. 1962).

under § 1983. (For a further discussion of the different types of damages, see p. 739.) It should be noted that under the controlling provisions of Rule 23 of the Federal Rules of Civil Procedure,[9] plaintiffs can bring *class actions* to vindicate § 1983 rights.

Anyone can sue for the deprivation of a civil right under 42 U.S.C. § 1983. One does not have to be a United States citizen to assert such a claim, and aliens can use § 1983 to vindicate their due process and equal protection rights, as well as their rights under federal statutes intended by Congress for their protection.[10] As the United States District Court for the Southern District of New York indicated in *Robeson* v. *Fanelli*, 94 F. Supp. 62 (1950), "This section [§ 1983] protects *all persons* within the jurisdiction of the respective states, whether citizens or not" (emphasis added).

Section 1983 provides for the protection of "rights, privileges, or immunities secured by the Constitution and laws." The rights to be protected are principally (1) due process rights, (2) equal protection rights, (3) privileges and immunities of citizens, (4) rights owing their existence to federal functions, and (5) rights created by federal statutes.[11] From a procedural standpoint, the existence of a state remedy does not bar a plaintiff's recovery under § 1983, nor is there a requirement that available state remedies be exhausted prior to the commencement of an action in federal district court. The United States Supreme Court noted in *Monroe* v. *Pape,* supra, that "it is no answer that the state has a law which . . . would give relief. The federal remedy is *supplementary* to the state remedy, and the latter need not first be sought and refused before the federal one is invoked" (emphasis added).

Before a person can be named a defendant in a § 1983 suit, he must be shown (1) to be a "person" within the meaning of the statute and (2) to have been "acting under color of" law or acting in concert with one who was acting under color of law, at the time of the alleged civil rights deprivation. Although it is true that under certain circumstances a private individual might be liable under the statute, the term "person" has generally been held to mean public servants employed by a state, a territory, or a political subdivision thereof; e.g., a state or city police officer or a county coroner. The political entity itself is not liable because it is not considered a "person" within the meaning of § 1983. For example, in *Monroe* v. *Pape,* supra, the Supreme Court noted that "Congress did not undertake to bring municipal corporations within the ambit of [§ 1983]." Likewise, the lower federal courts have held that a state, a city police department, and a county board of supervisors are not "persons" for purposes of the statute. However, state and quasi-state officials are "persons" and hence are liable under § 1983, provided the suit alleges that a deprivation of rights occurred as a result of their abuse of their power.[12]

The phrase "acting under color of law" has been interpreted to mean "carrying out the tasks or obligations assigned,"[13] and to refer to the "misuse of power, possessed by virtue of state law and made possible only because the wrongdoer is clothed with the authority of state law."[14] The Supreme Court held in *Screws* v. *United States,* 325 U.S. 91 (1945), that "acts of [state] officers who undertake to perform their official duties are included whether they hew to the line of their authority or overstep it." It should be noted that case law does not support the application of the doctrine of *respondeat superior* ("let the master [in this case the state's higher officials] be responsible") in civil rights actions: personal involvement in the unlawful activity is required.[15] Thus, police supervisory personnel are not liable under § 1983 for injuries done by their subordi-

---

[12]Kerper and Kerper, supra note 8, at 370, citing *Williford* v. *People of California*, 352 F.2d 474 (9th Cir. 1965); *United States ex rel. Lee* v. *People of State of Illinois,* 343 F.2d 120 (7th Cir. 1965); *Monroe* v. *Pape,* 365 U.S. 167 (1961); *Spampinato* v. *City of New York,* 311 F.2d 439 (2d Cir. 1962); *Roberts* v. *Williams,* 302 F. Supp. 972 (N.D. Miss. 1969); *Sostre* v. *McGinnis,* 442 F.2d 178 (2d Cir. 1971). See also *Marshall* v. *Sawyer,* 301 F.2d 639 (9th Cir. 1962).

[13]See *Monroe* v. *Pape,* 365 U.S. at 183.

[14] See *Williams* v. *United States,* 341 U.S. 97 (1951).

[15]See *Salazar* v. *Dowd,* 256 F. Supp. 220 (D. Colo. 1966).

---

[9]Antieau, supra note 3, at 51.
[10]Id. at 50.
[11]Id. at 75, 76.

nates unless the supervisors personally participated in the act.[16]

Public servants may be held to act under color of state law, and thus be liable under § 1983, even when they act in violation of established state law. For example, in *Marshall* v. *Sawyer,* 301 F.2d 639 (1962), the United States Court of Appeals for the Ninth Circuit concluded that "defendants' conduct . . . was under color of state law if they were clothed with the authority of the state and were purporting to act thereunder, whether or not the conduct was authorized, or, indeed, even if it was proscribed by state law."

Section 1983 also extends liability to persons who violate another's civil rights "under color of . . . any custom . . . of any State or Territory." The Supreme Court held in *Adickes* v. *S. H. Kress & Co.,* 398 U.S.

144 (1970), that for purposes of the federal statute, a custom "must have the force of law by virtue of the persistent practices of state officials." In *Adickes,* the plaintiff sought to show that the State of Mississippi enforced a custom of racial segregation in public restaurants.

As mentioned, a private citizen may also be named as a defendant in a § 1983 suit if he acts in concert with public employees to deprive another of his civil rights. In *Fulton* v. *Emerson Electric Co.,* 420 F.2d 527 (1969), the United States Court of Appeals for the Fifth Circuit stated: "Concerted action of private parties and state officials has consistently been held to be sufficient allegation of 'state action' for 42 U.S.C. § 1983."[17]

---

[16]See, e.g., *Jordan* v. *Kelly,* 233 F. Supp. 731 (D. Mo. 1963); *Sanburg* v. *Daley,* 306 F. Supp. 277 (D. Ill. 1969). In *Jordan* v. *Kelly,* supra, the district court stated: "[the police chief] is not responsible for their [officers'] acts unless he has directed such acts to be done, or has personally co-operated in the offense. . . ." See also *Nolen* v. *Fitzharris,* 450 F.2d 958 (9th Cir. 1971).

[17]See also *Johnson* v. *Crumlish,* 224 F. Supp. 22 (D. Pa. 1963). It should be noted that in addition to liability under § 1983, "if two or more persons conspire" to deprive an individual of his civil rights, they are also subject to a civil suit under 42 U.S.C. § 1985 and to criminal prosecution under 18 U.S.C. § 241. For an extended discussion of the liability of private persons under 42 U.S.C. § 1983, see Antieau, supra note 3, at 55–63. See also *Gillibeau* v. *City of Richmond,* 417 F.2d 426 (9th Cir. 1969).

10.02 THE CIVIL RIGHTS ACT

A. § 1983 ACTIONS

Acting "Under Color of" Law

MONROE v. PAPE

Supreme Court of the United States, 1961
365 U.S. 167, 81 S. Ct. 473, 5 L. Ed. 2d 492

Pursuant to 28 U.S.C. § 1343, the plaintiff, James Monroe, filed suit in federal district court against 13 Chicago police officers and the city of Chicago for violation of R.S. § 1979 (42 U.S.C. § 1983) of the federal Civil Rights Act. The complaint alleged, inter alia, that the officers broke into his home without a warrant, routed him and his family from bed, made them stand naked in the living room, and ransacked every room in his house. Monroe further claimed that he was taken to the police station and detained on "open charges" for ten hours and that during that period he was denied assistance of counsel. Plaintiff argued that such action constituted a deprivation of his civil rights and was done "under color of" state statutes and city ordinances. The District Court for the Northern District of Illinois dismissed the complaint and the United States Court of Appeals for the Seventh Circuit affirmed. The United States Supreme Court granted certiorari.

Mr. Justice DOUGLAS delivered the opinion of the Court.

* * *

I

Petitioners claim that the invasion of their home and the subsequent search without a warrant and the arrest and detention of Mr. Monroe without a warrant and without arraignment constituted a deprivation of their "rights, privileges, or immunities secured by the Constitution" within the meaning of R.S. § 1979 [42 U.S.C. § 1983]. It has been said that when 18 U.S.C. § 241, 18 U.S.C.A. § 241, made criminal a conspiracy "to injure, oppress, threaten, or intimidate any citizen in the free exercise or enjoyment of any right or privilege secured to him by the Constitution," it embraced only rights that an individual has by reason of his relation to the central government, not to state governments. . . . But the history of the section of the Civil Rights Act presently involved does not permit such a narrow interpretation.

Section 1979 came onto the books as § 1 of the Ku Klux Act of April 20, 1871. 17 Stat. 13. It was one of the means whereby Congress exercised the power vested in it by § 5 of the Fourteenth Amendment to enforce the provisions of that Amendment. . . . Its purpose is plain from the title of the legislation, "An Act to enforce the Provisions of the Fourteenth Amendment to the Constitution of the United States, and for other Purposes." 17 Stat. 13. Allegation of facts constituting a deprivation under color of state authority of a right guaranteed by the Fourteenth Amendment satisfies to that extent the requirement of R.S. § 1979. . . . So far petitioners are on solid ground. For the guarantee against unreasonable searches and seizures contained in the Fourth Amendment has been made applicable to the States by reason of the Due Process Clause of the Fourteenth Amendment. . . .

II

There can be no doubt at least since Ex parte Virginia, 100 U.S. 339, 346–347 (1880), that Congress has the power to enforce provisions of the Fourteenth Amendment against those who carry a badge of authority of a State and represent it in some capacity, whether they act in accordance with their authority or misuse it. . . . The question with which we now deal is the narrower one of whether Congress, in enacting § 1979, meant to give a remedy to parties deprived of constitutional rights, privileges and immunities by an official's abuse of his position. . . .

It is argued that "under color of" enumerated state authority excludes acts of an official or policeman who can show no authority under state law, state custom, or state usage to do what he did. In this case it is said that these policemen, in breaking into petitioners' apartment, violated the Constitution and laws of Illinois. It is pointed out that under Illinois law a simple remedy is offered for that violation and that, so far as it appears, the courts of Illinois are available to give petitioners that full redress which the common law affords for violence done to a person; and it is earnestly argued that no "statute, ordinance, regulation, custom or usage" of Illinois bars that redress.

* * *

. . . It is no answer that the State has a law which if enforced would give relief. The federal remedy is supplementary to the state remedy, and the latter need not be first sought and refused before the federal one is invoked. Hence the fact that Illinois by its constitution and laws outlaws unreasonable searches and seizures is no barrier to the present suit in the federal court.

We had before us in United States v. Classic, [313 U.S. 299 (1941)], § 20 of the Criminal Code, 18 U.S.C. § 242, 18 U.S.C.A. § 242, which provides a criminal punishment for anyone who "under color of any law, statute, ordinance, regulation, or custom" subjects any inhabitant of a State to the deprivation of "any rights, privileges, or immunities secured or protected by the Constitution or laws of the United States." . . . The right involved in the Classic case was the right of voters in a primary to have their votes counted. The laws of Louisiana required the defendants "to count the ballots, to record the result of the count, and to certify the result of the election." . . . But according to the indictment they did not perform their duty. In an opinion written by Mr. Justice (later Chief Justice) Stone, in which Mr. Justice Roberts, Mr. Justice

Reed, and Mr. Justice Frankfurter joined, the Court ruled, "Misuse of power, possessed by virtue of state law and made possible only because the wrongdoer is clothed with the authority of state law, is action taken 'under color of' state law." . . . There was a dissenting opinion; but the ruling as to the meaning of "under color of" state law was not questioned.

That view of the meaning of the words "under color of" state law, 18 U.S.C. § 242, 18 U.S.C.A. § 242, was reaffirmed in Screws v. United States, 325 U.S. 108–113 (1945). . . . The acts there complained of were committed by state officers in performance of their duties, viz., making an arrest effective. It was urged there, as it is here, that "under color of" state law should not be construed to duplicate in federal law what was an offense under state law.

It was said there, as it is here, that the ruling in the Classic case as to the meaning of "under color of" state law was not in focus and was ill-advised. . . . It was argued there, as it is here, that "under color of" state law included only action taken by officials pursuant to state law. . . . We rejected that view. We stated:

"The construction given § 20 [18 U.S.C. § 242, 18 U.S.C.A. § 242] in the Classic case formulated a rule of law which has become the basis of federal enforcement in this important field. The rule adopted in that case was formulated after mature consideration. . . ."

We adhered to that view in Williams v. United States, 341 U.S. 99 (1951). . . .

We conclude that the meaning given "under color of" law in the Classic case and in the Screws and Williams cases was the correct one; and we adhere to it.

In the Screws case we dealt with a statute that imposed criminal penalties for acts "wilfully"done. We construed that word in its setting to mean the doing of an act with "a specific intent to deprive a person of a federal right." . . . We do not think that gloss should be placed on § 1979 which we have here. The word "wilfully" does not appear in § 1979. Moreover, § 1979 provides a civil remedy, while in the Screws case we dealt with a criminal law challenged on the ground of vagueness. Section 1979 should be read against the background of tort liability that makes a man responsible for the natural consequences of his actions.

So far, then, the complaint states a cause of action. There remains to consider only a defense peculiar to the City of Chicago.

III

The City of Chicago asserts that it is not liable under § 1979. We do not stop to explore the whole range of questions tendered us on this issue at oral argument and in the briefs. For we are of the opinion that Congress did not undertake to bring municipal corporations within the ambit of § 1979.

* * *

. . . Accordingly we hold that the motion to dismiss the complaint against the City of Chicago was properly granted. But since the complaint should not have been dismissed against the officials the judgment must be and is reversed.

* * *

[Mr. Justice HARLAN joined Mr. Justice STEWART, concurring.]
[Mr. Justice FRANKFURTER dissented except insofar as the Court held that this action could not be maintained against the City of Chicago.]

Comments

1. The majority in *Monroe* v. *Pape,* supra, observed that the word "wilfully" does not appear in § 1983 as it does in its criminal counterpart, 18 U.S.C.A. § 242. Therefore, in § 1983 actions it is not necessary for the plaintiff to show that the defendant acted with "a specific intent to deprive [the plaintiff] of a federal right." Following the Supreme Court's lead, the United States Court of

Appeals (5th Cir.) held in *Whirl* v. *Kern,* 407 F.2d 781 (1968), that "the Supreme Court [has] noted that a complaint under the Civil Rights Act [§ 1983] should not be dismissed for failure to show 'specific intent' " (citing *Monroe* v. *Pape*). The court of appeals noted further: "We do not find in . . . the language of the [Civil Rights] Act itself any intimation that an invasion of constitutional rights *unaccompanied by an improper motive* lies beyond the reach of the statute" (emphasis added).

2. The United States Supreme Court held in *Pierson* v. *Ray,* 386 U.S. 547 (1967), that "the defense of good faith and probable cause, which [is] available in . . . common law action for false arrest and imprisonment, is also available . . . in the action under § 1983." However, the Court made it clear that such a holding did not mean that "the count based thereon should be dismissed." The Court suggested that such a defense is proper, but is a jury question: "If the jury . . . believed . . . and found that the officers reasonably believed in good faith that the arrest was constitutional, then a verdict for the officers would follow even though the arrest was in fact unconstitutional," supra at 557.

3. While it is true that in a common law tort suit a showing of absence of negligence may be a proper defense, it is still unclear whether or not a finding of nonnegligence will support a finding of good faith in a § 1983 action. For example, the court of appeals in *Whirl,* supra, noted: "While the issue of Sheriff Kern's 'good faith' in confining Whirl in prison was never . . . presented to the jury, we do not involve ourselves in the semantics of whether or not a finding of non-negligence is tantamount to a finding of good faith. As we read *Pierson* v. *Ray* and *Monroe* v. *Pape,* neither good faith nor non-negligence can exculpate Kern from liability." However, it is interesting to note that the United States Court of Appeals (2d Cir.) ruled that the good faith slaying of a fleeing felony suspect was not actionable under § 1983 because the Connecticut common law rule as stated in *Martyn* v. *Donlin,* 198 A.2d 700 (1964) "affords a *privilege* . . . to an officer using deadly force who *reasonably believes* such force is necessary to effect an arrest for a felony" (emphasis added). The court of appeals noted that although "a federal court interpreting the scope of [§ 1983] is not bound by the state law of torts or defenses of privilege which that law provides, . . . States must . . . be given some leeway with respect to officers' privilege for use of deadly force. . . ." *Jones* v. *Marshall,* 528 F.2d 132 (2d Cir. 1975).

4. As noted earlier, there is a federal statute, 42 U.S.C.A. § 242, that authorizes criminal prosecution for one who violates the constitutional rights of another. The statute, provides, inter alia: "Whoever, under color of any law, statute, ordinance, regulation, or custom, wilfully subjects any inhabitant of any State, Territory, or District to the deprivation of rights, privileges, or immunities secured . . . by the Constitution or laws of the United States . . . shall be fined not more than $1,000 or imprisoned not more than one year, or both; and if death results shall be subject to imprisonment for any term of years or for life."

Application to Federal Agents

BIVENS v. SIX UNKNOWN NAMED AGENTS OF THE FEDERAL BUREAU OF NARCOTICS

Supreme Court of the United States, 1971
403 U.S. 388, 91 S. Ct. 1999, 29 L. Ed. 2d 619

On July 7, 1967, the petitioner, Webster Bivens, filed suit in the federal District Court for the Eastern District of New York to recover damages in the amount of $15,000 from six agents of the Federal Bureau of Narcotics. Bivens' complaint alleged that the respondent agents, acting under color of federal law, made a warrantless entry of his apartment, searched it, and arrested him on a narcotics charge; all without probable cause. The district court dismissed the complaint on the ground, inter alia, that it failed to state a cause of action. The Court of Appeals (2d Cir.) affirmed, and the United States Supreme Court granted certiorari.

Mr. Justice BRENNAN delivered the opinion of the Court.

The Fourth Amendment provides that:

"The right of the people to be secure in their persons, houses, papers, and effects against unreasonable searches and seizures, shall not be violated. . . ."

In Bell v. Hood, 327 U.S. 678 (1946), we reserved the question whether violation of that command by a federal agent acting under color of his authority gives rise to a cause of action for damages consequent upon his unconstitutional conduct. Today we hold that it does.

* * *

I

Respondents do not argue that petitioner should be entirely without remedy for an unconstitutional invasion of his rights by federal agents. In respondents' view, however, the rights that petitioner asserts — primarily rights of privacy — are creations of state and not federal law. Accordingly, they argue, petitioner may obtain money damages to redress invasion of these rights only by an action in tort, under state law, in the state courts. In this scheme the Fourth Amendment would serve merely to limit the extent to which the agents could defend the state law tort suit by asserting that their actions were a valid exercise of federal power: if the agents were shown to have violated the Fourth Amendment, such a defense would be lost to them and they would stand before the state law merely as private individuals. Candidly admitting that it is the policy of the Department of Justice to remove all such suits from the state to the federal courts for decision, respondents nevertheless urge that we uphold dismissal of petitioner's complaint in federal court, and remit him to filing an action in the state courts in order that the case may properly be removed to the federal court for decision on the basis of state law.

We think that respondents' thesis rests upon an unduly restrictive view of the Fourth Amendment's protection against unreasonable searches and seizures by federal agents, a view that has consistently been rejected by this Court. Respondents seek to treat the relationship between a citizen and a federal agent unconstitutionally exercising his authority as no different from the relationship between two private citizens. In so doing, they ignore the fact that power, once granted, does not disappear like a magic gift when it is wrongfully used. An agent acting — albeit unconstitutionally — in the name of the United States possesses a far greater capacity for harm than an individual trespasser exercising no authority other than his own. . . . Accordingly, as our cases make clear, the Fourth Amendment operates as a limitation upon the exercise of federal power regardless of whether the State in whose jurisdiction that power is exercised would prohibit or penalize the identical act if engaged in by a private citizen. It guarantees to citizens of the United States the absolute right to be free from unreasonable searches and seizures carried out by virtue of federal authority. And "where federally protected rights have been invaded, it has been the rule from the beginning that courts will be alert to adjust their remedies so as to grant the necessary relief." . . .

First. Our cases have long since rejected the notion that the Fourth Amendment proscribes only such conduct as would, if engaged in by private persons, be condemned by state law. Thus in Gambino v. United States, 275 U.S. 310 (1927), . . . petitioners were convicted of conspiracy to violate the National Prohibition Act on the basis of evidence seized by state police officers incident to petitioners' arrest by those officers solely for the purpose of enforcing federal law. . . . Notwithstanding the lack of probable cause for the arrest . . . it would have been permissible under state law if effected by private individuals. It appears, moreover, that the officers were under direction from the Governor to aid in the enforcement of federal law. . . . Accordingly, if the Fourth Amendment reached only to conduct impermissible under the law of the State, the Amendment would have had no application to the case. Yet this Court held the Fourth Amendment applicable and reversed petitioners' convictions as having been based upon evidence obtained through an unconstitutional search and seizure. Similarly, in Byars v. United States, 273 U.S. 28 (1927), . . . the petitioner was convicted on the basis of evidence seized under a warrant issued, without probable cause under the Fourth Amendment, by a state court judge for a state law offense. At the invitation of state law enforcement officers, a federal prohibition agent participated in the search. This Court explicitly refused to inquire whether the warrant was "good under the state law . . . since in no event could it constitute the basis for a *federal* search and seizure." . . . And our recent decisions regarding electronic surveillance have made it clear beyond peradventure that the Fourth Amendment is not tied to the niceties of local trespass laws. . . . In light of these cases, respondents' argument that the Fourth Amendment serves only as a limita-tion on federal defenses to a state law claim, and not as an independent limitation upon the exercise of federal power, must be rejected.

Second. The interests protected by state laws regulating trespass and the invasion of privacy, and those protected by the Fourth Amendment's guarantee against unreasonable searches and seizures may be inconsistent or even hostile. Thus, we may bar the door against an unwelcome private intruder, or call the police if he persists in seeking entrance. The availability of such alternative means for the protection of privacy may lead the State to restrict imposition of liability for any consequent trespass. A private citizen, asserting no authority other than his own, will not normally be liable in trespass if he demands, and is granted, admission to another's house. . . . But one who demands admission under a claim of federal authority stands in a far different position. . . . The mere invocation of federal power by a federal law enforcement official will normally render futile any attempt to resist an unlawful entry or arrest by resort to the local police; and a claim of authority to enter is likely to unlock the door as well. . . . "In such cases there is no safety for the citizen, except in the protection of the judicial tribunals, for rights which have been invaded by the officers of the government, professing to act in its name. There remains to him but the alternative of resistance, which may amount to crime." United States v. Lee, 106 U.S. 196 (1882). Nor is it adequate to answer that state law may take into account the different status of one clothed with the authority of the Federal Government. For just as state law may not authorize federal agents to violate the Fourth Amendment, . . . neither may state law undertake to limit the extent to which federal authority can be exercised. . . . The inevitable consequence of this dual limitation on state power is that the federal question becomes not merely a possible defense to the state law action, but an independent claim both necessary and sufficient to make out the plaintiff's cause of action. . . .

Third. That damages may be obtained for injuries consequent upon a violation of the Fourth Amendment by federal officials should hardly seem a surprising proposition. Historically, damages have been regarded as the ordinary remedy for an invasion of personal interests in liberty. . . .

Of course, the Fourth Amendment does not in so many words provide for its enforcement by an award of money damages for the consequences of its violation. But "it is . . . well settled that where legal rights have been invaded, and a federal statute provides for a general right to sue for such invasion, federal courts may use any available remedy to make good the wrong done." . . . The present case involves no special factors counselling hesitation in the absence of affirmative action by Congress. . . . Finally, we cannot accept respondents' formulation of the question as whether the availability of money damages is necessary to enforce the Fourth Amendment. For we have here no explicit congressional declaration that persons injured by a federal officer's violation of the Fourth Amendment may not recover money damages from the agents, but must instead be remitted to another remedy, equally effective in the view of Congress. The question is merely whether petitioner, if he can demonstrate an injury consequent upon the violation by federal agents of his Fourth Amendment rights, is entitled to redress his injury through a particular remedial mechanism normally available in the federal courts. . . . "The very essence of civil liberty certainly consists in the right of every individual to claim the protection of the laws, whenever he receives an injury." . . . Having concluded that petitioner's complaint states a cause of action under the Fourth Amendment . . . we hold that petitioner is entitled to recover money damages for any injuries he has suffered as a result of the agents' violation of the Amendment.

II

In addition to holding that petitioner's complaint had failed to state facts making out a cause of action, the District Court ruled that in any event respondents were immune from liability by virtue of their official position. . . . This question was not passed upon by the Court of Appeals, and accordingly we do not consider it here. . . .

Judgment reversed and case remanded.

[Mr. Justice HARLAN concurred.]

Mr. Chief Justice BURGER, dissenting.

I dissent from today's holding which judicially creates a damage remedy not provided for by the Constitution and not enacted by Congress. We would more surely preserve the important values of the doctrine of separation of powers—and perhaps get a better result—by recommending a solution to the Congress as the branch of government in which the Constitution has vested the legislative power. Legislation is the business of the Congress, and it has the facilities and competence for that task—as we do not. . . .

* * *

I conclude, therefore, that an entirely different remedy is necessary but it is one that in my view is as much beyond judicial power as the step the Court takes today. Congress should develop an administrative or quasi-judicial remedy against the government itself to afford compensation and restitution for persons whose Fourth Amendment rights have been violated. The venerable doctrine of respondeat superior in our tort law provides an entirely appropriate conceptual basis for this remedy. If, for example, a security guard privately employed by a department store commits an assault or other tort on a customer such as an improper search, the victim has a simple and obvious remedy—an action for money damages against the guard's employer, the department store. . . . Such a statutory scheme would have the added advantage of providing some remedy to the completely innocent persons who are sometimes the victims of illegal police conduct—something that the suppression doctrine, of course, can never accomplish.

* * *

[Mr. Justice BLACK and Mr. Justice BLACKMUN filed dissenting opinions.]

Comment

1. Mr. Justice Douglas noted in *Monroe* v. *Pape*, 365 U.S. 167 (1961), supra: "It is abundantly clear that the legislation [Civil Rights Act of 1871] was passed to afford a federal right in federal courts because

. . . state laws might not be enforced and the claims of citizens to the enjoyment of rights . . . guaranteed by the Fourteenth Amendment might be denied by the state agencies." 42 U.S.C. § 1983, derived from that act, was intended as a remedy for persons injured by acts done "under color of" state or territorial law. Thus, it was not intended for application to federal officers. However, Mr. Justice Brennan, writing for the majority in *Bivens,* supra, found that a complaint alleging that the Fourth Amendment has been violated by federal agents acting "under color of" federal law does give rise to a cause of action for damages. The action is not unlike a simple tort suit between private citizens and is actionable under 28 U.S.C. § 1331(a), which provides: "The district courts shall have original jurisdiction of all civil actions wherein the matter in controversy exceeds the sum or value of $10,000, exclusive of interest and costs, and arises under the Constitution, laws, or treaties of the United States." Webster Bivens sought to recover damages in the amount of $15,000 from the six narcotics agents.

When a Person Is Falsely Named in a Police Flyer as an "Active Shoplifter"

PAUL v. DAVIS

Supreme Court of the United States, 1976
424 U.S. 693, 96 S. Ct. 1155, 47 L. Ed. 2d 405

In June, 1971, respondent, Edward Davis, was arrested on a charge of shoplifting. In December, 1972, petitioner police chiefs distributed a flyer to 800 area merchants containing names and photos of "active shoplifters" in Louisville, Kentucky. Respondent's picture and name appeared on page two of the flyer. Shortly after circulation of the flyer, the outstanding charge against respondent was dismissed by a judge of the Louisville Police Court. Respondent thereupon brought action under 42 U.S.C. § 1983 against petitioners. The District Court for the Western District of Kentucky dismissed the complaint. On appeal, the Court of Appeals (6th Cir.) concluded that respondent had set forth a claim under § 1983, basing its decision on *Wisconsin* v. *Constantineau,* 400 U.S. 433 (1971). The United States Supreme Court granted certiorari.

Mr. Justice REHNQUIST delivered the opinion of the Court.

We granted certiorari . . . in this case to consider whether respondent's charge that petitioners' defamation of him, standing alone and apart from any other governmental action with respect to him, stated a claim for relief under 42 U.S.C. § 1983 and the Fourteenth Amendment. For the reasons hereinafter stated, we conclude that it does not.

* * *

I

Respondent's due process claim is grounded upon his assertion that the flier, and in particular the phrase "Active Shoplifters" appearing at the head of the page upon which his name and photograph appear, impermissibly deprived him of some "liberty" protected by the Fourteenth Amendment. His complaint asserted that the "active shoplifter" designation would inhibit him from entering business establishments for fear of being suspected of shoplifting and possibly apprehended, and would seriously impair his future employment opportunities. Accepting that such consequences may flow from the flier in question, respondent's complaint would appear to state a classical claim for defamation actionable in the courts of virtually every State. Imputing criminal behavior to an individual is generally considered defamatory per se, and actionable without proof of special damages.

Respondent brought his action, however, not in the state court of Kentucky but in a United States District Court for that State. He asserted not a claim for defamation under the laws of Kentucky, but a claim that he had been deprived of rights secured to him by the Fourteenth Amendment of the United States Constitution. Concededly if the same allegations had been made about respondent by a private individual, he would have nothing more than a claim for defamation under state law. But, he contends, since petitioners are respectively an official of city and of county government, his action is thereby transmuted into one for deprivation by the State of rights secured under the Fourteenth Amendment.

In Greenwood v. Peacock, 384 U.S. 808 (1966), in the course of considering an important and not wholly dissimilar question of the relationship between the national and the state governments, the Court said that "it is worth contemplating what the result would be if the strained interpretation of § 1443(1) urged by the individual petitioners were to prevail." . . . We, too, pause to consider the result should respondent's interpretation of § 1983 and of the Fourteenth Amendment be accepted.

If respondent's view is to prevail, a person arrested by law enforcement officers who announce that they believe such person to be responsible for a particular crime in order to calm the fears of an aroused populace presumably obtains a claim against such officers under § 1983. And since it is surely far more clear from the language of the Fourteenth Amendment that "life" is protected against state deprivation than it is that reputation is protected against state injury, it would be difficult to see why the survivors of an innocent bystander mistakenly shot by a policeman or negligently killed by a sheriff driving a government vehicle would not have claims equally cognizable under § 1983.

It is hard to perceive any logical stopping place to such a line of reasoning. Respon-

dent's construction would seem almost necessarily to result in every legally cognizable injury which may have been inflicted by a state official acting under "color of law" establishing a violation of the Fourteenth Amendment. . . .

II

The result reached by the Court of Appeals, which respondent seeks to sustain here, must be bottomed on one of two premises. The first is that the Due Process Clause of the Fourteenth Amendment and § 1983 make actionable many wrongs inflicted by government employees which had heretofore been thought to give rise only to state law tort claims. The second premise is that the infliction by state officials of a "stigma" to one's reputation is somehow different in kind from the infliction by the same official of harm or injury to other interests protected by state law, so that an injury to reputation is actionable under § 1983 and the Fourteenth Amendment even if other such harms are not. We examine each of the premises in turn.

A

The first premise would be contrary to pronouncements in our cases on more than one occasion with respect to the scope of § 1983 and of the Fourteenth Amendment. In the leading case of Screws v. United States, 325 U.S. 91 (1945), the Court considered the proper application of the criminal counterpart of § 1983, likewise intended by Congress to enforce the guarantees of the Fourteenth Amendment. In his opinion for the Court plurality in that case, Mr. Justice Douglas observed that:

"Violation of local law does not necessarily mean that federal rights have been invaded. The fact that a prisoner is assaulted, injured, or even murdered by state officials does not necessarily mean that he is deprived of any right protected and secured by the Constitution or laws of the United States." . . .

After recognizing that Congress' power to criminalize the conduct of state officials under the aegis of the Fourteenth Amendment was not unlimited because that Amendment "did not alter the basic relation between the States and the national government," the plurality opinion observed that

Congress should not be understood to have attempted "to make all torts of state officials federal crimes. It brought within [the criminal provision] only specified acts 'under color' of law and then only those acts which deprived a person of some rights secured by the Constitution or laws of the United States." . . .

This understanding of the limited effect of the Fourteenth Amendment was not lost in the Court's decision in Monroe v. Pape, 365 U.S. 167 (1961). There the Court was careful to point out that the complaint stated a cause of action under the Fourteenth Amendment because it alleged an unreasonable search and seizure violative of the guarantee "contained in the Fourth Amendment [and] made applicable to the States by reason of the Due Process Clause of the Fourteenth Amendment." . . . Respondent, however, has pointed to no specific constitutional guarantee safeguarding the interest he asserts has been invaded. Rather he apparently believes that the Fourteenth Amendment's Due Process Clause should ex proprio vigore extend to him a right to be free of injury wherever the State may be characterized as the tortfeasor. But such a reading would make of the Fourteenth Amendment a font of tort law to be superimposed upon whatever systems may already be administered by the States. We have noted the "constitutional shoals" that confront any attempt to derive from congressional civil rights statutes a body of general federal tort law. Griffin v. Breckenridge, 403 U.S. 88, 101–102 (1971); a fortiori the procedural guarantees of the Due Process Clause cannot be the source for such law.

B

The second premise upon which the result reached by the Court of Appeals could be rested — that the infliction by state officials of a "stigma" to one's reputation is somehow different in kind from infliction by a state official of harm to other interests protected by state law — is equally untenable. The words "liberty" and "property" as used in the Fourteenth Amendment do not in terms single out reputation as a candidate for special protection over and above other interests that may be protected by state law. While we have in a number of our prior cases pointed out the frequently drastic effect of

the "stigma" which may result from defamation by the government in a variety of contexts, this line of cases does not establish the proposition that reputation alone, apart from some more tangible interests such as employment, is either "liberty" or "property" by itself sufficient to invoke the procedural protection of the Due Process Clause. As we have said, the Court of Appeals, in reaching a contrary conclusion, relied primarily upon Wisconsin v. Constantineau, 400 U.S. 433 (1971). We think the correct import of that decision, however, must be derived from an examination of the precedents upon which it relied, as well as consideration of the other decisions by this Court, before and after Constantineau, which bear upon the relationship between governmental defamation and the guarantees of the Constitution. While not uniform in their treatment of the subject, we think that the weight of our decisions establishes no constitutional doctrine converting every defamation by a public official into a deprivation of liberty within the meaning of the Due Process Clause of the Fifth or Fourteenth Amendments.

In United States v. Lovett, 328 U.S. 303 (1946), the Court held that an Act of Congress which specifically forbade payment of any salary or compensation to three named government agency employees was an unconstitutional bill of attainder. The three employees had been proscribed because the House of Representatives Subcommittee found them guilty of "subversive activity," and therefore unfit for government service. The Court, while recognizing that the underlying charges upon which Congress' action was premised "stigmatized [the employees'] reputation and seriously impaired their chance to earn a living," also made it clear that "what is involved here is a congressional proscription of [these employees] prohibiting their ever holding a government job." . . .

Subsequently, in Joint Anti-Fascist Refugee Committee v. McGrath, 341 U.S. 123 (1951), the Court examined the validity of the Attorney General's designation of certain organizations as "Communist" on a list which he furnished to the Civil Service Commission. There was no majority opinion in the case; Mr. Justice Burton, who announced the judgment of the Court, wrote an opinion which did not reach the petitioner's constitutional claim. Mr. Justice Frank-furter, who agreed with Mr. Justice Burton that the petitioners had stated a claim upon which relief could be granted, noted "that publicly designating an organization as within the proscribed categories of the Loyalty Order does not directly deprive anyone of liberty or property." . . .

* * *

In Wieman v. Updegraff, 344 U.S. 183 (1952), the Court again recognized the potential "badge of infamy" which might arise from being branded disloyal by the government. . . . But it did not hold this sufficient by itself to invoke the procedural due process guarantees of the Fourth Amendment; indeed, the Court expressly refused to pass upon the procedural due process claims of petitioners in that case. . . . The Court noted that petitioners would, as a result of their failure to execute the state loyalty oath, lose their teaching positions at a state university. It held such state action to be arbitrary because of its failure to distinguish between innocent and knowing membership in the associations named in the list prepared by the Attorney General of the United States. . . .

A decade after Joint Anti-Fascist Refugee Committee v. McGrath, supra, the Court returned to consider further the requirements of procedural due process in this area in the case of Cafeteria Workers v. McElroy, 367 U.S. 886 (1961). Holding that the discharge of an employee of a government contractor in the circumstances there presented comported with the due process required by the Fifth Amendment, the Court observed:

"Finally, it is to be noted that this is not a case where government action has operated to bestow a badge of disloyalty or infamy, *with an attendant foreclosure of other employment opportunity. . . .*"

Two things appear from the line of cases beginning with Lovett. The Court has recognized the serious damage that could be inflicted by branding a government employee as "disloyal," and thereby stigmatizing his good name. But the Court has never held that the mere defamation of an individual, whether by branding him disloyal or otherwise, was sufficient to invoke the guarantees of procedural due process absent an accompanying loss of government employment.

It is noteworthy that in Barr v. Mateo, 360 U.S. 564 (1959), and Howard v. Lyons, 360 U.S. 593 (1959), this Court had before it two actions for defamation brought against federal officers. But in neither opinion is there any intimation that any of the parties to those cases, nor any of the Members of this Court, had the remotest idea that the Due Process Clause of the Fifth Amendment might itself form the basis for a claim for defamation against federal officials.

It was against this backdrop that the Court in 1971 decided Constantineau. There the Court held that a Wisconsin statute authorizing the practice of "posting" was unconstitutional because it failed to provide procedural safeguards of notice and an opportunity to be heard, prior to an individual's being "posted." Under the statute "posing" consisted of forbidding in writing the sale or delivery of alcoholic beverages to certain persons who were determined to have become hazards to themselves, to their family, or to the community by reason of their "excessive drinking." The statute also made it a misdemeanor to sell or give liquor to any person so posted. . . .

There is undoubtedly language in Constantineau, which is sufficiently ambiguous to justify the reliance upon it by the Court of Appeals:

"Yet certainly where the state attaches 'a badge of infamy' to the citizen, due process comes into play. Wieman v. Updegraff, 344 U.S. 183, 191. '[T]he right to be heard before being condemned to suffer grievous loss of any kind, even though it may not involve the stigma and hardships of a criminal conviction, is a principle basic to our society.' Anti-Fascist Committee v. McGrath, 341 U.S. 123, 168 (Frankfurter, J., concurring).

"While a person's good name, reputation, honor or integrity is at stake *because of what the government is doing to him,* notice and an opportunity to be heard are essential. . . ."

The last paragraph of the quotation could be taken to mean that if a government official defames a person, without more the procedural requirements of the Due Process Clause of the Fourteenth Amendment are brought into play. If read that way, it would represent a significant broadening of the holdings of Wieman v. Updegraff, supra, and Anti-Fascist Committee v. McGrath, supra, relied upon by the Constantineau Court in its analysis in the immediately preceding paragraph. We should not read this language as significantly broadening those holdings without in any way adverting to the fact if there is any other possible interpretation of Constantineau's language. We believe there is.

We think that the [italicized] language in the last sentence quoted, "because of what the government is doing to him," referred to the fact that the governmental action taken in that case deprived the individual of a right previously held under state law — the right to purchase or obtain liquor in common with the rest of the citizenry. "Posting," therefore, significantly altered his status as a matter of state law, and it was that alteration of legal status which, combined with the injury resulting from the defamation, justified the invocation of procedural safeguards. The "stigma" resulting from the defamatory character of the posting was doubtless an important factor in evaluating the extent of harm worked by that act, but we do not think that such defamation, standing alone, deprived Constantineau of any "liberty" protected by the procedural guarantees of the Fourteenth Amendment.

This conclusion is reinforced by our discussion of the subject a little over a year later in Board of Regents v. Roth, 408 U.S. 564 (1972). There we noted that "the range of interests protected by procedural due process is not infinite . . ." and that with respect to property interests they are "of course . . . not created by the Constitution. Rather they are created and their dimensions defined by existing rules or understandings that stem from an independent source such as state law — rules or understandings that secure certain benefits and support claims of entitlements to those benefits." . . .

While Roth recognized that governmental action defaming an individual in the course of declining to rehire him could entitle the person to notice and an opportunity to be heard as to the defamation, its language is quite inconsistent with any notion that a defamation perpetrated by a government official but unconnected with any refusal to rehire would be actionable under the Fourteenth Amendment:

"The state in declining to rehire the respondent, did not make charge against him that might seriously damage his standing and associations in his community. . . .

"Similarly, there is no suggestion that the State, in declining to re-employ the respondent, imposed on him a stigma or other disability that foreclosed his freedom to take advantage of other employment opportunities." . . .

Thus it was not thought sufficient to establish a claim under § 1983 and the Fourteenth Amendment that there simply be defamation by a state official; the defamation had to occur in the course of the termination of employment. Certainly there is no suggestion in Roth to indicate that a hearing would be required each time the State in its capacity as employer might be considered responsible for a statement defaming an employee who continues to be an employee.

This conclusion is quite consistent with our most recent holding in this area, Goss v. Lopez, 419 U.S. 565 (1975), that suspension from school based upon charges of misconduct could trigger the procedural guarantees of the Fourteenth Amendment. While the Court noted that charges of misconduct could seriously damage the student's reputation . . . it also took care to point out that Ohio law conferred a right upon all children to attend school, and that the act of the school officials suspending the student there involved resulted in a denial or deprivation of that right.

III

It is apparent from our decisions that there exist a variety of interests which are difficult of definition but are nevertheless comprehended within the meaning of either "liberty" or "property" as meant in the Due Process Clause. These interests attain this constitutional status by virtue of the fact that they have been initially recognized and protected by state law, and we have repeatedly ruled that the procedural guarantees of the Fourteenth Amendment apply whenever the State seeks to remove or significantly alter that protected status. In Bell v. Burson, 402 U.S. 535 (1971), for example, the State by issuing drivers' licenses recognized in its citizens a right to operate a vehicle on the highways of the State. The Court held that the State could not withdraw this right without giving petitioner due process. In Morrissey v. Brewer, 408 U.S. 471 (1972), the State afforded parolees the right to remain at liberty as long as the conditions of their parole were not violated. Before the State could alter the status of a parolee because of alleged violations of these conditions, we held that the Fourteenth Amendment's guarantee of due process of law required certain procedural safeguards.

In each of these cases, as a result of the state action complained of, a right or status previously recognized by state law was distinctly altered or extinguished. It was this alteration, officially removing the interest from the recognition and protection previously afforded by the State, which we found sufficient to invoke the procedural guarantees contained in the Due Process Clause of the Fourteenth Amendment. But the interest in reputation alone which respondent seeks to vindicate in this action in federal court is quite different from the "liberty" or "property" recognized in those decisions. Kentucky law does not extend to respondent any legal guarantee of present enjoyment of reputation which has been altered as a result of petitioners' actions. Rather his interest in reputation is simply one of a number which the State may protect against injury by virtue of its tort law, providing a forum for vindication of those interests by means of damages actions. And any harm or injury to that interest, even where as here inflicted by an officer of the State, does not result in a deprivation of any "liberty" or "property" recognized by state or federal law, nor has it worked any change of respondent's status as theretofore recognized under the State's laws. For these reasons we hold that the interest in reputation asserted in this case is neither "liberty" nor "property" guaranteed against state deprivation without due process of law.

Respondent in this case cannot assert denial of any right vouchsafed to him by the State and thereby protected under the Fourteenth Amendment. That being the case, petitioners' defamatory publications, however seriously they may have harmed respondent's reputation, did not deprive him of any "liberty" or "property" interests protected by the Due Process Clause.

IV

Respondent's complaint also alleged a violation of a "right to privacy guaranteed by the First, Fourth, Fifth, Ninth, and Fourteenth Amendments." The Court of Appeals did not pass upon this claim since it found the allegations of a due process violation sufficient to require reversal of the District Court's order. As we have agreed with the District Court on the due process issue, we find it necessary to pass upon respondent's other theory in order to determine whether there is any support for the litigation he seeks to pursue.

While there is no "right of privacy" found in any specific guarantee of the Constitution, the Court has recognized that "zones of privacy" may be created by more specific constitutional guarantees and thereby impose limits upon government power. See Roe v. Wade, 410 U.S. 113, 152–153 (1973). Respondent's case, however, comes within none of these areas. He does not seek to suppress evidence seized in the course of an unreasonable search. . . . And our other "right of privacy" cases, while defying categorical description, deal generally with substantive aspects of the Fourteenth Amendment. In Roe the Court pointed out that the personal rights found in this guarantee of personal privacy must be limited to those which are "fundamental" or "implicit in the concept of ordered liberty" as described in Palko v. Connecticut, 301 U.S. 319, 325 (1937). The activities detailed as being within this definition were ones very different from that for which respondent claims constitutional protection — matters relating to marriage, procreation, contraception, family relationships, and child rearing and education. In these areas it has been held that there are limitations on the States' power to substantively regulate conduct.

Respondent's claim is far afield from this line of decisions. He claims constitutional protection against the disclosure of the fact of his arrest on a shoplifting charge. His claim is based not upon any challenge to the State's ability to restrict his freedom of action in a sphere contended to be "private," but instead on a claim that the State may not publicize a record of an official act such as an arrest. None of our substantive privacy decisions hold this or anything like this, and we decline to enlarge them in this manner.

None of respondent's theories of recovery were based upon rights secured to him by the Fourteenth Amendment. Petitioners therefore were not liable to him under § 1983. . . .

Reversed.

[Mr. Justice BRENNAN wrote a dissenting opinion in which Mr. Justice MARSHALL and Mr. Justice WHITE joined.]

[Mr. Justice STEVENS took no part in the consideration or decision of this case.]

Comments

1. In *Paul* v. *Davis,* supra, the respondent argued that the circulation of the flyer deprived him of some "liberty" protected by the Fourteenth Amendment. The majority, however, was careful to point out that no such deprivation occurred. Mr. Justice Rehnquist observed that "there exists a variety of interests . . . comprehended within the meaning of either 'liberty' or 'property' as meant in the Due Process Clause." Finding that maintenance of one's "reputation" involves neither "liberty" nor "property" interest, the majority concluded, "[H]owever seriously they [the publications] may have harmed respondent's reputation, [they] did not deprive him of any 'liberty' or 'property' interests protected by the Due Process Clause." Hence, respondent was not able to recover under § 1983. What about Davis' right to privacy claim? Why does the Court reject that specific theory of recovery under § 1983? Why does the Court refer to "zones" of privacy rather than a "right" of privacy?

2. In *Rizzo* v. *Goode,* 423 U.S. 362 (1976), the Supreme Court held that the plaintiffs' failure to establish that the named defendants had engaged in a pattern of conduct that resulted in the deprivation of constitutional rights precluded relief under 42 U.S.C. § 1983. The Court concluded that plaintiffs' claims of actual and immediate harm, based upon speculation that one of a small, unnamed minority of police officers *might* violate their civil rights, did not establish the "personal stake" in the outcome necessary for standing or for a showing that a case or controversy existed between the plaintiffs and the named city officials (the mayor and the police commissioner of Philadelphia, et al.).

Prosecutor's Immunity Under the Civil Rights Act

IMBLER v. PACHTMAN

Supreme Court of the United States, 1976
424 U.S. 409, 96 S. Ct. 984, 47 L. Ed. 2d 128

In 1962, petitioner, Imbler, was convicted in a California court of felony-murder. Thereafter, the district attorney, Pachtman, discovered new evidence to support Imbler's original alibi defense and wrote to the Governor of California describing the evidence. On the basis of the new evidence, Imbler in 1963 petitioned for state habeas corpus relief, charging that respondent, Pachtman, had knowingly used false testimony and suppressed material evidence at petitioner's trial. The Supreme

Court of California rejected these contentions and denied the writ. In 1968, petitioner filed a federal habeas corpus petition based on the same allegations and ultimately obtained his release in 1970. In April, 1972, petitioner filed a § 1983 action against Pachtman and others, seeking damages for loss of liberty caused by the allegedly unlawful prosecution. However, the district court held that respondent was immune against 42 U.S.C. § 1983 actions, and the Court of Appeals (9th Cir.) affirmed. The United States Supreme Court granted certiorari.

Mr. Justice POWELL delivered the opinion of the Court.

The question presented in this case is whether a state prosecuting attorney who acted within the scope of his duties in initiating and pursuing a criminal prosecution is amenable to suit under 42 U.S.C. § 1983 for alleged deprivations of the defendant's constitutional rights. . . .

* * *

II

Section 1983 provides that "every person" who acts under color of state law to deprive another of a constitutional right shall be answerable to that person in a suit for damages. The statute thus creates a species of tort liability that on its face admits of no immunities, and some have argued that it should be applied as stringently as it reads. But that view has not prevailed.

This Court first considered the implications of the statute's literal sweep in Tenney v. Brandhove, 341 U.S. 367 (1951). There it was claimed that members of a state legislative committee had called the plaintiff to appear before them not for a proper legislative purpose, but to intimidate him into silence on certain matters of public concern, and thereby had deprived him of his constitutional rights. Because legislators in both England and this country had enjoyed absolute immunity for their official actions, Tenney squarely presented the issue of whether the Reconstruction Congress had intended to restrict the availability in § 1983 suits of those immunities which historically, and for reasons of public policy, had been accorded to various categories of officials. The Court concluded that immunities "well-grounded in history and reason" had not been abrogated "by covert inclusion in the general language of § 1983. . . .

* * *

III

This case marks our first opportunity to address the § 1983 liability of a state prosecuting officer. The courts of appeals, however, have confronted the issue many times and under varying circumstances. Although the precise contours of their holdings have been unclear at times, at bottom they are virtually unanimous that a prosecutor enjoys absolute immunity from § 1983 suits for damages when he acts within the scope of his prosecutorial duties. These courts sometimes have described the prosecutor's immunity as a form of "quasi-judicial" immunity and referred to it as derivative of the immunity of judges recognized in Pierson v. Ray, 386 U.S. 547 (1967). . . . Petitioner focuses upon the "quasi-judicial" characterization, and contends that it illustrates a fundamental illogic in according absolute immunity to a prosecutor. He argues that the prosecutor, as a member of the Executive Branch, cannot claim the immunity reserved for the judiciary, but only a qualified immunity akin to that accorded other executive officials in this Court's previous cases.

* * *

A

The function of a prosecutor that most often invites a common-law tort action is his decision to initiate a prosecution, as this may lead to a suit for malicious prosecution if the State's case misfires. The first American case to address the question of a prosecutor's amenability to such an action was Griffith v. Slinkard, 146 Ind. 117, 44 N.E. 1001 (1896). The complaint charged that a local prosecutor without probable cause added the plaintiff's name to a grand jury true bill after the grand jurors had refused to indict him, with the result that the plaintiff was arrested and forced to appear in court repeatedly before the charge finally was nolle prossed. Despite allegations of malice, the Supreme Court of Indiana dismissed the action on the ground that the prosecutor was absolutely immune. . . .

The Griffith view on prosecutorial immunity became the clear majority rule on the issue. The question eventually came to this Court on writ of certiorari to the Court of Appeals for the Second Circuit. In Yaselli v. Goff, 12 F.2d 396 (2d Cir. 1926), the claim was that the defendant, a Special Assistant to the Attorney General of the United States, maliciously and without probable cause procured plaintiff's grand jury indictment by the willful introduction of false and misleading evidence. Plaintiff sought some $300,000 in damages for having been subjected to the rigors of a trial in which the court ultimately directed a verdict against the Government. The District Court dismissed the complaint, and the Court of Appeals affirmed. After reviewing the development of the doctrine of prosecutorial immunity . . . that court stated:

"In our opinion the law requires us to hold that a special assistant to the Attorney General of the United States, in the performance of the duties imposed upon him by law, is immune from a civil action for malicious prosecution based on an indictment and prosecution, although it results in a verdict of not guilty rendered by a jury. The immunity is absolute, and is grounded on principles of public policy. . . ."

After briefing and oral argument, this Court affirmed the Court of Appeals in a per curiam opinion. . . .

The common-law immunity of a prosecutor is based upon the same considerations that underlie the common-law immunities of judges and grand jurors acting within the scope of their duties. These include concern that harassment by unfounded litigation would cause a deflection of the prosecutor's energies from his public duties, and the possibility that he would shade his decisions instead of exercising the independence of judgment required by his public trust. . . .

* * *

B

The common-law rule of immunity is thus well settled. We now must determine whether the same considerations of public

policy that underlie the common-law rule likewise countenance absolute immunity under § 1983. We think they do.

If a prosecutor had only a qualified immunity, the threat of § 1983 suits would undermine performance of his duties no less than would the threat of common-law suits for malicious prosecution. A prosecutor is duty bound to exercise his best judgment both in deciding which suits to bring and in conducting them in court. The public trust of the prosecutor's office would suffer if he were constrained in making every decision by the consequences in terms of his own potential liability in a suit for damages. Such suits could be expected with some frequency, for a defendant often will transform his resentment at being prosecuted into the ascription of improper and malicious actions to the State's advocate. . . . Further, if the prosecutor could be made to answer in court each time such a person charged him with wrongdoing, his energy and attention would be diverted from the pressing duty of enforcing the criminal law.

Moreover, suits that survived the pleadings would pose substantial danger of liability even to the honest prosecutor. The prosecutor's possible knowledge of a witness' falsehoods, the materiality of evidence not revealed to the defense, the propriety of a closing argument, and—ultimately in every case—the likelihood that prosecutorial misconduct so infected a trial as to deny due process, are typical of issues with which judges struggle in actions for post-trial relief, sometimes to differing conclusions. The presentation of such issues in a § 1983 action often would require a virtual retrial of the criminal offense in a new forum, and the resolution of some technical issues by the lay jury. It is fair to say, we think, that the honest prosecutor would face greater difficulty in meeting the standards of qualified immunity than other executive or administrative officials. Frequently acting under serious constraints of time and even information, a prosecutor inevitably makes many decisions that could engender colorable claims of constitutional deprivation. Defending these decisions, often years after they were made, could impose unique and intolerable burdens upon a prosecutor responsible annually for hundreds of indictments and trials. . . .

The affording of only a qualified immunity

to the prosecutor also could have an adverse effect upon the functioning of the criminal justice system. Attaining the system's goal of accurately determining guilt or innocence requires that both the prosecution and the defense have wide discretion in the conduct of the trial and the presentation of evidence. The veracity of witnesses in criminal cases frequently is subject to doubt before and after they testify, as is illustrated by the history of this case. If prosecutors were hampered in exercising their judgment as to the use of such witnesses by concern about resulting personal liability, the triers of fact in criminal cases often would be denied relevant evidence.

The ultimate fairness of the operation of the system itself could be weakened by subjecting prosecutors to § 1983 liability. Various post-trial procedures are available to determine whether an accused has received a fair trial. These procedures include the remedial powers of the trial judge, appellate review, and state and federal post-conviction collateral remedies. In all of these the attention of the reviewing judge or tribunal is focused primarily on whether there was a fair trial under law. This focus should not be blurred by even the subconscious knowledge that a post-trial decision in favor of the accused might result in the prosecutor being called upon to respond in damages for his error or mistaken judgment.

We conclude that the considerations outlined above dictate the same absolute immunity under § 1983 that the prosecutor enjoys at common law. To be sure, this immunity does leave the genuinely wronged defendant without civil redress against a prosecutor whose malicious or dishonest action deprives him of liberty. But the alternative of qualifying a prosecutor's immunity would disserve the broader public interest. It would prevent the vigorous and fearless performance of the prosecutor's duty that is essential to the proper functioning of the criminal justice system. Moreover, it often would prejudice defendants in criminal cases by skewing post-conviction judicial decisions that should be made with the sole purpose of insuring justice. . . .

* * *

We emphasize that the immunity of prosecutors from liability in suits under § 1983 does not leave the public powerless to deter misconduct or to punish that which occurs.

This Court has never suggested that the policy considerations which compel civil immunity for certain governmental officials also place them beyond the reach of the criminal law. Even judges, cloaked with absolute civil immunity for centuries, could be punished criminally for willful deprivations of constitutional rights on the strength of 18 U.S.C. § 242, the criminal analog of § 1983. . . . The prosecutor would fare no better for his willful acts. Moreover, a prosecutor stands perhaps unique, among officials whose acts could deprive persons of constitutional rights, in his amenability to professional discipline by an association of his peers. These checks undermine the argument that the imposition of civil liability is the only way to insure that prosecutors are mindful of the constitutional rights of persons accused of crime.

IV

It remains to delineate the boundaries of our holding. As noted, the Court of Appeals emphasized that each of respondent's challenged activities was an "integral part of the judicial process." . . . The purpose of the Court of Appeals' focus upon the functional nature of the activities rather than respondent's status was to distinguish and leave standing those cases, in its circuit and in some others, which hold that a prosecutor engaged in certain investigatory activities enjoys not the absolute immunity associated with the judicial process, but only a good-faith defense comparable to the policeman's. . . . We agree with the Court of Appeals that respondent's activities were intimately associated with the judicial phase of the criminal process, and thus were functions to which the reasons for absolute immunity apply with full force. We have no occasion to consider whether like or similar reasons require immunity for those aspects of the prosecutor's responsibility that cast him in the role of an administrator or investigative officer rather than that of advocate. We hold only that in initiating a prosecution and in presenting the State's case, the prosecutor is immune from a civil suit for damages under § 1983. . . .

Affirmed.

[Mr. Justice WHITE wrote a concurring opinion in which Mr. Justice BRENNAN and Mr. Justice MARSHALL joined.]

[Mr. Justice STEVENS took no part in the consideration or decision of this case.]

Comments

1. In *Imbler,* supra, the respondent asserted that he, as a prosecutor, was subject to quasi-judicial immunity and argued that such immunity is derived from the immunity of judges recognized by the Supreme Court in *Pierson* v. *Ray,* 386 U.S. 547 (1967). In that case, the Court stated: "Few doctrines were more solidly established at common law than the immunity of judges from liability for damages for acts committed within their judicial jurisdiction, as this Court recognized when it adopted the doctrine in Bradley v. Fisher, 13 Wall. 335, 20 L. Ed. 646 (1872)." 386 U.S. at 553–554. The Court went on to note: "We do not believe that this settled principle of law was abolished by § 1983 . . . [T]he legislative record gives no clear indication that Congress meant to abolish whole-sale all common-law immunities. The immunity of judges for acts within the judicial role is . . . well established, and we presume that Congress would have specifically so provided had it wished to abolish the doctrine." Id. at 554, 555. See also *Roberts* v. *Williams,* 302 F. Supp. 972 (D. Miss. 1969); *Berg* v. *Cwiklinski,* 416 F.2d (7th Cir. 1969). It should be noted that state court judges can be prosecuted under 42 U.S.C. § 242, the criminal section of the Civil Rights Act. See *Ex parte Virginia,* 100 U.S. 339 (1879); *O'Shea* v. *Littleton,* 414 U.S. 488 (1974); *Lynch* v. *Johnson,* 420 F.2d 818 (6th Cir. 1970).

    What does the term "quasi-judicial" imply? Certainly it would seem to suggest, inter alia, a degree of similarity or likeness to judicial functions, while also implying that "judicial" should be interpreted with some flexibility. One writer has suggested that prosecutorial immunity from civil liability for official acts rests upon a "public policy" theory; i.e., the public interest dictates that the prosecutor have latitude in the performance of his official duties and be able to carry out his prosecutorial functions "freely and fearlessly." See LeGrande, *The Basic Processes of Criminal Justice* 74 (1973). Consider *United States* v. *Cox,* 342 F.2d 167 (5th Cir. 1965). See also *United States* v. *Falk,* 479 F.2d 616 (7th Cir. 1973) (en banc); *Littleton* v. *Berbling,* 468 F.2d 389 (7th Cir. 1972). One performing a judicial or quasi-judicial function would seem to be free to exercise some degree of discretion in making decisions, as opposed to one performing a "ministerial" function, who must act according to fixed rules without exercising any discretion.

2. In regard to state judges' immunity, consider Antieau, *Federal Civil Rights Act* 69 (1971): "Federal courts may be willing, notwithstanding *Pierson* v. *Ray,* to hold judges amenable to the Civil Rights Act when they perform non-judicial functions. For example, previous to the decision in *Pierson,* a federal court held a judge liable under § 1983 when he directed a police officer to arrest and take into custody a person not named in a warrant [*Yates* v. *Hoffman Estates,* 209 F. Supp. 757 (D. Ill. 1962)]. Furthermore, injunctive and declaratory relief are available in a § 1983 action against judges who interfere with citizens' civil rights [*Bramlett* v. *Peterson,* 307 F. Supp. 1311 (D. Fla. 1969)]."

3. Recent lower federal and state court decisions involving civil liability of criminal justice personnel include *Cox* v. *Stanton,* 529 F.2d 47 (4th Cir. 1975) (a county is not a "person" under 42 U.S.C. § 1983) (see also *Brault* v. *Town of Milton,* 527 F.2d 730 [2d Cir.

1975], and *Dahl* v. *City of Palo Alto,* 372 F. Supp. 647 [N.D. Calif. 1974]); *United States* v. *Senak,* 527 F.2d 129 (7th Cir. 1975) (civil rights conviction of former Indiana paupers' attorney who threatened his clients with inadequate representation unless they or their friends came up with payments upheld); *County of Champaign* v. *Anthony,* 337 N.E.2d 87 (Ill. App. 1975) (county may not recover money from convicted kidnapping defendant that was spent in providing his victim with protection during the time the defendant was free on bond); *Jones* v. *Marshall,* 528 F.2d 132 (2d Cir. 1975) (good-faith slaying of fleeing felon by police officer held not actionable under § 1983); *Bricker* v. *Michigan Parole Board,* 405 F. Supp. 1340 (E.D. Mich. 1975) (state parole board is not a "person" for purposes of a § 1983 action); *Fine* v. *City of New York,* 529 F.2d 70 (2d Cir. 1975) (attorney who accompanied his teenage client and police officer on an illegal search of an apartment held a proper defendant in a § 1983 action); *Martin* v. *Wainwright,* 526 F.2d 938 (5th Cir. 1975) (state prisoner who was denied visiting privileges with a woman because she was of a different race held to state a cause of action under § 1983); *City of Minneapolis* v. *Richardson,* 239 N.W.2d 197 (Minn. 1976) (city liable under state's Human Rights Act for police officers' racial slurs to a black youth); *Semler* v. *Psychiatric Institute of Washington,* 538 F.2d 121 (4th Cir. 1976) (psychiatrist and hospital civilly liable for prematurely releasing mental patient as outpatient without notifying the trial court and patient murdered another); *McNally* v. *Pulitzer Publishing Co.,* 532 F.2d 69 (8th Cir. 1976) (federal prisoner does not have a cause of action under § 1983 against a newsman and publisher who used the government's medical report on him for a newspaper article); *Covington* v. *Cole,* 528 F.2d 1365 (5th Cir. 1976) (§ 1983 plaintiff whose state conviction stands unchallenged but who alleges that law enforcement officers illegally engaged in a search of his house at the time of his arrest held to state a cause of action under § 1983); *Pate* v. *Alabama Board of Pardons and Paroles,* 409 F. Supp. 478 (M.D. Ala. 1976) (members of state board of pardons and paroles are absolutely immune from § 1983 suits); *Cicero* v. *Olgiati,* 410 F. Supp. 1080 (S.D.N.Y. 1976) (state prisoners' attack of parole release standards held to state a cause of action in § 1983 suit); *Qualls* v. *Parrish,* 534 F.2d 690 (6th Cir. 1976) (law of the situs state should be considered in determining the wrongful death liability of a police officer sued under § 1983) (see also *People* v. *Kilvington,* 37 P. 799 [1894], *Coldeen* v. *Reed,* 182 P. 599 [1919], *Union Indemnity Co.* v. *Webster,* 118 So. 794 [1928], *Fields* v. *City of New York,* 151 N.E.2d 188, 191 [1958], *Petrie* v. *Cartwright,* 70 S.W. 297 [1902], *Commonwealth* v. *Duerr,* 45 A.2d 235 [1945], and *Jones* v. *Marshall,* 528 F.2d 138 [1975]); *Bryan* v. *Jones,* 530 F.2d 1210 (5th Cir. 1976) (en banc) (good faith is a defense to a § 1983 suit against a sheriff who detained a prisoner more than a month because of a clerical error); *Sartin* v. *Commissioner,* 535 F.2d 430 (8th Cir. 1976) (plaintiff not barred from bringing a § 1983 action against a police officer who subjected him to a false arrest); *Brawer* v. *Horowitz,* 535 F.2d 830 (3d Cir. 1976) (witness who committed perjury at criminal trial held immune from § 1983 suit); *Sinwell* v. *Shapp,* 536 F.2d 15 (3d Cir. 1976) (improper venue is not sufficient ground to deny a prisoner's § 1983 petition to proceed in forma pauperis), overruling *Walker* v. *Weaver,* 266 F. Supp. 415 (M.D. Pa. 1967); *Tomko* v. *Lees,* 416 F. Supp. 1137 (W.D.Pa. 1976) (college student's claim that local prosecutors and a police officer compelled him to act as a police informer states a cause of action under § 1983); *Minns* v. *Paul,* 542 F.2d 899 (4th Cir. 1976) (court-appointed attorney whose job is to counsel and assist indigent inmates at a state prison enjoys absolute immunity from prisoners' damage suits brought under § 1983); *Hilliard* v. *Williams,* 540 F.2d 220 (6th Cir. 1976) (prosecutorial immunity doctrine of *Imbler* v. *Pachtman* protects a state district attorney who withheld exculpatory evidence from a murder defendant); *Shaw* v. *Briscoe,* 541 F.2d 489 (5th Cir. 1976) (although 42 U.S.C. § 1983 contains no statute of limitations, federal courts should look to state law for applicable limitations); *Dean* v. *Shirer,* 547 F.2d 227 (4th Cir. 1976) (judge enjoys judicial immunity under § 1983 with respect to his contempt adjudication against lawyer after the lawyer went onto the courtroom steps and said it was impossible to get a fair trial in the town); *Stadium Films, Inc.* v. *Baillargeon,* 542 F.2d 577 (1st Cir. 1976) (police officers not liable in damages under § 1983 for making negligent errors of law in seeking or executing a search warrant); *Edwards* v. *Garrison,* 544 F.2d 514 (4th Cir. 1976) (inmates' challenge to prison's use of racially coded prison identification numbers held to state a cause of action under § 1983); *Johnson* v. *Anderson,* 420 F. Supp. 845 (D. Del. 1976) (state prison warden's transfer of several prisoners to isolation section of maximum security prison without affording them hearings renders warden vulnerable to § 1983 action) (see also *Gray* v. *Creamer,* 465 F.2d 179 [3d Cir. 1972]); *Kimbrough* v. *O'Neil,* 545 F.2d 1059 (7th Cir. 1976) (en banc) (inmate who alleges that a deputy sheriff intentionally took his property and failed to return it states a cause of action under § 1983) (see also *Carroll* v. *Sielaff,* 514 F.2d 415 [7th Cir. 1975] [confiscation of inmate's typewriter]); *Bonner* v. *Coughlin,* 545 F.2d 565 (7th Cir. 1976) (en banc) (inmate cannot recover damages under § 1983 for loss of trial transcript due to guards' negligence) (in accord is *Page* v. *Sharpe,* 487 F.2d 561 [1st Cir. 1973], *Williams* v. *Vincent,* 508 F.2d 541 [2d Cir. 1974]) (contra is *McCray* v. *Maryland,* 456 F.2d 1 [4th Cir. 1972], *Whirl* v. *Kern,* 407 F.2d 781 [5th Cir. 1969], cert. denied, 396 U.S. 901); *Vosnos* v. *Perry,* 357 N.E.2d 614 (Ill. App. 1976) (evidence that a § 1983 defendant lacked capacity to form criminal intent to commit murder held not a complete defense to a wrongful death action) (see also *McIntyre* v. *Sholty,* 121 Ill. 660 [1887]); *Gonzalez* v. *Southern Methodist University,* 536 F.2d 1071 (5th Cir. 1976) (§ 1983 does not provide remedy for private acts of racial discrimination); *Fox* v. *Sullivan,* 539 F.2d 1065 (5th Cir. 1976) (§ 1983 gives remedy to state prisoners for prison officials' negligent acts that result in injuries to the prisoners); *Carter* v. *Cuyler,* 415 F. Supp. 852 (D. Pa. 1976) (verbal abuse or psychological stress may alone be sufficient to support § 1983 claim); *Hazo* v. *Geltz,* 537 F.2d 747 (3d Cir. 1976) (sheriff or his deputies are not necessarily immune from suit under the Civil Rights Act); *Bennett* v. *Passic,* 545 F.2d 1260 (10th Cir. 1976) (failure to give *Miranda* warnings does not necessarily subject police officers to liability under the Civil Rights Act); *Deas* v. *Potts* 547 F.2d 800 (4th Cir. 1976) (private attorney retained by state to represent criminal defendant is not acting "under color of" law and is therefore not amenable to suit by client under Civil Rights Act); *Walton* v. *Salter,* 547 F.2d 824 (5th Cir. 1976) (a city is not a "person" subject to suit under the Civil Rights Act); *Wyland* v. *James,* 426 F. Supp. 304 (D. Tex. 1977) (damages are recoverable under § 1983 for violations of a citizen's Fourth Amendment rights against unlawful arrest); *Miller* v. *Barilla,* 549 F.2d 648 (9th Cir. 1977) (public defender is accorded absolute immunity from damage claims under the Civil Rights Act for acts done as part of his judicial function as a public defender); *Vinnedge* v. *Gibbs,* 550 F.2d 926 (4th Cir. 1977) (a wilfull denial of medical treatment to a prisoner may give rise to a claim cognizable under § 1983); *Taken Alive* v. *Litzau,* 551 F.2d 196 (8th Cir. 1977) (Indian woman who sustained injuries as a result of a forceful arrest by police officer and who sued chief of police must prove some actual involvement of the chief in the alleged misconduct); *Stanford Daily* v. *Zurcher,* 550 F.2d 464 (9th Cir. 1977) (claimed good faith of police officers in securing what turned out to be an invalid warrant does not insulate them from liability under § 1983); *Sparkman* v. *McFarlin,* 552 F.2d 172 (7th Cir. 1977) (Indiana state court judge who ordered sterilization of a 15-year-old girl on her mother's petition is not judicially immune from liability under § 1983 when his action had no support in Indiana law); *Conner* v. *Pickett,* 552 F.2d 585 (5th Cir. 1977) (state judge who sentenced accused following his guilty plea is immune from liability under the Civil Rights Act); *Brooks* v. *Flagg Bros., Inc.,* 553 F.2d 764 (2d Cir. 1977) ("under color of" state law provision in Civil Rights Act is equivalent to "state action" requirement of Fourteenth Amendment); *Alexanian* v. *New York State Urban Development Corp.,* 554 F.2d 15 (2d Cir. 1977) (allegation that county jail warden confiscated inmate's money and personal possessions and refused to return them to him when he was released states a cause of action under § 1983); *Wolfel* v. *Sanborn,* 555 F.2d 583 (6th Cir. 1977) (police officers who were given permission by parolee's grandmother, in whose house parolee lived, to search unlocked room where parolee slept acted properly in searching and were not liable under § 1983); *Thompson* v. *Burke,* 556 F.2d 231 (3d Cir. 1977) (Pennsylvania Board of Parole and Pardon is not a "person" within the meaning of § 1983).

B. TITLE VII AND THE CORRECTIONAL SYSTEM

Physical Requirements for Prison Guards: Establishing a Prima Facie Case of Discrimination

DOTHARD v. RAWLINSON

Supreme Court of the United States, 1977
433 U.S. ___, 97 S. Ct. 2720, 53 L. Ed. 2d 786

The facts are stated in the opinion.

Mr. Justice STEWART delivered the opinion of the Court.

* * *

I

At the time she applied for a position as correctional counselor trainee, Rawlinson was a 22-year-old college graduate whose major course of study had been correctional psychology. She was refused employment because she failed to meet the minimum 120-pound weight requirement established by an Alabama statute. The statute also establishes a height minimum of 5 feet and 2 inches.

After her application was rejected because of her weight, Rawlinson filed a charge with the Equal Employment Opportunity Commission, and ultimately received a right to sue letter.[c] She then filed a complaint in the District Court on behalf of herself and other similarly situated women, challenging the statutory height and weight minima as violative of Title VII [of the 1964 Civil Rights Act] and the Equal Protection Clause of the Fourteenth Amendment.[d] A three-judge court was convened. . . . While the suit was pending, the Alabama Board of Corrections adopted Administrative Regulation 204, establishing gender criteria for assigning correctional counselors to maximum security institutions for "contact positions," that is, positions requiring continual close physical proximity to inmates of the institution.[f] Rawlinson amended her class-action complaint by adding a challenge to Regulation 204 as also violative of Title VII and the Fourteenth Amendment.

* * *

At the time this litigation was in the District Court, the Board of Corrections employed a total of 435 people in various

---

[c] See 42 U.S.C. § 2000$_e$-5(f) (Supp. V).

[d] A second plaintiff named in the complaint was Brenda Mieth, who, on behalf of herself and others similarly situated, challenged the 5'9" height and 160-pound weight requirements for the position of Alabama state trooper as violative of the Equal Protection Clause. The District Court upheld her challenge, and the defendants did not appeal from that aspect of the District Court's judgment.

[f] Administrative Regulation 204 provides in pertinent part as follows:

"I. GENERAL

"1. The purpose of this regulation is to establish policy and procedure for identifying and designating institutional Correctional Counselor I positions which require selective certification for appointment of either male or female employees from State Personnel Department registers.

"II. POLICY

"4. All Correctional Counselor I positions will be evaluated to identify and designate those which require selective certification for appointment of either a male or female employee. Such positions must fall within a bona fide occupational qualification stated in Title 45-2000$_c$ of the United States Code. . . .

"5. Selective certification from the Correctional Counselor Trainee register will be requested of the State Personnel Department whenever a position is being filled which has been designated for either a male or female employee only.

"III. PROCEDURE

"8. Institutional Wardens and Directors will identify each institutional Correctional Counselor I position which they feel requires

selective certification and will request that it be so designated in writing to the Associate Commissioner for Administration for his review, evaluation, and submission to the Commissioner for final decision.

"9. The request will contain the exact duties and responsibilities of the position and will utilize and identify the following criteria to establish that selective certification is necessary:

"A. That the presence of the opposite sex would cause disruption of the orderly running and security of the institution.

"B. That the position would require contact with the inmates of the opposite sex without the presence of others.

"C. That the position would require patroling dormitories, restrooms, or showers while in use, frequently, during the day or night.

"D. That the position would require search of inmates of the opposite sex on a regular basis.

"E. That the position would require that the Correctional Counselor Trainee not be armed with a firearm.

"10. All institutional Correctional Counselor I positions which are not approved for selective certification will be filled from Correctional Counselor Trainee registers without regard to sex."

Although Regulation 204 is not limited on its face to contact positions in maximum security institutions, the District Court found that it did not "preclude [women] from serving in contact positions in the all-male institutions other than the penitentiaries." 418 F. Supp., at 1176. Petitioners similarly defended the regulation as applying only to maximum security facilities.

correctional counselor positions, 56 of whom were women. Of those 56 women, 21 were employed at the Julia Tutwiler Prison for Women, 13 were employed in noncontact positions at the four male maximum security institutions, and the remaining 22 were employed at the other institutions operated by the Alabama Board of Corrections. Because most of Alabama's prisoners are held at the four maximum security male penitentiaries, 336 of the 435 correctional counselor jobs were in those institutions, a majority of them concededly in the "contact" classification. Thus, even though meeting the statutory height and weight requirements, women applicants could under Regulation 204 compete equally with men for only about 25% of the correctional counselor jobs available in the Alabama prison system.

II

In enacting Title VII, Congress required "the removal of artificial, arbitrary, and unnecessary barriers to employment when the barriers operate invidiously to discriminate on the basis of racial or other impermissible classification." Griggs v. Duke Power Co., 401 U.S. 424, 431 (1971). . . .

* * *

A

The gist of the claim that the statutory height and weight requirements discriminate against women does not involve an assertion of purposeful discriminatory motive. It is asserted, rather, that these facially neutral qualification standards work in fact disproportionately to exclude women from eligibility for employment by the Alabama Board of Corrections. We dealt in Griggs v. Duke Power Co., supra, and Albemarle Paper Co. v. Moody, 422 U.S. 405, with similar allegations that facially neutral employment standards disproportionately excluded Negroes from employment, and those cases guide our approach here.

Those cases make clear that to establish a prima facie case of discrimination, a plaintiff need only show that the facially neutral standards in question select applicants for hire in a significantly discriminatory pattern. Once it is thus shown that the employment standards are discriminatory in effect, the employer must meet "the burden of showing

that any given requirement [has] . . . a manifest relation to the employment in question." . . . If the employer proves that the challenged requirements are job related, the plaintiff may then show that other selection devices without a similar discriminatory effect would also "serve the employer's legitimate interest in 'efficient and trustworthy workmanship.'" . . .

Although women 14 years of age or older comprise 52.75% of the Alabama population and 36.89% of its total labor force, they hold only 12.9% of its correctional counselor positions. In considering the effect of the minimum height and weight standards on this disparity in rate of hiring between the sexes, the District Court found that the 5′2″ requirement would operate to exclude 33.29% of the women in the United States between the ages of 18–79, while excluding only 1.28% of men between the same ages. The 120-pound weight restriction would exclude 22.29% of the women and 2.35% of the men in this age group. When the height and weight restrictions are combined, Alabama's statutory standards would exclude 41.13% of the female population while excluding less than one percent of the male population. Accordingly, the District Court found that Rawlinson had made out a prima facie case of unlawful sex discrimination.

The appellants argue that a showing of disproportionate impact on women based on generalized national statistics should not suffice to establish a prima facie case. They point in particular to Rawlinson's failure to adduce comparative statistics concerning actual applicants for correctional counselor positions in Alabama. There is no requirement, however, that a statistical showing of disproportionate impact must always be based on analysis of the characteristics of actual applicants.

The application process might itself not adequately reflect the actual potential applicant pool, since otherwise qualified people might be discouraged from applying because of a self-recognized inability to meet the very standards challenged as being discriminatory. . . . A potential applicant could easily measure her height and weight and conclude that to make an application would be futile. Moreover, reliance on general population demographic data was not misplaced where there was no reason to suppose that physical height and weight characteristics of Alabama men and women differ markedly from those of the national population. . . .

* * *

B

We turn, therefore, to the appellants' argument that they have rebutted the prima facie case of discrimination by showing that the height and weight requirements are job related. These requirements, they say, have a relationship to strength, a sufficient but unspecified amount of which is essential to effective job performance as a correctional counselor. In the District Court, however, the appellants produced no evidence correlating the height and weight requirements with the requisite amount of strength thought essential to good job performance. Indeed, they failed to offer evidence of any kind in specific justification of the statutory standards.

If the job-related quality that the appellants identify is bona fide, their purpose could be achieved by adopting and validating a test for applicants that measures strength directly. Such a test, fairly administered, would fully satisfy the standards of Title VII because it would be one that "measure[s] the person for the job and not the person in the abstract." Griggs v. Duke Power Co., 401 U.S., at 436. But nothing in the present record even approaches such a measurement.

* * *

III

Unlike the statutory height and weight requirements, Regulation 204 explicitly discriminates against women on the basis of their sex. In defense of this overt discrimination, the appellants rely on § 703$_e$ of Title VII, which permits sex-based discrimination "in those certain instances where . . . sex . . . is a bona fide occupational qualification reasonably necessary to the normal operation of that particular business or enterprise."

The District Court rejected the bona fide occupational qualification (bfoq) defense, relying on the virtually uniform view of the federal courts that § 703$_e$ provides only the narrowest of exceptions to the general rule requiring equality of employment opportunities. . . .

We are persuaded — by the restrictive language of § 703$_e$, the relevant legislative history, and the consistent interpretation of the Equal Employment Opportunity Commission — that the bfoq exception was in fact meant to be an extremely narrow exception to the general prohibition of discrimination on the basis of sex. . . .

The environment in Alabama's penitentiaries is a peculiarly inhospitable one for human beings of whatever sex. Indeed, a federal district court has held that the conditions of confinement in the prisons of the State, characterized by "rampant violence" and a "jungle atmosphere," are constitutionally intolerable. James v. Wallace, 406 F. Supp. 318, 325 (M.D. Ala.). The record in the present case shows that because of inadequate staff and facilities, no attempt is made in the four maximum security male penitentiaries to classify or segregate inmates according to their offense or level of dangerousness — a procedure that, according to expert testimony, is essential to effective penological administration. Consequently, the estimated 20% of the male prisoners who are sex offenders are scattered throughout the penitentiaries' dormitory facilities.

. . . In the usual case, the argument that a particular job is too dangerous for women may appropriately be met by the rejoinder that it is the purpose of Title VII to allow the individual woman to make that choice for herself. More is at stake in this case, however, than an individual woman's decision to weigh and accept the risks of employment in a "contact" position in a maximum security male prison.

The essence of a correctional counselor's job is to maintain prison security. A woman's relative ability to maintain order in a male, maximum security, unclassified penitentiary of the type Alabama now runs could be directly reduced by her womanhood. There is a basis in fact for expecting that sex offenders who have criminally assaulted women in the past would be moved to do so again if access to women were established within the prison. There would also be a real risk that other inmates, deprived of a normal heterosexual environment, would assault women guards because they were women. In a prison system where violence is the order of the day, where inmate access to guards is facilitated by dormitory living arrangements, where every institution is understaffed, and where a substantial portion of the inmate population is composed of sex offenders mixed at random with other prisoners, there are few visible deterrents to inmate assaults on women custodians.

. . . The likelihood that inmates would assault a woman because she was a woman would pose a real threat not only to the victim of the assault but also to the basic control of the penitentiary and protection of its inmates and the other security personnel. The employee's very womanhood would thus directly undermine her capacity to provide the security that is the essence of a correctional counselor's responsibility.

There was substantial testimony from experts on both sides of this litigation that the use of women as guards in "contact" positions under the existing conditions in Alabama maximum security male penitentiaries would pose a substantial security problem, directly linked to the sex of the prison guard. On the basis of that evidence, we conclude that the District Court was in error in ruling that being male is not a bona fide occupational qualification for the job of correctional counselor in a "contact" position in an Alabama male maximum security penitentiary.

The judgment is accordingly affirmed in part and reversed in part, and the case is remanded to the District Court for further proceedings consistent with this opinion.

Mr. Justice REHNQUIST, with whom the CHIEF JUSTICE (BURGER) and Mr. Justice BLACKMUN join, concurring in the result and concurring in part.

I agree with, and join, Parts I and III of the Court's opinion in this case and with its judgment. While I also agree with the Court's conclusions in Part II of its opinion, holding that the District Court was "not in error" in holding the statutory height and weight requirements in this case to be invalidated by Title VII, . . . the issues with which that part deals are bound to arise so frequently that I feel obliged to separately state the reasons for my agreement with its result. I view affirmance of the District Court in this respect as essentially dictated by the peculiarly limited factual and legal justifications offered below by appellants on

behalf of the statutory requirements. For that reason, I do not believe—and do not read the Court's opinion as holding—that all or even many of the height and weight requirements imposed by States on applicants for a multitude of law enforcement agency jobs are pretermitted by today's decision.

* * *

Appellants, in order to rebut the prima facie case under the statute, had the burden placed on them to advance job-related reasons for the qualification. McDonnell Douglas Corp. v. Green, 411 U.S. 792, at 802 (1973). This burden could be shouldered by offering evidence or by making legal arguments not dependent on any new evidence. The District Court was confronted, however, with only one suggested job-related reason for the qualification—that of strength. Appellants argued only the job-relatedness of actual physical strength; they did not urge that an equally job-related qualification for prison guards is the *appearance* of strength. As the Court notes, the primary job of correctional counselor in Alabama prisons "is to maintain security and control of the inmates. . . ," . . . a function that I at least would imagine is aided by the psychological impact on prisoners of the presence of tall and heavy guards. If the appearance of strength had been urged upon the District Court here as a reason for the height and weight minima, I think that the District Court would surely have been entitled to reach a different result than it did. For, even if not perfectly correlated, I would think that Title VII would not preclude a State from saying that anyone under 5'2" or 120 pounds, no matter how strong in fact, does not have a sufficient appearance of strength to be a prison guard.

* * *

Mr. Justice MARSHALL, with whom Mr. Justice BRENNAN joins, concurring in part and dissenting in part.

I agree entirely with the Court's analysis of Alabama's height and weight requirements for prison guards, and with its finding that these restrictions discriminate on the basis of sex in violation of Title VII. Accordingly, I join Parts I and II of the Court's opinion. I also agree with much of the Court's general discussion in Part III of the bona fide occupational qualification exception contained in § 703(e) of Title VII.

* * *

What would otherwise be considered unlawful discrimination against women is justified by the Court, however, on the basis of the "barbaric and inhumane" conditions in Alabama prisons, conditions so bad that state officials have conceded that they violate the Constitution. . . . To me, this analysis sounds distressingly like saying two wrongs make a right. It is refuted by the plain words of § 706(e). The statute requires that a bfoq be "reasonably necessary to the normal operation of that particular business or enterprise." But no governmental "business" may operate "normally" in violation of the Constitution. Every action of government is constrained by constitutional limitations. While those limits may be violated more frequently than we would wish, no one disputes that the "normal operation" of all government functions takes place within them. A prison system operating in blatant violation of the Eighth Amendment is an exception that should be remedied with all possible speed. . . . In the meantime, the existence of such violations should not be legitimatized by calling them "normal." Nor should the Court accept them as justifying conduct that would otherwise violate a statute intended to remedy age-old discrimination.

The Court's error in statutory construction is less objectionable, however, than the attitude it displays toward women. Though the Court recognizes that possible harm to women guards is an unacceptable reason for disqualifying women, it relies instead on an equally speculative threat to prison discipline supposedly generated by the sexuality of female guards. There is simply no evidence in the record to show that women guards would create any danger to security in Alabama prisons significantly greater than already exists. All of the dangers—with one exception discussed below—are inherent in a prison setting whatever the gender of the guards.

The Court first sees women guards as a threat to security because "there are few visible deterrents to inmate assaults on women custodians." . . . In fact, any prison guard is constantly subject to the threat of attack by inmates and "invisible" deterrents are the guard's only real protection. No prison guard relies primarily on his or her ability to ward off an inmate attack to maintain order. Guards are typically unarmed and sheer numbers of inmates could overcome the normal complement. Rather, like all other law enforcement officers, prison guards must rely primarily on the moral authority of their office and the threat of future punishment for miscreants. As one expert testified below, common sense, fairness, and mental and emotional stability are the qualities a guard needs to cope with the dangers of the job. . . . Well qualified and properly trained women, no less than men, have these psychological weapons at their disposal.

* * *

The Court refers to the large number of sex offenders in Alabama prisons and to "the likelihood that inmates would assault a woman because she was a woman." In short, the fundamental justification for the decision is that women as guards will generate sexual assaults. With all respect, this rationale regrettably perpetuates one of the most insidious of the old myths about women—that women, wittingly or not, are seductive sexual objects. The effect of the decision, made I am sure with the best of intentions, is to punish women because their very presence might provoke sexual assaults. It is women who are made to pay the price in lost job opportunities for the threat of depraved conduct by prison inmates. . . .

The Court points to no evidence in the record to support the asserted "likelihood that inmates would assault a woman because she was a woman." . . . Perhaps the Court relies upon common sense, or "inmate recognition." . . . But the danger in this emotionally laden context is that common sense will be used to mask the "romantic paternalism" and persisting discriminatory attitudes that the Court properly eschews. . . . To me, the only matter of innate recognition is that the incidence of sexually motivated attacks on guards will be minute compared to the "likelihood that inmates will assault" a *guard* because he or she is a *guard*.

The proper response to inevitable attacks on both female and male guards is not to limit the employment opportunities of law-abiding women who wish to contribute to their community, but to take swift and sure punitive action against the inmate offenders. . . . To deprive women of job opportunities because of the threatened behavior of convicted criminals is to turn our social priorities upside down.

* * *

[Mr. Justice WHITE wrote a separate dissenting opinion.]

Comments

1. *Dothard* v. *Rawlinson,* supra, should not be read too broadly. The Court did not strike down the Alabama statute per se but rather limited its holding to a finding that (1) appellee Rawlinson did make out a prima facie case of employment discrimination by showing that the facially neutral standards in question (i.e., the height and weight standards) resulted in a significantly discriminatory pattern of applicant selection, and (2) that appellants failed to rebut the prima facie case of discrimination, offering no evidence to prove that the height and weight standards were job related. Isn't the Court saying that under the proper circumstances such standards could be justified with proper rebuttal evidence? Consider Mr. Justice Rehnquist's concurring opinion in this regard. Appellants were successful in justifying the gender criteria of Administrative Regulation 204; they were able to rebut the prima facie showing of sex discrimination by producing evidence that the gender qualification was bona fide and reasonable under the narrow exception of § 703(e) of Title VII.

2. The validity of a qualifying test administered to applicants for positions as police officers was the issue in the recent case of *Washington* v. *Davis,* 426 U.S. 229 (1976). Upon rejection of their applications to become police officers in the District of Columbia, respondents brought action against District of Columbia officials and others, alleging that the police department's personnel test was discriminatory and violated the Due Process Clause of the Fifth Amendment, under 42 U.S.C. § 1981 and under D.C. Code § 1-320. The test (Test 21) was designed to evaluate verbal ability, vocabulary, reading, and reading comprehension. Both parties filed cross-motions for summary judgment. The district court, noting the absence of any claim of intentional discrimination, found that a higher percentage of blacks failed the test than of whites but declined to hold that the test was designed to discriminate against otherwise qualified blacks. The Court of Appeals (D.C. Cir.) reversed, applying to the constitutional issue the statutory standards announced in *Griggs* v. *Duke Power Co.* (Comment 13, infra.) The court of appeals held that the lack of discriminatory intent was irrelevant; that four times as many blacks as whites failed the test and thus the test operated to exclude blacks in violation of Title VII of the Civil Rights Act of 1964. The Supreme Court held that the court of appeals erred when it resolved the constitutional issue (Fifth Amendment violation) by applying standards applicable to Title VII cases. The Supreme Court concluded that the Due Process Clause of the Fifth Amendment prohibits the government from invidious discrimination but that a law or practice can not be considered per se unconstitutional solely because it has a racially disproportionate impact. The Court found that petitioners had demonstrated "a positive relationship between the test and the Department's training program" and that the "disproportionate

impact of Test 21, which is neutral on its face, does not warrant the conclusion that the test was a purposely discriminatory device."

3. In *Griggs* v. *Duke Power Co.,* 401 U.S. 424 (1971), cited in *Dothard* v. *Rawlinson,* supra, black employees of the company brought a class action suit against their employer in federal court alleging that the employer violated Title VII of the 1964 Civil Rights Act by requiring a high school diploma or a satisfactory intelligence test score for certain jobs previously limited to white employees in order to preserve the longstanding practice of giving preference to whites. Title VII permits employers to give professionally developed ability tests provided such tests are "not designed or intended or used to discriminate because of race, color, religion, sex or national origin," § 703(h). In applying § 703(h) of the Civil Rights Act, a unanimous Supreme Court held that an employer may not require a high school diploma or the passing of a standardized intelligence test as a condition of employment or of job transfer unless they provide "a reasonable measure of job performance." If employment tests are shown to have a discriminatory effect, the employer has "the burden of showing that any given requirement has ... a manifest relation to the employment in question," at 432. The burden shifts only after the complaining party has made out a prima facie case of discrimination. The result of the use of the test must be shown to be a racially discriminatory pattern of selection of persons for hire or promotion. See *McDonnell Douglas Corp.* v. *Green,* 411 U.S. 792 (1973). If an employer does show that the tests are "job related," the complaining party may show that other tests without an undesirable racial effect would also serve the legitimate interests of the employer. In *Albemarle Paper Co.* v. *Moody,* 422 U.S. 405 (1975), cited in *Rawlinson,* the Supreme Court adopted the Equal Employment Opportunity Commission (EEOC) "Guidelines" for employees seeking to determine whether their employment tests are job related. Under these guidelines, discriminatory tests are impermissible unless shown, by professionally accepted methods, to be "predictive of or significantly correlated with important elements of work behavior which comprise or are relevant to the job or jobs for which candidates are being evaluated." 29 C.F.R. § 1607.4(c).

10.03 CONSTITUTIONAL RIGHTS OF LAW ENFORCEMENT AUTHORITIES

When a Police Officer Is the Accused

GARRITY v. NEW JERSEY

Supreme Court of the United States, 1967
385 U.S. 493, 87 S. Ct. 616, 17 L. Ed. 2d 562

The facts are stated in the opinion.

Mr. Justice DOUGLAS delivered the opinion of the Court.

Appellants were police officers in certain New Jersey boroughs. The Supreme Court of New Jersey ordered that alleged irregularities in handling cases in the municipal courts of those boroughs be investigated by the Attorney General, invested him with broad powers of inquiry and investigation, and directed him to make a report to the court. The matters investigated concerned alleged fixing of traffic tickets.

Before being questioned, each appellant was warned (1) that anything he said might be used against him in any state criminal proceeding; (2) that he had the privilege to refuse to answer if the disclosure would tend to incriminate him; but (3) that if he refused to answer he would be subject to removal from office.

Appellants answered the questions. No immunity statute was applicable in these circumstances. Over their objections, some of the answers given were used in subsequent prosecutions for conspiracy to obstruct the administration of the traffic laws. Appellants were convicted and their convictions were sustained over their protests that their statements were coerced, by reason of the fact that, if they refused to answer, they could lose their positions with the police department. . . .

We postponed the question of jurisdiction to a hearing on the merits. . . . The statute whose validity was sought to be "drawn in question," 28 U.S.C. § 1257(2), was the forfeiture statute. But the New Jersey Supreme Court refused to reach that question . . . deeming the voluntariness of the statements as the only issue presented. . . . The statute is therefore too tangentially involved to satisfy 28 U.S.C. § 1257(2), for the only bearing it had was whether, valid or not, the fear of being discharged under it for refusal to answer on the one hand and the fear of self-incrimination on the other was " 'a choice between the rock and the whirlpool' " which made the statements products of coercion in violation of the Fourteenth Amendment. We therefore dismiss the appeal, treat the papers as a petition for certiorari (28 U.S.C. § 2103), grant the petition and proceed to the merits.

We agree with the New Jersey Supreme Court that the forefeiture-of-office statute is relevant here only for the bearing it has on the voluntary character of the statements used to convict petitioners in their criminal prosecutions.

The choice imposed on petitioners was one between self-incrimination or job forfeiture. Coercion that vitiates a confession under Chambers v. State of Florida, 309 U.S. 227 (1948), and related cases can be "mental as well as physical"; "the blood of the accused is not the only hallmark of an unconstitutional inquisition." . . . Subtle pressures may be as telling as coarse and vulgar ones. The question is whether the accused was deprived of his "free choice to admit, to deny, or to refuse to answer.". . .

We adhere to Boyd v. United States, 116 U.S. 616 (1896), a civil forfeiture action against property. A statute offered the owner an election between producing a document or forfeiture of the goods at issue in the proceeding. This was held to be a form of compulsion in violation of both the Fifth Amendment and the Fourth Amendment. It is that principle that we adhere to and apply in Spevack v. Klein, 385 U.S. 511 (1967).

The choice given petitioners was either to forfeit their jobs or to incriminate themselves. The option to lose their means of livelihood or to pay the penalty of self-incrimination is the antithesis of free choice to speak out or to remain silent. That practice, like interrogation practices we reviewed in Miranda v. State of Arizona, 384 U.S. 436 (1966), is "likely to exert such pressure upon an individual as to disable him from making a free and rational choice." We think the statements were infected by the coercion inherent in this scheme of questioning and cannot be sustained as voluntary under our prior decisions.

It is said that there was a "waiver." That, however, is a federal question for us to decide. . . . The Court in Union Pac. R. R. Co. v. Public Service Comm. [248 U.S. 67, 69–70], in speaking of a certificate exacted under protest and in violation of the Commerce Clause, said:

"Were it otherwise, as conduct under duress involves a choice, it always would be possible for a State to impose an unconstitutional burden by the threat of penalties worse than it in case of a failure to accept it, and then to declare the acceptance voluntary. . . ."

Where the choice is "between the rock and the whirlpool," duress is inherent in deciding to "waive" one or the other.

"It always is for the interest of a party under duress to choose the lesser of two evils. But the fact that a choice was made according to interest does not exclude duress. It is the characteristic of duress properly so called."

In that case appellant paid under protest. In these cases also, though petitioners succumbed to compulsion, they preserved their objections, raising them at the earliest possible point. . . . The cases are therefore quite different from the situation where one who is anxious to make a clean breast of the whole affair volunteers the information.

Mr. Justice Holmes in McAuliffe v. New Bedford, 155 Mass. 216, 29 N.E. 517, stated a dictum on which New Jersey heavily relies:

"The petitioner may have a constitutional right to talk politics, but he has no constitutional right to be a policeman. There are few employments for hire in which the servant does not agree to suspend his constitutional right of free speech as well as of idleness by the implied terms of his contract. The servant cannot complain, as he takes the employment on the terms which are offered him. On the same principle the city may impose any reasonable condition upon holding offices within its control."

The question in this case, however, is not cognizable in those terms. Our question is whether a State, contrary to the requirement of the Fourteenth Amendment, can use the threat of discharge to secure incriminatory evidence against an employee.

We held in Slochower v. Board of Education, 350 U.S. 551 (1956), that a public school teacher could not be discharged merely because he had invoked the Fifth Amendment privilege against self-incrimination when questioned by a congressional committee:

"The privilege against self-incrimination would be reduced to a hollow mockery if its exercise could be taken as equivalent either to a confession of guilt or a conclusive presumption of perjury. . . . The privilege serves to protect the innocent who otherwise might be ensnared by ambiguous circumstances." . . .

We conclude that policemen, like teachers and lawyers, are not relegated to a watered-down version of constitutional rights.

There are rights of constitutional stature whose exercise a State may not condition by the exaction of a price. Engaging in interstate commerce is one. . . . Resort to the federal courts in diversity of citizenship cases is another. . . . Assertion of a First Amendment right is still another. . . . The imposition of a burden on the exercise of a Twenty-fourth Amendment right is also banned. . . . We now hold the protection of the individual under the Fourteenth Amendment against coerced statements prohibits use in subsequent criminal proceedings of statements obtained under threat of removal from office, and that it extends to all, whether they are policemen or other members of our body politic.

Reversed.

[Mr. Justice HARLAN, joined by Mr. Justice CLARK and Mr. Justice STEWART, dissented.]

[Mr. Justice WHITE filed a separate dissenting opinion.]

Police Hair Length Regulations

KELLEY v. JOHNSON

Supreme Court of the United States, 1976
425 U.S. 238, 96 S. Ct. 1440, 47 L. Ed. 2d 708

The facts are stated in the opinion.

Mr. Justice REHNQUIST delivered the opinion of the Court.

* * *

I

In 1971 respondent's predecessor, individually and as president of the Suffolk

County Patrolmen's Benevolent Association, brought this action under the Civil Rights Act of 1871, 42 U.S.C. § 1983, against petitioner's predecessor, the Commissioner of the Suffolk County Police Department. The Commissioner had promulgated Order No. 71-1, which established hair grooming standards applicable to male members of the police force.[a] The regulation

---

[a]Order No. 71-1, amending Chapter 2 of the Rules and Procedures, Police Department, County of Suffolk, N.Y., provided:

"2/75.0 Members of the Force and Department shall be neat and clean at all times while on duty. Male personnel shall comply with the following grooming standards unless excluded by the Police Commissioner due to special assignment:

"2/75.1 *Hair:* Hair shall be neat, clean, trimmed, and present a groomed appearance. Hair will not touch the ears or the collar except the closely cut hair on the back of the neck. Hair in front will be groomed so that it does not fall below the band of properly worn headgear. In no case will the bulk or length of the hair interfere with the proper wear of any authorized headgear. The acceptability of a member's hair style will be based upon the criteria in this paragraph and not upon the style in which he chooses to wear his hair.

"2/75.2 *Sideburns:* If an individual chooses to wear sideburns, they will be neatly trimmed and tapered in the same manner as his haircut. Sideburns will not extend below the lowest part of the exterior ear opening, will be of even width (not flared), and will end with a clean-shaven horizontal line.

"2/75.3 *Mustaches:* A short and neatly trimmed mustache may be worn, but shall not extend over the top of the upper lip or beyond the corners of the mouth.

"2/75.4 *Beards & Goatees:* The face will be clean-shaven other than the wear of the acceptable mustache or sideburns. Beards and goatees are prohibited, except that a Police Surgeon may grant a waiver for the wearing of a beard for medical reasons with the approval of the Police Commissioner. When a Surgeon prescribes that a member not shave, the beard will be kept trimmed symmetrically and all beard hairs will be kept trimmed so that they do not protrude more than one-half inch from the skin surface of the face.

"2/75.5 *Wigs:* Wigs or hair pieces will not be worn on duty in uniform except for cosmetic reasons to cover natural baldness or physical disfiguration. If under these conditions, a wig or hair piece is worn, it will conform to department standards."

---

was directed at the style and length of hair, sideburns, and mustaches; beards and goatees were prohibited, except for medical reasons; and wigs conforming to the regulation could be worn for cosmetic reasons. The regulation was attacked as violative of respondent patrolman's right of free expression under the First Amendment and his guarantees of due process and equal protection under the Fourteenth Amendment, in that it was "not based upon the generally accepted standard of grooming in the community" and placed "an undue restriction" upon his activities therein.

The Court of Appeals held that cases characterizing the uniform civilian services as "para-military," and sustaining hair regulations on that basis, were not soundly grounded historically. It said the fact that a police force is organized "with a centralized administration and a disciplined rank and file for efficient conduct of its affairs' " did not foreclose respondent's claim, but instead bore only upon "the existence of a legitimate state interest to be reasonably advanced by the regulation." Owen v. Barry, 483 F.2d 1126, 1128–1129 (1973). The Court of Appeals went on to decide that "choice of personal appearance is an ingredient of an individual's personal liberty" and is protected by the Fourteenth Amendment. It further held that the police department had "failed to make the slightest showing of the relationship between its regulation and the legitimate interest it sought to promote." . . . On the basis of this reasoning it concluded that neither dismissal nor summary judgment in the District Court was appropriate, since the department "has the burden of establishing a genuine public need for the regulation." . . .

Thereafter the District Court, under the compulsion of the remand from the Court of Appeals, took testimony on the question of whether or not there was a "genuine public need." The sole witness was the Deputy Commissioner of the Suffolk County Police Department, petitioner's subordinate, who testified as to the police department's concern for the safety of the patrolmen, and the need for some standards of uniformity in appearance. The District Court held that "no proof" was offered to support any claim of the need for the protection of the police officer, and that while "proper grooming" is an ingredient of a good police department's "esprit de corps," petitioner's standards did not establish a public need because they ultimately reduced to "[u]niformity for uniformity's sake." The District Court granted the relief prayed for by respondent, and on petitioner's appeal that judgment was affirmed without opinion by the Court of Appeals.

II

Section 1 of the Fourteenth Amendment to the United States Constitution provides in pertinent part:

"[No State] shall . . . deprive any person of life, liberty, or property, without due process of law."

This section affords not only a procedural guarantee against the deprivation of "liberty," but likewise protects substantive aspects of liberty against unconstitutional restriction by the State. . . .

The "liberty" interest claimed by respondent here, of course, is distinguishable from those protected by the Court in Roe v. Wade, 410 U.S. 113 (1973); Eisenstadt v. Baird, 405 U.S. 438 (1972); Stanley v. Illinois, 405 U.S. 645 (1972); . . . and Meyer v. Nebraska, 262 U.S. 390 (1923). Each of those cases involved a substantial claim of infringement on the individual's freedom of choice with respect to certain basic matters of procreation, marriage, and family life. But whether the citizenry at large has some sort of "liberty" interest within the Fourteenth Amendment in matters of personal appearance is a question on which this Court's cases offer little, if any, guidance. We can, nevertheless, assume an affirmative answer for purposes of deciding this case, because we find that assumption insufficient to carry the day for respondent's claim.

Respondent has sought the protection of the Fourteenth Amendment not as a member of the citizenry at large, but on the contrary as an employee of the police force of Suffolk County, a subdivision of the State of New York. While the Court of Appeals made passing reference to this distinction, it was thereafter apparently ignored. We think, however, it is highly significant. In Pickering v. Board of Education, 391 U.S. 563, 568 (1968), after noting that state employment may not be conditioned on the relinquishment of First Amendment rights, the Court stated that "[a]t the same time it cannot be gainsaid that the State has interests as an employer in regulating the speech of its employees that differ significantly from those it possesses in connection with regulation of the speech of the citizenry in general." More recently, we have sustained comprehensive and substantial restrictions upon activities of both federal and state employees lying at the core of the First Amendment. Civil Service Comm'n v. Letter Carriers, 413 U.S. 548 (1973); Broadrick v. Oklahoma, 413 U.S. 601 (1973). If such state regulations may survive challenges based on the explicit language of the First Amendment, there is surely even more room for restrictive regulations of state employees where the claim implicates only the more general contours of the substantive liberty interest protected by the Fourteenth Amendment.

The hair length regulation here touches respondent as an employee of the county and, more particularly, as a policeman. Respondent's employer has, in accordance with its well-established duty to keep the peace, placed myriad demands upon the members of the police force, duties which have no counterpart with respect to the public at large. Respondent must wear a standard uniform specific in each detail. When in uniform he must salute the flag. He cannot take an active role in local political affairs by way of being a party delegate or contributing or soliciting political contributions. He cannot smoke in public. All of these and other regulations of the Suffolk County Police Department infringe on respondent's freedom of choice in personal matters, and it was apparently the view of the Court of Appeals that the burden is on the State to prove a "genuine public need" for each and every one of these regulations.

This view was based upon the Court of Appeals' reasoning that the "unique judicial deference" accorded by the judiciary to regulation of members of the military was inapplicable because there was no historical or functional justification for the characterization of the police as "para-military." But the conclusion that such cases are inapposite, however correct, in no way detracts from deference due Suffolk County's choice of an organizational structure for its police force. Here the County has chosen a mode of organization which it undoubtedly deems the most efficient in enabling its police to carry out the duties assigned to them under state and local law. Such a choice necessarily gives weight to the overall need for discipline, esprit de corps, and uniformity.

The county's choice of an organizational structure, therefore, does not depend for its constitutional validity on any doctrine of historical prescription. Nor, indeed, has respondent made any such claim. His argument does not challenge the constitutionality of the organizational structure, but merely asserts that the present hair length regulation infringes his asserted liberty interest under the Fourteenth Amendment. We believe, however, that the hair length regulation cannot be viewed in isolation, but must be rather considered in the context of the county's chosen mode of organization for its police force.

The promotion of safety of persons and property is unquestionably at the core of the State's police power, and virtually all state and local governments employ a uniformed police force to aid in the accomplishment of that purpose. Choice of organization, dress, and equipment for law enforcement personnel is a decision entitled to the same sort of presumption of legislative validity as are state choices designed to promote other aims within the cognizance of the State's police power. . . . Having recognized in other contexts the wide latitude accorded the Government in the "dispatch of its own internal affairs," . . . we think Suffolk County's police regulations involved here are entitled to similar weight. Thus the question is not, as the Court of Appeals conceived it to be, whether the State can "establish" a "genuine public need" for the specific regulation. It is whether respondent can demonstrate that there is no rational connection between the regulation, based as it is on respondent's method of organizing its police force, and the promotion of safety of persons and property. . . .

We think the answer here is so clear that the District Court was quite right in the first instance to have dismissed respondent's complaint. Neither this Court, the Court of Appeals, or the District Court is in a position to weigh the policy arguments in favor of and against a rule regulating hair styles as a part of regulations governing a uniformed civilian service. This constitutional issue to be decided by these courts is whether petitioner's determination that such regulations should be enacted is so irrational that it may be branded "arbitrary," and therefore a deprivation of respondent's "liberty" interest in freedom to choose his own hair style. . . . The overwhelming majority of state and local police of the present day are uniformed. This fact itself testifies to the recognition by those who direct those operations, and by the people of the States and localities who directly or indirectly choose such persons, that similarity in appearance of police officers is desirable. This choice may be based on a desire to make police officers readily recognizable to the members of the public, or a desire for the esprit de corps which such similarity is felt to inculcate within the police force itself. Either one is a sufficiently rational justification for regulations so as to defeat respondent's claim based on the liberty guaranty of the Fourteenth Amendment.

The Court of Appeals relied on Garrity v. New Jersey, 385 U.S. 493 (1967), and amici in their brief in support of respondent elaborate an argument based on the language in Garrity that "policemen, like teachers and lawyers, are not relegated to a watered-down version of constitutional rights." . . . Garrity, of course, involved the protections afforded by the Fifth Amendment to the United States Constitution as made applicable to the States by the Fourteenth Amendment. . . . Certainly its language cannot be taken to suggest that the claim of a member of a uniformed civilian service based on the "liberty" interest protected by the Fourteenth Amendment must necessarily be treated for constitutional purposes the same as a similar claim by a member of the general public.

The regulation challenged here did not violate any right guaranteed respondent by the Fourteenth Amendment to the United States Constitution, and the Court of Appeals was therefore wrong in reversing the District Court's original judgment dismissing the action. The judgment of the Court of Appeals is

Reversed.

* * *

[Mr. Justice POWELL wrote a concurring opinion.]

Mr. Justice MARSHALL, with whom Mr. Justice BRENNAN joins, dissenting.

* * *

I

As the Court recognizes, the Fourteenth Amendment's guarantee against the deprivation of liberty "protects substantive aspects of liberty against unconstitutional restrictions by the State." ... And we have observed that "[l]iberty under law extends to the full range of conduct which the individual is free to pursue." ... It seems to me manifest that the "full range of conduct" must encompass one's interest in dressing according to his own taste. An individual's personal appearance may reflect, sustain, and nourish his personality and may well be used as a means of expressing his attitude and lifestyle. In taking control over a citizen's personal appearance, the Government forces him to sacrifice substantial elements of his integrity and identity as well. To say that the liberty guarantee of the Fourteenth Amendment does not encompass matters of personal appearance would be fundamentally inconsistent with the values of privacy, self-identity, autonomy, and personal integrity that I have always assumed the Constitution was designed to protect. ...

If little can be found in past cases of this Court or indeed in the Nation's history on the specific issue of a citizen's right to choose his own personal appearance, it is only because the right has been so clear as to be beyond question. When the right has been mentioned, its existence has simply been taken for granted. For instance, the assumption that the right exists is reflected in the 1789 congressional debates over which guarantees should be explicitly articulated in the Bill of Rights. Brant, The Bill of Rights 53–67 (1965). There was considerable debate over whether the right of assembly should be expressly mentioned. Congressman Benson of New York argued that its inclusion was necessary to assure that the right would not be infringed by the Government. In response, Congressman Sedgwick of Massachusetts indicated:

"If the committee were governed by that general principle ... they might have declared that *a man should have a right to wear his hat if he pleased* ... but [I] would ask the gentleman whether he thought it necessary to enter these trifles in a declaration of rights, *in a Government where none of them were intended to be infringed.*" Id., at 54–55 (emphasis added).

Thus, while they did not include it in the Bill of Rights, Sedgwick and his colleagues clearly believed there to be a right in one's personal appearance. And, while they may have regarded the right as a trifle as long as it was honored, they clearly would not have so regarded it if it were infringed.

This Court, too, has taken as an axiom that there is a right in one's personal appearance. Indeed, in 1958 we used the existence of that right as support for our recognition of the right to travel:

"The right to travel is a part of the 'liberty' of which the citizen cannot be deprived without due process of law under the Fifth Amendment. ... *It may be as close to the heart of the individual as the choice of what he eats, or wears, or reads.*" Kent v. Dulles, 357 U.S. 116, 125–126 (emphasis added).

To my mind, the right in one's personal appearance is inextricably bound up with the historically recognized right of "every individual to the possession and control of his own person," ... and, perhaps even more fundamentally, with "the right to be let alone — the most comprehensive of rights and the right most valued by civilized men." ... In an increasingly crowded society in which it is already extremely difficult to maintain one's identity and personal integrity, it would be distressing, to say the least, if the Government could regulate our personal appearance unconfined by any constitutional strictures whatsoever.

II

Acting on its assumption that the Fourteenth Amendment does encompass a right in one's personal appearance, the Court justifies the challenged hair length regulation on the grounds that such regulations may "be based on a desire to make police officers readily recognizable to the members of the public, or a desire for the esprit de corps which such similarity is felt to inculcate within the police force itself." ... While fully accepting the aims of "identifiability" and maintenance of esprit de corps, I find no rational relationship between the challenged regulation and these goals.

As for the first justification offered by the Court, I simply do not see how requiring policemen to maintain hair of under a certain length could rationally be argued to contribute to making them identifiable to the public as policemen. Surely, the fact that a uniformed police officer is wearing his hair below his collar will make him no less identifiable as a policeman. And one can not easily imagine a plainclothes officer being readily identifiable as such simply because his hair does not extend beneath his collar.

As for the Court's second justification, the fact that it is the President of the Patrolmen's Benevolent Association, in his official capacity, who has challenged the regulation here would seem to indicate that the regulation would if anything, decrease rather than increase the police force's esprit de corps. And even if one accepted the argument that substantial similarity in appearance would increase a force's esprit de corps, I simply do not understand how implementation of this regulation could be expected to create any increment in similarity of appearance among members of a uniformed police force. While the regulation prohibits hair below the ears or the collar and limits the length of sideburns, it allows the maintenance of any type of hair style, other than a pony tail. Thus, as long as their hair does not go below their collars, two police officers, one with an "Afro" hair style and the other with a crew cut, could both be in full compliance with the regulation.

The Court cautions us not to view the hair length regulation in isolation but rather to examine it "in the context of the county's chosen mode of organization of its police force." . . . While the Court's caution is well taken, one should also keep in mind, as I fear the Court does not, that what is ultimately under scrutiny is neither the overall structure of the police force nor the uniform and equipment requirements to which its members are subject but rather the regulation which dictates acceptable hair lengths. The fact that the uniform requirement, for instance, may be rationally related to the goals of increasing police officer "identifiability" and the maintenance of esprit de corps does absolutely nothing to establish the legitimacy of the hair length regulation. . . .

[Mr. Justice STEVENS took no part in the consideration or decision of this case.]

Comments

1. In *Garrity* v. *New Jersey,* supra, a majority of the Court held that coerced statements obtained under threat of the loss of employment may not be used in subsequent criminal proceedings. However, *Garrity* certainly does *not* stand for the proposition that an employee (e.g., a police officer) may not be fired for refusing to give possibly incriminating answers. The narrow holding of *Garrity* is that if the employee makes incriminating statements under a threat of discharge, the statements may not later be used in a criminal proceeding. Are any due process interests violated if a police officer is fired for refusing to answer incriminating questions even though a subsequent criminal investigation reveals no wrongdoing on his part? Does he have a constitutional right (e.g., due process property interest) to reinstatement? The answers are not clear. In his dissent in *Garrity,* Mr. Justice Harlan, joined by Justices Clark and Stewart, stated that the police officer's incriminating statements were voluntary both in fact and as a matter of law. Did the dissenters take this view in part because the new Jersey procedure was designed "to serve important public interests"?

2. In *Spevack* v. *Klein,* 385 U.S. 511 (1967), decided the same day as *Garrity,* a majority of the Court held that a lawyer may not be disbarred solely because he refused to testify at a disciplinary hearing at which he was charged with refusing to produce financial records pursuant to a subpoena. The following year, the Court held in *Gardner* v. *Broderick,* 392 U.S. 273 (1968), that a police officer who refuses to waive his privilege against self-incrimination may not

be fired for that reason alone. However, the Court noted that if a police officer refuses to answer questions relating specifically to the performance of his official duties and is not required to waive a grant of immunity from subsequent criminal prosecution, the Fifth Amendment would not bar his dismissal on those grounds. In *Gardner,* the Court found that the police officer had in fact been fired for refusing to waive his Fifth Amendment privilege even though he was entitled to immunity. Suppose a police officer waives immunity for fear of losing his job. Is that a valid waiver?

3. In *Kelley* v. *Johnson,* supra, a majority of the Court rejected the "genuine public need" test espoused by the court of appeals in determining the validity of police regulations. Instead, the *Kelley* Court held that a litigant challenging the validity of a police regulation must show that there is "no rational connection between the regulation . . . and the promotion of safety of persons and property"; the regulation must be shown to be "irrational" and "arbitrary." Given these criteria, would a police regulation forbidding female officers from wearing skirts or dresses while on duty violate the Fourteenth Amendment? Would an ordinance applicable to civilians that made it a misdemeanor to be "un-groomed," "unkempt," or not "properly groomed" be constitutional? It is unlikely that such a law could pass constitutional muster. The *Kelley* Court hinted that the "liberty" interests protected by the Fourteenth Amendment are different for members of uniformed civilian services (e.g., police officers) and members of the general public. Given this distinction, are "no smoking in public" police regulations constitutional? What about a city ordinance prohibiting smoking in public by anyone? Can it be argued that there is an esprit de corps in the community that would justify regulation of personal appearance? Do you agree with Justices Brennan and Marshall (dissenting) that the regulation would seem to "decrease rather than increase the police force's esprit de corps"?

4. What are the implications of Mr. Justice Douglas' statement in *Garrity* that "policemen, like teachers and lawyers, are not relegated to a watered-down version of constitutional rights"? Does that seem to be an accurate statement in light of the cases just discussed?

Firing Police Officers Without Cause

BISHOP v. WOOD

Supreme Court of the United States, 1976
426 U.S. 341, 96 S. Ct. 2074, 48 L. Ed. 2d 684

The facts are stated in the opinion.

Mr. Justice STEVENS delivered the opinion of the Court, in which the CHIEF JUSTICE (BURGER), Mr. Justice STEWART, Mr. Justice POWELL, and Mr. Justice REHNQUIST joined.

Acting on the recommendation of the Chief of Police, the City Manager of Marion, North Carolina, terminated petitioner's employment as a policeman without affording him a hearing to determine the sufficiency of the cause for his discharge. Petitioner brought suit contending that since a city ordinance classified him as a "permanent employee," he had a constitutional right to a pretermination hearing. During pretrial discovery petitioner was advised that his dismissal was based on a failure to follow certain orders, poor attendance at police training classes, causing low morale, and conduct unsuited to an officer. Petitioner and several other police officers filed affidavits essentially denying the truth of these charges. The District Court granted defendant's motion for summary judgment. The Court of Appeals affirmed and we granted certiorari. . . .

The questions for us to decide are (1) whether petitioner's employment status was a property interest protected by the Due Process Clause of the Fourteenth Amendment, and (2) assuming that the explanation for his discharge was false, whether that false explanation deprived him of an interest in liberty protected by that clause.

I

Petitioner was employed by the city of Marion as a probationary policeman on June 9, 1969. After six months he became a permanent employee. He was dismissed on March 31, 1972. He claims that he had either an express or an implied right to continued employment.

A city ordinance provides that a permanent employee may be discharged if he fails to perform work up to the standard of his classification or if he is negligent, inefficient or unfit to perform his duties. Petitioner first contends that even though the ordinance does not expressly so provide, it should be read to prohibit discharge for any other reason, and therefore to confer tenure on all permanent employees. In addition, he contends that his period of service, together with his "permanent" classification, gave him a sufficient expectancy of continued employment to constitute a protected property interest.

A property interest in employment can, of course, be created by ordinance, or by an implied contract. In either case, however, the sufficiency of the claim of entitlement must be decided by reference to state law. The North Carolina Supreme Court has held that an enforceable expectation of continued public employment in that State can exist only if the employer, by statute or contract, has actually granted some form of guarantee. Whether such a guarantee has been given can be determined only by an examination of the particular statute or ordinance in question.

On its face the ordinance on which petitioner relies may fairly be read as conferring such a guarantee. However, such a reading is not the only possible interpretation; the ordinance may also be construed as granting no right to continued employment but merely conditioning an employee's removal on compliance with certain specified procedures. We do not have any authoritative interpretation of this ordinance by a North Carolina state court. We do, however, have the opinion of the United States District Judge, who, of course, sits in North Carolina and practiced law there for many years. Based on his understanding of state law, he concluded that petitioner "held his position at the will and pleasure of the city." This construction of North Carolina law was upheld by the Court of Appeals for the Fourth Circuit, albeit by an equally divided Court. In comparable circumstances, the Court has accepted the interpretation of state law in which the District Court and the Court of Appeals have concurred even if an examination of the state law issue without such guidance might have justified a different conclusion.

In this case, as the District Court construed the ordinance, the City Manager's determination of the adequacy of the grounds for discharge is not subject to judicial review; the employee is merely given certain procedural rights which the District Court found not to have been violated in this case. . . .

Under that view of the law, petitioner's discharge did not deprive him of a property interest protected by the Fourteenth Amendment.

II

Petitioner's claim that he has been deprived of liberty has two components. He contends that the reasons given for his discharge are so serious as to constitute a stigma that may severely damage his reputation in the community; in addition, he claims that those reasons were false.

In our appraisal of petitioner's claim we must accept his version of the facts since the District Court granted summary judgment against him. His evidence established that he was a competent police officer; that he was respected by his peers; that he made more arrests than any other officer on the force; that although he had been criticized for engaging in high speed pursuits he had promptly complied with such criticism; and that he had a reasonable explanation for his imperfect attendance at police training sessions. We must therefore assume that his discharge was a mistake and based on incorrect information.

In Board of Regents v. Roth, 408 U.S. 564 (1972), we recognized that the nonretention of an untenured college teacher might make him somewhat less attractive to other employers but nevertheless concluded that it would stretch the concept too far "to suggest that a person is deprived of 'liberty' when he simply is not retained in one position but remains as free as before to seek another." ... This same conclusion applies to the discharge of a public employee whose position is terminable at the will of the employer when there is no public disclosure of the reasons for the discharge.

In this case the asserted reasons for the City Manager's decision were communicated orally to the petitioner in private and also were stated in writing in answer to interrogatories after this litigation commenced. Since the former communication was not made public, it cannot properly form the basis for a claim that petitioner's interest in his "good name, reputation, honesty, or integrity" was thereby impaired. And since the latter communication was made in the course of a judicial proceeding which did not commence until after petitioner had suffered the injury for which he seeks redress, it surely cannot provide retroactive support for his claim. A contrary evaluation of either explanation would penalize forthright and truthful communication between employer and employee in the former instance, and between litigants in the latter.

Petitioner argues, however, that the reasons given for his discharge were false. Even so, the reasons stated to him in private had no different impact on his reputation than if they had been true.... The truth or falsity of the City Manager's statement determines whether or not his decision to discharge the petitioner was correct or prudent, but neither enhances nor diminishes petitioner's claim that his constitutionally protected interest in liberty has been impaired. ...

The federal court is not the appropriate forum in which to review the multitude of personnel decisions that are made daily by public agencies. We must accept the harsh fact that numerous individual mistakes are inevitable in the day-to-day administration of our affairs. The United States Constitution cannot feasibly be construed to require federal judicial review for every such error. In the absence of any claim that the public employer was motivated by a desire to curtail or to penalize the exercise of an employee's constitutionally protected rights, we must presume that official action was regular and, if erroneous, can best be corrected in other ways. The Due Process Clause of the Fourteenth Amendment is not a guarantee against incorrect or ill-advised personnel decisions.

The judgment is affirmed.

Mr. Justice BRENNAN with whom Mr. Justice MARSHALL concurs, dissenting.

Petitioner was discharged as a policeman on the grounds of insubordination, "causing low morale," and "conduct unsuited to an officer." ... It is difficult to imagine a greater "badge of infamy" that could be imposed on one following petitioner's calling; in a profession in which prospective employees are invariably investigated, petitioner's job prospects will be severely constricted by the governmental action in this case. Although our case law would appear to require that petitioner thus be accorded an opportunity "to clear his name" of this calumny, ... the Court condones this governmental action and holds that petitioner was deprived of no liberty interest thereby.

* * *

The Court purports to limit its holding to situations in which there is "no public disclosure of the reasons for the discharge." ... [B]ut in this case the stigmatizing reasons have been disclosed, and there is no reason to believe that respondents will not convey these actual reasons to petitioner's prospective employers. The Court responds by asserting that since the stigma was imposed "after petitioner had suffered the injury for which he seeks redress, it surely cannot provide retroactive support for his claim.". . . But the "claim" does not arise until the State has officially branded petitioner in some way, and the purpose of the due process hearing is to accord him an opportunity to clear his name; merely because the derogatory information is filed in respondent's records and no "publication" occurs until shortly after his discharge from employment does not subvert the fact that a post-deprivation hearing to accord petitioner an opportunity to clear his name has been contemplated by our cases.

* * *

I also fully concur in the dissenting opinions of Mr. Justice WHITE and Mr. Justice BLACKMUN, which forcefully demonstrate the Court's error in holding that petitioner was not deprived of "property" without due process of law. I would only add that the strained reading of the local ordinance, which the Court deems to be "tenable," . . . cannot be dispositive of the existence vel non of petitioner's "property" interest. There is certainly a federal dimension to the definition of "property" in the Federal Constitution; cases such as Board of Regents v. Roth, supra, held merely that "property" interests encompass those to which a person has "a legitimate claim of entitlement," . . . and can arise from "existing rules or understandings" that derive from "an independent source such as state law." . . . But certainly, at least before a state law is definitively construed as not securing a "property" interest, the relevant inquiry is whether it was objectively reasonable for the employee to believe he could rely on continued employment. ("It is a purpose of the ancient institution of property to protect those claims upon which people rely in their daily lives, reliance that must not be arbitrarily determined.") . . .

* * *

Mr. Justice WHITE, with whom Mr. Justice BRENNAN, Mr. Justice MARSHALL, and Mr. Justice BLACKMUN join, dissenting.

I dissent because the decision of the majority rests upon a proposition which was squarely addressed and in my view correctly rejected by six members of this Court in Arnett v. Kennedy. . . .

Petitioner Bishop was a permanent employee of the Police Department of the City of Marion, N.C. The city ordinance applicable to him provides:

"*Dismissal.* A permanent employee whose work is not satisfactory over a period of time shall be notified in what way his work is deficient and what he must do if his work is to be satisfactory. If a permanent employee fails to perform work up to the standard of the classification held, or continues to be negligent, inefficient, or unfit to perform his duties, he may be dismissed by the City Manager. Any discharged employee shall be given written notice of his discharge setting forth the effective date and reasons for his discharge if he shall request such a notice." (Emphasis added.)

The second sentence of this ordinance plainly conditions petitioner's dismissal on cause—i.e., failure to perform up to standard, negligence, inefficiency, or unfitness to perform the job. The District Court below did not otherwise construe this portion of the ordinance. In the only part of its opinion rejecting petitioner's claim that the ordinance gave him a property interest in his job, the District Court said, in an opinion predating this Court's decision in Arnett v. Kennedy. . . . :

"It is clear from Article II, Section 6, of the City's Personnel Ordinance, that the dismissal of an employee does not require a notice or hearing. Upon request of the discharged employee, he shall be given written notice of his discharge setting forth the effective date and the reasons for the discharge. It thus appears that both the city ordinance and the state law have been complied with."

Thus in concluding that petitioner had no "property interest" in his job entitling him to a hearing on discharge and that he held his position "at the will and pleasure of the city," the District Court relied on the fact that the ordinance described its own procedures for determining cause, which procedures did not include a hearing. The majority purports . . . to read the District Court's opinion as construing the ordinance *not* to condition dismissal on cause, and if this is what the majority means, its reading of the District Court's opinion is clearly erroneous for the reasons just stated. . . . In the concluding paragraph of its discussion of petitioner's property interest, the majority holds that since neither the ordinance nor state law provides for a hearing or any kind of review of the City Manager's dismissal decision, petitioner had no enforceable property interest in his job. The majority concludes:

"In this case, as the District Court construed the ordinance, the City Manager's *determination of the adequacy of the grounds for discharge* is not subject to judicial review; the employee is merely given certain procedural rights which the District Court found not to have been violated in this case. The District Court's reading of the ordinance is tenable; . . . ." (Emphasis added.)

The majority thus implicitly concedes that the ordinance supplies the "grounds" for discharge and that the City Manager must determine them to be "adequate" before he may fire an employee. The majority's holding that petitioner had no property interest in his job in spite of the unequivocal language in the city ordinance that he may be dismissed only for certain kinds of cause rests then, on the fact that state law provides no *procedures* for assuring that the City Manager dismiss him only for cause. The right to his job apparently given by the first two sentences of the ordinance is thus redefined according to the majority by the procedures provided for in the third sentence and as redefined is infringed only if the procedures are not followed.

This is precisely the reasoning which was embraced by only three and expressly rejected by six Members of this Court in Arnett v. Kennedy. . . .

* * *

The views now expressed by the majority are thus squarely contrary to the views expressed by a majority of the Justices in Arnett. As Mr. Justice Powell suggested in Arnett, they are also "incompatible with the principles laid down in Roth and Sin-dermann." I would not so soon depart from these cases nor from the views expressed by a majority in Arnett. The ordinance plainly grants petitioner a right to his job unless there is cause to fire him. Having granted him such a right it is the Federal Constitution, not state law, which determines the process to be applied in connection with any state decision to deprive him of it.

Mr. Justice BLACKMUN, with whom Mr. Justice BRENNAN joins, dissenting.

* * *

. . . Still v. Lance, . . ., the only North Carolina case cited by the Court and by the District Court, is by no means the authoritative holding on state law that the Court . . . seems to think it is. In Still the Supreme Court of North Carolina considered a statute that contained no "for cause" standard for failure to renew a teacher's contract at the *end* of a school year. In holding that this provision did not create a continued expectation of employment, the North Carolina court noted that it "does not limit the right of the employer board to terminate the employment of a teacher at the end of a school year to a specified cause or circumstance." . . . This provision, the court observed, stood in sharp contrast with another provision of the statute relating to termination of employment *during* the school year and providing that when "it shall have been determined that the services of an employee are not *acceptable* for the remainder of a current school year" (emphasis added), . . . notice and hearing were required.

The Marion ordinance in the present case contains a "for cause" standard for dismissal and, it seems to me, is like that portion of the statute construed in Still pertaining to termination of employment during the year. As such, it plainly does not subject an employee to termination at the will and pleasure of the municipality but, instead, creates a proper expectation of continued employment so long as he performs his work satisfactorily. At this point, the Federal Constitution steps in and requires that appropriate procedures be followed before the employee may be deprived of his property interest.

Mandatory Retirement of Police Officers

MASSACHUSETTS BOARD OF RETIREMENT v. MURGIA

Supreme Court of the United States, 1976
427 U.S. 307, 96 S. Ct. 2562, 49 L. Ed. 2d 520

Robert Murgia, appellee, filed an action in the United States District Court (D. Mass.) alleging that a Massachusetts law, which requires that all uniformed state police officers retire at age 50, denied him the equal protection of the laws guaranteed by the Fourteenth Amendment. A three-judge district court was impaneled, and it declared the Massachusetts statute unconstitutional on the ground that "a classification based on age 50 alone lacks a rational basis in furthering any substantial state interest" and enjoined further enforcement of the statute. The United States Supreme Court noted probable jurisdiction of the retirement board's appeal.

PER CURIAM.

This case presents the question whether the provision of Mass. Gen. Laws Ann. c. 32, § 26(3)(a), that a uniformed State Police Officer "shall be retired . . . upon his attaining age fifty," denies appellee police officer equal protection of the laws in violation of the Fourteenth Amendment.

* * *

The primary function of the Uniformed Branch of the Massachusetts State Police is to protect persons and property and maintain law and order. Specifically, uniformed officers participate in controlling prison and civil disorders, respond to emergencies and natural disasters, patrol highways in marked cruisers, investigate crime, apprehend criminal suspects, and provide back-up support for local law enforcement personnel. As the District Court observed, "service in this branch is, or can be, arduous." 376 F. Supp., at 754. "[H]igh versatility is required, with few, if any, backwaters available for the partially superannuated." Ibid. Thus, "even [appellee's] experts concede that there is a general relationship between advancing age and decreasing physical ability to respond to the demands of the job." Id., at 755.

These considerations prompt the requirement that uniformed state officers pass a comprehensive physical examination bien-nially until age 40. After that, until mandatory retirement at age 50, uniformed officers must pass annually a more rigorous examination, including an electrocardiogram and tests for gastro-intestinal bleeding. Appellee Murgia had passed such an examination four months before he was retired, and there is no dispute that, when he retired, his excellent physical and mental health still rendered him capable of performing the duties of a uniformed officer.

The record includes the testimony of three physicians: that of the State Police Surgeon, who testified to the physiological and psychological demands involved in the performance of uniformed police functions; that of an associate professor of medicine, who testified generally to the relationship between aging and the ability to perform under stress; and that of a surgeon, who also testified to aging and the ability safely to perform police functions. The testimony clearly established that the risk of physical failure, particularly in the cardiovascular system, increases with age, and that the number of individuals in a given age group incapable of performing stress functions increases with the age of the group. . . . The testimony also recognized that particular individuals over 50 could be capable of safely performing the functions of uniformed officers. . . . We agree that rationality is the proper standard by which to test whether compulsory retirement at age 50 violates equal protection. We disagree, however, with the District Court's determination that the age 50 classification is not rationally related to furthering a legitimate state interest.

I

We need state only briefly our reasons for agreeing that strict scrutiny is not the proper test for determining whether the mandatory retirement provision denies appellee equal protection. San Antonio Independent School District v. Rodriguez, 411 U.S. 1, 16 (1973), reaffirmed that equal protection analysis required strict scrutiny of a legislative classification only when the classification impermissibly interferes with the exercise of a fundamental right or operates to the peculiar disadvantage of a suspect class. Mandatory retirement at age 50 under the Massachusetts statute involves neither situation.

This Court's decisions give no support to the proposition that a right of governmental employment per se is fundamental. . . . Accordingly, we have expressly stated that a standard less than strict scrutiny "has consistently been applied to state legislation restricting the availability of employment opportunities."

Nor does the class of uniformed state police officers over 50 constitute a suspect class for purposes of equal protection analysis. Rodriguez . . . observed that a suspect class is one "saddled with such disabilities, or subjected to such a history of purposeful unequal treatment, or relegated to such a position of political powerlessness as to command extraordinary protection from the majoritarian political process." While the treatment of the aged in this Nation has not been wholly free of discrimination, such persons, unlike, say, those who have been discriminated against on the basis of race or national origin, have not experienced a "history of purposeful unequal treatment" or been subjected to unique disabilities on the basis of stereotyped characteristics not truly indicative of their abilities. The class subject to the compulsory retirement feature of the Massachusetts statute consists of uniformed state police officers over the age of 50. It cannot be said to discriminate only against the elderly. Rather it draws the line at a certain age in middle life. . . .

Even if the statute could be said to impose a penalty upon a class defined as the aged, it would not impose a distinction sufficiently akin to those classifications that we have found suspect to call for strict judicial scrutiny.

Under the circumstances, it is unnecessary to subject the State's resolution of competing interests in this case to the degree of critical examination that our cases under the Equal Protection Clause recently have characterized as "strict judicial scrutiny."

II

We turn then to examine this state classification under the rational basis standard. This inquiry employs a relatively relaxed standard reflecting the Court's awareness that the drawing of lines that create distinctions is peculiarly a legislative task and an unavoidable one. Perfection in making the necessary classifications is neither possible nor necessary. . . . Such action by a legislature is presumed to be valid.

In this case, the Massachusetts statute clearly meets the requirements of the Equal Protection Clause, for the State's classification rationally furthers the purpose identified by the State: Through mandatory retirement at age 50, the legislature seeks to protect the public by assuring physical preparedness of its uniformed police. Since physical ability generally declines with age, mandatory retirement at 50 serves to remove from police service those whose fitness for uniformed work presumptively has diminished with age. This clearly is rationally related to the State's objective. There is no indication that § 26(3)(a) has the effect of excluding from service so few officers who are in fact unqualified as to render age 50 a criterion wholly unrelated to the objective of the statute.

That the State chooses not to determine fitness more precisely through individualized testing after age 50 is not to say that the objective of assuring physical fitness is not rationally furthered by a maximum age limitation. It is only to say that with regard to the interest of all concerned, the State perhaps has not chosen the best means to accomplish this purpose. But where rationality is the test, a State "does not violate the Equal Protection Clause merely because the classifications made by its laws are imperfect." Dandridge v. Williams, 397 U.S. 471, 485 (1970).

We do not make light of the substantial economic and psychological effects premature and compulsory retirement can have on an individual; nor do we denigrate the ability of elderly citizens to continue to contribute to society. The problems of retirement have been well documented and are beyond serious dispute. But "[w]e do not decide today that the [Massachusetts statute] is wise, that it best fulfills the relevant social and economic objectives that [Massachusetts] might ideally espouse, or that a more just and humane system could not be devised." Id., at 487. We decide only that the system enacted by the Massachusetts Legislature does not deny appellee equal protection of the law.

Reversed.

Mr. Justice MARSHALL, dissenting.

Today the Court holds that it is permissible for the Commonwealth of Massachusetts to declare that members of its state police force who have been proven medically fit for service are nonetheless legislatively unfit to be policemen and must be terminated—involuntarily "retired"—because they have reached the age of 50. Although we have called the right to work "of the very essence of the personal freedom and opportunity that it was the purpose of the [Fourteenth] Amendment to secure," Truax v. Raich, 239 U.S. 33, 41 (1915), the Court finds that the right to work is not a fundamental right. And, while agreeing that "the treatment of the aged in the Nation has not been wholly free of discrimination," . . . the Court holds that the elderly are not a suspect class. Accordingly, the Court undertakes the scrutiny mandated by the bottom tier of its two-tier equal protection framework, finds the challenged legislation not to be "wholly unrelated" to its objective, and holds, therefore, that it survives equal protection attack. I respectfully dissent.

I

Although there are signs that its grasp on the law is weakening, the rigid two-tier model still holds sway as the Court's articulated description of the equal protection test. Again, I must object to its perpetuation. The model's two fixed modes of analysis, strict scrutiny and mere rationality, simply do not describe the inquiry the Court has undertaken—or should undertake—in equal protection cases. Rather, the inquiry has been much more sophisticated and the Court should admit as much. It has focused upon the character of the classification in question, the relative importance to individuals in the class discriminated against of the governmental benefits that they do not receive, and the state interests asserted in support of the classification. . . .

Although the Court outwardly adheres to the two-tier model, it has apparently lost interest in recognizing further "fundamental" rights and "suspect" classes. See San Antonio School District v. Rodriguez, supra (rejecting education as a fundamental right); Frontiero v. Richardson, 411 U.S. 677 (1973) (declining to treat women as a suspect class). In my view, this result is the natural consequence of the limitations of the Court's traditional equal protection analysis. If a statute is subject to strict scrutiny, the statute always, or nearly always . . . is struck down. Quite obviously, the only critical decision is whether strict scrutiny should be invoked at all. It should be no surprise, then, that the Court is hesitant to expand the number of categories of rights and classes subject to strict scrutiny, when each expansion involves the invalidation of virtually every classification bearing upon a newly covered category.[a]

But however understandable the Court's hesitancy to invoke strict scrutiny, all remaining legislation should not drop into the

---

[a]Some classifications are so invidious that they should be struck down automatically absent the most compelling state interest, and by suggesting the limitations of strict scrutiny analysis I do not mean to imply otherwise. The analysis should be accomplished, however, not by stratified notions of "suspect" classes and "fundamental" rights, but by individualized assessments of the particular classes and rights involved in each case. Of course, the traditional suspect classes and fundamental rights would still rank at the top of the list of protected categories, so that in cases involving those categories analysis would be functionally equivalent to strict scrutiny. Thus, the advantages of the approach I favor do not appear in such cases, but rather emerge in those dealing with traditionally less protected classes and rights.

bottom tier, and be measured by the mere rationality test. For that test, too, when applied as articulated, leaves little doubt about the outcome; the challenged legislation is always upheld. . . .

While the Court's traditional articulation of the rational basis test does suggest just such an abdication, happily the Court's deeds have not matched its words. Time and again, met with cases touching upon the prized rights and burdened classes of our society, the Court has acted only after a reasonably probing look at the legislative goals and means, and at the significance of the personal rights and interests invaded. . . . These cases make clear that the Court has rejected, albeit sub silentio, its most deferential statements of the rationality standard in assessing the validity under the Equal Protection Clause of much noneconomic legislation.

But there are problems with deciding cases based on factors not encompassed by the applicable standards. First, the approach is rudderless, affording no notice to interested parties of the standards governing particular cases and giving no firm guidance to judges who, as a consequence, must assess the constitutionality of legislation before them on an ad hoc basis. Second, and not unrelatedly, the approach is unpredictable and requires holding this Court to standards it has never publicly adopted. Thus, the approach presents the danger that, as I suggest has happened here, relevant factors will be misapplied or ignored. All interests not "fundamental" and all classes not "suspect" are not the same; and it is time for the Court to drop the pretense that, for purposes of the Equal Protection Clause, they are.

II

The danger of the Court's verbal adherence to the rigid two-tier test, despite its effective repudiation of that test in the cases, is demonstrated by its efforts here. There is simply no reason why a statute that tells able-bodied police officers, ready and willing to work, that they no longer have the right to earn a living in their chosen profession merely because they are 50 years old should be judged by the same minimal standards of rationality that we use to test economic legislation that discriminates against business interests. . . . Yet, the Court today not

only invokes the minimal level of scrutiny, it wrongly adheres to it. Analysis of the three factors I have identified above — the importance of the governmental benefits denied, the character of the class, and the asserted state interests — demonstrates the Court's error.

Whether "fundamental" or not, "the right of the individual . . . to engage in any of the common occupations of life" has been repeatedly recognized by this Court as falling within the concept of liberty guaranteed by the Fourteenth Amendment. . . . As long ago as the Slaughterhouse Cases, Justice Bradley wrote that this right "is an unalienable right; it was formulated as such under the phrase 'pursuit of happiness' in the Declaration of Independence. . . . This right is a large ingredient in the civil liberty of the citizen." 111 U.S. 746, 762 (1884) (concurring opinion). And in Smith v. Texas, 233 U.S. 630 (1914), in invalidating a law that criminally penalized anyone who served as a freight train conductor without having previously served as a brakeman, and that thereby excluded numerous equally qualified employees from that position, the Court recognized that "all men are entitled to the equal protection of the law in their right to work for the support of themselves and families." Id., at 641. . . . Even if the right to earn a living does not include the right to work for the government, it is settled that because of the importance of the interest involved, we have always carefully looked at the reasons asserted for depriving a government employee of his job.

While depriving any government employee of his job is a significant deprivation, it is particularly burdensome when the person deprived is an older citizen. Once terminated, the elderly cannot readily find alternative employment. The lack of work is not only economically damaging, but emotionally and physically draining. Deprived of his status in the community and of the opportunity for meaningful activity, fearful of becoming dependent on others for his support, and lonely in his new-found isolation, the involuntarily retired person is susceptible to physical and emotional ailments as a direct consequence of his enforced idleness. Ample clinical evidence supports the conclusion that mandatory retirement poses a direct threat to the health and life expectancy of the retired person, and these consequences of termination for age are not disputed by appellant. Thus, an older person deprived of his job by the government loses not only his right to earn a living, but, too often, his health as well. . . .

Not only are the elderly denied important benefits when they are terminated on the basis of age, but the classification of older workers is itself one that merits judicial attention. Whether older workers constitute a "suspect" class or not, it cannot be disputed that they constitute a class subject to repeated and arbitrary discrimination in employment. . . .

Of course, the Court is quite right in suggesting that distinctions exist between the elderly and traditional suspect classes such as Negroes, and between the elderly and "quasi-suspect" classes such as women or illegitimates. The elderly are protected not only by certain anti-discrimination legislation, but by legislation that provides them with positive benefits not enjoyed by the public at large. Moreover, the elderly are not isolated in society, and discrimination against them is not pervasive but is centered primarily in employment. The advantage of a flexible equal protection standard, however, is that it can readily accommodate such variables. The elderly are undoubtedly discriminated against, and when legislation denies them an important benefit — employment — I conclude that to sustain the legislation the Commonwealth must show a reasonably substantial interest and a scheme reasonably closely tailored to achieving that interest. . . .

Turning, then, to the Commonwealth's arguments, I agree that the purpose of the mandatory retirement law is legitimate, and indeed compelling. The Commonwealth has every reason to assure that its state police officers are of sufficient physical strength and health to perform their jobs. In my view, however, the means chosen, the forced retirement of officers at age 50, is so overinclusive that it must fall.

All potential officers must pass a rigorous physical examination. Until age 40, this same examination must be passed every two years — when the officer re-enlists — and, after age 40, every year. The Commonwealth has conceded that "[w]hen a member passes his re-enlistment or annual physical, he is found to be qualified to perform all of the duties of the Uniformed Branch of the Massachusetts State Police." . . . If a member fails the examination, he is immediately terminated or refused re-enlistment. Thus, the only members of the state police still on the force at age 50 are those who have been determined — repeatedly — by the Commonwealth to be physically fit for the job. Yet, all of these physically fit officers are automatically terminated at age 50. . . . In these circumstances, I see no reason at all for automatically terminating those officers who reach the age of 50; indeed, that action seems the height of irrationality.

Accordingly, I conclude that the Commonwealth's mandatory retirement law cannot stand when measured against the significant deprivation the Commonwealth's action works upon the terminated employees. I would affirm the judgment of the District Court.

Comments

1. In *Bishop* v. *Wood,* supra, a majority of the Court rejected the petitioner's claim that his discharge denied him a "property interest" protected by the Fourteenth Amendment. The Court found that the ordinance under which the petitioner was hired did not grant a right to continued employment and that his dismissal was legal provided the employee-removal procedures were complied with. Wouldn't it have been more prudent for the Court to have dismissed the case as "improvidently granted" and vacated the decision of the court of appeals and obtained an authoritative interpretation of the ordinance by a North Carolina state court rather than to have relied on the opinion of the United States district judge, that was "based on his understanding of the state law"? An earlier decision by the North Carolina Supreme Court, *Still* v. *Lance,* 182 S.E.2d 403 (1971), held that "an enforceable expecta-

tion of continued employment" was a "property interest." However, under North Carolina law, that "expectation" can exist only if the employer (by statute or contract) has granted a guarantee of continued employment. A majority of the United States Supreme Court held that Bishop was not guaranteed a right to continued employment under the ordinance. Do you agree with Mr. Justice Brennan (dissenting) that Bishop was denied a "liberty interest" under the Fourteenth Amendment? According to the dissent, Bishop was denied a liberty interest because his ability to obtain other employment was diminished because the discharge damaged his reputation. Isn't this stretching the concept of "liberty" (within the meaning of the Fourteenth Amendment) a bit far? Should "liberty" refer only to imprisonment, or should it encompass economic liberties? Note that the *Bishop* majority is giving notice that federal courts should, in most instances, abstain from reviewing personnel decisions made by public agencies.

2. The *Bishop* decision makes reference to three earlier Supreme Court decisions involving property interests and continued employment. In *Board of Regents* v. *Roth*, 408 U.S. 564 (1972), the respondent was hired as an assistant professor of political science at Wisconsin State University at Oshkosh for one academic year. Subsequently, he was informed that he would not be rehired for the next academic year. Under university rules, Roth did not have to be given any reasons for the decision not to rehire him nor was he entitled to a hearing to challenge the decision since a nontenured professor has, under Wisconsin law, no right to continued employment. The district court granted summary judgment in favor of Roth and ordered the university to grant him a hearing and provide reasons for his nonrenewal. The United States Court of Appeals (7th Cir.) affirmed. The United States Supreme Court reversed and remanded. In a majority opinion written by Justice Stewart, the Court held that (1) procedural due process is applicable only to those interests encompassed by the Fourteenth Amendment's protection of life and property and the range of such interests is not infinite; (2) only those interests that a person has already acquired via specific employment benefits are protected by procedural due process; (3) the state, in declining to rehire Roth, did not impose on him any stigma that foreclosed other employment opportunities; (4) Roth was not denied any property interest since the terms of his employment specifically limited his employment to one academic year; and (5) Roth was not constitutionally entitled to a statement of reasons for or a hearing on the decision not to rehire him.

In *Perry* v. *Sindermann,* 408 U.S. 593 (1972), the respondent was employed as a professor in the Texas state college system for ten years at three different institutions and spent the last four years as a junior college professor under a series of one-year written contracts. In 1969, the board of regents declined to renew his contract for the next year without specifying any reasons or providing him with a prior hearing. Respondent challenged the nonrenewal decision in the United States district court, alleging that the decision not to rehire him was based on his public criticism of the college's administration and thus violated his right to free speech under the First Amendment. The district court granted summary judgment for the board of regents, concluding that Sindermann's contract had terminated and the junior college had not adopted a tenure system.

The United States Court of Appeals (5th Cir.) reversed on the ground that the respondent's due process rights were violated if the nonrenewal was in fact based on his protected free speech and if the respondent had an "expectation" of reemployment. The United States Supreme Court affirmed. In a majority opinion by Justice Stewart, the Court held that (1) the government may not deny a benefit to a person when such action infringes his constitutionally protected interest in free speech; (2) unless he can show that he has been deprived of some liberty or property interest protected by the Fourteenth Amendment, a nontenured professor is not constitutionally entitled to have a hearing or to receive reasons for his nonretention; (3) even though no explicit tenure system exists, a professor should be entitled to prove that a de facto tenure system does exist at an institution; (4) proof that a de facto tenure system exists entitles a professor to a hearing on the issue of nonretention, although he is not automatically entitled to reinstatement.

Bishop lost his appeal to the United States Supreme Court because his contract of employment contained no express or implied guarantee on which an expectation of continued employment could be based. Suppose a public employee has an "unreasonable" expectation of continued employment. Does procedural due process nevertheless require a hearing prior to discharge? In *Sindermann,* the Court held that a "mere subjective 'expectancy' [of continued employment] is not protected by procedural due process," at 603. Note that in this context, Fourteenth Amendment due process is applicable only to public employees, not private employees, since that amendment is directed at the states; likewise, Fifth Amendment due process governs only claims by federal employees.

Arnett v. *Kennedy,* 416 U.S. 124 (1974), the third case mentioned in *Bishop,* held that the Lloyd-LaFollette Act (5 U.S.C. § 7501), guaranteeing a nonprobationary federal employee continued employment absent "cause" for discharge, confers on the employee a property interest protected by Fifth Amendment procedural due process, and that the act's provisions authorizing discharge of an employee "for such cause as will promote the efficiency of the service" were not unconstitutionally vague or overbroad since constitutionally protected speech was not cause for discharge. Suppose a police officer publicly criticizes his superiors. Is that sufficient cause to fire him, or is that constitutionally protected speech? The *Bishop* case leaves open the issue of under what conditions, if any, a police officer may be fired without cause.

A broad reading of the *Roth-Sindermann-Bishop* decisions suggests that if a public employee has a reasonable expectancy of continued employment, he has a Fourteenth Amendment property interest that is governed by procedural due process, entitling him to a prior hearing at which the specific reasons for his discharge must be given. In view of *Bishop,* would it be a good idea, if permitted under state law, for a public agency to specify in its employment contracts that "this employment is terminable at the will and pleasure of the employer and does not create an expectancy of continued employment"?

3. In the *Murgia* decision, a majority of the Court held that mandatory retirement of state police officers at age 50 is a rational exercise of legislative judgment, even though 50-year-old officers may be

physically equipped to perform their duties. Interestingly, the Massachusetts 50-year-old retirement age is the lowest in the nation: no other state requires its police to retire before age 55. Suppose a state required its police to retire at age 45. Is that rational under the Fourteenth Amendment? At age 40?

4. The federal Constitution makes no reference to mandatory retirement of Supreme Court Justices. Article III, Sec. 1, states: "The Judges, both of the supreme and inferior Courts, shall hold their Offices during Good Behavior. . . ."—a lifetime job. Suppose the Constitution was amended to read, "No Justice of any federal court shall serve beyond age 50." Would the justices of the Supreme Court find this to be a rational exercise of official power? Of course, the Court would be bound by such an amendment regardless of its rationality. If such an age-50 scheme were implemented, all nine justices of the present Supreme Court would be forced to retire. A few observers of the Court might find such an amendment to be wholly rational.

5. The *Murgia* Court made it clear that a state classification based on age is not subject to "strict judicial scrutiny" under the Fourteenth Amendment. Rather, the proper test is whether the "state classification rationally furthers the purpose identified by the state." See Chapter Four, § 4.02, supra. Accordingly, the majority concluded that a classification based on *age* is not "suspect" and that the right to work is not "fundamental." Why? Do you agree with Mr. Justice Marshall's view (dissenting) that the Massachusetts statute exemplifies "the height of irrationality"? In view of the *Murgia* decision, how likely is it that the Supreme Court would strike down, as violative of the Equal Protection Clause, a state law requiring mandatory retirement of all college professors at age 65? Is *Murgia* distinguishable because college professors depend more on mental acuity than physical fitness? Suppose a state law required mandatory retirement at age 50 of all government employees. Could such a law withstand judicial scrutiny on the "rational basis" standard? What is the legitimate state interest in requiring mandatory retirement at age 50 (or 55 or 60) for holders of jobs in which physical fitness is of little or no importance? Are physical fitness and mental acuity sufficiently interrelated to justify any reasonable age for retirement regardless of the type of job? Many individuals have made their most significant contributions to society after the normal age of retirement. In the judicial realm, Mr. Justice Holmes was not appointed to the Supreme Court until he was 70—and he served until age 90. Mr. Justice Black served on the Court until he was 85. Surely no rational person would have accused these justices of senility or incompetency because of their advanced age.

6. In *Dandridge* v. *Williams,* 397 U.S. 471 (1970), cited in *Murgia,* the Court said: "In the area of economics and social welfare, a State does not violate the Equal Protection Clause merely because the classifications made by its laws are imperfect. If the classification has some 'reasonable basis,' it does not offend the Constitution simply because the classification 'is not made with mathematical nicety or because in practice it results in some inequality,'" at 485, quoting *Lindsley* v. *Natural Carbonic Gas Co.,* 220 U.S. 61, 78

(1911). *Dandridge* held that Maryland's administrative regulation limiting the amount of welfare to families with dependent children did not violate the Equal Protection Clause.

Mr. Justice Marshall, dissenting in *Murgia,* was quite correct in stating that application of "strict judicial scrutiny" ("compelling state interest" test) almost always results in invalidation of the statute and that when the "rational basis" test is utilized, the challenged legislation is almost always upheld. The Supreme Court has employed "strict judicial scrutiny" in the following cases: *Shapiro* v. *Thompson,* 394 U.S. 618 (1969) (right to travel); *Roe* v. *Wade,* 410 U.S. 113 (1973) (right to abortion); *Williams* v. *Rhodes,* 393 U.S. 23 (1968) (First Amendment rights); *McLaughlin* v. *Florida,* 379 U.S. 184 (1964) (classification based on race); *Levy* v. *Louisiana,* 391 U.S. 68 (1968) (classification based on lineage); *Harper* v. *Virginia Board of Elections,* 383 U.S. 663 (1966) (right to vote); *Graham* v. *Richardson,* 403 U.S. 365 (1971) (classification based on alienage); *Skinner* v. *Oklahoma,* 316 U.S. 535 (1942) (right to procreate); *Griffin* v. *Illinois,* 351 U.S. 12 (1956) (classification based on wealth); *Police Department of Chicago* v. *Mosley,* 408 U.S. 92 (1972) (freedom of speech); *Dunn* v. *Blumstein,* 405 U.S. 330 (1972) (one-year residence required prior to voter registration); and *Frontiero* v. *Richardson,* 411 U.S. 677 (1973) (classification based on sex — plurality opinion). The list is not inclusive. The Supreme Court has applied the less strict "reasonable basis" test in the following cases: *San Antonio School District* v. *Rodriguez,* 411 U.S. (1973) (right to education); *Lindsey* v. *Normett,* 405 U.S. 56 (1972) (right of tenant to possession of leased property); *Goldberg* v. *Kelly,* 397 U.S. 254 (1970) (right to welfare benefits); *Eisenstadt* v. *Baird,* 405 U.S. 438 (1972) (right to contraceptive devices); *Estelle* v. *Dorrough,* 420 U.S. 534 (1975) (right to appeal criminal conviction following escape by a felon); *James* v. *Strange,* 407 U.S. 128 (1972) (requiring indigent convicts to repay state for legal defense fees); *Kelly* v. *Johnson,* 425 U.S. 238 (1976) (supra), (hair and beard regulations for police officers); *McGowan* v. *Maryland,* 366 U.S. 420 (1961) (prohibiting sales of certain retail items on Sunday); *Douglas* v. *California,* 372 U.S. 353 (1963), and *Ross* v. *Moffitt,* 417 U.S. 600 (1974) (right to counsel on appeal); and *Massachusetts Board of Retirement* v. *Murgia,* 427 U.S. 307 (1976) (supra), (classification based on age). The list also is not inclusive.

7. Mr. Justice Marshall's opinion in *Murgia* (dissenting) is especially interesting in that he suggests that the Supreme Court has only paid lip service to the so-called "two-tier model" of the equal protection test; that the Court's analysis in equal protection cases has actually been more sophisticated and individualized. According to Justice Marshall, an analysis of equal protection involves a threefold test of " (1) character of the classification in question, (2) the relative importance to individuals in the class discriminated against of the governmental benefits they do not receive, and (3) the state interests asserted in support of the classification." Does that seem to be a better analysis than the "rational basis" test? Is it likely that many legislative classifications could withstand this threefold test? Or is this test simply an articulation of the Court's approach in equal protection cases? See Gunther, G., *The Supreme Court, 1971*

Term, Foreward: In Search of Evolving Doctrine on a Changing Court: A Model for a Newer Equal Protection, 86 Harv. L. Rev. 1 (1972). Finally, can (or should) a classification based on age ever be subjected to the "stricter judicial scrutiny" ("compelling state interest") test? What about restriction of the right to vote (a "fundamental" right) to those who have obtained a minimum age?

Recall that in sex discrimination cases, the Supreme Court has recently employed a third equal protection test: the challenged classification "must serve important governmental objectives and must be substantially related to achievement of those objectives." *Craig* v. *Boren,* 429 U.S. 190 (1976) (see Chapter Four, p. 131).

Part Four

SPECIAL PROBLEMS IN THE
ADMINISTRATION OF JUSTICE

11

CRUEL AND
UNUSUAL PUNISHMENT

11.01 INTRODUCTION

The Eighth Amendment to the United States Constitution provides: "Excessive bail shall not be required, nor excessive fines imposed, nor cruel and unusual punishments inflicted." In *Robinson* v. *California*, 370 U.S. 660 (1962) (infra, § 11.02), the Supreme Court held the Cruel and Unusual Punishments Clause to be applicable to the states.

Almost from the beginning the Supreme Court has stated that the terms "cruel" and "unusual" do not lend themselves to precise definition. As the Court noted in *Trop* v. *Dulles*, 356 U.S. 86 (1958), "The [Eighth] Amendment must draw its meaning from the evolving standards of decency that mark the progress of a maturing society" (Warren, C. J., at 101). Thus, "cruel and unusual punishments" is a fluid concept subject to reinterpretation over time, and is defined according to contemporary standards of decency. However, the Court has not had the same difficulty in defining "punishments." The Court has held that the term "punishment" includes (1) imprisonment,[1] (2) the death penalty,[2] and (3) deprivation of citizenship.[3]

The Supreme Court has indicated that at least four factors govern the applicability of the Cruel and Unusual Punishments Clause. These are (1) whether the method of punishment is inherently cruel or severe;[4] (2) whether the punishment is excessive;[5] (3) whether the punishment is unacceptable to society;[6] and (4) whether the punishment is arbitrarily inflicted.[7]

In other cases, the Supreme Court has held that (1) the imposition of the death penalty by means of electrocution is not cruel and unusual, *In re Kemmler*, 136 U.S. 436 (1890); (2) it is not cruel or unusual punishment to subject a defendant to electrocution a second time after the first attempt failed, *Louisiana ex rel. Francis* v. *Resweber*, 329 U.S. 459 (1947); (3) execution by "public shooting" is not cruel or unusual, *Wilkerson* v. *Utah*, 99 U.S. 130 (1878); (4) it is not cruel or unusual punishment in some instances for a judge to hold a person in contempt of court and order him jailed until he complies with an order of the court, *Uphaus* v. *Wyman*, 360 U.S. 72 (1959); (5) a state statute that authorizes more severe sentences for habitual criminals

---

[1] *Weemer* v. *United States*, 217 U.S. 349 (1910).

[2] *Furman* v. *Georgia*, 408 U.S. 238 (1972).

[3] *Trop* v. *Dulles*, 356 U.S. 86 (1958).

[4] *Wilkerson* v. *Utah*, 99 U.S. 130 (1878).

[5] Id.

[6] *Trop* v. *Dulles*, 356 U.S. 86 (1958).

[7] *Furman* v. *Georgia*, 408 U.S. 238 (1972).

is not unconstitutional, *McDonald* v. *Massachusetts,* 180 U.S. 311 (1901); (6) the loss of American citizenship as punishment for one who has been convicted of desertion and dishonorably discharged from military service is cruel and unusual, *Trop* v. *Dulles,* 356 U.S. 86 (1958); (7) a sentence of imprisonment *plus* a fine is not per se cruel and unusual, *Pervear* v. *Massachusetts,* 5 Wall. 475 (1867); (8) punishments of torture or unnecessary cruelty are unconstitutional, *Wilkerson* v. *Utah,* supra; and (9) the

imposition of a harsher sentence on one defendant than on his codefendants for the same offense is not cruel or unusual, *Howard* v. *Fleming,* 191 U.S. 126 (1903). The issue of cruel and unusual punishment also arose in *Estelle* v. *Gamble,* 429 U.S. 97 (1976) (Chapter Nine, § 9.03), in regard to denial of medical treatment to prisoners, and in *Ingraham* v. *Wright,* 97 S. Ct. 1401 (1977) (Chapter Eight, § 8.04), in regard to juveniles.

11.02 PUNISHMENT OF STATUS OFFENSES

Making Drug Addiction a Crime

ROBINSON v. CALIFORNIA

Supreme Court of the United States, 1962
370 U.S. 660, 82 S. Ct. 1417, 8 L. Ed. 2d 758

The facts are stated in the opinion.

Mr. Justice STEWART delivered the opinion of the Court.

A California statute makes it a criminal offense for a person to "be addicted to the use of narcotics.[a] This appeal draws into question the constitutionality of that provision of the state law, as construed by the California courts in the present case.

The appellant was convicted after a jury trial in the Municipal Court of Los Angeles. The evidence against him was given by two Los Angeles police officers. Officer Brown testified that he had had occasion to examine the appellant's arms one evening on a street

in Los Angeles some four months before the trial. The officer testified that at that time he had observed "scar tissue and discoloration on the inside" of the appellant's right arm, and "what appeared to be numerous needle marks and a scab which was approximately three inches below the crook of the elbow" on the appellant's left arm. The officer also testified that the appellant under questioning had admitted to the occasional use of narcotics.

Officer Lindquist testified that he had examined the appellant the following morning in the Central Jail in Los Angeles. The officer stated that at that time he had observed discolorations and scabs on the appellant's arms, and he identified photographs which had been taken of the appellant's arms shortly after his arrest the night before. Based upon more than ten years of experience as a member of the Narcotic Division of the Los Angeles Police Department, the witness gave his opinion that "these marks and the discoloration were the result of the injection of hypodermic needles into the tissue into the vein that was not sterile." He stated that the scabs were

---

[a]The statute is § 11721 of the California Health and Safety Code. It provides: "No person shall use, or be under the influence, or be addicted to the use of narcotics, excepting when administered by or under the direction of a person licensed by the State to prescribe and administer narcotics. It shall be the burden of the defense to show that it comes within the exception. Any person convicted of violating any provision of this section is guilty of a misdemeanor and shall be sentenced to serve a term of not less than 90 days nor more than one year in the county jail. . . .

CRUEL AND UNUSUAL PUNISHMENT 863

several days old at the time of his examination, and that the appellant was neither under the influence of narcotics nor suffering withdrawal symptoms at the time he saw him. This witness also testified that the appellant had admitted using narcotics in the past.

The appellant testified in his own behalf, denying the alleged conversations with the police officers and denying that he had ever used narcotics or been addicted to their use. He explained the marks on his arms as resulting from an allergic condition contracted during his military service. His testimony was corroborated by two witnesses.

The trial judge instructed the jury that the statute made it a misdemeanor for a person "either to use narcotics, or to be addicted to the use of narcotics. . . . That portion of the statute referring to the 'use' of narcotics is based upon a condition or status. They are not identical. . . . To be addicted to the use of narcotics is said to be a status or condition and not an act. It is a continuing offense and differs from most other offenses in the fact that [it] is chronic rather than acute; that it continues after it is complete and subjects the offender to arrest at any time before he reforms. The existence of such a chronic condition may be ascertained from a single examination, if the characteristic reactions of that condition be found present."

The judge further instructed the jury that the appellant could be convicted under a general verdict if the jury agreed *either* that he was of the "status" *or* had committed the "act" denounced by the statute. "All that the People must show is either that the defendant did use a narcotic in Los Angeles County, or that while in the City of Los Angeles he was addicted to the use of narcotics. . . ."

Under these instructions the jury returned a verdict finding the appellant "guilty of the offense charged." An appeal was taken to the Appellate Department of the Los Angeles County Superior Court, "the highest court of a State in which a decision could be had" in this case. . . . Although expressing some doubt as to the constitutionality of "the crime of being a narcotic addict," the reviewing court in an unreported opinion affirmed the judgment of conviction, citing two of its own previous unreported decisions which had upheld the constitutionality of the

statute. We noted probable jurisdiction of this appeal . . . because it squarely presents the issue whether the statute as construed by the California courts in this case is repugnant to the Fourteenth Amendment of the Constitution.

* * *

This statute . . . is not one which punishes a person for the use of narcotics, for their purchase, sale or possession, or for antisocial or disorderly behavior resulting from their administration. It is not a law which even purports to provide or require medical treatment. Rather, we deal with a state which makes the "status" of narcotic addiction a criminal offense, for which the offender may be prosecuted "at any time before he reforms." California has said that a person can be continuously guilty of this offense, whether or not he has ever used or possessed any narcotics within the State, and whether or not he had been guilty of any antisocial behavior there.

It is unlikely that any State at this moment in history would attempt to make it a criminal offense for a person to be mentally ill, or a leper, or to be afflicted with a venereal disease. A State might determine that the general health and welfare require that the victims of these and other human afflictions be dealt with by compulsory treatment, involving quarantine, confinement, or sequestration. But, in the light of contemporary human knowledge, a law which made a criminal offense of such a disease would doubtless be universally thought to be an infliction of cruel and unusual punishment in violation of the Eighth and Fourteenth Amendments. . . .

We cannot but consider the statute before us as of the same category. In this Court counsel for the State recognized that narcotic addiction is an illness. Indeed, it is apparently an illness which may be contracted innocently or involuntarily. We hold that a state law which imprisons a person thus afflicted as a criminal, even though he had never touched any narcotic drug within the State or been guilty of any irregular behavior there, inflicts a cruel and unusual punishment in violation of the Fourteenth Amendment. To be sure, imprisonment for ninety days is not, in the abstract, a punishment which is either cruel or unusual. But the question cannot be considered in the abstract. Even one day in prison would be a cruel and unusual punishment for the "crime" of having a common cold.

We are not ummindful that the vicious evils of the narcotics traffic have occasioned the grave concern of government. There are, as we have said, countless fronts on which those evils may be legitimately attacked. We deal in this case only with an individual provision of a particularized local law as it has so far been interpreted by the California courts.

Reversed.

* * *

[Mr. Justice DOUGLAS and Mr. Justice HARLAN wrote concurring opinions.]

Mr. Justice CLARK, dissenting.

* * *

Apart from prohibiting specific acts such as the purchase, possession, and sale of narcotics, California has taken certain legislative steps in regard to the status of being a narcotic addict—a condition commonly recognized as a threat to the State and to the individual. . . .

There was no suggestion that the term "narcotic addict" as here used included a person who acted without volition or who had lost the power of self-control. Although the section is penal in appearance—perhaps a carry-over from a less sophisticated approach—its present provisions are quite similar to those for civil commitment and treatment of addicts who have lost the power of self-control. . . .

Where narcotic addiction has progressed beyond the incipient, volitional stage, California provides for commitment of three months to two years in a state hospital. . . .

Thus, the "criminal" provision applies to the incipient narcotic addict who retains self-control, requiring confinement of three months to one year and parole with frequent tests to detect renewed use of drugs. Its overriding purpose is to cure the less seriously addicted person by preventing further use. On the other hand, the "civil" commitment provision deals with addicts who have lost the power of self-control, requiring hospitalization up to two years. Each deals with a different type of addict but with a common purpose. . . .

The majority strikes down the conviction primarily on the grounds that petitioner was denied due process by the imposition of criminal penalties for nothing more than being in a status. This viewpoint is premised upon the theme that § 11721 is a "criminal" provision authorizing a punishment, for the majority admits that "a State might establish a program of compulsory treatment for those addicted to narcotics" which "might require periods of involuntary confinement." I submit that California has done exactly that. The majority's error is in instructing the California Legislature that hospitalization is the *only treatment* for narcotics addiction—that anything less is a punishment denying due process. . . .

However, the case in support of the judgment below need not rest solely on this reading of California law. For even if the overall statutory scheme is ignored and a purpose and effect of punishment is attached to [the statute] that provision still does not violate the Fourteenth Amendment. The majority acknowledges, as it must, that a State can punish persons who purchase, possess or use narcotics. Although none of these acts are harmful to society *in themselves,* the State constitutionally may attempt to deter and prevent them through punishment because of the grave threat of future harmful conduct which they pose. Narcotics addiction—including the incipient, volitional addiction to which this provision speaks—is no different. . . .

It is no answer to suggest that we are dealing with an involuntary status and thus penal sanctions will be ineffective and unfair. The section at issue applied only to persons who use narcotics often or even daily but not to the point of losing self-control. When dealing with involuntary addicts California moves only through [its civil commitment procedure] which clearly is not penal. Even if it could be argued that § 11721 may not be limited to volitional addicts, the petitioner in the instant case undeniably retained the power of self-control and thus to him the statute would be constitutional. Moreover, "status" offenses have long been known and recognized in the criminal law. . . . A ready example is drunkenness, which plainly is as involuntary after addiction to alcohol as is the taking of drugs.

[Mr. Justice WHITE filed a separate dissenting opinion.]

[Mr. Justice FRANKFURTER took no part in the consideration or decision of this case.]

Comments

1. In *Robinson* v. *California,* supra, the Court made it clear that a defendant must engage in some criminal act before he may constitutionally be punished. "Status offenses," such as "being addicted to the use of narcotics," that involve no criminal act are unconstitutional. Is the other portion of the California statute (§ 11721 of the California Health and Safety Code) which provides that "no person shall use, or be under the influence of, . . . narcotics" constitutional? Mr. Justice Stewart, writing for the *Robinson* Court, stated, "Even one day in prison would be cruel and unusual punishment for the 'crime' of having a common cold." Is narcotic addiction equivalent to having a "common cold"? Suppose narcotic addiction was not viewed as a traditional "illness" but rather as the result of a character flaw. Would that cure the constitutional defect in the *Robinson* statute?

2. Although it was not explicitly stated by the Court, *Robinson* made the Eighth Amendment prohibition on cruel and unusual punishment applicable to the states. See *Woodson* v. *North Carolina,* 428 U.S. 280, 287 n.8 (1976).

Punishing Chronic Alcoholics

POWELL v. TEXAS

Supreme Court of the United States, 1968
392 U.S. 514, 88 S. Ct. 2145, 20 L. Ed. 2d 1254

The facts are stated in the opinion.

Mr. Justice MARSHALL announced the judgment of the Court and delivered an opinion in which the CHIEF JUSTICE [WARREN], Mr. Justice BLACK, and Mr. Justice HARLAN join.

In late December 1966, appellant was arrested and charged with being found in a state of intoxication in a public place, in violation of Texas Penal Code, Art. 477 (1952), which reads as follows:

"Whoever shall get drunk or be found in a state of intoxication in any public place, or at any private house except his own, shall be fined not exceeding one hundred dollars."

Appellant was tried in the Corporation Court of Austin, Texas, found guilty, and fined $20. He appealed to the County Court

at Law No. 1 of Travis County, Texas, where a trial de novo was held. His counsel urged that appellant was "afflicted with the disease of chronic alcoholism," that "his appearance in public [while drunk was] . . . not of his own volition," and therefore that to punish him criminally for that conduct would be cruel and unusual, in violation of the Eighth and Fourteenth Amendments to the United States Constitution.

The trial judge in the county court, sitting without a jury, made certain findings of fact, infra . . . but ruled as a matter of law that chronic alcoholism was not a defense to the charge. He found appellant guilty, and fined him $50. There being no further right to appeal within the Texas judicial system, appellant appealed to this Court. . . .

The principal testimony was that of Dr. David Wade, a fellow of the American Medical Association, duly certificated in psychiatry.... Dr. Wade sketched the outlines of the "disease" concept of alcoholism; noted that there is no generally accepted definition of "alcoholism"; alluded to the ongoing debate within the medical profession over whether alcohol is actually physically "addicting" or merely psychologically "habituating"; and concluded that in either case a "chronic alcoholic" is an "involuntary drinker," who is "powerless not to drink," and who "loses his self-control over his drinking." He testified that he had examined appellant, and that appellant is a "chronic alcoholic," who "by the time he has reached [the state of intoxication] ... is not able to control his behavior, and [who] ... has reached this point because he had an uncontrollable compulsion to drink," Dr. Wade also responded in the negative to the question whether appellant has "the willpower to resist the constant excessive consumption of alcohol." He added that in his opinion jailing appellant without medical attention would operate neither to rehabilitate him nor to lessen his desire for alcohol.

On cross-examination, Dr. Wade admitted that when appellant was sober he knew the difference between right and wrong, and he responded affirmatively to the question whether appellant's act of taking the first drink in any given instance when he was sober was a "voluntary exercise of his will." Qualifying his answer, Dr. Wade stated that "these individuals have a compulsion, and this compulsion, while not completely overpowering, is a very strong influence, an exceedingly strong influence, and this compulsion coupled with the firm belief in their mind that they are going to be able to handle it from now on causes their judgment to be somewhat clouded."

Appellant testified concerning the history of his drinking problem. He reviewed his many arrests for drunkenness; testified that he was unable to stop drinking; stated that when he was intoxicated he had no control over his actions and could not remember them later, but that he did not become violent; and admitted that he did not remember his arrest on the occasion for which he was being tried. On cross-examination, appellant admitted that he had had one drink on the morning of the trial and had been able to discontinue drinking. ...

* * *

Evidence in this case then closed. The State made no effort to obtain expert psychiatric testimony of its own, or even to explore with appellant's witness the question of appellant's power to control the frequency, timing, and location of his drinking bouts, or the substantial disagreement within the medical profession concerning the nature of the disease, the efficacy of treatment and the prerequisites for effective treatment.... Instead, the State contented itself with a brief argument that appellant had no defense to the charge because he "is legally sane and knows the difference between right and wrong."

Following this abbreviated exposition of the problem before it, the trial court indicated its intention to disallow appellant's claimed defense of "chronic alcoholism." Thereupon defense counsel submitted, and the trial court entered, the following "findings of fact":

"(1) That chronic alcoholism is a disease which destroys the afflicted person's will power to resist the constant, excessive consumption of alcohol.

"(2) That a chronic alcoholic does not appear in public by his own volition but under a compulsion symptomatic of the disease of chronic alcoholism."

"(3) That Leroy Powell, defendant herein, is a chronic alcoholic who is afflicted with the disease of chronic alcoholism."

Whatever else may be said of them, those are not "findings of fact" in any recognizable traditional sense in which that term has been used in a court of law; they are the premises of a syllogism transparently designed to bring this case within the scope of the Court's opinion in Robinson v. California, 370 U.S. 660 (1962). Nonetheless, the dissent would have us adopt these "findings" without critical examination; it would use them as the basis for a constitutional holding that "a person may not be punished if the condition essential to constitute the defined crime is part of the pattern of his disease and is occasioned by a compulsion symptomatic of the disease." ...

The difficulty with that position, as we shall show, is that it goes much too far on the basis of too little knowledge. In the first place, the record in this case is utterly inadequate to permit the sort of informed and responsible adjudication which alone can support the announcement of an important and wide-ranging new constitutional principle. We know very little about the circumstances surrounding the drinking which resulted in this conviction, or about Leroy Powell's drinking problem, or indeed about alcoholism itself. ... The State put on only one witness, the arresting officer. The defense put on three—a policeman who testified to appellant's long history of arrests for public drunkenness, the psychiatrist, and appellant himself.

Furthermore, the inescapable fact is that there is no agreement among members of the medical profession about what it means to say that "alcoholism" is a "disease." One of the principal works in this field states that the major difficulty in articulating a "disease concept of alcoholism" is that "alcoholism has too many definitions and disease has practically none."[b] This same author concludes that *a disease is what the medical profession recognizes as such.* In other words, there is widespread agreement today that "alcoholism" is a "disease," for the simple reason that the medical profession has concluded that it should attempt to treat those who have drinking problems. There the agreement stops. ...

* * *

It is one thing to say that if a man is deprived of alcohol his hands will begin to shake, he will suffer agonizing pains and ultimately he will have hallucinations; it is quite another to say that a man has a "compulsion" to take a drink, but that he also retains a certain amount of "free will" with which to resist. It is simply impossible, in the present state of our knowledge, to ascribe a useful meaning to the latter statement. ...

Despite the comparatively primitive state of our knowledge on the subject, it cannot be denied that the destructive use of alcoholic beverages is one of our principal social and public health problems. The lowest current informed estimate places the number of "alcoholics" in America (definitional problems aside) at 4,000,000, and most authorities are inclined to put the figure considerably higher. ...

There is as yet no known generally effective method for treating the vast number

of alcoholics in our society. Some individual alcoholics have responded to particular forms of therapy with remissions of their symptomatic dependence upon the drug. But just as there is no agreement among doctors and social workers with respect to the causes of alcoholism, there is no consensus as to why particular treatments have been effective in particular cases and there is no generally agreed-upon approach to the problem of treatment on a large scale. ...

* * *

One virtue of the criminal process is, at least, that the duration of penal incarceration typically has some outside statutory limit; this is universally true in the case of petty offenses, such as public drunkenness, where jail terms are quite short on the whole. "Therapeutic civil commitment" lacks this feature; one is typically committed until one is "cured." Thus, to do otherwise than affirm might subject indigent alcoholics to the risk that they may be locked up for an indefinite period of time under the same conditions as before, with no more hope than before of receiving effective treatment and no prospect of periodic "freedom." ...

Ignorance likewise impedes our assessment of the deterrent effect of criminal sanctions for public drunkenness. The fact that a high percentage of American alcoholics conceal their drinking problems, not merely by avoiding public displays of intoxication but also by shunning all forms of treatment, is indicative that some powerful deterrent operates to inhibit the public revelation of the existence of alcoholism. Quite probably this deterrent effect can be largely attributed to the harsh moral attitude which our society has traditionally taken toward intoxication and the shame which we have associated with alcoholism. Criminal conviction represents the degrading public revelation of what Anglo-American society has long condemned as a moral defect, and the existence of criminal sanctions may serve to reinforce this cultural taboo, just as we presume it serves to reinforce other, stronger feelings against murder, rape, theft, and other forms of antisocial conduct.

Obviously, chronic alcoholics have not been deterred from drinking to excess by the existence of criminal sanctions against public drunkenness. But all those who violate penal laws of any kind are by definition undeterred.

---

[b]E. Jellinek, *The Disease Concept of Alcoholism* 11 (1960).

The long-standing and still raging debate over the validity of the deterrence justification for penal sanctions has not reached any sufficiently clear conclusions to permit it to be said that such sanctions are ineffective in any particular context or for any particular group of people who are able to appreciate the consequences of their acts. Certainly no effort was made at the trial of this case, beyond a monosyllabic answer to a perfunctory one-line question, to determine the effectiveness of penal sanctions in deterring Leroy Powell in particular or chronic alcoholics in general from drinking at all or from getting drunk in particular places or at particular times.

Appellant claims that his conviction on the facts of this case would violate the Cruel and Unusual Punishment Clause of the Eighth Amendment as applied to the States through the Fourteenth Amendment. . . .

Appellant, however, seeks to come within the application of the Cruel and Unusual Punishment Clause announced in Robinson v. California, 370 U.S. 660 (1962), which involved a state statute making it a crime to "be addicted to the use of narcotics." . . .

On its face the present case does not fall within that holding, since appellant was convicted, not for being a chronic alcoholic, but for being in public while drunk on a particular occasion. The State of Texas thus has not sought to punish a mere status, as California did in Robinson; nor has it attempted to regulate appellant's behavior in the privacy of his own home. Rather, it has imposed upon appellant a criminal sanction for public behavior which may create substantial health and safety hazards, both for appellant and for members of the general public, and which offends the moral and esthetic sensibilities of a large segment of the community. This seems a far cry from convicting one for being an addict, being a chronic alcoholic, being "mentally ill, or a leper. . . ."

Robinson so viewed brings this Court but a very small way into the substantive criminal law. And unless Robinson is so viewed it is difficult to see any limiting principle that would serve to prevent this Court from becoming, under the aegis of the Cruel and Unusual Punishment Clause, the ultimate arbiter of the standards of criminal responsibility, in diverse areas of the criminal law, throughout the country.

It is suggested in dissent that Robinson stands for the "simple" but "subtle" principle that "[c]riminal penalties may not be inflicted upon a person for being in a condition he is powerless to change." . . . In that view, appellant's "condition" of public intoxication was "occasioned by a compulsion symptomatic of the disease" of chronic alcoholism, and thus apparently, his behavior lacked the critical element of mens rea. Whatever may be the merits of such a doctrine of criminal responsibility, it surely cannot be said to follow from Robinson. The entire thrust of Robinson's interpretation of the Cruel and Unusual Punishment Clause is that criminal penalties may be inflicted only if the accused has committed some act, has engaged in some behavior, which society has an interest in preventing, or perhaps in historical common law terms has committed some actus reus. It thus does not deal with the question of whether certain conduct cannot constitutionally be punished because it is, in some sense, "involuntary" or "occasioned by a compulsion."

Likewise, as the dissent acknowledges, there is a substantial definitional distinction between a "status" as in Robinson, and a "condition," which is said to be involved in this case. Whatever may be the merits of an attempt to distinguish between behavior and a condition, it is perfectly clear that the crucial element in this case, so far as the dissent is concerned, is whether or not appellant can legally be held responsible for his appearance in public in a state of intoxication. The only relevance of Robinson to this issue is that because the Court interpreted the statute there involved as making a "status" criminal, it was able to suggest that the statute would cover even a situation in which addiction had been acquired involuntarily. . . . That this factor was not determinative in the case is shown by the fact that there was no indication of how Robinson himself had become an addict.

Ultimately, then, the most troubling aspects of this case, were Robinson to be extended to meet it, would be the scope and content of what could only be a constitutional doctrine of criminal responsibility. In dissent it is urged that the decision could be limited to conduct which is "a characteristic and involuntary part of the pattern of the disease as it afflicts" the particular individual, and that "[i]t is not foreseeable" that it would be applied "in the case of offenses such as driving a car while intoxicated, assault, theft, or robbery." . . . That is limitation by fiat. In the first place, nothing in the logic of the dissent would limit its application to chronic alcoholics. If Leroy Powell cannot be convicted of public intoxication, it is difficult to see how a State can convict an individual for murder, if that individual, while exhibiting normal behavior in all other respects, suffers from a "compulsion" to kill which is an "exceedingly strong influence," but "not completely overpowering." Even if we limit our consideration to chronic alcoholics, it would seem impossible to confine the principle within the arbitrary bounds which the dissent seems to envision.

It is not difficult to imagine a case involving psychiatric testimony to the effect that an individual suffers from some aggressive neurosis which he is able to control when sober; that very little alcohol suffices to remove the inhibitions which normally contain these aggressions, with the result that the individual engages in assaultive behavior without becoming actually intoxicated; and that the individual suffers from a very strong desire to drink, which is an "exceedingly strong influence" but "not completely overpowering." Without being untrue to the rationale of this case, should the principles advanced in dissent be accepted here, the Court could not avoid holding such an individual constitutionally unaccountable for his assaultive behavior.

Traditional common-law concepts of personal accountability and essential considerations of federalism lead us to disagree with appellant. We are unable to conclude, on the state of this record or on the current state of medical knowledge, that chronic alcoholics in general, and Leroy Powell in particular, suffer from such an irresistible compulsion to drink and to get drunk in public that they are utterly unable to control their performance of either or both of these acts and thus cannot be deterred at all from public intoxication. And in any event this Court has never articulated a general constitutional doctrine in mens rea.

We cannot cast aside the centuries-long evolution of the collection of interlocking and overlapping concepts which the common law has utilized to assess the moral accountability of an individual for his antisocial deeds. The doctrines of actus reus, mens rea, insanity, mistake, justification, and duress have historically provided the tools for a constantly shifting adjustment of the tension between the evolving aims of the criminal law and changing religious, moral, philosophical, and medical views of the nature of man. This process of adjustment has always been thought to be the province of the States.

* * *

Affirmed.

* * *

[Mr. Justice BLACK, joined by Mr. Justice HARLAN, wrote a concurring opinion.]

Mr. Justice FORTAS, with whom Mr. Justice DOUGLAS, Mr. Justice BRENNAN, and Mr. Justice STEWART join, dissenting.

* * *

The sole question presented is whether a criminal penalty may be imposed upon a person suffering the disease of "chronic alcoholism" for a condition—being "in a state of intoxication" in public—which is a characteristic part of the pattern of his disease and which, the trial court found, was not the consequence of appellant's volition but of "a compulsion symptomatic of the disease of chronic alcoholism." We must consider whether the Eighth Amendment, made applicable to the States through the Fourteenth Amendment, prohibits the imposition of this penalty in these rather special circumstances as "cruel and unusual punishment." This case does not raise any question as to the right of the police to stop and detain those who are intoxicated in public, whether as a result of the disease or otherwise; or as to the State's power to commit chronic alcoholics for treatment. Nor does it concern the responsibility of an alcoholic for criminal *acts*. We deal here with the mere *condition* of being intoxicated in public.

* * *

Alcoholism is a major problem in the United States. In 1956 the American Medical Association for the first time designated alcoholism as a major medical problem and urged that alcoholics be admitted to general hospitals for care. This significant development marked the acceptance among the medical profession of the "disease concept of alcoholism." . . . Today most alcohologists and qualified members of the medical profession recognize the validity of this concept. Recent years have seen an intensification of medical interest in the subject. Medical groups have become active in educating the public, medical schools, and physicians in the etiology, diagnosis, and treatment of alcoholism.

Authorities have recognized that a number of factors may contribute to alcoholism. Some studies have pointed to physiological influences, such as vitamin deficiency, hormone imbalance, abnormal metabolism, and hereditary proclivity. Other researchers have found more convincing a psychological approach, emphasizing early environment and underlying conflicts and tensions. Numerous studies have indicated the influence of socio-cultural factors. It has been shown, for example, that the incidence of alcoholism among certain ethnic groups is far higher than among others.

The manifestations of alcoholism are reasonably well identified. . . . It is well established that alcohol may be habituative and "can be physically addicting." It has been said that "the main point for the nonprofessional is that alcoholism is not within the control of the person involved. He is not willfully drinking."

Although the treatment of alcoholics has been successful in many cases, physicians have been unable to discover any single treatment method that will invariably produce satisfactory results. . . .

The consequences of treating alcoholics, under the public intoxication laws, as criminals can be identified with more specificity. Public drunkenness is punished as a crime, under a variety of laws and ordinances, in every State of the Union. The Task Force on Drunkenness of the President's Commission on Law Enforcement and Administration of Justice has reported that "[t]wo million arrests in 1965 — one of every three arrests in America — were for the offense of public drunkenness." Drunkenness offenders make up a large percentage of the population in short-term penal institutions. Their arrest and processing place a tremendous burden upon the police, who are called upon to spend a large amount of time in arresting for public intoxication and in appearing at trials for public intoxication, and upon the entire criminal process.

It is not known how many drunkenness offenders are chronic alcoholics, but "[t]here is strong evidence . . . that a large number of those who are arrested have a lengthy history of prior drunkenness arrests." "There are instances of the same person being arrested as many as forty times in a single year on charges of drunkenness, and every large urban center can point to cases of individuals appearing before the courts on such charges 125, 150, or even 200 times in the course of a somewhat longer period."

It is entirely clear that the jailing of chronic alcoholics is punishment. It is not defended as therapeutic, nor is there any basis for claiming that it is therapeutic (or indeed a deterrent). The alcoholic offender is caught in a "revolving door" — leading from arrest on the street through a brief, unprofitable sojourn in jail, back to the street and, eventually, another arrest. The jails, overcrowded and put to a use for which they are not suitable, have a destructive effect upon alcoholic inmates.

* * *

Robinson stands upon a principle which, despite its subtlety, must be simply stated and respectfully applied because it is the foundation of individual liberty and the cornerstone of the relations between a civilized state and its citizens: Criminal penalties may not be inflicted upon a person for being in a condition he is powerless to change. In all probability, Robinson at some time before his conviction elected to take narcotics. But the crime as defined did not punish this conduct. The statute imposed a penalty for the offense of "addiction" — a condition which Robinson could not control. Once Robinson had become an addict, he was utterly powerless to avoid criminal guilt. He was powerless to choose not to violate the law.

In the present case, appellant is charged with a crime composed of two elements — being intoxicated and being found in a public place while in that condition. The crime, so defined, differs from that in Robinson. The statute covers more than a mere status. But the essential constitutional defect here is the same as in Robinson, for in both cases the particular defendant was accused of being in a condition which he had no capacity to change or avoid. The trial judge sitting as trier of fact found, upon the medical and other relevant testimony, that Powell is a "chronic alcoholic." He defined appellant's "chronic alcoholism" as "a disease which destroys the afflicted person's will power to resist the constant, excessive consumption of alcohol." He also found that "a chronic alcoholic does not appear in public by his own volition but under a compulsion symptomatic of the disease of chronic alcoholism." I read these findings to mean that appellant was powerless to avoid drinking; that having taken his first drink, he had "an uncontrollable compulsion to drink" to the point of intoxication; and that, once intoxi-

cated, he could not prevent himself from appearing in public places.

* * *

The findings in this case, read against the background of the medical and sociological data to which I have referred, compel the conclusion that the infliction upon appellant of a criminal penalty for being intoxicated in a public place would be "cruel and inhuman punishment" within the prohibition of the Eighth Amendment. This conclusion follows because appellant is a "chronic alcoholic" who, according to the trier of fact, cannot resist the "constant excessive consumption of alcohol" and does not appear in public by his own volition but under a "compulsion" which is part of this condition....

Comments

1. In *Powell* v. *Texas,* supra, a majority of the Supreme Court rejected the view that the punishment of a chronic alcoholic for being drunk in public constitutes cruel and unusual punishment. Why? Because Powell was convicted for his criminal *act* (public drunkenness) and not for the "status" of being an alcoholic? Why was the Court so willing in *Robinson* to find narcotic addiction to be an "illness" but unwilling in *Powell* to find chronic alcoholism to be one? Can it really be said that the drinking of liquor by a chronic alcoholic is a *"voluntary* exercise of the will"? If narcotic addiction is an "illness," may a heroin addict use his malady as a defense to a charge of unlawful sale of heroin on the ground that his act (the sale) was involuntary? In *United States* v. *Moore,* 486 F.2d 1139 (D.C. Cir.) (en banc) (per curiam), cert. denied, 414 U.S. 980 (1973), a divided court of appeals held that narcotics addiction is not a defense to the crime of possession. *Moore* involved a 40-year-old addict who had been a user for 24 years. The defendant's counsel raised the defenses of common law pharmacological duress, the applicability of *Robinson,* and the absence of congressional intent to punish addict-possessors under the federal narcotics laws. Psychiatric testimony at trial indicated that the defendant had no capacity to resist using the drug, although it was conceded that the defendant did not have any mental illness that would bring him within the traditional boundaries of the insanity defense. The court of appeals denied both the common law duress and the *Robinson* defenses. In an opinion written by Wright, J., the four dissenting judges recognized the common law defense of duress due to drug dependence but limited its application to the crimes of possession, use, and purchase for use (id. at 1208–1260). (Chief Judge Bazelon and Judges Tamm and Robinson joined in Judge Wright's dissent.)

2. Prior to the *Powell* decision, the Court of Appeals (D.C. Cir.) held in *Easter* v. *District of Columbia,* 361 F.2d 50 (1966), that a District of Columbia law forbid the imposition of criminal punishment for an alcoholic's public intoxication; that civil commitment is the

appropriate treatment. Easter, a chronic, skid-row alcoholic, had been arrested 70 times for public intoxication and alcohol-related offenses. His counsel, on the 70th arrest, argued that because of Easter's chronic alcoholism, he could not resist drinking and was therefore not capable of the voluntary acts or mens rea required for criminal liability. Although a majority of the judges of the court of appeals rejected this defense, four of the judges concluded that "one who is a chronic alcoholic cannot have the mens rea necessary to be held responsible criminally for being drunk in public" (id. at 53) and that punishment was therefore forbidden under the Eighth Amendment. In *Driver* v. *Hinnant*, 356 F.2d. 761 (4th Cir. 1966), the court of appeals reached the same result. Cf. *State* v. *Fearon*, 166 N.W.2d 720 (Minn. 1969).

11.03 THE DEATH PENALTY

Despite the amount of controversy and publicity it has generated, the death penalty has been imposed in a statistically insignificant number of cases in comparison to other sentencing alternatives. Table 11.1 indicates that 3,859 persons were executed in America between 1930 and 1967. To some commentators, the fact that more than half these executions were of nonwhites is prima facie evidence of discrimination based on race. Nevertheless, a Gallup poll taken in 1972 indicated that 57 per cent of Americans favored capital punishment.[8]

We will consider the various arguments made for and against the imposition of the death penalty.

Arguments for Capital Punishment

Bedau and Pierce[9] note that most support for capital punishment comes from law enforcement personnel—most notably the police and prosecutors. The major arguments in support of the death penalty are that (1) the Bible upholds this form of punishment ("He who kills a man shall be put to death," Leviticus 24:7; (2) it has a deterrent effect on murder and other serious crimes; (2) most states and the majority of nations provide for the death penalty; (4) certainty of punishment is an essential ingredient of deterrence; (5) it costs more to keep a man in prison for a long term than to execute him; (6) rehabilitation is not an effective substitute for the death penalty; (7) a life sentence is usually not for one's natural life, but rather for a varied term of years; (8) society has a right to seek revenge for vicious crimes; (9) intricate legal safeguards virtually preclude the execution of innocent persons; and (10) it is not "cruel and unusual" punishment.

Arguments Against Capital Punishment

A large number of social scientists, including criminologists, penologists, and social workers, are opposed to the death penalty. Opponents of capital punishment argue that (1) it violates the Biblical commandment, "Thou shall not kill"; (2) it is not

---

[8]*The New York Times,* November 25, 1972.

[9]Bedau, H., and Pierce, C. (eds.), *Capital Punishment in the United States* (1976).

TABLE 11.1   Executions in The United States By Race and Offense (1930–1967)*

	Murder	Rape	Other	Total
White	1664 (49.9%)	48 (10.6%)	39 (55.7%)	1751 (45.5%)
Black	1630 (48.9%)	405 (89.0%)	31 (44.3%)	2066 (53.4%)
Other	40 (1.2%)	2 (0.4%)	0 (0.0%)	42 (1.1%)
Total	3334 (100%)	455 (100%)	70 (100%)	3859 (100%)

*From *Cruel and Unusual Punishment: The Supreme Court and Capital Punishment*, by M. Meltsner. Copyright © 1973 by Random House, Inc. Reprinted by permission of Random House, Inc.

an effective (or measurable) deterrent to murder or other serious crimes; (3) it has been disproportionately imposed on the poor and nonwhite; (4) the per capita cost of execution is higher than imprisonment; (5) it is a primitive notion rooted in revenge; (6) innocent men could be executed; (7) a civilized society upholds the sanctity of human life; (8) paroled and pardoned murderers are the least likely to recidivate; (9) it undermines rehabilitative and other penologic goals; (10) it is unthinkable that death, as a legal sentence, should be subject to human discretion; and (11) it is "cruel and unusual" punishment.

It should be noted that some of these arguments and counterarguments are based more on emotion than on fact and thus are not susceptible to empirical corroboration.

The Constitutionality of the Death Penalty

Even a clear pronouncement on the constitutionality of the death penalty by the Supreme Court is not likely to end the public and academic debates over its imposition. In 1972 in *Furman* v. *Georgia,* 408 U.S. 238, the Court had an opportunity to rule on the constitutionality of the death penalty. Unfortunately, that case did not finally settle the issue.

In *Furman,* each of the three black defendants had been convicted by a jury in state court and sentenced to death. Two of the defendants were convicted of rape and the other of murder. The Supreme Court reversed the state court judgments in each case and held in a brief per curiam opinion expressing the views of five members of the Court that "the imposition and carrying out of the death penalty *in these cases* constitutes cruel and unusual punishment in violation of the Eighth and Fourteenth Amendments," at 239–240 (emphasis added). Each of the nine justices wrote a separate opinion. A close reading of these opinions, which covered 131 pages, indicates that the *Furman* decision did not close the issue of the constitutionality of capital punishment. Only Justices Brennan and Marshall were of the opinion that the imposition of the death penalty was per se cruel and unusual punishment. Four of the Justices (Burger, C. J., joined by Powell, Blackmun and Rehnquist, JJ.) were of the opinion that the death

penalty *as presently applied* was not cruel or unusual. Justices White, Stewart, and Douglas hinted in *Furman* that there might be circumstances in which the death penalty could be constitutionally imposed, but that the current procedures allowed the death penalty to be "arbitrarily" and "wantonly" imposed.

In reaction to *Furman,* 35 states and the federal government enacted revised capital punishment statutes designed to eliminate these constitutional problems. These statutes fall into two general categories: those that make the death penalty mandatory for certain crimes, and those that allow the judge or jury to decide, under legislative guidelines, whether to impose the penalty. On January 22, 1976, the Supreme Court granted certiorari in five cases to decide whether the imposition of the death penalty following a murder conviction constitutes cruel and unusual punishment in violation of the Eighth and Fourteenth Amendments. Oral arguments (infra) were heard on March 30 and 31, 1976, and the Court handed down its decisions in five separate opinions on July 2, 1976.

ORAL ARGUMENTS BEFORE THE U.S. SUPREME COURT ON CAPITAL PUNISHMENT*

Argued 3/30/76 and 3/31/76

The U.S. Supreme Court last week heard lengthy and, at times, impassioned argument over the most controversial issue of the Term — the constitutionality of the death penalty. Five cases involving six defendants are before the court, all from southern states and all involving first-degree murder convictions.

Jurek v. Texas, No. 75-5394 [†] and [Stanislaus] Roberts v. Louisiana, No. 75-5844 [‡]

---

*From 19 Crim. L. Rptr. 4005–4011. Reprinted by permission of the Bureau of National Affairs, Inc.

†This case is presented in Comment 2, p. 899.
‡This case is presented in Comment 1, p. 932.

Anthony Amsterdam, of Stanford, California, who presented argument in *Furman* v. *Georgia* . . . was on hand once again and spoke on behalf of petitioners Jurek and Roberts. He began by outlining the present state of capital punishment statutes around the country. Since the decision in *Furman* v. *Georgia*, 408 U.S. 238 (1972), 35 states have enacted new statutes and the federal government has provided for the death penalty in the narrow context of aircraft piracy. The pre-*Furman* statutes, Amsterdam noted, are largely out of the picture. The new laws break down into four categories, counsel said, and the five cases before the Court present a representative sampling. The first type is marked by the use of a two-stage trial in which the jury first determines the defendant's guilt or innocence. If a conviction for a capital crime is returned, the jury then considers a list of aggravating (and sometimes mitigating) circumstances to decide whether the defendant should be condemned or sentenced to life imprisonment. The Florida and Georgia statutes are of this type. The statutes of the second group, typified by the Texas law and the federal enactment on air piracy, require the finding of a specified fact, occurrence, or condition to support a death sentence. In contrast to the first type, there is no weighing or balancing involved. The third group is like the second in that a designated factor must be found, but that factor is built into the elements of the crime itself. Hence the death penalty applies not to all first-degree murders but to a narrower category. The Louisiana statute is representative of this group, Amsterdam said. Finally, there are statutes which, like that of North Carolina, simply make certain offenses punishable by death.

Amsterdam emphasized the necessity of examining the statutes not only as written but as put into practice by the states. The new laws are tidier in print than in operation, he asserted, and they will become even less tidy over time.

We make two separate Eighth Amendment arguments in these cases, Amsterdam said. First, despite the efforts of the states, these statutes still permit the arbitrary infliction of the death penalty in violation of *Furman*. The statutory schemes set up an "elaborate winnowing process" with many outlets for avoiding the infliction of the death penalty. Later in the argument counsel said the statutes provide an "avenue of death" intersected by side roads along which the ultimate penalty may be avoided.

Counsel's second argument went to the alleged unconstitutionality of the death penalty per se, but he did not reach this point until the subsequently argued North Carolina case.

Furman Fallout

When Amsterdam attempted to contrast the complexity of the capital punishment statutes with the simplicity of those covering life imprisonment, Mr. Justice Blackmun asked whether counsel was surprised that *Furman* resulted in complex laws. This sort of thing was forecast in my opinion, he said. [In his *Furman* dissent, Mr. Justice Blackmun expressed his fears "that statutes stricken down today will be reenacted by state legislatures to prescribe the death penalty for specific crimes without any alternative for the imposition of a lesser punishment and the discretion of the judge or jury as the case may be. This approach, it seems to me, encourages legislation that is regressive and of an antique mold, for it eliminates the element of mercy from the imposition of punishment." — ed.]

Nonetheless, Amsterdam replied, I am surprised that the new statutes are so narrow. I expected that the states would enact mandatory death penalty statutes, but the number of opportunities for evading the death penalty included in these statutes is surprising. Besides the "outs" that are unique to the capital punishment laws, there are others which are built into the system but assume a particular importance in the capital punishment context. An example is the traditional power of the jury to return a verdict upon a lesser included offense.

The life or death decision, Amsterdam maintained, is of such great magnitude that it is always out of proportion to the factual differences upon which capital and non-capital cases are allegedly distinguished. Also, the differences among these statutes are less important than the similarities. Amsterdam made the same point later when, in response to questioning from Mr. Justice Powell, he found himself unable to pick one of the five statutes as least objectionable. He did, however, indicate that mandatory schemes are particularly suspect.

The Chief Justice: "Do you say that no statute can meet the objections posed by the opinions [of Justices Stewart and White] in *Furman*?"

My first argument does not say so, Amsterdam replied, but the second does.

. . . One point, however, should be added. In responding to *Furman,* the legislatures set out to avoid the popular revulsion in which widespread application of the death penalty would result. The legislatures knew that, through the many avenues of discretion and evasion left in or added to the system, the random infliction of the death penalty would continue. Perhaps the most important function the Eighth Amendment serves is to step in where the normal pressures on the legislature against cruel and unusual punishments have been neutralized.

Amsterdam then described the Texas statute in more detail. Capital punishment is prescribed for five specific types of murder including a murder "committed in the course of the commission or attempted commission of kidnapping, burglary, robbery, forcible rape, or arson." If a guilty verdict is returned, the jury then considers three interrogatories, focusing on the deliberateness of the defendant's conduct, the probability that he will commit violent crimes in the future, and, in a proper case, whether he responded unreasonably to provocation. [For more detail, see *Jurek* v. *State,* 522 S.W.2d 934—ed.] In Amsterdam's view, the punishment phase of the trial shows little change from what went on before *Furman.* He charged that the judge here in effect invited the jury to decide that the defendant should be executed and instructed them how to reach that result through the interrogatories.

Attacking the contents of the interrogatories, counsel said that the first and third were, of necessity, already answered at the guilt phase. As for the second, an affirmative answer was returned in this case on nothing more than the fact of the murder itself and brief reputation evidence from four citizens. We can't challenge the jury's answers, Amsterdam said, because the interrogatories themselves are meaningless. The jury has unfettered power to make the life or death decision, and adequate appellate review is impossible.

What About McGautha?

Mr. Justice Stewart broached a question that recurred several times as the argument unfolded. Is counsel's position, he asked, consistent with *McGautha* v. *California?* [In *McGautha,* 402 U.S. 193 (1971), a majority of the Court held that the Fourteenth Amendment does not forbid a state to give juries absolute discretion in deciding whether to impose a death penalty. Noting that efforts to provide standards had been unsuccessful both in this country and in England, Mr. Justice Harlan said: "(W)e find it quite impossible to say that committing to the untrammelled discretion of the jury the power to pronounce life or death in capital cases is offensive to anything in the Constitution."—ed.]

Amsterdam asserted that both his position and *Furman* were consistent with *McGautha.* It became clear that, in Amsterdam's view, *McGautha* was predicated solely upon a due process test as applied to a single proceeding, rather than an Eighth Amendment test that looks across the board at all capital cases.

Amsterdam then turned to the Louisiana case, 319 So. 2d 317. Before *Furman,* Louisiana law did not distinguish degrees of murder. A jury in a capital case could return one of four responsive verdicts: guilty of murder with or without capital punishment, guilty of manslaughter, or innocent. All the state did after *Furman,* Amsterdam contended, was to abolish the first two verdicts and substitute two degrees of murder—thus perpetuating the old system. Moreover, instructions covering lesser included offenses are always given, whether or not a verdict upon a lesser included offense would be supported by the evidence. And the definitional differences between the greater and lesser offenses turn upon subjective jury conclusions such as determining the defendant's intention. [The Louisiana system is described in more detail in the leading state cases. *State* v. *Hill,* 297 So. 2d 660, and *State* v. *Selman,* 300 So. 2d 467.—ed.] As a result, Amsterdam said, Louisiana juries retain the kind of discretion outlawed in *Furman.*

Mr. Justice Stevens posed a question he asked again several times. Does the degree of discretion depend upon the number of crimes included in the definition of first-degree murder, and on the breadth of that definition?

That can be argued either way, Amsterdam replied. Narrowing the definition might be thought to limit the jury's discretion. On the other hand, retaining any discretion in the face of a narrow definition means that the distinctions made by the jury will be even more arbitrary.

Would the statutes be saved, Mr. Justice Stevens asked, if the defendant could insist on an all or nothing verdict—acquittal or guilty of murder one?

That would not cure the Eighth Amendment problem, Amsterdam said. Procedures which might help some defendants hurt others. We must focus not on the fairness of a single trial but upon overall results. This was the *Furman* approach.

Does your argument prove too much? Mr. Justice Stewart asked. We have prosecutor and jury discretion, appellate review, and executive clemency throughout the system. What would prevent any defendant, no matter what his sentence, from making your argument?

Our argument applies only in capital cases, Amsterdam replied. If the Court does not accept that death is different, we lose this case. The legislatures have recognized the uniqueness of the death penalty by hedging it about with many restrictions and avenues of escape; the statutes governing life imprisonment are simple in contrast. And death is factually different; a capital punishment statute represents a legislative decision to do we know not what.

Ultimate Deterrent

John L. Hill, Texas Attorney General, challenged Amsterdam's charge that the state statute continues to permit the selectivity condemned in *Furman*. But he added that no statute could or should remove all forms of discretion from the system.

Hill emphasized the particularly brutal and callous nature of the crime in this case. The defendant choked his victim, a 10-year-old girl, after she refused his sexual advances; he then threw her into a river. Moreover, the defendant ignored the victim's repeated cries for mercy, which were heard by several witnesses as the defendant drove through a Texas town. "Do you mean to tell me that our people have no means of taking care of such a crime?"

Hill acknowledged that the Court has the responsibility of interpreting the Eighth Amendment according to evolving standards of decency. However, he said, "this Court is not the keeper of the social values, the conscience, the moral values of the people."

Mr. Justice Stewart asked Hill to address the objections Amsterdam made to the three interrogatories considered by the jury in the punishment phase.

Hill used an example in his response. In another Texas case, he said, a gunman broke into a jail attempting to free a prisoner. In the shooting, a sheriff was killed by a bullet fired from the gun of a guard. The jury convicted the defendant of first-degree murder and had no trouble finding the requisite intent. But in the punishment phase the jury determined that the defendant did not have the intent required by the first interrogatory. This example makes clear that the interrogatories do not, as Amsterdam charged, merely repeat issues already decided. The cases show a real basis for distinguishing among defendants; it is not simply jury prejudice.

Hill also defended the jury's consideration of the crime itself in determining that Jurek was likely to commit more crimes of violence. A crime, he said, may itself show such incorrigibility and lack of remorse that a finding of likely recidivism is justified.

When Mr. Justice Marshall asked whether a sentence of life imprisonment would provide an adequate deterrent, the Chief Justice wondered how that would deter future crimes by a life prisoner.

Hill agreed that, in the absence of the death penalty, life prisoners have no reason not to commit further crimes.

Mr. Justice Stewart asked what evidence may be introduced at the punishment phase.

Subject to constitutional limitations, Hill replied, anything may be introduced, by either side.

Hill also defended Texas practice against the charge that the death penalty falls with disproportionate frequency on poor people and members of racial minorities.

Attack Upon Jury?

Louisiana's case was presented by James Babin, Assistant District Attorney, Fourteenth Louisiana Judicial District, who discerned in Amsterdam's argument an attack upon the jury system. Jurors, he said, as well as judicial and prosecutorial officers, are under oath to faithfully fulfill their duties. If the petitioners' argument is to be believed, juries are not dependable and nothing can be done to make them follow instructions. This argument, he warned, cannot be confined to the capital punishment context.

The Louisiana statute provides adequate guidelines for the jury, Babin asserted, and once a first degree murder verdict is returned, neither judge nor jury has any further control.

The Justices asked what knowledge the jury has of its verdict's consequences. As a practical matter, Babin said, jurors know that a first-degree murder conviction means death. Defense counsel is not permitted to point out, however, that a second-degree conviction will avert the death penalty.

As for prosecutorial discretion, counsel pointed out that Louisiana law requires an indictment for a capital crime, and the prosecutor loses any control once a guilty verdict is returned.

Mr. Justice Stewart asked what issues are open on appeal.

The state supreme court may not reduce the sentence, nor can it reduce the degree of offense, Babin replied. And while the governor can commute a sentence, this can only help a defendant; we do not see how the commutation power can affect the constitutionality of the statute.

Guidelines Requested

William E. James, Assistant California Attorney General, appeared as amicus curiae seeking affirmance of the sentences. Our concern, he said, is that the petitioners seek an all-encompassing decision which would effectively invalidate all the post-*Furman* statutes. We wish the Court to take this opportunity to affirm the constitutionality of capital punishment. James also suggested that the Court might find it appropriate to set forth guidelines to aid the legislature. Such action would also ease this Court's case load, he said.

California's experience in this area is unique, James continued. Within a few months after the state supreme court declared the death penalty violative of the state constitution [*People* v. *Anderson,* 493 P.2d 880], a million citizens signed an initiative petition to enact a constitutional amendment overruling the court. The amendment passed with 67 percent of the voters favoring it.

In his remaining time, James responded to questions concerning the new California capital punishment statute and the practice thereunder. . . .

What the Eighth Means

At the invitation of the Court, Solicitor General Robert H. Bork appeared as amicus on behalf of the United States. The words of the Fifth Amendment, he said, make clear that the Framers did not intend to outlaw capital punishment; the same is true of the authors of the Fourteenth Amendment. It is true, of course, that the Fifth Amendment also speaks of being put "in jeopardy . . . of limb" but the fact that disfigurement is not now an acceptable punishment does not permit us to ignore the Framers' original intention. The crucial difference is that society as a whole grew to regard disfigurement as cruel and unusual; it was not a judicial decision. The evolutionary principle of the Eighth Amendment is one of control, and it is not a grant of uncontrolled power to the judiciary.

The basic thrust of the Eighth Amendment, Bork said, is to outlaw punishments which are outside both the mainstream of penalties in our country and the moral judgments of the people. The Eighth Amendment had its genesis in charges by the Anti-Federalists that the national government would employ torture against defendants. Its purpose, then, was to prevent a return to the screw and the rack, not to outlaw any punishments then in common use. Indeed, the amendment lay dormant until the 1909 decision in *Weems* v. *U.S.,* 217 U.S. 349, a case from the Philippines, in which the Court struck down a sentence of Spanish origin involving "painful" labor, the wearing of chains, and the lifelong loss of certain rights—all for the offense of making false entries in official records. The language of the *Weems* majority is instructive, Bork said. The majority said such sentences "amaze those who have formed their conception of the relation of a state to even its offending citizens from the practice of the American commonwealths, and believe that it is a precept of justice that punishment for crime should be graduated and proportioned to the offense." Thus, the Eighth Amendment required two inquiries: is the punishment one that is employed by other states of the Union, and is it proportional in a very broad sense to the offense?

On the face of the legislative reaction to *Furman,* Bork continued, it simply cannot be said that capital punishment is out of step with current morality. Indeed, legislative action is the only reference point to which the court may look for the people's moral sense, "not to the writings of the more enlightened professors."

Mr. Justice White, a member of the *Furman* majority, asked whether that decision should be overruled.

I intend to suggest that, Bork answered, but you need not go so far to uphold the statutes in question here. What recent events show is that, pressed to the choice, state legislatures prefer mandatory death penalty laws to none at all. But such statutes are really only a second choice, and the legislatures should be free to enact the kind of statutes they prefer. Bork repeated the argument . . . that certain "empirical judgments" which underlay the *Furman* ruling have been refuted by subsequent events.

The meaning of "unusual," counsel continued, is ascertained by looking at " 'the practice of the American commonwealths' " and has nothing to do with the frequency of imposition. "I do not see how capital punishment can be unconstitutional just because it is used carefully."

Mr. Justice White questioned Bork about the Eighth Amendment's disproportionality test.

The *Weems* majority did not look simply at the offense itself, counsel emphasized; rather the majority looked also at the sentences imposed for similar offenses by the American states. This provides an objective standard. Bork was unwilling to guess what result the *Weems* Court would have reached had the offense been much more serious.

Too Much Discretion?

Like Amsterdam, Bork had devoted much of his time . . . to the discretion issue, and he referred the Court to that discussion. In summarizing, he asserted that discretion is worked into the Constitution itself. It is utterly implausible, he said, to argue that the mere ability of various individuals or groups to exercise discretion renders the death penalty unconstitutional.

Mr. Justice Stewart: "Are you attacking Amsterdam's argument or the *Furman* ruling?"

I'm attacking both, Bork replied. I don't think that *Furman* and *McGautha* can live together; I don't understand how procedures which reach intolerable results can satisfy due process. Moreover, the post-*Furman* move to mandatory statutes is unfortunate.

Mr. Justice Stevens: "Is the legal question posed by *Furman* the same if you have one narrowly defined capital offense or several hundred?"

The Chief Justice appeared troubled by Bork's answer that the discretion issue seemed the same.

Amsterdam appears to have argued, Bork continued, that any system involving discretion is unconstitutional. Apparently only a rigid, morally reprehensible standard would satisfy the Constitution as petitioners interpret it. Their real complaint is that certain murderers are spared. "The more counsel explains this argument, the less I understand it."

When Bork argued that Amsterdam's contentions could not be limited to the capital punishment context, Mr. Justice Stewart said "Death is different, isn't it?" For one thing, the Justice continued, it discards any idea of rehabilitation.

Death is not different in the constitutional sense, Bork insisted. But it is different in some ways—for instance, death deters better than any other punishment, and does the best job of upholding, in a symbolic way, the basic values of society. But the precautions surrounding its infliction, which Amsterdam appears to complain of, do not make it unconstitutional.

There is no reason to assume, Bork added, that the existence of discretion means that it will be exercised arbitrarily or capriciously. And if it were shown that juries are biased toward certain groups or that certain groups make poor jurors, these findings would affect all cases, not just capital ones. It is obvious that the solution would be to attack bias, not outlaw punishment altogether.

Ultimately, Bork asserted, these are cases about democratic government, about the right of the legislatures to choose the punishments they see fit.

Mr. Justice Powell: "While I recognize

that deterrence may not be the controlling factor here, I invite your attention to the 1973 report of the FBI showing that murder has increased 42 percent between 1968 and 1973. It is fairly obvious that we need some way to deter this slaughter of Americans. I say "slaughter" because that word was used in describing the American death toll during our involvement in Vietnam. Comparing the records of Vietnam and the FBI's figures, it appears that, on an annual basis, more Americans are murdered in this country than were killed in Vietnam. Do you care to comment?"

It cannot rationally be maintained, Bork responded, that capital punishment has no deterrent effect. Respectable academic authority can be cited on this point, but I think common sense is sufficient to tell us that as we raise the cost and risk of certain conduct, the incidence of that conduct decreases. This Court would take upon itself an awesome responsibility, Bork concluded, were it to condemn thousands of potential murder victims in order to save a few hundred guilty people.

Woodson v. North Carolina, No. 75-5491 [§]

Amsterdam returned to address the Court on behalf of the North Carolina petitioners Woodson and Waxton. In general outline, he said the arguments here are identical to those in the Texas and Louisiana cases. Before moving on to the per se argument, counsel summarized his earlier remarks. The predicate of my first argument, he said, is the arbitrary selectivity in the infliction of the death penalty. This is an Eighth Amendment issue because that amendment is concerned with the results of process rather than with process itself. This is why *Furman* and *McGautha* are consistent.

Responding to questioning from Mr. Justice Stevens, counsel said his position is that standardless discretion is equivalent to a lottery. Due process would distinguish between these two methods of selecting defendants to die, but the Eighth Amendment does not. Juries' alleged differentiation among defendants does not provide a rational basis.

Our second argument, he continued, does

not depend upon *Furman*. We assert that "capital punishment is atavistic butchery which has run its course." The discretionary element is important here again because it demonstrates how the legislatures react—while they insist on enacting capital punishment laws, they refuse to ensure that all equally guilty defendants will suffer the ultimate penalty. This case is a good example, Amsterdam said, pointing out that while four defendants participated in the armed robbery, two were permitted to plead guilty. . . . To trial counsel, Woodson appeared to have the most appealing case—he was drunk, he had been beaten by Waxton and was under some pressure to accompany the rest, he did not enter the store, and he was the first to make a statement to police. Accordingly, Woodson decided to exercise his right to trial. From a due process view, there can be no quarrel with the result; you take a risk, and you sometimes lose. But what purpose, Amsterdam asked, is served by Woodson's death if his codefendants live?

The Chief Justice: "Would you argue for abolishing the jury system because it sometimes works irrationally?"

No, counsel replied. But while we may tolerate a general looseness in the system, is the system acceptable in the context of life or death decisions?

Mr. Justice Powell asked whether Amsterdam could conceive of any crime meriting the death penalty. When counsel said no, Mr. Justice Powell asked whether the Commandant of Buchenwald might have deserved such punishment under an Eighth Amendment standard.

My instinctive reaction is to say yes, Amsterdam replied after some consideration, but applying the Eighth Amendment standard my answer is no.

Mr. Justice Powell: "Suppose a terrorist destroys New York City with a hydrogen bomb?"

The answer is still no, Amsterdam said, indicating such crimes can be prevented through police methods rather than the fear of punishment. Life imprisonment in solitary confinement and without possibility of parole would provide an effective deterrent and would be constitutional, he said in a reply to another question.

Reminded by the Chief Justice that some penologists consider life imprisonment to be

---

§This case is presented on p. 922.

the cruelest and most unusual punishment, Amsterdam replied "I have always thought that to be a good argument for giving the prisoner his choice."

For Tranquility's Sake

North Carolina's argument was presented by Sidney S. Eagles, Jr., Assistant Attorney General. Opposing counsel appears to argue, he said, that the jury system cannot be made rational in capital cases. But we submit that what the death penalty does is to make jurors even more serious about their duties. Nor can it be maintained that the mandatory death penalty has been repudiated either by this Court or by the people.

We must have the ultimate deterrent, Eagles asserted, to prevent crimes such as this which pose a threat to our system of government and to our people. We are governed by our consent, but "domestic tranquility" does not mean much to the victim of a heinous crime. Eagles also challenged Amsterdam's contention that defendant Woodson was the least culpable among the four participants. The defendants who were permitted to plead guilty were the youngest of the quartet and were the least experienced in crime. But the most important rationale behind the separate treatment of these defendants is the need to satisfy the reasonable doubt standard to obtain convictions. The state was forced to strike some sort of deal in this situation, and the prosecutor must be permitted to decide who should be offered a deal.

In responding to *Furman,* counsel continued, our legislature reduced the number of capital crimes but made the sentence mandatory. Instead of four capital crimes, there are now two—first-degree rape and first-degree murder.

Mr. Justice Stevens asked whether, as an overall result of the new legislation, death sentences in North Carolina have increased or decreased.

My assumption, Eagles replied, is that there have been more capital sentences. There are presently 106 prisoners on death row.

The North Carolina statute defines first-degree murder as one "which shall be perpetrated by means of poison, lying in wait, imprisonment, starving, torture, or by any other kind of willful, deliberate and premeditated killing, or which shall be committed in the perpetration or attempt to perpetrate arson, rape, robbery, kidnapping, burglary or other felonies. . . ." Mr. Justice Powell pointed to the language concerning "any other kind of willfull . . . killing"; this seems terribly broad, he said. Are there any qualifications?

The statute has been interpreted, counsel replied, to refer to offenses which are inherently dangerous to human life, or which carry a substantial risk of death and a death in fact results.

Mr. Justice Powell: "Is any other statute in the country as broad as this?"

Counsel was unable to say. Eagles went on to assert, in effect, that the death penalty can never be held unconstitutional. Even the evolving standards of decency, he said, can only be developed up to the plain language of the Constitution itself. The implied acceptance of the death penalty in the Fifth and Fourteenth Amendments would preclude a finding that the death penalty is unconstitutional.

Like Babin of Louisiana, Eagles stressed the oath and statutory and constitutional obligations under which jurors perform their duties. We are shocked, he said, at the contention because things are so fair and careful, capital punishment is inflicted arbitrarily. This reasoning requires the assumption that some person within the system acts in bad faith.

Opinion Polls

During Amsterdam's rebuttal argument, the Chief Justice asked: Suppose 90 percent of the people, as shown by the various polls, were in favor of capital punishment. Should we take this into our determination of constitutionality?

When Amsterdam replied in the negative, the Chief Justice said, I thought we have to evaluate the standards of decency in light of the public's moral views.

Amsterdam attacked Bork's contention that Eighth Amendment analysis ends with the finding that 35 states have adopted new capital punishment laws. Such a comparative analysis could not have been the initial intention of the Framers, he said, because at that time the Constitution did not apply to the states.

Gregg v. Georgia, No. 74-6257 [||]

The defendant in the Georgia case was convicted of murdering two men in whose car he had been riding. 210 S.E.2d 659. His counsel, G. Hughel Harrison, of Lawrenceville, Georgia, began by describing the capital punishment statute. A bifurcated trial is prescribed and, if a guilty verdict is returned, a sentencing hearing is conducted at which aggravating and mitigating evidence must be presented. The statute sets forth 10 aggravating circumstances for which the death penalty may be imposed in murder and armed robbery cases, but the statute is silent as to mitigating circumstances. [The statute is described in more detail in the leading Georgia decisions, the *Coley, House* and *Eberheart* cases: 204 S.E.2d 62, 205 S.E.2d 217, and 206 S.E.2d 12, respectively.—ed.]

While these changes in the law are desirable, they do not cure the *Furman* problem. Some discretion must be vested in the prosecutor, Harrison continued, but can this discretion be unlimited? Can it include the power to say that one defendant must die while his codefendant lives?

There was a codefendant in this case, counsel noted, who was allowed to plead guilty to armed robbery and received sentences of 10 years imprisonment and 10 years probation. This disparate treatment cannot be justified by the need to use the codefendant as a state witness—the codefendant did not testify at trial.

Harrison also complained of the fact that, despite the legislature's careful enumeration of statutory aggravating circumstances, juries have been permitted to note the presence of other aggravating circumstances in inflicting the death penalty.

We do not have to reach the ultimate Eighth Amendment question here, counsel concluded. The Georgia statute simply does not satisfy the *Furman* standard.

Distinction with a Difference

G. Thomas Davis, Senior Assistant Attorney General of Georgia, rejected opposing counsel's notion that the codefendant was just as guilty as petitioner Gregg. The codefendant was only 16 years old and could

not have been executed; nor was there any evidence that he had prior knowledge of Gregg's plan to kill the motorists. Davis asserted that the Georgia statute effectively controls the discretion of jurors and prosecutors. While the statute does contain the catch-all phrase "aggravating circumstances otherwise authorized by law," that phrase has been interpreted to cover only one circumstance, a prior conviction. In any event, capital punishment may not be imposed unless at least one of the statutory aggravating circumstances is found.

Counsel also pointed to the statute's provisions for swift appellate review. The state supreme court must determine "whether the sentence of death was imposed under the influence of passion, prejudice, or any other arbitrary factor," whether the evidence supports the finding of a statutory aggravating circumstance, and "whether the sentence of death is excessive or disproportionate to the penalty imposed in similar cases, considering both the crime and the defendant." Counsel suggested that, in order properly to evaluate the impact of the aggravating circumstance rule, reference must be made to state decisions thereunder. A review of the cases demonstrates that the system is operating rationally, he asserted, and that the distinctions made among defendants are supportable.

Proffitt v. Florida, No. 75-5706 [¶]

Clinton A. Curtis, of Bartow, Florida, presented petitioner's argument in the last of these cases. The Florida statute provides for a postconviction sentencing proceeding in which evidence relating to aggravating and mitigating circumstances may be presented. The jury renders an advisory sentence which is based upon a weighing of the aggravating and mitigating circumstances. The judge may accept or reject the jury's recommendation, but if a death sentence is imposed, findings must be set forth. [The leading Florida case is *State* v. *Dixon,* 283 So. 2d 1.—ed.] The statute sets forth eight aggravating and seven mitigating circumstances, and on its face does not permit others to be considered. Nonetheless, Curtis said, sentences are sometimes based on circumstances not listed

---

||This case is presented on p. 882.

¶This case is presented in Comment 1, p. 895.

in the statute. For example, this defendant was said to be "dangerous," a nonstatutory factor.

Pointing out that three other statutory aggravating circumstances were found, Mr. Justice Stevens wondered why the fourth could not simply be considered superfluous.

If the trial judge thought three circumstances were enough, Curtis replied, why did he add the fourth? This example makes clear that sentencing discretion simply cannot be controlled by statute. Nor does the statute explain how the weighing process is to be carried out. The relative weights of the various circumstances are not prescribed, and the jury is left to guess what constitutes "sufficient" weight to indicate life or death.

Curtis also alleged that the appellate review mandated by the statute is inadequate. The standards governing that review are meaningless, he said, particularly because the state supreme court does not have automatic review of cases in which life sentences are returned.

Death is Different

The proposition that death is different received support from Florida Attorney General Robert L. Shevin, but it did not lead him to the result Amsterdam had reached. It is precisely because death is different, Shevin said, that we surround its imposition with so many safeguards. Our sentencing procedure goes to the defendant himself, not just the crime, and our appellate review is full. Shevin mentioned that the state supreme court has added the requirement that trial judges include detailed findings of fact when life sentences are imposed. In this way, he said, there is developing a body of case law showing real distinctions between life prisoners and condemned defendants.

Shevin also made clear that he was not asking the Court to overrule the *Furman* decision. We are satisfied with our current procedure, he said. When *Furman* was decided, the Florida legislature considered a mandatory scheme but determined that such a law would be too harsh. It preferred to pass a law it thought good and take the chance that the statute would be held unconstitutional. We agree that mandatory death penalties represent a backward step.

Like the Attorney General of Texas, Shevin defended Florida practice against the charge that blacks and poor people are discriminated against. Over 50 percent of the death row prisoners are white, he said, although blacks arrested on capital charges outnumber whites by one-third. Also, over one-third of the prisoners on death row have retained rather than appointed counsel.

Death Is Constitutionally Different

GREGG v. GEORGIA

Supreme Court of the United States, 1976
428 U.S. 153, 96 S. Ct. 2909, 49 L. Ed. 2d 859

Troy Gregg, the petitioner, was charged with armed robbery and first degree murder. In accordance with Georgia law in capital cases, the trial was bifurcated, with a guilt stage and a sentencing stage. The evidence at the guilt trial established that Gregg and a traveling companion, Floyd Allen, were picked up by Fred Simmons and Bob Moore while hitchhiking north in Florida. The next morning the bodies of Simmons and Moore were discovered in a ditch near Atlanta. They had been shot and robbed. The next afternoon, Gregg and Allen were arrested in Simmons' car in Asheville, North Carolina. A .25 caliber pistol, later shown to be that used to kill Simmons and Moore, was found in Gregg's pocket. Subsequently, Gregg signed a statement in which he admitted shooting and then robbing Simmons and Moore. He justified the slayings on the ground of self-defense. Allen independently recounted to the police the events leading to the slayings; he subsequently pleaded guilty to armed robbery and was sentenced to 10 years' im-

prisonment. The jury found Gregg guilty of two counts of armed robbery and two counts of murder, and following the penalty stage, the jury recommended sentences of death on each count. The Georgia Supreme Court affirmed the convictions and the sentences of death for murder but vacated the death sentences for armed robbery on the ground, inter alia, that the death penalty had rarely been imposed in Georgia for that offense. The United States Supreme Court granted certiorari.

Mr. Justice STEWART, Mr. Justice POWELL, and Mr. Justice STEVENS, announced the judgment of the Court and filed an opinion delivered by Mr. Justice STEWART.

The issue in this case is whether the imposition of the sentence of death for the crime of murder under the law of Georgia violates the Eighth and Fourteenth Amendments.

* * *

II

. . . The Georgia statute, as amended after our decision in Furman v. Georgia, 408 U.S. 238 (1972), retains the death penalty for six categories of crime: murder and kidnapping for ransom or where the victim is harmed, armed robbery and rape, treason and aircraft hijacking. . . .

The capital defendants' guilt or innocence is determined in the traditional manner, either by a trial judge or a jury, in the first stage of a bifurcated trial.

If trial is by jury, the trial judge is required to charge lesser included offenses when they are supported by any view of the evidence. . . . After a verdict, finding, or plea of guilty to a capital crime, a presentence hearing is conducted before whomever made the determination of guilt. The sentencing procedures are essentially the same in both bench and jury trials. . . .

The defendant is accorded substantial latitude as to the types of evidence that he may introduce. . . . Evidence considered during the guilt stage may be considered during the sentencing stage without being resubmitted. . . .

In the assessment of the appropriate sentence to be imposed the judge is also required to consider or to include in his instructions to the jury "any mitigating circumstances or aggravating circumstances otherwise authorized by law and any of [10]

statutory aggravating circumstances which may be supported by the evidence. . . ." . . . The scope of the nonstatutory aggravating or mitigating circumstances is not delineated in the statute. Before a convicted defendant may be sentenced to death, however, except in cases of treason or aircraft hijacking, the jury, or the trial judge in cases tried without a jury, must find beyond a reasonable doubt one of the 10 aggravating circumstances specified in the statute.[i] The sentence of death may be imposed only if the jury (or judge) finds one of the statutory aggravating

---

[i]The statute provides in part:

"(a) The death penalty may be imposed for the offenses of aircraft hijacking or treason, in any case.

"(b) In all cases of other offenses for which the death penalty may be authorized, the judge shall consider, or he shall include in his instructions to the jury for it to consider, any mitigating circumstances or aggravating circumstances otherwise authorized by law and any of the following statutory aggravating circumstances which may be supported by the evidence:

"(1) The offense of murder, rape, armed robbery, or kidnapping was committed by a person with a prior record of conviction for a capital felony, or the offense of murder was committed by a person who has a substantial history of serious assaultive criminal convictions.

"(2) The offense of murder, rape, armed robbery, or kidnapping was committed while the offender was engaged in the commission of another capital felony, or aggravated battery, or the offense of murder was committed while the offender was engaged in the commission of burglary or arson in the first degree.

"(3) The offender by his act of murder, armed robbery, or kidnapping knowingly created a great risk of death to more than one person in a public place by means of a weapon or device which would normally be hazardous to the lives of more than one person.

"(4) The offender committed the offense of murder for himself or another, for the purpose of receiving money or any other thing of monetary value.

Footnote continued on page 884

circumstances and then elects to impose that sentence. . . . If the verdict is death the jury or judge must specify the aggravating circumstances(s) found. . . . In jury cases, the trial judge is bound by the jury's recommended sentence. . . .

In addition to the conventional appellate process available in all criminal cases, provision is made for special expedited direct review by the Supreme Court of Georgia of the appropriateness of imposing the sentence of death in the particular case. The court is directed to consider "the punishment as well as any errors enumerated by way of appeal." . . . If the court affirms a death sentence, it is required to include in its decision reference to similar cases that it has taken into consideration. . . .

A transcript and complete record of the trial, as well as a separate report by the trial judge, are transmitted to the court for its use in reviewing the sentence. . . . Under its special review authority, the court may either affirm the death sentence or remand the case for resentencing. In cases in which the death sentence is affirmed there remains the possibility of executive clemency.

III

We address initially the basic contention that the punishment of death for the crime of murder is, under all circumstances, "cruel and unusual" in violation of the Eighth and Fourteenth Amendments of the Constitution. . . .

[U]ntil Furman v. Georgia, 408 U.S. 238 (1972), the Court never confronted squarely the fundamental claim that the punishment of death always, regardless of the enormity of the offense or the procedure followed in imposing the sentence, is cruel and unusual punishment in violation of the Constitution. Although this issue was presented and addressed in Furman, it was not resolved by the Court. Four Justices would have held that capital punishment is not unconstitutional per se; two Justices would have reached the opposite conclusion; and three Justices, while agreeing that the statutes then before the Court were invalid as applied, left open the question whether such punishment may ever be imposed. We now hold that the punishment of death does not invariably violate the Constitution.

A

. . . The American draftsmen . . . in drafting the Eighth Amendment were primarily concerned, however, with proscribing "tortures" and other "barbarous" methods of punishment. . . .

In the earliest cases raising Eighth Amendment claims, the Court focused on particular methods of execution to determine whether they were too cruel to pass consti-

---

"(5) The murder of a judicial officer, former judicial officer, district attorney or solicitor or former district attorney or solicitor during or because of the exercise of his official duty.

"(6) The offender caused or directed another to commit murder or committed murder as an agent or employee of another person.

"(7) The offense of murder, rape, armed robbery, or kidnapping was outrageously or wantonly vile, horrible or inhuman in that it involved torture, depravity of mind, or an aggravated battery to the victim.

"(8) The offense of murder was committed against any peace officer, corrections employee or fireman while engaged in the performance of his official duties.

"(9) The offense of murder was committed by a person in, or who has escaped from, the lawful custody of a peace officer or place of lawful confinement.

"(10) The murder was committed for the purpose of avoiding, interfering with, or preventing a lawful arrest or custody in a place of lawful confinement, of himself or another.

"(c) The statutory instructions as determined by the trial judge to be warranted by the evidence shall be given in charge and in writing to the jury for its deliberation. The jury, if its verdict be a recommendation of death, shall designate in writing, signed by the foreman of the jury, the aggravating circumstance or circumstances which it found beyond a reasonable doubt. In non-jury cases the judge shall make such designation. Except in cases of treason or aircraft hijacking, unless at least one of the statutory aggravating circumstances enumerated in section 27-2534.1(b) is so found, the death penalty shall not be imposed." § 27-2534.1 (Supp. 1975).

The Supreme Court of Georgia, in Arnold v. State, 236 Ga. 534, 540, 224 S.E.2d 386, 391 (1976), recently held unconstitutional the portion of the first circumstance encompassing persons who have a "substantial history of serious assaultive criminal convictions" because it did not set "sufficiently 'clear and objective standards.'"

tutional muster. The constitutionality of the sentence of death itself was not at issue, and the criterion used to evaluate the mode of execution was its similarity to "torture" and other "barbarous" methods. . . .

But the Court has not confined the prohibition embodied in the Eighth Amendment to "barbarous" methods that were generally outlawed in the 18th century. Instead, the Amendment has been interpreted in a flexible and dynamic manner. . . . Thus the clause forbidding "cruel and unusual" punishments "is not fastened to the obsolete but may acquire meaning as public opinion becomes enlightened by a humane justice." . . .

[T]he Eighth Amendment has not been regarded as a static concept. As Chief Justice Warren said, in an oft-quoted phrase, "[T]he Amendment must draw its meaning from the evolving standards of decency that mark the progress of a maturing society." Trop v. Dulles, 356 U.S. 86, 101 (1958). . . . Thus, an assessment of contemporary values concerning the infliction of a challenged sanction is relevant to the application of the Eighth Amendment. . . . [A]ssessment does not call for a subjective judgment. It requires, rather, that we look to objective indicia that reflect the public attitude toward a given sanction.

But our cases also make clear that public perceptions of standards of decency with respect to criminal sanctions are not conclusive. A penalty also must accord with "the dignity of man," which is the "basic concept underlying the Eighth Amendment." Trop v. Dulles, supra at 100 (plurality opinion). This means, at least, that the punishment in the abstract (in this case, whether capital punishment may ever be imposed as a sanction for murder) rather than in the particular (the propriety of death as a penalty to be applied to a specific defendant for a specific crime) is under consideration, the inquiry into "excessiveness" has two aspects. First, the punishment must not involve the unnecessary and wanton infliction of pain. . . . Second, the punishment must not be grossly out of proportion to the severity of the crime. . . .

B

Of course, the requirements of the Eighth Amendment must be applied with an awareness of the limited role to be played by the courts. This does not mean that judges have no role to play, for the Eighth Amendment is a restraint upon the exercise of legislative power. . . .

But, while we have an obligation to insure that constitutional bounds are not overreached we may not act as judges as we might as legislators. . . .

Therefore, in assessing a punishment selected by a democratically elected legislature against the constitutional measure, we presume its validity. We may not require the legislature to select the least severe penalty possible so long as the penalty selected is not cruelly inhumane or disproportionate to the crime involved. And a heavy burden rests on those who would attack the judgment of the representatives of the people.

* * *

C

. . . We now consider specifically whether the sentence of death for the crime of murder is a per se violation of the Eighth and Fourteenth Amendments to the Constitution. We note first that history and precedent strongly support a negative answer to this question.

The imposition of the death penalty for the crime of murder has a long history of acceptance both in the United States and in England. The common-law rule imposed a mandatory death sentence on all convicted murderers. . . . And the penalty continued to be used into the 20th century by most American States, although the breadth of the common-law rule was diminished, intially by narrowing the class of murders to be punished by death and subsequently by widespread adoption of laws expressly granting juries the discretion to recommend mercy. . . .

It is apparent from the text of the Constitution itself that the existence of capital punishment was accepted by the Framers. At the time the Eighth Amendment was ratified, capital punishment was a common sanction in every State. Indeed, the First Congress of the United States enacted legislation providing death as the penalty for specified crimes. 1 Stat. 112 (1790). The Fifth Amendment, adopted at the same time as the Eighth, contemplated the continued existence of the capital sanction by imposing certain limits on the prosecution of capital cases:

"No person shall be held to answer for a capital, or otherwise infamous crime, unless on a presentment or indictment of a Grand Jury . . .; nor shall any person be subject for the same offence to be twice put in jeopardy of life or limb;... nor be deprived of life, liberty, or property, without due process of law...."

And the Fourteenth Amendment, adopted over three-quarters of a century later, similarly contemplates the existence of the capital sanction in providing that no State shall deprive any person of "life, liberty, or property" without due process of law.

For nearly two centuries, this Court, repeatedly and often expressly, has recognized that capital punishment is not invalid per se....

* * *

Four years ago, the petitioners in Furman and its companion cases predicated their argument primarily upon the asserted proposition that standards of decency had evolved to the point where capital punishment no longer could be tolerated.... This view was accepted by two Justices.[u] Three other Justices were unwilling to go so far; focusing on the procedures by which convicted defendants were selected for the death penalty rather than on the actual punishment inflicted, they joined in the conclusion that the statutes before the Court were constitutionally invalid.[v]

The petitioners in the capital cases before the Court today renew the "standards of decency" argument, but developments during the four years since Furman have undercut substantially the assumptions upon which their argument rested. Despite the continuing debate, dating back to the 19th century, over the morality and utility of capital punishment, it is now evident that a large proportion of American society continues to regard it as an appropriate and necessary criminal sanction.

The most marked indication of society's endorsement of the death penalty for murder is the legislative response to Furman. The legislatures of at least 35 States have enacted new statutes that provide for the death penalty for at least some crimes that result in

the death of another person. And the Congress of the United States, in 1974, enacted a statute providing the death penalty for aircraft piracy that results in death.... [A]ll of the post-Furman statutes make clear that capital punishment itself has not been rejected by the elected representatives of the people.

In the only statewide referendum occurring since Furman and brought to our attention the people of California adopted a constitutional amendment that authorized capital punishment, in effect negating a prior ruling by the Supreme Court of California in People v. Anderson, 6 Cal. 3d 628, 493 P.2d 880, cert. denied, 406 U.S. 958 (1972), that the death penalty violated the California Constitution.[y]

[The] relative infrequency of jury verdicts imposing the death sentence does not indicate rejection of capital punishment per se. Rather, the reluctance of juries in many cases to impose the sentence may well reflect the humane feeling that this most irrevocable of sanctions should be reserved for a small number of extreme cases.... Indeed, the actions of juries in many States since Furman is fully compatible with the legislative judgments, reflected in the new statutes, as to the continued utility and necessity of capital punishment in appropriate cases. At the close of 1974 at least 254 persons had been sentenced to death since Furman, and by the end of March 1976, more than 460 persons were subject to death sentences.

As we have seen, however, the Eighth

---

[u]See concurring opinions of Mr. Justice BRENNAN and Mr. Justice MARSHALL, 408 U.S. at 257 and 314.

[v]See concurring opinions of Mr. Justice DOUGLAS, Mr. Justice STEWART, and Mr. Justice WHITE, 408 U.S., at 240, 306, and 310.

---

[y]In 1968, the people of Massachusetts were asked "Shall the commonwealth ... retain the death penalty for crime?" A substantial majority of the ballots cast answered "Yes." Of 2,348,005 ballots cast, 1,159,348 voted "Yes," 730,649 voted "No," and 458,008 were blank. See Commonwealth v. O'Neal, 339 N.E.2d 676, 708 and n.1 (Mass. 1975) (Reardon, J., dissenting). A December 1972 Gallup poll indicated that 57% of the people favored the death penalty, while a June 1973 Harris survey showed support of 59%. Vidmar and Ellsworth, Public Opinion and the Death Penalty, 26 Stan. L. Rev. 1245, 1249 n.22 (1974). In a December 1970 referendum, the voters of Illinois also rejected the abolition of capital punishment by 1,218,791 votes to 676,320 votes. Report of the Governor's Study Commn. on Capital Punishment, p. 43 (Pa. 1973).

Amendment demands more than that a challenged punishment be acceptable to contemporary society. The Court also must ask whether it comports with the basic concept of human dignity at the core of the Amendment. Trop v. Dulles, 356 U.S. at 100 (plurality opinion).... [The] sanction imposed cannot be so totally without penological justification that it results in the gratuitous infliction of suffering....

The death penalty is said to serve two principal social purposes; retribution and deterrence of capital crimes by prospective offenders.[bb]

In part, capital punishment is an expression of society's moral outrage at particularly offensive conduct. This function may be unappealing to many, but it is essential in an ordered society that asks its citizens to rely on legal processes rather than self-help to vindicate their wrongs....

"Retribution is no longer the dominant objective of the criminal law," ... but neither is it a forbidden objective nor one inconsistent with our respect for the dignity of men.... Indeed, the decision that capital punishment may be the appropriate sanction in extreme cases is an expression of the community's belief that certain crimes are themselves so grievous an affront to humanity that the only adequate response may be the penalty of death.

Statistical attempts to evaluate the worth of the death penalty as a deterrent to crimes by potential offenders have occasioned a great deal of debate. The results simply have been inconclusive....

Although some of the studies suggest that the death penalty may not function as a significantly greater deterrent than lesser penalties, there is no convincing empirical evidence either supporting or refuting this view. We may nevertheless assume safely that there are murderers, such as those who act in passion, for whom the threat of death has little or no deterrent effect. But for many others, the death penalty undoubtedly is a significant deterrent. There are carefully contemplated murders, such as murder for hire, where the possible penalty of death may

well enter into the cold calculus that precedes the decision to act. And there are some categories of murder, such as murder by a life prisoner, where other sanctions may not be adequate.[hh]

The value of capital punishment as a deterrent of crime is a complex factual issue the resolution of which properly rests with the legislatures, which can evaluate the results of statistical studies in terms of their own local conditions and with a flexibility of approach that is not available to the courts.... Indeed, many of the post-Furman statutes reflect just such a responsible effort to define those crimes and those criminals for which capital punishment is most probably an effective deterrent.

In sum, we cannot say that the judgment of the Georgia legislature that capital punishment may be necessary in some cases is clearly wrong. Considerations of federalism, as well as respect for the ability of a legislature to evaluate, in terms of its particular state, the moral consensus concerning the death penalty and its social utility as a sanction, require us to conclude, in the absence of more convincing evidence, that the infliction of death as a punishment for murder is not without justification and thus is not unconstitutionally severe.

Finally, we must consider whether the punishment of death is disproportionate in relation to the crime for which it is imposed. There is no question that death as a punishment is unique in its severity and irrevocability.... When a defendant's life is at stake, the Court has been particularly sensitive to insure that every safeguard is observed.... But we are concerned here only with the imposition of capital punishment for the crime of murder, and when a life has been

---

[bb]Another purpose that has been discussed is the incapacitation of dangerous criminals and the consequent prevention of crimes that they may otherwise commit in the future....

[hh]... In 1964, reported murders totaled an estimated 9,250. During the ensuing decade, the number reported increased 123% until it totaled approximately 20,600 in 1974. In 1972, the year Furman was announced, the total estimated was 18,550. Despite a fractional decrease in 1975 as compared with 1974, the number of murders increased in the three years immediately following Furman to approximately 20,400, an increase of almost 10%. See Federal Bureau of Investigation, Crime in the United States, Uniform Crime Reports, for 1964, 1972, and 1974; 1975 Preliminary Annual Release, Uniform Crime Reports.

taken deliberately by the offender[ii] we cannot say that the punishment is invariably disproportionate to the crime. It is an extreme sanction, suitable to the most extreme of crimes.

We hold that the death penalty is not a form of punishment that may never be imposed, regardless of the circumstances of the offense, regardless of the character of the offender, and regardless of the procedure followed in reaching the decision to impose it.

IV

We now consider whether Georgia may impose the death penalty on the petitioner in this case.

A

While Furman did not hold that the infliction of the death penalty per se violates the Constitution's ban on cruel and unusual punishments, it did recognize that the penalty of death is different in kind from any other punishment imposed under our system of criminal justice. Because of the uniqueness of the death penalty, Furman held that it could not be imposed under sentencing procedures that created a substantial risk that it would be inflicted in an arbitrary and capricious manner. . . .

Furman mandates that where discretion is afforded a sentencing body on a matter so grave as the determination of whether a human life should be taken or spared, that discretion must be suitably directed and limited so as to minimize the risk of wholly arbitrary and capricious action.

It is certainly not a novel proposition that discretion in the area of sentencing be exercised in an informed manner. We have long recognized that "[f]or the determination of sentences, justice generally requires . . . that there be taken into account the circumstances of the offense together with the character and propensities of the offender." . . .

* * *

[ii]We do not address here the question whether the taking of the criminal's life is a proportionate sanction where no victim has been deprived of life—for example, when capital punishment is imposed for rape, kidnapping, or armed robbery that does not result in the death of any human being.

. . . When a human life is at stake and when the jury must have information prejudicial to the question of guilt but relevant to the question of penalty in order to impose a rational sentence, a bifurcated system is more likely to ensure elimination of the constitutional deficiencies identified in Furman.

But the provision of relevant information under fair procedural rules is not alone sufficient to guarantee that the information will be properly used in the imposition of punishment, especially if sentencing is performed by a jury. Since the members of a jury will have had little, if any, previous experience in sentencing, they are unlikely to be skilled in dealing with the information they are given. . . . To the extent that this problem is inherent in jury sentencing, it may not be totally correctible. It seems clear, however, that the problem will be alleviated if the jury is given guidance regarding the factors about the crime and the defendant that the State, representing organized society, deems particularly relevant to the sentencing decision.

The idea that a jury should be given guidance in its decision making is also hardly a novel proposition. Juries are invariably given careful instructions on the law and how to apply it before they are authorized to decide the merits of a lawsuit. . . .

. . . While such standards are by necessity somewhat general, they do provide guidance to the sentencing authority and thereby reduce the likelihood that it will impose a sentence that fairly can be called capricious or arbitrary. Where the sentencing authority is required to specify the factors it relied upon in reaching its decision, the further safeguard of meaningful appellate review is available to ensure that death sentences are not imposed capriciously or in a freakish manner.

In summary, the concerns expressed in Furman that the penalty of death not be imposed in an arbitrary or capricious manner can be met by a carefully drafted statute that ensures that the sentencing authority is given adequate information and guidance. As a general proposition these concerns are best met by a system that provides for a bifurcated proceeding at which the sentencing authority is apprised of the information relevant to the imposition of sentence and provided with standards to guide its use of the information.

We do not intend to suggest that only the above described procedures would be permissible under Furman or that any sentencing system constructed along these general lines would inevitably satisfy the concerns of Furman, for each distinct system must be examined on an individual basis. . . .

B

We now turn to consideration of the constitutionality of Georgia's capital-sentencing procedures. In the wake of Furman, Georgia amended its capital punishment statute, but chose not to narrow the scope of its murder provisions. . . .

Georgia did act, however, to narrow the class of murders subject to capital punishment by specifying 10 statutory aggravating circumstances, one of which must be found by the jury to exist beyond a reasonable doubt before a death sentence can ever be imposed. In addition, the jury is authorized to consider any other appropriate aggravating or mitigating circumstances. . . . The jury is not required to find any mitigating circumstance in order to make a recommendation of mercy that is binding on the trial court . . . but it must find a *statutory* aggravating circumstance before recommending a sentence of death.

These procedures require the jury to consider the circumstances of the crime and the criminal before it recommends sentence. No longer can a Georgia jury do as Furman's jury did: reach a finding of the defendant's guilt and then, without guidance or direction, decide whether he should live or die. Instead, the jury's attention is directed to the specific circumstances of the crime: Was it committed in the course of another capital felony? Was it committed for money? Was it committed upon a peace officer or judicial officer? Was it committed in a particularly heinous way or in a manner that endangered the lives of many persons? In addition, the jury's attention is focused on the characteristics of the person who committed the crime: Does he have a record of prior convictions for capital offenses? Are there any special facts about this defendant that mitigate against imposing capital punishment (e.g., his youth, the extent of his cooperation with the police, his emotional state at the time of the crime)? As a result, while some jury discretion still exists, "the discretion to

be exercised is controlled by clear and objective standards so as to produce nondiscriminatory application." Coley v. State, 231 Ga. 829, 834, 204 S.E.2d 612, 615.

As an important additional safeguard against arbitrariness and caprice, the Georgia statutory scheme provides for automatic appeal of all death sentences to the State's Supreme Court. That court is required by statute to review each sentence of death and determine whether it was imposed under the influence of passion or prejudice, whether the evidence supports the jury's finding of a statutory, aggravating circumstance, and whether the sentence is disproportionate compared to those sentences imposed in similar cases. . . .

In short, Georgia's new sentencing procedures require as a prerequisite to the imposition of the death penalty, specific jury findings as to the circumstances of the crime or the character of the defendant. Moreover, to guard further against a situation comparable to that presented in Furman, the Supreme Court of Georgia compares each death sentence with the sentences imposed on similarly situated defendants to ensure that the sentence of death in a particular case is not disproportionate. On their face these procedures seem to satisfy the concerns of Furman. . . .

The petitioner contends, however, that the changes in the Georgia sentencing procedures are only cosmetic, that the arbitrariness and capriciousness condemned by Furman continue to exist in Georgia—both in traditional practices that still remain and in the new sentencing procedures adopted in response to Furman.

1

First, the petitioner focuses on the opportunities for discretionary action that are inherent in the processing of any murder case under Georgia law. He notes that the state prosecutor has unfettered authority to select those persons whom he wishes to prosecute for a capital offense and to plea bargain with them. Further, at the trial the jury may choose to convict a defendant of a lesser included offense rather than find him guilty of a crime punishable by death, even if the evidence would support a capital verdict. And finally, a defendant who is convicted and sentenced to die may have his sentence commuted by the Governor of the State and the Georgia Board of Pardons and Paroles.

The existence of these discretionary stages is not determinative of the issues before us. At each of these stages an actor in the criminal justice system makes a decision which may remove a defendant from consideration as a candidate for the death penalty. Furman, in contrast, dealt with the decision to impose the death sentence on a specific individual who had been convicted of a capital offense. Nothing in any of our cases suggests that the decision to afford an individual defendant mercy violates the Constitution. Furman held only that, in order to minimize the risk that the death penalty would be imposed on a capriciously selected group of offenders, the decision to impose it had to be guided by standards so that the sentencing authority would focus on the particularized circumstances of the crime and the defendant.[xx]

The petitioner further contends that the capital-sentencing procedures adopted by Georgia in response to Furman do not eliminate the dangers of arbitrariness and caprice in jury sentencing that were held in

[xx]The petitioner's argument is nothing more than a veiled contention that Furman indirectly outlawed capital punishment by placing totally unrealistic conditions on its use. In order to repair the alleged defects pointed to by the petitioner, it would be necessary to require that prosecuting authorities charge a capital offense whenever arguably there had been a capital murder and that they refuse to plea bargain with the defendant. If a jury refused to convict even though the evidence supported the charge, its verdict would have to be reversed and a verdict of guilty entered or a new trial ordered, since the discretionary act of jury nullification would not be permitted. Finally, acts of executive clemency would have to be prohibited. Such a system, of course, would be totally alien to our notions of criminal justice.

Moreover, it would be unconstitutional. Such a system in many respects would have the vices of the mandatory death penalty statutes we hold unconstitutional today in Woodson v. North Carolina, [infra], and [Stanislaus] Roberts v. Louisiana, [infra]. The suggestion that a jury's verdict of acquittal could be overturned and a defendant retried would run afoul of the Sixth Amendment jury-trial guarantee and the Double Jeopardy Clause of the Fifth Amendment. In the federal system it also would be unconstitutional to prohibit a President from declining, as an act of executive clemency, to reprieve one sentenced to death. U.S. Const., Art. II § 2.

Furman to be violative of the Eighth and Fourteenth Amendments. He claims that the statute is so broad and vague as to leave juries free to act as arbitrarily and capriciously as they wish in deciding whether to impose the death penalty.... Specifically, Gregg urges that the statutory aggravating circumstances are too broad and too vague, that the sentencing procedure allows for arbitrary grants of mercy, and that the scope of the evidence and argument that can be considered at the presentence hearing is too wide.

The petitioner attacks the seventh statutory aggravating circumstance, which authorizes imposition of the death penalty if the murder was "outrageously or wantonly vile, horrible or inhuman in that it involved torture, depravity of mind, or an aggravated battery to the victim," contending that it is so broad that capital punishment could be imposed in any murder case. It is, of course, arguable that any murder involves depravity of mind or an aggravated battery. But this language need not be construed in this way, and there is no reason to assume that the Supreme Court of Georgia will adopt such an open-ended construction....

The petitioner also argues that two of the statutory aggravating circumstances are vague and therefore susceptible to widely differing interpretations, thus creating a substantial risk that the death penalty will be arbitrarily inflicted by Georgia juries. In light of the decisions of the Supreme Court of Georgia we must disagree....

The petitioner next argues that the requirements of Furman are not met here because the jury has the power to decline to impose the death penalty even if it finds that one or more statutory aggravating circumstances is present in the case. This contention misinterprets Furman.... Moreover, it ignores the role of the Supreme Court of Georgia which reviews each death sentence to determine whether it is proportional to other sentences imposed for similar crimes....

The petitioner objects, finally to the wide scope of evidence and argument allowed at presentence hearings. We think that the Georgia court wisely has chosen not to impose unnecessary restrictions on the evidence that can be offered at such a hearing and to approve open and far-ranging argument.... So long as the evidence introduced and the arguments made at the presentence hearing do not prejudice a defendant, it is preferable not to impose restrictions. We think it desirable for the jury to have as much information before it as possible when it makes the sentencing decision. . . .

3

Finally, the Georgia statute has an additional provision designed to assure that the death penalty will not be imposed on a capriciously selected group of convicted defendants. The new sentencing procedures require that the state Supreme Court review every death sentence to determine whether it was imposed under the influence of passion, prejudice, or any other arbitrary factor, whether the evidence supports the findings of a statutory aggravating circumstance, and "[w]hether the sentence of death is excessive or disproportionate to the penalty imposed in similar cases, considering both the crime and the defendant." . . . In performing its sentence review function the Georgia court has held that "if the death penalty is only rarely imposed for an act or it is substantially out of line with sentences imposed for other acts it will be set aside as excessive." Coley v. State, 231 Ga. 829, 834, 204 S.E.2d 612, 616 (1974). . . .

It is apparent that the Supreme Court of Georgia has taken its review responsibilities seriously. . . .

The provision for appellate review in the Georgia capital-sentencing system serves as a check against the random or arbitrary imposition of the death penalty. In particular, the proportionality review substantially eliminates the possibility that a person will be sentenced to die by the action of an aberrant jury. If a time comes when juries generally do not impose the death sentence in a certain kind of murder case, the appellate review procedures assure that no defendant convicted under such circumstances will suffer a sentence of death.

V

The basic concern of Furman centered on those defendants who were being condemned to death capriciously and arbitrarily. . . . The new Georgia sentencing procedures, by contrast, focus the jury's attention on the particularized nature of the crime and the particularized characteristics of the individual defendant. While the jury is permitted to consider any aggravating or mitigating circumstances, it must find and identify at least one statutory aggravating factor before it may impose a penalty of death. In this way the jury's discretion is channeled. No longer can a jury wantonly and freakishly impose the death sentence; it is always circumscribed by the legislative guidelines. In addition, the review function of the Supreme Court of Georgia affords additional assurance that the concerns that prompted our decision in Furman are not present to any significant degree in the Georgia procedure applied here.

For the reasons expressed in this opinion, we hold that the statutory system under which Gregg was sentenced to death does not violate the Constitution. Accordingly, the judgment of the Georgia Supreme Court is affirmed.

Mr. Justice WHITE, with whom the CHIEF JUSTICE [BURGER] and Mr. Justice REHNQUIST join, concurring in the judgment.

* * *

. . . The Georgia Legislature has made an effort to identify those aggravating factors which it considers necessary and relevant to the question whether a defendant convicted of capital murder should be sentenced to death. The jury which imposes sentence is instructed on all statutory aggravating factors which are supported by the evidence, and is told that it may not impose the death penalty unless it unanimously finds at least one of those factors to have been established beyond a reasonable doubt. The Georgia Legislature has plainly made an effort to guide the jury in the exercise of its discretion, while at the same time permitting the jury to dispense mercy on the basis of factors too intangible to write into a statute and I cannot accept a naked assertion that the effort is bound to fail. As the types of murders for which the death penalty may be imposed become more narrowly defined and are limited to those which are particularly serious or for which the death penalty is peculiarly appropriate as they are in Georgia by reason of the aggravating circumstance requirement, it becomes reasonable to expect that juries—even given discretion *not* to impose the death penalty—will impose the death penalty in a substantial portion of the cases so defined. If they do, it can no longer be said that the penalty is being imposed wantonly and freakishly or so infrequently that it loses its usefulness as a sentencing device. There is, therefore, reason to expect that Georgia's current system would escape the infirmities which invalidated its previous system under Furman. . . .

* * *

Petitioner's argument that prosecutors behave in a standardless fashion in deciding which cases to try as capital felonies is unsupported by any facts. Petitioner simply asserts that since prosecutors have the power not to charge capital felonies they will exercise that power in a standardless fashion. This is untenable. Absent facts to the contrary, it cannot be assumed that prosecutors will be motivated in their charging decision by factors other than the strength of their case and the likelihood that a jury would impose the death penalty if it convicts. Unless prosecutors are incompetent in their judgments, the standards by which they decide whether to charge a capital felony will be the same as those by which the jury will decide the questions of guilt and sentence. Thus defendants will escape the death penalty through prosecutorial charging decisions only because the offense is not sufficiently serious; or because the proof is insufficiently strong. This does not cause the system to be standardless any more than the jury's decision to impose life imprisonment on a defendant whose crime is deemed insufficiently serious or its decision to acquit someone who is probably guilty but whose guilt is not established beyond a reasonable doubt. Thus the prosecutor's charging decisions are unlikely to have removed from the sample of cases considered by the Georgia Supreme Court any which are truly "similar." If the cases really were "similar" in relevant respects, it is unlikely that prosecutors would fail to prosecute them as capital cases; and I am unwilling to assume the contrary.

Petitioner's argument that there is an unconstitutional amount of discretion in the system which separates those suspects who receive the death penalty from those who receive life imprisonment, a lesser penalty, or are acquitted or never charged, seems to be in final analysis an indictment of our entire system of justice. Petitioner has argued, in effect, that no matter how effective the death penalty may be as a punishment, government, created and run as it must be by humans, is inevitably incompetent to administer it. This cannot be accepted as a proposition of constitutional law. Imposition of the death penalty is surely an awesome responsibility for any system of justice and those who participate in it. Mistakes will be made and discriminations will occur which will be difficult to explain. However, one of society's most basic tasks is that of protecting the lives of its citizens and one of the most basic ways in which it achieves the task is through criminal laws against murder. I decline to interfere with the manner in which Georgia has chosen to enforce such laws on what is simply an assertion of lack of faith in the ability of the system of justice to operate in a fundamentally fair manner.

. . . [N]either can I agree with the petitioner's other basic argument that the death penalty, however imposed and for whatever crime, is cruel and unusual punishment.

I therefore concur in the judgment of affirmance.

Statement of the CHIEF JUSTICE [BURGER] and Mr. Justice REHNQUIST.

We join the opinion of Mr. Justice WHITE, agreeing with its analysis that Georgia's system of capital punishment comports with the Court's holding in Furman v. Georgia, 408 U.S. 238 (1972).

[Mr. Justice BLACKMUN concurred without opinion.]

Mr. Justice BRENNAN, dissenting.

The Cruel and Unusual Punishments Clause "must draw its meaning from the evolving standards of decency that mark the progress of a maturing society." The opinions of Mr. Justice STEWART, Mr. Justice POWELL, and Mr. Justice STEVENS today hold that "evolving standards of decency" require focus not on the essence of the death penalty itself but primarily upon the procedures employed by the state to single out persons to suffer the penalty of death. Those opinions hold further that, so viewed, the Clause invalidates the mandatory infliction of the death penalty but not its infliction under sentencing procedures that Mr. Justice STEWART, Mr. Justice POWELL, and Mr. Justice STEVENS conclude adequately safeguard against the risk that the death penalty was imposed in an arbitrary and capricious manner.

* * *

This Court inescapably has the duty, as the ultimate arbiter of the meaning of our Constitution, to say whether, when individuals condemned to death stand before our Bar, "moral concepts" require us to hold that the law has progressed to the point where we should declare that the punishment of death, like punishments on the rack, the screw and the wheel, is no longer morally tolerable in our civilized society. My opinion in Furman v. Georgia concluded that our civilization and the law had progressed to this point and that therefore the punishment of death, for whatever crime and under all circumstances, is "cruel and unusual" in violation of the Eighth and Fourteenth Amendments of the Constitution. I shall not again canvass the reasons that led to that conclusion. I emphasize only that foremost among the "moral concepts" recognized in our cases and inherent in the Clause is the primary moral principle that the State, even as it punishes, must treat its citizens in a manner consistent with their intrinsic worth as human beings — a punishment must not be so severe as to be degrading to human dignity. A judicial determination whether the punishment of death comports with human dignity is therefore not only permitted but compelled by the Clause. . . .

* * *

The fatal constitutional infirmity in the punishment of death is that it treats "members of the human race as nonhumans, as objects to be toyed with and discarded. [It is] thus inconsistent with the fundamental premise of the Clause that even the vilest criminal remains a human being possessed of common human dignity." . . . As such it is a penalty that "subjects the individual to a fate forbidden by the principle of civilized treatment guaranteed by the [Clause]." I therefore would hold, on that ground alone, that death is today a cruel and unusual punishment prohibited by the Clause. "Justice of this kind is obviously no less shocking than that crime itself, and the new 'official'

murder, far from offering redress for the offense committed against society, adds instead a second defilement to the first."

I concur in the judgments in No. 75-5491, Woodson v. North Carolina, and No. 75-5844, [Stanislaus] Roberts v. Louisiana, that set aside the death sentences imposed under the North Carolina and Louisiana death sentence statutes as violative of the Eighth and Fourteenth Amendments.

I dissent, however, from the judgments in No. 74-6257, Gregg. v. Georgia, No. 75-5706, Proffitt v. Florida, and No. 75-5394, Jurek v. Texas, insofar as each upholds the death sentences challenged in those cases. I would set aside the death sentences imposed in those cases as violative of the Eighth and Fourteenth Amendments.

Mr. Justice MARSHALL, dissenting.

In Furman v. Georgia, 408 U.S. 238, 314 (1972), I set forth at some length my views on the basic issue presented to the Court in these cases. The death penalty, I concluded, is a cruel and unusual punishment prohibited by the Eighth and Fourteenth Amendments. That continues to be my view.

* * *

In Furman, I concluded that the death penalty is constitutionally invalid for two reasons. First, the death penalty is excessive. . . . And second, the American people, fully informed as to the purposes of the death penalty and its liabilities, would in my view reject it as morally unacceptable. . . .

Since the decision in Furman, the legislatures of 35 states have enacted new statutes authorizing the imposition of the death sentence for certain crimes, and Congress has enacted a law providing the death penalty for air piracy resulting in death. . . . I would be less than candid if I did not acknowledge that these developments have a significant bearing on a realistic assessment of the moral acceptability of the death penalty to the American people. But if the constitutionality of the death penalty turns, as I have urged, on the opinion of an *informed* citizenry, then even the enactment of new death statutes cannot be viewed as conclusive. In Furman, I observed that the American people are largely unaware of the information critical to a judgment on the morality of the death penalty, and concluded that if they were better informed they would consider it shocking, unjust, and unacceptable. . . . A recent study, conducted after the enactment of the post-Furman statutes, has confirmed that the American people know little about the death penalty, and that the opinions of an informed public would differ significantly from those of a public unaware of the consequences and effects of the death penalty.[a]

Even assuming, however, that the post-Furman enactment of statutes authorizing the death penalty renders the prediction of the views of an informed citizenry an uncertain basis for a constitutional decision, the enactment of those statutes has no bearing whatsoever on the conclusion that the death penalty is unconstitutional because it is excessive. An excessive penalty is invalid under the Cruel and Unusual Punishments Clause "even though popular sentiment may favor" it. . . .

The two purposes that sustain the death penalty as nonexcessive in the Court's view are general deterrence and retribution. In Furman I canvassed the relevant data on the deterrent effect of capital punishment. . . . The available evidence, I concluded in Furman, was convincing that "capital punishment is not necessary as a deterrent to crime to our society. . . .

The Solicitor General in his amicus brief in these cases relies heavily on a study by Isaac Ehrlich,[d] reported a year after Furman, to support the contention that the death penalty does deter murder. Since the Ehrlich study was not available at the time of Furman and since it is the first scientific study to suggest that the death penalty may have a deterrent effect, I will briefly consider its import.

The Ehrlich study focused on the relationship in the Nation as a whole between the homicide rate and "execution risk"—the fraction of persons convicted of murder who were actually executed. Comparing the differences in homicide rate and execution risk for the years 1933 and 1969, Ehrlich found that increases in the execution risk were associated with increases in the homicide rate. But when he employed the statistical technique of multiple regression analysis to control for the influence of other variables posited to have an impact on the homicide rate, Ehrlich found a negative correlation between changes in the homicide rate and changes in execution risk. His tentative conclusion was that for the period from 1933 to 1967 each additional execution in the United States might have saved eight lives.

The methods and conclusions of the Ehrlich study have been severely criticized on a number of grounds. It has been suggested, for example, that the study is defective because it compares execution and homicide rates on a nationwide, rather than a State by State basis. . . .

The most compelling criticism of the Ehrlich study is that its conclusions are extremely sensitive to the choice of the time period included in the regression analysis. Analysis of Ehrlich's data reveals that all empirical support for the deterrent effect of capital punishment disappears when the five most recent years are removed from his time series—that is to say, whether a decrease in the execution risk corresponds to an increase or a decrease in the murder rate depends on the ending point of the sample period. . . .

The Ehrlich study, in short, is of little, if any, assistance in assessing the deterrent impact of the death penalty. . . . The evidence I reviewed in Furman remains convincing, in my view, that "capital punishment is not necessary as a deterrent to crime in our society." . . . The justification for the death penalty must be found elsewhere.

The other principal purpose said to be served by the death penalty is retribution. The notion that retribution can serve as a moral justification for the sanction of death finds credence in the opinion of my Brothers STEWART, POWELL, and STEVENS, and that of my Brother WHITE in [Stanislaus] Roberts v. Louisiana, [infra]. . . . It is this notion that I find to be the most disturbing aspect of today's unfortunate decision.

[O]ur recognition that retribution plays a crucial role in determining who may be punished by no means requires approval of

---

[a]Sarat and Vidmar, Public Opinion, The Death Penalty, and the Eighth Amendment: Testing the Marshall Hypothesis, 1976 Wisc. L. Rev. 171.

[d]I. Ehrlich, The Deterrent Effect of Capital Punishment: A Question of Life and Death (Working Paper No. 18, National Bureau of Economic Research, November 1973); Ehrlich, The Deterrent Effect of Capital Punishment: A Question of Life and Death, 65 Am. Econ. Rev. 397 (1975).

retribution as a general justification for punishment. It is the question whether retribution can provide a moral justification for punishment—in particular, capital punishment—that we must consider.

* * *

It simply defies belief to suggest that the death penalty is necessary to prevent the American people from taking the law into their own hands.

In a related vein, it may be suggested that the expression of moral outrage through the imposition of the death penalty serves to reinforce basic moral values—that it marks some crimes as particularly offensive and therefore to be avoided. . . . This contention, like the previous one, provides no support for the death penalty. It is inconceivable that any individual concerned about conforming his conduct to what society says is "right" would fail to realize that murder is "wrong" if the penalty were simply life imprisonment.

The foregoing contentions—that society's expression of moral outrage through the imposition of the death penalty pre-empts the citizenry from taking the law into its own hands and reinforces moral values—are not retributive in the purest sense. They are essentially utilitarian in that they portray the death penalty as valuable because of its beneficial results. These justifications for the death penalty are inadequate because the penalty is, quite clearly I think, not neces-

sary to the accomplishment of those results.

There remains for consideration, however, what might be termed the purely retributive justification for the death penalty—that the death penalty is appropriate, not because of its beneficial effect on society, but because the taking of the murderer's life is itself morally good. . . .

. . . The mere fact that the community demands the murderer's life in return for the evil he has done cannot sustain the death penalty, for as the plurality reminds us, "the Eighth Amendment demands more than that a challenged punishment be acceptable to contemporary society." . . . To be sustained under the Eighth Amendment, the death penalty must "[comport] with the basic concept of human dignity at the core of the Amendment"; . . . the objective in imposing it must be "[consistent] with our respect for the dignity of other men." . . . Under these standards, the taking of life "because the wrong-doer deserves it" surely must fall, for such a punishment has as its very basis the total denial of the wrong-doer's dignity and worth.

The death penalty, unnecessary to promote the goal of deterrence or to further any legitimate notion of retribution, is an excessive penalty forbidden by the Eighth and Fourteenth Amendments. I respectfully dissent from the Court's judgment upholding the sentences of death imposed upon the petitioners in these cases.

Comments

1. In *Proffitt* v. *Florida,* decided the same day as *Gregg* v. *Georgia,* supra, the Supreme Court decided the constitutionality of Florida's death penalty procedures. The decision is set out below.

PROFFITT v. FLORIDA
Supreme Court of the United States, 1976
428 U.S. 242, 96 S. Ct. 2960, 49 L. Ed. 2d 913

Mr. Justice STEWART, Mr. Justice POWELL, and Mr. Justice STEVENS announced the judgment of the Court and filed an opinion delivered by Mr. Justice POWELL.

* * *

The petitioner, Charles William Proffitt, was tried, found guilty, and sentenced to death for the first-degree murder of Joel Medgebow. The circumstances surrounding the murder were testified to by the decedent's wife, who was present at the time it was committed. On July 10, 1973, Mrs. Medgebow awakened around 5 A.M. in the bedroom of her apartment to find her husband sitting up in bed, moaning. He was holding what she took to be a ruler. Just then a third person jumped up, hit her several times with his fist, knocked her to the floor, and ran out of the house. It soon appeared that Medgebow had been fatally stabbed with a butcher knife. Mrs. Medgebow was not able to identify the attacker, although she was able to give a description of him.

The petitioner's wife testified that on the night before the murder the petitioner had gone to work dressed in a white shirt and gray pants, and that he had returned at about 5:15 A.M. dressed in the same clothing but without shoes. She said that after a short conversation the petitioner had packed his clothes and departed. A young woman boarder, who overheard parts of the petitioner's conversation with his wife, testified that the petitioner had told his wife that he had stabbed and killed a man with a butcher knife while he was burglarizing a place, and that he had beaten a woman. One of the petitioner's coworkers testified that they had been drinking together until 3:30 or 3:45 A.M. on the morning of the murder and that the petitioner at this time was wearing gray pants and a white shirt.

The jury found the defendant guilty as charged. Subsequently, as provided by Florida law, a separate hearing was held to determine whether the petitioner should be sentenced to death or to life imprisonment. Under the state law that decision turned on whether certain statutory aggravating circumstances surrounding the crime outweighed any statutory mitigating circumstances found to exist. At the hearing it was shown that the petitioner had one prior conviction, a 1967 charge of breaking and entering. The State also introduced the testimony of the physician at the jail where the petitioner had been held pending trial, Dr. Crumbley. He testified that the petitioner had come to him as a physician, and told him that he was concerned that he would harm other people in the future, that he had an uncontrollable desire to kill that had already resulted in his killing one man, that this desire was building up again, and that he wanted psychiatric help so he would not kill again. Dr. Crumbley also testified that, in his opinion, the petitioner was dangerous and would be a danger to his fellow inmates if imprisoned, but that his condition could be treated successfully.

The jury returned an advisory verdict recommending the sentence of death. The trial judge ordered an independent psychiatric evaluation of the petitioner, the results of which indicated that the petitioner was not, then or at the time of the murder, mentally impaired. The judge then sentenced the petitioner to death. In his written findings supporting the sentence, the judge found as aggravating circumstances that (1) the murder was premeditated and occurred in the course of a felony (burglary); (2) the petitioner has the propensity to commit murder; (3) the murder was especially heinous, atrocious, and cruel; and (4) the petitioner knowingly, through his intentional act, created a great risk of serious bodily harm and death to many persons. The judge also found specifically that none of the statutory mitigating circumstances existed. The Supreme Court of Florida affirmed. Proffitt v. State, 315 So. 2d 461 (1975). . . .

* * *

In response to Furman v. Georgia, 408 U.S. 238 (1972), the Florida Legislature adopted new statutes that authorize the imposition of the death penalty on those convicted of first-degree murder.... At the same time Florida adopted a new capital-sentencing procedure, patterned in large part on the Model Penal Code.... Under the new statute, if a defendant is found guilty of a capital offense, a separate evidentiary hearing is held before the trial judge and jury to determine his sentence. Evidence may be presented on any matter the judge deems relevant to sentencing and must include matters relating to certain legislatively specified aggravating and mitigating circumstances. Both the prosecution and the defense may present argument on whether the death penalty shall be imposed.

At the conclusion of the hearing the jury is directed to consider "[w]hether sufficient mitigating circumstances exist ... which outweigh aggravating circumstances found to exist; and ... [b]ased on those considerations, whether the defendant should be sentenced to life [imprisonment] or death." ...[f] The jury's verdict is determined by majority vote. It is only advisory; the actual sentence is determined by the trial judge. The Florida Supreme Court has stated, however, that "in order to sustain a sentence of death following a jury recommendation of life, the facts suggesting a sentence of death should be so clear and convincing that virtually

---

[f]The aggravating circumstances are:

"(a) The capital felony was committed by a person under sentence of imprisonment.

"(b) The defendant was previously convicted of another capital felony or of a felony involving the use or threat of violence to the person.

"(c) The defendant knowingly created a great risk of death to many persons.

"(d) The capital felony was committed while the defendant was engaged, or was an accomplice, in the commission of, or an attempt to commit, any robbery, rape, arson, burglary, kidnapping, or aircraft piracy or the unlawful throwing, placing, or discharging of a destructive device or bomb.

"(e) The capital felony was committed for the purpose of avoiding or preventing a lawful arrest or effecting an escape from custody.

"(f) The capital felony was committed for pecuniary gain.

"(g) The capital felony was committed to disrupt or hinder the lawful exercise of any governmental function or the enforcement of laws.

"(h) The capital felony was especially heinous, atrocious, or cruel." The mitigating circumstances are:

"(a) The defendant has no significant history of prior criminal activity.

"(b) The capital felony was committed while the defendant was under the influence of extreme mental or emotional disturbance.

"(c) The victim was a participant in the defendant's conduct or consented to the act.

"(d) The defendant was an accomplice in the capital felony committed by another person and his participation was relatively minor.

"(e) The defendant acted under extreme duress or under the substantial domination of another person.

"(f) The capacity of the defendant to appreciate the criminality of his conduct or to conform his conduct to the requirements of law was substantially impaired.

"(g) The age of the defendant at the time of the crime." § 921.141(6) (Supp. 1976–1977).

no reasonable person could differ." Tedder v. State, 322 So. 2d 908, 910 (1975). . . .

The trial judge is also directed to weigh the statutory aggravating and mitigating circumstances when he determines the sentence to be imposed on a defendant. The statute requires that if the trial court imposes a sentence of death, "it shall set forth in writing its findings upon which the sentence of death is based as to the facts. . . .

The statute provides for automatic review by the Supreme Court of Florida of all cases in which a death sentence has been imposed. . . . The law differs from that of Georgia in that it does not require the court to conduct any specific form of review. Since, however, the trial judge must justify the imposition of death sentence with written findings, meaningful appellate review of each such sentence is made possible, and the Supreme Court of Florida, like its Georgia counterpart, considers its function to be to "guarantee . . . that the aggravating and mitigating reasons present in one case will reach a similar result to that reached under similar circumstances in another case. . . . If a defendant is sentenced to die, this Court can review that case in light of the other decisions and determine whether or not the punishment is too great." State v. Dixon, 283 So. 2d 1, 10 (1973).

On their face these procedures, like those used in Georgia, appear to meet the constitutional deficiencies identified in Furman. The sentencing authority in Florida, the trial judge, is directed to weigh eight aggravating factors against seven mitigating factors to determine whether the death penalty shall be imposed. This determination requires the trial judge to focus on the circumstances of the crime and the character of the individual defendant. He must, inter alia, consider whether the defendant has a prior criminal record, whether the defendant acted under duress or under the influence of extreme mental or emotional disturbance, whether the defendant's role in the crime was that of a minor accomplice, and whether the defendant's youth argues in favor of a more lenient sentence than might otherwise be imposed. The trial judge must also determine whether the crime was committed in the course of one of several enumerated felonies, whether it was committed for pecuniary gain, whether it was committed to assist in an escape from custody or to prevent a lawful arrest, and whether the crime was especially heinous, atrocious, or cruel. . . .

The basic difference between the Florida system and the Georgia system is that in Florida the sentence is determined by the trial judge rather than by the jury. This Court has pointed out that jury sentencing in a capital case can perform an important societal function . . . but it has never suggested that jury sentencing is constitutionally required. And it would appear that judicial sentencing should lead, if anything, to even greater consistency in the imposition at the trial court level of capital punishment, since a trial judge is more experienced in sentencing than a jury, and therefore is better able to impose sentences similar to those imposed in analogous cases.

The Florida capital-sentencing procedures thus seek to assure that the death penalty will not be imposed in an arbitrary or capricious manner. Moreover, to the extent that any risk to the contrary exists, it is minimized by Florida's appellate review system, under which the evidence of the aggravating and mitigating circumstances is reviewed and reweighed by the Supreme Court of Florida. . . .

Under Florida's capital-sentencing procedures, in sum, trial judges are given specific and detailed guidance to assist them in deciding whether to impose a death penalty or imprisonment for life. Moreover, their decisions are reviewed to insure that they are consistent with other sentences imposed in similar circumstances. . . . On its face the Florida system thus satisfies the constitutional deficiencies identified in Furman.

* * *

Florida, like Georgia, has responded to Furman by enacting legislation that passes constitutional muster. That legislation provides that after a person is convicted of first-degree murder, there shall be an informed, focused, guided, and objective inquiry into the question whether he should be sentenced to death. If a death sentence is imposed, the sentencing authority articulates in writing the statutory reasons that led to its decision. Those reasons, and the evidence supporting them, are conscientiously reviewed by a court which, because of its statewide jurisdiction, can assure consistency, fairness, and rationality in the evenhanded operation of the state law. . . .

Affirmed.

[Justices WHITE, REHNQUIST, and BLACKMUN, and CHIEF JUSTICE BURGER concurred; Justices BRENNAN and MARSHALL dissented.]

2. In *Jurek* v. *Texas*, decided the same day as *Gregg* v. *Georgia* and *Proffit* v. *Texas*, the Court reviewed the constitutionality of the Texas procedures on capital homicides. The opinion is set out below.

JUREK v. TEXAS
Supreme Court of the United States, 1976
428 U.S. 262, 96 S. Ct. 2950, 49 L. Ed. 2d 929

Mr. Justice STEWART, Mr. Justice POWELL, and Mr. Justice STEVENS announced the judgment of the Court and filed an opinion delivered by Mr. Justice STEVENS.

* * *

The petitioner in this case, Jerry Lane Jurek, was charged by indictment with the killing of Wendy Adams 'by choking and strangling her with his hands, and by drowning her in the water, by throwing her into a river . . . in the course of committing and attempting to commit kidnapping of and forcible rape upon the said Wendy Adams.'

The evidence at his trial consisted of incriminating statements made by the petitioner, the testimony of several people who saw the petitioner and the deceased during the day she was killed, and certain technical evidence. This evidence established that the petitioner, 22 years old at the time, had been drinking beer in the afternoon. He and two young friends later went driving together in his old pickup truck. The petitioner expressed a desire for sexual relations with some young girls they saw, but one of his companions said the girls were too young. The petitioner then dropped his two friends off at a pool hall. He was next seen talking to Wendy, who was 10 years old, at a public swimming pool where her grandmother had left her to swim. Other witnesses testified that they later observed a man resembling the petitioner driving an old pickup truck through town at a high rate of speed, with a young blond girl standing screaming in the bed of the truck. The last witness who saw them heard the girl crying "help me, help me." The witness tried to follow them, but lost them in traffic. According to the petitioner's statement, he took the girl to the river, choked her, and threw her unconscious body in the river. Her drowned body was found downriver two days later.

At the conclusion of the trial the jury returned a verdict of guilty.

Texas law requires that if a defendant has been convicted of a capital offense, the trial court must conduct a separate sentencing proceeding before the same jury that tried the issue of guilt. Any relevant evidence may be introduced at this proceeding, and both prosecution and defense may present argument for or against the sentence of death. The jury is then presented with two (sometimes three) questions, the answers to which determine whether a death sentence will be imposed.

During the punishment phase of the petitioner's trial, several witnesses for the State testified to the petitioner's bad reputation in the community. The petitioner's father countered with testimony that the petitioner had always been steadily employed since he had left school and that he contributed to his family's support.

The jury then considered the two statutory questions relevant to this case: (1) whether the evidence established beyond a reasonable doubt that the murder of the deceased was committed deliberately and with the reasonable expectation that the death of the deceased or another would result, and (2) whether the evidence established beyond a reasonable doubt that there was a probability that the defendant would commit criminal acts of violence that would constitute a continuing threat to society. The jury unanimously answered yes to both questions, and the judge, therefore, in accordance with the statute, sentenced the petitioner to death. The Court of Criminal Appeals of Texas affirmed the judgment. Jurek v. State, 522 S.W.2d 934 (1975).

* * *

After this Court held Texas' system for imposing capital punishment unconstitutional . . . the Texas Legislature narrowed the scope of its laws relating to capital punishment. The new Texas Penal Code limits capital homicides to intentional and knowing murders committed in five situations: murder of a peace officer or fireman; murder committed in the course of kidnapping, burglary, robbery, forcible rape, or arson; murder committed for remuneration; murder committed while escaping or attempting to escape from a penal institution; and murder committed by a prison inmate when the victim is a prison employee. . . .

In addition, Texas adopted a new capital-sentencing procedure. . . . That procedure requires the jury to answer three questions in a proceeding that takes place subsequent to the return of a verdict finding a person guilty of one of the above categories of murder. The questions the jury must answer are these:

(1) whether the conduct of the defendant that caused the death of the deceased was committed deliberately and with the reasonable expectation that the death of the deceased or another would result;

(2) whether there is a probability that the defendant could commit criminal acts of violence that would constitute a continuing threat to society; and

(3) if raised by the evidence, whether the conduct of the defendant in killing the deceased was unreasonable in response to the provocation, if any, by the deceased. . . .

If the jury finds that the State has proved beyond a reasonable doubt that the answer to each of the three questions is yes, then the death sentence is imposed. If the jury finds that the answer to any question is no, then a sentence of life imprisonment results. . . . The law also provides for an expedited review by the Texas Court of Criminal Appeals. . . .

The Texas Court of Criminal Appeals has thus far affirmed only two judgments imposing death sentences under its post-Furman law. . . .

While Texas has not adopted a list of statutory aggravating circumstances the existence of which can justify the imposition of the death penalty as have Georgia and Florida, its action in narrowing the categories of murders for which a death sentence may ever be imposed serves much the same purpose. . . . In fact, each of the five classes of murders made capital by the Texas statute is encompassed in Georgia and Florida by one or more of their statutory aggravating circumstances. For example, the Texas statute requires the jury at the guilt determining stage to consider whether the crime was committed in the course of a particular felony, whether it was committed for hire, or whether the defendant was an inmate of a penal institution at the time of its commission. . . . Thus, in essence, the Texas statute requires that the jury find the existence of a statutory aggravating circumstance before the death penalty may be imposed. So far as consideration of aggravating circumstances is concerned, therefore, the principal difference between Texas and the other two States is that the death penalty is an available sentencing option — even potentially — for a smaller class of murders in Texas. Otherwise the statutes are similar. Each requires the sentencing authority to focus on the particularized nature of the crime.

But a sentencing system that allowed the jury to consider only aggravating circumstances would almost certainly fall short of providing the individualized sentencing determination that we today have held in Woodson v. North Carolina [infra] to be required by the Eighth and Fourteenth Amendments. For such a system would approach the mandatory laws that we today hold unconstitutional in Woodson and [Stanislaus] Roberts v. Louisiana, [infra]. A jury must be allowed to consider on the basis of all relevant evidence not only why a death sentence should be imposed, but also why it should not be imposed.

Thus, in order to meet the requirement of the Eighth and Fourteenth Amendments, a capital-sentencing system must allow the sentencing authority to consider mitigating circumstances. . . .

* * *

We conclude that Texas' capital-sentencing procedures, like those of Georgia and Florida, do not violate the Eighth and Fourteenth Amendments. By narrowing its definition of capital murder, Texas has essentially said that there must be at least one statutory aggravating circumstance in a first-degree murder case before a death sentence may even be considered. By authorizing the defense to bring before the jury at the separate sentencing hearing whatever mitigating circumstances relating to the individual defendant can be adduced, Texas has ensured that the sentencing jury will have adequate guidance to enable it to perform its sentencing function. By providing prompt judicial review of the jury's decision in a court with statewide jurisdiction, Texas has provided a means to promote the evenhanded, rational, and consistent imposition of death sentences under law. Because this system serves to assure that sentences of death will not be "wantonly" or "freakishly" imposed, it does not violate the Constitution. . . .

Affirmed.

[CHIEF JUSTICE BURGER and Justices WHITE, REHNQUIST, and BLACKMUN concurred; Justices BRENNAN and MARSHALL dissented.]

3. In *Gregg, Proffitt,* and *Jurek,* supra, a majority of the Court apparently accepted the "standards of decency" test of *Trop* v. *Dulles,* 356 U.S. 86, 101 (1958) (plurality opinion), and applying it, concluded that the death penalty for murder, under appropriate circumstances, is not cruel and unusual punishment. In *Gregg,* the Court noted that "it is now evident that a large proportion of American society continues to regard [the death penalty] as an appropriate and necessary criminal sanction." Would the death penalty have received the same support from the Court if public opinion polls had indicated that most Americans were opposed to capital punishment? Consider also the Court's statement that "public perceptions of standards of decency with respect to criminal sanctions are not conclusive." Is that an announcement that constitutional issues will not be decided by public opinion polls? If the majority of Americans were opposed to capital punishment, how difficult would it be for the Court to uphold the constitutionality of the death penalty under the "standards of decency" test? How much weight should the Court give to public opinion in deciding important constitutional issues? Should it be given more weight in regard to some issues than others? Are there certain issues in which public opinion should not be considered at all? If so, which issues?

4. Under the standards that (1) "punishment must not involve the unnecessary and wanton infliction of pain," and (2) "the punishment must not be grossly out of proportion to the severity of the crime," is the imposition of the death penalty for crimes that do not result in the loss of the victim's life constitutional? Several state statutes provide capital punishment for certain nonhomicide crimes: Ga. Code Ann. § 26-2001 (rape); Fla. Stat. Ann. § 794.011(2) (Supp. 1976–1977) (sexual battery of a child under 12 years of age); N.C. Gen. Stat. § 14-21 (Cum. Supp. 1975) (first-degree rape); La. Rev. Stat. Ann. § 14:44 (aggravated kidnapping). What about a statute authorizing the death penalty for

conspiracy to blow up Washington, D.C. or other large metropolitan areas? Suppose a defendant poisons the water supply in a large city and 100,000 persons become seriously ill but miraculously nobody dies. Would a statute permitting the death penalty for that act be upheld? Is the death of a victim required in all circumstances before capital punishment may be imposed? See *Coker* v. *Georgia,* infra.

5. The 35 state capital punishment statutes enacted post-*Furman* are: Ala. H. B. 212, §§ 2-4, 6-7 (1975); Ariz. Rev. Stat. Ann. §§ 13-452–13-454 (Supp. 1973); Ark. Stat. Ann. § 41-4706 (Cum. Supp. 1975); Cal. Penal Code §§ 190.1, 209, 219 (West Supp. 1974); Col. S. B. No. 46, § 4 (1974 Sess.); Gen. Stat. Conn. §§ 53a-25, 53a-35(b), 53a-46a, 53a-54b (1975); 11 Del. Code Ann. § 4209 (Cum. Supp. 1975); Fla. Stat. Ann. §§ 782.04, 921.141 (Cum. Supp. 1975–1976); Ga. Code Ann. §§ 26-3102, 27-2528, 27-2534.1, 27-2537 (Supp. 1975); Idaho Code § 18-4004 (Cum. Supp. 1975); Ill. Rev. Stat. c. 38, §§ 9-1, 1005-5-3, 1005-8-1A (1973); Burns Ind. Stat. Ann. § 35-13-4-1 (1975); 16 Ky. Rev. Stat. § 507.020 (1975); La. Rev. Stat. Ann. § 14:30 (Supp. 1974); Md. Code Ann., Art. 27, § 413 (Cum. Supp. 1975); Miss. Code Ann. §§ 97-3-19, 97-3-21, 97-25-55, 99-17-20 (Cum. Supp. 1975); Vernon's Mo. Stat. Ann. §§ 559.009, 559.05 (Supp. 1976); Mont. Rev. Codes Ann. § 94-5-105 (Spec. Crim. Code Supp. 1973), as amended, c. 262, 43d Legislative Assembly (Mar. 21, 1974); Neb. Rev. Stat. §§ 28-401, 29-2521–29-2523 (Cum. Supp. 1974); Nev. Rev. Stat. § 200.030 (1973); N. H. Rev. Stat. Ann. § 630:1 (1974); N. M. Stat. Ann § 40A-29-2 (Supp. 1973); N. Y. Penal Law § 60.06 (added by S. 21028 [Cal. No 1548] [Ass. B. 11474-A] N. Y. Laws 1974); N. C. Gen. Stat. § 14-17 (Cum. Supp. 1974); Ohio Rev. Code Ann. §§ 2929.02–2929.04 (Page Spec. Supp. 1973); 21 Okla. Stat. Ann. §§ 701.1–701.03 (Supp. 1973); Pa. Act. No. 46, 158th General Assembly (Mar. 26, 1974); R. I. Gen. Laws Ann. § 11-23-2 (Supp. 1975); S. C. Code § 16-52 (Cum. Supp. 1975); Tenn. Code Ann. §§ 39-2402, 39-2406 (1975); Vernon's Tex. Pen. Code Ann. § 19.03(a) (1974); Utah Code Ann. §§ 76-3-206-207, 76-5-202 (Supp. 1975); Va. Code §§ 18.2-10, 18.2-31 (1975); Wash. Rev. Code §§ 9A.32.046 (Supp. 1975); Wyo. Stat. Ann. § 6-54 (Cum. Supp. 1975). The federal statute is Antihijacking Act of 1974, 49 U.S.C. § 1472(i), (n) (Supp. IV).

6. Virtually all jurisdictions provide by statute for granting of executive clemency by either the governor or the board of pardons and paroles. Should a governor grant executive clemency in a death penalty case because he is personally opposed to capital punishment? Would such action usurp the proper functions of the jury, the courts, or the legislature? Should he sign the death warrant merely *because* capital punishment is provided for by law? Is the refusal of a governor to sign a death warrant arguably a form of civil disobedience? In most jurisdictions, executive clemency is usually not subject to judicial review. See, e.g., *Schick* v. *Reed,* 419 U.S. 256 (1974) (President has the power to grant a conditional pardon, or to commute a sentence with a no-parole condition). Could the warden of a prison be held in contempt of court for refusing to carry out a lawful death sentence? Suppose the warden refuses to do so on religious grounds.

7. Suppose a death penalty statute requires the jury to specify any mitigating circumstances before a recommendation of mercy will be binding on the trial court. Would that satisfy the concern of *Furman* that the death sentence not be arbitrarily and capriciously imposed? Consider the statement of the plurality in *Gregg* that "the concerns expressed in Furman . . . are best met by a system that provides for a bifurcated proceeding at which the sentencing authority is apprised of the information relevant to the imposition of sentence and provided with standards to guide its use of information." Is the Court hinting that any other type of system (e.g., a combined guilt and sentencing proceeding) will be difficult to justify? Under the Florida system, the recommendations of the jury are not binding on the sentencing judge. Is this system preferable to the Georgia and Texas procedures? Under what circumstances, if any, should a Florida judge impose the death sentence notwithstanding a recommendation of mercy by the jury? Suppose a sentencing procedure requires that a jury find only by a preponderance of the evidence that an aggravating circumstance sufficient to impose the death penalty exists (instead of by proof beyond a reasonable doubt as required under the Georgia, Florida, and Texas procedures). Would that be unconstitutional?

8. Consider the following statement of the Court in *Gregg* at n.47 (omitted in the text): "In McGautha v. California, 402 U.S. 183 (1971), this Court held that the Due Process Clause of the Fourteenth Amendment did not require that a jury be provided with standards to guide its decision whether to recommend a sentence of life imprisonment or death or that the capital-sentencing proceeding be separated from the guilt determination process. McGautha was not an Eighth Amendment decision, and to the extent it purported to deal with Eighth Amendment concerns, it must be read in light of the opinions in Furman v. Georgia. There the Court ruled that death sentences imposed under statutes that left juries with untrammeled discretion to impose or withhold the death penalty violated the Eighth and Fourteenth Amendments. While Furman did not overrule McGautha, it is clearly in substantial tension with a broad reading of McGautha's holding. In view of Furman, McGautha can be viewed rationally as a precedent only for the proposition that standardless jury sentencing procedures were not employed in the cases there before the Court so as to violate the Due Process Clause. We note that McGautha's assumption that it is not possible to devise standards to guide and regularize jury sentencing in capital cases has been undermined by subsequent experience. In view of that experience and the considerations set forth in the text, we adhere to Furman's determination that where the ultimate punishment of death is at issue a system of standardless jury discretion violates the Eighth and Fourteenth Amendments." If it was not overruled by *Furman,* what is left of the *McGautha* decision after *Gregg, Proffitt* and *Jurek?*

9. Suppose state procedures on capital punishment do not require mandatory appellate review by the state's highest court after a death sentence has been imposed. Does that violate the constitutional standards of *Furman?* The Court has stated on numerous occasions that appellate review of criminal convictions is not constitutionally required. See *Estelle* v. *Dorrough,* Chapter Four,

§ 4.04, and cases cited therein. Does the fact that the death penalty has been imposed make a constitutional difference?

10. Do you agree with Justice Brennan, dissenting in *Gregg,* that the majority failed to focus on the "essence of the death penalty itself" and instead concentrated on the "procedures employed by the State to single out persons to suffer the penalty of death"? Or is it immaterial how the Court reached its conclusions? Consider Justice Marshall's opinion in *Gregg* (dissenting) that the American people are largely unaware of the information critical to a judgment on the morality of the death penalty, and . . . if they were better informed they would consider it shocking, unjust, and unacceptable" and his statement in *Furman* (concurring) that "[the death penalty] is morally unacceptable to the people of the United States at this time in their history." Were the American people adequately informed about the morality of the death penalty in 1972 when *Furman* was decided but less informed four years later at the time of *Gregg?* If, as Justices Marshall and Brennan believe, the death penalty is "excessive" and per se unconstitutional, would the Eighth Amendment allow especially dangerous offenders to be sentenced to solitary confinement for life with no possibility of parole? Would Justices Brennan and Marshall permit capital punishment if compelling empirical evidence showed that the death penalty functions as a deterrent and thus saves lives? Such compelling evidence is not likely to be forthcoming because most studies concentrate on persons who have killed others, not on those who have not, for whatever reasons. It is often said that most persons are capable of killing under certain circumstances. Fortunately, most of us are not confronted with those circumstances. According to the FBI's Uniform Crime Reports, murder consistently accounts for less than one half of 1 per cent of all violent crimes although the rate of 20,000 murders a year in the United States is one of the highest in the world. Drunk drivers kill about 25,000 Americans a year—but that is not considered murder.

Death for Rape of Adult Women Is "Excessive"

ORAL ARGUMENTS BEFORE THE U.S. SUPREME COURT*

Coker v. Georgia, No. 75-5444; argued 3/28/77

While *Gregg. v. Georgia,* 428 U.S. 153 (1976), and its companion cases dealt with a variety of capital punishment statutes, those cases shared an important characteristic—all dealt with first-degree murder defendants and statutory enactments providing death for that particular crime. Georgia was back in the Court last week seeking approval of a

statute permitting the imposition of the death penalty for a different crime, the rape of an adult woman.

David E. Kendall, of New York, presented argument for defendant Ehrlich Anthony Coker. Coker was serving three life terms and other sentences for crimes including murder, rape, kidnapping, and aggravated assault, Kendall explained, when he escaped from prison in 1974. Several hours after the escape he entered a family dwelling, bound the husband in the bathroom, moved the three-week-old baby into the bathroom, and forced the wife to have intercourse with him. He then compelled his victim to enter the

*From 21 Crim. L. Rptr. 4003–4004. Reprinted by permission of the Bureau of National Affairs, Inc.

family car with him, telling her husband that she would be released at a certain city but killed if the police stopped them. Counsel emphasized that, despite the defendant's threats, the victim was eventually released when police surrounded the car. She suffered no harm, Kendall said, other than the effects of the rape.

The defendant was tried under the general provisions approved in *Gregg*. Besides the rape, he was also tried for armed robbery of the husband, a capital felony under state law. At the penalty phase, the state introduced evidence of the defendant's prior felonies that would have been capital under then-current law. The trial judge said the jury could find two aggravating circumstances as to the rape count—the prior convictions, and commission of the rape during the perpetration of the armed robbery. The jury found both factors to exist.

In response to a question from the Chief Justice, Kendall said the jury heard evidence of the defendant's alleged insanity and alcoholism, which could constitute mitigating factors.

Impact

The decision here will not have much impact on the criminal justice system, counsel asserted. The death penalty has been almost universally repudiated as a punishment for the rape of an adult woman. Georgia is virtually the only jurisdiction in the civilized world authorizing the punishment in non-homicide cases. The statute also lists kidnapping, treason, and aircraft hijacking as capital crimes; however, the state supreme court has rejected this punishment for armed robbery.

Even in Georgia, Kendall continued, only a small, arbitrarily selected fraction of rape defendants are chosen to suffer death.

Moreover, capital punishment in this context comes to the Court with a "notorious and unsavory reputation" for racial discrimination. Its origin as a punishment for rape is founded in invidious racial discrimination, counsel asserted. Since 1930, Georgia has executed 58 black men for rape, but only three whites—Coker would be the fourth.

In summary, counsel said, we argue that death is an excessive and disproportionate penalty for rape, and that the pattern of executions shows the same problems that proved decisive in *Furman* v. *Georgia*, 408 U.S. 238.

We must agree that rape is a serious crime, Kendall said. But death is different from any other punishment, as this Court's opinions have acknowledged.

The *Gregg* plurality eschewed "subjective" standards for evaluating the proportionality of punishment to crime and instead scrutinized objective indicia—legislation, jury verdicts, and history and traditional usage. Under all three standards, Kendall argued, capital punishment is disproportionate as a penalty for rape. No other American jurisdiction now authorizes it in this context. Even before *Furman* there was some movement toward abolition, with three states moving to abolish it.

Mr. Justice Rehnquist: "You don't argue that *Furman* represents a community consensus about the punishment's acceptability, do you?"

Furman does reflect the desuetude into which capital punishment has fallen, Kendall responded. After *Furman*, only six states reenacted the death penalty for rape; three of those statutes related to certain rapes committed on children, and two others, in Louisiana and North Carolina, covered only limited categories of rape. Only Georgia opted for broad coverage. The death-for-rape statutes have been overturned, by state or federal courts, in four of these states.

How long does a state have in which to react, once a statute has been overturned, before its inaction may be taken as a change of heart? Mr. Justice Rehnquist asked.

The post-*Gregg* era has not been with us long enough, counsel acknowledged. But he emphasized that the Louisiana legislature has enacted a new capital punishment statute for murder while defeating one for rape. In Tennessee, legislative committees have rejected a move to reenact this penalty for rape.

The Chief Justice asked why counsel emphasized the irreversibility of the death penalty in this particular case. Irreversibility is usually argued when there is a claim that the defendant may be innocent.

Kendall said he was using the concept in another sense. The irreversibility of death is a reason to apply a very high standard of review. Counsel also said that insanity or some other factor might raise a claim of innocence or mitigation here.

Deterrence

Mr. Justice Powell: "If we have a prisoner under life sentence without possibility of parole, and he escapes and commits a new capital crime, then what punishment is appropriate?"

Counsel emphasized that such is not the case here. But in any event, imprisonment is seen to be the appropriate punishment when one considers the punishments given other defendants. Such a defendant faces the added stigma of a new conviction if he commits a new crime.

Mr. Justice Powell did not think counsel's scheme offered society much protection. What deterrent exists for such a defendant? he asked.

Counsel responded by noting that Coker was not in maximum security at the time of his escape. Moreover, Georgia could enact a longer mandatory prison term for recidivists.

Mr. Justice Stewart: "Of course, anyone serving a life sentence without possibility of parole can commit any offense with impunity, unless you make death the punishment for any crime."

Counsel agreed. He added that this case was "not tried on a recidivism theory."

In response to a question from Mr. Justice Marshall, counsel indicated that statistics from states that have abolished the death penalty for rape are equivocal on the question of whether the incidence of rape increased after abolition.

Proportionality: A Different View

B. Dean Grindle, Jr., Assistant Attorney General of Georgia, summarized the state's argument as follows: First, the Constitution does not define what is or is not a capital crime. Second, condemning all convicted rapists to death would have far-reaching consequences. Finally, the problem of recidivism and violent crime makes it necessary for the states to have the option represented by Georgia's statute.

When counsel claimed an inability to see any constitutional difference between death for homicide and death for rape, Mr. Justice Stewart asked whether he recognized the proportionality principle. Under the Court's opinions, counsel replied, he had to recognize it.

The state's statutes are not designed to execute all murderers or all rapists, Grindle continued. Some rapes are viewed by society as calling for even more public condemnation than many murders. He pointed out that in many homicides, the victim is a friend or relative of the accused; this is rarely so in rape cases.

Georgia does not explicitly distinguish between rape and aggravated rape, counsel said in response to a question from Mr. Justice Powell. But the death penalty effectively makes this distinction.

The Chief Justice: "Doesn't this statutory scheme leave the jury at large to impose the death penalty on whomever it wishes?"

This could well be true, Grindle responded, but it is no less true in murder cases. A jury can always ignore the instructions given it.

Mr. Justice Stewart: "The jury cannot impose death without finding one or more aggravating circumstances, correct? On the other hand, the statute could apply even if the defendant and his victim are not strangers — if, for instance, a jilted boyfriend rapes his former girlfriend."

Grindle disputed Kendall's claim that the Court's decision will have little impact. Should the Court determine that death is an impermissible punishment for certain crimes, society's only recourse is a constitutional amendment. The decision here will surely be applied in all non-homicide cases.

Mr. Justice Stewart asked what other crimes counsel thought should be punishable by death.

Grindle distinguished two categories of crimes that could be capital. First, almost any violent crime committed by a recidivist could be so punished. Second are such "modern" crimes as aircraft hijacking, hostage taking, and terrorism, if accompanied by bodily harm or "disruption of governmental processes." He made reference to the recent siege in Washington involving a religious faction's takeover of three buildings, including the seat of the city government.

In response to a question from Mr. Justice Blackmun, Grindle added that treason and espionage could be capital, "if we put our freedom and form of government on a pedestal." We should not go back to a form of the simplistic "eye for an eye" formula, he said.

Invitation Not To Kill

Mr. Justice Stewart asked whether, under Georgia's statute, a rapist might decide he might as well kill his victim.

Perhaps he would under a mandatory system, counsel answered, but Georgia's statute encourages the rapist not to kill.

Grindle challenged Kendall's statement that the defendant was not tried under a recidivism theory. Evidence of his prior capital felonies was admitted at the penalty stage.

The states must be able to deter those who demonstrate their recidivist tendencies, Grindle asserted. For such a defendant, the constitutionality of the punishment should not hinge on what he did with his latest victim.

Counterproductive?

In rebuttal, Kendall noted that some women's groups oppose the death penalty for rape, saying that it is counterproductive.

On the question of whether the defendant was tried on a recidivism theory, counsel pointed out that the jury wasn't instructed to make findings on the defendant's future dangerousness. Assuming that death is an appropriate penalty in some rape cases, Georgia's statute does not draw a defensible line.

COKER v. GEORGIA

Supreme Court of the United States, 1977
433 U.S. ____, 97 Ct. 2861, 53 L. Ed. 2d 982

The petitioner, while serving sentences for murder, rape, kidnapping and aggravated assault, escaped from a Georgia prison and entered the house of Allen and Elnita Carver. He threatened the couple with a "board," tied up Mr. Carver, and obtained a kitchen knife, money, and keys to the Carver car. Brandishing the knife, he raped 16-year-old Mrs. Carver in the presence of her husband and their three-week-old infant, and then forced her to accompany him as he fled in the family auto. Mr. Carver was able to free himself and notify the police. Shortly afterwards, petitioner was apprehended and Mrs. Carver was freed unharmed. A jury convicted Coker of escape, armed robbery, motor vehicle theft, kidnapping, and rape, which was a capital crime in Georgia. At a separate sentencing hearing, the jury was instructed that it could consider in finding aggravating circumstances (1) whether the rape had been committed by a person with a prior record of conviction for a capital felony, and (2) whether it had been committed in the course of another capital felony (in this case the robbery of Mr. Allen). Pursuant to Georgia statute, the jury was also told that even if aggravating circumstances were found, it could still choose not to impose the death penalty if it found that the aggravating circumstances were outweighed by mitigating ones; i.e., circumstances "which in fairness and mercy, may be considered as extenuating or reducing the degree" of moral culpability. The jury returned a verdict on the rape count of death by electrocution. The Georgia Supreme Court affirmed both the conviction and sentence, and the United State Supreme Court granted certiorari.

Mr. Justice WHITE announced the judgment of the Court and filed an opinion in which Mr. Justice STEWART, Mr. Justice BLACKMUN, and Mr. Justice STEVENS joined.

* * *

II

* * *

In sustaining the imposition of the death penalty in Gregg [v. Georgia, 428 U.S. 153

(1976)] . . . the Court firmly embraced the holdings and dicta from prior cases, Furman v. Georgia [408 U.S. 238 (1972)]; Robinson v. California, 370 U.S. 660 (1963); Trop v. Dulles, 356 U.S. 86 (1958); and Weems v. United States, 217 U.S. 349 (1910), to the effect that the Eighth Amendment bars not only those punishments that are "barbaric" but also those that are "excessive" in relation to the crime committed. Under Gregg, a punishment is "excessive" and unconstitutional if it (1) makes no measurable contribution to acceptable goals of punishment and hence is nothing more than the purposeless and needless imposition of pain and suffering; or (2) is grossly out of proportion to the severity of the crime. A punishment might fail the test on either ground. Furthermore, these Eighth Amendment judgments should not be, or appear to be, merely the subjective views of individual Justices; judgment should be informed by objective factors to the maximum possible extent. To this end, attention must be given to the public attitudes concerning a particular sentence — history and precedent, legislative attitudes, and the response of juries reflected in their sentencing decisions are to be consulted. In Gregg, after giving due regard to such sources, the Court's judgment was that the death penalty for deliberate murder was neither the purposeless imposition of severe punishment nor a punishment grossly disproportionate to the crime. But the Court reserved the question of the constitutionality of the death penalty when imposed for other crimes. . . .

III

That question, with respect to rape of an adult woman, is now before us. We have concluded that a sentence of death is grossly disproportionate and excessive punishment for the crime of rape and is therefore forbidden by the Eighth Amendment as cruel and unusual punishment.

A

. . . At no time in the last 50 years has a majority of the States authorized death as a punishment for rape. In 1925, 18 States, the District of Columbia, and the Federal Government authorized capital punishment for the rape of an adult female. By 1971 just prior to the decision in Furman v. Georgia, that number had declined, but not substan-

tially, to 16 States plus the Federal Government. Furman then invalidated most of the capital punishment statutes in this country, including the rape statutes, because, among other reasons, of the manner in which the death penalty was imposed and utilized under those laws.

With their death penalty statutes for the most part invalidated, the States were faced with the choice of enacting modified capital punishment laws in an attempt to satisfy the requirements of Furman or of being satisfied with life imprisonment as the ultimate punishment of *any* offense. Thirty-five States immediately reinstituted the death penalty for at least limited kinds of crime. . . .

This public judgment as to the acceptability of capital punishment, evidenced by the immediate, post-Furman legislative reaction in a large majority of the States, heavily influenced the Court to sustain the death penalty for murder in Gregg v. Georgia. . . .

But if the "most marked indication of a society's endorsement of the death penalty for murder is the legislative response to Furman," Gregg v. Georgia, supra, at 179–180, it should also be a telling datum that the public judgment with respect to rape, as reflected in the statutes providing the punishment for that crime, has been dramatically different. In reviving death penalty laws to satisfy Furman's mandate, none of the States that had not previously authorized death for rape chose to include rape among capital felonies. Of the 16 States in which rape had been a capital offense, only three provided the death penalty for rape of an adult woman in their revised statutes — Georgia, North Carolina, and Louisiana. In the latter two States, the death penalty was mandatory for those found guilty, and those laws were invalidated by Woodson and Roberts. When Louisiana and North Carolina, responding to those decisions, again revised their capital punishment laws, they reenacted the death penalty for murder but not for rape; none of the seven other legislatures that to our knowledge have amended or replaced their death penalty statutes since July 2, 1976, including four States (in addition to Louisiana and North Carolina) that had authorized the death sentence for rape prior to 1972 and had reacted to Furman with mandatory statutes, included rape among the crimes for which death was an authorized punishment.

Georgia argues that 11 of the 16 states that authorized death for rape in 1972 attempted to comply with Furman by enacting arguably mandatory death penalty legislation and that it is very likely that aside from Louisiana and North Carolina, these States simply chose to eliminate rape as a capital offense rather than to *require* death for *each* and *every* instance of rape. The argument is not without force; but four of the 16 States did not take the mandatory course and also did *not* continue rape of an adult woman as a capital offense. Further, as we have indicated, the legislatures of six of the 11 arguably mandatory States have revised their death penalty laws since Woodson and Roberts without enacting a new death penalty for rape. And this is to say nothing of 19 other States that enacted nonmandatory, post-Furman statutes and chose not to sentence rapists to death.

It should be noted that Florida, Mississippi, and Tennessee also authorized the death penalty in some rape cases, but only where the victim was a child and the rapist an adult. The Tennessee statute has since been invalidated because the death sentence was mandatory. Collins v. State, 550 S.W. 2d 643 (1977). The upshot is that Georgia is the sole jurisdiction in the United States at the present time that authorizes a sentence of death when the rape victim is an adult woman, and only two other jurisdictions provide capital punishment when the victim is a child.

The current judgment with respect to the death penalty for rape is not wholly unanimous among state legislatures, but it obviously weighs very heavily on the side of rejecting capital punishment as a suitable penalty for raping an adult woman.

B

It was also observed in Gregg that "[t]he jury . . . is a significant and reliable index of contemporary values because it is so directly involved," 428 U.S., at 181, and that it is thus important to look to the sentencing decisions that juries have made in the course of assessing whether capital punishment is an appropriate penalty for the crime being tried. Of course, the jury's judgment is meaningful only where the jury has an appropriate measure of choice as to whether the death penalty is to be imposed. As far as execution for rape is concerned, this is now true only in Georgia and in Florida; and in the latter State, capital punishment is authorized only for the rape of children.

According to the factual submissions in this Court, out of all rape convictions in Georgia since 1973 — and that total number has not been tendered — 63 cases had been reviewed by the Georgia Supreme Court as of the time of oral argument; and of these, six involved a death sentence, one of which was set aside, leaving five convicted rapists now under sentence of death in the State of Georgia. Georgia juries have thus sentenced rapists to death six times since 1973. This obviously is not a negligible number; and the State argues that as a practical matter juries simply reserve the extreme sanction for extreme cases of rape and that recent experience surely does not prove that jurors consider the death penalty to be a disproportionate punishment for every conceivable instance of rape, no matter how aggravated. Nevertheless, it is true that in the vast majority of cases, at least nine out of 10, juries have not imposed the death sentence.

IV

These recent events evidencing the attitude of state legislatures and sentencing juries do not wholly determine this controversy, for the Constitution contemplates that in the end our own judgment will be brought to bear on the question of the acceptability of the death penalty under the Eighth Amendment. Nevertheless, the legislative rejection of capital punishment for rape strongly confirms our own judgment, which is that death is indeed a disproportionate penalty for the crime of raping an adult woman.

We do not discount the seriousness of rape as a crime. It is highly reprehensible, both in a moral sense and in its almost total contempt for the personal integrity and autonomy of the female victim and for the latter's privilege of choosing those with whom intimate relationships are to be established. Short of homicide, it is the "ultimate violation of self." It is also a violent crime because it normally involves force, or the threat of force or intimidation, to overcome the will and the capacity of the victim to resist. Rape is very often accompanied by physical injury to the female and can also inflict mental and psychological damage. Because it undermines the community's sense of security, there is public injury as well.

Rape is without doubt deserving of serious punishment; but in terms of moral depravity and of the injury to the person and to the public, it does not compare with murder, which does involve the unjustified taking of human life. Although it may be accompanied by another crime, rape by definition does not include the death or even the serious injury of another person. The murderer kills; the rapist, if no more than that, does not. Life is over for the victim of murderers; for the rape victim, life may not be nearly so happy as it was, but it is not over and normally is not beyond repair. We have the abiding conviction that the death penalty, which "is unique in its severity and revocability," 428 U.S. 187, is an excessive penalty for the rapist who, as such, does not take human life.

This does not end the matter, for under Georgia law, death may not be imposed for any capital offense, including rape, unless the jury or judge finds one of the statutory aggravating circumstances and then elects to impose that sentence. . . . For the rapist to be executed in Georgia, it must therefore be found not only that he committed rape but also that one or more of the following aggravating circumstances were present: (1) that the rape was committed by a person with a prior record of conviction for a capital felony; (2) that the rape was committed while the offender was engaged in the commission of another capital felony, or aggravated battery; or (3) the rape "was outrageously or wantonly vile, horrible or inhuman in that it involved torture, depravity of mind, or aggravated battery to the victim." Here, the first two of these aggravating circumstances were alleged and found by the jury.

Neither of these circumstances, nor both of them together, change our conclusion that the death sentence imposed on Coker is a disproportionate punishment for rape. Coker had prior convictions for capital felonies— rape, murder and kidnapping—but these prior convictions do not change the fact that the instant crime being punished is a rape not involving the taking of life.

It is also true that the present rape occurred while Coker was committing armed robbery, a felony for which the Georgia statutes authorize the death penalty. But Coker was tried for the robbery offense as well as for rape and received a separate life sentence for this crime; the jury did not deem the robbery itself deserving of the death penalty, even though accompanied by the aggravating circumstance, which was stipulated, that Coker had been convicted of a prior capital crime.

We note finally that in Georgia a person commits murder when he unlawfully and with malice aforethought, either express or implied, causes the death of another human being. He also commits that crime when in the commission of a felony he causes the death of another human being, irrespective of malice. But even where the killing is deliberate, it is not punishable by death absent proof of aggravating circumstances. It is difficult to accept the notion, and we do not, that the rape, with or without aggravating circumstances, should be punished more heavily than the deliberate killing as long as the rapist does not himself take the life of his victim. The judgment of the Georgia Supreme Court upholding the death sentence is reversed and the case is remanded to that court for further proceedings not inconsistent with this opinion.

Mr. Justice BRENNAN, concurring in the judgment.

Adhering to my view that the death penalty is in all circumstances cruel and unusual punishment prohibited by the Eighth and Fourteenth Amendments, Gregg v. Georgia, 428 U.S. 153, 227 (1976), I concur in the judgment of the Court setting aside the death sentence imposed under the Georgia rape statute.

Mr. Justice MARSHALL concurring in the judgment of the Court.

In Gregg v. Georgia, 428 U.S. 153, 231 (1976), I stated, "In Furman v. Georgia, 408 U.S. 238, 314 (1972) (concurring), I set forth at some length my views on the basic issue presented to the Court in these cases. The death penalty, I concluded, is a cruel and unusual punishment prohibited by the Eighth and Fourteenth Amendments. That continues to be my view."

I then explained in some detail my reasons for reaffirming my position. I continue to adhere to those views in concurring in the judgment of the Court in this case.

Mr. Justice POWELL, concurring in part and dissenting in part.

I concur in the judgment of the Court on the facts of this case, and also in its reasoning supporting the view that ordinarily death is disproportionate punishment for the crime of raping an adult woman. Although rape invariably is a reprehensible crime, there is no indication that petitioner's offense was committed with excessive brutality or that the victim sustained serious or lasting injury. The plurality, however, does not limit its holding to the case before us or to similar cases. Rather, in an opinion that ranges well beyond what is necessary, it holds that capital punishment *always*—regardless of the circumstances—is a disproportionate penalty for the crime of rape.

The Georgia statute, sustained in Gregg v. Georgia, 428 U.S. 153 (1976), specifies aggravating circumstances that may be considered by the jury when appropriate. With respect to the crime of rape, only three such circumstances are specified: (i) the offense was committed by a person with a prior record of conviction of a capital felony; (ii) the offense was committed while the offender was engaged in another capital felony or in aggravated battery; and (iii) the offense was "outrageously or wantonly vile, horrible or inhuman in that it involved torture, depravity of mind, or an aggravated battery to the victim." . . . Only the third circumstance describes in general the offense of aggravated rape, often identified as a separate and more heinous offense than rape. . . . That third circumstance was not submitted to the jury in this case, as the evidence would not have supported such a finding. It is therefore quite unnecessary for the plurality to write in terms so sweeping as to foreclose each of the 50 state legislatures from creating a narrowly defined substantive crime of aggravated rape punishable by death. . . .

* * *

Today, in a case that does not require such an expansive pronouncement, the plurality draws a bright line between murder and all rapes—regardless of the degree of brutality of the rape or the effect upon the victim. I dissent because I am not persuaded that such a bright line is appropriate. . . .

. . . [I]t may be that the death penalty is not disproportionate punishment for the crime of aggravated rape. Final resolution of the question must await careful inquiry into objective indicators of society's "evolving standards of decency," particularly legislative enactments and the responses of juries in capital cases. . . . In a proper case a more discriminating inquiry than the plurality undertakes well might discover that both juries and legislatures have reserved the ultimate penalty for the case of an outrageous rape resulting in serious, lasting harm to the victim. I would not prejudge the issue. To this extent, I respectfully dissent.

Mr. Chief Justice BURGER, with whom Mr. Justice REHNQUIST joins, dissenting.

* * *

My first disagreement with the Court's holding is its unnecessary breadth. The narrow issue here presented is whether the State of Georgia may constitutionally execute this petitioner for the particular rape which he has committed, in light of all the facts and circumstances shown by this record. The plurality opinion goes to great lengths to consider societal mores and attitudes toward the generic crime of rape and the punishment for it; however, the opinion gives little attention on the special circumstances which bear directly on whether imposition of the death penalty is an appropriate societal response to Coker's criminal acts: (a) On account of his prior offenses, Coker is already serving such lengthy prison sentences that imposition of additional periods of imprisonment would have no incremental punitive effect; (b) by his life pattern Coker has shown that he presents a particular danger to the safety, welfare, and chastity of women, and on his record the likelihood is therefore great that he will repeat his crime at first opportunity; (c) petitioner escaped from prison, only a year and a half after he commenced serving his latest sentences; he has nothing to lose by further escape attempts; and (d) should he again succeed in escaping from prison, it is reasonably predictable that he will repeat his pattern of attacks on women—and with impunity since the threat of added prison sentences will be no deterrent.

Unlike the Court, I would narrow the inquiry in this case to the question actually presented: Does the Eighth Amendment's ban against cruel and unusual punishment prohibit the State of Georgia from executing a person who has, within the space of three years, raped three separate women, killing one and attempting to kill another, who is serving prison terms exceeding his probable lifetime and who has not hesitated to escape confinement at the first available opportunity? Whatever one's view may be as to the State's constitutional power to impose the death penalty upon a rapist who stands before a court convicted for the first time, this case reveals a chronic rapist whose continuing danger to the community is abundantly clear.

* * *

In my view, the Eighth Amendment does not prevent the State from taking an individual's "well demonstrated propensity for life-endangering behavior" into account in devising punitive measures which will prevent inflicting further harm upon innocent victims. See Gregg v. Georgia, 428 U.S. 153, 183 n.28 (1976). Only one year ago Mr. Justice WHITE succinctly noted: "Death finally forecloses the possibility that a prisoner will commit further crimes, whereas life imprisonment does not." Roberts v. Louisiana, 428 U.S. 325, 354 (1976) (WHITE, J., dissenting). . . .

In sum, once the Court has held that "the punishment of death does not invariably violate the Constitution," Gregg v. Georgia, 428 U.S., at 169, it seriously impinges upon the State's legislative judgment to hold that it may not impose such sentence upon an individual who has shown total and repeated disregard for the welfare, safety, personal integrity and human worth of others, and who seemingly cannot be deterred from continuing such conduct. I therefore would hold that the death sentence here imposed is within the power reserved to the State and leave for another day the question of whether such sanction would be proper under other circumstances. . . . Since the Court now invalidates the death penalty as a sanction for all rapes of adults at all times under all circumstances, I reluctantly turn to what I see as the broader issues raised by this holding.

* * *

Despite its strong condemnation of rape, the Court reaches the inexplicable conclusion that "the death penalty . . . is an excessive penalty" for the perpetrator of this heinous offense.[g] This, the Court holds, is

---

[g]While only three Justices have joined Mr. Justice WHITE in this portion of his opinion, see separate opinion of Mr. Justice POWELL, ante, I take this to be the view of the Court in light of Mr. Justice BRENNAN's and Mr. Justice MARSHALL's statements joining the judgment.

true even though in Georgia the death penalty may be imposed only where the rape is coupled with one or more aggravating circumstances. The process by which this conclusion is reached is as startling as it is disquieting. It represents a clear departure from precedent by making this Court "under the aegis of the Cruel and Unusual Punishments Clause, the ultimate arbiter of the standards of criminal responsibility in diverse areas of the criminal law, throughout the country." Powell v. Texas, 392 U.S. 514, 533 (1968) (opinion of Marshall, J.). This seriously strains and distorts our federal system, removing much of the flexibility from which it has drawn strength for two centuries.

* * *

The plurality opinion bases its analysis, in part, on the fact that "Georgia is the sole jurisdiction in the United States at the present time that authorizes the sentence of death when the rape victim is an adult woman." . . .

Surely, however, this statistic cannot be deemed determinative, or even particularly relevant. As the opinion concedes . . . two other States—Louisiana and North Carolina—have enacted death penalty statutes for adult rape since this Court's 1972 decision in Furman v. Georgia, 408 U.S. 238 (1972). If the Court is to rely on some "public opinion" process does this not suggest the beginning of a "trend"?

* * *

In any case, when considered in light of the experience since the turn of the century, where more than one-third of American jurisdictions have consistently provided the death penalty for rape, the plurality's focus on the experience of the immediate past must be viewed as truly disingenuous. Having in mind the swift changes in positions of some Members of this Court in the short span of five years, can it rationally be considered a relevant indicator of what our society deems "cruel and unusual" to look solely to what legislatures have *refrained* from doing under conditions of great uncertainty arising from our less than lucid holdings on the Eighth Amendment? Far more representative of societal mores of the 20th Century is the accepted practice in a substantial number of jurisdictions preceding the Furman decision. "The problem . . . is the suddenness of the Court's perception of progress in the human attitude since decisions of only a short while ago." Furman v. Georgia, 408 U.S., at 410 (BLACKMUN, J., dissenting). Cf. Rudolph v. Alabama, 375 U.S. 889 (1963).

However, even were one to give the most charitable acceptance to the plurality's statistical analysis, it still does not, to my mind, support its conclusion. The most that can be claimed is that for the past year Georgia has been the only State whose adult rape death penalty statute has not otherwise been invalidated; two other state legislatures had enacted rape death penalty statutes in the last five years, but these were invalidated for reasons unrelated to rape under the Court's decisions last Term. Woodson v. North Carolina, 428 U.S. 280 (1976); [Stanislaus] Roberts v. Louisiana, 428 U.S. 325 (1976). Even if these figures could be read as indicating that no other States view the death penalty as an appropriate punishment for the rape of an adult woman, it would not necessarily follow that Georgia's imposition of such sanction violates the Eighth Amendment.

* * *

Statutory provisions in criminal justice applied in one part of the country can be carefully watched by other state legislatures, so that the experience of one State becomes available to all. Although human lives are in the balance, it must be remembered that failure to allow flexibility may also jeopardize human lives — those of the victims of undeterred criminal conduct. . . . Our concern for the accused ought not foreclose legislative judgments showing a modicum of consideration for the potential victims.

Three state legislatures have, in the past five years, determined that the taking of human life and the devastating consequences of rape will be minimized if rapists may, in a limited class of cases, be executed for their offenses. That these States are presently a minority does not, in my view, make their judgment less worthy of deference. Our concern for human life must not be confined to the guilty; a state legislature is not to be thought insensitive to human values because it acts firmly to protect the lives and related values of the innocent. In this area, the choices for legislatures are at best painful and difficult and deserve a high degree of deference. . . .

* * *

In order for Georgia's legislative program to develop it must be given time to take effect so that data may be evaluated for comparison with the experience of States which have not enacted death penalty statutes. Today, the Court repudiates the State's solemn judgment on how best to deal with the crime of rape before anyone can know whether the death penalty is an effective deterrent for one of the most horrible of all crimes. And this is done a few short years after Justice POWELL's excellent statement:

"In a period in our country's history when the frequency of [rape] is increasing alarmingly, it is indeed a grave event for the Court to take from the States whatever deterrent and retributive weight the death penalty retains." Furman v. Georgia, 408 U.S., at 459 (POWELL, J., dissenting) (footnote omitted).

To deprive States of this authority as the Court does, on the basis that "the current judgment with respect to the death penalty for rape . . . weighs very heavily on the side of an adult woman," . . . is impermissibly rash. The current judgment of some Members of this Court has undergone significant change in the short time since Furman. Social change on great issues generally reveals itself in small increments, and the "current judgment" of many States could well be altered on the basis of Georgia's experience, were we to allow its statute to stand.

The subjective judgment that the death penalty is simply disproportionate for the crime of rape is even more disturbing than the "objective" analysis discussed supra. The plurality's conclusion on this point is based upon the bare fact that murder necessarily results in the physical death of the victim, while rape does not. . . . However, no Member of the Court explains why this distinction has relevance, much less constitutional significance. It is, after all, not irrational — nor constitutionally impermissible — for a legislature to make the penalty more severe than the criminal act it punishes in the hope it would deter wrongdoing. . . . Until now, the issue under the Eighth Amendment has not been the state of any particular victim after the crime, but rather whether the punishment imposed is grossly disproportionate to the evil committed by the perpetrator. . . . As a matter of constitutional principle, that test cannot have the primitive simplicity of "life for life, eye for eye, tooth for tooth." Rather States must be permitted to engage in a more sophisticated weighing of values in dealing with criminal activity which consistently poses serious danger of death or grave bodily harm. If innocent life and limb is to be preserved I see no constitutional barrier in punishing by death all who engage in such activity, regardless of whether the risk comes to fruition in any particular instance. . . .

Only one year ago the Court held it constitutionally permissible to impose the death penalty for the crime of murder provided that certain procedural safeguards are followed. . . . Today, the Court readily admits that "[s]hort of homicide, [rape] is the 'ultimate violation of self.' " . . . Rape thus is not a crime "light-years" removed from murder in the degree of its heinousness; it certainly poses a serious potential danger to the life and safety of innocent victims — apart from the devastating psychic consequences. It would seem to follow therefore that, affording the States proper leeway under the broad standard of the Eighth Amendment, if murder is properly punishable by death, rape should be also, if that is the considered judgment of the legislators.

The Court's conclusion to the contrary is very disturbing indeed. The clear implication of today's holding appears to be that the death penalty may be properly imposed only as to crimes resulting in death of the victim. This casts serious doubt upon the constitutional validity of statutes imposing the death penalty for a variety of conduct which, though dangerous, may not necessarily result in any immediate death, e.g., treason, airplane hijacking, and kidnapping. In that respect, today's holding does even more harm than is initially apparent. We cannot avoid judicial notice that crimes such as airplane hijacking, kidnapping, and mass terrorist activity constitute a serious and increasing danger to the safety of the public. It would be unfortunate indeed if the effect of today's holding were to inhibit States and the Federal Government from experimenting with various remedies — including possibly imposition of the penalty of death — to prevent and deter such crimes.

* * *

Whatever our individual views as to the wisdom of capital punishment, I cannot agree that it is constitutionally impermissible for a state legislature to make the "solemn judgment" to impose such penalty for the crime of rape. Accordingly, I would leave to the States the task of legislating in this area of the law.

Comment

1. In *Coker,* supra, there appeared to be considerable disagreement between the plurality and the dissenters on two important aspects of the case: the scope of the question presented; and hence, the necessary breadth of the holding. The plurality prefaced the opinion by stating that the question was the constitutionality of the death penalty when imposed for the *rape of an adult woman.* They concluded, however, that "a sentence of death is grossly disproportionate and excessive punishment for the crime of *rape*" (emphasis added). The Court then proceeded to support its conclusion by relying on "objective evidence" of current public opinion, i.e., the attitude of juries and state legislatures concerning the acceptability of such a penalty. The Chief Justice, joined by Mr. Justice Rehnquist, argued in his dissent that the inquiry should have been narrowed to the issue of whether the State of Georgia may constitutionally execute a particular person (Coker) for a particular rape (the one in question) "in light of all the facts and circumstances shown by [the] record" (Coker's life pattern as a "chronic" rapist and his high risk of repeated escape and subsequent attacks on women).

Mr. Justice Powell took issue with what he termed the "expansive pronouncement" by the plurality that "ranges well beyond what is necessary." Although he supported the view that ordinarily death should be considered disproportionate punishment for the crime of raping an adult woman, he disagreed with the conclusion that such punishment is always disproportionate for rape, pointing out that "extreme variations" exist in the crime of rape and that some victims are so seriously injured that their lives are "beyond repair." He suggested at least two situations in which it might be proper to impose the death penalty on convicted rapists: (1) where the offense is committed with excessive brutality; and (2) when the victim sustains grievous physical and psychological injury. He did, however, concur in the result because there was no evidence that the rape of Mrs. Carver was "aggravated" under his proffered criteria. Mrs. Carver, a 16 year-old, was raped in the presence of her husband and infant, abducted, and threatened with death and serious bodily harm. What is the likelihood that long-term psychological harm resulted? How can the extent of psychological injury be measured in making the sentencing decision? Consider these questions in the context of the Chief Justice's dissent.

If the plurality opinion is to be interpreted as broadly as the dissenters suggested, what is likely to be the overall impact of *Coker?* For example, if the *Coker* decision limits the imposition of death to those crimes that result in the death of the victim, will we experience an increase in armed robbery, kidnapping, and other serious offenses that previously were capital felonies in certain states? What if the victim of a rape is a child? Do you believe the plurality would still adhere to the principles in *Coker?* Is it important that only three states (Florida, Mississippi, and Tennessee) now authorize capital punishment for the rape of a child by an adult? How important is this fact as an "objective indicator"? Finally, what do you suppose the reaction of women's groups will be to the *Coker* decision? Do you suppose that an organized group such as N.O.W. would be in agreement with the Court's pronouncement? Can you think of any way in which the decision might be viewed by women's liberation groups as being advantageous to their cause?

Ex Post Facto Laws and the Death Penalty

DOBBERT v. FLORIDA

Supreme Court of the United States, 1977
432 U.S. ____, 97 S. Ct. 2290, 53 L. Ed. 2d 344

The facts are stated in the opinion.

Mr. Justice REHNQUIST delivered the opinion of the Court.

Petitioner was convicted of murder in the first degree, murder in the second degree, child abuse, and child torture. The victims were his children. Under the Florida death penalty statute then in effect he was sentenced by the trial judge to death. The Florida Supreme Court affirmed and we granted certiorari to consider whether changes in the Florida death penalty statutes subjected him to trial under an ex post facto law or denied him equal protection of the laws, and whether the significant amount of pretrial publicity concerning the crime deprived petitioner of his right to a fair trial. . . .

I

Petitioner was convicted of murdering his daughter Kelly Ann, age 9, and his son Ryder Scott, age 7. He was also found guilty of torturing his son Ernest John, age 11, and of abusing his daughter Honore Elizabeth, age 5. The brutality and heinousness of these crimes are relevant both to petitioner's motion for a change of venue due to pretrial publicity and to the trial judge's imposition of the sentence of death. The trial judge, in his factual findings at the sentencing phase of the trial, summarized petitioner's treatment of his own off-spring as follows:

"The evidence and testimony showed premeditated and continuous torture, brutality, sadism and unspeakable horrors committed against all of the children over a period of time." App. 47.

The judge then detailed some of the horrors inflicted upon young Kelly Ann, upon which he relied to meet the statutory requirement that aggravating circumstances be found:

"Over the period of time of the latter portion of Kelly Ann's short, torturous life the defendant did these things to her on one or many occasions:

"1. Beat her in the head until it was swollen.

"2. Burned her hands.

"3. Poked his fingers in her eyes.

"4. Beat her in the abdomen until 'it was swollen like she was pregnant.'

"5. Knocked her against a wall and 'when she fell, kicked her in the lower part of the body.'

"6. Held her under water in both the bath tub and toilet.

"7. Kicked her against a table which cut her head — then defendant sewed up her wound with needle and thread.

"8. Scarred her head and body by beating her with a belt and board — causing marks from her cheek, across the neck and down her back — which injuries worsened without treatment 'until the body juices came out.'

"9. On one occasion beat her continuously for 45 minutes.

"10. On many occasions kicked her in the stomach with his shoes on, and on the night she died he kicked her a number of times.

"11. Kept her out of school so that the many scars, cuts and bruises on her body would not be seen by others.

"12. Defendant made no effort to get professional medical care and attention for the child and in fact actively prevented any out-siders from discovering her condition.

"13. Choked her on the night she died and when she stopped breathing he placed her body in a plastic garbage bag and buried her in an unmarked and unknown grave." App. 47.

This sordid tale began to unravel in early 1972 when Ernest John III was found battered and wandering in Jacksonville, Fla. An arrest warrant was issued for petitioner, who evidently fled the area. About a year later, Honore Elizabeth was found in a Ft. Lauderdale hospital with a note pinned to her clothing asking that she be sent to her mother in Wisconsin. Shortly thereafter petitioner's abandoned automobile was found near a bridge with a suicide note on the front seat. Petitioner, however, had fled to Texas, where he was eventually arrested and extradited to Florida.

Prior to trial, petitioner applied to the Supreme Court of Florida for a Constitutional Stay of Trial, alleging the application of an ex post facto law and a violation of equal protection. App. 81–86. The application was denied. Petitioner also moved in the lower court for a change of venue, alleging that he was charged with "inherently odious" acts, App. 17, and that extensive publicity regarding his flight, extradition, and arrest, as well as a search for bodies by the Jacksonville Police Department, had rendered impossible a fair and impartial trial in Duval County. App. 17–18. The trial judge took the motion under advisement and issued an order enjoining anyone connected with the trial from releasing any statement about the case to the news media. App. 25–26. The motion was later denied.

Trial was had and the jury found petitioner guilty of, inter alia, murder in the first degree. Pursuant to the Florida death penalty statute then in effect, a sentencing hearing was held before the judge and jury. The jury by a 10 to

2 majority found sufficient mitigating circumstances to outweigh any aggravating circumstances and recommended a sentence of life imprisonment. The trial judge, pursuant to his authority under the amended Florida statute, overruled the jury's recommendation and sentenced petitioner to death. The Florida Supreme Court affirmed over two dissents.

II

Petitioner makes three separate claims based on the prohibition against ex post facto laws, and a related claim based upon the Equal Protection Clause of the Fourteenth Amendment. His first ex post facto claim is addressed to the change in the function of judge and jury in the imposition of death sentences in Florida between the time he committed the acts charged and the time he was tried for them. The second ex post facto claim is grounded on his contention that at the time he acted there was no valid death penalty statute in effect in Florida. The third claim relates to the more stringent parole requirements attached to a life sentence under the new law. A discussion of the relevant changes in Florida death sentencing procedures brings these claims into focus.

The murders for which petitioner was convicted were alleged to have occurred on December 31, 1971 (Kelly Ann), and between January 1 and April 8, 1972 (Ryder Scott). During that period of time, F.S.A. § 775.082 (1971) and 921.141 (1971), as then written provided that a person convicted of a capital felony was to be punished by death unless the verdict included a recommendation of mercy by a majority of the jury.

On June 22, 1972, this Court struck down a Georgia death penalty statute as violative of the Eighth and Fourteenth Amendments. Furman v. Georgia, 408 U.S. 238 (1972). Shortly thereafter, on July 17, 1972, in Donaldson v. Sack, 265 So. 2d 499 (Fla. 1972), the Florida Supreme Court found the 1971 Florida death penalty statutes inconsistent with Furman. Late in 1972 Florida enacted a new death penalty procedure, Chapter 72-724, Laws of Florida (1972), amending, inter alia, § 775.082 and 921.141.

The opinion of Mr. Justice STEWART, Mr. Justice POWELL, and Mr. Justice STEVENS in Proffitt v. Florida, 428 U.S. 242 (1976), in which the constitutionality of this statute was upheld, details at length the operation of the revised § 921.141.

After a defendant is found guilty of a capital felony, a separate sentencing hearing is held before the trial judge and the trial jury. Any evidence that the judge deems relevant to sentencing may be admitted, and certain evidence relating to aggravating or mitigating circumstances must be admitted. The jury, by a majority vote, then renders an advisory decision, not binding on the court, based upon these aggravating and mitigating circumstances. The court must then also weigh the aggravating and mitigating circumstances. If the court imposes a sentence of death, it must set forth written findings of fact regarding the aggravating and mitigating circumstances. A judgment of conviction and sentence of death is then subject to an automatic, priority review by the Florida Supreme Court. It is in the light of these changes that we must adjudge petitioner's ex post facto claims.

A

Petitioner argues that the change in the role of the judge and the jury in the imposition of the death sentence in Florida between the time of the murders and the time of the trial constitutes an ex post facto violation. Petitioner views the change in the Florida death sentencing procedure as depriving him of a substantial right to have the jury determine, without review by the trial judge, whether that penalty should be imposed. We conclude that the changes in the law are procedural, and on the whole ameliorative, and that there is no ex post facto violation.

Article I, § 10, of the United States Constitution prohibits a State from passing any "ex post facto law." Our cases have not attempted to precisely delimit the scope of this Latin phrase, but have instead given it substance by an accretion of case law. In Beazell v. Ohio, 269 U.S. 167, 169 (1925), Mr. Justice Stone summarized for the Court the characteristics of an ex post facto law:

"It is settled, by decisions of this Court so well known that their citation may be dispensed with, that any statute which punishes as a crime an act previously committed, which was innocent when done; which makes more burdensome the punishment for a crime, after its commission, or which deprives one charged with crime of any defense available according to law at the time when the act was committed, is prohibited as ex post facto."

It is equally well settled, however, that "the inhibition upon the passage of ex post facto laws does not give a criminal a right to be tried, in all respects, by the law in force when the crime charged was committed." Gibson v. Mississippi, 162 U.S. 565, 590 (1896). "[T]he constitutional provision was intended to secure substantial personal rights against arbitrary and oppressive legislation, see Malloy v. South Carolina, 237 U.S. 180, 183, and not to limit the legislative control of remedies and modes of procedure which do not affect matters of substance." Beazell v. Ohio, supra, at 171.

Even though it may work to the disadvantage of a defendant, a procedural change is not ex post facto. . . .

* * *

In the case at hand, the change in the statute was clearly procedural. The new statute simply altered the methods employed in determining whether the death penalty was to be imposed; there was no change in the quantum of punishment attached to the crime. . . .

In this case, not only was the change in the law procedural, it was ameliorative. It is axiomatic that for a law to be ex post facto it must be more onerous than the prior law. Petitioner argues that the change in the law harmed him because the jury's recommendation of life imprisonment would not have been subject to review by the trial judge under the prior law. But it certainly cannot be said with assurance that, had his trial been conducted under the old statute, the jury would have returned a verdict of life.

Hence, petitioner's speculation that the jury would have recommended life were the prior procedure in effect is not compelling. We must compare the two statutory procedures in toto to determine if the new may be fairly characterized as more onerous. Under the old procedure, the death penalty was "presumed" unless the jury, in its unbridled discretion, made a recommendation for mercy. The Florida Legislature enacted the new procedure specifically to provide the constitutional procedural protections re-

quired by Furman, thus providing capital defendants with more, rather than less, judicial protection. These protections, upheld by this Court in Proffitt, provided are substantial. A separate hearing is held; the defendant is allowed to present any relevant mitigating evidence. The jury renders an advisory verdict based upon its perception of aggravating and mitigating factors in the case. The court makes the final determination, but may impose death only after making a written finding that there are insufficient mitigating circumstances to outweigh the aggravating circumstances.

Finally, in what may be termed a tripartite review, the Florida Supreme Court is required to review each sentence of death. This required review, not present under the old procedure, is by no means perfunctory; as we noted in Proffitt, as of that time the Florida Supreme Court had vacated eight of the 21 death sentences that it had reviewed to that date. Perhaps most importantly, the Florida Supreme Court has held that the following standard must be used to review a trial court's rejection of a jury's recommendation of life:

"In order to sustain a sentence of death following a jury recommendation of life, the facts suggesting a sentence of death should be so *clear and convincing that virtually no reasonable person could differ.*" Tedder v. State, 322 So. 2d 908, 910 (1975) (emphasis added). . . .

This crucial protection demonstrates that the new statute affords significantly more safeguards to the defendant than did the old. Death is not automatic, absent a jury recommendation of mercy, as it was under the old procedure. A jury recommendation of life may be overridden by the trial judge only under the exacting standards of Tedder.[i] Hence, defendants are not significantly disadvantaged vis-a-vis the recommendation of

---

[i]The fact that the trial judge imposed a death sentence after the jury had recommended life in this case in no way denigrates the procedural protections afforded by the new procedure. The judge did so in circumstances where there were obvious and substantial aggravating factors, and where there had been no significant mitigating factors adduced. To demonstrate that it was the nature of the crime, rather than the scope of the procedure, that resulted in the death sentence in

Footnote continued on page 920

life by the jury; on the other hand, unlike the old statute, a jury determination of death is not binding. Under the new statute, defendants have a second chance for life with the trial judge and a third, if necessary, with the Florida Supreme Court. No such protection was afforded by the old statute. Hence, viewing the totality of the procedural changes wrought by the new statute, we conclude that the new statute did not work in onerous application of an ex post facto change in the law. . . .

B

Petitioner's second ex post facto claim is based on the contention that at the time he murdered his children there was no death penalty "in effect" in Florida. This is so, he contends, because the earlier statute enacted by the legislature was, after the time he acted, found by the Supreme Court of Florida to be invalid under our decision in Furman v. Georgia, supra. Therefore, argues petitioner, there was no "valid" death penalty in effect in Florida as of the date of his actions. But this sophistic argument mocks the substance of the ex post facto clause. Whether or not the old statute would, in the future, withstand constitutional attack, it clearly indicated Florida's view of the severity of murder and of the degree of punishment which the legislature wished to impose upon murderers. The statute was intended to provide maximum deterrence, and its existence on the statute books provided fair warning as to the degree of culpability which the State ascribed to the act of murder.

* * *

Here the existence of the statute served as an "operative fact" to warn the petitioner of the penalty which Florida would seek to impose on him if he were convicted of first-degree murder. This was sufficient compliance with the ex post facto provision of the United States Constitution.

* * *

Petitioner's third ex post facto contention is based on the fact that the new Florida statute provides that anyone sentenced to life imprisonment under that section must serve at least 25 years before becoming eligible for parole. The prior section contained no such limitation. The Florida Supreme Court in Lee v. State, 294 So. 2d 305 (1974), found that this provision restricting parole could not constitutionally be applied to crimes committed prior to its effective date. Petitioner contends that nonetheless its enactment by the Florida Legislature amounts to an ex post facto law, and that because of this he may successfully challenge the death sentence imposed upon him.

Petitioner, of course, did not receive a life sentence, and so any added onus attaching to it as a result of the change in Florida law had no effect on him. . . .

* * *

[O]ne is not barred from challenging a change in the penal code on ex post facto grounds simply because the sentence he received under the new law was not more onerous than that which he might have received under the old. It is one thing to find an ex post facto violation where under

---

this case, we set forth in extenso the conclusions of the trial court at the sentencing phase:

"There are sufficient and great aggravating circumstances which exist to justify the sentence of death.

"In concluding my findings I would like to point out that my 22 years of legal experience have been almost exclusively in the field of criminal law.

"The Judge of this Court has been a defense attorney of criminal cases, a prosecutor for eight and one half years and a Criminal Court Judge and a Circuit Judge-Felony Division for three and one half years.

"During this 22 years I have defended, prosecuted and held trial of almost every type of

serious crime. During these years of legal experience I have never known a more heinous, atrocious and cruel crime than this one.

"My experience with the sordid, tragic and violent side of life has not been confined to the courtroom. During World War II, I was a United States paratrooper and served overseas in ground combat. I have had friends blown to bits and have seen death and suffering in every conceivable form.

"I am not easily shocked or affected by tragedy or cruelty—but this murder of a helpless, defenseless and innocent child is the most cruel, atrocious and heinous crime I have ever personally known of—and it is deserving of no sentence but death." App., at 49.

the new law a defendant *must* receive a sentence which was under the old law only the maximum in a discretionary spectrum of length; it would be quite another to do so in a case, such as this, where the change has had no effect on the defendant in the proceedings of which he complains. . . .

Under the new law, both life imprisonment and death remain as possible alternative sentences. . . . [W]e hold that petitioner, having been sentenced to death, may not complain of burdens attached to the life sentence under the law which may not have attached to it under the old.

D

After our Furman decision and its own decision in Donaldson v. Sack, supra, the Florida Supreme Court resentenced all prisoners under sentence of death pursuant to the old statute to life imprisonment. Anderson v. Florida, 267 So. 2d 8 (Fla. 1972); In re Baker, 267 So. 2d 331 (Fla. 1972). Petitioner argues that since his crimes were committed before our decision in Furman, the imposition of the death sentence upon him pursuant to the new statute which was in effect at the time of his trial denies him equal protection of the laws.

But petitioner is simply not similarly situated to those whose sentences were commuted. He was neither tried nor sentenced prior to Furman, as were they, and the only effect of the former statute was to provide sufficient warning of the gravity Florida attached to first-degree murder so as to make the application of this new statute to him consistent with the ex post facto clause of the United States Constitution. . . .

III

There was, understandably, extensive pretrial publicity concerning several aspects of this case. We accept petitioner's assertion . . . that there was substantial media coverage, including a number of television and radio stories regarding the various aspects of the case.

In Murphy v. Florida, 421 U.S. 794 (1975) [Chapter Seven, § 7.03], we reviewed a trial in which many jurors had heard of the defendant through extensive news coverage. Characterizing our previous cases in which we had overturned a state court conviction on these grounds as involving "a trial atmosphere that had been utterly corrupted by press coverage," id., at 798, we recognized that:

"Qualified jurors need not, however, be totally ignorant of the facts and issues involved.

"'To hold that the mere existence of any preconceived notion as to the guilt or innocence of an accused, without more, is sufficient to rebut the presumption of a prospective juror's impartiality would be to establish an impossible standard. It is sufficient if the juror can lay aside his impression or opinion and render a verdict based on the evidence presented in court. [Irvin v. Dowd, 366 U.S. 717, 723 (1961).]'" Id., at 799–800.

We concluded that the petitioner in Murphy had failed to show that the trial setting was inherently prejudicial or that the jury selection process permitted an inference of actual prejudice. Id., at 803.

The Florida Supreme Court in this case noted that 78 prospective jurors were interviewed, and that petitioner exercised only 27 of his 32 peremptory challenges. . . .

Petitioner's argument that the extensive coverage by the media denied him a fair trial rests almost entirely upon the quantum of publicity which the events received. He has directed us to no specific portions of the record, in particular the voir dire examination of the jurors, which would require a finding of constitutional unfairness as to the method of jury selection or as to the character of the jurors actually selected. But under Murphy, extensive knowledge of the community of neither the crimes nor the putative criminal is sufficient by itself to render a trial constitutionally unfair. Petitioner in this case has simply shown that the community was made well aware of the charges against him and asks us on that basis to presume unfairness of constitutional magnitude at his trial. This we will not do in the absence of a "trial atmosphere utterly corrupted by press coverage," Murphy v. Florida, supra. One who is reasonably suspected of murdering his children cannot expect to remain anonymous. Petitioner has failed to convince us that under the "totality of circumstances," Murphy, supra, the Florida Supreme Court was wrong in finding no constitutional violation with respect to the pretrial publicity. The judgment of the Supreme Court of Florida is therefore Affirmed.

[Chief Justice BURGER wrote a concurring opinion.]

[Mr. Justice STEVENS, with whom Mr. Justice BRENNAN and Mr. Justice MARSHALL joined, wrote a dissenting opinion.]

Comment

1. In *Dobbert* v. *Florida,* supra, the Supreme Court rejected appellant's argument that his sentence of death under the post-*Furman* statute, upheld in *Proffitt* v. *Florida,* 428 U.S. 242 (1976), supra, constituted an ex post facto law because his criminal acts occurred while the pre-*Furman* statute was operational. Do you agree with the Court's reasoning? Even though the change in the law was, in the words of Justice Rehnquist, "clearly procedural" and "ameliorative," Dobbert would not have received the death penalty under the prior Florida procedure because his jury had recommended life imprisonment. However, as the majority noted, Dobbert had received "fair warning" that a first degree murder conviction subjected an offender to a possible death sentence. As the Court pointed out, "There was no change in the quantum of punishment attached to the crime."

A leading case on ex post facto laws is *Calder* v. *Bull,* 3 U.S. (3 Dall.) 386 (1798), in which the Supreme Court defined such laws as: "1st. Every law that makes an action done before the passing of the law, and which was innocent when done, criminal; and punishes such action. 2d. Every law that aggravates a crime, or makes it greater than it was, when committed. 3d. Every law that changes the punishment, and inflicts a greater punishment, than the law annexed to the crime, when committed. 4th. Every law that alters the legal rules of evidence, and receives less, or different, testimony, than the law required at the time of the commission of the offense, in order to convict the offender," at 390. Is *Dobbert* compatible with the *Calder-Bull* rule? It should be noted that the restriction against ex post facto laws applies only to criminal cases; i.e., there must be a substantive change in a criminal law.

Mandatory Death Penalty for First-Degree Murder

WOODSON v. NORTH CAROLINA

Supreme Court of the United States, 1976
428 U.S. 280, 96 S. Ct. 2978, 49 L. Ed. 2d 944

The facts are stated in the opinion.

Mr. Justice STEWART, Mr. JUSTICE POWELL, and Mr. Justice STEVENS announced the judgment of the Court and filed an opinion delivered by Mr. Justice STEWART.

The question in this case is whether the imposition of a death sentence for the crime of first-degree murder under law of North Carolina violates the Eighth and Fourteenth Amendments.

I

The petitioners were convicted of first-degree murder as the result of their participation in an armed robbery of a convenience food store, in the course of which the cashier was killed and a customer was seriously wounded. There were four participants in the robbery; the petitioners Tyrone Woodson and Luby Waxton and two others, Leonard Tucker and Johnie Lee Carroll. At the petitioners' trial Tucker and Carroll testified for the prosecution after having been permitted to plead guilty to lesser offenses; the petitioners testified in their own defense.

The evidence for the prosecution established that the four men had been discussing a possible robbery for some time. On the fatal day Woodson had been drinking heavily. About 9:30 p.m., Waxton and Tucker came to the trailer where Woodson was staying. When Woodson came out of the trailer, Waxton struck him in the face and threatened to kill him in an effort to make him sober up and come along on the robbery. The three proceeded to Waxton's trailer where they met Carroll. Waxton armed himself with a nickel-plated derringer, and Tucker handed Woodson a rifle. The four then set out by automobile to rob the store. Upon arriving at their destination Tucker and Waxton went into the store while Carroll and Woodson remained in the car as lookouts. Once inside the store, Tucker purchased a package of cigarettes from the woman cashier. Waxton then also asked for a package of cigarettes, but as the cashier approached him he pulled the derringer out of his hip pocket and fatally shot her at point-blank range. Waxton then took the money tray from the cash register and gave it to Tucker, who carried it out of the store, pushing past an entering customer as he reached the door. After he was outside, Tucker heard a second shot from inside the store, and shortly thereafter Waxton emerged, carrying a handful of paper money. Tucker and Waxton got in the car and the four drove away.

The petitioners' testimony agreed in large part with this version of the circumstances of the robbery. It differed diametrically in one important respect: Waxton claimed he never had a gun, and that Tucker had shot both the cashier and the customer.

During the trial Waxton asked to be allowed to plead guilty to the same lesser offenses to which Tucker had pleaded guilty[a] but the solicitor refused to accept the pleas.[b] Woodson, by contrast, maintained throughout the trial that he had been coerced by Waxton, that he was therefore innocent, and that he would not consider pleading guilty to any offense.

The petitioners were found guilty on all charges,[c] and, as was required by statute, sentenced to death. The Supreme Court of North Carolina affirmed. State v. Woodson, 287 N.C. 578, 215 S.E.2d 607 (1975). We granted certiorari, 423 U.S. 1082 (1976), to consider whether the imposition of the death penalties in this case comports with the Eighth and Fourteenth Amendments to the United States Constitution.

II

The petitioners argue that the imposition of the death penalty under any circumstances is cruel and unusual punishment in violation of the Eighth and Fourteenth Amendments. We reject this argument for the reasons stated in Gregg v. Georgia, 428 U.S. 153 (1976).

III

* * *

North Carolina, unlike Florida, Georgia, and Texas, has thus responded to the Furman decision by making death the mandatory sentence for all persons convicted of first-degree murder. In ruling on the consti-

---

[a]Tucker had been allowed to plead guilty to charges of accessory after the fact to murder and to armed robbery. He was sentenced to 10 years imprisonment on the first charge, and to not less than 20 years nor more than 30 years on the second, the sentences to run concurrently.

[b]The solicitor gave no reason for refusing to accept Waxton's offer to plead guilty to a lesser offense. The Supreme Court of North Carolina, in finding that the solicitor had not abused his discretion, noted: "The evidence that Waxton planned and directed the robbery and that he fired the shots which killed Mrs. Butler and wounded Mr. Stancil is overwhelming. No extenuating circumstances gave the solicitor any incentive to accept the plea he tendered at the close of the State's evidence." . . .

[c]In addition to first-degree murder, both petitioners were found guilty of armed robbery. Waxton was also found guilty of assault with a deadly weapon with intent to kill, a charge arising from the wounding of the customer.

tutionality of the sentences imposed on the petitioners under this North Carolina statute, the Court now addresses for the first time the question whether a death sentence returned pursuant to a law imposing a mandatory death penalty for a broad category of homicidal offenses constitutes cruel and unusual punishment within the meaning of the Eighth and Fourteenth Amendments. The issue, like that explored in Furman, involves the procedure employed by the State to select persons for the unique and irreversible penalty of death.

A

The Eighth Amendment stands to assure that the State's power to punish is "exercised within the limits of civilized standards." Trop v. Dulles, 356 U.S. 86, 100 (1958) (plurality opinion). . . .

Central to the application of the Amendment is a determination of contemporary standards regarding the infliction of punishment. As discussed in Gregg v. Georgia, indicia of societal values identified in prior opinions include history and traditional usage, legislative enactments, and jury determinations.

In order to provide a frame for assessing the relevancy of these factors in this case we begin by sketching the history of mandatory death penalty statutes in the United States. At the time the Eighth Amendment was adopted in 1791, the States uniformly followed the common-law practice of making death the exclusive and mandatory sentence for certain specified offenses. Although the range of capital offenses in the American colonies was quite limited in comparison to the more than 200 offenses then punishable by death in England, the colonies at the time of the Revolution imposed death sentences on all persons convicted of any of a considerable number of crimes, typically including at a minimum, murder, treason, piracy, arson, rape, robbery, burglary, and sodomy. As at common law, all homicides that were not involuntary, provoked, justified, or excused constituted murder and were automatically punished by death. Almost from the outset jurors reacted unfavorably to the harshness of mandatory death sentences. The States initially responded to this expression of public dissatisfaction with mandatory statutes by limiting the classes of capital offenses.

* * *

Despite the broad acceptance of the divi-

sion of murder into degrees . . . juries continued to find the death penalty inappropriate in a significant number of first-degree murder cases and refused to return guilty verdicts for that crime.

The inadequacy of distinguishing between murderers solely on the basis of legislative criteria narrowing the definition of the capital offense led the States to grant juries sentencing discretion in capital cases. Tennessee in 1838, followed by Alabama in 1841, and Louisiana in 1846, were the first States to abandon mandatory death sentences in favor of discretionary death penalty statutes. This flexibility remedied the harshness of mandatory statutes by permitting the jury to respond to mitigating factors by withholding the death penalty. By the turn of the century, 23 States and the Federal Government had made death sentences discretionary for first-degree murder and other capital offenses. During the next two decades 14 additional States replaced their mandatory death statutes. Thus, by the end of World War I, all but eight States, Hawaii, and the District of Columbia either had adopted discretionary death penalty schemes or abolished the death penalty altogether. By 1963, all of these remaining jurisdictions had replaced their automatic death penalty statutes with discretionary jury sentencing.

The history of mandatory death penalty statutes in the United States thus reveals that the practice of sentencing to death all persons convicted of a particular offense has been rejected as unduly harsh and unworkably rigid. The two crucial indicators of evolving standards of decency respecting the imposition of punishment in our society—jury determinations and legislative enactments—both point conclusively to the repudiation of automatic death sentences. . . .

[L]egislative measures adopted by the people's chosen representatives weigh heavily in ascertaining contemporary standards of decency. The consistent course charted by the state legislatures and by Congress since the middle of the past century demonstrates that the aversion of jurors to mandatory death penalty statutes is shared by society at large.

Still further evidence of the incompatibility of mandatory death penalties with contemporary values is provided by the results of jury sentencing under discretionary statutes. . . . Various studies indicate that even in first-degree murder cases juries with sentencing discretion do not impose the death penalty "with any great frequency," H. Kalven and H. Zeisel, The American Jury 436 (1966).[ee] The actions of sentencing juries suggest that under contemporary standards of decency death is viewed as an inappropriate punishment for a substantial portion of convicted first-degree murderers.

Although the Court has never ruled on the constitutionality of mandatory death penalty statutes, on several occasions dating back to 1899 it has commented upon our society's aversion to automatic death sentences. . . .

* * *

Although it seems beyond dispute that, at the time of the Furman decision in 1972 mandatory death penalty statutes had been renounced by American juries and legislatures, there remains the question whether the mandatory statutes adopted by North Carolina and a number of other States following Furman evince a sudden reversal of societal values regarding the imposition of capital punishment. In view of the persistent and unswerving legislative rejection of mandatory death penalty statutes beginning in 1838 and continuing for more than 130 years until Furman, it seems evident that the post-Furman enactments reflect attempts by the States to retain the death penalty in a form consistent with the Constitution, rather than a renewed societal acceptance of mandatory death sentencing. The fact that some States have adopted mandatory measures following Furman while others have legislated standards to guide jury discretion appears attributable to diverse readings of this Court's multi-opinioned decision in that case.

* * *

It is now well established that the Eighth Amendment draws much of its meaning from "the evolving standards of decency that mark the progress of a maturing society." Trop v. Dulles, 356 U.S., at 101 (plurality opinion). As the above discussion makes clear, one of the most significant developments in our society's treatment of capital punishment has been the rejection of the

---

ee Data compiled on discretionary jury sentencing of persons convicted of capital murder indicate that the penalty of death is generally imposed in less than 20% of the cases. . . .

common-law practice of inexorably imposing a death sentence upon every person convicted of a specified offense. North Carolina's mandatory death penalty statute for first-degree murder departs markedly from contemporary standards respecting the imposition of the punishment of death and thus cannot be applied consistently with the Eighth and Fourteenth Amendments' requirement that the State's power to punish "be exercised within the limits of civilized standards." . . .

B

A separate deficiency of North Carolina's mandatory death sentence statute is its failure to provide a constitutionally tolerable response to Furman's rejection of unbridled jury discretion in the imposition of capital sentences. Central to the limited holding in Furman was the conviction that the vesting of standardless sentencing power in the jury violated the Eighth and Fourteenth Amendments. . . . When one considers the long and consistent American experience with the death penalty in first-degree murder cases, it becomes evident that mandatory statutes enacted in response to Furman have simply papered over the problem of unguided and unchecked jury discretion.

* * *

North Carolina's mandatory death penalty statute provides no standards to guide the jury in its inevitable exercise of the power to determine which first-degree murderers shall live and which shall die. And there is no way under the North Carolina law for the judiciary to check arbitrary and capricious exercise of that power through a review of death sentences. . . . Instead of rationalizing the sentencing process, a mandatory scheme may well exacerbate the problem identified in Furman by resting the penalty determination on the particular jury's willingness to act lawlessly. While a mandatory death penalty statute may reasonably be expected to increase the number of persons sentenced to death, it does not fulfill Furman's basic requirement by replacing arbitrary and wanton jury discretion with objective standards to guide, regularize and make rationally reviewable the process for imposing a sentence of death.

C

A third constitutional shortcoming of the North Carolina statute is its failure to allow the particularized consideration of relevant aspects of the character and record of each convicted defendant before the imposition upon him of a sentence of death.... A process that accords no significance to relevant facets of the character and record of the individual offender or the circumstances of the particular offenses excludes from consideration in fixing the ultimate punishment of death the possibility of compassionate or mitigating factors stemming from the diverse frailties of humankind. It treats all persons convicted of a designated offense not as uniquely individual human beings, but as members of a faceless, undifferentiated mass to be subjected to the blind infliction of the penalty of death.

* * *

While the prevailing practice of individualizing sentencing determinations generally reflects simply enlightened policy rather than a constitutional imperative, we believe that in capital cases the fundamental respect for humanity underlying the Eighth Amendment ... requires consideration of the character and record of the individual offender and the circumstances of the particular offense as a constitutionally indispensable part of the process of inflicting the penalty of death.

This conclusion rests squarely on the predicate that the penalty of death is qualitatively different from a sentence of imprisonment, however long. Death, in its finality, differs more from life imprisonment than a 100 year prison term differs from one of only a year or two. Because of that qualitative difference there is a corresponding difference in the need for reliability in the determination that death is the appropriate punishment in a specific case.

For the reasons stated, we conclude that the death sentences imposed upon the petitioners under North Carolina's mandatory death sentence statute violated the Eighth and Fourteenth Amendments and therefore must be set aside. The judgment of the Supreme Court of North Carolina is reversed insofar as it upheld the death sentences imposed upon the petitioners, and the case is remanded for further proceedings not inconsistent with this opinion.

Mr. Justice BRENNAN, concurring in the judgment.

For the reasons stated in my dissenting opinion in Gregg v. Georgia, 428 U.S. 153, 227 (1976), I concur in the judgment that sets aside the death sentences imposed under the North Carolina death sentence statute as violative of the Eighth and Fourteenth Amendments.

Mr. Justice MARSHALL, concurring in the judgment.

For the reasons stated in my dissenting opinion in Gregg v. Georgia, 428 U.S. 153, 231 (1976), I am of the view that the death penalty is a cruel and unusual punishment forbidden by the Eighth and Fourteenth Amendments. I therefore concur in the Court's judgment.

Mr. Justice WHITE, with whom The CHIEF JUSTICE [BURGER] and Mr. Justice REHNQUIST join, dissenting.

* * *

... I reject petitioners' arguments that the death penalty in any circumstances is a violation of the Eighth Amendment and that the North Carolina statute, although making the imposition of the death penalty mandatory upon proof of guilt and a verdict of first-degree murder, will nevertheless result in the death penalty being imposed so seldom and arbitrarily that it is void under Furman v. Georgia.... I also disagree with the two additional grounds which the plurality sua sponte offers for invalidating the North Carolina statute. I would affirm the judgment of the North Carolina Supreme Court.

Mr. Justice BLACKMUN, dissenting.

I dissent for the reasons set forth in my dissent in Furman v. Georgia, 408 U.S. 238, 405–414 (1972), and in the other dissenting opinions I joined in that case. Id., at 375, 414, and 465.

Mr. Justice REHNQUIST, dissenting.

* * *

... It is by no means clear that the prohibition against cruel and unusual punishments embodied in the Eighth Amendment, and made applicable to the States by the Fourteenth Amendment, Robinson v. California, 370 U.S. 660 (1962), was not limited to those punishments deemed cruel and unusual at the time of the adoption of the Bill of Rights. McGautha v. California, 402 U.S. 183, 225 (1971) (Black, J., concurring). ... Thus for the plurality to begin its analysis with the assumption that it need only demonstrate that "evolving standards of decency" show that contemporary "society" has rejected such provisions is itself a somewhat shaky point of departure. But even if the assumption be conceded, the plurality opinion's analysis nonetheless founders.

The plurality relies first upon its conclusion that society has turned away from the mandatory imposition of death sentences, and second upon its conclusion that the North Carolina system has "simply papered over" the problem of unbridled jury discretion which two of the separate opinions in Furman v. Georgia, 408 U.S. 238 (1972), identified as the basis for the judgment rendering the death sentences there reviewed unconstitutional. The third "constitutional shortcoming" of the North Carolina statute is said to be "its failure to allow the particularized consideration of relevant aspects of the character and record of each convicted defendant before the imposition upon him of a sentence of death." . . .

I do not believe that any one of these reasons singly, nor all of them together, can withstand careful analysis. Contrary to the plurality's assertions, they would import into the Cruel and Unusual Punishments Clause procedural requirements which find no support in our cases. Their application will result in the invalidation of a death sentence imposed upon a defendant con-victed of first-degree murder under the North Carolina system and the upholding of the same sentence imposed on an identical defendant convicted on identical evidence of first-degree murder under the Florida, Georgia, or Texas systems—a result surely as "freakish" as that condemned in the separate opinions in Furman.

* * *

. . . What the plurality opinion has actually done is to import into the Due Process Clause of the Fourteenth Amendment what it conceives to be desirable procedural guarantees where the punishment of death, concededly not cruel and unusual for the crime of which the defendant was convicted, is to be imposed. . . .

I agree with the conclusion of the plurality, and with that of Mr. Justice WHITE, that death is not a cruel and unusual punishment for the offense of which these petitioners were convicted. Since no member of the Court suggests that the trial which led to those convictions in any way fell short of the standards mandated by the Constitution, the judgments of conviction should be affirmed. The Fourteenth Amendment, giving the fullest scope to its "majestic generalities," Fay v. New York, 322 U.S. 261, 282 (1947), is conscripted rather than interpreted when used to permit one but not another system for imposition of the death penalty.

Mandatory Death Penalty for Murder of a Peace Officer

ORAL ARGUMENTS BEFORE THE U.S. SUPREME COURT*

Harry Roberts v. Louisiana, No. 76-5206; argued 4/28/77

On the same day that the Supreme Court heard argument on the question of whether capital punishment may be imposed for rape, *Coker* v. *Georgia*, 21 Cr.L. 4003, it was also presented with another case dealing with the

*From 21 Crim. L. Rptr. 4010–4012. Reprinted by permission of the Bureau of National Affairs, Inc.

death penalty. The state of Louisiana sought approval of a former statutory provision that established a mandatory death sentence for anyone who, with the requisite intent, killed "a peace officer or fireman who was engaged in the performance of his lawful duties." La. R.S. 14:30(2).

This provision, together with the rest of Louisiana's capital punishment statute, was changed by the legislature in the wake of *Stanislaus Roberts* v. *Louisiana,* 428 U.S. 325 (1976). The victim's status as a peace officer or fireman is now an aggravating circumstance which the jury, as sentencing authority, may consider. In *Stanislaus Roberts,* the Court dealt with Subsection 1 of the statute, which imposed the mandatory death sentence on anyone who killed "with a specific intent to kill or inflict great bodily harm" and was "engaged in the perpetration of aggravated kidnapping, aggravated rape or armed robbery." The Court struck down that subsection, saying that while it was not so broad as the provision condemned in *Woodson* v. *North Carolina,* 428 U.S. 280 (1976), it nonetheless suffered from the same infirmity — "lack of focus on the circumstances of the particular offense and the character and propensities of the offender. . . ."

Garland R. Rolling, of Metairie, Louisiana, began his presentation on behalf of defendant Harry Roberts by raising the possibility of a jurisdictional impediment to the Court's deciding this case. The Louisiana Supreme Court, which affirmed the conviction, 331 So. 2d 11 (1976), did so before *Stanislaus Roberts* was decided. Had the state court had the benefit of the Supreme Court's decision, Rolling suggested, its conclusion might have been different. The Louisiana Court considered the statute as a whole and did not focus on the question whether Subsection 1's invalidity has any bearing on Subsection 2.

Thus the question presently before the Court is one which the state court has not considered. For this reason, Rolling asserted, the Court has no power to decide it. In his brief, counsel cited *Street* v. *New York,* 394 U.S. 576 (1969); *Hill* v. *California,* 401 U.S. 797 (1971); *Monks* v. *New Jersey,* 398 U.S. 71 (1970); and *Cardinale* v. *Louisiana,* 394 U.S. 437 (1969), for this proposition.

Even if the Court has jurisdiction, it should decline to exercise it, Rolling continued. The state court may be able to dispose of the question on state law grounds.

Counsel also called the Court's attention to its action in *Washington* v. *Louisiana,* 19 Cr.L. 4098, a week after *Stanislaus Roberts* was decided. Johnson Washington was convicted for murdering a peace officer, and was sentenced under Subsection 2. The Court grouped his case with those of two other Louisiana murder defendants, and in a per curiam order, vacated his death sentence with a citation to *Stanislaus Roberts.* Thus we expected a perfunctory reversal when we petitioned for certiorari, Rolling said.

Counsel also expressed criticism of a statutory provision which defines "peace officer" as "any constable, sheriff, deputy sheriff, local or state policeman, game warden, federal law enforcement officer, jail or prison guard, parole officer, probation officer, judge, district attorney, assistant district attorney or district attorney's investigator." He commented, "As a lawyer, I personally feel slighted."

Waiver Alleged

Louise Korns, Assistant District Attorney for Orleans Parish, sought to minimize the jurisdictional complications raised by the defense. She theorized that Harry Roberts waived further proceedings in the state courts by seeking review in the Supreme Court.

In response to questioning by Mr. Justice Blackmun, Korns said that the *Washington* case is distinguishable. It was merely an order, and neither the Court nor the petitioner Washington in his papers addressed the narrow issue presented here. We cannot see how an order without opinion or reasons can be a binding precedent, she said. But she did agree with Mr. Justice Stevens that the operative facts of *Washington* were substantially identical to those here.

Counsel then asked the Court to distinguish the two *Roberts* cases. Unlike *Stanislaus Roberts,* she said, *Harry Roberts* concerns a narrowly drawn statutory provision. The aggravating circumstances requirement of *Gregg* v. *Georgia,* 428 U.S. 153 (1976), is satisfied by the victim's status. Moreover, we submit that no mitigating circumstances can justify a crime such as the defendant's. (In this brief, the state phrased this contention as follows: "The individual offender in such a case can have no worthwhile attributes which might redeem the heinous act of murdering a peace officer. If the rule of law and orderly conduct of our society are to be preserved and fostered, no violent physical attack of any kind on a peace officer engaged in the exercise of his duties can ever be tolerated, condoned, excused, or made acceptable.")

Finally, Korns continued, there is no need for appellate review of mandatory death sentences such as this one. In view of the narrowness of the statute, the sentence could not be the capricious result of an arbitrary exercise of unfettered jury discretion.

Korns emphasized that the question presented here was clearly reserved in last Term's capital punishment cases. Moreover, she pointed out that both the Florida and Georgia statutes approved last Term list the killing of a peace officer as an aggravating circumstance.

"If our society is to continue to exist, and a few policemen are to control dangerous situations, then no circumstances may excuse the killing of a uniformed policeman," she maintained. Besides, mitigating circumstances can always be shown during the guilt phase of the trial.

Mr. Justice Stevens asked whether the Louisiana Supreme Court has said that, to be convicted under Subsection 2, a defendant must know that his victim is a peace officer.

As far as I know, Korns answered, the question has never arisen. But it would seem that the victim's status would have to be reasonably apparent to the defendant.

Mr. Justice Blackmun asked about the current procedural stance of the *Washington* case.

Rehearing has been denied in this Court, Korns replied. See 20 Cr.L. 4032. The case is currently pending in the state supreme court, which is waiting to see what action is taken in this case.

Need for Protection

Jules E. Orenstein, Assistant Attorney General of New York, appeared on behalf of his state as amicus curiae and urged the Court to affirm the defendant's conviction. The killing of a peace officer, he said, "is one of those unique circumstances which under modern standards, permits imposition of the death penalty."

He referred to the recent decision in *Gardner* v. *Florida,* 20 Cr.L. 3083, in which

a plurality of the Court said, "It is of vital importance to the defendant and to the community that any decision to impose the death sentence be, and appear to be, based on reason rather than caprice or emotions." . . . The reasons are here, Orenstein declared.

Statistics on the murder of peace officers killed in the line of duty "scream and cry out for affirmance here," counsel continued. Between 1966 and 1975, 1,203 law enforcement officers were feloniously killed in this country. Significantly, the number is increasing annually. "This ought to tell us something."

Peace officers constitute a special group that requires special protection. Officers' exposure is constant. Some members of the Court have indicated that the killing of a correctional officer by a life prisoner presents a special case perhaps justifying a mandatory death sentence; see *Stanislaus Roberts* v. *Louisiana,* plurality opinion, footnote 9. Yet a policeman's exposure is far greater than that of a correctional officer.

Orenstein agreed with counsel for Louisiana that the crime itself provides sufficient information on the nature of the offender to pass muster under *Gregg.* The crime itself gives an idea of the defendant's character.

Asked by Mr. Justice Stewart about the Washington case, Orenstein suggested that the Court simply made a mistake. The fact that a peace officer was the victim might have been overlooked.

On rebuttal, Rolling disputed the state's contention that mitigating circumstances can be brought to the jury's attention at the guilt phase of the trial. He concluded by asking the Court to reject the mandatory scheme. Personal considerations must always be taken in view before the death penalty may be imposed, he argued.

HARRY ROBERTS v. LOUISIANA

Supreme Court of the United States, 1977
431 U.S. 633, 97 S. Ct. 1993, 52 L. Ed. 2d 637

The facts are stated in the opinion.

PER CURIAM.

Petitioner Harry Roberts was indicted, tried, and convicted of the first-degree

murder of Police Officer Dennis McInerney, who at the time of his death was engaged in the performance of his lawful duties. As required by Louisiana statute, petitioner was sentenced to death. La. Rev. Stat. Ann. § 14:30(2) (1974). On appeal, the Supreme Court of Louisiana affirmed his conviction and sentence. 331 So. 2d 11 (1976). Roberts then filed a petition for a writ of certiorari in this Court. The petition presented the question whether Louisiana's mandatory death penalty could be imposed pursuant to his conviction of first-degree murder as defined in subparagraph (2) of § 14:30.

Shortly before that petition was filed, we held in another case (involving a different petitioner named Roberts) that Louisiana could not enforce its mandatory death penalty for a conviction of first-degree murder as defined in subparagraph (1) of § 14:30 of the Louisiana Criminal Code. Stanislaus Roberts v. Louisiana, 428 U.S. 325 (1976) [infra, Comment 1]. In the plurality opinion in that case, the precise question presented in this case was explicitly answered.[b]

This precise question was again answered by the Court in Washington v. Louisiana, 428 U.S. 906 (1976). The petitioner in the Washington case had killed a policeman and was tried and sentenced to death under the

same provision of the Louisiana statute as was the petitioner in the present case. We vacated the death sentence, holding: "The imposition and carrying out of the death penalty [in this case] constitute cruel and unusual punishment in violation of the Eighth and Fourteenth Amendments. Roberts v. Louisiana. . . ." Ibid. See also Sparks v. North Carolina, 428 U.S. 905 (1976); Green v. Oklahoma, 428 U.S. 907 (1976).

Recognizing that this Court had already decided that a mandatory death sentence could not be imposed for the crime that Harry Roberts committed, the Attorney General of Louisiana initially conceded that "under this Court's decision in Stanislaus Roberts v. Louisiana, No. 75-5844, [the sentence of death in the present case] cannot be carried out unless, of course, this Court grants Louisiana's Application for Rehearing and modifies its former holding." Brief in Opposition to Certiorari, pp. 2–3. The Court nevertheless granted certiorari. . . .

In Woodson v. North Carolina, 428 U.S. 280, 304 (1976), this Court held that ". . . the fundamental respect for humanity underlying the Eighth Amendment . . . requires consideration of the character and record of the individual offender and the circumstances of a particular offense as a constitutionally indispensable part of the process of inflicting the penalty of death." In Roberts v. Louisiana, 428 U.S. 325 (1976), we made clear that this principle applies even where the crime of first-degree murder is narrowly defined. See n. [b], supra.

To be sure, the fact that the murder victim was a peace officer performing his regular duties may be regarded as an aggravating circumstance. There is a special interest in affording protection to those public servants who regularly must risk their lives in order to guard the safety of other persons and property.[c] But it is incorrect to suppose that no mitigating circumstances can exist when the

---

[b] "The diversity of circumstances presented in cases falling within the single category of killings during the commission of a specified felony, as well as the variety of possible offenders involved in such crimes, underscores the rigidity of Louisiana's enactment and its similarity to the North Carolina statute. Even the more narrowly drawn categories of first-degree murder in the Louisiana law (one of these being the wilful, deliberate, and premeditated homicide of a fireman or a police officer engaged in the performance of his lawful duties) afford no meaningful opportunity for consideration of mitigating factors presented by the circumstances of the particular crime or by the attributes of the individual offender."

"*Only* the third category of the Louisiana first-degree murder statute, covering intentional killing by a person serving a life sentence or by a person previously convicted of an unrelated murder, defines the capital crime at least in significant part in terms of the character or record of the individual offender. Although even this narrow category does not permit the jury to consider possible mitigating factors, a prisoner serving a life sentence presents a unique problem that may justify such a law. See Gregg v. Georgia, ante, at 186; Woodson v. North Carolina, ante, at 287 n.7, 292–293, n.25." 428 U.S., at 333–334 (emphasis added).

---

[c] We recognize that the life of a police officer is a dangerous one. Statistics show that the number of police officers killed in the line of duty has more than doubled in the last 10 years. In 1966, 57 law enforcement officers were killed in the line of duty; in 1975, 129 were killed. Uniform Crime Reporting Program of the Federal Bureau of Investigation. "Law Enforcement Officers Killed, Summary 1975."

victim is a police officer. Circumstances such as the youth of the offender, the absence of any prior conviction, the influence of drugs, alcohol or extreme emotional disturbance, and even the existence of circumstances which the offender reasonably believed provided a moral justification for his conduct are all examples of mitigating facts which might attend the killing of a peace officer and which are considered relevant in other jurisdictions.

As we emphasized repeatedly in Roberts and its companion cases decided last Term, it is essential that the capital sentencing decision allow for consideration of whatever mitigating circumstances may be relevant to either the particular offender or the particular offense.[e] Because the Louisiana statute does not allow consideration of particularized mitigating factors, it is unconstitutional.

Accordingly, we hold that the death sentence imposed upon this petitioner violates the Eighth and Fourteenth Amendments and must be set aside. The judgment of the Supreme Court of Louisiana is reversed insofar as it upholds the death sentence upon petitioner. The case is remanded for further proceedings not inconsistent with this opinion.

It is so ordered.

Mr. Chief Justice BURGER, dissenting.

I would sustain the Louisiana statute and I therefore dissent on the basis of my dissenting statement in Roberts v. Louisiana, 428 U.S. 325, 337 (1976) and that of Mr. Justice WHITE in Woodson v. North Carolina, 428 U.S. 280, 306 (1976).

Mr. Justice BLACKMUN, with whom Mr. Justice WHITE and Mr. Justice REHNQUIST join, dissenting.

* * *

In my view, the question of the constitutionality of Louisiana's mandatory death penalty for killing a peace officer was not answered in Stanislaus Roberts. Washington may be said to be a summary ruling on the

---

[e] We reserve again the question whether or in what circumstances mandatory death sentence statutes may be constitutionally applied to prisoners serving life sentences. See, n.[b], supra, quoting 428 U.S., at 334 n.9.

merits, but that case was decided without the benefit of plenary consideration, and without focusing on the identity and activity of the victim. I believe its result to be incorrect as a constitutional matter and I would disapprove and withhold its further application.

. . . It is indisputable that carefully focused consideration was not given to the special problem of a mandatory death sentence for one who has intentionally killed a police officer engaged in the performance of his lawful duties. I therefore approach this case as a new one, not predetermined and governed by the plurality in Stanislaus Roberts.

Washington may present a different problem. It did decide the issue now before the Court, but it did so without the benefit of full briefing and argument, and it was one of three pending Louisiana cases treated as a cluster and routinely remanded at the Term's end in the immediate wake of Stanislaus Roberts. . . .

On the merits, for reasons I have expressed before, I would not find § 14:30(2) constitutionally defective. See Furman v. Georgia, 408 U.S. 238, 405–414 (1972) (dissenting opinion). See also Stanislaus Roberts v. Louisiana, 428 U.S., at 337–363 (WHITE, J., dissenting). Furthermore, even under the plurality opinions of last Term, I would conclude that § 14:30(2) falls within that narrow category of homicide for which a mandatory death sentence is constitutional. See Gregg v. Georgia, 428 U.S. 153, 186 (1976); Woodson v. North Carolina, 428 U.S. 280, 287 n.7, 292–293 n.25 (1976); Stanislaus Roberts v. Louisiana, 428 U.S., at 334 n. 9. Since the decision in Washington is inconsistent with this view, I would overrule it.

I should note that I do not read the per curiam opinion today as one deciding the issue of the constitutionality of a mandatory death sentence for a killer of a peace officer for all cases and all times. Reference to the plurality opinion in Stanislaus Roberts reveals that the Louisiana statute contained what that opinion regarded as two fatal defects: lack of an opportunity to consider mitigating factors, and standardless jury discretion inherent in the Louisiana responsive verdict system. Without the latter, as here, a different case surely is presented. Furthermore, it is evident, despite the per curiam's general statement to the contrary, that mitigating factors need not be considered in every case; even the per curiam continues to reserve the issue of a mandatory death sentence for murder by a prisoner already serving a life sentence. . . .

Finally, it is possible that a state statute that required the jury to consider, during the guilt phase of the trial, both the aggravating circumstance of killing a peace officer and relevant mitigating circumstances would pass the pluarality's test. Cf. Jurek v. Texas, 428 U.S. 262, 270–271 (1976). For me, therefore, today's decision must be viewed in the context of the Court's previous criticism of the Louisiana system; it need not freeze the Court into a position that condemns every statute with a mandatory death penalty for the intentional killing of a peace officer.

[Mr. Justice REHNQUIST wrote a dissenting opinion in which Mr. Justice WHITE joined].

Comments

1. In *Stanislaus Roberts* v. *Louisiana*, decided the same day as *Woodson* v. *North Carolina*, supra, the Court reviewed the constitutionality of the Louisiana procedures for imposing the death sentence following a conviction for first-degree murder. The opinion is set out below.

STANISLAUS ROBERTS v. LOUISIANA
Supreme Court of the United States, 1976
428 U.S. 325, 96 S. Ct. 3001, 49 L. Ed. 2d 974

Judgment of the Court, and opinion of Mr. Justice STEWART, Mr. Justice POWELL, and Mr. Justice STEVENS, announced by Mr. Justice STEVENS.

* * *

On August 18, 1973, in the early hours of the morning, Richard G. Lowe was found dead in the office of the Lake Charles, La., gas station at which he worked. He had been shot four times in the head. Four men—the petitioner, Huey Cormier, Everett Walls, and Calvin Arcenaux—were arrested for complicity in the murder. The petitioner was subsequently indicted by a grand jury on a presentment that he "[d]id unlawfully with the specific intent to kill or to inflict great bodily harm, while engaged in the armed robbery of Richard G. Lowe, commit first degree murder by killing one Richard G. Lowe. . . .

At the petitioner's trial, Cormier, Walls, and Arcenaux testified for the prosecution. Their testimony established that just before midnight on August 17, the petitioner discussed with Walls and Cormier the subject of "ripping off that old man at the station," and that on the early morning of August 18, Arcenaux and the petitioner went to the gas station on the pretext of seeking employment. After Lowe told them that there were no jobs available they surreptitiously made their way into the office of the station, where Arcenaux removed a pistol from a desk drawer. The petitioner insisted on taking possession of the pistol. When Lowe returned to the office, the petitioner and Arcenaux assaulted him and then shoved him into a small back room. Shortly thereafter a car drove up. Arcenaux went out and, posing as the station attendant, sold the motorist about three dollars' worth of gasoline. While still out in front, Arcenaux heard four shots from inside the station. He went back inside and found the petitioner gone and

Lowe lying, bleeding on the floor. Arcenaux grabbed some empty "money bags" and ran.

The jury found the petitioner guilty as charged. As required by state law, the trial judge sentenced him to death. The Supreme Court of Louisiana affirmed the judgment. State v. Roberts, 319 So. 2d 317 (La. 1975). . . .

* * *

Louisiana, like North Carolina, has responded to Furman by replacing discretionary jury sentencing in capital cases with mandatory death sentences. Under the present Louisiana law, all persons found guilty of first-degree murder, aggravated rape, aggravated kidnapping, or treason are automatically sentenced to death. . . .

The history of mandatory death penalty statutes indicates a firm societal view that limiting the scope of capital murder is an inadequate response to the harshness and inflexibility of a mandatory death sentence statute. See Woodson v. North Carolina. . . . A large group of jurisdictions first responded to the unacceptable severity of the common-law rule of automatic death sentences for all murder convictions by narrowing the definition of capital homicide. Each of these jurisdictions found that approach insufficient and subsequently substituted discretionary sentencing for mandatory death sentences. . . .

The futility of attempting to solve the problems of mandatory death penalty statutes by narrowing the scope of the capital offense stems from our society's rejection of the belief that "every offense in a like legal category calls for an identical punishment without regard to the past life and habits of a particular offender." . . .

The constitutional vice of mandatory death sentence statutes — lack of focus on the circumstances of the particular offense and the character and propensities of the offender — is not resolved by Louisiana's limitation of first-degree murder to various categories of killings. The diversity of circumstances presented in cases falling within the single category of killings during the commission of a specified felony, as well as the variety of possible offenders involved in such crimes, underscores the rigidity of Louisiana's enactment and its similarity to the North Carolina statute. Even the other more narrowly drawn categories of first-degree murder in the Louisiana law afford no meaningful opportunity for consideration of mitigating factors presented by the circumstances of the particular crime or by the attributes of the individual offender.

Louisiana's mandatory death sentence statute also fails to comply with Furman's requirement that standardless jury discretion be replaced by procedures that safeguard against the arbitrary and capricious imposition of death sentences. The State claims that it has adopted satisfactory procedures by taking all sentencing authority from juries in capital murder cases. This was accomplished, according to the State, by deleting the jury's pre-Furman authority to return a verdict of guilty without capital punishment in any murder case. See La. Rev. Stat. Ann. § 14:30 (1974); La. Code Crim. Proc. Ann., Arts. 814, 817 (Supp. 1975).

Under the current Louisiana system, however, every jury in a first-degree murder case is instructed on the crimes of second-degree murder and manslaughter and permitted to consider those verdicts even if there is not a scintilla of evidence to support the lesser verdicts. See La. Code Crim. Proc. Ann., Arts. 809, 814 (Supp. 1975). And, if a lesser verdict is returned, it is treated as an acquittal of all greater charges. See La. Code Crim. Proc. Ann., Art. 598 (Supp. 1975). . . . The Louisiana procedure neither provides standards to channel jury judgments nor permits review to check the arbitrary exercise of the capital jury's de facto sentencing discretion. . . .

The Louisiana statute thus suffers from constitutional deficiencies similar to those identified in the North Carolina statute in Woodson v. North Carolina [supra]. As in North Carolina, there are no standards provided to guide the jury in the exercise of its power to select those first-degree murderers who will receive death sentences, and there is no meaningful appellate review of the jury's decision. As in North Carolina, death sentences are mandatory upon conviction for first-degree murder. Louisiana's mandatory death sentence law employs a procedure that was rejected by that State's legislature 130 years ago and that subsequently has been renounced by legislatures and juries in every jurisdiction in this nation. . . . The Eighth Amendment, which draws much of its meaning from "the evolving standards of decency that mark the progress of a maturing society," Trop v. Dulles, 356 U.S. 86, 101 (plurality opinion), simply cannot tolerate the reintroduction of a practice so thoroughly discredited.

Accordingly, we find that the death sentence imposed upon the petitioner under Louisiana's mandatory death sentence statute violates the Eighth and Fourteenth Amendments and must be set aside. The case is remanded for further proceedings not inconsistent with this opinion.

Reversed and remanded.

[Justices BRENNAN and MARSHALL concurred. Justices WHITE, REHNQUIST, and BLACKMUN dissented.]

2. In the absence of any public opinion polls, how did the majority of the Court conclude in *Woodson* and *Stanislaus Roberts,* supra, that mandatory death sentences are unacceptable to a majority of Americans? Was that conclusion reached because most jurisdictions do not have mandatory death statutes? Because the "evolving standards of decency" do not permit automatic sentences? Do mandatory prison sentences violate the Eighth Amendment, or is death constitutionally different?

3. In *Harry Roberts* v. *Louisiana,* supra, the Court said, "We reserve . . . the question whether or in what circumstances mandatory death sentence statutes may be constitutionally applied to prisoners serving life sentences," at n. e. Do prisoners stand on a different constitutional footing with regard to mandatory death sentences? Suppose an inmate serving a life sentence for arson-murder intentionally sets a fire and 100 fellow inmates are killed. Is there any need for a mandatory death statute, in this case, since a jury could easily find the act of arson to be an "aggravating circumstance"? Are mandatory death statutes more likely or less likely to have a

deterrent effect on inmates under life sentences than on other potential offenders?

4. At the time the North Carolina and Louisiana mandatory death statutes were struck down [see *Woodson, Stanislaus Roberts,* and *Harry Roberts,* supra], at least 12 other jurisdictions had similar statutes: Del. Ch. 284, 127th General Assembly (March 29, 1974); Ch. 276, [1973] Idaho Laws 588; Ind. Ann. Stat. § 10-3401 (Supp. 1973); Ky. Ch. 406, § 61.62, 275, 1974 General Assembly (April 2, 1974); Miss. Ch. 576, 1974 General Assembly (April 23, 1974); Nev. Rev. Stat. § 200.030 (1973); N. H. Ch. 34, 1974 General Court, Spec. Sess. (April 3, 1974); N. M. Stat. Ann. § 40A-29-2 (Supp. 1973); N. Y. Ch. 367, 1974 Legislative Assembly (May 6, 1974); Okla. Stat. Ann. Tit. 21, § 701.3 (Supp., 1973); R. I. Gen. Laws Ann. § 11-23-2 (Supp., 1973); Wyo. Stat. Ann. § 6-54 (Supp., 1973). See also Cal. Penal Code §§ 209, 219 (West Supp., 1974); Mont. Ch. 262, 43d Legislative Assembly (March 21, 1974). How likely is it, in view of *Woodson, Stanislaus Roberts,* and *Harry Roberts,* that these statutes will withstand judicial scrutiny? Some rewriting of all these death penalty statutes is likely. For a view that none of the death penalty statutes passed post-*Furman* are constitutional see Note, *Discretion and the Constitutionality of the New Death Penalty Statutes,* 87 Harv. L. Rev. 1690 (1974).

5. The inmates on death row in North Carolina and Louisiana were saved from the ultimate punishment by 5 to 4 decisions, whereas the death row inmates in Georgia, Florida, and Texas became immediate candidates for execution by 7–2 decisions. Were these arguably "wanton" and "freakish" impositions of the penalty that were condemned by the Court in *Furman*? The vote of a single justice saved the inmates in North Carolina and Louisiana.

6. The Supreme Court probably will have to review the death penalty statutes of all jurisdictions in which capital punishment is sought to be imposed. If so, will the Court be acting as a "superlegislature"? Such Supreme Court review doesn't necessarily require a full opinion: A denial of certiorari will judicially affirm a state supreme court decision. Obviously the Supreme Court is not going to write full opinions to decide the constitutionality of the death penalty procedures in the remaining 30 jurisdictions whose capital punishment schemes have not yet received plenary review, especially those that are constitutionally infirm. Questions on the constitutionality of aspects of the death penalty other than the procedures for imposing it (e.g., application to nonhomicide crimes) are likely to confront the Court in future years.

7. There seems little doubt that the Framers of the Constitution considered death to be a proper punishment. The federal Constitution mentions the death penalty in several places: The opening sentence of the Fifth Amendment provides, "No person shall be held to answer for a capital . . . crime, unless on a presentment or indictment of a Grand Jury." . . . The Fifth Amendment Double Jeopardy Clause is a prohibiton against being "twice put in jeopardy of life or limb." Likewise the Due Process Clauses of the Fifth and Fourteenth Amendments require "due process of law" before an accused can be "deprived of life, liberty, or property." However, in light of the "standards of decency" test formulated by

the Court in *Trop* v. *Dulles*, 356 U.S. 86 (1958), which apparently was accepted by the majority in *Gregg* v. *Georgia* and its progeny, supra, the Supreme Court can abolish or restrict the imposition of the death penalty.

8.

DAVIS v. GEORGIA

Supreme Court of the United States, 1976

429 U.S. 122, 97 S. Ct. 399, 50 L. Ed. 2d 339

PER CURIAM.

The petitoner in this case was convicted of murder and sentenced to death after trial by a jury selected in violation of the standards enunciated in Witherspoon v. Illinois, 391 U.S. 510 (1968), and applied in Boulden v. Holman, 394 U.S. 478 (1969), and Maxwell v. Bishop, 398 U.S. 262 (1970). The Witherspoon case held that "a sentence of death cannot be carried out if the jury that imposed or recommended it was chosen by excluding veniremen for cause simply because they voiced general objections to the death penalty or expressed conscientious or religious scruples against its infliction." Id., at 552–523.

The Supreme Court of Georgia found that one prospective juror had been excluded in violation of the Witherspoon standard. The Court nevertheless affirmed the conviction and death sentence, reasoning that the erroneous exclusion of one death-scrupled juror did not deny the petitioner a jury representing a cross-section of the community since other jurors sharing that attitude were not excused for cause: "The rationale of Witherspoon and its progeny is not violated where merely one of a qualified class or group is excluded where it is shown, as here, that others of such group were qualified to serve. This record is completely void of any evidence of a systematic and intentional exclusion of a qualified group of jurors so as to deny the appellant a jury of veniremen representing a cross section of the community." 236 Ga. 804, 809–810.

That, however, is not the test established in Witherspoon, and it is not the test that this Court has applied in subsequent cases where a death penalty was imposed after the improper exclusion of one member of the venire. See Wigglesworth v. Ohio, 403 U.S. 947, rev'g 18 Ohio St. 2d 171, 248 N.E. 2d 607; Harris v. Texas, 403 U.S. 947, rev'g 457 S.W. 2d 903; Adams v. Washington, 403 U.S. 947, rev'g 76 Wash. 2d 650, 458 P.2d 558. Unless a venireman is "irrevocably committed, before the trial has begun, to vote against the penalty of death regardless of the facts and circumstances that might emerge in the course of the proceedings" (391 U.S., at 522 n.21), he cannot be excluded; if a venireman is improperly excluded even though not so committed, any subsequently imposed penalty cannot stand.

Accordingly, the motion for leave to proceed in forma pauperis and the petition for certiorari are granted, the judgment is reversed, and the case is remanded for further proceedings not inconsistent with this opinion. It is so ordered.

Mr. Justice REHNQUIST, with whom the CHIEF JUSTICE [BURGER] and Mr. Justice BLACKMUN join, dissenting.

As is clear from the most cursory reading, Witherspoon v. Illinois, 391 U.S. 510 (1968), does not inexorably lead to the result this Court now reaches. Indeed, much of the language in that opinion would support the reasoning, and the result, reached by the Supreme Court of Georgia. The extension of Witherspoon to cover the case where a sole venireman is excluded in violation of its test deserves plenary consideration, not a per se rule that precludes application of even the harmless error test of Chapman v. California, 386 U.S. 18 (1967). There is no indication that the Supreme Court of Georgia was wrong when it observed that "[t]he record is completely void of any evidence of a systematic and intentional exclusion of a qualified group of jurors so as to deny the appellant a jury of veniremen representing a cross section of the community," 236 Ga. 804, 809–810.

It is, moreover, unclear whether the State was entitled to another peremptory challenge,* and surely Witherspoon does not decide whether the presence of unexercised peremptory challenges might render harmless the improper exclusion of a limited number of veniremen. Finally, the defect in this case is not that a juror was improperly excluded because she was not irrevocably opposed to the death penalty; rather the defect is a failure to question sufficiently to determine whether or not she was irrevocably opposed. It is not inconceivable that a hearing with the excluded juror could not be conducted to finish the aborted questioning and determine whether she would have, in fact, been excludable for cause.

The effects of the arguably improper exclusion, in short, are too murky to warrant summary reversal of the sentence imposed. Since I do not believe this case is controlled by our past decisions, I would grant certiorari and set the case for argument.

9. Do the following impose or constitute cruel and unusual punishment: State statute imposing mandatory jail terms for persons involved in accidents while driving with suspended licenses? See *State* v. *Fearick,* 350 A.2d 227 (N.J. 1976) (not cruel and unusual). A lack of rehabilitative programs in a state prison? See *French* v. *Heyne,* 547 F.2d 994 (7th Cir. 1977) (not cruel and unusual). State law providing mandatory one-year jail sentence for possession of unlicensed firearm? See *Commonwealth* v. *Jackson,* 344 N.E. 2d 166 (Mass. 1976) (not cruel and unusual). Sentencing admitted homosexual to five years' imprisonment with knowledge that homosexuals are frequently raped and assaulted in prison? See *United States* v. *Tolias,* 548 F.2d 277 (9th Cir. 1977) (not cruel and unusual). Mandatory sentence of imprisonment for minimum of 10 years to life without possibility of parole for 10 years for second-time drug offender convicted of selling marijuana? See *In re Grant,* 553 P.2d 590 (Calif. 1976) (held cruel and unusual). The death penalty for an aider and abettor to murder? See *State* v. *Perryman,* 358 N.E.2d 1040 (Ohio 1976) (not cruel and unusual). Mandatory three-year sentence, which must be served prior to eligibility for parole, on conviction of any offense in which a

---

*Normally, the defense, in a capital case, is entitled to 20 peremptory challenges, and the State is entitled to one-half as many as the defense. 59 Ga. Code 805. In this case, the defense utilized 21 peremptory challenges; the State, 10.

firearm is used? See *Sowell v. State*, 342 So. 2d 969 (Fla. 1977) (not cruel and unusual). Rectal and testicle searches of prisoners not based on reasonable belief or probable cause? See *Frazier v. Ward*, 426 F. Supp. 1354 (D.N.Y. 1977) (held cruel and unusual). Sentence of life imprisonment for armed robbery? See *Mydell v. State*, 233 S.E.2d 199 (Ga. 1977) (not cruel and unusual). Ordering defendant to prison upon revocation of probation for crime that occurred 17 years earlier? See *United States v. Albanese*, 554 F.2d 543 (2d Cir. 1977) (not cruel and unusual).

10. Some recent lower federal and state court decisions involving cruel and unusual punishment are *Inmates, D.C. Jail v. Jackson*, 416 F. Supp. 119 (D.D.C. 1976) (conditions of jail confinement can in themselves constitute cruel and unusual punishment); *State v. Jolla*, 337 So. 2d 197 (La. 1976) (sentence of 198 years' imprisonment with no possibility of parole, probation, or suspension of sentence not cruel and unusual); *Harris v. Chanclor*, 537 F.2d 203 (5th Cir. 1976) (warden's deliberate indifference to inmate's severe injuries held tantamount to cruel and unusual punishment); *State v. Gibson*, 553 P.2d 131 (Wash. App. 1976) (harsh punishment alone is not cruel and unusual punishment); *Martin v. Parratt*, 412 F. Supp. 544 (D. Neb. 1976) (state habitual criminal statute not unconstitutional because it punishes a status rather than a specific act); *People v. McDowell*, 130 Cal. Rptr. 839 (Cal. App. 1976) (probation requirement that convicted purse-snatcher wear shoes with metal heel and toe taps whenever he left his house held not cruel and unusual punishment); *Sims v. Waln*, 536 F.2d 686 (6th Cir. 1976) (imposition of reasonable corporal punishment to discipline school students is not cruel and unusual punishment); *State v. Defoe*, 241 N.W.2d 635 (Minn. 1976) (not cruel or unusual to sentence chronic alcoholic for a robbery that might be causally related to his condition); *Mathis v. Schnarr*, 404 F. Supp. 643 (D. Mo. 1975) (statutes permitting police officers to use deadly force in effecting an arrest of fleeing felon held not violative of Cruel and Unusual Punishments Clause); *People v. Shepherd*, 234 N.W.2d 502 (Mich. App. 1975) (not cruel and unusual to sentence an aider and abbettor to same term as principal); *United States v. Kahane*, 396 F. Supp. 687 (E.D.N.Y. 1975) (refusal to provide observant Orthodox Jewish rabbi with kosher food while imprisoned held cruel and unusual punishment); *People v. Jetter*, 540 P.2d 1217 (Calif. 1975) (indefinite involuntary confinement of civilly committed mentally disturbed sex offender in a prison setting is cruel and unusual punishment); *Jackson v. Werner*, 394 F. Supp. 805 (W.D. Pa. 1975) (conducting strip search of inmate pursuant to prison regulation held not cruel and unusual punishment); *Weatherford v. State*, 328 N.E. 2d 756 (Ind. App. 1975) (subjecting defendant to third trial following first mistrial due to procedural errors and second mistrial due to hung jury held not cruel and unusual); *Spencer v. State Dept. of Public Safety*, 315 So. 2nd 912 (La. App. 1975) (suspension of driver's license for refusal to submit to Intoximeter test held not cruel and unusual punishment); *State v. Lum*, 537 P.2d 672 (N.M. App. 1975) (fact that accused, who was convicted of murder, was tried four times held not to constitute cruel and unusual punishment); *State v. Dean*, 227 N.W.2d 712 (Wis. 1975) (imposition of five consecutive life sentences on defendant convicted of five counts of first-degree murder held not violative of Cruel and Unusual

Punishments Clause); *Esser* v. *Jeffes*, 416 F. Supp. 719 (D. Pa.) (denial of television and gym privileges for 15 days to inmate found guilty of stealing food from inmates' dining room held not cruel and unusual punishment); *Dyas* v. *State*, 539 S.W.2d 251 (Ark. 1976) (sentence of life imprisonment without parole on conviction of capital felony-murder not cruel and unusual); *Finney* v. *Hutto*, 548 F.2d 740 (8th Cir. 1977) (confinement of inmates in punitive isolation for more than 30 days held violative of Cruel and Unusual Punishments Clause); *Bennett* v. *Passic*, 545 F. 2d 1260 (10th Cir. 1976) (confinement of intoxicated defendant for three hours in small, unsanitary cell designated as "drunk tank" held not cruel and unusual punishment); *State* v. *Parker*, 558 P.2d 905 (Ariz. 1976) (statute prescribing death or life imprisonment without possibility of parole for the first 25 years for first-degree murder held not cruel and unusual); *State* v. *Jenkins*, 232 S.E.2d 648 (N.C. 1977) (when punishment does not exceed limits fixed by statute, it cannot be considered cruel and unusual in a constitutional sense); *State ex rel. Harris* v. *Alendine*, 233 S.E.2d 318 (W. Va. 1977) (state may not punish person in fact while alleging to rehabilitate or otherwise help him).

11.04 LIFE ON DEATH ROW: A POST-*FURMAN* PROFILE OF FLORIDA'S CONDEMNED*†

Various national polls indicate that most American citizens favor the imposition of the death penalty for some specified offenses.[1] But if one were to randomly ask persons on the street what they know about the history of capital punishment and the characteristics of death row inmates, their responses would likely be unilluminating and unsatisfactory.[2]

Even though the United States Supreme Court in 1976 upheld the constitutionality of the death penalty for the offense of first de-

*This profile is based on interviews with 83 death row inmates (nearly 25 per cent of the total in the United States) at the Florida State Prison. These interviews were conducted during weekly visits to the prison made between February and June, 1977. The assistance of Henry W. Mannle, Ph.D., Associate Professor of Sociology and Criminal Justice, Tennessee Technological University in participating in the study and in preparing this profile is gratefully acknowledged. We are also greatly indebted to the following graduate students who, at various times, accompanied us to death row and assisted in the collection of the data: Jerome Vermette, Gary Trichter, and Donald Nelson. Thanks is also extended to Harold J. Vetter, Ph.D., who accompanied us to death row on several occasions and provided valuable insights during the project and to Eric Carlton, Ph.D., and Harry E. Allen, Ph.D., who were instrumental in solving some of the theoretical and methodological problems that always accompany major research projects. Special thanks is extended to Louis Wainwright, Jr., Secretary of the Division of Offender Rehabilitation; Dave Bachman, Assistant Secretary of Operations, Division of Offender Rehabilitation; John Anderson, As-

sistant to the Superintendent, Florida State Prison; and S. R. Johns, counselor on death row, who granted permission to conduct this study and helped in its coordination. Finally, we wish to express our appreciation to the 83 inmates on Florida's death row without whose cooperation this study would not have been possible.

†A statistical summary of the findings from this study is presented in Appendix E.

[1]See, e.g., a December, 1972, Gallup Poll in which 57 per cent of those interviewed favored the death penalty. In a June, 1973, Harris Poll, 59 per cent of the persons sampled supported capital punishment. Seventy-three per cent of the respondents in a CBS-*New York Times* national poll (CBS Evening News, August 2, 1977) favored capital punishment.

[2]See, e.g., the dissenting opinion of Mr. Justice Marshall in *Gregg* v. *Georgia*, 428 U.S. 153 (1976) (supra), in which he stated, "The American people are largely unaware of the information critical to a judgment of the morality of the death penalty, and . . . if they were better informed they would consider it shocking, unjust, and unacceptable." See also *Furman* v. *Georgia*, 408 U.S. 238, 360 (1972) (Marshall, J., dissenting).

gree murder,[3] capital punishment remains a controversial issue among laymen and among scholars who have studied this unique penalty. The issue often gives rise to heated arguments among academicians,[4] although it is probably more fashionable in university circles than among criminal justice practitioners to be opposed to capital punishment on moral, legal or social grounds.

There is a plethora of literature on various aspects of the death penalty. Historically, the place of capital punishment within the framework of "enlightened" government has been debated on philosophical grounds.[5] As social and political currents have shifted since the eighteenth century, so has the thrust of ethical arguments on the validity of the death penalty.[6] Contemporary material on capital punishment, both in nature and in quantity, attests to the multifaceted dimensions of the subject. The most abundant material on capital punishment consists of position statements (occasionally accompanied by empirical research) that address the issues of the deterrent value, constitutionality (Eighth Amendment arguments), and equability of capital punishment. Also available are studies on attitudes toward the death penalty and, in significantly smaller number, typologies (profiles) of offenders sentenced to be executed.[7]

The nondeterrence argument looms at the forefront of the abolitionist's position—even though the question of the efficacy of capital punishment as a general deterrent remains unsettled in academic circles.[8] The argument

---

[3]*Gregg* v. *Georgia*, 428 U.S. 153 (1976) (supra); *Proffitt* v. *Florida*, 428 U.S. 242 (1976) (supra), and *Jurek* v. *Texas*, 428 U.S. 262 (1976) (supra). In *Woodson* v. *North Carolina*, 428 U.S. 280 (1976) (supra), and *Stanislaus Roberts* v. *Louisiana*, 428 U.S. 325 (1976) (supra), a majority of the Supreme Court struck down state statutes that imposed a mandatory death sentence following a conviction for first degree murder. In *Harry Roberts* v. *Louisiana*, 97 S. Ct. 1993 (1977) (per curiam) (supra), a 5–4 Supreme Court struck down a Louisiana statute that provided for mandatory death sentences for the intentional killing of police officers. In *Coker* v. *Georgia*, 97 S. Ct. 2861 (1977) (supra), a majority of the Supreme Court struck down a Georgia statute that permitted the imposition of the death penalty for the crime of rape of an adult woman. *Coker* suggests that unless the victim of a crime has lost his life, the death penalty is "grossly disproportionate and excessive punishment," at 2866.

[4]Compare, Ehrlich, *The Deterrent Effect of Capital Punishment: A Question of Life or Death*, 65 Am. Econ. Rev. 397, 414 (1975) ("an additional execution per year [over the period 1935–1969] may have resulted, on the average, in 7 or 8 fewer murders"), with Zeisel, *The Deterrent Effect of the Death Penalty: Facts v. Fiction*, in Kurland (ed.), *The Supreme Court Review* 317, 342 (1977) ("the deterrent effect, if it exists at all, can only be minute"). See also, Bedau and Pierce (eds.), *Capital Punishment in the United States* (1976).

[5]Beccaria, *Essay on Crimes and Punishment* (1764).

[6]Ancel, *The Problem of the Death Penalty*, in Sellin (ed.), *Capital Punishment* 6–9 (1967).

[7]See, e.g., Gallemore and Panton, *Inmate Responses to Lengthy Death Row Confinement*, 129 Am. J. Psychiat. 81 (1972) (study of eight North Carolina death row inmates convicted pre-*Furman*); Bluestone and McGahee, *Reaction to Extreme Stress: Impending Death by Execution*, 119 Am. J. Psychiat. 393 (1962) (study of 19 death row inmates at Sing Sing, New York); Swinburn, *Synopsis of Offenders Receiving the Death Sentence in Texas*, Research Report No. 8, Texas Department of Corrections (1972); Miller, *Massachusetts—Some Notes on Death Row and the Death Penalty*, Massachusetts Department of Corrections (1971).

[8]E.g., Sellin, *The Death Penalty* (1959); Zimiring and Hawkins, *Deterrence* (1973); Bowers, *Executions in America* (1974); Savitz, *A Study of Capital Punishment*, 49 J. Crim. L.C. & Pol. Sci. 416 (1974); Bailey, *Murder and the Death Penalty*, 65 J. Crim. L. & Crim. 416 (1974); Reckless, *The Use of the Death Penalty—A Factual Statement*, 15 Crime & Del. 43 (1969); Gibbs, *Crime, Punishment and Deterrence* (1975); Andenaes, *Punishment and Deterrence* (1974); Sellin, *Homicides in Retentionist and Abolitionist States*, in Sellin (ed.), *Capital Punishment* 135 (1967); Baldus and Cole, *A Comparison of the Work of Thorsten Sellin and Isaac Ehrlich on the Deterrent Effect of Capital Punishment*, 85 Yale L.J. 1987 (1975); Passell and Taylor, *The Deterrent Effect of Capital Punishment: Another View*, March, 1975 (unpublished Columbia University Discussion Paper 74-7509), cited in Zeisel, *The Deterrent Effect of the Death Penalty: Facts v. Fiction*, in Kurland (ed.), *The Supreme Court Review*, 317, 333 (1977); Passell, *The Deterrent Effect of the Death Penalty: A Statistical Test*, 28 Stan. L. Rev. 61 (1975); Klein, Forst, and Filatov, *The Deterrent Effect of Capital Punishment: An Assessment of the Estimates* (paper commissioned by the Panel on Research on Deterrence, Nat. Acad. of Sciences) (June, 1976);

that the death penalty has value as a specific deterrent has received only minimal scholarly support. The grave possibility that innocent persons may be executed[9] has received considerable attention in the professional literature. Even though the rehabilitation model has largely fallen into disrepute,[10] retribution as a justification for imposing the death penalty has recently received support from some noteworthy scholars.[11]

An equally pressing question concerns the fair and even-handed administration of the death penalty. The studies are too numerous to cite authority that demonstrate that the death penalty has been imposed arbitrarily and capriciously[12] on a disproportionate number of black and other minority group members,[13] young males, and members of the lower socioeconomic classes.[14] While no white male in the United States has ever

Avio, *Capital Punishment in Canada: A Time-Series Analysis of the Deterrent Hypothesis* (mimeo, 1976); Ehrlich, *Deterrence: Evidence and Inference*, 85 Yale L.J. 209 (1975); Forst, *The Deterrent Effect of Capital Punishment: A Cross-State Analysis of the 1960's* (mimeo, Sept. 1976), cited in Zeisel, *The Deterrent Effect of the Death Penalty: Facts v. Fiction,* in Kurland (ed.), *The Supreme Court Review,* 317, 336 (1977); Graves, *The Deterrent Effect of Capital Punishment in California,* in Bedau (ed.), *The Death Penalty in America* (1967); Fahah, *A Study of the Deterrent Effect of Capital Punishment with Special Reference to the Canadian Situation* (1972); Jayewardene, *Life or Death—Society's Reaction to Murder,* 15 Can. J. Crime & Corr. 265 (1973); Morrison, *Criminal Homicide and the Death Penalty in Canada—Time for Reassessment and New Directions—Toward a Typology of Homicide,* 15 Can. J. Crime & Corr. 367 (1973); Bailey, *Crime and Deterrence—A Correlational Analysis,* 11 J. Research Crime & Del. 124 (1974); Speaker, *Capital Punishment—Ineffective, Unjust, Unconstitutional,* 53 Prison J. 36 (1974); Glaser, *Response to Bailey: More Evidence on Capital Punishment as a Correlate of Tolerance or Murder,* 22 Crime & Del. 40 (1976); Zimiring & O'Malley, *Punishing Homicide in Philadelphia: Perspectives on the Death Penalty,* 43 Univ. Chicago L. Rev. 227 (1976); Bowers, *The Illusion of Deterrence in Isaac Ehrlich's Research on Capital Punishment,* 85 Yale L.J. 187 (1975); Clauncey, *Deterrence—Certainty, Severity, and Skyjacking,* 12 Criminology 447 (1975); Bailey, *Use of the Death Penalty Versus Outrage at Murder—Some Additional Evidence and Considerations,* 22 Crime & Del. 31 (1976).

[9]Black, *Capital Punishment: The Inevitability of Caprice and Mistake* (1974).

[10]E.g., Martinson, *What Works—Questions and Answers About Prison Returns,* 35 Public Interest 22 (1974); Kassebaum, et al., *Prison Treatment and Parole Survival: An Empirical Assessment* (1971); Lerman, *Community Treatment and Social Control: A Critical Analysis of Juvenile Correctional Policy* (1975); Lipton, Martinson, and Wilks, *The Effectiveness of Correctional Treatment: A Survey of Treatment Evaluation Studies* (1975); Morris, *The Future of Imprisonment* (1974); Fogel, *We Are the Living Proof* (1976).

[11]See Van Den Haag, *Punishing Criminals: Concerning a Very Old and Painful Question* (1975), arguing that retribution is a justified theory of punishment. See also statement of Mr. Justice Stewart in *Furman* v. *Georgia,* 408 U.S. 238, 308 (1972) (concurring), that "the instinct for retribution is a part of the nature of man, and channeling that instinct in the administration of criminal justice serves an important purpose in promoting the stability of a society governed by law," cited in *Gregg* v. *Georgia,* 428 U.S. 153 (1976) (supra). See also Von Hirsch, *Doing Justice: The Choice of Punishments* 45–55 (1976) (referring to retribution as "desert").

During oral arguments before the Supreme Court in *Woodson* v. *North Carolina,* 428 U.S. 280 (1976) (supra), in which North Carolina's mandatory death penalty statute was challenged as "cruel and unusual," Mr. Justice Powell asked Professor Anthony Amsterdam, who was representing the petitioners, whether he would impose the death penalty for a terrorist who destroyed New York City with a hydrogen bomb or for the commandant of Buchenwald. Professor Amsterdam responded that life imprisonment without the possibility of parole would be an acceptable punishment for such persons. 19 Crim. L. Rptr. 4010–4011. It seems to us that the existence of such extreme situations is central to the retributionist's position.

[12]*Furman* v. *Georgia,* 408 U.S. 238 (1972). See also, Meltsner, *Cruel and Unusual: The Supreme Court and Capital Punishment* (1973).

[13]See, e.g., Riedel, *Discrimination in the Imposition of the Death Penalty: A Comparison of the Characteristics of Offenders Sentenced Pre-Furman and Post-Furman,* 49 Temple L.Q. 261 (1976).

[14]Id. An additional issue is the "suicide through murder" theory. See Staub and Alexander, *The Criminal, the Judge, and the Public—A Psychological Analysis* (1951); Solomon, *Capital Punishment as Suicide and as Murder,* 45 Am. J. Orthopsychiat. 701 (1975); and Diamond, *Murder and the Death Penalty—A Case Report,* 45 Am. J. Orthopsychiat. 712 (1975).

been executed for raping a black female, almost 90 per cent of all persons executed for the crime of rape between 1930 and 1977 were black[15] – and most of them were executed for raping white females.[16] This form of unequal administration of the death penalty no longer exists, because the rape of an adult woman is no longer a capital offense.[17]

The philosophy of "life at any price" becomes especially problematic in regard to those offenders who intentionally kill multiple victims, children, police officers, or members of prison staffs,[18] who inflict torture, or who otherwise commit especially heinous crimes.

As criminologist-professors who were disturbed by the conflicting viewpoints in the professional literature, we decided to examine certain aspects of capital punishment from a perspective vastly different from that taken by most of our academic brethren.[19] We decided to spend time on Florida's death row to become familiar with the inmates and their case histories. Accordingly, we arranged to spend one day per week on Florida's death row interviewing inmates and examining their prison files.[20] After visiting the Florida State Prison for a period of five months (February through June, 1977), during which time 83 death row inmates (approximately one fourth of the total in the United States [see Table 11.1]) were exten-

sively interviewed[21] we developed the following typology of Florida's condemned.

Any discussion of the prototype inmate on death row must be qualified. Each inmate, like any other person, has a unique personality and life style. Nevertheless, there are some common denominators.

Characteristics of Death Row Inmates

As of August 1, 1977, 60 per cent of Florida's 85 death row inmates were white and 40 per cent black.[21] While the present racial composition may or may not be significant,[22] depending on one's research interests, historically blacks have always outnumbered whites on Florida's death row; and two thirds of all prisoners executed between 1930 and 1975 were black.[23] At the time of the *Furman* decision in 1972, two thirds of those on Florida's death row (N = 96) were black and one third white. Some implications of the present racial balance on death row will be explored later in this section. Tables 11.2 and 11.3 present a census of all death row inmates in the United States as of August 1, 1977.

The interviews and case history studies involved 46 white offenders (55.4% of the total), 34 black offenders (40.9%), and three inmates belonging to other minority groups

---

[15.] United States Department of Justice, Bureau of Prisons, National Prisoner Statistics, *Prisoners Executed Under Civil Authority in the United States by Race, Offense, and Year: 1930–75* (Bulletin, July, 1976), at 14.

[16] Meltsner, supra note 9, at 77.

[17.] *Coker* v. *Georgia*, 97 S. Ct. 2861 (1977) (supra). The Supreme Court left open the question of whether the death penalty may be imposed for the rape of a young child.

[18] Buffin, *Prison Killings and Death Penalty Legislation,* 53 Prison J. (1974); and Sellin, *Prison Homicides,* in Sellin (ed.), *Capital Punishment* 154 (1967).

[19] Most of the studies on death row inmates are based on data taken from the prisoners' files or on national statistics. See, e.g., Riedel, *Discrimination in the Imposition of the Death Penalty: A Comparison of the Characteristics of Offenders Sentenced Pre-Furman and Post-Furman,* 49 Temple L.Q. 261 (1976). We feel safe in stating that none of our colleagues has spent a comparable period of time on death row or interviewed more than 80 death row inmates.

[20] All interviews were conducted individually on

death row on a voluntary basis. They were done outside the presence of prison officials to enhance reliability. A lengthy questionnaire was devised, which elicited information on the sociological and criminological backgrounds of the offenders, as well as on the circumstances surrounding the murder(s), their trials, their attitudes toward capital punishment, and aspects of life on death row. In all, 145 variables were utilized. The average interview took about two hours, and in many instances, follow-up interviews were conducted. In addition, we had complete access to the inmates' prison files, which were a source of additional information. Only a few inmates declined to participate in the study.

[21] The racial composition of the 83 inmates studied was 55.4 per cent white (N = 46), 38.0 per cent black (N = 34), and 4.7 per cent other minority groups (N = 3). See Table 11.5, infra. During the study the population on Florida's death row reached a high of 96 inmates. See Table 11.2, infra.

[22] See Tables 11.4 and 11.5 infra.

[23] See note 15 supra, at 18. The last execution in Florida took place in 1964.

TABLE 11.2   Death Row Populations By Jurisdiction*

State	Black	White	Hispanic Surname	American Indian	Total
Alabama	3	4	—	—	7 (1.7%)
Alaska	—	—	—	—	0
Arizona	1	11	4	—	16 (4.0%)
Arkansas	4	3	—	—	7 (1.7%)
California	—	—	—	—	0
Colorado	2	3	—	—	5 (1.2%)
Connecticut	—	—	—	—	0
Delaware	—	—	—	—	0
Florida	34	50 (1F)†	1	—	85 (21.6%)‡
Georgia	32	27 (1F)	—	—	59 (15.0%)‡
Hawaii	—	—	—	—	0
Idaho	2	—	—	1	3 (0.7%)
Illinois	—	—	—	—	0
Indiana	4	5	—	—	9 (2.2%)
Iowa	—	—	—	—	0
Kansas	—	—	—	—	0
Kentucky	—	—	—	—	0
Louisiana	—	—	—	—	0
Maine	—	—	—	—	0
Maryland	—	—	—	—	0
Massachusetts	—	—	—	—	0
Michigan	—	—	—	—	0
Minnesota	—	—	—	—	0
Mississippi	18	4	—	—	22 (5.6%)
Missouri	—	—	—	—	0
Montana	1	4	—	—	5 (1.2%)
Nebraska	—	4	—	—	4 (1.0%)
Nevada	—	3	—	—	3 (0.7%)
New Hampshire	—	—	—	—	0
New Jersey	—	—	—	—	0
New Mexico	—	—	—	—	0
New York	2	—	—	—	2 (0.5%)
North Carolina	—	—	—	—	0
North Dakota	—	—	—	—	0
Ohio	43 (1F)	30 (2F)	—	—	73 (18.6%)‡
Oklahoma	1	3	—	—	4 (1.0%)
Oregon	—	—	—	—	0
Pennsylvania	12	6	—	—	18 (4.5%)
Rhode Island	2	—	—	—	2 (0.5%)
South Carolina	—	—	—	—	0
South Dakota	—	—	—	—	0
Tennessee	—	—	—	—	0
Texas	21	32	9	—	62 (15.8%)‡
Utah	2	3	—	—	5 (1.2%)
Vermont	—	—	—	—	0
Virginia	—	—	—	—	0
Washington	—	1	—	—	1 (0.2%)
West Virginia	—	—	—	—	0
Wisconsin	—	—	—	—	0
Wyoming	—	—	—	—	0
U.S. Code	—	—	—	—	0
U.C.M.J.	—	—	—	—	0
Dist. of Columbia	—	—	—	—	0
Totals	184 (46.9%) (1F)	193 (49.2%) (4F)	14 (3.6%)	1 (0.3%)	392 (98.9%) (5F)

*As of August 1, 1977. Data from Capital Punishment Project of the American Civil Liberties Union, New York, New York.

†F = female.

‡As of August 1, 1977, 71.1% of all persons on death row were in Florida, Georgia, Ohio, and Texas.

TABLE 11.3 National Death Row Census by Race and Sex*

	White	Black	Other	Total
Male	183 (46.7%)	189 (48.2%)	15 (3.8%)	387 (98.7%)
Female	4 (1.0%)	1 (0.3%)	0 (0.0%)	5 (1.3%)
Total	187 (47.7%)	190 (48.5%)	15 (3.8%)	392 (100.0%)

*As of August 1, 1977. Data from National Coalition Against the Death Penalty, New York, New York.

(3.7%). The sole female under a sentence of death refused to be interviewed.

The average inmate on Florida's death row was 28 years old at the time of sentencing (with a range of 17 to 58 years). This comports with official Florida statistics that indicate that the age group accounting for the highest percentage of persons arrested for murder during the years 1973 to 1976 was the 25 to 29-year-olds.[24]

Two thirds of the inmates stated that they are members of a Protestant denomination, most often Baptist, and 15 per cent are Catholic. Only one Jewish inmate was on death row during the period of the study. The remaining inmates claimed as their religious preference such faiths as Sunni, Buddhist, Holiness, Peyote, and Black Muslim, or indicated that they were agnostics or atheists. In all, over 20 different religious faiths are represented on death row. The 22 "born-again Christians" all were converted following their convictions and death sentences. All but a few of the inmates attended church only rarely both as adults and as children. (This is in no way meant to suggest a causal relation between criminality and church nonattendance.)

The average inmate completed the ninth grade in school; the range is no formal schooling to three years of college. Almost three fourths of the inmates did not complete high school. Thirteen per cent attended college, although no college graduates were on death row during the period of the study. Three inmates had no formal education. The inmates' performance levels on standardized tests were not consistent with their formal educational achievements: The mean score on the Gray-Votaw-Rogers educational scale was 6.8 years, and one third scored at the fifth grade level or lower. Two thirds of the inmates scored within the average cate-

gory on the Beta I.Q. Test. One sixth scored below average, and one sixth above average. The scores on the I.Q. tests ranged from 71 to 121.

Almost three fourths of the inmates were born in states other than Florida; 27 states, not including Florida, are represented on death row. A greater proportion of blacks than whites were Florida-born. Two thirds of the offenders were residents of the county in which the murder took place.

Slightly more than one half of the inmates claimed to have been raised by both parents (natural or adoptive); most had siblings. Slightly more than one half the inmates (55%) were single (never married, divorced, or widowed) at the time of the offense. Two thirds had been married at least once prior to their present incarceration, and one fourth had been married at least two times. Thirty-six per cent of the offenders had never married. Six per cent have children, and one inmate has 11 children.

Only one third of the inmates had previously served in the armed forces. Of these, about one half received less than honorable discharges.

With few exceptions, death row inmates are members of the working class. Almost two thirds claimed to have been employed (full or part-time) at the time of the capital offense. Their employment records were often spotty, and their occupations included truck driver, laborer, carpenter, dishwasher, mechanic, bartender, private security guard, and similar jobs not requiring extensive formal schooling or training. One inmate had been employed as a Florida correctional officer (he had been fired prior to the murder for which he is presently incarcerated). Few of the death row inmates were members of the middle class or had white-collar jobs. However, one inmate was the assistant manager of a motel belonging to a national chain of hotels and restaurants, and another owned a furniture store and was an apartment landlord. A few inmates supported

[24]See Annual Report, State of Florida, Department of Criminal Law Enforcement, *Crime in Florida*, 1973–1976.

themselves by selling drugs or stolen property or engaging in other property crimes, such as burglary and armed robbery. Several of these inmates had substantial incomes (tax free, of course).

About one third of the inmates were on probation or parole at the time of the murder for which they were incarcerated. Prior difficulty with the law is a common denominator, although some death row inmates are first offenders. Only one repeat murderer was found, but prior convictions for other violent or serious crimes (e.g., burglary, rape, robbery, assault) were not uncommon. Although one third of the offenders had two or more prior felony convictions, 42 per cent had not previously been convicted of a felony.

Most victims were killed by firearms (two thirds). The remainder were killed by a variety of methods, including stabbing, beating, and strangulation. Most killings were not of the "bizarre" type, although a few were especially heinous. One offender killed his victim by locking him in the trunk of his (the victim's) car, pouring gasoline over it, and setting it on fire. Another inmate stabbed a homosexual victim over 50 times after he discovered that the victim was an ordained minister. The inmate stated, "A man like that doesn't deserve to live."

A surprising finding was that about two thirds of the victims were total strangers to the offender. Although many studies have indicated that in three fourths of all homicides, the victim and the slayer know each other,[25] the inmates on Florida's death row most often killed strangers. These killings usually occurred during the course of some other felony, such as burglary, robbery, or rape, and the homicide was not premeditated in the usual sense of the word. Most inmates who admitted their involvement stated, "It just happened, that's all! I didn't plan to kill anybody!"

Several inmates indicated that they were unjustly convicted of first degree murder, because they had killed in the "heat of passion." As an example, one inmate killed a clerk in a convenience store because the clerk couldn't open a stuck cash register.

---

[25]See, e.g., Wolfgang, *Patterns in Homicide* (1958), and Federal Bureau of Investigation, *Uniform Crime Reports* (1975).

The inmate "got mad" and shot him in the head. Another inmate claimed self defense because he shot and killed a homeowner after the victim reached for a gun during an attempted burglary. When interviewed, the inmate said, "Look, if I didn't shoot him, he would have shot me. That's self-defense!"

One third of the killings took place in a residence, and about 20 per cent at a place of business. The remaining murders took place outdoors in streets, highways, woods, parking lots, or motor vehicles. About 60 per cent of the killings took place in counties with more than 200,000 residents; however, almost 58 per cent took place in cities or towns with populations of fewer than 100,000. It may be that some rural areas are less "tolerant" of murder than are larger metropolitan areas. For example, four death row inmates were convicted in a county having fewer than 70,000 residents.

Fourteen of the 96 death row inmates were involved in the killing of law enforcement officers. While the circumstances differed in each case, one inescapable fact seems to emerge from the records: police officers met their deaths when they suffered a lapse, however brief, in their vigilance toward the suspect.

Although almost two thirds of the offenders had one or more accomplices, most inmates have little or no understanding of accomplice liability under the criminal law that makes each participant equally responsible for a criminal act. In actual practice, however, the "triggerman" usually received a death sentence, and the accomplice(s), after plea bargaining, received life sentences or less in exchange for testifying against the death row inmate. Surprisingly, most inmates are not bitter toward their turn-coat accomplice(s), saying that "I would have done the same thing had the prosecutor offered me a deal." In some cases, however, the triggerman received a life sentence and the accomplice (who was present but did not shoot) received a death sentence. These inmates are understandably bitter toward our system of criminal justice.

Few inmates voluntarily expressed any remorse for the victim or the victim's family. Even when pressed on this point, many offenders seemed unable to muster any sympathy for the victim. A few inmates flatly expressed a view that "he (the victim) deserved to die"; or "everybody has to die sometime"; or "it just happened, that's all." Several inmates indicated that immediately after the killing they went home and slept. It is not suggested, however, that most inmates do not go through a period of remorse. Perhaps most or many did but were unable or unwilling to express such feelings for the following, or other, reasons: (1) most inmates had killed (or had been convicted of killing) total strangers; (2) most claimed to be innocent, and to express remorse for the acts of other "guilty" persons might appear to be inconsistent; (3) many inmates were told by their attorneys not to admit guilt during the pendency of their appeals—an expression of contrition might, from the inmate's viewpoint, compromise his claim of innocence; (4) many inmates are psychopathic, and a lack of remorse is compatible with this diagnosis; and (5) many inmates may have passed through a period of guilt and remorse by the time they were interviewed—many inmates have been on death row for three or four years.

An interesting finding was that 80 per cent of the offenders claimed to have been "high" at the time of the killing. The taking of drugs and alcohol immediately prior to the offense was a common occurrence. Most of the offenders who admitted to being "high" stated that they were "stoned" on marijuana and/or beer at the time of their offense, although some used other drugs, such as cocaine, barbiturates, and tranquilizers. Few scotch or champagne drinkers were found on death row. Some inmates intentionally got "high" prior to committing a burglary or robbery because it "gave them courage."

On the basis of prison psychological profiles, about 58 per cent of the inmates were classified as "normal." Diagnoses were made on the basis of personality tests, such as the Minnesota Multiphasic Personality Inventory (MMPI), and interviews with the staff psychiatrist and psychologist. Almost one fifth of the inmates were diagnosed as psychopathic, although it was felt that certain of these diagnoses were erroneously made on the basis of unusually high scores on the psychopathic scale of the MMPI. It should be noted that police officers often score high on this scale of the MMPI.[26]

---

[26]Shev, *Good Cops—Bad Cops* (1977) (psychiatric study concluding that 35 per cent of all police on duty are dangerous).

Attitudes of Death Row Inmates

Fairness of the Trial. About 80 per cent of the inmates interviewed felt that they had not received a fair trial, and most blamed the trial judge. The most common reasons given for the unfairness of the trial were that "he (the judge) denied all the defense motions," and "he wanted to see me convicted." Prosecutors were often seen as politically ambitious and in cahoots with the judge. Most inmates (three fourths) were represented by public defenders or court-appointed counsel. More than half indicated that their counsel (1) was not adequately prepared for the trial, and (2) had not previously tried a capital case. Even though 55% of the inmates rated the quality of their defense as average or above, almost 80 per cent indicated that, if retried, they would want a different attorney or would represent themselves. Surprisingly, 32 inmates (39%) rated their defense attorneys as "excellent" or "good."

Juries. Most inmates felt less hostile toward the jury than toward the judge and prosecutor. Most often, offenders saw the jury as merely reacting to the unfavorable (and "unfair") evidence presented by the overzealous and ambitious prosecutor. In some instances, the prosecutor did resort to questionable practices at trial, such as introducing glossy colored photographs of the victim or referring to the defendant as an "animal" or "beast."

Many of the black inmates convicted by all-white juries quickly pointed out that their convictions had racial implications. Most inmates, both black and white, feel that racism is prevalent in our judicial system. The facts that white jurors outnumber black jurors and that a black defendant is more likely to be convicted by an all-white jury are often cited as evidence. Almost all offenders believe that prosecutors try to obtain juries composed of elderly white persons, feeling that they are more conservative and more likely to convict than other groups. Some offenders reported that members of their jury slept during their trial, and one inmate stated that a juror was "drunk" during most of his trial. These claims could not be verified.

In about 92 per cent of the trials, between 9 and 12 of the jurors were white. About 36 per cent of the offenders were convicted by all-white juries. There were no all-black juries. The average jury in these capital cases had 4 to 5 female jurors.

Deliberations and Sentencing. In most cases (71%), the convicting jury deliberated one to three hours prior to rendering a guilty verdict; in one third of the trials, the jury reached a verdict in an hour or less. Slightly more than one half (52%) of the inmates expressed "surprise" at the guilty verdict even though they indicated that even before the verdict they felt that the proceedings had been unfair. At the sentencing phase, on the other hand, most juries recommended the death sentence after deliberating only 10 to 30 minutes; in three fourths of the cases the jury made the recommendation in less than an hour. Apparently, once the jurors decided that the accused was guilty, they had little difficulty in reaching a sentencing recommendation.[27] Two thirds of the offenders were "not surprised" at the jury's recommendation at sentencing.

In about 20 per cent of the cases, the jury recommended mercy (a life sentence), but the trial court imposed the death penalty, which is permitted under Florida law. This finding raises some serious questions about the fairness with which capital punishment is imposed. In Florida, except for sentencing, most decisions on substantive and proce-

dural questions in capital cases are group decisions involving the legislature, the grand jury, the prosecutor's office, the petit jury, the appellate courts, the Probation and Parole Commission on Clemency, and the decisions of the Executive Clemency Board, composed of the governor and his cabinet. A strong argument can be made that the initial sentencing decision in a death penalty case should rest with the petit jury, even though the judge must follow legislative guidelines in sentencing.[28] If a state intends to carry out the mandate of the legislature and execute some offenders, fairness and equity would seem to dictate that this ultimate penalty be the product of a collective decision (possibly by a group of professional jurors impaneled expressly to decide the fate of the convicted defendant) — not left to the discretion of a single judge whose personal feelings *could* play a role in the decision.

The race of the victim seems not to have been an irrelevant factor in the sentencing of the 83 Florida offenders studied. The data in Table 11.4 suggest that a disproportionate number of blacks and other minority group

[27]This is perhaps partly explained by the fact that the concurring votes of only 7 jurors are necessary for a sentencing recommendation, whereas a finding of guilt requires the concurring votes of all 12 jurors.

[28]The Florida procedure is described in *Proffitt* v. *Florida*, 428 U.S. 242 (1976), supra, § 11.03. See also Bedau, *Felony-Murder, Rape, and the Mandatory Death Penalty—A Study in Discretionary Justice*, 10 Suffolk L. Rev. 493 (1976) (arguing that the exercise of judicial discretion without adequate guidelines at the sentencing phase in capital cases is unconstitutional).

TABLE 11.4 Florida Homicides Reported 1973–1976 By Race of Victims, Offenders, and Death Row Inmates

	Florida Homicides Reported 1973–1976*	Florida Death Row Inmates: 1973–1976
Homicide Victims	Number of Victims (N = 4,406)	Killed by Death Row Inmates (N = 106)
White	2172 (49.3%)	98 (92.4%)
Black	2234 (50.7%)	8 (7.6%)
	$X^2 = 76.80$ p < .001	
Homicide Arrests	Number of Arrests (N = 3,623)	Number of Death Row Inmates (N = 80)
White	1522 (42.0%)	46 (57.5%)
Black	2101 (58.0%)	34 (42.5%)
	$X^2 = 7.081$ p < .01	

*Data from Department of Criminal Law Enforcement, State of Florida, *Crime in Florida* (1976 Annual Report) 18.

members who killed white victims received the death penalty.

During the years 1973 to 1976 whites accounted for 47.3, 48.0, 50.9, and 51.6 per cent, respectively, of murder victims; the corresponding rates for blacks were 52.7, 51.9, 49.1, and 48.1 per cent.[29] In the same period, 37.8, 38.2, 43.4, and 47.0 per cent, respectively, of persons arrested for murder were white; and 61.2, 60.9, 56.1, and 52.1 per cent were black.[30] The data in Table 11.5 indicate that while the number of blacks on death row is rather low in comparison to the number of blacks arrested for murder, the probability of receiving the death sentence is significantly higher for blacks who kill whites than for whites who kill blacks or blacks who kill blacks. However, if a white offender kills a white victim, the data implies that race does not play a significant role in sentencing.

These are tentative conclusions; the issue of racism in sentencing should be explored further. The fact that the number of blacks on Florida's death row has been substantially reduced since 1972 should not be interpreted as prima facie evidence that the State of Florida has resolved its pre-*Furman* problems.

Capital Punishment. Not surprisingly, few of the inmates interviewed had favorable attitudes toward capital punishment, although five inmates stated that they were in favor of the death penalty (although not in their own cases). Several inmates suggested that a particularly unpopular child-killer "should burn." When the inmates were asked if they had ever in the past favored capital punishment, 83.5 per cent said no, but these responses are questionable given

the lower class background of the offenders and the fact that most Americans favor the death penalty.[31]

Only 20 per cent of the inmates believe that they will eventually be executed. The responses of the remaining 80 per cent, in rating their chances, ranged from "no possibility," to "50-50 chance," to "I don't know." Surprisingly, few inmates openly expressed much anxiety about their pending executions. Most indicated that they sleep well at night and are not taking tranquilizers. Although more than half (58%) of the inmates indicated that they have considered suicide, two thirds had never attempted suicide. During the five months of this study, one inmate committed suicide by drug overdose. There were no other attempts at suicide.

When asked about methods of execution, 90 per cent indicated that electrocution is a "cruel and unusual" punishment. A few inmates pointed out that "we don't electrocute animals." More than half of the inmates indicated that, if given a choice, they would prefer to die by a drug overdose. The remaining inmates indicated that they would prefer to die by the electric chair (3.8%), gas (3.8%), shooting (11.5%), hanging (1.2%), and other methods. One inmate stated that "old age" is the most humane way to die. Two inmates wanted to fight the "Champion of the State" in hand-to-hand combat to the finish.

Rehabilitation as an Alternative to Death. The inmates were almost evenly divided over the question of whether rehabilitation is a workable goal in prisons. A common response was that rehabilitation "has never been tried" in the field of

[29] Supra note 24.
[30] Id.

[31] See note 1, supra.

TABLE 11.5   Florida Death Row Inmates By Race of Offenders and Victims Killed

Death Row Inmates	Victims Killed		
	White	*Black*	*Total*
White 46 (55.4%)	52 (49.0%)	1* (0.94%)	53 (50.0%)
Black 34 (40.9%)	40 (37.7%)	7 (6.60%)	47 (44.3%)
Others 3 (3.7%)	6 (5.7%)	0 (0.00%)	6 (5.7%)
Total N = 83 (100.0%)	98 (92.4%)	8 (7.5%)	106 (100%)
	$X^2 = 6.55$ p $< .01$		

*The sole white offender who killed a black victim also killed three white victims in a single instance.

corrections. Most inmates agreed that convicted murderers (those *actually* guilty) should spend some time in prison. Surprisingly, almost half felt that a sentence of 10 to 25 years is a just punishment for convicted murderers. However, many inmates believed a 5-year sentence would be appropriate.

Several inmates were frankly disgusted that no rehabilitation programs are employed on death row. As one inmate put it, "We need rehabilitation the most." However, few inmates could give any concrete suggestions for rehabilitation methods or goals beyond "having to work" and "learning some new skills." Several inmates are attempting to demonstrate their rehabilitation by taking Bible or other correspondence courses.

While some inmates are better candidates than others for rehabilitative programs, accurately predicting which are capable of leading productive, crime-free lives is a difficult, if not impossible, task. All but a few inmates see themselves as excellent rehabilitation candidates.

Are There Any Innocent Men on Death Row?

Because the case history of each inmate must be considered on an individual basis in terms of the factual and legal issues, and because this study was a criminological study (as opposed to a fact-finding legal research project), it is all but impossible to make any definitive conclusions regarding possibly unjust convictions of innocent inmates. We did learn that 10 inmates (12%) pleaded guilty at trial, and 16 inmates (20%) indicated during the interviews that they were guilty of first degree murder as charged. However, 63 of the inmates (74%) indicated that they were not guilty of first degree murder. Of these, a few indicated that they were guilty of, at most, second degree murder or manslaughter.

Several inmates evidenced a strong belief in their innocence. However, in most cases their "innocence" was less than convincing in light of the trial evidence. For example, one of these "innocent" inmates was convicted on the basis of the testimony of several eye witnesses and reliable physical evidence connecting him to the robbery-murder. Yet, despite his long record of violent offenses, he vehemently maintains his innocence.

It seems impossible, given the extralegal procedural safeguards attending capital cases,[32] that the criminal justice process in Florida has collapsed to the point where almost 75 per cent of the inmates on death row were wrongly convicted. Nevertheless, it cannot be stated with absolute confidence that there are no innocent inmates on death row. If there are, and if Professor Gelfand's statistical model is accurate that "for 12-member juries, the probability of convicting an innocent person is .0221" (see Chapter Seven, § 7.03) then the number of innocent inmates on death row must be quite small (statistically, fewer than two). In the event of erroneous convictions, the appellate process and executive clemency proceedings are available to right the wrong. Parenthetically, more than half the inmates believed that the percentage of erroneous convictions in capital cases is 10 per cent or less; and two inmates stated that "there are no innocent men on death row."

A Typical Week on Death Row

Death row at the Florida State Prison at Starke, Florida, consists of six rows of seventeen cells each, with two rows on each of the three floors. The rows are located on "R Wing" of the East Unit. As of August 1, 1977, 85 persons were under a death sentence in Florida (one female is held at the Women's Prison at Lowell, Florida).

A typical day begins at 5:45 A.M. when the lights are turned on. Breakfast is brought to the inmates by a "runner" (one inmate per row who lives on the row but is not under a death sentence) at around 6:30 A.M. The meals are served on metal trays and eaten

---

[32] Under Florida law, all capital cases must begin with the grand jury process. A quorum is 15 grand jurors, and the votes of 12 jurors are required for a true bill indictment. In addition, petit juries are composed of 12 persons in capital cases (6-member juries are used only in noncapital trials) and a unanimous verdict is required for conviction or acquittal. The sentencing phase is conducted at a separate hearing following conviction. The trial judge can, under legislative guidelines, overrule the recommendation of the sentencing jury. There is a mandatory appeal to the Florida Supreme Court following the imposition of the death sentence, and an automatic hearing before the Executive Clemency Board to review the sentence.

with plastic utensils. Powdered scrambled eggs and dry cereal are common breakfast items. The coffee is undrinkable.

Lunch is served at 11:30 A.M. and supper at 4:30 P.M. The diet is heavy in carbohydrates and starches. Potatoes, rice, and bread are served frequently. Common meat dishes are hamburger (solid as a brick), liver, canned ham, and beef stew. Frozen fish (sometimes literally cold) is often served on Fridays. One inmate has gained 60 pounds since he has been on the row, although some inmates who exercise in their cells are in excellent physical condition.

Each inmate is confined in an individual cell which measures 6 by 9 feet. Within the cells are a toilet (absent a seat), a small washbowl, and a bed. Each cell on death row contains a 15-inch black and white television set (supplied by the state). Many inmates keep their sets on all day even if they are not being watched. Television sets do not have to be turned off at any particular time although headphones are required after 11 P.M. In addition, inmates are allowed to have a variety of reading materials. The centerfolds of *Playboy Magazine* adorn many cell walls. Some inmates clean their cells on a regular basis; others do not.

Two times a week, inmates are permitted, one row at a time, to exercise in the recreation yard for two hours at a time. Once a week, the inmates on each row are permitted to visit with each other on the corridor (just outside their cells) for a two-hour period. Individual five-minute showers are permitted on alternate nights. Inmates spend the remainder of their time in their cells except for special occasions.

Death row inmates can see visitors in a special visitor's room from 9 A.M. to 3 P.M. on either Saturdays or Sundays. Members of the press can interview inmates in a press room (off the row) on Wednesday afternoons.

Razors and aluminum mirrors for shaving are supplied on Fridays and Mondays. Haircuts are given on the row by other inmates on request.

Each inmate is allowed to spend up to $15 a week for canteen items, such as sodas, cigarettes, and certain toilet articles. Because money is contraband in prison, such goods are bought with prison stamps. Each inmate is given 10 packs of nonfiltered "Florida Division of Corrections Industries" cigarettes per week. These cigarettes are unlike any found on the commercial market.

Death row is made of concrete and steel and is painted a dull green. In the winter it is cold. In the summer it is unbearably hot. No air conditioning or fans are available.

R Wing is generally understaffed. Usually only two or three correctional officers work the entire six rows during an eight-hour shift. Because of the staffing problem, "shakedowns" of individual cells are done only sporadically. This unhappy situation presents some security problems for the staff and researchers. Weapons such as pieces of mirror, razor blades, "shanks" (homemade knives), and "zip guns" (homemade guns) have occasionally been discovered on death row. In an isolated event, one inmate stabbed a guard in the face with a shank. During one visit we were threatened with death by an entire row of inmates for briefly speaking to an unpopular child-killer. Fortunately, the inmates were locked in their cells, although they tried to assault us with pieces of soap, feces, and several unidentified metal objects. Unhappily, the correctional officers were two floors away, and our pleas to be released from the row went unheard for 15 minutes. Needless to say, this was a traumatic experience, and it served as a reminder that life on death row can be dangerous, although assaults occur more often in other areas of the prison. No other incidents of this type occurred during the five months of the study.

Atmosphere on Death Row

One would expect the atmosphere on Death Row to be one of silent fear and introspection; however, this is not the case. Even though death row to an outsider seems grim and depressing, it isn't silent; in fact, the noise level is unusually high. Television sets and radios blare all day long. Cell doors are constantly slamming, and conversations among the inmates are often so loud that one has to shout to be heard.

As mentioned, most inmates believe that they will never be executed, and this, along with the fact that the last execution in Florida took place in 1964, helps to explain their guarded optimism. On September 12, 1977, Florida's Governor Askew signed the death warrant for inmate John Spinkellink, who was scheduled to die at 8:30 A.M. on September 19, 1977. At this writing, however, Spinkellink is under a stay of execution ordered by the federal courts. However, if an execution does take place, the atmosphere on death row is likely to become more tense and dangerous.

Cost of the Alternative of Life Imprisonment

Under Florida law, a person convicted of a capital felony and sentenced to life imprisonment must serve a minimum of 25 years before being eligible for parole.[33] In 1976, it cost the taxpayers of Florida an average of $17,000 per year to keep an inmate in prison. The present annual cost of maintaining the 85 death row inmates is $1.4 million; the cost for 25 years would exceed $36 million. Assuming a conservative 5 per cent rate of inflation, the cost of maintaining an inmate in the year 2002 could approach $50,000 per year. The cost to taxpayers of maintaining these 85 inmates (and that number could increase) over the next 25 years could well exceed $100 million. Current cost figures for execution of an inmate are not presently available. It is not suggested that a life can or should be measured in terms of dollars, even though the costs of maintaining death row inmates are substantial; the issue is raised because some proponents of capital punishment base their position on economic cost factors.

Conclusions

This study was undertaken because of a lack of information on death row inmates. It is offered neither in support nor in opposition to capital punishment; rather, it is anticipated that the reader will use this information to form his own opinion on this complex issue.

---

[33]Fla. Stat. Ann. § 775.082(1).

The facts that execution[34] will prevent a convicted murderer from ever killing again and that capital punishment, if administered rather swiftly, is less expensive than prolonged incarceration must be balanced against other considerations. The general deterrent effect of capital punishment has yet to be conclusively established and the costs of prosecution are a good deal higher for capital than for noncapital crimes. The uncertainty of behavioral predictions further confounds attempts to arrive at a consensual public opinion on the death penalty. Executing a condemned murderer denies any possibility of future societal contributions yet the alternative opens the door to potential future violence. As noted previously, this study revealed that about one third of the inmates on death row committed murder while on probation or parole. However, most of Florida's death row inmates, if resentenced to life terms, would not be eligible for parole until they are over 50 years of age. In 1976, only 6 per cent of persons arrested in Florida were over 50 and only 1 per cent were over 65.[35]

While much of the information in this "profile" is not flattering to the inmates and could provide fodder for capital punishment advocates, abolitionists and retentionists alike may draw upon an arsenal of moral and philosophical paradigms to support their contention that abolishing or retaining capital punishment does indeed comport with the "standards of decency that mark the progress of a maturing society."[36]

---

[34]For a vivid description of four Florida executions, see McLendon, *Deathwork* (1977).

[35]Supra note 24, at 107. Compare with national statistics for 1975 that indicate that 9.4 per cent of all arrests involved suspects over the age of 50, and only 1.2 per cent involved persons over age 65. Federal Bureau of Investigation, *Uniform Crime Reports* 189 (1976).

[36]*Trop* v. *Dulles,* 356 U.S. 86, 101 (1958) (opinion of Warren, C. J.).

12

EXCESSIVE BAIL AND FINES

12.01 INTRODUCTION

Bail is security, usually a sum of money, that the court requires arrested persons to post in exchange for their release from custody. Its purpose is to ensure the accused's appearance in court[1]; it is forfeited if he fails to appear. In the case of most jurisdictions and most offenses, if an accused has the cash for 10 per cent of the set bail, a professional bail bondsman will provide a surety bond (a guarantee), for the remaining 90 per cent, keeping the cash as his fee, and the accused will be released until trial.[2] State law governs the maximum fee chargeable by professional bondsmen, which may be as high as 20 per cent of the bail.[3] However, in addition to cash, bondsmen often require an accused to put up additional collateral (property subject to a lender's security interest that may be sold in the event of default) so that they will be financially protected in the event that the accused fails to appear at the next stage of the criminal process.[4] Often the accused's friends or relatives will have to put up the required collateral in the form of personal (e.g., a car) or real (e.g., land) property.[5]

Bail practices in the United States constitute a type of legal ransom.[6] Although the Supreme Court has consistently stated that the Equal Protection Clause of the Fourteenth Amendment protects the rich and poor alike (see, e.g., *Boddie* v. *Connecticut*, 401 U.S. 371 [1971]), the institution of bail illustrates most dramatically that the rich receive preferential treatment under our system of criminal justice. Bail practices provide the clearest examples of economic discrimination in the criminal process. Affluent defendants are not presumed to be more innocent than poor defendants, yet the poor, unable to purchase their freedom, languish in the often cruel environment of jail for weeks, months, or even years awaiting trial, while wealthier defendants buy their liberty and remain free to pursue their economic ventures. The familiar adage, "The rich get richer, and the poor get poorer," seems applicable when bail practices are scrutinized.

Bail Practices

If an accused is arrested for committing a misdemeanor, in most instances he can be

---

[1]See *Stack* v. *Boyle,* 342 U.S. 1 (1951), infra, § 12.02.

[2]President's Commission on Law Enforcement and the Administration of Justice, *The Courts* 37 (1967).

[3]Id.

[4]Johnson, P., *The Elements of Criminal Due Process* 57 (1975).

[5]Id.

[6]Goldfarb, R., *Ransom: A Critique of the American Bail System* (1965).

released on bail as soon as the booking process has been completed. The amount of bail is usually set according to a *bail schedule* (this is also known as *station-house bail*).[7] The amount of bail is based solely on the type of misdemeanor charged; differences in the ability of individuals to pay or the likelihood that they will appear at trial are often not taken into account. *Release on recognizance (R.O.R.)* (see Comment 4, p. 965) is available to misdemeant defendants in most jurisdictions.

If an accused is arrested without a warrant for a noncapital felony, in most instances only a magistrate may set bail. It is usually set at the initial appearance (see Chapter Two, § 2.01). Bail schedules are sometimes used by magistrates in felony cases.

If an accused is arrested for a felony under an arrest warrant, the warrant will usually specify the amount of bail. This enables defendants who can afford it to be released prior to their first appearance before a magistrate. An appeal based on "excessive bail" is permitted in most jurisdictions when it is alleged that the magistrate abused his discretion in setting bail.

Professional Bondsmen

The bondsman is a businessman whose financial success depends on his ability to predict which defendants will appear at trial. In the event of a default by the bailed accused, the bondsman can lose up to 90 per cent of the bail if he hasn't secured sufficient collateral from the accused. Because of this risk, bondsmen may refuse to post bond in doubtful cases. In the event that a bailed defendant unjustifiably fails to appear at trial, the bondsman may resort to extralegal methods and return him to the jurisdiction.[8] Failure to appear at trial is a distinct criminal charge in many jurisdictions.[9] Most defendants who fail to appear for trial and default on bail are eventually caught.

Bail in the Federal Courts

Rule 46(c) of the Federal Rules of Criminal Procedure, which governs the standards for admission to bail in the federal courts, provides:

If the defendant is admitted to bail, the amount thereof shall be such that as in the judgment of the commissioner or court or judge or justice will insure the presence of the defendant, having regard to the nature and circumstances of the offense charged, the weight of the evidence against him, the financial ability of the defendant to give bail, and the character of the defendant.

Thus in the federal courts, four factors determine the amount of bail to be set in an individual case: (1) the seriousness of the offense charged; (2) the amount of evidence in the prosecution's favor; (3) the economic resources of the defendant; and (4) the defendant's character. In actual practice, the magistrate who sets bail usually knows little about the defendant except what crime he is charged with and perhaps his police record. The recommendations of the prosecutor are accorded great weight, and little inquiry is made as to the defendant's character and circumstances.[10] In the federal system, as in most states, bail is denied in capital cases.[11]

12.02 THE SUPREME COURT AND BAIL

The Supreme Court has decided relatively few cases involving bail, mainly because the bail issue is usually moot by the time the case reaches the appellate stage of the criminal process; i.e., a verdict of guilt or innocence has already been rendered. The Eighth Amendment of the federal Constitution prohibits "excessive bail" in federal cases, but the Supreme Court has not held that guarantee to be applicable to the states through the Fourteenth Amendment Due Process Clause. However, virtually all states have a similar provision in their constitutions.

---

[7]Freed, D., and Wald, P., *Bail in the United States: 1964* (1964).

[8]Johnson, supra note 4.

[9]Federal Bail Reform Act, 18 U.S.C.A. § 3150 (infra, § 12.03).

[10]Freed and Wald, supra note 6.

[11]Federal Bail Reform Act, 18 U.S.C.A. § 3146 (infra, § 12.03).

"To Insure the Presence of the Accused"

STACK v. BOYLE

Supreme Court of the United States, 1951
342 U.S. 1, 72 S. Ct. 1, 96 L. Ed. 3

Twelve petitioners were indicted and arrested on charges of conspiring to violate the Smith Act, 18 U.S.C. (Supp. IV) §§ 371, 2385. Their initial bail was set in amounts varying from $2,500 to $100,000. Subsequently, the District Court (S.D. Calif.) fixed bail pending trial in the amount of $50,000 for each petitioner. The petitioners moved to reduce bail, arguing that it was "excessive" within the meaning of the Eighth Amendment. The only evidence offered by the government was a certified record showing that four other persons previously convicted under the Smith Act in another district (New York) had forfeited bail, and no evidence relating them to the petitioners was produced. The district court denied the motion, and the petitioners filed for habeas corpus relief in the same court. Those writs were also denied and the Court of Appeals (9th Cir.) affirmed. Petitioners then filed with Mr. Justice Douglas an application for bail and an alternative application for habeas corpus seeking interim relief. Both applications were referred to the Supreme Court. The Court granted review on a subsequent petition for certiorari.

Mr. Chief Justice VINSON delivered the opinion of the Court.

* * *

First. From the passage of the Judiciary Act of 1789, 1 Stat. 73, 91, to the present Federal Rules of Criminal Procedure, Rule 46(a)(1), federal law has unequivocally proved that a person arrested for a non-capital offense *shall* be admitted to bail. This traditional right to freedom before conviction permits the unhampered preparation of a defense, and serves to prevent the infliction of punishment prior to conviction. . . . Unless his right to bail before trial is preserved, the presumption of innocence, secured only after centuries of struggle, would lose its meaning.

The right to release before trial is conditioned upon the accused's giving adequate assurance that he will stand trial and submit to sentence if found guilty. . . . Like the ancient practice of securing the oaths of responsible persons to stand as sureties for the accused, the modern practice of requiring a bail bond or the deposit of a sum of money subject to forfeiture serves as additional assurance of the presence of an accused. Bail set at a figure higher than an amount reasonably calculated to fulfill this purpose is "excessive" under the Eighth Amendment. . . .

Since the function of bail is limited, the fixing of bail for any individual defendant must be based upon standards relevant to the purpose of assuring the presence of that defendant. The traditional standards as expressed in the Federal Rules of Criminal Procedure are to be applied in each case to each defendant. In this case petitioners are charged with offenses under the Smith Act and, if found guilty, their convictions are subject to review with the scrupulous care demanded by our Constitution. . . . Upon final judgment of conviction, petitioners face imprisonment of not more than five years and a fine of not more than $10,000. It is not denied that bail for each petitioner has been fixed in a sum much higher than that usually imposed for offenses with like penalties and yet there has been no factual showing to justify such action in this case. The Government asks the courts to depart from the norm by assuming, without the introduction of evidence, that each petitioner is a pawn in a conspiracy and will, in obedience to a superior, flee the jurisdiction. To infer from the fact of indictment alone a need for bail in an unusually high amount is an arbitrary act. Such conduct would inject into our own system of government the very principles of totalitarianism which Congress was seeking to guard against in passing the statute under which petitioners have been indicted.

If bail in an amount greater than that usually fixed for serious charges of crimes is required in the case of any of the petitioners, that is a matter to which evidence should be directed in a hearing so that the constitutional rights of each petitioner may be preserved. In the absence of such a showing, we are of the opinion that the fixing of bail before trial in these cases cannot be squared with the statutory and constitutional standards for admission to bail.

Second. The proper procedure for challenging bail as unlawfully fixed is by motion for reduction of bail and appeal to the Court of Appeals from an order denying such motion. Petitioner's motion to reduce bail did not merely invoke the discretion of the District Court setting bail within a zone of reasonableness, but challenged the bail as violating statutory and constitutional standards. As there is no discretion to refuse to reduce excessive bail, the order denying the motion to reduce bail is appealable as a "final decision" of the District Court under 28 U.S.C. (Supp. IV) §§ 1291. Cohen v. Beneficial Loan Corp., 337 U.S. 541, 545–547 (1949). In this case, however, petitioners did not take an appeal from the order of the District Court denying their motion for reduction of bail. Instead, they presented their claims under the Eighth Amendment in applications for writs of habeas corpus. While habeas corpus is an appropriate remedy for one held in custody in violation of the Constitution, 38 U.S.C. (Supp. IV) § 2241(c)(3), the District Court should withhold relief in this collateral habeas corpus action where an adequate remedy available in the criminal proceeding has not been exhausted. . . .

The Court concludes that bail has not been fixed by proper methods in this case and that petitioners' remedy is by motion to reduce bail, with right of appeal to the Court of Appeals. Accordingly, the judgment of the Court of Appeals is vacated and the case is remanded to the District Court with directions to vacate its order denying petitioners' applications for writs of habeas corpus and to dismiss the applications without prejudice. Petitioners may move for reduction of bail in the criminal proceeding so that a hearing may be held for the purpose of fixing reasonable bail for each petitioner.

* * *

Mr. Justice JACKSON, whom Mr. Justice FRANKFURTER joins.

I think the principles governing allowance of bail have been misunderstood or too casually applied in these cases and that they should be returned to the Circuit Justice or the District Courts for reconsideration in the light of standards which it is our function to determine. We have heard the parties on only four specific questions relating to bail before conviction — two involving considerations of law and of fact which should determine the amount of bail, and two relating to the procedure for correcting any departure therefrom. I consider first the principles which govern release of accused persons upon bail pending their trial.

The practice of admission to bail, as it has evolved in Anglo-American law, is not a device for keeping persons in jail upon mere accusation until it is found convenient to give them a trial. On the contrary, the spirit of the procedure is to enable them to stay out of jail until a trial has found them guilty. Without this conditional privilege, even those wrongly accused are punished by a period of imprisonment while awaiting trial and are handicapped in consulting counsel, searching for evidence and witnesses, and preparing a defense. To open a way of escape from this handicap and possible injustice, Congress commands allowance of bail for one under charge of any offense not punishable by death, Fed. Rules Crim. Proc. 46(a)(1) providing: "A person arrested for an offense not punishable by death shall by admitted to bail . . ." before conviction.

Admission to bail always involves a risk that the accused will take flight. That is a calculated risk which the law takes as the price of our system of justice. We know that Congress anticipated that bail would enable some escapes, because it provided a procedure for dealing with them. Fed. Rules Crim. Proc., 46(f).

In allowance of bail, the duty of the judge is to reduce the risk by fixing an amount reasonably calculated to hold the accused available for trial and its consequence. Fed. Rules Crim. Proc., 46(c). But the judge is not free to make the sky the limit, because the Eighth Amendment to the Constitution says: "Excessive bail shall not be required. . . ."

Congress has reduced this generality in providing more precise standards, stating that ". . . the amount thereof shall be such as in the judgment of the commissioner or court or judge or justice will insure the presence of the defendant, having regard to the nature and circumstances of the offense charged, the weight of the evidence against him, the financial ability of the defendant to give bail and the character of the defendant." Fed. Rules Crim. Proc., 46(c).

These statutory standards are not challenged as unconstitutional, rather the amounts of bail established for these petitioners are alleged to exceed these standards. We submitted no constitutional questions to argument by the parties, and it is our duty to avoid constitutional issues if possible. For me, the record is inadequate to say what amounts would be reasonable in any particular one of these cases and I regard it as not the function of this Court to do so. Furthermore, the whole Court agrees that the remedy pursued in the circumstances of this case is inappropriate to test the question and bring it here. But I do think there is a fair showing that these congressionally enacted standards have not been correctly applied.

It is complained that the District Court fixed a uniform blanket bail chiefly by consideration of the nature of the accusation and did not take into account the difference in circumstances between different defendants. If this occurred, it is a clear violation of Rule 46(c). Each defendant stands before the bar of justice as an individual. Even on a conspiracy charge defendants do not lose their separateness or identity. While it might be possible that these defendants are identical in financial ability, character and relation to the charge—elements Congress has directed to be regarded in fixing bail—I think it violates the law of probabilities. Each accused is entitled to any benefits due to his good record, and misdeeds or a bad record should prejudice

only those who are guilty of them. The question when application for bail is made relates to each one's trustworthiness to appear for trial and what security will supply reasonable assurance of his appearance.

Complaint further is made that the courts below have been unduly influenced by recommendations of very high bail made by the grand jury. It is not the function of the grand jury to fix bail, and its volunteered advice is not governing. Since the grand jury is a secret body, ordinarily hearing no evidence but the prosecution's, attended by no counsel except the prosecuting attorneys, it is obvious that it is not in a position to make an impartial recommendation. Its suggestion may indicate that those who have heard the evidence for the prosecution regard it as strongly indicative that the accused may be guilty of the crime charged. It could not mean more than that without hearing the defense, and it adds nothing to the inference from the fact of indictment. Such recommendations are better left unmade, and if made should be given no weight.

But the protest charges, and the defect in the proceedings below appears to be, that, provoked by the flight of certain Communists after conviction, the Government demands and public opinion supports a use of the bail power to keep Communist defendants in jail before conviction. Thus, the amount is said to have been fixed not as a reasonable assurance of their presence at the trial, but also as an assurance that they would remain in jail. There seems reason to believe that this may have been the spirit to which the courts below have yielded, and it is contrary to the whole policy and philosophy of bail. This is not to say that every defendant is entitled to such bail as he can provide, but he is entitled to an opportunity to make it in a reasonable amount. I think the whole matter should be reconsidered by the appropriate judges in the traditional spirit of bail procedure.

The other questions we have heard argued relate to the remedy appropriate when the standards for amount of bail are misapplied. Of course, procedural rights so vital cannot be without means of vindication. In view of the nature of the writ of habeas corpus, we should be reluctant to say that under no circumstances would it be appropriate. But that writ will best serve its purpose and be best protected from discrediting abuse if it is reserved for cases in which no other procedure will present the issues to the courts. Its use as a substitute for appeals or as an option alternative to other remedies is not to be encouraged. Habeas corpus is not, in the absence of extraordinary circumstances, the procedure to test reasonableness of bail.

* * *

It is my conclusion that an order denying reduction of bail is to be regarded as a final decision which may be applied to the Court of Appeals. But this is not because every claim of excessive bail raises a constitutional question. It is because we may properly hold appeal to be a statutory right. While only a sentence constitutes a final *judgment* in a criminal case, Berman v. United States, 302 U.S. 211, 212, it is a final *decision* that Congress has made reviewable. 28 U.S.C. § 1291. . . .

I cannot agree, however, that an order determining what amount of bail is reasonable under the standards prescribed does not call for an exercise of discretion. The Court of Appeals is not required to re-examine every order complained of. They represent exercises of discretion upon questions, usually, of fact. Trivial differences or frivolous objections would be dismissed. The Appellate Court should only reverse for clear abuse of discretion or other mistake of law. And it ought to be noted that this Court will not exercise its certiorari power in individual cases except where they are typical of a problem so important and general as to deserve the attention of the supervisory power.

* * *

Having found that the habeas corpus proceeding was properly dismissed by the District Court, in which its judgment was affirmed by the Court of Appeals, we should to that extent affirm. Having thus decided that the procedure taken in this case is not the proper one to bring the question of excessiveness of bail before the courts, there is a measure of inconsistency and departure from usual practice in our discussion of matters not before us. Certainly it would be inappropriate to say now that any particular amount as to any particular defendant is either reasonable or excessive. That concrete amount, in the light of each defendant's testimony and that of the Government, should be fixed by the appropriate judge or Justice upon evidence relevant to the standards prescribed. . . .

* * *

[Mr. Justice MINTON took no part in the consideration or decision of this case.]

The Illinois Cash-Deposit System

SCHILB v. KUEBEL

Supreme Court of the United States, 1971
404 U.S. 357, 92 S. Ct. 479, 30 L. Ed. 2d 502

John Schilb, the petitioner, was arrested and charged with (a) leaving the scene of an automobile accident, and (b) obstructing traffic. Bail was fixed at $500 on the first charge and $250 on the second charge. In accordance with the Illinois bail statutes of 1963, petitioner deposited $75 in cash with the clerk of the court. This amount was 10 per cent of the aggregate bail. At his trial, Schilb was acquitted of the first charge and convicted of the second. When he paid his fine, the amount petitioner deposited was returned to him less $7.50 retained as "bail bond costs" pursuant to the bail statute. The amount returned was 1 per cent of the total bail and 10 per cent of the amount actually deposited. In a subsequent class action, Schilb challenged the Illinois bail system on Fourteenth Amendment due process and equal protection grounds. The Circuit Court of St. Clair County upheld the statute and dismissed the complaint. The Supreme Court of Illinois affirmed, with two justices dissenting. Schilb appealed to the United States Supreme Court.

Mr. Justice BLACKMUN delivered the opinion of the Court.

* * *

I

* * *

Prior to 1964 the professional bail bondsman system with all its abuses was in full and odorous bloom in Illinois. Under that system the bail bondsman customarily collected the maximum fee (10% of the amount of the bond) permitted by statute, . . . and retained that entire amount even though the accused fully satisfied the conditions of the bond. . . . Payment of this substanial "premium" was required of the good risk as well as of the bad. The results were that a heavy and irretrievable burden fell upon the accused, to the excellent profit of the bondsman, and that professional bondsmen, and not the courts, exercised significant control over the actual workings of the bail system.

One of the stated purposes of the new bail provisions in the 1963 Code was to rectify this offensive situation. The purpose appears to have been accomplished. It is said that the bail bondsman abruptly disappeared in Illinois "due primarily to the success of the ten percent bail deposit provision." . . .

II

Article 110 of the 1963 Code, as it read at the time Schilb was arrested and charged, provided that an eligible accused could obtain pretrial release in one of three ways:

(1) Under § 110–2 he may be released, on his personal recognizance.

(2) Under § 110–7 he may execute a bail bond and deposit with the clerk cash equal to only 10% of the bail or $25, whichever is the greater. When bail is made in this way and the conditions of the bond have been performed, the clerk returns to the accused 90% of the sum deposited. The remaining 10% (1% of the bail) is retained by the clerk "as bail bond costs."

(3) Under § 110–8 he may execute a bail bond and secure it by a deposit with the clerk of the full amount of the bail in cash, or in stocks and bonds authorized for trust funds in Illinois, or by unencumbered nonexempt Illinois real estate worth double the amount of the bail. When bail is made in this way and the conditions of the bond have been performed, the clerk returns the deposit of cash or stocks or bonds, or releases the real estate, as the case may be, without charge or retention of any amount.

In each case bail is fixed by a judicial officer. Section 110–5 prescribes factors to be considered in fixing the amount of bail. Under § 110–6 either the State or the defendant may apply to the court for an increase or for a reduction in the amount of bail or for alteration of the bond's conditions.

The choice between § 110–7 and § 110–8 is reserved to the accused. . . .

The parties have stipulated that when bail in a particular case is fixed, the judge's "discretion in such respect is not guided by statute, rule of court or any definite, fixed standard; various and diverse judges in fact fix the amount of bail for the same types of offenses at various and diverse amounts, without relationship as to guilt or innocence of the particular defendant in a criminal charge, and without relationship of the particular offense charged and the bail fixed." They have also stipulated, "The actual cost of administering the provisions of said Sections 110–7 and 110–8 are substantially the same but there may probably be a slightly greater cost in the administration of Section 110–8."

III

The Court more than once has said that state legislative reform by way of classification is not to be invalidated merely because the legislative moves one step at a time. "The prohibition of the Equal Protection Clauses goes no further than the invidious discrimination." . . . "Legislatures are presumed to have acted constitutionally . . . and their statutory classifications will be set aside only if no grounds can be conceived to justify them. . . . With this much discretion, a legislature traditionally has been allowed to take reform 'one step at a time, addressing itself to the phase of the problem which seems most acute to the legislative mind.' " . . . The measure of equal protection has been described variously as whether "the distinctions drawn have some basis in practical experience," . . . or whether the legislature's action falls short of "the invidious discrimination," . . . or whether "any state of facts reasonably may be conceived to justify" the statutory discrimination, . . . or whether the classification is "on the basis of criteria wholly unrelated to the objective of [the] statute." . . . But the Court also has refined this traditional test and has said that a statutory classification based upon suspect criteria or affecting "fundamental rights" will encounter equal protection difficulties unless justified by a "*compelling* governmental interest." . . .

Bail, of course, is basic to our system of law, . . . and the Eighth Amendment's proscription of excessive bail has been assumed to have application to the States through the Fourth Amendment. Pilkinton v. Circuit Court, 324 F.2d 45, 46 (8th Cir. 1963). . . . But we are not at all concerned here with any fundamental right to bail or with any Eighth Amendment–Fourteenth Amendment question of bail excessiveness. Our concern, instead, is with the 1% cost-retention provision. This smacks of administrative detail and of procedure and is hardly to be classified as a "fundamental" right or as based upon any suspect criterion. The applicable measure, therefore, must be the traditional one: Is the distinction drawn by the statutes invidious and without rational basis? . . .

IV

With this background, we turn to the appellants' primary argument. It is three-fold: (1) that the 1% retention charge under § 110–7(f) is imposed on only one segment of the class gaining pretrial release; (2) that it is imposed on the poor and nonaffluent and not on the rich and affluent; and (3) that its imposition with respect to an accused found innocent amounts to a court cost assessed against the not-guilty person.

We are compelled to note preliminarily that the attack on the Illinois bail statutes, in a very distinct sense, is paradoxical. The benefits of the new system, as compared with the old, are conceded. And the appellants recognize that under the pre-1964 system Schilb's particular bail bond cost would have been 10% of his bail, or $75; that this premium price for his pretrial freedom, once paid, was irretrievable; and that, if he could not have raised the $75, he would have been consigned to jail until his trial. Thus, under the old system the cost of Schilb's pretrial freedom was $75, but under the new it was only $7.50. While acknowledging this obvious benefit of the statutory reform, Schilb and his coappellants decry the classification the statutes make and present the usual argument that the legislation must be struck down because it does not reform enough.

A

It is true that no charge is made to the accused who is released on his personal recognizance. We are advised, however, that this was also true under the old (pre-1964) system and that "Illinois has never charged people out on recognizance." Thus, the burden on the State with respect to a personal recognizance is no more under the new system than what the State had assumed under the old. Also, with a recognizance, there is nothing the State holds for safekeeping, with resulting responsibility and additional paperwork. All this provides a rational basis for distinguishing between the personal recognizance and the deposit situations.

There is also, however, no retention charge to the accused who deposits the full amount of cash bail or securities or real estate. Yet the administrative cost attendant upon the 10% deposit and that upon the full deposit are, by the stipulation, "substantially the same" with, indeed, any higher cost incurred with respect to the full deposit.

This perhaps is a more tenuous distinction, but we cannot conclude that it is constitutionally vulnerable. One who deposits securities or encumbers his real estate precludes the use of that property for other purposes. And one who deposits the full amount of his bail in cash is dispossessed of a productive asset throughout the period of the deposit; presumably, at least, its interim possession by the State accrues to the benefit of the State. Further, the State's protection against the expenses that inevitably are incurred when bail is jumped is greater when 100% cash or securities or real estate is deposited or obligated than when only 10% of the bail amount is advanced. The Joint Committee's and the State Legislature's decision in balancing these opposing considerations in the way that they did cannot be described as lacking in rationality to the point where equal protection considerations require that they be struck down.

* * *

B

The poor man–affluent-man argument centers, of course, in Griffin v. Illinois, 351 U.S. 12 (1956), and in the many later cases that "reaffirm allegiance to the basic command that justice be applied equally to all persons." . . .

In no way do we withdraw today from the Griffin principle. That remains steadfast. But it is by no means certain, as the appellants suggest, that the 10% deposit provision under § 110–7 is a provision for the benefit of the poor and the less affluent and that the full-deposit provision of § 110–8 is one for the rich and the more affluent. It should be obvious that the poor man's real hope and avenue for relief is the personal recognizance provision of § 110–2. We do not presume to say, as the appellants in their brief intimate, that § 110–2 is not utilized by Illinois judges and made available for the poor and the less affluent.

Neither is it assured, as the appellants also suggest, that the affluent will take advantage of the full-deposit provision of § 110–8, with no retention charge, and that the less affluent are relegated to the 10% deposit provision of § 110–7 and the 1% retention charge. The record is silent, but the flow indeed may be the other way. The affluent, more aware of and more experienced in the marketplace, may see the advantage, in these days of high interest rates, in retaining the use of 90% of the bail amount. A 5% or greater return on this 90% in a short period of time more than offsets the 1% retention charge. In other words, it is by no means clear that the route of § 110–8 is more attractive to the affluent defendant than the § 110–7 route. The situation, therefore, wholly apart from the fact that appellant Schilb himself has not pleaded indigency, is not one where we may assume that the Illinois plan works to deny relief to the poor man merely because of his poverty.

C

The court-cost argument is that the person found innocent but already "put to the expense, disgrace and anguish of a trial" is "then assessed a cost for exercising his right to release pending trial." Giaccio v. Pennsylvania, 382 U.S. 399 (1966), is cited. Giaccio was a holding that an ancient Pennsylvania statute that permitted the jury to impose court costs upon an acquitted defendant, in order to offset the expenses of prosecution, violated the Due Process Clause because of vagueness and the absence of any standards preventing the arbitrary imposition of costs. The Court thus did not reach the merits, although Mr. Justice STEWART and Mr. Justice FORTAS, each separately concurring, . . . felt that the very imposition of costs upon an acquitted defendant was violative of due process.

Giaccio is not dispositive precedent for the appellants here. Certainly § 110–7 is not subject to attack for vagueness or for lack of standards. Neither is it a vehicle for the imposition of costs of prosecution as was the Pennsylvania statute. Instead, § 110–7 authorizes retention of the 1% as "bail bond costs." This is what that description implies, namely, an administrative cost imposed upon all those, guilty and innocent alike, who seek the benefit of § 110–7. This conclusion is supported by the presence of the long-established Illinois rule against the imposition of costs of prosecution upon an acquitted or discharged criminal defendant, Wells v. McCullock, 13 Ill. 606 (1852), and by the Illinois court's own determination that the charge under § 110–7(f) is an administrative fee and not a cost of prosecution imposed under Ill. Rev. Stat., c. 38, § 180–3 (1969), only upon the convicted defendant.

V

Finally, the appellants would point out that Article 110 has its federal counterpart in § 3(a) of the Bail Reform Act of 1966, . . . and in particular in that portion now codified as 18 U.S.C. § 3146(a)(3). They note that S. 2840, 88th Cong., 2d Sess., contained a 1% retention provision "to defray bond costs" but that a parallel bill, S. 1357, 89th Cong., 1st Sess., as it progressed through Congress, at no time has a provision of that kind. . . .

The committee reports . . . accompanying the 1966 Act, and the debates . . . make no reference to this change from the earlier S. 2840. In the face of this silence, and without more, and being cognizant of the fact that the federal act, unlike the Illinois one was not directed against the professional bail bondsman, we are not inclined to read constitutional implications into the absence of the retention provision in the Bail Reform Act of 1966.

* * *

VI

We refrain from nullifying this Illinois statute that, with its companion sections, has brought reform and needed relief to the State's bail system. The judgment of the Supreme Court of Illinois is affirmed.

* * *

[Mr. Justice MARSHALL concurred in the result.]

Mr. Justice DOUGLAS, dissenting.

* * *

The commercial bail bondsman has long been an anathema to the criminal defendant seeking to exercise his right to pretrial release. In theory, courts were to set such amounts and conditions of bonds as were necessary to secure the appearance of defendants at trial. . . . Those who did not have the resources to post their own bond were at the mercy of the bondsman who could exact exorbitant fees and unconscionable conditions for acting as surety. . . . Criminal defendants often paid more in fees to bondsmen for securing their release than they were later to pay in penalties for their crimes. . . .

Moreover, the commercial bond system failed to provide an incentive to the defendant to comply with the terms of his bond. Whether or not he appeared at trial, the defendant was unable to recover the fee he had paid to the bondsman. . . .

It was in response to the abuses and inequities of the commercial bonding system that Illinois enacted the statutory scheme now under attack. The Supreme Court of Illinois indicated "that the central purpose of the legislature . . . was to severely restrict the activities of professional bail bondsmen who customarily collected 10% of the amount of a bond as a fee which was retained whether or not the conditions of the bond were met by the accused." . . .

Those defendants who under the old system had utilized the services of the profes-

sional bondsman are now required to post with the clerk of the court 10% of the face amount of their bonds in order to win their release. The significant difference, however, is that upon satisfaction of the terms of their bonds, § 110–7 now allows them to recover 90% of the amount deposited, while no such recovery was ever had from the commercial bondsman. Rather than paying a fee of 10% of the face amount of the bond, therefore, the cost is now only 1%.

* * *

I do not reach the question of equal protection but rest by decision on the issue stirred, but not decided in Giaccio v. Pennsylvania, 382 U.S. 399 (1966). . . . Giaccio involved a state statute which directed juries "in all cases of acquittals" to determine whether the government or the defendant should pay the costs. . . . We held the Act unconstitutional on grounds of vagueness. Mr. Justice STEWART, concurring, said: "In the present case it is enough for me that Pennsylvania allows a jury to punish a defendant after finding him not guilty. That, I think, violates the most rudimentary concept of due process of law." . . .

Mr. Justice Fortas also concurred, saying: "In my opinion, the Due Process Clause of the Fourteenth Amendment does not permit a State to impose a penalty or costs upon a defendant whom the jury has found not guilty of any offense with which he has been charged." . . . That is my view on the merits in the instant case.

Some costs are the unavoidable consequences of a system of government which is required to proceed against its citizens in a public trial in an adversary proceeding. Yet I see no basis for saying that an accused must bear the costs incurred by the Government in its unsuccessful prosecution of him. Imposition of costs upon individuals who have been acquitted has long been eschewed by our courts. . . . Where there is such uniform condemnation of a practice as onerous as the imposition of costs upon acquitted defendants, cf. Leland v. Oregon, 343 U.S. 790, 798 (1952), I would conclude, with Justices STEWART and Fortas in Giaccio, that it violates due process.

It is, however, said that the 1% charge is not "a vehicle for the imposition of costs of prosecution" and that it is merely "an administrative cost imposed upon all those, guilty and innocent alike, who seek the benefit of § 110-7.". . . The costs of administering the bail system occur, by definition, only during the course of criminal prosecutions. They are as much an element of the costs of conducting criminal cases as the prosecutor's salary, the fee for docketing an appeal, or the per diem paid to jurors. Nor does the rubric "administrative" require a contrary result. If this were the talisman through which a State could impose its costs upon acquitted defendants, I could see no stopping point and we might be left with a system in which an acquittal might be nearly as ruinous to the defendant as a conviction.

* * *

I would reverse this judgment insofar as it imposed bail bond costs under the criminal charges of which members of the class represented by appellant were acquitted and remand for further proceedings respecting the bail bond costs on the charges on which they were convicted.

Mr. Justice STEWART, with whom Mr. Justice BRENNAN concurs, dissenting.

* * *

It is common ground that the Illinois bail reform scheme reflects an admirable attempt to reduce the cost of liberty for those awaiting trial. Chapter 38, § 110-7(f), does arbitrarily discriminate, however, against the appellant and those similarly situated. As this Court said in Rinaldi v. Yeager, 384 U.S. 305 (1966):

"The Equal Protection Clause requires more of a state law than nondiscriminatory application within the class it establishes. It also imposes a requirement of some rationality in the nature of the class singled out. . . . [L]egislation may impose special burdens upon defined classes in order to achieve permissible ends. But the Equal Protection Clause does require that, in defining a class subject to legislation, the distinctions that are drawn have 'some relevance to the purpose for which the classification is made.'" Id., at 308–309 (citations omitted).

The Court assumes that the rationality of § 110-7(f)'s classification should be analyzed in relation to the purpose of ending the evils created by the bail bond system. However, while ending those evils is the aim of the whole bail reform, it is not the aim of §

110-7(f) itself. Rather, the appellees have acknowledged that the purpose of § 110-7(f) is to cover administrative costs; they have also acknowledged in oral argument that the financial burden on the State is probably as great or greater for those who use the other methods of obtaining pretrial release. Can the appellees constitutionally justify the selective imposition of administrative costs? I think not.

The Illinois Supreme Court held that there can be no unconstitutional discrimination in the state system of bail release, since each person accused has a choice of method for obtaining pretrial release. . . . Those who deposit 10%, said the court, "are not automatically placed in this class . . . by the law. They join only by the exercise of their own volition." Whether many persons accused of crime can really choose between paying 10% or paying the full amount (or securing double the amount in real estate) is highly debatable. But however that may be, it is clear that not every person accused of a crime is free to choose to be released on his own recognizance. Yet those who are fortunate enough to be so released need to pay no costs whatever.

The appellees argue that those who pay only 10% are being given a benefit that justifies imposing a burden. The appellees say that such persons are not required to put up the full amount of the bail set and that the 1% such persons do ultimately pay is a boon by comparison to the 10% of required bail that they would have automatically forfeited to the bondsman under the old procedures governing bail. This justification, however, also fails to distinguish between the "ten-percenters" and those who are released on their own recognizance. Obviously, those released on their own recognizance receive an even greater benefit than those who deposit 10%, since they give no money to the State at any time if they meet the conditions of release.

The appellees attempt to distinguish between those released on their own recognizance and the "ten-percenters" by noting that the recognizance practice is "historic," whereas the cost-retention provision was recently enacted to end the evils spawned by bail bondsmen. This distinction, however, does not confront the reality that both classes of persons receive benefits and only one class must pay administrative costs. A second attempt to distinguish between those released on their own recognizance and those who deposit 10% turns on the idea that the members of the former class are more "worthy" of the benefit they receive and therefore may rationally be required to pay less. But while the criteria used by judges to determine release on one's own recognizance—e.g., length of residence in the jurisdiction, marital status, employment record, or past criminal record—are obviously relevant to the recognizance decision, they are not rationally related to the decision to impose purely administrative costs, especially when such costs are at least as great for those released on their own recognizance as for those required to post bond.

Given the infirmities in the asserted justifications for § 110-7(f), I think the imposition of administrative costs on only one class of those persons seeking pretrial release violates the Equal Protection Clause of the Fourteenth Amendment. . . .

Comments

1. In *Stack* v. *Boyle,* supra, the Supreme Court held that "the fixing of bail for any individual defendant must be based upon standards relevant to the purpose of assuring the presence of the defendant." Since the magistrate in setting bail must, in effect, guess whether the accused will appear at trial, should the standards enumerated in Rule 46(c) Fed. R. Crim. Proc., supra, be given equal weight? Aren't most magistrates likely to give more consideration to the seriousness of the crime charged and the accused's prior criminal record than to the economic resources of the accused or the weight of the prosecutor's evidence? If a magistrate sets bail accordingly, has he necessarily denied the accused his right against "excessive bail"? What bail would be "excessive" for a group of radical Ph.D. physics professors charged with conspiracy to blow up New York City with a hydrogen bomb (a noncapital offense)? Suppose the professor-defendants had limited economic resources and no prior records and the prosecutor's evidence was, at the time of bail setting, entirely circumstantial. In all jurisdictions, forcible rape of an adult woman is not a capital offense. What bail would be "excessive" for a defendant accused of raping ten college coeds? Ten young children? Should a magistrate be required to state for the record his reasons for setting a particular bail? Few jurisdictions have such a requirement. Does an accused have a constitutional right to be given reasons for the specified bail?

The *Stack* Court held that $50,000 bail for each defendant was excessive in that case because the prosecution was unable to demonstrate the unreliability of the defendants. How would the prosecution go about showing a serious risk of flight by a defendant? By producing evidence of a prior flight? The vast majority of defendants released on bail appear at trial, Kaplan, J., and Waltz, J., *The Trial of Jack Ruby* (1965), principally because (1) the accused knows that he will probably be caught if he flees; (2) evidence of an accused's flight is relevant and admissible at trial to prove guilt; and (3) the accused knows that the probability of being acquitted will be substantially diminished if he flees.

Chief Justice Vinson, writing for the majority in *Stack,* noted that bail serves the following functions: (1) it allows a defendant an opportunity to adequately prepare his defense; (2) it preserves the presumption of innocence; and (3) it prevents the infliction of punishment prior to trial. May a court deny bail in capital cases? The constitutionality of forbidding bail for a capital offense has never been tested in the Supreme Court. Is a restriction constitutional when the Eighth Amendment makes no distinction between capital and noncapital crimes?

2. In *Schilb* v. *Kuebel,* supra, the Court upheld the constitutionality of the Illinois cash-deposit system on due process and equal protection grounds. Interestingly, the Court did not take the opportunity in *Schilb* to discuss bail practices and their needed reform, although the Court did express its approval of the Illinois legislation. Do you agree with Mr. Justice Douglas (dissenting) that assessment of the 1 per cent fee is a denial of due process because it amounts to an imposition of court costs against defendants subsequently acquitted? Wasn't the intent of the Illinois legislative bail reform to eliminate some of the abuses of the professional bondsmen system and to lower the costs of bail by tenfold to persons who were not released on recognizance or could not pay under the full-deposit provision? Isn't it stretching the point to label the § 110–7 1 per cent fee as "court costs" imposed on the acquitted? Was the majority of the Court in *Schilb* suggesting that the petitioner should not "look a gift horse in the mouth," since his costs under the former Illinois bail system would have been $75, while under the reform system they were only $7.50?

   What is the "rational basis" for the Illinois statute's classifying accused persons according to the method of release they employed, i.e., (1) personal recognizance (no fee), (2) full-deposit (no additional fee) and (3) § 110–7(f) (1% of deposit retained)? Does the classification amount to invidious discrimination as Justices Stewart and Brennan (dissenting) claimed?

3. In *Bandy* v. *United States,* 81 S. Ct. 197, 5 L. Ed. 2d 218 (1960), Mr. Justice Douglas, sitting as an individual circuit justice, considered an application for a reduction in bail. In criticizing the bail system, he wrote, "[T]his theory [of bail] is based on the assumption that a defendant has property. To continue to demand a substantial bond which the defendant is unable to secure raises considerable problems for the equal administration of the law. . . . It would be unconstitutional to fix excessive bail to assure that a defendant will not gain his freedom. . . . Yet in the case of an indigent defendant, the fixing of bail even in a modest amount may have the practical effect of denying him release. . . . Imprisoned, a man may have no opportunity to investigate his case, to cooperate with his counsel, to earn the money that is still necessary for the fullest use of his right to appeal."

4. In 1927, Arthur Lawton Beeley, in his classic study, *The Bail System in Chicago,* examined bail practices in the municipal court and criminal court of Cook County, Illinois. Beeley found that the setting of the amount of bail in Chicago was based on arbitrary standards; that consideration of individual factors in setting bail was rare. He also found that 50 per cent of the pretrial detainees were too poor to pay the required bail. Beeley's study revealed the following facts about these pretrial detainees who were unable to post bail: (1) 90 per cent were residents of Chicago at the time of arrest, and 33 per cent had lived in Chicago all their lives; (2) 60 per cent were living with their immediate families or close relatives at the time of arrest; (3) 50 per cent were first offenders; and (4) 50 per

cent were regularly employed. Beeley concluded that 28 per cent of these pretrial detainees were "good risks" and should have been released prior to trial because of their close ties to the community.

In 1954, a study of bail practices in Philadelphia was conducted by Caleb Foote. Note, 102 U. Pa. L. Rev. 1031. Professor Foote found that (1) three fourths of all defendants charged with a serious offense did not make bail; (2) 27 per cent of defendants not charged with serious offenses were unable to pay bail; (3) the majority (53%) of defendants unable to obtain pretrial release did not spend any time in jail after their trial; and (4) 20 per cent of those unable to pay bail were acquitted. Foote concluded that an inability to obtain pretrial release was closely correlated with a finding of guilt at trial.

In 1957, Professor Foote conducted another bail study, this time in New York City. 106 U. Pa. L. Rev. 693. The results were similar to those of the Philadelphia study. For example, 58 per cent of the pretrial detainees could not afford to pay the requisite bail; and 54 per cent of the defendants who were released prior to trial on bail received suspended sentences, while only 13 per cent of the pretrial detainees received suspended sentences.

Perhaps the best known study of bail practices is the Manhattan Bail Project undertaken by the Vera Foundation and staff members and law students from New York University. 38 N.Y.U. L. Rev. 67 (1963). The study sought to explore the feasibility of *release on one's own recognizance* (R.O.R.) in New York City (called "pretrial parole" in that city). The researchers hypothesized that substantially more defendants could be released on personal recognizance if certain verified information on these defendants was available to the courts at the time of bail determination. Offenders whose bail had not yet been set were interviewed to determine if they might be good risks for pretrial release. Five criteria were used to make the initial determination: (1) present or recent residence at the same address for six months or more; (2) current employment or recent employment for six months or more; (3) relatives in New York City with whom contact is maintained; (4) no previous criminal conviction; and (5) residence in New York City for ten years or more. If the defendant claimed to meet one of the five criteria (or to partially meet two of the five), the information was verified. A final determination and recommendation for R.O.R. was based on such factors as the defendant's past and present employment, family relationships, residence patterns, character references, present criminal charges, and previous criminal record.

Between October 16, 1961, and September 20, 1962, the researchers recommended 363 persons for R.O.R.; of these, the court released 215 (60 per cent). Only 14 per cent of the offenders in the control group were released (those about whom no information or recommendations were given to the court but who qualified for R.O.R. under the criteria for the study). Thus four times as many defendants were released on their own recognizance than would have been without the project's verified information. Of the 215 defendants released on the basis of the project's recommendations, only 3 failed to appear (less than 1 per cent). In contrast, of 1,395 bailed defendants randomly selected in 1960 prior to the project, 101, or 7 per cent, failed to appear at trial.

Other findings by the Manhattan Bail Project were similar to those of earlier studies. For example, 64 per cent of the detainees were convicted and imprisoned, in contrast to 53 per cent of those released prior to trial; and less than 1 per cent failed to show up at trial. The project's conclusions were that (1) bail is used to punish defendants; (2) the principal criterion used by the courts in setting bail is the present crime charged and factors relating to the defendant's ties to the community are largely ignored; (3) bail is used to insure detention in order to satisfy public demands; and (4) a defendant's ability to pay bail is one of the least important factors to the courts.

In another New York study, Anne Rankin found that only 17 per cent of bailed defendants were ultimately imprisoned, while 64 per cent of those unable to make bail were imprisoned following sentencing. In addition, 36 per cent of bailed defendants received suspended sentences, in contrast to 9 per cent of the detained defendants. 39 N.Y.U. L. Rev. 641 (1964).

These studies clearly indicate that many defendants are unnecessarily detained in jail prior to trial because they are unable to afford bail. Most defendants released prior to trial, whether on bail or on their own recognizance, appear at trial. The studies demonstrate that when certain background information on detainees is verified, they can be recommended as good risks to the court, and that these R.O.R. defendants have a substantially higher rate of appearance at trial than do cash-bailed defendants. Yet, as the Manhattan Bail Project noted, most judges put more weight on other factors than on likelihood of flight when setting bail.

5. In many instances the formal arrest of a defendant may not be necessary, especially if the crime charged is a relatively minor property offense or traffic or local code violation or there is little danger of flight by the accused. One such form of pretrial release is the *citation,* or *summons,* procedure, which allows the arresting officer to choose between giving an offender a citation or summons at the scene of the crime or formally arresting him. The procedure is used in several cities including, Oakland, California, New Haven, Connecticut, and Evanston, Illinois. Usually, the use of citations is restricted to nonviolent misdemeanors, and evidence of the defendant's ties to the community is the most important factor in deciding whether or not to give a citation in place of a formal arrest.

The advantages of a citation or summons procedure over formal arrest and its attendant consequences are that (1) it eliminates the economic discrimination inherent in the bail system; (2) it allows a defendant to be released shortly after his apprehension without judicial intervention; (3) it saves the many police man-hours required for arrests; and (4) it requires no cash deposit by the offender.

6. Under the present bail system, many defendants are detained in jail prior to trial without sufficient consideration of their background, likelihood of flight, or potential dangerousness. One study reported that only 17 per cent of all defendants released prior to trial were rearrested on other charges (counting both felony and misdemeanor bail recidivism charges), and most of these arrests occurred more than two months after pretrial release. *Preventive Detention: An Empirical Analysis,* Harv. Civil Rights L. Rev. 294 (1971).

A number of states and the federal government have taken

steps to reform bail practices. The Federal Bail Reform Act of 1966 (infra, § 12.03) is often cited as model legislation.

7. Consider the following bail problems: Should first-degree murder defendants who do not face capital punishment nevertheless be denied bail? See *State* v. *Pray*, 346 A. 2d 227 (Vt. 1975) (holding no). Should bail applicants be permitted to refute evidence of their dangerousness before bail is set? See *United States* v. *Wind*, 527 F.2d 672 (6th Cir. 1976) (holding yes). Should a county be permitted to retain 10 per cent of the cash bail bond sums posted by defendants? See *Board of Vanderburg County Commissioners* v. *Farris*, 342 N.E.2d 642 (Ind. App. 1976) (holding yes). May a state, under a bail reform act, abolish professional bail bondsmen? See *Stephens* v. *Bonding Assoc. of Kentucky*, 538 S.W.2d 580 (Ky. 1976) (yes). Is there a constitutional right to bail after conviction? See *Critchlow* v. *State*, 346 N.E.2d 591 (Ind. 1976) (holding no). In accord is *State* v. *Ryan*, 359 A.2d 657 (Vt. 1976). Before conviction, who should have the burden of proving why bail should or should not be granted — the prosecutor or the defendant? See *State* v. *Azure*, 241 N.W.2d 699 (N.D. 1976) (burden on prosecutor). In accord is *Martinez* v. *Superior Court*, 548 P.2d 1198 (Ariz. App. 1976) and *Ex parte Cevallos*, 537 S.W.2d 744 (Tex. Cr. App. 1976). May a defendant charged with aggravated robbery be denied bail because he had previously been convicted of two felonies? See *Ex parte Smith*, 548 S.W.2d 410 (Tex. Cr. App. 1977) (holding yes). May a trial court place the burden on the defendant to demonstrate that bail pending appeal is proper? See *State* v. *Marini*, 369 A.2d 202 (N.H. 1977) (yes). Is evidence that the accused presents a danger to the community relevant in determining the amount of bail? See *Carman* v. *State*, 564 P.2d 361 (Alaska 1977) (yes).

12.03 THE FEDERAL BAIL REFORM ACT OF 1966, 18 U.S.C.A. §§ 3146–3150

§ 3146. Release in noncapital cases prior to trial

(a) Any person charged with an offense, other than an offense punishable by death, shall, at his appearance before a judicial officer, be ordered released pending trial on his personal recognizance or upon the execution of an unsecured appearance bond in an amount specified by the judicial officer, unless the officer determines, in the exercise of his discretion, that such a release will not reasonably assure the appearance of the person as required. When such a determination is made, the judicial officer shall, either in lieu of or in addition to the above methods of release, impose the first of the following conditions of release which will reasonably assure the appearance of the person for trial or, if no single condition gives that assurance, any combination of the following conditions:

(1) place the person in the custody of a designated person or organization agreeing to supervise him;

(2) place restrictions on the travel, association, or place of abode of the person during the period of release;

(3) require the execution of an appearance bond in a specified amount and the deposit in the registry of the court, in cash or other security as directed, of a sum not to exceed 10 per centum of the amount of the bond, such deposit to be returned upon the performance of the conditions of release;

(4) require the execution of a bail bond with sufficient solvent sureties, or the deposit of cash in lieu thereof; or

(5) impose any other condition deemed reasonably necessary to assure appearance

as required, including a condition requiring that the person return to custody after specified hours.

(b) In determining which conditions of release will reasonably assure appearance, the judicial officer shall, on the basis of available information, take into account the nature and circumstances of the offense charged, the weight of the evidence against the accused, the accused's family ties, employment, financial resources, character and mental condition, the length of his residence in the community, his record of convictions, and his record of appearance at court proceedings or of flight to avoid prosecution or failure to appear at court proceedings.

(c) A judicial officer authorizing the release of a person under this section shall issue an appropriate order containing a statement of the conditions imposed, if any, shall inform such person of the penalties applicable to violations of the conditions of his release and shall advise him that a warrant for his arrest will be issued immediately upon any such violation.

(d) A person for whom conditions of release are imposed and who after twenty-four hours from the time of the release hearing continues to be detained as a result of his inability to meet the conditions of release, shall, upon application, be entitled to have the conditions reviewed by the judicial officer who imposed them. Unless the conditions of release are amended and the person is thereupon released, the judicial officer shall set forth in writing the reasons for requiring the conditions imposed. A person who is ordered released on a condition which requires that he return to custody after specified hours shall, upon application, be entitled to a review by the judicial officer who imposed the condition. Unless the requirement is removed and the person is thereupon released on another condition, the judicial officer shall set forth in writing the reasons for continuing the requirement. In the event that the judicial officer who imposed conditions of release is not available, any other judicial officer in the district may review such conditions.

(e) A judicial officer ordering the release of a person on any condition specified in this section may at any time amend his order to impose additional or different conditions of release: *Provided*, That, if the imposition of such additional or different conditions results in the detention of the person as a result of his inability to meet such conditions or in the release of the person on a condition requiring him to return to custody after specified hours, the provisions of subsection (d) shall apply.

(f) Information stated in, or offered in connection with, any order entered pursuant to this section need not conform to the rules pertaining to the admissibility of evidence in a court of law.

(g) Nothing contained in this section shall be construed to prevent the disposition of any case or class of cases by forfeiture of collateral security where such disposition is authorized by the court.

§ 3147. Appeal from conditions of release

(a) A person who is detained, or whose release on a condition requiring him to return to custody after specified hours is continued, after review of his application pursuant to section 3146(d) or section 3147(e) by a judicial officer, other than a judge of the court having original jurisdiction over the offense with which he is charged or a judge of a United States court of appeals or a Justice of the Supreme Court, may move the court having original jurisdiction over the offense with which he is charged to amend the order. Said motion shall be determined promptly.

(b) In any case in which a person is detained after (1) a court denies a motion under subsection (a) to amend an order imposing conditions of release, or (2) conditions of release have been imposed or amended by a judge of the court having original jurisdiction over the offense charged, an appeal may be taken to the court having appellate jurisdiction over such court. Any order so appealed shall be affirmed if it is supported by the proceedings below. If the order is not so supported, the court may remand the case for a further hearing, or may, with or without additional evidence, order the person released pursuant to section 3146(a). The appeal shall be determined promptly.

§ 3148. Release in capital cases or after conviction

A person (1) who is charged with an offense punishable by death, or (2) who has been convicted of an offense and is either awaiting sentence or has filed an appeal or a petition for a writ of certiorari, shall be treated in accordance with the provisions of section 3146 unless the court or judge has reason to believe that no one or more conditions of release will reasonably assure that the person will not flee or pose a danger to any other person or to the community. If such a risk of flight or danger is believed to exist, or if it appears that an appeal is frivolous or taken for delay, the person may be ordered detained. The provisions of section 3147 shall not apply to persons described in this section: *Provided,* That other rights to judicial review of conditions of release or orders of detention shall not be affected.

§ 3149. Release of material witnesses

If it appears by affidavit that the testimony of a person is material in any criminal proceeding, and if it is shown that it may become impracticable to secure his presence by subpena, a judicial officer shall impose conditions of release pursuant to section 3146. No material witness shall be detained because of inability to comply with any condition of release if the testimony of such witness can adequately be secured by deposition, and further detention is not necessary to prevent a failure of justice. Release may be delayed for a reasonable period of time until the deposition of the witness can be taken pursuant to the Federal Rules of Criminal Procedure.

§ 3150. Penalties for failure to appear

Whoever, having been released pursuant to this chapter, willfully fails to appear before any court or judicial officer as required, shall, subject to the provisions of the Federal Rules of Criminal Procedure, incur a forfeiture of any security which was given or pledged for his release, and, in addition, shall, (1) if he was released in connection with a charge of felony, or while awaiting sentence or pending appeal or certiorari after conviction of any offense, be fined not more than $5,000 or imprisoned not more than five years, or both or (2) if he was released in connection with a charge of misdemeanor, be fined not more than the maximum provided for such misdemeanor or imprisoned for not more than one year or both or (3) if he was

released for appearance as a material witness, shall be fined not more than $1,000 or imprisoned for not more than one year, or both.

12.04 EXCESSIVE FINES

The use of fines for punishment is quite common in the United States, not only for misdemeanor and traffic offenses, but also for many serious offenses. For example, a Missouri statute authorizes imprisonment or a fine of up to $500 following a manslaughter conviction. 40 Mo. R.S. § 559.140 (1939). Fines are used both to satisfy the community's desire for revenge against the offender and to provide additional revenue to the jurisdiction. Although the United States Supreme Court has often said that "there can be no equal justice where the kind of trial a man gets depends on the amount of money he has," *Griffin* v. *Illinois,* 351 U.S. 12, 19 (1956) (opinion by Black, J.), 47 states and the federal government provide for imprisonment of those offenders who cannot pay imposed fines. Failure to pay fines has become a major reason for imprisonment; most jurisdictions today operate on a philosophy of "pay or go to jail." Although debtor's prisons were long ago abolished in the United States, the imprisonment of those too poor to pay their fines produces quasi-debtor's prisons.

A few jurisdictions (e.g., California and New York) permit the payment of fines in installments; this avoids the expense of maintaining the offender in jail and his family on state welfare. In some countries, such as Cuba and Sweden, the amount of the fine is assessed according to the offender's ability to pay. If adopted in the United States, such an arrangement could result in a type of inverse discrimination wherein the rich would be fined a large amount and the poor little or nothing for the same offense. Ultimately, this could lead to an abolition of fines as punishment, and all offenders who did not receive suspended or probationary sentences would go to jail, further burdening our already overcrowded jails.

The United States Supreme Court has ruled on the constitutionality of fines on only a few occasions. *Williams* v. *Illinois,* 399 U.S. 235 (1970), infra, is one of these cases.

The "Statutory Ceiling" Limitation

WILLIAMS v. ILLINOIS

Supreme Court of the United States, 1970
399 U.S. 236, 90 S. Ct. 2018, 26 L. Ed. 2d 586

The appellant, Willie Williams, was convicted in an Illinois court for petty theft (a misdemeanor) and was sentenced to a maximum term of one year's imprisonment and a $500 fine. Court costs of $5 were also imposed. Under Illinois law if a defendant failed to pay the fine and court costs by the end of his prison term, he was required to remain in jail to "work off" the fine at a rate of $5 a day. Because Williams was unable to pay the $505 fine assessed, he was held in jail for an additional 101 days beyond the maximum term authorized for petty theft. The Illinois courts rejected Williams' allegation that he was denied the equal protection of the law because of his inability to pay. Williams appealed to the United States Supreme Court, which noted probable jurisdiction.

Mr. Chief Justice BURGER delivered the opinion of the Court.

This appeal from Illinois presents an important question involving a claim of discriminatory treatment based upon financial inability to pay a fine and court costs imposed in a criminal case. The narrow issue raised is whether an indigent may be continued in confinement beyond the maximum term specified by statute because of his failure to satisfy the monetary provisions of the sentence. . . .

The custom of imprisoning a convicted defendant for nonpayment of fines dates back to medieval England and has long been practiced in this country. At the present time almost all States and the Federal Government have statutes authorizing incarceration under such circumstances. Most States permit imprisonment beyond the maximum term allowed by law, and in some there is no limit on the length of time one may serve for nonpayment. While neither the antiquity of a practice nor the fact of steadfast legislative and judicial adherence to it through the centuries insulates it from constitutional attack, these factors should be weighed in the balance. Indeed, in prior cases this Court seems to have tacitly approved incarceration to "work off" unpaid fines. See Hill v. Wampler, 298 U.S. 460 (1936); Ex parte Jackson, 96 U.S. 727 (1878).

The need to be open to reassessment of ancient practices other than those explicitly mandated by the Constitution is illustrated by the present case, since the greatly increased use of fines as a criminal sanction has made nonpayment a major cause of incarceration in this country. Default imprisonment has traditionally been justified on the ground that it is a coercive device to ensure obedience to the judgment of the court. Thus, commitment for failure to pay has not been viewed as a part of the punishment or as an increase in the penalty; rather, it has been viewed as a means of enabling the court to enforce collection of money that a convicted defendant was obligated by the sentence to pay. The additional imprisonment, it has been said, may always be avoided by payment of the fine.

We conclude that when the aggregate imprisonment exceeds the maximum period fixed by the statute and results directly from an involuntary nonpayment of a fine or court costs we are confronted with an impermissible discrimination that rests on ability to pay, and accordingly, we vacate the judgment below.

Griffin v. Illinois, 351 U.S. 12 (1956), marked a significant effort to alleviate discrimination against those who are unable to meet the costs of litigation in the administration of criminal justice. . . . In the years since the Griffin case the Court has had frequent occasion to reaffirm allegiance to the basic command that justice be applied equally to all persons. Subsequent decisions of this Court have pointedly demonstrated that the passage of time has heightened rather than weakened the attempts to mitigate the disparate treatment of indigents in the criminal process. Applying the teaching of the Griffin case here, we conclude that an indigent criminal defendant may not be imprisoned in default of payment of a fine beyond the maximum authorized by the statute regulating the substantive offense.

A State has wide latitude in fixing the punishment for state crimes. Thus, appellant does not assert that Illinois could not have appropriately fixed the penalty, in the first instance, at one year and 101 days. Nor has the claim been advanced that the sentence imposed was excessive in light of the circumstances of the commission of this particular offense. However, once the State has defined the outer limits of incarceration necessary to satisfy its penological interests and policies, it may not then subject a certain class of convicted defendants to a period of imprisonment beyond the statutory maximum solely by reason of their indigency.

It is clear, of course, that the sentence was not imposed upon appellant because of his indigency but because he had committed a crime. And the Illinois statutory scheme does not distinguish between defendants on the basis of ability to pay fines. But, as we said in Griffin v. Illinois, supra, "a law nondiscriminatory on its face may be grossly discriminatory in its operation." Id., at 17 n.11. Here the Illinois statute as applied to Williams works an invidious discrimination solely because he is unable to pay the fine. On its face the statute extends to all defendants an apparently equal opportunity for limiting confinement to the statutory maximum simply by satisfying a money judgment. In fact, this is an illusory choice for Williams or any indigent who, by definition, is without funds. Since only a convicted person with access to funds can avoid the increased imprisonment, the Illinois statute in operative effect exposes only indigents to the risk of imprisonment beyond the statutory maximum. By making the maximum confinement contingent upon one's ability to pay, the State has visited different consequences on two categories of persons since the result is to make incarceration in excess of the statutory maximum applicable only to those without the requisite resources to satisfy the money portion of the judgment.

The mere fact that an indigent in a particular case may be imprisoned for a longer time than a non-indigent convicted of the same offense does not, of course, give rise to a violation of the Equal Protection Clause. Sentencing judges are vested with wide discretion in the exceedingly difficult task of determining the appropriate punishment in the countless variety of situations that appear. The Constitution permits qualitative differences in meting out punishment and there is no requirement that two persons convicted of the same offense receive identical sentences. Thus it was that in Williams v. New York, 337 U.S. 241, 247 (1949), we said: "The belief no longer prevails that every offense in a like legal category calls for an identical punishment without regard to the past life and habits of a particular offender."

Nothing in today's decision curtails the sentencing prerogative of a judge because, as noted previously, the sovereign's purpose in confining an indigent beyond the statutory maximum is to provide a coercive means of collecting or "working out" a fine. After having taken into consideration the wide range of factors underlying the exercise of his sentencing function, nothing we now hold precludes a judge from imposing on an indigent, as on any defendant, the maximum penalty prescribed by law.

It bears emphasis that our holding does not deal with a judgment of confinement for nonpayment of a fine in the familiar pattern of alternative sentence of "$30 or 30 days." We hold only that a State may not constitutionally imprison beyond the maximum duration fixed by statute a defendant who is financially unable to pay a fine. A statute permitting a sentence of both imprisonment and fine cannot be parlayed into a longer term of imprisonment than is fixed by the statute since to do so would be to accomplish indirectly as to an indigent that which cannot be done directly. We have no occasion to reach the question whether a State is precluded in any other circumstances from holding an indigent accountable for a fine by use of a penal sanction. We hold only that the Equal Protection Clause of the Fourteenth Amendment requires that the statutory ceiling placed on imprisonment for any substantive offense be the same for all defendants irrespective of their economic status.

The State is not powerless to enforce judgments against those financially unable to pay a fine; indeed, a different result would amount to inverse discrimination since it would enable an indigent to avoid both the fine and imprisonment for nonpayment whereas other defendants must alway suffer one or the other conviction.

It is unnecessary for us to canvass the numerous alternatives to which the State by legislative enactment—or judges within the scope of their authority—may resort in order to avoid imprisoning an indigent beyond the statutory maximum for involuntary nonpayment of a fine or court costs. Appellant has suggested several plans, some of which are already utilized in some States, while others resemble those proposed by various studies. The State is free to choose from among the variety of solutions already proposed and, of course, it may devise new ones.

We are not unaware that today's holding may place a further burden on States in administering criminal justice. Perhaps a fairer and more accurate statement would be that new cases expose old infirmities which apathy or absence of challenge has permitted to stand. But the consitutional imperatives of the Equal Protection Clause must have priority over the comfortable convenience of the status quo. "Any supposed administrative inconvenience would be minimal, since . . . [the unpaid portion of the judgment] could be reached through the ordinary processes of garnishment in the event of default." Rinaldi v. Yeager, 384 U.S. 305, 310 (1966).

Nothing we hold today limits the power of the sentencing judge to impose alternative sanctions permitted by Illinois law; the definition of such alternatives, if any, lies with the Illinois courts.

Vacated and remanded.

[Mr. Justice HARLAN wrote a concurring opinion.]

[Mr. Justice BLACKMUN took no part in the consideration or decision of this case.]

Comment

1. *Williams* v. *Illinois,* supra, makes it clear that an indigent cannot be sentenced to a term of imprisonment beyond the "statutory ceiling" for the offense because of inability to pay a fine. What if Williams had been sentenced to six months' imprisonment and a $500 fine and was incarcerated for an additional six months because of his inability to pay the fine? The *Williams* decision would not seem to impose a bar on this type of sentencing. Suppose Williams could pay the $505 fine but refused to do so on the ground that he was innocent. Does *Williams* preclude an aggregate sentence beyond the "statutory ceiling" under all conditions? What are the implications of Chief Justice Burger's statement in *Williams* that "the mere fact that an indigent in a particular case may be imprisoned for a longer time than a non-indigent convicted of the same offense does not, of course, give rise to a violation of the Equal Protection Clause"? Does that mean that a judge may sentence a defendant to $50 or 50 days in jail and imprison him if he cannot pay the fine? In *Tate* v. *Short*, 401 U.S. 395 (1971) (Chapter Four, § 4.04), the Court held that an indigent defendant may not be jailed solely because of his indigency. In light of the *Williams-Tate* decisions, may a judge consistent with the Equal Protection Clause impose a "pay the fine, or go to jail" sentence on indigent defendants?

13

GUILTY PLEAS AND THE
PLEA BARGAINING PROCESS

A plea of guilty . . . is itself a conviction. More is not required, the Court has nothing to do but give judgment and sentence.[1]

13.01 INTRODUCTION

Despite the controversy surrounding the plea bargaining process in the United States,[2] most criminal defendants (up to 95 per cent in some jurisdictions[3]) plead guilty—almost always in exchange for some benefit conferred by the prosecution. As Professor Lloyd Weinreb has noted, "Conviction by guilty plea is normal and a trial the exception."[4] Although the practice of plea bargaining originated in seventeenth century Engalnd, its widespread use in the United States was not officially acknowledged until the last dozen or so years.[5] Today the negotiated plea is the principal method of disposing of criminal cases in the United States.[6]

Legal Consequences of Pleading Guilty

Certain legal consequences follow a voluntary guilty plea by a criminal defendant. First, a plea of guilty results in a criminal conviction—as though the defendant had been adjudicated guilty at the conclusion of a

---

[1]*Kercheval* v. *United States,* 274 U.S. 220, 223 (1927).

[2]Rosett, A., and Cressey, D., *Justice by Consent* (1976).

[3]Kress, J., *The Agnew Case: Policy, Prosecution and Plea Bargaining,* 10 Crim. L. Bull. 80–82 (1974).

[4]Weinreb, L., *Denial of Justice* 71–72 (1977).

[5]Bond, J., *Plea Bargaining and Guilty Pleas* 11–12 (1975). See also Note, *Plea Bargaining in Historical Perspective,* 23 Buffalo L. Rev. 499, 512–524 (1974).

---

[6]The legal historian Sir James Stevens has described the early English plea bargaining system as follows: "If a person accused of any crime . . . chose to plead guilty and to offer up his accomplices he was handed over to the coroner before whom he confessed his guilt and accused a certain number of other persons and the king might grant him life and limb if he would deliver the country from a number of malefactors either 'by his body' (i.e., by killing them upon battle wages), or 'by the country' (i.e., by convicting them before a jury), or 'by flight.' If he failed to fulfill the conditions imposed upon him, he was hanged on his own condition." Stephen, J., *Criminal Procedure from the Thirteenth to the Eighteenth Century, 2 Select Essays in Anglo-American Legal History* 485 (1908).

trial. Second, the collateral consequences following a conviction, especially a felony, usually include the loss of certain civil rights.[7] Third, a guilty plea in most jurisdictions precludes the defendant from raising any nonjurisdictional defects (e.g., illegality of an arrest or search and seizure, involuntariness of a confession) in the proceedings on appeal.[8] As the Supreme Court has said:

> Once the defendant chooses to bypass the orderly procedure for litigating his constitutional claims in order to take the benefits, if any, of a plea of guilty, the State acquires a legitimate expectation of finality in the conviction thereby obtained.[9]

In the few states that permit such collateral attacks on appeal following a guilty plea (e.g., New York, California), such claims are cognizable in federal habeas corpus proceedings.[10] Finally, by pleading guilty a defendant waives his constitutional right to a jury trial, to present defense witnesses, to cross-examine prosecution witnesses, and to remain silent.[11]

Appellate review following a guilty plea is largely restricted to colorable claims by the defendant that the record fails to show that his plea was not "the product of such factors as misunderstanding, duress, or misrepresentation by others";[12] that the prosecutor did not fulfill an essential term of the plea bargaining agreement;[13] that the advice received amounted to a denial of the effective assistance of counsel;[14] that the plea was not voluntary or intelligent;[15] or that the sentence imposed exceeded the statutory limits of the crime for which the defendant was convicted.[16] By and large, appellate courts, and especially the Supreme Court, have not been receptive to collateral attacks following a guilty plea.[17]

Plea Bargaining Inducements

The successful implementation of the plea bargaining process requires a quid pro quo arrangement between the prosecutor and the defendant.[18] Frequently, the defendant does not bargain from a position of strength, and the only benefit he can confer by pleading guilty is saving the prosecution the time and expense of a trial and foreclosing any risk of acquittal. Sometimes, however, the prosecutor wants or needs the defendant's testimony at subsequent trials of accomplices, and he may be willing to accommodate the plea bargaining requests by a defendant in return for his testimony. But as every prosecutor knows, lapses of memory by defendant-witnesses at subsequent trials of accomplices are not uncommon, and as a safeguard, the trial judge will usually postpone sentencing of the defendant until the accomplices' trials have been completed.

The "benefit" most frequently offered a defendant by the prosecutor is a *charge reduction*, which in most cases automatically reduces the possible maximum sentence. As noted by one scholar:

> Such felonies as robbery, burglary, and rape are cut down to petty larceny, assault and battery, and contributing to the delinquency of a minor.

---

[7]See Chapter Nine, § 9.04.

[8]*Lefkowitz* v. *Newsome*, 420 U.S. 283, 289 (1975).

[9]*Lefkowitz* v. *Newsome*, 420 U.S. 283, 289 (1975). See also *Tollett* v. *Henderson*, 411 U.S. 258, 267 (1973): "A guilty plea represents a break in the chain of events which has preceded it in the criminal process. When a criminal defendant has solemnly admitted in open court that he is in fact guilty of the offense with which he is charged, he may not thereafter raise independent claims relating to the deprivation of constitutional rights that occurred prior to entry of the guilty plea."

[10]*Lefkowitz* v. *Newsome*, 420 U.S. 283 (1975).

[11]*Boykin* v. *Alabama*, 395 U.S. 238 (1969) (infra, § 13.02).

[12]*Blackledge* v. *Allison*, 97 S. Ct. 1621, 1629 (1977).

[13]*Santobello* v. *New York*, 404 U.S. 257 (1971) (infra, § 13.02).

[14]*Dukes* v. *Warden*, 406 U.S. 250 (1972); *Tollett* v. *Henderson*, 411 U.S. 258 (1973).

[15]*Boykin* v. *Alabama*, 395 U.S. 238 (1969) (infra, § 13.02). See also *McCarthy* v. *United States*, 394 U.S. 459 (1969).

[16]See Chapter Fourteen, § 14.01.

[17]See, e.g., *Brady* v. *United States*, 397 U.S. 742 (1970) (infra § 13.02); *McMann* v. *Richardson*, 397 U.S. 759 (1970); *Parker* v. *North Carolina*, 397 U.S. 790 (1970); *Tollett* v. *Henderson*, 411 U.S. 258 (1973); *Dukes* v. *Warden*, 406 U.S. 250 (1972); *North Carolina* v. *Alford*, 400 U.S. 25 (1970) (infra, § 13.02); *Hutto* v. *Ross*, 97 S. Ct. 202 (1976).

[18]Plea bargaining inducements are thoroughly discussed in Bond, J., *Plea Bargaining and Guilty Pleas* 15–21 (1975) and Newman, D., *Conviction: The Determination of Guilt or Innocence Without Trial* (1966).

Crimes which carry penalties such as twenty years or life ... are punished with as little as thirty days in the county jail.[19]

The *charge dismissal* is the second most commonly offered benefit. By obtaining dismissal of one or more related charges, the defendant avoids the possibility of multiple convictions and longer sentences. Sometimes the prosecutor will agree not to press additional criminal charges that could subject the defendant to more severe punishment under a habitual offender statute.

The *sentence recommendation* is the third most commonly offered benefit. The prosecutor agrees to recommend to the sentencing judge a particular sentence such as probation or a fine. Unless the judge has played a role in the plea negotiations, the recommendation is not binding on the court; however, judges usually follow the sentencing recommendations of prosecutors following plea negotiations.

Other prosecutorial plea bargaining inducements include (1) a promise not to prosecute the defendant's accomplices; (2) a stipulation that the defendant serve in the armed forces; (3) a promise not to oppose probation or a suspended sentence; (4) a promise to recommend that the defendant serve his sentence in a particular rehabilitation program; and (5) a promise that the defendant will be adjudicated in a juvenile court. The range of prosecutorial inducements is broad.

In exchange, the defendant may promise (1) to forego appeals; (2) to cooperate with the police; (3) to supply additional information to the prosecutor; or (4) to testify as a witness in a subsequent trial.

The average defendant who pleads guilty usually receives a lighter sentence than he would had he exercised his constitutional right to a trial and been convicted.[20] Many courts have concluded that such sentencing differentials have a "chilling effect" on the exercise of a defendant's constitutional rights.[21] The United States Supreme Court has not, to date, addressed this issue.

These sentencing differentials have been justified on various grounds: Some judges believe (often erroneously) that an acknowledgment of guilt by a defendant is the first step in his rehabilitation.[22] Many judges assume that most defendants who testify at trial commit perjury.[23] Others believe that sentencing differentials are deterrents to frivolous defenses in the face of overwhelming evidence of guilt.[24] Most important, the chance for a lighter sentence is the main inducement for plea bargaining: The overriding interest of most defendants who plead guilty is to minimize their punishment[25] — and most are successful.

It should be noted that the mitigation of punishment through plea bargaining may be of secondary importance to a defendant. For example, he may plead guilty because he wishes to begin serving his sentence immediately to avoid a possibly long preconviction delay and to hasten the date of his

---

[19]Dash, S., *Cracks in the Foundation of Criminal Justice*, 46 Ill. L. Rev. 385, 393 (1951). Having recently served as a Special Assistant State Attorney for the State of Florida, the senior author can state that the sentences imposed following a plea bargaining arrangement are often light: e.g., probation following conviction for vehicular homicide; armed robbery and assault reduced to simple robbery and sentence of 30 days in jail; 105 year maximum possible sentence for multiple burglaries but actual sentence of 3 years with 2 years suspended.

[20]See, e.g., Newman, D., *Conviction: The Determination of Guilt or Innocence Without Trial* 216 (1966); Bond., J., *Plea Bargaining and Guilty Pleas* 40 (1975); Ferguson, *The Role of the Judge in Plea Bargaining,* 15 Crim. L.Q. 26, 50–51 (1972). See also *Dewey* v. *United States,* 268 F.2d 124, 128 (8th Cir. 1959) (court takes "judicial notice of the fact that trial courts quite generally impose a lighter sentence on pleas of guilty than in cases where the accused pleaded not guilty but has been found guilty by a jury").

[21]E.g., *United States* v. *Stockwell,* 472 F.2d 1186, 1187 (9th Cir. 1973) (imposition of additional punishment "for taking the court's time with a trial" chills the defendant's constitutional rights). But see *People* v. *Merchant,* 283 N.E.2d 721 (Ill. 1972) (no coercion where judge admonished defendant that he might get more "time" if he went to trial).

[22]*Santobello* v. *New York,* 404 U.S. 260, 261 (1972) (infra, § 13.02) (pleading guilty "enhances whatever may be the rehabilitative prospects of the guilty when they are ultimately imprisoned").

[23]*Poteet* v. *Fauver,* 517 F.2d 393 (3d Cir. 1975) (sentencing judge may not increase defendant's sentence merely because judge believes defendant lied).

[24]Bond, J., supra note 5, at 44.

[25]Weinreb, L., supra note 4, at 75.

release or because he wants to avoid the social stigma that often attends a public trial.

If the defendant is out on bail pending trial, the prosecutor must offer a more attractive bargain. Such a defendant is often not willing to give up his freedom in exchange for a guilty plea because delaying the trial may have certain advantages for him: A substantial delay between arrest and trial may weaken the state's case as memories fade and witnesses disappear. Moreover, while on bail, the defendant may be able to build a good record of employment and behavior. Finally, most defendants who are able to make bail usually can afford retained counsel, who do not feel the administrative pressures to plea bargain as do public defenders, who must work with the prosecutors on a daily basis and are interested in maintaining good working relationships.

Whatever inducements are offered by the prosecutor, the bargain is usually attractive enough that the defendant will accept the offer. However, in most jurisdictions, a prosecutor is never required to plea bargain, and the policies of the prosecutor usually dictate the extent of plea bargaining in a particular jurisdiction.

The Constitutionality of Plea Bargaining

The precise question of the constitutionality of plea bargaining has not, to date, been addressed by the Supreme Court. However, dicta in its decisions have suggested that plea negotiations are an "essential component of the administration of justice"[26] and, under appropriate safeguards, do not run afoul of the Constitution.

The benefits of plea negotiations have been described recently by the Supreme Court:

The defendant avoids extended pre-trial incarceration and the anxieties and uncertainties of a trial; he gains a speedy disposition of his case, the chance to acknowledge his guilt, and a prompt start in realizing whatever potential there may be for rehabilitation. Judges and prosecutors conserve vital and scarce resources. The public is protected from the risks posed by those charged with criminal offenses who are at large on bail while awaiting completion of criminal proceedings.[27]

This and other pronouncements on plea negotiations seem to indicate that the Court favors curtailment of appellate review following a valid judgment and sentence. As noted by the Court, "To allow indiscriminate hearings in federal postconviction proceedings . . . would eliminate the chief virtues of the plea system—speed, economy, and finality."[28]

Although the National Advisory Commission on Criminal Justice Standards and Goals has recommended that the plea bargaining process be totally abolished by 1978,[29] it is likely that prosecutors, defendants, and the courts will continue to rely heavily on plea negotiations in the administration of justice. The increasing case loads and backlogs in the courts leave little room for bureaucratic autonomy, judicial efficiency, and significant judicial reform under our system of adversary justice without the use of plea bargaining. Perhaps if certain offenses were decriminalized and judicial resources were markedly increased, plea bargaining could be substantially reduced. Opponents of plea negotiations should remember that because of the safeguards which attend this process the defendant does have his "day in court." Nevertheless the question remains: Does "negotiated justice" promote judicial efficiency at the expense of constitutional rights?

---

[27]*Blackledge* v. *Allison*, 97 S. Ct. 1621, 1627 (1977). See also *Santobello* v. *New York*, 404 U.S. 257, 260–261 (1971) (infra, § 13.02); and *Brady* v. *United States*, 397 U.S. 742, 751–752 (1970) (infra, § 13.02).

[28]*Blackledge* v. *Allison*, 97 S. Ct. 1621, 1628 (1977).

[29]Standard 3.1, *Abolition of Plea Negotiations*, National Advisory Commission on Criminal Justice Standards and Goals: Courts 46 (1973). But see *Santobello* v. *New York*, 404 U.S. 257, 260 (1971) (infra, § 13.02) ("If every criminal charge were subjected to a full-scale trial, the States and the Federal Government would need to multiply by many times the number of judges and court facilities").

---

[26]*Santobello* v. *New York*, 404 U.S. 257, 260 (1971) (infra, § 13.02) ("'plea bargaining' is an essential component of the administration of justice. Properly administered it is to be encouraged") (opinion of Burger, C. J.); *Blackledge* v. *Allison*, 97 S. Ct. 1621, 1627 (1977) ("the guilty plea and . . . plea bargain are important components of this country's criminal justice system") (opinion of Stewart, J.).

Justice by Guilty Plea*

Most citizens have had some experience with the guilty plea, perhaps from appearing in court in response to a traffic ticket. Everyone knows the coercive inconvenience of pleading not guilty rather than guilty even to a minor traffic violation—the lines are longer, another trip to the courthouse is necessary, the procedures are more complex. It is easier to plead guilty, pay ten dollars, and go home. A few years ago all America watched as the vice president of the United States pleaded *nolo contendere* (largely equivalent to a guilty plea) to minor charges of income tax evasion rather than standing trial on a more serious set of charges. Once he pleaded guilty, he was allowed to pay a fine of ten thousand dollars and go home.

Whether the behind-the-scenes observer is a liberal or a conservative, a do-gooder or a law-and-order hard-liner, he is likely to be troubled by the guilty plea and the discretionary practices it exemplifies. Decisions should reflect policy, not the exercise of capricious whim. There should be equal justice under law, not haphazard and arbitrary punishment of the weak. There should be no browbeating of the guilty, not to mention the innocent. Guilty plea procedures seem capricious and unjust, and an explanation that the ordinary citizen can understand and accept has not been provided.

Perhaps it is the absence of understandable explanations of guilty plea practices that has lead to current uneasiness about what is happening in American courthouses. Perhaps it is also a lack of understanding that has precipitated sweeping calls for the abolition of discretionary guilty plea practices:

—In 1971, the Nixon administration established the National Advisory Commission on Criminal Justice Standards and Goals. This group was asked to recommend to the federal government ways of waging war on crime. More specifically, it was to suggest the kinds of projects and reforms on which the states were to spend the more than one billion dollars a year in federal anticrime grants that Congress had voted. After two years of studies and deliberations, the Com-

mission published its standards and goals. These were quickly embraced as policy by the national administration. The Commission claimed that its recommendation with respect to guilty plea negotiations, formulated at the last minute, was the most far-reaching of the more than one hundred recommendations it had made concerning court procedures, although the Commission discussion of it is only slightly more than three pages long. This recommendation calls for the total abolition of guilty plea negotiations by 1978.

—In 1973, at the urging of Governor Nelson Rockefeller, the New York Legislature acted in concert with the Nixon Commission's recommendation and passed laws to punish narcotic drug offenders more severely. One law is designed to prevent defendants from avoiding the harsh penalties stipulated for narcotics violators in other laws. It prohibits judges and prosecutors from accepting guilty pleas to reduced charges, thus letting drug offenders off lightly. For example, a man charged with selling drugs (heavily punished) shall not be permitted to plead guilty to possession of drugs or drug use (lightly punished). In July of 1975 the New York State Legislature substantially amended and effectively repealed the major provisions of the Rockefeller scheme.

—In July of 1975, President Gerald R. Ford sent a special crime message to Congress. This message called for the reduction of judges' sentencing discretion and mandatory laws requiring prison sentences for various offenses and offenders. The message did not explicitly endorse the Nixon Commission proposal for the total abolition of plea bargaining but is consistent with it.

—Early in 1974, the late District Attorney Joseph Busch of Los Angeles County, who headed the largest prosecutor's office in the nation, announced new guidelines for substantially limiting arranged pleas. Under these guidelines, one form of guilty plea negotiation is abolished. Defendants are no longer permitted to exchange a guilty plea for an understanding as to the sentence they will receive. The objective was to reduce the disparities in punishments ordered by the various courts in Busch's rather far-flung bailiwick.

—In August 1974, the Supreme Court of the United States published a number of

---

*From Rosett, A., and Cressey, D., *Justice by Consent* 5–8 (1976). Reproduced by permission of J. B. Lippincott Co.

amendments to the Federal Rules of Criminal Procedure. One pertains to guilty plea procedures. It is "designed to give recognition to the propriety of plea discussions, to bring the existence of a plea agreement out into the open in court, and to provide a method for court acceptance or rejection of a plea agreement." These new rules, which are similar to those recently adopted in some states, will apply to all criminal cases in the federal courts.

Our principal objective is to show that the first three proposals, and the versions of them that are proliferating in cities and counties across the country, are unrealistic and likely to reduce rather to improve the quality of justice. Guilty plea negotiations are negotiations about proper punishment, and our objective, stated positively, is to suggest how these negotiations may be improved. The last two proposals face in this direction, but we shall offer compelling reasons why they are unlikely to attain their stated goals in the absence of additional substantial reforms.

Abolishing the negotiated guilty plea in America would be disastrous. Plea negotiation is the central technique for settling cases in American courthouses. Without it, policemen, prosecutors, judges, defenders and probation officers would be unable to perform their crucial duty—to do justice.

One reason why there are so few trials in the courthouse is that Americans who favor government by law also favor government by men. They want strict rules that will restrain oppressors and bigots, but they also want flexible rules that will enable sensible officials to soften harsh laws in individual cases.

Further, Americans want full trials, but they also want low taxes—they expect courthouse workers to compromise, to save money by developing procedures that are less costly than trials. For reasons of both justice and economy, then, most of the handcuffed suspects who enter the courthouse are persuaded not to exercise their right to be tried. The majority who are convicted are persuaded to plead guilty.

Plea negotiation is the visible symbol of a discretionary system which serves important social goals. Prohibiting it by law, as the New York State Legislature did in drug cases, and as President Ford proposed in his crime message, merely evades the difficult question of why it is so prevalent and how it can be improved. When the New York State Legislature recognized this it substantially modified the Rockefeller laws relating to narcotics.

We share the critics' distaste for the devious and underhanded dealings that go on in guilty plea negotiations. We believe that many current practices are unacceptable and should be changed. We favor a system of justice more impartial than current plea-negotiating procedures allow. We want to prevent the travesty of the guilty escaping punishment for high crimes, as they now do by means of the plea-negotiating process. More generally, we want better procedures for ensuring that the punishment fits the crime. All informed Americans want these things. But before they can frame and bring sensible reforms into being, they must have a clear sense of what must be changed. Much more than mere "plea bargaining" is at stake. . . .

13.02 PROBLEMS IN PLEADING

Accepting the Plea

BOYKIN v. ALABAMA

Supreme Court of the United States, 1969
395 U.S. 238, 89 S.Ct. 1709, 23 L. Ed. 2d 274

The facts are stated in the opinion.

Mr. Justice DOUGLAS delivered the opinion of the Court.

In the spring of 1966, within the period of a fortnight, a series of armed robberies occurred in Mobile, Alabama. The victims, in each case, were local shopkeepers open at night who were forced by a gunman to hand over money. While robbing one grocery store, the assailant fired his gun once, sending a bullet through a door into the ceiling. A few days earlier in a drugstore, the robber had allowed his gun to discharge in such a way that the bullet, on ricochet from the floor, struck a customer in the leg. Shortly thereafter, a local grand jury returned five indictments against petitioner, a 27-year-old Negro, for common-law robbery—an offense punishable in Alabama by death.

Before the matter came to trial, the court determined that petitioner was indigent and appointed counsel to represent him. Three days later, at his arraignment, petitioner pleaded guilty to all five indictments. So far as the record shows, the judge asked no questions of petitioner concerning his plea, and petitioner did not address the court.

Trial strategy may of course make a plea of guilty seem the desirable course. But the record is wholly silent on that point and throws no light on it.

Alabama provides that when a defendant pleads guilty, "the court must cause the punishment to be determined by a jury" (except where it is required to be fixed by the court) and may "cause witnesses to be examined to ascertain the character of the offense." . . .

In the present case a trial of that dimension was held, the prosecution presenting its case largely through eyewitness testimony. Although counsel for petitioner engaged in cursory cross-examination, petitioner neither testified himself nor presented testimony concerning his character and background. There was nothing to indicate that he had a prior criminal record.

In instructing the jury, the judge stressed that petitioner had pleaded guilty in five cases of robbery, defined as "the felonious taking of money . . . from another against his will . . . by violence or by putting him in fear . . . (carrying) from ten years minimum in the penitentiary to the supreme penalty of death by electrocution." The jury, upon deliberation, found petitioner guilty and sentenced him severally to die on each of the five indictments.

Taking an automatic appeal to the Alabama Supreme Court, petitioner argued that a sentence of death for common-law robbery

was cruel and unusual punishment within the meaning of the Federal Constitution, a suggestion which that court unanimously rejected. . . . On their own motion, however, four of the seven justices discussed the constitutionality of the process by which the trial judge had accepted petitioner's guilty plea. From the order affirming the trial court, three justices dissented on the ground that the record was inadequate to show that petitioner had intelligently and knowingly pleaded guilty. The fourth member concurred separately, conceding that "a trial judge should not accept a guilty plea unless he has determined that such a plea was voluntarily and knowingly entered by the defendant," but refusing "[f]or aught appearing" "to presume that the trial judge failed to do his duty." . . . We granted certiorari.

Respondent does not suggest that we lack jurisdiction to review the voluntary character of petitioner's guilty plea because he failed to raise that federal question below and the state court failed to pass upon it. But the question was raised on oral argument and we conclude that it is properly presented. The very Alabama statute . . . that provides automatic appeal in capital cases also requires the reviewing court to comb the record for "any error prejudicial to the appellant, even though not called to our attention in brief of counsel." . . . The automatic appeal statute "is the only provision under the Plain Error doctrine of which we are aware in Alabama criminal appellate review." . . . In the words of the Alabama Supreme Court:

"Perhaps it is well to note that in reviewing a death case under the automatic appeal statute . . . we may consider any testimony that was seriously prejudicial to the rights of the appellant and may reverse thereon, even though no lawful objection or exception was made thereto. (Citations omitted.) Our review is not limited to the matters brought to our attention in brief of counsel." . . .

It was error, plain on the face of the record, for the trial judge to accept petitioner's guilty plea without an affirmative showing that it was intelligent and voluntary. That error, under Alabama procedure, was properly before the court below and considered explicitly by a majority of the justices and is properly before us on review.

A plea of guilty is more than a confession

which admits that the accused did various acts; it is itself a conviction; nothing remains but to give judgement and determine punishment. Admissibility of a confession must be based on a "reliable determination on the voluntariness issue which satisfies the constitutional rights of the defendant." The requirement that the prosecution spread on the record the prerequisites of a valid waiver is no constitutional innovation. In Carnley v. Cochran, 369 U.S. 506, 516 (1962), we dealt with a problem of waiver of the right to counsel, a Sixth Amendment right. We held: "Presuming waiver from a silent record is impermissible. The record must show, or there must be an allegation and evidence which show, that an accused was offered counsel but intelligently and understandingly rejected the offer. Anything less is not waiver."

We think that the same standard must be applied to determining whether a guilty plea is voluntarily made. For, as we have said, a plea of guilty is more than an admission of conduct; it is a conviction. Ignorance, incomprehension, coercion, terror, inducements, subtle or blatant threats might be a perfect cover-up of unconstitutionality. The question of an effective waiver of a federal constitutional right in a proceeding is of course governed by federal standards. . . .

Several federal constitutional rights are involved in a waiver that takes place when a plea of guilty is entered in a state criminal trial. First, is the privilege against compulsory self-incrimination guaranteed by the Fifth Amendment and applicable to the States by reason of the Fourteenth. . . . Second, is the right to trial by jury. . . . Third, is the right to confront one's accusers. . . . We cannot presume a waiver of these three important federal rights from a silent record.

What is at stake for an accused facing death or imprisonment demands the utmost solicitude of which courts are capable in canvassing the matter with the accused to make sure he has a full understanding of what the plea connotes and of its consequence. When the judge discharges that function, he leaves a record adequate for any review that may be later sought . . . and forestalls the spin-off of collateral proceedings that seek to probe murky memories.

The three dissenting justices in the Alabama Supreme Court stated the law accurately when they concluded that there was reversible error "because the record does not disclose that the defendant voluntarily and understandingly entered his pleas of guilty." . . .

Reversed.

Mr. Justice HARLAN, whom Mr. Justice BLACK joins, dissenting.

The Court today holds that petitioner Boykin was denied due process of law, and that his robbery convictions must be reversed outright, solely because "the record [is] inadequate to show that petitioner . . . intelligently and knowingly pleaded guilty." . . . The Court thus in effect fastens upon the States, as a matter of federal constitutional law, the rigid prophylactic requirements of Rule 11 of the Federal Rules of Criminal Procedure. It does so in circumstances where the Court itself has only very recently held application of Rule 11 to be unnecessary in the federal courts. See Halliday v. United States, 394 U.S. 831 (1969). Moreover, the Court does all this at the behest of a petitioner who has never at any time alleged that his guilty plea was involuntary or made without knowledge of the consequences. I cannot possibly subscribe to so bizarre a result.

I

* * *

The record does not show what inquiries were made by the arraigning judge to confirm that the plea was made voluntarily and knowingly.

Petitioner was not sentenced immediately after the acceptance of his plea. Instead, pursuant to an Alabama statute, the court ordered that "witnesses . . . be examined, to ascertain the character of the offense," in the presence of a jury which would then fix petitioner's sentence. . . . That proceeding occurred some two months after petitioner pleaded guilty. During that period, petitioner made no attempt to withdraw his plea. Petitioner was present in court with his attorney when the witnesses were examined. Petitioner heard the judge state the elements of common-law robbery and heard him announce that petitioner had pleaded guilty to that offense and might be sentenced to death. Again, petitioner made no effort to withdraw his plea.

On his appeal to the Alabama Supreme

Court, petitioner did not claim that his guilty plea was made involuntarily or without full knowledge of the consequences. In fact, petitioner raised no questions at all concerning the plea. In his petition and brief in this Court, and in oral argument by counsel, petitioner has never asserted that the plea was coerced or made in ignorance of the consequences.

II

Against this background, the Court holds that the Due Process Clause of the Fourteenth Amendment requires the outright reversal of petitioner's conviction. This result is wholly unprecedented. There are past holdings of this Court to the effect that a federal habeas corpus petitioner who makes sufficiently credible allegations that his state guilty plea was involuntary is entitled to a hearing as to the truth of those allegations. . . . These holdings suggest that if equally convincing allegations were made in a petition for certiorari on direct review, the petitioner might in some circumstances be entitled to have a judgment of affirmance vacated and the case remanded for a state hearing on voluntariness. . . . However, as has been noted, this petitioner makes no allegations of actual involuntariness.

The Court's reversal is therefore predicated entirely upon the failure of the arraigning state judge to make an "adequate" record. In holding that this is a ground for reversal, the Court quotes copiously from McCarthy v. United States, 394 U.S. 459 (1969), in which we held earlier this Term that when a *federal* district judge fails to comply in every respect with the procedure for accepting a guilty plea which is prescribed in Rule 11 of the Federal Rules of Criminal Procedure, the plea must be set aside and the defendant permitted to replead, regardless of lower-court findings that the plea was in fact voluntary. What the Court omits to mention is that in McCarthy we stated that our decision was based "solely upon our construction of Rule 11," and explicitly disavowed any reliance upon the Constitution. . . . Thus McCarthy can provide no support whatever for today's constitutional edict.

III

So far as one can make out from the Court's opinion, what is now in effect being held is that the prophylactic procedures of Criminal Rule 11 are substantially applicable to the States as a matter of federal constitutional due process. If this is the basis upon which Boykin's conviction is being reversed, then the Court's disposition is plainly out of keeping with a sequel case to McCarthy, decided only last month. For the Court held, Halliday v. United States, 394 U.S. 831 (1969), that "in view of the large number of constitutionally valid convictions that may have been obtained without full compliance with Rule 11, we decline to apply McCarthy retroactively." . . . The Court quite evidently found Halliday's conviction to be "constitutionally valid," for it affirmed the conviction even though Halliday's guilty plea was accepted in 1954 without any explicit inquiry into whether it was knowingly and understandingly made, as now required by present Rule 11. In justification, the Court noted that two lower courts had found in collateral proceedings that the plea was voluntary. The Court declared that:

"[A] defendant whose plea has been accepted without full compliance with Rule 11 may still resort to appropriate post-conviction remedies to attack his plea's voluntariness. Thus, if his plea was accepted prior to our decision in McCarthy, he is not without a remedy to correct constitutional defects in his conviction." . . .

It seems elementary that the Fifth Amendment due process to which petitioner Halliday was entitled must be at least as demanding as the Fourteenth Amendment process due petitioner Boykin. Yet petitioner Halliday's federal conviction has been affirmed as "constitutionally valid," despite the omission of any judicial inquiry of record at the time of his plea, because he initiated collateral proceedings which revealed that the plea was actually voluntary. Petitioner Boykin, on the other hand, today has his Alabama conviction reversed because of exactly the same omission, even though he too "may . . . resort to appropriate post-conviction remedies to attack his plea's voluntariness" and thus "is not without a remedy to correct constitutional defects in his conviction." In short, I find it utterly impossible to square today's holding with what the Court has so recently done.

* * *

Comments

1. In *Boykin* v. *Alabama,* supra, the Supreme Court held that a state conviction based on a guilty plea cannot stand unless the record of the proceedings affirmatively establishes that the defendant *voluntarily* and *intelligently* waived the right to a jury trial, the right to confront witnesses, and the privilege against self-incrimination. The same standard applies in the federal courts. *McCarthy* v. *United States,* 394 U.S. 459 (1969). Did the Supreme Court in *Boykin* vacate the guilty plea because it was "shocked" at the sentence imposed pursuant to the plea bargaining process? Because of the racial overtones? A sentence of five times in the electric chair is possibly the worst bargain ever received by a defendant who has engaged in plea bargaining. What do you suppose Boykin's counsel or the prosecutor told the defendant the likely sentence would be? Surely Boykin would not have pleaded guilty had he suspected such a sentence. An "intelligent" plea of guilty does not necessarily refer to the defendant's I.Q.; it generally means an "awareness of the risks" of pleading guilty. Suppose the trial judge had informed Boykin that there was a risk that the jury might sentence him to the electric chair and he nevertheless pleaded guilty. On what grounds, if any, could the Supreme Court have vacated the guilty plea? Would the Court have done so? *Boykin* does not indicate whether a trial judge must tell a defendant precisely which constitutional rights are lost by pleading guilty. Is such an explicit warning constitutionally required in light of several Supreme Court pronouncements that "there can be no presumption of a waiver of a constitutional right from a silent record"? See e.g., Carnley v. Cochran, 369 U.S. 506, 516 (1962). Should *Boykin* be applicable to misdemeanor pleas? Should the high volume of misdemeanor pleas be controlling, or is it irrelevant?

2. In the federal courts, Rule 11 of the Federal Rules of Criminal Procedure governs the plea bargaining process:

Rule 11.   Pleas

(a) *Alternatives* — A defendant may plead not guilty, guilty, or nolo contendere. If a defendant refuses to plead or if a defendant corporation fails to appear, the court shall enter a plea of not guilty.

(b) *Nolo contendere* — A defendant may plead nolo contendere only with the consent of the court. Such a plea shall be accepted by the court after due consideration of the views of the parties and the interest of the public in the effective administration of justice.

(c) *Advice to defendant* — The court shall not accept a plea of guilty or nolo contendere without first, by addressing the defendant personally in open court, informing him of and determining that he understands the following.
(1) the nature of the charge to which the plea is offered; and
(2) the mandatory minimum penalty provided by law, if any, and the maximum possible penalty provided by law for the offense to which the plea is offered; and
(3) that the defendant has the right to plead not guilty, or to persist in that plea if it has already been made; and

(4) that if he pleads guilty or nolo contendere there will not be a further of any kind, so that by pleading guilty or nolo contendere he waives the right to a trial.

(d) *Insuring that the plea is voluntary* — The court shall not accept a plea of guilty or nolo contendere without first, by addressing the defendant personally in open court, determining that the plea is voluntary and not the result of force, threats, or of promises apart from a plea agreement. The court shall also inquire as to whether the defendant's willingness to plead guilty or nolo contendere results from prior discussions between the attorney for the government and the defendant or his attorney.

(e) *Plea agreement procedure*

(1) *In general* — The attorney for the government and the attorney for the defendant or the defendant when acting pro se may engage in discussions with a view toward reaching an agreement that, upon the entering of a plea of guilty or nolo contendere to a charged offense or to a lesser or related offense, the attorney for the government will move for dismissal of other charges, or will recommend or not oppose the imposition of a particular sentence, or will do both. The court shall not participate in any such discussions.

(2) *Notice of such agreement* — If a plea agreement has been reached by the parties which contemplates entry of a plea of guilty or nolo contendere in the expectation that a specific sentence will be imposed or that other charges before the court will be dismissed, the court shall require the disclosure of the agreement in open court at the time the plea is offered. Thereupon the court may accept or reject the agreement, or may defer its decision as to acceptance or rejection until there has been an opportunity to consider the presentence report.

(3) *Acceptance of plea* — If the court accepts the plea agreement, the court shall inform the defendant that it will embody in the judgment and sentence the disposition provided for in the plea agreement or another disposition more favorable to the defendant than that provided for in the plea agreement.

(4) *Rejection of plea* — If the court rejects the plea agreement, the court shall inform the parties of this fact, advise the defendant personally in open court that the court is not bound by the plea agreement, afford the defendant the opportunity to then withdraw his plea, and advise the defendant that if he persists in his guilty plea or plea of nolo contendere the disposition of the case may be less favorable to the defendant than that contemplated by the plea agreement.

(5) *Time of plea agreement procedure* — Except for good cause shown, notification to the court of the existence of a plea agreement shall be given at the arraignment or at such other time, prior to trial, as may be fixed by the court.

(6) *Inadmissibility of plea discussions* — Evidence of a plea of guilty, later withdrawn, or a plea of nolo contendere, or of an offer to plead guilty or nolo contendere to the crime charged or any other crime, or of statements made in connection with any of the foregoing pleas or offers, is not admissible in any civil or criminal proceeding against the person who made the plea or offer.

(f) *Determining accuracy of plea* — Notwithstanding the acceptance of a plea of guilty, the court should not enter a judgement upon such plea without making such inquiry as shall satisfy it that there is a factual basis for the plea.

(g) *Record of proceedings* — A verbatim record of the proceedings at which the defendant enters a plea shall be made and, if there is a plea of guilty or nolo contendere, the record shall include, without limitation, the court's advice to the defendant, the inquiry into the voluntariness of the plea including any plea agreement, and the inquiry into the accuracy of a guilty plea.

3. In *McCarthy* v. *United States,* 394 U.S. 459, 465 (1969), the Supreme Court indicated that the purposes of Rule 11 of the Federal Rules of Criminal Procedure are twofold: (1) to assist the district judge in determining whether the defendant's guilty plea is truly voluntary; and (2) to produce a complete record at the time the plea is entered indicating the factors relevant to voluntariness. Thus, a judge must personally address a defendant who wishes to plead guilty and determine whether (1) the plea is made voluntarily, (2) the defendant understands the nature of the charge, and (3) the defendant is aware of the applicable minimum and maximum sentences. Failure of a district court to comply with the requisites of Rule 11 may constitute reversible error entitling the defendant to plead anew, even though he was represented by counsel. In *Halliday* v. *United States,* 394 U.S. 831 (1969), the Court held that the requirements of *McCarthy* are not to be made retroactive.

The "Voluntariness" Requirement

BRADY v. UNITED STATES

Supreme Court of the United States, 1970
397 U.S. 742, 90 S. Ct. 1463, 25 L. Ed. 2d 747

In 1959, petitioner was indicted for kidnapping and not releasing the victim unharmed in violation of 18 U.S.C. § 1201(a), which imposed a maximum penalty of death if the jury's verdict so recommended. When Brady learned that his co-defendant, who had confessed, would plead guilty and testify against him, petitioner changed his previous plea of not guilty to guilty. Brady was represented by competent counsel throughout the proceedings. After twice questioning petitioner as to the voluntariness of his plea, the trial judge accepted the guilty plea and sentenced Brady to imprisonment for 50 years, which was later reduced to 30 years. In 1967, petitioner sought relief in the United States District Court (D. N. Mex.), claiming that his plea of guilty was not voluntary because, inter alia, § 1201(a) operated to coerce his plea. The district court denied relief, finding that petitioner had pleaded guilty "by reason of other matters and not by reason of the statute." The Court of Appeals (10th Cir.) affirmed, and the Supreme Court granted certiorari to consider the claim that the court of appeals was in error in not reaching a contrary result on the authority of *United States* v. *Jackson*, 390 U.S. 570 (1968).

Mr. Justice WHITE delivered the opinion of the Court.

    *   *   *

I

In United States v. Jackson [390 U.S. 570 (1968)] . . . the defendants were indicted under § 1201(a). The District Courts dismissed the § 1201(a) count of the indictment, holding the statute unconstitutional because it permitted imposition of the death sentence only upon a jury's recommendation and thereby made the risk of death the price of a jury trial. This Court held the statute valid, except for the death penalty provision; with respect to the latter, the Court agreed with the trial court "that the death penalty provision ... imposes an impermissible burden upon the exercise of a constitutional right. ..." ... The problem was to determine "whether the Constitution permits the establishment of such a death penalty, applicable only to those defendants who assert the right to contest their guilt before a jury." ... The inevitable effect of the provision was said to be to discourage assertion of the Fifth Amendment right not to plead guilty and to deter exercise of the Sixth Amendment right to demand a jury trial. Because the legitimate goal of limiting the death penalty to cases in which a jury recommends it could be achieved without penalizing those defendants who plead not guilty and elect a jury trial, the death penalty provision "needlessly penalize[d] the assertion of a constitutional right," and was therefore unconstitutional.

Since the "inevitable effect" of the death penalty provision of § 1201(a) was said by the Court to be the needless encouragement of pleas of guilty and waivers of jury trial, Brady contends that Jackson requires the invalidation of every plea of guilty entered under that section, at least when the fear of death is shown to have been a factor in the plea. Petitioner, however, has read far too much into the Jackson opinion.

The Court made it clear in Jackson that it was not holding § 1201(a) inherently coercive of guilty pleas: "the fact that the Federal Kidnaping Act tends to discourage defendants from insisting upon their innocence and demanding trial by jury hardly implies that every defendant who enters a guilty plea to a charge under the Act does so involuntarily." ...

Moreover, the Court in Jackson rejected a suggestion that the death penalty provision of § 1201(a) be saved by prohibiting in capital kidnaping cases all guilty pleas and jury waivers, "however clear [the defendants'] guilt and however strong their desire to acknowledge it in order to spare themselves and their families the spectacle and expense of protracted courtroom proceedings." "[T]hat jury waivers and guilty pleas may occasionally be rejected" was no ground for automatically rejecting all guilty pleas under the statute, for such a rule "would rob the criminal process of much of its flexibility." ...

Plainly, it seems to us, Jackson ruled neither that all pleas of guilty encouraged by fear of a possible death sentence are involuntary pleas nor that such encouraged pleas are invalid whether involuntary or not. Jackson prohibits the imposition of the death penalty under § 1201(a), but that decision neither fashioned a new standard for judging the validity of guilty pleas nor mandated a new application of the text theretofore fashioned by courts and since reiterated that guilty pleas are valid if both "voluntary" and "intelligent." ...

... Central to the plea and the foundation for entering judgment against the defendants is the defendant's admission in open court that he committed the acts charged in the indictment. He thus stands as a witness against himself and he is shielded by the Fifth Amendment from being compelled to do so—hence the minimum requirement that his plea be the voluntary expression of his own choice. But the plea is more than an admission of past conduct; it is the defendant's consent that judgment of conviction may be entered without a trial—a waiver of his right to trial before a jury or a judge. Waivers of constitutional rights not only must be voluntary but must be knowing, intelligent acts done with sufficient awareness of the relevant circumstances and likely consequences. On neither score was Brady's plea of guilty invalid.

II

... Petitioner, advised by competent counsel, tendered his plea after his codefendant, who had already given a confession, determined to plead guilty and became available to testify against petitioner. It was this development that the District Court found to have triggered Brady's guilty plea.

The voluntariness of Brady's plea can be determined only by considering all of the relevant circumstances surrounding it. ... One of these circumstances was the possibility of a heavier sentence following a guilty verdict after a trial. It may be that Brady, faced with a strong case against him and recognizing that his chances for acquittal were slight, preferred to plead guilty and thus limit the penalty to life imprisonment rather than to elect a jury trial which could result in a death penalty. But even if we assume that Brady would not have pleaded guilty except for the death penalty provision of § 1201(a), this assumption merely identifies the penalty provision as a "but for" cause of his plea. That the statute caused the plea in this sense does not necessarily prove that the plea was coerced and invalid as an involuntary act.

* * *

Of course, the agents of the State may not produce a plea by actual or threatened physical harm or by mental coercion overbearing the will of the defendant. But nothing of the sort is claimed in this case; nor is there evidence that Brady was so gripped by fear of the death peanlty or hope of leniency that he did not or could not, with the help of counsel, rationally weigh the advantages of going to trial against the advantages of pleading guilty. Brady's claim is of a different sort: that it violates the Fifth Amendment to influence or encourage a guilty plea by opportunity or promise of leniency and that a guilty plea is coerced and invalid if influenced by the fear of a possibly higher penalty for the crime charged if a conviction is obtained after the State is put to its proof.

Insofar as the voluntariness of his plea is concerned, there is little to differentiate Brady from (1) the defendant, in a jurisdiction where the judge and jury have the same range of sentencing power, who pleads guilty because his lawyer advises him that the judge will very probably be more lenient than the jury; (2) the defendant, in a jurisdiction where the judge alone has sentencing power, who is advised by counsel that the judge is normally more lenient with defendants who plead guilty than with those who go to trial; (3) the defendant who is permitted by prosecutor and judge to plead guilty to a lesser offense included in the offense charged; and (4) the defendant who pleads guilty to certain counts with the understanding that other charges will be dropped. In each of these situations, as in Brady's case, the defendant might never plead guilty absent the possibility or certainty that the plea will result in a lesser penalty than the sentence that could be imposed after a trial and a verdict of guilty. We decline to hold, however, that a guilty plea is compelled and invalid under the Fifth Amendment whenever motivated by the defendant's desire to accept the certainty or probability of a lesser penalty rather than face a wider range of possibilities extending from acquittal to conviction and a higher penalty authorized by law for the crime charged. . . . For a defendant who sees slight possibility of acquittal, the advantages of pleading guilty and limiting the probable penalty are obvious—his exposure is reduced, the correctional processes can begin immediately, and the practical burdens of a trial are eliminated. For the State there are also advantages—the more promptly imposed punishment after an admission of guilt may more effectively attain the objectives of punishment; and with the avoidance of trial, scarce judicial and prosecutorial resources are conserved for those cases in which there is a substantial issue of the defendant's guilt or in which there is substantial doubt that the State can sustain its burden of proof. It is this mutuality of advantage that perhaps explains the fact that at present well over three-fourths of the criminal convictions in this country rest on pleas of guilty, a great many of them no doubt motivated at least in part by the hope or assurance of a lesser penalty than might be imposed if there were a guilty verdict after a trial to judge or jury.

Of course, that the prevalence of guilty pleas is explainable does not necessarily validate those pleas or the system which produces them. But we cannot hold that it is unconstitutional for the State to extend a benefit to a defendant who in turn extends a substantial benefit to the State and who demonstrates by his plea that he is ready and willing to admit his crime and to enter the correctional system in a frame of mind that affords hope for success in rehabilitation over a shorter period of time than might otherwise be necessary.

A contrary holding would require the States and Federal Government to forbid guilty pleas altogether, to provide a single invariable penalty for each crime defined by the statutes, or to place the sentencing function in a separate authority having no knowledge of the manner in which the conviction in each case was obtained. In any event, it would be necessary to forbid prosecutors and judges to accept guilty pleas to selected counts, to lesser included offenses, or to reduced charges. The Fifth Amendment does not reach so far.

Bram v. United States, 168 U.S. 532 (1897), held that the admissibility of a confession depended upon whether it was compelled within the meaning of the Fifth Amendment. To be admissible, a confession must be " 'free and voluntary: that is, must not be extracted by any sort of threats or violence, nor obtained by any direct or implied promises, however slight, nor by the exertion of any improper influence.' " . . . More recently, Malloy v. Hogan, 378 U.S. 1 (1964), carried forward the Bram definition of compulsion in the course of holding applicable to the States the Fifth Amendment privilege against compelled self-incrimination.

Bram is not inconsistent with our holding that Brady's plea was not compelled even though the law promised him a lesser maximum penalty if he did not go to trial. Bram dealt with a confession given by a defendant in custody, alone and unrepresented by counsel. In such circumstances, even a mild promise of leniency was deemed sufficient to bar the confession, not because the promise was an illegal act as such, but because defendants at such times are too sensitive to inducement and the possible impact on them too great to ignore and too difficult to assess. But Bram and its progeny did not hold that the possibly coercive impact of a promise of leniency could not be dissipated by the presence and advice of counsel, any more than Miranda v. Arizona, 384 U.S. 436 (1966), held that the possibly coercive atmosphere of the police station could not be counteracted by the presence of counsel or other safeguards.

Brady's situation bears no resemblance to Bram's. Brady first pleaded not guilty; prior to changing his plea to guilty he was subjected to no threats or promises in face-to-face encounters with the authorities. He had competent counsel and full opportunity to assess the advantages and disadvantages of a trial as compared with those attending a plea of guilty; there was no hazard of an impulsive and improvident response to a seeming but unreal advantage. His plea of guilty was entered in open court and before a judge obviously sensitive to the requirements of the law with respect to guilty pleas. Brady's plea, unlike Bram's confession, was voluntary.

The standard as to the voluntariness of guilty pleas must be essentially that defined by Judge Tuttle of the Court of Appeals for the Fifth Circuit:

" '[A] plea of guilty entered by one fully aware of the direct consequences including the actual value of any commitments made to him by the court, prosecutor, or his own counsel, must stand unless induced by threats (or promises to discontinue improper harrassment), misrepresentation (including unfulfilled or unfulfillable promises), or perhaps by promises that are by their nature improper as having no proper relationship to the prosecutor's business (e.g., bribes).' " . . .

Under this standard, a plea of guilty is not invalid merely because entered to avoid the possibility of a death penalty.

III

The record before us also supports the conclusion that Brady's plea was intelligently made. He was advised by competent counsel, he was made aware of the nature of the charge against him, and there was nothing to indicate that he was incompetent or otherwise not in control of his mental faculties; once his confederate had pleaded guilty and became available to testify, he chose to plead guilty, perhaps to ensure that he would face no more than life imprisonment or a term of years. Brady was aware of precisely what he was doing when he admitted that he had kidnapped the victim and had not released her unharmed.

It is true that Brady's counsel advised him that § 1201(a) empowered the jury to impose the death penalty and that nine years later in United States v. Jackson, supra, the Court held that the jury had no such power as long as the judge could impose only a lesser penalty if trial was to the court or there was a plea of guilty. But these facts do not require us to set aside Brady's conviction.

Often the decision to plead guilty is heavily influenced by the defendant's appraisal of the prosecution's case against him and by the apparent likelihood of securing leniency should a guilty plea be offered and accepted. . . . The rule that a plea must be intelligently made to be valid does not require that a plea be vulnerable to later attack if the defendant did not correctly assess every relevant factor entering into his decision. A defendant is not entitled to withdraw his plea merely because he discovers long after the plea has been accepted that his calculus misapprehended the quality of the State's case or the likely penalties attached to alternative courses of action. More particularly, absent misrepresentation or other impermissible conduct by state agents . . . a voluntary plea of guilty intelligently made in the light of the then applicable law does not become vulnerable because later judicial decisions indicate that the plea rested on a faulty premise. A plea of guilty triggered by the expectations of a competently counseled defendant that the State will have a strong case against him is not subject to later attack because the defendant's lawyer correctly advised him with respect to the then existing law as to possible penalties but later pronouncements of the courts, as in this case, hold that the maximum penalty for the crime in question was less than was reasonably assumed at the time the plea was entered.

The fact that Brady did not anticipate United States v. Jackson, supra, does not impugn the truth or reliability of his plea. We find no requirement in the Constitution that a defendant must be permitted to disown his solemn admissions in open court that he committed the act with which he is charged simply because it later develops that the State would have had a weaker case than the defendant had thought or that the maximum penalty then assumed applicable has been held inapplicable in subsequent judicial decisions.

Although Brady's plea of guilty may well have been motivated in part by a desire to avoid a possible death penalty, we are convinced that his plea was voluntarily and intelligently made and we have no reason to doubt that his solemn admission of guilt was truthful.

Affirmed.

[Mr. Justice BLACK, while adhering to his belief that *United States* v. *Jackson*, 390 U.S. 570 (1968), was wrongly decided, concurred in the judgment and in substantially all of the opinion in this case.]

[Mr. Justice BRENNAN, joined by Mr. Justice MARSHALL and Mr. Justice DOUGLAS, concurred in the result. For that opinion see the companion case of *McMann* v. *Richardson*, 397 U.S. 759, 799 (1970) (Comment 2, infra)].

Comments

1. In *Brady* v. *United States,* supra, the Supreme Court held that a plea of guilty is not invalid merely because a defendant might have been partially motivated to so plead by a fear of the death penalty. The Court noted that the voluntariness of a guilty plea is to be determined by "all of the relevant circumstances surrounding it" and that one of these circumstances is the possibility of a heavier sentence following a plea of guilty. In *United States* v. *Jackson*, 390 U.S. 570 (1968), the Supreme Court struck down the death penalty provision of the federal kidnapping statute (18 U.S.C. § 1201(a)) as unconstitutional because the death penalty could be imposed only on the recommendation of the jury. The statute was seen to place an impermissible burden upon the exercise of the right to a trial by jury because only those defendants who opted for a jury trial risked the death penalty. *Brady*, however, was distinguished because there was no evidence that the defendant pleaded guilty because he feared that the jury would impose the death penalty under the kidnapping statute. After *Brady*, can there be any doubt as to the constitutionality of plea bargaining when appropriate safeguards are provided?

2. In *McMann* v. *Richardson*, 397 U.S. 759 (1970), decided the same day as *Brady*, the Court was faced with the issue of the extent to which an otherwise valid guilty plea may be attacked by assertions

that the plea was motivated by a prior coerced confession. In each of the three consolidated cases decided in *McMann,* the defendants pleaded guilty in New York state courts to various felonies, including murder, rape and robbery, prior to the Supreme Court's decision in *Jackson* v. *Denno,* 374 U.S. 368 (1964). *Jackson* held that the judge, not the jury, must make a preliminary determination of the voluntariness of an allegedly coerced confession. The Court further held that the judge must hold a hearing (the so-called "*Jackson-Denno* hearing") outside the presence of the jury on the voluntariness of the confession, and that only if the judge finds the confession to be voluntary may the jury consider it as part of the state's evidence against the defendant. The *McMann* defendants claimed that their guilty pleas were tainted by coerced confessions, but the state courts denied relief. The district courts, without granting hearings, denied federal habeas corpus relief, but the Court of Appeals (2d Cir.) reversed and remanded each case back to the district courts for evidentiary hearings on the connection between the confessions and the guilty pleas, since the procedures employed by New York prior to *Jackson* v. *Denno* to determine the voluntariness of confessions were unconstitutional.

On certiorari, the United States Supreme Court vacated and remanded. In an opinion by Justice White, the Court held that a defendant is bound by his plea of guilty unless there is a showing of "serious derelictions on the part of counsel" resulting in a plea that was not knowing and intelligent. Id. at 774. As the Court said in *McMann*: "For the defendant who considers his confession involuntary . . . tendering a plea of guilty would seem a most improbable alternative. The sensible course would be to contest his guilt . . . at trial . . . and win acquittal, however guilty he may be. . . . If he nevertheless pleads guilty the plea can hardly be blamed on the confession which in his view was admissible evidence and no proper part of the State's case. . . . A guilty plea in such circumstances is nothing less than a refusal to present his federal claims to the state court. . . . Surely later allegations that the confession rendered his plea involuntary would appear incredible. . ." at 768.

The Court noted that a defendant who shows that his guilty plea was induced by ineffective or incompetent counsel is entitled to relief. However, the test is not whether counsel's advice was erroneous, but "whether the advice was within the range of competence demanded of attorneys in criminal cases"; and this decision should be left, for the most part, to the sound discretion of the trial judge.

In *Parker* v. *North Carolina,* 397 U.S. 790 (1970), decided the same day as *Brady* and *McMann,* the defendant was indicted for first degree burglary, an offense punishable by death under North Carolina law unless the jury recommended a penalty of life imprisonment. However, a competent plea of guilty to this offense carried a mandatory sentence of life imprisonment.

Parker confessed shortly after being taken to the police station. He informed his counsel that the confession was not prompted by threats or promises and was voluntary. Because his attorney believed that the defendant's confession would be admissible at trial, he recommended that Parker plead guilty. Parker signed written statements authorizing his plea of guilty and the prosecutor and the trial judge accepted the plea. On appeal, Parker asserted, inter alia, that his confession was invalid because it was induced by the North Carolina statute which authorized a lesser penalty for burglary for defendants who pleaded guilty than for those who went to trial and were convicted. This claim was rejected by the United States Supreme Court on the basis of the *Brady* decision. In addition, Parker asserted that he had received bad advice from his attorney with regard to the admissibility of his confession. This claim was also rejected. As Justice White said, writing for a majority Court in *Parker,* "Even if Parker's counsel was wrong in his assessment of Parker's confession, it does not follow that his error was sufficient to render the plea unintelligent and entitle Parker to disavow his admission in open court. . . . We think the advice he received was well within the range of competence required of attorneys representing defendants in criminal cases. Parker's plea of guilty was not open to attack on the grounds that counsel misjudged the admissibility of Parker's confession." Id. at 797–798.

The *Brady-McMann-Parker* trilogy indicates that a defendant who voluntarily pleads guilty is not entitled to federal relief merely because he claims that his plea was induced by the threat of a greater penalty on conviction at trial or that the plea was based on a prior coerced confession. Further, guilty pleas are not subject to collateral attack absent some showing that counsel was derelict in his duties; and a simple showing of "bad legal advice" is not sufficient to render a guilty plea invalid.

When the Defendant Maintains His Innocence

NORTH CAROLINA v. ALFORD

Supreme Court of the United States, 1970
400 U.S. 25, 91 S. Ct. 160, 27 L. Ed. 2d 162

The facts are stated in the opinion.

Mr. Justice WHITE delivered the opinion of the Court.

On December 2, 1963, Alford was indicted for first-degree murder, a capital offense under North Carolina law. The court appointed an attorney to represent him, and this attorney questioned all but one of the various witnesses who appellee said would substantiate his claim of innocence. The witnesses, however, did not support Alford's story but gave statements that strongly indicated his guilt. Faced with strong evidence of guilt and no substantial evidentiary support for the claim of innocence, Alford's attorney recommended that he plead guilty, but left the ultimate decision to Alford himself. The prosecutor agreed to accept a plea of guilty to a charge of second-degree murder, and on December 10, 1963, Alford pleaded guilty to the reduced charge.

Before the plea was finally accepted by the trial court, the court heard the sworn testimony of a police officer who summarized the State's case. Two other witnesses besides Alford were also heard. Although there was no eyewitness to the crime, the testimony indicated that shortly before the killing Alford took his gun from his house, stated his intention to kill the victim, and returned home with the declaration that he had carried out the killing. After the summary presentation of the State's case, Alford took the stand and testified that he had not committed the murder but that he was pleading guilty because he faced the threat of the death penalty if he did not do so. In response to the questions of his counsel, he acknowledged that his counsel had informed him of the difference between second- and first-degree murder and of his rights in case he chose to go to trial. The trial court then asked appellee if, in light of his denial of guilt, he still desired to plead guilty to second-degree murder and appellee answered, "Yes, sir. I plead guilty on—from the circumstances that he [Alford's attorney] told me." After eliciting information about Alford's prior criminal record, which was a long one, the trial court sentenced him to 30 years' imprisonment, the maximum penalty for second-degree murder.

Alford sought post-conviction relief in the state court. Among the claims raised was the claim that his plea of guilty was invalid because it was the product of fear and coercion. After a hearing, the state court in 1965 found that the plea was "willingly, knowingly, and understandingly" made on the advice of competent counsel and in the face of a strong prosecution case. Subsequently, Alford petitioned for a writ of habeas corpus, first in the United States District Court for the Middle District of North Carolina, and then in the Court of Appeals for the Fourth District. Both courts denied the writ on the basis of the state court's findings that Alford voluntarily and knowingly agreed to plead guilty. In 1967, Alford again petitioned for a writ of habeas corpus in the District Court for the Middle District of North Carolina. That court, without an evidentiary hearing, again denied relief on the grounds that the guilty plea was voluntary and waived all defenses and non-jurisdictional defects in any prior stage of the proceedings, and that the findings of the state court in 1965 clearly required rejection of Alford's claim that he was denied effective assistance of counsel prior to pleading guilty. On appeal, a divided panel of the Court of Appeals for the Fourth Circuit reversed on the ground that Alford's guilty plea was made involuntarily. . . . In reaching its conclusion, the Court of Appeals relied heavily on United States v. Jackson, 390 U.S. 570 (1968), which the Court read to require invalidation of the North Carolina statutory framework for the imposition of the death penalty because North Carolina statutes encouraged defendants to waive constitutional rights by the promise of no more than life imprisonment if a guilty plea was offered and accepted. Conceding that Jackson did not require the automatic invalidation of pleas of guilty entered under the North Carolina statutes, the Court of Appeals ruled that Alford's guilty plea was involuntary because its principal motivation was fear of the death penalty. By this standard, even if both the judge and the jury had possessed the power to impose the death penalty for first-degree murder or if guilty pleas to capital charges had not been permitted, Alford's plea of guilty to second-degree murder should still have been rejected because impermissibly induced by his desire to eliminate the possibility of a death sentence. We noted probable jurisdiction. . . . We vacate the judgment of the Court of Appeals and remand the case for further proceedings.

We held in Brady v. United States, 397 U.S. 742 (1970), that a plea of guilty which would not have been entered except for the defendant's desire to avoid a possible death penalty and to limit the maximum penalty to life imprisonment or a term of years was not for that reason compelled within the meaning of the Fifth Amendment. Jackson established no new test for determining the validity of guilty pleas. The standard was and remains whether the plea represents a voluntary and intelligent choice among the alternative courses of action open to the defendant. . . . That he would not have pleaded except for the opportunity to limit the possible penalty does not necessarily demonstrate that the plea of guilty was not the product of a free and rational choice, especially where the defendant was represented by competent counsel whose advice was that the plea would be to the defendant's advantage. The standard fashioned and applied by the Court of Appeals was therefore erroneous and we would, without more, vacate and remand the case for further proceedings with respect to any other claims of Alford which are properly before that court, if it were not for other circumstances appearing in the record which might seem to warrant an affirmance of the Court of Appeals.

As previously recounted, after Alford's plea of guilty was offered and the State's case was placed before the judge, Alford denied that he had committed the murder but reaffirmed his desire to plead guilty to avoid a possible death sentence and to limit the penalty to the 30-year maximum provided for second-degree murder. Ordinarily, a judgment of conviction resting on a plea of guilty is justified by the defendant's admission that he committed the crime charged against him and his consent that judgment be entered without a trial of any kind. The plea usually subsumes both elements, and justifiably so, even though there is no separate, express admission by the defendant that he committed the particular acts claimed to constitute the crime charged in the indictment. . . . Here Alford entered his plea but accompanied it with the statement that he had not shot the victim.

If Alford's statements were to be credited as sincere assertions of his innocence, there obviously existed a factual and legal dispute between him and the State. Without more, it might be argued that the conviction entered on his guilty plea was invalid, since his assertion of innocence negatived any admission of guilt, which, as we observed last Term in Brady, is normally "[c]entral to the plea and the foundation for entering judgment against the defendant. . . ."

In addition to Alford's statement, however, the court had heard an account of the events on the night of the murder, including information from Alford's acquaintances that he had departed from his home with his gun stating his intention to kill and that he had later declared that he had carried out his intention. Nor had Alford wavered in his desire to have the trial court determine his guilt without a jury trial. Although denying the charge against him, he nevertheless preferred the dispute between him and the State to be settled by the judge in the context of a guilty plea proceeding rather than by a formal trial. Thereupon, with the State's telling evidence and Alford's denial before it, the trial court proceeded to convict and sentence Alford for second-degree murder.

State and lower federal courts are divided upon whether a guilty plea can be accepted when it is accompanied by protestations of innocence and hence contains only a waiver of trial but no admission of guilt. Some courts, giving expression to the principle that "[o]ur law only authorizes a conviction where guilt is shown," Harris v. State, 172

S.W. 975, 977 (1915), require that trial judges reject such pleas. . . . But others have concluded that they should not "force any defense on a defendant in a criminal case," particularly when advancement of the defense might "end in disaster. . . ." Tremblay v. Overholser, 199 F. Supp. 569, 570 (D.C. 1961). They have argued that, since "guilt, or the degree of guilt, is at times uncertain and elusive," "[a]n accused, though believing in or entertaining doubts respecting his innocence, might reasonably conclude a jury would be convinced of his guilt and that he would fare better in the sentence by pleading guilty. . . ." McCoy v. United States, 363 F.2d 306, 308 (1966). As one state court observed nearly a century ago, "[r]easons other than the fact that he is guilty may induce a defendant to so plead, . . . [and] [h]e must be permitted to judge for himself in this respect." State v. Kaufman, 51 Iowa 578, 580, 2 N.W. 275, 276 (1879) (dictum). . . .

This Court has not confronted this precise issue, but prior decisions do yield relevant principles. In Lynch v. Overholser, 369 U.S. 705 (1962), Lynch, who had been charged in the Municipal Court of the District of Columbia with drawing and negotiating bad checks, a misdemeanor punishable by a maximum of one year in jail, sought to enter a plea of guilty, but the trial judge refused to accept the plea since a psychiatric report in the judge's possession indicated that Lynch had been suffering from "a manic depressive psychosis, at the time of the crime charged," and hence might have been not guilty by reason of insanity. Although at the subsequent trial Lynch did not rely on the insanity defense, he was found not guilty by reason of insanity and committed for an indeterminate period to a mental institution. On habeas corpus, the Court ordered his release, construing the congressional legislation seemingly authorizing the commitment as not reaching a case where the accused preferred a guilty plea to a plea of insanity. The Court expressly refused to rule that Lynch had an absolute right to have his guilty plea accepted, . . . but implied that there would have been no constitutional error had his plea been accepted even though evidence before the judge indicated that there was a valid defense.

The issue in Hudson v. United States, 272 U.S. 451 (1926), was whether a federal court has power to impose a prison sentence after accepting a plea of nolo contendere, a plea by which a defendant does not expressly admit his guilt, but nonetheless waives his right to a trial and authorizes the court for purposes of the case to treat him as if he were guilty. The Court held that a trial court does have such power, and, except for the cases which were rejected in Hudson, the federal courts have uniformly followed this rule, even in cases involving moral turpitude. . . . Implicit in the nolo contendere cases is a recognition that the Constitution does not bar imposition of a prison sentence upon an accused who is unwilling expressly to admit his guilt but who, faced with grim alternatives, is willing to waive his trial and accept the sentence.

These cases would be directly in point if Alford had simply insisted on his plea but refused to admit the crime. The fact that his plea was denominated a plea of guilty rather than a plea of nolo contendere is of no constitutional significance with respect to the issue now before us, for the Constitution is concerned with the practical consequences, not the formal categorizations, of state law. . . . Thus, while most pleas of guilty consist of both a waiver of trial and an express admission of guilt, the latter element is not a constitutional requisite to the imposition of criminal penalty. An individual accused of crime may voluntarily, knowingly, and understandingly consent to the imposition of a prison sentence even if he is unwilling or unable to admit his participation in the acts constituting the crime.

Nor can we perceive any material difference between a plea that refuses to admit commission of the criminal act and a plea containing a protestation of innocence when, as in the instant case, a defendant intelligently concludes that his interests require entry of a guilty plea and the record before the judge contains strong evidence of actual guilt. Here the State had a strong case of first-degree murder against Alford. Whether he realized or disbelieved his guilt, he insisted on his plea because in his view he had absolutely nothing to gain by a trial and much to gain by pleading. Because of the overwhelming evidence against him, a trial was precisely what neither Alford nor his attorney desired. Confronted with the choice between a trial for first-degree murder, on the one hand, and a plea of guilty to second-degree murder, on the other, Alford quite reasonably chose the latter and thereby limited the maximum penalty to a 30-year term. When his plea is viewed in light of the evidence against him, which substantially negated his claim of innocence and which further provided a means by which the judge could test whether the plea was being intelligently entered . . . its validity cannot be seriously questioned. In view of the strong factual basis for the plea demonstrated by the State and Alford's clearly expressed desire to enter it despite his professed belief in his innocence, we hold that the trial judge did not commit constitutional error in accepting it.

Relying on United States v. Jackson, supra, Alford now argues in effect that the State should not have allowed him this choice but should have insisted on proving him guilty of murder in the first degree. The States in their wisdom may take this course by statute or otherwise and may prohibit the practice of accepting pleas to lesser included offenses under any circumstances. But this is not the mandate of the Fourteenth Amendment and the Bill of Rights. The prohibitions against involuntary or unintelligent pleas should not be relaxed, but neither should an exercise in arid logic render those constitutional guarantees counterproductive and put in jeopardy the very human values they were meant to preserve.

The Court of Appeals for the Fourth Circuit was in error to find Alford's plea of guilty invalid because it was made to avoid the possibility of the death penalty. That court's judgment directing the issuance of the writ of habeas corpus is vacated and the case is remanded to the Court of Appeals for further proceedings consistent with this opinion. . . .

[Mr. Justice BLACK, while adhering to his belief that United States v. Jackson, 390 U.S. 570 (1968), was wrongly decided, concurred in the judgment and in substantially all of the opinion in this case.]

Mr. Justice BRENNAN, with whom Mr. Justice DOUGLAS and Mr. Justice MARSHALL join, dissenting.

Last Term, this Court held, over my dissent, that a plea of guilty may validly be induced by an unconstitutional threat to subject the defendant to the risk of death, so long as the plea is entered in open court and the defendant is represented by competent counsel who is aware of the threat, albeit not of its unconstitutionality. Brady v. United States, 397 U.S. 742, 745–758 (1970). . . . Today the Court makes clear that its previous holding was intended to apply even when the record demonstrates that the actual effect of the unconstitutional threat was to induce a guilty plea from a defendant who was unwilling to admit his guilt.

I adhere to the view that, in any given case, the influence of such an unconstitutional threat "must necessarily be given weight in determining the voluntariness of a plea." Parker v. North Carolina, 397 U.S., at 805 (dissent). And, without reaching the question whether due process permits the entry of judgment upon a plea of guilty accompanied by a contemporaneous denial of acts constituting the crime, I believe that at the very least such a denial of guilt is also a relevant factor in determining whether the plea was voluntarily and intelligently made. With these factors in mind, it is sufficient in my view to state that the facts set out in the majority opinion demonstrate that Alford was "so gripped by fear of the death penalty" that his decision to plead guilty was not voluntary but was "the product of duress as much so as choice reflecting physical constraint." . . . Accordingly, I would affirm the judgment of the Court of Appeals.

Comment

1. In *North Carolina* v. *Alford*, supra, a majority of the Court held that an assertion of innocence by a defendant does not invalidate an intelligent and voluntary guilty plea. Nevertheless, many trial judges will not accept a qualified guilty plea. Since a defendant in a criminal case does not have a constitutional right to have his guilty plea accepted by a court, should the trial court in *Alford* have refused the defendant's qualified plea? Are *Brady* and *Alford* distinguishable, or are they cut from the same cloth; i.e., the defendant is pleading guilty simply to avoid a greater sentence in the event of conviction? Must there be a *factual basis* for a finding of guilt pursuant to a guilty plea?

The Broken Promise

SANTOBELLO v. NEW YORK

Supreme Court of the United States, 1971
404 U.S. 257, 29 S. Ct. 495, 30 L. Ed. 2d 427

The facts are stated in the opinion.

Mr. Chief Justice BURGER delivered the opinion of the Court.

We granted certiorari in this case to determine whether the State's failure to keep a commitment concerning the sentence recommendation on a guilty plea required a new trial.

The facts are not in dispute. The State of New York indicted petitioner in 1969 on two felony counts, Promoting Gambling in the First Degree, and Possession of Gambling Records in the First Degree, N.Y. Penal Law §§ 225.10, 225.20. Petitioner first entered a plea of not guilty to both counts. After negotiations, the Assistant District Attorney in charge of the case agreed to permit petitioner to plead guilty to a lesser-included offense, Possession of Gambling Records in the Second Degree, N.Y. Penal Law § 225.15, conviction of which would carry a maximum prison sentence of one year. The prosecutor agreed to make no recommendation as to the sentence.

On June 16, 1969, petitioner accordingly withdrew his plea of not guilty and entered a plea of guilty to the lesser charge. Petitioner represented to the sentencing judge that the plea was voluntary and that the facts of the case, as described by the Assistant District Attorney, were true. The court accepted the plea and set a date for sentencing. A series of delays followed, owing primarily to the absence of a pre-sentence report, so that by September 23, 1969, petitioner had still not been sentenced. By that date petitioner acquired new defense counsel.

Petitioner's new counsel moved immediately to withdraw the guilty plea. In an accompanying affidavit, petitioner alleged that he did not know at the time of his plea that crucial evidence against him had been obtained as a result of an illegal search. The accuracy of this affidavit is subject to challenge since petitioner had filed and withdrawn a motion to suppress, before pleading guilty. In addition to his motion to withdraw his guilty plea, petitioner renewed the motion to suppress and filed a motion to inspect the grand jury minutes.

These three motions in turn caused further delay until November 26, 1969, when the court denied all three and set January 9, 1970, as the date for sentencing. On January 9 petitioner appeared before a different judge, the judge who had presided over the case to this juncture having retired. Petitioner renewed his motions, and the court again rejected them. The court then turned to consideration of the sentence.

At this appearance, another prosecutor had replaced the prosecutor who had negotiated the plea. The new prosecutor recommended the maximum one-year sentence. In making this recommendation, he cited petitioner's criminal record and alleged links with organized crime. Defense counsel immediately objected on the ground that the State had promised petitioner before the plea was entered that there would be no sentence recommendation by the prosecution. He sought to adjourn the sentence hearing in order to have time to prepare proof of the first prosecutor's promise. The second pros-

ecutor, apparently ignorant of his colleague's commitment, argued that there was nothing in the record to support petitioner's claim of a promise, but the State, in subsequent proceedings, has not contested that such a promise was made.

The sentencing judge ended discussion, with the following statement, quoting extensively from the pre-sentence report:

"Mr. Aronstein [Defense Counsel], I am not at all influenced by what the District Attorney says so that there is no need to adjourn the sentence, and there is no need to have any testimony. It doesn't make a particle of difference what the District Attorney says he will do, or what he doesn't do.

"I have here, Mr. Aronstein, a probation report. I have here a history of a long, long serious criminal record. I have here a picture of the life history of this man. . . .

" 'He is unamenable to supervision in the community. He is a professional criminal.' This is in quotes. 'And a recidivist. Institutionalization'—that means, in plain language, just putting him away—'is the only means of halting his anti-social activities,' and protecting you, your family, me, my family, protecting society. 'Institutionalization.' Plain language, put him behind bars.

"Under the plea, I can only send him to the New York City Correctional Institution for men for one year, which I am hereby doing."

The judge then imposed the maximum sentence of one year.

Petitioner sought and obtained a certificate of reasonable doubt and was admitted to bail pending an appeal. The Supreme Court of the State of New York, Appellate Division, First Department, unanimously affirmed petitioner's conviction, . . . and petitioner was denied leave to appeal to the New York Court of Appeals. Petitioner then sought certiorari in this Court. Mr. Justice Harlan granted bail pending our disposition of the case.

This record represents another example of an unfortunate lapse in orderly prosecutorial procedures, in part, no doubt, because of the enormous increase in the workload of the often understaffed prosecutor's offices. The heavy workload may well explain these episodes, but it does not excuse them. The disposition of criminal charges by agreement between the prosecutor and the accused, sometimes loosely called "plea bargaining," is an essential component of the administration of justice. Properly administered, it is to be encouraged. If every criminal charge were subjected to a full-scale trial, the States and the Federal Government would need to multiply by many times the number of judges and court facilities.

Disposition of charges after plea discussions is not only an essential part of the process but a highly desirable part for many reasons. It leads to prompt and largely final disposition of most criminal cases; it avoids much of the corrosive impact of enforced idleness during pretrial confinement for those who are denied release pending trial; it protects the public from those accused persons who are prone to continue criminal conduct even while on pretrial release; and, by shortening the time between charge and disposition, it enhances whatever may be the rehabilitative prospects of the guilty when they are ultimately imprisoned. . . .

However, all of these considerations presuppose fairness in securing agreement between an accused and a prosecutor. It is now clear, for example, that the accused pleading guilty must be counseled, absent a waiver. Moore v. Michigan, 355 U.S. 155 (1957). Fed. Rule Crim. Proc. 11, governing pleas in federal courts, now makes clear that the sentencing judge must develop, *on the record,* the factual basis for the plea, as, for example, by having the accused describe the conduct that gave rise to the charge. The plea must, of course, be voluntary and knowing and if it was induced by promises, the essence of those promises must in some way be made known. There is, of course, no absolute right to have a guilty plea accepted. A court may reject a plea in exercise of sound judicial discretion.

This phase of the process of criminal justice, and the adjudicative element inherent in accepting a plea of guilty, must be attended by safeguards to insure the defendant what is reasonbly due in the circumstances. Those circumstances will vary, but a constant factor is that when a plea rests in any significant degree on a promise or agreement of the prosecutor, so that it can be said to be part of the inducement or consideration, such promise must be fulfilled.

On this record, petitioner "bargained" and negotiated for a particular plea in order to secure dismissal of more serious charges, but also on condition that no sentence recommendation would be made by the prosecutor. It is now conceded that the promise to abstain from a recommendation was made, and at this stage the prosecution is not in a good position to argue that its inadvertent breach of agreement is immaterial. The staff lawyers in a prosecutor's office have the burden of "letting the left hand know what the right hand is doing" or has done. That the breach of agreement was inadvertent does not lessen its impact.

We need not reach the question whether the sentencing judge would or would not have been influenced had he known all the details of the negotiations for the plea. He stated that the prosecutor's recommendation did not influence him and we have no reason to doubt that. Nevertheless, we conclude that the interests of justice and appropriate recognition of the duties of the prosecution in relation to promises made in the negotiation of pleas of guilty will be best served by remanding the case to the state courts for further consideration. The ultimate relief to which petitioner is entitled we leave to the discretion of the state court, which is in a better position to decide whether the circumstances of this case require only that there be specific performance of the agreement on the plea, in which case petitioner should be resentenced by a different judge, or whether, in the view of the state court, the circumstances require granting the relief sought by petitioner, i.e., the opportunity to withdraw his plea of guilty. We emphasize that this is in no sense to question the fairness of the sentencing judge; the fault here rests on the prosecutor, not on the sentencing judge.

Vacated and remanded.

[Mr. Justice DOUGLAS wrote a concurring opinion.]

Mr. Justice MARSHALL, with whom Mr. Justice BRENNAN and Mr. Justice STEWART join, concurring in part and dissenting in part.

I agree with much of the majority's opinion, but conclude that petitioner must be permitted to withdraw his guilty plea. This is the relief petitioner requested, and, on the facts set out by the majority, it is a form of relief to which he is entitled.

There is no need to belabor the fact that the Constitution guarantees to all criminal defendants the right to a trial by judge or jury, or, put another way, the "right not to plead guilty." United States v. Jackson, 390 U.S. 570, 581 (1968). This and other federal rights may be waived through a guilty plea, but such waivers are not lightly presumed and, in fact, are viewed with the "utmost solicitude." ... Given this, I believe that where the defendant presents a reason for vacating his plea and the government has not relied on the plea to its disadvantage, the plea may be vacated and the right to trial regained, at least where the motion to vacate is made prior to sentence and judgment. In other words, in such circumstances I would not deem the earlier plea to have irrevocably waived the defendant's federal constitutional right to a trial.

Here, petitioner never claimed any automatic right to withdraw a guilty plea before sentencing. Rather, he tendered a specific reason why, in his case, the plea should be vacated. His reason was that the prosecutor had broken a promise made in return for the agreement to plead guilty. When a prosecutor breaks the bargain, he undercuts the basis for the waiver of constitutional rights implicit in the plea. This, it seems to me, provides the defendant ample justification for rescinding the plea. Where a promise is "unfulfilled," Brady v. United States, 397 U.S. 742, 755

(1970), specifically denies that the plea "must stand." Of course, where the prosecutor has broken the plea agreement, it may be appropriate to permit the defendant to enforce the plea bargain. But that is not the remedy sought here. Rather, it seems to me that a breach of the plea bargain provides ample reason to permit the plea to be vacated.[*]

It is worth noting that in the ordinary case where a motion to vacate is made prior to sentencing, the government has taken no action in reliance on the previously entered guilty plea and would suffer no harm from the plea's withdrawal. More pointedly, here the State claims no such harm beyond disappointed expectations about the plea itself. At least where the government itself has broken the plea bargain, this disappointment cannot bar petitioner from withdrawing his guilty plea and reclaiming his right to a trial. ...

---

*Mr. Justice DOUGLAS, although joining the Court's opinion (apparently because he believed that the remedy should be chosen by the state court), concluded that the state court "ought to accord a defendant's preference considerable, if not controlling, weight." Thus, a majority of the Court appeared to believe that, in cases like this, when the defendant seeks to vacate the plea, that relief should generally be granted. 404 U.S. 257, 263–267 (1971).

Comments

1. In *Santobello* v. *New York,* supra, the Court held that a broken promise (albeit inadvertent) by a prosecutor to make no sentencing recommendation pursuant to a guilty plea is sufficient to vacate the judgment and remand the case back to the state courts. Interestingly, the *Santobello* Court left it up to the New York courts to decide whether the defendant should be resentenced before a different judge or whether he should be entitled to withdraw his guilty plea and plead anew to the original charges. If a defendant is allowed to withdraw his plea of guilty, should he have a right to be tried before a different judge? If so, may the rejected plea arrangement be presented to the next judge? On what constitutional grounds was the judgment in *Santobello* vacated? Although the Court didn't specify, presumably the decision rested on Fourteenth Amendment due process grounds. In view of *Santobello,* could a prosecutor's good faith ever be sufficient to overcome a guilty plea that rested on a broken promise? How serious must a broken promise be to void a guilty plea? Suppose that a prosecutor promises a defendant that he will be sentenced on a particular day or by a certain judge, and fails to keep his promise. Suppose a

prosecutor assures a defendant that the sentencing judge will give "good time" credit (for pretrial jail time) or confidently predicts that the judge will sentence the defendant to probation and the judge does not. Are these broken promises sufficient to vacate a guilty plea notwithstanding the fact that the prosecutor had no control over the outcome?

2. In other cases relevant to the plea bargaining process the Supreme Court held that (1) a plea of guilty is subject to appeal if the defendant was unrepresented by counsel at the time of the plea, *Pennsylvania* v. *Claudy*, 350 U.S. 116 (1956); (2) a defendant who pleads guilty on the advice of counsel is not automatically entitled to federal habeas corpus relief because the indicting grand jury was unconstitutionally selected unless his attorney's advice was clearly incompetent, *Tollett* v. *Henderson*, 411 U.S. 258 (1973); (3) if a defendant pleads guilty to an offense, it is not error for the trial court to deny the defendant's motion to withdraw the plea prior to sentencing because his counsel was representing other co-defendants and there was an alleged conflict of interest, *Dukes* v. *Warden*, 406 U.S. 250 (1972); (4) when a state law permits a defendant to plead guilty and collaterally attack the conviction, such postconviction claims are cognizable in a federal habeas corpus proceeding, *Lefkowitz* v. *Newsome*, 420 U.S. 283 (1975); and (5) there is no constitutional right to have a guilty plea accepted, it being a matter of discretion for the trial judge, *Lynch* v. *Overholser*, 369 U.S. 705 (1962).

Pleas Made in Ignorance of an Essential Element of the Offense

HENDERSON v. MORGAN

Supreme Court of the United States, 1976
426 U.S. 637, 96 S. Ct. 2253, 49 L. Ed. 2d 108

Timothy Morgan, the respondent, was indicted in 1965 for first degree murder, but by agreement with the prosecution and on counsel's advice he pleaded guilty to second degree murder. He was sentenced by a New York state court to be imprisoned for 25 years to life. Subsequently, the New York state courts rejected his attempts to have his conviction vacated on the ground that his guilty plea was involuntary. In 1973, Morgan filed a petition for a writ of habeas corpus in federal District Court (N.D.N.Y.) alleging that his guilty plea was involuntary because he was not aware (1) of the sentence that might be imposed upon a conviction of second degree murder, and (2) that an intent to cause death was an element of the offense. The district court ultimately held an evidentiary hearing and concluded that although Morgan had been informed that he would be sentenced to 25 years' imprisonment if he pleaded guilty, he had not been advised by counsel or the state court that an intent to cause death was an essential element of second degree murder. On the basis of this finding, the district court held that the guilty plea was involuntary and must be set aside. The Court of Appeals (2d Cr.) affirmed, and the United States Supreme Court granted certiorari.

Additional facts are stated in the opinion.

Mr. Justice STEVENS delivered the opinion of the Court.

The question presented is whether a defendant may enter a voluntary plea of guilty to a charge of second-degree murder without being informed that intent to cause the death of his victim was an element of the offense.

* * *

. . . We review some of the facts developed at the evidentiary hearing.

I

On April 6, 1965, respondent killed Mrs. Ada Francisco in her home.

When he was in seventh grade, respondent was committed to the Rome State School for Mental Defectives where he was classified as "retarded." He was released to become a farm laborer and ultimately went to work on Mrs. Francisco's farm. Following an argument, she threatened to return him to state custody. He then decided to abscond. During the night he entered Mrs. Francisco's bedroom with a knife, intending to collect his earned wages before leaving; she awoke, began to scream, and he stabbed her. He took a small amount of money, fled in her car, and became involved in an accident about 80 miles away. The knife was found in the glove compartment of her car. He was promptly arrested and made a statement to the police. He was then 19 years old and substantially below average intelligence.

Respondent was indicted for first-degree murder and arraigned on April 15, 1965. Two concededly competent attorneys were appointed to represent him. The indictment, which charged that he "willfully" stabbed his victim, was read in open court. His lawyers requested, and were granted, access to his written statement and to earlier psychiatric reports. A new psychiatric examination was requested and ordered.

Respondent was found competent to stand trial. Defense counsel held a series of conferences with the prosecutors, with the respondent, and with members of his family. The lawyers "thought manslaughter first would satisfy the needs of justice." They therefore endeavored to have the charge reduced to manslaughter, but the prosecution would agree to nothing less than second-degree murder and a minimum sentence

of 25 years. The lawyers gave respondent advice about the different sentences which could be imposed for the different offenses, but, as the District Court found, did not explain the required element of intent.

On June 8, 1965, respondent appeared in court with his attorneys and entered a plea of guilty to murder in the second degree in full satisfaction of the first-degree murder charge made in the indictment. In direct colloquy with the trial judge respondent stated that his plea was based on the advice of his attorneys, that he understood he was accused of killing Mrs. Francisco in Fulton County, that he was waiving his right to a jury trial and that he would be sent to prison. There was no discussion of the elements of the offense of second-degree murder, no indication that the nature of the offense had ever been discussed with respondent, and no reference of any kind to the requirement of intent to cause the death of the victim.

At the sentencing hearing a week later his lawyers made a statement explaining his version of the offense, particularly noting that respondent "meant no harm to the lady" when he entered her room with the knife. The prosecutor disputed defense counsel's version of the matter, but did not discuss it in detail. After studying the probation officer's report, the trial judge pronounced sentence.

At the evidentiary hearing in the Federal District Court, respondent testified that he would not have pleaded guilty if he had known that an intent to cause the death of his victim was an element of the offense of second-degree murder. The District Judge did not indicate whether or not he credited this testimony.

II

Petitioner contends that the District Court applied an unrealistically rigid rule of law. Instead of testing the voluntariness of a plea by determining whether a ritualistic litany of the formal legal elements of an offense was read to the defendant, petitioner argues that the court should examine the totality of the circumstances and determine whether the substance of the charge, as opposed to its technical elements, was conveyed to the accused. We do not disagree with the thrust of petitioner's argument, but we are persuaded that even under the test which he espouses, this judgment finding respondent guilty of second-degree murder was defective.

We assume, as petitioner argues, that the prosecutor had overwhelming evidence of guilt available. We also accept petitioner's characterization of the competence of respondent's counsel and of the wisdom of their advice to plead guilty to a charge of second-degree murder. Nevertheless, such a plea cannot support a judgment of guilt unless it was voluntary in a constitutional sense. And clearly the plea could not be voluntary in the sense that it constituted an intelligent admission that he committed the offense unless the defendant received "real notice of the true nature of the charge against him, the first and most universally recognized requirement of due process." Smith v. O'Grady, 312 U.S. 329, 333 (1941).

The charge of second-degree murder was never formally made. Had it been made, it necessarily would have included a charge that respondent's assault was "committed with a design to effect the death of the person killed." . . .

There is nothing in this record that can serve as a substitute for either a finding after trial, or a voluntary admission, that respondent had the requisite intent. Defense counsel did not purport to stipulate to that fact; they did not explain to him that his plea would be an admission of that fact; and he made no factual statement or admission necessarily implying that he had such intent. In these circumstances it is impossible to conclude that his plea to the unexplained charge of second-degree murder was voluntary.

Petitioner argues that affirmance of the Court of Appeals will invite countless collateral attacks on judgments entered on pleas of guilty, since frequently the record will not contain a complete enumeration of the elements of the offense to which an accused person pleads guilty.[r] We think petitioner's fears are exaggerated.

Normally the record contains either an explanation of the charge by the trial judge,

or at least a representation by defense counsel that the nature of the offense has been explained to the accused. Moreover, even without such an express representation, it may be appropriate to presume that in most cases defense counsel routinely explain the nature of the offense in sufficient detail to give the accused notice of what he is being asked to admit. This case is unique because the trial judge found as a fact that the element of intent was not explained to respondent. Moreover, respondent's unusually low mental capacity provides a reasonable explanation for counsel's oversight; it also forecloses the conclusion that the error was harmless beyond a reasonable doubt, for it lends at least a modicum of credibility to defense counsel's appraisal of the homicide as a manslaughter rather than a murder.

Since respondent did not receive adequate notice of the offense to which he pleaded guilty, his plea was involuntary and the judgment of conviction was entered without due process of law.

Affirmed.

Mr. Justice WHITE, with whom Mr. Justice STEWART, Mr. Justice BLACKMUN, and Mr. Justice POWELL join, concurring.

There are essentially two ways under our system of criminal justice in which the factual guilt of a defendant may be established such that he may be deprived of his liberty consistent with the Due Process Clause of the Fourteenth Amendment to the United States Constitution. The first is by a verdict of a jury which or judge who concludes after trial that the elements of the crime have been proven beyond a reasonable doubt. The second is by the defendant's own solemn admission "in open court that he is *in fact guilty* of the offense with which he is charged," Tollett v. Henderson, 411 U.S. 258, 267 (1973), i.e., by plea of guilty. . . .

The problem in this case is that the defendant's guilt has been established neither by a finding of guilt beyond a reasonable doubt after trial nor by the defendant's own admission that he is in fact guilty. The defendant did not expressly admit that he intended the victim's death (such intent being an element of the crime for which he stands convicted); and his plea of guilty cannot be construed as an implied admission

---

[r]There is no need in this case to decide whether notice of the true nature, or substance, of a charge always requires a description of every element of the offense; we assume it does not. Nevertheless, intent is such a critical element of the offense of second-degree murder that notice of that element is required.

that he intended her death because the trial court has found that he was not told and did not know that intent to kill was an element of the offense with which he was charged.

* * *

In this case the defendant's factual guilt of second-degree murder has never been established in any fashion permitted by the Due Process Clause of the Fourteenth Amendment.

The dissent concedes that the conviction in this case was entered in violation of the United States Constitution. The dissent argues, however, that to set this defendant's conviction aside is to apply a new constitutional rule retroactively. The argument was not made by the State in this case and is, in any event, untenable. In order to escape application of a constitutional rule to a particular criminal case, on nonretroactivity grounds, the State must point to a judicial decision occurring after the operative facts of the case in question clearly establishing the rule. The constitutional rule relevant to this case is that the defendant's guilt is not deemed established by entry of a guilty plea, unless he either admits that he committed the crime charged, or enters his plea knowing what the elements of the crime charged are. If this is a new rule, created since the defendant entered his plea, I am at a loss to know what case, other than this one, established it. McCarthy v. United States, 394 U.S. 459 (1969), did not do so. That case involved only a construction of Fed. Rule Crim. Proc. 11, and has no application to the States. Boykin v. Alabama, 395 U.S. 238 (1969), did not do so. It does not mention the method of establishing the defendant's factual guilt. The only case which arguably addresses the issue in this case is Brady v. United States, 397 U.S. 742 (1970), which observed in dictum in a footnote "the importance of assuring that a defendant does not plead guilty except with a full understanding of the charges against him was at the heart of our recent decisions in McCarthy v. United States, supra, and Boykin v. Alabama, 395 U.S. 238 (1969)," p. 749 n.6. However, new rules of constitutional law are not established in dicta in footnotes. Either a new constitutional rule is being established in *this* case—in which event we will have to address at some future time the question whether this rule is ret-

roactive—or, as I believe to be true, this case rests on the long-accepted principle that a guilty plea must provide a trustworthy basis for believing that the defendant is in fact guilty. If so, then the principle will and should govern all similar cases presented to us in the future. In any event, the judgment of the court below should be affirmed, and I join the opinion of the Court.

Mr. Justice REHNQUIST, with whom the CHIEF JUSTICE [BURGER] joins, dissenting.

The Court's opinion affirms a judgment which directs the release on federal habeas of a state prisoner who, on advice of counsel, pleaded guilty in the New York State courts 11 years ago to a charge of second-degree murder. The Court declares its agreement with petitioner's contention that the test for reviewing the constitutional validity of a counselled plea of guilty should be "the totality of the circumstances.". . . But the Court's holding can be justified only if the Constitution requires that "a ritualistic litany of the formal legal elements of an offense [be] read to the defendant," . . . a requirement which it purports to eschew. The Court accomplishes this result by imposing on state courts, as a constitutional requirement, a definition of "voluntariness" announced by this Court in McCarthy v. United States, 394 U.S. 459 (1969), in which the Court interpreted a provision of the Federal Rules of Criminal Procedure. Yet that case has been held to have only prospective application even as to the federal courts. Halliday v. United States, 394 U.S. 831 (1969).

McCarthy extended the definition of voluntariness to include an "understanding of the essential elements of the crime charged, including the requirement of specific intent . . . ," 394 U.S. 459. But prior to McCarthy, and to this Court's decision of a related issue in Boykin v. Alabama, 395 U.S. 238 (1969), the generally accepted standard for a valid guilty plea in federal courts was set forth in Machibroda v. United States, 368 U.S. 487, 493 (1962), which in turn relied on Kercheval v. United States, 274 U.S. 220, 223 (1927). Though these were federal cases, certainly no more stringent a standard could be applied as a matter of constitutional law on federal habeas review of state convictions. The Court said in Machibroda: "Out of just consideration for persons accused of crime, courts are careful that a plea of guilty shall not be accepted unless made voluntarily after proper advice and with full understanding of the consequences."

These cases thus set forth a three-pronged test: the plea of guilty must be made voluntarily, it must be made after proper advice, and it must be made with full understanding of the consequences. There can be no doubt that respondent entered his plea "with full understanding of the consequences" because the District Court expressly so found. Nor can there be any serious doubt that respondent's plea was made "voluntarily" as that term is used in Machibroda and the previous cases upon which it relies.

There was no contention in the federal habeas court that respondent's guilty plea was not "voluntary" in the normal sense of that word. There was no hint of physical or psychological coercion, and respondent was represented by not one but two admittedly capable defense attorneys. While McCarthy v. United States, supra, expands the notion of "voluntariness" to include the concept that a defendant must have an "understanding of the essential elements of the crime charged, including the requirement of specific intent..." 394 U.S., at 471, in order for a plea in the federal courts to be valid under Fed. Rule Crim. Proc. 11, that decision was held prospective only in Halliday, supra. Even had it not been, Rule 11 by its terms applies only to proceedings in federal courts.

... Thus, unless the Court intends to establish a new and far more stringent standard for all guilty pleas entered before the 1969 decisions of this Court in Boykin and McCarthy, respondent's plea was "voluntary" as that term was understood before the decisions in those cases.

* * *

I do not see how this Court, or any court, could conclude on this state of the record that respondent was not "properly advised" at the time he entered his plea of guilty to the charge of second-degree murder.

His attorneys were motivated by the eminently reasonable tactical judgment on their part that he should plead guilty to second-degree murder in order to avoid the possibility of conviction for first-degree murder with its more serious attendant penalties. Since the Court concedes both the competence of respondent's counsel and the wisdom of their advice, that should be the end of the matter.

* * *

The "totality of the circumstances" in this case shows that respondent pleaded guilty to second-degree murder upon the advice of competent counsel. His plea was in no way the result of physical or psychological coercion or overreaching by the State, and he was fully advised as to the consequences of that plea. True, he was not expressly advised that the "design to effect death" was an element of the offense to which he was pleading, although the original first-degree murder indictment charging "malice aforethought" had been read to him. Given the finding of the habeas judge that there was more than ample evidence from which the jury could have found that respondent had the requisite intent, I cannot subscribe to the Court's invalidation of his pre-1969 guilty plea for such an extremely technical defect.

In adopting the rule it does, the Court opens the door to countless similarly situated prisoners to withdraw their guilty pleas many years after they were entered. Since it is unlikely that prosecutors will be able to reassemble witnesses and evidence at this late date to try these prisoners, the practical effect of the Court's ruling will be to release these prisoners who at one time freely admitted their guilt.

Comments

1. In *Henderson* v. *Morgan,* supra, a majority of the Court concluded that an otherwise voluntary plea of guilty to an offense will be set aside if the defendant did not receive "real notice of the true nature of the charges against him," and held that such notice includes an awareness of the essential elements of the offense. Did *Morgan* announce a new constitutional rule as Justice Rehnquist (dissenting) claimed? Or did it reaffirm the existing procedural rules from prior

cases as Justice White (concurring) suggested? If *Morgan* did announce a new constitutional rule, should it be made retroactive? The majority stated that the petitioner's (the Superintendent of the New York Auburn Correctional Facility) fears that *Morgan* will open the floodgates for prisoners' collateral attacks on guilty pleas are "exaggerated." Do you agree? The majority assumes that defendants need not *always* be given a description of every element of the offense (n.r). When is it not necessary? Intent is an essential element of many felonies (e.g., attempted felonies, larceny, robbery, conspiracy, burglary, kidnapping). Does *Morgan* mean that all defendants must be expressly informed that intent is an element of such felonies? If so, is *Morgan* applicable to misdemeanors that require intent as an essential element of the offense (e.g., simple assault)? Would the Court have reached a different result if the respondent had been of normal intelligence? Does *Morgan* have broad applications in light of the Court's statement that "it may be appropriate to presume that in most cases defense counsel routinely explain the nature of the offense in sufficient detail to give the accused notice of what he is being asked to admit"? Must a defendant be informed of all available defenses before a guilty plea will be accepted? Is the "totality of circumstances" test used by the Court the best measure of the voluntariness of a guilty plea?

2.   Recent lower federal and state court decisions involving the plea bargaining process and guilty pleas include *Selikoff* v. *N.Y. State Comm'r of Corrections*, 524 F.2d 650 (2d Cir. 1975) (defendant who pleaded guilty but misrepresented the extent of his criminal involvement to the judge is not entitled to a nonincarceration sentence even though the judge initially indicated he would not impose incarceration); *People* v. *Soto*, 233 N.W.2d 545 (Mich. App. 1975) (immediately after a guilty plea is accepted, the prosecution must move for a formal dismissal of other charges so that there is no threat to the defendant's exercise of the right to appeal on the charge to which he has pleaded guilty); *United States* v. *Smith*, 527 F.2d 692 (10th Cir. 1975) (statements made during plea bargaining are inadmissible in the government's case-in-chief at trial even though the defendant was warned of his rights) (in accord is *Burke* v. *Mancusi*, 425 F.2d 1061 [2d Cir. 1970]); *In re Arvedon*, 523 F.2d 914 (1st Cir. 1975) (under Fed. R. Crim. P. 20, Massachusetts federal judge erred in refusing to accept a guilty plea to a Florida federal indictment on the ground that the defendant desired not to return to Florida for trial); *State* v. *Gibson*, 348 A.2d 769 (N.J. 1975) (waiver of appeal rights as part of a plea bargaining arrangement upheld even though a defendant can nevertheless file a timely appeal); *Cruz* v. *State*, 530 S.W.2d 817 (Tex. Ct. Crim. App. 1975) (defendant does not have a right to withdraw a plea of guilty when the trial court refuses to follow the punishment recommendation of the prosecutor); *Faulis* v. *Daggett*, 527 F.2d 305 (7th Cir. 1975) (trial court's failure to advise a defendant offering to plead guilty that his sentence might be imposed consecutively to a state sentence he was already serving does not render the plea invalid) (see also *Hinds* v. *United States*, 429 F.2d 1322 [9th Cir. 1970]); *People* v. *Heral*, 342 N.E.2d 34 (Ill. 1976) (murder defendant who was found competent to stand trial is not entitled to a separate finding as to her competence to tender a guilty plea); *Cardenas* v. *Meacham*, 545 P.2d 632 (Wyo. 1976) (defendant who pleaded

guilty to rape and felonious assault held entitled to withdraw his plea because judge failed to advise him of the maximum sentence for felonious assault); *Kelleher* v. *Henderson,* 531 F.2d 78 (2d Cir. 1976) (defendant who had rejected a plea bargain offer of 6 to 18 years but who subsequently changed his plea to guilty held not entitled to withdraw his plea after being sentenced to 7 to 21 years despite the failure of defense counsel and the trial judge to inform him of the 25 year maximum sentence he faced); *Commonwealth* v. *Zuber,* 353 A.2d 441 (Pa. 1976) (parolee who pleaded guilty to murder but whose plea bargain was impossible to keep under state law held entitled to a modification of his sentence so that he could receive the benefit of the bargain); *Capri Adult Cinema* v. *State,* 537 S.W.2d 896 (Tenn. 1976) (defendants who waived their rights of appeal as a part of a plea bargain cannot obtain appellate review of their convictions); *State* v. *Allard,* 356 A.2d 671 (N.H. 1976) (burglary defendant's agreement to plead guilty, made without knowledge that he had a possible defense based on his asserted lack of intent to steal at the time he broke and entered, upheld); *United States* v. *Werker,* 535 F.2d 198 (2d Cir. 1976) (judge may not reveal sentence he would impose should the defendant plead guilty); *United States* v. *Crusco,* 536 F.2d 21 (3d Cir. 1976) (prosecutor's reneging on his promise not to take a position on sentencing pursuant to a plea negotiation requires that defendant be permitted to plead anew); *Hamlin* v. *Barrett,* 335 So. 2d 898 (Miss. 1976) (forgery defendant who received probation as a result of plea negotiations during which he concealed from the prosecution and the judge a prior New York robbery conviction, may have his probation revoked and be required to serve a prison sentence); *State* v. *Goodrich,* 363 A.2d 425 (N.H. 1976) (defendants whose sentences following their guilty pleas were much stiffer than those recommended by the prosecutor held entitled to withdraw their pleas and stand trial); *Jones* v. *Commonwealth,* 227 S.E.2d 701 (Va. 1976) (defendant who did not receive the benefit of a prosecution recommendation of leniency which had been agreed upon as a part of the plea bargain held entitled to relief in the nature of specific performance); *Wood* v. *Morris,* 554 P.2d 1032 (Wash. 1976) (failure of plea bargaining record to disclose on its face that a defendant was aware of the full consequences of his action held ground for setting aside the plea) (in accord is *United States* v. *Boone,* 543 F.2d 1090 [4th Cir. 1976]); *State* v. *Carlson,* 555 P.2d 269 (Ala. 1976) (trial judge exceeded his authority by accepting, over the prosecutor's objection, a murder defendant's plea of guilty to manslaughter) (see also *People* v. *Superior Court of Marin Co.,* 446 P.2d 138 [Calif. 1968], *People* v. *Sidener,* 375 P.2d 641 [Calif. 1962], cert. denied 374 U.S. 494 [1963], overruled on other grounds in *People* v. *Tenorio,* 473 P.2d 993 [Calif. 1970], *People* v. *Burke,* 301 P.2d 241 [Calif. 1956], and *People* v. *Smith,* 126 Cal. Rptr. 195 [Calif. App. 1975]); *Palermo* v. *Warden,* 545 F.2d 286 (2d Cir. 1976) (prosecutor's unfulfilled promise to defendant that he would receive parole in exchange for returning stolen jewelry requires specific performance); *Commonwealth* v. *Holmes,* 364 A.2d 259 (Pa. 1976) (failure of judge to explain elements of crime in understandable terms to defendant requires that guilty plea be set aside) (see also *Commonwealth* v. *Ingram,* 316 A.2d 77 [Pa. 1977], and *Commonwealth* v. *Sutton,* 350 A.2d 824 [Pa. 1976]); *People* v. *Matheson,* 245 N.W.2d 551 (Mich. App. 1976) (trial judge has an obligation to render a separate finding of competency at the time a plea bargain is offered); *United States* v. *Garcia*, 544 F.2d 681 (3d Cir. 1976) (trial court's imposition of harsh sentence on two guilty-pleading defendants because they refuse to give information about the drug trafficking in which they were involved set aside); *Hicks* v. *United States*, 362 A.2d 111 (D.C. App. 1976) (judge's failure to inform defendant of the consequences of his guilty plea does not require that the plea be set aside unless the defendant can show such failure was prejudicial to him); *Hicks* v. *State*, 552 P.2d 889 (Kan. 1976) (ineligibility for early parole or reduction of sentence is not a "consequence" of a guilty plea which a judge must advise a defendant of before accepting his guilty plea); *State* v. *Storbakken*, 246 N.W.2d 78 (N.D. 1976) (defendant is presumed to be competent to enter plea of guilty unless evidence to the contrary is produced); *People* v. *Watts*, 136 Cal. Rptr. 496 (Calif. App. 1977) (the law does not require that an offer to plead guilty be held open for any specified period of time); State v. *Stewart*, 250 N.W.2d 849 (Neb. 1977) (defendants have no absolute right to have guilty pleas accepted); *Cantu* v. *State*, 546 S.W.2d 621 (Tex. Cr. App. 1977) (possession of a trace of heroin is sufficient to support a plea of guilty); *Jackson* v. *Estelle*, 548 F.2d 617 (5th Cir. 1977) (defendant's fear of death penalty does not alone render guilty plea involuntary); *State* v. *LaRoche*, 370 A.2d 631 (N.H. 1977) (defendant's fear of a greater punishment should he go to trial is not a ground for finding guilty plea involuntary; *Commonwealth* v. *O'Donnell*, 370 A.2d 1209 (Pa. 1977) (guilty plea is not involuntary because counsel advised defendant of likely consequences if case were to go to trial); *State* v. *Nielson*, 547 S.W.2d 153 (Mo. App. 1977) (defendant who alleged that he pleaded guilty because of inadmissible confession is not, without more, entitled to relief); *State* v. *Kluge*, 251 N.W.2d 737 (Neb. 1977) (plea of nolo contendere is equivalent to, and places defendant in same position as, plea of guilty); *Jones* v. *Henderson*, 549 F.2d 995 (5th Cir. 1977) (length of time spent in consultation with counsel is only one factor in determining validity of guilty plea); *Butts* v. *State*, 346 So. 2d 497 (Ala. Cr. App. 1977) (a plea of guilty purges the record of error unless the defendant proves clearly that his plea was extorted by duress, fraud, intimidation, or deception); *Slay* v. *State*, 347 So.2d 730 (Fla. App. 1977) (when defendant pleaded nolo contendere pursuant to plea bargain whereby state recommended that he be placed on probation and trial judge concurred but judge later determined that incarceration was appropriate, defendant should have been allowed to withdraw plea).

14

SENTENCING, APPEALS, AND POSTCONVICTION REMEDIES

The almost wholly unchecked and sweeping powers we give to judges in the fashioning of sentences are terrifying and intolerable for a society that professes devotion to the rule of law.[1]
— Federal Judge Marvin E. Frankel

Our sentences . . . have consistently been two to three times as long as those found in most European countries.[2]
— Professor David Rothman

I warn you to stay unswerving to your task — that of standing by the man on the firing line — the practical, hard-headed, experienced honest policemen who have shown by their efforts that they, and they alone, know the answer to the crime problem. That answer can be summed up in one sentence — adequate detection, swift apprehension, and certain, unrelenting punishment. That is what the criminal fears. That is what he understands, and nothing else, and that fear is the only thing which will force him into the ranks of the law-abiding.[3]
— J. Edgar Hoover

14.01 INTRODUCTION TO THE SENTENCING PROCESS

Despite an abundance of professional literature on the underlying theories of criminal punishment[4] — especially on its value (or nonvalue) as a deterrent[5] — there is no similar wealth of scholarly writings and empirical studies on the sentencing process in the United States. However, some useful general statements can be made.

---

[4]Menninger, *The Crime of Punishment* (1966); Packer, *The Limits of the Criminal Sanction* (1968); Van den Haag, *Punishing Criminals — Concerning a Very Old and Painful Question* (1975); Von Hirsch, *Doing Justice: The Choice of Punishments* (1976); Chiricos and Waldo, *Punishment and Crime: An Examination of Some Empirical Evidence,* 18 Social Problems 200 (1970); Barnes, *The Story of Punishment* (2d ed. 1972); Walker, *Punishment: An Illustrated History* (1973); and Hart, *Punishment and Responsibility: Essays in the Philosophy of Law* (1968).

[5]Zimiring and Hawkins, *Deterrence* (1973); Gibbs, *Crime, Punishment, and Deterrence* (1975); Andenaes, *Punishment and Deterrence* (1974); Bailey, *Crime and Deterrence — A Correlational Analysis,* 11 J. Research Crime & Del. 124 (1974); Chamblis, *The Deterrent Influence of Punishment,* 12 Crime & Del. 70 (1966); Salem and Bowers, *Severity of Formal Sanctions as a Deterrent to Deviant Behavior,* 5 Law & Society Rev. 21 (1970); Levin, *Crime as a Deterrent,* 72 New Statesman 9 (1966); Gray and Martin, *Punishment and Deterrence: Another Analysis of Gibbs' Data,* 50 Soc. Sc. Q. 389 (1969); Bean and Cushing, *Criminal Homicide, Punishment and Deterrence: Methodological and Substantive Recommendations,* 52 Soc. Sci. Q. 277 (1971); Antunes and Hunt, *The Deterrent Impact of*

Footnote continued on opposite page

---

[1]Frankel, *Criminal Sentences* 5 (1972).
[2]In Orland and Tyler (eds.), *Justice in Sentencing* 46 (1974).
[3]Sutherland and Cressey, *Criminology* 347 (8th ed. 1970).

Although the sentencing is naturally of great importance to the convicted defendant, he enjoys few constitutional protections at this stage of the criminal justice process and is, in effect, left to the "mercy of the sentencing judge."[6] Yet few jurisdictions have developed legal standards to ensure that sentencing procedures are rational and fair.

At sentencing, a judge may have little or no information about the defendant before him, especially in misdemeanor cases. Even though a presentence report (PSI) may be available, the judge is not bound by the sentencing recommendations of the probation officer. An in general—except perhaps in capital cases[7]—neither the defendant nor his counsel has a constitutional right to see the information in the PSI to check its accuracy.[8]

In the absence of a mandatory sentencing statute, a judge can sentence a defendant to any term within the statutory range permitted for a particular crime, guided only by his own moral standards and sense of fairness. Sentences that are within statutory boundaries are not subject to appellate review in most jurisdictions.

Because of a lack of uniform sentencing standards and guidelines, gross disparities in sentencing have become an integral part of the criminal process, and such inequalities undermine what little rehabilitation occurs in the correctional field. As federal judge Marvin E. Frankel has noted, the sentencing practices in America are literally "lawless."[9]

Although American judges have the distinction of handing out some of the most severe sentences,[10] these lengthy sentences, despite their emotional appeal to many persons, seem to have little effect on the rate of recidivism, which has been estimated to be as high as 50 to 80 per cent, depending on the type of offense. The average inmate is returned to society within three years of the start of his incarceration and becomes a repeat offender within a year of his release.[11]

Criminal Sanctions: Some Implications for Criminal Justice Policy, 51 J. Urban Law 145 (1973); Zimiring, *Perspectives on Deterrence* (1971); Tittle, *Crime Rates and Legal Sanctions,* 16 Social Problems 409 (1969); Bailey and Lott, *Crime, Punishment and Personality: An Examination of the Deterrence Question,* 67 J. Crim. L. & Crim. 99 (1976); Ehrlich, *The Deterrent Effect of Criminal Law Enforcements,* 1 J. Legal Issues 259 (1972); Phillips and Votey, *An Economic Analysis of the Deterrent Effect of Law Enforcement on Criminal Activity,* 63 J. Crim. L. Crim. & Pol. Sci. 330 (1972); California Assembly Commission on Criminal Procedure, *Deterrent Effects of Criminal Sanctions* (1968); Andenaes, *General Prevention—Illusion or Reality,* 43 J. Crim. L. Crim. & Pol. Sci. 176 (1952); Ball, *The Deterrence Concept in Criminology and Law,* 46 J. Crim. L. Crim. & Pol. Sci. 347 (1955); Zimiring and Hawkins, *Deterrence and Marginal Groups,* 5 J. Research Crime & Del. 100 (1968); Morris and Zimiring, *Deterrence and Correction,* 381 The Annals 137 (1969); Doleschal, *The Deterrent Effect of Legal Punishment,* 1 Information Rev. Crime & Del. 1 (1969); Cooper, *Crime Control and the Deterrence Perspective,* 11 Criminology 161 (1973); Chauncey, *Deterrence: Certainty, Severity, and Skyjacking,* 12 Criminology 447 (1975); Decker, *Curbside Deterrence?* 10 Criminology 127 (1972).

[6]Singer and Statsky, *Rights of the Imprisoned* 271 (1974).

[7]See *Gardner* v. *Florida,* infra, § 14.02. It is unclear whether the holding of *Gardner* is applicable to noncapital offenses.

[8]*Williams* v. *New York,* 337 U.S. 241 (1949).

---

[9]Frankel, supra note 1, p. x. See also Hogarth, *Sentencing as a Human Process* (1971); Gaylin, *Partial Justice—A Study of Bias in Sentencing* (1974); Orland and Tyler (eds.), *Justice in Sentencing* (1974); Frankel, *Criminal Sentences* (1972); Hall and Sinkus, *Inequality in the Types of Sentences Received by Native Americans and Whites,* 13 Criminology 199 (1975); Chiricos, Jackson, and Waldo, *Inequality in the Imposition of a Criminal Label,* 19 Social Problems 553 (1972); Green, *Inter- and Intra-racial Crime Relative to Sentencing,* J. Crim. L. Crim. & Pol. Sci. 55 (1964); Thornberry, *Race, Socioeconomic Status in Sentencing in the Juvenile Justice System,* 64 J. Crim. L. & Crim. 90 (1973); Zumwalt, *The Anarchy of Sentencing in the Federal Courts,* Judicature 102 (1973); Cargan and Coates, *The Indeterminate Sentence and Judicial Bias,* 20 Crime & Del. 144 (1974); Hood and Sparks, *Key Issues in Criminology* 142 (1970); Johnson, *The Negro and Crime,* Annals of the American Academy of Political and Social Science 93 (1941).

[10]Zimiring and Hawkins, *Deterrence: The Legal Threat in Crime Control* 56 (1973).

[11]Goldfarb and Singer, *After Conviction: A Review of the American Correctional System* 11 (1973).

In his famous *Essay on Crimes and Punishments* (1764), Cesare Beccaria argued that swiftness and certainty in punishment best enhance the deterrence model and that the severity of punishment must be determined strictly in accordance with the social damage caused by the crime. Yet recent evidence suggests that while certainty and severity do have a moderate deterrent effect upon crime rates, increasing severity with low certainty has little deterrent value.[12] While Beccaria's swiftness-certainty-severity model is probably theoretically sound, there are serious practical and legal barriers to its implementation under our present system of justice. For example, it is well known that the rate of arrest for certain offenses is quite low (e.g., auto theft, larceny, burglary).[13] Thus, the certainty of punishment will have little relevance for such offenders. In addition, the swiftness component is limited by our adversary system of justice. While every defendant has a Sixth Amendment right to a "speedy trial," he also has a due process right to adequately prepare his defense, which takes time, sometimes many months. Moreover, the courts are not presently able to bring defendants swiftly to trial because of already crowded dockets.

Sentencing Alternatives

By law in most jurisdictions, convicted defendants must be sentenced reasonably soon after conviction. In the federal system, a sentence must be imposed "without unreasonable delay,"[14] and many jurisdictions specify time limits for the imposition of sentence.

Various sentencing alternatives are available to judges. (It should be noted here that 12 states permit jury sentencing for certain offenses,[15] and the Supreme Court has upheld the constitutionality of this practice.) Sentencing alternatives include (1) suspended sentences, (2) probation, (3) fines, (4) imprisonment, and, until recently, (5) capital punishment.

Suspended Sentences. The suspended sentence is available as a sentencing alternative for all but the most serious offenses (e.g., first degree murder), and it is frequently utilized. More often than not, when the suspended sentence is used, the judge will initially impose a sentence of imprisonment or a fine and then suspend the imposition of the sentence provided the defendant fulfills certain conditions. Such conditions might be to "stay out of trouble," or to make restitution to the victim, or to testify against an accomplice. The original sentence may be reinstated if the defendant fails to fulfill the conditions. Some conditions may be of questionable constitutionality (e.g., "stay out of this town" or "leave this state and never return").[17]

Probation. In recent years the use of probation as a sentencing alternative has increased dramatically.[18] Under this alternative a convicted defendant's sentence is suspended, and he remains at liberty, subject to conditions imposed by the court and under the control of the probation authorities. Today, this sentencing alternative is used in more than half of all criminal dispositions.[19] It generally is available to both adults and juveniles, and felons, and misdemeanants,

---

[12]Antunes and Hunt, *The Impact of Certainty and Severity of Punishment Levels of Crime in American States: An Extended Analysis*, 64 J. Crim. L. & Crim. 486, 492–493 (1973). See also Bailey and Smith, *Punishment: Its Severity and Certainty*, 63 J. Crim. L. Crim. & Pol. Sci. 530 (1972); and Scott, *The Use of Discretion in Determining the Severity of Punishment for Incarcerated Offenders*, 65 J. Crim. L. & Crim. 214 (1974).

[13]The F.B.I. reported that in 1975 the percentage of arrests for the crimes of auto theft, larceny-theft, and burglaries was 14, 20, and 18 per cent, respectively. Only 27 per cent of robberies were cleared by arrest. Uniform Crime Reports 37 (1976).

[14]Rule 32, Fed. R. Crim. P.

[15]*Chaffin* v. *Stynchcombe*, 412 U.S. 17, 21 n.7 (1973).

[16]*McGautha* v. *California*, 402 U.S. 183 (1971).

[17]But see *Shapiro* v. *Thompson*, 394 U.S. 618 (1969) (the right to travel is a fundamental constitutional right and cannot be restricted absent a "compelling government interest").

[18]The President's Commission on Law Enforcement and Administration of Justice, *Corrections* 27 (1967). See also Dressler, *Practice and Theory of Probation and Parole* 33–55 (1969).

[19]Goldfarb and Singer, *After Conviction: A Review of the American Correctional System* 209 (1973).

depending on the type of offense and the applicable statutes.[20]

Conditions usually accompany probationary sentences, and offenders can avoid imprisonment altogether by complying with them. The following conditions are typical:[21]

1. Report to the probation officer on a regular basis.

2. Maintain lawful behavior.

3. Make restitution to the victim.

4. Pay a fine.

5. Serve a short jail term prior to probation.

6. Have only restricted use of automobiles.

7. Not leave the jurisdiction without permission.

8. Abstain from the use of alcohol.

9. Avoid establishments where liquor is served.

10. Avoid contact with known criminals or ex-convicts.

11. Attend church regularly.

12. Marry the mother of the offender's unborn child.

Only a few conditions are usually imposed on a single probationer. One study reported that probation revocation rates increase as more conditions are imposed.[22] Failure to comply with the conditions of probation can result in a revocation of probation[23] (if the offender is caught, and many are not), and the offender may be imprisoned. However, some specified conditions of probation are flatly illegal (e.g., attending church on a regular basis).[24]

Fines. Most jurisdictions authorize fines for many serious crimes,[25] but more often than not, fines are imposed for misdemeanor offenses, traffic violations, and the less serious felonies. The constitutional problems involved in imposing fines as a punishment were discussed in Chapter Twelve, § 12.02.

Imprisonment. The term "imprisonment" refers to incarceration in jail or prison. The underlying premises upon which imprisonment is based are that some offenders are too dangerous to be at large in society; that they will commit further crimes if not incarcerated; and that such punishment is necessary to protect the public.[26] The offender needs to be isolated for the good of society. Yet, the validity of incarceration as a mode of punishment requires that these dangerous offenders can be identified with some accuracy. American judges tend to be overly cautious in assessing the dangerousness of offenders, with overcrowded prisons and overlong sentences resulting.[27] Unlike those in European countries, sentences in the United States for terms of more than five years are common, and sentences of more than ten years are far from rare.[28]

The American Bar Association's Advisory Committee on Sentencing and Review stated that long prison sentences are necessary in only a small number of cases (10 to 15 per cent). One study concluded that the longer an offender remains incarcerated, the more likely he is to commit crimes upon release.[29] Alternatives to institutional commitment are probably more effective for most offenders—at least in terms of recidivism. Many long sentences are probably nothing more than a disguise for vengeance and retribution. Unlike their counterparts in many European countries, American judges do not have to state to the defendant the reasons for the sentence imposed.[30] The judge at sentencing may refer, for the record, to the ideals of rehabilitation or to the dangerousness of the offender, but in many instances, a harsh sentence may actually reflect a judge's personal philosophy of punishment predicated on revenge. Unfortunately only limited remedies, if any, are available in most

---

[20]Dressler, *Practice and Theory of Probation and Parole* 45 (1969).

[21]Goldfarb and Singer, supra note 19, at 234–240. A probationary sentence is often made a part of a plea bargaining agreement.

[22]Davis, *A Study of Adult Probation Rates by Means of the Cohort Approach,* 55 J. Crim. L. Crim. & Pol. Sci. 70 (1964).

[23]See Chapter Nine, § 9.04.

[24]See Chapter Fifteen, § 15.04.

[25]40 Mo. Rev. Stat. § 559.140 (1939) (manslaughter conviction authorizes imprisonment or a fine of $500).

[26]Packer, *The Limits of the Criminal Sanction* 48–53 (1968).

[27]Id., at 49.

[28]Goldfarb and Singer, supra note 19, at 131.

[29]Eichmann, *Impact of the Gideon Decision Upon Crime and Sentencing in Florida: A Study of Recidivism and Socio-Cultural Change* (1966).

[30]Frankel, supra note 1, at 76–77.

jurisdictions to offenders to redress such sentences.

Because most state judges are elected, they must "please the public" to some degree, and their sentencing policies are one of the most "visible" and easily quantifiable measures of their work on the bench. The general public lacks the training to judge the correctness of a judge's day-to-day legal rulings, but the sentences he imposes, and especially those that are harsh, have high visibility. In a society hungry for "law and order," the imposition of long prison sentences can, and does, garner votes. This is not to suggest that federal judges, who are not elected, do not impose unusually harsh sentences; some do, but for reasons other than to gain reelection.

In the federal system and in two thirds of the states, sentencing decisions, no matter how harsh, are, for the most part, not subject to appellate review. Yet, in almost every jurisdiction in the United States, a $2000 judgment in a civil case is subject to at least one review by an appellate court, and in many cases to two appellate reviews. The sentencing power of American judges is the most unrestricted in the free world.[31]

Capital Punishment. This sentencing alternative is discussed in Chapter Eleven, § 11.03.

Factors in Sentencing

Sentencing decisions have been found to be based on such extra-legal factors as the socioeconomic and racial characteristics of the defendant,[32] with a resulting diversity of length and types of sentences that are handed out to the convicted.[33] Table 14.1 indicates that on the average, nonwhites receive longer sentences to federal prisons than whites. This disparity in sentencing is a blemish on our system of criminal justice.

---

[31]American Bar Association Project on Standards for Criminal Justice, *Standards Relating to Appellate Review of Sentences* 1–2 (1968).

[32]Thornberry, *Race, Socioeconomic Status and Sentencing in the Juvenile Justice System*, 64 J. Crim. L. & Crim. 90 (1973).

[33]Quinney, *Criminology: Analysis and Critique of Crime in America*, 209 (1975).

TABLE 14.1   Average Sentences of Court Commitments to Federal Prisons, by Race and Offense (Fiscal Year Ended June 30, 1972)*

	Average sentences (in months)	
	Whites	*Nonwhites*
Offenses in which nonwhites have longer average sentences than whites:		
Assault	51.1	81.2
Burglary	41.8	43.1
Drug laws	51.9	73.5
Embezzlement	26.9	31.0
Escape	20.1	46.0
Forgery	34.1	40.1
Immigration	10.4	14.0
Income tax	14.2	30.7
Juvenile delinquency	35.0	36.1
Selective Service acts	29.3	38.6
Offenses in which whites have longer average sentences than nonwhites:		
Counterfeiting	45.3	44.0
Extortion	56.0	51.4
Firearms	44.9	37.8
Fraud	34.5	33.0
Kidnapping	248.8	219.0
Larceny	39.5	33.3
Liquor laws	20.4	14.8
National security laws	66.9	24.0
Robbery	138.3	130.3
Securities	45.9	44.9
Average sentence for all offenses	43.3	58.7

*From United States Department of Justice, Federal Bureau of Prisons, *Statistical Report, Fiscal Years 1971 and 1972*, 60–61.

14.02 PROBLEMS IN SENTENCING

Imposing a Greater Sentence on Reconviction

NORTH CAROLINA v. PEARCE

Supreme Court of the United States, 1969
395 U.S. 711, 89 S. Ct. 2072, 23 L. Ed. 2d 656

The facts are stated in the opinion.

Mr. Justice STEWART delivered the opinion of the Court.

* * *

... The respondent Pearce was convicted in a North Carolina court upon a charge of assault with intent to commit rape. The trial judge sentenced him to prison for a term of 12 to 15 years. Several years later he initiated a state post-conviction proceeding which culminated in the reversal of his conviction by the Supreme Court of North Carolina, upon the ground that an involuntary confession had unconstitutionally been admitted in evidence against him. . . . He was retried, convicted, and sentenced by the trial judge to an eight-year prison term, which, when added to the time Pearce had already spent in prison, the parties agree amounted to a longer total sentence than that originally imposed. The conviction and sentence were affirmed on appeal. . . . Pearce then began this habeas corpus proceeding in the United States District Court for the Eastern District of North Carolina. That court held, upon the authority of a then very recent Fourth Circuit decision, Patton v. North Carolina, 381 F.2d 636, cert. denied, 390 U.S. 905, that the longer sentence imposed upon retrial was "unconstitutional and void." Upon the failure of the state court to resentence Pearce within 60 days, the federal court ordered his release. This order was affirmed by the United States Court of Appeals for the Fourth Circuit, 397 F.2d 253, in a brief per curiam judgment citing its Patton decision, and we granted certiorari. . . .

* * *

I

* * *

II

* * *

A

Long-established constitutional doctrine makes clear that ... the guarantee against double jeopardy imposes no restrictions upon the length of a sentence imposed upon reconviction. At least since 1896, when United States v. Ball, 163 U.S. 662, was decided, it has been settled that this constitutional guarantee imposes no limitations whatever upon the power to *retry* a defendant who has succeeded in getting his first conviction set aside. "The principle that this provision does not preclude the Government's retrying a defendant whose conviction is set aside because of an error in the proceedings leading to conviction is a well-established part of our constitutional jurisprudence." ... And at least since 1919, when Stroud v. United States, 251 U.S. 15, was decided, it has been settled that a corollary of the power to retry a defendant is the power, upon the defendant's reconviction, to impose whatever sentence may be legally authorized, whether or not it is greater than the sentence imposed after the first conviction. "That a defendant's conviction is overturned on collateral rather than direct attack is irrelevant for these purposes." ...

Although the rationale for this "well-established part of our constitutional jurisprudence" has been variously verbalized, it rests ultimately upon the premise that the original conviction has, at the defendant's behest, been wholly nullified and the slate wiped clean. . . . So far as the conviction itself goes, and that part of the sentence that has not yet been served, it is no more than a simple statement of fact to say that the slate *has* been wiped clean. The conviction *has* been set aside, and the unexpired portion of the original sentence will never be served. A new trial may result in an acquittal. But if it does result in a conviction, we cannot say that the constitutional guarantee against double jeopardy of its own weight restricts the imposition of an otherwise lawful single punishment for the offense in question. To hold to the contrary would be to cast doubt upon the whole validity of the basic principle enunciated in United States v. Ball, supra, and upon the unbroken line of decisions that have followed that principle for almost 75 years. We think those decisions are entirely sound, and we decline to depart from the concept they reflect.

B

The other argument advanced in support of the proposition that the Constitution absolutely forbids the imposition of a more severe sentence upon retrial is grounded upon the Equal Protection Clause of the Fourteenth Amendment. The theory advanced is that, since convicts who do not seek new trials cannot have their sentences increased, it creates an invidious classification to impose that risk only upon those who succeed in getting their original convictions set aside. The argument, while not lacking in ingenuity, cannot withstand close examination. In the first place, we deal here, not with increases in existing sentences, but with the imposition of wholly new sentences after wholly new trials. Putting that conceptual nicety to one side, however, the problem before us simply cannot be rationally dealt with in terms of "classifications." A man who is retried after his first conviction has been set aside may be acquitted. If convicted, he may receive a shorter sentence, he may receive the same sentence, or he may receive a longer sentence than the one originally imposed. The result may depend upon a particular combination of infinite variables peculiar to each individual trial. It simply cannot be said that a state has invidiously "classified" those who successfully seek new trials, any more than that the State has invidiously "classified" those prisoners whose convictions are *not* set aside by denying the members of that group the opportunity to be acquitted. To fit the

problem of this case into an equal protection framework is a task too Procrustean to be rationally accomplished.

C

We hold, therefore, that neither the double jeopardy provision nor the Equal Protection Clause imposes an absolute bar to a more severe sentence upon reconviction. A trial judge is not constitutionally precluded, in other words, from imposing a new sentence, whether greater or less than the original sentence, in the light of events subsequent to the first trial that may have thrown new light upon the defendant's "life, health, habits, conduct, and mental and moral propensities." Williams v. New York, 337 U.S. 241, 245 (1949). Such information may come to the judge's attention from evidence adduced at the second trial itself, from a new presentence investigation, from the defendant's prison record, or possibly from other sources. The freedom of a sentencing judge to consider the defendant's conduct subsequent to the first conviction in imposing a new sentence is no more than consonant with the principle, fully approved in Williams v. New York, supra, that a State may adopt the "prevalent modern philosophy of penology that the punishment should fit the offender and not merely the crime." . . .

To say that there exists no absolute constitutional bar to the imposition of a more severe sentence upon retrial is not, however, to end the inquiry. There remains for consideration the impact of the Due Process Clause of the Fourteenth Amendment.

It can hardly be doubted that it would be a flagrant violation of the Fourteenth Amendment for a state trial court to follow an announced practice of imposing a heavier sentence upon every reconvicted defendant for the explicit purpose of punishing the defendant for his having succeeded in getting his original conviction set aside. Where . . . the original conviction has been set aside because of a constitutional error, the imposition of such a punishment, "penalizing those who choose to exercise" constitutional rights, "would be patently unconstitutional." United States v. Jackson, 390 U.S. 570, 581 (1968). And the very threat inherent in the existence of such a punitive policy would, with respect to those still in prison, serve to "chill the exercise of basic constitutional rights." . . . But even if the first conviction has been set aside for nonconstitutional error, the imposition of a penalty upon the defendant for having successfully pursued a statutory right of appeal or collateral remedy would be no less a violation of due process of law. "A new sentence, with enhanced punishment, based upon such a reason, would be a flagrant violation of the rights of the defendant." Nichols v. United States, 106 F. 672, 679. A court is "without right to . . . put a price on an appeal. A defendant's exercise of a right of appeal must be free and unfettered. . . . [I]t is unfair to use the great power given to the court to determine sentence to place a defendant in the dilemma of making an unfree choice."

. . . "This Court has never held that the States are required to establish avenues of appellate review, but it is now fundamental that, once established, these avenues must be kept free of unreasoned distinctions that can only impede open and equal access to the courts. . . .

Due process of law, then, requires that vindictiveness against a defendant for having successfully attacked his first conviction must play no part in the sentence he receives after a new trial. And since the fear of such vindictiveness may unconstitutionally deter a defendant's exercise of the right to appeal or collaterally attack his first conviction, due process also requires that a defendant be freed of apprehension of such a retaliatory motivation on the part of the sentencing judge.

In order to assure the absence of such a motivation, we have concluded that whenever a judge imposes a more severe sentence upon a defendant after a new trial, the reasons for his doing so must affirmatively appear. Those reasons must be based upon objective information concerning identifiable conduct on the part of the defendant occurring after the time of the original sentencing proceeding. And the factual data upon which the increased sentence is based must be made part of the record, so that the constitutional legitimacy of the increased sentence may be fully reviewed on appeal.

. . . Neither at the time the increased sentence was imposed upon Pearce, not at any stage in this habeas corpus proceeding, has the State offered any reason or justification for that sentence beyond the naked power to impose it. We conclude that . . . the judgment should be affirmed.

Mr. Justice DOUGLAS, whom Mr. Justice MARSHALL joins, concurring.

Although I agree with the Court as to the reach of due process, I would go further. It is my view that if for any reason a new trial is granted and there is a conviction a second time, the second penalty imposed cannot exceed the first penalty, if respect is had for the guarantee against double jeopardy.

The theory of double jeopardy is that a person run the gantlet only once. The gantlet is the risk of the range of punishment which the State or Federal Government imposes for that particular conduct. It may be a year to 25 years, or 20 years to life, or death. He risks the maximum permissible punishment when first tried. That risk having been faced once need not be faced again. And the fact that he takes an appeal does not waive his constitutional defense of former jeopardy to a second prosecution. Green v. United States, 355 U.S. 184, 191–193 (1957).

In the Green case, the defendant was charged with arson on one count and on a second count was charged with either first-degree murder carrying a mandatory death sentence, or second-degree murder carrying a maximum sentence of life imprisonment. The jury found him guilty of arson and second-degree murder but the verdict was silent as to first-degree murder. He appealed the conviction and obtained a reversal. On a remand he was tried again. This time he was convicted of first-degree murder and sentenced to death—hence his complaint of former jeopardy. We held that the guarantee of double jeopardy applied and that the defendant, having been "in direct peril of being convicted and punished for first degree murder at his first trial" could not be "forced to run the gauntlet" twice. . . .

* * *

The ban on double jeopardy has its roots deep in the history of occidental jurisprudence. "Fear and abhorrence of governmental power to try people twice for the same conduct is one of the oldest ideas found in western civilization." . . . And its purposes are several. It prevents the State from using its criminal processes as an instrument of harassment to wear the accused out by a multitude of cases with accumulated trials. . . .

It serves the additional purpose of precluding the State, following *acquittal,* from successively retrying the defendant in the hope of securing a conviction. "The vice of this procedure lies in relitigating the same issue on the same evidence before two different juries with a man's innocence or guilt at stake" in the hope that they would come to a different conclusion." . . . "Harassment of an accused by successive prosecutions or declaration of a mistrial so as to afford the prosecution a more favorable opportunity to convict are examples when jeopardy attaches." . . .

And finally, it prevents the State, following *conviction,* from retrying the defendant again in the hope of securing a greater penalty.

"This case presents an instance of the prosecution being allowed to harass the accused with repeated trials and convictions on the same evidence, until it achieves its desired result of a capital verdict." Ciucci v. Illinois, 356 U.S. 571, 573 (1958) (DOUGLAS, J., dissenting).

It is the latter purpose which is relevant here, for . . . the Court allows the State a second chance to retry the defendant in the hope of securing a more favorable penalty.

* * *

Mr. Justice BLACK, concurring in part and dissenting in part.

* * *

. . . I . . . agree with the Court's rejection of respondents' claims that the increased sentences violate the Double Jeopardy and Equal Protection Clauses of the Constitution. It has been settled, as the Court correctly notes, that the double jeopardy provision does not limit the length of the sentence imposed upon reconviction. Nor is there any invidious discrimination in subjecting defendants who have had prior convictions set aside to the same punishment faced by people who have never been tried at all. . . .

The Court goes on, however, to hold that it would be a flagrant violation of due process for a "state trial court to follow an announced practice of imposing a heavier sentence upon every reconvicted defendant for the explicit purpose of punishing the defendant for his having succeeded in getting his original conviction set aside." This means, I take it, that a State cannot permit appeals in criminal cases and at the same

time make it a crime for a convicted defendant to take or win an appeal. That would plainly deny due process of law, but not, as the Court's opinion implies, because the Court believes it to be an "unfair" practice. In the first place, the very enactment of two statutes side by side, one encouraging and granting appeals and another making it a crime to win an appeal, would be contrary to the very idea of government by law. It would create doubt, ambiguity, and uncertainty, making it impossible for citizens to know which one of the two conflicting laws to follow, and would thus violate one of the first principles of due process. Due process, moreover, is a guarantee that a man should be tried and convicted only in accordance with valid laws of the land. If a conviction is not valid under these laws, statutory and constitutional, a man has been denied due process and has a constitutional right to have the conviction set aside, without being deprived of life, liberty, or property as a result. For these two reasons, I agree that a state law imposing punishment on a defendant for taking a permissible appeal in a criminal case would violate the Due Process Clause, but not because of any supposed "unfairness." Since such a law could take effect not only by state legislative enactment but also by state judicial decision, I also agree that it would violate the Constitution for any judge to impose a higher penalty on a defendant solely because he had taken a legally permissible appeal.

* * *

. . . For . . . there is not a line of evidence to support the slightest inference that the trial judge wanted or intended to punish Pearce for seeking post-conviction relief. Indeed the record shows that this trial judge meticulously computed the time Pearce had served in jail in order to give him full credit for that time.

* * *

Of course nothing in the Due Process Clause grants this Court any such power as it is using here. Punishment based on the impermissible motivation described by the Court is, as I have said, clearly unconstitutional, and courts must of course set aside the punishment if they find, by the normal judicial process of fact-finding, that such a motivation exists. But, beyond this, the courts are not vested with any general power to prescribe particular devices "[i]n order to assure the absence of such a motivation." Numerous different mechanisms could be thought of, any one of which would serve this function. Yet the Court does not explain why the particular detailed procedure spelled out in this case is *constitutionally* required, while other remedial devices are not. This is pure legislation if there ever was legislation.

I have no doubt about the power of Congress to enact such legislation under § 5 of the Fourteenth Amendment, which reads: "The Congress shall have power to enforce, by appropriate legislation, the provisions of this article." But should Congress enact what the Court has here enacted, a requirement that state courts articulate their reasons for imposing particular sentences, it would still be legislation only, and Congress could repeal it. In fact, since this is only a rule supplementing the Fourteenth Amendment, the Court itself might be willing to accept congressional substitutes for this supposedly "constitutional" rule which this Court today enacts. So despite the fact that the Court says that the judge's reasons "must be made part of the record, so that the constitutional legitimacy of the increased sentence may be fully reviewed on appeal," I remain unconvinced that this Court can legitimately add any additional commands to the Fourteenth Amendment or any other Amendment.

* * *

Mr. Justice HARLAN, concurring in part and dissenting in part.

... [T]he Court today, in Benton v. Maryland [395 U.S. 784 (1969)], has held, over my dissent, that the Double Jeopardy Clause of the Fifth Amendment is made applicable to the States by the Fourteenth Amendment Due Process Clause. ...

Given Benton, it is my view that the decision of this Court in Green v. United States, 355 U.S. 184 (1957), from which I dissented at the time, points strongly to the conclusion, also reached by my Brother DOUGLAS, . . . that the Double Jeopardy Clause of the Fifth Amendment governs . . . issues presently decided by the Court. Ac-

cordingly, I . . . concur in the result reached in Part II, except in one minor respect.[a]

Green v. United States, supra, held in effect that a defendant who is convicted of a lesser offense included in that charged in the orginal indictment, and who thereafter secures reversal, may be retried only for the lesser included offense. Mr. Justice Frankfurter observed, in a dissent which I joined, that: "As a practical matter, and on any basis of human values, it is scarcely possible to distinguish a case in which the defendant is convicted of a greater offense from one in which he is convicted of an offense that has the same name as that of which he was previously convicted but carries a significantly [increased] . . . punishment. . . ." Id., at 213.

Further reflection a decade later has not changed my view that the two situations cannot be meaningfully distinguished.

Every consideration enunciated by the Court in support of the decision in Green applies with equal force to the situation at bar. . . . Most significantly, perhaps, in each case a contrary rule would place the defendant considering whether to appeal his conviction in the same "incredible dilemma" and confront him with the same "desperate" choice. . . . His decision whether or not to appeal would be burdened by the consideration that success, followed by retrial and conviction, might place him in a far worse position than if he remained silent and suffered what seemed to him an unjust punishment. In terms of Green, that the imposition of a more severe sentence on retrial is a matter of pure *chance,* rather than the result of purposeful retaliation for having taken an appeal, renders the choice no less "desperate."

If, as a matter of policy and practicality,

---

[a]An outright affirmance . . . would carry the consequence of relieving the respondent Pearce from serving the remaining few months of his original state sentence. . . . There is no basis, whether the result in this case is governed by due process or double jeopardy, for such an interference with the State's legitimate criminal processes. I would therefore vacate the judgment of the Court of Appeals for the Fourth Circuit . . . and remand the case so that an order may be entered releasing Pearce at, but not before, the expiration of his first sentence. Cf. Peyton v. Rowe, 391 U.S. 54 (1968).

the imposition of an increased sentence on retrial has the same consequences whether effected in the guise of an increase in the degree of offense or an augmentation of punishment, what other factors render one route forbidden and the other permissible under the Double Jeopardy Clause? It cannot be that the provision does not comprehend "sentences"—as distinguished from "offenses"—for it has long been established that once a prisoner commences service of sentence, the Clause prevents a court from vacating the sentence and then imposing a greater one. . . .

The Court does not suggest otherwise, but in its view, apparently, when the conviction itself and not merely the consequent sentence has been set aside, or when either has been set aside at the defendant's behest, the "slate *has* been wiped clean" . . . and the Double Jeopardy Clause presents no bar to the imposition.

* * *

[United States v.] Ball [163 U.S. 662 (1896)] held, simply, that a defendant who succeeds in getting his first conviction set aside may thereafter be retried for the same offense of which he was formerly convicted. That is, indeed, a fundamental doctrine in our criminal jurisprudence, and I would be the last to undermine it. But Ball does not speak to the question of what *punishment* may be imposed on retrial. I entirely fail to understand the Court's suggestion, unless it assumes that Ball must stand or fall on the question-begging notion that, to quote the

majority today, "the original conviction has, at the defendant's behest, been wholly nullified and the slate wiped clean." . . .

In relying on this conceptual fiction, the majority forgets that Green v. United States, supra, prohibits the imposition of an increased punishment on retrial precisely *because* convictions are usually set aside only at the defendant's behest, and not in spite of that fact. [T]he defendant's choice to appeal an erroneous conviction is protected by the rule that he may not again be placed in jeopardy of suffering the greater punishment not imposed at the first trial. . . .

* * *

I therefore conclude that, consistent with the Fifth Amendment, a defendant who has once been convicted and sentenced to a particular punishment may not on retrial be placed again in jeopardy of receiving a greater punishment than was first imposed. Because the Double Jeopardy Clause has now been held applicable to the States, Benton v. Maryland, supra, I would . . . vacate and remand . . . so that respondent Pearce may finish serving his first, valid sentence. . . .

Mr. Justice WHITE, concurring in part.

I join the Court's opinion except that in my view Part II-C should authorize an increased sentence on retrial based on any objective, identifiable factual data not known to the trial judge at the time of the original sentencing proceeding.

Resentencing by a Different Judge

COLTEN v. KENTUCKY

Supreme Court of the United States, 1972
407 U.S. 104, 92 S. Ct. 1953, 32 L. Ed. 2d 584

The facts are stated in the opinion.

Mr. Justice WHITE delivered the opinion of the Court.

This case presents two unrelated questions. Appellant challenges his Kentucky

conviction for disorderly conduct on the ground that the conviction and the State's statute are repugnant to the First and Fourteenth Amendments. He also challenges the constitutionality of the enhanced penalty he received under Kentucky's two-tier system for adjudicating certain criminal cases, whereby a person charged with a misdemeanor may be tried first in an inferior court and, if dissatisfied with the outcome, may have a trial de novo in a court of general criminal jurisdiction but must run the risk, if convicted, of receiving a greater conviction.

Appellant Colten and 15 to 20 other college students gathered at the Blue Grass Airport outside Lexington, Kentucky, to show their support for a state gubernatorial candidate and to demonstrate their lack of regard for Mrs. Richard Nixon, then about to leave Lexington from the airport after a public appearance in the city. When the demonstration had ended, the students got into their automobiles and formed a procession of six to 10 cars proceeding along the airport access road to the main highway. A state policeman, observing that one of the first cars in the entourage carried an expired Louisiana license plate, directed the driver, one Mendez, to pull off the road. He complied. Appellant Colten, followed by other motorists in the procession, also pulled off the highway, and Colten approached the officer to find out what was the matter. The policeman explained that the Mendez car bore an expired plate and that a traffic summons would be issued. Colten made some effort to enter into a conversation about the summons. His theory was that Mendez may have received an extension of time in which to obtain new plates. In order to avoid Colten and to complete the issuance of the summons, the policeman took Mendez to the patrol car. Meanwhile other students had left their cars and additional policemen, having completed their duties at the airport and having noticed the roadside scene, stopped their cars in the traffic lane abreast of the students' vehicles. At least one officer took responsibility for directing traffic, although testimony differed as to the need for doing so. Testimony also differed as to the number of policemen and students present, how many students left their cars and how many were at one time or another standing in the roadway. A state police captain asked on four or five occasions that the group disperse. At least five times police asked Colten to leave. A state trooper made two requests, remarking at least once: "Now, this is none of your affair . . . get back in your car and please move on and clear the road."

In response to at least one of these requests Colten replied that he wished to make a transportation arrangement for his friend Mendez and the occupants of the Mendez car, which he understood was to be towed away. Another officer asked three times that Colten depart and when Colten failed to move away he was arrested for violating Kentucky's disorderly conduct statute, Ky. Rev. Stat. § 437.016 (Supp. 1968). The arresting officer testified that Colten's response to the order had been to say that he intended to stay and see what might happen. Colten disputed this. He testified that he expressed a willingness to leave but wanted first to make a transportation arrangement. At trial he added that he feared violence on the part of the police.

The complaint and warrant charging disorderly conduct, which carries a maximum penalty of six months in jail and a fine of $500, were addressed to the Quarterly Court of Fayette County, where Colten was tried, convicted, and fined $10. Exercising his right to a trial de novo in a court of general jurisdiction, Colten "appealed," as the Kentucky rules style this recourse, Ky. Rule Crim. Proc. 12.02, to the Criminal Division of the Fayette Circuit Court. By consent, trial was to the court and Colten was convicted of disorderly conduct and this time fined $50. The Kentucky Court of Appeals affirmed. Colten v. Commonwealth, 467 S.W.2d 374 (Ky. 1971). It rejected Colten's constitutional challenges to the statute and his claim that the punishment imposed was impermissible, under North Carolina v. Pearce, 395 U.S. 771, 23 L. Ed. 2d 656, 89 S. Ct. 2072 (1969). We noted probable jurisdiction. . . .

I

Colten was convicted of violating Ky. Rev. Stat. § 437.016(1)(f) (Supp. 1968), which states:

"(1) A person is guilty of disorderly conduct if, with intent to cause public inconvenience, annoyance or alarm, or recklessly creating a risk thereof, he:

* * *

"(f) Congregates with other persons in a public place and refuses to comply with a lawful order of the police to disperse. . . ."

* * *

Based on our own examination of the record, we perceive no justification for setting aside the conclusion of the state court that when arrested appellant was not engaged in activity protected by the First Amendment. Colten insists that in seeking to arrange transportation for Mendez and in observing the issuance of a traffic citation he was disseminating and receiving information. But this is a strained, near-frivolous contention and we have little doubt that Colten's conduct in refusing to move on after being directed to do so was not, without more, protected by the First Amendment. Nor can we believe that Colten, although he was not trespassing or disobeying any traffic regulation himself, could not be required to move on. He had no constitutional right to observe the issuance of a traffic ticket or to engage the issuing officer in conversation at that time. The State has a legitimate interest in enforcing its traffic laws and its officers were entitled to enforce them free from possible interference or interruption from bystanders, even those claiming a third-party interest in the transaction. Here the police had cause for apprehension that a roadside strip, crowded with persons and automobiles, might expose the entourage, passing motorists, and police to the risk of accident. We cannot disagree with the finding below that the order to disperse was suited to the occasion. We thus see nothing unconstitutional in the manner in which the statute was applied.

II

Neither are we convinced that the statute is either impermissibly vague or broad. We perceive no violation of "[t]he underlying principle ... that no man shall be held criminally responsible for conduct which he could not reasonably understand to be proscribed." United States v. Harriss, 347 U.S. 612, 617 (1954). ... We agree with the Kentucky court when it said: "We believe that citizens who desire to obey the statute will have no difficulty in understanding it...." Colten v. Commonwealth, 467 S.W. 2d at 378.

* * *

III

Kentucky, like many other States, has a two-tier system for adjudicating less serious criminal cases. In Kentucky, at the option of the arresting officer, those crimes classified under state law as misdemeanors may be charged and tried in a so-called inferior court, where, as in the normal trial setting, a defendant may choose to have a trial or to plead guilty. If convicted after trial or on a guilty plea, however, he has a right to a trial de novo in a court of general criminal jurisdiction ... as long as he applies within the statutory time. The right to a new trial is absolute. A defendant need not allege error in the inferior court proceeding. If he seeks a new trial, the Kentucky statutory scheme contemplates that the slate be wiped clean. Ky. Rule Crim. Proc. 12.06. Prosecution and defense begin anew. By the same token neither the judge nor jury that determines guilt or fixes a penalty in the trial de novo is in any way bound by the inferior court's findings or judgment. The case is to be regarded exactly as if it had been brought there in the first instance. A convicted defendant may seek review in the state appellate courts in the same manner as a person tried initially in the general criminal court. ... However, a defendant convicted after a trial or plea in an inferior court may not seek ordinary appellate review of the inferior court's ruling. His recourse is the trial de novo.

While by definition two-tier systems throughout the States have in common the trial de novo feature, there are differences in the kind of trial available in the inferior courts of first instance, whether known as county, municipal, police, or justice of the peace courts, or are otherwise referred to. Depending upon the jurisdiction and offense charged, many such systems provide as complete protection for a criminal defendant's constitutional rights as do courts empowered to try more serious crimes. Others, however, lack some of the safeguards provided in more serious criminal cases. Although appellant here was entitled to a six-man jury ... which he waived, some States do not provide for trial by jury, even in instances where the authorized punishment would entitle the accused to such tribunal. ... Some, including Kentucky, do not record proceedings and the judges may not be trained for their positions either by experience or schooling.

Two justifications are asserted for such tribunals: first, in this day of increasing burdens on state judiciaries, these courts are designed, in the interest of both the defendant and the State, to provide speedier and less costly adjudications than may be possible in the criminal courts of general jurisdiction where the full range of constitutional guarantees is available; second, if the defendant is not satisfied with the results of his first trial he has the unconditional right to a new trial in a superior court, unprejudiced by the proceedings or the outcome in the inferior courts. Colten, however, considers the Kentucky system to be infirm because the judge in a trial de novo is empowered to sentence anew and is not bound to stay within the limits of the sentence imposed by the inferior court. He bases his attack both on the Due Process Clause, as interpreted in North Carolina v. Pearce, 395 U.S. 711 (1969), and on the Fifth Amendment's Double Jeopardy Clause. The issues appellant raises have produced a division among the state courts that have considered them as well as a conflict among the federal circuits.

Colten rightly reads Pearce to forbid, following a successful appeal and reconviction, the imposition of a greater punishment than was imposed after the first trial, absent specified findings that have not been made here. He insists that the Pearce rule is applicable here and that there is no relevant difference between the Pearce model and the Kentucky two-tier trial de novo system. Both, he asserts, involve reconviction and resentencing, both provide the convicted defendant with the right to "appeal" and in both—even though under the Kentucky scheme the "appeal" is in reality a trial de novo—a penalty for the same crime is fixed twice, with the same potential for an increased penalty upon a successful "appeal."

But Pearce did not turn simply on the fact of conviction, appeal, reversal, reconviction, and a greater sentence. . . .

Our view of the Kentucky two-tier system of administering criminal justice, however, does not lead us to believe, and there is nothing in the record or presented in the briefs to show, that the hazard of being penalized for seeking a new trial, which underlay the holding of Pearce, also inheres in the de novo trial arrangement. Nor are we convinced that defendants convicted in Kentucky's inferior courts would be deterred from seeking a second trial out of fear of judicial vindictiveness. The possibility of vindictiveness, found to exist in Pearce, is not inherent in the Kentucky two-tier system.

We note first the obvious: that the court which conducted Colten's trial and imposed the final sentence was not the court with whose work Colten was sufficiently dissatisfied to seek a different result on appeal; and it is not the court that is asked to do over what it thought it had already done correctly. Nor is the de novo court even asked to find error in another court's work. Rather, the Kentucky court in which Colten had the unrestricted right to have a new trial was merely asked to accord the same trial, under the same rules and procedures, available to defendants whose cases are begun in that court in the first instance. It would also appear that, however understandably a court of general jurisdiction might feel that the defendant who has had a due process trial ought to be satisfied with it, the de novo court in the two-tier system is much more likely to reflect the attitude of the Kentucky Court of Appeals in this case when it stated that "the inferior courts are not designed or equipped to conduct error-free trials, or to insure full recognition of constitutional freedoms. They are courts of convenience, to provide speedy and inexpensive means of disposition of charges of minor offenses." Colten v. Commonwealth, 467 S.W.2d, at 379. We see no reason, and none is offered, to assume that the de novo court will deal any more strictly with those who insist on a trial in the superior court after conviction in the Quarterly Court than it would with those defendants whose cases are filed originally in the superior court and who choose to put the State to its proof in a trial subject to constitutional guarantees.

It may often be that the superior court will impose a punishment more severe than that received from the inferior court. But it no more follows that such a sentence is a vindictive penalty for seeking a superior court trial than that the inferior court imposed a lenient penalty. The trial de novo represents a completely fresh determination of guilt or innocence. It is not an appeal on the record. As far as we know, the record from the lower court is not before the superior court and is irrelevant to its proceedings. In all likelihood, the trial de novo court is not even informed of the sentence imposed in the inferior court and can hardly be said to have "enhanced" the sentence. In Kentucky, disorderly conduct is punishable by six months in jail and a fine of $500. The inferior court fined Colten $10, the trial de novo court $50. We have no basis for concluding that the latter court did anything other than invoke the normal processes of a criminal trial and then sentence in accordance with the normal standards applied in that court to cases tried there in the first instance. We cannot conclude, on the basis of the present record or our understanding, that the prophylactic rule announced in Pearce is appropriate in the context of the system by which Kentucky administers criminal justice in the less serious criminal cases.

It is suggested, however, that the sentencing strictures imposed by Pearce are essential in order to minimize an asserted unfairness to criminal defendants who must endure a trial in an inferior court with less-than-adequate protections in order to secure a trial comporting completely with constitutional guarantees. We are not persuaded, however, that the Kentucky arrangement for dealing with the less serious offenses disadvantages defendants any more or any less than trials conducted in a court of general jurisdiction in the first instance, as long as the latter are always available. Proceedings in the inferior courts are simple and speedy, and, if the results in Colten's case are any evidence, the penalty is not characteristically severe. Such proceedings offer a defendant the opportunity to learn about the prosecution's case and, if he chooses, he need not reveal his own. He may also plead guilty without a trial and promptly secure a de novo trial in a court of general criminal jurisdiction. He cannot, and will not, face the realistic threat of a prison sentence in the inferior court without having the help of counsel, whose advice will also be available in determining whether to seek a new trial, with the slate wiped clean, or to accept the penalty imposed by the inferior court. The state has no such options. Should it not prevail in the lower court, the case is terminated, whereas the defendant has the choice of beginning anew. In reality his choices are to accept the decision of the judge and the sentence imposed in the inferior court or to reject what in effect is no more than an offer in settlement of his case and seek the judgment of judge or jury in the superior court, with sentence to be determined by the full record made in that court. We cannot say that the Kentucky trial de novo system, as such, is unconstitutional or that it presents hazards warranting the restraints called for in North Carolina v. Pearce, particularly since such restraints might, to the detriment of both defendant and State, diminish the likelihood that inferior courts would impose lenient sentences whose effect would be to limit the discretion of a superior court judge or jury if the defendant is retried and found guilty.

Colten's alternative contention is that the Double Jeopardy Clause prohibits the imposition of an enhanced penalty upon reconviction. The Pearce Court rejected the same contention in the context of that case. . . . Colten urges that his claim is stronger because the Kentucky system forces a defendant to expose himself to jeopardy as a price for securing a trial that comports with the Constitution. That was, of course, the situation in Pearce, where reversal of the first conviction was for constitutional error. The contention also ignores that a defendant can bypass the inferior court simply by pleading guilty and erasing immediately thereafter any consequence that would otherwise follow from tendering the plea.

Affirmed.

Mr. Justice MARSHALL, dissenting.

In my view, North Carolina v. Pearce, 395 U.S. 711 (1969), requires a reversal of this case.

* * *

Even if the first conviction has been set aside for nonconstitutional error, the imposition of a penalty upon the defendant for having successfully pursued a statutory right of appeal or collateral remedy would be no less a violation of due process of law. "A new sentence, with enhanced punishment, based upon such a reason, would be a flagrant violation of the rights of the defendant." Nichols v. United States, 106 F. 672, 679. A court is "without right to . . . put a price on an appeal. A defendant's exercise of a right of appeal must be free and unfettered. . . . It is unfair to use the great power given to the court to determine sentence to place a defendant in the dilemma of making an unfree choice." Worcester v. Commissioner, 370 F.2d. 713, 718. . . . This Court has never held that the States are required to establish avenues of appellate review, but it is now fundamental that, once established, these avenues must be kept free of unreasoned distinctions that can only impede open and equal access to the courts. . . .

* * *

The record in this case also shows that the trial judge was informed of the lower $10 fine in the original trial and consequently knowingly increased it to $50. Finally, it should not be forgotten that under this Court's ruling today he could have increased it to $500 plus six months in jail.

The Court suggests that for some reason there is less danger of vindictive sentencing on the second trial in this context than after an ordinary appeal. Specifically, the Court faults the appellant for failing to present evidence that the danger of vindictiveness is as great here as in the precise context presented in Pearce. But Pearce did not rest on evidence that most trial judges are hostile

to defendants who obtain a new trial after appeal. Pearce was based, rather, on the recognition that whenever a defendant is tried twice for the same offense, there is inherent in the situation the danger of vindictive sentencing the second time around, and that this danger will deter some defendants from seeking a second trial. This danger, with its deterrent effect, is exactly the same even though the second trial takes place in a different court from the first. Certainly a defendant has good reason to fear that his case will not be well received by a second court after he rejects a disposition as favorable as the sentence originally imposed in this case.

Pearce was directed toward a new trial after an appellate reversal. This case involves a new trial without an appellate reversal. The core problem is the second trial. In both cases we have a second full and complete trial. Pearce should control.

[Mr. Justice DOUGLAS wrote a separate dissenting opinion.]

"Good Time" Credit

McGINNIS v. ROYSTER

Supreme Court of the United States, 1973
410 U.S. 263, 93 S. Ct. 1055, 35 L. Ed. 2d 282

Appellee state prisoners filed suit in the United States District Court (S.D.N.Y.) challenging the constitutionality of § 230(3) of the New York Correction Law. Appellees claimed that by disallowing them "good time" credit for their presentence incarceration in county jails while permitting credit up to the full period of ultimate incarceration for state prisoners who were released on bail prior to sentencing, the statute deprived appellees of equal protection of the laws. A three-judge district court upheld appellees' claim, finding that there was no rational basis for the statutory distinction between jail and nonjail defendants in awarding "good time" credit. The New York Commissioner of corrections, McGinnis, appealed to the United States Supreme Court.

Mr. Justice POWELL delivered the opinion of the Court.

The question before us concerns the constitutionality of § 230(3) of the New York Correction Law, which denied appellee state prisoners "good time" credit for their presentence incarceration in county jails. Ap-

pellees claim that disallowing such credit to them while permitting credit up to the full period of ultimate incarceration for state prisoners who were released on bail prior to sentencing deprived them of equal protection of the laws. . . .

The challenged New York sentencing system is a complex one, and some basic definitions are required at the outset. *Jail time* denotes that time an individual passes in a county jail prior to trial and sentencing. *Good time* is awarded for good behavior and efficient performance of duties during incarceration. Both good time and jail time figure variously in the calculations of a series of release dates that each prisoner receives upon his arrival at state prison. Each inmate has both a *minimum parole date,* which is the earliest date he *may* be paroled at the discretion of the Parole Board, and a *statutory release date* which is the earliest date he *must* be paroled by the Parole Board. The minimum parole date is calculated under §§ 230(2) and 230(3) by subtracting the greatest amount of good time that can be earned (10 days per month) from the *minimum* sentence of an indeterminate term. The statutory release date is calculated under § 230(4) by subtracting the greatest amount of good time that can be earned (5 days per month) from the maximum sentence of an indeterminate term.

Although appellees did receive jail-time credit for the period of their presentence incarceration in county jail, § 230(3) explicitly forbids, in calculating the *minimum parole date,* any good-time credit for the period of county jail detention served prior to transfer to state prison. Appellee Royster, being unable to post bail, served 404 days' jail time in the Nassau County Jail prior to his transfer to state prison to serve consecutive 5-to-10-year terms for burglary in the third degree and grand larceny in the first degree. Appellee Rutherford also failed to make bail and spent 242 days' jail time in Nassau County Jail prior to his trial, sentencing, and transfer to state prison for concurrent terms of 10 to 20 years for robbery in the first degree and two and one-half to five years for grand larceny in the second degree. It is undisputed that, were appellees Royster and Rutherford to receive good-time credit for their presentence confinement in county jail, they would be entitled to appear before the Parole Board approximately four and three months earlier, respectively, than under the computation required by § 230(3).

Two additional points merit mention. While New York does deny good-time credit for jail time in computing the minimum parole date under §§ 230(2) and (3), it allows such credit in calculating the statutory re-

lease date under § 230(4). Finally, § 230(3) itself provides that good-time credit for jail time shall be awarded to those prisoners confined after sentence in county penitentiaries, as opposed to those convicted of felonies, such as appellees, who are transferred after sentence to state prison.

I

Section 230(3) of the New York Correction Law does, as appellees note, draw a distinction "between the treatment of state prisoners incarcerated prior to sentencing and those who were not similarly incarcerated." Appellees contend that "denying state prisoners good-time credit for the period of their pre-sentence incarceration in a County Jail whereas those fortunate enough to obtain bail prior to sentence [receive] a full allowance of good time credit for the entire period which they ultimately spend in custody" violates the equal protection of the laws and discriminates against those state prisoners unable to afford or otherwise qualify for bail prior to trial.

We first note that any relative disadvantage the distinction works on appellees is lessened by the fact that New York on September 1, 1967, replaced § 230 of its Correction Law with §§ 803 and 805, which apply to all convictions for offenses after that date. Under the new scheme, "good time earned on the minimum sentence is abolished. A prisoner meets with the Parole Board at the expiration of his minimum term, regardless of how much good time he has earned or of how much time he spent in jail prior to arriving at state prison." New York has given appellees—and all those sentenced for offenses committed prior to September 1, 1967—a chance to elect the new procedure, but appellees declined to do so. Appellees thus enjoy at least as favorable a position as all state prisoners convicted for offenses committed subsequent to September 1, 1967, including those released on bail prior to sentence. Appellees thus are disadvantaged in the computation of time only in comparison with those who were convicted of offenses committed prior to September 1, 1967, and made bail prior to trial. Even the adverse impact of this difference is lessened, though not eliminated, by the fact that New York did not deprive appellees of credit for the full amount of *actual* time spent in jail prior to trial and sentencing but only of the potential *additional* 10 days per month of good time ordinarily available under § 230(2) to inmates for good conduct and efficient performance of duty.

We note, further, that the distinction of which appellees complain arose in the course of the State's sensitive and difficult effort to encourage for its prisoners constructive future citizenship while avoiding the danger of releasing them prematurely upon society. The determination of an optimal time for parole eligibility elicited multiple legislative classifications and groupings, which the court below rightly concluded require only some rational basis to sustain them. . . . Appellees themselves recognize this to be the appropriate standard. For this Court has observed that "the problems of government are practical ones and may justify, if they do not require, rough accommodations — illogical, it may be, and unscientific." . . . We do not wish to inhibit state experimental classifications in a practical and troublesome area, but inquire only whether the challenged distinction rationally furthers some legitimate, articulated state purpose. We conclude that it does.

II

The Commissioner defends the distinction by noting that "state prisons differ from county jails with respect to purpose, usage and availability of facilities." State prisons are "intended to have rehabilitation as a prime purpose and the facilities at these institutions are built and equipped to serve this purpose." The Commissioner cites the presence at state prisons of "educational and vocational services such as schools, factories, job-training programs and related activities."

* * *

We pass no judgment on the success or merits of the State's efforts, but note only that at state prisons a serious rehabilitative program exists. County jails, on the other hand, serve primarily as detention centers. The Commissioner asserts they are "neither equipped nor intended to do anything more than detain people awaiting trial and maintain no schools, run no factories and require no work from these inmates." While appellees do point to the existence of some rehabilitative or recreational facilities within

some county jails, it is clear that nothing comparable to the State's rehabilitative effort exists.

These significant differences afford the basis for a different treatment within a constitutional framework. We note that the granting of good-time credit toward parole eligibility takes into account a prisoner's rehabilitative performance. Section 230(2) of the New York Correction Law authorizes such credit toward the minimum parole date "for good conduct *and efficient and willing performance of duties assigned* [emphasis added]." The regulations of the New York Department of Correction, 7 N.Y.C.R.R. § 260.1(a), state that: "[T]he opportunity to earn good behavior allowances offers inmates a tangible reward for *positive efforts made during incarceration* [emphasis added]." As the statute and regulations contemplate state evaluation of an inmate's progress toward rehabilitation, in awarding good time, it is reasonable not to award such time for pretrial detention in a county jail where no systematic rehabilitative programs exist and where the prisoner's conduct and performance are not even observed and evaluated by the responsible state prison officials. Further, it would hardly be appropriate for the State to undertake in the pretrial detention period programs to rehabilitate a man still clothed with a presumption of innocence. In short, an inmate in county jail is neither under the supervision of the State Correction Department nor participating in the State's rehabilitative programs. Where there is no evaluation by state officials and little or no rehabilitative participation for anyone to evaluate, there is a rational justification for declining to give good-time credit.

III

We do not agree with the court below that the integrity of appellants' assertions as to rehabilitation is undermined by the fact that the State does grant under § 230(3) good-time credit for presentence trial time to county penitentiary inmates and under § 230(4) to state prisoners for the purpose of calculating their statutory release dates. The legislature could have concluded rationally that *county* penitentiary inmates, who are nonfelons with less than one-year sentences, required quantitatively and qualitatively less rehabilitation — with fewer risks of misevaluation—than inmates confined to state prisons for more serious crimes. And the legislature could rationally have distinguished between the minimum parole date and the statutory release date on the ground that an acceleration of the minimum parole date posed a greater danger that an inmate could be released without adequate exposure to rehabilitative programs and without adequate evaluation by prison officials. Thus, New York's decision to deny good-time credit for presentence jail time solely with respect to a state prisoner's minimum parole date is rationally justified on the ground that the risk of prematurely releasing unrehabilitated or dangerous criminals may well be greatest when the parole decision is made prior to expiration of the minimum sentence.

IV

Neither appellees nor the court below contend that increased opportunity for state evaluation of an inmate's behavior and rehabilitative progress was not a purpose of the challenged provison of § 230(3). Appellees state only that the rehabilitative purpose was not the "overriding" one, and the District Court noted that "the legislature's *primary* aim in enacting the good time statute was to foster and insure the maintenance of prison discipline." ... We do not dispute these statements: the disciplinary purpose is certainly an important and possibly the "primary" aim of the legislation. Yet, our decisions do not authorize courts to pick and choose among legitimate legislative aims to determine which is primary and which subordinate. Rather, legislative solutions must be respected if the "distinctions drawn have some basis in practical experience," South Carolina v. Katzenbach, 383 U.S. 301, 331 (1966), or if some legitimate state interest is advanced, Dandridge v. Williams, 397 U.S., at 486. So long as the state purpose upholding a statutory class is legitimate and nonillusory, its lack of primacy is not disqualifying.

When classifications do not call for strict judicial scrutiny, this is the only approach consistent with proper judicial regard for the judgments of the Legislative Branch. The search for legislative purpose is often elusive enough, Palmer v. Thompson, 403 U.S. 217 (1971), without a requirement that primacy be ascertained. Legislation is frequently multipurposed: the removal of even a "subordinate" purpose may shift altogether the consensus of legislative judgment supporting the statute. Permitting nullification of statutory classifications based rationally on a nonprimary legislative purpose would allow courts to peruse legislative proceedings for subtle emphases supporting subjective impressions and preferences. The Equal Protection Clause does not countenance such speculative probing into the purposes of a coordinate branch. We have supplied no imaginary basis or purpose for this statutory scheme, but we likewise refuse to discard a clear and legitimate purpose because the court below perceived another to be primary.

V

As the challenged classification here rationally promotes the legitimate desire of the state legislature to afford state prison officials an adequate opportunity to evaluate both an inmate's conduct and his rehabilitative progress before he is eligible for parole, the decision of the District Court is reversed.

Mr. Justice DOUGLAS, with whom Mr. Justice MARSHALL concurs, dissenting.

Under § 230(3) of the New York Correction Law, a prisoner loses "good time" as punishment for offenses against the discipline of the prison. The statutory appearance of inmates before a parole board is computed by allowance of up to 10 days for "good conduct" each month under the law governing appellees. No "good time" credit is allowed, however, for the period of their presentence incarceration in a county jail. Thus, two prisoners—one out on bail or personal recognizance pending trial and the other confined in jail while awaiting trial—are treated differently when it comes to parole, though each is convicted of the same crime and receives the identical sentence. The result, as the opinion of the Court makes plain, is that appellees are required to wait some months longer before they may appear before the Parole Board than do those who were out on bail or on personal recognizance pending trial but sentenced to the same term for the same crime.

The "good time" deduction is not based on progress toward rehabilitation but is an inducement to inhibit bad conduct. That is what the three-judge court held. . . . That construction accurately reflects New York's interpretation of § 230(3). . . .

That discipline—not rehabilitative progress—is the key to "good time" credit is evidenced in another way. Once a prisoner arrives at prison, his future "good time" is immediately computed and credited to his sentence. "In effect, then, a prisoner does not 'earn' good time credit as time goes on for exemplary performance in assorted prison programs but rather simply avoids being penalized for bad behavior." . . .

Moreover, under § 230(4) of the Act, jail time is *not* excluded from the computation of a prisoner's maximum good-time allowance from the maximum term of an indeterminate sentence. That is the earliest date on which an inmate *must* be paroled, unlike the one we have here which involves the earliest date on which a prisoner *may* be paroled. But no rational grounds have been advanced for allowing "good time" credit for jail time in one case but not in the other.

The claim that "good time" is correlated to rehabilitative programs that only prisons have is the red herring in this litigation. The District Court exposed the fallacy in that rationale. Since the "good time" credit is to induce good behavior by prisoners while they are confined, the place of their confinement becomes irrelevant. Jail-time allowance

is allowed those confined in county penitentiaries. § 230(3). And, as I have said, jail time is credited in computing a prisoner's statutory release date.

It would seem that the "good time" provision in § 230(3) is used capriciously, since it is allowed in cases not dissimilar to the present one.

* * *

If "good time" were related to rehabilitative progress, I would agree that the law passes muster under the Equal Protection Clause of the Fourteenth Amendment. But since "good time" is disallowed only to those who cannot raise bail or obtain release on personal recognizance, the discrimination is plainly invidious.

* * *

The important issue involved in this case is not when and whether a prisoner is released. It concerns only the time when the Parole Board may give a hearing. To speed up the time of that hearing for those rich and influential enough to get bail or release on personal recognizance and to delay the time of the hearing for those without the means to buy a bail bond or the influence or prestige that will give release on personal recognizance emphasizes the invidious discrimination at work in § 230(3).

Sentencing in Capital Cases

ORAL ARGUMENTS BEFORE THE U.S. SUPREME COURT*

Gardner v. Florida, No. 74-6593; argued 11/30/76.

Despite the examples of Utah's Gary Gillmore and Texas' Robert White, there are some condemned prisoners who would rather face life imprisonment than execution.

---

*From 20 Crim. Law Rptr. 4099–4101 (1976). Reprinted by permission of the Bureau of National Affairs, Inc.

Counsel for one such prisoner asked the U.S. Supreme Court last month for another chance at a life sentence. The Florida jury which convicted the defendant of murdering his wife recommended life imprisonment, but the judge overruled that recommendation, as he is permitted to do under the statute upheld in *Proffitt* v. *Florida*, 428 U.S. 242 (1976).

Charles H. Livingston, of Sarasota, Florida, told the Court the trouble with the sentence was that it was based in part on information to which neither the defendant nor his trial counsel had access. The trial judge ordered a presentence report and kept a portion of it confidential.

The Chief Justice: "What was the basis of the judge's determination? Wasn't it the nature of the crime itself?" [The defendant had been drinking heavily before his wife's murder, which came at the end of an argument about her refusal to tell him where their children were. Death resulted from a severe beating and attendant internal and external bleeding. — ed.]

The crucial problem, Livingston responded, is that we are simply not in a position to know the basis of the sentence, or what sort of impact the confidential portion of the report had. It was only three weeks ago that the state provided us with what it says is the report. We do not admit this document's authenticity.

Mr. Justice Brennan asked whether the defendant could contest any of the material contained in the report.

Counsel responded by giving reasons, grounded in procedure, why the report should not be used to shore up the sentence. When Mr. Justice Brennan repeated the question, counsel referred to a conclusory statement in the report that the defendant "beat on his wife" several times. This represents a "conviction" by the investigator, he said. The portion of the report that was disclosed contained a list of charges of assault and attacks upon the defendant's wife, but all these charges were dropped.

Mr. Justice Brennan continued to press his point. Would the defendant have offered testimony that the alleged incidents, or some of them, never occurred.

Counsel wasn't sure, pointing out that he was not the defendant's attorney at trial. But in any event, the defendant should have been given notice as to the report's contents.

Mr. Justice Stewart asked whether the investigator's statement about the defendant's wife beating would have been admissible at the sentencing proceeding.

Probably so, counsel said, as an aggravating circumstance.

The Chief Justice asked whether anything in the undisclosed material was exculpatory of the defendant or could be used as an argument against the imposition of the death penalty.

To answer that we would have to speculate on what went through the trial judge's mind, Livingston replied. Moreover, the report might contain information which changed the way the judge looked at the mitigating circumstances. [The jury found that the mitigating circumstances outweighed the aggravating circumstances here — Livingston suggested that the defendant's drinking and the couple's marital history itself constituted the strongest mitigating circumstances. The judge, however, found no mitigating circumstances at all. — ed.]

Jurisdictional Flaw?

A discussion then arose as to the Court's jurisdiction to decide the question in the context of this case. The Court appeared unsure whether the defendant raised the point early enough in the state proceedings.

The issue was first raised before the state supreme court, counsel said, and while it was not treated specifically by the majority there, neither was any other contention raised on appeal. Moreover, the state supreme court's practice is to consider any significant error revealed by its independent review of the record, whether or not a contemporaneous objection was made. And the two dissenting Florida justices discussed the point at issue here and said the trial judge committed reversible error in not disclosing the report.

Remedy

Mr. Justice Brennan asked what the proper remedy would be should the Court conclude there was error.

Livingston first said there should be a new sentencing proceeding before the jury, with the entire presentence report disclosed to the jury and defense if the trial judge wants to use it. But he later corrected himself, saying that the jury need not be involved. Instead there should be a remand for sentencing by a different judge.

Mr. Justice Rehnquist: "Have we ever, in a state case, specified that a different judge handle sentence proceedings?"

Not to my knowledge, Livingston replied. But this is a capital case, requiring the utmost procedural regularity. And it asks too much of human nature to expect that the trial judge, having once sentenced the defendant to die, would admit to having made a mistake.

Mr. Justice Stewart referred to *Tedder* v. *State*, 322 So. 2d 908, 910 (1975), where the Florida Supreme Court said that to justify overriding a jury's advisory recommendation of life imprisonment, "the facts suggesting a sentence of death should be so clear and convincing that virtually no reasonable person would differ." This assumes that the state supreme court will review the entire record, Mr. Justice Stewart said, but the undisclosed portion of the report was not before the state supreme court in this case, correct?

Counsel agreed, but he pointed out that this conviction predated *Tedder*.

The Chief Justice asked whether trial counsel presented any argument for upholding the jury's recommendation.

No, counsel said, but what the defense knew about the presentence report gave no cause for concern.

Retreat from Woodson?

The state's position was presented by Wallace E. Allbritton, Assistant Attorney General. He pointed out that one ground for the decision striking down the capital punishment law in *Woodson* v. *North Carolina*, 428 U.S. 280 (1976), was the absence of a way for the sentencing authority to consider personalized aspects of the defendant's character and record. The defendant here would have the Court retreat from *Woodson*, Allbritton said, by emasculating a Florida provision providing the judge with just such information.

The reason the state supreme court did not see the report, Allbritton said, was that counsel had not asked to see it at the trial level. If such a request had been made and denied, and an objection lodged, then the report would have been made part of the record on appeal.

Mr. Justice Stevens asked how this case can be squared with the holding in *Tedder*. That case seems to impose on the state supreme court an independent duty to resolve any issue that appears from the record, he said.

Counsel agreed that a defendant need not specifically raise a point in order to place it in issue. But he denied that the claim on which the defendant now relies was sufficiently raised in the Florida courts.

Mr. Justice Marshall: "How did the dissenting justices find out about it?"

Allbritton replied that the defendant mentioned what happened, but not in the context of a claim that the court erred in not disclosing the report.

Mr. Justice Brennan: "But under *Tedder* isn't a mention enough?"

The court cannot review what isn't before it, counsel responded.

The Chief Justice pointed out that *Tedder* was decided after this case and suggested that, since this is an evolving area of the law, *Tedder* might indicate some enlarging of the Florida court's views.

Counsel agreed that could well be the case.

The Chief Justice then asked what ought to happen if the Court reverses here.

"If the terrible event occurs," Allbritton said, the case should go back to the state supreme court with instructions to review the presentence report to see if there is anything that needed disclosing. Also, the court should decide whether the trial judge abused his discretionary power in failing to disclose the report without a request.

Undermining Proffitt?

Mr. Justice Stewart appeared concerned that the Court had been misled in *Proffitt*. "This Court upheld that statute on the representations of the State of Florida and the decisions of its courts that this was an open and above-board processing. This case gets here and it's apparent that it isn't." He saw nothing "discretionary" about the trial court's duty to conduct the sentencing hearing entirely in the open.

Allbritton disagreed. The decision on whether to disclose a presentence report is discretionary under Florida law, just as it is under F. R. Crim. P. 32(c).

But the Chief Justice pointed out that the federal rule has not been litigated in the capital context.

In contrast to Livingston, who presented this case as involving only a very narrow issue, Allbritton argued that a reversal here would limit a judge's power to withhold a presentence report in any case. The defendant's argument cuts across the whole criminal process, he said.

The Chief Justice asked whether there

were any grounds in this case for denying a motion to disclose the presentence report, had such a motion been made by trial counsel.

Allbritton said he saw none. I cannot say why the judge did not disclose the report himself, he continued. But the judge did not say he relied on the confidential part of the report, although he did say that he relied on the presentence report as a whole.

Policy Considerations

In the state's brief, three policy considerations were advanced against a rule requiring mandatory disclosure of presentence reports. First, it was said that mandatory disclosure would dry up the sources of information that would otherwise be available to an investigator. Second, such disclosure was seen as causing interminable delays. Finally, it was said that mandatory disclosure would inhibit efforts to rehabilitate defendants.

Addressing the first point, Allbritton said that needed sources of information would dry up completely. A presentence report would be nothing more than an abstract of public records, he said. Thus a sentencing judge would be denied the information which this Court has called a fundamental prerequisite to the imposition of the death penalty.

Once again he cited *Woodson* v. *North Carolina.*

Allbritton compared the confidentiality of presentence reports to the secrecy that surrounds grand jury investigations. Confidentiality and secrecy are the tools used by the judge and grand jury to get the information necessary to their decisions.

The defendant's premise here must be that the trial judge is incapable of separating the wheat from the chaff in the presentence report. I can't agree that judges are so unfair or inhumane, counsel said.

Counsel referred to the Court's 1949 opinion in *Williams* v. *New York,* 347 U.S. 241. There a death sentence was upheld even though the trial judge relied on information contained in a probation investigation report, the sources for which the defendant did not have the opportunity to confront and cross-examine. *Woodson* is an implicit reaffirmation of *Williams,* Allbritton said.

Mr. Justice White: "Suppose a judge looks at the presentence report and lists certain aggravating circumstances based upon it."

In that case, Allbritton replied, trial counsel should ask for disclosure.

Mr. Justice White: "But isn't your strongest point that an aggravating circumstance was found from the evidence before the jury, and that the judge found no mitigating circumstances?"

Counsel agreed this was so.

GARDNER v. FLORIDA

Supreme Court of the United States, 1977
430 U.S. 349, 97 S. Ct. 1197, 51 L. Ed. 2d 393

The facts are stated in the opinion.

Mr. Justice STEVENS announced the judgment of the Court and delivered an opinion in which Mr. Justice STEWART and Mr. Justice POWELL joined.

Petitioner was convicted of first-degree murder and sentenced to death. When the trial judge imposed the death sentence he stated that he was relying in part on infor-

mation in a presentence investigation report. Portions of the report were not disclosed to counsel for the parties. Without reviewing the confidential portions of the presentence report, the Supreme Court of Florida, over the dissent of two Justices, affirmed the death sentence. Gardner v. Florida, 313 So. 2d 675 (1975). We conclude that this procedure does not satisfy the constitutional command that no person shall be deprived of life without due process of law.

I

On June 30, 1973, the petitioner assaulted his wife with a blunt instrument, causing her death. On January 10, 1974, after a trial in the Circuit Court of Citrus County, Florida, a jury found him guilty of first-degree murder.

The separate sentencing hearing required by Florida law in capital cases was held later on the same day. The State merely introduced two photographs of the decedent, otherwise relying on the trial testimony. That testimony, if credited, was sufficient to support a finding of one of the statutory aggravating circumstances, that the felony committed by petitioner "was especially heinous, atrocious, or cruel."

In mitigation petitioner testified that he had consumed a vast quantity of alcohol during a day-long drinking spree which preceded the crime, and professed to have almost no recollection of the assault itself. His testimony, if credited, was sufficient to support a finding of at least one of the statutory mitigating circumstances.

After hearing this evidence the jury was instructed to determine by a majority vote (1) whether the State had proved one of the aggravating circumstances defined by statute, (2) whether mitigating circumstances outweighed any such aggravating circumstance, and (3) based on that determination, whether the defendant should be sentenced to life or death.

After the jury retired to deliberate, the judge announced that he was going to order a presentence investigation of petitioner. Twenty-five minutes later the jury returned its advisory verdict. It expressly found that the mitigating circumstances outweighed the aggravating circumstances and advised the Court to impose a life sentence. App., at 131.

The presentence investigation report was completed by the Florida Parole and Probation Commission on January 28, 1974. On January 30, 1974, the trial judge entered findings of fact and a judgment sentencing petitioner to death. His ultimate finding was that the felony "was especially heinous, atrocious or cruel; and that such aggravating circumstance outweighs the mitigating cir-

cumstance, to wit: none." App., at 138. As a preface to that ultimate finding, he recited that his conclusion was based on the evidence presented at both stages of the bifurcated proceeding, the arguments of counsel and his review of "the factual information contained in said presentence investigation." Ibid.

There is no dispute about the fact that the presentence investigation report contained a confidential portion which was not disclosed to defense counsel. Although the judge noted in his findings of fact that the State and petitioner's counsel had been given "a copy of that portion [of the report] to which they are entitled," App., at 138, counsel made no request to examine the full report or to be apprised of the contents of the confidential portion. The trial judge did not comment on the contents of the confidential portion. His findings do not indicate that there was anything of special importance in the undisclosed portion, or that there was any reason other than customary practice for not disclosing the entire report to the parties.

On appeal to the Florida Supreme Court, petitioner argued that the sentencing court had erred in considering the presentence investigation report, including the confidential portion, in making the decision to impose the death penalty. The per curiam opinion of the Supreme Court did not specifically discuss this contention, but merely recited the trial judge's finding, stated that the record had been carefully reviewed, and concluded that the conviction and sentence should be affirmed. The record on appeal, however, did not include the confidential portion of the presentence report.

Justice Ervin and Justice Boyd dissented on several grounds. They regarded the evidence as sufficient to establish a mitigating circumstance as a matter of law, and also concluded that it was fundamental error for the trial judge to rely on confidential matter not provided to the parties. . . .

Petitioner's execution was stayed pending determination of the constitutionality of the Florida capital sentencing procedure. Following the decision in Proffitt v. Florida, 428 U.S. 242 (1976), holding that the Florida procedure, on its face, avoids the constitutional deficiencies identified in Furman v. Georgia, 408 U.S. 238 (1972), the Court granted certiorari in this case, 428 U.S. 908 (1976) to consider the constitutionality of the trial judge's use of a confidential presentence report in this capital case.

II

The State places its primary reliance on this Court's landmark decision in Williams v. New York, 337 U.S. 241 (1949). In that case, as in this, the trial judge rejected the jury's recommendation of mercy and imposed the death sentence in reliance, at least in part, on material contained in a report prepared by the court's probation department. The New York Court of Appeals had affirmed the sentence, rejecting the contention that it was a denial of due process to rely on information supplied by witnesses whom the accused could neither confront nor cross-examine.

This Court referred to appellant's claim as a "narrow contention," 337 U.S., at 243, and characterized the case as one which "presents a serious and difficult question . . . relat[ing] to the rules of evidence applicable to the manner in which a judge may obtain information to guide him in the imposition of sentence upon an already convicted defendant." Id., at 244. The conviction and sentence were affirmed, over the dissent of two justices.

Mr. Justice Black's opinion for the Court persuasively reasons why material developed in a presentence investigation may be useful to a sentencing judge, and why it may not be unfair to a defendant to rely on such information even if it would not be admissible in a normal adversary proceeding in open court. . . . [However] the *holding* of Williams is not directly applicable to this case.

It is first significant that in Williams the material facts concerning the defendant's background which were contained in the presentence report were described in detail by the trial judge in open court. . . . In contrast, in the case before us, the trial judge did not state on the record the substance of any information in the confidential portion of the presentence report that he might have considered material. There was, accordingly, no similar opportunity for petitioner's counsel to challenge the accuracy or materiality of any such information.

It is also significant that Justice Black's opinion recognized that the passage of time justifies a re-examination of capital sentencing procedures. . . . Since [Williams] was written almost 30 years ago, this Court has acknowledged its obligation to re-examine capital sentencing procedures against evolving standards of procedural fairness in a civilized society.

III

In 1949, when the Williams case was decided, no significant constitutional difference between the death penalty and lesser punishments for crime had been expressly recognized by this Court. At that time the Court assumed that after a defendant was convicted of a capital offense, like any other offense, a trial judge had complete discretion to impose any sentence within the limits prescribed by the legislature. As long as the judge stayed within those limits, his sentencing discretion was essentially unreviewable and the possibility of error was remote, if, indeed, it existed at all. In the intervening years there have been two constitutional developments which require us to scrutinize a State's capital sentencing procedures more closely than was necessary in 1949.

Five members of the Court [Justices STEWART, POWELL, STEVENS, MARSHALL, and BRENNAN] have now expressly recognized that death is a different kind of punishment than any other which may be imposed in this country. From the point of view of the defendant, it is different in both its severity and its finality. From the point of view of society, the action of the sovereign in taking the life of one of its citizens also differs dramatically from any other legitimate state action. It is of vital importance to the defendant and to the community that any decision to impose the death sentence be, and appear to be, based on reason rather than caprice or emotion.

Second, it is now clear that the sentencing process, as well as the trial itself, must satisfy the requirements of the Due Process Clause. Even though the defendant has no substantive right to a particular sentence within the range authorized by statute, the sentencing is a critical stage of the criminal proceeding at which he is entitled to the effective assistance of counsel. . . . The defendant has a legitimate interest in the character of the procedure which leads to the imposition of sentence even if he may have no right to object to a particular result of the sentencing process. . . .

In the light of these developments we

consider the justifications offered by the State for a capital sentencing procedure which permits a trial judge to impose the death sentence on the basis of confidential information which is not disclosed to the defendant or his counsel.

The State first argues that an assurance of confidentiality to potential sources of information is essential to enable investigators to obtain relevant but sensitive disclosures from persons unwilling to comment publicly about a defendant's background or character. The availability of such information, it is argued, provides the person who prepares the report with greater detail on which to base a sentencing recommendation and, in turn, provides the judge with a better basis for his sentencing decision. But consideration must be given to the quality, as well as the quantity, of the information on which the sentencing judge may rely. Assurances of secrecy are conducive to the transmission of confidences which may bear no closer relation to fact than the average rumor or item of gossip, and may imply a pledge not to attempt independent verification of the information received. The risk that some of the information accepted in confidence may be erroneous, or may be misinterpreted, by the investigator or by the sentencing judge, is manifest.

If, as the State argues, it is important to use such information in the sentencing process, we must assume that in some cases it will be decisive in the judge's choice between a life sentence and a death sentence. If it tends to tip the scales in favor of life, presumably the information would be favorable and there would be no reason why it should not be disclosed. On the other hand, if it is the basis for a death sentence, the interest in reliability plainly outweighs the State's interest in preserving the availability of comparable information in other cases.

The State also suggests that full disclosure of the presentence report will unnecessarily delay the proceeding. We think the likelihood of significant delay is overstated because we must presume that reports prepared by professional probation officers, as the Florida procedure requires, are generally reliable. In those cases in which the accuracy of a report is contested, the trial judge can avoid delay by disregarding the disputed material. Or if the disputed matter is of critical importance, the time invested in ascertaining the truth would surely be well spent if it makes the difference between life and death.

The State further urges that full disclosure of presentence reports, which often include psychiatric and psychological evaluations, will occasionally disrupt the process of rehabilitation. The argument, if valid, would hardly justify withholding the report from defense counsel. Moreover, whatever force that argument may have in noncapital cases, it has absolutely no merit in a case in which the judge has decided to sentence the defendant to death. Indeed, the extinction of all possibility of rehabilitation is one of the aspects of the death sentence that makes it different in kind from any other sentence a State may legitimately impose.

Finally, Florida argues that trial judges can be trusted to exercise their discretion in a responsible manner, even though they may base their decisions on secret information. However acceptable that argument might have been before Furman v. Georgia, supra, it is now clearly foreclosed. Moreover, the argument rests on the erroneous premise that the participation of counsel is superfluous to the process of evaluating the relevance and significance of aggravating and mitigating facts. Our belief that debate between adversaries is often essential to the truth-seeking function of trials requires us also to recognize the importance of giving counsel an opportunity to comment on facts which may influence the sentencing decision in capital cases.

Even if it were permissible to withhold a portion of the report from a defendant, and even from defense counsel, pursuant to an express finding of good cause for nondisclosure, it would nevertheless be necessary to make the full report a part of the record to be reviewed on appeal. Since the State must administer its capital sentencing procedures with an even hand . . . it is important that the record on appeal disclose to the reviewing court the considerations which motivated the death sentence in every case in which it is imposed. Without full disclosure of the basis for the death sentence, the Florida capital sentencing procedure would be subject to the defects which resulted in the holding of unconstitutionality in Furman v. Georgia, supra. In this particular case, the only explanation for the lack of disclosure is the failure of defense counsel to request access to the full report. That failure cannot justify the submission of a less complete record to the reviewing court than the record on which the trial judge based his decision to sentence petitioner to death.

Nor do we regard this omission by counsel as an effective waiver of the constitutional error in the record. There are five reasons for this conclusion. First the State does not urge that the objection has been waived. Second, the Florida Supreme Court has held that it has a duty to consider "the total record," Swan v. State, 322 So. 2d 485, 489 (1975), when it reviews a death sentence. Third, since two members of that court expressly considered this point on the appeal in this case, we presume that the entire court passed on the question. Cf. Boykin v. Alabama, 395 U.S. 238, 240–242, and n.3 (1969). Fourth, there is no basis for presuming that the defendant himself made a knowing and intelligent waiver, or that counsel could possibly have made a tactical decision not to examine the full report, cf. Estelle v. Williams, 425 U.S. 501, 507–508 (1976). Fifth, since the judge found, in disagreement with the jury, that the evidence did not establish any mitigating circumstance, and since the presentence report was the only item considered by the judge but not by the jury, the full review of the factual basis for the judge's rejection of the advisory verdict is plainly required. For if the jury, rather than the judge, correctly assessed the petitioner's veracity, the death sentence rests on an erroneous factual predicate.

We conclude that petitioner was denied due process of law when the death sentence was imposed, at least in part, on the basis of information which he had no opportunity to deny or explain.

IV

There remains only the question of what disposition is now proper. Petitioner's conviction, of course, is not tainted by the error in the sentencing procedure. The State argues that we should merely remand the case to the Florida Supreme Court with directions to have the entire presentence report made a part of the record to enable that court to complete its reviewing function. That procedure, however, could not fully correct the error. For it is possible that full disclosure, followed by explanation or argument by defense counsel, would have caused the trial judge to accept the jury's advisory verdict. Accordingly, the death sentence is vacated and the case is remanded to the Florida Supreme Court with directions to order further proceedings at the trial court level not inconsistent with this opinion.

Reversed and remanded.

[Mr. Chief Justice BURGER concurred in the judgment.]

[Mr. Justice WHITE, Mr. Justice BLACKMUN, and Mr. Justice BRENNAN wrote concurring opinions.]

Mr. Justice MARSHALL, dissenting.

. . . While I continue to believe that the death penalty is unconstitutional in all circumstances . . . and therefore would remand this case for resentencing to a term of years; nevertheless, now that Florida may legally take a life, we must insist that it be in accordance with the standards enunciated by this Court. In this case I am appalled at the extent to which Florida has deviated from the procedures upon which this Court expressly relied. It is not simply that the trial judge, in overriding the jury's recommendation of life imprisonment, relied on undisclosed portions of the presentence report. Nor is it merely that the Florida Supreme Court affirmed the sentence without discussing the omission and without concern that it did not even have the entire report before it. Obviously that alone is enough to deny due process and require reversal as the Court now holds. But the blatant disregard exhibited by the courts below for the standards devised to regulate imposition of the death penalty calls into question the very basis for this Court's approval of that system in Proffitt [v. Florida, 428 U.S. 242 (1976)].

* * *

In Proffitt, a majority of this Court was led to believe that Florida had established capital sentencing procedures that would "assure that the death penalty would not be imposed in an arbitrary or capricious manner." . . . This case belies that promise and suggests the need to reconsider that assessment.

Mr. Justice REHNQUIST, dissenting.

. . . [I]f capital punishment is not cruel and unusual under the Eighth and Fourteenth

Amendments, as the Court [has held], the use of particular sentencing procedures, never previously held unfair under the Due Process Clause, in a case where the death sentence is imposed cannot convert that sentence into a cruel and unusual punishment. The prohibition of the Eighth Amendment relates to the character of the punishment, and not to the process by which it is imposed. I would therefore affirm the judgment of the Supreme Court of Florida.

Comments

1. In *North Carolina* v. *Pearce,* supra, the Supreme Court held that neither the Double Jeopardy Clause nor the Equal Protection Clause is an absolute bar to a more severe sentence upon reconviction. However, due process requires that whenever a judge imposes a more severe sentence following reconviction, his reasons for doing so must affirmatively appear in the record and the reasons must be based upon "objective information concerning identifiable conduct on the part of the defendant occurring after the time of the original sentencing proceeding." What "objective information" based on "factual data" would justify a more severe sentence? May a sentencing judge on reconviction impose a shorter term of imprisonment but a larger fine? Suppose a sentencing judge decides on reconviction that the defendant probably committed perjury because of a substantial variance in the defendant's testimony in the two trials. May the defendant receive a more severe sentence? Is that the type of objective-factual data contemplated in *Pearce*? See *United States* v. *Sanders,* 435 F.2d 165 (5th Cir. 1970), holding yes. Can a more severe sentence be justified on the ground that the defendant no longer reflects an attitude of remorse and lacks potential for rehabilitation?

   The concern of the *Pearce* Court with possible "vindictiveness" by a resentencing judge is well founded. Retribution ("an eye for an eye, a tooth for a tooth") is the oldest theory of punishment, and many judges still adhere to this judicial philosophy. Does the *Pearce* requirement of objective-factual data preclude disguised vindictiveness? What is there to prevent a resentencing judge from claiming to have been unaware of relevant factual data at the first sentencing and then imposing a more severe sentence following reconviction? Are the *Pearce* requirements applicable only to the conduct of the defendant *after* the initial sentencing? In *Michigan* v. *Payne,* 412 U.S. 47 (1973), the Supreme Court held that the requirements of *Pearce* are not to be applied retroactively.

2. In *Colten* v. *Kentucky,* supra, a majority of the Supreme Court refused to apply the "prophylactic rule" of *Pearce* to a trial de novo following a misdemeanor conviction. Suppose the prosecutor following a trial de novo informs the judge of the defendant's earlier sentence and recommends a heavier penalty. What result under the *Pearce-Colten* rationale? Are there any circumstances in which a judge, following a trial de novo, must affirmatively state objective data for imposing a more severe sentence? Suppose defendant's counsel has objective information that a sentencing judge always imposes the maximum sentence following a conviction de novo, which tends to show vindictiveness. Is the resentencing judge now limited under the *Pearce* rule? Suppose a defendant successfully appeals his conviction on the record (not a trial de novo) and is tried

and convicted before a different judge. May the second judge, consistent with *Pearce-Colten,* impose a more severe sentence without stating any objective reasons? Does it matter whether the resentencing judge is aware or unaware of the earlier sentence?

3. In *Chaffin* v. *Stynchcombe,* 412 U.S. 17 (1973), a divided Supreme Court (5–4) held that a jury that had not been informed of a defendant's prior sentence may impose a greater sentence following reconviction. The Court reasoned that since *Pearce* was premised on the need to guard against *vindictiveness* in the resentencing process, the potential for such abuse by a sentencing jury is de minimis. Four justices dissented, stating that "establishing one rule for resentencing by juries [unconstitutionally] burdens the defendant's right to choose to be tried by a jury after a successful appeal." Id. at 34 (Douglas, J., dissenting). May a sentencing jury impose a more severe sentence following reconviction if it has learned of the defendant's earlier sentence from the prosecutor or the mass media? Suppose defense counsel informs a sentencing jury of the defendant's earlier sentence. Is a more severe sentence permissible under the *Pearce-Colten-Chaffin* standards?

4. In *Blackledge* v. *Perry,* 417 U.S. 21 (1974), the Supreme Court held that a prosecutor may not substitute a more serious charge at a trial de novo following a misdemeanor conviction. In *Blackledge,* the defendant was convicted of assault with a deadly weapon (a misdemeanor) in a North Carolina court of inferior jurisdiction and was sentenced to six months' imprisonment. The defendant filed a notice of appeal to a court of general jurisdiction—an absolute right under North Carolina law. Prior to the trial de novo, the prosecutor obtained a grand jury indictment charging the defendant with the *felony* of assault with a deadly weapon, which covered the same conduct as the misdemeanor conviction. The defendant pleaded guilty to the felony charge and was sentenced to five to seven years' imprisonment. The District Court and the Court of Appeals (4th Cir.) granted federal habeas corpus relief. On certiorari, the United States Supreme Court affirmed. In an opinion by Justice Stewart, a majority of the Court held that on appeal from a misdemeanor conviction that entitles the defendant to a trial de novo, it is a violation of Fourteenth Amendment due process for the state to bring felony charges against him for the same conduct unless the state shows that it was impossible (for the prosecutor) to proceed on the felony charges at the first trial. The Court further held that a defendant so charged with a felony on retrial can bring federal habeas corpus proceedings notwithstanding his plea of guilty. Under what conditions would it have been "impossible" for the prosecution to initially proceed on the felony charge? What if important evidence was discovered after the first trial? Does *Blackledge* permit reprosecution on additional charges not included in the original indictment or information? See Borman, *The Chilled Right to Appeal From a Plea Bargain Conviction: A Due Process Cure,* 69 Nw. U.L. Rev. 663 (1975).

5. In *McGinnis* v. *Royster,* supra, a majority of the Supreme Court held that the New York system of applying "good time" credit in calculating the minimum parole date for bailed defendants but not for pretrial detainees who were unable to make bail was not a denial of equal protection of the laws. Why? Because there are no

systematic rehabilitative programs in New York jails? What type of rehabilitation services do bailed defendants receive prior to trial? Does the New York system meet the "rational basis" test for invidious discrimination? In light of *McGinnis,* could a state constitutionally deny "good time" credit to both pretrial detainees and bailed defendants? The question must be answered on due process rather than equal protection grounds. Why?

6. Three main types of sentences are employed in the American criminal justice system: the definite, the indefinite and the indeterminate.

Definite Sentence. Originally, and especially in the eighteenth century, the definite sentence was a set term of years that was fixed and invariable according to the established law. The definite sentence deprived judges of any discretion in sentencing. Mitigating or aggravating factors, such as a defendant's age, mental condition, prior criminal record, or social history, were deemed immaterial. Thus, in theory at least, the unfettered discretion and potential for abuse in sentencing by judges was eliminated. This classical criminological view soon gave way to a more "enlightened" view, espoused by the neoclassical school of criminology, that some variation in sentencing should be permitted at the discretion of the judge in light of the circumstances of the individual offender and the offense. The definite sentence, without possibility of parole, is rarely used today.

Indefinite Sentence. The indefinite sentence has a minimum and maximum set by the legislature (e.g., five to ten years), but the offender can be released before expiration of the minimum term by an administrative agency, usually a parole board. This type of sentence is a compromise between the definite sentence and the indeterminate sentence.

Indeterminate Sentence. The indeterminate sentence is a product of the late nineteenth century Italian positivistic school of criminology. Originally, no minimum or maximum term was set; the offender was sent to an institution to be "reformed," and the date of release was determined by physicians and correctional authorities. Today, most jurisdictions employ a partially indeterminate sentence: a minimum and maximum penalty is fixed by the legislature, but the offender can be released whenever the correctional authorities decide that the rehabilitation process has been effective.

Other variations are employed under indeterminate sentencing structures. The sentence is sometimes used for "sexual psychopaths" in lieu of fixed sentences, and, in theory, it can result in life imprisonment. In the most common variation of the indeterminate sentence, used in several western states, the trial judge sentences the offender to a maximum term set by statute but the release date is determined by a parole board or, in California, the Adult Authority. In some jurisdictions, the trial judge selects a minimum and maximum term, and the correctional authorities are given discretion to release the offender at any time within this range. In other jurisdictions, a minimum sentence must be served for all felonies, regardless of the maximum term imposed by the judge.

Today, 36 jurisdictions employ some form of indeterminate sentencing structure. Indeterminate sentences have been subject to a great deal of criticism since defendants in states that allow the greatest amount of indeterminancy serve the longest sentences.

7. At common law, and in most jurisdictions today, a convicted defendant has a right to personally address the court prior to the imposition of sentence. This practice, known as *allocution,* is available so (1) "that the defendant might be identified by the court as the real party adjudged guilty; (2) that he might have a chance to plead a pardon, or (3) move in arrest in judgment; (4) that he might have an opportunity to say why judgment should not be given against him; and (5) that the example of being brought up for the animadversion of the court and the open denunciation of punishment might tend to deter others from the commission of similar offenses." *Ball* v. *United States,* 140 U.S. 118 (1891).

Rule 32(a) of the Federal Rules of Criminal Procedure governs the sentencing of federal defendants. That rule provides, in part: "Before imposing sentence the court shall afford the defendant an opportunity to make a statement in his own behalf and to present any information in mitigation of punishment." The United States Supreme Court has held that federal judges, before imposing sentence, should afford a defendant an opportunity to make, in person and not merely through counsel, a statement in his own behalf. *Green* v. *United States,* 365 U.S. 301 (1961). However, a failure of a federal judge to personally address a defendant, prior to sentencing, is not an error of constitutional dimension and is not cognizable in federal habeas corpus proceedings. *Hill* v. *California,* 368 U.S. 424 (1962). Presumably, the substantive effect of a denial of allocution would be a remanding of the case for resentencing.

After judgment and sentencing is imposed, the defendant may appeal the sentencing decision of the trial court to a higher court.

8. In *Gardner* v. *Florida,* supra, the Supreme Court stopped short of holding that in a capital case defense counsel is automatically entitled to review the confidential portion of a presentence report. But as Mr. Justice Stevens noted, even if counsel can be kept in the dark, appellate courts must receive the full record so that they can take cognizance of the factors that motivated the judge to impose the death penalty. Under Florida law, a presentence report is not required in capital cases. What factors should the judge consider in deciding whether to order such a report? Under what circumstances would a prosecutor or a defense attorney want a presentence report? The Florida Supreme Court has stated, "In order to sustain a sentence of death following a recommendation of life, the facts suggesting a sentence of death should be so clear and convincing that virtually no reasonable person could differ," *Tedder* v. *State,* 322 So. 2d 908, 910 (1975). What facts appear in the record that justify the trial judge's overruling the jury's recommendation of life imprisonment? On remand, Daniel Gardner was resentenced to life imprisonment.

9. The following is a verbatim transcript of a sentence imposed upon a defendant convicted of murder in the federal District Court of the Territory of New Mexico many years ago by a United States judge, sitting at Taos in an adobe stable used as a temporary courtroom:

"Jose Manuel Miguel Xaviar Gonzales, in a few short weeks it will be spring. The snows of winter will flee away. The ice will vanish. And the air will become soft and balmy. In short, Jose Manuel Miguel Xaviar Gonzales, the annual miracle of the years will awaken and come to pass, but you won't be there.

"The rivulet will run its soaring course to the sea. The timid desert flowers will put forth their tender shoots. The glorious valleys of this imperial domain will blossom as the rose. Still, you won't be here to see.

"From every tree top some wild woods songster will carol his mating song. Butterflies will sport in the sunshine. The busy bee will hum happy as it pursues its accustomed vocation. The gentle breeze will tease the tissels of the wild grasses, and all nature, Jose Manuel Miguel Xaviar Gonzales, will be glad but you. You won't be here to enjoy it because I command the sheriff or some other officers of the country to lead you out to some remote spot, swing you by the neck from a knotting bough of some sturdy oak, and let you hang until you are dead.

"And then, Jose Manuel Miguel Xaviar Gonzales, I further command that such officer or officers retire quickly from your dangling corpse, that vultures may descend from the heavens upon your filthy body until nothing shall remain but bare, bleached bones of a cold-blooded, copper-colored, blood-thirsty, throat-cutting, chili-eating, sheep-herding, murdering son-of-a-bitch." *United States* v. *Gonzales* (1881), United States District Court, New Mexico Territory Sessions.

10. Some recent lower federal and state court decisions involving the sentencing process are *United States* v. *Floyd,* 519 F.2d 1031 (5th Cir. 1975) (rule of *North Carolina* v. *Pearce* is dependent upon the possibility of vindictiveness, not upon the sentencing authority's actual vindictiveness); *Lechuga* v. *State,* 532 S.W.2d 581 (Tex. Crim. App. 1975) (rule of *North Carolina* v. *Pearce* applies to second sentence of five years' probation following initial sentence of three years' imprisonment); *State* v. *Petersen,* 235 N.W.2d 801 (Minn. 1975) (state convict who was subsequently sentenced by a federal court for a federal offense of which he had been convicted prior to his state sentence held not entitled to have his state sentence run concurrently with his federal sentence); *United States* v. *Truelove,* 527 F.2d 980 (4th Cir. 1975) (federal conviction for transporting untaxed marijuana, in violation of a statute since repealed, is a prior conviction for purposes of sentencing under the 1970 Drug Act); *Shiflett* v. *State,* 530 S.W.2d 548 (Tex. Crim. App. 1975) (defendants have no statutory right to updated presentence reports prior to resentencing); *People* v. *Tidwell,* 338 N.E.2d 113 (Ill. App. 1975) (trial judge not unreasonable in conditioning probation for defendant convicted of damaging property upon his restitution of $200 to the victim, even though the defendant was unemployed, had three children, and had no way to pay the sum); *Hartwell* v. *Jackson,* 403 F. Supp. 1229 (D.D.C. 1975) (defendant is not entitled to sentencing credit under the Youth Corrections Act for the time he spent as an escapee); *Halliwell* v. *State,* 323 So. 2d 557 (Fla. 1975) (what a murderer does to his victim's body following the killing should not be taken into account in deciding whether the death penalty should be imposed); *Woofter* v. *O'Donnell,* 542 P.2d 1396 (Nev. 1975) (state legislature may constitutionally provide for increased sentences for defendants who use firearms during the commission of the offense) (in accord is *People* v. *Henry,* 91 Cal. Rptr. 841 [Calif. App. 1970], *State* v. *Rose,* 498 P.2d 897 [Wash. 1972], and *State* v. *Buffa,* 168 A.2d 49 [N.J. App. 1961]); *Scott* v. *State,* 326 So. 2d 165 (Fla. 1976) (following a new trial in which the defendant is placed on probation, trial judge who previously

sentenced defendant to a term less than the maximum allowed by law may, for violation of terms of probation, impose a sentence up to the maximum that could originally have been imposed); *United States v. Cunningham,* 529 F.2d 884 (6th Cir. 1976) (judge's imposing harsher sentence after conviction than he had imposed after the defendant's subsequently withdrawn guilty plea held not violative of *North Carolina v. Pearce*); *Klimas v. State,* 534 S.W.2d 202 (Ark. 1976) (when evidence of a prior conviction offered by the state for sentencing purposes is silent as to whether the defendant was represented by counsel, the state must first lay a foundation tending to show that the defendant had representation or had waived it); *Tanner v. State,* 532 S.W.2d 168 (Ark. 1976) (sentence of life imprisonment without possibility of parole held not unconstitutional); *United States v. Montecalvo,* 533 F.2d 1110 (9th Cir. 1976) (trial judge who read material on a bank robbery defendant prior to trial in violation of Fed. R. Crim. P. 32(c)(1) and presided over the defendant's trial held to have committed reversible error); *State v. Kamae,* 548 P.2d 632 (Hawaii 1976) (ordinary rules of evidence apply to an extended-term sentence hearing); *United States v. Cavazos,* 530 F.2d 4 (5th Cir. 1976) (judge, in sentencing heroin sale defendant, may not in imposing sentence take into account FBI statistics about the number of narcotics transactions a seller can get away with before being caught); *People v. Braithwaite,* 240 N.W.2d 293 (Mich. App. 1976) (defendant whose prison sentence was greatly enhanced because he had been convicted of a crime in Canada held entitled to resentencing); *Commonwealth v. LeBlanc,* 346 N.E.2d 874 (Mass. 1976) (judge at sentencing may not ask the defendant to tell his side of the story with respect to a pending criminal charge in another county); *Couser v. State,* 356 A.2d 612 (Md. Ct. Spec. App. 1976) (heroin-possession defendant's acquittal by judge at bench trial on charges of intent to sell did not preclude the judge, after finding the defendant guilty of possession, from taking into account for sentencing purposes various factors indicating the defendant was a pusher); *Pulliam v. State,* 345 N.E.2d 229 (Ind. 1976) (no constitutional requirement that a jury with sentencing responsibility be furnished the defendant's presentence report); *Gray v. State,* 538 S.W.2d 391 (Tenn. 1976) (consecutive sentences should be imposed only for purpose of protecting society from further criminal conduct by a dangerous or habitual offender); *Young v. State,* 551 P.2d 1133 (Okla. Ct. Crim. App. 1976) (sentencing judge entitled to consider the "hard-core" legal facts of an adult offender's juvenile record) (in accord is *People v. McFarlin,* 208 N.W.2d 504 [Minn. 1973]); *United States v. Wright,* 540 F.2d 1247 (4th Cir. 1976) (defendant who received an undetermined amount of money from a bank robbery in which $15,000 was stolen may be sentenced as a convicted felon despite the government's failure to prove he received more than $100 [receiving less than $100 from the proceeds of a bank robbery is a misdemeanor, 18 U.S.C. § 2131(c)]); *Baugh v. United States,* 540 F.2d 1245 (4th Cir. 1976) (under federal law, consecutive sentences may be imposed for receiving and possessing stolen money and transporting stolen money in interstate commerce); *United States v. Oliver,* 546 F.2d 1096 (4th Cir. 1976) (imposition of a fine as a condition of probation is permissible under the Youth Corrections Act) (contra is *United States v. Bowens,* 514 F.2d 440 [9th Cir.

1975], and *Cramer* v. *Wise,* 501 F.2d 959 [5th Cir. 1975]); *State* v. *Sanders,* 337 So. 2d 1131 (La. 1976) (defendant previously convicted of enumerated felonies who is sentenced under a state firearms statute cannot be charged as a habitual offender on the basis of the same prior convictions that formed the basis of his firearm possession conviction); *United States* v. *Robin,* 545 F.2d 775 (2d Cir. 1976) (trial court's refusal to allow counsel for guilty-pleading defendant adequate time to prepare a rebuttal to a lengthy presentence report held plain error); *State* v. *Murphy,* 555 P.2d 1110 (Ariz. 1976) (trial court may not order prosecution to present evidence about the circumstances surrounding a murder in order to decide if the death penalty should be imposed when the prosecution had recommended a life sentence as part of a plea bargain); *Graham* v. *State,* 560 P.2d 200 (Okla. Ct. Crim. App. 1976) (imposition of maximum one-year jail sentence for possession of marijuana against defendant who was a longtime law-abiding citizen, was gainfully employed, and was adequately supporting his two children held excessive); *United States* v. *McDuffie,* 542 F.2d 236 (5th Cir. 1976) (federal judge erred in relying on undisclosed interview defendant allegedly had given to FBI in imposing a harsher sentence following defendant's reconviction); *People* v. *Terminelli,* 243 N.W.2d 703 (Mich. App. 1976) (defendant who failed to meet term of probation that he make $20 per month payments on his $400 fine held entitled to have his counsel present his claim that he was financially unable to make payments, and to revoke his probation on this ground alone was unconstitutional); *Commonwealth* v. *Murray,* 351 N.E.2d 555 (Mass. App. 1976) (judge's statement at sentencing of robbery defendant that "I am not punishing this boy one minute for trying his case, but I am punishing him for coming up here and lying and for his whole attitude," held improper as tantamount to a summary finding of perjury without a separate trial); *Thomas* v. *Estelle,* 550 F.2d 1014 (5th Cir. 1977) (a sentencing recommendation by the prosecutor is not binding on the court); *Anderson* v. *State,* 251 N.W.2d 768 (Wis. 1977) (trial court is not required to follow recommendation of social investigator who conducted presentence investigation); *Collins* v. *State,* 548 S.W.2d 106 (Ark. 1977) (denial of right of allocution is error); *State* v. *Price,* 252 N.W.2d 165 (Neb. 1977) (trial court has no authority to change sentence after it has been pronounced and defendant has left courtroom); *State* v. *Sittig,* 249 N.W.2d 770 (Wis. 1977) (court's refusal to impose a mandatory sentence constitutes abuse of discretion); *State* v. *Craft,* 232 S.E.2d 282 (N.C. App. 1977) (condition of probation that defendant waive his right to be free from warrantless searches conducted in presence of his probation officer held not unreasonable); *Brown* v. *State,* 559 P.2d 107 (Alaska 1977) (a sentencing court has the authority to require a defendant to pay a fine as a condition of probation regardless of whether the statute upon which the defendant was convicted carries the sanction of a fine); *United States* v. *Remding,* 548 F.2d 1274 (6th Cir. 1977) (one convicted of an act of air piracy in which no loss of life occurred may be eligible for probation); *United States* v. *Hodges,* 556 F.2d 366 (5th Cir. 1977) (fundamental fairness requires that a defendant be given at least some opportunity to rebut information explicitly relied upon by sentencing judge).

14.03 APPEALS AND APPELLATE REVIEW

In all states and in the federal system, some type of appellate review is provided for those convicted of a crime. Although the right of appeal was unknown at common law, it is a statutory right today in every jurisdiction. Although the constitutionality of a denial of appellate review by a state has never been decided by the Supreme Court, in several cases it has suggested in dictum that appellate review is not constitutionally required.[34] However, even though appellate review is not constitutionally required, a state that does provide it may not discriminate on the basis of wealth by denying counsel[35] or transcripts[36] to indigents on first appeal because of their inability to pay for them.

In 1971, there were 14,163 state and local court systems operating in 16,460 court locations in America. Of these, 203 were appellate courts, 3621 courts of general jurisdiction, and 12,636 courts of limited or inferior jurisdiction. Eighty-seven per cent of all appellate courts, 95 per cent of all courts of general jurisdiction, and 89 per cent of all courts of limited jurisdiction exercise some criminal jurisdiction.[37]

In general, appeals in cases in which the death penalty may be imposed are automatically reviewed by a state's highest court.[38] All other felony convictions may be reviewed by that court or by an intermediate appellate court (e.g., district court of appeals). Following trial in a court of inferior jurisdiction such as a magistrates court, misdemeanor convictions are usually reviewed by a court of general jurisdiction (e.g., a court with both felony and misdemeanor jurisdiction) in a trial de novo. Many jurisdictions require that a convicted defendant be expressly informed of his right to appeal, usually by the judge at sentencing, unless he has made a valid plea of guilty.

In general, if a defendant is acquitted at trial, the Double Jeopardy Clause of the Fifth Amendment bars appeal by the prosecution. However, in a few jurisdictions, a prosecutor's appeal is allowed following a defendant's acquittal to determine the law for future cases, but the judgment of acquittal cannot be reversed. Prosecutor's appeals are also allowed, in most jurisdictions, from a pretrial dismissal of charges (e.g., judge dismisses charges because the statute upon which the indictment is based is held to be unconstitutional). Because the actual trial has not begun, jeopardy has not attached and the Fifth Amendment Double Jeopardy Clause is not applicable.[39] In many jurisdictions, if the court sustains the defense's motion to suppress evidence, no prosecutor's appeal is permitted, and in many instances, the prosecutor is "forced" to dismiss the charges because other admissible evidence is lacking. However, in the federal system and in some states, an interlocutory appeal by the prosecutor is permitted from such rulings. However, the defendant usually may not take such an interlocutory appeal from an overruled motion to suppress because he can still be acquitted at trial.

As noted in Chapter Thirteen, most defendants plead guilty via the plea bargaining process, and a valid guilty plea effectively eliminates most legal grounds upon which an appeal could be based. Therefore, collateral

---

[34]See *McKane* v. *Durston*, 153 U.S. 684, 687 (1894); *Ross* v. *Moffitt*, 417 U.S. 600, 606 (1974) (Chapter Seven, § 7.02) ("a State is not obliged to provide any appeal at all for criminal defendants"); *Estelle* v. *Dorrough*, 420 U.S. 534, 536 (1975) (Chapter Four, § 4.04) ("there is no federal constitutional right to state appellate review of state criminal convictions").

[35]*Douglas* v. *California*, 372 U.S. 353 (1963) (counsel required on indigent defendant's first appeal). But see *Ross* v. *Moffitt*, 417 U.S. 600 (1974) (indigents have no constitutional right to appointed counsel on discretionary appeals).

[36]*Griffin* v. *Illinois*, 351 U.S. 12 (1956) (Chapter Four, § 4.02). See also Chapter Four, Comments, pp. 137–138.

[37]U.S. Dept. of Justice, Law Enforcement Assistance Administration, *National Survey of Court Organization 1971* (June, 1972). See generally Frank, *Courts on Trial* (1949); Robertson, *Rough Justice: Perspectives on Lower Criminal Courts* (1974); Carrington, Meador, and Rosenberg, *Justice on Appeal* (1976); Rubin, *The Courts* (1976); Klein, *Federal and State Court Systems—A Guide* (1977).

[38]See, e.g., Fla. Stat. Ann. § 921.141(4) (Supp. 1976–1977); and *Gregg* v. *Georgia*, 428 U.S. 153, 166 (1976) (Chapter Eleven, § 11.03).

[39]See Chapter Six, § 6.02.

attacks on judgments of conviction based on guilty pleas are not subject to appellate review in most jurisdictions. Consequently, most convicted defendants do not appeal their cases to higher courts, and the convictions of those who do are usually affirmed. Even so, the dockets of our appellate courts are crowded with appeals from criminal convictions and civil judgments.

All jurisdictions have procedural rules that require that objections to the admission or exclusion of evidence be made by the defendant either at a pretrial hearing or at the time the evidence is offered at trial. Failure of a defendant to make these *timely objections* results in an automatic forfeiture of the claim for appeal purposes. In general, appellate courts will not review claims not properly raised at trial.[40] The courts require claims to be raised at trial because only in that way can the trial judge make a ruling and develop facts so the appellate court will have a record of the events below upon which to conduct an adequate appellate review.

The "Plain Error" Rule

There is one notable exception to the general rule requiring timely objections by the defendant: this is the so-called "plain error" rule. In the federal system, "plain errors or defects affecting substantial rights" of defendants are subject to appellate review even though they were not properly raised at trial or on appeal (e.g., involuntary confession admitted without objection).[41] In all jurisdictions, appellate review of "plain error" or its equivalent is permitted. Less than 1 per cent of convictions are reversed on a finding of plain error.

The "Harmless Error" Rule

At the other end of the legal spectrum, some errors (even some of a constitutional dimension) are not of sufficient magnitude to require a reversal of a conviction on appeal regardless of the timeliness of objection. These fall under the "harmless error," or *Chapman,* rule.

Today, all jurisdictions prohibit appellate reversals predicated upon errors that do not affect the substantial rights of the defendant. The leading case decided by the Supreme Court in this area is *Chapman* v. *California,* 386 U.S. 18 (1976).[42]

In *Chapman,* in an opinion by Justice Black, a majority of the Supreme Court held that a denial of a federal constitutional right can be a "harmless error," and that federal law, rather than state law, governs whether a federal constitutional error is harmless. As the *Chapman* Court stated:

> We cannot leave to the States the formulation of the authoritative laws, rules, and remedies designed to protect people from infractions by the States of federally guaranteed rights. We have no hesitation in saying that the right of these petitioners not to be punished for exercising their Fifth and Fourteenth Amendment right to be silent . . . is a federal right which, in the absence of appropriate congressional action, it is our responsibility to protect by fashioning the necessary rule.[43]

The Court refused to hold that all constitutional errors require an automatic reversal of conviction. But before a constitutional error can be deemed harmless, the state must prove (1) that the error was harmless beyond a reasonable doubt, and (2) that it did not contribute to the defendant's conviction.

The Court went on to hold that a violation of the *Griffin* rule, which forbids comment by a prosecutor on a defendant's silence at trial,[44] can be harmless error, but in the instant case the prosecutor's repeated references to the defendant's silence were not harmless.

The "Automatic Reversal" Rule

The Supreme Court has held in several cases that certain constitutional errors are of such magnitude as to require an *automatic reversal* of a conviction. For example, the erroneous introduction of a defendant's involuntary confession at trial requires an

---

[40]See *Wainwright* v. *Sykes,* 97 S. Ct. 2497 (1977) (infra, § 14.04).

[41]Rule 52(b), Fed. R. Crim. P.

[42]See Chapter Six, Comment 2, p. 515, for a listing of cases applying the harmless error doctrine.

[43]*Chapman* v. *California,* 386 U.S. 18, 21 (1967).

[44]*Griffin* v. *California,* 380 U.S. 609 (1965).

automatic reversal.[45] Likewise, when a defendant has been denied counsel at trial,[46] or has been convicted by a partial judge,[47] such errors can *never* be harmless and there must be an automatic reversal of conviction.

14.04 POSTCONVICTION REMEDIES

Although most defendants who plead guilty do not appeal their convictions because of the legal constraints on such appeals, some defendants continue their legal attacks upon their conviction beyond the normal appellate process.

These *collateral attacks* (challenges against the legality of the confinement as opposed to appeals on the merits of the conviction) are made through one of several postconviction remedies. While traditional avenues of appeal are used to establish finality in criminal prosecutions, postconviction remedies are extraordinary judicial remedies that allow courts to review, under some circumstances, alleged violations of fundamental rights in the trial process. Most often, but not always, federal habeas corpus relief is sought. Although such relief is available to federal prisoners, most criminal cases decided by the United States Supreme Court on federal habeas corpus petitions involve state prisoners. Because the legal rules surrounding postconviction remedies are often very complex, this discussion will be restricted to a general overview of these extraordinary methods of judicial review.[48]

The writ of federal habeas corpus is recognized in the United States Constitution and is often referred to as the "great writ." Article I, § 9 of the Constitution provides, inter alia:

The Privilege of the Writ of Habeas Corpus shall not be suspended, unless when in Cases of Rebellion or Invasion the Public Safety may require it.

The writ of habeas corpus, found at common law, is a judicial order that requires a government official, usually the prison warden or director of corrections, to bring a defendant in his custody before the court to determine the legality of that custody. Thus, habeas corpus is a constitutional remedy for unlawful detention or imprisonment. In some instances, the granting of habeas corpus relief can result in a convicted defendant's outright release from imprisonment. Although any person restrained of his liberty in violation of the Constitution may apply for federal habeas corpus relief, state habeas corpus is also provided for in every state constitution. The implementing federal habeas corpus statutes, 28 U.S.C. §§ 2241–2255, are presented in Appendix A.

Federal Habeas Corpus and State Prisoners—Dual Review

The writ of federal habeas corpus is today the principal method used by state prisoners to obtain review of their convictions in the federal courts. This is largely due to a 1953 United States Supreme Court decision, *Brown* v. *Allen*, 344 U.S. 443,[49] which expanded the scope of federal habeas corpus jurisdiction to include state prisoners. In *Brown*, the Court held that a convicted state defendant whose conviction had been affirmed on direct appeal in the state courts could apply to a federal district court for federal habeas corpus relief on his claim that his federal constitutional rights had been denied in the state proceedings. The Court further held that if the federal district court denied him habeas corpus relief, he could appeal that denial to the higher federal courts. As a result of *Brown* v. *Allen*, a state prisoner has two avenues of review for his conviction—state appellate review and, if that is unsuccessful, federal review via habeas corpus.

Ten years later, in 1963, the Court further broadened the scope of federal habeas corpus relief in *Fay* v. *Noia*, 372 U.S. 391, and *Townsend* v. *Sain*, 372 U.S. 293. In *Fay* v. *Noia*, the Supreme Court relaxed the federal requirement that state defendants

---

[45] *Haynes* v. *Washington*, 373 U.S. 503 (1963).

[46] *Gideon* v. *Wainwright*, 372 U.S. 335 (1963) (Chapter Seven, § 7.02).

[47] *Tumey* v. *Ohio*, 273 U.S. 510 (1927).

[48] For in-depth discussions of postconviction remedies, see Hart and Wechsler, *The Federal Courts*, and Bator, Mishkin, Shapiro, and Wechsler, *The Federal System* (2d ed. 1973); McCormick, Chadbourne, and Wright, *Federal Courts* 544–572 (1976); Wright, *Law of Federal Courts* 236–248 (3d ed. 1976).

---

[49] See also *Henry* v. *Mississippi*, 379 U.S. 443 (1965); *Francis* v. *Henderson*, 425 U.S. 536 (1976).

must "exhaust all available remedies" in the state system before a writ of habeas corpus may be heard in a federal court. While the Court noted that a "deliberate by-pass" of available state remedies would preclude federal review, it held that if a state defendant failed to take a state appeal and if because of state procedural requirements that appeal was no longer available, a petition for federal habeas corpus relief could still be entertained. Thus, only the deliberate by-pass of available state remedies would preclude habeas corpus relief.

Townsend v. *Sain* further increased the availability of federal habeas corpus to state prisoners. In that case, the Court held that in reviewing a habeas corpus petition a federal court must hold an evidentiary hearing whenever an applicant has not received a "full and fair evidentiary hearing in a state court." As noted by the Court in *Townsend*, "A federal evidentiary hearing is required unless the state-court trier of fact has after a full hearing reliably found the relevant facts."[50] The *Townsend* Court said that if a federal judge concludes that the applicant did receive a full and fair hearing in a state court on a habeas application, which resulted in reliable findings of fact, the federal judge should ordinarily accept the facts as found by the state court. However, he is not required to, and in his discretion, he may reach other conclusions of fact. Thus, every federal court may, under certain conditions, reverse the findings of any state criminal court as to either the law or the facts. However, certain other requirements must be fulfilled by a state prisoner before he will be given an evidentiary hearing in federal court on a habeas corpus application.

First, the federal statute implementing habeas corpus requires that the state prisoner be "in custody in violation of the Constitution, laws, or treaties of the United States." 28 U.S.C. § 2254. The Court has held that persons "in custody" include parolees,[51] and defendants released on bail or on their own recognizance, because their freedom of movement is still subject to legal constraints.[52] Second, the state detention must be "in violation of" federal law. Therefore illegal detentions not violative of federal law (e.g., false imprisonment by a private person) are not subject to habeas corpus relief. Third, the application for habeas corpus must be in writing and signed by the person for whom relief is sought or his agent (e.g., counsel). No particular form is required—the habeas application can be written on a scrap of paper.[53] Fourth, the petition must allege facts regarding the alleged illegal detention and they must be sworn to under oath. In summary, the basic legal requirements for an application for federal habeas corpus by a state prisoner are few: (1) all presently available state remedies must be exhausted; (2) the prisoner must be in custody; (3) the custody must be in violation of federal law; and (4) the facts of the alleged illegal detention must be in writing and sworn to.

This extension of federal habeas corpus to state prisoners has been the subject of much criticism by prosecutors, legal scholars, and federal judges, including Chief Justice Burger.[54] According to the Chief Justice, this dual state-federal review of state criminal convictions has resulted in a "procedural nightmare"[55] and caused "unhappy tensions"[56] between the states and federal courts. Recent court statistics bear out these criticisms.

In 1960, 868 state-prisoner habeas corpus petitions were filed in federal district courts, of which 2.6 per cent resulted in evidentiary hearings. In 1964 (one year after *Townsend* v. *Sain*), 4243 such cases were filed in federal courts, of which 11 per cent resulted in evidentiary hearings. In 1970, 9063 state-prisoner habeas applications were filed in federal district courts—but the number of cases reaching trial was only 4.8 per cent because of the accelerating caseload.

---

[50]*Townsend* v. *Sain*, 372 U.S. 293, 312–313 (1963).

[51]*Jones* v. *Cunningham*, 371 U.S. 236 (1963).

[52]*Hensley* v. *Municipal Court*, 411 U.S. 354 (1973).

[53]*Johnson* v. *Avery*, 393 U.S. 483, 500 (1969) (dissenting opinion of White, J.).

[54]Burger, *Post-Conviction Remedies: Eliminating Federal-State Friction*, 61 J. Crim. L. Crim. & Pol. Sci. 148 (1970).

[55]Id., at 148.

[56]Id., at 151.

If all petitions by federal and state prisoners are included, 15,997 habeas corpus applications were filed in 1970, compared to 2177 in 1960. Although most habeas petitions do not result in an evidentiary hearing, some judicial consideration must be given to each case—and this is often a waste of effort. Former Associate Supreme Court Justice Tom C. Clark has said that 98 per cent of these claims are "frivolous,"[57] and Chief Justice Burger believes that the vast majority of habeas petitions have "no merit."[58] Judge Macklin Fleming of the California Court of Appeals noted:

As a consequence of this dual review, state enforcement of criminal law has fallen into a condition that may charitably be described as chaotic. With parallel systems of courts operating on identical subject matter, a defendant can switch back and forth from one system to another as his interests dictate, and if fortune smiles, he may succeed in getting one system of courts in contention with the other.[59]

Viable solutions to the expanded use of federal habeas corpus by state prisoners do not come easily, since the "great writ" is given constitutional recognition. Federal Judge Henry J. Friendly has called for restrictions on the use of federal habeas corpus. He suggested that the writ be used only when plausible (colorable) claims of innocence are presented (most defendants on appeal or habeas do not claim that they are innocent but rather that their convictions were illegal) or when the attack concerns fundamental rights in the criminal process.[60] Chief Justice Burger has pointed to the system used in some European countries, such as Holland, in which a trained team of experts in law, psychology, and counselling make routine visits to penal institutions,

listen to inmates' grievances, and report to the minister of justice on those cases that appear to call for a remedy.[61] Others have suggested that states adopt a postconviction remedy at least as broad in scope as the federal habeas corpus remedy for state prisoners.

In 1974 Chief Justice Burger and Justices Powell and Rehnquist suggested that federal collateral review of a state prisoner's Fourth Amendment claims "should be confined solely to the question of whether the petitioner was provided a fair opportunity to raise and have adjudicated the question in state courts."[62]

The justices went on to criticize the excessive use of federal habeas corpus by state prisoners. During the 1975–1976 Term, the Court began to reduce the availability of federal habeas corpus to state prisoners. In *Stone* v. *Powell*, 428 U.S. 465 (1975) (Chapter Five, § 5.03), a majority of the Court held that on a petition for habeas corpus relief a state inmate may not raise the claim that his conviction was based upon evidence obtained by an unconstitutional search when he had previously been afforded an opportunity for "full and fair litigation" of his claim in the state courts. More recently, in *Wainwright* v. *Sykes*, 433 U.S. ___ (1977) (infra), a majority of the Court held that federal habeas corpus is barred when a state inmate fails to object to the admissibility at trial of his confession, and other evidence of guilt was substantial enough to negate any possibility of actual prejudice resulting from the admission of the inculpatory statement.

Whatever "solutions" to the increased use of federal habeas corpus petitions by state prisoners are ultimately adopted by the Supreme Court, it seems likely, in light of *Stone* v. *Powell* and *Wainwright* v. *Sykes*, that the trend toward broadening the scope of habeas corpus evidenced in *Brown* v. *Allen*, *Fay* v. *Noia*, and *Townsend* v. *Sain* will not be continued by the Burger Court.

---

[57]*Fay* v. *Noia*, 372 U.S. 391, 445 (Clark, J., dissenting).

[58]Burger, supra, note 54, at 148.

[59]Fleming, *The Price of Perfect Justice* 23–24 (1974).

[60]Friendly, *Is Innocence Irrelevant? Collateral Attack on Criminal Judgments*, 38 U. Chi. L. Rev. 142 (1970).

---

[61]Burger, supra note 54.

[62]*Schneckloth* v. *Bustamonte*, 412 U.S. 218, 250 (1974) (concurring opinion).

The "Cause and Prejudice" Test in Federal Habeas Corpus Proceedings

ORAL ARGUMENTS BEFORE THE U.S. SUPREME COURT*

Wainwright v. Sykes, No. 75-1578; Argued 3/29/77

For the second time this Term, the Court was asked to determine whether a state defendant's failure to raise a constitutional claim at trial precludes later federal habeas relief. *Henderson* v. *Kibbe,* argued 20 Cr.L. 4186, raised this question earlier this Term.

The State of Florida urged the Court to overturn a U.S. Court of Appeals for the Fifth Circuit grant of habeas relief to a third-degree murder defendant who now claims that his inculpatory statements to police came during a drunken spell that rendered him unable to intelligently and knowingly waive his *Miranda* rights; see 528 F.2d 55.

Charles Corces, Jr., Assistant Attorney General of Florida, told the Court that Florida Rule of Criminal Procedure 3.190 (1972) requires a defendant to raise his suppression motion before or at trial. But the respondent made no such challenge. Even when he appealed his third-degree murder conviction, he did not raise his voluntariness claim. Thus the state courts never had a chance to rule on this point.

Is he raising an issue of ineffectiveness of counsel? a Justice asked.

"No, sir," Corces replied. There is no question of the trial lawyers' competency. This point is conceded by the respondent.

Mr. Justice White: "What if the defendant had raised the voluntariness claim on state appeal? Would that claim have been subject to the plain error doctrine?"

Counsel thought not. Invocation of the plain error doctrine depends on the situation. There was no such error apparent here.

The Chief Justice: "Did he raise any claim that he was intoxicated?"

Some evidence that Sykes was intoxicated at the time of his arrest did come out, Corces responded.

Mr. Justice Blackmun: "Then is the respondent claiming that he was intoxicated at the time, or that he didn't understand *Miranda?*"

The defendant claims that he was too drunk to understand what he was doing, Corces said.

Mr. Justice Rehnquist: "The federal habeas judge ordered a new hearing on this point. That would suggest that all the evidence necessary to resolve the admissibility point had not been presented."

Corces agreed. But he again noted that no plain error is apparent on the face of this record.

Continuing, counsel noted that the Fifth Circuit affirmed the district judge's order directing the state to conduct the *Jackson* v. *Denno* voluntariness hearing even though the statement's admissibility had not been challenged. The federal courts concluded that since the state had not proved that the procedural default was tactical, the defendant was not bound by it.

Florida, of course, does not question the power of the federal district court to consider federal claims "even when a procedural default exists. But we are talking about the appropriate exercise of that power," Corces submitted. Principles of comity and federalism require foregoing of habeas relief where an inexcusable procedural default has been made. "In the case of such procedural defaults, denial of habeas relief should be the rule instead of the exception."

This may conflict with dicta in *Fay* v. *Noia,* 372 U.S. 39 (1963), Corces acknowledged. But even in *Fay,* there was a timely objection and historical facts had been developed at the trial level. In *Fay,* there was an intentional, albeit coerced, bypass.

*From 21 Crim. L. Rptr. 4012–4014 (1977). Reprinted by permission of the Bureau of National Affairs, Inc.

Davis Analysis

Fay does not establish the only criteria for determining the effects of a procedural default, Corces asserted. *Davis* v. *U.S.*, 411 U.S. 233 [1973], articulates the guidelines for determining the consequences of Sykes' waiver. In *Davis* v. *U.S.*, the Court recognized that a failure to timely raise a substantive constitutional issue, as required by procedural rules, can constitute a waiver which precludes habeas review. True, *Davis* involved a federal inmate's untimely challenge but as this Court indicated in *Francis* v. *Henderson* [425 U.S. 536 (1976)], principles of comity and federalism require application of the *Davis* rule to state inmates, too. *Davis*, coupled with *Francis* v. *Henderson*, suggests that it takes both cause and actual prejudice to excuse a defendant's waiver. However, Sykes has demonstrated neither cause nor actual prejudice to excuse his failure to raise the voluntariness question.

Mr. Justice White: "In this case, there wouldn't be much question about prejudice would there?"

"No, sir."

Mr. Justice White: "What about cause?"

None has been shown, Corces responded.

Mr. Justice White: "Was the failure to raise the claim 'just a plain mistake'?"

Even if it were, that alone would not be enough to entitle the defendant to federal habeas relief. *Estelle* v. *Williams* [425 U.S. 501 (1976)], indicates that much.

Mr. Justice White: "Would the guidelines that you suggest take into consideration ineffectiveness of counsel?"

Counsel thought so.

Mr. Justice White: "How would you state the ineffectiveness rule? Suppose counsel said, 'I just made a mistake.'"

Corces answered that he would review the entire case to determine if counsel has been reasonably effective.

Mr. Justice White: "Would your guidelines permit a 'plain error' exception?"

"Yes, sir; if the error was plain enough."

Mr. Justice White: "Would your plain error rule depend on state law?"

Not necessarily, counsel submitted. The federal plain error rule would govern claims premised on federal law, Corces added.

Mr. Justice Stevens: "Suppose a defendant had been given *Miranda* warnings by an arresting officer. This defendant also told police he had drunk two quarts of gin and killed another person. Would his statements be admissible at trial if objected to?"

This determination, Corces responded, is best left to the trial judge, who can resolve whether the defendant understood the *Miranda* warnings.

Mr. Justice Stevens: "Assume that the defendant did not understand the warnings."

Then the statements would be inadmissible, Corces responded.

Focusing on Issues

Returning to his *Davis* v. *U.S.* point, Corces argued that *Davis* forces a defendant to timely assert his constitutional claims so that the state can focus clearly on the issues.

If the prosecution has not been effectively put on notice as to the issues, the trial evidence cannot be focused. Thus the state may be forced to deal with an unarticulated issue later. The *Davis* rule, Corces maintained, would tend to simplify the federal habeas proceeding—only a state transcript would then be needed to review the federal constitutional issue. The Fifth Circuit erred in holding that *Jackson* v. *Denno*, 378 U.S. 368 [1964], mandated a hearing for this defendant in the absence of a challenge to the statements' admissibility. To require a trial judge to conduct a voluntariness hearing sua sponte interferes with the defense strategy, Corces argued. Florida satisfied *Jackson* v. *Denno's* commandments by providing the defendant with a forum to air his challenges; see Rule 3.109. *Lego* v. *Twomey*, 404 U.S. 477 (1972), indicates that the *Jackson* v. *Denno* hearing is only mandated when a defendant challenges his confession.

Mr. Justice Rehnquist: "Even if the Fifth Circuit is right that a trial judge must initiate inquiry into voluntariness under certain circumstances, the defendant can still waive the *Jackson* v. *Denno* hearing, right?"

Counsel thought so. For tactical or strategic reasons the defense may not want the state to focus on the problem, Corces added.

Overwhelming Evidence

Edward R. Korman joined the State of Florida as amicus curiae for the United States in urging reversal of the Fifth Circuit.

The evidence is fairly simple here, he told the Court. Police officers placed Sykes under arrest after the shooting death of another man. The *Miranda* issue was quite evident to the arresting officers. At trial, the defense did everything but make a formal *Miranda* objection.

Even without Sykes' confession, there was overwhelming evidence to convict him, Korman submitted. The confession became relevant in light of the respondent's self-defense claim at trial. However, nothing indicated that this confession was involuntary. In fact, trial counsel may have felt it was pointless to raise the objection.

Mr. Justice Stevens: "What in the confession was inconsistent with the self-defense claim?"

The confession indicates that the defendant may have lost his temper. The confession could have been used to impeach his self-defense claim.

Mr. Justice Marshall: "There was never any question that he shot the victim?"

That was correct, Korman replied.

The Chief Justice: "Sykes' wife's testimony that 'John shot him' might tend to undermine the self-defense claim, too."

Korman agreed.

Mr. Justice Marshall: "What was the defendant charged with?"

Originally, he was charged with second-degree murder, Korman replied. However, he was convicted of third-degree murder.

Interpreting F. R. Crim. P. 12(f) in *Davis v. U.S.*, this Court concluded that absent "cause" for relief from procedural defaults, a federal prisoner could not get habeas relief. A state prisoner can do no better, Korman further submitted, absent cause. Cause means prejudice in the sense of a denial of the right to a fair trial.

Mr. Justice White: "Then you wouldn't permit a habeas petitioner to benefit from plain error unless the error went to the integrity of the proceeding."

That's right, counsel said.

Mr. Justice Stevens: "Did the prosecutor, in fact, use the inculpatory statements to impeach the defendant's testimony?"

Counsel thought that the prosecutor had done this.

State Rule Ignored

William F. Casler, of St. Petersburg, Florida, began his argument by asserting that both the state and the amicus have practically ignored Florida Rule 3.109 which deals specifically with admissions of confession. This rule, Casler submitted, mandates that upon the court's or defense's motion, a trial court shall suppress an illegally obtained confession or admission.

The Chief Justice: "But doesn't that assume that someone is going to call the trial judge's attention to the matter?"

No, Casler replied, nothing in this rule says that the failure to do so results in a waiver.

Mr. Justice Rehnquist: "Must some evidence have been adduced that would lead to the motion? Why didn't the judge hold a hearing here?"

Casler thought that enough evidence existed to spark the sua sponte motion here. The trial transcript highlights the voluntariness issue vividly, he said. However, he suggested that the trial judge may have been unaware of the rule.

Mr. Justice Marshall: "Why have a motion by the defense at all if the judge must hold the hearing anyway?"

As Casler construed the state rule, this sua sponte procedure was mandatory. If the Florida trial court had followed this rule, no need would have existed for federal habeas on this point, he added.

Mr. Justice White: "Are you also arguing that the Constitution requires a judge to conduct a hearing on his own motion?"

"No, sir."

Mr. Justice Brennan: "Are you saying that when the prosecution offered the confession, the trial judge should have ordered a voluntariness hearing?"

"Yes, sir."

Mr. Justice White: "How was the federal Constitution violated?"

By the introduction of the inculpatory statements, Casler answered.

Mr. Justice White: "Then you do argue that the Constitution requires a judge to hold a hearing on his own—even absent objection by the defendant?"

"Yes, sir."

Mr. Justice Brennan: "In your own practice, what do you do when the state offers a confession?"

"I file a motion to suppress."

Mr. Justice Brennan: "Even if you knew you were going to put your defendant on the stand and subject him to impeachment?"

Then it would depend on the circumstances, Casler said.

The Chief Justice: "On your theory, suppose that a defendant were sentenced to 35 years, and you came in 25 years later. Your argument is that the federal courts could do what they did here?"

"I suppose so," Casler said. He saw no reason why a voluntariness hearing could not be held here.

Mr. Justice Rehnquist: "If the trial court failed to follow the state rule, there would be [federal] habeas, in your view."

Casler agreed. He also emphasized that the Florida rule differed in material respect from F. R. Crim. P 12(f).

The Chief Justice: "When the defendant went into subsequent state proceedings, he never made the voluntariness claim. Does that mean that trial counsel wasn't aware of Florida's practice?"

"I don't know, sir."

Mr. Justice White: "Did your appeal the denial of state habeas?"

I was appointed at the federal habeas level, Casler replied.

Mr. Justice White: "Did the defendant take his state habeas claim to the state supreme court?"

Yes, Casler said, but his claim was not reviewed by that court; it found a lack of jurisdiction.

Mr. Justice Brennan: "Did you negotiate the stipulation that trial counsel was competent?"

Counsel answered affirmatively.

Mr. Justice Brennan: "Why would you want to stipulate to something like that?"

Without that stipulation, we would have had to return to the state courts and litigate the effectiveness issue.

The Chief Justice: "Do you acknowledge that the defendant's statement could be used for impeachment under *Harris* v. *New York,* 403 U.S. 573 (1971)?"

Counsel agreed that this was so.

Finally, nothing in this record establishes a deliberate bypass by the respondent, Casler stated.

On rebuttal, Corces again called for reversal.

Mr. Justice Marshall: "Do you have a Florida case that says if you don't make a suppression motion, you waive it?"

Yes, Corces replied, the Florida courts have ruled on this point.

Mr. Justice White: "What do you do with *Henry* v. *Mississippi*?"

Henry was concerned with the adequacy of the state grounds, Corces answered.

WAINWRIGHT v. SYKES

Supreme Court of the United States, 1977
433 U.S. ___, 97 S. Ct. 2497, 53 L. Ed. 2d 594

Respondent, John Sykes, was convicted in 1972 of third degree murder in a Florida State court. During his trial inculpatory statements made by him to police officers were admitted into evidence. At no time during the trial was the admissibility of any of respondent's statements challenged by his counsel on the ground that respondent had not understood the *Miranda* warnings, nor did the trial judge question their admissibility. Respondent appealed his conviction but did not challenge the admissibility of the inculpatory statements, although he later challenged the statements on the grounds of involuntariness in a motion to vacate the conviction and in state habeas corpus petitions. The respondent was unsuccessful in all these actions. Respondent then filed a federal habeas corpus action under 28 U.S.C. § 2254, asserting the inadmissibility of his statement by reason of his lack of understanding of the *Miranda* warnings. The District Court (M.D. Fla.) ruled that *Jackson* v. *Denno*, 378 U.S. 368 (1964), requires a hearing in a state criminal trial prior to the admission of inculpatory statements by a defendant, and that he had not lost this right by failing to assert his claim at trial or on appeal. The Court of Appeals (5th Cir.) agreed that respondent was entitled to a *Jackson-Denno* hearing, and held that respondent's failure to comply with Florida's "contemporaneous objection rule," which requires a defendant to make a motion to suppress prior to trial, did not bar review of the suppression claim unless the right to object was deliberately bypassed for tactical reasons. The United States Supreme Court granted certiorari.

Mr. Justice REHNQUIST delivered the opinion of the Court.

We granted certiorari to consider the availability of federal habeas to review a state convict's claim that testimony was admitted at his trial in violation of his *Miranda* rights, a claim which the Florida courts have previously refused to consider on the merits because of noncompliance with a state contemporaneous objection rule. . . .

* * *

The simple legal question before the Court calls for a construction of the language of 28 U.S.C. § 2254(a), which provides that the federal courts shall entertain an application for a writ of habeas corpus "in behalf of a person in custody pursuant to the judgment of the state court only on the ground that he is in custody in violation of the Constitution or laws or treaties of the United States." . . .

. . . Where the habeas petitioner challenges a final judgment of conviction rendered by a state court, this Court has been called upon to decide no fewer than four different questions, all to a degree interrelated with one another: (1) What types of federal claims may a federal habeas court properly consider; (2) Where a federal claim is cognizable by a federal habeas court, to what extent must that court defer to a resolution of the claim in prior state proceedings; (3) To what extent must the petitioner who seeks federal habeas exhaust state remedies before resorting to the Federal court; (4) In what instances will an adequate and independent state ground bar consideration of otherwise cognizable federal issues on federal habeas review?

* * *

There is no need to consider here . . . these first three areas of controversy attendant to federal habeas review of state convictions. Only the fourth area—the adequacy of state grounds to bar federal habeas review—is presented in this case. . . .

As to the role of adequate and independent state grounds, it is a well-established principle of federalism that a state decision resting on an adequate foundation of state substantive law is immune from review in the federal courts. Fox Film Corp. v. Muller, 296 U.S. 207 (1935); Murdock v. Memphis, 87 U.S. (20 Wall.) 590 (1875). The application of this principle in the context of a federal habeas proceeding has therefore excluded from consideration any questions of state *substantive law,* and thus effectively barred federal habeas review where questions of that sort are either the only ones raised by a petitioner or are in themselves dispositive of his case. The area of controversy which has developed has concerned the reviewability of federal claims which the state court has declined to pass on because not presented in the manner prescribed by its *procedural* rules. The adequacy of such an independent state procedural ground to prevent federal habeas review of the underlying federal issue has been treated very differently than where the state law ground is substantive. The pertinent decisions marking the Court's somewhat tortuous efforts to deal with this problem are: Ex parte Spencer, 228 U.S. 652 (1913); Daniels v. Allen, 344 U.S. 443 (1953); Fay v. Noia, supra [372 U.S. 391 (1963)]; Davis v. United States, 411 U.S. 233 (1973); and Francis v. Henderson, 425 U.S. 536 (1976).

In Daniels, supra, petitioners' lawyer had failed to mail the appeal papers to the state supreme court on the last day provided by law for filing, and hand delivered them one day after that date. Citing the state rule requiring timely filing, the Supreme Court of North Carolina refused to hear the appeal. This Court, relying in part on its earlier decision in Ex parte Spencer, supra, held that federal habeas was not available to review a constitutional claim which could not have been reviewed on direct appeal here because it rested on an independent and adequate state procedural ground. 344 U.S., at 486–487.

In Fay v. Noia, supra, respondent Noia sought federal habeas to review a claim that his state court conviction had resulted from the introduction of a coerced confession in violation of the Fifth Amendment to the United States Constitution. While the convictions of his two codefendants were reversed on that ground in collateral proceedings following their appeals, Noia did not appeal and the New York courts ruled that his subsequent coram nobis action was barred on account of that failure. This Court held that petitioner was nonetheless entitled to raise the claim in federal habeas, and thereby overruled its decision 10 years earlier in Daniels v. Allen, supra:

"[T]he doctrine under which state procedural defaults are held to constitute an adequate and independent state law ground barring direct Supreme Court review is not to be extended to limit the power granted the federal courts under the federal habeas statute." 372 U.S. at 399.

As a matter of comity but not of federal power, the Court acknowledged "a limited discretion in the federal judge to deny relief . . . to an applicant who had deliberately by-passed the orderly procedure of the state courts and in so doing has forfeited his state remedies." Id., at 438. In so stating, the Court made clear that the waiver must be knowing and actual—"an intentional relinquishment or abandonment of a known right or privilege." Id., at 439, quoting Johnson v. Zerbst, [304 U.S. 458 (1938)] at 464. Noting petitioner's "grisly choice" between acceptance of his life sentence and pursuit of an appeal which might culminate in a sentence of death, the Court concluded that there had been no deliberate bypass of the right to have the federal issues reviewed through a state appeal.[h]

---

[h]Not long after Fay, the Court in Henry v. Mississippi, 379 U.S. 442 (1965), considered the question of the adequacy of a state procedural ground to bar Supreme Court review on direct review, and concluded that failure to comply with a state contemporaneous objection rule applying the admission of evidence did not necessarily foreclose consideration of the underlying Fourth Amendment claim. The state procedural ground would be "adequate," and thus dispositive of the case on direct appeal to the United States Supreme Court, only where "the State's insistence on compliance with its procedural rule serves a legitimate state interest." Id., at 447. Because, the Court reasoned, the purposes of the contemporaneous objection rule were largely served by the motion for a directed verdict at the close of the State's case, enforcement of the contemporaneous objection rule was less than essential and therefore lacking in the necessary "legitimacy" to make it an adequate state ground.

Rather than searching the merits of the constitutional claim, though, the Court remanded for determination whether a separate adequate state ground might exist—that is, whether petitioner had knowingly and deliberately waived his right to object at trial for tactical or other reasons. This was the same type of waiver which the Court in Fay had said must be demonstrated in order to bar review on state procedural grounds in a federal habeas proceeding.

A decade later we decided Davis v. United States, 411 U.S. 233 (1973), in which a federal prisoner's application under § 2255 sought for the first time to challenge the makeup of the grand jury which indicted him. The Government contended that he was barred by the requirement of Fed. Rule Crim. Proc. 12(b)(2) providing that such challenges must be raised "by motion before trial." The rule further provides that failure to so object constitutes a waiver of the objection, but that "the Court for cause shown may grant relief from the waiver." . . . Referring to previous constructions of Rule 12(b)(2), we concluded that review of the claim should be barred on habeas, as on direct appeal, absent a showing of cause for the noncompliance and some showing of actual prejudice resulting from the alleged constitutional violation.

Last Term, in Francis v. Henderson, 425 U.S. 536 (1976), the rule of Davis was applied to the parallel case of a state procedural requirement that challenges to grand jury composition be raised before trial. The Court noted that there was power in the federal courts to entertain an application in such a case, but rested its holding on "considerations of comity and concerns for orderly administration of criminal justice. . . ." Id., at 538–539. While there was no counterpart provision of the state rule which allowed an exception upon some showing of cause, the Court concluded that the standard derived from the federal rule should nonetheless be applied in that context since "[t]here is no reason to . . . give greater preclusive effect to procedural defaults by federal defendants than to similar defaults by state defendants." Id., at 542, quoting Kaufman v. United States, 394 U.S. 217, 218 (1969). As applied to the federal petitions of state convicts, the Davis cause and prejudice standard was thus incorporated directly into the body of law governing the availability of federal habeas corpus review.

To the extent that the dicta of Fay v. Noia may be thought to have laid down an all-inclusive rule rendering state timely objection rules ineffective to bar review of underlying federal claims in federal habeas preceedings—absent a "knowing waiver" or a "deliberate bypass" of the right to so object—its effect was limited by Francis, which applied a different rule and barred a habeas challenge to the makeup of a grand jury. . . .

* * *

Respondent . . . urges that a defendant has a right under Jackson v. Denno, 378 U.S. 368 (1964), to a hearing as to the voluntariness of a confession, even though the defendant does not object to its admission. But we do not read Jackson as creating any such requirement. In that case the defendant's objection to the use of his confession was brought to the attention of the trial court, . . . and nothing in the Court's opinion suggests that a hearing would have been required even if it had not been. Language in subsequent decisions of this Court has reaffirmed the view that the Constitution does not require a voluntariness hearing absent some contemporaneous challenge to the use of the confession.

We therefore conclude that the Florida procedure did, consistently with the United States Constitution, require that petitioner's confession be challenged at trial or not at all, and thus his failure to timely object to its admission amounted to an independent and adequate state procedural ground which would have prevented direct review here. See Henry v. Mississippi, 379 U.S. 442 (1965). We thus come to the crux of this case. Shall the rule of Francis v. Henderson, supra, barring federal habeas review absent a showing of "cause" and "prejudice" attendant to a state procedural waiver, be applied to a waived objection to the admission of a confession at trial?[k] We answer that question in the affirmative.

As earlier noted in the opinion, since Brown v. Allen, supra, it has been the rule that the federal habeas petitioner who claims he is detained pursuant to a final judgment of a state court in violation of the U.S. Constitution is entitled to have the federal habeas court make its own independent determination of his federal claim, without being bound by the determination on the merits of that claim reached in the state proceedings. This rule of Brown v. Allen is in no way changed by our holding today. Rather, we deal only with contentions of federal law which were *not* resolved on the merits in the state proceeding due to the petitioner's failure to raise them there as required by state procedure. We leave open for resolution in future decisions the precise definition of the "cause" and "prejudice" standard, and note here only that it is narrower than the standard set forth in dicta in Fay v. Noia, supra, which would make federal habeas review generally available to state convicts absent a knowing and deliberate waiver of the federal constitutional contention. It is the sweeping language of Faye v. Noia, supra, going far beyond the facts of the case eliciting it, which we today reject.[1]

The reasons for our rejection of it are several. The contemporaneous objection rule itself is by no means peculiar to Florida, and deserves greater respect than Fay gives it, both for the fact that it is employed by a coordinate jurisdiction within the federal system and for the many interests which it serves in its own right. A contemporaneous objection enables the record to be made with respect to the constitutional claim when the recollections of witnesses are freshest, not years later in a federal habeas proceeding. It enables the judge who observed the de-

---

[k]Petitioner does not argue, and we do not pause to consider whether a bare allegation of a Miranda violation, without accompanying assertions going to the actual voluntariness or reliability of the confession, is a proper subject for consideration on federal habeas review, where there has been a full and fair opportunity to raise the argument in the state proceeding. See Stone v. Powell, 428 U.S. 465 (1976). We do not address the merits of that question because of our resolution of the case on alternative grounds.

---

[1]We have no occasion today to consider the Fay rule as applied to the facts there confronting the Court. Whether the Francis rule should preclude federal habeas review of claims not made in accordance with state procedure where the criminal defendant has surrendered, other than for reasons of tactical advantage, the right to have all of his claims of trial error considered by a state appellate court, we leave for another day.

The Court in Fay stated its knowing and deliberate waiver rule in language which applied not only to the waiver of the right to appeal, but to failures to raise individual substantive objections in the state trial. Then, with a single sentence in a footnote, the Court swept aside all decisions of this Court "to the extent that [they] may be read to suggest a standard of discretion in federal habeas corpus proceedings different from what we lay down today. . . ." 372 U.S., at 439 n. 44. We do not choose to paint with a similarly broad brush here.

meanor of those witnesses to make the factual determinations necessary for properly deciding the federal constitutional question. . . .

A contemporaneous objection rule may lead to the exclusion of the evidence objected to, thereby making a major contribution to finality in criminal litigation. Without the evidence claimed to be vulnerable on federal constitutional grounds, the jury may acquit the defendant, and that will be the end of the case; or it may nonetheless convict the defendant, and he will have one less federal constitutional claim to assert in his federal habeas petition. If the state trial judge admits the evidence in question after a full hearing, the federal habeas court pursuant to the 1966 amendment to § 2254 will gain significant guidance from the state ruling in this regard. Subtler considerations as well militate in favor of honoring a state contemporaneous objection rule. An objection on the spot may force the prosecution to take a hard look at its whole card, and even if the prosecutor thinks that the state trial judge will admit the evidence he must contemplate the possibility of reversal by the state appellate courts or the ultimate issuance of a writ of federal habeas corpus based on the impropriety of the state court's rejection of the federal constitutional claim.

We think that the rule of Fay v. Noia, broadly stated, may encourage "sand bagging" on the part of defense lawyers, who may take their chances on a verdict of not guilty in a state trial court and intend to raise their constitutional claims in a federal habeas court if their initial gamble does not pay off. The refusal of federal habeas courts to honor contemporaneous objection rules may also make state courts themselves less stringent in their enforcement. Under the rule of Fay v. Noia, supra, state appellate courts know that a federal constitutional issue raised for the first time in the proceeding before them may well be decided in any event by a federal habeas tribunal. Thus their choice is between addressing the issue notwithstanding the petitioner's failure to timely object, or else face the prospect that the federal habeas court will decide the question without the benefit of their views.

The failure of the federal habeas courts generally to require compliance with a contemporaneous objection rule tends to detract from the perception of the trial of a criminal case in state court as a decisive and portentous event. A defendant has been accused of a serious crime, and this is the time and place set for him to be tried by a jury of his peers and found either guilty or not guilty by that jury. To the greatest extent possible all issues which bear on this charge should be determined in this proceeding: the accused is in the court room, the jury is in the box, the judge is on the bench, and the witnesses, having been subpoenaed and duly sworn, await their turns to testify. Society's resources have been concentrated at that time and place in order to decide, within the limits of human fallibility, the question of guilt or innocence of one of its citizens. Any procedural rule which encourages the result that those proceedings be as free of error as possible is thoroughly desirable, and the contemporaneous objection rule surely falls within this classification.

We believe the adoption of the Francis rule in this situation will have the salutary effect of making the state trial on the merits the "main event," so to speak, rather than a tryout on the road for what will later be the determinative federal habeas hearing. There is nothing in the Constitution or in the language of § 2254 which requires that the state trial on the issue of guilt or innocence be devoted largely to the testimony of fact witnesses directed to the elements of the state crime, while only later will there occur in a federal habeas hearing a full airing of the federal constitutional claims which were not raised in the state proceedings. If a criminal defendant thinks that an action of the state trial court is about to deprive him of a federal constitutional right there is every reason for his following state procedure in making known his objection.

The "cause" and "prejudice" exception of the Francis rule will afford an adequate guarantee, we think, that the rule will not prevent a federal habeas court from adjudicating for the first time the federal constitutional claim of a defendant who in the absence of such an adjudication will be the victim of a miscarriage of justice. Whatever precise content may be given those terms by later cases, we feel confident in holding without further elaboration that they do not exist here. Respondent has advanced no explanation whatever for his failure to object at trial, and, as the proceeding unfolded, the trial judge is certainly not to be faulted for failing to question the admission of the confession himself. The other evidence of guilt presented at trial, moreover, was substantial to a degree that would negate any possibility of actual prejudice resulting to the respondent from the admission of his inculpatory statement.

We accordingly conclude that the judgment of the Court of Appeals for the Fifth Circuit must be reversed, and the cause remanded to the United States District Court for the middle District of Florida with instructions to dismiss respondent's petition for a writ of habeas corpus.

[Mr. Chief Justice BURGER, Mr. Justice WHITE, and Mr. Justice STEVENS each wrote concurring opinions.]

Mr. Justice BRENNAN, with whom Mr. Justice MARSHALL joins, dissenting.

Over the course of the last decade, the deliberate bypass standard announced in Fay v. Noia, 372 U.S. 391, 438–439 (1963), has played a central role in efforts by the federal judiciary to accommodate the constitutional rights of the individual with the States' interests in the integrity of their judicial procedural regimes. The Court today decides that this standard should no longer apply with respect to procedural defaults occurring during the trial of a criminal defendant. In its place, the Court adopts the two-part "cause" and "prejudice" test originally developed in Davis v. United States, 411 U.S. 233 (1973), and Francis v. Henderson, 425 U.S. 536 (1976). As was true with these earlier cases, however, today's decision makes no effort to provide concrete guidance as to the content of those terms. More particularly, left unanswered is the thorny question that must be recognized to be central to a realistic rationalization of this area of law: How should the federal habeas court treat a state procedural default that is attributable purely and simply to the error or negligence of a defendant's trial counsel?

* * *

[A]ny realistic system of federal habeas corpus jurisdiction must be premised on the reality that the ordinary procedural default is borne of the inadvertence, negligence, inexperience, or incompetence of trial counsel. See, e.g., Hill, The Inadequate State Ground, 65 Colum. L. Rev. 941, 997 (1965). The case under consideration today is typi-

cal. The court makes no effort to identify a tactical motive for the failure of Sykes' attorney to challenge the admissibility or reliability of a highly inculpatory statement. . . . Indeed, there is no basis for inferring that Sykes or his state trial lawyer were even aware of the existence of his claim under the Fifth Amendment; for this is not a case where the trial judge expressly drew the attention of the defense to a possible constitutional contention or procedural requirement, . . . or where the defense signals its knowledge of a constitutional claim by abandoning a challenge previously raised. . . . Rather, any realistic reading of the record demonstrates that we are faced here with a simple lawyer's error.

Fay's answer thus is plain: the bypass test simply refuses to credit what is essentially a lawyer's mistake as a forfeiture of constitutional rights. I persist in the belief that the interests of Sykes and the State of Florida are best rationalized by adherence to this test, and by declining to react to inadvertent defaults through the creation of an "airtight system of forfeitures."

* * *

Punishing a lawyer's unintentional errors by closing the federal courthouse door to his client is both a senseless and misdirected method of deterring the slighting of state rules. It is senseless because unplanned and unintentional action of any kind generally is not subject to deterrence; and, to the extent that it is hoped that a threatened sanction addressed to the defense will induce greater care and caution on the part of trial lawyers, thereby forestalling negligent conduct or error, the potential loss of all valuable state remedies would be sufficient to this end. And it is a misdirected sanction because even if the penalization of incompetence or carelessness will encourage more thorough legal training and trial preparation, the habeas applicant, as opposed to his lawyer, hardly is the proper recipient of such a penalty. Especially with fundamental constitutional rights at stake, no fictional relationship of principal-agent or the like can justify holding the criminal defendant accountable for the naked errors of his attorney. This is especially true when so many indigent defendants are without any realistic choice in selecting who ultimately represents them at trial. Indeed, if responsibility for error must be apportioned between the parties, it is the

State, through its attorney's admissions and certification policies, that is more fairly held to blame for the fact that practicing lawyers too often are ill-prepared or ill-equipped to act carefully and knowledgeably when faced with decisions governed by state procedural requirements.

* * *

In short, I believe that the demands of our criminal justice system warrant visiting the mistakes of a trial attorney on the head of a habeas corpus applicant only when we are convinced that the lawyer actually exercised his expertise and judgment in his client's service, and with his client's knowing and intelligent participation where possible. This, of course, is the precise system of habeas review established by Fay v. Noia.

* * *

[I]t is accurate to assert that most courts, this one included, traditionally have resisted any realistic inquiry into the competency of trial counsel. There is nothing unreasonable, however, in adhering to the proposition that it is the responsibility of a trial lawyer who takes on the defense of another to be aware of his client's basic legal rights and of the legitimate rules of the forum in which he practices his profession. If he should unreasonably permit such rules to bar the assertion of the colorable constitutional claims of his client, then his conduct may well fall below the level of competence that can fairly be expected of him. . . . If the scope of habeas jurisdiction previously governed by Fay v. Noia is to be redefined so as to enforce the errors and neglect of lawyers with unnecessary and unjust rigor, the time may come when conscientious and fair-minded federal and state courts, in adhering to the teaching of Johnson v. Zerbst, will have to reconsider whether they can continue to indulge the comfortable fiction that all lawyers are skilled or even competent craftsmen in representing the fundamental rights of their clients.

Federal Habeas Corpus and Federal Prisoners

In the 1948 revision of the Judicial Code, Congress provided that federal prisoners may petition the sentencing court to vacate, set aside, or correct any sentence subject to collateral attack under a motion to vacate sentence (28 U.S.C. § 2255). Federal habeas corpus relief is also available under § 2255, but the federal prisoner must first file a motion to vacate sentence before a writ of habeas corpus can issue. However, a denial of the motion to vacate under § 2255 usually precludes habeas corpus relief.

Section 2255 was enacted in response to the proliferation of federal habeas corpus petitions by federal prisoners. The congressional purpose was to provide a remedy commensurate with that formerly available by habeas corpus. Accordingly, the Supreme Court has held that issues cognizable under the general habeas corpus statute (§ 2254) may be raised in a § 2255 motion. In addition to constitutional issues such as the legality of a search and seizure, nonconstitutional issues may also be raised under § 2255, provided the alleged error of law was a fundamental defect that caused a miscarriage of justice.[63]

Most states have postconviction remedies that are often modeled on the general federal habeas corpus statute (§ 2254). But as Judge Friendly has pointed out, prisoners who are unsuccessful in the state postconviction remedy process are likely to pursue their claims in federal habeas corpus, and "dual review" under the guise of "perfectibility" is likely to remain a major source of controversy in our system of criminal justice.[64]

---

[63]*Davis* v. *United States*, 417 U.S. 333 (1974).

[64]For discussions of the historic role of federal habeas corpus, see Hart, *Forward: The Time Chart of the Justices*, 73 Harv. L. Rev. 84 (1959); Reitz, *Federal Habeas Corpus: Impact of an Abortive State Proceeding*, 74 Harv. L. Rev. 1315 (1961); Brennan, *Federal Habeas Corpus and State Prisoners: An Exercise in Federalism*, 7 Utah L. Rev. 423 (1961); Bator, *Finality in Criminal Law and Federal Habeas Corpus for State Prisoners*, 76 Harv. L. Rev. 441, 468 (1963); Oaks, *Legal History in the High Court— Habeas Corpus*, 64 Mich. L. Rev. 451 (1966); Friendly, *Is Innocence Irrelevant? Collateral Attack on Criminal Judgments*, 38 U. Chi. L. Rev. 142, 170–171 (1970); and Note, *Developments in the Law—Federal Habeas Corpus*, 83 Harv. L. Rev. 1938 (1970).

15

THE FIRST AMENDMENT IN ITS CRIMINAL CONTEXT: FREEDOM OF THE PRESS, SPEECH, RELIGION, AND ASSEMBLY

15.01 INTRODUCTION

The First Amendment to the federal Constitution contains six guarantees that are fundamental to the American system of justice: These are the prohibitions against (1) governmental establishment of religion, known as the "Establishment Clause," and (2) governmental interference in the free exercise of religion, known as the "Free Exercise Clause"; and the guarantees of (3) freedom of speech, (4) freedom of the press, (5) the right to peaceful assembly, including the right of association, and (6) the right to petition the government for a redress of grievances.

Most United States Supreme Court decisions interpreting the First Amendment have not involved the criminal process, since the parties usually have not been subjected to criminal liability by virtue of the First Amendment issues presented. However, some First Amendment issues, such as obscenity and pornography, are inextricably intertwined with the criminal process (see Table 15–1, pp. 1070–1071), and certain problems of free speech, assembly, and establishment and free exercise of religion may also involve the criminal law.

In the following sections, eight Supreme Court decisions involving the First Amendment and the criminal process are presented. The cases were selected to demonstrate the broad range of interests that the First Amendment is designed to protect. Five other cases dealing with First Amendment issues were presented earlier in the text: *Branzburg* v. *Hayes*, Chapter Six, § 6.04; *Nebraska Press Association* v. *Stuart*, Chapter Seven, § 7.03; and *Procunier* v. *Martinez*, *Pell* v. *Procunier*, and *Jones* v. *North Carolina Prisoners' Labor Union, Inc.*, Chapter Nine, § 9.03.

15.02 FREEDOM OF THE PRESS

"Congress shall make no law . . . abridging the
freedom . . . of the press . . . .

Obscenity and Pornography — Developing a Standard

ROTH v. UNITED STATES

ALBERTS v. CALIFORNIA

Supreme Court of the United States, 1957
354 U.S. 476, 77 S. Ct. 1304, 1 L. Ed. 2d 1498

Samuel Roth was convicted by a jury in federal District Court (S.D.N.Y.) on 4 counts of a 26-count indictment that charged him with mailing obscene circulars and other advertising and an obscene book in violation of the federal obscenity statute (18 U.S.C. § 1461), which provides that obscene, lewd, lascivious, filthy, or indecent material is nonmailable and that anyone who knowingly deposits such material for mailing shall be fined not more than $5000 or imprisoned not more than five years, or both. Roth's conviction was affirmed by the United States Court of Appeals (2nd Cir.), and the United States Supreme Court granted certiorari.

David Alberts was convicted by a California municipal court of violating a California statute that provides that every person who wilfully and lewdly writes or otherwise produces obscene or indecent material, or who writes or otherwise produces any notice or advertisement of any such material, shall be guilty of a misdemeanor. Albert's conviction was affirmed by the Appellate Department of the California Superior Court, and he appealed to the United States Supreme Court.

Mr. Justice BRENNAN delivered the opinion of the Court.

* * *

The dispositive question is whether obscenity is utterance within the area of protected speech and press. Although this is the first time the question has been squarely presented to this Court, either under the First Amendment or under the Fourteenth Amendment, expressions found in numerous opinions indicate that this Court has always assumed that obscenity is not protected by the freedoms of speech and press. . . .

The guaranties of freedom of expression in effect in 10 of the 14 States which by 1792 had ratified the Constitution gave no absolute protection for every utterance. Thirteen of the 14 States provided for the prosecution of libel, and all of those States

made either blasphemy or profanity, or both, statutory crimes. As early as 1712, Massachusetts made it criminal to publish "any filthy, obscene, or profane song, pamphlet, libel or mock sermon" in imitation or mimicking of religious services. . . . Thus, profanity and obscenity were related offenses.

In light of this history it is apparent that the unconditional phrasing of the First Amendment was not intended to protect every utterance. This phrasing did not prevent this Court from concluding that libelous utterances are not within the area of constitutionally protected speech. Beauharnais v. Illinois, 343 U.S. 250, 266 (1952).

At the time of the adoption of the First Amendment, obscenity law was not as fully developed as libel law, but there is sufficiently contemporaneous evidence to show that obscenity, too, was outside the protection intended for speech and press.

The protection given speech and press was fashioned to assure unfettered interchange of ideas for the bringing about of political and social changes desired by the people. . . .

All ideas having even the slightest redeeming social importance — unorthodox ideas, controversial ideas, even ideas hateful to the prevailing climate of opinion — have the full protection of the guaranties, unless excludable because they encroach upon the limited area of more important interests. But implicit in the history of the First Amendment is the rejection of obscenity as utterly without redeeming social importance. This rejection for that reason is mirrored in the universal judgment that obscenity should be restrained, reflected in the international agreement of over 50 nations, in the obscenity laws of all of the 48 States, and in the 20 obscenity laws enacted by the Congress from 1842 to 1956. This is the same judgment expressed by this Court in Chaplinsky v. New Hamsphire, 315 U.S. 568, 571 (1942):

". . . There are certain well-defined and narrowly limited classes of speech, the prevention and punishment of which have never been thought to raise any Constitutional problem. *These include the lewd and obscene. . . . It has been well observed that such utterances are no essential part of any exposition of ideas, and are of such slight social value as a step to truth that any benefit that may be derived from them is clearly outweighed by the social interest in order and morality. . . ."* (Emphasis added.)

We hold that obscenity is not within the area of constitutionally protected speech or press.

It is strenuously urged that these obscenity statutes offend the constitutional guaranties because they punish incitation to impure sexual *thoughts*, not shown to be related to any overt antisocial conduct which is or may be incited in the persons stimulated to such *thoughts.* In Roth, the trial judge instructed the jury: "The words 'obscene, lewd and lascivious' as used in the law, signify that form of immorality which has relation to sexual impurity and has a tendency to excite lustful *thoughts.*" (Emphasis added.) In Alberts, the trial judge applied the test . . . whether the material has "a substantial

tendency to deprave or corrupt its readers by inciting lascivious *thoughts* or arousing lustful desires." (Emphasis added.) It is insisted that the constitutional guaranties are violated because convictions may be had without proof either that obscene material will perceptibly create a clear and present danger of antisocial conduct, or will probably induce its recipients to such conduct. But, in light of our holding that obscenity is not protected speech, the complete answer to this argument is in the holding of this Court in Beauharnais v. Illinois, supra (343 U.S. at 266):

"Libelous utterances not being within the area of constitutionally protected speech, it is unnecessary, either for us or for the State courts, to consider the issues behind the phrase 'clear and present danger.' Certainly no one would contend that obscene speech, for example, may be punished only upon a showing of such circumstances. Libel, as we have seen, is in the same class."

However, sex and obscenity are not synonymous. Obscene material is material which deals with sex in a manner appealing to prurient interest.[1] The portrayal of sex, e.g., in art, literature and scientific works, is not itself sufficient reason to deny material the constitutional protection of freedom of speech and press. Sex, a great and mysterious motive force in human life, has indisputably been a subject of absorbing interest to mankind through the ages; it is one of the vital problems of human interest and public concern. . . .

The fundamental freedoms of speech and press have contributed greatly to the development and well-being of our free society and are indispensable to its continued growth. Ceaseless vigilance is the watchword to prevent their erosion by Congress or

---

[1] I.e., material having a tendency to excite lustful thoughts. Webster's New International Dictionary (Unabridged, 2d ed., 1949) defines *prurient,* in pertinent part, as follows:

". . . Itching; longing; uneasy with desire or longing; of persons, having itching, morbid, or lascivious longings; of desire, curiosity, or propensity, lewd. . . ."

Pruriency is defined, in pertinent part, as follows:

". . . Quality of being prurient; lascivious desire or thought. . . ." . . .

by the States. The door barring federal and state intrusion into this area cannot be left ajar; it must be kept tightly closed and opened only the slightest crack necessary to prevent encroachment upon more important interests. It is therefore vital that the standards for judging obscenity safeguard the protection of freedom of speech and press for material which does not treat sex in a manner appealing to prurient interest.

The early leading standard of obscenity allowed material to be judged merely by the effect of an isolated excerpt upon particularly susceptible persons. Regina v. Hicklin (1868) L.R. 3, Q.B. 360. Some American courts adopted this standard but later decisions have rejected it and substituted this test: whether to the average person, applying contemporary community standards, the dominant theme of the material taken as a whole appeals to prurient interest. The Hicklin test, judging obscenity by the effect of isolated passages upon the most susceptible persons, might well encompass material legitimately treating with sex, and so it must be rejected as unconstitutionally restrictive of the freedoms of speech and press. On the other hand, the substituted standard provides safeguards adequate to withstand the charge of constitutional infirmity.

Both trial courts below sufficiently followed the proper standard. Both courts used the proper definition of obscenity. . . .

It is argued that the statutes do not provide reasonably ascertainable standards of guilt and therefore violate the constitutional requirements of due process. Winters v. New York, 333 U.S. 507 (1948).

The federal obscenity statute makes punishable the mailing of material that is "obscene, lewd, lascivious, or filthy . . . or other publication of an indecent character." The California statute makes punishable, inter alia, the keeping for sale or advertising material that is "obscene or indecent." The thrust of the argument is that these words are not sufficiently precise because they do not mean the same thing to all people, all the time, everywhere.

Many decisions have recognized that these terms of obscenity statutes are not precise. This Court, however, has consistently held that lack of precision is not itself offensive to the requirements of due process. ". . . (T)he Constitution does not require impossible standards"; all that is required is that the language "conveys sufficiently definite

warning as to the proscribed conduct when measured by common understanding and practices. . . ." . . . These words, applied according to the proper standard for judging obscenity, already discussed, give adequate warning of the conduct proscribed and mark ". . . boundaries sufficiently distinct for judges and juries fairly to administer the law. . . . That there may be marginal cases in which it is difficult to determine the side of the line on which a particular fact situation falls is no sufficient reason to hold the language too ambiguous to define a criminal offense. . . ." . . .

In summary, then, we hold that these statutes, applied according to the proper standard for judging obscenity, do not offend constitutional safeguards against convictions based upon protected material, or fail to give men in acting adequate notice of what is prohibited.

Roth's argument that the federal obscenity statute unconstitutionally encroaches upon the powers reserved by the Ninth and Tenth Amendments to the States and to the people to punish speech and press where offensive to decency and morality is hinged upon his contention that obscenity is expression not excepted from the sweep of the provision of the First Amendment that *Congress* shall make *no law* . . . abridging the freedom of speech, or of the press. . . ." (Emphasis added.) That argument falls in light of our holding that obscenity is not expression protected by the First Amendment. We therefore hold that the federal obscenity statute punishing the use of the mails for obscene material is a proper exercise of the postal power delegated to Congress by Art. 1, § 8, cl. 7. . . .

Alberts argues that because his was a mail-order business, the California statute is repugnant to Art. 1, § 8, cl. 7, under which the Congress allegedly pre-empted the regulatory field by enacting the federal obscenity statute punishing the mailing or advertising by mail of obscene material. The federal statute deals only with actual mailing; it does not eliminate the power of the state to punish "keeping for sale" or "advertising" obscene material. The state statute in no way imposes a burden or interferes with the federal postal functions. . . .

Affirmed.

Mr. Chief Justice WARREN, concurring in the result.

I agree with the result reached by the Court in these cases, but, because we are operating in a field of expression and because broad language used here may eventually be applied to the arts and sciences and freedom of communication generally, I would limit our decision to the facts before us and to the validity of the statutes in question as applied.

* * *

The line dividing the salacious or pornographic from literature or science is not straight and unwavering. Present laws depend largely upon the effect that the materials may have upon those who receive them. It is manifest that the same object may have a different impact, varying according to the part of the community it reached. But there is more to these cases. It is not the book that is on trial; it is a person.

The conduct of the defendant is the central issue, not the obscenity of a book or picture. The nature of the materials is, of course, relevant as an attribute of the defendant's conduct, but the materials are thus placed in context from which they draw color and character. A wholly different result might be reached in a different setting.

The defendants in both cases were engaged in the business of purveying textual or graphic matter openly advertised to appeal to the erotic interest of their customers. They were plainly engaged in the commercial exploitation of the morbid and shameful craving for materials with prurient effect. I believe that the State and Federal Governments can constitutionally punish such conduct. That is all that these cases present to us, and that is all we need to decide.

* * *

[Mr. Justice HARLAN concurred in the result in *Alberts* and dissented in *Roth*.]

[Mr. Justice DOUGLAS, joined by Mr. Justice BLACK, dissented in both *Alberts* and *Roth*.]

Comments

1. *Roth* v. *United States,* supra, provided the first constitutional definition of obscenity developed by the Supreme Court. Prior to *Roth,* many American courts embraced the English *Hicklin* test: "The test of obscenity is this, whether the tendency of the matter charged as obscenity is to deprave and corrupt those whose minds are open to such immoral influences, and into whose hands a publication (such as a pamphlet purporting to expose the errors and practices of the Roman Catholic Church) of this sort might fall." *Regina* v. *Hicklin,* L.R. 3, Q.B. 360, 8 E.R.C. 60 (1868) (opinion of Cockburn, C. J.) As Mr. Justice Brennan noted in *Roth*, the *Hicklin* test allowed material to be judged by the "effect of an isolated excerpt upon particularly susceptible persons [which] might well encompass material legitimately treating with sex." Some American courts had rejected the *Hicklin* test prior to *Roth.* For example, in *United States* v. *One Book Entitled "Ulysses,"* 72 F.2d 705 (2d Cir. 1934), the court of appeals held that the book *Ulysses* by James Joyce was not obscene within the meaning of the federal statute prohibiting the importation of obscene books.

2. Some legal scholars feared that the lack of specificity of the *Roth* test ("Whether to the average person, applying contemporary community standards, the dominant theme of the material taken as a whole appeals to the prurient interest") would invite undue censorship. Do you agree? Although the *Roth* test is hardly a model of precision, can you (or any one) draft a more definitive test for obscenity? One solution (perhaps the easiest) would be to adopt the "absolutist" position of Justices Douglas and Black that the First Amendment forbids any limitations on sexual expression.

However, a majority of the Court has steadfastly maintained to the present (e.g., *Miller* v. *California*, 413 U.S. 15 [1973] [infra]), that "obscenity is not within the area of constitutionally protected speech or press."

3. The "contemporary community standards" test suggests that certain materials found to be obscene in one geographical area might be constitutionally protected in another and that those materials that are obscene today might be constitutionally protected at a later time. Does "community" refer to a single town? An entire state? A region of the country? Is the *Roth* court suggesting that producers and distributors of allegedly lewd materials "assume the risk" that they might be subject to criminal sanctions? After *Roth*, do writers and producers of sexually explicit materials know "how far they can go" without fear of a criminal prosecution? Under *Roth*, would a book or movie which graphically describes or portrays cunnilingus or fellatio be per se obscene? What about sodomy? Bestiality?

4. When a case involving material challenged as obscene is granted review by the Supreme Court, the members of the Court gather in the projection room in the basement of the Supreme Court building to view the evidence. While this procedure is quite proper and arguably necessary, isn't the Court to some extent playing the role of ultimate censor? Or is the Court merely determining whether there is substantial evidence to uphold or reverse the lower court decisions?

5. Following *Roth*, the Supreme Court in a series of per curiam decisions reversed lower court decisions that had found the following materials obscene: the motion picture *The Game of Love, Times Film Corp.* v. *City of Chicago*, 355 U.S. 35 (1957); a book called *One—The Homosexual Magazine, One, Inc.* v. *Olesen*, 355 U.S. 371 (1958); two nudist magazines, *Sunshine and Health* and *Sun, Sunshine Book Co.* v. *Summerville*, 355 U.S. 372 (1958); and a collection of art-student publications, *Mounce* v. *United States*, 355 U.S. 180 (1957). In 1959, the Court reversed the New York Supreme Court's holding that *Lady Chatterly's Lover* by D. H. Lawrence was obscene, *Kingsley International Picture Corp.* v. *Regents of the University of New York*, 360 U.S. 684.

6. In Smith v. California, 361 U.S. 147 (1959), the Supreme Court held that *scienter* (knowledge by the defendant of the contents of the book or other material for the possession of which he was convicted) is constitutionally required in obscenity-possession cases. As Mr. Justice Brennan said in writing for the Court in *Smith*, "If the bookseller is criminally liable without knowledge of the contents . . . he will tend to restrict the books he sells to those he inspected; and thus the State will have imposed a restriction upon the distribution of constitutionally protected as well as obscene literature" at 153. The Court implied that actual knowledge of the contents of a book may not be constitutionally required; that circumstantial evidence may imply an awareness (i.e., constructive knowledge of what a book contains despite the denial of the bookseller.) Mr. Justice Black, concurring in *Smith*, reiterated his view that obscene materials are protected by the First Amendment: "I think it timely to suggest again that there are grave doubts in my mind as to the desirability or constitution-

ality of this Court's becoming a Supreme Board of Censors—reading books and viewing television performances to determine whether, if permitted, they might adversely affect the morals of the people throughout the many diversified local communities in this vast country," at 159–160. Interestingly, Mr. Justice Black stated in a famous television interview that he refused to view the evidence in obscenity cases because, in his view, such materials are constitutionally protected by the First Amendment. "Mr. Justice Black and the Bill of Rights," CBS, December 4, 1968. See "Text of Historic TV Interview of Justice Black, "*Congressional Quarterly Report* 29 (1969); and Dunn, *Hugo Black and the Judicial Revolution* (1977).

7. Following *Roth* and during the next seven years, the battle lines across the First Amendment became quiet until 1964, when *Jacobellis* v. *Ohio,* 378 U.S. 184 (1964), was decided. There, a plurality of the Court stated that the *Roth* standard requires in the first instance a finding that material alleged to be obscene "goes substantially beyond customary limits of candor in description or representation" of sexual behavior, at 191, and that the contemporary community standards contemplated in *Roth* are national rather than local.

8. In *Memoirs* v. *Attorney General of Massachusetts,* 383 U.S. 413 (1966), a plurality Court introduced a new criterion for determining whether materials are obscene: "whether the material is utterly without redeeming social value." Thus, a work could be constitutionally protected even though it was found to be patently offensive and met the prurient interest requirement. Did the "utterly without redeeming social value" test add specificity to the constitutional criteria for obscenity?

9. In *Ginzburg* v. *United States,* 383 U.S. 463 (1966), and *Mishkin* v. *New York,* 383 U.S. 502 (1966), decided the same day as *Memoirs,* the Supreme Court affirmed the convictions of Ginzburg and Mishkin. Ralph Ginzburg, who boasted of the sexual content of his publications, was convicted in federal court for sending through the mail the magazine *Eros,* the biweekly newsletter *Liaison,* and the *Housewifes' Handbook on Selective Promiscuity* in violation of the federal obscenity statute. Ginzburg had unsuccessfully sought mailing privileges from the postmasters of Intercourse and Blue Ball, Pennsylvania; he finally deposited his materials with the postmaster at Middlesex, New Jersey. The Supreme Court in a 5–4 decision held that even if the materials involved were not obscene, the publications offended the federal obscenity statute because the defendant was engaged in the sordid business of "pandering," that is, purveying graphic matter openly advertised to appeal to the erotic interests of customers. Ginzburg advertised that his publications were sordid and the Supreme Court took him at his word without deciding whether the materials were in fact obscene. Interestingly, the Supreme Court has not since invoked the rule involving pandering.

   In *Mishkin* v. *New York,* supra, the defendant was convicted in New York City of manufacturing and selling a wide variety of books dealing with sexual aberrations in violation of New York law. The Supreme Court affirmed, holding that the "prurient interest" test was satisfied when it could be shown that materials are designed for and disseminated to a well-defined deviant sexual group.

10. By 1967, the docket of the Supreme Court had become clogged with obscenity cases. In a little known per curiam decision, *Redrup* v. *New York,* 386 U.S. 767 (1967), the Supreme Court reversed the New York courts' determination that two paperbacks, *Lust Pool* and *Shame Agent,* were obscene. In a 7–2 decision, the Supreme Court suggested that materials not sold to minors, not foisted on unwilling audiences, or not pandered were constitutionally protected. *Redrup* gave hope to many observers that the Court was finally on the road to relaxing the obscenity laws by constitutionally protecting most sexually oriented material. This turned out to be a false hope, however, as *Miller* v. *California,* infra, proved. Nevertheless, *Redrup* was the basis for reversing 35 obscenity convictions during the following years.

Possession of Obscene Materials

STANLEY v. GEORGIA

Supreme Court of the United States, 1969
394 U.S. 557, 89 S. Ct. 1243, 22 L. Ed. 2d 542

Robert Stanley was convicted in a Georgia state court of knowingly possessing obscene matter in violation of a Georgia statute. The obscene matter in question consisted of three reels of 8 mm. film, which federal and state law enforcement agents found in Stanley's home under authority of a search warrant during an investigation of alleged bookmaking activities. The Georgia Supreme Court affirmed the conviction, and the United States Supreme Court noted probable jurisdiction on appeal.

Mr. Justice MARSHALL delivered the opinion of the Court.

* * *

Appellant raises several challenges to the validity of his conviction. We find it necessary to consider only one. Appellant argues here, and argued below, that the Georgia obscenity statute, insofar as it punishes mere private possession of obscene matter, violates the First Amendment, as made applicable to the States by the Fourteenth Amendment. For reasons set forth below, we agree that the mere private possession of obscene matter cannot constitutionally be made a crime.

* * *

The State and appellant both agree that the question here before us is whether "a statute imposing criminal sanctions upon the mere [knowing] possession of obscene matter" is constitutional. In this context, Georgia concedes that the present case appears to be one of "first impression . . . on this exact point," but contends that since "obscenity is not within the area of constitutionally protected speech or press," Roth v. United States, 354 U.S. 476, 485 (1957), the States are free, subject to the limits of other provisions of the Constitution, to deal with it any way deemed necessary, just as they may deal with possession of other things thought to be detrimental to the welfare of their citizens. If the State can protect the body of a citizen, may it not, argues Georgia, protect his mind?

It is true that Roth does declare, seemingly without qualification, that obscenity is not protected by the First Amendment. That statement has been repeated in various forms in subsequent cases. . . . However, neither

Roth nor any subsequent decision of this Court dealt with the precise problem involved in the present case.... Moreover, none of this Court's decisions subsequent to Roth involved prosecution for private possession of obscene materials. Those cases dealt with the power of the State and Federal Governments to prohibit or regulate certain public actions taken or intended to be taken with respect to obscene matter....

In this context, we do not believe that this case can be decided simply by citing Roth. Roth and its progeny certainly do mean that the First and Fourteenth Amendments recognize a valid governmental interest in dealing with the problem of obscenity. But the assertion of that interest cannot, in every context, be insulated from all constitutional protections. Neither Roth nor any other decision of this Court reaches that far....

It is now well established that the Constitution protects the right to receive information and ideas. "This freedom [of speech and press] ... necessarily protects the right to receive...." ... This right to receive information and ideas, regardless of their social worth ... is fundamental to our free society. Moreover, in the context of this case—a prosecution for mere possession of printed or filmed matter in the privacy of a person's own home—that right takes on an added dimension. For also fundamental is the right to be free, except in very limited circumstances, from unwanted governmental intrusions into one's privacy.

"The makers of our Constitution undertook to secure conditions favorable to the pursuit of happiness. They recognized the significance of man's spiritual nature, of his feelings and of his intellect. They knew that only a part of the pain, pleasure and satisfactions of life are to be found in material things. They sought to protect Americans in their beliefs, their thoughts, their emotions and their sensations. They conferred, as against the Government, the right to be let alone—the most comprehensive of rights and the right most valued by civilized man." Olmstead v. United States, 277 U.S. 438, 478 (1928) (Brandeis, J., dissenting). ...

These are the rights that appellant is asserting in the case before us. He is asserting the right to read or observe what he pleases—the right to satisfy his intellectual and emotional needs in the privacy of his own home. He is asserting the right to be free from state inquiry into the contents of his library. Georgia contends that appellant does not have these rights, that there are certain types of materials that the individual may not read or even possess. Georgia justifies this assertion by arguing that the films in the present case are obscene. But we think that mere categorization of these films as "obscene" is insufficient justification for such a drastic invasion of personal liberties guaranteed by the First and Fourteenth Amendments. Whatever may be the justifications for other statutes regulating obscenity we do not think they reach into the privacy of one's own home. If the First Amendment means anything, it means that a State has no business telling a man, sitting alone in his own house, what books he may read or what films he may watch. Our whole constitutional heritage rebels at the thought of giving government the power to control men's minds.

And yet, in the face of these traditional notions of individual liberty, Georgia asserts the right to protect the individual's mind from the effects of obscenity. We are not certain that this argument amounts to anything more than the assertion that the State has the right to control the moral content of a person's thoughts. To some, this may be a noble purpose, but it is wholly inconsistent with the philosophy of the First Amendment. ... Nor is it relevant that obscene materials in general, or the particular films before the Court, are arguably devoid of any ideological content. The line between the transmission of ideas and mere entertainment is much too elusive for this Court to draw, if indeed such a line can be drawn at all. ... Whatever the power of the state to control public dissemination of ideas inimical to the public morality, it cannot constitutionally premise legislation on the desirability of controlling a person's private thoughts.

Perhaps recognizing this, Georgia asserts that exposure to obscene materials may lead to deviant sexual behavior or crimes of sexual violence. There appears to be little empirical basis for that assertion. But more important, if the State is only concerned about printed or filmed materials inducing antisocial conduct, we believe that in the context of private consumption of ideas and information we should adhere to the view that "[a]mong free men, the deterrents ordinarily to be applied to prevent crime are education and punishment for violations of the law...." Whitney v. California, 274 U.S. 357, 378 (1927) (Brandeis, J., concurring).... Given the present state of knowledge, the State may no more prohibit mere possession of obscene matter on the ground that it may lead to antisocial conduct than it may prohibit possession of chemistry books on the ground that they may lead to the manufacture of homemade spirits.

It is true that in Roth this Court rejected the necessity of proving that exposure to obscene material would create a clear and present danger of antisocial conduct or would probably induce its recipients to such conduct.... But that case dealt with public distribution of obscene materials and such distribution is subject to different objections. For example, there is always the danger that obscene material might fall into the hands of children ... or that it might intrude upon the sensibilities or privacy of the general public.... No such dangers are present in this case.

Finally, we are faced with the argument that prohibition of possession of obscene materials is a necessary incident to statutory schemes prohibiting distribution. That argument is based on alleged difficulties of proving the intent to distribute or in producing evidence of actual distribution. We are not convinced that such difficulties exist, but even if they did we do not think that they would justify infringement of the individual's right to read or observe what he pleases. Because that right is so fundamental to our scheme of individual liberty, its restriction may not be justified by the need to ease the administration of otherwise valid criminal laws....

We hold that the First and Fourteenth Amendments prohibit making mere private possession of obscene material a crime. Roth and the cases following that decision are not impaired by today's holding. As we have said, the States retain broad power to regulate obscenity; that power simply does not extend to mere possession by the individual in the privacy of his own home.

Reversed and remanded.

Mr. Justice STEWART, with whom Mr.

Justice BRENNAN and Mr. Justice WHITE join, concurring in the result.

Before the commencement of the trial in this case, the appellant filed a motion to suppress the films as evidence upon the ground that they had been seized in violation of the Fourth and Fourteenth Amendments. The motion was denied, and the films were admitted in evidence at the trial. In affirming the appellant's conviction, the Georgia Supreme Court specifically determined that the films had been lawfully seized. The appellant correctly contends that this determination was clearly wrong under established principles of constitutional law. But the Court today disregards this preliminary issue in its hurry to move on to newer constitutional frontiers. I cannot so readily overlook the serious inroad upon Fourth Amendment guarantees countenanced in this case by the Georgia courts.

* * *

For what happened here was that a search that began as perfectly lawful became the occasion for an unwarranted and unconstitutional seizure of the films.

* * *

This is not a case where agents in the course of a lawful search came upon contraband, criminal activity, or criminal evidence in plain view. For the record makes clear that the contents of the films could not be determined by mere inspection. And this is not a case that presents any questions as to the permissible scope of a search made incident to a lawful arrest. For the appellant had not been arrested when the agents found the films. After finding them, the agents spent some 50 minutes exhibiting them by means of the appellant's projector in another upstairs room. Only then did the agents return downstairs and arrest the appellant.

* * *

To condone what happened here is to invite a government official to use a seemingly precise and legal warrant only as a ticket to get into a man's home, and, once inside, to launch forth upon unconfined searches and indiscriminate seizures as if armed with all the unbridled and illegal power of a general warrant.

Because the films were seized in violation of the Fourth and Fourteenth Amendments, they were inadmissible in evidence at the appellant's trial. Mapp v. Ohio, 367 U.S. 643

(1961). Accordingly, the judgment of conviction must be reversed.

[Mr. Justice BLACK wrote a separate concurring opinion.]

Comment

1.   Does *Stanley* protect the right of a person to receive obscene materials outside his home? Suppose pornographic materials are mailed or delivered to one's place of business or to a private club to which the addressee belongs. Does a student have a right to keep obscene materials in his school locker? Can a person keep them in his car? Suppose one "lives" in his vehicle (e.g., long distance truck driver or owner of a Winnebago). Apparently, *Stanley* does not undermine statutes making it unlawful to sell or distribute obscene materials. Suppose obscene materials are sold to a buyer in the latter's home. Is only the seller criminally liable?

The Demise of the "National Standard" Test

MILLER v. CALIFORNIA

Supreme Court of the United States, 1973
413 U.S. 15, 93 S. Ct. 2607, 37 L. Ed. 2d 419

The facts are stated in the opinion.

Mr. Chief Justice BURGER delivered the opinion of the Court.

This is one of a group of "obscenity-pornography" cases being reviewed by the Court in a reexamination of standards enunciated in earlier cases involving what Mr. Justice Harlan called "the intractable obscenity problem." Interstate Circuit, Inc. v. Dallas, 390 U.S. 676, 704 (1968) (concurring and dissenting).

Appellant conducted a mass mailing campaign to advertise the sale of illustrated books, euphemistically called "adult" material. After a jury trial, he was convicted of violating California Penal Code § 311.2(a), a misdemeanor, by knowingly distributing obscene matter, and the Appellate Department, Superior Court of California, County of Orange, summarily affirmed the judgment without opinion. Appellant's conviction was specifically based on his conduct in causing five unsolicited advertising brochures to be

sent through the mail in an envelope addressed to a restaurant in Newport Beach, California. The envelope was opened by the manager of the restaurant and his mother. They had not requested the brochures; they complained to the police.

The brochures advertise four books entitled "Intercourse," "Man-Woman," "Sex Orgies Illustrated," and "An Illustrated History of Pornography," and a film entitled "Marital Intercourse." While the brochures contain some descriptive printed material, primarily they consist of pictures and drawings very explicitly depicting men and women in groups of two or more engaging in a variety of sexual activities, with genitals often prominently displayed.

I

This case involves the application of a State's criminal obscenity statute to a situation in which sexually explicit materials have been thrust by aggressive sales action upon unwilling recipients who had in no way indicated any desire to receive such materials. This Court has recognized that the States have a legitimate interest in prohibiting dissemination or exhibition of obscene material when the mode of dissemination carries with it a significant danger of offending the sensibilities of unwilling recipients or of exposure to juveniles.... It is in this context that we are called on to define the standards which must be used to identify obscene material that a State may regulate without infringing on the First Amendment as applicable to the States through the Fourteenth Amendment.

* * *

Apart from the initial formulation in the Roth case, no majority of the Court has at any given time been able to agree on a standard to determine what constitutes obscene, pornographic material subject to regulation under the States' police power. ... We have seen "a variety of views among the members of the Court unmatched in any other course of constitutional adjudication." Interstate Circuit, Inc. v. Dallas, 390 U.S., at 704–705 (1968) (Harlan, J., concurring and dissenting) (footnote omitted). This is not remarkable, for in the area of freedom of speech and press the courts must always remain sensitive to any infringement of genuinely serious, literary, artistic, political or scientific expression. This is an area in which there are few eternal verities.

The case we now review was tried on the theory that the California Penal Code § 311 approximately incorporates the three-stage Memoirs test.... But now the Memoirs test has been abandoned as unworkable by its author,* and no member of the Court today supports the Memoirs formulation.

---

* In *A Book Named "John Cleland's Memoirs of a Woman of Pleasure"* v. *Attorney General of Massachusetts,* 383 U.S. 413 (1966), Justice Brennan discussed the threefold test that had evolved following *Roth* v. *United States,* 354 U.S. 476 (1957) (supra): "It must be established that (a) the dominant theme of the material taken as a whole appeals to a prurient interest in sex; (b) the material is patently offensive because it affronts contemporary community standards relating to the description or representation of sexual matters; and (c) the material is utterly without redeeming social value."

II

This much has been categorically settled by the Court, that obscene material is unprotected by the First Amendment.... "The First and Fourteenth Amendments have never been treated as absolutes (footnote omitted)." Breard v. Alexandria, 341 U.S. at 642 (1951), and cases cited. ... We acknowledge, however, the inherent dangers of undertaking to regulate any form of expression. State statutes designed to regulate obscene materials must be carefully limited. ... As a result, we now confine the permissible scope of such regulation to works which depict or describe sexual conduct. That conduct must be specifically defined by the applicable state law, as written or authoritatively construed. A state offense must also be limited to works which, taken as a whole, appeal to the prurient interest in sex, which portray sexual conduct in a patently offensive way, and which, taken as a whole, do not have serious literary, artistic, political, or scientific value.

The basic guidelines for the trier of fact must be: (a) whether "the average person, applying contemporary community standards" would find that the work, taken as a whole, appeals to the prurient interest ...; (b) whether the work depicts or describes, in a patently offensive way, sexual conduct specifically defined by the applicable state law; and (c) whether the work, taken as a whole, lacks serious literary, artistic, political, or scientific value. We do not adopt as a constitutional standard the "utterly without redeeming social value" test of Memoirs v. Massachusetts, 383 U.S., at 419 (1966); that concept has never commanded the adherence of more than three Justices at one time....

If a state law that regulates obscene material is thus limited, as written or construed, the First Amendment values applicable to the States through the Fourteenth Amendment are adequately protected by the ultimate power of appellate courts to conduct an independent review of constitutional claims when necessary. ...

We emphasize that it is not our function to propose regulatory schemes for the States. That must await their concrete legislative efforts. It is possible, however, to give a few plain examples of what a state statute could define for regulation under part (b) of the standard announced in this opinion, supra:

(a) Patently offensive representations or descriptions of ultimate sexual acts, normal or perverted, actual or simulated.

(b) Patently offensive representations or descriptions of masturbation, excretory functions, and lewd exhibition of the genitals.

Sex and nudity may not be exploited without limit by films or pictures exhibited or sold in places of public accommodation any more than live sex and nudity can be exhibited or sold without limit in such public places. At a minimum, prurient, patently offensive depiction or description of sexual conduct must have serious literary, artistic, political, or scientific value to merit First Amendment protection.... For example, medical books for the education of physicians and related personnel necessarily use graphic illustrations and descriptions of human anatomy. In resolving the inevitably sensitive questions of fact and law, we must continue to rely on the jury system, accompanied by the safeguards that judges, rules of evidence, presumption of innocence, and other protective features provide, as we do with rape, murder, and a host of other offenses against society and its individual members.

Mr. Justice BRENNAN, author of the opinions of the Court, or the plurality opinions, in Roth v. United States [354 U.S. 476 (1959)]; Jacobellis v. Ohio [378 U.S. 184 (1964)]; Ginzburg v. United States, 383 U.S. 463 (1966); Mishkin v. New York, 383 U.S. 502 (1966); and Memoirs v. Massachusetts, supra, has abandoned his former position and now maintains that no formulation of this Court, the Congress, or the States can adequately distinguish obscene material unprotected by the First Amendment from protected expression, Paris Adult Theatre I v. Slaton, 413 U.S. 49, 73 (1973) (BRENNAN, J., dissenting). Paradoxically, Mr. Justice BRENNAN indicates that suppression of unprotected obscene material is permissible to avoid exposure to unconsenting adults, as in this case, and to juveniles, although he gives no indication of how the division between protected and nonprotected materials may be drawn with greater precision for these purposes than for regulation of commercial exposure to consenting adults. Nor does he indicate where in the Constitution he finds the authority to distinguish between a willing "adult" one month past the state law age of majority and a willing "juvenile" one month younger.

Under the holdings announced today, no one will be subject to prosecution for the sale or exposure of obscene materials unless these materials depict or describe patently offensive "hard core" sexual conduct specifically defined by the regulating state law, as written or construed. We are satisfied that these specific prerequisites will provide fair notice to a dealer in such materials that his public and commercial activities may bring prosecution.... If the inability to define regulated materials with ultimate, god-like precision altogether removes the power of the States or the Congress to regulate, then "hard core" pornography may be exposed without limit to the juvenile, the passerby, and the consenting adult alike, as, indeed, Mr. Justice DOUGLAS contends. As to Mr. Justice DOUGLAS' position ... [he] now stands alone.

Mr. Justice BRENNAN also emphasizes "institutional stress" in justification of his change of view. Noting that "[t]he number of obscenity cases on our docket gives ample testimony to the burden that has been placed upon this Court," he quite rightly remarks that the examination of contested materials "is hardly a source of edification to the members of this Court." Paris Adult Theatre I v. Slaton, supra, 413 U.S., at 92, 93.

He also notes, and we agree, that "uncertainty of the standards creates a continuing source of tension between state and federal courts...." "The problem is...that one cannot say with certainty that material is obscene until at least five members of this Court, applying inevitably obscure standards, have pronounced it so." Id., at 92, 93.

It is certainly true that the absence, since Roth, of a single majority view of this Court as to proper standards for testing obscenity, has placed a strain on both state and federal courts. But today, for the first time since Roth was decided in 1957, a majority of this Court has agreed on concrete guidelines to isolate "hard core" pornography from expression protected by the First Amendment. Now we may ... attempt to provide positive guidance to federal and state courts alike.

This may not be an easy road, free from difficulty. But no amount of "fatigue" should lead us to adopt a convenient "institutional" rationale—an absolutist, "anything goes" view of the First Amendment—because it will lighten our burdens. . . .

III

Under a national Constitutional, fundamental First Amendment limitations on the powers of the States do not vary from community to community, but this does not mean that there are, or should or can be fixed, uniform national standards of precisely what appeals to the "prurient interest" or is "patently offensive." These are essentially questions of fact, and our nation is simply too big and too diverse for this Court to reasonably expect that such standards could be articulated for all 50 States in a single formulation, even assuming the prerequisite consensus exists. When triers of fact are asked to decide whether "the average person, applying contemporary community standards" would consider certain materials "prurient," it would be unrealistic to require that the answer be based on some abstract formulation. The adversary system, with lay jurors as the usual ultimate factfinders in criminal prosecutions, has historically permitted triers of fact to draw on the standards of their community, guided always by limiting instructions on the law. To require a State to structure obscenity proceedings around evidence of a *national* "community standard" would be an exercise in futility.

As noted before, this case was tried on the theory that the California obscenity statute sought to incorporate the tripartite test of Memoirs. This, a "national" standard of First Amendment protection enumerated by a plurality of this Court, was correctly regarded at the time of trial as limiting state prosecution under the controlling case law. The jury, however, was explicitly instructed that, in determining whether the "dominant theme of the material as a whole . . . appeals to the prurient interest" and in determining whether the material "goes substantially beyond customary limits of candor and affronts contemporary community standards of decency," it was to apply "contemporary community standards of the State of California."

* * *

We conclude that neither the State's alleged failure to offer evidence of "national standards," nor the trial court's charge that the jury consider state community standards, were constitutional errors. Nothing in the First Amendment requires that a jury must consider hypothetical and unascertainable "national standards" when attempting to determine whether certain materials are obscene as a matter of fact. . . .

It is neither realistic nor constitutionally sound to read the First Amendment as requiring that the people of Maine or Mississippi accept public depiction of conduct found tolerable in Las Vegas or New York City. . . .

People in different States vary in their tastes and attitudes, and this diversity is not to be strangled by the absolutism of imposed uniformity. . . . We hold that the requirement that the jury evaluate the materials with reference to "contemporary standards of the State of California" serves this protective purpose and is constitutionally adequate.

IV

The dissenting Justices sound the alarm of repression. But, in our view, to equate the free and robust exchange of ideas and political debate with commercial exploitation of obscene material demands the grand conception of the First Amendment and its high purposes in the historic struggle for freedom. It is a "misuse of the great guarantees of free speech and free press. . . ." Breard v. Alexandria, 341 U.S. at 645 (1951). The First Amendment protects works which, taken as a whole, have serious literary, artistic, political, or scientific value, regardless of whether the government or a majority of the people approve of the ideas these works represent. . . . But the public portrayal of hard core sexual conduct for its own sake, and for the ensuing commercial gain, is a different matter.

There is no evidence, empirical or historical, that the stern 19th century American censorship of public distribution and display of material relating to sex . . . in any way limited or affected expression of serious literary, artistic, political, or scientific ideas. On the contrary, it is beyond any question that the era following Thomas Jefferson to Theodore Roosevelt was an "extraordinary vigorous period," not just in economics and politics, but in belles lettres and in "the outlying fields of social and political philosophies." We do not see the harsh hand of censorship of ideas—good or bad, sound or unsound—and "repression" of political liberty lurking in every state regulation of commercial exploitation of human interest in sex.

Mr. Justice BRENNAN finds "it is hard to see how state-ordered regimentation of our minds can ever be forestalled." Paris Adult Theatre I v. Slaton, at 110 (BRENNAN, J., dissenting). These doleful anticipations assume that courts cannot distinguish commerce in ideas, protected by the First Amendment, from commercial exploitation of obscene material. Moreover, state regulation of hard core pornography so as to make it unavailable to nonadults, a regulation which Mr. Justice BRENNAN finds constitutionally permissible, has all the elements of "censorship" for adults; indeed even more rigid enforcement techniques may be called for with such dichotomy of regulation.... One can concede that the "sexual revolution" of recent years may have had useful byproducts in striking layers of prudery from a subject long irrationally kept from needed ventilation. But it does not follow that no regulation of patently offensive "hard core"

materials is needed or permissible; civilized people do not allow unregulated access to heroin because it is a derivative of medical morphine.

In sum, we (a) affirm the Roth holding that obscene material is not protected by the First Amendment; (b) hold that such material can be regulated by the States, subject to the specific safeguards enunciated above without a showing that the material is *"utterly* without redeeming social value"; and (c) hold that obscenity is to be determined by applying "contemporary community standards,"... not "national standards." The judgment of the Appellate Department of the Superior Court, Orange County, California, is vacated and the case remanded to that court for further proceedings not inconsistent with the First Amendment standards established by this opinion.

Vacated and remanded.

[Mr. Justice DOUGLAS dissented.]
[Mr. Justice BRENNAN, joined by Mr. Justice STEWART and Mr. Justice MARSHALL, dissented.]

Comments

1. A majority of the Supreme Court continued to apply the *Roth–Memoirs* test for obscenity until 1973. See, e.g., *Blount* v. *Rizzi,* 400 U.S. 410 (1971); *Kois* v. *Wisconsin,* 408 U.S. 229 (1972). In *Miller* v. *California,* supra, which involved a challenge of a California obscenity statute, a majority of the Supreme Court reformulated the test for the determination of obscenity. In *Miller* the Court held that (1) the permissible scope of state regulation must be confined to works that depict or describe sexual conduct; (2) the proper standards to be applied in determining whether particular materials are obscene and subject to regulation are (a) whether the average person applying contemporary community standards would find that the work, taken as a whole, appealed to prurient interests, (b) whether the work depicted or described, in a patently offensive way, sexual conduct specifically defined by the applicable state law, as written or authoritatively constructed, and (c) whether the work, taken as a whole, lacked serious literary, artistic, political, or scientific value; (3) there is no requirement that the material be shown to be "utterly without redeeming social value"; and (4) obscenity is to be determined by applying "contemporary [local] community standards," not the "national standards" of *Roth.* Thus, the *Miller* test elaborates on and redefines, but does not overrule, the *Roth* test. Interestingly, the *Miller* Court omitted the "dominant theme" criterion of *Roth.* An important feature of the *Miller* deci-

TABLE 15.1 Two Decades of Supreme Court Decisions Involving "The Intractable Obscenity Problem*—1957–1977

Case	Holding	Vote	Dissenting
Roth v. United States, 354 U.S. 476 (1957)	The test for obscenity is whether to the average person applying contemporary standards the dominant theme of the material in question, when taken as a whole, appeals to prurient interests.	6–3	Douglas Black, Harlan (in part)
Kingsley Books, Inc. v. Brown, 354 U.S. 436 (1957)	State statute making it a crime to keep for sale booklets found to be obscene held constitutional.	5–4	Warren, Douglas, Black, Brennan
Kingsley International Pictures Corp. v. Regents of Univ. of New York, 360 U.S. 684 (1959)	State statute requiring the denial of a license to any motion picture which approvingly portrays an adulterous relationship regardless of the manner of its portrayal held violative of the First Amendment.	9–0	—
Smith v. California, 361 U.S. 147 (1959)	Municipal ordinance making it unlawful to possess obscene materials without requiring any knowledge by the defendant of the contents of the materials held violative of the First Amendment.	8–1	Harlan (in part)
Times Film Corp. v. Chicago, 365, U.S. 43 (1961)	City ordinance requiring submission to censor of all motion pictures prior to their public exhibition held constitutional.	5–4	Warren, Black, Douglas, Brennan
Bantam Books v. Sullivan, 372 U.S. 58 (1963)	Activities and practices of commission created by state legislature and given power to notify distributors that certain books and magazines were obscene or objectionable to youths under 18 years of age resulting in a halting of the circulation of the listed publications held violative of the First Amendment.	8–1	Harlan
Jacobellis v. Ohio, 378 U.S. 184 (1964)	Obscenity is excluded from constitutional protection if it is "utterly without redeeming social importance" or has no "literary or scientific or artistic value or any other form of social importance"; the test for obscenity is based on national standards.	6–3	Warren, Clark. Harlan
A Quantity of Books v. Kansas, 378 U.S. 205 (1964)	State's seizure of allegedly obscene paperback novels, without a prior adversary determination of their obscenity, and a subsequent court order directing the sheriff to stand ready to destroy them held unconstitutional.	7–2	Harlan, Clark
Freedman v. Maryland, 380 U.S. 51 (1965)	State motion picture censorship statute held invalid because of its failure to provide adequate safeguards against undue inhibition of protected expression.	9–0	—
Memoirs v. Attorney General of Massachusetts, 383 U.S. 413 (1966)	For material to be obscene, it must be shown that (1) the dominant theme of the material taken as a whole appeals to a prurient interest in sex, (2) the material is patently offensive because it affronts contemporary standards for the description or representation of sexual matters, and (3) the material is utterly without redeeming social value.	6–3	Clark, Harlan, White
Ginzburg v. United States, 383 U.S. 463 (1966)	Convictions for mailing obscene materials affirmed even though literature not obscene on its face when defendant engaged in the business of pandering.	5–4	Black, Douglas, Harlan, Stewart
Mishkin v. New York, 383 U.S. 502 (1966)	First Amendment not violated by state criminal obscenity statute that has been interpreted by the courts to cover only "hard-core pornography," that definition being more stringent than the definition required by federal constitutional standards.	6–3	Black, Douglas, Stewart
Redrup v. New York, 386 U.S. 767 (1967) (per curiam)	Distribution of books and magazines attacked as obscene held protected by the First Amendment when there is no claim that the applicable statute reflects a specific concern for juveniles; there is no suggestion of an assault upon individual privacy as to make it impossible for an unwilling person to avoid exposure to it; there is no evidence of pandering; the publications are not "hard-core" pornography; and they are not obscene under the coalescing three elements required for a determination of obscenity (see Memoirs v. Attorney General of Massachusetts, supra).	7–2	Harlan, Clark
Teitel Film Corp. v. Cusack, 390 U.S. 139 (1968) (per curiam)	City ordinance held unconstitutional that required the prior submission of a motion picture to a censor but did not provide for a prompt judicial decision if the license was not issued	9–0	—
Ginsburg v. New York, 390, U.S. 629 (1968)	State criminal statute prohibiting sale to minors of material defined as obscene on the basis of its appeal to them held constitutional.	6–3	Douglas, Black, Fortas
Interstate Circuit v. Dallas, 390 U.S. 676 (1968)	City ordinance authorizing administrative board to classify motion pictures as "not suitable for young persons" held unconstitutionally vague.	8–1	Harlan
Lee Art Theatre v. Virginia, 392 U.S. 636 (1968) (per curiam)	Seizure of allegedly obscene motion pictures under the authority of a warrant issued by a justice of the peace based on the strength of the conclusions of a single police officer, held unconstitutional.	8–1	Harlan
Stanley v. Georgia, 394 U.S. 557 (1969)	First Amendment violated by statute that imposes criminal sanctions for the mere knowing private possession of obscene materials.	9–0	—

Case	Holding	Vote	Justices
Blount v. Rizzi, 400 U.S. 410 (1971)	Federal statutes authorizing postmaster general to return mail to the sender or to forbid the payment of postal money orders in connection with the sale of allegedly obscene materials held violative of the First Amendment because of a lack of adequate procedural safeguards.	9–0	—
Kois v. Wisconsin, 408 U.S. 229 (1972) per curiam	Newspaper photos of nude persons rationally related to article and sex poem representing attempt at serious art held constitutionally protected expression.	9–0	—
California v. LaRue, 409 U.S. 109 (1972)	State liquor department regulations prohibiting certain sexually explicit live entertainment or films in bars and night clubs held constitutional on their face.	6–3	Douglas, Brennan, Marshall
Rabe v. Washington, 405 U.S. 313 (1972) (per curiam)	State criminal statute prohibiting exhibition of obscene movies held unconstitutional as applied to drive-in theatre operator showing film not obscene to audience of consenting adults.	9–0	—
Papish v. University of Missouri, 410 U.S. 667 (1973) (per curiam)	Expulsion of state university student for distribution of newspaper held violative of First Amendment when contents of newspaper could not be constitutionally labeled obscene.	6–3	Burger, Rehnquist, Blackmun
Miller v. California, 413 U.S. 15 (1973)	The proper First Amendment standards for determining whether particular material is obscene are (1) whether the average person, applying contemporary community standards, would find that the work, taken as a whole, appealed to the prurient interest; (2) whether the work depicted or described, in a patently offensive way, sexual conduct specifically defined by the applicable state law; and (3) whether the work, taken as a whole, lacked serious literary, artistic, political, or scientific value. The "utterly without redeeming social value" test and the "national standards" test are no longer applicable.	5–4	Douglas, Brennan, Stewart, Marshall
Paris Adult Theatre I v. Slaton, 413. U.S. 49 (1973)	State regulations prohibiting the exhibition of obscene motion pictures valid even though films are exhibited in "adults-only" theatres.	5–4	Douglas, Brennan, Stewart, Marshall
Kaplan v. California, 413 U.S. 115 (1973)	Obscene materials not protected by the First Amendment merely because they contain no pictures or were sold only to consenting adults.	5–4	Douglas, Brennan, Stewart, Marshall
United States v. 12 200-ft. Reels, 413 U.S. 123 (1972)	The government may constitutionally prohibit the importation of obscene material against a claim that the material was for private, personal use in importer's home.	5–4	Douglas, Stewart, Brennan, Marshall
United States v. Orito, 413 U.S. 139 (1973)	The First Amendment right to possess obscene material in the privacy of one's home does not create a correlative right to transport such material.	5–4	Douglas, Brennan, Stewart, Marshall
Heller v. New York, 413 U.S. 483 (1973)	State's seizure, without prior adversary hearing, of obscene movie film pursuant to warrant issued by judicial officer after viewing film made to preserve film as evidence in obscenity prosecution held not violative of the First Amendment.	5–4	Douglas, Brennan, Stewart, Marshall
Roaden v. Kentucky, 413 U.S. 496 (1973)	State seizure, without warrant, of allegedly obscene movie film as incident to arrest of theatre manager held violative of the Fourth Amendment.	9–0	—
Hamling v. United States, 418 U.S. 87 (1974)	Federal statute prohibiting the use of mails for sending "obscene" material or advertisements held not violative of the First Amendment.	5–4	Douglas, Brennan, Stewart, Marshall
Jenkins v. Georgia, 418 U.S. 153 (1974)	In state obscenity prosecutions juries could properly be instructed to apply "community standards" of obscenity without specifying which community; film "Carnal Knowledge" not obscene and protected by First Amendment.	9–0	—
Erznoznik v. City of Jacksonville, 422 U.S. 205 (1975)	City ordinance that prohibits showing of films containing nudity at drive-in movie theatres where screen is visible from public areas held violative of the First Amendment.	7–2	Burger, Rehnquist
McKinney v. Alabama, 424 U.S. 669 (1976)	State procedures whereby defendant is precluded from litigating the obscenity of materials that are the subject of his criminal prosecution because they were previously determined to be obscene in a civil proceeding held violative of the First Amendment.	8–0	Stevens did not participate.
Young v. American Mini Theatres, 427 U.S. 50 (1976)	City ordinances restricting the location of adult movie theatres to regulate obscenity held not violative of the First Amendment.	5–4	Stewart, Brennan, Marshall, Blackmun
Marks v. United States, 97 S. Ct. 990 (1977)	Standards announced in Miller v. California, 413 U.S. 15 (1973), are not to be applied retroactively to the potential detriment of defendants in criminal cases.	5–4	Brennan, Stewart,]in Marshall, Stevens]part
Smith v. United States, 97 S. Ct. 1756 (1977)	State law cannot define the "contemporary community standards" test under Miller v. California, supra, as these standards are a matter of federal law.	5–4	Brennan, Stewart, Marshall, Stevens
Splawn v. California 97 S. Ct. 1170 (1977)	State trial court's instruction that jury could consider "circumstances" of sale and distribution" of allegedly obscene material in determining its "social importance" under the then applicable obscenity test held not violative of First Amendment.	5–4	Brennan, Marshall, Stewart, Stevens
Ward v. Illinois, 97 S. Ct. 2085 (1977)	Earlier construction of state obscenity statute gave bookstore operator ample notice that sale of sado-masochistic materials were banned by statute even though U.S. Supreme Court failed to list sado-masochistic materials among examples of regulable material in Miller v. California, supra.	5–4	Brennan, Stewart, Marshall, Stevens

*Interstate Circuit, Inc. v. Dallas, 390 U.S. 676,704 (1968) (opinion of Hartan, J., concurring and dissenting).

sion is the rejection of the *Memoirs* "utterly without redeeming social value" criterion, which was replaced by the criterion of whether the work, "taken as a whole, lacks serious literary, artistic, political, or scientific value." Materials appealing to the "prurient interest" have been defined as "having a tendency to excite lustful thoughts." See *Roth* v. *United States,* supra, at n.20. The term "patently offensive" is generally held to refer to "hard-core" pornography. The term "average person" excludes both a particularly susceptible or sensitive person and a totally insensitive person, but does not preclude a finding of obscenity by virtue of a prurient-interest appeal to specific groups, such as homosexuals or minors. See, e.g., *Mishkin* v. *New York,* 838 U.S. 502 (1966).

2. Decisions following *Miller* include *Paris Adult Theatre I* v. *Slaton,* 413 U.S. 49 (1973) (obscene, pornographic motion pictures are not exempt from state regulation even though they are exhibited only for consenting adults); *Kaplan* v. *California,* 413 U.S. 115 (1973) (an obscene book is not protected by the First Amendment merely because it contains no pictures); *United States* v. *12 200-Ft. Reels of Super 8 mm. Film,* 413 U.S. 123 (1973) (government may prohibit the importation of obscene materials even though the importer claimed that such material was for his private personal use and possession only); *United States* v. *Orito,* 413 U.S. 139 (1973) (the right to possess obscene material in the privacy of one's home does not create a correlative right to transport such material); *Hamling* v. *United States,* 418 U.S. 87 (1974) (federal statute prohibiting the use of mails for "obscene materials or advertisements" not violative of the First Amendment or void for vagueness); *Jenkins* v. *Georgia,* 418 U.S. 153 (1974) (juries in state obscenity cases may be instructed to apply "community standards" of obscenity without specifying which community); *McKinney* v. *Alabama,* 424 U.S. 669 (1976) (Alabama procedure that precluded bookseller prosecuted for selling pornography from litigating the issue of the obscenity of a magazine after the magazine had been declared obscene in an in rem action (i.e., prosecution of the magazine rather than the publisher, seller, or buyer) is violative of the First Amendment); *Erznoznik* v. *City of Jacksonville,* 422 U.S. 205 (1975) (city ordinance that prohibits showing of films containing nudity on drive-in movie screens visible from public areas violates the First Amendment); *Hicks* v. *Miranda,* 422 U.S. 332 (1975) (require-ment of showing exceptional circumstances for federal court interference in pending state obscenity prosecution held applicable when there is no showing of bad faith or harassment); *Young* v. *American Mini Theatres,* 427 U.S. 50 (1976) (Detroit zoning ordinances restricting location of adult movie theatres not violative of First Amendment).

3. The development of the constitutional standards for obscenity has been marked by vicissitudes. Table 15–1, pp. 1070–1071, provides an overview of the tortuous path taken by the Supreme Court in attempting to solve what Mr. Justice Harlan called the "intractable obscenity problem."

15.03 FREEDOM OF SPEECH

Congress shall make no law . . . abridging the freedom of speech. . . .

Speech Versus Conduct and "Fighting Words"

COHEN v. CALIFORNIA

Supreme Court of the United States, 1971
403 U.S. 15, 91 S. Ct. 1780, 29 L. Ed. 2d 284

Paul Cohen was observed in the corridor of the Los Angeles County courthouse wearing a jacket bearing the plainly written words "Fuck the draft." There were women and children in the corridor. Cohen was arrested under § 415 of the California Penal Code, which prohibits "maliciously and willfully disturbing the peace or quiet of any neighborhood or person . . . by . . . offensive conduct. . . ." Cohen testified that he wore the jacket knowing that the words were on the back as a means of informing the public of the depth of his feelings against the Vietnam War and the draft. He was convicted in Los Angeles Municipal Court and sentenced to 30 days' imprisonment. The California Court of Appeal affirmed the conviction and rejected Cohen's argument that the statute infringed his right to freedom of expression guaranteed by the First and Fourteenth Amendments of the federal Constitution. The California Supreme Court denied review, and Cohen appealed directly to the United States Supreme Court.

Mr. Justice HARLAN delivered the opinion of the Court.

This case may seem at first blush too inconsequential to find its way into our books, but the issue it presents is of no small constitutional significance.

* * *

The conviction quite clearly rests upon the asserted offensiveness of the *words* Cohen used to convey his message to the public. The only "conduct" which the State sought to punish is the fact of communication. Thus, we deal here with a conviction resting solely upon "speech" . . . not upon any separately identifiable conduct which allegedly was intended by Cohen to be perceived by others as expressive of particular views but which, on its face, does not necessarily convey any message and hence arguably could be regulated without effectively repressing Cohen's ability to express himself. . . . Further, the State certainly lacks power to punish Cohen for the underlying content of the message the inscription conveyed. At least so long as there is no showing of an intent to incite disobedience to or disruption of the draft, Cohen could not, consistently with the First and Fourteenth Amendments, be punished for asserting the evident position on the inutility or immorality of the draft his jacket reflected. . . .

Appellant's conviction, then, rests squarely upon his exercise of the "freedom of speech" protected from arbitrary governmental interference by the Constitution and can be justified, if at all, only as a valid regulation of the manner in which he exercised that freedom, not as a permissible prohibition on the substantive message it conveys. This does not end the inquiry, of course, for the First and Fourteenth Amendments have never been thought to give absolute protection to every individual to speak whenever or wherever he pleases, or to use any form of address in any circumstances that he chooses. . . .

. . .[C]ohen was tried under a statute applicable throughout the entire State. Any attempt to support this conviction on the ground that the statute seeks to preserve an appropriately decorous atmosphere in the courthouse where Cohen was arrested must fail in the absence of any language in the statute that would have put appellant on notice that certain kinds of otherwise permissible speech or conduct would nevertheless, under California law, not be tolerated in certain places. . . . No fair reading of the phrase "offensive conduct" can be said sufficiently to inform the ordinary person that distinctions between certain locations are thereby created.

In the second place, as it comes to us, this case cannot be said to fall within those relatively few categories of instances where prior decisions have established the power of government to deal more comprehensively with certain forms of individual expression simply upon a showing that such a form was employed. This is not, for example, an obscenity case. . . . It cannot plausibly be maintained that this vulgar allusion to the Selective Service System would conjure up such psychic stimulation in anyone likely to be confronted with Cohen's crudely defaced jacket.

This Court has also held that the States are free to ban the simple use, without a demonstration of additional justifying circumstances, of so-called "fighting words," those personally abusive epithets which, when addressed to the ordinary citizen, are, as a matter of common knowledge, inherently likely to provide violent reaction. Chaplinsky v. New Hampshire, 315 U.S. 568, 86 L. Ed. 1031, 62 S. Ct. 766 (1942). While the four-letter word displayed by Cohen in relation to the draft is not uncommonly employed in a personally provocative fashion, in this instance it was clearly not "directed to the person of the hearer." . . . No individual actually or likely to be present could reasonably have regarded the words on appellant's jacket as a direct personal insult. Nor do we have here an instance of the exercise of the State's police power to prevent a speaker from intentionally provoking a given group to hostile reaction. . . . There is, as noted above, no showing that anyone who saw Cohen was in fact violently

aroused or that appellant intended such a result.

. . . [T]he mere presumed presence of unwitting listeners or viewers does not serve automatically to justify curtailing all speech capable of giving offense. . . . While this Court has recognized that government may properly act in many situations to prohibit intrusion into the privacy of the home of unwelcome views and ideas which cannot be totally banned from the public dialogue . . . , we have at the same time consistently stressed that "we are often 'captives' outside the sanctuary of the home and subject to objectionable speech." . . . The ability of government, consonant with the Constitution, to shut off discourse solely to protect others from hearing it is, in other words, dependent upon a showing that substantial privacy interests are being invaded in an essentially intolerable manner. Any broader view of this authority would effectively empower a majority to silence dissidents simply as a matter of personal predilections.

In this regard, persons confronted with Cohen's jacket were in a quite different posture, than, say, those subjected to the raucous emissions of sound trucks blaring outside their residences. Those in the Los Angeles courthouse could effectively avoid further bombardment of their sensibilities simply by averting their eyes. And, while it may be that one has a more substantial claim to a recognizable privacy interest when walking through a courthouse corridor than, for example, strolling through Central Park, surely it is nothing like the interest in being free from unwanted expression in the confines of one's own home. . . .

* * *

. . . [W]e cannot overemphasize that, in our judgment, most situations where the State has a justifiable interest in regulating speech will fall within one or more of the various established exceptions, discussed above but not applicable here, to the usual rule that governmental bodies may not prescribe the form or content of individual expression. . . .

. . . [W]e discern certain more particularized considerations that peculiarly call for reversal of this conviction. First, the principle contended for by the State seems inherently boundless. How is one to distinguish this from any other offensive word? Surely the State has no right to cleanse public debate to the point where it is grammatically palatable to the most squeamish among us. Yet no readily ascertainable general principle exists for stopping short of that result were we to affirm the judgment below. For, while the particular four-letter word being litigated here is perhaps more distasteful than most others of its genre, it is nevertheless often true that one man's vulgarity is another's lyric. Indeed, we think it is largely because governmental officials cannot make principled distinctions in this area that the Constitution leaves matters of taste and style so largely to the individual.

* * *

It is, in sum, our judgment that, absent a more particularized and compelling reason for its actions, the State may not, consistently with the First and Fourteenth Amendments, make the simple public display here involved of this single four-letter expletive a criminal offense. Because that is the only arguably sustainable rationale for the conviction here at issue, the judgment below must be
Reversed.

Mr. Justice BLACKMUN, with whom the CHIEF JUSTICE [BURGER] and Mr. Justice BLACK join.

I dissent, and I do so for two reasons:

1. Cohen's absurd and immature antic, in my view, was mainly conduct and little speech. . . . The California Court of Appeal appears so to have described it . . . and I cannot characterize it otherwise. Further, the case appears to me to be well within the sphere of Chaplinsky v. New Hampshire, 315 U.S. 568 (1942). . . . As a consequence, this Court's agonizing over First Amendment values seems misplaced and unnecessary.

2. I am not at all certain that the California Court of Appeal's construction of § 415 is now the authoritative California construction. . . .

Inasmuch as this Court does not dismiss this case, it ought to be remanded to the California Court of Appeal for reconsideration in the light of the subsequently rendered decision by the State's highest tribunal. . . .

[Mr. Justice WHITE concurred in Paragraph 2 of Mr. Justice BLACKMUN's dissenting opinion.]

Comments

1. In *Cohen* v. *California,* supra, the Court reversed the defendant's conviction for disturbing the peace because the California law did not limit the scope of the statute to "fighting words" (see Comment 2, infra). The Court in *Cohen* also reaffirmed the view that freedom of speech is not an absolute and may, under certain circumstances, be restricted by the government. As Justice Harlan noted in *Cohen,* "The First and Fourteenth Amendments have never been thought to give absolute protection to every individual to speak whenever or wherever he pleases, or to use any form of address in any circumstances that he chooses." The Court said that Cohen could not be punished for the *content* of the message inscribed on his jacket so long as there was no showing of an "intent to incite disobedience to or disruption of the draft." Could Cohen have been punished if the inscription on his jacket read, "Goddamn the draft" or "Refuse to serve in the army"? Suppose a sensitive passerby, upon reading the "prose" on Cohen's jacket, became extremely upset and had a heart attack or stroke. Any criminal or civil liability? Suppose the message on Cohen's jacket caused several members of the military to physically attack him. Has Cohen disturbed the peace? After *Cohen,* what kinds of epithets on clothing could a state outlaw consistent with the First Amendment?

2. The term "fighting words" originated in *Chaplinsky* v. *New Hampshire,* 315 U.S. 568 (1942), where the Supreme Court held

that the utterance of fighting words is beyond the protection of the First Amendment. Fighting words are those words "that by their very utterance inflict injury or tend to incite an immediate breach of the peace," at 572. Accordingly, a state law that seeks to punish fighting words must, by its own terms or its construction by the state courts, be limited in its application to "fighting words" and must not be susceptible of application to speech that is protected by the First Amendment, *Terminiello* v. *Chicago,* 337 U.S. 1, 4–5 (1949), and only state courts can supply the requisite construction since the Supreme Court lacks jurisdiction to construe state legislation, *United States* v. *Thirty-seven Photographs,* 402 U.S. 363 (1971).

State statutes or ordinances that punish the use of "opprobrious words or abusive language tending to cause a breach of the peace" or "disorderly conduct" have been held to be unconstitutionally vague and overbroad when they were not limited in application to fighting words. However, a state statute construed by the state courts to punish only fighting words tending to cause a breach of the peace was held valid by the Supreme Court. *Chaplinsky* v. *New Hampshire,* supra (defendant called a police officer a "goddamned racketeer" and a "damned fascist").

The words involved in the following cases were held by the Supreme Court not to be "fighting words": *Street* v. *New York,* 394 U.S. 576 (1969) ("We don't need no damn flag"); *Bachellar* v. *Maryland,* 397 U.S. 564 (1970) ("Make love not war"); *Cohen* v. *California,* supra ("Fuck the draft"); and *Hess* v. *Indiana,* 414 U.S. 105 (1973) ("We'll take the fucking street again" — spoken during an antiwar demonstration on a university campus).

In the following cases, a state statute or ordinance was held unconstitutional by the Supreme Court as violative of the freedom of speech: *Terminiello* v. *Chicago,* 337 U.S. 1 (1949) ("all persons who shall make, aid, countenance or assist in making any improper noise, riot, disturbance, breach of the peace or diversion tending to a breach of the peace"); *Gooding* v. *Wilson,* 405 U.S. 518 (1972) ("for any person, without provocation, to use to or of another, and in his presence opprobrious words or abusive language, tending to cause a breach of the peace"); *Plummer* v. *City of Columbus,* 414 U.S. 2 (1973) ("no person shall abuse another by using menacing, insulting, slanderous, or profane language"); *Lewis* v. *City of New Orleans,* 415 U.S. 130 (1974) (making it unlawful "for any person wantonly to curse or revile or use obscene or opprobrious language toward or with reference to any member of the city police while in the actual performance of his duties"); *Street* v. *New York,* 394 U.S. 476 (1969) (making it a crime "to publicly cast contempt upon an American flag either by words or act").

Symbolic Speech and Misuse of the Flag

SPENCE v. WASHINGTON

Supreme Court of the United States, 1974
418 U.S. 405, 94 S. Ct. 2727, 41 L. Ed. 2d 842

Harold Spence, a college student, hung a United States flag, which he owned, from the window of his apartment on private property in Seattle, Washington. The

flag was upside down, and attached to both sides of the flag was a large peace symbol made of removable black tape. The flag measured 3 by 5 feet and was plainly visible to passersby. Three Seattle police officers observed the flag, entered the apartment house, and by invitation of Spence, entered the apartment. The flag was seized and Spence was arrested under a Washington statute that made it a misdemeanor to "desecrate or misuse" a flag. Spence was convicted, but the Washington Court of Appeals reversed. However, the Washington Supreme Court reversed and reinstated the conviction, rejecting Spence's contention that the statute violated the First Amendment and was void for vagueness. On appeal, the United States Supreme Court noted probable jurisdiction.

PER CURIAM.

* * *

Appellant was not charged under Washington's flag-desecration statute.... Rather, the State relied on the so-called "improper use" statute. Wash. Rev. Code § 9.86.020. This statute provides, in pertinent part:

"No person shall, in any manner, for exhibition or display:

"(1) Place or cause to be placed any word, figure, mark, picture, design, drawing or advertisement of any nature upon any flag, standard, color, ensign or shield of the United States or of this state . . . or

"(2) Expose to public view any such flag, standard, color, ensign or shield upon which shall have been printed, painted or otherwise produced, or to which shall have been attached, appended, affixed or annexed any such word, figure, mark, picture, design, drawing or advertisement. . . ."

* * *

A number of factors are important in the instant case. First, this was a privately owned flag. In a technical property sense it was not the property of any government. We have no doubt that the State or National Governments constitutionally may forbid anyone from mishandling in any manner a flag that is public property. But this is a different case. Second, appellant displayed his flag on private property. He engaged in no trespass or disorderly conduct. Nor is this a case that might be analyzed in terms of reasonable time, place, or manner restraints on access to a public area. Third, the record is devoid of proof of any risk of breach of the peace. It was not appellant's purpose to incite violence or even stimulate a public demonstration. There is no evidence that any crowd gathered or that appellant made any effort to attract attention beyond hanging the flag out of his own window. Indeed, on the

facts stipulated by the parties there is no evidence that anyone other than the three police officers observed the flag.

Fourth, the State concedes . . . that appellant engaged in a form of communication. Although the stipulated facts fail to show that any member of the general public viewed the flag, the State's concession is inevitable on this record. The undisputed facts are that appellant "wanted people to know that I thought America stood for peace." To be sure, appellant did not choose to articulate his views through printed or spoken words. It is therefore necessary to determine whether his activity was sufficiently imbued with elements of communication to fall within the scope of the First and Fourteenth Amendments.... [T]he nature of appellant's activity, combined with the factual context and environment in which it was undertaken, lead to the conclusion that he engaged in a form of protected expression.

The Court for decades has recognized the communicative connotations of the use of flags.... In many of their uses flags are a form of symbolism comprising a "primitive but effective way of communicating ideas . . . ," and "a short cut from mind to mind." . . . On this record there can be little doubt that appellant communicated through the use of symbols. The symbolism included not only the flag but also the superimposed peace symbol.

Moreover, the context in which a symbol is used for purposes of expression is important, for the context may give meaning to the symbol.... In this case, appellant's activity was roughly simultaneous with and concededly triggered by the Cambodian incursion and the Kent State tragedy, also issues of great public moment.... A flag bearing a peace symbol and displayed upside down by a student today might be interpreted as nothing more than bizarre behavior, but it would have been difficult for the great majority of citizens to miss the drift of appellant's point at the time that he made it.

It may be noted, further, that this was not an act of mindless nihilism. Rather, it was a pointed expression of anguish by appellant about the then-current domestic and foreign affairs of his government. An intent to convey a particularized message was present, and in the surrounding circumstances the likelihood was great that the message would be understood by those who viewed it.

We are confronted then with a case of prosecution for the expression of an idea through activity. Moreover, the activity occurred on private property, rather than in an environment over which the State by necessity must have certain supervisory powers unrelated to expression.... Accordingly, we must examine with particular care the interests advanced by appellee to support its prosecution.

* * *

[W]e think it appropriate to review briefly the range of varous state interests that might be thought to support the challenged conviction.... The first interest at issue is prevention of breach of the peace. In our view, the Washington Supreme Court correctly rejected this notion. It is totally without support in the record.

We are also unable to affirm the judgment below on the ground that the State may have desired to protect the sensibilities of passersby. "It is firmly settled that under our Constitution the public expression of ideas may not be prohibited merely because the ideas are themselves offensive to some of their hearers." Street v. New York, 394 U.S. 576, 592 (1969). Moreover, appellant did not impose his ideas upon a captive audience. Anyone who might have been offended could easily have avoided the display.... Nor may appellant be punished for failing to show proper respect for our national emblem....

We are brought, then, to the state court's thesis that Washington has an interest in preserving the national flag as an unalloyed symbol of our country. The court did not define this interest; it simply asserted it.... Mr. Justice REHNQUIST's dissenting opinion today ... adopts essentially the same approach. Presumably, this interest might be seen as an effort to prevent the appropriation

of a revered national symbol by an individual, interest group or enterprise where there was a risk that association of the symbol with a particular product or viewpoint might be taken erroneously as evidence of governmental endorsement. Alternatively, it might be argued that the interest asserted by the state court is based on the uniquely universal character of the national flag as a symbol. For the great majority of us, the flag is a symbol of patriotism, of pride in the history of our country, and of the service, sacrifice, and valor of the millions of Americans who in peace and war have joined together to build and to defend a Nation in which self-government and personal liberty endure. It evidences both the unity and diversity which are America. For others the flag carries in varying degrees a different message.... It might be said that we all draw something from our national symbol, for it is capable of conveying simultaneously a spectrum of meanings. If it may be destroyed or permanently disfigured, it could be argued that it will lose its capability of mirroring the sentiments of all who view it.

But we need not decide in this case whether the interest advanced by the court below is valid. We assume, arguendo, that it is. The statute is nonetheless unconstitutional as applied to appellant's activity. There was no risk that appellant's acts would mislead viewers into assuming that the Government endorsed his viewpoint. To the contrary, he was plainly and peacefully protesting the fact that it did not. Appellant was not charged under the desecration statute ... nor did he permanently disfigure the flag or destroy it. He displayed it as a flag of his country in a way closely analogous to the manner in which flags have always been used to convey ideas. Moreover, his message was direct, likely to be understood, and within the contours of the First Amendment. Given the protected character of his expression and in light of the fact that no interest the State may have in preserving the physical integrity of a privately owned flag was significantly impaired on these facts, the conviction must be invalidated.

Mr. Justice DOUGLAS, concurring.

I would reverse the judgment for substantially the same reasons given by the Iowa Supreme Court in State v. Kool, 212 N.W.2d 518. In that case the defendant hung a peace symbol made of cardboard and wrapped in tinfoil in the window of his home and hung a replica of the United States flag behind the peace symbol but in an upside-down position. The state statute made it a crime to "cast contempt upon, satirize, deride or burlesque (the) flag." Iowa Code 32.1. The court held that defendant's conduct constituted "symbolic speech." . . .

That view is precisely my own. Hence I concur in reversing this judgment of conviction.

[Mr. Justice BLACKMUN concurred in the result.]

Mr. Chief Justice BURGER, dissenting.

If the constitutional role of this Court were to strike down unwise laws or restrict unwise application of some laws, I could agree with the result reached by the Court. That is not our function, however, and it should be left to each State and ultimately the common sense of its people to decide how the flag, as a symbol of national unity, should be protected.

Mr. Justice REHNQUIST, with whom the CHIEF JUSTICE [BURGER] and Mr. Justice WHITE join, dissenting.

* * *

Although I agree with the Court that appellant's activity was a form of communication, I do not agree that the First Amendment prohibits the State from restricting this activity in furtherance of other important interests. And I believe the rationale by which the Court reaches its conclusion is unsound.

* * *

This Court has long recognized, for example, that some forms of expression are not entitled to any protection at all under the First Amendment, despite the fact that they could reasonably be thought protected under its literal language. . . . The Court has further recognized that even protected speech may be subject to reasonable limitation when important countervailing interests are involved. Citizens are not completely free to commit perjury, to libel other citizens, to infringe copyrights, to incite riots or to interfere unduly with passage through a public thoroughfare. The right of free speech, though precious, remains subject to reasonable accommodation to other valued interests.

Since a State concededly may impose some limitations on speech directly, it would seem to follow a fortiori that a State may legislate to protect important state interests even though an incidental limitation on free speech results. Virtually any law enacted by a State, when viewed with sufficient ingenuity, could be thought to interfere with some citizen's preferred means of expression. But no one would argue, I presume, that a State could not prevent the painting of public buildings simply because a particular class of protesters believed their message would best be conveyed through that medium. Had appellant here chosen to tape his peace symbol to a federal courthouse, I have little doubt that he could be prosecuted under a statute properly drawn to protect public property.

Yet the Court today holds that the State of Washington cannot limit use of the American flag, at least insofar as its statute prevents appellant from using a privately owned flag to convey his personal message. Expressing its willingness to assume, arguendo, that Washington has a valid interest in preserving the integrity of the flag, the Court nevertheless finds that interest to be insufficient in this case. To achieve this result the Court first devalues the State's interest under these circumstances, noting that "no interest the State may have in preserving the physical integrity of a privately owned flag was significantly impaired on these facts. . . ." The Court takes pains to point out that appellant did not "permanently disfigure the flag or destroy it," and emphasizes that the flag was displayed "in a way closely analogous to the manner in which flags have always been used to convey ideas." The Court then restates the notion that such state interests are secondary to messages which are "direct, likely to be understood, and within the contours of the First Amendment." . . . In my view the first premise demonstrates a total misunderstanding of the State's interest in the integrity of the American flag, and the second premise places the Court in the position either of ultimately favoring appellant's message because of its subject matter, a position about which almost all members of the majority have only recently expressed doubt, or, alternatively, of making the flag available for a limitless succession of political and commercial messages. . . .

*　*　*

What appellant here seeks is simply license to use the flag however he pleases, so long as the activity can be tied to a concept of speech, regardless of any state interest in having the flag used only for more limited purposes. I find no reasoning in the Court's opinion which convinces me that the Constitution requires such license to be given.

The fact that the State has a valid interest in preserving the character of the flag does not mean, of course, that it can employ all conceivable means to enforce it. It certainly could not require all citizens to own the flag or compel citizens to salute one. . . . It presumably cannot punish criticism of the flag, or the principles for which it stands, any more than it could punish criticism of this country's policies or ideas. But the statute in this case demands no such allegiance. Its operation does not depend upon whether the flag is used for communicative or noncommunicative purposes; upon whether a particular message is deemed commercial or political; upon whether the use of the flag is respectful or contemptuous; or upon whether any particular segment of the State's citizenry might applaud or oppose the intended message. It simply withdraws a unique national symbol from the roster of materials that may be used as a background for communications. Since I do not believe the Constitution prohibits Washington from making that decision, I dissent.

Comments

1. In *Spence* v. *Washington,* supra, the defendant's conviction under the state "improper use" statute was reversed because the flag was privately owned and displayed on private property, there was no evidence of any risk of a breach of the peace, and Spence was engaging in a form of communication. Suppose Spence had displayed on government property (e.g., Army recruitment center) his privately owned flag bearing the epithet "Fuck the draft." Would his conviction have been upheld by the Supreme Court? Is it significant that a peace symbol was displayed on the flag? In a case involving related issues, the Supreme Court held that the wearing of black armbands in a school environment to protest the Vietnam War was protected speech. *Tinker* v. *Des Moines School District,* 393 U.S. 503 (1969).

2. *Misuse of Flag Cases.* The Congress and all states have passed laws prohibiting the public mutilation, defacing, defiling, misuse, defying, or trampling of an American flag. See, e.g., 18 U.S.C. § 700(a) and Uniform Flag Act § 3 (1917). The validity of the prohibitions depends upon the nature of the specified conduct proscribed.

   Destruction or Mutilation of the Flag. In *Street* v. *New York,* supra, a majority of the Court did not reach the issue of whether it is constitutional to convict a person for publicly burning an American flag. However, four justices were of the view that the destruction or mutilation of an American flag was not protected by the First Amendment. In *Street,* the Court held it was unconstitutional to punish a person merely for making disrespectful remarks about an American flag ("We don't need no damn flag"). The Court held that a person has a constitutional right to express publicly his opinion about the flag.

   In *Smith* v. *Goguen,* 415 U.S. 566 (1974), a majority of the Supreme Court struck down a Massachusetts statute that imposed criminal liability on anyone who publicly "treats contemptuously" an American flag. The defendant in *Smith* was convicted for wearing a small cloth version of a flag sewn onto the seat of his pants. The Supreme Court held the statute to be void for vagueness because it did not give fair and adequate notice of what acts were prohibited and did not set reasonable standards to guide law enforcement officers and juries. Although *Smith* was not decided on First Amendment grounds, the Court noted that some important issues on the freedom of speech had been raised.

Refusal to Salute the Flag. Prohibitions against the refusal to salute or pledge allegiance to the American flag have been held unconstitutional since *West Virginia State Board of Education* v. *Barnette,* 319 U.S. 624 (1943) (overruling *Minersville School District* v. *Gobitis,* 310 U.S. 586 [1940]). In *Barnette,* the children of Jehovah's Witnesses had been expelled from school because they refused to salute the flag. The Court struck down the actions of the school board because the power to compel the salute of the flag could be justified only if remaining passive during the salute ritual created a "clear and present danger" of a kind that the state was empowered to prevent and punish. In *Taylor* v. *Mississippi,* 319 U.S. 583 (1943), the Supreme Court reversed the defendant's conviction for advocating and teaching refusal to salute the flag in violation of a state statute.

Use of the Flag for Advertising and Commercial Purposes. The Supreme Court has upheld laws that prohibit the use of the American flag for advertising and commercial purposes. The leading case is *Halter* v. *Nebraska,* 205 U.S. 34 (1907), in which the defendants were convicted for selling bottles of beer upon which were printed representations of the American flag. The Court stated that the use of the flag for commercial purposes was wholly foreign to the purposes of the flag and tended to degrade and cheapen the flag.

3. *Freedom of Speech—General Principles.* The First Amendment freedom of speech is a preferred right. Despite the fact that the First Amendment is written in absolute terms, i.e., "Congress shall make *no* law abridging the freedom of speech . . .," the Supreme Court has never held that an individual may say anything he pleases in any place he pleases. Whether one adopts an absolutist interpretation or reads restrictions into the Amendment, the issue is always how much freedom of speech the Court is willing to read into the First Amendment. A number of decisions have recognized that freedom of speech, and acts done in the exercise of that freedom, are subject to reasonable governmental regulation under appropriate circumstances. The Supreme Court has over the years developed a number of principles for application of the right of free speech: (1) the First Amendment right of free speech is applicable to the states through the Due Process Clause of the Fourteenth Amendment; (2) the right of free speech is one of the most precious liberties safeguarded by the Bill of Rights; (3) freedom of expression needs "breathing space" to survive and to allow open discussion of public policy issues; (4) streets, sidewalks, parks, and other public places are so important to the exercise of First Amendment rights that access to them cannot be broadly and absolutely denied; (5) First Amendment rights are available to teachers and students in public school environments; (6) the First Amendment protects some false statements as well as true ones; (7) teaching and espousing revolution—as opposed to committing overt acts—are within the

scope of the First Amendment; and (8) the right to free speech is not absolute.

Some Restrictions on the Freedom of Speech. The Supreme Court, on a number of occasions, has accepted the view that some limited restrictions on the freedom of speech may be justified. Accordingly, in *Walker* v. *Birmingham,* 388 U.S. 307 (1967), the Supreme Court upheld the contempt convictions of persons who disobeyed an injunction against participating in mass street parades and civil rights marches even though the parade ordinance, which required a permit to parade, raised substantial constitutional questions. The Court said in *Walker,* "We . . . reject the notion . . . that the First and Fourteenth Amendments afford the same kind of freedom to those who would communicate ideas by conduct such as patrolling, marching, and picketing on streets and highways, as these amendments afford to those who communicate ideas by pure speech," at 316 (quoting *Cox* v. *Louisiana,* 379 U.S. 536, 555 [1965]). In *United States* v. *O'Brien,* 391 U.S. 367 (1968), the Supreme Court upheld the criminal conviction of a defendant who intentionally burned his selective service registration certificate in violation of a federal law. In *O'Brien,* the Court noted that "not every kind of conduct can be labeled 'speech' whenever the person engaging in the conduct intends thereby to express an idea," at 376. The Court in *O'Brien* further stated that whenever the elements of "speech" and "nonspeech" are combined in the same course of conduct, the governmental regulation on the nonspeech element can justify incidental limitations on First Amendment freedoms, provided "(1) it is within the constitutional power of the government; (2) it furthers an important or substantial governmental interest; (3) the governmental interest is unrelated to the suppression of free expression; and (4) the incidental restriction on alleged First Amendment freedoms is no greater than is essential to the furtherance of that interest," at 377. In *Cameron* v. *Johnson,* 390 U.S. 611 (1968), and *Shuttlesworth* v. *Birmingham,* 394 U.S. 147 (1968), the Supreme Court held that states have the right and duty to control public streets and public places in the interest of traffic and public safety and that a citizen's right to use public streets and parks to communicate his views on national questions must be subordinated to the interests of maintaining the peace and good order of society. In *Brandenburg* v. *Ohio,* 395 U.S. 444 (1969), the Supreme Court held that a state may not prohibit advocacy of the use of force or law violations unless such advocacy is directed to inciting or producing imminent lawless activity which is likely to incite or produce such action. In *Amalgamated Food Employees Union* v. *Logan Valley Plaza, Inc.,* 391 U.S. 308 (1968), the Supreme Court held that access to private property for the purpose of exercising First Amendment rights may be denied altogether; that even access to public property may be restricted so as to prevent interference with the use to which the property is ordinarily put by the state; and that access to private property to which the public is generally invited may be restricted when the exercise of First Amendment rights will unduly interfere with the normal public use of such property. In *Pickering* v. *Board of Education,* 391 U.S. 563 (1968), the Supreme Court held that a teacher's dismissal for writing a letter to the editor of a local newspaper, which was published, violated the teacher's right to free speech. In *Time, Inc.* v. *Hill,* 385 U.S. 374 (1974), the Court held that calculated falsehood is not protected by the First Amendment. In *Watts* v. *United States*, 394 U.S. 705 (1969), the Supreme Court, while upholding a federal statute making it a crime to make a "threat" upon the President of the United States, reversed the conviction of the defendant, who told a discussion group that he was not going to report for military induction and that "if they ever make me carry a rifle the first man I want to get in my sights is L.B.J." A majority of the Supreme Court held that the defendant's conditional statement was "political hyperbole" rather than a true threat within the meaning of the statute.

Other Supreme Court Pronouncements Involving Speech. Other cases decided by the Supreme Court dealing with the freedom of speech include *Red Lion Broadcasting Co.* v. *FCC*, 395 U.S. 367 (1969) (Federal Communication Commission's rules requiring broadcasters to afford equal time to individuals personally attacked on the air and to political opponents of those endorsed by a station do not violate freedom of speech and press); *NLRB* v. *Gissel Packing Co.*, 395 U.S. 575 (1969) (an employer is free to communicate to his employees any of his general views about unionism so long as the communications do not contain a threat of reprisal or force or promise of benefit); *Carroll* v. *President and Commissioners of Princess Anne County*, 393 U.S. 175 (1968) (ex parte orders in the area of First Amendment rights are not permitted when there is no showing that it is impossible to serve or to notify the opposing parties and give them an opportunity to participate); *Adderly* v. *Florida*, 385 U.S. 39 (1966) (First Amendment rights not violated by protesters' state convictions for refusing to leave jail grounds upon request by sheriff); *Bond* v. *Floyd*, 385 U.S. 116 (1966) (First Amendment violated by refusal of Georgia House of Representatives to seat duly elected black because of his statements attacking government's Vietnam policy; *Pittsburgh Press Co.* v. *Pittsburgh Comm'n on Human Relations*, 413 U.S. 376 (1973) (help-wanted advertisements in newspapers are commercial speech that is unprotected by the First Amendment); *Police Department of City of Chicago* v. *Mosley*, 408 U.S. 92 (1972) (a state's specifically permitting picketing for the dissemination of labor union views while prohibiting other sorts of picketing violates the First Amendment); *Lloyd Corp.* v. *Tanner*, 407 U.S. 551 (1972) (privately owned shopping center that was not dedicated to public use is entitled to prohibit handbilling unrelated to shopping center's operations); *Kleindienst* v. *Mandel*, 408 U.S. 753 (1972) (attorney general's refusal to waive alien's ineligibility for visa does not violate American professor's First Amendment right to communicate with alien, an author who advocated Communist doctrines); *Connell* v. *Higginbotham*, 403 U.S. 207 (1971) (state loyalty oath requiring public employees to pledge support to federal and state constitutions does not violate the First Amendment); *Flower* v. *United States*, 407 U.S. 197 (1972) (First Amendment protects right to distribute leaflets on public street on open military post); *Greer* v. *Spock*, 424 U.S. 828 (1976) (military reservation's regulations prohibiting political speeches, public demonstrations, and distribution of literature without prior approval within the confines of the reservation does not violate First Amendment); *Cole* v. *Richardson*, 405 U.S. 676 (1972) (Massachusetts loyalty oath requiring public employees to swear to "uphold and defend" federal and state constitutions and to "oppose the overthrow" of the federal or state governments by force or unconstitutional methods does not violate First Amendment); *Schact* v. *United States,* 398 U.S. 58 (1970) (clause in federal statute restricting authorization of actors' wearing of American military uniforms to portrayals that do not "tend to discredit" armed forces violates freedom of speech); *Rowan* v. *U.S. Post Office,* 397 U.S. 728 (1970) (federal statute permitting householder to have his name removed from mailing lists for pandering advertisements does not violate freedom of speech); *Communist Party of Indiana* v. *Whitcomb,* 414 U.S. 441 (1974) (state statute requiring members of political party to take loyalty oath in order to have their candidates placed on ballot violates freedom of speech); *Norwell* v. *Cincinnati,* 414 U.S. 14 (1973) (conviction for disorderly conduct based on defendant's nonprovocative, verbal protest to questioning by policemen violative of defendant's freedom of speech); *Broadrick* v. *Oklahoma,* 413 U.S. 601 (1973) (state statute forbidding political activities by state employees not violative of First Amendment); *Arnett* v. *Kennedy,* 416 U.S. 134 (1974) (federal statute authorizing administrative removal of nonprobationary federal government employees "for cause" authorizes dismissal for speech or conduct but not constitutionally protected speech); *Procunier* v. *Martinez,* 416 U.S. 396 (1974) (Chapter Nine, § 9.03) (inmates' mail may be censored under regulations that further one or more of the substantial government interests in maintaining prison security and order or rehabilitating prisoners; *Parker* v. *Levy,* 417 U.S. 733 (1974) (Chapter Sixteen, § 16.02) (Article 133 of the Uniform Code of Military Justice, which prohibits "conduct unbecoming an officer or gentleman," and Article 134, which prohibits "all disorders and neglects to the prejudice of good order and discipline in the armed forces" do not violate freedom of speech); *Pell* v. *Procunier,* 417 U.S. 817 (1974) (Chapter Nine, § 9.03) (prison regulation prohibiting news media interviews with specific individual inmates does not violate freedom of speech); *Lehman* v. *City of Shaker Heights,* 418 U.S. 298 (1974) (policy of refusing to sell space for political advertising on city-operated transit system does not violate First Amendment); *Hynes* v. *Mayor,* 425 U.S. 610 (1976) (municipal ordinance requiring those who solicit house to house for a "recognized charitable cause" or a "political campaign or cause" to "notify the police department in writing," for identification purposes only, held violative of First Amendment).

4. *"Clear and Present Danger" and Free Speech.* Despite the fact that the free speech guarantee is written as an absolute, i.e., "Congress shall make *no* law . . . abridging freedom of speech," the Supreme Court has never held that a person can say whatever he pleases in any place he pleases. Even Justices Black and Douglas, who tended to interpret the First Amendment in absolute terms, agreed that freedom of speech is not absolute. See, e.g., *Terminiello* v. *Chicago,* 337 U.S. 1 (1949) (opinion by Douglas, J.). Accordingly, the cases involving restrictions on free speech are exceedingly numerous and complex.

Although Congress first set limitations on free speech seven years after the adoption of the First Amendment in the Sedition Act of 1798, the constitutionality of the Sedition Act was never decided by the Supreme Court, and, in fact, no important decisions on free speech were decided by the Court until after World War I. Following the war, an important group of cases came before the Court involving convictions under the Espionage Act of 1917. The first and perhaps most significant of these decisions was *Schneck* v. *United States,* 249 U.S. 47 (1919), in which the Supreme Court attempted to establish a standard of free speech by formulating the "clear and present danger" rule. In a unanimous opinion written by Mr. Justice Holmes, the Court disregarded the possibility that freedom of speech could be absolute. Instead, the Court adopted a "balancing of interests" philosophy in *Schneck:* "The question in every case is whether the words are used in such circumstances and are of such a nature as to create a clear and present danger that they will bring about the substantive evils that Congress has a right to prevent. It is a question of proximity and degree. When a nation is at war many things that might be said in time of peace are such a hindrance to its effort that their utterance will not be endured so long as men fight and that no Court could regard them as protected by a constitutional right." This test was used to justify convictions under the Espionage Act for the publication of twelve newspaper articles attacking the war and for a speech attacking American involvement in the war. See *Frohwerk* v. *United States,* 249 U.S. 204 (1919); *Debs* v. *United States,* 249 U.S. 211 (1919). See also *Abrams* v. *United States,* 250 U.S. 616 (1919); *Schaefer* v. *United States,* 251 U.S. 400 (1920); and *Pierce* v. *United States,* 252 U.S. 239 (1920).

The *"Bad Tendency" Test.* In *Gitlow* v. *New York,* 268 U.S. 652 (1925), the Supreme Court substituted the "bad tendency" test for the "clear and present danger" rule. Under this rule, a state could suppress speech that *tended* to be injurious to the government. Thus, the proximity of the speech to the substantive evil was no longer the test for free speech; under the "bad tendency" test all that had to be shown was that the speech had a tendency to threaten the peace or safety of society. The "bad tendency" test was used again two years later in *Whitney* v. *California,* 274 U.S. 357 (1927), in which the defendant was convicted under California's criminal syndicalism statute for helping to form the Communist Labor Party, which advocated the commission of crimes, sabotage, and unlawful acts of force as a means of producing a change in industrial ownership and control. The "bad tendency" test remained the predominant test for free speech until 1937, when a more "liberal" Roosevelt Court resurrected the "clear and present danger" test and began to strike down governmental restrictions on First Amendment rights. See, e.g., *Thornhill* v. *Alabama,* 310 U.S. 88 (1940); *Hague* v. *Committee for Industrial Organization,* 307 U.S. 496 (1939); *Bridges* v. *California,* 314 U.S. 252 (1941); *Pennekamp* v. *Florida,* 328 U.S. 331 (1946); *Terminiello* v. *Chicago,* 337 U.S. 1 (1949).

Balancing of Interests. During the early 1950's a judicial philosophy of self-restraint dominated the Court. The constitutionality of limitations on speech was measured by balancing the social interests protected by the statute (e.g., national security) against the degree of infringement on speech. If the social interests were sufficiently paramount, free speech could be suppressed. See, e.g., *Dennis* v. *United States,* 341 U.S. 494 (1951) (Smith Act forbidding advocating overthrow of the government upheld); *Barenblatt* v. *United States,* 360 U.S. 109 (1959).

In 1950, in an attempt to control Communist organizations in the

United States, Congress passed the Internal Security Act (McCarran Act), which required Communist organizations to register with the Department of Justice and forbid Communists from obtaining federal employment and passports. Later, Congress passed the Communist Control Act of 1954 which was designed to outlaw the Communist Party. In *American Communications Association* v. *Douds,* 339 U.S. 382 (1959), the Supreme Court upheld a provision of the Taft-Hartley Act of 1947 that required union officers to take an oath disavowing membership in or support of the Communist Party. See also *Yates* v. *United States,* 354 U.S. 298 (1957); *Scales* v. *United States,* 367 U.S. 203 (1961); *Adler* v. *Board of Education,* 342 U.S. 485 (1952); and *United States* v. *Robel,* 389 U.S. 258 (1967).

Following the appointment of Earl Warren as Chief Justice in 1953, the Court began to demonstrate a marked concern for the First Amendment rights of individuals. For example, in *Pennsylvania* v. *Nelson,* 350 U.S. 497 (1956), the Court held that the states cannot prosecute persons who advocate the violent overthrow of the government because the field of antisubversive activities was preempted by federal law. See also *Cole* v. *Young,* 351 U.S. 536 (1955); *Watkins* v. *United States,* 354 U.S. 178 (1957); *Sweeny* v. *New Hampshire,* 354 U.S. 234 (1956); *Wilkinson* v. *United States,* 365 U.S. 399 (1961); *Braden* v. *United States,* 369 U.S. 749 (1962); *Deutsch* v. *United States,* 367 U.S. 456 (1961); *Communist Party* v. *Subversive Activities Control Board,* 367 U.S. 1 (1961); *Albertson* v. *Subversive Activities Control Board,* 382 U.S. 70 (1965); *Aptheker* v. *Secretary of State,* 378 U.S. 500 (1964); *United States* v. *Brown,* 381 U.S. 437 (1965); *Gibson* v. *Florida Legislative Investigation Comm.,* 372 U.S. 539 (1963); *Lamont* v. *Postmaster General,* 381 U.S. 301 (1965); *Brandenburg* v. *Ohio,* 395 U.S. 444 (1969) (overruling *Whitney* v. *California,* supra).

During the 1960's, the Warren Court continued to utilize the "preferred position" doctrine, under which laws restricting First Amendment rights are not presumed to be valid but must be proved constitutional by the proponent because of the importance of First Amendment rights. See, e.g., *Brandenburg* v. *Ohio,* supra, and *Gibson* v. *Florida Legislative Investigation Committee,* supra. In addition, the Warren Court struck down statutes that infringed upon free speech if they were vague or could have been more narrowly drawn. See, e.g., *Cox* v. *Louisiana,* 379 U.S. 536 (1965); *Wright* v. *Georgia,* 373 U.S. 274 (1963); *Edwards* v. *South Carolina,* 372 U.S. 229 (1963); *Brown* v. *Louisiana,* 383 U.S. 131 (1966); *Garner* v. *Louisiana,* 368 U.S. 157 (1961); *Dombrowski* v. *Pfister,* 380 U.S. 479 (1965); *Bell* v. *Maryland,* 378 U.S. 226 (1964); *Hamm* v. *Rock Hill,* 379 U.S. 306 (1964). Many of these "speech" cases arose from the civil rights and other social protest movements. Although the Supreme Court continued to utilize the balancing test, it became clear that the constitutional right to free speech does not include the right to trespass and disrupt the normal operations of business and government. See, e.g., *Cox* v. *Louisiana,* 379 U.S. 536 (1965) (state law prohibiting demonstrations near a courthouse upheld); *Adderly* v. *Florida,* 385 U.S. 39 (1967) (state not required to open up all public property for demonstrations); *Walker* v. *Birmingham,* 388 U.S. 307 (1967) (freedom of speech does not protect persons who deliberately violate valid laws during the course of social protest).

The Burger Court, while generally not willing to extend Warren

Court rulings in the area of free speech, has continued to uphold First Amendment rights as fundamental. However, the Burger Court seems reluctant to decide whether the words in a statute are objectionable; rather, the Court seems to concentrate on whether the speech rights of specific persons have been violated. See *Branzburg* v. *Hayes,* 408 U.S. 665 (1972) (Chapter Six, § 6.04); *Laird* v. *Tatum,* 408 U.S. 1 (1972); *Pittsburgh Press Co.* v. *Pittsburgh Comm'n on Human Relations,* 413 U.S. 376 (1973); *Kleindienst* v. *Mandel,* 408 U.S. 753 (1972); *Lloyd Corp.* v. *Tanner,* 407 U.S. 551 (1972); *Coates* v. *Cincinnati,* 402 U.S. 611 (1971); *Civil Service Comm'n* v. *Letter Carriers,* 413 U.S. 548 (1973); *Broadrick* v. *Oklahoma,* 413 U.S. 601 (1973); *Organization for a Better Austin* v. *Keefe,* 402 U.S. 514 (1971); *Papish* v. *Board of Curators,* 410 U.S. 667 (1973).

15.04 FREEDOM OF RELIGION

Congress shall make no law respecting an establishment of religion, or prohibiting the free exercise thereof. . . .

Compulsory Education

WISCONSIN v. YODER

Supreme Court of the United States, 1972
406 U.S. 205, 92 S. Ct. 1526, 32 L. Ed. 2d 15

The respondents, members of the Amish faith, refused to send their children, aged 14 and 15, to public school after the children had completed the eighth grade, in violation of a Wisconsin law that requires a child to attend school until age 16. On complaint of a school district administrator, the parent-respondents were charged, tried, and convicted of violating the Wisconsin compulsory school attendance law and fined $5 each. The evidence showed that the Amish sincerely believed that high school attendance was contrary to their religious beliefs and way of life. The Wisconsin Supreme Court reversed the convictions, sustaining the defendant's claims that the Wisconsin law violated their First Amendment right to free exercise of religion. The United States Supreme Court granted certiorari.

Mr. Chief Justice BURGER delivered the opinion of the Court.

* * *

Amish objection to formal education beyond the eighth grade is firmly grounded in these central religious concepts. They object to the high school, and higher education generally, because the values they teach are in marked variance with Amish values and the Amish way of life; they view secondary school education as an impermissible exposure of their children to a "wordly" influence in conflict with their beliefs. The high school tends to emphasize intellectual and scientific accomplishments, self-distinction, competitiveness, worldly success, and social life with other students. Amish society emphasizes informal learning-through-doing; a life of "goodness," rather than a life of intellect; wisdom, rather than technical knowledge; community welfare, rather than competition;

and separation from, rather than integration with, contemporary worldly society.

Formal high school education beyond the eighth grade is contrary to Amish beliefs, not only because it places Amish children in an environment hostile to Amish beliefs with increasing emphasis on competition in class work and sports and with pressure to conform to the styles, manners, and ways of the peer group, but also because it takes them away from their community, physically and emotionally, during the crucial and formative adolescent period of life. During this period, the children must acquire Amish attitudes favoring manual work and self-reliance and the specific skills needed to perform the adult role of an Amish farmer or housewife. They must learn to enjoy physical labor. Once a child has learned basic reading, writing, and elementary mathematics, these traits, skills, and attitudes admittedly fall within the category of those best learned through example and "doing" rather than in a classroom. And, at this time in life, the Amish child must also grow in his faith and his relationship to the Amish community if he is to be prepared to accept the heavy obligations imposed by adult baptism. In short, high school attendance with teachers who are not of the Amish faith—and may even be hostile to it—interposes a serious barrier to the integration of the Amish child into the Amish religious community. . . .

The Amish do not object to elementary education through the first eight grades as a general proposition because they agree that their children must have basic skills in the "three R's" in order to read the Bible, to be good farmers and citizens, and to be able to deal with non-Amish people when necessary in the course of daily affairs. They view such a basic education as acceptable because it does not significantly expose their children to worldly values or interfere with their development in the Amish community during the crucial adolescent period. . . . In the Amish belief higher learning tends to develop values they reject as influences that alienate man from God.

On the basis of such considerations [an expert witness] testified that compulsory high school attendance could not only result in great psychological harm to Amish children, because of the conflicts it would produce, but would also, in his opinion, ultimately result in the destruction of the Old Order Amish church community as it exists in the United States today. . . . [Another expert witness] described their system of learning through doing the skills directly relevant to their adult roles in the Amish community as "ideal" and perhaps superior to ordinary high school education. The evidence also showed that the Amish have an excellent record as law-abiding and generally self-sufficient members of society.

* * *

There is no doubt as to the power of a State, having a high responsibility for education of its citizens, to impose reasonable regulations for the control and duration of basic education. See, e.g., Pierce v. Society of Sisters, 268 U.S. 510, 534 (1925). Providing public schools ranks at the very apex of the function of a State. Yet even this paramount responsibility was, in Pierce, made to yield to the right of parents to provide an equivalent education in a privately operated system. There the Court held that Oregon's statute compelling attendance in a public school from age eight to age 16 unreasonably interfered with the interest of parents in directing the rearing of their offspring, including their education in church-operated schools. As that case suggests, the values of parental direction of the religious upbringing and education of their children in their early and formative years have a high place in our society. . . . Thus, a State's interest in universal education, however highly we rank it, is not totally free from a balancing process when it impinges on fundamental rights and interests, such as those specifically protected by the Free Exercise Clause of the First Amendment. . . .

It follows that in order for Wisconsin to compel school attendance beyond the eighth grade against a claim that such attendance interferes with the practice of a legitimate religious belief, it must appear either that the State does not deny the free exercise of religious belief by its requirement, or that there is a state interest of sufficient magnitude to override the interest claiming protection under the Free Exercise Clause. . . .

The essence of all that has been said and written on the subject is that only those interests of the highest order and those not otherwise served can overbalance legitimate claims to the free exercise of religion. We can accept it as settled, therefore, that, however strong the State's interest in universal compulsory education, it is by no means absolute to the exclusion or subordination of all other interests. . . .

. . . In evaluating those claims we must be careful to determine whether the Amish religious faith and their mode of life are, as they claim, inseparable and interdependent. A way of life, however virtuous and admirable, may not be interposed as a barrier to reasonable state regulation of education if it is based on purely secular considerations; to have the protection of the Religion Clauses, the claims must be rooted in religious belief. Although a determination of what is a "religious" belief or practice entitled to constitutional protection may present a most delicate question, the very concept of ordered liberty precludes allowing every person to make his own standards on matters of conduct in which society as a whole has important interests. Thus, if the Amish asserted their claims because of their subjective evaluation and rejection of the contemporary secular values accepted by the majority, much as Thoreau rejected the social values of his time and isolated himself at Walden Pond, their claims would not rest on a religious basis. Thoreau's choice was philosophical and personal rather than religious, and such belief does not rise to the demands of the Religion Clauses.

Giving no weight to such secular considerations, however, we see that the record in this case abundantly supports the claim that the traditional way of life of the Amish is not merely a matter of personal preference, but one of deep religious conviction, shared by an organized group, and intimately related to daily living. . . .

The unchallenged testimony of acknowledged experts in education and religious history, almost 300 years of consistent practice, and strong evidence of a sustained faith pervading and regulating respondents' entire mode of life support the claim that enforcement of the State's requirement of compulsory formal education after the eighth grade would gravely endanger if not destroy the free exercise of respondents' religious beliefs.

* * *

We turn, then, to the State's broader contention that its interest in its system of compulsory education is so compelling that even the established religious practices of the Amish must give way. Where fundamental claims of religious freedom are at stake, however, we cannot accept such a sweeping claim; despite its admitted validity in the generality of cases, we must searchingly examine the interests that the State seeks to promote by its requirement for compulsory education to age 16, and the impediment to those objectives that would flow from recognizing the claimed Amish exemption. . . .

The State advances two primary arguments in support of its system of compulsory education. It notes, as Thomas Jefferson pointed out early in our history, that some degree of education is necessary to prepare citizens to participate effectively and intelligently in our open political system if we are to preserve freedom and independence. Further, education prepares individuals to be self-reliant and self-sufficient participants in society. We accept these propositions.

However, the evidence adduced by the Amish in this case is persuasively to the effect that an additional one or two years of formal high school for Amish children in place of their long-established program of informal vocational education would do little to serve those interests. . . . It is one thing to say that compulsory education for a year or two beyond the eighth grade may be necessary when its goal is the preparation of the child for life in modern society as the majority live, but it is quite another if the goal of education be viewed as the preparation of the child for life in the separated agrarian community that is the keystone of the Amish faith. . . .

* * *

Contrary to the suggestion of the dissenting opinion of Mr. Justice DOUGLAS, our holding today in no degree depends on the assertion of the religious interest of the child as contrasted with that of the parents. It is the parents who are subject to prosecution here for failing to cause their children to attend school, and it is their right of free exercise, not that of their children, that must determine Wisconsin's power to impose criminal penalties on the parent. The dissent argues that a child who expresses a desire to attend public high school in conflict with the wishes of his parents should not be prevented from doing so. There is no reason for the court to consider that point since it is not an issue in the case. The children are not parties to this litigation. The State has at no point tried this case on the theory that respondents were preventing their children from attending school against their expressed desires, and indeed the record is to the contrary. . . .

Our holding in no way determines the proper resolution of possible competing interests of parents, children, and the State in an appropriate state court proceeding in which the power of the State is asserted on the theory that Amish parents are preventing their minor children from attending high school despite their expressed desires to the contrary. Recognition of the claim of the State in such a proceeding would, of course, call into question traditional concepts of parental control over the religious upbringing and education of their minor children recognized in this Court's past decisions. It is clear that such an intrusion by a State into family decisions in the area of religious training would give rise to grave questions of religious freedom. . . .

On this record we neither reach nor decide those issues.

* * *

For the reasons stated we hold, with the Supreme Court of Wisconsin, that the First and Fourteenth Amendments prevent the State from compelling respondents to cause their children to attend formal high school to age 16. Our disposition of this case, however, in no way alters our recognition of the obvious fact that courts are not school boards or legislatures, and are ill-equipped to determine the "necessity" of discrete aspects of a State's program of compulsory education. . . .

* * *

Affirmed.

Mr. Justice DOUGLAS, dissenting in part.

I agree with the Court that the religious scruples of the Amish are opposed to the education of their children beyond the grade schools, yet I disagree with the Court's conclusion that the matter is within the dispensation of parents alone. The Court's analysis assumes that the only interests at stake in the case are those of the Amish parents on the one hand, and those of the State on the other. The difficulty with this approach is that, despite the Court's claim, the parents are seeking to vindicate not only their own free exercise claims, but also those of their high-school-age children.

* * *

. . . If the parents in this case are allowed a religious exemption the inevitable effect is to impose the parents' notions of religious duty upon their children. Where the child is mature enough to express potentially conflicting desires, it would be an invasion of the child's rights to permit such an imposition without canvassing his views. . . . As the child has no other effective forum, it is in this litigation that his rights should be considered. And, if an Amish child desires to attend high school, and is mature enough to have that desire respected, the State may well be able to override the parents' religiously motivated objections.

Religion is an individual experience. It is not necessary, nor even appropriate, for every Amish child to express his views on the subject in a prosecution of a single adult. Crucial, however, are the views of the child whose parent is the subject of the suit. Frieda Yoder has in fact testified that her own religious views are opposed to high-school education. I therefore join the judgment of the Court as to respondent Jonas Yoder. But Frieda Yoder's views may not be those of [other children].

* * *

On this important and vital matter of education, I think the children should be entitled to be heard. While the parents, absent dissent, normally speak for the entire family, the education of the child is a matter on which the child will often have decided views. He may want to be a pianist or an astronaut or an oceanographer. To do so he will have to break from the Amish tradition.

It is the future of the student, not the future of the parents, that is imperiled by today's decision. If a parent keeps his child out of school beyond the grade school, then the child will be forever barred from entry into the new and amazing world of diversity that we have today. The child may decide that this is the preferred course, or he may rebel. It is the student's judgment, not his parents', that is essential if we are to give full meaning to what we have said about the Bill of Rights and of the right of students to be masters of their own destiny. If he is harnessed to the Amish way of life by those in authority over him and if his education is truncated, his entire life may be stunted and deformed. The child, therefore, should be given an opportunity to be heard before the State gives the exemption which we honor today.

* * *

[Mr. Justice POWELL and Mr. Justice REHNQUIST took no part in the consideration or decision of this case.]

Comments

1. *Wisconsin* v. *Yoder,* supra, is one of the few Supreme Court decisions on the freedom of religion that involve the criminal process. In *Yoder,* what did the Supreme Court mean by a "legitimate religious belief" or "sincere religious belief"? Suppose the Amish religion prohibited public school attendance altogether. Suppose two parents, both of whom hold Ph.Ds, decide not to send their children to public schools but rather to teach them at home (1) in order to prevent them from being bused 20 miles away, (2) because the public school district in which they reside provides an "inferior education" (which they can prove), and (3) their personal religion (although not an identifiable religious sect) requires that their children receive the "best possible education." Is *Yoder* any aid to them? Could the parents prevail on any of the three points just mentioned in order to escape a state's compulsory school attendance law? Virtually every jurisdiction has such attendance laws although they often are not enforced, especially when the child is near the permissible age of withdrawing from school. Can inmates be forced to attend educational classes in prison?

2. The First Amendment has two Religion Clauses: The Establishment Clause forbids the government from requiring by law acceptance of any particular creed or form of worship, and the Free Exercise Clause forbids governmental interference with any citizen's religious beliefs. In short, the First Amendment reflects a philosophy that church and state should be separated. The First Amendment would not permit the establishment of a national church, such as the Church of England, yet total separation in every conceivable respect is not required. The major requirement is that the government stand neutral, favoring no religion (including nonbelief), and not become entangled in religious affairs. Accordingly, while laws giving direct aid to religions are prohibited, laws that incidentally benefit religions are not per se invalid. Thus, religious groups may use the courts to resolve legal disputes as long as the issues are not doctrinal in nature.

3. *The Establishment Clause.* The First Amendment provides, in part, that "Congress shall make no law respecting an establishment of religion. . . ." Over the years, the Supreme Court has struggled to define the parameters of this "opaque" clause. See *Lemon* v. *Kurtzman,* 403 U.S. 602, 612 (1971) (opinion by Burger, C. J.). In many decisions, the Supreme Court has made it clear that the Clause forbids more than simply the establishment of a national church; it prohibits the government from giving preferential

treatment to any religion, or in some manner favoring religion over nonbelief. See, e.g., *Cantwell* v. *Connecticut*, 310 U.S. 296 (1940), and *United States* v. *Ballard*, 322 U.S. 78 (1944).

In *Everson* v. *Board of Education*, 330 U.S. 1 (1947), the Supreme Court for the first time (in modern times) defined the meaning of the Establishment Clause. A majority of the Court upheld a state statute that reimbursed the parents of parochial school children for bus transportation expenses, holding that the prohibition against "establishment of religion" means the government (federal or state) cannot (1) set up a religion; (2) pass laws aiding one religion, or aiding all religions; (3) force a person to profess a belief or nonbelief; (4) punish a person for professing a particular belief or nonbelief; (5) levy tax in any amount to support any religious activity or organization; or (6) participate in the affairs of any religious organization or group.

In *Walz* v. *Tax Commission*, 397 U.S. 664 (1970), the Court stated that the establishment clause was designed to afford protection against three "evils": "sponsorship, financial support, and active involvement of the sovereign in religious activity," at 668. Over the years, the Court has developed three tests for statutory compliance with the Establishment Clause: (1) the statute must have a secular *purpose;* (2) the principal or primary effect of the statute must be one that "neither advances nor inhibits religion," *Board of Education* v. *Allen,* 392 U.S. 236, 243 (1968); and (3) the statute must not foster "an excessive government entanglement with religion." *Walz,* supra, at 674. Accordingly, the Supreme Court has held that a state cannot release pupils from class to attend religious instruction classes in the public school building, *McCollum* v. *Board of Education,* 333 U.S. 203 (1948); a state law permitting public school students to be released on parental request to attend religious services during school hours involving neither public school classrooms nor the expenditure of public funds is valid, *Zorach* v. *Clauson,* 343 U.S. 306 (1952); the government may not suppress real or imagined attacks on a particular religion whether they appear in publications, speeches, or motion pictures, *Joseph Burstyn, Inc.* v. *Wilson,* 343 U.S. 495 (1952); the courts may not approve, disapprove, classify, regulate, or control in any manner sermons delivered at a religious meeting, *Fowler* v. *Rhode Island,* 345 U.S. 67 (1953); a public school system may not encourage the recitation of a prayer composed by a state board of regents, *Engel* v. *Vitale,* 370 U.S. 421 (1962), or Bible readings in public schools, *School District of Abington Township* v. *Schempp,* 374 U.S. 203 (1963); state laws under which state aid for secular instruction was furnished to church-related elementary and secondary schools are violative of the Establishment Clause, *Lemon* v. *Kurtzman,* 403 U.S. 602 (1971); state laws under which textbooks were lent free of charge to all students in certain grades in all schools, including parochial schools, are valid, *Board of Education* v. *Allen,* 392 U.S. 236 (1968); a state's loaning free textbooks to students attending racially discriminatory private schools is unconstitutional, *Norwood* v. *Harrison,* 413 U.S. 455 (1973); federal law granting aid to religious institutions of higher learning by way of construction grants for buildings and facilities to be used for secular educational purposes is constitutional, *Tilton* v. *Richardson,* 403 U.S. 672 (1971); state aid encompassing the construction of secular buildings at sectarian schools is not violative of the First Amendment, *Hunt*

v. *McNair*, 413 U.S. 734 (1973); states may, under limited circumstances, assist church-related schools in performing their secular functions, *Norwood* v. *Harrison*, 413 U.S. 455 (1973); a state law under which the state reimbursed all schools, including private and parochial schools, for costs of testing and record keeping is violative of the First Amendment, *Levitt* v. *Committee for Public Education and Religious Liberty*, 413 U.S. 472 (1973); a state authority's proposed financing of secular project at Baptist college not violative of First Amendment, *Hunt* v. *McNair*, 413 U.S. 734 (1973); a state law providing funds to reimburse parents for part of tuition expenses incurred in sending their children to nonpublic schools held violative of the First Amendment, *Sloan* v. *Lemon*, 413 U.S. 825 (1973); state court's resolution of a church property dispute proper where the court did no more than consider the language in the deeds in the dispute, *United States* v. *Mary Elizabeth Blue Hull Memorial Presbyterian Church*, 393 U.S. 440 (1969) (to the same effect is *Maryland and Virginia Eldership of Churches of God, Inc.* v. *Church of God, Inc.*, 396 U.S. 367 [1970]); tax exemptions granted to religious organizations do not constitute "establishment" of religion, *Walz* v. *Tax Comm'n of New York*, 397 U.S. 664 (1970); state law granting cash reimbursements or tax credits to parents who paid tuition for their children to attend private, including parochial, schools is violative of the First Amendment, *Committee for Public Education and Religious Liberty* v. *Nyquist*, 413 U.S. 756 (1973); Sunday closing laws, although in agreement with the dictates of Christian religions, are not violative of the Establishment Clause, *McGowan* v. *Maryland*, 366 U.S. 420 (1961) (see also *Gallagher* v. *Crown Kosher Super Market, Inc.*, 366 U.S. 617 [1961] and *Two Guys from Harrison–Allentown, Inc.* v. *McGinley*, 366 U.S. 582 [1961]); state may not require school children or anyone else to salute the American flag if it violates their beliefs, whether religious or not, *West Virginia State Board of Education* v. *Barnette*, 319 U.S. 624 (1943); state law authorizing state aid to school children enrolled in nonpublic schools for "auxiliary services," including counseling, testing, psychological services, and instructional materials, is violative of Establishment Clause, *Meek* v. *Pittenger*, 421 U.S. 349 (1975); state statute authorizing grants of state funds to private colleges and universities of which one third are church-related, but forbidding their use for sectarian purposes is not violative of Establishment Clause, *Roemer* v. *Maryland Board of Public Works*, 426 U.S. 736 (1976).

In summary, the First Amendment Establishment Clause, made applicable to the states in *Cantwell* v. *Connecticut*, 310 U.S. 296, 303 (1940), and *Murdock* v. *Pennsylvania*, 319 U.S. 105, 108 (1943), is governed by the following principles: (1) a state law that protects a valid secular interest is not invalid simply because it also incidentally benefits one or more (or all) religions—the "incidental benefit" rule; (2) the government need not be hostile to religious institutions, only neutral, and the required neutrality need not result in a callous indifference to religion—the "government neutrality" rule; (3) the government may "accommodate" religion as long as the end result does not excessively entangle government in the affairs of religion—the "excessive entanglement" rule; (4) religious organizations may use the civil courts to decide disputes (e.g., church property disputes), but in doing so the civil courts may not become involved in deciding ecclesiastical or doctrinal questions.

4. *The "Free Exercise" Clause.* The First Amendment prohibits laws
    that interfere with the "free exercise" of religion. This clause has a
    double aspect: "freedom to believe and freedom to act. The first is
    absolute, but, in the nature of things, the second cannot be,"
    Cantwell v. *Connecticut,* 310 U.S. 296, 300 (1940) (opinion by
    Roberts, J.). Although freedom to act in following one's beliefs may
    be somewhat restricted, infra, the government may not interfere in
    or attempt to regulate any citizen's religious beliefs or penalize him
    for holding religious views repugnant to those held by other
    members of society. In general, laws that are necessary for the
    common good of society and that place only an incidental burden on
    the free exercise of religion will be upheld. Thus, one may be
    prosecuted for following religious practices that violate criminal
    statutes. See, e.g., *Reynolds* v. *United States,* 98 U.S. 145 (1878)
    (Mormons in Utah must abide by criminal laws prohibiting polyg-
    amy).

    In cases involving the "Free Exercise" Clause of the First Amend-
    ment, the Supreme Court has made the following pronouncements:
    a striking down of state laws requiring Bible readings in public
    schools does not infringe on the free exercise of religion, *School
    District of Abington Township* v. *Schempp,* 374 U.S. 203 (1963); a
    state may not deny unemployment benefits to Seventh-Day
    Adventists whose religious beliefs prevent their working on
    Saturday, *Sherbert* v. *Verner,* 374 U.S. 398 (1963); a state law that
    regulates church administration or the operation of churches inhibits
    the free exercise of religion, *Kedroff* v. *St. Nicholas Cathedral of
    Russian Orthodox Church,* 344 U.S. 94 (1952); freedom of religion
    includes the freedom to disseminate one's religious beliefs through
    the distribution of religious literature and personal visitations from
    door to door, *Murdock* v. *Pennsylvania,* 319 U.S. 105 (1943); the
    freedom of religion is not restricted to orthodox religious practices,
    Follett v. *McCormick,* 321 U.S. 573 (1944); freedom of religion
    includes the right of persons to believe what they cannot prove,
    United States v. *Ballard,* 322 U.S. 78 (1944); members of the
    Orthodox Jewish faith who are also merchants are not denied free
    exercise of religion by Sunday closing laws, *Gallagher* v. *Crown
    Kosher Super Market, Inc.,* 366 U.S. 617 (1961), and *Braunfield* v.
    Brown, 366 U.S. 599 (1961); control of religious parades by means
    of municipal ordinances regulating their time, place, and manner is a
    proper exercise of state police powers, *Cox* v. *New Hampshire,* 312
    U.S. 569 (1941); a municipal ordinance requiring that a license be
    obtained from city before religious ceremonies are permitted in a
    public park is valid, *Poulos* v. *New Hampshire,* 345 U.S. 395
    (1953); city ordinance absolutely prohibiting the distribution of
    leaflets or handbills on city streets is unconstitutional, *Jamison* v.
    Texas, 318 U.S. 413 (1943); ordinances completely prohibiting the
    distribution of religious literature in a company town are invalid,
    Marsh v. *Alabama,* 326 U.S. 501 (1946); a municipality may
    control the use of public streets for the expression of religious
    views, *Kunz* v. *New York,* 340 U.S. 290 (1951); state child labor
    law does not violate the free exercise rights of a 9-year-old girl who
    distributed religious literature on the street, *Prince* v. *Massachu-
    setts,* 321 U.S. 158 (1944); Free Exercise Clause does not
    invalidate criminal convictions of Mormons who practiced polyg-
    amy, *Reynolds* v. *United States,* 98 U.S. 145 (1878) (see also *Davis*
    v. *Beason,* 133 U.S. 333 [1890], *Late Corp. of Church of Jesus*

Christ v. *United States*, 136 U.S. 1 [1890], *Cleveland* v. *United States*, 329 U.S. 14 [1946]); Congress may exempt conscientious objectors to all wars while not exempting objectors to particular wars, *Gillette* v. *United States*, 401 U.S. 437 (1971); denial of VA educational benefits to conscientious objectors who performed alternative civilian service upheld, *Johnson* v. *Robison*, 415 U.S. 361 (1974); World War I Selective Service Act exempting from the draft regular or duly ordained ministers and theological students is valid, *Arver* v. *United States*, 245 U.S. 366 (1918); defendant's willingness to participate in a theocratic war is not inconsistent with Military Selective Service Act requirement of opposition to participation in war "in any form," *Sicurella* v. *United States*, 348 U.S. 385 (1955) (to the same effect is *Clay* v. *United States*, 403 U.S. 698 [1971]); state law requiring university students to take a course in military science and tactics does not inhibit free exercise of religion, *Hamilton* v. *Regents of the University of California*, 293 U.S. 245 (1934); conscientious objectors seeking exemption from military service not required to hold orthodox beliefs as to a Supreme Being, *United States* v. *Seeger*, 380 U.S. 163 (1965); the test for determining whether an individual's conscientious objection to all wars is "religious" is whether his opposition to war stems from moral, ethical, or religious beliefs and whether such beliefs have the strength of traditional religious convictions, *Welsh* v. *United States*, 398 U.S. 333 (1970); Arkansas statute prohibiting teachers in public schools from teaching the theory of evolution is violative of Free Exercise Clause, *Epperson* v. *Arkansas*, 393 U.S. 97 (1968); requiring religious oath as condition for state employment infringes on the free exercise of religion, *Torcaso* v. *Watkins*, 367 U.S. 488 (1961); teacher could be compelled, in spite of her religious reliefs, to take a constitutionally prescribed loyalty oath to government as a condition of public employment, *Biklen* v. *Board of Education*, 406 U.S. 951 (1972); it is proper for Congress to deny a tax exemption to a church for land owned by the church but not used for religious purposes, *Gibbons* v. *District of Columbia*, 116 U.S. 404 (1886) (see also *Walz* v. *Tax Comm'n of New York*, 397 U.S. 664 [1970]); license tax levied against person who distributed religious literature as a method of spreading his religious beliefs is invalid, *Jones* v. *Opelika*, 319 U.S. 103 (1943); taxpayer has standing to challenge expenditure of federal funds to finance instruction in religious schools provided he can show a nexus between his status as a taxpayer and the constitutional infringement, *Flast* v. *Cohen*, 392 U.S. 83 (1968).

In summary, the following principles govern the application of the Free Exercise Clause of the First Amendment: (1) religious organizations are entitled to the same right to be free from government interference in the exercise of religion as are individuals; (2) the Free Exercise Clause protects both orthodox and unorthodox religious beliefs; (3) a law advancing a legitimate governmental interest is not invalid simply because it has an incidental detrimental effect on the free exercise of religion; (4) the states have an inherent police power, in spite of the Free Exercise Clause, to regulate religious activities in a reasonable manner to protect society; (5) the government may not regulate religious activities in an arbitrary manner; (6) any laws beyond the mere regulation of religious activities will not be justified unless the infringement serves a compelling state interest; (7) the government is permitted to go further in regulating the religious activities of children than it could in regulating the same actions by adults; and (8) the right to free exercise of religion does not include the right to commit crimes in the name of religion.

15.05　FREEDOM OF ASSEMBLY (AND ASSOCIATION)

Congress shall make no law ... abridging ... the right of the people peaceably to assemble....

The SDS and Colleges and Universities

HEALY v. JAMES

Supreme Court of the United States, 1972
408 U.S. 169, 92 S. Ct. 2338, 33 L. Ed. 2d 266

Catherine Healy and a group of college students at Central Connecticut State College (CCSC) organized a local chapter of the SDS (Students for a Democratic Society), but were denied recognition as a campus organization. Recognition would have permitted the group to place announcements regarding meetings, rallies, and other activities in the student newspaper, to use various college bulletin boards, and to use campus facilities for meetings. The college president, Dr James, denied recognition because he was not satisfied that the local chapter was independent of the national SDS, which he concluded had a philosophy of disruption and violence in conflict with the school's policies. Thereafter, the petitioners filed suit in the United States District Court (D. Conn.) seeking declaratory and injunctive relief against the college president, other administrators, and trustees on the ground that their First Amendment rights of expression and association had been violated. The district court dismissed the case. The United States Court of Appeals (2d Cir.) affirmed on the grounds that the petitioners had failed to meet their burden of complying with the prevailing standards at the college for recognition of "campus organizations." The United States Supreme Court granted certiorari.

Mr. Justice POWELL delivered the opinion of the Court.

* * *

We mention briefly at the outset the setting in 1969–1970. A climate of unrest prevailed on many college campuses in this country. There had been widespread civil disobedience on some campuses, accompanied by the seizure of buildings, vandalism, and arson. Some colleges had been shut down altogether, while at others files were looted and manuscripts destroyed. SDS chapters on some of those campuses had been a catalytic force during this period. Although the causes of campus disruption were many and complex, one of the prime consequences of such activities was the denial of the lawful exercise of First Amendment rights to the majority of students by the few. Indeed, many of the most cherished characteristics long associated with institutions of higher learning appeared to be endangered. Fortunately, with the passage of time, a calmer atmosphere and a greater maturity now pervade our campuses. Yet, it was in this climate of earlier unrest that this case arose.

* * *

State colleges and universities are not enclaves immune from the sweep of the First Amendment. "It can hardly be argued that either students or teachers shed their constitutional rights to freedom of speech or expression at the school house gate." Tinker v. Des Moines Independent School District, 393 U.S. 503, 506, 731, 737 (1969). Of course ... First Amendment rights must always be applied "in light of the special characteristics of the ... environment" in the particular case.... And, where state-operated educational institutions are involved, this Court has long recognized "the need for affirming the comprehensive authority of the States and of school officials consistent with fundamental safeguards to prescribe and control conduct in the schools." ...

Among the rights protected by the First Amendment is the right of individuals to associate to further their personal beliefs. While the freedom of association is not explicitly set out in the Amendment, it has long been held to be implicit in the freedoms of speech, assembly, and petition. ... There can be no doubt that denial of official recognition, without justification to college organizations burdens or abridges that associational right. The primary impediment to free association flowing from nonrecognition is the denial of use of campus facilities for meetings and other appropriate purposes. The practical effect of nonrecognition was demonstrated in this case when, several days after the President's decision was announced, petitioners were not allowed to hold a meeting in the campus coffee shop because they were not an approved group.

* * *

... [I]t is appropriate to discuss the several bases of President James' decision. Four possible justifications for nonrecognition, all closely related, might be derived from the record and his statements. Three of those grounds are inadequate to substantiate his decision: a fourth, however, has merit.

From the outset the controversy in this case has centered in large measure around the relationship, if any, between petitioners' group and the national SDS. The Student Affairs Committee meetings, as reflected in its minutes, focused considerable attention on this issue; the court-ordered hearing also was directed primarily to this question. Despite assurances from petitioners and their counsel that the local group was in fact independent of the national organization, it is evident that President James was significantly influenced by his apprehension that there was a connection. Aware of the fact that some SDS chapters had been associated with disruptive and violent campus activity, he apparently considered that affiliation itself was sufficient justification for denying recognition.

Although this precise issue has not come before the Court heretofore, the Court has consistently disapproved governmental action imposing criminal sanctions or denying rights and privileges solely because of a citizens' association with an unpopular organization.... [I]t has been established that "guilt by association alone, without [establishing] that an individual's association poses the threat feared by the Government," is an impermissible basis upon which to deny First Amendment rights. ... The Government has the burden of establishing a knowing affiliation with an organization possessing unlawful aims and goals, and a specific intent to further those illegal aims.

Students for a Democratic Society, as conceded by the College ... is loosely organized, having various factions and promoting a number of diverse social and political views, only some of which call for unlawful action. Not only did petitioners proclaim their complete independence from this organization but they also indicated that they shared only some of the beliefs its leaders have expressed. On this record it is clear that the relationship was not an adequate ground for the denial of recognition.

* * *

[P]resident James attributed what he believed to be the philosophy of that organization to the local group. He characterized the petitioning group as adhering to "some of the major tenets of the national organization," including a philosophy of violence and disruption. Understandably he found that philosophy abhorrent. ...

The mere disagreement of the President with the group's philosophy affords no reason to deny it recognition. As repugnant as these views may have been, especially to one with President James' responsibility, the mere expression of them would not justify the denial of First Amendment rights. Whether petitioners did in fact advocate a philosophy of "destruction" thus becomes immaterial. The College, acting here as the instrumentality of the State, may not restrict speech or association simply because it finds the views expressed [408 U.S. 188] by any group to be abhorrent. . . .

As the litigation progressed . . . a third rationale for President James' decision — beyond the questions of affiliation and philosophy — began to emerge. His second statement . . . indicates that he based rejection on a conclusion that this particular group would be a "disruptive influence at CCSC." . . .

If this reason, directed at the organization's activities rather than its philosophy, were factually supported by the record, this Court's prior decisions would provide a basis for considering the propriety of nonrecognition. The critical line heretofore drawn for determining the permissibility of regulation is the line between mere advocacy and advocacy "directed to inciting or producing imminent lawless action and . . . likely to incite or produce such action." Brandenburg v. Ohio, 395 U.S. 444, 447 (1969) (unanimous per curiam opinion). . . .

In the context of the "special characteristics of the school enviornment," the power of the government to prohibit "lawless action" is not limited to acts of a criminal nature. Also prohibitable are actions which "materially and substantially disrupt the work and discipline of the school." . . . Associational activities need not be tolerated where they infringe reasonable campus rules, interrupt classes, or substantially interfere with the opportunity of other students to obtain an education.

. . . [I]f there were an evidential basis to support the conclusion that CCSC–SDS posed a substantial threat of material disruption in violation of that command the President's decision should be affirmed.

The record, however, offers no substantial basis for that conclusion. . . .

. . . [R]eferences in the record to the group's equivocation regarding how it might respond to "issues of violence" and whether it could ever "envision . . . interrupting a class," suggest a fourth possible reason why recognition might have been denied to these petitioners. These remarks might well have been read as announcing petitioners' unwillingness to be bound by reasonable school rules governing conduct. The College's Statement of Rights, Freedoms, and Responsibilities of Students contains . . . an explicit statement with respect to campus disruption. The regulation, carefully differentiating between advocacy and action, is a reasonable one, and petitioners have not questioned it directly. Yet their statements raise considerable question whether they intend to abide by the prohibitions contained therein.

. . . [T]he critical line for First Amendment purposes must be drawn between advocacy, which is entitled to full protection, and action, which is not. Petitioners may, if they so choose, preach the propriety of amending or even doing away with any or all campus regulations. They may not, however, undertake to flout these rules. . . .

Just as in the community at large, reasonable regulations with respect to the time, the place, and the manner in which student groups conduct their speech-related activities must be respected. A college administration may impose a requirement, such as may have been imposed in this case, that a group seeking official recognition affirm in advance its willingness to adhere to reasonable campus law. Such a requirement does not impose an impermissible condition on the students' associational rights. Their freedom to speak out, to assemble, or to petition for changes in school rules is in no sense infringed. It merely constitutes an agreement to conform with reasonable standards respecting conduct. This is a minimal requirement, in the interest of the entire academic community, of any group seeking the privilege of official recognition.

. . . Because respondents failed to accord due recognition to First Amendment principles, the judgments below approving respondents' denial of recognition must be reversed. Since we cannot conclude from this record that petitioners were willing to abide by reasonable campus rules and regulations, we order the case remanded for reconsideration. We note, in so holding, that the wide latitude accorded by the Constitution to the freedoms of expression and association is not without its costs in terms of the risk to the maintenance of civility and an ordered society. Indeed, this latitude often has resulted, on the campus and elsewhere, in the infringement of the rights of others. Though we deplore the tendency of some to abuse the very constitutional privileges they invoke, and although the infringement of rights of others certainly should not be tolerated, we reaffirm this Court's dedication to the principles of the Bill of Rights upon which our vigorous and free society is founded.

Reversed and remanded.

Mr. Chief Justice BURGER, concurring.

Student organizations seeking the privilege of official campus recognition must be willing to abide by valid rules of the institution applicable to all such organizations. This is a reasonable condition insofar as it calls for the disavowal of resort to force, disruption and interference with the rights of others.

... It is within ... the academic community that problems such as these should be resolved. The courts, state or federal, should be a last resort. Part of the educational experience of every college student should be an experience in responsible self-government and this must be a joint enterprise of students and faculty. It should not be imposed unilaterally from above, nor can the terms of the relationship be dictated by students. ...

The relatively placid life of the college campus of the past has not prepared either administrators or students for their respective responsibilities in maintaining an atmosphere in which divergent views can be asserted vigorously, but civilly, to the end

that those who seek to be heard accord the same right to all others. ... [I]t is impossible to know from the record in this case whether the student group was willing to acknowledge an obligation to abide by that "Bill of Rights."

Against this background, the action of the Court in remanding on this issue is appropriate.

Mr. Justice DOUGLAS, concurring.

* * *

The First Amendment does not authorize violence. But it does authorize advocacy, group activities, and espousal of change.

The present case is minuscule in the events of the 60's and 70's. But the fact that it has to come here for ultimate resolution indicates the sickness of our academic world, measured by First Amendment standards. Students as well as faculty are entitled to credentials in their search for truth. If we are to become an integrated, adult society, rather than stubborn status quo opposed to change, students and faculties should have communal interests in which each age learns from the other. Without ferment of one kind or another, a college or university (like a federal agency or other human institution) becomes a useless appendage to a society which traditionally has reflected the spirit of rebellion.

* * *

[Mr. Justice REHNQUIST concurred in the result.]

Comments

1. Although the word "association" is not mentioned in the First Amendment, *Healy* v. *James,* supra, makes it clear that among the rights protected by the First Amendment is the right of individuals to associate to further their personal beliefs. The freedom of association is implicit in the freedoms of speech, assembly, and petition and is a necessary penumbral right: the effective exercise of the freedoms of speech, press, and petition frequently requires group or associational activity.

2. Always an essential freedom, the right of association has assumed increasing importance in a society of increasing size and complexity as individuals find it advisable to join with others to voice mutual concerns. See Emerson, T., *Freedom of Association and Freedom of Expression,* 74 Yale L. J. 1 (1964). Yet it was not until 1958 in *NAACP* v. *Alabama,* 357 U.S. 449 (1958) that the Supreme Court

elevated the freedom of association to its present status as a separate First Amendment right. In that case, the Supreme Court reviewed a contempt conviction based upon the NAACP's refusal to fully comply with a state court order requiring it to provide its membership lists. In reversing the conviction, the Supreme Court, per Mr. Justice Harlan, held that freedom to engage in association for the advancement of beliefs and ideas was an inseparable aspect of "liberty" that embraced freedom of speech and was secured by the Due Process Clause of the Fourteenth Amendment. The Court stated, "It is immaterial whether the beliefs sought to be advanced by association pertain to political, economic, religious or cultural matters, and state action which may have the effect of curtailing the freedom to associate is subject to the closest scrutiny," at 460–461.

3. Like other First Amendment rights, the freedom of association is not absolute. See, e.g., *Konigsberg* v. *State Bar of California*, 366 U.S. 36 (1961). Before the government can curtail the right, it must demonstrate a substantial or compelling state interest in doing so. Compare *Williams* v. *Rhodes*, 393 U.S. 23 (1968) (compelling state interest required before state may require a new party to obtain petitions signed by qualified electors totaling 15 per cent of the number of ballots cast in the last preceding gubernatorial election), with *Uphaus* v. *Wyman*, 360 U.S. 72 (1959) (state attorney general investigating subversive activities within a state may infringe associational rights if public interests outweigh the need to protect the right). The Supreme Court has held that the government may not require an individual to give up his associational right in order to receive governmental benefits to which he is otherwise entitled. See, e.g., *Camp* v. *Board of Public Instruction*, 368 U.S. 278 (1961); *Aptheker* v. *Secretary of State*, 378 U.S. 500 (1964); *Keyishian* v. *Board of Regents*, 385 U.S. 589 (1967); *Schneider* v. *Smith*, 390 U.S. 17 (1968); *Baird* v. *State Bar of Arizona*, 401 U.S. 1 (1971); *In re Stolar*, 401 U.S. 23 (1971); *Law Students Civil Rights Research Council, Inc.* v. *Wadmond*, 401 U.S. 154 (1971); and *Cole* v. *Richardson*, 405 U.S. 676 (1972) (government may not condition employment on taking oaths that interfere with First Amendment rights) (dictum).

4. From the Supreme Court's decisions in the area of freedom of association some basic principles have emerged: (1) The right to freedom of association protects groups having lawful goals, whether or not these goals are popular with the majority of the populace. See, e.g., *NAACP* v. *Button*, 371 U.S. 415 (1963); *Gibson* v. *Florida Legislative Committee*, 372 U.S. 539 (1963). However, the right to freedom of association does not extend to the protection of groups pursuing unlawful goals. See, e.g., *Barenblatt* v. *United States*, 360 U.S. 109 (1959); *Wilkinson* v. *United States*, 365 U.S. 399 (1961); *Braden* v. *United States*, 365 U.S. 431 (1961); *Scales* v. *United States*, 367 U.S. 203 (1961); *Noto* v. *United States*, 367 U.S. 290 (1961); *Elfbrandt* v. *Russell*, 384 U.S. 11 (1966); *United States* v. *Robel*, 389 U.S. 258 (1967); *Communist Party of the United States* v. *Subversive Activities Control Board*, 367 U.S. 1 (1961). (2) Absent a showing by the government of a substantial interest (compelling state interest in some cases), an individual need not disclose his associational ties, nor must an organization disclose its membership lists. See, e.g., *Beilan* v. *Board of Public Instruction*,

357 U.S. 399 (1958); *Barenblatt* v. *United States,* supra; *Shelton* v. *Tucker,* 364 U.S. 479 (1960); *De Gregory* v. *Attorney General of New Hampshire,* 383 U.S. 825 (1966); *NAACP* v. *Alabama,* 357 U.S. 449 (1958); *Bates* v. *Little Rock,* 361 U.S. 516 (1960); *Louisiana ex rel. Gremillion* v. *NAACP,* 366 U.S. 293 (1961). (3) An individual may not be presumed guilty merely because he belongs to an organization that has members who commit or advocate unlawful acts without a showing that he personally advocated the commission of illegal acts. See, e.g., *Healy* v. *James,* 408 U.S. 169 (1972) (supra). (4) The government may require or prohibit association when a substantial interest is involved and when the required or prohibited association is not fundamentally political in nature. See, e.g., *Railway Employees' Dept.* v. *Hanson,* 351 U.S. 225 (1951); *Lathrop* v. *Donohue,* 367 U.S. 820 (1961); *International Assoc. of Machinists* v. *Street,* 367 U.S. 740 (1961); *Cox* v. *Louisiana,* 379 U.S. 559 (1965); *Cameron* v. *Johnson,* 390 U.S. 611 (1968); *Arciniega* v. *Freeman,* 404 U.S. 4 (1971).

5. The Supreme Court has decided cases involving the freedom of association as it applies to bar associations, e.g., *Baird* v. *State Bar of Arizona,* 401 U.S. 1 (1971); labor unions, e.g., *United Transportation Union* v. *State Bar of Michigan,* 401 U.S. 576 (1971); minority group organizations, e.g., *NAACP* v. *Alabama,* 357 U.S. 449 (1958); the Communist Party and other subversive groups, e.g., *Communist Party of Indiana* v. *Whitcomb,* 414 U.S. 441 (1974); non-Communist political parties, e.g., *Rosario* v. *Rockefeller,* 410 U.S. 752 (1973), *Storer* v. *Brown,* 415 U.S. 724, (1974), *American Party of Texas* v. *White,* 415 U.S. 767 (1974); social organizations, e.g., *Moose Lodge* v. *Irvis,* 407 U.S. 163 (1972); student organizations, e.g., *Healy* v. *James,* 408 U.S. 169 (1972) (supra); and tenant associations, e.g., *Thorpe* v. *Housing Authority of Durham,* 386 U.S. 670 (1967).

A Democratic Sheriff, Republican Employees, and the Patronage System

ELROD v. BURNS

Supreme Court of the United States, 1976
427 U.S. 347, 96 S. Ct. 2673, 49 L. Ed. 2d 547

In December, 1970, the sheriff of Cook County, Illinois, a Republican, was replaced by Richard Elrod, a Democrat. Respondents, John Burns et al., were discharged from their employment solely because they neither supported nor were members of the Democratic Party. Respondents were non–civil-service employees and were therefore not protected by any statute, ordinance, or regulation from arbitrary discharge. John Burns was chief deputy of the process division and the other respondents held the positions of bailiff and security guard, process server, and employee in the Sheriff's Office. Respondents filed suit in federal district court against petitioners Elrod et al., alleging that their discharge was in violation of the First and Fourteenth Amendments and various provisions of the 1871 Civil Rights Act. The District Court (N.D. Ill.) ultimately dismissed the complaint for failure to

state a claim upon which relief could be granted, but the Court of Appeals (7th Cir.) reversed and remanded, holding that respondents' complaint stated a legally cognizable claim and ordering the district court to enter appropriate preliminary injunctive relief. The United States Supreme Court granted certiorari.

Mr. Justice BRENNAN announced the judgment of the Court and delivered an opinion in which Mr. Justice WHITE and Mr. Justice MARSHALL joined.

This case presents the question whether public employees who allege they were discharged or threatened with discharge solely because of their partisan political affiliation or nonaffiliation state a claim for deprivation of constitutional rights secured by the First and Fourteenth Amendments.

*   *   *

The Cook County Sheriff's practice of dismissing employees on a partisan basis is but one form of the general practice of political patronage. The practice also includes placing loyal supporters in government jobs that may or may not have been made available by political discharges. Nonofficeholders may be the beneficiaries of lucrative government contracts for highway construction, buildings, and supplies. Favored wards may receive improved public services. Members of the judiciary may even engage in the practice through the appointment of receiverships, trusteeships, and refereeships. Although political patronage comprises a broad range of activities, we are here concerned only with the constitutionality of dismissing public employees for partisan reasons.

Patronage practice is not new to American politics. It has existed at the federal level at least since the presidency of Thomas Jefferson, although its popularization and legitimization primarily occurred later, in the presidency of Andrew Jackson. The practice is not unique to American politics. It has been used in many European countries, and in darker times, it played a significant role in the Nazi rise to power in Germany and other totalitarian states. More recent times have witnessed a strong decline in its use, particularly with respect to public employment.

The cost of the practice of patronage is the restraint it places on freedoms of belief and association. In order to maintain their jobs, respondents were required to pledge their political allegiance to the Democratic Party, work for the election of other candidates of the Democratic Party, contribute a portion of their wages to the Party, or obtain the sponsorship of a member of the Party, usually at the price of one of the first three alternatives. Regardless of the incumbent party's identity, Democractic or otherwise, the consequences for association and belief are the same. An individual who is a member of the out-party maintains affiliation with his own party at the risk of losing his job. He works for the election of his party's candidates and espouses its policies at the same risk. The financial and campaign assistance that he is induced to provide to another party furthers the advancement of that party's policies to the detriment of his party's views and ultimately his own beliefs, and any assessment of his salary is tantamount to coerced belief. . . . Even a pledge of allegiance to another party, however ostensible, only serves to compromise the individual's true beliefs. Since the average public employee is hardly in the financial position to support his party and another, or to lend his time to two parties, the individual's ability to act according to his beliefs and to associate with others of his political persuasion is constrained, and support for his party is diminished.

It is not only belief and association which are restricted where political patronage is the practice. The free functioning of the electoral process also suffers. . . . Patronage . . . tips the electoral process in favor of the incumbent party, and where the practice's scope is substantial relative to the size of the electorate, the impact on the process can be significant.

Our concern with the impact of patronage on political belief and association does not occur in the abstract, for political belief and association constitute the core of those activities protected by the First Amendment. Regardless of the nature of the inducement, whether it be by denial of public employment or . . . by the influence of a teacher over students, . . . "[t]he First Amendment protects political association as well as political expression." . . .

Particularly pertinent to the constitutionality of the practice of patronage dismissals are Keyishian v. Board of Regents, 385 U.S. 589 (1967), and Perry v. Sindermann, 408 U.S. 593 (1972). In Keyishian, the Court invalidated New York statutes barring employment merely on the basis of membership in a "subversive" organization. Keyishian squarely held that political association alone could not, consistently with the First Amendment, constitute an adequate ground for denying public employment. In Perry, the Court broadly rejected the validity of limitations on First Amendment rights as a condition to the receipt of a governmental benefit, stating that the Government "may not deny a benefit to a person on a basis that infringes his constitutionally protected interests — especially, his interest in freedom of speech. For if the government could deny a benefit to a person because of his constitutionally protected speech or associations, his exercise of those freedoms would in effect be penalized and inhibited. . . .

Patronage practice falls squarely within the prohibitions of Keyishian and Perry. Under that practice, public employees hold their jobs on the condition that they provide, in some acceptable manner, support for the favored political party. The threat of dismissal for failure to provide that support unquestionably inhibits protected belief and association, and dismissal for failure to provide support only penalizes its exercise. The belief and association which Government may not ordain directly are achieved by indirection. And regardless of how evenhandedly these restraints may operate in the long run, after political office has changed hands several times, protected interests are still infringed and thus violation remains.

Although the practice of patronage dismissals clearly infringes First Amendment interests, our inquiry is not at an end, for the prohibition on encroachment of First Amendment protections is not an absolute. Restraints are permitted for appropriate reasons. . . . Perry and Keyishian properly recognize one such impermissible reason: the denial of a public benefit may not be used by the Government for the purpose of creating an incentive enabling it to achieve what it may not command directly. . . .

While the right–privilege distinction furnishes no ground on which to justify patronage, petitioners raise several other justifica-

tions requiring consideration. . . . It is firmly established that a significant impairment of First Amendment rights must survive exacting scrutiny. . . . Thus encroachment "cannot be justified by a mere showing of some legitimate governmental interest." Kusper v. Pontikes, 414 U.S. 51, 58 (1973). The interest advanced must be paramount, one of vital importance, and the burden is on the Government to show the existence of such an interest. . . . [I]f conditioning the retention of public employment on the employee's support of the in-party is to survive constitutional challenge, it must further some vital government end by a means that is least restrictive of freedom of belief and association in achieving that end, and the benefit gained must outweigh the loss of constitutionally protected rights.

One interest which has been offered in justification of patronage is the need to insure effective government and the efficiency of public employees. It is argued that employees of political persuasions not the same as that of the party in control of public office will not have the incentive to work effectively and may even be motivated to subvert the incumbent administration's efforts to govern effectively. We are not persuaded. The inefficiency resulting from the wholesale replacement of large numbers of public employees every time political office changes hands belies this justification. And the prospect of dismissal after an election in which the incumbent party has lost is only a disincentive to good work. Further, it is not clear that dismissal in order to make room for a patronage appointment will result in replacement by a person more qualified to do the job since appointment often occurs in exchange for the delivery of votes, or other party service, not job capability. More fundamentally, however, the argument does not succeed because it is doubtful that the mere difference of political persuasion motivates poor performance; nor do we think it legitimately may be used as a basis for imputing such behavior. The Court has consistently recognized that mere political association is an inadequate basis for imputing disposition to ill-willed conduct. . . . [L]ess drastic means for insuring government effectiveness and employee efficiency are available to the State. Specifically, employees may always be discharged for good cause, such as insubordination or poor job performance, when those bases in fact exist.

Even if the first argument that patronage serves effectiveness and efficiency be rejected, it still may be argued that patronage serves those interests by giving the employees of an incumbent party the incentive to perform well in order to insure their party's incumbency and thereby their jobs. Patronage, according to the argument, thus makes employees highly accountable to the public. But the ability of officials more directly accountable to the electorate to discharge employees for cause and the availability of merit systems, growth in the use of which has been quite significant, convince us that means less intrusive than patronage still exist for achieving accountability in the public work force and, thereby, effective and efficient Government. The greater effectiveness of patronage over these less drastic means, if any, is at best marginal, a gain outweighed by the absence of intrusion on protected interests under the alternatives.

* * *

A second interest advanced in support of patronage is the need for political loyalty of employees, not to the end that effectiveness and efficiency be insured, but to the end that representative government not be undercut by tactics obstructing the implementation of policies of the new administration, policies presumably sanctioned by the electorate. The justification is not without force, but is nevertheless inadequate to validate patronage wholesale. Limiting patronage dismissals to policymaking positions is sufficient to achieve this governmental end. Nonpolicymaking individuals usually have only limited responsibility and are therefore not in a position to thwart the goals of the in-party.

No clear line can be drawn between policymaking and nonpolicymaking positions. While nonpolicymaking individuals usually have limited responsibility, that is not to say that one with a number of responsibilities is necessarily in a policymaking position. The nature of the responsibilities is critical.... In determining whether an employee occupies a policymaking position, consideration should also be given to whether the employee acts as an adviser or formulates plans for the implementation of broad goals.... Since ... it is

the Government's burden to demonstrate an overriding interest in order to validate an encroachment on protected interests, the burden of establishing this justification as to any particular respondent will rest on the petitioners on remand, cases of doubt being resolved in favor of the particular respondent.

It is argued that a third interest supporting patronage dismissals is the preservation of the democractic process. According to petitioners, "'we have contrived no system for the support of party that does not place considerable reliance on patronage. The party organization makes a democratic government work and charges a price for its service.'" The argument is thus premised on the centrality of partisan politics to the democratic process.

Preservation of the democratic process is certainly an interest protection of which may in some instances justify limitations on First Amendment freedoms.... But however important preservation of the two-party system or any system involving a fixed number of parties may or may not be ... we are not persuaded that the elimination of patronage practice or, as is specifically involved here, the interdiction of patronage dismissals, will bring about the demise of party politics. Political parties existed in the absence of active patronage practice prior to the administration of Andrew Jackson, and they have survived substantial reduction in their patronage power through the establishment of merit systems.

Patronage dismissals thus are not the least restrictive alternative to achieving the contribution they may make to the democratic process. The process functions as well without the practice, perhaps even better, for patronage dismissals clearly also retard that process. Patronage can result in the entrenchment of one or a few parties to the exclusion of others. And most indisputably, as we recognized at the outset, patronage is a very effective impediment to the associational and speech freedoms which are essential to a meaningful system of democratic government.... [P]atronage dismissals severely restrict political belief and association. Though there is a vital need for government efficiency and effectiveness, such dismissals are on balance not the least restrictive means for fostering that end. There is also a need to insure that policies which the electorate has sanctioned are effectively implemented. That interest can be fully satisfied by limiting patronage dismissals to policymaking positions. Finally, patronage dismissals cannot be justified by their contribution to the proper functioning of our democratic process through their assistance to partisan politics since political parties are nurtured by other, less intrusive and equally effective methods. More fundamentally, however, any contribution of patronage dismissals to the democratic process does not suffice to override their severe encroachment on First Amendment freedoms. We hold, therefore, that the practice of patronage dismissals is unconstitutional under the First and Fourteenth Amendments. . . .

* * *

Affirmed.

Mr. Justice STEWART, with whom Mr. Justice BLACKMUN joins, concurring in the result.

* * *

This case does not require us to consider the broad contours of the so-called patronage system, with all its variations and permutations. In particular, it does not require us to consider the constitutional validity of a system that confines the hiring of some governmental employees to those of a particular political party, and I would intimate no views whatever on that question.

The single substantive question involved in this case is whether a nonpolicymaking, nonconfidential government employee can be discharged from a job that he is satisfactorily performing upon the sole ground of his political beliefs. I agree with the Court that he cannot. . . .

Mr. Chief Justice BURGER, dissenting.

* * *

The Illinois Legislature has pointedly decided that roughly half of the Sheriff's staff shall be made up of tenured career personnel and the balance left exclusively to the choice of the elected head of the department. The Court strains the rational bounds of First Amendment doctrine and runs counter to

longstanding practices that are part of the fabric of our democratic system to hold that the Constitution *commands* something it has not been thought to require for 185 years. For all that time our system has wisely left these matters to the States and, on the federal level, to the Congress. The Court's action is a classic example of trivializing constitutional adjudication—a function of the highest importance in our system.

* * *

Mr. Justice POWELL, with whom the CHIEF JUSTICE [BURGER] and Mr. Justice REHNQUIST join, dissenting.

The Court holds unconstitutional a practice as old as the Republic, a practice which has contributed significantly to the democratization of American politics. This decision is urged on us in the name of First Amendment rights, but in my view the judgment neither is constitutionally required nor serves the interest of a representative democracy. It also may well disserve—rather than promote—core values of the First Amendment. I therefore dissent.

* * *

The question is whether it is consistent with the First and Fourteenth Amendments for a State to offer some employment conditioned, explicitly or implicitly, on partisan political affiliation and on the political fortunes of the incumbent officeholder. This is to be determined, as the plurality opinion agrees, by whether patronage hiring practices sufficiently advance important state interests to justify the consequent burdening of First Amendment interests. . . . It is difficult to disagree with the view, as an abstract proposition, that government employment ordinarily should not be conditioned upon one's political beliefs or activities. But we deal here with a highly practical and rather fundamental element of our political system, not the theoretical abstractions of a political science seminar. . . .

[P]atronage hiring practices have contributed to American democracy by stimulating political activity and by strengthening parties, thereby helping to make government accountable. It cannot be questioned seriously that these contributions promote important state interests. . . . We also have recognized the strong government interests in encouraging stable political parties and avoiding excessive political fragmentation. Through the medium of established parties the "people ... are presented with understandable choices and the winner in the general election with sufficient support to govern effectively," Storer v. Brown, 415 U.S. 724, 735 (1974), while "splintered parties and unrestrained factionalism [might] do significant damage to the fabric of government." ...

* * *

Patronage hiring practices also enable party organizations to persist and function at the local level. Such organizations become visible to the electorate at large only at election time, but the dull periods between elections require ongoing activities: precinct organizations must be maintained; new voters registered; and minor political "chores" performed for citizens who otherwise may have no practical means of access to officeholders. In some communities, party organizations and clubs also render helpful social services.

Patronage hiring practices sufficiently serve important state interests, including some interests sought to be advanced by the First Amendment, to justify a tolerable intrusion on the First Amendment interests of employees or potential employees.

... The principal intrusion of patronage hiring practices on First Amendment interests ... arises from the coercion on associational choices that may be created by one's desire initially to obtain employment. This intrusion, while not insignificant, must be measured in light of the limited role of patronage hiring in most government employment. The pressure to abandon one's beliefs and associations to obtain government employment—especially employment of such uncertain duration—does not seem to me to assume impermissible proportions in light of the interests to be served.

* * *

I would hold that a state or local government may elect to condition employment on the political affiliation of a prospective employee and on the political fortunes of the hiring incumbent. History and long prevailing practice across the country support the view that patronage hiring practices make a sufficiently substantial contribution to the practical functioning of our democratic system to support their relatively modest intrusion on First Amendment interests. ...

[Mr. Justice STEVENS did not participate in the consideration or decision of this case.]

Comment

1. Is the patronage system unconstitutional with regard to policy-making employees? A majority of the Court declined to answer that question, although Justices Brennan, White, and Marshall apparently would extend the holding of *Elrod* to these employees. What practical impact, if any, is *Elrod* likely to have on the political process? Of course, the Court notes, employees may be fired for "good cause, such as insubordination or poor job performance...." Are many employees of the minority political party likely to be discharged under the guise of "good cause"? Do non–civil-service employees now enjoy the same protection against being discharged as civil service employees?

16

THE MILITARY
JUSTICE PROCESS

16.01 INTRODUCTION

The conduct of persons in the armed forces is governed by the Uniform Code of Military Justice (U.C.M.J.), enacted by Congress in 1950 and revised and made part of Title 10 of the United States Code in 1956 (10 U.S.C. §§ 801–940, Art. 1–140). Most of the punitive offenses of the code are the familiar substantive common law offenses (e.g., murder), but certain military offenses have no common law or civil statutory counterpart, for example, absence without leave, desertion, disrespect to superiors, and disobedience to lawful orders. The constitutionality of most of these military offenses has been upheld by the United States Supreme Court even though the proscribed behavior is somewhat broadly defined (i.e., disrespect to superiors). See, e.g., *Parker* v. *Levy,* 417 U.S. 733 (1974) infra, § 16.02. The military defends these code offenses on the basis of "military necessity," and although the Supreme Court has stated that servicemen are not to be denied their federal constitutional rights, the Court has at the same time stressed the unique status of servicemen and the fundamental differences between civilian and military courts.

MILITARY JUSTICE AND THE UNIFORM CODE*

* * *

The Constitution

The constitutional sources of military law stem from two provisions: those vesting certain powers in the legislative branch (Section 8, Article I) and those granting certain authority to the executive branch (Sections 2 and 3, Article II). In addition, the Fifth Amendment, in effect, recognizes that service-connected offenses in the Armed Forces will be dealt with in accordance with military law.

Powers granted to Congress. Under Section 8, Article I, Congress is empowered to define and punish offenses against the Law of Nations; to declare war, grant letters of

---

*Reprinted by permission from *Military Law*: published 1974 by Air Force Reserve Officers Training Corps, Maxwell AFB, AL 36112.
1107

marque and reprisal, and make rules concerning captures on land and water; to raise and support armies; to provide and maintain a navy; to make rules for the government and regulation of the land and naval forces; to provide for calling forth the militia to execute the laws of the union, suppress insurrections and repel invasions; to provide for organizing, arming, and disciplining the militia, and for governing such part of them as may be employed in the service of the United States; and, in general, to make all laws which shall be necessary and proper for carrying into execution the foregoing powers, and all other powers vested by the Constitution in the Government of the United States, or in any department or officer thereof.

Authority vested in the President. Section 2, Article II, constitutes the President commander in chief of the Army and Navy of the United States, and of the militia of the several states, when called into the actual service of the United States. It further empowers the President (with the concurrence of the Senate) to appoint the officers of the services. Section 3 of the same article, in fact, requires that the President commission all of the officers of the United States and makes it his duty to see that the laws of his country are faithfully executed.

The Fifth Amendment. The framers of the Constitution recognized that cases arising in the military services would be handled differently from cases arising in civilian life. In the Fifth Amendment, it was provided that *no* person should be held to answer for a capital or otherwise infamous crime, unless on a presentment or indictment of a grand jury, *except in cases arising in the land or naval forces, or in the Militia when in actual service in time of war or public danger. . . .*

* * *

Protection of Personal Liberties

The Fifth Amendment guarantees personal freedom of the individual. It provides that no person shall be deprived of liberty without due process of law. In effect, it means that an American citizen cannot be thrown into jail or otherwise confined without reasonable cause and then only in a legal manner. In military law, this doctrine is explicitly stated in, and strictly enforced under, the *Uniform Code* [of Military Justice (UCMJ)].

Three methods of restraining an individual under military law are known as "apprehen-

sion," "arrest," and "confinement." Definitions of these terms are necessary to explain the distinctions.

Apprehension is the act of taking a person into custody. It is accomplished by notifying the person that he is being taken into custody. This notification may be written or verbal. A physical securing of the person taken into custody, such as handcuffing, is not mandatory. However, any reasonable measure of securing and maintaining custody is authorized.

In contrast, *arrest* is the restraint of a person by an order directing him to remain within certain specified limits. It is moral restraint. Arrest is imposed by notifying the person to be restrained that he is under arrest and informing him of the limits of his arrest. The notification may be written or verbal.

"Confinement" is defined in the *Manual for Courts-Martial* [MCM] as the physical restraint of a person. In such confinement, military law prescribes a definite procedure. The accused is taken to the place of confinement and placed under guard. The person who authorized the restraint must furnish a written statement to the individual directly in charge of the place of confinement, giving the name, grade, and organization of the accused and the offense with which he is charged. This statement is usually presented with the accused or within 24 hours after his confinement. The prison officer must make a written report of the confinement to the base commander within 24 hours. It is a general rule that no person can be placed in confinement for minor offenses. Arrest and confinement are ordered as circumstances require. The latter normally is imposed only when the accused is charged with a very serious crime or when it is necessary to insure his presence in court.

* * *

Protection Against Self-Incrimination

The second fundamental area in safeguarding the rights of both civilian and military personnel in America is the protection afforded by the Constitution against arbitrary methods. Under military law, an accused person has at least three rights which, in general, cannot be denied him. They are:

1. The right to refuse to incriminate himself.
2. The right to legal counsel.
3. The right to plead "not guilty."

Everyone knows in a vague sort of way that these rights protecting a person accused of crime exist in civil life, but many people do not realize that these same rights are upheld to an even greater degree by military law. The statement, "Anything you say may be used against you," has its roots in the Constitution. A part of the Fifth Amendment states that no person shall be compelled in any criminal case to be a witness against himself. Article 31 of the *Uniform Code* extends the right of personal silence not only to one accused of crime but even to one merely under suspicion or investigation. Furthermore, the Article expressly prohibits the use in a court-martial of any statement obtained from an accused without first explaining to him this right of silence.

Another right given an accused by civil law is that of counsel. A person charged with committing a serious crime is entitled to be defended by a lawyer during the trial. In the event the accused cannot afford to hire a lawyer, the judge who is to preside at the trial will appoint a lawyer for the defense of such a person. The pay of this defense counsel is provided by a court fund supplied by taxes. In military law, Article 27 provides for the automatic appointment of a defense counsel for all special and general courts-martial. The accused does not have to do a thing to secure such counsel. In addition, the accused may have his own civilian defense counsel, but at his own expense.

A third general principle of civilian law allows the accused person to plead as he desires — "guilty" or "not guilty" — in court. The *Uniform Code* protects the accused even more than civilian law. It not only allows him to plead "not guilty" in any case; it actually prohibits a plea of guilty whenever the accused is tried for an offense for which the death penalty may be given.

Right to Remain Silent and Right to an Attorney*

In accordance with Article 31(b) of the *Uniform Code* and current Supreme Court decisions, a suspect must be advised of the following prior to interrogation.

---

*Failure to advise a suspect in accordance with Article 31(b) and as to his right to an attorney will render any subsequent confession inadmissible in trial by court-martial.

1. Of the nature of the offense
2. That he does not need to make any statement
3. That any statement he does make may be used as evidence against him in trial by court-martial
4. That he can retain a civilian attorney at his own expense
5. That a military attorney will be provided free of charge
6. That he can consult with an attorney prior to the interrogation
7. That he can have an attorney present during the interrogation
8. That he can terminate the interrogation at anytime.

Article 31(d), UCMJ, also provides that statements obtained by coercion, unlawful influence, or unlawful inducement are inadmissible in trial by court-martial.

Fundamental Elements of Military Due Process

Basic Rights of Every Member of the Armed Forces of the United States.

(a) To be informed of the charges against him
(b) To have a formal pretrial hearing prior to trial by general court-martial
(c) To be confronted by witnesses testifying against him
(d) To cross-examine witnesses for the Government
(e) To challenge court members for cause or peremptorily*
(f) To challenge the military judge for cause
(g) To have a specified number of members compose courts-martial
(h) To be represented by counsel*
(i) Not to be compelled to incriminate himself
(j) To have an involuntary confession excluded from consideration
(k) To have the court instructed on the elements of the offense, presumption of innocence, and burden of proof*
(l) To be found guilty of an offense only when designated number of members concur*
(m) To be sentenced only when certain number of members vote in the affirmative*
(n) To have a speedy trial

---

*These rights are waived when an accused elects trial by military judge alone.

(o) To have an appellate review

(p) To be free from unreasonable search and seizure

Fair Trial

In the final area of safeguarding an accused's fundamental rights, he is specifically guaranteed a fair hearing held without delay. This simply means that the accusation of crime must either be dropped entirely or the accused must be given a fair public trial, with no unnecessary delay in either event. The source of this right is the Sixth Amendment to the Constitution. It states: "In all criminal prosecutions, the accused shall enjoy the right to a speedy and public trial." The *Uniform Code* provides that "the proper authority shall take immediate steps to determine what disposition should be made [of the charges] in the interest of justice and discipline. . . ." It is a punishable offense for any person subject to the code to cause unnecessary delay in bringing an accused to trial.

In military law, the guarantee of a speedy public trial is assured from the moment that a specific criminal accusation is made against a particular person. Protection of the right begins with notice to such person. Under the code, the immediate commander of the accused informs him of the exact crime with which he is charged. If the accused is not available, his immediate commander must make a full written report of the circumstances, stating completely the reasons why such notice could not be made. Again, any unnecessary delay in making the notification or in explaining why it was not made may be punished as a separate offense under the *Uniform Code*.

As a further safeguard, the Manual forbids the withholding or accumulation of accusations against the accused. Only in exceptional situations will any delay be allowed and then generally only when the person concerned is not deprived of his personal liberty. For example, such a person may be allowed to continue a certain course of misconduct, such as disposing of stolen Government property, for the purpose of identifying any associates in the crime. The same principle may be used by the Federal Bureau of Investigation in trying to round up a spy ring by delaying the arrest of one spy in order to locate all his co-conspirators.

The protection against delay in bringing the accused to trial has already been mentioned in the general consideration of the accused's fundamental right to a speedy trial. There are two specific time limits that further spell out this right. The ordinary effect of these limits, relating to the trial of an accused, is to place a floor and a ceiling on the meaning of "speedy" in reference to trial. The Court of Military Appeals has established a limitation of 90 days between the date of placing an accused in pretrial confinement and the trial. Extraordinary circumstances, such as operational demands or a complicated investigation or requests for delay by the accused, are the only matters that will permit a delay beyond 90 days. Failure of the Government to prove that the delay between confinement and trial was reasonable will result in a dismissal of the charges and specifications. There is also a minimum time expressly suggested. Article 35 of the code provides that, in time of peace, no person may, against his objection, be brought to trial before a general court-martial within a period of five days after the service of the charges upon him or before a special court-martial within a period of three days after the service of the charges upon him. This protects an accused from the danger of too speedy a trial; that is, one in which insufficient time for preparing a proper legal defense has been allowed.

As a matter of general practice, counsel for the accused often requests and receives additional time delays in order to conduct further legal research, to conduct further investigation, or to obtain additional witnesses, all of which may be necessary for the proper defense of the accused.

Formal Pretrial Investigation—Article 32

Another important protection under military law assuring an accused of a fair public trial is provided by Article 32. This article calls for a careful, formal pretrial investigation into accusations of crime, or serious misconduct, made against anyone subject to the *Uniform Code* before and when such accusations may result in trial by general court-martial. The *Manual* specifies that the investigating officer be mature and preferably hold the rank of major or higher or have legal training and experience. The purpose of the investigation is to find out whether the crime charged against an accused rests on facts or reasonable inferences (i.e., logical conclusions drawn from facts). It is not the task of the investigating officer to prosecute an accused. He is given an accusation. All that he must do is to look thoroughly and impartially into all the available facts on which the accusation is based. The conclusion that he draws from such an examination of the facts serves as the basis for his recommendation to the commander who ordered the investigation. He recommends whether the accused should be tried or cleared; and, if he recommends trial, whether it should be by summary, special, or general court-martial.

At the start of such an investigation, the accused must be informed of the specific accusation against him and the name of the person who made it. He has a right to be represented by legal counsel during the investigation, to hear what witnesses have to say against him, and to call witnesses in his own behalf during the investigation. All of these rights must be disclosed to him. There is no legal presumption that he knows them unless he is told at the beginning of the investigation.

The formal pretrial investigation is somewhat like the grand jury under the criminal law of civil life, but it offers more protection to the accused person. Thus, an accused being investigated by a grand jury in civil life is not assured of representation by counsel. Ordinarily, he is not present at the meetings of the grand jury looking into the charge of criminal conduct against him. The *Uniform Code* makes it the legal right of a person subject to the code to be present at all hearings conducted by the investigating officer. This presence means that the accused may be there in person, be represented by counsel, or both. The right of an accused person to a pretrial investigation into criminal accusation against him is a practical guarantee against a general court-martial based on flimsy, ill-considered, or trumped-up charges. The fundamental right to a fair trial is guarded at the very outset by this process of investigation.

* * *

Summary Court-Martial

The summary court-martial (Table 16.1) is discussed in three phases: (1) a summary court-martial and its purpose; (2) the limits of its power; and (3) its description of the activities before trial, during trial, and after trial.

The specific authority in law establishing this court is found in Articles 16 and 20 of the *Uniform Code*. Article 16 fixes the basic "what," stating that, for the summary court-martial, one officer is judge, trial counsel and defense counsel all wrapped into one. . . .

The summary court-martial is somewhat like the civilian traffic court or police court. By definition, it is a court without a jury, just as the civilian police court is. It is established to try less serious criminal charges almost immediately after detection of the offense. The ordinary city police court, for example, hears cases dealing with offenses that have occurred for the most part within the 24 hours preceding trial. The summary court-martial usually holds trial of an accused person within two to five days of the time that charges are formally made. For example, in the usual case of absence without leave—perhaps where the accused was AWOL five days—when charges are sent to a summary court for trial, the accused would very likely be tried not later than three or four days after his return to duty. Thus, this court acts promptly after accusation of crime is sent to it for trial, generally very soon after the offense is committed.

In conducting the trial itself, the summary court-martial also acts promptly. The trial usually lasts no more than several hours. This feature of promptness, based on a simplified procedure, gives the court its distinguishing name. In law, "summary" means a short, concise trial process following in relatively immediate sequence after a crime. Thus, the summary court-martial exercises justice promptly under a simplified procedure.

The three-sided role of the summary court-martial in representing both the accused and the Government and in acting as judge dictates a technical qualification in addition to the desirable personal characteristics just discussed. It is this: ordinarily an officer who is the accuser in a case will not act as summary court-martial in the trial of that case.

. . . The summary court-martial is restricted as to whom it may try. It may lawfully try airmen who consent to trial by summary court-martial. Article 20, UCMJ, provides that any airman, whether he has previ-

TABLE 16.1 Composition, Appointment, and Jurisdiction of Courts-Martial*

Court	Required Membership	Convening Authority	Persons Triable	Offenses Triable	Maximum Punishment
Summary	1 commissioned officer (Art. 16).	Commander of a detached squadron or other detachment, or higher command of the Air Force (Art. 24).	Enlisted men; unless they object to trial by SCM (Art. 20), in which event they may be tried by SpCM or GCM.	Any offense not capital made punishable by the Uniform Code (Art. 20).	E-4 and below: confinement at hard labor for 1 month, forfeiture of ⅔ of 1 month's pay (Art. 20), and reduction to airman basic. E-5 and above: one grade reduction, restriction for 2 months and forfeiture of ⅔ of 1 month's pay.
Special	3 or more members and a military judge; or a military judge alone, if requested; or 3 or more members without a military judge (normally may not impose a bad conduct discharge) (Art. 16).	Commander of a wing, base, or separate squadron (Art. 23).	Any person subject to the Uniform Code (Art. 19).	Any offense not capital made punishable by the Uniform Code (Art. 19).	Enlisted men: bad conduct discharge, confinement at hard labor for 6 months, forfeiture of ⅔ pay per month for 6 months (Art. 19), and reduction to airman basic. Officers: reprimand, forfeiture of ⅔ pay per month for 6 months, and 2 months' restriction.
General	5 or more members and a military judge; or a military judge alone, if requested in noncapital cases (Art. 16).	Commander of an air command, air force, air division, or separate wing of the Air Force, and commanders designated by the Secretary of the Air Force (Art. 22).	Any person subject to the Uniform Code (Art. 18).	Any offense made punishable by the Uniform Code (Art. 18).	Any punishment authorized by law or customs of service, not forbidden by the code (Art. 18).

*Reprinted by permission from *Military Law:* published 1974 by Air Force Reserve Officers Training Corps, Maxwell AFB, AL 36112.

ously been offered and refused punishment under Article 15, may refuse to be tried by a summary court-martial. Under Air Force policy, an accused must first be offered and have refused an Article 15 before he can be offered a summary court-martial. The summary court-martial has no power to try officers, warrant officers, cadets, aviation cadets, or midshipmen because the law (Article 20) specifically excepts these persons. However, the summary court-martial does have the power under law (Article 46) to compel civilian witnesses, as well as military, to appear and testify. This latter power is similar to that of our Federal courts and covers all the United States, its territories, and possessions. The authority to compel witnesses to testify in a trial by any court-martial is backed by a penalty for refusal to appear. Article 47 of the code provides punishment by a fine of $500, six months in jail, or both.

The power of the court with respect to offenses is described by Article 20 in broad terms. It is given as the authority to try certain cases involving "any noncapital offense made punishable" by the *Uniform Code*. Does this mean that this court could try an airman accused of any offense, under the code, except those for which the death sentence may be given? If this is taken literally, the summary court could try all cases, except murder, treason, spying, and a few other crimes punishable by death. However, custom and Air Force policy, as well as the *Manual for Court-Martial* act to restrict the apparently broad power of the summary court-martial to relatively minor offenses.

The limits on this court's power to punish convicted offenders are fixed expressly in Article 20 and paragraph 16b of the Manual. The law generally limits the maximum power of the summary court-martial to these punishments:

1. Confinement at hard labor for one month.
2. Hard labor without confinement for 34 days.
3. Restriction for two months.
4. Forfeiture or detention of two-thirds pay for one month.
5. Reduction to next lower grade for staff sergeant and above; reduction to airman basic for any grade below staff sergeant.

* * *

When the summary court-martial is satisfied that the charge is correct and in proper form, together with all supporting papers, he makes arrangements for the trial. He reserves the use of a courtroom or other proper place to serve as a courtroom. He notifies all witnesses whose presence is required at the trial. Finally, he makes reasonably certain that the accused will be present at the time fixed for trial.

The trial begins, as a matter of procedure, at the time set by the summary court-martial. As soon as the accused presents himself, the first action taken by the court is to inform the accused of the following:

1. What the general accusation is.
2. That the accusation is before summary court-martial.
3. Who appointed the court.
4. Who the accuser is.
5. Who will be witnesses against the accused.
6. That the accused has a right to cross-examine all witnesses
7. That the accused may call all witnesses in his favor.
8. That the accused may make a sworn statement on the issue of his guilt or innocence, or may remain silent.
9. What the maximum sentence could be if the accused is found guilty.
10. That it is the duty of the court to help the accused in every way possible; for instance, in cross-examining witnesses against the accused.

The second step of procedure following advice by the court is very important. It actually is a test of the legal authority of the court to try the case. The summary court-martial must obtain a written statement from the accused that he does not object to trial by summary court-martial. A provision for this is made on the charge sheet. If the accused objects to trial by summary court-martial, the trial may not proceed. In such an event, the charges are returned to the convening authority. At the latter's discretion, the charges may be sent to a special court-martial or referred to an Article 32 investigating officer for possible trial by a general court-martial. Or, again at his discretion, they may be dropped entirely. The accused will not be put in the position of being able to demand specific trial as a matter of individual right. The right to prosecute belongs to the Government; it alone may exercise that right. The point is that, here again, by provision of Article 20, there is a strong protection of the individual's prerogative of justice and fair play.

If the accused consents to trial, the summary court-martial will proceed with the trial.

* * *

After the accused has been acquitted or convicted, the summary court-martial is responsible for preparing an official record of the trial. This record is prepared in five copies. If the trial resulted in an acquittal, no entry is made in the service record of the accused, nor can the record of trial be used in any way to prejudice a person found innocent.

The record is the basis for review by higher authority. This review is significant principally in the case of a conviction. If the summary court-martial finds an accused guilty, the convening authority (usually the groups or wing commander) will examine the record to see that the trial was lawful and just and that the sentence given was legal. If the convening authority finds the trial illegal, he may do one of two things: dismiss the charges or order a rehearing. If he finds the trial legal, the sentence legal, and everything in order, he may again do one of two things: disapprove the sentence or approve the sentence in whole or in part. He cannot increase the punishment. Even though the sentence is legal, the convening authority may want to reduce it. He may do this by approving only a part of the sentence. This partial approval, in effect, cuts down the severity of a sentence, and it is a prerogative of the commander. This right is known as the clemency power.

But review does not stop at the wing base level in the case of a finding of guilty by summary court-martial. Two copies of the record of trial are sent to the officer exercising general court-martial authority. This officer has a trained military lawyer, his staff judge advocate, who reviews the record for legal sufficiency. If it was an illegal or incomplete trial according to the record, the officer having general court-martial authority may do one of three things: he may set aside all or part of the sentence, order a rehearing, or send the record back to the authority who convened the court, informing him that he is authorized to withdraw approval of the finding of guilty. If the latter is the course taken, the convening authority must either dismiss the charges or order a rehearing. This is the last step in the review of a record of trial by summary court-martial involving a conviction.

Special and General Courts-Martial

The special and general courts-martial are the other two forums for determining the innocence or guilt of an accused under military law (see Table 16.1). These courts-martial are normally composed of several members and are somewhat similar in their composition to the civilian courts under the judge and jury system.

Although, normally, the special and general courts-martial consist of several members, an accused may be tried by a special or general court-martial consisting of only a military judge. This one-officer special or general court-martial is authorized only in noncapital cases, if the accused requests trial by judge alone in writing after consultation with defense counsel and if the military judge approves the request. This procedure is somewhat related to the right in civilian courts to waive a jury trial and to be tried by a judge alone.

The special court-martial normally consists of three or more members and may, in addition, include a military judge. . . .

The general court-martial normally consists of five or more members and a military judge. However, as indicated above, the general court-martial may consist of a military judge alone but only when the accused so requests. The one-officer general court-martial does not have jurisdiction to try a person for an offense in which the death penalty could be adjudged unless the case has previously been referred to trial as a noncapital case.

The authority of a court to hear and decide cases is known as the jurisdiction of the court. Criminal jurisdiction, as it relates to special and general courts-martial, is the power and authority given a court to try certain persons to determine whether a crime has been committed and to determine the guilt or innocence of the accused.

Jurisdiction of the Courts

Jurisdiction consists of three elements: the authority to try the accused, the authority to hear the offense, and the power to sentence the accused. Jurisdiction, then, is related to courts-martial because courts-martial have authority to try persons accused of committing crimes and power to impose a sentence. In the development of both the special and general courts-martial, the degree of authority or jurisdiction over offenses and persons can be seen as the distinguishing feature of these two courts. The authority, or jurisdiction, of each is responsible for the differences in the composition and in the qualifications of the members and officials of the two courts.

The authority of these courts over persons is identical; that is, any person subject to the *Uniform Code* may be tried by either the special or general court-martial. The special court-martial, however, does not have the broad power of the general court-martial over offenses. Specifically, the special court-martial has jurisdiction only over noncapital offenses punishable by the code (Article 19), whereas a general court-martial has jurisdiction over both noncapital and capital offenses. (A capital offense is one for which the death penalty *may* be imposed.)

Under the *Uniform Code,* the imposition of the death sentence is mandatory upon conviction of spying (Article 106), and imposition of either death or life imprisonment is mandatory upon conviction of premeditated or felony murder [Article 118(1) and (4)]. Because of this, a person accused of one of these crimes could never be tried by a special court-martial. There are other capital offenses, however, for which the death sentence, while permissible, is not mandatory. Persons accused of these offenses could be tried by a special court-martial if the officer who has the power to convene a general court-martial refers such a case for trial by a special court-martial. Further limitations to the severity and types of punishment that each court-martial may impose are discussed below.

The special court-martial, under such limitations as the President of the United States may prescribe (Article 56 of the UCMJ), may adjudge any sentence not forbidden by the code, except death, dismissal (in the case of an officer), or dishonorable discharge. The *Manual for Courts-Martial* allows a special court-martial to impose the following sentences:

1. Bad conduct discharge.
2. Confinement for not more than six months.
3. Hard labor without confinement for not more than three months.
4. Restriction to certain limits for a period of time not to exceed two months.
5. Forfeiture of up to two-thirds pay per month not to exceed six months.
6. Detention of up to two-thirds pay per month not to exceed three months.
7. Reduction.

However, reduction in grade, confinement, hard labor without confinement, or a bad conduct discharge may only be adjudged against enlisted personnel. A bad conduct discharge may not be adjudged by a special court-martial unless a complete record of the proceedings and testimony has been made, certified counsel provided to the accused, and a military judge detailed to the trial. The only exception to the requirement for a military judge before a bad conduct discharge can be imposed by a special court-martial is in case a military judge could not be detailed to a trial because of physical conditions or military exigencies. The bad conduct discharge is less severe than a dishonorable discharge, and it is designed as a punishment for bad conduct. It is a means of punishment for those who should be separated punitively under conditions other than honorable. These limitations on the power of the special court-martial to prescribe punishment are consistent with its limitations of jurisdiction over offenses.

The general court-martial has no such limitations on its power over offenses, except that the general court-martial consisting of a military judge only may not try a person for a capital offense unless the case has been referred to trial as a noncapital case. Under Article 18 of the code, the general court-martial has jurisdiction to try any person subject to the code for any offense made punishable by the code. It may, under such limitations as the President may prescribe [see Table 16–1], adjudge any punishment not forbidden by the code, including dismissal, dishonorable discharge, or bad conduct discharge. A dishonorable discharge is reserved for those who should be separated under conditions of dishonor. A sentence to dismissal of an officer is, in general, the equivalent of a dishonorable discharge of an airman or warrant officer. The authority of general courts-martial to adjudge sentences and punishments of a much greater degree of severity determines the relative importance of the two courts. The special court-martial may be thought of as an intermediate court, and the general court-martial as the highest trial court of the military.

Composition of the Courts

The difference in the degree of importance of the two courts is reflected in their composition. The special court-martial, as we have indicated, consists of three or more members and a military judge, or it may consist of a military judge, or it may consist of a military judge only if the accused requests trial by military judge alone and if the judge approves the request. In addition to the composition of the court as indicated above, the code (Article 27) requires a trial counsel who acts as prosecutor of the case for the United States and a defense counsel for the accused. Assistant counsel may be appointed as necessary.

The general court-martial consists of a military judge and five or more members of the court. The general court-martial may consist of a military judge alone if the accused requests it and if the military judge alone approves the request. In addition, counsel for the Government and counsel to defend the accused are provided. Both trial and defense counsel must belong to the bar of a Federal court or of the highest court of a state and be certified as competent counsel by the Judge Advocate General of the Air Force. An accused may, however, be represented by individual defense counsel, such as a civilian attorney provided at his own expense. If at any time the membership of a general or special court is reduced below the statutory number, i.e., general court – 5, special court – 3, the court will adjourn until a new member or members are detailed and qualified to sit on the Court.

The *Manual for Courts-Martial* requires that court reporters, clerks, and orderlies be provided whenever their services are necessary. While the general court-martial is in session, a reporter is always present. Reporters must also be present at special court-martial trials if a bad conduct discharge could be given as punishment. They are not supplied for trial by summary court-martial. Occasionally, the services of an interpreter are required during a trial. If such a need is anticipated, arrangements should be completed before the trial to insure the presence of such an individual.

The eligibility rules for members of either the special or general court-martial are few and simple. The following four rules indicate that eligibility is determined in a large measure by the rank or status of the accused:

1. Ordinarily no member of a court will be of lower rank than the accused.
2. A commissioned officer must be tried by commissioned officers.
3. A warrant officer must be tried by warrant officers or commissioned officers.
4. If an enlisted person requests enlisted members on the court that tries him, at least one-third of the court must be enlisted persons, but they may not be members of the same unit as the accused.

The senior member in rank among the members sitting at the trial is the president of the court. The *Manual for Courts-Martial* provides that, whenever possible, the president of a general or special court-martial should be an officer whose rank is not below that of an Air Force Captain.

The duties of the president of a court-martial with a military judge are different from those of a president of a special court-martial without a military judge. The president of a court-martial with a military judge has the same duties as other members of a court. In addition, he consults with the military judge as to the time of assembling the court, prescribes the uniform, administers oaths as required, presides over closed sessions of the court, and speaks for the members of the court in conferring with or requesting instructions from the military judge.

The president of a special court-martial without a military judge is in a position of far greater responsibility. The reason is that he not only presides during closed sessions of the court but also performs the duties that would normally be performed by the military judge, i.e., presiding at the hearings in open session. He rules on all questions of law and on procedural questions except challenges. He has the primary responsibility of declaring whether a point of evidence or a step in procedure is correct in law, but his greatest responsibility, perhaps, occurs near the end of the trial before the court closes to make its determination of the guilt or innocence of the accused. At that time, he is required by law to instruct the members of the court on the law that will guide them during their deliberations in closed sessions. These instructions are given in open court in the presence of counsel and the accused. The instructions to the court must thoroughly and completely cover the elements of each offense charged, the meaning and application of the presumption of innocence, reasonable doubt, and burden of proof.

* * *

A feature of the special and general courts-martial that distinguishes them from the summary court-martial is advocacy, or "taking sides." For the special and general courts, a trial counsel (the Government advocate) and the defense counsel and whatever assistants are needed are appointed to represent both sides. The members of the courts and the military judge, of course, remain impartial.

Ordinarily, no one who has acted as investigating officer may be either trial or defense counsel. However, if the accused so chooses, he may request as defense or assistant defense counsel an officer who has previously investigated the case. But with or without the consent of the accused, no person who has acted for the prosecution shall subsequently act in the same case for the defense, and no person who has acted for the defense shall act in the same case for the prosecution.

As previously mentioned, in a general court-martial, both trial and defense counsel must belong to the bar of a Federal court or of the highest court of a state and must be certified as competent counsel by the Judge Advocate General of the Air Force. . . .

If counsel are not so qualified, a bad conduct discharge may not be adjudged by the court. The law requires that counsel for opposing sides in a special court-martial be evenly matched professionally. This exemplifies another way in which military justice safeguards individual's rights

Appellate Review

* * *

The appeal and review process which is automatically provided for in the *Uniform Code of Military Justice* (Articles 65, 66, 67, 69, and 70) is very elaborate. It is a positive illustration of the strong safeguards for justice to the individual which the Congress has enacted as an integral part of military law.

Appellate review can never cause a sentence to be increased in severity nor can an acquittal ever be changed to a conviction. Practically speaking, appellate review gives the accused person tremendous safeguards of liberty and freedom.

Historical Background

Historically, military law was regarded as summary in nature. The term "summary" did not mean that trial procedure was unfair, hasty, or unsolicitous of the rights of the accused but, rather, meant that the institution of the proceedings was relatively more swift than in civilian procedure and that punishment swiftly followed a sentence.

* * *

The *Uniform Code of Military Justice,* enacted on May 1950, established the United States Court of Military Appeals in addition to continuing the Board of Review. The code was amended in 1968 to change the name of the Boards of Review to Courts of Military Review.

Initial Review of Records of Trial

After every trial by court-martial, the record of trial is reviewed for legal sufficiency and appropriateness of the sentence by the authority who convened the court. No trial by court-martial is complete without such review and written approval or disapproval of the findings and sentence by the convening authority. A sentence of a court-martial may not be executed until approved by the convening authority. The convening authority has the power to approve any portion of the findings or sentence that he finds to be correct in law. He may disapprove any findings or sentence in whole or in part which he believes to be inappropriate. In this connection, he has the power to rewrite any portion of the sentence that he believes to be inappropriate and to suspend the execution of any sentence that he has approved, except a sentence of death. He may, in certain instances, order a rehearing of the case.

* * *

Records of trial by special court-martial involving an approved sentence to a bad conduct discharge and all records of trial by general court-martial are reviewed by the officer exercising general court-martial jurisdiction. He must take action to approve or disapprove the findings and sentence as approved by the convening authority. He also has the power of remission or suspension. Before acting upon the record, the

officer exercising general court-martial jurisdiction receives the formal written review of
the record and advice of his staff judge
advocate. This review and the action then
become a part of the record, which is
forwarded to the Judge Advocate General of
the Air Force.

Every record of trial by a general court-
martial must be examined in the office of the
Judge Advocate General, USAF. This examination is made by thoroughly qualified
judge advocates, usually field grade officers.
All records of trial involving a sentence to a
bad conduct discharge (including those imposed by special court-martial), a dishonorable discharge, or confinement for one year
or more are examined by the Court of Military Review.

Court of Military Review

Article 66 of the code requires the Judge
Advocate General to establish a Court of
Military Review. This court may consist of
several panels, and each panel is composed
of not less than three appellate military
judges who are military lawyers normally in
the rank of colonel and lieutenant colonel.
However, civilian lawyers could also be
appointed to this court. There are as many
panels in existence at any given time as the
needs of the Air Force demand. The court
may sit in panels or as a whole. The Court of
Military Review is required to review the
record of trial in every case in which the
sentence affects a general officer or extends
to death, dismissal, dishonorable or bad
conduct discharge, or confinement for one
year or more.

The Court of Military Review acts only
with respect to the findings and sentences as
approved by proper authority. It has generally the same powers with respect to modification of a sentence as does the convening
authority. In considering the record, the
court weighs the evidence, judges the credibility of witnesses, and determines controverted questions of fact, recognizing that the
trial court saw and heard witnesses. The
Court of Military Review has authority to
dismiss the charges completely against a
person convicted by a court-martial and
order him to be released as though he had
originally been acquitted. A Court might

take such action, for example, if it found that
a conviction had been based on evidence
insufficient to prove the offense charged. The
Court of Military Review also has the power
to approve any record of trial that it
examines and finds legally sufficient.

The accused may be represented before
the Court of Military Review by a civilian
attorney retained by him or by appellate
defense counsel detailed by the Judge Advocate General. The Government is in turn
represented by appellate Government counsel appointed by the Judge Advocate General.

Unless further action is required by the
President, Secretary of the Air Force, or
Court of Military Appeals, the Judge Advocate General instructs the convening authority to take action in accordance with the
decision of the Court of Military Review.
Sentences extending to death or involving a
general officer must also be approved by the
President. Sentences involving the dismissal
of an officer may not be executed until
approved by the Secretary of the Air Force.
Action by the Court of Military Appeals is
necessary under the conditions specified in
the next section.

The United States Court of Military Appeals

The United States Court of Military Appeals is located in Judiciary Square, Washington, D.C. It is a civilian court consisting
of three civilian judges appointed by the
President, by and with the advice and
consent of the Senate, for terms of 15 years.
If any judge of the court is temporarily
unable to perform his duties because of
illness or other disability, the President may
designate a judge of the United States Courts
of Appeals to fill the office for the period of
disability.

In addition to the three judges, the court
has a staff of approximately 40 employees,
all civilians.

Although the court is located in the
Department of Defense for administrative
purposes, it is judicially independent. The
court officially started operating on 25 July
1951, at which time, in an open session, the
court admitted the first members to its bar.

In its first 22 years of existence, the court

reviewed over 28,000 cases. The code provides that review of cases by the court may occur in three different ways:

(1) All cases in which the sentence, as affirmed by the Court of Military Review, affects a general or flag officer or extends to death.

(2) All cases reviewed by the Court of Military Review which the Judge Advocate General orders forwarded to the Court of Military Appeals for review.

(3) All cases reviewed by a Court of Military Review in which, upon petition of the accused and on good cause shown, the Court of Military Appeals has granted a review.

In any case reviewed by it, the United States Court of Military Appeals acts only with respect to the findings and sentence as approved by the convening authority and as affirmed or set aside as incorrect in law by the Court of Military Review. The court may take action only with respect to matters of law.

* * *

Review of the Judge Advocate General

The Judge Advocate General, in accordance with Article 69 of the *Uniform Code,* has authority to review cases not otherwise reviewed by the Court of Military Review. Prior to the Military Justice Act of 1968, his Article 69 review power was limited to certain general courts-martial. Article 69 now gives the Judge Advocate General the power to review and to vacate or modify in whole or in part the findings or sentence, or both, in any court-martial involving a finding of guilt and a sentence which has been finally reviewed but has not been reviewed by the Court of Military Review. Such action is instituted by petition and must be based on newly discovered evidence, fraud in the court, lack of jurisdiction over the accused or the offense, or error prejudicial to the substantial rights of the accused. Thus, whether tried by summary, special, or general court-martial, a convicted and sentenced accused now has an avenue of appeal to the Judge Advocate General.

16.02 THE MILITARY JUSTICE PROCESS

Courts-Martial of Ex-Servicemen

UNITED STATES ex rel. TOTH v. QUARLES

Supreme Court of the United States, 1955
350 U.S. 11, 7 S. Ct. 1, 100 L. Ed. 8

Robert Toth served with the United States Air Force in Korea and was honorably discharged. He returned to his home in Pittsburgh and began work in a steel plant. Five months later he was arrested by military authorities on charges of committing murder and conspiring to commit murder while serving in the armed forces in Korea in violation of the Uniform Code of Military Justice. At the time of his arrest he had no relationship with the military. He was taken to Korea to stand trial before a court-martial under authority of Article 3(a) of the Uniform Code of Military Justice (U.C.M.J.), which authorized courts-martial of former servicemen for all crimes punishable by five years' or more imprisonment and for which an accused could not be tried in any federal district court. Toth's sister, Audrey Toth, filed a petition for habeas corpus in the federal District Court (D.D.C.), which ordered Toth released from custody on the ground that the military authorities had no jurisdiction to remove him to Korea for trial without a prior hearing. The United States Court of Appeals (D.C. Cir.) reversed, and in sustaining the act, held that ex-servicemen could be tried by court-martial. The United States Supreme Court granted certiorari.

Mr. Justice BLACK delivered the opinion of the Court.

* * *

... The Government's contention is that the Act is a valid exercise of the power granted Congress in Article 1 of the Constitution "To make Rules for the Government and Regulation of the land and naval Forces," as supplemented by the Necessary and Proper Clause.

This Court has held that the Article 1 Clause just quoted authorizes Congress to subject persons actually in the armed service to trial by court-martial for military and naval offenses. Later it was held that court-martial jurisdiction could be exerted over a dishonorably discharged soldier then a military prisoner serving a sentence imposed by a prior court-martial. It has never been intimated by this Court, however, that the Article 1 military jurisdiction could be extended to civilian ex-soldiers who had severed all relationship with the military and its institutions. To allow this extension of military authority would require an extremely broad construction of the language used in the constitutional provision relied on. For given its natural meaning, the power granted Congress "To make Rules" to regulate "the land and naval Forces" would seem to restrict court-martial jurisdiction to persons who are actually members of part of the armed forces. There is a compelling reason for construing the clause this way: any expansion of court-martial jurisdiction like that in the 1950 Act necessarily encroaches on the jurisdiction of federal courts set up under Article 3 of the Constitution where persons on trial are surrounded with more constitutional safeguards than in military tribunals.

Article 3 provides for the establishment of a court system as one of the separate but coordinate branches of the National Government. It is the primary, indeed the sole, business of these courts to try cases and controversies between individuals and between individuals and the Government. This includes trial of criminal cases. These courts are presided over by judges appointed for life, subject only to removal by impeachment. Their compensation cannot be diminished during their continuance in office. The provisions of Article 3 were designed to give judges maximum freedom from possible coercion or influence by the executive or legislative branches of the Government. But the Constitution and the Amendments in the Bill of Rights show that the Founders were not satisfied with leaving determination of guilt or innocence to judges, even though wholly independent. They further provided that no person should be held to answer in those courts for capital or other infamous crimes unless on the presentment or indictment of a grand jury drawn from the body of the people. Other safeguards designed to protect defendants against oppressive governmental practices were included. One of these was considered so important to liberty of the individual that it appears in two parts of the Constitution. Article 3, § 2, commands that the "Trial of all Crimes, except in Cases of Impeachment, shall be by Jury; and such Trial shall be held in the State where the said Crimes shall have been committed; but when not committed within any State, the Trial shall be at such Place or Places as the Congress may by Law have directed." And the Sixth Amendment provides that "In all criminal prosecutions, the accused shall enjoy the right to a speedy and public trial, by an impartial jury of the state and district wherein the crime shall have been committed. . . ." This right of trial by jury ranks very high in our catalogue of constitutional safeguards.

We find nothing in the history of constitutional treatment of military tribunals which entitles them to rank along with Article 3 courts as adjudicators of the guilt or innocence of people charged with offenses for which they can be deprived of their life, liberty or property. . . .

. . . There is a great difference between trial by jury and trial by selected members of the military forces. It is true that military personnel because of their training and experience may be especially competent to try soldiers for infractions of military rules. Such training is no doubt particularly important where an offense charged against a soldier is purely military, such as disobedience of an order, leaving post, etc. But whether right or wrong, the premise underlying the constitutional method for determining guilt or innocence in federal courts is that laymen are better than specialists to perform this task. This idea is inherent in the institution of trial by jury.

Juries fairly chosen from different walks of

life bring into the jury box a variety of different experiences, feelings, intuitions and habits. Such juries may reach completely different conclusions than would be reached by specialists in any single field, including specialists in the military field. . . .

The 1950 Act here considered deprives of jury trial and sweeps under military jurisdiction over 3,000,000 persons who have become veterans since the Act became effective. That number is bound to grow from year to year; there are now more than 3,000,000 men and women in uniform. These figures point up what would be the enormous scope of a holding that Congress could subject every ex-serviceman and woman in the land to trial by court-martial for any alleged offense committed while he or she had been a member of the armed forces. Every veteran discharged since passage of the 1950 Act is subject to military trial for any offense punishable by as much as five years' imprisonment unless the offense is now punishable in a civilian court. And one need only glance at the Military Code to see what a vast number and variety of offenses are thus brought under military jurisdiction. . . . Under the present law courts-martial have jurisdiction only if no civilian court does. But that might also be changed by Congress. Thus there is justification for treating the Act as a mere minor increase of congressional power to expand military jurisdiction. It is a great change both actually and potentially.

Fear has been expressed that if this law is not sustained discharged soldiers may escape punishment altogether for crimes they commit while in the service. But that fear is not warranted and was not shared by the Judge Advocate General of the Army. . . . He asked Congress to "confer jurisdiction upon Federal courts to try any person for an offense denounced by the [military] code if he is no longer subject thereto. This would be consistent with the fifth amendment of the Constitution." . . . It is conceded that it was wholly within the constitutional power of Congress to follow this suggestion and provide for federal district court trials of discharged soldiers accused of offenses committed while in the armed services. This concession is justified. U.S. Const. Art. 3, § 2; . . . There can be no valid argument, therefore, that civilian ex-servicemen must be tried by court-martial or not tried at all. If that is so it is only because Congress has not seen fit to subject them to trial in federal district courts.

* * *

There are dangers lurking in military trials which were sought to be avoided by the Bill of Rights and Article 3 of our Constitution. Free countries of the world have tried to restrict military tribunals to the narrowest jurisdiction deemed absolutely essential to maintaining discipline among troops in active service. . . . [A]rmy discipline will not be improved by court-martialing rather than trying by jury some civilian ex-soldier who has been wholly separated from the service for months, years or perhaps decades. Consequently considerations of discipline provide no excuse for new expansion of court-martial jurisdiction at the expense of the normal and constitutionally preferable system of trial and jury.

Determining the scope of the constitutional power of Congress to authorize trial by court-martial presents another instance calling for limitation to *"the least possible power adequate to the end proposed."* We hold that Congress cannot subject civilians like Toth to trial by court-martial. They, like other civilians are entitled to have the benefit of safeguards afforded those tried in the regular courts authorized by Article 3 of the Constitution.

Reversed.

Mr. Justice REED, with whom Mr. Justice BURTON and Mr. Justice MINTON join, dissenting.

* * *

The judgment just announced turns loose, without trial or possibility of trial, a man accused of murder. In future similar cases among the military, if Congress enacts the substitute law as the Court suggests, . . . the accused must face a jury far removed from the scene of the alleged crime and before jurors without the understanding of the quality and character of a military crime possessed by those accustomed to administer the Uniform Code of Military Justice. Or perhaps those accused will be extradited and tried by foreign law.

The congressional power under Article 1 of the Constitution to regulate the armed forces is conceded by the Court to embrace the power to provide for trial by court-martial and military punishment for violations of the Military Code. But the Court holds that that power ceases when the serviceman becomes a civilian. Nothing, we think, in the words of Article 1 or in the history of that congressional power justifies limiting trial and punishment by the military, for crimes committed by members of the armed services, to the period of service. Certainly the power of Congress to provide for a military trial and punishment for a breach of the Military Code on charges brought before the end of enlistment or discharge may continue thereafter. . . .

* * *

Mr. Justice MINTON, whom Mr. Justice BURTON joins, dissenting.

* * *

A civilian not under the jurisdiction of the Military Code has a right to be tried in a civil court for an alleged crime as a civilian. My trouble is that I don't think Toth was a full-fledged civilian. By 50 U.S.C. § 553 Congress had retained jurisdiction to try Toth for a crime he had committed while a soldier and for which admittedly he could have been tried by court-martial if the United States had discovered his crime one minute before discharge.

He was not a full-fledged civilian under his discharge. He was still a soldier to answer to court-martial for the crime he had committed while a soldier. He had a conditional discharge only. The United States clearly reserved the right to charge and try him by court-martial for a crime committed while in the status of a soldier. This is the way Congress had provided for his trial. No other way was provided. That it may have provided another way is not to say the way provided is invalid.

I know of no reason why Congress could not pass this statute, 50 U.S.C. § 553, retaining court-martial jurisdiction over Toth to answer for a crime he allegedly committed when he was clearly subject to court-martial. . . .

Comments

1. "Ex rel.," or "ex relatione," means "on relation" and indicates that the government is bringing suit on behalf of one party against another. The legal proceedings are usually instituted by the attorney general in the name and on behalf of the federal government (or state) on the basis of information given by an individual who has a private interest in the matter. The case is said to be taken "on the relation" of this interested party, who is called the "relator." In the *Toth* case, Toth's sister was the relator.

   In *Toth*, the Court held that ex-servicemen are not subject to military jurisdiction for offenses they committed while in the service. Are any of the following "civilians" within the meaning of *Toth*: Retired military personnel? Weekend reservists? One who is AWOL beyond the normal statute of limitations? Can there ever be a "military necessity" for subjecting an ex-serviceman to military jurisdiction? After reading the introductory section of the chapter, would you prefer trial by a military or a civilian court?

2. In *Reid* v. *Covert*, 354 U.S. 1 (1957), the Supreme Court held that civilian dependents of members of the armed forces stationed overseas could not be constitutionally tried by a court-martial in times of peace for capital offenses committed abroad. Three years later, in *Kinsella* v. *United States ex rel. Singleton*, 361 U.S. 234 (1960), the Supreme Court reached the same result in a noncapital case. In companion cases to *Kinsella*, the Supreme Court held that civilian employees of the armed forces overseas are not subject to military jurisdiction for their criminal offenses. *Grisham* v. *Hagan*,

361 U.S. 278 (1960) (capital offense); *McElroy* v. *United States,* 361 U.S. 281 (1960) (noncapital case).

3.   Do you agree with Justices Minton and Burton (dissenting in *Toth*) that a discharge from the service is only "conditional"? Since only military courts had jurisdiction to try Toth, he had to be released without any possibility of a civilian trial for murder. Today ex-servicemen can be tried in civilian courts for their crimes committed while in the service.

"Service-Connected" Crimes

O'CALLAHAN v. PARKER

Supreme Court of the United States, 1969
395 U.S. 258, 89 S. Ct. 1683, 23 L. Ed. 2d 291

The facts are stated in the opinion.

Mr. Justice DOUGLAS delivered the opinion of the Court.

Petitioner, then a sergeant in the United States Army, was stationed in July 1956, at Fort Shafter, Oahu, in the Territory of Hawaii. On the night of July 20, while on an evening pass, petitioner and a friend left the post dressed in civilian clothes and went into Honolulu. After a few beers in the bar of a hotel, petitioner entered the residential part of the hotel where he broke into the room of a young girl and assaulted and attempted to rape her. While fleeing from her room into Waikiki Beach, he was apprehended by a hotel security officer who delivered him to the Honolulu city police for questioning. After determining that he was a member of the Armed Forces, the city police delivered petitioner to the military police. After extensive interrogation, petitioner confessed and was placed in military confinement.

Petitioner was charged with attempted rape, housebreaking, and assault with intent to rape, in violation of Articles 80, 130, and 134 of the Uniform Code of Military Justice. He was tried by court-martial, convicted on all counts, and given a sentence of 10 years' imprisonment at hard labor, forfeiture of a-1 pay and allowances, and dishonorable discharge. His conviction was affirmed by the Army Board of Review and, subsequently, by the United States Court of Military Appeals.

Under confinement at the United States Penitentiary at Lewisburg, Pennsylvania, petitioner filed a petition for writ of habeas corpus in the United States District Court for the Middle District of Pennsylvania alleging, inter alia, that the court-martial was without jurisdiction to try him for nonmilitary offenses committed off-post while on an evening pass. The District Court denied relief without considering the issue on the merits, and the Court of Appeals for the Third Circuit affirmed. This Court granted certiorari limited to the question:

"Does a court-martial, held under the Articles of War, Title 10, U.S.C. § 801 et seq., have jurisdiction to try a member of the Armed Forces who is charged with commission of a crime cognizable in a civilian court and having no military significance, alleged to have been committed off-post and while on leave, thus depriving him of his constitutional rights to indictment by a grand jury and trial by a petit jury in a civilian court?"

The Constitution gives Congress power to "make Rules for the Government and Regulation of the land and naval Forces," Art. I, § 8, cl. 14, and it recognizes that the exigencies of military discipline require the existence of a special system of military courts in which not all of the specific procedural protections deemed essential in Art. III trials need apply. The Fifth Amendment specifically exempts "cases arising *in the land or naval forces* or in the Militia, when in actual service in time of War or public danger" from the requirement of prosecution by indictment and inferentially, from the right to trial by jury. . . . The result has been the establishment and development of a system of military justice with fundamental differences from the practices in the civilian courts.

If the case does not arise *"in the land or naval forces,"* then the accused gets *first,* the benefit of an indictment by a grand jury and *second,* a trial by jury for a civilian court as guaranteed by the Sixth Amendment and by Art. III, § 2, of the Constitution. . . .

Those civil rights are the constitutional stakes in the present litigation. . . .

A court-martial is tried, not by a jury of the defendant's peers which must decide unanimously, but by a panel of officers empowered to act by a two-thirds vote.

The presiding officer at a court-martial is not a judge whose objectivity and independence are protected by tenure and undiminishable salary and nurtured by the judicial tradition, but is a military law officer. Substantially different rules of evidence and procedure apply in military trials. Apart from those differences, the suggestion of the possibility of influence on the actions of the court-martial by the officer who convenes it, selects its members and the counsel on both sides, and who usually has direct command authority over its members is a pervasive one in military law, despite strenuous efforts to eliminate the danger.

A court-martial is not yet an independent instrument of justice but remains to a significant degree a specialized part of the overall mechanism by which military discipline is preserved.

That a system of specialized military courts, proceeding by practices different from those obtaining in the regular courts and in general less favorable to defendants, is necessary to an effective national defense establishment, few would deny. But the justification for such a system rests on the special needs of the military, and history teaches that expansion of military discipline beyond its proper domain carries with it a threat to liberty. . . .

While the Court of Military Appeals takes cognizance of some constitutional rights of the accused who are court-martialed, courts-martial as an institution are singularly inept in dealing with the nice subtleties of constitutional law. Article 134, . . . punishes as a crime "all disorders and neglects to the prejudice of good order and discipline in the armed forces." Does this satisfy the standards of vagueness as developed by the civil courts? It is not enough to say that a court-martial may be reversed on appeal. One of the benefits of a civilian trial is that the trap of Article 134 may be avoided by a declaratory judgment proceeding or otherwise. . . . A civilian trial, in other words, is held in an atmosphere conducive to the protection of individual rights, while a military trial is marked by the age-old manifest destiny of retributive justice.

* * *

We have held in a series of decisions that court-martial jurisdiction cannot be extended to reach any person not a member of the Armed Forces at the times of both the offense and the trial. Thus, discharged soldiers cannot be court-martialed for offenses committed while in service. . . . Similarly, neither civilian employees of the Armed Forces overseas . . . nor civilian dependents of military personnel accompanying them overseas . . . may be tried by court-martial.

These cases decide that courts-martial have no jurisdiction to try those who are not members of the Armed Forces, no matter how intimate the connection between their offense and the concerns of military discipline. From these cases, the Government invites us to draw the conclusion that once it is established that the accused is a member of the Armed Forces, lack of relationship between the offense and identifiable military interests is irrelevant to the jurisdiction of a court-martial.

The fact that courts-martial have no jurisdiction over nonsoldiers, whatever their offense, does not necessarily imply that they have unlimited jurisdiction over soldiers, regardless of the nature of the offenses charged. Nor do the cases of this Court suggest any such interpretation. . . .

* * *

We have concluded that the crime to be under military jurisdiction must be service connected, lest "cases arising in the land or naval forces, or in the Militia, when in actual service in time of War or public danger," as used in the Fifth Amendment, be expanded to deprive every member of the armed services of the benefits of an indictment by a grand jury and a trial by a jury of his peers. . . .

In the present case petitioner was properly absent from his military base when he committed the crimes with which he is charged. There was no connection — not even the remotest one — between his military duties and the crimes in question. The crimes were not committed on a military post or enclave; nor was the person whom he attacked performing any duties relating to the military. Moreover, Hawaii, the situs of the crime, is not an armed camp under military control, as are some of our far-flung outposts.

* * *

. . . Since petitioner's crimes were not service connected, he could not be tried by court-martial but rather was entitled to trial by the civilian courts.

Reversed.

[Mr. Justice HARLAN, with whom Mr. Justice STEWART and Mr. Justice WHITE joined, wrote a dissenting opinion.]

Comment

1. In light of *O'Callahan*, can an offense be "service connected" if it takes place off military property? Suppose a serviceman rapes a general's daughter or wife in town or assaults the general on civilian property. Are all crimes committed on military property necessarily "service connected"? Suppose a serviceman rapes a civilian employee on base, or a civilian rapes a servicewoman either on base or off base. Suppose a military prisoner who has been discharged assaults a military guard in the stockade. The *O'Callahan* Court did not indicate the possible reach of that decision to military installations in foreign countries, but overseas crimes that clearly are not "service connected" would fall under the primary jurisdiction of the host country. Suppose the foreign tribunal decided not to prosecute a serviceman for a non–service-connected crime. How feasible would it be to try the serviceman in an American civilian court since (1) there is no way to compel the attendance of foreign citizens, and (2) the American jury would be totally unfamiliar with the scene of the crime? Few foreign countries provide procedural safeguards commensurate with the constitutional protections afforded American citizens, and there are undoubtedly many instances in which servicemen stationed overseas wish they could be tried by American military or civilian courts.

Crimes on Military Property

RELFORD v. COMMANDANT

Supreme Court of the United States, 1971
401 U.S. 355, 91 S. Ct. 649, 28 L. Ed. 2d 102

In 1961, when Isiah Relford was a corporal on active duty with the United States Army, he was tried and convicted by a general court-martial of kidnapping and raping two women. At the time of the incidents, Relford was in civilian clothes.

Both offenses took place on a military reservation. Relford was sentenced to death, which was later reduced to 30 years' hard labor, total forfeiture of all pay and allowances, and a dishonorable discharge. The conviction was sustained by the Army Board of Review, and the Court of Military Appeals denied review. In 1967, Relford's application for a federal writ of habeas corpus was denied by a United States District Court (D. Kan.), and the United States Court of Appeals (10th Cir.) affirmed. Several weeks thereafter, the United States Supreme Court decided *O'Callahan* **v.** *Parker***, 395 U.S. 258 (1969) (supra), which held that a court-martial may not try a member of the armed forces unless the alleged offenses were sufficiently "service connected." Relford was granted certiorari by the United States Supreme Court limited to the retroactivity and scope of** *O'Callahan* **v.** *Parker***.**

Mr. Justice BLACKMUN delivered the opinion of the Court.

* * *

This case, as did O'Callahan, obviously falls within the area of stress between the constitutional guarantee contained in the Constitution's Art. III, § 2, cl. 3, in the Sixth Amendment, and possibly in the Fifth Amendment on the one hand, and, on the other, the power vested in the Congress, by the Constitution's Art. I, § 8, cl. 14, "To make Rules for the Government and Regulation of the land and naval Forces," with its supportive Necessary and Proper provision in cl. 18, and the Fifth Amendment's correlative exception for "cases arising in the land or naval forces."

Relford argues that O'Callahan's requirement that the crime be "service connected" before a court-martial may sit demands that the crime itself be military in nature, that is, one involving a level of conduct required only of servicemen and, because of the special needs of the military, one demanding military disciplinary action. He further states that the charges against him—like those against O'Callahan—do not involve a level of conduct required only of servicemen. He maintains that occurrence of the crimes on a military reservation and the military dependent identity of one of his victims do not substantially support the military's claim of a special need to try him.

In further detail, it is stated that the Court in O'Callahan recognized that a court-martial "remains to a significant degree a specialized part of the overall mechanism by which military discipline is preserved," . . . that military courts, of necessity, are not impartial weighers of justice, but have as their primary consideration the enforcement of the unique discipline required of a fighting force; and that, as a consequence, the court-martial must be limited to the "least possible power adequate to the end proposed." . . .

It is then said that the level of conduct Relford is alleged to have violated, that is, intercourse only with consent, is the very same level required in the civilian community and is not altered by considerations of military dependency; that his alleged crimes are no more military than were O'Callahan's; that the ability of the military to perform its mission remains the same whether the crimes with which he was charged were committed on base or off base; that any interest in the maintenance of order on the base is adequately served by apprehension of the offender and trial in a civilian court; that the on-post/off-post distinction has little meaning; that it is the nature of the crime that is important; that the crimes charged to Relford stand in contrast to purely military crimes such as desertion, absence without leave, missing movement, assaulting a superior commissioned officer, and being drunk on duty, . . . and that only crimes of the latter type have "an immediate adverse impact upon the ability of the military to perform its mission," and are "proper subjects for the exercise of military jurisdiction."

In evaluating the force of this argument, the facts of O'Callahan and the precise holding in that case possess particular significance. We repeat: O'Callahan was in military service at the time and was stationed at a base in American territory. His offenses, however, took place off base in a civilian hotel while he was on leave and not in uniform.

* * *

We stress seriatim what is thus emphasized in the [O'Callahan] holding:

1. The serviceman's proper absence from the base.

2. The crime's commission away from the base.

3. Its commission at a place not under military control.

4. Its commission within our territorial limits and not in an occupied zone of a foreign country.

5. Its commission in peacetime and its being unrelated to authority stemming from the war power.

6. The absence of any connection between the defendant's military duties and the crime.

7. The victim's not being engaged in the performance of any duty relating to the military.

8. The presence and availability of a civilian court in which the case can be prosecuted.

9. The absence of any flouting of military authority.

10. The absence of any threat to a military post.

11. The absence of any violation of military property.

12. The offense's being among those traditionally prosecuted in civilian courts.

This listing of factors upon which the Court relied for its result in O'Callahan reveals, of course, that it chose to take an ad hoc approach to cases where trial by court-martial is challenged. We therefore turn to those factors in Relford's case that, as spelled out in O'Callahan's, bear upon the court-martial issue.

It is at once apparent that elements 4, 6, 8, 11 and 12, and perhaps 5 and 9, operate in Relford's favor as they did in O'Callahan's: The offenses were committed within the territorial limits of the United States; there was no connection between Relford's military duties and the crimes with which he was charged; courts in New Jersey were open and available for the prosecution of Relford; despite the Vietnam conflict we may assume for present purposes that the offenses were committed in peacetime and that they were unrelated to any problem of authority stemming from the war power; military authority, directly at least, was not flouted; the integrity of military property was not [violated; and rape and] kidnapping are traditionally cognizable in the civilian courts.

Just as clearly, however, the other elements, present and relied upon in O'Callahan's case, are not at hand in Relford's case. These are elements 1, 2, 3, 7, and 10; Relford was not absent from the base; the crimes were committed on the military enclave; the second victim, because of her duties at the post exchange and because of the fact that her abduction and the attack upon her took place as she was returning to the PX at the end of a short and approved break in her work, was engaged in the performance of a duty relating to the military; and the security of two women properly on the post was threatened and, indeed, their persons were violated.

There are still other significant aspects of the Relford offenses: The first victim was the sister of a serviceman who was then properly at the base. The second victim was the wife of a serviceman stationed at the base; she and her husband had quarters on the base and were living there. Tangible property properly on the base, that is, two automobiles, were forcefully and unlawfully entered.

With the foregoing contrasting comparison of the pertinent factual elements of O'Callahan with those of Relford's case, we readily conclude that the crimes with which Relford was charged were triable by a military court. We do not agree with petitioner when he claims that the "apparent distinctions" between this case and O'Callahan "evaporate when viewed within the context of the 'service-connected' test." We stress: (a) the essential and obvious interest of the military in the security of persons and of property on the military enclave. Relford concedes the existence of this vital interest. (b) The responsibility of the military commander for maintenance of order in his command and his authority to maintain that order. . . . Relford also concedes this. (c) The impact and adverse effect that a crime committed against a person or property on a military base, thus violating the base's very security, has upon morale, discipline, reputation and integrity of the base itself, upon its personnel and upon the military operation and the military mission. (d) The conviction that Art. I, § 8, cl. 14, vesting in the Congress the power, "To make Rules for the Government and Regulation of the land and naval Forces," means, in appropriate areas beyond the purely military offense, more than the mere power to arrest a serviceman offender and turn him over to the civil authorities. The term "Regulation" itself implies, for those appropriate cases, the power to try and to punish. (e) The distinct possibility that civil courts, particularly non-federal courts, will have less than complete interest, concern, and capacity for all the cases that vindicate the military's disciplinary authority within its own community. . . . (f) The very positive implication in O'Callahan itself, arising from its emphasis on the absence of service-connected elements there, that the presence of factors such as geographical and military relationships have important contrary significance. (g) The recognition of O'Callahan that, historically, a crime against the person of one associated with the post was subject even to the General Article. . . . (h) The misreading and undue restriction of O'Callahan if it were interpreted as confining the court-martial to the purely military offenses that have no counterpart in nonmilitary criminal law. (i) Our inability appropriately and meaningfully to draw any line between a post's strictly military areas and its nonmilitary areas, or between a serviceman-defendant's on-duty and off-duty activities and hours on the post.

This leads us to hold, and we do so hold, that when a serviceman is charged with an offense committed within or at the geographical boundary of a military post and violative of the security of a person or of property there, that offense may be tried by a court-martial. Expressing it another way: a serviceman's crime against the person of an individual upon the base or against property

on the base is "service connected," within the meaning of that requirement as specified in O'Callahan. . . . This delineation, we feel, fully comports with the standard of "the least possible power adequate to the end proposed" referred to in O'Callahan. . . .

By this measure, Relford's alleged offenses were obviously service connected. There is, therefore, no constitutional or statutory barrier and Relford was properly tried by a court-martial.

We recognize that any ad hoc approach leaves outer boundaries undetermined. O'Callahan marks an area, perhaps not the limit, for the concern of the civil courts and where the military may not enter. The cast today marks an area, perhaps not the limit, where the court-martial is appropriate and permissible. What lies between is for decision at another time.

Having reached this result on the court-martial issue, the additional issue that the parties have argued, of O'Callahan's retrospectivity, need not be decided. . . .

We recognize that the retroactivity question has important dimensions, both direct and collateral, and that the Government strongly urges that the question be decided here and now. We have concluded, however, that the issue is better resolved in other litigation where, perhaps, it would be solely dispositive of the case. We take some comfort in the hope that the present decision shou d eliminate at least some of the confusion that the parties and commentators say has emerged from O'Callahan.

Affirmed.

Comments

1. In *Relford,* the Court held that crimes committed by a serviceman on military property are sufficiently "service connected" to permit a trial by military courts. Does it make any difference whether a serviceman is wearing civilian clothes at the time of the offense? Suppose a serviceman in uniform rapes a servicewoman who is also in uniform off base. Is that a "service connected" crime? Suppose the rape took place off base at a time when both parties were (or were supposed to be) engaged in military duties. For example, suppose a sergeant recruiter rapes a civilian off base during his regular duty hours, or rapes a servicewoman-recruiter in the recruiting office (off base). In *Relford,* the Court listed 12 factors used in *O'Callahan* to determine whether a crime is "service connected." The *Relford* Court noted that 7 of these 12 factors operated in the defendant's favor; yet Relford's argument that his

crimes were not "service connected" ultimately failed. How many factors does a defendant need in his favor before he will prevail under the *O'Callahan-Relford* analysis? Obviously a majority of favorable factors is no guarantee of success on appeal.

2. In *Gosa* v. *Mayden,* 413 U.S. 665 (1973), the Supreme Court divided 4–4 on the issue of whether *O'Callahan* should be made retroactive. The Court also did not resolve the question whether a rape committed by a serviceman off base on a civilian victim or the theft by a serviceman of an automobile owned by a civilian are "service-connected" crimes. The courts of appeals had held they were not. The *O'Callahan-Relford* decisions are sufficiently confusing to invite future litigation in this area.

3. Consider whether any of the following situations are sufficiently "service connected" to warrant military jurisdiction: Army captain charged with attempted rape while off base and off duty and dressed in civilian clothes. See *United States* v. *Borys,* 18 U.S.C.M.A. 547 (1969) (held not service connected). Serviceman strikes taxicab driver over head on post and forces him to drive off base and then robs him. See *United States* v. *Crapo,* 18 U.S.C.M.A. 594 (1969) (held service connected). Serviceman rapes daughter of fellow serviceman on post. See *United States* v. *Smith,* 18 U.S.C.M.A. 609 (1969) (held service connected). Marine accused of being drunk and disorderly while off base. See *United States* v. *Sharkey,* 19 U.S.C.M.A. 26 (1969) (held service connected). Serviceman commits assault off base on fellow serviceman. See *United States* v. *Everson,* 19 U.S.C.M.A. 70 (1969) (service connected). Serviceman escapes from post stockade dressed in fatigues and steals car in a neighboring community. See *United States* v. *Shockley,* 18 U.S.C.M.A. 610 (1969) (held service connected). Marine forges check off base and uses his military identification card in presenting the check. See *United States* v. *Frazier,* 19 U.S.C.M.A. 40 (1969) (held service connected). Serviceman in uniform registers in a hotel under a fictitious name and fails to pay the hotel bill. See *United States* v. *Fryman,* 19 U.S.C.M.A. 71 (1969) (held service connected). Serviceman cashes bad check at a civilian grocery store. See *United States* v. *Williams,* 18 U.S.C.M.A. 605 (held not service connected). The off-base sale of marijuana to a serviceman-informer. See *United States* v. *Sexton,* 23 U.S.C.M.A. 101 (1974) (held service connected). GI's arrest for possession of marijuana. See *Lyle* v. *Kincaid,* 344 F. Supp. 223 (M.D. Fla. 1972) (not service connected). Possession of narcotics paraphernalia by serviceman in a civilian bar. See *United States* v. *Teasley,* 22 U.S.C.M.A. 131 (1973) (not service connected). Serviceman's offenses committed in a foreign country. See *United States* v. *Newvine,* 23 U.S.C.M.A. 208 (1974) (held service connected). Serviceman steals automobile on base in California and drives to Arizona. See *United States* v. *Wills,* 20 U.S.C.M.A. 208 (1974) (held service connected). Serviceman commits manslaughter and assaults his military dependents while off base. See *United States* v. *Snyder,* 20 U.S.C.M.A. 102 (1970) (not service connected). Officer cashes bad check at civilian department store and uses civilian credit card for identification. See *United States* v. *Wolfson,* 21 U.S.C.M.A. 549 (1972) (held not service connected). See also Rice, *Court Martial Jurisdiction — The Service Connection Standard in Confusion,* 61 J. Crim. Law Crim. & Pol. Sci. 339 (1970).

"Conduct Unbecoming an Officer or Gentleman"

PARKER v. LEVY

Supreme Court of the United States, 1974
417 U.S. 733, 94 S. Ct. 2547, 41 L. Ed. 2d 439

Captain Howard Levy, an Army officer and physician, refused to train Special Forces medical aide men and made public statements urging black enlisted men not to go to Viet Nam if ordered to do so. He characterized Special Forces personnel as liars, thieves, killers of peasants, and murderers of women and children. Levy was convicted by a general court-martial of three violations of the Uniform Code of Military Justice: (1) "willfully disobeying a lawful order of a superior officer" (Art. 90), (2) "disorders and neglects to the prejudice of good order and discipline in the armed forces" (Art. 134), and (3) "conduct unbecoming an officer or gentleman" (Art. 133). He was sentenced to dismissal from the service, forfeiture of all pay and allowances, and confinement for three years at hard labor. After exhausting avenues of relief under military law, Levy sought federal habeas corpus relief in the United States District Court (M.D. Pa.), which denied relief. The United States Court of Appeals (3d Cir.) reversed, holding Articles 133 and 134 of the U.C.M.J. unconstitutional as void for vagueness. Appellants appealed to the United States Supreme Court pursuant to 28 U.S.C. § 1252, which permits such review when any court of the United States holds an act of Congress unconstitutional.

Mr. Justice REHNQUIST delivered the opinion of the Court.

* * *

This Court has long recognized that the military is, by necessity, a specialized society separate from civilian society. We have also recognized that the military has, again by necessity, developed laws and traditions of its own during its long history. The differences between the military and civilian communities result from the fact that "it is the primary business of armies and navies to fight or be ready to fight wars should the occasion arise." . . .

Just as military society has been a society apart from civilian society, so "[m]ilitary law . . . is a jurisprudence which exists separate and apart from the law which governs in our federal judicial establishment." . . . And to maintain the discipline essential to perform its mission effectively, the military has developed what "may not unfitly be called the customary military law" or "general usage of the military service." . . .

* * *

The differences . . . between the military community and the civilian community, and second between military law and civilian law, continue in the present day under the Uniform Code of Military Justice. That Code cannot be equated to a civilian criminal code. It, and the various versions of the Articles of War, which have preceded it, regulate aspects of the conduct of members of the military which in the civilian sphere are left unregulated. While a civilian criminal code carves out a relatively small segment of potential conduct and declares it criminal, the Uniform Code of Military Justice essays more varied regulation of a much larger segment of the activities of the more tightly knit military community. In civilian life there is no legal sanction—civil or criminal—for failure to behave as an officer and a gentleman; in the military world, Art. 133 imposes such a sanction on a commissioned officer. The Code likewise imposes other sanctions for conduct that in civilian life is not subject to criminal penalties: disrespect toward superior commissioned officers, Art. 89; cruelty toward or oppression or maltreatment of subordinates, Art. 93; negligent damaging, destruction, or wrongful disposition of military property of the United States, Art. 108; improper hazarding of a vessel, Art. 110; drunkenness on duty, Art. 112; and malingering, Art. 115.

* * *

In short, the Uniform Code of Military Justice regulates a far broader range of the conduct of military personnel than a typical state criminal code regulates of the conduct of civilians; but at the same time the enforcement of that Code in the area of minor offenses is often by sanctions which are more akin to administrative or civil sanctions than to civilian criminal ones.

* * *

Appellee urges that both Art. 133 and Art. 134 (the general article) are "void for vagueness" under the Due Process Clause of the Fifth Amendment and overbroad in violation of the First Amendment. We have recently said of the vagueness doctrine:

"The doctrine incorporates notions of fair notice or warning. Moreover, it requires legislatures to set reasonably clear guidelines for law enforcement officials and triers of fact in order to prevent 'arbitrary and discriminatory enforcement.' Where a statute's literal scope, unaided by a narrowing state court interpretation, is capable of reaching expression sheltered by the First Amendment, the doctrine demands a greater degree of specificity than in other contexts." Smith v. Goguen, 415 U.S. 566, 572–573 (1974).

Each of these articles has been construed by the United States Court of Military Appeals or by other military authorities in such a manner as to at least partially narrow its otherwise broad scope.

* * *

The effect of these constructions of Arts. 133 and 134 by the Court of Military Appeals and by other military authorities has been twofold: It has narrowed the very broad reach of the literal language of the articles, and at the same time has supplied considerable specificity by way of examples of the conduct which they cover. It would be idle to pretend that there are not areas within the general confines of the articles' language

which have been left vague despite these narrowing constructions. But even though sizable areas of uncertainty as to the coverage of the articles may remain after their official interpretation by authoritative military sources, further content may be supplied even in these areas by less formalized custom and usage. And there also cannot be the slightest doubt under the military precedents that there is a substantial range of conduct to which both articles clearly apply without vagueness or imprecision. It is within that range that appellee's conduct squarely falls. . . .

. . . This Court has on more than one occasion invalidated statutes under the Due Process Clause of the Fifth or Fourteenth Amendment because they contained no standard whatever by which criminality could be ascertained, and the doctrine of these cases has subsequently acquired the shorthand description of "void for vagueness." Lanzetta v. New Jersey, 306 U.S. 451 (1939); Winters v. New York, 333 U.S. 507 (1948). In these cases, the criminal provision is vague "not in the sense that it requires a person to conform his conduct to an imprecise but comprehensible normative standard, but rather in the sense that no standard of conduct is specified at all." Coates v. City of Cincinnati, 402 U.S. 611, 614 (1971).

But the Court of Appeals found in this case, and we agree, that Arts. 133 and 134 are subject to no such sweeping condemnation. Levy had fair notice from the language of each article that the particular conduct which he engaged in was punishable. . . .

* * *

Because of the factors differentiating military society from civilian society, we hold that the proper standard of review for a vagueness challenge to the articles of the Code is the standard which applies to criminal statutes regulating economic affairs. Clearly, that standard is met here, for as the Court stated in United States v. National Dairy Corporation, 372 U.S. 29, 32–33 (1963):

"The strong presumptive validity that attaches to an Act of Congress has led this Court to hold many times that statutes are not automatically invalidated as vague simply because difficulty is found in determining whether certain marginal offenses fall within their language." . . . Indeed, we have consistently sought an interpretation which supports the constitutionality of legislation. . . .

"Void for vagueness simply means that criminal responsibility should not attach where one could not reasonably understand that his contemplated conduct is proscribed. United States v. Harriss, 347 U.S. 612, 617 (1954). In determining the sufficiency of the notice a statute must of necessity be examined in the light of the conduct with which a defendant is charged. Robinson v. United States, 324 U.S. 282 (1945)."

Since appellee could have had no reasonable doubt that his public statements urging Negro enlisted men not to go to Vietnam if ordered to do so were both "unbecoming an officer and a gentleman," and "to the prejudice of good order and discipline in the armed forces," in violation of the provisions of Arts. 133 and 134, respectively, his challenge to them as unconstitutionally vague under the Due Process Clause of the Fifth Amendment must fail.

We likewise reject appellee's contention that Arts. 133 and 134 are facially invalid because of their "overbreadth."

* * *

While the members of the military are not excluded from the protection granted by the First Amendment, the different character of the military community and of the military mission require a different application of those protections. The fundamental necessity for obedience, and the consequent necessity for imposition of discipline, may render permissible within the military that which would be constitutionally impermissible outside it. Doctrines of First Amendment overbreadth asserted in support of challenges to imprecise language like that contained in Arts. 133 and 134 are not exempt from the operation of these principles.

* * *

This Court has, however, repeatedly expressed its reluctance to strike down a statute on its face where there were a substantial number of situations to which it might be validly applied. Thus, even if there are marginal applications in which a statute would infringe on First Amendment values, facial invalidation is inappropriate if the "remainder of the statute . . . covers a whole

range of easily identifiable and constitutionally proscribable . . . conduct. . . ."

* * *

There is a wide range of the conduct of military personnel to which Arts. 133 and 134 may be applied without infringement of the First Amendment. While there may lurk at the fringes of the Articles, even in the light of their narrowing construction by the United States Court of Military Appeals, some possibility that conduct which would be ultimately held to be protected by the First Amendment could be included within their prohibition, we deem this insufficient to invalidate either of them at the behest of appellee. His conduct, that of a commissioned officer publicly urging enlisted personnel to refuse to obey orders which might send them into combat, was unprotected under the most expansive notions of the First Amendment. Articles 133 and 134 may constitutionally prohibit that conduct, and a sufficiently large number of similar or related types of conduct so as to preclude their invalidation for overbreadth.

Appellee urges that should we disagree with the Court of Appeals as to the constitutionality of Arts. 133 and 134, we should nonetheless affirm its judgment by invalidating his conviction under Art. 90. He contends that to carry out the hospital commandant's order to train aide men in dermatology would have constituted participation in a war crime, and that the commandant gave the order in question, knowing that it would be disobeyed, for the sole purpose of increasing the punishment which could be imposed upon appellee. The Court of Appeals observed that each of these defenses was recognized under the Uniform Code of Military Justice, but had been resolved against appellee on a factual basis by the court-martial which convicted him. The court went on to say that: "In isolation, these factual determinations adverse to appellant under an admittedly valid article are not of constitutional significance and resultantly, are beyond our scope of review." 478 F.2d, at 797. . . . We agree with the Court of Appeals.

* * *

Reversed.

[Mr. Justice BLACKMUN, with whom Mr.

Chief Justice BURGER joined, concurred.]

Mr. Justice STEWART, joined by Mr. Justice DOUGLAS and Mr. Justice BRENNAN, dissenting.

. . . I find it hard to imagine criminal statutes more patently unconstitutional than these vague and uncertain general articles, and I would, accordingly, affirm the judgment before us.

* * *

Article 133 has been recently employed to punish such widely disparate conduct as dishonorable failure to repay debts, selling whiskey at an unconscionable price to an enlisted man, cheating at cards, and having an extramarital affair. Article 134 has been given an even wider sweep, having been applied to sexual acts with a chicken, window peeping in a trailer park, and cheating while calling bingo numbers. Convictions such as these leave little doubt that "[a]n infinite variety of other conduct, limited only by the scope of a commander's creativity or spleen, can be made the subject of court-martial under these articles." . . .

In short, the general articles are in practice as well as theory "catchalls," designed to allow prosecutions for practically any conduct that may offend the sensibilities of a military commander. . . .

* * *

It may be that military necessity justifies the promulgation of substantive rules of law that are wholly foreign to civilian life, but I fail to perceive how any legitimate military goal is served by enshrouding these rules in language so vague and uncertain as to be incomprehensible to the servicemen who are to be governed by them. Indeed, I should suppose that vague laws, with their serious capacity for arbitrary and discriminatory enforcement, can in the end only hamper the military's objectives of high morale and esprit de corps.

In short, I think no case has been made for finding that there is any legitimate military necessity for perpetuation of the vague and amorphous general articles. . . .

. . . I do not for one moment denigrate the importance of our inherited tradition that the commissioned officers of our military forces are expected to be men of honor, nor do I doubt the necessity that servicemen generally must be orderly and dutiful. An efficient and effective military organization depends in large part upon the character and quality of its personnel, particularly its leadership. The internal loyalty and mutual reliance indispensable to the ultimate effectiveness of any military organization can exist only among people who can be counted on to do their duty. It is, therefore, not only legitimate but essential that in matters of promotion, retention, duty assignment and internal discipline, evaluations must repeatedly be made of a serviceman's basic character as reflected in his deportment, whether he be an enlisted man or a commissioned officer. But we deal here with criminal statutes. And I cannot believe that such meaningless statutes as these can be used to send men to prison under a Constitution that guarantees due process of law.

[Mr. Justice STEVENS took no part in the consideration or decision of this case.]

Comment

1. Could civilian criminal statutes as broadly written as Articles 133 and 134 of the U.C.M.J. withstand constitutional scrutiny under the void-for-vagueness doctrine? Suppose a local ordinance made it a misdemeanor to engage in behavior "unbecoming a civilian" or for an employee to "willfully disobey a reasonable order of his employer." In *Parker* v. *Levy,* supra, a majority of the Court upheld the U.C.M.J. articles in question because of (1) "military necessity," and (2) the narrow reach given the articles by the United States Court of Military Appeals. Mr. Justice Rehnquist, writing for the Court in *Levy,* went to great lengths to point out the differences between civilian and military life. Is *Levy* affected by the fact that

we now have an all-volunteer Army? Does this tend to undermine the "military necessity" argument? Is it really true that the Court of Military Appeals has taken a narrow view of the articles in question in light of the dissenting opinion, which pointed out that these articles have been used to punish "dishonorable failure to repay debts, selling whiskey at an unconscionable price to an enlisted man, cheating at cards, and having an extramarital affair," as well as "sexual acts with a chicken, window peeping in a trailer park, and cheating while calling bingo numbers"? Can it really be said that military personnel are given "fair notice" of what conduct is proscribed subject to criminal sanctions? Does one "assume the risk" that his behavior may be "criminal" by joining the military?

The Right to Counsel at Summary Courts-Martial

MIDDENDORF v. HENRY

Supreme Court of the United States, 1976
425 U.S. 25, 96 S. Ct. 1281, 47 L. Ed. 2d 556

The facts are stated in the opinion.

Mr. Justice REHNQUIST delivered the opinion of the Court.

In February 1973 plaintiffs — then enlisted members of the United States Marine Corps — brought this class action in the United States District Court for the Central District of California challenging the authority of the military to try them at summary courts-martial without providing them with counsel. Five plaintiffs had been charged with "unauthorized absences" in violation of Art. 86, U.C.M.J. (10 U.S.C. § 886), convicted at summary courts-martial and sentenced, inter alia, to periods of confinement ranging from 20 to 30 days at hard labor. The other three plaintiffs, two of whom were charged, inter alia, with unauthorized absence and one with assault, Art. 134, U.C.M.J. (10 U.S.C. § 934), had been ordered to stand trial at summary courts-martial which had not been convened. Those who were convicted had not been provided counsel — those who were awaiting trial had been informed that counsel would not be provided. All convicted plaintiffs were informed prior to trial that they would not be afforded counsel and that they could refuse trial by summary court-martial if they so desired. In the event of such refusal their case would be referred to a special court-martial at which counsel would be provided. All plaintiffs consented in writing to proceed to trial by summary court-martial, without counsel. Plaintiffs' court-martial records were reviewed and approved by the Staff Judge Advocate. . . . Plaintiffs did not file a petition for review with the Judge Advocate General of the Navy. . . .

In the District Court, plaintiffs brought a class action seeking habeas corpus (release from confinement), an injunction against future confinement resulting from uncounseled summary courts-martial convictions, and an order vacating the convictions of those previously convicted.

The District Court allowed the suit to proceed as a class action, expunged all of plaintiffs' convictions, released all plaintiffs and all other members of their class from confinement, and issued a worldwide injunction against summary courts-martial without counsel. Because of our disposition of this case on the merits, we have no occasion to reach the question of whether Fed. Rule Civ. Proc. 23, providing for class actions, is applicable to petitioners for habeas corpus, see Harris v. Nelson, 394 U.S. 286 (1969), or whether the District Court properly determined that its remedial order was entitled to be enforced outside of the territorial limits of the district in which the court sat.

The Court of Appeals vacated the judgment of the District Court, and remanded the case for reconsideration in light of the Court of Appeals' opinion in Daigle v. Warner, 490 F.2d 358 (9th Cir. 1973). Daigle had held that there was no Sixth Amendment right to counsel in summary courts-martial, and likewise held that there was no absolute Fifth Amendment due process right to counsel in every case in which a military defendant might be imprisoned. However, citing Gagnon v. Scarpelli, 411 U.S. 778 (1973), it did hold that counsel was required where the "accused makes a request based on a timely and colorable claim (1) that he has a defense and (2) that there are mitigating circumstances and the assistance of counsel is necessary in order adequately to present the defense of mitigating circumstances." Daigle made an exception from this general rule for cases in which counsel "is not reasonably available," in which case it would not be required. 490 F.2d, at 365. We granted certiorari. . . .

The Uniform Code of Military Justice provides four methods for disposing of cases involving offenses committed by servicemen: the general, special, and summary courts-martial, and disciplinary punishment administered by the commanding officer pursuant to Art. 15, U.C.M.J. (10 U.S.C. § 815). General and special courts-martial resemble judicial proceedings, nearly always presided over by lawyer judges with lawyer counsel for both the prosecution and the defense. General courts-martial are authorized to award any lawful sentence, including death. Art. 18, U.C.M.J. (10 U.S.C. § 818). Special courts-martial may award a bad-conduct discharge, up to six months' confinement, and forfeiture of two-thirds pay for six months. Art. 19 U.C.M.J. (10 U.S.C. § 819). Article 15 punishment, conducted personally by the accused's commanding officer, is an administrative method of dealing with the most minor offenses. Parker v. Levy, 417 U.S. 733, 750 (1974).

The summary court-martial occupies a position between informal nonjudicial disposition under Art. 15 and the courtroom-type procedure of the general and special courts-martial. Its purpose, "is to exercise justice promptly for relatively minor offenses under a simple form of procedures." . . . It is an informal proceeding conducted by a single commissioned officer with jurisdiction only over noncommissioned officers and enlisted personnel. . . . The presiding officer acts as judge, factfinder, prosecutor, and defense counsel. The presiding officer must inform the accused of the charges and the name of the accuser and call all witnesses whom he or the accused desires to call. . . . The accused must consent to trial by summary court-martial, or the case will be either dismissed or referred to a special or general court-martial.

The maximum sentences which may be imposed by summary courts-martial are: 30 days' confinement at hard labor; 45 days' hard labor without confinement; two months' restrictions to specified limits; reduction to the lowest enlisted pay grade; and forfeiture of two-thirds pay for one month. . . .

The question of whether an accused in a court-martial has a constitutional right to counsel has been much debated and never squarely resolved. . . .

We find it unnecessary in this case to finally resolve the broader aspects of this question, since we conclude that even were the Sixth Amendment to be held applicable to court-martial proceedings, the summary court-martial provided for in these cases was not a "criminal prosecution" within the meaning of that Amendment.

This conclusion of course, does not answer the ultimate question of whether the plaintiffs are entitled to counsel at a summary court-martial proceeding, but it does shift the frame of reference from the Sixth Amendment's guarantee of counsel "[i]n all criminal prosecutions" to the Fifth Amendment's prohibition against the deprivation of "life, liberty, or property, without due process of law."

Argersinger v. Hamlin, 407 U.S. 25 (1972), held that the Sixth Amendment's provision for the assistance of counsel extended to misdemeanor prosecutions in civilian courts if conviction would result in imprisonment. A summary court-martial may impose 30 days' confinement at hard labor, which is doubtless the military equivalent of imprisonment. Yet the fact that the outcome of a proceeding may result in loss of liberty does not by itself, even in civilian life, mean that the Sixth Amendment's guarantee of counsel is applicable. In Gagnon v. Scarpelli, 411 U.S. 778 (1973), the respondent faced the prospect of being sent to prison as a result of the revocation of his probation, but we held that the revocation proceeding was nonetheless not a "criminal proceeding." . . .

In re Gault, 387 U.S. 1 (1967), likewise involved a proceeding in which a juvenile was threatened with confinement. The Court, although holding counsel was required, went on to say:

"We do not mean . . . to indicate that the hearing to be held must conform with all of the requirements of a criminal trial or even of the usual administrative hearing; but we do hold that the hearing must measure up to the essentials of due process and fair treatment." Id., at 30.

The Court's distinction between various civilian proceedings, and its conclusion that, notwithstanding the potential loss of liberty, neither juvenile hearings nor probation revocation hearings are "criminal proceedings," are equally relevant in assessing the role of the summary court-martial in the military.

The summary court-martial is, as noted above, one of four types of proceedings by which the military imposes discipline or punishment. If we were to remove the holding of Argersinger from its civilian context and apply it to require counsel before a summary court-martial proceeding simply because loss of liberty may result from such a proceeding, it would seem all but inescapable that counsel would likewise be required for the lowest level of military proceeding for dealing with the most minor offenses. For even the so-called Art. 15 "nonjudicial punishment," which may be imposed administratively by the commanding officer, may result in the imposition upon an enlisted man of "correctional custody" with hard labor for not more than 30 consecutive days. . . .

It seems to us indisputably clear, therefore, that even in a civilian text the fact that a proceeding will result in loss of liberty does not ipso facto mean that the proceeding is a "criminal prosecution" for purposes of the Sixth Amendment. Nor does the fact that confinement will be imposed in the first instance as a result of that proceeding make it a "criminal prosecution." When we consider in addition the fact that a summary court-martial occurs in the military community, rather than the civilian community, we believe that the considerations supporting the conclusion that it is not a "criminal prosecution" are at least as strong as those which were held dispositive in Gagnon and Gault.

* * *

[A] summary court-martial is procedurally quite different from a criminal trial. In the first place, it is not an adversary proceeding. Yet the adversary nature of civilian criminal proceedings is one of the touchstones of the Sixth Amendment's right to counsel which we extended to petty offenses in Argersinger v. Hamlin, 407 U.S. 25 (1972).

* * *

The function of the presiding officer is quite different from that of any participant in a civilian trial. He is guided by the admonition in paragraph 79 of the MCM [Manual for Court Martial] that "[t]he function of a summary court-martial is to exercise justice promptly for relatively minor offenses under a simple form of procedure. The summary court will thoroughly and impartially inquire into both sides of the matter and will assure that the interests of both the Government and the accused are safeguarded." . . .

We believe there are significant parallels between the Court's description of probation and parole revocation proceedings in Gagnon and the summary court-martial, which parallels tend to distinguish both of these proceedings from the civilian misdemeanor prosecution upon which Argersinger focused. When we consider in addition that the court-martial proceeding takes place not in civilian society, as does the parole revocation proceedings, but in the military community with all of its distinctive qualities, we conclude that a summary court-martial is not a "criminal prosecution" for purposes of the Sixth Amendment.

The Court of Appeals likewise concluded that there was no Sixth Amendment right to counsel in summary court-martial proceedings such as this, but applying the due process standards of the Fifth Amendment adopted a standard from Gagnon v. Scarpelli, supra, which would have made the right to counsel depend upon the nature of the serviceman's defense. We are unable to agree that the Court of Appeals properly applied Gagnon in this military context.

We recognize that plaintiffs, who have either been convicted or are due to stand trial before a summary court-martial, may be subjected to loss of liberty or property, and consequently are entitled to the due process of law guaranteed by the Fifth Amendment.

However, whether this process embodies a right to counsel depends upon an analysis of the interests of the individual and those of the regime to which he is subject. . . .

In making such an analysis we must give particular deference to the congressional determination, made under its authority to regulate the land and naval forces, United States Constitution, Art. I, § 8, that counsel should not be provided in summary courts-martial. . . .

". . . [T]he rights of men in the armed forces must perforce be conditioned to meet certain overriding demands of discipline and duty, and the civil courts are not the agencies which must determine the precise balance to be struck in this adjustment. The Framers especially entrusted that task to Congress."

The United States Court of Military Appeals has held that Argersinger is applicable to the military and requires counsel at summary courts-martial. United States v. Alderman, 22 U.S.C.M.A. 298 (1973). Dealing with areas of law peculiar to the military branches, the Court of Military Appeals' judgments are normally entitled to great deference. But the 2-to-1 decision, in which the majority itself was sharply divided in theory, does not reject the claim of military necessity. . . .

We thus need only decide whether the factors militating in favor of counsel at summary court-martial are so extraordinarily weighty as to overcome the balance struck by Congress.

We first consider the effect of providing counsel at summary courts-martial. As we observed in Gagnon v. Scarpelli, supra, at 787:

"The introduction of counsel into a . . . proceeding will alter significantly the nature of the proceeding. If counsel is provided for the (accused), the State in turn will normally provide its own counsel; lawyers by training and disposition are advocates and bound by professional duty to present all available evidence and arguments in support of their clients' positions and to contest with vigor all adverse evidence and views."

Presence of counsel will turn a brief, informal hearing which may be quickly convened and rapidly concluded into an attenuated proceeding which consumes the resources of the military to a degree which Congress could properly have felt to be beyond what is warranted by the relative insignificance of the offenses being tried. Such a lengthy proceeding is a particular burden to the armed forces because virtually all the participants, including the defendant and his counsel, are members of the military whose time may be better spent than in possibly protracted disputes over the imposition of discipline.

* * *

The Court of Appeals did not find counsel necessary in all proceedings but only, . . . when the accused makes

"A timely and colorable claim (1) that he has a defense or (2) that there are mitigating circumstances, and the assistance of counsel is necessary in order to adequately present the defense or mitigating circumstances." 409 F.2d, at 365.

But if the accused has such a claim, if he feels that in order to properly air his views and vindicate his rights, a formal, counseled proceeding is necessary he may simply refuse trial by summary court-martial and proceed to trial by special court-martial at which he may have counsel. Thus, he stands in a considerably more favorable position than the probationer in Gagnon, who, though subject to the possibility of longer periods of incarceration, had no such absolute right to counsel.

It is true that by exercising this option the accused subjects himself to greater possible penalties imposed in the special court-martial proceeding. However, we do not find that possible detriment to be constitutionally decisive. . . . In such a case the defendant gives up, not only his right to counsel but his right to any trial at all. Furthermore, if he elects to exercise his right to trial he stands to be convicted of a more serious offense which will likely bear increased penalties.

Such choices are a necessary part of the criminal justice system. . . .

We therefore agree with the federal parties that neither the Sixth nor the Fifth Amendments to the United States Constitution empower us to overturn the congressional determination that counsel is not required in summary courts-martial. The judgment of the Court of Appeals is therefore reversed.

[Mr. Justice POWELL, joined by Mr. Justice BLACKMUN, wrote a concurring opinion.]

[Mr. Justice MARSHALL, joined by Mr. Justice BRENNAN, dissented.]

[Mr. Justice STEWART dissented, believing that the Due Process Clause of the Fifth Amendment requires that a defendant be accorded the assistance of counsel in a summary court-martial proceeding.]

[Mr. Justice STEVENS took no part in the consideration or decision of this case.]

Comment

1. In *Middendorf* v. *Henry,* supra, a majority of the Supreme Court held that there is no Sixth Amendment right to counsel in summary court-martial proceedings, even though 30 days' confinement at hard labor may be imposed. In light of this possible punishment, why did the Court conclude that a summary court-martial is not a "criminal prosecution" within the meaning of the Sixth Amendment? Does this do violence to the English language? If a summary court-martial is not "criminal" in nature, what type of proceeding is it? An administrative hearing that incidentally provides 30 days' confinement at hard labor? How does *Middendorf* square with the holding of *Argersinger* v. *Hamlin,* 407 U.S. 25 (1972) (Chapter Seven, § 7.02), that "the denial of the assistance of counsel will preclude the imposition of a jail sentence"; and that "every judge will know when the trial of a misdemeanor starts that no imprisonment may be imposed . . . unless the accused is represented by counsel"? Isn't a proceeding whereby an accused can receive up to 30 days' imprisonment a "critical stage" requiring the assistance of counsel? What, if any, is the "military necessity" for the holding in *Middendorf*? Should any provisions of the Sixth Amendment be applicable to court-martial proceedings?

APPENDIX A

Selected Provisions Relating to Federal Habeas Corpus 28 U.S.C.A. §§ 2241–2255

28 U.S.C.A. § 2241. Power to grant writ

(a) Writs of habeas corpus may be granted by the Supreme Court, any justice thereof, the district courts and any circuit judge within their respective jurisdictions. The order of a circuit judge shall be entered in the records of the district court of the district wherein the restraint complained of is had.

(b) The Supreme Court, any justice thereof, and any circuit judge may decline to entertain an application for a writ of habeas corpus and may transfer the application for hearing and determination to the district court having jurisdiction to entertain it.

(c) The writ of habeas corpus shall not extend to a prisoner unless—

(1) He is in custody under or by color of the authority of the United States or is committed for trial before some court thereof; or

(2) He is in custody for an act done or omitted in pursuance of an Act of Congress, or an order, process, judgment or decree of a court or judge of the United States; or

(3) He is in custody in violation of the Constitution or laws or treaties of the United States; or

(4) He, being a citizen of a foreign state and domiciled therein is in custody for an act done or omitted under any alleged right, title, authority, privilege, protection, or exemption claimed under the commission, order or sanction of any foreign state, or under color thereof, the validity and effect of which depend upon the law of nations; or

(5) It is necessary to bring him into court to testify or for trial.

(d) Where an application for a writ of habeas corpus is made by a person in custody under the judgment and sentence of a State court of a State which contains two or more Federal judicial districts, the application may be filed in the district wherein such person is in custody or in the district court for the district within which the State court was held which convicted and sentenced him and each of such district courts shall have concurrent jurisdiction to entertain the application. The district court for the district wherein such application is filed in the exercise of its discretion and in furtherance of justice may transfer the application to the other district court for hearing and determination.

28 U.S.C.A. § 2242. Application

Application for a writ of habeas corpus shall be in writing signed and verified by the person for whose relief it is intended or by someone acting in his behalf.

It shall allege the facts concerning the applicant's commitment or detention, the name of the person who has custody over him and by virtue of what claim or authority, if known.

It may be amended or supplemented as provided in the rules of procedure applicable to civil actions.

If addressed to the Supreme Court, a justice thereof or a circuit judge it shall state the reasons for not making application to the district court of the district in which the applicant is held.

28 U.S.C.A. § 2243. Issuance of writ; return; hearing; decision

A court, justice or judge entertaining an application for a writ of habeas corpus shall forthwith award the writ or issue an order directing the respondent to show cause why the writ should not be granted, unless it appears from the application that the applicant or person detained is not entitled thereto.

The writ, or order to show cause shall be directed to the person having custody of the person detained. It shall be returned within three days unless for good cause additional time, not exceeding twenty days, is allowed.

The person to whom the writ or order is directed shall make a return certifying the true cause of the detention.

When the writ or order is returned a day shall be set for hearing, not more than five days after the return unless for good cause additional time is allowed.

Unless the application for the writ and the return present only issues of law the person to whom the writ is directed shall be required to produce at the hearing the body of the person detained.

The applicant or the person detained may, under oath, deny any of the facts set forth in the return or allege any other material facts.

The return and all suggestions made against it may be amended, by leave of court, before or after being filed.

The court shall summarily hear and determine the facts, and dispose of the matter as law and justice require.

28 U.S.C.A. § 2244. Finality of Determination

(a) No circuit or district judge shall be required to entertain an application for a writ of habeas corpus to inquire into the detention of a person pursuant to a judgment of a court of the United States if it appears that the legality of such detention has been determined by a judge or court of the United States on a prior application for a writ of habeas corpus and the petition presents no new ground not theretofore presented and determined, and the judge or court is satisfied that the ends of justice will not be served by such inquiry.

(b) When after an evidentiary hearing on the merits of a material factual issue, or after a hearing on the merits of an issue of law, a person in custody pursuant to the judgment of a State court has been denied by a court of the United States or a justice or judge of the United States release from custody or other remedy on an application for a writ of habeas corpus, a subsequent application for a writ of habeas corpus in behalf of such person need not be entertained by a court of the United States or a justice or judge of the United States unless the application alleges and is predicated on a factual or other ground not adjudicated on the hearing of the earlier application for the writ, and unless the court, justice, or judge is satisfied that the applicant has not on the earlier application deliberately withheld the newly asserted ground or otherwise abused the writ.

(c) In a habeas corpus proceeding brought in behalf of a person in custody pursuant to the judgment of a State court, a prior judgment of the Supreme Court of the United States on an appeal or review by a writ of certiorari at the instance of the prisoner of the decision of such State court shall be conclusive as to all issues of fact or law with respect to an asserted denial of a Federal right which constitutes ground for discharge in a habeas corpus proceeding, actually adjudicated by the Supreme Court therein, unless the applicant for the writ of habeas corpus shall plead and the court shall find the existence of a material and controlling fact which did not appear in the record of the proceeding in the Supreme Court and the court shall further find that the applicant for the writ of habeas corpus could not have caused such fact to appear in such record by the exercise of reasonable diligence.

* * *

28 U.S.C.A. § 2254. State custody; remedies in Federal courts

(a) The Supreme Court, a justice thereof, a circuit judge, or a district court shall entertain an application for a writ of habeas corpus in behalf of a person in custody pursuant to the judgment of a State court only on the ground that he is in custody in violation of the Constitution or laws or treaties of the United States.

(b) An application for a writ of habeas corpus in behalf of a person in custody pursuant to the judgment of a State court shall not be granted unless it appears that the applicant has exhausted the remedies available in the courts of the State, or that there is either an absence of available State corrective process or the existence of circumstances rendering such process ineffective to protect the rights of the prisoner.

(c) An applicant shall not be deemed to have exhausted the remedies available in the courts of the State, within the meaning of this section, if he has the right under the law of the State to raise, by any available procedure, the question presented.

(d) In any proceeding instituted in a Federal court by an application for a writ of habeas corpus by a person in custody pursuant to the judgment of a State court, a determination after a hearing on the merits of a factual issue, made by a state court of competent jurisdiction in a proceeding to which the applicant for the writ and the State or an officer or agent thereof were parties, evidenced by a written finding, written opinion, or other reliable and adequate written indicia, shall be presumed to be correct, unless the applicant shall establish or it shall otherwise appear, or the respondent shall admit—

(1) that the merits of the factual dispute were not resolved in the State court hearing;

(2) that the factfinding procedure employed by the State court was not adequate to afford a full and fair hearing;

(3) that the material facts were not adequately developed at the State court hearing;

(4) that the State court lacked jurisdiction of the subject matter or over the person of the applicant in the State court proceeding;

(5) that the applicant was an indigent and the State court, in deprivation of his constitutional right, failed to appoint counsel to represent him in the State court proceeding;

(6) that the applicant did not receive a full, fair, and adequate hearing in the State court proceeding; or

(7) that the applicant was otherwise denied due process of law in the State court proceeding;

(8) or unless that part of the record of the State court proceeding in which the determination of such factual issue was made, pertinent to a determination of the sufficiency of the evidence to support such factual determination, is produced as provided for hereinafter, and the Federal court on a consideration of such part of the record as a whole concludes that such factual determination is not fairly supported by the record:

And in an evidentiary hearing in the proceeding in the Federal court, when due proof of such factual determination has been made, unless the existence of one or more of the circumstances respectively set forth in paragraphs numbered (1) to (7), inclusive, is shown by the applicant, otherwise appears, or is admitted by the respondent, or unless the court concludes pursuant to the provisions of paragraph numbered (8) that the record in the State court proceeding, considered as a whole, does not fairly support such factual determination, the burden shall rest upon the applicant to establish by convincing evidence that the factual determination by the State court was erroneous.

(e) If the applicant challenges the sufficiency of the evidence adduced in such State court proceeding to support the State court's determination of a factual issue made therein, the applicant, if able, shall produce that part of the record pertinent to a determination of the sufficiency of the evidence to support such determination. If the applicant, because of indigency or other reason, is able to produce such part of the record, then the State shall produce such part of the record and the Federal court shall direct the State to do so by order directed to an appropriate State official. If the State cannot provide such pertinent part of the record, then the court shall determine under the existing facts and circumstances what weight shall be given to the State court's factual determination.

(f) A copy of the official records of the State court, duly certified by the clerk of such court to be a true and correct copy of a finding, judicial opinion, or other reliable written indicia showing such a factual determination by the State court shall be admissible in the Federal court proceeding.

28 U.S.C.A. § 2255. Federal custody; remedies on motion attacking sentence

A prisoner in custody under sentence of a court established by Act of Congress claiming the right to be released upon the ground that the sentence was imposed in violation of the Constitution or laws of the United States, or that the court was without jurisdiction to impose such sentence, or that the sentence was in excess of the maximum authorized by law, or is otherwise subject to collateral attack, may move the court which imposed the sentence to vacate, set aside or correct the sentence.

A motion for such relief may be made at any time.

Unless the motion and the files and records of the case conclusively show that the prisoner is entitled to no relief, the court shall cause notice thereof to be served upon the United States attorney, grant a prompt hearing thereon, determine the issues and make findings of fact and conclusions of law with respect thereto. If the court finds that the judgment was rendered without jurisdiction, or that the sentence imposed was not authorized by law or otherwise open to collateral attack, or that there has been such a denial or infringement of the constitutional rights of the prisoner as to render the judgment vulnerable to collateral attack, the court shall vacate and set the judgment aside and shall discharge the prisoner or resentence him or grant a new trial or correct the sentence as may appear appropriate.

A court may entertain and determine such motion without requiring the production of the prisoner at the hearing.

The sentencing court shall not be required to entertain a second or successive motion for similar relief on behalf of the same prisoner.

An appeal may be taken to the court of appeals from the order entered on the motion as from a final judgment on application for a writ of habeas corpus.

An application for a writ of habeas corpus in behalf of a prisoner who is authorized to apply for relief by motion pursuant to this section, shall not be entertained if it appears that the applicant has failed to apply for relief, by motion, to the court which sentenced him, or that such court has denied him relief, unless it also appears that the remedy by motion is inadequate or ineffective to test the legality of his detention.

APPENDIX B

Rating Supreme Court Justices*

Albert P. Blaustein and Roy M. Merskey

How good have our Supreme Court Justices been? Who are the ones acknowledged to be great? Who are the failures? What characteristics raise some above the others?

Sixty-five law school deans and professors of law, history and political science who deal with constitutional law attempted to evaluate the Justices with service on the High Court from its establishment until just before the appointment of Chief Justice Burger in 1969.[†] They were invited to do so in the hope that a study of those picked by these men as (a) great, (b) near great, (c) average, (d) below average or (f) failure might point up some patterns that would help in the selection of Supreme Court Justices in the future. They were given no criteria. They were asked to pick their own and to rate all the Justices in a continuum from "A" to "E."

Included in our roster of "judges of the judges" are specialists in fields of law with which the Court deals. While the Court attains most of its glamour in dealing with the Bill of Rights, it is also involved in—and its members must be judged for competence in—public utilities law, antitrust law, bankruptcy proceedings, contract actions, corporation law, copyright, trademark and patent cases, international law, admiralty law, family law, alien, citizenship and immigration cases, libel law, labor-management actions and elections law, to name but some. They also must be able to deal with matters of procedure, evidence, administrative law, Congressional committee hearings problems and other questions.

Here is the list of those selected as "great" in our survey, with names recorded in chronological order. The dates indicate years of service on the Court.

John Marshall	1801–1835
Joseph Story	1811–1845
Roger B. Taney	1836–1864
John M. Harlan I	1877–1911
Oliver W. Holmes, Jr.	1902–1932
Charles E. Hughes	1910–1916 and 1930–1941
Louis D. Brandeis	1916–1939
Harlan F. Stone	1925–1946
Benjamin N. Cardozo	1932–1938
Hugo L. Black	1937–1971
Felix Frankfurter	1939–1962
Earl Warren	1953–1969

*From 58 A.B.A.J. 1183 (1972). Reprinted by permission of the American Bar Association Journal.

†The survey was taken prior to the appointments of Chief Justice Burger and Associate Justices Blackmun, Powell, Rehnquist, and Stevens.

Marshall Alone Unanimously Classified as "A"

John Marshall alone is unanimously classified as "A" by all participants in the poll. It was Marshall who created the modern Court. In 1803 in *Marbury* v. *Madison,* he had the audacity, temerity or courage (choose one) to declare an act of Congress unconstitutional—and, by the sheer force of his argument and personality, make it stick. Although the Court did not declare another Congressional act unconstitutional for more than half a century—not until *Dred Scott* in 1857—it was this precedent, more than any other, that has made the Supreme Court a co-ordinate partner with the legislative and executive branches in the governance of the United States.

Two others are *near-unanimous choices: Brandeis and Holmes* with votes of sixty-two and sixty-one. They served together on the bench for more than sixteen years. They voted together in numerous decisions in which they expressed the minority view—in opinions which have made their dissenting votes of yesterday the majority position of today.

The remaining eight "greats" are bunched in the voting. Three served as Chief Justice—Stone, Hughes and Warren. Stone often joined Holmes and Brandeis in both majority opinions and dissents. They brought their different backgrounds to play in discussing the issues brought before them and, if they agreed on the outcome, they did not always agree on how to arrive at it.

Stone is known for the creativity of his opinions and for his zeal for social justice but not particularly for his role as "Chief." On the other hand, it is precisely for their outstanding qualities of leadership that Marshall, Hughes, and Warren are so highly rated. Hughes wrote the majority opinion in several key decisions that brought the Court in tune with the postdepression times of Franklin D. Roosevelt. Warren, of course, placed emphasis on individual liberty. This meant new rights and freedoms for black citizens, "one man, one vote" apportionment and a new judicial watchfulness over police procedure.

Hugo Black is the last on the list of greats to leave the Court. And he is the Justice who served third longest: thirty-four years, less nine days. Black was probably the most influential of the strong figures on the Court in the past thirty years. A man of intense moral commitment he is revered as a defender of personal liberties, of freedom of speech, of the rights of the "weak, the helpless and the outnumbered," to use John P. Frank's words.

Frankfurter is known for his deep love of the Supreme Court as a judicial body only, fulfilling the constitutional mandate of deciding cases and controversies. He was the exponent of judicial restraint in the most activist period the modern court has experienced. It is for this preoccupation with "restraint" that one of the law professors rates Frankfurter not great but a failure. He termed Frankfurter "consistently overrated," the point being that he used his brilliance to restrict the development of law.

Roger B. Taney is also a "great"—despite the *Dred Scott* case. This is a view shared by most commentators on the Court, conservative and liberal alike. For example, Norman Dorsen, a professor of law at New York University who is director of the Arthur Garfield Hays civil liberties program and one of the chief counsels for the American Civil Liberties Union, strongly disapproves of Taney's vote in the *Dred Scott* case, yet rates him great. While admitting that that particular vote gave him pause, Professor Dorsen credits Taney with being a jurist of outstanding skill, competence in the varied business of the Court, and long and conspicuous service.

Story—The Great Common Law Judge

Story's name is less well known to the general public. Undoubtedly this is because he served with Marshall for most of the thirty-three years of his tenure and was overshadowed by him. Yet many students of the Court still consider Story the greatest scholar the Court has seen, a virtuoso who contributed to equity jurisprudence, substantially creating American law on copyrights and patents, stamped his mark on property, trusts, partnership and insurance law and helped formulate commercial and maritime law.

Harlan I is most widely known today, perhaps as the Justice who dissented in *Plessy* v. *Ferguson* and said: "The Constitution is colorblind." He provides a good example of the disparity of viewpoint among the academicians. He rates an "A" from such men as Walter Gellhorn of Columbia (once law clerk to Chief Justice Stone), John P. Roche of Brandeis (distinguished for his studies of Justices John Marshall, Murphy and Rutledge) and Alpheus T. Mason, now at the University of Virginia (biographer of Stone, Brandeis, Taft and others). Yet, Gerald Gunther of Stanford Law School, once clerk to Chief Justice Warren, gives Harlan a "C." And Charles Alan Wright of the University of Texas gives him a lowly "D."

Justice Benjamin Cardozo provokes wide disagreement as to his greatness as a Supreme Court Justice, although the total vote clearly places him among the "select" dozen greats. Professor Gellhorn rates him "A," but Robert McKay, Dean of New York University Law School, limits him to a "C," while Professor Wright provides another "D." The question is whether the lofty esteem in which Cardozo is held (and that esteem is virtually unanimous) can fairly be attributed to a tenure on the Supreme Court of only six years. Cardozo was unquestionably one of the greatest of the common law judges, which he demonstrated as Chief Judge of the New York Court of Appeals. But fate denied him the opportunity to exploit fully his talents on the Supreme Bench.

Great Justices are Easier to Select

It is easier for students of the Court to select the great Justices than it is to differentiate between the near-great and the average. The task is a difficult and complicated one, for one can get confused between viewing members of the Supreme Court as judges and as historical personages. A good example is Jay, the first Chief Justice, whose greatness is more attributable to his prior roles as a diplomat and as one of the authors of *The Federalist*. On the Court he accomplished little. Taft received a "B" minus rating, a mark that undoubtedly is affected by his image as an adequate but not outstanding President. James Byrnes, who was rated near the bottom, may have suffered even more in the public mind because of his postjudicial career. He was a cold war warrior as Secretary of State under President Truman, and he fought vigorously against school desegregation as Governor of South Carolina.

Selecting the great Justices is more difficult, for example, than selecting the great Presidents. The President has a solo role. His impact is more obvious. The Justices are assembled nine at a time; their impact in discussion is not always revealed by their written opinions. Presidents have more or less a standard period of time in which to make their reputation. With the exception of Franklin D. Roosevelt, who was elected four times, all Presidents served one or two terms. And this makes for easier comparisons. But many of the Justices, and predominantly those acclaimed great, served long periods of time—ten served for more than thirty years. It is open to argument whether others, like Justices Moody and Goldberg, had like potential but were not rated highly and emerge with a grade of average because they did not have the time to become great.

Yet, it cannot be claimed that time alone can produce greatness: Wayne and McLean, both appointed by President Jackson, each served more than three decades but remained undistinguished. High rating seems to hinge on long service coupled with conspicuous attainments.

To rate the Justices, it was necessary to look behind the impact they made on the Supreme Court to make sure that great scholarship, learning, effort and judgment were not overlooked because they were expressed in support of minority positions. This is extremely difficult for educators, as much as anyone, are impressed by end results. So the dissentient may not fare as well in the rating as the spokesman for the Court.

Many of those questioned for this study admitted frankly that they did not even recognize the names of some of the pre-Marshall Justices, much less have an informed opinion about them. An exception to the handicap of era, perhaps, is Wilson (1789–1798), who did achieve a "B" minus rating. Such was Wilson's reputation as a lawyer in colonial times that George Washington paid him one hundred guineas tuition to permit his nephew, Bushrod Washington, himself later a member of the Court, to clerk in the Wilson office although the first President saw fit to turn a deaf ear to Wilson's application to become Chief Justice. Wilson's reputation is undoubtedly tarnished by his land speculations which led to his spending the closing years of his life ducking imprisonment for nonpayment of debts.

Fifteen Justices are Rated "Near Great"

Fifteen Justices are rated "near great" by the deans and professors. These are chronologically:

William Johnson	1804–1834
Benjamin R. Curtis	1851–1857
Samuel F. Miller	1862–1890
Stephen J. Field	1863–1897
Joseph P. Bradley	1870–1892
Morrison R. Waite	1874–1888
Edward D. White	1894–1921
William H. Taft	1921–1930
George Sutherland	1922–1938
William O. Douglas	1939–[1975]
Robert H. Jackson	1941–1954
Wiley B. Rutledge	1943–1949
John M. Harlan II	1955–1972
William J. Brennan, Jr.	1956–
Abe Fortas	1965–1969

This brings the list of those above "average" to twenty-seven of ninety-six. One can understand then Assistant Attorney General, now Associate Justice, Rehnquist's observation at the time of George H. Carswell's nomination that the standards of competence being applied to Carswell "would have excluded a good number of Supreme Court Justices throughout our history."

Johnson, like Story, was overshadowed by Marshall, but Johnson was more of a humanitarian than Marshall. He often objected to Marshall's "bossing" the Justices and protested against what he viewed as Marshall's excessive tenderness for property rights at the expense of human values.

Curtis was considered brilliant in admiralty and commercial law and cast one of the two dissenting votes in *Dred Scott,* but he did not like the routine of being a Justice and resigned after six years—in part because of his dislike of Taney's behavior in the publication of the *Dred Scott* decision.

Miller, Field and Bradley served at approximately the same time—the middle period of the Court. They dominated intellectually the post-Civil War Court, sharing the spotlight for a number of years with another remarkable judge, the first John M. Harlan. They are three who might easily have been rated as "great." Waite, White and Taft, all Chief Justices, received high marks for leadership and administrative ability.

Jackson, prosecutor at the Nuremberg Trials, was not well known for his pronouncements on the Bill of Rights, but was a highly knowledgeable, technically proficient lawyer. The second John Harlan, the Wall Street lawyer, was also greatly respected for his knowledge and craftsmanship. Rutledge, on the other hand, wrote his most brilliant opinions in the field of civil rights. He was a hard worker—he wrote 170 opinions in six years.

The incumbents on the list are Douglas[*] and Brennan. There is a wide difference of opinion about Douglas varying from those who rate him among the greatest to those who feel that his craftsmanship and technical competence do not match his courage or the correctness of his views. Brennan, the author of some of the most important opinions in the Warren years, is today the major spokesman for the Warren tradition.

It is particularly significant to see Sutherland chosen as near-great by so many "liberal" professors. Sutherland was the leader of the conservative bloc that attempted to obstruct so much of Franklin Roosevelt's New Deal legislation. His three close judicial allies (Van Devanter, McReynolds and Butler) were all ranked as "failures" in this survey. Yet Sutherland earns respect; if he was an obstructionist, he was, nonetheless, a learned judge. Some of his opinions endure. His opinion in the *Scottsboro Boys* case marks the beginning of Supreme Court modernization of criminal justice.

And finally, the assessment of Fortas seemed to give many of the academic raters some trouble. Professor Lindsay Cowen of the University of Georgia refused to rate him at all, simply commenting: "He could have been great." Professor Wright gave Fortas an "A," and Professor Dorsen gave him a "C," noting it would have been "B" if not for his "troubles and resignation."

In selecting those rated "below average" and "failure" the academicians made a distinction between judges who are obscure and those who are viewed in a negative way.

Moore (1799–1804) is a good example of those rated "below average." He served a short tenure before resigning in an unimportant judicial period and is written off merely as "unbelievably unimportant" but not as a failure. Six men are rated "below average." Besides Moore, they are:

Thomas Johnson	1791–1793
Robert Trimble	1826–1828
Philip P. Barbour	1836–1841
William B. Woods	1881–1887
Howell B. Jackson	1893–1895

Eight are Listed as Failures

The eight men named as failures reflect a more definite negative reaction among the raters. The professors' comments, added to their ratings, indicated that these are the judges thought to be of least accomplishment:

Willis Van Devanter	1911–1937
James C. McReynolds	1914–1941
Pierce Butler	1922–1939
James F. Byrnes	1941–1942
Harold Burton	1945–1958
Fred M. Vinson	1946–1953
Sherman Minton	1949–1956
Charles E. Whittaker	1957–1962

*Mr. Justice Douglas resigned in 1975.

This appraisal of Vinson and Van Devanter is likely to surprise some Court watchers. Vinson was at least an average administrative "Chief"; Van Devanter is a much respected technician.

McReynolds and Whittaker share the dubious distinction of being voted at the bottom of the list. McReynolds may suffer from an understandable distaste for his pettiness and prejudice.

Commonly accepted legal gossip has it that President Wilson appointed the crotchety, cantankerous McReynolds because he could not stand working with him as Attorney General and wanted to get him out of the way. McReynolds did not write his share of opinions and was hypercritical of the opinions of others.

Whittaker cast the deciding vote in forty-one crucial decisions—each time standing on the side that would deny civil rights or the extension of liberty. A Whittaker biographer says of him: "He was neither a judicial thinker nor a legal technician. None of his opinions showed any new insights. They were pedestrian."

Three of the bottom group were in the four-member anti-New Deal bloc headed by the respected Sutherland. They were McReynolds, Van Devanter and Butler. Byrnes, already mentioned in the context of his post-Court career, never wrote an individual dissenting or concurring opinion while on the bench and never participated in debate, except to agree. He only wrote sixteen opinions in all during his less than one year on the bench.

Of the ninety-six Justices rated, fifty-five were "average." There are four Chief Justices in this group: John Rutledge, Oliver Ellsworth, Salmon P. Chase and Melville Fuller. "Chief" Fred Vinson was placed with the "failures." Among the Associate Justices who were graded "average" are Peter Daniels, Stanley Matthews, Horace Gray, Brewer, Roberts, Reed, Murphy, Tom Clark, Potter Stewart, Byron White, and Thurgood Marshall.

Can Guidelines be Drawn for Selection of Justices?

Where then does an evaluation of great, good, so-so and bad lead? Can standards be drawn that will guide Presidents in sending the best possible judicial talent to the Court?

The Constitution does not help in that respect. Article III, Section 1, says nothing about the qualifications of judges or about the mechanics of choice. A Supreme Court Justice can be foreign born (as was Frankfurter) or wholly without legal training or experience. The able Jackson did not have a law degree, although his appointment was as late as 1941. Justice Samuel Miller, who sat for twenty-eight years, commencing in 1862, earned a medical degree and practiced medicine for more than a decade. Finding medicine tedious, he turned to law, picking up his legal training by browsing in the lawbooks of the lawyer with whom he shared office space. He was 31 when admitted to the Bar and 46 when named to the Court.

One of the difficulties in trying to formulate a rule is that one can almost always think of an exception that disproves it. President Eisenhower, in *Mandate for Change: The White House Years,* set up four rules he felt should be observed in selecting a Justice: The candidate should be investigated by the Federal Bureau of Investigation, should be approved by the American Bar Association, should hold no extreme legal or philosophical views and should be drawn from the inferior federal and state courts.

Ridiculing these criteria, historian Henry Steele Commager, a student of the Court, expressed astonishment that any President would substitute the FBI's judgement of a person's character and qualifications for his own or that he might permit any private organization—such as a bar association—to have veto power.

It should be recalled that former President Eisenhower—who appointed

Whittaker—also selected one "great" in Warren and two "near greats" in Harlan and Brennan, while his other appointee, Stewart, now classified as "average," may well move up before his service ends.

As far as extremist views are concerned, every important Justice has been accused of them at one time or another. Thomas Jefferson thought Marshall was a "dangerous extremist" and there were those who would have branded Brandeis with the same words.

President Nixon, as did Eisenhower, has stated that prior judicial experience is a prerequisite. Chief Justice Burger and Justice Blackmun, as well as Carswell and Haynsworth, met this test, although Justices Powell and Rehnquist did not.

Fifty of the ninety-six jurists included in this study had prior judicial experience, but for the most part that might be considered more of an argument against than for. Frankfurter, who came from professional ranks, once made a study of the relevance and value of this particular attribute and concluded: "One is entitled to say without qualification that the correlation between prior judicial experience and fitness for the functions of the Supreme Court is zero."

It is easier for the analyst to come up with a list of what is not relevant than what is. One ought to be able to say without question—given the examples of Vinson, Burton and Minton—that cronyism is undesirable. One can check the record and say that emphasizing such factors as geographical origin (as for Whittaker) or attitude (as in the case of Chief Justice Salmon P. Chase) will lead to unsatisfactory results. But then one must consider the counter results in the ultimately acclaimed appointments of Field (a geographical appointee) and Hugo Black (a close friend of Franklin Roosevelt).

Political Parties Have Provided Good and Bad Justices

No political party can lay claim to being the party of judicial greatness. Republicans and Democrats (and Federalists, for that matter) have provided good and bad justices. Nor are there any guarantees that the judges appointed for political reasons will pursue the philosophies of the Presidents who appointed them. Madison, who together with Jefferson disliked Marshall, appointed Story, but Story turned into a judicial ally of Marshall. Stone was even more of a liberal than the conservative Calvin Coolidge feared he was becoming, while Warren certainly surprised Eisenhower.

How about government experience? Dean McKay once summed up this subject by writing: "Indeed, if an "understanding" of government were an important criterion of success, surely Chief Justice Vinson (appointed by Truman) would deserve top experience honors for his service as a Congressman, judge of the Court of Appeals for the District of Columbia, Director of the Office of Economic Stabilization and Secretary of the Treasury." Chief Justice Taft, the only former President to sit on the Court, had a uniquely rich and distinguished background, but he did not reach greatness on the Court.

Fourteen Justices were law professors for significant periods of their lives, and for six or seven of them law teaching was their principal occupation. Five justices were law school deans.

Justice Frankfurter gained his greatest reputation as a Harvard Law School professor; Holmes taught at Harvard prior to his appointment. Stone was best known for his years as Dean of the Columbia Law School; Douglas spent most of his pre-judicial career as a law professor, first at Columbia and then at Yale. Chief Justice Taft was Dean of Cincinnati Law School prior to his election to the Presidency and a professor of law at Yale between his term as President and his appointment as Chief Justice. Fortas followed Taft and Douglas to become the third Yale Law School professor to serve as Justice. Chief Justice Hughes was a Cornell Law School professor for two years. And the remarkable Story, the youngest appointee in the history of the Supreme Court, served as the first professor of law at Harvard College during his service on the bench from 1811 to 1845, while he was also engaged in a third career, composing his celebrated legal poems. Wiley Rutledge, rated a "near-great," held law deanships at both Washington University in St. Louis and Iowa University.

But other law professors made average or less than average records on the Court. Roberts was a professor of law at the University of Pennsylvania before his selection to the Court and was named dean after leaving the bench. Burton was dean of the law school at Vanderbilt. Strong taught law at Columbia College (later George Washington University), Murphy spent a few years teaching law at the University of Detroit, and McReynolds was once a professor of law at Vanderbilt.

Many of the great judges were "well-born"—Holmes and Taft came from aristocratic families. But Stone was the son of a New Hampshire farmer, and Black was the eighth son of an Alabama storekeeper. The youngest Justice appointed was Story (at thirty-two), and he made the roster of greats. Near-great Douglas was appointed at forty, yet Warren was sixty-two when appointed and seventy-eight when he retired; Oliver Wendell Holmes was sixty-three when he was appointed and ninety when he retired.

If the statistics indicate anything, it is that law professors make the best Supreme Court Justices, although it may seem self-serving for a group of academics to reach that conclusion. Murphy, when Attorney General for F.D.R., urged him to make federal court appointments from the universities, from among those who view the law from a background of philosophy, history and public welfare rather than from among those who think as practitioners. His advice opened the way for the appointments of Frankfurter, Douglas and Rutledge.

But all this still does not provide criteria. What can be said of all those labeled great and, to some extent certainly, those labeled near-great? Their biographies show them to be men of broad intelligence, of wide-ranging interests. This means they are informed on more than their narrow field of the law. They are men who are steeped in diverse fields, among them literature, history, political science, economics, the physical sciences, philosophy and religion. The key would seem to lie in the realm of character and temperament. This may furnish a reliable guide as to whether a potential appointee is a man vested with a love of learning and the capacity to assimilate, digest and apply.

Great Justices must be men of dispassion and integrity. They must be men of resourcefulness and imagination. Perhaps one of the best tests is one of courage. President Kennedy's conclusion in his choice of great politicians in *Profiles in Courage* may be equally applicable to Supreme Court Justices.

Frankfurter showed his courage early in his career by serving on the board of the National Association for the Advancement of Colored People when it was not popular to do so and by being among the founders of the American Civil Liberties Union. Holmes was born in the purple and yet fought consistently for the rights of the common man. Hughes and Stone represented members of the New York legislature who were accused of being Communists after World War I. Brandeis is known as the "poor man's lawyer." Equally, Marshall did not hesitate to stand up against Jefferson, and Taney held his ground against Lincoln, while Hughes heroically and successfully opposed Franklin Roosevelt's Court Packing bill.

By and large, it can be said that it is far easier to diagnose a lack of integrity and courage than the contrary manifestation. Perhaps what history shows is that while it is difficult for everyone to be able to foretell who will be the great men, perhaps it is possible for the experts to determine who will not be.

APPENDIX C

Supreme Court Decisions Involving the Criminal Process Overruled By Subsequent Decisions

---

It is difficult to compile a comprehensive list of Supreme Court decisions involving the criminal process that have been subsequently overruled, in part because the Court does not always state explicitly that it is overruling a prior decision. As of June, 1969, the Court had overruled itself in 133 cases (criminal and civil). See Freidman and Israel, *The Justices of the United States Supreme Court: 1789–1969,* 3257–3265 (Vol. IV, 1969). The authors have discovered an additional 14 decisions (criminal and civil) that were overruled by the Burger Court between June, 1969, and January, 1977. The following compilation of those cases involving the criminal process that have been subsequently overruled by the Supreme Court is presented with the knowledge that legal scholars are unlikely to agree on a single list. The authors bear the responsibility for any erroneous inclusions or exclusions.

OVERRULING CASE AND HOLDING	*CASE(S) OVERRULED*
1. *Garland* v. *United States,* 232 U.S. 642, 646 (1914) (due process not violated when no arraignment or plea taken from defendant after prior conviction set aside and new trial granted).*	1. *Crain* v. *United States,* 162 U.S. 625 (1896).
2. *Rosen* v. *United States,* 245 U.S. 467, 470 (1918) (previous conviction for forgery does not disqualify the person convicted from testifying on behalf of the government in a federal criminal trial).	2. *United States* v. *Reid,* 12 How. 361 (1851).
3. *Funk* v. *United States,* 290 U.S. 371 (1933) (the wife of a defendant on trial in a federal criminal trial is not incompetent as a witness on his behalf).	3. *Stein* v. *Bowman,* 13 Pet. 209 (1839) (in part).

---

*This is the earliest overruling decision involving the criminal process that we could discover.

4. *Tigner* v. *Texas,* 310 U.S. 141 (1940) (exemption of agriculture activities from criminal liability under state antitrust act not violative of the equal protection of the laws).

4. *Connolly* v. *Union Sewer Pipe Co.,* 184 U.S. 540 (1902).

5. *Edwards* v. *California,* 314 U.S. 160 (1941) (use of police powers of state to prohibit the bringing in or transportation of known indigents held unconstitutional).

5. *City of New York* v. *Miln,* 11 Pet. 102 (1837).

6. *Nye* v. *United States,* 313 U.S. 33 (1941) (contempt of court is considered "civil" only when the punishment is wholly remedial, and is not intended as a deterrent to offenses against the public).

6. *Toledo Newspaper Co.* v. *United States,* 247 U.S. 402 (1918).

7. *Jones* v. *Opelika,* 319 U.S. 103 (1942) (reargument) (state may not impose license tax, subject to criminal penalties, on persons canvassing or soliciting within a municipality). In accord is *Murdock* v. *Pennsylvania,* 319 U.S. 105 (1943).

7. *Jones* v. *Opelika,* 316 U.S. 584 (1941).

8. *United States* v. *Rabinowitz,* 339 U.S. 56, 66 85 (1950) (warrantless search does not violate the Fourth Amendment merely because the officers who conducted the search failed to secure a warrant, although they had time to do so).

8. *Trupiano* v. *United States,* 334 U.S. 699 (1948).

9. *Reid* v. *Covert,* 354 U.S. 1 (1957) (civilian dependents of members of armed forces overseas may not be constitutionally tried by court-martial in times of peace for capital offenses committed abroad).

9. *Kinsella* v. *Krueger,* 351 U.S. 470 (1956).

10. *Ladner* v. *United States,* 358 U.S. 169 (1958) (on rehearing) (single discharge of a shotgun wounding two federal officers constitutes only a single violation of federal assault statute).

10. *Ladner* v. *United States,* 355 U.S. 282 (1958).

11. *Elkins* v. *United States,* 364 U.S. 206, 212–213 (1960) (evidence illegally seized by state officials is not admissible in a federal criminal trial). In accord is *Rios* v. *United States,* 364 U.S. 253 (1960).

11. *Weeks* v. *United States,* 232 U.S. 383, 398 (1914) (in part).

12. *James* v. *United States,* 366 U.S. 213, 215, 221, 223, 241 (1961) (embezzled funds are included as the "gross income" of the embezzler in the year in which the funds are misappropriated).

12. *Commissioner* v. *Wilcox,* 327 U.S. 404 (1946).

13. *Mapp* v. *Ohio,* 367 U.S. 643 (1961) (evidence illegally seized is not admissible in state criminal trials).

13. *Wolf* v. *Colorado,* 338 U.S. 25 (1949) (in part).

14. *Fay* v. *Noia*, 372 U.S. 391, 435 (1963) (state prisoners not required to seek certiorari in the U.S. Supreme Court as a precondition to applying in federal district court for habeas corpus).

14. *Darr* v. *Burford*, 339 U.S. 200 (1959) (in part).

15. *Ferguson* v. *Skrupa*, 372 U.S. 726, 731 (1963) (state statute making it a crime for any person except a lawyer to engage in the business of debt adjusting held not violative of the equal protection of the laws).

15. *Adams* v. *Turner*, 244 U.S. 590 (1917).

16. *Gideon* v. *Wainwright*, 372 U.S. 335 (1963) (Sixth Amendment right to counsel held applicable to state felony trials).

16. *Betts* v. *Brady*, 316 U.S. 455 (1942).

17. *Malloy* v. *Hogan*, 378 U.S. 1 (1964) (Fifth Amendment privilege against self-incrimination held applicable to state criminal proceedings).

17. *Twining* v. *New Jersey*, 211 U.S. 78 (1908).

18. *Murphy* v. *Waterfront Commission*, 378 U.S. 52 (1964) (privilege against self-incrimination protects a state witness against incrimination under federal as well as state law).

18. *Jack* v. *Kansas*, 199 U.S. 373 (1905).

19. *Escobedo* v. *Illinois*, 378 U.S. 478 (1964) (suspect has a constitutional right to the presence of his retained counsel during custodial interrogation).

19. *Crooker* v. *California*, 357 U.S. 433 (1958).

20. *Pointer* v. *Texas*, 380 U.S. 415 (1965) (Sixth Amendment right to confront witnesses held applicable to state criminal proceedings).

20. *West* v. *Louisiana*, 194 U.S. 258 (1904).

21. *United States* v. *Brown*, 381 U.S. 437 (1965) (federal statute making it a crime for a Communist Party member to serve as a union officer or employee held to constitute a bill of attainder).

21. *American Communications Association* v. *Douds*, 339 U.S. 382 (1950); *Communist Party of the U.S.* v. *Subversive Activities Control Board*, 367 U.S. 1 (1961).

22. *Harris* v. *United States*, 382 U.S. 162 (1965) (witness' refusal to comply with federal district court order to answer grand jury's questions held not within Fed. R. Crim. P. 42(a) authorizing summary punishment for contempt).

22. *Brown* v. *United States*, 359 U.S. 41 (1959).

23. *Griffin* v. *California*, 380 U.S. 609 (1965) (prosecutor may not directly comment on defendant's silence at trial).

23. *Adamson* v. *California*, 332 U.S. 46 (1947).

24. *Spevack* v. *Klein*, 385 U.S. 511 (1967) (attorney may not be disbarred for invoking privilege against self-incrimination).

24. *Cohen* v. *Hurley*, 366 U.S. 177 (1961).

25. *Warden* v. *Hayden*, 387 U.S. 294 (1967) (mere evidence admissible in criminal trial providing there is a nexus between the item seized and criminal behavior).

25. *Gouled* v. *United States*, 255 U.S. 298 (1919).

26. *Camara* v. *Municipal Court*, 387 U.S. 541 (1967) (administrative search of home requires search warrant if the owner refuses to consent to warrantless inspection).

26. *Frank* v. *Maryland*, 359 U.S. 360 (1959).

27. *Katz* v. *United States*, 389 U.S. 347 (1967) (electronic surveillance comes within ambit of Fourth Amendment protections). In accord is *Berger* v. *New York*, 388 U.S. 41 (1967).

27. *Olmstead* v. *United States*, 277 U.S. 438 (1928); *Goldman* v. *United States*, 316 U.S. 129 (1942).

28. *Peyton* v. *Roe*, 391 U.S. 54 (1968) (prisoner-petitioner serving consecutive sentences is "in custody" for purposes of federal habeas corpus even though he challenges future sentence not yet served).

28. *McNally* v. *Hill*, 293 U.S. 131 (1934).

29. *Bruton* v. *United States*, 391 U.S. 123 (1968) (in joint trial of co-defendants, admission by one co-defendant implicating other co-defendant held not admissible unless the co-defendant making admission testifies at trial).

29. *Delli Paoli* v. *United States*, 352 U.S. 232 (1957).

30. *Duncan* v. *Louisiana*, 391 U.S. 145 (1968) (Sixth Amendment right to jury trial applicable to state criminal trials).

30. *Maxwell* v. *Dow*, 176 U.S. 581 (1900)

31. *Carafas* v. *LaVallee*, 391 U.S. 234 (1968) (unconditional release from custody of prisoner pending Supreme Court review does not render case moot).

31. *Parker* v. *Ellis*, 362 U.S. 574 (1960).

32. *Lee* v. *Florida*, 392 U.S. 378 (1968) (illegal electronic surveillance by state police violates the Federal Communications Act).

32. *Schwartz* v. *Texas*, 344 U.S. 199 (1952).

33. *Brandenburg* v. *Ohio*, 395 U.S. 444 (1969) (Ohio criminal syndicalism statute prohibiting, inter alia, the advocating of crime, sabotage, or violence and assembling with persons advocating such acts, held unconstitutional).

33. *Whitney* v. *California*, 274 U.S. 357 (1927).

34. *Chimel* v. *California*, 395 U.S. 752 (1969) (scope of search incident to arrest restricted to area of arrestee's immediate control).

34. *Harris* v. *United States*, 331 U.S. 145 (1947); *United States* v. *Rabinowitz*, 339 U.S. 56 (1950).

35. *Benton* v. *Maryland,* 395 U.S. 784 (1969) (Double Jeopardy Clause applicable to state criminal trials).

35. *Palko* v. *Connecticut,* 302 U.S. 319 (1937).

36. *Miller* v. *California,* 413 U.S. 15 (1973) (test of "utterly without redeeming social value" rejected in obscenity prosecutions).

36. *Memoirs* v. *Massachusetts,* 383 U.S. 413 (1966) (in part).

37. *Cardwell* v. *Lewis,* 417 U.S. 583 (1974) (not unreasonable for police to tow arrestee's car to impoundment area and without warrant to take paint samples from the exterior of the car).

37. *Preston* v. *United States,* 376 U.S. 364, 367 (1964).

38. *Taylor* v. *Louisiana,* 419 U.S. 522 (1975) (women may not be excluded from jury service or given automatic exemptions solely on basis of sex).

38. *Hoyt* v. *Florida,* 368 U.S. 57 (1961).

39. *Dove* v. *United States,* 423 U.S. 325 (1976) (petitioner's death pending Supreme Court review held to require dismissal of petition).

39. *Durham* v. *United States,* 401 U.S. 481 (1971).

40. *Gregg* v. *Georgia,* 428 U.S. 153 (1976) (standardless jury procedures in sentencing for capital offense held unconstitutional). See also *Proffitt* v. *Florida,* 428 U.S. 242 (1976); *Jurek* v. *Texas,* 428 U.S. 262 (1976); *Woodson* v. *North Carolina,* 428 U.S. 280 (1976); and *Roberts* v. *Louisiana,* 428 U.S. 325 (1976).

40. *McGautha* v. *California,* 402 U.S. 183 (1971). See also *Furman* v. *Georgia,* 408 U.S. 238 (1972) (plurality opinion).

41. *Stone* v. *Powell,* 428 U.S. 465 (1976) (when a state has provided an opportunity for a full and fair hearing on a Fourth Amendment claim, a state prisoner may not be granted federal habeas corpus relief on the ground that illegally seized evidence was introduced at his trial).

41. *Kaufmann* v. *United States,* 394 U.S. 217 (1969) (in part).

APPENDIX D

Sample Petition for Certiorari

IN THE

SUPREME COURT OF THE UNITED STATES
October Term, 1974
No. 74–6377

———

ROBERT AUSTIN SULLIVAN,

Petitioner,

-v.-

STATE OF FLORIDA,

Respondent.

———

PETITION FOR WRIT OF CERTIORARI TO THE
SUPREME COURT OF FLORIDA

———

ATTORNEYS FOR PETITIONER

———

INDEX

———

*Corresponding text page.

TABLE OF CASES

* * *

STATUTES

* * *

OTHER AUTHORITIES

* * *

IN THE
SUPREME COURT OF THE UNITED STATES
October Term, 1974
No. 74–6377

———

ROBERT AUSTIN SULLIVAN,

Petitioner,

-v.-

STATE OF FLORIDA,

Respondent.

———

PETITION FOR WRIT OF CERTIORARI TO THE
SUPREME COURT OF FLORIDA

Petitioner prays that a writ of certiorari issue to review the judgment of the
Supreme Court of the State of Florida entered on November 27, 1974.

CITATIONS TO OPINIONS BELOW

The opinion of the Supreme Court of Florida is reported at 303 So. 2d 632
(1974) and is set out in Appendix A, hereto, pp. 1a–7a, infra [omitted].

JURISDICTION

The judgment of the Supreme Court of the State of Florida was entered on November 27, 1974, and is set out in Appendix A hereto [omitted]. Jurisdiction of this Court is invoked under 28 U.S.C. § 1257(3), petitioner having asserted below and asserting here deprivation of rights secured by the Constitution of the United States.

QUESTIONS PRESENTED

1. Whether the imposition and carrying out of the sentence of death for the crime of first degree murder under the law of Florida violates the Eighth or Fourteenth Amendment to the Constitution of the United States?

2. Whether a prosecutor's knowing, calculated and intentional introduction at a criminal trial in the jury's presence of manifestly inadmissible and prejudicial testimony suggesting that a state's witness has taken and passed a polygraph test is "harmless error" under the due process clause of the Fourteenth Amendment in a capital case where petitioner was subsequently convicted and sentenced to death?

CONSTITUTIONAL AND STATUTORY PROVISIONS INVOLVED

1. This case involves the Eighth and Fourteenth Amendments to the Constitution of the United States.

2. This case also involves the following provisions of the statutes of Florida:

* * *

STATEMENT OF THE CASE

This is a petition for a writ of certiorari to review the judgment of the Supreme Court of Florida, entered on November 27, 1974, affirming the petitioner's conviction and sentence of death.

On November 12, 1973, in the Circuit Court of Dade County, Florida, petitioner, Robert Austin Sullivan, an indigent white male, was sentenced to die upon conviction for the first degree murder of Donald Schmidt, a white male.

The State's evidence showed that on April 10, 1973, the body of Donald Schmidt was found by two hunters in a remote marshy area in the western part of Dade County, Florida. Sgt. Arthur Felton, of the Dade County Public Safety Department, testified that the body was lying face down, that the hands were bound behind the back with white surgical tape, that one shoe was missing, and that there was a large wound in the back of the head, R. [trial record] 1240–1242; 1245.

Sgt. Felton obtained information that the petitioner frequented Keith's Cruise Lounge in Hallandale, Broward County, Florida, and on April 17, 1973, Sgt. Felton, together with three other Dade County detectives went in two cars to that location. Prior to going to Keith's Lounge, Felton obtained knowledge about outstanding felony warrants from New Hampshire, where the petitioner had been prior to coming to Miami, R. 1256.

The detectives arrived at the Lounge at about midnight and shortly thereafter observed a Cadillac (previously described as having belonged to petitioner); a person whom they believed to be petitioner left the car together with two other individuals, and the three remained in the Lounge for approximately three hours. They then left, stood talking in the parking lot for 15 or 20 minutes, and got back in the car and headed toward Miami, R. 1331–1335.

After the petitioner had driven a few blocks into Dade County, Sgt. Felton stopped the car and arrested the petitioner on the outstanding felony warrants from New Hampshire, R. 1256–1257.

The police seized various items in the automobile which were later introduced at petitioner's trial, including a shotgun, hand gun, and white adhesive tape. The State also introduced at trial a watch the petitioner was wearing at the time of his arrest which had belonged to the victim and two credit cards belonging to the victim found in the petitioner's wallet at the time of his arrest, R. 1262–1265. The two persons in the car with petitioner, a juvenile and one Reid McLaughlin, were also taken into custody, although the juvenile was released by the police a few hours later.

After petitioner's arrest, he was transported to the Public Safety Department Building, where he gave a statement to the police, R. 1253–1254. In this statement, which was introduced at petitioner's trial, R. 1279–1289, petitioner admitted that Reid McLaughlin and he went to the Homestead Howard Johnson's on the night of April 8, 1973, with the intention of robbing it, that McLaughlin and he counted the customers and employees as they left until they were certain the assistant manager, Donald Schmidt, was inside alone, that McLaughlin and he entered through the back door, that McLaughlin held the assistant manager at gunpoint while he took money from the safe, that McLaughlin taped Schmidt's hands behind him as petitioner drove him to a deserted and swampy area of Dade County, that McLaughlin and he planned to "dispose" of Schmidt by murdering him, that they stopped the car and walked Schmidt into the swamp, that petitioner struck Schmidt twice on the head with a tire iron, and taking the shotgun that McLaughlin was carrying, then shot Schmidt four times in the head, and that McLaughlin and he took Schmidt's watch and credit cards and used the cards several times in Dade County. After the police took petitioner's statement, they described it to McLaughlin, who also made a statement admitting complicity in the murder of Schmidt and implicating petitioner in this crime. Both McLaughlin and petitioner were subsequently indicted for the first degree murder and robbery of Schmidt.

McLaughlin was the State's chief witness against petitioner. Prior to petitioner's trial, he had agreed to plead nolo contendere to a second degree murder charge in return for a life sentence and his testifying against petitioner.[5] McLaughlin testified that petitioner and he had discussed committing "[t]he perfect crime," R. 1360,[6] and had determined to rob the Howard Johnson's restaurant where petitioner had once served as assistant manager, R. 1362. McLaughlin entered the restaurant, ordered food, and counted the customers and employees. He and petitioner waited until all of these persons had left except the assistant manager and then entered and held Donald Schmidt at gunpoint; McLaughlin took his jewelry and wallet, and petitioner took the cash from the safe. The two then abducted Schmidt in petitioner's car. McLaughlin taped Schmidt's hands behind him, and since "[h]e was looking kind of worried, . . . I said, 'Don't worry about it, we will leave you in the woods and tie you up,' " R. 1376. McLaughlin described how he and petitioner stopped the car in a swampy area and led Schmidt away, how petitioner hit Schmidt on the head twice with a tire iron, and how he gave petitioner the shotgun, R. 1377–1378. McLaughlin testified that he then started to walk away and heard petitioner fire the shotgun four times, R. 1378. The two men left the swamp and returned to Miami; on the drive back, according to McLaughlin, R. 1379, petitioner remarked "I don't feel no different," ibid.

---

[5]McLaughlin received a sentence of life imprisonment on the day after petitioner's death sentence was imposed, R. 1706. The robbery charge against him was dismissed. Ibid.

[6]Sgt. Arthur Felton testified that petitioner told him, after giving the statement concerning the crime, "that he always wanted to commit a murder." R. 1276.

Near the conclusion of the cross examination of McLaughlin by petitioner's attorney, McLaughlin was asked:

"Q. [Defense counsel] Did anyone tell you that your sentence would depend on how your testimony turned out?
A. Yes." (R. 1390).

Upon redirect examination by the State, McLaughlin was asked:

"Q. [Assistant State Attorney] Now, sir, when you say that your sentence is going to be determined by your testimony is there any question in your mind what your sentence is going to be?
A. No.
Q. Has there been an agreement as to what your sentence is going to be?
A. Yes.
Q. What is that?
A. Life." (R. 1392).

The State continued:

"Q. Now, Reid, I believe you just indicated that the sentence is going to be life.
A. Yes, it is.
Q. Was there any agreement if you testified any particular way that you would get anything other than life?
A. No.
Q. When you said that your sentence is going to be determined by your testimony would you explain to the jury what you meant?
A. That I would have to have taken a polygraph test and passed it." (R. 1393–1394).

An immediate defense motion for a mistrial was denied on the grounds, inter alia, that "the reply of the witness was not calculated by the question," R. 1397, asked by the State. On the following day, the State admitted that the "question was intended to elicit that answer," R. 1425. A renewed mistrial motion by petitioner was denied.

Petitioner presented witnesses in his defense and testified at some length, denying complicity in the murder and robbery of Donald Schmidt, repudiating the statement he had given to the police, and directly controverting McLaughlin's testimony about petitioner's involvement in these crimes.

The jury was instructed that on the first degree murder charge, it could return a verdict of guilty to first degree murder, guilty to second degree murder, guilty to third degree murder, guilty to manslaughter or not guilty.[7] It found petitioner guilty of first degree murder. A sentencing hearing was subsequently convened, and petitioner introduced the testimony of five witnesses in mitigation of sentence. A majority of the jury recommended the death sentence,[8] and the trial judge made

---

[7]Petitioner admitted having used Schmidt's credit cards, but claimed that McLaughlin had given them to him, along with Schmidt's watch, R. 1472–1475, and that McLaughlin had said " 'He had ripped them [the cards and watch] off from a trip the previous night,' " R. 1474. Petitioner had stipulated that the watch, Master Charge credit card, and Playboy Club credit card in his possession when he was arrested belong to Donald Schmidt and that he had signed the name "Donald Schmidt" to a number of credit card receipts used to purchase goods with these two credit cards. R. 1213.

[8]The verdict stated: "We, a majority of the jury, in Miami, Dade County, Florida, this 9th day of November, A.D., 1973, recommend that the Court impose a sentence of death by electrocution as authorized by the Florida Statute 775.0821. So say the majority." R. 1885.

the formal findings required by Fla. Stat. Ann. § 921.141 (1974–1975 supp.), that three "aggravating circumstances" were present (the murder was committed during the course of a felony, robbery; for a pecuniary motive; and in a "heinous, atrocious and cruel" fashion, R. 1694–1695) and two "mitigating circumstances" were present (petitioner's age; the fact that he had no prior criminal convictions, R. 1697). The court concluded that the "aggravating circumstances in this case purely outweigh beyond and to the exclusion of every reasonable doubt in the court's mind the mitigating circumstances," ibid., and imposed a sentence of death upon petitioner. . . .

On November 27, 1974, the Supreme Court of Florida affirmed petitioner's conviction and sentence of death, with two Justices dissenting in regard to the death penalty. *Sullivan* v. *State,* 303 So. 2d 632 (Fla. 1974) (attached as App. A [omitted]).[10]

HOW THE FEDERAL QUESTIONS WERE RAISED AND DECIDED BELOW

I. A motion to dismiss the indictment, on the grounds of the unconstitutionality of the Florida capital punishment statute, was filed, R. 1764–1765, and after a hearing the trial court denied it. R. 431.[11] Petitioner's motion for new trial, R. 1814–1815, which was denied on November 12, 1973, R. 1700, raised the denial of the motion to dismiss.

Petitioner's assignments of error, R. 1820–1821, and brief filed with the Supreme Court of Florida again raised the claim that the statute under which petitioner was convicted and sentenced to death violated the Eighth and Fourteenth Amendments to the United States Constitution in that it authorized the imposition of cruel and unusual punishment and the arbitrary infliction of punishment.

The Court tacitly rejected this claim by stating: "We have examined the other assignments of error urged by appellant, and find them to be without merit. Accordingly, no reversible error appearing, the decision appealed from is hereby affirmed." *Sullivan* v. *State,* 303 So. 2d 632, 637 (Fla. 1974) (App. A, infra at 6a [omitted]).

II. Petitioner's counsel made an ore tenus motion during the trial for a mistrial at the first instance of the introduction of testimony by state's witness Reid McLaughlin pertaining to a polygraph test; however, the motion for mistrial was denied, R. 1397. Petitioner renewed the mistrial motion when the State admitted that the elicitation of this testimony was calculated and intentional, but the motion was again denied, R. 1429, 1524–1525. Petitioner's motion for new trial, R. 1814–1815, which was denied, raised as error the denial of the motion for mistrial, R. 1700.

Petitioner briefed this issue on appeal, but the Supreme Court of Florida rejected the claim:

> We conclude that, under the peculiar circumstances presented here, the trial court did not commit reversible error in denying appellant's motion for mistrial.

---

[10]Petitioner did not file for rehearing. On December 9, 1974, the Supreme Court of Florida stayed the issuance of the mandate and further proceedings until January 9, 1975, in order to allow a petition for certiorari to be filed in this Court. On January 7, 1975, Mr. Justice Powell stayed the execution and enforcement of sentence pending a timely filing and disposition by the Court of a petition for writ of certiorari. On February 18, 1975, Mr. Justice Powell signed an order extending the time to file a petition for certiorari to and including April 20, 1975.

[11]The Supreme Court of Florida on July 26, 1973, in the case of *State* v. *Dixon,* 283 So. 2d 1, upheld the constitutionality of the Florida capital punishment statute which is here under attack and which was enacted by the Florida legislature after this Court's opinion in *Furman* v. *Georgia,* 408 U.S. 238 (1972).

Sullivan v. *State,* 303 So. 2d 632, 636 (Fla. 1974) (App. A, infra, at 5a [omitted]).

REASONS FOR GRANTING THE WRIT

I. The court should grant certiorari to consider whether the imposition and carrying out of the sentence of death for the crime of first degree murder under the law of Florida violates the eighth or fourteenth amendment to the Constitution of the United States.

In order to avoid burdening the Court with lengthy and repetitious matter, petitioner adopts the "Reasons for Granting the Writ" section of the Petition for Writ of Certiorari to the Supreme Court of Florida, *Hallman* v. *Florida,* No. 74–6168 (filed March 11, 1975) at 19–59 (attached as App. B, infra [omitted]).

II. The Court should grant certiorari to consider whether a prosecutor's knowing, calculated, and intentional introduction at a criminal trial in the jury's presence of manifestly inadmissible and prejudicial testimony suggesting that a state's witness had taken and passed a polygraph test is "harmless error" under the due process clause of the Fourteenth Amendment in a capital case where petitioner was subsequently convicted and sentenced to death.

* * *

CONCLUSION

Petitioner prays that the petition for a writ of certiorari be granted.

Respectfully submitted,

ATTORNEYS FOR PETITIONER

Note: On July 6, 1976, the United States Supreme Court denied certiorari. 428 U.S. 911.

APPENDIX E

Statistical Summary of Findings of Florida Death Row Study

Below is a summary of the major findings of the Florida Death Row study. In some instances, data were not available, so that the sample size is less than 83 inmates. The accuracy of the inmates' answers to certain factual, qualitative questions (e.g., number of accomplices, length of jury deliberations) could not be independently verified. This was also the case with opinion questions (e.g., fairness of trial, feasibility of prisoner rehabilitation).

PLACE OF BIRTH ($N = 81$)

	N	%
Florida	22	27.1
Other	59	72.9

AGE AT SENTENCING ($N = 83$)

Mode* = 23 yrs.
Median = 28.2
Range = 17–58
$\bar{x}$ age = 28.0 yrs.

RELIGIOUS PREFERENCE ($N = 82$)

Faith	N	%
Traditional Protestant	47	57.3
Catholic	15	18.2
Other	9	10.9
None	11	13.4

BORN-AGAIN CHRISTIAN? ($N = 81$)

	N	%
Yes	22	27.1
No	59	72.9

*Mode = the value of maximum frequency.

WHEN REBORN? ($N = 22$)

	N	%
Before conviction	3	13.6
After conviction	19	86.3

I.Q. TESTS (BETA) ($N = 57$)

Score	N	%
71–79	2	3.5
80–89	7	12.2
90–109	39	68.4
110–119	8	14.0
120–128	1	1.7

FORMAL EDUCATION COMPLETED ($N = 83$)

Grade-years	N	%
0–5	8	9.6
6–12	64	77.1
13+	11	13.2

$\bar{x} = 9.7$ yrs.

EDUCATIONAL PERFORMANCE LEVEL ($N = 39$)

Gray-Votaw-Rogers Scale

Grade-years	N	%
0–5	13	33.3
6–12	25	66.7

$\bar{x} = 6.8$ yrs.

Marital Status at Time of Offense (N = 83)

	N	%
Married	35	42.1
Single	48	57.8

Present Marital Status (N = 83)

	N	%
Married	27	32.5
Single	56	67.4

No. of Marriages (N = 83)

	N	%
None	30	36.1
1	32	38.5
2 or more	21	25.3

No. of Children (N = 83)

	N	%
None	34	40.9
1-2	30	36.1
3-4	13	15.6
5 or more	6	7.2

Living with Children at Time of Offense? (N = 51)

	N	%
Yes	17	33.3
No	34	66.7

No. of Brothers (N = 83)

	N	%
None	16	19.2
1-2	29	34.9
3 or more	38	45.7

No. of Sisters (N = 83)

	N	%
None	12	14.4
1-2	38	45.7
3 or more	33	39.7

Raised as a Child by Whom? (N = 83)

	N	%
Both parents (natural or adoptive)	48	57.8
Mother only	18	21.6
Father only	5	6.0
Grandparents	5	6.0
Other	7	8.4

Employed at Time of Offense (Full- or Part-time)? (N = 83)

	N	%
Yes	54	65.0
No	29	34.9

Prior Military Service? (N = 83)

	N	%
Yes	28	33.7
No	55	66.3

Type of Discharge (N = 28)

	N	%
Honorable	15	53.5
Less than honorable	13	46.6

Psychological Diagnosis (N = 58)

	N	%
Normal	34	58.6
Manic Depressive	7	12.0
Psychopath	11	18.9
Other (abnormal)	6	10.3

On Probation or Parole at Time of Offense? (N = 83)

	N	%
Yes	27	32.5
No	56	67.5

Prior Juvenile Arrests (N = 83)

	N	%
None	32	38.5
1-2	29	34.9
3 or more	22	26.5
Range = 0-50		

PRIOR ADULT FELONY ARRESTS
(N = 83)

	N	%
None	10	12.0
1–2	26	31.3
3 or more	47	56.6
Range = 0–77		

PRIOR FELONY CONVICTIONS
(N = 80)

	N	%
None	34	42.5
1–2	33	41.2
3 or more	13	16.2
Range = 0–8		

PRIOR MISDEMEANOR CONVICTIONS
(N = 78)

	N	%
None	45	57.6
1–2	22	28.2
3 or more	11	14.1

PLEA AT TRIAL (N = 83)

	N	%
Guilty	10	12.0
Not Guilty	70	84.3
N.G. — Insanity	3	3.6

GUILTY OR INNOCENT OF PRESENT OFFENSE? (N = 82)

	N	%
Guilty	16	19.5
Not Guilty	63	76.8
Don't know	3	3.6

TIME OF OFFENSE (N = 65)

	N	%
Between 12 P.M. and 12 A.M.	32	49.2
Between 12 A.M. and 12 P.M.	33	50.8
Mode = 1 A.M.		
Between 10 P.M. and 4 A.M.	32	49.2

DAY OF OFFENSE (N = 78)

	N	%
Monday	13	16.6
Tuesday	18	23.0
Wednesday	5	6.4
Thursday	3	1.2
Friday	12	15.3
Saturday	12	15.3
Sunday	15	19.2

Friday, Saturday, Sunday } 49.8

METHOD USED TO KILL VICTIM
(N = 83)

	N	%
Shooting	51	61.4
Stabbing	8	9.6
Beating	10	12.0
Strangulation	7	8.4
Other	7	8.4

WEAPON USED (N = 83)

	N	%
Handgun	40	48.1
Shotgun	8	9.6
Rifle	3	3.6
Blunt Instrument	6	7.2
Hatchet	8	9.6
Fists	7	8.4
Other	11	13.2

NO. OF ACCOMPLICES (N = 83)

	N	%
None	31	37.3
1	19	22.8
2	19	22.8
3 or more	14	16.8

KNOWN DISPOSITION OF ACCOMPLICES (N = 83)

	N	%
Death sentence	12	13.3
Life sentence	23	25.5
Imprisonment less than life	20	22.2
Not apprehended	11	12.2
Killed	5	5.5
Other (including acquittal, dismissal, probation)	19	21.1

Drugs or Alcohol Taken Prior to Offense (N = 78)

	N	%
Marijuana, THC	15	17.9
Narcotics	4	5.1
Other drugs	3	3.8
Combination of drugs	9	11.5
Beer	11	14.1
Liquor	14	17.9
Wine	1	1.2
Alcohol and drugs	7	8.9
None	15	19.2

No. of Victims Killed (N = 83)

	N	%
1	65	78.3
2	12	14.4
3	4	4.8
4	1	1.2

Age of Victims (N = 65)

Range = 7–81 yrs.
47.6% of victims aged 25–40

Race of Victims (N = 83)

	N	%
White	8	7.5
Black	98	92.4

Sex of Victims (N = 65)

	N	%
Male	63	59.4
Female	43	46.5

Victim-Offender Relationship (N = 83)

	N	%
Total strangers (including police)	65	61.3
Acquaintances	25	23.5
Close friends (including lovers)	8	7.5
Relatives (including wife and ex-wife)	8	7.5

Place of Offense (N = 83)

	N	%
Home	28	33.7
Business	20	24.0
Outdoors (street, parking lot, woods, etc.)	34	40.9
Other	1	1.2

Size of Place of Offense (N = 76)

Pop.	N	%
250,000+	18	23.6
100,000–250,000	3	3.9
50,000–99,000	11	14.4
10,000–50,000	22	28.9
Under 10,000	15	19.7
Rural	7	9.2

Did Offender Reside in Locality of Offense? (N = 76)

	N	%
Yes	52	68.4
No	24	31.6

Was Judge Fair at Trial? (N = 76)

	N	%
Yes	11	14.4
No	62	81.5
Don't know	3	3.9

How Was Judge Unfair? (N = 60)

	N	%
Denied defense motions	31	51.6
Prejudiced against all defendants	9	15.0
Racially prejudiced	7	8.4
Other	13	15.6

Sex of Judge (N = 81)

	N	%
Male	78	96.2
Female	3	3.8

RACE OF JUDGE (N = 81)

	N	%
White	81	100.0
Black	0	0.0

DID JUDGE HAVE PERSONAL VENDETTA AGAINST OFFENDER? (N = 79)

	N	%
Yes	60	75.9
No	15	18.9
Don't know	4	1.2

WAS JUDGE POLITICALLY MOTIVATED? (N = 67)

	N	%
Yes	29	43.2
No	21	31.3
Don't know	17	25.3

NO. OF WHITE JURORS (N = 80)

	N	%
5–8	5	6.2
9–10	25	31.2
11–12	49	61.2

NO. OF BLACK JURORS (N = 80)

	N	%
None	29	36.2
1–2	37	46.2
3–4	10	12.5
5 or more	4	5.0
Range = 0–7		

NO. OF MALE JURORS (N = 79)

	N	%
2–5	17	21.5
6–9	55	69.6
10–11	7	8.8
Range = 2–11		

NO. OF FEMALE JURORS (N = 79)

	N	%
1–4	26	32.9
5–8	50	63.2
9–10	3	3.7
Range = 1–10		

WAS JURY'S VERDICT FAIR? (N = 73)

	N	%
Yes	16	21.9
No	53	72.6
Don't know	4	5.4

LENGTH OF TRIAL (N = 68)

Days	N	%
1–3	22	32.3
4–5	30	44.1
6 or more	16	23.5

LENGTH OF JURY DELIBERATIONS (N = 73)

Hours	N	%
1 or less	24	32.8
1–3	28	38.3
4–6	9	12.3
7–9	5	6.8
More than 12	7	9.5

WAS OFFENDER SURPRISED AT GUILTY VERDICT? (N = 73)

	N	%
Yes	38	52.0
No	35	48.0

LENGTH OF JURY DELIBERATIONS AT SENTENCING (N = 77)

	N	%
Under 30 min.	39	50.6
30 min.–1 hr.	18	23.3
1–2 hr.	12	15.5
2 hr. or more	18	23.3
Range = 10 min.–9 hr.		

JURY RECOMMENDATION AT SENTENCING (N = 81)

	N	%
Death	66	81.4
Life imprisonment	15	18.6

WAS OFFENDER SURPRISED AT DEATH SENTENCE? (N = 81)

	N	%
Yes	27	33.3
No	54	66.7

Did Judge Follow Jury's Sentencing Recommendation? (N = 82)

	N	%
Yes	65	79.2
No	17	20.8

Was Jury Sequestered During Trial? (N = 76)

	N	%
Yes	20	26.3
No	50	65.7
Don't know	6	7.8

Did Offender Request Jury Sequestration? (N = 64)

	N	%
Yes	20	31.2
No	36	56.2
Don't know	8	12.5

Are Black Jurors Dominated by White Jurors? (N = 80)

	N	%
Yes	38	47.5
No	31	38.7
Don't know	11	13.8

Percentage of Erroneous Convictions for Every 100 Capital Trials? (N = 72)

	N	%
10% or less	28	38.8
10–33%	10	13.8
34–50%	10	13.8
51–75%	9	12.5
75% or more	15	20.8

Is an All-white Jury More Likely to Convict a Black Defendant? (N = 81)

	N	%
Yes	64	79.0
No	14	17.2
Don't know	3	3.7

Was Prosecutor Fair During Trial? (N = 79)

	N	%
Yes	14	17.7
No	65	82.3

Was Prosecutor Politically Motivated? (N = 77)

	N	%
Yes	53	68.8
No	13	16.8
Don't know	11	14.2

Did Prosecutor Have Personal Vendetta Against Offender? (N = 78)

	N	%
Yes	39	50.0
No	38	48.7
Don't know	1	1.3

Type of Counsel Representing Offender (N = 83)

	N	%
Public defender	37	44.6
Court-appointed	26	31.3
Privately retained	20	24.1

Was Defense Counsel Experienced in Capital Cases? (N = 82)

	N	%
Yes	25	30.4
No	41	50.0
Don't know	16	19.5

Performance of Defense Counsel (N = 82)

	N	%
Excellent	13	15.8
Good	19	23.1
Average	13	15.8
Below average	9	10.9
Poor	28	34.1

If Retried, Would Offender Want Same Defense Counsel? (N = 82)

	N	%
Yes	18	21.9
No	64	78.1

BEHAVIOR OF POLICE AT TIME OF ARREST (N = 77)

	N	%
Fair	49	62.6
Unfair	27	35.0
Don't remember	1	1.3

HOW WERE POLICE UNFAIR? (N = 48)

	N	%
Beatings	14	29.1
Psychological tricks	12	25.0
Lies and/or threats	7	14.5
Long interrogations	6	12.5
Other	9	18.7

DOES OFFENDER PRESENTLY SUPPORT CAPITAL PUNISHMENT? (N = 81)

	N	%
Yes	5	6.1
No	76	93.8

DID OFFENDER EVER SUPPORT CAPITAL PUNISHMENT? (N = 79)

	N	%
Yes	13	16.4
No	66	83.5

UNDER WHAT CIRCUMSTANCES COULD OFFENDER SUPPORT CAPITAL PUNISHMENT? (N = 74)

	N	%
Child killers	7	9.4
Terrorists	2	2.7
Other	3	4.0
None	62	83.7

HOW SHOULD SOCIETY PUNISH CONVICTED MURDERERS? (N = 76)

	N	%
1–10 years' imprisonment	4	5.2
10–25 years' imprisonment	31	40.7
Minimum 25 years' imprisonment	8	10.5
Life imprisonment	15	19.7
Death	1	1.3
Mental hospital	4	5.2
Other	13	17.1

IN GENERAL, IS REHABILITATION FEASIBLE IN PRISONS? (N = 81)

	N	%
Yes	38	46.9
No	39	48.1
Don't know	4	4.9

IS DEATH BY ELECTROCUTION CRUEL AND UNUSUAL PUNISHMENT? (N = 80)

	N	%
Yes	71	89.8
No	8	10.1
Don't know	1	1.2

WHY IS ELECTROCUTION CRUEL AND UNUSUAL? (N = 67)

	N	%
All intentional deaths are cruel	16	23.8
Mental stress of waiting	7	10.4
Painful	17	25.3
Disfiguring	7	10.4
Lacks dignity	7	10.4
Ritualistic	6	8.9
Other	7	10.4

MOST HUMANE METHOD OF EXECUTING CONVICTED OFFENDERS? (N = 78)

	N	%
Drug overdose	38	48.7
Shooting	9	11.5
Electrocution	3	3.8
Gassing	3	3.8
Hanging	1	1.2
Fight to death	2	2.5
Other	12	15.3
None	10	12.8

PERCENTAGE OF "INNOCENT" MEN ON FLORIDA'S DEATH ROW? (N = 61)

	N	%
0–5%	26	42.6
5–10%	9	14.7
11–33%	15	24.5
34% or more	11	18.0

Ever Seriously Consider Suicide? (N = 81)

	N	%
Yes	47	58.0
No	34	41.9

Ever Attempt Suicide? (N = 80)

	N	%
Yes	28	35.0
No	52	65.0

Number of Suicide Attempts (N = 26)

	N	%
One	19	73.0
Two	3	11.5
Three or more	4	15.3

Why Not Suicide, Given Death Sentence? (N = 45)

	N	%
Have to live	14	31.1
Always a chance death sentence will be vacated	8	17.7
Love myself	6	13.3
Not a coward	4	8.8
Other	13	28.8

Does Offender Still Have Hope of Not Being Executed? (N = 79)

	N	%
Yes	73	92.4
No	6	7.6

Why Hope? (N = 47)

	N	%
Pending appeals	22	46.8
Faith in God	4	8.5
Innocent	5	10.6
Other	16	34.0

Does Offender Believe He Will Be Executed? (N = 79)

	N	%
Yes	17	21.5
No	46	58.2
Don't know	6	7.5
50–50 chance	10	12.6

Why Won't Offender Be Executed? (N = 47)

	N	%
Courts will intervene	16	34.0
Capital punishment will be abolished	5	10.6
Innocent	6	12.7
Will first commit suicide	6	12.7
Other	14	29.7

Who Will Prevent Execution? (N = 68)

	N	%
Courts	50	73.5
Governor	3	4.4
Clemency board	3	4.4
Other	12	17.6

In General, Does Offender Have Faith in the American Legal System? (N = 76)

	N	%
Yes	31	40.7
No	44	57.8
Don't know	1	1.3

Period of Time from Date of Offense to Sentence of Death (N = 83)

	N	%
1–6 months	38	45.7
7–12 months	21	25.3
More than 1 year	24	28.9

Range = 1–39 months
Mean = 8.2 months

Florida Murder Victims by Sex (1973–1976)

	Total Murder Victims*	Victims of Death Row Inmates†
Male	3,214 (72.9%)	63 (59.4%)
Female	1,192 (27.1%)	43 (40.5%)
	4,406 (100.0%)	106 (99.9%)
	$x^2 = 9.36$	
	$p < .01$	

*Data from Department of Criminal Law Enforcement, State of Florida, *Crime in Florida* (Annual Reports, 1973–1976).
†As of September 15, 1977.

Florida Arrests for Murder by Sex (1973–1976)

	Total Arrests for Murder*	Sex of Death Row Inmates†
Male	2,967 (81.9%)	90 (98.9%)
Female	656 (18.1%)	1 (1.1%)
	3,623 (100.0%)	91 (100.0%)
	$x^2 = 17.634$	
	$p < .001$	

*Data from Department of Criminal Law Enforcement, State of Florida, *Crime in Florida* (Annual Reports, 1973–1976).
†As of September 15, 1977.

Florida Homicide Arrests Reported by Race (1973–1976)

	Total Homicide Arrests*	Death Row Inmates†
White	1,522 (42.0%)	55 (60.4%)
Black	2,101 (57.9%)	36 (39.5%)
	3,623 (99.9%)	91 (99.9%)
	$x^2 = 12.34$	
	$p < .001$	

*Data from Department of Criminal Law Enforcement, State of Florida, *Crime in Florida* (Annual Reports, 1973–1976).
†As of September 15, 1977.

INDEX

Note: Page numbers in *italic* indicate illustrations; those followed by (t) indicate tables.

DATE DUE
